THE
MOTION PICTURE
GUIDE

THIS VOLUME IS DEDICATED TO
CHARLIE CHAPLIN
BUSTER KEATON
W. C. FIELDS
WOODY ALLEN
and all the great funny
people who made us laugh

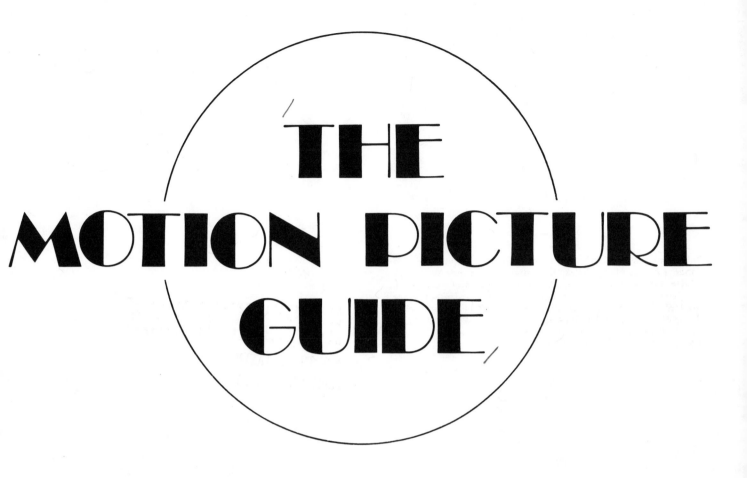

THE MOTION PICTURE GUIDE

S

1927-1983

Jay Robert Nash
Stanley Ralph Ross

CINEBOOKS, INC.
Chicago, 1987
Publishers of THE COMPLETE FILM RESOURCE CENTER

Publishers: Jay Robert Nash, Stanley Ralph Ross; **Associate Publisher:** Kenneth H. Petchenik; **Executive Editor:** Jim McCormick; **Senior Editor:** David Tardy; **Associate Editors:** Oksana Lydia Creighton, Jeffrey H. Wallenfeldt; **Senior Staff Writer:** James J. Mulay; **Staff Writers:** Arnie Bernstein, Daniel Curran, Phil Pantone, Michael Theobald; **Director of Production:** William Leahy; **Production Editor:** Shelby Payne; **Production Assistants:** Jeanette Hori, Michaela Tuohy; **Chief Researcher:** William C. Clogston.

Editorial and Sales Offices: CINEBOOKS, 990 Grove, Evanston, Illinois 60201.

Library of Congress Catalog Card Number: 85-071145
ISBN: 0-933997-00-0 THE MOTION PICTURE GUIDE (10 Vols.)
    0-933997-07-8 THE MOTION PICTURE GUIDE, Vol. VII (S)

Printed in the United States
First Edition
This volume contains 3,448 entries.

1 2 3 4 5 6 7 8 9 10

HOW TO USE INFORMATION IN THIS GUIDE

ALPHABETICAL ORDER

All entries have been arranged alphabetically throughout this and all subsequent volumes. In establishing alphabetical order, all articles (A, An, The) appear after the main title (AFFAIR TO REMEMBER, AN). In the case of foreign films the article precedes the main title (LES MISERABLES appears in the letter L) which makes, we feel, for easier access and uniformity. Contractions are grouped together and these will be followed by non-apostrophized words of the same letters. B.F.'s DAUGHTER is at the beginning of the letter B, not under BF.

TITLES

It is important to know what title you are seeking; use the *complete* title of the film. The film ADVENTURES OF ROBIN HOOD, THE, cannot be found under merely ROBIN HOOD. Many films are known under different titles and we have taken great pains to cross-reference these titles. (AKA, also known as) as well as alternate titles used in Great Britain (GB). In addition to the cross-reference title only entries, AKAs and alternate titles in Great Britain can be found in the title line for each entry. An alphabetically arranged comprehensive list of title changes appears in the Index volume (Vol. X).

RATINGS

We have rated each and every film at critical levels that include acting, directing, script, and technical achievement (or the sad lack of it). We have a *five-star* rating, unlike all other rating systems, to signify a film superbly made on every level, in short, a masterpiece. At the lowest end of the scale is *zero* and we mean it. The ratings are as follows: *zero* (not worth a glance), °(poor), °°(fair), °°°(good), °°°°(excellent), °°°°°(masterpiece, and these are few and far between). Half-marks mean almost there but not quite.

YEAR OF RELEASE

We have used in all applicable instances the year of United States release. This sometimes means that a film released abroad may have a different date elsewhere than in these volumes but this is generally the date released in foreign countries, not in the U.S.

FOREIGN COUNTRY PRODUCTION

When possible, we have listed abbreviated names of the foreign countries originating the production of a film. This information will be found within the parenthesis containing the year of release. If no country is listed in this space, it is a U.S. production.

RUNNING TIME

A hotly debated category, we have opted to list the running time a film ran at the time of its initial U.S. release but we will usually mention in the text if the film was drastically cut and give the reasons why. We have attempted to be as accurate as possible by consulting the most reliable sources.

PRODUCING AND DISTRIBUTING COMPANIES

The producing and/or distributing company of every film is listed in abbreviated entries next to the running time in the title line (see abbreviations; for all those firms not abbreviated, the entire firm's name will be present).

COLOR OR BLACK-AND-WHITE

The use of color or black-and-white availability appears as c or bw following the producing/releasing company entry.

CASTS

Whenever possible, we give *the complete cast and the roles played* for each film and this is the case in 95% of all entries, the only encyclopedia to ever offer such comprehensive information in covering the entire field. The names of actors and actresses are in Roman lettering, the names of the roles each played in Italic inside parentheses.

SYNOPSIS

The in-depth synopsis for each entry (when such applies) offers the plot of each film, critical evaluation, anecdotal information on the production and its personnel, awards won when applicable and additional information dealing with the production's impact upon the public, its success or failure at the box office, its social significance, if any. Acting methods, technical innovations, script originality are detailed. We also cite other productions involving an entry's personnel for critical comparisons and to establish the style or genre of expertise of directors, writers, actors and technical people.

REMAKES AND SEQUELS

Information regarding films that have sequels, sequels themselves or direct remakes of films can be found at the very end of each synopsis.

DUBBING AND SUBTITLES

We will generally point out in the synopsis when a foreign film is dubbed in English, mostly when the dubbing is poor. When voices are dubbed, particularly when singers render vocals on songs mimed by stars, we generally point out these facts either in the cast/role listing or inside the synopsis. If a film is in a foreign language and subtitled, we signify the fact in a parenthetical statement at the end of each entry (In Italian, English subtitles).

CREDITS

The credits for the creative and technical personnel of a film are extensive and they include: p (producer, often executive producer); d (director); w (screenwriter, followed by adaptation, if any, and creator of original story, if any, and other sources such as authors for plays, articles, short stories, novels and non-fiction books); ph (cinematographer, followed by camera system and color process when applicable, i.e., Panavision, Technicolor); m (composer of musical score); ed (film editor); md (music director); art d (art director); set d (set decoration); cos (costumes); spec eff (special effects); ch (choreography); m/l (music and lyrics); stunts, makeup, and other credits when merited. When someone receives two or more credits in a single film the credits may be combined (p&d, John Ford) or the last name repeated in subsequent credits shared with another (d, John Ford; w, Ford, Dudley Nichols).

GENRES/SUBJECT

Each film is categorized for easy identification as to genre and/or subject and themes at the left-hand bottom of each entry. (Western, Prison Drama, Spy Drama, Romance, Musical, Comedy, War, Horror, Science-Fiction, Adventure, Biography, Historical Drama, Children's Film, Animated Feature, etc.) More specific subject and theme breakdowns will be found in the Index (Vol. X).

PR AND MPAA RATINGS

The Parental Recommendation provides parents having no knowledge of the style and content of each film with a guide; if a film has excessive violence, sex, strong language, it is so indicated. Otherwise, films specifically designed for young children are also indicated. The Parental Recommendation (**PR**) is to be found at the right-hand bottom of each entry, followed, when applicable, by the **MPAA** rating. The PR ratings are as follows: **AAA** (must for children); **AA** (good for children); **A** (acceptable for children); **C** (cautionary, some objectionable scenes); **O** (completely objectionable for children).

KEY TO ABBREVIATIONS

Foreign Countries:

Arg.	Argentina
Aus.	Australia
Aust.	Austria
Bel.	Belgium
Braz.	Brazil
Brit.	Great Britain (GB when used for alternate title)
Can.	Canada
Chi.	China
Czech.	Czechoslovakia
Den.	Denmark
E. Ger.	East Germany
Fin.	Finland
Fr.	France
Ger.	Germany (includes W. Germany)
Gr.	Greece
Hung.	Hungary
Ital.	Italy
Jap.	Japan
Mex.	Mexico
Neth.	Netherlands
Phil.	Philippines
Pol.	Poland
Rum.	Rumania
S.K.	South Korea
Span.	Spain
Swed.	Sweden

Key to Abbreviations (continued)

Switz.	Switzerland
Thai.	Thailand
USSR	Union of Soviet Socialist Republics
Yugo.	Yugoslavia

Production Companies, Studios and Distributors (U.S. and British)

AA	ALLIED ARTISTS
ABF	Associated British Films
AE	Avco Embassy
AEX	Associated Exhibitors
AH	Anglo-Hollandia
AIP	American International Pictures
AM	American
ANCH	Anchor Film Distributors
ANE	American National Enterprises
AP	Associated Producers
AP&D	Associated Producers & Distributors
ARC	Associated Releasing Corp.
Argosy	Argosy Productions
Arrow	Arrow Films
ART	Artcraft
Astra	Astra Films
AY	Aywon
BA	British Actors
B&C	British and Colonial Kinematograph Co.
BAN	Banner Films
BI	British Instructional
BIFD	B.I.F.D. Films
BIP	British International Pictures
BJP	Buck Jones Productions
BL	British Lion
Blackpool	Blackpool Productions
BLUE	Bluebird
BN	British National
BNF	British and Foreign Film
Boulting	Boulting Brothers (Brit.)
BP	British Photoplay Production
BPP	B.P. Productions
BRIT	Britannia Films
BRO	Broadwest
Bryanston	Bryantston Films (Brit.)
BS	Blue Streak
BUS	Bushey (Brit.)
BUT	Butchers Film Service
BV	Buena Vista (Walt Disney)
CAP	Capital Films
CC	Christie Comedy
CD	Continental Distributing
CHAD	Chadwick Pictures Corporation
CHES	Chesterfield
Cineguild	Cineguild
CL	Clarendon
CLIN	Clinton
COL	COLUMBIA
Colony	Colony Pictures
COM	Commonwealth
COMM	Commodore Pictures
COS	Cosmopolitan (Hearst)
DE	Dependable Exchange
DGP	Dorothy Gish Productions
Disney	Walt Disney Productions
DIST	Distinctive
DM	DeMille Productions
DOUB	Doubleday
EAL	Ealing Studios (Brit.)
ECF	East Coast Films
ECL	Eclectic
ED	Eldorado
EF	Eagle Films
EFF & EFF	E.F.F. & E.F.F. Comedy
EFI	English Films Inc.
EIFC	Export and Import Film Corp.
EL	Eagle-Lion
EM	Embassy Pictures Corp.

EMI	EMI Productions
EP	Enterprise Pictures
EPC	Equity Pictures Corp.
EQ	Equitable
EXCEL	Excellent
FA	Fine Arts
FC	Film Classics
FD	First Division
FN	First National
FOX	20TH CENTURY FOX (and Fox Productions)
FP	Famous Players (and Famous Players Lasky)
FRP	Frontroom Productions
Gainsborough	Gainsborough Productions
GAU	Gaumont (Brit.)
GEN	General
GFD	General Films Distributors
Goldwyn	Samuel Goldwyn Productions
GN	Grand National
GOTH	Gotham
Grafton	Grafton Films (Brit.)
H	Harma
HAE	Harma Associated Distributors
Hammer	Hammer Films (Brit.)
HD	Hagen and Double
HM	Hi Mark
HR	Hal Roach
IA	International Artists
ID	Ideal
IF	Independent Film Distributors (Brit.)
Imperator	Imperator Films (Brit.)
IP	Independent Pictures Corp.
IN	Invincible Films
INSP	Inspirational Pictures (Richard Barthelmess)
IV	Ivan Film
Javelin	Javelin Film Productions (Brit.)
JUR	Jury
KC	Kinema Club
KCB	Kay C. Booking
Knightsbridge	Knightsbridge Productions (Brit.)
Korda	Alexander Korda Productions (Brit.)
Ladd	Ladd Company Productions
LAS	Lasky Productions (Jesse L. Lasky)
LFP	London Films
LIP	London Independent Producers
Lorimar	Lorimar Productions
LUM	Lumis
Majestic	Majestic Films
Mascot	Mascot Films
Mayflowers	Mayflowers Productions (Brit.)
Metro	Metro
MFC	Mission Film Corporation
MG	Metro-Goldwyn
MGM	METRO-GOLDWYN-MAYER
MON	Monogram
MOR	Morante
MS	Mack Sennett
MUT	Mutual
N	National
NG	National General
NGP	National General Pictures (Alexander Korda, Brit.)
NW	New World
Orion	Orion Productions
Ortus	Ortus Productions (Brit.)
PAR	PARAMOUNT
Pascal	Gabriel Pascal Productions (Brit.)
PDC	Producers Distributors Corp.

Key to Abbreviations (continued)

PEER	Peerless
PWN	Peninsula Studios
PFC	Pacific Film Company
PG	Playgoers
PI	Pacific International
PIO	Pioneer Film Corp.
PM	Pall Mall
PP	Pro Patria
PRC	Producers Releasing Corporation
PRE	Preferred
QDC	Quality Distributing Corp.
RAY	Rayart
RAD	Radio Pictures
RANK	J. Arthur Rank (Brit.)
RBP	Rex Beach Pictures
REA	Real Art
REG	Regional Films
REN	Renown
REP	Republic
RF	Regal Films
RFD	R.F.D. Productions (Brit.)
RKO	RKO RADIO PICTURES
Rogell	Rogell
Romulus	Romulus Films (Brit.)
Royal	Royal
SB	Samuel Bronston
SCHUL	B.P. Schulberg Productions
SEL	Select
SELZ	Selznick International (David O. Selznick)
SF	Selznick Films
SL	Sol Lesser
SONO	Sonofilms
SP	Seven Pines Productions (Brit.)
SRP	St. Regis Pictures
STER	Sterling
STOLL	Stoll
SUN	Sunset
SYN	Syndicate Releasing Co.
SZ	Sam Zimbalist
TC	Two Cities (Brit.)
T/C	Trem-Carr
THI	Thomas H. Ince
TIF	Tiffany
TRA	Transatlantic Pictures
TRU	Truart
TS	Tiffany/Stahl
UA	UNITED ARTISTS
UNIV	UNIVERSAL (AND UNIVERSAL INTERNATIONAL)
Venture	Venture Distributors
VIT	Vitagraph
WAL	Waldorf
WB	WARNER BROTHERS (AND WARNER BROTHERS-SEVEN ARTS)
WEST	Westminster
WF	Woodfall Productions (Brit.)
WI	Wisteria
WORLD	World
WSHP	William S. Hart Productions
ZUKOR	Adolph Zukor Productions

Foreign

ABSF	AB Svensk Film Industries (Swed.)
Action	Action Films (Fr.)
ADP	Agnes Delahaie Productions (Fr.)
Agata	Agata Films (Span.)
Alter	Alter Films (Fr.)
Arch	Archway Film Distributors
Argos	Argos Films (Fr.)
Argui	Argui Films (Fr.)
Ariane	Les Films Ariane (Fr.)
Athos	Athos Films (Fr.)
Belga	Belga Films (Bel.)

Beta	Beta Films (Ger.)
CA	Cine-Alliance (Fr.)
Caddy	Caddy Films (Fr.)
CCFC	Compagnie Commerciale Francais Einematographique (Fr.)
CDD	Cino Del Duca (Ital.)
CEN	Les Films de Centaur (Fr.)
CFD	Czecheslovak Film Productions
CHAM	Champion (Ital.)
Cinegay	Cinegay Films (Ital.)
Cines	Cines Films (Ital.)
Cineriz	Cinerez Films (Ital.)
Citel	Citel Films (Switz.)
Como	Como Films (Fr.)
CON	Concordia (Fr.)
Corona	Corona Films (Fr.)
D	Documento Films (Ital.)
DD	Dino De Laurentiis (Ital.)
Dear	Dear Films (Ital.)
DIF	Discina International Films (Fr.)
DPR	Films du Palais-Royal (Fr.)
EX	Excelsa Films (Ital.)
FDP	Films du Pantheon (Fr.)
Fono	Fono Roma (Ital.)
FS	Filmsonor Productions (Fr.)
Gala	Fala Films (Ital.)
Galatea	Galatea Productions (Ital.)
Gamma	Gamma Films (Fr.)
Gemma	Gemma Cinematografica (Ital.)
GFD	General Film Distributors, Ltd. (Can.)
GP	General Productions (Fr.)
Gray	(Gray Films (Fr.)
IFD	Intercontinental Film Distributors
Janus	Janus Films (Ger.)
JMR	Macques Mage Releasing (Fr.)
LF	Les Louvre Films (Fr.)
LFM	Les Films Moliere (Fr.)
Lux	Lux Productions (Ital.)
Melville	Melville Productions (Fr.)
Midega	Midega Films (Span.)
NEF	N.E.F. La Nouvelle Edition Francaise (Fr.)
NFD	N.F.D. Productions (Ger.)
ONCIC	Office National pour le Commerce et L'Industrie Cinematographique (Fr.)
Ortus	Ortus Films (Can.)
PAC	Production Artistique Cinematographique (Fr.)
Pagnol	Marcel Pagnol Productions (Fr.)
Parc	Parc Films (Fr.)
Paris	Paris Films (Fr.)
Pathe	Pathe Films (Fr.)
PECF	Productions et Editions Cinematographique Francais (Fr.)
PF	Parafrench Releasing Co. (Fr.)
PIC	Produzione International Cinematografica (Ital.)
Ponti	Carlo Ponti Productions (Ital.)
RAC	Realisation d'Art Cinematographique (Fr.)
Regina	Regina Films (Fr.)
Renn	Renn Productions (Fr.)
SDFS	Societe des Films Sonores Tobis (Fr.)
SEDIF	Societe d'Exploitation ed de Distribution de Films (Fr.)
SFP	Societe Francais de Production (Fr.)
Sigma	Sigma Productions (Fr.)
SNE	Societe Nouvelle des Establishments (Fr.)
Titanus	Titanus Productions (Ital.)
TRC	Transcontinental Films (Fr.)
UDIF	U.D.I.F. Productions (Fr.)
UFA	Deutsche Universum-Film AG (Ger.)
UGC	Union Generale Cinematographique (Fr.)
Union	Union Films (Ger.)
Vera	Vera Productions (Fr.)

S

S.O.B.**   (1981) 121m Lorimar/PAR c

Julie Andrews (*Sally Miles*), William Holden (*Tim Culley*), Marisa Berenson (*Mavis*), Larry Hagman (*Dick Benson*), Robert Loggia (*Herb Maskowitz*), Stuart Margolin (*Gary Murdock*), Richard Mulligan (*Felix Farmer*), Robert Preston (*Dr. Irving Finegarten*), Craig Stevens (*Willard*), Loretta Swit (*Polly Reed*), Robert Vaughn (*David Blackman*), Robert Webber (*Ben Coogan*), Shelley Winters (*Eva Brown*), Jennifer Edwards (*Lila*), Katherine MacMurray (*Tommy Taylor*), Benson Fong (*Chinese Chef*), John Pleshette, John Lawlor (*Capitol Studios Vice Presidents*), Larry Storch (*Guru*), Ken Swofford (*Guard*), Bert Rosario (*Gardner*), Hamilton Camp (*Lab Manager*), Stiffe Tanney (*Jogger*), David Young (*Sam Marshall*), Virginia Gregg (*Mortician's Wife*), Byron Kane (*Mortician*), Paddy Stone (*Barker*), Rosanna Arquette (*Babs*), Gene Nelson (*Clive Lytell*), Marisa Berenson, Paul Stewart, Joe Penny, Mimi Davis, Stephen Johnson, Erica John, Charles Lampkin, Kevin Justrich, Kimberly Woodward, Scott Arthur Allen, Corbin Bernsen, Joseph Benti, Rebecca Edwards, Neil Flanagan, Todd Howland, Jill Jaress, Alexandra Johnson, Len Lawson, Shelby Leverington, Gisele Lindley, Dominick Mazzie, Fay McKenzie, Bill McLaughlin, Tony Miller, Dave Morick, Charles Parks, Charles Rowe, James Purcell, Gay Rowan, Borah Silver, Ken Smolka, Henry Sutton, Noel Toy, Howard Vann, Sharri Zak.

Blake Edwards' satirical attack on Hollywood and the film industry doesn't have the biting edge or fresh characters needed to make it stand out. The film opens with a successful director, Mulligan, trying to commit suicide. It seems his most recent film, a $30 million picture, has bombed and the movie critics have already written him off as a "has-been." In the process of his attempted suicide, a beachfront jogger dies of a heart attack, while both men go unnoticed by everyone. After his wife, Andrews, leaves him, Mulligan decides to fight back by turning his family musical failure into a porno film. This requires Andrews to bare her breasts, which she does for financial reasons. (At the time, Andrews was trying to shed her virginal image, and so really does go buff, which in a twisted way, makes this film a parody of itself). The fact is, most people probably went to see this picture in order to see Andrews strip; ditto for the story-line, in which Andrews' stripping becomes the draw for Mulligan's movie. The catch, though, is that for Mulligan to remake his picture, he must buy it back from the studio. In the end, the studio regains control of the film and Mulligan is killed while trying to steal his negatives. The director's three friends, Holden, Preston, and Loggia, want to give their friend a decent burial at sea, not the hyped extravaganza the studio and Andrews have planned. The film does have its moments; unfortunately, the Hollywood stereotypes are all to a prevalent to make this an interesting and sharp satire. This would be the last film for Holden.

p, Blake Edwards, Tony Adams; d&w, Edwards; ph, Harry Stradling (Panavision, Metrocolor); m, Henry Mancini; ed, Ralph E. Winters; prod d, Roger Maus; art d, William Craig Smith; cos, Theadora Van Runkle; ch, Paddy Stone.

Comedy   Cas.   (PR:O MPAA:R)

S.O.S. ICEBERG**½   (1933) 77m UNIV bw

Rod La Rocque (*Dr. Carl Lawrence*), Leni Riefenstahl (*Ellen Lawrence*), Sepp Rist (*Dr. Johannes Brand*), Gibson Gowland (*John Dragan*), Dr. Max Hoisboer (*Dr. Jan Matushek*), Walter Rimi (*Fritz Kuemmel*), Ernst Udet (*Maj. Udet*).

A realistic, gripping drama that has La Rocque searching for the records of the lost Alfred Lothar Wegener expedition to Greenland. La Rocque is joined on the perilous journey by three experienced explorers and a financial backer who has gone along for the "adventure." This film was praised for its authenticity in its use of the Greenland landscape, and the scene where the group is trapped on an iceberg illustrates that point. The financial backer is driven mad by the dangers and wants to stay back, but La Rocque keeps pushing on. His wife, Riefenstahl, is a noted flier and goes after them, but ends up crashing the plane and becoming marooned with the others. As members of the group slowly start to die, they are rescued by major Udet and a group of kayaking Eskimoes. When making this picture, Universal called on the advice of Knud Rasmussen, considered to be the expert on the polar regions, as well as two members of the actual, ill-fated Wegener expedition of 1929-30.

p, Carl Laemmle; d, Tay Garnett; w, Tom Reed, Edwin H. Knopf (based on the story by Dr. Arnold Fanck); ph, O. Hans Schneeberger, Richard Angst; m, Paul Dessau; ed, Andrew Marton; technical advisors, Dr. Fritz Loewe, Dr. Ernst Sorge.

Adventure   (PR:A MPAA:NR)

S.O.S. PACIFIC**   (1960, Brit.) 91m Rank/UNIV bw

Eddie Constantine (*Mark*), Pier Angeli (*Teresa*), Richard Attenborough (*Whitey*), John Gregson (*John Bennett*), Eva Bartok (*Maria*), Jean Anderson (*Miss Shaw*), Cec Linder (*Willy*), Clifford Evans (*Peterson*), Gunnar Moller (*Dr. Strauss*), Harold Kasket (*Monk*), Andrew Faulds (*Sea Captain*), Cyril Shaps (*Louis*), Tom Bowman (*Alberte*).

A diverse group of people on a seaplane flight crashes on a deserted island. They soon discover that they have just five hours to get off the island because it is the site for a nuclear bomb test. While there is plenty of action, gun fights, hurricanes, a battle with sharks, and a fire on the plane, the crux of the story deals with character development. In the tense ending, the hero lives in the British version, while the U.S. version has him die. Attenborough shines above the rest of the cast, but all fit perfectly into their respective roles.

p, John Nasht, Patrick Filmer-Sankey; d, Guy Green; w, Robert Westerby (based on a story by Gilbert Travers Thomas); ph, Wilkie Cooper; m, Georges Auric; ed, Arthur Stevens; art d, George Provis; cos, Jim Donlevy.

Suspense   (PR:A MPAA:NR)

S.O.S. TIDAL WAVE**   (1939) 62m REP bw (GB: TIDAL WAVE)

Ralph Byrd (*Jeff Shannon*), George Barbier (*Uncle Dan*), Kay Sutton (*Laurel Shannon*), Frank Jenks (*Peaches Jackson*), Marc Lawrence (*Sutter*), Dorothy Lee (*Mable*), Oscar O'Shea (*Mike Halloran*), Mickey Kuhn (*Buddy Shannon*), Ferris Taylor (*Farrow*), Donald Barry (*Curley*), Raymond Bailey (*Roy Nixon*).

An early film that shows the potential of television as a powerful medium. Byrd is a news reporter who exposes a crooked candidate in the mayoral race. At the same time, New York is clobbered by a tidal wave and earthquake, both hitting the earth at once. The underlying message is that television can be a powerful weapon in the hands of the wrong people.

p, Armand Schaefer; d, John H. Auer; w, Maxwell Shane, Gordon Kahn (based on the story by James Webb); ph, Jack Marta; m, Cy Feuer; ed, Ernest Nims; md, Feuer; art d, John Victor MacKay.

Drama   (PR:A MPAA:NR)

**S*P*Y*S*   (1974) 87m FOX c

Elliott Gould (*Griff*), Donald Sutherland (*Brulard*), Zouzou (*Sybil*), Joss Ackland (*Martinson*), Kenneth Griffith (*Lippet*), Vladek Sheybal (*Borisenko*), Russian Spy Chief, Kenneth J. Warren (*Grubov*), Yuri Borienko (*Yuri*), Michael Petrovitch (*Sevitsky, Defector*), Pierre Oudry (*Gaspar*), Jacques Marin (*Lafayette*), Shane Rimmer (*Hessler*), Xavier Gelin (*Paul*), George Pravda (*Russian Coach*), Alf Joint (*Stunt Man/KGB Agent*), Andy Ho (*Toy Ling*), Melanie Ackland (*Ellie*), James Woolley (*Alan*), Michael Anthony (*Priest*), Robert Cawdron (*Vet*), Raf De La Torre (*King of Swobodia*), Andre Charisse (*Clerk*), John Bardon (*Evans*), Norman Atkyns (*Head Waiter*), Jeffry Wickham (*Seely*), Nigel Hawthorne (*Croft*), Larry Taylor (*Lippet's Bodyguard*), Marian Desmond (*Russian-Speaking Lady*), Phillip Ross (*KGB Agent*), Hella Petri (*Prostitute*).

A satire on international espionage has Gould and Sutherland playing two bumbling agents whom the CIA would like to get rid of. When they bungle the defection of a Russian ballet dancer, the pair incur the wrath of both the CIA and the Russians. They are sheltered by French revolutionaries, then are tortured, shot at, and chased by weird characters. The title S*P*Y*S was an attempt to cash in on the success of the similarly titled M*A*S*H, which also starred Gould and Sutherland, but this attempt at comedy doesn't even come close to the well-written script of the latter.

p, Irwin Winkler, Robert Chartoff; d, Irvin Kershner; w, Mal Marmorstein, Laurence J. Cohen, Fred Freeman; ph, Gerry Fisher (DeLuxe Color); m, Jerry Goldsmith; ed, Keith Palmer; prod d, Michael Seymour; art d, Richard Rambeau; set d, Harry Cordwell; cos, Sue Yelland.

Comedy   Cas.   (PR:C MPAA:PG)

S.T.A.B.* (1976, Hong Kong/Thailand) 100m Paragon/Golden Harvest c

Greg Morris (*Richard Hill*), Sombat Metanee (*Chuck*), Krung Srivilai (*Zak*), Tham Thuy Hang (*Suzie*), Anoma Palalak (*Joanne*), Krisana Amnueyporn (*Johnnie*), Darm Daskorn (*Santana*), Dolna Sopir (*Donna*).

Ridiculous action film has Morris an adventurer-for-hire contracted by a well-heeled government anti-drug force to recover a large amount of lost gold in return for a $5 million finder's fee. Morris recruits the usual bunch of Southeast Asian hero types and a couple of sexy but tough women in tight shorts and sets off into the jungle to wreak havoc on dope peddlers. Enough fight scenes to maintain interest, and a generous helping of R-rated sex scenes make this one okay for mindless entertainment, but no more. Tham Thuy Hang, one of the sexy but tough women in tight shorts mentioned above, allegedly disappeared after production only to emerge later in Hanoi, a spy for the Communists.

p&d, Chalong Pakdivijit (English-language version produced by Leonard K.C. Ho); w, Andre Morgan; m, Noel Quinlan.

Adventure   **(PR:O MPAA:NR)**

S.W.A.L.K.   (SEE: MELODY, 1971, Brit.)

SAADIA*½   (1953) 81m MGM c

Cornel Wilde (Si Lahssen), Mel Ferrer (Henrik), Rita Gam (Saadia), Michel Simon (Bou Rezza), Cyril Cusack (Khadir), Wanda Rotha (Fatima), Marcel Poncin (Moha), Anthony Marlowe (Capt. Sabert), Helene Vallier (Zoubida), Mahjoub Ben Brahim (Ahmed), Jacques Dufilho (Bandit Leader), Bernard Farrel (Lt. Camuzac), Richard Johnson (Lt. Girard), Peter Copley (Leader Mokhazenis), Marne Maitland (Horse Dealer), Edward Leslie (Villager), Harold Kasket (Cheikh of Inimert), Peter Bull (Village Potentate), Abdullah Mennebhi (Brahim).

A slow-mover that relies more on flash than substance. A French doctor (Ferrer) saves a young girl (Gam) under a witch's (Rotha) spell as the film becomes witchcraft against modern technology. Gam is grateful to the doctor but her real love is for Wilde. Wilde is too gracious as he realizes that Ferrer is in love with his former patient. While weaving in and out of the romantic tangle, the village is attacked by bandits, with Gam proving smarter than they when she saves the doctor's sought-after serum. Finally, Ferrer realizes where Gam's heart is and gives the pair his approval at the end.

p,d&w, Albert Lewin (based on the novel Echeck au Destin by Francis D' Autheville); ph, Cristopher Challis (Technicolor); m, Bronislau Kaper; ed, Harold F. Kress; art d, John Hawkesworth.

Drama   **(PR:A MPAA:NR)**

SABAKA   (SEE: HINDU, THE, 1953)

SABALEROS   (SEE: PUT UP OR SHUT UP, 1968, Arg.)

SABATA½**   (1969, Ital.) 106m P.E.A.-Produzioni Associate Delphos/UA c (EHI, A MICO...C'E SABATA, HAI CHIUSO)

Lee Van Cleef (Sabata), William Berger (Banjo), Franco Ressel (Stengel), Linda Veras (Jane), Pedro Sanchez [Ignazio Spalla] (Carrincha), Gianni Rizzo (Judge O'Hara), AnthonyGradwell [Antonio Gradoli] (Fergusson), Nick Jordan (Alley Cat/Indio), Robert Hundar [Claudio Undari] (Oswald), Spanny Convery [Spartaco Conversi] (Slim), Marco Zuanelli (Sharky), Gino Marturano (McCallum), Joseph Mathews [Pino Mattei] (Frankie), Franco Ukmar (Cutty), Bruno Ukmar (Jumping Kid), Rodolfo Lodi (Fr. Brown), Alan Collins [Luciano Pigozzi] (False Fr. Brown), Vittorio Andre (Logan), Romano Puppo (Rocky Bendato), Andrew Ray [Andrea Aurell] (Daniel), Franco Marletta (Captain), John [Janos] Bartha (Sheriff), Charles Tamblyn [Carlo Tamberlani] (Nichols), Mimmo Poli (Hotel Workman).

Ressel plays a rich man who decides to get richer by planning the heist of a shipment of US Army gold from a Texas bank. Once the robbery is completed, Ressel arranges to have a $5000 reward offered for the capture of the robbers so that he can avoid sharing the loot. Van Cleef is the stranger who rides into town and kills the robbers, then collects the reward. When he learns Ressel was behind the robbery, he attempts to blackmail the mastermind. Ressel responds by hiring a series of gunslingers to do away with Van Cleef, but they are no match for the stranger. Eventually, Van Cleef kills Ressel and rides off into the desert. Some wild characterizations and well-handled action sequences make this a fast-moving and entertaining spaghetti western. Sequel: ADIOS, SABATA.

p, Alberto Grimaldi; d, Frank Kramer [Gianfranco Parolini]; w, Kramer, Renato Izzo; ph, Sandro Mancori (Techniscope, Technicolor); m, Marcelo Giombini; ed, Edmondo Lozzi; art d&cos, Carlo Simi; spec eff, Stacchini; makeup, Gianfranco Mecacci.

Western   **(PR:C MPAA:GP)**

SABINA, THE*   (1979, Span./Swed.) 105m El Iman-Svenska Filminstitutet c (LA SABINA)

Carol Kane (Daisy), Jon Finch (Michael), Harriet Andersson (Monica), Simon Ward (Philip), Angela Molina (Pepa), Ovidi Montllor (Manolin), Fernando Sanchez Polac (Felix), Francisco Sanchez (Antonio).

A poorly conceived film about a contemporary British writer living in a Spanish village while he does research on a 19th-Century traveler. The mysterious traveler, according to legend, was killed by a female dragon named La Sabina. Things get real strange and melodramatic from there. Writer Finch sleeps with American Kane until he falls for local beauty Molina. Finch's friend Ward arrives with his wife and everyone starts sleeping around, except Finch, who isn't able to seduce Molina. In a rage he kills his friend and then himself, leaving the audience to wish he'd done it sooner.

p,d&w, Jose Luis Borau; ph, Lars-Goran Bjorne (Eastmancolor); m, Paco de Lucia; ed, Jose Salcedo; set d, Wolfgang Burmann.

Drama   **(PR:O MPAA:NR)**

SABOTAGE, 1932, Brit.   (SEE: WHEN LONDON SLEEPS, 1932, Brit.)

SABOTAGE*½**   (1937, Brit.) 76m GAU/GAU-Janus bw (AKA: THE WOMAN ALONE; A WOMAN ALONE)

Sylvia Sidney (Sylvia Verloc), Oscar Homolka (Carl Verloc), John Loder (Sgt. Ted Spencer), Desmond Tester (Steve), Joyce Barbour (Renee), Matthew Boulton (Supt. Talbot), S.J. Warmington (Hollingshead), William Dewhurst (A.S. Chatman), Austin Trevor (Vladimir), Torin Thatcher (Yunct), Aubrey Mather (Greengrocer), Peter Bull (Michaelis), Charles Hawtrey (Studious Youth), Pamela Bevan, Sara Allgood, Martita Hunt, Sam Wilkinson, Clare Greet, Arnold Bell, Albert Chevalier, Frederick Piper, Hal Gordon.

Based on Joseph Conrad's thrilling novel The Secret Agent, SABOTAGE (the name being changed from the novel so as not to confuse moviegoers with Hitchcock's earlier film, SECRET AGENT, based on stories by W. Somerset Maugham) is a carefully constructed chiller dealing with terrorism and bombs that might go off at any minute. Sidney, a shy woman, is married to moody, sullen Homolka who is a saboteur using his movie theater as a front for his dark activities. Tester, Sidney's young brother, lives with her and her surly husband, running errands. Next to the theater is a grocery where clerk Loder works; he is not a clerk at all but a Scotland Yard detective who has been assigned to get evidence against Homolka. Just as he is about to be exposed, Homolka gives Tester a package to deliver and the boy goes off dutifully, not knowing he's carrying a bomb. The boy is delayed several times from delivering the package, once by a man giving a demonstration of new toothbrushes who uses Tester as a guinea pig before a curious throng of passersby. Meanwhile, Loder, who has befriended the unhappy Sidney, has gotten enough evidence from her to believe her husband is a saboteur working for a nameless organization. Then Sidney hears the news that a bomb went off in a bus killing her young brother and other passengers. She quickly pieces together events and confronts Homolka who more or less admits his guilt but tells her to keep her mouth shut. Sidney becomes hysterical and, grabbing a butcher knife, attacks her beast-like husband, killing him. Sidney is about to confess her crime when Loder discovers other terrorists have entered the theater, knowing it is now pinpointed by the authorities as a center of their activities. They blow up the theater just before Sidney murdering Homolka and she is half prevented from admitting her guilt by Loder, who has become her protector and is in love with her. SABOTEUR, though painstakingly constructed by Hitchcock to build monumental suspense, backfired on the director. The public and critics alike criticized him mightily for allowing the bomb to go off and kill a child. Homolka is terrific as the brooding terrorist but it is never explained why he and his mysterious henchmen are busy planting bombs all over London and killing innocent people. Hitchcock later admitted he was wrong in showing this scene and allowing the boy, not to mention the passengers, to be blown up. When the film was shown in England for the press, one elderly critic became so incensed at the boy's death that he had to be restrained from punching the director right then and there. Hitchcock also perversely played with Sidney's reaction to the death of her brother. She hears the news while watching a Silly Symphony cartoon in the theater, WHO KILLED COCK ROBIN? (which Hitchcock got permission from Walt Disney to show). She cannot help but laugh with the audience, even though her brother has just been killed. Hitchcock had to work hard to get a stage-trained stage-trained wordlessly kill Homolka with the knife after staring at his back for the longest time. She was convinced the scene wouldn't play well but the director begged her to do it his way and watch the scene later which, she admitted, was one of the most powerful she ever performed. When she left the screening, Sidney stated: "Hollywood must hear of this." The detail of SABOTAGE is rich in that Hitchcock shows the London of his childhood. The grocery where Loder works was similar to the one his own father owned and the theater was almost an exact replica of the East End movie theater Hitchcock himself attended as a youth. Loder was not the director's first choice for the role of the detective. He had signed Robert Donat to the part but, at the last minute, Alexander Korda–to whom Donat was under contract– withdrew his permission to use the actor. Hitchcock settled for the solid if not inspiring Loder. Hitchcock showed his flair for expensive sets in SABOTAGE, ordering a streetcar line built for some distance just to show it for a few minutes on film. This cost more than $30,000 and Gaumont executives thought it a foolish expense. At the time Hitchcock knew he was being watched by all the major American studios and he wanted the moguls in the U.S. to see that he knew how to do things in a big way, given the kind of budgets available in America. There were problems with SABOTAGE abroad with several countries initially refusing to show it, particularly Brazil, which outright banned the film, claiming it was nothing more than a handbook for terrorists on the building and planting of bombs. When the film was released in the U.S. it bore the nondescript title THE WOMAN ALONE, a title that far from suggested the kind of film Hitchcock had made. This title was quickly forgotten and the film, as seen in the U.S. today, is shown under the original British title, SABOTAGE.

p, Michael Balcon, Ivor Montagu; d, Alfred Hitchcock; w, Charles Bennett,

Ian Hay, Alma Reville, Helen Simpson, E.V.H. Emmett (based on the novel *The Secret Agent* by Joseph Conrad); ph, Bernard Knowles; m, Louis Levy; ed, Charles Frend; set d, Otto Werndorff, Albert Jullion.

Suspense/Mystery   Cas.   **(PR:O MPAA:NR)**

SABOTAGE**   (1939) 69m REP bw (GB: SPIES AT WORK)

Arleen Whelan (*Gail*), Gordon Oliver (*Tommy Grayson*), Charley Grapewin (*Maj. Grayson*), Lucien Littlefield (*Eli*), Paul Guilfoyle (*Barsht*), J. M. Kerrigan (*Mel*), Dorothy Peterson (*Edith*), Don Douglas (*Joe*), Joseph Sawyer (*Gardner*), Maude Eburne (*Mrs. Hopkins*), Horace MacMahon (*A. Kruger*), Johnny Russell (*Matt*), Wade Boteler (*Cop*), Frank Darien (*Smitty*).

Another in a large batch of WW II films that waved the flag and called on preservation of the "American Way." In this picture, the spies are from no specific country; but with names like Barsht and Kruger, it's easy to figure out where they're supposed to be from. When a plane crashes during a test and kills three aboard, the townsfolk accuse the aircraft engineer, Oliver, of sabotaging the plane and working for spies. This prompts Oliver's father, Grapewin, to investigate the matter himself and he uncovers the real spy ring. He gives the community a piece of his mind, telling them off about their rash, so-called patriotic judgments. Unfortunately, the script is a little too heavy-handed in spouting its American-way propaganda.

p, Herman Schlom; d, Harold Young; w, Lionel Houser, Alice Altschuler; ph, Reggie Lanning; ed, William Morgan; md, Cy Feuer.

Action   **(PR:A MPAA:NR)**

SABOTAGE AT SEA*½   (1942, Brit.) 74m BN-Shaftesbury/Anglo American bw

Jane Carr (*Diane*), David [Dave] Hutcheson (*Capt. Tracey*), Margaretta Scott (*Jane Dighton*), Wally Patch (*Steward*), Ronald Shiner (*Cook*), Felix Aylmer (*John Dighton*), Martita Hunt (*Daphne Faber*), Ralph Truman (*Chandler*), Billy [William] Hartnell (*Digby*), Arthur Maude (*Engineer*), Ian Fleming.

Poorly contrived high-seas drama stars Hutcheson as the ship's captain faced with the arduous task of discovering who aboard his ship is a saboteur. When a crew member is murdered, he tracks down the guilty party and finds that he also is the saboteur. The cast is handicapped by an uneventful, wordy script.

p, Elizabeth Hiscott; d, Leslie Hiscott; w, Michael Barringer; ph, Gunther Krampf.

War/Drama   **(PR:A MPAA:NR)**

SABOTAGE SQUAD*   (1942) 64m COL bw

Bruce Bennett (*Lt. John Cronin*), Kay Harris (*Edith Cassell*), Eddie Norris (*Eddie Miller*), Sidney Blackmer (*Carlyle Harrison*), Don Beddoe (*Chief Hanley*), John Tyrrell (*Robert Fuller*), George McKay (*Chuck Brown*), Robert Emmett Keane (*Conrad*), Eddie Laughton (*Felix*), Byron Foulger (*Suspect*), Edward Hearn (*Foreman*), Pat Lane (*Sam*), John Dilson (*Mr. Guthrie*), Ethan Laidlaw (*Strong-Arm Man*), Hugh Prosser (*Saboteur*), Cy Ring (*Jefferson*), Lester Dorr (*Harry*), Bill Lally (*Cop*), Richard Bartell (*Gunner*), George Magrill (*Workman*), Al Hill (*Police Clerk*), Connie Evans (*Attendant*), Stanley Brown (*Clerk*), Edmund Cobb (*Policeman*), Ernie Adams (*Customer*), Al Herman (*Bookmaker*), Jack Gardner (*Bettor*), Eddie Bruce (*Clancy*), Brick Sullivan (*Cop*), Kenneth MacDonald (*Medical Examiner*), Max Wagner (*Recruiting Sergeant*).

Bennett is in the Army's subversion investigation outfit fighting spies and saboteurs. In between chasing down Nazi spies, the lieutenant helps get Harris' boy friend, Norris, out of the stockade. Bennett breaks the spy ring and sacrifices his life to steer a truck full of dynamite away from an aviation plant.

p, Jack Fier; d, Lew Landers; w, Bernice Petkere, Wallace Sullivan, David Silverstein (based on a story by Petkere, Sullivan); ph, Franz F. Planer; ed, William Lyon; md, M.W. Stoloff; art d, Lionel Banks.

Action Adventure   **(PR:A MPAA:NR)**

SABOTEUR****   (1942) 108m UNIV bw

Priscilla Lane (*Patricia Martin*), Robert Cummings (*Barry Kane*), Otto Kruger (*Charles Tobin*), Alan Baxter (*Freeman*), Clem Bevans (*Neilson*), Norman Lloyd (*Frank Fry*), Alma Kruger (*Mrs. Henrietta Sutton*), Vaughan Glaser (*Phillip Martin*), Dorothy Peterson (*Mrs. Mason*), Ian Wolfe (*Robert the Butler*), Frances Carson (*Society Woman*), Murray Alper (*Mac the Deputy Driver*), Kathryn Adams (*Young Mother, Mrs. Brown*), Pedro de Cordoba (*Bones the Human Skeleton*), Billy Curtis (*"Major" the Midget*), Marie LeDeaux (*Tatania the Fat Woman*), Jeanne Romer, Lynn Romer (*Marigold, Annette/Siamese Twins*), Samuel S. Hinds (*Foundation Leader*), Charles Halton (*Sheriff*), John Eldredge (*Footman*), Selmer Jackson (*FBI Chief*), Emory Parnell (*Husband in Movie*), Lou Lubin, Torin Thatcher, Oliver Prickett 'Blake' (*Men*), Will Lee (*Worker*), Will Wright (*Company Official*), James Flavin, Archie Twitchell 'Michael Brandon' (*Motorcycle Cop/Voices*), Margaret Moffat (*Neighbor*), Hans Conried (*Edward*), Paul

Everton (*Bus Man*), Pat Flaherty (*Navy Man*), Barton Yarbrough (*1st FBI Man at Mason's House*), Anita Sharp-Bolster (*Esmeralda the Bearded Lady/Lorelei*), Virgil Summers (*Ken Mason*), Lee Phelps (*Plant Policeman*), George Offerman, Jr. (*Worker*), Harry Strang (*Cop*), Matt Willis (*Deputy*), Marjorie Wood (*Farmer's Wife*), Paul E. Burns (*Farmer*), Belle Mitchell (*Adele the Maid*), Ed Foster (*Driver for Saboteurs*), William Ruhl (*Deputy Marshal*), Gene Garrick (*Worker*), Dick Midgley, Don Cadell (*FBI Men*), Milton Kibbee (*Husband in Movie Audience*), Gene O'Donnell (*Jitterbug*), Paul Phillips (*Driver*), William Gould (*Stranger*), Ralph Dunn (*FBI Man at Mason's House*), Jack Arnold (*Other Man in Movie*), Margaret Hayes (*Wife in Movie*), Rex Lease (*Plant Counterman*), Duke York (*Deputy*), Nancy Loring (*Young Mother*), Claire Whitney (*Wife in Movie Audience*), Frank Marlowe (*George the Truck Driver*), Alan 'Al' Bridge (*Marine Sergeant MP*), Norma Drury (*Refugee Mother*), Charles Sherlock (*Barry's Taxi Driver*), Jack Cheatham (*Detective*), Jack Gardner (*Pat's Taxi Driver*), Alex Lockwood (*Marine*), Kernan Cripps (*Man in Movie Audience*), Jean Trent (*Blonde Aircraft Worker*), Jim Lucas (*Taxi Driver*), Dale Van Sickel (*FBI Assistant/Phone Operator*), Walter Miller, Mary Curtis (*Midgets*), Margaret Ann McLaughlin (*Baby Susie Brown*), Kermit Maynard (*Cow Hand*), Gerald Pierce (*Elevator Operator*), Carol Stevens (*Deaf Man's Companion*), Alfred Hitchcock (*Deaf and Dumb Man Outside Drug Store*), Tar, Grey, Shadow, Smokey (*Dogs*), Cyril Ring (*Party Guest*), Jeffrey Sayre (*Henchman*), Ralph Brooks (*Dance Extra*).

This film was Hitchcock's first contribution to wartime American propaganda and it's as polished and suspenseful as any the great director would ever make. The film is actually a forerunner to the director's masterpiece, NORTH BY NORTHWEST, in that it depicts an innocent man accused of mass murder and he must clear himself by chasing a bunch of insidious spies across the country, but this time going from west to east. Cummings is a simple factory worker laboring in an airplane plant, making bombers. He and his best friend, Summers, are shown with hundreds of others leaving the main plant and heading for a huge dining area. En route Cummings stoops and picks up a $100 bill and a letter addressed to a Frank Fry. He hands the letter to a thin, wiry, man who dropped these items. The man forgets the $100 bill and Cummings races after him, finding him at one of the lunch tables, asking him, Lloyd, if he's Fry. He hesitantly admits he is and Cummings hands him the bill. Moments later, black smoke comes curling out of the huge doors to the main plant and the cloud billows upward so that it becomes a wall of smoke. The factory workers turn en masse, horrified, and some of them, including Lloyd, Cummings, and Summers, race for the partly open factory doors leading to the main plant. Lloyd grabs a fire extinguisher, hands it to Cummings, and he begins to run to the fire, but Summers, almost like a small boy participating in a game, grabs the extinguisher and runs ahead of Cummings, spraying the fire which, to Cummings' horror, shoots upward, engulfing and roasting his friend who has obviously sprayed a flammable liquid from a doctored extinguisher. The entire factory begins to burn and later Cummings explains what happened to investigators, mentioning that Lloyd gave him the extinguisher, and then goes to see Summers' mother, Peterson. Detectives come to Peterson's door, ask for Cummings, and tell Peterson that the extinguisher her son used was full of gasoline. Peterson, on the verge of hysteria, tells the detectives that she can't talk about the fire and when Cummings returns after going on an errand for her, she tells him that the detectives were looking for him, that they wanted to arrest him, that the extinguisher was full of gasoline, and that Cummings killed her son. Moreover, Peterson tells him, there is no such person as Lloyd working at the plant. Cummings is in shock and asks Peterson if she believes he had nothing to do with the obvious sabotage. She tells him she has told the police nothing, but is confused. Cummings realizes he must find Lloyd to clear his own name. He remembers the address of a ranch in a western state which was on the envelope he handed Lloyd and Cummings hitches a ride with eastbound trucker, Alper. The garrulous truckdriver drones on and on about his wife and defense work, until a traffic cop stops him, asking him to get out of his cab. Cummings thinks he is about to be arrested when the cop has only stopped Alper because one of his taillights has gone out. Just after the truck continues onward, the cop hears an alert for Cummings over his radio. He looks up the road at the fast-disappearing and then turns his cycle around and goes the other way. Cummings gets off near a huge spread called Deep Springs Ranch and proceeds to the luxurious ranch house. He is shown in to see Kruger after asking for Frank Fry. Kruger is playing in a large pool with his grandchild and he is gracious and cordial in welcoming Cummings. Kruger says he knows no one by the name of Frank Fry. Kruger excuses himself to make a phone call while Cummings plays with the baby who picks up some mail just delivered to Kruger. One of the missives is a telegram, Cummings discovers, from Frank Fry. Kruger walks in just as Cummings is putting the letters back into Kruger's pocket. Cummings again asks the whereabouts of Frank Fry and Kruger tells him that he already knows, having read a telegram from Fry in Soda City. Cummings is perplexed, asking why a man of Kruger's wealth and prestige would be associated with a ruthless saboteur. Kruger smiles, lights his pipe, and tells him, "you have the makings of an outstanding boor." Cummings tells him he can't get away with his anti-American activities and that if he can't stop him others will. "A man like you can't last in a country like this." Kruger takes a puff on his pipe and says calmly: "Very pretty speech—youthful, passionate, idealistic." He tells him that he has already sent for the police and then adds: "Need I remind you that *you* are the fugitive from justice, not *I*. I'm a prominent citizen, widely respected. You are an obscure young workman wanted for the committing of an extremely unpopular crime. Now which of us do you think the police will believe?" Before the police arrive, Cummings makes a break, followed on horseback by Kruger's wranglers who lasso Cummings and turn him over to the police. Detectives drive Cummings along a mountain road and come to a bridge where Alper's truck is stalled. Cummings jumps from the police car and runs to the middle of the bridge, then, in handcuffs, leaps into the river, hiding beneath the rocky ledges of a nearby waterfall as detectives comb the area. Alper, who has recognized him, does him a good turn by shouting to the other detectives to follow the struggling body of a detective Cummings has pulled into the water and the fugitive escapes once more, exchanging a friendly wave with Alper. In a rainstorm, Cummings makes his way to the comfortable cottage of an elderly blind pianist, Glaser, who makes him welcome. Later, Glaser's niece, Lane, appears and immediately suspects Cummings of being the much wanted fugitive. Then she sees his handcuffs, but Glaser, who has heard the clanking of the handcuffs earlier, tells her that he doesn't believe Cummings is dangerous and that he is innocent because he can see "intangible things." He tells Lane to take Cummings to a local blacksmith where he can have the handcuffs removed. Once in the car, Lane tricks Cummings, looping his handcuffed arms over the steering wheel and tells him she's driving him to the police. Cummings jams down the accelerator and drives into the desert. When Cummings stops the car, Lane jumps out and tells him that she will stop the first car she sees. Cummings lifts the hood of the car and spreads the handcuffs over the fan belt ring and grinds the links away, then gets into the car and picks up Lane who has walked off and stopped another car. As they drive off, the woman in the other car smiles and says: "My, they must be terribly in love." The police later find the car abandoned on the desert road. Cummings and Lane wait for a lift farther down the road. They spot a caravan of slow-moving trucks and stop them. It turns out to be a carnival on the move and the sideshow performers take them into their cabin. Here they meet Siamese twins, who are always in conflict with each other, a bearded lady with her beard in curlers, a grumpy little midget, a fat lady, and a thin acrobat, de Cordoba, who is their spokesman. The performers look upon Lane and Cummings as young lovers until they hear police sirens and see the cuffs on Cummings. He tells them he's wanted for a crime he has not done. The performers are undecided about believing him but they vote and the majority agree to hide the couple. Lane has come to believe in Cummings' innocence but lets the performers express her feelings for her, later telling Cummings she is sorry for not believing in him. Hundreds of miles north, Cummings and Lane get off at a junction that takes them to Soda City, a western ghost town. Here, inside a shack, they find a shortwave radio and a telescope trained on Boulder Dam. They've uncovered a spy nest. They hear someone coming and Cummings hides Lane in a closet as Bevans and Baxter enter the shack. Cummings shows them his photo in the newspaper and insists that he has been sent there by Kruger and that they take care of him, that police heat is too great in the West. Baxter tells him he'll take Cummings back East. By the time they leave Lane has vanished. She goes to another town and tells a local sheriff, Halton, the whole story, and he promises to help. But Halton is in league with the saboteurs and he informs Kruger, who has Lane taken to New York. Baxter and Cummings drive to New York, and Baxter talks about his little boy smashing his toys to bits and how he doesn't want to cut his little boy's hair. He goes on to state dreamily how "when I was a child I had long blond curls. People used to stop on the street to admire me." Once in New York, Cummings is deposited at the mansion of millionairess Alma Kruger right in the middle of a charity ball she is throwing. Cummings finds Lane at the mansion and Kruger is also present, stating that he has been exposed and is now a refugee thanks to Cummings and Lane. Kruger goes on to explain to all the spies that Cummings is not one of their number, which gives Lane joy since she has, after being taken East as a prisoner, believed that Cummings was one of the saboteurs. Kruger announces that he's heading for Central America and Alma Kruger attends to a guest complaining about the catering service. Cummings uses this interruption to drag Lane out into the main ball room where he and she mingle with the guests, trying to explain that they are being held prisoner. Everywhere they look Kruger's men lurk with guns, standing in hallways, on balconies, behind curtains. Cummings approaches one distinguished man in a tuxedo and tells him that "this whole house is a hotbed of spies and saboteurs." The elderly gentleman looks at Cummings as if he were a stumblebum, saying he's "either crazy or drunk...you're not even dressed!" and moves away, affronted. Other guests think Cummings is kidding when he tries to tell them the truth about their hostess and her friends. Cummings and Lane dance on the main floor and she asks him what the spies are up to. "Right now," Cummings replies, "they're probably haggling over the price 'for us' with Murder Incorporated." Cummings kisses Lane and then she is whisked off by one of Kruger's spies to disappear into the crowd. Cummings later surrenders and goes upstairs to ask Kurger where he has taken Lane. The master spy tells Cummings that Lane has become Cumming's soft spot and has made him vulnerable, something he can't afford "when you're trying to *save* your country." Defiantly, Cummings says: "Why is it that you sneer every time you refer to this country? You've done pretty well here. I don't get it." Replies Kruger: "No, you wouldn't. You're one of the ardent believers–a good American. Oh, there are millions like you, people who plod along, without asking questions. I hate to use the word *stupid* but it seems to be the only one that applies. The great masses, the moron millions. Well, there are a few of us who are unwilling to just troop along, a few of us who are clever enough to see that there's much more to be done than just live small, complacent lives, a few of us in America who desire a more profitable type of government. When you think about it, Mr. Kane, the competence of totalitarian nations is much higher than ours. They get things done." "Yeah," responds Cummings, "they get things done. They bomb cities, sink ships, torture and murder so you and your friends can eat off gold plates. A great philosophy." Kruger ignores the remark and brags that he will come back some day and get what he wants: "Power, yes, I want that as much as you want your job, or that girl. We all have different tastes as you can see, only I'm willing to back my tastes with the necessary force." Cummings tells Kruger that millions believe as he does and that they will "win if it takes from now until the cows come home." Kruger, tired of the conversation, orders a butler standing by, Wolfe, to see that Cummings is put to sleep and with that Wolfe zaps Cummings into unconsciousness. Meanwhile, Baxter and other spies prepare to sink a battleship at the Brooklyn Navy Yards about to be launched, using a newsreel company as a front to get close enough to set off the charge. Baxter laconically states that "it's a shame to lose a good camera" even though hundreds will die. Lane is being held in a skyscraper office and Cummings in a basement room of the mansion but both manage to escape through clever ruses. Cummings discovers that the saboteurs are to blow up the battleship in about an hour and makes his way to the launching site. There he recognizes Lloyd in the newsreel truck and dives in after him, struggling with him as Lloyd tries to reach the button that will set off the bomb, his finger getting closer and closer, finally setting off the bomb, but too late as the bomb explodes only part of the launching pad the ship has already cleared. (Hitchcock shows the reaction of the crowd by running up the faces of horrified witnesses almost frame by slow frame, coming to a halt to show the ship safely sliding down the pad.) Meanwhile, Lloyd escapes and races into Radio City Music Hall where he runs behind a screen showing a movie. During a shootout on the screen Lloyd shoots it out with pursuing police in the theater, with several persons in the audience being shot. The audience panics and viewers dash for the exits, including Lloyd, who escapes in a taxi. Cummings tries to follow him but he is stopped by police. Lane follows Lloyd by cab after Cummings tells her Lloyd is escaping. Lloyd sits back in the cab and goes by the shipyards, looking with a sinister smile on the sight of the *Normandie*, sunk and on its side. He takes the ferry to the Statue of Liberty. There Lane, whom Lloyd does not know, makes a play for him and he responds to her when they are at the top of the statue, looking down from the windows in the statue's head. Lane engages Lloyd in conversation, reading to him from a brochure the stirring words of Emma Lazarus which are on the base of the statue. She stalls him long enough so that FBI agents pour onto the island. "They're coming for you," Lane tells him, and Lloyd pulls a gun, running down the spiral staircase. He climbs into the statue's arm and goes out onto the platform where the torch is held. Cummings arrives and chases Lloyd. On the platform he struggles with Lloyd who falls over the railing but catches hold of the statue's hand. Cummings climbs down to him, reaches out his hand, and grabs his coat sleeve as police prepare to throw down a rope. Lloyd looks up, terrified. He says, "I'll cling," but the threads of his coat begin to separate stitch by agonizing stitch at the shoulder as Hitchcock cuts to many different angles of the statue, as if it is about to shrug him off. The sleeve separates from the coat and Lloyd falls and falls and falls downward to his ignominious death while the horrified Cummings is left clutching an empty sleeve. Cummings climbs back up the hand to the platform where Lane awaits him. They embrace for the finale. SABOTEUR ends as it began, with a spectacular scene, one which shows justice and freedom triumphant over evil and tyranny. Though its characters are sharply drawn as black and white, good and bad guys, the film offers one exciting scene after another with Hitchcock using his cameras brilliantly to encompass the vastness of America. At some times he placed his cameras as far away from his actors as a mile, using a telescopic lens to show the tiny figures and the overwhelming landscape of the West. This was a technical masterpiece as well, with the director ordering more than 1,000 scenes and requiring 4,500 camera setups. This was the first of many Hitchcock films to use monuments and historical sites to thoroughly identify the majestic aspects of the chase–Boulder Dam, Radio City Music Hall (where most of Hitchcock's films premiered), the Statue of Liberty. The end of evildoer Lloyd on the Statue of Liberty was an incredible visual, the saboteur's fall achieved by his falling a short distance and then telescoping backward backward rapidly to increase the appearance of Lloyd's depth of fall. The stars of this film were not Hitchcock's choices, despite the fact that he was promised by Universal that he would decide on all casting. He wanted Gary Cooper to play the victimized factory worker and Barbara Stanwyck to play the girl who falls in love with him. Both stars said no and he was more or less assigned pleasant but comic-faced Cummings and plump Lane. He did the best he could with what was available and that was excellent. Kruger played a menacing heavy but Hitchcock wanted Harry Carey, Sr. to play the masterspy, thinking this kindly faced man, the hero of every school boy in America, would be the perfect two-faced villain. Mrs. Carey exploded at the very thought of her husband enacting such a hideous part and she answered Hitchcock for her husband, saying that since the death of Will Rogers her husband was the number one idol of every child in America. It was out of the question. As usual Hitchcock spent lavishly on this production, creating the New York mansion for $45,000 on Universal's enormous back lot and much more on the reproductions of the Statue of Liberty's head and outstretched arm and hand holding the torch, albeit the director masked the rest of the statue beneath these massive sets. He shot most of the film at Universal but did take his cast and crew to certain western sites and New York. What caused him trouble, similar to that with the FBI concerning atom bomb ingredients mentioned in NOTORIOUS, was his inclusion of short newsreel footage showing the *S.S. Normandie* which had been renamed the *U.S.S. Lafayette* and was to have been used as a troop transport, a ship which had suddenly suffered a mysterious fire which caused her to capsize on a Manhattan pier on February 9, 1942. "I cut to the hulk of the *Normandie*," the director later stated. "I cut back to a closeup of the saboteur, who, after staring at the wreck, turns around with a slightly smug smile on his face. The Navy raised hell with Universal about these shots because I implied that the *Normandie* had been sabotaged, which was a reflection on their lack of vigilance in guarding it." Over the objections of the Navy, the shot was kept in the movie and can be seen to this day. There is no doubt that the Navy's original assumption was correct.

p, Frank Lloyd, Jack H. Skirball; d, Alfred Hitchcock; w, Peter Viertel, Joan Harrison, Dorothy Parker (based on an original story by Hitchcock); ph, Joseph Valentine; m, Charles Previn, Frank Skinner; ed, Otto Ludwig; art d, Jack Otterson.

Spy   **Cas.**   **(PR:A MPAA:NR)**

SABOTEUR, CODE NAME MORITURI   (SEE: MORITURI, 1965)

SABRA**½   (1970, Fr./Ital./Israel) 100m
Comacico-Israfilm-Fonoroma-Copernic/Ci ne Globe (AKA: DEATH OF A JEW)

Akim Tamiroff (*Inspector Mehdaloun*), Assaf Dayan (*David Shimon*), Jean Claudio (*Kassik*), Azaria Rappaport (*Doctor*).

Two Israeli spies are caught bugging an Arab phone exchange. One is killed outright and the other, Dayan, is tortured to reveal his accomplices. When these measures have failed, he is turned over to Tamiroff, a kindly, aging police inspector who tries kindness, even taking the youthful spy into his home. Finally, the boy softens and agrees to give Tamiroff the names if he lets him escape. Tamiroff agrees and at the border Dayan makes a run for it. He is shot dead by Tamiroff's superiors, who have had their distrusting eyes on the policeman and his prisoner all the time. Tamiroff cries when he learns that the list of names Dayan gave him were false. A simple and well-meaning film. (In English.)

d, Denys de la Patelliere; w, Vahe Katcha, de la Patelliere (based on a novel by Katcha); ph, Alain Levent (Eastmancolor); ed, Claude Durand.

Spy Drama   **(PR:C MPAA:PG)**

SABRE AND THE ARROW, THE
         (SEE: LAST OF THE COMANCHES, THE, 1952)

SABRE JET*½   (1953) 96m UA c

Robert Stack (*Col. Gil Manton*), Coleen Gray (*Jane Carter*), Richard Arlen (*Gen. Robert E. Hale*), Julie Bishop (*Mrs. Marge Hale*), Leon Ames (*Lt. Col. Eckert*), Amanda Blake (*Helen Daniel*), Reed Sherman (*Lt. Crane*), Tom Irish (*Lt. Bill Crenshaw*), Michael Moore (*Sgt. Klinger*), Lucille Knoch (*Lee Crane*), Kathleen Crowley (*Susan Crenshaw*), Jerry Paris (*Capt. Bert Flanagan*), Jan Shepard (*Betty Flanagan*), Ray Montgomery (*Maj. James Daniel*), Johnny Sands (*Sgt. Cosgrove*), Frank Kamagi (*Fuji*).

American jet pilots headed by Stack fly missions during the Korean conflict and find as many problems back at the base as in the air. With the wives living with their husbands on the base, the stress of the daily waiting begins to be too much for some couples. Stack is married to reporter Gray, and wants her to quit her job to wait every day with the other wives. In the end, she gives up her reporter job. Most of the action sequences are stock footage from the war, but the pilots and wives' stories are simplistic and melodramatic.

p, Carl Krueger; d, Louis King; w, Dale Eunson, Katherine Albert (based on a story by Krueger); ph, Charles Van Enger (Cinecolor); m, Herschel Burke Gilbert; ed, Arthur Nadel; art d, Jerry Pycha, Jr.

War Drama   **(PR:A MPAA:NR)**

SABRINA****   (1954) 112m PAR bw (GB: SABRINA FAIR)

Humphrey Bogart (*Linus Larrabee*), Audrey Hepburn (*Sabrina Fairchild*), William Holden (*David Larrabee*), Walter Hampden (*Oliver Larrabee*), John Williams (*Thomas Fairchild*), Martha Hyer (*Elizabeth Tyson*), Joan Vohs (*Gretchen Van Horn*), Marcel Dalio (*Baron*), Marcel Hillaire (*The Professor*), Nella Walker (*Maude Larrabee*), Francis X. Bushman (*Mr. Tyson*), Ellen Corby (*Miss McCardle*), Marjorie Bennett (*Margaret the Cook*), Emory Parnell (*Charles the Butler*), Kay Riehl (*Mrs. Tyson*), Nancy Kulp (*Jenny the Maid*), Kay Kuter (*Houseman*), Paul Harvey (*Doctor*), Emmett Vogan, Colin Campbell (*Board Members*), Harvey Dunn (*Man with Tray*), Marion Ross (*Spiller's Girl*), Charles Harvey (*Spiller*), Greg Stafford (*Man with David*), Bill Neff (*Man with Linus*), Otto Forrest (*Elevator Operator*), David Ahdar (*Ship Steward*), Rand Harper.

Three recent Oscar winners and the sure guidance of Wilder helped make this familiar Cinderella story into something more than it might have been under other auspices. Holden was 36 at the time, a bit ancient to convince us he was a dissolute playboy. Further, he was more than eclipsed by

Bogart's performance as his older brother, an unaccustomed comedy role that showed Bogie could play for laughs as well as sneers. Wilder had already won an Oscar and co-author Lehman was to be the recipient of the coveted statuette later, so this was a formidable team. The story isn't much but it's the treatment and the witty dialog that set it apart from the ordinary. Holden and Bogart are the sons of Hampden and Walker, two very rich people in the Long Island horsey set. Holden is the devilish one who lives for fast cars and faster women, while Bogart is the hard-headed businessman who has inherited his father's acumen. Also living on the estate (which was the real Glen Cove acreage owned by Barney Balaban, the president of Paramount) are Williams, the chauffeur, and his young, impressionable daughter, Hepburn. Hepburn is mad about Holden, who only thinks of her as a slightly addled adolescent and pays just enough attention to make her think there might be a chance. When Hepburn realizes that Holden is only toying with her, she attempts suicide by turning on the ignitions of eight of the family cars in the garage and inhaling the exhaust. After she is rescued, Williams sends her to France where she attends a Parisian school to learn the chef's trade. Once in France, Hepburn meets Dalio, an aged and kindly baron who finds her naivete charming and performs a Pygmalion to her Galatea, thereby transforming the sweet young thing into a sophisticated woman who knows the right clothes to wear, the right wine to drink, and who automatically says the right things for all occasions. In the U.S., Bogart seeks to enhance the family's wealth by marrying Holden off to Hyer, an heiress to yet another huge fortune overseen by her father, Bushman. Hepburn returns to Long Island, and once Holden gets a look at and listen to this new version, he falls madly in love with her, despite his engagement to Hyer. Hepburn is determined to win Holden, who has been the man of her dreams for so long, but Bogart and Hampden realize that Holden must marry Hyer, as it would be in the family's best interests. Bogart tells Hepburn she would be wise to keep out of Holden's grasp but she won't hear of it. In order to get her mind off Holden, bachelor Bogart pretends to be courting her. Bogart has been concentrating on business for so many years that Hampden wonders if his eldest son can still hold a conversation with a woman that's not about loans or debentures. Bogart assures him that he can and reverts to his youth by donning an old Yale sweater and reaching for a phonograph and the one record he owns, a copy of "Yes, We Have No Bananas" (Frank Silver, Irving Conn). Bogart manages to talk Hepburn aboard an ocean liner and promises her that he'll be on board. What he really wants to do is get her out of the way so she won't foul up the marriage plans of Holden and Hyer. It's only when Holden points out to his older brother that the truth is that Bogart loves Hepburn and should admit it, that Bogart wakes up. He races to the dock, hires a tugboat, and makes it to the ocean liner before it clears the port. Bogart and Hepburn are united, much to the surprise of anyone who thought the younger, more handsome brother would nab the female star. A charming, if often-seen, tale, paced with alacrity by Wilder from the adaptation of Taylor's hit play which had starred Margaret Sullavan. This was a resounding hit at the box office and with the critics and proved that silk purses were still possible from less than perfect sources. Bogart had been making movies for more than two decades and this was his first effort for Paramount. He and Wilder did not get along and had differing views of what was funny. Whoever won those battles will never be known but the results were satisfying, as Bogart was played drawing-room comedy with aplomb.

p&d, Billy Wilder; w, Wilder, Samuel Taylor, Ernest Lehman (based on the play "Sabrina Fair" by Taylor); ph, Charles Lang, Jr.; m, Frederick Hollander; ed, Arthur Schmidt; art d, Hal Pereira, Walter Tyler; set d, Sam Comer, Ray Moyer; cos, Edith Head; spec eff, John P. Fulton, Farciot Edouart; m/l, Wilson Stone, Richard Rodgers, Lorenz Hart, Harold Lewis, John Cope; makeup, Wally Westmore.

Comedy   **Cas.**   **(PR:A MPAA:NR)**

SABRINA FAIR   (SEE: SABRINA, 1954)

SABU AND THE MAGIC RING*   (1957) 61m AA c

Sabu, Daria Massey, Robert Shafto, Peter Mamakos, John Doucette, William Marshall, George Khoury, Vladimir Sokoloff, Robin Morse, Bernie Rich, Kenneth Terrell, John Lomma.

Sabu gets hold of a genie in this ripoff of THE THIEF OF BAGHDAD. The film is really an unsuccessful TV series that never made it to the tube and was edited for local movie theaters. Marshall is the black genie who gives Sabu a hand in getting rid of the bad guys.

p, Maurice Duke; d, George Blair; w, Sam Roeca; ph, Harry Neumann; m, Harry Sukman; ed, William Austin; art d, David Milton; cos, Eileen Younger.

Adventure   **(PR:A MPAA:NR)**

SACCO AND VANZETTI***   (1971, Ital./Fr.) 120m
Jolly-Unidis-Theatre Le Rex/UMC c (SACCO E VANZETTI)

Gian Maria Volonte (*Bartolomeo Vanzetti*), Riccardo Cucciolla (*Nicola Sacco*), Cyril Cusack (*Frederick Katzmann*), Milo O'Shea (*Fred Moore*), Geoffrey Keen (*Judge Webster Thayer*), William Prince (*William Thompson*), Rosanna Fratello (*Rosa Sacco*), Claude Mann (*Journalist*), Edward

Jeuesbury, Armenia Balducci, Valentino Orfeo, Lewis Ciannelli, Piero
Archisi, Desdemond Perry, John Harvey, Felicity Mason, Marisa Fabbri,
Maria Grazia Marescalchi, Paul Sheriff, Anthony Stergar, William Kenn,
John Gray, Claudio Sora, Sergio Serafini, Giorgio Dolfini, Giacomo Piperno,
Giorgio Paoletti, Franco Odoardi, Raimondo Penne, Carlo Sabatini, Raffaele
Triggia, Page Jones, Romano Moschini, Charles Crowder, Riccardo Ven-
tura, William Packer, Francesco Conversi, Luchiano Palermo.

The American judicial system has a long and spotted history of convicting
and executing those whose political views defy the status quo. One of the
most notorious such trials was that of Sacco and Vanzetti, two Italian
immigrants and admitted anarchists who were convicted and sent to the
electric chair as a result of the 1920s red scare. This English-dubbed version
of the tale accurately portrays the facts, with clear sympathy shown towards
the two defendants. Cucciolla and Volonte (the latter from A FISTFUL OF
DOLLARS and FOR A FEW DOLLARS MORE) portray the duo, who are
brought up on charges of murder when two employees of a shoe store are
killed in a robbery. After a sham trial in which Cucciolla and Volonte are
tried more for their politics than for the actual crime, they are found guilty
and sentenced to death. The case causes worldwide commotion as literally
thousands of people rally behind them over the course of the next six years.
However, despite overwhelming evidence of their innocence, Cucciolla and
Volonte are executed on August 23, 1927. Though overall an impressive and
accurate retelling of this miscarriage of justice, the film is not without its
faults. The major problem is length. Considering the scope of actual time and
the myriad events that took place over those seven years, two hours is
simply insufficient for the story. Worst of all is an annoying theme song by
Joan Baez which is packed with such insincere (and ultimately condescend-
ing) lyrics as, "Here's to you, Sacco and Bart/Something, something forever
in my heart." The film is at its strongest when allowed to simply speak for
itself. This is a story fraught with natural emotion, portrayed with sincerity
and genuine sympathy for its doomed heros. In the end, SACCO AND
VANZETTI becomes an eloquent portrait of two simple men swept up in the
fury of political self-righteousness; a portrait which is not flattering to the
American way of justice, to say the least.

p, Arrigo [Harry] Colombo, Giorgio Papi; d, Giuliano Montaldo; w, Montal-
do, Fabrizio Onofri, Ottavio Jemma; ph, Silvano Ippoliti (Technicolor); m,
Ennio Morricone; ed, Nino Baragli; art d, Aurelio Crugnola; cos, Enrico
Sabatini; m/l, "The Ballad of Sacco and Vanzetti," Morricone, Joan Baez.

Historical Drama   **Cas.**   **(PR:C MPAA:GP)**

SACRED FLAME, THE*½   (1929) 65m WB bw

Conrad Nagel (Col. Maurice Taylor), Lila Lee (Stella Taylor), Pauline
Frederick (Mrs. Taylor), William Courtenay (Maj. Laconda), Walter Byron
(Colin Taylor), Alec B. Francis (Dr. Harvester), Dale Fuller (Nurse Wayland).

Early talky adapted from W. Somerset Maugham's play which suffers from
the inexperience of the director's handling of dialog. The film is no more
than a stiff rendition of the stage play. Some of the major problems at the
time were the cumbersome soundproof cameras and stationary micro-
phones that limited actors' movement. Nagel plays a WW I vet crippled in
a plane crash on the day of his wedding to Lee. The veteran is confined to
a wheelchair and his wife begins an affair with his brother, Byron.
Frederick, Nagel's mother, ends her crippled son's life so he won't discover
what has been going on behind his back.

d, Archie L. Mayo; w, Harvey Thew (based on the play by W. Somerset
Maugham); ph, James Van Trees; ed, James Gaibbou; titles, De Leon
Anthony.

Drama   **(PR:A MPAA:NR)**

SACRED FLAME, THE, 1935   (SEE: RIGHT TO LIVE, THE, 1935)

SACRED KNIVES OF VENGEANCE, THE*
                    (1974, Hong Kong) 94m WB c (AKA: THE KILLER)

Chin Han (Ma I), Wang Ping (Yu Chiao), Tsung Hua (Hsieh Chun), Ku Feng
(Ruffian), Ching Miao (Wang), Yang Che Ching (Yun), Chiang Nan (Chiao),
Cheng Lei (Kao), Li Hao (Jen).

Mundane chop-socky about a couple of brothers who stop the feuding
between themselves to combat much more threatening evils existing in their
village. Not only do these two guys have some very nimble feet, but they
throw knives too. The appearance of martial arts expert Tsung Hua was an
attempt to find a successor to the famed Bruce Lee, but Tsung was not to
have this throne.

p, Run Run Shaw; d, Chu Yuan; w, Kuo Chia; ph, Wu Cho-hua (Technicolor);
m, Chen Yung-shu; ed, Chiang Hsing-Lung; art d, Chen Ching Shen.

Martial Arts   **(PR:O MPAA:R)**

SACRIFICE OF HONOR**   (1938, Fr.) 80m Imperial/Tri-National bw
                                          (SACRIFICE D'HONNEUR)

Annabella (Jeanne de Corlaix), Victor Francen (Capt. de Corlaix), Signoret
(Adm. Morbraz), Robert Vidalin (Lt. d'Artelle), Pierre Renoir (Comdr.
Brambourg), Roland Toutain (Leduc), Rosine Derean (Alice).

An engaging tale that has a sea captain (Francen) attempt to save his
battleship from an attack by an enemy cruiser and then to save his honor
in a court martial. The film moves slowly through the battle scenes and picks
up pace as Annabella, who is having an affair with a younger officer, plays
a more prominent part in the story. It climaxes at Francen's court martial
with Annabella's indiscreet activities enabling her to testify in his favor and
save his rank. (In French; English Subtitles.)

d, Marcel L'Herbier; w, L'Herbier, Charles Spaak (based on a story by
Claude Farrere, Lucien Nepoty); m, Jean Lenoir; ed, Forrest Izard.

Drama   **(PR:A MPAA:NR)**

SAD HORSE, THE**½   (1959) 78m FOX c

David Ladd (Jackie Connors), Chill Wills (Capt. Connors), Rex Reason (Bill
MacDonald), Patrice Wymore (Leslie MacDonald), Gregg Palmer (Bart
Connors), Leslie Bradley (Jonas), David De Paul (Sam), Eve Brent (Sheila),
William Yip (Ben).

Wymore owns a horse that has a dog for its best friend and when the dog
is lost, the nag goes into a deep depression. Young Ladd comes to his
grandfather's ranch while the boy's father remarries. The dog and Ladd
have a run-in with a rattlesnake and a puma, and then they meet Wymore
and her horse. Ladd's dog and the horse become instant friends and the
horse is lifted out of it's depression. Wymore begs the boy to give her the
dog and in the end Ladd realizes that it would be best if his dog stayed with
its new companion.

p, Richard E. Lyons; d, James B. Clark; w, Charles Hoffman (based on a story
by Zoe Akins); ph, Karl Struss (CinemaScope, DeLuxe Color); m, Paul
Sawtell, Bert Shefter; ed, Richard C. Meyer; m/l, Walter Kent, Tom Walton.

Drama   **(PR:AA MPAA:NR)**

SAD SACK, THE***   (1957) 98m PAR bw

Jerry Lewis (Bixby), David Wayne (Dolan), Phyllis Kirk (Maj. Shelton),
Peter Lorre (Abdul), Joe Mantell (Pvt. Stan Wenaslawsky), Gene Evans (Sgt.
Pulley), George Dolenz (Ali Mustapha), Liliane Montevecchi (Zita), Shep-
perd Strudwick (Gen. Vanderlip), Abraham Sofaer (Hassim), Mary Treen
(Sgt. Hansen), Drew Cahill (Lt. Wilson), Michael G. Ansara (Moki), Don
Haggerty (Capt. Ward), Jean Del Val (French General), Dan Seymour (Arab
Chieftain), Yvette Vickers (Hazel).

Based on the famous cartoon character, Lewis plays the bumbling hero with
two left feet, only this time he's gifted with a photographic memory. When
he throws the whole base he's stationed at into chaos, he's transferred to
Morocco to guard the army's new secret weapon. There, Lewis falls in love
with cafe singer Montevecchi but, as usual, he mistakenly believes she
wants nothing to do with him. Heartbroken, he deserts the army to join the
french Foreign Legion. In typical Lewis fashion, he hooks up with a band
of renegade Arabs led by Lorre, who have stolen a weapon but are at a loss
on how to assemble it. When they discover that Lewis has memorized the
instruction manual, they pretend to be the Foreign Legion and talk Lewis
into helping them put it together. The army, guided by Montevecchi, arrives
soon after to rescue Lewis. He's made a hero but is soon messing up again,
and it doesn't take long for the private to be back on K.P. duty. This was
Lewis' second film without ex-partner Martin. He was so successful at the
box office that most of the critics wondered aloud what he ever needed
Martin for in the first place.

p, Hal B. Wallis; d, George Marshall; w, Edmund Beloin, Nate Monaster
(based on the cartoon character by George Baker); ph, Loyal Griggs (Vista
Vision); m, Walter Scharf; ed, Archie Marshek; md, Scharf; art d, Hal
Pereira, John Goodman; cos, Edith Head; ch, Charles O'Curran; m/l "The
Sad Sack," Hal David, Burt F. Bacharach .

Comedy   **Cas.**   **(PR:A MPAA:NR)**

SAD SACK, THE, 1963   (SEE: ARMY GAME, THE, 1963, Fr.)

SADDLE BUSTER, THE*½   (1932) 59m RKO-Pathe bw

Tom Keene, Helen Foster, Charles Quigley, Ben Corbett, Fred Burns, Marie
Quillan, Richard Carlyle, Robert Frazer, Harry Bowen, Al Taylor, Charles
"Slim" Whitaker, .

Keene is a cowboy on the rodeo circuit who is almost killed by a wild bronco
named Black Pearl. This incident causes him to give up riding because he's
too afraid to get on another horse. In the end, Keene jumps back on "Black
Pearl, wins prize money to pay the hospital bills of a friend injured by the
animal, and wins Foster. These Keene westerns were so low-budget that it
was nearly impossible for them not to turn a profit. SADDLE BUSTER was
made for $38,000 and made a profit of $25,000.

d, Fred Allen; w, Oliver Drake (based on a story by Cherry Wilson); ph, Ted
McCord; ed, William Clements; md, Arthur Lange; art d, Carroll Clark.

Western   **(PR:A MPAA:NR)**

SADDLE LEGION   (1951) 61m RKO bw

Tim Holt (*Dave Saunders*), Dorothy Malone (*Dr. Ann Rollins*), Robert Livingston (*Regan*), Mauritz Hugo (*Kelso*), James Bush (*Gabe*), Movita Castaneda (*Mercedes*), Cliff Clark (*Warren*), Stanley Andrews (*Chief Layton*), George Lewis (*Rurales Captain*), Dick Foote (*Sandy*), Bob Wilke (*Hooker*), Richard Martin (*Chito Rafferty*).

Holt and Martin are cowboys on Clark's ranch. When cattle inspector Livingston tells the rancher that his herd has blackleg disease, Holt becomes suspicious. With the help of doctor Malone, the cowboys discover that Livingston is using the disease as a scam to rustle ranchers' herds. The inspector and his gang take the cattle under the pretense they are to be killed, and sell them in Mexico. Holt saves Clark's herd and brings the rustlers to justice after a fair amount of chases and gunfights. Livingston, one of the original "Three Mesquiteers," does a turnaround here and plays a bad guy.

p, Herman Schlom; d, Lesley Selander; w, Ed Earl Repp; ph, J. Roy Hunt; m, C. Bakaleinikoff; ed, Desmond Marquette; art d, Albert S. D'Agostino.

Western   **(PR:A   MPAA:NR)**

SADDLE MOUNTAIN ROUNDUP   (1941) 60m MON bw

Ray Corrigan (*Crash*), John King (*Dusty*), Max Terhune (*Alibi*), Lita Conway (*Nancy*), Jack Mulhall (*Freeman*), Willie Fung (*Fang Way*), John Elliott (*"Magpie" Harper*), George Chesebro (*Blackie*), Jack Holmes (*Sheriff*), Steve Clark (*Henderson*), Carl Mathews (*Bill*), Cousin Herald Goodman (*Himself*), Al Ferguson, Slim Whitaker, Tex Palmer.

The Range Busters, Corrigan, King, and Terhune (the comedian of the trio), are driving old man Elliott's cattle to be sold when they get a message from him saying that his life and money are in danger. Corrigan and King race back to the ranch, where they find Elliott murdered. At this point the western turns into a murder mystery, and everyone associated with Elliott is a suspect. The Range Busters play detective and unmask lawyer Mulhall as the culprit. (See RANGE BUSTERS series, Index.)

p, George W. Weeks; d, S. Roy Luby; w, William L. Nolte. ph, Robert Cline; m, Frank Sanucci; ed, Ray Claire.

Western   **(PR:A   MPAA:NR)**

SADDLE PALS   (1947) 72m REP bw

Gene Autry (*Gene*), Lynne Roberts (*Shelly Brooks*), Sterling Holloway (*Waldo T. Brooks, Jr.*), Iving Bacon (*Thaddeus Bellweather*), Damian O'Flynn (*Brad Collins*), Charles Arnt (*William Schooler*), Jean Van (*Robin Brooks*), Tom London (*Dad Gardner*), Charles Williams (*Leslie*), Francis McDonald (*Sheriff*), George Chandler (*Dippy*), Edward Gargan (*Jailer*), Cass Country Boys, Carl Sepulveda, Paul E. Burns, Joel Friedkin, LeRoy Mason, Larry Steers, Edward Keane, Maurice Cass, Nolan Leary, Minerva Urecal, John S. Roberts, James Carlisle, Sam Ash, Frank O'Connor, Neal Hart, Frank Henry, Edward Piel, Sr, Bob Burns, Joe Yrigoyen, Johnny Day, Champion, Jr. the Horse.

This Autry western is full of singing cowboys but lacks the standard amount of western action. Holloway is a wealthy land owner who has someone trying to drive him into bankruptcy. Autry arrives on the scene, and Holloway asks him to uncover the bad guys. Songs sung by Autry include "I Wish I Had Never Met Sunshine," "Amapola," "You Stole My Heart." The Cass Country Boys croon "Which Way Did They Go", "The Covered Wagon Rolled Right Along." (See GENE AUTRY Series, Index.)

p, Sidney Picker; d, Lesley Selander; w, Bob Williams, Jerry Sackheim (based on a story by Dorrell and Stuart E. McGowan); ph, Bud Thackery; ed, Harry Keller; md, Morton Scott; art d, Fred Ritter; m/l, Harry Sosnik, Stanley Adams, Ray Allen, Perry Botkin, Britt Wood, Hy Heath, Gene Autry.

Western   **(PR:A   MPAA:NR)**

SADDLE THE WIND   (1958) 84m MGM c

Robert Taylor (*Steve Sinclair*), Julie London (*Joan Blake*), John Cassavetes (*Tony Sinclair*), Donald Crisp (*Mr. Deneen*), Charles McGraw (*Larry Venables*), Royal Dano (*Clay Ellison*), Richard Erdman (*Dallas Hansen*), Douglas Spencer (*Hamp Scribner*), Ray Teal (*Brick Larson*), Jay Adler (*Hank*), Stanley Adams, Nacho Galindo, Irene Tedrow.

Taylor, an ex-gunfighter enjoying a peaceful existence on his ranch, finds his life suddenly turned upside down when kid brother Cassavetes arrives. Cassavetes, who has brought dance hall girl London and a gun along, proceeds to get himself and his brother in a peck of trouble when his temper and quick draw result in killing a man who has threatened Taylor. Enjoying the power a gun gives him, he terrorizes a group of squatters and this brings a visit from landowner Crisp, who wants Taylor and his unstable brother to leave before there is any more killing. Instead, Cassavetes gets into a gun fight with Crisp's men and is wounded. Taylor goes out to find his brother but before he can help him Cassavetes shoots himself. A solid western that takes few chances, but overall finely done and entertaining.

p, Armand Deutsch; d, Robert Parrish; w, Rod Serling (based on the screen story by Thomas Thompson); ph, George J. Folsey (CinemaScope, Metrocolor); m, Jeff Alexander; ed, John McSweeney, Jr.; art d, William A. Horning, Malcolm Brown; set d, Henry Grace, Otto Siegel; cos, Helen Rose; m/l, "Saddle the Wind," Jay Livingston, Ray Evans (sung by Julie London).

Western   **(PR:A   MPAA:NR)**

SADDLE TRAMP   (1950) 77m UNIV c

Joel McCrea (*Chuck Conner*), Wandra Hendrix (*Della*), John Russell (*Rocky*), John McIntire (*Hess Higgins*), Jeanette Nolan (*Ma Higgins*), Russell Simpson (*Pop*), Ed Begley, Jimmy Hunt, Orley Lindgren, Gordon Gebert, Gregory Moffett, Antonio Moreno, John Ridgely, Walter Coy, Joaquin Garay, Peter Leeds, Michael Steele, Paul Picerni.

McCrea is a carefree cowboy who inherits four kids after their father, a friend of McCrea, dies. He also takes on Hendrix, who has run away from her vicious uncle. The cowboy has his hands full keeping his employer, who dislikes children, from discovering the little ones, while trying to feed and tend to them. On top of that, there's a land war going on between his boss and another rancher, and McCrea finds himself caught in the middle of it. An enjoyable family western, thanks to McCrea's charm and a witty script.

p, Leonard Goldstein; d, Hugo Fregonese; w, Harold Shumate; ph, Charles P. Boyle (Technicolor); m, Joseph Gershenson; ed, Frank Gross; art d, Bernard Herzbrun, Richard H. Riedel.

Western   **(PR:A   MPAA:NR)**

SADDLEMATES   (1941) 56m REP bw

Robert Livingston (*Stony Brooke*), Bob Steele (*Tucson Smith*), Rufe Davis (*Lullaby Joslin*), Gale Storm (*Susan Langley*), Forbes Murray (*Col. Langley*), Cornelius Keefe (*Lt. Manning*), Peter George Lynn (*LeRoque/Wanechee*), Marin Sais (*Mrs. Langley*), Matty Faust (*Thunder Bird*), Glenn Strange (*Little Bear*), Ellen Lowe (*Aunt Amanda*), Iron Eyes Cody (*Black Eagle*), Chief Yowlachie, Bill Hazlett, Henry Wills, Maj. Bill Keefer.

The Three Mesquiteers, Livingston, Steele and Davis, become Army scouts to help hunt down Indian chief Lynn. The trio gets thrown in the stockade for getting into a fight with an Army interpreter, who turns out to be Lynn. The Mesquiteers and the U.S. Cavalry arrive at the last minute to save a wagon train from Lynn and his braves. (See THREE MESQUITEERS series, Index.)

p, Louis Gray; d, Lester Orlebeck; w, Albert DeMond, Herbert Dalmasx (based on an original screen story by Bernard McConville, Karen DeWolf, and characters created by William Colt MacDonald); ph, William Nobles; m, Cy Feuer; ed, Tony Martinelli.

Western   **(PR:A   MPAA:NR)**

SADIE MCKEE   (1934) 90m MGM bw

Joan Crawford (*Sadie McKee*), Gene Raymond (*Tommy Wallace*), Franchot Tone (*Michael Alderson*), Esther Ralston (*Dolly*), Edward Arnold (*Jack Brennon*), Earl Oxford (*Stooge*), Jean Dixon (*Opal*), Leo Carroll (*Phelps*), Akim Tamiroff (*Riccori*), Zelda Sears (*Mrs. Craney*), Helen Ware (*Mrs. McKee*), Gene Austin, Candy & Coco (*Cafe Entertainers*), Charles Williams (*Cafe Pest*), Mary Forbes (*Mrs. Alderson*), Francis MacDonald, Lee Phelps (*Chauffeurs*), Harry Bradley (*Dr. Taylor*), Wyndham Standing (*Butler at Alderson House*), Minerva Urecal (*Cook's Assistant at Brennon Home*), Ethel Griffies (*Woman in Subway*).

A well-crafted melodrama featuring Crawford as a maid working in the home of a wealthy family that also employs her mother, Ware, as the cook. Though encouraged by her mother to engage in a coy flirtation with the heir to the family fortune, Tone (her soon-to-be third husband), Crawford really loves Raymond, a ne'er-do-well who works in the local factory. When Raymond is fired from his job, he deserts Crawford and moves to New York City. Unable to face life without her love, Crawford follows Raymond to the big city. Upon her arrival, she discovers that Raymond has taken up with vaudevillian sweetie Ralston and has no intention of continuing their relationship. Crushed, Crawford decides to stay in New York and make the best of it. She lands a job in a nightclub and there meets kindly, alcoholic millionaire Arnold, who falls in love with her and asks her to marry him. Though she does not love him, Crawford marries Arnold out of convenience and settles down to a miserable life. Meanwhile, Raymond has slipped into a pattern of self-destruction which has begun to consume him. Learning that he is seriously ill, Crawford, who still loves him, goes to Raymond and he dies in her arms. Feeling hopeless, Crawford resigns herself to a loveless existence with Arnold. Luckily, Tone arrives on the scene and re-establishes his relationship with her. At the end Crawford realizes that she has loved Tone since the days she worked in his home as a maid and she decides to divorce Arnold to pursue true happiness. While the plot is pure hokum, SADIE MCKEE is filmed and acted with a professional flair that elevates the material. Crawford is fine as the near-tragic small town girl looking for love, but Arnold steals the movie with his detailed, sympathetic portrayal of a happy but pathetic alcoholic. Fans of director Frank Capra who fondly remember Arnold's villainous performances in MR. SMITH GOES TO WASHINGTON (1939) and MEET JOHN DOE (1941) will find his moving performance a revelation.

p, Lawrence Weingarten; d, Clarence Brown; w, John Meehan (based on the story "Pretty Sadie McKee" by Vina Delmar); ph, Oliver T. Marsh; ed, Hugh Wynn; cos, Adrian; m/l, "All I Do Is Dream of You," Arthur Freed, Nacio Herb Brown. (sung by Gene Raymond).

Drama (PR:A MPAA:NR)

SADIST, THE*½ (1963) 95m Fairway-International bw (AKA: THE PROFILE OF TERROR)

Arch Hall, Jr (*Charley Tibbs*), Helen Hovey (*Doris Page*), Richard Alden (*Ed Stiles*), Marilyn Manning (*Judy Bradshaw*), Don Russell (*Carl Oliver*).

An innocent trip to Dodger Stadium ends up a terrifying nightmare for three naive teachers. After their car breaks down, they come across what appears to be a deserted garage, only to be captured by psychopathic killer Hall and his companion, Manning. After discovering their occupations, Hall kills Russell because of his hatred of teachers. Hall also kills two policemen, and in the confusion Alden blinds him with gasoline. Manning is killed by Hall, who then hunts down and shoots Alden. Hovey, the only survivor of the ordeal, becomes Hall's next target and is on the brink of insanity. She escapes when Hall falls into a pit of rattlesnakes. Plenty of bloodshed. First-rate photography by Zsigmond.

p, L. Steven Snyder; d&w, James Landis; ph, William [Vilmos] Zsigmond; ed, Anthony M. Lanza; md, Rod Moss; art d, Mark Von Berblinger; makeup, Lynn Noonkester.

Horror (PR:A MPAA:NR)

SADKO (SEE: MAGIC VOYAGE OF SINBAD, THE, 1962, USSR)

SAFARI*½ (1940) 80m PAR bw

Madeleine Carroll (*Linda Stewart*), Douglas Fairbanks, Jr (*Jim Logan*), Tullio Carminati (*Baron de Courland*), Muriel Angelus (*Fay Thorne*), Lynne Overman (*Jock McPhall*), Billy Gilbert (*Mondehare, Trader*), Thomas Louden (*Dr. Phillip's*), Clinton Rosemond (*Mike*), Jack Carr (*Wamba*), Frank Godoy (*Steward*), Fredrik Vogeding, Hans Von Morhart, Darby Jones, Henry Rowland, George Melford, James Davis, Al Duval, John B. Washington, Hasson Said, Maj. Sam Harris, Jeffe Graves, Ernest Wilson, Mme. Sul-Te-Wan, Ben Carter.

Fairbanks portrays an American adventurer hired by millionaire Carminati and his fiance, Carroll, to lead them on a hunting expedition into the jungle. The typical love triangle develops as Carroll longs for the adventuresome type she once loved. Discovering money and security aren't everything, she follows her heart and ends up in the arms of Fairbanks.

p, Anthony Veiller; d, Edward H. Griffith; w, Delmer Daves based on a story by Paul Hervey Fox); ph, Ted Tetzlaff; m, Frederick Hollander; ed, Eda Warren; art d, Hans Dreier, Ernst Fegte.

Adventure (PR:A MPAA:NR)

SAFARI** (1956) 90m COL c

Victor Mature (*Ken Duffield*), Janet Leigh (*Linda Latham*), John Justin (*Brian Sinden*), Roland Culver (*Sir Vincent Brampton*), Liam Redmond (*Roy Shaw*), Earl Cameron (*Jeroge*), Orlando Martins (*Jerusalem*), Juma (*Odongo*), Lionel Ngakane (*Kakora*), Slim Harris (*Renegade*), Harry Quashie (*O'Keefe*), Cy Grant (*Chief Massai*), John Wynn (*Charley*), Arthur Lovegrove (*Blake*), May Estelle (*Augy*), Christopher Warbey (*Kenny*), John Cook (*District Commissioner*), Bob Isaacs (*Henderson*), John Harrison (*Wambut*), Frank Singuineau (*Kikuyu*), Charles Hayes (*Police Inspector*), Bartholomew Sketch (*Special Mau Mau*).

Another jungle hunt where the rich guy loses out to the man with a sense of adventure, but this one has a twist. This time the hunter is after more than just big game: he wants the killer of his son. Mature, the leader of the expedition whose own son has been killed by an African tribe, wants revenge but is prevented by a tangled mass of red tape. He is hired by the wealthy but eccentric Culver and his fiance, Leigh, to take them on a hunt. Mature succeeds with this hunt on all counts, avenging his son's death and winning Leigh.

p, Adrian D. Worker; d, Terence Young; w, Anthony Veiller (based on a story by Robert Buckner); ph, John Wilcox (CinemaScope, Technicolor); m, William Alwyn; ed, Michael Gordon; md, Muir Mathieson; art d, Elliot Scott; m/l, "We're on Safari," Alwyn, Paddy Roberts.

Adventure (PR:A MPAA:NR)

SAFARI DRUMS** (1953) 71m AA bw (GB: BOMBA AND THE SAFARI DRUMS)

Johnny Sheffield (*Bomba*), Barbara Bestar (*Peggy*), Emory Parnell (*Conrad*), Paul Marion (*Steve*), Douglas Kennedy (*Brad Morton*), Leonard Mudie (*Barnes*), Robert "Smoki" Whitfield (*Eli*), James Adamson (*Sumbo*), Carleton Young (*Collins*), Rory Mallinson (*Murphy*), Jack Williams (*Native*), Russ Conway.

A strictly-by-the budget film in which a group comes to Africa to make a

movie about wildlife. One of the bunch has killed a geologist, and it's up to jungle boy Sheffield to bring the killer to justice. As the animals fight around them, Sheffield helps the group complete the picture and find out who the killer is. But in keeping with the laws of the jungle, a lion finishes off the killer. Sheffield grabs his trusty vine and swings back into the jungle, ready for another adventure. (See BOMBA series, Index)

p,d&w, Ford Beebe (based on characters created by Roy Rockwood); ph, Harry Neumann; m, Marlin Skiles; ed, Walter Hannemann; art d, David Milton.

Adventure (PR:A MPAA:NR)

SAFARI 3000** (1982) 92m MGM-UA c

David Carradine (*Eddie*), Stockard Channing (*J.J. Dalton*), Christopher Lee (*Count Borgia*), Hamilton Camp (*Feodor*), Ian Yule (*Freddie*), Hugh Rouse (*Hawthorne*), Mary Ann Berold (*Victoria*), Peter J. Elliott (*Stewart*), Cocky Two Bull, Ben Masinga, James White, Mackson Ngobeni, Sam Williams, Fanyana H. Sidumo, Eric Flynn, Kerry Jordan, Albert Raphael, John Leslie, Ann Courtneidge, Anthony Fridjhon, Ian Hamilton, Anne Power, Eddie Stacey, Craig Gardner.

A trans-African auto race is the background for this amateurishly written adventure. Carradine is the top driver, forced to take Playboy photographer Channing with him for the ride. Along the way they encounter lots of nice wildlife footage, and foil the various attempts of villian Lee (a Borgia, no less) to stop Carradine and win the race himself. Carradine is an interesting actor, but he only plays two roles, the martial arts expert of the "Kung Fu" television series (LONE WOLF McQUADE, CIRCLE OF IRON) and the ace race car driver (DEATH RACE 2000, CANNONBALL). SAFARI 3000, as its title suggests, is mostly a rip-off of DEATH RACE 2000. Strictly for the nondiscriminating.

p, Arthur Gardner, Jules V. Levy; d, Harry Hurwitz; w, Michael Harreschou (based on a story by Levy, Gardner, Harreschou); ph; Adam Greenberg (Panavision, Technicolor); m, Ernest Gold; ed, Samuel E. Beetley; art d, Peter Williams; set d, Pat Bergh; stunts, Eddie Stacey.

Adventure **Cas.** (PR:A-C MPAA:PG)

SAFE AFFAIR, A*½ (1931, Brit.) 52m Langham/MGM bw

Franklin Dyall (*Rupert Gay*), Jeanne Stuart (*Olga Delgaroff*), Nancy Welford (*Mary Bolton*), J.H. Roberts (*Judd*), J. Neil More (*Otto Crann*), George Turner (*Jim*), James Knight (*Tom*), Douglas Jeffries (*Henry*), Connie Emerald (*Blonde*).

A weak British entry about a millionaire, Dyall, who gets mixed up in a search for secret documents while fending off the attacks of a malicious financier. With the help of his secretary and valet, Dyall overcomes *Re Financier* by the picture's finale. Dyall and Roberts apparently felt strongly enough about this film to produce it themselves, but whatever good they saw in the script never made it to the screen.

p, Franklin Dyall, J.H. Roberts; d, Herbert Wynne; w, Eliot Stannard (based on a story by Douglas Hoare).

Crime (PR:A MPAA:NR)

SAFE AT HOME** (1962) 84m COL bw

Mickey Mantle, Roger Maris (*Themselves*), William Frawley (*Bill Turner*), Patricia Barry (*Johanna Price*), Don Collier (*Ken Lawton*), Bryan Russell (*Hutch Lawton*), Eugene Iglesias (*Mr. Torres*), Flip Mark (*Henry*), Scott Lane (*Mike Torres*), Charles G. Martin (*Henry's Father*), Ralph Houk, Whitey Ford (*Themselves*), Desiree Sumarra (*Mrs. Torres*), Joe Hickman (*Joe*), Chris Hughes (*Phil*), James R. Argyras (*Jackie*), Fred A. Schwarb (*Coach Benton*), Joe Morrison (*Hank*).

A young boy (Russell), trying to impress his new Little League team, crows that his father is best buddies with New York Yankee superstars Mickey Mantle and Roger Maris. As the lies build, Russell is forced by his new friends to produce the goods or face humiliation. Russell treks down to spring training and confesses his lies to his heroes. Aimed at the younger fans, the two lecture Russell that honesty is the best policy. Heartbroken, Russell returns home, ready to face the music. But lo and behold, guess who invites the whole group to spring training?

p, Tom Naud; d, Walter Doniger; w, Robert Dillon (based on a story by Naud, Steve Ritch); ph, Irving Lippman; m, Van Alexander; ed, Frank P. Keller; set d, James M. Crowe.

Drama (PR:A MPAA:NR)

SAFE IN HELL** (1931) 65m FN-WB bw (GB: LOST LADY, THE)

Dorothy Mackaill (*Gilda Carlson*), Donald Cook (*Carl Bergen*), Ralf Harolde (*Piet Van Saal*), Morgan Wallace (*Bruno*), Victor Varconi (*Gomez*), Ivan Simpson (*Crunch*), John Wray (*Egan*), Nina Mae McKinney (*Leonie*), Gustav Von Seyffertitz (*Larson*), Cecil Cunningham (*Angie*), Charles Middleton (*Jones*), Noble Johnson (*Bobo*), George Marion, Sr (*Jack*), Clarence Muse (*Newcastle*).

A hard-bitten story that carried a "not for children" tag. Mackaill is a tough call girl, who thinks she killed one of her "dates" after a fight that subsequently starts a fire. A sailor gets sweet on her and takes her away to a tropical island that has no extradition laws. On the island are other seedy-looking fugitives, all of whom put the make on Mackaill. The man she thought she had killed turns up, after which she finishes him off for good. A winding story with no real direction ends with Mackaill turning over a new leaf on the way to her execution. It wasn't for children, and many adults didn't take to it either.

d, William A. Wellman; w, Maude Fulton, Joseph Jackson (based on a story by Houston Branch); ph, Sid Hickox; ed, Owens Marks; art d, Jack Okey; cos, Earl Luick.

Drama   **(PR:A MPAA:NR)**

SAFE PLACE, A**   (1971) 94m BBS/COL c

Tuesday Weld (*Susan/Noah*), Orson Welles (*The Magician*), Jack Nicholson (*Mitch*), Philip Proctor (*Fred*), Gwen Welles (*Bari*), Dov Lawrence (*Larry*), Fanny Birkenmaier (*Maid*), Richard Finnochio, Barbara Flood, Roger Garrett, Jordon Hahn, Francesca Hilton, Julie Robinson, Jennifer Walker (*The Friends*), Rhonda Alfaro (*Little Girl in Rowboat*), Sylvia Zapp (*Susan age 5*).

A hippie-like fantasy has Weld reverting to her childhood to a place where she feels safe. Almost no character development leaves plenty of questions about Weld's life. Film is set only in a few locations and doesn't provide much explanation for anything. Plenty of color and flashing images, which leave the audience confused in the end. Writer-actor-editor Jaglom made his directorial debut with A SAFE PLACE, which was a critical and box-office disaster. Originally written as a play and performed at New York's Actors Studio (with Karen Black, Proctor, and Jaglom himself), the film's cast was comprised entirely of Jaglom's friends, with the exception of Orson Welles. Most of the picture was filmed in Jaglom's parents' apartment and, just before its premiere, the director admitted it was autobiographical, taken primarily from his and Weld's real-life experiences. The 94-minute print was culled from more than 50 hours of footage, leading the critics to charge that unorthodox editing techniques resulted in the film's becoming confusing and incoherent. Recordings used in the film include: "La Vie En Rose" (Edith Piaf), "It's a Big, Wide Wonderful World," "Passing By," (Buddy Clark), "Give Me Something to Remember You By," (Helen Forrest), "Lavender Blue" (Vera Lynn), "Vous Qui Passer Sans Me Voir," "Le Mer," (Charles Trenet), "As Time Goes By" (Dooley Wilson), "Someone to Watch Over Me" (Dinah Shore), "I'm Old-Fashioned" (Fred Astaire).

p, Harold Schneider; d&w, Henry Jaglom; ph, Dick Kratina (Technicolor); ed, Pieter Bergema [uncredited] Jaglom; cos, Barbara Flood.

Drama   **(PR:A MPAA:GP)**

SAFECRACKER, THE½   (1958, Brit.) 96m Coronado/MGM bw

Ray Milland (*Colley Dawson*), Barry Jones (*Bennett Carfield*), Jeannette Sterke (*Irene*), Victor Maddern (*Morris*), Ernest Clark (*Maj. Adbury*), Cyril Raymond (*Inspector Frankham*), Melissa Stribling (*Angela*), Percy Herbert (*Sgt. Harper*), Barbara Everest (*Mrs. Dawson*), Anthony Nicholls (*Gen. Prior*), David Horne (*Herbert Fenwright*), Colin Gordon (*Dakers*), Clive Morton (*Sir George Turvey*), John Welsh (*Inspector Owing*), Pamela Stirling (*Belgian Messenger*), Colin Tapley (*Col. Charles Mercer*), Henry Vidon (*Lonsen*), Ian MacNaughton (*Thomson*), Bernard Fox (*Shafter*), Richard Shaw (*Bailey*), Charles Lloyd Pack (*Lambert*), Barry Keegan (*Squadron Leader Hawkes*), Sam Kydd (*McCullers*), Ferdy Mayne (*Greek Ship Owner*), Jackie Collins (*Fenwright's Secretary*), John Robinson (*Assistant Chief of Staff*), David Lodge (*Parachute Instructor*), Wolf Frees (*German Commandant*), Ernest Walder (*German Security Policeman*), Arnold Bell (*Detective*), Gerald Case (*Car Salesman*), Basil Dignam (*Air Vice Marshal*), Hilda Fenemore (*Mrs. McCullers*), Bernard Foreman (*Foreman*), Eddie Eddon (*Eddon*), Richard Marner (*German NCO*), Carl Conway (*German Sergeant*).

Two thinly connected stories with a weak link in the middle. Milland is an expert safecracker for a London safe-making company who unknowingly falls in with a disreputable antique dealer. This association lands him in jail. The story picks up a couple of years later during the war, when England needs the services of an expert safecracker. Milland is freed from jail and the drama follows him into German territory on his mission.

p, John R. Sloan; d, Ray Milland; w, Paul Monash (based on the book *The Willy Gordon Story* by Lt. Col. Rhys Davies (ret.), Bruce Thomas); ph, Gerald Gibbs; m, Richard Rodney Bennett; ed, Ernest Walter; art d, Muir Mathieson; art d, Elliot Scott; makeup, Bill Lodge; tech adv, Capt. J.I.H. Owen.

War Drama   **(PR:A MPAA:NR)**

SAFETY IN NUMBERS**   (1930) 69m PAR bw

Charles "Buddy" Rogers (*William Butler Reynolds*), Josephine Dunn (*Maxine*), Roscoe Karns (*Bertram Shipiro*), Carole Lombard (*Pauline*), Kathryn Crawford (*Jacqueline*), Francis McDonald (*Phil Kempton*), Richard Tucker (*F. Carstair Reynolds*), Raoul Paoli (*Jules*), Lawrence Grant (*Commodore Brinker*), Virginia Bruce (*Alma McGregor*), Louise Beavers (*Messaline*), Geneva Mitchell (*Cleo Careine*).

Sprightly, fluffy musical comedy casts Rogers as a songwriter aspiring to make it on Broadway. To "show him the ways of the world," his wealthy uncle hires three follies girls to show him the sights of New York. All three become attracted to Rogers, who is set to inherit $350 million. In the end, he chooses Crawford. Songs include "My Favorite Just Passed," "The Pickup," "Business Girl," "Pepola," "I'd Like to Be a Bee in Your Boudoir," "You Appeal to Me," "Do You Play, Madame?" (George Marion, Jr., Richard A. Whiting, sung by Buddy Rogers;).

d, Victor Schertzinger; w, Marion Dix, George Marion, Jr. (based on a story by Marion, Percy Heath); ph, Henry Gerrard; ed, Robert Bassler; ch, David Bennett.

Musical   **(PR:A MPAA:NR)**

SAFETY IN NUMBERS**   (1938) 58m FOX bw

Jed Prouty (*John Jones*), Shirley Deane (*Bonnie Thompson*), Spring Byington (*Mrs. John Jones*), Russell Gleason (*Herbert Thompson*), Ken Howell (*Jack Jones*), George Ernest (*Roger Jones*), June Carlson (*Lucy Jones*), Florence Roberts (*Granny Jones*), Billy Mahan (*Bobby Jones*), Marvin Stephens (*Tommy McGuire*), Iva Stewart (*Toni Stewart*), Helen Freeman (*Mrs. Stewart*), Henry Kolker (*Dr. Lawrence Edmonds*), Paul McVey (*Mr. Hensley*).

The Jones family gets in trouble again in this lighthearted family comedy. A group of con men convince the mayor (Prouty) that the local swamp is worth plenty of money because it contains valuable minerals. After a series of yuk-it-up routines, some of the Jones kids take a tumble into the swamp and discover the mineral claim by the cons is untrue. Their efforts to stop dad from making a mistake provide the laughs for the whole family. (See JONES FAMILY series, Index.)

p, John Stone; d, Malcolm St. Clair; w, Joseph Hoffman, Karen DeWolf, Robert Chapin (based on a story by Dorothy Manney, Zena George, from characters created by Katherine Kavanaugh); ph, Charles Clarke; ed, Harry Reynolds; md, Samuel Kaylin; cos, Helen A. Myron.

Comedy   **(PR:A MPAA:NR)**

SAFFO, VENERE DE LESBO   (SEE: WARRIOR EMPRESS, THE, 1961, Fr./Ital.)

SAGA OF DEATH VALLEY**   (1939) 58m REP bw

Roy Rogers (*Roy*), George "Gabby" Hayes (*Gabby*), Donald Barry (*Jerry*), Doris Day (*Ann Meredith*), Frank M. Thomas (*Tasker*), Hal Taliaferro (*Rex*), Jack Ingram (*Brace*), Tommy Baker (*Roy as a Boy*), Buz Buckley (*Jerry as a Boy*), Lew Kelly, Fern Emmett, Horace Murphy, Lane Chandler, Fred Burns, Jimmy Wakely, Johnny Bond, Dick Rinehart, Peter Frago, Ed Brady, Bob Thomas, Matty Roubert, Pasquel Perry, Cactus Mack, Art Dillard, Horace B. Carpenter, Hooper Atchley, Frankie Marvin, Jess Cavan, Trigger the Horse.

A middle-of-the roader for Rogers: not his best, nor his worst. Story focuses on a group of bad guys who cut off the water supply to local ranchers. The film casts Rogers and Barry as long-lost brothers who became separated when, as a youth, Barry was kidnaped. Just after Barry and Rogers discover their kinship, the crooks kill Barry, setting the stage for Rogers to gain revenge and get the water flowing again. (See ROY ROGERS series, Index.)

p&d, Joseph Kane; w, Karen DeWolf, Stuart Anthony; ph, Jack Marta; ed, Lester Orlebeck.

Western   **Cas.**   **(PR:A MPAA:NR)**

SAGA OF DRACULA, THE*   (1975, Span.) 90m
Profilmes/International Amusements c (LA SAGA DE LOS DRACULA)

Narciso Ibaniz Menta (*Count Dracula*), Tina Sainz, Tony Isbert, Maria Koski, Cristina Suriani, Helga Line, J.J. Paladino.

A Spanish vampire tale which bears some similarity to Polanski's ROSEMARY'S BABY (1968). Menta is an aging vampire who needs to assure himself that his bloodline will live on. His only son is an incompetent fool, so Menta extends an invitation to his pregnant niece. He hopes to convert the newborn to vampirism, but succeeds only in turning her mortal husband into one. The baby is born dead, sending its mother into a murderous rage, driving stakes into the hearts of all her relatives. A macabre ray of hope is given to the dead child, however, when fresh blood touches its lips. THE SAGA OF DRACULA, like many other Spanish or Mexican horrors, will appeal to certain diehard horror fans.

p, Ricardo Munoz Suay, Jose Antonio Perez Giner; d, Leon Klimovsky; w, Lazarus Kaplan, Erika Zsell; ph, Francisco Sanchez (Technicolor); ed, Antonio Ramirez.

Horror   **(PR:O MPAA:R)**

SAGA OF HEMP BROWN, THE**   (1958) 80m UNIV c

Rory Calhoun (*Hemp Brown*), Beverly Garland (*Mona Langley*), John Larch (*Jed Givens*), Russell Johnson (*Hook*), Fortunio Bonanova (*Serge Bolanos, Medicine Man*), Allan Lane (*Sheriff*), Trevor Bardette (*Judge*), Morris Ankrum (*Bo Slauter*), Addison Richards (*Colonel*), Victor Sen Yung (*Chang*), Theodore Newton (*Murphy*), Francis MacDonald (*Prosecutor*), Yvette Vickers (*Amelia Smedley*), Marjorie Stapp (*Mrs. Ford*), Charles Boaz (*Alf Smedley*).

A slight twist is added to this basic shoot-em-up. Calhoun is a down-on-his luck U.S. Cavalry officer, stripped of his rank and uniform after being wrongly accused of allowing an ambush in which several troopers and his colonel's wife are killed. Out to redeem his honor, he joins forces with a quirky medicine man and his assistant, Garland. He finally finds the real killers after Garland rescues him from a lynch mob. The medicine man character gives a unique touch to this otherwise gun-blazing western.

p, Gordon Kay; d, Richard Carlson; w, Bob Williams (based on a story by Bernard Girard); ph, Philip Lathrop (CinemaScope, Eastmancolor); m, Joseph Gershenson; ed, Tony Martinelli; md, Joseph Gershenson; art d, Alexander Golitzen, Robert E. Smith; cos, Bill Thomas.

Western   (PR:A   MPAA:NR)

SAGA OF THE FLYING HOSTESS   (SEE: GIRL GAME, 1968, Fr./Ital.)

SAGA OF THE ROAD, THE   (SEE: PATHER PANCHALI 1958, India)

SAGA OF THE VAGABONDS***   (1964, Jap.) 115m Toho c
(SENGOKU GUNTO-DEN)

Koji Tsuruta (*Taro Tarao*), Toshiro Mifune (*Rokuro Kai*), Misa Uehara (*Princess Koyuki*), Takashi Shimura (*Toki Saemon-no-jo*), Akihiko Hirata (*Jiro Hidekuni*), Seizaburo Kawazu (*Hyoe Yamano*), Yoko Tsukasa (*Tazu*).

Mifune leads a group of bandits bent on taking control of the provinces and rich lords in feudal Japan. Tsuruta, on his way to deliver funds for the war against the bandits, is attacked, and the money is stolen. While Tsuruta goes after the bandits to clear his name, his younger brother, Hirata, is encouraged by evil family friend Kawazu to tell everyone his brother took the money. Tsuruta joins forces with the bandits and sets out after his brother upon learning his father has been killed and his fiancee has committed suicide. Tsuruta storms the castle with his fellow thieves, kills Kawazu and looks on as his brother jumps to his death.

p, Sanezumi Fujimoto, Kazuo Nishino; d, Toshio Sugie; w, Sadao Yamanaka, Akira Kurosawa (based on a story by Juro Miyoshi); ph, Akira Suzuki (Tohoscope, Agfacolor); m, Ikuma Dan.

Drama   (PR:A   MPAA:NR)

SAGA OF THE VIKING WOMEN AND THEIR VOYAGE TO THE WATERS OF THE GREAT SEA SERPENT, THE zero
(1957) 70m Malibu/AIP bw (AKA: THE VIKING WOMEN AND THE SEA SERPENT)

Abby Dalton, Susan Cabot, Betsy Jones-Moreland, Brad Jackson, Richard Devon, Jonathan Haze, Gary Conway, June Kenney, Jay Sayer, Michael Forest.

One of the strangest films to emerge from the fertile imagination of Roger Corman, THE SAGA OF THE VIKING WOMEN AND THEIR VOYAGE TO THE WATERS OF THE GREAT SEA SERPENT details the story of a band of Nordic women concerned over the prolonged absence of their menfolk. They set out in a longboat to look for them but soon the boat is destroyed by a whirlpool and all but four of the women are drowned. The survivors make their way to an island where they are captured by a tribe of moron warriors. These slobbering spearmen, the Grimaults, place the women in a quarry along with the long-missing Viking men and when a storm comes up they all escape and steal a boat. The Grimaults take off after them in another boat, but they encounter the whirlpool and a sea serpent which lunches on the pursuing villains. One of the Viking men slays the big lizard and they all reach their home safely. Made on a 10-day schedule for $110,000, the film was plagued by difficulties. On the first day of shooting the leading lady called in sick, so Corman took the second lead, Dalton, and promoted her to lead Viking woman, then bumped each of the other Viking women up a notch and added an extra at the bottom. When the film was finished Corman still didn't have a title for it. Stuck for a concise title, he decided to go completely the other way and give it the longest title he could come up with. It was later shortened when it was found it wouldn't fit on theater marquees.

p&d, Roger Corman; w, Louis Goldman (based on a story by Irving Block); ph, Monroe P. Askins; m, Albert Glasser; ed, Ronald Sinclair; art d, Robert Kinoshita.

Science Fiction/Adventure   (PR:A   MPAA:NR)

SAGEBRUSH FAMILY TRAILS WEST, THE*   (1940) 62m PDC bw

Bobby Clark (*Bobby Sawyer*), Earle Hodgins ("*Doc" Sawyer*), Nina Guilbert (*Minerva Sawyer*), Joyce Bryant (*Nellie Sawyer*), Minerva Urecal (*Widow Gail*), Archie Hall (*Jim Barton*), Kenne Duncan (*Bart Wallace*), Forrest Taylor (*Len Gorman*), Carl Mathews (*Zeke*), Wally West (*Hank*), Byron Vance (*Seth*), Augie Gomez (*Bart*).

A laughable western whose main hero is a 13-year-old boy. A directionless plot has Clark taking care of bank robbers and making sure an invention and secret formula are safe. Clark also has to battle a jealous sheriff's deputy and a newspaperman, who turns out to be a crooked cowboy's spy. Stilted action and outdated dialog drag this one down to the depths.

p, Sigmund Neufeld; d, Peter Stewart [Sam Newfield; w, William Lively.

Western   (PR:A   MPAA:NR)

SAGEBRUSH LAW*½   (1943) 56m RKO bw

Tim Holt, Cliff "Ukulele Ike" Edwards, Joan Barclay, John Elliott, Ed Cassidy, Karl Hackett, Roy Barcroft, Ernie Adams, John Merton, Bud McTaggart, Edmund Cobb, Otto Hoffman, Cactus Mack, Ben Corbett, Frank McCarroll, Bob McKenzie, Merrill Rodin, Dick Rush.

Holt's father is wrongly accused of stealing from the bank of which he was president, and the loyal son sets out to clear his name in this weak-scripted effort. Holt, of course, eventually tracks down the real thieves and makes them face the music. Barclay plays the mandatory love interest and the ukulele-playing Edwards provides the needed comedic relief and music.

p, Bert Gilroy; d, Sam Nelson; w, Bennett Cohen; m, Paul Sawtell; ed, John Lockert; m/l, "Crazy Old Trails," "Rockin' Down the Cherokee Train," Fred Rose, Ray Whitley.

Western   (PR:A   MPAA:NR)

SAGEBRUSH POLITICS*   (1930) 50m Art Mix/Hollywood bw

Art Mix, Lillian Bond, Jim Campbell, Tom Forman, William Ryno, Pee Wee Holmes, Jack Gordon, Wally Merrill.

Mix is a drifter making his way through the West who meets up with sheriff's daughter Bond. Mix learns that Bond's brother has been captured by an outlaw gang and helps the sheriff get him back. A substandard offering which borders on the fine line between featurette and full-length film.

p&d, Victor Adamson.

Western   (PR:A   MPAA:NR)

SAGEBRUSH TRAIL**   (1934) 55m Lone Star/MON bw

John Wayne (*John Brant*), Nancy Shubert (*Sally Blake*), Lane Chandler (*Bob Jones*), Yakima Canutt (*Ed Walsh*), Wally Wales (*Deputy Sheriff*), Art Mix (*Henchman*), Robert E. Burns (*Sheriff Parker*), Henry Hall (*Dad Blake*), Earl Dwire (*Bind Pete*), Hank Bell, Slim Whitaker, Hal Price.

Plenty of shoot-em-up action is offered in Waynes' second western for Monogram. Wrongly convicted of murder, he escapes from prison and heads out to find the man he was mistaken for. His travels take him out west, where he eventually teams up with the real killer. Shubert is the love interest provided for Wayne, and Chandler is the murderer, who is killed in a shoot-out with some bad guys.

p, Paul Malvern; d, Armand Schaefer; w, Lindsley Parsons; ph, Archie Stout.

Western   **Cas.**   (PR:A   MPAA:NR)

SAGEBRUSH TROUBADOR**   (1935) 68m REP bw

Gene Autry (*Himself*), Smiley Burnette (*Frog*), Barbara Pepper (*Joan*), J. Frank Glendon (*John Martin*), Denny Meadows (*Lon*), Hooper Atchley (*Henry Nolan*), Fred Kelsey (*Hank Polk*), Julian Rivero (*Pablo*), Dennis Moore, Tom London, Wes Warner, Frankie Marvin, Bud Pope, Tommy Gene Fairey, Art Davis, Champion the Horse.

Typical afternoon western casts Autry as a ranger who, with faithful sidekick Burnette, is on the trail of a murderer. He comes across the murdered man's granddaughter and spends most of the movie professing his love to her in song. The man who committed the murder is revealed in a muddled ending.

p, Nat Levine; d, Joseph Kane; w, Oliver Drake, Joseph Poland (based on a story by Drake); ph, Ernest Miller, Jack Marta; ed, Lester Orlebeck; m/l, Gene Autry, Smiley Burnette.

Western   **Cas.**   (PR:A   MPAA:NR)

SAGINAW TRAIL**   (1953) 56m COL bw

Gene Autry, Smiley Burnette (*Themselves*), Connie Marshall (*Flora Tourney*), Eugene Borden (*Jules Brissac*), Ralph Reed (*Randy Lane*), Henry Blair (*Phillip Brissac*), Myron Healey (*Miller Webb*), Mickey Simpson (*Jean Leblanc*), John War Eagle (*Red Bird*), Rod Redwing (*The Huron*), Billy

Wilkerson *(The Fox)*, Gregg Barton *(Lin Oakes)*, John Parrish *(Walt Curry)*, Champion, Jr, the Horse.

Autry is back in the saddle again, but the focus is more on the plot this time, rather than his singing. Autry is the leader of Hamilton's Rangers, a group brought into the northern Michigan territory (circa 1827) to stop the Indians from attacking the settlers. It turns out the Indians have been hired by fur-trapping king Borden to keep settlers out of his little empire. While everyone else blames the Indians, Autry knows Borden is behind the trouble and sets out to prove it. More of a detective movie, with just a handful of trademark barroom brawls and gunfights. Autry sings "Beautiful Dreamer," and Burnette performs "Learn I Love You." (See GENE AUTRY series, Index.)

p, Armand Schaefer; d, George Archainbaud; w, Dorothy Yost, Dwight Cummings; ph, William Bradford; ed, James Sweeney; art d, Ross Bellah.

Western **(PR:A MPAA:NR)**

SAHARA***** (1943) 97m COL bw

Humphrey Bogart *(Sgt. Joe Gunn)*, Bruce Bennett 'Herman Brix' *(Waco Hoyt)*, Lloyd Bridges *(Fred Clarkson)*, Rex Ingram *(Sgt. Tambul)*, J. Carrol Naish *(Giuseppe)*, Dan Duryea *(Jimmy Doyle)*, Richard Nugent *(Capt. Jason Halliday)*, Patrick O'Moore *(Ozzie Bates)*, Louis Mercier *(Jean Leroux)*, Carl Harbord *(Marty Williams)*, Guy Kingsford *(Peter Stegman)*, Kurt Kreuger *(Capt. Von Schletow)*, John Wengraf *(Maj. Von Falken)*, Hans Schumm *(Sgt. Krause)*, Frank Lackteen *(Arab Guide)*, Frederick Worlock *(Radio Newscaster Voice)*.

A stirring and gripping WW II film, SAHARA was one of Bogart's first starring films (other than CASABLANCA) where he was a good, decent man, fighting for democracy and upholding the honor and dignity of the common man. His enemy was universal at the time– the German army, the Nazi tyranny. It is 1942 and Tobruk has fallen to the Germans who are busy mopping up elements of the British Eighth Army, including some American tank units attached to it. On the littered battlefield sits an American 28-ton M-3 tank, which Bogart and what is left of his crew, Duryea and Bennett, are hurriedly attempting to repair as artillery shells fall all around them, German gunners trying to get their range. As Bogart repairs the tank, Duryea hears a British officer on the tank's shortwave radio ordering all Allied forces to retreat to the south, through the barren stretches of the Libyan desert, the only escape route left open. Bogart finishes his repairs and asks Duryea what the orders are. "He said scram," reports Duryea and Bogart quickly pulls his tank out of line and drives it southward. At dusk, Bogart comes upon a British officer, Nugent, whose tent hospital has been destroyed by German shellfire, killing all his 42 patients. Standing behind Nugent are stragglers, a mixed lot of British troopers. Bogart offers to take them along with him but Harbord tells him that he doesn't care to be pinpointed by the Germans while riding a "tin hearse." Bogart takes offense, telling the British soldier just how efficient and reliable his tank is and that it is no hearse: "She's an M-3 air-cooled job that can cross two hundred miles of desert as easy as you'd walk around that Picadilly Circus of yours." Harbord snorts at this and Bogart snaps back: "Stick around and let the Germans mop you up and spend the rest of the war in a prison camp in Berlin. But when I go into Berlin I'm gonna be riding that tank, the same one you see standing there with the name *Lulubelle* written on her!" He reminds Nugent that the only way out is south and that's the way he's going. The foot soldiers quickly agree to go with Bogart and pile onto his tank, Mercier, a Free French soldier; Nugent, an Irish doctor; Bridges, a Scottish soldier; Harbord and O'Moore, soldiers from England; Kingsford, a South African volunteer. Even the Americans are from diversified areas of the U.S., Duryea from Brooklyn, Bennett from Waco, Texas, and Bogart from "just the Army," as he later states. When the tank later stalls and Bogart once again repairs it, two men are seen struggling along a distant sand dune. Nugent identifies them through field glasses as "a British Sudanese with an Italian prisoner." The men–Ingram, the Sudanese sergeant, and Naish, the Italian soldier–come forward and Bogart asks Ingram to find a remote well he knows of in the deep desert. He throws some rations in Naish's direction and prepares to leave him. Naish begs not to be left in the desert to die under the blistering sun. (Vultures are shown hovering high above.) Nugent, who has turned over nominal control to Bogart, asks the tanker to reconsider, but Bogart is worried about their water supply and tells Nugent: "I got to take the Sudanese because he's a British soldier and he's entitled to share with the rest of us, but I'm not taking on a load of spaghetti! He walked this far and he can walk back." Naish begs and cries to be taken along but Bogart turns his back on the pathetic soldier in rags and grinds the tank away. Naish stumbles blindly after the tank, up and down dunes, falling inside the deep tracks left by the tank, getting up, following, following. Inside the tank Duryea bets Bennett $10 that Bogart will stop for him. Bogart looks around to see Naish following and orders the tank stopped as the men happily wave Naish forward to join them. Bennett pays the $10 to Duryea. As the tank grinds its way into the southwestern Libyan desert, heading into uncharted areas, a German fighter plane spots the tank and dives on it. The men riding on top of the tank jump off and crawl beneath it for cover while Bogart "plays dead," keeping the tank's guns silent. "Let 'em think that we're out of ammunition," he tells O'Moore. The plane makes several passes over the tank, strafing it, and then Bogart opens fire, hitting the plane and causing the pilot to parachute to safety and his plane crashes and burns. The pilot, Kreuger, a vicious Nazi, is taken along as a prisoner-of- war. Kreuger comes close to being left behind to die in the desert after making derogatory remarks about Bogart's "curious detachment," and objects to being searched by Ingram, explaining in German through Nugent who acts as an interpreter that he doesn't want to be touched by someone of "an inferior race." Bogart tells Nugent: "Tell him not to worry about him being black, it won't come off on his pretty uniform." Bogart orders Ingram to search Kreuger. When the Nazi pilot calls Ingram a "nigger" and smirks (in a fractured German-English pronunciation), Bogart explodes, telling the Nazi, "Wipe that smile off your puss or I'll knock your teeth through the top of your head!" Bridges is discovered to be wounded by the German and later dies, calling out his sweetheart's name. He is buried in the desert. The well the men so desperately searched for is dry and they move on to another well Ingram believes might yield some water. They find the ruins of Bir Acroma during a violent sandstorm and take refuge inside the old mosque. When the storm subsides, the men conduct a search of the area and the old well is found. It appears dry but Ingram is lowered into the well and finds some water still dripping. Containers are sent down and the slow process of collecting the tiny dribble of water ensues, smaller containers filling up and poured in larger ones. While Ingram watches the water in the well, Bennett joins him below and asks him if it is true what he has heard of Mohammedan customs, that each man can have more than one wife. Ingram tells him that it is true and that four wives is the general figure. Then he asks Bennett if his wife would honor such a custom in the U.S. and Bennett tells him no, that his wife would not like it. "It is the same in my country, my friend," remarks Ingram, and admits that he only has one wife because "my wife would not like it" if he had more. A mechanized column of German troops is also looking for the well at Bir Acroma and its colonel, Wengraf, sends a half-track to see if the well is active. While all the water that can be drained from the well is accumulated, Bogart repairs his tank with the help of the friendly Naish who cannot stop talking about his wife and child in Italy. He is a simple soul who has never had any heart in going to war and thinks Mussolini is not really good for Italy but, he tells Bogart, he is only a little man who has no voice in matters of government. "Mussolini–he speaks like a thunderstorm...everywhere he writes his mottos on the walls...obey, believe, work!" "Well," Bogart says, "don't you worry–some day that guy's gonna blow up and bust." The German half-track is sighted and the little Allied command takes cover. When the half-track gets close enough, Bogart's men fire on the occupants, including fire from the tank which has been camouflaged with the parachute taken from Kreuger. Two of the German soldiers are taken captive and are offered water but only if they will tell what kind of unit they've come from and its strength. One of the German breaks down as Bogart tantalizes him by pouring water from a canteen into a cup, telling Bogart and Nugent that he is from a mechanized battalion which is running out of water. Just before the German cracks, Kreuger shouts from inside the mosque where he and Naish are held prisoner that the German is to say nothing. Bogart orders Kreuger to shut up and later upbraids Naish for not telling him that Kreuger spoke English. Naish with quavering voice says: "I was afraid...I am like a man who fights his shadow..." Bogart lies to the two Germans, saying that his men are starving and that they are to tell their commander to come on, that he will trade water for food. When they are let go, the German sergeant, Schumm, who did not cooperate, kills his companion and goes on alone to his battalion. The Americans and British joke about the bitter lesson the Germans will learn when they get to the well and find it dry. "I wouldn't half mind seeing their faces," O'Moore says. This gives Bogart an idea and he proposes that they see the faces of the Germans, that they wait for them and destroy as many of them as possible. Harbord objects, saying that there are only nine of them facing an entire battalion of the Germans. He asks why they should do such a suicidal thing. "Why?" Bogart repeats. "Why did your people in London go about their business when the Germans were throwing everything in the book at them? Why did your little boats take the men off the beach at Dunkirk? Why did the Russians make a stand at Moscow? Why did the Chinese move whole cities thousands of miles inland when the Japs attacked them? Why Bataan? Why Corregidor? Maybe they were all nuts! There was one thing they did do–they delayed the enemy until we got strong enough to hit him harder than he was hitting us. I ain't no general, but it seems to me that's one way to win. If all I've said don't answer your question then somebody tell me why." All of the men agree with Bogart and decide to make a stand against the Germans. The Allied soldiers dig in while Bennett takes the German half-track and goes for help. The Germans, parched and exhausted, arrive at Bir Acroma and Bogart and his men unleash a withering fire that kills scores of the weakened enemy. Wengraf calls a truce and meets with Bogart, telling him that as an American, he has "come a long way to pull British chestnuts out of the fire." "I dunno," replies Bogart. "We kinda like chestnuts. Don't like to see them burn." Bogart then gives Wengraf his real terms–he will trade guns for water, for every weapon the Germans turn over, they will get one pint of water. Wengraf dismisses the idea and returns to his lines and a terrible battle ensues with Germans attempting to advance against fortified hills. One by one the Allied soldiers are killed. Another truce is held, this time between Wengraf and Mercier. During their talk between the lines the German, whose lips are split with thirst, looks up the hill to the ruins to see what appears to be an Allied soldier bathing. (This is a clever trick where one soldier pours water into a can unseen at his feet and right between the outstretched hands of another soldier without spilling a drop.) Again the German gets nowhere and calls off the talk, hurrying back to the lines and telling his machinegunners to open up on Mercier who has not reached the ruins. Bogart opens up with a machine gun and kills Wengraf. But Mercier is hit and falls dead as Duryea and Bogart pull his body into a trench, Duryea saying: "Frenchie was right–we don't know the Nazis. They *did* shoot him in the back." Bennett, meanwhile, has abandoned the broken-down half-track and is now out of water, crawling slowly up the side of a sand dune, half unconscious with lack of thirst. (A marvelous closeup of the sand he claws shows it falling toward his open eyes as if it were slow, lapping waves of water.) Kreuger, during a German mortar attack, decides to reach the German lines and tell Wengraf that there is really no water at the ruins. When Naish refuses to help him and tells him that he "likes these men," Krueger threatens to denounce him. "Denounce me then," Naish says, suddenly finding new courage. "Italians are not like Germans–only the body wears the uniform and not the soul! Mussolini is not so clever like Hitler. He can dress his Italians up only to *look* like thieves, cheats, murderers. He cannot, like Hitler, make them feel like that. He cannot like Hitler scrape from the conscience the knowledge that right is right and wrong is wrong, or dig holes in their heads to plant his own ten commandments: Steal from thy neighbor! Cheat thy neighbor! Kill thy neighbor!" Krueger is livid and spits out: "You Italian swine–you dare to insult the Fuhrer?" Naish shrugs: "That would take an artist; I am but a mechanic. But are my eyes blind that I must fall to my knees to worship a maniac who has made of my country a concentration camp? Who has made of my people slaves? Must I kiss the hand that beats me, lick the boot that kicks me? No! I'd rather spend my whole life living in this dirty hole than to escape to fight again for things I do not believe! Against people I do not hate! For your Hitler! It's because of a man like him that God–my God–created hell!" Kreuger knocks Naish down and drives a knife he has been secreting into the Italian's back. Naish staggers outside and tells Bogart that Kreuger has escaped and is going to tell the Germans that there is no water. He falls dead. Kreuger is running across the open ground between the lines when Ingram goes after him, racing wildly up and down the sand dunes until knocking the German to the ground and grinding his head into the sand, suffocating him. Ingram then tries to make it back to his own lines, running just ahead of the German fire tracing his steps, running until the bullets catch up to him and cut him down. Bogart sees him coming and says to Duryea: "He hasn't got a chance." Ingram lies silent atop a sand dune but then his left arm raises in a dying gesture to show thumbs up. "He got the Heinie," Duryea says. Bennett, meanwhile, has collapsed and is found by a British patrol car; water is poured over his face and he is revived. At Bir Acroma Nugent and Bogart have a last conference and Bogart says that when they run out of ammunition they will use bayonets and gun butts to fight. Nugent believes that holding off several hundred Germans is nothing short of a miracle. He says: "Do you know why we're able to do it? Because we're stronger than they are...I don't mean in numbers. I mean something else. You see, those men out there have never known the dignity of freedom." More German shells explode and Duryea cries out that he is wounded and Nugent takes him into the mosque to bandage his wounds. "It's going to take a lot more than this to kill me," Duryea says. "That's the spirit–never say die," Nugent replies. At that second a mortar shell strikes the mosque and both men are killed. Only O'Moore and Bogart are now left defending the ruins when the last haggard German attack is made against them. They open fire on the stumbling, half-dead German troops who begin to throw away their weapons, crying out for water. Soon, what's left of the battalion is pouring forth to claim the water for their guns and Bogart stands up with a submachine gun on the parapet, sneering at them, pointing to the well. "Go ahead–drink your fill!" He looks down amazed to see the Germans herding into the well which is now gushing water; the old well has been opened up by an exploding shell. O'Moore and Bogart gather up the enemy's guns and herd the German prisoners in front of their tank, the *Lulubelle*, which is later met by Bennett and a British column of troops. O'Moore happily rejoins his British companions. Bennett asks about Duryea and the others, saying, "I see you whittled them down a bit." Bogart pulls out a handful of dogtags, identification tags signifying the dead of his little command. "They whittled us down, too." (The symbol of the metal identification tages worn around the necks of servicemen was employed through many WW II films. In OBJECTIVE BURMA Errol Flynn holds up a handful of dogtags to his commander to show him what a completed mission cost.) Bennett then tells Bogart the great news that "the Limies held the Jerries at El Alamein. Too bad they didn't know about it." As the strains of Rozsa's magnificent score rise, Bogart, after glancing down at the dogtags, talks and the images of the graves of his dead command are shown, hats and helmets atop upturned rifles jammed in the sand: "Yeah, they'd want to know–Halliday, Doyle, Tambul, Williams, Stegman, Frenchie, Clarkson–they stopped 'em at El Alamein!" Zoltan Korda directed SAHARA with swift, sure expertise, his story unraveling without a hitch. His scenes are taut, well edited to each succeeding scene, and he loses neither cohesion nor character development. His characters are wonderful and inspiring and each part in this all-male cast is well balanced. The superb Lawson script is literate and as tough as the desert campaigners it represents. Mate's photography is simply great as he captures the gritty feel of the desert with its barren, vast wasteland and its endless skies. There are countless scenes where the camera itself moves with every gesture and posture of the characters it is capturing, a result of both Korda's and Mate's brilliant setups. Bogart's character, of course, the sheer force of his indomitable presence, overshadows all in the film, for he is the man who holds it all together, the compelling force behind the heroic story. The idea of nine men holding back 500 Germans is made graphically feasible by showing the strong position held by the Allied soldiers and the poor condition of the Germans who are already on their last legs due to lack of water. Korda had no lack of men to play the hordes of German troops; he simply borrowed an American battalion that was presently in training near Camp Young, California. Bogart was loaned out to Columbia for this film, one which he always thought was one of his better achievements, as did studio boss Harry Cohn. The scriptwriter for this stirring drama, Lawson, was later part of the Hollywood Ten and when officials tried to pressure Cohn into firing him, he refused, much to his credit, defying the McCarthyites of the day. The portrayal by Naish, a memorable one like so many in this film, was designed to show Italians in a favorable light, that Italy was not a "serious" enemy, that Italians were fun-loving, family-oriented people who had no real interest in "Hitler's war." This was a recurrent theme in WW II films, one designed to impress upon the huge Italian-American community that the actual evil was in Berlin, not Rome, and that their countrymen were merely misled and hoodwinked. Naish's incredible denunciation of the Nazis and Hitler spoke for the Italians at large, Hollywood felt. It was a speech that would be repeated or reflected by Italian actors in many a WW II film such as FIVE GRAVES TO CAIRO where Fortunio Bonanova portrays an Italian general more interested in singing snippets from operas than in conquering other people, or VON RYAN'S EXPRESS where, without the help of ordinary Italian citizens, hundreds of Allied prisoners would not have escaped the clutches of the insidious Germans.

p, Harry Joe Brown; d, Zoltan Korda; w, John Howard Lawson, Korda, James O'Hanlon (based on a story by Philip MacDonald from an incident in the film THE THIRTEEN 'USSR'); ph, Rudolf Mate; m, Miklos Rozsa; ed, Charles Nelson; md, M.W. Stoloff; art d, Lionel Banks, Eugene Lourie; set d, William Kiernan.

War Drama **Cas.** **(PR:C MPAA:NR)**

SAID O'REILLY TO MACNAB (SEE: SEZ O'REILLY TO MACNAB 1938, Brit.)

SAIGON*** (1948) 93m PAR bw

Alan Ladd *(Maj. Larry Briggs)*, Veronica Lake *(Susan Cleaver)*, Douglas Dick *(Capt. Mike Perry)*, Wally Cassell *(Sgt. Pete Rocco)*, Luther Adler *(Lt. Keon)*, Morris Carnovsky *(Alex Maris)*, Mikhail Rasumny *(Clerk)*, Luis Van Rooten *(Simon)*, Eugene Borden *(Boat Captain)*, Griff Barnet *(Surgeon)*, Frances Chung *(Chinese Nurse)*, Betty Bryant *(Singer at Waterfront Cafe)*, Dorothy Eveleigh *(Portuguese Woman)*, Harry Wilson *(Stevedore)*, William Yip *(Cafe Proprietor)*, Lester Sharpe *(Barman at Cafe)*, Allan Douglas *(American Soldier/Vendor)*, Kenny O'Morrison *(Air Corps Lieutenant)*, Lee Tung Foo *(Chinese Farmer)*, Leo Abbey *(Sinister Driver)*, Oie Chan *(Farmer's Wife/Flower Vendor)*, Charles Stevens *(Driver of Susan's Car)*, Thomas Quon Woo, Rito Punay, Quon Gong, Joe R. Bautista *(Natives)*, Tommy Lee *(Ox Cart Driver/Farmer at Rice Paddy)*, Eddie Lee *(Tea House Merchant)*, Billy Louie *(Woman in Tea House)*, Moy Ming *(Proprietor of Tea House)*, George Chan *(Tea House Customer)*, Perry Ivins *(Prisoner at Hotel)*, Kanza Omar *(Russian Entertainer)*, Mary Chan *(Farmer's Wife)*, Angel Cruz *(Boat Pilot)*, Anthony Barredo *(Boat Mechanic)*, Philip Ahn *(Boss Merchant)*, Luke Chan, Ralph R. Sencuya *(Tailors)*, Jean De Briac, Jack Chefe *(Hotel Clerks)*, Harold G. Fong *(Bartender)*, George Sorel *(Travel Agent)*, Andra Verne, Renee Randall, Hazel Shon *(Girls)*, Jimmy Dundee *(Stunt Man)*, Andre Charlot *(Priest)*.

Two WW II buddies, Ladd and Cassell, learning that a third friend, Dick, is dying of some disease, decide to keep it a secret from him and show him a good time during his final weeks. To raise some money they agree to fly a shady financier, Carnovsky, out of Shanghai to Saigon for $10,000, no questions asked. While they wait at the airport, Carnovsky's secretary, Lake, shows up, but he is late. When he does arrive, it is with the police in hot pursuit and Ladd and the others decide it would be best not to get involved so they take off without him, over Lake's protests. She turns out to have half a million dollars in a briefcase that belongs to Carnovsky, his takings as a war profiteer. Over the Indo-Chinese jungle the plane develops engine trouble and Ladd is forced to crash-land. As the four make their way out of the jungle by boat and ox cart, Dick falls in love with Lake, and Ladd, who doesn't trust her because of her connections to Carnovsky, threatens to turn her over to Adler, a detective who has been following them, unless she pretends to reciprocate Dick's love. Gradually, though, Ladd finds himself falling in love with Lake, a sentiment she returns. Eventually the four reach Saigon and find Carnovsky waiting and wanting his ill-gotten money back. Dick and Cassell are killed in the ensuing gunplay and in a final scene at the cemetery, Lake and Ladd leave their funerals to begin a life together. The fourth and last teaming of Ladd and Lake–not counting three all-star revues in which they appeared separately, STAR-SPANGLED RHYTHM (1942), DUFFY'S TAVERN (1945), and VARIETY GIRL (1947)–is nowhere near the quality of the other three, THIS GUN FOR HIRE (1942), THE GLASS KEY (also 1942), and THE BLUE DAHLIA (1946). The plot and dialog were ridiculous and Lake, never any great shakes as an actress, has her deficiencies fully shown off here. Her career came to a grinding halt very soon thereafter. Today she and Ladd are remembered as one of the great love teams of the 1940s, but SAIGON does little to advance that reputation.

p, P.J. Wolfson; d, Leslie Fenton; w, Wolfson, Arthur Sheekman (based on a story by Julian Zimet); ph, John F. Seitz; m, Robert Emmett Dolan; ed, William Shea; md, Dolan; art d, Hans Dreier, Henry Bumstead; set d, Sam V.Comer, Bertram Granger; cos, Edith Head; spec eff, Gordon Jennings; makeup, Wally Westmore.

Drama   (PR:A   MPAA:NR)

SAIKAKU ICHIDAI ONNA   (SEE: LIFE OF OHARU, 1964, Jap.)

SAIL A CROOKED SHIP**   (1961) 88m COL bw

Robert Wagner (*Gilbert Barrows*), Dolores Hart (*Elinor Harrison*), Carolyn Jones (*Virginia*), Ernie Kovacs (*Bugsy F. "Captain" Foglemeyer*), Frankie Avalon (*Rodney*), Frank Gorshin (*George Wilson*), Jesse White (*McDonald*), Harvey Lembeck (*Nickels*), Sid Tomack (*Sammy*), Guy Raymond (*Helmut*), Buck Kartalian (*Finster*), Wilton Graff (*Simon J. Harrison*), Marjorie Bennett (*Mrs. Chowder*), Terry Huntingdon (*Young Lady Pilgrim*), Graeme Ferguson (*1st Man*), Tom Symonds (*2nd Man*), Howard Wendell (*Mr. Caldingham*), Mary Young (*Woman*), Bru Mysak (*Newsboy*), Hope Sansberry (*Biddy*), Mark Myer (*Cop*).

This comedy, heavy on sight gags, has a bunch of crooks taking advantage of a naive, ex-Navy officer Wagner. Wagner sails a group of vessels from the scrap heap in an effort to impress the boss' daughter. Petty thief Kovacs, who fools Wagner into believing he is a ship builder, plans to use the ship for a bank heist. Wagner and girl friend Hart are captured, and Wagner is forced to skipper the ship. Gorshin tries to take control of the ship, but Wagner signals the Coast Guard for rescue by using Hart's brassiere as a slingshot. Veteran comedians stand out in their roles, but others have trouble pulling off the laughs.

p, Philip Barry Jr.; d, Irving Brecher; w, Ruth Brooks Flippen, Bruce Geller (based on the novel by Nathaniel Benchley); ph, Joseph Biroc; m, George Duning; ed, William A. Lyon; art d, Robert Peterson; set d, James M. Crowe; m/l, "Opposites Attract," Bob Marcucci, Russ Faith (sung by Frankie Avalon).

Comedy   (PR:A   MPAA:NR)

SAIL INTO DANGER**   (1957, Brit.) 72m Patria/GN bw

Dennis O'Keefe (*Steve Ryman*), Kathleen Ryan (*Lana*), James Hayter (*Monty*), Ana Luisa Peluffo (*Josafina*), Pedro de Cordoba (*Luis*), Barta Barry (*Emil*), Felix de Pommes (*Inspector Gomez*), John Bull (*Angel*), Miguel Fleta.

O'Keefe is an American boat owner and former smuggler who is forced by Ryan's gang to sail them from Barcelona to Tangiers. The gang kills O'Keefe's son and injures his shipmate, Hayter, sending O'Keefe into an avenging rage. He kills two members of the gang and gains police assistance in capturing the other two.

p, Steven Pallos; d&w, Kenneth Hume; ph, Phil Grindrod.

Crime   (PR:A   MPAA:NR)

SAILING ALONG**   (1938, Brit.) 80m GAU bw

Jessie Matthews (*Kay Martin*), Barry Mackay (*Steve Barnes*), Jack Whiting (*Dicky Randall*), Roland Young (*Anthony Gulliver*), Noel Madison (*Windy*), Frank Pettingell (*Skipper Barnes*), Alastair Sim (*Sylvester*), Athene Seyler (*Victoria Gulliver*), Margaret Vyner (*Stephanie*), William Dewhurst (*Winton*), Peggy Novak (*Jill*), Patrick Barr, Bruce Winston, Edward Cooper, Leslie Laurier, Charles Paton, D. Hay Plumb, Arthur Denton, Cot d' Ordan, Yvonne Dulac, Frank Fox, Bombardier Billy Wells, Clement Dutto, Eve Chipman, Alexander Ramsay, Edna Searle, Simeta Marsden, Mabel Silvester.

This British musical stars Matthews as a woman who gives up all the trappings of stardom for the love of Mackay. This was Matthews' last musical. Matthews, who made her first professional stage appearance at age 10, went on to appear in the chorus line of London musicals in her teens and play bit roles in a few films. She rose to stardom in the late 1920s and early 1930s in musical revues. Her popularity as a film star during pre-WW II lasted for several years. Considered one of the most graceful dancers of her time, she was promoted as "The Dancing Divinity."

p, Michael Balcom; d, Sonnie Hale; w, Lesser Samuels, Hale (based on a story by Selwyn Jepson); ph, Glen MacWilliams; ed, Al Barnes; cos, Norman Hartnell; m/l, "My River," "Your Heart Skips a Beat," "Trusting My Luck," Arthur Johnston, Maurice Sigler.

Musical   (PR:A   MPAA:NR)

SAILOR BE GOOD*½   (1933) 68m Jefferson/RKO bw

Jack Oakie (*Kelsey Jones*), Vivienne Osborne (*Red Dale*), George E. Stone (*Murphy*), Lincoln Stedman (*Slim*), Max Hoffman, Jr (*Hartigan*), Gertrude Michael (*Kay Whitney*), Huntley Gordon (*Mr. Whitney*), Gertrude Sutton (*Priscilla*), Charles Coleman (*Butler*), Louise Mackintosh, Crauford Kent, Carlos Alvarado.

Osborne, a dance-hall hostess who is the toast of every ship that comes to

port, becomes the object of Oakie's affections. He's supposed to be in training for the boxing championship of the fleet but, after an all-night binge, ends up marrying a wealthy society girl. Oakie just can't cut the society scene and gets a divorce from his social-climbing wife, allowing him to return to Osborne and beat the champ.

d, James Cruze; w, Viola Brothers Shore, Ethel Doherty, Ralph Spence; ph, Charles F. Schoenbaum; ed, Viola Lawrence.

Comedy   (PR:A   MPAA:NR)

SAILOR BEWARE**   (1951) 108m PAR bw

Dean Martin (*Al Crowthers*), Jerry Lewis (*Melvin Jones*), Corinne Calvet (*Guest Star*), Marion Marshall (*Hilda Jones*), Robert Strauss (*Lardoski*), Leif Erickson (*Cdr. Lane*), Don Wilson (*Mr. Chubby*), Vincent Edwards (*Blayden*), Skip Homeler (*Mac.*), Dan Barton (*'Bama*), Mike Mahoney (*Tiger*), Mary Treen (*Ginger*), Betty Hutton (*Betty*), Dick Stabile (*Band Leader*), Donald MacBride (*Chief Bos'n Mate*), Louis Jean Heydt (*Naval Doctor*), Elaine Stewart (*Lt. Saunders*), Danny Arnold (*Turk*), Drew Cahill (*Bull*), James Flavin (*Petty Officer*), Dan Willis, James Dean (*Sailors*), Irene Martin, Mary Murphy (*Pretty Girls*), Darr Smith (*Jeff Spencer*), Bobby and Eddie Mayo (*Themselves*), Eddie Simms (*Killer Jackson*), Marshall Reed, John V. Close (*Hospital Corpsmen*), Jimmie Dundee (*Bartender*), Larry McGrath (*Referee*), The Marimba Merry Makers, Richard Karlan (*Guard*), Robert Carson (*Naval Captain*).

A drawn-out but frantic musical comedy that tries to use Lewis' antics and Martin's singing to the utmost. The boys play a couple of sailors assigned to a submarine, a situation that lends itself to Lewis' getting into one tight situation after another, including the inflation of a life raft. Every sailor gag in historical memory is used, many revolving around all the pretty girls available for Lewis and Martin to chase. Even with one gag after another, the movie is still a bit hard on the senses. Tunes include "Sailors' Polka," "Never Before," "Merci Beaucoup," "The Old Calliope," and "Today, Tomorrow, Forever" (Mack David, Jerry Livingston; sung by Martin). Remake of THE FLEET'S IN

p, Hal B. Wallis; d, Hal Walker; w, James Allardice, Martin Rackin (based on a play by Kenyon Nicholson); ph, Daniel L. Fapp; ed, Warren Low; md, Joseph J. Lilley; art d, Hal Pereira, Henry Bumstead.

Comedy   (PR:A   MPAA:NR)

SAILOR BEWARE!   (SEE: PANIC IN THE PARLOUR, 1956, Brit.)

SAILOR FROM GIBRALTAR, THE*   (1967, Brit.) 89m
                                                          Woodfall/Lopert bw

Jeanne Moreau (*Anna*), Ian Bannen (*Alan*), Vanessa Redgrave (*Sheila*), Zia Mohyeddin (*Noori*), Hugh Griffith (*Legrand*), Orson Welles (*Louis of Mozambique*), Umberto Orsini (*Postcard Vendor*), Erminio Spalla (*Eolo*), Eleanor Brown (*Carla*), Gabriella Pallotta (*Girl at Dance*), Arnoldo Foa (*Man on Train*), Claudio De Renzi (*Jeannot*), Fausto Tozzi (*Captain*), John Hurt (*John*), Theo Roubanis (*Theo*), Brad Moore (*Brad*), Massimo Sarchielli (*Massimo*), Guglielmo Spoletini (*Guglielmo*), Wolf Hillinger (*Wolf*).

For one fleeting moment, a wealthy Frenchwoman experiences true happiness with an elusive sailor. After her husband commits suicide and leaves her his estate, she begins an endless port-to-port search for her true love. Along the way, she meets the young Englishman Bannen. The two go from one seedy place to another searching for the sailor. But on the journey, Bannen finds himself falling in love with the woman. Finale has them sailing off together, still searching for the sailor.

p, Oscar Lewenstein, Neil Hartley; d, Tony Richardson; w, Richardson, Christopher Isherwood, Don Magner (based on the novel *Le Marin de Gibraltar* by Marguerite Duras); ph, Raoul Coutard; m, Antoine Duhamel; ed, Antony Gibbs; set d, Marilena Aravantinou; cos, Jocelyn Richards; m/l, "Jo le Rouge," Duhamel, Bassiak (sung by Jeanne Moreau); makeup, Simone Knapp

Drama   (PR:O   MPAA:NR)

SAILOR OF THE KING**   (1953, Brit.) 85m FOX bw (GB:
                                        SINGLE-HANDED; AKA: ABLE SEAMAN BROWN)

Jeffrey Hunter (*Signalman Andrew Brown*), Michael Rennie (*Capt. Richard Saville*), Wendy Hiller (*Lucinda Bentley*), Bernard Lee (*Petty Officer Wheatley*), Peter Van Eyck (*Kapitan von Falk*), Victor Maddern (*Signalman Earnshaw*), John Horsley (*Cmdr. Willis*), Patrick Barr (*Capt. Ashley*), Robin Bailey (*Lt. Stafford*), James Copeland (*Cmdr. Laughton*), Sam Kydd (*Naval Rating*), Nicholas Bruce (*Hesse*), Martin Boddey, Guido Lorraine, Lockwood West, James Drake, Robert Dean, John Schlesinger, Derek Prentice.

A British sailor, Hunter, is the only survivor when the ship he is on is sunk. He ends up on a desert island, where he manages to disable a German cruiser long enough to give the British fleet time to come in and destroy it. He is killed without ever knowing that the commander of the cruiser squadron is the father he never met. Or maybe he survives and is decorated at Buckingham Palace; Fox couldn't seem to decide how to end the picture, so they showed it in New York with both endings and asked the audience

to vote. Neither ending saves the film from its wooden acting and
unbelievable action.

p, Frank McCarthy; d, Roy Boulting; w, Valentine Davies (based on the
novel *Brown on Resolution* by C.S. Forester); ph, Gilbert Taylor; m, Clifton
Parker; ed, Alan Obiston; md, Muir Mathieson; art d, Alec Vetchinsky.

War Drama   (PR:A   MPAA:NR)

SAILOR TAKES A WIFE, THE**   (1946) 92m MGM bw

Robert Walker *(John)*, June Allyson *(Mary)*, Hume Cronyn *(Freddie)*,
Audrey Totter *(Lisa)*, Eddie "Rochester" Anderson *(Harry)*, Reginald Owen
(Mr. Amboy), Gerald Oliver Smith *(Butler)*.

Allyson meets Walker one night, and thinking she's found a navy hero,
decides to marry him right then and there. But he gets discharged (to her
disappointment) and the adjustment to civilian life starts to provide all the
laughs. He becomes an innocent target for Totter, who has more than just
friendship in mind. While he's dodging her, Allyson has to elude her still
amorous boss (Cronyn). With all the wriggling out of comedic situations, the
two never get a chance to consummate the marriage, which keeps the
audience interested until the end.

p, Edwin H. Knopf; d, Richard Whorf; w, Chester Erskine, Anne Morrison
Chapin, Whitfeld Cook (based on a play by Erskine); ph, Sidney Wagner; m,
Johnny Green; ed, Irvine Warburton; art d, Cedric Gibbons, Edward
Carfagno; cos, Irene; spec eff, Warren Newcombe.

Comedy   (PR:A   MPAA:NR)

SAILOR WHO FELL FROM GRACE WITH THE SEA, THE**
                                            (1976, Brit.) 105m AE c

Sarah Miles *(Anne Osborne)*, Kris Kristofferson *(Jim Cameron)*, Jonathan
Kahn *(Jonathan Osborne)*, Margo Cunningham *(Mrs. Palmer)*, Earl Rhodes
(Chief), Paul Tropea *(Number Two)*, Gary Lock *(Number Four)*, Stephen
Black *(Number Five)*, Peter Clapham *(Richard Pettit)*, Jennifer Tolman
(Mary Ingram).

The Japanese author of the book used as the basis for this very English
movie was a unique person. He was profiled in a movie in 1985 that only told
part of the story of his complexity. Six years before this film was released,
Yukio Mishima, who was about the size of a tall dwarf, was leading a
right-wing coup attempt in Japan, and, when his pleas failed, he punished
everyone by disemboweling himself in front of witnesses, then had his head
cut off by one of his trusted aides who then bared his neck and had *his* head
separated from his body. *That* is strict. You can guess from the way in which
Mishima chose to die that he was not a writer of light or breezy material.
This most oriental story loses nearly everything in the occidental translation
by director-writer Carlino. Like many Japanese films, it is excruciatingly
slow. The only problem is that Carlino has made a Japanese movie with
English actors and the cultural differences between East and West never get
close to having their twains meet. Miles is a sex-starved widow with a weird
son, Kahn. They live in Dartmouth, England, where Kahn pals around with
some boys left over from BLESS THE BEASTS AND CHILDREN or LORD
OF THE FLIES. Kristofferson is a sailor who has been at sea so long that
the sound of a voice higher than a baritone is almost orgasmic. The two meet
and their sexual scenes are as explicit as you will ever see outside the local
porno movie house. Once that's out of the way, Kahn likes Kristofferson and
the fact that he is a sailor represents something important in the twisted
youth's mind. Once Kahn learns that the sailor has chosen to stay on land
to marry Miles, he gathers his compatriots around him and they attempt to
kill and castrate Kristofferson in order to bring him back to his state of
grace. It's all very Asian and the words don't work in the mouths of
Caucasians. Symbolism reigns less than supreme. The movie looks good but
a snail races down a road faster. A few shocking scenes, plus the sexually
graphic ones, but they do not compensate for the fuzziness of the concept.

p, Martin Poll; d&w, Lewis John Carlino (based on the novel by Yukio
Mishima); ph, Douglas Slocombe (Eastmancolor); m, John Mandel; ed,
Anthony Gibbs; prod d, Ted Haworth; art d, Brian Ackland-Snow; cos, Lee
Poll.

Drama   **Cas.**   (PR:O   MPAA:R)

SAILOR'S DON'T CARE**   (1940, Brit.) 79m But bw

Tom Gamble *(Nobby Clark)*, Edward Rigby *(Joe Clark)*, Jean Gillie *(Nancy)*,
Michael Wilding *(Dick)*, Marion Gerth *(Mimi)*, Mavis Villiers *(Blondie)*, G.H.
Mulcaster *(Adm. Reynolds)*, John Salew *(Henri)*, Henry B. Longhurst *(Adm.
Drake)*, Denis Wyndham *(Capt. Raleigh)*, Ian Maclean.

A silly comedy about a father and son shipbuilding team (Rigby and Gamble)
who enlist in the River Patrol Service. They get tangled up in a spy ring, and
discover that a man has parachuted into the river with a time bomb. The
comic finale has the bomb exploding and drenching Rigby and Gamble, as
well as all of Scotland Yard.

p, F.W. Baker; d&w, Oswald Mitchell (based on a story by W.W. Jacobs); ph,
Stephen Dade.

Comedy   (PR:A   MPAA:NR)

SAILORS' HOLIDAY*½   (1929) 58m Pathe bw

Alan Hale *(Adam Pike)*, Sally Eilers *(Molly Jones)*, George Cooper *(Shorty)*,
Paul Hurst *(Jimmylegs)*, Mary Carr *(Mrs. Pike)*, Charles Clary, Jack
Richardson *(Captains)*, Natalie Joyce *(The Fast Worker)*, Phil Sleeman *(Her
Secretary)*.

Hale and Cooper are fun-loving, rambunctious sailors who get involved in
one mixup after another in this lighthearted comedy with a dash of
suspense. The boys get involved with a girl, Eilers, who wants them to help
her find her brother. With a parrot continuously perched on his shoulder,
Hale, along with buddy Cooper, dodges the mean boatswain, Clary, who is
always on their tail. After the boys conclude Eilers' story is a fake, it turns
out that their enemy the boatswain is her brother.

d, Fred Newmeyer; w, Joseph Franklin Poland, Ray Harris (based on a story
by Poland); ph, Arthur Miller; ed, Claude Berkeley.

Comedy   (PR:A   MPAA:NR)

SAILOR'S HOLIDAY**   (1944) 60m COL bw

Arthur Lake *(Marble Head Tomkins)*, Jane Lawrence *(Clementine Brown)*,
Bob Haymes *(Bill Hayes)*, Shelley Winters *(Gloria Flynn)*, Lewis Wilson
(Iron Man Collins), Edmund MacDonald *(Ferd Baxter)*, Pat O'Malley
(Studio Guide), Herbert Rawlinson *(Director)*, Buddy Yarus *(Assistant
Director)*, Vi Athens *(Maid)*, George Ford *(Ronald Blair)*.

Lake, Haymes, and Wilson are a trio of merchant marines. Two of them
have broken off engagements after meeting other women, but all is righted
after a few fights, laughs, and a self-serving tour through Columbia Studios.
Some funny moments here but nothing exceptional. Winters and Lawrence
are the female interests, both appearing fresh from Broadway shows:
Winters from "Rosalinda" and Lawrence from "Oklahoma."

p, Wallace MacDonald; d, William Berke; w, Manny Seff; ph, Burnett
Guffey; ed, Paul Borofsky; md, M.W. Stoloff; art d, Lionel Banks, Victor
Greene.

Comedy   (PR:A   MPAA:NR)

SAILOR'S LADY**   (1940) 66m FOX

Nancy Kelly *(Sally Gilroy)*, Jon Hall *(Danny Malone)*, Joan Davis *(Myrtle)*,
Dana Andrews *(Scrappy Wilson)*, Mary Nash *(Miss Purvis)*, Larry "Buster"
Crabbe *(Rodney)*, Katherine [Kay] Aldridge *(Georgine)*, Harry Shannon
(Father McGann), Wally Vernon *(Goofer)*, Bruce Hampton *("Skipper")*,
Charles D. Brown *(Capt. Roscoe)*, Selmer Jackson *(Executive Officer)*, Edgar
Dearing *(Chief Master-at-Arms)*, Edmund MacDonald *(Barnacle)*, William
B. Davidson *(Judge Hinsdale)*, Kane Richmond *(Division Officer)*, Lester
Dorr *(Assistant Paymaster)*, Don Barry *(Paymaster)*, George O'Hanlon
(Sailor), Matt McHugh *(Cabby)*, Ward Bond *(Shore Patrolman)*, Barbara
Pepper *(Maude)*, Gaylord [Steve] Pendleton *(Information)*, Eddie Acuff
(Guide), Edward Earle *(Navigator)*, Pierre Watkin, Paul Harvey *(Captains)*,
Emmett Vogan *(Medical Officer)*, Harry Strang *(Messenger)*, Edward Keane
(Captain's Aide), Charles Trowbridge *(Aide)*, William Conselman, Jr,
Charles Tannen, Murray Alper, John Kellogg *(Sailors)*, Irving Bacon
(Storekeeper), Peggy Ryan *(Ellen, the High School Girl)*, Cyril Ring *(Lt.
Cmdr of Arizona)*, Bernadene Hayes *(Babe)*, Ruth Clifford *(Maid)*, James
Flavin *(Motorcycle Cop)*, Billy Wayne *(Sail Maker)*, Ruth Warren *(Mother)*,
Marie Blake, Gladys Blake, Frances Morris *(Beauty Operators)*.

Hall is a Navy man who is engaged to Kelly. They plan to marry after he
returns from a tour of duty but complications arise when he discovers that
she's adopted a 10-month-old baby (Hampton) in his absence. Seems the
tyke's parents were killed in an accident and Kelly took it upon herself to
raise the child. Crisis arises when the babe is accidentally left aboard Hall's
ship. Hampton isn't discovered until the ship is engaged in practice war
maneuvers but, of course, all ends happily. This so-so B programmer never
quite makes it, and it goes for the obvious laugh every time. Some moments
are good but others are completely witless. Hampton is a natural scene
stealer. Production values are typical.

p, Sol M. Wurtzel; d, Allan Dwan; w, Frederick Hazlett Brennan, Lou
Breslow, Owen Francis (based on a story by Lt. Cdr. Frank "Spig" Wead);
ph, Ernest Palmer; ed, Fred Allen; md, Samuel Kaylin.

Comedy   (PR:A   MPAA:NR)

SAILOR'S LUCK**   (1933) 64m FOX bw

James Dunn *(Jimmy Harrigan)*, Sally Eilers *(Sally Brent)*, Sammy Cohen
(Barnacle Benny), Frank Moran *(Bilge)*, Victor Jory *(Barron Darrow)*,
Esther Muir *(Minnie Broadhurst)*, Will Stanton *(J. Felix Hemingway)*,
Curley Wright *(Angelo)*, Jerry Mandy *(Rico)*, Lucien Littlefield *(Elmer
Brown)*, Buster Phelps *(Elmer Brown, Jr.)*, Frank Atkinson *(Attendant)*.

Dunn is a sailor who accidentally ends up with unemployed dame Eilers. He
gets into a couple of fights on her account and ends up marrying her. Cohen
and Moran are a pair of sailors who provide the comic relief. A minor
programmer comedy that has its moments but never amounts to much. An
early directoral effort from Walsh, who went on to much better things.

d, Raoul Walsh; w, Marguerite Roberts, Charlotte Miller, Bert Hanlon, Ben

Ryan (based on a story by Roberts, Miller); ph, Arthur Miller; ed, Jack Murray; cos, William Lambert.

Comedy   **(PR:A   MPAA:NR)**

SAILORS ON LEAVE**   (1941) 71m REP bw

William Lundigan (*Chuck Stephens*), Shirley Ross (*Linda Hall*), Chick Chandler (*Swifty*), Ruth Donnelly (*Aunt Navy*), Mae Clarke (*Gwen*), Cliff Nazarro (*Mike*), Tom Kennedy (*Dugan*), Mary Ainslee (*Sadie*), Bill Shirley (*Bill Carstairs*), Garry Owen (*Thompson*), William Haade (*Sawyer*), Jane Kean (*Sunshine*).

Lundigan is a navy man hopelessy in debt to the other crew members on board a battleship. He hates women but his buddies jokingly fake a marriage between him and cafe singer Ross. But other crew members, who have it in for Lundigan, fix it so the marriage is the real thing. There's a mix-up involving some stolen jewels, but all is naturally righted by the film's end. The problem here lies with the plotting. There are too many threads, some of which get tangled and others of which lead nowhere. Lundigan and Ross are okay but limited by the material. The direction isn't much help in solving the confusions, and the result is a boring mess. At the time there was a spate of Navy-based musicals coming from the studios, but this wasn't one of the better ones. Ross and Bill Shirley sing four tunes, including "Because We Are Americans."

p, Albert J. Cohen; d, Albert S. Rogell; w, Art Arthur, Malcolm Stuart Boylan (based on a story by Herbert Dalmas); ph, Ernest Miller; ed, Edward Mann; cos, Adele Palmer; m/l, Jule Styne, Frank Loesser, Emily Robinson Head.

Musical/Comedy   **(PR:A   MPAA:NR)**

SAILOR'S RETURN, THE*   (1978, Brit.) 112m
                                                  Euston-Ariel-NFFC/Osprey c

Tom Bell (*William Targett*), Shope Shodeinde (*Tulip*), Mick Ford (*Tom*), Paola Dionisotti (*Lucy*), George Costigan (*Harry*), Clive Swift (*The Rev. Pottock*), Ray Smith (*Fred Leake*), Ivor Roberts (*Molten*), Bernard Hill (*Carter*), Anthony Langdon (*Jack Sait*).

During Queen Victoria's reign a sailor returns home from duty in West Africa, bringing with him a native bride. With her dowry the couple set up an inn in the English countryside, but the locals don't want a black woman around. Bell fights with his sister and the local pastor over his love for Shodeinde, and the couple slowly drifts apart. Soon their money runs out and their lives are visited with tragedy when their newborn son dies. Finally, Bell is killed in a fight with a local and Shodeinde is forced to send her surviving son back to Africa. She herself is denied passage, however, and lives out her days as a maidservant in the inn she formerly owned. THE SAILOR'S RETURN is based on a novel by David Garnett, one of the many fine British novelists of the pre-WW I "Bloomsbury Group." His contemporaries included such noted men and women of letters as E.M. Forster, Virginia Woolf, Lytton Strachey, Clive Bell, and Roger Fry. The original novel is well-told and deceptively simple. The film, on the other hand, is a bit too simple and agonizingly slow-paced. The countryfolk's prejudice is played so overdramatically that it overwhelms the slight story. There's little style to the direction, making this more a soap opera than anything else. THE SAILOR'S RETURN had difficulty finding any theater bookings and eventually made its debut on British television in 1980.

p, Otto Plaschkes; d, Jack Gold; w, James Saunders (based on the novel by David Garnett); m, Carl Davis.

Drama   **(PR:O   MPAA:NR)**

SAILORS THREE   (SEE: THREE COCKEYED SAILORS, 1940, Brit.)

ST. BENNY THE DIP**½   (1951) 80m UA bw (GB: ESCAPE IF YOU
                                                                  CAN)

Dick Haymes (*Benny*), Nina Foch (*Linda Kovacs*), Roland Young (*Matthew*), Lionel Stander (*Monk*), Freddie Bartholomew (*Rev. Wilbur*), Oscar Karlweis (*Mr. Kovacs*), Dort Clark (*Lt. Saunders*), Will Lee (*Sgt. Monahan*), Verne Colette (*Walter*), Richard Gordon (*Rev. Miles*).

Three confidence men (Haymes, Young, and Stander) are on the lam and disguise themselves as clergymen in order to fool the cops. Unfortunately, the cops are not the only people fooled when the trio gets mistaken for real ministers in a skid row mission. Gradually they let the Roman collars get to them and end up going straight. Former child star Bartholomew plays a young minister who encounters the three. This predictable comedy does have some good moments even though you can see every joke a mile off. The cast is terrific under unexceptional direction.

p, Edward J. Danziger, Harry Lee Danziger; d, Edgar G. Ulmer; w, George Auerbach, John Roeburt (based on a story by Auerbach); ph, Don Malkames; m, Robert Stringer.

Comedy   **Cas.**   **(PR:A   MPAA:NR)**

ST. GEORGE AND THE 7 CURSES
                                      (SEE: MAGIC SWORD, THE, 1962)

ST. HELENS**   (1981) 90m Parnell c

Art Carney (*Harry Truman*), David Huffman (*Geologist*), Cassie Yates (*His Girl Friend*), Ron O'Neal (*Helicopter Pilot*), Bill McKinney, Albert Salmi, Tim Thomerson, Henry Darrow, Nehemiah Persoff.

On May 18, 1980, after much anticipation Mt. St. Helen's, an active volcano, finally erupted. Filmmakers were quick to jump on the disaster bandwagon, and this cheap quickie came out just a year after the event. Carney plays Harry Truman, the real-life man who refused to leave from his vacation cabin despite the coming disaster. He's really what makes this film as the rest of the roles are the usual set of stock characters found in disaster films. Best reason to watch this film is the fantastic footage of the volcano's eruption. Other than that, the film is highly fictionalized melodrama without much substance. It's an unfortunate waste of some fine talents.

p, Michael Murphy; d, Ernest Pintoff; w, Peter Bellwood, Larry Ferguson; ph, Jacques Haitkin (DeLuxe Color); m, Goblin and Buckboard; ed, George Berndt; spec eff, Magic Lantern.

Disaster Drama   **Cas.**   **(PR:A   MPAA:PG)**

SAINT IN LONDON, THE**½   (1939, Brit.) 72m RKO

George Sanders (*Simon Templar*), Sally Gray (*Penelope Parker*), David Burns (*Dugan*), Gordon McLeod (*Inspector Teal*), Henry Oscar (*Bruno Lang*), Ralph Truman (*Kussella*), Carl Jaffe (*Stengler*), Ben Williams (*Wilkins*), Nora Howard (*Mrs. Morgan*), Charles Carson (*Mr. Morgan*), Ballard Berkeley (*Richard Blake*), Hugh McDermott (*Tim*), John Abbott (*Count Duni*), Athene Seyler (*Mrs. Buckley*), Charles Paton.

Sanders returns as "The Saint" in the third outing for the RKO series. This time he's off to London to crack a gang that wants to pass off $5 million worth of counterfeit banknotes. Gray is a society girl who becomes enamoured of Sanders and horns her way into the investigation, and Burns is a wisecracking underworld ringleader. As usual for the series, this is an enjoyable mystery with a taut script and intelligent direction. The society girl forcing her way into the hero's investigation is reminiscent of THE THIN MAN, but Gray does so well in the part that you're willing to forgive RKO for stealing the idea from MGM's series. Carstairs directed this film as part of a quota agreement for RKO. THE SAINT IN LONDON initially earned $140,000 for the studio, a fairly handsome sum for the times. (See: SAINT series, Index.)

p, William Sistrom; d, John Paddy Carstairs; w, Lynn Root, Frank Fenton (based on the novel *The Million Pound Day* by Leslie Charteris); ph, Claude Friese-Greene.

Mystery   **Cas.**   **(PR:A   MPAA:NR)**

SAINT IN NEW YORK, THE*   (1938) 71m RKO

Louis Hayward (*The Saint/Simon Templar*), Kay Sutton (*Fay Edwards*), Sig Rumann (*Hutch Rellin*), Jonathan Hale (*Inspector Henry Fernack*), Jack Carson (*Red Jenks*), Paul Guilfoyle (*Hymie Fanro*), Frederick Burton (*William Valcross*), Ben Welden (*Papinoff*), Charles Halton (*Vincent Nather*), Cliff Bragdon (*Sebastian Lipke*), Frank M. Thomas (*Prosecutor*), George Irving (*Judge*), Paul Fix (*Hoodlum*), Lee Phelps (*Cassidy, Detective*).

"The Big Fellow" is the evil underworld king who just about runs New York City. It's up to Hayward as "The Saint" to use all of his super sleuthing talents to stop the bad man and his henchmen. Stylish and witty, this was the first film in the popular SAINT series adapted from the stories of Charteris. The entire production is slick and brimming with imagination. Hayward, who played the sleuth only in this and the final film in the series (THE SAINT'S GIRL FRIDAY), is just a touch over-eager, but otherwise he's fine in the role. Direction is zippy, matched with a sharp script that remained quite faithful to the novel. THE SAINT IN NEW YORK proved to be a popular release and RKO immediately bought the rights to the rest of the Saint novels. The series, which spawned nine films, was one of the studio's most important and brought them good financial success. (See SAINT series, Index.)

p, William Sistrom; d, Ben Holmes; w, Charles Kaufman, Mortimer Offner (based on the novel by Leslie Charteris); ph, Joseph August, Frank Redman; ed, Harry Marker; art d, Van Nest Polglase; cos, Edward Stevenson.

Mystery   **Cas.**   **(PR:A   MPAA:NR)**

SAINT IN PALM SPRINGS, THE*   (1941) 65m RKO

George Sanders (*Simon Templar, The Saint*), Wendy Barrie (*Elna Johnson*), Paul Guilfoyle (*Clarence "Pearly" Gates*), Jonathan Hale (*Inspector Henry Fernack*), Linda Hayes (*Margaret Forbes*), Ferris Taylor (*Mr. Evans*), Harry Shannon (*Chief Graves*), Eddie Dunn (*Detective Barker*), Richard Crane (*Whitey*), Charles Quigley (*Mr. Fletcher*), Gene Rizzi (*Bartender*), Joey Ray (*Hoodlum*), Vinton Haworth (*Hotel Clerk*), Robert Carson (*Mystery Man*), Chester Tallman, Gayle Mellott (*Guests*), James Harrison (*Bellhop*), Frank O'Connor (*Brady*), Norman Mayes (*Club Car Bartender*), Edmund

Elton (*Peter Masson*), Lee Bonnell (*Tommy*), Henry Roquemore (*Mr. Flannery*), Betty Farrington, Mary MacLaren (*Women*), Chick Collins (*Callahan*), Ed Thomas (*Waiter*), Peter Lynn (*Jimmy the Henchman*).

This was Sanders' last appearance as "The Saint" in one of the series' lesser entries. Three rare postage stamps are smuggled out of England and Sanders is asked by his police friends to solve the mystery. Along the way he deals with three murders, a kidnap attempt, and a few attempts on his own life. Realizing the gangsters are tailing him from England to Palm Springs, Sanders gives them the slip and fights back in his usual suave, sophisticated manner. Barrie and Hale, two series vets, were back for this one, and Guilfoyle appears in a reprise of his role "Pearly" Gates. The direction is suspenseful and clever as usual, but the script lacks the characteristic gleam. Still, it's not a bad little mystery and turned the studio a good-sized profit of $90,000. From this Sanders went on to THE FALCON, a SAINT-like series that was also produced by RKO. (See: SAINT series, Index.)

p, Howard Benedict; d, Jack Hively; w, Jerry Cady (based on a story by Leslie Charteris); ph, Harry Wild; m, Roy Webb; ed, George Hively; cos, Renie.

Mystery   **(PR:A   MPAA:NR)**

ST. IVES**   (1976) 93m WB c

Charles Bronson (*Raymond St. Ives*), John Houseman (*Abner Procane*), Jacqueline Bisset (*Janet Whistler*), Maximilian Schell (*Dr. John Constable*), Harry Guardino (*Detective Deal*), Harris Yulin (*Detective Oller*), Dana Elcar (*Charlie Blunt*), Michael Lerner (*Myron Green*), Dick O'Neill (*Hesh*), Elisha Cook (*Eddie the Bell Boy*), Val Bisoglio (*Finley Cummins*), Burr DeBenning (*Officer Frann*), Daniel J. Travanti (*Johnny Parisi*), Joe Roman (*Seymour*), Robert Englund, Mark Thomas, Jeff Goldblum (*Hoods*), Tom Pedi (*Fat Angie Polaterra*), Joseph De Nicola (*No Nose*), George Memmoli (*Shippo*), Don Hanmer (*Punch*), Bob Terhune (*Mike Kluszewski*), Norman Palmer (*McDuff*), Walter Brook (*Mickey*), Jerome Thor (*Chasman*), George Sawaya (*Arab Bagman*), Glenn Robards (*Procane Butler*), Jerry Brutsche (*Jack Boykins*), Dar Robinson (*Jimmy Peskoe*), Lynn Borden (*Party Girl*), Stanley Brock (*Night Clerk*), Larry Martindale, Olan Soule (*Station Men*), Louis H. Kelly (*Croupier*), Rosalyn Marshall (*Girl at Table*), Owen Hith Pace (*Slim*), Morris Buchanan (*Police Sergeant*), Ben Young (*Detective*), John Steadman (*Willie*), Benjie Bancroft (*Patrolman*), Gayla Gallaway, Jill Stone (*Nurses*), Edward Cross (*Orderly*).

Bronson plays a former crime reporter who turns to novel writing. He's contacted by Houseman for a private job. It seems some ledgers have been stolen that could potentially set off a gang war between two rival mob factions. Bronson is asked to recover the ledgers, a job he reluctantly accepts. This leads him into a labyrinth of betrayal and murder, all played in a boring, plodding style, and very confusing for the audience. Surprisingly, the violence is toned down in ST. IVES, unusual for a Bronson film. This gives Bronson more of a chance to act, which he does in decidedly better form than in most of his films. For once Bronson gets to show he knows more than three facial expressions. However, the film's merits are few, and it is hampered by the many confusions within the plot. At points a little violence might be a welcome relief from the tedium. Bisset has a minor role as the love interest, conveying a volatile eroticism simply by unzipping her dress. Watch for Daniel J. Travanti (of TV's "Hill Street Blues") in an early appearance. Jeff Goldblum, who would later score in THE BIG CHILL, also has a bit appearance.

p, Pancho Kohner, Stanley Canter; d, J. Lee Thompson; w, Barry Beckerman (based on the novel *The Procane Chronicle* by Oliver Bleeck); ph, Lucien Ballard (Technicolor); m, Lalo Schifrin; ed, Michael F. Anderson; prod d, Philip M. Jeffries; set d, Robert De Vestel; spec eff, Gene Grigg.

Crime   **Cas.**   **(PR:O   MPAA:PG)**

SAINT JACK**½   (1979) 112m Playboy-Shoals Creek-Copa de Oro/
                                                                    New World c

Ben Gazzara (*Jack Flowers*), Denholm Elliott (*William Leigh*), James Villiers (*Frogget*), Joss Ackland (*Yardley*), Rodney Bewes (*Smale*), Mark Kingston (*Yates*), Lisa Lu (*Mrs. Yates*), Monika Subramaniam (*Monika*), Judy Lim (*Judy*), George Lazenby (*Senator*), Peter Bogdanovich (*Eddie Schuman*), Joseph Noel (*Gopi*), Ong Kian Bee (*Hing*), Tan Yan Meng (*Little Hing*), Andrew Chua (*Andrew*), Ken Wolinski (*Australian Businessman*), Peter Tay (*Mike*), Osman Zailani (*Bob*), Elizabeth Ang (*Shirley*), S.M. Sim (*Mr. Tan*), Peter Pang, Ronald Ng, Seow Teow Keng (*Triad Gang*).

In Singapore circa 1971, Gazzara is an American pimp who tries to become an independant operator. This arouses the anger of the local mobsters who want to put him out of business. He finally knuckles under after heavy pressure and goes to work for an American mobster (played by director Bogdanovich in a good quirky performance). He's forced to photograph an important senator in the arms of a young male prostitute, but eventually Gazzara's conscience catches up with him. The film uses the locations well and Gazzara's performance is an actor's dream. But SAINT JACK never quite becomes the "important" film it seems to aspire to be. The story is told in too meandering a style and the many well-acted characterizations never mesh together. This was Bogdanovich's first film in many years. He had

been a boy wonder but destroyed his career creating films for his various mistresses and trying to recapture dead genres (DAISY MILLER and AT LONG LAST LOVE are two of the worst modern films imaginable, real disappointments considering they were made by the director of THE LAST PICTURE SHOW). SAINT JACK helped Bogdanovich regain his critical strength, but it wasn't until 1985's MASK that he was accepted by the public again. SAINT JACK was produced by Roger Corman, who had given the director his start in 1964 with THE WILD ANGELS. Serving as executive producer was Playboy's Hugh Hefner, which may explain some of the film's unnecessary steamier moments.

p, Roger Corman; d, Peter Bogdanovich; w, Bogdanovich, Howard Sackler, Paul Theroux (based on the novel by Theroux); ph, Robby Muller; ed, William Carruth; art d, David Ng.

Drama   **Cas.**   **(PR:O   MPAA:R)**

SAINT JOAN**½   (1957) 110m Wheel/UA bw

Jean Seberg (*Joan*), Richard Widmark (*Charles the Dauphin*), Richard Todd (*Dunois*), Anton Walbrook (*Cauchon, Bishop of Beauvais*), John Gielgud (*The Earl of Warwick*), Felix Aylmer (*The Inquisitor*), Harry Andrews (*John de Stognumber*), Barry Jones (*de Courcelles*), Finlay Currie (*The Archbishop of Rheims*), Bernard Miles (*The Master Executioner*), Patrick Barr (*Capt. Le Hire*), Kenneth Haigh (*Brother Martin Ladvenu*), Archie Duncan (*Robert de Baudricourt*), Margot Grahame (*Duchesse de la Tremouille*), Francis de Wolff (*La Tremouille, Lord Chamberlain*), Victor Maddern (*English Soldier*), David Oxley (*Gilles de Rais/"Bluebeard"*), Sydney Bromley (*Baudricourt's Steward*), David Langton (*Captain of Warwick's Guard*), David Hemmings.

After a talent hunt which sifted through 18,000 applicants and took director Preminger to more than 20 cities, the final choice for the plum role in Shaw's classic was Jean Seberg, a young Iowa lass whose only acting experience had been in amateur productions. As soon as this film was released, Seberg was set on fire by almost everyone who saw her inexperienced attempts at the famed dialog. Shaw's play was somewhat anticlerical and it was a surprise when Greene, an ardent converted Catholic, was chosen to adapt the work for the screen. The picture begins with a portion of the play's epilog and goes back in time as a flashback. It's France in the 15th Century and the country is divided and ruled by Britons and Burgundians. Seberg is a teenager from the country who comes to the palace of Widmark carrying a letter of introduction from Duncan, a captain in the service. It is said that Seberg has heard the angels speak and has a particular acquaintance with Saints Margaret and Catherine, as well as Michael the Archangel. Through them, she has received her mission in life: to help Widmark assume the throne as king. Widmark is suitably impressed by her zealousness and makes her the commander of his army. At Orleans, there is a battle between the British and Widmark's forces, led by Seberg. Widmark is made king and orders an end to the fighting, but Seberg wants to continue and rid the country of the invaders from across the Channel. Seberg rallies her forces but no longer has the blessing of Widmark. She is captured at Compiegne by the Burgundians, who sell her to Gielgud, the Earl of Warwick, who commands the forces of the English. Seberg is held in jail for nine months and relentlessly questioned. The church officials refuse to acknowledge that this upstart could have been on speaking terms with saints, so she is tried for heresy in Rouen. Rather than face torture, she signs a confession but recants and tears it up when she learns that her sentence will be one of solitary confinement for life. Gielgud, in a fit of pique similar to Pilate's, wants to put an end to this and orders Seberg's burning at the stake in a market place for all to see. The date was May 30, 1431, and the young woman was 19. In the 1923 play, Dame Sybil Thorndike played Joan at the age of 41. The stage is kinder to age than the screen, and although many actresses with more experience wanted the role, Preminger opted for the newcomer and all the attendant publicity, which included Seberg's introduction on Ed Sullivan's TV show. It didn't help and the picture was a failure on many levels. The fervency of the child-soldier is lost on the screen and she appears to be sweet and naive and not the calculating person Shaw intended and wrote of in the play's prolog. Preminger always uses the best actors he can hire and the supporting cast reflects that policy. In later years, Seberg would improve greatly before her tragic death.

p&d, Otto Preminger; w, Graham Greene (based on the play by George Bernard Shaw); ph, Georges Perinal; m, Mischa Spoliansky; ed, Helga Cranston; prod d, Roger Furse; art d, Raymond Simm; historical consultant, Dr. Charles Beard.

Period Drama   **Cas.**   **(PR:A-C   MPAA:NR)**

ST. LOUIS BLUES**½   (1939) 92m PAR bw

Dorothy Lamour (*Norma Malone*), Lloyd Nolan (*Dave Guerney*), Tito Guizar (*Rafael San Ramos*), Jerome Cowan (*Ivan DeBrett*), Jessie Ralph (*Aunt Tibbie*), William Frawley (*Maj. Martingale*), Mary Parker (*Punkins*), Maxine Sullivan (*Ida*), Cliff Nazarro (*Shorty*), Victor Kilian (*Sheriff Burdick*), Walter Soderling (*Mr. Hovey*), The King's Men (*Deck Hand Quartette*), Virginia Howell (*Mrs. Hovey*), Matty Malneck and his Orchestra (*Themselves*), Spencer Charters, Emmett Vogan (*Judges*), Joseph Crehan (*Simpson*), Billy Arnold (*Hotel Clerk*), George Guhl (*Turnkey*), Archie Twitchell (*Cameraman*), Florence Dudley (*Secretary*), Gene Morgan (*Pub-

licity Man), Emory Parnell (*Police Officer White*), Ernie Adams, Eddie Borden, Edward Hearn, Carl Harbaugh (*Actors*), Clarence Harvey (*Old Man*), Sterling Holloway (*Boatman*), Nora Cecil (*Storekeeper*), Wade Boteler (*Police Lieutenant*), Lane Chandler (*Man in Audience*), James Burtis (*Sailor in Boiler Room*).

A Broadway singing star (Lamour) is tired of her sarong-girl image as well as the manager (Cowan) who put her in that garb in the first place. She runs off to Missouri and meets a showboat owner (Nolan). They hit it off and she gets a job singing in his new review. It seems to be smooth sailing but the show is dealt a blow when Frawley, a rival carnival owner, discovers Lamour's true identity. He tries to keep the new show from opening by proving that Nolan's new singer is violating an old contract. This is a hit-or-miss effort with some parts working better than others. The musical numbers are what the film is all about and Lamour gets to vocalize plenty. Her tunes include "Junior" and the title number (by the great W.C. Handy), "Blue Nightfall" (Frank Loesser, Burton Lane), "I Go for That" (Loesser, Matty Malneck), and "Let's Dream in the Moonlight" by none other than director Walsh (who would make his name for his excellent action features) and Malneck. Sullivan's numbers include "Otchichornya," "Loch Lomond," and "Kinda Lonesome" (Leo Robin, Sam Coslow, Hoagy Carmichael). Loesser and Lane also contributed one other song, "The Song in My Heart is a Rhumba." Nolan's part had originally been offered to George Raft but the star turned it down.

p, Jeff Lazarus; d, Raoul Walsh; w, John C. Moffitt, Malcolm Stuart Boylan, Frederick Hazlitt Brennan, Virginia Van Upp (based on a story by Eleanore Griffin, William Rankin); ph, Theodor Sparkuhl; m, Frank Loesser; ed, William Shea; art d, Hans Dreier; ch, LeRoy Prinz.

Musical   **(PR:A   MPAA:NR)**

ST. LOUIS BLUES**   (1958) 93m PAR bw

Nat "King" Cole (*W.C. Handy*), Eartha Kitt (*Gogo Germaine*), Pearl Bailey (*Aunt Hagar*), Cab Calloway (*Blade*), Ella Fitzgerald (*Herself*), Mahalia Jackson (*Bessie May*), Ruby Dee (*Elizabeth*), Juano Hernandez (*Charles Handy*), Billy Preston (*W.C. Handy as a Boy*), Teddy Buckner, Barney Bigard, George "Red" Callender, Lee Young, George Washington (*Musicians*).

Cole is featured as the famed black composer of immortal blues tunes. His father (Hernandez) is a minister who feels his son is playing "the devil's music," but Cole finally chooses the music he knows he does best. Kitt is a New Orleans singer who encourages him, and Dee a local girl who simply wants to make him happy. Tragedy strikes when psychosomatic blindness sets in, but Cole eventually overcomes this, becomes widely admired for his music, and wins grudging acceptance by his father. ST. LOUIS BLUES is short on fact and conviction with an unimaginative direction that merely records the action. The only reason to see this film is its wonderful cast of popular musicians and their renditions of Handy's work. Cole's voice is at its lyrical best, and there are fine performances by Calloway, Jackson, and Fitzgerald. Watch for future pop star Preston playing Handy as a child. What's really significant about ST. LOUIS BLUES is its almost exclusive use of black talent. Blacks have been ignored or mistreated by Hollywood from the beginning of the movie industry and an all-black cast of this quality is a rarity. Songs include "Hesitating Blues," "Chantez Les Bas," "Beale Street Blues," (W.C. Handy), "Careless Love" (based on folk music by Handy; lyrics by Spencer Williams, Martha Koenig), "Morning Star," "Way Down Sou Where the Blues Began," "Mr. Bayle," "Aunt Hagar's Blues" (Handy; lyrics by Tim Brymn), "They that Sow" (hymn), and "Going to See My Sarah" (spiritual).

p, Robert Smith; d, Allen Reisner; w, Smith, Ted Sherdeman (based on the life and music of W. C. Handy); ph, Haskell Boggs (Vistavision); ed, Eda Warren; md, Nelson Riddle (based on themes and songs by Handy); art d, Hal Pereira, Roland Anderson; cos, Edith Head; spec eff, John P. Fulton.

Musical Biography   **(PR:A   MPAA:NR)**

ST. LOUIS KID, THE***   (1934) 67m WB bw (GB: A PERFECT WEEKEND)

James Cagney (*Eddie Kennedy*), Patricia Ellis (*Ann Reid*), Allen Jenkins (*Buck Willetts*), Robert Barrat (*Farmer Benson*), Hobart Cavanaugh (*Richardson*), Spencer Charters (*Merseldopp*), Addison Richards (*Brown*), Dorothy Dare (*Gracie*), Arthur Aylesworth (*Judge Jones*), Charles Wilson (*Harris*), William Davidson (*Joe Hunter*), Harry Woods (*Louie*), Gertrude Short (*The Girl Friend*), Eddie Shubert (*Pete*), Russell Hicks (*Gorman*), Guy Usher (*Sergeant*), Cliff Saum, Bruce Mitchell (*Cops*), Wilfred Lucas (*Policeman*), Mary Russell (*Office Girl*), Ben Hendricks (*Motor Cop*), Harry Tyler (*Mike*), Milton Kibbee (*Paymaster*), Tom Wilson (*Cook*), Alice Marr, Victoria Vinton (*Secretaries*), Lee Phelps (*Farmer*), Louise Seidel (*Girl in Car*), Mary Treen (*Giddy Girl*), Rosalie Roy, Nan Grey, Virginia Grey, Martha Merrill (*Girls*), Charles B. Middleton (*Sheriff*), Douglas Cosgrove (*Prosecutor*), Monte Vandergrift, Jack Cheatham (*Deputies*), Stanley Mack (*Driver*), Grover Liggen (*Attendant*), Frank Bull (*Broadcast Officer*), Wade Boteler (*Sergeant*), Frank Fanning, Gene Strong (*Policemen*), Edna Bennett (*Flora*), Clay Clement (*Man*), James Burtis (*Detective*), Eddie Fetherstone, Joan Barclay.

Cagney's last film of 1934 dealt with striking dairymen, a topical issue of the year. He plays a rough-and-tumble truck driver whose route takes him between St. Louis and Chicago. A group of strikers want no milk delivered into their district and are determined to stop any strikebreaking drivers. Cagney gets into a fight with some of the dairymen and ends up in jail as a result. He manages to escape one evening and heads off to visit his girl friend Ellis. While Cagney is free one of the strikers is killed by a trucking company goon. Cagney is fingered as the killer and consequently must prove his innocence. When Ellis tries to provide Cagney's alibi, she is kidnaped by some of the trucking company's agents who don't want the truth revealed. Eventually Cagney is able to outwit the villainous agents through a mixture of brains and brawn, rescuing Ellis and clearing his name of the murder charge. Despite the timeliness of the subject the story never delves into the issues raised by headlines of the era. Using the milk wars as a starting point, the film delivers another tough-guy Cagney portrait that rarely fails to entertain. The film is full of energy, led by Cagney's vigorous performance. Right from the beginning one knows just what sort of man Cagney is. He is introduced with his hands wrapped in bandages, souvenirs from a previous night's fisticuffs. Cagney's hands remained bandaged throughout the film but this hardly impedes his fighting abilities. Instead of pounding foes with clenched fists, the ever resourceful Cagney takes to butting antagonists with his head. This was a deliberate choice by the actor who was tired of merely punching out his foes in movie after movie. "...I just whipped my head around and hit the guy with my forehead. Down he went. For the rest of the picture I went around hitting people with my head, all of this in a specific attempt to vary the old punching formula," he wrote in his autobiography, *Cagney By Cagney.* What audiences missed in seeing Cagney's fists fly was more than made up in the rare opportunity of seeing his leading lady actually take a smack at him. Ellis is a good counterpart for Cagney, proving herself to be just as feisty as Cagney when it counts. Enright took over the direction after Robert Florey was dismissed from the assignment and does a fine job keeping the action filled story moving. The film was shot in a brisk two weeks at a cost of only $80,000 and made a whopping box-office profit of $1.8 million. A few years later, during a legal battle over film costs and earnings, Cagney brought up the financial statistics of THE ST. LOUIS KID as an example of studios making tremendous profits while failing to properly compensate actors for their work.

p, Samuel Bischoff; d, Ray Enright; w, Warren Duff, Seton I. Miller (based on a story by Frederick Hazlitt Brennan); ph, Sid Hickox; ed, Clarence Kolster; md, Leo F. Forbstein; art d, Jack Okey; cos, Orry-Kelly; makeup, Perc Westmore.

Drama   **(PR:A   MPAA:NR)**

ST. MARTIN'S LANE   (SEE: SIDEWALKS OF LONDON, 1940, Brit.)

SAINT MEETS THE TIGER, THE**   (1943, Brit.) 70m RKO/REP bw

Hugh Sinclair (*Simon Templar, the Saint*), Jean Gillie (*Pat Holmes*), Gordon McLeod (*Inspector Teal*), Clifford Evans (*Sidmarsh*), Wylie Watson (*Horace*), Dennis Arundell (*Bentley*), Charles Victor (*Bittle*), Louise Hampton (*Aunt Agatha*), John Salew (*Merridon*), Arthur Hambling (*Police Constable*), Amy Veness (*Mrs. Jones*), Claude Bailey (*Mr. Jones*), Noel Dainton (*Burton*), Eric Clavering (*Frankie*), Ben Williams (*Joe*), Tony Quinn (*Paddy*), John Slater (*Eddie*), Alf Goddard (*Tailor*).

After a two-year hiatus THE SAINT was revived by RKO, though this film was not considered part of the highly successful series. Sinclair returns once more as the hero who finds a man murdered on his doorstep. This begins a string of murders, involving Sinclair in a chase after a gold smuggler who also dabbles in phony mine shares. The dialog is as lame as the plot, inspiring more laughs than anything else. The British cast contributed below-par performances and often unintelligible accents. RKO knew they had a turkey on their hands and handed it over to Republic Studios for U.S. distribution. The direction is far below the standards set by the other SAINT films, and the script has more holes than a bullet-ridden corpse. All in all THE SAINT MEETS THE TIGER is a disappointing return for the popular detective. (See: SAINT series, Index.)

p, William Sistrom; d, Paul Stein; w, Leslie Arliss, James Seymour, Wolfgang Wilhelm (based on the novel *Meet the Tiger* by Leslie Charteris); ph, Bob Krasker; ed, Ralph Kemplen; art d, Paul Sheriff.

Mystery   **(PR:A   MPAA:NR)**

SAINT STRIKES BACK, THE***½   (1939) 67m RKO bw

George Sanders (*Simon Templar, the Saint*), Wendy Barrie (*Val Travers*), Jonathan Hale (*Inspector Henry Fernack*), Jerome Cowan (*Cullis, Criminologist*), Neil Hamilton (*Allan Breck*), Barry Fitzgerald (*Zipper Dyson, Burglar*), Robert Elliott (*Chief Inspector Webster*), Russell Hopton (*Harry Donnell*), Edward Gargan (*Pinky Budd*), Robert Strange (*Commissioner*), Gilbert Emery (*Martin Eastman, Philanthropist*), James Burke (*Secretary*), Nella Walker (*Mrs. Lucy Fernack*), Paul E. Burns (*Organ Grinder*), Willie Best (*Algernon, Saint's Butler*).

Sanders plays the Robin Hood-like sleuth in this second adventure in THE SAINT series, having taken over the role from Louis Hayward that he would play in the majority of the SAINT pictures. In this one, Sanders is bound for San Francisco to prove that Barrie's murdered father was not the brains behind a series of clever murders. Sanders, on loan from 20th Century-Fox, takes the role and makes it his own. Until this film he had been slowly working his way into the Hollywood system after coming from England. Hale returns as a police detective and Barrie is fine as the female lead. Good support is provided in the secondary roles and spine-tingling direction makes the most of clever script. After this film THE SAINT was a guaranteed winner in the public eye and RKO had a monster hit on their hands. (See SAINT series, Index.)

p, Robert Sisk; d, John Farrow; w, John Twist (based on the novel *Angels of Doom* by Leslie Charteris); ph, Frank Redman; ed, Jack Hively; md, Roy Webb.

Mystery   **Cas.**   **(PR:A MPAA:NR)**

SAINT TAKES OVER, THE*   (1940) 68m RKO bw

George Sanders (*Simon Templar, the Saint*), Wendy Barrie (*Ruth*), Jonathan Hale (*Inspector Henry Fernack*), Paul Guilfoyle (*Clarence "Pearly" Gates*), Morgan Conway (*Sam Reese*), Robert Emmett Keane (*Leo Sloan*), Cyrus W. Kendall (*Max Bremer*), James Burke (*Mike*), Robert Middlemass (*Capt. Wade*), Roland Drew ("*Rocky*" *Weldon*), Nella Walker (*Lucy Fernack*), Pierre Watkin (*Egan*), Theodore Von Eltz (*Shipboard Card Cheater*).

This entry in RKO's series had the first original story created for a SAINT film without using a Charteris novel as a source. The film works just as well as its predecessors, with Sanders once again helping out hapless police inspector Hale. The story involves a group of race track gamblers who've been framing Hale. Sanders comes in to help and stumbles across a few murders before wrapping up the case. Guilfoyle is a gang member who goes straight and helps Sanders, while Barrie returns to the series in a minor role as a mob hit-woman. The original script is witty and clever with some good twists, nicely handled by the direction. The supporting cast is good and Sanders, as usual is superb. (See SAINT series, Index.)

p, Howard Benedict; d, Jack Hively; w, Lynn Root, Frank Fenton (based on characters created by Leslie Charteris); ph, Fred Redman; ed, Desmond Marquette.

Mystery   **Cas.**   **(PR:A MPAA:NR)**

ST. VALENTINE'S DAY MASSACRE, THE*½** (1967) 100m FOX c

Jason Robards, Jr. (*Al "Scarface" Capone*), George Segal (*Peter Gusenberg*), Ralph Meeker (*George "Bugs" Moran*), Jean Hale (*Myrtle Nelson*), Clint Ritchie ("*Machinegun Jack*" *McGurn*), Frank Silvera (*Nicholas Sorello*), Joseph Campanella (*Al Wienshank*), Richard Bakalyan (*John Scalise*), David Canary (*Frank Gusenberg*), Bruce Dern (*John May*), Harold J. Stone (*Frank "The Enforcer" Nitti*), Michele Guayini (*Patsy Lolordo*), Kurt Kreuger (*James Clark*), Paul Richards (*Charles Fischetti*), Joseph Turkel (*Jake "Greasy Thumb" Guzik*), Milton Frome (*Adam Heyer*), Mickey Deems (*Reinhart Schwimmer*), John Agar (*Dion O'Bannion*), Celia Lovsky (*Josephine Schwimmer*), Tom Reese (*Ted Newberry*), Jan Merlin (*Willie Marks*), Alex D'Arcy (*Joey Aiello*), Reed Hadley (*Earl "Hymie" Weiss*), Gus Trikonis (*Rio*), Charles Dierkop (*Salvanti*), Tom Signorelli (*Bobo Borotto*), Rico Cattani (*Albert Anselmi*), Alex Rocco (*Diamond*), Leo Gordon (*James Morton*), Barboura Morris (*Jeanette Landsman*), Mary Grace Canfield (*Mrs. Doody, Landlady*), Daniel Ades (*Little Jerry Molina*), Richard Krisher (*Desk Clerk*), Paul Frees (*Narrator*), Jack Nicholson (*Gino*), Ron Gans (*Chapman*), Jack Del Rio, Phil Haran, Bob Brandin, Ernesto Moralli, Nick Borgaini (*Capone's Board Members*), Ken Scott (*Policeman*), Joan Shawlee (*Edna, Frank's Girl Friend*), Dale Van Sickel (*Stunt Double*).

As to be expected of this Corman produced bloodbath, the violence is excessive and the viewer must choose a hero from an army of death-dealing thugs, yet, surprisingly, this film has not only high production values but it does a good job depicting the gangland events and personalities as they really were at the end of America's most reckless decade. Even though he's all wrong as Capone, too thin and too old and certainly too intelligent, Robards gives a bravura performance as Scarface, Chicago's public menace No.1. With Frees narrating a blow-by-blow description of events, heralding the carnage to follow as if he were giving the background to the Declaration of Independence, the story of Chicago's gangland wars unfolds quickly under Corman's rapid-fire direction. The crime wars between Robards and his rivals on the North Side of Chicago reach epic proportions, especially when Meeker, essaying George "Bugs" Moran, decides to eliminate the dreaded Robards and his seemingly all-powerful Mafia-backed South Side gang. He kills Guayini, playing Mafia don Patsy Lolordo, and this throws Robards into a frenzy. He tells his top aides– Turkel, Stone, Richards–that he plans on wiping out Meeker's entire mob once and for all, even though they counsel against it, urging truce, peace. Robards tells them that Meeker and his gang will stop at nothing and reminds them of the bloody years that have gone before when he tried to be conciliatory toward the North Siders and we see in flashback a long series of events and ruthless personalities recounting Robards' first days in Chicago. He is shown meeting with Agar, playing the feared Irish gangleader Dion O'Bannion, Hadley, as Earl "Hymie" Weiss, and Meeker, trying to establish boundaries to their competing bootleg empires, agreeing on a nonviolent arrangement only to see the truce broken again and again by both sides. We see in flashback how

Robards' men are slain and even he is attacked in broad daylight while sitting in the coffee shop of the Hawthorn Inn in Cicero (Capone's private fiefdom, 1924-28), as 10 cars full of Hadley's men rake the place with machine guns, driving Robards to cower on the restaurant floor. This spectacular raid (which really occurred in 1925) is visually captioned by Segal, playing Pete Gusenberg, Moran's most feared gunsel, stepping from one of the slowly passing cars, kneeling on the cement in front of the hotel, and methodically emptying his machine gun into its foyer, destroying its interior as he guns down chandeliers, candelabra, furniture, walls, all to show his contempt for Robards and his power. The reprisals by Robards are shown: the gunning down of Agar in his flower shop by Bakalyan and Cattani, Robards' top killers (Scalise and Anselmi) as they ostensibly arrive to pick up a floral arrangement for a funeral of a prominent gangland figure (this was known as the "handshake murder," in that one of the killers held O'Bannion's hand to prevent him from reaching for one of the three guns he always wore while the other assassin gunned him down) and the killing of Hadley and a group of his men as they step from their auto on Clark Street, all machine-gunned to death. (Weiss was mowed down in 1926 in front of Chicago's famed Holy Name Cathedral, sprayed with so many bullets that these tore through the gangster's body and smacked into the facade of the church, chipping away the words of its cornerstone.) Having summarized the awful gang wars and convinced his henchmen that the only way to deal with Meeker is with force, Robards goes about the planning of Meeker's destruction. First, he personally locates D'Arcy, playing turncoat Joey Aiello, who arranged the Lolordo killing, on a train about to leave the Windy City, and slits his throat while the mobster prays on his knees in his compartment. Robards holds many meetings to work out how to eradicate his North Side rivals and adopts a plan put forth by his top killer, Ritchie, playing the infamous "Machinegun Jack" McGurn. (His real name was Vincenzo DeMora and he took the name McGurn from an old time boxer he admired, DeMora being a novice pugilist in his early days.) Ritchie explains that something must occur to compel all of Meeker's gang members to be present at their headquarters at a garage on North Clark Street. (The front for the Moran Gang was the S-M-C Cartage Company at 2122 N. Clark Street.) He proposes that a decoy, Silvera, call Meeker, telling him that he has a truckload of hijacked imported booze for sale and the Robards gang actually stages a hijacking of the truck by Silvera to make sure Meeker accepts Silvera's story as the truth. Silvera delivers the hijacked truck of booze and is shorted on his payment by Segal who slaps him around and sends him on his way. Though most of Meeker's gang is present during the delivery, Silvera notices that Meeker himself is not there. Some time later, just before February 14, 1929, St. Valentine's Day, Silvera calls Meeker again, telling him he has another hijacked truckload of excellent Canadian booze. Meeker by now accepts Silvera as genuine and he tells him that he will take the shipment. Silvera, however, tells Meeker that the last time he delivered a shipment of booze to Meeker's garage his boys slapped him around and paid him less than the agreed-upon price. He insists that Meeker be present personally when he arrives with the truckload of booze so that he will be treated fairly. Meeker agrees. Ritchie then posts men in rooming houses around the gangland garage to make sure the entire gang, particularly Meeker, is present before he springs his trap. The day demonically selected by Robards for the delivery is St. Valentine's Day. (Capone reportedly supervised the entire plan and chuckled when it was ready to go, saying to Guzik: "I'm gonna deliver a Valentine to Bugs he will never forget.") On the appointed day, Ritchie's lookouts report via phone as each member of the Meeker gang enters the garage. They wait anxiously for the boss, Meeker, to arrive. Then they spot a man of Meeker's height and build, and report to Ritchie that Meeker is present in the garage. (They, like their real-life counterparts, erred, seeing instead Weinshank, played here by Campanella, who bore a close resemblance to Moran.) Ritchie and his other top gunners then get into an auto that has been made over to look like a police car, two of his men wearing policemen's uniforms. They arrive at the garage, the two cops going in first and lining up the seven gangsters inside against a wall, as if they are making a routine arrest. The gangsters inside, including mechanic Dern, meekly line up against the wall, facing the naked brick, telling the uniformed gunmen that they will probably lose their badges for such effrontery, that Meeker's paid-off politicians will be sending them to remote stations for not checking with "downtown." As the Meeker gangsters are being lined up, weapons removed from their pockets by the fake cops, Meeker turns a corner and sees the police car parked outside his headquarters; he steps inside a coffee shop with his two bodyguards, Reese and Merlin, intending to wait until the routine raid is over. (This actually happened; had not Moran, Newberry, and Marks ducked inside the restaurant, there would have been, undoubtedly, *ten* bullet-torn bodies on the floor of the garage instead of seven.) With the seven gangsters facing the wall, their hands spread high against the brick, helpless, the fake cops nod toward a door leading into the garage and Ritchie, Bakalyan, and Cattani step inside, withdrawing machine guns and shotguns from beneath their long coats, sauntering smugly to stand behind the men lined up against the wall, who cannot see them, and then open fire, cutting the men to pieces, firing their machine guns with devastating accuracy, spraying the wall head high, chest high, waist high, and knee high until all the rival gangsters topple, chopped, vivisected, one of them decapitated at the forehead by the riveting fusillade. Quickly, the killers depart their methodical gore, the phony cops grabbing the machine guns and training them on their fellow assassins in civilian clothes, stepping outside to the fake squad car with what appears to be prisoners being taken into custody. The car roars away and

soon cries are heard by Meeker in the street that "they just killed Bugs
Moran and his whole gang." Robards, knowing he will be blamed for the
crime, is at his Palm Island, Florida, estate, enjoying the sunshine when he
hears the news. He laughs loudly and goes back to a party he is giving for
his upstanding neighbors who will later serve as witnesses that he was in
Florida during the awful killing. Meeker, terrified, retreats to a hospital bed
where reporters later find him, nervously explaining that the dead men did
not work for him, that he is only a businessman taking a rest. When pushed
by reporters, Meeker blurts, "Only Capone kills like that!" Narration
finishes off the rest of the film with the stentorian Frees stating that the St.
Valentine's Day Massacre aroused an apathetic public into pressuring its
political and law enforcement representatives into waging a crusade against
the gangsters and this brought down Capone and all of the crime kingpins
of Chicago, ending with the grossly inaccurate statement that "though no
one is ever brought to trial for the slaughter, the killers all die violent deaths
within 22 months." Capone, the mastermind of the slaughter, did not die
until 1947 (his nemesis Moran dying of cancer in Leavenworth 10 years later
while serving time for bank robbery). The actual machine-gunners, according
to Jay Robert Nash's *Bloodletters and Badmen*, were McGurn, who did not
die until 1936, gunned down in a Chicago bowling alley with a comic
Valentine pinned to his shirt as a gruesome prank, and Scalise and Anselmi,
both personally killed by Capone about a year later–he took a baseball bat
to their heads–for attempting to usurp him. The man who actually did the
firing of the machine guns that mowed down the Moran gangsters was Fred
R. "Killer" Burke, an out-of-town gunman. He kept the weapon which did
the killing and this was found by Chicago police during a search of his rented
house. In the first significant case where ballistics played a major role, the
gun was matched to bullets dug out of the bodies of Moran's men. Burke,
tipped that the police had irrefutable evidence to convict him of the mass
killing, drove madly into Michigan, looking for a policeman to kill. He
spotted a traffic cop, started an argument, and gunned him down in full view
of witnesses, knowing he would be quickly convicted and sent to prison for
life, which is exactly what Burke wanted, for he also knew that Michigan
had no death penalty and that, if convicted of the St. Valentine's Day
Massacre, he would be sent to the electric chair in Illinois. Corman
admittedly does a good job with a complex story (at least the element of how
the massacre was engineered). This production looks expensive but had a
budget of only $1.5 million. Corman's documentary approach often goes
awry, especially when Frees must try to give credence to a slugfest between
Segal and his whore, Hale, as the blonde pavement pounder cavorts about
in a skimpy nightgown. Robards seems to have little direction and is allowed
to gnaw on everything during his incessant tirades, including his automatic.
The actor obviously attempts to make up for his lack of Latin persona by
growling his way through the part of Capone. Segal is good as the psychotic
killer Gusenberg and Capone's advisors, Richards, Stone, and Turkel are
convincingly oily. Meeker shines as the stubborn Bugs Moran and so does
the slippery Silvera as the Judas goat who sets up the slaughter. Jack
Nicholson was offered a strong supporting role in this film but turned it
down after figuring out that he would stay with the production longer and
receive more money if he took a bit part. Look for him as one of Ritchie's
henchmen setting up the massacre. He has one line of dialog. He is asked
what he is rubbing on his bullets and Nicholson replies: "It's garlic.... If the
bullets don't kill ya, ya die of blood poisoning." Actually, this was a
technique of Scalise and Anselmi, two uneducated Sicilian thugs who
brought such Mafia beliefs with them when they migrated to Chicago to kill
exclusively for Capone. This was the best production in the many films
chronicling the tawdry history of gangsters Corman produced or directed
over the years. Others include MACHINE GUN KELLY (1959), starring
Charles Bronson, and BLOODY MAMA, starring an excessively overweight
Shelley Winters as Ma Barker, in 1970, both as loaded with blood, guts, and
gore as THE ST. VALENTINE'S DAY MASSACRE.

p&d, Roger Corman; w, Howard Browne; ph, Milton Krasner (Panavision,
DeLuxe Color); m, Fred Steiner; ed, William B. Murphy; md, Lionel
Newman; art d, Jack Martin Smith, Phil Jeffries; set d, Walter M. Scott,
Steven Potter; spec eff, L.B. Abbott, Art Cruickshank, Emil Kosa, Jr.;
makeup, Ben Nye ; tech adv, Chicago Historical Society.

Crime   Cas.   (PR:O MPAA:NR)

SAINTED SISTERS, THE**   (1948) 89m PAR bw

Veronica Lake (*Letty Stanton*), Joan Caulfield (*Jane Stanton*), Barry
Fitzgerald (*Robbie McCleary*), William Demarest (*Vern Tewilliger*), George
Reeves (*Sam Stoaks*), Beulah Bondi (*Hester Rivercomb*), Chill Wills (*Will
Twitchell*), Darryl Hickman (*Jud Tewilliger*), Jimmy Hunt (*David Frisbee*),
Kathryn Card (*Martha Tewilliger*), Ray Walker (*Abel Rivercomb*), Harold
Vermilyea (*Lederer*), Clancy Cooper (*Cal Frisbee*), Dorothy Adams (*Widow
Davitt*), Hank Worden (*Taub Beasley*), Don Barclay (*Dr. Benton*), Edwin
Fowler (*Rev. Hallrock*), Dick Elliott (*Milt Freeman*), Eddie Parks (*Clem
Willis*), Rudolf Erickson, Sidney D'Albrook, Perc Launders, Douglas Spenc-
er, Max Wagner, Jack Woody, Jimmie Dundee (*Townsmen*), June Smaney,
Maria Tavares (*Townswomen*), Eula Guy (*Emmy Lou*), Beulah Hubbard
(*Mrs. Prentiss*), Frances Sandford (*Mrs. Grigsby*), Gigi Perreau (*Beasley
Girl*), Alex Gerry (*District Attorney*), Hal Rand (*Assistant District Attorney*),
David McMahon (*Policeman*), Richard Bond (*Detective*).

Lake and Caulfield are a pair of con artists who take a banker for $25,000.
They head out of New York City and cross the border to Canada, but a storm

forces them to seek shelter and they end up with Fitzgerald. He introduces
them around the little town on the Maine-Canada border and gradually the
pair reform their ways. They learn a thing or two about humanity and end
up donating their money to various needy people in the town. The film is
meant to be a comedy, but the premise is so far-fetched that it doesn't work
on any level. There are a few minor laughs, but the picture is permeated
with a feeling of unreality that inhibits the players. Fitzgerald, in one of his
patented good-natured characterizations, just about carries the film. Direction is credible with standard production values.

p, Richard Maibaum; d, William D. Russell; w, Harry Clork, N. Richard
Nash, Mindret Lord (based on a play by Elisa Bialk, Alden Nash); ph, Lionel
Lindon; m, Van Cleave; ed, Everett Douglass; art d, Hans Dreier, Henry
Bumstead.

Comedy   (PR:A MPAA:NR)

SAINTLY SINNERS**½   (1962) 78m Harvard/UA bw

Don Beddoe (*Father Dan*), Paul Bryar (*Duke*), Stanley Clements (*Slim*),
Ellen Corby (*Mrs. McKenzie*), Ron Hagerthy (*Joe Braden*), Erin O'Donnell
(*Sue*), Clancy Cooper (*Idaho*), William Fawcett (*Horsefly*), Addison Richards
(*Monsignor*), Willis Bouchey (*Harrihan*), Earle Hodgins (*Uncle Clete*),
Norman Leavitt (*Phineas*), Marjorie Bennett (*Mrs. Madigan*), Tommy
Farrell (*Mike*), Max Mellinger (*Sam*), Robert B. Williams (*Hank*), David
Tyrell (*Tubber*), Bobs Watson (*Attendant*), Bob Hopkins (*Honest Jim*), Marla
Craig (*Maybelle*).

A pair of minor con artists (Bryar and Clements) grab a car that belongs to
Hagerthy, an ex-con trying hard to make it as a salesman. The pair rob a
bank and put the swag in the car's spare tire. Before they can retrieve the
money a collection agency repossesses the car. It's then bought by Beddoe,
a parish priest who drives off on a fishing trip. But a sharp-eyed cop stops
him en route and, not realizing the man garbed in fisherman's outfit is really
a priest, arrests Beddoe for bank robbery. He's let go the next day and
Hagerthy is arrested for the crime. The cops complain that Beddoe is using
his church to harbor a criminal, so the priest is transferred to another parish
by his monsignor. This upsets the parishoners and fills Bryar and Clements
with guilt. They finally confess to the crime and Beddoe is returned to his
old parish. Hagerthy benefits as well, for this new-found fame helps him in
his sales career. This is a sweet, minor comedy with humanistic values. The
players are good, making the slightly far-out plot line believable. The
direction isn't bad, though it could be tighter.

p, Robert E. Kent; d, Jean Yarbrough; w, Kevin Barry; ph, Gilbert
Warrenton; m, Richard LaSalle; ed, Robert Carlisle; set d, Harry Reif; spec
eff, Barney Wolff.

Comedy   (PR:A MPAA:NR)

SAINTS AND SINNERS**   (1949, Brit.) 85m LFP/Lopert bw

Kieron Moore (*Michael Kissane*), Christine Norden (*Blanche*), Sheila
Manahan (*Sheila Flaherty*), Michael Dolan (*Canon*), Maire O'Neill (*Ma
Murnaghan*), Tom Dillon (*O'Brien*), Noel Purcell (*Flaherty*), Pamela Arliss
(*Betty*), Tony Quinn (*Berry*), Eddie Byrne (*Morreys*), Liam Redmond (*O'Dris-
coll*), Eric Gorman (*Madigan*), Cecilia McKevitt (*Maeve*), Austin Meldon
(*Auctioneer*), Minnie McKittrick (*Brigid Madden*), Godfrey Quigley (*Colin*),
Edward Byrne (*Barney Downey*), Sheila Ward (*Clothing Woman*), Joe
Kennedy (*Guard*), Dave Crowley (*Barman*), Vincent Ellis (*Paddy*), Gabrielle
Daye (*Maeve's Mother*), Harry Hutchinson (*Doctor*), James Neylin, Sam
Kydd, Glenville Darling, Vic Hagan (*Men in Bar*), Maurice Keary (*Flaher-
ty's Hotel Barman*), Maureen Delaney (*Postmistress*).

A small Irish town is the setting for this English production. Moore is a
resident who has served two years in prison for theft. But he's innocent and
is determined to prove it to the town's residents. Manahan, his former
fiancee, has become engaged to a local banker in the wake of his disgrace,
but Moore vows to win her back. The film showcases an unusual mix of Irish
traditions, folktales, and superstitions, all within the confines of an ordinary
plot line. However, it never quite achieves the level it aims for, and the
result is a disappointing comedy.

p&d, Leslie Arliss; w, Arliss, Paul Vincent Carroll, Mabbie Poole; ph,
Osmond Borradaile; m, Philip Green; ed, David Newhouse; prod d, Wilfred
Shingleton; md, Dr. Hubert Clifford; cos, Honoria Plesch.

Comedy   (PR:A MPAA:NR)

SAINT'S DOUBLE TROUBLE, THE**½   (1940) 68m RKO bw

George Sanders (*Simon Templar, the Saint/Duke Piato*), Helene Whitney
(*Anne Bitts*), Jonathan Hale (*Inspector Henry Fernack*), Bela Lugosi
(*Partner*), Donald MacBride (*Inspector John H. Bohlen*), John F. Hamilton
(*Limpy*), Thomas W. Ross (*Prof. Bitts*), Elliott Sullivan (*Monk*), Pat O'Malley
(*Express Man*), Donald Kerr (*Card Player*), Byron Foulger (*Jewel Cutter*),
William Haade, Walter Miller, Ralph Dunn.

In the fourth outing for RKO's SAINT series, Sanders finds himself in hot
water when the jewel thief he is after, known as "The Boss," is his exact
double. Sanders, of course, played a double role. As the crook, Sanders takes
to smuggling gems via an Egyptian mummy being shipped to a college

professor. Lugosi is the crook's assistant, an Egyptian smuggler. This is probably the weakest of Sanders' SAINT performances. As the sleuth he's his usual witty self, but fails to achieve the proper tone as a jewel thief. He appears in scenes with himself through the aid of rear screen projection. While the technique looks good, things are often confused as to who is who. One scene has good guy Sanders impersonating bad guy Sanders meeting up with bad guy Sanders impersonating good guy Sanders! This schizophrenic atmosphere is explained without the usual style and wit found in SAINT screenplays and the plot quickly becomes muddled. As the smuggler's assistant, Lugosi had hoped to break his "monster movie" image but this was not to be. His performance here is lacklustre, never becoming the believable villain that he is intended to be. On the set (done on RKO's back lot in only 19 days), Lugosi had a tendency to speak quite loudly in his familiar voice. After being reminded by the director that movies didn't require such boisterous vocalization, he toned down the vocals. Whitney, as the socialite romantic interest for Sanders made her film debut here. (See SAINT series, Index.)

p, Cliff Reid; d, Jack Hively; w, Ben Holmes (based on a story by Leslie Charteris); ph, J. Roy Hunt; m, Roy Webb; ed, Theron Warth; spec eff, Vernon Walker.

Mystery   **Cas.**   **(PR:A MPAA:NR)**

SAINT'S GIRL FRIDAY, THE*½   (1954, Brit.) 70m Hammer/RKO
                                   bw (GB: SAINT'S RETURN, THE)

Louis Hayward (Simon Templar, the Saint), Sydney Tafler (Max Lennar), Naomi Chance (Lady Carol Denby), Charles Victor (Chief Inspector Teal), Harold Lang (Jarvis), Thomas Gallagher (Hoppy Uniatz), Jane Carr (Katie French), Russell Enoch (Keith Merton), Diana Dors (Margie), Fred Johnson (Irish Cassidy).

After an 11-year absence, THE SAINT was revived one last time for the movies, and appropriately enough, Hayward, who originated the part in THE SAINT IN NEW YORK (1938), again plays the famous sleuth. In this picture, Hayward returns to London to visit an old girl friend, only to discover that she's been murdered. He tracks down the killers to gamblers aboard a luxury yacht to whom the victim was indebted. Hayward cracks the ring before they can murder their next intended victim, Chance, a woman who also is deep in debt to the killers. This final attempt to breathe new life into the famous sleuth character maintains all the style and grace present in the best of THE SAINT films. Although this was the end of the character's movie career, THE SAINT was successfully revived once more for television in the 1960s. This time Mr. Templar was played by Roger Moore, who later went on to play James Bond after Connery. But it was in this role as "The Saint," where he first achieved international fame. (See SAINT series, Index.)

p, Julian Lesser, Anthony Hinds; d, Seymour Friedman; w, Allan MacKinnon (based on a story by MacKinnon from characters created by Leslie Charteris); ph, Walter Harvey; m, Ivoy Slanley; ed, James Needs.

Mystery   **(PR:A MPAA:NR)**

SAINT'S RETURN, THE   (SEE: SAINT'S GIRL FRIDAY, THE, 1954,
                                                                    Brit.)

SAINT'S VACATION, THE*   (1941, Brit.) 60m RKO bw

Hugh Sinclair (Simon Templar, the Saint), Sally Gray (Mary Langdon), Arthur Macrae (Monty Hayward), Cecil Parker (Rudolph Hauser), Leueen MacGrath (Valerie), Gordon McLeod (Insp. Teal), John Warwick (Gregory), Ivor Barnard (Emil), Manning Whiley (Marko), Felix Aylmer (Leighton).

Sinclair takes over the title role of RKO's noted international sleuth. In this adventure, The Saint finds himself coupled with a sidekick, played by Macrae. The pair are in Switzerland on vacation and soon become involved in a hunt for a music box containing a secret code wanted by a group of international spies. Murder, torture, and mail robbery ensue in the usual SAINT style. The direction is up to par, a fast style that works well with the hide-and-seek plot. Unfortunately, Sinclair lacks that charm and finesse of his predecessor, Sanders. Still, he gives it his best shot with Gray, a series vet who makes a return appearance. This was the last of RKO's films of the SAINT series, although in several years the character would be revived for two more films. THE SAINT'S VACATION also marked the first time Charteris, the sleuth's creator, contributed to the screenplay. (See SAINT series, Index.)

p, William Sistrom; d, Leslie Fenton; w, Jeffry Dell, Leslie Charteris (based on the novel Getaway by Charteris); ph, Bernard Knowles; m, Bretton Byrd; ed, Al Barnes, R. Kemplin; md, Byrd; art d, Paul Sheriff.

Mystery   **Cas.**   **(PR:A MPAA:NR)**

SAL OF SINGAPORE**½   (1929) 70m Pathe bw

Phyllis Haver (Sal), Alan Hale (Capt. Erickson), Fred Kohler, Sr (Capt. Sunday), Noble Johnson (Erickson's 1st Mate), Dan Wolheim (Erickson's 2nd Mate), Jules Cowles (Cook), Pat Harmon (Sunday's 1st Mate), Harold William Hill (Baby).

Early programmer about a rough and tough waterfront saloon harpie who's collared by a skipper to keep her eye on a baby he's found in a'life boat. It's just a re-working of SCARLET SEAS with Richard Barthelmess, but SAL OF SINGAPORE works well for what it is. Though talkies were a staple by 1929, this had only 18 minutes of dialog which took up the final moments of the film. The actors make the transition from silent to speech without much trouble, although the dialog is creaky by modern standards. However, the various "ain'ts" and "lousys" that get tossed around were considered quite daring by Hollywood standards of dialog. In today's anything-goes era SAL OF SINGAPORE'S "rough launguage" has a sort of quaintness about it.

d, Howard Higgin; w, Elliot Clawson, Pierre Gendron, Higgin (based on the story "The Sentimentalists" by Dale Collins); ph, John J. Mescall; m, Josiah Zuro; ed, Claude Berkeley; titles, Edwin Justus Mayer.

Drama   **(PR:A MPAA:NR)**

SALAMANDER, THE*   (1983, U.S./Ital./Brit.) 101m Lew
                                   Grade-William R. Forman/ITC c

Franco Nero (Dante Matucci), Anthony Quinn (Bruno Manzini), Martin Balsam (Stefanelli), Sybil Danning (Lili Anders), Christopher Lee (Director Baldassare), Cleavon Little (Maj. Malinowsky), Eli Wallach (Leporello), Claudia Cardinale (Elena), Paul Smith (The Surgeon), John Steiner (Roditi), Renzo Palmer (Girgione), Anita Strindberg (Princess), Marino Mase, Jacques Herlin, Gita Lee.

When an Italian general is killed, counter-intelligence officer Nero begins an investigation. This leads to the uncovering of a planned fascist over-throw of the existing Italian government, spearheaded by Wallach. Quinn plays what can only be termed an over-sized cameo with his role as a rich industry king who tracks down war criminals. Despite the uniformly talented cast and potentially exciting material, THE SALAMANDER is a suspense film with more laughs than thrills. The dialog is pure hokum delivered in a lacklustre style by the majority of the cast. The director previously won an Oscar as best film editor, but fails to score in his new job with a heavy-handed style. Among the cast members only Lee instills any sort of life to his part. This was initially released in Europe before it's American debut, but the producers, realizing what a bomb they had on their hands sold the film to Home Box Office, a cable television system, before a limited theatrical release. It was also originally adapted by West from his own novel and titled THE DEVIL'S ADVOCATE, but failed to receive U.S. distribution.

p, Paul Maslansky; d, Peter Zinner; w, Robert Katz (based on a novel by Morris West); ph, Marcello Gatti; m, Jerry Goldsmith; ed, Claudio Cutry; art d, Giantito Burchiellaro; cos, Fabrizio Caracciolo.

Thriller   **(PR:O MPAA:NR)**

SALAMMBO   (SEE: LOVE OF SALAMMBO, THE, 1962, Fr./Ital.)

SALARIO PARA MATAR   (SEE: MERCENARY, THE, 1970,
                                                             Ital./Span.)

SALESLADY**½   (1938) 65m MON bw

Anne Nagel (Mary), Weldon Heyburn (Bob), Harry Davenport (Cannon), Harry Hayden (Steele), Ruth Fallows (Lillian), Kenneth Harlan (Bigelow), Doris Rankin (Matron), John St. Polis (Crane).

Low budget picture stars Nagel as a rich girl who wants a man to marry her for love, not daddy's money. She disregards her wealthy background and finds a mate in Heyburn. Soon they are up to their necks in financial troubles. But when Heyburn loses his job, he refuses to take another job, or money, from Nagel's millionaire father.

p, Ken Goldsmith; d, Arthur Greville Collins; w, Marion Orth (based on the story "Nothing Down" by Kubec Glasmon); ph, Gilbert Warrenton; m, Abe Meyers; ed, Russell Schoengarth.

Romance   **(PR:A MPAA:NR)**

SALLAH**½   (1965, Israel) 105m Sallah Ltd./Palisades International
                                          bw (SALLAH SHABATI)

Haym Topol [Topol] (Sallah Shabati), Geula Noni (Habbubah Shabati), Gila Almagor (Bathsheva Sosialit), Arik Einstein (Ziggi), Shraga Friedman (Neuman), Zaharira Harifai (Frieda), Shaika Levi (Shimon Shabati), Nathan Meisler (Mr. Goldstein), Esther Greenberg (Sallah's Wife), Mordecai Arnon (Mordecai).

An oriental Jew, played by the gifted actor Topol, immigrates with his family to the newly formed state of Israel in 1949. They take up housing in a run-down camp until they can afford better living conditions. But Topol is forever lazy and will only work up a sweat to scheme his way out of real work. He sells his vote in elections several times over as one way to raise some easy cash. His lovely daughter Noni falls in love with Einstein, a resident of a kibbutz. Topol fools a cab driver into buying Noni for Einstein. Topol's son Levi has problems with his love life when he falls for another kibbutz member, Almagor. The kibbutz director wants some money from Topol, but through his constant scheming, he exposes Israel's housing problems and finagles an apartment for his family at last.

p, Menahem Golan; d&w, Ephraim Kishon (based on the story by Kishon); ph, Floyd Crosby; m, Yohanan Zarai; ed, Dani Schick, Jacques Erlich, Roberto Cinquini; art d, Joseph Carl; cos, Gina Rosenbach; makeup, Rachel Golan.

Comedy   **Cas.**   **(PR:C MPAA:NR)**

SALLY**½   (1929) 103m FN-WB c

Marilyn Miller *(Sally)*, Alexander Gray *(Blair Farrell)*, Joe E. Brown *(Connie)*, T. Roy Barnes *(Otis Hooper)*, Pert Kelton *(Rosie)*, Ford Sterling *("Pops" Shendorff)*, Maude Turner Gordon *(Mrs. Ten Brock)*, E.J. Ratcliffe *(John Farquar)*, Jack Duffy *(The Old Roue)*, Nora Lane *(Marcia)*, Albertina Rasch Ballet.

One of the first color musicals to be lensed and released in both silent and talkie versions, SALLY is a tuneful extravaganza based on the Kern-Bolton 1920 stage show which also featured Miller. It had been done as a silent in 1925 with Colleen Moore and Leon Errol and that version, while lacking songs and color, was far funnier. Miller is a waitress who dances and sings her way into our hearts as she ascends the staircase to the heights of Broadway stardom. That's about the size of the story. On this slim tale, they hung a cast which included Joe E. Brown for comic relief, Gray for male sex appeal, Chaplin veteran Sterling for a bit of villainy, 150 gorgeous showgirls, 36 superb Albertina Rasch dancers, 110 musicians in the orchestra, and some of the largest sets ever built at that time. Instead of taking the story outside, the producers constructed exterior-interior sets so they could better control the new sound technology as well as the color film exposure. Tiny Miller was a very important star in theaters, although her charm seemed to elude the cameras, despite an energetic attitude and her winsome ways. Many of the Kern songs were tossed aside in favor of some new ones by studio writers Al Dubin and Joe Burke. The remaining Kern melodies were "Look for the Silver Lining" (lyrics by B.G. De Sylva) and "Wild Rose" (lyrics by Clifford Grey). Dubin and Burke reworked Kern's "Sally" and also wrote "What Will I Do Without You?" "If I'm Dreaming, Don't Wake Me Up Too Soon," "All I Want to Do Do Do Is Dance," "Walking Off Those Balkan Blues," and "After Business Hours." Even by 1929 standards, this story had been seen many times before. It wasn't long before the studios got wise and decided that they needn't spend a lot of cash for stage rights. Rather, they commenced making original musicals for the screen, hired the best song writers they could find, built their own stables of stars, and began a trend which lasted for decades.

d, John Francis Dillon; w, Waldemar Young (based on the musical play by Guy Bolton, Jerome Kern); ph, Dev Jennings, C. Edgar Schoenbaum (Technicolor); ed, Leroy Stone; md, Leo Forbstein; art d, Jack Stone; cos, Edward Stevenson; ch, Larry Ceballos.

Musical/Comedy   **(PR:A MPAA:NR)**

SALLY AND SAINT ANNE***   (1952) 90m UNIV bw

Ann Blyth *(Sally O'Moyne)*, Edmund Gwenn *(Grandpa)*, John McIntire *(Goldsooth McCarthy)*, Palmer Lee [Gregg Palmer] *(Johnny Evans)*, Hugh O'Brian *(Danny O'Moyne)*, Jack Kelly *(Mike O'Moyne)*, Frances Bavier *(Mom O'Moyne)*, Otto Hulett *(Pop O'Moyne)*, Kathleen Hughes *(Lois Foran)*, George Mathews *(Father Kennedy)*, Lamont Johnson *(Willie)*, King Donovan *(Hymie)*, Robert Nichols, Alix Talton, George Mathews.

Blyth is a young woman with a fervent belief in Saint Anne, the mother of Mary and patron saint of young girls. It seems St. Anne answers all of Blyth's prayers, such as her brother O'Brian's boxing debut, Blyth's boy-girl romances, and the fight against an alderman who wants to tear down the family home to make room for an apartment complex. Gwenn steals the show as Blyth's grandfather, a man who thought he was dying twenty years prior to the storys commencement. He's kept up the charade for his own amusement and somehow has gotten away with it for two decades. Mathews is fine in a bit part as the priest who's tired of the old man's games. The script has a homey quality to it that works nicely with some good humanistic comic moments. But the film occasionally panders to sugary sweetness, often overplaying its simplicity. The performances of the cast overcome this handicap, however, making SALLY AND SAINT ANNE perhaps better than it should have been.

p, Leonard Goldstein; d, Rudolph Mate; w, James O'Hanlon, Herb Meadow (based on a story by O'Hanlon); ph, Irving Glassberg; m, Frank Skinner; ed, Edward Curtiss; art d, Bernard Herzbrun, Hilyard Brown.

Comedy   **(PR:A MPAA:NR)**

SALLY BISHOP***   (1932, Brit.) 80m BL bw

Joan Barry *(Sally Bishop)*, Harold Huth *(John Traill)*, Isabel Jeans *(Dolly Durlacher)*, Benita Hume *(Evelyn Standish)*, Kay Hammond *(Janet Hallard)*, Emlyn Williams *(Arthur Montague)*, Anthony Bushell *(Bart)*, Annie Esmond *(Landlady)*, Diana Churchill *(Typist)*.

Barry is a typist and mistress of a wealthy individual. After three years as

his lover, she is thrown over for a rich socialite. Unlike many cheap soap operas of this period, SALLY BISHOP is a cut above most with its high production values and nicely conceived script. Rather than go for the obvious, this film leaves much unsaid with a subtlety rarely found in films of this nature. In the end, Barry finds new romance, but when her lover begs for forgiveness, she takes him back.

p, S.W. Smith; d, T. Hayes Hunter; w, John Drinkwater, G. E. Wakefield (based on the novel by E. Temple Thurston); ph, Alex Bryce.

Drama   **(PR:O MPAA:NR)**

SALLY FIELDGOOD & CO.*   (1975, Can.) 91m Image Flow Centre
Film c

Hagan Beggs, Liza Creighton, Lee Broker, Valerie Ambrose, Brian Brown, Lloyd Berry, Keith Pepper.

Inferior Canadian western about a wandering prostitute working out of the back of her wagon in mining camps. Outlaws show up and give the miners trouble, but the hooker-with-the-heart-of-gold saves the miners, appeases the desperados, and fixes up her virginal sidekick with a cute guy from town. Shot on a tiny budget largely provided by the Canadian government, the film is unlikely to resurface, but stay away if it does.

p, Werner Aellen; d, Boon Collins; w, Collins, Barry Pearson; ph, Doug McKay; m, Valdy; ed, George Johnson.

Western   **(PR:C-O MPAA:NR)**

SALLY IN OUR ALLEY**½   (1931, Brit.) 75m Associated Talking
Pictures/RKO bw

Gracie Fields *(Sally Winch)*, Ian Hunter *(George Miles)*, Florence Desmond *(Florrie Small)*, Ivor Barnard *(Tod Small)*, Fred Groves *(Alf Cope)*, Gibb McLaughlin *(Jim Sears)*, Ben Field *(Sam Bilson)*, Barbara Gott *(Mrs. Pool)*, Renee Macready *(Lady Daphne)*, Helen Ferrers *(Duchess of Wexford)*.

When her boy friend is wounded in the war, Fields suddenly stops hearing from him. She thinks he's dead, but it is really because Hunter doesn't want her to know that he's crippled. Desmond has the role of the woman trying to break up their romance once Fields and Hunter reunite. Eventually all is resolved and a party is held at the cafe where Fields works as a singer. This is an early talkie short on believability, but with enough sincerity to make it work. SALLY IN OUR ALLEY was enough to make vaudeville performer, Fields, a film star. Songs include: "Sally," "Fall In and Follow the Band," sung by Fields.

p, Basil Dean; d, Maurice Elvey; w, Miles Malleson, Alma Reville, Archie Pitt (based on the play "The Likes of 'Er" by Charles McEvoy); ph, Robert G. Martin, Alex Bryce.

Drama/Musical   **(PR:A MPAA:NR)**

SALLY, IRENE AND MARY***   (1938) 86m Fox bw

Alice Faye *(Sally Day)*, Tony Martin *(Tommy Reynolds)*, Fred Allen *(Gabriel "Gabby" Green)*, Jimmy Durante *(Jefferson Twitchell)*, Gregory Ratoff *(Baron Zorka)*, Joan Davis *(Irene Keene)*, Marjorie Weaver *(Mary Stevens)*, Louise Hovick [Gypsy Rose Lee] *(Joyce Taylor)*, J. Edward Bromberg *(Pawnbroker)*, Barnett Parker *(Oscar)*, Raymond Scott Quintette *(Themselves)*, Eddie Collins *(Captain)*, Andrew Tombes *(Judge)*, Brian Sisters *(Themselves)*, Mary Treen *(Miss Barkow)*, Charles Wilson *(Cafe Manager)*.

Although Darryl Zanuck is listed as the producer of this, Gene Markey did much of the on-line production work while DFZ was running the studio. The play by Eddie Dowling and Cyrus Wood was only a suggestion for this screenplay which departed greatly from the stage musical. Faye, Davis, and Weaver do manicures at the shop owned by Parker. It's just a way station for the trio who want to make it in musical comedy. They get a chance to sing for Ratoff, a big-time investor, but that opportunity falls apart when Ratoff hassles with the girls' agent, Allen (in his second film and proving he could rattle off comedy lines in films as well as on radio). Allen feels awful about what's happened and finds them work (but not as performers) at a Greenwich Village night club where Martin is the star singer. Allen brings in rich widow Hovick (if that name sounds familiar, it's Gypsy Rose Lee before she changed her monicker) to put up some money for a show starring Martin and the trio. Hovick sees that Martin and Faye are getting too close (they were husband and wife in real life at the time), and since she has her chapeau set on Martin, she agrees to put up the cash if Faye is fired. When Faye gets the axe, Martin decides to quit as well. They are all out of money in a hurry, but Weaver learns that a relative has passed away and left her a ferry in his will. It's a terrible boat that barely stays afloat, but Allen thinks it can be whipped into shape and made into a New York version of a Mississippi River show-boat for about $25,000. Meanwhile, Ratoff proposes marriage to Faye, and Hovick indicates the same to Martin. Unbeknown to each other, Faye and Martin accept the offers with the stipulation that $25,000 be paid (sort of an O. Henry twist from "The Gift Of The Magi"). Allen and his partner, Durante, a one-time janitor, use the money to make the old boat look like a million. The floating theater-restaurant is due to open with Martin and Faye headlining; Durante goes into the ship's innards, hits the wrong lever, and the ship takes off right in the middle of the busy Hudson. A wild chase occurs until the boat is taken back to the dock. Customers arrive, the show's a hit, and the ship's captain, Collins, marries Martin and Faye on stage. Ratoff and Hovick have, by this time, noticed each other, realized they've been fooled but that they will get their money back, and we are led to believe they will wind up together. Songs from a multitude of writers include: "Minuet in Jazz" (Raymond Scott, performed by Raymond Scott Quintette), "Hot Potata" (Jimmy Durante, sung by Durante), "Help Wanted Male," (Walter Bullock, Jack Spina, sung by Davis), "Who Stole the Jam?" (Bullock, Spina, sung by Faye, Weber, Davis, the Brian Sisters), "I Could Use a Dream" (Bullock, Spina, sung by Martin), "Sweet As A Song" (Mack Gordon, Harry Revel, sung by Martin), "This Is Where I Came In," "Half Moon on the Hudson" (Bullock, Spina), "Got My Mind on Music" (Gordon, Revel, sung by Faye).

p, Darryl F. Zanuck; d, William S. Seiter; w, Harry Tugend, Jack Yellen (based on a story by Karl Tunberg, Don Ettinger, from a play by Edward Dowling, Cyril Wood); ph, Peverell Marley; ed, Walter Thompson; md, Arthur Lange; art d, Bernard Herzbrun, Rudolph Sternad; set d, Thomas Little; cos, Gwen Wakeling; ch, Nick Castle, Geneva Sawyer.

Musical/Comedy   **(PR:A   MPAA:NR)**

SALLY OF THE SUBWAY*½   (1932) 63m Action bw

Jack Mulhall, Dorothy Revier, Blanche Mehaffey, Huntley Gordon, Harry Semels, Crauford Kent, John Webb Dillon, Bill Burke.

Mediocre drama involves a crooked gang out to swindle some jewelery from under the nose of a visiting grand duke. The title is misleading for there's no underground action. "Sally of the Subway" is simply a character's nickname. There are some okay action scenes, but the threadbare plot can only go so far on that. Despite the film's weaknesses, it does have some good looking sets that show a budget not usually found in a film of this quality.

d&w, George B. Sietz; ph, Jules Cronjager; ed, Byron Robinson.

Drama   **(PR:C   MPAA:NR)**

SALLY'S HOUNDS*   (1968) 90m Edgeville bw

Robin Woodard (Sally), Eric Sherman (John), Hope Wilson (Kate), Robert Edelstein (Paul), Harvey Bellin (Gary), Al Rubottom (Matt), Richard Kutner, Richard Moore, Tim Hunter, Nora Paley, The Hard Corps, Reynold Frutkin (Narrator).

Pretentious student film that actually got serious consideration in "Cahiers Du Cinema." Sherman wanders through his own existential crisis ignoring the girl who really loves him for a mysterious, strong-willed woman. Painfully slow and afflicted with a voiceover narration and no dialog– a technique that grons tiresome very quickly.

p,d,w&ph, Robert Edelstein; m, Roy Gould; ed, Edelstein; m/l, The Hard Corps.

Drama   **(PR:C   MPAA:NR)**

SALLY'S IRISH ROGUE   (SEE: POACHER'S DAUGHTER, THE, 1958, Brit.)

SALOME***   (1953) 103m Beckworth/COL c

Rita Hayworth (Princess Salome), Stewart Granger (Commander Claudius), Charles Laughton (King Herod), Judith Anderson (Queen Herodias), Sir Cedric Hardwicke (Caesar Tiberius), Alan Badel (John the Baptist), Basil Sydney (Pontius Pilate), Maurice Schwartz (Ezra), Rex Reason (Marcellus Fabius), Arnold Moss (Micha), Sujata, Asoka (Oriental Dance Team), Robert Warwick (Courier), Carmen D'Antonio (Salome's Servant), Michael Granger (Capt. Quintus), Karl "Killer" Davis (Slave Master), Joe Schilling, David Wold, Ray Beltram, Joe Sawaya, Anton Northpole, Carlo Tricoli, Franz Roehn, William McCormick (Advisors), Mickey Simpson (Herod's Captain of the Guards), Eduardo Cansino (Roman Guard), Lou Nova (Executioner), Fred Letuli, John Wood (Sword Dancers), William Spaeth (Fire Eater), Abel Pina, Jerry Pina, Henry Pina, Henry Escalante, Gilbert Marques, Richard Rivas, Miguel Gutierez, Ramiro Rivas, Ruben T. Rivas, Hector Urtiaga (Acrobats), Duke Johnson (Juggling Specialty), Earl Brown, Bud Cokes (Galilean Soldiers), George Khoury, Leonard George (Assassins), Eva Hyde (Herodias' Servant), Charles Wagenheim (Simon), Italia De Nublia, David Ahdar, Charles Soldani, Dimas Sotello, William Wilkerson, Mario Lamm, Tina Menard (Converts), Leslie Denison (Court Attendant), Henry dar Boggia, Michael Couzzi, Bobker Ben Ali, Don De Leo, John Parrish, Eddy Fields, Robert Garabedion, Sam Scar (Politicians), Tris Coffin, Bruce Cameron, John Crawford (Guards), Michael Mark (Old Farmer), David Leonard, Maurice Samuels, Ralph Moody (Old Scholars), Saul Martell (Dissenting Scholar), Paul Hoffman (Sailmaster), Stanley Waxman (Patrician), Franz Roehn, Jack Low, Bert Rose, Tom Hernandez (Townsmen), Trevor Ward (Blind Man), Barry Brooks (Roman Guard), Roque Barry (Slave), George Keymas, Fred Berest, Rick Vallin (Sailors), Carleton Young, Guy Kingsford (Officers).

An overwrought and often downright silly Biblical story which is given the standard lavish mounting and amounts to nothing but second-rate C. B. DeMille, lacking any real energy or Roman decadence. Here Columbia head

Harry Cohn combined two of the sauciest, most erotic femme fatales the world has known– Salome New Testament flame famed for the revealing Dance of the Seven Veils, and Rita Hayworth, famed for the passionate "Put the Blame on Mame" dance of GILDA (1946). In this version of the Bible According to Cohn, Hayworth's Salome tries to save John the Baptist (Badel) from losing his head to the sword of King Herod (played with marvelous scene-chewing by Laughton) rather than following the common belief that she was responsible for his death. Set, of course, in biblical Galilee under Roman occupation, Hayworth plays the stepdaughter of king Laughton, who has been promised by his evil wife, queen Anderson, that the girl will be his if John the Baptist's head is presented on a silver platter. Laughton is deathly fearful of a prophecy that Badel is a holy man, and must fight against Anderson who insists Badel be killed for speaking out against the throne. While Laughton drools over Hayworth, she is making a play for Stewart Granger even though the two were, initially, at odds. Anderson tries to further upset life in Galilee by pressuring Stewart Granger to kill Badel, though he refuses, secretly citing his recent discovery of Christianity as his reason. Eventually, Hayworth is persuaded to dance for Laughton, performing a jaw-dropping strip-tease strip-tease Hayworth can. The eroticism then turns macabre when Badel's head is brought in on a platter. Disgusted, Hayworth retreats from Galilee with her true love, Stewart Granger, and heads for the Sermon on the Mount. Grossly bending the original events, the film still presents its tale in a moderately entertaining fashion. Without Hayworth, however, SALOME would have been a long-forgotten Columbia flop. As if waiting for the invention of cinema in order to be liberated from the pages of the Bible, Salome quickly found a home on the screen. Finding her way from the pages of Oscar Wilde (written as a Sarah Bernhardt vehicle) to the operatic score of Richard Strauss, Salome was first memorably portrayed by the ultimate vamp Theda Bara in 1918, then in 1923 by the legendary Russian actress Nazimova, before Hayworth took the honors. Although the story was completely distorted to fit Hollywood guidelines, at least it could boast some authentic location footage–18,000 feet of the Holy Land. With SALOME it was Harry Cohn's hope to regenerate the DeMille style epic, so he hired former DeMille scriptwriter Jesse Lasky, Jr. to bang out, over a weekend, a vehicle for Hayworth. Unfortunately, however, Cohn handed the final scriptwriting chores over to Harry Kleiner, who was unfamiliar with the essential exploitative and lusty ingredients of the biblical epic.

p, Buddy Adler; d, William Dieterle; w, Harry Kleiner (based on a story by Jesse Lasky, Jr., Kleiner); ph, Charles Lang (Technicolor); m, George Duning, Daniele Amfitheatrof; ed, Viola Lawrence; md, Morris W. Stoloff; art d, John Meehan; set d, William Kiernan; cos, Jean Louis, Emile Santiago; ch, Valerie Bettis; makeup, Clay Campbell; religious tech adv, Millard Sheets.

Biblical Epic   **(PR:C   MPAA:NR)**

SALOME, WHERE SHE DANCED*   (1945) 90m Walter Wanger/UNIV
c

Yvonne De Carlo (Salome), Rod Cameron (Jim), David Bruce (Cleve), Walter Slezak (Dimitrioff), Albert Dekker (Von Bohlen), Marjorie Rambeau (Madam), J. Edward Bromberg (Prof. Max), Abner Biberman (Dr. Ling), John Litel (Gen. Robert E. Lee), Kurt Katch (Prince Otto von Bismarck), Arthur Hohl (Bartender), Nestor Paiva (Panatela), Gavin Muir (Henderson), Will Wright (Sheriff), Joseph Haworth (Henry), Matt McHugh (Lafe), Jane Adams, Barbara Bates, Daun Kennedy, Kathleen O'Malley, Karen Randle, Jean Trent, Kerry Vaughn (Salome Girls), Jan Williams, Doreen Tryden, Bert Dole, Emmett Casey (Specialties), Eddie Dunn (Lineman), Charles Wagenheim (Telegrapher), Gene Garrick (German Sergeant), Eric Feldary (Uhlan Sergeant), Sylvia Field (Maid), Richard Ryen (Theater Manager), Colin Campbell (Mate), George Sherwood (Bartender), Charles McAvoy (Policeman), Al Ferguson (Deputy), Alan Edwards (Bret Harte), George Leigh (Bayard Taylor), Ina Ownbey (Girl), Eddie Cobb (Stage Driver), Jimmy Lung (Chinese Guard), Jack Clifford (Messenger), Peter Seal (Russian Chasseur), Bud Osborne (Gambler), George Chesebro, George Morrell (Miners), Jasper Palmer, Hank Bell (Cowhands), Budd Buster (Desert Rat), Dick Alexander (Shotgun), Cecelia Callejo (Bar Girl).

During the Franco-Prussian War De Carlo is a Viennese dancer. She meets Cameron, an American reporter, and helps him fool one of Bismarck's top officers. This Mata Hari type stunt forces De Carlo and her man to head off to America, ending up in a small Arizona town. The locals of Drinkman's Wells are a group of assorted outlaws who are straightened out by DeCarlo. They're so entranced by her and her dancing that they rename their town "Salome." From there it's off to San Francisco for the tempting lady where she hooks up with the wealthy Russian, Slezak. He too becomes entranced by her various skills and ends up building an opera house for her, a la CITIZEN KANE. De Carlo becomes the toast of San Francisco and, to no one's surprise, the film ends on a happy note. SALOME, WHERE SHE DANCED is one of those films that defies criticism. Without a doubt, it is a bad film complete with a rambling, mostly unbelievable script and some awful performances by the leads (De Carlo in one of her first film appearances was picked for this film after a nationwide search). There's plenty of action and romance with good Technicolor scenery as well, but all poorly connected by the thinnest of plot threads. But like many films of this nature, SALOME, WHERE SHE DANCED is a member of the "So bad it's good" club, a film so undeniably awful one can't help but enjoy it. Over the years it has achieved some minor cult status. De Carlo worked her way around Hollywood before achieving some recognition as Lily of the 1960s television sitcom "The Munsters."

p, Alexander Golitzen; d, Charles Lamont; w, Laurence Stallings (based on a story by Michael J. Phillips); ph, Hal Mohr, W. Howard Greene (Technicolor); m, Edward Ward; ed, Russell Schoengarth; md, Ward; art d, Golitzen, John B. Goodman; set d, Russell A. Gausman, Victor A. Gangelin; cos, Vera West; ch, Lester Horton; m/l, Everett Carter.

Drama   **Cas.**   (PR:C   MPAA:NR)

SALOON BAR***   (1940, Brit.) 80m EAL/ABF bw

Gordon Harker (*Joe Harris*), Elizabeth Allan (*Queenie*), Mervyn Johns (*Wickers*), Joyce Barbour (*Sally*), Anna Konstam (*Ivy*), Cyril Raymond (*Harry Small*), Judy Campbell (*Doris*), Al Millen (*Fred*), Norman Pierce (*Bill Hoskins*), Alec Clunes (*Eddie Graves*), Mavis Villiers (*Joan*), Felix Aylmer (*Mayor*), O. B. Clarence (*Sir Archibald*), Aubrey Dexter (*Major*), Helena Pickard (*Mrs. Small*), Manning Whiley (*Evangelist*), Laurence Kitchin (*Peter*), Al Millen (*Fred*), Roddy Hughes (*Doctor*), Torin Thatcher, Gordon James, Annie Esmond, Eliot Makeham, Julie Suedo, Roddy McDowall, Robert Rendel.

An innocent man is about to be hanged. His fiancee, Allan, is a barmaid who's naturally distraught over this turn of events. Her friends at the bar, led by Harker a part-time bookie, play some mental gymnastics and in the course of the evening figure out the real murderer. This clever little piece is an imaginative exercise. The dialog is sharp and well handled by the ensemble. Based on a popular West End play, there are a few holes in the plot, but these are covered to some degree with fast-paced direction. Overall, an enjoyable effort that will appeal to mystery fans.

p, Culley Forde; d, Walter Forde; w, Angus Macphail, John Dighton (based on a play by Frank Harvey, Jr.); ph, Ronald Neame; m, Ernest Irving; ed, Ray Pitt; art d, Wilfred Shingleton.

Mystery   (PR:C   MPAA:NR)

SALT & PEPPER**   (1968, Brit.) 102m Chrislaw-Trace-Mark/ UA c

Sammy Davis, Jr (*Charles Salt*), Peter Lawford (*Christopher Pepper*), Michael Bates (*Inspector Crabbe*), Ilona Rodgers (*Marianne Renaud*), John Le Mesurier (*Col. Woodstock*), Graham Stark (*Sgt. Walters*), Ernest Clark (*Col. Balsom*), Jeanne Roland (*Mai Ling*), Robert Dorning (*Club Secretary*), Robertson Hare (*Dove*), Geoffrey Lumsden (*Foreign Secretary*), William Mervyn (*Prime Minister*), Llewellyn Rees ("*Fake*" *Prime Minister*), Mark Singleton ("*Fake*" *Home Secretary*), Michael Trubshawe ("*Fake*" *First Lord*), Francisca Tu (*Tsai Chan*), Oliver MacGreevy (*Rack*), Peter Hutchins (*Straw*), Jeremy Lloyd (*Lord Ponsonby*), Sean Lynch (*Black Jack Player*), Ivor Dean (*Police Commissioner*), Brian Harrison (*1st Policeman*), Harry Hutchinson (*Manservant*), Max Faulkner (*Lieutenant*), Beth Rogan (*Greta*), Rifat Shenel (*Mario*), Calvin Lockhart (*Jones*), Nicholas Smith (*Constable*), Susan Blair (*Janice*), Christine Pocket (*Jill*), Cassandra Mowan (*Jean*), Joe Wadham (*Col. Woodstock's Aide*).

A black man (Davis) named Salt and his white partner (Lawford) named Pepper are the owners of a Soho nightclub. When a man and woman are murdered at the club, the partners are pointed to as the killers by an anonymous source. They finally are released and find themselves caught up in the middle of some intrigue. Seems the dead woman was a British secret service agent. They find her diary with names of four men marked for murder. The club owners turn amatuer sleuths and try to solve the crimes. But three men are murdered and the trail leads to Le Messurier, a madman who wants to overthrow the English government using nuclear blackmail. Davis and Lawford can't get anyone to believe them, but eventually stop the plan with the appropriate amount of hijinks and dangerous situations. After stopping the bad guys with an ancient army tank, the pair find themselves heroes and are taken to Buckingham Palace to be knighted by the Queen. SALT & PEPPER suffers from a lack of imagination, using broad comedy and over-indulgent slapstick as a substitute for plot development and humor. The result is a mostly unfunny film without creativity other than to provide a film vehicle for its two stars. This film was followed by a sequel, ONE MORE TIME.

p, Milton Ebbins; d, Richard D. Donner; w, Michael Pertwee; ph, Ken Higgins (DeLuxe Color); m, John Dankworth; ed, Jack Slade; prod d, Bill Constable; art d, Don Mingaye; set d, Scott Slimon, Andrew Low; cos, Cynthia Tingey, Charles Glenn; ch, Lionel Blair; m/l, "I Like the Way You Dance," George Rhodes, Sammy Davis, Jr., "Salt & Pepper," Leslie Bricusse (sung by Davis, Jr.); makeup, Jimmy Evans.

Comedy   (PR:C   MPAA:G)

SALT AND THE DEVIL   (SEE: SALT TO THE DEVIL, 1949, Brit.)

SALT LAKE RAIDERS***   (1950) 60m REP bw

Allan "Rocky" Lane (*Himself*), Eddy Waller (*Nugget Clark*), Roy Barcroft (*Brit Condor*), Martha Hyer (*Helen Thornton*), Byron Foulger (*John Sutton*), Myron Healey (*Fred Mason*), Clifton Young (*Luke Condor*), Stanley

Andrews (*Head Marshal*), Rory Mallinson (*Sheriff*), Kenneth MacDonald (*Deputy Marshal*), George Chesebro (*Stage Driver*), Black Jack.

Healey plays a cowboy falsely accused of murder. But before he can prove his innocence he, along with Lane and Waller, are held captive by outlaws who believe Healey has stashed a cache of gold away. They constantly force the trio to search for the gold, but because none of them actually knows where it's hidden, they can't find the fortune. In the end, the three escape, locate the gold, bring the outlaws to justice, and Healey clears his name.

p, Gordon Kay; d, Fred C. Brannon; w, M. Coates Webster; ph, John MacBurnie; m, Stanley Wilson; ed, Richard L. Van Enger.

Western   (PR:A   MPAA:NR)

SALT OF THE EARTH*****   (1954) 94m International Union of Mine, Mill and Smelter Workers/Independent Productions bw

Rosaura Revueltas (*Esperanza Quintero*), Will Geer (*Sheriff*), David Wolfe (*Barton*), Melvin Williams (*Hartwell*), David Sarvis (*Alexander*), , Non-professional actors: Juan Chacon (*Ramon Quintero*), Henrietta Williams (*Teresa Vidal*), Ernest Velasquez (*Charley Vidal*), Angela Sanchez (*Consuelo Ruiz*), Joe T. Morales (*Sal Ruiz*), Clorinda Alderette (*Luz Morales*), Charles Coleman (*Antonio Morales*), Virginia Jencks (*Ruth Barnes*), Clinton Jencks (*Frank Barnes*), E.A. Rockwell (*Vance*), William Rockwell (*Kimbrough*), Frank Talavera (*Luis Quintero*), Mary Lou Castillo (*Estella Quintero*), Floyd Bostick (*Jenkins*), Victor Torres (*Sebastian Prieto*), E.S. Conerly (*Kalinsky*), Elivira Molano (*Mrs. Salazar*), Adolfo Barela, Albert Munoz (*Miners*), the Brothers and Sisters of Local 890, International Union of Mine, Mill and Smelter Workers, Bayard, New Mexico.

SALT OF THE EARTH is, historically as well as artistically, a landmark film. It took a realistic look at society's inequalities, portraying them in an honest manner. In the anti-Communist heat of the 1950s Cold War such sentiments, the legitimate children of the nation's founding principles, were considered anti-American Red propaganda. The film, told in a flashback narration by its heroine, opens with Revueltas, a Mexican-American woman, expecting her third child. Her husband Chacon – the real-life president of Local 890 – is a zinc miner in the New Mexico hills and his union is considering a strike. The poverty-ridden miners anger their wives by sacrificing hot water and indoor plumbing as a union demand. Though Chacon forgets his wife's Saint's day, his son reminds him. Chacon gives Revueltas a small party and she temporarily forgets her anger. Then a mine worker is injured and the threatened strike finally comes. The workers take up picket signs and form a line, refusing to let any scabs cross over to work the zinc mines. The local sheriff (Geer, later to play Grandpa on TV's "The Waltons") and mine foreman Williams decide that Chacon is the ringleader and have a pair of deputies beat and arrest the man. At the moment of her husband's beating Revueltas gives birth to a daughter. The two call each others' names, linked by some sort of emotional psyche. On the day of his release from jail Chacon's daughter has her christening. Soon a Taft-Hartley injunction is served, preventing the men from picketing. A meeting is held and their wives insist they take over the picketing. Some men laugh this off while others, including Chacon, are shocked by their wives' boldness. A non-union community voice vote of both men and women approves the call and the women take their place in line. Though Chacon will not allow his wife to participate, Revueltas disobeys and joins her sisters-in-arms. Despite much abuse the women stick to their places in line and the strike continues. In a desperate, move Geer has several of the women arrested. Revueltas is among this group and brings her infant and other daughter with her so Chacon will not have to worry about them at home. The baby needs nourishment and the women drive Geer and his deputies mad with their chant for "The formula! The formula!" The children are finally taken back home by Chacon. He becomes overwhelmed by the housework and comes to realize how hard his wife's work really is. He vows to a neighbor that the demand by the women for better sanitation will be put back with the other union demands. Revueltas returns from jail, feeling exhilarated by her experience. Chacon tells her that she should stay home and not go back to the picket line. Revueltas counters him by saying his arguments for a "woman's place" are no different from his Caucasian bosses telling Chicanos to stay in their place. Everyone must unite and work together for the common good, she explains. The next morning an angry Chacon does not fulfill his job of watching the women as they picket. He goes hunting with a few friends but finally, the truth of Revuelta's words sinks in and he hurries back to the line, fearful that the authorities may do something terrible. Upon arrival his worst fears are realized, for Geer and his goons are removing the furniture from his home on an eviction notice. But this is stopped when the women, men, and children of both the union and the community arrive in droves and begin putting back the furniture. The legal authorities are frightend by the mob and wisely back off. Williams must concede to the strikers. Chacon thanks his fellow miners and their wives, a united camaraderie of brothers and sisters. The victory is not just theirs but also their children's, the real "salt of the earth." The film is one of enormous power, taking on several subjects that were highly taboo in the early 1950s. The rights of Chicanos was a relatively ignored topic. Other minorities such as blacks and Jews were portrayed in an occasional film that gave the Hollywood version of racial inequality. However, most of these films were sanitized versions of reality, with caricatures more than characters. SALT OF THE EARTH was filmed with actual participants of the real-life struggle on which it was based (Chacon, a non-professional actor, does an amazing job in his true-life role). These are actual people going through a real-life struggle. Unlike so many left-wing propaganda pieces, SALT OF THE EARTH educates without having to resort to weary sloganeering. These are not the words of Lenin or Marx, rather the everyday speech of the common man. What makes SALT OF THE EARTH even more progressive is the struggle shown for women's equality. The women openly defying their husbands, the protrayal of how difficult housework really is, the women taking an equal place with their men: all of this is far ahead of its time, filmed well before "feminism" became a household word. Naturally a film of such liberal leanings would be a cause of controversy in the 1950s. SALT OF THE EARTH was doubly cursed, for both its content and its background. Producer Paul Jarrico had been banned from Hollywood, but this could not stop him. He joined with director Herbert Biberman, a member of the infamous "Hollywood Ten", who had served a 5-month prison sentence for being an uncooperative House Un-American Activities Committee (HUAC) witness. They wanted to create a film company which would give work to blacklisted members of the film industry (Geer himself was blacklisted at the time). Their intent was to create stories, as the two wrote 20 years later, "drawn from the living experiences of people long ignored in Hollywood – the working men and women of America." As it turns out, this was their only production, made in association with the International Mine, Mill and Smelter Workers. They were lucky to make this film at all. Shortly after production began in early 1953 the pro-McCarthy establishment press sought to discredit the film and filmmakers. Hollywood actor Walter Pidgeon, then president of the Screen Actors Guild, upon receiving a letter from a New Mexico schoolteacher warning of "Hollywood Reds...shooting a feature-length anti-American racial-issue propaganda movie" alerted his contacts in government ranging from members of HUAC to officials of the FBI and CIA Donald Jackson, a member of HUAC, claimed he would do everything he could to prevent the screening of "this Communist-made film," citing non-existent scenes as examples of the film's Red leanings. Even billionaire Howard Hughes, head of RKO, got on the bandwagon and came up with a plan to stop the film's processing and distribution. The local population near the shooting site also got into the act. Vigilante groups took action, picking fights with crew members, setting fire to real union headquarters, and local merchants refused to do business with anyone in the production. One group threatened to take out the company "in pine boxes" and finally the New Mexico State Police came in to protect the filmmakers. Problems were compounded when Revueltas, a Mexican actress, was arrested by immigration officials for a minor passport violation. She returned to Mexico and the film had to be completed with a double. Some of her scenes were also shot in her native country on the pretext of being test shots for a future production. (Sadly, the Red fever of this country spilled over into Mexico as Revueltas was blacklisted there for her work in this film. The talented actress would never work again.) Revuelta's role was originally to have been played by Hollywood actress Gale Sondergaard, director Biberman's wife. Sondergaard withdrew from the project, feeling that the part should be played by a Hispanic actress. Troubles continued to plague the filmmakers after the shooting was completed. Apparently Hughes' campaign had worked, for eight labs refused to process the negative. The union-made film also ran into trouble from a sister union, the International Alliance of Theatrical and Stage Employees (IATSE), which refused to allow its technician members to work on the project. Ironically, the film was shot with a nonunion crew. The producer was forced to rely on cunning to get the processing done, including submitting parts of the negative to labs under the title VAYA CON DIOS. Editing proved equally difficult. It was done in great secrecy in numerous (and unlikely) locations. One editing room was the women's bathroom of an abandoned movie theater! In March of 1954 SALT OF THE EARTH made its debut, which was limited to only 13 theaters nationwide. Newspapers refused to carry ads for it, with exhibitors being threatened by pickets. Critical reaction was surprisingly good. Most felt that the anti-American message was nonexistent. This was a film about human rights rather than Communist revolutions. Biberman filed a lawsuit claiming that his film was systematically kept from the American public, though this proved to be a futile effort when the case was lost. It was overseas where SALT OF THE EARTH finally triumphed. It played for ten straight months in France and received wide distribution in China and the U.S.S.R. It also was seen on television in some countries like West Germany and Canada, prompting Jarrico to state, "It has been seen, probably, by more people than any film in history." SALT OF THE EARTH finally did receive some American screenings, mostly on college campuses during the politically liberal era of the 1960s. (At one point in the independent feature THE RETURN OF THE SECAUSUS 7, a comedy dealing with the reunion of some former 1960s radicals, one character recalls SALT OF THE EARTH and the chant of "The formula!" as a rallying point for their political activism.)" SALT OF THE EARTH's power has not diminished with age. Indeed, its portrait of the dignity of men and women unifying for a cause with little bloodshed remains without comparison. Its framework of a simple plot line permeated with important themes continues to maintain a powerful relevance. While history has passed judgment on the people who tried to stop this important work, SALT OF THE EARTH continues to walk hand-in-hand with real American ideals.

p, Paul Jarrico, Sonja Dahl Biberman, Adolfo Barela; d, Herbert J. Biberman; w, Michael Wilson Biberman; ph, Leonard Stark, Stanley Meredith; m, Sol Kaplan; ed, Ed Spiegel, Joan Laird; prod d, Sonja Dahl, Adolfo Bardela.

Drama   (PR:C   MPAA:NR)

SALT TO THE DEVIL*   (1949, Brit.) 120m Plantagenet/RANK-EL
                                               bw (GB: GIVE US THIS DAY)

Sam Wanamaker (*Geremio*), Lea Padovani (*Annunziata*), Kathleen Ryan (*Kathleen*), Charles Goldner (*Luigi*), Bonar Colleano (*Julio*), Bill [William] Sylvester (*Giovanni*), Nino Pastellides (*The Lucy*), Philo Hauser (*Head of Pig*), Sidney James (*Murdin*), Karel Stapanek (*Jaroslav*), Ina De La Haye (*Dame Katarina*), Rosalie Crutchley (*Julio's Wife*), Ronan O'Casey (*Bastian*), Robert Rietty (*Pietro*), Charles Moffat (*Pasquale*).

Grim and powerful drama starring Wanamaker as an Italian immigrant bricklayer whose life is in ruins when he can't find work. He and his wife have dreamed of owning their own house, and have frugally saved nearly enough cash to do it when the Depression hits, forcing them to spend their savings. Desperate, Wanamaker accepts a job in an unsafe workplace against his better judgment. An accident strikes and he is entombed alive in a slab of concrete. In a grim and ironic twist, the life insurance compensation given to his widow is just enough to pay for the house she always dreamed of. One of three films Dmytryk directed in England after serving a year in prison for alleged un-American activities.

p, Rod Geiger, Nat A. Bronsten, Edward Dmytryk; d, Dmytryk; w, Ben Barzman (based on the novel *Christ in Concrete* by Pietro Di Donato); ph, C. Pennington Richards; m, Benjamin Frankel; ed, John Guthridge; art d, Alex Vetchinsky; set d, Arthur Taksen.

Drama   (PR:A   MPAA:NR)

SALTO*   (1966, Pol.) 104m KADR Film Unit-Film Polski/Kanawha
                                                                    Films bw

Zbigniew Cybulski (*Kowalski/Malinowski*), Gustaw Holoubek (*The Host*), Marta Lipinska (*Helena*), Irena Laskowska (*Cecylia, a Fortune Teller*), Wojciech Siemion (*The Poet*), Wlodzimierz Borunski (*Blumenfeld*), Zdzislaw Maklakiewicz (*The Captain*), Andrzej Lapicki (*The Drunkard*), Jerzy Blok (*The Mayor*), Iga Cembrzynska (*Kowalski's Wife*).

A stranger leaps from a train and ends up in a small Polish village. To the bewilderment of the residents, he claims to have lived there once before. No one recognizes him, but one family takes him in. However, the stranger refuses to reveal his past. All he says is that he changed his name from Kowalski to Malinowski as certain people following him would prefer him dead. The stranger's presence creates a weird aura that affects the entire population and soon the normally blase villagers are opening up their innermost feelings. The stranger seemingly cures two sick children by a miracle, then seduces his host's daughter. At a village gathering he teaches a special dance called the salto. This throws the villagers into a strange hypnotic trance. But suddenly everything is wrenched into the open when a woman with her two children arrives and announces she is the man's wife. She claims her husband is little more than a womanizing faker and the villagers respond by stoning the stranger. He grabs the next train leaving town. Ironically, actor Cybulski–the frog-mouthed, sunglasses-wearing angry young man of such films as Andrzej Wajda's ASHES AND DIAMONDS (1958) – died in a railway accident a year following the U.S. release of SALTO, which begins and ends with scenes of a railway.

d&w, Tadeusz Konwicki; ph, Kurt Weber; m, Wojciech Kilar.

Comedy/Drama   (PR:O   MPAA:NR)

SALTY*   (1975) 90m Saltwater c

Clint Howard (*Tim*), Mark Slade (*Taylor*), Nina Foch (*Mrs. Penninger*), Julius W. Harris (*Clancy*), Linda Scruggs (*Girl*).

Wretched children's film has the insufferably cute Howard adopting an intelligent sea lion. Apparently the sea lion wasn't intelligent enough to let this awful script go by (there are so few good parts written for sea lions). Writer-director Browning is best known for playing THE CREATURE FROM THE BLACK LAGOON.

p, Kobi Jaeger; d, Ricou Browning; w, Browning, Jack Cowden.

Children   (PR:A   MPAA:G)

SALTY O'ROURKE*   (1945) 97m PAR bw

Alan Ladd (*Salty O'Rourke*), Gail Russell (*Barbara Brooks*), William Demarest (*Smitty*), Stanley "Stash" Clements (*Johnny Cates*), Bruce Cabot (*Doc Baxter*), Spring Byington (*Mrs. Brooks*), Rex Williams (*Babe*), Darryl Hickman (*Sneezer*), Marjorie Woodworth (*Lola*), Don Zelaya (*Hotel Proprietor*), Lester Matthews (*Dignified Salesman*), William Forrest (*Racing Secretary*), William Murphy (*Bennie*), Denis Brown (*Murdock*), David Clyde, Jean Willes.

Ladd is at his best in another hard-boiled role, this time as a lowlife who hangs around race horses. In this, as in THIS GUN FOR HIRE, Ladd excels as a sort of villain who winds up having the audience root for him, despite everything he's done before. Ladd and Demarest owe a bundle to Cabot, a tough cookie. If they don't come up with the money in 30 days, it might mean curtains. Ladd is aware of a seemingly unrideable race horse that he can buy for a song, but he has to find a jockey who can handle the steed. There's only one, Clements, a smart-talking kid who has been banned from riding in the U.S. due to some questionable races. Ladd and Demarest get the horse and convince 22-year-old Clements (he was actually 18 at the time) to use his teenage brother's birth certificate and masquerade as the younger boy in order to qualify for the race. Clements is appalled when he learns that he must now go to the school run by the track for under-18 jockeys. Clements wants to back out, but the promise of a big payoff gets him back in the fold. At the school, he meets Russell, the attractive teacher. He is a wise guy and she tosses him out on his ear when he begins mouthing off to her. Ladd has to convince Russell to allow Clements back in the school or he won't qualify for the race. Ladd begins to put the make on Russell and to pay attention to her flighty mother, Byington. Clements starts to get jealous of Ladd's attention to Russell, as he likes her himself. Ladd arranges for Clements to squire Russell to the Jockey's Ball where the youth confesses his love for the teacher. She responds by admitting she loves Ladd, which sends Clements off on a drunken toot with Woodworth, a local hanger-on. Ladd realizes that he is in love with Russell, despite her reading him out for having arranged this situation with Clements. The jockey decides to exact revenge by throwing the race, thereby allowing Cabot to come in and claim the horse as payment for the debt. Russell learns of Clements' duplicity and asks that he run a legit race, which he does, and the horse wins. When Cabot sees he's been double-crossed, he orders one of his men to shoot Clements, who dies in Ladd's grasp. In the denouement Ladd shoots it out with Cabot and his gang. The cops arrive but Ladd, Russell, and Demarest race away in his car and Ladd closes the door on his old wicked ways by throwing his gun out the window. (That weapon had been his close associate throughout the film, a pal he referred to as "my friend John Roscoe," adding, "He persuades my enemies."). A tough movie with sharp dialog, SALTY O'ROURKE is a good example of Ladd's screen charisma, as he dominates every scene, although Clements almost steals the ones he's in. Clements was one of Gloria Grahame's many husbands and later appeared as one of the Bowery Boys.

p, E.D. Leshin; d, Raoul Walsh; w, Milton Holmes; ph, Theodor Sparkuhl; m, Robert Emmett Dolan; ed, William Shea; art d, Hans Dreier, Haldane Douglas; spec eff, Farciot Edouart.

Sports Drama   (PR:A-C   MPAA:NR)

SALUTE**½   (1929) 83m FOX bw

George O'Brien (*Cadet John Randall*), William Janney (*Midshipman Paul Randall*), Frank Albertson (*Midshipman Albert Edward Prince*), Helen Chandler (*Nancy Wayne*), Joyce Compton (*Marion Wilson*), Clifford Dempsey (*Maj.-Gen. Somers*), Lumsden Hare (*Rear Adm. Randall*), Stepin Fetchit (*Smoke Screen*), David Butler (*Navy Coach*), Rex Bell (*Cadet*), John Breeden (*Midshipman*), Ward Bond, John Wayne (*Football Players*), Lee Tracy (*Announcer*).

It's the old story of the Army versus the Navy on a gridiron battlefield. O'Brien is the freshman player for the Army who's a whizz on the football field and dance floor. Janney's his younger brother, who's the Navy's dream boy. When they meet at the final climactic game it's a 6-6 tie with both brothers scoring the only touchdown for their respective teams. A standard outing with typical production values and some good use of newsreel footage. Fetchit plays his shuffling, mumbling Uncle Tom character that got big laughs in 1929 but plays as degrading and racist today. This was unfortunately typical of the majority of Hollywood's attitudes towards blacks; it gave Fetchit a career, at that. Look for a minor appearance by Wayne as O'Brien's other brother. This was one of his earliest film roles. He would later do some of his finest work with the director of SALUTE, Ford. This was also a first film role for character actor Bond, who was to become a Ford regular. Bond and Wayne, at the time, were both on the football team at the University of Southern California. Ford had brought the entire USC football team with him to Annapolis; when a pair of speaking parts were called for, he gave the small roles to Bond and Wayne (the latter had worked for Ford during school vacations as a laborer and prop man, and was well liked by the director, the crew, and O'Brien, the star). Ford had the advantage of extreme cooperation from the superintendent of the Naval Academy, who had been a great friend of his father (they were both from Peak's Island, Maine). Ford was to say, "The admirals' daughters were all in the picture–you know, 10 bucks a day–and we had a lot of fun."

d, John Ford, David Butler; w, John Stone, James Kevin McGuinness (based on a story by Tristram Tupper); ph, Joseph H. August; ed, Alex Troffey.

Sports Drama   (PR:A   MPAA:NR)

SALUTE FOR THREE**   (1943) 74m PAR bw

Betty Rhodes (*Judy Ames*), MacDonald Carey (*Buzz McAllister*), Marty May (*Jimmy Gates*), Cliff Edwards (*Foggy*), Minna Gombell (*Myrt*), [Jeanne] Lorraine and [Roy] Rognan (*Themselves*), Dona Drake (*Dona*), Charles Smith, Charles Williams, Doodles Weaver, Harry Barris, Jack Gardner, Walter Sande (*Sailors*), Tony Hughes (*Col. Rennick*), Robert Emmett Keane (*Patton*), Linda Brent, Patti Brilhante, DeDe Barrington (*Girls in Canteen*), Frank Moran (*Sleepy Soldier*), Frederic Henry, Frank Wayne (*M.P.'s*), Emmett Vogan (*Radio Announcer*), Eddie Dew (*Marine in Broadcasting Station*), Noel Neill (*Gracie*), Edna Bennett (*Woman*), Franklin Parker (*Radio Official*), Blanche Payson (*Taxi Driver*), Isabel Withers (*Nurse*),

Frank Faylen (*Soldier Friend with Buzz*), Eddie Coke (*Corporal*), Billy Wayne, George Sherwood (*Marines*), Lynda Grey, Louise La Planche, Maxine Ardell, Christopher King (*Hostesses*), Marcella Phillips, Marjorie Deanne, Yvonne De Carlo, Alice Kirby (*Quartette Girls*), Tom Seidel (*Roy Ward, the Soldier*), Ralph Montgomery (*Sergeant in Hospital*).

Rhodes is a perky radio singer who just can't get a break. Her agent (May) comes up with a guaranteed public relations scheme, announcing Rhodes as the sweetheart of Carey, a recently returned hero of World War II. Of course no such romance exists, but you can bet it does by the film's end. The simplistic plot is just an excuse for numerous musical numbers by Jule Styne and Gannon including "My Wife's a WAAC," "What Do You do When It Rains?" and "I'd Do It For You." The songs are the best things going for the film, which never can decide whether it's a comedy, a farce, a musical, or a drama. Consequently, this wartime programmer is lesser fare for the genre with an innocuous script and some wooden performances that fight the dialog as best they can. The exotic DeCarlo, in her second year as a bit player, had previously used her real name, Peggy Middleton, in her small roles. Roy Rognan, of the ballroom dance team of Lorraine and Rognan, died in a crash of the luxurious Yankee Clipper transatlantic passenger plane prior to the film's release. Other songs include "Left, Right" (Styne, Gannon, Sol Meyer) and "Valse Continental" (Victor Young).

p, Walter MacEwen; d, Ralph Murphy; w, Doris Anderson, Curtis Kenyon, Hugh Wedlock, Jr., Howard Snyder (based on a story by Art Arthur); ph, Theodor Sparkuhl; m, Kim Gannon; ed, Arthur Schmidt; md, Victor Young; art d, Hans Dreier, Haldane Douglas; ch, Jack Donohue.

Musical/Drama/Comedy   (PR:A   MPAA:NR)

SALUTE JOHN CITIZEN**½   (1942, Brit.) 96m BN/Anglo-American
                                                                                      bw

Edward Rigby (*Mr. Bunting*), Mabel Constanduros (*Mrs. Bunting*), Stanley Holloway (*Oskey*), George Robey (*Corder*), Jimmy Hanley (*Ernest Bunting*), Henry Hallett (*Mr. Bickerton*), Christine Silver (*Mrs. Bickerton*), Eric Micklewood (*Chris Bunting*), Peggy Cummins (*Julie Bunting*), Stewart Rome (*Col. Saunders*), Dinah Sheridan (*Evie*), Charles Deane (*Bert Rollo*), David Keir (*Turner*), Jonathan Field (*Young Brockley*), June Willock, Gordon Begg, Ian Fleming, Valentine Dunn, Harry Fowler.

Rigby, is an elderly, unemployed former store clerk who is re-hired during WWII. His son Hanley is a pacifist but after the London blitz the wayward youth realizes he must do his part for the war effort. Though clearly a propaganda piece designed to support the war effort, SALUTE JOHN CITIZEN is a nice little film, a simple telling of a modest family's attempts to cope with the ongoing conflict.

p, Wallace Orton; d, Maurice Elvey; w, Elizabeth Baron, Clemence Dane (based on the novels *Mr. Bunting, Mr. Bunting at War* by Robert Greenwood); ph, James Wilson

Drama   (PR:A   MPAA:NR)

SALUTE THE TOFF**   (1952, Brit.) 75m Nettlefold/BUT bw

John Bentley (*Hon. Richard Rollison*), Carol Marsh (*Fay Gretton*), Valentine Dyall (*Inspector Grice*), Shelagh Fraser (*Myra Lorne*), June Elvin (*Lady Anthea*), Arthur Hill (*Ted Harrison*), Michael Golden (*Benny Kless*), Jill Allen (*Singer*), Roddy Hughes (*Jolly*), Wally Patch (*Bert Ebbutt*), John Forbes-Robertson (*Gerald Harvey*), Tony Britton (*Draycott*), Andrea Malandrinos, Ian Fleming.

Entertaining mystery plot has Marsh enlisting the aid of amateur detective and man-about-town Bentley, who does his sleuthing under the alias "The Toff", to find her missing boss. After a number of incidents, Bentley finds the man, who is hiding out from an insurance cheat who plans to murder him. Nice comedy bits keep this one from disappearing into the mass of British programmers.

p, Ernest G. Roy; d, Maclean Rogers; w, (based on a novel by John Creasey); ph, Geoffrey Faithfull.

Crime   (PR:A   MPAA:NR)

SALUTE TO A REBEL   (SEE: PATTON, 1972)

SALUTE TO COURAGE   (SEE: NAZI AGENT, 1942)

SALUTE TO ROMANCE   (SEE: ANNAPOLIS SALUTE, 1937)

SALUTE TO THE MARINES**½   (1943) 101m MGM c

Wallace Beery (*Sgt. Maj. William Bailey*), Fay Bainter (*Jennie Bailey*), Reginald Owen (*Mr. Caspar*), Keye Luke (*"Flashy" Logaz*), Ray Collins (*Col. Mason*), Marilyn Maxwell (*Helen Bailey*), William Lundigan (*Rufus Cleveland*), Donald Curtis (*Randall James*), Noah Beery, Sr (*Adjutant*), Dick Curtis (*Corporal*), Russell Gleason (*Pvt. Hanks*), Rose Hobart (*Mrs. Carson*), James Davis (*Saunders*), Mark Daniels (*Myers*), Leonard Strong (*Karitu*), Fritz Leiber (*Mr. Agno*), Charles Trowbridge (*Mr. Selkirk*), Bobby Blake (*Small Boy*), Mary Field (*Mrs. Riggs*), William Bishop (*Cpl. Anderson*), Hugh

Beaumont, Dave O'Brien (Sergeants), Myron Healey (Gunner), Tom Yuen (Filipino), Chester Gan, Kaem Tong (Japanese Officers).

Beery at his most butch as a swaggering, multi-hashmarked marine sergeant major in the Philippines near the start of WW II, growling at his men, getting things done. His terrible secret, one that plagues him, is that he's a peacetime patriot, one who's never seen combat. When his unit ships out to see action in China, Beery is refused permission to go with them. Dejected, he drinks, and starts an altercation with some merchant sailors. Committed to the brig, and with wife Bainter urging his retirement, he complies with her wishes and turns disgruntled civilian. When the Japanese – the "mustard-colored monkeys," he calls them (remember, this was shortly after Pearl Harbor, when such adjectives were de rigeur in films with patriotic fervor) – invade the islands, Beery organizes the civilian withdrawal, and he and Bainter both heroically lose their lives. Daughter Maxwell – a pacifist at the outset of the picture, but now uniformed herself – accepts a posthumous medal for her father at the conclusion of the film. Owen makes an unlikely villain as an English-accented undercover Nazi agent.

p, John W. Considine, Jr.; d, S. Sylvan Simon; w, George Bruce, Wells Root (based on a story by Robert D. Andrews); ph, Charles Schoenbaum, W. Howard Greene (Technicolor); m, Lennie Hayton; ed, Frederick Y. Smith; art d, Cedric Gibbons, Stanley Rogers, Lynden Sparhawk; set d, Edwin B. Willis, Glen Barner.

War Drama/Comedy   (PR:C   MPAA:NR)

SALVAGE GANG, THE½** (1958, Brit.) 52m World Wide-Children's Film Foundation/BL bw

Christopher Warbey (Borer), Ali Allen (Ali), Amanda Coxell (Pat), Fraser Hines (Kim), Richard Molinas (Mr. Caspanelli).

Better than average children's film has four children trying various money-raising schemes to repair a broken saw. They sell an iron bed to a junk dealer, then discover they have to get it back. Even adults may like this creative effort.

p, P. Hindle Edgar; d&w, John Krish (based on a story by Mary Cathcart Borer); ph, James Allen.

Children   (PR:AA   MPAA:NR)

SALVARE LA FACCIA   (SEE: PSYCHOUT FOR MURDER, 1971, Arg./Ital.)

SALVATION NELL½** (1931) 84m James Cruze/TIF bw (GB: MEN WOMEN LOVE)

Ralph Graves (Jim Platt), Helen Chandler (Nell Saunders), Sally O'Neil (Myrtle), Jason Robards, Sr (Maj. Williams), DeWitt Jennings (McGovern), Charlotte Walker (Margie), Matthew Betz (Mooney), Rose Dione (Madame Cloquette), Wally Albright (Jimmy).

Graves plays a nice guy involved with Chandler. Pregnant, she wants to marry her man. But when he defends her honor and accidentally kills the man, he gets five years in the slammer. After he's released, Chandler joins the Salvation Army to support the now slovenly Graves. In the end, he sees the light and joins up with her cause. Though clearly a propaganda piece for the Salvation Army (based on the popular play of the time), SALVATION NELL tells its story without being dogmatic. Chandler and Graves are both good in the leads, giving this a livelier quality than most films of this nature.

p, Samuel Zierler; d, James Cruze; w, Selma Stein, Walter Woods (based on the play by Edward B. Sheldon); ph, Charles Schoenbaum; ed, R.E. Loewinger.

Drama   (PR:A   MPAA:NR)

SALVATORE GIULIANO*** (1966, Ital.) 125m Lux-Vides-Galatea/Royal bw

Frank Wolff (Gaspare Pisciotta), Salvo Randone (President of Viterbo Assize Court), Federico Zardi (Pisciotta's Defense Counsel), Pietro Cammarata (Salvatore Giuliano), Fernando Cicero (Bandit), Sennuccio Benelli (Reporter), Bruno Ekmar (Spy), Max Cartier (Francesco), Giuseppe Calandra (Minor Official), Cosimo Torino (Frank Mannino), Giuseppe Teti (Priest of Montelepre), Ugo Torrente.

This film is based on the true story of Salvatore Giuliano, an important Sicilian Mafia chieftain who was found shot full of holes on July 5, 1950. The film opens with the bullet-ridden remains found in a sunny courtyard. After his wake and funeral begin, the mobster's career is portrayed in flashbacks. Cammarata is the gangster who becomes involved with some guerrilla activities in post war Sicily. When the group breaks up, a number of his men continue to follow Cammarata as he stages a minor war against legal authorities. He has a group of peasants slaughtered at a Communist rally, which triggers violent confrontations between gangsters and the law. Slowly his men grow disillusioned with him and they abandon the man. Wolff, Cammarata's second-in-command, also abandons his boss but like many of the outlaws, is tried and thrown in jail. There Wolff is poisoned by members of the Mafia, a group he joined after leaving Cammarata. This is an

interesting gangster picture, made in the heart of the Mafia's birthplace. The use of camera technique is excellent, coupled with a strong sense of direction. The acting is equally good, making full use of the cast's respective talents. Non-professional actors as well as professionals were used with fine results. However the film is severely hampered for American audiences by the confusing plot line that was clearly designed with more local audiences in mind. The political, historical, and social references are not always clear, which can be distracting, yet this still works and works well.

p, Franco Cristaldi; d, Francesco Rosi; w, Rosi, Suso Cecchi D'Amico, Enzo Provenzale, Franco Solinas; ph, Gianni Di Venanzo; m, Piero Piccioni; ed, Mario Serandrei; art d, Sergio Canevari, Carlo Egidi; cos, Marilu Carteny.

Crime/Historical Drama   (PR:O   MPAA:NR)

SALZBURG CONNECTION, THE* (1972) 93m FOX c

Barry Newman (William Mathison), Anna Karina (Anna Bryant), Klaus-Maria Brandauer (Johann Kronsteiner), Karen Jensen (Elissa Lang), Joe Maross (Chuck), Wolfgang Preiss (Felix Zauner), Helmut Schmid (Grell), Udo Kier (Anton), Michael Haussermann (Lev Benedescu), Whit Bissell (Newhart), Raoul Retzer (Large Man), Elisabeth Felchner (Trudi Seidl), Bert Fortell (Rugged Man), Alf Beinell (Anton's Companion), Patrick Jordan (Richard Bryant), Edward Linkers (Tour Guide), Gene Moss (Tourist), Karl Otto Alberty, Rudolf Bary (Stocky Men), Christine Buchegger (Waitress), The Wiener Spatzen Boys' Choir.

While vacationing in Austria, an American lawyer, Newman, gets mixed up with the CIA and various agents from different countries. A chest containing names of Nazi collaborators has been dredged from a lake and no one can decide whether to destroy it or reveal the contents. The result is a boring and confusing plot that loses interest very quickly. The preponderance of freeze-frames and slow motion is annoying and fails to achieve the intended stylized look. The Austrian locales are beautiful, though, probably the most interesting parts of the film.

p, Ingo Preminger; d, Lee H. Katzin; w, Oscar Millard (based on a novel by Helen MacInnes); ph, Wolfgang Treu (DeLuxe Color); m, Lionel Newman; ed, John M. Woodcock; md, Newman; art d, Herta Hareiter-Pischinger; cos, Lambert Hofer, Jr.

Spy Drama   **Cas.**   (PR:C   MPAA:PG)

SAM COOPER'S GOLD   (SEE: RUTHLESS FOUR, THE, 1969, Ital./Ger.)

SAM MARLOW, PRIVATE EYE   (SEE: MAN WITH BOGART'S FACE, THE, 1980)

SAM SMALL LEAVES TOWN** (1937, Brit.) 79m British Screen Service bw (AKA: IT'S SAM SMALL AGAIN)

Stanley Holloway (Richard Manning), June Clyde (Sally Elton), Fred Conyngham (Jimmy West), Harry Tate (Camper), Johnnie Schofield (Sam Small), Robert English (Robert Harrison), James Craven (Steve Watt), Brookins and Van, Aubrey Pollock, Molly Fisher.

Actor Holloway bets a publisher friend that he can disappear for a week. At a vacation spot he meets Schofield, the resort handyman, and switches identities with him. The ruse is quite a success until Holloway allows himself to be identified by a young reporter so that the newsman can win the reward money and marry his girl friend. Mediocre comedy made palatable by Holloway.

p, Maurice J. Wilson; d, Alfred Goulding.

Comedy   (PR:A   MPAA:NR)

SAM WHISKEY½** (1969) 97m Brighton Pictures/UA c

Burt Reynolds (Sam Whiskey), Clint Walker (O. W. Bandy), Ossie Davis (Jedidiah Hooker), Angie Dickinson (Laura Breckinridge), Rick Davis (Fat Henry Hobson), Del Reeves (Fisherman), William Schallert (Mint Superintendent Perkins), Woodrow Parfrey (Thornton Bromley, Mint Inspector), Virgil Warner (Narrator), Anthony James (Cousin Leroy), John Damler (Hank), Bud Adler (Pete), Chubby Johnson (The Blacksmith), Ayllene Gibbons (Big Annie), Amanda Harley (Mrs. Perkins), Sidney Clute, William Boyett, Tracey Roberts.

The Civil War has ended and Reynolds is seduced away from his career as a gambler by the lovely Dickinson. She wants him to help her recover a quarter of a million dollars worth of gold bars her late husband has stolen. The gold now lies on the bottom of Colorado's Platte River aboard a sunken river boat and must be recovered before the Denver mint it was stolen from discovers it's missing, potentially destroying Dickinson's family's reputation. Reynolds agrees to do the job for $20,000 and teams up with Ossie Davis, a local blacksmith, and Walker, a buddy from the war who now works as an inventor. The team heads for the Platte, unaware that they are being followed by Rick Davis, an outlaw who wants the gold for himself. Walker creates a diving helmet that will allow Reynolds to go beneath the river, but after the heroes retrieve the loot, Rick Davis steals it from them. With the help of a Walker-created machine gun, however, Reynolds manages to recover the gold and with his cohorts rejoins Dickinson in Denver. Reynolds then poses as a government inspector, enters the mint, and then "accidentally" damages a bust of George Washington. He insists upon having it repaired and takes it back to Ossie Davis' blacksmith shop. The gold is recast into the shape of the bronze bust by the blacksmith and when the outlaw Rick Davis catches up with the trio, he mistakenly steals the bronze bust. Reynolds and his cohorts pose as plumbers to gain entrance to the mint and there re-cast the bust into gold bars. The next morning Dickinson rewards the men with the promised $20,000 and Reynolds has her heart as well. This is an amiable enough film with some fine comic acting by Reynolds. At the time, he was beginning the transition from TV to movies. The chemistry between Reynolds (playing a virgin of all things!) and Dickinson works well. Shortly after the film was completed he took a still picture from the romantic bedroom scene with Dickinson and had it enlarged. He hung it up over his bar at home with a caption under it that read "An Actor's Life is Pure Hell!" Support from the other cast members works fine, but the direction is the film's downfall, with pacing that moves too slowly for good comedic effect. The odd mixture of light comedy and western action could have become a cult favorite under better hands; as it is, SAM WHISKEY is enjoyable enough, but forgettable.

p, Jules Levy, Arthur Gardner, Arnold Laven; d, Laven; w, William W. Norton (based on a story by Norton); ph, Robert Moreno (DeLuxe Color); m, Herschel Burke Gilbert; ed, John Woodcock; art d, Lloyd S. Papez; set d, Charles Thompson; cos, William T. Zacha, Helen Colvig; m/l, Norton; makeup, Dan Greenway.

Comedy/Western   **(PR:C-O MPAA:M)**

SAMANTHA   (SEE: A NEW KIND OF LOVE, 1963)

SAMAR**½**   (1962) 89m Winchester-MAM/WB c

George Montgomery (*Dr. John Saunders*), Gilbert Roland (*Col. Salazar*), Ziva Rodann (*Ana*), Joan O'Brien (*Cecile Salazar*), Nico Minardos (*De Guzman*), Mario Barri (*Sgt. Nanding*), Tony Fortich, Carmen Austin, Danny Jurado, Pedro Faustino, Henry Feist, Johnny Cortez, Esperanza Garcia, Luciano Lasam, Pam Saunders, Rita Moreno.

It is the 1870s and Montgomery is a soldier of fortune. He's sent to a Spanish penal colony in the Philippines which is run by Roland, a real humanitarian. He tries to make the colony of Samar more a model community than a prison. Also arriving is Rodann, the daughter of a Spanish official. Montgomery has killed a man in a duel over the man's wife and has been sentenced to five years. Minardos is a Spanish inspector who disapproves of the model setting and demands Roland explain himself to his superiors. Instead, Roland destroys the camp, takes Minardos hostage, and, with the prisoners, heads for a secluded valley hidden within the jungle. En route they are attacked by headhunters and Minardos is killed. Fighting off the overwhelming forces of nature, including storms and high mountains, the group pushes onward. Roland is hit by a poison dart and Montgomery, who is a doctor, is forced to amputate his benefactor's arm so that the man might live. They finally reach the secluded valley and there set up a new community. Plenty of action and adventure to be found in this one, steeped in macho tradition. Montgomery, in addition to starring, also produced, directed, and co-wrote the feature. His weakest point is the writing, which never really fleshes out the characters.

p&d, George Montgomery; w, Montgomery, Ferde Grofe, Jr. (based on a story by Montgomery, Grofe); ph, Emmanuel Rojas (Technicolor); m, Harry Zimmerman; ed, Walter Thompson; md, Zimmerman.

Adventure   **(PR:C MPAA:NR)**

SAMARITAN, THE   (SEE: SOUL OF THE SLUMS, 1931)

SAME TIME, NEXT YEAR***½**   (1978) 119m Mirisch-Mulligan/UNIV
c

Ellen Burstyn (*Doris*), Alan Alda (*George*), Ivan Bonar (*Chalmers*), Bernie Kuby (*Waiter*), Cosmo Sardo (*2nd Waiter*), David Northcutt (*Pilot No. 1*), William Cantrell (*Pilot No. 2*).

Moving comedy-drama written by Bernard Slade from his play that ran nearly 1500 performances on Broadway. The stage producer, Morton Gottlieb, also co-produced the picture. Gottlieb has long specialized in small character plays and also did Slade's ROMANTIC COMEDY as well as Tony Shaffer's SLEUTH. They've opened it up somewhat here to add a few characters but it never loses the stagebound feeling or the intimacy, which is both a good and a bad quality. At the start, it's 1951 and Burstyn (age 24) and Alda (age 27) meet at a Northern California resort. They are both married to other spouses, but there is a magnetism between this Oakland housewife and the New Jersey accountant. They have an affair but both realize it can go no further because their own marriages are still fresh and neither is about to alter the situation. However, they make a pact to meet, every five years, at this same resort to commemorate the splendor and passion of their first tryst. It is these reunions which are the basis for the remainder of the film. The two grow, progress (and in Alda's case, regress) and change. Alda questions the meaning of life, leaves New Jersey, moves

to California, gets a psychiatrist, and decides to become a piano player. Burstyn becomes a hippie, then a successful businesswoman and a grandmother. The changes they go through are the film's assets and liabilities because Alda's sudden conversion to California hipness is a bit shocking and Burstyn's radical move to the Berkeley world is equally abrupt. Alda endures a personal tragedy and Slade does his best to make the audience root for these people, even though what they are doing is conducting a clandestine affair, engaging in infidelity. It's contrived but Slade opts for some touching moments and wisely forgoes the cheap one-liners that he is capable of writing. Mulligan's direction is seamless and Gausman's sets are superbly subtle as they reflect the time passing in the hotel suite. Special plaudits to makeup man Tuttle, who manages to age Alda and Burstyn in a believable fashion. Good music from Hamlisch and a boring song sung by Jane Oliver and Johnny Mathis that somehow managed an Oscar nomination. Nominations also went to Slade, Surtees, and Burstyn. SAME TIME, NEXT YEAR goes by very quickly, is filled with good jokes and just as many insights.

p, Walter Mirisch, Morton Gottlieb; d, Robert Mulligan; w, Bernard Slade (based on his play); ph, Robert Surtees (Panavision, Technicolor); m, Marvin Hamlisch; ed, Sheldon Kahn; prod d, Henry Bumstead; set d, Hal Gausman; cos, Theadora Van Runkle; spec eff, Tim Moran; m/l, "The Last Time I Felt Like This," Hamlisch, Alan and Marilyn Bergman (sung by Johnny Mathis, Jane Oliver); makeup, William Tuttle.

Comedy/Drama   **Cas.**   **(PR:A-C MPAA:PG)**

SAMMY GOING SOUTH   (SEE: BOY TEN FEET TALL, A, 1965,
                                              Brit.)

SAMMY STOPS THE WORLD zero (1978) 105m Ed Rood, Sr./Special Events Entertainmen t c (AKA: STOP THE WORLD–I WANT TO GET OFF)

Sammy Davis, Jr (*Littlechap*), Dennis Daniels (*Baton Twirler*), Donna Lowe (*Schoolgirl*), Marian Mercer (*Evie*), Debora Masterson, Joyce Nolen, Wendy Edmead, Patrick Kinser-Lau, Shelly Burch, Charles Willis, Jr, Edwetta Little.

Updated version of the musical "Stop the World–I Want to Get Off," rewritten for Davis in what amounts to little more than an ego-fest for the talented singer. The simple story is of Davis as a poor coffee vendor who rises to the top by getting the boss' daughter pregnant and marrying her. He becomes a big wheeler-dealer in the business world, dabbles in politics, has a few affairs, and otherwise sings and dances up a storm until he realizes that his wife is the only girl for him. Davis' hipster black man characterization panders to the worst of stereotypes about blacks with a touch of Las Vegas glitz mixed in. This is a filmed version of the stage production and there are occasional shots of the audience which appears to be enjoying the show. The direction is completely inept with a camera that remains rooted in place for nearly the entire film.

p, Mark Travis, Del Jack; d, Mel Shapiro; w, Leslie Bricusse, Anthony Newley; ph, David Myers (DeLuxe Color); ed, William H. Yahraus; set d, Santo Loquasto; cos, Loquasto; ch, Billy Wilson; m/l, Bricusse, Newley.

Musical   **(PR:C MPAA:NR)**

SAMPO   (SEE: DAY THE EARTH FROZE, THE, 1964, USSR/Fin.)

SAM'S SONG*   (1971) 120m Cannon c (AKA: THE SWAP)

Robert DeNiro (*Sam*), Jarred Mickey (*Andrew*), Jennifer Warren (*Erica*), Terrayne Crawford (*Carol*), Martin Kelley (*Mitch*), Phyllis Black (*Marge*), Viva (*Girl with the Hourglass*), Anthony Charnota (*Vito*), Lisa Blount, Sybil Danning, John Medici, James Brown, Sam Anderson, Tony Brande, Matt Green, Alvin Hammer, Jack Slater.

A pretentious picture about a New York film buff's attempt to complete a documentary about Nixon. He gets involved with a crowd of wealthy characters during a weekend on Long Island. He is disenchanted with the vacuous people he meets and decides to return to his life of films. Interesting only to see a young Robert DeNiro in the lead role, though fans of Arthur Penn's 1975 film NIGHT MOVES may find Jennifer Warren's performance a treat. Re-released theatrically and on video as THE SWAP in 1980, with additional footage added by John C. Broderick.

p, Christopher C. Dewey; d, Jordan Leondopoulos, John C. Broderick; ph, Alex Phillips, Jr.; m, Gershon Kingsley; ed, Arline Garson.

Drama   **(PR:O MPAA:R)**

SAMSON*   (1961, Ital.) 90m Telewide-Medallion c (AKA: SANSONE)

Brad Harris (*Samson*), Brigitte Corey (*Jasmine*), Alan Steel [Sergio Ciani], Serge Gainsbourg, Walter Reeves, Mara Berni, Carlo Tamberlani, Irene Prosen.

A fairly incompetent version of the age-old Samson tale with Harris playing the hero whose strength lies in his long hair. He offers his assistance to the king and must fend off countless enemies who would prefer him dead.

d, Gianfranco Parloni; w, Georgio C. Simonelli, Parloni (based on the story by Simonelli, C. Madison); ph, Francesco Izzarelli; m, Carlo Innocenzi; ed, Mario Sansoni; art d, Oscar D'Amico.

Adventure **(PR:A MPAA:NR)**

SAMSON AND DELILAH*½** (1949) 131m PAR c

Hedy Lamarr *(Delilah)*, Victor Mature *(Samson)*, George Sanders *(Saran of Gaza)*, Angela Lansbury *(Semadar)*, Henry Wilcoxon *(Ahtur)*, Olive Deering *(Miriam)*, Fay Holden *(Hazel)*, Julia Faye *(Hisham)*, Rusty Tamblyn *(Saul)*, William Farnum *(Tubal)*, Lane Chandler *(Teresh)*, Moroni Olsen *(Targil)*, Francis J. McDonald *(Story Teller)*, William "Wee Willie" Davis *(Garmiskar)*, John Miljan *(Lesh Lakish)*, Arthur Q. Bryan *(Fat Philistine Merchant)*, Laura Elliot *(Spectator)*, Victor Varconi *(Lord of Ashdod)*, John Parrish *(Lord of Gath)*, Frank Wilcox *(Lord of Ekron)*, Russell Hicks *(Lord of Ashkelon)*, Fritz Leiber *(Lord Sharif)*, Mike Mazurki *(Leader of Philistine Soldiers)*, Davison Clark *(Merchant Prince)*, George Reeves *(Wounded Messenger)*, Pedro de Cordoba *(Bar Simon)*, Frank Reicher *(Village Barber)*, Charles Evans *(Manoah, Samson's Father)*, George Zoritch, Hamil Petroff *(Sword Dancers)*, Frank Mayo *(Master Architect)*, Lloyd Whitlock *(Chief Scribe)*, Crauford Kent *(Court Astrologer)*, Harry Woods *(Gammad)*, Stephen Robets *(Bergam at Feast)*, Ed Hinton *(Makon at Feast/Double for Victor Mature)*, Carl Saxe *(Slave)*, James Craven, Nils Asther, Harry Cording, Colin Tapley *(Princes)*, Charles Meredith *(High Priest)*, Pierre Watkin, Fred Graham, Boyd Davis *(Priests)*, John "Skins" Miller *(Man with Burro)*, Lester Sharpe *(Saddle Maker)*, Edgar Dearing, Hugh Prosser *(Tax Collectors)*, John Merton *(Assistant Tax Collector)*, Al Ferguson *(Villager)*, Fred Kohler, Jr. *(Soldier)*, Tom Tyler *(Philistine Captain of Gristmill)*, Ray Bennett *(Overseer at Gristmill)*, Charles Judels *(Danite Merchant)*, Brahm van den Berg *(Temple Dancer)*, Eric Alden *(Courtier)*, Bob Kortman *(Vendor)*, Philo McCullough *(Merchant)*, Ted Mapes *(Captain Killed by Jawbone)*, Gertrude Messinger, Betty Boyd, Dorothy Adams, Betty Farrington, Calire DuBrey, Greta Granstedt *(Women)*, Byron Foulger, Stanley Blystone, Crane Whitley, Kenneth Gibson *(Men)*, Jeff York, Bert Moorhouse, Margaret Field, John Kellogg *(Spectators)*, Charles Dayton *(Midget at Arena)*, Henry Wills *(Saran's Charioteer)*, Karen Morley *(Woman)*.

This was one of DeMille's blockbusters and an all-time money maker, a fantasy fable of ancient time strongman Samson, essayed with beefy pride by Mature, and the vixen Delilah, played by a steaming Lamarr, whose soft curves vanquished the muscled arms of the titan. Everything about this film was lavish, from its wondrous sets to its ornate costumes, all shown in rich color upon which millions of viewers feasted their anxious eyes. Mature, the champion of the oppressed Danite tribe, is enamored of golden-haired Lansbury, beauteous daughter of a wealthy Philistine merchant. He plans to marry her despite the warnings of his own elders and the hostility of the Philistines. In the land of Dan, circa 1100 B.C., the Danites pray that shepherd Mature will come to his senses and oppose the evil tyranny of the Philistines, instead of taking to bed one of its harlots. Deering, who is Mature's betrothed, wordlessly allows her fellow Danite to pursue his pleasures, believing that he will someday see the light and return to her arms. Mature visits Lansbury at her estate and tells her he plans to wed her, his conversation overheard by the family's younger daughter, Lamarr, a wild and reckless young woman who admires Mature's strength. Philistine general Wilcoxon, who vies with Mature for Lansbury's hand, insults him and Mature grabs an iron spear. Instead of throwing it at warrior Wilcoxon, he slowly bends it double, shocking Wilcoxon, frightening Lansbury, and enthralling Lamarr. Later, the king of the Philistines, Sanders, conducts a lion hunt which Mature attends, driving ahead of the main party of hunters in a chariot with Lammarr at this side. He finds the lion they are seeking and, in a fierce struggle, breaks its neck with his bare hands. Sanders comes upon the scene and is amazed at the shepherd's incredible strength, telling him he wishes to reward him. Mature boldly asks for the hand of princess Lansbury. The honor-bound Sanders grants the request and plans are made for the Danite and Philistine to marry, a situation which incenses Lamarr who wants Mature for herself. But during the pre-wedding ceremonies, Danite guests at Lansbury's estate insult the impoverished Mature, stating that he is ignorant. He responds by giving them a riddle to solve, and a time limit in which to respond with the correct answer. Wilcoxon goes to Lansbury and, telling her that her allegiance is to her own people, the Philistines, says that she must learn the secret of the riddle and tell him so that he and his friends can win the wagers they have bet with Mature. Lansbury worms the secret out of Mature and tells Wilcoxon who, in turn, tells his countrymen. The Philistines smugly answer Mature in the dining hall, compelling him to settle with them, all demanding expensive cloaks. Mature angrily departs after realizing that his bride-to-be has betrayed him. He waylays a number of well-to-do travelers, taking their cloaks and returning to the dining hall where he throws them out to the jeering Philistines. Then he discovers Wilcoxon with the half-naked Lansbury and states that Wilcoxon would never have learned the secret to the riddle "had you not ploughed with my heifer!" Wilcoxon and the others attack Mature but he drives them off, a dozen of the best Philistine warriors, killing several, until one throws a spear at him and accidentally pierces Lansbury, killing her. Using his massive strength, Mature lifts tons of marble slabs and urns, hurling these as one would small stones at his charging enemies, slaying them and departing, promising Wilcoxon and the few other survivors that he will take vengeance on all Philistines thereafter. He burns Lansbury's crops and estate to the ground, making Lamarr homeless. The raven-haired vixen vows to have her own revenge against Mature. Goading her is the thought, more than the death of her sister and the destruction of her home, that when she offered herself to Mature he rejected her. Mature goes on a rampage against the tax collectors of the king, as well as destroying whole companies of soldiers Sanders sends against him. Lamarr, now the favorite courtesan of Sanders, suggests that he starve and tax the Danites until they deliver Mature into the hands of Sanders' troops. Sanders approves the idea and soon Mature, unable to bear the suffering of his people, delivers himself into the hands of his enemies. Wilcoxon and a whole army escort the massive Mature to the Philistine capital but en route, as he is being dragged along, chained to the back of a chariot, a dwarf jester taunting him with the skull of a jackass, Mature stops and begs for water. He is given a drink and then, as strange purple clouds gather about him in the mountain pass where he has stopped, he asks, "Is this the place known as Leehigh?" When he is told it is, Mature grabs the skull of the ass, breaks his bonds, and hurls the chariot to which he was bound in the air, killing its occupants. Wilcoxon's heavily armed soldiers advance upon him, but Mature steps into a narrow crevice where only a few can attack him at one time and, using the jawbone of the ass, smashes their skulls, despite the fact that they are wearing armor-plated helmets. He breaks their spears and swords and hurls them back upon each other, phalanx by phalanx, hundreds of the soldiers dying. The slaughter is incredible as a strange wind and dust storm rises and swirls about the bizarre battle. The Philistine army is destroyed, with only a few survivors, Wilcoxon included, reporting the cataclysmic battle to an astounded Sanders who finds it hard to believe that one man could kill more than 1,000 of his best mounted cavalry and hand-picked infantrymen. Listening to this tale is Lamarr, who asks Sanders and an assembly of visiting chieftans to pay her an enormous amount of gold to conquer Mature alone. They agree but doubt she will have an effect on what is apparently a superhuman creature. Lamarr, traveling with only servants, pitches her tents alongside a tranquil lagoon and soon Mature finds her. At first, all he wants is to loot her treasures but she soon vamps him into her arms and he becomes her love pawn. Days and nights pass while Lamarr subtly attempts to learn the secret of Mature's strength and he lies to her repeatedly but she learns that nothing he has told her reveals the true source of his might. Then, in a moment of weakness, he tells her that his long luxuriant black hair is the source of his strength. After he drinks his fill of wine, Lamarr cuts his hair short and he awakes to find himself surrounded by Philistine soldiers and powerless against them. Wilcoxon has promised Lamarr that not one sword will pierce Mature's flesh. (Lamarr is still enamored of the proud Mature and wants no harm to ever come to him.) Wilcoxon agrees to the request but wounds the strong man in another way, passing a white-hot sword so close to his eyes that he blinds Mature. Taken away, Mature is used like an ox, pulling a huge wheel to grind wheat, on display where Philistines stop to jeer and make fun of him. Lamarr, unable to stay away from him, visits her conquered Danite lover to find that she still loves him and always will love him. She begs his forgiveness and offers to plan an escape; they will flee together and make a new life in another country. The blind Mature is still full of rage and reaches out for her, suddenly lifting her in the air, ready to hurl her through the air to her death, but when he does so he realizes that he has broken his shackles with a single movement. Lamarr points to his hair. It has grown long again and he has regained his unworldly strength. Mature thanks God for restoring his power. He takes Lamarr in his arms and tells her that he loves her also but that he must appear the following day at the mammoth Philistine temple where he is to be put on display for the edification of the fun-poking populace. The next day, after Lamarr struts around the arena of the temple, leading Mature by the end of a rope, she takes him to the great pillars supporting the entire temple. He begs her to run away as he must do God's bidding and begins to put his great strength against the pillars of the Minoan temple. The Philistines roar with laughter at the attempt. Lamarr stands nearby silently, vowing to die with the man she loves. Suddenly, striking the thousands present into silence, one of the pillars begins to move under Mature's arm. Then the other. The stunned Philistines, including Sanders and his royal court, watch in horror as the one pillar collapses under pressure from Mature, bringing down the enormous structure and then the other so that the towering pagan idol of the god Dagon burning huge fires in its belly also topples forth, crashing right into Sanders and the royal box as he lifts a goblet of wine in a final toast to Lamarr and accepts his death in resignation. Thousands of Philistines die as the entire temple crashes downward, killing its occupants, and Mature and Lamarr. Deering and a small shepherd boy who has always admired Mature, Tamblyn, are left to witness the devastation and sadly turn away to tell their tribesmen of the death of their hero whose fame "will live for a thousand years." SAMSON AND DELILAH is tried and true ground for DeMille, who, unlike any great film director before or after him, felt he was the world's greatest film historian. DeMille had reached for historical themes in 12 of his 18 sound films, but he is best remembered for dipping his hoary hands into the Bible and drawing forth his extravagant tales– KING OF KINGS (1927), SIGN OF THE CROSS (1932), THE TEN COMMANDMENTS (1923 and 1956)–or dwelling in other ancient times such as CLEOPATRA (1933) and THE CRUSADES (1935). Of all his majestic Biblical epics, nothing compares with SAMSON AND DELILAH. The master of the crowd scene flourishes here by expertly managing thousands of extras in stunning scenes that are both pleasurable to see and awesome in their scope. Mature's battle scenes when destroying the Philistine army with the jawbone of an ass are savage and traumatic. Here DeMille took an excerpt from the Old Testament, Judges 13-16, and made a spectacular epic that had a $3 million price tag but a film that saw enormous and immediate returns, filling Paramount's coffers with more than $12 million from its initial release, the largest box-office release that studio had up to that time. The studio had serious doubts about SAMSON AND DELILAH when DeMille proposed the project. One studio executive queried: "Put millions of dollars into a Sunday school story?" It was really a boy meets girl story with bizarre and exotic trappings scooped up from the long ago. The director was a perfectionist when it came to researching his subject matter and he spent $100,000 on background information for this story, learning for instance that Samson, in his defeating of the Philistine army, was always depicted in ancient drawings with *a half of a jawbone of an ass*. He tried that as a weapon and realized that it would require a *full jawbone* for a man to have a lethal weapon, holding it in the area of the chin, and so Mature uses a full jawbone, not a half, in the film. In his quest for the perfect specimen to play the strong man, DeMille considered Burt Lancaster, one-time circus acrobat. But he dismissed Lancaster after learning that he had a bad back and thought him a bit too young for the role. Others came to mind but then DeMille saw a hulking tough-looking actor named Victor Mature in a Ben Hecht crime melodrama, KISS OF DEATH, and decided Mature would be his Samson. He could not have chosen a more unlikely candidate. He had Mature test in costume and almost suffered an apoplectic attack. The actor was outright flabby and overweight, his muscle tone gone. DeMille ordered the actor to go into intensive training with the athletic Wilcoxon, DeMille's right-hand production assistant, ordering Mature to take off 30 pounds of fat. The actor worked hard and took off the weight but, when shooting got underway, DeMille discovered that Mature possessed every phobia known to man. He feared wild animals, water, and weapons, especially swords. The wind machine used in the battle with the Philistines was turned on and, right in the middle of this expensive scene, Mature shook in terror of the machine and fled to his dressing room where no amount of pleading could dislodge him. Finally, fearing DeMille's wrath more than the wind machine, Mature meekly stepped forth and stepped back onto the set. Sneering his disgust for such cowardice, DeMille snatched up one of his many monogrammed megaphones and shouted through it for the entire cast and crew to hear: "I have met a few men in my time! Some have been afraid of heights, some have been afraid of water, some have been afraid of fire, some have been afraid of closed spaces! Some have even been afraid of open spaces–or themselves! But in all my 35 years of picture-making experience, Mr. Mature, I have not until now met a man who was 100 percent yellow!" Lamarr, on the other hand, feared nothing but made life difficult for DeMille since she admitted she still thought in German and had never really mastered the English language and learned her lines (which she knew to the letter) by rote. He also realized early that she acted like a fashion model posing for still photography and always ended each scene in a frozen pose designed to capture her best profile. Lamarr, however, comes across as the perfect Delilah, a scheming, scratching, clawing creature of such rare and exquisite beauty that DeMille was content to let her vamp her way through his magnificent sets and let it go at that. (It is odd to think that the director had actually thought in preproduction to cast Betty Hutton in the role of Delilah, which proves he was no master at types.) DeMille was ever the showman and, when discussing his film after its release, told newsmen that he collected almost 2,000 peacocks on his ranch so that the feathers would make up a single costume for the exotic Lamarr. The peacock feathers he did use came from the Paramount prop department and had been used on his original silent film, THE TEN COMMANDMENTS. The destruction of the temple, however, was no joke, but a colossal set that was actually destroyed by 200 of DeMille's best technicians. The pillars of the temple, tapered at the bottom, as was the original according to legend, were made of light plaster that gave way under Mature's lightweight pressure and the rest of the huge set, duplicated by a scaled-down model the cameras cut to occasionally, was brought down like an old skyscraper, amazingly without a single injury to the thousands of extras inside it. The film was an enormous success and even the Kellogg Company put out Samson-like cornflakes with the flakes twice as big as usual, and Parisian designers mimicked Lamarr's ancient gowns which sold to countless women for exhorbitant prices. Hans Dreier and Walter Tyler won Oscars for Best Art Direction and Edith Head and Company took home a deserved Oscar for the fabulous costumes.

p&d, Cecil B. DeMille; w, Vladimir Jabotinsky, Harold Lamb, Jesse L. Lasky, Jr., Frederic M. Frank (based on the history of Samson and Delilah in the Holy Bible and the book *Judge and Fool* by Jabotinsky); ph, Dewey Wrigley, George Barnes (Technicolor); m, Victor Young; ed, Anne Bauchens; md, Young; art d, Hans Dreier, Walter Tyler; set d, Sam Comer, Ray Moyer; cos, Edith Head, Gus Peters, Dorothy Jeakins, Gwen Wakeling, Elois Jenssen; spec eff, Gordon Jennings, Paul Lerpae, Devereaux Jennings; ch, Theodore Kosloff; m/l, Ray Evans, Jay Livingston, Young; makeup, Wally Westmore, Harold Lierly, William Wood.

Biblical Epic   Cas.   (PR:C MPAA:NR)

SAMSON AND THE SEVEN MIRACLES OF THE WORLD**
(1963, Fr./Ital.) 80m Panda-Gallus-Agiman/AIP c (MACISTE ALLA CORTE DEL GRAN KHAN; LE GEANT A LA COUR DE KUBLAI KHAN; AKA: MACISTE AT THE COURT OF THE GREAT KHAN; GOLIATH AND THE GOLDEN CITY)

Gordon Scott *(Samson)*, Yoko Tani *(Princess Lei-ling)*, Gabriele Antonini *(Cho)*, Leonardo Severini *(Garak)*, Valery Inkijinoff *(High Priest)*, Helene Chanel *(Liutai)*, Dante Di Paolo *(Bayan)*, Chu-Lai-Chit, Luong-Ham-Chau, Franco Ressel, Antonio Cianci, Ely Yeh, Giacomo Tchang.

During the 13th century ex-TARZAN star Scott saves a young prince and princess after their father is murdered by a Tartar. The princess is taken to a safe spot by rebels, only to be kidnaped by the cruel Tartar who has matrimony on his mind. Scott rescues her again and takes her to the rebels' monastery hideout. But this hideout is attacked and the prince is killed. Scott sounds "The Gong of Freedom" that causes enslaved Chinamen to rise up against the Tartars, but gets knocked down by the swinging bell and ends up being buried alive in an underground vault created by the enemy. Using all his might, Scott causes an earthquake and escapes. Everything is resolved when the Tartars are defeated and the princess takes her rightful place on the throne. In foreign versions, Scott's character was known by the proper name "Maciste," which was changed to "Samson" in the dubbed American prints, undoubtedly to cash in on the semi-popular SAMSON films released here.

p, Ermanno Donati, Luigi Carpentieri; d, Riccardo Freda; w, Oreste Biancoli, Duccio Tessari (based on a story by Biancoli); ph, Riccardo Pallottini (Colorscope, Technicolor); m, Les Baxter; ed, Ornella Micheli; art d, Piero Filippone; cos, Massimo Bolongaro; ch, Wilbert Bradley.

Adventure   (PR:A MPAA:NR)

SAMSON AND THE SLAVE QUEEN**
(1963, Ital.) 86m Romana/AIP c (ZORRO CONTRA MACISTE; AKA: ZORRO AGAINST MACISTE)

Pierre Brice *(Zorro/Ramon)*, Alan Steel [Sergio Ciani] *(Samson)*, Moira Orfei *(Malva)*, Maria Grazia Spina *(Isabella)*, Andrea Aureli *(Rabek)*, Massimo Serato *(Garcia)*, Aldo Bufi Landi, Andrea Scotti, Loris Gizzi, Rosy De Leo, Nazzareno Zamperla, Gaetano Scala, Attilio Dottesio.

In 15th Century Navarre the king dies and his two nieces must struggle for power. One is good (Spina), the other evil (Orfei). The only way to find out the chosen successor is to get hold of a treasure chest that carries the king's will, which states his heir. Orfei is ambitious and fears the will she holds her rival's name. She hires Steel to bring the chest to her so she can change the name and take the throne. Meanwhile Spina hires Brice, a great swordsman, on the advice of a poet she loves. Steel and Brice go through numerous conflicts before Steel finally gets the chest and takes it to Orfei. He stops short of giving it to her though, realizing that Spina should be the ruler. He and Brice team up after reconciling differences and the two fight off Serato, who is Orfei's lover and the leader of the palace guards. Spina becomes queen and she discovers that the masked swordsman is also her poet. This is typical beefcake action, full of gleaming pectorals and swashbuckling galore. It liberally mixes historical legends, eras, and heroes. Steel was called "Samson" in dubbed American prints, but was "Maciste" in the Italian version. Production values are okay for what this is, though the color processing is not up to par. At some points blonde-haired Spina looks like a victim of yellow jaundice!

p, Fortunato Misiano; d, Umberto Lenzi; w, Guido Malatesta, Lenzi; ph, Augusto Tiezzi (Colorscope, Eastmancolor); m, Angelo Francesco Lavagnino; ed, Iolanda Benvenuti; md, Lavagnino; set d, Peppino Piccol o; cos, Walter Patriarca.

Adventure   (PR:A MPAA:NR)

SAMSON IN THE WAX MUSEUM
(SEE: SANTO EN EL MUSEO DE CERA, 1963, Mex.)

SAMSON VS. THE GIANT KING
(SEE: ATLAS AGAINST THE CZAR, 1965, Ital.)

SAMURAI*   (1945) 78m Cavalcade bw

Paul Fung *(Dr. Ken Morey)*, Luke Chan *(Priest)*, David Chow *(Japanese Secret Service Man)*, Barbara Woodell *(Mrs. Morey)*, Fred C. Bond *(Mr. Morey)*, Larry Moore *(Frank Morey)*, Ronald Siu *(Dr. Ken Morey as a Boy)*, Joseph Kim, Beal Wong *(Engineers)*, Sung Lee *(Gen. Sugiama)*, Frances Chan *(Chinese Girl Prisoner)*, Mary Ellen Butler *(White Girl Prisoner)*.

Lurid propaganda picture mixes newsreels with re-enacted atrocities to prove that the Japanese are not to be trusted. Ironically, the film didn't make it into release until after the Japanese surrendered to the Americans in WW II.

p, Ben Mindenburg; d&w, Raymond Cannon (based on a story by Mindenburg).

War   (PR:A-C MPAA:NR)

SAMURAI   (SEE: SAMURAI ASSASSIN, 1965, Jap.)

SAMURAI*   (1955, Jap.) 92m Toho/FA c (MIYAMOTO MUSASHI; AKA: THE LEGEND OF MUSASHI; MASTER SWORDSMAN)

Toshiro Mifune (*Takeso/Miyamoto Musashi*), Kaoru Yachigusa (*Otsu*), Rentaro Mikuni (*Matahachi*), Mariko Okada (*Akemi*), Kuroemon Onoe (*Takuan*), Mitsuko Mito (*Oko*), Eiko Miyoshi (*Osugi*), Daisuke Kato, Kusuo Abe, Yoshio Kosugi, Sojin Kamiyama, Kanta Kisaragi, Akihiko Hirata, William Holden (*Narrator*).

Mifune is a young man of 17th Century Japan. He wants to elevate himself from his low caste in a poor village to the high status of the powerful samurai warriors. He is faced with numerous temptations and setbacks but sticks to his dream and becomes a great samurai by the film's end. This is an intelligent, well-made action piece that handles the drama well. The color photography nicely captures the forest scenery, giving the film a mythical look and feeling. Mifune is fine in the lead, going from youngster to noble warrior with believability and skill. The supporting cast is equally fine. For the American release a narration was provided with Holden as the narrator. Though probably unnecessary, this sets up the story nicely and never interferes with the on-screen action.

p, Kazuo Takimura; d, Hiroshi Inagaki; w, Tokuhei Wakao, Inagaki, Hideji Hojo (based on the novel *Miyamoto Musashi* by Eiji Yoshikawa); ph, Jun Yasumoto (Eastmancolor); m, Ikuma Dan; ed, Robert Homel, William Holden; art d, Makoto Sono.

Adventure   (PR:O   MPAA:NR)

SAMURAI ASSASSIN½   (1965, Jap.) 123m Toho-Toshiro Mifune/Toho International bw (SAMURAI)

Toshiro Mifune (*Niino*), Keiju Kobayashi (*Kurihara*), Michiyo Aratama (*Okiko Kukuhime*), Yunosuke Ito (*Hoshino*), Koshiro Matsumoto (*Lord Naosuke Li*), Nami Tamura, Kaoru Yachigusa, Haruko Sugimura, Takashi Shimura, Chusha Ichikawa, Susumu Fujita.

Because he doesn't know the identity of his father, Mifune is denied entrance to a house of nobility despite his keen swordsmanship. He grows frustrated in his attempts at becoming a great warrior and ends up joining a band of outlaws. Their plan is to assassinate the chief minister who wants more open relations with Western countries. The outlaws turn on Mifune but he escapes. Fighting off palace guards, he at last gains admission to the palace he so wanted to enter. He succeeds in assassinating the minister, only to discover that this man was his father all along. This high-action Japanese film has no relationship to any of Mifune's SAMURAI films made in the late 1950s.

p, Tomoyuki Tanaka, Reiji Miwa; d, Kihachi Okamoto; w, Shinobu Hashimoto (based on the story "Samurai Nippon" by Jiromasa Gunji); ph, Hiroshi Murai (Tohoscope); m, Masaru Sato.

Adventure/Action   (PR:O   MPAA:NR)

SAMURAI BANNERS   (SEE: UNDER THE BANNER OF SAMURAI, 1964, Jap.)

SAMURAI FROM NOWHERE½   (1964, Jap.) 93m Shochiku/Shochiku Films of America bw (DOJO YABURI; KEMPO SAMURAI)

Isamu Nagato (*Ihei Misawa*), Tetsuro Tamba (*Gunjuro Ohba*), Shima Iwashita (*Tae*), Chieko Baisho (*Chigusa*), Seiji Miyaguchi (*Tatewaki Komuro*).

During the 17th century, Iwashita is being held captive by an evil Japanese lord. Nagato, an unemployed samurai, rescues the woman, saving her from a life as a concubine. They are pursued by the kidnaper's underlings, but manage to get some menial work in order to earn the money needed to pay off debts and bribe border guards. Nagato decides to supplement the income by challenging a local fencing ace to a duel, not revealing his samurai background. He defeats the man and blackmails him for more money, breaking the honored samurai code of not using skills for monetary gain. The local governor hears of Nagato's abilities and offers him a post as master of martial arts. However when the governor learns that Nagato earned money through his fencing, the offer is withdrawn. The couple continues on its way, but is finally caught by the evil lord's henchmen. But thanks to the aid of Tamba, a fellow unemployed samurai, as well as the man Nagato defeated in the tournament, the two escape once more and proceed on their journey.

p, Gin-ichi Kishimoto; d, Seiichiro Uchikawa; w, Hideo Oguni (based on a story by Shoguro Yamamoto); ph, Yoshiharu Ota (Shochiku GrandScope); m, Masaru Sato; art d, Jun-ichi Osumi.

Martial Arts   (PR:C   MPAA:NR)

SAMURAI (PART II)   (1967, Jap.) 102m Toho/Toho International c (ICHIJOJI NO KETTO; ZOKU MIYAMOTO MUSASHI)

Toshiro Mifune (*Musashi Miyamoto*), Koji Tsuruta (*Kojiro Sasaki*), Sachio Sakai (*Matahachi Honiden*), Akihiko Hirata (*Seijuro Yoshioka*), Yu Fujiki (*Denshichiro Yoshioka*), Daisuke Kato (*Toji Gion*), Eijiro Tono (*Baiken*

Shishido), Kuninori Kodo (*Old Priest Nikkan*), Kenjim Iida (*Jotaro*), Kaoru Yachigusa (*Otsu*), Mariko Okada (*Akemi*), Mitsuko Mito (*Oko*), Michiyo Kogure (*Yoshino*), Kuroemon Ono.

A follow-up to the 1955 film SAMURAI continues the adventures of Mifune, the man of humble beginnings who becomes a great samurai warrior. In this picture he wanders through feudal Japan and continues to learn the ways of a warrior. He once more comes upon temptations from several women, but must sacrifice any romantic involvement to the discipline his life demands. Though released in the U.S. in 1967, this was originally released in Japan in 1955. The third film of the SAMURAI trilogy was released in the U.S. again in 1967, with the Japanese date being 1956.

p, Kazuo Takimura; d, Hiroshi Inagaki; w, Inagaki, Tokuhei Wakao (based on the novel *Miyamoto Musashi* by Eiji Yoshikawa); ph, Asushi Atumoto, Jun Yasumoto (Eastmancolor); m, Ikuma Dan.

Adventure   (PR:C-O   MPAA:NR)

SAMURAI (PART III)**   (1967, Jap.) 102m Toho/Toho International c (KETTO GANRYU JIMA; AKA: DUEL AT GANRYU ISLAND)

Toshiro Mifune (*Musashi Miyamoto*), Koji Tsuruta (*Koijiro Sasaki*), Kaoru Yachigusa (*Otsu*), Michiko Saga (*Omitsu*), Mariko Okada (*Akemi*), Takashi Shimura (*Court Official*), Kyo Shimura.

The final film in the SAMURAI series from Japan's Toho studios finds Mifune being challenged to a duel by his rival, Tsuruta. However, Mifune asks that the duel be put off temporarily, and his foe agrees. Mifune's woes continue as he is followed by two women who love the warrior. He settles in a farming village that has been overrun by bandits and attempts to teach the locals a few things about self-defense. But the bandits kidnap one of Mifune's women and attack the village using her to fool everyone. She dies and Mifune decides to settle down with Yachigusa, the other woman. However, his brief moment of happiness is interrupted when Tsuruta returns for the challenge. They meet on Ganryu Island for the long-awaited duel which Mifune wins. He returns home hoping that his troubles are over.

p, Kazuo Takimura; d, Hiroshi Inagaki; w, Inagaki, Tokuhei Wakao (based on the story by Eiji Yoshikawa); ph, Kazuo Yamada (Eastmancolor); m, Ikuma Dan; art d, Kisaku Ito.

Adventure   (PR:C-O   MPAA:NR)

SAMURAI PIRATE   (SEE: LOST WORLD OF SINBAD, THE, 1965, Jap.)

SAN ANTONE**   (1953) 90m REP bw

Rod Cameron (*Carl Miller*), Arleen Whelan (*Julia Allerby*), Forrest Tucker (*Brian Culver*), Katy Jurado (*Mistania Figueroa*), Rodolfo Acosta (*Chino Figueroa*), Roy Roberts (*John Chisum*), Bob Steele (*Bob*), Harry Carey, Jr (*Dobe*), James Lilburn (*Jim*), Andrew Brennan (*Ike*), Richard Hale (*Abraham Lincoln*), Martin Garralaga (*Mexican*), Argentina Brunetti (*Mexican Woman*), Douglas Kennedy (*Capt. Garfield*), Paul Fierro (*Bandit Leader*), George Cleveland (*Col. Allerby*).

During the Civil War Cameron is a Texas rancher who won't choose up sides. Tucker is an ex-Confederate officer who goes bananas and becomes a bandit. He murders Cameron's father and the rancher swears revenge. Though the action sequences are nicely handled and directed with energy, the explanatory passages drag. This was quite a surprise from Kane, once one of Republic's better veteran directors. The actors are passable in their roles, though Whelan as the love interest for Tucker overplays her part with gusto. Songs include: "South of San Antone," "Ten Thousand Cattle," "The Cowboy's Lament" (sung by Steele, Carey, Lilburn).

p&d, Joseph Kane; w, Steve Fisher (based on the novel *The Golden Herd* by Curt Carroll); ph, Bud Trackery; m, R. Dale Butts; ed, Tony Martinelli; art d, Frank Arrigo; cos, Adele Palmer.

Western   (PR:C   MPAA:NR)

SAN ANTONE AMBUSH**   (1949) 60m REP bw

Monte Hale (*Lt. Ross Kincaid*), Bette Daniels (*Sally Wheeler*), Paul Hurst (*Happy Daniels*), Roy Barcroft (*Roberts*), James Cardwell (*Clint Wheeler*), Trevor Bardette (*Wade Shattuck*), Lane Bradford (*Al*), Francis Ford (*Maj. Farnsworth*), Tommy Coats (*Joe*), Tom London (*Bartender*), Edmund Cobb (*Marshal Kennedy*), Carl Sepulveda.

A group of outlaws is holding up stagecoaches. The army sends out Hale to stop the gang from stealing the government funds carried along the line. Cardwell is an honest rancher being framed by the gang and a dishonest government official. After being tricked with a counterfeit note, Hale is arrested and tried by a court martial. But the plucky officer escapes, captures the real outlaws, and clears both his name and Cardwell's. Routine western with typical thesping and production values.

p, Melville Tucker; d, Philip Ford; w, Norman S. Hall (based on a story by Hall); ph, John MacBurnie; m, Stanley Wilson; ed, Tony Martinelli; art d, Frank Hotaling; set d, John McCarthy, Jr., James Redd; spec eff, Howard Lydecker, Theodore Lydecker.

Western   (PR:A   MPAA:NR)

SAN ANTONIO***   (1945) 111m WB c

Errol Flynn (Clay Hardin), Alexis Smith (Jeanne Starr), S.Z. Sakall (Sacha Bozic), Victor Francen (Legare), Florence Bates (Henrietta), John Litel (Charlie Bell), Paul Kelly (Roy Stuart), John Alvin (Pony Smith), Monte Blue (Cleve Andrews), Robert Shayne (Capt. Morgan), Robert Barrat (Col. Johnson), Pedro de Cordoba (Ricardo Torreon), Tom Tyler (Lafe McWilliams), Chris-Pin Martin (Hymie Rosas), Charles Stevens (Sojer Harris), Poodles Hanneford (San Antonio Stage Driver), Doodles Weaver (Square Dance Caller), Dan White (Joey Sims), Ray Spiker (Rebel White), Al Hill (Hap Winters), Wallis Clark (Tip Brice), Harry Cording (Hawker), Chalky Williams (Poker Player), Bill Steele (Roper), Howard Hill, Allen E. Smith (Clay's Henchmen), Arnold Kent (Dancer), Don McGuire, John Compton (Cowboys), Eddie Acuff (Gawking Cowboy), Si Jenks (Station Boss), Denver Dixon (Barfly), Snub Pollard (Dance Extra), Cliff Lyons (Errol Flynn's Double), Harry Semels (Mexican), Francis Ford (Old Cowboy Greeting Coach), William Gould, Jack Mower (Wild Cowmen), Brandon Hurst (Gambler), Dan Seymour (Laredo Border Guard), Brad King, Johnny Miles, Lane Chandler, Hal Taliaferro (Cowboys), Harry Seymour (Bartender), Norman Willis (Jay Witherspoon), Eddy Waller, Henry Hall, James Flavin (Cattlemen).

Until Richard Harris came along with A MAN CALLED HORSE, Errol Flynn was the only foreign actor to ever have any success in U.S. westerns. This one is an okay oater that borrowed a lot from many other pictures, including Max Steiner's main title from DODGE CITY. Flynn's previous western was THEY DIED WITH THEIR BOOTS ON, a far superior effort. This time around, they toss in color and a few tunes to add some spice to an otherwise ordinary movie that is distinguished only by a good shoot-out at the deserted Alamo. It's the late 1870s and Flynn is a cattle man who has just come back from Mexico to San Antonio. While south of the border, Flynn uncovered some evidence that Kelly, who owns the local saloon-dance hall-whatever, is also the head of a rustling organization that has made cattle stealing a state-of-the-art project in those parts. Smith is an Eastern entertainer who has come to San Antonio to work at Kelly's place and Flynn thinks that she must be part of the crooked group. Sakall provides the comic relief as Smith's manager as the story unfolds. Flynn and Kelly have been at odds for a long time and Francen, who runs the bar, becomes Flynn's rival for Smith's attention. There's the standard break-up-the-bar brawl and the final gunplay at Texas' most famous shrine. Before everything ends satisfactorily, we've been treated to a bit of action, a little sparking and three tunes by Smith: "Some Sunday Morning" (Ray Heindorf, M.K. Jerome, Ted Koehler), "Put Your Little Foot Right Out" (Larry Spier), "Somewhere In Monterey" (Charles Kisco, Jack Scholl). Flynn's name in the picture is Hardin, which may or may not have been a tribute to John Wesley Hardin, who'd been the subject of a few other westerns. For SAN ANTONIO, both Raoul Walsh and Robert Florey are said to have added uncredited directorial aid. Location shooting was done in Calabasas, California.

p, Robert Buckner; d, David Butler; w, Alan LeMay, W.R. Burnett; ph, Bert Glennon (Technicolor); m, Max Steiner; ed, Irene Morra; md, Leo F. Forbstein; art d, Ted Smith; set d, Jack McConaghy; cos, Milo Anderson; spec eff, Willard Van Enger; ch, LeRoy Prinz; makeup, Perc Westmore.

Western   Cas.   (PR:A-C   MPAA:NR)

SAN ANTONIO KID, THE**½   (1944) 59m REP bw

Bill Elliott (Red Ryder), Bobby Blake (Little Beaver), Alice Fleming, Linda Stirling, Tom London, Earle Hodgins, Glenn Strange, Duncan Renaldo, LeRoy Mason, Jack Kirk, Bob Wilke, Cliff Parkinson, Jack O'Shea, Tex Terry, Bob Woodward, Herman Hack, Henry Wills, Tom Steele, Joe Garcia, Billy Vincent, Bud Geary.

Mason and Strange are a pair of outlaws plotting to drive ranchers off their oil-saturated land. Elliott tries to save the day but must tangle with hired killer Renaldo before all is resolved. A routine entry in Republic's popular RED RYDER series. (See RED RYDER series, Index.)

p, Stephen Auer; d, Howard Bretherton; w, Norman S. Hall; ph, William Bradford; m, Joseph Dubin; ed, Tony Martinelli; art d, Gano Chittenden.

Western   (PR:A   MPAA:NR)

SAN ANTONIO ROSE**½   (1941) 63m UNIV bw

Jane Frazee (Hope Holloway), Robert Paige (Con Conway), Eve Arden (Gabby Trent), Lon Chaney, Jr (Jigsaw Kennedy), Shemp Howard (Benny the Bounce), Richard Lane (Willoughby), Louis DaPron (Alex), Charles Lang (Ralph), Roy Harris (Jimmy), Peter Sullivan (Don), Richard Davie (Eddie), Luis Alberni (Nick Ferris), The Merry Macs, Mary Lou Cook (Mona Mitchell), Joe McMichael (Harry), Ted McMichael (Ted), Judd McMichael (Phil), Tim Ryan (Gus), Hal K. Dawson (Farnsworth), William "Billy" Newell (Headwaiter), Rolfe Sedan (Henry), Ferris Taylor (Keller), Jason Robards, Sr (Radio Station Man), Cyril Ring (Man at Bar), Major Sam Harris (Fitzgerald).

The flimsy story for this film involves the goings-on between two rival roadhouses. Actually this was little more than an excuse to pack nine songs

into a little over an hour. Universal was known at this time for taking a hit song and giving it the thinnest of plots in order to create, it was hoped, a hit movie. The results here are pretty much what one would expect: long on musical delights and short on any acting or script developments. The title tune (by Bob Willis; sung by The Merry Macs), "Hi Neighbor" (by Jack Owens), and "The Hut Sut Song" (by Leo Killion and Ted McMichael; sung by The Merry Macs) became popular hits of the day. The rest were standard, musical numbers with typical staging for the period. These include: "Once Upon a Summertime" (by Jack Brooks, Norman Berens), "Mexican Jumping Bean" (by Don Raye and Gene De Paul; sung by The Merry Macs), "You've Got What it Takes" (by Raye and De Paul), "You're Everything Wonderful," "Bugle Woogie Boy" (by Henry Russell), and "Sweep It" (by Frank Skinner).

p, Ken Goldsmith; d, Charles Lamont; w, Hugh Wedlock, Jr., Howard Snyder, Paul Gerard Smith (based on a story by Jack Lait, Jr.); ph, Stanley Cortez; ed, Milton Carruth; ch, Nick Castle.

Musical   (PR:A   MPAA:NR)

SAN DEMETRIO, LONDON**½   (1947, Brit.) 76m EAL bw

Walter Fitzgerald (Chief Engineer Charles Pollard), Mervyn Johns (Greaser John Boyle), Ralph Michael (2nd Officer Hawkins), Robert Beatty ("Yank" Preston), Charles Victor (Deckhand), Frederick Piper (Bosun W.E. Fletcher), Gordon Jackson (John Jamieson), Arthur Young (Capt. George Waite), Barry Letts (Apprentice John Jones), James McKechnie (Colum McNeil), Nigel Clarke (R.J.E. Dodds), Lawrence O'Madden (Capt. Fogarty Fegan), David Horne (Mr. Justice Langton), Neville Mapp (3rd Engineer Willey), Michael Allen (Cadet Roy Housden), James Knight, John Coyle, Herbert Cameron, Duncan McIntyre, Diana Decker, Rex Holt, James Donald, James Sadler, Peter Miller Street.

It is 1940 and the San Demetrio, a merchant marine tanker, is crippled at sea. It's up to the crew to bring it in which of course is managed after a few harrowing adventures. For its time, SAN DEMETRIO, LONDON served its purpose well as war propaganda. However, a different era has really aged this film. What could once be accepted by audiences now plays as a story riddled with plot holes and unbelievable sequences. Based on a true story.

p, Robert Hamer; d, Charles Frend; w, Hamer, Frend (based on a story by F. Tennyson Jesse); ph, Ernest Palmer; m, John Greenwood; ed, Sidney Cole, Eily Boland; md, Ernest Irving; art d, Duncan Sutherland.

Drama/Adventure   (PR:C   MPAA:NR)

SAN DIEGO, I LOVE YOU***½   (1944) 83m UNIV bw

Jon Hall (John Caldwell), Louise Allbritton (Virginia McCooley), Edward Everett Horton (Philip McCooley), Eric Blore (Nelson, Butler), Buster Keaton (Bus Driver), Irene Ryan (Miss Jones), Rudy Wissler (Walter McCooley), Gerald Perreau [Peter Miles] (Joey McCooley), Charles Bates (Larry McCooley), Don Davis (Pete McCooley), Florence Lake (Miss Lake), Chester Clute (Percy Caldwell), Sarah Selby (Mrs. Lovelace), Fern Emmett (Mrs. Callope), Mabel Forrest (Mrs. Fresher), George Lloyd (Moving Man), Jack Rice (Hotel Clerk), Bill Davidson (General), John Gannon (Soldier), Jerry Shane (Sailor), Clarence Muse (Porter), Jan Wiley (Receptionist), Matt McHugh (Man on street), Harry Barris (Clarinetist), George Meader (Mr. Applewaite), Almira Sessions (Mrs. Mainwaring), Leon Belasco (Violinist), Sarah Padden (Mrs. Gulliver), Vernon Dent (Mr. Fitzmaurice), Harry Tyler (Mr. Carruthers), Victoria Horne (Mrs. Allsop), Hobart Cavanaugh (Mr. McGregor), Esther Howard (Mother), Teddy Infuhr (Brat), Gene Stutenroth [Gene Roth] (Stevedore).

Horton is the father of a good-sized brood in wartime San Diego. He has invented a new collapsible life raft that he believes will help the war effort. While trying to sell his invention it's up to his daughter, Allbritton, to watch her four younger brothers. She also helps sell the life raft to a research institute owned by Hall, the third richest man in America. SAN DIEGO, I LOVE YOU is a fine comedy with a quality that rises above its B film budget. At its comic heart is Allbritton, a wonderful comic actress. Her performance is a fine combination of wit and charm that ranks alongside any major comedian. (Allbritton had a seven-year contract with Universal and surely would have gone on to a fine career had she not retired to devote herself to marriage to reporter Charles Collingwood.) This was her favorite film of all and for good reason. The laughs are well maintained with a good comic direction and a delightful script by producers Fessier and Pagano. In addition to Allbritton's performance the film is filled with excellent supporting players. Horton (later the narrator of "Fractured Fairy Tales" one of Jay Ward's TV cartoon creation) is a delight as the inventor/high school professor. He has a great chemistry with Blore, the butler who is hired as many times as he is fired. Best of all is a memorable performance by Keaton as a bus driver. His career had taken a much undeserved trouncing with the advent of sound, and Keaton had bounced around Hollywood working as part of a comic team with Jimmy Durante and writing gags for the lesser Marx Brothers' film GO WEST. He made a few bit appearances in pictures during the 1940s and this ranks as one of the best. His bored attitude and the sudden abandonment of his 10-year-old bus route are indeed memorable. All in all, this film is one of those minor gems that broke through B filmmaking, an excellent study in comic acting, writing and direction with results that pleased audiences.

p, Michael Fessier, Ernest Pagano; d, Reginald LeBorg; w, Fessier, Pagano (based on a story by Ruth McKenney, Richard Bransten); ph, Hal Mohr; m, Hans J. Salter; ed, Charles Maynard; md, Don George; art d, John B. Goodman, Alexander Golitzen; cos, Vera West; spec eff, John P. Fulton.

Comedy **(PR:A MPAA:NR)**

SAN FERNANDO VALLEY** (1944) 74m REP bw

Roy Rogers *(Roy)*, Dale Evans *(Dale Kenyon)*, Jean Porter *(Betty Lou)*, Andrew Tombes *(John "Cyclone" Kenyon)*, Charles Smith *(Oliver Griffith)*, Edward Gargan *(Keno)*, Dot Farley *(Hattie O'Toole)*, LeRoy Mason *(Matt)*, Pierce Lyden, Maxine Doyle, Helen Talbot, Pat Starling, Kay Forrester, Marguerite Blount, Mary Kenyon, Hank Bell, Vernon and Draper, Morell Trio, Bob Nolan and the Sons of the Pioneers, Trigger.

In this age-old plot Rogers is brought into an area that is not the San Fernando Valley (despite the title) to clean it up of some bad guys and sing a few songs along the way. Definitely a lesser effort for the singing cowboy with unsure direction by English, a serial veteran. This was the first of three films he did with Rogers and the first film (after 1942) in which Rogers didn't use his regular director, Joseph Kane. SAN FERNANDO VALLEY is also notable for Rogers' first on-screen kiss, which he receives in a dream sequence. Ironically it's not his off-screen love Evans who delivers the smooch but kid sister Porter who is the cowboy's osculatory de-flowerer. Songs include "San Fernando Valley," "I Drotled a Drit Drit," and "They Went That A-Way." (See Roy Rogers series, Index)

p, Edward J. White; d, John English; w, Dorrell and Stuart McGowan; ph, William Bradford; ed, Ralph Dixon; md, Morton Scott; ch, Larry Ceballos; m/l, Gordon Jenkins, Ken Carson, Tim Spencer, Charles Henderson, William Lava, Alyce Walker

Western **Cas.** **(PR:A MPAA:NR)**

SAN FERRY ANN** (1965, Brit.) 55m Dormar/BL bw

Wilfrid Brambell *(Grandad)*, David Lodge *(Dad)*, Ron Moody *(German)*, Joan Sims *(Mum)*, Graham Stark *(Gendarme)*, Ronnie Stevens, Barbara Windsor *(Hikers)*, Rodney Bewes *(Loverboy)*, Catherine Feller *(Lover Girl)*, Lynn Carol *(Grandma)*, Warren Mitchell *(Maitre d'Hotel)*, Aubrey Woods *(Immigration Officer)*, Hugh Paddick *(Traveler)*, Joan Sterndale Bennett *(Madame)*.

A group of British folks heads for France on a holiday and encounters a number of humorous people and happenings. Starring as Grandad is Brambell, the same snippy old fellow who played Paul McCartney's granddad in A HARD DAY'S NIGHT (1964).

p, John G. Barry, Bob Kellett; d, Jeremy Summers; w, Kellett.

Comedy **(PR:A MPAA:NR)**

SAN FRANCISCO***** (1936) 115m MGM bw

Clark Gable *(Blackie Norton)*, Jeanette MacDonald *(Mary Blake)*, Spencer Tracy *(Father Tim Mullin)*, Jack Holt *(Jack Burley)*, Ted Healy *(Matt)*, Margaret Irving *(Della Bailey)*, Jessie Ralph *(Maisie Burley)*, Harold Huber *(Babe)*, Al Shean *(Professor)*, William Ricciardi *(Baldini)*, Kenneth Harlan *(Chick)*, Roger Imhof *(Alaska)*, Frank Mayo *(Dealer)*, Charles Judels *(Tony)*, Russell Simpson *(Red Kelly)*, Bert Roach *(Freddy Duane)*, Warren B. Hymer *(Hazeltine)*, Edgar Kennedy *(Sheriff Jim)*, Shirley Ross *(Trixie)*, Tandy MacKenzie *(Faust)*, Tudor Williams *(Mephistopheles)*, Spec O'Donnell *(Man Praying)*, Bob McKenzie *(Messenger)*, Adrienne d'Ambricourt *(Mme. Albani)*, Nigel deBrulier *(Old Man)*, Mae Digges, Nyas Berry *(Dancers)*, John Kelly *(Kelly)*, Jim Farley *(Charlie, Police Captain)*, Pat O'Malley, Ortho Wright *(Firemen)*, Gertrude Astor *(Drunk's Girl)*, Tom Dugan, Vince Barnett *(Drunks)*, Belle Mitchell *(Mary's Maid, Louise)*, Fred M. Fagan, Bill O'Brien *(Waiters)*, James Brewster, Samuel Glasser, John Pearson *(Stooges)*, Jason Robards, Sr. *(Father)*, William 'Billy' Newell *(Man in Breadline)*, James Macklin *(Young Man)*, Tom McGuire, Wilbur Mack *(Bartenders)*, Harry C. Myers *(Reveler)*, Edward Hearn *(Parishioner)*, Henry Roquemore *(Drinker)*, C. Pat Collins *(Bartender)*, Harry Strang *(Soldier)*, Vernon Dent *(Fat Man)*, Irving Bacon *(Picnicker)*, Orrin Burke *(Pompous Man)*, David Thursby *(Man)*, John "Skins" Miller *(Man on Stretcher)*, Helen Shipman *(Bit)*, George Gohl, Edward Earle *(Bit Men)*, Maude Allen *(Elderly Woman)*, Jack Baxley *(Kinko)*, Carl Stockdale *(Salvation Army Man)*, Anthony Jowitt *(Society Man)*, Jane Barnes *(Girl)*, Richard Carle, Oscar Apfel, Frank Sheridan, Ralph Lewis *(Members of Founders' Club)*, Chester Gan *(Jowl Lee)*, Jack Kennedy *(Mike, Old Irishman in Church)*, Cy Kendall *(Headwaiter)*, Don Rowan *(Coast Type)*, Sherry Hall *(Well-Wisher)*, Ben Taggart *(Cop)*, Long Beach Boys' Choir *(Choir)*, Dennis O'Keefe *(New Year's Celebrant)*, Charles Sullivan *(Fire Spectator)*, Beatrice Roberts *(Forrestal Guest)*, Bruce Mitchell *(Heckler)*, Sidney Bracy *(Burley's Butler)*, Tommy Bupp *(Bill, a Newsboy)*, Sam Ash *(Orchestra Leader)*, Bud Geary *(Man Restraining Blackie after Quake)*, George Magrill *(A Marine)*, King Baggott, Rhea Mitchell, Flora Finch, Fritzi Brunette, Helene Chadwick, Naomi Childers, Rosemary Theby, Jean Acker, Donald Hall.

This film left no doubt that MGM was the most omnipotent studio in Hollywood. Star power, a great, rowdy story, and one of the most awesome special effects sequences in the history of film made SAN FRANCISCO a masterpiece. Here is a picture any film lover can see once a year and enjoy as completely as if seeing it for the first time. It sparkles and explodes, a tremendous firecracker whose loud bang has been echoing for five decades. The electric duo of Gable and Tracy, typifying the turbulent time in which they live, is more than memorable in this picture; it is historic. This idea is underscored with the words rolling up at the opening credits: "San Fransisco, guardian of the Golden Gate, stands today as a queen among seaports...industrious...mature...respectable...but perhaps she dreams of the queen and city she was...splendid and sensuous, vulgar and magnificent...-that perished suddenly with a cry still heard in the hearts of those who knew her at exactly 5:13 a.m., April 18, 1906." The first raucous scenes of the film show Gable, the brassy, colorful boss of the infamous Paradise gambling hall and beer garden, celebrating New Year's Eve, 1906. Into the boss' presence is shown pretty, shy MacDonald looking for a job. "Well, sister," Gable says, "what's your racket?" She tells him she's a singer. "Let's see your legs," he tells her. "I said I'm a singer," MacDonald replies indignantly. "All right," Gable repeats, "let's see your legs." MacDonald lifts her ankle-length skirt demurely, only a few inches so that her ankles show, but Gable, growing annoyed, tells her, "Well, come on! Let's see 'em!" MacDonald raises her skirt a few more inches and Gable studies her legs. He has her sing a song and tells her, "You've got a pretty fair set of pipes, kid." He then offers her $75 a week to sing in his place but MacDonald doesn't respond, only swoons and collapses to the floor. Gable doesn't make a move to help her, but remains seated and says laconically, "I guess she fainted." Healy, one of Gable's cronies, exclaims, "Give me 75 bucks a week and I'll drop dead!" Later, MacDonald is shown eating a large meal in the parlor of Gable's apartment, her famished state the reason for her fainting spell. When Gable enters she thanks him and he tells her to "never mind the etiquette" and then asks her name, which she tells him. Pretending to be impressed, Gable says, "Mary Blake, eh? That's catchy." Gable goes into another room, puts on a dressing gown, and returns to hear MacDonald tell him that she is the daughter of a preacher who died four years earlier. He cannot find enough enthusiasm to seduce this attractive but obviously refined young woman so he retreats to a couch and grumbles "the orphan child of a country parson!" MacDonald snaps back, "After all, Mr. Norton, there are *such* men as country parsons and they do have daughters." He later half-heartedly to seduce MacDonald but realizes that she's not the run-of-the-mill saloon girl, and he gives her some money and tells her that she can sleep in his parlor. He goes to his bedroom, returns, and puts a key *on her side* of the door. Inside of his bedroom, before turning off the light, Gable looks at himself in the mirror and grimaces, saying to his own image, "Goodnight, sucker." MacDonald prepares a bed on the floor of the parlor, tossing down a pillow which has an embroidered inscription on it reading: "WELCOME TO SAN FRANCISCO." Next morning Gable is shown boxing in a gym with a robust man of his own age, Tracy, when Healy comes in and tells Gable that MacDonald never showed up for rehearsal. He tells Healy to forget about her and goes on jabbing and punching Tracy, who is later revealed to be a priest. As he boxes he talks with Tracy, telling him that a new girl he hired was a good singer but gave him the stagnant line about her father being a preacher. Laughs Tracy, "That's an old one!" Gable makes a few wisecracks and Tracy lands a haymaker on Gable's jaw that sends him to the canvas. Both Gable and Tracy laugh about it but Gable refuses to get up until his opponent is "out of the building." Later, at his emporium, Gable sees that MacDonald has shown up and is rehearsing but he demands that she pick up her tempo, replacing her piano player and banging out a tune, making MacDonald sing faster, "That's it–heat it up!" MacDonald stops and tells him she cannot sing that way and Gable storms, "Well, that's the way you're *going* to sing it or you don't sing it for me!" That night, dressed in a gaudy costume, MacDonald is on stage singing the way Gable wants her to, as he gloats with pride over his new prize on stage, admiring her from his private box. Wealthy Nob Hill socialite Holt appears in tuxedo and is shown to a special table where he, too, instantly admires MacDonald. With Holt is the maestro from the city opera house, Ricciardi, who becomes intrigued with MacDonald's voice and, after being persuaded to listen to her sing by her voice coach, Shean, tells Holt that she would make an excellent operatic singer. Holt and Ricciardi try to sign MacDonald up for the opera but Gable tells them he has the young singer under a two-year contract (which he was smart enough to have her sign before she stepped onto the stage). MacDonald tells Holt that she will live up to her contract with Gable, but she's obviously unhappy about the arrangement now that she has an opportunity to advance herself with a real musical future. Holt tells Gable that he won't give up on MacDonald. When he leaves Gable tells MacDonald not to "sing any more of that highbrow stuff. I don't like it." He then asks her to go around the corner and sing a little number for a friend of his who operates "a joint...on Kearney Street." It turns out to be St. Anne's Mission and the friend is priest Tracy. Tracy calls Gable later and thanks him for the new organ he has sent to the mission and asks him to attend evening services. Gable refuses. That evening Tracy is astounded at MacDonald's beautiful voice as she sings with the choir. Later MacDonald talks with Tracy and tells him she has just started singing at the Paradise and that she's afraid of boss Gable. "I don't think Blackie ever knew your kind of woman before," Tracy tells her. "But you needn't be afraid of him unless...you're afraid of yourself." He likens the tough, brawling city to Gable and adds, "you're in probably the wickedest, most corrupt, most Godless city in America. Sometimes it frightens *me* and I wonder what the end is going to be. But nothing can harm you if you don't allow it to. Because nothing in the world...*no one* in the world is *all* bad." Then he asks her if she knows who gave the mission its new organ and when she doesn't reply, Tracy says, "The most godless and scoffing and unbelieving soul in San Francisco...Blackie Norton." He explains that Gable has a good heart but squanders his money and he, Tracy, has been trying to turn him toward the path of good for years without luck, explaining that he and Gable were "kids together-born and brought up on the Coast. We used to sell newspapers in the joints along Pacific Street. Blackie was the leader of all the kids in the neighborhood and I was his pal." He goes on to tell MacDonald that their parents tried to get him and Gable to go to Sunday School but they evaded going until "I *wanted* to go. And Blackie thought I was crazy." He tells her that when he decided to become a priest he could not get Gable to listen and that all his friend said at the time was, "Good luck, sucker." His friend, Tracy says, is "ashamed of his *good deeds* as other people are ashamed of their sins." He shows MacDonald a photo of himself and Gable as newsboys, their arms about each other's shoulders, and says, "But nobody will ever convince me that there's not a whole lot more good than there is bad in Blackie Norton." The next scene shows Gable on a reviewing stand about to make a speech; he's running for the office of supervisor and he has hired a band and is giving away free beer to get elected. Healy leads a large crowd in singing a song of praise for Gable while Gable's goons circulate through the crowd to muscle those into singing who have remained mute. Irving, one of Gable's old flames and chief singing attraction at his club until MacDonald arrived, stands up and gives Gable an endorsement, her lusty sentiments echoed mightily by girls from Gable's club who stand in the crowd. Baxley, a barker, jumps up and heralds Gable by shouting, "Ladies and gentlemen, I want to introduce that great guy, our candidate-born on the Coast-raised on the Coast-lives on the Coast-our champion, Blackie Norton!" Gable stands up and says he will institute new fire laws to prevent the clapboard buildings in the Barbary Coast from catching fire. When a heckler accuses him of shilling for a construction company, Gable leaps down from the stand, knocks the man out, and climbs back up on the reviewing stand, shouting, "We've tried long enough to get a square deal from a lot of pot-bellied pot-bellied up on Nob Hill-now we're going after it on our own!" He gets big applause and then Gable pulls a youngster to the platform and says with deep concern, "This is Jim Sullivan's kid. Last New Year's Eve he and his sister had to jump two floors out of a burning building. Are we going to go on letting these Nob Hill stiffs make *fire dancers* out of our women and kids? Not if I can help it!" The reaction is thunderous applause and shouts of support. Gable calms the crowd, his speech over. He steps down from the platform after saying, "Now-free beer on me!" MacDonald witnesses the good-hearted Gable in action and finds herself growing fond of him. The two later take a carriage ride in the country where they talk about Tracy and his work and Gable tells her that "I don't go in for that sucker competition," referring to God. "Blackie's got to be No. 1 boy." She responds by saying, "It isn't competition! I think that people who believe in something can love each other more!" She is growing deeper in love with the man she also fears. Later Holt arrives at Gable's club and asks to buy MacDonald's contract. But, with MacDonald present, Gable has his star singer personally but reluctantly reject the offer. Holt then tells MacDonald that "I'd like to show you another side of San Francisco sometime" and leaves. Gable tells the disheartened MacDonald that the Tivoli Opera House, her real goal, isn't anything compared with his Paradise gambling hall and beer garden and then proudly tells her that every year for three years his saloon has won the $10,000 top prize at the annual "Chicken's Ball," the greatest event on the Barbary Coast, "and for *artistic achievement,* that's what they said every time they slipped me the trophy, *artistic achievement*!" He says that when he wins next time he'll give all the money to "the little mugs 'children' down here on the Coast." He looks deep into MacDonald's eyes and says: "I like to look into those big lamps of yours...I'm stuck on you, kid. You know it?" He kisses her and she responds warmly. Then Gable proudly pulls out a surprise, a poster showing MacDonald in tights. He admires his handiwork- "I've been working on this for weeks-I'll have it on every billboard in San Francisco"-while MacDonald recoils with a stunned look. "I wanted it to be a surprise," continues Gable, "so I got Della Bailey to pose for the figure. Then they slapped your head on top of it. Clever art work, eh?" He then looks at her, puzzled when she doesn't respond, but MacDonald recognizes the gesture as one of boyish enthusiasm and tells him she appreciates the thought, although she is crying. MacDonald later leaves the Paradise without notifying Gable and takes Holt's offer to appear at the Tivoli Opera House. Gable, upon hearing of this betrayal, goes to the Tivoli on opening night with a process server, intent upon serving an injunction on Holt to prevent MacDonald's performance, stating that he has exclusive rights to her talent. But when Gable hears MacDonald sing the part of Marguerite in "Faust" he stops the process server by knocking him out. Later, he asks MacDonald to marry him and she accepts, returning to the Paradise. There she agrees to be the kind of singer Gable wants, donning black tights and preparing to sizzle the rowdy audiences hooting and hollering for her first stage appearance in her "new image." But Tracy appears in MacDonald's dressing room. She embarrassedly covers her exposed legs with the long cape hanging from her shoulders. Tracy approaches Gable and says: "Have you gone out of your mind? Showing Mary-like this- to that mob out there?" Gable is baffled and says he doesn't know what Tracy is talking about. He tells Tracy that "I'm making her Queen of the Coast. See that poster? Five thousand of them will be plastered all over Frisco by tomorrow...and ten thousand little ones for ash cans and the front of trolley cars!" Tracy tells Gable that he will not let him exploit MacDonald and Gable asks MacDonald to speak up. She tells Tracy that she loves Gable. "That isn't *love,*" Tracy replies. "It isn't love to let him drag you down to his level!" Gable tells Tracy that he's going to marry MacDonald. Tracy juts his jaw and says: "Not if I can stop you....You can't take a woman in marriage and then sell her immortal soul!" Now Gable is angry and shouts: "I don't go for that kind of talk, Tim! Don't believe that nonsense and never have! You'd better go back to the half-wits that do!" The stage manager begins to call for MacDonald; the customers are becoming so anxious that they are threatening to tear the place apart unless MacDonald appears on stage. But in the dressing room Tracy tells Gable that she will not appear, ordering MacDonald to go with him. "Wait a minute!" Gable shouts at Tracy, "I'm running this place! You take care of your suckers, I'll take care of mine!" Tracy stands between Gable and MacDonald, as if to shield her, saying resolutely, "She's not going out there!" Gable is dark with rage: "I've stood for this psalm-singing blather of yours for years and never squawked. But you can't drag it in here! This is *my* joint!" In the hall the orchestra has struck up again the introductory notes of MacDonald's song, "San Francisco." The stage manager is shouting frantically for her to come on stage. Tracy bars the door of the dressing room and says solemnly, "*She's not going out there!*" Gable lets loose with a powerhouse punch to the jaw that rocks and brings a trickle of blood flowing out of the corner of his mouth. He will not move. Gable orders MacDonald out on stage but she takes one look at how Gable has injured his best friend and refuses. She says she will leave with Tracy and does, Gable telling her, "If you leave now, you're never coming back!" Policemen, who have been sent under Holt's orders, are breaking up the Paradise but Gable does not react, only looks in a daze after the retreating MacDonald and Tracy. MacDonald goes to Holt and is soon the star attraction at the Tivoli. She has thrown over Gable and is now engaged to Holt, as Gable learns by reading a newspaper. Holt has closed his place and Gable is on the skids. But, on the night of the "Chicken's Ball," with Gable absent, MacDonald makes a sudden appearance at the Lyric Hall to sing for the Paradise club, belting out a fast- tempoed "San Francisco" which brings down the house and wins the first prize. Gable, who is told that his protegee has appeared for him, rushes to the Lyric Hall and dashes on stage to stand next to MacDonald who holds the gold cup with $10,000 in gold pieces in it. He tells the master of ceremonies, "I never told that woman she could appear for me!" He takes the cup out of MacDonald's hands and dumps it at her feet. "You've got me all wrong, sister! I don't need this kind of dough!" Gable leaves the stage, a stunned MacDonald looking wordlessly after him. Humiliated, MacDonald steps down from the stage and is being escorted from the theater when a low, protracted rumble is heard. A door flies open, its frame bending out of plumb as the rumble increases. Holt shouts, "It's an earthquake!" As Holt escorts MacDonald out of the club which is now crumbling to pieces about the hysterical customers, she cries out for Gable but he is nowhere to be seen. The walls of the theater begin to crack, and then crash downward. Gable is in the crowd, the wall falling on him. Plaster and chandeliers collapse and everywhere in the theater there is destruction with people crushed or running for their lives. "Oh, God, save him!" MacDonald cries out as Holt manages to get her to an exit where a huge balcony is wrenched from a wall and comes crashing down, dust and debris obliterating the image on the screen. In a montage, the great old historic sites of San Francisco are shown breaking to pieces under the strain of the tremendous earthquake. City Hall collapses, fountains disintegrate, and office and residence buildings sway and tumble as the quake grips the entire city. Inside the wrecked theater, Gable stands up, his tuxedo torn, a gash on his forehead. He begins a frantic search for MacDonald and finds only the injured and the dying. He discovers a musician staring dumbly at his cello and asks if he has seen MacDonald and he replies in a monotone that he saw her flee with Holt. He rushes to the street and finds Holt dead, partly buried under the rubble of the Lyric Hall. Everywhere is ruination as Gable goes along the street looking for his beloved MacDonald. A hotel behind him splits wide open and collapses, a man falling out of a bed and through the open portion of the building to his death. A mother grabs a child about to fall through the opening. People call out for help. Gable moves along almost in a stupor. He asks everyone he knows if they've seen MacDonald but they have their own woes, one man mumbling out prayers, another telling Gable that "I lost my old lady, Blackie...my house is in the street!" Live wires are shown leaping about and these soon cause fires to break out. Gable goes to MacDonald's hotel but it is nothing but rubble. Everywhere there are people looking for lost loved ones. A long view of the city shows fires breaking out everywhere and a series of quick shots show firemen helpless to combat them, discovering that the water mains are broken and there is no water with which to fight the fires. A second tremor begins and this time the very streets through which Gable staggers split wide open, sucking people into the black chasms. One hangs on by his fingertips and Gable pulls him to safety. He spots some feathers that look like part of the gown MacDonald was wearing and he begins to dig frantically, begging anyone passing by to help him, but a wall begins to collapse and a man who has been helping Gable pull away a mountain of bricks yanks Gable to safety just before the wall collapses on the spot. Through the night Gable wanders the city, looking for MacDonald, staggering as if living a nightmare, walking past troops who have entered the city and are now dynamiting whole blocks in a desperate attempt to put out the fires with man-made backfires. Gable goes to Tracy's mission and asks where the priest has gone. He is told that Tracy is working with the wounded in a nearby stable and there Gable is overjoyed to find his friend alive. He asks if he has seen MacDonald and Tracy says, "What do you want her for, Blackie-the Paradise?" Gable says with genuine apology, "I don't want her for the Paradise." Tracy tells Gable to follow him and the two begin to look for MacDonald together. A soldier Gable has stopped earlier asks Gable if he's still "looking for a red-haired girl," and points to a stretcher where a figure is completely covered with a sheet, dead. Gable trembles as Tracy kneels, pulls back the sheet, and then tells Gable that it's not MacDonald. As they continue their search, Gable appears sincerely contrite, mumbling to Tracy: "I don't know why you want to help me, Tim....I thought you and I had gotten awfully far apart..." Then, climbing a distant hill, Gable hears the high, soft voice of MacDonald singing "Nearer My God to Thee," and follows the sound of it to see her standing with a group of refugees, her hair falling about her shoulders, her white dress in rags. Next to her is a mother weeping over the death of her child. Gable is overcome by the sight of his great love being alive. He turns to Tracy. "I want to thank God, Tim. What do I say?" Replies Tracy, "Say what's in your heart, Blackie." Gable, tears welling in his eyes, sinks to his knees and says in a low, quavering voice: "Thanks, God. Thanks! I really mean it!" MacDonald sees him and he her. Gable stands up and the couple walk to each other and embrace just as someone joyfully shouts, "The fire's out!" The survivors gather, thousands of them, streaming up the hill to look down on old San Francisco which lies in ashes and rubble before them, but they are singing "The Battle Hymn of the Republic" to show their thanks for surviving and their spirit which is captioned in other cries of "we'll build a new San Francisco!" As Gable, Tracy, and MacDonald, backed by countless citizens, look over the city, the strains of "San Francisco" can be heard and the devastating ruin shown on camera dissolves to show a shining new city, a modern San Francisco will all its great skyscrapers, the Bay Bridge, and the newly-constructed Golden Gate Bridge.

SAN FRANCISCO is undoubtedly the greatest film director Van Dyke ever helmed, one which he directed at a fantastic pace, hustling along his actors to keep time with the gaudy, bawdy era he presented in the background. All of his principals, even the usually anemic MacDonald, render extraordinary performances under Van Dyke's insistent hand. Although Van Dyke certainly earned the credit for his astounding, technically flawless film, his mentor and the father of American silent film (and creator of almost all the techniques used thereafter in the sound era), D.W. Griffith, appeared at MGM one day and Van Dyke asked "the master" if he cared to direct any of the scenes in the film. He did, but just which scene the great Griffith directed is still in debate. One report had it that he directed one of MacDonald's operatic scenes, another had it that he directed one of the mob scenes at the Paradise club. But it was also rumored that the great Griffith directed the gem of this golden film, the incredible 20- minute earthquake and fire sequence, or that portion which was not achieved by the special effects of Gillespie and the uncredited James Basevi (who would work wonders for THE GOOD EARTH in showing the plague of locusts devasting the Chinese countryside, and in THE HURRICANE, which graphically detailed the most awesome storm filmed to date). Much of the earthquake scenes dealing with the fleeing, frantic crowds, the runaway horse-drawn carts and wagons and, in particular, the spinning wheel of a destroyed wagon, which goes round and round to finally come to a stop and signal the end of the quake, has the mark of the master and very well may have been Griffith's own doing, yet the fabulous editing job of intercutting myriad lightning-quick shots of the disaster to compound the terror and accelerate the short-lived moment short-lived earthquake, is all Van Dyke. One of the most devastating and realistic scenes is where the earth opens up, cracking the street wide open, sections of pavement pulling away from each other. This was achieved by Basevi and others with two hydraulic platforms pulled apart by cables with hoses underneath gushing water to simulate the breaking of water pipes. Van Dyke's gracious gesture toward Griffith was merely his salute to the man for whom he had once worked as an assistant director. (Van Dyke had organized and kept together the enormous crowds in the Babylonian sequences of Griffith's mammoth INTOLERANCE.) Van Dyke later admitted that Griffith had taught him just about everything he knew in the making of films. The director did not forget others of the silent era and tried to put to work many of the silent stars who were then unemployed and financially suffering during that year of the Great Depression, including Flora Finch; one-time Vitagraph star Naomi Childer; Jean Acker, who had been Rudolph Valentino's first wife and a leading lady in her own right during the silent days; King Baggott and Rhea Mitchell, whom Van Dyke had directed in the 1918 silent film THE HAWK'S LAIR. Even silent film director Erich von Stroheim got into the act, writing some additional dialog for Loos' script. Loos and Hopkins, who did the original story, had long envisioned writing SAN FRANCISCO, both being natives of San Francisco and wanting to capture that vital city's personality, particularly as it used to be before the Great Earthquake. Their deep feeling for their city, as opposed to the historically and culturally nomadic Los Angeles, is shown early in SAN FRANCISCO. Bouncer Harold Huber is having a hard time with a drunk in the Paradise but he tries to placate the man who continues to make terrible remarks about the ladies singing on stage. Huber finally asks the drunk, "Where are you from?" "Los Angeles," replies the loud-mouth drunk. With that Huber snorts "I thought so!" and knocks the man cold before dragging him out. Hopkins was employed in MGM's writing department by Thalberg just to write gags and jokes to be inserted into scripts. When Loos went to work there as a scriptwriter the two got along well and Hopkins would regale Loos with tales of the Barbary Coast in San Francisco before it was destroyed by the quake, and how he used to be a Western Union messenger boy delivering messages to characters in all the fabulous saloons along its tumultuous way. One man, Hopkins remembered, stood out in that era, a handsome, devil-may-care gambler whose adventures, from Alaska during the Gold Rush to Florida during the Land Boom, were the stuff of legend (and wound up in many films) The character was the inventive and colorful Wilson Mizner, and it was Mizner upon whom Loos and Hopkins built their character of Blackie Norton, an unforgettable rowdy whose wickedness was only skin deep, even though it took an earthquake to crack the tough veneer. Loos later got into trouble with the Hollywood censors for showing a Catholic priest being slammed in the face by king Gable. She remarked in a 1967 interview with *Film Fan Monthly* that she had to be clever to outwit the censors regarding the priest-hitting scene. Said Ms. Loos: "The Johnson Office said you cannot have Clark Gable sock a priest, it's unthinkable. So I went away and got to pondering about how I could fix the scene...I figured out that we would prove at the beginning that the priest could floor Gable any time he wanted to. He was a much cleverer boxer than Gable. That proved that when Clark hit him he could have killed Clark, but didn't do it, which made his character stronger as a priest, and it was accepted by the censor. In order to prove this situation, I opened with a scene of two men boxing and you saw Spencer Tracy sock Gable and knock him out. And then, when they got dressed, you saw that one of them was a priest. That scene wouldn't have been in if I hadn't had to outsmart the censor." The Loos- Hopkins script is rich in humor and wit, and its vigor splashed over and onto the screen to put muscle in the arms of Gable and Tracy, appearing together for the first time. The offbeat brand of humor exercised by Loos, really mimicking the hard-boiled Mizner, is summed up in a line by Gable when he tries to convince Holt just how rotten and miserable process-server Edgar Kennedy really is: "Why, he's so mean he'd shut off the air in a baby's incubator, just to watch the little sucker squirm!" So well did the chemistry between Gable and Tracy work (Gable admired Tracy for his great acting ability and Tracy admired, grudgingly, Gable's enormous popularity), that MGM would pair them again in two more blockbusters, TEST PILOT (1938), and BOOM TOWN (1940). But even before these two stellar stars were signed for SAN FRANCISCO, MacDonald was approached by Loos and Hopkins. She was then riding high with several successes, the most recent being the musical smash, (MAYTIME.) In that (MAYTIME.) MacDonald appeared with long-time partner Nelson Eddy and a man very strange to musicals, John Barrymore. The Great Profile, as Barrymore was known, hated appearing in MAYTIME but did so for the money he so desperately needed to fund his extravagant way of life. So annoyed in one scene was Barrymore with MacDonald as she flourished a handkerchief, he shouted, "If you don't refrain from waving that infernal kerchief in front of my face I will ram it down your gurgling throat!") After reading the Loos script, MacDonald went to Irving Thalberg, head of MGM production and persuaded him to make the film. But he insisted that Gable and only Gable could play the villain-hero, Blackie Norton. Thalberg pointed out that he was perfect for the role with his tall, muscular body, dark thick hair, dark eyes and flashing smile, elegant mustache, and a voice that was deep and delivered lines with rapid fire, the perfect Barbary Coast gambler. He was busy at the time so MacDonald had to bide her time waiting for Gable's schedule to allow for the production. Gable was approached and he reacted negatively to the idea of playing a gambler in SAN FRANCISCO where he would have to stand and let MacDonald sing at him. "It's one thing if you have a voice and can sing back and defend yourself. It's another if you don't and I don't." Moreover, Gable had been hanging around with his good friend Nelson Eddy and had learned that the soprano was a prima donna. He also didn't like the part as originally written. Loos went back to the script and beefed up his part with a lot of business that put blood in the character's veins and still Gable wasn't persuaded to play the role. MGM executive Eddie Mannix then went to the superstar and told him that MacDonald had been standing by waiting for him *without salary* and this impressed Gable, whose concern for a dollar was legendary. Anyone who would sacrifice money to wait for him to make up his mind deserved to have him, he felt, and finally accepted the role. He was also eager to play Blackie Norton when he learned that "Woody" Van Dyke would be directing. Gable considered Van Dyke "a man's man," as did costar Tracy. Still, there was little conversation between Gable and MacDonald during the production of SAN FRNACISCO. As soon as scenes were over, Gable stepped away from his leading lady and often ignored her when she casually spoke to him. She got so upset on one occasion that she broke into tears when Gable turned his back on her. She asked a friend in the MGM publicity department to find out why Gable disliked her so. The question was put to Gable who would not admit he just did not like high-toned ladies (as would be the case with Greer Garson when they appeared together a decade later in ADVENTURE). At the time Gable gave a ridiculous excuse for not talking to MacDonald, saying lamely, "She eats too much garlic." Yet, it was reported, Gable himself showed contempt for the warbling soprano (whose vibrato was the most famous in filmdom) during their first scene together. He arrived to play a love scene with her while reeking of garlic, which may explain the strange look of surprise on MacDonald's face after she kisses Gable for the first time in the picture. Tracy, who was brought together with Gable for the first time, was personally offered his role by Van Dyke, a supporting role but, the director emphasized, a strong one that held the moral fibre of the film together. Reportedly, the director pleaded with Tracy to take the role, stating to him that the film would be a smash hit "but there's one important thing it has to have...and that's humanity. Father Tim has to supply it, and, so help me, Spencer, you're the only actor I know who can bring humanity into a part. I don't know where you got it, but you have it." He took the role and did more with it than any actor of his generation could have made of it. Of the many other standout performances by the great cast is a little character part marvelously rendered by Al Sheen as the Professor, another old-timer whose career even predated films, silent or otherwise, when he was part of the famous comic partnership of Gallagher and Sheen in early vaudeville. A few changes occurred to this masterpiece film along its production route. A prolog showing Gable and Tracy as newsboys in the Barbary Coast of an earlier era was cut before the film was released. And when the film was premiered in San Francisco, the manager of the Paramount Theater there, Allen Warshauer, became worried that his customers might take exception to San Francisco being wiped out with nothing much more to go on than a wall of humanity peering over a cliff at the ruins, so he had local cinematographers take pan shots of the San Francisco of 1936, which showed the Golden Gate still under construction, the modern city his viewers then lived in. Warshauer tacked this on to the ending of SAN FRANCISCO, and when his audiences saw the new city, viewers stood up and cheered. Warshauer called Van Dyke in Hollywood and asked him to come up to San Francisco and see the effect the epilog had on audiences. Van Dyke and other MGM officials went to San Francisco, viewed the audience reaction to Warshauer's photographic addition to his creation, and wisely agreed to have it tacked on to all release prints. When the film was re-released in 1948, the shots of modern San Francisco, 1936, were eliminated since it was felt San Franciscans would be embarrassed to see their beloved Golden Gate Bridge still under construction at that late date. The epilog was put back in later and is now seen on most prints. Rarely do any commercial TV stations show SAN FRANCISCO uncut; invariably the scenes edited out for reasons of running time (which is no excuse) are the scenes involving Gable and the Chinese cook, Gable's brief romance with Ross, and sometimes the carriage ride he takes into the country with MacDonald. It is amazing to realize that in all the pandemonium and destruction occurring in SAN FRANCISCO, not one extra was scratched. MacDonald turned out to be the only injured party, her pride wounded, not her flesh. During a rehearsal of her operatic number, in "La Traviata," MacDonald took a curtain bow and when the curtain was pulled back to allow her to step forth her dress got caught in the curtain and went up with it, showing her backside to scores of extras playing the chorus, all of whom broke into such hysterical laughter while the actress struggled to cover herself that MacDonald was reduced to tears. Regaining her composure and dress, MacDonald said to Van Dyke, "Maybe they can use this situation for the next Marx Brothers picture." Much as MGM boss Louis B. Mayer hoped SAN FRANCISCO would be a hit, he was banking on the studio's recently released THE GREAT ZIEGFELD to make the millions that year. It did, grossing more than $4 million but three months later the newly released SAN FRANCISCO outstripped THE GREAT ZIEGFELD and every other MGM film in box-office receipts, gleaning box-office before the year was out, which staggered the studio chieftains. Mayer visited the studio's sales department himself and heard the news, then beamed broadly and half-shouted in glee, "Now that's my idea of a prestige picture!" Songs include: "Happy New Year," "San Francisco" (Bronislau Kaper, Walter Jurmann, Gus Kahn), "Noontime" (Ted Healy), "Love Me and the World is Mine" (Ernest R. Ball, David Reed, Jr.), "A Heart That's Free" (A.J. Robyn, T. Railey), "The Holy City" (Stephen Adams, F.E. Weatherly), "Would You?" (Arthur Freed, Nacio Herb Brown) "Nearer My God to Thee" (Lowell Mason, Sarah F. Adams), "The Battle Hymn of the Republic" (William Steffe, Julia Ward Howe), "At a Georgia Camp Meeting" (Kerry Mills), "The Philippine Dance," "A Hot Time in the Old Town Tonight" (Joe Hayden, Theodore Metz), "The Jewel Song," "Soldiers' Chorus," "Il Se Fait Tard," "Anges Purs," "Me Voila Toute Seule" (taken from Gounod's "Faust"), "Sempre Libera" (from Giuseppe Verdi's opera "La Traviata").

p, John Emerson, Bernard H. Hyman; d, W.S. Van Dyke II, (uncredited) D.W. Griffith; w, Anita Loos, (uncredited) Erich Von Stroheim (based on a story by Robert Hopkins); ph, Oliver T. Marsh; m, Edward Ward; ed, Tom Held; md, Herbert Stothart; art d, Cedric Gibbons, Arnold Gillespie, Harry McAfee; set d, Edwin B. Willis; cos, Adrian; ch, Val Raset; spec eff, Arnold Gillespie, (uncredited) James Basevi.

Adventure/Romance/Disaster   Cas.   **(PR:A   MPAA:NR)**

SAN FRANCISCO DOCKS   (1941) 66m UNIV bw

Burgess Meredith (*Johnny Barnes*), Irene Hervey (*Kitty Tracy*), Raymond Walburn (*Admiral Andy Tracy*), Robert Armstrong (*Father Cameron*), Lewis Howard (*Sanford*), Barry Fitzgerald (*The Icky*), Ed Gargan (*Hank*), Esther Ralston (*Frances March*), Edward Pawley (*Monte March*), Floyd Criswell (*Traffic Cop*), William B. Davidson (*District Attorney Craig*), Don Zelaya (*Felipe*), Joe Downing (*Cassidy*), Colin Campbell (*Dr. Conway*), Ralf Harolde (*Hawks*), Esther Howard (*Jean*), Harold Daniels (*Cab Driver*), Ken Christy, Lou Hicks (*Cops*), Billy Mitchell (*Black Man*), Harry Cording (*Collins*), Glenn Strange (*Mike*), Kernan Cripps (*First Guard*), Max Wagner (*Second Guard*), Ed Cassidy (*Dock Foreman*), Minerva Urecal (*Landlady*), Ralph Dunn (*Guard*), William Ruhl (*Forkild*), Harold [Hal] Gerard (*Interne*), Charles Sullivan (*First Longshoreman*), Tom London (*Second Longshoreman*), Branford Hatton, Charles McMurphy, Jimmy O'Gatty, Art Miles, Jimmie Lucas, Charles Sherlock (*Longshoremen*).

On the docks of San Francisco's waterfront Meredith is a longshoreman who's studying to be an aviation mechanic. He's in love with Hervey, the barmaid at a saloon owned by her father (Walburn). Meredith gets into a fight with Downing who later turns up dead. Though the real murderer is

Alcatraz escapee Pawley, Meredith is believed guilty and arrested for the crime. Only three men can prove he wasn't the killer and they are of no help since the trio comprises Pawley and the two longshoremen who aided his escape (Cording and Zelaya). Hervey, along with priest Armstrong, drunk Fitzgerald (who would win an Oscar in a few years with GOING MY WAY), and Walburn tries to prove Meredith's innocence. They find Pawley's wife Ralston, the bleachiest of blondes, and after a terrific cat fight between Hervey and Ralston, Pawley gets what's coming to him in a wrestling match with the priest. This film is plagued by a talky script and mediocre direction that never lets the characters develop as well as they might. Certainly the cast has the talent for a good drama (this was Meredith's follow-up to his terrific performance in OF MICE AND MEN) but unfortunately the actors never get to show their abilities. As it is, SAN FRANCISCO DOCKS is just another tough-talking, forgettable B programmer that never lives up to its potential.

p, Marshall Grant; d, Arthur Lubin; w, Stanley Crea Rubin, Edmund L. Hartman; ph, Art Lasky; ed, Bernard W. Burton; md, H. J. Salter.

Crime Drama   **(PR:A   MPAA:NR)**

SAN FRANCISCO STORY, THE½**   (1952) 80m Fidelity-Vogue/WB bw

Joel McCrea (*Rick Nelson*), Yvonne De Carlo (*Adelaide McCall*), Sidney Blackmer (*Andrew Cain*), Richard Erdman (*Shorty*), Florence Bates (*Sadie*), Onslow Stevens (*Jim Martin*), John Raven (*Lessing*), O.Z. Whitehead (*Alfey*), Ralph E. Dumke (*Winfield Holbert*), Robert Foulk (*Thompson*), Lane Chandler (*Morton*), Trevor Bardette (*Miner*), John Doucette (*Slade*), Peter Virgo (*Meyers*), Frank Hagney (*Palmer*), Tor Johnson (*Buck*), Fred Graham (*Scud*).

McCrea is a wealthy California miner based in San Francisco, circa 1856. He's pals with Stevens, a newspaper editor who asks the miner for help in getting rid of Blackmer, an unscrupulous politician. De Carlo plays Blackmer's girl friend who ends up falling for McCrea. The film finishes with a climactic shotgun duel between McCrea and Blackmer as they ride astride their respective horses. This is a routine political melodrama punched up with some fine performances by the leads. The direction is good with some nicely handled fight sequences.

p, Howard Welsch; d, Robert Parrish; w, D. D. Beauchamp (based on the novel *Vigilante* by Richard Summers); ph, John Seitz; m, Emil Newman, Paul Dunlap; ed, Otto Ludwig; md, Joseph Gershenson; Prod d, George Jenkins; art d, Bernard Herzbrun, Robert Clatworthy; cos, Yvonne Wood; ch, Harold Belfaer.

Drama   **(PR:A   MPAA:NR)**

SAN QUENTIN*   (1937) 70m WB-FN bw

Pat O'Brien (*Capt. Stephen Jameson*), Humphrey Bogart (*Joe "Red" Kennedy*), Ann Sheridan (*May Kennedy*), Barton MacLane (*Lt. Druggin*), Joseph Sawyer ("*Sailor Boy" Hansen*), Veda Ann Borg (*Helen*), James Robbins (*Mickey Callahan*), Joseph King (*Warden Taylor*), Gordon Oliver (*Captain*), Garry Owen (*Dopey*), Marc Lawrence (*Venetti*), Emmett Vogan (*Lieutenant*), William Pawley, Al Hill, George Lloyd, Frank Faylen (*Convicts*), Max Wagner (*Prison Runner*), Ernie Adams (*Fink*), Raymond Hatton (*Pawnbroker*), Hal Neiman (*Convict No. 38216*), Glen Cavender (*Convict Hastings*), William Williams (*Convict Conklin*), George Offenman, Jr. (*Young Convict*), Lane Chandler (*Guard*), Edward Piel, Sr. (*Deputy*), Dennis Moore (*Convict Simpson*), John Ince (*Old Convict*), Ralph Byrd (*Policeman on Phone*), Ray Flynn (*Police Officer*), Claire White, Jack Mower (*Couple in Car*), Douglas Wood (*Chairman of Prison Board*), Ernest Wood (*Attorney*), Saul Gorss (*Clerk*), Jerry Fletcher (*Hoffman*), Ralph Dunn (*Head Guard*), Frank Fanning (*Cop in Radio Car*), Bob Wilkie (*Young Convict in Riot*).

One of a rash of prison reform movies that hit the screens in the last half of the 1930s (at least 27 appeared in 1937-39), SAN QUENTIN was blessed with a top-name cast that made the ordinary (and consequently cliched) plot worthwhile. O'Brien is a former Army captain who is sent to San Quentin to bring some military-style order to the rowdy prison yard. He quickly employs a method of reform that separates the hardened criminals from first-time offenders. The night before he is to begin O'Brien visits a nightclub where he watches singer Sheridan perform her act. He falls for Sheridan but keeps his job secret when she admits that her brother, Bogart, was recently imprisoned in San Quentin. Bogart isn't easily converted to O'Brien's new methods and does all he can to make reform difficult. After a prison-yard brawl, Bogart gets sent into solitary. On his release he is visited by Sheridan, who wrongly tries to sneak her brother some money. She is hauled into O'Brien's office where she discovers his secret. She bitterly refuses to further involve herself with him, remaining loyal to her brother. When O'Brien begins paying special attention to Bogart and making concessions for him, Sheridan changes her opinion. To further prove his dedication to the prison population, O'Brien daringly saves some convicts from a crazed, machine gun-wielding inmate. Jealous of O'Brien's success, MacLane, the old guard superintendent, decides to stir up trouble. He sends a stoolie, Sawyer, into the ranks to work beside Bogart on a road gang. When Sawyer begins blabbing about O'Brien's romance with Sheridan, ideas of escape form in Bogart's head. With help from Sawyer's tough moll, Borg, Bogart manages to get away, heading straight for his sister's apartment. There he confronts O'Brien, wounding him with a gunshot before Sheridan can explain that they are in love. Now convinced that O'Brien's methods of reform are a step in the right direction, Bogart plans to surrender himself. On the way back to San Quentin, however, he is gunned down. He makes his way to the front gate before collapsing, pleading with the prisoners to give O'Brien a chance. In the same way that 20,000 YEARS IN SING SING (1933) and ALCATRAZ ISLAND (1937, also starring Sheridan) captured the realistic atmosphere of the respective prisons, so did SAN QUENTIN. Because much of the film was shot in and around the California penitentiary, one can almost feel the prison walls closing in. Adding another degree of authenticity was Bacon's decision to employ an actual criminal as technical advisor. Instead of scouting prisons to fill the position Bacon asked O'Brien if any of his "con pals" would be interested. O'Brien offered the name of Doc Stone, a con who had been in and out of prison for some 50 years. Stone was hired at $300 a week simply to offer information on prison life and dialog. Soon Stone found himself in high demand and not only did SAN QUENTIN benefit from his knowledge, but so did a number of other pictures.

p, Samuel Bischoff; d, Lloyd Bacon; w, Peter Milne, Humphrey Cobb (based on a story by Robert Tasker, John Bright); ph, Sid Hickox; m, Heinz Roemheld, Charles Maxwell, David Raksin; ed, William Holmes; md, Joseph Nussbaum, Ray Heindorf; art d, Esdras Hartley; cos, Howard Shoup; spec eff, James Gibbons, H.F. Koenekamp; m/l, "How Could You," Harry Warren, Al Dubin; tech adv, Doc Stone.

Prison Drama   **(PR:C MPAA:NR)**

SAN QUENTIN**½   (1946) 66m RKO bw

Lawrence Tierney (Jim), Barton MacLane (Nick Taylor), Marian Carr (Betty), Harry Shannon (Warden Kelly), Carol Forman (Ruthie), Richard Powers [Tom Keene] (Schaeffer), Joe Devlin (Broadway), Tony Barrett (Marlowe), Lee Bonnell (Carzoni), Robert Clarke (Tommy), Raymond Burr (Torrance).

At San Quentin's famous prison a group of inmates creates "The Inmate's Welfare League," an organization which maintains order and helps prisoners prepare for parole. MacLane is one of the most trustworthy members, but when he breaks out and starts a crime spree, the League is almost dashed by officials. The League's members feel it is their duty to see their wayward brother caught and punished; a former founding member (Tierney) who's on the outside now hunts MacLane. Competently acted and directed, the film was perhaps a bit far-fetched, but any disbelievers will be overwhelmed by the action, quickly forgetting any complaints they might have. Stage and radio actor Burr made his film debut with this one, which was also Carr's first leading-lady role.

p, Martin Mooney; d, Gordon M. Douglas; w, Lawrence Kimble, Arthur A. Ross, Howard J. Green; ph, Frank Redman; m, Paul Sawtell; ed, Marvin Coil; art d, Albert A. D'Agostino, Lucius O. Croxton; set d, Darrell Silvera, Tom Oliphant.

Prison Drama/Crime   **(PR:A MPAA:NR)**

SANCTUARY*   (1961) 90m Darryl F. Zanuck/FOX bw

Lee Remick (Temple Drake), Yves Montand (Candy Man), Bradford Dillman (Gowan Stevens), Harry Townes (Ira Bobbitt), Odetta (Nancy Mannigoc), Howard St. John (Governor Drake), Jean Carson (Norma), Reta Shaw (Miss Reba), Strother Martin (Dog Boy), William Mims (Lee), Marge Redmond (Flossie), Jean Bartel (Swede), Hope Du Bois (Mamie), Enid James (Jackie), Dana Lorenson (Connie), Pamela Raymond (Cora), Linden Chiles (Randy), Robert Gothie (Gus), Wyatt Cooper (Tommy), Kim Hector (Bucky Stevens), Voltaire Perkins (The Judge), Wilton Felder (Musician).

Darryl F. Zanuck allowed his son Richard (who was still in his 20's) to produce this for Fox in the grand old Hollywood tradition of nepotism. Based on two Faulkner books (Sanctuary and Requiem for a Nun) and the stage adaptation of the latter by Ruth Ford, it's a Grecian tragedy set in Mississippi in the late 1920s. Odetta, a black woman in her early 30's, is sentenced to death for having murdered Remick's baby by her husband, Dillman. Odetta has scant hours left and Remick tells her father, St. John, who is the governor of Mississippi, the truth about what's gone on in the past few years as she attempts to get St. John to pardon Odetta. Flash back to see Remick six years earlier as a happy college co-ed romantically involved with Dillman. Dillman is a spoiled college boy who wants Remick's body and when he gets plastered one night, he takes her to a corncrib but is never quite up to the task. She is later raped by Montand, a Cajun bootlegger (in the book, the character was not a Cajun but since they'd signed Montand, there had to be some way to account for that accent) and experiences a sexual excitement unlike anything she's ever had before. The next day, she is so enthralled by Montand that she doesn't fight his advances, but welcomes them. Soon after, they go to New Orleans to live in a brothel together (the set of this bordello is ludicrous to the point of being a parody) where Remick adores her life. Odetta becomes Remick's maid and everything is jake until Remick hears that Montand has died in a car crash. She shrugs, sighs, and seeks sanctuary back home in her little town. Hardly any time passes before she marries Dillman and settles into a ho-hum existence, a far cry from the excitement of New Orleans. To remind her of those days, she hires Odetta to stay with her so they can reminisce together. Two

children arrive quickly and so does Montand, who didn't die at all. Remick is tempted to toss aside her secure life and run off with Montand, but Odetta, sensing that, thinks there is but one way to shock Remick into reality, so she smothers the baby. Flash forward and St. John is stunned to hear all this, but the fact remains that Odetta did kill his own grandchild and he won't stay the execution. Remick pays her last call on the doomed Odetta and realizes that it's her maid's sacrifice that has brought her back to her senses. Phew! Not a picture for children. This was first made in 1933 as THE STORY OF TEMPLE DRAKE and is so filled with degradation and degeneracy that it makes most of the works by Tennessee Williams look like Aesop's Fables. Julie London sings the title song. In a nutshell, the feeling about this so-called "adult" film is "Sanctuary much, but no thank you."

p, Richard D. Zanuck; d, Tony Richardson; w, James Poe (based on the novels Sanctuary and Requiem for a Nun by William Faulkner and the stage adaptation of the latter by Ruth Ford); ph, Ellsworth Fredricks (Cinema-Scope); m, Alex North; ed, Robert Simpson; art d, Duncan Cramer, Jack Martin Smith; set d, Walter M. Scott, Fred Maclean; cos, Donfeld; makeup, Ben Nye.

Drama   **(PR:O MPAA:NR)**

SAND**½   (1949) 77m FOX c (AKA: WILL JAMES' SAND)

Mark Stevens (Jeff Keane), Coleen Gray (Joan Hartley), Rory Calhoun (Chick Palmer), Charley Grapewin (Doug), Bob Patten (Boyd), Mikel Conrad (Tony), Tom London (Clem), Paul Hogan (Don), Jack Gallagher (Bill), William "Bill" Walker (Sam), Davison Clark (Jim Gannon), Ben Erway (Dr. Dunlap), Harry Cheshire (Logan), Iron Eyes Cody, Joseph Cody, Jay Silverheels (Indians).

During a railroad accident Stevens loses his valuable show horse. The stallion goes off into the Colorado wilderness and soon comes to love its freedom. Meanwhile Stevens enlists the help of fellow horse-lover Gray in an effort to track down his animal. The horse has been pursued by others, though, and has become quite dangerous. Stevens and Gray catch up with it, fearing the stallion has become a killer. In the climactic scene, Stevens talks to his steed and finally coaxes the horse into coming back. After a re-training period the horse is back in competitions, restored to its former manner. The location photography is beautiful to look at in this well-told horse story. There's some good action and suspenseful treatment of the subject, though SAND will probably have more appeal for children and horse lovers than any other audience.

p, Robert Bassler; d, Louis King; w, Martin Berkeley, Jerome Cady (based on the novel by Will James); ph, Charles G. Clarke (Technicolor); m, Daniele Amfitheatrof; ed, Nick De Maggio; md, Amfitheatrof; art d, Lyle Wheeler, Chester Gore; set d, Thomas Little, Ernest Lansing.

Sports Drama   **(PR:A MPAA:NR)**

SAND CASTLE, THE***   (1961) 70m Noel/Louis de Rochemont
                    Associates-Barney Pitkin Associates-Contemporary Films bw-c

Barry Cardwell (Boy), Laurie Cardwell (Girl), George Dunham (Artist), Alec Wilder (Fisherman), Maybelle Nash (Shade Lady), Erica Speyer (Sun Lady), Charles Rydell (Young Man), Allegra Ahern (Young Girl), Lester Judson (Fat Man), Martin Russ (Frogman), Ghislain Dussart (Priest), Mabel Mercer (Voice of the Shell).

Barry and Laurie Cardwell are a brother and sister left on the beach while their mother goes shopping. After being snubbed by a group of older boys the pair wanders to the water's edge where the boy finds a seashell. He pretends to hear a voice that tells him to build a sand castle. His work attracts a horde of visitors ranging from a fat woman loaded down with useless items to an artist. Also visiting are a drunk, a bikini-draped sun goddess, some muscle men, a skindiver and some soft ball-playing nuns. A rainstorm begins and the two children seek the shelter of a beach umbrella. Falling asleep, the boy dreams of the people who visited his castle. In the dream they take the form of paper cutouts stop-motion animated against a real model of the castle. The dream is interrupted by his mother's cry and the two children head home. The sand castle is swept away as the tide rolls in. This highly imaginative piece is a neat exercise in filmmaking. The live-action sequences are shot in black-and-white with the dream portrayed in wonderful contrasting color. The paper cutouts are well animated, inspired by the paper cutout theater for children presented in the 19th Century. The director handles the material nicely, wisely underplaying the story with moments of great subtlety. Originally released in 16mm but subsequent releases were in 35mm.

p,d&w, Jerome Hill; ph, Lloyd Ahern (partial Eastmancolor); m, Alec Wilder; ed, Julia Knowlton, Henry A. Sundquist; art d, Hill; spec eff, Francis Thompson.

Fantasy   **(PR:AAA MPAA:NR)**

SAND PEBBLES, THE**** (1966) 195m Argyle-Solar Productions/FOX
                                                                      c

Steve McQueen (Jake Holman), Richard Attenborough (Frenchy Burgoyne), Richard Crenna (Capt. Collins), Candice Bergen (Shirley Eckert), Marayat Andriane, , 'Emmanuelle Arsan' (Maily), Mako (Po-han), Larry Gates

(Jameson), Charles Robinson *(Ens. Bordelles)*, Simon Oakland *(Stawski)*, Ford Rainey *(Harris)*, Joseph Turkel *(Bronson)*, Gavin MacLeod *(Crosley)*, Joseph Di Reda *(Shanahan)*, Richard Loo *(Maj. Chin)*, Barney Phillips *(Chief Franks)*, Gus Trikonis *(Restorff)*, Shepherd Sanders *(Perna)*, James Jeter *(Farren)*, Tom Middleton *(Jennings)*, Paul Chinpae *(Cho-jen)*, Tommy Lee *(Chien)*, Beulah Quo *(Mama Chunk)*, James Hong *(Victor Shu)*, Stephen Jahn *(Haythorn)*, Alan Hopkins *(Wilsey)*, Steve Ferry *(Lamb)*, Ted Fish *(CPO Wellbeck)*, Loren Janes *(Coleman)*, Glen Wilder *(Waldron)*, Henry Wang *(Lop-eye Shing)*, Ben Wright *(Englishman)*, Walter Reed *(Bidder)*, Gil Perkins *(Customer)*.

A powerful and spectacular film, THE SAND PEBBLES saw McQueen at his finest and director Wise at his most persuasive in this panoramic story of a U.S. Navy gunboat cruising China's Yangtze River in 1926. McQueen, a loner but a technical wizard with cranky engines, is assigned to the *U.S.S. San Pablo*, its crew members dubbed the Sand Pebbles. A tight-lipped machinist with eight years' service behind him, McQueen is put in charge of the engine room where Chinese coolies operate everything under the command of an elderly Chinese boss. McQueen alienates himself from the rest of the crew members by getting rid of the Chinese crew which also did all the on-board duties for the American sailors, who lived in ease. Forced to go back to their regular chores, the Americans are openly hostile to McQueen and the one Chinese assistant, Mako, McQueen keeps on board, showing Mako the intricacies of the engine and how to get up steam when the captain calls for speed. McQueen's only friend on board is Attenborough, who is in love with English-bred Chinese girl, Andriane, who has been sold into prostitution. Attenborough intends to buy her back from her saloon-operating masters. To get the money, Mako, who has been insulted by overweight Oakland, fights Oakland and heavy bets are put down. McQueen teaches Mako the rudiments of boxing and acts as his manager during the one-sided where Oakland pummels the little Chinaman about. But then Mako begins to hammer Oakland in the stomach, his most vulnerable spot, and he systematically reduces his opponent to a gasping, blubbering wreck, winning the fight and enough money for Attenborough to buy Andriane. Attenborough and Andriane have a common law marriage since, under Chinese law, they cannot legally wed. Meanwhile, McQueen visits with Bergen, daughter of fanatical missionary Gates, when the gunboat makes a trip to the mission station at China Light. They had earlier met when McQueen was en route to join the *San Pablo*. Civil war breaks out in China when Chiang Kai-Shek moves against the feudal war lords. The U.S. policy is to remain neutral but this is difficult, particularly when Robinson must carry a dispatch to a local U.S. consulate and he and his men are pelted with garbage en route and escorted back to the ship under guard by Nationalist troops commanded by Loo. All of this is by government design to humiliate all foreigners and drive them from Chinese soil, a policy Gates also advocates, considering himself more Chinese than Caucasian. (He and his daughter will later take out Chinese citizenship.) A crisis develops when Mako is chased by insurgent Chinese irregulars to the docks. There he is held prisoner and the men on board the *San Pablo*, lying offshore, witness his torture at the hands of sadistic fanatics, who slowly slice up the screaming coolie. McQueen begs his captain, Crenna, to do something, but, when nothing is done about Mako, McQueen grabs a rifle and, rather than see the brave coolie suffer more, he fires a bullet into his friend's head, killing him. Crenna decides to sit out the crisis and the *San Pablo* rusts through the winter in Shanghai as it undergoes a sort of siege. Attenborough hears that Andriane is ill and he goes AWOL each night, swimming through the icy waters to see her. He develops pneumonia and McQueen hears that he is deathly ill. He goes ashore and finds Attenborough dead in a dirty little room where he has been living with Andriane. He is just about to help the grieving Andriane when Chinese soldiers appear and abduct her, later murdering her. After McQueen is back aboard ship, several Chinese boats row out to the *San Pablo*, Chinese officials holding up signs demanding that McQueen be turned over to them to answer charges of murdering Andriane. They send his cap, the one left behind when McQueen tried to fight Andriane's abductors, as proof that he was present when the woman was killed. Crenna believes McQueen is innocent and refuses to turn him over, training machine guns on the Chinese boats and ordering them to stand away from his ship. The Chinese move off but are persistent, returning again and again to demand McQueen be turned over to them. Crenna realizes that they are trying to create an international incident and use one of his sailors as a scapegoat. He is resolute in defying the Chinese but his men begin to grumble and each time they are called on deck to grab arms and prepare to fend off a possible Chinese attack, they are less and less enthusiastic until they begin, on one occasion, to chant McQueen's name, demanding he turn himself over to the Chinese. Crenna orders MacLeod to fire his machine gun just ahead of the Chinese boat closing in on the *San Pablo* but MacLeod shrugs, telling Crenna it's jammed. None of his men will obey his orders and the frustrated Crenna mans a machine gun himself and fires a burst just ahead of the boat, which brings it to a halt. His action silences his near-muntinous men, who go back to their posts. Crenna then goes to his cabin and locks himself inside. When the tide rises, Crenna moves his ship into deeper waters. When Crenna hears that U.S. Marines have landed in Shanghai to quell outbreaks of violence against Americans and other foreigners, Crenna decides to sail the *San Pablo* to glory in an effort to remove the stain of a cowardly posture. The ship is cleaned up and sails for China Light where Crenna intends to evacuate the American missionaries, Gates and Bergen. En route, he sees that the Chinese have blocked a narrow waterway with many junks tied together with a heavy rope, serving as a barrier. The gunboat sails forward at full steam, firing its heavy gun, and the sailors battle fiercely with the Chinese once they come abreast of one of the junks. McQueen and Crenna lead a raiding party that boards a junk while other sailors chop the heavy rope so that their ship can sail through the blockade. Many sailors are killed but even more Chinese die under withering automatic fire from the Americans. After breaking through the blockade, Crenna leads a party of men, including McQueen, to the remote mission at China Light. But once there Gates tells Crenna that they don't wish to leave China and that Crenna and his men are the culprits, not the Chinese. Meanwhile, Chinese troops surround the walled mission and begin sniping at those inside. When Gates goes forward, waving his new Chinese citizenship papers, the unseen enemy shoot him down. The fight is on, with the sailors trying to battle their way out of the place. Crenna is killed and McQueen takes over, ordering Bergen, the woman he loves and with whom he has decided to live (he intended to quit the Navy and stay in China as a missionary), to leave with MacLeod and the others while he stays behind to delay the enemy. Alone in the high-walled compound, McQueen conducts a running battle with the Chinese, pretending to be several sailors, running from position to position and shouting to himself, killing several troopers who fall from the high walls. He is finally hit and slammed into a wall. He is hit again and says, staring down at the bullet wound in his chest: "I was almost home!" He slumps sideways, dead. The final scene shows the *San Pablo* steaming away from China Light and to safe waters. THE SAND PEBBLES proved once and for all that McQueen was a superb actor, not merely a matinee idol, and he would deservedly receive an Oscar nomination for Best Actor because of his intense portrayal of the introspective sailor (he would lose to Paul Scofield for A MAN FOR ALL SEASONS). Wise's direction is excellent, as he carefully unravels an almost gothic tale in exotic China, his scenes beautifully crafted and photographed by MacDonald. His direction is as sensitive and personal as was his WEST SIDE STORY and THE SOUND OF MUSIC. The script is intelligent and delivers dialog authentic to the day and age depicted. The sets and the crowd scene are awesome and even the sweaty saloon-bordello where the sailors drink and fight is marvelous, a seedy, dirty place clouded with blue smoke and deep shadows where real dangers lurk. Though overlong, THE SAND PEBBLES presents an intriguing story of a forgotten episode in American foreign involvement. U.S. gunboats continued to patrol Chinese waters until 1937 when the *U.S.S. Panay* was sunk by Japanese artillery that "accidentally" shelled it, an incident that caused the Japanese government to issue its notorious "So sorry" statement. (At the time the Japanese had invaded mainland China and purposely sank the *Panay* as a warning to the U.S. to get out of China once and for all.) Crenna is outstanding as the captain of the *San Pablo*, resolute and duty-bound, and slightly mad toward the end when he decides to uphold American honor at any price. Attenborough is empathic, as is Andriane (also known as Emmanuelle Arsan). Mako is both funny and tragic as the coolie struggling to learn English and the mysterious boiler room ruled by McQueen. Gates is rather stereotyped in his predictable role of do-gooder missionary and so too is Bergen, although she makes a fetching soul-saver. Not to be forgotten is the lush and exotic score by Goldsmith which captures the mood and menace of that long ago, reckless era. THE SAND PEBBLES was scheduled to be an expensive picture from the start, budgeted at $8 million; it would top $12 million before being completed. On-location shooting was done in Hong Kong but mostly in Taiwan (formerly Formosa), with principal photography done in Keelung Harbor. Hordes of Fox technicians spent weeks converting two miles of the harbor to represent Shanghai as it looked during the 1920s. The 150-foot, steel-hulled gunboat *San Pablo* was built for $250,000, an exact replica of the U.S. gunboats America had in service during the period, right down to the 41,000-pound antique engine McQueen personally learned how to operate. McQueen was as much an enigma to fellow cast members as he was on screen. Crenna tried to befriend him but found it difficult, later stating (in *McQueen* by William F. Nolan): "When I first talked to him his jargon was so odd it was like conversing with a Zulu warrior. Eventually we got along okay, but I found him to be extremely cautious about friendship, about allowing people to enter his life. You had to sustain the relationship on *his* terms." Wise, who had, years earlier given McQueen a bit part in SOMEBODY UP THERE LIKES ME which starred Paul Newman, was amazed at McQueen's drive and the fact that, like the character he was playing, he learned everything there was to know about the ancient engine he had to operate. Wise and McQueen, while in Taiwan, contributed $12,500 to a local mission so that a home for female waifs could be established, a fact purposely never publicized at the request of the contributors. The tough, taciturn McQueen returned from Taiwan after several months of shooting to state that THE SAND PEBBLES was "the roughest film I ever made. I had my skull twisted a couple of times, got sick, inhaled tear gas, worked myself dingy, and ended up exhausted." He also gave the performance of his life as a lone wolf who ever so slowly transfers his love from inanimate machinery to a flesh-and-blood flesh-and-blood he symbolically dies next to new uncrated farm equipment at the missionary station. His cerebral vigor is present in every scene and it is often electrifying to watch the man. Other than the original 195-minute running time, THE SAND PEBBLES has undergone several editings which caused the film to later be released with different running times, including 155, 162, 182, 188, 191, and 193 minutes. The film received additional honors, with an Oscar nomination for Best Picture, a nomination for Mako for Best Supporting Actor, and nominations for Best Color Cinematography and Art Direction, Best Editing, Best Musical Score, and Best Sound. Producer-director Wise was given the Irving

G. Thalberg Memorial Award at the annual ceremony.

p&d, Robert Wise; w, Robert W. Anderson (based on the novel by Richard McKenna); ph, Joseph MacDonald (Panavision, DeLuxe Color); m, Jerry Goldsmith; ed, William Reynolds; md, Lionel Newman; prod d, Boris Leven; set d, Walter M. Scott, John Sturtevant, William Kiernan; cos, Renie; spec eff, Jerry Endler; makeup, Ben Nye, Bill Turner, Del Acevedo.

Adventure   Cas.   (PR:C-O MPAA:M)

SANDA TAI GAILAH   (SEE: WAR OF THE GARGANTUAS, THE, 1970, U.S./Jap.)

SANDAI KAIJU CHIKYU SAIDAI NO KESSEN
  (SEE: GHIDRAH, THE THREE-HEADED MONSTER, 1965, Jap.)

SANDERS**   (1963, Brit.) 83m Big Ben-Hallam/Planet bw-c (AKA: DEATH DRUMS ALONG THE RIVER)

Richard Todd (*Inspector Harry Sanders*), Marianne Koch (*Dr. Inge Jung*), Vivi Bach (*Marlene*), Walter Rilla (*Dr. Schneider*), Jeremy Lloyd (*Hamilton*), Robert Arden (*Hunter*), Bill Brewer (*Pearson*), Albert Lieven (*Dr. Weiss*).

Todd is a British police investigator whose search for murder clues in an African hospital leads him to a hidden diamond mine. Based on an Edgar Wallace novel and co-written by Nicolas Roeg, whose career also encompasses cinematography (FAHRENHEIT 451, PETULIA) and direction (DON'T LOOK NOW, WALKABOUT). Sequel: COAST OF SKELETONS (1964).

p, Harry Alan Towers; d, Lawrence Huntington; w, Towers, Nicolas Roeg, Kevin Kavanagh, Huntington (based on the novel *Sanders Of The River* by Edgar Wallace).

Crime   (PR:A MPAA:NR)

SANDERS OF THE RIVER**   (1935, Brit.) 96m LFP/UA bw (AKA: BOSAMBO)

Leslie Banks (*R.G. Sanders*), Paul Robeson (*Bosambo*), Nina Mae McKinney (*Lilongo*), Robert Cochran (*Tibbets*), Martin Walker (*Ferguson*), Richard Grey (*Hamilton*), Tony Wane (*King Mofolaba*), Marquis de Portago (*Farini*), Eric Maturin (*Smith*), Allan Jeayes (*Father O'Leary*), Charles Carson (*Governor of the Territory*), Oboja (*Chief of the Acholi Tribe*), Orlando Martins (*K'Lova*), Luao, Kilongalonga (*Chiefs of the Wagenia Tribe*), Bertrand Frazer (*Makara*), Anthony Popafio (*Bosambo's Son*), Beresford Gale (*Topolaka*), James Solomons (*Kaluba*), John Thomas (*Obiboo*), Members of the Acholi, Sesi, Tefik, Juruba, Mendi, and Kroo tribes.

Edgar Wallace wrote a series of stories about a British man in Africa and they (along with his novel of the same name) served as the basis for this spectacular film which starred two Americans, Robeson and McKinney. Banks is the Brit who is on his way back to England for a vacation, leaving the territory where he rules as commissioner. While he's away, his temporary replacement is slain. Banks is to be married in England and two trouble-makers spread the word that he's been killed. Banks had been running the area with impartiality, and although he is respected, he is not feared. For 10 years, everything has been running smoothly and, now that the word is out that Banks is dead, trouble erupts. Banks has only gotten as far as the coast when the news reaches him and he returns to his domain. Robeson is a minor chief who has had trouble with the law in the past, but Banks realizes he is a good man and enlists his aid to quell the rebellion begun by Wane, the old king who wants to regain his power. With Robeson as his aide, the two men break up the cabal and Robeson is installed as the new king, with his wife, McKinney, at his side. Lots of authentic native rites and rituals and a trio of songs that almost make this adventure into a musical. (Given Robeson's powerful voice, how could they have cast him without finding something for him to sing?) MacKinney, who scored in HALLELUJAH, also does a song, so it begins to look like KING SOLOMON'S MINES with tunes. The movie was popular in England, where the colonial rule of Africa was accepted. In the U.S., however, it failed to get more than a passing glance from any theaters other than art houses, as it was the equivalent of showing THE BABE RUTH STORY in London. The working title was, for some reason, "Kongo Raid." It was Robeson's second film, after his triumph in THE EMPEROR JONES. His subsequent visits to the Soviet Union and his acceptance of some leftist ideologies made him a pariah in later years, thereby cutting his film career to just a few movies. His passport was revoked by the State Department in 1950 and it was eight years later when he went again to Russia to accept the Stalin Peace Prize he'd been awarded in 1952. Robeson apparently never totally espoused communism and was merely seeking a way to achieve equality for blacks and thought that the Russians might have had an answer, something that has since been disproven by their treatment of Jews and other minorities within their country.

p, Alexander Korda; d, Zoltan Korda; w, Lajos Biro, Jeffrey Dell (based on the stories by Edgar Wallace); ph, Georges Perinal, Bernard Browne, Osmund Borradaile, Louis Page; m, Michael [Mischa] Spoliansky; ed, William Hornbeck, Charles Crichton; prod d, Vincent Korda; md, Muir

Mathieson; m/l, Spoliansky, Arthur Wimperis; technical advisers, C.O. Lemon, Cecil Gross, Major C. Wallace.

Adventure   Cas.   (PR:A-C MPAA:NR)

SANDFLOW***   (1937) 58m UNIV bw

Buck Jones (*Buck Hallett*), Lita Chevret (*Rose Porter*), Bob Kortman (*Quayle*), Arthur Aylsworth (*Tex*), Robert Terry (*Lane Hallett*), Enrique DeRosas (*Joaquin*), Josef Swickard (*Mr. Porter*), Lee Phelps (*The Kid*), Harold Hodge (*Rillito*), Tom Chatterton (*Sheriff*), Arthur Van Slyke (*Santone*), Malcolm Graham (*Parable*), Ben Corbett, Silver.

Jones plays the son of a man who has cheated many ranchers. He's out to build a new life for himself and avenge all of his father's misdeeds as well by repaying each rancher who was rustled. Before he can pay back the last rancher, Jones' younger brother Terry gets mixed up in a murder, but all is righted when Jones uncovers the real killer. A good outing for Jones and a well-made programmer western. The story is not sacrificed for action and the plot is more than a re-hash of a hundred other Westerns. Desert sand dune locations are used with good effect, as well.

p, Buck Jones; d, Lesley Selander; w, Frances Guihan (based on a story by Cherry Wilson); ph, Allen Thompson, Herbert Kirkpatrick; ed, Bernard Loftus.

Western   (PR:A MPAA:NR)

SANDOKAN THE GREAT**   (1964, Fr./Ital./Span.) 110m Comptoir Francais du Film-Filmes Cinematografica-Ocean Film/MGM c (SANDOKAN, LE TIGRE DE BORNEO; SANDOKAN, LA TIGRE DI MOMPRACEM; SANDOKAN; I PIRATI DELLA MALESIA; AKA: SANDOKAN, THE TIGER OF MOMPRACEM)

Steve Reeves (*Sandokan*), Genevieve Grad (*Mary Ann*), Andrea Bosic (*Yanez*), Maurice Poli (*Giro Batol*), Rik Battaglia (*Sambigliong*), Leo Anchoriz (*Lord Hillock*), Joaquin Oliveras (*Lt. Appleton*), Mario Valdemarin (*Lt. Ross*), Ananda Kumar (*Tuang Olong*), Antonio Molino Rojo (*Lt. Tollbee*), Enzo Fiermonte (*Sgt. Mitchell*), Gino Marturano (*Tananduriam*), Wilbert Bradley, Pietro Capanna, Nazzareno Zamperla, Giovanni Cianfriglia, Mimmo Palmara, Jacqueline Sassard.

Anchoriz is a British commander during the reign of Queen Victoria. While occupying the East Indian village of Tapuah, Anchoriz and his troops win the hearts and minds of the people by killing off the population en masse. Of course he makes a major mistake when Reeves' family is included amongst the victims. Reeves organizes a rebel cell that attacks the Englishmen but Anchoriz retaliates by threatening to hang Reeves' father, an important sultan. Reeves manages to get into Anchoriz's home and kidnaps Grad, the British commander's niece. In good tradition that is a hallmark in films of this nature, Grad is at first indignant but soon comes to love her captor. Reeves and company meet up with some headhunters but overpower the brutes only to find themselves surrounded by Anchoriz's troops. An agreement which calls for Reeves and his rebels to be exiled in return for Grad's release is substantiated but of course this is immediately broken by Anchoriz. He throws the revolutionaries in prison and plans for executions. But they escape and are rejoined by Grad. They get together with Kumar, a local chieftain, and overcome the British forces at last. Plenty of action here, not all of it exciting. Reeves is good, though covering his much-acclaimed frame with clothing hurt a lot of the ex-Mr. Universe's drawing power. This was the 12th film he made for cheap Italian production companies aimed at the younger filmgoer, though he went on to make A LONG RIDE FROM HELL, an R-rated western which was certainly an unusual move for the muscleman. Despite this film's simplistic plot and routine action sequences, SANDOKAN THE GREAT did good business, particularly at movie houses which specialized in action films.

p, Solly V. Bianco, Joseph Fryd; d, Umberto Lenzi; w, Lenzi, Fulvio Gicca, Victor A. Catena (based on the novel *Le Tigri di Mompracem* by Emilio Salgari); ph, Angelo Lotti, Giovanni Scarpellini, Aurelio Gutierrez Larraya (Techniscope, Technicolor); m, Giovanni Fusco; ed, Iolanda Benvenuti, Antonietta Zita; set d, Arrigo Equini, Juan Alberto Soler; cos, Giancarlo Bartolini Salimbeni; makeup, Raoul Ranieri.

Action/Drama   (PR:A MPAA:NR)

SANDPIPER, THE*   (1965) 115m Venice-Filmways/MGM c

Elizabeth Taylor (*Laura Reynolds*), Richard Burton (*Dr. Edward Hewitt*), Eva Marie Saint (*Claire Hewitt*), Charles Bronson (*Cos Erickson*), Robert Webber (*Ward Hendricks*), James Edwards (*Larry Brant*), Torin Thatcher (*Judge Thompson*), Tom Drake (*Walter Robinson*), Doug Henderson (*Phil Sutcliff*), Morgan Mason (*Danny Reynolds*), Dusty Cadis, John Hart (*Troopers*), Jan Arvan (*1st Trustee*), Mary Benoit (*Trustee's Wife*), Tom Curtis (*2nd Trustee*), Paul Genge (*Architect*), Rex Holman (*1st Celebrant*), Kelton Garwood (*2nd Celebrant*), Jimmy Murphy (*3rd Celebrant*), Mel Gallagher (*4th Celebrant*), Ron Whelan (*Poet Celebrant*), Diane Sayer (*6th Celebrant*), Joan Connors (*7th Celebrant*), Peggy Adams Laird (*8th Celebrant*), Shirley Bonne (*9th Celebrant*), Peter O'Toole (*Voice*).

A hot-blooded woman meets a repressed and married Episcopalian minister. Take the premise and give it to Somerset Maugham and you have RAIN.

Give it to the wrong people and you have this picture, which was named for the wrong bird. As dreary and dull and contrived as this was, it still managed to earn well over $7 million the first time around, a tribute to the drawing power of Taylor and Burton because it couldn't have had anything to do with the quality of their performances, the dismal script or the tiresome direction. Taylor is a bohemian artist living with her out-of-wedlock son, Mason, in a fabulous house in Big Sur, one of the most spectacular areas along the California coastline. How she has managed to afford such a gorgeous home after it is established that she doesn't care a whit about money is not sufficiently explained. Taylor eschews the usual educational opportunities afforded to U.S. citizens and wants to tutor her son in her own fashion, which causes a problem with the local school authorities. Mason is always in trouble because he is a wild, unfettered child who has no idea of morality other than what his immoral mother has taught him. When the judge, Thatcher, states that Mason must either go to school or be taken from her custody, Taylor relents and sends Mason to a private institution run by Episcopalian Burton, who is married to Saint and has twin sons. Mason astounds Burton and Saint with his facility in several subjects and eases his way into the school with no problems. Taylor resents the fact that she's had to give up educating Mason and is, at first, angry at Burton, but that turns into passionate love as everyone in the audience must have known it would. Taylor surrounds herself with hippie friends who include Bronson as a sculptor who does a nude statue of her, Webber, her one-time lover, and Edwards. Burton is wracked with guilt about the affair he's having with Taylor (this is close to their actual story and amounts to a *"romance" a clef*). He can't take it and confesses to Saint. Now he battles with the local politicians and lets everyone know what he's been up to so Taylor gives him the air. Burton decides to leave both his wife and his mistress, quits his job, and goes off to renew his faith in his faith. Taylor got a million for her work, Burton 3/4ths of that and audiences should have been paid part of the money for being asked to watch. The exteriors were done in California and took about eight weeks, then Taylor and Burton had to leave the U.S. for tax reasons and shoot all of the interiors in Paris (where she insisted they shoot a Las Vegas-based film, THE ONLY GAME IN TOWN, so she could be near Burton while he was doing STAIRCASE). Taylor was getting porky by this time but that didn't stop her from showing a great deal of her overweight body in various shots. It was the first passionate pairing of the two since the scandal of their divorces from Eddie Fisher and Sybil Burton and audiences clamored to see them hugging and fondling. Taylor had worked for Minnelli 15 years before in FATHER OF THE BRIDE and my, how the times had changed (as well as the subject matter). She'd been off the screen for a couple of years while Burton was busily doing BECKETT, NIGHT OF THE IGUANA, and his version of HAMLET. THE SANDPIPER opened at Radio City and broke records, despite the brickbats hurled at the movie. Mason is the son of James and Pamela and does a good job as the child. He has since gone into political public relations. The best part of this movie was the Oscar-winning song "The Shadow Of Your Smile" by Johnny Mandel and Paul Francis Webster. There was some nice trumpet-playing by Jack Sheldon, and solos by Howard Roberts, Bud Shank, and Vic Feldman. Otherwise, it must rank as one of the most expensive and pretentious loads of garbage ever foisted upon an adoring public.

p, Martin Ransohoff; d, Vincente Minnelli; w, Dalton Trumbo, Michael Wilson, Irene Kamp, Louis Kamp (based on a story by Ransohoff); ph, Milton Krasner (Panavision, Metrocolor); m, Johnny Mandel; ed, David Bretherton; art d, George W. Davis, Urie McCleary; set d, Henry Grace, Keogh Gleason; cos, Irene Sharaff; m/l, "The Shadow Of Your Smile," Mandel, Paul Francis Webster; makeup, William Tuttle.

Drama   **Cas.**   **(PR:C-O   MPAA:NR)**

SANDPIT GENERALS, THE   (SEE: WILD PACK, THE, 1972)

SANDRA**½   (1966, Ital.) 100m Vides/Royal bw (VAGHE STELLE
                        DELL'ORSA; GB: OF A THOUSAND DELIGHTS)

Claudia Cardinale *(Sandra)*, Jean Sorel *(Gianni)*, Michael Craig *(Andrew)*, Marie Bell *(Mother)*, Renzo Ricci *(Gilardini)*, Fred Williams *(Pietro Fornari)*, Amalia Troiani *(Fosca)*, Vittorio Manfrino, Renato Moretti, Giovanni Rovini, Paolo Pescini, Isacco Politi.

Cardinale is a 25-year-old woman who, along with her American husband Craig, returns to her home town of Volterra. Volterra dates back to the Etruscan era, a city of crumbling, aging ruins. Craig is more practical than his wife and is confounded by the highly emotional nature of Cardinale's family. Sorel is her younger brother, a suicidal would-be author who has been stopped from killing himself in the past by Cardinale. He also harbors passionate emotional feelings for his sister, which has left Cardinale with feelings of guilt. Another family member is Bell, Cardinale's mother. She was once a proud woman of great beauty, but physical and psychological woes have diminished her former self. Cardinale is returning for a ceremony honoring her late father, a Jewish scientist killed by Nazis during the war. However her real reason for coming to Volterra is to confirm her suspicion that Bell arranged her husband's deportation to certain death in a concentration camp in order to marry Ricci, the ex-administrator of her father's estate. Craig tries to reconcile Cardinale with her stepfather but does not succeed. He leaves for the United States while Sorel ultimately destroys his autobiographical novel and finally succeeds at suicide. Cardinale stays for the ceremony then leaves to rejoin her husband in America.

Filmed on location in Volterra, Italy as well as locations in the Swiss Alps, Geneva, Switzerland, and Florence, Italy.

p, Franco Cristaldi; d, Luchino Visconti; w, Suso Cecchi D'Amico, Visconti, Enrico Medioli; ph, Armando Nannuzzi; m, Cesar Franck; ed, Mario Serandrei; art d, Mario Garbuglia; cos, Bice Brichetto; makeup, Michele Trimarchi.

Drama   **(PR:O   MPAA:NR)**

SANDS OF BEERSHEBA**½   (1966, U.S./Israel) 90m David/AIP bw
                                              (MORDEI HA'OR)

Diane Baker *(Susan)*, David Opatoshu *(Daoud)*, Tom Bell *(Dan)*, Paul Stassino *(Salim)*, Didi Ramati *(Naima)*, Theodore Marcuse *(Nuri)*, Wolfe Barzell *(Ayub)*, Oded Kotler, Avraham Ben-Yosef.

Baker, an American gentile woman, goes to Israel to look at the site of her Jewish fiance's death in the 1948 war. She meets the late man's best friend (Bell) and the two fall in love. Bell works in a potash factory but is a gun runner for Israel as well. Bell is ambushed by Stassino, an Arab terrorist, but is taken in by the terrorist's father (Opatoshu). Stassino discovers this information and attacks the house. Stassino is killed and Bell is wounded, left to the comforting arms of his beloved Baker. Somewhat pretentious with its attempts at analyzing the philosophies behind the Arab-Israeli conflict, but this does have a few moments of interest. Hollywood-born actress Baker went on to try her hand at directing; in the early 1970s, she filmed a documentary, ASHYANA. Opatoshu, born in New York City, had been active in Yiddish theater in his teens.

p,d&w, Alexander Ramati (based on *Rebel Against the Light* by Ramati); ph, Wolfgang Suschitzky; m, Mel Keller; ed, Helga Cranston; m/l, Naomi Shemer (sung by Shoshana Damari).

Drama   **(PR:O   MPAA:NR)**

SANDS OF IWO JIMA****   (1949) 110m REP bw

John Wayne *(Sgt. John M. Stryker)*, John Agar *(Pfc. Peter Conway)*, Adele Mara *(Allison Bromley)*, Forrest Tucker *(Pfc. Al Thomas)*, Wally Cassell *(Pfc. Benny Regazzi)*, James Brown *(Pfc. Charlie Bass)*, Richard Webb *(Pfc. Shipley)*, Arthur Franz *(Cpl. Robert Dunne/Narrator)*, Julie Bishop *(Mary)*, James Holden *(Pfc. Soames)*, Peter Coe *(Pfc. Hellenpolis)*, Richard Jaeckel *(Pfc. Frank Flynn)*, Bill Murphy *(Pfc. Eddie Flynn)*, George Tyne *(Pfc. Harris)*, Hal Fieberling 'Hal Baylor' *(Pvt. "Ski" Choynski)*, John McGuire *(Capt. Joyce)*, Martin Milner *(Pvt. Mike McHugh)*, Leonard Gumley *(Pvt. Sid Stein)*, William Self *(Pvt. L.D. Fowler, Jr.)*, Dick Wessel *(Grenade Instructor)*, I. Stanford Jolley *(Forrestal)*, David Clarke *(Wounded Marine)*, Gil Herman *(Lt. Baker)*, Dick Jones *(Scared Marine)*, Don Haggerty *(Colonel)*, Bruce Edwards *(Marine)*, Dorothy Ford *(Tall Girl)*, John Whitney *(Lt. Thompson)*, Col. D.M. Shoup, USMC, Lt. Col. H.P. Crowe, USMC, Capt. Harold G. Schrier, USMC, Pfc. Rene A. Gagnon, Pfc. Ira H. Hayes, PM 3/C John H. Bradley.

Unlike many of Wayne's superman films of WW II where he single-handedly destroys whole Japanese armies, SANDS OF IWO JIMA provides an intelligent look at warfare and at Wayne, though he is no less heroic than in his other films. He is a believable and vulnerable human being here who can bleed, feel pain, and die. He is also a martinet sergeant who inherits a new group of raw recruits at Camp Packakariki, in New Zealand, 1943, and must turn them into crack Marines within a few weeks, no easy chore. He drills them hard, marches them hard, and doesn't care whether he makes any friends. He doesn't, and when Brown and Franz, survivors of his old squad. When one of them tells a complaining recruit that Wayne "knows his business," the grumpy recruit retorts, "So did Jack the Ripper!" Agar, the son of a military hero who is one of Wayne's old friends, despises Wayne for his insensitive ways of disciplining the men. On one occasion, Fieberling makes an awkward thrust with his bayonet and Wayne, pretending to be his enemy, smashes the gun butt into his jaw, breaking it. But Wayne later gets the same recruit to coordinate his footwork by practicing with a phonograph. When the men get a pass and go on the town, Wayne runs into the recruits in a bar and learns that Agar has received a letter from his wife telling him that he has a new-born son. Wayne congratulates Agar and tells him that the Marines can always use more good men, like his infant son. Agar lectures him: "I won't insist he be tough. Instead, I'll try to see that he's intelligent. And I won't insist that he read the Marine Corps manual. Instead I'll get him a set of Shakespeare. In short, I don't want him to be a Sergeant John M. Stryker. I want him to be intelligent, considerate, cultured, and a gentleman." Wayne takes this upbraiding off-duty and goes on a bender, and is later found by the squad and hidden until MPs pass by. The recruits turn over the boozed-up Wayne to Brown, who acts as Wayne's protector, and gets him back to the base in tact. During training, Agar is too busy to see that a live grenade has slipped out of the hands of another recruit, Milner, and has rolled into his direction while reading a letter from his wife. Wayne sees the grenade and dives for Agar, knocking him out of the way and taking a piece of shrapnel in the shoulder. "You ought to get a medal for that," an impressed corpsman attending to Wayne's wound tells the sergeant. Replies Wayne with a grimace, "Aw, knock it off." The men are finally ready and they land on Tarawa some days later to get into one of the worst battles of the Pacific. Tucker, a Marine who has served with Wayne before and lost his sergeant stripes thanks to Wayne's code of discipline, is with Brown and Coe when the three are separated and pinned down by Japanese fire. They are running out of ammunition when Tucker is selected to go for more. Tucker gets the ammunition but then stops to drink some hot coffee that some mortar men have made and, in his prolonged absence, Brown and Coe are overrun by the Japanese who bayonet them and leave them for dead. When Tucker returns he finds Coe dying and asking him, "What kept you, sport?" Brown has crawled away and is heard crying Wayne's name by the squad throughout the night. Wayne will not answer his best friend, knowing that he might give away his position, and so he goes on with the agony of listening to his friend suffer while his men, chiefly Agar, hate him for not rescuing Brown. The men are finally pulled out of Tarawa after the island is secured and they head for Hawaii for rest and recuperation. (In the Tarawa battle scenes, cleverly interspersed with actual combat footage, Wayne destroys a built-up bunker containing Japanese machine guns by throwing a satchel full of explosives into the narrow opening.) Once in Hawaii, Wayne is delighted to learn that Brown has survived and is back with him. He goes on the town to get drunk again and runs into hooker Bishop who invites him up to her room for a drink. He joins her but she holds up an empty bottle and tells him she's out. He gives her some money to buy more booze and when she's gone he discovers in another room a little child in a crib. Bishop returns and pulls out a bottle but Wayne looks into the shopping bag to find to containers of baby food. He questions Bishop and finds out that her husband has deserted her, leaving her to make a living as a prostitute. He nods and helps her prepare the baby's food. She smiles at him and says, "So you know about babies?" He answers in a tender but deep voice that has memory running through it: "Yeah, I know about babies." He walks into the little bedroom where the baby is playing and dumps all of his money into the crib. When Bishop sees this she expresses her gratitude, and is ready to perform but Wayne tells her he's leaving. At the door Bishop kisses him and says "God bless you, sergeant. You're a fine man." He gives her a little salute and a smile as he begins to walk away, saying: "You'd get odds on that in the Marine Corps." Outside he meets Brown, his faithful friend who has been following him. Happier than he has been in years, Wayne goes off to have a friendly drink with Brown. The squad is called back to duty once more, this time landing on the most infamous island in the Pacific, Iwo Jima, and participating in the worst battle the Marines had to endure during WW II. The men are picked off by the hidden enemy as they inch their way up Mount Suribachi, the commanding mountain on the island and focal point of the attack. Most of the men eventually reach the summit and sit with Wayne to have a smoke. He hands an American flag to another squad that has been assigned to raise Old Glory. (Three of the men in this squad, Hayes, Gagnon, and Bradley, were the real-life Marines who raised the flag at Iwo Jima and were caught in the historic photograph from which the great monument in Washington D.C., was created.) As Wayne begins to talk to his squad, now loyal to him as a man, a Japanese sniper shoots Wayne in the back and kills him. From his pocket is taken an unfinished letter Wayne had been writing to his son, which Agar slowly reads aloud, one in which Wayne tells his young son that he was a failure in many things, except at being a good Marine. Agar vows to finish the incompleted mission and assumes Wayne's personality by harshly ordering the men into war. Atop the mountain, the other squad raises the American flag (in a shivering patriotic setting). This film, directed with marvelous restraint by old hand Dwan, portrays Wayne in more human terms than ever before and when he dies, his death is genuinely shocking. A single bullet cuts him down without a farewell speech or a heroic act to go with it, unlike many another Wayne film. It is as shocking as the scene he plays with Bishop is tender. These two scenes, most likely, earned Wayne his Oscar nomination for Best Actor. He lost out to Broderick Crawford for ALL THE KING'S MEN. Ironically, Wayne had been asked to play a role in the Crawford film and angrily turned it down, stating that the Robert Penn Warren novel disgusted him as did the story for the film. Wayne had been told years earlier that he would win no awards playing roles in westerns, yet it would be a western, TRUE GRIT, made 20 years later, that would win him his one and only Oscar. But there was some compensation for the Duke. During the year SANDS OF IWO JIMA enjoyed great popularity, 1950, he became the No. 1 box office attraction in America. His gentle but tough role in this superb war film did that for him.

p, Edmund Grainger; d, Allan Dwan; w, Harry Brown, James Edward Grant (based on a story by Brown); ph, Reggie Lanning; m, Victor Young; ed, Richard L. Van Enger; art d, James Sullivan

War Drama   Cas.   (PR:C   MPAA:NR)

SANDS OF THE DESERT*½   (1960, Brit.) 92m ABF/Warner-Pathe c

Charlie Drake (Charlie Sands), Peter Arne (Sheikh El Jabez), Sara Branch (Janet Brown), Raymond Huntley (Bossom), Peter Illing (Sheikh Ibrahim), Harold Kasket (Abdullah), Marne Maitland (Adviser to Sheikh), Neil McCarthy (Hassan), Paul Stassino (Pilot), Derek Sydney (Mamud), Alan Tilvern (Mustafa), Martin Benson (Selim), Eric Pohlmann (Scrobin), Rebecca Dignam (Nerima), Charles Carson (Philpots), Judith Furse (Yasmin), Robert Brown (1st Tourist), William Kendall (British Consul), Inia te Wiata (Fahid).

A mild-mannered British travel agency clerk gets the brilliant idea of opening up a desert resort. He goes out to the Mideast and immediately gets himself into trouble with a local sheikh. Drake wants to put his resort on

some oil-rich land, which the sheikh won't allow. This leads to a near war between two rival groups, but Drake unwittingly stops them from fighting and gets the land. Of course, it's clogged with oil, which pleases his boss no end. SANDS OF THE DESERT is a mildly amusing comedy that never really delivers its laugh quota with success. The scripting is uneven with various comic highs and lows. Drake, a popular British television comic of the day, is good though the movies are clearly not his metier.

p, Gordon L. T. Scott; d, John Paddy Carstairs; w, Carstairs, Charlie Drake (based on a story by Robert Hall, Anne Burnaby, Stafford Byrne); ph, Gilbert Taylor (Technicolor); m, Stanley Black; ed, Richard Best.

Comedy   (PR:A   MPAA:NR)

SANDS OF THE KALAHARI**½   (1965, Brit.) 119m Pendennis/PAR c

Stuart Whitman (O'Brien), Stanley Baker (Bain), Susannah York (Grace Monckton), Harry Andrews (Grimmelman), Theodore Bikel (Dr. Bondarah-kai), Nigel Davenport (Sturdevant), Barry Lowe (Detjens).

A flight to Johannesburg, South Africa is delayed. Bikel, one of the stranded passengers, decides to hire a small private plane. Joining him on the charter is a stock ensemble including York as a recent divorcee trying to rebuild her life; Baker, a failed mining engineer; Andrews, an older German man; and Davenport, the smarmy pilot. Just before the plane takes off, the little group is joined by Whitman. He has two gun cases for luggage and bribes Davenport to head for Capetown rather than the intended destination. En route, the plane encounters a cloud of locusts – a Biblical portent? – which splatter against the windshield and clog up the plane's engines. Ultimately the plane is forced down in a fiery crash that kills Davenport's co-pilot. The group is forced to go it alone out on the desert and immediately arguments for the best survival tactics come up. Davenport tries to rape York but after failing heads out onto the desert by himself. Whitman takes over as group leader and forces Bikel to go off alone as well. He orders the German to do the same, but when Andrews refuses, Whitman kills him. Baker sees this and convinces York to steal the man's rifle, even though she is attracted to the rogue. Baker knocks out Whitman and throws him into a hole, but a handy rainstorm floods the hole that night, permitting the villain an escape device. He hides among some rocks and, enmeshed in the survival game, decides to stay in the desert rather than join the two other remaining members in a rescue helicopter. But as York and Baker fly off, Whitman gets what's coming to him. He's surrounded by a group of baboons that have been annoying him ever since the crash. They attack him and begin to devour the hapless man. This could have been a terribly funny bit of hokum but the script and direction never pander to the overly melodramatic potential inherent in the plot. Rather it becomes a well-crafted string of action scenes that use the African locations with good effect. The ensemble is a good group, never getting into the ham acting with which these sorts of pictures are usually sprinkled. Rather, it's – on the whole – quite entertaining and often suspenseful. The ending is as eerie as they come, wholly unexpected and well handled. At worst, SANDS OF THE KALAHARI is a bit too long, which causes it to drag at certain points. Otherwise, this is a good bit of entertainment that overcomes the seemingly cliched material.

p, Cy Endfield, Stanley Baker; d&w, Endfield (based on the novel by William Mulvihill); ph, Erwin Hillier (Panavision, Technicolor); m, John Dankworth; ed, John Jympson; art d, Seamus Flannery; cos, James Smith; spec eff, Cliff Richardson; makeup, Wally Schneiderman.

Adventure   (PR:O   MPAA:NR)

SANDU FOLLOWS THE SUN**½   (1965, USSR) 66m
Moldova-Film/Artkino c (CHELOVEK IDYOT ZA SOLNTSEM; AKA: MAN FOLLOWING THE SUN)

Nika Krimnus (Sandu), Tatyana Bestayeva, N. Volkov, G. Georgiu, M. Grekov, L. Dolgorukova, Yevgeniy Yevstigneyev, Valentin Zubkov, L. Kruglyy, N. Kavunovskiy, I. Levyanu, Larisa Luzhina, V. Markin, Anatoliy Papanov, G. Svetlani, G. Sovchis, Valentina Telegina, S. Troitskiy, I. Unguryanu, D. Fusu, S. Andreyev, G. Belov, V. Bogatyy, V. Grigoryeva, I. Gurzo-Gubanova, N. Doni, B. Yermolayev, L. Zimina, P. Zavtoni, V. Kulik, K. Kramarchuk, V. Minin, N. Nikitich, L. Namuov, A. Nagits, L. Panova, V. Filina, Yu. Khaso, Viktor Chetverikov, I. Shkurya, I. Shatokhin, A. Yurchak.

Krimnus is a five-year-old Russian lad who decides to follow the sun in its trek around the earth. He begins rolling his hoop around his city, taking time to look at things through bits of tinted glass. Arriving at a maternity hospital, Krimnus stops to see the process of birth. Next he meets a variety of characters including a shoeshine man with a passion for soccer who has lost his legs in the war and a new arrival to the city, a young woman who works as a gardener. She takes care of a flower bed which reminds her of her own childhood and explains to the boy how a sunflower will turn its head to follow the sun. But when a park attendant cuts down the beautiful sunflower, Krimnus must suddenly confront man's wicked nature for the first time in his young life. After sharing a meal with some friendly workers, Krimnus watches a funeral procession, then meets a truck driver. After watching some gymnasts work out, he falls asleep next to a stone lion. He has a wonderful dream wherein the park attendant buries the sunflower in a somber ceremony, then turns into a mannequin. Next arrives the shoeshine man who now has his legs again. He takes Krimnus to a beautiful street where they meet the sun. Krimnus awakens and a military musician takes the young wanderer home. The Russian version of this pathos-filled children's film ran about five minutes longer than its American release. Director Kalik and cameraman Derbenev, schoolmates at Moscow's All-Union State Institute of Cinematography, worked together on three such lyrical films; the others were ATAMAN KODR and CRADLE SONG. In 1963, Derbenev became a director himself.

d, Mosei Kalik; w, Valeriu Gazhiu, Kalik; ph, Vadim Derbenev (Sovcolor); m, Mikhail Tariverdiyev; ed, K. Blinova; md, E. Kachaturyan; art d, S. Bulgakov, A. Roman; makeup, P. Klimov

Children's Comedy-Drama   **(PR:AAA   MPAA:NR)**

SANDWICH MAN, THE½**   (1966, Brit.) 95m Titan
                                                         International/Rank c

Michael Bentine (Horace Quilby), Dora Bryan (Mrs. DeVere), Harry H. Corbett (Stage-Doorkeeper), Bernard Cribbins (Photographer), Diana Dors (Billingsgate Woman), Ian Hendry (Motorcycle Cop), Stanley Holloway (Gardener), Wilfrid Hyde-White (Lord Uffingham), Michael Medwin (Sewer Man), Ron Moody (Coach), Anna Quayle (Billingsgate Woman), Terry-Thomas (Scoutmaster), Norman Wisdom (Father O'Malley), Donald Wolfit (Manager), Tracey Crisp (Girl in Mac), Suzy Kendall (Sue), Alfie Bass (Yachtsman), Earl Cameron (Conductor), Max Bacon (Chef), Michael Chaplin (Artist), Fred Emney (Sir Arthur Moleskin), Sid and Max Harrison (Zoo Men), Peter Jones (Escapologist), John le Mesurier (Sandwich Man), Tony Tanner (Ferryman), Peter Arne (Gentleman), Warren Mitchell (Gypsy Syd), Sidney Tafler (Billingsgate Porter).

A sandwich-board man wanders around London and in the course of the day meets a variety of different characters. The two largest stories involve a romance between a car salesman and a model; and the adventures of Bentine as he is about to enter his racing pigeon in an important competition. Other players (most lasting only a few minutes apiece) include Holloway as a park gardener; Terry Thomas as a rather inept scout leader; and Chaplin (son of Charlie) as a beatnik artist. The film is a mixed effort with some moments working better than others. The comedy is played out with a free-moving camera, giving this a documentary look. For the most part THE SANDWICH MAN is silent, an interesting if not always proper choice. The on-location London shooting works well with a mise-en-scene that often has a dream-like quality to it. Bentine, who co-wrote the screenplay with the film's director, was a popular English television comedian of the day.

p, Peter Newbrook; d, Robert Hartford-Davis; w, Hartford-Davis, Michael Bentine; ph, Newbrook (Eastmancolor); m, Mike Vickers; ed, Peter Taylor

Comedy   **(PR:A   MPAA:NR)**

SANDY GETS HER MAN½**   (1940) 65m UNIV bw

Baby Sandy (Sandy), Stuart Erwin (Bill), Una Merkel (Nan), William Frawley (Police Chief O'Hara), Edgar Kennedy (Fire Chief Galvin), Edward Brophy (Junior), Wally Vernon (Bagshaw), Jack Carson (Tom), William B. Davidson (Councilman Clark), John Sheehan (Justice), Isabel Randolph (Justice's Wife), Mira McKinney (Woman), Bert Roach (Clerk), Lillian Yarbo (Hattie), Frances Morris (Secretary).

The lovable little tyke of Universal Studios, Baby Sandy, takes on city departments in one of her better outings. The police department and fire department are slugging it out for the better portion of a major municipal contract. Davidson is the councilman who must choose between the two and, by no mean coincidence, is also Sandy's grandfather. Erwin is the fireman who competes for the affections of Sandy's mother (Merkel) with Carson, a cop. Merkel has difficulty choosing but Davidson doesn't after Sandy crawls into a burning building and is rescued by the fire department. Guess who gets the contract. Kennedy does a few slow burns of his own in the role of fire chief while Frawley plays his rival on the police department. Though this is no great comedy, it has some funny moments of slapstick and the cast members do give it their best. (See SANDY series, Index.)

p, Burt Kelly; d, Otis Garrett, Paul Gerard Smith; w, Sy Bartlett, Jane Storm (based on the story "Fireman, Save My Child" by Bartlett and Smith); ph, Elwood Bredell; ed, Phillip Cahn; Cos, Vera West.

Comedy   **(PR:AAA   MPAA:NR)**

SANDY IS A LADY**   (1940) 62m UNIV bw

Baby Sandy (Baby Sandy), Butch and Buddy (Pat and Mike, the Little Tornadoes), Eugene Pallette (P.J. Barnett), Nan Grey (Mary Phillips), Tom Brown (Joe Phillips), Mischa Auer (Felix Lobo Smith), Billy Gilbert (Billy Pepino), Edgar Kennedy (Officer Rafferty), Fritz Feld (Mario), Anne Gwynne (Millie), Richard Lane (Philip Jarvis), Charles Wilson (Sergeant), Joseph Downing (Nick Case).

Little more than a rehash of old comedy routines fitted for the talents of Universal's precocious two-year-old star Baby Sandy. Watch Sandy as she is nearly run over when she crawls into traffic! Thrill at the danger when

she climbs a bell tower! Smile and wipe a tear from the eye as she helps the wonderful people around her! The cast is good and the direction quite competent but SANDY IS A LADY, like most of the Hollywood baby films, suffers from a self-conscious cuteness. (See SANDY series, Index.)

p, Burt Kelly; d, Charles Lamont; w, Charles Grayson; ph, Milton Krasner; ed, Phillip Cahn; md, Charles Previn; art d, Jack Otterson; cos, Vera West.

Comedy   **(PR:AAA   MPAA:NR)**

SANDY TAKES A BOW   (SEE: UNEXPECTED FATHER, 1939)

SANDY THE SEAL**   (1969, Brit.) 70m Towers of London/Tigon c

Heinz Drache (Jan Van Heerden), Marianne Koch (Karen Van Heerden), David Richards (David), Anne Mervis (Anne), Bill Brewer (Lowenstein), Gabriel Bayman (Lofty), Gert Van Den Berg (Jacobson).

A standard children's tale of the heart-warming sort in which a darling group of youngsters finds a baby seal and takes care of it. In the meantime, the kids turn their energies to ridding their town of some inconsiderate poachers who pay no attention to animal rights.

p, Oliver Unger, Harry Alan Towers; d, Robert Lynn; w, Peter Welbeck [Towers].

Children   **(PR:AAA   MPAA:NR)**

SANG D'UN POETE   (SEE: BLOOD OF A POET, THE, 1930, Fr.)

SANG ET LUMIERES   (SEE: LOVE IN A HOT CLIMATE, 1958)

SANGAREE**   (1953) 94m PAR c

Fernando Lamas (Dr. Carlos Morales), Arlene Dahl (Nancy Darby), Patricia Medina (Martha Darby), Francis L. Sullivan (Dr. Bristol), Charles Korvin (Felix Pagnol), Tom Drake (Dr. Roy Darby), John Sutton (Harvey Bristol), Willard Parker (Gabriel Thatch), Charles Evans (Judge Armstrong), Lester Mathews (Gen. Darby), Roy Gordon (Dr. Tyrus), Lewis L. Russell (Capt. Bronson), Russell Gaige (McIntosh), William Walker (Priam), Felix Nelson (Billy), Voltaire Perkins (Crowther).

Lamas is the son of an indentured servant in the Old South. When the owner of a Georgia estate passes away, Lamas inherits the place, helped by the late man's son, Drake. But Dahl, the man's daughter, is furious that this freed slave has the plantation. Of course their differences are resolved and the fiery woman softens her stance by the picture's end for the eventual marriage. Mixed up in this tale are various subplots involving blockades, the plague, and the attempt by Medina, as Drake's wife, to seduce Lamas. SANGAREE is hollow, with a dull plot and an acting style typical of potboilers. What make this film better than expected are the lush locations and period costumes, filmed in wide-screen 3-D with good effect. The visual beauty, however, comes at the expense of believable dialog and a credible plot.

p, William H. Pine, William C. Thomas; d, Edward Ludwig; w, David Duncan, Frank Moss (based on the novel by Frank G. Slaughter); ph, Lionel Lindon, Wallace Kelley (3-D, Technicolor); m, Lucien Cailliet; ed, Howard Smith; art d, Hal Pereira, Earl Hedrick; cos, Edith Head.

Historical Drama   **(PR:C   MPAA:NR)**

SANITORIUM   (SEE: TRIO, 1950, Brit.)

SANJURO½**   (1962, Jap.) 96m Toho bw (TSUBAKI SANJURO)

Toshiro Mifune (Sanjuro), Tatsuya Nakadai (Muroto), Takashi Shimura (Kurofuji), Yuzo Kayama (Iori Izaka), Reiko Dan (Koiso, the Chamberlain's Daughter), Masao Shimizu (Kukui), Yunosuke Ito (Mutsuta the Chamberlain), Takako Irie (Chamberlain's Wife), Kamatari Fujiwara (Takebayashi), Keiju Kobayashi (Spy), Akihiko Hirata, Kunie Tanaka, Hiroshi Tachikawa, Tatsuhiko Hari, Tatsuyoshi Ehara, Kenzo Matsui, Yoshio Tsuchiya, Akira Kubo (Young Samurai).

Kayama is the nephew of Ito, a powerful mid-19th-Century Japanese chamberlain. Kayama suspects his uncle of causing political unrest and joins eight samurai for a meeting with Shimizu, one of Ito's superintendents. But they are warned by Mifune, a renegade samurai, that Shimizu is really the man to be feared. He's shown to be correct when a group of Shimizu's men attacks the empty shrine where the meeting is to take place. Mifune fights them off and agrees to help the other samurai end the political strife. They discover that Ito and his family have been kidnaped and set out to rescue his wife and daughter with the aid of information supplied by Shimura, a comrade of Shimizu's. Mifune pretends to join Shimizu to learn of the chamberlain's whereabouts. He persuades Nakadai, one of Shimizu's head men, to lead his warriors away from the hiding place but he is captured before he can tell his own samurai when to attack. Mifune finally manages to float white camellias downstream (the signal for attack) and his men rescue the kidnaped chamberlain. The victorious samurai celebrate but Mifune does not attend, instead choosing to face Nakadai in a duel which Mifune wins. He ignores the congratulations from Kayama and company, leaving them to go off alone once more. Mifune gives his usual stoic performance in this mildly satirical action-adventure tale from noted director Kurosawa. SANJURO can be seen as a comic-book style film, which is actually a sequel to the much better YOJIMBO.

p, Ryuzo Kikushima, Tomoyuki Tanaka; d, Akira Kurosawa; w, Kikushima, Kurosawa, Hideo Oguni (based on the short story "Hibi Heian" by Shugoro Yamamoto); ph, Fukuzo Koizumi, Kozo Saito (Tohoscope); m, Masaru Sato; ed, Kurosawa; art d, Yoshiro Muraki; swordplay advisor, Ryu Kuze.

Action/Adventure Drama   Cas.   (PR:C MPAA:NR)

SANSHO THE BAILIFF*** (1969, Jap.) 125m Daiei-Kyoto/Brandon bw (SANSHO DAYU; AKA: THE BAILIFF)

Yoshiaki Hanayagi (*Zushio*), Kyoko Kagawa (*Anju*), Kinuyo Tanaka (*Tamaki*), Eitaro Shindo (*Sansho*), Akitake Kono (*Taro*), Masao Shimizu (*Masauji Taira*), Ken Mitsuda (*Prime Minister Morozane Fujiwara*), Chieko Naniwa (*Ubatake, Woman Servant*), Kikue Mori (*Priestess*), Kazukimi Okuni (*Norimura*), Yoko Kosono (*Kohagi*), Kimiko Tachibana (*Namiji*), Ichiro Sugai (*Minister Of Justice*), Masashiko Tsugawa (*Zushio as a Boy*), Naoki Fujiwara (*Zushio as an Infant*), Keiko Enami (*Anju as a Girl*), Ryosuke Kagawa (*Ritsushi Kumotake*), Kanji Koshiba (*Kaikudo Naiko*), Shinobu Araki (*Sadaya*), Reiko Kongo (*Shiono*), Shozo Nambu (*Masasue Taira*), Ryonosuke Azuma (*Manager of a Brothel*), Teruko Omi (*The Other Nakagimi*).

A classic of Japanese cinema, SANSHO THE BAILIFF (released in Japan in 1954) is set in the 11th Century Heian era and tells the tale of Hanayagi and his struggle with the limits of feudal society. The picture opens with Hanayagi as a young boy, traveling through the woods with his mother (Tanaka) sister (Kagawa) and a guide, in search of his exiled father. They are soon assaulted by kidnapers. Tanaka is sold into prostitution and exiled to Sado Island, while the children are sold as slaves to a powerful and cruel bailiff (Shindo). Ten years pass and Hanayagi prepares his escape. In order to keep from burdening her brother, or risk having to confess his whereabouts, Kagawa drowns herself in a lake. Hanayagi eventually reaches his destination, Kyoto, and discovers that his father (now dead) has become a folk legend, immortalized in song. In recognition of his father's important role, Hanayagi is granted the post of governor and takes it upon himself to abolish slavery and banish the bailiff from his land. Having done his service to humanity, Hanayagi resigns and renews his search for his mother. He finds her sitting beside her hut, looking weary and blind, and facing towards the sea. SANSHO THE BAILIFF is an awesomely photographed picture which pays great attention to nature and environment. Mizoguchi, in an attempt to film life as he sees it, captures a scene in a painterly way—one which uses the entire palette of contrasts and colors in order to create an atmosphere.

p, Masaichi Nagata; d, Kenji Mizoguchi; w, Yahiro Fuji, Yoshikata Yoda (based on the story "Sansho Dayu" by Ogai Mori); ph, Kazuo Miyagawa; m, Fumio Hayasaka, Kanahichi Odera, Tamekichi Mochizuki; ed, Mitsuji Miyata; art d, Kisaku Ito.

Drama   Cas.   (PR:A MPAA:NR)

SANSONE   (SEE: SAMSON, 1961, Ital.)

SANTA*   (1932, Mex.) 86m Compania Nacional Productora de Peliculas/Rafael Calderon bw

Carlos Orellana, Mimi Derba, Ernesto Guillen, Rosita Arriaga, Juan Martinez Casado, Lupita Tovar.

A blind piano player in a Mexican brothel falls for one of the girls who works there. She needs an operation to save her life and the piano player manages to pay for the surgery. Based on a popular Mexican novel, the film was a critical success in that country. By American standards, however, SANTA suffers from poor production values. The story is sentimental, and the directorial style seems inadequate, using far more close-ups than necessary. The sound is atrocious and often unintelligible. Actors can only do so much under such circumstances and the ensemble here could not compensate for production standards far below those of Hollywood. The film's interest lies in the fact that it is an early example of Latin American filmmaking, and its technical inadequacies reflect the problems poorer nations experienced in establishing a national cinema.

d, Antonio Moreno; w, Carlos Noriega Hope (based on the novel by Don Federico Gamboa).

Drama   (PR:O MPAA:NR)

SANTA AND THE THREE BEARS**   (1970) 63m R&S Film Enterprises/Ellman Enterprises c

The Voices of: Hal Smith, Jean Vanderpyl, Annette Ferra, Bobby Riha.

Two bear cubs are told the story of Santa Claus by a kindly forest ranger at Yellowstone National Park. Naturally the furry tykes want to see Santa for themselves and stay up half-past hibernation time to do so. Their mother wants to go to bed, though, and talks the ranger into impersonating Santa so she can get some sleep. A minor animated film for the holiday season

aimed at the youngest in the family. Anyone over age six will be bored by the syrupy, padded story.

p,d&w, Tony Benedict; ph, (Colorscope, Eastmancolor); md, Joe Leahy; art d, Walt Peregoy; m/l, Doug Goodwin, Leahy, Benedict (sung by Joyce Taylor); animation, Bill Hutten, Tony Love, Volus Jones.

Children's Animation   Cas.   (PR:AAA MPAA:G)

SANTA CLAUS*   (1960, Mex.) 94m Walter Calderon/K. Gordon Murray c

Joseph Elias Moreno (*Santa Claus*), Ken Smith (*Narrator*).

Everybody's favorite stout man is given the camp treatment in this poorly produced, badly dubbed Mexican quickie. Moreno is jolly old St. Nick who puts together his toys with the help of children from around the world, even from places like China where there is no Santa. Problems arise when the devil arrives to induce temptation in the hids. But with the help of Merlin the magician Moreno defeats the cheaply costumed spirit and spreads his good cheer once more. This minor camp classic proved to be a substantial money maker when it was released in the early 1960s. For some reasons, the judges of the 1959 San Francisco International Film Festival saw fit to bestow "Best Family Film" honors on SANTA CLAUS. If this was the best they could pick, heaven help the competition.

p, William Calderon; d, Rene Cardona; w, Cardona, Adolpho Portillo; ph, (Colorscope, Eastmancolor); md, Anthony Diaz.

Holiday Fantasy   (PR:AAA MPAA:NR)

SANTA CLAUS CONQUERS THE MARTIANS zero
(1964) 81m Jalor/EM c

John Call (*Santa Claus*), Leonard Hicks (*Kimar*), Vincent Beck (*Voldar*), Victor Stiles (*Billy*), Donna Conforti (*Betty*), Bill McCutcheon (*Dropo*), Christopher Month (*Bomar*), Pia Zadora (*Girmar*), Leila Martin (*Momar*), James Cahill (*Rigna*), Charles G. Renn (*Hargo*), Carl Don (*Von Green/ Chochem*), Al Nesor (*Stobo*), Josip Elic (*Shim/ Torg*), Jim Bishop (*Lomas*), Doris Rich (*Mrs. Claus*), Ned Wertimer (*Andy Henderson*), Lin Thurmond (*Children's Announcer*), Don Blair (*News Announcer*), Ivor Bodin (*Winky*), Gene Lindsey (*Polar Bear*), Glenn Schaffer, Ronald Rotholz, Tony Ross, Scott Aronesty (*Santa's Helpers*).

Without exaggeration, one of the single worst films ever made. The unhappy children of Mars watch a TV news conference of the jolly, fat man that they monitor from Earth. Martian leaders decide to kidnap St. Nick (Call) and they send off an expedition to Earth. The outer-space visitors are confused by the proliferation of street corner Santas, and two disgustingly adorable children take them to their leader at the North Pole. Beck, the Martian leader, decides that the children (Stiles and Conforti) must be taken back to the red planet along with Call. On the way Beck tries to throw the trio off the ship and is punished by being exiled upon his arrival home. He holes up in a cave and plots revenge. Call sets up a Martian workshop which is invaded by Beck and hench-Martians Elic and Nesor, and they kidnap McCutcheon, a happy Martian dressed in a Santa suit. Beck tries to negotiate his release but is arrested and a fight ensues at the workshop. Using toy weapons, Stiles, Conforti, and their Martian counterparts, Month and Zadora (yes, that Zadora] She began her career of bad filmmaking with this garbage. Befittingly most of her adult work ranks on par with her child actress debut). blows a lot of soap bubbles (nice action there, Santa) and the Martian head decides it's time to send the Earthlings home. He's been touched with the Christmas spirit (and perhaps by other spirits as well). Call has introduced automation to Mars (which doesn't explain how they were technologically advanced enough to build space ships and Earth-monitoring televisions, but never mind) and makes it home just in time to deliver toys on Christmas eve. The film ends with the psuedo-rousing song, "Hooray for Santa Claus," with titles that encourage the audience to sing along. This mush was produced by an ex-unit manager for the popular TV kiddie show of the 1950s, "Howdy Doody." Apparently he learned nothing from Buffalo Bob, for SANTA CLAUS CONQUERS THE MARTIANS is an ugly, poorly produced work that can be easily dismissed by adults but that unintentionally frightened much of its child audience. It was shot on just $200,000 in a studio converted out of an old airport hanger. Using TV technicians, this nonsense actually gave employment to some of Broadway's best rejects. Call was a minor character from the hit show "Oliver]" as was youngster Stiles. Conforti was also a denizen from Broadway, discovered in a minor holiday themed musical called "Here's Love." Despite its amateurish production and worthless acting, SANTA CLAUS turned a good profit and was annually re-released at Christmastime year after year. As Chico Marx so wisely put it, "There ain't no Sanity Clause]"

p, Paul L. Jacobson; d, Nicholas Webster; w, Glenville Mareth (based on a story idea by Jacobson); ph, David Quaid (Eastmancolor); art d, Maurice Gordon; cos, Rames Mostoller; m/l "Hurray for Santa Claus," Milton De Lugg, Roy Alfred; makeup, George Fiala.

**Christmas Story/Science Fic-
tion   Cas.   (PR:C-O MPAA:NR)**

SANTA FE**½ (1951) 89m COL c

Randolph Scott (*Britt Canfield*), Janis Carter (*Judith Chandler*), Jerome Courtland (*Terry Canfield*), Peter Thompson (*Tom Canfield*), John Archer (*Clint Canfield*), Warner Anderson (*Dave Baxter*), Roy Roberts (*Cole Sanders*), Billy House (*Luke Plummer*), Olin Howlin (*Dan Dugan*), Allene Roberts (*Ella Sue*), Jock O'Mahoney [Jock Mahoney] (*Crake*), Harry Cording (*Moore Legrande*), Sven Hugo Borg (*Swede Swanstrom*), Frank Ferguson (*Marshal Bat Masterson*), Irving Pichel (*Harned*), Harry Tyler (*Rusty*), Chief Thundercloud (*Chief Longfeather*), Paul E. Burns (*Uncle Dick Wootton*), Reed Howes, Charles Meredith, Paul Stanton, Richard Cramer, William Haade, Francis McDonald, Frank O'Connor, Harry Tenbrook, James Mason, Guy Wilkerson, Frank Hagney, William Tannen, James Kirkwood, Stanley Blystone, Edgar Dearing, Al Kunde, Art Loeb, Blackie Whiteford, Bud Fine, Richard Fortune, Lane Chandler, Charles Evans, Chuck Hamilton, George Sherwood, Louis Mason, Roy Butler, Ralph Sanford, William McCormack.

The Civil War has ended and Scott, a Confederate soldier, heads West to forget the defeat. He has broken ties with his three brothers (Courtland, Thompson, and Archer) and takes a job with the Santa Fe railroad. But his brothers refuse to take money from Northern businesses and instead get mixed up with some gamblers, led by Roberts. As the railroad progresses Roberts convinces the brothers, along with henchman O'Mahoney (a former stunt man for B-western cowpoke Charles Starrett) to rob the Iron Horse. This leads to an on-train fight climax with Scott naturally coming out the winner. Though this was nowhere near the quality of Scott's later work, SANTA FE has its moments in its grim, action-packed screenplay. Scott is fine as the stoica hero and the color photography uses the locations well.

p, Harry Joe Brown; d, Irving Pichel; w, Kenneth Gamet (based on a story by Louis Stevens and the novel by James Marshall); ph, Charles Lawton, Jr. (Technicolor); ed, Gene Havlick; md, Morris Stoloff; art d, Walter Holscher.

Western (PR:A MPAA:NR)

SANTA FE BOUND** (1937) 58m Reliable bw

Tom Tyler (*Tom Cranshaw*), Jeanne Martel (*Molly Bates*), Richard Cramer (*Stanton*), Charles "Slim" Whitaker (*Morgan*), Edward Cassidy (*Logan*), Lafe McKee (*Sheriff*), Dorothy Woods (*Bridget*), Charles King (*Denton*), Earl Dwire (*Tobbets*), Wally West.

Cramer knocks off Martel's old man in an effort to get his money, ranch, and daughter. Somehow Tyler is thought to be the guilty party and is forced to play the outlaw. But Martel knows all along that he's a nice guy and the two end up together. An entertaining but mostly forgettable independent western.

p, Bernard B. Ray; d, Henri Samuels [Harry S. Webb]; w, Rose Gordon (based on a story by Carl Krusada); ph, William Hyer; ed, Carl Himm.

Western (PR:A MPAA:NR)

SANTA FE MARSHAL** (1940) 66m PAR bw

William Boyd (*Hopalong Cassidy*), Russell Hayden (*Lucky Jenkins*), Marjorie Rambeau (*Ma Burton*), Bernadene Hayes (*Paula Bates*), Earle Hodgins (*Doc Bates*), Britt Wood (*Axel*), Kenneth Harlan (*Blake*), William Pagan, George Anderson, Jack Rockwell, Eddie Dean, Fred Graham, Matt Moore, Duke Green, Billy Jones, Tex Phelps, Cliff Parkinson.

A town in the Old West is overrun by outlaws and U.S. Marshal Boyd is called in to straighten things out. He disguises himself as a member of a medicine show and discovers the ringleader for the outlaws is sweet little old lady Rambeau. Of course she's behind bars by the film's end as everyone expects. Nothing out of the ordinary in this plot though the film plays up humor more than the action end of the western. It's not a successful choice, making this a lesser outing – the 27th – in the HOPALONG CASSIDY series. (See HOPALONG CASSIDY series, Index.)

p, Harry Sherman; d, Lesley Selander; w, Harrison Jacobs (based on characters created by Clarence E. Mulford); ph, Russell Harlan; m, John Leopold; ed, Sherman A. Rose; art d, Lewis Rachmil.

Western (PR:A MPAA:NR)

SANTA FE PASSAGE*** (1955) 91m REP c

John Payne (*Kirby Randolph*), Faith Domergue (*Aurelie St. Clair*), Rod Cameron (*Jess Griswold*), Slim Pickens (*Sam Beekman*), Irene Tedrow (*Ptewaquin*), George Keymas (*Satank*), Leo Gordon (*Tuss McLawery*), Anthony Caruso (*Chavez*).

After being accused of betraying a wagon train to Apache Indians, Payne is rebuffed by his employers. But Cameron gives him another chance, hiring him to guide a large cargo of guns and other munitions through hostile Apache territory. The cargo is owned by Domergue, who's being wooed by both men. She's a half-breed who hates her mixed heritage. When Payne learns of her background, he, too, has to face his prejudices. The interesting themes and exciting action in this late western from Republic are handled well by director Witney. Payne's performance is stoica and powerful while Cameron, who is cast against type, and Domergue are also appealing in their

roles.

p, Sidney Picker; d, William Witney; w, Lillie Hayward (based on a short story by Clay Fisher); ph, Bud Thackery (Trucolor); m, R. Dale Butts; ed, Tony Martinelli; md, Butts; art d, Frank Arrigo; cos, Adele Palmer.

Western (PR:O MPAA:NR)

SANTA FE SADDLEMATES** (1945) 56m REP bw

Sunset Carson, Linda Stirling, Olin Howlin, Roy Barcroft, Rex Lease, Bud Geary, Kenne Duncan, George Chesebro, Bob Wilke, Forbes Murray, Henry Wills, Frank Jaquet, Josh [John] Carpenter, Edmund Cobb, Nolan Leary, Fred Graham, George Magrill, Jack O'Shea, Carol Henry, Billy Vincent.

A group of smugglers is tailed by Carson, a U.S. marshal operating incognito as an outlaw. He's assisted by reporter Stirling and plenty of action later the bad guys are in the pokey. Routine fare for Republic's would-be star Carson. His baby face and high vocal timbre just weren't right for a cowboy hero but somehow he worked for two years grinding out Republic westerns. This was the first of 11 pictures Carson would make with director Carr.

p&d, Thomas Carr; w, Bennett Cohen; ph, William Bradford; ed, Ralph Dixon; md, Richard Cherwin; art d, Frank Hotaling.

Western (PR:A MPAA:NR)

SANTA FE SATAN (SEE: CATCH MY SOUL, 1974)

SANTA FE SCOUTS** (1943) 55m REP bw

Bob Steele (*Tucson Smith*), Tom Tyler (*Stony Brooke*), Jimmie Dodd (*Lullaby Joslin*), Lois Collier (*Claire Robbins*), John James (*Tim Clay*), Elizabeth Valentine (*Minerva Clay*), Tom Chatterton (*Neil Morgan*), Tom London (*Billy Dawson*), Budd Buster (*Wid Neighton*), Jack Ingram (*Frank Howard*), Kermit Maynard (*Ben Henderson*), Rex Lease, Ed Cassidy, Yakima Canutt, Jack Kirk, Curley Dresden, Reed Howes, Bud Geary, Carl Sepulveda, Al Taylor, Kenne Duncan.

Lesser entry in "The Three Mesquiteers" series finds the trio of Steele, Tyler, and Dodd saving a rancher framed for murder and stopping outlaw squatters from unfairly taking over some ranch land and watering their cattle with the rancher's water. The action is fair but there's not enough of it, causing the film to drag. (See THREE MESQUITEERS series, Index.)

p, Louis Gray; d, Howard Bretherton; w, Morton Grant, Betty Burbridge (based on characters created by William Colt MacDonald); ph, Reggie Lanning; m, Mort Glickman; ed, Charles Craft; art d, Russell Kimball.

Western (PR:A MPAA:NR)

SANTA FE STAMPEDE**½ (1938) 58m REP bw

John Wayne (*Stony Brooke*), Ray Corrigan (*Tucson Smith*), Max Terhune (*Lullaby Joslin*), William Farnum (*Dave Carson*), June Martel (*Nancy Carson*), LeRoy Mason (*Gil Byron, Mayor*), Martin Spellman (*Billy Carson*), Genee Hall (*Julie Jane Carson*), Ferris Taylor (*Judge*), Tom London (*Marshal Wood*), Walter Wills (*Harris*), James F. Cassidy (*Newton*), Dick Rush (*Sheriff*), George Chesebro, Bud Osborne, Yakima Canutt, Dick Alexander, Nelson McDowell, Curley Dresden, Duke Lee, Bill Wolfe, Charles King, Ralph Peters.

An old prospector (Farnum) invites the Three Mesquiteers (Wayne, Corrigan, and Terhune) to share a claim with him. Upon arrival the trio discovers Mason, a crooked politician who also wants a piece of the gold and will do anything he can to get it. Farnum is killed and Wayne is framed for the murder but the Mesquiteers right everything by the film's end. The story and direction are fairly routine but the cinematography is better than usual for the series. SANTA FE STAMPEDE also breaks new ground in the history of B westerns with a disturbing scene in which two children are killed on screen when the buckboard they are riding in gets loose and crashes. (See THREE MESQUITEER series, Index.)

p, William Berke; d, George Sherman; w, Luci Ward, Betty Burbridge (based on a story by Ward and characters created by William Colt MacDonald); ph, Reggie Lanning; m, William Lava; ed, Tony Martinelli.

Western Cas. (PR:C MPAA:NR)

SANTA FE TRAIL, THE** (1930) 80m PAR bw (GB: THE LAW RIDES WEST)

Richard Arlen (*Stan Hollister*), Rosita Moreno (*Maria Castinado*), Eugene Pallette (*"Doc" Brady*), Mitzi Green (*Emily*), Junior Durkin (*"Old Timer"*), Hooper Atchley (*Marc Collard*), Luis Alberni (*Juan Castinado*), Lee Shumway (*Slaven*), Chief Standing Bear (*Chief Sutanek*), Blue Cloud (*Eagle Feather*), Chief Yowlachie (*Brown Beaver*), Jack Byron (*Webber*).

Minor western features Arlen as a sheep rancher who stops a land grabber in New Mexico and wins the heart of Moreno as well. Notable mainly for its use of Spanish, something not found in most B westerns. At times, Mexican characters speak their native tongue without any translating subtitles. Though it works cinematically, audiences didn't buy it, which is probably why Spanish is little-used in westerns. The action is only fair and the Indians sound too well-educated to be believed.

p, Sam Mintz; d, Edwin H. Knopf, Otto Brower; w, Mintz, E. E. Paramore, Jr. (based on the novel *Spanish Acres* by Hal Evarts); ph, David Abel; ed, Verna Willis.

Western   (PR:A MPAA:NR)

SANTA FE TRAIL* ½   (1940) 110m FN/WB bw

Errol Flynn *(Jeb Stuart)*, Olivia de Havilland *(Kit Carson Halliday)*, Raymond Massey *(John Brown)*, Ronald Reagan *(George Armstrong Custer)*, Alan Hale *(Barefoot Brody)*, Guinn Williams *(Tex Bell)*, Van Heflin *(Rader)*, Henry O'Neill *(Cyrus Halliday)*, William Lundigan *(Bob Halliday)*, John Litel *(Harlan)*, Gene Reynolds *(Jason Brown)*, Alan Baxter *(Oliver Brown)*, Moroni Olsen *(Robert E. Lee)*, Erville Alderson *(Jefferson Davis)*, Suzanne Carnahan, 'Susan Peters' *(Charlotte Davis)*, Charles D. Brown *(Maj. Sumner)*, David Bruce *(Phil Sheridan)*, Frank Wilcox *(James Longstreet)*, William Marshall *(George Pickett)*, George Haywood *(John Hood)*, Russell Simpson *(Shoubel Morgan)*, Joseph Sawyer *(Kitzmiller)*, Hobart Cavanaugh *(Barber Doyle)*, Spencer Charters *(Conductor)*, Ward Bond *(Townley)*, Wilfred Lucas *(Weiner)*, Charles Middleton *(Gentry)*, Russell Hicks *(J. Boyce Russell)*, Napoleon Simpson *(Samson)*, Cliff Clark *(Instructor)*, Harry Strang *(Sergeant)*, Emmett Vogan *(Lieutenant)*, Selmer Jackson, Joseph Crehan, William Hopper *(Officers)*, Clinton Rosemond, Bernice Pilot, Libby Taylor, Mildred Gover *(Blacks)*, Roy Barcroft, Frank Mayo *(Engineers)*, Grace Stafford *(Farmer's Wife)*, Louis Jean Heydt *(Farmer)*, Lane Chandler *(Adjutant)*, Richard Kipling *(Army Doctor)*, Jack Mower *(Surveyor)*, Trevor Bardette, Nestor Paiva *(Agitators)*, Mira McKinney *(Woman)*, Harry Cording, James Farley, Alan Bridge, Eddy Waller *(Men)*, John Meyer *(Workman)*, Maris Wrixon, Lucia Carroll, Mildred Coles *(Girls)*, Georgia Caine *(Officer's Wife)*, Arthur Aylesworth, Walter Soderling, Henry Hall *(Abolitionists)*, Theresa Harris *(Maid)*, Jess Lee Brooks *(Doorman)*, Eddy Chandler, Edmund Cobb, Ed Peil, Ed Hearn *(Guards)*, Victor Kilian *(Dispatch Rider)*, Creighton Hale *(Telegraph Operator)*, Alec Proper *(Townsman)*, Rev. Neal Dodd, Lafe McKee *(Ministers)*, Addison Richards *(Sheriff)*.

Despite its misleading title, this roaring, action-packed film, directed with great vigor by Curtiz, is not a western and has little to do with the Santa Fe Trail. And though it purports to deal with a serious segment of American history, even that is inaccurate. Flynn is his ever dashing self as he appears at West Point, playing the southern-born J.E.B. Stuart, who later became the South's greatest cavalryman during the Civil War. He arrives, along with mule and dog, wearing an outlandish uniform of his own design which so confuses the sentinels at the post that they mistakenly call out an honor guard to salute what appears to be a high-ranking officer of a foreign power. This auspicious arrival is soon ended when it is learned that Flynn is nothing more than a new cadet reporting to the Point for training. Other than his academic studies, Flynn's real enemy at the Point is Heflin, a wild-eyed radical abolitionist who is out to change the class and caste system of America. He is a secret follower of the fanatic, John Brown, and his political activities finally get Heflin cashiered from the Point. Flynn and his friends, Reagan, playing George Armstrong Custer, Bruce, essaying Phil Sheridan, Wilcox, playing Longstreet, Marshall, enacting the role of George Pickett, and Haywood, playing John Hood, all graduate from the Point in 1854 and are assigned to a western post in Kansas where they must combat the illegal activities of the dreaded Brown, played by Massey. (The collecting of all these gentlemen at West Point at the same time is grossly inaccurate historically. Stuart did graduate in 1854, as the film shows, but not the other future generals of the Civil War; Custer was only 15 years old and living on an Ohio farm when Stuart took his diploma at the Point.) Flynn and Reagan meet and fall in love with perky de Havilland once they are stationed at Fort Leavenworth with the 2nd U.S. Cavalry; she is the daughter of O'Neill, who owns a successful freighting company. Flynn, Reagan, and the other West Pointers are assigned to escort an important shipment of freight but, before reaching their destination, they are stopped by Massey, who tells them that he will pick up his shipment on the open plains and orders his own wagon drivers forward to transfer the shipment. A box breaks open to reveal hidden illegal rifles, which is not specified on the manifest. When Flynn tells Massey that he cannot turn over such an illegal shipment to him, Massey gives a signal and the main body of his fanatical followers swoops down on the small cavalry detachment, taking the guns. Flynn leads his men in a charge to overtake the wagons and one of Massey's sons, Reynolds, is captured when his wagon turns over on him. Reynolds, nursed at Leavenworth by de Havilland, tells how he has wanted to escape his father's emotional stranglehold, that Massey is such an ardent abolitionist that he has committed wholesale slaughter of slave owners in Kansas. (This is based on fact; Brown '1800-1859' ordered the mass executions of proslavers at Osawatomie, Kansas, in 1859.) Reynolds later dies and Flynn, donning civilian clothes and taking along his freight-driving pals, Hale and Williams, goes to town to try to learn about Massey's secret operations. He is captured and taken to Massey's hidden headquarters, a farm where runaway slaves are kept and where Massey is collecting an army in order to take over the state. Reagan and the other West Pointers lead a raid against the remote farm, and, after a pitched battle, free Flynn. Massey and his top aides escape but his Kansas operation is smashed once and for all. Fleeing with Massey is the renegade Heflin and these fanatics later seize Harper's Ferry, the U.S. arsenal in Virginia, planning to start a revolution, but the expected

thousands of supporters do not rally to Massey's standard and Heflin, who has not received the pay Massey has promised, betrays the abolitionist to authorities. Federal troops under the command of Olsen, playing Robert E. Lee (this is historically correct), lay siege to the arsenal while Massey and his followers put up a terrific fight. Massey, realizing Heflin has betrayed him, shoots the turncoat. Flynn, Reagan, and the West Pointers lead a wild charge against the arsenal and it is captured, with Massey taken prisoner. He is later hanged for his crimes, with Olsen stating, "So perish all enemies of the Union!" This is an odd statement in an oddity-glutted movie, in that Olsen, playing Lee, would certainly become an enemy of the Union six years later when the South split from the Union and that Civil War ensued. This film, directed with frantic fury by Curtiz, is really a split-level affair, one which proposes to present American history and does so in a fractured, inaccurate fashion, peopling the production with historical figures, most of whom never knew each other, and on the other hand simply being a rousing adventure yarn. As the latter, SANTA FE TRAIL is a huge success, offering a great romp for Flynn and providing a bevy of colorful characterizations. When scriptwriter Buckner inserts his notion of history into the script, it runs afoul of the facts but Warner Bros., like most studios of that era, concerned itself little with facts, only box office receipts, and this film yielded much for the studio coffers. De Havilland is her feisty, attractive self, playing more of a tomboy than a radiant woman, while Reagan has the "best friend" role who loses her to the handsome Flynn. Exceptional is Massey, whose overacting fits well here with the fanatic Brown whom he would essay again in the low-budgeted SEVEN ANGRY MEN (1955). Baxter, as one of his sons, also gives a weird performance that is attention-getting, and Heflin, a superb actor, here essays the kind of sniveling, conniving coward he expanded upon in THEY DIED WITH THEIR BOOTS ON, ironically a film where Flynn played George Armstrong Custer, not unlike the character of Stuart he presents in SANTA FE TRAIL, and far from the reserved Custer which Reagan offers in this film. The gratuitous patriotism which is certainly pro-South in this film is countered by the softly spoken sympathies Reagan and a few others utter on behalf of Massey, stating that he may be misdirected but his ambition of freeing the slaves is correct. Thus the film straddles the fence and alienates as few viewers as possible. The film was premiered in Santa Fe, New Mexico, five days before its Broadway opening. Flynn received good notices but he was reportedly unhappy with his leading lady, de Havilland, who had refused to return his offscreen affection and he asked that Warners not cast her in this film. After de Havilland got the part over his objections, Flynn made the best of it but knew his personal relationship would never go beyond friendship. De Havilland would later involve herself with director John Huston and this led to a terrific fistfight at a Hollywood party between Flynn and the director, neither besting the other but bloodying some expensive imported clothes.

p, Jack L. Warner, Hal B. Wallis; d, Michael Curtiz; w, Robert Buckner; ph, Sol Polito; m, Max Steiner; ed, George Amy; art d, John Hughes; cos, Milo Anderson; spec eff, Byron Haskin, H.D. Koenekamp; makeup, Perc Westmore.

Adventure   Cas.   (PR:C MPAA:NR)

SANTA FE UPRISING**   (1946) 56m REP bw

Allan "Rocky" Lane, Bobby Blake, Martha Wentworth, Barton MacLane, Jack LaRue, Tom London, Dick Curtis, Forrest Taylor, Emmett Lynn, Hank Patterson, Edmund Cobb, Pat Michaels, Kenne Duncan, Edythe Elliott, Frank Ellis, Art Dillard, Lee Reynolds, Forrest Burns.

Lane is sent out West to help a lady fight off some malicious highwaymen who kidnap little Blake in the process. Lane's gun-toting overpowers the gang and insures little Blake's safe return. (See RED RYDER series, Index.)

p, Sidney Picker; d, R.G. Springsteen; w, Earle Snell; ph, Bud Thackery; ed, William P. Thompson; md, Mort Glickman; art d, Fred A. Ritter; set d, John McCarthy, Jr., Earl Woodin; spec eff, Howard and Theodore Lydecker.

Western   Cas.   (PR:A MPAA:NR)

SANTA'S CHRISTMAS CIRCUS*½   (1966) 60m Gold Star/Mercury c

Frank Wiziarde *(Whizzo, the Clown)*, John Bilyeu *(Santa Claus)*, Dancing Children *(Themselves)*.

Wiziarde was a popular television clown in Kansas City, Missouri and this minor effort is just an expansion of his show, released around the Midwest. First some students of the Johnny Miller Dance Studio in K.C. entertain everyone in "Whizzoland." One little girl remains unhappy so Wiziarde takes her and the others to see some Christmas displays. From there it's off to the North Pole via a chintzy magic carpet ride. There they meet the jolly man in the red suit as interpreted by Bilyeu. He shows them around his toy factory, then explains the true meaning of Christmas. Everyone leaps back onto the carpet and it's a quick ride home to Whizzoland and the film's end. This local personality's holiday special might have looked better if it had been kept on the tube rather than shown in theaters. On the small screen, Wiziarde's little fans, and possibly even their parents, would have had an easier time overlooking the silly plot and bargain basement special effects.

p, Byers Jordan; d, Frank Wiziarde (based on an idea by Jordan); m, Harry Jenks.

Children's Fantasy (PR:AAA MPAA:NR)

SANTEE½ (1973) 93m Vagabond/Crown International c

Glenn Ford *(Santee)*, Michael Burns *(Jody)*, Dana Wynter *(Valerie)*, Jay Silverheels *(John Crow)*, Harry Townes, John Larch, Robert Wilke, Bob Donner, Taylor Lacher, Lindsay Crosby, Charles Courtney, X. Brands, John Hart, Russ McCubbin, Robert Mellard, Boyd "Red" Morgan, Ben Zeller, Brad Merhege.

Ford plays a horse breeder who becomes a bounty hunter. He kills an outlaw and adopts the man's son despite the boy's vow of revenge. Gradually the two become close and a father-son relationship blossoms between them. It is revealed that Ford first took up bounty hunting when his own son was killed by o utlaws years earlier. Finding happiness, he retires from the business but when the local sheriff is shot, the adopted son blames his father. It turns out the real killers are the gang that killed Ford's son. Ford and Burns take them on and successfully wipe out the gang, but at the cost of the youngster's life. Twice the victim of the gang's murderous ways, Ford is left alone and psychologically tormented. This was director Nelson's screen debut after a somewhat successful career as television director. It's not a bad Western though it never reaches the higher levels it aims for; the script with its stiff dialog and unrealistic sequences is too limiting. However, the team of Ford and Burns overcomes script handicaps and creates a fine chemistry that is honest and works well. Watch for Silverheels (Tonto of the "Lone Ranger" television series of the 1950s) in a bit part as a horse tender.

p, Deno Paoli, Edward Platt; d, Gary Nelson; w, Tom Blackburn (based on a story by Brand Bell); ph, Donald Morgan; m, Don Randi; ed, George W. Brooks; art d, Mort Rabinowitz.

Western **Cas.** (PR:O MPAA:PG)

SANTIAGO*** (1956) 92m WB c (GB: THE GUN RUNNERS)

Alan Ladd *(Cash Adams)*, Rossana Podesta *(Isabella)*, Lloyd Nolan *(Clay Pike)*, Chill Wills *(Sidewheel)*, Frank De Kova *(Jingo)*, L.Q. Jones *(Digger)*, Paul Fix *(Trasker)*, George J. Lewis *(Pablo)*, Royal Dano *(Lobo)*, Don Blackman *(Sam)*, Francisco Ruiz *(Juanito)*, Clegg Hoyt *(Dutch)*, Ernest Sarracino *(Jose Marti)*, Natalie Masters *(Governess)*, Willard Willingham *(Keiffer)*, Russ M. Saunders *(Ferguson)*, Edward Colmans *(Lorenzo)*, Rico Alaniz *(Dominguez)*.

Ladd plays a hardened gun runner whose only cares are selfish ones as he takes a shipment to Cuba for use in its fight for independence from Spain. He plans to drop the guns in Florida and take off with the gains but finds that the only way to get paid is to make the trek through the Spanish blockade to the revolutionaries. Furthermore, the only available boat is a rickety old paddle-wheel operated by Wills, whose other passengers include rival gun runner Nolan and Podesta. Nolan is Ladd's old nemesis from the days before Ladd was dishonorably discharged from the cavalry and Nolan was supplying the Apaches with weapons. Podesta is Cuba's Joan of Arc, returning from her attempts to raise U.S. support for her countrymen. Old tensions between Ladd and Nolan quickly flair, given a new spark by the presence of the beautiful Podesta. While defending Podesta's honor against Nolan's passionate advances, Ladd finds his cynicism softened by her high ideals. Finally reaching the revolutionaries, Ladd and Nolan discover that the Cubans are unable to pay for the guns. When Nolan wants to sell out to the Spanish, Ladd faces one last encounter with his adversary before devoting himself to Podesta and her cause. Directed with standard flash by hack Douglas, the film is most entertaining when it concentrates on the comrade-adversary tension, punctuated by snappy insults, between Nolan and Ladd. Both actors expend a great deal of energy in their roles and Nolan makes an almost charming villain. Wills supplies additional laughs and Podesta does not have to do much more than look lovely.

p, Martin Rackin; d, Gordon Douglas; w, Rackin, John Twist (based on the novel *The Great Courage* by Rackin); ph, John Seitz (Warner Color); m, David Buttolph; ed, Owen Marks; art d, Edward Carrere; cos, Marjorie Best, Moss Mabry.

Adventure/Drama (PR:A MPAA:NR)

SANTO AND THE BLUE DEMON VS. THE MONSTERS
(SEE: SANTO Y BLUE DEMON CONTRA LOS MONSTROUS, 1968, Mex.)

SANTO CONTRA BLUE DEMON EN LA ATLANTIDA*
(1968, Mex.) 89m Producciones Sotomayor bw

Santo, Alejandro Cruz, Jorge Rado, Rafael Banquella, Silvia Pasquel, Magda Giner, Rosa Maria Pineiro, Griselda Mejia.

Rado uses mind control to have Santo fight the Blue Demon, in their first picture before teaming up for a number of entries in the wrestling series. But the former Nazi can't keep the two heroes in his power for too long a time. Rado's stomping grounds consist mostly of stock shots borrowed from Inoshiro Honda's KAIJU DAISENSO (1965), so much so that Honda's cinematographer, Eiji Tsuburaya, should have been given credit for SANTO's special effects.

p, Jesus Sotomayer; d, Julian Soler; w, Soler, Rafael Garcia Traversi; ph, spec eff, Raul Martinez Solares.

Adventure (PR:O MPAA:NR)

SANTO CONTRA EL CEREBRO DIABOLICO zero
(1962, Mex.) 85m Peliculas Rodriguez bw

Santo, Fernando Casanova, Ana Bertha Lepe, Roberto Ramirez, Luis Aceves Castaneda, Celia Viberos, Augustino Benedico.

Follow-up to SANTO CONTRA EL REY DEL CRIMEN and SANTO EN EL HOTEL DE LA MUERTE, Curiel's other additions to the SANTO series, the masked wrestler, who always seems a bit heavy to be much of a super-hero. The setting for this installment is the hacienda of Santo's sister, who has been killed by a mysterious woman trying to get at the gold on the hacienda.

p, J. Rodriguez; d, Federico Curiel; w, Curiel, Antonio Orellana, Fernando Oses; ph, Fernando Alvarez Carces Colin.

Horror (PR:C MPAA:NR)

SANTO CONTRA EL DOCTOR MUERTE* (1974, Span./Mex.) 96m Cinematografia Pelimex c

Carlos Romero Marchent, Helga Line, George Rigaud, Antonio Pica, Mirta Miller.

One in many of the series in which the masked wrestler and enforcer of good opposes some evil force, none of which has a decipherable plot or aesthetics beyond the horribly mundane. This time it's a scientist killing beautiful models with a secret virus that can be removed from the dead bodies to produce a chemical that allows for perfect reproductions of paintings. A rather burdensome way to make forgeries, but Santo ends the trivialities soon enough.

d, Rafael Romero Marchent; w, Jose Luis Merino, Marchent; ph, Godofredo Pacheco.

Horror (PR:O MPAA:NR)

SANTO CONTRA LA HIJA DE FRANKENSTEIN*
(1971, Mex.) 97m Cinematografica Calderon (SANTO VS. LA HIJA DE FRANKENSTEIN; LA HIJA DE FRANKENSTEIN; AKA: SANTO VS. FRANKENSTEIN'S DAUGHTER; THE DAUGHTER OF FRANKEN-STEIN) c

Santo, Gina Romand, Roberto Cadendo, Carlos Agosti, Sonia Fuentes, Lucy Gallardo, Jorge Casanova, Anel.

Santo destroys the monster only to combat the daughter of the scientist who created the monster. The daughter is trying to keep herself looking beautiful with a formula that requires the blood of young women, but Santo quickly puts an end to that.

p, Guillermo Calderon; d, Miguel M. Delgado; w, Fernando Oses; ph, Raul Martinez Solares.

Horror (PR:O MPAA:NR)

SANTO CONTRA LA INVASION DE LOS MARCIANOS*
(1966, Mex.) 85m Producciones Cinematograficas (AKA: SANTO VER-SUS THE MARTIAN INVASION) bw

Santo, Maura Monti, Eva Norvind, Wolf Ruvinskis, Belinda Corell, Gilda Miros, El Nazi, Benny Galan, Natanael Leon Frankenstein.

Martians who look strangely like wrestlers come to Earth under the guise of a peaceful mission to warn earthlings against nuclear testing and exploiting outer space. But with their superior powers, particularly a ray-emitting astral eye, they take advantage of the weaker people, including several people they kidnap for purposes of biological investigation. Santo comes to the rescue and blows up the alien vessel, but not before romancing Martians Norvind and Monti, a couple of female wrestlers. Plot doesn't make much sense, but at least it tries to make a point or two about nuclear hazards.

p, Alfonso Rosas Priego; d, Alfredo B. Crevenna; w, Rafael Garcia Traversi; ph, Jorge Stahl, Jr.

Fantasy (PR:O MPAA:NR)

SANTO EN EL MUSEO DE CERA* (1963, Mex.) 92m Filmadora Panamericana (AKA: SAMSON IN THE WAX MUSEUM; SANTO IN THE WAX MUSEUM) bw

Santo, Claudio Brook, Rueben Rojo, Norma Mora, Roxana Bellini, Fernando Oses, Jose Luis Jimenez, Jorge Mondragon, Conception Martinez.

Santo, the masked wrestler, foils the plans of a mad scientist who has found the secret for making wax monsters come alive. Investigating the disappear-ance of photographer Bellini, Santo stumbles across the mad man's creatures, who apparently don't like their master—they finally do him in. There is no plot here, but interesting visual work is achieved.

p, Alberto Lopez; d, Alfonso Corona Blake; w, Fernando Galiana, Julio Porter; ph, Jose Ortez Ramos.

Horror   (PR:O MPAA:NR)

SANTO VS. FRANKENSTEIN'S DAUGHTER
(SEE: SANTO CONTRA LA HIJA DE FRANKENSTEIN, 1971, Mex.)

SANTO VERSUS THE MARTIAN INVASION
(SEE: SANTO CONTRA LA INVASION DE LOS MARCIANOS, 1966, Mex.)

SANTO Y BLUE DEMON CONTRA LOS MONSTRUOS ZERO
(1968, Mex.) 84m Producciones Sotomayor (AKA: SANTO CONTRA LOS MONSTRUOS DE FRANKENSTEIN; SANTO AND THE BLUE DEMON VS. THE MONSTERS) bw

Santo, Alejandro Cruz [Blue Demon], Hedi Blue, Jorge Rado, Carlos Ancira (Bruno Halder), Adalberto Martinez, Vicente Lara, David Alvizu, Gerardo Cepeda, Manuel Leal, Fernando Rosales, Elsa Maria Tako, Yolanda Ponce.

Every classic monster of the cinema that could be remembered, apparently, was brought in to try to deter the wrestling duo of Santo and Cruz (as the Blue Demon). These creatures were vampires, a werewolf, a mummy, a cyclops, and, of course, Frankenstein's monster complete with beard and mustache who can even drive a car. At one point all the monsters make it into the ring at the same time, but still can't defeat the heroes, who eventually make their ways to the mastermind behind the whole thing, a certain crazed scientist. When director Solares couldn't make a living making social commentary pictures, he did a complete about-face and started making wrestling and horror pictures.

p, Jesus Sotomayor; d, Gilberto Martinez Solares; w, Rafael Garcia Traversi; ph, Raul Martinez Solares.

Horror   (PR:O MPAA:NR)

SAP, THE*½
(1929) 80m WB bw

Edward Everett Horton (The Sap), Alan Hale (Jim Belden), Patsy Ruth Miller (Betty), Russell Simpson (The Banker), Jerry Mandy (The Wop), Edna Murphy (Jane), Louise Carver (Mrs. Sprague), Franklin Pangborn (Ed Mason).

An almost-funny spoof portrays daydreamer Horton, who finally gets his chance to make it big, and to everyone's surprise, succeeds. It comes about when Horton takes the rap for an embezzlement scheme set up by his brother-in-law, giving Horton a chance to make a killing at the stock market and cover up the crime before anyone notices. Silent version had been made in 1926, in which Kenneth Harlan took the Horton role. Although he tries very hard, Horton is unable to overcome the wretched material.

d, Archie L. Mayo; w, Robert Lord (based on the play by William A. Grew); ph, Dev Jennings; ed, Desmond O'Brien.

Comedy   (PR:A MPAA:NR)

SAP FROM ABROAD, THE   (SEE: SAP FROM SYRACUSE, THE, 1930)

SAP FROM SYRACUSE, THE**½
(1930) 68m PAR bw (GB: THE SAP FROM ABROAD)

Jack Oakie (Littleton Looney), Ginger Rogers (Ellen Saunders), Granville Bates (Hycross), George Barbier (Senator Powell), Sidney Riggs (Nick Pangolos), Betty Starbuck (Flo Goodrich), Verree Teasdale (Dolly Clark), J. Malcolm Dunn (Capt. Barker), Bernard Jukes (Bells), Walter Fenner (Henderson), Jack Daley (Hopkins), Kathryn Reese.

This was only Rogers' third screen appearance, and the first in a strictly dramatic part which didn't depend on her dancing and singing. Her performance produced some interest in her, and she soon had an illustrious career in Hollywood. She plays a wealthy heiress on board a Europe-bound luxury liner. Also on board is Jack Oakie, a laborer who is mistaken for a famous engineer. Romance quickly develops between Rogers and Oakie, as Oakie soaks up all the praise and attention he receives because of his mistaken identity. He also saves Rogers from a plot by Starbuck and Teasdale to get at her money. With the charming smiles of Rogers and Oakie, and directer Sutherland around to liven up the flat material, this project couldn't go wrong. Songs include: "Ah, What's the Use," "How I Wish I Could Sing a Love Song," and "Capitalize That Thing Called IT" (E.Y. Harburg, Johnny Green).

d, A. Edward Sutherland; w, Gertrude Purcell (based on the play by John Wray, Jack O'Donnell, John Hayden); ph, Larry Williams; ed, Helene Turner; art d, William Saulter; cos, Aileen Hamilton.

Musical/Comedy   (PR:A MPAA:NR)

SAPHO   (SEE: WARRIOR EMPRESS, THE, 1961, Fr./Ital.)

SAPPHIRE***
(1959, Brit.) 92m Artna/UNIV c

Nigel Patrick (Supt.), Yvonne Mitchell (Mildred), Michael Craig (Inspector Learoyd), Paul Massie (David Harris), Bernard Miles (Ted Harris), Olga Lindo (Mrs. Harris), Earl Cameron (Dr. Robbins), Gordon Heath (Paul Slade), Jocelyn Britton (Patsy), Harry Baird (Johnny Fiddle), Orlando Martins (Barman), Rupert Davies (Ferris), Freda Bamford (Sgt. Cook), Robert Adams (Horace Big Cigar), Yvonne Buckingham (Sapphire).

Good detective yarn starring Patrick and Craig as detectives of Scotland Yard who are investigating the murder of a young black woman whose light-colored skin allowed her to pass as white. Suspects range from Massie, as the girl's white boyfriend, and his parents, who feared for their son's career, to the black youths the girl tosses aside when she is accepted by whites. Craig's prejudice, as well as just about everyone else's, adds a good deal of tension to the sleuthing, which Patrick pursues in a highly dignified, professional manner despite the additional obstacles. Material stays on safe ground about shedding light on the problem of racial prejudice which was rampant in England in the late 1950s. The picture was made shortly after race riots occurred in London and Nottingham.

p, Michael Relph; d, Basil Dearden; w, Janet Green, Lukas Heller (based on the screenplay by Green); ph, Harry Waxman (Eastmancolor); m, Philip Green; ed, John Guthridge; art d, Carmen Dillon.

Drama   (PR:A MPAA:NR)

SAPS AT SEA**½
(1940) 57m UA bw

Oliver Hardy (Oliver Hardy), Stan Laurel (Stan Laurel), James Finlayson (Dr. J.H. Finlayson), Ben Turpin (Mixed-Up Plumber), Dick Cramer (Nick Grainger), Eddie Conrad (Professor O'Brien), Harry Hayden (Mr. Sharp), Charlie Hall (Apartment Desk Clerk), Patsy Moran (Switchboard Operator), Gene Morgan, Charles A. Bachman, Bud Geary, Jack Greene (Officers), Eddie Borden (Berserk Victim), Robert McKenzie (Capt. McKenzie), Ernie Alexander (Newsboy), Mary Gordon (Mrs. O'Riley), Jack Hill (Man Beneath Auto), Walter Lawrence (Pedestrian), Carl Faulkner (Harbor Police Officer), Harry Evans, Ed Brady (Store Dress Extras), Patsy O'Byrne (Mother), Francesca Santoro/ Jackie Horner (shared role of Girl with Doll), Harry Bernard (Harbor Patrol Captain), Sam Lufkin, Constantine Romanoff (Workmen at Horn Factory), Narcissus the Goat.

This was the last film Laurel and Hardy made with Hal Roach before breaking away in the name of artistic freedom but things didn't go as planned for the successful comic duo. They were also separated from several of the many characters, such as James Finlayson and Charlie Hall, who added life to their features. SAPS AT SEA is an uneven picture. In one sense it offers some of the duo's most ingenuous routines, but when the four writers fail to come up with a good gag, the comedy lapses into forced slapstick. Thin plot has Laurel and Hardy as employees at a horn manufacturing company, their jobs being to test the horns. When Hardy suffers a nervous breakdown because of all the noise, Doc Finlayson suggests a quiet cruise. But, since Hardy is afraid of water, they settle for staying in a small boat docked securely at the harbor. They're adrift very soon, however, when an escaped convict, Cramer, sneaks on board and sets them out to sea. Cramer takes over the ship and forces the boys to be his servants. The saving grace against the vicious criminal is Hardy's temper tantrums at the sound of a horn, one of which Laurel just happens to have aboard. Hardy knocks Cramer cold, then ends up in jail himself, when displaying to the police the tactics he used in apprehending the prisoner. One of the highlights is the dinner of shoestrings, lamp-wicks, and other odds and ends Laurel and Hardy put together to serve Cramer when there is no food on the ship. (SEE LAUREL AND HARDY series, Index.)

p, Hal Roach; d, Gordon Douglas; w, Charles Rogers, Felix Adler, Gil Pratt, Harry Langdon; ph, Art Lloyd; m, Marvin Hatley; ed, William Ziegler; art d, Charles D. Hall; set d, William L. Stevens; spec eff, Roy Seawright.

Comedy   Cas.   (PR:A MPAA:G)

SARABA MOSUKUWA GURENTAI
(SEE: GOODBYE MOSCOW, 1968, Jap.)

SARABAND***
(1949, Brit.) 96m EAL/EL c (GB: SARABAND FOR DEAD LOVERS)

Stewart Granger (Count Philip Konigsmark), Joan Greenwood (Sophie Dorothea), Francoise Rosay (Electress Sophie), Flora Robson (Countess Platen), Frederick Valk (Elector Ernest Augustus), Peter Bull (Prince George-Louis), Anthony Quayle (Durer), Megs Jenkins (Frau Busche), Michael Gough (Prince Charles), Jill Balcon (Knesbeck), Cecil Trouncer (Major Eck), David Horne (Duke George William), Mercia Swinburne (Countess Eleanore), Miles Malleson (Lord Of Misrule), Allan Jeayes (Governor at Ahlden), Guy Rolfe (Envoy), Barbara Leake (Maria), Noel Howlett (Count Platen), Anthony Lang (Young Prince George), Rosemary Lang (Young Princess Sophie), Edward Sinclair (Nils), Aubrey Mallalieu, Victor Adams, Margaret Vines, Peter George, W. E. Holloway, Myles Eason, Janet Howe, Peter Albrecht, Anthony Steel, Christopher Lee, John Gregson,

Sandra Dorne, Barbara Murray.

A lush period piece garnished with lavish costumes and luxurious settings that tells the story of a doomed romance between Greenwood and Granger. Forced into a marriage with a young Prince, who soon becomes King George I of England, Greenwood leads a life of romantic disillusionment. Her heart is healed, however, when she falls in love with Granger, a Swedish Count. Their plans to flee are overheard by Robson, a jealous countess who is also Granger's former mistress. Robson informs the King of Greenwood's plan and Granger is soon found dead. Ending on a sombre note, Greenwood is sent to a remote castle to live a life of broken hearted isolation. For fans of this sort of spectacle, SARABAND is one that will border on a teary-eyed experience. Ealing Studios, best known for its superb comedies, attempted to broaden its image with SARABAND. Not only was the film an exercise in romanticism, it was also the studio's first color film.

p, Michael Relph; d, Basil Dearden, Relph; w, John Dighton, Alexander Mackendrick (based on the novel by Helen Simpson); ph, Douglas Slocombe (Technicolor); m, Alan Rawsthorne; ed, Michael Truman; md, Ernest Irving; art d, Relph, Jim Morahan, William Kellner; cos, Georges Benda.

Romance/Historical Drama   **(PR:A MPAA:NR)**

SARABAND FOR DEAD LOVERS   (SEE: SARABAND, 1949, Brit.)

SARACEN BLADE, THE½**   (1954) 77m COL c

Ricardo Montalban (Pietro), Betta St. John (Iolanthe), Rick Jason (Enzio), Carolyn Jones (Elaine of Siniscola), Whitfield Conner (Frederick II), Michael Ansara (Count Siniscola), Edgar Barrier (Baron Rogliano), Nelson Leigh (Isaac), Pamela Duncan (Zenobia), Frank Pulaski (Donati), Leonard Penn (Haroun), Nyra Monsour (Maria), Edward Coch (Giuseppi), Gene D'Arcy (Italian Prince), Poppy Deluando (Gina).

Plenty of action adorns the screen as Montalban plays a common man who has risen in status in order to go through with his plans for revenge against Ansara and Jason, the count and son responsible for the death of Montalban's father. To carry out his scheme, Montalban marries Jones, while really in love with St. John, the wife of Jason. His stubbornness pays off when his revenge is fulfilled. In the end he wins the hand of St. John, his true love. Performed and directed in standard fashion, placing most of the emphasis on the action sequences. The lush backgrounds add to the flavor of the times, although several scenes are tinted black-and- white footage instead of color. This vengeance theme is an almost exact replica of that from the John Wayne vehicle KING OF THE PECOS (1936), only with a different setting and time period.

p, Sam Katzman; d, William Castle; w, DeVallon Scott, George Worthing Yates (based on the novel by Frank Yerby); ph, Henry Freulich (Technicolor); ed, Gene Havlick.

Drama/Adventure   **(PR:A MPAA:NR)**

SARAGOSSA MANUSCRIPT, THE½**
    (1972, Pol.) 155m Kamera-Film Polski/Amerpol bw (REKOPIS ZNALEZIONY W SARAGOSSIE; AKA: ADVENTURES OF A NOBLE-MAN; MANUSCRIPT FOUND IN SARAGOSSA)

Zbigniew Cybulski (Capt. Alfons van Worden), Kazimierz Opalinski (Hermit), Iga Cembrzynska (Princess Emina), Joanna Jedryka (Princess Zibelda), Slawomir Linder (van Worden's Father), Miroslawa Lombardo (van Worden's Mother), Aleksander Fogiel (Spanish Nobleman), Franciszek Pieczka (Pascheco), Ludwik Benoit (Pascheco's Father), Barbara Krafftowna (Camilla), Pola Raksa (Inezilla), August Kowalczyk (Envoy of the Holy Inquisition), Adam Pawlikowski (Cabalist), Beata Tyszkiewicz (Dona Rebeca Uzeda), Gustaw Holoubek (Don Pedro Velasquez), Leon Niemczyk (Don Avadoro), Krzysztof Litwin (Don Lopez Soarez), Stanislaw Igar (Don Gaspar Soarez), Bogumil Kobiela (Toledo), Juliusz Jablczynski (Aquillar), Elzbieta Czyzewska (Frasquetta), Janusz Klosinski (Frasquetta's Husband), Jan Machulski (Count Pena Flor), Zdzislaw Maklakiewicz (Don Roque Busqueros), Henryk Hunko (Thug from the Holy Inquisition), Feliks Chmurkowski (Father of Don Lopez), Jerzy Przybylski (Don Moro), Jadwiga Krawczyk (Donna Inez Moro), Edmund Fetting.

Army captain Cybulski finds himself in the company of beautiful princesses and ghosts, and among complex and mysterious happenings, as he travels in the mountains outside of Madrid. Although the film is not without its humor, an aura of unpleasantness lurks about the captain. The author, Potocki, committed suicide a year after finishing this novel. This film was released in Poland in 1965, and was three hours long. It was to be the last film of Cybulski (known in Europe as the Polish James Dean); he was killed in a train accident in Poland in 1967 at the age of 41. (In Polish; English subtitles.)

d, Wojciech J. Has; w, Tadeusz Kwiatkowski (based on the novel by Jan Potocki); ph, Mieczyslaw Jahoda (Dyaliscope); m, Krzysztof Penderecki; art d, Jerzy Skarzyns ki, Tadeusz Myszorek.

Mystery   **(PR:A MPAA:NR)**

SARAH AND SON½**   (1930) 86m PAR bw

Ruth Chatterton (Sarah Storm), Fredric March (Howard Vanning), Fuller Mellish, Jr (Jim Gray), Gilbert Emery (John Ashmore), Doris Lloyd (Mrs. Ashmore), William Stack (Cyril Belloc), Philippe de Lacy (Bobby).

Early drama starring Chatterton, who finds herself family-less after her shiftless husband sells their child to a rich couple, then leaves her. Though Chatterton begs Emery and Lloyd to give her child back, they slam the door in her face. Several years later, after Chatterton has established herself as an opera star, she once again makes a call for her son, this time meeting with success. March plays a lawyer and brother of the couple that bought the child; it is due to his change of heart and growing fondness for Chatterton that the child is returned to his rightful mother. The director, Dorothy Arzner, was the only commercial female director at the time; she did a creditable job, but it was the skill of Chatterton that gave the rather overly sentimental material the needed momentum.

d, Dorothy Arzner; w, Zoe Akins (based on the novel by Timothy Shea); ph, Charles Lang; ed, Vera Willis.

Drama   **(PR:A MPAA:NR)**

SARATOGA*½**   (1937) 94m MGM bw

Jean Harlow (Carol Clayton), Clark Gable (Duke Bradley), Lionel Barrymore (Grandpa Clayton), Walter Pidgeon (Hartley Madison), Frank Morgan (Jesse Kiffmeyer), Una Merkel (Fritzi O'Malley), Cliff Edwards (Tip O'Brien), George Zucco (Dr. Beard), Jonathan Hale (Frank Clayton), Hattie McDaniel (Rosetta), Frankie Darro (Dixie Gordon), Carl Stockdale (Boswell), Henry Stone (Hard Riding Hurley), Ruth Gillette (Mrs. Hurley), Charley Foy (Valet), Robert Emmett Keane (Auctioneer), Edgar Dearing (Medbury the Trainer), Frank McGlynn, Sr. (Kenyon), Margaret Hamilton (Maizie), Lionel Pape, Pat West, John Hyams (Horse Owners), Sam Flint (Judge), Harrison Greene (Clipper), Irene Franklin, Bill Carey, Ernie Stanton, Franklyn Ardell, John "Skins" Miller, Hank Mann, Nick Copeland, Bert Roach (Passengers on Train), Forbes Murray (Pullman Steward), George Reed, Billy McLain (Butlers), Si Jenks (Gardener), George Chandler, Drew Demarest (Cameramen), Mel Ruick (Tout), Patsy O'Connor (Hurley's Kid), Charles R. Moore, Herbert Ashley (Bartenders), Fred "Snowflake" Toones (Train Porter), Hooper Atchley (Bidder), Gertrude Simpson (Bit), Joseph E. Bernard (Attendant), Walter Robbins (Limpy), Edward "Bud" Flanagan 'Dennis O'Keefe' (Steve, a Bidder), Mary Dees, Geraldine Dvorak (Harlow's Doubles), Paula Winslow (Harlow's Voice Double).

A sharp-witted and charming comedy set amidst a background of horse stables and racing tracks which, sadly, marked the final film appearance for its platinum blonde star, Jean Harlow, who died before the film's completion. Harlow stars as the daughter of an impoverished horse breeder, Hale, who loses his Saratoga breeding farm to gambler and friend, Gable, as payment for a pile of debts that have accrued. Harlow, after an absence in New York where she became engaged to wealthy stockbroker Pidgeon, returns to Saratoga, only to have her father die soon afterwards of a heart attack. Pidgeon, as it turns out, also has lost a great deal of money to Gable and hopes to win it back. Harlow, however, refuses to let him gamble as she has been sheltered, at her father's insistence, from the evils of the race track. Although Gable and Harlow make as if they hate each other, there is an obvious attraction between the pair. Gable has, in the meantime, hooked up with Merkel, an old friend, whose husband, Morgan, is jealous of Gable's indefatigable charms. Gable sets a plan into motion to win another wad of money from Pidgeon, this time with the help of Merkel who has recently purchased a horse and, with it, the contract of top jockey Darro. With Darro riding, Gable is sure to beat Pidgeon's horse. By now Harlow has completely fallen for the gambler and has written a note to her fiance announcing the end of their engagement. Gable, at his most noble, breaks off the budding romance with Harlow in order to abide by her father's wishes and keep her away from a future at the race track. Heartbroken, Harlow purchases Darro's contract from Merkel. Unaware of the change in riders, Gable bets a fortune against Pidgeon. Trying to save Gable from ruin, Merkel quickly hires a replacement jockey and seals Gable's victory. Overlooking what Harlow did, Gable realizes that he still loves her and Harlow, realizing the same, agrees to run off with him, planning their future around the next race. SARATOGA was, in its earliest stages, to have been a vehicle which would again team Gable and Lombard, but contractual difficulties put Lombard on the set of NOTHING SACRED opposite Fredric March instead. Although Harlow had been suffering from faltering physical health (just prior to shooting she underwent severe oral surgery) and a disastrous personal life–1932 saw the pathetic suicide of husband Paul Bern, 1934 saw the end of a one-year marriage to director Robert Rossen, and in 1936 lover William Powell left her–MGM head Louis B. Mayer decided to cast her in the lead. Harlow may not have been in the best of health, but her performance was still a superb one, perhaps the best of her career, and perhaps because she knew it would be her last. With the film nearly completed Harlow collapsed on the set. After being revived, she was sent home to rest (everyone thought she was merely fatigued) under the care of her mother, an overprotective woman whose severe belief in faith-healing kept the 26-year-old platinum beauty at a safe distance from doctors. When she was finally admitted into the hospital it was too late, Harlow had died of cerebral edema, a complication caused by uremic poisoning, on June 7, 1937. Thousands paid their respects at Forest Lawn Cemetery to bid farewell to their favorite starlet. The problem still existed, however, of finishing SARATOGA. A statement released by Mayer announced: "The story SARATOGA in the form it was photographed up to this time is no more. In accordance with our policy it was written for two distinct, strong personalities, Clark Gable and Jean Harlow. Jean Harlow has passed on. Therefore production on the picture will be indefinitely delayed until we can rewrite the story to fit some other feminine personality. All that has been photographed to date, and we were within a week of the picture's completion, will be discarded." Mayer quickly dismissed this idea, however (or perhaps never intended to abide by it at all), when letters poured into MGM begging for the studio to release the star's final effort. A search was then begun to find an actress who could stand in for Harlow. Mary Dees was chosen for the majority of the scenes (which were hastily rewritten and reduced to a minimum of dialog for "Harlow"), with Geraldine Dvorak appearing in others. By photographing the double from behind while wearing a large floppy hat, the illusion was, to some extent, preserved. To duplicate Harlow's voice (which was disguised by a cold and cough that the screenwriters had devised) one Paula Winslow was hired. However unorthodox or immoral, this was not the only time for a lead actor to have a double in a film--Tyrone Power died during SOLOMON AND SHEBA and all of his scenes were reshot with Yul Brynner in his place; a sickly W.C. Fields was replaced by a double for numerous scenes in POPPY, after David Niven's death during THE CURSE OF THE PINK PANTHER Rich Little dubbed the actor's voice in many scenes; and in the cult film PLAN 9 FROM OUTER SPACE the director's wife's chiropractor doubled for the dead Bela Lugosi. On July 23, 1937, just over a month after Harlow's death, SARATOGA was released to a resounding box-office success, becoming one of the largest moneymakers of the year. Although money rolled into MGM, the studio still suffered from the thought of having to cancel or recast the films that Harlow was still scheduled for--TELL IT TO THE MARINES which would have cast her opposite Spencer Tracy and Robert Taylor, THE BEST DRESSED WOMAN IN PARIS penned by Edgar Selwyn (the "wyn" half of Goldwyn Pictures), two Hunt Stromberg productions, MAIDEN VOYAGE and SPRING TIDE, and IN OLD CHICAGO, a Tyrone Power-Dom Ameche starrer in which she was replaced by Alice Faye. SARATOGA includes a pair of tunes for the soundtrack, "The Horse with the Dreamy Eyes" and the title tune "Saratoga" (Walter Donaldson, Bob Wright, Chet Forrest).

p, Bernard H. Hyman; d, Jack Conway; w, Anita Loos, Robert Hopkins; ph, Ray June; m, Edward Ward; ed, Elmo Veron; art d, Cedric Gibbons, John Detlie; set d, Edwin B. Willis; cos, Dolly Tree.

Comedy   **(PR:A   MPAA:NR)**

SARATOGA TRUNK***   (1945) 135m WB bw

Gary Cooper (*Col. Clint Maroon*), Ingrid Bergman (*Clio Dulaine*), Flora Robson (*Angelique Buiton*), Jerry Austin (*Cupidon*), John Warburton (*Bartholomew Van Steed*), Florence Bates (*Mrs. Coventry Bellop*), Curt Bois (*Augustin Haussy*), John Abbott (*Roscoe Bean*), Ethel Griffies (*Mme. Clarissa Van Steed*), Marla Shelton (*Mrs. Porcelain*), Helen Freeman (*Mrs. Nicholas Dulaine*), Sophie Huxley (*Charlotte Dulaine*), Fred Essler (*Mons. Begue*), Louis Payne (*Raymond Soule*), Sarah Edwards (*Miss Diggs*), Adrienne D'Ambricourt (*Grandmother Dulaine*), Jacqueline DeWit (*Guilia Forosini*), Minor Watson (*J.P. Reynolds*), J. Lewis Johnson, Libby Taylor, Lillian Yarbo (*Servants*), Geneva Williams (*Blackberry Woman*), Ruby Dandridge (*Turbaned Vendor*), Paul Bryant, Shelby Bacon (*Urchins*), Peter Cusanelli (*Coffee Proprietor*), George Humbert (*Jambalya Proprietor*), Bertha Woolford (*Flower Woman*), George Reed (*Carriage Driver*), Amelia Liggett (*Mme. Begue*), George Beranger (*Leon the Head Waiter*), John Sylvester (*Young Man Escort*), Edmond Breon (*McIntyre*), William B. Davidson (*Mr. Stone*), Edward Fielding (*Mr. Bowers*), Thurston Hall (*Mr. Pound*), Alice Fleming (*Woman on Piazza*), Ralph Dunn (*Engineer*), Lane Chandler (*Al*), Glenn Strange (*Cowboy*), Chester Clute (*Hotel Clerk*), Theodore Von Eltz (*Hotel Manager*), Monte Blue (*Fireman on Train*), Franklyn Farnum (*Gambler*), Bob Reeves (*Bodyguard*), Al Ferguson, Hank Bell (*Cowhands*), Dick Elliott (*Politician*), Frank Hagney (*Leader of Soule's Gang*), Alan Bridge (*Engineer of Soule's Gang*), Georges Renavent (*Ship's Captain*), Robert Barron (*Officer*), Louis Mercier (*1st Mate*), Gino Corrado (*Diner*), Major Sam Harris, Franklyn Farnum (*Gamblers*).

After Cooper and Bergman scored in FOR WHOM THE BELL TOLLS at Paramount, this was rushed into production in February 1943 and finished in late May, with Wood shooting hundreds of thousands of feet of film. The picture, along with several others, was not released to the general public until after the end of WW II but had been seen for almost two years by members of the armed forces. It was one of several movies made but not released during the war by Warner Brothers. The others were DEVOTION, MY REPUTATION, and THE TWO MRS. CARROLLS, which didn't come out until 1947. Here, screenwriter Robinson took Ferber's best seller, an essentially shallow romance novel, and adapted it well enough for the two stars to merit a huge box-office return for the time, upwards of $5 million. It's 1875 in New Orleans. Bergman is the half-creole illegitimate daughter of a Louisiana man who'd slept with a local woman. After Bergman's mother's death, she vowed to wreak havoc on her late father's family. Bergman sweeps into town from Paris with her bizarre retinue, which includes Austin, a dwarf, and Robson, a mulatto maid. (Robson's performance gained the film's only Oscar nomination for the movie as Best Supporting Actress.) Bergman is in the French market area near the docks when she meets Cooper, a lanky Texan. They flirt with each other and Robson makes her feelings clear about what Bergman is doing. She'd prefer her mistress stay away from this drawling gambler. Since New Orleans is such a small town, it's not long before tongues are wagging over their romance, essentially the same sort of malicious rumors which attended the love affair between Bergman's deceased parents. Cooper has to go north to Saratoga Springs on business and thinks this might be an opportunity to disengage himself from Bergman, whom he has correctly assessed to be a gold digger, although his heart is in her hands. Saratoga Springs was the watering hole for the wealthiest easterners of the era and it isn't long before Bergman follows Cooper there with the express purpose of finding herself a rich man to marry. Upon arriving, Bergman pretends she is a rich French woman, carrying the ruse off with the $10,000 she's received from her father's snobbish family in return for leaving New Orleans. In her anger, she also stipulated that her mother be buried in the crypt of her father's family. (There are no graves in New Orleans because of the water table and everyone must be interred above ground, as the city is actually below the level of the Gulf and only kept dry by a series of levees.) Bates, who knows everyone in Saratoga, is quick to spot Bergman as a phony. She checks up on Bergman's simulated background and confronts her with it, offering to arrange an introduction to Warburton, a big-bucks railroad man, in return for some cash if a marriage is made. Bergman refuses Bates and says she'll do it herself. Bates laughs and likes Bergman's spunk and tosses the money arrangement aside, agreeing to make the introduction anyhow. Cooper is observing all of this with some amusement but he hates the thought of Bergman being so money-hungry, especially since he does love her. Meanwhile, Cooper is involved in business with Warburton and some other wealthy men, and they hope to get control of the railroad to Saratoga (the Saratoga Trunk Line, which is how the title came to pass) over a rival group. Austin becomes an aide to Cooper and there's a physical battle between the two groups, during which Austin is hurt. Warburton's mother, Griffies, comes to Saratoga and doesn't believe a word of Bergman's background, but Bates, who is sort of the Elsa Maxwell of her day, speaks on Bergman's behalf and Griffies is somewhat mollified. Warburton is not fooled by Bergman but he loves her anyhow and asks her to marry. The battle between the two railroad groups winds up in a crash between two trains, and Cooper comes back to town with Austin in his arms just as Bergman and Warburton are about to announce their marriage at a fancy-dress ball. Upon seeing Cooper, who was also injured, Bergman forgets about her arranged romance with Warburton and races to Cooper in front of a horde of astonished guests attending the party. Wallis had left Warner Brothers a while before to take up residence at Paramount as an independent, and although this was not nearly one of his best productions, it still is remembered fondly by devotees of Cooper and Bergman, who wore a dark wig for the role and whose innate sexiness was allowed to run rampant in this picture, a great change from the noble women she'd usually essayed. It was not a great movie, just a good one.

p, Hal B. Wallis; d, Sam Wood; w, Casey Robinson (based on the novel by Edna Ferber); ph, Ernest Haller; m, Max Steiner; ed, Ralph Dawson; md, Leo F. Forbstein; prod d, Joseph St. Amaad; art d, Carl Jules Weyl; set d, Fred MacLean; cos, Leah Rhodes; spec eff, Lawrence Butler; m/l, "As Long as I Live," "Goin' Home" (Steiner, Charles Tobias), "Ah Suzette Chere" (sung by Ingrid Bergman); makeup, Perc Westmore.

Period Drama   **(PR:A-C   MPAA:NR)**

SARDINIA: RANSOM***   (1968, Ital.) 110m Clesi-Euro International c
(SEQUESTRO DI PERSONA)

Franco Nero (*Gavino*), Charlotte Rampling (*Cristina*), Frank Wolff (*Osilo*), Pier Luigi Apra (*Marras Francesco*).

Former documentarist Mingozzi brought his skill for discerning facts to this dramatized version of the internal conflict on the rugged terrain of Sardinia. The peasants have an ancient custom of kidnaping and exchanging the victim for land. In this case the victim is a student, son of wealthy merchants. His kidnaping creates a stir among the police and his family, and friend Nero comes up with a plan that exposes the criminal who has been taking advantage of the peasant custom. A hand-held camera adds a realistic atmosphere to the story. A fine job is done of integrating the legend and folklore of the island into the story.

p, Silvio Clementelli; d, Gianfranco Mingozzi; w, Mingozzi, Ugo Pirro; ph, Ugo Piccone; m, Riz Ortolani; art d, Sergio Canevari.

Drama   **(PR:C   MPAA:NR)**

SARDONICUS   (SEE: MR. SARDONICUS, 1961)

SARGE GOES TO COLLEGE*½   (1947) 63m MON bw

Freddie Stewart (*Freddie Trimball*), June Preisser (*Dodie Rogers*), Frankie Darro (*Roy Donne*), Warren Mills (*Lee Watson*), Noel Neill (*Betty Rogers*), Arthur Walsh (*Arthur Walsh*), Alan Hale, Jr (*Sarge*), Russ Morgan (*Russ Morgan*), Monte Collins (*Dean McKinley*), Frank Cady (*Professor Edwards*), Margaret Brayton (*Miss Koregmeyer*), Selmer Jackson (*Capt. Handler*), Earl Bennett (*Eddie*), Margaret Burt (*Mrs. Rogers*), Harry Tyler (*Mr. Rogers*), Pat Goldin (*Landlord*), William Forrest (*Col. Winters*), Irwin Kaufman (*George*), Russ Morgan Orchestra, Jack McVea Orchestra, Jam Session, Candy

Candido, Abe Lyman, Wingy Manone, Les Paul, Jess Stacy, Joe Venuti, Jerry Wald.

Barren plot is about a tough and not-very-bright marine sergeant (Hale) taking it easy, before undergoing a serious operation, by going to college (of all places). This sets the stage for the Sarge to go through dramatics more typical of a high school student. It's all just an excuse for a musical display anyway, which is integrated quite well into the meager story. Guitar great Les Paul is among the many performers. Songs include: "I'll Close My Eyes" (Buddy Kaye, Billy Reid); "Penthouse Serenade" (Will Jason, Val Burton); "Somebody Else is Taking My Place" (Dick Howard, Bob Ellsworth, Russ Morgan); "Open the Door, Richard" (Dusty Fletcher, John Mason, Jack McVea, Don Howell, performed by Jack McVea and His Orchestra), "Two Are the Same as One," "Blues In B Flat." Other numbers include those by Henry Nemo, Sid Robin.

p&d, Will Jason; w, Hal Collins (based on a story by Henry Edwards); ph, Mack Stengler; ed, Jason Bernie; md, Edward Kay; art d, Dave Milton; m/l.

Musical   (PR:A   MPAA:NR)

SARONG GIRL**   (1943) 70m MON bw

Ann Corio (*Dixie Barlow*), Tim Ryan (*Tim Raynor*), Irene Ryan (*Irene Raynor*), Mantan Moreland (*Maxwell*), Bill Henry (*Jeff Baxter*), Damian O'Flynn (*Gil Gailord*), Johnny "Scat" Davis (*Scat Davis*), Mary Gordon (*Mattie*), Henry Kolker (*Mr. Jefferson Baxter*), Gwen Kenyon (*Barbara*), Charles Jordan (*Sgt. O'Brien*), Betty Blythe (*Miss Ellsworth*), Charles Williams (*Mr. Chase*), Lorraine Krueger, Paul Bryer.

Corio, in a role not too dissimilar from her own beginnings as a stripper, plays a burlesque queen who is busted, and through the aid of her lawyer, O'Flynn, cooks up a scheme to get her off on probation. They dig a woman out of the old people's home to pose as Corio's mother, thus vying for sympathy on the elderly woman's behalf. Free again, Corio decides to get revenge on the cop who busted her by putting the make on his son. But problems arise when the old lady who posed as the mother decides to disclose her true identity. The Ryan husband and wife team (at the time recently from radio fame, with Irene later known for her TV role as "Granny" in THE BEVERLY HILLBILLIES) supply a spark in their comic and musical routines. Musical numbers are also performed by Corio and Davis, backed by the Johnny "Scat" Davis Band.

p, Philip N. Krasne; d, Arthur Dreifuss; w, Charles R. Marion, Arthur Hoerl, Tim Ryan; ph, Mack Stengler; ed, Carl Pierson; md, Edward Kay; art d, Dave Milton; m/l, "Woogie Hula," Lou Hercher, Andy Iola Long, "Darling Nellie," Gray Benjamin, Russell Hanby.

Musical/Comedy   (PR:A   MPAA:NR)

SARUMBA*½   (1950) 65m EL bw

Michael Whalen (*Senor Valdez*), Doris Dowling (*Hildita*), Tommy Wonder (*Joe Thomas*), Dolores Tatum (*Maria*), Rodriguez Molina (*Rodriguez*), Shelia Garret (*Helen*), Manuel Folgoso (*The Beggar*), Red Davis (*"La Paloma" Manager*), Collins Hay, John D. Bonin, Ira Wolfer (*Sailors*), Laurette Campeau (*Laurie*).

Shot in Havana, Cuba, most of the action takes place inside the local nightclubs, with sailor Wonder going AWOL, setting the stage for the time-worn plot of "boy meets girl." Only this time Whalen also has an interest in the girl, Dowling, which just serves as a ploy to prolong the happy ending a little longer. Added feature has Wonder and Dowling performing the title song, combining portions of samba and rhumba for one hot little number.

p, Marion Gering, George P. Quigley, Julian Roffman; d, Gering; w, Jay Victor; ph, Don Malkames.

Musical/Drama   (PR:A   MPAA:NR)

SASAKI KOJIRO   (SEE: KOJIRO, 1967, Jap.)

SASAYASHI NO JOE   (SEE: WHISPERING JOE, 1969, Jap.)

SASKATCHEWAN***   (1954) 87m UNIV c (GB: O'ROURKE OF THE
                                                                   ROYAL MOUNTED)

Alan Ladd (*Sgt. Thomas O'Rourke*), Shelley Winters (*Grace Markey*), J. Carroll Naish (*Batoche*), Hugh O'Brian (*Marshal Smith*), Robert Douglas (*Inspector Benton*), George Lewis (*Lawson*), Richard Long (*Scanlon*), Jay Silverheels (*Cajou*), Antonio Moreno (*Chief Dark Cloud*), Frank Chase (*Keller*), Lowell Gilmore (*Banks*), Anthony Caruso (*Spotted Eagle*), John Cason (*Cook*), Henry Wills (*Merrill*), Robert D. Herron (*Brill*).

Ladd had already played a very different "O'Rourke" in SALTY O'ROURKE than he did this big-budget western that had a *deja-vu* feeling about it. He's a Mountie in Canada (it was shot around Banff in the Canadian Rockies) who has been out trapping with Silverheels. The two men were raised together in a Cree village and are blood brothers. Ladd is going back to work at Mountie headquarters in Saskatchewan and Silverheels is returning to the village. They come upon a massacre. A wagon train has

been decimated and the only survivor is Winters, who says that it was a tribe of Indians who killed everyone. Ladd will take her to safety at his fort, but she seems to not want to go. At the fort, Ladd learns that the only Indians reported in the area are the Cree, the same ones who raised him, and he knows that they are nonviolent. Now he discovers that the warlike Sioux have come up from the U.S. side and have been raiding various areas. They are also responsible for a slaughter of cavalrymen from the U.S. Seventh Cavalry. The Sioux are attempting to incite the docile Cree Indians into forming an alliance and attacking the infidels who've come to take away what they feel is their rightful property. Someone up high in the Canadian government has ordered that the Crees be divested of their weapons, but Ladd is against that and understands it will only force the Cree nation into joining the Sioux. Douglas is the new commander at headquarters, a martinet who goes by the book, and since he has his orders, he means to carry them out to the nth degree. Now we learn why Winters didn't want to be rescued. O'Brian, a Montana marshal, arrives with a warrant for her arrest for having committed murder. A message to Douglas indicates that the vicious Sioux are nearby and planning to sweep down on the fort. Douglas, Ladd, and several Mounties load up with ammo and supplies and will travel south to the Canadian-U.S. border where the Sioux are. O'Brian and Winters, who are heading in the same direction, will travel with the Mounties. O'Brian is attracted to Winters and one wonders what might happen, but she likes Ladd and that is immediately evident. (There is not one scintilla of subtlety in Winters' acting here and she is as miscast as Burt Reynolds doing Disraeli.) Douglas is one of the new breed of commanders, all noise and no experience. He is leading his men through large open areas where they will make a great target for the Sioux. Ladd won't stand for it and seems to mutiny, taking the other Mounties with him into the dense brush. Along the way, O'Brian makes a pass at Winters and her honor is protected by Ladd in a fist fight. Now O'Brian admits that the charges against Winters are false and he only wants her as his mistress. O'Brian grabs a gun to shoot Ladd but Douglas saves Ladd's life by shooting O'Brian. The group makes it to the fort near the border and Ladd and the others are immediately arrested for not following Douglas' orders. There are very few men at the fort, but that doesn't deter the commander, Gilmore, from planning to attack the Indians, which would be a Siouxicide mission. Ladd pleads with his superiors to free the imprisoned men but they won't listen and go off to fight. The Sioux quickly surround Douglas, Gilmore, and the small band and another massacre is in the works. Meanwhile, Silverheels helps Ladd escape. The peaceful Crees are given weapons and, together, they arrive in the nick of time to save the Mounties. Ladd is forgiven for what he did and the picture ends with Ladd and Winters making eyes at each other. Ladd is a larger-than-life type who is always right. Everything he predicts comes to pass, and after it happens a couple of times, there is no suspense. Lots of action and beautiful photography but the entire thing is ultimately unsatisfying. O'Brian makes a good villain and J. Carroll Naish plays an Indian scout with the same professionalism he always brought to every role.

p, Aaron Rosenberg; d, Raoul Walsh; w, Gil Doud; ph, John Seitz (Technicolor); ed, Frank Gross; md, Joseph Gershenson; art d, Bernard Herzbrun, Richard H. Reidel; cos, Bill Thomas.

Western   (PR:A-C   MPAA:NR)

SASOM I EN SPEGEL   (SEE: THROUGH A GLASS DARKLY, 1962,
                                                                              Swed.)

SASQUATCH*½   (1978) 102m North American Film Enterprises c
                                      (AKA: SASQUATCH, THE LEGEND OF BIGFOOT)

George Lauris (*Chuck Evans*), Steve Boergadine (*Hank Parshall*), Jim Bradford (*Barney Snipe*), Ken Kenzle (*Josh Bigsby*), William Emmons (*Dr. Paul Markham*), Joe Morello (*Techka Blackhawk*).

A semi-documentary attempt to capitalize on the popularity of the "Big Foot" legend has a group of scientists stalk the beast in the northern woods of the U.S. and Canada. Burdened with heavy equipment, their goal is to track down Sasquatch, the Indian name for Big Foot, a creature that may provide a link with man's ancient past. But amateurish photography, including California sets that are supposed to be northwestern woods and supposedly real, but blurry, footage of the monster, take away from an authentic attempt to convince the audience that this legend is real.

p, John Fabian; d, Ed Ragozzini; w, Edward H. Hawkins (based on the story by Ronald B. Olson); ph, Fabian, Bill Farmer (DeLuxe Color); ed, Fabian, Farmer.

Adventure   **Cas.**   (PR:A   MPAA:G)

SATAN BUG, THE²   (1965) 114m Mirisch-Kappa/UA c

George Maharis (*Lee Barrett*), Richard Basehart (*Dr. Hoffman/Ainsley*), Anne Francis (*Ann*), Dana Andrews (*The General*), Edward Asner (*Veretti*), Frank Sutton (*Donald*), John Larkin (*Michaelson*), Richard Bull (*Cavanaugh*), Martin Blaine (*Martin*), John Anderson (*Reagan*), Russ Bender (*Mason*), Hari [Harry] Rhodes (*Johnson*), John Clarke (*Raskin*), Simon Oakland (*Tasserly*), Henry Beckman (*Dr. Baxter*), Harold Gould (*Dr. Ostrer*), James Hong (*Dr. Yang*), Harry Lauter (*Fake SDI agent*), John Newton.

Not one of director Sturges' better efforts, this science fiction thriller has Maharis as a former government agent called in to investigate the mysterious murder of a scientist, as well as the disappearance of several flasks of a killer virus. His findings uncover millionaire Basehart as the culprit, who also poses as the head assistant in the original experiments. Basehart's reason for stealing the germs and threatening to spread a plague upon L.A., is his protest against the U.S.'s engagement in germ warfare. After Basehart has let loose a dose of his virus on a small Flordia community, wiping it out, Maharis tracks him down just before L.A. is exposed to the bug. An exciting helicopter fight ensues in which Basehart falls to his death. Sturges' direction is shaky in handling the suspense aspects, but a good cast performs in a customary manner. This includes Ed Asner as one of Basehart's henchmen.

p&d, John Sturges; w, James Clavell, Edward Anhalt (based on the novel by Ian Stuart (Alistair MacLean)); ph, Robert Surtees (Panavision, DeLuxe Color); m, Jerry Goldsmith; ed, Ferris Webster; md, Goldsmith; art d, Herman Blumenthal; set d, Charles Vassar; cos, Wes Jeffries; spec eff, Paul Pollard; makeup, Emile Lavigne.

Science Fiction/Thriller   Cas.   (PR:A MPAA:NR)

SATAN IN HIGH HEELS zero   (1962) 89m Vega/Cosmic bw

Meg Myles (*Stacey Kane*), Grayson Hall (*Pepe*), Mike Keene (*Arnold Kenyon*), Robert Yuro (*Laurence Kenyon*), Sabrina (*Herself*), Nolia Chapman (*Felice*), Earl Hammond (*Rudy*), Del Tenney (*Paul*), Ben Stone (*Louie*), Paul Scott (*Vincent*), John Nicholas (*Peter*), Pat Hamer (*Stripper*), Sandra Dale (*Cigarette Girl*).

An unintelligent story about a sleazy stripper, Myles, who leaves her junkie husband by escaping to New York. She finds work at a ritzy club and has an affair with both the owner and his playboy son. When her husband tracks her down, she persuades him to kill the owner. Instead, however, he explains the situation to the owner's son. All three men see Myles clearly for the first time, leaving her alone to fend for herself.

p, Leonard M. Burton; d, Jerald Intrator; w, John T. Chapman (based on a story by Harold Bonnett, Chapman); ph, Bernard Herschensen; m, Mundell Lowe; ed, Armond Lebowitz; md, Lowe; m/l, Jack Lawrence, Walter Marks, Lowe, Bobby Weil.

Crime Drama   (PR:O MPAA:NR)

SATAN MET A LADY**½   (1936) 75m WB bw

Bette Davis (*Valerie Purvis*), Warren William (*Ted Shayne*), Alison Skipworth (*Mme. Barabbas*), Arthur Treacher (*Anthony Travers*), Winifred Shaw (*Astrid Ames*), Marie Wilson (*Murgatroyd*), Porter Hall (*Mr. Ames*), Maynard Holmes (*Kenneth*), Charles Wilson (*Pollock*), Olin Howland (*Dunhill*), Joseph King (*McElroy*), Barbara Blane (*Babe*), Eddie Shubert, Stuart Holmes, James P. Burtis, Francis Sayles (*Detectives*), Billy Bletcher, Alice La Mont (*Parents of Sextuplets*), May Beatty (*Mrs. Arden*), John Alexander (*Black Porter*), Alphonse Martell (*Headwaiter*), Huey White (*Taxi Driver*), John Elliott (*City Father*), Saul Gorss (*Farrow*), Cliff Saum (*Night Watchman*), Douglas Williams (*Dock Walloper*), Kid Herman, J.H. Allen (*Bootblacks*), Edward McWade (*Richards*).

The second filming of Dashiell Hammett's classic detective story is probably the least true to the book and the least successful. William plays the Sam Spade role, here called Ted Shayne. He is hired by Davis to locate a certain Mrs. Barrabas (equivalent to Casper Gutman in the other films, and played by Alison Skipworth), but she will not tell him why. Skipworth finds out she is being sought and sends one of her minions to find out why from William's none-too-clever secretary, Wilson. Later William calls on Skipworth and she offers him money to tell her where Davis is, further explaining that Davis used to work for her and stole a fabulously valuable ram's horn filled with jewels. William goes back to Davis and questions her. When she gives him yet another story, he sets his partner to follow her. She spots the tail and, thinking it one of Skipworth's men, kills him. She asks William to collect the treasure when it arrives on board a ship from the orient the next day, but Skipworth and her associates show up as well and take it away from him. Davis then emerges with a gun and takes the horn for herself. Suddenly, though, the police swarm in, called by William's secretary, and they arrest the whole sordid crew. Played largely for laughs that never really come off and needlessly tampering with its characters, this film would be all but forgotten today except as a piece of interesting trivia. Davis had just finished THE PETRIFIED FOREST when she was told this (then under the working title of THE MAN IN THE BLACK HAT) was her next film. She looked at the script and refused to have any part of it, telling the studio lawyer sent to remind her of her contractual obligations, "Valerie Purvis in HAT is wrong for me. There are hundreds of artists you can select for the part. I'm exhausted from this picture–*can't you see I'm exhausted?* I need a rest–my nerves are bad." Jack Warner would not accept this and sent a studio doctor to examine Davis. When he arrived she was not at home, and more threats and counter-threats went via telegram between the star and the studio. Eventually, though, she was forced to relent. She had too many bills and could not afford to take a suspension. Davis' judgment of the film was correct, it was savaged by the critics on its release and never found an audience. Five years had passed since the first MALTESE FALCON had appeared. Five more would elapse before John Huston would bring it to the

screen definitively.

p, Henry Blanke; d, William Dieterle; w, Brown Holmes (based on the novel *The Maltese Falcon* by Dashiell Hammett); ph, Arthur Edeson; ed, Max Parker; md, Leo F. Forbstein; art d, Max Parker; cos, Orry-Kelly.

Crime   (PR:A MPAA:NR)

SATAN NEVER SLEEPS**   (1962) 126m FOX c (GB: THE DEVIL
                                        NEVER SLEEPS; AKA: FLIGHT FROM TERROR)

William Holden (*Father O'Banion*), Clifton Webb (*Father Bovard*), France Nuyen (*Sin Lan*), Athene Seyler (*Sister Agnes*), Martin Benson (*Kuznietsky*), Edith Sharpe (*Sister Theresa*), Robert Lee (*Chung Ren*), Marie Yang (*Ho San's Mother*), Andy Ho (*Ho San's Father*), Burt Kwouk (*Ah Wang*), Weaver Lee (*Ho San*), Lin Chen (*Sister Mary*), Anthony Chinn (*Ho San's Driver*), Ronald Adam (*Father Lemay*), Noel Hood (*Sister Justine*), Eric Young (*Junior Officer*).

SATAN NEVER SLEEPS but most of the audience did in this rehash of GOING MY WAY. McCarey liked making pictures with Catholic themes like the Bing Crosby-Barry Fitzgerald film as well as THE BELLS OF ST. MARY'S, but he came a cropper here with miscasting and an ill-advised story. It's 1949 and priests Holden and Webb are living in China where the local Communists won't leave them alone. They are at a quiet village on the edge of nowhere and Lee, the leader of the Reds, is causing trouble. The mission's cook, Nuyen, has a crush on Holden and her feelings are obvious. Lee and his thugs come into the mission, smash up the hospital area, wreck the chapel, and top it off when Lee ties Holden to a seat and makes him watch helplessly as Lee rapes Nuyen. Phew! The requisite number of months later, Nuyen delivers Lee's son. He is thrilled by the cute little Communist and celebrates by continuing his harassment of Holden and Webb (who was far too effete to play a missionary priest and looked more at home with a martini than a glass of sacramental wine). The local people rise up against the Reds and Lee gets the order from on high that he must kill all the Christians in the area, including the priests and his own converted parents, Yang and Ho. That puts a damper on his allegiance to Mao and he decides that it's time to get away from the hammer and sickle. Lee takes Nuyen, their son, Holden, and Webb and plans to find sanctuary in Hong Kong. Before they can get too far, a helicopter arrives to stop them from escaping. Webb does the heroic thing by putting on Lee's identifiable hat and coat, getting into Lee's car, and driving in a different direction. Bullets rain down from the chopper and kill Webb, but his diversionary tactic gives the others the chance to cross the border. At Hong Kong, the baby is given a proper baptism and Holden marries Lee to Nuyen as the picture ends. Cloying, filled with homilies, and then one action sequence after another to wake up the viewers. England and Wales doubled as China in the location shots and only a few could tell the difference, as in those days, nobody was allowed in mainland China, so who knew? The villains, except for Lee, are painted in such black tones that the politicizing of the movie is far too strong for the subject matter. The rape scene and the violence make this a cautionary choice for youngsters.

p&d, Leo McCarey; w, Claude Binyon, McCarey (based on the novel *The China Story* by Pearl Buck); ph, Oswald Morris (CinemaScope, DeLuxe Color); m, Richard Rodney Bennett; ed, Gordon Pilkington; md, Muir Mathieson; prod d, Tom Morahan; art d, Jim Jorahan, John Hoesli; set d, Jack Stephens; m/l, "Satan Never Sleeps," Harry Warren, Harold Adamson, Leo McCarey, (sung by Timi Yuro); makeup, George Frost.

Drama   (PR:C MPAA:NR)

SATANIC RITES OF DRACULA, THE
      (SEE: COUNT DRACULA AND HIS VAMPIRE BRIDE, 1978, Brit.)

SATAN'S BED*½   (1965) 72m Promotheus Ventures-Sam Lake
                                            Enterprises bw

Yoko Ono (*Ito*), Val Avery, Glen Nielson, Gene Wesson, Robert Williams, Steve Shaw, Lydia Martin, Cathy Stevens, Judy Young, Sarah Gold, William Stein, Marvin Holtz, Philip Dunn, Franklyn Clark, Ruth Rawson, Juanita Rodriguez, Thomas O'Reilly, Michael Ryan, Anna Riva [Roberta Findley], Madison Arnold, Neil Merk, Judy Adler, Norman Berliner [Jerry Burke], Robert Renfield [Roger Wilson], Wally Martin [Marshall Smith], Michael Findley [Julian Marsh, Michael Fenway].

Before hooking up with John Lennon, among other things, Ono made cheap independent features like this. Story has Ono as the girl friend of a local pusher, with her becoming the pawn in a deadly game when her beau decides to stop dealing in drugs. On the one hand are the three punks who depend on him for their heroin; on the other is the local supplier wanting to keep him in business for the steady income. Both groups are after Ono to use her as bait to keep her boy friend in business. While the punks go after the wrong girl, the supplier kidnaps Ono and takes advantage of her until he is ready to make his move. In the end Ono winds up dead, and her boy friend returns to drug trafficking.

p, Jerry Burke, Roger Wilson; d, Marshall Smith; ph, Julian Marsh; m, Thomas J. Valentino; ed, Michael Fenway; makeup, Lem Amero.

Crime/Drama   (PR:O MPAA:NR)

SATAN'S CHEERLEADERS zero   (1977) 92m World Amusements c

John Ireland *(Sheriff Bub/High Priest)*, Yvonne De Carlo *(Emm Bub, Sheriff's Wife/ High Priestess)*, Jack Kruschen *(Billy the Janitor)*, John Carradine *(Bum)*, Sydney Chaplin *(Mond, Devil Worshipper)*, Jacquelin Cole *(Ms. Johnson, Teacher)*, Kerry Sherman *(Patti)*, Hillary Horan *(Chris)*, Alisa Powell *(Debbie)*, Sherry Marks *(Sharon)*, Lane Caudell *(Stevie)*, Joseph Carlo *(Coach)*, Michael Donavon O'Donnell *(Farmer)*, Robin Greer *(Baker Girl)*.

Wretched drive-in fare that doesn't even live up to the potential for unintentional laughs promised by the title. Kruschen is the strange Benedict High School janitor angered by smarty-pants teenage cheerleaders (Sherman, Marks, Horan, and Powell) who make fun of him. Seeking vengeance, Kruschen decides to impress the members of the satanic cult he's just joined by sacrificing these nubile young big mouths to the devil himself. Using his evil powers to detain the cheerleaders' bus as they travel to a football game, Kruschen arrives on the scene in his car and volunteers to drive the stranded girls to their destination. The girls climb in the car only to panic when the friendly janitor takes a wrong turn into the dark and lonely woods. Once again employing his satanic powers, Kruschen "freezes" the girls before a stone slab and prepares to sexually sacrifice Sherman to Satan. Upon awakening from their trance, the girls discover Kruschen dead on the slab and Sherman explains that he died while trying to rape her. The cheerleaders then wander into the woods for help and meet Carradine, a bum who directs them to the sheriff's house. Unfortunately, sheriff Ireland and his wife, De Carlo, happen to be the high priest and priestess of the satanic cult. After several attempts to capture the girls for sacrifice, it turns out that cheerleader Sherman has secretly become satan's favorite girl and she sends the hounds of hell to rip out Ireland and De Carlo's respective throats. Keeping her new high priestess identity a secret from the other girls, Sherman and her cheerleaders finally make it to the big football game where she uses her newly acquired powers to help their team win. Obnoxious and irritating in all respects, SATAN'S CHEERLEADERS is just another embarrassing entry in the filmographies of Ireland, Carradine, and De Carlo.

p, Alvin L. Fast; d, Greydon Clark; w, Clark, Fast; ph, Dean Cundy (Movielab Color); m, Gerald Lee.

Horror   **(PR:O   MPAA:R)**

SATAN'S CLAW   (SEE: BLOOD ON SATAN'S CLAW, 1970, Brit.)

SATAN'S CRADLE**   (1949) 60m Duncan Renaldo/UA bw

Duncan Renaldo *(Cisco Kid)*, Leo Carrillo *(Pancho)*, Ann Savage *(Lil)*, Douglas Fowley *(Steve Gentry)*, Byron Foulger *(Henry Lane)*, Buck Bailey *(Rocky)*, George De Normand *(Idaho)*, Wes Hudman *(Peters)*, Claire Carleton.

The CISCO KID saves the day again as Renaldo and his sidekick Carrillo are up against Fowley and Savage, a couple of real smoothies who have almost taken total control of a small mining town. Savage is the saloon girl pretending to be the widow of the town's big boss, with Fowley as the lawyer, making all their illegalities appear legal. Renaldo breezes through his role with his usual good nature, with Carrillo around to take care of the laughs. (See CISCO KID series, Index.)

p, Philip N. Krasne; d, Ford Beebe; w, Jack Benton [Cheney] (based on the "Cisco Kid" character created by O. Henry); ph, Jack Greenhalgh; m, Albert Glasser; ed, Marty Cohn; art d, Frank Sylos; set d, Helen Hansard.

Western   **(PR:A   MPAA:NR)**

SATAN'S MISTRESS zero   (1982) 91m Diversified Film Ventures-B.J. Creators/Motion Picture Marketing c (AKA: FURY OF THE SUC-CUBUS; DEMON RAGE; DARK EYES)

Britt Ekland *(Anne-Marie)*, Lana Wood *(Lisa)*, Kabir Bedi *(The Spirit)*, Don Galloway *(Carl)*, John Carradine *(Father Stratten)*, Sherry Scott *(Michelle)*, Elise-Anne *(Belline)*, Chris Polakof *(Cissy)*, Howard Murphy *(The Beast)*, Tom Hallick *(Burt)*, John Simon *(Police Sergeant)*, Alan Harris *(Dave)*, Michael Blackburn *(Ambulance Driver)*, Bennett Waxman *(Ambulance Attendant)*, Rick Alan, La Donna, K. Starchuk, Rheya Ferrooh, Michaelle Waxman *(Demons)*.

A highly contrived story has Wood (Natalie's kid sister) being raped by a spirit, Bedi, whose soul is lost in limbo. Ekland plays a mystic called in to aid in figuring out the reasons for Wood's strange behavior, with Carradine as the friendly, advising priest. But things don't return to normal until husband Galloway, who has done his job in neglecting Wood, gets his head chopped off by Bedi. The latter then promptly makes his way to hell. This film is mainly an excuse to show off Wood's body.

p, James Polakof, Beverly Johnson; d, Polakof; w, Polakof, Johnson; ph, James L. Carter (CFI color); m, Roger Kellaway; ed, George Trirogoff; art d, Fred Cutter, John Flaherty; spec eff, Karen Kubeck, Dennis Dion, Tom Shouse; makeup, Kubeck, Donna Lyons.

Horror   **(PR:O   MPAA:R)**

SATAN'S SADIST zero   (1969) 86m
Kennis-Frazer/Independent-International c

Russ Tamblyn *(Anchor)*, Scott Brady *(Charles Baldwin)*, Kent Taylor *(Lew)*, John Cardos *(Firewater)*, Robert Dix *(Willie)*, Gary Kent *(Johnny Martin)*, Greydon Clark *(Acid)*, Regina Carrol *(Gina)*, Jackie Taylor *(Tracy Stewart)*, William Bonner *(Muscle)*, Bobby Clark *(Romero)*, Evelyn Frank *(Nora Baldwin)*, Yvonne Stewart *(Carol)*, Cheryl Anne *(Jan)*, Randee Lynn *(Rita)*, Bambi Allen *(Lois)*, Breck Warwick *(Ben)*.

In this violence-for-violence-sake picture, a gang of motorcycle desert rats, led by Tamblyn, cause terror and a string of murders as they ride through the Southwest. They wind up destroying Taylor's truck stop and killing him and several customers after Taylor makes a remark about Tamblyn's girl friend, Carrol. One of the customer's, Kent, a Vietnam Vet, survives long enough to escape into the desert with waitress Stewart, and then uses Army tactics to stop the killers. This includes flushing one gang member's head down a toilet, and throwing a rattlesnake around another's neck. Carrol, as Tamblyn's motorcycle mama, drives her cycle off a cliff after being dumped by him. In the end, the gang is wiped out and peace returns to the Southwest. When this picture was released, it was said to have capitalized on the recent Sharon Tate murders, although in all actuality the only similarities between the murders were in the number of people being senselessly wiped out. Tamblyn made his comeback in this film, a complete reversal to the shiny-faced roles audiences were used to seeing him play. Songs include: "Satan," "Gotta Stop that Feeling," "I Like the Way You Work," "I'm on My Way Out," "Is it Better to Have Loved and Lost?," "Baby How I Fell for You."

p&d, Al Adamson; w, Dennis Wayne; ph, Gary Graver (DeLuxe Color); m, Harley Hatcher; ed, Graver; m/l, Hatcher (performed by The Nightriders); makeup, Susan Arnold.

Crime/Drama   **Cas.**   **(PR:O   MPAA:R)**

SATAN'S SATELLITES*½   (1958) 70m REP bw (AKA: ZOMBIES OF THE STRATOSPHERE)

Judd Holdren *(Larry Martin)*, Aline Towne *(Sue Davis)*, Wilson Wood *(Bob Wilson)*, Lane Bradford *(Marex)*, John Crawford *(Roth)*, Craig Kelly *(Mr. Steele)*, Ray Boyle *(Shane)*, Leonard Nimoy *(Narab)*, Tom Steele *(Truck Driver)*, Dale Van Sickel *(Telegraph Operator)*, Roy Engel *(Lawson)*, Jack Harden *(Kerr)*, Paul Stader *(Fisherman)*, Gayle Kellogg *(Dick)*, Jack Shea *(Policeman)*, Robert Garabedian *(Elah)*, Stanley Waxman.

This feature was a chopped-up version of Republic's last serial, the twelve part ZOMBIES OF THE STRATOSPHERE (1952). Holdren, an ever present minor space opera hero, is a caped rocketeer who heads off to Mars in order to stop an evil plot of destroying the earth with atomic weapons. The plot is old hat with a robot borrowed from THE MYSTERIOUS DR. SATAN and footage from KING OF THE ROCKET MEN (which also featured Holdren) tossed in as well. Perhaps the only thing of note in this poorly made film was the presence of Nimoy, here playing an evil Martian henchman, in his pre "Star Trek" days.

p, Franklin Adreon; d, Fred C. Brannon; w, Ronald Davidson; ph, John MacBurnie; m, Stanley Wilson; ed, Cliff Bell; spec eff, Howard Lydecker, Theodore Lydecker.

Science Fiction   **Cas.**   **(PR:AA   MPAA:NR)**

SATAN'S SKIN   (SEE: BLOOD ON SATAN'S CLAW, 1970, Brit.)

SATAN'S SLAVE zero   (1976, Brit.) 84m Crown c

Michael Gough *(Alexander Yorke)*, Candace Glendenning *(Catherine Yorke)*, Martin Potter *(Stephen Yorke)*, Barbara Kellerman *(Frances)*, Michael Grace *(John)*, James Bree *(Malcolm)*, Celia Hewitt *(Elizabeth)*.

A vile shocker which has Gough involved with an evil cult of, witches. Fortunately, the boiling and bubbling of the witches cauldron barely made an appearance on American shores. SATAN'S SLAVE is full of unappetizing gore effects and, like most films in the genre, is lacking in characterizations that aren't completely wooden.

p, Les Young, Richard Crafter; d, Norman J. Warren; w, David McGillivray; m, John Scott.

Horror   **(PR:O   MPAA:R)**

SATELLITE IN THE SKY*½   (1956) 84m WB c

Kieron Moore *(Michael)*, Lois Maxwell *(Kim)*, Donald Wolfit *(Merrity)*, Bryan Forbes *(Jimmy)*, Jimmy Hanley *(Larry)*, Thea Gregory *(Barbara)*, Barry Keegan *(Lefty)*, Alan Gifford *(Col. Galloway)*, Shirley Lawrence *(Ellen)*, Walter Hudd *(Blandford)*, Donald Gray *(Capt. Ross)*, Peter Neil *(Tony)*, Rick Rydon, Ronan O'Casey, Robert O'Neil *(Reporters)*, Carl Jaffe *(Bechstein)*, Charles Richardson *(Gen. Barnett)*, Trevor Reid *(Expert)*, Alastair Hunter *(Expert)*, John Baker *(Official)*.

Trite and talky science fiction film pushes believability to the limit. Plot involves a reporter who stows away aboard a satellite where scientists are studying the effects of a tritonium bomb that's supposed to explode above the Earth's atmosphere. A mishap causes the bomb to attach itself to the satellite instead, leaving the entire crew certain that they are about to die. When the inventor of the bomb, Wolfit, goes berserk, two of his own scientists sacrifice their lives for that of the crew. They climb outside the spacecraft and dislodge the bomb from the ship, exploding with it. Special effects stand up to the expected, but the script, especially in the dialog department, is superficial.

p, Edward J. Danziger, Harry Lee Danziger; d, Paul Dickson; w, John C. Mather, J.T. McIntosh, Edith Dell; ph, Georges Perinal, Jimmy Wilson (CinemaScope, Warner Color); m, Albert Elms; ed, Sydney Stone; art d, Erik Blakemore; cos, Rene Coke; spec eff, Wally Veevers.

Fantasy   **(PR:A   MPAA:NR)**

SATIN MUSHROOM, THE*½   (1969) 78m Grads PRC c (AKA: A SOFT WARM EXPERIENCE)

Matla Bridgestone (Gail), Jan Kent (Pam), John DeWar (Gitano), Vic Lance (Manolo), Vince Render (Pepe), Don Auld (Jim), Lynda Prish (Hooker), Dick Osmun, Bethel Buckalew (Bartenders), Briggette Weihnstraume (Stripper), Stuart Lancaster (Mexican Lawyer), Rachel Jablonski (Manolo's Girl friend), Natasha Steele (Secretary), Terry Hart (Drummer), Vivian David, Don Hallstrom, Mark Lowhead, The Matadors Band.

Kent arrives in Mexico as the heir to her uncle's estate. She brings along her girl friend, Bridgestone, only to discover that the estate is being held in suspension until Kent is cleared as the rightful heir. While waiting for clearance, she and Bridgestone decide to travel and meet DeWar, a local guitar player who falls for Bridgestone. He takes the two girls to see his friend, famed matador Lance, who winds up romancing Kent.

d, Don Brown; w, Van Zurich; ph, Ray Nadeau; ed, Don Hallstrom; prod d, Bethel Buckalew.

Drama   **(PR:C   MPAA:NR)**

SATURDAY ISLAND   (SEE: ISLAND OF DESIRE, 1952, Brit.)

SATURDAY NIGHT AND SUNDAY MORNING*****
                                    (1961, Brit.) 90m Woodfall/CD bw

Albert Finney (Arthur Seaton), Shirley Ann Field (Doreen Gretton), Rachel Roberts (Brenda), Hylda Baker (Aunt Ada), Norman Rossington (Bert), Bryan Pringle (Jack), Robert Cawdron (Robboe), Edna Morris (Mrs. Bull), Elsie Wagstaff (Mrs. Seaton), Frank Pettitt (Mr. Seaton), Avis Bunnage (Blowsy Woman), Colin Blakely (Loudmouth), Irene Richmond (Doreen's Mother), Louise Dunn (Betty), Peter Madden (Drunken Man), Cameron Hall (Mr. Bull), Alister Williamson (Policeman), Anne Blake (Civil Defense Officer).

Young directors and writers should be strapped into their seats and forced to watch this film several times before attempting to make movies on their own. In 89 minutes, Sillitoe and Reisz create a world, plunge the viewer into it, and make the audience feel happy they can walk away from the movie house and not have actually been a part of the dismal existence of one young man in the Midlands area of England. This was 23-year-old Finney's first major film (he'd done a bit in THE ENTERTAINER earlier that year) and the trio of John Osborne, Tony Richardson, and Harry Saltzman decided to give him his break with this. Finney is so good that he won the British Film Academy award in the role, and the picture also took the accolade as Best Film of the year. It's another of the "angry young men" pictures on the order of ROOM AT THE TOP and LOOK BACK IN ANGER, but this one stays in the mind long after others have faded. Sillitoe, who also wrote THE LONELINESS OF THE LONG DISTANCE RUNNER, adapted his own novel here with major results. Finney is a lathe operator in a small town near Nottingham. He is a lively young man devoted to pleasure and thumbing his nose at authority. As he says, "All I want is a good time. The rest is propaganda." To that end, he spends his weekends boozing and brawling and bedding down any woman he can. He makes a good wage; he has plenty of discretionary money to spend. He hates his job but is willing to put in his week at the lathe in return for the fun he can have with his pay envelope. He's having an affair with Roberts, who is married to his fellow worker, Pringle. Finney enjoys the sexual liaisons with Roberts but that's as far as he will go with her and she wants more. At the same time, Finney meets Field, a beautiful, old-fashioned young woman with strict morals. Finney finds himself falling in love with Field, but she won't sleep with him unless there is a commitment, something Finney cannot bear to make. When Roberts announces that she's pregnant, Finney immediately brings her to see his aunt, Baker, in the hope that an abortion can be arranged. The attempt fails, Finney shrugs, and offers to make Roberts an honest woman by proposing to arrange for her divorce from Pringle and marrying her himself. Roberts senses that it's only a gesture, albeit a brave one from someone constituted as Finney is, so she thanks him but decides that she'll have the child and take whatever comes with it. When Pringle learns that his wife is carrying Finney's child, he has Finney beaten to a pulp by his brother and a hoodlum pal. Finney seems to accept this pain as just another side of his life, and when he recovers from his wounds, he returns to work but now feels he is ready for marriage. He proposes to Field and they will move into a block of newly built workers' flats where he will

probably spend the rest of his life in the same dull, dreary way his friends and ancestors have. And yet, there is still the spark of independence in Finney when he tells his prospective mate that she should never take him for granted, as there is still some life in the old boy yet. The story seems slim at best, but Reisz's sharp direction and the superb editing combine with Sillitoe's grasp of the argot to make this a compelling, if somewhat difficult to understand, movie. The accents in that area of England are almost impossible for U.S. ears (and even many London auricles) to fathom, so it had to be looped in places where the words blurred. Sillitoe, who used to work in a Midlands factory, captures the nuances perfectly in his script, and Reisz, who was in his early thirties at the time, does a smashing job in his first feature after having worked in the documentary field. SATURDAY NIGHT FEVER owes a great deal to this brilliant film. There are so many similarities that it seems to be a New York remake. Despite Finney's youth, he was already a veteran Shakespearean actor and had once taken over for Olivier when Sir Larry was felled by injury on the eve of a performance of "Corialanus" at Stratford. It was a sensational outing for Finney and great things were in store. Roberts was excellent and her role (not unlike that of Simore Signoret in ROOM AT THE TOP) also won a BFA Award. One of the best of the "kitchen sink" pictures of the era, SATURDAY NIGHT AND SUNDAY MORNING has more than its share of humor to temper the highly charged drama and it stands out in every department. The sex is steamy, the language is raw, the emotions are strong, and the result is a movie that should not be seen by children under 16. To anyone who can take the experience, it's a must-watch.

p, Tony Richardson; d, Karel Reisz; w, Alan Sillitoe (based on his novel); ph, Freddie Francis; m, John Dankworth; ed, Seth Holt; art d, Ted Marshall; md, Dankworth; m/l, "Let's Slip Away," Dankworth (performed by Dankworth and His Orchestra).

Drama   **(PR:O   MPAA:NR)**

SATURDAY NIGHT AT THE BATHS**   (1975) 86m Mammoth c

Ellen Sheppard (Tracy), Robert Aberdeen (Michael), Don Scotti (Himself), Steve Ostrow (Steve), Caleb Stone (Judy Garland), J.C. Gaynor (Shirley Bassey), Toyia (Diana Ross), Janie Olivor, Phillip Ownes, R. Douglas Brautigham, Paul J. Ott, Paul Vanase, Lawrence Smith, Pedro Valentino.

Taking place almost entirely at the Continental Baths, a New York gay hang-out, story tries to make some headway in the relations between gays and straights. Super straight piano player Aberdeen gets a job at the nightclub, and learns to throw over some of his stereotyped perspectives toward gays, as his girl friend, Sheppard, pushes him on to accept changes. Overly contrived ending has Aberdeen sleeping with a gay, only to have his heterosexuality confirmed. Highlight is the female impersonator acts, which offers some great renditions of Diana Ross, Judy Garland, and Carmen Miranda.

p, David Buckley, Steve Ostrow; d, Buckley; w, Buckley, Franklin Khedouri; ph, Ralf Bode (Movielab Color); ed, Jackie Raynal, Suzanne Fenn.

Drama/Comedy   **(PR:O   MPAA:R)**

SATURDAY NIGHT BATH IN APPLE VALLEY
                (SEE: SATURDAY NIGHT IN APPLE VALLEY, 1965)

SATURDAY NIGHT FEVER***½   (1977) 119m PAR c

John Travolta (Tony Manero), Karen Lynn Gorney (Stephanie), Barry Miller (Bobby C.), Joseph Call (Joey), Paul Pape (Double J), Donna Pescow (Annette), Bruce Ornstein (Gus), Julie Bovasso (Flo), Martin Shakar (Frank, Jr.), Sam J. Coppola (Fusco), Nina Hansen (Grandmother), Lisa Peluso (Linda), Denny Dillon (Doreen), Bert Michaels (Pete), Robert Costanza (Paint Store Customer), Robert Weil (Becker), Shelly Batt (Girl in Disco), Fran Drescher (Connie), Donald Gantry (Jay Langhart), Murray Moston (Haberdashery Salesman), William Andrews (Detective), Ann Travolta (Pizza Girl), Monti Rock III (Deejay), Val Bisoglio (Frank Sr.), Ellen Marca (Bartender), Helen Travolta (Woman in Paint Store).

While not actually a musical version of SATURDAY NIGHT AND SUNDAY MORNING, this film owes a great deal to that one, although the grosses on this far exceed the former. When one adds the ticket sales to the astounding 27 million records sold of the soundtrack, the cash brought in by this modern-day version of MARTY was nearly $200 million! It's a slick look at a genre of movie that was limned by Arkoff and Nicholson in the 1960s with their AIP teenage epics and even before that by Sam Katzman in the 1950s. The difference is the Oscar-nominate performance by Travolta who electrified audiences with his charisma, a quality he has yet to show again in any of his followup movies. It's not much more than what he showed to TV audiences as "Vinnie" on "Welcome Back, Kotter," and, judging by his two previous roles in CARRIE and THE DEVIL'S RAIN, it took great foresight on the part of the producers to cast him in this after he did not catch fire in the other two movies. Travolta is a teenage clerk in a paint store in Brooklyn where he toils weekly in boredom as he awaits Saturday night, which is his chance to show off at the local disco, "2001 Odyssey" (a real place). As in the case of MEAN STREETS (a far superior film about growing up Italian in New York), Travolta's family does not approve of his ways and wishes that he would be more like his brother, Shakar, who is preparing to be a priest and is the favorite of the family patriarch, Bisoglio. Travolta meets Gorney at the disco. She is an excellent dancer with ambitions to move out of Brooklyn and get her own place in "the city" (Manhattan) where she works as a secretary in public relations. Gorney likes Travolta and wishes he would have just one scintilla of her ambition but he is content to be a big fish in a little pond. They practice for an upcoming dance contest at the disco and Travolta decides that he's outgrown his regular sexual partner, Pescow. Travolta's best friends in the neighborhood are Call, Pape, Miller, and Ornstein and when Miller tells the others that he's gotten a girl pregnant, the boys get together to try and figure some way to extricate him. The dance contest takes place and Travolta and Gorney are superb but not nearly as good as a visiting Puerto Rican couple. The judges are bigoted against the carpetbaggers and give Gorney and Travolta the prize but they realize it's not rightfully theirs so they hand it over to the Latin duo. Later, Travolta tries to put the make on Gorney but she resists and runs away. He is despondent and goes out with Pescow, Miller and some other pals. They drive around and wind up on the Verrazano Bridge, the span that connects Brooklyn with Staten Island. Pescow is hurt that Travolta has thrown her over for Gorney and decides to get him jealous by allowing all of the others to have sex with her. Suddenly, Pescow comes to her senses and resists while Miller begins acting strangely when he realizes that he may have to marry the girl he's impregnated. He climbs up on the bridge's cables and begins acting like a high wire performer with a daredevil attitude. He slips and falls to his death, sobering everyone there in a hurry. Later, Travolta goes to see Gorney, who has now moved into Manhattan. He tells her he's sorry for doing what he did, explains why he's shaken and the two of them begin a friendship that may, or may not, bear fruit. It doesn't sound like much of a story, and it wasn't. But the whole film had such high energy, a pulsing beat underscoring every scene, and it captured the 1970s generation in an urban setting. It began as a documentary story by Nik Cohn in the June, 1976 issue of "New York" magazine entitled "Tribal Rites of the New Saturday Night." Although not technically a musical, because nobody in the cast sang, there was more music in this picture than in most musicals. The Bee Gees (Barry Gibb, Robin Gibb, Maurice Gibb) wrote and sang: "Night Fever," "Jive Talkin'," "How Deep Is Your Love?," "Stayin' Alive," "You Should Be Dancin'," They also wrote "If I Can't Have You" (sung by Yvonne Elliman), "More than a Woman" (Tavares), and "K-Jee" (M.F.S.B.). "A Fifth of Beethoven" was adapted by Walter Murphy from Beethoven's Fifth Symphony. More songs include: "Open Sesame" (R. Bell, performed by Kool And The Gang), "Calypso Breakdown" (R. Bell, sung by Ralph MacDonald), "Disco Inferno" (Leo Green, Ron Kersey, performed by The Trammps), "Boogie Shoes" (H.W. Casey, R. Finch, performed by K.C. and the Sunshine Band), and "Disco Duck" (performed by Rick Dees, who became one of the country's highest-paid disc jockeys in the 1980s). David Shire, former husband of Talia Shire, did the score and wrote the following originals: "Barracuda Hangout," "Salsation," "Manhattan Skyline," and "Night on Disco Mountain," which was adapted from Modest Petrovich Mussorgski's "Night on Bare Mountain." The picture was shot in the predominately Italian neighborhood of Bay Ridge, with other scenes in Manhattan. To read the screenplay by Wexler (who coauthored SERPICO with Waldo Salt) is to see how slim it actually is and how little Travolta's role is plumbed. Credit then must be given to Badham as the director as well as to the costumes by Von Brandenstein (who made white suits into a national fad) for erecting a myth around Travolta. Producer Stigwood would later be the man who brought "Evita" to the stage and it's a toss-up as to which project earned more millions for him. The four-letter words and sexual scenes make this inadvisable for children, although a PG version was later released. The sequel STAYING ALIVE did not come close to the success of the original.

p, Robert Stigwood; d, John Badham; w, Norman Wexler (based on the *New York* magazine article "Tribal Rites of the New Saturday Night" by Nik Cohn); ph, Ralf D. Bode (Panavision, Movielab Color); m, Barry Robin, Maurice Gibb, David Shire; ed, David Rawlins; prod d, Charles Bailey; set d, George Detitta, John Godfrey; cos, Patrizia Von Brandenstein, Jennifer Nichols; ch, Lester Wilson (Lorraine Fields); stunts, Paul Nuckles; dance consultant, Jo-Jo Smith; tech adv., James Gambina; makeup, Max Herriquez.

Drama   **Cas.**   **(PR:C-O   MPAA:PG)**

SATURDAY NIGHT IN APPLE VALLEY*½
                             (1965) 80m Empire/Emerson bw

Phil Ford (*Big Man*), Mimi Hines (*Mimi Madison*), Cliff Arquette (*Charley Weaver/Mama Coot*), Shanton Granger (*Beau Coot*), Joan Benedict (*Poopsie Patata*), Marvin Miller, Anthony Dexter.

A spoof on the classic Hollywood romantic cliche, has Ford as the macho dude who comes to romance and protect the virginal Hines. Filled with sight gags and obvious symbolic jokes about movie making that lose power as the film goes on.

p,d&w, John Myhers; ph, Alan Stensvold; m, Foster Wakefield; ed, Myhers.

Comedy   **(PR:C   MPAA:NR)**

SATURDAY NIGHT KID, THE**   (1929) 62m FP-PAR bw

Clara Bow (*Mayme*), James Hall (*Bill*), Jean Arthur (*Janie*), Charles Sellon (*Lem Woodruff*), Ethel Wales (*Ma Woodruff*), Frank Ross (*Ken*), Edna May Oliver (*Miss Streeter*), Hyman Meyer (*Ginsberg*), Eddie Dunn (*Jim*), Leone Lane (*Pearl*), Jean Harlow (*Hazel*), Getty Bird (*Riche Ginsberg*), Alice Adair (*Girl*), Irving Bacon (*McGonigle the Sales Manager*), Mary Gordon (*Reducing Customer*), Ernie S. Adams (*Gambler*).

This was the second time around for the popular play by Abbott and Weaver. The first, a silent, was made in 1926 and starred Louise Brooks, Lawrence Gray, and Evelyn Brent. This one was released with sound and in a silent version that had titles written by 20-year-old Joseph Mankiewicz. The original silent film carried that play's title and they used another name for this so as not to confuse audiences who'd seen the other one just three years before. Bow, who was renowned as "The IT Girl," and her sister, Arthur, work as sales clerks in the department store owned by Meyer. Another clerk is Harlow, in a small bit before she gained stardom. Hall also works in the store and the three of them live at the same rooming house. Arthur has eyes for Hall, who is to marry Bow, and she steals him away by getting Bow in trouble. Arthur is in charge of the store's welfare fund and she uses the money to bet on a losing horse, then she puts the blame on Bow. Bow is a sweet, selfless type and goes to the bookie and gets him into a crap game in which she wins back all the money her sister lost. Bow learns that Hall has sold his prized possession, a radio, to help pay back the money to the employee fund. Bow finally gets disgusted with her sister, tells her what for, and when Hall learns that Bow is innocent and that Arthur is the conniver, he dumps Arthur and returns to his senses, proposing to Bow. Some very funny scenes, including a rally at the department store where all the employees sing "Hallelujah" to Meyer in a satirical bit aimed at some of the New York department stores. Odd that vamp Bow turned out to be the innocent one while Arthur is the sleazy sister. It might have worked better if they switched roles. A pleasant love comedy, little more.

d, A. Edward Sutherland; w, Lloyd Corrigan, Ethel Doherty, Edward E. Paramore, Jr. (based on the play "Love 'Em and Leave 'Em" by George Abbott, John V.A. Weaver); ph, Harry Fishbeck; ed, Jane Loring.

Comedy/Romance   **(PR:A   MPAA:NR)**

SATURDAY NIGHT OUT**   (1964, Brit.) 84m Michael Klinger-Tony
                                   Tenser-Tekli/Compton Cameo bw

Heather Sears (*Penny*), Bernard Lee (*George Hudson*), Erika Remberg (*Wanda*), John Bonney (*Lee*), Francesca Annis (*Jean*), Colin Campbell (*Jamie*), Toni Gilpin (*Margaret*), Inigo Jackson (*Harry*), Nigel Green (*Paddy*), Caroline Mortimer (*Marlene*), Vera Day (*Arlene*), David Burke (*Manager*), Freddie Mills (*Joe*), David Lodge (*Arthur*), Wendy Newton (*Cathy*), Barry Langford (*Barman*), Margaret Nolan (*Julie*), Derek Bond (*Paul*), Shirley Cameron (*Edie*), Patsy Fagan (*Barmaid*), Barbara Roscoe (*Miss Bingo*), Gerry Gibson (*Doorman*), Patricia Hayes, The Searchers.

An interesting conception concerns the separate adventures of five sailors during their 15-hour stay-over in London. Unfortunately, nothing new is offered as the sailors go for the chase of a skirt or the comfort of a bottle. One of the sailors, Campbell, is the shy and sensitive sort, and manages to meet a girl that is perfect for him. So perfect, in fact, that he decides to jump ship in order to be with her. Performances are all adequate, but little material beyond the predictable type of sailors-on-leave is given the cast with which to work.

p&d, Robert Hartford-Davis; w, Donald Ford, Derek Ford; ph, Peter Newbrook; m, Bobby Richards; ed, Alastair McIntyre, John Poyner; md, Richards; art d, Peter Proud; cos, Harry Haynes, Tina Swanson; makeup, Jimmy Evans.

Drama   **(PR:A   MPAA:NR)**

SATURDAY NIGHT REVUE**   (1937, Brit.) 77m Welwyn/Pathe bw

Billy Milton (*Jimmy Hanson*), Sally Gray (*Mary Dorland*), John Watt (*Himself*), Betty Lynne (*Ann*), Edward Ashley (*Duke O'Brien*), Georgie Harris (*Plug*), Julien Vedey (*Monty*), Charles Carson (*Mr. Dorland*), Mary Jerrold (*Mrs. Dorland*), Douglas Stuart, Gerry Fitzgerald, John Turnbull, Alvin Conway, Reg Bolton, Webster Booth, The Hillbillies, Bennett & Williams, Stanford & McNaughton, Sydney Kyte and His Band, Scots Kilties Band, John Reynders and The BBC Orchestra, Billy Reid and His Band, Strad and His Newsboys.

Milton is a singer who befriends gangster Ashley and saves him from his gun-toting girlfriend Gray, who also happens to be Milton's singing partner. When Milton loses his eyesight in an accident, Ashley pays for treatment which saves him from permanent blindness. Ashley does his best to avoid Gray, but she finds him when he pretends to be Milton during a radio broadcast. He wears a mask to avoid identification, but she recognizes his voice. Instead of killing him, however, she falls back in love with him. Besides this potent melodrama, SATURDAY NIGHT REVUE offers a wide selection of songs and variety acts.

p, Warwick Ward; d, Norman Lee; w, Vernon Clancey.

Musical   **(PR:A   MPAA:NR)**

SATURDAY THE 14TH*   (1981) 75m New World Pictures c

Richard Benjamin (John), Paula Prentiss (Mary), Severn Darden (Van Helsing), Jeffrey Tambor (Waldemar), Kari Michaelsen (Debbie), Kevin Brando (Billy), Nancy Lee Andrews (Yolanda), Craig Coulter (Duane, the Delivery Boy), Roberta Collins (Cousin Rhonda), Thomas Newman (Cousin Phil), Rosemary De Camp (Aunt Lucille), Carol Androsky (Marge, the Real Estate Broker), Annie O'Donnell (Annette, the Next Door Neighbor), Michael Miller (Ernie, the Cop), Stacy Keach, Sr (Attorney), Paul "Mousie" Garner (Major), Patrick Campbell (Mailman), Irwin Russo (Truck Driver).

Uninspired farce that has Benjamin and Prentiss inheriting a haunted house. They move in, and their son Brando manages to conjure up a number of grotesque playmates. A satire on horror films that has little suspense and even fewer laughs.

p, Julie Corman, Jeff Begun; d&w, Howard R. Cohen (based on a story by Begun); ph, Daniel LaCambre (DeLuxe Color); ed, Joanne D'Antonio, Kent Beyda; art d, Arlene Alen.

Comedy/Horror   Cas.   (PR:A MPAA:PG)

SATURDAY'S CHILDREN***   (1929) 90m FN-WP bw

Corinne Griffith (Bobby Halvey), Grant Withers (Jim O'Neill), Albert Conti (Mr. Mengle), Alma Tell (Florrie), Lucien Littlefield (Willie), Charles Lane (Mr. Halvey), Ann Schaefer (Mrs. Halvey), Marcia Harris (Mrs. Gorlick).

An early talkie for director La Cava (MY MAN GODFREY) offers only partial dialog, but is filled with subtle visual touches and characterizations found throughout the director's light comedies. Story evolves around the simple love affair between Griffith and lady's man Withers, which begins in a harmless enough fashion, then develops as the two temporarily drift apart. Griffith resorts to the tactics she originally felt herself above, the use of cunning techniques to bag a man, to win Withers back and get him to the altar. Except for her voice, Griffiths proves to have talent for light comedy of this type, with Withers offering a manly stereotype La Cava can play off of.

p, Walter Morosco; d, Gregory La Cava; w, Forrest Halsey, Paul Perez (based on the play by Maxwell Anderson); ph, John Seitz; ed, Hugh Bennett; song, "I Still Believe in You."

Comedy   (PR:A MPAA:NR)

SATURDAY'S CHILDREN***   (1940) 101m WB bw

John Garfield (Rimes Rosson), Anne Shirley (Bobby Halevy), Claude Rains (Mr. Halevy), Lee Patrick (Florrie Sands), George Tobias (Herbie Smith), Roscoe Karns (Willie Sands), Dennie Moore (Gertrude Mills), Elizabeth Risdon (Mrs. Halevy), Berton Churchill (Mr. Norman), Tom D'Andrea (Cab Driver).

Maxwell Anderson's Pulitzer Prize-winning play had already been filmed by Greg La Cava in 1929 and would be made again as MAYBE IT'S LOVE in 1935 before this one was attempted. Garfield was sick of playing louts and gangsters and begged for a role he could sink his teeth into. He did an admirable job here, but the movie sunk quickly and the studio bosses gave him a lot of "I Told You Sos." Warner Bros. liked stories about average joes and this is a good example. Shirley – who replaced Jane Bryant when she retired and de Havilland when she refused the role and went on suspension – is the daughter of Rains, an amiable if dull man. She takes a job at Rains office, then meets Garfield, a slow-witted but likable inventor who has a penchant for devising strange contraptions that no one wants. Garfield has big dreams of going to the Philippines to make his fortune. There's a big party thrown for him by his pals and Shirley is angry that he's going to leave when she'd planned to marry him. With the help of her sister Patrick, Shirley tricks Garfield into marrying her. The couple marry but she soon loses her job and his wages aren't enough to support them. Garfield gets another chance at the job in the Philippines and is going to go there – without her. Rains knows the kids need money and he plans to stage an accident so he can give them the insurance money, but that's thwarted. Then the couple learn that they are to be parents and, despite all the hassles, they decide to stay together and try to make it work. Karns does well as Patrick's henpecked husband and Moore brings lots of comedy to her role as a daffy office worker. Garfield's early death has long been the subject of interest. Legend has it that he had a problem with his teeth but refused to consult a Los Angeles dentist, preferring to wait until he was finished shooting HE RAN ALL THE WAY so he could go back to New York and see the man who'd always tended his molars. His mouth was aching and he popped aspirin like they were jellybeans until he overdosed and caused fibrillation. He is alleged to have died of a heart attack in a Hollywood house while in bed with a woman. Other speculation is that he was so tensed by the accusations made for so-called Leftist leanings by HUAC that he died because of the covert blacklist against them.

p, Jack L. Warner, Hal B. Wallis; d, Vincent Sherman; w, Julius J. Epstein, Philip G. Epstein (based on the play by Maxwell Anderson); ph, James Wong Howe; ed, Owen Marks; cos, Milo Anderson.

Drama   (PR:A MPAA:NR)

SATURDAY'S HERO***   (1951) 109m Sidney Buchman/COL bw (GB: IDOLS IN THE DUST)

John Derek (Steve Novak), Donna Reed (Melissa), Sidney Blackmer (T.C. McCabe), Alexander Knox (Megroth), Elliott Lewis (Eddie Abrams), Otto Hulett (Coach Tennant), Howard St. John (Belfrage), Aldo DaRe [Ray] (Gene Hausler), Alvin Baldock (Francis Clayborne), Wilbur Robertson (Bob Whittier), Charles Mercer Barnes (Moose Wagner), Bill Martin (Joe Mestrovic), Mickey Knox (Joey Novak), Sandro Giglio (Poppa), Tito Vuolo (Manuel), Don Gibson (Red Evans), Peter Virgo (Vlatko), Don Garner (Jamieson), Robert Foulk (Butler), John W. Bauer (Turner Wylie), Mervin Williams (Dr. Comstock), Peter Thompson (John Fitzhugh), Noel Reyburn (Toby Peterson), Steven Clark (Ted Bricker).

A subtle cut at the businesslike ethics that have almost made a shambles of sportmanship in college sports, has Derek (mostly known for the films he's produced with wife Bo) as the high school football star who goes to college via a scholarship in the hopes of rising above the immigrant surroundings of his New Jersey home. When his third year comes along, and he finds that an injury keeps him from playing football, he also discovers that the man who has taken such an interest in his future, Blackmer, is really a two-bit hustler, only out to benefit himself. But the determined Derek doesn't give up too easily. He settles down with girl friend Reed, also niece of Blackmer, and continues his education by attending night school while working during the day. A cynical attitude is kept under the surface throughout this film, but the theme of college sports taking precedence over education is as timely today as it was then.

p, Buddy Adler; d, David Miller; w, Millard Lampell, Sidney Buchman (based on the novel The Hero by Lampell); ph, Lee Garmes; m, Elmer Bernstein; ed, William Lyon; md, Morris Stoloff; art d, Robert Peterson; cos, Jean Louis.

Drama   (PR:A MPAA:NR)

SATURDAY'S HEROES**   (1937) 58m RKO bw

Van Heflin (Val), Marian Marsh (Frances), Richard Lane (Red Watson), Alan Bruce (Burgeson), Minor Watson (Doc Thomas), Frank Jenks (Dubrowsky), Willie Best (Sam), Walter Miller (Coach Banks), Crawford Weaver (Baker), George Irving (President Hammond), John Arledge (Calkins), Dick Hogan (Freshman), Al St. John (Andy Jones), Charles Trowbridge (President Mitchell), Jack Mulhall (Desk Clerk), Frank Coghlan, Jr (Student).

A college football tale that almost offers something new when it shows Heflin as the college star who refuses to put up with the patronage he receives because of his status. He wants to get through his classes through hard work and development of his mental faculties, just like everyone else. But this angle is tossed to the side to allow for the customary heroics and to give Heflin a chance to romance Marsh. Awkward handling of an awkward script is given a lift by Heflin's capable performance.

p, Robert Sisk; d, Edward Killy; w, Paul Yawitz, David Silverstein, Charles Kaufman (based on the story by George Templeton); ph, Nicholas Musuraca; ed, Frederic Knudston; cos, Renie.

Drama   (PR:A MPAA:NR)

SATURDAY'S MILLIONS**½   (1933) 76m UNIV bw

Robert Young (Jim Fowler), Leila Hyams (Joan Chandler), Johnny Mack Brown (Alan Barry), Andy Devine (Andy Jones), Grant Mitchell (Ezra "Scoot" Fowler), Mary Carlisle (Thelma Springer), Joe Sauers [Sawyer] (Coach), Mary Doran (Marie), Paul Porcasi (Felix), Lucille Lund (Myra Blaine, Society Reporter), Richard Tucker (Mr. Chandler), Paul Hurst (Doc Maloney), Herbert Corthell (Baldy), William "Billy" Kent (Sam), Robert Allen [Craig Reynolds]] (Football Player), Ralph Brooks (Student in Locker Room), Sidney Bracey (Butler), Al Richmond, Charles K. French, Phil Dunham (Old Grads), Walter Brennan, Don Brodie, Sam Godfrey, Eddie Phillips, Dick [Richard] Cramer, Harrison Greene (Reporters), Alan Ladd (Student).

Young is a college football star with a cocky attitude toward the many fans who make fools of themselves over the game. To support himself while playing football and studying at the same time, Young resorts to numerous jobs, including delivering laundry. The girl he is after, Hyams, can sit around and do nothing, as she is rich and needn't worry. The surprise downbeat ending has Young disobeying his coach's orders and fumbling the game-winning play. Young's performance is given a shade of realism through his cynical attitude, though the plot nevers drifts too far from the stereotype. Devine is around for much-needed laughs. Sharp-eyed moviegoers may be able to spot Alan Ladd in a bit part as a student during his lean early years in Hollywood.

p, Carl Laemmle, Jr.; d, Edward Sedgwick; w, Dale Van Every (based on the story by Lucian Cary); ph, Charles Stumar; ed, Dave Berg, Robert Carlisle; art d, Thomas F. O'Neill.

Drama   (PR:A MPAA:NR)

SATURN 3*   (1980) 88m Associated Film Distributors c

Farrah Fawcett *(Alex)*, Kirk Douglas *(Adam)*, Harvey Keitel *(Benson)*, Douglas Lambert *(Capt. James)*, Ed Bishop *(Harding)*, Christopher Muncke *(2nd Crewman)*.

Futuristic setting takes place entirely on a space station located on the third moon of Saturn, where Fawcett and Douglas are making synthetic food for consumption on Earth. Along comes Keitel, with an ill-advised British accent dubbed over his Brooklynese, as a crazed scientist fleeing from Earth. In his company is an 8-foot tall robot, Hector, who has the same basic personality as Keitel but because of his size is more forceful, causing problems for everyone, especially Fawcett, who the robot lusts after. Set designer Barry, who conceived the story, was taken off the project as director two weeks into production because of disagreements with the producers. He then joined the crew of a sequel to STAR WARS and died of spinal meningitis before it was completed. Douglas grins and grimaces through his role as the ultimate defender of beautiful Fawcett, who, it must be mentioned in the interest of historical factuality, bares her right breast in one sequence of this fantasy.

p&d, Stanley Donen; w, Martin Amis (based on the story by John Barry); ph, Billy Williams; m, Elmer Bernstein; ed, Richard Marden; prod d, Stuart Craig; art d, Norman Dorme; spec eff, Colin Chilvers, Roy Spencer, Terry Schubert, Jeff Luff.

Fantasy   **Cas.**   **(PR:C MPAA:R)**

SATYRICON   (SEE: FELLINI SATYRICON 1969, Fr./Ital.)

SAUL AND DAVID½**   (1968, Ital./Span.) 105m San Paolo Film-San Pablo Films/Riz zoli c (SAUL E DAVID; SAUL Y DAVID)

Norman Wooland *(King Saul)*, Gianni Garko *(David)*, Elisa Cegani *(Akhinoam)*, Luz Marquez *(Abigail)*, Pilar Clemens *(Michal [Mikol])*, Virgilio Teixeira *(Abner)*, Antonio Mayans *(Jonathon)*, Carlos Casaravilla *(Samuel)*, Marco Paoletti *(David as a Boy)*, Stefy Lang *(Goliath)*, Paolo Gozlino *(Joab)*, Dante Maggio *(Abdon)*, Jose Jaspe, Nino Parsello.

Bible epic that focuses on the relationship between the Goliath-slaying hero, David, and the King of the Israelites, Saul. Saul has instilled into him through his wife's jealousy that David's only interest after killing the giant is to become successor to the throne over her son. Saul feels so threatened by David that he attempts to have him killed though he loves him deeply. But throughout David remains devoted to his King. A moving story of loyalty and the great wars between the Philistines and Israelites.

p, Emilio Cordero, Toni De Carlo; d, Marcello Baldi; w, Ottavio Jemma, Flavio Nicolini, Tonino Guerra, Baldi (based on a story by Cordero); ph, Marcello Masciocchi, Juan Ruiz Romero (Eastmancolor); m, Teo Usuelli; ed, Giuliana Attenni; art d, Ottavio Scotti, Sigfrido Burman.

Religious/Drama   **Cas.**   **(PR:A MPAA:NR)**

SAUTERELLE   (SEE: FEMMINA, 1968, Fr./Ital./Ger.)

SAUVE QUI PEUT/LA VIE   (SEE: EVERY MAN FOR HIMSELF, 1980, Fr.)

SAVAGE, THE½**   (1953) 95m PAR c

Charleton Heston *(Warbonnet/Jim Ahern)*, Susan Morrow *(Tally Hathersall)*, Peter Hanson *(Lt. Weston Hathersall)*, Joan Taylor *(Luta)*, Richard Rober *(Capt. Arnold Vaugant)*, Donald Porter *(Running Dog)*, Ted De Corsia *(Iron Breast)*, Ian MacDonald *(Yellow Eagle)*, Milburn Stone *(Cpl. Martin)*, Angela Clarke *(Pehangi)*, Orley Lindgren *(Whopper Aherne)*, Larry Tolan *(Long Mane)*, Howard Negley *(Col. Ellis)*, Frank Richards *(Sgt. Norris)*, John Miljan *(White Thunder)*.

One of the few pre-1960s westerns that concentrate on the plight of the Indians. Though never overcoming stereotypes, it takes a stab at offering a humanist approach. Heston plays the martyr figure again, a white man brought up by Sioux Indians after the enemy Crow have besieged the wagon train his family was traveling west on. The inevitable encroachment of whites forces questions from other members of the tribe as to Heston's loyalties. To prove himself, he must infiltrate the cavalry fort, which he does, discovering that whites can be good people as well as bad. When the warring Crow kill several soldiers, minor feuds break out in which Taylor, the Indian maiden companion to Heston, is killed. A major attack is planned in which Heston is given the job of leading the cavalry soldiers to their doom. At the last moment he decides he doesn't want to see any more blood shed, and because of this action is ostracized from his tribe. He leaves, but not before warning the tribe not to battle the white man because of the great numbers that are sure to soon journey westward. Heston is convincing, though the material he is given is pretty flat, something that the other members of the cast can't seem to overcome either.

p, Mel Epstein; d, George Marshall; w, Sydney Boehm (based on the novel *The Renegade* by L.L. Foreman); ph, John F. Seitz; m, Paul Sawtell; ed, Arthur Schmidt; art d, Hal Pereira, William Flannery; set d, Sam Comer, Ray Moyer. Cos, Edith Head.

Western   **(PR:A MPAA:NR)**

SAVAGE!*   (1962) 84m Jones-Carpenter c (AKA: MISSION TO HELL)

Bill Carpenter, Roy Hurst, Peter Hankins, Francis Lindsey.

This well-meaning environmental piece has a group of white hunters going to the aid of endangered crocodiles in South Africa. Because of a new dam being built, the natives had to be moved to a new locality, where the vicious creatures got in their way. So one group starts to trap the crocodiles, forcing the government to worry about the fate of these animals. Carpenter and company help move the animals to a safer place, but in the process almost incite a native rebellion. Lots of animal action and some beautiful African scenery.

p,d&w, Arthur A. Jones; ph, (Ultrascope, Eastmancolor); m, Ed Richard; ed, Herbert Prechtel.

Adventure   **(PR:A MPAA:NR)**

SAVAGE, THE*   (1975, Fr.) 110m Lira-PAI/GAU c (LE SAUVAGE; AKA: LOVERS LIKE US)

Catherine Deneuve *(Nelly)*, Yves Montand *(Martin)*, Luigi Vanucchi *(Vittorio)*, Tony Roberts *(Alex)*, Dana Wynter *(Wife)*.

Deneuve and Montand play roles far from their normal coolness in this farce that has them meeting in Venezuela and winding up on a desert island as they flee pursuers. Deneuve is about to marry an Italian but runs off at the last moment. The groom chases her, causing a fracas in the room next to Montand's, getting the perfume maker involved. Montand is running from his wife, as well as business commitments, so the two decide to take off together on Montand's boat before they finally give in to their pursuers. Montand and Deneuve are convincing and entertaining, but the material given them is too dry to evoke many laughs.

d, Jean-Paul Rappeneau; w, Jean-Paul and Elizabeth Rappeneau, Jean-Loup Dabadie; ph, Pierre Lhomme (Eastmancolor); m, Michel Legrand; ed, Marie-Josephe Yoyotte.

Comedy   **(PR:C MPAA:PG)**

SAVAGE ABDUCTION zero   (1975) 82m Cinemation c

Tom Drake, Stephen Oliver, Joseph Turkel.

A worthless, amateurish production about a couple of girls who are abducted en route to Los Angeles. Their disappearance leads to a search for them and their demented kidnaper.

p,d&w, John Lawrence.

Horror   **Cas.**   **(PR:O MPAA:R)**

SAVAGE AMERICAN, THE   (SEE: TALISMAN, THE, 1966)

SAVAGE BRIGADE½**   (1948, Fr.) 87m Franco-London Films/Distinguished Films bw

Charles Vanel *(Col. Kalatjeff)*, Vera Korene *(Marie Kalatjeff)*, Roger Duchesne *(Grand Duke)*, Lisette Lanvin *(Natasha)*, Troubetskoy *(Boris Mirsky)*, Jean Galland *(Maximovich)*.

Heavy-handed dramatics from the French hack L'Herbier takes place in Russia during WW I. Vanel is a Cossack colonel who is feuding with Troubetskoy over a woman. But the war gets in the way of the duel they mean to fight in the name of honor, forcing them to wait 20 years before they can pick up where they left off. The conclusion is not worth the wait.

d, Marcel L'Herbier; w, Arnold Lipp; ph, Gerald Perrin; ed, Walter Klee.

Drama/War   **(PR:A MPAA:NR)**

SAVAGE DRUMS*   (1951) 73m Lippert bw

Sabu *(Tipo)*, Lita Baron *(Sari)*, H.B. Warner *(Maou)*, Sid Melton *(Jimmy)*, Steven Geray *(Chang)*, Bob Easton *(Max)*, Margia Dean *(Tania)*, Francis Pierlot *(Aruna)*, Paul Marion *(Rata)*, Ray Kinney *(Rami)*, John Mansfield *(John)*, Edward Clark *(Tabuana)*, Harold Fong *(Officer)*, Nick Thompson *(Spy)*.

Even Sabu [Dastagir! got into the anti-Communist arena of the early 1950s in this trying story which has the young jungle hero studying in the U.S. and a boxer as well, leaving his island home open to the plans of no-good "Reds" Paul Marion and Steven Geray. Trite story runs dully to its conclusion over some very tired attempts at comedy. SAVAGE DRUMS was the last film the former child star made in the U.S. for five years, as the vogue for Eastern films ran its course and Sabu had grown into a chunky-cheeked young man. Thereafter, he tried unsuccessfully to salvage his career in foreign films, until he returned to Hollywood in 1956.

p&d, William Berke; w, Fenton Earnshaw; ph, Jack Greenhalgh; m, Darrell Calker; ed, Carl Pierson; art d, F. Paul Sylos.

Adventure   **(PR:A MPAA:NR)**

SAVAGE EYE, THE***
(1960) 67m Kingsley/Trans-Lux bw

Barbara Baxley (Judith McGuire), Gary Merrill (The Poet), Herschel Bernardi (Kirtz), Jean Hidey (Venus the Body), Elizabeth Zemach (The Nurse).

Baxley stars in this semi-documentary about a woman, divorced after nearly 10 years of marriage, who arrives for a new start in Los Angeles. She struggles to find her own identity and adjust to her new independence, all the while living off her husband's alimony checks. She becomes involved with the married Bernardi but, unfulfilled, she continues to wander. It takes a serious accident to sober Baxley and shake her out of her unmotivated pace. THE SAVAGE EYE, for all its fictional elements, emerges as a remarkably realistic portrayal of one woman and her transition to an unfamiliar facet of modern-day living. Photographed over a number of years by three cameramen (including Haskell Wexler), the film's authenticity was well rewarded by the festival juries of Venice, Edinburgh, and Mannheim, as well as receiving England's Robert Flaherty Award.

p,d&w, Ben Maddow, Sidney Myers, Joseph Strick; ph, Jack Couffer, Haskell Wexler, Helen Levitt; m, Leonard Roseman.

Drama (PR:C-O MPAA:NR)

SAVAGE FRONTIER*½
(1953) 54m REP bw

Allan "Rocky" Lane (Himself), Eddy Waller (Nugget Clark), Bob Steele (Sam Webb), Dorothy Patrick (Elizabeth Webb), Roy Barcroft (William Oakes), Richard Avonde (Cherokee Kid), Bill Phipps (Johnny Webb), Jimmy Hawkins (Davie), Lane Bradford (Tulsa Tom), John Cason (Buck Madsen), Kenneth MacDonald (Bradley), Bill Henry (Dan Longley), Gerry Flash (Pete), Lee Shumway, Blackjack the Horse.

"Rocky" is a U.S. marshal tracking down two killers. His investigation leads to none other than standard western villain Barcroft as the real culprit posing as a civic leader in the town of Bitter Springs. In the process Lane helps out an ex-con and a young robber, setting them straight as to what road to follow from now on.

p, Rudy Ralston; d, Harry Keller; w, Dwight Babcock, Gerald Geraghty; ph, Bud Thackery; ed, Harold Minter; art d, Frank Arrigo.

Western (PR:A MPAA:NR)

SAVAGE GIRL, THE*
(1932) 64m Freuler/Monarch bw

Rochelle Hudson (The Goddess), Walter Byron (The Scientist), Harry F. Myers (The Millionaire), Theodore Adams (The Valet), Adolph Milar (The German), Floyd Schackleford (The Chauffeur), Charles Gemora (The Gorilla).

Silly picture that has wealthy Byron going to Africa to hunt animals and instead coming upon beautiful Hudson, a white girl considered a goddess by the natives. A feud over the girl between Byron and his companion hunter, Milar, almost leads to a bloody battle. But Byron takes the girl back with him. Unbelievable story given less credibility by the insertion of numerous jungle shots that do nothing to advance the story. For Hudson, then 18 years old, it was her first leading role, and she comes across in a brief leopard-skin outfit (precursor to Dorothy Lamour's sarong in her native garb), as an innocent and engaging ingenue, far from the tough lady dame types she was later to portray.

p, Henry R. Freuler; d, Harry S. Fraser; w, N. Brewster Morse; ph, Edward S. Kull; m, Lee Zahler; ed, Fred Bain.

Adventure Cas. (PR:A MPAA:NR)

SAVAGE GOLD**½
(1933) Harold Auten bw

George M. Dyott (Himself), John Martin (Narrator), the Jivaro Indians of Ecuador.

Deep in the jungles of the Amazon basin, near the Ecuador and Brazil border, live the Jivaro Indians, a fierce people noted for their practice of shrinking human heads. In 1928, Dyott discovered a German explorer who had lost his life in the territory of the Jivaro and he came to the conclusion that the explorer was a victim of the bizarre practices of the Jivaro. When Brazilian government officials would not believe him, he decided to make a film to prove his point. Playing himself, Dyott is on another journey through South America when he meets an anxious German prospector who ignores warnings about traveling inside the Jivaro's territory in search of gold. A short while later Dyott learns that the German has been captured by the Jivaro, so he sets out with a small party of white explorers and native scouts to bring the German back. Traveling through the densest portions of the jungle into a territory which scares even the accompanying natives, the group eventually descends upon a Jivaro village. At first they are greeted by war drums, warning them to stay away, but this quickly changes and the group is welcomed by the Jivaro. A bit of snooping about by Dyott leads him to discover that he and his party are too late to save the German. His body is found without a head, and fearful that the same fate awaits them, the white men make a quick exit with the Indians chasing them. SAVAGE GOLD may not be a totally true-to-life depiction of the Jivaros, but it does capture many of their cultural practices on film. These shots alone make this

picture extremely rare and valuable. The Jivaro did in fact shrink heads, a ritual they practiced after the killing of an enemy. They believed the shrinking would keep the dead person's soul trapped so that it could not escape and cause further harm. Occasionally a white person – usually a missionary who offended the Jivaro – would make himself an enemy and thus meet the same fate as the traditional victims. Fearful of losing their ethnic homogenity like neigboring tribes, since the 1950s the Jivaro have severed almost all ties with whites, including ethnographers who want to record their tribal practices. This makes SAVAGE GOLD one of the few films which captured rare footage of the Jivaro in their everyday practices, and a treat for any person who takes pleasure in witnessing events not easily understood by a civilized mentality.

p, George M. Dyott; w, Burnett Hershey, Richard Mack (based on the story by Dyott and Harold Auten); ph, Dyott; ed, L.F. Kennedy; md, James C. Bradford.

Adventure (PR:C MPAA:NR)

SAVAGE GUNS, THE**½
(1962, U.S./Span.) 84m Capricorn-TECISA/MGM c (TIERRA BRU TAL)

Richard Basehart (Steve Fallon), Don Taylor (Mike Summers), Alex Nicol (Danny Post), Paquita Rico (Franchea), Maria Granada (Juana), Jose Nieto (Ortega), Fernando Rey (Don Hernan), Felix Fernandez (Paco), Francisco Camoiras (Manola), Antonio Fuentes (Capt. Baez), Sergio Mendizabal (Mayor), Rafael Albaicin (Gonzales), Jose Manuel Martin (Segura), Victor Bayo (Sanchez), Pilar Caballero (Sanchez' Wife).

Basehart plays a wounded gunslinger who finds a home to recuperate in at the humble ranch of Taylor, an ex-Confederate officer who has seen enough of bloodshed. He grows fond of Taylor's sister, Granada, and develops a deep respect for the peaceful ways of the man who has given him shelter. When greedy rancher Nieto hires sadistic Nicol and a bunch of henchman to drive the smaller ranchers, including Taylor, from the valley, Basehart is quick to come to Taylor's aid. He outguns and outfights Nicol and his gang of no-gooders, which forces the cowardly villain to disappear, to return only to take advantage of his former boss, Nieto. Nicol murders Nieto, then decides to finish off what Nieto had begun. A badly beaten Basehart is rescued from the gun of Nicol by Taylor, who forsakes his nonviolent views one last time to save his friend's life. Shot in Spain, this is an offbeat western that offers some interesting characterizations but doesn't vary too much from an old western formula. Basehart made THE SAVAGE GUNS in another effort to test his versatility. He has frequently appeared in European films in a career-long fight to escape Hollywood typecasting and its pitfalls, and in the process has become adept in playing a wide range of roles.

p, Jimmy Sangster, Jose Maesso; d, Michael Carreras; w, Edmund Morris; ph, Alfredo Fraille (MetroScope, Metrocolor),; m, Anton Garcia Abril; ed, David Hawkins, Pedro Del Rey; art d, Francisco Canet; Makeup, Paco Puyol.

Western (PR:A MPAA:NR)

SAVAGE HARVEST*
(1981) 87m FOX c

Tom Skerritt (Casey), Michelle Phillips (Maggie), Shawn Stevens (Jon), Anne-Marie Martin (Wendy), Derek Partridge (Derek), Arthur Malet (Dr. MacGruder), Tana Helfer (Kristie), Vincent Issac (Jurogi), Eva Kiritta (Halima), Rene LeVant (Alayo), Bill Okwirry (Yumadi), Abdullah Sunado (Katinga), Levit Tereria (Asian), Philip Chege (Customs Officer), Greg Odhambo (Wireless Operator).

Guide Skerritt outwits a horde of lions made hungry by a severe drought in Kenya, and saves his former wife, daughter, his son, and the son's girl friend from a plantation the cunning lions have surrounded. In spite of the excitement promised by that succinct story, very little of it develops. One of the few interesting features of the film is the scene showing the smart way the lions find to reach their prey, actually using what seems like Indian warfare tactics in surrounding the plantation and girding for the attack. Obviously the work of a skilled animal trainer or trainers, nowhere mentioned in the credits.

p, Ralph Helfer, Sandy Howard, Lamar Card; d, Robert Collins; w, Collins, Robert Blees (based on a story by Helfer, Ken Noyle); ph, Ronnie Taylor (DeLuxe Color); m, Robert Folk; ed, Patrick Kennedy, Scott Wallace; prod d, Brian Eatwell; art d, Alan Roderick-Jones, cos, Ellis Cohen.

Adventure (PR:A MPAA:PG)

SAVAGE HORDE, THE**
(1950) 90m REP bw

William Elliott (Ringo), Adrian Booth (Livvy Weston), Grant Withers (Proctor), Barbara Fuller (Louise Cole), Noah Berry, Jr (Glenn Larrabee), Jim Davis (Lt. Mike Baker), Douglas Dumbrille (Col. Price), Will Wright (Judge Cole), Roy Barcroft (Fergus), Earle Hodgins (Buck Yallop), Stuart Hamblen (Stuart), Hal Taliaferro (Sgt. Gowdy), Bob Steele (Dancer), Lloyd Ingraham, Marshall Reed, Crane Whitley, Charles Stevens, James Flavin, Edward Cassidy, Kermit Maynard, George Chesbro, Jack O'Shea, Monte Montague, Bud Osborne, Reed Howes.

Talky oater has Ringo (Elliott), the noted fast man with a gun of the Old West, fleeing the law because of his self-defense killing of an Army officer.

With a posse on his trail, the hero risks capture to aid a group of small-time ranchers at the mercy of cattle baron Withers, who is trying to increase his empire at the expense of the other ranchers. "Three Mesquiteer" fans will be surprised to see Steele, who played the hero Tucson Smith in the series through 1940 and 1941, as a sneaky, totally unlikable heavy in THE SAVAGE HORDE.

p&d, Joseph Kane; w, Kenneth Gamet (based on the story by Thames Williamson, Gerald Geraghty); ph, Reggie Lanning; m, Dale Butts; ed, Arthur Roberts; art d, Frank Arrigo; m/1, Stuart Hamblen.

Western   **(PR:A MPAA:NR)**

SAVAGE INNOCENTS, THE*   (1960, Brit.) 111m Magic
                                          Film-Playart-Gray-Pathe Cinema-Appia/PAR c

Anthony Quinn (Inuk), Yoko Tani (Asiak), Carlo Giustini (2nd Trooper), Marie Yang (Powtee), Peter O'Toole (1st Trooper), Andy Ho (Anarvik), Kaida Horiuchi (Imina), Yvonne Shima (Iulik), Lee Montague (Itti), Francois De Wolff (Trading Post Boss), Anthony Chin (Kidak), Anna May Wong (Hiko), Michael Chow (Undik), Ed Devereaux (Pilot), Marco Guglielmi (Missionary), Andy Ho (Anarvik), Francis De Wolff (Trading Post Proprietor).

In one of his many portrayals of exotic and odd people, Quinn plays an Eskimo in what might be the toughest role of his career since he was required to perform a number of feats from hunting and fishing Eskimo-style, to their peculiar forms of mating. Quinn is quite convincing, which is essential in making this picture work, as it concentrates on the differences between Western and Eskimo culture. The first portion of the film shows Quinn going about his daily tasks and coming in contact with a northern trading post. He takes his wife and mother-in-law to try swap some skins, but winds up killing a priest when he offers the priest his wife, a custom which, when refused, leaves Quinn deeply offended. A fugitive from the law (a theme common throughout Nick Ray's films) is forced to send his mother-in-law out to die, otherwise she would be too much of a burden. Quinn is arrested by two Canadian Mounties, but in their attempt to bring him back one freezes to death while the other is saved by Quinn. The Mountie then lets the Eskimo go free as he realizes, through his contact with Quinn, that a different set of laws is at work in his mind. A realistic and stark picture that makes the Eskimo lifestyle almost seem cruel, yet Quinn and the other players who portray the Eskimos exude a certain simple quality that makes them likable. THE SAVAGE INNOCENTS was one of the first of Quinn's international films and also was the earliest screen appearance of Peter O'Toole, who caused a minor flap on the set because he objected to his voice being dubbed into pidgin English. The producers won, of course. This stunning pictorial account of the way Eskimos live and hunt and love and die was filmed in the northernmost part of Canada, and the scenes of Eskimos fighting for survival are truly magnificent and deeply moving. However, in spite of the critics being respectful when the film came out, the public gave it a wide berth.

p, Joseph Janni, Maleno Malenotti; d, Nicholas Ray; w, Ray, Hans Ruesch, Franco Solinas (based on the novel Top of the World by Ruesch); ph, Alsdo Tonti, Peter Hennessy (Technirama, Technicolor); m, Angelo Francesco Lavagnino; ed, Ralph Kemplen, Eraldo Da Roma; art d, Don Ashton, Dario Cecchi; cos, Vittorio Nino Novarese; makeup, Geoffrey Rodway; arctic consultant, Douglas Wilkinson.

Drama/Adventure   **(PR:A MPAA:NR)**

SAVAGE IS LOOSE, THE½   (1974) 115m Campbell-Devon c

George C. Scott (John), Trish Van Devere (Maida), John David Carson (David), Lee H. Montgomery (Young David).

A turn-of-the-century ship is wrecked off a small tropical desert island, with scientist Scott, his wife Van Devere, and their son the only survivors. The faith that a rescue ship will arrive gradually wanes and Scott decides that it is useless to train their son in the manner of refined society. Instead he pushes for a training that will allow the boy to fend for himself in the wilds, a hunter at home with the beasts of the jungle. The boy becomes a young man, and, the only woman on the island being his mother, incestual feelings arise, with resulting tensions between the father and son. A slow-moving story that is realistic in showing the changes in hope that evolve as the family stays on the island and is forced to resign itself to being part of the island. But it seems a bit contrived, especially in the incest theme, which is not touched upon in any depth.

p&d, George C. Scott; w, Max Ehrlich, Frank De Felitta; ph, Alex Phillips, Jr. (Panavision, Technicolor); m, Gil Melle; ed, Michael Kahn; art d, Agustin Ytuarte; set d, Enrique Estevez.

Adventure/Drama   **Cas.**   **(PR:C MPAA:R)**

SAVAGE MESSIAH*   (1972, Brit.) 100m Russ-Arts/MGM c

Dorothy Tutin (Sophie Brzeska), Scott Antony (Henri Gaudier-Brzeska), Helen Mirren (Gosh Smith-Boyle), Lindsay Kemp (Angus Corky), Peter Vaughan (Louvre Attendant), Michael Gough (Mons. Gaudier), John Justin (Lionel Shaw), Judith Paris (Kate), Imogen Claire (Mavis Coldstream), Ben Aris (Thomas Buff), Otto Diamant (Mr. Saltzman), Alex Jawdokimov (Library Student), Paul McDowell (Agitator), Howard Goorney, Henry

Woolf (Gendarmes), Claire Marshall (Maid), Robert Lang (Maj. Boyle), Susanna East (Pippa), Maggy Maxwell (Tart), Aubrey Richards (Mayor), Eleanor Fazan (Mme. Gaudier).

Another highly stylized outing from Ken Russell, enfant terrible of the British cinema, has few of the excesses found in his other films, but is not without moments of visual highlights that at times are oppressive and detract from the story, which centers on the relationship between a talented young sculptor, Scott Antony (portraying the French artist Henri Gaudier), and a Polish woman 20 years his senior. The youth's wild ways are rounded off by the more refined mannerisms of the older woman, which develop inner qualities in the young man. Russell conveys the magnetism between the two characters in a highly visual and rare manner, capturing the mood of the pre-WW I time in a richly endowed atmosphere. Shirley Russell, the director's first wife, did the costuming for the film.

p&d, Ken Russell; w, Christopher Logue (based on a biography by H.S. Ede); ph, Dick Bush (Metrocolor); m, Michael Garrett; ed, Michael Bradsell; art d, George Lack; set d, Ian Whittaker; cos, Shirley Russell; m/1, "Two Fleas," Dorothy Tutin; makeup, Freddie Williamson.

Drama   **(PR:O MPAA:R)**

SAVAGE MUTINY*½   (1953) 73m COL bw

Johnny Weissmuller (Jungle Jim), Angela Stevens (Joan Harris), Lester Matthews (Maj. Walsh), Nelson Leigh (Dr. Parker), Charles Stevens (Chief Wamai), Paul Marion (Lutembi), Gregory Gay (Carl Kroman), Leonard Penn (Emil Bruno), Ted Thorpe (Paul Benek), George Robotham (Johnson), Tamba the Chimp.

Jungle Jim Weissmuller is called upon by the U.S. and British governments to help remove the natives from a small island that is to be used as an atom bomb testing ground. Enemy agents have other plans, as they try to coerce the natives to remain, and thus take photographs of the tests as propaganda against the two nations. Of course Tamba the Chimp, a near relative to Cheetah from Weissmuller's "Tarzan" days, hangs around for moments of comic relief, along with Jungle Jim's host of other pets, in this exotically campy outing which takes a childish approach to the bleak cold war situation. Here again, as in most "Jungle Jim" outings in the 12-picture series, ample stock footage from the Columbia Pictures library was used, notably from old Frank Buck travel documentaries. (See JUNGLE JIM series, Index)

p, Sam Katzman; d, Spencer Gordon Bennett; w, Sol Shor; (based on characters from the comic strip by Alex Raymond); ph, William Whitley; ed, Henry Batista; m, Mischa Bakaleinikoff; art d, Paul Palmentola.

Adventure   **(PR:A MPAA:NR)**

SAVAGE PAMPAS*   (1967, Span./Arg.) 108m Samuel
                                          Bronston-Dasa/Comet c (PAMPA SALVAJE)

Robert Taylor (Capt. Martin), Marc Lawrence (Sgt. Barril), Ron Randell (Padron), Ty Hardin (Carreras), Rosenda Monteros (Rucu), Felicia Roc (Camila), Angel Del Pozo (Lt. Del Rio), Mario Lozano (Santiago), Enrique Avila (Petizo), Laura Granados (Carmen), Milo Quesada (Alfonso), Hector Quiroga (Pepe), Juan Carlos Galvin (Isidro), Charles Fawcett (El Gato), Julio Pena (Chicha), Jose Nieto (Gen. Chavez), Jose Jasp (Luis), Jose Maria Cafarell (Vigo), Lucia Prado (Chiquito), Barta Barry (Priest), Pastora Ruiz (Magnolia), Sancho Gracia (Carlos), George Rigaud (Old Man), Isabel Pisano (Lucy), Laya Raki (Mimi).

Taylor plays a tough captain at an outpost in the Argentine pampas in the mid-1800s. Fearing an Indian attack, and given a helping hand by a vengeful ex-soldier, the captain resorts to using his enemies' tactics. Randell, the renegade soldier, comes up with the plan to coerce Taylor's soldiers away and plunder villages by offering them captive women. His numbers dwindling, Taylor drags a bunch of prostitutes out of prison to reside at the fort, thus keeping his men content. His plan works, making for some of the film's amusing moments. Taylor is comfortable in his role as a rugged and hardened soldier who goes about taking what he wants. Remake of PAMPA BARBARA (1946).

p, Jaime Prades; d, Hugo Fregonese; w, Fregonese, John Melson (based on the novel Pampa Barbara by Ulises Petit De Murat, Homero Manzi); ph, Manuel Berenguer (Super-Panorama, Eastmancolor); m, Waldo de los Rios; ed, Juan Serra; art d, Gil Parrondo, Angel Canizares; set d, Roberto Carpio; cos, Marian Ribas; ch, Alberto Masulli; makeup, Juan Farsac.

Western   **(PR:C MPAA:NR)**

SAVAGE SAM*   (1963) 103m Walt Disney/BV c

Brian Keith (Uncle Beck Coates), Tommy Kirk (Travis Coates), Kevin Corcoran (Arliss Coates), Dewey Martin (Lester White), Jeff York (Bud Searcy), Royal Dano (Pack Underwood), Marta Kristen (Lisbeth Searcy), Rafael Campos (Young Warrior), Slim Pickens (Wily Crup), Rodolfo Acosta (Bandy Legs), Pat Hogan (Broken Nose), Dean Fredericks (Comanche Chief), Brad Weston (Ben Todd).

Only the Disney studios could produce a film that portrays a group of Indians as a marauding bunch of savages, targeted for attack by the white men, and give it an air of good, clean fun. That's exactly what has been accomplished in what is supposed to be a sequel to the successful OLD YELLER, though any kinship between the two films is hard to find. "Savage Sam," the offspring of "Old Yeller," is instrumental in tracking down a group of Apaches who have kidnaped Kirk, Corcoran and Kristen. Keith heads the posse pursuing the Indians. Little sympathy is shown toward the Indians, many of whom meet with harsh treatment and violence bestowed on them by the other characters. Direction is well-paced, with ample amounts of action, but the unsympathetic treatment of the characters makes for some ambiguity. High points include Keith's performance and the scenic photography.

p, Bill Anderson; d, Norman Tokar; w, Fred Gipson, William Tunberg (based on the book by Gipson); ph, Edward Colman (Technicolor); m, Oliver Wallace; ed, Grant K. Smith, art d, Carroll Clark, Marvin Aubrey Davis; set d, Emile Kuri, Hal Gausman; cos, Chuck Keehne, Gertrude Casey; spec eff, Eustace Lycett, Jim Fetherolf; m/l, "Savage Sam and Me," "The Land of the Wild Countree," Terry Gilkyson; makeup, Pat McNalley.

Western   (PR:A   MPAA:NR)

SAVAGE SEVEN, THE**½   (1968) 94m AIP c

Robert Walker, Jr *(Johnnie Little Hawk)*, Larry Bishop *(Joint)*, Joanna Frank *(Maria Little Hawk)*, John Garwood *(Stud)*, Adam Roarke *(Kisum)*, Max Julien *(Grey Wolf)*, Richard Anders *(Bull)*, Duane Eddy *(Eddie)*, Chuck Bail *(Taggert)*, Mel Berger *(Fillmore)*, Billy Rush *(Seely)*, John Cardos *(Running Back)*, Susannah Darrow *(Nancy)*, Beach Dickerson *(Bruno)*, Eddie Danno *(Fat Jack)*, Alan Gibbs *(Stunt Man)*, Fabian Gregory *(Tommy)*, Gary Kent *(Lansford)*, Gary Littlejohn *(Dogface)*, Penny Marshall *(Tina)*, Walt Robles *(Walt)*.

A semi-underground classic from American International has the white man pitted against the Indian once again; only in this version everyone turns out a loser. Roarke is the head of a motorcycle gang who rides into a small Indian shanty town, which has been at the mercy of corrupt businessmen. Taken by pretty Indian waitress Frank, Roarke helps out her brother, Walker (son of the late star by the same name, famous for his role as Bruno in Alfred Hitchcock's STRANGERS ON A TRAIN) in a disagreement he has with Berger, whose store has been torn apart by both Indian and motorcycle gangs. The cops come in and make several arrests, with Berger agreeing to drop charges against the motorcyclists if they rough up the Indians. A feud develops between the two groups, though Roarke and Frank are eventually able to resolve their differences. When an Indian girl is raped, someone murders one of Roarke's boys. A full-fledged battle develops, with the real culprit, Berger, getting off scot-free. Very violent, but with its share of golden moments.

p, Dick Clark; d, Richard Rush; w, Michael Fisher (based on the story by Rosalind Ross); ph, Laszlo [Leslie] Kovacs (Perfect Color); m, Mike Curb, Jerry Styner; ed, Renn Reynolds; art d, Leon Erikson; m/l, "Anyone for Tennis," Cream, "The Ballad of the Savage Seven," Valjean Johns, Guy Hemric (performed by the American Revolution).

Drama   (PR:O   MPAA:NR)

SAVAGE SISTERS*   (1974) 89m AIP c

Gloria Hendry *(Lynn Jackson)*, Cheri Caffaro *(Jo Turner)*, Rosanna Ortiz *(Mei Ling)*, John Ashley *(W.P. Billingsley)*, Eddie Garcia, Sid Haig, Rita Gomez.

A baffling picture about a group of rifle-wielding women who back a revolution on some faceless banana-republic island. Luckily, it doesn't take itself too seriously and emerges as just another of director Romero's exploitative island entries.

p, John Ashley, Eddie Romero; d, Romero; w, H. Franco Moon, Harry Corner; ph, Justo Paulino; m, Bax; ed, Isagani V. Pastor.

Adventure   (PR:O   MPAA:R)

SAVAGE WEEKEND zero   (1983) 83m Upstate Murder Co./Cannon c
(AKA: THE KILLER BEHIND THE MASK; THE UPSTATE MURDERS)

Christopher Allport *(Nicky)*, James Doerr *(Robert)*, Marilyn Hamlin *(Marie)*, Kathleen Heaney *(Shirley)*, David Gale *(Mac)*, Devin Goldenberg *(Jay)*, Jeffrey David Pomerantz *(Greg)*, William Sanderson *(Otis)*.

Originally shot in 1976, released in 1981 and re-released in 1983, this picture is a very, very bad soft-core pornography/horror film, with a few other distasteful things thrown in for good measure. The basic premise has a couple of families visiting upstate New York for a weekend, where they are building a wooden ship. Eventually, members of the group start getting killed off one by one.

p, John Mason Kirby, David Paulsen; d&w, Paulsen; ph, Zoli Vidor (Technicolor, Berkey/Pathe Humphreys Color); m, Dov Seltzer; ed, Zion Avrahamian, Jonathan Day.

Horror   **Cas.**   (PR:O   MPAA:R)

SAVAGE WILD, THE*½   (1970) 103m AIP c

Gordon Eastman *(Gordon)*, Carl Spore *(Red)*, Maria Eastman *(Maria)*, Arlo Curtis *(Arlo)*, Jim Timiaough *(Jim)*, Robert Wellington Kirk *(Bob)*, John Payne *(John)*, Charles Abou *(Cha-Lay)*, Alex Dennis *(Cha-Lay's Brother)*, Charley Davis *(Charley)*, Wilber O'Brian *(Helicopter Pilot)*, Yukon, Teton, Missy *(Wolves)*.

A docu-drama set in Northern Canada about a nature photographer, Eastman, who raises three timber wolf cubs to save them from bounty hunters. One hunter, Spore, who kills the animals from his airplane, is justly dealt with when his plane crashes during a hunt. Eventually, the cubs become adults and are freed in the wild. Similar in many respects to the far superior NEVER CRY WOLF (1983).

p,d&w, Gordon Eastman; ph, Eastman, Wes Marks, Brad Eastman, Rod Eastman, Art Bothum (Techniscope, Technicolor); m, Jaime Mendoza-Nava; ed, Tom Boutross; m/l Title song, Earl Smith, Gordon Eastman (sung by Cris Quesada).

Nature Drama   (PR:A   MPAA:G)

SAVAGE WILDERNESS   (SEE: LAST FRONTIER, THE, 1955)

SAVAGES***   (1972) 105m Angelika-Merchant-Ivory/Angelika c

Lewis J. Stadlen *(Julian Branch)*, Anne Francine *(Carlotta)*, Thayer David *(Otto Nurder)*, Susie Blakely *(Cecily)*, Russ Thacker *(Andrew)*, Salome Jens *(Emily Penning)*, Margaret Brewster *(Lady Cora)*, Neil Fitzgerald *(Sir Harry)*, Eva Saleh *(Zia)*, Ultra Violet *(Iliona)*, Kathleen Widdoes *(Leslie)*, Sam Waterston *(James)*, Martin Kove *(Archie)*, Asha Puthili *(Forest Girl)*, Paulita Sedgwick *(Penelope)*, Christopher Pennock *(Hester)*, Lilly Lessing, Claus Jurgen *(Narrators)*.

A satrical jab at modern civilization and its development from primitive cultures. A group of natives from an unnamed place stumble upon an old mansion. They inhabit the mansion, adorning the clothing and other refined characteristics of what they take to be civilization. The culmination is a party in which all sorts of heavies are invited. The natives' personalities, while not deviating entirely, do take on certain "civilized" traits. The strong tribe members evolve into their 20th century counterparts, while the weak still find themselves the victims. The natives' party eventually degenerates, the participants tire of the game, and everyone reverts back to his primitive ways. Lassally photographs the primitive scenes in black and white, with "civilization" filmed in color. The color scenes are given a hueing that captures an atmosphere reminiscent of the early 1900s.

p, Ismail Merchant; d, James Ivory; w, George Swift Trow, Michael O'Donoghue, Ivory (based on an idea by Ivory); ph, Walter Lassally; m, Joe Raposo; ed, Kent McKinney; art d, James Rule, Jack Wright; cos, Susan Schlossman, Joan Hanfling; makeup, Gloria Natale.

Comedy   **Cas.**   (PR:O   MPAA:NR)

SAVAGES FROM HELL* (1968) 79m Trans-International c (AKA: BIG ENOUGH AND OLD ENOUGH)

Cyril Poitier *(Reuben)*, Bobbie Byers *(Lucy)*, Diwaldo Myers *(Marco)*, Viola Lloyd *(Teresa)*, William P. Kelley *(High Test)*.

Biker Kelley lusts after the teenage Lloyd, the daughter of a Mexican migrant worker. Kelley then finds his regular girl flirting with Poitier, a black friend of Lloyd's. He beats the daylights out of Poitier and then attempts to rape Lloyd. She fights back, however, and kills her greasy nemesis.

p, K. Gordon Murray; d&w, Joseph Prieto; w, Reuben Guberman; ph, J.R. Remy (Colorscope).

Crime   (PR:O   MPAA:R)

SAVANNAH SMILES**½   (1983) 104m Gold Coast c

Mark Miller *(Alvie)*, Donovan Scott *(Boots)*, Bridgette Andersen *(Savannah Driscoll)*, Peter Graves *(Harland Dobbs)*, Chris Robinson *(Richard Driscoll)*, Michael Parks *(Lt. Savage)*, Barbara Stanger *(Joan Driscoll)*, Pat Morita *(Father O'Hara)*, Philip Abbott *(Chief Pruitt)*, Fran Ryan *(Farmer Wilma)*, John Fiedler *(Grocery Clerk)*, Ray Anzalone *(Mr. Greenblatt)*, Carol Wayne *(Doreen)*.

A perfect Shirley Temple-type story brought up to date has Andersen running away from her rich parents because they won't give her enough attention. During her travels she is picked up by a pair of escaped convicts, who decide to kidnap her and ask for $100,000 in ransom. But after just a short time with the lovable little girl, the hardened criminals prove to be all right underneath and return the girl to her parents free of charge. In the process a strong relationship builds between Miller and Scott, as the crooks, and the young girl, giving the men a chance to display the type of affection they've seldom had. During the girl's absence, her father decides to have a brutal and militaristic cop pursue the kidnapers, but his methods don't prove to be worthwhile. A strain is also placed on the parents' marriage; the mother finds it impossible to contend with her husband and leaves. The film was made with a naive energy that is quite charming. Andersen is effective as the little girl, but a few less sugar lumps would do.

p, Clark L. Paylow; d, Pierre DeMoro; w, Mark Miller (based on a story by Miller); ph, Stephen W. Gray (CFI Color); m, Ken Sutherland; ed, Eva Ruggiero; prod d, Charles Stewart; art d, Allen Terry; set d, Linda Kiffe; m/l, "Another Dusty Road," "Out of the Shadows," "When Savannah Smiles," "Pretty Girl," "Love Will Never Be the Same Again" (Sutherland).

Drama/Comedy   Cas.   (PR:AA MPAA:PG)

SAVE A LITTLE SUNSHINE*½   (1938, Brit.) 75m Welwyn/Pathe bw

Dave Willis (Dave Smalley), Pat Kirkwood (Pat), Tommy Trinder (Will), Max Wall (Walter), Ruth Dunning (Miss Dickson), Peggy Novak (Clara Timpson), Roger Maxwell (Hector Stanley), Annie Esmond (Mrs. Melworthy), Marian Dawson (Mrs. Winterbottom), Aubrey Mallalieu (Official), Annabel Maule, Rosemary Scott, Charles Lefeaux.

Willis invests some reward money in a dilapidated boarding house which fails to turn anything that even resembles a profit. He must resort to working there when all his other money-making options fail. When Kirkwood, his enterprising sweetheart, comes up with the idea of turning the house into a ritzy restaurant, business takes off like Willis never imagined. A harmless entry which offers nothing of value but a few hummable tunes.

p, Warwick Ward; d, Norman Lee; w, Victor Kendall, Vernon J. Clancey, Gilbert Gunn (based on the play "Lights Out at Eleven" by W. Armitage Owen); ph, Ernest Palmer.

Comedy/Musical   (PR:A MPAA:NR)

SAVE THE TIGER***   (1973) 100m Filmways-Jalem-Cirandinha/PAR
                                                                  c

Jack Lemmon (Harry Stoner), Jack Gilford (Phil Greene), Laurie Heineman (Myra the Hitchhiker), Norman Burton (Fred Mirrell), Patricia Smith (Janet Stoner), Thayer David (Charlie Robbins), William Hansen (Meyer), Harvey Jason (Rico), Liv Von Linden (Ula), Lara Parker (Margo the Prostitute), Eloise Hardt (Jackie), Janina (Dusty), Ned Glass (Sid Fivush), Pearl Shear (Cashier), Biff Elliott (Tiger Man), Ben Freedman (Taxi Driver), Madeline Lee (Receptionist).

Director John Avildsen has a knack for taking small budgets and making big movies. First it was JOE, then this, then his triumph with ROCKY. SAVE THE TIGER was the first screenplay sold by producer Steve Shagan (who also wrote a number of novels including The Formula), a one-time advertising and public relations man for Universal. Shagan also produced the film. It's the 1970s DEATH OF A SALESMAN, in that it's a story of a good man who cannot cope with what's happening around him. Just as Willy Loman represented so many salesmen, Lemmon's Harry Stoner will be familiar to anyone who has ever had to meet a payroll. In many ways, SAVE THE TIGER also resembles the Reginald Rose, Paddy Chayefsky, Rod Serling, and Horton Foote TV dramas that blessed the tube in the 1950s ... which is not to say it's anything less than a superb movie. The action takes place in about a day and a half in the life of a man who is trapped by his own indulgences. In 1986, Paul Mazursky would do the comedy side of this story, emphasizing the protagonist's home life, and call it DOWN AND OUT IN BEVERLY HILLS. Lemmon is the managing partner in Capri Casuals, a Los Angeles garment manufacturing company. Business is rotten and Lemmon finds himself dropping off into reveries about his youth, the baseball players he loved, the days he spent in WW II, etc. One morning, after a hellish night filled with dreams, he rises in his sumptuous Beverly Hills home; mentions that it costs him $200 a day just to get up every morning; says goodbye to his wife, Smith, who is leaving to go to a relative's funeral; and gets into his Lincoln for the long drive downtown. On the street, he picks up a Sunset Boulevard young woman, Heineman, who is so open about sex that she suggests they eventually get together. Lemmon doesn't know how to handle it and stalls the situation; he thanks her for the offer but is certain "it just wouldn't work out." Heineman doesn't take it personally and exits the car at her stop. Lemmon gets to his office and talks with his partner, Gilford. They owe a bundle of money and are on the brink of collapse. There's not a bank in town who will lend them the needed cash and their straits are dire. The company owns a warehouse in nearby Long Beach that would not cause them any great distress if it should "happen" to burn down. Lemmon makes the suggestion that they go the route taken by many of their compatriots and have a controlled fire raze the building. Gilford won't hear of it, condemns the whole idea, and Lemmon retorts, "Everyone does it," as if that might be reason enough for such a crime. Burton, an out-of-town client, arrives from Illinois to see the new line from Capri. Burton's a conservative man who lets his hair down when he comes to swinging Los Angeles and Lemmon arranges for a call girl to service Burton. This is Parker, and she's obviously done this before for other Lemmon buyers. Then Lemmon meets David in a porno movie house in a tacky area of Los Angeles where they talk about David's taking care of the Lemmon-Gilford situation with some well-placed matches. Lemmon hears the terms and tells David he'll let him know. On the street outside the movie house, Elliott is raising funds to save wildlife, particularly lions and tigers. That night, Capri is to host a fashion show of the new line at a local hotel. Before departing for the hotel, Lemmon receives a frantic message from Parker that Burton has had a heart attack. When he gets to the man's hotel,

it's obvious that the two were engaging in some kinky sexual escapades and Lemmon is enraged. Once Lemmon is assured that Burton will recover, he takes Parker out for a drink and says he's sorry about yelling at her. At the hotel, the buyers are gathered to see the Capri clothing and Lemmon is slated to give the opening speech. It is at this moment that Lemmon begins to have a mental breakdown. He's named his company after the island where he fought in the war and the assembled clients begin to appear as the buddies who died on that island so long ago fighting against the Axis. Lemmon can't control himself and begins to sob when he thinks about his pals whom he feels died for no reason. He makes his way off the stage, muddled and tearful, then tries to gather himself to make the decision about the arson. He calls David and tells him to apply the torch. Later in the afternoon, Lemmon is driving home and again sees Heineman. He picks her up and she takes him out to Malibu, where she's staying in a cottage that's barely standing. They are decades apart but he is willing to see her side of life and takes a marijuana cigarette for the first time in his life. The two have a long (too long) dialog whereby they each name an important person or thing from their own generation and we can see that the twain is far from meeting intellectually, although physically they finally do get together. In the morning, Lemmon rises and goes into town and walks into a park where some youngsters are playing baseball. Lemmon picks up the ball that's gotten away from one of the boys and wants to know if he can play with them. The kids think he's nuts and say that he can't. He responds by taking a big wind-up, emulating Cleveland's Bob Feller, and tossing the ball 200 feet away, then walking off at the conclusion. The picture asks many questions and answers hardly any of them, but that's not the reason for the movie at all. It's a character study, a portrait of a desperate man who would seem, from the outside, to have it all. He's lost his conscience and his ability to reason as he lusts after success, and despite all of his illegal, immoral, and unethical practices, we are drawn to him and wish him luck. Lemmon won an Oscar for this role, beating out Brando for LAST TANGO IN PARIS, Pacino in SERPICO, Redford in THE STING, and Nicholson in THE LAST DETAIL. Gilford and Shagan were nominated. Heineman's screen debut was excellent and a great career was predicted but never realized. The picture only cost a bit over a million, and though it received some acclaim, it was a disappointment at the turnstiles. Lemmon was never better as a basically decent man who was seduced by circumstance and his inability to give up his expensive life style, thus plunging him into his predicament. He was a man who had everything, and let it slip away. Songs include: "Air Mail Special" (Jimmie Mundy, Benny Goodman, Charlie Christian), "Stompin' at the Savoy" (Goodman, Chick, Webb, Edgar Sampson), "I Can't Get Started" (Vernon Duke, Ira Gershwin).

p, Steve Shagan; d, John G. Avildsen; w, Shagan; ph, Jim Crabe (Movielab Color); m, Marvin Hamlisch; ed, David Bretherton; md, Hamlisch; art d, Jack Collis; set d, Ray Molyneaux; makeup, Harry Ray.

Drama   Cas.   (PR:C-O MPAA:R)

SAWDUST AND TINSEL   (SEE: THE NAKED NIGHT, 1956, Swed.)

SAXON CHARM, THE*½   (1948) 88m UNIV bw

Robert Montgomery (Matt Saxon), Susan Hayward (Janet Busch), John Payne (Eric Busch), Audrey Totter (Alma), Henry Morgan (Hermy), Harry Von Zell (Zack Humber), Cara Williams (Dolly Humber), Chill Wills (Capt. Chatham), Heather Angel (Vivian Saxon), John Baragrey (Peter Stanhope), Addison Richards (Abel Richman), Barbara Challis (Ingenue), Curt Conway (Jack Bernard), Fay Baker (Mrs. Noble), Philip Van Zandt (Chris), Martin Garralaga (Manager), Max Willenz (Proprietor), Fred Nurney (Headwaiter), Archie Twitchell (Mr. Maddox), Barbara Billingsley (Mrs. Maddox), Eula Guy (Harassed Secretary), Al Murphy (Bald Man), Clarence Straight (Mr. McCarthy), Bert Davidson (Mr. Noble), Maris Wrixon (Mrs. McCarthy), Peter Brocco (Cyril Leatham), Donna Martell (Flower Girl), Mauritz Hugo (Designer), Anthony Jochim (Agent), Kathleen Freeman (Nurse), Blanche Obronska (Soubrette), Laura Kasley Brooks (Buxom Nurse), Vivian Mason (Blonde), Basil Tellou (Character Man), Robert Spencer (Leading Man), Paul Rochin (Waiter), Lomax Study (Headwaiter), Robert Cabal (Bus Boy).

Screen adaptation of Claude Binyon's novel casts Montgomery as an egomaniacal producer out to ruin anyone who gets in his path. Payne, who plays a novelist, finds this out the hard way after ignoring advice from his wife, Hayward. The famous producer has agreed to stage Payne's play on Broadway. Hayward's attitude toward Montgomery sours after she and her husband are invited to a party given in honor of Payne's new play. The arrogant producer is a bit too pushy for Hayward's taste, and she warns Payne to back out before it is too late. Montgomery then goes on to destroy the career of his girlfriend, Totter, by spreading rumors over which she loses her contract. Disagreement between Payne and Hayward over Montgomery's methods eventually leads to a separation. Payne is forced to rewrite most of the play, and the new version fails to attract a much-desired actor. Hayward gets her jabs at Montgomery, however, when she shows the original play to the actor and another producer, and finds willing backers. Payne, immediately informed of the turn of events, rushes back to his wife's side, but not before leaving Montgomery with a black eye. Montgomery mustered all the nastiness he could to turn in a convincing portrayal of the phony producer. Hayward, cast in a role to which she was not accustomed, gave it her best shot. The script is very witty, but is besmirched by an overabundance of talk and not enough action.

p, Joseph Sistrom; d&w, Claude Binyon (based on the novel by Frederic Wakeman); ph, Milton Krasner; m, Walter Scharf; ed, Paul Weatherwax; art d, Alexander Golitzen; set d, Russell A. Gausman, Ted Offenbacker; cos, Mary K. Dodson; spec eff, David S. Horsley; ch, Nick Castle; m/1, "I'm in the Mood for Love," Jimmy McHugh, Dorothy Fields (sung by Audrey Totter); makeup, Bud Westmore.

Drama   **(PR:A MPAA:NR)**

SAY HELLO TO YESTERDAY*   (1971, Brit.) 91m Cinerama c

Jean Simmons (*Woman*), Leonard Whiting (*Boy*), Evelyn Laye (*Woman's Mother*), John Lee (*Woman's Husband*), Jack Woolgar (*Boy's Father*), Constance Chapman (*Boy's Mother*), Richard Pescaud (*Labor Exchange Official*), Gwen Nelson (*Char*), Laraine Humphreys (*Teenager*), Ben Aris (*Floor Walker*), Nora Nicholson (*Aged Lady*), Jimmy Gardner (*Balloon Seller*), Caria Chaloner (*Au Pair Girl*), Roy Evans (*Father's Friend*), Ronald Lacey (*Car Park Attendant*), Peter Stephens (*Businessman*), Derek Francis (*Park Keeper*), Geoffrey Bayldon (*Estate Agent*), James Cossins (*Policeman*), Frank Middlemass, Edward Atienza.

Shoddy production in many respects, including scripting and direction, make this overly contrived story about the affair between middle-aged housewife Simmons and rowdy youth Whiting, almost totally worthless. During her afternoon shopping spree in London, Simmons is harassed to an excessive degree by a very obnoxious Whiting. She responds to his strange type of mating call by going to bed with him. What could have been an thought-provoking study of the sexual desires and uncertainties confronted by an aging woman, as well as budding youth, is handled in a blase and trite manner.

p, Josef Shaftel; d, Alvin Rakoff; w, Rakoff, Peter King (based on the story by Rakoff, Ray Mathew); ph, Geoffrey Unsworth (Eastmancolor); m, Riz Ortolani; ed, Ralph Sheldon; prod d, Wilfred Shingleton; art d, Fred Carter; set d, Bryan Graves; cos, Sandy Moss; m/1, title song, Ortolani, Norman Newell (sung by Mark Wynter), "Hello Happiness, Goodbye Misery," Ortolani; makeup, Harry Frampton.

Drama   **(PR:C MPAA:GP)**

SAY IT IN FRENCH**   (1938) 70m PAR bw

Ray Milland (*Richard Carrington, Jr.*), Olympe Bradna (*Julie*), Irene Hervey (*Auriol Marsden*), Janet Beecher (*Mrs. Carrington*), Mary Carlisle (*Phyllis Carrington*), Holmes Herbert (*Richard Carrington, Sr.*), William Collier, Sr (*Howland*), Walter Kingsford (*Hopkins*), Erik Rhodes (*Irving*), Mona Barrie (*Lady Westover*), George P. Huntley (*Lord Westover*), Gertrude Sutton (*Daisy*), Forbes Murray (*Dr. Van Gulden*), Billy Daniels (*Messenger Boy*), Billy Lee (*Boy with Lollipop*), Jean Fenwick (*Nursemaid*), Joseph Swickard (*Old Man*), Grace Goodall (*Miss Briggs*), Gus Glassmire (*Mr. Nolan*), George Hickman (*Messenger*), Walter Soderling (*Commodore Simms*), Maj. Sam Harris (*Commodore Chapman*), Billy Benedict (*Red-Haired Boy*), George Magrill, George Cooper (*Taxi Drivers*), Marek Windheim (*Headwaiter*), Archie Twitchell (*Elevator Operator*), Richard Denning, Ruth Rogers (*Elevator Passengers*), Bert Roach, Max Barwyn (*Waiters*), Byron Foulger (*Swedish Janitor*), Bernice Pilot (*Washerwoman*), Clara Mackin Blore (*Dowager*), Edward Earle, Hooper Atchley (*men*), Paul Newlan (*Customs Inspector*), George Davis (*Steward*), Ed Cecil (*Lift Boy*), Hayden Stevenson (*Elevator Boy*), Luana Walters (*Hat Check Girl*), Gwen Kenyon, Joyce Matthews, Harriette Haddon, Dolores Casey, Marie Burton, Sheila Darcy, Paula de Cardo, Norah Gale, Helaine Moler, Dorothy White, Judith King (*Girls*), Ethel Clayton (*Woman*).

Basically a vehicle for Bradna, a French actress Paramount was trying its hardest to promote at the time. The comedy offers very few laughs, despite a script that had potential were it to have been handled properly. Milland, in a tiresome portrayal, plays a golf pro who meets and falls in love with Bradna. They quickly marry, only to return to the States and find Milland's folks have arranged a society marriage for him to acquire financial backing for family business. Hiding his true marriage from his parents, Milland goes through with an engagement to rich girl Hervey. Not wishing to drop a bomb on his bride-to-be, Milland informs Hervey that he is already married to Bradna. Hervey doesn't mind at all, and for that matter goes along with the plan for the fun of it. By the time the picture ends nobody really cares how Milland's wedding plans will turn out; neither does he.

p&d, Andrew L. Stone; w, Frederick Jackson (based on the play by Jacques Deval); ph, Victor Milner; ed, LeRoy Stone; md, Boris Morros; m/1, "April In My Heart," Hoagy Carmichael, Helen Meinardi.

Comedy   **(PR:A MPAA:NR)**

SAY IT WITH DIAMONDS*½   (1935, Brit.) 64m Davis/MGM bw

Frank Pettingell (*Ezra Hopkins*), Eva Becke (*Sylvia*), Vera Bogetti (*Kay*), Gerald Rawlinson (*Richard*), Eileen Munro (*Fanny Hopkins*), Ernest Sefton (*Mocket*), Arther Finn (*Montana*).

Pettingell turns in a likable performance as a brassworker who thwarts the attempts of a gang of crooks trying to steal a valuable necklace. The thieves pose as detectives, but aren't smart enough to dupe Pettingell.

p&d, Redd Davis; w, Jack Marks.

Comedy   **(PR:A MPAA:NR)**

SAY IT WITH FLOWERS**   (1934, Brit.) 71m REA/RKO bw

Mary Clare (*Kate Bishop*), Ben Field (*Joe Bishop*), George Carney (*Bill Woods*), Mark Daly (*Scotty MacDonald*), Edgar Driver (*Titch*), Freddie Watts (*Steve*), Edwin Ellis (*Ted*), Florrie Forde, Charles Coburn, Marie Kendall, Tom Costello, Percy Honri, Kearney & Browning, Wilson Coleman.

A passable music hall picture which serves as nothing but a stage for numerous cockney variety acts. Clare and Field are a pair of flower sellers who are in dire financial straits and failing health. Some friends help them out by staging a benefit, which enables them to take a much-needed seaside holiday.

p, Julius Hagen; d, John Baxter; w, Wallace Orton, H. Fowler Mear (based on a story by Baxter); ph, Sydney Blythe.

Musical   **(PR:A MPAA:NR)**

SAY IT WITH MUSIC**½   (1932, Brit.) 69m British and Dominions/Woolf and Freedm an bw

Jack Payne (*Himself*), Percy Marmont (*Philip Weston*), Joyce Kennedy (*Mrs. Weston*), Evelyn Roberts (*Dr. Longfellow*), Sybil Summerfield (*Betty Weston*), Freddy Schweitzer, Anna Lee, Billy [William] Hartnell, The BBC Dance Band.

Payne is a bandleader who befriends a composer and long-time friend who has lost his memory after a near-fatal plane crash. Payne's music and recollecting of the past help bring his buddy around, finishing the picture on a positive note.

p, Herbert Wilcox; d, Jack Raymond; w, William Pollock.

Musical   **(PR:A MPAA:NR)**

SAY IT WITH SONGS**½   (1929) 95m WB bw

Al Jolson (*Joe Lane*), Davey Lee (*Little Pal*), Marian Nixon (*Katherine Lane*), Fred Kohler (*Joe's Cellmate*), Holmes Herbert (*Dr. Robert Merrill*), John Bowers (*Surgeon*).

Trying to cash in on Jolson's success in THE JAZZ SINGER and THE SINGING FOOL, Warner Bros. was so sure of his box office potential it paid him $500,000, an astronomical figure in 1929, to star in this film. Little Davey Lee was even thrown in, a la "Sonny Boy." The result was a familiar story and plot that was to become a formula for Jolson. He plays a radio singer who tends to neglect his wife, Nixon, and son, Lee. Despite the wandering ways of her husband, Nixon remains the devoted spouse, even when Jolson's boss and best friend makes advances toward her and promises "big success" for her husband if she cooperates. Jolson gets wind of his friend's antics and gives him a swift hook to the jaw. The man's skull hits the pavement and he dies. Given a life sentence for manslaughter, Jolson goes to jail, leaving Nixon to become a nurse to support the family. She also attracts the attention of surgeon Bowers. Eventually Jolson is paroled, and as he exits from the prison, Lee is hit by a car. The skilled hands of Bowers save the boy. Jolson proved to be a more polished actor than in his other two vehicles, although the formula material had become a bit tiresome. Direction and all phases of production were top-notch; nonetheless, the film flopped, even with the great Jolson voice. Some of Jolson's songs include "Little Pals," "Why Can't You," "I'm In Seventh Heaven," "One Sweet Kiss" (Buddy De Sylva, Lew Brown, Ray Henderson, Al Jolson); "Back In Your Own Backyard," "I'm Ka-razy About You" (Dave Dreyer, Jolson, Billy Rose).

d, Lloyd Bacon; w, Joseph Jackson (based on the story by Darryl F. Zanuck, Harvey Gates); ph, Lee Garmes; ed, Owen Marks.

Musical/Drama   **(PR:A MPAA:NR)**

SAY ONE FOR ME*   (1959) 119m FOX c

Bing Crosby (*Father Conroy*), Debbie Reynolds (*Holly*), Robert Wagner (*Tony Vincent*), Ray Walston (*Phil Stanley*), Les Tremayne (*Harry LaMaise*), Connie Gilchrist (*Mary Manning*), Frank McHugh (*Jim Dugan*), Joe Besser (*Joe Greb*), Alena Murray (*Sunny*), Stella Stevens (*Chorine*), Nina Shipman (*Ray Flagg*), Sebastian Cabot (*Monsignor*), Judy Harriet (*June January*), Dick Whittinghill (*Lou Christy*), Robert Montgomery, Jr (*Hotel Clerk*), Murray Alper (*Otto*), Richard Collier (*Capt. Bradford*), David Leonard (*Rabbi Berman*), Thomas B. Henry (*Dr. Leventhal*), Wilkie de Martel (*Rev. Kendall*), Alexander Campbell (*Pastor Johnson*), Bruce McFarlane (*Detective Minelli*).

This was the third time Crosby donned the clerical collar for a movie and, by far, the least impressive. It can best be described as a religious musical comedy that owes a lot to Damon Runyon, but it fails to come close to the Broadway characters chronicled by the man who inspired GUYS AND DOLLS. Crosby runs a show business church (there really was one, St. Malachy's, in the theater district in New York) where just about all the devout are in some way aligned with the entertainment field. Crosby reads the show-biz trade papers and runs his services like Fat Jack Leonard monologues. Enter Reynolds, a naive collegian who wants to make a lot of money in show business because her father needs an operation. Crosby knows Reynolds' father, so he agrees to play surrogate daddy while she's in the big city. Reynolds gets a job at a tawdry nightclub managed by Wagner, a "Pal Joey"-type rat who wants to take advantage of Reynolds. Crosby tells him to lay off. Crosby takes on the job of producing a charity show for TV and brings in several other clergymen. Wagner arrives and asks that he be allowed to appear in the show. Crosby has no intention of letting that happen, then Wagner says he's charmed Reynolds into agreeing to marry him, and Crosby is willing to let Wagner be on the show if he promises to forget about Reynolds. The show is a mish mash of songs, and when Wagner comes center stage, he goes through a remarkable conversion and tells the millions watching that he's a heel. Crosby is touched by this and gives his approval for Wagner and Reynolds to marry, then performs the service. The couple go to Florida for their honeymoon and the end title reads "The Beginning." A dull movie that is also tasteless, with a drunk scene, a seduction scene, Reynolds shaking her behind while Crosby and a nun watch, plus several songs that are unhummable, unwhistleable, and unmemorable. It is also heavy-handed, with cuts between singing and Jesus on the cross, just in case anyone should forget that religion is a part of show people's lives. Tunes by the normally reliable Sammy Cahn and Jimmy Van Heusen include "The Girl Most Likely to Succeed" (sung by Wagner, Reynolds), "Chico's Choo Choo" (sung by Wagner, Reynolds), "The Secret of Christmas" (sung by Crosby), "The Night Rock n Roll Died" (sung by Judy Harriet a former Mouseketeer), plus "I Couldn't Care Less," "You Can't Love 'Em All," "Hanoveh." The studio knew they had a turkey and tried a "semi-preview" by showing half the film to the press. It didn't help. Good comedians Walston, McHugh, Cabot and Besser were wasted. Stella Stevens does a bit as a chorine. By this time, Crosby was becoming hard to cast, as he was too old to play romantic leads. A sappy film with unsympathetic characters and a poor score. Other than that, it was terrific.

p&d, Frank Tashlin; w, Robert O'Brien; ph, Leo Tover (CinemaScope, DeLuxe Color); ed, Hugh S. Fowler; md, Lionel Newman; art d, Lyle R. Wheeler, Leland Fuller; set d, Walter M. Scott, Eli Benneche; cos, Adele Palmer; ch, Alex Romero; m/l, James Van Heusen, Sammy Cahn.

Musical/Comedy   Cas.   (PR:C   MPAA:NR)

SAYONARA**   (1957) 147m Goetz-Pennebaker/WB c

Marlon Brando (*Maj. Lloyd Gruver*), Ricardo Montalban (*Nakamura*), Red Buttons (*Joe Kelly*), Patricia Owens (*Eileen Webster*), Martha Scott (*Mrs. Webster*), James Garner (*Capt. Mike Bailey*), Miiko Taka (*Hana-ogi*), Miyoshi Umeki (*Katsumi*), Kent Smith (*Gen. Webster*), Douglas Watson (*Col. Craford*), Reiko Kuba (*Fumiko-san*), Soo Young (*Teruko-san*), Harlan Warde (*Consul*), Shochiku Kagekidan Girls Revue.

This beautifully photographed and often moving story of racial prejudice features Brando as an Army major reassigned to a Japanese air base in the midst of the Korean conflict. This assignment has come in part due to the work of his supposed future father-in-law Smith, a general married to Scott. Scott and her daughter Owens join Smith and Brando at the air base where the prim matron is highly upset when Garner, a captain, tries to get his Japanese girl friend admitted to the officer's club. Buttons, an enlisted man buddy of Brando's from Korea, has fallen in love with a Japanese woman and is fighting official policies which forbid interracial marriage. One night Brando and Owens attend an evening of Kabuki theater where they meet Japanese actor Montalban. The engaged couple later quarrel about Owens, apparent interest in Montalban and her plans for a married life with Brando. Brando agrees to be the best man at Buttons' wedding, which angers Smith. Brando responds in anger as well, telling Smith he did not want to leave the conflict in Korea in the first place. After meeting Garner in a bar, Brando joins the captain on a sightseeing tour. While on this jaunt Brando notices Taka, a beautiful member of the Matsubayashi dancers. This highly praised troupe is made up of Japanese women so devoted to dance that they must limit their contact with any outsiders so as not to stray from their talents. Brando goes back day after day in hope of catching Taka's eye, then appeals to Buttons when he learns that his friend's fiancee (Umeki) knows some of the Matsubayashi troupe. A meeting is arranged between the major and the dancer where each admits to a mutual attraction. The two realize that their love will come under fire from both the American military and the Japanese dance troupe. Watson, a colonel fueled by his prejudices, finds out about the romance and informs Smith. Thoroughly against miscegenation, Watson issues an order sending all military men who have married Japanese women back home without spouses. The sympathetic Owens tells Brando and Buttons of the forthcoming edict after realizing she has lost her fiance's heart to another. Brando tries to help out Buttons now that Umeki is pregnant, but to no avail. His emotions go through further turmoil when Taka will not break the American rules because she would lose respect among her own people. Brando and Buttons take their respective loves to a puppet show in what they want to be a fond farewell. The show–by the noted Bunraku Mitsuwa puppets, featuring oversized figures–is entitled "The Love Suicides of Amijima." Buttons and his wife go home to find their dwelling now boarded up and considered off-limits to Americans, while Brando is arrested. Buttons is also arrested but manages to escape. He is again reunited with Umeki and the two commit suicide. Brando and Garner later discover the bodies after pushing their way through a crowd of people.

Shocked by what has happened, Brando looks at the bodies and murmers quietly to himself, "Oh, God." After asking Garner to report the deaths, Brando tries to find Taka at the theater, where he learns that she has left for Tokyo. Smith, now more understanding, tells Brando that regulations will soon be changed on interracial marriages. Brando then follows his love to Tokyo and proposes. Taka accepts, telling reporters that she doesn't care what others think. Brando and Taka prepare to leave, but are asked one final question. Brando tells the inquisitive reporter that his only statement for the American Far East Command is "Sayonara." SAYONARA is a sensitive work, sparing neither American nor Japanese cultures in condemning prejudice. Performances are uniformly excellent, matched by Logan's caring direction. The film received 10 Oscar nominations including Best Picture, Best Director, Best Actor, Best Cinematography, Best Screenplay, and Best Editing. Oscars went to the film for sound, art, and set decoration as well as to Buttons and Umeki for their supporting roles. (In her memoirs *Brando for Breakfast*, Brando's ex-wife Kashfi, related that her husband met fellow Oscar loser Anthony Quinn in the parking lot outside the hall. "Both had lost the Best Actor award to Alec Guinness for BRIDGE ON THE RIVER KWAI. The two men gazed ruefully at one another. 'I'll read you my acceptance speech if you read me yours', yours', Marlon.") The film was just as popular with the public, grossing a whopping $10 million in box office receipts, quite a sum for the time. Logan had originally tossed around the idea with James Michener, envisioning the project as a musical. (Logan would later direct the film version of a similarly themed Michener-inspired musical, SOUTH PACIFIC). After penning his novel, Michener offered Logan first rights to the property, but various legal problems prevented the director from bringing it to the Broadway stage. Later, Logan recalled in his book *Josh, My Up and Down, In and Out Life*, while hospitalized for some mental troubles the director came across an installment of Michener's novel in a magazine. Turning to a nun who cared for him, Logan wrote "...I pointed to the magazine and said, 'I own the movie rights to that story, you know.' 'No, I didn't know–but I'm very happy for you,' she said, with the overly sweet voice nuns use to mean, 'Who are you kidding, Mac?' " Eventually Logan was able to get the story before the cameras, but even then problems continued, this time coming in the form of his leading man. Brando was initially impressed with Logan as a director ("I like the tender way you took the leaves off that plant while we were talking yesterday. I didn't know you were sensitive enough to care for flowers..." Brando reportedly told Logan on accepting the part) but the two strong-minded artists entered into arguments soon after production began. The original ending had Brando leaving his Japanese love behind but the actor insisted that the racial prejudice be overcome in the climax. Once Logan agreed to this Brando immediately took the rest of the script to task. In a controversial interview during the filming done with the actor by Truman Capote, Brando related some rather inflammatory vodka-induced comments. Brando claimed Logan had told him " '...We welcome any suggestions you have, Marlon...If there's anything you don't like–why, rewrite it...write it your own way.' Rewrite, hell. I rewrote the whole damn script. And now they're going to use maybe eight lines." Brando and Logan continued the arguments throughout filming, but in her book Kashfi maintained it was two dedicated artists fighting for what they believed in. The pair had other incidents of a more unusual nature. Brando was fond of jokes on the set and during the last days of shooting showed up with his arm in a sling. Claiming that if he moved it at all he'd be maimed for life, Brando turned down every possible suggestion of Logan's to shoot around this seemingly broken arm. "Too bad I can't move it like this," said the star as he waved the arm above his head. Logan was severely shocked by the gag and exclaimed to associates "One more picture with Brando and I'll be an old man." Despite these differences the film was eventually finished to both men's satisfaction. This updating of the "Madam Butterfly" theme remains a powerful story, well told with a statement on racial prejudice that remains timeless. The story was certainly topical; when filming began in 1956 (the picture was a year in the making), more than 10,000 American servicemen had defied extant regulations and married Japanese women (as author Michener had done during an earlier period). This was the debut film of each of the Oriental leading ladies, Taka and Umeki. Taka, a nisei, had been discovered in Los Angeles after a lengthy talent search.

p, William Goetz; d, Joshua Logan; w, Paul Osborn (based on the novel by James A. Michener); ph, Ellsworth Fredricks (Technirama, Technicolor); m, Franz Waxman; ed, Arthur P. Schmidt, Philip W. Anderson; art d, Ted Haworth; set d, Robert Priestly; cos, Norma Koch; ch, LeRoy Prinz; m/l, "Sayonara," Irving Berlin.

Drama   Cas.   (PR:C   MPAA:NR)

SAYS O'REILLY TO MCNAB   (SEE: SEZ O'REILLY TO MCNAB, 1938, Brit.)

SCALAWAG*½   (1973, Yugo.) 93m Inex-Oceania-Byrna/PAR c

Kirk Douglas (*Peg*), Mark Lester (*Jamie*), Neville Brand (*Brimstone/Mudhook*), George Eastman (*Don Aragon*), Don Stroud (*Velvet*), Lesley-Anne Down (*Lucy-Ann*), Danny DeVito (*Fly Speck*), Mel Blanc (*Barfly the Parrot*), Phil Brown (*Sandy*), Davor Antolic (*Rooster*), Stole Arandjelovic (*Beanbelly*), Fabijan Sovagovic (*Blackfoot*), Shaft Douglas, Beau the Dog.

This directorial debut by veteran actor Douglas was shot in Yugoslavia. In it, Douglas plays the part of a peg-legged pirate whose men bury treasure on an island, then are all killed. The only one who knows the whereabouts of the gold is an alcoholic parrot who isn't telling. Douglas befriends two youngsters he finds, Lester and Down, and together they battle mutinous cutthroats, hostile Indians, and deadly rapids. The Douglas family dog also stars.

p, Anne Douglas; d, Kirk Douglas; w, Albert Maltz, Sid Fleischman (based on the story by Robert Louis Stevenson); ph, Jack Cardiff (Technicolor); m, John Cameron; ed, John Howard; art d, Sjelko Senecic.

Adventure   **(PR:A MPAA:G)**

SCALPEL** (1976) 95m P.J. Productions/United International c (AKA: FALSE FACE)

Robert Lansing (*Dr. Phillip Reynolds*), Judith Chapman (*Heater/Jane*), Arlen Dean Snyder (*Uncle Bradley*), David Scarroll (*Dr. Robert Dean*), Sandy Martin (*Sandy*), Bruce Atkins (*Plumber*).

Lansing is a plastic surgeon who tries to collect an inheritance by reconstructing a go-go dancer's face in the image of his missing daughter. Before long the pseudo-daughter delivers bedroom favors on the way to a surprise ending. Tolerable idea poorly executed on a shoestring budget.

p, Joseph Weintraub, John Grissmer; d&w, Grissmer (based on a story by Weintraub); ph, Edward Lachman, Jr. (Movielab Color); m, Robert Cobert; ed, Weintraub; prod d, William DeSeta.

Drama   **(PR:O MPAA:PG)**

SCALPHUNTERS, THE***   (1968) 103m Bristol-Norlan/UA c

Burt Lancaster (*Joe Bass*), Shelley Winters (*Kate*), Telly Savalas (*Jim Howie*), Ossie Davis (*Joseph Winfield Lee*), Armando Silvestre (*Two Crows*), Dan Vadis (*Yuma*), Dabney Coleman (*Jed*), Paul Picerni (*Frank*), Nick Cravat (*Ramon*), John Epper, Jack Williams, Chuck Roberson, Tony Epper, Agapito Roldan, Gregorio Acosta, Marco Antonio Arzate (*Scalphunters*), Nestor Dominguez, Francisco Oliva, Benjamin Ramos, Enrique Tello, Raul Martinez, Jose Martinez, Rodolfo Toledo, Jose Salas, Cuco Velazquez, Alejandro Lopez, Raul "Pin" Hernandez, Pedro Aguilar (*Kiowas*), Angela Rodriguez, Amelia Rivera, Alicia del Lago (*Scalphunters' Women*).

A comical western with more than a hint of social satire starring Lancaster as an illiterate trapper who has a run-in with a band of Kiowa Indians. They force him to "trade" his year's cache of pelts in exchange for an educated slave, Davis. Lancaster follows the Kiowas, only to see them get ambushed by a gang of scalphunters led by Savalas. Later Savalas captures Davis, giving Lancaster another reason to continue his pursuit. Traveling with Savalas is Winters, a weathered sexpot whose wagon is decorated with a brass bed. She takes a liking to Davis, convincing Savalas to free the slave of his restraints. Since the gang is heading for Mexico, where slavery has been outlawed, there is no reason for Davis to leave. Lancaster refuses to give up his possessions, and little by little wages war on Savalas' men. The sneaky Savalas tries to make peace, but Lancaster isn't fooled and kills the scalphunter. By now the Kiowas have regrouped and ambush Savalas' band of marauders. Only Lancaster, Davis, and Winters and the other women are spared, with Winters offering herself to the Kiowa chieftain. While the movie is a bit dated and suffers from the cultural climate of the 1960s, it remains watchable thanks to some shining performances, especially from Winters and Davis, who steal the picture whenever they're on the screen. In response to the racial tension of the time, THE SCALPHUNTERS contains one truly memorable scene in which a quarreling Lancaster and Davis wrestle each other to the ground in a mud pond. Covered head to toe with mud, the racial lines are blurred and both men are placed on an equal plane. Filmed in Mexico, THE SCALPHUNTERS was constantly the subject of blistering rumors about fights and tension on the set between Lancaster and former flame Winters, and between Lancaster and director Pollack. Whatever the truth, the hard feelings were eventually resolved by the time Pollack and Lancaster began work on their next picture, CASTLE KEEP.

p, Jules Levy, Arthur Gardner, Arnold Laven; d, Sydney Pollack; w, William Norton (based on a story by Norton); ph, Duke Callaghan, Richard Moore (Panavision, DeLuxe Color); m, Elmer Bernstein; ed, John Woodcock; art d, Frank Arrigo; cos, Joe Drury; spec eff, Herman Townsley; ch, Alex Ruiz; stunts, Tony Epper.

Western/Comedy   **(PR:C-O MPAA:NR)**

SCALPS zero   (1983) 82m American Panther/21st Century c

Kirk Alyn (*Dr. Howard Machen*), Carroll Borland (*Dr. Reynolds*), Jo Ann Robinson (*D.J.*), Richard Hench (*Randy*), Roger Maycock (*Kershaw*), Barbara Magnusson (*Ellen*), Frank McDonald (*Ben*), Carol Sue Flockhart (*Louise*), George Randall (*Billy Iron Wing*), Forrest J. Ackerman (*Prof. Treatwood*).

A truly pathetic and embarrassing splatter picture which barely resembles a professional film at all. A group of teenagers poke their noses around a sacred Indian burial ground and stir up a warrior's spirit. What follows is the bloody removal of the kids' scalps (hence the title). The film does boast the casting of Alyn, of 1948's Superman serials, and Borland, of Tod Browning's 1935 MARK OF THE VAMPIRE. "Famous Monsters" magazine

editor Forrest J. Ackerman makes a cameo with his magazine in hand. You can see him in the same role in THE HOWLING (1981).

p, The Eel [T.L. Lankford]; d&w, Fred Olen Ray; ph, Brett Webster, Larry van Loon (Quality Color); m, Drew Neumann, Eric Rasmussen; ed, John Barr; makeup, Chris Biggs.

Horror   **(PR:O MPAA:R)**

SCAMP, THE   (SEE: STRANGE AFFECTION, 1957, Brit.)

SCANDAL**   (1929) 70m UNIV bw

Laura La Plante (*Laura Hunt*), Huntley Gordon (*Burke Innes*), John Boles (*Maurice*), Jane Winton (*Vera*), Julia Swayne Gordon (*Mrs. Grant*), Eddie Phillips (*Pancho*), Nancy Dover (*Janet*).

An early talkie, beset with problems of crude recording methods, offers only 22 of its 70 minutes in dialog form; the rest is in the standard silent mode. La Plante, in her sound debut, is a former socialite who must get a job after coming on hard times. Her new position brings her contact with several old acquaintances, including former lover Boles, now married to a woman who later turns up murdered. Though still infatuated with Boles, La Plante rejects his advances and marries Gordon instead. On the night of Boles' wife's death, Boles had visited La Plante, and only she can provide him with an alibi. She does so, and saves him from the death penalty. The musical arrangement from an early Universal talkie was also used in this film.

p, Harry L. Decker; d, Wesley Ruggles; w, Paul Schofield, Tom Reed, Walter Anthony (based on the story "The Haunted Lady" by Adela Rogers St. John); ph, Gilbert Warrenton; ed, Ray Curtiss, Maurice Pivar.

Drama   **(PR:A MPAA:NR)**

SCANDAL***   (1964, Jap.) 104m Shochiku Co./Shochiku Films of America bw (SHUBUN)

Toshiro Mifune (*Ichiro Aoye*), Yoshiko Yamaguchi (*Miyako Saigo*), Takashi Shimura (*Hiruta*), Yoko Katsuragi (*Masako*), Noriko Sengoku (*Sumie*), Sakae Ozawa (*Hori*), Bokuzen Hidari (*Drunk*), Kuninori Kodo (*Farmer*).

In a rare appearance out of samurai garb, Mifune plays a painter who sues a magazine for printing a picture and scandalous story about him and a famous pop singer. Troubles erupt when Mifune's lawyer takes a bribe to lose the case from the magazine, so he can get money to treat his ill daughter. But the lawyer's guilt forces him to confess, and his daughter dies shortly thereafter. Done with Kurosawa's subtle touch of irony. The film was first released in Japan in 1950.

p, Takashi Koide; d, Akira Kurosawa; w, Ryuzo Kikushima, Kurosawa; ph, Toshio Ubukata; m, Fumio Hayasaka; art d, Tatsuo Hamada.

Drama   **(PR:A MPAA:NR)**

SCANDAL AT SCOURIE**   (1953) 90m MGM c

Greer Garson (*Mrs. Patrick McChesney*), Walter Pidgeon (*Patrick J. McChesney*), Agnes Moorehead (*Sister Josephine*), Donna Corcoran (*Patsy*), Arthur Shields (*Father Reilly*), Philip Ober (*B.G. Belney*), Rhys Williams (*Bill Swazey*), Margalo Gillmore (*Alice Hanover*), John Lupton (*Artemus*), Philip Tonge (*Mr. Gogarty*), Wilton Graff (*Mr. Leffington*), Ian Wolfe (*Councilman Hurdwell*), Michael Pate (*Rev. Williams*), Tony Taylor (*Edward*), Patricia Tiernan (*Nun*), Victor Wood (*James Motely*), Perdita Chandler (*Sister Dominique*), Walter Baldwin (*Michael Hayward*), Ida Moore (*Mrs. Ames*), Maudie Prickett (*Mrs. Holahan*), Ivis Goulding (*Mrs. O'Russell*), Alex Frazer (*Womsley*), Matt Moore (*Kenston*), Charles Watts (*Barber*), Roger Moore, Al Ferguson, Jack Bonigul (*Ad Libs*), Eugene Borden (*Old Man*), Rudy Lee (*Donald*), Max Willenz (*Vidocq*), Ivan Triesault (*Father Barrett*), Wayne Farlow, Linda Greer, Kathleen Hartnagel, Warren Farlow (*Children*), Joann Arnold (*Sister Maria*), Peter Roman (*Freddie*), George Davis (*Bartender*), Vicki Joy Kreutzer (*Edith*), Gary Lee Jackson (*Other Boy*), Jill Martin (*Isabella*), Coral Hammond (*Cecilia*), Nolan Leary (*Conductor*), Owen McGiveney (*Clark*), Archer McDonald (*Barber Apprentice*), Earl Lee (*Tweedy Man*), Howard Negley (*Duggin*), Robert Ross (*Dr. Parker*), John Sherman (*Mr. Pringle*).

The wrong title, the wrong script, and the right actors couldn't help this bathetic tearjerker. It was the ninth and final duet for Garson and Pidgeon and the only picture they made which did not open at New York's prestigious Radio City. Set in Canada, SCANDAL AT SCOURIE tells the story of little Corcoran, a Catholic orphan who inadvertently starts a fire that destroys her Quebec orphanage. The children are now homeless and must be placed, so the nuns take them across the country on a train, dropping kids off at good homes. They arrive at the Protestant town of Scourie where Corcoran meets Garson, wife of one of the town's leading political lights and owner of the department store. Garson has no children and would like to adopt the cute tyke, but Pidgeon is against it, as the child is from a different faith. The nuns also think it's a bad idea, but Garson assures them that Corcoran will be raised a Catholic with no attempt to convert her to Protestantism. With that assurance, Corcoran is placed in the Garson-Pidgeon home. Pidgeon intends to run for office and his rival, newspaperman Ober, decides to turn the situation against Pidgeon and writes that his only reason for adopting this child was to garner the Catholic vote in the election on the horizon. Ober is in the local barber shop when Garson walks in and whacks him with a wet towel. Pidgeon is speaking at a political convention and has to use force to quell some hecklers. Ober's words are believed by the townspeople and Pidgeon is soon looked upon with scorn and advised to return Corcoran to the nuns if he wants any sort of office in the town. All of this serves to get Pidgeon's dander up and he absolutely refuses to think of giving up this little girl he's come to love. There's a fire at the school, and when Corcoran's past history is uncovered, the townspeople assume she started it. Pidgeon is livid at the accusations, resigns his office, and quits his high position in the local church. Corcoran feels that she has ruined the lives of Garson and Pidgeon and decides to run away and allow them to regain their stature in the town. The rain pours down as Garson, Pidgeon, and a few of the villagers, who have since learned that Corcoran is innocent of the arson charge, begin to search the countryside for her. She is finally found, cold, wet, but unharmed. At the finale, the local people realize the folly of their ways and endorse Pidgeon and Garson for their pluck and faith in the little girl. Movies about religious intolerance and racial problems had been coming out with regularity since Dore Schary did CROSSFIRE in 1947. This was a mild attempt at showing the schism between Protestantism and Catholicism and it never gathered enough steam to make a dent in the public's sensibilities. Beautifully photographed by Planck. Moorehead does a cameo as a nun at the beginning of the film, then disappears, and Arthur Shields plays a priest again. There is a bit of comedy, but not as much as there should have been, which is odd when one considers the three screenwriters, all of whom are noted for their wit and erudition, little of which came through in this.

p, Edwin H. Knopf; d, Jean Negulesco; w, Norman Corwin, Leonard Spigelgass, Karl Tunberg (based on a story by Mary McSherry); ph, Robert Planck; m, Daniele Amfitheatrof; ed, Ferris Webster; art d, Cedric Gibbons, Wade B. Rubottom; cos, Walter Plunkett; songs, "Green Sleeves," "Frere Jacques."

Drama/Comedy   (PR:A   MPAA:NR)

SCANDAL FOR SALE**   (1932) 75m UNIV bw

Charles Bickford (Jerry Strong), Rose Hobart (Claire Strong), Pat O'Brien (Waddell), Claudia Dell (Dorothy Pepper), J. Farrell MacDonald (Treadway), Berton Churchill (Bunnyweather, Publisher), Glenda Farrell (Stella), Tully Marshall (Simpkins), Mitchell Harris (Carrington), Heinrich [Hans] von Twardowsky (Affner the Aviator), Mary Jane Graham (Mildred Strong), Buster Phelps (Bobby Strong), Harry Beresford (Brownie), Paul Nicholson (Detective), James Farley (Police Lieutenant), Lew Kelly, Jack Richardson (Compositors), Angie Norton (Nurse).

For the most part an uninteresting and choppy newspaper yarn, with Bickford as a dedicated newsman who raises from humble small-town origins to become editor of a large New York daily. After her son dies, neglected wife Hobart decides to leave her husband. A totally out-of-character ending has Bickford bucking his career to give another go at marriage in more tame surroundings. O'Brien plays a reporter who takes to the bottle, has a brief affair with Hobart and is killed in a plane crash while pursuing an assignment Bickford gave him. No one involved seemed to care too much about this production.

p, Carl Laemmle, Jr.; d, Russell Mack; w, Ralph Graves, Robert Keith (based on the novel Hot News by Emile Gauvreau); ph, Karl Freund.

Drama   (PR:A MPAA:NR)

SCANDAL IN DENMARK*½   (1970, Den.) 90m Novaris/Cinetex
                                                Industries c (DER KOM EN SOLDAT)

Willy Rathnov (The Soldier), Hanne Borchsenius (The Witch), Poul Bundgaard (Dobbermann), Olaf Ussing (Pinchier), Karl Stegger (Schaefer), Ove Sprogoe (Baron Royal King von Konig), Astrid Villaume (Baroness Regina King von Konig), Ullabella Johansson (Countess Elise), Inger Bagger (Governess), Paul Hagen (Hotel Porter).

A modern version of Hans Christian Andersen's classic "The Tinder-Box," that switches elements and plot details around to provide a story aimed more at adults. Some of these changes include the introduction of a gambling casino and a seductress in place of a princess.

p,d&w, Peer Guldbrandsen (based on the fairy tale "The Tinder-Box" by Hans Christian Andersen); ph, Erik Wittrup Willumsen (Eastmancolor); m, Sven Gyldmark; ed, Edith Nisted.

Drama   Cas.   (PR:O MPAA:R)

SCANDAL IN PARIS, A**   (1946) 100m UA bw (AKA: THIEVES
                                                                    HOLIDAY)

George Sanders (Vidocq), Signe Hasso (Therese), Carole Landis (Loretta), Akim Tamiroff (Emile), Gene Lockhart (Richet), Jo Ann Marlowe (Mimi), Alma Kruger (Marquise), Alan Napier (Houdon), Vladimir Sokoloff (Uncle Hugo), Pedro De Cordoba (Priest), Leona Maricle (Owner of Dress Shop), Fritz Leiber (Painter), Skelton Knaggs (Cousin Pierre), Fred Nurney (Cousin Gabriel), Gisella Werbiseck (Aunt Ernestine), Marvin Davis (Little Louis).

Based on the exploits of real-life criminal Francois Eugene Vidocq, A SCANDAL IN PARIS stars Sanders in the lead role. Set during the Napoleonic era, the film begins with Sanders and Tamiroff escaping from prison after serving time for theft. Sanders, a charismatic and enterprising criminal, engineers a number of crimes before joining Napoleon's army for a short while. Later, when Sanders meets Hasso and discovers that her father is an important official, he sets his sights on becoming chief of police. Under the name Lt. Rousseau, Sanders becomes the police chief, heading the French Surete, filling vacant posts with his crooked friends. He makes plans for his ultimate crime- the burglary of The Bank of Paris-but is dissuaded by Hasso. Sanders then turns his back on a life of crime and devotes himself to a life of honesty. Although attacked by the critics upon its release, A SCANDAL IN PARIS has become one of director Sirk's most thematically and stylistically telling films- providing insight into the "Sirk hero" who would later be embodied most prominently in the Rock Hudson vehicles MAGNIFICENT OBSESSION (1954), ALL THAT HEAVEN ALLOWS (1956), and the masterpiece WRITTEN ON THE WIND (1957). A SCANDAL IN PARIS was originally planned as one of two Sanders-Tamiroff vehicles, the other to be called "Cagliostro," based on the Alexandre Dumas pere novel Memoirs of a Physician. "Cagliostro," however, fell through so Sirk went ahead with the adaptation of the Memoirs of Vidocq. Sirk's film is not the only work to be based on Vidocq. Novelist Honore de Balzac's character Inspector Vautrin from his classic Le Pere Goriot and Edgar Allan Poe's The Murders in the Rue Morgue also took Vidocq as their model. A SCANDAL IN PARIS was co-photographed by the brilliant Eugen Schuftan who, because of his German background and union regulations, had to work uncredited. Schuftan also went unbilled on two previous Sirk Films, HITLER'S MADMAN (1942) and SUMMER STORM (1944).

p, Arnold Pressburger; d, Douglas Sirk; w, Ellis St. Joseph (based on the Memoirs of Francois Eugene Vidocq); ph, Guy Roe, (uncredited) Eugen Schuftan; m, Hanns Eisler, Heinz Roemheld; ed, Al Joseph; md, Eisler, David Chudnow; art d, Gordon Wiles, Frank Sylos; set d, Emile Kuri; m/l, Eisler, Roemheld, Paul Webster.

Crime   (PR:A   MPAA:NR)

SCANDAL IN SORRENTO**   (1957, Ital./Fr.) 85m
        Gala-Titanus-S.G.C./Distributors Corporation of America c (PANE,
                                                                    AMORE E...)

Sophia Loren (Donna Sofia), Vittorio De Sica (Marasciallo Carotenuto), Lea Padovani (Donna Violante Ruotolo), Antonio Cifariello (Nicolino), Mario Carotenuto (Don Matteo), Joka Berretty (Erika), Tina Pica (Caramella the Housekeeper), Antonio La Raina (Mayor of Sorrento).

An unimpressive Loren picture (released in Italy in 1955) which casts her as a fish-seller nicknamed "The Heckler" in the coastal Italian town of Sorrento. She lives in a rented home belonging to De Sica, a Casanova type who is returning to his home town after a 30-year absence to become the local police chief. Loren, however, selfishly refuses to vacate. De Sica turns on the charm and before long he wants her to stay--as his wife. Loren nearly agrees, spurning the love of her fiance Cifariello. When De Sica realizes that he is the wedge between Loren's love for Cifariello, he backs off from the marriage. He then turns his amorous attentions to his charming landlady Padovani. Nothing more here than the usual Loren love adventures, this time with the gorgeous Bay of Naples providing the only picturesque scenery in the film. This third in a series of frothy but extremely popular (in Italy) comedies starring De Sica as the fatuous, androgen-ridden policeman was the first to use the statuesque Loren; Gina Lollobrigida had played the chaste but much-chased heroine of the previous two. Loren and Lollobrigida, at the time the two most celebrated mammals in cinema (for obvious reasons), were engaged in a vocal, highly publicized feud at the time of the picture's 1955 release in Italy. De Sica completed the cycle of four films in the series by personally producing the last one in Spain in 1958. Neither Loren nor Lollobrigida played the part of the pursued beauty in the latter; this was Loren's lone essay into the series. Only one other film in the group was released in English-speaking countries: BREAD, LOVE AND DREAMS (1953, Italy). Dubbed in English.

p, Marcello Girosi; d, Dino Risi; w, Ettore Margadonna, Girosi, Vincenzo Talarico, Risi; ph, Giuseppe Rotunno (CinemaScope, Technicolor); ed, Mario Serandrei; art d, Gastone Medin.

Romance   (PR:O MPAA:NR)

SCANDAL INCORPORATED*   (1956) 79m REP bw

Robert Hutton (Brad Cameron), Paul Richards (Marty Ellis, Attorney), Claire Kelly (June Trapping), Patricia Wright (Marge Cameron), Robert Knapp (Jess Blancher), Havis Davenport (Billie Wayne), Reid Hammond (Jerry Dexter), Nestor Paiva (Leland Miller, Publisher), Gordon Wynn (Herman Todd), Guy Prescott (Mr. James), Donald Kirke (Sidney Woods), Marjorie Stapp (Alice Yoland), Enid Baine (Martha Collum), Mauritz Hugo (Lewis Adams), Joe Breen (Champ Winter), Allen O'Locklin (Bob Hamilton), George Cisar (Willie Anderson), Tracey Morgan (Gracie), Mimi Simpson (Marie Ryan).

Very dull film that attempts to take shots at Hollywood scandal magazines. Hutton is a star whose name is dirtied through the efforts of an unscrupulous reporter. When the reporter turns up dead, all suspicion turns to

Hutton, who loses his contract with a studio. It takes Richards to clear the actor's name and give this picture the only performance worthy of being called acting.

p, Milton Mann; d, Edward Mann; w, M. Mann; ph, Brydon Baker; m, Paul Sawtell, Bert Shefter; ed, E. Mann; m/l, sid Shrager, Al Chorney, Hal Shrager.

Drama/Crime (PR:A MPAA:NR)

SCANDAL SHEET*½ (1931) 77m PAR bw (GB: THE DARK PAGE)

George Bancroft (*Mark Flint, the Editor*), Clive Brook (*Noel Adams, the Banker*), Kay Francis (*Mrs. Flint*), Gilbert Emery (*Franklin, the Publisher*), Lucien Littlefield (*McCloskey, the City Editor*), Regis Toomey (*Regan, the Reporter*), Mary Foy, Jackie Searl, James Kelsey, Harry Beresford.

Plot of this film, which features Bancroft as a rag-sheet editor, seems to have been inspired by the story of a real-life city editor who had died at Sing Sing. Bancroft's character is a tyrant who prints the news, no matter what it takes and who it harms. He gets his just deserts, however, when he becomes the subject of some juicy gosip: A photographer takes a picture of a banker with his arm around Bancroft's wife. The banker is later murdered, and the audience is led to believe that it was Bancroft who killed his wife's lover. The film ends with scenes of Bancroft in prison, editing a convict newspaper.

d, John Cromwell; w, Vincent Lawrence, Max Marcin (based on the story by Oliver H.P. Garrett); ph, David Abel; ed, George Nichols.

Drama (PR:A MPAA:NR)

SCANDAL SHEET*½ (1940) 67m COL bw

Otto Kruger (*Jim Stevenson*), Ona Munson (*Kitty Mulhane*), Edward Norris (*Petty Haynes*), John Dilson (*Chris Durk*), Don Beddoe (*Chick Keller*), Eddie Laughton (*Hal Lunny*), Linda Winters (*Marjorie Lawe*), Nedda Harrigan (*Seena Haynes*), Selmer Jackson (*Douglas Haynes*), Frank M. Thomas (*District Attorney*), Edward Marr (*Bert Schroll*).

Hard-to-swallow newspaper yarn casts Kruger as the powerful tabloid publisher who gives his illegitimate son, Norris, a job as a reporter. The kid, who doesn't know Kruger is his father, quits after one week and goes to work for another paper. While investigating a murder, he pins the crime on Kruger - who committed the crime to keep his true identity from his son. Kruger, who has appeared to be a real louse all along, turns out to be a man of some honor. There is little of worthwhile value in this shoddy production.

d, Nick Grinde; w, Joseph Carole; ph, Benjamin Kline; ed, William Lyon.

Crime/Drama (PR:A MPAA:NR)

SCANDAL SHEET***½ (1952) 82m COL bw (GB: THE DARK PAGE)

John Derek (*Steve McCleary*), Donna Reed (*Julie Allison*), Broderick Crawford (*Mark Chapman*), Rosemary DeCamp (*Charlotte Grant*), Henry O'Neill (*Charlie Barnes*), Henry Morgan (*Biddle*), James Millican (*Lt. Davis*), Griff Barnett (*Judge Hacker*), Jonathan Hale (*Frank Madison*), Pierre Watkin (*Baxter*), Ida Moore (*Needle Nellie*), Ralph Reed (*Joey*), Luther Crockett (*Jordan*), Charles Cane (*Heeney*), Jay Adler (*Bailey*), Don Beddoe (*Pete*), Shirlee Allard, Pat Williams (*Telephone Operators*), Raymond Largay (*Conklin*), Edna Holland (*Mrs. Penwick*), Kathryn Card (*Mrs. Rawley*), Cliff Clark (*O'Hanlon*), Victoria Horne (*Mary*), Matt Willis (*Joe*), Eugene Baxter (*Edwards*), Helen Brown (*Woman*), Katherine Warren (*Mrs. Allison*), Mike Mahoney, Peter Virgo, Ric Roman, Tom Kingston, Charles Colean (*Reporters*), Harry Hines, Harry Wilson, Ralph Volkie, John "Skins" Miller, Gary Owen (*Bums*), Guy Wilkerson (*Janitor*), Duke Watson (*Policeman*).

When ambitious editor Crawford is put in charge of saving the well respected *New York Express* newspaper, he decides to ignore its noble reputation and instead turn it into a tabloid. Using an outrageous series of sensational stunts, Crawford propels the paper's sagging circulation through the roof. His protege, Derek, looks up to his mentor and wishes to emulate him. Unfortunately, Derek's girl friend, Reed, a feature writer, hates Crawford's tactics and thinks he has ruined a once great newspaper. To promote reader participation, Crawford creates a Lonely Hearts Club for the paper and sponsors a huge ball to celebrate. At the bash, Crawford is shocked to discover DeCamp, the wife he deserted years ago who is now penniless and alone. The powerful editor hustles his wife out of the party and back to her apartment where she threatens to blackmail him. Enraged, Crawford beats her to death and then puts her body in the bathtub to make it look like an accident. Before leaving, he takes all clues to her identity and destroys them. When the body is found the coroner concludes that her death was murder. Wanting to impress his mentor, Derek energetically investigates the killing. He discovers an old pawn ticket that belonged to DeCamp and he accidentally turns it over to his friend, O'Neill, an aging ex-reporter. O'Neill redeems the ticket and finds a photograph of Crawford and the dead woman. Before he can tell Derek the news, he is murdered by Crawford. Meanwhile, Derek and Reed have traced the judge that married the murder victim and they are shocked to learn that Crawford was the groom. Crawford has followed the reporters and bursts into the room with a gun, threatening to shoot. The police arrive in the nick of time and kill Crawford

in a shootout. His illusions shattered, Derek writes Crawford's obituary for the front page. SCANDAL SHEET is an intense, gripping crime drama that hurtles along like an express train. Based on a novel entitled *The Dark Page* written by film director-writer Samuel Fuller, which was picked by the Book Critics of America as the outstanding psychological novel of 1944, the film is an examination of the dark side of American journalism. Fuller culled the material for the novel from his experiences as a writer for various tabloids and it illustrates how basically honorable men can be warped by their obsession to be on top. Crawford's character is a villain, but he is also understandable and sympathetic. We watch as this ambitious, hard-working man disintegrates into a cynical, cold-hearted murderer, and at the end there is a tragic sense of loss. The mentor-protege relationship between Crawford and Derek is especially ironic because Crawford created the monster that ultimately destroyed him. Fuller had originally written the screenplay himself for director Howard Hawks but the project lay dormant until 1951 when it was rewritten, retitled, and produced. Director Karlson does a fine job at the helm and was well attuned to this sort of material. He would go on to direct such memorable crime films as 99 RIVER STREET (1953), THE PHENIX CITY STORY (1955), and THE BROTHERS RICO (1957), but one must wonder what *SCANDAL SHEET* might have been like if directed by the masterful Howard Hawks or its obsessed and passionate creator, Samuel Fuller.

p, Edward Small; d, Phil Karlson; w, Ted Sherdeman, Eugene Ling, James Poe (based on the novel *The Dark Page* by Samuel Fuller); ph, Burnett Guffey; m, George Duning; ed, Jerome Thoms; md, Morris Stoloff; art d, Robert Peterson; set d, William Kiernan; cos, Jean Louis; makeup, Clay Campbell.

Crime (PR:C MPAA:NR)

SCANDAL '64 (SEE: CHRISTINE KEELER AFFAIR, THE, 1964)

SCANDAL STREET** (1938) 62m PAR bw

Lew Ayres (*Joe McKnight*), Louise Campbell (*Nora Langdon*), Roscoe Karns (*Austin Brown*), Porter Hall (*James Wilson*), Virginia Weidler (*Wilma Murphy*), Cecil Cunningham (*Maybelle Murphy*), Edgar Kennedy (*Daniel Webster Smith*), Elizabeth Patterson (*Ada Smith*), Jan Duggan (*Vera Venzey*), Laraine Johnson [Day] (*Peg Smith*), Lois Kent (*Marilyn Smith*), George Offerman, Jr (*Jerome Murphy*), Esther Howard (*Birdie Brown*), Lucien Littlefield (*Robert Johnson*), Louise Beavers (*Clarice*), Carl "Alfalfa" Switzer (*Bennie Johnson*).

An uneven story centers on the small-town gossip that develops when new girl Campbell comes to town. While all the young ruffians are trying to impress the girl with their virility, the old ladies spread rumors about her at their bridge parties. A murder occurs in the peaceful town, and what earlier sounded like harmless tripe now approaches vicious slander. A homey look at small-town Americana, but plot gets to be a bit trying.

d, James Hogan; w, Bertram Millhauser, Eddie Welch (based on the story by Vera Caspary); ph, Henry Sharp; ed, James Smith.

Drama (PR:A MPAA:NR)

SCANDALOUS ADVENTURES OF BURAIKAN, THE** (1970, Jap.) 104m Ninjin Club-Toho/Toho International c (BURAIKAN)

Tatsuya Nakadai (*Naojiro*), Suisen Ichikawa (*Naojiro's Mother*), Shima Iwashita (*Michitose*), Tetsuro Tamba (*Soshun*), Shoichi Ozawa (*Ushimatsu*), Masakane Yonekura (*Ichinojo Kaneko, the Killer*), Kiwako Taichi (*Namiji*), Fumio Watanabe (*Seizo Moritaya*), Hiroshi Akutagawa (*Mizuno Echizen-nokami*), Sakatoshi Yonekura (*Kaneko Ichinojo*).

During the mid-19th century, an extremely repressive period in Japanese culture, a young actor attempts to defy tradition and his mother's wishes by marrying a prostitute. He must also battle a powerful figure who has his own designs for the young girl. An unusual look at knavery and backstabbing, as well as rare glimpses of honor, in Japanese culture.

p, Ninjin Kurabu; d, Masahiro Shinoda; w, Shuji Terayama (based on the play by Mokuami Kawatake); ph, Kozo Okazaki (Panavision, Eastmancolor); m, Masaru Sato; art d, Shigemasa Toda.

Drama (PR:C MPAA:NR)

SCANDALOUS JOHN**½ (1971) 114m Disney/BV c

Brian Keith (*John McCanless*), Alfonso Arau (*Paco Martinez*), Michele Carey (*Amanda McCanless*), Rick Lenz (*Jimmy Whittaker*), Harry Morgan (*Sheriff Pippin*), Simon Oakland (*Barton Whittaker*), Bill Williams (*Sheriff Hart*), Christopher Dark (*Card Dealer*), Fran Ryan (*Farm Woman*), Bruce Glover (*Sludge*), Richard Hale (*Old Indian*), James Lydon (*Grotch*), John Ritter (*Wendell*), Iris Adrian (*Mavis*), Larry D. Mann (*Bartender*), Jack Raine (*Switchman*), Booth Colman (*Gov. Murray*), Edward Faulkner (*Hillary*), Bill Zuckert (*Abernathy*), John Zaremba (*Wales*), Robert Padilla (*Paco's Cousin*), Alex Tinne (*Clerk*), Ben Baker (*Dr. Kropak*), Paul Koslo (*Pipes*), William O'Connell (*Men's Store Clerk*), Sam Edwards (*Bald Head*), Leonore Stevens (*Girl*), Jose Nieto, Margarito Mendoza, Joseph Gutierrez, Freddie Hernandez (*Mariachi Band*).

In a role somewhat reminiscent of Cervantes' Don Quixote, Keith plays a 79-year-old rancher who upholds the honor and codes of the Old West. When land developer Oakland wants to buy Keith's land for a dam project, the old man fights instead of giving in to development. Aided by Oakland's son, Lenz, and his own daughter Carey, Keith decides to make one last great cattle drive with his lone, gangly steer. Instead he lands in jail, but is later sprung by Carey. In a manner fitting his code of valor, Keith dies by the gun, thus living his myth to the end. Keith gives a heartwarming performance as the old cowpoke. Unfortunately the direction slips into slapstick routines a bit too often in its quest for laughs.

p, Bill Walsh; d, Robert Butler; w, Walsh, Don DaGradi (based on the book by Richard Gardner); ph, Frank Phillips (Panavision, Technicolor); ed, Cotton Warburton; prod d, Robert Clatworthy; art d, John B. Mansbr idge; set d, Emile Kuri, Frank R. McKelvy; cos, Chuck Keehne, Emily Sundby; spec eff, Robert A. Mattey; m/l, "Pastures Green," Rod McKuen (sung by McKuen); makeup, Robert J. Schiffer.

Western/Comedy   **(PR:AA MPAA:G)**

SCANDALS   (SEE: GEORGE WHITE'S SCANDALS, 1934)

SCANDALS OF PARIS**   (1935, Brit.) 63m Pathe-Stafford-BIP/Regal bw (GB: THERE GOES SUSIE)

Gene Gerrard (Andre Cochet), Wendy Barrie (Madeleine Sarteaux), Zelma O'Neal (Bunny), Gus McNaughton (Brammell), Henry Wenman (Otto Sarteaux), Bobbie Comber (Uncle Oscar), Gibb McLaughlin (Manager), Mark Daly (Sunshine).

Silly comedy starring Gerrard as an artist who paints model Barrie in a scanty outfit. His domestic sells the painting to the manager of a big soap firm for advertising purposes. The campaign goes into motion and is a smashing success, much to the dismay of the soap company owner, who looks up at one of the billboards and recognizes the scantily clad girl as his daughter. In the end, things are set straight when it is determined that the artist and the model are in love.

p,d&w, John Stafford, W. Victor Hanbury (based on the novel by Charlotte Roellinghoff, Hans Jacoby; ph, Jack Beaver; m/l, Otto Stransky, Niklos Schwalb, Sonny Miller.

Comedy   **(PR:A MPAA:NR)**

SCANNERS***   (1981, Can.) 102m Filmplan International/AE c

Stephen Lack (Cameron Vale), Jennifer O'Neill (Kim), Patrick McGoohan (Dr. Paul Ruth), Lawrence Dane (Keller), Charles Shamata (Gaudi), Adam Ludwig (Crostic), Michael Ironside (Darryl Revok), Victor Desy (Dr. Gatineau), Mavor Moore (Trevellyan), Robert Silverman (Pierce).

This "explosive" film revolves around McGoohan's efforts to do away with a group of people endowed with the ability to lock into others' nervous systems and take control of their bodies. The "scanners" use their powers for evil purposes and, in some of the film's more repulsive scenes, explode peoples' heads. These so-called mutants had these powers bestowed on them as a result of their pregnant mothers being given a thalidomide-like drug. In the original experiment, Lack and his twin brother Ironside had been conceived. Ironside, who sees his superior powers as a means of taking over the world, amasses a whole slew of "scanners" to undertake the scheme. Lack is enlisted by McGoohan to try and put an end to his brother's plot. The film's climax is a literal "battle of the minds," as Lack and Ironside use their powers in an effort to outdo each other. A striking film that has more than its share of heads blowing up and faces taking on grotesque configurations, convincingly handled through superb special effects.

p, Claude Heroux; d&w, David Cronenberg; ph, Mark Irwin (CFI Color); m, Howard Shore; ed, Ron Sanders; art d, Carol Spier; spec eff, Dick Smith, Gary Zeller, Henry Pierrig, Chris Walas; Makeup, Smith.

Fantasy/Horror   **Cas.**   **(PR:O MPAA:R)**

SCAPEGOAT, THE**½ (1959, Brit.) 92m Guinness-du. Maurier/MGM bw

Alec Guinness (Jacques De Gue/John Barrett), Bette Davis (The Countess), Nicole Maurey (Bella), Irene Worth (Francoise De Gue), Pamela Brown (Blanche), Annabel Bartlett (Marie-Noel), Geoffrey Keen (Gaston, Chauffeur), Noel Howlett (Dr. Aloin), Peter Bull (Aristide), Leslie French (Lacoste), Alan Webb (Inspector), Maria Britneva (Maid), Eddie Byrne (Barman), Alexander Archdale (Gamekeeper), Peter Sallis (Customs Official).

Guinness plays a dual role as an English teacher visiting France and a wealthy French count. The count's family of crazed eccentrics includes Davis as his mother, a bed-ridden morphine addict. When Guinness as the count comes across the schoolteacher, he convinces the latter to take on his identity . This allows the count to go through with a scheme to murder his wife, Worth, and run off with his Italian mistress, Maurey. The deception fools almost everyone, including Davis, but not Maurey. After Worth is murdered, the count intends to do away with his double. But a deliberately confusing ending has what appears to be the English teacher running off

with Maurey, who is equally unsure of her partner's true identity. Guinness was convincing in both portrayals, as was Davis in her role. But the script unfortunately does a poor job of determining motivation and developing plot.

p, Michael Balcon; d, Robert Hamer; w, Hamer, Gore Vidal (based on the novel by Daphne du Maurier); ph, Paul Beeson; m, Bronislau Kaper; ed, Jack Harris; art d, Elliott Scott; makeup, Harry Frampton.

Mystery   **(PR:A MPAA:NR)**

SCAPPAMENTO APERTO   (SEE: BACKFIRE, 1965)

SCAR, THE   (SEE: HOLLOW TRIUMPH, 1948)

SCARAB*   (1982, U.S./Span.) 92m Tesauro and Alloi c

Rip Torn, Robert Ginty, Cristina Hachuel, Don Pickering.

The combination of devil worshipers, Nazis, and ancient Egyptian gods in one picture can have no other effect than to drown the viewer in an overabundance of occult rituals and accompanying sadistic practices. Such is the case with SCARAB, in which an evil Nazi is brought back to life with the soul of an Egyptian god. The premise is intriguing, but once it's established the picture unfolds in a routine and uninteresting manner. Worth a glimpse just to catch Torn in another of his strange roles.

d, Steven-Charles Jaffe; w, Robert Jaffe, Steven-Charles Jaffe; Ned Miller, Jim Block; ph, Fernando Arribas; m, Miguel Morales.

Horror   **(PR:O MPAA:NR)**

SCARAB MURDER CASE, THE*   (1936, Brit.) 68m British and Dominions/PAR bw

Kathleen Kelly (Angela Hargreaves), Wilfrid Hyde-White (Philo Vance), Wally Patch (Inspector Moor), Henri de Vries (Dr. Bliss), John Robinson (Donald Scarlett, Archeologist), Wallace Geoffrey (Salveter), Stella Moya (Meryt Amen), Grahame Chesewright (Makeham), Rustum Medora (Hani), Shaun Desmond (Detective).

An inferior portrayal of the popular sleuth Philo Vance (best done by the convincing Basil Rathbone in THE BISHOP MURDER CASE, 1930) has White as the American detective in London to uncover the murderer of a millionaire. An interesting twist has archeologist Robinson, who appears to be an innocent victim accused of the crime, actually turning out to be the killer. Pretty boring, with White making a poor detective, much less an American. (See: PHILO VANCE Series, Index)

p, Anthony Havelock-Allan; d, Michael Hankinson; w, Selwyn Jepson (based on the novel by S.S. Van Dine); ph, Claude Friese-Greene.

Mystery   **(PR:A MPAA:NR)**

SCARAMOUCHE***½   (1952) 118m MGM c

Stewart Granger (Andre Moreau/Scaramouche), Eleanor Parker (Lenore), Janet Leigh (Aline de Gavrillac), Mel Ferrer (Noel, Marquis de Maynes), Henry Wilcoxon (Chevalier de Chabrillaine), Nina Foch (Marie Antoinette), Richard Anderson (Philippe de Valmorin), Robert Coote (Gaston Binet), Lewis Stone (Georges de Valmorin), Elizabeth Risdon (Isabelle de Valmorin), Howard Freeman (Michael Vanneau), Curtis Cooksey (Fabian), John Dehner (Doutreval), John Litel (Dr. Dubuque), Jonathan Cott (Sergeant), Dan Foster (Pierrot), Owen McGiveney (Punchinello), Hope Landin (Mme. Frying Pan), Frank Mitchell (Harlequin), Carol Hughes (Pierrette), Richard Hale (Perigore), Henry Corden (Scaramouche the Drinker), John Eldredge (Clerk), Mitchell Lewis (Major Domo), Ottola Nesmith (Lady-In-Waiting), Dorothy Patrick (Dorie), John Sheffield (Flunky), Douglas Dumbrille (President), Frank Wilcox (DeCrillion), Anthony Marsh (Capelier), John Crawford (Vignon), Bert LeBaron (Fencing Opponent).

An audience-pleasing swashbuckler which benefits from one of MGM's most lavish mountings and a jaw-dropping six-and-a-half minute finale of swordplay. Granger stars as a handsome and adventurous young nobleman during the French Revolution who thinks he learns the identity of his previously unknown father. He sets out to meet the wealthy and influential Duc de Gavrillac, only to find that he has died. Along the way, Granger falls in love with the beautiful Leigh but ends the romance when he is told her last name–de Gavrillac–making her his sister. Later, while in a tavern with friend Anderson, a revolutionary newspaper editor, there is a confrontation with a renowned royalist marquis, Ferrer, who is feared as the most skilled swordsman in the country. Ferrer kills Anderson and threatens to do the same to Granger. A complete amateur at swordfighting, Granger flees, vowing to return one day and avenge the death of his friend. Further adding to Granger's dismay about Leigh, he learns that she is about to be married to Ferrer at the wish of the queen, Foch. In his travels, Granger joins a theater troupe where he is able to hide behind the role of "Scaramouche" and spend his hours learning to fence from the masterful Dehner. When not acting or fencing, Granger spends his time with actress Parker, with whom he soon falls in love. Ferrer, however, learns of Granger's whereabouts, forcing the nobleman to continue his studies under Dehner's instructor,

Hale. Granger then enters the political arena as a minister on the side of the revolutionary forces. Opposite him is Ferrer. Eventually the pair meet at the theater while Granger is on stage as Scaramouche. Granger peels away his mask and challenges Ferrer to a duel. What follows is one of the finest sword battles in movie history. Choreographed by a former Belgian fencing champion, Jean Heremans, the fight establishes both Granger and Ferrer as impressive sword handlers who are able to convince the audience of the danger their battle involves. The dueling swords of Granger and Ferrer carry the two foes from the box seats, onto the balcony ledges, swinging across the auditorium, down the grand staircase and into the foyer, through the theater seats, and finally onto the stage. After this colorful, heart-stopping flurry of parries, lunges, thrusts, and feints, Granger corners the defeated Ferrer. He is unable, however, to deliver the fatal thrust. Granger is then informed that Ferrer is really his half-brother. This fact not only reunites the two brothers, but also frees Granger to marry Leigh, whom he now knows is not his sister. A marvelously eventful picture in the most traditional of Hollywood styles, SCARAMOUCHE thrilled the audiences but failed to convince many critics of the day. Most were upset by the film's inability to live up to its 1923 silent predecessor that starred Ramon Novarro as the nobleman and Lewis Stone (who appears in the 1952 version as Anderson's father) as the rival swordsman. The chief difference between the two versions is the original's concentration on the French Revolution (which is barely referred to in 1952) and the revelation that the hero's nemesis is actually his father instead of his half-brother. Based on a novel by Rafael Sabatini, SCARAMOUCHE is just one of many of that writer's swashbuckling epics to hit the screen, including the Errol Flynn vehicles CAPTAIN BLOOD (1935) and THE SEA HAWK (1940), and Tyrone Power's vehicle THE BLACK SWAN (1942). Sabatini's *Scaramouche* again hit the screens in the 1964 French production ADVENTURES OF SCARA-MOUCHE.

p, Carey Wilson; d, George Sidney; w, Ronald Millar, George Froeschel (based on the novel by Rafael Sabatini); ph, Charles Rosher (Technicolor); m, Victor Young; ed, James E. Newcom; art d, Cedric Gibbons, Hans Peters; set d, Edwin P. Willis, Richard Pefferle; cos, Gile Steele; spec eff, A. Arnold Gillespie, Warren Newcombe, Irving G. Ries; makeup, William Tuttle; montages, Peter Ballbusch; dueling ch, Jean Heremans.

Adventure　　　　　　　　　　　　　　　(PR:A　MPAA:NR)

SCARAMOUCHE, 1964　　(SEE: ADVENTURES OF SCARAMOUCHE, THE, 1964, Fr./Ital./Sp.)

SCARECROW***　　　　　　　　　　　　(1973) 112m WB c

Gene Hackman *(Max)*, Al Pacino *(Lion)*, Dorothy Tristan *(Coley)*, Ann Wedgeworth *(Frenchy)*, Richard Lynch *(Riley)*, Eileen Brennan *(Darlene)*, Penny Allen *(Annie)*, Richard Hackman *(Mickey)*, Al Cingolani *(Skipper)*, Rutanya Alda *(Woman in Camper)*.

This is a good look at a pair of losers that suffers from being slightly too episodic as it examines the characters of Pacino and Hackman. Basically an EASY RIDER type of film, it follows the protagonists as they hit the road, leaving California to go to Pittsburgh. The fact that they are reversing the usual trend of leaving the East for the West makes them slightly suspect in the common sense department. Hackman has recently been released from San Quentin where he did some hard time for assault. He's on his way to Pittsburgh where he hopes to open a car wash on the modest savings he's accumulated. Pacino is a drifter on land and on sea, a man who has just come off the briny, where he successfully avoided seeing the wife and child he left back in Detroit. The two men hit it off and decide to team up for their voyage. On the trip, they have adventures in bars, diners, and various residences belonging to former loves and/or old pals. Brennan does well as a barroom floozie and Tristan scores as one of Hackman's ex-girl friends. As they cross the country and near their destinations, Pacino become jumpy about again seeing his wife, Allen, whom he left while she was pregnant. Hackman does his best to encourage Pacino, but Pacino is beginning to crumble. He's never seen his child, and when he phones ahead to Detroit and talks to Allen (in a very sensitive portrayal), she lies, telling him in a semimonolog (Pacino's answers are little more than grunts and "uh huhs") that the child he'd thought she had was never born. She says she miscarried early and all of his trepidation about meeting his child was for naught. The child doesn't exist. Pacino goes into what appears to be some sort of epileptic seizure but turns out to be a violent form of nervous breakdown. The final scenes show Hackman using his savings to pay for Pacino's hospital care, his hopes of opening his own business tossed aside in favor of helping his only friend. Hackman gives another splendid and compelling performance. We suspend disbelief and he becomes the bawdy, foul-mouthed ex-con who made a mistake a long time ago and is destined to pay for it again and again. There is no doubt that his trigger temper could flare up at any moment and land him into violence. Pacino, however, is not given enough characterization by the script or the direction or even his own abilities. His roles in DOG DAY AFTERNOON and THE GODFATHER are better indications of his talents than this or the unfortunate AUTHOR, AUTHOR. There are moments when writer White has created unrealistic lines for Pacino instead of allowing the character to emerge subtly and become part of the story. The picture looks wonderful and captures the grittiness of the road. Schatzberg had been a photographer and his collaboration with Zsigmond is fruitful in that respect for much of the film. The bad side of things is that they both

add a bit of Hollywood gloss to a few of the scenes which pop up and punch one in the eye. The ending is a cheat and not consistent with Hackman's behavior all the way through. They seemed to be attempting a denouement similar to that in MIDNIGHT COWBOY. Stories about the relationship of two men and their camaraderie have been seen often in pictures like BUTCH CASSIDY AND THE SUNDANCE KID and the wonderful Michael Caine-Sean Connery triumph THE MAN WHO WOULD BE KING. This doesn't quite reach those heights but is a good enough attempt. Given the box office potency of the two stars, the receipts were disappointing, although the movie eventually did recoup its cost and made a few bucks. No four-letter word seems to have been omitted.

p, Robert M. Sherman; d, Jerry Schatzberg; w, Garry Michael White; ph, Vilmos Zsigmond (Panavision, Technicolor); m, Fred Myrow; ed, Evan Lottman; prod d, Al Brenner; cos, Jo Ynocencio.

Drama　　　　　　　Cas.　　　　　(PR:C-O　MPAA:R)

SCARECROW, THE**　　　　　(1982, New Zealand) 87m New Zealand
　　　　　　　　　　　　　　　　　　　National Film Unit/Oasis c

John Carradine *(Salter)*, Tracy Mann *(Prudence Poindexter)*, Jonathan Smith *(Ned Poindexter)*, Daniel McLaren *(Les Wilson)*, Denise O'Connell *(Angela Potroz)*, Anne Flannery *(Mrs. Poindexter)*, Des Kelly *(Mr. Poindexter)*, Bruce Allpress *(Uncle Athol)*, Jonathan Hardy *(Charlie Dabney)*, Philip Holder *(Constable Len Ramsbottom)*, Ted Coyle *(Alf Yerby)*, Elizabeth Moody *(Mabel)*, Mark Hadlow *(Sam Finn)*, Greg Naughton *(Victor Lynch)*, John Kempt *(Peachy Blair)*, Stephen Taylor *(Herbert Poindexter)*, Sarah Smuts-Kennedy *(Daphne Moran)*, Duncan Smith *(Skin Hughson)*, Bill Walker *(Clem Walker)*, Roy Billing *(Mr. Potroz)*, Paul Owen-Lowe *(Jim Coleman)*, Margaret Blay *(Mrs. Breece)*, Greer Robson *(Lynette)*, Yvonne Lawley *(Miss Fitzherbert)*, Doug Hastings *(Channing Fitzherbert)*, Simon Phillips *(Chote Fitzherbert)*, Elizabeth McRae *(Mrs. Peacock)*, Norm Keesing *(Mr. Lynch)*, Norm Forsey *(Old Man)*.

An unusual and entertaining piece of filmmaking from New Zealand takes place in a small backwoods town in the 1950s, where a number of mysterious events lead to the discovery that Carradine is an estranged killer, guilty of not just one murder but a slew of them. Carradine was never better as the weird murderer, a role he approached with gusto and obviously enjoyed. Attempts at humor seem a bit forced and out of place, but a keen sense of visual awareness helps sustain the atmosphere. Further proof of the existence of a struggling film industry, worthy of international attention, existing in New Zealand.

p, Rob Whitehouse; d, Sam Pillsbury; w, Pillsbury, Michael Heath (based on the novel by Ronald Hugh Morrieson); ph, Jim Bartle; m, Schtung; ed, Ian John; prod d, Neil Angwin; cos, Glenys Hitchins.

Horror/Mystery　　　　　　　　　　　(PR:C　MPAA:PG)

SCARECROW IN A GARDEN OF CUCUMBERS**½
　　　　　　　　　　　(1972) 82m Sliding Pond/Maron-New Line c

Holly Woodlawn *(Eve Harrington/Rhett Butler)*, Tally Brown *(Mary Poppins)*, Suzanne Skillen *(Ninotchka)*, Yafa Lerner *(Margo Channing)*, David Margulies *(Walter Mitty)*, Jennifer Laird *(Blanche DuBois)*, Katherine Howell, Margret Howell *(Baby and Jane Hudson)*, Jane Kutler *(Marjorie Morningstar)*, Sonny Boy Hayes *(Joe Buck)*, Michael Sklar *(Noel Airman)*, Joe Malanga *(Ratso Rizzo)*, Johnny Jumpup *(Stanley Kowalski)*, Meg Winters, Judy Martin, Joe Palmieri, Dori Brenner.

A spoof on Hollywood with "camp" written all over it, the story focuses on a young girl, Woodlawn, who goes by the name Eve Harrington (the name of the ambitious young actress from ALL ABOUT EVE). On her way to New York to make it big as a Broadway actress, she runs into eccentric people with names of characters from novels and famous Hollywood movies. These include Mary Poppins, a very hefty blues singer; Blanche Dubois, sister to a midget wrestler; and Rhett Butler, an independent film producer. Though this name game and the interesting personalities depicted are of some amusement, the absence of plot makes it all tiresome after awhile. Transvestite Woodlawn's appearance marks her first in a non-Warhol film. Shot for $100,000 in 16mm color blown up to 35mm, the film's production values were surprisingly good considering the small budget. Songs, written by Jerry Blatt and Marshall Barer, include "Scarecrow" (sung by Emmaretta Marks), "Get It On" (sung by Bette Midler, Mike Lincoln), "Bethesda" (sung by The Enchanters), "Nothing Goin' Down at All" (sung by Middler, Lincoln), "The Dusty Rose Hotel" (sung by Tally Brown), "Lost in My Dreams of Heaven" (sung by Holly Woodlawn), "Love Theme" (sung by Midler), "Strawberry, Lilac and Lime" (sung by Midler), "The Up Number" (sung by entire cast).

p, Henry J. Alpert, Robert J. Kaplan; d, Kaplan; w, Sandra Scoppettone; ph, Paul Glickman (DuArt Color); ed, Dick Cohen.

Comedy　　　　　　　　　　　　　　(PR:C　MPAA:NR)

SCARED STIFF**** (1945) 65m PAR bw (AKA: TREASURE OF FEAR)

Jack Haley (*Larry Elliot*), Ann Savage (*Sally Warren*), Barton MacLane (*Deacon Markham*), Veda Ann Borg (*Flo Rosson*), Arthur Aylesworth (*Emerson Cooke*), George E. Stone (*Mink*), Lucien Littlefield (*Charles Waldeck/Preston Waldeck*), Paul Hurst (*Sheriff*), Robert Emmett Keane (*Prof. Wisner*), Eily Malyon (*Mrs. Cooke*), Buddy Swan (*Oliver Waldeck*), Roger Pryor (*Richardson*).

Thin plot has Haley as a newspaper reporter who knows beans about news. When an escaped convict has the entire staff of the paper booked, Haley is assigned to cover a wine festival. He goes to the wrong place, gets on a bus in which a murder is committed and becomes a suspect. Forced to stop at an inn, Haley's girl friend Savage and detective Borg also turn up. The owners of the inn have a pair of jeweled chessmen that have peaked several people's interest, including the escaped convict. Haley winds up catching the crook when he tries to make claim to the chessmen. Far-fetched plot and the numerous coincidences stretch the imagination a bit too far. Remake of GHOST BREAKERS.

p, William Pine, William Thomas; d, Frank McDonald; w, Geoffrey Homes, Maxwell Shane; ph, Fred Jackman, Jr.; ed, Howard Smith, Henry Adams; art d, F. Paul Sylos.

Comedy   (PR:A   MPAA:NR)

SCARED STIFF**½**   (1953) 106m PAR bw

Dean Martin (*Larry Todd*), Jerry Lewis (*Myron Myron Mertz*), Lizabeth Scott (*Mary Carroll*), Carmen Miranda (*Carmelita Castina*), George Dolenz (*Mr. Cortega*), Dorothy Malone (*Rosie*), William Ching (*Tony Warren*), Paul Marion (*Carriso Twins*), Jack Lambert (*Zombie*), Tom Powers (*Police Lieutenant*), Tony Barr (*Trigger*), Leonard Strong (*Shorty*), Henry Brandon (*Pierre*), Hugh Sanders (*Cop on Pier*), Frank Fontaine (*Drunk*), Bob Hope, Bing Crosby (*Themselves*).

Basically a remake of the successful Hope-Crosby vehicle THE GHOST BREAKERS, made in 1940, the scripters reworked the original to allow a part for Carmen Miranda and a walk-on bit for Hope and Crosby. Lewis and Martin play their usual roles: Martin as the sly ladyies' man and Lewis as the nincompoop sidekick around to carry the laughs, which he does somewhat successfully. Lewis' most memorable moment comes in his Carmen Miranda imitation, in which he squeaks out a rendition of "Mamie." Martin gets in trouble with the mob after he is pursued by Malone, a gangster's girl friend. The duo splits with heiress Scott to the desert island she has just inherited, which houses a large old castle that is supposedly haunted. In reality, villain Ching just wants it to appear haunted to scare off the new owners and have free access to the gold that lies there. Lewis' antics when he comes up against the spooks take little imagination to figure out. Songs include: "San Domingo," "Song of The Enchilada Man" (Jerry Livingston, Mack David; Sung by Martin, Lewis, Miranda), "Mama Yo Quiero" (Al Stillman, Jarca and Vincente Paiva; mimed by Lewis to a Miranda recording), "You Hit The Spot" (Mack Gordon, Harry Revel), "I Don't Care If The Sun Don't Shine" (David; sung by Martin), "I'm Your Pal" (David, Livingston), "When Somebody Thinks You're Wonderful" (Harry Woods).

p, Hal Wallis; d, George Marshall; w, Herbert Baker, Walter De Leon, Ed Simmons, Norman Lear (based on the play "Ghost Breakers" by Paul Dickey, Charles W. Goddard); ph, Ernest Lazlo; m, Leith Stevens; ed, Warren Low; md, Joseph J. Lilley; art d, Hal Pereira, Franz Bachelin; cos, Edith Head; spec eff, Gordon Jennings, Paul Lerpae; ch, Billy Daniels; m/l, Mack David, Jerry Livingston.

Musical/Comedy   (PR:A   MPAA:NR)

SCARED TO DEATH*½**   (1947) 65m Screen Guild c

Bela Lugosi (*Leonide*), Douglas Fowley (*Terry Lee*), Joyce Compton (*Jane*), George Zucco (*Dr. Van Ee*), Nat Pendleton (*Raymond*), Roland Varno (*Ward Van Ee*), Molly Lamont (*Laura Van Ee*), Angelo Rossitto (*Indigo*), Gladys Blake (*Lilybeth*), Lee Bennett (*Rene*), Stanley Andrews, Stanley Price (*Autopsy Surgeons*).

Perhaps one of the only Bela Lugosi films to be made in color, using an inexpensive process, since discontinued, known as Cinecolor. It was shot in 1946 but not released for a full year after production. Story is told entirely in flashbacks from the point of view of a corpse, killed without any identifiable marks. (A dead person as a narrator was later to be used in SUNSET BOULEVARD, where William Holden played a murdered gigolo). The story takes place entirely in a sanitarium, where a girl relates the incidentes that led to her death. As it turns out, the title gives the clue to how she died. Lugosi plays a mysterious figure accompanied by an eerie dwarf, Rossitto. Very slack production values, with an almost incoherent script, makes for a project that has some interesting moments despite its flaws. Lugosi has little more to do than just take his standard pose and look scary.

p, William B. David; d, Christy Cabanne; w, W. J. Abbott; ph, Marcel Le Picard (Cinecolor); m, Carl Hoefle; ed, George McGuire; art d, Harry Reif.

Mystery   Cas.   (PR:A   MPAA:NR)

SCARED TO DEATH*** (1981) 95m Lone Star c (AKA: THE TERROR FACTOR)

John Stinson (*Ted Lonergan*), Diana Davidson (*Jennifer Stanton*), Jonathon David Moses (*Lou Capell*), Toni Jannotta (*Sherry Carpenter*), Kermit Eller (*Syngenor*), Walker Edmiston, Pamela Bowman.

Cheaply made science fiction film has a synthetic creature made through DNA experiments, appropriately named "Syngenor." When the creature's creator dies, it goes on a rampage, killing humans by sucking fluid out of their spinal columns. The police try to pin the murders on a psychotic killer, leaving Stinson and Jannotta to scrounge around sewers to look for the beast. Not much of a story here, but lots of fun.

p, Rand Marlis, Gil Shelton; d&w, William Malone; ph, Patrick Prince (Getty Color); m, Tom Chase, Ardell Hake; ed, Warren Chadwick; spec eff, Malone, Robert Short.

Science Fiction/Horror   (PR:O   MPAA:R)

SCAREHEADS*** (1931) 67m CAP bw (GB: THE SPEED REPORTER)

Richard Talmadge, Gareth Hughes, Jacqueline Wells [Julie Bishop], Joseph Girard, Virginia True Boardman, King Baggott, Lloyd Whitlock, Walter James, Edward Lynch, Nancy Caswell.

Poorly scripted and performed production has Talmadge as a hard-nosed reporter struggling to free himself of a murder charge, a case he is immersed in because of his articles against the mayor and in support of the opposition. Put behind bars, Talmadge manages to escape and then clears his name. Hardly worth a glimpse.

p, Richard Talmadge; d, Noel Mason.

Crime   (PR:A   MPAA:NR)

SCARF, THE**½**   (1951) 93m Gloria/UA bw

John Ireland (*John Barrington*), Mercedes McCambridge (*Connie Carter*), Emlyn Williams (*David Dunbar*), James Barton (*Ezra Thompson*), Lloyd Gough (*Dr. Gordon*), Basil Ruysdael (*Cyrus Barrington*), David Wolfe (*Level Louie*), Harry Shannon (*Warden*), David McMahon (*State Trooper*), Chubby Johnson (*Sam*), Frank Jenks (*Tom*), Frank Jaquet (*Sheriff*), Emmett Lynn (*Jack the Waiter*), John Merrick (*Deputy*), Lyle Talbot (*Detective*), King Donovan (*Tiger*), O.Z. Whitehead (*Woopie*), Frank Richards (*Gargantua*), Sue Casey (*Receptionist*), Celia Lovsky (*Mrs. Barrington*), Dick Wessel (*Sid*).

Thriller has Ireland breaking out of an asylum for the criminally insane, where he has been committed for strangling a girl with a scarf. Psychiatrist Williams turns out to be the real murderer, who has convinced Ireland he really is crazy. After he meets McCambridge, who is wearing a scarf identical to the supposed murder weapon, Ireland realizes he is innocent. He hides out at Barton's turkey farm, where he eventually is traced. Borrows some of the elements from SPELLBOUND, though it does have a few of its own moments, including Ireland's performance.

p, I. G. Goldsmith; d&w, E.A. Dupont (based on a story by Goldsmith, E.A. Rolfe); ph, Frank [Franz] F. Planer; m, Herschel Burke Gilbert; ed, Joseph Gluck; art d, Rudolph Sternad.

Crime/Thriller   (PR:A   MPAA:NR)

SCARFACE******* (1932) 99m Caddo Company/UA bw (AKA: SCARFACE, SHAME OF A NATION)

Paul Muni (*Tony Camonte*), Ann Dvorak (*Cesca Camonte*), Karen Morley (*Poppy*), Osgood Perkins (*Johnny Lovo*), Boris Karloff (*Gaffney*), George Raft (*Guido Rinaldo*), Vince Barnett (*Angelo*), C. Henry Gordon (*Inspector Guarino*), Inez Palange (*Tony's Mother*), Edwin Maxwell (*Commissioner*), Tully Marshall (*Managing Editor*), Harry J. Vejar (*Big Louis Costillo*), Bert Starkey (*Epstein*), Henry Armetta (*Pietro*), Maurice Black (*Sullivan*), Purnell Pratt (*Publisher*), Charles Sullivan, Harry Tenbrook (*Bootleggers*), Hank Mann (*Worker*), Paul Fix (*Gaffney Hood*), Howard Hawks (*Man on Bed*), Dennis O'Keefe (*Dance Extra*).

Gangsters in the 1930s received more press than the President of the United States. Grim, gruesome creatures that the gangsters were, the financially downtrodden public during the Great Depression oddly identified with the gangster who was either a home-grown product or an immigrant, their twisted careers, which the press itself promoted, were thought to be glamorous and sophisticated. Gangsters had money, fast cars, luscious women, and they thumbed their noses at all authority. For the uneducated and the unemployed, the gangster was sort of a folk hero, no worse than the slightly tipsy Minute Men who stepped out of a pub at dawn on April 19, 1775, Lexington Green, Massachusetts, and "fired the shot heard round the world." SCARFACE changed that quaint and misconceived notion. Though the gangster cycle had begun with a tremendous explosion with such films as LITTLE CAESAR and PUBLIC ENEMY, it was SCARFACE (originally entitled SCARFACE, THE SHAME OF A NATION) that depicted the glorious gangster for the murdering beast that he really was. In earlier films of the genre, a great deal of attention was paid to developing the background of the criminal and placing much of the blame for his antisocial activities on environment, poverty, bad home life, and unthinking parents. But with

SCARFACE, all of that was dispensed with as viewers saw for the first time an adult, fully developed monster who thrived on death and power. The first scene of the powerful SCARFACE shows Muni only in shadow, whistling a few bars of an Italian aria before shooting a victim and then, his shadow long on a wall, walking calmly away. The remainder of the film shows Muni rise from gunman to crime boss of the city, obviously Chicago, and it's also blatantly obvious that his career as shown on the screen is that of the notorious Al Capone. Muni is honestly portrayed as the typical gangster of the era, irrespective of his being an Italian immigrant. He is brutal, arrogant, unsophisticated, vulgar, stupid, a homicidal maniac who revels in gaudy clothes, fast cars, and machine guns because their rapid fire allows him to kill more people at a single outing. (The number of deaths recorded in this ultra-violent film is 28, with many more occurring off-camera which are referred to, a record for any gangster film.) But beyond these less than ingratiating traits, Muni is also insanely jealous of his slinky sister, Dvorak, to the point where his feelings toward her are obliquely incestuous, though he is too stupid to know it. Muni works for Perkins, a more sophisticated and clever hoodlum who, in turn, is the chief lieutenant of Vejar, the city's nominal crime boss. (Perkins' role is based on Johnny Torrio, the creator of organized crime in America, and Vejar is an exact duplicate of Chicago's old-time crime czar, Big Jim Colosimo.) After his latest killing, Muni goes to a barber shop and with him is his pal and enforcer, Raft, who has the habit of tossing a coin in the air, a cocky gesture that seems to suggest contempt for money while flaunting it. Muni is arrested for the murder by Gordon and taken to the police station but the mob lawyer soon has him free on a special writ and Muni brags of his downtown political connections through his boss, Perkins. When meeting with Perkins later, Muni encourages him to kill the old-time boss Vejar since Vejar will not take advantage of the new Prohibition law and go into bootlegging liquor. Vejar is killed while celebrating in his lavish restaurant (the killing is almost a duplication of the murder of Colosimo in Chicago at his Wabash Avenue nightclub on May 11, 1920). Perkins calls a meeting of all the mob bosses in the city and lectures them about the wild shootouts that have drawn too much attention from the press and heat from the police. He is told that North Side boss Karloff has no intention of obeying Perkins' dictates about dividing up the city in mob zones and Muni states he'll take care of Karloff. Later, Perkins has the ambitious Muni come to his swanky apartment where the bodyguard gets a good look at cool blonde Morley, Perkins' sexy mistress. Muni walks into the parlor and Perkins, as he steps from the bedroom, leaves the door open; Morley sits at her vanity, primping, wearing only a short slip which reveals her attractive legs. When Morley catches Muni gaping at her body, she lets him have a long look before covering herself. It's obvious that the ruthless thug covets her from that moment on, and she is ready to reciprocate. Perkins warns Muni that his strong-arm methods must be curbed, that he should use restraint in running the bootleg territory the mob has cut out for itself. Muni gives him an empty promise of caution. He goes his own way, strong-arming and killing at will. In one scene he enters a saloon not serving the beer the mob is distributing and goes behind the bar to twist the owner's arm behind his back while, at the same time, propelling him like a ball out of a cannon into the back room for a proper beating, one long, continuous take by director Hawks which instantly shows the physical danger of Muni and his ability to employ his brawn like a panther. Muni himself is not invulnerable. After shooting down one of Karloff's men, he himself is ambushed while driving down the street. Grinning–he *enjoys* the threat of death–Muni drives with one hand and fires back with his free hand, shooting his assailants while both cars crash. He survives. (This is a re-creation of the Chicago killing of Angelo Genna on May 25, 1925, when he was shot to pieces while driving his roadster in a running gun battle with George "Bugs" Moran, Earl "Hymie" Weiss, and Vincent "The Schemer" Drucci all in another car firing shotguns and pistols at him, seeking vengeance for the recent killing of their boss, Dion O'Bannion.) He first believes that he has been attacked by his North Side opponents. By then he has taken Morley over as his own girl, she responding to his animal tactics and knowing he has a thirst for power that will not be slaked until he controls the entire city. Morley is the real reason Muni has been attacked, he learns, the gunmen having been sent by Perkins who believes Muni, now his junior partner, is too dangerous to work with and because he has stolen Morley away from him. In a rage, Muni goes to Perkins' headquarters and kills him while Raft and another goon, Barnett, who is even more stupid that Muni, stand in an outer office and chant nonchalantly. Once Perkins has been removed, Muni is in full control of the South Side, but Karloff's men keep trying to kill him. He, Raft, Morley, and Barnett are sitting in a coffee shop when the place, a known Muni hangout, is fired upon by several cars moving slowly by on the street led by a hearse in a phony funeral procession. The place is riddled with submachine-gun fire and the patrons, including Muni and his clan, press themselves to the floor. Barnett, too idiotic to know better, stands up and answers a phone during the prolonged attack, holding a comic phone conversation with someone he cannot understand (he himself talks with such a thick Italian accent that *he* cannot be understood). As the coffee urns behind him are punctured, Barnett is sprayed by hot coffee and dances around while trying to converse with the phone caller all through the roaring attack. Almost as if playing a game, the smiling Muni, acting like a boy envious of another child having a toy he does not have, asks Raft to get one of "them new guns" and Raft slips outside during the raid and kills one of the gangsters hanging on the running board of a passing car (it's a whole slow-moving caravan, duplicating the attack Earl "Hymie" Weiss made against Capone's headquarters in Cicero in 1926), and grabbing the machine gun the dead man drops, running back to the restaurant to present it to Muni like a new plaything. Following the attack, Muni, grinning maniacally, practices with the submachine gun, shouting: "Look out, I'm gonna spit!" and he shoots up the wall. Morley gapes as Muni fires the gun, with an ecstatic look on her face, almost as though she were enjoying the sex act, and, if one logically construes Muni's act and the gun he holds in his hand as an extension of himself, she is. Muni has Perkins' office made over as his own, having his name lettered on the glass door, stepping up his image as gang boss by changing his loud plaid suits to wide pinstripes. He now wears expensive fedora hats and is surrounded wherever he goes by an army of bodyguards, all packing guns. Symbolizing Muni's rise to power is a rooftop sign across from his lavish apartments (which have armor-plated steel window shutters and doors), one that blinks on and off constantly, advertising the words: "The World is Yours, Cook's Tours." But at home, the monied Muni is thought of as a fallen child by his mother, Palange, who will accept no cash from her murdering son (much the way Beryl Mercer, Cagney's mother in THE PUBLIC ENEMY, refuses *his* bootleg money), and she makes the statement, "Once I have a son...I have a daughter!" The daughter, Dvorak, however, who hero-worships her brother at the beginning of the film, though he is always running off any man who pays any attention to her, slowly turns on Muni. He catches her dancing in a nightclub and barrels his way through the crowd to knock her dancing partner to the floor as a sea of his gunmen swell around the fallen man in case he's lunatic enough to protest. Muni drags Dvorak out to a terrace and upbraids her for being with a man, any man. She is half out of her mind at the prospect of becoming an old maid because of her brother's rabid jealousy. Meanwhile, Karloff remains as Muni's only significant enemy, raiding his warehouses, killing his men, and waging all-out war against him. Muni finally corners Karloff's gang in a garage and they are cut down with machine guns (a re-creation of the infamous St. Valentine's Day Massacre, 1929), a slaughter which finally brings down the wrath of the public and the police on Muni. Here, as with every killing shown in the film, the symbol of an X is shown (as used in "X marks the spot," a symbol also used by detectives in investigation charts marking the spot where a murder victim is killed). Karloff himself is later gunned down in a bowling alley by Muni's henchmen and this is ironic in that he is killed the same way real-life "Machine Gun Jack" McGurn, one of the machine gunners responsible for the St. Valentine's Day Massacre, would be slain in Chicago four years later, in 1936. Muni, now hunted by police and his power almost gone, along with his depleted gang, next learns that his sister is living with his best friend Raft. He goes to Raft's apartment, not knowing that Dvorak and Raft are married (as if that would make a difference) and, when Raft opens the door wearing a silk bathrobe with the skimpily clad Dvorak in the background, Muni shoots and kills him. Dvorak, hysterically screaming that she and Raft have wed, begins cursing Muni as he walks dumbly away in a daze. The police are closing in on Muni now, and trap him at his apartment where Dvorak has gone to seek revenge for the killing of Raft. The place is surrounded and the army of police outside begin raking the place with machine gun fire. Excitedly and almost happy to be in another fight, Muni grabs a machine gun and fires back, running from window to window, shouting to Dvorak as he begins closing the steel shutters specially made for such an occasion that they can hold out indefinitely against the police. She is hysterical by now and, telling him that she's just like him, a killer, she joins him in his lunatic defense, handing him weapons to fire, blubbering and weeping, until a stray police bullet strikes her, killing her. Muni goes berserk with the death of his sister, an event that turns his swaggering braggadocio character into a sniveling, whining coward. He runs down the stairs just as the police burst through the door and begs them not to shoot him. But when he steps into the street, sees the squads of heavily armed police, the squad cars, the search lights trained on the building that had been his fortress, Muni makes a dash for freedom and is shot down, his body landing in the gutter. Above him flashes the ironic sign, "The World is Yours," and from an ornate street lamp a shadow of an X crosses his body. SCARFACE, under Hawks' iron grip, was the most violent, bloody gangster film of the genre and remains a *film noir* classic to this day, a totally uncompromising story. Hawks pulled no punches in this exciting but shocking film, unravelling Muni's character as that of a thoroughly corrupt, utterly lethal creature, running his cameras with the incredible action in truck and dolly shots that were mostly unheard of in the early talkie period of stationary cameras and static scenes. Aiding Hawks greatly in his intricate construction of the picture was one of filmdom's greatest cameramen, Garmes, whose low-key and sharp contrasts lent a sinister look to the film, and, in the glaring gangster daylight he created, images that are stark and brutal. The script, written by Hecht and drawing most of its characters and events from real-life Chicago gangsters and the shooting gallery they had turned the city into in the 1920s, was completed in Hecht's usual whirlwind fashion–finished in 11 days–though Hawks took six months to complete the expensive production. Hughes spared no expense in presenting the greatest gangster film of the era, but he also interfered with Hawks as he would with other directors after him, insisting that he approve of the casting of all leading players. Hughes viewed screen tests for the role of the animalistic Tony Camonte and watched James Cagney enact the role. "No," Hughes said to Hawks about Cagney, "he's a little runt." When he saw Clark Gable's test for the gangster role, Hughes, never a good judge of talent, snorted and said no again, cracking: "Look at that guy's ears, will you? He looks like a taxicab with the doors open!" The Hawks-Hughes production was almost cancelled because of the incessant squabbling between the producer and director. In fact, it's a wonder that the liaison even existed in the first place. In 1930, when Hughes decided to make SCARFACE from an awful novel by Armitage Trail, he concluded that the only man to direct the film was Hawks. But he was suing Hawks at the time, claiming that the director's 1930 DAWN PATROL was a direct lift of his production, HELL'S ANGELS. (The two would be involved with lawsuits for decades, with Hughes later suing Hawks for making RED RIVER, whick he claimed lifted important scenes from his production of THE OUTLAW, and it did, as Hawks was forever borrowing ideas from Hughes-produced films in which he, Hawks, had had a hand, thinking that he was entitled to take whatever he liked from Hughes' projects because Hughes never paid him enough money for his work and vexed him endlessly while working for him, and that borrowing those ideas was merely the compensation that he, Hawks, was entitled to for putting up with the machinations of Howard Hughes.) Hawks was playing golf at the Lakeside Country Club one day when a golf pro ran out to a green to tell him that Hughes was on the line and calling for him, that Hughes wanted to come over to the club and play golf with him. Hawks stared dumbfounded at the golf pro and then blurted: "Hell, no! Tell him that I don't want to play golf with him. The S.O.B. is suing me!" But on the next green the golf pro was waiting for Hawks to say that Hughes was coming over anyway. Hughes appeared and played golf with Hawks that afternoon (Hawks won), and before they reached the 18th green, Hawks had agreed to direct SCARFACE. He immediately hired Ben Hecht to write the story (almost nothing but the original title was used of the Trail novel) and oversee the shooting script, and a bevy of crime writers, including Burnett, who had written LITTLE CAESAR, and Fred Palsey, who had authored the excellent *Al Capone, The Story of a Self-Made Man*, were added to the writing staff. It was Hecht who suggested that the story be a modernization of "Macbeth," and profiling Camonte and his tempestuous sister as modern day Borgias was Hawks' idea, throwing in the incest relationship which is really what Hawks and Hecht intended to serve as the emotional trauma that destroys the unthinking Camonte. Hawks later commented: "Capone was supposed to have staged a big party for a gangland enemy. First Capone made a long, polite speech about the man. Toward the end of the speech, he became angry and zeroed in on how the man had deceived him. At that point, filled with rage, Capone was supposed to have beaten the man to death with a baseball bat. (This incident really occurred in 1929 but Capone, after feting *three* of his turncoat followers, used the baseball bat to crush the heads of his guests of honor, John Scalise, Albert Anselmi, and Giuseppe "Hop Toad" Guinta.) That was to me an act so lunatic and duplicitous that it seemed a modern version of Cesare Borgia and the Borgia family. Hecht and I researched the whole Borgia family. Cesare Borgia and his sister Lucretia were supposed to have been lovers. We copied that." Hecht had been offered $20,000 by Hawks to write the script but the writer insisted that he receive $1,000 a day instead and in cash. His own speed was Hecht's undoing. At the end of 11 days he looked up at Hawks and said, amazed, "We're through, aren't we?" Hawks laughed and told Hecht: "You made $11,000–and you could have had 20. You're the lousiest businessman I ever met in my life!" But Hawks allowed Hecht another $1,000 a day while he accompanied the director to New York on a three-day car trip, and lost another $6,000 to him in backgammon so Hecht wound up with the $20,000 after all. Hughes read the script before Hecht and Hawks left for the East, believing they were following the Trail novel he had purchased, a banal story about two brothers, one becoming a cop, the other going bad. After reading the script, Hughes said to Hawks, "Where's the brother, the cop?" Replied Hawks, "There isn't any." Hughes let out a laugh and said, "You threw away the whole book but you have one hell of a story here!" Hecht had been using Chicago gangsters, which he knew from his days as a journalist in Chicago, as movie characters for years. His character in Josef von Sternberg's silent crime classic UNDERWORLD is based upon "Terrible Tommy" O'Connor; the script won Hecht an Oscar for Best Screenplay. (It is interesting to note that George Bancroft, playing the crime boss in UNDERWORLD, takes refuge in his apartment which is equipped with steel shutters, and battling the cops with a submachine gun in the same way Muni does in SCARFACE.) The character essayed by Muni is obviously Al Capone and it was obvious to anyone who saw the film when it was originally released in 1932, including Al Capone and some of his goons. Some Capone men visited Hollywood only a few months after SCARFACE was completed and called unexpectedly on Hecht. They had known Hecht a decade or more earlier in Chicago and they wanted to know if the character portrayed in SCARFACE was based on their boss, Capone. Hecht nervously poured his two callers a drink, noticing that they had guns in their pockets and also carried a copy of the SCARFACE script, having gotten it from some mysterious source. Finally, one of them pulled out the script and brandished it menacingly, as if it were a writ about to be served. "This stuff about Al Capone?" "God, no," Hecht replied. "I don't even know Al." Hecht went on to say that he had left Chicago just as Capone was rising in power and had never met him, explaining that he knew Big Jim Colosimo, and gangsters like Mossy Enright, Pete Gentleman, and Dion O'Bannion. The gangsters stood up and one said, "Okay, we'll tell Al this stuff you wrote is about them other guys." Hecht watched them anxiously head toward the door and then froze as they turned and the one who had done all the talking said with plenty of menace in his voice: "If this stuff ain't about Al Capone, why are you callin' it SCARFACE? Everybody'll think it's him." Hecht thought fast and replied: "That's the reason. Al is one of the most famous and fascinating men of our time. If we call the movie SCARFACE, everybody will want to see it, figuring it's about Al. That's part of the racket we call showmanship." The two goons looked at each other, confused, then the one mumbled, "We'll tell Al." He added as an afterthought, "Say, who's this fella Howard Hughes?" This time Hecht spoke the truth: "He's got nothing to do with anything. He's the sucker with the money!" The gangsters finally left, mumbling incoherently about Hecht's gobbledegook explanations. Hecht, who became the highest paid screenwriter in Hollywood in years to come, vowed to himself that night that he would never again write a movie about real life gangsters, at least any scripts that had to do with Capone. The real Scarface, Capone, saw the film and laughed through most of it, especially the murder scenes, scoffing at the way Hollywood killed off thugs. "What a bunch of dopes they think we are," he commented to Jake Guzik, "to go around bumping off guys in the open like that." He did not object to Muni's portrayal of him, if he did admit that the portrayal was based upon him, but he did object to the way Muni, early in the film, wolfs down spaghetti by cramming his mouth with noodles, forking great gobs of it into his cavernous mouth. "Look at that," Capone said when witnessing the scene. "The guy's a real slob. Somebody should tell them Hollywood jerks that you spoon the spaghetti with your fork before you eat it."

Muni, of course, is superlative in his role of the maniac killer Camonte, moving sluggishly as if only the part of his brain that is evil generates his physical movements. He acts with his entire body and his face is contorted into the expression of an ape at times. Muni was an unknown actor when Hawks selected him for the part, having been trained in the Yiddish theater. Morley is perfect as the ice-cool blonde gun moll, appropriately named Poppy, a violence-craving chippie who is turned on by power and killing, all embodied by Muni. Karloff's appearance in SCARFACE is strange in that he incongruously speaks with his natural British accent crawling out the side of his mouth in an oddball interpretation of how a Chicago gangster is supposed to talk. Karloff, who had a tremendous success a year earlier by playing the monster in Universal's FRANKENSTEIN, had appeared once before as a gangster, essaying a small role in SMART MONEY where Warner Bros. tough guys Edward G. Robinson and James Cagney ran all over him. In SCARFACE he plays a part based on Chicago's George "Bugs" Moran and he looks his part, with his staring deep-socketed eyes and stiff, lethargic movements, a gaunt, almost ghoulish-looking gangster. He was not one of Hawks' favorite actors. The director later stated (in *Hawks on Hawks* by Joseph McBride), "Boris Karloff was utterly unknown, and he played just a little part. After that, I had an awful time with him. Every time I made a picture he insisted on having a part in it." The dumbbell gunsel who acts as Muni's secretary, Barnett, had never acted before Hawks gave him his role in SCARFACE. Barnett was a lowbrow type who used to hire himself out to Hollywood parties as a joke waiter; he would purposely spill soup on a guest the host did not like and start such a row with the offended person that he would drive the unwanted guest from the house while the host merely shrugged as if to say that good help was really hard to find. Barnett did about the same thing to Muni in SCARFACE, Hawks allowing the little bald-headed man to do just about whatever he thought was funny. And this drove consummate actor Muni crazy to the point where he insisted that Barnett be taken off the film. But Hawks got around Muni by telling him that he was a great actor and no stooge could undo his marvelous concentration. Muni explained that in every important scene where Barnett was present the little character tried to upstage him with pieces of business that Barnett had picked up from burlesque performers he had hired as coaches. "He stinks, he's awful," cried Muni to Hawks, but the director explained that Barnett's bad acting only made Muni look that much better on screen. Muni later told a friend that the director's explanation for keeping Barnett in the film was "a perverse notion, something a director does, even one as talented as Hawks, when he wishes to be before the camera himself." Barnett, who is all ham and not as funny as Hawks thought he was, would go on being the bane of Muni's life in Hollywood, appearing in other films with him, almost as if he were assigned to spill the soup on the great actor's spectacular Hollywood career throughout the 1930s. As the crafty sub-boss, Perkins is slick but not as smooth as Raft with his silk nightgown, tuxedo, and pomaded hair parted in the middle. Raft is excellent as Muni's right-hand man, loyal unto death, a killer who does Muni's bidding without question. After killing one gangster rival (ostensibly Dion O'Bannion, in his flower shop), Raft hands Muni a single rose to signify the fact that he has made the hit as ordered. Muni later gives this same rose to his mistress Morley; the eternal symbol of great love, the rose, is thusly shown to be perverted by nightmare humans to whom it really has no significance other than as an expression of cynicism. Muni and Raft would become stars overnight because of SCARFACE and both would receive long-term, high-paying contracts from studios, Muni at Warners where he would see enormous success with such films as I AM A FUGITIVE FROM A CHAIN GANG, JUAREZ, THE GOOD EARTH, THE LIFE OF EMILE ZOLA, and THE STORY OF LOUIS PASTEUR for which he would win an Oscar as Best Actor; he would become one of the greatest actors on film in the 1930s, bar none. Raft, on the other hand, got a seven-year contract with Paramount thanks to SCARFACE and appeared in a host of rather mediocre films, but was nevertheless a solid leading man for two decades to come. Raft himself was never a full-fledged gangster but, in the 1920s, before his dancing act caught on along Broadway, he drove a beer truck for bootlegger Owney Madden who was his lifelong friend (among many gangsters, including the notorious Benjamin "Bugsy" Siegel) and it was Madden who was directly responsible for Raft getting his part in SCARFACE. He and Madden went to a boxing match in Hollywood one night and ran into Hawks. They spent the rest of the evening with the director and Hawks and Madden left Raft and went up to Madden's hotel room to have a serious talk. The next day Hawks called Raft and offered him the role of Guido "Little Boy" Rinaldo in SCARFACE, which he accepted immediately. (Obviously, Owney "The Killer" Madden– unlike most gangsters in that he was urbane and well-read–had talked Hawks into giving his protege Raft the big break.) What made Raft memorable in the film was his constant flipping of a coin, something Raft later admitted he had seen another gangster do. Raft had hung around several New York gangs in the 1920s, including the Dutch Schultz mob. He had been fascinated by one of Schultz's lieutenants, Bo Weinberg, who had the habit of flipping a coin just before he shot someone. Where Weinberg invariably flipped a quarter, Raft later insisted he was flipping only a nickel, yet inspection of the film shows him flipping a much-larger coin in his hand while he stands at an organ-grinder's stand and plays with a monkey, a half dollar or a silver dollar. On other occasions he appears to be flipping a quarter or a nickel or even a dime. In a later meeting with Capone, the real Scarface thought he was flipping a "four-bit piece," and Raft corrected him, telling him it was a nickel. "That's worse," Capone reportedly said to Raft. "You tell 'em that if any of my boys are tossin' coins, they'll be $20 gold pieces, see?" The part essayed by Raft was that of Capone's bodyguard, Frankie Rio, a loyal gunsel who died for the likes of Al Capone but who wasn't murdered by him as Raft is by Muni in SCARFACE. The death scene rendered by Raft in the film is outstanding and it brought Raft critical raves for its realism but the actor later admitted that he achieved that realism quite by accident. "In doing the fall after the shooting, Raft stated (as quoted in *The George Raft File* by James Robert Parish), "I slipped and hit my head on the door. The pain made my eyes roll, and the cameras were on. They shot the scene only once, and I couldn't have done it again without another crack on the head." Almost everything Raft did in the film was drawn from real life, including the scene where vixen Dvorak entices him at the nightclub, getting him to dance by doing a sultry, shimmying dance before him, snaking her body around. This come-hither ploy by Dvorak had happened before Dvorak was cast in her role of Camonte's sister. She attended a large party at Hawks' home. Raft was sitting in a chair. Since he was a nondrinker and poor at small talk, he appeared to be having a boring time. Dvorak, an unknown actress at the time, approached the handsome Raft, wearing what Hawks later described as "a black silk gown almost cut down to her hips. I'm sure that's all she had on...Ann asked him to dance with her but he said he'd rather not. She was a little high and right in front of him starts to do this sexy, undulating dance, sort of trying to lure him on to dance with her...After a while, George couldn't resist her suggestive dance and in no time they were doing a sensational number which stopped the party..." Hawks cast Dvorak as the sex-starved sister that night and had her repeat what she had done at the party in SCARFACE. "The scene played like a million dollars," Hawks stated, "because it was something that really happened between George and Ann." Authenticity was Hawks' middle name during the filming of SCARFACE. He even insisted on using real bullets when the coffee shop is riddled by the passing caravan of gangsters trying to kill Muni, Raft, and his pals. First, all the actors were called off the set, and then the machine gunners, using real bullets, shot the set to pieces. The actors were then brought back onto the set and the shot was superimposed as if they are right in the middle of the murderous fusillade. One visitor at that time, Harold Lloyd's brother, was warned not to go on the set while the machine gunners (veterans from WW I) were firing into it. But he slipped behind the set to see what was going on and a bullet slammed into him; he lost an eye for the sake of his curiosity. Hawks had one car smashup in a running gun battle during a gang shootout, and when the director saw the rushes of this shot he insisted that more cars be wrecked in a mob war which was shown in a dazzling montage to caption the gang battles between Muni and Karloff, until Hawks had supervised the crashing of 19 cars that smashed into buildings, lampposts, and uprooted fire hydrants. Hawks later claimed that some real gangsters, members of the Capone mob (perhaps the same two goons who paid the lightning call on Hecht), somehow got into the studio and demanded that Hawks show them the film. The feisty director shouted at them, "You can pay a dollar when it shows in a movie house and then you can look at the picture!" The thugs backed away, one of them saying, "Oh, hell, you didn't scare, did you?" Hawks used Fred Palsey, then the top crime reporter for the Chicago *Tribune* as a sort of long-distance researcher (he received credit in the screenplay), checking almost daily with Palsey by phone to verify crime personalities and underworld techniques and procedures. When real gangsters heard that Hawks was making SCARFACE they applied for jobs as extras or "advisors." One man named White appeared and asked Hawks for a job and the director told him to return the following day. He called Palsey and the reporter told him that the gangster was 'Puggy' White, carried a gun, was a pimp for Capone at one time, and had killed so-and-so and so-and-so. The next day when White returned, Hawks sat him down and said, "Your real name is "Puggy" White and you were a pimp for Capone and shot so-and-so and so-and-so." The gangster turned red in the face and got indignant, snapping, "I was never no pimp!" He didn't deny the murders. Several of these underworld types were used to supply additional information on how the gangs operated. According to Hawks the gangsters "would usually tell me exactly how something was done...and we would do that very thing in the movie. We did scenes of killings that actually happened. For example, in one scene we put guns in a hearse, then drove it by the windows of a cafe and shot the devil out of the place. That was something that actually happened in Chicago." Capone himself, according to the director, later gave him a special party in Chicago, honoring him for making SCARFACE. It was a formal affair and Scarface himself wore a morning coat and striped trousers. He had the ballroom where the fete was held filled with the most attractive whores from his hundreds of brothels and even asked Hawks if he thought a few of them wouldn't make good movie stars. "All of Capone's friends and associates, the cream of Chicago's gangster society," Hawks recalled (as quoted by Lewis Yablonsky in *George Raft*), "were there, all very cordial and polite. The high point of the evening came after dinner when Capone presented me with a small machine gun as a special gift." (Not only did Capone, according to Hawks, see SCARFACE "five or six times" but "he had his own print of it. He thought it was great. He'd say, 'Jesus Christ, you guys got a lot of stuff in that picture! How'd you know about that?' ") Many of the lines Muni and the other actors delivered were straight out of the mouths of real gangsters. At one time, Perkins bristles when his own protege, Muni, tells him what to do and Perkins says: "Don't give me orders, you murdering ape!" Muni pats the machine gun in his hand and replies, as Frankie McErlane (first to use a Thompson submachine gun in the Chicago gang wars, 1925) once said, "This is the only thing that gives orders!" SCARFACE remained Hawks' favorite film as it was Hughes'. The producer, as was his usual fate, ran into censorship problems with SCARFACE right from the beginning. Hollywood, which had practiced every conceivable excess on the screen had still never experienced anything like SCARFACE, an utterly ferocious film of bloodshed and violence, not to mention the ultimate taboo, incest, even though that carnal image is obtuse and only occurs to Muni's murky mind at the very end when he is surrounded by the cops and Morley calls him (wanting to be as close to the gore as possible) during the gun battle, with Barnett, his illiterate secretary shot dead while trying to converse again on the phone and the arrival of Dvorak to fight his last gunfight with him and die with him. Muni shouts "I got nobody...I'm all alone...my steel shutters don't work!" To Morley, when he is dazed with the thought that he actually covets the sister he has been protecting, he can only say limply on the phone: "...I didn't know..." before hanging up. Of course, all this and all the gunfights and cynical murders were objected to by the Hollywood censors. They started with such scenes as the killing of a helpless gangster in a hospital bed who had survived a Muni-Raft extermination attempt and who is visited by Muni and Raft, both men carrying flowers. They shove nurses and doctors out of the way to barge into the man's room to find him almost wholly in bandages and casts, his legs and arms strung up in traction (to form the ever-present X symbol), shooting him to death, and thus completing their job and retaining their professional standing, throwing the flowers they carry on the corpse as a final act of contempt. Scene by scene the censors chopped away at SCARFACE, the organization then acting as Hollywood's moral janitor being the powerful Motion Picture Producers and Distributors of America. This agency insisted upon dozens of cuts and a whole new ending. Muni's flagrant crimes, graphically shown, deserved to be atoned for, the censors said, in a manner more suitable to the workings of the law. He could not merely be gunned down in the gutter at the end. Another ending was called for but Hawks refused to shoot it. Hughes ordered more scenes shot, showing Muni (a stand-in, shown in silhouette, since Muni himself had left the production and returned to the Broadway stage at the time), being tried and sentenced and then hanged as a mass murderer. This method of execution would not have been shown if Hawks, the ever-careful researcher, had been in charge of these scenes; the Muni character would have been *electrocuted* since the State of Illinois had abandoned the gallows in 1922 and gone over to the electric chair. Moreover, disclaiming speeches of a high moral tone which tried to depict the Hawks movie as a "social lesson" instead of the stark and realistic profile the director always intended, were delivered by newspaper editor Marshall and police commissioner Maxwell in a prolog and epilog. This watered down version of SCARFACE finally received a Seal of Approval but when prints were shipped East for the film's premiere, the State Board of Censors in New York refused to let the movie be shown, demanding even more cuts and changes. Hughes exploded and released a statement to the press that made him appear to be the champion of free speech: "It has become a serious threat to the freedom of honest expression in America when self-styled guardians of the public welfare, as personified by our film censor boards, lend their aid and their influence to the abortive efforts of selfish and vicious interests to suppress a motion picture simply because it depicts the truth about conditions in the United States which have been front page news since the advent of Prohibition. I am convinced that the determined opposition to SCARFACE is actuated by political motives. The picture, as originally filmed eight months ago, has been enthusiastically praised by the foremost authorities on crime and law enforcement and by leading screen reviewers. It seems to be the unanimous opinion of these authorties that SCARFACE is an honest and powerful indictment of gang rule in America and, as such, will be a tremendous force in compelling our state and Federal governments to take more drastic action to rid the country of gangsterism." In frustration, Hughes released both the original print as Hawks had shot it and the doctored, revised print with the prolog and epilog tacked on (these have long since disappeared from prints seen today), showing either print wherever in the U.S. there was the least objection to what was shown. This resulted in confusion among film enthusiasts and endless arguing over how Muni dies at the end of the film, either by being shot down in the gutter by police or being hanged. Depending on where the film was seen at the initial time of release, both conceptions were correct. Almost all prints available today show Muni ending his bullet-laden career in the gutter. Hughes had spent well over $1 million to make SCARFACE and he saw that returned double after all the commotion died down, his censorship problems greatly aiding his cause at the box office. This discovery led the producer to use censorship in the future like an unpaid public relations department working for almost every one of his films, particularly the Jane Russell opuses, THE OUTLAW and UNDERWATER, where Hughes showed on screen as much as possible of this lady's large breasts, and, in the case of THE FRENCH LINE, as much of her Amazonian body as the skimpiest costume of the day would permit. But SCARFACE was no flesh-peddling production, rather the most innovative, shocking gangster film ever made. Hughes would forever consider it, as would Hawks, his most creative and cherished film product. Hughes so zealously guarded its future releases that once the billionaire removed it from distribution, he refused to sell the rights to the story or allow exhibitors to show the classic *film noir* production. In 1974 a producer offered Hughes $2 million for the rights to the movie and Hughes laughed at him and hung up the phone. Oddly, the prints Hughes kept locked up in his vaults at 7000 Romaine Street in Hollywood were only copies. Hawks somehow got his hands on the original negative and refused to give it up to Hughes, hiding it. Upon Hughes' death the executors of his will were posthumously instructed by Hughes to confiscate all copies of SCARFACE, meaning that they were to get their hands on Hawks' negative. Not until 1979 did Hughes' Summa Corporation sell all the rights to SCARFACE to Universal Studios, thus making the film available once more to the public (present release having a 91-minute running time), which could only see this classic in pirated editions up to that time, a 47-year hiatus between showings. In 1983, Universal allowed goremaster Brian De Palma to get his hands on the property and he turned it into a perverted and abysmal slaughterhouse through which Al Pacino waded with maniacal glee. This disgusting remake is obviously the reason why Hughes and Hawks never wanted to allow anyone else to get their hands on SCARFACE.

p, Howard Hughes, Howard Hawks; d, Hawks; w, Ben Hecht, Seton I. Miller, John Lee Mahin, W.R. Burnett, Fred Palsey (based on the novel by Armitage Trail); ph, Lee Garmes (additional scenes for censor), L. William O'Connell; m, Adolph Tandler, Gus Arnheim; ed, Edward D. Curtis; prod d, Harry Olivier.

Crime Drama   Cas.   (PR:O   MPAA:NR)

SCARFACE zero   (1983) 170m UNIV c

Al Pacino *(Tony Montana)*, Steven Bauer *(Manny Ray)*, Michelle Pfeiffer *(Elvira)*, Mary Elizabeth Mastrantonio *(Gina)*, Robert Loggia *(Frank Lopez)*, Miriam Colon *(Mama Montana)*, F. Murray Abraham *(Omar)*, Paul Shenar *(Alejandro Sosa)*, Harris Yulin *(Bernstein)*, Angel Salazar *(Chi Chi)*, Arnaldo Santana *(Ernie)*, Pepe Serna *(Angel)*, Michael P. Moran *(Nick the Pig)*, Al Israel *(Hector the Toad)*, Dennis Holahan *(Banker)*, Mark Margolis *(Shadow)*, Michael Alldredge *(Sheffield)*, Ted Beniades *(Seidelbaum)*, Richard Belzer *(M.C. at Babylon Club)*, Paul Espel *(Luis)*, John Brandon, Tony Perez, Garnett Smith *(Immigration Officers)*, Loren Almaguer *(Dr. Munoz)*, Gil Barreto *(Cuban Refugee)*, Heather Benna *(Gutierrez Child)*, Dawnell Bowers *(Miriam)*, Tina Leigh Cameron *(Saleslady)*, Victor Campos *(Ronnie Echevierra)*, Robert Hammer Cannerday *(Marielito)*, Rene Carrasco, Gary Cervantes, Gregory N. Cruz *(Shooters)*, Albert Carrier *(Pedro Quinn)*, John Carter *(Vic Phillips)*, Richard Caselnova *(Driver)*, Carlos Cestero *(Matos)*, John Contardo *(Miguel Echevierra)*, Roberto Contreras *(Rebenga)*, Caesar Cordova *(Cook)*, Dante D'Andre *(Gen. Strasser)*, Richard Delmonte *(Fernando)*, Wayne Doba *(Octavio the Clown)*, Michel Francois *(Maitre d')*, Ben Frommer *(Male Patron)*, Edward R. Frommer *(Taco Stand Customer)*, John Gamble *(Helicopter Pilot)*, Troy Isaacs *(Cuban Refugee)*, Ronald Joseph *(Car Salesman)*, Mario Machado *(Interviewer)*, Joe Marmo *(Nacho "El Gordo")*, Ray Martel *(Nacho's Bodyguard)*, John McCann *(Bank Spokesman)*, Richard Mendez *(Gina's Killer)*, Victor Millan *(Ariel Bleyer)*, Santos Morales *(Waldo)*, Mike Moroff *(Gaspar's Bodyguard)*, Angela Nisi *(Gutierrez Child)*, Arnold Tafolla *(1st Kid)*, Manuel Padilla, Jr. *(2nd Kid)*, Tony Pann *(Driver)*, Ilka Payan *(Mrs. Gutierrez)*, Barbra Perez *(Marta)*, Michael Rougas *(Monsignor)*, Anthony Saenz, Jim Towers *(Cuban Refugees)*, Gino Silva *(The Skull)*, Charles Tamburro *(Helicopter Pilot)*, Robert Van Den Berg *(Gaspar Gomez)*, Bob Yanez *(Cuban Man)*.

In what is probably the most bloody film ever made, Sam Peckinpah's THE WILD BUNCH being no exception, De Palma's monument to human gore is doubly repugnant in that it postures itself as a remake of the Hughes-Hawks-Hecht classic of 1932, when nothing could be further from the truth. It seems, as this disgusting film strongly testifies, that Universal only wished to obtain the rights to the Hughes property so that it could vivisect it in front of viewers, its foul-speaking star, Pacino, gleefully toying with the film's entrails like some mad ghoul let loose in a Hollywood cemetery. Hardly a frame sprockets by without showing a splash of blood, a bit of exposed brain, a piece of crushed bone. The fact that every character profiled in this scum-producing potboiler deserves to die and does cannot mitigate the film's existence. Pacino is one of the alleged 25,000 hardened criminals who were dumped onto Florida's shores during Castro's 1980 expulsion of those Cubans who did not or could not support his failed revolution. He quickly goes to work for dope-distributor Loggia, makes a fortune, and soon rises in the Miami-based Cuban-American underworld. He covets Loggia's blonde mistress, coke-snorting Pfeiffer, and, after making his own connection with suave Bolivian dope king Shenar, he kills Loggia, marries drug addict Pfeiffer, and, only toward the end of the film, realizes that his secret dream is to sleep with his sister, Mastrantonio, killing best

friend Bauer when he and his sister get together. Pacino dies in a gun battle with rival dopesters that makes the Normandy Invasion look like a tea party. Everywhere there are rapid-fire gun battles and so many bodies litter the screen for the almost three painful hours of this abattoir film that the average filmgoer will not be able to count or realize–if not having the good sense to walk away from this expensive vomit in the first 20 minutes–that this ultra-cynical film is designed to assault all human sensibilities while preposterously calling itself art. Pacino's performance is laughable as he clutters his phony Cuban accent with a foul American word per second, a perverse transference from Italian godfather to Cuban crime lord. Not for man, woman, or child, this film is an insult to the profession of both criminals and filmmakers. The most insulting aspect of this dungheap movie is the audacity and pomposity of its exploitative director De Palma to dedicate it to Howard Hawks and Ben Hecht, the creators of the 1932 classic. It's about the same as murdering your mother, then dumping her corpse on your father's doorstep and calling it affection. This was a film that should never have been made. Besides dragging the viewer along through an endless mire of guts and blood, it repeats its theme over and over again until it bores, despite the fact that De Palma tries to get a jump on the action by early on showing several of Pacino's coke-pushing pals dismembered with a chain saw during a gang struggle for drug distribution. This, of course, is De Palma's kind of "meat," and he gnaws on it for another two-plus hours. Millions were pumped into this ghastly, stinking cesspool of a picture and it enjoyed only brief popularity when released, mostly by those seeking sadistic thrills or mental-outpatients needing to be wither shocked out of their euphoric states or reduced from manic conditions to stupors for their own protection. The only redeeming aspects of this overbearing slush are Alonzo's lush lensing and some notable art direction by Richardson. That's not enough to offset the mental and emotional pistol-whipping this film will administer to any viewer with half a brain. This film should definately NOT be seen by children, nor by any intelligent viewer seeking entertainment. For sickies only. De Palma's SCARFACE was originally scheduled to receive an "X" MPAA rating, but producers argued that such a rating would hurt the film at the box office (which it should have), and it got a "hard R" rating instead (which it shouldn't have), and what is a "hard R" rating anyway, other than an "X" rating that has been bullied into something it isn't? So much for the sincerity and credibility of the MPAA rating system. Songs include "Scarface (Push It to the Limit)," "Turn Out the Light," "She's on Fire" (Giorgio Moroder, Pete Bellotte), "Shake It Up," "Dance Dance Dance," "I'm Hot Tonight" (Morodor, Arthur Barrow), "Vamos a Bailar" (Morodor, Maria Conchita), and the hit single "Rush, Rush" (Morodor, Deborah Harry).

p, Martin Bregman, Peter Saphier; d, Brian De Palma; w, Oliver Stone (based on the 1932 film script by Ben Hecht); ph, John A. Alonzo (Panavision, Technicolor); m, Giorgio Morodor; ed, Jerry Greenberg, David Ray; art d, Ed Richardson; set d, Blake Russell, Steve Schwartz, Geoff Hubbard, Bruce Weintraub; cos, Patricia Norris; spec eff, Ken Pepiot, Stan Parks.

Crime   Cas.   (PR:O   MPAA:R)

SCARFACE MOB, THE½**   (1962) 105m Desilu/Cari Releasing-Desilu bw (TUEUR DE CH ICAGO)

Robert Stack *(Eliot Ness)*, Keenan Wynn *(Joe Fuselli)*, Barbara Nichols *(Brandy La France)*, Patricia Crowley *(Betty Anderson)*, Neville Brand *(Al Capone)*, Bill Williams *(Martin Flaherty)*, Joe Mantell *(George Ritchie)*, Bruce Gordon *(Frank Nitti)*, Peter Leeds *(Lamarr Kane)*, Eddie Firestone *(Eric Hansen)*, Robert Osterloh *(Tom Kopka)*, Paul Dubov *(Jack Rossman)*, Abel Fernandez *(William Youngfellow)*, Paul Picerni *(Tony Liguri)*, John Beradino *(Johnny Giannini)*, Wolfe Barzell *(Picco)*, Frank Wilcox *(Beecher Asbury)*, Peter Mamakos *(Bomber Belcastro)*, Wally Cassell *(Phil D'Andrea)*, Herman Rudin *(Mops Volpe)*, Richard Benedict *(Furs Sammons)*, Bern Hoffman *(Jake Guzik)*, Frank De Kova *(Jimmy Napoli)*, James Westerfield *(Ed Marriatt)*, Walter Winchell *(Narrator)*.

A theatrical release of the popular television series from the early 1960s, THE UNTOUCHABLES, which concentrated on the efforts of police to thwart the antics of powerful Chicago underworld figures. Stack, as government agent Eliot Ness, targets the Capone mob. After several stills run by the gang are closed down, the notorious gangland figure makes a declaration of war against Stack and his men, and hires a hitman to bump off Stack. But Capone winds up in jail with a long sentence before anything comes of his threats.

p, Quinn Martin; d, Phil Karlson; w, Paul Monash (based on the novel *The Untouchables* by Eliot Ness, Oscar Fraley); ph, Charles Straumer; m, Wilbur Hatch; ed, Robert L. Swanson; art d, Ralph Berger, Frank T. Smith; set d, Sandy Grace; ch, Jack Baker; makeup, Ed Butterworth.

Crime   (PR:A   MPAA:NR)

SCARLET ANGEL**   (1952) 81m UNIV c

Yvonne De Carlo *(Roxy McClanahan)*, Rock Hudson *(Frank Truscott)*, Richard Denning *(Malcolm Bradley)*, Bodil Miller *(Linda Caldwell)*, Amanda Blake *(Susan Bradley)*, Henry O'Neill *(Morgan Caldwell)*, Henry Brandon *(Pierre)*, Maude Wallace *(Eugenia Caldwell)*, Dan Riss *(Walter Frisby)*, Whitfield Connor *(Norton Wade)*, Tol Avery *(Phineas Calhoun)*,

Arthur Page (*Edwards*), George Hamilton (*Gus*), Dale Van Sickel (*Jeb*), Mickey Pfleger (*Bobbie Caldwell*), Harry Harvey (*Doctor Corbin*), George Spaulding (*Trowbridge*), Tom Browne Henry (*Jason Mortimer*), Fred Graham (*Cass Walters*), Fred Coby, Eddie Dew (*Soldiers*), Nolan Leary (*Apothecary*), Elizabeth Root (*Trixie*), Wilma Francis (*Daisy*), Betty Allen (*Another Girl*), Leo Curley (*Sheriff Jasper*), Dabbs Greer, John Roy, Martin Clichy, Jack Perry, Buddy Sullivan (*Men*), Sally Corner, Ada Adams (*Sisters*), Joe Forte, Vera Marshe (*Hotel Clerks*), Fred Berest (*Hamlet*), Coleman Francis (*Deckhand*), Jack Daley (*Jepson*), Jean Andren (*Flora*), George Ramsey, Charles Horvath (*Crewmen*), Bud Wolfe (*Bartender*), Frankie Van, Carl Saxe, Edwin Parker (*Waiters*), Mil Patrick (*Dolly*), Creighton Hale (*Judge Ames*), Ed Hinkle (*Longshoreman*), Bert LeBaron (*Philippe*), Lila Finn (*Girl*), Louis G. Hart (*Ad Lib Waiter*).

De Carlo plays an unscrupulous New Orleans saloon girl who takes advantage of Hudson's admiration to make off with his earnings as a sea captain. Further opportunities arise when a wealthy widow dies in the saloon where De Carlo works. She poses as the rich woman and takes the dead woman's baby to San Francisco to take over the woman's estate. The sharp cookie that De Carlo is, she quickly gains a prominent position in San Francisco society, but not without arguments with the family of the dead woman's husband. De Carlo has a change of heart when Hudson sails into port. She gives up her riches and assumed identity to be with the man she really loves. An overly talky script, filled with redundant scenes, mars any possibilities this project may have had.

p, Leonard Goldstein; d, Sidney Salkow; w, Oscar Brodney; ph, Russell Metty (Technicolor); ed, Ted J. Kent; md, Joseph E. Gershenson; art d, Bernard Herzbrun, Robert Clatworthy; cos, Rosemary Odell; ch, Harold Belfer.

Drama   (PR:A MPAA:NR)

SCARLET BLADE, THE   (SEE: CRIMSON BLADE, THE, 1964, Brit.)

SCARLET BRAND**½*   (1932) 59m Big 4 bw

Bob Custer, Betty Mack, Duke Lee, Nelson McDowell, Blackie Whiteford, William Nolte, Robert Walker, Frederick Ryter, Jack Long, Frank Ball.

Custer is up against a bunch of angry ranchers when he is accused of rustling. He eventually clears his name with the help of a stranger who believes in his innocence but not before he has his chest branded with a hot iron, in one of the more gruesome scenes in an early oater. Repetitive use of scenery begs for a little change.

p, Burton King; d, J.P. McGowan; w, Ethel Hill (based on a story by Hill); ph, Edward Kull; ed, Fred Bain.

Western   (PR:A MPAA:NR)

SCARLET BUCCANEER, THE   (SEE: SWASHBUCKLER, 1976)

SCARLET CAMELLIA, THE**½*   (1965, Jap.) 117m
Shochiku/Shochiku Films of America -Shiro Kido c (GOBEN NO TSUBAKI)

Shima Iwashita (*Oshino*), Yoshi Kato (*Kihei Musashiya*), Sachiko Hidari (*Osono*), Takahiro Tamura (*Chodayu*), Yunosuke Ita (*Unno*), Shoichi Ozawa (*Seiichi*), Ko Nishimura (*Sakichi*), Eiji Okada (*Gen Maruu*), Go Kato (*Aoki*).

In order to avenge her dying father, Iwashita goes on a vicious killing spree, first setting fire to the villa of her parents, then murdering all the lovers of her promiscuous mother. A sweet girl who is discounted as a suspect by the investigating detective, Kato, Iwashita has every intention of turning herself in once she has completed her revenge. However, the last man she plans to kill turns out to be her real father; she decides to spare him, but the man's wife commits suicide after learning of her husband's faithlessness.

p, Shino Kido; d, Yoshitaro Nomura; w, Masato Ide (based on the novel *Goben No Tsubaki* by Shugoro Yamamoto); ph, Ko Kawamata (Shochiku GrandScope, Eastmancolor); m, Yasushi Akutagawa; art d, Takashi Matsuyama, Chiyoo Umeda.

Crime   (PR:C MPAA:NR)

SCARLET CLAW, THE***   (1944) 74m UNIV bw (AKA: SHERLOCK HOLMES AND THE SCARLET CLAW)

Basil Rathbone (*Sherlock Holmes*), Nigel Bruce (*Dr. John H. Watson*), Gerald Hamer (*Potts, Postman/Tanner/Alistair Ransom*), Paul Cavanagh (*Lord William Penrose*), Arthur Hohl (*Emile Journet, Innkeeper*), Kay Harding (*Marie Journet, his Daughter*), Miles Mander (*Judge Brisson*), David Clyde (*Sgt. Thompson, Village Constable*), Ian Wolfe (*Drake, Lord Penrose's Butler*), Victoria Horne (*Nora*), Judge Brisson's Housekeeper, George Kirby (*Father Pierre*), Frank O'Connor (*Cab Driver*), Harry Allen (*Taylor the Storekeeper*), Olaf Hytten (*Hotel Desk Clerk*), Gertrude Astor (*Woman*).

One of the better films in the series of HOLMES features in which Rathbone starred. This one takes place in Canada, where the sleuth and his side kick Watson (Nigel Bruce) are attending a seminar on the supernatural. The foggy marshes differ little from the usual setting, and the inhabitants of the

village are fearful of a legendary monster that stalks the marshes and is apparently responsible for a number of murders. But Rathbone astutely relates these killings to a former actor who had been madly in love with the first victim, the wife of Cavanagh. The actor, played by Hamer, has taken on a number of disguises and become a trusted member of the small community. Posing as the local innkeeper, Hohl, Rathbone allows himself to be prey for the killer, in this case under the guise of the local postman. The second and final time Rathbone and Bruce are to cross the Atlantic, the journey back to their homeland is marked by yet another speech Rathbone credits to Winston Churchill. He praises Canadians for their "relations of friendly intimacy with the United States on the one hand and their unswerving fidelity to the British Commonwealth and the motherland on the other. Canada, the link which joins together these great branches of the Human family." (See SHERLOCK HOLMES Series, Index.)

p&d, Roy William Neill; w, Neill, Edmund L. Hartmann (based on a story by Paul Gangelin, Brenda Weisberg; based on characters created by Sir Arthur Conan Doyle); ph, George Robinson; ed, Paul Landres; md, Paul Sawtell; art d, John B. Goodman, Ralph M. DeLacy; spec eff, John P. Fulton.

Mystery   (PR:A MPAA:NR)

SCARLET CLUE, THE**½*   (1945) 65m MON bw

Sidney Toler (*Charlie Chan*), Benson Fong (*Tommy Chan*), Mantan Moreland (*Birmingham Brown, Chan's Chauffeur*), Helen Devereaux (*Diane Hall*), Robert E. Homans (*Capt. Flynn*), Virginia Brissac (*Mrs. Marsh*), I. Stanford Jolley (*Ralph Brett*), Reid Kilpatrick (*Wilbur Chester*), Jack Norton (*Willie Rand*), Charles Sherlock (*Sgt. McGraw*), Janet Shaw (*Gloria Bayne*), Milt Kibbee (*Herbert Sinclair*), Ben Carter (*Ben*), Victoria Faust (*Hulda Swenson*), Charles Jordan (*Nelson*), Leonard Mudie (*Horace Carlos*), Kernan Cripps (*Detective*).

Evenly paced and suspenseful thriller has the Oriental supersleuth, played here by Toler, investigating the mysterious deaths of several people. His meanderings uncover a plot to make off with government radar plans. Number-one son helps out in the clue gathering, with Moreland around for humor's sake. A tighter and faster-moving script than the usual CHAN outing. (See CHARLIE CHAN series, Index.)

p, James B. Burkett; d, Phil Rosen; w, George Callahan (based on the character created by Earl Derr Biggers); ph, William A. Sickner; ed, Richard Currier; md, Edward Kay; art d, Dave Milton.

Mystery   (PR:A MPAA:NR)

SCARLET COAT, THE**½*   (1955) 101m MGM c

Cornel Wilde (*Maj. John Bolton*), Michael Wilding (*Maj. John Andre*), George Sanders (*Dr. Jonathan Odell*), Anne Francis (*Sally Cameron*), Robert Douglas (*Benedict Arnold*), John McIntire (*Gen. Robert Howe*), Rhys Williams (*Peter*), John Dehner (*Gen. Nathanael Greene*), James Westerfield (*Col. Jameson*), Ashley Cowan (*Mr. Brown*), Paul Cavanagh (*Sir Henry Clinton*), John Alderson (*Mr. Durkin*), John O'Malley (*Col. Winfield*), Bobby Driscoll (*Ben Potter*), Robin Hughes (*Col. Tarleton*), Anthony Dearden (*Capt. De Lancey*), Vernon Rich (*Colonel*), Dabbs Greer (*Capt. Brewster*), Olaf Hytten (*Butler*), Gordon Richards (*Mr. Cameron*), Leslie Denison (*Capt. Sutherland*), Harlan Warde, John Blackburn (*Captains*), Tristram Coffin (*Col. Varick*), Byron Foulger (*Man*), Wilson Benge (*Servant*), Dennis King, Jr (*Boatswain's Mate*), Robert Dix (*Lt. Evans*), Charles Watts (*Will Potter*), Peter Adams (*Lt. Blair*), Wesley Hudman (*Capt. Sheldon*), Robert Forrest (*Stout Man*), Tom Cound (*English Soldier*), Keith McConnell (*Lieutenant*), Phyllis Coghlan (*Woman*), Gil Stuart (*Officer*), Owen McGiveney (*Servant*), Charles R. Keane, Richard Simmons (*Sergeants*), Jim Hayward (*Joshua Smith*), Rush Williams (*Soldier*), Ivan Hayes (*Mr. Nyby*), Michael Fox (*Maj. Russell*), Don C. Harvey (*Captain*), Barry Regan, Rick Vallin, Ronald Green, Joe Locke (*Lieutenants*), Jennifer Raine (*Miss Trumbull*), Guy Kingsford (*Officer*), Richard Peel (*Sailor*), Vesey O'Davoren (*Butler*), Anne Kunde (*Cook*), George Peters (*Staff Officer*), Ethan Laidlaw (*Executioner*).

A behind-the-scenes look at the events of the Revolutionary War that concentrates on the espionage efforts of both the Redcoats and the Continentals. Wilde is a devoted American who plays the part of an unscrupulous materialist who doesn't care which side wins in order to infiltrate the British staff. Despite the efforts of the suave Sanders to convince his superiors that Wilde is a spy, the latter uncovers the infamous plot of Benedict Arnold. Filmed in the Hudson Bay area, the picture is bolstered by CinemaScope photography and realistic settings which support the efficient direction and convincing cast.

p, Nicholas Nayfack; d, John Sturges; w, Karl Tunberg; ph, Paul C. Vogel (CinemaScope, Eastmancolor); m, Conrad Salinger; ed, Ben Lewis; md, Salinger; art d, Cedric Gibbons, Merrill Pye; cos, Walter Plunkett.

Spy/Drama   (PR:A MPAA:NR)

SCARLET DAWN**½*   (1932) 58m WB bw

Douglas Fairbanks, Jr (*Nikiti*), Nancy Carroll (*Tanyusha*), Earle Fox (*Boris*), Lilyan Tashman (*Vera*), Sheila Terry (*Marjorie Murphy*), Betty Gillette (*The Girl*), Guy Kibbee (*Marjorie's Father*), Ivan Linow (*Ivan*), Dewey Robinson (*Sergeant*), Richard Alexander (*Pyotyr*), Frank Reicher

(Plotsky), Arnold Korff *(Kalin)*, Hadji Ali *(Turkish Landlord)*, Mae Busch *(Landlord's Wife)*, Lee Kohlmar *(German Tailor)*, Alphonse Kohlmar *(Minister)*, William Ricciardi *(Kitchen Boss)*, C. Henry Gordon *(Headwaiter)*, Yola D'Avril *(Girl)*, John Marston *(Bilkerson)*, Maurice Black *(Cafe Manager)*, Mischa Auer *(Serge)*.

Lavishly adorned costume epic set during the Russian Revolution has Fairbanks playing a young aristocrat who flees his Russian home with his maid Carroll. The two find themselves in Constantinople, where they marry and settle into a life of common labor. But Fairbanks' aristocratic ways make him discontented in his new life, and when he meets up with the vampish Tashman he forsakes his humble bride. After attempting to make it as a swindler he goes back to Carroll just as she is about to be deported back to Russia. Plot drags and is uneven in parts, but the great sets of the aristocratic homes, as well as the lowly Turkish ones, are worth a glimpse.

p, Hal B. Wallis; d, William Dieterle; w, Niven Busch, Edwin Gelsey, Douglas Fairbanks, Jr. (based on the novel *Revolt* by Mary McCall); ph, Ernest Haller; art d, Anton Grot; cos, Orry-Kelly.

Drama **(PR:A MPAA:NR)**

SCARLET EMPRESS, THE**** (1934) 110m PAR bw

Marlene Dietrich *(Sophia Frederica, Catherine II)*, John Lodge *(Count Alexei)*, Sam Jaffe *(Grand Duke Peter)*, Louise Dresser *(Empress Elizabeth)*, Maria Sieber *(Sophia as a Child)*, C. Aubrey Smith *(Prince August)*, Ruthelma Stevens *(Countess Elizabeth)*, Olive Tell *(Princess Johanna)*, Gavin Gordon *(Gregory Orloff)*, Jameson Thomas *(Lt. Ostvyn)*, Hans Von Twardowski *(Ivan Shuvolov)*, Davison Clark *(Archimandrite Simeon Tevedovsky/Arch-Episcope)*, Erville Alderson *(Chancellor Alexei Bestuchef)*, Marie Wells *(Marie)*, Jane Darwell *(Mlle. Cardell)*, Harry Woods *(Doctor)*, Edward Van Sloan *(Herr Wagner)*, Philip G. Sleeman *(Count Lestocq)*, John B. Davidson *(Marquis De La Chetardie)*, Gerald Fielding *(Officer, Lt. Dimitri)*, James Burke *(Guard)*, Belle Stoddard Johnstone, Nadine Beresford, Eunice Moore, Petra McAllister, Blanche Rose *(Aunts)*, James Marcus *(Innkeeper)*, Thomas C. Blythe, Clyde Davis *(Narcissuses)*, Richard Alexander *(Count Von Breummer)*, Jay Boyer, Bruce Warren, Eric Alden *(Lackeys)*, George Davis *(Jester)*, Agnes Steele, Barbara Sabichi, May Foster, Minnie Steele *(Elizabeth's Ladies-in-Waiting)*, Katerine Sabichi, Julanne Johnston, Elinor Fair, Dina Smirnova, Anna Duncan, Patricia Patrick, Elaine St. Maur *(Catherine's Ladies-in-Waiting.)*.

The same year that this striking and audacious Dietrich-Sternberg opus was released saw another film starring Elisabeth Bergner, the breathless Viennese actress, vying with Dietrich in profiling one of the most sensational women who ever lived, Catherine the Great of Russia. Where Bergner, under the delicate hand of husband-director Paul Czinner, appeared to be an innocent, suffering at the hands of a slightly deranged husband-tyrant, Douglas Fairbanks, Jr., Dietrich plays the royal lady as she was, a beautiful schemer outwitting a maniacal husband whose lunacy was lethal and fully captured by Jaffe in an incredible but memorable-to-this-day performance. Before CITIZEN KANE rocked critics, the film industry, and the public, Sternberg's THE SCARLET EMPRESS stood as undoubtedly the most innovative film of the sound era. Dietrich is shown as a child in the royal household in Germany at age seven (as played by Dietrich's own daughter, Maria Sieber), suddenly taken away from her toys and told that she must prepare to live in another royal house, preparation for becoming the wife of some foreign prince she has never met. As a teenager, she is whisked off to Russia, married to an insane prince, Jaffe, and ordered by the Empress Elizabeth, played by Dresser, to change her name from Sophia to Catherine, to never have her natural parents–German foreigners–visit her, to never speak her native tongue, to learn Russian immediately and, most importantly, to produce a male child as soon as possible so there will be an heir to the throne. Dresser plays the Empress as an illiterate, vulgar, carnal creature whose manners are equivalent to a sow (the Empress Elizabeth could speak many languages and was well-read but her manners and morals were atrocious). In no time, Dietrich discovers that her husband, pop-eyed, wig-wearing Jaffe, is an utter madman who spends most of his time playing with his toy soldiers and ignores his attractive young wife. At one point he catches a rat in the palace that has chewed away part of one of his soldiers and he orders the rat ceremoniously hanged with officials and an honor guard in attendance. On another occasion, when Dietrich attempts to fulfill her wifely duties, she entices him into the boudoir only to have him thrust a saber in her direction; she boldly parries this thrust with her feather boa, earning Jaffe's halfwit admiration for courage. Her marriage never consummated, Dietrich is repulsed by Dresser's treatment of her simple-minded son, the empress ordering him about as if he were a barnyard beast. Still, Smith, a nobleman of the old school, and one of Dietrich's fellow countrymen, visits the Russian court to remind her of her duties as a royal wife, telling her: "Be obedient, and be worthy of a glorious destiny." But slowly Dietrich withdraws from her lunatic husband–who prefers the company of his new mistress, Stevens–and she takes up with Lodge, a self-assured count who throws her over for the slatternly and crone-like Empress, Dresser, a betrayal Dietrich cannot abide. She has an affair with the captain of the guards, and is later pregnant. The child is denounced as a bastard by Jaffe but the court accepts the newborn as the heir-apparent. Then Dresser dies and Jaffe is proclaimed emperor, earning quickly the sobriquet, "Peter the Mad." Jaffe toys with Dietrich as one would a mouse but she is equal to the challenge, knowing that he plans to kill her after embarrassing and humiliating her at court. During a wild dinner party Jaffe, sitting with mistress Stevens, mercilessly taunts his wife, but Dietrich is unflappable, no longer the shy young girl who came to the Russian court years earlier. She has demonstrated her sexual prowess and manifests her self-assuredness by donning uniforms worn by her palace guards, which endears her to these stalwarts who–as she knows they will–adopt a protective attitude toward her. Then Jaffe orders his soldiers and tax collectors to oppress the very peasants who keep him on the throne. Further, he insults the church and the throne itself by publicly announcing Dietrich's execution and his intention to make his sluttish mistress Stevens his new empress. Lodge, meanwhile, sensing that Dietrich's power is increasing, begins to side with her, but she rejects him as he rejected her for Dresser. With Gordon, playing the insidious and duplicitous Gregory Orloff, Dietrich plans to wrest control of Russia from her mad husband. Later Jaffe is taken by guards to his room and strangled while Dietrich is proclaimed empress of Russia. In a magnificent scene, she is shown racing down the enormous palace stairway, surrounded by the bric-a-brac of this most ornate of royal households, for the first time in her repressed life a free soul. Sternberg portrays Dietrich in the final scene riding her favorite horse with her loyal guardsmen as she accepts the throne. (Showing Dietrich with the horse, it was later pointed out by film historians, was Sternberg's ironic last statement about Catherine the Great, as if he were commenting on her future sexual escapades in a long and notoriously profligate reign. It is well-known that this empress died at the age of 67 while attempting to have sex with a stallion.) Sternberg made of this tale great pomp and pageantry and it is a feast for the eye as he moves his cameras, under the able hand of Glennon, to achieve splendid, fluid movements, tracking through the marvelous sets created by Dreier, using dollies and boom shots, trucking and panning his sequences so that the whole film is visually alive. Director Clarence Brown later admitted that Sternberg's shot which rolls down the long, long dinner table to show the royal couple and their courtiers and courtesans choosing sides between Jaffe and Dietrich, inspired an equally famous shot in ANNA KARENINA, 1935. There is so much that is inventive in the film that the viewer can easily get lost in Sternberg's Byzantine creativity, for each set is swimming in decor so rich as to stagger the imagination. The arms of chairs are sculpted in the form of either human arms or animal paws, as are the legs of tables. Sternberg fussed over every little detail of the film, working closely with Dreier and importing painter Ballbasch to sculpt statues and gargoyles of immense proportions, checking the drawings for these and changing them to suit his own self-conceived images. Kollorsz created paintings and ikons with equal exactitude and along Sternberg's perfectionist specifications. Where he was visually correct in his historical presentation of the Russian court, Sternberg took some liberties with the actual backgrounds of the lusty Russian royalty, compressing many years into a short period of time but this was an understandable summarization for a film which actually captures the feel of the corrupt Russian monarchy if not the decades of its existence. Dietrich is superb as Catherine, especially when enacting her early years, but Dresser, who appeared much more regal in such silent classics as THE EAGLE, is disappointingly common as the dowager empress. Jaffe (who could almost double for Harpo Marx in some of his scenes) is a wild man, chewing up the baroque sets with the vigor of a rodent desperate to wear down weighty fangs. He truly appears mad and perhaps this is the result of Sternberg's relentless demand for perfection. At one point, where Jaffe goes into a screaming fit, Sternberg ordered 50 takes before the actor walked off the set, furious, stumbling exhausted through a maze of cuckoo clocks, bells, statues, and ikons so fierce-looking as to give even the strongest heart palpitations. Lodge, grandson of the esteemed senator from Massachusetts, Henry Cabot Lodge, appears here in one of his few starring roles; he is striking and forceful, and possesses a commanding voice equal to his towering frame. Lodge would later quit films and return to the political fold of his family, becoming governor of Massachusetts and later ambassador to Spain and Argentina. Lodge delivers a line in the film that caused some snickers in the audience, reminding a naive Dietrich when arriving at the Russian court that they are living in an enlightened age: "This is the 18th Century!" Playing Dietrich as a child is her own daughter, Maria Sieber, whom she "loaned" to Sternberg for the film. The director, who had discovered Dietrich and made a superstar of her, creating the mystique that hovered about her personality, still maintained an iron hand on his sensuous protege. When she flubbed a line before the cameras, he practiced little tyrannies, such as demanding she raise her skirt a little more, which she obediently did. (This was an apparent statement to her that she was acting not with her head or heart but with her body, and the skirt-raising told her that she was relying on her legs–the same fabulous legs that had made her famous in THE BLUE ANGEL–rather than her most distinctive face and voice.) As the teenager who is about to be sent to the Russian court, Sternberg made her look as young as possible, adorning her with ribbons and childlike garb, moving Cecil Beaton to state that she looked "as if she had fallen into a baby's bassinet." A master of lighting, Sternberg himself arranged the "tender" lights and soft focus that give the actress her youthfulness, aging her ever so slowly through additional makeup until she appears a mature, aggressive woman, looking like the empress she is playing, a girl transformed into a woman who is no longer the pawn of men, but one who manipulates men. Still it was Sternberg who did the manipulating behind the cameras. Sternberg later wrote in his strange memoirs, *Fun in a Chinese Laundry*: "I completely subjected my bird of paradise 'Dietrich' to my peculiar tendency to prove that a film might well be an art medium." That the film was a commercial failure worried Sternberg not one bit. He said: "THE SCARLET EMPRESS, the penultimate film, deserved to be successful by any standard then existing or now prevalent, but with few exceptions it was greeted as an attempt to assassinate a superb actress. The film was, of course, a relentless excursion into style, which, taken for granted in any work of art, is considered to be unpardonable in this medium." Like all great directors, Sternberg copied from others. His long tracking shot down the banquet table is almost a direct lift from THE EAGLE, and he took a crowd shot almost verbatim from THE PATRIOT, which angered his friend Ernst Lubitsch who directed that silent film. Though Sternberg's marvelously baroque film did not do well at the box office, much of this was due to the fact that the Czinner film, CATHERINE THE GREAT, was released eight months before Sternberg's production and much of the thunder for the subject was stolen, swallowed at the box office and coughed back into the coffers of another studio. Sternberg had originally thought to call his film CATHERINE THE GREAT but the Czinner picture canceled that notion. It is fortunate for the final release that his next-to-last title was also abandoned, one that would never have gotten past the censors anyway: HER REGIMENT OF LOVERS.

d, Josef von Sternberg; w, Manuel Komroff (based on the diary of Catherine the Great); ph, Bert Glennon; m, Felix Mendelssohn, Pyotr Ilich Tchaikovsky, Richard Wagner, von Sternberg; ed, von Sternberg; art d, Hans Dreier, (statues) Peter Ballbasch, (ikons and paintings) Richard Kollorsz; cos, Travis Banton; spec eff, Gordon Jennings.

Biography/Historical Drama   **(PR:C MPAA:NR)**

SCARLET HOUR, THE**   (1956) 95m PAR bw

Carol Ohmart (*Paulie*), Tom Tryon (*Marsh*), Jody Lawrence (*Kathy*), James Gregory (*Ralph*), Elaine Stritch (*Phyllis Rycker*), E.G. Marshall (*Jennings*), Edward Binns (*Sgt. Allen*), Scott Marlowe (*Vince*), Billy Gray (*Tom Rycker*), Jacques Aubuchon (*Fat Boy*), David Lewis (*Sam Lynbury*), Johnstone White (*Tom Raymond*), James F. Stone (*Dean Franklin*), Maureen Hurley (*Mrs. Lynbury*), James Todd (*Inspector Paley*), Benson Fong, Joe Conley, Barry Atwater, Richard Collier, Almira Sessions, Richard Deacon, Harry Hickox, Peter Gray, Bill Tischer, Autumn Russell, Theron Jackson, Enid Baine, Bill Anders, Gilmore Bush, Max Power, Nat "King" Cole.

Contrived plot has Ohmart playing the femme fatale, using Tryon to help her sabotage a jewelry heist planned by her husband and his cohorts. The woman is utterly selfish, as Tryon soon learns, but not until Ohmart's husband is killed and Tryon is sent to jail. Tryon's consolation prize is the devoted Lawrence, who promises to wait for him. Filmed using Fujinon lenses, a major cinematographic development which allowed shooting at lower light levels because of larger aperture openings. Added bonus is a nightclub scene in which Nat "King" Cole sings "Never Let Me Go" (Jay Livingston, Ray Evans).

p&d, Michael Curtiz; w, Rip Von Ronkel, Frank Tashlin, John Meredyth Lucas (based on the story "The Kiss Off" by Von Ronkel, Tashlin); ph, Lionel Linden (VistaVision); m, Leith Stevens; ed, Everett Douglas; art d, Hal Pereira, Tambi Larsen; cos, Edith Head.

Crime   **(PR:A MPAA:NR)**

SCARLET LETTER, THE**   (1934) 70m Darmour/Majestic bw

Colleen Moore (*Hester Prynne*), Hardie Albright (*Arthur Dimmesdale*), Henry B. Walthall (*Roger Chillingworth*), William Farnum (*Gov. Billingham*), Alan Hale (*Bartholomew Hockins*), Virginia Howell (*Abigail Crakstone*), Cora Sue Collins (*Pearl*), William Kent (*Samson Goodfellow*), Betty Blythe, Al C. Henderson, Jules Cowles, Mickey Rentschler, Shirley Jean Rickert, Flora Finch, Dorothy Wolbert.

Adaptation of the early American classic by Hawthorne has Moore playing the woman forced to wear a letter on her chest in order to set her apart from the community outraged by her illegitimate pregnancy. She plays the part with appropriate humility, and the other members of the cast are equally fitting in their Puritan roles. Script has added a dimension of comedy to an otherwise somber story, which doesn't detract from plot development but hampers the tension.

d, Robert G. Vignola; w, Leonard Fields, David Silverstein (based on the novel by Nathaniel Hawthorne); ph, James S. Brown, Jr.; ed, Charles Harris.

Drama   **Cas.**   **(PR:A MPAA:G)**

SCARLET PAGES**½   (1930) 65m FN bw

Elsie Ferguson (*Mary Bancroft*), John Halliday (*John Remington*), Marion Nixon (*Nora Mason*), Grant Withers (*Bob Lawrence*), Daisy Belmore (*Sister Beatrice*), DeWitt Jennings (*Judge*), William B. Davidson (*Gregory Jackson*), Wilbur Mack (*Mr. Mason*), Charlotte Walker (*Mrs. Mason*), Helen Ferguson (*Miss Hutchison, Secretary*), Donald MacKenzie (*Callahan*), Jean Bary (*Carlotta*), Neely Edwards (*Barnes*), Fred Kelsey (*Judge*).

Courtroom dramatics are offered in abundance in this early soaper that has successful female attorney Ferguson assigned the job of defending cabaret singer Nixon, who has killed her foster father. The victim turns out to have been a real louse, and Ferguson discovers that Nixon is the baby she had left in an orphanage twenty years earlier. The cold setting of the courtroom puts a bit of a damper on things.

d, Ray Enright; w, Walter Anthony, Maude Fulton (based on the play by Samuel Shipman, John B. Hymer); ph, William Rees.

Drama   **(PR:A MPAA:NR)**

SCARLET PIMPERNEL, THE****   (1935, Brit.) 85m LFP/UA bw

Leslie Howard (*Sir Percy Blakeney*), Merle Oberon (*Lady Marguerite Blakeney*), Raymond Massey (*Chauvelin*), Nigel Bruce (*The Prince of Wales*), Bramwell Fletcher (*The Priest*), Anthony Bushell (*Sir Andrew Ffoulkes*), Joan Gardner (*Suzanne de Tournay*), Walter Rilla (*Armand St. Just*), Mabel Terry-Lewis (*Countess de Tournay*), O.B. Clarence (*Count de Tournay*), Ernest Milton (*Robespierre*), Edmund Breon (*Col. Winterbottom*), Melville Cooper (*Romney*), Gibb McLaughlin (*The Barber*), Morland Graham (*Treadle*), John Turnbull (*Jellyband*), Gertrude Musgrove (*Jellyband's Daughter, Sally*), Allan Jeayes (*Lord Grenville*), Bromley Davenport (*French Innkeeper*), Hindle Edgar (*Lord Hastings*), William Freshman (*Lord Wilmot*), Lawrence Hanray (*Burke*), Bruce Belfrage (*Pitt*), Edmund Willard (*Bibot*), Roy Meredith (*Viscount de Tournay*), Billy Shine (*An Aristocrat*), Brember Wills (*Doman*), Kenneth Kove ("*Codlin, a Fisherman*"), Renee Macredy (*Lady Q*), Philip Strange, Carl Harbord, Philip Desborough, Hugh Dempster, Peter Evan Thomas, Derrick de Marney (*Members of the Pimpernel League*), Harry Terry ("*Renad*"), Douglas Stewart ("*Merieres*"), Arthur Hambling (*Captain of the Guard*).

One of the greatest adventure films ever made, THE SCARLET PIMPERNEL is based on a romantic novel written in England by the daughter of deposed Hungarian aristocrats writing about deposed French aristocrats. If anything, this is one of the few examples of the film being better than the novel, and certainly this film is one of the ones that keeps Leslie Howard forever in the mind while the Baroness Orczy is all but forgotten. Howard is a foppish courtier in the court of the Prince of Wales. While the Reign of Terror executes large numbers of aristocrats in France, Howard loses the respect of his wife (Oberon) for being so ineffectual and he actually thinks she was responsible for the arrest of some old friends of hers. Meanwhile, Robespierre (Milton) and the rest of the revolutionary government are troubled by a series of daring rescues of condemned nobles. Leaving only a small, common, red flower behind him, the Scarlet Pimpernel adopts a variety of disguises as he saves the gentry from the guillotine. The French send one of their most capable individuals, Massey, to London to serve as ambassador, but really to discover the identity of the Pimpernel. He is a clever foe and he persuades Oberon to help bait a trap for the Pimpernel in return for the lives of her arrested friends. She is amazed when the trap succeeds and she learns that the heroic Pimpernel is her own despised husband. Howard makes a deal with Massey, her life in return for his own. Massey agrees and listens with pleasure to the firing squad outside ridding him of his nemesis for the last time. Moments later, though, Howard is back, having paid off the entire firing squad. Although ostensibly directed by Harold Young, the film is much more the work of its producer, another transplanted Hungarian (and Howard, for that matter, was the son of Hungarian immigrants). The first director hired was Rowland Brown, director of QUICK MILLIONS (1931), BLOOD MONEY (1933), and author of several well-regarded screenplays. He also had a reputation for getting fired. Massey, in his autobiography, recalls Brown beginning shooting the first day when Korda came to the set. After watching a short while, Korda told Brown that he was directing the film like it was a gangster picture. Brown told his employer that he would direct the film his own way or he would walk. "Please walk" was Korda's answer, and the producer immediately took over the directing that day, and Young was hired the next day, although Korda kept a tight rein on him the whole time. The production skills of Korda's studio are much evident and very impressive. Much of the film was shot outdoors, contrary to the general practice in England at the time. Korda imported Hal Rosson from Hollywood to shoot the film, and the cinematographer was ecstatic. "I can make sunlight anytime with a few arcs," he said, "but I can't make clouds like that–look at them!" Howard gives a wonderful performance, languid and almost effeminate as Sir Percy, and richly deserving of his wife's contempt, but dashing and daring as the Pimpernel. The other parts are similarly well played, especially Massey's, who called his villainous character "the most wicked and the most fun to do." The novel served as the basis of several silent films and it was remade as a talker in 1950 with David Niven in the title role of THE ELUSIVE PIMPERNEL. Perhaps the best remembered thing about this classic adventure yarn, though, is the little bit of doggerel that Howard makes up to throw off suspicion: They seek him here, they seek him there/The Frenchies seek him everywhere/Is he in Heaven? Is he in Hell?/That damned elusive Pimpernel.

p, Alexander Korda; d, Harold Young (Rowland V. Brown, Korda, uncredited); w, S.N. Behrman, Robert Sherwood, Arthur Wimperis, Lajos Biro (based on the novel by Baroness Emma Magdalena Rosalia Maria Josepha Barbara Orczy); ph, Harold 'Hal' Rosson; m, Arthur Benjamin; ed, William Hornbeck; prod d, Vincent Korda; md, Muir Mathieson; set d, Francis Hallam; cos, John Armstrong, Oliver Messel; spec eff, Ned Mann.

Adventure   **Cas.**   **(PR:A MPAA:NR)**

SCARLET RIVER**½   (1933) 62m RKO bw

Tom Keene, Dorothy Wilson, Creighton Chaney [Lon Chaney, Jr.], Edgar Kennedy, Betty Furness, Hooper Atchley, Roscoe Ates, Yakima Canutt, James Mason, Jack Raymond, Billy Butts, Myrna Loy, Rochelle Hudson, Joel McCrea, Julie Haydon, Bruce Cabot.

An interesting western, of sorts, which stars Keene as an actor in a western directed by Kennedy. The film's production takes them to the Scarlet River Ranch, where Wilson is trying to keep her malevolent foreman, Chaney, from taking over her property. Keene steps off the set to prove that he's just as brave off the screen as on. The opening sequence has Keene strolling through the RKO commissary and meeting such notables as Loy, Hudson, McCrea, Haydon, and Cabot–all of whom play themselves and just happened to be on the set at the time of shooting. One of the more exciting moments of this early B Western is the appearance of stuntman Yakima Canutt doing the same stunt which would amaze viewers several years later in John Ford's STAGECOACH. With the stage traveling at high speed, Canutt fell off the horse team so that the wagon rolled over him, then grabbed hold of the back of the wagon.

p, David O. Selznick; d, Otto Brower; w, Harold Shumate (based on a story by Shumate); ph, Nick Musuraca; ed, Fred Knudtson; art d, Al Sherman.

Western   (PR:A   MPAA:NR)

SCARLET SPEAR, THE*   (1954, Brit.) 78m Present Day/UA c

John Bentley (*Jim Barneson*), Martha Hyer (*Christine*), Morasi (*Himself*).

Replete with travelog footage, this adventure set deep in Africa's foliage stars Bentley as a local commissioner who fears that chieftain Morasi's need to prove his manhood will be the catalyst of a tribal war. Morasi must show that he is as accomplished as his father by performing feats of bravery and combatting jungle creatures.

p, Charles Reynolds; d&w, George Breakston, Ray Stahl; ph, Bernard Davies (Technicolor); m, Ivor Slaney; ed, John Shirley.

Adventure   (PR:A   MPAA:NR)

SCARLET STREET***   (1945) 103m Diana/UNIV bw

Edward G. Robinson (*Christopher Cross*), Joan Bennett (*Kitty March*), Dan Duryea (*Johnny Prince*), Margaret Lindsay (*Millie*), Rosalind Ivan (*Adele Cross*), Jess Barker (*Janeway*), Arthur Loft (*Dellarowe*), Samuel S. Hinds (*Charles Pringle*), Vladimir Sokoloff (*Opo Lejon*), Charles Kemperer (*Patch-eye*), Russell Hicks (*Hogarth*), Lou Lubin (*Tiny*), Anita Bolster (*Mrs. Michaels*), Cyrus W. Kendall (*Nick*), Fred Essler (*Marchetti*), Edgar Dearing (*Policeman*), Tom Dillon (*Policeman*), Chuck Hamilton (*Chauffeur*), Gus Glassmire, Ralph Littlefield, Sherry Hall, Howard Mitchell, Jack Statham (*Employees*), Rodney Bell (*Waiter*), Milton Kibbee (*Saunders*), Tom Daly (*Penny*), George Meader (*Holliday*), Lee Phelps, Matt Willis (*Policemen*), Clarence Muse (*Ben*), John Barton (*Hurdy Gurdy Man*), Emmett Vogan (*Prosecution Attorney*), Robert Malcolm (*Policeman*), Horace Murphy (*Milk-man*), Will Wright (*Loan Officer Manager*), Syd Saylor (*Crocker*), Dewey Robinson (*Derelict*), Fritz Leiber (*Evangelist*), Byron Foulger (*Jones*), Dick Wessel (*2nd Detective*), Dick Curtis (*3rd Detective*), Joe Devlin (*Williams*), George Lloyd (*Conway*), Herbert Heywood (*Bellboy*), Charles C. Wilson (*Watchman*), Constance Purdy (*Matron*), Wally Scott (*Drunk*), Edward Keane (*Detective*), Arthur Gould Porter, Boyd Irwin, Richard Abbott (*Critics*), Thomas Jackson (*Chief of Detectives*), Richard Cramer (*Principal Keeper*), Rev. Neal Dodd (*Priest*), Kerry Vaughn (*Blonde Girl*), Beatrice Roberts (*Secretary*), William Hall, Ralph Dunn (*Policemen*), Byron Foulger (*Apartment House Manager Jones*), Henri de Soto (*Waiter*).

Fritz Lang brings his bleak eye to this *Film noir* story that was done before in a 1931 French film named LA CHIENNE that featured Michel Simon and was directed by Jean Renoir. Robinson is a cashier for a large New York city clothing retailer. He spends his spare time painting (which Robinson was quite interested in, having amassed an important collection over the years). He's being feted for two decades of employment at the company banquet in his honor and is immediately characterized as one of those faceless people who make things tick but never receive their due, except at dinners like this when gold watches are presented. Robinson has a bit too much to drink, and when he leaves the party, he is reeling slightly and finds Bennett being attacked in the street. He fends off the mugger by using his umbrella as a saber and takes Bennett to have a quiet drink at a bar. Robinson finds this young woman fascinating and can't bear to tell her what he really does for a living, so he lies about it and lets her think he is a renowned artist. Robinson is married to Ivan, a shrewish woman who heckles him unmercifully for his lack of ambition. It isn't long before he thinks he is in love with Bennett, who continues to lead him on and doesn't make him aware of her relationship with Duryea, a hoodlum living on the edge of legality. Since they reckon Robinson is a good mark, Bennett and Duryea conspire to have him rent a studio where he can meet Bennett for their trysts. Robinson does that and hauls several of his art works to the studio. Duryea brings in a professional critic, Barker, to look at the work and he is impressed. The cost of maintaining the separate residence is cutting into Robinson's savings and he is at a loss to figure how to pay for his passion. Duryea removes Robinson's name from the art and puts Bennett's signature on the work. Robinson is annoyed at this, but when the pictures are acknowledged to be

the work of a talented person, Robinson takes solace in the fact that someone appreciates him. Robinson begins to embezzle cash from the company he works for, then learns that Ivan's first husband, long thought dead, is actually still alive. That means he can divorce Ivan and marry Bennett. When he races to the studio to tell Bennett the good news, he finds her and Duryea in each other's arms. He watches surreptitiously until Duryea exits, then walks in, has a confrontation with Bennett, and when she taunts him with the news that he's been a patsy all along, he reaches for an ice pick and plunges it into Bennett's heart. Now he painstakingly arranges the evidence to throw guilt on Duryea and leaves. Duryea is arrested, tried, and convicted and Robinson's embezzlement is discovered, so he loses his job. He suffers a mental breakdown and becomes one of the flotsam who inhabit the streets, and on the night when Duryea is to be executed, he climbs a power pole in his desire to hear the electrical surge go through the wires as it rushes into Duryea's body. He can't paint anymore because his recognizable style has been credited to the late Bennett, he can't get a reference from the only job he ever had, and so he is doomed to walk the city forever. His pain is even deeper when he notes that the portrait he did of Bennett has just sold for $10,000. The paintings for the film were done by John Decker, the artist who palled around with Errol Flynn, John Barrymore, W.C. Fields, et al., and whose life was chronicled by Gene Fowler in Minutes Of The Last Meeting. It is Decker's portrait of W.C. Fields as Queen Victoria which sits in the entry at Chasen's Restaurant on the corner of Doheny Drive and Beverly Boulevard in West Los Angeles.

p&d, Fritz Lang; w, Dudley Nichols (based on the novel and play *La Chienne* by Georges de la Fouchardiere, Mouezy-Eon); ph, Milton Krasner; m, Hans J. Salter; ed, Arthur Hilton; art d, Alexander Golitzen; John B. Goodman; set d, Russell A. Gausman, Carl Lawrence; cos, Travis Banton; spec eff, John P. Fulton.

Crime Drama   **Cas.**   (PR:C   MPAA:NR)

SCARLET THREAD**   (1951, Brit.) 84m Nettlefold-International
                                                            Realist/BUT bw

Kathleen Byron (*Josephine*), Laurence Harvey (*Freddie*), Sydney Tafler (*Marcon*), Arthur Hill (*Shaw*), Dora Bryan (*Maggie*), Eliot Makeham (*Jason*), Harry Fowler (*Sam*), Cyril Chamberlain (*Mason*), Renee Kelly (*Eleanor*), Bill Shine, Hylton Allen, Vi Kaley, Ben Williams, Joyce Boorman, Gerald Rex, John Powe, Sheila Aza.

Decent British programmer in which small-time crook Harvey hooks up with hood Tafler to pull off a jewelry robbery. During the robbery an innocent man is accidentally shot and killed. This same man proves to be the father of the woman Harvey later falls in love with. Harvey is quite convincing as the hard-up crook anxious to make the big score, with Tafler lending his support to the role of the unfeeling criminal who takes pleasure in killing. Their believable performances make this film worthwhile, though it's hard to find any likable qualities in either of their characters.

p, Ernest G. Roy; d, Lewis Gilbert; w, A.R. Rawlinson (based on the play by Rawlinson, Moie Charles); ph, Geoffrey Faithfull.

Crime/Drama   (PR:A   MPAA:NR)

SCARLET WEB, THE**   (1954, Brit.) 63m Fortress/Eros bw

Griffith Jones (*Jake Winter*), Hazel Court (*Susan Honeywell*), Zena Marshall (*Laura Vane*), Robert Percival (*Charles Dexter*), Molly Raynor (*Miss Riggs*), Ronald Stevens (*Simpson*), John Fitzgerald (*Bert*), Stuart Douglass, Johnnie Schofield, Michael Balfour.

Insurance investigator Jones is framed for murder after a pretty lady hires him to recover a letter from a man who wants to blackmail her. His boss, Court, saves him by discovering that the dead woman's husband and the pretty lady know each other quite well, and then she herself almost is murdered before the cops come and save the day. A nice, taut presentation of a familiar story by B-bracket thriller expert, director Saunders.

p, Frank Bevis; d, Charles Saunders; w, Doreen Montgomery; ph, Hone Glendining.

Crime   (PR:A   MPAA:NR)

SCARLET WEEKEND, A*   (1932) 58m Maxim/Irving bw

Dorothy Revier, Theodore Von Eltz, Phyllis Barrington, Niles Welch, Douglas Cosgrove, Virginia Bruce, William Desmond, Eddie Phillips, Charles K. French, Sheila Mannors, Aber Twins, Nora Hayden, Vance Farroll, Chubby Colman.

A laborious mystery which sticks close to familiar formulas. A young woman is accused of murder but her noble boyfriend takes the rap for her. The detective, who suspects nearly everyone, eventually brings the real culprit to justice. A poor script with even worse production values.

d, George Melford; w, Willis Kent (based on the novel *A Woman In Purple Pajamas*) ph, William Nobles; ed, Ruth Wright.

Mystery   (PR:A   MPAA:NR)

SCARS OF DRACULA, THE*½

(1970, Brit.) 96m
Hammer-EMI/Anglo-EMI/American Continental c

Christopher Lee (Count Dracula), Dennis Waterman (Simon Carlson), Jenny Hanley (Sarah Framsen), Christopher Matthews (Paul Carlson), Patrick Troughton (Klove), Michael Gwynn (Priest), Wendy Hamilton (Julie), Anoushka Hempel (Tania), Delia Lindsay (Alice), Bob Todd (Burgomaster), Toke Townley (Elderly Wagon Master), Michael Ripper (Landlord), David Leland, Richard Durden (Officers), Morris Bush (Farmer), Margot Boht (Landlord's Wife), Clive Barrie (Fat Young Man).

The usually competent Hammer horror series slacks off in this lame vampire picture with Lee in a role he had played countless times before. After a midnight sex romp with a femme vampire, Matthews gets fanged in Lee's castle. Matthews' brother Waterman and the latter's girlfriend Hanley begin to look for him and have the stock encounters with bats, cobwebs, and garlic before meeting ol' Drac face-to-face. Instead of the usual stake-in-the-heart routine, Lee gets zapped by a bolt of lightning which strikes in the proverbial nick of time. Gory, but not very scary unless you've never heard of vampires before. (See: Dracula Series, Index.)

p, Aida Young; d, Roy Ward Baker; w, John Elder [Anthony Hinds] (based on the characters created by Bram Stoker); ph, Moray Grant (Technicolor); m, James Bernard; ed, James Needs; md, Philip Martell; art d, Scott MacGregor; spec eff, Roger Dicken; makeup, Wally Schneiderman.

Horror   **Cas.**   **(PR:O MPAA:R)**

SCATTERBRAIN**

(1940) 74m REP bw

Judy Canova (Judy Hull), Alan Mowbray (J.R. Russell), Ruth Donnelly (Miss Stevens), Eddie Foy, Jr (Eddie MacIntyre), Joseph Cawthorn (Nicolas Raptis), Wallace Ford (Sam Maxwell), Isabel Jewell (Esther Harrington), Luis Alberni (Prof. DeLemma), Billy Gilbert (Hoffman), Emmett Lynn (Pappy Hull), Jimmy Starr (Joe Kelton), Cal Shrum's Gang (Themselves), Matty Malneck and Orchestra (Themselves).

Canova is an Ozark Mountain girl who mistakenly gets "discovered" by a Hollywood film producer who arranged a scam in which a real actress is planted in the hills, and then is reported to be a new discovery. Some signals get mixed up and the unsuspecting Canova is mistakenly whisked off to Hollywood and stardom. Musical numbers include: "Scatterbrain" (Johnny Burke, Frankie Masters, Kahn Keene, Carl Bean) and "Benny the Beaver" (Johnny Lange, Lew Porter).

p&d, Gus Meins; w, Jack Townley, Val Burton, Paul Conlon; ph, Ernest Miller; ed, Ernest Nims; md, Cy Feuer; art d, John Victor MacKay.

Musical Comedy   **(PR:A MPAA:NR)**

SCATTERGOOD BAINES**½

(1941) 69m Pyramid/RKO bw

Guy Kibbee (Scattergood Baines), Carol Hughes (Helen Parker), John Archer (Johnny Bones), Francis "Dink" Trout (Pliny Pickett), Emma Dunn (Mirandy Baines), Lee "Lasses" White (Ed Potts), Fern Emmett (Clara Potts), Edward Earle (Crane), Bradley Page (McKettrick), Joseph Crehan (Keith), Willie Best, Paul White.

The profitable radio series is brought to the screen with Kibbee in the likable role of Scattergood. He works his way up the economic ladder of Coldriver, a small New England village, while still staying in the good graces of his neighbors. Of course there are those who try to make his life tough, but Kibbee comes out on top. (See SCATTERGOOD BAINES series, Index.)

p, Jerrold T. Brandt; d, Christy Cabanne; w, Michael L. Simmons, Edward T. Lowe (based on Clarence Budington Kelland's "Scattergood Baines" stories); ph, Jack Mackenzie; m, Constantin Bakaleinikoff; ed, Henry Berman.

Drama/Comedy   **(PR:A MPAA:NR)**

SCATTERGOOD MEETS BROADWAY**

(1941) 68m Pyramid/RKO bw

Guy Kibbee (Scattergood Baines), Emma Dunn (Mirandy Baines), Joyce Compton (Diana), Bradley Page (Bard), Frank Jenks (Bent), William Henry (Davy), Mildred Coles (Peggy), Paul White (Hipp), Chester Clute (Quentin), Carl Stockdale (Squire), Charlotte Walker (Elly), Sharon Mackie (Rhumba Dancer), Morgan Wallace, Donald Brodie, Herbert Rawlinson.

Kibbee takes his down-home philosophizing to New York when a local boy who is an aspiring playwright gets mixed up with some crooked promoters and the blonde floozy they use as bait. Kibbee helps the kid get on his feet by finding a leading lady and bankrolling the show. Edited by John Sturges, who went on to become a notable western director. (See SCATTERGOOD BAINES series, Index.)

p, Jerrold T. Brandt; d, Christy Cabanne; w, Michael L. Simmons, Ethel B. Stone (based on the "Scattergood" stories by Clarence Budington Kelland); ph, Jack Mackenzie; ed, John Sturges.

Drama/Comedy   **(PR:A MPAA:NR)**

SCATTERGOOD PULLS THE STRINGS**

(1941) 69m Pyramid/RKO bw

Guy Kibbee (Scattergood Baines), Bobs Watson (Jimmy Jordan), Susan Peters (Ruth Savage), James Corner (Urban Downs), Emma Dunn (Mirandy Baines), Francis "Dink" Trout (Pliny Pickett), Monte Blue (Ben Mott), Carl Stockdale (Squire Pettibone), Paul White (Hipp), Fern Emmett (Clara Potts), Lee 'Lasses' White (Ed Potts), Ann Shoemaker (Mrs. Downs), Gordon Hart (Homer Savage), Howard Hickman (Withers), Earle Hodgins (Deputy), Rex (Emperor).

Kibbee, the lovable humanist, helps straighten out the lives of a couple of his Coldriver neighbors. He comes to the aid of a runaway boy, securing a governor's pardon for the kid's father, who has been wrongly accused of murder; plays Cupid for a pair of young lovers; and brings success to a struggling inventor. Kibbee's Scatterbrain is unbelievably sugar-coated, but he still can win over the audience. (See SCATTERGOOD BAINES series, Index.)

p, Jerrold T. Brandt; d, Christy Cabanne; w, Cabanne, Bernard Schubert (based on the "Scattergood Baines" stories by Clarence Budington Kelland), ph, Jack Mackenzie; m, Constantin Bakaleinikoff; ed, Desmond Marquette; art d, Bernard Herzbrun.

Drama/Comedy   **(PR:A MPAA:NR)**

SCATTERGOOD RIDES HIGH**

(1942) 63m Pyramid/RKO bw

Guy Kibbee (Scattergood Baines), Jed Prouty (Mr. Van Pelt), Dorothy Moore (Helen Van Pelt), Charles Lind (Dan Knox), Kenneth Howell (Phillip Dane), Regina Wallace (Mrs. Van Pelt), Frances Carson (Mrs. Dane), Arthur Aylesworth (Cromwell), Paul White (Hipp), Phillip Hurlic (Toby), Walter S. Baldwin, Jr (Martin Knox), Lee Phelps (Trainer).

Kibbee offers his rural wisdoms to a young neighbor who might lose his father's horse stable to a big city millionaire. Things look bad until Kibbee steps in, secures the youngster's inheritance, and sparks a romance between the boy and a gal from the city. This is the fourth in the "Scattergood Baines" series. (See SCATTERGOOD BAINES series, Index.)

p, Jerrold T. Brandt; d, Christy Cabanne; w, Michael L. Simmons (based on the "Scattergood Baines" stories by Clarence Budington Kelland); ph, Jack Mackenzie; ed, Henry Berman.

Drama/Comedy   **(PR:A MPAA:NR)**

SCATTERGOOD SURVIVES A MURDER**

(1942) 66m Pyramid/RKO bw

Guy Kibbee (Scattergood Baines), John Archer (Dunker Gilson), Margaret Hayes (Gail Barclay), Wallace Ford (Wally Collins), Spencer Charters (Sheriff), Eily Malyon (Mrs. Grimes), John Miljan (Rolfe), George Chandler (Sam Caldwell), Dick Elliot (Mathew Quentin), Florence Lake (Phoebe Quentin), Sarah Edwards (Selma Quentin), Willie Best (Hipp), George Guhl (Deputy), Eddy Waller (Lafe Allen), Margaret Seddon (Cynthia Quentin), Margaret McWade (Lydia Quentin), Frank Reicher (Thaddeus Quentin), Earle Hodgins (Coroner), Alfred Hall (Surrogate).

The fifth and final installment in the SCATTERGOOD BAINES series for RKO, delivering exactly what the revealing title promises. A pair of Coldriver spinsters kick off and leave their fortune to their cat, raising a few suspicious eyebrows. Just about everyone in town is suspected, but a slew of newspapermen from small towns and cities alike eventually get to the bottom of the mystery. (See SCATTERGOOD BAINES series, Index.)

p, Jerrold T. Brandt; d, Christy Cabanne; w, Michael Simmons (based on the "Scattergood Baines" stories by Clarence Budington Kelland); ph, Jack Mackenzie m, Paul Sawtell; ed, Richard Cahoon; art d, Bernard Herzbrun.

Drama/Comedy/Mystery   **(PR:A MPAA:NR)**

SCAVENGER HUNT*

(1979) 116m Melvin Simon/FOX c

Richard Benjamin (Stuart), James Coco (Henri), Scatman Crothers (Sam), Ruth Gordon (Arvilla), Cloris Leachman (Mildred Carruthers), Cleavon Little (Jackson), Roddy McDowall (Jenkins), Robert Morley (Bernstein), Richard Mulligan (Marvin Dummitz), Tony Randall (Henry Motley), Dirk Benedict (Jeff Stevens), Willie Aames (Kenny Stevens), Stephanie Faracy (Babette), Stephen Furst (Merle), Richard Masur (Georgie Carruthers), Meat Loaf (Scum), Pat McCormick (Barker), Vincent Price (Milton Parker), Avery Schreiber (Zoo Keeper), Liz Torres (Lady Zero), Carol Wayne (Nurse), Stuart Pankin (Duane), Maureen Teefy (Lisa), Missy Francis, Julie Anne Haddock, David Hollander, Shane Sinutko, Henry Polic II, Hal Landon, Jr, Emory Bass.

An all-star, all-stupid comedy attempt that proves, once again, no actor can triumph over bad material. Price is a multimillionaire games manufacturer, who has nobody to leave his estate to (worth about $200 million), so he devises a scavenger hunt and assigns his various pals and heirs to find a bunch of silly items, with the winner being the recipient of the fortune. Price dies and the hunt begins. It's a series of absurdities just in there to put the performers into unbelievable situations. Whereas IT'S A MAD, MAD, MAD, MAD WORLD had some wit and telling comments about greed, this one has not an iota of intelligence and it is directed at such a breakneck pace that there is not a moment when we get to know anyone in the large cast. Every minority is scathed, including those with physical problems and the only taste evidenced is in Goldenberg's music. Benjamin is an unscrupulous attorney. Leachman is a noisy shrew whose son, Masur, is a disgusting spoiled brat. The servants are McDowall, Coco, Little, and Faracy, all of whom should have been slain at birth and...it is just too painful to describe. Even Avery Schreiber, who can do almost anything and make it look funny, is wasted here. Schultz, when given the right script, can do good work, as in CAR WASH, although you'd never know it from this dull, dense, and depressing picture. How all of these funny actors could have been seduced into working on such a waste of time, money, and effort is a mystery. Could it have been that multimillionaire Mel Simon offered them more than they usually got? Simon, who also executive produced THE STUNT MAN, made all his cash in real estate development, mostly in Indiana. If he keeps making bombs like this, that fortune will soon disappear. And yet, despite all of the movie's shortcomings, one should watch it, strictly for research, just to see how bad good actors can be.

p, Steven A. Vail, Paul Maslansky; d, Michael Schultz; w, Steven A. Vail, Henry Harper, John Thompson, Gerry Woolery (based on a story by Vail); ph, Ken Lamkin (DeLuxe Color); m, Billy Goldenberg; ed, Christopher Holmes; art d, Richard Berger; set d, Ed Baer; spec eff, Phil Cory, Ray Svedin; stunts, Jon Parker Ward.

Comedy   **Cas.**   **(PR:C MPAA:PG)**

SCAVENGERS, THE**   (1959, U.S./Phil.) 79m
                              Lynn-Romero/Valiant-Roach bw (AKA: CIT Y OF SIN.)

Vince Edwards (*Stuart Allison*), Carol Ohmart (*Marion Allison*), Tamar Benamy (*Marissa*), Efren Reyes (*Puan*), John Wallace (*Taggert*), Vic Diaz (*O'Hara*).

A one-time smuggler, Edwards ventures to Hong Kong, where he runs into his missing wife, Ohmart. He does all he can to pick up the pieces of her life, which has become a tangle of addictions, drug trafficking, and other crime. Edwards' efforts prove futile when Ohmart and others eventually meet their death, but he takes comfort in the waiting arms of another woman.

p, Edgar Romero; d, John Cromwell; w, Romero (based on a story by Romero); ph, Felipe Sacdalan; ed, Gervasio Santos; art d, Vincente Tomas.

Crime/Adventure.   **(PR:A MPAA:NR)**

SCAVENGERS, THE zero   (1969) 111m Cresse-Forst/Republic
                              Amusements-Grads c (AKA: THE GRABBERS)

John Bliss (*The Captain*), Maria Lease (*Faith*), Michael Dikova (*Sgt. West*), Roda Spain (*Nancy*), John Riazzi, Wes Bishop, Bruce Kemp, Sanford Mitchell, Tom Siegel, Jody Berry, Paul Wilmoth, Uschi Digart, James E. McLarty, Claudia Siefried, Karen Swanson, Warren James, Paul Hunt, James K. Shea, Freddy Mizrahi, Ben Adams, Tom Bowden, Jr, Fig Blackman, Ben Cadlett, Robert Jones, James Gorden.

Offensive, brainless oater about a band of Confederate soldiers who plan to rob a Union payroll, not knowing the Civil War has ended since they set out on their mission. They ride into a small town, rape and kill for a while, then settle down to wait for the money wagon to pass through. The Negro servant of a woman held by the rebels escapes and makes her way to a nearby squatter camp of recently freed slaves. They arm themselves and attack the soldiers, and a bloody battle follows that sees most of the men on both sides killed. Bliss, the demented commander of the Confederates, tries to escape but his horse is shot out from under him and he is pinned down by the fall. His cries for help are ignored as vultures circle above him. Badly acted, written, and directed, the film exists largely as an excuse for its sex scenes, which were boosted with additional footage for an X-rated release as THE GRABBERS.

p, R.W. Cresse; d, R.L. Frost; w, Cresse; ph, Bob Maxwell (Eastman color); ed, B. Richard Conners; art d, John Fry; set d, Joe Anthony; cos, Steve Mooni; spec eff, Joe Zomar; makeup, Dennis Marsh; m/l, "The Scavengers are Coming," Lee Frost, Paul Hunt, Tom Bowden, Jr., Cresse, performed by Jody Berry; stunts, Chuck Bail; makeup, Dennis Marsh.

Western   **(PR:O MPAA:R)**

SCENE OF THE CRIME**   (1949) 94m MGM bw

Van Johnson (*Mike Conovan*), Gloria De Haven (*Lili*), Tom Drake (*C.C. Gordon*), Arlene Dahl (*Gloria Conovan*), Leon Ames (*Capt. A.C. Forster*), John McIntire (*Fred Piper*), Norman Lloyd (*Sleeper*), Donald Woods (*Herkimer*), Anthony Caruso (*Tony Rutzo*), Anthony Benedict (*Turk Kingby*), Tom Powers (*Umpire Menafoe*), Jerome Cowan (*Arthur Webson*), Mickey Kuhn (*Ed Monigan*), William Haade (*Lafe Douque*), Caleb Peterson (*Loomis*), Robert Gist (*Pontiac*), Romo Vincent (*Hippo*), Tom Helmore (*Norrie Lorfield*), Thomas E. Breen (*Boy*), Mary Jane Smith, Bette Arlen (*Girls*), G. Pat Collins (*Monigan*), Ray Teal (*Patrolman*), Don Haggerty, Allen Mathews, Gregg Barton, Mickey McCardle, James Scott, William J. Tannen, Paul Fierro, Anthony Merrill, George Magrill, Ralph Montgomery (*Detectives*), Forrest Taylor (*Captain of Detectives*), Minerva Urecal, Margaret Bert (*Women*), Charles Wagenheim (*Nervous Man*), William McCormick (*Older

Man), Victor Paul (*Young Punk*), Guy Kingsford (*Ballistics Man*), Ray [Raphael] Bennett (*Sheriff Kiesling*), Jack Shea, Cameron Grant (*Fighters*), Jean Carter (*Marlene*), Jimmy Dundee (*Captain of Waiters*), Douglas Carther (*Sanitation Man*), Lucille Barkley (*Corrine*), Gladys Balke, Sarah Berner (*Girl Voices*), Mack Chandler, Fred Murray (*Men On Table*), William Phipps (*Young Man*), Richard Irving, Harris Brown, John Phillips (*Doctors*), Wilson Wood (*Gateman*), Billy Snyder, Eddie Foster, Zon Murray, Michael Jordan, Michael Barrett, Billy Dix (*Gangsters*), Jeffrey Sayre (*Manager of the Fol De Rol*), Erin Selwyn (*Hat Check Girl*), Sam Finn, Charles Regan, Jimmy Dunn (*Patrons*), John McKee (*Recorder*), Robert Strong (*Police Stenographer*), Allan Ray (*Wounded Officer*).

A tough *Film noir* about a cop, Johnson, who is determined to track down his partner's killers. He gets a tip on a couple of bookies from one of their molls, pursuing and eventually killing one and getting injured himself. Hampering his efforts is the concern of his wife, Dahl, who fears for his safety, urging him to quit the force. He finally gives in to her and turns in his badge. An officer who takes his place, however, gets killed and Johnson returns to the beat, even more intent on revenge than before. He gets tipped off on a planned robbery attempt, hops in the armored car and smashes into the killer's vehicle, which is reduced to a flaming pile of rubble. Thoughtful characterizations and a tightly-knit script put this one on a plateau above the average B-crime movies of the day. Producer Harry Rapf, while he receives credit for the film, actually died early on in the production.

p, Harry Rapf; d, Roy Rowland; w, Charles Schnee (based on the story "Smashing the Bookie Gang Marauders" by John Bartlow Martin); ph, Paul C. Vogel; m, Andre Previn; ed, Robert J. Kern; art d, Cedric Gibbons, Leonid Vasian; set d, Edwin B. Willis, Alfred E. Spencer; Cos, Irene; makeup, Jack Dawn.

Crime   **(PR:A MPAA:NR)**

SCENES FROM A MARRIAGE***   (1974, Swed.) 168m
                              Cinematograph AB Sweden/Cinema 5 c

Liv Ullmann (*Marianne*), Erland Josephson (*Johan*), Bibi Andersson (*Katarina*), Jan Malmsjo (*Peter*), Anita Wall (*Mrs. Palm*), Gunnel Lindblom (*Eva*), Barbro Hiort AF Ornas (*Mrs. Jacobi*).

Bergman's finest film of the 1970's, SCENES FROM A MARRIAGE was originally conceived as a six-episode, 300-minute Swedish television series, cut by Bergman for U.S. release. He again proves that he is film's best, and most theatrical, director of women by giving the inimitable Ullmann a superb script from which to work. She is cast as the scorned woman who is forced to deal with her husband's involvement with a younger woman. Filmed almost entirely in extreme close-ups (adapted for the TV screen) by the masterful Sven Nykvist, the picture has Ullman's face conveying a variety of expressions similar to these of Maria Falconetti in Carl Dreyer's silent THE PASSION OF JOAN OF ARC. The film is not without its faults; however, these are faults that strict Bergman fans are always, inexplicably, able to overlook. Despite the use of close-ups, the film sinks to its knees in theatricality. With the few locations, the film may well have been performed on the stage. Bergman simply gives his die-hard audience more of what it wants to see, relaxing the curiousity through watching characters deal with emotional trauma. On its most basic level, the film is nothing more than a Swedish soap opera/mini-series brought to the screen for the whole world to see.

p,d&w, Ingmar Bergman; ph, Sven Nykvist (Eastmancolor); ed, Siv Lundgren; set d, Bjorn Thulin; cos, Inger Pehrsson.

Drama   **Cas.**   **(PR:C-O MPAA:PG)**

SCENIC ROUTE, THE**   (1978) 76m New Line Cinema c

Randy Danson (*Estelle*), Marilyn Jones (*Lena*), Kevin Wade (*Paul*).

A minimalist, avant-garde tale about Danson, a New Yorker into Orpheus, who meets Wade after a local stabbing. They carry on an affair and chatter endlessly about art. Jones moves in, turning the relationship into a trio. Producer, writer, and director Rappaport, unfortunately, falls into the trap of believing that in order for a film to be artistic, its characters must be as well. Stagey, but well-executed.

p,d&w, Mark Rappaport; ph, Fred Murphy; ed, Rappaport; art d, Lilly Kilvert.

Drama   **(PR:A MPAA:NR)**

SCENT OF A WOMAN½**   (1976, Ital.) 100m UA c

Vittorio Gassman (*Blind Captain*), Allessandro Momo (*Ciccio*), Agostina Belli (*Sara*), Moira Orsei.

In an odyssey redolent of such classics as "Don Quixote" or "Jacques le Fataliste", an Italian army captain, Gassman, blinded in an accidental explosion during maneuvers, journeys to Turin, Genoa, Rome, and Naples with his army-assigned Sancho Panza, Momo. Proud, arrogant, and aristocratic, the blinded captain turns hyperaesthetic with his handicap; his short-term mission is the seduction and subjection of beautiful women. But beauty is in the eye of the beholder, and he is eyeless in these oases of pulchritude. Momo, his seeing-eye private, must describe to him the physical attractions of the women he meets. His other senses sharpened, the captain is suspicious of his temporary aide's judgments in such matters; he can, he attests, smell a beautiful woman. In each of the cities they visit, such women prove to be most receptive to the handsome, handicapped hero; his vanity much assuaged by his encounters, the journey turns almost delightful. But fulfillment to Gassman is something entirely different, as one might be led to suspect from the items in his travelling case: a pistol and a portrait of a woman. The tour is to end in Naples, after all: "See Naples and die." Too proud to pursue the woman of the portrait because of his handicap, Gassman has arranged to meet a similarly wounded fellow officer at this terminal town, their object mutual suicide. Well acted and extremely entertaining. Gassman won the Best Actor prize at Cannes in 1975 for his portrayal of the capricious captain.

p, Pio Angeletti, Andriano, De Micheli; d, Dino Risi; w, Ruggero Maccari, Risi (based on a novel by Giovanni Arpino); ph, Claudio Cirillo (Technicolor); m, Armando Trovaioli; ed, Alberto Gallitti.

Drama/Comedy   **(PR:O MPAA:R)**

SCENT OF MYSTERY**½   (1960) 125m Michael Todd, Jr. c (AKA: HOLIDAY IN SPAIN)

Denholm Elliott (*Oliver Larker*), Peter Lorre (*Smiley, Chauffeur*), Beverly Bentley (*The Decoy Sally*), Paul Lukas (*Baron Saradin*), Liam Redmond (*Johnny Gin, Derelict*), Leo McKern (*Tommy Kennedy*), Peter Arne (*Robert Fleming*), Diana Dors (*Winifred Jordan*), Mary Laura Wood (*Margharita*), Judith Furse (*Miss Leonard*), Maurice Marsac (*Pepi, Storekeeper*), Michael Trubshawe (*English Aviator*), Juan Olaguivel (*Truck Driver*), Billie Miller (*Constance Walker*), Elizabeth Taylor (*The Real Sally Kennedy*).

This beautifully photographed mystery/chase film takes its cast through the Spanish landscape, but the real star of the picture is "Smell-O-Vision," a process by which real scents are pumped into the theater. The story, which stands on its own, is about "scrutable" Englishman Elliott, who gets involved with a search for a mysterious woman who will inherit $3 million at midnight the following evening. Originally a project his father planned to film, SCENT OF MYSTERY was brought to the eyes, ears, and noses of its Chicago, New York, and Los Angeles audiences by Michael Todd, Jr. He employed osmologist Hans Laube to further develop a system he had been working on since the 1930s. Laube and Todd, Jr. equipped Chicago's Cinestage Theater with over a mile of plastic tubing, each piece running to an outlet for every seat. More than 30 different smells were stored in vials which, on an audio cue from the soundtrack, would disperse throughout the theater. Seconds later, a neutralizing scent was then sprayed. The scents corresponded to visuals on the screen–garlic, gunpowder, wine, peppermint, shoe polish, lemon, seafood, bananas, pipe tobacco, perfume, and about 20 others. Occasionally, however, the scent would be the gag–Lorre would be seen drinking coffee, but instead of smelling that aroma, the audience would get a whiff of brandy–adding a cue which is entirely dependent on your nose. One week earlier, a different system, AromaRama, was developed and added to an already-existing film, BEHIND THE GREAT WALL, a documentary on China (a rather odd choice) which sprayed scents through the air-conditioning vents. Another odoriferous process was first explored by Michael Todd, Sr., who financed further experimental research in the hope that the system might be used for AROUND THE WORLD IN 80 DAYS (1956), but it was not to be. Todd, Jr., was the son of Elizabeth Taylor's third husband, and the sought-after star helped him finance the movie which, in addition to its other technical innovations, featured eight-channel sound. Taylor made an unpublicized and unbilled cameo appearance at the film's conclusion as the true sought-after heiress, identified nasally by her expensive perfume. This fad was forgotten for 21 years, when John Waters decided to make the stinky POLYESTER, in Odorama.... But what if you have a cold? SCENT OF MYSTERY was a box-office failure, which augurs ill for processes that might expose audiences to the delights of taste and touch, as outlined in Aldous Huxley's *Brave New World* The "feelies" are probably a long way off.

p, Michael Todd, Jr.; d, Jack Cardiff; w, William Roos, Gerald Kersh (based on a story by Kelley Roos); ph, John Von Kotze (Todd Color); m, Mario Nascimbene, Jordan Ramin, Harold Adamson; ed, James Newcom; md, Franco Ferrara; prod d, Vincent Korda; art d, Korda; set d, Dario Simoni; cos, Charles Simminger; spec eff, Cliff Richardson; osmologist, Hans Laube (Smell-O-Vision).

Mystery   **(PR:A MPAA:NR)**

SCHATTEN UBER TIRAN-KOMMANDO SINAI
                    (SEE: SINAI COMMANDOES, 1968, Israel/Ger.)

SCHEHERAZADE*½   (1965, Fr./Ital./Span.) 115m
Speva-Cine-Alliance-Filmsonor-Dea r-Tecisa/Shawn International c (LA SCHIAVA DI BAGDAD; SHEHERAZADE)

Anna Karina (*Scheherazade*), Gerard Barray (*Renaud de Villecroix*), Antonio Vilar (*Haroun-al-Raschid*), Marilu Tolo (*Shirin*), Jorge Mistral (*Grand Vizier Zaccar*), Fausto Tozzi (*Barmak*), Giuliano Gemma (*Didier*), Gil Vidal (*Thierry*), Joelle Latour (*Anira*), Fernando Rey, Jose Manuel Martin.

Just another sand opera, this one without music, and with Karina an unlikely Arabian princess (she seems better suited to the boulevards of Paris). Barring camels, caliphs, and wicked viziers, the plot line has little to do with the classical heroine of the traditional Persian/Indian/Arabian "A Thousand-and-One Nights". Instead, it mixes cultures, with Barray the emissary of his uncle, Emperor Charlemagne, dispatched to attempt to ensure safe transit for European pilgrims to the Holy Land ruled by caliph Vilar. On his trip, he saves Karina from Bedouin bandits and bears her to Baghdad, where she is to compete for the honor of joining Vilar's harem. Those same qualities of looks, guts, and brains that are to win her that honor prove to be overwhelming to the youthful Christian, who beds her in the Sultan's harem, where they are discovered through the ministrations of the jealous Tolo. When Karina is condemned to death, Barray offers to exchange his life for hers. Vilar agrees, but tosses his unfaithful near-bride to Baghdad's beggars to use for their pleasure. In the nick of time, both are rescued by Barray's retinue, and seek refuge in the arid desert. Forced by thirst from their barren sanctuary, they are recaptured, but the recalcitrant caliph decides to pardon them both if Karina will be his bride. As the ceremony nears, wicked vizier Mistral foments a rebellion in which Vilar is wounded. Barray assists in undoing the uprising, and the lovers are blessed by the dying Vilar. Released in Europe in sumptuous 70 mm Superpanorama, a first there, the film lost scope in its journey abroad; it played in the U. S. in a diminished 35 mm version.

p, Michael Safra, Serge Silberman; d, Pierre Gaspard-Huit, Jacques Bourdon; w, Marc-Gilbert Sauvajon, Gaspard-Huit, Jose G. Maesso; ph, Christian Matras, Andre Domage (Eastmancolor); m, Andre Hossein; ed, Louisette Hautecoeur; art d, Georges Wakhevitch, Francisco Canet; cos, Wakhevitch; ch, Janine Charrat.

Adventure   **(PR:A MPAA:NR)**

SCHIZO*   (1977, Brit.) 105m Niles International c (AKA: AMOK; BLOOD OF THE UNDEAD)

Lynne Frederick (*Samantha*), John Leyton (*Alan*), Stephanie Beacham (*Beth*), John Fraser (*Leonard*), Victoria Allum (*Samantha as a Child*), Jack Watson (*Haskin*), Paul Alexander (*Peter*), Queenie Watts (*Mrs. Wallace*), Trisha Mortimer (*Joy*), John McEnery (*Stephens*), Colin Jeavons (*Commissioner*), Raymond Bowers (*Manager*), Terry Duggan (*Editor*), Robert Mill (*Maitre d'*), Diana King (*Mrs. Falconer*), Lindsay Campbell (*Falconer*), Victor Winding (*Sergeant*), Pearl Hackney (*Lady at Seance*), Primi Townsend (*Secretary*), Wendy Gilmore (*Samantha's Mother*).

A mindless slasher picture which has Frederick being pursued by an axe-wielding nut case who killed her mother. She was unlucky enough to witness the murder and now has to pay. Comes complete with its own shower scene, not to mention a title that is a bit reminiscent of PSYCHO. At some showings, publicists promised free smelling salts for squeamish theater patrons. Sexy starlet Frederick was upgraded after this one by playing Princess Flavia, the feminine lead in the spoof THE PRISONER OF ZENDA (1979) with Peter Sellers. And why not? She was married to him at the time.

p&d, Peter Walker; w, David McGillivray; ph, Peter Jessop (Technicolor); m, Stanley Myers; ed, Alan Brett.

Horror   **Cas.**   **(PR:O MPAA:R)**

SCHIZOID**   (1980) 91m Cannon c (AKA: MURDER BY MAIL)

Klaus Kinski (*Dr. Peter Fales*), Mariana Hill (*Julie*), Craig Wasson (*Doug*), Donna Wilkes (*Alison Fales*), Richard Herd (*Donahue*), Joe Regalbuto (*Jake*), Christopher Lloyd (*Gilbert*), Flo Gerrish (*Pat*), Kiva Lawrence (*Rosemary*), Claude Duvernoy (*Francoise*), Cindy Dolan (*Sally*), Danny Assael (*Barney*), Jon Greene (*Archie*), Richard Balin (*Freddy*), Kathy Garrick (*Maxine*), Tobar Mayo (*Francis*), Fredric Cook (*Willy*), Jonathan Millner (*Francis' Friend*), Gracie Lee (*Bruce*), Frances Nealy (*Housekeeper*), Jay May (*Boy*), Kimberly Jensen (*Girl*), Cindy Riegel (*Secretary*), Tony Swartz (*Bartender*).

Transplanted Israelis Golan and Globus, a talented team with astute business sense, forged a fortune making low-budget films both good and bad which exploited current crazes. Here they have super-face Kinski as their draw in a PSYCHO-like shocker sans Hitchcock's superb direction. A succession of murderer's-point-of-view slashing scenes serve to alleriate the boredom in an otherwise slow-paced plot line involving psychiatrist Kinski, whose group-therapy patients (all nubile women, oddly enough) are being sheared by scissors wielded by a maniac. Those self-same scissors may be the very ones used for the cut-out, paste-up letters portending the crimes posted to advice columnist Hill (who, as a member of the therapy group, herself appears to be at risk). Who is the crazy cut-up? Is it the kinky shrink, Kinsky, who likes to look at daughter Wilkes as she showers (in a possible tribute to Hitchcock)? Let's not be too obvious. For all of the flesh and fantasy, this picture–set in sunny Southern California–is a clean movie, despite its ratings; it has hot tubs and showers, after all. The gorgeous Hill began her sparse career 15 years earlier in Howard Hawks' RED LINE 7000 (1965), the great director's cheapest and tawdriest film (this possibly a result of its being badly re-edited before its final release).

p, Menahem Golan, Yoram Globus; d&w, David Paulsen; ph, Norman Leigh

(TVC Color); m, Craig Hundley; ed, Robert Fitzgerald, Dick Brummer; art d, Kathy Curtis Cahill.

Horror   **Cas.**   **(PR:O MPAA:R)**

SCHLAGER-PARADE**   (1953) 100m Melodie-Herzog bw

Germaine Damar, Walter Giller, Nadja Tiller, Karl Schonbock, Loni Heuser, Walter Cross, Renate Danz, Bully Buhlan, Willi Schaeffers, Margot Hielscher, Johannes Heesters, Lya Assia, Gitta Lind, Rita Paul, Renate Holm, Rudi Schuricke, Friedel Hensch and the Cyprys, The Sunshine Quartet, The Cornel Trio, Tatjana Gsovsky and Her Dancers, Robby Gay, Michael Jary, Peter Kreuder, Friedrich Schroder, Peter Igelhoff, The Rias Dance Orchestra Conducted by Werner Muller, Stan Kenton and His Orchestra, Maurice Chevalier.

Giller is a struggling songwriter in Germany whose devoted sweetheart, Damar, sends one of his songs to a publisher, claiming it's the work of a big-time composer. As expected, the song becomes a hit. Complications follow on who actually penned the tune, and Giller becomes famous. Filled with a number of unfamiliar names to anyone outside Germany, except for Chavalier, Tiller, and Kenton, who perform on par with expectations. The translation of this film's title is HIT PARADE, and it borrows freely from the 1943 U.S. film of the same name which, incidentally, had been released there as late as 1951.

p, H.J. Ewert; d, Eric Ode; w, Aldo von Pinelli, H.F. Kollner; ph, Richard Angst; m, Heino Gaze; ed, Wolfgang Wehrums; set d, Karl Walter; m/l, Gaze, von Pinelli, Gunther Schwenn.

Musical   **(PR:A MPAA:NR)**

SCHLOCK**   (1973) 77m Gazotskie Films/Jack Harris c (AKA: THE BANANA MONSTER)

John Landis *(The Schlockthropus)*, Saul Kahan *(Detective/Sgt. Wino)*, Joseph Piantadosi *(Prof. Shlibovitz)*, Eliza Garrett *(Mindy Binerman)*, Eric Allison *(Joe Puzman)*, Enrica Blankey *(Mrs. Binerman)*, Charles Villiers *(Cal)*, John Chambers *(National Guard Captain)*, Richard Gillis, Alvici, Forrest J. Ackerman, Jack Harris.

Completed in 1971, SCHLOCK is the feature debut of John Landis. A sometimes hilarious, more often silly spoof of science-fiction and horror films, it ended up taking the top prize at the prestigious science-fiction festival at Trieste. The film has Landis dressed in an ape suit as a Rip-Van-Winkle missing link known as Schlockthropus. He wanders around town, killing and leaving banana peels behind him, watches THE BLOB and hates the ending, and becomes the subject of a TV contest whose viewers must guess how many he'll kill before he's stopped. He also is befriended by a blind girl who thinks he's a dog–that is, until she regains her sight. The makeup was done with great expertise by Rick Baker, who would go on to save Landis' AN AMERICAN WEREWOLF IN LONDON.

p, James C. O'Rourke; d&w, John Landis; ph, Bob Collins (DeLuxe Color); m, David Gibson; ed, George Folsey, Jr.; spec eff, Ivan Lepper; makeup Rick Baker.

Satire/Horror   **Cas.**   **(PR:A MPAA:PG)**

SCHNEEWEISSCHEN UND ROSENROT
                    (SEE: SNOW WHITE AND ROSE RED, 1966, Ger.)

SCHNEEWITTCHEN UND DIE SIEBEN ZWERGE
                    (SEE: SNOW WHITE, 1965, Ger.)

SCHNOOK, THE (SEE: SWINGIN' ALONG, 1962)

SCHOOL FOR BRIDES**   (1952, Brit.) 73m Hoffberg bw (GB: TWO ON THE TILES)

Herbert Lom *(Ford)*, Hugh McDermott *(Dick Lawson)*, Brenda Bruce *(Janet Lawson)*, Humphrey Lestocq *(Jimmy Bradley)*, Ingeborg Wells *(Madeleine)*, G.A. Guinle *(Pierre)*, Les Compagnons de la Chanson.

An innocuous comedy which has butler Lom scheming to blackmail his husband-and-wife employers. McDermott is the head of the household who takes a trip to Paris and takes up with Wells, Lom's wife. In the meantime Bruce, the lady of the house, gets under way with a man of her own. Lom's plan goes haywire when McDermott and Bruce catch on, causing them to give up his plan. Enjoyable.

p, Roger Proudlock; d, John Guillermin; w, Alec Coppel; ph, Ray Elton.

Comedy   **(PR:A MPAA:NR)**

SCHOOL FOR DANGER*   (1947, Brit.) 68m Central Office of Information/UA bw

Captain Harry Ree *(Felix)*, Jacqueline Nearne *(Cat)*, Edward Baird *(Henri Pickard)*, Members of the French Resistance.

British agent Ree and his civilian cohort Nearne reenact their WW II roles

as special trained saboteurs who were parachuted into occupied France. The methods of training and sabotage are given detailed treatment in a documentary reenactment. Not surprisingly, it is a weak picture with weak performances, but still has interest for its factual information.

d, Wing Comdr. Edward Baird; w, Baird, Squadron Officer J. Woolaston; ph, Flight/Officer W. Pollard; m, John Greenwood; md, Muir Mathieson.

War   **(PR:A MPAA:NR)**

SCHOOL FOR GIRLS*½   (1935) 66m Liberty bw

Sidney Fox *(Annette Eldridge)*, Paul Kelly *(Garry Waltham)*, Lois Wilson *(Miss Cartwright)*, Lucille La Verne *(Miss Keeble)*, Dorothy Lee *(Dorothy Bosworth)*, Toby Wing *(Hazel Jones)*, Dorothy Appleby *(Florence Burns)*, Lona Andre *(Peggy)*, Russell Hopton *(Elliott Robbins)*, Barbara Weeks *(Nell Davis)*, Kathleen Burke *(Gladys Deacon)*, Anna Q. Nilsson *(Dr. Anne Galvin)*, Purnell Pratt *(Inspector Jameson)*, Robert Warwick *(Governor)*, William Farnum *(Charles Waltham)*, Charles Ray *(Duke)*, Mary Foy *(Miss Gage)*, Dawn O'Day [Anne Shirley] *(Catherine Fogarty)*, Myrtle Stedman *(Mrs. Winters)*, Edward Kane *(Ted)*, Gretta Gould *(Mrs. Smoot)*, George Cleveland *(Reeves)*, Helene Chadwick *(Larson)*, Helen Foster *(Eleanor)*, Fred Kelsey, Harry Woods *(Detectives)*, Edward LeSaint *(Judge)*, Jack Kennedy *(Hansen)*.

An abundance of soap boxing on the necessity of reform hampers this tedious tale of young girl Fox, who though innocent, gets sent to reform school. When Mr. Right–Kelly–comes along, he gets her paroled into his custody and follows with the usual marriage proposal. A school for screenwriting may be in order here. An ancillary plot deals with cruel headmatron La Verne and her murder by inmate sympathizer-assistant Wilson, with the appropriate police investigation. This was one of a number of films of the time which capitalized on the success of the German-made MAEDCHEN IN UNIFORM (1932). The formula of nubile adolescent girls within difficult institutional settings appeared to be a great draw for a secretly concupiscent public when combined with a conscience-salving message of social reform. The trend continued with a succession of women's-prison pictures.

p, M.H. Hoffman; d, William Nigh; w, Albert DeMond (based on the story "Our Undisciplined Daughters" by Reginald Wright Kauffman); ph, Harry Neumann; ed, Mildred Johnston.

Drama   **(PR:A MPAA:NR)**

SCHOOL FOR HUSBANDS**   (1939, Brit.) 71m Wainwright/J.H. Hoffberg bw

Rex Harrison *(Leonard Drummond)*, Diana Churchill *(Marion Carter)*, June Clyde *(Diana Cheswick)*, Henry Kendall *(Geoffrey Carter)*, Romney Brent *(Morgan Cheswick)*, Roxie Russell *(Kate)*, Phil Thomas *(Chauffeur)*, Richard Goolden *(Whittaker)*, Judith Gick *(Joan)*, Joan Kemp-Welsh *(Maid)*.

Harrison turns in a first rate performance as a philandering novelist who is palling around with a pair of married women – Churchill and Clyde. Meanwhile, both their husbands are testing how faithful their mates be. A bit risque for the time, especially a bubble-bath scene in which the water gets shared.

p, Richard Wainwright; d, Andrew Marton; w, Frederick Jackson, Austin Melford, Gordon Sherry (based on the play by Jackson); ph, Phil Tannura.

Comedy   **(PR:A MPAA:NR)**

SCHOOL FOR RANDLE**   (1949, Brit.) 89m Film Studios Manchester/Mancunian bw

Frank Randle *(Flatfoot Mason)*, Dan Young *(Clarence)*, Alec Pleon *(Blackhead)*, Terry Randal *(Betty Andrews)*, Maudie Edwards *(Bella Donna)*, John Singer *(Ted Parker)*, Hilda Bayley *(Mrs. Andrews)*, Jimmy Clitheroe *(Jimmy)*, Elsa Tee *(Miss Weston)*.

The popular lowbrow series of comedies starring Randle (SOMEWHERE IN CAMP, SOMEWHERE IN CIVVIES, etc.) continued with this mediocre offering. Randle is the janitor at a girl's school where his long-lost daughter is enrolled. For the ever-diminishing number of Randle fans only.

p&d, John E. Blakeley; w, Blakeley, Anthony Toner, Frank Randle; ph, Ernest Palmer.

Comedy   **(PR:A MPAA:NR)**

SCHOOL FOR SCANDAL, THE*½   (1930, Brit.) 76m Albion Film/PAR c

Basil Gill *(Sir Peter Teazle)*, Madeleine Carroll *(Lady Teazle)*, Ian Fleming *(Joseph Surface)*, Henry Hewitt *(Charles Surface)*, Edgar K. Bruce *(Sir Oliver Surface)*, Hayden Coffin *(Sir Harry Bumper)*, Hector Abbas *(Moses)*, Anne Grey *(Lady Sneerwell)*, John Charlton *(Benjamin Backbite)*, Stanley Lathbury *(Crabtree)*, Henry Vibart *(Squire Hunter)*, May Agate *(Mrs. Candour)*, Maurice Braddell *(Careless)*, Gibb McLaughlin *(William)*, Wallace Bosco *(Rawley)*, Rex Harrison *(Bit)*, Dodo Watts *(Maria)*, Constance Stevens [Sally Gray], Anna Neagle.

A faithful rendering of Sheridan's famed restoration comedy about the doings at Lady Sneerwell's Grey is backbiting salon where the gossipmongers gather to do in their friends and acquaintances. A host of fine performers – including the youthful Carroll and the yet more youthful Harrison in a bit role – do justice to the several subplots of the classic, although the film is more stagey than cinematic.

p&d, Maurice Elvey; w, Jean Jay (based on the play by Richard Brinsley Sheridan); ph, (Raycol Color).

Comedy   **(PR:A   MPAA:NR)**

SCHOOL FOR SCOUNDRELS**   (1960, Brit.) 94m Guardsman/CD bw

Ian Carmichael (Henry Palfrey), Terry-Thomas (Raymond Delauney), Alastair Sim (Stephen Potter), Janette Scott (April Smith), Dennis Price (Dunstan Dorchester), Peter Jones (Dudley Dorchester), Edward Chapman (Gloatbridge), John Le Mesurier (Headwaiter), Irene Handl (Mrs. Stringer), Kynaston Reeves (General), Hattie Jacques (1st Instructress), Hugh Paddick (Instructor), Barbara Roscoe (2nd Instructress), Gerald Campion (Proudfoot), Monty Landis (Fleetsnod), Jeremy Lloyd (Dingle), Charles Lamb (Carpenter), Anita Sharp-Bolster (Maid).

A delicious satire of life, this film is subtitled "How To Win Without Actually Cheating" and that should tell it all. One needn't have read Potter's books on "gamesmanship," "lifemanship," and "oneupmanship" to appreciate all the humor in the movie, but it is advised that your library include those books and that you refer to them regularly. This film is similar HOW TO SUCCEED IN BUSINESS WITHOUT REALLY TRYING, in that both movies are cinematic handbooks for moving up the ladder, but the tacks they take are quite different. SCHOOL FOR SCOUNDRELS is a delicate adaptation of Potter's books that concern a mythical school at Yeovil that teaches losers to be winners. We meet Carmichael, a bumbling fool who is the type that walks into a 200-foot-long room, closes the door gently, and a priceless Ming vase falls off the table at the other end. We've all met this poor soul and laughed at his plight. He's the one the passing car shoots mud on, the man who gets to the station just as the train is pulling out, etc. Carmichael loves Scott and would like to make her his own, but Terry-Thomas, the boorish master of all he surveys, succeeds in winning Scott away. When Carmichael goes to a used car lot, he is gulled by sharpies Price and Jones. After finally acknowledging that he needs help, Carmichael registers at Sim's College of Lifemanship to rectify his situation. This is a school unlike any other, as it teaches students practical lessons in important subjects like "woomanship" (how to get to the woman you love), "partymanship" (how to behave at functions and come off looking top-hole), "gamesmanship" (how to win at every sport despite being not as adept at the game as the person you're playing against), and, of course, "oneupmanship" (how to always be one-up on the other person). Carmichael goes through the various courses taught by Jacques, Paddick, Roscoe, and others and comes out totally metamorphosed into a smiling, confident young man who is no longer a victim. Upon his return to London, Carmichael puts his new-found knowledge to work and begins exacting his revenge on his rival. He gets Terry-Thomas to wreck his beloved vintage sports car, and beats him in a hilarious tennis match which he causes Terry-Thomas to lose by subtly injecting various comments and moves, none of which look untoward to the casual viewer and all of which are calculated to drive a man mad. Everyone whom Carmichael encountered before his education at Sim's school is dealt with. Carmichael gets even with Le Mesurier, a snobbish headwaiter; the two used car salesmen; and, in the end, wins Scott away from Terry-Thomas as Sim, who has been watching Carmichael's progress, nods approvingly. The final sequence shows a whipped Terry-Thomas entering Sim's college as a new student in the hopes that he can rise to a higher level in "lifemanship". Except for the used car sequences, which go on a few beats too long, this is a nonstop comedy with the laughs delivered in quick succession by a cast of adept comic actors who play it so straight that you can't help but wipe your eyes from the tears of laughter. Jacques and Le Mesurier married, and when he died, he'd ordered an ad run in the local show-business trade-paper which read (and these may not be the precise words but the idea is correct): "John Le Mesurier Would Like All His Friends To Know That He's Kicked Off." Jacques is the heavy-set actress who played in many CARRY ON films and was so good as the "mannish-depressive" in MAKE MINE MINK. In a small role, note rubber-faced Monty Landis who'd been a mime in the "Le Crazy Horse" cafe in Paris, then came to the U.S. and appeared in many TV shows including "The Monkees" and "Columbo". In another small role, it's Jeremy Lloyd, who began as an actor before he started singing as part of the team of Chad and Jeremy a few years after this film. The courses taught at Sim's school (and he has Potter's name in the picture so there is no mistaking who he is) are so honest and believable that if someone actually did open this type of higher educational institution, they could make millions. Like so many of the 1950s and 1960s British comedies, this one is clean enough for grandmothers and grandchildren to see, although some of the bits may be over pre-teeners' heads.

p, Hal E. Chester, Douglas Rankin, d, Robert Hamer; w, Chester, Patricia Moyes (based on the books Theory and Practice Gamesmanship, Same Some Notes on Lifemanship and Oneupmanship by Stephen Potter); ph, Edwin Hillier; m, John Addison; ed, Richard Best; art d, Terence

Verity.

Comedy   **(PR:AA   MPAA:NR)**

SCHOOL FOR SECRETS½   (1946, Brit.) 108m Two Cities/GFD bw (AKA: SECRET FLIGH T)

Ralph Richardson (Prof. Heatherville), Raymond Huntley (Prof. Laxton-Jones), Richard Attenborough (Jack Arnold), Marjorie Rhodes (Mrs. Arnold), John Laurie (Dr. McVitie), Ernest Jay (Dr. Dainty), David Hutcheson (Squadron Leader Sowerby), Finlay Currie (Sir Duncan Wills), David Tomlinson (Mr. Watlington), Michael Hordern (Lt. Comdr. Lowther), Pamela Matthews (Mrs. Watlington), Joan Young (Mrs. McVitie), Cyril Smith (Flight Sgt. Cox), Hugh Dempster (Squadron Leader Slatter), Peggy Evans (Daphne Adams), Edward Lexy (Sir Desmond Prosser), Bill Rowbotham (Sergeant), Paul Carpenter (Flight Leader Argylle), Robin Bailey (Billeting Officer), Joan Haythorne (Mrs. Laxton Jones), Ann Wilton (Mrs. Dainty), Patrick Waddington (Cpl. Aspinall), Joseph Almas (Dr. Klemmerhahn), Dagenham Girl Pipers, Alvar Liddell, Norman Webb, D. Bradley Smith, Kenneth Buckley, Anthony Dawson, Robert Lang, Richard Mantell, Murray Matheson, Anthony Wyckham, Ingrid Forrest, Geraldine Keyes, Vida Hope, Sonia Elverson [Holm], Robert Wyndham, Andrew Blackett, Tony Arpino, Peter March, Robert Elson, Roger Keyes, Trevening Hill, Edward Lodge, Arthur Rieck, Ernest Urbank, Karl Morel, Hugh Pryse, Kenneth More, O.B. Clarence, Aubrey Mallalieu, Desmond Roberts, Guy Belmore.

An absorbing but at times badly flawed actioner detailing the efforts of a group of British scientists to perfect radar at the outset of WW II. Five scientists bicker among themselves over how to achieve their goal, but ultimately they pull together and make the necessary sacrifices to get the job done. Top-billed Richardson plays a meek, slightly eccentric scientist who winds up heading a nighttime test raid into Cologne in order to bomb a German-held radio station. The mission is a success, the Allies have perfected radar, and the reluctant soldier is hailed a hero upon his return to England. As would be expected from young writer-director Ustinov (he was 25 years old at the time) the film manages to integrate a nice sense of humor into the proceedings, which is a refreshing change from the deadly serious propaganda films that dominated the screen at the time. Unfortunately, portions of SCHOOL FOR SECRETS are too talky and tend to drag on past the point of interest, but the action scenes are excitingly handled and manage to keep the narrative aloft.

p, Peter Ustinov, George H. Brown; d&w, Ustinov; ph, Jack Hildyard; m, Alan Rawsthorne; ed, Russell Loyd.

War   **(PR:A   MPAA:NR)**

SCHOOL FOR SEX½   (1966, Jap.) 95m Toho bw (NIKUTAI NO GAKKO) (AKA: SCHOOL OF LOVE)

Kyoko Kishida (Taeko), Tsutomu Yamazaki (Senkichi), Yuki Nakagawa, So Yamamura.

A stylish adaptation of a story by famed Japanese novelist Yukio Mishima about a lonely divorcee, Kishida, who falls in love with a male prostitute, Yamazaki, who is half her age. Their relationship grows stronger and she invites him to live with her. When he is introduced to the daughter of one of Kishida's friends, the pair begin dating and soon become engaged. The jilted Kishida plans revenge and obtains some incriminating photos of Yamazaki. She threatens to show his fiancee if he doesn't break the engagement. The pressure proves too much for Yamazaki and he begins to deteriorate emotionally. Realizing the pain she has caused, Kishida loosens her grip over Yamazaki and destroys the pictures. She then returns to her uneventful existence as a dress shop owner. Kishida is electric as the lonely, tortured woman,–a role she familiarized herself with in the 1964 Japanese classic WOMAN IN THE DUNES.

p, Masakatsu Kaneko; d, Ryo Kinoshita; w, Toshiro Ide (based on the book Nikutai No Gukko by Yukio Mishima); ph, Jo Aizawa; m, Shigeru Ikeno.

Drama   **(PR:O   MPAA:NR)**

SCHOOL FOR SEX   (1969, Brit.) 80m Miracle c

Derek Aylward (Giles Wingate), Rose Alba (Duchess of Burwash), Hugh Latimer (Berridge), Nosher Powell (Hector), Bob Andrews (Sgt. Braithewaite), Vic Wise (Horace Clapp), Wilfred Babbage (Judge), Robert Dorning (Official), Dennis Castle (Col. Roberts), Edgar K. Bruce (Fred), Julie May (Ethel), Cathy Howard (Sue Randall), Gilly Grant (Stripper).

Sophomoric sex comedy has Aylward opening an institute where attractive young girls are trained in the art of marrying men for their money. Scarcely a laugh to be found here.

p,d&w, Pete Walker.

Comedy   **Cas.**   **(PR:O   MPAA:NR)**

SCHOOL FOR STARS* (1935, Brit.) 70m British and Dominions/PAR British bw

Fred Conyngham (*Frank Murray*), Jean Gillie (*Joan Martin*), Torin Thatcher (*Guy Mannering*), Peggy Novak (*Phyllis Dawn*), Ian Fleming (*Sir Geoffrey Hilliard*), Frank Birch (*Robert Blake*), Winifred Oughton (*Mrs. Dealtry*), Victor Stanley (*Bill*), Rosamund Greenwood, Effie Atherton, Phyllis Calvert, Geraldo and His Music.

Waitress Gillie attends drama school, where she becomes a dancer and falls in love. Not terribly interesting, but Gillie is nice to look at.

p, Anthony Havelock-Allan; d&w, Donovan Pedelty (based on a story by Arthur Austin).

Drama   (PR:A MPAA:NR)

SCHOOL FOR UNCLAIMED GIRLS**
(1973, Brit.) 95m GN c (AKA: HOUSE OF UNCLAIMED WOMEN; GB: THE SMASHING BIRD I USED TO KNOW)

Madeline Hinde (*Nicki Johnson*), Renee Asherson (*Anne Johnson*), Dennis Waterman (*Peter*), Patrick Mower (*Harry Spenton*), Faith Brook (*Dr. Sands*), Janina Faye (*Susan*), David Lodge (*Richard Johnson*), Maureen Lipman (*Sarah*), Derek Fowlds (*Geoffrey*), Colette O'Nell (*Miss Waldron*), Megs Jenkins (*Matron*), Cleo Sylvestre (*Carlien*), Lesley-Anne Down.

Film focuses on the problems confronted by a young girl who thinks she was responsible for her father's death several years earlier. When her lonely mother, Asherson, takes on another lover, Mower, Hinde winds up stabbing him when he tries to molest her. The girl is sent to a reform school, where she eventually is seduced by a lesbian who helps her escape. Looking for a place to turn, Hinde looks up her old boy friend, Waterman. Tragedy strikes when Hinde is killed in a car crash. Unique British entry to the women's prison film genre is highlighted by Lipman's moving performance.

p, Peter Newbrook; d, Robert Hartford-Davis; w, John Peacock; ph, Newbrook (Eastmancolor); m, Bobby Richards; ed, Don Deacon; art d, Bruce Grimes.

Drama   (PR:O MPAA:NR)

SCHOOL FOR VIOLENCE (SEE: HIGH SCHOOL HELLCATS, 1958)

SCHOOL OF LOVE   (SEE: SCHOOL FOR SEX, 1966, Jap.)

SCHOOLBOY PENITENTIARY
(SEE: LITTLE RED SCHOOLHOUSE, THE, 1936)

SCHOOLGIRL DIARY*½   (1947, Ital.) 95m Film Distributor bw
(LEZIONE DI CHIMICA)

Alida Valli (*Anna*), Irasema Dilian (*Maria*), Andrea Checchi (*Prof. Marini*), Giuditta Rissone (*Principal*), Ada Dondini (*Miss Mattel*), Carlo Campanini (*Campanelli*), Sandro Ruffini (*Maria's Father*), Nino Micheluzzi (*Campolmi*), Blanca della Corte (*Luisa*), Olga Solbelli (*Miss Bottelli*), Giuliana Pitti (*Marcella*), Tatiana Farnese (*Teresa*), Dedi Montano (*Music Teacher*), Diana Franci (*Caria*).

Valli turns in a virtuoso performance as a snobbish student who comes from a wealthy family. She heads her sorority, but doesn't do so well in her classes, failing almost every subject she takes. She tries to make amends by making a play for chemistry professor Checchi. When she suspects that fellow classmate Dilian also has her sights on Checchi, tensions flare. Everything is sweetly cleaned up for the finale, however, as Valli gives Dilian a life saving blood transfusion. Valli's expert handling of her acting duties got her signed by David O. Selznick, appearing the following year in THE PARADINE CASE and shortly afterwards in THE THIRD MAN. Dilian, whose performance was thought by many viewers to surpass that of Valli, remained in Europe taking secondary roles in a few films. (In Italian: English Subtitles.)

p,d&w, Mario Mattoli; ph, Jan Stallich; ed, Ferdinando Tropea; set d, Mario Rappini.

Drama   (PR:A MPAA:NR)

SCHOOLMASTER, THE   (SEE: HOOSIER SCHOOLMASTER, THE, 1935)

SCHOONER GANG, THE*   (1937, Brit.) 72m New Garrick/BUT bw

Vesta Victoria (*Mrs. Truman*), Billy Percy (*Freddie Fellowes*), Gerald Barry (*Carleton*), Percy Honri (*Adam*), Mary Honri (*Mary*), Betty Norton (*Mary Truman*), Basil Broadbent (*Jack Norris*), Frank Atkinson (*Ben Worton*), Iris Terry, Ralph Dawson, John Rowal, Tubby Hayes.

Poor crime drama has Atkinson trying to go straight after a stretch in jail. His sister, Victoria, gives him a job at her pub, but a gang of thieves comes along and forces him to help crack a safe. He double-crosses his associates and runs off with the money after leaving a valuable necklace hidden in the pub. The angry robbers kill Atkinson, but Victoria finds the necklace and

claims the reward.

p&d, W. Devenport Hackney; w, Frank Atkinson, Ralph Dawson, Iris Terry (based on a story by W. Devenport Hackney, M.L. Hackney); ph, Jack Parker, Gerald Gibbs.

Crime   (PR:A MPAA:NR)

SCHWARZE NYLONS-HEISSE NACHTE
(SEE: INDECENT, 1962, Ger.)

SCHWEIK'S NEW ADVENTURES*½   (1943, Brit.) 84m Eden/Coronet
bw (AKA: IT STARTED AT MIDNIGHT)

Lloyd Pearson (*Schweik*), Margaret McGrath (*Madame Karova*), Julian Mitchell (*Gestapo Chief*), Richard Attenborough (*Railway Worker*), George Carney (*Gendarme*), Jan Masaryk (*Narrator*).

Basically a sequel to Jaroslav Hasek's famed comic novel *The Good Soldier Schweik*, but without a British-made forerunner–(a German production, THE GOOD SOLDIER SCHWEIK, was made later and released in the U.S. in 1963–) this updated the silly-shrewd soldier's adventures to WW II, with the invasion of Czechoslovakia by the Nazis. Hasek had actually published a pamphlet subsequent to the occupation of his country which bore the title "How to Speak German". Inside, the pamphlet contained the story "Schweik against the Gestapo". It was a best seller in the occupied land. The film is introduced by Czech elder statesman Masaryk, who explains that the low slapstick tone is intentional, planned to make the invaders seem less than invincible. Pearson, as Schweik, is detailed to locate a playing card that will pinpoint the position of a German ammunition dump. He gets a job as butler to besotted Gestapo Chief Mitchell and, after numerous pratfalls and perils, does what he set out to do. All of the players, with the sole exception of statesman Masaryk, are extremely British in this flawed attempt at wartime political satire.

p, Walter Sors, Edward G. Whiting; d, Karel Lamac; w, Lamac, Con West (based on characters created by Jaroslav Hasek); m, Clifton Parker.

Comedy   (PR:A MPAA:NR)

SCHWESTERN, ODER DIE BALANCE DES GLUECKS
(SEE: SISTERS, OR THE BALANCE OF HAPPINESS, 1979, Ger.)

SCIENTIFIC CARDPLAYER, THE**   (1972, Ital.) 113m DD/CIC c
(LO SCOPANE SCIENTIFICO)

Alberto Sordi (*Peppino*), Silvana Mangano (*Antonia*), Joseph Cotten (*George*), Bette Davis (*Millionairess*), Domenico Modugno (*Gighetto*), Mario Carotenuto (*Professor*).

Davis is a millionairess from the States who, with her cardplaying partner Cotten, heads for Rome to beat some money out of Sordi and Mangano, an impoverished couple who play cards with her once a year. One's enjoyment of this picture is correlated with one's understanding of "scopa," an Italian card game.

d, Luigi Comencini; w, Rodolfo Sonego; ph, Giuseppe Ruzzolini (Eastmancolor); m, Piero Piccioni; art d, Luigi Scaccianoce.

Comedy   (PR:A MPAA:NR)

SCINTILLATING SIN (SEE: VIOLATED PARADISE, 1963, Ital./Jap.)

SCIPIO   (SEE: DEFEAT OF HANNIBAL, THE, 1937, Ital.)

SCOBIE MALONE**   (1975, Aus.) 98m Kingcroft/Cemp-Regent c

Jack Thompson (*Scobie Malone*), Judy Morris (*Helga Brand*), Shane Porteous (*Constable Clements*), Jacqueline Kott (*Norma Helidon*), James Condon (*Walter Helidon*), Joe Martin (*Jack Savanna*), Cul Cullen (*Captain Bixby*), Noel Ferrier ("*Mr. Sin*"), Walter Sullivvan (*Inspector*), Max Meldrum (*Scientific Officer*), Ken Goodlett (*Premier*), Joe James (*Attorney General*).

Thompson is a private eye investigating the mysterious death of Morris, who was involved in a blackmailing scheme against both cabinet minister Condon and gangster Ferrier, who may or may not be smuggling drugs. Both men are suspect, but Thompson has a hard time coming up with any evidence. Marred by an excessive reliance on flashbacks and almost no development of action.

p, Casey Robinson; d, Terry Ohlsson; w, Robinson, Graham Woodlock (based on the novel *Helga's Web* by Jon Cleary); ph, Keith E. Lambert (Eastmancolor); m, Peter Clark, Alan Johnston; ed, Bill Stacey; art d, Bill Hutchinson.

Mystery   (PR:O MPAA:NR)

SCOOP, THE, (1932) (SEE: HONOR OF THE PRESS, 1932)

SCOOP, THE* (1934 , Brit.) 68m British and Dominions/PAR British bw

Anne Grey (*Mrs. Banyon*), Tom Helmore (*Scoop Moreton*), Peggy Blythe (*Marion Melville*), Wally Patch (*Harry Humphries*), Arthur Hambling (*Inspector Stephenson*), Reginald Bach (*Daniels*), Roland Culver (*Barney Somers*), Cameron Carr (*Douglas Banyon*), Marjorie Shotter (*Reporter*), Moore Marriott (*Jim Stewart*), Gordon Bailey.

Boring crime drama has Grey's husband found murdered just as she's about to elope with her lover. Reporter Helmore covers the case and clears Grey's lover by admitting that he himself killed the victim, albeit in self-defense. Unbelievable premise badly put over.

p&d, Maclean Rogers; w, Gerald Geraghty, Basil Mason, (based on a play by Jack Heming).

Crime **(PR:A MPAA:NR)**

SCOOP, THE* (1934, Brit.) 68m British and Dominions/PAR British bw

Anne Grey (*Mrs. Banyon*), Tom Helmore (*Scoop Moreton*), Peggy Blythe (*Marion Melville*), Wally Patch (*Harry Humphries*), Arthur Hambling (*Inspector Stephenson*), Reginald Bach (*Daniels*), Roland Culver (*Barney Somers*), Cameron Carr (*Douglas Banyon*), Marjorie Shotter (*Reporter*), Moore Marriott (*Jim Stewart*), Gordon Bailey.

Boring crime drama has Grey's husband found murdered just as she's about to elope with her lover. Reporter Helmore covers the case and clears Grey's lover by admitting that he himself killed the victim, albeit in self-defense. Unbelievable premise badly put over.

p&d, Maclean Rogers; w, Gerald Geraghty, Basil Mason (based on a play by Jack Heming).

Crime **(PR:A MPAA:NR)**

SCORCHY zero (1976) 99m Hickmar/AIP c

Connie Stevens (*Sgt. Jackie Parker*), Cesare Danova (*Philip Bianco*), William Smith (*Carl Heinrich*), Normann Burton (*Chief Frank O'Brien*), John David Chandler (*Nicky*), Joyce Jameson (*Mary Davis*), Greg Evigan (*Alan*), Nick Dimitri (*Steve*), Nate Long (*Charlie*), Ingrid Cedergren (*Suzi*), Ellen Thurston (*Maria*), Ray Sebastian (*Counterman*), Mike Esky (*Dimitri*), Gene White (*Big Boy*), Marlene Schmidt (*Claudia Bianco*).

A lame cop action picture which is nothing more than an R-rated version of TV's POLICE WOMAN, with Stevens falling far below Angie Dickinson's barely average characterization. The nemesis of Stevens' tough-broad cop is heroin dealer Danova, but after peeling tons of rubber off her patrol cars tires, she serves him his just desserts. Sleazy, full of bad taste, with scenes of Stevens naked in a shower, which is where the whole film belongs.

p,d&w, Hikmet Avedis; ph, Laszlo Pal (Movielab Color); m, Igo Kantor; ed, Michael Luciano; spec eff, Roger George.

Crime **(PR:O MPAA:R)**

SCORPIO* (1973) 114m Mirisch-Scimitar/UA c

Burt Lancaster (*Cross*), Alain Delon (*Laurier*), Paul Scofield (*Zharkov*), John Colicos (*McLeod*), Gayle Hunnicutt (*Susan*), J.D. Cannon (*Filchock*), Joanne Linville (*Sarah Cross*), Melvin Stewart (*Pick*), Vladek Sheybal (*Zametkin*), Mary Maude (*Anne*), Jack Colvin (*Thief*), James Sikking (*Harris*), Burke Byrnes (*Morrison*), William Smithers (*Mitchell*), Shmuel Rodensky (*Lang*), Howard Morton (*Heck Thomas*), Celeste Yarnall (*Helen Thomas*), Sandor Eles (*Malkin*), Frederick Jaeger (*Novins*), George Mikell (*Dor*), Robert Emhardt (*Man in Hotel*), Bill Nagy (*Man at Animal Home*).

SCORPIO starts like a house on fire and quickly burns to the ground. In the wake of many superior spy thrillers, this one looks awful by comparison. The pretentious script was made even worse by Winner's insistence at letting the audience know he was directing. After having done so many movies, one would have thought Winner might have matured and tired of the Sydney Furie techniques of whip pans, zooms, close-ups, rack focus, jump cuts, and various angle shots, all of which detract from the storytelling. Lancaster is a heavyweight CIA agent who has arranged for the death of a radical Arab. He and his hired killer, Delon, leave Paris to go to Washington, where they go about their business like manufacturers home from a selling trip to Europe. Lancaster returns to his wife, Linville, and Delon goes to live with his *femme*, Hunnicutt. Colicos is the boss man at Langley and he asks for Delon's presence. When the killer (code-named "Scorpio") doesn't answer the summons, Colicos orders Delon arrested and incarcerated on a phony narcotics rap, then has him brought to Colicos' office. Colicos wants to know why Delon did not kill Lancaster while on the trip. It turns out that Lancaster is suspected of having become a double agent for the U.S.S.R., although that's not been proven. Delon tells Colicos he doesn't think Lancaster has pulled a Benedict Arnold and hands Colicos back the advance fee he received for supposedly doing the job. Colicos is certain Lancaster is a spy and keeps upping the offer to Delon, who finally acquiesces when

Colicos agrees to pay him $25,000 and give him Lancaster's high-ranking job. That agreed upon, Delon prepares to fulfill the hard contract. Lancaster gets wind of the plot to assassinate him and flees to Austria disguised as a priest. Once in Vienna, Lancaster locates Scofield, now a KGB official. Lancaster and Scofield had served side by side in the fight against the Nazis and retain a warm friendship, despite being on opposite sides of the ideological fence. Scofield helps Lancaster disappear for a while and the two men decry that the once-honorable profession of spying has now become a money business, with little caring for patriotism. Lancaster would like to give it all up and retire quietly to spend his life with the woman he loves, Linville. Those hopes are dashed when Lancaster hears that Linville has been killed, probably by a CIA murderer. Lancaster comes back to the States, murders Colicos, and when the other members of the CIA discover that Lancaster has not been selling secrets, the heat comes off. Delon, who could have killed Lancaster a few times, decides that spying is no business for a nice French boy and he plans to go home to Paris with Hunnicutt. Those thoughts are erased when Delon sees some motion pictures taken by long lenses which show Hunnicutt in league with Lancaster on a spying mission. Delon can't believe his eyes, but he knows what he must do and kills Hunnicutt. Later, Delon faces Lancaster in an underground garage. Lancaster warns Delon that he won't live much longer, as the CIA is after him because he knows too much. Lancaster says they'd be better off if they joined forces and both could escape. Delon shakes it off as the pleadings of a doomed man, unholsters his gun, and shoots Lancaster dead. Delon exits the garage, stops for a moment to pet a pussycat (thus showing that even cold-blooded killers like warm-blooded animals), and is himself shot down by an unidentified CIA assassin. Made in Washington, London, Paris, and Vienna, SCORPIO is undone by the absurd dialog, Winner's demonstrating his camera versatility and the miscasting of Hunnicutt, who is dull as a dishrag and Colicos, who exhibits more ham than the entire output of the Hormel factory. Scofield, one of the English-speaking world's best actors, doesn't make many movies. It's too bad that this empty exercise is one of his few film credits. Tired, pointless, and using plot confusion to substitute for characterization, SCORPIO disappeared faster than a pickpocket at a nudist camp.

p, Walter Mirisch; d, Michael Winner; w, David W. Rintels, Gerald Wilson (based on a story by Rintels); ph, Robert Paynter (DeLuxe Color); m, Jerry Fielding; ed, Freddie Wilson; art d, Herbert Westbrook; stunts, Alan Gibbs; makeup, Richard Mills.

Spy Thriller **(PR:C MPAA:PG)**

SCOTCH ON THE ROCKS½ (1954, Brit.) 77m Group 3/Kingsley International bw (GB: LAXDALE HALL)

Ronald Squire (*Gen. Matheson*), Kathleen Ryan (*Catriona Matheson*), Raymond Huntley (*Samuel Pettigrew, M.P.*), Sebastian Shaw (*Hugh Marvell, M.P.*), Fulton Mackay (*Andrew Flett*), Jean Colin (*Lucy Pettigrew*), Jameson Clark (*Roderick McLeod*), Grace Gavin (*Mrs. McLeod*), Keith Faulkner (*Peter McLeod*), Prunella Scales (*Morag McLeod*), Kynaston Reeves (*Rev. Ian Macaulay*), Andrew Keir (*McKellaig*), Neil Ballantyne (*Nurse Connachy*), Roddy McMillan (*Willie John Watt*), Rikki Fulton (*Poacher*), Meg Buchanan, Ian MacNaughton, Tom Baird-Ferguson, Eric Woodburn, James Gilbert, Howard Connell, James Copeland, Archie Duncan, Margaret Boyd, Norman MacOwan, James Anderson, Julian D'Albie, Walter Horsbrugh, Anthony Kilshawe, Lionel Harris.

Parliament gets a bit upset with some Scotsmen in this charming comedy about five locals who refuse to pay their road tax because the road is impassable. The humor is subtle and gentle, but often very funny, in much the same way as in Bill Forsythe's pictures (LOCAL HERO, COMFORT AND JOY). One of a handful of features produced by documentarian John Grierson.

p, John Grierson, Alfred Shaughnessy; d, John Eldridge; w, Shaughnessy, Eldridge (based on the novel *Laxdale Hall* by Eric Linklater); ph, Arthur Grant; m, Frank Spencer.

Comedy **(PR:A MPAA:NR)**

SCOTLAND YARD★★ (1930) 65m FOX bw

Edmund Lowe (*Sir John Lasher/Dakin Barrolles*), Joan Bennett (*Xandra, Lady Lasher*), Donald Crisp (*Charles Fox*), Georges Renavent (*Dr. Paul Dean*), Lumsden Hare (*Sir Clive Heathcote*), David Torrence (*Capt. Graves*), Barbara Leonard (*Nurse Cecilia*), Halliwell Hobbes (*Lord St. Arran*), J. Carrol Naish (*Dr. Remur*), Arnold Lucy (*McKillop*).

A highly implausible tale about a crook wanted by Scotland Yard who gets plastic surgery after a war wound. He ends up looking like a dead banker, fooling the detectives and the banker's wife. To prove that he is a man of honor, and to demonstrate his love for her, he turns himself in to the Yard, who then mercifully let him go free.

p, Ralph Block; d, William K. Howard; w, Garrett Fort (based on the play by Denison Clift); ph, George Schneiderman; ed, Jack Murray; art d, Duncan Cramer; cos, Sophie Wachner.

Drama/Romance **(PR:A MPAA:NR)**

SCOTLAND YARD** (1941) 67m FOX bw

Nancy Kelly (*Lady Sandra Lasher*), Edmund Gwenn (*Inspector Cork*), John Loder (*Sir John Lasher*), Henry Wilcoxon (*Dakin Barrolles*), Melville Cooper (*Dr. Crownfield*), Gilbert Emery (*Sir Clive Heathcote*), Norma Varden (*Lady Heathcote*), Leyland Hodgson (*Henderson*), Lionel Pape (*Hugh Burnside*), Lilian Bond (*Lady Constance*), Leo G. Carroll (*Craven*), Frank Dawson (*Kinch, Butler*), Eugene Borden (*Tony*), Edward Fielding (*Pickering*), Robert de Bruce (*Jeffries*), Denis Green (*Scott-Bishop*), Jimmy Aubrey (*Cockney*), Yorke Sherwood (*Lorry Driver*), Lester Matthews (*Dr. Gilbert*), Doris Lloyd (*Miss Harcourt*), Sidney Bracey (*Train Attendant*), Billy Bevan (*Porter*), Herbert Evans (*Footman*), Marga Ann Deighton (*Lady Doakes*), Leonard Mudie (*Clerk*), Holmes Herbert (*Dr. Woodward*), Reginald Barlow (*Messenger*), Lilyan Irene (*Maid*), John Rogers (*Newsboy*), Reginald Sheffield (*Hat Clerk*), Wright Kramer (*Dr. Scott*), Forrester Harvey (*Air Raid Warden*), Dave Thursby (*Laundry Man*), Frank Benson (*Newsboy*).

Loder takes over Edmund Lowe's role from the 1930 version of this picture as the bank robber who undergoes plastic surgery after being injured in the war. He begins to lead the life of the banker he now resembles (who is actually a Pow in Germany) and carries on with the banker's wife while planning a heist. It doesn't take Scotland Yard inspector Gwenn too long to figure out that something's wrong. Loder straightens out his act when he exposes a scheme by a German spy ring to clean out the bank.

p, Sol M. Wurtzel; d, Norman Foster; w, Samuel G. Engel, John Balderston (based on a play by Denison Clift); ph, Virgil Miller; ed, Al de Gaetano; md, Emil Newman.

Drama/Romance　　　　　　　　　　　　　　(PR:A   MPAA:NR)

SCOTLAND YARD COMMANDS* (1937, Brit.) 61m GN bw (GB: THE LONELY ROAD)

Clive Brook (*Comdr. Malcolm Stevenson*), Victoria Hopper (*Molly Gordon*), Nora Swinburne (*Lady Anne*), Malcolm Keen (*Professor*), Cecil Ramage (*Maj. Norman*), Charles Farrell (*Palmer*), Lawrence Hanray (*Jenkinson*), Frederick Peisley (*Bill Gordon*), Ethel Coleridge (*Mrs. Rogers*), Warburton Gamble (*Fedden*), Dennis Wyndham (*The Satellite*).

Brook stars as a retired naval commander whose marriage proposal to a society woman is turned down. Feeling rejected, he decides to take an automobile trip and along the way, runs into a gang of men who are smuggling machine guns. They knock Brook out and arrange the scene to convince Brook that his head injury is due to a car crash. After a stint in the hospital, Brook meets Hopper at a dance hall. As the evening progresses, he unwittingly discovers that her brother is the truck driver for the gang. Having fallen in love with her, he's not sure if he should go to the police with the information, but in the end he does the right thing and the gang is picked up by Scotland Yard.

p, Basil Dean; d, James Flood; w, Flood, Gerard Fairlie, Anthony Kimmins (based on the novel by Nevil Shute); ph, Jan Stallich.

Crime/Drama　　　　　　　　　　　　　　　(PR:A   MPAA:NR)

SCOTLAND YARD DRAGNET*½ (1957, Brit.) 74m Merton Park/REP bw (GB: THE HYPNOTIST)

Roland Culver (*Dr. Francis Pelham*), Patricia Roc (*Mary Foster*), Paul Carpenter (*Val Neal*), William Hartnell (*Inspector Rose*), Kay Callard (*Susie*), Ellen Pollock (*Barbara Barton*), Gordon Needham (*Sgt. Davies*), Martin Wyldeck (*Dr. Bradford*), Oliver Johnston (*Dr. Kenyon*), Mary Jones (*Mrs. Neal*), John Serret (*Psychiatrist*), Helene Gilmer, Patricia Wellum (*Nurses*), Edgar Driver (*Atkins*), Robert Sansom (*Chief Designer*), Douglas Hayes (*Mechanic*), Salvin Stewart (*Engineer*), Gordon Harris (*Control Officer*), Jill Nicholls (*Nurse*), Jessica Cairns (*Secretary*), Hilda Barry (*Mrs. Briggs*), Tim Fitzgerald (*Val as a lad*), Tom Tann (*Manservant*), Dennis McCarthy (*Police Constable Green*), Richard Stewart (*Constable*).

Culver is a psychiatrist who uses hypnotism to treat his patients. When Carpenter, a test pilot, comes to see him complaining of blackouts that make his job difficult, Culver tries to mesmerize him into killing his wife. Carpenter fails to commit the crime for Culver, so the evil doctor kills his wife himself and frames Carpenter. Roc, as Carpenter's fiancee, finally uncovers the truth and clears her love. Drags on and on, going nowhere and taking too long to get there.

p, Alec C. Snowden; d&w, Montgomery Tully (based on a play by Falkland Cary); ph, Philip Grindrod; m, Trevor Duncan; ed, Geoffrey Muller; md, Richard Taylor; art d, Wilfred Arnold.

Crime　　　　　　　　　　　　　　　　　　(PR:A   MPAA:NR)

SCOTLAND YARD HUNTS DR. MABUSE**½ (1963, Ger.) 90m CCC-Film bw (SCOTLAND YARD JAGT DR. MABUSE)

Peter Van Eyck, Werner Peters, Sabine Bethmann, Dieter Borsche, Walter Rilla, Klaus Kinski [Claus Guenther Nakszynski], Agnes Windeck, Hans Nielsen, Ruth Wilbert.

The fourth in the series begun by Fritz Lang in 1960. This time the spirit of the murderous villain takes over the body of a psychiatrist and begins a reign of terror. Van Eyck is determined to capture the killer, but runs into an obstacle in the form of the evil Kinski. Well-acted, but the disinterested direction adds nothing. One cannot help but wonder how master director Lang would have overseen the acting of Kinski and Van Eyck, who both have a fine edge of pathological violence that would have lent itself nicely to a more expressionistic, Langian treatment. (See DR. MABUSE series, Index)

p, Artur Brauner; d, Paul May [Ostrmayer]; w, Ladislas Fodor; ph, Nenad Jovicic.

Crime　　　　　　　　　　　　　　　　　　(PR:A   MPAA:NR)

SCOTLAND YARD INSPECTOR*½ (1952, Brit.) 73m Hammer/Lippert bw (GB: LADY IN THE FOG)

Cesar Romero (*Philip Odell*), Lois Maxwell (*Peggy*), Bernadette O'Farrell (*Heather*), Geoffrey Keen (*Hampden*), Campbell Singer (*Inspector Rigby*), Lloyd Lamble (*Sorroway*), Mary Mackenzie (*Marilyn*), Alastair Hunter (*Sgt. Reilly*), Frank Birch (*Boswell*), Lisa Lee (*Donna Devore*), Wensley Pithey, Reed de Rouen, Bill Fraser, Peter Swanwick, Lionel Harris, Betty Cooper, Katie Johnson, Clare James, Stuart Sanders, Robert Moore, Jacques Cey, Jean Bayliss, Richard Johnson, Robert Dorning, Jack Howarth, Laurie Taylor, Stuart Nichol, Josephine Douglas, Marguerite Brennan, Terry Carney, Christina Forrest, Hazel Sutton, Dorinda Stevens, Robert Adair.

When her brother is killed in what appears to be a freak auto accident, O'Farrell suspects that he is actually the victim of foul play. Her suspicions prove to be correct after the real murderer is uncovered through the efforts of American reporter Romero. A decent job was done in recreating London nightlife, but the script was brought to the screen in a confusing and mangled manner. Director Newfield is best known for the hundreds of poverty row westerns he made in conjunction with his brother, Sigmund Neufeld.

p, Anthony Hinds; d, Sam Newfield; w, Orville H. Hampton (based on a radio serial by Lester Powell); ph, Jimmy Harvey; ed, Jimmy Needs; art d, Wilfred Arnold.

Mystery　　　　　　　　　　　　　　　　　(PR:A   MPAA:NR)

SCOTLAND YARD INVESTIGATOR*** (1945, Brit.) 68m REP bw

Sir C. Aubrey Smith (*Sir James Collison*), Erich Von Stroheim (*Carl Hoffmeyer*), Stephanie Bachelor (*Tony Collison*), Forrester Harvey (*Sam Todworthy*), Doris Lloyd (*Ma Todworthy*), Eva Moore (*Mary Collison*), Richard Fraser (*Inspector Cartwright*), Victor Varconi (*Jules*), Frederick Worlock (*Col. Brent*), George Metaxa (*Henri*), Emil Rameau (*Prof. Renault*), Colin Campbell (*Waters*).

Stroheim is superb as an obsessed art collector who, through faked papers, gets his hands on what he thinks is the Mona Lisa, but really is an expert forgery. Meanwhile, the original is held by Harvey, who wants to sell the painting back to its museum for a profit. On both their trails is museum curator Smith whose reputation depends on recovering the canvas. Stroheim leaves a trail of corpses which the authorities follow to his private gallery, where he had hoped to hang the Mona Lisa. An average British crime thriller, which is saved by all-around sterling performances.

p&d, George Blair; w, Randall Faye; ph, Ernest Miller, William Bradford; m, Charles Maxwell; ed, Fred Allen; md, Richard Cherwin; art d, Frank Hotaling; spec eff, Howard Lydecker, Theodore Lydecker.

Crime　　　　　　　　　　　　　　　　　　(PR:A   MPAA:NR)

SCOTLAND YARD MYSTERY, THE
(SEE: LIVING DEAD, THE 1936, Brit.)

SCOTT JOPLIN*** (1977) 96m Motown/UNIV c

Billy Dee Williams (*Scott Joplin*), Art Carney (*John Stark*), Clifton Davis (*Louis Chauvin*), Margaret Avery (*Belle Joplin*), Eubie Blake (*Will Williams*), Godfrey Cambridge (*Tom Turpin*), Seymour Cassel (*Dr. Jaelki*), De Wayne Jessie (*John the Baptist*), Mabel King (*Madam Amy*), Taj Mahal (*Poor Alfred*), Spo-De-Odee (*Left Hand of God*), Denise Gordy (*Prostitute*), Samuel Fuller (*Theater Impresario*), David Healy, Leon Charles, Fred Pinkard, Delos W. Smith Jr, Marcus Grapes, Rita Ross, The Commodores, David Hubbard.

There is a great movie to be made about the life of Scott Joplin. Unfortunately, this is only a good one. Joplin died at the age of 49 at the Manhattan State Hospital in 1917. It was in 1973 that his music was used as the score for THE STING but the Oscar went to Marvin Hamlisch and Joplin's original contribution was mostly overlooked. In 1975, his second opera "Treemonisha" was done on Broadway and he was posthumously given the Pulitzer Prize. His first opera, "Guest Of Honor", never found a publisher. In this Motown production, the second of their films honoring important black Americans in music (The first was LADY SINGS THE BLUES), Williams is Joplin, a musical giant reduced to tinkling the ivories in sleazy 1900s bars and whorehouses. He meets Davis, an excellent musician who can't read notes, and the two men travel to a small town in

Missouri for a "piano-cutting" contest. (That's when players are in direct competition with each other and take alternate choruses.) Davis and Williams plan to split the $100 prize if either wins. Davis plays an original by his friend, "Maple Leaf Rag," and music publisher Carney offers money for the work. It's a low price and Williams is reluctant to sell but Davis convinces him that when he is a published composer, his performing price will rise and they will get much better fees at the various New Orleans brothels in which they play. Williams is hard at work on a new opus when a local hooker, Gordy (related to the man who owns Motown), seduces him. Carney works on Williams until the young composer agrees to join forces with the white publisher. It isn't long before "ragtime" is the national fad and Williams rides the crest of the tidal wave. He meets Avery, a young and beautiful widow. They fall in love, get married and move to St. Louis, where Carney has his headquarters. It's not long before Williams notices that he's lost some of the speed in his fingers in what appears to be advancing arthritis or some such thing. Williams is a bit concerned that his kind of music might have a short life in the fickle public's fancy. There's a gala honoring Williams as the man who started ragtime and he is unable to play well. Later he learns that Gordy gave him something besides a good time; she gave him syphilis, a then fatal disease that would begin taking its toll very soon. Williams is hurt when his works are bypassed at the St. Louis World's Fair (the same exposition where MEET ME IN ST. LOUIS was set) in favor of the music of John Phillip Sousa. (To show this on screen, they used black-and-white footage of Clifton Webb when he played the bandmaster in STARS AND STRIPES FOREVER.) Life keeps going in a downward spiral as his daughter dies, Avery leaves him and Davis admits that he has the same disease. Williams begins work on his opera "Treemonisha" hoping it will be important enough to take him out of the realm of "pop" and allow the serious critics to consider his work. (A similar desire is what inspired Gershwin.) Davis dies and Williams, now in his last days, goes to New York, where Carney has moved his offices, and shows him the finished opera. Carney, by this time, is out of money and can't find anyone willing to put up backing for the expensive opera. Williams arranges for a bare-bones reading of the opera in an uptown warehouse but the performers are not up to the task. Carney gets Fuller, a theatrical producer of note, to agree to listen to the work but Williams can no longer handle the piano chores and the result is a disaster. Outside the auditorium where Williams has just finished playing, Carney tries to buck up his spirits but Williams, a defeated man, says goodbye and walks away into the cold as the picture concludes. SCOTT JOPLIN was shot in a scant 20 days as a TV movie and one can see the places for commercial breaks in the way it was constructed. Kagan was making his feature debut and did quite well when one considers his breakneck pace and the short budget he was given to do a period piece. Godfrey Cambridge appeared in his final film here. Soon after, he was shooting the TV show "Victory At Entebbe" when he died of a heart attack at 43. Cambridge, Avery and Jessie had worked together before when they did the pilot episode of ABC's "That's My Mama." ABC turned thumbs down on Cambridge for the lead and he was replaced by another member of the SCOTT JOPLIN cast, Clifton Davis, who appeared on the show during the years it played. Davis later discovered religion and became a minister. Avery achieved nationwide prominence as Shug Avery in the 1985 movie THE COLOR PURPLE which brought her an Oscar nomination. In a small role as the impresario, Samuel Fuller, director of THE BIG RED ONE and many more, does a fine job. The redoubtable Eubie Blake is seen as a judge in the "piano-cutting" contest. Blake began performing in the last century and continued until his death, shortly before his 100th birthday. All of the music is by Joplin, with the exception of one song by Harold Johnson. The movie was released in selected locations and didn't engender enough box office business to warrant a full promotional campaign so it eventually wound up where it was supposed to have been from the start, on television. The Motown company, which made millions in the popular record business, also produced one of the best sports films about life in the old Negro leagues, THE BINGO LONG TRAVELING ALL-STAR AND MOTOR KINGS. Considering the tight schedule, SCOTT JOPLIN was an excellent job on everyone's part.

p, Stan Hough; d, Jeremy Paul Kagan; w, Christopher Knopf; ph, David M. Walsh (Technicolor); m, Scott Joplin (arranged and performed by Richard Hyman); ed, Patrick Kennedy; art d, William M. Hiney; set d, James W. Payne; cos, Bernard Johnson; ch, Michael Peters; m/l, "Hangover Blues," Harold Johnson; makeup, Mike Hancock.

Musical/Biography   **(PR:C   MPAA:PG)**

SCOTT OF THE ANTARCTIC***½   (1949, Brit.) 111m
                                            EAL/EL-Pyramid c

John Mills (*Capt. Robert Falcon Scott*), Derek Bond (*Capt. L.E.G. Oates*), Harold Warrender (*Dr. E.A. Wilson*), James Robertson Justice (*Petty Officer Taffy Evans*), Reginald Beckwith (*Lt. H.R. Bowers*), Kenneth More (*Lt. Teddy Evans*), James McKechnie (*Lt. Atkinson*), John Gregson (*Petty Officer Green*), Norman Williams (*Stoker Lashley*), Barry Lettes (*Apsley Cherry-Garrard*), Clive Morton (*Herbert Ponting*), Anne Firth (*Oriana Wilson*), Diana Churchill (*Kathleen Scott*), Dennis Vance (*Charles Wright*), Larry Burns (*Kilhane*), Edward Lisak (*Dmitri*), Melville Crawford (*Cecil Mears*), Christopher Lee (*Bernard Day*), John Owerns (*E.J. Hooper*), Bruce Seton (*Canell*), Sam Kydd (*McKenzie*), Mary Merritt (*Helen Field*), Percy Walsh (*Chairman of Meeting*), Noel Howlett (*1st Questioner*), Philip Stainton (*2nd*

Questioner), Desmond Roberts (*Admiralty Official*), Dandy Nichols (*Caroline*), David Lines (*Telegraph Boy*).

Although Captain Scott failed to reach the South Pole first (the Norwegians under Roald Amundsen won that prize), and although all five expedition members in Scott's party died on the way back– as much due to faulty planning as to bad luck and bad weather– Scott is revered to this day as a hero of the British Empire. This film is a fairly accurate account of that doomed expedition of 1911-1912, opening with Mills (as Scott) trying to raise money for a second expedition after his first failed to reach its goal. He finally gets the money from the British government and sets about organizing his expedition, which will utilize motor sledges, Siberian ponies, and dogs. From the start, though, misfortunes plague the expedition. One of the motor sledges falls through the ice; the ponies prove to not be rugged enough for the Antarctic rigors. The expedition loses time due to these and other delays and slowly its timetable becomes more and more impossible. Finally, through superhuman efforts, five men make it to the pole, where they are heartbroken to find Amundsen's Norwegian flag already flying. They set out on the return journey, but more disasters befall them as the weather turns very bad. Two men die along the way as the party makes less and less distance every day. A blizzard confines them to their tent for some days, during which Bond, suffering from frostbite and holding up the expedition, makes the famous statement, "I am just going outside and may be some time," after which he exits the tent into the raging blizzard, never to be seen again. His sacrifice is in vain, though, and the men are still unable to travel; eventually they all freeze to death in their tent, not to be found until a relief expedition arrives months later. The men were buried under a cairn of ice on the spot where they died, and recent calculations on the movement of the ice pack indicate that the bodies are now 50 feet below the surface and some 15 miles nearer the sea. Eventually Scott and his compatriots will break off in an iceberg and drift north. The film was a major success and was the royal-command performance of 1948. Everyone is good in the stiff-upper-lip style of British heroics, and the actors were partly chosen on the basis of their resemblance to the real participants in the events. Current counsel holds that Scott's party might have made the mere 11 miles back to its base camp but for the public-school prejudices which prevented its upper-caste members from eating their sled dogs (the method of preventing starvation and subsequent frostbite employed by the Amundsen expedition). The actors represented these attitudes well. Scott's log was discovered nearly a year after his death; the log and many of the personal effects of the real-life explorers–then in the coffers of the British Museum–were loaned to the producers for use in this faithful near-documentary. Mills carried Scott's own pocket watch and played the gramophone that accompanied the explorer. Actor Lee–in his first film role of any great moment, before he became Hammer Films' resident horror menace–recounted some of the difficulties of the production, which had the befurred actors sweating in the studio in the heat of summer while choking on artificial snow crafted of salt and plastic, propelled at them by an engine-driven propeller. Composer Vaughan Williams' fine musical score was later transmuted into his seventh symphony, the "Sinfonia Antarctica." Producer Balcon had recruited Vaughan Williams against his will by showering the famed composer with photographs of expedition members and memorabilia, finally gaining his attention and interest. Much of the filming was done in the Swiss Alps, and there Mills had a narrow brush with disaster. The company could not rehearse many scenes beforehand because of the danger of leaving footprints in the snow, so they would simply receive directions, then carry them out. Mills was instructed to pull his sled a short distance, then turn to wave the others along. When he turned back around to keep walking, he fell through a snow bridge and into a chasm hundreds of feet deep. Only the harness attached to the sled and some other actors kept him from meeting the same kind of fate that befell several Antarctic explorers.

p, Michael Balcon; d, Charles Frend; w, Walter Meade, Ivor Montagu, Mary Hayley Bell; ph, Jack Cardiff, Osmond Borradaile, Geoffrey Unsworth (Technicolor); m, Ralph Vaughan Williams; ed, Peter Tanner; md, Ernest Irving; art d, Arne Akermark, Jim Morahan; cos, Anthony Mendelson; spec eff, Richard Bendy, Norman Ough, Geoffrey Dickinson, Sydney Pearson; makeup, Ernest Taylor, Harry Frampton.

Historical Adventure   **Cas.**   **(PR:A   MPAA:NR)**

SCOUNDREL, THE***½   (1935) 76m PAR bw

Noel Coward (*Anthony Mallare*), Julie Haydon (*Cora Moore*), Stanley Ridges (*Paul Decker*), Rosita Moreno (*Carlotta*), Martha Sleeper (*Julia Vivian*), Hope Williams (*Margie*), Ernest Cossart (*Jimmy Clay*), Everley Gregg (*Mildred Langwiter*), Eduardo Ciannelli (*Maurice Stern*), Helen Strickland (*Mrs. Rollinson*), Lionel Stander (*Rothenstein*), Harry Davenport (*Slevack*), William Ricciardi (*Luigi*), Isabelle Foster (*Scrub Woman*), Madame Shushkina (*Fortune Teller*), Alexander Woollcott (*Vanderveer Veyden*), Richard Bond (*Howard Gillette*), Frank Conlan (*Massey*), O.Z. Whitehead (*Calhoun*), Raymond Bramley (*Felix Abrams*), Uhei Hasegawa, Carl Schmidt.

Coming off their sensational debut as co-authors-directors-producers of CRIME WITHOUT PASSION, Hecht and MacArthur made the virtually unreleasable ONCE IN A BLUE MOON with sweet-faced Jimmy Savo (it was held for a year before they let it slip out) and followed up with this, what must be one of the earliest existential films produced. To star in their original work, which owes a bit to a Hecht novel, *Fantazius Mallare*, and his well-known A Jew In Love, they chose Noel Coward, who was making his talking picture debut after having done a silent juvenile bit in Griffith's HEARTS OF THE WORLD in 1918. This movie was made at the Astoria, Long Island, lot and was a favorite of sophisticates, pseudo-sophisticates, and anyone who could recognize the real-life people upon whom the screenplay was based. It's a smart-set literati piece starring Coward as a New York publisher who is a marionette master, dangling and pulling the strings of everyone around him as he delights himself by his manipulations, scattering bon mots like rose petals from a wedding flower girl. He is a charming heel who loves 'em, leaves 'em, and remains the main topic of conversation at swank hotels, various watering spots, and brittle cocktail parties. Haydon, a young author, is in love with Ridges, and Coward means to break them up and make her his own. Meanwhile, he meets his female counterpart in Williams, who is just as world-weary, cynical, and cunning as he is. Coward gets aboard a Bermuda-bound flight and it crashes, killing him and everyone else aboard. But he gets a new lease when, by some magical means, he is allowed to return to this world, never to rest until he finds someone, anyone, who mourns his passing. Coward goes searching for that person who will free his soul by shedding one tear. In the end, Coward makes his peace with his Maker and is allowed to have eternal salvation. The metaphysical conclusion left many in the audience wondering what it all meant. Some of the actors were mystified as well. The picture is all talk and little action or even movement. Hecht and MacArthur were not true directors who knew how to make the screen dance with images and their lack of expertise is evident throughout. And yet, if one listens to the wonderful words spoken by almost everyone in the cast, there is much to chew upon and more substantial ideas in each scene than in a handful of many 1980s movies. Hecht and MacArthur had earlier adapted Coward's play into the movie DESIGN FOR LIVING and he must have forgiven them because he agreed to make this picture. The main reason to keep children away from THE SCOUNDREL is that they won't understand a word and will probably be snoring within minutes of the opening credits.

p,d&w, Ben Hecht, Charles MacArthur; ph, Lee Garmes; ed, Arthur Ellis; md, Frank Tours; art d, Walter E. Keller; set d, Albert Johnson.

Drama/Comedy   **(PR:C MPAA:NR)**

SCOUNDREL IN WHITE   (SEE: DOCTEUR POPAUL, 1972, Fr.)

SCOUTS OF THE AIR   (SEE: DANGER FLIGHT, 1939)

SCRAMBLE**   (1970, Brit.) 61m Eady-Barnes/Children's Film Foundation c

Ian Ramsey (*Jimmy Riley*), Stuart Lock (*Colin Buxton*), Stephen Mallett (*Brian Buxton*), Lucinda Barnes (*Vicky*), Gareth Marks (*Oscar Heppelwhite*), Robin Askwith (*Lennie*), Carling Paton (*Cliff*), Alfred Marks (*Mr. Heppelwhite*), James Hayter, David Lodge, William Lucas, Graham Stark.

While his father is in prison a boy is diverted from following the same path by joining a motorbike club and learning a different set of social rules. His final test comes when he thwarts a couple of would-be car thieves. Designed for children's tastes, but also worthwhile for an adult.

p, Tom Lyndon-Haynes; d, David Eady; w, Michael Barnes.

Childrens Drama   **(PR:AAA MPAA:NR)**

SCRATCH HARRY**   (1969) 94m Cannon/CG c

Harry Walker Staff (*Harry*), Victoria Wilde (*Erica*), Christine Kelly (*Christine*).

An interesting tale about the title character (Staff) who lives life to the fullest, driving a fast car, spending money like mad, and hopping into bed with a couple of different girls while his bisexual wife is away on vacation. When the wife returns, she jumps into bed with Staff's girl, who afterward kills herself. Staff and his wife get into an argument and end up killing each other. Staff's guardian angel, watching from the sidelines, tells Staff that he blew it and scratches him off the list. A few moral insights, but not enough to make the film memorable.

d, Alex Matter; w&ph, Matter, Stephen Winsten (Eastmancolor); m, Ken Lauber.

Satire/Fantasy   **(PR:O MPAA:NR)**

SCREAM AND DIE   (SEE: HOUSE THAT VANISHED, THE 1974, Brit.)

SCREAM AND SCREAM AGAIN***   (1970, Brit.) 94m Amicus-American International/AIP c

Vincent Price (*Dr. Browning*), Christopher Lee (*Fremont, British Agent*), Peter Cushing (*Maj. Benedek Heinrich*), Judy Huxtable (*Sylvia*), Alfred Marks (*Superintendent Bellaver*), Anthony Newlands (*Ludwig*), Peter Sallis (*Schweitz*), David Lodge (*Detective Inspector Strickland*), Uta Levka (*Jane*), Christopher Matthews (*David Sorel, Pathologist*), Judi Bloom (*Helen Bradford*), Clifford Earl (*Detective Sgt . Jimmy Joyce*), Kenneth Benda (*Prof.*

Kingsmill), Michael Gothard (*Keith*), Marshall Jones (*Konratz*), Julian Holloway (*Griffin*), Edgar D. Davies (*Rogers*), Yutte Stensgaard (*Erika*), Lincoln Webb (*Wrestler*), Nigel Lambert (*Ken Sparten*), Steve Preston (*Fryer*), Lee Hudson (*Matron*), Leslie Ewin (*Tramp*), Kay Adrian (*Nurse*), Rosalind Elliot (*Valerie*), The Amen Corner.

An excellent example of the successful British horror films made from the days of Hammer to the early 1970s. This time out AIP gathered Price, Lee and Cushing for the eerie tale of a mad scientist who is building a super race by attaching other people's limbs to his creations. Cushing is the sadistic mastermind behind the project, while Lee is the intelligence agent investigating a string of murders. The film's construction is (excuse the pun) choppy; it cuts from the investigation to a military plot by Jones to Price's experiments and, finally, to a hospital bed where a patient is slowly becoming a living stump as Cushing amputates his limbs one by one. The film's most gruesome scene has one of the master race who is captured and handcuffed ripping his arm off to escape, only to jump into a vat of bubbling acid.

p, Max J. Rosenberg, Milton Subotsky; d, Gordon Hessler; w, Christopher Wicking (based on the novel *The Disoriented Man* by Peter Saxon); ph, John Coquillon (Eastmancolor); m, David Whitaker; ed, Peter Elliott; md, Shel Talmy; prod d, Bill Constable; art d, Don Mingaye; m/l, title song, Dominic King, Tim Hayes, "When We Make Love," King; makeup, Jimmy Evans.

Horror/Science-Fiction   **Cas.**   **(PR:O MPAA:M/PG)**

SCREAM, BABY, SCREAM*   (1969) 83m Westbury Films c

Ross Harris (*Jason Grant*), Eugenie Wingate (*Janet Wells*), Chris Martell (*Scotty*), Suzanne Stuart (*Marika Gold*), Larry Swanson (*Charles Butler*), Jim Vance (*Garrison*), Naomi Fink (*Laura*), Phil Philbin (*Doctor*), Gordon Walsh (*Detective*), Brad F. Grinter (*Instructor*), Jerry DeGennaro (*Nightclub Comic*), Leona Resnick (*Nurse*), Candy Ernst, Bunny Ware (*Models*).

Swanson plays a demented artist in this screamer who disfigures his model's faces as inspiration for his art. Harris is a rock musician in love with Wingate and jealous of her relationship with fellow rocker, Martell. He tries to break them up by provoking a fight between the two, but this only sends them off to the deserted beach where Swanson lives. Once at the beach, Martell is strangled by Swanson. After murdering her boyfriend, Swanson takes Wingate as his next victim. Harris, concerned because his two friends have been gone for quite some time, decides to try to locate them, and stumbles upon Swanson's mansion. He is taken prisoner, but soon escapes, only to wind up in a disfiguring automobile accident.

p&d, Joseph Adler; w, Laurence Robert Cohen (based on a story by Cohen); ph, Julio C. Chavez; m, The Charles Austin Group; ed, Adler; set d, David Trimble; m/l, Chris Martell (performed by The Odyssey); makeup, Doug Hobart.

Horror   **Cas.**   **(PR:O MPAA:R)**

SCREAM BLACULA SCREAM**   (1973) 95m AIP c

William Marshall (*Manuwalde*), Don Mitchell (*Justin*), Pam Grier (*Lisa*), Michael Conrad (*Sheriff Dunlop*), Richard Lawson (*Willis*), Lynn Moody (*Denny*), Jane Michelle (*Gloria*), Barbara Rhoades (*Elaine*), Bernie Hamilton (*Ragman*), Arnold Williams (*Louis*), Van Kirksey (*Prof. Walston*), Bob Minor (*Pimp No.1*), Al Jones (*Pimp No.2*), Eric Mason (*Milt*), Sybil Scotford (*Librarian*), Beverly Gill (*Maggie*), Don Blackman (*Doll Man*), Judith Elliotte (*Prostitute*), Dan Roth (*Cop*), Nicholas Worth (*Dennis*), Kenneth O'Brien (*Joe*), Craig Nelson (*Sarge*), James Payne (*Attendant*), Richard Washington (*Cop No.1*), Bob Hoy (*Cop No.2*), James Kingsley (*Sgt. Williams*), Arnita Bell (*Woman*).

Set in L.A. and Africa, this weak follow-up to BLACULA is nothing more than your standard blacxploitation picture. Marshall returns in the title role after his bones are brought back to life, enabling him to drink all the blood he can sink his teeth into. Grier, a voodoo princess, gets the unenviable job of putting the vampire back in the ground. This sequel lacks the originality of its predecessor, mostly due to Kelljan's unimaginative direction. Good for laughs.

p, Joseph T. Naar; d, Bob Kelljan; w, Joan Torres, Raymond Koenig, Maurice Jules (based on the story by Koenig, Torres); ph, Isidore Mankofsky (Movielab Color); m, Bill Marx; ed, Fabian Tordjmann; art d, Alfeo Bocchicchio.

Horror   **(PR:O MPAA:PG)**

SCREAM BLOODY MURDER zero   (1972) 90m Indepix c

Paul Vincent, Marlena Lustik, Nick Kleinholz III, Paul Ecenta, Nancy Whetmore.

Released from an insane asylum where he was placed after killing his father with a tractor, a man with a hook for one of his hands takes up where he left off before his incarceration. First he kills his mother and stepfather, then he terrorizes the small town he left behind, leaving a string of corpses in his path. As a gimmick, theaters gave out blindfolds for patrons to hide behind during some of the more gruesome sequences. Rock bottom gore.

p,d&w, Robert J. Emery.

Horror   **Cas.**   **(PR:O MPAA:R)**

SCREAM FREE   (SEE: FREE GRASS, 1969)

SCREAM IN THE DARK, A**   (1943) 53m REP bw

Robert Lowery *(Mike Brooker)*, Marie McDonald *(Joan Allen)*, Edward S. Brophy *(Eddie Tough)*, Wally Vernon *(Clousky)*, Hobart Cavanaugh *(Leo Starke)*, Jack LaRue *(Cross)*, Elizabeth Russel *(Muriel)*, Frank Fenton *(Lackey)*, William Haade *(Gerald Messenger)*, Linda Brent *(Stella)*, Arthur Loft *(Norton)*, Kitty McHugh *(Maisie)*.

A well-handled mystery about Lowery's attempt to discover the identity of a woman suspected of killing her many husbands with a spiked umbrella. Not all the scenes are played seriously, with an edge of humor sneaking in occasionally, but not detracting from the sleuthing.

p&d, George Sherman; w, Gerald Schnitzer, Anthony Coldeway (based on the novel *The Morgue Is Always Open* by Jerome Odlum); ph, Reggie Lanning; ed, Arthur Roberts.

Mystery   **(PR:A MPAA:NR)**

SCREAM IN THE NIGHT*½   (1943) 58m Astor bw (AKA: MURDER IN MOROCCO)

Lon Chaney, Jr *(Jack Wilson/Butch Curtain)*, Zara Tasil *(Mora)*, Sheila Terry *(Edith Bentley)*, Manuel Lopez *(Johnny Fly)*, Philip Ahn *(Wu Ting)*, Richard Cramen *(Inspector Green)*, John Ince *(Bentley)*, Merrill McCormick *(Arab)*, John Lester Johnson.

Chaney plays a dual role in this picture, first that of a detective and then the deformed assistant to a famous jewel thief and killer, Lopez. Chaney as the detective, along with fellow dicks Cramen and Ahn, track at of a down the thief in Singapore, where his next marks are Chaney's old friend, Terry, and her uncle, Ince. Terry winds up getting kidnapped by Lopez, and so Chaney impersonates his assistant in a successful attempt to free her and bring down the international jewel thief. Director Newmeyer had been a top director during the silent era, but after two decades of failure in talkies, SCREAM IN THE NIGHT was his unsuccessful attempt at a comeback. This film also precluded Chaney's rise to fame as a major "horror" actor. Originally filmed in 1935.

p, Ray Kirkwood; d, Fred Newmeyer; w, Norman Springer; ph, Bert Longenecker; ed, Fred Bain.

Crime   **(PR:A MPAA:NR)**

SCREAM OF FEAR***½   (1961, Brit.) 82m Hammer/COL bw (GB: TASTE OF FEAR)

Susan Strasberg *(Penny Appleby)*, Ronald Lewis *(Bob, Chauffeur)*, Ann Todd *(Jane Appleby)*, Christopher Lee *(Dr. Gerrard)*, John Serret *(Inspector Legrand)*, Leonard Sachs *(Spratt)*, Anne Blake *(Marie)*, Fred Johnson *(Father)*, Bernard Brown *(Gendarme)*, Richard Klee *(Plainclothes Sergeant)*, Madame Lobegue *(Swiss Air Hostess)*.

Full of mysterious twists and turns, this expertly crafted thriller casts Strasberg as the wheelchair-bound step daughter of Todd. Strasberg pays a visit to her father's Riviera resort, having never met Todd before, and learns that her dad is away on business. She gets a bit suspicious, however, when in the middle of the night she finds her father's corpse propped up in the backyard. Of course everyone thinks she's crazy, but the same thing happens the next night. She suspects a plot to drive her mad and enlists the aid of chauffeur Lewis. The tricky end reveals, among other things, that Strasberg isn't really the daughter, but a friend of the dead girl investigating the shady Todd. More mistaken identities are uncovered in a climactic scene which takes place at the edge of a cliff. The perfect film to show those people that always seem to figure out the ending after the first half hour.

p, Jimmy Sangster; d, Seth Holt; w, Sangster; ph, Douglas Slocombe; m, Clifton Parker; ed, Eric Boyd-Perkins; md, John Hollingsworth; prod d, Bernard Robinson; art d, Thomas Goswell; cos, Dora Lloyd; makeup, Basil Newall.

Mystery/Drama   **(PR:C MPAA:NR)**

SCREAM OF THE BUTTERFLY*½   (1965) 76m Emerson bw (AKA: THE PASSION PIT)

Nelida Lobato *(Marla Williams)*, Nick Novarro *(David)*, William Turner *(Paul Williams)*, Leona Gage, Britt Nelson.

Novarro kills his nymphomaniac lover, Lobato, during an insane outburst when she tells him she no longer needs him and she is content to stay with her millionaire husband. The reasons behind the murder come out during the court case when Novarro relates that Lobato married Turner, but had to find a lover to quench her passion. She decides that she really does love her husband only after she devises a scheme to murder him, but is unsuccessful. Once these facts are disclosed the question is whether Novarro should be sent to an asylum or to jail. Trashy drama that will leave viewers

opting for an asylum themselves.

d, Ebar Lobato; ph, Ray Dennis Steckler; ed, Don Snyder.

Crime/Drama   **(PR:O MPAA:NR)**

SCREAMERS*½   (1978, Ital.) 91m Dania-Medusa/New World bw (L'ISOLA DEGLI UOMINI PESCE) (AKA: ISLAND OF THE FISHMEN, THE; SOMETHING WAITS IN THE DARK)

Barbara Bach *(Amanda)*, Claudio Cassinelli *(Claude)*, Richard Johnson *(Edmund)*, Joseph Cotten *(Prof. Marvin)*, Beryl Cunningham *(Shakira)*, Mel Ferrer *(Radcliffe)*, Cameron Mitchell *(Decker)*, Eunice Bolt *(Samantha)*, Tom J. Delaney *(Patterson)*, Charles Cass.

Cotton stars as the proverbial mad scientist on a deserted island, who creates a race of fishmen mutants. He trains these "fishmen" to recover the lost fortune of Atlantis. Bach satisfies the perversions of the exploitation audience by appearing in soaking wet clothes and communicating telepathically with the gilled creatures.

p, Lawrence Martin; d, Sergio Martino, Dan T. Miller; w, Sergio Donati, Cesare Frugoni, Martino; ph, Giancarlo Ferrando (Eastmancolor); m, Luciano Michelini, Sandy Berman; ed, Eugenio Alabiso; prod d, Massimo A. Geleng; spec eff, Christopher Wilas.

Science Fiction   **(PR:A MPAA:R)**

SCREAMING EAGLES**   (1956) 80m AA bw

Tom Tryon *(Pvt. Mason)*, Jan Merlin *(Lt. Pauling)*, Alvy Moore *(Grimes)*, Martin Milner *(Corliss)*, Jacqueline Beer *(Marianne)*, Joe di Reda *(Dubrowski)*, Mark Damon *(Lambert)*, Paul Burke *(Dreef)*, Pat Conway *(Forrest)*, Edward G. Robinson, Jr *(Smith)*, Ralph Votrian *(Talbot)*, Paul Smith *(Foley)*, Bobby Blake *(Hernandez)*, Bob Roark *(Torren)*, Bob Dix *(Peterson)*, Wayne Taylor *(Nolan)*, Robert Boon *(Hans Schacht)*, Peter Michaels *(Gustav Bormann)*.

A routine war picture about a group of young soldiers who parachute into France in preparation for D-Day. Before they hit the beaches of Normandy, they do battle with Nazi troops, run into some Resistance fighters, and take rescued femme prisoner Beer along for the invasion. One of famed novelist Tryon's early leading roles, well before he gave up stardom to become a scrivener.

p, Samuel Bischoff, David Diamond; d, Charles Haas; w, David Lang, Robert Presnell, Jr. (based on a story by Virginia Kellogg); ph, Harry Neumann; m, Harry Sukman; ed, Robert S. Eisen; md, Sukman; art d, Jack Okey.

War   **(PR:A MPAA:NR)**

SCREAMING HEAD, THE   (SEE: HEAD, THE, 1969, Ger.)

SCREAMING MIMI**½   (1958) 79m Sage/COL bw

Anita Ekberg *(Virginia Wilson)*, Phil Carey *(Bill Sweeney)*, Gypsy Rose Lee *(Joann Mapes)*, Harry Townes *(Dr. Greenwood)*, Linda Cherney *(Ketti)*, Romney Brent *(Charlie Wilson)*, Alan Gifford *(Capt. Bline)*, Oliver McGowan *(Walter Krieg)*, Red Norvo *(Red Yost)*, Stephen Ellsworth *(Dr. Joseph Robinson)*, Vaughn Taylor *(Roal Reynarde)*, Frank Scannell *(Paul)*.

Bizarre psychological thriller which sees Ekberg get attacked while taking a shower by a knife-wielding killer a full two years before Hitchcock did the same scene in PSYCHO (1960). Ekberg, who works as a dancer at a sleazy nightclub called the "El Madhouse," emerges from the attack with superficial wounds (her stepbrother, Brent, shot and wounded the assailant), but the experience has so unnerved her that she goes to a psychiatrist, Townes, for therapy. Meanwhile, a local reporter, Carey, learns of the attack and connects it with similar crimes that ended in murder. Frustrated with the slow-moving police and in pursuit of a hot story, Carey begins to investigate the crimes on his own. While counseling Ekberg, Towne falls in love with the voluptuous dancer and begins exerting great influence over her and even becomes her manager. Carey's digging uncovers that Ekberg has had a past history of mental illness, and he begins to suspect her as the killer. Carey also learns that each of the victims was given a strange sculpture of a woman contorted in a horrible scream (thus, "Screaming Mimi") and the artist turns out to be Ekberg's stepbrother. Eventually Carey puts all the pieces of the puzzle together and the mystery is solved. A weird, very obscure thriller that holds interest for fans of the strange cinema for several reasons. Ekberg, an actress who now has something of a cult following, performs some rather risque strip-tease numbers backed by the Red Norvo Trio. Famed stripper Gypsy Rose Lee–who has a cult following of her own–plays the owner of the sleazy nightclub. The film has some very effective scenes, and was directed by Oswald, who later would direct several episodes of the superior television science-fiction series "Outer Limits" which was known for its frequently chilling stories and expressionist visual style.

p, Harry Joe Brown, Robert Fellows; d, Gerd Oswald; w, Robert Blees (based on the book by Frederic Brown); ph, Burnett Guffey; m, Mischa Bakaleinikoff; ed, Gene Havlick, Jerome Thoms; md, Bakaleinikoff; art d, Cary Odell; ch, Lee Scott.

Suspense Drama   (PR:O MPAA:NR)

SCREAMING SKULL, THE**   (1958) 68m AIP bw

John Hudson [William Hudson] *(Eric)*, Peggy Webber *(Jenni)*, Toni Johnson *(Mrs. Snow)*, Russ Conway *(Rev. Snow)*, Alex Nicol *(Mickey, the Gardener)*.

Hudson plots to drive his new wife crazy in order to get his grubby hands on her fortune. He places skulls all around the house, in the hope of sending her back to the mental asylum where she had once been treated. At first the gardener seems to be the culprit, but eventually the finger is pointed at Hudson. On another level the old adage "the butler did it" fits here – Nicol cast himself as the butler as well as directed the film.

p, John Kneubuhl; d, Alex Nicol; w, Kneubuhl; ph, Frank Crosley; m, Ernest Gold; ed, Betty Lane.

Horror   (PR:A MPAA:NR)

SCREAMS OF A WINTER NIGHT zero

                                      (1979) 91m Full Moon/Dimension c

Matt Borel *(John)*, Gil Glascow *(Sam)*, Patrick Byers *(Carl)*, Mary Agen Cox *(Elaine)*, Robin Bradley *(Sally)*, Ray Gaspard *(Harper)*, Beverly Allen *(Jookie)*, Brandy Barrett *(Liz)*, Charles Rucker *(Alan)*, Jan Norton *(Lauri)*.

Ten fun-loving teenagers head for Louisiana's backwoods (film was shot in Natchitoches) to an area which is supposed to be haunted by a devil wind. While waiting for something scary to happen, the kids sit around the campfire and tell ghost stories, ineptly visualized to form the bulk of the film. The most frightening thing about the film is that someone actually spent money making it.

p, Richard H. Wadsack, James L. Wilson; d, Wilson; w, Wadsack; ph, Robert E. Rogers (PSI Color); m, Don Zimmers; ed, Gary Ganote, Craig Mayes; set d & cos, Mar Sue Wilson; spec eff, William T. Cherry III.

Horror   **Cas.**   (PR:A MPAA:PG)

SCREWBALLS zero   (1983) 80m New World c

Peter Keleghan *(Rick McKay)*, Lynda Speciale *(Purity Busch)*, Alan Daveau *(Howie Bates)*, Kent Deuters *(Brent Van Dusen III)*, Jason Warren *(Melvin Jerkovski)*, Linda Shayne *(Bootsie Goodhead)*, Jim Coburn *(Tim Stevenson)*, Raven De La Croix *(Miss Anna Tommical)*, Donnie Bowes *(Principal Stuckoff)*, Terrea Foster *(Chesty Colgate)*, Carolyn Tweedle *(Librarian)*, Nicky Flan *(Vince)*, Astrid Hildebrandt *(Blonde Cheerleader)*, Kim Cayer *(Brunette Cheerleader)*, Kimberly Brooks *(Rhonda Rockett)*, Nancy Chambers *(Trisha)*, Arnie Miller *(American Legionnaire)*, Angela Jenson, Allison Smith, Shannon McMahon, Stephanie Murgaski.

Trying to jump on the PORKY'S train, the makers of SCREWBALLS came up with another teen sex comedy – the type that gives movies a bad name, teens a bad name, and sex a bad name. The girls are given degrading names, the boys have only one thing on their minds and the producers obviously have no sense of moral responsibility. Only one code is evident – "If it sells, do it." The young leads in this picture pose as doctors during a breast checkup, play strip bowling, and drool over the only virgin left in school. Made only for indiscriminate animals.

p, Maurice Smith; d, Rafal Zielinski; w, Linda Shayne, Jim Wynorski; ph, Miklos Lente; m, Tim McCauley; ed, Brian Ravok; art d, Sandra Kybartas; cos, Nancy Kaye; m/l, Johnny Dee Fury.

Comedy   **Cas.**   (PR:O MPAA:R)

SCROOGE***   (1935, Brit.) 72m Twickenham/PAR bw

Sir Seymour Hicks *(Ebenezer Scrooge)*, Donald Calthrop *(Bob Cratchit)*, Robert Cochran *(Fred)*, Mary Glynne *(Belle)*, Garry Marsh *(Belle's Husband)*, Oscar Asche *(Spirit of Christmas Present)*, Marie Ney *(Spirit of Christmas Past)*, C.V. France *(Spirit of Christmas Future)*, Athene Seyler *(Scrooge's Charwoman)*, Maurice Evans *(A Poor Man)*, Mary Lawson *(His Wife)*, Barbara Everest *(Mrs. Cratchit)*, Eve Grey *(Fred's Wife)*, Morris Harvey *(Poulterer)*, Philip Frost *(Tiny Tim)*, D.J. Williams *(Undertaker)*, Margaret Yarde *(Scrooge's Laundress)*, Hugh E. Wright *(Old Joe)*, Charles Carson *(Middlemark)*, Hubert Harben *(Worthington)*.

A well-executed adaptation of the classic Dickens tale which remains brilliantly faithful to the original. The familiar story has Hicks playing the greedy old man Ebenezer Scrooge, who has a change of heart on Christmas eve when he looks into his lonely past and future. Hicks had played the Scrooge role many times in the previous quarter-century, and had grown into it remarkably by 1935, when this film was made.

p, Julius Hagen, Hans [John] Brahm; d, Henry Edwards; w, Seymour Hicks, H. Fowler Mear (based on Charles Dickens' *A Christmas Carol*); ph, Sydney Blythe, William Luff; ed, Brahm.

Fantasy   **Cas.**   (PR:AA MPAA:NR)

SCROOGE, 1951, Brit.   (SEE: CHRISTMAS CAROL, A, 1951, Brit.)

SCROOGE***½   (1970, Brit.) 118m Waterbury/NG c

Albert Finney *(Ebenezer Scrooge)*, Alec Guinness *(Jacob Marley's Ghost)*, Edith Evans *(Ghost of Christmas Past)*, Kenneth More *(Ghost of Christmas Present)*, Laurence Naismith *(Fezziwig)*, Michael Medwin *(Nephew)*, David Collings *(Bob Cratchit)*, Anton Rodgers *(Tom Jenkins)*, Suzanne Neve *(Isabel)*, Frances Cuka *(Mrs. Cratchit)*, Derek Francis, Roy Kinnear *(Portly Gentlemen)*, Mary Peach *(Nephew's Wife)*, Paddy Stone *(Ghost of Christmas Yet To Come)*, Kay Walsh *(Mrs. Fezziwig)*, Gordon Jackson *(Nephew's Friend)*, Richard Beaumont *(Tiny Tim)*, Geoffrey Bayldon *(Toyshop Owner)*, Molly Weir, Helena Gloag *(Women Debtors)*, Reg Lever *(Punch and Judy Man)*, Keith Marsh *(Well Wisher)*, Marianne Stone *(Party Guest)*, Philip Da Costa, Raymond Hoskins, Gaynor Hodgson, Nicholas Locise, Peter Lock, Joy Leigh, Sara Gibson, Clive Moss, John O'Brien, David Peacock, Michael Reardon, Karen Scargill, Terry Winter, Stephen Garlick.

A good, but not great, musicalization of Dickens' 1843 classic story which had already been made eight previous times (five of them were one-reelers back in the silent era). *A Christmas Carol* is the most widely read work by Dickens and it was herein entrusted to a director who had already produced (but not directed) two of the master's works, OLIVER TWIST and GREAT EXPECTATIONS. This same year, 1970, there was yet another Dickens novel musicalized and it swept the Oscars and did enormous box-office business. That was, of course, OLIVER! Had these two pictures not been released the same year, this might have achieved greater success. Finney is Scrooge, a misanthropic Londoner who abhors the idea of Christmas and his reaction to any mention of the holiday is an abrupt "Bah, humbug!" He is visited by the ghost of his former partner, Guinness, who tells him that he will have to host three more ghosts during the course of the evening. Guinness vanishes and Finney now faces the Ghost of Christmas Past, Evans, who takes him back to his childhood when he was a young man wooing Neve and gave up his love for her in favor of amassing a fortune. Evans disappears and is replaced by the Ghost of Christmas Present, More, who whisks Finney to the home of one of Finney's overworked and underpaid employees at the counting house, Collings. The family is one step away from abject poverty but that doesn't seem to matter as they happily prepare for their Christmas dinner. There are five children that Cuka has born to Collings and Finney casts a particular eye on the one who is crippled, Beaumont. Finney finds the child adorable and seems to be melting at the sight of the lame little boy. Later, the Ghost of Christmas Future (also referred to as the Ghost of Christmas Yet To Come), Stone, takes Finney to a grave site at a local cemetery, where Finney is stunned to see that Beaumont has been buried. If that's not enough, Stone now shows Finney the way he will spend eternity, chained and damned in Hell forever. Finney wakes up Christmas morning after having had these nightmares and is suddenly excited about the holiday and all it stands for. He races out and purchases several gifts, including a large turkey, and runs to the Collings' residence to share everything with them. They are stunned by his appearance at their door, but, in the true spirit of Christmas, welcome him with smiles and set another place at the table. The picture accurately visualized the period and Neame is to be congratulated for his well-paced work. Neame had been a cinematographer on some superb movies – PYGMALION, IN WHICH WE SERVE, and MAJOR BARBARA – before turning to producing and, later, directing. Leslie Bricusse wrote the adaptation, the music, and the songs, an amazing feat when one learns that he doesn't really play any instrument other than a small wooden flute. Bricusse and his erstwhile partner Anthony Newley would bring their ideas for melodies to musical director Ian Fraser, who would write down the notes, add the chords, and turn the simple tunes into several hits. On this film, there were no outstanding songs because Bricusse chose to stay within the context of the story, rather than obviously attempt to go for a popular tune. His songs included: "The Beautiful Day" (sung by Beaumont), "Happiness" (Neve), "Thank You Very Much" (Finney), "A Christmas Carol" (the company), "Christmas Children" (Collings), "I Hate People" (Finney), "Farver Chris'mas" (Urchins), "See the Phantoms" (the company), "December the 25th" (Naismith), "You...You..." (Finney), "I Like Life" (More), "I'll Begin Again" (Finney). The acting was excellent, especially Finney and Guinness. Bricusse was nominated for Oscars for his music and the song "Thank You Very Much." Cartwright, Furse, Fraser, and Spencer also received Academy nominations. Finney demonstrated ability singing and dancing and again proved he could handle himself musically when he appeared as Daddy Warbucks in ANNIE. Dame Edith Evans was 83 when she made this film and followed it with DAVID COPPERFIELD and five more before her death in 1976. Neve was making her theatrical debut. This G-rated picture was never accorded the applause it merited and should be played every year at Christmas, instead of some of the other movies of the story. The U.S. version in 1938 was actually far superior to the British remake in 1951 which starred Alastair Sim as Scrooge. Given a choice of the three, and even including the George C. Scott TV show, this one takes the cake for technical expertise and sheer delight. Richard Harris was supposed to star but dropped out to take another job. Then Rex Harrison was called in, learned the score, and was ready to star, but had to depart due to personal reasons. Only three weeks before production, Finney accepted the role and did a smashing rendition. One oddity is that he sang "I'll Begin Again" "live" instead of pre-recorded. He felt that he couldn't do it properly unless he segued from the dialog to the singing. In order to accomplish that, a mini-speaker was concealed under Finney's wig. In another area, Fraser played the piano to give Finney his key as well as the tempo and Finney sang the song. Later, the orchestral arrangements were added and recorded to conform to Finney's performance. It's the reverse of what usually happens in such cases but the results were gratifying.

p, Robert H. Solo; d, Ronald Neame; w, Leslie Bricusse (based on the novel *A Christmas Carol* by Charles Dickens); ph, Oswald Morris (Panavision, Technicolor); m, Bricusse; ed, Peter Weatherley; prod d, Terence Marsh; md, Ian Fraser, Herbert Spencer; art d, Bob Cartwright; set d, Pamela Cornell; cos, Margaret Furse; spec eff, Wally Veevers, Jack Mills; makeup, George Frost.

Musical   **Cas.**   **(PR:AAA MPAA:G)**

SCRUFFY**   (1938, Brit.) 61m Vulcan/British Independent bw

Jack Melford (*Jim*), Billy Merson (*Golly*), Tonie Edgar Bruce (*Mrs. Pottinger*), Michael Gainsborough (*Michael*), McArthur Gordon (*Hoskins*), Chris McMaster (*Adam*), Peter Gawthorne (*Chairman*), Joan Ponsford (*Judy*), Roddy McDowall, Winifred Willard, Valentine Rooke, Michael Rae, E.J. Kennedy, Jenny Barclay, Scruffy the Dog.

Another soppy boy-and-his-dog story, with little Gainsborough an orphan separated from his beloved dog when a wealthy woman, who doesn't care much for the furry animal, adopts him. Without his dog, Gainsborough finds life dull with the old lady and runs away. He finds sanctuary on a barge, where crooks Melford and Merson take him and his dog under their wings. When it looks as though the two men will go to jail, the dog comes to the rescue by getting rid of the incriminating evidence. Melford and Merson have become so attached to Gainsborough that they are willing to give up their life of crime if allowed to retain custody of the boy. Unabashed sentimentalism but good for a heartfelt tear or two.

p&d, Randall Faye; w, Margaret Houghton; ph, Desmond Dickinson.

Drama   **(PR:AA MPAA:NR)**

SCUDDA-HOO! SCUDDA-HAY!***½
     (1948) 95m Fox c (GB: SUMMER LIGHTNING)

June Haver (*Rad McGill*), Lon McCallister (*Snug Dominy*), Walter Brennan (*Tony Maule*), Anne Revere (*Judith Dominy*), Natalie Wood (*Bean McGill*), Robert Karnes (*Stretch Dominy*), Henry Hull (*Milt Dominy*), Tom Tully (*Roarer McGill*), Lee MacGregor (*Ches*), Geraldine Wall (*Mrs. McGill*), Ken Christy (*Sheriff Bursom*), Matt McHugh (*Jim*), Edward Gargan (*Ted*), C. Pat Collins (*Malone*), Eugene Jackson (*Stable Hand*), Marilyn Monroe (*Girl friend*), Robert Adler (*Lumberjack*), Colleen Townsend (*Girl in Canoe*), Tom Moore (*Judge Stillwell*), Charles Wagenheim (*Barber*), Herbert Heywood (*Dugan*), Guy Beach (*Elmer*), Charles Woolf (*Jeff*).

Who'd ever thought a good movie could be made about training mules? Well, it was, and this is it. The title refers to the yells trainers make while putting the beasts through their paces, sort of like "sooey" to a pig. McCallister is a young man who has just bought two mules from farmer Tully and now has to go to work for the man in order to pay off the purchase price. McCallister's stepmother, Revere, is a hard-bitten woman who has no sympathy for her stepson and showers her attentions on her own son, Karnes. McCallister's father is Hull, but he is at a loss to control the relationship between his son and Revere, which is rapidly disintegrating. Brennan is a veteran muler who befriends the youth and helps him stave off Tully's attempts to get the animals back. Tully's daughter is the attractive Haver and it isn't long before she and McCallister are in love and she sides with him against her father and gives the old man a piece of her mind in one particularly good sequence. Tully's other daughter is Wood who was appearing in her eigth movie at the age of 10. Marilyn Monroe had just signed a contract with the studio and her bit was shipped from the film, although there is a brief cut to her and Colleen Townsend as they row a canoe, however, their faces cannot be discerned. The fun in the movie is in the good-natured way rural Americana is handled. Veteran scripter F. Hugh Herbert was directing his first movie in 15 years and did a crackerjack job of keeping the action rolling, the love story sweet, and the villains menacing. This was an original idea for a film and not the sort of thing they remake, so if you can get a chance to see it, do.

p, Walter Morosco; dbw, F. Hugh Herbert; (based on the novel by George Agnew Chamberlain); ph, Ernest Palmer (Technicolor); m, Cyril Mockridge; ed, Harmon Jones; md, Lionel Newman; art d, Lyle Wheeler, Albert Hogsett; cos, Bonnie Cashin.

Period Comedy/Drama   **(PR:A MPAA:NR)**

SCUM***   (1979, Brit.) 96m Boyd's Company/World Northal c

Ray Winstone (*Carlin*), Mick Ford (*Archer*), John Judd (*Sands*), Phil Daniels (*Richards*), John Blundell (*Banks*), Ray Burdis (*Eckersley*), Julian Firth (*Davis*), Alrick Riley (*Angel*), John Fowler (*Woods*), Nigel Humphreys (*Taylor*), Philip Jackson (*Greaves*), Peter Howell (*Governor Baildon*), Jo Kendall (*Miss Biggs*), John Grillo (*Goodyear*), Alan Igpon (*Meakin*).

Intense drama set in a British reform school follows Winstone as he is brutalized by the system until he fights back, rising to the top of the prisoner

hierarchy and becoming a hardened criminal, probably for life, along the way. Thick, slang-laden accents make comprehension difficult in the early stretches of the movie, but after the audience grows used to the rhythms of speech it all becomes intelligible. Originally commissioned by the BBC for television, then refused for showing because of its unpleasantness and "bias," it was then released theatrically and received a great deal of praise. The performances are mostly good and the direction and editing work wonders in the tight gray interiors of the juvenile prison. Not for everyone, but worthwhile viewing for the not easily shocked.

p, Davina Belling, Clive Parsons; d, Alan Clarke; w, Roy Minton; ph, Phil Meheux; ed, Mike Bradsell; art d, Mike Porter.

Drama   **Cas.**   **(PR:O MPAA:R)**

SCUM OF THE EARTH zero   (1963) 71m Box Office Spectaculars bw
     (AKA: DEVIL'S CAME RA)

Vickie Miles (*Kim*), Thomas Sweetwood (*Harmon*), Sandra Sinclair (*Sandy*), Lawrence Wood (*Lang*), Mal Arnold (*Larry*), Craig Maudsley, Jr (*Ajax*), Edward Mann (*Mr. Sherwood*), Toni Calvert (*Marie*).

Herschel Gordon Lewis' precursor to BLOOD FEAST (1963), the picture that would begin a string of wretched gore films. This one starred Miles as an innocent teenager who gets blackmailed into posing for pornographic materials. She fights back, pits two gang leaders against each other, and manages to survive the ordeal. An amateurish, uninvolving waste of 71 minutes which was advertised as "Depraved, Loathsome, Nameless, and Shameless."

p, Davis Freeman [David Friedman]; d, Lewis H. Gordon [H.G. Lewis]; ph, Marvin L ester; m, Manuel Ortiz; ed, Patrick Murphy.

Crime   **(PR:O MPAA:NR)**

SCUM OF THE EARTH zero   (1976) 83m Dimension c (AKA: POOR
     WHITE TRASH II)

Norma Moore, Gene Ross, Ann Stafford, Charlie Dell, Camilla Carr, Joel Cole.

A crazed Viet Nam veteran returns to his backwoods home and starts killing off members of an incestuous hillbilly family. Not surprisingly, SCUM OF THE EARTH failed to show any box office strength–that is, until a producer named Mike Ripps took over. Having already made a small fortune by re-releasing BAYOU (1957) as POOR WHITE TRASH, Ripps decided to try the same trick with this picture. He tagged on the title POOR WHITE TRASH II and presented it with a new ad campaign: "In the tradition of GODFATHER II and WALKING TALL II." He even added that the film had an "abnormal subject matter," thereby necessitating the need for "Special Uniformed Police" to supervise admissions. The only tradition that POOR WHITE TRASH II followed was luring in audiences with a slick ad campaign and then showing them an unwatchable film.

p, M.A. Ripps; d, S.F. Brownrigg; w, Mary Davis, Gene Ross; m, Robert Farrar.

Horror   **(PR:O MPAA:R)**

SCUSI, FACCIAMO L'AMORE? (SEE: LISTEN LET'S MAKE LOVE, 1969, Fr./Ital.)

SE PERMETTETE, PARLIAMO DI DONNE
     (SEE: LET'S TALK ABOUT WOMEN, 1964, Fr./Ital.)

SE TUTTE LE DONNE DEL MONDO
     (SEE: KISS THE GIRLS AND MAKE THEM DIE, 1967, U.S./Ital.)

SEA BAT, THE**½   (1930) 74m MGM bw

Raquel Torres (*Nina*), Charles Bickford (*Rev. Sims*), Nils Asther (*Carl*), George F. Marion (*Antone*), John Miljan (*Juan*), Boris Karloff (*Corsican*), Gibson Gowland (*Limey*), Edmund Breese (*Maddocks*), Mathilde Comont (*Mimba*), Mack Swain (*Dutchy*).

Long before people feared sharks in the movies there were sea bats (aka sting rays) that did the dirty work. Torres plays the sister of a man who, while sponge-diving, has his breathing apparatus tampered with and becomes lunch for a giant sea bat. A priest comes to the island to console Torres and restore her waning faith. Actually, he isn't really a man of the cloth at all, but an escaped convict from Devil's Island. The man who killed her brother plans to turn the priest in, but while traveling to the prison in a motor boat, the sea bat attacks. The boat is overturned and dragged through the waters by the harpooned creature, sparing only the priest's life. A well photographed, exciting change of pace.

d, Wesley Ruggles; w, Bess Meredyth, John Howard Lawson (based on the story by Dorothy Yost); ph, Ira Morgan; ed, Harry Reynolds, Jerry Thoms; art d, Cedric Gibbons; m/l, "Lo-Lo," Al Ward, Reggie Montgomery.

Adventure   **(PR:A MPAA:NR)**

SEA CHASE, THE** (1955) 117m WB c

John Wayne (*Capt. Karl Erlich*), Lana Turner (*Elsa Keller*), Lyle Bettger (*Krichner*), David Farrar (*Comdr. Napier*), Tab Hunter (*Cadet Wesser*), James Arness (*Schlieter*), Wilton Graff (*Hepke*), Richard [Dick] Davalos (*Cadet Walter Stemme*), John Qualen (*Chief Schmidt*), Paul Fix (*Max Heinz*), Luis Van Rooten (*Matz*), Peter Whitney (*Bachman*), Alan Hale, Jr (*Wentz*), Lowell Gilmore (*Capt. Evans*), John Doucette (*Bo'sun*), Alan Lee (*Brounck*), Claude Akins (*Winkler*), Adam Williams (*Kruger*), Gil Perkins (*Baldhead*), Fred Stromsoe (*Mueller*), James Lilburn, Tony Travers, John Indrisano, Joey Ray (*Sub Lieutenants*), Cameron Grant (*Kruse*), Gavin Muir (*Officer-of-the-Watch*), Gloria Dea, Josephine Para, Lucita (*Spanish Girls*), Isabel Dwan, Theresa Tudor, Renata Huy (*Frauleins*), John Sheffield (*Patron in Dining Room*), Anthony Eustrel (*British High Official*), Tudor Owen (*Trawler Survivor*), Jean de Briac (*French Governor*), Patrick O'Moore (*Warship Officer*), Gail Robinson, Gilbert Perkins.

What's this? John Wayne as a German sea captain and Lana Turner as a Teutonic adventuress? Yep, it's true, but the result was exactly what one might have expected: a trite, dull, and uneventful picture that was ill-conceived from the start. Director Farrow knew something about the sea, having once served as a sailor as well as having directed TWO YEARS BEFORE THE MAST and BOTANY BAY. Naturally, Wayne could never portray a Nazi, so he is one of those Germans who opposed the Hitler regime and paid for his lack of adherence to the fascist cause by being given command of a rickety freighter. He's in the Australian area and wants to return home via Chile. On the ship are Turner, a spy who loves him; Bettger, the first mate; Hunter and Davalos, also mates. Farrar, a one-time pal of Wayne's, heads a British ship assigned to blow Wayne out of the water. Wayne's ship docks off New Zealand and he sends his men on a foray for food and gear. There are several fishermen on the island and Bettger kills them on his own, without any orders from Wayne. When Farrar finds the slaughter, it makes him all the more determined to catch Wayne. Further, Turner is engaged to Farrar, although he doesn't know she was acting on behalf of her government. When Wayne learns what Bettger has done, he is enraged. The ship makes it to Valparaiso where they get a huge welcome from the expatriate Germans who live there. Farrar, in a much faster ship, is getting closer. Wayne forces Bettger to write of his foul murders in the ship's log. At sea, there is a series of occurrences which include: a storm, a shark attack which takes the life of Davalos, and an attempt to convince other boats that this German freighter is a banana boat from Panama. In the end, Farrar catches up with the boat and a battle rages which results in the German boat sinking with Wayne and Turner still aboard. One lifeboat gets away, and on that boat, Turner has placed the ship's log that will eventually absolve Wayne of the crime of killing the fishermen. At the film's conclusion, we're never sure of the fate of the two leads, as Farrar, who is narrating the picture, states some words to the effect that: "We looked as hard as we could. Had they died at sea or were they able to reach the fjords nearby? Only two people can answer that question but, knowing (Wayne) Ehrlich the way I do, I have my own opinion." This was Turner's first film for Warner Brothers in 17 years and a poor choice for her return to the Burbank lot. There have been other films about the same subject: The British picture PURSUIT OF THE GRAF SPEE, which was a semi-true story about the *Graf Spee* and then, of course, THE ENEMY BELOW. Wayne never used a German accent, so it sounded odd against the others who attempted to do something different. Moss Mabry did a fine job designing Turner's clothing, all of which miraculously fit into a small bag she toted on board. She had enough clothing and accessories for a trip around the world... Hollywood magic at its best. It was shot from the end of September through the middle of December of 1964. In a small role, note the man who took a TV job when Wayne turned it down and became one of the richest and most recognizable actors ever, James Arness.

p&d, John Farrow; w, James Warner Bellah, John Twist (based on the novel by Andrew Geer); ph, William Clothier (CinemaScope, Warner Color); m, Roy Webb; ed, William Ziegler; art d, Franz Bachelin; set d, William Wallace; cos, Moss Mabry; makeup, Gordon Bau.

War/Adventure (PR:A-C MPAA:NR)

SEA DEVILS* (1931) 77m Standard/CD bw

Walter Long, Edmund Burns, Molly O'Day, Paul Panzer, Theodore Strohbach, Henry Otto, James Donnelly, Jules Cowles.

Routine adventure drama about a man sentenced to jail for a crime he did not commit who escapes from prison and joins a group of cutthroat treasure seekers aboard a boat where a mutiny is about to take place. The reason for the mutiny is not that the captain is a bad sort. Rather, he has a girl the first mate would like for himself. Picture looks as though it were made in a day or two, including time for extended lunch breaks.

d, Joseph Levering; w, Scott Littleton; ph, James Brown; ed, Dwight Caldwell.

Adventure (PR:A MPAA:NR)

SEA DEVILS**½ (1937) 85m RKO bw

Victor McLaglen (*Medals Malone*), Preston Foster (*Mike O'Shay*), Ida Lupino (*Doris Malone*), Donald Woods (*Steve Webb*), Helen Flint (*Sadie*), Gordon Jones (*Puggy*), Pierre Watkin (*Commander*), Murray Alper (*Seaman*), Billy Gilbert (*Cop*), Barbara Pepper.

Coast Guard tough guy McLaglen plans to marry his daughter, Lupino, to a gentlemanly seaman, Woods, under his command. Instead, she has her heart set on the rough-and-ready Foster, a fellow her dad violently dislikes. McLaglen has Foster transferred to his command, hoping to knock some sense into him during a tough dynamiting operation. A mishap occurs and McLaglen's intended son-in-law dies, leaving Foster as the one for Lupino. Fast-paced, authentic Coast Guard action.

p, Edward Small; d, Ben Stoloff; w, Frank Wead, John Twist, P.J. Wolfson; ph, J. Roy Hunt, Joseph August; ed, Arthur Roberts; md, Roy Webb; art d, Van Nest Polglase; spec eff, Vernon L. Walker; tech adv, Lt. H.C. Moore.

Drama/Adventure (PR:A MPAA:NR)

SEA DEVILS** (1953) 91m Coronado/RKO c

Yvonne De Carlo (*Drouette*), Rock Hudson (*Gilliatt*), Maxwell Reed (*Rantaine*), Denis O'Dea (*Lethierry*), Michael Goodliffe (*Ragan*), Bryan Forbes (*Willie*), Jacques Brunius (*Fouche*), Ivor Barnard (*Benson*), Arthur Wontner (*Baron de Vaudrec*), Gerard Oury (*Napoleon*), Laurie Taylor (*Blasquito*), Keith Pyott (*Gen. Latour*), Rene Poirer, Reed de Rouen, Michael Mulcaster.

Set against the backdrop of the Napoleonic Wars, this costumed adventure stars De Carlo as a British agent pretending to be a French countess, to whom she happens to bear a strong resemblance. Hudson, a smuggler, helps her sail to France, where he believes she is going to rescue her royal brother. Eventually she is caught by the French authorities and Hudson stages a daring rescue. Strong action scenes tend to camouflage the stock script.

p, David E. Rose, John R. Sloan (uncredited); d, Raoul Walsh; w, Bordon Chase (based on the novel *The Toilers Of The Sea* by Victor Hugo); ph, Wilkie Cooper (Technicolor); m, Richard Addinsell; ed, John Seabourne; art d, Wilfred Shingleton.

Adventure (PR:A MPAA:NR)

SEA FURY*½ (1929) 57m H.H. Rosenfield bw

James Hallet, Mildred Harris, George Rigas, Frank Campeau, George Godfrey, Bernard Siegel.

Adventure on the high seas has the crew aboard a ship involved in illegal smuggling activities throwing the captain and his officers, except for the navigator, overboard. The one remaining officer, then undertakes to steer the ship to safety, but threatens not to in order to keep the mutinous crew in check and away from the young woman who had earlier been rescued from a wrecked ship. Originally released as a silent, sound was added a couple of months later to try and stimulate the box office.

p, Tom White; d, George Melford; w, Melford, Elmer Ellsworth.

Adventure (PR:A MPAA:NR)

SEA FURY**½ (1959, Brit.) 97m RANK-Aqua/Lopert bw

Stanley Baker (*Abel Hewson*), Victor McLaglen (*Capt. Bellew*), Luciana Paluzzi (*Josita*), Gregoire Aslan (*Fernando*), Francis de Wolff (*Mulder*), David Oxley (*Blanco*), George Murcell (*Loudon*), Percy Herbert (*Walker*), Rupert Davies (*Bosun*), Robert Shaw (*Gorman*), Roger Delgado (*Salgado*), Barry Foster (*Vincent*), Joe Robinson (*Hendrik*), Dermot Walsh (*Kelso*), Richard Pearson (*Kershaw*), Fred Johnson (*Doc*), Jack Taylor (*Donkeyman*), Julian Bream (*Guitarist*).

Heavy on crashing waves and clashing fists, this sea adventure stars McLaglen as the captain of the *Fury*, a ship which makes its fortune by salvaging sunken vessels. Baker is promoted to second in command, competing with McLaglen for power and the love of a lovely senorita, Paluzzi. Baker is the one who ends up in her arms, against the wishes of her father. Tensions flare, until Baker proves his worth during a daring, stormy rescue of explosive sodium from a wrecked freighter.

p, S. Benjamin Fisz; d, C. Raker Endfield; w, Endfield, John Kruse; ph, Reginald Wyer; m, Philip Green; ed, Arthur Stevens.

Romance/Adventure (PR:A MPAA:NR)

SEA GHOST, THE** (1931) 73m Peerless bw

Laura La Plante, Alan Hale, Clarence Wilson, Claud Allister, Peter Erkelenz.

A Yankee skipper lets a German submarine officer live after he is discovered at the end of WW I. The German's secret is soon revealed however, as the American discovers that his wife went down on a ship the German's submarine had sunk. The film was one of the last made by La Plante, a silent screen star, before she retired.

p, Alfred T. Mannon; d, William Nigh; w, Nigh, Jo Von Ronbeo (based on a story by Burnet Hershey); ph, Sidney Hickox; ed, Thomas Persons.

Drama   **(PR:A MPAA:NR)**

SEA GOD, THE**   (1930) 73m PAR bw

Richard Arlen (Phillip "Pink" Barker), Fay Wray (Daisy), Eugene Pallette (Square Deal McCarthy), Robert Gleckler (Big Schultz), Ivan Simpson (Pearly Nick), Maurice Black (Rudy), Robert Perry (Abe), Fred Wallace (Bill), Willie Fung (Sin Lee), Sol K. Gregory (Duke), Mary De Bow (Mary), James Spencer (Sanaka Joe).

While diving for a sunken treasure, Arlen's underwater airline is cut by attacking island natives. He then simply walks to shore and the cannibalistic island dwellers assume him to be a sea god, bowing down before him. Sharing the little island is a gang led by Glecker, Arlen's nemesis. When Wray is kidnaped, Arlen hops back into his deep sea suit, stirs up the natives who kill Gleckler, and then is free to go. More interesting than the film itself is the fact that well-known writer and director of Broadway musicals George Abbott served as both director and writer for this adventure tale. Abbott directed eight films for Paramount between 1929 and 1931, this being one of the last. Here he made extensive use of outdoor scenery, with footage shot on Catalina Island, which was not the norm at this time. Scenes using studio-built jungle sets were then combined with the location footage, giving the film a more naturalistic look.

d&w, George Abbott (based on the story "The Lost God" by John Russell); ph, Archie J. Stout.

Adventure   **(PR:A MPAA:NR)**

SEA GULL, THE*½   (1968) 141m WB c

James Mason (Trigorin), Vanessa Redgrave (Nina), Simone Signoret (Arkadina), David Warner (Konstantin), Harry Andrews (Sorin), Denholm Elliott (Dorn), Eileen Herlie (Polina), Alfred Lynch (Medvedenko), Ronald Radd (Shamraev), Kathleen Widdoes (Masha), Frej Lindqvist (Yakov), Karen Miller (Housemaid).

When Ira Gershwin wrote about "more clouds of gray than any Russian play could guarantee," he must have been thinking about THE SEA GULL. This is a good version of Chekhov's "Chayka" and stays true to the play, even pausing after each act for a long fade to black. It's Russia in the late 1800s and Signoret, a well-known actress, is paying a visit to the huge estate where Andrews, her brother, has retired after years of public service. Signoret's son is Warner, a sensitive youth who yearns to write and lives with Andrews, helping to tend him in his waning days. Signoret pays little attention to her grown son and would prefer people didn't even know she had a child of that age. Warner's plays are unique and don't follow a dramatic pattern, so Signoret is only vaguely interested in his labors. Warner loves Redgrave, who lives on the property that abuts Andrews' estate (a large country home in Sweden is where it was shot). Signoret's current lover is Mason, a suave novelist who reeks charm and whom Redgrave finds increasingly attractive, much to the pain of the pining Warner. Meanwhile, Widdoes, the daughter of Radd, who works for Andrews, loves Warner from afar. At the same time, she is beloved by the local schoolteacher, Lynch, but she can't return his affection, as she finds him repulsive. To make his point about the shortness of life to Redgrave, Warner kills a sea gull, gives it to Redgrave, and says that he will be in the same position soon. Widdoes can't bear the attention Warner pays Redgrave, so she drinks too much, dresses in mourning black, and mopes around. Redgrave announces her intention to go to Moscow and follow a career on the stage, and Mason gives her his address so they can meet there. Two years go by and Redgrave delivers a child to Mason, without benefit of clergy. When the child does not survive, Mason departs. During this period, Andrews has become quite sick and Widdoes has finally bowed to Lynch's pleas and married him. Another weekend, and the same people come together again. Despite being tossed aside by Mason, Redgrave still won't accept Warner's affections. There's a card game in the house and Signoret, almost proudly, mentions that she still hasn't read any of Warner's plays. Outside the house, Warner makes one more play for Redgrave but she spurns him once again and says she will always love Mason. Warner's response to that is to walk to the lake and put a bullet through his head. The picture was made for less than $1 million and the mood is properly sombre, but Signoret is far too Gallic for the complex role she plays and Redgrave would seem more at home in Sussex than St. Petersburg. All the actors treat the words as though they were classic when the opposite should have taken place. By making it more realistic and not stentorian, Chekhov's meaning would have come across more clearly. Long at 141 minutes, and with a few rewrites by Woody Allen, it would have almost been a comedy.

p&d, Sidney Lumet; w, Moura Budberg (based on the play by Anton Chekhov translated by Budberg); ph, Gerry Fisher (Technicolor); ed, Alan Heim; prod d, Tony Walton; set d, Rune Hjelm, Rolf Larsson; cos, Walton; makeup, Tina Johansson, Kjell Gustavsson.

Historical Drama   **(PR:A-C MPAA:G)**

SEA GYPSIES, THE***   (1978) 101m WB c (GB: SHIPWRECK!)

Robert Logan (Travis), Mikki Jamison-Olsen (Kelly), Heather Rattray (Courtney), Cjon Damitri Patterson (Jesse), Shannon Saylor (Samantha).

A satisfying family adventure produced independently with kids in mind. Logan is about to set sail for Jamaica with his two daughters, and they are anxiously awaiting the arrival of a journalist from the magazine putting up some of the money for the trip. When it turns out that the writer is a beautiful woman, he is a bit put off, but eventually they fall in love. An orphaned boy joins the group as well after he stows away and is not discovered until the ship is at sea. Survival plays its part when they are shipwrecked off the coast of Alaska, with a variety of animals, including a killer whale, some Kodiak bears, and a pack of wolves, threatening the hearty group. Of course, rescue is imminent. Great fun for the young ones, with some excellent nature footage.

p, Joseph C. Rafill; d&w, Stewart Rafill; ph, Thomas McHugh (CFI Color); m, Fred Steiner; ed, Dan Greer, R. Hansel Brown, Art Stafford; animal trainers, Hubert Wells, Lloyd Beebe, Cheryl Shawver, George Toth, Gwen Johnson, Marinho Correia, Mickey Bailey, Helena Walsh, Sonny Allen.

Children's Film/Adventure   **(PR:AAA MPAA:G)**

SEA HAWK, THE***   (1940) 126m WB bw

Errol Flynn (Capt. Geoffrey Thorpe), Brenda Marshall (Donna Maria Alvarez de Cordoba), Claude Rains (Don Jose Alvarez de Cordoba), Flora Robson (Queen Elizabeth), Donald Crisp (Sir John Burleson), Henry Daniell (Lord Wolfingham), Alan Hale (Carl Pitt), Una O'Connor (Martha, Miss Latham), William Lundigan (Danny Logan), James Stephenson (Abbott), J.M. Kerrigan (Eli Matson), Gilbert Roland (Capt. Lopez), Julien Mitchell (Oliver Scott), David Bruce (Martin Burke), Frank Wilcox (Martin Barrett a Galley Slave), Herbert Anderson (Eph Winters), Clifford Brooke (William Tuttle), Charles Irvin (Arnold Cross), Clyde Cook (Walter Boggs), Edgar Buchanan (Ben Rollins), Ellis Irving (Monty Preston), Montagu Love (King Phillip II), Francis McDonald (Samuel Kroner), Pedro de Cordoba (Capt. Mendoza), Ian Keith (Peralta), Jack La Rue (Lt. Ortega), Fritz Leiber (Inquisitor), Halliwell Hobbes (Astronomer), Alec Craig (Chartmaker), Frank Lackteen (Capt. Ortiz), Victor Varconi (Gen. Aguerra), Lester Matthews (Lieutenant, Palace Officer), Leonard Mudie (Officer), Robert Warwick (Capt. Frobisher), Harry Cording, Nestor Paiva (Slavemasters), Frederic Worlock (Darnell), David Thursby (Driver), Michael Harvey (Sea Hawk), Gerald Mohr (Spanish Officer), Leyland Hodgson, Colin Kenny (Officers), Crauford Kent (Lieutenant), Elizabeth Sifton, Mary Anderson (Maids of Honor).

Audiences were waiting for this picture, the greatest swashbuckling film of the decade starring the inimitable Flynn. He and Warner Bros. were, in producing this kind of style and grandeur, at their creative peaks, and this film shows it in every frantic frame constructed by dynamo director Curtiz. Everything worked here, thanks to the studio's great facilities and the superior technical and creative talents–producer Blanke, the master studio photographer, Polito, one of the cinematographic pioneers of the silent era, the lush scoring of master composer Korngold (who provided, undoubtedly, his best film score ever for THE SEA HAWK), and a cast of character actors hard to match in any era. In an enormous throne room which shows a map of the 16th Century world, Love, enacting the scheming and ambitious King Phillip II of Spain, casts his shadow long over the map, and instructs his military advisors to devise a plan to conquer not only England but all of the European continent. But, to placate the nervous Queen Elizabeth of England, Love directs his ambassador, the crafty Rains, to journey to England and soothe the British sovereign's fears about Love's intentions. The Spanish galleon carrying Rains and his attractive niece Marshall is attacked en route to England by the British ship Albatross, commanded by privateer Flynn, and sunk, with the dashing British captain freeing the English prisoners who have worked the galleon's oars as galley slaves. He takes an indignant Rains and angry Marshall on board, promising to see them safely to England. Despite his gentlemanly manners, Flynn is a dedicated "Sea Hawk," along with a half-dozen other British ship captains, who foresee an inevitable war with Spain and have been busy raiding Spanish coastal forts and seizing Phillip's treasures to fund the building of a British fleet to combat the Spanish Armada which is under construction. All of this is done with the cautious secret sanction of Elizabeth, nobly played by Robson, although her "Sea Hawks" often cause political embarrassment through their actions. Such is the case when Flynn escorts Rains and Marshall into her throne room after arriving in England. Robson patiently hears out Rains' loud complaint about the sinking of his ship, but Robson flares up when he makes demands that Flynn and others be punished. Robson rebukes Flynn publicly and tells him that she sees him later in her chambers. Flynn points out to Robson that he freed 20 English sailors who had been laboring on the galleon's oars as galley slaves. Rains interrupts to state that these men had been tried and sentenced in a Spanish court. "I submit, your Highness," Flynn responds, "that the Court of the Inquisition is not qualified to pass fair judgment on English seamen or subject them to the cruel indignities of the Spanish galleys." Such gallantry and nobility of purpose arouses admiration (which later turns to love) from Marshall, who stands with her father in the court. When Rains attempts to seek retribution from her for the sinking of his ship, Robson cuts him off, rendering her apology for Flynn's action and letting it go at that. In her chambers Robson's attitude toward the devil-may-care Flynn is entirely different. She and Flynn have a close relationship, and, instead of treating her like a woman, it was decided at the start of the production that Flynn would treat his sovereign Robson like a man, talking to her straight from the shoulder. This often causes embarrassment for the queen. At one point in front of the court with Rains smugly looking on as she upbraids her corsair, she asks Flynn: "Did you think you could make war on Spain?" His unfearful response is: "Your majesty, Spain is at war with the world." He presents her with a precocious little simian which does tricks and the queen is charmed, although she cautions Flynn to be more careful in selecting ships to sink. Marshall, who sees through the machinations of her conspiratorial father and sides with Flynn for his humanitarian views, falls in love with him. Flynn is off to the Americas for more Spanish booty but before leaving he sees Marshall in a garden picking roses and goes to her. He then is in love with the Spanish noblewoman and tells her so poetically: "Maria, in the garden of a convent in Peru, there's a beautiful statue. The Spanish nuns call it *Nuestra Senora de las Rosas*. This is how I will remember you, as my Lady of the Roses." He tells her he is off on a voyage but will return for her. Meanwhile, Daniell, a member of Robson's court, has been intriguing with Rains and both of them learn from a chartmaker who has mapped Flynn's charts for his new voyage that the Sea Hawk is bound for Panama. Marshall later overhears her father and Daniell plotting to send the Armada against England and waylay England's finest seaman, Flynn, in Panama, before he can attack the Spanish garrisons there. Marshall takes a coach to Dover but she is too late to warn the love of her life, Flynn's ship already having sailed. She tearfully watches its sails billow and carry the vessel into the dusk. Alerted to Flynn's destination, Rains and Daniell set a trap for the adventurer in Panama. Flynn and his men are ambushed by a large Spanish force as they approach the Spanish forts in Panama, and the survivors–Flynn leading the way–retreat way– retreat the swamps, cutting their way through the jungle growth back to the sea where they row out to the *Albatross*. Flynn, Hale, and other seamen find their ship deserted and they discover the few sailors left on board are all dead. The ship is suddenly alive with scores of Spanish soldiers under the command of Roland, who orders Flynn and the others to surrender or be shot to death. Rather than see more of his men uselessly killed, Flynn surrenders. He is dragged before a judge of the Inquisition, Lieber, who sentences Flynn and his followers to life on board a Spanish galleon, to serve as galley slaves. Flynn and his men slave at the oars of a galleon for months, starved, beaten, exhausted, and without much hope of surviving under such merciless conditions. But Flynn obtains a knife and begins to chop away at the wood around the pin holding the chains which link him and his followers to the oars and, once free, he soon leads a daring escape while his ship is in a Spanish port. He overhears a conference of Spanish captains in which they boast of how the Armada is to sail against England. Following a fierce sword fight, Flynn obtains a secret dispatch sent from Daniell to Love in which the British turncoat promises to lead a revolt against the British throne. Flynn and his men sail for England and he manages to slip into the palace with Marshall's aid, fighting his way to see the highly protected queen. Daniell bars his path and the two men duel to the death in a savage fight, with Flynn running the traitor through in the throne room before a half dozen guards surround him and he begins to fight a losing battle. At that moment, Robson bursts into the throne room and orders the fighting stopped. Flynn kneels at her feet to explain that Daniell, lying dead on the floor before Robson, is "one less enemy of England." He hands her the dispatches Daniell had sent to Love, which alert her to the approaching Armada. Now Robson has the evidence she needs to declare war against her insidious enemy, Love, and she quickly orders a new war fleet built, to be commanded by the Sea Hawks, Flynn at their head. In a final crowd-cheering scene, Robson knights Flynn and announces that he will lead the British fleet to glorious triumph over the Spanish. Marshall is smiling at Flynn's side when the last scene dissolves to the credits. Jack Warner spared no expense in making THE SEA HAWK, lavishing a then-staggering $1.7 million on the film, and he saw his investment return twice that much before the year was out. The 31-year-old Flynn, then at the apex of his spectacular career, is magnificent in his swashbuckling role. He had become an overnight sensation four years earlier with CAPTAIN BLOOD and the public had been crying for a reprise of that role ever since. THE SEA HAWK was it. He was never more handsome or gracious than he appears in this film and his charm and athletic prowess are very much in evidence (although some of his fencing scenes were doubled by Don Turner; Daniell, a poor swordsman, was doubled by Ralph Faulkner and Ned Davenport). Marshall was never more radiant and is convincing as the beautiful daughter of Spanish ambassador Rains (her voice dubbed when singing by Sally Sweetland). Rains is the epitome of evil here; with his heavy arched eyebrows, mustache, and goatee, he easily passes–when Polito's shadows cross his face–for Mephistopheles. Robson does a fine job with her regal chore of essaying Elizabeth the Queen, a restrained performance, far superior to the histrionic portrayal of that tempestuous monarch by Bette Davis in THE PRIVATE LIVES OF ELIZABETH AND ESSEX, filmed two years earlier. This was Robson's second outing as the British queen, having scored heavily in the role in FIRE OVER ENGLAND in 1937. When this film was reissued (with THE SEA WOLF on a double bill) in 1947 about 10 minutes were edited out, most of the scenes dealing with Crisp, who is billed fourth, being deleted, especially a long scene with Flynn where Crisp visits the adventurer in Dover before he sails for Panama, warning him to be careful. Without these scenes, Crisp's role is reduced to an almost walk-on status but the missing scenes were restored in the 1960s and the original running length of the film, 126 minutes, is now present in most prints shown on TV or available on cassette. Warners provided a new sound stage for this splendid adventure yarn, one with its own lake offering 12 feet of rippling water, and two full-scale sailing vessels which were used in the film, one 165 feet long, the other 135 feet. In the astounding sea battle between the *Albatross* and the Spanish galleon, Curtiz managed some brilliant editing, using footage he shot for the film and the two marvelous full-scale reproductions at his disposal, while cleverly intercutting miniature shots (far superior to CAPTAIN BLOOD, where the vessels look like miniatures), and using footage from the 1936 CAPTAIN BLOOD, from that picture's silent predecessor, and from the silent version of THE SEA HAWK which had been filmed by First National in 1924, directed by Frank Lloyd and starring Milton Sills. Curtiz, a work-obsessed director, thought little of his actors' safety and pushed Flynn to his physical limits in making this film. Neither director not star had much use for the other. Flynn does his own swinging on ropes from ship to ship and sword play during the sea battles but for the final duel between Flynn and Daniell, Curtiz wanted almost a dance of death, and had fencing master Fred Davens come in and choreograph doubles for the actors who are shown in silhouettes as they battle down stairs and through cavernous halls, lopping off the tops of chairs and candles, smashing furniture in their deadly paths, intercuttting Flynn and Daniell at points. It's one of the most exciting duels ever filmed and is accompanied by lively, old-world music written by the brilliant Korngold, who scored each scene as it was completed. Delmer Daves was initially assigned to write a script from the Sabatini novel *The Sea Hawk* after Flynn scored his great success with the earlier swashbuckler, CAPTAIN BLOOD, but the project was tabled for a while. Then Miller submitted a script entitled BEGGARS OF THE SEA, which loosely profiled the career of Sir Francis Drake and other privateers who raided Spanish cities and sank Spanish fleets. These corsairs were called "sea dogs" in their day but the name was changed for this film which finally got underway in 1939 when Warners kept the Sabatini title but dropped the story about the Cornish gentleman who is a secret privateer in favor of the Miller script. Howard Koch, who had shocked America by writing "The War of the Worlds" script for Orson Welles' 1938 radio broadcast, was brought in to work on the script, his first screenplay. The script, as written, is a good example of how Hollywood distorted history, although Drake–upon whom Miller based his character Capt. Thorpe–did raid Panama at one time. Miller and the studio bosses decided not to draw too close a parallel between the character enacted by Flynn and Drake, lest they antagonize the British public, then a large segment of the Hollywood market. Moreover, the script was purposedly designed to align England's plight during the 16th Century with England in 1940, besieged and surrounded by the Spanish then and, in 1940, threatened with extinction by Hitler's Nazi Germany, creating as much sympathy for England as possible. The script is literate and witty, thanks to both Miller and Koch. (Koch at one time demanded sole screen credit for the script but this was denied when Miller proved his considerable contribution to the shooting script.) Curtiz and Flynn came almost to the breaking point with each other during the production, even though this indefatigable team created some of the most memorable adventure films ever made (CAPTAIN BLOOD, 1936, CHARGE OF THE LIGHT BRIGADE, 1936, THE ADVENTURE OF ROBIN HOOD, 1938, DODGE CITY, 1939, THE PRIVATE LIVES OF ELIZABETH AND ESSEX, 1939, VIRGINIA CITY, 1940, THE SANTA FE TRAIL, 1940). But the director, according to one report, proved himself the half-mad half-mad always claimed him to be in one of the most dramatic scenes, where Flynn and a host of extras are rowing oars as galley slaves. The bit player shipping the galley slaves was instructed by Curtiz, for the sake of the realism the director wanted, to actually lash the bare backs of the actors. As the actors winced in pain–but not moving from their positions so as not to spoil the shot–Curtiz laughed at their agony. Flynn, who had earlier collapsed on the set and was ill throughout most of the film, was running a high temperature during this scene but he forgot his illnss when the slavemaster went to work. He jumped up from his oar, threw off his chains, grabbed the bit player using the whip, and smashed him so hard he bled all over Flynn and had to be replaced. Then Flynn sent for Curtiz, who saw the look of mayhem in the swashbuckler's eyes and ran from the set, forgetting to yell "Cut!" and letting the cameras roll. Flynn and Robson got along famously on and off the set; the actor, to show how much he liked the refined British actress, took her to his favorite Hollywood bordello and introduced her to the heavily made-up madam, who, in turn, showed Robson her prized possession, a photo showing her top girls surrounding Flynn and George Sanders, both actors symbolically holding cricket bats and grinning like little boys.

p, Jack L. Warner, Hal B. Wallis, Henry Blanke; d, Michael Curtiz; w, Howard Koch, Seton I. Miller; ph, Sol Polito; m, Erich Wolfgang Korngold; ed, George Amy; md, Leo F. Forbstein; art d, Anton Grot; cos, Orry-Kelly; spec eff, Byron Haskin, H.F. Koenekamp; fencing master, Fred Cavens.

Adventure **Cas.** **(PR:A MPAA:NR)**

SEA HORNET, THE*½ (1951) 84m REP bw

Rod Cameron *(Gunner McNeil)*, Adele Mara *(Suntan Radford)*, Adrian Booth *(Ginger)*, Chill Wills *(Swede)*, Jim Davis *(Tony Sullivan)*, Richard Jaeckel *(Johnny Radford)*, Ellen Corby *(Mrs. Drinkwater)*, James Brown *(Pete Hunter)*, Grant Withers *(Rocky Lowe)*, William Ching *(Sprowl)*, William Haade *(Condor)*, Hal Taliaferro *(Bone)*, Emil Sitka *(Waiter)*, Byron

Foulger (Clerk), Monte Blue (Lt. Drake), Jack Pennick (Salty).

An uninspired action picture which has Cameron leading a search for a sunken ship full of gold. His buddy, Brown, was killed when the ship went under. Cameron finds the vessel, but it has been emptied of the gold already by Davis. After some underwater fisticuffs, Cameron learns that the treasure is hidden in Davis' hotel and brings the murderous thief to justice. Slow-moving and overrun with too many tunes sung by Booth.

p&d, Joseph Kane; w, Gerald Drayson Adams; ph, Bert Glennon (special ph, Ellis F. Thackery); m, R. Dale Butts; ed, Tony Martinelli; art d, Frank Arrigo; m/l, Jack Elliott, Nathan Scott.

Adventure (PR:A MPAA:NR)

SEA LEGS** (1930) 63m PAR bw

Jack Oakie ("Searchlight" Doyle), Lillian Roth (Adrienne), Harry Green (Gabriel Grabowski), Eugene Pallette (Hyacinth Nitouche), Jean Del Val (Crosseti), Albert Conti (Captain), Andre Cheron (High Commissioner), Charles Sellon (Adm. O'Brien), Tom Ricketts (Commander).

Oakie lives it up on board a European naval ship which is captained by a fellow with a number of lovely daughters. Romance is tossed in when Oakie goes for daughter Roth, and the comedic intrigue concerns an heir to a $2 million fortune. Silly but fun.

d, Victor Heerman; w, Marion Dix (based on the story by George Marion); ph, Allen Siegler; ed, Doris Drought.

Comedy (PR:A MPAA:NR)

SEA NYMPHS (SEE: VIOLATED PARADISE, 1963, Ital./Jap.)

SEA OF GRASS, THE**½ (1947) 131m MGM bw

Spencer Tracy (Col. Jim Brewton), Katharine Hepburn (Lutie Cameron), Melvyn Douglas (Brice Chamberlain), Robert Walker (Brock Brewton), Phyllis Thaxter (Sarah Beth Brewton), Edgar Buchanan (Jeff), Harry Carey (Doc Reid), Ruth Nelson (Selina Hall), William "Bill" Phillips (Santy), Robert Armstrong (Floyd McCurtin), James Bell (Sam Hall), Robert Barrat (Judge White), Charles Trowbridge (George Cameron), Russell Hicks (Maj. Harney), Trevor Bardette (Andy Boggs), Morris Ankrum (Crane), Dan White (Ike Randall), Glenn Strange (Bill Roach), Douglas Fowley (Joe Horton), Guy Wilkerson (Wake), Buddy Roosevelt, Earle Hodgins, Robert Bice, John Rice, Hank Worden (Cowboys), Larry Lathrop (Messenger), George Reed (Uncle Nat), Dorothy Vaughan (Mrs. Hodges), Marietta Canty (Rachael), Vernon Dent (Conductor), Erville Alderson (Station Agent), Jack Davis (Foreman), Irving Smith (Black Servant), Jessie Graves (Luke), Bernice Pilot, Myrtle Anderson, Helen Dickson, Ruth Cherrington, Laura Treadwell, Leota Lorraine (Bits), Henry Adams, Wyndham Standing, William Holmes (Gamblers), Mickey Martin (Newsboy), Joseph Crehan (Sen. Graw), John Hamilton (Forrest Cochran), John Vosper (Hotel Clerk), Bud Fine (Brakeman), Many Treaties (Indian), James O'Rear (Piano Tuner), Nora Cecil (Mrs. Ryan), Gertrude Chorre (Indian Nurse), Pat Henry (Brock at 1), Ann Gowland (Sarah Beth at 2 ½), Polly Bailey, Vangie Beolby, Margaret Bert, Naomi Childers, Rose Langdon (Women), Sid D'Albrook, Franz Dorfler, Obed "Dad" Pickard, Henry Sylvester, J. L. Palmer, Robert Malcolm, Jack Stoney, Fred Graham, Frank Hagney (Men), Frank Austin (Station Agent), Howard Mitchell (Conductor's Voice), Patty Smith (Sarah Beth at 4 ½), Duncan Richardson (Brock at 3), Frank Pharr, Bob Ingersoll (Station Loafers), Ray Teal, Eddie Acuff, Davison Clark, Joe Brockman, Rocky Wood, Fred Gilman, Dick Rush (Cattlemen), Charles Middleton (Charley), Carol Nugent (Sarah Beth at 7), Jimmie Hawkins (Brock at 5 ½), Skeets Noyes (Beady-Eyed Man), Wheaton Chambers (Dean), George Magrill, Charles McAvoy, Nolan Leary, Eddy Waller, Forrest Taylor, Gene Stutenroth, Joe Bernard, Ralph Littlefield (Homesteaders), Frank Darien (Minister), William Challee (Deputy Sheriff), Stanley Andrews (Sheriff), Dick Baron (Newsboy), Mike Donovan, Bill Van Vleck (Nestors).

At 131 minutes, this sprawling western was long on talk and short on action. The title was a definite liability and should have been changed, as not enough people had read the novel to make it an asset. Tracy had just come home from a semi-failure on the Broadway stage in Robert Sherwood's "The Rugged Path" (it ran 81 performances) and went into this film at the beginning of 1946. It took 75 days to shoot and Tracy and Kazan were at each other the entire time. When the picture was done, the studio held it back for about a year before they attempted a media blitz to hype it, but the public was hip and kept off THE SEA OF GRASS as though there was a sign warning them against it. Tracy is a tough cattle baron who owns a huge tract in the New Mexico Territory known as "The Sea of Grass." (It was actually shot near Valentine, Nebraska.) Tracy resents the intrusion of hundreds of homesteaders but loses a court case to keep them off the land. He is married to Hepburn, a sweet St. Louis woman who has borne him a lovely daughter (played at various ages by Patty Smith, Carol Nugent, Ann Gowland, and Phyllis Thaxter). Tracy becomes obsessed with keeping these interlopers out of his gray hair and eventually becomes more and more ruthless. Tracy's behavior has become illegal; Hepburn can't bear it, leaves him, and goes to Denver. There she meets Douglas, an attorney who sided with the homesteaders. Hepburn finds him attractive because of his gentle ways, the antithesis of what her husband has become. Douglas and Tracy have been

angry enemies in court and Hepburn seals that enmity by having a brief fling with Douglas, getting pregnant in the process. She goes home to Tracy and delivers a son (played at various ages by Pat Henry, Duncan Richardson, and Jimmy Hawkins). As she's giving birth, she admits that the child is by Douglas. Nevertheless, Tracy takes her back into his life. He attempts to give the little boy a good home and accept him, despite the parentage. The boy grows up to be Robert Walker and is, at best, an irresponsible youth. Tracy and Hepburn argue again and she leaves once more. Walker has problems because his history is known and slurs are tossed at him. Because of that, he fights back and gets into legal trouble. He goes to hide in the hills that surround the spread, is shot by the law, and dies in the arms of the only father he ever knew. Thaxter, now grown, persuades Hepburn to come back to Tracy at the end and the two are finally reconciled. Tracy underplays and Hepburn overacts and the twain is too far apart to meet. He spends a great deal of time contemplating the sea of grass while she struts like a peacock in her frippery and finery. (Yes, we know that it's the male bird that has all the colors, but the peahen is a plain creature and you know what we mean.) The script was far too long, had no action, and Kazan vainly attempted to breathe some life into it but he was, as yet, too inexperienced to make this effective. A tedious film that spent most of its' time on the back lot and in front of the rear screen process contraption, this was the lamest of the Tracy-Hepburn collaborations. Lots of money spent, beautiful photography, but it again proves, you can't make dichondra out of weeds.

p, Pandro S. Berman; d, Elia Kazan; w, Marguerite Roberts, Vincent Lawrence (based on the novel by Conrad Richter); ph, Harry Stradling; m, Herbert Stothart; ed, Robert J. Kern; art d, Cedric Gibbons, Paul Groesse; set d, Edwin B. Willis, Mildred Griffiths; cos, Walter Plunkett; spec eff, Arnold Gillespie, Warren Newcombe; makeup, Jack Dawn.

Western (PR:A-C MPAA:NR)

SEA OF LOST SHIPS**½ (1953) 85m REP bw

John Derek (Grad Matthews), Wanda Hendrix (Pat), Walter Brennan (Chief O'Malley), Richard Jaeckel (Hap O'Malley), Tom Tully (Capt. Holland), Barton MacLane (Capt. Matthews), Erin O'Brien-Moore (Mrs. O'Malley), Ben Cooper (3rd Crewman), Darryl Hickman (Pete Bennett), Roy Roberts (Captain of the Eagle), Tom Powers (Rear Admiral), Richard Hale (Capt. Welch), James Brown (Executive Officer), Douglas Kennedy (Copter Pilot), Steve Brodie (Lt. Rogers), John Hudson (Pilot).

A Coast Guard drama which features Brennan as a father rearing his own son, Jaeckel, as well as the orphaned Derek. Both boys enter the Coast Guard Academy to begin their training, but after a boozing brawl over Hendrix, Derek gets the boot, and loses Jaeckel's friendship. Derek works his way back to the top rung, becoming a hero to both Hendrix and his foster dad, as well as reaffirming his friendship with Jaeckel. The film makes good use of location shooting in the North Atlantic as well as stock footage supplied by the Coast Guard.

p&d, Joseph Kane; w, Steve Fisher (based on the story by Norman Reilly Raine); ph, Reggie Lanning; m, R. Dale Butts; ed, Richard L. Van Enger; art d, Frank Arrigo; spec eff, Howard Lydecker, Theodore Lydecker; m/l, "Just One Kiss," Victor Young, Ned Washington.

Drama (PR:A MPAA:NR)

SEA OF SAND (SEE: DESERT PATROL, 1962, Brit.)

SEA PIRATE, THE* (1967, Fr./Span./Ital.) 83m Edic-Arco-Balcazar/PAR c (SURCOUF, LE TIGRE DES SEPT MERS; EL TIGRE DE LOS SIETE MARES; SURCOUF L'EROE DEI SETTE MARI)

Gerard Barray (Capt. Robert Surcouf), Antonella Lualdi (Margaret Carruthers), Terence Morgan (Lord Blackwood), Genevieve Casile (Marie Catherine), Frank Oliveras (Nicolas), Armand Mestral (Capt. Fell), Gerard Tichy (Kernan), Alberto Cevenini (Garneray), Giani Esposito (Napoleon), Fernando Sancho (Jailer), Vidal Molina (Andre Chambles), Gonzalo Esquiroz (Capt. Toward), Jorge Rigaud (Admiral), Monica Randal (Josephine), Aldo Sambrell, Tomas Blanco, Rossella Bergamonti.

A swashless swashbuckler that is a mishmash of SON OF CAPTAIN BLOOD, a European product helmed by Bergonzelli and a dubbed-English language version of the same with Rowland credited as director. The Napoleonic War is the setting, as state-employed pirate Barray splits his time between saving captured islands and carrying on with Lualdi while trying to rescue his fiancee Casile. Barray is nothing more than a cardboard cut-out of Errol Flynn placed against an endless string of implausible actions and coincidences.

p, Roy Rowland; d, Sergio Bergonzelli, Rowland; w, Grandiere, Jose Antonio de la Loma, Giovanni Simonelli, Georges Farrel, Jacques Severac; ph, Juan Gelpi (Techniscope, Eastmancolor); m, Georges Garvarentz; ed, Jean-Michel Gautier; art d, Juan Alberto Soler; spec eff, John P. Fulton; m/l, "Surcouf," Georges Garvarentz, Joe Juliano (sung by Les Compagnons de la Chanson).

Adventure (PR:A MPAA:NR)

SEA RACKETEERS*   (1937) 64m REP bw

Weldon Heyburn (Jim), Jeanne Madden (Pat), Warren Hymer (Spud), Dorothy McNulty (Toots), J. Carroll Naish (Durant), Joyce Compton (Blondie), Charles Trowbridge (Maxwell Gordon), Syd Saylor (Weasel), Lane Chandler (McGrath), Benny Burt (Maxie), Ralph Sanford (Turk), Don Rowan (Lew), Bryant Washburn (Mr. Crane).

A waterlogged attempt to bring the glory of the Coast Guard to the screen, but instead the film turns out to be nothing more than an average "good guys show the bad guys who's boss" picture. Heyburn is the supposedly tough seaman who saves Madden from the murderous clutches of a gang that terrorizes a floating nightclub.

p, Armand Schaefer; d, Hamilton McFadden; w, Dorrell McGowan, Stuart McGowan; ph, Ernest Miller; ed, William Morgan; md, Alberto Colombo; m/l, Ned Washington, Sam H. Stept, Lou Handman, Walter Hirsch, Raoul Kraushaar, William Lava.

Crime/Drama   (PR:A MPAA:NR)

SEA SHALL NOT HAVE THEM, THE***   (1955, Brit.) 91m UA bw

Michael Redgrave (Air Commodore Waltby), Dirk Bogarde (Flight Sgt. Mackay), Anthony Steel (Flying Officer Treherne), Nigel Patrick (Flight Sgt. Slingsby), Bonar Colleano (Sgt. Kirby), James Kenney (Cpl. Skinner), Sydney Tafler (Capt. Robb), Ian Whittaker (Air Crewman Milliken), George Rose (Tebbitt), Victor Maddern (Gus Westover), Michael Ripper (Botterill), Gly Houston (Knox), Jack Taylor (Robinson), Michael Balfour (Dray), Paul Carpenter (Lt. Pat Boyle), Eddie Byrne (Porter), Anton Diffring (German Pilot), Rachel Kempson (Mrs. Waltby), Joan Sims (Mrs. Tebbitt), Ann Gudrun (Kirby's Fiancee), Griffith Jones (Group Commander Todd), Jack Watling (Flight Officer Harding), Guy Middleton (Squadron Leader Scott), Jack Lambert, Moultrie Kelsall, Nigel Green.

What might have been a gripping saga of men against the sea settles into being just an average story and little more. It's 1944 and a plane is making its way across the North Sea in an attempt to get back to Great Britain after a stay behind enemy lines. Aboard the Hudson airship are Redgrave, a VIP in the air force; Bogarde, the flight commander; Colleano, a sergeant; and Watling, a flying officer. Redgrave carries with him some super-secret documents that might help stop the rain of terror from the skies brought on by the Nazi rockets (updates of the infamous V-25). The aircraft is involved in a dogfight with a German plane and knocked out of the sky. It makes a forced descent and smoothly alights on the sea. The aforementioned quartet climbs aboard an inflatable raft and begins to drift. Once the plane is overdue, the Air-Sea Rescue Units sweep into action. The last third of the picture concerns the efforts to save the men and the important documents. There's the usual foul weather, a couple of abortive rescue attempts, the resignation of the victims, etc. At the conclusion, the raft drifts dangerously close to German gun emplacements on the Belgian coast and the rescuers must make a heroic effort to get in and get out before they are shot out of the sea. Needless to say, the mission is a success, as Steel and Patrick brave the shelling and the sea to effect the rescue. The suspense wasn't very much, as most of the film was predictable and not enough time was spent developing the personalities of the characters for the audience to care about them. Redgrave and Bogarde are wasted. For a better British sea story, watch IN WHICH WE SERVE. In a small role as a German pilot, note Anton Diffring, a Koblenz-born actor who played Nazis so often and so well we're surprised he wasn't tried at Nuremberg.

p, Daniel M. Angel; d, Lewis Gilbert; w, Gilbert, Vernon Harris (based on the novel by John Harris); ph, Stephen Dade; m, Malcolm Arnold; ed, Russell Lloyd; md, Muir Mathieson; art d, Bernard Robinson; spec eff, Cliff Richardson.

War/Sea Adventure   Cas.   (PR:A-C MPAA:NR)

SEA SPOILERS, THE*½   (1936) 63m UNIV bw

John Wayne (Bob Randall), Nan Grey (Connie Dawson), William Bakewell (Lt. Mays), Fuzzy Knight (Hogan), Russell Hicks (Phil Morgan), George Irving (Commander Mays), Lotus Long (Marie), Harry Worth (Nick Austin), Ernest Hilliard (Reggie), George Humbert (Hop Scotch), Ethan Laidlaw (Louie), Chester Gan (Oil), Cy Kendall (Detective), Harrison Green (Fats).

Wayne tries to prevent THE SEA SPOILERS from sinking into the ocean's depths, but even his Coast Guard persona can't do the trick. He is the skipper of a cutter who smokes out a gang of seal poachers from their hideout. They retaliate by kidnaping Grey, Wayne's girl, but the heroic skipper rescues her and stops the poachers from finishing their killing spree.

p, Trem Carr; d, Frank Strayer; w, George Waggner (based on the story by Dorrell McGowan, Stuart McGowan); ph, Archie J. Stout, John P. Fulton; ed, H.T. Fritch, Ray Lockhart; md, Herman S. Heller.

Drama   (PR:A MPAA:NR)

SEA TIGER**   (1952) 71m MON bw

John Archer (Ben McGrun), Marguerite Chapman (Jenine), Harry Lauter (Jon Edmun), Ralph Sanford (Fat Harry), Marvin Press (Quick Boy), John Mylong (Hennick), Mara Corday (Alola), Paul McGuire (Bendy), Lyle Talbot (Williams), Sam Flint (Klavier), Chad Mallory (1st Seaman), John Reese (2nd Seaman).

Archer is a sea captain who has to prove that he wasn't an agent for the Japanese during the war. When he comes into co-ownership of a freighter with Chapman, they are pitted against some crooked thiefs and an equally unlawful insurance agent who all want their hands on a shipment of jewels hidden on board. Archer comes out on top in terms of his spotted past, and his romance with Chapman. Barely average.

p, Wesley E. Barry; d, Frank McDonald; w, Sam Roeca (based on the story "Island Freighter" by Charles Yerkow); ph, John Martin; m, Edward J. Kay; ed, Ace Herman; art d, David Milton.

Drama/Adventure   (PR:A MPAA:NR)

SEA WALL, THE   (SEE: THIS ANGRY AGE, 1958, US/Ital.)

SEA WIFE**   (1957, Brit.) 82m Sumar/FOX c (GB: SEA WYF AND BISCUIT)

Joan Collins (Sea Wife), Richard Burton (Biscuit), Basil Sydney (Bulldog), Cy Grant (No. 4), Ronald Squire (Teddy), Harold Goodwin (Daily Telegraph Clerk), Joan Hickson (Scribe), Gibb McLaughlin (Club Porter), Roddy Hughes (Club Barman), Lloyd Lamble (Capt. "San Felix"), Ronald Adam (Army Padre), Nicholas Hannen (Elderly Passenger), Otokichi Ikeda (Submarine Commander), Tenji Takagi (Submarine Interpreter), Beatrice Varley (Elderly Nun), Eileen Way (Mrs. Giass), Nora Nicholson, Edith Saville, John Wood, Vilma Ann Leslie, Sandra Caron, Yvette Wyatt.

Unconvincing performances mar this desert island melodrama about four survivors of a ship torpedoed after the evacuation of Singapore by the British in 1942. Collins plays a nun; Burton, the RAF officer; Sydney, the prejudiced, atheistic business magnate; and Grant, the black purser who is referred to by a number, rather than his name. After drifting about, the four are washed up on the shore of an uncharted island. Grant gets eaten by a shark, leaving only three to try to escape on the raft Grant had built. Burton falls in love with Collins, but her devotion to God is never revealed. After the rescue, Burton searches for Collins throughout England. He passes her on the street in London, but fails to recognize her in her habit.

p, Andre Hakim; d, Bob McNaught; w, George K. Burke (based on the novel Sea-Wyf and Biscuit by J.M. Scott); ph, Ted Scaife (DeLuxe Color, CinemaScope); m, Kenneth V. Jones, Leonard Salzedo; ed, Peter Taylor; art d, Arthur Lawson; m/l, "I'll Find You" (sung by David Whitfield).

Adventure/Romance   Cas.   (PR:A MPAA:NR)

SEA WOLF, THE**½   (1930) 87m FOX bw

Milton Sills (Wolf Larson), Jane Keith (Lorna Marsh), Raymond Hackett (Allen Rand), Mitchell Harris (Death Larson), Nat Pendleton (Smoke), John Rogers (Mugridge), Harold Kinney (Leach), Harry Tenbrook (Johnson), Sam Allen (Neilson).

An able adaptation of Jack London's swashbuckling adventure novel about a sea captain (Sills) who battles the voracious appetite of the ocean with one fist, and the malevolant Harris with the other, while leaving his heart open for Keith. Michael Curtiz directed the even more spectacular remake in 1941. THE SEA WOLF proved to be the second and last talking feature for Sills, a silent screen actor known for his wide range of roles. Sills died of a heart attack at age 48 in the same year as the film's release.

d, Alfred Santell; w, Ralph Block, S.N. Behrman (based on the novel by Jack London); ph, Glen MacWilliams, William Abbott; ed, Paul Weatherwax; art d, Joseph Wright.

Adventure   (PR:A MPAA:NR)

SEA WOLF, THE****   (1941) 100m WB bw

Edward G. Robinson (Wolf Larsen), John Garfield (George Leach), Ida Lupino (Ruth Webster), Alexander Knox (Humphrey Van Weyden), Gene Lockhart (Dr. Louie Prescott), Barry Fitzgerald (Cooky), Stanley Ridges (Johnson), Francis McDonald (Svenson), David Bruce (Young Sailor), Howard da Silva (Harrison), Frank Lackteen (Smoke), Ralf Harolde (Agent), Louis Mason, Dutch Hendrian (Crew Members), Cliff Clark, William Gould (Detectives), Ernie Adams (Pickpocket), Jeanne Cowan (Singer), Wilfred Lucas (Helmsman), Ethan Laidlaw, George Magrill (Sailors), Charles Sullivan (1st Mate).

A ferryboat capsizes in a fog-shrouded sea, and the scavenger ship Ghost picks up survivors Knox—an author-scholar—and sad, sick Lupino. Captained by the brutal, callous Robinson—who rules his seagoing fiefdom both by physical might and cerebral strategies—the ship is crewed by shanghaied sailors, pressed into service in the old British way, with belaying pins and Mickey Finns, except for Garfield. The surly young sailor has signed on this ship of horror voluntarily to escape the clutches of the law. Robinson refuses to sail the two survivors to shore. Instead, he presses them both into service, telling the reluctant–but somewhat fascinated–Knox, "You're soft, like a woman. This voyage ought to do you a lot of good." To humiliate the scholar, but also to gain his company–for the cruel captain is a secret intellectual, a man who reads incessantly when closeted in his cabin alone, reads from the classics, reads poetry, reads philosophy–Robinson appoints Knox the cabin boy for the duration of the voyage. In his servitor role, Knox functions as intellectual echo sounder for Robinson, who espouses his Nietzchean superman theories–"Better to reign in Hell than to serve in Heaven"–to his captive audience of one. During one of these discourses, Robinson is suddenly seized with a blinding–a *literally* blinding–headache, which incapacitates him. He attempts to hide this weakness, both because he despises weakness, and because his condition threatens the absolute control he wields over his crew. Robinson plays the latter in the manner of a chess master rather than a ship's master, manipulating them mentally, divining their weaknesses, dividing them in order to conquer them. The toadying ship's cook, Fitzgerald, attempts to curry favor with the cruel captain who, despising this maladroit attempt at manipulation on the part of one he considers to be so far beneath him, lets the crew know of Fitzgerald's role as an informer. Shrieking for mercy, Fitzgerald is keelhauled, dropped on a rope into the sea, prey to the sharks that feasted on the scraps he dumped overboard. Fitzgerald loses a leg to an attacking shark before his shipmates retrieve his mutilated body. Sullen seaman Garfield forms an attachment to Lupino which somewhat softens his demeanor. His lost idealism partly restored, Garfield is looked to by the other sufferers as a possible unifying force in their struggle against their absolute domination by cruel captain Robinson. Lockhart, the ship's bibulous doctor, is humiliated beyond endurance by Robinson, and seeks what seems his only respite from the torment. He drunkenly, agonizingly hauls himself up the ship's masthead and leaps to his death. Scholar Knox studies Robinson, fascinated, finding him as arresting as a rattlesnake's gaze. Robinson's piercing headaches become more frequent; he cloisters himself in his cabin to conceal his periodical infirmity, of which only his attendant Knox knows. Finally, the newly unified crew members learn the true extent of their captain's problem: "HE'S BLIND!" But even without his vision, the megalomaniac ship's master is nearly a match for his adversaries, taunting them with their weaknesses, Samson-like, blind but still powerful. Cast into the shark-infested waters by the mutinous men, he survives, regaining the haven of the *Ghost*, locking himself in his cabin. Garfield, Lupino, and Knox elect to leave the ship no matter what the peril; launching a lifeboat, they escape, drifting for days, only to find themselves approaching the apparently sinking *Ghost* once again, their route a circular one. The sinister ship appears to be deserted. In desperate need of water, Garfield opts to board the vessel. When he fails to return, Knox and Lupino follow. The searching Knox finds Robinson still in his cabin, and learns from him that he has trapped Garfield, locking the latter in the vessel's galley, already low in the water, where he is certain to quickly drown. Knox attempts to leave the cabin to save his friend, but Robinson pulls a revolver, his sharpened nonvisual senses alerting him to Knox's position. Aware of his unsighted enemy's penchant for mental tussles, Knox strikes a bargain with Robinson: he will remain with him in the cabin voluntarily in return for the key to the galley which serves as Garfield's death chamber. His curiosity about Knox's motivation whetted, the captain agrees and gives the key to the scholar. Knox passes the key under the cabin door to the waiting Lupino, telling her to free Garfield and leave the sinking ship. The scholar and the mad, blind egomaniac await their mutual doom as the *Ghost* sinks ever lower into the fog-shrouded sea, their contemplative postures reflecting each one's fascination with the character of the other, each hoping to the last for revelation. Garfield and Lupino set their course for an island, redemption now a possibility for both. THE SEA WOLF contains little of the verbosity of author London's most philosophically oriented novel, yet it is true to the spirit of the book. The megalomanic madness of the ship's master–a big frog in a small confine within an enormous pond–is wonderfully expressed by the contemptuous captain in Robinson's fine portrayal. Knox's reserved performance forms a perfect foil for Robinson's sneering bombast; in his screen debut, this fine stage actor is beautifully restrained. Lupino, in her role as a loser, gives one of her best screen performances. Garfield is fine as her masculine counterpart. Supporting the leads is as laudable an assemblage of Warner Bros. stock-company character actors as has ever been assembled. Writer Rossen, required to work a romance into London's all-male work to satisfy the studio's formula, did very well at the forbidding task. His added characters–played by Garfield and Lupino–actually helped carry the substance of the story, successfully substituting for un-cinematic dialog. Warner's all-purpose director, Curtiz, does a flawless job in this location-free film, which was photographed entirely in studio tanks and set pieces. Composer Korngold's score melds well with the excellent sound effects–the constant creaking of timbers under stress, the whipping of ratlines–which create the ambience of a ship at sea. Players Lupino and Garfield had worked together in OUT OF THE FOG, released the same year. For this film, they walked *into* the fog, a thick, pervasive vapor that suffused the ship, created by the studio's brand new fog machines (making their own cinematic debut). Robinson was delighted to be able to play the part of Wolf Larsen, a role that had originally been offered to Paul Muni. As an 11-year-old immigrant boy, Robinson had sharpened his skills with a new language–English–by reading author London's novel, as serialized in *The Saturday Evening Post*, his first such experience with fiction (if we except his obsessive perusal of the Hearst newspapers of the time). In his

ghostwriter-assisted autobiography *All My Yesterdays*, Robinson stated, "I had no idea at the time that the domineering Captain Wolf Larsen was to be characterized by critics as a Nietzche superman; I just considered him to be a wonderful character. And that's how I played him, decades later." Garfield actively campaigned for his role, which had been offered to–and refused by–George Raft, who wrote producer Wallis, stating that the part was "little better than a bit." Author London was one of Garfield's heroes, and the actor prevailed on writer Rossen to agree to rewrite the role to better suit his personal screen image, whereupon the studio executives bought the strategy. (Curtiz had directed Garfield in his screen debut; producer Wallis and associate producer Henry Blanke had had those respective tasks in that picture, FOUR DAUGHTERS, released in 1938.) THE SEA WOLF is generally regarded as the finest film ever made of a Jack London story; with only a few other selected fine films, it was re-released by the studio to theaters over a 10-year period starting in 1943. The story has, to this date, been filmed six times (twice as a silent)–by Bosworth (1913), Paramount (1920), PDC (1925), Fox (1930), and the remakes BARRICADE (Warner Bros., 1950), WOLF LARSEN (AA, 1958), and WOLF LARSEN (1975, Ital.). This one remains the definitive version of the story. The picture cost more than $1 million to make, a substantial sum at the time, and it earned good returns for the studio.

p, Jack L. Warner, Hal B. Wallis; d, Michael Curtiz; w, Robert Rossen (based on the novel by Jack London); ph, Sol Polito; m, Erich Wolfgang Korngold; ed, George Amy; art d, Anton Grot; spec eff, Byron Haskin, H.F. Koenekamp.

Drama   Cas.   (PR:C MPAA:NR)

SEA WOLVES, THE***   (1981, Brit.) 120m Lorimar/PAR c

Gregory Peck (*Col. Lewis Pugh*), Roger Moore (*Capt. Gavin Stewart*), David Niven (*Col. Bill Grice*), Trevor Howard (*Jack Cartwright*), Barbara Kellermann (*Mrs. Cromwell*), Patrick MacNee (*Maj. Yogi Crossley*), Patrick Allen (*Colin MacKenzie*), Bernard Archard (*Underhill*), Martin Benson (*Montero*), Faith Brook (*Doris Grice*), Allan Cuthbertson (*Melborne*), Kenneth Griffith (*Wilton*), Donald Houston (*Hilliard*), Glyn Houston (*Peters*), Percy Herbert (*Dennison*), Patrick Holt (*Barker*), Wolf Kahler (*Trompeta*), Terence Longdon (*Malverne*), Michael Medwin (*Radcliffe*), John Standing (*Finley*), Graham Stark (*Manners*), Jack Watson (*MacLean*), Moray Watson (*Breene*), Brook Williams (*Butterworth*), Mark Zuber (*Ram Das Gupta*), George Mikell (*Capt. Rofer*), Morgan Sheppard (*Lovecroft*), Edward Dentith (*Lumsdaine*), Clifford Earl (*Sloane*), Robert Hoffmann (*U-Boat Captain*), Dan Van Husen (*1st Officer*), Jurgen Andersen (*German First Officer*), Rusi Ghandhi (*Governor*), Victor Langley (*Williamson*), Keith Stevenson (*Manuel*), Scot Finch (*Croupier*), Farid Currim (*Waiter*), Mohan Agashe (*Brothel Keeper*), Martin Grace (*Kruger*).

This attempt to return to the films of days gone by turns out to be a moderately successful wartime adventure. The voluntary members of the Calcutta Light Horse regiment come together in a mission to explode three German ships docked in a neutral Indian port. With the usual amount of intrigue, the post-draft fighters, aided by spy Kellermann, hit their destined target. There are no surprises among the cast, with only Peck's bad British accent faltering.

p, Euan Lloyd; d, Andrew V. McLaglen; w, Reginald Rose (based on the novel *The Boarding Party* by James Leasor); ph, Tony Imi (Panavision); m, Roy Budd; ed, John Glen; prod d, Syd Cain; art d, Maurice Cain; cos, Elsa Fennell; m/l, "Warsaw Concerto," Richard Addinsell.

War   Cas.   (PR:A MPAA:PG)

SEA WYF AND BUSCUIT   (SEE: SEA WIFE 1957, Brit.)

SEABO*½   (1978) 88m E.O. Corp. c (AKA: BUCKSTONE COUNTY PRISON)

Earl Owensby (*Seabo*), David Allan Coe, Don Barry, Ed Parker, Leonard Dixon, Sunset Carson, Holly Conover, Rod Sachanrnoski, Ron Lampkin.

A standard independent exploitation picture similar in some respects to BILLY JACK, with producer Owensby starring as a peaceful, but angry half-breed. He gets tough with those folks who don't take kindly to Indian blood, winds up on a chain gang, and eventually escapes when the sadistic warden plans a massacre. Owensby has produced several films in North Carolina, similar to SEABO in the use of nonactors, often locals, or performers from other fields. Here country western singer David Allen Coe is cast in a major supporting role. Other interesting cast members include former B-western stars Don "Red" Barry and Sunset Carson in small character parts. Owensby's films are made in the South and contain characters and story lines peculiar to that area of the country. For that reason they most frequently are exhibited through the southern drive-in circuit, and receive little attention elsewhere.

p, Earl Owensby; d, Jimmy Huston; w, Tom McIntyre; ph, Darrell Cathcart; m, David Allen Coe, Clay Smith, Arthur Smith; ed, Huston.

Drama   (PR:O MPAA:NR)

SEAFIGHTERS, THE　　　　(SEE: OPERATION BIKINI, 1963)

SEAGULLS OVER SORRENTO
　　　　　　(SEE: CREST OF THE WAVE, 1954, Brit.)

SEALED CARGO*　　　　　　(1951) 90m RKO bw

Dana Andrews (*Pat Bannon*), Carla Balenda (*Margaret McLean*), Claude Rains (*Skalder*), Philip Dorn (*Conrad*), Onslow Stevens (*McLean*), Skip Homeier (*Steve*), Eric Feldary (*Holger*), J.M. Kerrigan (*Skipper Ben*), Arthur Shields (*Dolan*), Morgan Farley (*Caleb*), Dave Thursby (*Ambrose*), Henry Rowland (*Anderson*), Charles A. Browne (*Smitty*), Don Dillaway (*Owen*), Al Hill (*Tom*), Lee MacGregor (*Lt. Cameron*), William Andrews (*Holtz*), Richard Norris (*2nd Mate*), Kathaleen Ellis, Karen Norris, Harry Mancke (*Villagers*), Whit Bissell (*Schuster*), Kay Morley (*Wharf Official*), Bert Kennedy (*Old Seaman*), Larry Johns (*Mark*), George Ovey, Carl Sklover (*Men*), Bessie Wade (*Woman*), Bruce Cameron, Ned Roberts (*Nazi Machine Gunners*), Dick Crockett, Bob Morgan, Wes Hopper (*Nazis*), Art Dupuis (*Bit*), Zachary Berger, Bob Smitts, John Royce (*Nazi Sailors*), Peter Bourne (*Lieutenant*), William Yetter (*German*), Geza De Rosner (*German Sub Officer*), Robert Boon (*Sailor with Rating*).

When a damaged vessel is found floating off the coast of Newfoundland, fisherman Andrews thinks he is doing the honorable thing by towing the boat ashore so it can be repaired. Only he catches a glimpse of the cargo the ship is carrying, namely torpedos and other war materials, and correctly supposes the boat is actually a supplier for Nazi U-boats hiding off the coast. It then becomes Andrews' duty to design a method of sinking the boat without destroying the entire fishing village. Overcoming the obstacles of a Nazi spy among his own crew and a female hostage in Rains' (skipper of the German boat) custody, Andrews inventively destroys the ship, adding his small part in the fight against his country's enemy. Director Werker seems more comfortable with action scenes, particularly when the German boat is blown up, than in handling drama, though Rains, and to a point Andrews, still give convincing portrayals. This was the first production under RKO head Samuel Bischoff.

p, William Duff; d, Alfred Werker; w, Dale Van Every, Oliver H.P. Garrett, Roy Huggins (based on the novel *The Gaunt Woman* by Edmund Gilligan); ph, George E. Diskant; ed, Ralph Dawson; md, C. Bakaleinikoff; art d, Albert S. D'Agostino.

War/Drama　　　　　　**(PR:A MPAA:NR)**

SEALED LIPS, 1933　　　(SEE: AFTER TOMORROW, 1933)

SEALED LIPS**　　　　　(1941) 62m UNIV bw

William Gargan (*Lee Davis*), June Clyde (*Lois Grant*), John Litel (*Mike Rofano/Fred Morton*), Anne Nagel (*Mary Morton*), Mary Gordon (*Mrs. Morton*), Ralf Harolde (*"Lips" Haggarty*), Joseph Crehan (*Dugan*), Addison Richards (*Gary Benson*), Russell Hicks (*Evans*), Ed Stanley (*Warden*), Charles Lane (*Dixon*), William Gould (*Slater*), Walter Sande (*Blake*), Joe Downing (*Trigger*), Paul Bryar (*Spike*).

Entertaining and artfully conceived picture has detective Gargan putting his wits to their maximum use in uncovering the scheme of a big-time hood (Litel) to have a double serve his prison term. The low budget does not hinder the effects of the inventive script and good performances.

p, Jack Bernhard; d&w, George Waggner; ph, Stanley Cortez; ed, Arthur Hilton.

Crime　　　　　　**(PR:A MPAA:NR)**

SEALED VERDICT**　　　　　(1948) 82m PAR bw

Ray Milland (*Maj. Robert Lawson*), Florence Marly (*Themis DeLisle*), Broderick Crawford (*Capt. Kinsella*), John Hoyt (*Gen. Otto Steigmann*), John Ridgely (*Capt. Lance Nissen*), Ludwig Donath (*Jacob Meyersohn*), Paul Lees (*Priv. Clay Hockland*), Olive Blakeney (*Camilla Cameron*), Marcel Journet (*Capt. Gribemont*), Celia Lovsky (*Emma Steigmann*), Dan Tobin (*Lt. Parker*), James Bell (*Elmer Hockland*), Elizabeth Risdon (*Cora Hockland*), Frank Conroy (*Col. Pike*), Charles Evans (*Gen. Kirkwood*), June Jeffery (*Erika Wagner*), Patricia Miller (*Maria Romanek*), Selmer Jackson (*Dr. Bossin*), Ann Doran (*Ellie Blaine*), Dorothy Granger (*Edna Brown*), John Eldredge (*Col. Macklin*), Eric Alden (*Man, M.P. in Corridor*), Archie Twitchell (*Medical Captain*), Otto Reichow (*German Soldier*), Carole Mathews (*Nurse*), Edward Van Sloan (*Priest*), Torben Meyer (*Interpreter*), Norbert Schiller (*Slava Rodal*).

An interesting but lamely executed Nazi drama about a suspected SS man (Hoyt), who Milland believes may be innocent. Even after a guilty verdict is secured, Milland, the Army prosecutor, hunts for the evidence that will save the German's skin. Marly offers her aid in proving Hoyt's innocence. As expected, a number of angry Nazi-haters throw accusations at Milland and Marly for being sympathizers, but in the end the pair are treated like heroes. This was the first U.S. film for Czechoslovakian actress Marly.

p, Robert Fellows; d, Lewis Allen; w, Jonathan Latimer (based on the novel by Lionel Shapiro); ph, Leo Tover; m, Hugo Friedhofer; ed, Alma Macrorie;

art d, Hans Dreier, John Meehan; set d, Sam Comer, Ray Moyer; cos, Mary Kay Dodson; spec eff, Gordon Jennings; process ph, Farciot Edouart; makeup, Wally Westmore.

Drama　　　　　　**(PR:A MPAA:NR)**

SEANCE ON A WET AFTERNOON**　　　(1964 Brit.) 115m
Beaver-Allied/Artixo bw

Kim Stanley (*Myra Savage*), Richard Attenborough (*Billy Savage*), Mark Eden (*Charles Clayton*), Nanette Newman (*Mrs. Clayton*), Judith Donner (*Amanda Clayton*), Patrick Magee (*Supt. Walsh*), Gerald Sim (*Sgt. Beedle*), Margaret Lacey (*Woman at 1st Seance*), Maria Kazan (*Other Woman at Seance*), Lionel Gamlin (*Man at Seances*), Marian Spencer (*Mrs. Wintry*), Ronald Hines (*Policeman at Clayton's*), Hajni Biro (*Maid at Clayton's*), Diana Lambert (*Clayton's Secretary*), Godfrey James (*Clayton's Chauffeur*), Arnold Bell (*Mr. Weaver*), Stanley Morgan (*Man in Trilby*), Michael Lees (*Plainclothes Policeman*), Margaret McGrath (*Woman at 2nd Seance*), Frank Singuineau (*Bus Conductor*).

This is one of the rare and wonderful appearances by Kim Stanley, whose film career credits could be etched on the head of a pin and have room left over for every baseball player who hit more than 50 home runs in a season. In Stanley's case, each performance on screen has been a round-tripper and this is one of her best. Forbes has written an excellent script from McShane's novel and his tense direction is as good as his dialog. Stanley is a medium who claims contact with "the other side" through her late son. The boy was stillborn but she won't discuss that and says that he manages to help her reach the beings who inhabit the nether world. Her husband, Attenborough, does his best to keep her happy, knowing well that she is walking the tightrope between insanity and rationality. He is a weak man and adores Stanley, so he can deny her nothing. Stanley would like some publicity for her flagging business, so she creates a plan she believes will do that and enlists Attenborough. It calls for him to pretend to kidnap a wealthy child, and, after the ransom money has been forwarded, Stanley will offer her services to the bereaved family and, of course, "find" the child and restore her to the parents. Attenborough nabs Donner, the daughter of industrialist Eden and his wife, Newman (Forbes' real wife off screen). In this scene, Donner is particularly good as she cowers in a locked car, while Attenborough patiently waits outside to get her. She is taken back to the Victorian house where Stanley has fixed up their dead child's room like a small hospital. Newman attends one of Stanley's seances over the disapproval of her husband. The ransom money is paid, then Donner falls ill with a fever. Attenborough is all for sending the child back to Newman and Eden right away, but Stanley announces that she's been in touch with their dead son and he wants a playmate, Stanley's indication that Attenborough must kill Donner. Instead, Attenborough takes Donner to a wooded area he knows is frequented by Boy Scouts in the hopes that she'll be found. Police officer Magee has learned about Stanley's contact with Newman and knows that many kidnapings are done by women who have lost children early in life. Armed with that modus operandi, Magee contacts Stanley and asks her to hold a senace that might help find the child. Once the session begins, Stanley falls into her trance and, instead of using the carefully prepared story she has rehearsed with Attenborough, she tells the truth and Attenborough can only stand by and watch as she falls into insanity and reveals the facts that will put her into a mental institution and Attenborough into a jail. It doesn't sound like much of a tale, but the execution is so superior that it overcomes any banality in the tale. Stanley is a revelation, going through many alterations in character, subtly changing from moment to moment, the way an irrational person often does. Her performance was good enough to secure an Oscar nomination but she lost to Julie Andrews in MARY POPPINS. Attenborough, wearing a patently false nose for some unknown reason, makes the transition here from youthful comic actor to character man. Simone Signoret was originally asked to play the role but declined, as she felt the subject was distasteful. Then Margaret Lockwood was turned down by the financiers as not having enough appeal to a general audience. Forbes rewrote the script for two men and Alec Guinness and Tom Courtenay were considered. The script was again rewritten (Forbes should know about such matters, as he once wrote a book called *The Rewrite Man*). Stanley eventually took the job despite the fact that, as a stage actress, she didn't enjoy the stop-and-start film process which doesn't allow for sustaining a characterization. Despite that, she won the New York Film Critics Best Actress Award over Andrews. Much of the film has a deliberately documentary approach and hidden cameras were used in public places. There are three seances shown and only one takes place on a wet afternoon and none are terribly exciting or important to the plot. Lots of tension and suspense although there is virtually no violence. Smaller children will be very frightened if they are imaginative.

p, Richard Attenborough, Bryan Forbes; d&w, Forbes (based on the novel by Mark McShane); ph, Gerry Turpin; m, John Barry; ed, Derek York; md, Barry; art d, Ray Simm; set d, Peter James; makeup, Stuart Freeborn.

Drama　　　　Cas.　　　　**(PR:C MPAA:NR)**

SEARCH, THE**   (1948) 105m Prasens-Film/MGM bw

Montgomery Clift (Ralph Stevenson), Aline MacMahon (Mrs. Murray), Jarmila Novotna (Mrs. Malik), Wendell Corey (Jerry Fisher), Ivan Jandl (Karel Malik), Mary Patton (Mrs. Fisher), Ewart G. Morrison (Mr. Crookes), William Rogers (Tom Fisher), Leopold Borkowski (Joel Makowsky), Claude Gambier (Raoul Dubois).

Clift was making his first movie, RED RIVER, when approached by Zinnemann to take this role. Clift read the first draft by Peter Viertel and liked it enough to commit. As it turned out, THE SEARCH was released before RED RIVER, so this was the first time his handsome face was on any screen. When Swiss producer Wechsler hired his son to help rewrite the screenplay, Clift became angered and began to substitute his own words for those in the script. Attorneys were called in to mediate the hassles and, in the end, Wechsler (fils) and co-author Schweizer, won an Oscar for a screenplay that contained many of Clift's own words. Schweizer also wrote the previous film by Wechsler (pere), a good semidocumentary named THE LAST CHANCE. THE SEARCH begins with those downtrodden children who have been left homeless and parentless by WW II and have continued to roam in the wreckage of the conflagration. They have been taken to a camp for displaced children in Germany. Jandl is a 9-year-old Czech who hasn't seen his mother since he was torn from her arms at the age of 5. He is wary of everyone at the camp because it resembles all the other camps he's lived in for the past four years. The terrible experiences have left him an amnesiac with no knowledge of his name, his background, nothing. All he can do is mutter "I don't know" in German. Jandl and some of the others fear that they will be harmed, so they escape from a Red Cross ambulance (they recall how their parents were ferried to gas chambers on trains and in buses). Jandl's hat is later found floating in the river and the authorities think he must have drowned, but he is actually living like a frightened animal in the burnt-out houses of the city while foraging for food in trash cans and anywhere else he can find a morsel. He is nearly dead of starvation when Clift, an American soldier, finds him and takes him home. Jandl is hostile, fearful, and makes attempts to leave, but Clift manages to convince the boy that he loves him and wishes him no harm as he teaches him various words in English like "tomato," meaning "pretty girl." Clift is very patient and relaxed with the damaged boy and they are soon like father and son as Jandl's defenses start to melt. Clift attempts to trace Jandl's history with the help of Corey, a pal, but it's a brick wall. Meanwhile, Jandl's mother, Novotna, is still alive and has spent the last few years trying to find her son by begging, borrowing, and stealing enough money to pay her way across Europe to visit the various camps for displaced children. She arrives at the one where Jandl had been and learns that he's drowned. She won't accept that without proof of a body and continues her search. Clift would like to arrange to take Jandl to the U.S. with him, as he presumes the boy has no living relatives. He is about to go home and arranges to place Jandl in the camp until he can finish all the paper work needed to officially adopt Jandl. MacMahon is a worker at the camp, recognizes the boy from Novotna's description, and recalls Jandl having been there. She locates Novotna, and mother and son are soon united. The happy ending occurs on a bit of circumstance, as Novotna inadvertently returns to the camp. This saccharine addition mars the essential believablity of the plot and audiences, who were wiping their eyes with lots of hankies, might have even liked it better if Novotna's character were not so wonderful and if Jandl got a new lease on life by going to the U.S. with Clift. Zinnemann and Clift received Oscar nominations and Jandl won a special juvenile Oscar for his haunting portrayal of the tragic child seeking a wisp of happiness. Jandl had been discovered singing with a youth choir in Prague, and after this picture it was just assumed that he would stay in films, but his parents voted against it and he's disappeared from sight. Zinnemann had been with MGM, then they dropped his contract while he was shooting this, so he signed with RKO. However, after the picture was released and Zinnemann's star rose, they re-signed him for a great deal more money. THE SEARCH was shot entirely in the American Occupied Zone of Germany, the first such movie to be made there after the war. With THE SEARCH and RED RIVER released the same year, Clift became a huge star and was given the Life Magazine cover for the week of December 6, 1948. Only four professional actors appeared in the movie: Clift, who was under contract to Howard Hawks; Corey, on loan from Hal Wallis; Novotna, an opera star at the Met; and MacMahon. The others were locals recruited for the job and their unfamiliar presence lent an air of credibility to the project. Clift, only 27, received $75,000 for the job and brought along his friend and mentor, Mira Rostova, who stood behind the camera and gave her approval on each scene. Zinnemann objected to this, so she stayed away but spent almost every night before shooting going over each nuance of the next day's pages. This superior movie made the world aware of the plight of these children and money poured in to UNRRA to help their plight.

p, Lazar Wechsler; d, Fred Zinnemann; w, Richard Schweizer, David Wechsler, Paul Jarrico; ph, Emil Berna; m, Robert Blum; ed, Hermann Haller; tech adv., Therese Bonney, Robert D. Mockler, Eva Landesberg.

Drama   (PR:A   MPAA:NR)

SEARCH AND DESTROY*½   (1981) 93m Eabee/Film Ventures
                                                        International c

Perry King (Kip Moore), Don Stroud (Buddy Grant), Tisa Farrow (Kate), Park Jong Soo (Assassin), George Kennedy (Anthony Fusqua), Tony Sheer (Frank Malone).

A variation on the "Let's Win Vietnam" theme which emerged in the years following America's loss. This picture has an angry Vietnamese official who was left behind by U.S. troops during an evacuation, returning to the States to get revenge. After killing two of the soldiers responsible, he ambushes the remaining pair, King and Stroud, at Niagara Falls. Stroud is paralyzed and King turns into the proverbial one-man fighting army. Mindless.

p, James Margellos; d, William Fruet; w, Don Enright; ph, Rene Verzier (DeLuxe Color); m, FM; ed, Donald Ginsberg; stunts, Buddy Joe Hooker.

Drama   (PR:C   MPAA:PG)

SEARCH FOR BEAUTY*½   (1934) 78m PAR bw

Larry "Buster" Crabbe (Don Jackson), Ida Lupino (Barbara Hilton), Toby Wing (Sally), James Gleason (Dan Healey), Robert Armstrong (Larry Williams), Gertrude Michael (Jean Strange), Roscoe Karns (Newspaper Reporter), Verna Hillie (Susie), Pop Kenton (Caretaker), Frank McGlynn, Sr (Rev. Rankin), Clara Lou Sheridan [Ann Sheridan] (Beauty Contestant), Nora Cecil, Virginia Hammond, Eddie Gribbon, Phil Dunham, Bradley Page, Del Henderson, Tammany Young.

An oddity which couldn't be saved by all the beauty in Hollywood, SEARCH FOR BEAUTY stars the unlikely pair of bodies, Crabbe and Lupino, as winners of a U.S.-British beauty pageant. The two get mixed up in a power struggle initiated by a magazine about physiques, edited by some Olympic swim team members. The money-hungry publishers want to show off more skin while the Olympians want a publication devoted to health. After the decent folk nearly get framed at the hands of the publishers, the police intervene and the magazine is saved from decadence. It's amazing what some people would pay to see. Then again, 1985 had PERFECT.

d, Erle Kenton; w, David Boehm, Maurine Watkins, Frank Butler, Claude Binyon, Sam Hellman (based on the play "Love Your Body" by Schuyler Grey, Paul Milton); ph, Harry Fischbeck; ed, James Smith; ch, Leroy Prinz; m/l, Ralph Rainger, Leo Robin.

Drama/Crime   (PR:A   MPAA:NR)

SEARCH FOR BRIDEY MURPHY, THE**   (1956) 84m PAR bw

Teresa Wright (Ruth Simmons), Louis Hayward (Morey Bernstein, Hypnotist), Nancy Gates (Hazel Bernstein), Kenneth Tobey (Rex Simmons), Richard Anderson (Dr. Deering), Tom McKee (Catlett), Janet Riley (Lois Morgan), Charles Boaz (Jerry Thomas), Lawrence Fletcher (Cranmer), Charles Maxwell (Father Bernard), Walter Kingsford (Professor), Noel Leslie (Edgar Cayce), William J. Barker (Himself), Eilene Janssen (Bridey at 15), Bradford Jackson (Brian at 17), James Kirkwood (Brian at 68), Hallene Hill (Bridey at 66), Denise Freeborn (Bridey at 8), Ruth Robinson (Bridey at 4), James Bell (Hugh Lynn Cayce), Flora Jean Engstrom, Marion Gray, Jeane Wood, HughCorcoran, Thomas P. Dillon, Dick Ryan.

Right up there with hula-hoops and flagpole sitting was the 1950s fad of hypnosis. This picture, based on a fluke best selling novel, jumped the train by casting Wright as an average housewife (the only people who would believe this gibberish). Through Hayward's hypnosis, she goes back in time to become a 19th Century Irish lass. The picture's well done, but about as believable as an issue of the National Inquirer.

p, Pat Duggan; d&w, Noel Langley (based on the book The Search For Bridey Murphy by Morey Bernstein); ph, John F. Warren (VistaVision); ed, Floyd Knudtson; md, Irvin Talbot; art d, Hal Pereira, Arthur Lonergan; cos, Edith Head; spec ph eff, John P. Fulton.

Drama/Fantasy   (PR:A   MPAA:NR)

SEARCH FOR DANGER*½   (1949) 63m Falcon/FC bw

John Calvert (Falcon), Albert Dekker (Kirk), Myrna Dell (Wilma), Ben Welden (Gregory), Douglas Fowley (Inspector), Michael Mark (Perry), Anna Cornell (Elaine), James Griffith (Cooper), Mauritz Hugo (Larry Andrews), Peter Brocco (Morris Jason), Peter Michael (Jailer), Jack Daly (Drunk), Billy Nelson (Thug).

One of the three pictures in the FALCON series which don't really have anything to do with the previous 13 George Sanders-Tom Conway vehicles. Calvert plays the debonaire private eye, hired to track a pair of gamblers who've kidnaped one of their partners and stolen $100,000. The abducted man is killed, then a second murder is committed, placing all concerned under Calvert's suspicious eye. A confusing whodunit which isn't worth the trouble of figuring out. (See FALCON series, Index.)

p&d, Jack Bernhard; w, Don Martin (based on the story by Jerome Epstein; based on the characters created by Michael Arlen); ph, Paul Ivano; m, Karl Hajos; ed, Asa Boyd Clark; art d, Boris Leven.

Mystery   (PR:A   MPAA:NR)

SEARCH FOR THE MOTHER LODE   (SEE: MOTHER LODE, 1982)

SEARCH OF THE CASTAWAYS   (SEE: IN SEARCH OF THE CASTAWAYS, 1967, US/Brit.)

SEARCHERS, THE***   (1956) 119m WB c**

John Wayne (*Ethan Edwards*), Jeffrey Hunter (*Martin Pawley*), Vera Miles (*Laurie Jorgensen*), Ward Bond (*Capt. Rev. Samuel Clayton*), Natalie Wood (*Debbie Edwards*), John Qualen (*Lars Jorgensen*), Olive Carey (*Mrs. Jorgensen*), Henry Brandon (*Chief Scar*), Ken Curtis (*Charlie McCorry*), Harry Carey, Jr. (*Brad Jorgensen*), Antonio Moreno (*Emilio Figueroa*), Hank Worden (*Mose Harper*), Lana Wood (*Debbie as a Child*), Walter Coy (*Aaron Edwards*), Dorothy Jordan (*Martha Edwards*), Pippa Scott (*Lucy Edwards*), Pat Wayne (*Lt. Greenhill*), Beulah Archuletta (*Look*), Jack Pennick (*Private*), Peter Mamakos (*Futterman*), Bill Steele (*Nesby*), Cliff Lyons (*Col. Greenhill*), Chuck Roberson (*Man at Wedding*), Ruth Clifford (*Deranged Woman at Fort*), Mae Marsh (*Woman at Fort*), Dan Borzage (*Accordionist at Funeral*), Billy Cartledge, Chuck Hayward, Slim Hightower, Fred Kennedy, Frank McGrath, Dale Van Sickel, Henry Wills, Terry Wilson (*Stuntmen*), Away Luna, Billy Yellow, Bob Many Mules, Exactly Sonnie Betsuie, Feather Hat, Jr., Harry Black Horse, Jack Tin Horn, Many Mules Son, Percy Shooting Star, Pete Grey Eyes, Pipe Line Begishe, Smile White Sheep (*Comanches*).

The darkness is broken by the door of a cabin being opened to the dry, arid wilderness that lies outside. The silhouette of a frontier woman blocks the doorway. Beyond her we see a tiny figure on a horse approaching the house. The man stops and dismounts. As he walks toward the house we see that he looks somewhat haggard, as if he's been on the trail for quite some time. His clothes are filthy. He wears a faded Confederate coat. "Ethan? Is that you, Ethan?" the woman (Jordan) asks. Jordan is joined on the porch by her husband, Coy, their two daughters, Scott, who is a teenager, and Lana Wood, who is 10, and their son, Lyden, who is in his early teens. They excitedly chant, "Uncle Ethan! Uncle Ethan!" Ethan (Wayne) has finally come home–three years after the end of the Civil War. After ushering him into the tiny, somewhat cramped cabin, the family gathers around Wayne. Jordan takes his coat and puts it in her hope chest. Wayne, who has not seen the children in years, mistakes Wood for the older Scott. "I'm Debbie!," the little girl declares as Wayne gently lifts her up to get a good look at the child who was just an infant the last time he saw her. While her uncle and father talk (and it is hinted that Wayne has robbed a few banks since the war), Wood interrupts and asks Wayne if she could have a locket like the one he gave Scott on his last visit. Instead of a locket, Wayne produces a war medal and gives it to the child. When Jordan protests giving the child such an honored item, Wayne undercuts her reservations and declares, "It don't amount to much." As the family sits down to dinner, Hunter arrives. Almost grown, Hunter is a one-eighth Cherokee boy whom Wayne had saved after the child's parents were slaughtered years before. Wayne left the boy with his brother, who has raised him as his own son. Because Hunter is part Indian, Wayne treats him as a boarder and not like one of the family. Dinner is interrupted by Bond, a reverend and captain of the Texas Rangers. With him is a small posse of Rangers who have come to enlist Coy's help in finding the cattle that Indians had driven off Qualen's nearby farm. Wayne makes Coy stay with the women while he and Hunter join the Rangers. Everyone goes outside except Bond, who stays to take one last sip of coffee. Out of the corner of his eye, he notices Jordan getting Wayne's Confederate coat out of her hope chest. She looks lovingly at the garment and strokes it gently. Wayne walks in behind Bond and Jordan goes to him. She hands him his coat and he kisses her tenderly on the forehead. Keeping his back to them, Bond stares straight ahead, fully realizing the implications of the intimate moment he has just witnessed. Wayne, Hunter, the Rangers, Qualen, his son Carey, Jr. (who is Scott's boy friend), and a slightly mad old Indian scout, Worden, race off into the desert in search of Qualen's cattle. Several miles out, the tiny band finds Qualen's prize bull dead. Wayne realizes that the cattle were stolen by the Indians as a diversion to get the men away from the cabins. Qualen's farm is closer so the majority of the men gallop off, leaving Wayne, Hunter, and Worden. Hunter immediately jumps on his horse, but Wayne tells him the horses need rest. Impatient because the lives of his family may be in danger, Hunter rides off despite Wayne's warning. Meanwhile, tension grips Coy's farmhouse. As the red sun sets, both parents sense that the house is surrounded by Indians but they put up a front of normality so as not to panic the children. Scott, however, suddenly realizes the truth and lets out a blood-curdling scream. In an attempt to spare little Wood the horror, her parents give her a blanket and her doll and send the child to hide behind her grandmother's tombstone nearby. No sooner has the child taken to her hiding place when the shadow of Comanche chief Scar (Brandon) falls across her. When Wayne and Worden finally do ride back to his brother's farm, they gallop past Hunter, whose horse has died from exhaustion. The farm is a smoldering ruin. Wayne looks inside what is left of the cabin and is horrified by what he sees. Coy, Jordan, and Lyden have all been killed and mutilated. Scott and little Wood have been kidnaped. All that is left behind of Wood is her rag doll. Wayne, Hunter, and Worden meet up with the rest of the Rangers (Qualen's home was spared) and they take off in search of the missing girls. The Rangers engage the Comanches in one brief skirmish and Bond is forced to retreat. "You want to quit, Ethan?" Bond asks. "That'll be the day," Wayne growls. Wayne, Hunter, and the grief-stricken Carey, Jr. continue the search on their own. While investigat-

ing a rock cleft, Wayne discovers Scott's raped and mutilated body. When Wayne reveals what he has seen, Carey, Jr., goes mad and rides into the nearby Comanche camp alone. He is killed instantly. Wayne and Hunter continue the search for Wood. As the months drag on, Hunter is amazed by Wayne's knowledge of the Indians and his ability to read their signs and speak their language, but comes to realize that the racist Wayne intends to kill Wood if they find her because she has by now become a squaw. After years of fruitless wandering, Wayne and Hunter return to Qualen's farm for a rest. Miles, Qualen's daughter, is thrilled to see Hunter (she's had a crush on him since they were children) and tries to persuade him to give up the search. Qualen, however, gives Wayne a letter from a trader named Futterman (Mamakos) who claims that an Indian sold him a little girl's dress. Enclosed is a piece of fabric and Hunter identifies it as Wood's. Determined to protect his sister from Wayne, Hunter leaves Miles to continue the search. Miles is heartbroken when Hunter once again rides off with Wayne and she tells him that she won't wait for him again. The searchers show up at Mamakos' trading post and ask him what he knows. The man demands a $1,000 reward and Wayne plunks down a handful of coins to pay him back for the dress, letter, and postage, saying that he'll get the rest later. Mamakos tells them that a Comanche chief named Scar has the girl. That night, Mamakos and two other men try to ambush Wayne and Hunter, but Wayne smells it coming and is forced to shoot all three in the back. The events are all detailed by Hunter who describes them in a letter to Miles which is delivered to the farm by Curtis, a bumpkin-like cowboy trying to court Miles. In addition to the killings, Hunter relates how he accidentally bought himself an Indian bride when he thought he was trading for a blanket. Miles is shocked and outraged by the news, while Curtis gleefully drives the point home by droning on in his slow, southern drawl, "So he got himself a Comanche squaw! Hawh! Hawh! Hawh!" As the letter continues, Hunter tells how the Indian woman (Archuletta) ran off when asked about chief Scar, only later to be found dead in a Comanche village whose residents were slaughtered by the U.S. Cavalry. Hunter wonders if she was trying to warn her people or help him find Wood, ending the letter with, "I guess we'll never know." At the fort Wayne and Hunter are shown three white women who were held captive by the tribe–all of them now insane–but none of them is Wood. The sight of the crazed women adds fuel to the homicidal fire burning within Wayne. The searchers then turn their attention to New Mexico Territory where they meet up with goofy Indian scout Worden again. Worden tells Wayne he has been looking for Wood during the last five years as well. A Mexican man in the bar, Moreno, overhears the conversation and declares that he knows where chief Scar is camped and will take Wayne there for a price. Finally, after five years, Wayne and Brandon face each other. Wayne and Hunter pose as traders, but they don't fool anybody. Wayne tells Brandon that he speaks "...good American for a Comanch'. Someone teach ya?" Brandon shoots back, "You speak good Comanch'–someone teach you?" While sitting in his tepee, Wayne notices the military medal he had given Wood hanging on Brandon's neck. Brandon declares that the white man had killed his sons and for vengeance he took many scalps. Brandon orders one of his wives to show his guests the lance full of scalps. As Wayne and Hunter look at the grisly trophies they glance up to see Natalie Wood (taking over for sister Lana as the older Debbie), now a young woman and in full Indian dress, holding the lance. Their search is over, but they have to bide their time before rescuing the girl. Wayne and Hunter return to their camp and agree to trade with Brandon the next day. As the pair argue over the fate of the girl, Wood runs toward them down a large sand dune. Hunter is the first to see her and he dashes to her calling her name. She speaks to him in Comanche, telling him to leave. Hunter eventually gets her to speak English. She tells him she remembers everything, "for always," but the Comanches are her people now and he must go before they kill him. At that moment Wayne, with his pistol drawn, barks for Hunter to stand aside so that he can kill Wood. Hunter refuses and shields his sister with his body. Before Wayne can pull the trigger, dozens of Comanches appear on the ridge and attack. Wayne is hit in the shoulder with an arrow and the two men barely escape with their lives. Wood returns to the Indians. Once hidden safely among the rocks, Wayne tends to his wound. Hunter viciously condemns Wayne for trying to kill Wood and even goes so far as to pull a knife on him, but he is too civilized for murder and breaks into sobs, telling Wayne, "I hope you die!" "That'll be the day," is Wayne's response. Unable to rescue Wood without assistance, Wayne and Hunter return to Qualen's farmhouse to find help. They arrive just as Miles is about to marry Curtis. The ceremony is interrupted as Miles explains to Hunter that she didn't want to end up an old maid. Hunter understands and tells her he'll leave, but she surprises him by saying, "If you do, I'll just die!" They embrace just as Curtis enters the room. The slow-witted cowboy throws down the gauntlet by declaring "I'll thank you to unhand my fie-ants- see." A comic brawl ensues between the two and the wedding is called off. Meanwhile, Bond informs Wayne that he'll have to arrest him for the murder of Mamakos and the two other men. Their departure is interrupted by a young cavalry trooper, Patrick Wayne (son of John), who brings with him the exhausted Worden, who had been captured by the Comanches but managed to escape. As they sit him in a rocking chair by the fire, Worden tells the group that he made the Indians "...think I was crazy. Chewed grass, ate dirt..." When Wayne asks where the Indians are camped Worden defiantly sneers, "Won't tell ya!" and sticks his tongue out (knowing that Wayne wants to kill Wood). The crazed old scout then turns to Hunter and tells him. Refusing to wait for the soldiers, Wayne, Hunter, Bond, and his Rangers depart. When the camp is in sight, Hunter volunteers to sneak in and rescue Wood so that she won't be killed in the ensuing cavalry charge. He finds her tent, and just as he is about to whisk Wood away, Brandon appears. Hunter whirls and shoots the Indian chief dead. The sound of gunfire sends Bond, Wayne, and the Rangers riding into the village. During the brief battle Wayne finds Brandon's dead body, and, robbed of his vengeance, he scalps the Indian. Bloody scalp in hand, Wayne mounts his horse and goes off after Wood, who has seen him and is running to the rocks for shelter. Hunter sees Wayne riding off after Wood and tries to stop him but fails. Wood almost reaches the rocks but trips and falls. Wayne rides up on her, dismounts, grabs her by the shoulders, and looks her in the eye. As she stares defiantly back at him, all his ingrained prejudice and bigotry melts and he lifts her up and cradles her in his arms: "Let's go home, Debbie," he softly tells her. Once again we look at the foreboding wilderness from inside a dark doorway. Wayne brings Wood to the porch where Qualen and Olive Carey are waiting. As the farmers bring Wood into the house, Miles runs past them and hugs Hunter. Wayne stands on the porch in front of the door looking inside. He moves to enter, but then hesitates to let Hunter and Miles walk in before him. Wayne stands alone–looking in–holding his left elbow with his right hand. He then breaks this stance, turns around, and walks back into the wilderness. The door closes, leaving the viewer in darkness. THE SEARCHERS is yet another masterpiece from a director whose resume brims with artistic triumphs. While no one but Ford could have brought this magnificent film to the screen, much of the credit deserves to go to John Wayne, who turns in the greatest performance of his career. Ethan Edwards is the most detailed and complex character ever created by the Ford-Wayne team and it is a tribute to their brilliance that THE SEARCHERS continues to show the beholder new facets upon each viewing. Ford's visual structuring of the film is flawless. The film begins with a door opening and ends with a door closing–seven years of deep emotion play out in between. Ford never limits us to the point of view of the main character. He shifts the point of view using devices like Hunter's letter to Miles so that the viewer can see several different perspectives of the same series of events. We share Bond's unease at seeing an intimate moment between brother-in-law and sister-in-law that must forever remain secret. Wayne's character is an obsessed man whose perceptions are distorted by mixed feelings of prejudice, respect, rage, fear, and love. For Ford to let the viewer just follow Wayne would limit our understanding to his confused perspective. By balancing the points of view, Ford deepens our perceptions and lets us see all aspects of the situation. The balance between drama and humor is honed to perfection as well. THE SEARCHERS is essentially a tragedy. Without passages of humor the film would have been much too grim to bear (as was the novel). However, the humor is not at all gratuitous and serves to further illuminate aspects of character. Even Wayne demonstrates a sense of irony and humor. Ford's brilliant sense of narrative structure and visual composition is still overpowered by his superb direction of actors. THE SEARCHERS is one of the tiny handful of sound films where more is told by facial expressions, physical stance, and subtle gesture than any line of dialog. Ford is a master of the unspoken emotion and his skill reaches its zenith here. Deep, complex, and detailed character insights are all beautifully conveyed through body language. It is Wayne's unspoken love for Jordan that drives him on his quest and it is the memory-jarring gesture of lifting Wood up that brings all Wayne's suppressed compassion and love for the dead Jordan flooding back. He could bring himself to shoot the girl from a distance, but physical contact with what remains of the woman he loved crumbles the hate he has been carrying with him for seven years. Ford fills in the details of Wayne's relationship with his brother's wife through the characters of Hunter and Miles. It is easy to imagine that Jordan once waited for Wayne to return, but then grew desperate for the security she knew she'd never have with him and married his stable, less complex, brother. Part of Hunter yearns for the nomadic life style of Wayne, but he is lucky enough to be able to embrace hearth and home and benefit from the fruits of civilization. The tragedy of the Wayne character in THE SEARCHERS is that America needed men like him–half man, half savage–to tame the West, but for that very reason he is unable to share in its bounty. Early in the film Wayne shoots out the eyes of an Indian corpse. Bond and his men are horrified by the apparently gratuitous act of violence, but Wayne knows that the Comanche believe that a corpse without eyes is condemned to forever "wander between the winds." Wayne lives on that thin line between savagery and civilization and because he possesses the key to both, he can never fully participate in one or the other and is condemned to wander between the winds. The West of THE SEARCHERS is one filled with such contradictions. Wayne's initial attitude toward Wood after she has been kidnaped is shared by the majority of the so-called Christian settlers but left unspoken; only Miles vocalizes it when she suggests to Hunter that Wood would be better off dead than remain "...the leavings of a Comanche buck." It takes Wayne to decide that she is worthy of salvation. Bond's character is a literal embodiment of contradiction–both reverend and military man. Both the Indians and the whites are shown capable of committing acts of compassion and savagery. There are no easy answers here, nothing as simple as good or evil. Ford does not want us to judge his West, but merely to understand it and ourselves. THE SEARCHERS is a deeply felt emotional experience that manages to be wholly entertaining as well. It is a magnificent film, and a true American masterpiece.

p, Merian C. Cooper, C.V. Whitney; d, John Ford; w, Frank S. Nugent (based on the novel by Alan LeMay); ph, Winton C. Hoch (VistaVision, Technicolor); m, Max Steiner; ed, Jack Murray; art d, Frank Hotaling, James Basevi;

set d, Victor Gangelin; cos, Frank Beetson, Ann Peck; spec eff, George Brown; m/l, title song, Stan Jones (sung by The Sons of the Pioneers).

Western   Cas.   **(PR:C MPAA:NR)**

SEARCHING WIND, THE*½   (1946) 108m PAR bw

Robert Young (*Alex Hazen*), Sylvia Sidney (*Cassie Bowman*), Ann Richards (*Emily Hazen*), Douglas Dick (*Sam*), Dudley Digges (*Moses*), Albert Basserman (*Count Von Stammer*), Dan Seymour (*Torrone*), Marietta Canty (*Sophronia*), Charles D. Brown (*Carter*), Don Castle (*David*), William Trenk (*Ponette*), Mickey Kuhn (*Sam as a Boy*), Ann Carter (*Sarah*), Dave Willock (*Male Attendant*), Fred Gierman (*Eppler*), Henry Rowland (*Capt. Heyderbreck*), Arthur Loft (*Dr. Crocker*), Frank Ferguson (*Embassy Attendant*), John Mylong (*Hotel Manager*), Eva Heyde (*Woman Customer*), Daniel De Jonghe, Adolph Freeman (*Jewish Waiters*), Albert Ferris (*German Officer*), Al Winters, Hans Hoebus (*German Agents*), Eugene Borden, Maurice Marsac (*French Reporters*), Reginald Sheffield (*Prissy Little Man*), Harry Semels (*Waiter in Madrid*), Elmer Serrano (*Spanish Major*), Jack Mulhall, Frank Arnold (*Reporters*), Louis Lowy (*French Bartender*), Norman Varden (*Mrs. Hayworth*), William Yetter, Jr, Otto Reichow, Jon Gilbreath (*German Gangsters*).

A lot of talk, albeit most of it brilliant, is what this film will be remembered for. Hellman's play of 1944 was adapted by the author for the screen and she did an even better job with the script the second time, perhaps because she'd seen what worked and what didn't work on Broadway. It takes place over many years and is the story of three generations in love and war. Young is a Europe-based U.S. diplomat, a weak-willed man who is the epitome of career government employees, in that he won't take a stand on anything and protects his position at all costs. The Italians have marched on Rome in 1922 and Mussolini is *Il Duce* Young is one of those appeaser types who thinks the political situation will go away if nobody makes waves. He doesn't realize that a firm stance must be taken, as all the Fascists understand is might. Young is married unhappily to Richards. There's nothing wrong with either of them, but there is also no passion in the relationship and he yearns for the arms of Sidney, the sharp and principled newspaperwoman he should have wed. But since Young is presented as a man who cannot make decisions, it's a sure bet that he would have chosen the wrong woman. Their illicit romance takes them through several years in many countries and serves to fuzzy up the sharp political comments the author makes. (Hellman also wrote "Watch on the Rhine," which may have been the definitive political drama of the times). Digges is Young's father, a retired publisher who can't understand how his son waffles when the world is changing, Italy is becoming a joke, and Germany is on the verge of dictatorship. Dick, Young's son, fights in the war and has to have his leg amputated, thereby triggering the best scene in the film. He gives a brilliant speech about the folly of war and says that all the blood spilled, the legs gone, the faces crushed have been for nil, because wars are made by people who never die in them. (Dick's speech is not unlike the scene in COMING HOME when the wheelchaired John Voight talks to some young men who are considering serving in Vietnam.) Basserman plays a Prussian diplomat, Young's counterpart, who hears the thunder of guns and decides to retire to neutral Switzerland at the moment when the British are giving in to Hitler at Munich. THE SEARCHING WIND is a message picture and therein lies its failure. After half a decade of war, nobody seemed to want a picture about it. War movies had been a success while the battles were raging, but peace had settled on the world and people wanted entertainment. As good as Hellman's writing and Dieterle's direction was, it was released at the wrong time. The studio knew they had a hard sell on their hands and tried to market the picture as a love triangle between Young, Richards, and Sidney but it didn't help. Digges was outstanding in the role he first did in the play. Most of the film takes place in the 1930s and it would have been a much more successful movie if made and shown at that time, when reality and fiction were blending into newspaper headlines.

p, Hal B. Wallis; d, William Dieterle; w, Lillian Hellman (based on her play); ph, Lee Garmes; m, Victor Young; ed, Warren Low; art d, Hans Dreier, Franz Bachelin; set d, Sam Comer, John McNeil; cos, Michael Woulfe, Dorothy O'Hara; spec eff, Farciot Edouart.

Drama   **(PR:A-C MPAA:NR)**

SEAS BENEATH, THE*½   (1931) 99m FOX bw

George O'Brien (*Comdr. Bob Kingsley*), Marion Lessing (*Anna-Maria Von Steuben*), Mona Maris (*Lolita*), Walter C. Kelly (*Chief Mike Costello*), Walter McGrail (*Chief Joe Cobb*), Larry Kent (*Lt. McGregor*), Gaylord Pendleton (*Ens. Dick Cabot*), Henry Victor (*Ernst Von Steuben, U-Boat Commandant*), John Loder (*Franz Schiller*), Ferdinand Schumann-Heink (*Adolph Brucker, U-Boat Engineer*), Warren Hymer (*Lug Kaufman*), William Collier, Sr (*Mugs O'Flaherty*), Nat Pendleton (*Butch Wagner*), Harry Tenbrook (*Winkler*), Terry Ray (*Reilly*), Hans Furberg (*Fritz Kampf, 2nd. Officer, U-172*), Francis Ford (*Trawler Captain*), Kurt Furberg (*Hoffman*), Ben Hall (*Harrigan*), Harry Weil (*Jevinsky*), Maurice Murphy (*Merkel*).

After MEN WITHOUT WOMEN, director John Ford, scenarist Dudley Nichols, and cameraman Joseph August teamed up again to film THE SEAS BENEATH, practically making them honorary naval officers. This time Ford adds a couple of women–Lessing as the German spy, and Maris as a spy who doubles as a singer at a waterfront night spot. O'Brien is cast as a tough officer who tries to lure a German sub into a battle, soon learning that Lessing's brother is the commander and her fiance, an officer. Gunfire eventually follows, with Lessing and her German counterparts being sent off to a prison camp. Shot off of Catalina Island, the movie called for Ford and his tight-knit crew to enlist the assistance of the U.S. Navy. The group also made use of two submarines and a mine sweeper, adding a welcome air of authenticity to the production.

d, John Ford; w, Dudley Nichols (based on the story by James Parker, Jr.); ph, Joseph H. August, ed, Frank E. Hull.

War   **(PR:A   MPAA:NR)**

SEASIDE SWINGERS*½   (1965, Brit.) 94m Fitzroy-Maycroft/EM c
                                       (GB: EVERY DAY'S A HOLIDAY)

John Leyton (*Gerry Pullman*), Michael Sarne (*Timothy Gilbin*), Freddie and The Dreamers (*The Chefs*), Ron Moody (*Prof. Bastinado*), Liz Fraser (*Miss Slightly*), Grazina Frame (*Christina Barrington De Witt*), Jennifer Baker (*Jennifer*), Susan Baker (*Susan*), The Mojos (*Themselves*), Nicholas Parsons (*Julian Goddard*), Hazel Hughes (*Mrs. Barrington De Witt*), Michael Ripper (*Mr. Pullman*), Richard O'Sullivan (*Jimmy*), Tony Daines (*Mike*), Peter Gilmore (*Kenneth*), Patrick Newell (*Mr. Hoskins*), Charles Lloyd Pack (*Mr. Close*), Gaby Vargas (*Anne*), Nicola Riley (*Little Girl*), Marion Grimaldi (*Vision Mixer*), Coral Morphew (*Serena*), The Leroys (*Themselves*), The Gillian Lynne Dancers.

A bizarre collection of kids, from rock"n"roll singers to snobby opera students to identical twins, work together to win a televised talent competition. By some cinematic miracle, the bunch takes the top prize. Includes the British pop tunes "All I Want Is You," "A Girl Needs a Boy" (Clive Westlake, Kenny Lynch), "Second Time Around" (Westlake). "Indubitably Me" (Lynch), "Love Me, Please" (Westlake, Lynch, Michael Sarne), "Now Ain't That Somethin'– Caw Blimey," "Romeo Jones" (Mort Shuman, J. Leslie McFarland), "What's Cookin'?" (Jackie Rae, Tony Osborne). Photographed by Nicolas Roeg, whose credits include several popular films of the 1960s and whose directing talent was revealed in some early 1970s films.

p, Ronald J. Kahn; d, James Hill; w, Anthony Marriott, Jeri Matos, Hill (based on the story by Marriott); ph, Nicolas Roeg (Techniscope, Technicolor); m, Tony Osborne; ed, Tristam Cones; art d, Edward Carrick; ch, Gillian Lynne.

Musical/Comedy   **(PR:AA   MPAA:NR)**

SEASON FOR LOVE, THE** (1963, Fr.) 100m Jad/Gaston Hakim bw
                                       (LA MORTE-SAISON DES AMOURS)

Daniel Gelin (*Jacques Saint-Ford*), Francoise Arnoul (*Genevieve*), Pierre Vaneck (*Sylvain*), Francoise Prevost (*Francoise*), Alexandra Stewart (*Sandra*), Anne-Marie Bauman (*Anne-Marie*), Hubert Noel (*Hubert*), Edouard Molinaro (*New Male Secretary*), Michele Verez (*Michele*), Ursula Vian (*Ursula*), Anne Colette, Claudie Bourlon, Frederic Lambre, Andre Certes, Christiane Breaud.

A fair, overly intellectual sampling of minor New Wave director Kast that tells the story of a pair of lovers–failed writer Vaneck and his newlywed wife Arnoul–living amongst ruins. When Gelin comes on the scene, Arnoul has packed her bags and is ready to leave. Before she does, though, she realizes that Vaneck still needs her. The inevitable JULES AND JIM road is taken, and the three live happily together. Released in Paris in 1961.

p, Clara d'Ovar, Peter Oser; d, Pierre Kast; w, Kast, Alain Aptekman; ph, Sacha Vierny; m, Georges Delerue; ed, Yannick Bellon; prod d, Georges Charlot; art d, Jacques Saulnier.

Drama   **(PR:A-C   MPAA:NR)**

SEASON OF PASSION***   (1961, Aus./Brit.) 93m
Hecht-Hill-Lancaster/UA bw (SUMMER OF THE SEVENTEENTH DOLL)

Ernest Borgnine (*Roo*), Anne Baxter (*Olive*), John Mills (*Barney*), Angela Lansbury (*Pearl*), Vincent Ball (*Dowd*), Ethel Gabriel (*Emma*), Janette Craig (*Bubba*), Deryck Barnes (*Spruiker*), Tom Lurich (*"The Atomic Bomber"*), Dana Wilson (*Little Girl*), Al Garcia, Al Thomas, Frank Wilson (*Cane-Cutter*), Jessica Noad (*Nancy*).

A stark drama about friendship and romance that stars Borgnine and Mills as Australian sugar cane cutters. The two spend their annual five-month vacations by heading to Sydney and carrying on with their mistresses, Baxter and Lansbury. After 16 years, however, things change–Borgnine loses his job and cannot afford his annual habit of buying Baxter a doll souvenir, while Lansbury has married and sent another woman in her place. The changes prove difficult to realize, and tensions rise between Borgnine and Mills. Finally, in an attempt to recapture their youth, Borgnine and Baxter decide to become husband and wife. A pleasant, powerfully acted surprise.

p&d, Leslie Norman; w, John Dighton (based on the play "Summer of the Seventeenth Doll" by Ray Lawler); ph, Paul Beeson; m, Benjamin Frankel;

ed, Gordon Hales; art d, Jim Morahan.

Drama/Comedy   **(PR:C   MPAA:NR)**

SEASON OF THE WITCH   (SEE: HUNGRY WIVES, 1973)

SEATED AT HIS RIGHT**   (1968, Ital.) 100m Ital Noleggio/Castoro
                                       bw (SEDUTO ALLA SUA DESTRA)

Woody Strode (*Maurice Lalubi*), Franco Citti (*Oreste*), Jean Servais (*Commander*), Pier Paolo Capponi (*Officer*), Stephen Forsyth.

Bogged down in religious symbolism, this tale of ex-Congo rebel chief Patrice Lumumba has Strode playing the Christ-like figure, here tagged Lalubi. He and his numerous armed followers are taken prisoner by mercenaries and brutally beaten; still, he finds those who are sympathetic to his beliefs. Eventually the government, upset with his rebellious nature, orders his execution and that of his followers. Strode turns in a fine performance in one of his few starring roles.

d, Valerio Zurlini; w, Zurlini, Franco Brusati; ph, Aiace Parolin; m, Ivan Vandor; ed, Franco Arcalli; art d, cos, Franco Bottari.

Biography   **(PR:O   MPAA:NR)**

SEAWEED CHILDREN, THE   (SEE: MALACHI'S COVE, 1973, Brit.)

SEBASTIAN**½   (1968, Brit.) 100m Maccius/PAR c

Dirk Bogarde (*Sebastian*), Susannah York (*Becky Howard*), Lilli Palmer (*Elsa Shahn*), John Gielgud (*Head Of Intelligence*), Margaret Johnston (*Miss Phillips*), Nigel Davenport (*Gen. Phillips*), John Ronane (*Jameson*), Susan Whitman (*Tilly*), Ann Beach (*Pamela*), Ann Sidney (*Naomi*), Veronica Clifford (*Ginny*), Jeanne Roland (*Randy*), Lyn Pickney (*Joan*), Louise Pernell (*Thelma*), Janet Munro (*Carol Fancy*), Ronald Fraser (*Toby*), Donald Sutherland (*American*), Portland Mason (*"UG" Girl*), Alan Freeman (*TV Disc Jockey*), Charles Lloyd Pack (*Chess Player*).

Bogarde shines as the title character, a mathematics wizard who is employed by the British government to decipher enemy codes. Besides his involvement with espionage, he starts up a romance with new code-breaking recruit York. Gielgud turns in his usual brilliant performance as the stout chief of the cryptography bureau. Inventive and amusing, but never really rising above the norm for long.

p, Herbert Brodkin, Michael Powell; d, David Greene; w, Gerald Vaughn-Hughes (based on a story by Leo Marks); ph, Gerry Fisher (Technicolor); m, Jerry Goldsmith; ed, Brian Smedley-Aston; prod d, Wilfrid Shingleton, art d, Fred Carter; set d, Terence Morgan II; m/l, "Here Comes the Night," Goldsmith, Hal Shaper (sung by Anita Harris); makeup, Bob Lawrence.

Spy/Comedy   **(PR:A   MPAA:NR)**

SECOND BEST BED**½   (1937, Brit.) 74m CAP/GFD bw

Tom Walls (*Victor Garnett*), Jane Baxter (*Patricia Lynton*), Veronica Rose (*Jenny Murdoch*), Carl Jaffe (*Georges Dubonnet*), Greta Gynt (*Yvonne*), Edward Lexy (*Murdoch*), Tyrell Davis (*Whittaker*), Mai Bacon (*Mrs. Whittaker*), Ethel Coleridge (*Mrs. Knuckle*), Davy Burnaby (*Lord Kingston*), Martita Hunt (*Mrs. Mather*), Gordon James (*Judge*), Charlotte Leigh, C. Denier Warren.

An enjoyable British romp which has the middle-aged, conservative Walls marrying the lively, younger Baxter. She's upset by his desire to make her a subordinate, causing her to rebel when she is expected to take the "second best bed." When he starts devoting time to a friendly girl villager, Baxter escapes to Monte Carlo with her younger friends. By the finale, however, the newlyweds reach a workable compromise.

p, Max Schach; d, Tom Walls; w, Ben Travers; ph, Jack Cox.

Comedy   **(PR:A   MPAA:NR)**

SECOND BEST SECRET AGENT IN THE WHOLE WIDE WORLD, THE*½   (1965, Brit.) 97m Ali stair/EM c (GB: LICENSED TO KILL)

Tom Adams (*Charles Vine*), Karel Stepanek (*Henrik Jacobsen, Swedish Scientist*), Veronica Hurst (*Julia Lindberg*), Peter Bull (*Masterman*), John Arnatt (*Rockwell*), Francis De Wolff (*Walter Pickering*), Felix Felton (*Tetchnikov*), George Pastell (*Russian Commissar*), Judy Huxtable (*Computer Center Girl*), Gary Hope (*Army Officer*), Denis Holmes (*Maltby*), Billy Milton (*Wilson*), Carole Blake (*Crossword Puzzle Girl*), Tony Wall (*Sadistikov*), Oliver MacGreevy (*1st Russian Commissar*), Stuart Saunders (*Police Inspector*), Paul Tann (*Vladimir Sheehee*), Shelagh Booth (*Governess*), John Evitts (*"Killer"*), Robert Marsden (*August Jacobsen*), Mona Chong (*Chinese Girl*), Michael Godfrey (*Roger*), Julian Strange (*Hotel Clerk*), Claire Gordon (*Hospital Doctor*), Sarah Maddern (*Hotel Maid*), J.A.B. Dubin-Behrmann (*Slavonic Official*).

A silly spoof on the Bond series that casts Sean Connery clone Adams in the title role, which is just as obnoxious as the character he plays. A bumbling spy who can't shoot straight, he's assigned to protect a Swedish scientist who supposedly has invented an anti-gravity device. It seems that the sneaky scientist and his late partner have sold the plans for the nonexistent device to both Russia and Great Britain. The film has a number of funny moments, but like all 007 spoofs, its time has come and gone. A title song, warbled by Sammy Davis, Jr. was added to the U.S. version. Why?

p, S.J.H. Ward; d, Lindsay Shonteff; w, Shontoff, Howard Griffiths; ph, Terry Maher (Pathe Color); ed, Ron Pope; m/l "The Second Best Secret Agent In the Whole Wide World, " Sammy Cahn, James Van Heusen (sung by Sammy Davis, Jr.)

Comedy/Spy   **(PR:A-C MPAA:NR)**

SECOND BUREAU**   (1936, Fr.) 105m C.S.F. Cie Francaise Cinematographie/World bw (DEUXIEME BUREAU)

Jean Murat (*Capt. Benoit*), Vera Korene (*Erna Flieder*), Jeanne Crispin (*Dorothee*), Jean-Max (*Comte Brusilot*), Pierre Alcover (*Weygelmann*), Pierre Magnier (*Col. Gueraud*), Georges Prieur (*Gen. Von Rauguitz*), Gildes (*An Old Stranger*), Moreau (*Nageberger*), Bonvallet (*Schaffingen*), Georges Ferney (*The Innkeeper*), Pierre Larquey (*Colleret*), Jean Galland (*Lt. Von Strammer*).

Against the backdrop of German vs. French spy intrigue, a romance between French agent Murat and German spy Crispin blossoms into marriage. Korene also shares camera time as Murat's counterpart, turning on the charm in order to get the secret information that she needs. Aptly directed and acted, but ultimately forgettable. (In French; English subtitles.)

d, Pierre Billon; w, Bernard Zimmer (based on the novel Second Bureau by Charles Robert-Dumas); ph, Marcel Lucien, Robert Asselin, Raymond Clumy; m, Jean Lenoir.

Spy/Romance   **(PR:A MPAA:NR)**

SECOND BUREAU**   (1937, Brit.) 75m Premier-Stafford/RKO bw

Marta Labarr (*Erna Fielder*), Charles Oliver (*Paul Benoit*), Arthur Wontner (*Col. Gueraud*), Meinhart Maur (*Gen. Von Rauguitz*), Joan White (*Dorothy Muller*), G.H. Mulcaster (*Yvanne Brosilow*), Bruno Barnabe (*Commissaire Of Police*), Fred Groves (*Sgt. Colleret*), Fewlass Llewellyn (*Director Of Schaffingen*), Leo Von Porkony (*Dr. Weygelmann*), Anthony Eustrel (*Lt. Von Stranmer*).

A remake of the French picture of the previous year, this version stars Oliver as the French secret agent who falls in love with German spy Labarr. She is sent to find out how the French Intelligence (aka, Second Bureau) wound up with a German invention. Instead of killing Oliver, however, she runs away with him. The couple leaves in a car which has been booby-trapped to fire a bullet into the driver when it reaches a certain velocity, but Labarr is aware of the trick. She is soon killed by a pursuing German spy and dies in the arms of Oliver.

p, John Stafford; d, Victor Hanbury; w, Akos Tolnay, Reginald Long (based on the novel Second Bureau by Charles Robert-Dumas); ph, James Wilson.

Spy/Romance   **(PR:A MPAA:NR)**

SECOND CHANCE**   (1947) 62M FOX bw

Kent Taylor (*Kendal Wolf*), Louise Currie (*Joan Summers*), Dennis Hoey (*Roger Elwood*), Larry Blake (*Detective Sgt. Sharpe*), Ann Doran (*Doris*), John Eldredge (*Conrad Martyn*), Paul Guilfoyle (*Nick*), William "Billy" Newell (*Pinky*), Guy Kingsford (*Jerry*), Charles Flynn (*Sam*), Eddie Fetherston (*Bart*), Francis Pierlot (*Montclaire*), Betty Compson (*Mrs. Davenport*), Edwin Maxwell, Michael Brandon.

Taylor and Currie team up to pull off a jewel heist, but they find that the police are always a step ahead of them. The two thieves fall in love and Currie reveals that she is a detective hired by an insurance company. She begs him to go straight and when he doesn't, she blows the whistle on him. An average, well-crafted melodrama.

p, Sol M. Wurtzel; d, James S. Tinling; w, Arnold Belgard (based on a story by Lou Breslow, John Patrick); ph, Benjamin Kline; m, Dale Butts; ed, Frank Baldridge; art d, Eddie Imazu; set d, Fay C. Babcock.

Crime/Romance   **(PR:A MPAA:NR)**

SECOND CHANCE***   (1953) 82m Edmund Grainger/RKO c

Robert Mitchum (*Russ Lambert*), Linda Darnell (*Clare Shepard*), Jack Palance (*Cappy Gordon*), Sandro Giglio (*Cable Car Conductor*), Rodolfo Hoyos, Jr (*Vasco*), Reginald Sheffield (*Mr. Woburn*), Margaret Brewster (*Mrs. Woburn*), Roy Roberts (*Charley Malloy*), Salvador Baguez (*Hernandez*), Maurice Jara (*Fernando*), Jody Walsh (*Maria*), Dan Seymour (*Felipe*), Fortunio Bonanova (*Hotel Manager*), Milburn Stone (*Edward Dawson*), Abel Fernandez (*Rivera*), Michael Tolan (*Antonio*), Richard Vera (*Pablo*), Virginia Linden (*Blonde in Bar*), Manuel Paris (*Waiter*), Eddie Gomez (*Bellhop*), Martin Garralaga (*Don Pasqual*), Jose Dominguez (*Rug Dealer*), Luis Alvares (*Hotel Clerk*), Oresta Seragnoli (*Priest*), Tony Martinez, Tina Menard, Orlando Beltran, Judy Landon, Marc Wilder, Pere Rand, Max Wagner, Ricardo Alba, Dan Bernaducci, Bob Castro, John Cliff, Henry Escalanate, Joe Herrara, Eddie Kerrant, Eddie LeBaron, David

Morales, George Navarro, Shirley Patterson, Tony Roux.

SECOND CHANCE is a 3-D movie with 2-D characterizations, the least of which is Mitchum. Presenter Howard Hughes decided that the third dimension and stereophonic sound might enhance this typical crime story and director Mate infused it with all the verve he could, but Mitchum's usual laconic performance worked against anything memorable. It was his last film for RKO (although he'd made SHE COULDN'T SAY NO earlier, it was not released until after this one) and his boredom was evident. Shot in Taxco and Cuernavaca, Mexico, it's the story of two people looking for a second chance from life. Mitchum is a boxer battling his way around Mexico and trying to forget that he once killed an opponent in the ring. Darnell is on the run because a Senate crime committee would like to find her and have her testify against her former lover, a heavyweight in crime. Palance has been sent to kill Darnell so she won't open her mouth. The two meet and she doesn't tell him her story. Love happens and they wind up on a cable car that has it's cables break. So the car sways in the wind and aboard it are Darnell, Mitchum, Palance, plus several others. It's a bang-up climax as Mitchum escapes the car by hanging from a rope. When he gets back, he has a device that will take all but one of the passengers to safety, and since the cables keep snapping, it looks like curtains for whomever is left over. There's a battle between Mitchum and Palance, with the villain falling to his death and the two lovers getting out of the cable car and into the auxiliary baskets just before the last cable snaps. The writing was good, Darnell was beautiful, Palance was his usual mean-spirited self, and sweating palms were the order of the day. It was also sent out in flat-screen format and was not nearly as effective. The final sequence looked more like the Rockies or the Andes than Mexico.

p, Sam Wiesenthal; d, Rudolph Mate; w, Oscar Millard, Sydney Boehm, D.M. Marshman, Jr. (based on a story by Marshman); ph, William E. Snyder (3-D, Technicolor); m, Roy Webb; ed, Robert Ford; md, Constantin Bakaleinikoff; art d, Albert S. D'Agostino, Carroll Clark; cos, Michael Woulfe.

Crime/Romance   Cas.   **(PR:A-C MPAA:NR)**

SECOND CHANCES   (SEE: PROBATION, 1932)

SECOND CHOICE**   (1930) 66m WB bw

Dolores Costello (*Vallery Grove*), Chester Morris (*Don Warren*), Jack Mulhall (*Owen Mallery*), Edna Murphy (*Beth Randall*), Charlotte Merriam (*Madge Harcourt*), Edward Martindel (*Herbert Satterlee*), Ethlyne Clair (*Edith Pemberton*), James Clemmons (*Ned Pemberton*), Henry Stockbridge (*Mr. Grove*), Anna Chance (*Mrs. Grove*).

A typical melodrama which has Costello and Mulhall in a tizzy after being jilted by Morris and Murphy, whom they are respectively romancing. Emotions run high, causing Morris to draw a gun on his competitor. All the confusion is finally sorted out, but not until Costello and Mulhall give the other two a run for their money.

d, Howard Bretherton; w, Joseph Jackson (based on the story by Elizabeth Alexander); ph, John Stumar; ed, Robert Crandall.

Drama   **(PR:A MPAA:NR)**

SECOND CHORUS***   (1940) 83m PAR bw

Fred Astaire (*Danny O'Neill*), Paulette Goddard (*Ellen Miller*), Burgess Meredith (*Hank Taylor*), Charles Butterworth (*Mr. Chisholm*), Artie Shaw and His Band (*Themselves*), Frank Melton (*Stu*), Jimmy Conlon (*Mr. Dunny*), Adia Kuznetzoff (*Boris*), Michael Visaroff (*Sergai*), Joseph Marievsky (*Ivan*), Don Brodie (*Hotel Clerk*), Billy Benedict (*Ticket Taker*), Ben Hall (*Western Union Boy*).

Not even the 10 tapping toes of Astaire or the 10 twinkling fingers of Artie Shaw could breathe much life into this effort. Astaire and Meredith (at ages 41 and 32) are college students who keep flunking their tests so they can stay in school and evade responsibilities. Both men are trumpeters and have a love-hate-jealousy relationship with each other. They meet Goddard who agrees to be their manager and both men begin to vie for her affections as she seeks to get them jobs with Artie Shaw and his aggregation. They leave school, get involved in a few sequences in New York, and Goddard eventually chooses Astaire to be her lawful-wedded dance partner. In real life, she selected Meredith and they were married four years later. The comedy is mild but shows that Meredith can deliver wit well, something that no one was sure of because he'd been appearing in some heavy dramas until then. Charlie Butterworth, as a wealthy patron of jazz, does a neat turn. Astaire only dances three times and not for any extended length of time, a loss to anyone who came to see him trip the light fantastic. Goddard is gorgeous, but as a dancer, she's a good actress. Astaire had many partners and Goddard ranks somewhere near the bottom, where Joan Fontaine dwells, having appeared with Astaire in DAMSEL IN DISTRESS. Songs from several writers include: the Oscar-nominated "Would You Like to Be the Love of My Life?" (Artie Shaw, Johnny Mercer, sung by Astaire), "Poor Mr. Chisholm" (Mercer, Bernie Hanighen, sung by Astaire), "(I Ain't Hep to that Step) But I'll Dig It" (Mercer, Hal Borne, sung by Astaire), "Swing Concerto" (Shaw, performed by Shaw and His Orchestra), "Sweet Sue" (Will Harris, Victor Young, performed by Shaw and His Orchestra), "I'm Yours" (E.Y. Harburg, Johnny Green). This was producer Morros' first independent production for Paramount after having done Laurel and Hardy's FLYING DEUCES. It wasn't until years later that he was revealed to have had another occupation during the war years as a secret agent for the U.S. government. He wrote a book published in 1957 titled *My Ten Years As A Counterspy* which was filmed three years later as MAN ON A STRING and starred Ernest Borgnine as the Russian-born musical director-producer-spy.

Hunter, Frank Cavett, Johnny Mercer (based on a story by Cavett); ph, Theodor Sparkuhl; ed, Jack Dennis; md, Ed Paul; art d, Boris Levin; ch, Hermes Pan.

Musical/Comedy   **(PR:A MPAA:NR)**

SECOND COMING, THE   (SEE: DEAD PEOPLE, 1974)

SECOND COMING OF SUZANNE, THE*½   (1974) 90m Barry c

Sondra Locke (*Suzanne*), Paul Sand (*Artist*), Jared Martin (*Film Maker*), Richard Dreyfuss (*Clavius*), Gene Barry (*TV Commentator*).

A well-photographed but ultimately empty and pretentious Christ-like tale which casts the unexciting Locke as the gal destined to be crucified. Includes an excess of film-within-a-film nonsense, which has become a typical trap for young, debuting filmmakers. Director Barry is the 28-year-old son of Gene Barry, whose acting is a positive contribution here.

p, Ralph Burris; exec p, Gene Barry; d&w, Michael Barry; ph, Isidore Mankofsky; m, Don Caverhill; ed, Frank Mazzola; art d, Elayne Ceder.

Drama   **Cas.**   **(PR:C MPAA:NR)**

SECOND FACE, THE*   (1950) 77m EL bw

Ella Raines (*Phyllis Holmes*), Bruce Bennett (*Paul Curtis*), Rita Johnson (*Claire Elwood*), John Sutton (*Jerry Allison*), Patricia Knight (*Lynn Hamilton*), Roy Roberts (*Allan Wesson*), Jane Darwell (*Mrs. Lockridge*), Pierre Watkin (*Mr. Hamilton*).

Raines is a grotesquely disfigured dress designer, as homely as she is ugly. After countless cold shoulders resulting from her appearance, she resorts to plastic surgery. She comes out of the operation looking like a million and hooks her employer. Not too unbelievable!

p, Edward J. Leven; d, Jack Bernhard; w, Eugene Vale; ph, Paul Ivano; m, Raoul Kraushaar; ed, Chris Nyby.

Drama   **(PR:A MPAA:NR)**

SECOND FIDDLE***   (1939) 86m Fox bw

Sonja Henie (*Trudi Hovland*), Tyrone Power (*Jimmy Sutton*), Rudy Vallee (*Roger Maxwell*), Edna May Oliver (*Aunt Phoebe Hovland*), Mary Healy (*Jean Varick*), Lyle Talbot (*Willie Hogger*), Alan Dinehart (*George "Whit" Whitney*), Minna Gombell (*Jenny*), Stewart Reburn (*Skating Partner*), Spencer Charters (*Joe Clayton*), Brian Sisters (*Specialty*), George Chandler (*Taxi Driver*), Irving Bacon (*Justice of the Peace Harvey Vaughan*), Maurice Cass (*Justice of the Peace Alex Blank*), A. S. Byron (*Bit*), Lillian Porter (*Jimmy's Girl*), Robert Lowery (*Orchestra Leader*), Charles Lane (*Voice of the Chief of the Studio*), Minerva Urecal (*Miss Bland the School Principal*), Cyril Ring (*Florist*), Dale Van Sickel (*Musician*), Ralph Brooks (*Dining Extra*), Gertrude Sutton, Fern Emmett (*Women*), Frank Coghlan, Jr (*Call Boy*), Purnell Pratt (*Abbott the Editor*), Dick Redman (*Freddie the Boy Skater*), Leyland Hodgson (*Henry the Maitre d'Hotel*), Don Douglas (*Director*), King Sisters Quartette (*Themselves*), Harold Goodwin (*Photographer*), Charles Tannen (*Assistant Director*), Charles Brokaw.

SECOND FIDDLE begins with a very amusing idea, then peters out. The huge publicity campaign to find Scarlett O'Hara is satirized as Power, a studio employee of Consolidated Pictures is given the job of mounting a huge campaign to make the public aware of the hunt for "Violet" who is to star in the new epic "Girl of the North." (The parallels are quite clear.) Boss of the studio's tub-thumping department is Dinehart and he sends Power to Minnesota to interview Henie, one of several hundred women who have applied for the role. Henie lives with her aunt, Oliver, who is not so sure she wants the comely Henie to leave the small town where she leads a quiet life as a schoolteacher. Power uses all his considerable charm to convince Oliver that Hollywood is not filled with lechers and orgiasts, and Henie is allowed to come west for a screen test. She gets the part in the picture and Power's new task is to make her a well-known item, so he creates a bogus romance between Henie and Vallee, her co star in "Girl Of The North," whose real girl, Healy, is miffed over the whole thing. The campaign will realize two goals: it will make Henie a household name and get Vallee's flagging popularity back up to snuff. Henie doesn't know that it's all for show and begins to believe that the love notes Vallee writes (all written by Power) and the daily delivery of flowers mean something. (In essence, Power is acting Cyrano to Vallee's Christian as they both woo Henie's Roxanne.) Henie has never had this kind of romantic attention and is mooning over Vallee, not knowing that in Hollywood the minute the job ends it's "I love you, honey, but the picture's over." Power has fallen for Henie and the notes he writes are sincere and touching. The movie is about to end when Healy, who has taken about as much of this as she can stand, tells Henie how she's had her

emotions abused and that it's all a ruse on the part of Vallee and Power. Henie leaves immediately and returns to Minnesota with Oliver. The picture opens and is a smash, with Henie being lauded as the greatest new star to be discovered since Alpha Centauri. Dinehart, at the behest of the barking studio chief who is never seen (existing only as a voice on the intercom), tells Power that they must have Henie back to send her out on a tour to promote the film, plus they want to sign her to a contract. If Power can't accomplish this, he's out of a job and, as the saying has often been in movies, "will never work in this town again." Meanwhile, in the little town where Henie lives, she's about to marry local yokel Bettger, a childhood swain. Power arrives just in time and admits to Henie that it was he who wrote those love letters and that he meant every word. Henie is on the fence about her feelings but Oliver convinces her niece that Power is a lovely young man, sincere about his feelings, and that she would be wise to snap him up right away. Some very funny shots at the movie Ben business and had they stayed with the satire, it might have been a Hecht-Charlie MacArthur-type movie. Instead, they opted for a mushy love story and the satire soon disappeared. Irving Berlin's songs were only adequate, and when the two stars don't sing (Power and Henie), it's not easy to sustain a musical. Tunes include: "Back to Back," "I'm Sorry for Myself," the Oscar-nominated "I Poured My Heart Into Song" (sung by Healy), "An Old-Fashioned Tune Is Always New," "When Winter Comes" (sung by Vallee), "Song of the Metronome" (sung by Henie, children's chorus, reprise by Vallee). Henie, the 1936 Olympic-Gold-Medal winner, skates a few times and does one excellent routine with Reburn. Earl Carroll's nightclub on Sunset Boulevard receives a nice plug as the place where Healy sings. The club is still there, across from the Hollywood Palladium, having gone through several changes from nightspot to TV studio to theater.

ex p, Darryl F. Zanuck; p, Gene Markey; d, Sidney Lanfield; w, Harry Tugend (based on a story by George Bradshaw); ph, Leon Shamroy; ed, Robert Simpson; md, Louis Silvers; art d, Richard Day, Hans Peter; set d, Thomas Little; cos, Royer; ch, Harry Losee.

Musical/Comedy   **(PR:A MPAA:NR)**

SECOND FIDDLE**   (1957, Brit.) 73m Association of Cinema Technicians/BL bw

Adrienne Corri (*Deborah*), Thorley Walters (*Charles*), Lisa Gastoni (*Pauline*), Richard Wattis (*Bill Turner*), Bill Fraser (*Nixon*), Aud Johansen (*Greta*), Madoline Thomas (*Fenny*), Brian Nissen (*Jack Carter*), Ryck Rydon (*Chuck*), Jill Melford (*Dolly*), Joy Webster (*Joan*), Dino Galvani (*Dino*), John Briggs (*Jimmy*), Launce Maraschal (*Pontifex*), Frederick Piper (*Potter*), Beckett Bould (*General*), Frederick Victor (*Wallace*), Christina Lubicz (*"Tahiti" Waitress*), Yah Ming (*Chinese Waiter*), Ian Whittaker (*Delivery Boy*), Dorren Dawn (*Geraldine*), Cyril Renison (*Jenkins*).

Corri and Walters are a newly married pair of ad agency employees whose post-wedding bliss must be postponed when she goes off to work in the States. Meantime, Walters falls for Gastoni, the seductive new secretary. His marriage is saved when he realizes his mistake and he decides to remain faithful to Corri.

p, Robert Dunbar; d, Maurice Elvey; w, Dunbar, Allan Mackinnon (based on a story by Dunbar, Mary Cathcart Borer); ph, Arthur Graham.

Comedy   **(PR:A MPAA:NR)**

SECOND FIDDLE TO A STEEL GUITAR** (1965) 107m Marathon c

Arnold Stang (*Jubal A. Bristol*), Pamela Hayes (*Mrs. Bristol*), Leo Gorcey, Huntz Hall (*Stagehands*), Homer and Jethro, Kitty Wells, Webb Pierce, Faron Young, Minnie Pearl, Lefty Frizzell, Sonny James, Bill Monroe, George Hamilton IV, Del Reeves, Carl Butler, Pearl Butler, Merle Kilgore, Little Jimmy Dickens, Johnnie Wright, Dottie West, Billy Walker, Connie Smith, The Cheatin' Hearts, Old Joe Clark, Delores Smiley, Marilyn Gallo, Pete Drake, Bill Phillips, Buddy Spiker, Murv Shiner, Curly Fox, Clyde Smith, Lamar Morris, Dave Lewis, Bob Perry.

Stang is put in a bind when the Italian opera company hires his wife for a benefit that cancels at the last minute. Being a fan of country music, he gathers up a number of C.W performers. Things get out of hand when Gorcey and Hall cause some confusion by dressing up in the Italians' wardrobe. Songs include: "Young Love," "Don't Let Me Cross Over," "Hello Walls," "Columbus Stockade Blues," "John Henry," "Born to Lose," "Honky Tonk Angels," "Abilene," "Ain't that a Shame," and "Careless Love."

d, Victor Duncan; w, Seymour D. Rothman; ph, Gary Galbraith, (SuperScope, Eastmancolor); m, Audrey Williams; ed, John Mullin; makeup, Allie Clayton.

Comedy/Musical   **(PR:A MPAA:NR)**

SECOND FLOOR MYSTERY, THE**   (1930) 58m WB bw

Grant Withers (*Geoffrey West*), Loretta Young (*Marian Ferguson*), H.B. Warner (*Inspector Bray*), Claire McDowell (*Aunt Hattie*), Sidney Bracey (*Alfred*), Crauford Kent (*Capt. Fraser*), John Loder (*Lt. Norman Fraser*), Claude King (*Enright*), Judith Voselli (*Mystery Woman*).

An absorbing little mystery which has Withers and Young writing to each other through a London newspaper's "personal" columns under the aliases of Lord Strawberries and Lady Grapefruit (the names come from their favorite breakfast fruit). When Withers' upstairs neighbor is found dead, the letter writers are held suspect by an inspector who really is a murderer and tries to frame them.

d, Roy Del Ruth; w, Joseph Jackson (based on the novel *The Agony Column* by Earl Derr Biggers).

Mystery/Comedy   **(PR:A   MPAA:NR)**

SECOND GREATEST SEX, THE   (1955) 87m UNIV c

Jeanne Crain (*Liza McClure*), George Nader (*Matt Davis*), Kitty Kallen (*Katy Connors*), Bert Lahr (*Job McClure*), Mamie Van Doren (*Birdie Snyder*), Keith Andes (*Rev. Peter Maxwell*), Kathleen Case (*Tilda Bean*), Paul Gilbert (*Roscoe Dobbs, traveling salesman*), Tommy Rall (*Alf Connors*), Edna Skinner (*Cassie Slater, Spinster*), Jimmy Boyd (*Newt McClure*), Cynthia May Carver (*Cousin Emmy*), The Midwesterners (*Themselves*), Ward Ellis (*Zach Bean*), Mary Marlo (*Sarah McClure*), Sheb Wooley (*Jones, City Leader*), George Wallace (*Simon Clegghorn*), Sharon Bell (*Sally McClure*).

A moderately entertaining musical, not unlike MGM's SEVEN BRIDES FOR SEVEN BROTHERS of the previous year, which centers on the feuds between the men of a little town in Kansas called Osawkie and the neighboring villages. It seems they all want to get possession of a safe full of county records. The women, however, have had enough of placing second to the men's brawling and barricade themselves in a fort, cutting off all bedroom activities. Love is more powerful than war, and the feuding stops. Songs include: "Lysistrata," "Send Us a Miracle" (sung by Keith Andes) "My Love Is Yours," "Travellin' Man," "What Good Is a Woman without a Man?" "There's Gonna Be a Wedding" (Pony Sherrell, Phil Moody), "The Second Greatest Sex" (Jay Livingston, Ray Evans, sung by Bert Lahr), "How Lonely Can I Get?" (Joan Whitney, Alex Kramer, sung by Kitty Kallen).

p, Albert J. Cohen; d, George Marshall; w, Charles Hoffman (based on the theme suggested by "Lysistrata" by Aristophanes); ph, Wilfrid M. Cline (CinemaScope, Technicolor); ed, Frank Gross; md, Joseph Gershenson; art d, Alexander Golitzen, Robert Clatworthy; cos, Jay A. Morley Jr.; ch, Lee Scott.

Musical   **(PR:A   MPAA:NR)**

SECOND-HAND HEARTS*   (1981) 102m Caribou-Northstar/PAR c
                                    (AKA: HAMSTERS OF HAPPINESS)

Robert Blake (*Loyal Muke*), Barbara Harris (*Dinette Dusty*), Collin Boone (*Human*), Amber Rose Gold (*Iota*), Jessica Stansbury, Erica Stansbury (*Sandra Dee*), Bert Remsen (*Voyd*), Sondra Blake (*Ermy*), Shirley Stoler (*Maxy*), Woodrow Chambliss (*Deaf Attendant*), Gwen Van Dam (*Waitress*), Joe Wilson (*Snake Rustler*), Louis Williams (*Carwash Employer*), James Steven Beverly (*Alton*), Spencer Quinn (*Swollen Boy*), Antonio Abeyta (*Chicano Youth*), Carol Cox (*Diesel Driver*), Beege Barkette (*Waitress*), Sherry Lowell (*Cook*), David Welch (*Cop*), Elisa Martinez (*Chicano Mother*), Ron Spivey (*God-Fearing Customer*), Kenneth Osman (*Master of Ceremonies*), Patsy Wilcox (*Cashier*), Larry Bettis (*Macon Billy*), Billie Joe Marlin (*Billie Jo*).

The only reason for anyone to see this is Haskell Wexler's sensational cinematography, which was far too good for the story, almost like putting a silk blouse on a skeleton. The original title of the film was "The Hamster of Happiness" which made about as much sense as this title. Blake and Harris are two dumb Texans who meet, fall in love, travel, and work it out. She's a terrible nightclub singer (not unlike the role she did in NASHVILLE) with a trio of young kids and he's a dull-witted car washer. They get married one night when he's had too much to drink and decide that life might be better in California. So they leave their Texas home and begin a hegira to the Golden State. They meet a few interesting people along the way (Bert Remsen, who is one of the better casting directors in Hollywood, plays a gentle shopkeeper who helps them) and eventually get to their goal. The highway scenes would have been boring without Wexler's intelligent lenses making them appear beautiful. New Jersey-born Blake and Chicago-born Harris vainly try to affect Texas accents, but they put too much into it and a great deal of the dialog is unlistenable. In a small role as Macon Billy, is former ad-man Larry Bettis, who spent years producing commercials in Hollywood, desperately wanting to be an actor, then went back to the Oklahoma city where he was born and did his first, and perhaps only, role in this forgettable exercise.

p, James William Guercio; d, Hal Ashby; w, Charles Eastman; ph, Haskell Wexler (Movielab Color); m, Willis Alan Ramsey; ed, Amy Holden Jones; prod d, Peter Wooley; art d, Richard Carter.

Romance/Comedy   **(PR:A-C   MPAA:PG)**

SECOND HAND WIFE*   (1933) 70m FOX bw (GB: THE ILLEGAL DIVORCE)

Sally Eilers (*Sandra Trumbell*), Ralph Bellamy (*Carter Cavendish*), Helen Vinson (*Betty Cavendish*), Clay Clement (*Peter Cavendish*), Karol Kay (*Patsy Cavendish*), Esther Howard (*Mrs. Trumbull*), Nella Walker (*Mrs. Cavendish*), Victor Jory (*Lotzi Vadja*), Dorothy Christy (*Rose Bray*), Ara Haswell (*Miss Curtis*), Effie Ellsler (*Mrs. Hough*).

A domestic drama with a husband and wife, Bellamy and Vinson, splitting when Eilers, Bellamy's secretary, enters the scene. Cliche after cliche, tossed in with poor technical credits, make for a low-interest production.

d&w, Hamilton MacFadden (based on the novel by Kathleen Norris); ph, Charles Clarke; ed, Alex Troffey; art d, Paul Crowley; cos, David Cox.

Drama   **(PR:A   MPAA:NR)**

SECOND HONEYMOON   (1931) 76m Continental/RAY bw

Josephine Dunn (*Mary Huntley*), Edward Earle, Ernest Hilliard, Bernice Elliott, Fern Emmett, Harry Allen, Henry Roquemore.

Dunn is married to a devoted businessman, but wants more excitement out of life. She decides to take a lover and makes a play for her hubby's best friend, planning to elope to a mountain cottage. Her lover-to-be tips off the husband, who follows Dunn to the cabin and wins her back. An amusing romantic comedy.

d, Phil Rosen; w, Harry O. Hoyt (based on the story by Ruby M. Ayres); ph, H. J. Kirkpatrick; ed, Charles Hunt.

Romance/Comedy   **(PR:A   MPAA:NR)**

SECOND HONEYMOON½   (1937) 79m FOX bw

Tyrone Power (*Raoul McLish*), Loretta Young (*Vicki*), Stuart Erwin (*Leo McTavish*), Claire Trevor (*Marcia*), Marjorie Weaver (*Joy*), Lyle Talbot (*Bob Benton*), J. Edward Bromberg (*Herbie*), Paul Hurst (*Dennis Huggins*), Jayne Regan (*Paula*), Mary Treen (*Elsie*), Hal K. Dawson (*Andy*), William Wagner (*Dr. Sneed*), Robert Kellard, Lon Chaney, Jr, Charles Tannen, Arthur Rankin, Robert Lowery, Fred Kelsey (*Reporters*), Major McBride (*Croupier*), Sarah Edwards (*Woman in Airplane*), Wade Boteler, Stanley Blystone (*Policemen*), Joseph King (*Lieutenant*), Herbert Fortier (*Lawyer*), Henry Roquemore, Alex Novinsky (*Bondsmen*), Harry Burkhardt, Thomas Pogue, Arthur Stuart Hull (*Lawyers*), Troy Brown (*Piano Player*), Phil Smalley (*Banker*), Don Marion (*Bellboy*), Phillipa Hilbere, Lillian Porter (*Telephone Operators*).

Usually dour author Phillip Wylie (The Disappearance, Opus 21, etc.) turned in a lightweight, giddy Redbook story that's given appropriate treatment by the screenwriters, director, and actors. These were the days when the rich were treated with disdain and satire by writers. Heiresses were always wealthy but unhappy, scions were forever seeking a real meaning in life, etc. Power and Young were making their fourth film together in less than a year and this wisp about infidelity is typical of the material they were given. Young has been divorced from Power because he was an irresponsible playboy who was exciting, but much too erratic for her sensibilities. So she's married Talbot, a stolid, conservative businessman who runs a large belt company. He's dull, but predictable, and that is what she evidently needs at this point in her life. While on holiday in Florida, Young meets her ex-husband and the spark that once was there ignites again, but both are attempting to deny it. Power wants to be friends with Young's husband, so he tosses a soiree in their honor and the guest list includes Young's friend, Trevor, and her husband, Bromberg. The two are Miami millionaires who spend much time being social. To indicate that he is not after Young, Power brings Weaver to the party, a pert brunette who never shuts up, taking over every conversation and being the cutest thing anyone's ever seen. Weaver is in Florida to nab a wealthy husband and makes no bones about her quest, which disturbs some of the guests at the party. Erwin is Power's valet, a man who has taken and passed almost 100 correspondence school courses but still has the personality of an otter. Weaver sees something in Erwin and their romance begins in earnest, although Young is disturbed when she sees Weaver going to the apartment on several occasions, thinking that Weaver has come to see Power. There's a fishing party aboard a boat and Talbot is pushed overboard fully clothed and towed out to sea by a sting ray that has been harpooned. Talbot gets a message that he has to go north to conclude some important business matters and leaves Young in the care of Power, never dreaming that she could have an affair with her ex-husband (it just isn't done in the best circles). Once the cat's out of the way, the mice begin to play and Power turns on his high-powered woomanship. Talbot makes several phone calls to convince Young to leave Florida but she insists on staying. He comes south and gets into a mean spat with her, and both are hauled off to Dade County Jail. After their release, Young tries to find Power and learns that he's at the local airport. When she arrives there, she sees that he is with Weaver and thinks they are going off together, but the truth is that Power is about to ferry Erwin and Weaver to the justice of the peace who will legalize their relationship. Young goes back to Talbot, resigned that she's lost Power to Weaver. It isn't long before she and Talbot are battling once more and she tells Talbot that she wants her freedom, thereby branding her a two-time loser in the marriage game at the age of 24 (which is how old she was at the time this was made). When Trevor tells her that Power did not marry Weaver, Young is thrilled, runs back to him, and in the last scene, the happy couple fly off in Power's plane for their second honeymoon. Some lovely moments, snappy dialog, terrific costumes, and lots of money lavished on production values. Great things were predicted for Weaver after scoring in this, her fifth movie and by far her largest role. It never came to pass and she spent most of her career in low-budget Fox films.

p, Darryl F. Zanuck, Raymond Griffith; d, Walter Lang; w, Kathryn Scola, Darrell Ware (based on a story by Philip Wylie); ph, Ernest Palmer; ed, Walter Thompson; md, David Buttolph; art d, Bernard Herzbrun, David Hall; set d, Thomas Little; cos, Gwen Wakeling.

Romance/Comedy   (PR:C MPAA:NR)

SECOND HOUSE FROM THE LEFT
                              (SEE: NEW HOUSE ON THE LEFT, THE,

SECOND MATE, THE*½   (1950, Brit.) 76m Elstree/ABF bw

Gordon Harker (Bill Tomkins), Graham Moffatt (Paddy), David Hannaford (Bobby), Beryl Walkley (Kate), Charles Sewell (Joe), Anne Blake (Fortune Teller), Charles Heslop (Hogan), Jane Welsh (Mrs. Mead), Howard Douglas (Dusty), Hamilton Keene, Sam Kydd, Johnnie Schofield, Pat Keogh, Pauline Drewett, Tom Fallon.

Harker stars as a barge worker who joins a gang of smugglers in the hopes of avenging his friend's murder. The gang soon figures out his real identity and kidnaps his son and second mate, Hannaford. A bomb almost kills Harker, but Hannaford's heroics save the day.

p&d, John Baxter; w, Barbara K. Emary, Jack Francis (based on the story by Anson Dyer); ph, Arthur Grant.

Crime   (PR:A MPAA:NR)

SECOND MR. BUSH, THE*½   (1940, Brit.) 56m BN/Anglo-American
                                                                        bw

Wallace Evennett (Mr. Bush), Evelyn Roberts (Maj. Dawson), Kay Walsh (Angela Windel-Todd), Derrick de Marney (Tony), Barbara Everest (Mrs. Windel-Todd), Ruth Maitland (Mrs. Bush), Kenneth Buckley (David), A. Bromley Davenport (Col. Barlow), Hal Walters (Joe), Margaret Yarde, Robert Rendel, Vi Kaley.

A stagey comedy about a millionaire (Evennett) who trades places with de Marney, a hungry author, in the hopes of finding some privacy. De Marney moves into a boarding house, where the inhabitants try to soak him for all the cash they can. Maitland, the real millionaire's wife, blows her husband's set-up by unexpectedly arriving at the boarding house. Too stiff to be anything more than mildly amusing.

p, John Corfield; d, John Paddy Carstairs; w, Doreen Montgomery, Leslie Arliss (based on the play by Stafford Dickens); ph, Jimmy Wilson.

Comedy   (PR:A MPAA:NR)

SECOND MRS. TANQUERAY, THE**½
                                   (1952, Brit.) 75m Vandyke/ABF bw

Pamela Brown (Paula Tanqueray), Hugh Sinclair (Aubrey Tanqueray), Ronald Ward (Cayley Drummle), Virginia McKenna (Ellean Tanqueray), Andrew Osborn (Capt. Ardale), Mary Hinton (Mrs. Cortellion), Peter Haddon (Sir George Orreyed), Peter Bull (Misquith), Bruce Seton (Gordon Jayne), Shelagh Frazer, Charles Perry.

An intriguing drama which stars Brown as a woman with a secret past who wants to marry Sinclair. Though Sinclair receives numerous warnings about his new love, he ignores them and goes forward with the wedding. Not only does he lose his friends, but he also has trouble keeping his own daughter's loyalty. She is the victim of constant abuse by Brown until one day it is revealed that the daughter's fiance is one of Brown's many lovers. Humiliated and broken, Brown decides to end her own life. While overly melodramatic (making Douglas Sirk look like a documentarian), this one does have its moments.

p, Roger Proudlock; d, Dallas Bower (based on a play by Arthur Wing Pinero); ph, Gerald Gibbs.

Drama   (PR:A MPAA:NR)

SECOND STORY MURDER, THE
                              (SEE: SECOND FLOOR MYSTERY, 1930)

SECOND THOUGHTS, 1938 (SEE: CRIME OF PETER FRAME, THE,
                                                            1938, Brit.)

SECOND THOUGHTS zero   (1983) 98m EMI/UNIV c

Lucie Arnaz (Amy), Craig Wasson (Will), Ken Howard (John Michael), Anne Schedeen (Janis), Arthur Rosenberg (Dr. Eastman), Peggy McCay (Dr. Martha Carpenter), Tammy Taylor (Sharon), Alan Stock (Hondo), James

O'Connell (Chief Staab), Louis Giambalvo (Sgt. Cabrillo), Alex Kubik (Officer Behncke), Charles Lampkin (Judge Richards), Michael Prince (Alfred Venable), Susan Duvall (Trudy), Larry David (Monroe Clark), Joseph Whipp (Jailer), Bert Hinchman (Deputy), Ernie Banks, Raleigh Gardenhire, Mark Anderson (Cowboys), Trinidad Silva, Gary Cervantes (Latinos), Dehl Berti (Indian), Philip L. Mead (Harry the Cop), Gene Ross (Cop), Gwen Van Dam (Matron), Ina Gould (Mrs. Devargas), Sheldon Feldner (Roger Porter), Gina Alvarado (Mrs. Padilla), Gay Rowan (Annie), Howard Vann (Bank Guard), Kim Terry (Woman Teller), Jerry Fujikawa (Yamashiro), George Maquire (VIP), Jesse Goins (Security Guard), Meg Wyllie (Mrs. Gardner), Elsa Raven (Large Nurse), Janice Carroll (Head Nurse), Haunani Minn (Scrub Nurse), Annette McCarthy (Nurse), Ralph Anderson (Intern), Joe Mantegna (Orderly), Brett Richman (Anesthesiologist), Douglas Doran (Counterman), Jon Cedar (Prosecutor), Vincent Duke Milana (Bailiff), Nancy Vawter (Court Reporter), Christina Hutter (Janey), Bumper Yothers (Phil), George Nason (Dog Owner), Gary Kanin (Head FBI Agent), Janice Sena-Shannon, Jacqueline A. Lewis (Receptionists).

A pretty pathetic melodrama starring Arnaz as a frustrated female attorney who decides to change her dull life by divorcing her stuffy husband, Howard, a banker, and then shacking up with wacked-out hippie Wasson. Eventually the sappy lawyer realizes that she's being used by the hippie just as much as by her ex-husband, and so she dumps him. Unfortunately Arnaz soon learns that she's pregnant, but since she cannot deal with Wasson for the rest of her life, she opts for abortion. Wasson, however, learns of the pregnancy, kidnaps Arnaz and holds her prisoner (he chains her to a bed]) in a tumble-down shack in the middle of the Arizona desert, with the intent of keeping her there until the baby is far enough along to prevent an abortion. The rest of the film wallows in a right-to-life debate that is neither informative, insightful nor dramatic.

p, Lawrence Turman, David Foster; d, Turman; w, Steve Brown (based on a story by Brown, Terry Louise Fisher); ph, King Baggot (Technicolor); m, Henry Mancini; ed, Neil Travis; prod d, Paul Peters; set d, Robert Goldstein, Linda DeScenna; cos, Julie Weiss.

Drama   Cas.   (PR:C MPAA:PG)

SECOND TIME AROUND, THE**½   (1961) 99m FOX c

Debbie Reynolds (Lucretia Rogers), Steve Forrest (Dan Jones), Andy Griffith (Pat Collins), Juliet Prowse (Rena, a Dancehall Girl), Thelma Ritter (Aggie), Ken Scott (Sheriff John Yoss), Isobel Elsom (Mrs. Rogers), Rudolph Acosta (Rodriguez), Timothy Carey (Bonner), Tom Greenway (Shack), Eleanor Audley (Mrs. Trask), Blossom Rock (Mrs. Collins), Tracy Stratford (Cissie), Jimmy Garrett (Tobey), Lisa Pons (Mrs. Rodriguez), Nicky Blair (Mr. Stone), Jack Orrison (Editor), Tom Fadden (Feed Store Owner), Joe Yrigoyen (Bonner's Pal).

Reynolds is a young widow who packs up her two children and moves out to Arizona in 1912 in search of a new beginning. She becomes a cowgirl, is wooed by ranchers Forrest and Griffith (Forrest wins), and eventually works her way up to sheriff, vowings vows to clean the town of all nasty varmints. Pleasant enough.

p, Jack Cummings; d, Vincent Sherman; w, Oscar Saul, Cecil Dan Hansen (based on the novel Star in the West by Richard Emery Roberts); ph, Ellis W. Carter (CinemaScope, DeLuxe Color); m, Gerald Fried; ed, Betty Steinberg; art d, Jack Martin Smith, Walter M. Simonds; set d, Walter M. Scott, Stuart A. Reiss; cos, Don Feld; m/1, title song, Henry Mancini; makeup, Ben Nye.

Western   (PR:A MPAA:NR)

SECOND WIFE**   (1930) 67m RKO bw

Conrad Nagel (Walter Fairchild), Lila Lee (Florence Wendell), Hugh Huntley (Gilbert Gaylord), Mary Carr (Mrs. Rhodes), Freddie Burke Frederick (Junior).

Despite fine performances from Lee and Nagel, SECOND WIFE is nothing but an uninspired melodrama that suffers from some contrived scripting. Lee stars as an eligible young lady who chooses to marry widower Nagel instead of Huntley, despite the latter's warnings that she'll never measure up to Nagel's first wife. It appears as if the warnings were true when Nagel leaves Lee when his young son takes ill in Switzerland. Lee, now pregnant with Nagel's child, is upset by this lack of attention, and decides to take off with former suitor Huntley. Huntley, however, wants nothing to do with the kid, and it slowly dawns on her that she should return to Nagel and her stepson. He, of course, takes her back and all is resolved. In 1936, a remake of the film by RKO starred Gertrude Michael, Walter Abel, and Erik Rhodes.

d, Russell Mack; w, Hugh Herbert, Bert Glennon (based on the play "All the King's Men" by Fulton Oursler); ph, William Marshall.

Drama   (PR:A MPAA:NR)

SECOND WIFE zero   (1936) 59m RKO bw

Gertrude Michael (*Virginia Howard*), Walter Abel (*Kenneth Carpenter*), Erik Rhodes (*Dave Bennett*), Emma Dunn (*Mrs. Brown*), Lee Van Atta (*Junior*), Florence Fair (*Mrs. Stevenson*), Brenda Fowler (*Mrs. Anderson*), Frank Reicher (*Headmaster*), George Breakston (*Jerry Stephenson*), Ward Bond, Bentley Hewlett, Edward Stanley.

For some reason only known to RKO, the studio decided to remake the overwrought and fairly weak 1930 melodrama SECOND WIFE. Failing to recognize that what little power existed in the first version was due to a pair of fine performances by the leads, RKO left the lame script alone and cast the film with equally lame actors, rendering the film totally helpless. The now all too familiar story has Michael as the young woman who marries widower Abel, only to discover that Abel cares more about his 10-year-old son from his first marriage than he does about her. He dashes off to Europe to be by the ill boy's side (in the *Hindenburg* no less), leaving her alone, frustrated, and pregnant. She gets her revenge by running around behind his back, but eventually they both see the light and reunite.

p, Lee Marcus; d, Edward Killy; w, Thomas Lennon (based on the play "All the King's Men" by Fulton Oursler); ph, Nicholas Musuraca; ed, George Crane; cos, Edward Stevenson.

Drama   (PR:A MPAA:NR)

SECOND WIND**   (1976, Can.) 92m Olympic/Ambassador c

James Naughton (*Roger*), Lindsay Wagner (*Linda*), Kenneth Pogue (*Pete*), Tedde Moore (*Paula*), Tom Harvey (*Frank*), Louis Del Grende (*Howie*), Gerard Parkes (*Packard*), Jonathan Welsh (*Simon*), Cec Linder (*Graham*), Alan Levson (*Kevin*).

The rather dull, but harmless, saga of a bored stockbroker, Naughton, who changes his routine existence by preparing himself for some competitive long distance running. Naughton decides to compete in the mile and run every day, but for some reason never really made clear, he refuses to explain to his wife, Wagner (soon to become TV's "Bionic Woman"), the importance of his obsession. The wife soon gets fed up and walks, but all works out well when the fleet-of-foot stockbroker wins both the mile-long race and the return of his bride.

p, James Margellos; d, Donald Shebib; w, Hal Ackerman; ph, Reginald Morris; m, Hagood Hardy; ed, Shebib.

Drama   (PR:A MPAA:NR)

SECOND WIND, A**   (1978, Fr.) 101m Cinepole-Janus-TFI/GAU c (UN SECOND SOUFFLE)

Robert Stack (*Francois*), Anicee Alvina (*Catherine*), Sophie Desmarets (*Helene*), Marieke Carrierre (*Sophie*), Frederic Meisner (*Marc*).

Stack stars in this minor French effort directed by former "New Wave" actor, Blain. Stack (who speaks halting French) plays a middle-aged dentist who seeks to invigorate his life by deserting his wife, Desmarets, and taking up with a young woman, played with little spunk or emotion by Alvina. Stack gets a bit upset, however, when he discovers that his mistress also has a lover closer to her own age. The swinging dentist tries to remain cool about the three-way relationship, but he eventually breaks up with the gal and tries return to his wife. At this point Desmarets is no longer interested in Stack because she has since built herself an existence without him, leaving Stack middle-aged and alone. (In French.)

d, Gerard Balin; w, Blain, Michel Perez; ph, Emmanuel Machuel (Eastmancolor); m, Jean-Pierre Stora; ed, Jean Phillipe Berger.

Drama   (PR:C MPAA:NR)

SECOND WOMAN, THE**½   (1951) 91m Harry M. Popkin/UA bw (AKA: HERE LIES LOVE; E LLEN; TWELVE MILES OUT)

Robert Young (*Jeff Cohalan*), Betsy Drake (*Ellen Foster*), John Sutton (*Keith Ferris*), Florence Bates (*Amelia Foster*), Morris Carnovsky (*Dr. Hartley*), Henry O'Neill (*Ben Sheppard*), Jean Rogers (*Dodo Ferris*), Raymond Largay (*Maj. Badger*), Shirley Ballard (*Vivian Sheppard*), Vici Raaf (*Secretary*), John Galludet (*Mac*), Jason Robards, Sr (*Stacy Rogers*), Steven Geray (*Balthazar Jones*), Jimmy Dodd (*Mr. Nelson*), Smokey Whitfield (*Porter*), Cliff Clark (*Police Sergeant*).

Psychological opus that strives to be more than it is. Young is a bright young architect given to a teetering mental state due to the loss of his fiancee the night before they were to be wed. He's staying at the home of his aunt, Bates, on a barren section of the Pacific Coast, when he tries to take his own life. His new girl friend, Drake, tells Bates that she met Young on a train while back and he told her he'd been working for real estate developer O'Neill and was engaged to his daughter, Ballard. When Ballard was killed in the car accident that also injured him slightly, Young began to have dizzy spells, total lapses of memory, and fainting incidents. Young has begun to wonder about his rationality due to several inexplicable incidents which have since taken place. Young's house is right out of Architectural Digest, a gorgeous, modern home that he planned to live in with his wife. When it burns down for no apparent cause, Young's pal, Carnovsky, a psychiatrist, thinks that

Young may have inadvertently caused the fire as well as a few other unexplained incidents because he may be suffering from guilt over Ballard's death. Drake continues to investigate and learns that Sutton, who works for O'Neill, hates Young because Ballard and Sutton were, in fact, lovers and were running off together before the alleged marriage to Young was to take place. Young had been in the car behind them, and when the accident happened, Young, in order to keep his fiancee's name unsullied, said that he was in the car with the dead woman. O'Neill, believing that lie, is the person who caused all the accidents and burned down Young's house. Drake and Young go to O'Neill and have a confrontation. O'Neill pulls a gun and says that his wife had been a tramp. (Obviously, he is confusing his late spouse with his late daughter.) Now, O'Neill's mind bends even further as he begins to think Drake is his daughter and fires the gun, hitting Young. Carnovsky escourts O'Neill to the hospital and tells Drake that this trauma will probably shock Young out of his frequent depressions. Young and Drake will be able to spend the rest of their lives together. Young is a very quiet psychotic, underplaying almost to the point of somnambulism. This actually works in the context of the film, as it is highly suspenseful and any emoting on Young's part would have destroyed the moody believability slowly built by Smith's screenplay and Kern's direction.

p, Mort Briskin, Robert Smith; d, James V. Kern; w, Smith, Briskin; ph, Hal Mohr; m, Nat W. Finston, Peter Ilyich Tchaikovsky; ed, Walter Thompson; prod d, Boris Leven; md, Joseph Nussbaum; set d, Jacques Mapes; cos, Maria Donovan; makeup, Henry Vilardo.

Thriller   Cas.   (PR:A-C MPAA:NR)

SECONDS***½   (1966) 106m PAR bw

Rock Hudson (*Antiochus "Tony" Wilson*), Salome Jens (*Nora Marcus*), John Randolph (*Arthur Hamilton*), Will Geer (*Old Man*), Jeff Corey (*Mr. Ruby*), Richard Anderson (*Dr. Innes*), Murray Hamilton (*Charlie Evans*), Karl Swenson (*Dr. Morris*), Khigh Dhiegh (*Davalo*), Frances Reid (*Emily Hamilton*), Wesley Addy (*John*), John Lawrence (*Texan*), Elisabeth Fraser (*Plump Blonde*), Dody Heath (*Sue Bushman*), Robert Brubaker (*Mayberry*), Dorothy Morris (*Mrs. Filter*), Barbara Werle (*Secretary*), Frank Campanella (*Man in Station*), Edgar Stehli (*Tailor Shop Presser*), Aaron Magidow (*Meat Man*), De De Young (*Nurse*), Francoise Ruggieri (*Girl in Boudoir*), Thom Conroy (*Dayroom Attendant*), Kirk Duncan (*Mr. Filter*), William Richard Wintersole (*Operating Room Doctor*), Tina Scala (*Young Girl*), Ned Young (*Mr. Filter*).

This film was savaged by critics but deserved much better. Looking at it today, many carpers find much to like although the holes in the story are large enough to drive a 16-wheeler through. Frankenheimer's direction is somewhat self-serving (in the cinematography and use of oddball lenses) but there is no faulting the narrative. A middle-aged banker, Randolph, is followed through Grand Central Station in New York as he goes about his routine trip to his Scarsdale home and a boring marriage to his aging wife, Reid. An unknown man slips him a note at the Station, he rides home, Reid picks him up in the family car, and they exchange banalities. Randolph later receives a call from Hamilton, a man who he thought was dead. Hamilton's call takes Randolph to the headquarters of a mysterious company headed by Geer, an old, sly Southerner. For the sum of $32,000, this company offers select individuals a second chance in life. They will arrange for an individual's "death," make certain that any survivors are taken care of, have a corpse that has been either burned or disfigured enough so identification will prove impossible, and settle the prospect into a new life, after suitable plastic surgery has altered the person's appearance. Corey is the guidance counselor who leads Randolph through until he becomes, through the miracle of medical science, a taller, trimmer Hudson. (It is here that the picture becomes unbelievable. If they had Randolph become Kirk Douglas, it might have made more sense but Hudson's 6-foot-6 height is hard to handle since Randolph, even wearing elevator shoes, is nowhere near that altitude.) Hudson emerges as a painter with a Malibu, California, home after Randolph is conveniently burned beyond recognition in a hotel fire. Hudson moves into the house with Addy as his valet, to help him adjust to the new surroundings, and a horde of paintings (executed by artist John Hunter) provided by Geer's company. He is soon part of the local scene. Hudson finds it difficult to step outside the house wearing his new face and persona. He meets Jens on the beach, not knowing that she has been sent by the company. With Jens and Addy to prod him, Hudson tosses a party to meet everyone in the neighborhood. It turns into a disaster as he drinks too much. Now he learns that all of the guests, who have been chosen by Addy, are also "seconds" and they are fearful that Hudson will betray the secret. Hudson returns to Scarsdale to see Reid, tells her that he's an old pal of Randolph's and he is surprised to see that her grieving is over though she is content to remain in widow's weeds. Hudson returns to the headquarters of the company and says that he is uncomfortable in his new face and body and he wants to be restored to the boring, although contented, life he had before. He is told that in order to have that happen, he must recommend another client, the way Hamilton did in reel one. When he can't do that, and the company won't waste a perfectly good body, Hudson is tied, gagged, and wheeled down a hall to be killed in order to provide a corpse for another client. While this happens, a nondenominational clergyman reads him the last rites. It was a fascinating premise and Hudson gives one of his best performances. Howe's camerawork was eerie, and a bit mannered (no doubt, it was under Frankenheimer's prodding). Howe was 66 at the time and had been working in movies since 1923 when he was DeMille's "slate boy" at this very same studio. The main problem with the picture was a failure to motivate Hudson's disappointment with his new existence. It was vague and did not force the picture forward. Two songs were featured, "That Old Black Magic" (Harold Arlen, Johnny Mercer) and "Love Is Just Around the Corner" (Leo Robin, Lewis E. Gensler). This is one of those movies that plays better on a small screen. It was treated so poorly at the Cannes Film Festival that Frankenheimer, who was shooting GRAND PRIX nearby, refused to go there and Hudson had to face the blistering press alone.

p, Edward Lewis; d, John Frankenheimer; w, Lewis John Carlino (based on the novel *Seconds* by David Ely); ph, James Wong Howe; m, Jerry Goldsmith; ed, Ferris Webster, David Webster; art d, Ted Haworth; set d, John Austin; makeup, Jack Petty, Mark Reedall.

Mystery/Thriller (PR:C MPAA:NR)

SECRET, THE** (1955, Brit.) 80m Laureate-Golden Era/Eros c

Sam Wanamaker (*Nick Delaney*), Mandy Miller (*Katie Martin*), Andre Morell (*Inspector Lake*), Harold Berens (*Frank Farmer*), Jan Miller (*Margaret*), Wyndham Goldie (*Dr. Scott*), Marian Spencer (*Aunt Doris*), Richard O'Sullivan (*John Martin*), Henry Caine (*Superintendent*), Aimee Delamain, John Miller.

Wanamaker, a broke American stranded in England, meets a woman who has smuggled diamonds into the country inside a stuffed teddy bear. His hope for financial assistance is shattered when she is pushed from a cliff. Naturally, Wanamaker is blamed. He finally gets his hands on the gems but loses them to a gang of crooks. By the picture's end, however, Wanamaker is able to prove his innocence and dish up the crooks to the police. Slow going, but with a couple of high moments.

p, S. Benjamin Fisz; d&w, C. Raker "Cy" Endfield (based on the play by Robert Brenon); ph, Jack Asher (Eastmancolor).

Crime (PR:A MPAA:NR)

SECRET, THE**½ (1979, Hong Kong) 100m Unique c

Sylvia Chiang (*Nurse and Victim's Friend*), Chiu Ah Chi (*Female Victim*), Tsui Siu Keung (*The Madman*), Man Chi Leung (*Male Victim*), Li Hai Suk (*Male Victim's Mistress*).

A surprisingly well directed suspense film based on an actual 1970 double-murder case in which a young medical student and his girl were found with their faces bludgeoned and tied to a tree. After the discovery of the bodies by some schoolchildren, the film winds a strange path through darkness and the supernatural until it reaches its climax, which is somewhat contrived and disappointing. (In Cantonese; English subtitles.)

p, Lo K.M., S.Y. Wu; d, Ann Hui; w, Joyce Chan; ph, C.M. Chung; m, Violet Lam; ed, C.F. Yu.

Mystery (PR:C-O MPAA:NR)

SECRET AGENT**½ (1933, Brit.) 89m BIP/Alliance bw (GB: ON SECRET SERVICE; AKA : SPY 77)

Greta Nissen (*Marchesa Marcella*), Carl Ludwig Diehl (*Hauptmann von Hombergk*), Don Alvarado (*Valenti*), Lester Matthews (*Coronello Ramenelli*), Esme Percy (*Bleuntzli*), C.M. Hallard (*Waldmuller*), Austin Trevor (*ADC Larco*), Cecil Ramage (*De Villa*), Wallace Geoffrey (*B 18*).

Set against a WW I backdrop, SECRET AGENT tells the romantic tale of an Austrian officer who becomes enamored of an Italian girl, only to discover that she is a spy. He later becomes a counter espionage officer and she gets into the habit of rescuing him from near-certain capture. A tragic end comes to the romance, however, when she gives up her own life to save his.

p, John Maxwell; d, Arthur Woods; w, Frank Vosper, Max Kimmich, Herbert Juttke, Woods (based on the novel *Spione Am Werk* by Georg Kloren, Robert Baberske); ph, Cyril Bristow, Jack Parker; ed, E.B. Jarvis.

War/Romance (PR:A MPAA:NR)

SECRET AGENT THE***½ (1936, Brit.) 83m GAU bw

Madeleine Carroll (*Elsa Carrington*), John Gielgud (*Edgar Brodie/Richard Ashenden*), Peter Lorre (*The General*), Robert Young (*Robert Marvin*), Percy Marmont (*Caypor*), Florence Kahn (*Mrs. Caypor*), Lilli Palmer (*Lilli*), Charles Carson ("*R*"), Michel Saint-Denis (*Coachman*), Andrea Malandrinos (*Manager*), Tom Helmore (*Capt. Anderson*), Michael Redgrave.

One of a string of British espionage thrillers Hitchcock directed in the mid-1930s–THE 39 STEPS preceded it in 1935 and SABOTAGE followed in 1936–and often referred to as his "spy trilogy." The film begins in England, 1916, with the funeral of war hero and famed novelist, Edgar Brodie. When the mourners finally file out, the one-armed funeral director wrestles with the coffin as he tries to move it, revealing that it is empty. Brodie, played by a dashing young Gielgud, arrives in the office of a British intelligence officer and questions why there is a photo of himself in that morning's paper, accompanied with a story of his death. The officer, Carson, who is known

only as "R," explains to Gielgud that he must go to Switzerland and terminate an enemy agent–although no one knows the identity or description of the agent. "Do you love your country?" Carson asks. Gielgud comes backs with a snappy retort, "I just died for it." Gielgud is issued a new passport, under the name Richard Ashenden, and is issued a "wife," in Carroll, also a secret agent. Also assigned to the operation is Lorre, a demented, sexually charged, professional killer with a head of curly hair and an earring, who is referred to both as "the hairless Mexican" and "the General," though he is neither. When Gielgud arrives for his first meeting with Carroll in his room at the Hotel Excelsior in Saint Moritz, he finds a talkative American, Young, munching on grapes and wooing Carroll, who is in the next room. Gielgud makes his presence known and begins his charade as Carroll's husband. Young charms his way out of the embarrassing situation and Carroll emerges from the bathroom to greet Gielgud. There is an instant intimacy between the pair, as if they'd been married for years–Carroll allowing him to see her in just a bath towel and with her face covered, unflatteringly, with cold cream. She tells Gielgud that she is a fan of his writing and explains that she became a secret agent for the thrill and the adventure–an expression of dilettantism which Gielgud doesn't seem to respect. As she pretties herself Carrol asks, "What do you think of me?" Gielgud replies, "I don't know. I'll tell you when you're done putting on your face," only to then accuse her of being vain. Gielgud's loyalty is clearly to his country, with the thought of romance lagging far behind. Lorre arrives, after "knocking and barking" at the door, and he and Gielgud follow their first clue to a small local church. As they enter, they hear a sustained organ chord filling the church. To avoid suspicion, they pretend to be parishioners, lighting candles and maintaining an aura of reverence. "Do you know any prayers?" Gielgud asks Lorre, to which the demented assassin answers, "Do not insult me." They decide to question and, if necessary, kill the organist who they believe may be their informant. When Lorre taps him on the shoulder, however, the organist slowly falls back, his hands limply coming off the keys with an unintentional, cryptic chord change as he drops to the ground. Lorre, morbidly impressed with the murder, responds in his broken English, "That's work...neat...very neat....Someone very much did not want we should speak to him." When a coat button is found clutched in the dead man's hand, Lorre realizes the murder is "not so neat after all." When someone arrives unexpectedly, Lorre and Gielgud retreat to the chapel's bell tower. The visitor finds the corpse and furiously rings the bell, deafening the two spies who cannot leave the bell tower for fear of discovery. When they finally get away, Lorre humorously complains, "I'm still blind in this ear." Later, at a casino, Gielgud and Lorre deduce that the button belongs to Marmont, a tourist traveling with his yapping dachshund. Meantime, Young continues making passes at Carroll, who also is the object of Lorre's desires. The only one who doesn't seem interested in her is her "husband," Gielgud. Upon talking with Marmont and meeting his quiet, matronly German wife Kahn (a stage actress who had never even seen a movie until Hitchcock cast her here), Lorre and Gielgud plan to murder their suspect on a climbing expedition in the Alps, while Carroll keeps Marmont's wife and dachshund occupied. Gielgud loses his nerve and stays behind while Lorre, anxious to kill, continues the ascent. Approaching the edge of a cliff, Lorre pushes Marmont to his death. Meantime, Marmont's dachsund is whipped into a wimpering frenzy, sensing its master's death. Only after the murder do they learn that they killed the wrong man, Marmont being merely an innocent vacationer. Riddled with guilt, Carroll and Gielgud plan to hand in their resignations. Lorre, however, will not allow Gielgud to quit just yet, and when Gielgud agrees to carry out his mission, Carroll takes it personally. A secret message leads Lorre and Gielgud to a chocolate factory which is used as a meeting place for German spies. They are spotted by an informer who then calls the police. Before they can be apprehended, however, Lorre and Gielgud create a diversion which allows them to slip away. A factory employee chases them down and supplies them with the identity of the spy they must kill–Young. Gielgud calls the hotel to warn Carroll of Young's identity, but it is too late–she has just left for Greece with Young, turning to him for companionship on the rebound from Gielgud. When Gielgud learns from the hotel clerk that Carroll has left with Young, he is impressed with her skills as an agent. Lorre responds by calling Carroll "the first-classest bloodhound of us all." On board the train to Greece, Carroll is unaware of the danger she is in, even when Young begins to suspect her. Luckily, Lorre and Gielgud are also on the train, and eventually find their way to Young's compartment. An edgy Lorre stands with his knife in hand, ready to plunge it into the deceptive Young, but a sudden attack on the train by British fighter pilots (a precaution ordered by British intelligence, in case Gielgud failed) causes a derailment. After a monumental crash, Young lies pinned under the wreckage near death, with Lorre, Gielgud, and Carroll safe and nearby. As Lorre sits down to rest near Young, he is shot by the dying agent and both men collapse. Newsreel footage depicts the outcome of future battles, and proves that Gielgud's operation was a success. British intelligence head Carson then receives a wire which informs him of Gielgud's and Carroll's resignation reading: "Home safely but never again, Mr. and Mrs. Asherton." A followup to Hitchcock's successful, and superior, espionage thriller, THE 39 STEPS, SECRET AGENT reunited the director with his previous film's star, Carroll, and screenwriter, Bennett; the villain of his 1934 picture THE MAN WHO KNEW TOO MUCH, Lorre; and his producers at British Gaumont, Balcon and Montagu. By adding American star Young to the cast, Hitchcock further insured success abroad. Rounding out the cast was Gielgud in the lead, who portayed a dapper, adventurous hero who still conveyed a sense of being a real person with real guilt for killing someone (though he never actually committed a murder). It is Lorre, however, who steals the show, chewing up every scene like a hyperactive child determined to raise hell. This was due more, unfortunately, to his full-blown morphine addiction than to any great acting virtuosity–an addiction which caused a certain amount of tension on the set between himself and consummate stage actor Gielgud. In spite of having Gielgud and Lorre to work with, Hitchcock found himself concentrating almost exclusively on Carroll, whose unconvincing, flighty character is the weakest of the three. As the director would so many times in his films, he became obsessed with Carroll and her on-screen appearance, pampering her at every opportunity, and yet exhibiting his manic control over her. "Nothing gives me more pleasure than to knock the lady-likeness out...," Hitchcock is quoted in Donald Spoto's biography of him. "That is why I deliberately deprived Madeleine Carroll of her dignity and glamor in THE 39 STEPS. I have done exactly the same thing with her in SECRET AGENT–in which the first shot of her you see is with her face covered with cold cream." Based on two Maugham stories (for the espionage angle) and a Dixon play (for the romance), SECRET AGENT did not perform at the box office as well as Hitchcock had hoped. Although the director has cited this film among his favorites (probably for its perverse comic touches and its not-so-hidden sexual innuendoes) he felt that its fault was in having a main character with whom the audience could not identify and said, "In an adventure drama your central figure must have a purpose...that's vital for the progression of the film, and it's also a key factor in audience participation. The public must be rooting for the character; they should almost be helping him to achieve his goal. In SECRET AGENT, John Gielgud has an assignment, but the job is distasteful and he is reluctant to do it." SECRET AGENT also marked a rarity for Hitchcock–being pressured into changing an ending. Originally, after the train wreck, Lorre was to have given the injured and thirsty Young a drink from his flask, a humane gesture which is quickly erased when Lorre shoots and kills the agent. This was apparently too cold-blooded and fearing the negative reaction to American Young being murdered, censors requested an alteration and Hitchcock complied. One other change occurred during a preview screening in which London-based animator Len Lye (who had, in 1934, invented a technique for painting directly on film) had created, for the train crash scene, a piece of brightly colored film which was to make it appear as if the film itself had burst into flames. Proving too much of a distraction, the effect was eliminated.

p, Michael Balcon, Ivor Montagu; d, Alfred Hitchcock; w, Charles Bennett, Ian Hay, Jesse Lasky, Jr., Alma Reville (based on the play by Campbell Dixon, from the stories "Triton" and "The Hairless Mexican" in the book *Ashenden* by W. Somerset Maugham); ph, Bernard Knowles; m, Louis Levy; ed, Charles Frend; set d, Otto Werndorff, Albert Julian; cos, J. Strasser.

Spy Drama   **Cas.**   **(PR:C MPAA:NR)**

SECRET AGENT FIREBALL**   (1965, Fr./Ital.) 89m
Nike-Devon-Radius/AIP c (LES ESPI ONS MEURENT A BEYROUTH;
LE SPIE UCCIDONO A BEIRUT; AKA: KILLERS ARE CHAL-
LENGED)

Richard Harrison (*Robert Fleming*), Dominique Boschero (*Liz*), Wandisa Guida (*Elena*), Alcide Borik (*Taxi Driver*), Jim Clay (*Aldo Cecconi*), Alan Collins [Luciano Pigozzi] (*Russian Agents*), Audry Fisher, Franklyn Fred, Clement Harari, Caroll Brown [Bruno Carotenuto], Jean Ozenne, Freddy Unger.

American CIA agent Harrison is hot on the trail of some highly important microfilm that was smuggled over from Russia by two brave, but now dead, scientists who attempted to defect. The microfilm found its way into the hands of a Lebanese financier, but he too is killed, leaving Harrison to convince the dead man's niece, Boschero, of his noble intentions. She reveals that the microfilm was buried along with her uncle, and so the body is exhumed. A Russian agent grabs the goods, reveals that he is a double-agent working in cahoots with a third world, power and then steals a speed boat and Boschero. Harrison jumps in a handy helicopter, catches up to the Russian, and gets the girl and the microfilm, once again saving the Western world from the commie hordes.

p, Mino Loy, Luciano Martino; d, Martin Donan [Mario Donen]; w, Julian Barry [Sergio Martino]; ph, Richard Thierry [Riccardo Pallottini] (Eastman-color); m, Carlo Savina; ed, Robert Quintley [Roberto Cinquini]; art d, Rick Sommers [Riccardo Domenici].

Spy Drama   **(PR:A-C MPAA:NR)**

SECRET AGENT OF JAPAN**   (1942) 72m FOX bw

Preston Foster (*Roy Bonnell*), Lynn Bari (*Kay Murdock*), Noel Madison (*Saito*), Victor Sen Yung (*Fu Yen*), Janis Carter (*Doris Poole*), Steve Geray (*Alecsandri*), Kurt Katch (*Traeger*), Addison Richards (*Remsen*), Ian Wolfe (*Capt. Larsen*), Hermine Sterler (*Mrs. Alecsandri*), Selmer Jackson (*American Naval Captain*), Frank Puglia (*Eminescu*), Leyland Hodgson, Leslie Denison (*English Secret Service*), Jean Del Val (*Solaire*), Noel Cravat, Wilfred Hari (*Japanese Detectives*), Cyril Ring, Harry Denny, ArthurLoft (*American Businessmen*), Florence Shirley (*American Woman*), Tim Ryan (*Bartender*), Tom O'Grady (*Man at Bar*), Al Kikume (*Sikh Policeman*), Bud Fine (*American Detective*), Bob Okazaki (*Japanese Lieutenant*), Don Forbes

(*Radio Announcer*), Daisy Lee (*Chinese Landlady*), Gino Corrado (*Gambler*).

Typical WW II propaganda film starring Bari as a lovely British agent who convinces cynical American nightclub owner Foster (who has set up shop in Shanghai) to help her in her fight against Japanese spies. Worth watching for the laughable makeup job on Madison, who plays an evil Japanese.

p, Sol M. Wurtzel; d, Irving Pichel; w, John Larkin; ph, Lucien Andriot; ed, Alfred Day; md, Emil Newman.

Spy Drama/War   **(PR:A MPAA:NR)**

SECRET AGENT SUPER DRAGON zero
(1966, Fr./Ital./Ger./Monaco) 95m Ramofilm-Fono-Borderie-Gloria/Unit-
ed Screen c (NEW YORK APPELLE SUPER DRAGON; NEW YORK
CHIAM A SUPERDRAGO; HOLLENJAGD AUF HEISSE WARE; AKA:
SUPER DRAGON)

Ray Danton (*Byran Cooper, "Super Dragon"*), Marisa Mell (*Charity Farrell*), Margar et Lee (*Cynthia Fulton*), Jess Hahn (*Baby Face*), Carlo D'Angelo (*Fernand Lamas*), Adriana Ambesi (*Verna*), Marco Guglielmi (*Prof. Kurge*), Solvi Stubing (*Elizabeth*), Gerhard Haerter (*Coleman*), Jacques Herlin (*Dumont*), Carlo Hintermann, Pinkas Braun, Christia Hester.

A really poor, dubbed spy movie starring Danton as a CIA agent known in the trade as "Super Dragon" who becomes embroiled in the insidious plot of a mysterious Venezuelan crime kingpin to destroy the U.S. By spiking chewing gum and candy with a strange and dangerous drug, the villain immobilizes his victims. The Venezuelan test-markets his confections in a Michigan college town and the evil stuff works. Danton leaps into action to find the villain and get the antidote for his deadly drug. Ridiculous premise, execution, and performances provide a few unintentional laughs.

p, Roberto Amoroso; d, Calvin Jackson Padgett; w, Bill Coleman, Mike Mitchell, Remigio del Grosso, Amoroso, Padgett (based on a story by Padgett); ph, Antonio Secchi (Technicolor); m, Benedetto Ghiglia; set d, Arrigo Equini.

Spy Drama   **(PR:A MPAA:NR)**

SECRET BEYOND THE DOOR, THE***   (1948) 98m Diana/UNIV bw

Joan Bennett (*Celia Lamphere*), Michael Redgrave (*Mark Lamphere*), Anne Revere (*Caroline Lamphere*), Barbara O'Neil (*Miss Robey*), Natalie Schafer (*Edith Potter*), Paul Cavanagh (*Rick Barrett*), Anabel Shaw (*Intellectual Sub-Deb*), Rosa Rey (*Paquita*), James Seay (*Bob Dwight*), Mark Dennis (*David*), Virginia Brissac (*Sarah*), Houseley Stevenson (*Andy*), Marie Harmon, Kay Morley (*Sub-Debs*), Crane Whitley, Virginia Farmer (*Lavender Falls Couple*), Lucio Villegas (*Priest*), Eddy C. Waller (*Lem*), Paul Fierro (*Fighter*), Julian Rivero (*Proprietor*), Paul Scardon (*Owl Eyes*), Danny Duncan (*Ferret-Faced Man*), Frank Dae (*Country Squire*), Pedro Regas (*Waiter*), Donne Martell (*Young Mexican Girl*), David Cota (*Knife Fighter*), Tom Chatterton (*Judge*), Ralph Littlefield (*Gothic Man*), Nolan Leary (*Station Agent*), Wayne Treadway (*Beefy Man*), Watson Downs (*Conductor*), Jessie Graves (*Porter*), Donald Kerr (*Ticket Man*), Robert Espinosa, Robert Barber, Tony Rodriquez (*Altar Boys*), Peggy Remington (*Dean of Women*), Harry Denny (*College President*).

After a whirlwind romance while on vacation in Mexico, young and beautiful heiress Bennett decides to marry Redgrave, the publisher of an architectural journal. They are married in a Mexican church, but during the ceremony Bennett panics momentarily when she realizes that she barely knows Redgrave. Swallowing her reservations, she goes through with the marriage. During their honeymoon Bennett playfully locks the bedroom door on Redgrave, who reacts badly and returns without her to New York. The shocked and confused Bennett follows her husband to his large home in Lavender Falls. There she is surprised to discover that Redgrave has a sister, Revere, a jealous secretary, O'Neil, and a son from a previous marriage, Dennis, all of whom live under his roof. Probing his past, Bennett discovers that Redgrave is a widower who didn't really love his first wife, but blames himself for her death. Dennis has been cold and distant since the day his mother died and the boy resents Bennett's presence. To add further tension, secretary O'Neil has been in love with Redgrave for years and once saved Dennis' life during a fire which horribly scarred her face. Hoping to marry Redgrave, O'Neil has had the scars fixed with plastic surgery but the arrival of Bennett dashed all her hopes and she continues to cover the area with a scarf. In addition to Redgrave's strange "family," the house itself is forbidding and intimidating. Redgrave has an architectural theory which states that the manner in which a place is built determines what happens in it. To illustrate this thesis, he has built replicas of rooms where famous murders have taken place. On a tour of the rooms, Bennett becomes dismayed with her husband's obsession. At the end of the hall is a locked room and, though the display is completed, Redgrave refuses to open it. The curious Bennett decides that the locked room is the secret to Redgrave's mental turmoil over the death of his first wife and that if she can open the door to his mind, she can cure him. She manages to enter the locked room and discovers that it is a replica of the room of Redgrave's first wife. By all obvious appearances the room is complete, but upon closer examination tiny details are missing, as though Redgrave himself isn't convinced a murder has taken place. Realizing that this room is also an exact duplicate of her own room, Bennett becomes distraught and suddenly fears for her life. Running from the house in a panic, she spots the figure of a man blocking her way and all turns black. We then see Redgrave clutching Bennett's scarf. He hallucinates a mock trial where he is both the prosecutor and defendant. The discourse reveals that Redgrave is torn with guilt over the death of his first wife and feels he has murdered her. His other half, however, repudiates the guilt and claims that a man can't be responsible for his unconscious impulses. At the end of the trial, Redgrave declares an impulse to kill Bennett. The next morning we see that Bennett is very much alive and has returned to Redgrave because she loves him and wants to try and cure his mental problems. While alone in a locked room with her, Redgrave reveals that he was once locked in his home by his mother and he watched as she drove off with another man. From that day on he has hated his mother and wished he could have killed her. Bennett instantly psychoanalyzes Redgrave and, with a plethora of simplified Freudian mumbo-jumbo, cures him. Ecstatic at finally having found true happiness, the couple tries to leave the room but discover the door locked and the house burning. Redgrave breaks the door down and saves Bennett, only to discover that the jealous O'Neil had thought Bennett alone in the room and tried to kill her. With the house burned to the ground, freeing Redgrave of his obsession, the couple return to Mexico for a second honeymoon. THE SECRET BEYOND THE DOOR is a frustrating film for fans of director Fritz Lang. While filled with stunning visuals and amazing camera moves, it suffers from bad scripting and trite, dated, laughable psychological analysis of character. The structure is overcomplicated and deceiving with flashbacks, voice-overs, and dishonesty (making the audience believe Redgrave has murdered Bennett when that simply isn't the case) covering the holes and weakening the base of the whole film. Despite these problems, Lang does manage to create a fairly engrossing film. This was his last film starring the wonderful Joan Bennett (MAN HUNT, THE WOMAN IN THE WINDOW, and SCARLET STREET being the others) and they try desperately to rise above the overly melodramatic material. The most successful aspect of the production is the expressionist cinematography which creates a shadowy world of false appearances, hidden meanings, and elusive truths. The musical score by Miklos Rozsa also is fascinating. In the screening room Lang suggested that Rozsa compose the music in reverse and then when the backward score was recorded it could be played back forward, making the music sound normal but retaining an intangible, odd quality. The trick worked and Rozsa's score adds an eerie and disturbing facet to the overall effect. Unfortunately, cinematography and music do not alone make great films. THE SECRET BEYOND THE DOOR is crippled by its naive and simplistic melodramatic meanderings, dating it badly and preventing it from attaining the masterful quality that marks most of Lang's work.

p&d, Fritz Lang; w, Silvia Richards (based on the story "Museum Piece No. 13" by Rufus King); ph, Stanley Cortez; m, Miklos Rozsa; ed, Arthur Hilton; prod d, Max Parker; set d, Russell Gausman, John Austin.

Drama   **Cas.**   **(PR:C   MPAA:NR)**

SECRET BRIDE, THE*½   (1935) 76m WB bw (GB: CONCEALMENT)

Barbara Stanwyck (Ruth Vincent), Warren William (Robert Sheldon), Glenda Farrell (Hazel Normandie), Grant Mitchell (Willie Martin), Arthur Byron (Gov. Vincent), Henry O'Neill (Jim Lansdale), Douglas Dumbrille (Dave Bredeen), Arthur Aylesworth (Lt. Nygard), William B. Davidson (Sen. McPherson), Willard Robertson (Sen. Grosvenor), Russell Hicks (Holdsteck), Vince Barnett (Drunk), Frank Darien (Justice of the Peace), Gordon "Bill" Elliott (Governor's Secretary), Spencer Charters (Messenger), Purnell Pratt (District Attorney), Mary Russell (Girl), Milton Kibbee (Judge's Secretary), Wallis Clark (Defense Attorney), Samuel S. Hinds (Clerk), Joseph Crehan (Senator), John Larkin (Janitor), Emmett Vogan (Teller), Frank Dawson (Butler), Billy Ray (Radio Announcer), James Burtis (Taxi Driver), James Burke (Counterman), Wade Boteler (Police Officer), Thomas E. Jackson (Daniels), Charles C. Wilson (Lt. Forrest), Katherine Clare Ward (Matron), Cliff Saum (Policeman), Florence Fair (Woman Secretary), Wilfred Lucas (Bailiff), Davison Clark (Sergeant at Arms), Selmer Jackson (Vincent's Counsel).

Attorney general William and his fiancee, Stanwyck, are secretly married out of state in order to keep their names out of the papers. Upon their return home they are shocked to learn that Stanwyck's father, Byron, the governor, has been accused of taking a $10,000 bribe from a rich and powerful criminal businessman who was convicted and sent to prison. Byron had recently pardoned the man and the money appears to have been the motivation, but when the story hit the papers the shady businessman killed himself. Knowing that his marriage to the governor's daughter would bring a public outcry, William keeps it a secret and sets out to investigate the case. Convinced of her father's innocence, Stanwyck aids her husband in uncovering the true facts. Soon impeachment proceedings begin against Byron and it is a race against time. When Byron's chief investigator is murdered it appears the culprit was an old girl friend, but Stanwyck finds the real killer and discovers that her father's chief advisor and the dead investigator plotted the up. Having cleared her father's name, Stanwyck and William finally find time to announce their marriage. Despite its solid cast, THE SECRET BRIDE is nothing more than a routine programmer with a fairly ludicrous plot. Director Dieterle had taken over the production from director Archie Mayo and finished the film in a workman like fashion that kept the pace moving so fast that the audience had no time to question

the incongruities. While certainly not a bad film, THE SECRET BRIDE is a disappointment for Stanwyck devotees.

p, Henry Blanke; d, William Dieterle; w, Tom Buckingham, F. Hugh Herbert, Mary McCall, Jr. (based on the play by Leonard Ide); ph, Ernest Haller; ed, Owen Marks; art d, Anton Grot; cos, Orry-Kelly.

Drama   **(PR:A   MPAA:NR)**

SECRET BRIGADE, THE*   (1951 USSR) 77 m Bielorussian Film Studios/Artkino bw

Vladimir Druzhnikov (Zaslonov), A. Khvilya (Secretary), G. Glebov (Kropylyar), V. Dorofeyev (Shurmin), G. Michurin (Hirt), V. Solovyov (Neuchaus), A. Fenin (Gammer), Z. Stomma (Buravchik), V. Balashov (Dokutovich), V. Maryev (Semenikhin), I. Kondratyeva (Galina), Y. Malyutin (Kube).

Yet another Russian movie detailing the struggle with the Nazis for Moscow during WW II. This time out, a brave railroad technician who heads up the local partisan group goes undercover and wins the Nazis' confidence in order to find out their battle plans. The trick works and the partisans manage to destroy the Nazis' transportation into Moscow. As reviewed by American critics in 1951, THE SECRET BRIGADE was dismissed without a second thought. One suspects that some of this ill will was due to the Red-baiting attitude of the times.

d, A. Feinzimmer, V. Korsh-Sablin; w, A. Movzon; ph, A. Gintsburg; m, A. Bogatyrov.

War   **(PR:A   MPAA:NR)**

SECRET CALL, THE*   (1931) 70m PAR bw

Richard Arlen (Tom Blake), Peggy Shannon (Wanda Kelly), William B. Davidson (Jim Blake), Charles Trowbridge (Phil Roberts), Jane Keith (Grace Roberts), Selmer Jackson (Matt Stanton), Ned Sparks (Bert Benedict), Jed Prouty (Jim Neligan), Charles D. Brown (Bob Barnes), Harry Beresford (Frank Kelly), Larry Steers (Fillmore), Elaine Baker (Vera Lorraine), Frances Moffett (Gwen), Claire Dodd (Maisie), Patricia Farr (Ellen).

Shannon plays the daughter of a wealthy politician who is forced by her father's suicide to take a job as a switchboard operator in a big hotel. The switchboard then becomes the center of action for the film as we glimpse various stories dealing with clandestine affairs, crime, and politics with the switchboard serving to intersect the parts.

d, Stuart Walker; w, Arthur Kober, Eve Unsell (based on the play "The Woman" by William C. DeMille); ph, David Abel.

Drama   **(PR:A   MPAA:NR)**

SECRET CAVE, THE*   (1953, Brit.) 62m Merton Park-Children's Film Foundation/ABF bw

David Coote (Steve Draycott), Susan Ford (Margaret Merriman), Nicholas Emdett (Lennie Hawkins), Lewis Gedge (Miller Griffin), Johnny Morris (Charlie Bassett), Trevor Hill (Job Tray).

A downright boring children's film based on a Thomas Hardy novel about two boys who are nearly killed when they try to divert a stream. With their mother facing eviction they route the water to her property in the hopes that the land value will rise. Although they get trapped in a cave in the process, danger is evaded and all ends well.

p, Frank A. Hoare; d, John Durst; w, Joe Mendoza (based on the novel Our Exploits at West Poley by Thomas Hardy); ph, Martin Curtis.

Children's Film   **(PR:A   MPAA:NR)**

SECRET CEREMONY*   (1968, Brit.) 109m UNIV-World Film Services-Paul M. Heller/UNI V c

Elizabeth Taylor (Leonora), Mia Farrow (Cenci), Robert Mitchum (Albert), Peggy Ashcroft (Hannah), Pamela Brown (Hilda), Michael Strong (Dr. Walter Stevens), Robert Douglas (Sir Alex Gordon).

A murky, moody psychological scare story that has more holes than a swiss cheese, SECRET CEREMONY was so ill-conceived that a few scenes had to be shot later for the TV version, using actors who were not in the film, to straighten out the story line. Made at Elstree Studios in London, it features Taylor in a banshee parody of her role in WHO'S AFRAID OF VIRGINIA WOOLF, Farrow in a macabre follow-up to ROSEMARY'S BABY, and Mitchum in an unusual satyr-like role, wearing an Uncle Sam beard. Based on a short story by an Argentine civil servant who won $5,000 for writing it, the movie had to be edited severly when shown on TV, and Taylor's role, that of an aging whore, was rinsed to make her a wig model now employed by a London department store as a seamstress. All of that was handled by the additional scenes which featured Strong and Douglas as a psychiatrist and an attorney. They were there to explain some of the plot contrivances. Many scenes were deleted later because they were too steamy. Particularly, a massage sequence, a nude bath, and the suggestion that Farrow and Taylor were having an affair and that Mitchum was a child molester. The screen version and the TV version bear as much resemblance as Dom De

Luise to Tiny Tim. For the record, the feature story begins as Taylor, a blowsy hooker, is on a London bus; she sees Farrow (wearing a black wig to hide her light hair) and is stunned by the resemblance between Farrow and her late child. Taylor is on her way to the graveyard to visit her daughter's final resting place and Farrow follows her there. Once they begin talking, Farrow admits that Taylor more than resembles her late mother and a symbiosis begins between the women. Farrow asks if Taylor would like to stay at the house where Farrow resides, an old dark place Vincent Price might have enjoyed. In the house, Taylor and Farrow become even closer and wind up in a mother-daughter relationship, thereby satisfying each's needs. Farrow's two aunts are Brown and Ashcroft, and Farrow tells them that Taylor is her late mother's sister, hence the resemblance. The two greedy women accept that Taylor becomes more comfortable in her role as Farrow's mother. She thinks Farrow is about 14 and is surprised to learn that she's actually 22. Further, Farrow's step-father had been chased from the house for attempting to seduce her and Farrow's mother was nuttier than a two-pound jar of Skippy's. Taylor is out one day and comes home to find Farrow shivering with fear. Her stepfather, Mitchum, has returned and Farrow claims that the old goat has raped her. Taylor immediately takes her new "daughter" to the sea shore to get away from the mansion. Mitchum catches up with them and tells Taylor that Farrow is as crazy as her mother was and that she is a nymphomaniac who actually tried to seduce him. Taylor is confused by the conflicting stories, but when she sees Farrow stuff the front of her dress with a toy doll in an attempt to appear pregnant, she realizes that Farrow's elevator stops several floors short of the penthouse. Farrow finds Mitchum on the beach, uses her wiles to seduce him, and later tells Taylor that she doesn't want to see her any longer. Heartbroken, Taylor leaves, but not for long. Soon afterward, Taylor comes back, desperately wanting to continue the mother-daughter life she'd been so happy leading. Farrow won't hear of it, tells Taylor to exit, then overdoses on sleeping pills and dies. At the funeral, Mitchum is there to pay his last respects when Taylor walks in, pulls out a knife, and stabs Mitchum in the chest. The picture ends and not soon enough for almost everyone. Mitchum's role was more a cameo than a co-starring one and the scene he'd done with Farrow in a bathtub was later altered to put Taylor in the water to give the picture a lesbian slant. Evidently the producers knew they had a huge turkey on their hands and were attempting to change the stuffing.

p, John Heyman, Norman Priggen; d, Joseph Losey; w, George Tabori (based on the short story "Ceremonia Secreta" by Marco Denevi); ph, Gerald Fisher (Technicolor); m, Richard Rodney Bennett; ed, Reginald Beck; md, Marcus Dods; prod d, Richard MacDonald; art d, John Clark; set d, Jill Oxley; cos, Marc Bohan, Christian Dior, Susan Yelland; makeup, Alex Garfath.

Drama (PR:O MPAA:R)

SECRET COMMAND**½ (1944) 82m Torneen/COL bw

Pat O'Brien (Sam Gallagher), Carole Landis (Jill McCann), Chester Morris (Jeff Gallagher), Ruth Warrick (Lea Damaron), Barton MacLane (Red Kelly), Tom Tully (Brownell), Wallace Ford (Miller), Howard Freeman (Max Lessing), Erik Rolf (Ben Royall), Matt McHugh (Curly), Frank Sully (Shawn), Frank Fenton (Simms), Charles D. Brown (James Thane), Carol Nugent (Joan), Richard Lane (Paul), Richard Lyon, Cyril Ring.

O'Brien stars as a Naval Intelligence agent who is sent to the planned Nazi sabotage of a big American shipyard. His home office sets him up with a "wife," Landis, and two kids in a small house near the shipyard. Coincidentally, O'Brien's brother Morris works at the shipyard and thinks this new "family" is a bit suspicious. O'Brien eventually locates the Nazi saboteurs and learns that they plan to blow up the yard and a newly-built aircraft carrier. While O'Brien has a knock-down-drag-out with the lead baddie, the rest of the Naval Intelligence agents arrive and corral the other Nazis. Having saved the shipyard, O'Brien looks forward to further battles against the huns, as well as making Landis and the kids his "real" family.

p, Phil L. Ryan; d, A. Edward Sutherland; w, Roy Chanslor (based on the story "The Saboteurs" by John Hawkins, Ward Hawkins); ph, Franz F. Planer; m, Paul Sawtell; ed, Viola Lawrence; md, Morris Stoloff; art d, Lionel Banks, Edward Jewell; set d, Robert Priestley; spec eff, Robert Wright.

Espionage/War Drama (PR:A MPAA:NR)

SECRET DOCUMENT -- VIENNA**½ (1954, Fr.) 90m Arthur Davis bw

Renee Saint-Cyr (Florence Henning), Frank Villard (Rudolph Henning), Howard Vernon (Col. Von Pennwitz), Nathalie Nattier (Marika), George Galley (Spy), Andre Valmy (Inspector Braun), Oliver Hussenot (Steward).

Villard plays a WW I Austrian soldier who is accused of double-crossing his government and sentenced to die before a firing squad. Seeking revenge on the Germans whom she is convinced framed her innocent husband, the soldier's French wife, Saint-Cyr, leaves their home in Switzerland and joins French counter-intelligence in an effort to sabotage the Kaiser. While on a mission she learns that her husband is alive after all, and with his help she completes her assignment and dashes into Switzerland to await his arrival. (In French; English subtitles.)

p, Helene Davis; d, Andre Haguet; w, Andre Legrand (based on the novel by

Maurice Dekobra); ph, Charles Bauer; m, Van Hoorebeke.

Espionage/War Drama (PR:A MPAA:NR)

SECRET DOOR, THE** (1964) 72m Dorton-Fifeshire/AA bw

Robert Hutton (Joe Adams), Sandra Dorne (Sonia), Peter Illing (Buergher), Peter Allenby (Edward Brentano), George Pastell (Antonio), Shirley Lawrence (Gretchen), Bob Gallico (Lt. Ted Avery), Peter Elliott (Japanese Ambassador), Tony Arpino (Freighter Captain), James Dyrenforth (Prison Warden), Chris Lawrence (Capt. Hastings), Martin Benson (Edmundo Vara), Joel Aldred (Narrator), Ed Parker, Moises Batista, Carlos Rodriguez, Antonio Faira, Yoshio Hikida.

Hutton and Allenby play two convicted safecrackers who are released to the custody of Naval Intelligence following the attack on Pearl Harbor so they can steal top-secret Japanese documents stored in the Japanese embassy in Lisbon. Once in Lisbon, the pair discover that the documents are worth $1 million. Once the documents have been obtained, Allenby tries to grab them for himself, but he is killed by their Lisbon contact, Illing, who takes off with them. Illing, however, is killed in a car crash. The Navy recovers the papers, but Hutton is captured by the Japanese and held prisoner on a freighter. Eventually Hutton is rescued when the freighter is sunk. He then receives a presidential pardon for his crimes.

p, Charles Baldour; d, Gilbert L. Kay; w, Charles Martin (based on the story "Paper Door" by Stephen Longstreet); ph, Robert Moss, Aurelio Rodriguez; m, Tony Osborne; ed, David Capey; md, Osborne; m/l, "Lisboa," Baldour.

Espionage/War Drama (PR:A MPAA:NR)

SECRET ENEMIES** (1942) 57m WB bw

Craig Stevens (Carl Becker), Faye Emerson (Paula Fengler), John Ridgely (John Trent), Charles Lang (Jim Jackson), Robert Warwick (Dr. Woodford), Frank Reicher (Henry Bremmer), Rex Williams (Hans), George Meeker (Rudolph), Roland Drew (Fred), Addison Richards (Travers), Cliff Clark (Capt. Jarrett), Monte Blue (Hugo), Stuart Holmes (Adolph), Ray Teal (Motor Cop), Ruth Ford (Miss Charlton), Sol Gross (Joe), Leah Baird (Maid), Jack Mower (Medical Examiner), Frank Mayo (Patrolman's Voice), Marian Hall (Secretary), Ernst Hausman (Bellhop), Rudolf Steinbeck, Robert Stevenson (Spies), Bill Hopper (Ensign), Rolf Lindau (Spy Radio Operator), Harry Lewis (Radio Operator), Stacy Keach, Victor Zimmerman, Frank Wilcox, Lane Chandler, Lee Powell (Counter-Espionage Men).

Stevens joins the FBI during WW II when one of his buddies is murdered by Nazi secret agents working in America. After a few more G-Men are bumped off, the Federal agents trace the Nazis to a hotel in New York City where they have set up headquarters. The FBI successfully raids the joint, but some of the head Nazis escape to an upstate hunting lodge. Stevens is right on their heels of course, and they capture the remaining goose-steppers after a rousing gunfight.

p, William Jacobs, d, Ben Stoloff; w, Raymond L. Schrock; ph, James Van Trees; ed, Douglas Gould; art d, Hugh Reticker; spec eff, Edwin A. DuPar.

Espionage (PR:A MPAA:NR)

SECRET ENEMY (SEE: ENEMY AGENT, 1940)

SECRET EVIDENCE** (1941) 68m PRC bw

Marjorie Reynolds (Linda), Charles Quigley (David), Ward McTaggart (Baxter), Kenneth Harlan (Billings), Donald Curtis (Murphy), Howard Masters (Jerry), Bob White (Sniffy), Kitty McHugh (Mazie), Budd Buster (Frank), Charles Phipps (Dad), Dorothy Vaughan (Mother), Boyd Irwin (Judge).

Secretary Reynolds is in love with McTaggart, a no good crook – only she doesn't know he's a hood until he's hauled off to jail for four years. While he stews in prison, the overly-cautious Reynolds marries an assistant district attorney and settles down. (she really wants to make sure her beau is no gangster this time. McTaggart serves his time and upon his release seeks to reunite with Reynolds. Before he gets too far, however, McTaggart is shot to death by a hoodlum associate and the crime is blamed on Reynolds' kid brother. This leads to the inevitable courtroom scene where Reynolds must convince the court and her husband of her brother's innocence.

p, E.B. Derr; d, William Nigh; w, Brenda Kline (based on a story by Edward Bennett); ph, Arthur Martinelli; ed, Elaine Turner.

Crime (PR:A MPAA:NR)

SECRET FILE: HOLLYWOOD* (1962) 85m Crown International bw
(AKA: SECRET FILE OF HOLLYWOOD)

Robert Clarke (Maxwell Carter), Francine York (Nan Torr), Syd Mason (Hap Grogan), Maralou Gray (Gay Shelton), John Warburton (James Cameron).

An inept little crime drama starring Clarke as an out-of-work private detective who reluctantly takes a job with a sleazy Hollywood tabloid as a photographer. York sends him out to snap sensational photos of movie director Warburton and his new starlet Gray. Clarke gets the pictures and then stands by helpless as York and her associate Mason blackmail the director. He pays, but the slimy crooks publish the pictures anyway which causes the director's wife to commit suicide. Gray is cleared of any wrongdoing, and she teams up with Clarke to find out who's behind the blackmail ring. When both York and Mason are found dead, Clarke digs deeper and finds tape-recorded instructions from the mysterious head of the organization to York which reveal the big bad guy to be an old radio actor. Clarke soon finds the blackmailer/murderer and brings him to justice.

p, Rudolph Cusumano, James Dyer; d, Ralph Cushman; w, Jack Lewis; ph, Gregory Sandor.

Crime (PR:A-C MPAA:NR)

SECRET FILE OF HOLLYWOOD
(SEE: SECRET FILE: HOLLYWOOD 1962)

SECRET FLIGHT (SEE: SCHOOL FOR SECRETS, 1951, Brit.)

SECRET FOUR, THE½** (1940, Brit.) 79m EAL/MON bw (GB: THE FOUR JUST MEN)

Hugh Sinclair (*Humphrey Mansfield*), Griffith Jones (*James Brodie*), Francis L. Sullivan (*Leon Poiccard*), Frank Lawton (*Terry*), Anna Lee (*Ann Lodge*), Alan Napier (*Sir Hamar Ryman, M.P.*), Basil Sydney (*Frank Snell*), Lydia Sherwood (*Myra Hastings*), Edward Chapman (*B. J. Burrell*), Athole Stewart (*Police Commissioner*), George Merritt (*Inspector Falmouth*), Garry Marsh (*Bill Grant*), Ellaline Terriss (*Lady Willoughby*), Roland Pertwee (*Mr. Hastings*), Eliot Makeham (*Simmons*), Frederick Piper (*Pickpocket*), Arthur Hambling (*Constable*), Percy Walsh (*Prison Governor*), Henrietta Watson, Jon Pertwee, Liam Gaffney, Manning Whiley, Neal Arden, Basil Radford, Edward Rigby, Paul Sheridan.

Another Edgar Wallace adaptation, this time with Lawton as a Britisher who is killed by traitors. The other three of the four seek revenge and in the process foil an attempt to block the Suez Canal. Typically dry, stilted, and dull presentation of one of the prolific Wallace's best novels.

p, Michael Balcon; d, Walter Forde; w, Angus MacPhail, Sergei Nolbandov, Roland Pertwee (from the novel by Edgar Wallace); ph, Ronald Neame; m, Ernest Irving; ed, Stephen Dalby; art d, Wilfred Shingleton.

Drama (PR:A MPAA:NR)

SECRET FOUR, THE, 1952 (SEE: KANSAS CITY CONFIDENTIAL, 1952)

SECRET FURY, THE½** (1950) 86m RKO bw

Claudette Colbert (*Ellen*), Robert Ryan (*David*), Jane Cowl (*Aunt Clara*), Paul Kelly (*Eric Lowell*), Philip Ober (*Kent*), Elisabeth Risdon (*Dr. Twining*), Doris Dudley (*Pearl*), Dave Barbour (*Lucian Randall*), Vivian Vance (*Leah*), Percy Helton (*Justice of the Peace*), Dick Ryan (*Postman*), Ann Godee (*Tessa*), Joseph Forte (*Martin*), Edith Angold (*Flora*), Adele Rowland (*Mrs. Palmer*), Howard Quinn (*Bellhop*), John Mantley (*Hotel Clerk*), Marjorie Babe Kane (*Maid*), Ralph Dunn (*McCafferty*), Ruth Robinson (*Mrs. Updyke*), Pat Barton (*Louise*), Charmienne Harker (*Ethel*), Eddie Dunn (*Mike*), Willard Parker (*Smith*), Vivien Oakland (*Mrs. Brownley*), Abe Dinovitch (*Man*), Paul Picerni (*Dr. Roth*), Wheaton Chambers (*District Attorney*), Bert Moorhouse (*Deputy Assistant Attorney*), Vangie Beilby, June Benbow, Sonny Boyne, Connie Van (*Patients*), Gail Bonney (*Nurse*), Frank Scannell (*Wilson*), Margaret Wells (*Mrs. May*), Burk Symon (*Judge*), Gene Brown (*Hospital Nurse*).

A hopelessly contrived mystery saved by a good cast and a fast pace. Colbert and Ryan star as a happy couple about to get married when a stunning announcement that she is already wed halts the ceremony. Disbelieving the accusation, Ryan accompanies Colbert to the records office and both are shocked to find that her "wedding" is fully documented, including witnesses who claim they were there. The confused couple attempt to trace Colbert's "husband" and succeed, but he is murdered and she is arrested for the crime. Colbert snaps under all this pressure and she is tossed into a loony bin. Ryan still stands by his fiancee however, and he continues to investigate. In the end it is revealed that Colbert's lawyer has been trying to drive her nuts because her father had wronged him years ago.

p, Jack H. Skirball, Bruce Manning; d, Mel Ferrer; w, Lionel Houser (based on a story by Jack R. Leonard, James O'Hanlon); ph, Leo Tover; m, Roy Webb; ed, Harry Marker; md, Constantin Bakaleinikoff; art d, Albert S. D'Agostino, Carroll Clark .

Mystery (PR:A MPAA:NR)

SECRET GARDEN, THE** (1949) 92m MGM bw-c

Margaret O'Brien (*Mary Lennox*), Herbert Marshall (*Archibald Craven*), Dean Stockwell (*Colin Craven*), Gladys Cooper (*Mrs. Medlock*), Elsa Lanchester (*Martha*), Brian Roper (*Dickon*), Reginald Owen (*Ben Weatherstaff*), Aubrey Mather (*Dr. Griddlestone*), George Zucco (*Dr. Fortescue*), Lowell Gilmore (*British Officer*), Billy Bevan (*Barney*), Dennis Hoey (*Mr.

Pitcher), Matthew Boulton (*Mr. Bromley*), Isobel Elsom (*Governess*), Norma Varden (*Nurse*).

A strange and wonderful little film starring a 12-year-old O'Brien as an orphan sent to live with her grouchy uncle Marshall who lives in a spooky Victorian mansion. Marshall has grown cold and uncaring ever since the death of his wife in the estate garden and he refuses to allow anyone to touch the area. Upstairs, Marshall keeps his son Stockwell a virtual prisoner due to the boy's paralysis of the legs which his father has decided is untreatable. O'Brien's arrival, however, begins to change things. She finds the key to the locked up garden and secretly tends to the long-dead flowers. Aided by neighbor boy Roper, O'Brien soon transforms the sickly brown garden into a lush, green hideaway. She and her pal sneak Stockwell into the garden for daily visits and as a result of the friendship of others, combined with the outdoor air, he is soon able to take his first few steps. This miracle snaps Marshall out of his depression and he decides to let himself and his son live again. Most of the film is in black and white, but the sequences in the revived garden are in Technicolor. O'Brien retired briefly after THE SECRET GARDEN, but eventually returned to an apathetic audience.

p, Clarence Brown; d, Fred M. Wilcox; w, Robert Ardrey (based on the novel by Frances Hodgson Burnett); ph, Ray June (Technicolor); m, Bronislau Kaper; ed, Robert J. Kern; md, Andre Previn; art d, Cedric Gibbons, Urie McCleary; set d, Edwin B. Willis, Richard Pefferle; cos, Walter Plunkett; Makeup, Jack Dawn.

Drama (PR:AA MPAA:NR)

SECRET HEART, THE** (1946) 97m MGM bw

Claudette Colbert (*Lee Addams*), Walter Pidgeon (*Chris Matthews*), June Allyson (*Penny Addams*), Robert Sterling (*Chase Addams, Jr.*), Marshall Thompson (*Brandon Reynolds*), Elizabeth Patterson (*Mrs. Stover*), Richard Derr (*Larry Addams, Sr.*), Patricia Medina (*Kay Burns*), Eily Malyon (*Miss Hunter*), Ann Lace (*Penny as a Child*), Nicholas Joy (*Dr. Rossiger*), Anna Q. Nilsson (*Miss Fox*), Frank Darien (*Mr. Wiggins*), Donald Dewar (*Page Boy*), Chester Clute (*Old Man*), Harry Hayden (*Minister*), Wyndham Standing, Alex Pollard (*Butlers*), Audrey Totter (*Brittle Woman's Voice*), Hume Cronyn (*Man's Voice*), Hall Hankett (*Young Man's Voice*), Boyd Davis (*Sheriff*), Ruth Brady, Barbara Billingsley (*Saleswomen*), Virginia Randolph (*Salesgirl*), Joan Beeks (*Woman Customer*), John Webb Dillon (*Conductor*), Dwayne Hickman (*Chase as a Child*), Drew Demarest (*Cab Driver*).

Excellent cast helps this fairly unusual drama starring Allyson as the college-aged stepdaughter of young widow Colbert, who is obsessed with the memory of her late father who had committed suicide. Her brother, Sterling, and Colbert are disturbed by Allyson's behavior (she locks herself in her room and plays piano for her dead father) so they seek the advice of a psychiatrist. He advises that they move Allyson to the family farmhouse and force her to face up to the fact that her father killed himself there. Once at the farm however, Allyson becomes disillusioned with her father's myth and tries to kill herself the same way he did. Luckily she is stopped, and eventually things work out for a happy ending.

p, Edwin H. Knopf; d, Robert Z. Leonard; w, Whitfield Cook, Anne Morrison Chapin, Rose Franken (based on the story by Franken, William Brown Meloney); ph, George Folsey; m, Bronislau Kaper; ed, Adrienne Fazan; art d, Cedric Gibbons. Edward Carfagno; set d, Edwin B. Willis, Henry W. Grace.

Drama (PR:C MPAA:NR)

SECRET INTERLUDE, 1936 (SEE: PRIVATE NUMBER, 1936)

SECRET INTERLUDE, 1955 (SEE: VIEW FROM POMPEY'S HEAD, 1955)

SECRET INVASION, THE½** (1964) 95m San Carlos/UA c

Stewart Granger (*Maj. Richard Mace*), Raf Vallone (*Roberto Rocca*), Mickey Rooney (*Terrence Scanlon*), Edd Byrnes (*Simon Fell*), Henry Silva (*John Durell*), Mia Massini (*Mila*), William Campbell (*Jean Saval*), Helmo Kindermann (*German Fortress Commandant*), Enzo Fiermonte (*Gen. Quadri*), Peter Coe (*Marko*), Nan Morris (*Stephana*), Helmut Schneider (*German Patrol Boat Captain*), Giulio Marchetti (*Italian Garrison Officer*), Nicholas Rend (*Fishing Boat Captain*), Craig March (*Petar*), Todd Williams (*Partisan Leader*), Charles Brent (*1st Monk*), Richard Johns (*Wireless Operator*), Kurt Bricker (*German Naval Lieutenant*), Katrina Rozan (*Elderly Peasant Farm Woman*).

Roger Corman directed this precursor to Robert Aldrich's THE DIRTY DOZEN in Yugoslavia and was given the largest budget of his career, $590,000, for this WW II tale starring Granger as a British Intelligence officer who must draft five unwilling criminals: Vallone, Rooney, Silva, Burns, and Campbell (all experts in a variety of the criminal arts) for a secret mission. Their mission: infiltrate Dubrovnik and rescue an imprisoned Italian general who has soured on the Nazis, and then bring him to his troops so he can convince them to turn against Hitler. Once in Dubrovnik however, the small band of soldiers is captured and thrown into prison. Coincidentally, they are thrown into the same prison which houses the

Italian general they seek, and so they escape, dragging the strangely resistant general with them. They soon learn that the general is an impostor who replaced the real general after he was murdered by the Nazis. Determined to complete their mission, the soldiers haul the impostor in front of the Italian troops and force him to tell them to fight against Hitler. Halfway through the speech, the imposter begins shouting pro-Nazi propaganda, so Silva, dressed as a Nazi, spouts his own Third Reich rhetoric and guns the general down in front of his troops. The angry troops decide that the Nazis cannot be trusted and pick up arms against the Axis, making the mission a success.

p, Gene Corman; d, Roger Corman; w, R. Wright Campbell; ph, Arthur E. Arling (Panavision, DeLuxe Color); m, Hugo Friedhofer; ed, Ronald Sinclair; art d, John Murray; set d, Ian Love; spec eff, George Blackwell; makeup, Sandra James.

War   (PR:A   MPAA:NR)

SECRET JOURNEY   (SEE: AMONG HUMAN WOLVES, 1939, Brit.)

SECRET LIFE OF AN AMERICAN WIFE, THE***
(1968) 93m Charleston/FOX c

Walter Matthau *("Charlie" the Movie Star)*, Anne Jackson *(Victoria Layton)*, Patrick O'Neal *(Tom Layton)*, Edy Williams *(Suzie Steinberg)*, Richard Bull *(Howard)*, Paul Napier *(Herb Steinberg)*, Gary Brown *(Jimmy)*, Albert Carrier *(Jean-Claude)*, Todd Baron *(Peter Layton)*, Christy Hall *(Susan Layton)*.

Whenever George Axelrod writes a screenplay, it somehow looks as though it were a stage play that he couldn't get produced so he adapted it for pictures. Such is the case again in this. Jackson is the 34 year-old wife of O'Neal, a New York press agent (she was actually about 42 when she played this role). He says something about the fact that she could never have been a successful hooker and she resents that. One of O'Neal's jobs is to arrange sexual favors for his major client, movie star Matthau, at a hundred bucks per. The realization that she may have lost her attraction comes when a delivery boy fails to notice that she is totally nude when he comes to their suburban home. Jackson is determined to change matters, so she infuses her body with a few brandies, screws up her courage, calls Matthau, who is in town from Hollywood, and says that she's a call girl. When she arrives at his hotel, Jackson sees that the "Great Lover" of the screen is not that at all. He's lonely, subject to attacks of sinusitis, and just needs someone to be his pal. Jackson is slightly miffed that Matthau prefers her company to any hanky-panky but she eventually enjoys listening to Matthau's tales of woe. They tell each other their deepest secrets and Matthau admits that his prowess is largely a matter of public relations rather than intimate ones. Jackson and Matthau finally make love, then O'Neal arrives at the hotel and calls upstairs to Matthau's suite. He enters the suite, Jackson hides in the other room, O'Neal decides that he cannot be a lackey any longer and punches Matthau in the snoot, then exits. Jackson emerges from the bedroom, puts a cold compress on Matthau's proboscis, and is about to leave for her Connecticut home when Matthau gives her $100 for cab fare. She brightens up as she realizes she's fulfilled her ambitions and can now return to her domestic tranquility. It's an immoral story but made somewhat palatable by Jackson's plight and her desire to be desirable. Edy Williams, the one-time wife of Russ Meyer, plays the sexy girl who walks in and out of the fantasies of Jackson as she relates her problems directly to the camera in a very stagy fashion. The same subject matter was handled better and with more taste in BELLE DU JOUR, the Catherine Deneuves tarrer about a married woman who spent her afternoons working in a brothel. A good idea that goes somewhat awry because the author-producer-director couldn't make up his mind if he was doing a French farce or a British satire.

p,d&w, George Axelrod; ph, Leon Shamroy (DeLuxe Color); m, Billy May; ed, Harry Gerstad; art d, Jack Martin Smith, Ed Graves; set d, Walter M. Scott, Raphael Bretton; cos, Travilla; spec eff, L.B. Abbott, Art Cruickshank; makeup, Dan Striepeke.

Comedy   (PR:C-O   MPAA:R)

SECRET LIFE OF WALTER MITTY, THE****
(1947) 105m Goldwyn/RKO c

Danny Kaye *(Walter Mitty)*, Virginia Mayo *(Rosalind van Hoorn)*, Boris Karloff *(Dr. Hugo Hollingshead)*, Fay Bainter *(Mrs. Mitty)*, Ann Rutherford *(Gertrude Griswold)*, Thurston Hall *(Bruce Pierce)*, Konstantin Shayne *(Peter van Hoorn)*, Florence Bates *(Mrs. Griswold)*, Gordon Jones *(Tubby Wadsworth)*, Reginald Denny *(RAF Colonel)*, Henry Corden *(Hendrick)*, Doris Lloyd *(Mrs. Follinsbee)*, Fritz Feld *(Anatole)*, Frank Reicher *(Maasdam)*, Milton Parsons *(Butler/Tyler)*, Mary Brewer, Betty Carlyle, Lorraine DeRome, Jackie Jordan, Martha Montgomery, Sue Casey, Pat Patrick, Irene Vernon, Karen X. Gaylord, Mary Ellen Gleason, Georgia Lane, Michael Mauree, Lynn Walker *(Goldwyn Girls)*, Bess Flowers *(Illustrator)*, Donna Dax *(Stenographer)*, George Magrill *(Wolfman)*, Joel Friedkin *(Grimsby)*, John Tyrrell, Raoul Freeman *(Department Heads)*, Sam Ash *(Art Editor)*, Dorothy Granger, Harry L. Woods *(Wrong Mr. and Mrs. Follinsbee)*, Lumsden Hare *(Mr. Pritchard-Mitford)*, Hank Worden *(Western Character)*, Vernon Dent *(Bartender)*, John Hamilton *(Dr. Remington)*, Henry Kolker *(Dr. Benbow)*, Frank LaRue *(Conductor)*, Brick Sullivan

(Cop), Charles Trowbridge *(Dr. Renshaw)*, Minerva Urecal *(Woman with Hat)*, Maude Eburne *(Fitter)*, George Chandler *(Mate)*, Vincent Pelletier *(Narrator for Dream Sequence)*, Harry Harvey, Mary Anne Baird, Jack Gargan, Harry Depp, Dick Earle, Broderick O'Farrell, Wilbur Mack, Ralph Dunn, Jack Cheatham, Mary Forbes, Pierre Watkin, Ernie Adams, George Lloyd, Syd Saylor, Billy Bletcher, Eddie Acuff, Wade Crosby, Dorothy Christy, Dick Rush, William Haade, Billy Newell, Paul Newlan, Chris Pin Martin, Sam McDaniel, Betty Blythe, Ethan Laidlaw, Moy Ming, Beal Wong.

Though Thurber himself offered to give producer Sam Goldwyn $10,000 *not to* film his classic short story for which Goldwyn had bought the film rights, THE SECRET LIFE OF WALTER MITTY is still an outstanding production and undoubtedly the best film Kaye ever made. Thurber's tale (first appearing in the *New Yorker* on March 18, 1939) about a middle-aged, hen-pecked who escapes desperately from reality by imagining himself in all sorts of heroic situations doesn't lose much in the film adaptation. Kaye, who is hilarious throughout, is single but still henpecked by his dominating mother Bainter and by his grasping fiancee, Rutherford. He works for a pulp magazine firm, an unlikely proofreader in that the company publishes gory crime stories that terrify the timid Kaye. In an uproariously funny scene, his publisher, Hall, storms into Kaye's office and holds up a mock-up cover of a forthcoming magazine edition, showing someone being brutally attacked in lurid color. Kaye lets out a little scream of terror just looking at the graphic gore while Hall indignantly asks, "What's the meaning of this, Mitty?" Kaye denies all responsibility for the cover and Hall goes on to say that he objects to the cover, too, because it's not gory *enough*! "See here, Mitty," Hall intones, "I don't want this fellow merely killed. I want him stabbed from the front, from the side, from the back!" As Hall describes each angle of assault, Kaye lets out a yelp of fright. Hall, like Bainter and Rutherford, acts as another oppressor in the milquetoast's miserable life. He is forever running errands like some handyman for mother Bainter and in Rutherford's pushy presence Kaye can only stammer and awkwardly stumble about. To escape his dilemma, Kaye envisions himself a confident heroic figure in a number of very funny sequences. These imaginary adventures are sprinkled throughout the film, used as supportive sequences to a main plot that involves spies and jewel thieves. Kaye's zany imagination thrusts him into the role of a sea captain bravely navigating his ship through a typhoon; a fast-drawing western gunslinger called "The Perth Amboy Kid;" a gambler on a Mississippi riverboat who bets against the villain to save the honor of a southern belle; a brilliant surgeon performing an incredible operation to save the life of a patient; a dashing pilot in the RAF who shoots down countless Nazi fighters; and a rather effeminate fashion designer, "Anatole of Paris," wherein he presents one of his famous sing-song numbers (in rapid-fire recitative, as he does with an even more famous patter number, "Symphony for Sunstrung Tongues"). In all his daydreams, the same luscious blonde heroine appears, the leggy Mayo, the girl with whom he is subconsciously seeking to spend the rest of his humdrum life. Lo and behold, Mayo does appear in Kaye's real life, asking a confused Kaye to help her escape a villainous character who has been following her. She explains that she is an heiress and that the fabulous jewels she has inherited from her family, entrusted to Uncle Denny, are now being sought by an infamous gang of international jewel thieves. Kaye aids Mayo and soon the thieves are chasing him about Manhattan and into the country. At one point his chief antagonist even climbs the skyscraper in which he works and appears outside his office window, attempting to push him off a ledge. With danger lurking everywhere, Kaye's offbeat behavior becomes even more strange, so much so that Bainter and Rutherford convince Hall that Kaye is going crazy and he is taken to psychiatrist Karloff. The psychiatrist, however, turns out to be the secret head of the jewel thieves and, to throw Kaye off the track, convinces him that his recent experiences with Mayo have been nothing more than his usual fantasies. Kaye accepts this as fact and goes ahead with his plans to marry Rutherford. But at the altar Kaye reaches into his pocket and finds a memento from Mayo which proves her to be real. He rushes to her uncle's estate and, in a wild chase, manages to round up Karloff and gang and win the heart of his blonde goddess. Though the film slips downward toward the end into slapstick (which is pretty funny as is), THE SECRET LIFE OF WALTER MITTY is enjoyable and presents more hilarious scenes than most comedies. It is sumptuously produced--Goldwyn sank more than $3 million into this great showcase for Kaye--and it is directed with the pace of a lunatic running ahead of his keepers. And even in a few of Kaye's big numbers, producer Goldwyn got to parade his statuesque Goldwyn Girls, a treat for those males who admire voluptuous women on the large side. Thurber didn't like Kaye's gibberish and commented, after seeing the film, "It began to be bad with the first git- gat-gittle." But the author was in the minority, most critics and the public universally endorsing this wild romp. Mayo, with her voluptuous body and creamy skin, is alluring, and Bainter is terrific as the overbearing mom. Hall stands out as the blood-craving blood-craving Karloff does a great burlesque of himself as the monster from FRANKENSTEIN but without the aid of makeup. And throughout the film there is that memorable sound of Kaye's imaginary life-saving machine--"pucketa, pucketa, pucketa." Thurber disclaimed the film until his dying days, putting up such a battle about the original script that Goldwyn submitted to him that the producer actually canceled the film, then rescheduled its production while he and Englund reworked the script. Kaye, always Goldwyn's choice ever since he performed so well in Goldwyn's UP IN ARMS, vexed author Thurber no end; he hated Kaye's routines and general personality. When the film was released the August 18, 1947, edition of *Life* magazine carried two letters pro and con about the movie, one from Goldwyn, a gentle missive saying he had done his best with the film and that writers rarely realize what it takes to bring their work into another medium, the other from a very angry Thurber, objecting to the film in sarcastic terms and ending with an apology to the meek hero of his story, "Sorry, Walter, sorry for Everything." But the average viewer was delighted with the film and accepted Goldwyn's theory that the story was only a good basis for a spectacular Kaye vehicle. THE SECRET LIFE OF WALTER MITTY was a heavy winner at the box office.

p, Sam Goldwyn; d, Norman Z. McLeod; w, Ken Englund, Everett Freeman (based on the story by James Thurber); ph, Lee Garmes (Technicolor); m, David Raksin; ed, Monica Underwood; md, Emil Newman; art d, George Jenkins, Perry Ferguson; set d, Casey Roberts; cos, Irene Sharoff; spec eff, John Fulton; m/l, Sylvia Fine.

Comedy   **Cas.**   **(PR:A   MPAA:NR)**

SECRET LIVES   (SEE: I MARRIED A SPY 1938)

SECRET MAN, THE**   (1958, Brit.) 68m Producers
                                         Associates-Amalgamated/BUT bw

Marshall Thompson (*Dr. Cliff Mitchell*), John Loder (*Maj. Anderson*), Anne Aubrey (*Jill Warren*), Magda Miller (*Ruth*), John Stuart (*Dr. Warren*), Henry Oscar (*John Manning*), Murray Kash (*Waldo*), Michael Mellinger (*Tony*), Robert MacKenzie, Bernard Archard, Tom Bowman, Peter Elliott, Stan Simmons, Shirley Thieman, Robert Dorning, Harcourt Curacao.

Thompson is an American physicist living in England who is called on to locate a secret agent who is working at his research station. Thompson goes undercover to learn the spy's identity and, with the help of Aubrey, his wife and assistant, digs up some answers. Loder, an army major, then comes in to help round up the perpetrator, who will surprise the viewer. Rather tired overall, though.

p&d, Ronald Kinnoch; w, Tony O'Grady; ph, Geoffrey Faithfull.

Spy Drama   **(PR:A   MPAA:NR)**

SECRET MARK OF D'ARTAGNAN, THE**   (1963, Fr./Ital.) 95m
Liber-Agiman/Medallion c (LE SECRET DE D'ARTAGNAN; IL COLPO
                                         SEGRETO DI D'ARTAGNAN)

George Nader (*d'Artagnan*), Magali Noel (*Carlotta, Maid*), Georges Marchal (*Duke de Montserant*), Mario Petri (*Porthos*), Alessandra Panaro (*Diana*), Massimo Serato (*Cardinal Richelieu*), Franco Fantasia, Raf Baldassarre, Giulio Marchetti.

A minor Musketeers drama which sees Nader and Petri sent out by Serato to smash a ring of assassins intent on killing the king. Nader learns that Marchal is the leader of the gang and he uses Marchal's niece Panaro to infiltrate the gang and the pair fall in love. Eventually, the Musketeers stage a swordfight with the evil Duke and his conspirators, and the assassins are routed.

p, Ottario Poggi; d, Siro Marcellini; w, Poggi, Milton Krims, Marcellini; ph, Alvaro Mancori (Totalscope, Eastmancolor); m, Carlo Rustichelli; ed, Renato Cinquini; art d, Amedeo Mellone; set d, Ernesto Kromberg.

Adventure   **(PR:A   MPAA:NR)**

SECRET MENACE*   (1931) 59m Cardinal/Imperial bw

Glenn Tryon, Virginia Brown Faire, Arthur Stone, Margaret Mann, Edward Cecil, John Elliott, Jules Cowles, Pat Harmon, Joe Savage, Charles Balda, Vera McGinnis.

Bad guys kill an old prospector who just struck gold, but their plans are held up when the owner of the property, which is in the middle of a dude ranch, won't sell. The owner stages a rodeo to attract customers, so the bad guys set out to wreck his business so he'll have to sell. The stubborn owner still refuses to sell, puts two and two together and calls in the sheriff who runs the villains out of town.

d, Richard C. Kahn; w, B. Wayne Lamont (based on a story by Kahn); ph, Bert Baldridge; ed, Arthur Brooks.

Western   **(PR:A   MPAA:NR)**

SECRET MISSION**½   (1944, Brit.) 82m Independent
                                         Producers-Excelsior/GFD bw

Hugh Williams (*Peter Garnett*), Carla Lehmann (*Michele de Carnot*), James Mason (*Raoul de Carnot*), Roland Culver (*Red Gowan*), Michael Wilding (*Nobby Clark*), Nancy Price (*Violette*), Percy Walsh (*Fayolle*), Anita Gombault (*Estelle*), David Page (*Child Rene*), Betty Warren (*Mrs. Nobby Clark*), Nicholas Stuart (*Capt. Mackenzie*), Brefni O'Rorke (*Father Jouvet*), Karel Stepanek (*Maj. Lang*), F.R. Wendhausen (*Gen. von Reichmann*), John Salew (*Capt. Grune*), Herbert Lom (*Medical Officer*), Beatrice Varley (*Mrs. Donkin*), Yvonne Andre (*Martine*), Stewart Granger (*Sub-Lt. Jackson*), Oscar Ebelsbacher (*Provost Officer*), Marcel Hellman.

British Intelligence agents Culver, Wilding, and Frenchman Mason are led by Williams into occupied France to assess the strength of the Nazi invasion forces. Once in France they learn that the information they seek can only be obtained at Nazi headquarters. Williams and Culver gain entry to the building by posing as champagne sellers. They obtain the information, but the Nazis catch on quickly and give chase. With the help of the French Resistance, the vital information is given to British troops who then destroy the Nazis' supplies and munitions. As the intelligence force makes their escape, Mason is killed, leaving his sister Lehmann determined to help defeat the Nazis no matter how long it may take.

p, Marcel Hellman; d, Harold French; w, Anatole de Grunwald, Basil Bartlett (based on a story by Shaun Terence Young); ph, Bernard Knowles, Cyril Knowles; m, Mischa Spoliansky; ed, E.B. Jarvis; art d, Carmen Dillon; spec eff, Percy Day, Desmond Dickinson, John Mills.

War   **(PR:A   MPAA:NR)**

SECRET MISSION**   (1949, USSR) 95m Kiev/Artkino bw

Pavel Kadochnikov (*Fedotov*), Ambrosi Buchma (*Leschuk*), V. Dobrovolsky (*Chief*), D. Miliutenko (*Berezhnol*), S. Martinson (*Willi Pommer*), M. Romanov (*Rummelsburg*), P. Arjanov (*Shtubing*), Boris Barnet (*Kuhn*), Elena Izmailova (*Theresa*), Vera Ulesova (*Nina*).

Russian WW II spy film stars Kadochnikov as a master spy whose mission is to obtain the Nazis' secret plans for the invasion of the Ukraine. With the aid of some partisans, the Russian spy kidnaps a German general and learns what he needs to know. Barnet, who plays the German general, also directed the movie. (In Russian; English Subtitles.)

d, Boris Barnet; w, M. Bleman, K. Ivayev, M. Maklyarsky; ph, D. Demutsky.

War   **(PR:A   MPAA:NR)**

SECRET MOTIVE   (SEE: LONDON BLACKOUT MURDERS, 1942)

SECRET OF BLOOD ISLAND, THE**½
                                         (1965, Brit.) 84m Hammer/UNIV bw-c

Barbara Shelley (*Elaine*), Jack Hedley (*Sgt. Crewe*), Charles Tingwell (*Maj. Dryden*), Bill Owen (*Bludgin*), Peter Welch (*Richardson*), Lee Montague (*Levy*), Edwin Richfield (*O'Reilly*), Michael Ripper (*Lt. Tojoko*), Patrick Wymark (*Capt. Jocomo*), Philip Latham (*Capt. Drake*), Glyn Houston (*Berry*), Ian Whittaker (*Mills*), John Southworth (*Leonard*), David Saire (*KEMPI Chief*), Peter Craze (*Red*), Henry Davies (*Taffy*).

A fairly silly WW II film starring Shelley as a British secret agent who finds herself hiding in a POW camp in Malaya after her plane was shot down by the Japanese. Though the Japanese know she is somewhere on the island, Shelley is kept right under their noses by prisoner of war Hedley and his cell mates. The Japanese suspect they know something, so they begin to torture the prisoners for information. Two of them crack and Shelley is captured and tortured. Realizing that she's more important to them alive, the Japanese decide to ship her to Singapore for expert interrogation. Luckily, the other prisoners cause a diversion allowing her to escape, but they are killed in the progress. Once again, though this British film was shot in Eastmancolor and released that way in England, the American prints are all black & white.

p, Anthony Nelson Keys; d, Quentin Lawrence; w, John Gilling; ph, Jack Asher (Eastmancolor); m, James Bernard; ed, Tom Simpson; prod d, Bernard Robinson; spec eff, Syd Pearson; makeup, Roy Ashton.

War   **(PR:A   MPAA:NR)**

SECRET OF CONVICT LAKE, THE**½   (1951) 83m FOX bw

Glenn Ford (*Canfield*), Gene Tierney (*Marcia Stoddard*), Ethel Barrymore (*Granny*), Zachary Scott (*Greer*), Ann Dvorak (*Rachel*), Barbara Bates (*Barbara Purcell*), Cyril Cusack (*Limey*), Richard Hylton (*Clyde Maxwell*), Helen Westcott (*Susan Haggerty*), Jeanette Nolan (*Harriet*), Ruth Donnelly (*Mary*), Harry Carter (*Rudy*), Jack Lambert (*Matt Anderson*), Mary Carroll (*Millie Gower*), Houseley Stevenson (*Pawnee Sam*), Charles Flynn (*Steve Gower*), David Post (*Mike Fancher*), Max Wagner (*Jack Purcell*), Raymond Greenleaf (*Tom Fancher*), William Leicester (*Luke Haggerty*), Frances Endfield (*Tess*), Bernard Szold (*Bartender*), Ray Teal (*Sheriff*), Tom London (*Jerry*).

Criminal Ford leads a small band of escaped convicts from a Nevada prison to the tiny Sierra town of Diablo Lake. Once there, the assorted rapists, robbers, and killers are delighted to find that all the men have left on a silver strike and just women populate the town. Ford, who isn't all that bad, tries to keep the men from raping and marauding, but is less than successful. When the escapees learn that there's $40,000 of loot to be had, they steal the money and decide to blow town. Unfortunately, they run into the returning male townsfolk. A bloody battle ensues and all the convicts are killed. Ford is vindicated by the women and found innocent of his crimes. He then returns to Diablo Lake to marry Tierney.

p, Frank P. Rosenberg; d, Michael Gordon; w, Oscar Saul, Victor Trivas (based on a story by Anna Hunger, Jack Pollexfen); ph, Leo Tover; m, Sol

Kaplan; ed, James B. Clark; md, Lionel Newman; art d, Lyle Wheeler, Richard Irvine.

Western   (PR:A   MPAA:NR)

SECRET OF DEEP HARBOR*½   (1961) 70m Harvard/UA bw

Ron Foster (*Skip Hanlon*), Barry Kelley (*Milo Fowler*), Merry Anders (*Janey Fowler*), Norman Alden (*Barney Hanes*), James Seay (*Travis*), Grant Richards (*Rick Correll*), Ralph Manza (*Frank Miner*), Billie Bird (*Mama Miller*), Elaine Walker (*Rita*), Max Mellinger (*Doctor*).

Bad reworking of 1933's I COVER THE WATERFRONT starring Foster as the tough newshound who learns that his girl friend Anders' father, old sea captain Kelley, is being paid by the mob for transporting gangsters out of the country. Things get sticky when it appears Kelley has murdered one of his charges, and Foster tips the cops. Thinking that he only went out with her to get a story about her father, Anders dumps Foster and tries to get her old man to Mexico. Foster catches up with them however, and kills Kelley in a gunfight. Anders realizes her father was a crook and reconciles with Foster.

p, Robert E. Kent; d, Edward L. Cahn; w, Owen Harris, Wells Root (based on the novel *I Cover the Waterfront* by Max Miller); ph, Gilbert Warrenton; m, Richard La Salle; ed, Kenneth Crane; set d, Morris Hoffman; cos, Einar Bourman, Sabine Manela; spec eff, Barney Wolff.

Crime   (PR:C   MPAA:NR)

SECRET OF DR. ALUCARD, THE
                              (SEE: TASTE OF BLOOD, A, 1967)

SECRET OF DR. KILDARE, THE**½   (1939) 84m MGM bw

Lew Ayres (*Dr. James Kildare*), Lionel Barrymore (*Dr. Leonard Gillespie*), Lionel Atwill (*Paul Messenger*), Laraine Day (*Mary Lamont*), Helen Gilbert (*Nancy Messenger*), Nat Pendleton (*Joe Wayman*), Sara Haden (*Nora*), Samuel S. Hinds (*Dr. Stephen Kildare*), Emma Dunn (*Mrs. Martha Kildare*), Grant Mitchell (*John Archley*), Walter Kingsford (*Dr. Walter Carew, Hospital Head*), Alma Kruger (*Molly Byrd, Head Nurse*), Robert Kent (*Charles Herron*), Nell Craig (*Nurse Parker "Nosey"*), George Reed (*Conover*), Marie Blake (*Sally*), Martha O'Driscoll (*Mrs. Roberts*), Donald Barry (*Collins*), Frank Orth (*Mike Ryan*), Byron Foulger (*Attendant*).

The third DR. KILDARE outing sees Ayres curing blind heiress Gilbert of her affliction (it turns out to be psychosomatic) and tricking the grouchy, overworked Barrymore into taking a long-needed vacation. Considered by some critics to be a superior entry in the series, THE SECRET OF DR. KILDARE also stands out as the vehicle which starred an actress who worked her way up in an unusual way. Helen Gilbert first joined the MGM studio orchestra as a cellist before she was tapped for an on-screen appearance. Though exceedingly attractive, her acting skills left something to be desired. (See DR. KILDARE series, Index.)

d, Harold S. Bucquet; w, Willis Goldbeck, Harry Ruskin (based on a story by Max Brand); ph, Alfred Gilks; m, David Snell; ed, Frank Hull; md, Snell; art d, Cedric Gibbons.

Drama   (PR:A   MPAA:NR)

SECRET OF DORIAN GRAY, THE   (SEE: DORIAN GRAY, 1970, Ital./Ger./Lichtenstein)

SECRET OF G.32   (SEE: FLY BY NIGHT, 1942)

SECRET OF LINDA HAMILTON (SEE: SECRETS OF A SORORITY GIRL, 1946)

SECRET OF MADAME BLANCHE, THE**½   (1933) 67m MGM bw

Irene Dunne (*Sally*), Lionel Atwill (*Aubrey St. John*), Phillips Holmes (*Leonard St. John*), Una Merkel (*Ella*), Douglas Walton (*Leonard Junior*), C. Henry Gordon (*State's Attorney*), Jean Parker (*Eloise*), Mitchell Lewis (*Duval*).

Another reworking of the well-trod MADAME X territory starring Dunne as the outcast widow of Holmes who committed suicide after his father, Atwill, wouldn't approve his marriage because his bride was a showgirl. Dunne gives birth to a son and they are separated. Walton is the boy grown up who is ignorant of his mother's identity until he commits a murder and she shows up to take the rap for him. The film encompasses a time span from the 1890s until WW I and is given a decent production, but the material is all too familiar and stale despite a fine cast. The film does give Dunne an opportunity to sing a few tunes, which may for some be a mixed blessing.

d, Charles Brabin; w, Frances Goodrich, Albert Hackett (based on the play "The Lady" by Martin Brown); ph, Merritt B. Gerstad; m, Dr. William Axt; ed, Blanche Sewell.

Drama   (PR:A   MPAA:NR)

SECRET OF MAGIC ISLAND, THE**   (1964, Fr./Ital.) 63m Del Duca-Cino del Duco-Tourane/EM c (UNE FEE PAS COMME LES AUTRES; IL PAESE DI PAPERINO; AKA: SECRET OF OUTER SPACE ISLAND)

Phil Tonkin (*Narrator*), Robert Lamoureux (*Narrator, French Version*).

A children's fantasy film which uses live animals as its cast. The story involves the theft of a magic wand from a Good Fairy by an evil monkey who uses its power to become master of all the elements. A pair of brave ducks travel in a balloon to the Land of the Doves where they become immune to the monkey's evil magic. They then track down the monkey and trick him into turning himself to stone. The ducks then return the wand to the Good Fairy. (English version.)

p, Jack Dunn Trop; w, Jean Tourane, Frank Scully, Richard Lavigne, Trop (based on an adaptation by Trop); m, Richard Cornu, Warren Baker; French Version: p, Pierre Bochart; d, Jean Tourane; w, Louise de Vilmorin (based on a story by Tourane); ph, Maurice Fellous (Eastmancolor); m, Richard Cornu; ed, Albert Jurgenson; art d, Rene Thevenet.

Children's Fantasy   (PR:AAA   MPAA:NR)

SECRET OF MONTE CRISTO, THE**   (1961, Brit.) 83m Mid-Century/MGM c (GB: THE TREASURE OF MONTE CRISTO)

Rory Calhoun (*Capt. Adam Corbett*), John Gregson (*Renato*), Patricia Bredin (*Pauline Jackson*), Peter Arne (*Count Boldini*), Gianna Maria Canale (*Lucetta Di Marca*), Ian Hunter (*Col. Jackson*), Sam Kydd (*Albert*), David Davies (*Van Ryman*), Francis Matthews (*Louis Auclair*), Endre Muller (*Carlo*), Tutte Lemkow (*Gino*), Tony Thawnton (*Militia Officer*), C. Denier Warren (*French Cafe Proprietor*), Michael Balfour (*Beppo*), George Street (*English Innkeeper*), Walter Randall (*Sailor*), John Sullivan (*Jenkins*), Bill Cummings (*Ben*), Derek Prentice (*Groom*).

Calhoun plays a brave soldier in Italy circa 1815 who becomes embroiled in an adventure to find a treasure hidden on the island of Monte Cristo. He accompanies Bredin, the daughter of a murdered adventurer, on a quest which sees several unscrupulous characters in possession of different sections of the treasure map. Bredin doesn't trust Calhoun, and it is only after he has killed quite a few bandits, ruffians, and hoodlums for her that she decides he's all right. Eventually the treasure is found, and when the chest is opened it is nothing more than some chain and ropes. The real treasure had gone down in a different ship. Though left with no material wealth, Calhoun and Bredin have found love.

p&d, Robert S. Baker, Monty Berman; w, Leon Griffiths; ph, Baker, Berman (Dyaliscope, Eastmancolor); m, Clifton Parker; ed, John Jympson; md, Muir Mathieson; art d, Allan Harris.

Adventure   (PR:A   MPAA:NR)

SECRET OF MY SUCCESS, THE*   (1965, Brit.) 112m MGM c

Shirley Jones (*Marigold Marado*), Stella Stevens (*Violet Lawson*), Honor Blackman (*Baroness von Lukenburg*), James Booth (*Arthur Tate*), Lionel Jeffries (*Inspector Hobart/Baron von Lukenburg/President Esteda/Earl of Aldershot*), Amy Dolby (*Mrs. Tate*), Joan Hickson (*Mrs. Pringle*), Robert Barnete (*Col. Armandez*), Nicolau Breyner (*Pallazio*), Richard Vernon, David Davenport, Peadar Lamb, Ann Lancaster, Martin Benson, Reginald Beckwith, Ernest Clark, Robert Harris.

An inane British comedy starring Booth as a naive young "nebbish" who follows his mother's advice about having faith in mankind and rises from a lowly British policeman to the ruler of a South American country. Booth gets his first break while investigating the murder of the husband of sexy dressmaker Stevens. Unbeknownst to Booth, his mother Dolby suspects an illicit connection between Stevens and the magistrate and uses her knowledge to get her son promoted to inspector. While inspector, Booth begins an affair with a baroness (Blackman) who is breeding giant spiders in her basement and once more his mother's conniving gets him appointed liaison officer to a dictator of a small South American country. Once there Booth falls in with revolutionary Jones and accidentally winds up as the new leader of the country. Moronic and unfunny.

p, Andrew L. Stone, Virginia Stone; d&w, Andrew L. Stone; ph, Davis Boulton (Panavision, Technicolor); m, Lucien Cailliet; ed, Noreen Ackland; md, Roland Shaw; cos, John Cavanagh; m/l, "Guandurian Anthem," "No Secrets," Derek New, "Mangerico Verdi," Joao Baptista Laurenco, "Music Box Waltz, Bicycle and Guitar Themes," Christopher Stone; makeup, Tom Smith.

Comedy   (PR:A-C   MPAA:NR)

SECRET OF NIMH, THE***   (1982) 82m MGM-UA c

Voices: Derek Jacobi (*Nicodemus*), Elizabeth Hartman (*Mrs. Brisby*), Arthur Malet (*Ages*), Dom DeLuise (*Jeremy*), Hermione Baddeley (*Auntie Shrew*), John Carradine (*Great Owl*), Peter Strauss (*Justin*), Paul Shenar (*Jennar*), Tom Hattan (*Farmer Fitzgibbons*), Shannen Doherty (*Teresa*), Wil Wheaton (*Martin*), Jodi Hicks (*Cynthia*), Ian Fried (*Timmy*), Lucille Bliss, Aldo Ray.

A superbly animated but weakly scripted tale produced by Don Bluth, who left Disney Studios when he got fed up with the quality of their animated films in the 1970s and took a dozen of Disney's frustrated top animators with him. The result is a return to the lush, finely detailed animation seen in the best of Disney. This is the story of a mother mouse, desperately trying to move her family to a new location before they are killed by the farmer who is soon to plow his field. Hindered by her ill son, the mother mouse is aided by some escaped laboratory rats with superior intelligence. The assembled voice talent is outstanding, but the film is strangely uninvolving.

p, Don Bluth, Gary Goldman, John Pomeroy; exec p, Rich Irvine, James L. Stewart; d, Bluth; w, Bluth, Goldman, Pomeroy, Will Finn (based on the novel *Mrs. Frisby and the Rats of N.I.M.H.* by Robert C. O'Brien); ph, Joe Jiuliano, Charles Warren, Jeff Mellquist (Technicolor); m, Jerry Goldsmith; ed, Jeffrey Patch; directing animators, Pomeroy, Goldman; animators, Lorna Pomeroy, Skip Jones, Dave Spafford, Finn, Linda Miller, Dan Kuenster, Heidi Guedel, David Molna, Emily Jiuliano, Kevin M. Wurzer; spec eff, D.A. Lanpher, Tom Hush.

Fantasy   Cas.   **(PR:AA MPAA:G)**

SECRET OF OUTER SPACE ISLAND
(SEE: SECRET OF MAGIC ISLAND, THE, 1964, Fr./Ital.)

SECRET OF ST. IVES, THE½   (1949) 75m COL bw

Richard Ney *(Anatole de Keroual)*, Vanessa Brown *(Floria Gilchrist)*, Henry Daniell *(Maj. Edward Chevenish)*, Edgar Barrier *(Sgt. Carnac)*, Aubrey Mather *(Daniel Romaine)*, Luis Van Rooten *(Clausel)*, John Dehner *(Couguelat)*, Paul Marion *(Amiot)*, Douglas Walton *(Allan St. Ives)*, Jean Del Val *(Count St. Ives)*, Phyllis Morris *(Annie Gilchrist)*, Maurice Marsac *(Portuguese Joe)*, Harry Cording *(Innkeeper)*, Alex Fraser *(Swindow)*, Tom Stevenson *(Flint)*, Billy Bevan *(Douglas)*, Guy de Vestal *(Dubois)*, Charles Andre *(Rene)*.

Robert Louis Stevenson-inspired tale starring Ney as a brave French prisoner of war who escapes a British prison camp and is accompanied by his English fiancee, Brown, as he makes his way back to Napoleon. Unnecessary subplots and an overly talky script bog down this swashbuckler.

p, Rudolph C. Flothow; d, Philip Rosen; w, Eric Taylor (based on a story by Robert Louis Stevenson); ph, Henry Freulich; m, Mischa Bakaleinikoff; ed, James Sweeney; art d, Cary Odell; set d, Sidney Clifford; makeup, Bob Shiffer.

Adventure   **(PR:A MPAA:NR)**

SECRET OF SANTA VITTORIA, THE*½   (1969) 134m UA c

Anthony Quinn *(Italo Bombolini)*, Anna Magnani *(Rosa Bombolini)*, Virna Lisi *(Contessa Caterina Malatesta)*, Hardy Kruger *(Sepp Von Prum, German Commander)*, Sergio Franchi *(Tufa)*, Renato Rascel *(Babbaluche)*, Giancarlo Giannini *(Fabio)*, Patrizia Valturri *(Angela)*, Valentina Cortese *(Gabriella)*, Eduardo Ciannelli *(Luigi Lunghetti)*, Leopoldo Trieste *(Vittorini)*, Gigi Ballista *(Padre Polenta)*, Quinto Parmeggiani *(Copa)*, Carlo Caprioli *(Giovanni Pietrosanto)*, Francesco Mule *(Francocci)*, Wolfgang Jansen *(Sgt. Zopf)*, Aldo De Carellis *("Old Vines")*, Marco Tulli *(Mazzola)*, Chris Anders *(Cpl. Heinsick)*, Peter Kuiper *(Sgt. Traub)*, Dieter Wilken *(Hans)*, Karl Otto Alberty *(Otto)*, Gigi Bonos *(Benedetti)*, Clelia Matania *(Julietta)*, Pippo Lauricella *(Pulci)*, Carlo Capannelle *(Capoferro)*, Renato Chiantoni *(Bracolini)*, Pino Ferrara *(Dr. Bara)*, Curt Lowens *(Col. Scheer)*, Tim Donnelly *(Pvt. Holtzmann)*.

An amusing WW II story starring Quinn as a boozy Italian who becomes installed as mayor of his small wine-making village when he erases a Mussolini slogan off a wall upon pronouncement of the death of Il Duce. Despite his new title, Quinn continues his ways as a bumbling drunk much to the dismay of his impatient wife Magnani, who throws him out of the house. News arrives that the Nazis are headed for the village to plunder its vast stores of vintage wine. If the Nazis take the wine, the village will starve, as wine is its only source of income. Thinking quickly, Quinn and Magnani decide to hide the wine in an old cave on the outskirts of town. The villagers form a line and pass the bottles one by one from the wine cellars to the cave. They work day and night and finally one million bottles of wine are hidden safely away only an hour before the Germans arrive. Quinn has left 300,000 bottles for the Nazis. The Nazi commander, Kruger, suspects that there is more wine than what is in the cellar and tries to trick Quinn into revealing the location. After a lengthy battle of wits, Kruger gives up and pulls his troops out, but not before Quinn gives him a bottle of wine as a souvenir.

p&d, Stanley Kramer; w, William Rose, Ben Maddow (based on the novel by Robert Crichton); ph, Giuseppe Rotunno (Panavision, Technicolor); m, Ernest Gold; ed, William Lyon, Earle Herdan; prod d, Robert Clatworthy; set d, Ferdinando Ruffo; cos, Joe King; spec eff, Danny Lee.

Comedy/Drama   **(PR:A MPAA:M)**

SECRET OF STAMBOUL, THE* *   (1936, Brit.) 93m GFD bw (AKA: THE SPY IN WHITE)

Valerie Hobson *(Tania)*, Frank Vosper *(Kazdim)*, James Mason *(Larry)*, Kay Walsh *(Diana)*, Peter Haddon *(Peter)*, Laura Cowie *(Baroness)*, Cecil Ramage *(Prince Ali)*, Robert English *(Sir George)*, Emilio Cargher *(Renouf)*, Leonard Sachs *(Arif)*, Andrea Malandrinos *(Moltov)*.

Guard officers Mason and Haddon are fired from the service for starting a brawl with Arab prince Ramage when the foreign visitor tries to seduce Mason's girlfriend Walsh. Walsh's father is grateful, however, and gives Mason a job managing his tobacco warehouse in Turkey. Mason meets a beautiful Russian girl, Hobson, and falls in love, but she is an unwitting pawn of Ramage who is planning to overthrow the Turkish government. Joined in Turkey by Haddon and Walsh, Mason works to prevent the overthrow. He is nearly killed in the attempt, but is saved by Hobson, and eventually the insurgents are captured. This was re-issued as THE SPY IN WHITE in 1940.

p, Richard Wainwright; d, Andrew Marton; w, Wainwright, Howard Irving Young, Noel Langley (based on the novel *Eunuch of Stamboul* by Dennis Wheatley); ph, Henry Harris.

Drama   **(PR:A MPAA:NR)**

SECRET OF THE BLUE ROOM*½   (1933) 66m UNIV bw

Lionel Atwill *(Robert von Hellsdorf)*, Gloria Stuart *(Irene von Hellsdorf)*, Paul Lukas *(Capt. Walter Brink)*, Edward Arnold *(Commissioner Foster)*, Onslow Stevens *(Frank Faber)*, William Janney *(Thomas Brandt)*, Robert Barrat *(Paul, the Butler)*, Muriel Kirkland *(Betty)*, Russell Hopton *(Max)*, Elizabeth Patterson *(Mary)*, Anders van Haden *(Stranger)*, James Durkin Kruger, *(Foster's Assistant)*.

A good haunted house mystery starring Stuart as a strange woman who forces her three suitors Janney, Stevens, and Lukas to prove their bravery by each spending a night alone in the mysterious blue room of an old castle owned by Atwill where three people were murdered twenty years ago. Remade twice, as THE MISSING GUEST (1938) and again as MURDER IN THE BLUE ROOM (1944).

d, Kurt Neumann; w, William Hurlbut (based on a story by Erich Phillipi); ph, Charles Stumar; ed, Philip Cohn.

Mystery   **(PR:A MPAA:NR)**

SECRET OF THE CHATEAU*½   (1935) 67m UNIV bw

Claire Dodd, Clark Williams, William Faversham, Osgood Perkins, Ferdinand Gottschalk, Alice White, Jack LaRue, George E. Stone, DeWitt Jennings, Helen Ware, Frank Reicher, Alphonse Ethier, Paul Nicholson, Olaf Hytten, Cecile Elliott, Tony Merlo, Frank Thornton.

Mystery tale starring Williams as a young man who has inherited a priceless Guttenberg Bible. He spends the night in a chateau where the other guests are crooked characters trying to get their hands on the valuable book. After lots of pointless chatter, creepy shadows and a few corpses, the thief/murderer is revealed, though the viewer is long past caring.

p, Lou L. Ostrow; d, Richard Thorpe; w, Albert DeMond, Harry Behn, Llewellyn Hughes (based on a story by Lawrence G. Blochman); ph, Robert Planck; ed, Harry Marker.

Mystery   **(PR:A MPAA:NR)**

SECRET OF THE FOREST, THE* *   (1955, Brit.) 61m Rayant-Children's Film Foundation/BL bw

Kit Terrington *(Henry)*, Diana Day *(Mary)*, Jacqueline Cox *(Caroline)*, Barry Knight *(Johnny)*, Vincent Ball *(Mr. Lawson)*, Michael Balfour *(Len)*, Arthur Lovegrove *(Wally)*.

A forester's two children, Knight and Day, become friends with two spoiled rich kids, Terrington and Cox, when the latter two come to the woods for a visit. The quartet get involved with a gang of crooks when a valuable gold cup is stolen. The crooks then kidnap Terrington and Cox, but Knight and Day rescue them and help the cops nab the crooks. First film directed by actor Conyers, who went on to make many other children's pictures and some good farces.

p, Anthony Gilkison; d, Darcy Conyers; w, Conyers, Gerry [Gerard] Bryant (based on the story by George Ewart Evans); ph, Sydney Samuelson.

Children's Film   **(PR:AA MPAA:NR)**

SECRET OF THE INCAS*½   (1954) 100m PAR c

Charlton Heston *(Harry Steele)*, Robert Young *(Dr. Stanley Moorehead)*, Nicole Maurey *(Elena Antonescu)*, Yma Sumac [Amy Camus] *(Kori-Tica)*, Thomas Mitchell *(Ed Morgan)*, Glenda Farrell *(Mrs. Winston)*, Michael Pate *(Pachacutec)*, Leon Askin *(Anton Marcu)*, William Henry *(Phillip Lang)*, Kurt Katch *(Man with Rifle)*, Edward Colmans *(Col. Emilio Cardoza)*, Grandon Rhodes *(Mr. Winston)*, Geraldine Hall *(Mrs. Richmond)*, Harry Stanton *(Mr. Richmond)*, Booth Colman *(Juan Fernandez)*, Rosa Rey,

Robert Tafur, Martin Garralaga, Alvy Moore, Rodolfo Hoyos, Zacharias Yaconelli, Marion Ross, John Marshall, Carlos Rivero, Delmar Costello, Dimas Sotello, Miguel Contreras, Anthony Numkena.

SECRET OF THE INCAS looks terrific. The sweeping vistas and wide expanses of Peru's Machu Picchu area are reason enough to see this. Machu Picchu was discovered in the late 1910s and is a real Inca city that has yielded many important archaeological treasures. It is only when the actors begin to talk that the movie starts to lose momentum as the dialogue is trite and predictable and the characters are of a stereotypical nature. And who better to carry off the familiar role of the avaricious-swindler-destined-to-come-around-and-prove-he's-not-such-a-bad-guy-after-all than Heston? Heston has been stone-faced before but this time he's positively granite and shows as much vulnerability as a female black widow spider on her wedding night. He's shacked up in Cuzco where he spends his time bilking tourists out of their vacation money to raise the funds to secure an airplane so he can fly up to the Andes. There he believes he'll find the fabled treasure of the Incas, a jewel-laden ritual mask known as the "Sunburst." At the same time, a man of equally-dubious morals, Mitchell, is also after the same relic. Farrell is a tourist and Heston gets her to help him nab the plane. Several groups descend on Machu Picchu at the same time. Young is after the mask for quite another reason – he hopes that its discovery might help the local natives get their heritage back. At the site, the various groups get into a fracas. To add to the complications, Maurey, a knockout who happens to be along on the trip, falls for Heston. In the end, Heston gives the antique to the natives, confesses his love for Maurey, and the two of them leave to spend their lives together. Heston's character change is totally out of whack with what we've seen. He wants the mask, engages in all sorts of derring-do to get it, then throws it aside for the love of a good woman. Sumac (whom everyone at the time thought was a real South American but who was actually one Amy Camus, a native of New York) has a remarkable five-octave singing voice and does three tunes by Moises Vivanco, "High Andes," "Virgin Of The Sun God," and "Earthquake." Fans of Robert Young should be prepared for what amounts to a cameo. Though they would be better off watching old "Marcus Welby" reruns to slake their thirst for this latter-day Sanka Brand salesman. All technical credits are good and particular applause goes to the second unit photography by Roberts.

p, Mel Epstein; d, Jerry Hopper; w, Ranald MacDougall, Sydney Boehm (based on the story "Legend of the Incas" by Boehm); ph, Lionel Lindon, Irma Roberts (Technicolor); m, David Buttolph; ed, Eda Warren; art d, Hal Pereira, Tambi Larsen.

Adventure   **(PR:A   MPAA:NR)**

SECRET OF THE LOCH, THE*½   (1934, Brit.) 80m Wyndham/ABF
                                                                   bw

Seymour Hicks (Prof. Heggie), Nancy O'Neil (Angela Heggie), Gibson Gowland (Angus), Frederick Peisley (Jimmy Andrews), Eric Hales (Diver), Ben Field (Piermaster), Hubert Harben (Prof. Fothergill), Stafford Hilliard (Macdonald), Rosamund Jones [Rosamund John] (Maggie), Robb Wilton, John Jamieson, Elma Reid.

Another crackpot scientist in Scotland, former farceur and then fine character actor Hicks, swears that he has seen the Loch Ness monster. A London reporter, Peisley, believes him and offers assistance, falling in love with O'Neil, Hicks' granddaughter. Peisley eventually finds the courage to scout the waters himself and comes face to face with the monster. A trite programmer which doesn't make one believe in the humans' actions, much less the sea serpent's. First film outing for gentle redhead John, who went on to a long movie career in England.

p, Bray Wyndham; d, Milton Rosmer; w, Charles Bennett, Billie Bristow.

Fantasy   **(PR:A   MPAA:NR)**

SECRET OF THE PURPLE REEF, THE**   (1960) 81m FOX c

Jeff Richards (Mark Christopher), Margia Dean (Rue Amboy), Peter Falk (Tom Weber), Terence de Marney (Ashby), Richard Chamberlain (Dean Christopher), Robert Earl (Tobias), Gina Petrushka (Grandmere), Frank Ricco (Henri), Phil Rosen (Twine), Ben Blum (Priest), Larry Markow (Kilt), Jerry Mitchell.

Mystery starring Richards and Chamberlain as two brothers intent on finding out why the family fishing boat sank during calm weather. Crime kingpin Falk seems to be responsible, and the brothers are surprised to be aided by Falk's girlfriend Dean in their search for evidence. Nothing special, but the Caribbean locations help.

p, Gene Corman; d, William N. Witney; w, Harold Yablonsky, Corman (based on a "Saturday Evening Post" serial by Dorothy Cottrell); ph, Kay Norton (CinemaScope, DeLuxe Color); m, Buddy Bregman; ed, Peter C. Johnson; art d, Juan Viguie.

Crime   **(PR:A   MPAA:NR)**

SECRET OF THE SACRED FOREST, THE*½   (1970) 87m William
                                        Copeland-Sari-Manok/She rmart c

Gary Merrill (Mike Parks), Jon Provost (Jimmy), Henry Duval (Garcia), Leo Martinez (Bayani), Michael Parsons (Chris Carpenter), Dave Harvey (Brownie), Laurie Agudo (Annie), Christina Ponce-Enrile (Fely), Vic Silayan, Rolf Bayer, Mona Morena, Lola Boy, Louis Florentino, Joseph de Cordova, Carol Varga, Bruno Punzalan, Poch Apostol, Fred Viray, Don Smith, Zenaida Amador, Gami Virray, Vincente Sempio.

Provost plays a brave teenager who sneaks into the Philippines in order to search for his brother, Parsons, a famed investigative reporter whose plane crashed in the middle of the jungle while he was trying to expose the movements of a drug-smuggling ring. American Embassy official Merrill learns the boy has entered the country illegally and heads off into the bush after him. In the meantime, Provost has found a guide, native boy Martinez, to help him in his search. Pursued by black marketeers, unsympathetic government agents, headhunters, and Merrill, Provost finds his brother and is shocked to learn that he is a member of the drug-smuggling ring. The confusion ends, however, when Parsons explains that he staged his disappearance in order to join the smugglers so that he could expose them.

p, William Copeland; d, Michael Du Pont; w, Copeland; ph, Vincente Sempio (Eastmancolor); m, Herschel Burke Gilbert; ed, Tony Di Marco; m/l, "Has Any One Seen Chris?" Copeland, Gilbert, Ernest Hughes, "Filipina Filipina" Copeland, Angel Pena (sung by Maurice Santa Lucia.)

Adventure   **(PR:A   MPAA:G)**

SECRET OF THE TELEGIAN, THE**½   (1961, Jap.) 85m
          Toho/Herts-Lion c (DENSO NINGEN; AKA: THE TELEGIAN)

Koji Tsuruta, Yumi Shirakawa, Akihiko Hirata, Tadao Nakamaru, Seizaburo Kawazu, Yoshio Tsuchiya, Sachio Sakai.

Toho Studios took a break from giant monster movies to produce a few interesting sci-fi films dealing with matter-transformation. In THE SECRET OF TELEGIAN, the police become concerned when a number of ex-soldiers in the Imperial Japanese Army are found dead with mysterious glass coils and dog tags at their sides. The cops track down a potential victim, and the panicked veteran tells them that during the war, he and his unit (members of which have now been murdered) were given the task of hiding a brilliant scientist vital to the war effort. When the greedy soldiers learned that gold bars were among the scientist's research materials, they decided to steal them. One of their number, a corporal, protested the theft and was sealed up in the cave along with the scientist. As it turns out, the scientist was developing a way to teleport soldiers from one area to another, and the police surmise that he succeeded. The entombed corporal had been using the scientist's invention to get revenge on those who tried to kill him by teleporting himself to the victim, murdering him, and then teleporting back to his hideout.

p, Tomoyuki Tanaka; d, Jun Fukuda; w, Shinichi Sekizawa; ph, Kazuo Yamada (Tohoscope, Eastmancolor); spec eff, Eiji Tsuburaya.

Science Fiction   **(PR:A   MPAA:NR)**

SECRET OF THE WHISTLER***   (1946) 65m COL bw

Richard Dix, Leslie Brooks, Mary Currier, Michael Duane, Mona Barrie, Ray Walker, Claire DuBrey, Charles Trowbridge, Arthur Space, Jack Davis, Barbara Wooddell.

The eighth and final entry in the excellent "The Whistler" series, SECRET OF THE WHISTLER tells the story of a crazed artist (Dix) who has killed his first wife and is preparing to do in his second. The police have cleared him of the first murder, but can prove that he's the killer. With the help of some expert clue-finding, Dix's murderous nature is revealed. Engrossing as usual and well-acted. (See WHISTLER series, Index.)

p, Rudolph C. Flothow; d, George Sherman; w, Raymond L. Schrock (based on the story by Richard H. Landau); ph, Allen Siegler; ed, Dwight Caldwell; md, Mischa Bakaleinikoff; art d, Hans Radon; set d, Robert Bradfield.

Crime   **(PR:A   MPAA:NR)**

SECRET OF TREASURE MOUNTAIN*½   (1956) 68m COL bw

Valerie French (Audrey Lancaster), Raymond Burr (Cash Larsen), William Prince (Robert Kendall), Lance Fuller (Juan Alvarado), Susan Cummings (Tawana), Pat Hogan (Vahoe), Reginald Sheffield (Edward Lancaster), Rodolfo Hoyos (Francisco Martinez), Paul McGuire (Sheriff), Tom Hubbard (Sam), Boyd Stockman (Stub McCurdy).

Buried Spanish gold is the excuse for action in this run-of-the-mill Western. Years ago a Spaniard buried the loot on Apache land. The Apaches killed him, threw a curse on the ground and gold, and posted a guard. Enter the villainous Burr and his henchmen 200 years later. They try to get the fabled gold, but they too fall victim to the curse, and the gold stays buried.

p, Wallace MacDonald; d, Seymour Friedman; w, David Lang; ph, Benjamin H. Kline; ed, Edwin Bryant; md, Mischa Bakaleinikoff; art d, Carl Anderson.

Western   **(PR:A   MPAA:NR)**

SECRET PARTNER, THE** (1961, Brit.) 92m MGM bw (AKA: THE STREET PARTNER)

Stewart Granger (*John Brent*), Haya Harareet (*Nicole Brent*), Bernard Lee (*Detective Supt. Hanbury*), Hugh Burden (*Charles Standish*), Lee Montague (*Detective Inspector Henderson*), Melissa Stribling (*Helen Standish*), Conrad Phillips (*Alan Richford*), John Lee (*Clive Lang*), Norman Bird (*Ralph Beldon, Dentist*), Peter Illing (*Strakarios*), Basil Dignam (*Lyle*), William [James] Fox (*Brinton*), George Tovey (*Vickers*), Sydney Vivian (*Dock Foreman*), Paul Stassino (*Man in Soho Street*), Colette Wilde (*Girl in Car*), Willoughby Goddard (*Hotelkeeper*), Peter Welch (*P.C. McLaren*), Joy Wood (*Brent's Secretary*), Dorothy Gordon (*Dentist's Receptionist*).

Granger plays a London shipping tycoon being blackmailed by Bird, an evil dentist who threatens to expose the businessman's former conviction for embezzlement. Granger pays but his wife Harareet wonders why the family bank account is dwindling. Granger refuses to discuss it so Harareet decides that there's another woman and leaves him. Meanwhile, Bird is visited by a mysterious hooded man who tells the dentist that his blackmail scheme will be exposed unless he obtains the combination to Granger's office safe. Bird gets Granger in his dentist chair, drugs him, and extracts the proper numbers. The safe is robbed and Scotland Yard suspects Granger. Granger escapes and forces Bird to confess. This is good enough for the police, but they also suspect Harareet's new lover as Bird's accomplice. Granger confesses that he was the hooded stranger and it was he and Harareet who stole the money.

p, Michael Relph; d, Basil Dearden; w, David Pursall, Jack Seddon; ph, Harry Waxman; m, Philip Green; ed, Raymond Poulton; prod d, Elliot Scott; md, Green; art d, Alan Withy; makeup, Bob Lawrence.

Crime (PR:A MPAA:NR)

SECRET PASSION, THE (SEE: FREUD, 1962)

SECRET PATROL*½ (1936) 60m COL bw

Charles Starrett (*Alan*), Henry Mollison (*Gene*), Finis Barton (*Ann*), J.P. McGowan (*Blacksmith*), LeStrange Millman (*McCord*), James McGrath (*Arnold*), Arthur Kerr (*Jordan*), Reginald Hincks (*Superintendent*), Ted Mapes.

Starrett plays an agent sent out to the Northwest territory to investigate a rash of logging accidents at a lumber camp. Eventually it is learned that McGowan is behind the deaths because he wants control of the company.

d, David Selman; w, J.P. McGowan, Robert Watson (based on a story by Peter B. Kyne); ph, George Meehan, William Beckway; ed, William Austin.

Western (PR:A MPAA:NR)

SECRET PEOPLE*½ (1952, Brit.) 96m Ealing/Lippert bw

Valentina Cortesa (*Maria Brentano*), Serge Reggiani (*Louis*), Charles Goldner (*Anselmo*), Audrey Hepburn (*Nora Brentano*), Angela Fouldes (*Nora as a child*), Megs Jenkins (*Penny*), Irene Worth (*Miss Jackson*), Reginald Tate (*Inspector Eliot*), Norman Williams (*Sgt. Newcome*), Michael Shepley (*Pavillion Manager*), Athene Seyler (*Mrs. Reginald Kellick*), Sydney Tafler (*Syd Burnett*), Geoffrey Hibbert (*Steenie*), John Ruddock (*Daly*), Michael Allan (*Rodd*), John Field (*Fedor Luki*), Bob Monkhouse (*Barber*), Hugo Schuster (*Gen. Galbern*), Charlie Cairoli & Paul (*Speciality*), Lionel Harris, Rollo Gamble, John Penrose, John Chandos, Michael Ripper, Yvonne Coulette, John Mansi, John Gabriel, Olga Landiak, Frederick Schiller, Phaedros Antonio, Gaston Richer, Derek Elphinstone, Edward Evans, Ingeborg Wells, Helen Ford, Ann Lancaster, Grace Draper, Bertram Shuttleworth, Pamela Harrington, John Allen, Joe Linnane, Bay White, Sam Kydd, Simone Silva.

A tale of political assassination that follows the lives of two sisters, Cortesa and Hepburn, who are orphaned and forced to move to London after their father is murdered by a brutal European ruler in 1930. Seven years later, Cortesa meets up with the boyfriend she left behind, Reggiani and the two plot to assassinate the evil ruler with a time bomb. Their plot goes awry, however, and the pair kill an innocent bystander. Cortesa confesses her crime to the police, and is able to prevent her little sister being corrupted.

p, Sidney Cole; d, Thorold Dickinson; w, Dickinson, Wolfgang Wilhelm, Christianna Brand (based on a story by Dickinson, Joyce Carey); ph, Gordon Dines; m, Roberto Gerhard; ed, Peter Tanner; art d, William Kellner; cos, Anthony Mendleson; ch, Andree Howard.

Crime (PR:A MPAA:NR)

SECRET PLACE, THE** (1958, Brit.) 81m RANK of America bw

Belinda Lee (*Molly Wilson*), David McCallum (*Mike Wilson*), Anne Blake (*Mrs. Wilson*), Ronald Lewis (*Gerry Carter*), Michael Gwynn (*Stephen Waring*), George Selway (*Paddy*), George A. Cooper (*Harry*), John Welsh (*Mr. Christian*), Michael Brooke (*Freddie Haywood*), Maureen Pryor (*Mrs. Haywood*), Geoffrey Keen (*Mr. Haywood*), Brendon Hanley (*Johnnie Haywood*), Hugh Manning (*Sgt. Paynter*), Philip Ray (*Mr. Venner*), Wendy Craig (*Receptionist*).

An uneven crime drama with a great start: a small-time gang of hoodlums plan and perform a daring diamond robbery. The film then slides to a grinding halt as the gems fall into the hands of a policeman's young son (Brooke), leaving a desperate gang to try to get them back. The first part of the film is fast-paced and well developed, while the second half is contrived and drags.

p, John Bryan; d, Clive Donner; w, Linette Perry; ph, Ernest Steward; m, Clifton Parker; ed, Peter Bezencenet; md, Muir Mathieson; m/l, "But You," Lester Powell, Danny Maule (sung by Jimmy Parkinson), additional music by Ray Martin, Eric Jupp.

Crime (PR:A MPAA:NR)

SECRET SCROLLS (PART I)**½ (1968, Jap.) 106m Toho/Toho International c (YAGYU BUGEICHO; AKA: YAGYU SECRET SCROLLS)

Toshiro Mifune (*Tasaburo*), Koji Tsuruta (*Senshiro*), Yoshiko Kuga (*Yuhime*), Kyoko Kagawa (*Oki*), Mariko Okada (*Rika*), Denjiro Okochi (*Lord Yagyu*), Jotaro Togami (*Jubei*), Senjaku Nakamura (*Matajuro*), Hanshiro Iwai (*Iyemitsu*), Eijiro Tono (*Fugetsusai*), Akihiko Hirata (*Tomonori*).

Released in Japan in 1957, SECRET SCROLLS (PART I) is set in 17th Century Japan and details the saga of three sacred scrolls that are kept apart by three families. If the scrolls are ever assembled at one location, the reader could destroy the current ruling family and overthrow the government, which would start a long and bloody war in peaceful Japan. There are greedy and evil clans after the scrolls, and a lengthy and confusing battle for the powerful items ensues. Mifune plays a samurai/magician hired by one of the clans to collect the scrolls. More talk than action, the film has a sequel, SECRET SCROLLS (PART II).

d, Hiroshi Inagaki; w, Inagaki, Takeshi Kimura (based on the novel *Yagyu Bugeicho* Kosuke Gomi); ph, Tadashi Iimura (Agfacolor); m, Akira Ifukube; art d, Takeo Kita, Hirochi Ueda.

Adventure (PR:A-C MPAA:NR)

SECRET SCROLLS (PART II)**½ (1968, Jap.) 106m Toho/Toho International c (NINJUTSU, SORYU HIKEN)

Toshiro Mifune (*Tasaburo*), Koji Tsuruta (*Senshiro*), Nobuke Otawa (*The Princess*), Jotaro Togami (*Jubei*), Senjaku Nakamura (*Matajuro*), Eijiro Tono (*Fugetsusai*), Hanshiro Iwai (*Iyemitsu*), Yoshiko Kuga (*Yuhime*), Mariko Okada (*Rika*), Denjiro Okochi (*Lord Yagyu*), Kyoko Kagawa (*Oki*), Akihiko Hirata (*Tomonori*).

Released in 1958, this sequel to SECRET SCROLLS (PART I) picks up where the last film left off. Samurai/magician Mifune and his brother (Tsuruta) find one of the scrolls, but it is torn in half when they argue over who shall possess it. The family from whom it was stolen pursue the brothers, who split up, and the rest of the film follows the members of the Yagyu clan as they attempt to retrieve the parts of the scroll. Mifune isn't on screen as much in this film as he was in the first, but the film has more action and moves more quickly, although it is pointless for anyone who hasn't seen Part I to try to decipher Part II.

d, Hiroshi Inagaki; w, Inagaki, Takeshi Kimura, Tokuhei Wakao (based on the novel *Yagyu Bugeicho* by Kosuke Gomi); ph, Tadashi Iimura, Asaichi Nakai (Tohoscope, Agfacolor); m, Akira Ifukube; art d, Takeo Kita, Hiroshi Ueda.

Adventure (PR:A-C MPAA:NR)

SECRET SERVICE** (1931) 69m RKO bw

Richard Dix (*Lewis Dumont*), Shirley Grey (*Edith Varney*), William Post, Jr (*Lt. Dumont*), Gavin Gordon (*Archford*), Fred Warren (*Gen. U.S. Grant*), Nance O'Neil (*Mrs. Varney*), Virginia Sale (*Miss Kittridge*), Florence Lake (*Caroline*), Clarence Muse (*Jonas*), Harold Kinney (*Howard Varney*), Eugene Jackson (*Israel*), Frederick Burton (*Gen. Randolph*), Carl Gerard (*Lt. Foray*), Gertrude Howard (*Martha*), Emma Reed.

Dix plays a Union officer, who, along with his brother, Post, Jr., is sent behind Confederate lines to gather intelligence information about rebel troops strength, in this remake of the 1919 silent Civil War epic. Once in Dixie, however, Dix falls in love with Grey, the daugher of a Confederate general, and his sense of honor is put to the test. Eventually Dix is captured by the Confederates and thrown in the brig, but he meets his fate willingly, knowing that Grey will be waiting with a mint julep in her hand when the war is over.

p, Louis Sarecky; d, J. Walter Ruben; w, Gerrit J. Lloyd, Bernard Schubert (based on a play by William Gillette); ph, Edward Cronjager; ed, John Kitchin; art d, Max Ree.

War (PR:A MPAA:NR)

SECRET SERVICE INVESTIGATOR★★   (1948) 60m REP bw

Lynne Roberts *(Susan Lane)*, Lloyd Bridges *(Steve Mallory/Dan Redfern)*, George Zucco *(Otto Dagoff)*, June Storey *(Laura Redfern)*, Trevor Bardette *(Henry Witzel)*, John Kellogg *(Benny Deering)*, Jack Overman *(Herman)*, Roy Barcroft *(Al Turk)*, Douglas Evans *(Inspector Crahan)*, Milton Parsons *(Miller)*, James Flavin *(Police Inspector)*, Tommy Ivo *(Teddy Lane)*, Sam McDaniel *(Porter)*, Billy Benedict *(Counterman)*, Minerva Urecal *(Mrs. McGiven)*.

Fast-paced programmer starring Bridges as an unemployed WW II veteran who is conned by counterfeiter Zucco and his gang, posing as Secret Service agents, into participating in their evil schemes. Eventually Bridges wises up and calls real Treasury agents in to round up the baddies.

p, Sidney Picker; d, R.G. Springsteen; w, John K. Butler; ph, John MacBurnie; m, Mort Glickman; ed, Arthur Roberts; md, Glickman; art d, Frank Arrigo; set d, John McCarthy, Jr., Charles Thompson; cos, Adele Palmer.

Crime   (PR:A MPAA:NR)

SECRET SERVICE OF THE AIR★★½   (1939) 61m WB bw

Ronald Reagan *(Lt. "Brass" Bancroft)*, John Litel *(Saxby)*, Ila Rhodes *(Pamella Schuyler)*, Rosella Towne *(Zelma Warren)*, James Stephenson *(Jim Cameron)*, Eddie Foy, Jr *(Gabby Watters)*, Larry Williams *(Dick Wayne)*, John Ridgely *(Joe Leroy)*, Anthony Averill *(Hafer)*, Bernard Nedell *(Hemrich)*, Frank M. Thomas *(Doc)*, Joe Cunningham *(Dawson)*, Morgan Conway *(Ed Powell)*, Raymond Bailey *(Klume)*, John Harron *(Cliff Durell)*, Sidney Bracey *(John Vicary)*, Pierre Watkin *(Morrow)*, Herbert Rawlinson *(Schuyler)*, John Hamilton *(Warden Jackson)*, Davison Clark *(Deputy Warden)*, George Sorel *(Capt. Cortez)*, Alberto Morin *(Pedro the Bartender)*, Richard Bond *(Buzz)*, Jack Mower *(Aldrich)*, Frank Mayo *(Manning)*, Henry Otho *(Turnkey)*, Nat Carr *(Convict)*, Pat O'Malley, Jeffrey Sayre, Harry Hollingshead *(Guards)*, Albert Lloyd *(Bartell)*, Edgar Edwards *(Crowley)*, Cliff Saum *(Loudspeaker Announcer)*, Duke Green, John Sinclair *(Toughs)*, Jack Wise *(Alien)*, Glen Cavender *(Waiter)*, Sol Gorss *(Pilot)*, Paul Panzer *(Ivan)*, Don Turner *(Harper)*, Carlyle Moore, Jr *(Radio Operator)*, Eddy Chandler *(Capt. King of the Highway Patrol)*, Emilio Blanco *(Mexican)*, Lane Chandler *(Border Patrol Officer)*.

Seeking to capitalize on Reagan's new popularity after his appearance in BROTHER RAT, Warner Brothers bought the rights to the memoirs of former Secret Service chief William H. Moran, and threw away most of the factual information to create a surprisingly well-done (and fairly outrageous) series of adventures, starring Reagan as "Brass" Bancroft, Secret Service agent extraordinaire. This, the first in the series, sees Reagan as a former army pilot, making a comfortable living as a commercial airline pilot, who, for reasons only known to himself, decides to join the Secret Service for a life of danger. He is assigned to investigate a gang of evildoers suspected of smuggling illegal aliens into the U.S. in airplanes. The rotten, cheap labor-runners easily dispose of their cargo when in trouble, by simply opening a hatch underneath the aliens and letting them drop. This angers Reagan, and his investigation leads to a thrilling fight with the villainous Stephenson in the cockpit of a plane, as it nose dives toward the earth. Reagan did his own stunts in the series because of his good health and a low budget that only allowed a double for the bad guys.

p, Bryan Foy; d, Noel Smith; w, Raymond Schrock (based on the story "Murder Plane" by Schrock from the files of the ex-chief of the Secret Service, William H. Moran); ph, Ted McCord; ed, Doug Gould.

Crime   (PR:A MPAA:NR)

SECRET SEVEN, THE★★   (1940) 62m COL bw

Florence Rice *(Lola Hobbs)*, Barton MacLane *(Sam O'Donnell)*, Bruce Bennett *(Pat Norris)*, Joseph Crehan *(Chief Hobbs)*, Joseph Downing *(Lou Bodie)*, Howard Hickman *(Dr. Talbot)*, Edward Van Sloan *(Prof. Holtz)*, Don Beddoe *(Maj. Blinn)*, P.J. Kelly *(Prof. Cordet)*, William Forrest *(Brooks)*, Danton Ferrero *(De Soto)*, George Anderson *(Bennett)*.

Silly, but fun crime drama starring Bennett as a former crook turned scientific crime investigator. Forming a secret society of forensic scientists, he decides to convince police departments nation-wide that detective work through chemistry is the answer to their crime-solving problems. The seven scientists pick a large American city at random, and with the help of the chief of police's daughter, Rice, the plucky forensics prove that a gang led by the nasty MacLane are connected to a series of unsolved murders. Hooray for test-tubes!

d, James Moore; w, Robert Tasker (based on a story by Dean Jennings, Tasker); ph, John Stumar; ed, Charles Nelson.

Crime   (PR:A MPAA:NR)

SECRET SEVEN, THE★½   (1966, Ital./Span.) 92m
Columbus-Atenea/MGM c (GLI INVINCIBILI SETTE; LOS INVENCI-
BLES

Tony Russell *(Leslio)*, Helga Line *(Lydia)*, Massimo Serato *(Axel)*, Gerard Tichy *(Rabirio)*, Renato Baldini *(Kadem)*, Livio Lorenzon *(Rubio)*, Barta

Barri *(Baxo)*, Joseph Marc [Jose Marco] *(Luzar)*, Kris Huerta *(Gular)*, Gianni Solaro *(Nakassar)*, Frank Sorman [Francesco Sormano] *(Aristocrat)*, Emma Baron *(Mother)*, Pedro Mari *(Ario)*, Tomas Blanco *(Panuzio)*, Renato Montalbano *(Aristocrat)*, Nando Gazzolo, Piero Lulli, Pietro Capanna, Paola Pitti, Walter Maestosi, Caetano Quarraro, Fernando Maria Sanchez.

An Italian sandal epic set in 4th century B.C. stars Russell and Serato as two brave brothers, who, along with five equally brave ex-galley slaves, fight nobly against the tyrannical rule of an unnamed Middle Eastern country. Russell goes undercover as the lead tyrant's architect and learns of the evil despot's battle plans. When no one is looking, he then dons a disguise and joins his brother and their merry band to battle against the rampaging armies. Okay for fans of this stuff. This film could make a good case for the theory that all movie themes are basically a rehash of earlier themes. The one used here comes from the popular Western THE MAGNIFICENT SEVEN, which in turn has its roots in Akira Kurosawa's THE SEVEN SAMURAI.

p, Cleto Fontini, Italo Zingarelli; d, Alberto De Martino; w, De Martino, Sandro Continenza, Tonino Guerra, Natividad Zaro; ph, Eloy Mella (Techniscope, Eastmancolor); m, Carlo Franci; ed, Otello Colangeli; art d, Piero Poletto, Anthony Guere [Antonio de la Guerra]; cos, Mario Giorsi; makeup, Romolo Demartino.

Adventure   (PR:A MPAA:NR)

SECRET SINNERS★   (1933) 70m Mayfair bw

Jack Mulhall, Sue Carol, Nick Stuart, Cecilia Parker, Armand Kaliz, Natalie Moorehead, Bert Roach, Gertrude Short, Eddie Kane, William Humphries, Tom Ricketts, Paul Ellis, Lillian Leighton, Phillips Smalley, The Harmonettes, Lee Zahler.

Rich married man falls in love with chorus girl and fully intends to divorce his wife to marry the hoofer, but she misunderstands his intentions and runs off with some sap to make the playboy jealous. Rich guy tells her the truth and she returns.

p & d, Wesley Ford; W, F. McGrew Willis (based on a story by Willis); ph, James S. Brown, Jr.; ed, Fred Bain.

Drama   (PR:A MPAA:NR)

SECRET SIX, THE★★★½   (1931) 83m MGM bw

Wallace Beery *(Louis Scorpio)*, Lewis Stone *(Richard Newton)*, John Mack Brown *(Hank Rogers)*, Jean Harlow *(Anne Courtland)*, Marjorie Rambeau *(Peaches)*, Paul Hurst *(Nick Mizoski the Gouger)*, Clark Gable *(Carl Luckner)*, Ralph Bellamy *(Johnny Franks)*, John Miljan *(Smiling Joe Colimo)*, DeWitt Jennings *(Chief Donlin)*, Murray Kinnell *(Dummy Metz)*, Fletcher Norton *(Jimmy Delano)*, Louis Natheaux *(Eddie)*, Frank McGlynn *(Judge)*, Theodore Von Eltz *(District Attorney)*, Tom London *(Hood)*.

Though the gangster film was hardly MGM's metier, THE SECRET SIX is a well-made genre piece marked by some excellent performances. It is the Prohibition era and Beery, along with partners Hurst and Bellamy, decides to enter the bootlegging racket. Stone, an alcoholic lawyer, gives them advice, and soon their underhanded business is thriving. The group sets its horizons on the more lucrative market of the big city, ruffling the feathers of mob boss Miljan. Bellamy and some thugs decide to pay a call on Miljan's brother at the nightclub he works at. After bumping him off, Bellamy pins the murder on Beery, hoping Miljan's organization will act accordingly. Beery is wounded by a gunshot, then learns of Bellamy's double cross. He has Bellamy killed, then murders Miljan for good measure. Brown and Gable are two newspapermen assigned to investigate these gang wars. They spend some time in Beery's cafe, which causes the mob boss to grow suspicious. He has Harlow work as a cashier in the cafe to keep a watch on the two men. Later, a group of businessmen who go only by the name "The Secret Six," talk to Brown, and ask him to get some evidence against Beery's activities. Brown gets hold of the gun Beery used in the killings. Harlow learns of this, then finds that Beery's thugs are out to kill the reporter. She tries to catch up with Brown on the subway train in hopes of warning him, but Harlow is not in time and Brown is murdered. Harlow decides to retaliate against her former employer and turns witness against Beery at his trial. However, the powerful crime lord has rigged the jury, thus assuring him an acquittal. Beery fires back at Harlow's treachery by having her kidnaped. Gable learns where she is being held and goes to rescue her. He ends up being taken hostage himself, but "The Secret Six" arrive with the law in tow. They swoop in on the hideout, while Gable is able to escape with Harlow. Beery and Stone, who is the controlling mind behind the gang, also manage to escape, but argue over how they will split up their money. Beery shoots Stone, but before he dies Stone is able to fire back, killing the man who is murdering him. THE SECRET SIX is a well-crafted film, with gritty, realistic dialog and some excellent performances. Beery is a powerhouse, an angry performance showing the ruthless character for everything he is. Screenwriter Marion later said she based Beery's character on Al Capone's image. Stone is fine in support as the failed, booze-riddled lawyer, a far cry from the image he would attain in a few years with the ANDY HARDY films. Both Gable and Harlow were up-and-comers when this was made. They show distinctive talents, though there is little chemistry between the two. This would develop in time and they would go on to make five films together. Brown, who was billed above Gable, was slowly declining at MGM and would soon leave the austere studio for Poverty Row stardom with a series of successful B westerns. Beery and Harlow loathed one another, and made this no secret during production. Beery would take any chance he could to insult the actress and her performance. Harlow responded in kind, which made for many on-set histrionics. Though they would continue to appear in films together, their deeply rooted dislike for one another never ceased. THE SECRET SIX was a subject of some controversy, as many considered it to be an excessively violent portrait. The film was banned in many areas, including the entire state of New Jersey, while other local censors excised what they felt to be the more objectionable moments.

d, George Hill; w, Frances Marion (based on a story by Marion); ph, Harold Wenstrom; ed, Blanche Sewell.

Crime   (PR:C   MPAA:NR)

SECRET STRANGER, THE   (SEE: ROUGH RIDING RANGER, 1935)

SECRET TENT, THE*½   (1956, Brit.) 69m Forward/BL bw

Donald Gray (Chris Martyn), Andree Melly (Ruth Martyn), Jean Anderson (Mrs. Martyn), Sonia Dresdel (Miss Mitchum-Browne), Andrew Cruickshank (Inspector Thornton), Dinah Ann Rogers (Sally), Peter Hammond (Smith), Conrad Phillips (Sergeant), Shirley Jacobs.

Melly, a former criminal, is happily married to Gray and leads a law-abiding life. When a neighborhood burglary is reported and she mysteriously drops from sight, Gray and the authorities suspect Melly. Gray combs the streets for her and discovers that she has been forced to help her brother–the one guilty of the crime. Melly and Gray reunite by the film's end, however, and resume their life of clean living.

p, Nat Miller, Frank Bevis; d, Don Chaffey; w, Jan Read (based on the play by Elizabeth Addeyman); ph, Harry Waxman.

Crime   (PR:A   MPAA:NR)

SECRET VALLEY   (1937) 60m FOX bw (GB: GANGSTER'S BRIDE)

Richard Arlen (Lee Rogers), Virginia Grey (Jean Carlo), Jack Mulhall (Russell Parker), Norman Willis (Slick Collins), Syd Saylor (Paddy), Russell Hicks (Austin Martin), Willie Fung (Tobasco), Maude Allen.

City gal Grey high-tails it to Arlen's Nevada ranch when she discovers that her rich husband Mulhall is actually a big-time gangster. Mulhall and his goons pursue her out west of course, and Arlen is forced to defend the fair lady from the crooks.

p, Sol Lesser; d, Howard Bretherton; w, Paul Franklin, Dan Jarrett, Earle Snell (based on a story by Harold Bell Wright); ph, Charles Schoenbaum; ed, Charles Craft.

Western   (PR:A   MPAA:NR)

SECRET VENTURE*½   (1955, Brit.) 68m REP bw

Kent Taylor (Ted O'Hara), Jane Hylton (Joan Butler), Kathleen Byron (Renee l'Epine), Karel Stepanek (Zelinsky), Frederick Valk (Otto Weber), Maurice Kaufmann (Dan Fleming), Martin Boddey (Squire Marlowe), Arthur Lane (Bob Hendon), Michael Balfour (Stevens), John Boxer (Inspector Dalton), Hugo Schuster, John Warren, Fred Griffiths, Terence Brook, Patrick Dowling, Arthur Bentley, Michael Ripper, Vivienne Martin, Alexander Field.

Taylor is an American in England who gets mixed up in an espionage ring. Spies kidnap a renowned scientist, but in the process Taylor gains possession of a briefcase containing a secret formula. Instead of working with Scotland Yard, Taylor decides to crack the case by himself. The Yard eventually gets involved and together they apprehend the perpetrators. One of a couple of pictures that Americans Springsteen and Taylor made in England.

p, William N. Boyle; d, R.G. Springsteen; w, Paul Erickson, Kenneth R. Hayles; ph, Basil Emmott; m, Lambert Williamson; ed, John Seabourne; md, Williamson; art d, John Stoll.

Spy Drama   (PR:A   MPAA:NR)

SECRET VOICE, THE*½   (1936, Brit.) 68m British and
                                                Dominions/PAR bw

John Stuart (Jim Knowles), Diana Beaumont (Helen Allinson), John Kevan (Dick Allinson), Henry Victor (Brandt), Ruth Gower (Joan Grayson), Monte de Lyle (Perez), Charles Carew (Scotty), Susan Bligh.

A typical espionage thriller about a scientist who photographs his formula for nonflammable fuel and sends it off to the League of Nations for safekeeping. Foreign spies intervene and kidnap his sister to acquire the formula. The malicious plans are soon foiled, however, and the formula remains in the League's hands.

p, Anthony Havelock-Allan; d, George Pearson; w, Margaret McDonnell (based on the story by Frances Warren).

Spy Drama   (PR:A   MPAA:NR)

SECRET WAR, THE   (SEE: DIRTY GAME, THE, 1965, Fr./Ger./Ital.)

SECRET WAR OF HARRY FRIGG, THE½**
                                            (1968) 110m Albion/UNIV c

Paul Newman (Harry Frigg), Sylva Koscina (Countess di Montefiore), Andrew Duggan (Gen. Armstrong), Tom Bosley (Gen. Pennypacker), John Williams (Gen. Mayhew), Charles D. Gray (Gen. Cox-Roberts), Vito Scotti (Col. Ferrucci), Jacques Roux (Gen Rochambeau), Werner Peters (Maj. Von Steignitz), James Gregory (Gen. Homer Prentiss), Fabrizio Mioni (Lt. Rossano), Johnny Haymer (Sgt. Pozzallo), Norman Fell (Capt. Stanley), Buck Henry (Stockade Commandant), Horst Ebersberg (Lt. Gruber), Richard X. Slattery (M.P. Sergeant), George Ives (Major).

The first time screenwriters Tarloff and Stone shared a credit was on FATHER GOOSE, which won them an Oscar, even though they'd never met in person until the moment they ascended the stairs to collect their statuettes. In that picture, they had Cary Grant to carry the plot along with his inimitable insouciance. Here, they have been saddled with a muffed performance by mugging Paul Newman, who again proves that comedy is not his metier. The offensive title is an indication of the nature of the piece and the extra g in the hero's name must have been as a sop to any censors who knew what the word meant in Army parlance. It's the middle of WW II when five Allied officers are captured in a Turkish bath house in Tunisia and hied to an Italian mansion where they are under the watchful eye of Scotti, the Italian colonel in charge of their incarceration. The officers, Bosley, Duggan, Williams, Gray, and Roux are vital to the war effort but they argue so much about a means to escape that they can't agree on one. (It's a case of "all chiefs and no Indians.") Newman is a private who has spent more time in the guardhouse than in action and he is known for his ability to escape from jails, so he is tapped to get these men out. They are living in incredible luxury, far from the front, and there is a question as to whether or not they want to escape. Newman is vaulted to the rank of major general, so the others must take his commands. He is flown to Italy, parachuted behind enemy lines near the villa, and allows himself to be taken there. Once inside, he attempts to convince the quintet to escape. The owner of the villa is Koscina, a woman who espouses no political beliefs and has nothing to do with the Fascists who are occupying her home. The moment Newman meets her, he stalls the escape attempt in order to get to know her better. All of the Allies have come to like Scotti, who is a decent man. The night they are to flee they hold off because Scotti is to be promoted to general and they don't want to endanger his opportunity for advancement. Just then, Nazi officers show up and say that Italy is now under the Allied thumb, so all prisoners of the Italians are to be transferred to German prison camps, which are, of course, a good deal less sumptuous than this mansion. Once in a German camp, Newman decides he doesn't like it, plans the escape, and they all get away. In reward for his derring-do, Newman accepts a commission and his new assignment is to run a radio station at the villa of Koscina. The location scenes were done east of Los Angeles in the Sierra Madre area, which effectively doubled for Italy. Some interesting casting includes writer Buck Henry (THE GRADUATE, etc), commercials actors Haymer and Slattery, and long-time farceur Fell, who was a leading TV comedy actor in the 1970s. Koscina is absolutely scrumptious to look at as the only woman in the otherwise all-male cast. Some of the jokes are tedious but would have been far more effective in mouth of anyone else but Newman, who has demonstrated over and over that his ability with comedy is about on a par with Al Pacino's capacity for slam-dunking a basketball.

p, Hal E. Chester; d, Jack Smight; w, Peter Stone, Frank Tarloff (based on a story by Tarloff); ph, Russell Metty (Techniscope, Technicolor); m, Carlo Rustichelli; ed, J. Terry Williams; art d, Alexander Golitzen, Henry Bumstead; set d, John McCarthy, John Austin; cos, Edith Head; makeup, Bud Westmore.

Comedy   **Cas.**   (PR:A-C   MPAA:NR)

SECRET WAYS, THE**   (1961) 112m Heath/UNIV bw

Richard Widmark (Michael Reynolds), Sonja Ziemann (Julia Jansci), Charles Regnier (The Count), Walter Rilla (Prof. Jansci), Howard Vernon (Col. Hidas), Senta Berger (Elsa), Heinz Moog (Minister Sakenov), Hubert von Meyerinck (Hermann Sheffler), Oskar Wegrostek (The Fat Man), Stefan Schnabel (Border Official), Elisabeth Newmann-Viertel (Olga), Helmuth Janatsch (Janos), John Horsley (Jon Bainbridge), Walter Wilz (Peter), Raoul Retzer (Special Agent), Georg Kovary (Language Professor), Adi Berber (Sandor), Jochen Brockmann (The Commandant), Brigitte Brunmuller (Waitress), Reinhard Kolldehoff, Rudolf Rosner (The Count's Men).

Sluggish, laughable, spy movie produced by and starring Widmark as an American soldier-of-fortune, hired by an international anti-Communist league to retrieve brilliant professor Rilla out of communist controlled Hungary where he is hiding. Widmark enlists the aid of Rilla's daughter, Ziemann, and is brought to her father's secret laboratory by Hungarian freedom fighters. The communist authorities manage to pinpoint the location of the hideout, and they throw Widmark, Rilla, and Ziemann in prison where they are tortured by Vernon (who would have given the same characterization as a sadistic Nazi guard in 1942). The trio are rescued by mysterious freedom fighter Regnier, but before they can make good their escape, their savior is killed, allowing the three to flee out of Hungary.

p, Richard Widmark; d, Phil Karlson; w, Jean Hazelewood (based on the novel by Alistair MacLean); ph, Max Greene; m, Johnny Williams; ed, Aaron Stell; art d, Werner & Isabella Schlichting; cos, Leo Bei; makeup, Rudolf Ohlschmidt; stunts, Bob Simmons.

Espionage   **(PR:A-C MPAA:NR)**

SECRET WEAPON, THE   (SEE: SHERLOCK HOLMES AND THE
                                           SECRET WEAPON, 1942)

SECRET WITNESS, THE*   (1931) 65m COL bw (AKA: TERROR BY
                                                            NIGHT)

Una Merkel (*Lois Martin*), William Collier, Jr (*Arthur Jones*), ZaSu Pitts (*Bella*), Purnell Pratt (*Capt. McGowan*), Clyde Cook (*Larson*), Ralf Harolde (*Lewis Leroy*), June Clyde (*Tess*), Rita LaRoy (*Sylvia Folsom*), Paul Hurst (*Brannigan, Cop*), Clarence Muse (*Building Engineer*), Nat Pendleton (*Gunner, Folsom's Bodyguard*), Hooper Atchley (*Herbert Folsom*), Greta Grandstedt (*Moll*), Mike Donlin.

Rich cad strings naive mistress along, while refusing to divorce his wife. Distraught, she commits suicide and her vengeance-seeking brother goes after the cold-hearted playboy, who caused all the trouble.

d, Thornton Freedland; w, Samuel Spewack (based on his novel, *Murder in the Gilded Cage*); ph, Robert Planck; ed, Louis H. Sackin.

Drama   **(PR:A MPAA:NR)**

SECRET WORLD**½   (1969, Fr.) 111m Fox Europa-Les Films Du
                                  Siecle-FOX c (L'ECHE LLE BLANCHE)

Jacqueline Bisset (*Wendy*), Giselle Pascal (*Florence*), Pierre Zimmer (*Philippe*), Marc Porel (*Olivier*), Jean-Francois Maurin (*Francois*), Paul Bonifas (*Gustave*), Guy D'Avout (*Malevar*), Jacques Riberolles (*Norbert*), Judith Magre (*Eliane*), Chantal Goya (*Monique*), Yves Lefebvre (*Alain*).

English girl Bisset travels to France to visit her former lover Zimmer and his family, who live in a beautiful chateau. Her presence causes a great disturbance in the household especially to Zimmer's wife, Pascal, who feels old and threatened by this gorgeous young woman. Porel, the couple's son, seeks to seduce Bisset, but becomes frustrated when she does not respond. Trying to hide from this madness, Bisset turns her interest to Zimmer's young nephew, Maurin, who has shut himself off from the family ever since his parents died in a car crash. The beautiful woman's attention brings the boy out of his shell (and arouses some definite sexual feelings), but he is crushed when she returns to London without him. Potentially powerful material is diffused by an overly complicated visual style, and some badly drawn characterizations.

p, Jacques Strauss; d, Robert Freeman, Paul Feyder; w, Gerard Brach, Jackie Glass; ph, Peter Biziou (DeLuxe Color); m, Antoine Duhamel; ed, Richard Bryan; art d, Jacques Dugied; cos, Colette Baudot; makeup, Michel Dervelle, Fernande Hugi.

Drama   **(PR:C MPAA:M)**

SECRETS**   (1933) 90m Mary Pickford/UA bw

Mary Pickford (*Mary Marlow/Mary Carlton*), Leslie Howard (*John Carlton*), C. Aubrey Smith (*Mr. Marlowe*), Blanche Frederici (*Mrs. Marlowe*), Doris Lloyd (*Susan Channing*), Herbert Evans (*Lord Hurley*), Ned Sparks ("*Sunshine*"), Allan Sears (*Jake Houser*), Mona Maris (*Senora Martinez*), Lyman Williams (*William Carlton as a Child*), Huntley Gordon (*William Carlton as an Adult*), Virginia Grey (*Audrey Carlton as a Child*), Ethel Clayton (*Audrey Carlton as an Adult*), Ellen Johnson (*Susan Carlton as a Child*), Bessie Barriscale (*Susan Carlton as an Adult*), Randolph Connelly (*Robert Carlton as a Child*), Theodore Von Eltz (*Robert Carlton as an Adult*).

Mary Pickford's last movie, which her company also produced, was a great disappointment. After the first version was edited, she tossed it into the round file and re-shot the whole thing. It wasn't much better. Norma Talmadge had already made a silent version of the play from whence this sprung and that was a bit more pleasing. Pickford is a New England miss in love with handsome Howard, but her domineering father, Smith, does not approve of Howard and wants her to marry Evans, a peer of the realm in England and a man for whom boredom is a step up in excitement. Rather than be trapped in a loveless marriage, Pickford and Howard leave the East and jump aboard a wagon train to California where they will be far enough away from Smith's anger and can begin their lives anew. They arrive, show their mettle, and in no time at all are wealthy cattle ranchers. They become so successful at getting their little dogies along that Howard is thought to be gubernatorial fodder. It looks as though everything is going smoothly; then the truth comes out: Howard, who has appeared to be a solid husband, has been dallying with temptress Lloyd for several years. Once that's uncovered, it marks the end of his political plans. As it turns out, Pickford has been aware of Howard's peccadillos and turned the other cheek because

she loved him so much. In the end, she takes him back and all is forgiven. It's a mixed bag and suffers from miscasting. Howard, who had been known for his effete drawing-room types, is not quite right as the sturdy rancher. Pickford and Howard were both the same age, 40, when they made the movie and might have been a good team, given the right material. Half of this is urban, the other half is frontier, and the two genres don't seem to blend well. The picture opened on a dismal day for the U.S. as it was on that morning that Roosevelt declared a "bank holiday" and people were not allowed to remove their money for a short time. In the atmosphere of gloom and doom, not many people wanted to see this kind of melodrama and the picture was one of the biggest secrets of the year. A couple of action scenes, including one with Howard, Pickford, and hired hand Sparks holding off a passel of desperate crooks who want to take over their spread. Other than that, it's fairly static.

d, Frank Borzage; w, Frances Marion, Salisbury Field, Leonard Praskins (based on the play by Rudolf Besier, May Edington); ph, Ray June; ed, Hugh Bennett; cos, Adrian.

Western Drama   **(PR:A-C MPAA:NR)**

SECRETS, 1941   (SEE: SECRETS OF THE LONE WOLF, 1941)

SECRETS*   (1971) 92m Lone Star c

Jacqueline Bisset (*Jacky*), Per Oscarsson (*Raoul*), Shirley Knight Hopkins (*Beatrice*), Robert Powell (*Allan*), Tarka Kings (*Josy*), Martin C. Thurley (*Raymond*), Stephen Martin (*Dominique*).

A boring and amateurish production about a married couple and their daughter who have each had their own sexual interlude that day. Naturally, their attempt to keep secrets from one another fails. The film was re-released in 1978 after Bisset's much publicized wet T-shirt appearance in THE DEEP. SECRETS, however, isn't one of those pictures made by a hungry starlet looking for work and forced into low-budget sleaze. Bisset had already appeared in a number of quality films: CUL-DE-SAC (1966), CASINO ROYALE (1967), BULLITT (1968), and AIRPORT (1970). SE-CRETS is simply a third-rate film that will satisfy certain fans' desires to see Bisset naked for five minutes.

p, John Hanson; d, Philip Saville; w, Rosemary Davies (based on a story by Saville); ph, Nic Knowland, Harry Hart; m, Mike Gibbs; ed, Tony Woolard.

Drama   **Cas.**   **(PR:O MPAA:R)**

SECRETS D'ALCOVE**½   (1954, Fr./Ital.) 110m
                                  Terra-Cormoran/Pathe bw

Jeanne Moreau (*Mother*), Richard Todd (*Soldier*), Dawn Addams (*Janet*), Vittorio De Sica (*Bob*), Mouloudji (*Ricky*), Francoise Arnoul (*Martine*), Martine Carol (*Agnes*), Bernard Blier (*President*), Francois Perier (*Alfred*).

European anthology film which sees a group of businessmen forced to cohabit a tiny cabin with only one bed when dense fog waylaid their journey to an important conference. The bed spurs memories in the men and they swap stories about sharing beds with strangers. De Sica relates a story about how he sought divorce from his wife by hiring a beautiful American girl, Addams, to sleep with him. Unexpectedly, the business-like coupling turns to love, and Addams and De Sica are soon married. In another story, Mouloudji plays a lonely truckdriver who helps snobby rich girl, Arnoul, change a flat. After he helps her, Mouloudji dreams of being in bed with the girl. The last story, set at the turn of the century, sees courtesan, Carol, accidentally receiving a fancy bed from the President of the country, which was intended for a rich madame. Carol soon finds herself in a position of power in the country.

d, Henri Decoin, Jean Delannoy, Ralph Habib, G. Franciolini; w, Maurice Auberge, Roland Laudenbach, Antoine Blondin, Sergio Amedel, Janet Wolf; ph, Christian Matras, L.H. Burel; m, Georges Van Parys; ed, Denis Reis, James Cuenet.

Comedy   **(PR:C MPAA:NR)**

SECRETS OF A CO-ED*½   (1942) 67m PRC bw (GB: SILENT
                                                          WITNESS)

Otto Kruger (*Reynolds*), Tina Thayer (*Brenda*), Rick Vallin (*Nick*), Russell Hoyt (*Bille*), Marcia Mae Jones (*Laura*), Geraldine Spreckels (*Tessie*), Diana Del Rio (*Maria*), Herbert Vigran (*Soapy*), Patricia Knox (*Flo*), Claire Rochelle (*Miss Wilson*), Addison Richards (*District Attorney*), Isabelle La Mal (*Dean Sophie*).

Kruger plays a successful criminal lawyer who leads a double-life as the head of a powerful crime syndicate. His college-age daughter, Thayer, causes him nothing but trouble and forces him to take action, when she falls in love with one of his goons. Not wanting her to marry a crook, Kruger has the goon bumped off, but the plan backfires and Thayer is arrested for murder. Kruger then puts on his lawyer cap to defend his daughter, but in the end is forced to reveal his other identity and take the rap for her benefit. Though material here is of the sketchiest kind, it provided director Lewis a chance to perform some wizardry as a B director. Shot in only six days, this film contains an unbelievable 10-minute crane shot in the courtroom.

It's impossible to believe that Lewis managed to pull off such a feat, given the time restrictions.

p, Leon Fromkess, Albert Stern, Arthur Alexander; d, Joseph H. Lewis; w, George W. Sayre; ph, Robert Cline; ed, Charles Henkel, Jr.; md, Lee Zahler; m/l, J. Jay Levinson, Ray Evans, Harol d Lobo, Milton De Oliviera.

Drama   **(PR:A   MPAA:NR)**

SECRETS OF A MODEL*   (1940) 60m Continental-Times bw

Sharon Lee (*Rita Wilson*), Harold Daniels (*Jack Thorndyke*), Julien Madison (*Bob Grey*), Phyllis Barry (*Sally Adams*), Bobby Watson (*Stuart Bannerman*), Eddie Borden (*Customer*), Grace Lenard (*Jo Jo*).

Small-town girl Lee moves to the big city looking for work as a model. She gets a job as a waitress at a hamburger stand and hopes to be discovered. At first she is only discovered by wholesome milkman Madison, but she's not too interested. Then the suave but sleazy Daniels moves in on her, and tells young Lee that he can make her a star. Before she knows it she's posing practically naked (by 1940 standards) for a friend of Daniels who is an artist. Lee thinks she's in love with Daniels and he promises he'll marry her, but she eventually gets fed up with his excuses and goes back to the honorable but safe milkman. If that isn't enough, Daniels decides to force his attentions on Lee's unwitting roommate, but the villain is killed in a car crash before he gets too far.

p, J.D. Kendis; d, Sam Newfield; w, Sherman Lowe, Arthur St. Claire; ph, Jack Greenhalgh; ed, George Merrick.

Drama   **(PR:C   MPAA:NR)**

SECRETS OF A NURSE*   (1938) 69m UNIV bw

Edmund Lowe (*John Dodge*), Helen Mack (*Katherine MacDonald*), Dick Foran (*Lee Burke*), Samuel S. Hinds (*Judge Corrigan*), Paul Hurst (*Slice Cavanaugh*), Leon Ames (*Joe Largo*), David Oliver (*Spud Williams*), Frances Robinson (*Nurse*), Clarence Muse (*Tiger*), Stanley Hughes (*Intern*), Horace MacMahon (*Larry Carson*), Dorothy Arnold (*Secretary*), George Chandler (*Dopey*), Clyde Dilson (*Churchill*), Virginia Brissac (*Farlinger*).

Ridiculously plotted crime film starring Foran as an unfortunate boxer who is the victim of a big-shot gambler, McMahon, who sets it up so that the pugilist is practically beaten to death in the ring. Nursed back to health by the lovely Mack, Foran begins to get jealous when she begins to pay too much attention to another patient, dashing criminal attorney Lowe, who is convalescing from an illness. His boxing career over, Foran takes a job as a bellhop and is soon framed for the murder of his former manager and sent to death row. Though they are rivals for Mack's affections, Lowe comes to the aid of Foran and gets an eleventh-hour confession from McMahon.

p, Burt Kelly; d, Arthur Lubin; w, Tom Lennon, Lester Cole (based on the story "West Side Miracle" by Quentin Reynolds); ph, Elwood Bredell; ed, Ed Curtis; md, Charles Previn; art d, Jack Otterson.

Crime/Drama   **(PR:A   MPAA:NR)**

SECRETS OF A SECRETARY*   (1931) 71m PAR bw

Claudette Colbert (*Helen Blake*), Herbert Marshall (*Lord Danforth*), George Metaxa (*Frank D'Agnoli*), Betty Lawford (*Sylvia Merritt*), Mary Boland (*Mrs. Merritt*), Berton Churchill (*Mr. Merritt*), Averell Harris (*Dan Marlow*), Betty Garde (*Dorothy White*), Hugh O'Connell (*Charlie Rickenbacker*), H. Dudley Hawley (*Mr. Blake*), Joseph Crehan (*Reporter*), Charles Wilson (*Police Captain*), Edward Keane (*Albany Hotel Manager*), Porter Hall, Millard Mitchell (*Drunks*).

One of the last films produced by Long Island's Astoria Studios which was desperately trying for a big hit before the doors slammed shut. SECRETS OF A SECRETARY did little to halt the inevitable. Colbert stars as a flighty rich girl who impulsively marries a South American gigolo while on a cruise. After the death of Colbert's wealthy daddy, the gigolo takes off when he realizes she's broke. Forced to work, Colbert takes a job as the social secretary to her father's best friend's wife. Though the daughter of her boss treats her like dirt, Colbert soon finds herself trying to cover up the kid's involvement in a rather messy murder which leads to predictable results.

d, George Abbott; w, Dwight Taylor, Abbott; (based on a story by Charles Brackett); ph, George Folsey; ed, Helene Turner.

Drama   **(PR:A   MPAA:NR)**

SECRETS OF A SORORITY GIRL*½
                    (1946) 58m PRC bw (GB: SECRET OF LINDA HAMILTON)

Mary Ware, Rick Vallin, Addison Richards, Ray Walker, Marie Harmon, Caren Marsh, Mary Kenyon, Marilyn Johnson, Rosemonde James, Mauritz Hugo, Emmett Vogan, Frank Ferguson, Anthony Warde, Bill Murphy, Pierre Watkin.

Sorority girl Ware begins hanging around with the criminal element and is photographed in a number of gambling dens. The photos are then sent to her district attorney father who is pressured into a blackmail scheme. Ware is then made to believe she is guilty of murder in a hit-and-run case. With the

help of her father, she is able to prove her innocence and pin the crime on the real culprits.

p, Max Alexander, Alfred Stern; d, Lew Landers; w, George Wallace Sayre; ph, Robert Cline; ed, Roy Livingston; md, Karl Hajos; art d, Edward Jewell.

Crime   **(PR:A   MPAA:NR)**

SECRETS OF A SOUL   (SEE: CONFESSIONS OF AN OPIUM
                                                            EATER, 1962)

SECRETS OF A WINDMILL GIRL*½   (1966, Brit.) 86m
                                          Searchlight-Markten/Compton c

April Wilding (*Linda Grey*), Pauline Collins (*Pat Lord*), Renee Houston (*Dresser*), Derek Bond (*Inspector Thomas*), Harry Fowler (*Larry*), Howard Marion Crawford (*Producer*), Peter Swanick (*Len Mason*), Martin Jarvis (*Mike*), Leon Cortez (*Agent*), Dana Gillespie, George Rutland, Deirdre O'Dea, Sadie Eddon, Pat Patterson, Jill Millard.

An exploitative crime story about a stripper who is gang-raped and murdered. The events that lead up to her grisly death are told by a singer who was the dead girl's best friend. A sensational subject which is given an empty-headed treatment.

p, Arnold Miller, Stanley Long; d&w, Miller; ph (Eastmancolor).

Crime   **(PR:O   MPAA:NR)**

SECRETS OF A WOMAN'S TEMPLE**   (1969, Jap.) 79m Daiei bw

Michiyo Yasudo (*Oharu*), Shigako Shimegi (*Shigetsuin*), Sanae Nakahara, Machiko Hasegawa, Naomi Kobayashi, Yasuyo Matsumura.

Yasudo investigates the mysterious disappearance of her brother and joins a convent in the area where he vanished in hopes of finding him. She discovers that Shimegi, an evil cousin to the Shogun, is the mother superior and is responsible for a series of murders of young men she has lured into the convent and seduced. Before Yasudo can kill her, Shimegi sets the temple afire and kills herself.

d, Tokuzo Tanaka; w, Shozaburo Asai; ph, Chishi Makiura (Daieiscope); m, Hajime Kaburagi; art d, Yoshinobu Nishioka.

Crime Drama   **(PR:O   MPAA:NR)**

SECRETS OF AN ACTRESS*   (1938) 71m WB bw

Kay Francis (*Ray Carter*), George Brent (*Dick Orr*), Ian Hunter (*Peter Snowden*), Gloria Dickson (*Carla Orr*), Isabel Jeans (*Marian Plantagenet*), Penny Singleton (*Miss Reid*), Dennie Moore (*Miss Blackstone*), Selmer Jackson (*Thompson*), Herbert Rawlinson (*Harrison*), Emmett Vogan (*Spencer*), James B. Carson (*Carstairs*).

Francis was one of the stars at Warner Bros., earning the princessly salary of more than $200,000 per year. When she lost the plum role in TOVARICH to Claudette Colbert, she was irked enough to call in her lawyers and state to the bosses that she wouldn't renew *them* after her current contract expired. To get even with that kind of sassiness, Warners cast her in several dull programmers, all of which caused her career to wane quickly. Francis is an actress who has been on the stage since her diaper days but still hasn't gotten the big break. She meets Hunter, a laconic but rich architect and he likes her well enough to plan financing a play, for which he will design the sets, something he's always wanted to do. Hunter's associate, Brent, tries to convince him that it's a pipe dream but Hunter remains steadfast in his desires. Brent's attitude melts when he finally meets Francis. The two of them fall in love but that's complicated by the fact that Brent is married to Dickson. The two have been apart for a couple of years and Brent doesn't consider himself married any longer, so he omits telling Francis of his situation. Brent goes to Dickson and pleads with her to set him free, promising her a huge settlement and custody of her mother. Dickson does not give in so easily, though, and when Francis finds out Brent is still wed, she feels terrible and goes back to Hunter, agreeing to marry him. Hunter is a gentleman and sees that it's a rebound and that she is mad for Brent, so he helps convince Dickson to let Brent go, thereby bringing Brent and Francis together. The best performance in this otherwise lackluster picture is by Isabel Jeans as Francis' inebriated roommate. In an early scene, after having had too much to drink in a bar, Jeans punches Hunter out and that leads to Francis meeting him. She stands out like a diamond in a mudhole. British-born Jeans began in movies in 1917, came to the U.S. and made her debut in TOVARICH, then worked in pictures in the U.S. before returning to England after WW II and appearing in several films, the last of which was THE MAGIC CHRISTIAN with Peter Sellers and Ringo Starr. She was married to Claude Rains for a time.

p, David Lewis; d, William Keighley; w, Milton Krims, Rowland Leigh, Julius J. Epstein (based on the story "Lovely Lady" by Krims, Leigh, Epstein); ph, Sid Hickox; ed, Owen Marks; md, Leo F. Forbstein; art d, Anton Grot; cos, Orry-Kelly.

Comedy/Love Story   **(PR:A-C   MPAA:NR)**

SECRETS OF CHINATOWN*   (1935) 63m Northern/SYN bw

Nick Stuart (Robert Rand), Lucille Browne (Zenobia), Raymond Lawrence (Donegal Dawn), James Flavin (Brandhma), Harry Hewitson (Chan Tow Ling), James McGrath (Commissioner), Reginald Hincks (Dr. Franklin), John Barnard (Doverscourt), Arthur Legge-Willis (Yogi of Madrada).

Stuart is the enthusiastic friend of famous detective Lawrence, both of whom are involved in a strange rash of Chinatown crimes. Stuart falls for Browne and tries to take her away from her dangerous surroundings. Upon further investigation, Stuart finds that secret rituals are being carried out in the basement of Browne's work place. During one of these meetings Browne is hypnotized and dressed up as the cult's high priestess. Stuart is captured and taken to the cult's mountaintop hideout. Lawrence follows and, in the nick of time, saves both Stuart and the glassy-eyed Browne. A bottom-of-the-barrel programmer which itself should have been kept a secret.

p, Kenneth J. Bishop; d, Fred Newmeyer; w, Guy Morton (based on his novel); ph, William Beckway; ed, William Austin

Mystery/Crime   (PR:A   MPAA:NR)

SECRETS OF MONTE CARLO**   (1951) 60m REP bw

Warren Douglas (Bill Whitfield), Lois Hall (Susan Reeves), June Vincent (Stella), Stephen Bekassy (Otto Von Herzen), Robin Hughes (Charles Reeves), Otto Waldis (Louis Gunther), Charles LaTorre (Tony Retella), Philip Ahn (Wong), Isabel Randolph (Mrs. Gussy), Charles Lung (Rajah of Bandore), Sue Casey (Wife of Rajah), Georges Renavent (Inspector Marcel Remy), Bruce Lester (British Inspector), George Davis (Pierre), Howard Chuman (Ah Fong).

Competent programmer starring Douglas as an innocent American businessman visiting Monte Carlo who finds himself embroiled in the theft of valuable jewels belonging to a rajah. Seduced into the role by evil femme gang leader Vincent, Douglas finds himself reluctantly on the run from British insurance investigator Hughes. Hughes' sister, Hall, is in love with the wronged man.

p, William Lackey; d, George Blair; w, John K. Butler; ph, Walter Strenge; m, Stanley Wilson; ed, Irving M. Schoenberg; art d, Fred A. Ritter.

Crime   (PR:A   MPAA:NR)

SECRETS OF SCOTLAND YARD**   (1944) 68m REP bw

Edgar Barrier (John Usher/Robert Usher), Stephanie Bachelor (Sudan Ainger), C. Aubrey Smith (Sir Christopher Belt), Lionel Atwill (Waterlow), Henry Stephenson (Sir Reginald Meade), John Abbott (Mortimer Cope), Walter Kingsford (Roylott Bevan), Martin Kosleck (Josef), Forrester Harvey (Alfred Morgan), Frederick Worlock (Mason), Matthew Boulton (Col. Hedley), Bobby Cooper (David Usher), William Edmunds (Isaiah Thom), Louis V. Arco (Col. Eberling), Frederick Giermann (Hans Koebig), Sven-Hugo Borg (Nazi Messenger), Leslie Vincent (Hardy the Copilot), Arthur Stanning (Inspector Collins), Keith Hitchcock (Inspector Chambers), Leonard Carey (Butler), Mary Gordon (Libby the Housekeeper), Jordan Shelley (Larkworthy the Pilot), Jack George (Wine Waiter), Ed Biby (Sir Philip Gough), Arthur Mulliner (Lt. Col. Jardine), Maj. Sam Harris (Undersecretary Borden), Eric Wilton (Gen. Eric Holt), Carey Harrison (British Navy Officer), Larry Steers (Adm. Langley), William Nind (English Waiter), Carl Ekberg (German Cook), Antonio Filauri (Waiter), Richard Ryen (Herr Friedrich Eberling), Frank Brand (Carl Eberling), Nigel Horton (Official of Communications), Richard Woodruff (Radio Man), Kenne Duncan (Steward).

The trials and tribulations of decoders of Nazi secret messages for the British are detailed in this wartime drama featuring Barrier in a brief dual role as twin brothers (one of whom is killed off after deciphering an important Nazi message). Nazi agents operating in England under the supervision of the evil Atwill provide the appropriate amount of villainy as dedicated but luckless decoders are bumped off for being too good at their jobs. Eventually the staffers figure out that there's a spy in their midst, and they round up the foreign agents.

p&d, George Blair; w, Denison Clift (based on the novel Room 40, O.B. by Clift); ph, William Bradford; ed, Fred Allen; md, Morton Scott; art d, Gano Chittenden.

Espionage   (PR:A   MPAA:NR)

SECRETS OF SEX zero   (1970, Brit.) 91m Noteworthy/Balch c

Richard Schulman, (Judge), Janet Spearman (Wife), Dorothy Grumbar (Photographer), Anthony Rowlands (Model), George Herbert (Steward), Kenneth Benda (Sacha Seramona), Yvonne Quenet (Mary-Clare), Reid Anderson (Dr. Rilke), Cathy Howard (Burglar), Mike Britton (Burglary Victim), Maria Frost (Lindy Leigh), Peter Carlisle (Colonel X), Sue Bond (Call Girl), Elliott Stein (Strange Man).

A silly soft-core fantasy which is a collection of sex tales told by a mummified Arabian. Yes, a mummified Arabian. Relatively harmless, but worthless.

p, Richard Gordon, Anthony Balch; d, Balch; w, Martin Locke, John Eliot,

Maureen Owen, Elliott Stein, Balch (based on a story by Alfred Mazure).

Fantasy   (PR:O   MPAA:NR)

SECRETS OF THE CITY   (SEE: CITY OF SECRETS, 1963, Ger.)

SECRETS OF THE FRENCH POLICE*½   (1932) 59m RKO bw

Gwili Andre (Eugenie Dorain), Frank Morgan (Francois St. Cyr), Gregory Ratoff (Gen. Moloff), Murray Kinnell (Bertillon), John Warburton (Leon Renault), Lucien Prival (Baron Lomzoi), Julia Swayne Gordon (Mme. Danton), Kendall Lee (Rena), Christian Rub (Anton Dorain), Arnold Korff (Grand Duke), Rochelle Hudson, Guido Trento.

A nearly incoherent mystery film stars Ratoff as an evil hypnotist who has poor Andre under his spell. He has her believing she's a Russian princess so that he can use her to commit his criminal acts. When a few of the seven corpses in this film pop up, French detective Kinnell jumps into action to solve the strange crimes.

d, Edward Sutherland; w, Samuel Ornitz, Robert Tasker (based on magazine series "Secrets of Surete" by H. Ashton-Wolfe, Ornitz); ph, Al Gilks, m, Max Steiner; art d, Carroll Clark.

Crime   (PR:A   MPAA:NR)

SECRETS OF THE LONE WOLF***   (1941) 62m COL bw (GB: SECRETS)

Warren William (Michael Lanyard), Ruth Ford (Helene de Leon), Roger Clark (Paul Benoit), Victor Jory (Dapper Dan Streever), Eric Blore (Jamison the Butler), Thurston Hall (Inspector Crane), Fred Kelsey (Dickens), Victor Kilian (Col. Costals), Marlo Dwyer (Bubbles Deegan), Lester Scharff (Deputy Duval), Irving Mitchell (Benjamin Evans), John Harmon (Bernard), Joe McGuinn (Bob Garth).

One of the best of the LONE WOLF series of detective films, and the first directed by Edward Dmytryk who injected some clever humor into the series. This time out, William is hired to advise the police on how to prevent the priceless Napoleon jewels from being stolen once they arrive on a steamship. Meanwhile, William's loyal butler Blore is mistaken for his boss by a gang of international jewel thieves who draft him to assist in their theft of the very jewels William is supposed to be guarding. Blore decides to go along with the plan in order to get enough evidence to capture the notorious criminals. He cons the crooks into coming to William's apartment where his boss can capture them, but William screws up and the thieves escape, leaving him the most likely suspect in the eyes of the law. Eventually he clears himself by chasing after the crooks and discovering where they've hidden the jewels. (See LONE WOLF series, Index.)

p, Jack Fier; d, Edward Dmytryk; w, Stuart Palmer (based on a story by Louis Joseph Vance); ph, Philip Tannura; ed, Richard Fantl; md, Morris W. Stoloff.

Mystery   (PR:A   MPAA:NR)

SECRETS OF THE MARIE CELESTE, THE   (SEE: MYSTERY OF THE MARIE CELESTE, 1935, Brit.)

SECRETS OF THE UNDERGROUND**   (1943) 70m REP bw

John Hubbard (P. Cadwallader Jones), Virginia Grey (Terry), Lloyd Corrigan (Maurice Vaughn), Robin Raymond (Marianne Panois), Miles Mander (Paul Panois), Olin Howlin (Oscar), Ben Welden (Joe), Marla Shelton (Mrs. Perkins), Neil Hamilton (Kermit), Ken Christy (Cleary), Dick Rich (Maxie), Pierre Watkin (District Attorney Winton), Eule Morgan (Mrs. Calhoun), George Sherwood (Window Dresser), Herbert Vigran (Street Photographer), Nora Lane (Woman Clerk), Charles Williams (Hypo), Bobby Stone (Messenger), Francis Sayles (Station Agent), Roy Gordon (Mr. Perkins), Connie Evans (Telephone Operator), George Chandler (Lynch the Hotel Clerk), Eddie Kane (Bradley the Reporter), Joey Ray (Harrison the Reporter), Max Wagner (Baggage Man), Pauline Drake (Receptionist), Eddy Chandler (Dan the Detective), Ben Taggart (Bob the Detective).

Corrigan is an undercover Nazi stationed in the U.S. to run a fancy gown shop as a front for an insidious counterfeiting operation in which he and fellow agents churn out bogus war savings stamps. They hope to shatter the morale of the loyal Americans who have been plunking down their hard-earned dollars for the stamps and will now find out that their investments are worthless. Of course more than a few of Corrigan's customers get suspicious. (To the 1940s audiences, the mere idea of a male speaking the language of high fashion was suspicious as well as humorous). These alert but unfortunate customers end up murdered, their corpses incorporated into the shop's patriotic window displays. Eventually, glib reporter Grey and district attorney Hubbard gather enough evidence to expose the Nazis.

p, Leonard Fields; d, William Morgan; w, Robert Tasker, Geoffrey Homes (based on a story by Homes); ph, Ernest Miller; ed, Arthur Roberts; md, Walter Scharf; art d, Russell Kimball; set d, Otto Siegel.

Spy Drama   (PR:A   MPAA:NR)

SECRETS OF THE WASTELANDS**   (1941) 66m PAR bw

William Boyd (Hopalong Cassidy), Brad King (Johnny Nelson), Andy Clyde (California), Barbara Britton (Jennifer Kendall), Douglas Fowley (Salters), Keith Richards (Clay Elliott), Soo Young (May Soong), Gordon Hart (Prof. Birdsall), Hal Price (Prof. Stubbs), Lee Tung Foo (Doy Kee), Earl Gunn (Clanton), Ian McDonald (Hollister), John Rawlings (Williams), Richard Loo (Quan), Roland Got (Yeng), Jack Rockwell (Sheriff).

East meets West as Boyd and his cowpoke pals help a group of Chinese immigrants defend their farms against an evil gang of landgrabbers. In this far-fetched 39th episode of the Hopalong Cassidy series, Boyd also finds time to lead an archaeological expedition into some rough California territory. (See HOPALONG CASSIDY series, Index.)

p, Harry Sherman; d, Derwin Abrahams; w, Gerald Geraghty (based on a story by Bliss Lomax, characters created by Clarence E. Mulford); ph, Russell Harlan; m, Irvin Talbot, John Leopold; ed, Fred Feitshans, Jr.

Western   (PR:A   MPAA:NR)

SECRETS OF WOMEN***½   (1961, Swed.) 114m Svensk/Janus bw
(KVINNORS VANTAN; GB: WAITING WOMEN)

Anita Bjork (Rakel), Karl-Arne Holmsten (Eugen Lobelius), Jarl Kulle (Kaj), Maj-Britt Nilsson (Marta), Eva Dahlbeck (Karin), Gunnar Bjornstrand (Fredrik Lobelius), Birger Malmsten (Martin), Gerd Andersson (Maj), Bjorn Bjelvenstam (Henrik), Aino Taube (Annette), Hakan Westergren (Paul), Naima Wifstrand (Family Matriarch), Ingmar Bergman (Street Character), Kjell Nordenskold, Carl Strom, Marta Arbin.

This light-hearted comedy, made by Bergman in 1952 but not released in America until nine years later, was written by the director during what he considered a darker period of his life. One might never guess this, considering how much fun the film is both as entertainment and cinematic technique. The story, an episodic one, is told in flashback as three sisters-in-law chat about past experiences. The first episode relates a past affair which dramatically changed one of the women's relationship with her husband. The second tells of the often difficult courtship another woman had with her husband when he was a struggling young artist. The last episode, drawn from a real life experience of Bergman's, is more comical, involving the story of the third woman and the night she was trapped with her husband in a stalled elevator. At the conclusion of these three stories, a fourth woman, who had been quietly listening to them, decides marriage is for her and runs off with her boy friend to elope. The film marked some deliberate attempts by Bergman to advance his filmic style. The elevator sequence in particular was, according to Bergman, heavily influenced by some of the experiments of Alfred Hitchcock. At one point within the sequence very little dialog goes on between Nilsson and Malmsten. "This really was an experiment, an attempt on my part to tell a story in pictures," Bergman later told an interviewer, "... but it was a secret experiment, too. We didn't dare tell anyone we were experimenting." Like so many of these Bergman experiments, the scene works well. It adds a dimension of lightness and life to a man who's body of work may best be remembered for his genius in dealing with darker themes.

p, Allan Ekelund; d&w, Ingmar Bergman; ph, Gunnar Fischer; m, Erik Nordgren; ed, Oscar Rosander; md, E. Eckert-Lundin; art d, Nils Svenwall; set d, Svenwall.

Drama/Comedy   **Cas.**   (PR:C   MPAA:NR)

SECRETS OF WU SIN*½   (1932) 65m Invincible Pictures/Chesterfield bw

Lois Wilson (Nona Gould, Writer), Grant Withers (Jim Manning, Editor), Dorothy Revier (Margaret King), Robert Warwick (Roger King), Toschia Mori (Miao Lin), Eddie Boland (Eddie Morgan, Reporter), Tetsui Komai (Wu Sin), Richard Loo (Charlie San), Luke Chan (Luke), Jimmy Wang (Wang), Lafe McKee (Minister), Henry Hall (Informant).

Wilson plays a suicidal writer who is saved from death by friendly newspaper editor Withers and given a job on his paper. She soon becomes involved in a mysterious plot that involves the smuggling of Chinese workers. The clues take her to the heart of Chinatown, where she gets her scoop. The merger of Invincible Pictures and Chesterfield Motion Picture Corp. in 1932 created a company which, in its heyday, turned out one picture a month. The team's movies usually were filmed on rented sets at Universal City. Use of Universal's collection of authentic Oriental properties gave SECRETS OF WU SIN an elaborate appearance beyond what its budget would have allowed.

p, George R. Batcheller; d, Richard Thorpe; w, William McGrath, Basil Dickey (based on a story by Dickey); ph, M.A. Anderson; ed, Roland C. Reed; md, Abe Meyer; art d, Edward C. Jewell.

Crime   **Cas.**   (PR:A   MPAA:NR)

SECURITY RISK**   (1954) 69m AA bw

John Ireland (Ralph Payne), Dorothy Malone (Donna Weeks), Keith Larsen (Ted), Dolores Donlon Peggy, John Craven (Dr. Lanson), Suzanne Ta Fel (Joan Weeks), Joe Bassett (Malone), Burt Wenland (Burke), Steven Clark (Johnny), Murray Alper (Mike), Harold Kennedy (Sheriff).

FBI agent Ireland tries to thwart a communist plot while vacationing at Big Bear resort. The trouble begins when atomic scientist Craven is murdered by his traitorous assistant Larsen who steals the doc's important papers to further the Russian cause. Ireland's girl friend Malone's evil sister, Donlon, witnesses the crime and grabs the papers to sell herself. She is killed by Larsen, who is eventually killed himself, while Ireland wraps up the case.

p, William F. Broidy; d, Harold Schuster; w, Jo Pagano, Frank McDonald, John Rich (based on a story by Rich); ph, John Martin; ed, Ace Herman.

Spy Drama   (PR:A   MPAA:NR)

SEDDOK, L'EREDE DI SATANA
(SEE: ATOM AGE VAMPIRE, 1963, Ital.)

SEDMI KONTINENT   (SEE: SEVENTH CONTINENT, THE, 1968, Czech./Yugo.)

SEDMIKRASKY   (SEE: DAISIES, 1967, Czech.)

SEDUCED AND ABANDONED**   (1964, Fr./Ital.) 118m
Lux-Ultra-Vides-C.C.F. Lux/CD bw (SEDUITE ET ABBANDONNEE; SEDOTTA E ABBANDONATA)

Stefania Sandrelli (Agnese Ascalone), Aldo Puglisi (Peppino Califano), Saro Urzi (Vincenzo Ascalone), Lando Buzzanca (Antonio Ascalone), Leopoldo Trieste (Baron Rizieri), Rocco D'Assunta (Orlando Califano), Lola Braccini (Amalia Califano), Paola Biggio (Matilde Ascalone), Umberto Spadaro (Cousin Ascalone), Oreste Palella (Police Chief Potenza), Lina La Galla (Francesca Ascalone), Roberta Narbonne (Rosaura Ascalone), Rosetta Urzi (Consolata the Maid), Adelino Campardo (Bisigato, Policeman), Vincenzo Licata (Profumo the Undertaker), Italia Spadaro (Aunt Carmela), Gustavo D'Arpe (Ciarpetta the Lawyer), Salvatore Fazio (Father Mariano), Bruno Scipioni, Attilio Martella.

Another Sicilian slice of life drama which sees the trouble brought on an innocent family by an unscrupulous lothario played by Puglisi. Puglisi, who is Engaged to marry Biggio, seduces his fiancee's 15-year-old sister Sandrelli and gets her pregnant. Her father, Urzi, is outraged and breaks off the engagement demanding that Puglisi marry Sandrelli. He refuses and leaves town. The police drag him back telling him that if he does not marry the girl, he'll be thrown in jail for seducing a minor. The clever Puglisi forces the girl's family to beg him to marry her, and the shamed girl refuses his hand out of embarrassment. This only makes things worse for the family as their neighbors ostracize them for allowing a daughter with an illegitimate baby in the house. Urzi dies from a heart attack, Biggio becomes a nun, and Sandrelli nobly decides to restore the family honor by agreeing to marry the cad. (In Italian; English subtitles.)

p, Franco Cristaldi; d, Pietro Germi; w, Germi, Luciano Vincenzoni, Age and Scarpelli (based on an original idea by Germi, Vincenzoni); ph, Aiace Parolin; m, Carlo Rustichelli; ed, Roberto Cinquini; md, Pierluigi Urbini; art d, Carlo Egidi; set d, Andrea Fantacci; cos, Angela Sammaciccia, Egidi; makeup, Raffaele Cristini; English subtitles, Herman G. Weinberg.

Drama   **Cas.**   (PR:C   MPAA:NR)

SEDUCERS, THE*½   (1962) 88m Boar's Head-Quest/Joseph Brenner bw

Nuella Dierking (Jean Wells), Mark Saegers (Joe), Robert Milli (Robert Wells), Sheila Britt (Wilma), John Coe (Hank).

Confusing, contrived, and hopelessly complicated mystery drama starring Dierking as a distraught heiress who is convinced she killed a man with her car while driving home from a party. Her suspicions appear to be confirmed when a mysterious man, Saegers, appears at the door asking for blackmail money in exchange for his silence about the hit-and-run killing. Dierking decides to kill herself instead of paying the money, but a panicked Saegers declares that the man isn't dead, that he got up and walked away from the accident. Dierking is not convinced and returns to the scene of the accident. There she discovers the muddy corpse of her lawyer and this nearly snaps her mind. Eventually it is revealed by Saegers (who has taken a liking to the heiress and investigated the strange crime on her behalf) that Dierking's good-for-nothing husband and his lover staged the whole thing to drive her insane. The plan nearly works, but the evil husband is foiled by Dierking and Saegers.

p, Wilson Ashley; d, Graeme Ferguson; w, Ashley; ph, Baird Bryant; m, Mort Lindsey; ed, Bernard Leslie.

Mystery   (PR:C   MPAA:NR)

SEDUCTION, THE zero   (1982) 104m AE c

Morgan Fairchild *(Jamie)*, Michael Sarrazin *(Brandon)*, Vince Edwards *(Maxwell)*, Andrew Stevens *(Derek)*, Colleen Camp *(Robin)*, Kevin Brophy *(Bobby)*, Wendy Smith Howard *(Julie)*, Woodrow Parfrey *(Salesman)*, Betty Kean *(Mrs. Caluso)*, Joanne Linville *(Dr. Weston)*, Marri Mak *(Lisa)*, Richard Reed *(Floor Manager)*, Robert DeSimone *(Photographer)*, Michael Griswold *(Anchorman)*, Marilyn Staley *(Newscaster)*, Diana Rose *(Mrs. Wilson)*, Shailar Schmoeller *(Ricky)*, Marilyn Wolf *(Waitress)*, Jeffrey Richman *(Technical Director)*, Kathryn Hart, Deborah Koppel *(Teleprompter Girls)*.

Fairchild, noted mainly for her portrayal of various powerful and nasty women on all too numerous insipid television programs of the 1970s and 1980s, makes her theatrical film debut in this none too thrilling thriller. She's a beautiful newscaster being pursued by Stevens, an overzealous and psychotic fan who wants to possess his favorite broadcaster. After the usual predictable psuedo-suspense elements that are staples of the woman-in-danger film, Fairchild stops her pursuer with a handy blast of a shotgun. The only thing that separates this trash from the quality of a made-for-television feature are Fairchild's nude scenes, worked in undoubtedly to please the average drooling misogynist filmgoer. They add no artistic merit to the story, though "artistic merit" and THE SEDUCTION are definitely a contradiction in terms.

p, Irwin Yablans, Bruce Cohn Curtis; d&w, David Schmoeller; ph, Mac Ahlberg (CFI Color); m, Lalo Schifrin; ed, Tony DiMarco.

Drama   Cas.   (PR:O MPAA:R)

SEDUCTION BY THE SEA**   (1967, Ger./Yugo.) 80m
Alfa-Avala/Europix-Consolidated c (VERFUHRUNG AM MEER; OST-RVA)

Peter Van Eyck *(Peter)*, Elke Sommer *(Girl)*.

Van Eyck leaves his wife and job for the peacefulness of an island in the Adriatic Sea. Distraught over the absence of her son, Van Eyck's mother employs beautiful Sommer to fetch him and lure him back. Love takes charge, however between Van Eyck and Sommer ignoring the impassioned pleas of Van Eyck's mother the pair marry. Originally released in 1963.

d, Jovan Zivanovic; w, Yug Grizely, Rolf Schulz; ph, Miskovic.

Drama/Romance   (PR:C MPAA:NR)

SEDUCTION OF JOE TYNAN, THE***½   (1979) 107m UNIV c

Alan Alda *(Joe Tynan)*, Barbara Harris *(Ellie)*, Meryl Streep *(Karen Traynor)*, Rip Torn *(Sen. Kittner)*, Melvyn Douglas *(Sen. Birney)*, Charles Kimbrough *(Francis)*, Carrie Nye *(Aldena Kittner)*, Michael Higgins *(Sen. Pardew)*, Blanche Baker *(Janet)*, Adam Ross *(Paul Tynanl)*, Maureen Anderman *(Joe's Secretary)*, Chris Arnold *(Jerry)*, John Badila *(Reporter on TV)*, Robert Christian *(Arthur Briggs)*, Maurice Copeland *(Edward Anderson)*, Lu Elrod *(Congresswoman at Party)*, Clarence Felder *(Golf Pro)*, Gus Fleming *(Eric)*, Merv Griffin *(Himself)*, Marian Hailey-Moss *(Sheila Lerner)*, Dan Hedaya *(Alex Heller)*, Bill Moor *(Barry Traynor)*, Ronald Hunter, Walter Klavun, Norman La Rochelle, Kaiulani Lee, Charles Levin, Christopher McHale, Ron Menchine, M.B. Miller, Novella Nelson, Stephen D. Newman, Eric Pederson, Wyman Pendleton, Don Plumley, Ben Prestbury, Frederick Rolf, Peter Schroeder, William Shust, Martha Sherill, Ben Slack, Leon B. Stevens, Frank Stoegerer, Suzanne Stone, Kay Todd, Nathan Wilansky.

A fine political drama with lots of comedy on the order of THE CANDIDATE, THE BEST MAN, and several others in the genre. Alda proved he's a good writer with this intelligent and observant screenplay that's vaguely based on the supposed life of Ted Kennedy, although that might be denied by anyone who was involved with the movie. The seduction referred to in the title is not so much a sexual situation (although Alda's senatorial character does have a fling with attorney Streep) as it is a depiction of the power-and-success goddess that beckons to people in the political arena. Alda is a liberal senator married to Harris, with two children, Ross and Baker. Harris hates being in the limelight and Alda revels in it. He is a darling of the press and his basically nice nature is seen to change as he rises higher in the national scene. He dallies with labor lawyer Streep, but it's only a trapping of power and he eventually returns to Harris, who gives a sensational performance, doing more with a look than many actresses can give with 10 pages of dialog. Torn is a powerful solon and plays it to the hilt as he deals in raw power. Douglas, who made a career out of essaying public figures (he was the President's adviser in BEING THERE) near the end of his life, is superb as a man who's seen his best days and is now looking forward bleakly to his last days. It's a character study that reveals the phony smiles, the hearty handshakes and all that is bad about the people who run for office. There are no solutions offered in the movie, just a presentation of the way things are. After seeing this film, you may never believe a candidate's speech again. Kudos for all concerned and caution to any children because the language and some of the sex is too raw for young eyes.

p, Martin Bregman; d, Jerry Schatzberg; w, Alan Alda; ph, Adam Holender (Technicolor); m, Bill Conti; ed, Evan Lottman; art d, David Chapman; set d, Alan Hicks; cos, Jo Ynocencio.

Political Drama   Cas.   (PR:C-O MPAA:R)

SEE AMERICA THIRST**   (1930) 71m UNIV bw

Harry Langdon *(Wally)*, George "Slim" Summerville *(Slim)*, Bessie Love *(Ellen)*, Mitchell Lewis *(Screwy O'Toole)*, Matthew Betz *(Inspector McGann)*, Stanley Fields *(Spumoni)*, Lloyd Whitlock *(O'Toole's Henchman)*, Dick Alexander *(McGann's Henchman)*, Tom Kennedy *(Shivering Smith)*, Lew Hearn *(Inventor)*, LeRoy Mason *(The Attorney)*.

Silent comedian Harry Langdon's first feature length talkie (he had done several sound shorts), which heralded his quick fade from a motion picture comedian once considered on apar with Keaton and Chaplin to minor roles opposite the likes of Slim Summerville. Langdon and Summerville play two wandering buddies who are mistaken by gangsters for two brutal gunmen and are drafted by the crooks to help in their fight against a rival gang. The film wallows in dated, badly staged slapstick and Langdon, who had made a career of playing impish, shy characters, is nearly inaudible as he mumbles and whispers his dialog.

d, William James Craft; w, Henry Lacossitt, C. Jerome Horwin (based on a story by Vin Moore, Edward I. Luddy); ph, Arthur Miller, C. Allyn Jones; ed, W. Harry Lieb.

Comedy   (PR:A MPAA:NR)

SEE HERE, PRIVATE HARGROVE**½   (1944) 101m MGM bw

Robert Walker *(Pvt. Marion Hargrove)*, Donna Reed *(Carol Halliday)*, Robert Benchley *(Mr. Halliday)*, Keenan Wynn *(Pvt. Mulvehill)*, Bob Crosby *(Bob)*, Ray Collins *(Brody S. Griffith)*, Chill Wills *(Sgt. Cramp)*, Marta Linden *(Mrs. Halliday)*, Grant Mitchell *(Uncle George)*, George Offerman, Jr *(Pvt. Orrin Esty)*, Edward Fielding *(Gen. Dillon)*, Donald Curtis *(Sgt. Heldon)*, William "Bill" Phillips *(Pvt. Bill Burk)*, Douglas Fowley *(Capt. Manville)*, Morris Ankrum *(Col. Forbes)*, Mickey Rentschler *(Sergeant)*, Frank Faylen *(M.P.)*, Jack Luden *(Doctor)*, Clarence Straight *(Capt. Hamilton)*, William "Billy" Newell *(Mr. Smith)*, Michael Owen *(Officer of Day)*, John Kelly *(Exercise Sergeant)*, Joe Devlin *(Mess Sergeant)*, Louis Mason *(Farmer)*, Connie Gilchrist *(Farmer's Wife)*, Harry Tyler *(Old Man)*, Mantan Moreland *(Porter)*, Mary McLeod *(Girl Clerk)*, Eddie Acuff *(Capt. Hammond)*, Ken Scott, Stephen Barclay *(Corporals)*, Dennis Moore, James Warren *(Executive Officers)*, Rod Bacon, Blake Edwards *(Field Operators)*, Harry Strang, Louis Jean Heydt *(Captains)*, Fred Kohler, Jr, Myron Healey, Maurice Murphy *(Lieutenants)*.

Walker stars in this lively screen adaptation of Marion Hargrove's funny memoirs of his troubles in boot camp. Walker plays Hargrove, a bumbling cub reporter who drives his editor crazy. When WW II breaks out, Walker finds himself in the Army driving his commanders crazy and doing a lot of K.P. duty. Reed plays Walker's girl friend who lives in New York. The goofy soldier sells huckster Wynn a percentage of his future earnings as a writer in order to raise enough money to visit her. A pleasant, well-cast war-time comedy that, oddly enough, originally had a fairly serious ending because the studio feared presenting a too flip view of WW II, which was currently waging. After preview audiences disapproved of the mixture of seriousness and comedy, the studio reconsidered. As director Ruggles was engaged on a project in London, Tay Garnett was designated to direct a new upbeat, comic ending, which resulted in much critical praise for the film upon its official release. Its success resulted in a sequel the next year, WHAT NEXT, CORPORAL HARGROVE? Film director Blake Edwards (S.O.B., VICTOR/VICTORIA) can be seen in a bit role as a field operator. Writer Hargrove went on to become a screenwriter in Hollywood.

p, George Haight; d, Wesley Ruggles, Tay Garnett (uncredited); w, Harry Kurnitz (based on the book by Marion Hargrove); ph, Charles Lawton; m, David Snell; ed, Frank E. Hull; art d, Cedric Gibbons, Stephen Goosson; set d, Edwin B. Willis, Ralph Hurst; m/l, "In My Arms," Frank Loesser, Ted Grouya.

Comedy   (PR:A MPAA:NR)

SEE HOW THEY RUN**   (1955, Brit.) 84m Winwell/BL bw

Ronald Shiner *(Wally Winton)*, Greta Gynt *(Penelope Toop)*, James Hayter *(Bishop of Lax)*, Wilfrid Hyde-White *(Brigadier Buskin)*, Dora Bryan *(Ida)*, Richard Wattis *(Rev. Lionel Toop)*, Viola Lyel *(Miss Skilton)*, Charles Farrell *(Basher)*, Michael Brennan *(Sgt. Maj. Towers)*, Ballard Berkeley *(Col. Warrington)*, Roddy Hughes *(Rev. Arthur Humphrey)*, Ian Wilson, Gloria Haig, Stuart Latham, Hamilton Keene, Fred Griffiths, Will Cruft, Tony Quinn, George Roderick, Ken Buckle, Johnnie Schofield, Arthur Cortez.

A zany British comedy which stars comic Cockney Shiner as a corporal hoping to get promoted in order to receive an inheritance. He gets his chance when he dresses as a priest and spends a night out with the vicar's wife, blonde glamor girl Gynt. Before long, however, there are nearly half a dozen priests running around – some real, some fake. It turns out that one, Farrell, is an escaped convict, who is apprehended by Shiner. The corporal is then promoted and made eligible to receive his inheritance. Crazy antics surprisingly get few laughs, a grievance the audience must lay to director Arliss, son of the legendary actor George Arliss.

p, Bill Luckwell; d, Leslie Arliss; w, Arliss, Philip King, Val Valentine (based on a play by King).

Comedy   (PR:A   MPAA:NR)

SEE MY LAWYER   (1945) 69m UNIV bw

Ole Olsen (Ole), Chic Johnson (Chic), Alan Curtis (Charlie), Grace McDonald (Betty), Noah Beery, Jr (Arthur), Franklin Pangborn (B.J. Wagenhorn), Edward S. Brophy (Otis Fillmore), Richard Benedict (Joe), Lee Patrick (Sally), Gus Schilling (Winky), William B. Davidson (Judge), Stanley Clements (Willie), Mary Gordon (Mrs. Fillmore), Ralph Peters (O'Brien), Yvette, Carmen Amaya, The King Cole Trio, The Cristianos Troupe, The Rogers Adagio Trio, The Six Willys, The Hudson Wonders, The Four Teens.

The last of the Olsen and Johnson comedies sees the pair as nightclub comedians trying desperately to get out of their contract. Fussy club owner Pangborn won't let them loose however, so the boys are forced to wander about the club spraying soda water and slinging mud at the patrons until Pangborn relents and fires them. They think their troubles are over until they are slapped with a series of lawsuits from angry patrons seeking damages. The laughs are few and far between, and the film is crowded with a variety of specialty acts that pad the action. Songs include: "Fuzzy Wuzzy" (Bob Bell, Roy Branker), "Penny Arcade" (Dave Franklin), "We're Making a Million," "Take It Away," "It's Circus Time" (Everett Carter, Milton Rosen), "Man on the Little White Keys" (Joe Greene, Nat King Cole), "I'll Be Seeing You" (Sammy Fain).

p, Edmund L. Hartmann; d, Edward Cline; w, Hartmann, Stanley Davis (based on the play by Richard Maibaum, Harry Clork); ed, Paul Landres; md, H.J. Salter.

Comedy/Musical   (PR:A   MPAA:NR)

SEE NO EVIL*   (1971, Brit.) 87m Filmways-Genesis/COL c (Gb: BLIND TERROR)

Mia Farrow (Sarah), Dorothy Alison (Betty Rexton), Robin Bailey (George Rexton), Diane Grayson (Sandy Rexton), Brian Rawlinson (Barker), Norman Eshley (Steve Reding), Paul Nicholas (Jack "Jacko" Osgood), Christopher Matthews (Frost), Lila Kaye (Gypsy Mother), Barrie Houghton (Gypsy Jack), Michael Elphick (Gypsy Tom), Donald Bisset (Doctor), Max Faulkner (Steve's Man No. 1), Scott Fredericks (Steve's Man No. 2), Reg Harding (Steve's Man No. 3).

A creepy, effective thriller starring Farrow as a recently blinded girl who goes to her uncle Bailey's mansion to convalesce. Unbeknown to Bailey or Farrow, they splash a young, psychopathic man's boots with mud when driving past him on their way home. While Farrow is out horseback riding with her fiancee Eshley, the strange young man sneaks into the house and murders Bailey, his wife, their daughter, and the gardener. When Farrow returns to the house alone, she slowly realizes that all her relatives have been killed. Panicked, she tries to call for help, but the killer has returned to reclaim a lost bracelet. The blind girl bravely overcomes her handicap and cleverly defeats the young killer. Very suspenseful, with a terrific performance from Farrow and atmospheric direction by veteran helmsman Richard Fleischer.

p, Martin Ransohoff, Leslie Linder; d, Richard Fleischer; w, Brian Clemens; ph, Gerry Fisher (Eastmancolor); m, Elmer Bernstein; ed, Thelma Connell; art d, John Hoesli; set d, Hugh Scaife; makeup, Stuart Freeborn.

Mystery/Thriller   (PR:C   MPAA:GP)

SEE YOU IN HELL, DARLING   (SEE: AMERICAN DREAM, AN, 1966)

SEED*½   (1931) 96m UNIV bw

John Boles (Bart Carter), Genevieve Tobin (Mildred), Lois Wilson (Peggy Carter), Raymond Hackett (Junior Carter), Bette Davis (Margaret Carter), Frances Dade (Nancy), ZaSu Pitts (Jennie), Richard Tucker (Bliss), Jack Willis (Dicky Carter), Bill Willis (Danny Carter), Dick Winslow (Johnny Carter), Kenneth Seiling (Junior Carter as a Child), Don Cox (Dicky Carter as a child), Terry Cox (Danny Carter as a Child), Helen Parrish (Margaret Carter as a Child), Dickie Moore (Johnny Carter as a Child).

Maudlin tear-jerker starring Boles as a would-be writer who leaves his wife, Wilson, and his five children to pursue his career under the guidance of Tobin, who works for a publishing company. In the decade that follows, Boles becomes a big success, but the literary critics have singled him out for harsh criticism because he has fallen into writing trashy mystery novels to support Tobin's extravagant lifestyle. Wilson, who still loves Boles, seeks to help him stabilize his life by inviting him to see their now-grown children. The experience leaves Boles longing for a family again, and he begs Wilson to let the children live with him. Wilson agrees and brings his family to New York where Tobin, now threatened by Boles' love for his children, feels like an outcast. Soppy, trite, and rife with unrealistic character motivations, SEED's only current day interest is the brief and early appearance of Bette Davis as Boles' grown daughter.

p&d, John M. Stahl; w, Gladys Lehman (based on the novel by Charles G.

Norris); ph, Jackson Rose; ed, Ted J. Kent.

Drama   (PR:A   MPAA:NR)

SEED OF INNOCENCE*   (1980) 90m Cannon c (AKA: TEEN MOTHERS)

Timothy Wead (Danny), Mary Cannon (Alice), Vincent Schiavelli (Leo), T.K. Carter (Captain), Azizi Johari (Denise), Julianna McCarthy (Nadine), Sonja O. Menor (Teacher), Mary Ellen O'Neill (Sister Mary), Monika Ramirez (Jane), John Miranda (Dr. Walthour), Brad Gorman (Barney), Shirley Stoler (Corky), Gloria Stroock (Sophie), Robert Alan Brown (Dale), Bonnie Bartlett (Velma), Jane Drennan (Marie), Russ Marin (Marv), Bart Burns (Ray), William J. Sanderson, Scott Edmund Lane, Art Bradford, John Wheeler, Jeremy West, Tony Plana, Lanny Duncan, Earl Montgomery, Barbara Lyle, Hillary Horan.

A teenaged girl gets pregnant, runs away with her boy friend, and experiences the pain and emptiness of living on her own in New York City. This kind of plot is usually saved for the cliched "rights of passage" films of the late 1960s and early 1970s, and at this time it seems completely out of date. The only reason to watch is Shirley Stoler, the stout murderer of THE HONEYMOON KILLERS (1970) and the evil concentration camp guard in SEVEN BEAUTIES (1976).

p, Yoram Globus; d, Boaz Davidson; w, Stuart Krieger; ph, Adam Greenberg; m, Shalom Chanach; ed, Jon Koslowsky; prod d, Brent Swift; art d, Dan Linkmeyer.

Drama   (PR:O   MPAA:R)

SEED OF MAN, THE**   (1970, Ital.) 101m Polifilm/SRL c (IL SEME DELL'UOMO)

Marco Margine (Ciro), Anne Wiazemsky (Dora), Annie Girardot (Anna), Milva [Deanna] Frosini, Rada Rassimov, Maria Teresa Piaggio, Angela Pagano.

A pretentious look at the apocalypse from Italian director Ferreri which sees Margine and Wiazemsky seeking shelter at the seashore after most of the Earth has been wiped out by war and plague. Margine feels that it is his duty to repopulate the world and he demands that Wiazemsky bear him a child. Not seeing any point to repopulating such a horrid world, Wiazemsky refuses, even after government authorities arrive and decree that it is her obligation to do so. Soon another woman, Girardot, arrives and agrees to have children with Margine. That night the pair make love in the same bed where Wiazemsky pretends to sleep. Seeking to secure her position with Margine, Girardot attacks Wiazemsky the next morning and tries to kill her. Wiazemsky counters, however, and kills Girardot. Angered, she cuts off the dead girl's leg and serves it to the shocked Margine for dinner. The days drag on and soon Margine resumes his requests for children. Wiazemsky continues to refuse, but a frustrated and enraged Margine finally drugs the woman and rapes her. When she awakes Margine informs Wiazemsky that she is pregnant, but before she can react they are both blown to bits in an accident. For a film that pretends to warn of man's stupidity and inhumanity, THE SEED OF MAN is hard to take seriously. Overbearing and obvious symbolism coupled with a coy sense of humor and self-importance tend to annoy any audience that possesses a better than seventh grade understanding of metaphor and dramatic irony. This is a simple-minded film made by an immature filmmaker whose overriding obsession is a fear of men losing their potency to a society of women who don't need them.

p, Roberto Giussani; d, Marco Ferreri; w, Ferreri, Sergio Bazzini; ph, Mario Vulpiani (Eastmancolor); m, Teo Usuelli.

Science Fiction   (PR:C-O   MPAA:NR)

SEED OF TERROR   (SEE: GRAVE OF THE VAMPIRE, 1972)

SEEDS OF DESTRUCTION*   (1952) 84m Astor bw

Kent Taylor, Gene Lockhart, Gloria Holden, David Bruce.

Out of the midsts of the Cold War came this interesting piece of propaganda about a Russian spy (Taylor), who comes to America to spread the seeds of Commie thought. He sees the light, however, and renounces his former beliefs in favor of Democracy.

d, Frank Strayer.

Drama   (PR:A   MPAA:NR)

SEEDS OF EVIL zero   (1981) 81m KKI c (AKA: THE GARDENER)

Katharine Houghton (Ellen Bennett), Joe Dallesandro (Carol the Gardener), Rita Gam (Helena Boardman), James Congdon (John Bennett), Teodorino Bello, Anne Meacham.

Rotten horror film shot in Puerto Rico in 1972 and not released until 1981, starring Warhol-favorite Dallesandro as a nutty gardener who works for rich women, who have a nasty habit of dying soon after he is hired. His latest victim er, employer...is Houghton (Katharine Hepburn's less-than-talented niece who is best remembered for her role in GUESS WHO'S COMING TO

DINNER?), who looks to the hulking Dallesandro as a distraction from her uncaring and cold husband, Congdon. Little does she know that the big gardener breeds orchids that emit poisonous fumes that kill off his wealthy clients. In the end, Dallesandro gets his just desserts by being turned into a tree via some very bad special effects makeup. Almost too bad to be laughable.

p, Tony Belletier; d&w, Jim Kay; ph, Michael Zingale (TVC Labs Color); m, Marc Fredericks; ed, Cal Schultz.

Horror　　　　　**Cas.**　　　　　**(PR:O MPAA:R)**

SEEDS OF FREEDOM**　　　　(1943, USSR) 67m Potemkin bw

Cast of POTEMKIN: A. Antonov, G. Alexandrov, V. Barsky, Mikhail Goronorov, Sailors of the Red Navy, Citizens of Odessa, American Cast: Henry Hull, Martin Wolfson, Wendell Philips, Grover Burgess, John Berry, Peter Frye, Aline MacMahon, Lucy Helm, Louis Sorin, Russell Collins, Stanley Phillips, James Elliot, Speakers: Julius Matthews, Charles Henderson, Martin Wolfson, John Boyd, Harry Kadison, Hester Sondergaard, Lou Polen, Jack Lambert, Jay Meredith, William Beach.

A *very* odd WW II propaganda film that takes Russian director Sergei Eisenstein's silent masterpiece POTEMKIN, dubbed with dialog and sound effects, and surrounds it with a bracket story which sees Russian freedom fighter Hull trying to inspire his downtrodden troops with the story of when he served on the battleship Potemkin at the time of the glorious revolution. The 1943 footage then "flashes back" to the 1925 masterpiece and stays there for most of the film. When we return to 1943, the Russian soldiers have been so inspired by Hull's tale that they happily plan an attack on the Nazis that will liberate their village. Someone had an incredible amount of nerve to dare this one, and pressure during war time is no excuse. A real oddity.

p, William Sekely (revised production); d, Hans Burger (contemporary scenes); w, Albert Maitz (original story by N. Agedzanov, Sergei Eisenstein); ph, K. Tisse, William Kelly; ed, Marc Sorkin.

War　　　　　　　　　**(PR:A MPAA:NR)**

SEEING IS BELIEVING***　　　　(1934, Brit.) 70m British and
　　　　　　　　　　　　　　　　Domenions/PAR bw

Billy [William] Hartnell (*Ronald Gibson*), Gus NcNaughton (*Geoffrey Cooper*), Faith Bennett (*Marion Harvey*), Vera Boggetti (*Nita Leonard*), Fewlass Llewellyn (*Sir Robert Gibson*), Joan Periera (*Mme. Bellini*), Elsie Irving (*Lady Mander*), Pat Baring.

A slow-moving comedy about an aspiring detective, Hartnell, who nearly gets two other detectives arrested for a jewel theft. After that mixup he goes on to accuse Bennett, a young girl with whom he falls in love, of stealing a bracelet. Hartnell's watchful father intervenes and before long everyone's name is cleared.

d, Redd Davis; w, Donovan Pedelty.

Comedy　　　　　　　　　**(PR:A MPAA:NR)**

SEEING IT THROUGH　　　　(SEE: MOTH, THE, 1934)

SEEKERS, THE　　　　(SEE: LAND OF FURY, 1955, Brit.)

SEEMS LIKE OLD TIMES***　　　　(1980) 102m COL c

Goldie Hawn (*Glenda*), Chevy Chase (*Nick*), Charles Grodin (*Ira*), Robert Guillaume (*Fred*), Harold Gould (*Judge*), George Grizzard (*Governor*), Yvonne Wilder (*Aurora*), T.K. Carter (*Chester*), Judd Omen (*Dex*), Marc Alaimo (*Bee Gee*), Joseph Running Fox (*Thomas*), Ray Tracey (*Robert*), Ray Hauser (*Anne*), Carolyn Fromson (*Bank Teller*), Sandy Lipton (*Jean*), Herb Armstrong (*Jack*), Natividad Rios Kearsley (*Rosita*), Dolores Aguirre (*Conchita*), Edmund Stoiber (*Ezra*), Alice Sachs (*Mrs. Ezra*).

A thin plot, heavily laden with many of Neil Simon's best one-liners, makes this a pleasant way to spend 102 minutes. Chase is Hawn's ex-husband and when he is forced to help some bank robbers, the cops are soon after him. She's a liberal lawyer who is married to nerd Grodin, the local district attorney. When Chase arrives at their home seeking shelter, she takes him in (it's established that she is one of those people who gives of herself and takes in strays of all shapes, sizes, and persuasions). The expected thing happens, Hawn and Chase eventually reawaken the passion they once had for each other, and Grodin is out in the cold. After their success in FOUL PLAY, it seemed natural to reteam Chase and Hawn and this picture has the feeling that it was written and shot with only that in mind. Director Sandrich, who has won many awards for his TV work, was making his feature debut and kept the pace moving in the same fashion that he's become famous for on the tube. Some nice work from the secondary players including Gould as a local judge, Guillaume as Grodin's aide, and Wilder in a funny but, by this time, almost insulting role as a Latino maid. Lots of jokes, somewhat frantic acting on the part of Chase, and the usual cuteness from Hawn make this one of those movies that's fun to watch but with as much substance as a bowl of heavily aerated whipped cream.

p, Ray Stark; d, Jay Sandrich; w, Neil Simon; ph, David M. Walsh

(Metrocolor); m, Marvin Hamlisch; ed, Michael A. Stevenson; prod d, Gene Callahan; art d, Pete Smith; set d, Lee Poll; cos, Betsy Cox.

Comedy　　　　**Cas.**　　　　**(PR:A-C MPAA:PG)**

SEGRETI CHE SCOTTANO　　　(SEE: DEAD RUN, 1969, Fr./Ital./Ger.)

SEI DONNE PER L'ASSASSINO　　　(SEE: BLOOD AND BLACK LACE,
　　　　　　　　　　　　　　　　1965, Fr./Ital./Ger.)

SEISHUN MONOTOGARI　　　(SEE: NAKED YOUTH, 1961, Jap.)

SEISHUN ZANKOKU MONOTOGARI
　　　　　　　　　　　　　　(SEE: NAKED YOUTH, 1961, Jap.)

SEIZURE*½　　　　(1974) 93m Cinerama/AIP c

Jonathan Frid (*Edmund Blackstone*), Martine Beswick (*Queen of Evil*), Joe Sirola (*Charlie*), Christina Pickles (*Nicole Blackstone*), Herve Villechaize (*The Spider*), Anne Meacham (*Eunice*), Roger De Koven (*Serge*), Troy Donahue (*Mark*), Mary Woronov (*Mikki*), Henry Baker (*Jackal*).

Frid, the star of television's only horror soap opera, "Dark Shadows," appears in this fairly lame excuse for a horror film as a mystery writer who conjures up living characters from his novels and has them kill his wife and her guests. The materialized beings are a hairy dwarf played by "Fantasy Island" regular Villechaize, an evil queen played by Beswick, and a giant played by Baker. The victims are Pickles, Donahue, Sirola, Meacham, De Koven, and Woronov (not even she can save this). In the end it was all a dream! A bad cop-out to a very bad movie. This was the feature debut of director/writer Stone who would later direct another unintentionally laughable horror film, THE HAND.

p, Garrard Glenn, Jeffrey Kapelman; d, Oliver Stone; w, Edward Mann, Stone (based on a story by Stone); ph, Roger Racine (Deluxe Precision Color); m, Lee Gagnon; ed, Nobuko Oganesoff, Stone; art d, Najwa Stone; set d, Michelle Marchand; spec eff, Thomas Brumberger.

Horror　　　　　　　　**(PR:C MPAA:PG)**

SELF-MADE LADY*½　　　　(1932, Brit.) 68m George King/UA bw

Heather Angel (*Sookey*), Harry [Henry] Wilcoxon (*Bert Taverner*), Amy Veness (*Old Sookey*), A. Bromley Davenport (*Duke of Alchester*), Louis Hayward (*Paul Geneste*), Charles Cullum (*Lord Mariven*), Ronald Richie (*Alf Naylor*), Doris Gilmour (*Claudine*), Oriol Ross (*Lady Poppy*), Lola Duncan (*Mrs. Stoach*), Violet Hopson (*Assistant*).

Routine bootstraps melodrama starring fragile beauty Angel as a poor slum girl who works long and hard to escape her oppressive environment and becomes a successful fashion designer. A ghost from her past surfaces and threatens to reveal her impoverished past to her rich suitors unless she forks over some of her savings. She is saved by Wilcoxon, a boxer and long-time secret admirer. Though she welcomes the fighter's intervention, Angel marries Hayward, the son of a doctor, instead. Trite and unremarkable, though Angel is outstanding. By "king of the quickies" producer King.

p, George King; d, George Brown; w, Billie Bristow (based on the novel *Sookey* by Douglas Newton); ph, Geoffrey Faithfull.

Drama　　　　　　　　**(PR:A MPAA:NR)**

SELF-PORTRAIT zero　　　　(1973, U.S./Chile) 74m Art in Motion
　　　　　　　　　　　　　　Pictures-Peliculas/Inte rnacionales de Chile/ CCN c

Joby Baker, Pamela Hensley, Alicia Quiroga, Norman Day, Maria E. Cavieres, Patricio Castilla.

An inept U.S.-Chilean coproduction about a successful magazine photographer whose life takes an emotional turn for the worse after snapping pictures of dying children in Vietnam. He returns to Chile where he broods over the suffering he saw, while becoming involved with some local ladies. A worthless entry which has more interesting production notes than it does a plot. The film's associate producer, Gregory Roberts, had to leave the picture when it was discovered that he had an international arrest record. Changes at the helm also occurred when director James Mobley left the film after one week to be replaced by the equally ineffective McEndree. If that's not enough evidence that this movie is a dog, no writer claims credit for the script.

p, Robert Faust; d, Maurice McEndree, James Mobley; ed, Steve Michael; m/l, Angel Parra, Isabel Parra.

Drama　　　　　　　　**(PR:O MPAA:NR)**

SELL OUT, THE***　　　　(1976) 88m Hemdale/Distrib Venture c

Richard Widmark (*Sam Lucas*), Oliver Reed (*Gabriel Lee*), Gayle Hunnicutt (*Deborah*), Sam Wanamaker (*Sickles*), Vladek Sheybal (*The Dutchman*), Ori Levy (*Maj. Benjamin*), Assaf Dayan (*Lt. Elan*), Shmuel Rodensky (*Zafron*), Peter Frye (*Kasyan*).

Boring espionage drama starring Widmark as a CIA agent retired and living in Jerusalem who is dragged back into the business by his former protege Reed, who had defected to the Soviets, but now returns to his mentor begging for help. It seems that not only the U.S., but now the Russians have taken out assassination contracts on Reed, and he is desperate to survive. This leads to lots of gunplay and car chases, much to the dismay of Israeli major Levy who is sick and tired of watching the Americans and Soviets play hardball in his country.

p, Josef Shaftel; d, Peter Collinson; w, Murray Smith, Judson Kinberg (based on a story by Smith); ph, Arthur Ibbetson; m, Mick Green, Colin Frichter.

Spy Drama   **Cas.**   **(PR:C   MPAA:PG)**

SELLERS OF GIRLS**   (1967, Fr.) 100m CFPC/American bw
                               (MARCHANDS DE FILLES; AKA: GIRL MERCHANTS)

Georges Marchal (*Mister John*), Agnes Laurent (*Josette*), Daniela Rocca (*Bettina*), Saro Urzi (*Mottia*), Roger Duchesne (*Gofferi*), Richard Winckler (*Henri*), Pascale Roberts (*Gaby*), Jacques Dynam (*Mister Jean*), Evelyne Dandry (*Vera*), Renee Cosima, Florence Arnaud, Robert Porte, Luce Aubertin, Anne-Marie Mersen, Catherine Romane, Claude Cerval, Georges Lycan, Henri-Jacques Huet, Roger Coggio, Jorge Matthews, Clement Harari, Pierre Massimi.

After a series of hardships in Paris, young Laurent falls into the hands of a nefarious white slavery-narcotics ring. She's sent by boat to South America, but manages to get engaged to a crewman Winckler en route. The hapless Laurent rebels against her slavery, which of course is dealt with in appropriately evil manners. Eventually it's discovered that Marchal, seemingly a mysterious stranger causing dissent between rival bad guys, is actually an Interpol agent who had been assigned to break up the ring. Laurent goes back to her fiance with all resolved nicely.

p, Jean Maumy; d&w, Maurice Cloche; ph, Jacques Mercanton; m, Guy Magenta; ed, Franchette Mazin; art d, Raymond Negre; set d, Belin; cos, Monique Naussac, Luce Scatena; makeup, Gisele Jacquin.

Crime Drama   **(PR:O   MPAA:NR)**

SELLOUT, THE**   (1951) 83m MGM bw

Walter Pidgeon (*Haven D. Allridge, Editor*), John Hodiak (*Chick Johnson*), Audrey Totter (*Cleo Bethel*), Paula Raymond (*Peggy Stauton*), Thomas Gomez (*Sheriff Kellwin C. Burke*), Cameron Mitchell (*Randy Stauton*), Karl Malden (*Buck Maxwell, Cop*), Everett Sloane (*Nelson S. Tarsson, Attorney*), Jonathan Cott (*Ned Grayton*), Frank Cady (*Bennie Amboy*), Hugh Sanders (*Judge Neeler*), Griff Barnett (*J.R. Morrisson*), Burt Mustin (*Elk M. Ludens*), Whit Bissell (*Wilfred Jackson*), Roy Engel (*Sam F. Slaper*), Jeff Richards (*Truck Driver*), Vernon Rich (*Court Clerk*), Bob Stevenson (*Bailiff*), Cy Stephens (*Court Stenographer*), Frankie Darro (*Little Jake*), Ann Tyrell (*Jennie Nova*), Benny Rubin (*Smoke Shop Proprietor*), Robert Williams (*Barney the Taxi Driver*), Jack Sherman (*Bartender*), John Dierkes (*Big Jake*), Roy Butler (*Prisoner*), Cliff Clark (*Police Chief*), Mabel Smaney (*Fat Woman*).

Preachy film starring Pidgeon as a crusading newspaper editor out to smash corrupt sheriff Gomez by detailing his dirty deeds. Soon Pidgeon is kidnaped, but state's attorney Hodiak picks up the torch and continues the fight. Unfortunately, all witnesses against Gomez refuse to talk, including Pidgeon when he resurfaces. As it turns out Pidgeon has learned that his weak-willed son-in-law, Mitchell, is involved with Gomez, therefore the silence. Nevertheless, justice triumphs.

p, Nicholas Nayfack; d, Gerald Mayer; w, Charles Palmer (based on a story by Matthew Rapf); ph, Paul G. Vogel; m, David Buttolph; ed, George White; art d, Cedric Gibbons, Arthur Longergan.

Crime   **(PR:A   MPAA:NR)**

SEMBAZURU   (SEE: THOUSAND CRANES, 1969, Jap.)

SEMI-TOUGH***   (1977) 108m UA c

Burt Reynolds (*Billy Clyde Puckett*), Kris Kristofferson (*Shake Tiller*), Jill Clayburgh (*Barbara Jane Bookman*), Robert Preston (*Big Ed Bookman*), Bert Convy (*Friedrich Bismark*), Roger E. Mosley (*Puddin*), Lotte Lenya (*Clara Pelf*), Richard Masur (*Phillip Hooper*), Carl Weathers (*Dreamer Tatum*), Brian Dennehy (*T.J. Lambert*), Mary Jo Catlett (*Earlene*), Joe Kapp (*Hose Manning*), Ron Silver (*Vlada*), Jim McKrell (*McNair*), Peter Bromilow (*Interpreter*), Norm Alden (*Coach Parks*), Fred Stuthman (*Minister*), Janet Brandt (*Dressmaker*), William Wolf (*Fitter*), Jenifer Shaw (*Stewardess*), Kevin Furry (*Puddin, Jr.*), Ava Roberts (*Puddin's Wife*), Melonie Magruder (*Linda*), Michelle Griffin (*Little Girl*), Mark Franklin (*Attendant Tom*), Mary Rae Hoskins, Charlotte Stanton, Niki Flacks, Rose Pearson (*BEAT Women*), Thom Phillips, Hugh Gorian (*BEAT Men*), Mickey Caruso (*Curtis*), Edward Jones, Kevin Grady, Tim Guy (*Football Players*), Dick Schaap, Lindsay Nelson, Paul Hornung (*Themselves*).

Broadway producer David Merrick doesn't like Hollywood because so many decisions are made by committee while he is accustomed to risking his own money and making all the moves. This time, he's made quite a few of them

and the casting of game show host Bert Convy is a *tour de force*. Convy shows never-before-seen talents as he does a scathing satire of Werner Erhard, the guru of the self-help craze of the 1970s. Convy, working in some high-powered acting company, steals every scene in which he appears. Dan Jenkins wrote a funny book about football but by the time director Ritchie got through with it, another dimension was added, although not necessarily a plus. Reynolds and Kristofferson are football players, roommates and best friends as they toil for a Miami team owned by Preston, a loudmouthed Texas oilman who discovers Convy's self-help cult and tries to get all of his employees to take the course, which is known as BEAT (an obvious reference to Erhard's "est," using all upper-case rather than all lower-case lettering. Preston has arranged his office according to the precepts of Convy's teachings so the entrance is so low that one must crawl in on one's knees, there is a desk with no legs, all the art works are hung one foot from the floor, etc. Clayburgh is Preston's free-thinking daughter. She's just come back from a trip to Africa and Europe and she is the Moreau to the men's Serre and Werner (from JULES AND JIM) in that this menage is strictly friendly with no sexual overtones. Clayburgh is "one of the boys" to the men and she has already shed two husbands and is paying alimony to both of them. Clayburgh, Kristofferson, and Reynolds are long-time pals from high school and she notices that while Reynolds is still the same looney he's always been, Kristofferson seems to have matured. He tells her that he has indeed changed and it's all due to Convy and his methods. Reynolds really loves Clayburgh but she is drawn to Kristofferson, although it is plain from the start which guy she'll be with at the film's end. There's a big football game (shot at the Super Bowl) and when Clayburgh and Kristofferson are standing at the altar at the end, Kristofferson answers "no" when asked if he'll take Clayburgh as his lawful wedded wife. He strolls off and best man Reynolds takes Clayburgh's arms and walks her along the beach in Miami where passing senior citizens thinks that it's cute to see a newlywed couple walking on the sand in their formal clothing. This kind of three-way love story has been seen often -- in THE PHILADELPHIA STORY, JULES AND JIM and many others. This is the first time it's set against professional football, and what could have been a devastating comedy about the game wanders off, taking too many pot shots at too many cows, both sacred and not-so-sacred. Lotte Lenya is on hand for a cameo as a woman who manipulates muscles (a take-off on "rolfing") and such topics as "pyramid power" and other fads of the era are raked. Several Gene Autry songs serve as the background music. It is said that Ritchie's decision to use the Convy character was due to his reading the non-fiction book *Powers Of Mind* by Adam Smith which reported the wave of consciousness-raising organizations that ran rampant at the time. Despite the hit-or-miss nature of the picture, it was a big winner at the theaters and made well over $20 million. An attempt at a TV series by ABC on the same subject failed miserably and Merrick went back to New York still annoyed at the way things happen in Hollywood. Lots of gratuitous four-letter words where six-letter words would have served just as well.

p, David Merrick; d, Michael Ritchie; w, Walter Bernstein (based on the novel by Dan Jenkins); ph, Charles Rosher, Jr. (Panavision, DeLuxe Color); m, Jerry Fielding; ed, Richard A. Harris; prod d, Walter Scott Herndon; set d, Cheryal Kearney; cos, Theoni V. Aldredge; m/l Gene Autry; stunts, Hal Needham.

Football Comedy   **Cas.**   **(PR:C-O   MPAA:R)**

SEMINOLE**½   (1953) 87m UNIV c

Rock Hudson (*Lt. Lance Caldwell*), Barbara Hale (*Revere Muldoon*), Anthony Quinn (*Osceola/John Powell*), Richard Carlson (*Maj. Harlan Degan*), Hugh O'Brian (*Kajeck*), Russell Johnson (*Lt. Hamilton*), Lee Marvin (*Sgt. Magruder*), Ralph Moody (*Kulak*), Fay Roope (*Zachary Taylor*), James Best (*Cpl. Gerard*), Don Gibson (*Capt. Streller*), John Day (*Scott*), Howard Erskine (*Cpl. Smiley*), Frank Chase (*Trooper*), Duane Thorsen (*Hendricks*), Walter Reed (*Farmer*), Robert Karnes (*Corporal*), Robert Dane (*Trader Taft*), John Phillips (*Maj. Lawrence*), Soledad Jimenez (*Mattie Sue Thomas*), Don Garrett (*Officer*), Robert Bray (*Capt. Sibley*), Earl Spainard, Scott Lee (*Troopers*), Peter Cranwell (*Sentry*), Alex Sharp (*Officer*), Jack Finlay, Jody Hutchinson (*Guards*), William Janssen, Dan Poore.

Hudson is a graduate of West Point assigned to an outpost near the Everglades because of his expertise in both the area and the local Seminole Indians. Upon arriving at his new position the lieutenant looks up Hale, his girl friend from childhood who is now in love with Quinn. Quinn, leader of the Seminoles, was also a boyhood friend of Hudson's. Hudson plans to use Hale to help arrange a peace treaty between the Indians and the white men but this is foiled by a scouting party sent out by Hudson's commander, Carlson. Carlson has ill feelings towards the Seminoles, feelings intensified when a member of the scouting party kills an Indian chief. Quinn's son O'Brian vows that the death will be avenged. Though Hudson tries to warn his commander about possible consequences, Carlson orders a surprise raid on the Indian tribes, which is a resounding failure. Carlson grows incensed and has Hudson and Hale bring Quinn to him under the guise of a truce. Once alone with the Seminole leader, Carlson inflicts a savage beating on Quinn before throwing him into a detention pit. After Hudson hears of this he confronts Carlson, who arrests the lieutenant. O'Brian, in an attempt to replace his father as the tribe's leader, sneaks into the fort and murders Quinn. Hudson is blamed for the death and Carlson orders him to be shot. Before the orders are carried out O'Brian and his men stage a raid on the fort. Hudson is freed and Carlson is arrested, charged with deceit. As the story closes, Hudson and O'Brian arrange a peace treaty with the understanding that Carlson be brought to trial. Though only about average for a Boetticher western, the film has some good action sequences, making use of the Florida swamp land. Particularly good is the surprise attack on the Indians which leaves Carlson's men floundering around in the Everglades marsh knowing they are surrounded by the enemy but not knowing how it happened. Performances are good considering the slight sketches the script offers, particularly by Marvin in an early supporting role. Entertaining enough, though certainly not the best of what its participants could offer. Though the picture deals with real historical characters and events, it deviates substantially from what really occurred. In 1837, Gen. Thomas S. Jesup arrested the real Osceola and a number of other Seminoles under a flag of truce. Osceola was transported to Fort Moultrie in South Carolina, where he died the following year. The Seminoles never signed a peace treaty, and technically are still at war with the government of the U.S. (what few of them remain, that is; most were wiped out in a genocidal campaign of attrition by the perfidious whites over the following few years).

p, Howard Christie; d, Budd Boetticher; w, Charles K. Peck, Jr.; ph, Russell Metty (Technicolor); m, Joseph Gershenson; ed, Virgil Vogel; art d, Alexander Golitzen, Emrich Nicholson; set d, Russell A. Gausman, Joseph Kish; cos, Rosemary Odell; makeup, Bud Westmore.

Western (PR:C MPAA:NR)

SEMINOLE UPRISING*½ (1955) 74m COL c

George Montgomery (*Lt. Cam Elliott*), Karin Booth (*Susan Hannah*), William Faucett (*Cubby Crouch, Scout*), Steve Ritch (*Black Cat, Seminole Chief*), Ed Hinton (*Capt. Phillip Dudley*), John Pickard (*Sgt. Chris Zanoba*), Jim Moloney (*Tony Zanoba*), Rory Mallinson (*Toby Wilson*), Howard Wright (*Col. Hannah*), Russ Conklin (*High Cloud*), Jonni Paris (*Malawa*), Joanne Rio (*Tasson Li*), Richard Cutting (*Col. Robert E. Lee*), Paul McGuire (*Spence*), Kenneth MacDonald (*Dinker*), Rube Schaffer (*Wood*), Edward Coch (*Marsh*).

Montgomery plays an army lieutenant assigned to retrieve a tribe of Seminole Indians who fled their Florida reservation in 1855 and headed for Texas. A bit of old-fashioned racism occurs when Booth, the lovely daughter of the post's commander who had been flirting with Montgomery, drops him when she hears that he's part Indian. In the end Montgomery gets the Seminoles back to Florida and wins the hand of Booth.

p, Sam Katzman; d, Earl Bellamy; w, Robert E. Kent (based on the novel *Bugle's Wake* by Curt Brandon); ph, Henry Freulich (Technicolor); ed, Jerome Thoms; md, Mischa Bakaleinikoff; art d, Paul Palmentola.

Western (PR:A MPAA:NR)

SEN NOCI SVATOJANSKE (SEE: MIDSUMMER NIGHT'S DREAM, A, 1961, Czech.)

SENATOR WAS INDISCREET, THE***½
(1947) 81m UNIV bw (GB: MR. ASHTON WAS INDISCREET)

William Powell (*Sen. Melvin G. Ashton*), Ella Raines (*Poppy McNaughton*), Peter Lind Hayes (*Lew Gibson*), Arleen Whelan (*Valerie Shepherd*), Ray Collins (*Houlihan*), Allen Jenkins (*Farrell*), Charles D. Brown (*Dinty*), Hans Conried (*Waiter*), Whitner [Whit] Bissell (*Oakes*), Norma Varden (*Woman at Banquet*), Milton Parsons (*Joe, "You Know Who"*), Francis Pierlot (*Frank*), Cynthia Corley (*Helen*), Oliver Blake, Chief Thundercloud, Chief Yowlachie, Iron Eyes Cody (*Indians*), Boyd B. Davis, Rodney Bell, Tom Coleman, John Alban (*Politicos*), Edward Clark (*Eddie*), William Forrest (*U.S. Officer*), Douglas Wood (*University President*), Tom Dugan (*Attendant at Stand*), George K. Mann (*Texas*), Claire Carleton (*Ingrid*), William H. Vedder (*Book Dealer*), Nina Lunn (*Girl in Elevator*), John R. Wald (*Broadcaster*), Vincent Pelletier (*Quiz Master*), Alex Davidoff, Forrest Dickson, Howard Mitchell (*Guests*), Don Wilson (*Commentator*), Beatrice Roberts (*Woman*), Martin Garralaga, John Bagni (*Italian Waiters*), Leon Lenoir (*French Waiter*), Billy Newell (*Elevator Operator*), Billy Bletcher (*Newsboy*), John A. Butler, John O'Connor, Franklin Parker, Clarence Straight (*Reporters*), Mervin Williams (*Newsreel Man*), Eddie Coke (*Ticket Buyer*), Bruce Riley, Ethan Laidlaw, Richard Gordon, Walton DeCardo, Watson Downs, Cedric Stevens, Rex Dale, Oliver Prickett (*Men*), Sven Hugo Borg (*Swedish Waiter*), John Valentine (*Desk Clerk*), Walter Soderling (*Hotel Clerk*), Jimmy Clark, Russ Whiteman (*Bellboys*), Mike Stokey (*Night Clerk*), Laura R. Parrish (*Aunt Abby*), Dutch Schlickenmeyer (*Ticket Buyer*), Gene Fowler, Sr (*Charlie*), Myrna Loy (*Mrs. Ashton*).

A broad satire on politics that would have been much better if the barbs were more directly pointed at the people whom they were satirizing. George S. Kaufman's directorial debut was a good one but it also needed some of his writing to sharpen the jokes. Loy and Powell were making their last appearance together and her role is a tiny cameo done more as a favor than as a legit part. Powell is a pompous boor of a senator who is too dumb to be true. If you can recall Kenny Delmar's portrayal of Senator Klaghorn on Fred Allen's brilliant radio show, this is about what it would have looked like onscreen. After two decades of fooling his constituents, Powell thinks that he might make a fine U.S. President, so he begins a campaign for the

office with Hayes as his press agent. The political bosses of his party, led by Brown, would like Powell to go away, but he has an ace up his sleeve, a diary he's kept over the years that will blow the lid off the party if it ever gets into journalists' hands. Powell's nonsensical campaign promises include such silliness as all letters being written on tissue paper so mailmen's backs won't hurt, a three-day work week with eight days pay, every person in the U.S. being able to go Harvard for their educations, all prescriptions being written in English so they can be understood by lay people, cows being altered so they produce malted milk, etc. When Powell's hot diary suddenly disappears, the politicians begin to book airplanes to Little America in the Antarctic, Patagonia, and anywhere else there is no extradition treaty with the U.S. Hayes finds the diary and can't make up his mind about what to do with it. If he gives it back to Powell, he'll be doing the country a disservice. If he gives it to his sweetheart, newspaperwoman Raines, he'll be out of a job when the spit hits the fan. Hayes chooses to do the decent thing, hands the diary to Raines, who prints the truth, and all the party members flee, with Powell and his wife, Loy, leading the way. The picture ends with Powell and spouse in Hawaii (remember, this was well before Hawaii was a state), wearing South Seas garb. A few very funny scenes, including one where candidate Powell is inducted into an Indian tribe by Cody and the others. A few years after this, film studios took a larger chance and began making political comedies that were able to be sharper and more telling. No political party was named and any coincidental resemblance between the characters and the truth was inadvertent because they laundered the comedy very carefully.

p, Nunnally Johnson; d, George S. Kaufman; w, Charles MacArthur (based on a story by Edwin Lanham); ph, William Mellor; m, Daniele Amfitheatrof; ed, Sherman A. Rose; art d, Bernard Herzbrun, Boris Levin; set d, Russell A. Gausman, Ken Swartz; cos, Grace Houston; spec eff, David S. Horsley.

Comedy Cas. (PR:A MPAA:NR)

SEND FOR PAUL TEMPLE** (1946, Brit.) 83m BUT bw

Anthony Hulme (*Paul Temple*), Joy Shelton (*Steve Trent, Reporter*), Tamara Desni (*Diana Thornley*), Jack Raine (*Sir Graham Forbes*), Beatrice Varley (*Miss Marchmont*), Hylton Allen (*Dr. Milton*), Maire O'Neill (*Mrs. Neddy*), Phil Ray (*Horace Daley*), Olive Sloane (*Ruby*), Michael Golden, Richard Shayne, Edward V. Robson, Leslie Weston, Victor Weske, Norman Pierce, Melville Crawford, Charles Wade.

The film debut of popular radio detective Paul Temple suffers from a bargain-basement production. Hulme stars as the novelist-amateur detective who is called in by Scotland Yard to help investigate a murder committed by a gang of diamond thieves. Shelton, a lady reporter whose brother was murdered by the gang, helps Hulme track down the leader of the gang, who turns out to be masquerading as a police inspector.

p&d, John Argyle; w, Francis Durbridge, Argyle (based on characters created by Durbridge); ph, Geoffrey Faithfull.

Crime (PR:A MPAA:NR)

SEND ME NO FLOWERS**½ (1964) 100m UNIV c

Rock Hudson (*George Kimball*), Doris Day (*Judy Kimball*), Tony Randall (*Arnold Nash*), Paul Lynde (*Mr. Akins*), Hal March (*Winston Burr*), Edward Andrews (*Dr. Ralph Morrissey*), Patricia Barry (*Linda Bullard*), Clive Clerk (*Vito*), Dave Willock (*Milkman*), Aline Towne (*Cora*), Helen Winston (*Woman Commuter*), Christine Nelson (*Nurse*), Clint Walker (*Bert Power*), John Melfi (*Caddy*), Herb Vigran (*TV Announcer*), Shep Houghton (*Sam Scheffing*), Forrest Draper (*Cheating Golfer*), Tommy Cook (*Tennis Player*), Maureen Jantzen (*Hat Check Girl*), Lou Byrne (*Secretary*), Jean Paul King (*Waiter*).

The last and weakest Hudson/Day outing is lame from the starting gate because the film opens with the couple already married, preventing any of the funny, somewhat risque sexual escapades that marked the first two films. Instead, SEND ME NO FLOWERS relies on the hackneyed convention of mistaken identity as hypochondriac Hudson enters the hospital for chest pains and overhears his doctor discussing the terminal illness of another patient and assumes the illness is his own. Hudson takes the news with aplomb and nobly sets out to find a new husband for Day who will provide the lifestyle she's grown accustomed to. He digs up her old college beau, Walker, now a rich oil man, and practically forces him on her. She knows nothing about the "illness" and begins to suspect Hudson is doing this out of guilt from an illicit affair. When she confronts him, he discloses the news of his illness. She asks the family doctor, who insists that Hudson is fine, so she angrily prepares to divorce him. Eventually the bugs are worked out and the couple reunite.

p, Harry Keller; d, Norman Jewison; w, Julius V. Epstein (based on the play by Norman Barasch, Carroll Moore); ph, Daniel Fapp (Technicolor); m, Frank DeVol; ed, J. Terry Williams; md, Joseph Gershenson; art d, Alexander Golitzen, Robert Clatworthy; set d, John McCarthy, Oliver Emert, John Austin; cos, Jean Louis; ch, David Winters; m/l, "Send Me No Flowers," Hal David, Burt Bacharach; makeup, Bud Westmore.

Comedy (PR:A MPAA:NR)

SENDER, THE* (1982, Brit.) 91m PAR c

Kathryn Harrold (Gail Farmer), Zeljko Ivanek (The Sender), Shirley Knight (Jerolyn), Paul Freeman (Dr. Denman), Sean Hewitt (The Messiah), Harry Ditson (Dr. Hirsch), Olivier Pierre (Dr. Erskine), Tracy Harper (Young Girl), Al Matthews (Vietnam Veteran), Marsha Hunt (Nurse Jo), Angus MacInnes (Sheriff Prouty), Jana Shelden (Nurse Reimbold), Monica Buferd (Dr. Warren), Colin Bruce (Computer Technician), Jerry Harte (Security Guard), Darcy Flynn (TV Anchorwoman).

Underrated psychological horror thriller that bombed at the box office because the studio had no idea how to sell a crisply directed shocker that didn't wallow in pointless gore effects. Ivanek plays a 20-year-old attempted suicide who is brought to a psychiatric clinic for treatment. Refusing to divulge his identity, pretty young psychiatrist Harrold dubs him "John Doe." It soon becomes apparent that Ivanek possesses the ability to telepathically send his disturbed nightmares and feelings into the minds of others. Unfortunately Ivanek cannot control these powers and his dreams involving hideous bugs, rats, and fires are invading the brains of most people in the hospital. Soon after, Ivanek's mysterious mother, Knight, arrives, and it is obvious that mother and son have shared this power since birth. Knight has always thought her son was the second coming of Christ and has dominated him his whole life. She turns up dead shortly thereafter and Ivanek is the only suspect. Director Christian (who was the set decorator for STAR WARS and the art director for ALIEN) slowly builds the suspense, keeping the performances calm and underplayed, so that when the fairly simple effects sequences do arrive, they are all the more horrifying and powerful. An intelligent film that refuses to resort to the kind of bloody, overblown direction that marks the work of other horror film directors. Worth seeing.

p, Edward S. Feldman; d, Roger Christian; w, Thomas Baum; ph, Roger Pratt (Rank Color); m, Trevor Jones; ed, Ian Crafford; prod d, Malcolm Middleton; art d, Steve Spence, Charles Bishop; set d, Roy Stannard; cos, Shari Feldman, Ian Hickenbotham; spec eff, Nick Allder, Allan Bryce; makeup, Sarah Monzani, stunts, Colin Skeaping.

Horror   Cas.   (PR:O   MPAA:R)

SENGOKU GUNTO-DEN (SEE: SAGA OF THE VAGABONDS, 1964, Jap.)

SENGOKU YARO (SEE: WARRING CLANS, 1963, Jap.)

SENIOR PROM* (1958) 82m COL bw

Jill Corey (Gay Sherridan), Paul Hampton (Tom Harper), Jimmie Komack (Dog), Barbara Bostock (Flip), Tom Laughlin (Carter Breed III), Frieda Inescort (Mrs. Sherridan), Selene Walters (Caroline), Francis De Sales (Carter Breed, Sr.), Peggy Moffit (Girl with Holder), Louis Prima, Keely Smith, Sam Butera & The Witnesses, Ed Sullivan, Mitch Miller, Connee Boswell, Bob Crosby, Toni Arden, Freddy Martin & His Orchestra, Jose Melis, Les Elgart, Howard Miller (Themselves), Marvin Miller (Narrator).

Uninteresting musical starring Corey as a college girl trying to decide between rich bore Laughlin and poor-but-nice singer Hampton. Not to ruin the suspense, but she opts for Hampton. The boring assemblage of musical talent doesn't help much. Songs include: "One Year Older" (Don Gohman, Hal Hackady), "Big Daddy" (Lee Pockriss, Peter Udell), and "That Old Black Magic." Laughlin later became famous for his portrayal of Billy Jack in the film series of the same name.

p, Harry Romm; d, David Lowell Rich; w, Hal Hackady; ph, Fred Jackman; ed, Al Clark; md, Morris Stoloff; art d, Carl Anderson; m/l, Don Gohman, Hackady, Peter Udell, Lee Pockriss.

Musical   (PR:A   MPAA:NR)

SENIORS, THE* (1978) 87m Cinema Shares c

Jeffrey Byron, Gary Imhoff, Dennis Quaid, Lou Richards, Priscilla Barnes, Rockey Flintermann, Edward Andrews, Ian Wolf, Robert Emhardt, Alan Hewitt, Lynn Cartwright, Woodrow Parfrey, Troy Hoskins, David Haney, Alan Reed.

A quartet of collegians decide to open a sex clinic as a joke but end up surprising themselves when the business becomes a multi-million dollar operation. There are some mildly amusing moments but certainly nothing to make this memorable. Surprisingly, the film was written and co-produced by the Oscar-winning writer of PILLOW TALK.

p, Stanley Shapiro, Carter DeHaven; d, Rod Amateau; w, Shapiro; ph, Robert Jessup; m, Pat Williams; ed, Guy Scarpita; m/l, Williams (sung by Gene Cotton).

Comedy   Cas.   (PR:O   MPAA:R)

SENJO NI NAGARERU UTA (SEE: WE WILL REMEMBER, 1966, Jap.)

SENOR AMERICANO* (1929) 71m UNIV bw

Ken Maynard (Michael Banning), Kathryn Crawford (Carmelita), Gino Corrado (Ramirez), J.P. McGowan (Maddux), Frank Yaconelli (Manana), Frank Beal (Don Manuel), Tarzan the Horse.

Early Maynard talkie sees our hero kicking all the bad guys out of California territory so that it can be annexed by the U.S. Maynard also produced, and long-time colleague Brown served as director.

p, Ken Maynard; d, Harry Joe Brown; w, Bennett Cohen, Lesley Mason (based on a story by Helmer Bergman, Henry McCarthy); ph, Ted McCord; ed, Fred Allen; titles, Mason.

Western   (PR:A   MPAA:NR)

SENORA CASADA NECEISITA MARIDO* (1935) 72m FOX bw (A MARRIED WOMAN NEEDS A HUSBAND)

Catalina Barcena, Antonio Moreno, Barbara Leonard, Jose Crespo, Romualdo Tirado.

Another in the series of Spanish-language films produced by 20th Century Fox. This one is a comedy and stars Barcena as a housewife seeking to liven up her marriage by making her husband jealous. He, of course, gets her back by pulling the same trick, and after the standard series of misunderstandings they are once again a happy couple. Barcena possesses a modicum of Latin charm, making this one worth sitting through if you speak Spanish. (In Spanish.)

p, John Stone; d, James Tinling.

Comedy   (PR:A   MPAA:NR)

SENORITA FROM THE WEST* (1945) 63m UNIV bw

Allan Jones (Phil Bradley), Bonita Granville (Jeannie Blake), Jess Barker (Tim Winters), Olin Howlin (Justice of the Peace), Danny Mummert (Kid), Emmett Vogan (Producer), Oscar O'Shea (Dusty), George Cleveland (Cap), Renny McEvoy (William Wylliams), Fuzzy Knight (Rosebud), Bob Merrill (Elmer), Billy Nelson (Taxi Driver), Jack Clifford (Motor Cop), Gwen Donovan (Elevator Starter), Ralph Dunn (Man), Ann Lawrence (Girl), Dick Alexander (Masseur), Al Ferguson, Frank Hagney (Moving Men), Betty McDonough, Peggy Leon (Women), Martin Lowell (Bellhop), Jerome Sheldon, Carey Harrison (Men), Lane Chandler (Cop), Douglas Carter (Technician), Cy Ring (Bystander), Spade Cooley and His Orchestra.

Small-town girl Granville travels to the Big Apple looking for fame and fortune as a singer. Little does she know that she's heir to a massive gold fortune, a secret kept by her smart relatives who don't want an evil gigolo latching onto their little girl just for her money. She falls in love with dopey singer Jones who "dubs" the singing voice of fading crooner Barker. Barker gets wind of Granville's fortune and tries to weasel in between the sweethearts. He fails and all works out well in the end. Songs include: "Lonely Love" (Everett Carter, Ray Sinatra), "Lou Lou Louisiana" (Carter, Milton Rosen), "What A Change In The Weather" (Kim Gannon, Walter Kent), "These Hazy, Lazy Old Hills" and "All the Things I Wanna Say."

p, Philip Cahn; d, Frank Strayer; w, Howard Dimsdale; ph, Paul Ivano; ed, Paul Landres; art d, John B. Goodman, Abraham Grossman; m/l, Kim Gannes, Walter Kent, Jack Gardens, Mark Levant, John Blackburn, Les Huntley, Everett Carter, Milton Rosen, Buddy Pepper, Inez James, Ray Sinatra.

Musical   (PR:A   MPAA:NR)

SENSATION*½ (1936, Brit.) 54m ABF/Film Alliance bw

John Lodge (Pat Heaton), Diana Churchill (Maisie Turnpit), Francis Lister (Richard Grainger), Joan Marion (Mrs. Grainger), Margaret Vyner (Claire Lindsay), Jerry Verno (Spikey), Richard Bird (Henry Belcher), Athene Seyler (Madame Henry), Dennis Wyndham (Spurge), Henry Oscar (Superintendent Stainer), Antony Holles (Blake), Martin Walker (Dimmitt), Sybil Grove (Mrs. Spurge), Leslie Perrins (Strange), Felix Aylmer (Lord Bouverie), Arthur Chesney (Ernie Turnpit), James Hayter (Jock), Billy Shine (Quick), Brian Herbert (Inspector Hoggett), Joe Cunningham (D.D.I. Proctor), Michael Gainsborough (Dick Grainger).

A typical news-hound film starring Lodge as a tough reporter who risks ruining his love life in order to get the low-down on a hot scoop. After extensive digging, Lodge is able to unearth some damning evidence in the form of love letters to nail a murder wrap on the man who killed a waitress.

p, Walter C. Mycroft; d, Brian Desmond Hurst; w, Dudley Leslie, Marjorie Deans, William Freshman (based on the play "Murder Gang" by Basil Dean, George Munro); ph, Walter Harvey.

Crime   (PR:A   MPAA:NR)

SENSATION, 1970 (SEE: SEDUCERS, THE, 1970, Ital.)

SENSATION HUNTERS**   (1934) 73m MON/FD bw

Arline Judge, Preston Foster, Kenneth MacKenna, Marion Burns, Juanita Hansen, Creighton Hale, Cyril Chadwick, Nella Walker, Harold Minjir, Finis Barton.

Judge is the tough-talking thrush in a Panama clip joint run by Hansen who befriends youthful, innocent newcomer Burns. When the jaded Judge falls ill, bosom-buddy Burns elects to barter her body to gain some much-needed cash to help her friend. She leaves her first trick unturned, as he proves to be nice fellow Foster. Just in time, Judge's errant husband – an admiral in the Chinese navy – steams into the canal to help her in her hour of need. Typically snappy dialog by DeMond keeps this from dragging.

p, Robert Welsh; d, Charles Vidor; w, Albert E. DeMond, Paul Schofield (based on a story by Whitman Chambers); ph, Sid Hickox; m, Harold Lewis, Bernie Grossman.

Drama   (PR:A MPAA:NR)

SENSATION HUNTERS*½   (1945) 62m MON bw

Robert Lowery (*Danny Burke*), Doris Merrick (*Julie Rodgers*), Eddie Quillan (*Ray Lawson*), Constance Worth (*Irene*), Isabel Jewell (*Mae*), Wanda McKay (*Helen*), Nestor Paiva (*New Davis*), Byron Foulger (*Mark Rogers*), Vince Barnett (*Agent*), Minerva Urecal (*Edna Rodgers*), The Rubenettes.

An innocent, hard-working girl goes head-over-heels for cad Lowery. Her father tosses her out of the house when she is an innocent victim of a gambling raid involving Lowery. Merrick's life goes downhill from there, as she cons her way into a chorus-line job at the club where Lowery hangs out. But as she slowly lets her life turn downward, he dumps her for her best friend. She freaks and pulls out a gun and both die during the fight at the depressing end.

p, Joseph Kaufman; d, Christy Cabanne; w, Dennis Cooper (based on a story by John Faxon); ph, Ira Morgan; ed, Martin Kohn; m/l, Jack Kenney, Lewis Bellin; ch, Phyllis Avery.

Drama   (PR:A MPAA:NR)

SENSATIONS   (SEE: SENSATIONS OF 1945, 1944)

SENSATIONS OF 1945**   (1944) 86m UA bw (AKA: SENSATIONS)

Eleanor Powell (*Ginny Walker*), Dennis O'Keefe (*Junior Crane*), C. Aubrey Smith (*Dan Lindsay*), Eugene Pallette (*Gus Crane*), Mimi Forsythe (*Julia Westcott*), Lyle Talbot (*Randall*), Hubert Castle (*The Great Gustafson*), Richard Hageman (*Pendergast*), Marie Blake (*Miss Grear*), Stanley Andrews (*Mr. Collins*), Louise Currie (*English Girl*), Betty Wells (*Girl in Penny Arcade*), Bert Roach (*Photographer*), Grandon Rhodes (*Doctor*), Earle Hodgins (*Detective*), Constance Purdy (*Mme. Angostina*), Joe Devlin (*Silas Hawkins*), George Humbert (*Martinelli*), Anthony Warde (*Moroni*), Ruth Lee (*Mrs. Gustafson*), W.C. Fields, Sophie Tucker, Dorothy Donegan, The Christianis, Pailenberg's Bears, Cab Calloway and Woody Herman Bands, David Lichine, Wendell Niles, Gene Rodgers, Les Paul 3, The Flying Copelands, Mel Hall, Johnson Brothers, Willie Pratt.

Basically an excuse for a potpourri of vaudeville acts and musical numbers, the plot of this entertaining musical deals with the conflict between Pallette, an old-fashioned, anything-goes press agent, and his conservative son, O'Keefe. The latter wants to make deals with dignity, while Pallette is all flair and bombast. To confound his progeny and teach him a lesson, Pallette turns over the operating reins of his firm to a client, dancer Powell, who has even wilder notions than he. Her promotional peregrinations get her into a great deal of trouble, finally landing her in jail, where junior bails her out. A fun show-business saga featuring an amazing variety of turns, from rope-walkers through performing horses, with lots of dancing and music. W.C. Fields is superb in an all-too-short cameo in this, his last film appearance. Powell went into virtual retirement following this film; she had gotten married to actor Glenn Ford the year prior to its release. She did dancing cameos in THE GREAT MORGAN (1946) (but her appearance in that film was comprised of out-takes from an earlier film), and in THE DUCHESS OF IDAHO (1950), an Esther Williams vehicle. Songs by Al Sherman and Harry Tobias include "Mister Hepster's Dictionary," "Wake Up Man You're Slippin'," "One Love," "Kiss Serenade," "No Never," "Spin Little Pin Ball," and the Sophie Tucker standard "You Can't Sew a Button On a Heart."

p&d, Andrew L. Stone; w, Dorothy Bennett (based on a story by Frederick Jackson, Stone); ph, Peverell Marley; John Mescall; m, Al Sherman; ed, Jimmy Smith; md, Mahlon Merrick; art d, Charles Odds; set d, Maurice Yates; cos, Eleanor Behm; m/l, Sherman, Harry Tobias; ch, David Lichine, Charles O'Curran.

Musical   Cas.   (PR:A MPAA:NR)

SENSO***½   (1968, Ital.) 125m Lux/Fleetwood c (AKA: THE WANTON CONTESSA)

Alida Valli (*Contessa Livia Serpieri*), Farley Granger (*Lt. Franz Mahler*), Massimo Girotti (*Marquis Roberto Ussoni*), Heinz Moog (*Count Serpieri*),

Rina Morelli (*Laura*), Marcella Mariani (*Prostitute*), Christian Marquand (*Bohemian Officer*), Tonio Selwart (*Col. Kleist*), Sergio Fantoni (*Patriot*), Cristoforo De Hartungen (*Commander at Venetian Square*), Tino Bianchi (*Meucci*), Marianna Leibl (*Wife of Austrian General*), Ernst Nadherny, Goliarda Sapienza.

Visconti counterposes romance and rebellion in this historical tale of love and betrayal set against the Italian *risorgimento* in 1866. Both the aristocracy and Garibaldi's partisan patriots battle the Austro-Hungarian Empire for Italian independence. During a performance of Giuseppe Verdi's "Il Trovatore" in Venice, as the operatic chorus chants *"All'armi, all'armi"* (to arms, to arms) the patriots in the stalls and the Italian aristocrats in the boxes take up the chant, unfurling the Italian national colors, to the alarm of the occupying Austrian officers. A young Austrian lieutenant, Granger, makes a disparaging remark about the Italians and is challenged to a duel by the fiery young Girotti, an underground leader. His cousin, the beautiful contessa–Valli–is in attendance with a group of Austrian officers. Realizing Girotti's peril if he is discovered, she protects him by sending for Granger and pointing out that the stage, not life, is the appropriate place for such a drama as a duel. Granger defers to her wishes, but later secretly denounces Girotti, who is arrested and exiled. Valli is attracted to the handsome, cynical young officer, and the two become lovers. When the evasive Granger disappears for a time, she awaits his return. A message arrives for her, bearing only an address; she rushes to meet her lover, but is intercepted by her husband, Moog, at the meeting place. Trapped, she begins to confess her infidelity when the door bursts open to reveal not Granger, but the newly returned Girotti. Her husband elects to disbelieve her confession, assuming it to be a diversion to throw him off Girotti's track (Moog had been sympathetic to the Austrian cause, but now, sensing a turn of fate, seeks an alliance with the partisans. Girotti has raised money for the cause and entrusts it to Valli. However, she gives the money to the returned Granger so that he can buy his way out of military service in the forthcoming shooting war, sending him to Verona. Against his explicit instructions, the love-struck Valli then follows Granger to Verona, where she finds him ridden with guilt, drinking heavily, and supporting an attractive young woman on the funds that had been intended for the partisans. Betrayed, and herself guilty of betraying her national cause, she denounces him as a deserter. He is shot, and Valli cries his name through streets crowded with besotted soldiers celebrating a victory. A visually beautiful, well-crafted, disarmingly cynical set-piece in which the motives of the prideful patriots seem as banal and petty as those of the selfishly lustful. Cinematographer Graziata died during production.

p, Domenico Forges Davanzanti; d, Luchino Visconti; w, Visconti, Suso Cecchi d'Amico, Giorgio Prosperi, Carl Alianello, Giorgio Bassani, Tennessee Williams, Paul Bowles (based on the short story "Senso, Scartafaccio Segreto della Contessa Livia" by Camillo Boito); ph, Aldo Graziata [G. R. Aldo], Robert Krasker, Giuseppe Rotunno; m, Anton Bruckner, Giuseppe Verdi; ed, Mario Serandrei; md, Franco Ferrara; art d, Ottavio Scotti; set d, Gino Brosio; cos, Marcel Escoffier, Piero Tosi.

Drama   (PR:A MPAA:NR)

SENSUALITA**½   (1954, Ital.) 93m Ponti-DD/PAR bw (AKA: BAREFOOT SAVAGE)

Eleonora Rossi-Drago (*Franca*), Amedeo Nazzari (*Riccardo*), Marcello Mastroianni (*Carlo*), Francesca Liddi (*Nidia*), Corrado Nardi (*Bosci*), Clorindo Cerato (*Cowhand*), Maria Zanoli (*Maid*), Angelo Binarelli (*Marco*).

Simmering Italian drama has Drago as the main angle in a love triangle involving two brothers. She is a Slav immigrant who, in trying to get out of working the fields, goes after one of the brothers who own the farm. When he rejects her, she goes after the other brother and is welcomed with open arms. After the honeymoon, the first brother decides he wants her after all. He realizes he can't compete with his own brother and starts to leave the farm, with Drago in hot pursuit. Her husband catches them and a struggle ensues. Unbelievable finish has Drago shooting her lover, then being shot by her husband.

d, Clemente Fracassi; w, Alberto Moravia, Ennio De Concini (based on a story by Fracassi, De Concini); ph, Aldo Tonti; m, Enzio Masetti.

Drama   (PR:A MPAA:NR)

SENSUOUS VAMPIRES   (SEE: VAMPIRE HOOKERS, THE 1979, Phil.)

SENTENCE SUSPENDED   (SEE: MILITARY ACADEMY WITH THAT 10TH AVENUE GANG, 1950)

SENTENCED FOR LIFE*½   (1960, Brit.) 64m Danzigers/UA bw

Francis Matthews (*Jim Richards*), Jill Williams (*Sue Thompson*), Basil Dignam (*Ralph Thompson*), Jack Gwillim (*John Richards*), Lorraine Clewes (*Mrs. Richards*), Mark Singleton (*Edward Thompson*), Nyree Dawn Porter (*Betty*), Arnold Bell (*Williams*), John M. Moore, Garard Green, Norah Gordon, Jack Taylor, Eric Dodson, Vernon Smythe, Reginald Hearne, Jack Melford, Charles Maunsell.

Engineer Gwillim is wrongly convicted of selling secrets to enemy agents and sentenced to life in prison. Suspecting that his former partner, Dignam, may have framed him, he enlists the aid of his law student son, Matthews, to investigate the case. Standard crime drama with a touch of espionage thrown in to spice up the incredibly bland stew. Perhaps hot sauce would have worked better.

p, Edward J. Danziger, Harry Lee Danziger; d, Max Varnel; w, Eldon Howard, Mark Grantham; ph, S.D. Onions.

Crime   **(PR:A MPAA:NR)**

SENTENZA DI MORTE   (SEE: DEATH SENTENCE, 1967, Ital.)

SENTIMENTAL BLOKE**   (1932, Aus.) 65m Efftee/Hoyts bw

Cecil Scott, Ray Fisher.

A very early romantic comedy from the Australian film industry is a remake of a silent film made several years before. Based on a book of poems by C.J. Dennis, the film chronicles the romance of a pugnacious tough guy with a sweet young girl. Better than average for early Australian cinema.

p, F.W. Thring.

Romance/Comedy   **(PR:A MPAA:NR)**

SENTIMENTAL JOURNEY***   (1946) 94m FOX bw

John Payne (Bill), Maureen O'Hara (Julie), William Bendix (Donnelly), Sir Cedric Hardwicke (Dr. Miller), Glenn Langan (Judson), Mischa Auer (Lawrence Ayres), Connie Marshall (Hatty), Kurt Kreuger (Wilson), Trudy Marshall (Ruth), Ruth Nelson (Mrs. McMasters), Dorothy Adams (Martha), Mary Gordon (Agnes), Lillian Bronson (Miss Benson), Olive Blakeney (Mrs. Deane), James Flavin (Detective), William Haade (Bus Driver), Mary Field (Chaperon), Byron Foulger (Clerk in Toy Shop), George E. Stone (Toy Hawker), John Davidson (Floorwalker), Mary Ann Bricker, Peggy Miller, Carol Coombs, Carol Ann Beekly, Shirley Barton, Donna Cooke (Girls), Bert Hicks (Actor).

Grab the hankies for this one, which is just full of cliches. Payne, a producer, and O'Hara, a famous actress, are a married couple that cannot have children. Both desperately want a child when O'Hara meets Marshall, a cute, lovable orphan who is ready for adoption. As the child brings joy to their lives, O'Hara has a fatal heart attack and Payne is left alone to raise the child. The slow-moving film deals with Marshall's problem of filling the gap left by her mother, and with Payne's struggle to accept the child as a real part of his life. Remade as THE GIFT OF LOVE.

p, Walter Morosco; d, Walter Lang; w, Samuel Hoffenstein, Elizabeth Reinhardt (based on a story by Nelia Gardner White); ph, Norbert Brodine; m, Cyril J. Mockridge; ed, J. Watson Webb; art d, Lyle Wheeler, Albert Hogsett; set d, Thomas Little; cos, Kay Nelson; m/l, Bud Green, Les Brown, Ben Homer; makeup, Ben Nye.

Drama   **(PR:A MPAA:NR)**

SENTINEL, THE*   (1977) 91m UNIV c

Chris Sarandon (Michael Lerman), Cristina Raines (Alison Parker), Martin Balsam (Professor), John Carradine (Halliran), Jose Ferrer (Robed Figure), Ava Gardner (Miss Logan), Arthur Kennedy (Franchino), Burgess Meredith (Chazen), Sylvia Miles (Gerde), Deborah Raffin (Jennifer), Eli Wallach (Gatz), Christopher Walken (Rizzo), Jerry Orbach (Director), Beverly D'Angelo (Sandra), Hank Garrett (Brenner), Robert Gerringer (Hart), Nana Tucker (Girl At End), Tom Berenger (Man At End), William Hickey (Perry), Gary Allen (Malcolm Stinnett), Tresa Hughes (Rebecca Stinnett), Kate Harrington (Mrs. Clark), Jane Hoffman (Lillian Clotkin), Elaine Shore (Emma Clotkin), Sam Gray (Dr. Aureton), Reid Shelton (Priest), Fred Stuthman (Alison's Father), Lucie Lancaster (Alison's Mother), Anthony Holland (Party Host), Jeff Goldblum (Jack), Zane Lasky (Raymond), Mady Heflin (Professor's Student), Diane Stilwell (Brenner's Secretary), Ron McLarty (Real Estate Agent).

Sick, cliche-ridden horror film that gets very boring very fast. Raines, an actress, moves into a nice-looking apartment that turns out to be what separates hell from the earth above. Weird things start to happen and weird characters make up the film, which finishes with an ending that will turn away most people. Even this cast of recognizable faces and names can't save the audience from boredom and from just plain feeling sick.

p, Michael Winner, Jeffrey Konvitz; d, Winner; w, Winner, Konvitz (based on novel The Sentinel by Konvitz); ph, Dick Kratina (Technicolor); m, Gil Melle; ed, Bernard Gribble, Terence Rawlings; prod d, Philip Rosenberg; set d, Ed Stewart; cos, Peggy Farrell; spec eff, Albert Whitlock; makeup, Dick Smith, Bob Laden.

Horror   **Cas.**   **(PR:O MPAA:R)**

SEPARATE PEACE, A*   (1972) 105m PAR c

John Heyl (Finny), Parker Stevenson (Gene), William Roerick (Mr. Patchwithers), Peter Brush (Leper), Victor Bevine (Brinker), Scott Bradbury (Chet), John E.A. Mackenzie (Bobby), Mark Trefethen (John), Frank Wilich Jr (Quackenbush), Elizabeth B. Brewster (Mrs. Patchwithers), Edward Echols (Mr. Ludsbury), Don Schultz (Dr. Stanpole), Paul Sadler (Naval Officer).

An offbeat drama that grappled with the years bridging adolescence and adulthood of seven male students at a stuffy east coast prep school. Heyl and Stevenson are roommates who share an especially close relationship. Set in 1942, how the young men deal with their feelings about the war is the focal point of the story. One of the group, Brush, joins the service and eventually becomes a deserter. The others are in a quandary about what to do after their impending graduation. The school's justice system finds Stevenson guilty of causing an accident that has injured Heyl. A disbelieving Heyl falls down a staircase and later dies during an operation on his leg. The story is told by Stevenson in flashbacks after he has returned from the war. He tells it under the tree that was the site of the first tragedy that befell his friend.

p, Robert Goldston, Otto Plaschkes; d, Larry Peerce; w, Fred Segal (based on the novel A Separate Peace by John Knowles); ph, Frank Stanley (Eastmancolor); m, Charles Fox; ed, John C. Howard; art d, Charles Rosen; set d, Philip Abramson; cos, Ron Talsky; makeup, Fred Blau, Mike Hancock.

Drama   **Cas.**   **(PR:A MPAA:PG)**

SEPARATE TABLES***   (1958) 98m Clifton-Joanna/UA bw

Deborah Kerr (Sibyl Railton-Bell), Rita Hayworth (Ann Shankland), David Niven (Maj. Pollack), Wendy Hiller (Miss Pat Cooper), Burt Lancaster (John Malcolm), Gladys Cooper (Mrs. Railton-Bell), Cathleen Nesbitt (Lady Matheson), Felix Aylmer (Mr. Fowler), Rod Taylor (Charles), Audrey Dalton (Jean), May Hallatt (Miss Meachum), Priscilla Morgan (Doreen), Hilda Plowright (Mabel).

Terence Rattigan's original play consisted of two one-acts set in the same Bournemouth, England locale. It was a tour de force for Eric Portman and Margaret Leighton, who played it successfully in London, then in New York during the fall of 1956. Rattigan collaborated with John Gay to blend the two stories into one that used four actors instead of two. The result was a rewarding drama that received nominations from the Motion Picture Academy as Best Picture, for Best Actress (Kerr), Best Screenplay (from another medium), Best Cinematography (black-and-white), and Best Music. It won Oscars for Niven as Best Actor and Hiller as Best Supporting Actress. Lancaster's partnership with Harold Hecht and James Hill produced the film that saw two of the major characters having their nationalities altered from British to American in order to make it a starring vehicle for Lancaster and Hayworth. The title refers to the practice of seating solo guests at their dining room tables when they have arrived alone. The small hotel is at the seashore and the dining room is filled with a host of lonely people. Niven is the ultimate Englishman, peppering his dialog with all the Major Blimp cliches like "ekshully," and "I say!" and "Good show!"–almost the way Terry-Thomas played it in MAKE MINE MINK. He is a one-time military man who waxes on and on about his experiences in the war's North African campaign, but his stories have the ring of prevarication about them. Cooper is a stern and forceful matriarch with a shy daughter, Kerr, a mousey spinster fascinated by Niven but far too shy to let him know that. The third at the Cooper table is Cooper's friend, Nesbitt, a peeress of the realm. Aylmer is a former schoolteacher who talks about his glory days when he guided young persons' lives. Hallatt is a racing enthusiast and Taylor and Dalton are unmarried lovers. The hotel is run by Hiller, a plain but pleasant woman who wants to make sure all her guests are happy, but she is not all that happy herself, as her lover, Lancaster, has not popped the question yet. Lancaster is a reclusive American writer who drinks more than he creates and spends much of his time in his room getting acquainted with Haig and Haig. Kerr and Niven begin a halting relationship but Cooper does her best to put an end to that before it can blossom. Lancaster's former wife, Hayworth, arrives at the hotel. She is a blowsy, sad social type with a penchant for histrionics. Then the truth about Niven comes out. He wasn't a major at all, just a noncombatant supply officer. Further, Niven is arrested by the local cops for harassing women at the small movie house in Bournemouth's center, then released. Cooper suggests that Niven leave this genteel hotel immediately but Hiller springs to his defense and says that decision is Niven's. Hayworth is a needy woman and fearful that she may never find another man and makes it subtly clear that she might like to renew her life with Lancaster, but he is becoming more enamored of Hiller, who is as sweet as a dessert trifle. Niven decides that he is not going to leave the hotel but will tough it out in the face of the grim visages on the guests' faces. In the morning, Niven enters the dining room and the other guests are pleasant enough, offering their "good mornings" but little else. Cooper tries to get Kerr away from Niven, but when the quiet daughter asserts herself, ignores her mother, and begins a conversation with Niven, Cooper must realize that she no longer can can pull Kerr's strings and the picture concludes with the hope that Niven and Kerr will eventually get together and that the same will happen for Lancaster and Hiller. It's adult, intelligent, and every role is marvelously shaded. The idea of bringing various types to a hotel setting had been done before in GRAND HOTEL and other films but seldom as touchingly as in this film. To anyone who saw the play, the screen adaptation is a marvel of interweaving, so it appears to be one ensemble tale rather than two disparate stories. The addition of Vic Damone crooning the title song over the titles was not needed.

p, Harold Hecht; d, Delbert Mann; w, Terence Rattigan, John Gay (based on the play by Rattigan); ph, Charles Lang, Jr.; m, David Raksin; ed, Marjorie Fowler, Charles Ennis; prod d, Harry Horner; art d, Edward Carrere; set d, Edward G. Boyle; cos, Edith Head, Mary Grant; m/l, "Separate Tables," Harry Warren, Harold Adamson (sung by Vic Damone); makeup, Harry Maret, Frank Prehoda.

Drama   Cas.   (PR:A-C MPAA:NR)

SEPARATE WAYS½   (1981) 92m 13 Valentine Associates/Crown International c

Karen Black (Valentine Colby), Tony LoBianco (Ken Colby), Arlene Golonka (Annie), David Naughton (Jerry), Jack Carter (Barney), Sharon Farrell (Karen), William Windom (Huey), Robert Fuller (Woody), Walter Brooke (Lawrence), Jordan Charney (Harry), Sybil Danning (Mary), Angus Duncan (Allen), Bob Hastings (Jack), Noah Hathaway (Jason), Katherine Justice (Sheila), Josh Taylor (Jim), Cissy Wellman (Darlene), Howard Avedis (Director), Marc Bentley (Allen, Jr.), Pamela Bryant (Waitress), Doris Dowling (Rebecca), Monte Markham.

A light-weight love story about housewife Black, unhappy as her former race car driver husband allows the family car dealership to slide downhill. She starts an innocent affair with art student Naughton and discovers her husband having an affair of his own, on the boat he named after Black. She moves out and takes a waitress job in a sleazy club, managed by low-life Carter. Expectant ending has the couple getting back together at the same time that LoBianco goes back on the race track to win the big race.

p&d, Howard Avedis; w, Leah Appet (based on the story by Appet, Avedis and Marlene Schmidt); ph, Dean Cundy (DeLuxe); m, John Cacavas; ed, John Wright; art d, Chuck Seaton; m/l, Bonnie Becker, Cacavas; stunts, Gene Hartline.

Drama   Cas.   (PR:O MPAA:R)

SEPARATION½   (1968, Brit.) 92m Bond/CD bw/c

Jane Arden (Jane), David De Keyser (Husband), Ann Lynn (Woman), Iain Quarrier (Lover), Terence De Marney (Old Man), Fay Brook, Leslie Linder, Joy Bang, Neil Holmes, Ann Norman, Malou Pantera, Theo Aygar, Kathleen Saintsbury, Peter Thomas, Donald Sayer, Tom Corbett.

A fuzzy, muddled plot with no direction makes this British film a basic blob. Arden, the subject of this mess, is a woman going through the stages of a nervous breakdown after her marriage ends. A collage of scenes shows her in a series of real or imaginary confrontations with her husband, her new young lover and her psychiatrist. This is supposed to show all the sides of her personality as she tries to contend with each one's demands. Some flashes of nudity; the story line is obscure and self-indulgent.

p&d, Jack Bond; w, Jane Arden (based on her story); ph, David Muir, Aubrey Dewar (Eastmancolor); m, Stanley Myers, Procol Harum; ed, Michael Johns; m/l, Matthew Fisher.

Drama   (PR:A MPAA:NR)

SEPIA CINDERELLA   (1947) 70m Herald bw

Billy Daniels (Bob), Sheila Guyse (Barbara), Tondeleyo (Vivian), Ruble Blakey (Barney), Jack Carter (Ralph), Dusty Freeman (Mooney), George Williams (Sonny), Fred Gordon (Press Agent), Harold Norton (M.C.), Lora Pierre (Evelyn), Emory Richardson (Great Joseph), Gertrude Saunders (Mrs. Dryden), Hilda Offley Thompson (Mama Keyes), Percy Verwayen (MacMilliam), Al Young (Chinaman), Jimmy Fuller (Collins), Apus and Estellita, Deek Watson and His Brown Dots, Leonard and Zolo (Themselves), Ray C. Moore (Preacher), Freddie Bartholomew (Himself), Walter Fuller's Orchestra, John Kirby's Band.

An old, worn-out story, about a struggling young artist who strays from his roots, features several well-known black entertainers. Daniels is a songwriter who finally has a hit song. However, all the money that comes with fame colors his glasses and causes him to abandon his true love, Guyse. But after finding neither high society women nor the fast lane to his liking, he comes running back to her. Songs by Deek Watson's Brown Dots add some pizzazz, as does the singing by Ruble Blakey.

p, Jack Goldberg, Arthur Leonard; d, Leonard; w, Vincent Valentini; ph, George Webber; m, Charlie Shavers; ed, Jack Kemp; art d, Frank Namczy; m/l, Elaine and Leona Blackman, Deek Watson, Herman Fairbanks, Willie Best.

Drama   (PR:A MPAA:NR)

SEPPUKU   (SEE: HARAKIRI, 1963, Jap.)

SEPT FOIS FEMME   (SEE: WOMAN TIMES SEVEN, 1967, US/Fr./Ital.)

SEPT HOMMES EN OR   (SEE: SEVEN GOLDEN MEN, 1969, Fr./Ital./Ger.)

SEPTEMBER AFFAIR   (1950) 91m PAR bw

Joan Fontaine (Manina Stuart), Joseph Cotten (David Lawrence), Francoise Rosay (Maria Salvatini), Jessica Tandy (Catherine Lawrence), Robert Arthur (David Lawrence, Jr.), Jimmy Lydon (Johnny Wilson), Fortunio Bonanova (Grazzi), Grazia Narciso (Bianca), Anna Demetrio (Rosita), Lou Steele (Vittorio Portini), Frank Yaconelli (Mr. Peppino), Charles Evans (Charles Morrison), Jimmy Frasco (Francisco), Michael Frasco (Boy), Charles LaTorre (Captain of Plane), Gilda Oliva (Mail Girl), Saverio Lomedico (Italian Man), George Nardelli, Nick Borgani (Italian Workmen), Jeanne Lafayett (French Woman), Dino Bolognese (Flower Vendor), Georgia Clancey (Stewardess), Dick Elliott (Fat Gentleman), Rudy Rama, Franz F. Foehm (Draymen), George Humbert (Waiter), Harry Cheshire (Jim the Butler), Iphigenie Castiglioni (Maid), Inez Palange (Concierge), Zacharias Yaconelli (Ricardo), Victor Desny (Hotel Clerk), James R. Scott, Stan Johnson, Douglas Grange (Reporters), Larry Arnold (Italian Waiter), Walter Merrill (Taxi Driver), Christopher Dark (Passport Clerk).

Italian film locations add immensely to this simple romance. Fontaine and Cotten are on their way to New York from Rome: she to play the piano, he to patch up a shaky marriage and see the son he hardly knows. Engine trouble puts them in Naples, and they manage to miss their plane while sightseeing. They go back to reserve another plane and find out their original one had crashed. Sensing they are already in love and unhappy with their other lives, and knowing they are listed among the dead in the wreckage, they start a new life together. However, Cotten's wife shows up in Italy, and both he and Fontaine realize they cannot run from reality. Both return to New York and their respective lives, with just some memories to keep them going.

p, Hal B. Wallis; d, William Dieterle; w, Robert Thoeren (based on a story by Fritz Rotter); ph, Charles B. Lang, Victor Milner; m, Victor Young; ed, Warren Low; art d, Hans Dreier, Franz Bachelin; m/l, "September Song," "Kurt Weill, Maxwell Anderson (sung by Walter Huston).

Drama   (PR:A MPAA:NR)

SEPTEMBER STORM   (1960) 99m FOX c

Joanne Dru (Anne Traymore), Mark Stevens (Joe Balfour), Robert Strauss (Ernie Williams), Asher Dann (Manuel del Rio Montoya), M. Jean Pierre Kerien (LeClerc), Vera Valmont (Yvette), Claude Ivry, Charito Leon, Ernesto Lapena.

An entry in the 3-D sweepstakes, this one features not monsters, but a simple love story set in Majorca. Dru is a model from New York who crosses paths with local kid Dann. Trying to impress Dru, he tells her he owns a yacht when actually he just works on one. Stevens, an adventurer, and his sullen buddy Strauss get Dann to take them looking for treasure. While battling the seas, which make way for the 3-D effects, the model and adventurer fall in love and leave Dann out in the cold.

p, Edward L. Alperson; d, Byron Haskin; w, W.R. Burnett (based on a story by Steve Fisher); ph, Jorge Stahl, Jr., Lamar Boren (Stereovision, Cinema-Scope, DeLuxe Color); m, Edward L. Alperson, Jr., Raoul Kraushaar; ed, Alberto Valenzuela; art d, Boris Leven; spec eff, Jack Cosgrove; m/l, Edward L. Alperson, Jr., Jerry Winn; underwater director, Paul Stader.

Drama   (PR:A MPAA:NR)

SEPTEMBER 30, 1955   (SEE: 9/30/55, 1978)

SEQUOIA   (1934) 75m MGM bw (AKA: MALIBU)

Jean Parker (Toni Martin), Samuel S. Hinds (Mathew Martin), Russell Hardie (Bob Alden), Paul Hurst (Bergman), Ben Hall (Joe), Willie Fung (Sang Soo), Harry Lowe, Jr (Feng Soo).

Actual stars of the film are a deer and a mountain lion in a surprisingly good suspense movie. It's a story of two animals who should be natural enemies, but have the same human owner and so share the same dish. The film focuses on the relationship between the two and how they must survive against ruthless hunters. Photography of the animal-loving epic is sharp and to the point. Nothing is hidden. Hurst is the determined bad guy who is always pursuing the pair. Happily, the two can live in peace at the film's end because the government finally posts a "No Hunting" sign at the site of their habitat. Unusual for its time, SEQUOIA posed a problem to the MGM publicity people when it came time to promote it. They tried to romance the tame subject matter in an attempt to make it attractive to a wider audience. Nevertheless, the film found receptive viewers, and charmed the critics as well.

p, John W. Considine, Jr.; d, Chester M. Franklin; w, Anne Cunningham, Sam Armstrong, Carey Wilson (based on the novel Malibu by Vance Joseph Hoyt); ph, Chester A. Lyons; m, Herbert Stothart; ed, Charles Cochberg.

Adventure (PR:A MPAA:G)

SERAFINO½** (1970, Fr./Ital.) 94m R.P.A.-Rizzoli-Francoriz/Royal c (SERAFINO OU L'AMOUR AUX CHAMPS)

Adriano Celentano (*Serafino Fiorin*), Ottavia Piccolo (*Lidia*), Saro Urzi (*Uncle Agenore*), Francesca Romana Coluzzi (*Asmara*), Benjamin Lev (*Armido*), Nazareno Natale (*Silio*), Giosue Ippolito (*Rocco*), Ermelinda De Felice (*Aunt Armida*), Nerina Montagnani (*Aunt Gesuina*), Luciana Turina (*Aunt Lucia*), Oreste Palella (*Lawyer*), Piero Gerlini (*1st Policeman*), Goffredo Canzano (*Uncle Olmo*), Gino Santercole (*Sergeant*), Nestor Garay (*Priest*), Amedeo Trilli (*Pasquale*), Orlando D'Ubaldo (*Uncle Felicetto*), Gustavo D'Arpe (*Medical Officer*), Vittorio Fanfoni (*2nd Policeman*), Mara Oscuro (*4th Aunt*), Gianni Pulone (*Corporal of the Guard*), Clara Colosimo (*1st Washerwoman*), Nazzareno D'Aquilio (*Town Policeman*), Lidia Mancani (*2nd Washerwoman*).

Celentano is a shepherd in the mountains who simply seeks pleasure in his life. He gets thrown out of the army and takes up with his 17-year-old cousin who allows him to have his way with her. She wants to get married, but since he got what he wanted, he refuses and takes up with the local prostitute. When his dotty aunt passes away and leaves him with a substantial sum of money, he uses it for wine, women, and song. His uncle then wants him declared mentally incompetent so he can gain control of the estate. He forces Celentano to the altar to marry his daughter Piccolo, but the young man's friends come to the rescue. Celentano heads for the mountains with the prostitute and her children. (In Italian and French; English subtitles.)

p&d, Pietro Germi; d, Lee Kresel (English version); w, Leo Benvenuti, Piero De Bernardi, Tullio Pinelli, Germi (based on a story by Alfredo Giannetti, Pinelli, Germi); ph, Aiace Parolin (Technicolor); m, Carlo Rustichelli; ed, Sergio Montanari; md, Bruno Nicolai; art d, Carlo Egidi; set d, Andrea Fantacci; cos, Angela Sammaciccia; English subtitles, Harold J. Salemson.

Comedy Drama (PR:A MPAA:GP)

SERDTSE MATERI (SEE: SONS AND MOTHERS, 1967, USSR)

SERENA** (1962, Brit.) 62m BUT bw

Patrick Holt (*Inspector Gregory*), Emrys Jones (*Howard Rogers*), Honor Blackman (*Ann Rogers*), Bruce Beeby (*Sgt. Conway*), John Horsley (*Mr. Fisher*), Robert Perceval (*Bank Manager*), Wally Patch (*Barman*).

Holt plays a police inspector who discovers that the wife of artist Jones has been murdered by one of his models, and that the killer has been posing as her victim. Basic programmer with a plot more clever than most.

p, John I. Phillips; d, Peter Maxwell; w, Edward Abraham, Reginald Hearne (based on a story by Edward Abraham, Valerie Abraham).

Crime (PR:A-C MPAA:NR)

SERENADE** (1956) 121m WB c

Mario Lanza (*Damon Vincenti*), Joan Fontaine (*Kendall Hale*), Sarita Montiel (*Juana Montes*), Vincent Price (*Charles Winthrop*), Joseph Calleia (*Maestro Marcatello*), Harry Bellaver (*Monte*), Vince Edwards (*Marco Roselli*), Silvio Minciotti (*Lardelli*), Frank Puglia (*Manuel*), Edward Platt (*Carter*), Frank Yaconelli (*Giuseppe*), Mario Siletti (*Sanroma*), Maria Serrano (*Rosa*), Eduardo Noriega (*Felipe*), Jean Fenn (*Soprano*), Joseph Vitale (*Baritone*), Victor Romito (*Bass*), Norma Zimmer (*Mimi in "La Boheme"*), Licia Albanese (*Desdemona in "Otello"*), Francis Barnes (*Iago in "Otello"*), Lilian Molieri (*Tosca in "Tosca"*), Laura Mason (*Fedora in "Fedora"*), Richard Cable (*Shepherd Boy in "L'Arlesiana"*), Richard Lert (*Conductor in "L'Arlesiana"*), Jose Govea (*Paco*), Antonio Triano (*Man in the Bull*), Nick Mora (*Luigi the Waiter*), Joe DeAngelo, William Fox, Jack Santora (*Busboys*), Mickey Golden (*Cabdriver*), Elizabeth Flournoy (*Elevator Operator*), Creighton Hale (*Assistant Stage Manager*), Martha Acker (*American Woman*), Joe Torvay (*Mariachi Leader*), Don Turner (*Bus Driver*), Johnstone White (*Hughes the Butler*), Ralph Volkie (*Cop*), Vincent Padula (*Pagnil*), Stephen Bekassy (*Hanson*), Leo Mostovoy (*Chief*), Martin Garralaga (*Romero*), Perk Lazelle, April Stride, Diane Gump (*Party Guests*).

If you like Mario Lanza, you'll love this film because he does 15 tunes and occupies about half the screen time with his tenor on a host of operatic arias and other songs. The James M. Cain story concerned a homosexual relationship between a singer and his benefactor but that was tossed aside in favor of this more conventional telling. Lanza works in a California vineyard when he is heard by wealthy Fontaine, who decides that she can make him a star. (This was the role that had the gender switch.) She's just finished toying with a boxer and wants new flesh. She's a dilettante and it isn't long before she is bored by Lanza and takes off with a sculptor. Meanwhile, Lanza has come to love her, and when she dumps him, his heart is broken and he blows his big chance for success playing Otello at the Metropolitan Opera. His career in a shambles, Lanza goes down to Mexico (it was shot beautifully at San Miguel de Allende) where he gets sick with some sort of disease that only screenwriters can concoct. He meets Montiel, the attractive daughter of an ex-bullfighter. She helps him get well and the remainder of the film is a love triangle between Lanza, Montiel, and Fontaine, who now wants to come back and help Lanza regain his operatic

career. Calleia does well as Lanza's vocal coach and Price is properly oily as a concert booker, a role that could have also been played to perfection by George Sanders, who specialized in first-rate snideness. Along the way, Lanza gets the chance to exercise his pipes for the first time in three years. He does two pop songs by Sammy Cahn and Nicholas Brodszky, "Serenade" and "My Destiny," then tackles the classics, which include: "Torna A Sorrento" (Ernesto de Curtis, Claude Aveling), "Nessun Dorma," (from "Turandot," Giacomo Puccini), "Ave Maria," (Franz Schubert), "Italian Tenor Aria," (from "Der Rosenkavalier," Richard Strauss), "Lamento di Federico" (from "L'Arlesiana," by Francesco Cilea), "Amor Ti Vieta" (from "Fedora," Umberto Giordano), "Il Mio Tesoro" (from "Don Giovanni," Wolfgang Amadeus Mozart), "La Danza" (Gioacchino Antonio Rossini), "Di Quella Pira" (from "Il Trovatore," Giuseppe Verdi), "O Paradis" "Sorti De L'Onde" (from "L'Africaine," Giacomo Meyerbeer), "O Soave Fanciulla" (from "La Boheme," Puccini, sung with Jean Fenn), and "Dio Ti Giocondi" (from "Otello," Verdi, sung with Licia Albanese). One of Vince Edwards' earliest movie appearances, long before he became nationally famous as Ben Casey on TV. Lanza would only make 2 more films before his early death at 38.

p, Henry Blanke; d, Anthony Mann; w, Ivan Goff, Ben Roberts, John Twist (based on the novel by James M. Cain); ph, J. Peverell Marley (CinemaScope, Warner Color); ed, William Ziegler; art d, Edward Carrere; set d, William Wallace; cos, Howard Shoup; operatic advisers, Walter Ducloux, Giacomo Spadoni.

Musical/Drama Cas. (PR:A MPAA:NR)

SERENADE FOR TWO SPIES½** (1966, Ital./Ger.) 90m Modern Art-Metheus/United c (SINFONIA PER DUE SPIE; SERENADE FUR ZWEI SPIONE)

Helmut Lange (*John Krim*), Tony Kendall [Luciano Stella] (*Pepino*), Barbara Lass (*Tamara*), Heidelinde Weis (*Goldfeather*), Wolfgang Neuss (*Secret Service Chief*), Dick Palmer [Mimmo Palmara] (*Cormoran*), Annie Giess.

A send-up look at the spy game. A group of international smugglers nab a laser from a German lab. Palmer, who used to be with the FBI, now seems to be with the group. Enter Lange, agent 006½ (get the satire?). After several brushes with some crooks that allow him to show off some brilliant escapes, he meets with female agents, Lass and Weis for some romantic escapades. Lange is pursued across the U.S. before being caught and abandoned in the Nevada desert. He's saved by Lass and eventually gets his hands on the laser. Lass, meanwhile, snares him with a lasso and flies him off to Venice where she tells him they will be married. A satire without much bite; just a few laughs at the sheer stupidity of it all.

p, Hansjurgen Pohland; d, Michael Pfleghar; w, Pfleghar, Klaus Munro; ph, Ernst Wild (Franscope, Eastmancolor); m, Francesco De Masi; ed, Margot von Schlieffen; art d, Peter Scharff.

Comedy (PR:A MPAA:NR)

SERENADE OF THE WEST, 1937
(SEE: GIT ALONG LITTLE DOGIE, 1937)

SERENADE OF THE WEST, 1942
(SEE: COWBOY SERENADE, 1942)

SERENITY½** (1962) 90m Serenity c

Norma Valdi (*Eirene Veni*), Constantine Baldimas (*Dimitri Veni*), Vivian Verrilli (*Anna*), George Foundas (*Photis Glaros*), Nina Bobbie (*Eleni Glaros*), Koula Agagiotou (*Aunt Maria*), Athena Mihalidou (*Aunt Sophia*), Dimitri Maras (*Andreas, her son*), Pandopoulos (*A Water-Diviner*), Lili Yannikaki (*Zambeta*), Margarita Goumas (*Widow*), Thanas Veloudios (*Barba-Stathys*), Byron Pallia (*Mechanic*), Takis Cabouras (*Haritos*), Dimitri Stamos (*A Boy*), Mike Papalexis (*Greek Narrator*), Brian Clark (*English Narrator*), Peter Schreicher (*German Narrator*), Mr. Kozowski (*Russian Narrator*).

Made in Greece, this was considered a very experimental film for its time. After Greece and Turkey have signed new boundary agreements, the two countries exchange nationals. The new boundaries mean the Greeks of Ionia must leave their homeland. Valdi is the wife of a physician (Baldimas) who is much older than she. Instead of growing wheat and grapes as the government suggested, she grows roses as her husband's family once did. Recurring scenes pop up throughout the film, including one in which Baldimas ponders his failing marriage and his control over the group of Ionian immigrants. Valdi, reflecting her husband's dissatisfaction, tears apart the rose garden. This unusual film ends with a flashback of the film shown in a 30-second sequence.

p,d&w, Gregory J. Markopoulos; m, Peter Hartman.

Drama (PR:A MPAA:NR)

SERGEANT, THE zero   (1968) 108m Robert Wise/WB c-bw

Rod Steiger (*Master Sgt. Albert Callan*), John Phillip Law (*Pfc. Tom Swanson*), Ludmila Mikael (*Solange*), Frank Latimore (*Capt. Loring*), Elliott Sullivan (*Pop Henneken*), Ronald Rubin (*Cpl. Cowley*), Philip Roye (*Aldous Brown*), Jerry Brouer (*Sgt. Komski*), Memphis Slim (*Night Club Singer*), Gabriel Gascond (*Solange's Brother-in-Law*).

A flatulent attempt at social relevance and sexual frankness, THE SERGEANT comes off as nothing more than a misfired attempt which is supposed to be appreciated for its subject matter, regardless of its ineptitude. Steiger, who is normally a fine and perceptive actor, resorts to militaristic ham in his role as an American sergeant stationed in France in 1952. In a useless black-and-white prolog Steiger is shown at his most heroic and inhumane, strangling a German soldier when his gun jams. After the war's end, Steiger brings this cold, impenetrable exterior to a camp run by the boozing Latimore. Steiger takes over the command and strongly asserts his military ways on the lazy and unmotivated young soldiers. In turn, the soldiers resent the camp's strict new policies. Steiger soon finds himself taking notice of a handsome young private, Law. Before long Law has become the sergeant's personal clerk, naively interpreting his possessiveness as loneliness. Steiger struggles with his latent homosexuality and continuously tries to repress it. When Steiger refuses to issue Law a pass to see his girl friend, Mikael, the private grows more distressed. Life gets worse for Law when Steiger boldly kisses him. The private finally gets the hint and bucks the sergeant's orders to stop seeing Mikael. Steiger, once the rugged distinguished career man, now begins to disintegrate. Having discovered his true sexuality he resorts to the bottle. After wallowing in some booze-induced sexual suffering, Steiger puts a gun to his head and ends his miserable existence (something the German soldier from the prolog should have done 108 minutes earlier). Where THE SERGEANT fails most grossly is in its supposed understanding of its subject–attempting to portray its characters with sensitivity but instead painting them as cardboard idiots in search of love and sex. Because of the director's insistence on ridiculous phallic symbols, Steiger seems most comfortable caressing a beer bottle (or maybe that's the point). Whatever the case, THE SERGEANT merely panders to audiences who want simple clear-cut answers to the complexities of human nature and sexuality. The picture was shot entirely in France, with interiors using the facilities of Paris' Studios de Boulogne. A number of French players were recruited, including Comedie Francaise actress Mikael in what was inaccurately described as her first film role (this *was* director Flynn's feature film debut). One critic described Steiger's bravura performance as resembling the inflection and delivery of James Cagney.

p, Richard Goldstone; d, John Flynn; w, Dennis Murphy (based on his novel); ph, Henri Persin (Technicolor); m, Michel Magne; ed, Francoise Diot; prod d, Willy Holt; art d, Marc Frederix; makeup, Michel Deruelle.

Drama   **Cas.**   **(PR:O MPAA:R)**

SERGEANT BERRY**   (1938, Ger.) 113m Tobis Filmkunst bw

Hans Albers, Roni von Bukovics, Peter Vob, Gerda Hochst, Alexander Engel, Herbert Hubner.

Crude humor is the trademark of this German film that attempts to show off the talents of German swashbuckler Albers. Silly plot has Albers as a master detective who travels west to break up a band of Mexican hash smugglers while at the same time romancing Bukovics. Of course, he wins on all counts. Movie stoops so low to create excitement that at one point it has Albers prancing around nude. The Italian desert serves to simulate the American West.

p, Hans Albers; d, Herbert Selpin; w, Walter Wasserman, C.H. Diller; ph, Franz Koch.

Drama   **(PR:A MPAA:NR)**

SERGEANT DEADHEAD*½   (1965) 90m AIP c (AKA: SERGEANT DEADHEAD THE ASTRONUT)

Frankie Avalon (*Sgt. O.K. Deadhead/Sgt. Donovan*), Deborah Walley (*Col. Lucy Turner*), Cesar Romero (*Adm. Stoneham*), Fred Clark (*Gen. Rufus Fogg*), Gale Gordon (*Capt. Weiskopf*), Harvey Lembeck (*Pvt. McEvoy*), John Ashley (*Pvt. Filroy*), Buster Keaton (*Pvt. Blinken*), Reginald Gardiner (*Lt. Cmdr. Talbott*), Eve Arden (*Lt. Kinsey*), Pat Buttram (*The President*), Donna Loren (*Susan*), Romo Vincent (*Tuba Player*), Tod Windsor (*Sgt. Keeler*), Norman Grabowski, Mike Nader (*Air Police*), Edward Faulkner (*Radioman*), Bobbi Shaw (*Gilda*), Patti Chandler (*Patti*), Salli Sachse (*Sue Ellen*), Luree Holmes (*Luree*), Sue Hamilton (*Ivy*), Jo Collins (*Gail*), Bob Harvey (*Bellhop*), Jerry Brutsche (*Newsman*), Andy Romano, John Macchia (*Marine MPs*), Sallie Dornan (*Secretary*), Mary Hughes.

Avalon undergoes a personality change after accidentally launching himself into space. He's supposed to marry Wally, but has been sent to the guardhouse because he threatens to expose the Air Force mistake that caused his space trip. Sgt. Donovan (Avalon in a dual role) becomes his replacement at the altar. Deadhead Avalon escapes from prison, gets to the honeymoon suite, and turns into his charming self just in time to win back his woman. Avalon, Walley, and Arden even get a chance to sing a number of songs along the way, including: "Sergeant Deadhead," "The Difference in Me is You," "Let's Play Love," "Two-Timin' Angel," "How Can You Tell,"

"You Should Have Seen the One That Got Away," "Hurry Up and Wait" (Guy Hemric, Jerry Styner).

p, James H. Nicholson, Samuel Z. Arkoff; d, Norman Taurog; w, Louis M. Heyward; ph, Floyd Crosby (Panavision, Pathe Color); m, Les Baxter; ed, Ronald Sinclair, Fred Feitshans, Eve Newman; md, Al Simms; art d, Howard Campbell; ch, Jack Baker.

Musical Comedy   **(PR:A MPAA:NR)**

SERGEANT DEADHEAD THE ASTRONAUT
                        (SEE: SERGEANT DEADHEAD, 1965)

SERGEANT JIM***   (1962, Yugo.) 82m Triglav/Cain bw (DOLINA MIRA; AKA: MR. JIM–AMERICAN, SOLDIER, AND GENTLEMAN)

John Kitzmiller (*Sgt. Jim*), Evelyne Wohlfeiler (*Lotti*), Tugo Stiglic (*Marko*), Boris Kralj, Maks Furijan, Janez Cuk.

Two orphans, Stiglic and Wohlfeiler, befriend a black American airman whose plane has been shot down. The two children are on run from the Germans and are searching for a "valley of peace." The trio finds it, but a battle breaks out when the Germans arrive and the American is killed. The two children hit the road again, searching for a peaceful existence–somewhere.

d, France Stiglic; w, Ivan Ribic; ph, Rudi Vavpotic; m, Marijan Kozina.

War Drama   **(PR:A MPAA:NR)**

SERGEANT MADDEN½**   (1939) 82m MGM bw

Wallace Beery (*Shaun Madden*), Tom Brown (*Al Boylan, Jr.*), Alan Curtis (*Dennis Madden*), Laraine Day (*Eileen Daly*), Fay Holden (*Mary Madden*), Marc Lawrence (*"Piggy" Ceders*), Marion Martin (*Charlotte*), David Gorcey (*"Punchy"*), Donald Haines (*Milton*), Ben Welden (*Stemmy*), Etta McDaniel (*Dove*), John Kelly (*Nero*), Horace MacMahon (*Philadelphia*), Neil Fitzgerald (*Casey*), Dickie Jones (*Dennis Madden as a Boy*), Drew Roddy (*Al Boylan, Jr., as a Boy*), Charles Trowbridge (*Commissioner 1912*), George Irving (*Police Commissioner*), Donald Douglas (*Al Boylan, Sr.*), Ivan "Dusty" Miller (*Frawley*), Mary Field (*Woman*), Esther Dale (*Mrs. McGillivray*), Reed Hadley (*Lawyer*), Wade Boteler (*Niles*), Harold Minjir (*Couturier*), James Flavin, Lee Phelps, Harry Strang (*Cops*), Jack Pennick, Charles Sullivan (*Prisoners*), E. Alyn Warren (*Judge*), Milton Kibbee (*Foreman*), Claire Rochelle (*Phone Operator*), Clayton Moore (*Interne*), Dale Van Sickel (*Rookie/Alan Curtis' Double*), John Webb Dillon (*Court Attendant*), Barbara Bedford (*Nurse*), Bess Flowers, Nell Craig (*Reception Nurses*).

A long-drawn-out tale with just enough plot twists to make it interesting. Beery is the typical Irish policeman who is the pride of the force and plays strictly by the book. His boy Curtis also becomes a policeman, but is more interested in getting promoted than he is in being a good cop. His attitude turns off many of his fellow cops, and when he shoots a kid caught stealing, he's set up and sent to prison. Prison does not rehabilitate him, but rather makes him worse. He escapes and goes on a robbery binge. A trap is set for him at the hospital where his son has just been born. Setting the trap is his father, who places justice ahead of his own blood.

p, J. Walter Ruben; d, Josef von Sternberg; w, Wells Root (based on the story "A Gun in His Hand" by William A. Ullman); ph, John F. Seitz; m, Dr. William Axt; ed, Conrad A. Nervig; art d, Cedric Gibbons, Randall Duell; set d, Edwin B. Willis; spec eff, Peter Ballbusch.

Drama   **(PR:A MPAA:NR)**

SERGEANT MIKE**   (1945) 60m COL bw

Larry Parks (*Allen*), Jeanne Bates (*Terry*), Loren Tindall (*Simms*), Jim Bannon (*Patrick Henry*), Robert Williams (*Sgt. Rankin*), Richard Powers (*Reed*), Larry Joe Olsen (*S.K. Arno*), Eddie Acuff (*Monohan*), John Tyrrell (*Rogers*), Charles Wagenheim (*Hall*), Mike (*Himself*), Pearl (*Herself*).

A typical patriotic war film that grinds out the action for the youth audiences. Parks is the disgruntled soldier, moved from a tough machine gun unit to the canine corps. He has a change of heart when he finds out that Mike (the dog) is a present from an 8-year-old child whose father was killed in the war. Parks goes all out to make Mike the best army dog ever. Pearl is the other dog paired with Mike and the two together are great at finding Japanese machine gun nests. Pearl is killed in the line of duty, but Mike carries on to help the American soldiers battle the Japanese.

p, Jack Fier; d, Henry Levin; w, Robert Lee Johnson; ph, L.W. O'Connell; ed, Reg Browne; md, Mischa Bakaleinikoff; art d, Edward Jewell.

War Drama   **(PR:A MPAA:NR)**

SERGEANT MURPHY*½   (1938) 57m WB bw

Ronald Reagan (*Pvt. Dennis Riley*), Mary Maguire (*Mary Lou Carruthers*), Donald Crisp (*Col. Carruthers*), Ben Hendricks (*Corp. Kane*), William B. Davidson (*Maj. Gruff*), Max Hoffman, Jr (*Sgt. Connors*), David Newell (*Lt. Duncan*), Emmett Vogan (*Maj. Smythe*), Tracey Lane (*Texas*), Edmund Cobb (*Adjutant*), Ellen Clancy (*Joan*), Rosella Towne (*Alice*), Helen Valkis (*Bess*),

Sam McDaniel *(Henry)*, Henry Otho, Artie Ortega, Art Mix, Kansas Moehring, Chad Trower, Jack Shannon, Lloyd Lane, James D. Green *(Cavalrymen)*, Edward Keane *(Maj. Biddle)*, Douglas Wood *(Maj. Gen. Truson)*, Fred Miller *(Quartermaster)*, Walter Miller *(Superintendent Dairy)*, Raymond Brown *(Turner)*, Lee Prather *(Slaughterhouse Foreman)*, William Worthington *(Judge at Horse Show)*, Jack Richardson *(Hawkins)*, Boyd Irwin *(Veterinary Inspector)*, Wilfred Lucas *(Captain)*, Cyril Thornton *(Assistant Inspector)*, Alec Harford *(Clerk)*, Dave Thursby *(Attendant)*, John Graham Spacey *(Thornby)*, Reginald Sheffield *(English Radio Commentator)*.

It's tough to separate a man from his horse, even during wartime. Reagan is a young private whose horse, Sergeant Murphy of the title, is pegged unfit for active duty. But the two persevere and win the Grand National in their efforts to prove their worth. In so doing, Reagan also manages to impress the daughter of the post colonel (Maguire). The Reagan role was originally offered to James Cagney who turned it down. In so doing, he helped turn SERGEANT MURPHY from an "A" picture to a "B." Regardless of its classification, however, this film is a good example of the kind of competent second feature Hollywood could turn out in the 1930s and 1940s. As an interesting historical footnote, it also offers a glimpse at what U.S. Army life was like just before WW II when a soldier's main concern could be his beloved horse. Filmed in the Monterey Peninsula, SERGEANT MURPHY is an unusual "B" film because of its extensive location shooting.

p, Bryan Foy; d, B. Reeves Eason; w, William Jacobs (based on the story "Golden Girl" by Sy Bartlett); ph, Ted McCord; ed, James Gibbons; cos, Howard Shoup.

Drama   **(PR:A   MPAA:NR)**

SGT. PEPPER'S LONELY HEARTS CLUB BAND zero
(1978) 111m Geria/UNIV c

Peter Frampton *(Billy Shears)*, Barry Gibb *(Mark Henderson)*, Robin Gibb *(Dave Henderson)*, Maurice Gibb *(Bob Henderson)*, Frankie Howerd *(Mean Mr. Mustard)*, Paul Nicholas *(Dougie Shears)*, Donald Pleasence *(B.D. Brockhurst)*, Sandy Farina *(Strawberry Fields)*, Dianne Steinberg *(Lucy)*, Steve Martin *(Dr. Maxwell Edison)*, Aerosmith *(Future Villain)*, Alice Cooper *(Father Sun)*, Earth, Wind, & Fire *(Benefit Performers)*, Billy Preston *(Sgt. Pepper)*, Stargard *(The Diamonds)*, George Burns *(Mr. Kite)*, Carel Struycken *(The Brute)*, Patti Jerome *(Saralinda Shears)*, Max Showalter *(Ernest Shears)*, John Wheeler *(Mr. Fields)*, Jay W. MacIntosh, Eleanor Zee, Scott Manners, Stanley Coles, Stanley Sheldon, Bob Mayo, Woodrow Chambliss, Hank Worden, Morgan Farley, Delos V. Smith, Pat Cranshaw, Teri Lynn Wood, Tracy Justrich, Anna Rodzianko, Rose Aragon, Peter Allen, Stephen Bishop, Keith Carradine, Donovan, Jose Feliciano, Peter Noone, Helen Reddy, Chita Rivera, Johnny Rivers, Sha-Na-Na, Del Shannon, Connie Stevens, Carol Channing, George Benson, Wilson Pickett, Jack Bruce, Jim Dandy, Sarah Dash, Rick Derringer, Barbara Dickson, Randy Edelman, Yvonne Elliman, Leif Garrett, Adrian Gurvitz, Eddie Harris, Heart, Nona Hendryx, Etta James, Dr John, Bruce Johnston, Joe Lala, D.C. LaRue, Marcy Levy, Mark Lindsay, Nils Lofgren, Jackie Lomax, John Mayall, Curtis Mayfield, Alan O'Day, Lee Oskar, The Paley Brothers, Robert Palmer, Anita Pointer, Bonnie Raitt, Minnie Riperton, Monte Rock III, Joe Simon, Seals and Croft, Al Stewart, John Stewart, Tina Turner, Frankie Valli, Grover Washington, Jr, Wolfman Jack, Bobby Womack, Alan White, Gary Wright.

Pitiful, pitiful attempt at turning the classic Beatles album, "Sgt. Pepper's Lonely Hearts Club Band," into a story. A scattered plot and pathetic acting kill this film. Peter Frampton and the Bee Gees, the central characters, are quickly forgotten. Updating the songs sunk the film deeper. The story about a group of bizarre characters out to steal the band's instruments, was bad even on a small scale. It just proved that only the Beatles could make movies with Beatle songs. Among the 20-plus compositions by John Lennon, Paul McCartney and George Harrison were "Sgt. Pepper's Lonely Hearts Club Band" (sung by the Bee Gees, Paul Nicholas), "With a Little Help from My Friends" (sung by Peter Frampton, the Bee Gees), "Fixing a Hole" (sung by George Burns), "Getting Better" (Frampton, Bee Gees), "Here Comes the Sun" (Sandy Farina), "I Want You (She's So Heavy)" (Bee Gees, Dianne Steinberg, Nicholas, Donald Pleasence, Stargard), "Good Morning, Good Morning" (Nicholas, Frampton, Bee Gees), "Nowhere Man" (Bee Gees), "Polythene Pam" (Bee Gees), "She Came Through the Bathroom Window" (Frampton, Bee Gees), "Mean Mr. Mustard" (Frankie Howerd), "She's Leaving Home" (Bee Gees, Jay MacIntosh, John Wheeler), "Lucy in the Sky With Diamonds" (Steinberg, Stargard), "Oh Darling" (Robin Gibb), "Maxwell's Silver Hammer" (Steve Martin), "Because" (Alice Cooper, Bee Gees), "Strawberry Fields Forever" (Farina), "Being for the Benefit of Mr. Kite" (Maurice Gibb, Frampton, Bee Gees, Burns), "You Never Give Me Your Money" (Nicholas, Steinberg), "Got to Get You Into My Life" (Earth, Wind and Fire), "When I'm 64" (Farina), "Come Together" (Aerosmith), "Golden Slumbers" (Frampton), "Carry That Weight" (Bee Gees), "The Long and Winding Road" (Frampton), "A Day in the Life" (Barry Gibb, Bee Gees), "Get Back" (Preston).

p, Robert Stigwood; d, Michael Schultz; w, Henry Edwards; ph, Owen Roizman (Panavision, Technicolor); ed, Christopher Holmes; md, George Martin; prod d, Brian Eatwell; set d, Marvin March; cos, May Routh; ch, Patricia Birch.

Musical   **Cas.**   **(PR:A   MPAA:PG)**

SERGEANT RUTLEDGE***½
(1960) 111m WB c

Jeffrey Hunter *(Lt. Thomas Cantrell)*, Constance Towers *(Mary Beecher)*, Billie Burke *(Mrs. Cordelia Fosgate)*, Woody Strode *(1st Sgt. Braxton Rutledge)*, Juano Hernandez *(Sgt. Matthew Luke Skidmore)*, Willis Bouchey *(Col. Otis Fosgate)*, Carleton Young *(Capt. Shattuck)*, Judson Pratt *(Lt. Mulqueen)*, Bill Henry *(Capt. Dwyer)*, Walter Reed *(Capt. MacAfee)*, Chuck Hayward *(Capt. Dickinson)*, Mae Marsh *(Nellie)*, Fred Libby *(Chandler Hubble)*, Charles Seel *(Dr. C.J. Eckner)*, Toby Richards *(Lucy Dabney)*, Jan Styne *(Chris Hubble)*, Cliff Lyons *(Sam Beecher)*, Jack Pennick *(Sergeant)*, Estelle Winwood, Eva Novak *(Spectators)*, Shug Fisher *(Mr. Owens)*, Chuck Roberson *(Juror)*, Hank Worden *(Laredo)*.

This was the first time in the history of the mainstream western that a black man was given the chance to be the central heroic figure, and it was done in no less hallowed a place than among the magnificent buttes of John Ford's beloved Monument Valley. There had been black westerns before, from the 1923 silent THE BULL-DOGGER to items like BRONZE BUCKAROO (1938) and HARLEM ON THE PRAIRIE (1939), but these were low-budget, all-black-cast affairs that segregated from white audiences. SERGEANT RUTLEDGE was the first such film of true stature, produced by a major studio, and directed by one of the greatest and most respected talents in filmmaking. The film begins as Strode, a black sergeant of the 9th Cavalry (an all-black unit under white command that fought some of the bravest battles during the Indian wars) is put on trial for the murder of his commanding officer and the rape and murder of the dead man's daughter. Through flashbacks the stories begin to converge and form a picture of the events. Towers, a young Western woman who has just returned home after 12 years in eastern schools, relates how she met Cavalry lieutenant Hunter on the train. That evening, Towers finds the body of the murdered stationmaster, and is shocked when Strode, who is wounded, arrives to protect her. The soldier goes into the stationhouse and removes the body so that the woman doesn't have to view it. She watches him through the window, unsure that he can be trusted. When Strode askes for whiskey, Towers is again very apprehensive about his intentions. Strode uses the whiskey on his wound, making Towers feel guilty for harboring suspicious thoughts about the black man. She decides to trust him. The next morning, Hunter and the rest of the 9th Cavalry arrive to arrest Strode for the murders. Upon seeing Strode and Towers together, Hunter–who views himself as one of Strode's best friends–blurts out, "He didn't hurt you, did he?" The previous day, Strode's commanding officer had been murdered and the man's daughter, who was a friend of Strode's, had been raped and strangled. When Strode was found to be missing, Hunter immediately assumed he was the guilty party. Through the testimony of Burke, the wife of the court-martial general, a sinister, openly racist light is cast on the "friendly" relationship between Strode and the dead girl. This merely confirms the already deep suspicions of Strode harbored by those in the court. The prosecutor, Young, provokes racist sentiment even further by driving home the fact that Strode is a *"negro"* (i.e. *animal*), and the doctor, Seel, inflames things even further by emotionally relating how the girl was "violated" before she was killed, all the time staring at Strode. When Hunter takes the stand--at this point he has come to be one of Strode's defenders--we are brought back to the morning after the murders. On the ride back to the fort, with Strode in chains, the soldiers are attacked by Indians. Strode manages to escape, but he returns to the group when he sees that they are about to ride into an Indian ambush. Strode bravely rides into the fray and with his help the company is saved. In a moving moment, Strode comforts a dying comrade and tells him not to worry about his family's future because he has given his little girls memories of a father who commanded respect and dignity. Due to Strode's efforts the company survives the attack, but Hunter still must bring Strode in to stand trial. Eventually Strode is given the chance to testify on his own behalf. Under brutal grilling from the prosecution, the soldier finally loses his reserved demeanor when Young questions his devotion to the 9th Cavalry and ridicules his return to the unit after he had escaped. Strode rises up out of his chair and makes a powerful, very emotional speech declaring he returned "Because the 9th Cavalry was my home, my real freedom, and my self-respect. The way I was deserting it, I was nothin' but a swamp-running nigger, and I ain't that. Do you hear me? I'm a man!" His speech shocks the racist courtroom into silence. In those brief moments, Strode has demonstrated greater devotion, honor, and dignity than anyone else in the courtroom could ever hope to possess. Though his speech has affected the tribunal, it is obvious that Strode is going to be found guilty. Suddenly a spectator, Styne, the father of a boy friend of the dead girl, breaks down and confesses to the crimes. Finally cleared, Strode rejoins the proud 9th Cavalry while Hunter and Towers embrace. SERGEANT RUTLEDGE is a fascinating, detailed look at racism. Contrasted with the obvious, unashamed racism demonstrated by Burke, Young, Seel, and most of the people in the courtroom is the more subtle, repressed racism demonstrated by Strode's friends, Hunter and Towers. If a white cavalry soldier had come to her rescue at the train station, Towers wouldn't have hesitated to tend the man's wounds and help him in any way she could. But because the soldier was a black man, she immediately distrusted him and feared that he might harm her sexually. Hunter, who had known Strode and watched him become the best soldier in the outfit, instantly assumed the worst of his friend upon discovering the double murder and rape, and also suspected him of attacking Towers. Though both these white people rise to the black man's defense when reason overcomes emotion, one cannot help but feel that they do so out of guilt for suspecting him in the first place. Through it all, Strode knows who he is and what it is all about. The 9th Cavalry is his identity. It separates him from other men, black or white, and gives him self-respect, pride, and honor. When he is accused of the crimes he is not surprised. Strode even goads Hunter by sarcastically playing up his racial stereotypes and tells the lieutenant not to worry about his wound because, "...we heal fast." While the film's heart is in the right place, it proves a bit of a disappointment as a John Ford film because the courtroom structure forces a claustrophobic, static perspective. Except for the flashbacks, the film takes place entirely on one tight set, with action being related more through dialog than visuals. Ford, who is a master of the unspoken emotion, must fall back on people making speeches to get his points across. He succeeds brilliantly, however, with Strode's final statement of identity. Playing his old tricks, the director told the inexperienced black actor that the shooting schedule had been changed and he wouldn't be needed the next day. To ensure that Strode would relax, Ford threw a party for his star, making sure the actor got good and drunk. At six the next morning a groggy and hung-over Strode got a call to be on the set in an hour for his big scene. Strode performed his moving and emotional speech with his head pounding and nausea sweeping over him. Ford had pulled the same trick on Victor McLaglen 25 years before on the set of THE INFORMER. Though the courtroom drama and character study are at times quite powerful, perhaps the most significant aspect of the film is the visual portrayal of the 9th Cavalry itself. Shot in just as stunning a manner as any John Wayne picture, the men of the 9th strike giant, heroic figures against the buttes of Ford's Monument Valley, giving them a place of immortal respect and honor in the western genre.

p, Patrick Ford, Willis Goldbeck; d, John Ford; w, Goldbeck, James Warner Bellah (based on the novel *Captain Buffalo* by Bellah); ph, Bert Glennon (Technicolor); m, Howard Jackson; ed, Jack Murray; art d, Eddie Imazu; set d, Frank M. Miller; cos, Marjorie Best; m/l, "Captain Buffalo," Mack David, Jerry Livingston.

Western   **Cas.**   **(PR:C MPAA:NR)**

SERGEANT RYKER*   (1968) 86m Roncom/UNIV c

Lee Marvin (*Sgt. Paul Ryker*), Bradford Dillman (*Capt. David Young*), Vera Miles (*Ann Ryker*), Peter Graves (*Maj. Whitaker*), Lloyd Nolan (*Gen. Amos Bailey*), Murray Hamilton (*Capt. Appleton*), Norman Fell (*Sgt. Max Winkler*), Walter Brooke (*Col. Arthur Merriam*), Francis DeSales (*President of Court Martial*), Don Marshall (*Cpl. Jenks*), Charles Aidman (*Maj. Kitchener*).

Marvin is about to be executed for being a traitor to his country. Miles is the persistent wife who thinks her husband's trial was handled wrong and convinces prosecutor Dillman to conduct a personal investigation. After checking Marvin's story that he was sent behind enemy lines by a general who has since died, Nolan grants a stay of execution and appoints Dillman to defend Marvin. Dillman falls in love with Miles, causing Marvin to lose his temper at the trial. Two witnesses testify against Marvin, who tells those present that he received better treatment from the enemy. However, it is proven that the dead leader frequently gave secret orders, and Marvin is acquitted. At the same time, Miles decides to stay with her husband. The film originally was presented on NBC TV's "Kraft Suspense Theater" as a two-part episode, titled "The Case Against Paul Ryker," in 1963. Footage was expanded somewhat for the film version.

p, Frank Telford; d, Buzz Kulik; w, Seeler Lester, William D. Gordon (based on a story by Lester); ph, Walter Strenge (Technicolor); m, Johnny Williams; ed, Robert B. Warwick; md, Stanley Wilson; art d, John J. Lloyd; set d, John McCarthy; makeup, Bud Westmore.

Drama   **(PR:A MPAA:NR)**

SERGEANT STEINER   (SEE: BREAKTHROUGH, 1978, Ger.)

SERGEANT WAS A LADY, THE   (1961) 72m Twincraft/UNIV bw

Martin West (*Cpl. Gale Willard*), Venetia Stevenson (*Sgt. Judy Fraser*), Bill Williams (*Col. House*), Catherine McLeod (*Maj. Hay*), Roy Engel (*Sgt. Bricker*), Gregg Martell (*Red Henning*), Chickie Lind (*Lenore Bliss*), Jomarie Pettitt (*Marge McKay*), Mari Lynn (*Rose Miller*), Joan Barry (*Rita Waters*), Francine York (*Tina Baird*), Rhoda Williams (*Lt. Witt*), Doris Fisette (*Lt. Read*), Lonnie Blackman (*Capt. Beal*), Ric Turner (*Cy Turner*), Richard Emory (*Maj. Zilker*), James Dale (*Sgt. Thomas*), Dan White (*Gen. Payson*), Hal Torey (*Col. Burns*), John Mitchum (*1st M.P.*), Mike Masters (*2nd M.P.*).

Despite having Bernard Glasser direct, write and produce this low budget product shows its shortcomings. A simple story that had some promise: women are trying to show they are just as good as the men when it comes to missile tactics. West is accidentally assigned to an island containing 125 of these women and is run by Stevenson. West helps the women compete against some men at a neighboring island and the women treat him as a hero. At his farewell party, the stern, but now turning soft Stevenson, tells him they definitely will meet again someday.

p,d&w, Bernard Glasser; ph, Hal McAlpin; ed, John F. Link; art d, Frank

Sylos; set d, William Stevens; ch, Noel Parenti; makeup, Larry Butterworth.

Comedy   **(PR:A MPAA:NR)**

SERGEANT YORK***   1941 134m WB bw

Gary Cooper (*Alvin C. York*), Walter Brennan (*Pastor Rosier Pile*), Joan Leslie (*Gracie Williams*), George Tobias (*Michael T. "Pusher" Ross*), Stanley Ridges (*Maj. Buxton*), Margaret Wycherly (*Mother York*), Ward Bond (*Ike Botkin*), Noah Beery, Jr. (*Buck Lipscomb*), June Lockhart (*Rose York*), Dickie Moore (*George York*), Clem Bevans (*Zeke*), Howard Da Silva (*Lem*), Charles Trowbridge (*Cordell Hull*), Harvey Stephens (*Capt. Danforth*), David Bruce (*Bert Thomas*), Charles 'Carl' Esmond (*German Major*), Joseph Sawyer (*Sgt. Early*), Pat Flaherty (*Sgt. Harry Parsons*), Robert Porterfield (*Zeb Andrews*), Erville Alderson (*Nate Tompkins*), Joseph Girard (*Gen. Pershing*), Frank Wilcox (*Sergeant*), Donald Douglas (*Capt. Tillman*), Lane Chandler (*Cpl. Savage*), Frank Marlowe (*Beardlsey*), Jack Pennick (*Cpl. Cutting*), James Anderson (*Eb*), Guy Wilkerson (*Tom*), Tully Marshall (*Uncle Lige*), Lee "Lasses" White (*Luke the Target Keeper*), Jane Isbell (*Gracie's Sister*), Frank Orth (*Drummer*), Arthur Aylesworth (*Bartender*), Rita La Roy, Lucia Carroll, Kay Sutton (*Saloon Girls*), Elisha Cook, Jr. (*Piano Player*), William Haade (*Card Player*), Jody Gilbert (*Fat Woman*), Victor Kilian (*Andrews*), Frank Faylen, Murray Alper (*Gunnery Spotters*), Gaylord "Steve" Pendleton, Charles Drake (*Scorers*), Theodore Von Eltz (*Prison Camp Commander*), Roland Drew (*Officer*), Russell Hicks (*General*), Jean Del Val (*Marshal Foch*), Selmer Jackson (*Gen. Duncan*), Creighton Hale (*AP Man*), George Irving (*Harrison*), Ed Keane (*Oscar of the Waldorf*), Gig Young (*Soldier*), Walter Sande (*Sergeant*), Si Jenks, Ray Teal, Kit Guard.

At dawn, October 8, 1918, a poorly educated, God-fearing, simple man from the hill country of eastern Tennessee, Alvin C. York, went over the top in the Meuse-Argonne offensive. He worked his way with Company G, 328th Infantry of the 82nd (All-American) Division, across a wide stretch of no-man's land, under heavy German fire which decimated the doughboys all around him. Most were forced to take cover but York and a small contingent of men found a ravine separating two ridges and worked their way through it and behind the German lines. It was the beginning of one of the most incredible feats in military history. York alone raced up a ridge and flanked the German machine gun nests, killing 20 men and then capturing the remaining enemy troops singlehandedly. By the time he was done, this great hero had captured 132 soldiers, the largest bagging of prisoners by a single soldier in history. And he was a pacifist. Hawks brought the life of this incredible man to the screen with forceful integrity, and Cooper is simply wonderful as the country fellow who gets religion and holds onto it, even through the nightmare of WW I. The film opens in 1916 with Cooper and fellow hell-raisers Beery and Bond getting drunk in a clapboard saloon after disturbing a church session with a shooting match. Moore, Cooper's younger brother, arrives at the saloon, which is just across the state line in Kentucky, to fetch him, telling him that his mother, Wycherly, wants him. When another hillbilly, Haade makes fun of Cooper, a grown man, beckoning to the call of his mother, Cooper knocks Haade across the room and a donnybrook explodes, with Bond and Beery pitching in to help Cooper. Moore is nonchalant about the wild battle and when Cooper lands upside down next to him after a blow from an opponent, all Moore can do is repeat laconically: "Ma wants ya, Alvin." The next morning, Moore delivers Cooper to their mountain home; he stands before Wycherly sheepishly; she throws a pail of water on him and he sits down to breakfast. Wycherly tells him the fields need plowing. Cooper is shown struggling with a hand plow drawn by a horse, striking rocks which dot the farm on which he lives. Brennan, the local pastor, goes to Cooper in the field and lectures him, saying that "the Devil's got you by the shirttail, Alvin," telling him he has to "rassle old Satan." Cooper replies that he has prayed but it does no good. Brennan tells him that "a fellow has got to have roots outside his own self." The pastor's colorful lecture falls on deaf ears as Cooper goes about his careless way. Some time later he is hunting a fox when he runs through Leslie's farm, the pretty young Leslie pointing and telling Cooper which way the fox went. He stops, enthralled by the girl. Cooper tells brother Moore to go after the fox while he visits with Leslie and she tells him that she knew it was him hunting because of the sound of his hounds, "one of them having a hook to the end of his bay you could be hanging a bucket on." The barking of the hounds interrupts them and he races off to the hunt but both of them give each other long, lingering looks before Cooper leaves. Later his mother sees Cooper combing his hair. He asks her to sew a tear in his worn-out overalls, and then tells her that he's planning on "setting up" (getting married) and mentions Leslie's name. When he visits Leslie's farmhouse that night, Cooper finds Porterfield, son of a wealthy farmer, sitting on the porch wooing Leslie. The snide Porterfield insults Cooper by interrupting him every time he tries to speak. When Leslie gets up to get some cider for them, Cooper takes Porterfield aside and, by the time Leslie returns, Porterfield is hobbling away. Leslie accuses Cooper of fighting with Porterfield and driving him off and he admits it. He next tells her that he's going to marry her. "You might have told me about it," she says. "A fine husband you'd make. Folks say you're not good 'ceptin' for fighting and hellraising." Cooper believes Leslie likes Porterfield better because he has "bottom land," and Cooper's farm is high in the rocky hills, one that bears meager crops. He tells Leslie that he will get some bottom land, fertile, rock-free land to prove that he's worthy of marrying her. He brings home some bottom land soil which his mother recognizes and she states, "Queer how the folks that lives on the bottom looks down on the folks that lives on the top." Cooper says he will "get me some bottom land," and Wycherly tells him that his father tried to get some bottom land once and "it nearly killed him." Cooper tells her he knows where some land is available. He goes to Alderson who has land for sale, trading his mule, pelts, skins, and an old clock for $50 against the price of the land, $120, telling Alderson that he will pay the balance, $70, within 60 days. Alderson tells him that if he isn't paid within that time, Cooper will forfeit his payments and lose the land. "Sixty days is all ya got," Alderson tells him. "Sixty days and 60 nights," Cooper replies, planning to work night and day. He takes any kind of job he can get, uprooting rocks for other farmers, splitting rails, baling hay, working like a slave, returning home exhausted to put his change into a jar and diligently mark down his savings on a samll calendar. Even Brennan, the pastor who owns the general store, helps out by buying a fox fur for $3, a top price, knowing Cooper's ambition. At dusk one day, while he is plowing a field, Leslie comes to him instead of going to a dance and, almost speechless, kisses him, then says before she runs away: "That's what I was wanting to tell ya." Day and night Cooper labors to earn the money, seeing the deadline looming and not obtaining enough money for the payment. Wycherly prays one night, "Lord, ifen ya can, help him to be gettin' his land." Some nights later Cooper yells that "I can't do it," his voice echoing over the Tennessee hills. "How, how am I gonna do it?" He sees Alderson and begs him for four extra days on the deadline, telling him that the sharpshooting match the following Saturday, where he expects to "cut five targets and win the beef critter and put it up for sale," will provide the extra money he needs. Alderson is skeptical, but allows him the extra time. During the match Cooper does the impossible, hitting five targets dead center and winning a prize steer which he offers as a prize in another shooting match, collecting all the money he needs for the bottom land. Alderson shows up at the match and Cooper rushes forward to pay for the land but the double-dealing farmer, who has Porterfield with him, tells him that he sold the land to Porterfield, and that he didn't believe Cooper could win the entire shooting match and, "Besides," Alderson says, "your time was up." Cooper stares with murderous eyes and begins to advance on Alderson but he is restrained by friends Beery and Bond while Porterfield and Alderson run for their lives. Later Cooper gets drunk and thinks only of murdering Alderson. He rides slowly through a thunderstorm towards Alderson's home, but lightning strikes and knocks him from his horse. He turns to see that a lightning bolt has struck his rifle and split it. Cooper considers this a sign from the Lord and he soon joins Brennan's flock. He does penance for his murderous thoughts by apologizing to Alderson and Porterfield, and both men, stunned, apologize to him for cheating him out of his land. Porterfield tells Cooper that if he works the bottom land for a few seasons, he will give it to him. Cooper puts away his gun, condemns drinking and violence, and even begins teaching Sunday school, keeping as his constant companion his Bible. Then the war engulfs America and tens of thousands of men join the Army. Cooper refuses to enlist, believing that killing of any sort is evil. He is drafted and refuses to report for duty, claiming to be a pacifist and conscientious objector. Brennan tries to convince a local draft board that Cooper's religion does not allow him to go into battle but the board does not recognize Brennan's back country church as a legitimate religious sect. Reluctantly, Cooper enters the Army, the noncommissioned officers commanding him, Sawyer, Flaherty, Wilcox, distrusting him because of his religious beliefs. But Cooper does what he is told, and makes friends with Tobias, Bruce, and others. From Tobias, who had worked in New York as a subway conductor, he learns of the marvels of the big city. During target practice, Cooper's instructors are amazed to see him strike dead center on every target he shoots at; he earns a marksman's medal and is promoted to the rank of corporal before being sent to France. Before going overseas, Cooper's superior officers, Ridges and Stephens, call him into their office and quiz him about his attitude toward going into battle. He tells them that killing is against the word of the Lord and cites his Bible. Ridges gives him another book, the history of the United States, and asks him to study it, telling him that many men have hated killing but have defended their country in its time of need. He gives Cooper a furlough and Cooper returns to his home, pondering his dilemma. He finally comes to believe that though he is against killing, he must serve his country, finding a single line in the Bible that enlightens him: "Therefore render unto Caesar the things that are Caesar's and unto God the things that are God's." Once in France, Cooper sees his friend Bruce killed and then, during the battle of Argonne, he performs his incredible acts of courage, rounding up scores of Germans. After the battle, Cooper escorts Ridges and his commanding general, Hicks, through the now silent battlefield and tells them how he flanked the entire ridgeline of German machine gun nests and trenches filled with German infantry. He astounds Ridges by telling him that "I'm as much agin killin' as ever but when I heard them machine guns...well, them guns was killin' hundreds, maybe thousands, and there weren't nothin' anybody could do but to stop them guns. That's what I done." Ridges stares at him and says, "You mean to tell me you did it to *save* lives?" Cooper nods, "Yes, sir, that was why." Replies Ridges, "York, what you've just told me is the most extraordinary thing of all." Cooper is shown being decorated with the Distinguished Service Cross, the Medaille Militaire, and the coveted Croix de Guerre from France, awarded to him by Marshal Foch (Del Val), and the highest American decoration, the Congressional Medal of Honor, given to him by Gen. Pershing (Girard). (When Cooper is given his medal by Del Val, the Frenchman kisses him, which causes the hardened mountaineer to wince.) Cooper returns to New York and a ticker tape parade while Trowbridge, playing Cordell Hull of Tennessee, escorts him about the city, Cooper asking to ride on the subway, the Bronx Express, in honor of Tobias, who was killed in France. Cooper, while he is being housed at the Waldorf, talks to his mother, Brennan, and Leslie on the phone, a modern convenience that surprises both Cooper and his people in backward Tennessee. Later, Trowbridge presents Cooper with offers for more than $250,000 if he will endorse certain products, or appear in the Ziegfeld Follies, or in movies. "Are they offering that money because of what happened over there?" Cooper asks. "That's it," replies Trowbridge, who tells him to think it over. "I done thought it over, Mr. Hull," Cooper says, "I ain't proud of what I done over there. What we done in France is something we had to do. Some fellows done it ain't a-comin' back. So, the way I figure, things like that ain't for buyin' and sellin'...I reckon I'll have to refuse 'em." All Cooper really wants is to go home and he finally returns to his beloved Three Forks of the Valley of the Wolf, outside of Pall Mall, Tennessee, arriving to be greeted by the entire population of his district. Leslie, Wycherly, Brennan, Moore, and his sister Lockhart, accompany Cooper, driving him toward home. Brennan stops his car and Leslie and Cooper get out. Leslie takes him by the hand and leads him to the bottom land in Tompkins' Hollow, asking him to "keep lookin' down" after they cross a small bridge. She leads him up a hill and then tells him to look up. There, before them, is a beautiful new house and a barn. Leslie bubbles: "It's yours, Alvin, all yours, they give it to you, it's from the people of Tennessee." Cooper, in a daze, replies, "The Lord sure do move in mysterious ways." He and Leslie, hand in hand, run to their new home and life. Hawks, though he is true to the facts of York's prosaic life, achieves a great artistic success here for the very reason of being constrained by a larger-than-life true hero and still conveying the simple virtues of the man, his sincerity, his sublime nobility of spirit, while splendidly dealing with significant moral issues. With an absence of sophisticated dialog, Hawks achieves in wordless and brilliant interaction between his characters a great and telling story of a man of purpose, first dark purposes, then lofty aims, but all emanating from a fierce dedication. This is a basic story of good and evil, told in the simplest and yet most profound terms, with Hawks bringing all of his superior talents to a much underrated film. Technically, the production is without fault, Hawks keeping his cameras fluid and utilizing Polito's magnificent photographic skills at every turn. The WW I battle scenes are sweeping and grimly realistic and the opening tracking shots that accompany Cooper's first scramble through no-man's-land are stunning (almost duplicated foot by foot by Stanley Kubrick when depicting the attack scenes in PATHS OF GLORY). But where Hawks excels at the spectacular in his war scenes, he shines in his gentle profiles of community life in backwoods Tennessee, from the small white church where Brennan and his psalm-singing flock gather to atone for their sins, to the raw log cabin where Wycherly, her children around her, thanks the Lord for giving them their meager food. The heroism shown by Hawks is not only on the battlefield, but in hearts of a valiant rural people struggling to maintain lives just above the poverty level. Stylishly beautiful, from its open boom shot running down a Tennessee river behind the credits to the idyllic portrait of Cooper's new farm at the end, SERGEANT YORK is a courageous work by a savant director who risked being attacked for refusing to adopt a patronizing pose in filming this story as he was in later years by so-called critics who snickered at the sincerity and simplicity of another age for the lack of it in themselves. (There are but a few film critics who understand human history as well as they purport to understand the making of any film.) SERGEANT YORK would probably never have gotten on film had not a young Jesse Lasky been standing on Fifth Avenue, watching the Armistice Day Parade of 1919, and witnessing Sergeant Alvin C. York being honored by a million people, a shy man who could hardly bring himself to look at the crowds cheering him. Lasky vowed to make a film of the hero's life then and there. Over the years, while the producer prospered, he often wrote to York in Tennessee, requesting permission to film his life. The answer was always a polite no. Finally, Lasky traveled to the remote Tennessee valley where the hero lived and got him to agree to the making of the film but only on the proviso that all proceeds he was to receive be given to various religious charities. There was one other requirement: York would not allow anyone to play him except Gary Cooper. The actor turned down the role when asked to play it by coproducer Wallis, but when Lasky *and* York called him to request his talent for the film, he agreed. But Cooper, before signing to do the role, also visited York and spent a great deal of time talking to him, walking through the mountainous terrain with him and learning about his simple way of life and the sound character of the war hero, one who did not drink, smoke, or swear. When it was announced that Cooper would play the hero, Cordell Hull, then secretary of state, wired the actor, stating, "I know you will do full justice to the life and achievements of a most remarkable person." Gen. John Pershing, who had labeled York America's "greatest civilian soldier," also wired Cooper, "Wish you every success in your portrayal of this fine soldier of the World War." The lanky actor, who won his first Oscar for his sterling performance, enjoyed everything about the production except Leslie, who was only 16 at the time, and he was embarrassed to play across from this mere teenager. He seriously joked when saying, "I can see how I'm going to really feel like a hillbilly with a child bride." Hawks, according to Wallis, writing in his memoirs, *Starmaker*, wanted "to play Mrs. York as a sexy Jane Russell type, and even suggested that Jane play the part. I wanted a simple, country girl, and chose Joan Leslie." Hawks was not the first choice of producers Lasky and Wallis. They wanted Michael Curtiz but Cooper would not work with this frantic Hungarian director. Universal refused to release Henry Koster, Paramount said they could not have Henry Hathaway, and when the producers asked for either Victor Fleming or Norman Taurog, their parent studio, MGM, said no. Wallis finally hired Hawks from Samuel Goldwyn "for an exorbitant price." Hawks spent a great deal of time getting releases from almost every man in York's squad who had witnessed his incredible feats and many of these WW I veterans were invited to the Broadway premiere of the film. York himself appeared, shy and reticent as ever. Mayor Fiorello LaGuardia, also in attendance, ordered Broadway to dim its lights for a minute in his honor, which the Great White Way did. York was given another ticker tape parade, sitting with Cooper, and a private train brought scores of U.S. senators from Washington to attend the premiere. The patriotic Jazz Singer Al Jolson took out a full page ad in *Variety* to congratulate Wallis and Lasky for making this superlative film. Cooper later stated: "Sergeant York and I had quite a few things in common, even before I played him on the screen. We both were raised in the mountains–Tennessee for him, Montana for me–and learned to ride and shoot as a natural part of growing up. SERGEANT YORK won me an Academy Award, but that's not why it's my favorite film. I liked the role because of the background of the picture, and because I was portraying a good, sound American character." Brennan, Leslie, Wycherly, Tobias, and the great characters peopling this marvelous cast, brought the era and rural people to life, giving Cooper great support. (Wallis had to pay Goldwyn $150,000 for Cooper's services.) Cooper was too old to serve in WW II, plus he had an old hip injury that would have prevented him from serving had he been young enough. But he did more to build WW II morale among American soldiers by his great performance in SERGEANT YORK and by traveling 23,000 miles during the war to entertain soldiers throughout the Pacific. Ironically, crew members on board the aircraft carrier U.S.S. *Enterprise* watched SERGEANT YORK on the night of December 6, 1941, only hours before leaving Pearl Harbor; the Japanese sneak attack occurred at dawn the next day with the aircraft carrier then at sea. SERGEANT YORK was the top moneymaker of 1941 and put Cooper at the top of the most popular film star lists everywhere. In addition to Cooper, Holmes won an Oscar for his top-notch editing of the film which also received nine other nominations. (See Index.)

p, Jesse L. Lasky, Hal B. Wallis; d, Howard Hawks; w, Abem Finkel, Harry Chandlee, Howard Koch, John Huston (based on *War Diary of Sergeant York* by Sam K. Cowan, *Sergeant York and His People* by Cowan, and *Sergeant York--Last of the Long Hunters* by Tom Skeyhill); ph, Sol Polito, (war sequences) Arthur Edeson; m, Max Steiner; ed, William Holmes; md, Leo F. Forbstein; art d, John Hughes; set d, Fred MacLean; tech adv, Donoho Hall, Paul Walters, Capt. F.A.R. William Yettes; makeup, Perc Westmore.

War Drama   Cas.   (PR:A MPAA:NR)

SERGEANTS 3*   (1962) 113m Essex-Claude/UA c

Frank Sinatra (*1st Sgt. Mike Merry*), Dean Martin (*Sgt. Chip Deal*), Sammy Davis, Jr (*Jonah Williams*), Peter Lawford (*Sgt. Larry Barrett*), Joey Bishop (*Sgt. Maj. Roger Boswell*), Henry Silva (*Mountain Hawk*), Buddy Lester (*Willie Sharpknife*), Ruta Lee (*Amelia Parent*), Phillip Crosby (*Cpl. Ellis*), Dennis Crosby (*Pvt. Page*), Lindsay Crosby (*Pvt. Wills*), Hank Henry (*Blacksmith*), Richard Simmons (*Col. William Collingwood*), Michael Pate (*Watanka*), Armand Alzamora (*Caleb*), Richard Hale (*White Eagle*), Mickey Finn (*Morton*), Sonny King (*Corporal*), Madge Blake (*Mrs. Parent*), Dorothy Abbott (*Mrs. Collingwood*), Eddie Littlesky (*Ghost Dancer*), Rodd Redwing (*Irregular*), James Waters (*Colonel's Aide*), Walter Merrill (*Telegrapher*), Ceffie (*Herself*).

The "Rat Pack" takes to the saddle in this sanitized, lukewarm version of Rudyard Kipling's "Gunga Din." The guys are sergeants in charge of establishing an outpost at the rugged edge of the prairie. Comedic actions have them counter Indian attacks by Silva. The laughs quickly diminish and the group should have loped off into the sunset much sooner in the film.

p, Frank Sinatra; d, John Sturges; w, W.R. Burnett; ph, Winton C. Hoch (Panavision, Technicolor); m, Billy May; ed, Ferris Webster; art d, Frank Hotaling; set d, Victor Gangelin; cos, Wesley V. Jefferies, Angela Alexander; spec eff, Paul Pollard; m/l, "And the Night Wind Sang," Johnny Rotella, Franz Steininger.

Western   (PR:A MPAA:NR)

SERIAL*   (1980) 91m PAR c

Martin Mull (*Harvey*), Tuesday Weld (*Kate*), Jennifer McAlister (*Joan*), Sam Chew, Jr (*Bill*), Sally Kellerman (*Martha*), Anthony Battaglia (*Stokeley*), Bill Macy (*Sam*), Nita Talbot (*Angela*), Pamela Bellwood (*Carol*), Barbara Rhoades (*Vivian*), Ann Weldon (*Rachel*), Peter Bonerz (*Leonard*), Jon Fong (*Wong*), Christopher Lee (*Luckman/Skull*), Patch MacKenzie (*Stella*), Stacey Nelkin (*Marlene*), Tom Smothers (*Spike*), Clark Brandon (*Spenser*), Paul Rossilli (*Paco*), Clyde Ventura (*Donald*), Rosana Soto, Kevin O'Brien, Mark Taylor, Donna Ponteretto, Lee Wilkof, John Thompson, Kevyn Howard, Robin Sherwood, Bob Balhatchet, Victoria Huxtable, George American Horse, Peter Horton, Kenny Endoso, Jay Currin, Buddy Joe Hooker, Billy Sands, Sam Denoff, Melanie Workhoven, Mark Rasmussen, Bill Jelliffe, Scott Paulin, Anthony Fusco.

Nothing is sacred in this scathingly, funny film that sends up the fads of the 1970s. Everything is fair game. Mull, playing the head of the family, remains

at a distance from all this insanity. Quickly paced, it parodies vegetarianism, oriental sex techniques, disco dancing, and "rap" sessions. Much of the comedy comes from the interaction between Mull's family and his neighbor's, Macy. Director Bill Persky, who previously worked strictly in TV, makes his switch to the big screen with no problem.

p, Sidney Beckerman; d, Bill Persky; w, Rich Eustis, Michael Elias (based on the novel by Cyra McFadden); ph, Rexford Metz (Movielab Color); m. Lalo Schifrin; ed, John W. Wheeler; art d, Bill Sandell; set d, Bob Gould, Paul Dal Porto; m/l, "A Changing World," Schifrin, Norman Gimbel.

Comedy   Cas.   (PR:O MPAA:R)

SERIOUS CHARGE   (SEE: IMMORAL CHARGE, 1962, Brit.)

SERPENT, THE*½**   (1973, Fr./Ital./Ger.) 113m La Boetie-Euro International-Ria lto/AE c (LE SERPENT; AKA: NIGHT FLIGHT FROM MOSCOW)

Yul Brynner (*Vlassov*), Henry Fonda (*Allan Davies*), Dirk Bogarde (*Philip Boyle*), Philippe Noiret (*Lucien Berthon*), Michel Bouquet (*Tavel*), Martin Hel (*Lepke*), Farley Granger (*Computer Programming Chief*), Virna Lisi (*Annabel Lee*), Guy Trejean (*Deval*), Marie Dubois (*Suzanne*), Elga Andersen (*Kate Cross*), Robert Alda (*Interrogator*), Nathalie Nerval (*Tatiana*), Andre Falcon (*French Diplomat*), Paola Pitagora (*Duty Free Shop Salesgirl*), Francois Maistre (*Airport Police Inspector*), Luigi Diberti (*Lefevre*), William Sabatier (*Mercadier*), Robert Party (*Debecourt*), Larry Dolgin (*Atamian*).

A solid international espionage story that eschews flashiness and goes for authenticity, THE SERPENT is based on a true story and the details will be of interest to anyone who sees through the JAMES BOND glitter and prefers reality. Brynner is a cool colonel in the Soviet spy hierarchy. He defects to the other side and asks for asylum, not unlike a 1985 Russian spy who came to the U.S., then went back to Russia, and wound up getting executed for his behavior. CIA chief Fonda is not so sure he isn't being gulled, so he runs a series of tests on Brynner that include a go against a lie detector. When little hints come up that Brynner may be holding back, Fonda keeps a watchful eye. Brynner claims to have a list of all Kremlin agents operating in Europe. The Russian begins to tell of the spies he knows in France and Germany, and Noiret, the French minister of the interior, is implicated. There are several suicides but they are later determined to be murders. (The Kremlin is trying to clean house while pulling the wool over the West's eyes.) The boss of the operation is Bogarde, No. 2 man for British Intelligence, and a longtime mole inside their secret service. Bogarde, code-named "The Serpent" is doing all the killing. In the end, Fonda finds out that Brynner has been planted and the Russian is eventually swapped for an American pilot who'd been downed behind the Iron Curtain. Bogarde's role is brief, but telling, and he gets a chance to play something more macho than his usual part. Producer Verneuil's previous two films were THE SICILIAN CLAN and THE BURGLARS, both of which were a bit more successful than this, a thinking man's spy film. A good cast from several countries leads us to suspect that this was one of those "sell the movie by country" deals.

p&d, Henri Verneuil; w, Verneuil, Gilles Perrault, Tom Rowe (based on the novel Le *13e Suicide* by Pierre Nord); ph, Claude Renoir (Panavision, DeLuxe Color); m, Ennio Morricone; ed, Pierre Gillette; prod d, Jacques Saulnier; md, Bruno Nicolai.

Spy Drama   (PR:A-C MPAA:PG)

SERPENT ISLAND*½   (1954) 65m Medallion-TV bw

Sonny Tufts, Mary Munday.

Obscure voodoo thriller from the man who would soon bring out THE AMAZING COLOSSAL MAN (1957), the king of cheap science fiction, Bert I. Gordon. This one chronicles an expedition into the dark Caribbean led by everyone's favorite hero, Tufts, who witnesses such exciting events as actual voodoo rituals and a battle with a giant jungle snake. While never brilliant cinema, Gordon's films are always a lot of fun.

p,d&w, Bert I. Gordon.

Adventure   Cas.   (PR:A MPAA:NR)

SERPENT OF THE NILE   (1953) 81m COL c

Rhonda Fleming (*Cleopatra*), William Lundigan (*Lucilius*), Raymond Burr (*Mark Anthony*), Jean Byron (*Charmion*), Michael Ansara (*Florus*), Michael Fox (*Octavius*), Conrad Wolfe (*Assassin*), John Crawford (*Domitius*), Jane Easton (*Cytheris*), Robert Griffin (*Brutus*), Fredric Berest (*Marculius*), Julie Newmeyer [Newmar] (*Golden Girl*).

No one is the good guy in this tale of Mark Antony's rise to power, who succumbs to the evil ways of Cleopatra and falls from power just as quickly as he ascended. Wooden dialog hurts all the participants. (Burr) proposes a merger between Rome and Egypt. (Fleming) agrees, and quickly plans Burr's death so she can take over the entire empire. But her plan is killed by Lundigan. Lundigan brings in the Roman army and becomes the reason Fleming commits suicide. Burr comes off too weak to portray a powerful leader and Fleming's dialog does not suit an Egyptian empress: if the set looks familiar, its because it was used in SALOME, 1953.

p, Sam Katzman; d, William Castle; w, Robert E. Kent; ph, Henry Freulich (Technicolor); m, Mischa Bakaleinikoff; ed, Gene Havlick; art d, Paul Palmentola; cos, Jean Louis.

Drama   **(PR:A   MPAA:NR)**

SERPENT'S EGG, THE**   (1977, Ger./U.S.) 120m Rialto-DD/PAR c
                                              (DAS SCHLANGENEI)

Liv Ullmann (*Manuela Rosenberg*), David Carradine (*Abel Rosenberg*), Gert Frobe (*Inspector Bauer*), Heinz Bennent (*Doctor Hans Vergerus*), James Whitmore (*The Priest*), Toni Berger (*Mr. Rosenberg*), Christian Berkel (*Student*), Paula Braend (*Mrs. Hemse*), Edna Bruenell (*Mrs. Rosenberg*), Paul Buerks (*Cabaret Comedian*), Gaby Dohm (*Woman with Baby*), Emil Feist (*Cupid*), Kai Fischer, Georg Hartmann, Edith Heerdegen, Klaus Hoffmann, Grischa Huber, Volkert Kraeft, Gunther Malzacher, Lisi Mangold, Guenter Meisner, Kyra Mladeck, Heide Picha, Hans Quest, Charles Regnier, Walter Schmidinger, Irene Steinbeisser, Fritz Strassner, Glynn Turman, Ellen Umlauf, Wolfgang Wieser, Ralf Wolter.

Ingmar Bergman's trademark look is evident at the start of his first English-language film, made outside of his home country. Again Bergman collaborates with famed cinematographer Sven Nykvist. The story involves Ullmann and Carradine, who are struggling to survive in the turbulent, poverty-stricken Berlin of the 1920s. He used to be a trapeze artist in an act with his sister-in-law (Ullmann) and his late brother, who has recently committed suicide. To make ends meet, she works in a whorehouse by day and a dive bar at night. They befriend a doctor who runs a clinic that performs experiments on humans, which eventually drive the patients insane or to suicide. Both enter the clinic, with only Carradine coming out again, but not before he wrecks the clinic in a rage on the night of an early failure by Hitler to stage a *coup d'etat* in another German city. Carradine then disappears. A heavy film, without the depth of Bergman's other work, which failed critically and at the box office.

p, Dino DeLaurentiis; d&w, Ingmar Bergman; ph, Sven Nykvist (Eastmancolor); m, Rolf Wilhelm; ed, Petra Von Oelffen; prod d, Rolf Zehetbauer; art d, Werner Achmann, Friedrich Thaler; cos, Charlotte Flemming; ch, Heino Hallhuber; m/l, "Sweet Bon Bons," Wilhelm.

Drama   **Cas.**   **(PR:O   MPAA:R)**

SERPENTS OF THE PIRATE MOON, THE**½
                                              (1973) 93m NEF-Planfilm c

Sylvia Morales (*Girl*), Sahdji (*Transvestite*), Jean-Philippe Carson (*Boss*), Juliette Graham (*Woman*).

Morales is a young woman trying to hold on to reality as she fights her overwhelming obsessions and neuroses. Dividing her time between her home and job in a local semi-decadent nightclub, Morales is eventually able to overcome her psychological disturbances with renewed hope in her life. An atmospheric work, the film has a fine hold on its characters and the world they populate. The parallels between Morales' problems and the show business life at the cabaret are well drawn. This project was a thesis film by a UCLA student from Santo Domingo and was highly praised in addition to winning the grand prize at France's Toulon Young Cinema Festival.

p,d&w, Jean-Louis Jorge; ph, David Garcia (DeLuxe Color); m, Judith Bell.

Drama   **(PR:O   MPAA:NR)**

SERPICO****   (1973) 129m DD-Artists Entertainment Complex PAR c

Al Pacino (*Frank Serpico*), Tony Roberts (*Bob Blair*), John Randolph (*Chief Sidney Green*), Jack Kehoe (*Tom Keough*), Biff McGuire (*Capt. McClain*), Barbara Eda-Young (*Laurie*), Cornelia Sharpe (*Leslie*), John Medici (*Pasquale Serpico*), Allan Rich (*D.A. Tauber*), Norman Ornellas (*Rubello*), Ed Grover (*Lombardo*), Al Henderson (*Peluce*), Hank Garrett (*Malone*), Damien Leake (*Joey*), Joe Bova (*Potts*), Gene Gross (*Capt. Tolkin*), John Stewart (*Waterman, Arresting Officer*), Woodie King (*Larry*), James Tolkin (*Steiger*), Ed Crowley (*Barto*), Bernard Barrow (*Palmer*), Sal Carollo (*Mr. Serpico*), Mildred Clinton (*Mrs. Serpico*), Nathan George (*Detective Smith*), Gus Fleming (*Dr. Metz*), Richard Foronjy (*Corsaro*), Alan North (*Brown*), Lewis J. Stadlen (*Berman*), John McQuade (*Kellogg*), Ted Beniades (*Sarno*), John Lehne (*Gilbert*), M. Emmet Walsh (*Gallagher*), George Ede (*Daley*), Franklin Scott (*Black Prisoner*), Don Billett (*Detective Threatening Serpico*), Tim Pelt, Willie Pelt (*Black Hoods*), F. Murray Abraham (*Detective Partner*), Charles White (*Commissioner Delaney*), Mary Louise Weller (*Girl*).

In 1970, police officer Frank Serpico electrified the Knapp Commission investigating the New York City Police Department by testifying that there were as many cops taking money illegally as there were crooks. Peter Maas wrote a biography of Serpico that was turned into a script by Waldo Salt (MIDNIGHT COWBOY) and Norman Wexler (SATURDAY NIGHT FEVER) which was nominated for an Oscar. John Avildsen was the first director of the project and was replaced by Lumet, who did a fine job, although he might have paid more attention to trimming about 15 minutes from the opening hour in order to hook viewers into the story. Pacino's Oscar-nominated performance proved that his work in THE GODFATHER

was not a one-shot. Pacino won an Obie in 1966 for his work in "The Indian Wants the Bronx." In 1966, he took a Tony for "Does a Tiger Wear a Necktie?" which led to a film job in ME, NATALIE then PANIC IN NEEDLE PARK. In order to prepare for his portrayal, Pacino and the real Serpico spent many weeks together and became good friends before the latter moved to Europe, where he lived for many years. Pacino is an honest cop who refuses to be one of the many who supplement their incomes by taking money from the criminals in their area. One of Pacino's fellow officers is Kehoe, who states "Who can trust a cop that won't take money?" and that about sums up the attitude of the men on the force with whom Pacino works Pacino is told several times that he cannot remain above the corruption and that if he insists on staying clean, his life won't be worth much. Pacino stays aloof, keeps doing his job, and refuses his share of the booty. It begins to stick in his craw and his life away from work is also disintegrating. His affair with Sharpe comes to an end and he has more domestic woes with another woman whom he loves, Eda-Young. When the situation becomes unbearable Pacino tells his friend, Roberts, about what's going on. Roberts is a cop close to the Mayor's investigating committee. Inspector Grover also feels that the truth must be told. Pacino tries to blow the whistle to Commissioner White through McGuire, one of the men who handles police department investigations, but when nothing happens there, he goes to the New York Times editors (It seems everyone does that. Redford did the same in THREE DAYS OF THE CONDOR), who print the story. Until this time, Pacino has been transferred from precinct to precinct where the other officers have shown him no support as they are all, in one way or another, suspect. After the investigation begins, Pacino is sent to Brooklyn to work on the Narcotics Squad. He welcomes the change of venue and is then seriously wounded by an unseen sniper when his pals, who were supposed to cover him, seem to vanish. While recovering from his wounds, Pacino is offered a detective's job but he realizes it's little more than a bribe, so he quits the Force and completes his testimony. Excellent acting from everyone. It's a pleasure to see Roberts in a role outside a Woody Allen movie and he does well as Pacino's pal. An exciting, raw picture in which every role, no matter how small, is wonderfully cast. Note Oscar-winner F. Murray Abraham (AMADEUS) as one of the cops, Mary Louise Weller (ANIMAL HOUSE) in a small role, character man M. Emmet Walsh (STRAIGHT TIME) and Hank Garrett, the killer postman in THREE DAYS OF THE CONDOR. Former boxer Garrett was born Hank Greenberg and changed his name for acting purposes because he didn't want to be confused with the great Detroit and Pittsburgh slugger. Despite all the good work in smaller roles, it is Pacino's riveting presence that is the force behind the movie and it would be difficult to imagine any other actor in the part. The language is very graphic and the violence is realistic. Parents are advised to keep children away. A fair-sized success at the box office, SERPICO earned nearly $20 million when all receipts were in.

p, Martin Bregman; d, Sidney Lumet; w, Waldo Salt, Norman Wexler (based on the book by Peter Maas); ph, Arthur J. Ornitz (Panavision, Technicolor); m, Mikis Theodorakis; ed, Dede Allen, Richard Marks; md, Bob James; prod d, Charles Bailey; art d, Douglas Higgins; set d, Thomas H. Wright; cos, Anna Hill Johnstone; makeup, Redge Tackley.

Crime Biography   **Cas.**   **(PR:C-O   MPAA:R)**

SERVANT, THE***   (1964, Brit.) 115m Springbok/Landau bw

Dirk Bogarde (*Hugo Barrett*), Sarah Miles (*Vera*), Wendy Craig (*Susan*), James Fox (*Tony*), Catherine Lacey (*Lady Mounset*), Richard Vernon (*Lord Mounset*), Ann Firbank (*Society Woman*), Doris Knox (*Older Woman*), Patrick Magee (*Bishop*), Jill Melford (*Younger Woman*), Alun Owen (*Curate*), Harold Pinter (*Society Man*), Derek Tansley (*Headwaiter*), Brian Phelan (*Irishman in Pub*), Hazel Terry (*Woman in Big Hat*), Philippa Hare (*Girl in Bedroom*), Dorothy Bromiley (*Girl Outside Phone Box*), Colette Martin, Joanna Wake, Harriet Devine (*Her Friends*), Alison Seebohm (*Girl in Pub*), Chris Williams (*Cashier in Coffee Bar*), Gerry Duggan (*Waiter*), John Dankworth (*Jazz Band Leader*), Davy Graham (*Guitarist*), Bruce Wells (*Sidewalk Painter*).

An interesting but flawed examination of the master-servant relationship in modern England, this picture had a spot of aggravation in getting off the ground. Based on Robin Maugham's novel, it took a while for Pinter, Losey, and Bogarde to find the money. Losey, an American, had been in England since the early 1950's, the result of having run afoul of the various witch-hunters who were functioning during that time and finding Communists under every bed. This movie was overlooked by the Oscars, but it did manage to garner awards from the British Film Academy for Bogarde as the Best Actor, Fox as the Most Promising Newcomer, Slocombe for his cinematography. Fox is a bored, rich, and lazy playboy who, like Miniver Cheevy yearns for the days of yore. He comes home from a long holiday in Europe, buys a magnificent Georgian townhouse, and decides that he needs a Jeeves to his Bertie Wooster. He meets Bogarde, a Cockney valet, and hires him to run the house. Fox is engaged to upper-cruster Craig, a woman of his own caste, but a marriage date is still to be set. Under Bogarde's prodding, Fox spends a fortune furnishing the house and it is soon a most posh place that reeks of elegance. Craig sees through Bogarde's influence over Fox and hates the fact that Fox is relying more and more upon Bogarde in every way. Craig feels that Bogarde has an insidious side that will soon manifest itself, despite his seemingly perfect behavior. Bogarde realizes that his job is in danger if Craig ever succeeds in undermining his hold over Fox.

To forestall that, Bogarde brings in his mistress, Miles (who had won a great deal of approval for her earlier role as the student opposite Laurence Olivier in TERM OF TRIAL), but introduces her as his sister and offers her services as a maid. Bogarde's plan is to push Craig out of the way and, to that end, he sends Miles to seduce the naive Fox, something she manages quite easily. Later, Fox comes home one night and discovers Bogarde and Miles making love. He is shocked at this incestuous behavior, then learns that they are not siblings at all. Enraged by this, Fox discharges both of them and it isn't long before the house begins to run down without the efficient Bogarde to supervise matters. To further complicate matters, Craig walks out on Fox and his life is rapidly disintegrating. At a chance encounter in a pub (that is instead, rather a calculated move on the part of Bogarde), Fox and Bogarde meet again and Fox is only too happy to bring Bogarde back into the house. Once Bogarde is inside, the balance of power changes and Fox becomes subservient to his man. Fox begins drinking and his already weak spine starts to vanish entirely as Bogarde continues pulling Fox's strings. If this is an incipient homosexual situation it is suggested rather than demonstrated. Craig comes back in an attempt to repair her life with Fox, but by this time, the youth is too far gone into a dream world of drugs, booze, and debauchery. The servant has become the master and the corruption is complete, with the class distinction between the two men now having been erased. Pinter's adaptation was his usual melange of wit and silence. He does a cameo as a society man and proves himself a worthy actor. After appearing in PERFORMANCE and THE SERVANT, Fox experienced a religious conversion and retired from movies for a while, then returned in the 1980's. He is the younger brother of Edward Fox (DAY OF THE JACKAL, A BRIDGE TOO FAR among others) and they are often confused because of their resemblance to one another.

p, Joseph Losey, Norman Priggen; d, Losey; w, Harold Pinter (based on the novel by Robin Maugham); ph, Douglas Slocombe; m, John Dankworth; ed, Reginald Mills; prod d, Richard MacDonald; md, Dankworth; art d, Ted Clements; cos, Beatrice Dawson; m/l, "All Gone," Dankworth, Pinter (sung by Cleo Laine); makeup, Bob Lawrence.

Drama   **Cas.**   **(PR:C   MPAA:NR)**

SERVANTS' ENTRANCE**   (1934) 88m FOX bw

Janet Gaynor (Hedda Nilsson), Lew Ayres (Eric Landstrom), Ned Sparks (Hjalmar Gnu), Walter Connolly (Viktor Nilsson), Louise Dresser (Mrs. Hansen), G.P. Huntley, Jr (Karl Berghoff), Astrid Allwyn (Sigrid Hansen), Siegfried Rumann (Hans Hansen), John Qualen (Detective), Josephine Whittell (Christina), Greta Meyer (Anna), Jerry Stuart (Olfa), Ruth Marion (Olga), Buster Phelps (Tommy), Ann Gibbons (Gretchen), Ann Doran (Maid), Gladys Blake (Telephone Operator), John Marston (Newspaper Editor), Catherine Doucet, Dorothy Christy, Harold Minjir, Paul Parry.

The film's main premise here is too hard to believe as Gaynor chooses to be a maid rather than enjoy life with her wealthy father. The most interesting aspect is an animated sequence contributed by Walt Disney in which a barrage of kitchen utensils haunt Gaynor on her first night as a maid. The sugar-coated action takes place in Sweden.

p, Winfield Sheehan; d, Frank Lloyd; w, Samson Raphaelson (based on a novel by Sigrid Boo); ph, Hal Mohr; md, Arthur Lange; cos, Rene Hubert; cartoon sequence, Walt Disney.

Comedy/Drama   **(PR:A   MPAA:NR)**

SERVICE   (SEE: LOOKING FORWARD, 1933)

SERVICE DE LUXE**½   (1938) 85m UNIV bw

Constance Bennett (Helen Murphy), Vincent Price (Robert Wade), Charlie Ruggles (Scott Robinson), Helen Broderick (Pearl), Mischa Auer (Bibenko), Joy Hodges (Audrey Robinson), Halliwell Hobbes (Butler), Chester Clute (Chester Bainbridge), Frances Robinson (Secretary), Raymond Parker, Frank Coghlan, Jr (Bell Hops), Lawrence Grant (Voroshinsky), Nina Gilbert (Mrs. Devereaux), Crauford Kent (Mr. Devereaux), Lionel Belmore (Wade), Ben Hall (Yokel).

A fast-paced comedy/drama that marks Vincent Price's film debut. Bennett runs a service bureau for the wealthy taking care of everything from writing checks to staging weddings. Ruggles employs her services to keep his country-bumpkin nephew, Price, from visiting him in New York. But as expected, Bennett and Price become romantically involved and the two eventually marry. She first battles Hodges for him, winning him over with her big-city charm, while Hodges makes due with Auer.

p, Edmund Grainger; d, Rowland V. Lee; w, Gertrude Purcell, Leonard Spigelgass (based on a story by Bruce Manning, Vera Caspary); ph, George Robinson; ed, Ted J. Kent; art d, Jack Otterson; cos, Irene.

Comedy/Drama   **(PR:A   MPAA:NR)**

SERVICE FOR LADIES (SEE: RESERVED FOR LADIES, 1932, Brit.)

SERYOZHA   (SEE: SUMMER TO REMEMBER, A, 1961, USSR)

SESSION WITH THE COMMITTEE (SEE: COMMITTEE, THE, 1968, Brit.)

SET, THE*   (1970, Aus.) 108m Mawson Continental bw

Sean McEuan (Paul), Rodney Mullinar (Tony), Hazel Phillips (Peggy), Denis Doonan (Bronoski), Julie Rodgers (Cara), Elsa Jacoby, Tracy Lee, Ann Aczel, Michael Charnley, Ken Johnson, Muriel Hopkins.

The film opens with a young woman admitting to her male lover on a beach that she has had only lesbian encounters before. This opening scene reflects the nature of the rest of this Australian film, which was thoroughly trashed in its own country, and rightly so. There is no character development whatsoever, with sex being the one and only subject throughout the entire film. The final scene has everyone swimming in a pool fully clothed. The absurdity of the scene sums up the film as a whole. It was made Down Under and should have stayed there.

p&d, Frank Brittain; w, Dianne Brittain, Roger Ward (based on a novel by Ward); ph, Sandor Siro; m, Sven Libaek.

Drama   **(PR:O   MPAA:NR)**

SETTE CONTRO LA MORTE (SEE: CAVERN, THE, 1965, Ital./Ger.)

SETTE DONNE PER I MAC GREGOR (SEE: UP THE MAC GREGORS, 1967, Ital./Span.)

SETTE PISTOLE PER I MAC GREGOR (SEE: SEVEN GUNS FOR THE MAC GREGORS, 1968, Ital./Span.)

SETTE UOMINI D'ORO   (SEE: SEVEN GOLDEN MEN, 1969, Fr./Ital./Span.)

SETTE VOLTE DONNA   (SEE: WOMAN TIMES SEVEN, 1967, U.S./Fr./Ital.)

SETTE WINCHESTER PER UN MASSACRO (SEE: PAYMENT IN BLOOD, 1968, Ital.)

SET-UP, THE****   (1949) 72m RKO bw

Robert Ryan (Bill "Stoker" Thompson), Audrey Totter (Julie), George Tobias (Tiny), Alan Baxter (Little Boy), Wallace Ford (Gus), Percy Helton (Red), Hal Fieberling (Tiger Nelson), Darryl Hickman (Shanley), Kenny O'Morrison (Moore), James Edwards (Luther Hawkins), David Clarke (Gunboat Johnson), Phillip Pine (Souza), Edwin Max (Danny), Dave Fresco (Mickey), William E. Green (Doctor), Abe Dinovitch (Ring Caller), Jack Chase (Hawkin's Second), Mike Lally, Arthur Sullivan, William McCather, Gene Delmont (Handlers), Herbert Anderson, Jack Raymond (Husbands), Helen Brown, Constance Worth (Wives), Walter Ridge (Manager), Jess Kirkpatrick, Paul Dobov (Gamblers), Frank Richards (Bat), Jack Stoney (Nelson's Second), Archie Leonard (Blind Man), John Butler, Ralph Volke, Tony Merrill, Carl Sklover, Sam Shack, Herman Bodel, Andy Carillo, Charles Sullivan, Al Rehin, Tom Noonan, Dan Foster, Everett Smith, Brian O'Hara, Donald Kerr (Men), Lillian Castle, Frances Mack, Ruth Brennan (Women), Lynn Millan (Bunny), Bernard Gorcey (Tobacco Man), Charles Wagenheim (Hamburger Man), Billy Snyder (Barker), W.J. O'Brien (Pitchman), Frank Mills (Photographer), Bobby Henshaw (Announcer), Dwight Martin (Glutton), Noble "Kid" Chissel (Handler), Ben Moselle (Referee), Arthur Weegee Fellig (Timekeeper).

One of the most realistic and gripping boxing films ever made, THE SET-UP is a tautly constructed, emotionally charged examination of one night in the life of an aging boxer, Ryan. Played out in real time (the action on screen takes as long as it would in real life–there are no editing transitions to advance the narrative ahead in time as would be found in a film where the story spans several days or even years–THE SET-UP is 72 uninterrupted minutes of a man's life), the film begins as the crowd gathers in front of the fight arena in anticipation of the evening's bouts. Two men look over the schedule and note that Ryan is fighting a bout after the main event–a space reserved for unimportant fights. "Stoker Thompson! Is he still fightin'? I remember him when I was a kid!" Across the street in a cheap hotel, Ryan packs his gear and gets ready to go to the arena. His wife, Totter, informs him that she will not be watching him fight tonight. Shocked because she always attends his bouts, Ryan asks why. Totter tearfully tells him that he's getting too old and that "two hours after the 'last' fight you still didn't know who I was!" She begs him to quit before he gets himself beaten punchy or killed, but he tells her that if he can win tonight's bout he'll be back on the road to the top. "Just one punch away" from being able to collect a big purse, open their own "beer joint," and retire. Ryan leaves Totter her ticket and heads down to the arena's locker room. Meanwhile, Ryan's seedy manager, Tobias, has taken $50 from a hood, Max, as payment for Ryan throwing the fight. Max's boss, Baxter, is a local gangster who has invested a large sum of money in Ryan's opponent, Fieberling. Tobias gives Ryan's little toady of a trainer, Helton, $5 of the $50. Helton asks Tobias when he's going to inform Ryan that he has to lay down after the second round. Tobias says he won't have to since as of late Ryan has been getting knocked out regularly after the second round. Helton disagrees and says that Ryan's still got enough left in him to win, but Tobias ignores him. While Ryan prepares for his bout in a cramped locker room crowded with other fighters, the featured bouts go on in the arena before a sweating, smoky mass of humanity that screams like animals possessed by the bloodlust. An obese man sits by himself stuffing his face with food while intently watching the contest. A wealthy blind man gets seats as close to the ring as possible so that he can hear the gruesome pummeling while his sighted friend vividly describes the action in gory detail. Another man winces as his wife jumps to her feet screaming, "Kill 'em!" Also in the audience is Baxter and his blonde moll who makes side bets with strangers during the bout. Back in the locker room, Ryan watches as fighters–ranging ranging in age from fresh-out-of-high-school to punchy veterans–psych veterans–psych for their bouts. Back in the hotel, Totter finally decides to go to the fight, but as she approaches the door to the arena she can hear the primal grunts and yells of the crowd and the horrible din drives her away. She spends the bout walking the streets by herself. In the locker room, the fighter for the main event, Edwards, a powerful, sleek, and confident young black man who seems destined for the world championship, prepares for his bout. Ryan admires Edwards for he represents everything Ryan has ever dreamed of being, and Edwards respects Ryan for having stuck with it for so long. Finally no one is left in the locker room but Ryan. Edwards wins his fight easily and wishes Ryan good luck. Ryan climbs into the ring and faces his opponent, Fieberling, who is a young, dumb, curly-headed blonde. Tobias gives Ryan some insincere encouragement, while Helton begs Ryan to "stay away from him." As the fight begins Ryan notices that his wife's seat is empty. The disappointment seems to fuel a fire within him and his vicious fighting in the first round takes his opponent–and all the parties involved in the setup–by surprise. Helton seems convinced Ryan will win, while Tobias pretends not to be concerned. Round two plays much the same, with both fighters punching savagely. Both Max and Baxter begin to worry. Helton begs Tobias to tell Ryan about the setup and make him fall down. Tobias gives in, but Ryan refuses. He knows he can win this fight. Meanwhile, Totter stops at a food stand and buys some groceries. She returns to the hotel and makes dinner for herself and Ryan. Round three sees both boxers slamming away at each other. Ryan goes down a few times, but he comes back up to continue. The bloodlust of the crowd soars to new heights. Round four is a brutal contest as the exhausted fighters beat each other senseless. Fieberling finally goes down and Ryan wins the fight. Tobias and Helton dash out of the arena before Max and Baxter can find them. Ryan is confronted in his dressing room by the pair, and when he tells them he was ignorant of the setup, Baxter tells him to get dressed, "We'll talk about it later." Ryan knows that they'll be waiting for him outside, so he gets dressed quickly and goes out the alley door. Unfortunately, Baxter and his goons spot him, and he is cornered. Ryan tries to fend off the four men, but there are too many of them and he is too tired. Baxter tells them to hold Ryan down. The gangster leans forward and Ryan manages to get his right arm loose and punch Baxter right in the face. The shocked, hurt look of a little boy (which happens to be Baxter's nickname) momentarily sweeps across the gangster's face. He then recovers his cold demeanor and calmly tells Ryan, "You'll never hit anyone with that hand again." The gangster grabs a brick and pounds Ryan's right hand to a pulp. When Ryan awakens the men are gone. He struggles to his feet and drags himself out of the alley. Totter looks out the window of their hotel room and sees Ryan collapse on the sidewalk. She runs to him and cradles her husband's head in her arms. He tells her that they have ruined his right hand forever–he can no longer box–but that it doesn't matter because "I won tonight." With tears in her eyes Totter tells him, "Yes, Bill. We both won tonight." THE SET-UP is an amazingly powerful film. Within this very simple format (the screenplay was based on a poem) director Wise and his performers present a myriad of hopes, fears, criticism, and emotions. THE SET-UP is one of the most brutal condemnations of boxing ever filmed, but no one makes speeches. Wise simply lets the sport and its fans speak for themselves. The fighting is shown as dehumanizing and cruel, while the audience is seen as a mass of animalistic maniacs who satisfy their bloodlust by living vicariously through the boxers. Everyone from the trainers, promoters, and gangsters are shown to be seedy, uneducated opportunists. Only the fighters themselves are shown to have any self-respect. Ryan gives the best performance of his career as the quiet, inarticulate fighter who is determined to stick with the brutal game because he feels that he's "just one punch away" from success. Ryan, who actually boxed for four years undefeated during his days at Dartmouth College, handles his role with great subtlety–always soft-spoken and sincere–the man clings to his simple set of beliefs and will take whatever punishment is necessary to retain his self-respect and dignity. He wins at the end because he took the worst the world had to dish out and survived with his pride intact. The fight scenes in THE SET-UP are among the best ever filmed and are only surpassed by those in Martin Scorsese's incredible RAGING BULL (1980). Cinematographer Krasner's work in THE SET-UP is outstanding. The lighting is in the best *film noir* tradition and the camera work is incredibly mobile and fluid. Enhanced by Gross' flawless editing, the film is a fast-moving, totally fast-moving, that will have viewers on the edge of their seats. A unique and fascinating film.

p, Richard Goldstone; d, Robert Wise; w, Art Cohn (based on the poem by Joseph Moncure March); ph, Milton Krasner; ed, Roland Gross; md,

Constanin Bakaleinikoff; art d, Albert S. D'Agostino, Jack Okey; set d, Darrell Silvera, James Altwies; makeup, Gordon Bau, Joe Norrin, Bill Phillips; tech adv, John Indrisano.

Sports Drama   **Cas.**   **(PR:C   MPAA:NR)**

SET-UP, THE**   (1963, Brit.) 58m Merton Park/Anglo-Amalgamated
                                                                                          bw

Maurice Denham (*Theo Gaunt*), John Carson (*Inspector Jackson*), Maria Corvin (*Nicole Romain*), Brian Peck (*Arthur Payne*), Anthony Bate (*Ray Underwood*), John Arnatt (*Supt. Ross*), Manning Wilson (*Sgt. Bates*), Billy Milton (*Simpson*).

Routine Edgar Wallace-inspired crime story about a wealthy businessman who tries to frame an ex-con for the murder of his wife by hiring him to steal his wife's jewelry and then trapping him in his house with the body.

p, Jack Greenwood; d, Gerard Glaister; w, Roger Marshall (based on a story by Edgar Wallace).

Crime   **(PR:A   MPAA:NR)**

SEVEN**   (1979) 100m Melvin Simon/AIP c

William Smith (*Drew*), Barbara Leigh (*Alexa*), Guich Koock (*Cowboy*), Art Metrano (*Kinsella*), Martin Kove (*Skip*), Richard Le Pore (*Professor*), Christopher Joy (*T.K.*), Susan Kiger (*Jennie*), Robert Relyea (*Harris*), Little Egypt (*Malie*), Lenny Montana (*Kahyuna*), Reggie Nalder (*Hermit*), Ed Parker (*Himself*), Terry Kiser (*Senator*), Tadashi Yamashita, Seth Sakai, Kwam Hi Lim, Tino Tuiolosega, Henry Ayau, John-Alderman, Terry Jastrow, Russ Howell, Peter Knecht, Red Johnson, John Thorp.

Though the film is supposed to be satirical, it's actually too real to qualify. The muddled plot doesn't help either. Smith is hired by the government to wipe out some Hawaiian gangsters. The title refers to either the number of mobsters he is supposed to kill or the $7 million dollars he is to collect if he succeeds. Plenty of violence packs the film as Smith kills mobsters in large numbers. Leigh and Kiger are his female distraction when he is not wiping out villains.

p&d, Andy Sidaris; w, William Driskill, Robert Baird (based on a story by Sidaris); prod d, Sal Grasso; spec eff, Joe Lombardi.

Comedy   **(PR:O   MPAA:R)**

SEVEN AGAINST THE SUN**½   (1968, South Africa) 115m South
                                                    African Screen Prod./Emerson Film c

Gert van den Bergh (*Corp. Smit*), John Hayter (*Lt. Mitchell*), Brian O'Shaughnessy (*Sgt. MacCarthy*), Patrick Mynhardt (*Pvt. Peters*), James White (*Pvt. Irving*), Chris Robinson (*Pvt. Louw*), Morne Coetzer, Jr (*Pvt. Harley*), Elizabeth Meyer (*Nursing Sister Bowley*).

A war drama set and filmed in South Africa. The time is 1941 and South African troops are at the northern part of the country trying to turn back the Italian Army. The army wants to set up phony broadcasts to trick the Italians into thinking there are more troops at the site than are actually there. A diverse group of seven is assigned this task. Meyer, a nurse, is picked up along the way. Troubles crop up as van den Bergh threatens to disrupt Hayter's command; O'Shaughnessy and Meyer become romantically involved; and white mixes his water with medicinal alcohol. However, when the chips are down during the fighting, all rise to the occasion.

p, David Millin, Roscoe C. Behrmann; d, Millin; spec eff, Ike Honeyball; adv, George Duxbury.

Drama   **(PR:A   MPAA:NR)**

SEVEN ALONE**   (1975) 96m Doty-Dayton c (AKA: HOUSE
                                                                      WITHOUT WINDOWS)

Dewey Martin (*Henry*), Aldo Ray (*Dr. Dutch*), Anne Collings (*Naome*), Dean Smith (*Kit*), James Griffith (*Billy*), Stewart Petersen (*John*), Dehl Berti (*White Elk*), Bea Morris (*Sally*), Scott Petersen, Debbie van Orden, Diane Petersen, Suzanne Petersen, Julie Petersen, Christy Clark, Kliss Sparks, Pat Wilde, Craig Larson, Roger Pancake, Ann David, Riley Morgan, Ann Seymour (*Narrator*).

Another entry in the rash of substandard children's films set during the westward pioneer push of the 1800's. This one tells the tale of a family of seven children who suddenly find themselves orphaned while on the Oregon Trail. Stranded, the kids decide to continue the lengthy journey on their own, helped, and sometimes obstructed, by the eccentric group of wilderness characters they meet on the way. Though inoffensive and harmless, the film is also bland and uninteresting for children as well as adults. The innocuous theme song is sung by Pat Boone.

p, Lyman D. Dayton; d, Earl Bellamy; w, Douglas Stewart, Eleanor Lamb (based on the book *On to Oregon* by Honore Morrow); ph, Robert Stumm; m, Robert O. Ragland; ed, Dan Greer; prod d, Ray Markham.

Western/Adventure   **Cas.**   **(PR:AA   MPAA:G)**

SEVEN ANGRY MEN***   (1955) 90m AA bw

Raymond Massey (John Brown), Debra Paget (Elizabeth), Jeffrey Hunter (Owen), Larry Pennell (Oliver), Leo Gordon (White), John Smith (Frederick), James Best (Jason), Dennis Weaver (John, Jr.), Guy Williams (Salmon), Tom Irish (Watson), James Anderson (Thompson), James Edwards (Green), John Pickard (Wilson), Smoki Whitfield (Newby), Jack Lomas (Doyle), Robert Simon (Col. Washington), Dabbs Greer (Doctor), Ann Tyrrell (Mrs. Brown), Robert Osterloh (Col. Robert E. Lee).

A heavy, gut-wrenching story about abolitionist John Brown and his attempt to free the slaves. Massey is the strong, dominant father who, with his six sons, gets more and more violent in his cause. The story rings somewhat true, neither making Brown a hero nor ignoring his fanatic views. Brown was eventually caught and hanged in Harper's Ferry, Virginia (later West Virginia), for attempting to lead a revolt of slaves and followers against the U.S.

p, Vincent M. Fennelly; d, Charles Marquis Warren; w, Daniel B. Ullman; ph, Ellsworth Fredericks; m, Carl Brandt; ed, Lester A. Sansom, Richard C. Meyer; md, Brandt; art d, David Milton.

Drama   (PR:A   MPAA:NR)

SEVEN BAD MEN   (SEE: RAGE AT DAWN, 1955)

SEVEN BEAUTIES***½   (1976, Ital.) 115m Medusa/Cinema 5 c
(PASQUALINO SETTEBELLEZZE; AKA: PASQUALINO: SEVEN BEAUTIES)

Giancarlo Giannini (Pasqualino Frafuso), Fernando Rey (Pedro), Shirley Stoler (Commandant), Elena Fiore (Concettina), Enzo Vitale (Don Raffaele), Mario Conti (Totonno), Piero Di Orio (Francesco), Ermelinda De Felice (Mother), Francesca Marciano (Carolina), Lucio Amelio (Lawyer), Roberto Herlitzka (Socialist), Doriglia Palmi (Doctor).

The grotesque casting, the surrealistic shooting, and the entire production make one think that Federico Fellini was in charge of this movie. But it was Wertmuller who handled the writing and directing (and garnered Oscar nominations for both). Giannini is a small-time crook in Naples during the dark days of WW II. He has seven ugly sisters, none of whom will probably ever get married, and he is busily supporting them doing whatever he can do to keep their fat bodies and souls together. Giannini is subjected to the terrors of a German prison camp, where gross Shirley Stoler is the matron and forces him to do unspeakable things to her body. In an all-out attempt to survive, Giannini does whatever it is that's necessary to keep from being killed and, finally, manages to live through the war. It's a vast picture with many memorable scenes that are each brilliant. Where the picture falters is that it bites off more than it can show so it becomes too episodic, racing from one disaster to another in an attempt to show how far a man will go to stay alive. Giannini received an Oscar nomination for his work and deserved it, if only for the amount of time he had on screen, virtually every scene. It's sad, funny, silly, and frightening and Wertmuller's message of individual anarchy is hammered across too often. It must have cost a pretty lira to make this movie, but the general feeling of having watched it is like being force fed about two more portions of your favorite pasta than you can handle. The sexual scenes and the violence are too explicit for children. (In Italian; English subtitles.)

p, Lina Wertmuller, Giancarlo Giannini, Arrigo Colombo; d&w, Wertmuller; ph, Tonino Delli Colli (Eastmancolor); m, Enzo Iannacci, ed, Franco Fraticelli; art d, Enrico Job.

War Drama   Cas.   (PR:O   MPAA:R)

SEVEN BRAVE MEN**   (1936, USSR) 91m Lenfilm/Amkino bw

N. Boguliubov (Ilya Letnikov), T. Makarova (Dr. Genia Ochrimenko), I. Novoseltzev (Pilot Bogun), O. Jakov (Radio Operator), A. Absolon (Korfunkel, Metallurgist), I. Kuznetzov (Sasha Ribnikov), P. Oleinikov (Maliboga, Cook).

Slow-moving Russian film that takes a firm grip in the final half. It follows the travels of seven Soviet explorers who set out north searching for rich mineral deposits. A blizzard takes one of their lives and a romance develops between the doctor Kuznetzov and pilot Novoseltzev. The government steps in at the end, terminating the expedition, but lets the doctor stay and minister to the barely surviving captain of the journey. (In Russian; English subtitles.)

d, S. Gerasimov; ph, G. Vellchko.

Drama   (PR:A   MPAA:NR)

SEVEN BRIDES FOR SEVEN BROTHERS***** (1954) 102m MGM c

Jane Powell (Milly), Howard Keel (Adam Pontabee), Jeff Richards (Benjamin Pontabee), Russ Tamblyn (Gideon Pontabee), Tommy Rall (Frank Pontabee), Howard Petrie (Pontabee), Ian Wolfe (Rev. Elcott), Marc Platt (Daniel Pontabee), Matt Mattox (Caleb Pontabee), Jacques d'Amboise (Ephraim Pontabee), Julie Newmeyer [Newmar] (Dorcas), Nancy Kilgas (Alice), Betty Carr (Sarah), Ruta Kilmonis [Lee] (Ruth),

Norma Doggett (Martha), Earl Barton (Harry), Dante DiPaolo (Matt), Kelly Brown (Carl), Matt Moore (Ruth's Uncle), Dick Rich (Dorcas' Father), Marjorie Wood (Mrs. Bixby), Russell Simpson (Mr. Bixby), Anna Q. Nilsson (Mrs. Elcott), Larry Blake (Drunk), Phil Rich (Prospector), Lois Hall (Girl), Russ Saunders (Swains), Terry Wilson, George Robotham (Swains), Walter Beaver (Lem), Jarma Lewis (Lem's Girl Friend), Sheila James (Dorcas' Sister), Stan [I. Stanford] Jolley, Tim Graham (Fathers).

MGM had spent a great deal of money acquiring the screen rights for stage musicals like SHOWBOAT, KISS ME KATE and others when they decided to try a few original musicals. In 1952, they had a smash with SINGIN' IN THE RAIN, and two years later attempted another original that would partially repeat the box-office success of the former. Benet's story "The Sobbin' Women" had been optioned by director-producer Josh Logan who wanted to make it into a Broadway musical and held the property for several years until he abandoned the idea and it was bought for the movies. Twenty-four years later, it would become a stage musical with new tunes by Oscar-winning songwriters Al Kasha and Joel Hirschhorn. It starred Howard Keel and Jane Powell and was produced by Kasha's brother, Lawrence ("Applause"). The talented husband-wife team of Hackett and Goodrich joined with Dorothy Kingsley to write a splendid script that had all the elements necessary for enjoyment. It was a rousing film that grossed many millions and will be remembered for years in the same category as OKLAHOMA! and CAROUSEL! for being uniquely American. The time is the middle 1800s. Keel is one of seven brothers who live and work on a huge ranch in Oregon. Keel is lonely and yearns for a voice that's higher than his so he rides into the nearest burg in search of feminine companionship. Powell is a waitress at the local eatery and when Keel shyly pops the question, she agrees to quit the hash house and become his wife, not knowing that their honeymoon cottage is filled with six more men. When she gets to the ranch, she is horrified to discover the truth and is further aghast when she sees that Keel's brothers are slovenly, boorish, ill-mannered and disrespectful. She spends the next reel or so teaching these louts how to behave in front of a lady. There's a barn-raising (all the neighbors combine to build a barn) and the brothers, Richards, Tamblyn, Rall, d'Amboise, Mattox, and Platt are there to help. The boys get bug-eyed when they see a bevy of beautiful women, including Newmeyer (Julie Newmar), Carr, Kilgas, Gibson, Kilmonis (Ruta Lee), and Doggett. When the local townboys poke fun at the brothers, there's a huge scuffle that the brothers win. Later, at the ranch, the brothers can't get those gorgeous women out of their minds and they tell Keel, the oldest, how they feel. Keel responds by relating the tale of The Sabine Women ("The Sobbin' Women") which he just read about in one of Powell's books. If the boys want these women, there's nothing to do but emulate the story, sneak into town and kidnap the beauties. The boys do just that and when the local villagers come after them, fate sends a hand and sends an avalanche down to halt the pursuit. The 12 of them arrive at the ranch and Powell can't believe that her dear husband, Keel, actually suggested such a plot. When she reads Keel off, he is hurt and leaves the ranch to spend the cold winter at his remote cabin in the mountains. He has no idea that Powell is now expecting and disappears for a few months, while Powell makes sure that the other brothers don't do anything untoward to their captives. The boys ogle the girls and vice versa but it's all as squeaky clean as a church picnic. Winter ends and the brothers embark on some wooing. The townspeople have been unable to come to the ranch to rescue the girls because the snow is as high as a giraffe's eye and there is no way they can get through until the thaw. Keel comes home to learn that he is a father and shortly thereafter, the townspeople, armed with guns, arrive–and it looks as though blood will be spilled. The sound of the baby is heard and when the girls are asked whose child it is, all six of them shout, "Mine." That occasions a shotgun wedding for the half-dozen couples as they are all happily married by the local minister, Wolfe. It was a magical blend of the right story, a corking good score, and the brilliant choreography of Michael Kidd as he handled a coterie of dancers culled from the best in Hollywood. Never mind that it was produced on MGM's extensive back lot (now a real estate development in Culver City) and that the Ansco Color process was not nearly as good as Technicolor or Eastmancolor, it is still a rollicking film with a breathless pace, well-defined characters and, an incredible vitality under Donen's direction. At the age of 30, he had already co-directed ON THE TOWN and SINGIN' IN THE RAIN with Gene Kelly, directed ROYAL WEDDING, LOVE IS BETTER THAN EVER, FEARLESS FAGAN and GIVE A GIRL A BREAK and was a show business veteran, having begun as a chorus boy at 16 in "Pal Joey," where he began his long association with Kelly. Dancer Rall is acknowledged to be one of the best and surely one of the very few who can do a triple "tour" in the air. Tamblyn's dancing was a revelation for those who thought he only played troubled teenagers. Platt came from the Radio City Music Hall and d'Amboise from the New York City Ballet. Dancer Mattox had his vocals looped by Bill Lee; and the one brother who was not heavy in the dance department was Richards, a rugged young man who never skipped a handsome lesson. Newmeyer was in her fourth film at the age of 18. She later changed her name to Newmar, appeared in many Broadway shows and films as well as her own TV series, "My Living Doll," and the recurring role as "Catwoman" on "Batman." Kilmonis changed her name to Ruta Lee, had some success on TV and stage. Townsperson Earl Barton later became a choreographer and handled dance chores for many TV shows and Las Vegas presentations. In 1970, there was an attempt to do a TV series that was loosely based on this film, although not credited. It was "Here Come the Brides" and starred Robert Brown, Joan Blondell, and Bobby Sherman. Keel's work in this film was for a mere pittance, something around $10,000, but he became instantly popular and was later signed by MGM on a long-term contract. The picture won an Oscar for Deutsch and Chaplin's scoring and took nominations for Best Picture, Best Script, and Best Cinematography. The Johnny Mercer/Gene de Paul score included: "When You're In Love" (sung by Keel, Powell), "Spring, Spring, Spring" (sung by Powell, Brothers, Brides), "Sobbin' Women" (sung by Keel, Brothers), "Bless Your Beautiful Hide" (sung by Keel), "Goin' Co'tin'" "Wonderful, Wonderful Day" (sung by Powell), "June Bride" (sung by Gibson, Brides), "Lonesome Polecat Lament" (dance number). One hundred and four minutes has seldom been packed with more effervescence.

p, Jack Cummings; d, Stanley Donen; w, Albert Hackett, Frances Goodrich, Dorothy Kingsley (based on the story "The Sobbin' Women" by Stephen Vincent Benet); ph, George Folsey (CinemaScope, Ansco Color); ed, Ralph E. Winters; md, Adolph Deutsch, Saul Chaplin; art d, Cedric Gibbons, Urie McCleary; set d, Edwin B. Willis, Hugh Hunt; cos, Walter Plunkett; ch, Michael Kidd.

Musical/Comedy   **Cas.**   **(PR:AA   MPAA:G)**

SEVEN BROTHERS MEET DRACULA, THE
(SEE: DRACULA & THE GOLDEN VAMPIRES, 1974, Brit./Hong Kong)

SEVEN CAPITAL SINS*   (1962, Fr./Ital.) 113m Gibe-Franco London-Titanus/EM bw (LES SEPT PECHES CAPITAUX; I SETTE PECCATI CAPITALI)

"Anger": Marie-Jose Nat (Young Wife), Dominique Patural (Young Husband), Jean-Marc Tennberg (Gendarme), Perrette Pradier (TV Announcer), Genevieve Casile (Rita Gerly), Claude Brasseur (Riri), Jean Murat (M. Duchemin), Jacques Monod (Mons. Jasmin, Innkeeper), Paulette Dubost (Mme. Jasmin), Paul Demange; "Gluttony": George Wilson (Valentin), Marcelle Arnold (His Wife), Magdelaine Berubet (His Mother-in-Law), Paul Preboist (Postman), Henri Virlojeux; "Lust": Laurent Terzieff (Bernard), Jean-Louis Trintignant (Paul), Paul Desailly (Father), Micheline Presle (Mother), Corinne Marchand (Girl on the Street), Nicole Mirel (Herself), Jean-Pierre Aumont (Her Husband), Sami Frey (Her Lover), Michele Girardon (Her Husband's Mistress), Daniele Barraud (Girl), Jean-Claude Brialy, Jean-Pierre Cassell, Claude Rich, Sacha Briquet, Jean-Claude Massoulier, Andre Jocelyn, Claude Berri, Michel Benoist, Andre Chanal, Serge Bento (Students).

An enjoyable, light-hearted episode film which combines the talents of many top "New Wave" directors with the seven capital sins–Anger, Envy, Gluttony, Lust, Laziness, Pride, and Greed. The most enjoyable skit is De Broca's "Gluttony," a tale of a family driving to a funeral. They stop to eat once too often, however, and arrive too late for mass, but are just on time for the funeral banquet. Vadim's "Pride" also packs a satiric punch in its telling of an adulterous wife, Vlady, who decides not to run off with her lover when she discovers that her husband, Aumont, is having an affair. More important than her lover is the need to defend her household and marriage from another woman. Godard's "Laziness" is very matter-of-fact in its story of a famous movie idol, Constantine (playing himself), who is too lazy to pay attention to the sexual advances of young starlet Mirel. Chabrol's "Greed" has a group of young men pooling their money in a raffle for a high-priced prostitute. A shy virgin wins the drawing and is befriended by the hooker, who thoughtfully refunds his portion of the money. Demy's "Lust" is set at the usual Parisian sidewalk cafe with two men talking about the girls around them. One of them, however, is lucky enough to be able to see through the girls' clothes. Molinaro's "Envy" has a chambermaid falling in love with a millionaire who spends the evening at her hotel. He takes her away, but later she returns and is jealous of the new chambermaid's romance with a coworker. The least interesting is Dhomme's "Anger" which occurs one strange day in France when flies pop up in a number of bowls of soup around town. The crazed Frenchmen get so angry they destroy the whole country. As with so many compilation films, SEVEN CAPITAL SINS is quick moving, has a couple of gems ("Gluttony" and "Pride"), a couple of average segments ("Laziness," "Greed," and "Lust") and a couple of dogs ("Envy" and "Anger"). (In French; English subtitles.)

Presented in the U.S. by Joseph Levine; "Anger": d, Sylvain Dhomme, Eugene Ionesco, Max Douy; w, Ionesco; ph, Jean Penzer; m, Michel Legrand; ed, Jacques Gaillard, Jean Feyte; "Envy": d, Edouard Molinaro; w, Claude Mauriac; ph, Louis Miaille; m, Legrand; ed, Gaillard, Feyte; "Gluttony": d, Philippe de Broca; w, Daniel Boulanger; ph, Penzer; m, Legrand; ed, Gaillard, Feyte; "Lust": d, Jacques Demy; w, Demy, Roger Peyrefitte; ph, Henri Decae; m, Legrand; ed, Gaillard, Feyte; art d, Bernard Evein; "Laziness": d&w, Jean-Luc Godard; ph, Decae; m, Legrand; ed, Gaillard, Feyte; "Pride": d, Roger Vadim; w, Vadim, Felicien Marceau; ph, Decae; m, Sacha Distel; ed, Gaillard, Feyte; "Greed": d, Claude Chabrol; w, Marceau; ph, Jean Rabier; m, Jansen; ed, Gaillard, Feyte. (Entire picture in Dyaliscope.)

Comedy   **(PR:O   MPAA:NR)**

SEVEN CITIES OF GOLD*   (1955) 103m FOX c

Richard Egan (Jose), Anthony Quinn (Capt. Portola), Michael Rennie (Father Junipero Serra), Jeffrey Hunter (Matuwir), Rita Moreno (Ula), Eduardo Noriega (Sergeant), Leslie Bradley (Galves), John Doucette (Juan Coronel), Victor Juncos (Lt. Faces), Julio Villareal (Pilot Vila), Miguel Inclan (Schrichak), Carlos Musquiz (Dr. Pratt), Pedro Galvan (Father Vizcaino), Angelo De Stiffney (Capt. Rivera), Ricardo Adalid Black (Pilot Perez), Fernando Wagner (Blacksmith), Guillermo Calles (Miscomi), Eduardo Gonzales Pliego (Axajui), Yerye Beirute (Atanuk), Anna Maria Gomez (Kukura), Jaime Gonzalez Quinones (Indian Boy), Luciel Nieto (Rano), Olga Gutierrez (Dira), Juan Jose Hurtado (Guitar Player), Jack Mower (Father), Kathleen Crowley (Mother).

The husband-and-wife team of Webb and McLean were behind this ambitious project that mixed fiction and history in an engaging adventure. There is a legend that the Indians had seven cities filled with gold and it is this story that brings Quinn and his men to the area in Mexico in the year 1769. Quinn is from Spain and doesn't know the territory so he takes Rennie, a lame Catholic priest, along with him. Rennie's goal is to establish a series of missions in the area. (In real life, the priest, Junipero Serra, actually did that and his name is seen on many streets in Southern California. There is even a real estate subdivision in Malibu called "Serra Retreat.") After several setbacks, the group finds a place to rest at what is today San Diego. Quinn leaves a group of soldiers there in the command of Egan while he travels north looking for the fabled seven cities. Hunter is the leader of some natives who attack the soldiers and when Hunter is wounded in the fracas, Rennie oversees his medical attention. Soon enough, the Indians abandon their hostile ways and Rennie sets out to convert them to his faith. Hunter's sister is Moreno and Egan finds her attractive so he goes after the Indian woman and successfully has his way with her. Meanwhile, they are running out of supplies and when Quinn returns after his unsuccessful expedition, he wants to take them all to the mountaintop where Mexico City sits. Rennie asks Quinn to reconsider for just nine days (a religiously significant period of time as it represents the novena) and wait for the possibility of supply ships to arrive from Spain. Quinn nods his approval. Moreno wants to marry Egan and is shocked when he won't do it, thereby angering Hunter and injuring the Indian's honor. Hunter insists that Egan be given to the tribe for having compromised Moreno. Quinn won't hear of it and Rennie thinks it's savage. It looks like another battle will kill all of them; then Egan sacrifices himself and gives his life in order to save the others. The ninth day arrives and Quinn readies the men to leave but stops the exodus when he sees a Spanish ship arrive in the harbor and San Diego is established as the picture fades. Some good action, more than a bit of humor and a strong performance by Quinn who plays the proud Spanish captain as though he was born to it, which, incidentally, he was. Quinn was born in Mexico in 1915 of Irish-Mexican ancestry.

p, Robert D. Webb, Barbara McLean; d, Webb; w, Richard L. Breen, John C. Higgins, Joseph Petracca (based on a novel by Isabelle Gibson Ziegler); ph, Lucien Ballard (CinemaScope, DeLuxe Color); m, Hugo Friedhofer; ed, Hugh S. Fowler; md, Lionel Newman; art d, Lyle R. Wheeler, Jack Martin Smith; cos, Adele Balkan; spec eff, Ray Kellogg.

Biography/Adventure   **(PR:A-C   MPAA:NR)**

SEVEN CITIES TO ATLANTIS   (SEE: WARLORDS OF ATLANTIS, 1978, Brit.)

SEVEN DARING GIRLS½   (1962, Ger.) 76m Rapid Film/Manson bw (INSEL DER AMAZONEN)

Adrian Hoven (Manuel), Ann Smyrner (Liz), Jan Hendriks (Murdok), Dorothee Glocklen (Colette), Beatrix Norden (Trixi), Demeter Bitenc (Leblanc), Kurt Ludwig (Muhazzin), Slavo Schwaiger (Felipe), Dora Carras (Sonja), Karin Heske (Katrin), Hertha Riedle (Pat), Nina Semona (Merci).

Seven women take off on a cargo boat for a cruise, after graduating from an exclusive boarding school in Switzerland. They party with the ship's crew, but in port they meet up with Hoven, who runs a meteorological station with his father on a remote Amazon island. While out there, Manuel's father has found a crashed airplane carrying gold ignots. Manuel goes to the mainland to tell of his father's finding and is overheard by a gangster. The gangsters head over to the island and shoot Manuel's father, but Manuel escapes. Hendriks captures some of the girls who must fight off some of the gang members' evil intentions. Eventually the rest of the girls and Manuel arrive to the rescue, but Murdok gets away only in time to be shot by the police.

p, Wolfgang Hartwig; d, Otto Meyer; w, Johannes Kai; ph, Georg Krause; m, Karl Bette; cos, Anna Hanoszek; makeup, Ladislaus Valicek.

Crime Drama   **(PR:A   MPAA:NR)**

SEVEN DAYS ASHORE*½   (1944) 74m RKO bw

Wally Brown (Monty), Alan Carney (Orval), Marcy McGuire (Dot), Gordon Oliver (Dan Arland), Virginia Mayo (Carol), Amelita Ward (Lucy), Elaine Shepard (Annabelle), Dooley Wilson (Jason), Marjorie Gateson (Mrs. Arland), Alan Dinehart (Mr. Arland), Miriam LaVelle (Hazel), Margaret Dumont (Mrs. Croxton-Lynch), Emory Parnell (Capt. Harvey), Ian Wolfe

(Process Server), Freddie Slack and Orchestra, Freddie Fisher Band *(Themselves)*, Dorothy Malone *(Betty)*, Patti Brill, Daun Kennedy, Elaine Anderson, Elaine Riley, Shirley O'Hara *(Girls in Band)*, William Haade, Charles Cane *(Bosun's Mates)*, Ruth Cherrington, Helen Dickson *(Dowagers)*, Bill Dyer *(Soldier)*, Michael St. Angel *(Marine)*.

Low-budget all the way, this is a happy tale of a sailor with too many girl friends. Oliver's boat comes in at San Francisco and he is greeted by three women, ready for his charms. He gets out of his predicament by conning two friends into helping him. After his buddies initially turn on him and then rescue him, everyone comes up happily singing at the end. Songs include: "The Poor Little Fly on the Wall," "Apple Blossoms in the Rain," "Hail and Farewell," "Sioux City Sue," "Ready, Aim, Kiss," "Jive Samba" (Mort Greene, Lew Pollack), "Improvisation in B Flat" (Freddie Fisher).

p&d, John H. Auer, W, Edward Verdier, Irving Phillips, Lawrence Kimble (based on a story by Jacques Deval); ph, Russell Metty; ed, Harry Marker; md, C. Bakaleinikoff; art d, Albert S. D'Agostino; set d, Darrell Silvera, william Stevens; spec eff, Vernon L. Walker; ch, Charles O'Curran.

Musical/Drama   **Cas.**   **(PR:A MPAA:NR)**

SEVEN DAYS IN MAY**   (1964) 120m Seven Arts-Joel/PAR bw

Burt Lancaster *(Gen. James M. Scott)*, Kirk Douglas *(Col. Martin "Jiggs" Casey)*, Fredric March *(President Jordan Lyman)*, Ava Gardner *(Eleanor Holbrook)*, Edmond O'Brien *(Sen. Raymond Clark)*, Martin Balsam *(Paul Girard)*, George Macready *(Christopher Todd)*, Whit Bissell *(Sen. Prentice)*, Hugh Marlowe *(Harold McPherson)*, Bart Burns *(Arthur Corwin)*, Richard Anderson *(Col. Murdock)*, Jack Mullaney *(Lt. Hough)*, Andrew Duggan *(Col. "Mutt" Henderson)*, John Larkin *(Col. Broderick)*, Malcolm Atterbury *(White House Physician)*, Helen Kleeb *(Esther Townsend)*, John Houseman *(Adm. Barnswell)*, Colette Jackson *(Bar Girl)*, Fredd Wayne, Rodolfo Hoyos, Clegg Hoyt.

A taut, gripping, and suspenseful political thriller which sports superb performances from the entire cast. Based on the best-selling 1962, SEVEN DAYS IN MAY begins as the President of the U.S., March, signs a nuclear disarmament treaty with the Soviets in the year 1974. This diplomatic move angers Lancaster, the head of the Joint Chiefs of Staff, who feels that March has handcuffed the military, and he plans a coup to overthrow March. With help from the other members of the Joint Chiefs, Lancaster sets the date for the revolt during the early days of May. Lancaster's loyal aide Douglas (who knows nothing of the plot) begins to notice some strange coincidences that make him suspicious of his boss. He discovers a secret Air Force base in Texas, and finds some cryptic messages being passed between Lancaster and the other Joint Chiefs. Fearing the worst, Douglas meets with March and tells him that he suspects a military coup. March dispatches one of the few men he can trust, senator O'Brien, to visit the secret air base and see what he can learn. O'Brien finds the base, but is held a captive (he eventually escapes). Meanwhile, another presidential aide, Balsam, is sent to Gibraltar to get the statement of an admiral, Houseman, who has become disillusioned with the coup and is willing to sign a statement revealing its existence and purpose. Unfortunately, Balsam is killed in a plane crash while returning to Washington with the document and Houseman denies everything. To further help uncover the plot, Douglas meets with Lancaster's former mistress, Gardner, and gets her to turn over some personal letters that will incriminate the general. Armed with the letters, March confronts Lancaster with his knowledge of the plot and demands his resignation. Lancaster refuses and claims that the public will support the coup, but March cannot bring himself to use the personal letters to hang the general. Instead, March goes on television and informs the public of the planned coup and demands the resignations of the Joint Chiefs. Though Lancaster still plans to proceed with the coup, the other Joint Chiefs back down. During his speech, March is given a note revealing that Houseman's statement was recovered among the wreckage of Balsam's plane. With proof of the conspiracy now in his hands, March is able to force Lancaster to resign and the coup is dismantled. Filmed in stark black and white and proceeding to unravel its complicated plot at a rapid clip, SEVEN DAYS IN MAY is a surprisingly exciting film that also packs a grim warning. In 1964 the world's movie screens were filled with grim dramas fretting over the deadly influence of the military-industrial complex. From the black comedy DR. STRANGELOVE to the ultra-ultra-serious SAFE, the American military was shown to be crazy, impulsive, arrogant, dangerous, and just plain stupid for relying on technology to prevent an accidental nuclear war. Instead of portraying the military as buffoons or incompetent, SEVEN DAYS IN MAY takes the premise one step further and shows the military ready to take over an entire government whose policies they cannot abide. Actor Douglas initiated the film project after reading the galley pages of the novel and decided to buy the film rights for the production company he had formed with partner Edward Lewis. Because of his work on THE MANCHURIAN CANDIDATE, Douglas approached director Frankenheimer to helm the project. Frankenheimer agreed, and it was on the strength of his participation that Lancaster was signed (the actor had worked with Frankenheimer twice before–THE YOUNG SAVAGES and BIRDMAN OF ALCATRAZ). Needless to say, the Pentagon would never have approved of the project and the filmmakers never bothered asking for their help. The Kennedy administration was enthusiastic abrut the film and offered assistance. Press Secretary Pierre Salinger even arranged for the president to take a trip to Hyannisport while

Frankenheimer shot a small riot scene in front of the White House. Salinger also allowed the filmmakers to tour the interior of the White House and take notes on the decor so it could be accurately reproduced in the studio. The Pentagon was used for one brief sequence, however, and in Gerald Pratley's book *The Cinema of John Frankenheimer*, the director explains, "We had the camera in the back of a station wagon with a black cloth over it. We put Kirk Douglas in a car, and brought him to a motel right near the Pentagon where he changed into his Marine colonel's outfit...He drove up and parked his car, got out and walked into the Pentagon. Three men saluted him. Three other officers saluted him. They really thought he was a colonel. He walked into the Pentagon. We had two cameras, each with a different lens. He turned right around, walked out, and got back into his car and drove off. This gave us entrance and exit shots. We were gone in about five minutes." Despite the successful skullduggery, the footage was deemed unnecessary and was never used. The performances in SEVEN DAYS IN MAY are stunning. Lancaster underplays the part of the slightly crazed general and makes him seem quite rational and persuasive. It is a frightening performance. Douglas is also quite good as the loyal aide who uncovers the fantastic plot that could destroy the entire country. March, Balsam, O'Brien, Bissell, and Houseman all turn in topnotch performances and it is through their conviction that the viewer becomes engrossed in this outlandish tale. Douglas and Lancaster had appeared in four films together (I WALK ALONE, GUNFIGHT AT THE O.K. CORRAL, THE DEVIL'S DISCIPLE, and THE LIST OF ADRIAN MESSENGER) and after SEVEN DAYS IN MAY there would be a 22-year hiatus until the fall of 1986 when they engaged in a bit of charming self-parody in the gangster comedy TOUGH GUYS. Thirteen years after SEVEN DAYS IN MAY Lancaster played another renegade general toying with the nuclear button in Robert Aldrich's equally gripping TWILIGHT'S LAST GLEAMING.

p, Edward Lewis; d, John Frankenheimer; w, Rod Serling (based on the novel by Fletcher Knebel, Charles Waldo Bailey II); ph, Ellsworth Fredricks; m, Jerry Goldsmith; ed, Ferris Webster; art d, Cary Odell; set d, Edward G. Boyle; makeup, Art Jones.

Drama   **Cas.**   **(PR:C MPAA:NR)**

SEVEN DAYS LEAVE**   (1930) 80m PAR bw (GB: MEDALS)

Gary Cooper *(Kenneth Dowey)*, Beryl Mercer *(Sarah Ann Dowey)*, Daisy Belmore *(Emma Mickelham)*, Nora Cecil *(Amelia Twymley)*, Tempe Piggott *(Mrs. Haggerty)*, Arthur Hoyt *(Mr. Willings)*, Arthur Metcalfe *(Colonel)*, Basil Radford *(Corporal)*, Larry Steers *(Aide-de-Camp)*.

Kind-hearted Canadian soldier Cooper lets himself be adopted by a flighty spinster in 1916, who is unhappy that she has never produced an offspring to help the boys who are fighting in WW I. Eventually they grow fond of each other and he accepts her as his "mother." When he is sent behind enemy lines and never returns, she receives his medals and, in a great tear-jerking close, she puts them carefully away and proudly resumes her former life. Cooper appropriately thoughtthe film mushy.

p, Louis D. Lighton; d, Richard Wallace; w, John Farrow, Dan Totheroh (based on the play "The Old Lady Shows Her Medals" by Sir James M. Barrie); ph, Charles Lang; m, Frank Terry; ed, George Nicholls, Jr.; art d, Bernard Herzbrun.

Drama   **(PR:A MPAA:NR)**

SEVEN DAYS LEAVE**   (1942) 87m RKO bw

Victor Mature *(Johnny Grey)*, Lucille Ball *(Terry)*, Harold Peary *(The Great Gildersleeve)*, Mapy Cortes *(Mapy)*, Ginny Simms *(Ginny)*, Marcy McGuire *(Mickey)*, Peter Lind Hayes *(Jackson)*, Walter Reed *(Ralph Bell)*, Wallace Ford *(Sgt. Mead)*, Arnold Stang *(Bitsy)*, Buddy Clark *(Clarky)*, Charles Victor *(Charles)*, King Kennedy *(Gifford)*, Charles Andre *(Andre)*, Harry Holman *(Justice of Peace)*, Addison Richards *(Capt. Collins)*, Sergio Orta *(Himself)*, Jack Gardner *(Announcer)*, Willie Fung *(Houseboy)*, Ronnie Rondell *(Miller the Chauffeur)*, Richard Martin, Frank Martinelli, Russell Hoyt *(The Financial Trio)*, Henry DeSoto *(Maitre d'Hotel)*, Charles Hall, Ed Thomas *(Waiters)*, Max Wagner *(Military Police)*, Ralph Dunn *(Cop)*, Allen Wood *(Groom)*, Charles Flynn *(Guard)*, Freddy Martin and His Orchestra, Les Brown and His Orchestra, Lynn Royce and Vanya *(Themselves)*, Cast of The Court of the Missing Heirs, Ralph Edwards and Company of Truth or Consequences.

Plenty of talent here, but no one could coordinate it. Mature is an army private in line for a tidy inheritance if he marries socialite Ball. He has seven days leave in which to win her affections, and runs into the usual problems before finally succeeding. The premise is good, but too many disjointed scenes leave it out of whack. This was the first film work for choreographer Charles Walters, who would soon climb the ladder to the top rung among MGM's musical directors. Victor Mature at the conclusion of this mixed bag joined the Coast Guard, where he remained for the rest of WW II. Songs include: "Can't Get Out of This Mood" (sung by Ginny Simms), "I Get the Neck of the Chicken" (sung by Marcy McGuire), "A Touch of Texas," "Please Won't You Leave My Girl Alone?" "Baby, You Speak My Language," "Puerto Rico," "Soft Hearted" (Frank Loesser, Jimmy McHugh).

P&d, Tim Whelan; w, William Bowers, Ralph Spence, Curtis Kenyon, Kenneth Earl; ph, Robert De Grasse; ed, Robert Wise; md, C. Bakaleinikoff;

art d, Albert S. D'Agostino, Carroll Clark; cos, Renie; spec eff, Vernon L. Walker; ch, Charles Walters.

Comedy   **(PR:A   MPAA:NR)**

SEVEN DAYS TO NOON***½   (1950, Brit.) 93m LFP-Boulting Bros./Mayer- Kingsley-Distinguished bw

Barry Jones (*Prof. Willingdon*), Olive Sloane (*Goldie*), Andre Morell (*Supt. Folland*), Sheila Manahan (*Ann Willingdon*), Hugh Cross (*Stephen Lane*), Joan Hickson (*Mrs. Peckett*), Ronald Adam (*Prime Minster*), Marie Ney (*Mrs. Willingdon*), Merrill Mueller (*American Commentator*), Geoffrey Keen, Russell Waters, Wyndham Goldie, Martin Boddey, Frederick Allen, Victor Maddern, Ian Wilson, and the People of London.

A gripping British thriller which stars the relatively unknown Jones as an atomic scientist who becomes distraught over the ignorance of the public, his fellow scientists, and his government on the subject of atomic weaponry. A chief contributor to the development of the A-bomb, Jones is driven mad and one Monday sends a letter to the prime minister, Adam. Jones' demand is that the government cease production of atomic weaponry by noon the following Sunday, or else he will obliterate London with a bomb he has stolen. Adams and his staff respond coolly, failing to see the seriousness of Jones' threat. Scotland Yard head Morell gets to work on the investigation, but there seems to be no real urgency. As the suspense and anticipation builds, so does the sense of danger. London is evacuated, leaving streets and homes deserted. The hunt is on for Jones, who scampers around clutching in his briefcase the bomb which could bring about the death of London. The clock ticks away and the doomsday deadline of 12:00 Sunday nears quickly. Suspense builds to an unbearable level. Scotland Yard watches the final minutes tick away. Madman Jones, with tufts of hair protruding from the sides of his head, prepares to detonate the bomb. But a nuclear holocaust is averted when Jones is located and his bomb defused. Using as a basis the real-life fears of the public, SEVEN DAYS TO NOON attempts to teach a lesson to its audience–the same lesson that Jones preaches but without the fatal consequences. In lesser hands, the fine story (which won an Oscar for Dehn and Bernard) would have become little more than an anti-nuclear propaganda picture or, at very least, a poor suspense film, but the talented Boulting brothers manage to sustain interest throughout. By combining a brilliant creation of suspense, a stark newsreel-style evacuation sequence, and a superb cast of unknown actors, SEVEN DAYS TO NOON exudes a frightening sense of urgency. Jones is truly compelling as the scientist (real-life physicist Robert J. Oppenheimer taken to the dramatic extreme) whose mind is numbed by his sense of moral indignation. The film's supporting cast is also worth mention, especially Manahan as the daughter who tries to bring Jones to his senses, and Sloane as the aging music hall entertainer who innocently harbors the scientist. A topical subject in 1950 (only five years after the first atomic attack), the threat of nuclear war was still a relevant subject for films three decades later with such pictures as TESTAMENT and the television films THE DAY AFTER and SPECIAL BULLETIN (all 1983).

p, Roy Boulting; d, John Boulting; w, Roy Boulting, Frank Harvey (based on a story by Paul Dehn, James Bernard); ph, Gilbert Taylor, Ray Sturgess; m, John Addison; ed, Roy Boulting; md, Dr. Hubert Clifford; art d, John Elphick.

Drama   **(PR:C   MPAA:NR)**

SEVEN DEADLY SINS, THE***   (1953, Fr./Ital.) 124m Arlan bw

"Avarice and Anger": Eduardo de Filippo (*Eduardo*), Isa Miranda (*Mme. Alvaro*), Paolo Stoppa (*Alvaro*), Jacqueline Plessis (*Laziness*), Louis de Funes (*The Frenchman*), Madeleine Barbulee (*1st Secretary*), Frank Villard (*Ravila*), Francette Vernillat (*Chantel*), Jacques Fabbrias (*Julien*), Maurice Ronetas (*The Cure*), Orfeo Tamburi (*Oliver*), Claudine Dupuis (*The Wife*), Jean Richard (*The Husband*), Francoise Rosay (*The Mother*), Jean Debucourt (*M. Signac*), Marcelle Praince (*The President*), Louis Seigner (*Uncle Henri*).

A compilation by some of the highest names in Italian and French filmmaking put together this seven part movie. Five parts are in French and two are in Italian. All are well-edited and contain clear, clean dialog. They all deal with some sort of human emotion, lust, greed, gluttony, laziness, etc. One shows a miser losing not only his money, but also his wife. Another shows the difference between puppy love and pure passion by adults. In one, a cat becomes the object of a woman's affection, rather than her husband, while another shows how a haughty mother and daughter, once on the social register, fall into poverty. The eighth and final sin? Philipe dresses up this surprise ending with his legendary masculine charm.

"Avarice and Anger": d, Eduardo de Filippo; w, Charles Spaak; ph, Enzo Serafin; "Sloth": d, Jean Dreville; w, Carlo Rim; ph, Andre Thomas; "Lust": d, Yves Allegret; w, Pierre Bost, Jean Aurenche; ph, Roger Hubert; "Envy": d, Roberto Rossellini; w, Rossellini (based on a story by Colette); ph, Serafin; "Gluttony": d&w, Rim; ph, Robert Le Fevre; "Pride": d, M. Autant-Lara; w, P. Bost, J. Aurenche, Claude Autant-Lara; "The Eighth Sin": d, Georges Lacombe; w, P Bost, Aurenche; ph, Andre Bac.

Drama   **(PR:A   MPAA:NR)**

SEVEN DIFFERENT WAYS   (SEE: QUICK, LET'S GET MARRIED, 1965)

SEVEN DOORS TO DEATH*½   (1944) 64m PRC bw

Chick Chandler (*Jimmy McMillan*), June Clyde (*Mary Rawling*), George Meeker (*Charles Eaton*), Michael Raffetto (*Capt. William Jaffe*), Gregory Gaye (*Henry Butler*), Edgar Dearing (*Claude Burns*), Rebel Randall (*Mable De Rose*), Milton Wallace (*Donald Adams*), Casey MacGregor (*Timothy Green*).

A poorly made tale with little to offer. Chandler is a young architect entangled in a crime who solves it to avoid being placed under suspicion himself. All the characters act and look suspicious. The seven doors to death are six shop entrances and one courtyard entrance from an apartment building where the other key people in the stagey drama go through the motions of acting guilty until the tame denouement.

p, Alfred Stern; d&w, Elmer Clifton (based on a story by Helen Kiely); ph, Robert Cline; ed, Charles Henkle, Jr.; md, Lee Zahler.

Murder Mystery   **Cas.**   **(PR:A   MPAA:NR)**

SEVEN DWARFS TO THE RESCUE, THE**½
(1965, Ital.) 84m P.W.T. Produzione/Childhood Productions bw (I SETTE NANI ALLA RISCOSSA)

Rossana Podesta (*Snow White*), Roberto Risco (*Prince Charming*), Georges Marchal (*Prince of Darkness*), Ave Ninchi, Salvatore Furnari, Francesco Gatto, Ulisse Lorenzelli, Mario Mastrantonio, Giovanni Solinas, Arturo Tosi, Domenico Tosi, Rossana Martini, Guido Celano, Pietro Tordi, Amedeo Trilli.

Almost an Italian sequel to Disney's "Snow White and the Seven Dwarfs." Snow White and her Prince Charming have gone on to rule the kingdom where her former buddies live. The Prince of Darkness arrives and begins to scare the people who live there. Prince Charming and his army ride off to stop him but are captured. Snow White goes to the rescue and gets herself caught by the evil prince. The Seven Dwarfs, using all kinds of charming tricks, come to the aid of Prince Charming, who in turn rescue Snow White.

p,d&w, Paolo William Tamburella; (based on characters from the Grimm Brothers fairy tale); ph, Aldo Giordani; ed, Giuseppe Vari.

Fantasy   **(PR:A   MPAA:NR)**

711 OCEAN DRIVE***   (1950) 102m Essaness/COL bw

Edmond O'Brien (*Mal Granger*), Joanne Dru (*Gail Mason*), Donald Porter (*Larry Mason*), Sammy White (*Chippie Evans*), Dorothy Patrick (*Trudy Maxwell*), Barry Kelley (*Vince Walters*), Otto Kruger (*Carl Stephans*), Howard St. John (*Lt. Pete Wright*), Robert Osterloh (*Gizzi*), Bert Freed (*Marshak*), Carl Milletaire (*Joe Gish*), Charles La Torre (*Rocco*), Fred Aldrich (*Peterson*), Charles Jordan (*Tim*), Sidney Dubin (*Mendel Weiss*).

711 OCEAN DRIVE was one of those pictures that had more success than it deserved because it was released at precisely the right time. The U.S. newspapers were filled with bookmaking scandals in several cities and this movie was noted by some lawmakers in Washington for its documentary realism. O'Brien is an average Joe who works hard at his telephone company repair job. One of his calls is to a large bookmaking establishment where he meets Kelley and Walters, the two men who run the operation. Both are slick operators and are taken by O'Brien's ingenious ways around wires. They realize that a telephone repairman can't earn all that much money, so they offer him some cash if he'll fix up a system that will bring them the race results of faraway tracks. O'Brien is seduced by the thought of riches and goes in with Kelley and Porter. It isn't long before O'Brien has eyes for Kelley's position and Porter's wife, Dru. When Kelley is mysteriously killed, O'Brien takes over. Soon enough, he is involved with Dru, and Kruger, who heads a larger bookie operation, wants a piece of the action. Porter is killed and O'Brien seems to have everything he wants until Kruger decides that he wants to muscle O'Brien out. By this time, O'Brien has murdered, cheated, and been an all-around nogoodnick and so we don't much care when he gets his in an exciting climax filmed at Hoover Dam. When he tries to cross the dam on foot while being chased by syndicate killers, he is shot and falls to his death in the raging waters. Kruger is excellent as the oily mob chief and St. John does his usual good work as a police detective. O'Brien's character is not unlike the undercover cop he played in WHITE HEAT, except that this time he is an unregenerate crook and killer and gets what's coming to him. Films where the protagonists are criminals are hard to engender sympathy for, so it just makes Francis Ford Coppola's work in both GODFATHERs that much more outstanding.

p, Frank N. Seltzer; d, Joseph M. Newman; w, Richard English, Francis Swan; ph, Franz F. Planer; m, Sol Kaplan; ed, Bert Jordan; md, Emil Newman; prod d, Perry Ferguson; set d, Howard Bristol; cos, Odette Myrtil, Athena; makeup, Jack Byron; tech adv, Lt. William Burns (Los Angeles Police Department), Edwin Block.

Crime   **(PR:C   MPAA:NR)**

SEVEN FACES*½   (1929) 78m FOX bw

Paul Muni (*Papa Chibou*), Marguerite Churchill (*Helene Berthelot*), Lester Lonergan (*Judge Berthelot*), Russell Gleason (*Georges Dufeyel*), Gustav von Seyffertitz (*Mons. Pratouchy*), Eugenie Besserer (*Mme. Vallon*), Walter Rogers (*Henri Vallon*), Walka Stenermann (*Wax - "Catherine of Russia"*).

Muni's second starring feature – he'd gotten an Academy Award nomination for his first, THE VALIANT, released the same year – has the great character actor essaying seven different roles. Muni is the aged caretaker of a bankrupt wax museum in Paris. When the figures in the museum are auctioned off, he makes a bid for his favorite, Napoleon Bonaparte. Outbid, he steals the figure and is tried for the crime before austere magistrate Lonergan. Defended by young attorney Gleason (the son of actors James and Lucille Gleason, in his first year as a featured player), who had used the wax museum as a trysting place in his romance with Lonergan's daughter Churchill, Muni is ultimately exonerated. In attempting to further the romance of the young lovers, Muni dreams that he is six of the historical figures represented by waxen images in the defunct museum, including Napoleon, Franz Schubert, Don Juan, and Svengali, each of whom offers advice anent *amour*. The dreams include a multiply exposed ballet sequence in this tour de force for the great actor of the Yiddish theater, who had come to Hollywood's attention only after his first English-speaking Broadway stage role three years previously. Muni made many brief personal appearances in theaters to promote this production. He was discouraged by studio press reports which compared him with Lon Chaney, the great master of monsters. Muni stated, "I'm an actor. I play *any* part." Muni, unaccustomed to the speed of Hollywood production, was disappointed in this film; he felt that he had not been allowed enough time to develop either his characterizations or his makeup. He went back to the Broadway stage after this, returning to Hollywood and ultimate triumph in two major releases of 1932, SCARFACE and I AM A FUGITIVE FROM A CHAIN GANG. This was also lovely actress Churchill's first year as a featured player; she had worked with Muni in THE VALIANT, released earlier that year. The studio thought well enough of her charms to include a brief, utterly gratuitous shot of her in her lingerie in this one. Like many early talkies, this one had dual direction; the directors who were experienced with the visuals of the silents were unfamiliar with the requirements of dialog. The dialog direction was handled by actor Lonergan, the visual by codirector Viertel.

p, George Middleton; d, Berthold Viertel; w, Dana Burnett (based on the story "Friend of Napoleon" by Richard Connell); ph, Joseph August, Al Brick; ed, Ed Robbins; set d, William S. Darling; cos, Sophie Wachner.

Drama   (PR:A MPAA:NR)

SEVEN FACES OF DR. LAO***½ (1964) 100m Galaxy-Scarus/MGM
                                                                             c

Tony Randall (*Dr. Lao/Merlin the Magician/Pan/The Abominable Snowman/Medusa/The Giant Serpent/Apollonius of Tyana*), Barbara Eden (*Angela Benedict*), Arthur O'Connell (*Clint Stark*), John Ericson (*Ed Cunningham*), Noah Beery, Jr (*Tim Mitchell*), Lee Patrick (*Mrs. Howard T. Cassan*), Minerva Urecal (*Kate Lindquist*), John Qualen (*Luther Lindquist*), Frank Kreig (*Peter Ramsey*), Peggy Rea (*Mrs. Peter Ramsey*), Eddie Little Sky (*George G. George*), Royal Dano (*Carey*), Argentina Brunetti (*Sarah Benedict*), John Doucette (*Lucas*), Dal McKennon (*Lean Cowboy*), Frank Cady (*Mayor James Sargent*), Chubby Johnson (*Fat Cowboy*), Douglas Fowley (*Toothless Cowboy*), Kevin Tate (*Mike Benedict*).

A wonderful fantasy from puppeteer Pal, whose futurist fancies have delighted so many, this one is set in the Oold West. Randall is Dr. Lao, the oriental prestidigitator who rides into the town of Abalone with his strange circus. He finds the welfare of the good citizens threatened by the land-grabbing activities of villain O'Connell, who knows that the railroad is soon to come to the area. The major recipient of the wretch's wrath is young crusading newspaper editor Ericson, who tries to prevent O'Connell's takeover of the town while simultaneously wooing lovely widow Eden. Randall, as Lao, attempts to foster both these commendable aspirations by exposing the citizens to some homely truths. He does this through the medium of the bizarre creations that populate his strange circus tent, all played by Randall who, despite his virtuoso multiple performances, disliked the film. A reformed O'Connell, shown the error of his grasping ways, recants, but not so his henchmen. They savage Ericson's newspaper, but Randall magically redeems it. Frustrated, they shoot at what they believe to be Randall's pet fish, which proves to be a sea monster reduced in size through Randall's strange powers. The monster grows, acquiring seven heads in the process, and pursues the bad band. Randall saves them at his own risk and again reduces the monster to pet-like proportions. Excellent performances and special effects, including a few scenes from Pal's ATLANTIS, THE LOST CONTINENT (1961). Makeup man William Tuttle won the first of only two special Academy Awards for his work on this film, before the category was permanently established in 1981 (the second went to PLANET OF THE APES in 1968).

p&d, George Pal; w, Charles Beaumont (based on the novel *The Circus of Dr. Lao* by Charles G. Finney); ph, Robert Bronner (Metrocolor); m, Leigh Harline; ed, George Tomasini; art d, George W. Davis, Gabriel Scognamillo; set d, Henry Grace, Hugh Hunt; spec eff, Paul Byrd, Wah Chang, Jim Danforth, Ralph Rodine, Robert R. Hoag; makeup, William Tuttle.

Fantasy   Cas.   (PR:A MPAA:NR)

SEVEN FOOTPRINTS TO SATAN*½   (1929) 60m FN bw

Thelma Todd (*Eve*), Creighton Hale (*Jim*), Sheldon Lewis (*The Spider*), William V. Mong (*The Professor*), Sojin (*Himself*), Laska Winters (*Satan's Mistress*), Ivan Christy (*Jim's Valet*), De Witt Jennings (*Uncle Joe*), Nora Cecil (*Old Witch*), Kalla Pasha (*Prof. Von Viede*), Harry Tenbrook (*Eve's Chauffeur*), Cissy Fitzgerald (*Old Lady*), Angelo Rossitto (*The Dwarf*), Thelma McNeil (*Tall Girl*).

This strange item has Hale, a collector of curios, in love with Todd, a jewel collector's daughter. When a valuable gem is missing from a reception in Todd's home under strange circumstances, the two set out in search of it. They end up taking a wild ride en route to the police, with their final destination being the abode of a man known only as Satan. The place is populated by a variety of unusual characters, including Rossitto, a dwarf who befriends the pair. A masked ball is held and Satan's henchmen make off with Todd, demanding the jewel under threat of torture. After some further harrowing adventures the lovers are reunited, though their respective mental conditions are less than intact. Bizarre, to say the least, and a forgotten classic for fans of the "so-bad-it's-good" genre. Todd later proved to be a comedian of some merit in her work with the Marx Brothers. Rossitto undoubtedly was one of cinema's most prolific little people. Beginning with his debut in 1927's THE BELOVED ROGUE (featuring John Barrymore), Rossitto appeared in over 200 different films including FREAKS (1932) and his featured role as "Master" in MAD MAX BEYOND THUNDERDOME (1985). He also served as a double for Shirley Temple in several of her features, operated a Hollywood newstand (customers included Charlie Chaplin and the Barrymores), ran an unsuccessful campaign for mayor of Los Angeles in 1941, and was one of the founding fathers of the Little People of America.

p, Wid Gunning; d, Benjamin Christensen; ph, Sol Polito; ed, Frank Ware.

Mystery/Drama   (PR:C MPAA:NR)

SEVEN GOLDEN MEN*½   (1969, Fr./Ital./Span.) 87m Atlantica
     Cinematografica-Pari s Union-As Film Produccion/WB c (SEPT
     HOMMES EN OR; SETTE UOMINI D'ORO; SIETE HOMBRES DE
                                                          ORO)

Rossana Podesta (*Giorgia*), Philippe Leroy (*Albert*), Gastone Moschin (*Adolf*), Gabriele Tinti (*Aldo*), Jose Suarez (*Bank Manager*), Giampiero Albertini (*August*), Dario De Grassi (*Anthony*), Manuel Zarzo (*Alfonso*), Maurice Poli (*Alfred*), Ennio Balbo (*Police Chief*), Alberto Bonucci (*Radio Ham*), Renzo Palmer, Renato Terra, Juan Luis Gagliardo, Juan Cortez, Gianni Di Benedetto.

The devilish devices and methods used to extract seven tons of gold bars from the Swiss National Bank, plus the charms of the pulchritudinous Podesta, are the making of this multinational heist picture. Mastermind Leroy and his six selected outside accomplices pose as a crew of city workers to tunnel their way into the Geneva water system and scuba to a spot under the vault, guided by a radar device positioned by inside-woman Podesta. The gold, recast as brass, is shipped to Rome. Leroy turns his comrades in to border guards, pointing out that their passports are fake; Podesta, in turn, tries to double-cross him while on the journey to Rome. All arrive safely, however, and agree to split the gold fairly. Before they can do so, the truck transporting the gold meets with an accident and spreads the goodies on a public thoroughfare. The robbers regroup and plan to loot the Bank of Rome.

p&d, Marco Vicario; w, Vicario, Mariano Ozores, Noelle Gillmor, ph, Ennio Guarnieri (Eastmancolor); m, Armando Trovajoli; ed, Roberto Cinquini, Pedro del Rey; md, Trovajoli; prod d, Jaime Perez Cubero; art d, Piero Poletto, Arrigo Equini; set d, Dario Micheli; cos, Gaia Romanini; makeup, Michele Trimarchi.

Crime Drama   (PR:A MPAA:G)

SEVEN GRAVES FOR ROGAN   (SEE: TIME TO DIE, A, 1983)

SEVEN GUNS FOR THE MACGREGORS**½ (1968, Ital./Span.) 94m
     Produzione D. S.-Jolly Film-Estela Films/COL c (7 PISTOLE PER I
     MACGREGOR; SIETE PISTOLAS PARA LOS MACGREGOR)

Robert Woods (*Gregor MacGregor*), Manuel Zarzo (*David MacGregor*), Nick Anderson [Nazareno Zamperla] (*Peter MacGregor*), Paul Carter [Paolo Magalotti] (*Kenneth MacGregor*), Julio Perez Tabernero (*Mark MacGregor*), Saturnino Cerra (*Johnny MacGregor*), Albert Waterman [Alberto Dell'Acqua] (*Dick MacGregor*), Agatha Flory [Agata Flori] (*Rosita Carson*), Leo Anchoriz (*Santillana*), Perla Cristal (*Perla*), Georges Rigaud (*Alastair MacGregor*), Harry Cotton (*Harold MacGregor*), Fernando Sancho (*Miguel*), Anne-Marie Noe [Ana Maria Noe] (*Mamie MacGregor*), Margaret Horowitz [Margherita Orowitz] (*Annie MacGregor*), Raphael Bardem (*Justice Garland*), Antonio Molino Rojo (*Sheriff*), Cris Huerta (*Crawford*), Max Dean [Massimo Righi], Peter Cross [Pierre Cressoy], Jesus Puente.

This Italian-Spanish western comedy is entertaining and well written. Story has the MacGregors as ranchers of Scottish descent living on the Mexican border. They find themselves at odds with the town's corrupt sheriff, Rojo, the town's horse dealer, played by Huerta, and some Mexican bandits. When Huerta doesn't give them a fair deal for their horses, the seven brothers start a fight and wind up in jail. Upon their release, they find that their horses have been stolen by some Mexican bandits. They call upon the help of Sheriff Rojo, only to find that he's in cahoots with Anchoriz, leader of the bandits. The seven brothers set out to get their horses back, but wind up getting captured by the outlaws. They are freed by their bagpipe-playing elderly MacGregors, who kill or capture the bandits and sheriff. Anchoriz is killed by his discarded mistress, Cristal, and Woods comes home to marry his betrothed, Flory. (Sequel: UP THE MAC GREGORS.)

p, Ted O'Darsa [Dario Sabatello]; d, Frank Garfield [Franco Giraldi]; w, Vincent Eagle [Enzo Dell'Aquila], Fernando Lion [Fernando di'Leo], David Moreno, Duccio Tessari (based on a story by Moreno); ph, Alejandro Ulloa (Techniscope, Technicolor); m, Ennio Morricone; ed, Nino Baragli, Mario Morra, Antonio Ramirez; md, Bruno Nicolai; art d, Jaime Perez Cubero; cos, Karl Kinds.

Western Comedy   **(PR:A   MPAA:NR)**

SEVEN GUNS TO MESA*½   (1958) 69m AA bw

Charles Quinlivan (*John Trey*), Lola Albright (*Julie Westcott*), James Griffith (*Clellan*), Jay Adler (*Ben Avery*), Burt Nelson (*Bear*), John Merrick (*Brown*), Charles Keane (*Marsh*), Jack Carr (*Sam Denton*), Don Sullivan (*Louis Middleton*), Rush Williams (*Duncan*), Reed Howes (*Stage Driver*), Mauritz Hugo (*Lt. Franklin*), Dan Sheridan (*Simmons*), Gerald Frank (*Grandall*), Harvey Russell.

A mediocre western about a group of stagecoach passengers who are held hostage by an outlaw gang. The gang decides to use them as leverage until they can pull off the robbery of a gold shipment. Guns are fired, outlaws are felled, and the passengers are freed before it is all over with a bang.

p, William F. Broidy; d, Edward Dein; w, Myles Wilder, Edward Dein, Mildred Dein (based on the story by Wilder); ph, John J. Martin; m, Leith Stevens; ed, Thor Brooks; art d, George Troast; cos, Byron Munson.

Western   **(PR:A   MPAA:NR)**

SEVEN HILLS OF ROME, THE** (1958) 107m LeCloud-Titanus/MGM
                                                                                              c

Mario Lanza (*Marc Revere*), Renato Rascel (*Pepe Bonelli*), Marisa Allasio (*Rafaella Marini*), Peggie Castle (*Carol Ralston*), Clelia Matania (*Beatrice*), Rossella Como (*Anita*), Amos Davoli (*Carlo*), Guido Celano (*Luiggi*), Carlo Rizzo (*Director of Ulpia Club*), Marco Tulli (*Romoletto*), Giorgio Gandos (*Commissario Rugarello*), Carlo Guiffre (*Franco Cellis*), Adriana Hart (*Landlady*), Patrick Crean (*Mr. Fante*), Pennachi (*Helicopter Pilot*), April Hennessy (*Mrs. Stone*), Stuart Hart (*Miller*), Luisa DiMeo (*Street Singer*).

Purely a showcase for Lanza's big screen comeback, with a bare storyline as a basis to show off his fantastic singing talents. Plot involves Lanza as a big TV star whose girl friend, Castle, takes off to Rome after they have a lovers' quarrel. He follows in an attempt to woo her back, but instead meets up with local girl, Alassio, and before the film ends they fall in love. The photography of Rome is more dazzling than the plot, although Lanza does do some clever impersonations of Dean Martin, Frankie Laine, Louis Armstrong, and Perry Como. Songs include: "Arrivederci Roma" (Renato Rascel, Carl Sigman), "Seven Hills of Rome," "Never Till Now" (John Green, Paul Francis Webster), "Earthbound" (Jack Taylor, Clive Richardson, Bob Muset), "Come Dance With Me," "Lolita," "There's Gonna Be a Party Tonight," "Italian Calypso," "Questa o Quella" (from "Rigoletto" by Guiseppe Verdi), "Imitation Routine," "Temptation" (Arthur Freed, Nacio Herb Brown), "Jezebel" (Wayne Shanklin), "When the Saints Go Marching In" (traditional), "Memories Are Made of This" (Terry Gilkyson, Richard Dehr, Frank Miller).

p, Lester Welch; d, Roy Rowland; w, Art Cohn, Giorgio Prosperi (based on a story by Giuseppi Amato); ph, Tonino Delli Colli, Franco Delli Colli (Technirama, Technicolor); m, George Stoll; ed, Gene Ruggiero; md, Irving Aaronson; set d, Piero Filippone; cos, Maria Barony Cecchi; ch, Paul Steffen; makeup, Otello Fava.

Musical   **(PR:A   MPAA:NR)**

SEVEN KEYS*½   (1962, Brit.) 57m Independent Artists/AA bw

Jeannie Carson (*Shirley Steele*), Alan Dobie (*Russell*), Delphi Lawrence (*Natalie Worth*), John Carson (*Norman*), John Lee (*Jefferson*), Anthony Nicholls (*Governor*), Robertson Hare (*Mr. Piggott*), Fabia Drake (*Mrs. Piggott*), Alan White (*Warder*), Colin Gordon (*Mr. Barber*), Peter Barkworth (*Estate Agent*).

A well-worn crime picture about an ex-convict who sets out to locate his dead cellmate's hidden cache. A tame entry directed by former WW II documentarian, Jackson, whose later works failed to make any impact on audiences.

p, Julian Wintle, Leslie Parkyn; d, Pat Jackson; w, Jack Davies, Henry Blyth; m, Alan Clare.

Crime   **(PR:A   MPAA:NR)**

SEVEN KEYS TO BALDPATE**   (1930) 72m RKO bw

Richard Dix (*William Magee*), Miriam Seegar (*Mary Norton*), Margaret Livingston (*Myra Thornhill*), Joseph Allen (*Peters*), Lucien Littlefield (*Thomas Hayden*), De Witt Jennings (*Mayor Cargan*), Carleton Macy (*Kennedy*), Nella Walker (*Mrs. Rhodes*), Joe Herbert (*Max*), Alan Roscoe (*Bland*), Harvey Clark (*Elijah Quimby*), Edith Yorke (*Mrs. Quimby*), Crauford Kent (*Hal Bentley*).

This picture was the third of five adaptations of Earl Derr Biggers' novel. The first version was made in 1917 with George M. Cohan, who had also written a successful stageplay version of the book, with the second silent adaptation done in 1925 starring Douglas MacLean. RKO would go on to make two more versions after this, with Gene Raymond in 1935 and Phillip Terry in 1947. Story centers on Dix, as a writer who is soon to be married, but must first complete an overdue novel. He locks himself away in the Baldpate Inn and sets out to complete the book in one day. But his peace and quiet are disrupted when $200,000 is stolen, causing a beehive of activity at the inn. The local police arrest everyone except Dix, and after the money is recovered and the criminal apprehended, the audience discovers that everything that has happened is just part of Dix's novel. A trite ending, but overall an enjoyable, undemanding mystery comedy.

p, Louis J. Sarecky; d, Reginald Barker; w, Jane Murfin (based on the play by George M. Cohan, from the story by Earl Derr Biggers'; ph, Edward Cronjager.

Comedy/Mystery   **(PR:A   MPAA:NR)**

SEVEN KEYS TO BALDPATE**½   (1935) 80m RKO bw

Gene Raymond (*Magee*), Margaret Callahan (*Mary*), Eric Blore (*Bolton*), Erin O'Brien-Moore (*Myra*), Moroni Olsen (*Cargan*), Grant Mitchell (*Hayden*), Ray Mayer (*Bland*), Henry Travers (*The Hermit*), Murray Alper (*Max*), Erville Alderson (*Police Chief*), Harry Beresford (*Quimby*), Emma Dunn (*Mrs. Quimby*), Monte Vandergrift (*Deputy*), Walter Brennan (*Station Agent*), Philip Morris.

The fourth version of Earl Derr Biggers' novel and RKO's second remake. Raymond steps into the role of the writer and soon-to-be husband who must finish an over-due manuscript. Raymond sets out to do it in 24 hours and makes his camp in the Baldpate Inn. $200,000 is stolen and a long list of crazy characters keep interrupting Raymond's concentration. Blore is the detective trying to solve the crime with Callahan, the writer's female distraction, and Alper the culprit of the crime. Walter Brennan has a small but funny bit part at the beginning of the film.

p, William Sistrom; d, William Hamilton, Edward Killy; w, Wallace Smith, Anthony Veiller (based on the play by George M. Cohan, from the novel by Earl Derr Biggers); ph, Robert de Grasse; ed, Desmond Marquette.

Comedy/Mystery   **(PR:A   MPAA:NR)**

SEVEN KEYS TO BALDPATE**   (1947) 68m RKO bw

Phillip Terry (*Magee*), Jacqueline White (*Mary*), Eduardo Ciannelli (*Cargan*), Margaret Lindsay (*Connie Lane*), Arthur Shields (*Bolton*), Jimmy Conlin (*Hermit*), Tony Barrett (*Max*), Richard Powers (*Bland*), Jason Robards, Sr (*Hayden*).

The fifth and last version of the Earl Derr Biggers novel about a writer who must finish his novel in 24 hours and sets up shop in the remote Baldpate Inn to do it. But peace and quiet are not to be found for Terry. He's made a bet with White, the inn's secretary, that he'll finish the book, and White sets out to make sure he doesn't. While she's trying to frighten Terry into writer's block, a gang of jewel thieves arrive at the inn to split the profits of their latest heist. With all this going on around him, Terry finds himself in a number of situations that keep him from his typewriter. Jack Haley was supposed to play the writer, but refused to do so, which caused the cancellation of his contract with RKO. RKO's two earlier versions of this film were released in 1930 and 1935, with the first two silent versions filmed in 1917 and 1925.

p, Herman Schlom; d, Lew Landers; w, Lee Loeb (based on the play by George M. Cohan, from the novel by Earl Derr Biggers); ph, Jack MacKenzie; m, Paul Sawtell; ed, J.R. Whittredge; md, C. Bakaleinikoff; art d, Albert S. D'Agostino, Lucius O. Croxton.

Comedy/Mystery   **(PR:A   MPAA:NR)**

SEVEN LITTLE FOYS, THE***½   (1955) 95m PAR c

Bob Hope (*Eddie Foy*), Milly Vitale (*Madeleine Morando*), George Tobias (*Barney Green*), Angela Clarke (*Clara*), Herbert Heyes (*Judge*), Richard Shannon (*Stage Manager*), Billy Gray (*Brynie*), Lee Erickson (*Charley*), Paul De Rolf (*Richard Foy*), Lydia Reed (*Mary Foy*), Linda Bennett (*Madeleine Foy*), Jimmy Baird (*Eddie, Jr.*), James Cagney (*George M. Cohan*), Tommy Duran (*Irving*), Lester Matthews (*Father O'Casey*), Joe Evans, George Boyce (*Elephant Act*), Oliver Blake (*Santa Claus*), Milton Frome (*Driscoll*), King Donovan (*Harrison*), Jimmy Conlin (*Stage Doorman*), Marian Carr (*Soubrette*), Harry Cheshire (*Stage Doorman at Iroquois*), Renata Vanni (*Italian Ballerina Mistress*), Betty Uitti (*Dance Specialty Double*), Noel Drayton (*Priest*), Jack Pepper (*Theater Manager*), Dabbs Greer (*Tutor*), Billy Nelson

(Customs Inspector), Joe Flynn *(2nd Priest)*, Jerry Mathers *(Brynie at Age 5)*, Lewis Martin *(Presbyterian Minister)*, Eddie Foy, Jr *(Narrator)*.

Engaging musical biography based on the life of vaudevillian actor Eddie Foy. Funny and heart-warming account but just a little too contrived for its own good. Hope tried vainly to bring a different persona to the screen than had been previously seen, but, with two of his old radio writers doing the script, the one-liners came thick and fast. Hope marries Vitale, an Italian beauty, after decreeing to one and all that he'll always do a "single," both on stage and in his domestic life. They have seven children in no time at all and Vitale pays the price for her efforts by dying and inconveniently leaving Hope with the septet: Gray, Bennett, De Rolf, Reed, Duran, Erickson, and Baird. Hope is not a sensational father, preferring to spend his time doing his act and cavorting with his cronies. When Vitale passes on, Hope is forced to pay more attention to the kids and he forges them into a vaudeville act, which they immediately begin to steal. With Foy's son, Eddie, Jr., doing the narrating, we are taken through the various episodes of the family's life, including the famous night when Foy saved a packed theater from panic as he helped usher them out of the Iroquois in Chicago. The highlight of the film occurs near the end when the legendary Friars Club tosses a dinner for Hope and his great pal Cagney (reprising his Oscar-winning role as George M. Cohan) gets on stage with him. The two men throw some fast and furious jokes back and forth, then wind up in a splendid dance routine to cap the proceedings. Cagney was excellent and gave a lift to the movie just when it needed it, because the cuteness was beginning to pall. Cagney reportedly did the role for no pay, even though the two men rehearsed for 10 days in preparation for the dance routine. Two of the real Foy boys went into show business. Eddie, Jr. became a comedian and comic actor who may be best remembered for his role in PAJAMA GAME and his brief TV series "Fair Exchange." His son, Eddie, III, became a casting director and later a TV producer. Bryan Foy (...Brynie...), the oldest, wrote "Mr. Gallagher and Mr. Shean" routines for the comedians of the same name. Later, Bryan Foy became an enormously prolific producer of low-budget pictures which included GUADALCANAL DIARY, HOUSE OF WAX, THE MIRACLE OF FATIMA, PT 109, and many, many more. Eddie Foy, Jr., was impersonated by Eddie, Jr. in YANKEE DOODLE DANDY, BOWERY TO BROADWAY, WILSON, and others. Foy, Sr., made a few silent films including A FAVORITE FOOL but died just as sound was arriving on the cinema scene. In a small role, note Joe Flynn ("McHale's Navy"). Vitale could not sing, so her notes were looped by Viola Vonn. Songs from several sources included George M. Cohan's "Mary's a Grand Old Name" and "I'm a Yankee Doodle Dandy" (performed by Cagney and Hope), plus "I'm the Greatest Father of Them All" (William Jerome, Joseph J. Lilley, Eddie Foy, Sr., sung by Hope), "Row, Row, Row" (Jerome, James V. Monaco), "Nobody" (Bert Williams, Alex Rogers), "Comedy Ballet" (Lilley), "I'm Tired," and "Chinatown, My Chinatown" (Jean Schwartz, Jerome). George Tobias chimes in with a good portrayal of Foy's agent and little Billy Gray is properly obnoxious as the young Bryan, but it is the energetic Cagney who sparkles in a cameo and brings the audience out of its seats. It was only after seeing the video obituary all the TV stations ran when Cagney died in April 1986 that many younger people were able to fathom the depths of his talent and the versatility that made him, at once, a *film noir*, a musical, comic, western, and dramatic star, something that no other actor has yet to match. He was a one-of-a-kind person and you might spend years interviewing people he worked with to find anyone who might even say a mildly reproving word about him. Shavelson and Rose were Oscar-nominated for their script. It was Shavelson's directorial debut and he made the most of it.

p, Jack Rose; d, Melville Shavelson; w, Shavelson, Rose; ph, John F. Warren (VistaVision, Technicolor); ed, Ellsworth Hoagland; md, Joseph J. Lilley; art d, Hal Pereira, John Goodman; cos, Edith Head; ch, Nick Castle; tech adv, Charley Foy.

Musical/Biography **(PR:AAA MPAA:NR)**

SEVEN MEN FROM NOW*½ (1956) 77m BATJAC/WB c

Randolph Scott *(Ben Stride)*, Gail Russell *(Annie Greer)*, Lee Marvin *(Big Masters)*, Walter Reed *(John Greer)*, John Larch *(Pate Bodeen)*, Donald Barry *(Clete)*, Fred Graham *(Henchman)*, John Barradino *(Clint)*, John Phillips *(Jed)*, Chuck Roberson *(Mason)*, Steve Mitchell *(Fowler)*, Pamela Duncan *(Senorita)*, Stuart Whitman *(Cavalry Lieutenant)*.

A strong Scott western with a typical revenge theme that is worked well by director Boetticher and screenwriter Kennedy. Scott is an ex-lawman who tracks down the seven men who killed his wife during the robbery of a Wells Fargo office. During his search, Scott is joined by Reed and his wife, Russell, and bad guy Marvin. Marvin has hooked up with Scott in the hopes of snatching the bounty from the bounty and the gold Reed is carrying. His performance is one of the highlights of the film. The showdown between the ex-sheriff and the men responsible for his wife's death moves with the pace of an attacking rattlesnake. Scott kills Marvin in the end, after an Indian attack in which Reed is killed. In the final moments the lawman and Russell ride off together. This was the first of many westerns that teamed Scott, director Boetticher, and writer Kennedy (who would go on to direct). Boetticher later went on to become one of the leading directors of westerns in the 1950s.

p, Andrew V. McLaglen, Robert E. Morrison; d, Budd Boetticher; w, Burt Kennedy (based on a story by Kennedy); ph, William H. Clothier (Warner-

Color); m, Henry Vars; ed, Everett Sutherland; art d, Leslie Thomas; cos, Carl Walker, Rudy Harrington, Edward Sebaster; m/l, By Dunham, Vars.

Western **(PR:A MPAA:NR)**

SEVEN MILES FROM ALCATRAZ* (1942) 62m RKO bw

James Craig *(Champ Larkin)*, Bonita Granville *(Anne Porter)*, Frank Jenks *(Jimbo)*, Cliff Edwards *(Stormy)*, George Cleveland *(Capt. Porter)*, Erford Gage *(Paul Brenner)*, Tala Birell *(Baroness)*, John Banner *(Fritz Weinermann)*, Otto Reichow *(Max)*.

Craig and Jenks are cons who escape from the infamous Alcatraz "Rock" and find their way to a lighthouse off San Francisco Bay. The two soon discover that their hide-out is also a haven for Nazi spies who are preparing a U-boat attack on San Francisco. The two cons are convinced by the lighthouse owner, Cleveland, and his daughter, Granville, that they must stop the spies from getting information to one of their subs. Craig and Jenks forgo their freedom, with Craig brawling with the Nazis while Jenks sends for a naval patrol. This was director Dmytryk's first film for RKO and shows why he became one of the studio's top directors.

p, Herman Schlom; d, Edward Dmytryk; w, Joseph Krumgold (based on a story by John D. Klorer); ph, Robert de Grasse; ed, George Crone; art d, Albert S. d'Agostino, Feild M. Gray.

Spy Drama Cas. **(PR:A MPAA:NR)**

SEVEN MINUTES, THE* (1971) 115m FOX c

Wayne Maunder *(Mike Barrett)*, Marianne McAndrew *(Maggie Russell)*, Philip Carey *(Elmo Duncan)*, Jay C. Flippen *(Luther Yerkes)*, Edy Williams *(Faye Osborn)*, Yvonne De Carlo *(Constance Cumberland)*, Lyle Bettger *(Frank Griffith)*, Jackie Gayle *(Norman Quandt)*, Ron Randell *(Merle Reid)*, Charles Drake *(Sgt. Kellog)*, John Carradine *(Sean O'Flanagan)*, Harold J. Stone *(Judge Upshaw)*, Tom Selleck *(Phil Sanford)*, James Iglehart *(Clay Rutherford)*, John Sarno *(Jerry Griffith)*, Stanley Adams *(Irwin Blair)*, Billy Durkin *(George Perkins)*, Yvonne D'Angers *(Sheri Moore)*, Robert Moloney *(Ben Fremont)*, Olan Soule *(Harvey Underwood)*, Jan Shutan *(Anna Lou White)*, Alex D'Arcy *(Christian Leroux)*, David Brian *(Cardinal McManus)*, Berry Kroeger *(Paul Van Fleet)*, Ralph Story *(TV Commentator)*, Charles Napier *(Officer Iverson)*, Kay Peters *(Olivia St. Clair)*, Richard Angarola *(Father Sarfatti)*, Baby Doll Shawn Devereaux *(Yerkes' Girl friend)*, Regis J. Cordic *(Louis Polk)*, John Lawrence *(Howard Moore)*, Barry Coe *(Court Clerk)*, Mora Gray *(Donna Novick)*, Wolfman Jack *(Himself)*, Calvin Bartlett *(Olin Adams)*, Ken Jones *(Charles Wynter)*, Bill Baldwin *(Commentator)*, Robin Hughes *(Ashcroft)*, Vince Williams, Jim Bacon *(Reporters)*, John Gruber *(Dr. Quigley)*, Chris Marks *(Dr. Eberhart)*, Stuart Lancaster *(Dr. Roger Trimble)*, Peter Shrayder *(Merle Reid's Cameraman)*, Lynn Hamilton *(Avis)*, Patrick Wright *(1st Detective)*, Lillian Lehman *(Librarian)*, Judy Baldwin *(Fremont's Girl Friend)*, Paul Stader *(Thug)*, Henry Rowland *(Yerkes' Butler)*, George De Normand, Jeffrey Sayre *(Jurors)*, Barry Coe *(Court Bailiff)*.

Meyers better known for his soft porn films, tried unsuccessfully to make a serious picture about censorship. It fails, unfortunately, because of his own heavy handedness. The box office success of BEYOND THE VALLEY OF THE DOLLS gave Meyers a chance to do this straightforward film in which De Carlo plays an actress who writes a novel under a pseudonym that throws her into the center of the pornography issue. She decides to come forward as the "true" author after a bookstore owner is arrested for selling her book to a teenager who is later held for a girl's rape. But the film is too talky to make the audience really care about its censorship issue. In fact, many critics at the time claimed that THE SEVEN MINUTES gave free speech a bad name, after stagnantly dividing the world up between the "censorship squares" and the "with-it free speechers." The film was based on the novel by Irving Wallace, who chose "Seven minutes" as its title because that was supposed to be the time it takes for a woman to reach an orgasm.

p&d, Russ Meyer; w, Richard Warren Lewis (based on the novel by Irving Wallace); ph, Fred Mandl (DeLuxe Color); m, Stu Phillips; ed, Dick Wormell; md, Phillips; art d, Rodger Maus; set d, Walter M. Scott, Raphael Bretton; cos, Bill Thomas; spec eff, Howard A. Anderson Co.; m/l, "Seven Minutes" (sung by B. B. King), "Love Train" (sung by Don Reed), "Midnight Tricks" (sung by Merryweather, Carey), Bob Stone, Phillips; makeup, Dan Striepeke, Del Acevedo, Lynn Reynolds.

Drama **(PR:O MPAA:R)**

SEVEN NIGHTS IN JAPAN (1976, Brit./Fr.) 104m EMI-PAR/PAR c

Michael York *(Prince George)*, Hidemi Aoki *(Somi)*, Charles Gray *(Ambassador Hollander)*, Ann Lonnberg *(Jane Hollander)*, Eleonore Hirt *(Mrs. Hollander)*, James Villiers *(Finn)*, Yolande Donlan *(American Wife)*, Peter Jones *(Balcon)*, Lionel Murton *(American Tourist)*.

Excellent lighting effects show off Tokyo, but lackluster performances drag it down. The story is simple, with York a prince in the navy who strikes up a romance with bus driver Aoki. Not only do they have to battle class differences, but a sub-plot of a bunch of killers after York is also thrown in.

Both get away and enjoy each other's company at a secluded lake where photographer Henri Decae's work shines, particularly with the moonlight and rising sun shots. Lighting is nice, but story is dull. This was Aoki's first English-speaking role.

p&d, Lewis Gilbert; w, Christopher Wood; ph, Henri Decae (Technicolor); m, David Hentschel; ed, John Glen; prod d, John Stoll.

Drama   **(PR:C   MPAA:NR)**

SEVEN-PER-CENT SOLUTION, THE***   (1977, Brit.) 113m UNIV c

Alan Arkin *(Sigmund Freud)*, Vanessa Redgrave *(Lola Deveraux)*, Robert Duvall *(Dr. Watson)*, Nicol Williamson *(Sherlock Holmes)*, Laurence Olivier *(Prof. Moriarty)*, Joel Grey *(Lowenstein)*, Samantha Eggar *(Mary Watson)*, Jeremy Kemp *(Baron von Leinsdorf)*, Charles Gray *(Mycroft Holmes)*, Georgia Brown *(Mrs. Freud)*, Regine *(Madame)*, Anna Quayle *(Freda)*, Jill Townsend *(Mrs. Holmes)*, John Bird *(Berger)*, Alison Leggatt *(Mrs. Hudson)*, Frederick Jaeger *(Marker)*, Erik Chitty *(The Butler)*, Jack May *(Dr. Schultz)*, Gertan Klauber *(The Pasha)*, Leon Greene *(Squire Holmes)*, Michael Blagdon *(Young Holmes)*, Ashley House *(Young Freud)*, Sheila Shand Gibbs *(Nun)*, Erich Padalewsky *(Station Master)*, John Hill *(Train Engineer)*.

By all rights a film that should be an embarrassment to the memory of Sherlock Holmes, THE SEVEN-PER-CENT SOLUTION works in spite of its contrivances. Williamson is the great detective, but when his old associate and chronicler, Watson (Duvall) goes to see him for the first time in months, he finds him deep in the throes of cocaine addiction, paranoid and incoherent (the title refers to the concentration of cocaine to water that Holmes mainlines). Williamson gibbers about the evil genius, Prof. Moriarty: "His agents may be caught and their crimes forestalled, but he–*he* is never so much as suspected! Until now, that is! Until I, his arch enemy, managed to deduce his existence and penetrate his perimeters. And now his minions, having discovered my success, are on my track." Duvall asks him what he is going to do. "Do?" Williamson answers, his mood suddenly shifting. "Why, for the moment, I think I shall nap." After Duvall is thrown out of 221-B Baker Street, he receives a message to meet Prof. Moriarty (Olivier). With some trepidation he goes, and finds Williamson's evil genius to be an old man who tells Duvall that he is constantly being harassed and followed and his only connection with Holmes was as his math tutor when he was a boy. Deeply concerned about his friend's health, Duvall recalls an article in a medical journal about cures for cocaine addiction being achieved by a young Viennese doctor, Sigmund Freud (Arkin). Duvall confers with Williamson's older brother, Gray, and together they work out a scheme to tell Williamson that Olivier has fled to the continent and that he must pursue. They work out a trail to follow right up to Arkin's door, and when Williamson bursts in demanding his enemy surrender, Arkin begins talking to him and persuades him to undergo therapy. After a hellish withdrawal the detective is thrown in a deep depression. Arkin tries to get him interested in something new so he takes him along to meet another patient, Redgrave, also addicted to cocaine. When they visit her in her hospital room, Williamson discovers through his keen observation and deduction that she has been bound hand and foot and forcibly injected with the drug. Soon after, she is kidnaped from the hospital, and Williamson, Duvall, and Arkin set off on a chase. Redgrave has been abducted by Kemp, an anti-Semite (we have earlier seen him being defeated in a game of tennis by Arkin after insulting the doctor) who plans to sell her to an Arab sheik who collects redheads. Williamson and the good guys commandeer a train and pursue Kemp's train, and when they catch up Williamson leaps across to the roof of the other locomotive. There he and Kemp fight with sabers until Williamson runs him through. Later, as Williamson thanks Arkin for curing him, Arkin asks to hypnotize him one last time. Williamson at first resists, but eventually submits, and Arkin learns from his subconscious that as a boy his father found his math tutor in bed with his mother and shot her, as Olivier escaped through the window. This explains Williamson's fixation on Olivier, and why he has chosen a life of bringing justice to wrongdoers. Arkin clears this from Williamson's mind, and when he brings him out of his trance, the detective can remember nothing. As the film ends, Williamson is about to take a leisurely cruise along the Danube. On deck he meets Redgrave, and the implication that romance is about to spring up is unmistakable. Williamson is a Holmes unlike any other, a man of genius, but a man tormented by things he cannot recall. He actually cries at one point, something Basil Rathbone would never have done. Duvall is a breath of fresh air as well, his Watson far from the Nigel Bruce bumbler, he is a capable man and a devoted friend. In one of the more fascinating exchanges of the film, Arkin asks Duvall what his motivations are in helping Williamson. "He is the best and wisest man I have ever known," answers Duvall. Arkin analyzes further, "And you have become his chronicler, his Boswell. Your place in the great scheme of things is to record his life, whatever happens. Your motives, then, for coming with him to Vienna, are not pure altruism, but a sense of destiny that tells you to be at his side, always. Mixed motives." Arkin's Freud on the verge of fame, Redgrave's entertainer "not long ago the toast of four continents," Grey's villainous toady, and Kemp's aristocratic heavy are all wonderful parts well played. The only drawback is the somewhat thin story, and one wishes that Holmes would have gotten something a little meatier to sink his detecting teeth into. Production design is nothing short of marvelous, conveying the gentility of the late Victorian

era in splendid detail. The train chase was shot with real steam locomotives on a small stretch of track in the Severn Valley in the English Midlands. The music was originally to be composed by Bernard Herrmann, but he died before completing it. The score by John Addison is more than serviceable, and the witty song that Stephen Sondheim contributed for French chanteuse Regine to sing is another pleasure. While not as good as a real Conan Doyle story, THE SEVEN-PER-CENT SOLUTION is the next best thing.

p&d, Herbert Ross; w, Nicholas Meyer (based on his novel); ph, Oswald Morris (Panavision, Technicolor); m, John Addison; ed, Chris Barnes; prod d, Ken Adam; art d, Peter Lamont; set d, Peter James; cos, Alan Barrett; m/l, "The Madam's Song," Stephen Sondheim.

Crime   **Cas.**   **(PR:C   MPAA:PG)**

SEVEN REVENGES, THE*   (1967, Ital.) 92m Adelphia/AE c

Ed Fury, Elaine Stewart, Bella Cortez, Roldano Lupi, Paola Barbara, Furio Meniconi, Gabriele Antonini.

Another "sword and sandle" epic which has two tribal chiefs serving Genghis Khan facing seven deadly challenges in order to prove their worth. Released in 1961 in Italy and notable only for Sergio Leone's involvement.

d, Primo Zeglio; w, Sabatino Ciuffini, Sergio Leone, Zeglio, Emimmo Salvi, G. Taffarel, Roberto Natale (based on the story by Salvi); ph, Adalberto Albertini (Totalscope, Eastmancolor); m, Carlo Innocenzi.

Adventure   **(PR:C   MPAA:NR)**

SEVEN SAMURAI, THE***   (1956, Jap.) 200m Toho/COL-Landmark bw (SHICHININ NO SAMURAI; AKA: THE MAGNIFICENT SEVEN)

Takashi Shimura *(Kambei, Leader of Samurai)*, Toshiro Mifune *(Kikuchiyo, Would-Be Samurai)*, Yoshio Inaba *(Gorobei, Wise Warrior)*, Seiji Miyaguchi *(Kyuzo, Swordsman)*, Minoru Chiaki *(Heihachi, Good-Natured Samurai)*, Daisuke Kato *(Shichiroji, Kambei's Friend)*, Ko [Isao] Kimura *(Katsushiro, Young Samurai)*, Kunihori Kodo *(Gisaku, Village Elder)*, Kamatari Fujiwara *(Manzo, Shino's Father)*, Yoshio Tsuchiya *(Rikichi, Militant Villager)*, Bokuzen Hidari *(Yohei, Frightened Villager)*, Yoshio Kosugi *(Mosuke)*, Keiji Sakakida *(Gosaku)*, Jiro Kumagai *(Gisaku's Son)*, Haruko Toyama *(Gisaku's Daughter-in-Law)*, Fumiko Homma *(Peasant Woman)*, Ichiro Chiba *(Priest)*, Tsuneo Katagiri, Yasuhisa Tsutsumi *(Peasants)*, Keiko Tsushima *(Shino)*, Toranosuke Ogawa *(Grandfather)*, Noriko Sengoku *(Wife from Burned House)*, Yu Akitsu *(Husband from Burned House)*, Gen Shimizu *(Masterless Samurai)*, Jun Tasaki *(Big Samurai)*, Isao Yamagata *(Samurai)*, Jun Tatari *(Laborer)*, Atsushi Watanabe *(Vendor)*, Yukiko Shimazaki *(Rikichi's Wife)*, Sojin Kamiyama *(Minstrel)*, Shimpei Takagi *(Bandit Chief)*, Eijiro Higashino, Kichijiro Ueda, Akira Tani, Naruo Nakajima, Takashi Narita, Senkichi Omura, Shuno Takahara, Masanobu Okubo, Eijiro Tono *(Bandits)*.

Simply one of the best movies ever made, THE SEVEN SAMURAI covers so much ground, assaults almost every emotion in one's makeup, and is so totally satisfying that it must be viewed many times to glean the full weight of the message. The original (and since restored) version runs nearly 3 and a half hours, though various Shorter versions of 161, 155, and 148 have been released. in the 1600s was a dangerous place. It was the Sengoku era when the once-powerful samurai were coming to the end of their days. These men had been in the service of wealthy or royal masters and that fashion was over. (Masterless samurai are actually called "Ronin.") A small village is being regularly pillaged by murderous thieves and they are unable to protect themselves. Along comes Shimura, the veteran warrior who doesn't have enough for a good meal in his *obi*. When the villagers appeal to him for help, Shimura gathers up six more men and they proceed to teach the townspeople how to defend themselves. Each of the samurai is quickly limned so we know who they are, what they do, and whatever personal quirks they may have. The villagers welcome the warriors and some relationships begin. Kimura falls in love with one of the local women, although the other fighters keep their distance from the farmers as though they were barred from fraternization with their employers. In return for three small meals daily, the town is drilled on how to fight back, but both groups are battling for different reasons. The townspeople are desperate to keep their lives and property intact and the warriors are in it for honor alone. The last of the samurai is Mifune, a loudmouth who pretends that he is qualified but is, in reality, a farmer's son who would hope to be accepted by the others. The bandits arrive, there is a huge battle that is so violent it jars the eyes, and, in the end, the villains are defeated, but only a trio of warriors manage to live. They look down at the grave of their late comrades as the people in the town start planting rice for the next season. A simple enough tale but so rich with underlying meaning and cinematic technique that any synopsis will sound puny compared to the power of the film. The picture was released in the U.S. as THE MAGNIFICENT SEVEN but had to be renamed because of the John Sturges film of the same title. Kurosawa admitted that he wanted to make a western and there are many ways in which one can compare his style with those of John Ford, Howard Hawks, and others. It never flags, not for an instant. Action-lovers will be thrilled by the staging of the raid on the town, the violence, the epic horse scenes. (It took more than a year to film because they were hampered by a lack of funds and a lack of horses.) Never is the action strictly for its own sake and all of the characters are so carefully etched that we sincerely grieve when they are killed. When Mifune is unmasked as a farmer's son, he delivers a powerful speech to the warriors that reveals the true nature of the peasants as greedy, selfish, and grasping people who would lie and cheat and pretend to be poor and oppressed but who are, in fact, vicious, cunning, and untrustworthy. He speaks the words while going through a panoply of emotion which sees him laugh, cry, scream, love, hate, and several other gradations in between. The remake rights for this remarkable film were secured for a pittance by American producer Lou Morheim who then took the associate producer's position when Sturges insisted on being both producer and director on THE MAGNIFICENT SEVEN. The titles translation was excellent, but even if you should see this in Japanese, with no titles, everything is so clear that you don't need a word, which is how movies should be made. (In Japanese; English subtitles.)

p, Shojiro Motoki; d, Akira Kurosawa; w, Shinobu Hashimoto, Hideo Oguni, Kurosawa; ph, Asakasu Nakai; m, Fumio Hayasaka; ed, Kurosawa; art d, So Matsuyama; wrestling & sword stunts, Yoshio Sugino; archery masters, Ienori Kaneko, Shigeru Endo; English subtitles, Frederick Lang.

Historical/Drama   **Cas.**   **(PR:C MPAA:NR)**

SEVEN SEAS TO CALAIS★★   (1963, Ital.) 99m Adelphia Compagnia Cinematografica/MGM c (IL DOMINATORE DEI SETTE MARI)

Rod Taylor (Sir Francis Drake), Keith Michell (Malcolm Marsh), Irene Worth (Queen Elizabeth), Hedy Vessel (Arabella), Basil Dignam (Sir Francis Walsingham), Anthony Dawson (Burleigh), Gianni Cajafi (Tom Moone), Mario Girotti (Babington), Esmeralda Ruspoli (Mary of Scotland), Marco Guglielmi (Fletcher), Arturo Dominici (Mendoza), Gianni Solaro (Admiral Medina Sidonie), Adriano Vitale (Recalde), Bruno Ukmar (Emmanuel), Franco Ukmar (Francisco), Aldo Bufi-Landi (Vigeois), Umberto Raho (King Philip of Spain), Luciano Melani (Winter), Jacopo Tecchi (Garcia), Giuseppe Abbrescia (Chester), Rossella D'Aquino (Potato), Anna Santarsiero, Luciana Gilli (Other Indian Wives).

Adventure story about the travels and conquests of famous pirate Sir Francis Drake. Drake, despite his pirating, is still the undisputed leader of the English fleet. Taylor leads his swashbuckling men in raid after raid against the ships of Spain. He also thwarts an attempt on the Queen's life by King Philip of Spain. The action-packed ending has Drake and his sailors turning back the mighty Spanish Armada.

p, Paolo Moffa; d, Rudolph Mate, Primo Zeglio; w, Filippo Sanjust, George St. George, Lindsay Galloway; ph, Giulio Gianini (Cinemascope, Eastmancolor); m, Franco Mannino; ed, Franco Fraticelli; md, Mannino; art d, Nicola Cantatore; set d, Antonio Martini, Brunello Serena, Adele Tosi; cos, Sanjust; spec eff, Eros Bacciucchi; makeup, Maurizio Giustini.

Drama   **(PR:A MPAA:NR)**

SEVEN SECRETS OF SU-MARU, THE
     (SEE: RIO 70, U.S./Ger./Span.)

SEVEN SINNERS, 1936   (SEE: DOOMED CARGO, 1936, Brit.)

SEVEN SINNERS★★★½   (1940) 87m UNIV bw (GB: CAFE OF THE SEVEN SINNERS)

Marlene Dietrich (Bijou Blanche), John Wayne (Lt. Bruce Whitney), Broderick Crawford (Little Ned 'Edward Patrick Finnegan'), Mischa Auer (Sasha), Albert Dekker (Dr. Martin), Billy Gilbert (Tony), Oscar Homolka (Antro), Anna Lee (Dorothy Henderson), Samuel S. Hinds (Governor), Reginald Denny (Capt. Church), Vince Barnett (Bartender), Herbert Rawlinson (1st Mate), James Craig, William Bakewell (Ensigns), Willie Fung (Shopkeeper), Richard Carle (District Officer), William Davidson (Police Chief), Russell Hicks (1st Governor), Antonio Moreno (Rubio).

The first of Dietrich's three films with Wayne finds her a cabaret singer in the South Seas. Trouble seems to follow her from island to island, as do former Navy man Crawford and pickpocket-cum-magician Auer. After a fight breaks out in Dietrich's latest place of employ, the three are once again kicked off an island. They board the first ship out, where Dekker, the ship's doctor, falls hard for the beautiful torch singer. Dietrich will have nothing to do with him, though, as Dekker's drinking problem recalls an unhappy period in the singer's life. Dietrich entertains first-class passengers as she sings amidst a crate of chickens. Lee, the daughter of an island governor (Hinds), is enchanted by Dietrich's voice, and shows her appreciation by tossing the singer some money. Dietrich takes this the wrong way, angrily cutting her performance short. Later Dekker informs Dietrich Lee only meant to pay a compliment. After learning Lee is Hinds' daughter, Dietrich is overjoyed. Now she can be readmitted to an island she had been tossed off three years before. Upon arriving, Dietrich meets Wayne, a handsome Navy man. Wayne gives her a hand getting off, then takes Lee for a tour of the Navy base. Dietrich, with Crawford and Auer in tow, heads to the Seven Sinners Cafe. She confronts her old boss, Gilbert, and convinces him to rehire her. Gilbert reluctantly agrees, knowing full well that he is courting disaster. At the Seven Sinners Dietrich runs into Homolka, another man from her past. Homolka and Dietrich have been involved in some illegal activities, something Dietrich does not care to remember. That night, a naval reception is held for Lee but the men attending cut out to see

Dietrich's return. Lee brings the angered Wayne to the cafe, where he reprimands the ensigns. Dietrich continues to sing her song, decked out in Navy garb, and Wayne's heart is lost. Wayne makes sure she is invited to sing at a party for his men, despite Hinds' displeasure. Dietrich is a hit but Hinds demands she be put off the ship. Wayne escorts her home and nearly quits the Navy after spending the evening with Dietrich. Hinds confronts Dietrich, telling the singer he'll deport her unless she leaves Wayne alone. Crawford then angrily tells Dietrich the only place for a Navy man is the sea, and she agrees to leave. However, she tries to sing just one last time, and a fight breaks out. In the end, Wayne pulls some strings, allowing Crawford to rejoin the Navy as Dietrich and Auer head off to another island. Once more she meets Dekker, who has stopped drinking, giving Dietrich some hope for the future. Dietrich is marvelous in the role, parodying every South Seas island siren ever to hit the screen. Her throaty voice caresses her numbers with her own brand of enticing sexuality. Her three Frederick Hollander and Frank Loesser-penned include: "I've Been in Love Before," "I Fall Overboard," and "The Man's in the Navy." Wayne is a fine, rugged counterpart to Dietrich's sultry image. His part originally was created with Tyrone Power in mind, but Wayne has an on-screen chemistry with Dietrich that gives their romance some real passion. Director Garnett liked Wayne for the role at the very start. He took advantage of Wayne's vacation from Republic to get the star without having to pay a loan fee, then made arrangements for Dietrich to meet her potential costar. After making sure Wayne would be at the Universal commissary at a prearranged time, Garnett took Dietrich to lunch. In his autobiography, Light Your Torches and Pull Up Your Tights, Garnett recalled: "Dietrich, with that wonderful floating walk, passed Wayne as if he were invisible, then paused, made a half-turn half-turn him from cowlick to cowboots. As she moved on, she said in her characteristic basso whisper, 'Daddy, buy me THAT.' I said, 'Honey, you've gotta deal. That's our boy.'" Wayne came over at Garnett's signal, and casting was set. The film is further complemented by Dietrich's delightfully camp outfits and some rousing stunt choreography in the fight sequences. The musical score was later used in the serial DON WINSLOW OF THE NAVY. In 1949 this was remade as SOUTH SEA SINNER with Shelley Winters and MacDonald Carey in the lead roles.

p, Joe Pasternak; d, Tay Garnett; w, John Meehan, Harry Tugend (based on a story by Ladislaus Fodor, Laslo Vadnay); ph, Rudolph Mate; m, Frank Skinner; ed, Ted Kent; md, Charles Previn; art d, Jack Otterson; cos, Vera West, Irene.

Drama   **(PR:A MPAA:NR)**

SEVEN SISTERS   (SEE: HOUSE ON SORORITY ROW, 1983)

SEVEN SLAVES AGAINST THE WORLD★★   (1965, Ital.) 96m Leone Film/PAR c (GLI SCHIAVI PIU FORTI DEL MONDO)

Roger Browne (Marcus), Gordon Mitchell (Balisten), Scilla Gabel (Claudia), Giacomo Rossi Stuart (Gaius), Germano Longo (Lucius Emilius), Alfredo Rizzo (Efrem), Carlo Tamberlani (Lucius Terentius), Arnaldo Fabrizio (Goliath), Pietro Ceccarelli, Aldo Pini, Alfio Caltabiano, Adriano Vita, Luciana Vincenzi.

Browne plays a Roman sent to Asia to make sure the project of building an aqueduct is being done properly. He takes over for Stuart, who had been ruthless in his treatment of the slaves, and instead uses the soft approach to get the job done. Browne then tops Stuart in a duel for supremacy, leaving him steaming and plotting for revenge. Stuart gets the slaves to start an insurgency and all the Romans are slain except for Browne, who is taken in by another slave, Mitchell. The slaves who have revolted are captured and executed for their crimes and the blame falls on Browne. He and Mitchell sneak off to the city and band with Rizzo to make themselves masked gladiators to hide their identities from the Romans. They discover that Stuart is planning to stage another revolt, this time to take over the government, and they foil his plans. For their good deeds, the slaves are freed and Browne preserves his reputation as a full-fledged Roman citizen.

p, Elio Scardamaglia; d, Michele Lupo; w, Roberto Gianviti, Lupo; ph, Guglielmo Mancori (Techniscope, Technicolor); m, Francesco De Masi; ed, Alberto Gallitti, art d, Pier Vittorio Marchi; cos, Walter Patriarca; fencing ch, Alfio Caltabiano.

Adventure   **(PR:A MPAA:NR)**

SEVEN SWEETHEARTS★★   (1942) 98m MGM bw

Kathryn Grayson (Billie Van Maaster), Van Heflin (Henry Taggart), Marsha Hunt (Regina), Cecilia Parker (Victor), Peggy Moran (Albert), Diana Lewis (Mrs. Nugent), S.Z. Sakall (Mr. Van Maaster), Isobel Elsom (Miss Robbins), Carl Esmond (Jan Randall), Louise Beavers (Petunia), Donald Meek (Minister), Lewis Howard (Mr. Nugent), Dorothy Morris (Peter), Frances Rafferty (George), Frances Raeburn (Cornelius), Michael Butler, Cliff Danielson, William Roberts.

Lightweight story revolves around the set ways of a Dutch family in Michigan during the famed tulip festival. Grayson is the youngest daughter of seven and falls in love with visiting reporter Heflin. But tradition, which must be followed closely, her parents say, is that no other child can be wed before the oldest one is. Problem comes up is because the oldest, Hunt, is so bossy no one wants her. Songs include: "Tulip Time," "You and the Waltz and I," "Little Tingle Tangle Toes."

p, Joe Pasternak; d, Frank Borzage; w, Walter Reisch, Leo Townsend; ph, George Folsey; m, Franz Waxman; ed, Blanche Sewell; art d, Cedric Gibbons; cos, Howard Shoup; m/l, Walter Jurmann, Paul Francis Webster, Burton Lane, Ralph Freed; ch, Ernst Matray.

Musical   **(PR:A   MPAA:NR)**

SEVEN TASKS OF ALI BABA, THE**   (1963, Ital.) 95m
                                               Avis/Medallion c (LE 7 FATICHE DI ALI BABA)

Rod Flash [Rod Flash Ilush] (*Ali Baba*), Bella Cortez (*Lota*), Furio Meniconi (*Mustapha*), Amedeo Trilli (*Hassam Bey*), Mario Polletin, Omero Gargano, Liliana Zagra, Salvatore Furnari, Aristide Massari.

Meniconi has taken over Trilli's kingdom and is ruling the town with his evil ways, so it is up to Flash to come to the rescue. He gets arrested and is sentenced to perform seven impossible tasks, which of course he pulls off. Helping him get away is Cortez, the one that Meniconi also wants for his wife. But she is also caught, so Flash and his 40 thieves get the townspeople to raise arms against the ruthless leader, Killing him and restoring Trilli back to the throne. Flash and Lota return the sacred crown back to the genie of Sesame.

d, Emimmo Salvi; w, Salvi, Ambrogio Molteni, Benito Ilforte; ph, Mario Paradetti(Totalscope, Eastmancolor); art d, Giovanni Amadei.

Adventure   **(PR:A   MPAA:NR)**

SEVEN THIEVES****   (1960) 102m Fox bw

Rod Steiger (*Paul Mason*), Edward G. Robinson (*Theo Wilkins*), Joan Collins (*Melanie*), Eli Wallach (*Poncho*), Michael Dante (*Louis*), Alexander Scourby (*Raymond Le May*), Berry Kroeger (*Hugo Baumer*), Sebastian Cabot (*Director of Casino*), Marcel Hillaire (*Duc di Salins*), John Berardino (*Chief of Detectives*), Alphonse Martell (*Governor*), Jonathan Kidd (*Seymour*), Marga And Deighton (*Governor's Wife*).

There have been many copies of RIFIFI since the early 1950s, some of which have been awful and some excellent. This falls into the latter category. Robinson was beginning his fourth decade as a hoodlum star and not many actors could do it any better. This time he's a former scientist-professor who realizes he doesn't have much time left and wants to commit the perfect crime. Perfect crimes had been attempted often before and usually ended with the perpetrators getting away with it, up to a point, then adding a twist at the end, so the censors would be appeased. So it was with this film. Robinson enlists six accomplices to help him carry out his plan. Steiger is a recently released crook who arrives on the Riviera in France to meet Robinson, a man he'd known before his incarceration. In the first scene, Robinson and Steiger spar verbally in a funny scene that shows both men jockeying for position but Steiger not finding out what's happening until the end. Once Steiger is committed to the project, the robbery of millions from the casino at Monte Carlo, they gather the remainder of the septet, who include: Collins, a sexpot chorine; Wallach, her boy friend; Dante, a jumpy safe-cracking expert; Kroeger, an expert wheel man; and Scourby, the insider who works as the right-hand man to the boss of the casino, Cabot. The first half of the film is devoted to gathering the conspirators and planning the robbery. The second half is the robbery itself and the plot-twist ending. Collins supposedly seduces Scourby; Wallach fakes a suicide in the casino to divert the security guards. While this goes on, Steiger and Dante make their way to the money rooms. The heist is successful but the money is in huge denominations that are registered, so the crooks can not pass the cash. Robinson is so thrilled by having pulled it off that his heart gives out, and when the other six realize that there is no way they can spend the money, they return it to the casino. It's a bit of a cheat at the end because the characters are so engaging that we want them to succeed, especially since no one is hurt or killed and they are obviously thieves, not murderers. Until the conclusion, it's a tight, taut, and superior heist film with well-drawn characters. Collins and Steiger fall in love and the others part company and the air goes out of the picture in the last few minutes. Well-directed by Hathaway and beautifully photographed by Levitt, it would have benefitted greatly by being shot in color. Frontiere's score adds to the tension. The chief of detectives was played by John Berardino, who went on to great success in "General Hospital" but whom sports fans will remember as being the light-hitting infielder for the St. Louis Browns in the American League.

p, Sydney Boehm; d, Henry Hathaway; w, Boehm (based on the novel *Lions at the Kill* by Max Catto); ph, Sam Leavitt (CinemaScope); m, Dominic Frontiere; ed, Dorothy Spencer; art d, Lyle R. Wheeler, John De Cuir; set d, Walter M. Scott, Stuart A. Reiss; cos, Bill Thomas; makeup, Ben Nye.

Crime   **(PR:A-C   MPAA:NR)**

SEVEN THUNDERS   (SEE: BEASTS OF MARSEILLES, THE, 1959, Brit.)

SEVEN UPS, THE***   (1973) 103m FOX c

Roy Scheider (*Buddy Manucci*), Tony Lo Bianco (*Vito*), Larry Haines (*Max Kalish*), Victor Arnold (*Barilli*), Jerry Leon (*Mingo*), Ken Kercheval (*Ansel*), Richard Lynch (*Moon*), Bill Hickman (*Bo*), Ed Jordan (*Bruno*), David Wilson (*Bobby*), Robert Burr (*Lt. Hanes*), Rex Everhart (*Gilson*), Matt Russo (*Festa*), Lou Polan (*Coltello*), Joe Spinell (*Toredano*), William Shust (*Henry Parten*), Roger Serbagi (*Mickey Parten*), Frances Chaney (*Sara Kalish*), Louis Yaccarino (*Chef*), Benedetto Marino (*Besta's Son*), Tom Signorelli (*Fitz*), Thomas Rand (*Fat Man*), Adeline Leonard (*Nurse*), Frank Mascetta (*Barber*), Mary Multari (*Mrs. Pugliese*).

D'Antoni had already produced two action films, BULLITT and THE FRENCH CONNECTION and must have thought he could do better than the directors of the former so he assumed those reins here. The results were good. The chase scenes were excellent but the humanity was left behind in favor of screeching cars and an attempt at gritty realism that never quite convinced. Scheider runs an unorthodox division of the N.Y.P.D. that uses local hoods as finks. In Scheider's unit are Arnold, Leon, and Kercheval, and Lo Bianco is Scheider's chief informant on the streets. The group is after crooks whose crimes will result in them getting more than seven years in jail. Lo Bianco has his own plan and uses Scheider's confidential list of loan sharks to set up a kidnaping ring to nab these Shylocks and hold them for ransom. Scheider isn't hip to this until Kercheval is killed, which sends Scheider into a frenzy of unlawful assaults on criminals in an attempt to get to the bottom of things. One of these includes a sequence in which the chased car drives under a truck trailer which takes the top of the car clean off and decapitates the passengers. This was the most exciting scene in the film and everything else was wan by comparison, At the end of the movie, Scheider gets to Lo Bianco but doesn't kill him. Instead, he promises to tell all the mobsters who was behind the kidnapings and let them do the job that the cops won't. D'Antoni and Furrer, in a vain try at making the picture look real, have photographed it so dimly that squinting is needed and it becomes an example of *Cinema Irrite*. Nothing much special about the acting. Don Ellis's score helps immensely to buck up what would have been an otherwise undistinguished cops-and-robbers tale. Lots of violence and tough language.

p&d, Philip D'Antoni; w, Albert Ruben, Alexander Jacobs (based on a story by Sonny Grosso); ph, Urs Furrer (DeLuxe Color); m, Don Ellis; ed, Jerry Greenberg, Stephen A. Rotter, John C. Horger; prod d, Ed Wittstein; set d, John Godfrey; cos, Joseph G. Aulisi; stunts, Bill Hickman.

Crime   **Cas.**   **(PR:C   MPAA:PG)**

SEVEN WAVES AWAY   (SEE: ABANDON SHIP, 1957, Brit.)

SEVEN WAYS FROM SUNDOWN*½   (1960) 86m UNIV c

Audie Murphy (*Seven Jones*), Barry Sullivan (*Jim Flood*), Venetia Stevenson (*Joy Karrington*), John McIntire (*Sgt. Hennessey*), Kenneth Tobey (*Lt. Herly*), Mary Field (*Ma Kerrington*), Ken Lynch (*Graves*), Suzanne Lloyd (*Lucinda*), Ward Ramsey (*Fogarty*), Don Collier (*Duncan*), Jack Kruschen (*Becker*), Claudia Barrett (*Gilda*), Teddy Rooney (*Jody*), Don Haggerty (*Dorton*), Robert Burton (*Eavens*), Fred Graham (*Chief Waggoner*), Dale Van Sickle (*2nd Waggoner*).

An uninteresting western about the young upstart who outshines his elder. Murphy is a neophyte Texas Ranger assigned to work with hard-crusted McIntire. The pair are after the clever and dashing outlaw Sullivan, who eventually kills McIntire but not the guileful Murphy. Murphy proves he is wise beyond his years as a Ranger as he tracks Sullivan down, finally captures him, and brings him to justice.

p, Gordon Kay; d, Harry Keller; w, Clair Huffaker (based on the novel by Huffaker); ph, Ellis Carter (Eastmancolor); m, William Lava, Irving Gertz; ed, Tony Martinelli; art d, Alexander Golitzen, William Newberry.

Western   **(PR:A   MPAA:NR)**

SEVEN WERE SAVED*   (1947) 72m PAR bw

Richard Denning (*Capt. Allen Danton*), Catherine Craig (*Susan Briscoe*), Russell Hayden (*Capt. Jim Willis*), Ann Doran (*Mrs. Rollin Hartley*), Byron Barr (*Lt. Martin Pinkert*), John Eldredge (*Mr. Rollin Hartley*), Richard Loo (*Col. Yamura*), Keith Richards (*Smith*), Don Castle (*Lt. Pete Sturdevant*).

Though plenty of real-life footage was supplied by the Air-Sea Rescue Service, nothing could bail out this boring film. The plot concerns a generalized cast of characters thrown together in a life raft after their plane goes down in the ocean. Two had done time in a Japanese prison camp, one is a ranking Japanese official on his way to trial, along with the two pilots and a nurse. Of course some of the characters break down and panic, while the others get stronger and keep the crew together until help arrives. The climax is supposed to be when a power boat is dropped from a plane for the people to use.

p, William H. Pine, William Thomas; d, Pine; w, Maxwell Shane (based on a story by Shane, Julian Harmon); ph, Jack Greenhalgh; ed, Howard Smith; art d, F. Paul Sylos.

War Drama   **(PR:A   MPAA:NR)**

SEVEN WOMEN***   (1966) 87m Ford-Smith/MGM c

Anne Bancroft *(Dr. D.R. Cartwright)*, Sue Lyon *(Emma Clark)*, Margaret Leighton *(Agatha Andrews)*, Flora Robson *(Miss Binns)*, Mildred Dunnock *(Jane Argent)*, Betty Field *(Florrie Pether)*, Anna Lee *(Mrs. Russell)*, Eddie Albert *(Charles Pether)*, Mike Mazurki *(Tunga Khan)*, Woody Strode *(Lean Warrior)*, Jane Chang *(Miss Ling)*, Hans William Lee *(Kim)*, H.W. Gim *(Coolie)*, Irene Tsu *(Chinese Girl)*.

It's a shame that John Ford's final picture had to be less than satisfying, but even adequate Ford is better than many others' bests. The lead role was to be played by Patricia Neal and they began shooting with her, but when she suffered her strokes and almost passed away, Bancroft was brought in to replace Neal and those scenes were re-shot. It was an odd choice for Ford, who made his reputation helming the most macho males. Going far afield from the Old West, Ford must have wanted to show that after 48 years behind the lense, he could do something distinctly feminine. It's 1935 in China and Mazurki is a Mongolian warlord who is pillaging the area near the China-Mongolia border. (This was not the first time that Austrian-born Mazurki-of Ukrainian ancestry–had portrayed an Asian. He was the Japanese jiu-jitsu expert in BEHIND THE RISING SUN 17 years before.) The American religious mission is run by stern Leighton, a prissy, repressed lesbian who lives by the rules and is solid as granite. Her aides are young Lyon, Dunnock, and the one male, Albert, who is married to Field, a nervous, pregnant woman. Bancroft, a physician, joins the mission staff and she and Leighton are immediately at loggerheads because Bancroft's character is loose, easy-going, and a trifle cynical, while Leighton is as flexible as ebony. The two women can't seem to agree on anything and chaos erupts in the mission when cholera sufferers arrive, led by Robson, who has brought them over from the British mission nearby. Field is due to give birth and needs to go to a hospital, but Leighton holds the purse strings and won't give the necessary money to check Field in for professional help in delivering. The mission is being guarded by Chinese soldiers, and when they have to leave, the place is now vulnerable to Mazurki and his men. Albert departs to see if he can get help and is killed. Just as Field begins her labor, Mazurki and his hordes crash into the compound. Bancroft successfully delivers Field's child, then offers her body to Mazurki to calm him down. Once he is under her seductive spell, she wields her sexual power over him to get Mazurki to make some concessions to the other women and children who are unprotected. Leighton, who we think may just have designs on Bancroft herself, is outraged by the way Bancroft has used her wiles on Mazurki and lets her know it in no uncertain terms. The other women, however, fathom that Bancroft has sacrificed herself and her morals in order to keep them alive. She turns on all her charms and gets Mazurki to allow all the women to exit and be safely escorted to a haven. Once they are out of the way, Bancroft and Mazurki will share a glass of wine and toast their new-found relationship. What the Mongol doesn't know is that Bancroft has poisoned the wine and the two of them will be united in death. Some good character touches are all through the film, such as Leighton's disgust at Field's pregnant condition, as well as the tension caused by her desire to embrace Lyon and establish a woman-to-woman situation. One of the problems is that the women of the mission are so concerned with their own semi-soap opera stories that we hardly see them doing what they are there to do, teach children. Ford used an interesting technique for the first part of the film; he shot it in dull, muted tones to emphasize the quiet lives these people were leading. It was only when Mazurki burst in wearing red and gold that color invaded the screen. Lots of violence and heavy religious overtones make this a bad bet for youngsters and sometimes incomprehensible for adults.

p, Bernard Smith; d, John Ford; w, Janet Green, John McCormick (based on the story "Chinese Finale" by Norah Lofts); ph, Joseph La Shelle (Panavision, Metrocolor); m, Elmer Bernstein; ed, Otho S. Lovering; art d, George W. Davis, Eddie Imazu; set d, Henry Grace, Jack Mills; cos, Walter Plunkett, spec eff, J. McMillan Johnson; makeup, William Tuttle.

Historical Drama   **(PR:C MPAA:NR)**

SEVEN WOMEN FROM HELL*   (1961) 88m AP/FOX bw

Patricia Owens *(Grace Ingram)*, John Kerr *(Bill Jackson)*, Denise Darcel *(Claire Oudry)*, Cesar Romero *(Luis Hullman)*, Margia Dean *(Mara Shepherd)*, Yvonne Craig *(Janet Cook)*, Pilar Seurat *(Mai-Lu Ferguson)*, Sylvia Daneel *(Ann Van Laer)*, Richard Loo *(Sgt. Takahashi)*, Bob Okazaki *(Capt. Oda)*, Lloyd Kino *(Rapist Guard)*, Evadne Baker *(Regan)*, Yuki Shimoda *(Dr. Matsumo)*, Kam Fong Chun *(House Guard)*, Yankee Chang *(Guard)*.

Inadequate wartime drama that is unintentionally funny. The film intends to be a heavy story about a group of women escaping from a Japanese prison camp in New Guinea. All the women look nice, but what comes out of their mouths is strictly absurd. Some of the women die along the way, and one takes up with a wealthy planter, Romero, who attempts to turn the girls back over to the Japanese. When the women discover his true nature, they kill him. The dialog is so pitiful that when the women finally see American soldiers, the encounter goes as follows: Women, "Yanks]" Soldiers, "Broads]"

p, Harry Spalding; d, Robert D. Webb; w, Jesse Lasky, Jr., Pat Silver; ph, Floyd Crosby (CinemaScope); m, Paul Dunlap; ed, Jodie Copelan; art d, Duncan Cramer; set d, Morris Hoffman; spec eff, Lee Zavitz; makeup,

George Lane.

War Drama   **(PR:A MPAA:NR)**

SEVEN YEAR ITCH, THE****   (1955) 105m FOX c

Marilyn Monroe *(The Girl)*, Tom Ewell *(Richard Sherman)*, Evelyn Keyes *(Helen Sherman)*, Sonny Tufts *(Tom McKenzie)*, Robert Strauss *(Kruhulik)*, Oscar Homolka *(Dr. Brubaker)*, Marguerite Chapman *(Miss Morris)*, Victor Moore *(Plumber)*, Roxanne *(Elaine)*, Donald MacBride *(Mr. Brady)*, Carolyn Jones *(Miss Finch)*, Butch Bernard *(Ricky)*, Doro Merande *(Waitress)*, Dorothy Ford *(Indian Girl)*, Mary Young *(Woman in Railroad Station)*, Ralph Sanford *(Railroad Station Gateman)*.

A funny commercial film based on an even funnier commercial play. In the original stage presentation, Ewell played a man who ultimately gained his sexual fantasies with the woman. For the film, they have toned it down and there is no completion, sort of like *comedus interruptus*. If you want to have a little fun, find someone who loves this movie and ask what Monroe's name was in it. The answer is that she had no name, and was only referred to as "The Girl," which is sort of like Lot's Wife in the Bible, who also had no name of her own. Paperback book publisher Ewell has a lively imagination, due in great part to the books he issues. (There was a similarity here to Danny Kaye's character in THE SECRET LIFE OF WALTER MITTY.) He and wife Keyes have been married for seven years, a period which is established early as the time when married men begin to look in other directions for frivolity. Ewell has to stay in Manhattan on business for the summer so Keyes and their son, Bernard, leave on a vacation. The small building has an upstairs apartment which has been sublet to Monroe, a commercial actress-model who, while not dumb, is at least flighty. Monroe forgets her building key and hits Ewell's buzzer so she can get in. She has her apartment key but two keys are necessary to enter most of these residences. Ewell's lively imagination sends him into flights of fancy as he often talks directly to the camera in monologues imagining passionate flings with women he has a bare acquaintance with. Ewell stands on his small balcony and Monroe accidentally tips over a flower pot that nearly crashes on his head. Ewell sees this as an opening and asks her down to have something tall and cool. While he waits for her to arrive, Ewell imagines everything that will happen. Monroe enters and is delighted that Ewell is married as she feels at home with men who have wives. While both are seated at Ewell's piano, he muffs a pass, the antithesis of the suavity he's shown in his imaginings, and both of them wind up on the floor with Ewell pleading that it was all a mistake. Monroe shrugs it off. After she leaves, Ewell's mind runs at maximum speed as he pictures her spreading the word around the area that he is a pervert. In his mind, he sees Monroe in her bathtub, getting her toe stuck in a faucet and waiting to have little Victor Moore extricate her in his role as the plumber. (This "toe in faucet" has been copied over and over in many TV shows.) Ewell's fevered worries continue as he imagines Moore telling everyone in the neighborhood about his advances while Monroe appears on a local television station to warn women about Ewell's proclivities. Meanwhile, Keyes is up at a resort and when Ewell learns that her old beau, Tufts, is also there, he fantasizes that Keyes has learned about his behavior with Monroe and has retaliated by having a fling with Tufts. In real life, Ewell takes Monroe out to dinner and a local movie on a sultry summer evening. When Monroe complains about the stifling heat, she stands over a subway grating and her white dress is sent up by the cool air from beneath. Monroe tries to keep her dress down and Ewell stands there watching, like a male dog in a state of tumescence. (It was the still photo from this scene that served as the advertising picture for the movie. It is also the most recalled photo of Monroe, aside from the nude calendar she made early in her career and the "Playboy" centerfold which appeared in the very first edition of that magazine.) Monroe informs Ewell that she's just done a toothpaste TV spot and demonstrates her flawless breath by kissing him. They return to Ewell's air-conditioned apartment and since her place upstairs does not have the benefit of cooling, she innocently asks if she could stay with him, as there is no way she can get her beauty sleep in the hot, humid sublet above. Ewell offers her the bedroom while he'll sleep on the couch in the living room. Again, his imagination takes over his sensibilities and he sees Monroe and the building's janitor, Strauss, conspire to extract money from him in a blackmail plot. The dream continues and he sees Keyes learn about his dalliance and prove the truth about Hell having no fury like a woman scorned by killing him! The next day, Ewell is back to normal, moping around, and he informs Monroe of his self-doubt and how it would be impossible for any woman, other than his wife, to find him attractive. Monroe sees that his ego needs repairing so she tells him that she finds him very sexy, much more so than many *handsome* men. Ewell is not sure how to take that but he decides it's a compliment. Monroe goes into the small kitchen to make something and Tufts arrives. He's been sent by Keyes to bring back an item belonging to Bernard. When Ewell sees Tufts, all of his anger comes out, as do his suspicions about Keyes and Tufts having had an affair, so he knocks the burly Tufts out with a well-placed punch. Strauss walks in and carts Tufts out and Ewell figures he'd better race up to the resort where Keyes and Bernard are right away. He gives Monroe the key to the air-conditioned apartment and tells her to look after it while he's up North. Ewell kisses Monroe in a sisterly fashion and he runs out to catch a train. He has left the house without his shoes, which she tosses out the window to him. The picture ends with no adultery having been committed, except in the wild thoughts of Ewell. This was Monroe's 23rd movie and

Ewell's eighth, since he broke in opposite Judy Holliday in ADAM'S RIB. Ewell had flown back and forth between Hollywood and New York before making a deep impression in this 1952 play and managing to convince the producers that he was the man to do it in the movie. Monroe seemed to be having a wonderful time while making the movie but she was in and out of depression as her marriage to Yankee slugger Joe DiMaggio was ending. THE SEVEN YEAR ITCH is, of course, a fantasy, but there is enough believability in it to make it close to home to any husband who has watched his wife go off on a vacation, leaving him alone in a world inhabited by beautiful women. It was filmed on location in New York, with the interiors being shot at Fox. Oscar Homolka does a small bit as a psychiatrist that could have been edited out, despite his usual convincing portrayal. Even though the movie is titillating, there's hardly a thing in it that's tawdry.

p, Charles K. Feldman, Billy Wilder; d, Wilder; w, Wilder, George Axelrod (based on the play by Axelrod); ph, Milton Krasner (CinemaScope, DeLuxe Color); m, Alfred Newman; ed, Hugh S. Fowler; md, Newman; art d, Lyle Wheeler, George W. Davis; set d, Walter M. Scott, Stuart A. Reiss; cos, William Travilla, Charles LeMaire; spec eff, Ray Kellogg.

Comedy   **Cas.**   **(PR:A-C   MPAA:NR)**

SEVENTEEN**½   (1940) 78m PAR bw

Jackie Cooper *(William Sylvanus Baxter)*, Betty Field *(Lola Pratt)*, Otto Kruger *(Mr. Sylvanus Baxter)*, Ann Shoemaker *(Mrs. Mary Baxter)*, Norma Nelson *(Jane Baxter)*, Betty Moran *(May Parcher)*, Thomas Ross *(Edward P. Parcher)*, Peter [Lind] Hayes *(George Crooper)*, Buddy Pepper *(Johnnie Watson)*, Donald Haines *(Joe Bullitt)*, Richard Denning *(Jack)*, Jody S. Gilbert *(Ethel Boke)*, Paul E. Burns *(McGrill)*, Hal Clements *(Wally Banks)*, Edward Earle *(Headwaiter)*, Stanley Price *(Waiter)*, Joey Ray *(Orchestra Leader)*, Fred "Snowflake" Toones *(Genesis)*, Hattie Noel *(Adella)*.

Originally made in 1916 as a silent film, Paramount produced this talking version of Booth Tarkington's story about the growing pains of adolescence 25 years later. Cooper is excellent as an average high-school boy worrying about if his grades will get him into college. But when sophisticated Field arrives on the scene, the boy forgets why he is in school. He pays for her dates with other fellows, puts out the money for a car to impress her, and basically does everything to please his new-found object of infatuation. But she leaves, and he learns she was just using him to have fun and that his parents are really his friends. The corny story is handled in a skillful manner.

p, Stuart Walker; d, Louis King; w, Agnes Christine Johnston, Stuart Palmer (based on a story by Booth Tarkington and a play by Stuart Walker, Hugh Stanislaus Strange, Stanford Mears); ph, Victor Miller; ed, Arthur Schmidt; art d, Hans Dreier, Franz Bachelin.

Drama   **(PR:A   MPAA:NR)**

1776**   (1972) 141m COL c

William Daniels *(John Adams)*, David Ford *(John Hancock)*, Howard Da Silva *(Benjamin Franklin)*, Donald Madden *(John Dickinson)*, Emory Bass *(James Wilson)*, Ken Howard *(Thomas Jefferson)*, Ronald Holgate *(Richard Henry Lee)*, Rex Robbins *(Roger Sherman)*, Peter Forster *(Oliver Wolcott)*, Frederic Downs *(Samuel Huntington)*, Howard Caine *(Lewis Morris)*, John Myhers *(Robert Livingston)*, Richard McMurray *(Francis Lewis)*, John Cullum *(Edward Rutledge)*, Gordon De Vol *(Thomas Lynch, Jr.)*, William H. Bassett *(Thomas Heyward, Jr.)*, Jonathan Moore *(Lyman Hall)*, William Engle *(Button Gwinnett)*, Barry O'Hara *(George Walton)*, William Hansen *(Caesar Rodney)*, Ray Middleton *(Thomas McKean)*, Leo Leyden *(George Read)*, Patrick Hines *(Samuel Chase)*, Heber Jentzsch *(Charles Carroll)*, Andy Albin *(William Paca)*, Charles Rule *(Joseph Hewes)*, Jack De Mave *(John Penn)*, Jordan Rhodes *(William Hooper)*, Roy Poole *(Stephen Hopkins)*, James Noble *(John Witherspoon)*, Richard O'Shea *(Francis Hopkinson)*, Fred Slyter *(Richard Stockton)*, Daniel Keyes *(Josiah Bartlett)*, John Holland *(William Whipple)*, Ralston Hill *(Secretary Charles Thomson)*, Stephen Nathan *(Courier)*, William Duell *(Custodian Andrew McNair)*, Mark Montgomery *(Leather Apron)*, Blythe Danner *(Martha Jefferson)*, Virginia Vestoff *(Abigail Adams)*.

1776 is almost an insult to anyone who knows American history. The Broadway play ran more than 1,200 performances from its March 16, 1969, opening. Jack Warner had retired from the company that bore his name and, even at the age of 80, still had plenty of fire in him, so he coughed up well over $1 million to buy the rights and released the film through Columbia (who now share the same studio facilities on the lot that Jack built). Stage director Peter H. Hunt (making his film debut), choreographer White, and more than 20 members of the cast came from various stage versions and they probably were too reverential to the Tony Award-winning show. The script suffered from fallen archness as it combined a retelling of history (some of which was painfully inaccurate) with sexual innuendos, toilet humor, and a general feeling of relief in the audience that the States managed to be united despite the clods who ran the country, not because of them. It was often tedious and never caught fire, but Stradling's photography was good enough to secure an Oscar nomination, the only notice taken of this $5 million flop. It's June of the momentous year of our Lord 1776, and the original 13 colonies have had it with the domineering behavior of England. There's a rebellion and the British navy has been sent to this side

of the pond to put an end to the fracas. In Philadelphia, Daniels stands committed to detachment from England, but the others in the 2nd Continental Congress don't rally behind him because of his personality. Da Sylva thinks that Daniels might get his points across if he allows the more popular Holgate to present them. When Holgate announces that he is about to leave Philadelphia to become Virginia's governor, Da Sylva and Daniels must find an equally charming replacement to submit the proposals. If they don't do it right away, they feel sure the other members of Congress will vote down the measures Daniels espouses. They call upon Howard to use his wise pen to write a Declaration. Howard agrees but he is lonesome for his wife, Danner, and can't keep his attention span on the work. Da Sylva arranges to bring Danner to Philadelphia to take care of Howard's sexual needs and allow him to get down to business on the document. Now Da Sylva and Daniels leave to pay a call on George Washington (who is not seen), and when they come back, they see that the Congress is divided over what Howard has written. Howard is all for abolishing slavery, but there are so many southerners in the Congress that the entire Declaration is in danger of being defeated unless the anti-slavery clause is deleted. Cullum is the senator from South Carolina and Da Sylva manages to talk Daniels and Howard out of their desire to put an end to slavery in order to bring unification to the men voting. Reluctantly, Daniels agrees to remove the offending material and a vote is taken. There are a few detractors but they come around when Hansen, a dying Delaware representative, makes the trip to Philadelphia despite his illness and gives his assent. Caine, a New Yorker, has steadfastly remained impartial, but when his home is destroyed by soldiers from Britain, he joins in. Soon enough, everybody agrees, even the shy Bass who had stayed above it all until that moment. July 4th rolls around, the Liberty Bell peals, and the men sign the Declaration of Independence, led by Ford. 1776 had some cheap shots going for it that included the aforementioned toilet jokes, anachronistic dialog, and 1970s slang that got laughs, but at the expense of intelligence. Almost every one of the signers was shown to be either a buffoon or a rakehell. Howard's portrayal of Jefferson was the most restrained, and therefore the most effective, but even he was hampered by having to essay a man who was too sexually frustrated to be able to write the words that would change the course of history. Composer Edwards was credited on the stage for having originated the "concept." If what they meant by that was changing history to fit a pale set of words and music, so be it. Eddie Sauter and Peter Howard did the arrangements for the limp Sherman Edwards tunes that included: "The Lees of Old Virginia" (sung by Holgate), "He Plays the Violin" (Danner), "But, Mr. Adams" (Daniels and the members of Congress), "Sit Down John" (Congress), "Till Then" (Daniels, Virginia Vestoff), "Piddle, Twiddle and Resolve" (Daniels), "Yours, Yours, Yours" (Daniels, Vestoff), "Mama, Look Sharp" (Stephen Nathan), "The Egg" (Da Sylva, Howard, Daniels), "Is Anybody There?" (Daniels), and "Molasses To Rum" (Cullum). Mistakes abound in the script and any student will tell you there were 56 signers of the Declaration of Independence, whereas this film allows only 35. Although written earlier, the first signature wasn't on the document until August and there are many more errors. Don't confuse this Peter Hunt with the other one, the man who edited many JAMES BOND films and directed ON HER MAJESTY'S SECRET SERVICE. The only other American history film to do such damage to memory was the disastrous REVOLUTION, in 1985, that starred Al Pacino as a Scotsman with an accent that was strictly Bronx.

p, Jack L. Warner; d, Peter H. Hunt; w, Peter Stone (based on the musical play by Stone, Sherman Edwards); ph, Harry Stradling, Jr. (Panavision, Eastmancolor); m, Sherman Edwards; ed, William Ziegler; Florence Williamson; md, Ray Heindorf; art d, George Jenkins; set d, George James Hopkins; cos, Patricia Zipprodt; ch, Onna White; m/l, Edwards; makeup, Allan Snyder.

Musical   **Cas.**   **(PR:A   MPAA:G)**

SEVENTH CAVALRY**½   (1956) 75m COL c

Randolph Scott *(Capt. Tom Benson)*, Barbara Hale *(Martha Kellogg)*, Jay C. Flippen *(Sgt. Bates)*, Jeanette Nolan *(Mrs. Reynolds)*, Frank Faylen *(Krugger)*, Leo Gordon *(Vogel)*, Denver Pyle *(Dixon)*, Harry Carey, Jr *(Cpl. Morrison)*, Michael Pate *(Capt. Benteen)*, Donald Curtis *(Lt. Bob Fitch)*, Frank Wilcox *(Maj. Reno)*, Pat Hogan *(Young Hawk)*, Russell Hicks *(Col. Kellogg)*, Peter Ortiz *(Pollock)*, William Leslie, Jack Parker, Edward F. Stidder, Al Wyatt.

Custer's last stand at the Little Big Horn is handled a little differently this time. Here the story revolves around Scott, a soldier branded a coward because he wasn't at the famous battle which had no survivors. To get over his guilt he heads up the detail that is sent out to bury the dead and return with the officers' bodies. The convoluted ending depicts the Indians as being afraid of Custer's horse. Hale stands by her man throughout the painful ordeal.

p, Harry Joe Brown; d, Joseph H. Lewis; w, Peter Packer (based on a story by Glendon F. Swarthout); ph, Ray Rennahan (Technicolor); m, Mischa Bakaleinikoff; ed, Gene Havlick; art d, George Brooks.

Western   **(PR:A   MPAA:NR)**

7TH COMMANDMENT, THE*½   (1961) 82m Irvmar/Crown
International bw

Jonathan Kidd (*Ted Mathews/Tad Morgan*), Lyn Statten (*Terry James*),
Frank Arvidson (*Noah Turnbull*), John Harmon (*Pete*), John Carpenter.

Too many twists and easy solutions make this crime drama monotonous.
Kidd falls into amnesia after being in an auto accident in which he thinks
he killed the other driver. He becomes Tad Morgan and falls under the wing
of preacher Arvidson, who guides him into the life of a successful evangelist.
His old girlfriend, Statten, wants some of his new wealth and decides to
concoct a blackmail scheme with her new boy friend, Harmon. Instead, she
shocks Kidd's memory into returning. He still doesn't know the other driver
was not killed, so Statten pushes her blackmail scheme further and marries
him in a fake wedding ceremony. He tries to get rid of her by shoving her
off of a bridge, and then returns to his congregation, thinking his problems
are over forever. But she has lived through the fall, returns home, and
accidentally kills Harmon, thinking it is Kidd. Almost insane by now, she
hurries off to kill Kidd; they fight, and he chokes her to death. Distraught,
his life comes to an end when he is stricken with a heart attack at the altar.

p&d, Irvin Berwick; w, Jack Kevan, Berwick; ph, Robert C. Jessup.

Crime Drama   (PR:A   MPAA:NR)

SEVENTH CONTINENT, THE***   (1968, Czech./Yugo.) 84m
Jadran-Koliba/U-M c (SEDMY KONTINENT; SIEDMA PEVNINA; SED-
MI KONTINENT)

Iris Vrus (*Yellow Girl*), Tomislav Pasaric (*White Boy*), Abdoulaye Seck
(*Black Boy*), Hermina Pipinic (*White Boy's Mother*), Demeter Bitenc (*White
Boy's Father*), Oudy Rachmat Endang (*Yellow Girl's Father*), Mikulas Huba
(*General*), Karla Chadimova (*General's Wife*), Viktor Starcic (*Expert at
Conference*), Vanja Drach (*Diplomat*), Dano Zivojinovic, Jindrich Laznicka.

Yugoslavian film similar in story line to Britain's LORD OF THE FLIES.
This animated tale concerns a white boy and a yellow girl who go off and
create their own society on a deserted island. Instead of the authoritarian,
cruel world of LORD OF THE FLIES, however, the two create a nonracist,
harmonious place to live. All types of people reside there, but the new
inhabitants are strictly children, leaving the parents alone in their old world.
A multicolored group returns to see if they can help the adults get along
better, but the plan doesn't work, and they head back for their idyllic
paradise.

p, Sidney Glazier; d, Dusan Vukotic; w, Vukotic; Andro Lusicic (based on a
story by Ruzena Fiserova); ph, Karol Krska (CinemaScope, Eastmancolor);
m, Tomislav Simovic; ed, Lidija Branis; art d, Rudolf Kovac, Branko Hundic;
cos, Ivan Stefan; English subtitles, Herman G. Weinberg.

Fantasy   (PR:A   MPAA:NR)

SEVENTH CROSS, THE***½   (1944) 110m MGM bw

Spencer Tracy (*George Heisler*), Signe Hasso (*Toni*), Hume Cronyn (*Paul
Roeder*), Jessica Tandy (*Liesel Roeder*), Agnes Moorehead (*Mme. Marelli*),
Herbert Rudley (*Franz Marnet*), Felix Bressart (*Poldi Schlamm*), Ray
Collins (*Wallau*), Alexander Granach (*Zillach*), Katherine Locke (*Mrs.
Sauer*), George Macready (*Bruno Sauer*), Paul Guilfoyle (*Fiedler*), Steven
Geray (*Dr. Lowenstein*), Kurt Katch (*Leo Herman*), Kaaren Verne (*Leni*),
Konstantin Shayne (*Fuellgrabe*), George Suzanne (*Bellani*), John Wengraf
(*Overkamp*), George Zucco (*Fahrenburg*), Steven Muller (*Hellwig*), Eily
Malyon (*Fraulein Bachmann*), Fay Wall, William Challee.

Seven prisoners escape from a Nazi concentration camp in the years
preceding WW II. The commandant has crosses nailed to seven trees for the
prisoners to be nailed to and left to die when they are recaptured. One by
one they are recaptured, until only one cross remains, the one intended for
Tracy. He has been embittered by his years of captivity and has lost all faith
in mankind (although, some critics pointed out, he didn't seem to have lost
much weight during those years). He narrowly escapes the Gestapo time
and again, and various friends and strangers help him as he makes his way
for neutral Holland, and, although he meets with a great deal of betrayal
from those he thought he could trust, his faith in mankind gradually returns
and he reaches safety a much better man than the hollow shell that survived
the death camp. Tracy's performance is almost unbearably strong as he
watches everything he thought he could believe in destroyed with the
acquiescence of the population to Adolf Hitler's brutal regime. Tracy was
depressed throughout the shooting of this dark film. Several friends and his
mother died in a short period before shooting began, and during shooting
a telegram arrived informing Tracy that an orphan he had met while filming
BOYS TOWN had been killed in battlefield action. The boy had listed Tracy
as his next of kin. Tracy surprised everyone by agreeing to do a series of
publicity interviews for the film and praised novice director Zinnemann
lavishly, leading to Zinnemann quickly establishing a reputation as a
top-drawer director. Many of the small parts are beautifully and subtly
played, especially Cronyn's, as an old friend who helps Tracy along, and the
role played by Cronyn's wife both on the screen and in real life, Tandy, in
her first film. When released the film was attacked in some quarters for
taking too soft a view toward a nation with whom we were at war, but now
the film can be seen in clearer light and it stands as one of the best of the
swarms of anti-Nazi films Hollywood was to produce during the war years.

p, Pandro S. Berman; d, Fred Zinnemann; w, Helen Deutsch (based on the
novel by Anna Seghers); ph, Karl Freund; m, Roy Webb; ed, Thomas
Richards; art d, Cedric Gibbons, Leonid Vasian; set d, Edwin B. Willis, Mac
Alper; cos, Irene; spec eff, A. Arnold Gillespie, Danny Hall; makeup, Jack
Dawn.

Drama   (PR:C   MPAA:NR)

SEVENTH DAWN, THE**   (1964) 123m Holdean/UA c

William Holden (*Ferris*), Susannah York (*Candace*), Capucine (*Dhana*),
Tetsuro Tamba (*Ng*), Michael Goodliffe (*Trumphey*), Allan Cuthbertson
(*Cavendish*), Maurice Denham (*Tarlton*), Sidney Tafler (*C.P.O.*), Beulah Quo
(*Ah Ming*), Hugh Robinson (*Judge*), Tony Price (*Morley*), Griffiths Alun
(*Sedgwick*), Christopher Allen (*C.I.D.*), Yap Mook Fui (*Lim*), David Keith
(*Aide*), James Massong (*Malay Engineer*), R. William Koh (*Gen. Osaki*),
Allan Wong (*Col. Hsai*), Ibrahim Bin (*Capt. Chey*), Noel Chow (*Capt. Kiat*),
Hew Thian Choy (*Lt. Nelson*), David Weinman (*Tamil Cyclist*), George
Zakhariah (*Indian Unionist*), Seow (*Chinese Unionist*), Tony Cheng (*Wal-
ter*), Kip Bahadun (*Japanese Prisoner*).

Holden and Capucine had been conducting an off-screen affair ever since
they met while filming THE LION in Kenya. They must have saved all their
passion for their private moments because very little of it is on the screen
in this cliche-laden adventure made in and around Kuala Lumpur in
Malaysia. It's a compendium of every steamy Eurasian action drama ever
made and the dialog could have come from half a dozen other pictures. It's
1945 and the war has just ended. Holden had been running a guerrilla force
against the Japanese and now that the battles are done, he elects to stay on
and becomes a wealthy real estate owner. His old comrade, Tamba, takes off
for Moscow where he is indoctrinated into the Red terrorist ways. Holden's
mistress is Capucine and they have shared love and war together. She
remains at his side. Goodliffe is the new local British governor and York is
his sexy daughter, mad for Holden. Tamba returns some time later with an
eye toward converting Malaysia to communism. He gathers a cadre of men
and begins attacking all the landowners, notably leaving Holden safe from
his tactics. Goodliffe's people want Holden to trap Tamba but he refuses.
Capucine is also above turning in her pal, so she is framed by the authorities
and sentenced to be executed. To forestall that, York becomes Tamba's
hostage and word gets back that she will be killed unless Capucine is
released. Holden senses that it's time to toss loyalty out the window, so he
goes in bravely, rescues York, and sends Tamba's aides running. He's not
fast enough to get back before Capucine is executed. When Tamba gets the
drop on Holden, York shoots the terrorist after a struggle between the two.
With his mistress gone, York thinks she can step into Holden's affections,
but he thanks her and wearily suggests that she find love in the arms of a
younger man (he was 46 when he made this, York was 23). The working
titles for the movie were "The Third Road" and Wherever Love Takes Me."
A tired movie with little vitality, THE SEVENTH DAWN disappeared
quickly.

p, Charles K. Feldman; d, Lewis Gilbert; w, Karl Tunberg (based on the novel
The Durian Tree by Michael Koen); ph, Frederick Young (Technicolor); m,
Riz Ortolani; ed, John Shirley; md, Ortolani; prod d, John Stoll; art d,
Herbert Smith; set d, Jose MacAvin; cos, Hylda Gilbert; spec eff, Cliff
Richardson. makeup, John O'Gorman.

Adventure   (PR:A-C   MPAA:NR)

SEVENTH HEAVEN**½   (1937) 100m FOX bw

Simone Simon (*Diane*), James Stewart (*Chico*), Gale Sondergaard (*Nana*),
Gregory Ratoff (*Boul*), Jean Hersholt (*Father Chevillon*), J. Edward
Bromberg (*Aristide*), Victor Kilian (*Gobin*), John Qualen (*Sewer Rat*), Mady
Christians (*Marie*), Thomas Beck (*Bissac*), Sig Rumann (*Durand*), Rafaela
Ottiano (*Mme. Frisson*), Georges Renavent (*Gendarme Sergeant*), Edward
Keane, John Hamilton, Paul Porcasi (*Gendarmes*), Evelyn Selbie (*Old
Slattern*), John Picorri (*Proprietor*), Rollo Lloyd (*Mateot*), Leonid Snegoff
(*Officer*), Gene Massett (*Wounded Soldier*), Frank Puglia (*Postman*), Mar-
celle Corday (*Woman*), Constant Franke, Alphonse Martell, Joseph De
Stefani (*Men*), Eugene Borden (*Young Man*), John Bleifer (*Lamplighter*),
Adrienne d'Ambricourt (*Nurse*), Will Stanton, Irving Bacon (*Young Sol-
diers*).

This version of SEVENTH HEAVEN is an uneven remake of the Janet
Gaynor-Charles Farrell 1927 picture which had been brought to the screen
after the play, which starred Helen Menken, took Broadway by storm in
1922. Stewart never quite convinced anyone he was a Parisian sewer worker
living in the slums and Simon couldn't get a handle on her character under
King's uneven direction. Stewart is the sewer man who is a cynic, rejecting
the concept of God and never dreaming he could ever fall in love. Simon is
a prostitute who is dominated by her cruel sister, Sondergaard. When
Sondergaard tosses Simon out into the streets, she meets Stewart and he
gives her a haven in his slum apartment. She is struck by his kindliness and
is soon in love with him, an emotion he doesn't return. Hersholt is a priest
who is disturbed by Stewart's inability to embrace God and, in an attempt
to show him that other people care what happens, he arranges for Stewart
to get a new job as a street washer. Stewart and Simon become closer and
he eventually thinks about marrying her but WW I breaks out and he is
drafted. Rather than go through a formal ceremony, they swear their vows

cyclops, a fire-breathing dragon, and in the most memorable scene of all, Mathews has a thrilling swordfight with a living skeleton. After a breathtaking amount of never-before-seen action, all ends well with Grant restored to her normal size, the evil Thatcher defeated, and the survivors sailing home to Baghdad. While Harryhausen's contribution to the film is nothing less than stunning, the acting unfortunately is very weak. Though critics usually cluck their tongues over the stiff handling of the inherently unspeakable dialog, what they ignore is the actors' ability to pretend they are actually fighting creatures that don't exist until Harryhausen mattes them in. This is no easy task and the success of these movies depends on the actors being able to convey a sense of astonishment and fear, but the most difficult aspect of the actor's performance is "shadow-boxing" with these imaginary creatures. To film the fight with the skeleton, Mathews had to practice the carefully choreographed swordfight with Enzo Musomeci-Greco, an Olympic fencing master. Once Mathews had the moves memorized, Musomeci-Greco would withdraw from the scene, leaving the actor to perform the fight solo for the cameras. Months later, Harryhausen would animate his 8-inch skeleton to match Mathews' moves, using footage of Musomeci-Greco as a reference for his stop-motion model, and eventually combine the two sequences onto one piece of film, perfectly matched. After weeks of shooting in Spain and months of tedious special-effects work back in the States, THE SEVENTH VOYAGE OF SINBAD was ready for release. Hollywood skeptics quickly retracted their former negativity about the project because the film soon went on to become one of the top grossers of 1958 (on a re-release in 1968 the film grossed nearly $6 million), paving the way for Harryhausen to make more magic in such outstanding fantasy features as MYSTERIOUS ISLAND (1961), JASON AND THE ARGONAUTS (1963), THE VALLEY OF GWANGI (1969), THE GOLDEN VOYAGE OF SINBAD (1973), SINBAD AND THE EYE OF THE TIGER (1977), and CLASH OF THE TITANS (1981).

p, Charles H. Schneer; d, Nathan Juran; w, Kenneth Kolb; ph, Wilkie Cooper (Dynamation, Technicolor); m, Bernard Herrmann; art d, Gi Parrendo; ed, Edwin Bryant, Jerome Thoms; spec eff, Ray Harryhausen.

Fantasy   **Cas.**   **(PR:AA   MPAA:NR)**

SEVENTY DEADLY PILLS**   (1964, Brit.) 55m Children's Film
                                                     Foundation bw

Gareth Robinson (Brian), Len Jones (Phil Streaker), John Ross (Rusty), Sally Thomsett (Gerty), Linda Hansen (Nellie), Ronnie Johnson (Dickie Goodwin), Edward Cast (Police Constable Weaver), Leslie Dwyer (Police Constable Robinson), Warren Mitchell (Lofty), Timothy Bateson (Goldstone), Ronald Leigh-Hunt (Sergeant), Newton Blick (Sergeant), Ian Fleming (Doctor).

A group of children cause a panic when they mistake deadly poison for candy. The police conduct a wide-scale search and track down the kids before tragedy strikes.

p, Derick Williams; d&w, Pat Jackson (based on the story by Frank Wells).

Children   **(PR:AA   MPAA:NR)**

77 PARK LANE   (1931, Brit.) 82m Famous Players Guild/UA bw

Dennis Neilson-Terry (Lord Brent), Betty Stockfeld (Mary Connor), Malcolm Keen (Sherringham), Ben Welden (Sinclair), Cecil Humphreys (Paul), Esmond Knight (Philip Connor), Molly Johnson (Eve Grayson), Roland Culver (Sir Richard Carrington), W. Molesworth Blow (George Malton), John Turnbull (Superintendent).

An English melodrama, replete with the customary lords and earls to give it that distinct English flavor. Neilson-Terry is out on the town one night, grabs a taxi and spirits Stockfeld off to what he thinks is his empty house. When he arrives, he finds out the house is now a gambling center. He lets the crooks get away with it because they are blackmailing Stockfeld's brother for a murder of one of their associates. It was based on the play by Walter Hackett which enjoyed a decent following on the stage in London. A French version of this film was also directed by de Courville in the same year, starring Jean Murat and a French cast.

p, John Harding; d, Albert de Courville; w, Michael Powell, Reginald Berkeley (based on a play by Walter Hackett); ph, Matz Greenbaum, Geoffrey Faithfull; ed, Arthur Seabourne.

Drama   **(PR:A   MPAA:NR)**

70,000 WITNESSES**   (1932) 71m PAR bw

Phillips Holmes (Buck Buchanan), Dorothy Jordan (Dorothy Clark), Charlie Ruggles (Johnny Moran), Johnny Mack Brown (Wally Clark), J. Farrell MacDonald (State Coach), Lew Cody (Slip Buchanan), David Landau (Dan McKenna), Kenneth Thomson (Dr. Collins), Guinn "Big Boy" Williams (Connors), George Rosener (Ortello), Walter Hiers (Old Grad), Paul Page (Greenwood), Reed Howes (Southard), John David Horsley (Griffith).

The plot here, which takes some time to establish, is about a murder that occurs in the middle of a football game, hence, the 70,000 witnesses. Holmes is the big football star, who is framed by gamblers because his brother is a noted point shaver. When the quarter in which the death occurred is played

over again at the request of the police, Holmes slowly becomes exonerated for the crime. The sharp dialog drops hints about his innocence and who is guilty along the way. One drawback is that Holmes is far from being built like a football player and it takes a good stretch of the imagination to think of him lugging the ball time after time.

p, Charles R. Rogers; d, Ralph Murphy; w, Garret Fort, Robert N. Lee, P.J. Wolfson, Allen Rivkin (based on a novel by Cortland Fitzsimmons); ph, Henry Sharp.

Mystery   **(PR:A   MPAA:NR)**

7254 zero   (1971) 87m SHA c

Alan Midgette (Alan), Ruth Ford (Mother), Phoebe McAdams (Wife), Paul Gallan (Paul).

Midgette is a man filled with angst over the meaning of life in a world wracked by war. This gives him a handy excuse to run off from his usually naked wife, McAdams, loving mother Ford, and his friend, Gallan. Midgette usually ends up by himself, spouting incoherent dialog that when decipherable offers such sage wisdom as, "This war is a crime against nature." A good rule of thumb for film-going is to avoid anything where the actors use their own names for their characters. This movie is no exception. It has an improvisational style for just about everything, making for a disjointed effort that is impossible to sit through. The title comes from the designation set by Kodak for color negative film with significance only to the filmmaker. Director Stember was a fashion photographer who turned to cinema with this effort and hopefully went back to the still camera after its debut.

d, John Stember.

Drama   **(PR:O   MPAA:NR)**

SEVERED HEAD, A*½   (1971, Brit.) 98m Winkast/COL c

Lee Remick (Antonia Lynch-Gibbon), Richard Attenborough (Palmer Anderson, Psychiatrist), Ian Holm (Martin Lynch-Gibbon, Wine Merchant), Claire Bloom (Honor Klein), Jennie Linden (Georgie Hands), Clive Revill (Alexander Lynch-Gibbon), Ann Firbank (Rosemary Lynch-Gibbon), Rosamunde Greenwood (Miss Seelhaft), Constance Lorne (Miss Hernshaw), Robert Gillespie (Winking Patient), Katherine Parr (Nurse), Ann Jameson, Yvette Rees (Women at Party).

A black comedy about the sexual escapades of the upper crust in Britain. Remick, who is married to wine taster Holm, falls in love with Attenborough, the family's best friend and a psychologist, who is sexually involved with his half-sister, Bloom. All of them romp in the sack along the way, and enjoy each other's company in the meantime. After some trading around with various partners, each settles into a sexual, peaceful bliss. The film takes a few stabs at satire, with Holm playing the fall guy to perfection. He is the only one who does not enjoy all of the sexual freedom.

p, Alan Ladd, Jr.; d, Dick Clement; w, Frederic Raphael (based on the novel by Iris Murdoch and the play by Murdoch and J.B. Priestley); ph, Austin Dempster (Technicolor); m, Stanley Myers; ed, Peter Weatherley; prod. d, Richard MacDonald; art d, John Clark; set d, Hugh Scaife; cos, Sue Yelland; makeup, Freddie Williamson.

Comedy   **(PR:O   MPAA:R)**

SEX AGENT (SEE: THERE IS A STILL ROOM IN HELL, 1963, Ger.)

SEX AND THE SINGLE GIRL***   (1964) 114m WB c

Tony Curtis (Bob Weston), Natalie Wood (Dr. Helen Brown), Henry Fonda (Frank Broderick), Lauren Bacall (Sylvia Broderick), Mel Ferrer (Rudy DeMeyer), Fran Jeffries (Gretchen), Leslie Parrish (Susan), Edward Everett Horton (The Chief), Larry Storch (Motorcycle Cop), Stubby Kaye (Helen's Cabbie), Otto Kruger (Dr. Anderson), Howard St. John (George Randall), Max Showalter (Holmes), William Lanteau (Sylvester), Count Basie and His Orchestra (Themselves), Helen Kleeb (Hilda), Barbara Bouchet (Frannie), Burt Mustin (Harvey), Cheerio Meredith (Elderly Woman), Sharon Johnson (Sonia), Paul Bryar (Toll Gate Guard), Edmund Glover (Dr. Chickering), Taggart Casey (Guard), Fredd Wayne (Production Man), Charles Morton, Irving Steinberg, Tom Harkness, Jerry Martin, Sheila Stephenson, George Carey, Tom Quine (Board Members), Paddi O'Hara (Strange Woman), William Fawcett (Bum), Frank Baker (Pretzel Vendor), Curly Klein (Sylvia's Cabbie), Claire Carleton, Yvonne White, Mary Kovacs (Women), Philip Garris (Young Man).

Other than the title, the movie does not resemble Helen Gurley Brown's hit nonfiction book in any form. Joe Hoffman wrote the story and it was Joe Heller's agreeing to write the script that got Henry Fonda to join the cast. Fonda's favorite book was Heller's Catch-22 (perhaps because Heller wrote that one of his characters, "Major Major" looked like Fonda) and that's what finally convinced him to appear here, even after he'd declined the offer of a lot of money and the chance to play comedy after a long hiatus from the form. Curtis works as an editor for a scandal magazine run by Horton, who says that he wants to make his publication "the most disgusting scandal sheet the mind can recall." Curtis notes that psychologist Wood, who runs an organization called "The International Institute of Advanced Marital and

Pre-Marital Studies" might be a good subject for an expose. He suspects that this youngish woman (about 23) may just be a virgin and is using her position to alleviate her sexual frustrations. In order to get close to Wood, Curtis poses as another person and uses Fonda's name. Fonda is a neighbor of Curtis and in a constant harangue with his wife, Bacall, that is pocked with knock-down, drag-out verbal battles that everyone on their street is privy to. Curtis applies for help at Wood's organization and she thinks he's cute so she agrees to help, not knowing that he's there to write a follow-up smear article to the first one he's already written. Curtis consults Wood professionally on a number of occasions, then suggests they have an affair, something she soundly turns down. He calls her one day and claims that he's going to drown himself unless she agrees to make love and she races to the boat basin where the two of them accidentally fall into the water. They repair to Wood's apartment to get out of their wet clothes and into a dry martini (a quote from Robert Benchley) and he mixes some strong booze and puts a heavy make on Wood, which she continues to repel. Then Curtis tells her that he and his wife are not legally wed, just living together. Wood doesn't believe him and wants to consult with his wife, Bacall. Since Wood has never met Bacall, Curtis enlists the aid of his one-time lover, Jeffries, and his secretary, Parrish. When one says she can't make it, he tries the other. As it stands, both women show up to impersonate Bacall at Wood's office and, at the same time, Wood calls Bacall and asks her to come in. All three women arrive and Bacall is furious, then has Fonda thrown in jail for having two too many wives. Wood finally sees through Curtis' ploy and decides to go out of town with Ferrer, a colleague-psychiatrist who admits that he became a shrink because "I like to hear dirty stories." Wood and Ferrer are on their way to the airport and Curtis, who has just been fired by Horton for refusing to write a scurrilous article on Wood, is after them. At the same time, Fonda is trying to get away to Hawaii and Bacall is pursuing him in a cab. There's a mad chase in taxis that winds up at the airport where everything is finally sorted out. Curtis and Wood find each other, Ferrer and Jeffries fall madly in love and Fonda and Bacall decide that they can't live a moment apart from each other. Ferrer and Jeffries get on the plane to Hawaii and it all ends up in a predictable smile. Count Basie appears with his orchestra (including Marshall Royal, Frank Foster, Freddie Green, Lou Blackburn, Sonny Payne) and plays the title tune by Quine and Hefti as well as "What Is This Thing Called Love?" by Cole Porter from "Wake Up And Dream." In a small role as a production man note Fredd Wayne, who spends his night-times playing Benjamin Franklin in a superb one-man show around the world. Larry Storch also turns in a neat cameo as a motorcycle cop driven to distraction by the chase along the San Diego Freeway that precedes the final scenes at the airport. Ms. Brown's husband, David, was a studio executive who later teamed up with Richard Zanuck to produce many hits such as THE STING as well as both JAWS films.

p, William T. Orr; d, Richard Quine; w, Joseph Heller, David R. Schwartz (based on the book by Helen Gurley Brown, story by Joseph Hoffman); ph, Charles Lang (Panavision, Technicolor); m, Neal Hefti; ed, David Wages; md, Hefti; art d, Cary O'Dell; set d, Edward G. Boyle; cos, Edith Head, Norman Norell; m/l, Cole Porter, Hefti, Quine; makeup, Gordon Bau.

Comedy   **(PR:C   MPAA:NR)**

SEX AND THE TEENAGER   (SEE: TO FIND A MAN, 1972)

SEX AT NIGHT   (SEE: LOVE AT NIGHT, 1961, Fr.)

SEX IS A WOMAN   (SEE: LOVE IS A WOMAN, 1967, Brit.)

SEX KITTENS GO TO COLLEGE*
(1960) 94m AA bw (AKA: BEAUTY AND THE ROBOT; BEAUTY AND THE BRAIN)

Mamie Van Doren (Dr. Mathilda West), Tuesday Weld (Jody), Mijanou Bardot (Suzanne), Mickey Shaughnessy (Boomie), Louis Nye (Dr. Zorch), Pamela Mason (Dr. Myrtle Carter), Marty Milner (George Barton), Conway Twitty (Himself), Jackie Coogan (Wildcat MacPherson), John Carradine (Prof. Watts), Vampira (Etta Toodie), Allan Drake (Legs Raffertino), Woo Woo Grabowski (Himself), Irwin Berke (Prof. Towers), Babe London (Miss Cadwallader), Arlene Hunter (Nurse), Jody Fair (Bartender), Buni Bacon (Night Club Hostess), Charles Chaplin, Jr (Fire Chief), Harold Lloyd, Jr (Policeman).

Some big names can't save this farce about beauty and brains. Van Doren is a stripper selected by a robot because of her high I.Q. to run a college science department. Strutting their stuff in tight sweaters along with Doren are Weld, Bardot (Brigitte's sister), and Vampira. Coogan, a child star of the 1920s, stars as a Texas millionaire, and Conway Twitty appears and croons a couple of songs. The interesting cast also includes the sons of two great silent comedians, Charles Chaplin and Harold Lloyd.

p&d, Albert Zugsmith; w, Robert Hill (based on a story by Zugsmith); m, Dean Elliott; m/l, Conway Twitty.

Drama   **(PR:A   MPAA:NR)**

SEX RACKETEERS, THE   (SEE: MAN OF VIOLENCE, 1970, Brit.)

SEXORCISTS, THE   (SEE: TORMENTED, THE, 1978, Ital.)

SEXTETTE*   (1978) 91m Crown International c

Mae West (Marlo Manners), Timothy Dalton (Sir Michael Barrington), Dom DeLuise (Dan Turner), Tony Curtis (Alexei Karansky), Ringo Starr (Laslo Karolny), George Hamilton (Vance), Alice Cooper (Waiter), Keith Allison (Waiter in Alexei's Suite), Rona Barrett (Herself), Van McCoy (Delegate), Keith Moon (Dress Designer), Regis Philbin (Himself), Walter Pidgeon (The Chairman), George Raft (Himself), Harry Weiss (The Don), Gil Stratton (Himself).

The original sex kitten's last film. West should have never come out of her retirement for this role, which could almost be biographical for some Hollywood starlets of the past. West plays a fading star who marrys an English nobleman. She's all set to consummate the marriage (her sixth) but is flooded with interruptions – a gymnastics team, Rona Barrett, news reporters, and some international diplomats. While doing all this, she is dictating her memoirs when the tape accidentally gets lost. She searches frantically for the tape because it could ruin her marriage, since her past could create international havoc. Too much camp from West in a film that should never have been made. Rock singers Alice Cooper and Ringo Starr appear in small roles, while various Hollywood personalities appear as themselves.

p, Daniel Briggs, Robert Sullivan; d, Ken Hughes; w, Herbert Baker (based on the play by Mae West); ph, James Crabe (Metrocolor); m, Artie Butler, Gene Cantamessa; ed, Argyle Nelson; prod d, Thad Prescott; art d, James F. Clayton; set d, Reg Allen; cos, Edith Head (gowns); ch, Marc Breaux.

Musical/Comedy   **Cas.**   **(PR:C   MPAA:PG)**

SEXTON BLAKE AND THE BEARDED DOCTOR*
(1935, Brit.) 64m FOX British/MGM bw

George Curzon (Sexton Blake), Henry Oscar (Dr. Gibbs), Tony Sympson (Tinker), Gillian Maude (Janet), Phil Ray (Jim Cameron), John Turnbull (Inspector Donnell), Edward Dignon (Hawkins), James Knight (Red), Donald Wolfit (Percy), Johnnie Schofield, Ben Williams.

Curzon is a renowned detective studying the case of a murdered violinist. He meticulously combs the clues until he uncovers a plot engineered by Oscar to defraud an insurance company. Curzon exposes Oscar's plan and saves the life of a pressured young insurance agent. One of Curzon's three appearances as Sexton Blake, though David Farrar brought back the role one more time in MEET SEXTON BLAKE (1944). (See SEXTON BLAKE series, Index.)

p&d, George A. Cooper; w, Rex Hardinge (based on his novel The Blazing Launch Murder).

Crime   **(PR:A   MPAA:NR)**

SEXTON BLAKE AND THE HOODED TERROR½**
(1938, Brit.) 70m MGM bw

George Curzon (Sexton Blake), Tod Slaughter (Michael Larron), Greta Gynt (Mlle. Julie), Charles Oliver (Max Fleming), Tony Sympson (Tinker), Marie Wright (Mrs. Bardell), Norman Pierce (Inspector Bramley), David Farrar (Granite Grant), Carl Melene, Alex Huber, Philip Holles, Len Sharpe, H.B. Hallam.

An entertaining crime drama which stars Curzon as Sexton Blake, a poor man's Sherlock Holmes. He is hot on the trail of an international gang of crooks known as "The Hooded Terror," led by a notorious person known only as "The Snake." Curzon's sleuthing leads him to the doorstep of millionaire Slaughter, who turns out to be "The Snake." Curzon's goal of snaring Slaughter goes unrealized when the detective must divert his energies to save the lovely Gynt from a premature death. Slaughter escapes and the possibility of a sequel is left wide open. In fact, the possibility is still there since an expected fourth entry in the series never came. In a bit role is David Farrar who resurrected the Sexton Blake character in the unrelated and less-successful MEET SEXTON BLAKE (1944). (See SEXTON BLAKE series, Index.)

p&d, George King; w, A.R. Rawlinson (based on the novel by Pierre Quiroule); ph, Hone Glendinning.

Crime   **Cas.**   **(PR:A   MPAA:NR)**

SEXTON BLAKE AND THE MADEMOISELLE**
(1935, Brit.) 63m FOX British/MGM bw

George Curzon (Sexton Blake), Lorraine Grey (Mlle. Roxanne), Tony Sympson (Tinker), Edgar Norfolk (Inspector Thomas), Raymond Lovell (Captain), Ian Fleming (Henry Norman), Vincent Holman (Carruthers), Wilson Coleman (Pierre), Ben Williams, Henry Peterson, William Collins.

Curzon is hired by a financier to uncover some stolen bonds. He puts his supersleuth sense to work and digs up proof that the culprit is the daughter

(Grey) of a former employee, ruined by the financier's tactics. A likable film with the enjoyable Curzon again tackling his SEXTON BLAKE role. (See SEXTON BLAKE series, Index)

p, Michael Barringer; d, Alex Bryce; w, Barringer (based on a novel They Shall Repay by G.H. Teed); ph, Bryce.

Crime   (PR:A MPAA:NR)

SEXY GANG   (SEE: MICHELLE, 1970, Fr.)

SEZ O'REILLY TO MACNAB***   (1938, Brit.) 83m
        GAU-Gainsborough/GFD bw (GB: SAID O 'REILLY TO MACNAB)

Will Mahoney (Timothy O'Reilly), Will Fyffe (Malcolm MacNab), Ellis Drake (Mrs. MacNab), Sandy McDougal (Jock McKay), Jean Winstanley (Mary MacNab), James Carney (Terry O'Reilly), Marianne Davis (Sophie), Robert Gall (Jock MacNab).

Charming picture with Mahoney and Fyffe doing their best to swindle each other. Mahoney plays a businessman who leaves the U.S. so he doesn't end up in prison. Taking his secretary, Davies, he winds up in Scotland in the home of wealthy Fyffe. The stage is set for the pair to show off their skills at one-upmanship, ending with the marriage of Mahoney's son to Fyffe's daughter. All in good fun.

p, Edward Black; d, William Beaudine; w, Leslie Arliss, Marriott Edgar (based on the story by Howard Irving Young); ph, Arthur Crabtree.

Comedy/Drama   (PR:A MPAA:NR)

SFIDA A RIO BRAVO   (SEE: GUNMEN OF THE RIO GRANDE, 1965, Fr./Ital./Span.)

SH! THE OCTOPUS*½   (1937) 54m FN-WB bw

Hugh Herbert (Kelly), Allen Jenkins (Dempsey), Marcia Ralston (Vesta Vernoff), John Eldredge (Paul Morgan), George Rosener (Capt. Hook), Brandon Tynan (Mr. Cobb), Eric Stanley (A Stranger), Margaret Irving (Polly Crane), Elspeth Dudgeon (Nanny).

Even an octopus doesn't have enough arms to choke off this one. Lame attempt at a thriller with Herbert reprising his role as an idiot detective with able companion Jenkins. They stumble through the investigation of some strange goings-on at a lighthouse. The film is supposed to evoke scares, but is so poor, it only elicits laughter, and applause – when it's finally mercifully over. Based on the play, "The Gorilla," with an octopus substituting for the gorilla. A zoo full of animals couldn't make this one scary.

p, Bryan Foy; d, William McGann; w, George Bricker (based on a play by Ralph Spence, Ralph Murphy, Donald Gallagher); ph, Arthur Todd; ed, Clarence Kolster.

Mystery/Comedy   (PR:A MPAA:NR)

SHABBY TIGER, THE   (SEE: MASQUERADE, 1965, Brit.)

SHACK OUT ON 101*½   (1955) 80m AA bw

Terry Moore (Kotty the Waitress), Frank Lovejoy (Professor), Keenan Wynn (George), Lee Marvin (Slob the cook), Whit Bissell (Eddie), Jess Barker (Artie), Donald Murphy (Pepe), Frank De Kova (Dillon), Len Lesser (Perch), Fred Gabourie (Lookout).

Some decent actors suffer their way through this film, which just crawls along, losing the audience on the way. The "shack" of the title refers to the restaurant where Moore works. Lovejoy plays a scientist who works in the area. Along with pursuing Moore, he trades government secrets with foreign agent Marvin. After too much talking and not enough action, it is revealed that Lovejoy is on the right side and is trying to snare Marvin for the U.S. government while keeping Moore away from him.

p, Mort Millman; d, Edward Dein; w, Edward Dein, Mildred Dein; ph, Floyd Crosby; m, Paul Dunlap; ed, George White; art d, Lou Croyton; m/l, "A Sunday Kind of Love," Barbara Belle, Louis Prima, Anita Leonard, Stan Rhodes.

Drama   **Cas.**   (PR:A MPAA:NR)

SHADES OF SILK½** (1979, Can.) 65m John and Mary Production c

Alexandra Brouwer, Mary Stephen, John Cressey, Isabel Beers.

In Shanghai during the 1930s two women become close friends. The intense friendship borders on the sexual, though this is left ambiguous. Finally one of the two marries, leaving her companion to choose her own path. This film was put together in a slightly surrealistic style to suggest memories rather than actual events, and, using music with a unique visual style, conveys a strong sense of emotion. Director Stephen, who plays one of the protagonists, was originally from Hong Kong but emigrated to Canada. Though shot on location in Paris, Stephen created an authentic look of the Orient within that city, a true measure of skill if ever there was one.

d, Mary Stephen; w, Stephen, Ann Martin; ph, John Cressy; m, Alain Leroux; ed, Stephen Martin.

Drama   (PR:O MPAA:NR)

SHADOW, THE*½   (1936, Brit.) 63m Real Art/UA bw

Henry Kendall (Reggie Ogden/The Shadow), Elizabeth Allan (Sonya Bryant), Jeanne Stuart (Moya Silverton), Felix Aylmer (Sir Richard), Cyril Raymond (Silverton), Viola Compton (Mrs. Bascomb), John Turnbull (Inspector), Sam Livesey (Sir Richard Bryant).

Too much dialog at the expense of action and a middle-of-the-road plot puts no light on "The Shadow." A blackmailing killer is on the loose and its up to Scotland Yard to track him down. Kendall is the novelist who finally helps them unveil the murderer. Allan is herded in, seemingly against her will, as the romantic interest.

p, Julius Hagen; d, George A. Cooper; w, H. Fowler Mear, Terence Egan (based on a play by Donald Stuart); ph, Sydney Blythe; ed, Jack Harris.

Crime Drama   (PR:A MPAA:NR)

SHADOW, THE½**   (1937) 59m COL bw

Rita Hayworth (Mary Gillespie), Charles Quigley (Jim Quinn), Marc Lawrence (Kid Crow), Arthur Loft (Sheriff Jackson), Dick Curtis (Carlos), Vernon Dent (Dutch Schultz), Marjorie Main (Hannah Gillespie), Donald Kirke (Senor Peter Martinet), Dwight Frye (Vindecco), Bess Flowers (Marianne), Bill Irving (Mac), Eddie Fetherston (Woody), Sally St. Clair (Dolores), Sue St. Clair (Rosa), John Tyrrell (Mr. Moreno), Beatrice Curtis (Mrs. Moreno), Ann Doran, Beatrice Blinn (Shaw Sisters), Bud Jamison, Harry Strang (Ticket Sellers), Francis Sayles (Mr. Shaw), Edward Hearn (Circus Doctor), Edward J. LeSaint (Bascomb), Mr. and Mrs. Clemens (Knife-Throwing Act), Ted Mahgean (Masked Figure), Harry Bernard (Watchman), George Hickman (Messenger Boy), Ernie Adams (Roustabout).

The alluring Hayworth plays a woman who inherits a debt-ridden circus after her father dies in this better-than-average murder-melodrama. Her father owed $60,000 to the horseman in the riding act, who also happens to be a hated by almost everyone in the show. After the film sets up all the characters with a motive for murder, the horseman turns up with a knife sticking out of his back. The film is most interesting for the fact that it is the first film in which Hayworth received top billing.

p, Wallace MacDonald; d, Charles C. Coleman, Jr.; w, Arthur T. Horman (based on a story by Milton Raison); ph, Lucien Ballard; ed, Byron Robinson; md, Morris W. Stoloff; art d, Lionel Banks, Stephen Goosson; cos, Ray Howell, Robert Kalloch.

Mystery   (PR:A MPAA:NR)

SHADOW AND THE MISSING LADY, THE
        (MISSING LADY, THE, 1946) 22130 SHADOW BETWEEN, THE**½
                                                (1932, Brit.) 86m BIP/Powers bw

Godfrey Tearle (Paul Haddon), Kathleen O'Regan (Margaret Haddon), Olga Lindo (Nell Baker), Ann Casson (Betty Fielder), Haddon Mason (Philip), Mary Jerrold (Mrs. Maddox), Hubert Harben (Rev. Simon Maddox), Henry Wenman (Sgt. Blake), Henry Caine (Wincher), Morton Selten (Sir George Fielder), Arthur Chesney (Pug Wilson), Jerrold Robertshaw (Mr. Haddon).

A British prison film with an offbeat plot. Tearle is sent to prison for a crime he never committed. His wife, O'Regan, rather than wait on the outside for her innocent man, decides to commit a crime to join him in jail, so he doesn't feel inferior to her when he is released. When he finally gets out, he discovers she is also under suspicion for a crime she didn't do. Seems like guilty looks run in the family.

p, John Maxwell; d, Norman Walker; w, Walker, Dion Titheradge (based on a story by Titheradge); ph, Claude Friese-Greene.

Drama   (PR:A MPAA:NR)

SHADOW BETWEEN, THE½**   (1932, Brit.) 86m BIP/Powers bw

Godfrey Tearle (Paul Haddon), Kathleen O'Regan (Margaret Haddon), Olga Lindo (Nell Baker), Ann Casson (Betty Fielder), Haddon Mason (Philip), Mary Jerrold (Mrs. Maddox), Hubert Harben (Rev. Simon Maddox), Henry Wenman (Sgt. Blake), Henry Caine (Wincher), Morton Selten (Sir George Fielder), Arthur Chesney (Pug Wilson), Jerrold Robertshaw (Mr. Haddon).

A British prison film with an offbeat plot. Tearle is sent to prison for a crime he never committed. His wife, O'Regan, rather than wait on the outside for her innocent man, decides to commit a crime to join him in jail, so he doesn't feel inferior to her when he is released. When he finally gets out, he discovers she is also under suspicion for a crime she didn't do. Seems like guilty looks run in the family.

p, John Maxwell; d, Norman Walker; w, Walker, Dion Titheradge (based on a story by Titheradge); ph, Claude Friese-Greene.

Drama   (PR:A MPAA:NR)

SHADOW IN THE SKY½   (1951) 78m MGM bw

Ralph Meeker (*Burt*), Nancy Davis (*Betty*), James Whitmore (*Lou*), Jean Hagen (*Stella*), Gladys Hurlbut (*Mrs. Lehner*), Eduard Franz (*The Doctor*), Dennis Ross (*Chris*), Nadene Ashdown (*Nina*), John Lupton (*Clayton*), Jonathan Cott (*Doug*).

Meeker returns from WW II with a problem. He has been shell-shocked during the war, and becomes suddenly afraid every time it begins to rain. Davis is his big-hearted sister who wants him to live with her and her family in the bucolic suburbs. She and her husband must face the question of whether to allow Meeker around their two young children. Meeker conquers his neurosis when his nephew falls into a large body of water during a rainstorm. The story line gets too melodramatic, with Hagen thrown in to provide Meeker's love interest.

p, William H. Wright; d, Fred M. Wilcox; w, Ben Maddow (based on the story by Edward Newhouse); ph, George J. Folsey; m, Bronislau Kaper; ed, Ben Lewis; art d, Cedric Gibbons, Randall Duell.

Drama   (PR:A   MPAA:NR)

SHADOW MAN   (1953, Brit.) 76m Anglo Amalgamated/Lippert bw
(GB: STREET OF SHADOWS)

Cesar Romero (*Luigi*), Kay Kendall (*Barbara Gale*), Edward Underdown (*Inspector Johnstone*), Victor Maddern (*Limpy*), Simone Silva (*Angele Abbe*), Liam Gaffney (*Fred Roberts*), Robert Cawdron (*Sgt. Hadley*), John Penrose (*Capt. Gerald Gale*), Bill Travers (*Nigel Langley*), Molly Hamley Clifford (*Starry Darrell*), Eileen Way (*Mrs. Toms*), Paul Hardtmuth (*Poppa*), Annaconda (*Darrell*).

Fair drama with Romero running a casino in London. He is framed for the killing of an old flame, Silva, who was found stabbed in his apartment. He unwittingly asks the crippled Maddern for help in finding the real murderer, not knowing that his buddy is the actual killer. The tension builds nicely with Underdown investigating the case step by step, finally clearing Romero in the climactic scene when Maddern confesses to all. Nice touch of suspense throughout, with Romero trying to outwit the police while Maddern tries to set a trap for Romero to get himself off the hook.

p, W.H. Williams; d,w, Richard Vernon (based on the novel *The Creaking Chair* by Lawrence Meynall); ph, Phil Grindrod; m, Eric Spear; ed, Geoffrey Muller.

Crime/Drama   (PR:A   MPAA:NR)

SHADOW OF A DOUBT   (1935) 71m MGM bw

Ricardo Cortez (*Sim*), Virginia Bruce (*Trenna*), Constance Collier (*Aunt Melissa*), Isabel Jewell (*Inez*), Arthur Byron (*Bellwood*), Betty Furness (*Lisa*), Regis Toomey (*Reed Ryan*), Ivan Simpson (*Morse*), Bradley Page (*Hayworth*), Edward Brophy (*Wilcox*), Samuel S. Hinds (*Mr. Granby*), Richard Tucker (*Mark Torrey*), Bernard Siegel (*Ehrhardt*), Paul Hurst (*Lt. Sackville*).

A run-of-the-mill murder story, which featured the first film appearance by well-known Shakespearean actress Collier, who had been coaching MGM stars in drama and diction. The story involves an actress, Bruce, who is charged with murder. Cortez wants to marry her, but Collier, his wealthy aunt, will disown him and cut him out of her will if he keeps chasing Bruce. Suddenly, she has a change of heart, believes her nephew, and works at getting Bruce declared innocent. The actual killer is revealed to be Toomey.

p, Lucien Hubbard; d, George B. Seitz; w, Wells Root (based on a story by Arthur Somers Roche); ph, Charles Clarke; ed, Basil Wrangell.

Thriller   (PR:A   MPAA:NR)

SHADOW OF A DOUBT***   (1943) 108m UNIV bw

Teresa Wright (*Young Charlie*), Joseph Cotten (*Uncle Charlie*), Macdonald Carey (*Jack Graham*), Henry Travers (*Joseph Newton*), Patricia Collinge (*Emma Newton*), Hume Cronyn (*Herbie Hawkins*), Edna Mae Wonacott (*Ann Newton*), Wallace Ford (*Fred Saunders*), Irving Bacon (*Station Master*), Charles Bates (*Roger Newton*), Clarence Muse (*Railroad Porter*), Janet Shaw (*Louise*), Estelle Jewell (*Girl Friend*), Minerva Urecal (*Mrs. Henderson*), Isabel Randolph (*Mrs. Green*), Earle S. Dewey (*Mr. Norton*), Eily Malyon (*Librarian*), Edward Fielding, Sarah Edwards (*Doctor and Wife on Train*), Vaughn Glaser (*Dr. and Mrs. Phillips*), Grandon Rhodes, Ruth Lee (*Rev. and Mrs. MacCurdy*), Edwin Stanley (*Mr. Green*), Frances Carson (*Mrs. Poetter*), Byron Shores, John McGuire (*Detectives*), Constance Purdy (*Mrs. Martin*), Shirley Mills (*Young Girl*).

This was Hitchcock's favorite film, one based on a real-life "Merry Widow Murderer," Earle Leonard Nelson, mass strangler of the 1920s. The sly Hitchcock made this chiller all the more frightening by having his crafty homicidal maniac intrude into the tranquility of a warm, middle-class family living in a small town, deeply developing his characters and drawing forth from soft-spoken Cotten one of that actor's most remarkable and fascinating performances. Cotten is shown at the beginning of the film wooing and then murdering a woman for her riches, and escaping just ahead of the pursuing detectives who chase him through the back alleys of an eastern city. He

boards a train after wiring his sister Collinge in Santa Rosa, California, that he is coming for an extended stay with the only family he has. (On board the train, as a passenger in his cameo appearance, is director Hitchcock.) Wright, a vivacious and warm-hearted young lady, is delighted to hear that her urbane, witty, and adventurous uncle, Cotten, will be visiting her and her family. She and her father, Travers, and young brother and sister, Wonacott and Bates, greet Cotten at the train station and are shocked to see him alight with the help of porters, limping on a cane. He claims to be ill and the family quickly takes him home where his sister dotes on him. Wright is totally charmed by the suave and sophisticated Cotten who compliments her on her wit and attractiveness. She accompanies him about the little town of Santa Rosa. Cotten stops at a bank and makes a scene while depositing $40,000, but his strange behavior is explained as an idiosyncracy by the adoring Wright. Collinge thinks her younger brother is the "better half" of the family with his intelligence and intellectual wit and she is protective of him, even when thinking back to Cotten's childhood. Collinge recalls for the family as they sit in their comfortable middle-class house how Cotten was "such a quiet boy, always reading." She turns to Cotten who gives her a benign smile and continues, "I always said that Papa never should have bought you that bicycle. You didn't know how to handle it." She turns to Wright, eager for any background information on the uncle she admires, and tells her: "He took it right out onto the icy road and skidded into a streetcar. We thought he was going to die. He was laid up so long. And then, when he was getting well, there was no holding him. It was just as though all the rest he had was too much and he had to get into mischief to blow off steam." (Hitchcock himself wrote this particular speech and it is reportedly based on an incident of his own life, but it is an almost verbatim accident that occurred to mass murderer Earle Leonard Nelson whose head was opened when he was struck by a streetcar as a child and, it was later thought, his brain was damaged, the accident making him a lunatic from childhood.) This nostalgic talk warms Cotten's heart and he responds to his sister's statements by saying: "I keep remembering those things—all the old things....Everybody was sweet and pretty then, the whole world. A wonderful world. Not like the world today. Not like the world now. It was great to be young then." Cotten hates the present and, as Wright sadly learns later, all the women in it, (except for his sister, a surrogate mother image). Meanwhile, as a peripheral goad to Cotten's real character, the strangler lurking beneath his thin veneer of charm, is a running dialog that Travers has with oddball next-door-neighbor Cronyn. Both of them are obsessed with murder, a typical small town preoccupation to stimulate otherwise drab existences, and are constantly proposing to each other types of murders that could not be detected but the other always finding a way of quickly solving the so-called perfect crime. (Here Hitchcock is able to parade a number of ingenious killings before the viewer, mostly by 19th Century British killers who fascinated him.) The director does not fail to interject his offbeat brand of humor, having the younger daughter, Wonacott, complain to her father Travers about her mother's misuse of the telephone (a trait of Hitchcock's own mother, after whom he named Collinge's character): "Really, Papa, you'd think Mama had never seen a phone. She makes no allowance for science. She thinks she has to cover the distance by sheer lung power!" Both of the smaller children are absorbed by science, Wonacott being a voracious reader and the small boy, Bates, totally obsessed with mathematics. But into this tranquil backwater setting the world and Cotten's awful past begin to intrude. Carey, a detective, comes upon the scene and begins to make inquiries about Cotten to Wright, arousing her suspicions, but she battles this compunction to think that her beloved uncle could ever be a mass killer, as Carey has suggested. She tries to draw closer to her uncle to learn about his past and allay her fears. He tells her that they are family and must stick together, already suspicious himself that Carey, pretending to be just another of Wright's beaus, is really the cop he is and on his trail. "The same blood runs through our veins." Cotten reminds Wright. She responds by telling him that "I'm glad that mother named me after you, and that she thinks we're both alike. I think we are, too. I know it.... We're not just an uncle and a niece. It's something else. I know you. I know you don't tell people a lot of things. I don't either. I have a feeling that inside you somewhere there's something nobody knows about...something secret and wonderful. I'll find out....We're sort of like twins, don't you see? We have to know." These words are like red warning flags to the apprehensive Cotten. He finds a newspaper article about himself, describing the nationwide manhunt to capture the "Merry Widow Murderer," and tears it from the daily paper. When Wright discovers the newspaper mutilated and later finds the clipping hidden in Cotten's room, she begins to investigate on her own. Cotten quickly discerns her suspicions of him, almost as if a weird telepathy existed between the pair. The two are very much alike, but where Wright is good, Cotten is simply evil. And the evil in the man begins to burst from him. At one dinner he suddenly explodes when the subject of rich widows is brought up and he sneers, spitting out words coated with venom, "You see these women everywhere—useless women, drinking the money, eating the money, smelling of money!" His outburst brings tears to Wright's eyes, as her preconceived image of her noble uncle begins to evaporate. Later, when Wright has definitely decided that Cotten is the mass killer Carey the police everywhere are seeking, she agonizes over what to do. She is not only afraid for herself and her family but still clings to the love she had for Cotten and fears for him also. She nevertheless grows cold toward him and they exchange long, knowing glances while Cotten decides that he must kill Wright to keep her silent. Before that, he takes her to a smoke-filled bar and, sitting in a booth, tries to convince her that the little lies she has caught him telling mean nothing. But in his talk Cotten does nothing more than reveal his own hideous nature, convincing Wright that her suspicions are correct. Says Cotten: "We're old friends, Charlie. More than that...we're like twins. You said so yourself. You think you know something, don't you? You think you're the clever little girl who knows something. There's so much you don't know. So much. What do you know, really? You're just an ordinary little girl living in an ordinary little town. You wake up every morning of your life and you know perfectly well that there's nothing in the world to trouble you. You go through your ordinary little day and at night, you sleep your untroubled, ordinary little sleep filled with peaceful stupid dreams. And I brought your nightmares. Or did I? Or was it a silly inexpert little lie? You live in a dream. You're a sleepwalker, blind! How do you know what the world is like?" Here Cotten's demeanor changes to a man so full of hatred that he cannot help but expose it, his eyes narrowing, his voice growing hoarse with the fierce anger that possesses him: "Do you know the world is a foul sty? Do you know if you ripped the fronts off houses you'd find swine? The world's a hell! What does it matter what happens in it?" Unable to bear Cotten's invective further, Wright runs home. Later, when the family is preparing to go out, Cotten inveigles Wright into starting the family car in the garage, making sure that she cannot turn off the ignition and escape; he closes the garage doors, knowing that the family has been having problems opening these doors. While Wright begins to succumb to carbon monoxide poisoning, the family dawdles about, Travers going back up the stairs to get his overcoat so many times that Hitchcock was later accused of playing sadistic games with the audience, viewers literally screaming in the theaters: "She's in the garage! Hurry up!" Neighbor Cronyn passes the garage at the last minute and notices the car's exhaust smoke and calls the family. Cotten, to cover his own devilish machinations, races to the garage and saves Wright. He had already tried to kill her earlier by fixing a step on a steep stairway so that she would fall and kill herself but Wright managed to survive this trap. After the garage incident, Wright plots with Carey on how to expose her uncle but is still having a hard time bringing herself to hurt her family. Cotten is now like a caged animal and realizes that the law is closing in on him. It's time to flee. He tells the family members that he must leave to attend to business, and asks them to see him off at the train station. He entices Wright on board the train to say a final farewell and, between cars, as the train begins to pull out of the station and get up lethal speed, he confronts her with her own suspicions about him, more or less admitting that he is the mass killer and that, because she knows it, she must die. He will make her death look like an accident. He grabs her and is about to throw her through the open door, waiting for another train approaching in the opposite direction, to come abreast of the train on which they are riding so that she will be crushed by the oncoming train. Here Hitchcock shows only the legs of his two stars, Cotten and Wright, struggling, moving for balance and position on the little platform of the moving car. "Not yet, Charlie," Cotten says, gauging the distance being shortened by the oncoming train, "just a little longer..." The train suddenly lurches just as Wright pushes away from Cotten and he, not his intended victim, goes pitching off the train directly in the path of the on-coming engine and is killed instantly. Wright winds up with Carey at her side but does not expose the horrid past of her dead uncle, preferring for her family's sake to let the world believe her cherished Cotten died in an accident. He is buried after an impressive funeral, the little town of Santa Rosa unwittingly paying tribute to one of the country's worst mass killers. Some film analysts have tried, and miserably so, to connect this film with the inner workings of Hitchcock's mind, claiming that he put so much of himself into this film that it is a mirror image of his own worst side, showing, as he meticulously does, the underside of the worst in human beings, particularly one human being. Nothing could be further from the truth. Hitchcock was merely telling a good story, based not on himself but on a real-life killer who intrigued him; he went about his skilful way in examining the character and personality of that killer. This is Hitchcock's most penetrating analysis of a murderer, including his psychological thriller SPELLBOUND, and, as such, it is a masterpiece profile. Cotten is superb as the subtle killer who cannot escape his own dark passions, despite an iron-willed intellect that tells him he is superior to all comers. The construction of the film is adroit and very calculated, letting the viewer know early on just what kind of man Cotten really is but presenting him in such a way that his own family cannot think of him as anything other than a gentle and kind man. All the while Hitchcock presents a cat-and-mouse game between Cotten and Wright that is full of chilling *angst*. He is at his story-telling here, creating a down-to-earth thriller that discards all the impossible, wild exploits his characters would experience in such entertaining but fanciful films as NORTH BY NORTHWEST. The director took his time with this film, getting Wilder to write the screenplay, accurately figuring that the author of "Our Town" would be the perfect scriptwriter to profile the small town of Santa Rosa and give the right kind of ambience and characterization to such a close-knit community. He was correct, although Hitchcock wrote some scenes Wilder never saw. This was his method of constructing a film, first doing his story boards to place his own ideas into firm visuals, depicting with his own stick drawings exactly how he envisioned each scene, and then working closely with the writer to develop the script. He was to say later (in Jay Robert Nash's *The Innovators*): "I work on it 'the script' from the beginning with the writer. It's not so much that I'm doing the writing, like dialog and character, it's the fact that I'm bringing the writer into the direction of the picture. I'm making him aware of how we ought to see certain things, how it should be shot. It's not a

question of my taking his script and interpreting it. If the writer goes to see the picture, he will see exactly on the screen what we have decided on ahead of time. Many writers turn in a script and when they look at the picture, it's all different from what they wrote." Wilder did not stay put for long with Hitchcock in the same room, but wandered about Hollywood with a little notebook, writing bits and pieces of the screenplay when he could. He and the director took their time developing this intricate story and Wilder had not yet finished the film play when he enlisted to serve in the psychological Warfare Division of the Army. The director simply got on a train going cross-country to Florida where Wilder was to begin his training, and patiently sat in the next compartment while Wilder emerged to give him another few pages of copy. The great playwright finished the last page of SHADOW OF A DOUBT just as the train was coming to his stop, and he used the very train upon which he and Hitchcock were traveling as a role model for the last scenes in the script. Except for the interiors, Hitchcock shot all of SHADOW OF A DOUBT in Santa Rosa, using the townspeople as extras and even recruiting one of his supporting cast members, Wonacott, to play the younger daughter, she being the offspring of a local grocer where Hitchcock shopped when on location. The director, never one to let a good idea slip past him, admired Welles' productions of CITIZEN KANE and THE MAGNIFICENT AMBERSONS and used Welles' technique of having characters talk across one another and interrupt dialog in this film, filling in the sound with background conversation and small talk by passersby. The traffic cop who is friendly toward Wright was an actor but he was coached so expertly by the real cop who was assigned to that corner that he appeared genuine. During the production, an out-of-town woman approached the actor, thinking him a real policeman, and asked for directions, only to be shocked when the actor replied, "Lady, I'm a stranger here myself." The funeral procession through Santa Rosa's main square at the end of the film was so authentic that hundreds of passersby, not knowing Hitchcock's cameras were grinding from second-story perches, stopped and removed their hats as the hearse crept past them. Remade in 1958 as STEP DOWN TO TERROR.

p, Jack H. Skirball; d, Alfred Hitchcock; w, Thornton Wilder, Sally Benson, Alma Reville (based on a story by Gordon McDonnell); ph, Joseph Valentine; m, Dimitri Tiomkin; ed, Milton Carruth; md, Charles Previn; art d, John B. Goodman, Robert Boyle; set d, R.A. Gausman, E.R. Robinson.

Crime Drama/Thriller (PR:C MPAA:NR)

SHADOW OF A MAN** (1955, Brit.) 69m New Realm bw

Paul Carpenter (*Gene*), Rona Anderson (*Linda*), Jane Griffiths (*Carol*), Ronald Leigh Hunt (*Norman*), Tony Quinn (*Inspector*), Jack Taylor (*Sgt. McBride*), Robert O'Neill (*Max*), Rose Alba (*Singer*).

After the town drunk has a fight with a local nightclub manager and turns up dead, the authorities settle on heart failure as the cause of death. The case is reopened however, when a friend of the victim, a writer, uncovers the truth and reveals that his pal was murdered. The killer, a diabetic, is caught when a hypodermic needle he used to give himself insulin is discovered near the scene of the crime.

p, E.J. Fancey; d, Michael McCarthy; w, Paul Erickson, McCarthy (based on the play by Erickson); ph, Geoffrey Faithfull.

Crime (PR:A-C MPAA:NR)

SHADOW OF A WOMAN** (1946) 78m WB bw

Helmut Dantine (*Dr. Eric Ryder*), Andrea King (*Mrs. Ryder*), Don McGuire (*Johnnie*), Dick [Richard] Erdman (*Joe*), John Alvin (*Carl*), William Prince (*David MacKellar*), Becky Brown (*Genevieve Calvin*), Peggy Knudsen (*Mrs. Louise Ryder*), Lisa Golm (*Emma*), Larry Geiger (*Philip Ryder*), Monte Blue (*Police Lieutenant*), Jack Smart (*Freeman*), Leah Baird (*Mrs. Calvin*), Lottie Williams (*Sarah*), Paul Stanton (*Dr. Nelson Norris*), Elvira Curci.

A slightly unrealistic story line hinders this drama that deals with a bride's terror. King is a young woman who blissfully weds a doctor after a whirlwind romance. As time goes by, she slowly realizes that he murders people through his questionable medical practices. Of particular concern is his son, who may be slowly starving to death as a result of the doctor's deeds. If the child dies, the doctor will receive a substantial amount of money. King eventually catches on. The story is related via flashback.

p, William Jacobs; d, Joseph Santley; w, Whitman Chambers, C. Graham Baker (based on a novel *He Fell Down Dead* by Virginia Perdue); ph, Bert Glennon; m, Adolph Deutsch; ed, Christian Nyby; md, Leo F. Forbstein; art d, Hugh Reticker; spec eff, Edwin DuPar.

Drama (PR:A MPAA:NR)

SHADOW OF CHIKARA (SEE: WISHBONE CUTTER, 1978)

SHADOW OF EVIL** (1967, Fr./Ital.) 92m P.A.C.-C.I.C.C.-DA.MA./Seven Arts c (BANCO A BANGKOK POUR OSS 117; OSS 117 MINACCIA BANGKOK)

Kerwin Mathews (*OSS 117*), Robert Hossein (*Dr. Sinn*), Pier Angeli (*Lila*), Dominique Wilms (*Eva Davidson*), Akom Mokranond (*Sonsak*), Sing Milintrasai (*Prasit*), Henri Virlojeux (*Leasock*), Jacques Mauclair, Gamil Ratib.

A deadly epidemic breaks out in Southeast Asia and Mathews is sent to solve the mystery. At a party, he meets Hossein and his sister Angeli. Hossein captures Mathews and imprisons him with Angeli, who has now fallen in love with him. He finds out that Hossein is masterminding a plan to wipe out "inferior races" and become the leader of his own supergroup of humans. He and Angeli escape and his adventure leads him to the lab where the deadly virus is being made. He is captured again, but rescued by Angeli and Wilms. They manage to torch the lab but Wilms is killed during a struggle. The world is safe once again, however, when Hossein tumbles into a pit full of rats that have been given the deadly virus. An Italian version of a James Bond film without all the gimmicks, this movie is actually part of a series starring different actors for each film.

p, Paul Cadeac; d, Andre Hunebelle; w, Pierre Foucard, Raymond Borel, Hunebelle, Michel Lebrun, Richard Caron, Patrice Rondard; ph, Raymond Lemoigne (Franscope, Eastmancolor); m, Michel Magne; ed, Jean Feyte; art d, Rene Moulaert.

Adventure (PR:A MPAA:NR)

SHADOW OF FEAR** (1956, Brit.) 76m Roxbury-Gilbraltar/UA bw
(GB: BEFORE I WAKE)

Mona Freeman (*April Haddon*), Jean Kent (*Florence Haddon*), Maxwell Reed (*Michael Elder*), Hugh Miller (*Mr. Driscoll*), Gretchen Franklin (*Elsie*), Frederick Leister (*Dr. Elder*), Alexander Gauge (*Police Sergeant*), Josephine Middleton (*Mrs. Harrison*), Frank Forsyth (*Jack Storey*), Stanley Van Beers (*Harry*), Frank Atkinson (*Taxi Driver*), Philip Ray (*Station Master*), Robert Sansom (*Parson*), Phyllis Cornell (*Dr. Elder's Receptionist*).

Decent suspense mystery stars Freeman as a woman returning to England because of the death of her mother and father. The deaths seem to be from natural causes but Freeman's intuition tells her that her stepmother, Kent, who was a nurse to the late pair, had something to do with it. But she can't convince the authorities, especially because Kent is a well-respected member of the town and completely above suspicion. Freeman is in line for a hefty inheritance from her late father as soon as she turns 21, and while investigating the deaths, she realizes her own life is in danger. Every bit of information Freeman finds seems to fit her stepmother's story but, finally, her stepmother slips up and the truth is revealed. Strong point of the story is the credibility Kent gives the story; for all intents and purposes, she is innocent and even the viewer thinks so. Well-crafted, but a little rushed at the end.

p, Steven Pallos, Charles A. Leeds; d, Albert S. Rogell; w, Robert Westerby (based on a novel by Hal Debrett); ph, Jack Asher; m, Leonard Salzedo; ed, Jim Connock; art d, Scott McGregor.

Mystery (PR:A MPAA:NR)

SHADOW OF FEAR**½ (1963, Brit.) 60m BUT bw

Paul Maxwell (*Bill Martin*), Clare Owen (*Barbara*), Anita West (*Ruth*), Alan Tilvern (*Warner*), John Arnatt (*Sharp*), Eric Pohlmann (*Spiroulos*), Reginald Marsh (*Oliver*), John Sutton (*Halliday*), Colin Tapley (*John Bowen*), Edward Ogden (*Chase*), Anthony Wager (*Carter*), John H. Watson (*Baker*), Robert Russell (*Ransome*), John Murray (*Scott Endacott*), Jack Taylor (*Holt*), Cecil Waters (*Kalik*), Mia Karam (*Dancey*), Eugene Stylianou (*Hotel Clerk*).

On a trip to Baghdad Maxwell is given the task of delivering a coded message to a man in London. When word leaks out that Maxwell has a photographic memory and that he has seen the message, every enemy agent with an interest in the material comes after him. Asked by M15 to assist, Maxwell and his girl allow themselves to be captured so that the British agents can catch the foreign spies. A competent thriller possessing a few excellent moments.

p, John I. Phillips; d, Ernest Morris; w, Ronald Liles, James O'Connolly (based on the novel *Decoy Be Damned* by T.F. Fotherby); ph, Walter J. Harvey; m, Martin Stairn; ed, Henry Richardson; art d, Wilfred Arnold.

Spy/Drama (PR:A MPAA:NR)

SHADOW OF MIKE EMERALD, THE** (1935, Brit.) 61m GS
Enterprises/RAD bw

Leslie Perrins (*Mike Emerald*), Marjorie Mars (*Lucia Emerald*), Martin Lewis (*Lee Cooper*), Vincent Holman (*John Ellman*), Atholl Fleming (*Clive Warner*), Neville Brook (*Ryder March*), Basil Langton (*Rollo Graham*), Iris Parnell, Miss Messina, Bruce Seton.

A group of financiers have been bilked out of a tidy sum of money by their associate, Perrins. One of the men commits suicide, and the others unjustly go to prison for their supposed involvement in the crime. Perrins goes to jail as well, but escapes. After his former associates are released, they go off to find Perrins, the partner that cheated them. Perrins is found through his wife, Fleming, but her new lover takes care of Perrins and his former associates.

p, A George Smith; d, P. Maclean Rogers; w, Kathleen Butler, Anthony Richardson (based on a story by Richardson); ph, Geoffrey Faithfull.

Drama (PR:A MPAA:NR)

SHADOW OF SUSPICION** (1944) 68m MON bw

Marjorie Weaver (*Claire*), Peter Cookson (*Jimmy*), Tim Ryan (*Northup*), Pierre Watkin (*Randall*), Anthony Warde (*Bill*), Frank Scanell (*Red*), George Lewis (*Paul*), Ralph Lewis (*Steve*), J. Farrell MacDonald (*Dolan*), Clara Blandick (*Mrs. Randall*), Tom Herbert (*Holman*), Lester Dorr (*Reporter*), Frank Stephens (*Express Guard*), Wilbur Mack (*Mr. Vanderbrook*), Charlotte Treadway (*Mrs. Vanderbrook*).

Cookson and Ryan are a couple a goofy private detectives who come up with an ingenious scheme to trap the people who stole a valuable necklace. Cookson makes himself appear as a possible suspect, which allows him to do his tracking unhampered. Weaver is the gal who leads him to the culprits, through her own innocent involvement as a messenger in the case. The chase is more rewarding than the actual capture.

p, A.W. Hackel; d, William Beaudine; w, Albert DeMond, Earle Snell (based on the story by Harold Goldman); ph, Marcel Le Picard; ed, William Austin; md, Lee Zahler.

Comedy/Crime (PR:A MPAA:NR)

SHADOW OF TERROR** (1945) 60m PRC bw

Richard Fraser (*Jim*), Grace Gillern (*Joan*), Cy Kendall (*Maxwell*), Emmett Lynn (*Elmer*), Kenneth MacDonald (*McKenzie*), Eddie Acuff (*Walters*), Sam Flint (*Sheriff*).

Rushed into production when the atomic bomb was released over Hiroshima, this film stars Fraser as a scientist chased by gangsters because he has a formula to make the A-bomb. The villains knock him out and toss him off a train, where he staggers on to Gillern's ranch. While recuperating from amnesia, he and Gillern must foil the crooks and make contact with the government to tell them of his formula. In the final fight scene he regains his memory, takes off with his girl, and is saved by the local authorities after being chased across the desert. The world is safe once again.

p, Jack Grant; d, Lew Landers; w, Arthur St. Claire (based on a story by Sheldon Leonard); ph, Jack Greenhalgh; ed, Ray Livingston; md, Karl Hajos; art d, Edward C. Jewell; set d, Glenn P. Thompson.

Thriller (PR:A MPAA:NR)

SHADOW OF THE CAT, THE** (1961, Brit.) 79m BHP/UNIV bw

Andre Morell (*Walter Venable*), Barbara Shelley (*Beth Venable*), William Lucas (*Jacob*), Freda Jackson (*Clara, Servant*), Conrad Phillips (*Michael Latimer*), Alan Wheatley (*Inspector Rowles*), Andrew Crawford (*Andrew, Servant*), Catherine Lacey (*Ella Venable*), Vanda Godsell (*Louise*), Richard Warner (*Edgar*), Kynaston Reeves (*Grandfather*), Charles Stanley (*Dobbins*), Vera Cook (*Mother*), Howard Knight (*Boy*), Kevin Stoney (*Father*), Angela Crow (*Daughter*), Henry Kendall (*Doctor*), John Dearth (*Constable Hamer*), Fred Stone, George Doonan (*Ambulance Men*), Rodney Burke (*Workman*).

Morell plays the conniving husband of wealthy Lacey. He and the servants want a slice of her money, so they kill her and hide the body, which is all witnessed by her pet cat. Seeing the murderous act transforms the cat into a vicious animal. The members of the guilty group decide to kill it, but the crafty feline sets out to do them all in. Morell panics and persuades his niece, Shelley, that both the cat and Ella's will must be done away with. But soon after Morell is stricken by a heart attack, being literally scared to his death by the cat. The pretty kitty then leads the innocent Shelley and her boy friend to the body of its previous owner. All three enjoy the benefits of Lacey's money.

p, Jon Penington; d, John Gilling; w, George Baxt; ph, Arthur Grank; m, Mikis Theodorakis; ed, James Needs, John Pomeroy; prod d, Bernard Robinson; art d, Don Mingaye; spec eff, Les Bowie; makeup, Roy Ashton; cat trainer, John Holmes.

Thriller (PR:A MPAA:NR)

SHADOW OF THE EAGLE**½ (1955, Brit.) 93m Valiant/UA bw

Richard Greene (*Count Alexei Orloff*), Valentina Cortesa (*Princess Tarakanova*), Binnie Barnes (*Empress Catherine of Russia*), Greta Gynt (*Countess Camponiello*), Charles Goldner (*Gen. Korsakov*), Walter Rilla (*Prince Radziwill*), Hugh French (*Capt. Sergei Nikolsky*), Dennis Vance (*Vaska*).

The Russia of Catherine the Great serves as the setting for this costume drama in which Greene is ordered by the Empress to kill her rival, Cortesa (most known for her portrayal as the fading star in Francois Truffaut's DAY FOR NIGHT). But when Greene meets the intended victim he falls in love with her, much to the Empress's displeasure. The lovers are captured and threatened with execution. Some nifty heroics on Greene's part allow them to escape and find sanctuary in Switzerland. The action is well-paced, with the cast turning in a grand performance.

p, Anthony Havelock-Allan; d, Sidney Salkow; w, Doreen Montgomery,

Hagar Wilde (based on the story by Jacques Companeez); ph, Edwin Hillier, Cecil Cooney; m, Hans May; ed, Peter Graham Scott; md, Mays; art d, Wilfred Shingleton; cos, Nino Novarese.

Adventure   **(PR:A MPAA:NR)**

SHADOW OF THE HAWK*½   (1976, Can.) 92m COL c

Jan-Michael Vincent (*Mike*), Marilyn Hassett (*Maureen*), Chief Dan George (*Old Man Hawk*), Pia Shandel (*Faye*), Marianne Jones (*Dsonoqua*), Jacques Hubert (*Andak*), Cindi Griffith (*Secretary*), Anna Hagan (*Desk Nurse*), Murray Lowry (*Intern*).

To learn something about his Indian ancestory, Vincent takes off for the wilderness. The legends he encounters are not the ones from films and books but evil spirits, and, with the help of his reporter girl friend and an Indian chief, he has to fight his way back to the present.

p, John Kemeny; d, George McGowan; w, Norman Thaddeus Vane, Herbert J. Wright (based on the story by Vane, Peter Jensen, Lynette Cahill); ph, John Holbrook, Reginald Morris (Panavision, Eastmancolor); m, Robert McMullin; ed, O. Nicholas Brown; art d, Keith Pepper; cos, Ilse Richter, Bobby Watts.

Fantasy   **(PR:A MPAA:PG)**

SHADOW OF THE LAW*   (1930) 69m PAR bw

William Powell (*John Nelson/Jim Montgomery*), Marion Shilling (*Edith Wentworth*), Natalie Moorehead (*Ethel Barry*), Regis Toomey (*Tom Owen*), Paul Hurst (*Pete Shore*), George Irving (*Col. Wentworth*), Frederic Burt (*Detective Lt. Mike Kearney*), James Durkin (*Warden*), Richard Tucker (*Lew Durkin*), Walter James (*Captain of the Guards*), Oscar Smith (*Elevator Operator*), Edward LeSaint (*Judge*), Allan Cavan (*Juror*), Harry Strang (*Barber*), Harry Wilson (*Convict*), Leo Willis (*Engineer*), Ed Piel, Sr (*Usher*), Frank O'Conner (*Doctor*).

Trying to protect a lady from her irate husband Powell inadvertantly kills the man. She leaves and Powell is given a life sentence. Through the efforts of his con-artist cell mate, Hurst, Powell escapes and makes his way to a small southern town, where he changes his identity and makes a go of it working in a mill. This includes placing his fingers in a milling machine in order to remove fingerprints. When cell-mate Hurst manages to escape, Powell sends him to New York to find the woman who can clear Powell's name. But she is now a notorious blackmailer, and turns Hurst into the cops, before coming after Powell to blackmail him. Powell does not buy, however, eventually proving his innocence when a New York cop travels to the South to nab Powell, but latches onto the blackmailer instead. Powell is his usual suave self in his portrayal of the convicted man. Though the story suffers from some illogical moments, it moves well and keeps the suspense. Hurst does a good job in adding comedy to the plot.

d, Louis Gasnier, Max Marcin; w, John Farrow (based on the novel *The Quarry* by John A. Morosco and the play "The Quarry" by Marcin) ph, Charles Lang; ed, Robert Bassler.

Crime Drama   **(PR:A MPAA:NR)**

SHADOW OF THE PAST**   (1950, Brit.) 83m Anglofilm/COL bw

Joyce Howard (*Lady in Black*), Terence Morgan (*John Harding*), Michael Medwin (*Dick Stevens*), Andrew Osborn (*George Bentley*), Wylie Watson (*Caretaker*), Marie Ney (*Mrs. Bentley*), Ella Retford (*Daily Help*), Ronald Adam (*Solicitor*), Louise Gainsborough (*Susie*), Ian Fleming, W.E. Holloway, Eve Ashley, Meadows White, Willoughby Gray, Francis Roberts, John Warren, Richard Neller, Anthony Pendrell, Dervis Ward.

Modest murder mystery about a woman, Howard, posing as the ghost of her murdered sister in an effort to capture her killer. With the help of a stranger who has discovered the woman's secret, she learns that her brother-in-law is the murderer and enacts her revenge. Tightly paced with several highly tense sequences.

p, Mario Zampi, Mae Murray; d, Zampi; w, Aldo di Benedetti, Ian Stuart Black (based on a story by Benedetti); ph, Hone Glendinning.

Crime   **(PR:A MPAA:NR)**

SHADOW OF THE THIN MAN*   (1941) 97m MGM bw

William Powell (*Nick Charles*), Myrna Loy (*Nora Charles*), Barry Nelson (*Paul Clarke*), Donna Reed (*Molly Ford*), Sam Levene (*Lt. Abrams*), Alan Baxter (*Whitey Barrow*), Dickie Hall (*Nick Charles, Jr.*), Loring Smith (*Link Stephens*), Joseph Anthony (*Fred Macy*), Henry O'Neill (*Maj. Jason I. Sculley*), Stella Adler (*Claire Porter*), Lou Lubin (*"Rainbow" Benny Loomis*), Louise Beavers (*Stella*), Will Wright (*Maguire*), Edgar Dearing (*Motor Cop*), Noel Cravat (*Baku*), Tito Vuolo (*Luis*), Oliver Blake (*Fenster*), John Dilson, Arthur Aylesworth (*Coroners*), James Flavin, Edward Hearn, Art Belasco, Bob Ireland, Robert Kellard (*Cops*), Cliff Danielson, J. Louis Smith, Jerry Jerome, Roger Moore, Buddy Roosevelt, Hal Le Sueur (*Reporters*), Cardiff Giant (*Bouncing Tschekov*), Richard Frankie Burke (*Buddy Burns*), Tor Johnson (*Jack the Ripper*), Johnnie Berkes (*Paleface*), John Kelly (*Meatballs Murphy*), Jody Gilbert (*Lana*), Dan Tobey (*Announcer*), Tommy Mack

(*Soft Drink Vendor*), Joe Devlin (*Mugg*), Bill Fisher, Aldrich Bowker (*Watchmen*), Charles Calvert (*Referee*), Joey Ray (*Stephen's Clerk*), Inez Cooper (*Girl in Cab*), Adeline De Walt Reynolds (*Landlady*), Duke York (*Valentino*), Seldon Bennett (*Mario*), Sidney Melton (*Fingers*), George Lloyd (*Pipey*), Patti Moore (*Lefty's Wife*), Jerry Mandy (*Waiter*), Hard-boiled Haggerty, Eddie Sims, Abe Dinovitch, Wee Willie Davis, Sailor Vincent, Jack Roper, Harry Wilson (*Muggs*), Ray Teal (*Cab Driver*), Sam Bernard (*Counterman*), Ken Christy (*Detective*), David Dornack (*Lefty's Kid*), Lyle Latell, Matt Gilman, Fred Graham (*Waiters with Steaks*), Harry Burns (*Greek Janitor*), Fred Walburn (*Kid on Merry-go-Round*), Arch Hendricks (*Photographer*), Pat McGee (*Handler*).

The fourth THIN MAN film isn't nearly as good as the first ones, but it has its own rewards thanks to the inimitable by-play of Powell and Loy. This time the sleuthing socialites are visiting the track when a jockey is murdered. Despite the pleas of the police and Loy, Powell refuses to investigate the baffling case. Later, though, a reporter is also murdered and Powell can no longer resist. While he investigates, he is constantly trying to lose Loy, who always finds him again, bringing their baby and dog along. They turn up a number of suspects, including assorted gangsters, molls, and track officials. Powell deduces that the first death was accidental, but he lets on that he believes it was committed by the same person who killed the reporter. All the suspects are called into one room for the denouement, and it turns out to be the kindly O'Neill, chairman of the state athletic commission, who killed the reporter who was getting close to uncovering a scandal. By this time the series was definitely on the downslide, and MGM took advantage of its low cost and sure success to show off some of its new contract players, such as Reed and Nelson. More comedy was injected into the series, watering down the impact of what had once been sparkling wit, as well as leaving less time to intelligently develop the mystery at hand. Still, any pairing of Powell and Loy is worth watching again and again for those moments when it all clicks into place and they become the ideal couple.

p, Hunt Stromberg; d, W.S. Van Dyke II; w, Irving Brecher, Harry Kurnitz (based on a story by Kurnitz and characters created by Dashiell Hammett); ph, William Daniels; m, David Snell; ed, Robert J. Kern; art d, Cedric Gibbons.

Crime   **(PR:A MPAA:NR)**

SHADOW ON THE WALL½**   (1950) 84m MGM bw

Ann Sothern (*Dell Faring*), Zachary Scott (*David I. Starrling*), Gigi Perreau (*Susan Starrling*), Nancy Davis (*Dr. Caroline Canford*), Kristine Miller (*Celia Starrling*), John McIntire (*Pike Ludwell*), Tom Helmore (*Crane Weymouth*), Helen Brown (*Miss Burke*), Barbara Billingsley (*Olga*), Marcia Van Dyke (*Secretary*), Anthony Sydes (*Bobby*), Jimmy Hunt (*Boy*).

When his wife is killed all evidence points to Scott. His 8-year-old daughter, the slain woman's stepdaughter, is the only witness. The child has gone into a state of shock, leaving Davis (later to become the nation's First Lady) as the psychologist who tries to discover the truth before Scott dies in the electric chair. The real killer turns out to be Sothern, jealous over her sister's fling with Sothern's future husband. Sothern tries to drown and poison the child to no avail. The shadow of Sothern's profile on a wall is the image that jogs the child's memory. A fairly taut drama that maintains an evenly paced level of suspense right up to the conclusion.

p, Robert Sisk; d, Patrick Jackson; w, William Ludwig (based on the story "Death in the Doll's House" by Hannah Lees, Lawrence P. Bachmann); ph, Ray June; m, Andre Previn; ed, Irvine Warburton; art d, Cedric Gibbons, Eddie Imazu.

Mystery   **(PR:A MPAA:NR)**

SHADOW ON THE WINDOW, THE½**   (1957) 73m COL bw

Phil Carey (*Tony Atlas*), Betty Garrett (*Linda Atlas*), John Barrymore, Jr (*Jess Reber*), Corey Allen (*Gil Ramsby*), Gerald Sarracini (*Joey Gomez*), Jerry Mathers (*Petey*), Sam Gilman (*Sgt. Paul Denke*), Rusty Lane (*Capt. McQuade*), Ainslie Pryor (*Dr. Hodges*), Paul Picerni (*Bigelow*), William Leslie (*Stuart*), Doreen Woodbury (*Molly*), Ellie Kent (*Girl*), Angela Stevens (*Myra*), Mort Mills (*Husband*), Carl Milletaire (*Sgt. Nordli*), Julian Upton (*Bergen*), Nesdon Booth (*Conway*), Jack Lomas (*Warren*).

Taut little crime programmer featuring "Leave It to Beaver" star Mathers as a young boy shocked into silence after witnessing three crooks; Barrymore, Allen, and Sarracini, commit a murder and then kidnap his mother. Though police know that his mother has been kidnaped, Mathers' mute state leaves them helpless in looking for clues. Finally, by following Mathers around and piecing the events together through tedious detail work, the investigators track down the criminals.

p, Jonie Taps; d, William Asher; w, Leo Townsend, David P. Harmon (based on a story by John and Ward Hawkins); ph, Kit Carson; m, George Duning; ed, William A. Lyon; art d, Robert Peterson.

Crime   **(PR:A MPAA:NR)**

SHADOW RANCH** (1930) 64m COL bw

Buck Jones (Sim Baldwin), Marguerite De La Motte (Ruth), Kate Price (Maggie Murphy), Ben Wilson (Tex), Al Smith (Dan Blake), Frank Rice (Williams), Ernie Adams (Joe), Slim Whitaker (Curley), Robert McKenzie (Fatty), Lafe McKee, Fred Burns, Ben Corbett, Frank Ellis, Hank Bell.

Jones rides into town and comes to the aid of ranch owner De La Motte. She has been fighting a losing battle against the opportunistic Smith, who is trying to pressure her into selling her land. His plan of securing water rights is quickly foiled when Jones catches some of his men rustling cattle. Blazing guns color a showdown which ends in Smith's death.

p, Harry Cohn; d, Louis King; w, Frank Howard Clark, Clarke Silvernail (based on a story by George M. Johnson, Silvernail); ph, Ted McCord; ed, James Sweeney; art d, Edward Jewell.

Western   (PR:A   MPAA:NR)

SHADOW RETURNS, THE** (1946) 61m MON bw

Kane Richmond (Lamont Cranston), Barbara Reed (Margo Lane), Tom Dugan (Shevvier the Chauffeur), Joseph Crehan (Inspector Cardona), Pierre Watkin (Commissioner Weston), Robert Emmett Keane (Charles Frobay), Frank Reicher (Michael Hasdon), Lester Dorr (William Monk), Rebel Randall (Lenore Jessup), Emmett Vogan (Brock Yomans), Sherry Hall (Robert Buell), Cyril Delevanti (John Adams).

Richmond, as "The Shadow," solves the case of jewels stolen from a grave when police inspector Crehan cannot make heads or tales of it. The jewels actually contain a secret formula for plastics, the clue which leads Richmond to the culprit. Mystery is solved in pretty routine fashion, making for a boring outing.

p, Joe Kaufman; d, Phil Rosen; w, George Callahan (based on Shadow Magazine characters); ph, William Sickner; ed, Ace Herman; md, Edward Kay; art d, Dave Milton.

Mystery   (PR:A   MPAA:NR)

SHADOW STRIKES, THE*½ (1937) 61m GN bw

Rod La Rocque ("The Shadow"), Lynn Anders (Marcia Delthern), Walter McGrall (Winstead Comstock), James Blakely (Jasper Delthern), Kenneth Harlan (Capt. Breen), Norman Ainsley (Kendricks), John Carnavale (Warren Berrenger).

The producers tried to create an atmosphere of suspense and mystery in this adaptation of the popular radio program, but ultimately fails because of a straining plot and an overly cliched script. La Rocque plays the sleuth-lawyer as he pursues a mysterious killer and a gangster chief. All the while the police are on La Rocque's tail, trying to pin a robbery on him. Neither performance nor situations are believable.

p, Max Alexander, Arthur Alexander; d, Lynn Shores; w, Al Martin (based on characters created by Maxwell Grant); ph, Marcel Picard; ed, Charles Henkel.

Mystery   **Cas.**   (PR:A   MPAA:NR)

SHADOW VALLEY*½ (1947) 59m PRC Pictures/EL bw

Eddie Dean (Eddie), Roscoe Ates (Soapy), Jennifer Holt (Mary Ann), George Chesebro (Gunnison), Eddie Parker (Foster), Lee Morgan (Sheriff), Lane Bradford (Bob), Carl Mathews (Tucker), Budd Buster (Grimes), The Plainsmen, Andy Parker, Earl Murphy, Paul Smith, George Bamby, Charles Morgan, White Cloud the Horse.

When lawyer Holt's father and uncle are killed by a gang of crooks led by, who else but, Chesebro, the crooks bother her for the gold on her property. But galloping in on his white stallion comes Dean to make life safe for Holt. A few songs and the comedy antics of Ates are interspersed between the action.

p, Jerry Thomas; d, Ray Taylor; w, Arthur Sherman; ph, Ernest Miller; m, Pete Gates; ed, Joe Gluck.

Western   (PR:A   MPAA:NR)

SHADOW VERSUS THE THOUSAND EYES OF DR. MABUSE, THE
(SEE: THOUSAND EYES OF DR. MABUSE, THE, 1960, Fr./Ital./Ger.)

SHADOW WARRIOR, THE (SEE: KAGEMUSHA, 1980, Jap.)

SHADOWED*½ (1946) 70m COL bw

Anita Louise, Lloyd Corrigan, Michael Duane, Robert Scott, Doris Houck, Helen Koford, [Terry Moore], Wilton Graff, Eric Roberts, Paul E. Burns, Fred Graff (Graham), Jack Lee, Sarah Edwards, Jack Davis.

An uninspired programmer which sees a brave millionaire put his fortune and reputation on the line in an effort to wipe out a gang of dangerous counterfeiters. A quickie that can be dispensed with the same way.

p, John Haggott; d, John Sturges; w, Brenda Weisberg (based on a story by

Julian Harman); ph, Henry Freulich; ed, James Sweeney; md, Mischa Bakaleinikoff; art d, Hans Radon; set d, Bill Calvert.

Crime   (PR:A   MPAA:NR)

SHADOWED EYES*½ (1939, Brit.) 68m Savoy-Greenspan and Seligman Enterprises/RK O bw

Basil Sydney (Dr. Zander), Patricia Hilliard (Dr. Diana Barnes), Stewart Rome (Sir John Barnes), Ian Fleming (Dr. McKane), Tom Helmore (Ian), Dorothy Calve (Marjorie), Ruby Miller (Mrs. Clarke-Fenwick), Dorothy Boyd, Brian Buchel, Sidney Monckton.

A ludicrous crime melodrama starring Sydney as a world famous eye surgeon who goes temporarily insane and kills his wife's lover. Captured and sentenced to life in an asylum, Sydney's situation looks hopeless until a bizarre turn of events leads to his freedom. As it turns out, his assistant's father, Rome, a man in desperate need of Sydney's surgical skills, just happens to be the prosecuting attorney who got him his sentence. Unable to get Sydney released, the assistant breaks him out of the asylum to perform the operation. Though Sydney suffers a brief relapse of his insanity which causes a few moments of tension, the surgery is a success and leads to a vow from his assistant to work diligently for his official release.

p, Kurt Sternberg, A. George Smith; d, Maclean Rogers; w, Roy Carter, Herbert Hill (based on a story by Arnold Ridley); ph, Gerald Gibbs.

Crime   (PR:A-C   MPAA:NR)

SHADOWMAN*** (1974, Fr./Ital.) 105m Terra Film-SOAT/New Line Cinema c (L'HOMME SANS VISAGE; NUITS ROUGES; THE MAN WITHOUT A FACE)

Jacques Champreux (The Man), Gayle Hunnicutt (The Woman), Gert Frobe (Sorbier), Josephine Chaplin (Martine), Ugo Pagliai (Paul), Patrick Prejean (Seraphin), Clement Harari (Dutreuil), Henry Lincoln (Prof. Petri).

A legendary secret sect and an ancient treasure serve as the elements in this Parisian crime drama. Champreux is a mysterious thief, face hidden by a red cloth, out to get the treasure of a 12th century sect that guarded the Crusaders. Though outlawed in the Middle Ages, this sect has members still in Paris and serves as the obstacle the masked man must overcome. Direction and scripting keep the suspense going. Performances are lifeless but fitting for this project.

p, Raymond Froment; d, Georges Franju; w, Jacques Champreux; ph, Guido Bertoni (Eastmancolor); m, Franju, Hector Berlioz.

Mystery   (PR:A   MPAA:PG)

SHADOWS*½ (1931, Brit.) 57m BIP/FN-Pathe bw

Jacqueline Logan (Fay Melville), Bernard Nedell (Press Rawlinson), Gordon Harker (Ear'ole), Derrick de Marney (Peter), Molly Lamont (Jill Dexter), D.A. Clarke-Smith (Gruhn), Wally Patch (Cripps), Mary Clare (Lily), Mark Lester (Herb), Roy Emerton (Capt.).

Vicious gangster Nedell kills his moll and kidnaps an heiress, holding her hostage aboard his boat. An intrepid reporter, De Marney, is hot on his trail and traces him to his hideout. He then rescues the girl, while Nedell kills himself rather than be captured. Routine in all respects.

p&d, Alexander Esway; w, Frank Miller.

Crime   (PR:A-C   MPAA:NR)

SHADOWS**** (1960) 81m Lion bw

Hugh Hurd (Hugh), Lelia Goldoni (Lelia), Ben Carruthers (Ben), Anthony Ray (Tony), Dennis Sallas (Dennis), Tom Allen (Tom), David Pokitillow (David), Rupert Crosse (Rupert), David Jones (David), Pir Marini (Pir), Victoria Vargas (Victoria), Jack Ackerman (Jack), Jacqueline Walcott (Jacqueline), Cliff Carnell, Jay Grecco, Ronald Maccone, Bob Rech, Joyce Miles, Nancy Deale, Gigi Brooks, Lynn Hamelton, Marilyn Clark, Joanne Sages, Jed McGarvey, Greta Thyssen.

An episodic, moving, and powerful first directorial effort from actor John Cassavetes that unveiled a fresh and vital new talent behind America's cameras. Based on a series of improvisations created by members of the Variety Arts Studio in New York of which Cassavetes was the director, SHADOWS brings us into the lives of a parentless black family struggling to carve out an identity in the mean streets of Manhattan. Herd, a would-be jazz musician, is the father-figure of the clan and he watches over his brother, Carruthers, and his sister, Goldoni, both of whom can pass as white. Herd grows frustrated because his artistic potential is being wasted in the dives and strip joints he is forced to blow a trumpet in to survive. Being the only obviously black member of the family, Herd has become bitter due to his limited opportunities. Meanwhile, his sister, Goldoni, hooks up with the pretentious pseudo-intellectual New York art crowd and moves among them, teasing and flirting. She starts an affair with Ray, a young white man who is unaware that she is a mulatto, and she loses her virginity to him. The experience is a disappointment to Goldoni, as is the relationship, for when Ray learns that she is of partly black heritage he leaves her. The last member of the family, Carruthers, lives a carefree life, hanging out with his friends Allen and Sallas. The boys drift along drinking, carousing, and getting into trouble. One night they are caught in a vicious street fight and lose. We leave the family as Herd grows more determined to win over one of the catatonic strip joint audiences, Goldoni has taken refuge with friends, and Carruthers is abandoned by his buddies and left alone to lick his wounds. Having casually mentioned his desire to film the improvisation project while on a radio talk show hosted by Jean Shepherd, Cassavetes was surprised to find the public sending him donations totaling nearly $20,000. Inspired, he scraped together another $20,000 and armed with $40,000 and a 16mm camera, he shot SHADOWS, which was then blown up and printed on 35mm stock. Failing to interest American distributors who were put off by the fact that the film was technically spotty, somewhat unusual, and directed by a man heretofore known only as an actor, Cassavetes took his movie to Europe and entered it in the Cannes Film Festival where it won the Critics Award. Soon after, SHADOWS was picked up for distribution by a British firm, Lion International, and did quite well. The film finally made its way to the shores that spawned it and to Hollywood's surprise was a minor hit. Suddenly Cassavetes was receiving directing offers from major studios and being hailed as a genius by the critics. The new director accepted Hollywood's embrace, but after making only two films for major studios (TOO LATE BLUES, A CHILD IS WAITING) he became frustrated by the limitations imposed on him by producers and returned to independent filmmaking where he could have complete control over his art. While SHADOWS has become dated over the years and Cassavetes has gone on to make greater films, its importance in the development of the American independent film cannot be overstated, nor can the unique power it still retains. SHADOWS perfectly captured a specific time and place, illuminating simple truths regarding the human condition, while unveiling an important, powerful, and visionary new force in the American cinema.

p, Maurice McEndree; d, John Cassavetes; w, (improvised by cast and director); ph, Erich Kollmar; m, Charlie Mingus, Shifi Hadi; ed, McEndree, Len Appelson; set d, Randy Liles, Bob Rech; m/l, "Beautiful," Jack Ackerman, Hunt Stevens, Eleanor Winters.

Drama   **(PR:O   MPAA:NR)**

SHADOWS GROW LONGER, THE**½   (1962, Switz./Ger.) 91m
Praesens CCC-Filmkunst/Times Film bw (DIE SCHATTEN WERDEN
LANGER; DEFIANT DAUGHTERS)

Luise Ulrich (Frau Diethelm), Barbara Rutting (Christa Andres), Hansjorg Felmy (Max), Loni von Friedl (Erika Schoner), Fred Tanner (Dr. Barner), Helga Sommerfield (Helena), Renja Gill (Anni), Margot Philipp (Barbara), Carola Rasch (Bessie), Iris Erdmann (Hilde), Heidi Pawellek (Paula), Brit von Thiesenhausen (Ruth), Elizabeth Roth (Steffie), Erika Wolf (Susanne), Gabriele Adam (Vera), Bella Neri (Yvette), Michael Paryla, Anneliese Betschart, Hans Gaugler, Max Haufler.

A girls' reform school is the setting for a former prostitute's self-sacrifice. Rutting now works as a mistress in the school. A young girl comes along who reminds her of her own beginnings on the streets, but the girl, Friedl, does not want to be bothered. Friedl escapes from the school and Rutting hunts for her. Along the way she meets her former pimp, who threatens to reveal Rutting's past unless she gives him information about the girls. But she kills the man, is taken to jail for her crime, and finally makes an impression on Friedl.

p, Lazar Wechsler, Artur Brauner; d, Ladislao Vajda; w, Vajda, Heinz Pauck, Istvan Bekeffi; ph, Enrique Gaertner; m, Robert Blum; ed, Hermann Haller; art d, Max Rothlisberger.

Drama   **(PR:A   MPAA:NR)**

SHADOWS IN AN EMPTY ROOM
(SEE: STRANGE SHADOWS IN AN EMPTY ROOM, 1977, Can./Ital.)

SHADOWS IN THE NIGHT**   (1944) 67m COL bw

Warner Baxter (Dr. Robert Ordway), Nina Foch (Lois Garland), George Zucco (Frank Swift), Minor Watson (Frederick Gordon), Lester Matthews (Stanley Carter), Ben Welden (Nick Kallus), Edward Norris (Jess Hilton), Charles Wilson (Sheriff), Charles Halton (Doc Stacey), Jeanne Bates (Adele Carter).

A fairly eerie and suspenseful thriller based on the popular radio program "Crime Doctor," has Foch as a wealthy heiress slowly being driven to madness and suicide. Baxter plays the psychologist with his own technique for solving crimes, who wades through seemingly supernatural phenomena before reaching his conclusion through scientific methods. (See CRIME DOCTOR series, Index)

p, Rudolph C. Flothow; d, Eugene J. Forde; w, Eric Taylor (based on the radio program "Crime Doctor" by Max Marcin); ph, James S. Brown, Jr.; ed, Dwight Caldwell; art d, John Datu; set d, Sidney Clifford.

Mystery   **(PR:A   MPAA:NR)**

SHADOWS OF DEATH*½   (1945) 60m PRC bw

Buster Crabbe, Al "Fuzzy" St. John, Donna Dax, Charles King, Karl Hackett, Edward Piel, Sr, Bob Cason, Frank Ellis, Frank McCarroll, Ed Hall, Emmett Lynn.

Crabbe and sidekick St. John foil a gang of outlaws who have murdered a man to find out the route of a new railroad planned for the territory. With the information gained from their victim, the gang had planned to buy up the soon-to-be-valuable land at a cheap price and then sell it to the railroad for a big profit. (See BILLY CARSON series, Index.)

p, Sigmund Neufeld; d, Sam Newfield; w, Fred Myton; ph, Jack Greenhalgh; ed, Holbrook N. Todd.

Western   **(PR:A   MPAA:NR)**

SHADOWS OF FORGOTTEN ANCESTORS***   (1967, USSR) 100m
Dovzhenko/Artkino Pictures bw/c (TINI ZABUTYKH PREDKIV;
SHADOWS OF OUR ANCESTORS; SHADOWS OF OUR FORGOTTEN
ANCESTORS)

Ivan Mikolaychuk (Ivan), Larisa Kadochnikova (Marichka), Tatyana Bestayeva (Palagna), Spartak Bagashvili (Yurko), N. Grinko (Batag), L. Yengibarov (Miko), Nina Alisova, A. Gay (Paliychuks), N. Gnepovskaya, A. Raydanov (Gutenyuks), I. Dzyura (Ivan as a child), V. Glyanko (Marichka as a child).

A deeply heartfelt story set during the early part of the 20th century in rural Russia, centering on a man whose life is marred with sadness. First his brother is killed while saving him from a falling tree. Then his father is murdered, forcing the boy and his mother to live in poverty. He falls in love with the daughter of the man responsible for his father's death. The lovers cannot marry and she eventually falls to her death. The man becomes obsessed with memories of his past. In a feeble attempt to prove family devotion, he is struck dead by a sorcerer and the whole village mourns his death.

d, Sergey Paradzhanov; w, Paradzhanov, Ivan Chendey (based on the story "Tini Zabutykh Predkiu" by Mikhaylo Mikhaylovich Koysyubinskiy); ph, V. Ilyenko (Sovcolor); m, M. Skorik; ed, M. Ponomarenko; art d, M. Rakovskiy, G. Yakutovich.

Drama   **(PR:A   MPAA:NR)**

SHADOWS OF OUR FORGOTTEN ANCESTORS
(SEE: SHADOWS OF FORGOTTEN ANCESTORS, 1967, USSR)

SHADOWS OF SING SING*½   (1934) 63m COL bw

Mary Brian (Muriel), Bruce Cabot (Bob Martel), Grant Mitchell (Joe Martel), Harry Woods (Rossi), Claire DuBrey (Angela), Bradley Page (Slick), Irving Bacon (Highbrow), Dewey Robinson (Dumpy), Fred Kelsey (Murphy).

A crime drama concerning the attempts of Brian and Cabot to have a romance against the odds. She is sister to a gangster boss. Cabot is the son of a prominent detective and the victim of a frame-up by Page. But dad comes to the rescue, giving Cabot a second chance with Brian. But first he, and the audience, must sit through an overdrawn courtroom scene. At times the actors exhibit some semblance of realistic behavior.

d, Phil Rosen; w, Albert De Mond (based on the story by Katherine Scola, Doris Maloy); ph, Benjamin Kline; ed, John Rawlins.

Crime/Drama   **(PR:A   MPAA:NR)**

SHADOWS OF SINGAPORE   (SEE: MALAY NIGHTS, 1933)

SHADOWS OF THE ORIENT*   (1937) 70m MON bw

Esther Ralston (Viola Avery), Regis Toomey (Baxter), J. Farrell MacDonald (Sullivan), Oscar Apfel (Judge Avery), Sidney Blackmer (King Moss), Eddie Featherston (Flash), Kit Guard (Nolan), Matty Fain (Gangster), James Leong (Chin Chu).

A miscast and misdirected attempt at producing a rather obvious story about Chinese being smuggled into the U.S. Blackmer is the smuggler, Toomey the immigrations official, and Ralston the woman who unknowingly gets mixed up with and winds up falling in love with Toomey.

p, Larry Darmour; d, Burt Lynwood; w, Charles Francis Royal (based on a story by L.E. Heifetz); ph, James S. Brown, Jr.; ed, Dwight Caldwell.

Crime/Drama   **Cas.**   **(PR:A   MPAA:NR)**

SHADOWS OF THE WEST**   (1949) 59m MON bw

Whip Wilson (Whip), Andy Clyde (Winks), Riley Hill (Bud), Reno Browne (Ginny), Bill Kennedy (Ward), Pierce Lyden (Jordon), Keith Richards (Steve), William H. Ruhl (Sheriff), Ted Adams (Davis), Lee Phelps (Hart), Bert Hamilton (Clerk), Bud Osborne (Jones), Donald Kerr (Baker), Billy Hammond (Ranson), Clem Fuller (Ed Mayberry), Carol Henry (Lee), Bob Woodward (Gus), Edmund Glover (Keefe), Dee Cooper (Joe), Curt Barrett, Red Egner (Singers), Kenne Duncan.

Wilson once again proves the six-shooter is no match for his whip, as he rounds up a gang of crooks who are trying to pin the murder of a rancher on an innocent former convict. The deputy sheriff, Wilson, was supposed to be on vacation, but he proves that a true lawman never rests. Some of the action scenes are handled in an interesting fashion for a western; concentration is on reaction to violence rather than the actual violence. This not only saves time in setting up shots, but also keeps from displaying Wilson's limited talents.

p, Barney A. Sarecky; d, Ray Taylor; w, Adele Buffington; ph, Harry Neumann; m, Edward Kay; ed, John C. Fuller; song "Red River Valley" (sung by Whip Wilson and chorus).

Western   (PR:A MPAA:NR)

SHADOWS OF TOMBSTONE*½   (1953) 54m REP bw

Rex Allen (Himself), Slim Pickens (Slim), Jeanne Cooper (Marge), Roy Barcroft (Mike), Emory Parnell (Sheriff Webb), Ric Roman (Delgado), Richard Avonde (Deputy Todd), Julian Rivero (Peon), Koko the Horse.

A crooked sheriff and the local saloonkeeper have taken over a small town, making life miserable for its inhabitants. Allen and Pickens come along to try and bring justice, but take a bit too much time in doing so. Cooper plays the diehard reporter who wants to tell the tale of political corruption.

p, Rudy Ralston; d, William Witney; w, Gerald Geraghty; ph, Bud Thackery; m, R. Dale Butts; ed, Richard L. Van Enger; art d, Frank Hotaling.

Western   (PR:A MPAA:NR)

SHADOWS ON THE SAGE**   (1942) 58m REP bw

Bob Steele (Tucson Smith), Tom Tyler (Stony Brooke), Jimmie Dodd (Lullaby Joslin), Cheryl Walker (Doris Jackson), Harry Holman (Lippy), Bryant Washburn (John Carson), Griff Barnett (Steve Jackson), Freddie Mercer (Johnny), Tom London (Franklin), Yakima Canutt (Red), Rex Lease, Curley Dresden, Eddie Dew, Horace B. Carpenter, Frank Brownlee, John Cason, Pascale Perry.

THE THREE MESQUITEERS are after the gang responsible for continually knocking off a small-town sheriff. Old-timer Holman eventually takes the job when everyone else is afraid to; he gets little Mercer to trail him all over the place so as to practice his draw. A trick in plot development has Steele also playing the gangleader the three boys are after. They bring him to justice after the appropriate number of chases and shoot-outs. (See THREE MESQUITEERS series, Index.)

p, Louis Gray; d, Les Orlebeck; w, J. Benton Cheney (based on characters created by William Colt MacDonald); ph, Edgar Lyons; m, Mort Glickman; ed, William Thompson; art d, Russell Kimball; m/l, "Happy Cowboy," "The Cowboy's Voice Lesson," Jimmie Dodd (sung by Dodd).

Western   (PR:A MPAA:NR)

SHADOWS ON THE STAIRS**   (1941) 63m FN-WB bw

Freida Inescort (Mrs. Armitage), Paul Cavanagh (Reynolds), Heather Angel (Sylvia), Bruce Lester (Bromilow), Miles Mander (Armitage), Lumsden Hare (Inspector), Turhan Bey (Ram Singh), Charles Irwin (Constable), Phyllis Barry (Lucy), Mary Field (Miss Snell), Paul Benay (Sailor), Sidney Bracey (Watchman).

A number of mysterious murders occur in the boarding house of Inescort and Mander, whose inhabitants include young lovers Lester and Angel; Cavanagh, a man with a mysterious past; and Bey as the ever present Oriental. Lester makes all sorts of wild accusations as he becomes more entrenched in the mystery novel he is reading. Direction and performances are all adequate, but can do little to overcome the implausabilities in the script.

p, William Jacobs, d, D. Ross Lederman; w, Anthony Coldeway (based on the play "Murder on the 2nd Floor" by Frank Vosper); ph, Allen G. Siegler; ed, Thomas Pratt.

Mystery   (PR:A MPAA:NR)

SHADOWS OVER CHINATOWN**   (1946) 64m MON bw

Sidney Toler (Charlie Chan), Mantan Moreland (Birmingham Brown), Victor Sen Young (Jimmy Chan), Tanis Chandler (Mary Conover), Paul Bryar (Mike Rogan, Fake Bus Driver), Bruce Kellogg (Jack Tilford), Alan Bridge (Capt. Allen), Mary Gordon (Mrs. Conover), Dorothy Granger (Joan Mercer), Jack Norton (Cosgrove), John Gallaudet (Jeff Hay), Charlie Jordan (Jenkins), Mira McKinney, George Eldredge, Harry Depp, Gladys Blake, Jack Mower, Tyra Vaughn, Lyle Latell, John Hamilton.

San Francisco's Chinatown serves as the setting for this Chan outing in which Toler investigates murders related to insurance fraud. Chandler plays a girl who assists Toler to free her fiance from gangsters. Action is kept at an even pace, with a moderate amount of suspense maintained. Of course Moreland and Yong are around for their support, and to provide the laughs. (See CHARLIE CHAN series, Index.)

p, James S. Burkett; d, Terry Morse; w, Raymond Schrock (based on stories by Earl Derr Biggers); ph, William Sickner; ed, Ralph Dixon; art d, Dave Milton.

Mystery   (PR:A MPAA:NR)

SHADOWS OVER SHANGHAI*½   (1938) 66m GN bw

James Dunn (Johnny McGinty), Ralph Morgan (Howard Barclay, Arms Buyer), Linda Gray (Irene Roma), Robert Barrat (Igor Sargoza), Paul Sutton (Fuji Yokahama), Edward Woods (Peter Roma), Edwin Mordant (Dr. Adams), Chester Gan (Lun Sat Li), Victor Wong (Wu Chang), Edward Keane (American Consul), Billy Bevan (Gallcuddy), William Haade (Capt. Murphy), Richard Loo (Fong), Victor Young (Wang).

This confusing and uneven tale set in Shanghai during the Chinese-Japanese War of 1937-1945 centers on four people's attempts to get an amulet that holds the secret to a Chinese treasure which has been shipped to the United States. These characters include a Russian secret service man, a Russian school teacher, a reporter, and a Chinese weapons buyer. It is hard to figure out what is going on, and the stock footage of Shanghai being bombed does not make things any easier. There are also some moments of very unfitting comedy.

p, Franklyn Warner; d, Charles Lamont; w, Joseph Hoffman (based on a story by Richard B. Sale); ph, Arthur Martinelli; ed, Bernard Loftus, art d, Ralph Berger.

Spy Drama   (PR:A MPAA:NR)

SHADY LADY, THE**   (1929) 60m Pathe bw

Phyllis Haver (Lola Mantell), Robert Armstrong (Blake), Louis Wolheim (Prof. Holbrook), Russell Gleason (Haley).

The addition of dialog in the last 10 minutes did little to aid this rather obvious and unrealistic yarn. Armstrong and Wolheim are rival gunrunners working out of Cuba to get guns to Central American revolutionaries. The plot has them at each others necks, with Wolheim using Haver as bait for Armstrong. But Haver, a woman wrongly accused of a murder, soon falls in love with her prey.

p, Paul Block; d, Edward H. Griffith; w, Jack Jungmeyer, Griffith (based on a story by Leonard Praskins, Richard L. Thorpe); ph, John Mescall; ed, Doane Harrison.

Crime/Drama   (PR:A MPAA:NR)

SHADY LADY**½   (1945) 94m UNIV bw

Charles Coburn ("Colonel" Appleby), Robert Paige (Bob Wendell), Ginny Simms (Lee), Alan Curtis (Marty), Martha O'Driscoll (Gloria), Kathleen Howard (Butch), James Burke (Crane), John Gallaudet (Rappaport), Joe Frisco (Tramp), Thomas Jackson (Bowen), Billy Wayne (Fred), William Hall (Clarence), Bill Hunt (Warren), Erno Verebes (Proprietor), George Lynn, Bert Moorehouse (Card Players), Stuart Holmes (McNeil), Billy Green (Norton), Emmett Smith (Porter), Chuck Hamilton (Carlson).

Coburn plays a card shark, recently released from jail, with a devoted niece in nightclub singer Simms. The two move to Chicago to have a clean go of it. Simms gets a job at a club run by mobster Curtis, while Coburn decides to go behind his niece's back and make a killing at the tables. Investigating attorney Paige is soon involved in a romance with Simms, though his main job is to put her boss behind bars because of illegal gambling activities. Frisco handles a bit of comedy as a bum who gives advice on love. Songs include: "In Love with Love," "Mam'selle Is on Her Way" (George Waggner, Milton Rosen), "Tango" (Edgar Fairchild), "Cuddle Up a Little Closer" (Karl Hoschna, Otto Harbach).

p&d, George Waggner; w, Curt Siodmak, Gerald Geraghty, M.M. Musselman, Monty Collins; ph, Hal Mohr; m, Milton Rosen; ed, Edward Curtiss; md, Rosen; art d, John B. Goodman, Richard H. Riedel; set d, Russell A. Gausman, Ralph Sylos; ch, Lester Horton.

Crime Drama   (PR:A MPAA:NR)

SHAFT***   (1971) 98m Stirling Silliphant-Roger Lewis/MGM c

Richard Roundtree (John Shaft), Moses Gunn (Bumpy Jonas), Charles Cioffi (Lt. Vic Androzzy), Christopher St. John (Ben Buford), Gwenn Mitchell (Ellie Moore), Lawrence Pressman (Sgt. Tom Hannon), Victor Arnold (Charlie), Sherri Brewer (Marcy), Rex Robbins (Rollie), Camille Yarbrough (Dina Greene), Margaret Warncke (Linda), Joseph Leon (Byron Leibowitz), Arnold Johnson (Cul), Dominic Barto (Patsy), George Strus (Carmen), Edmund Hashim (Lee), Drew Bundini Brown (Willy), Tommy Lane (Leroy), Al Kirk (Sims), Shimen Ruskin (Dr. Sam), Antonio Fargas (Bunky), Gertrude Jeannette (Old Lady), Lee Steele (Blind Vendor), Damu King (Mal), Donny Burks (Remmy), Tony King (Davies), Benjamin R. Rixson (Bey Newfield), Ricardo Brown (Tully), Alan Weeks (Gus), Glenn Johnson (Char), Dennis Tate (Dotts), Adam Wade, James Hainesworth (Brothers), Clee Burtonya (Sonny), Ed Bernard (Peerce), Ed Barth (Tony), Joe Pronto (Dom), Robin Nolan (Waitress), Ron Tannas (Billy), Betty Bresler (Mrs. Androzzi), Jon Richards (Elevator Starter), Paul Nevens (Elevator Man),

Gonzalo Madurga *(Counterman)*.

This was the second feature of the longtime still photographer Parks, in which he brought the talent for capturing an image and his personal knowledge of life on the streets to create a hard-hitting action thriller. Roundtree plays a private detective hired by Harlem mobster Gunn to find his kidnaped daughter. This requires infiltrating the mob before finding the girl. St. John plays the black militant who assists Roundtree, and Cioffi is the cop who helps keep a gangland war from escalating. Although obvious racial tensions are created, these are kept under check by Parks, who concentrated on the humanistic elements in his character. Shaft is presented in some depth beyond that of a super-slick detective, showing other sides to his personality. One thing for sure he is one tough cookie, something to which the Academy Award winning song by Isaac Hayes will attest.

p, Joel Freeman; d, Gordon Parks, Sr.; w, John D.F. Black, Ernest Tidyman (based on the novel by Tidyman); ph, Urs Furrer (Metrocolor); m, Isaac Hayes; ed, Hugh A. Robertson; art d, Emanuel Gerard; set d, Robert Drumheller; cos, Joe Aulisi; m/l, "Theme from Shaft," Hayes (performed by Hayes with the Bar-Kays and Movement); makeup, Martin Bell.

Crime   Cas.   (PR:O   MPAA:R)

SHAFT IN AFRICA**   (1973) 112m MGM c

Richard Roundtree *(John Shaft)*, Frank Finlay *(Amafi the Slave Dealer)*, Vonetta McGee *(Aleme)*, Neda Arneric *(Jazar)*, Debebe Eshetu *(Wassa)*, Spiros Focas *(Sassari)*, Jacques Herlin *(Perreau)*, Jho Jhenkins *(Ziba)*, Willie Jonah *(Oyo)*, Adolfo Lastretti *(Piro)*, Marne Maitland *(Col. Gondar)*, Frank McRae *(Osiat)*, Zenebech Tadesse *(Prostitute)*, A.V. Falana *(Ramila's Son)*, James E. Myers *(Detective Williams)*, Nadim Sawalha *(Zubair)*, Thomas Baptiste *(Kopo)*, Jon Chevron *(Shimba)*, Glynn Edwards *(Vanden)*, Cy Grant *(Emir Ramila)*, Jacques Marin *(Inspector Cusset)*, Nick Zaran *(Sadi)*, Aldo Sambrell *(Angelo)*.

Third in the SHAFT series, and the first without Gordon Parks' direction or Tidyman's scripting. The lack of these two talents is quite obvious. The heart is gone from the project making it little more than flashy entertainment. As the title implies Roundtree, as the tough New York detective, leaves the ghetto to uncover a slave smuggling ring in Africa. Finlay is the mastermind behind the ring, which makes for cheap employment in Europe. His trusted aide, Eshetu, is really a spy and helps Roundtree get Finlay. But first he must deal with numerous henchman, who are taken care of in pretty creative manners.

p, Roger Lewis; d, John Guillermin; w, Stirling Silliphant (based on characters created by Ernest Tidyman); ph, Marcel Grignon (Panavision, Metrocolor); m, Johnny Pate; ed, Max Benedict; prod d, John Stoll; art d, Jose Maria Tapiador; m/l, "Are You Man Enough?," Dennis Lambert, Brian Potter (sung by the Four Tops).

Crime   (PR:O   MPAA:R)

SHAFT'S BIG SCORE**½   (1972) 105m MGM c

Richard Roundtree *(John Shaft)*, Moses Gunn *(Bumpy Jonas)*, Drew Bundi Brown *(Willy)*, Joseph Mascolo *(Gus Mascola)*, Kathy Imrie *(Rita)*, Wally Taylor *(Kelly)*, Julius W. Harris *(Capt. Bollin)*, Rosaland Miles *(Arna Ashby)*, Joe Santos *(Pascal)*, Angelo Nazzo *(Al)*, Don Blakely *(Johnson)*, Melvin Green, Jr *(Junior Gillis)*, Thomas Anderson *(Preacher)*, Evelyn Davis *(Old Lady)*, Richard Pittman *(Kelly's Hood No.1)*, Robert Kya-Hill *(Cal Ashby)*, Thomas Brann *(Mascola's Hood)*, Bob Jefferson *(Harrison)*, Dan P. Hannafin *(Cooper)*, Jimmy Hayeson *(Caretaker)*, Henry Ferrentino *(Detective Salmi)*, Frank Scioscia *(Rip)*, Kitty Jones *(Cabaret Dancer)*, Gregory Reese *(Foglio)*, Marilyn Hamlin *(Mascola's Girl)*, John Foster *(Jerry)*, Joyce Walker *(Cigarette Girl)*, Gordon Parks *(Croupier)*.

Follow-up to the extremely successful SHAFT, lacks the energy of its predecessor, with a plot and performances that seems overly contrived. Yet it is still a well-paced and finely tuned actioner featuring a chase in Brooklyn harbor involving cars, boats, and helicopters. Roundtree is the stylish detective left to sort out the problems created in a feud between mobsters Taylor and Mascolo, the latter looking to expand his territory. Gangster Gunn is also around to add to the problems. Songs include: "Blowin' Your Mind," "Don't Misunderstand," "Move on In" (Gordon Parks; sung by O.C. Smith), "Type Thang" (Isaac Hayes; sung by Hayes).

p, Roger Lewis, Ernest Tidyman; d, Gordon Parks, Sr.; w, Tidyman (based on characters created by Tidyman); ph, Urs Furrer (Panavision, Metrocolor); m, Parks; ed, Harry Howard; art d, Emanuel Gerard; set d, Robert Drumheller; cos, Joe Aulisi; spec eff, Tony Parmalee; makeup, Martin Bell; stunts, Alex Stevens, Marvin Walters.

Crime   (PR:O   MPAA:R)

SHAGGY**½   (1948) 71m PAR c

Brenda Joyce *(Laura Calvin)*, George Nokes *(Robbie Calvin)*, Robert Shayne *(Bob Calvin)*, Jody Gilbert *(Tessie)*, Ralph Sanford *(Fuzzie)*, Alex Fraser *(Mac)*, William Haade *(Gonnell)*, Dan White *(Joe)*, Ian McDonald, Shaggy the Dog.

Warm-hearted boy and his dog story has the dog accused of killing

neighboring sheep. The real culprit is a large wolf, which the dog kills. The boy, Nokes, must also contend with a new stepmother who is unhappy with her surroundings.

p, William Pine, William Thomas; d, Robert Emmett Tansey; w, Maxwell Shane; ph, Ellis W. Carter (Cinecolor); m, Ralph Stanley; ed, Howard Smith; art d, F. Paul Sylos; set d, John MacNeil, William Magginetti.

Drama/Adventure   (PR:AA   MPAA:NR)

SHAGGY D.A., THE**   (1976) 91m Walt Disney/BV c

Dean Jones *(Wilby Daniels)*, Suzanne Pleshette *(Betty Daniels)*, Tim Conway *(Tim)*, Keenan Wynn *(District Attorney John Slade)*, Jo Anne Worley *(Katrinka Muggelberg)*, Dick Van Patten *(Raymond)*, Shane Sinutko *(Brian Daniels)*, Vic Tayback *(Eddie Roschak)*, John Myhers *(Adm. Brenner)*, Dick Bakalyan *(Freddie)*, Warren Berlinger *(Dip)*, Ronnie Schell *(T.V. Director)*, Jonathan Daly *(T.V. Interviewer)*, John Fiedler *(Howie Clemmings)*, Hans Conried *(Prof. Whatley)*, Michael McGreevey *(Sheldon)*, Richard O'Brien *(Desk Sergeant)*, Dick Lane *(Roller Rink Announcer)*, Benny Rubin *(Waiter)*, Ruth Gillette *(Song Chairman)*, Hank James *(Policeman)*, Iris Adrian *(Manageress)*, Pat McCormick *(Bartender)*, George Kirby *(Dog Character Voices)*, Henry Slate, Milton Frome, Walt Davis, Albert Able, Mary Ann Gibson, Helene Winston, Joan Crosby, Sarah Fankboner, Danny Wells, Herb Vigran, Olan Soule, Vern Rowe, Karl Lukas, John Hayes, Christina Anderson, Liam Dunn.

One of the few sequels to come nearly 20 years after the original, and prove every bit as good. Following in the same footsteps as THE SHAGGY DOG, Jones plays a lawyer who comes across the ancient ring that changes him into a large sheep dog (the same thing happened to Tommy Kirk several years earlier). Jones is running for district attorney against Wynn, a villainous sort who gets his comeuppance when he turns into a bulldog in the end. It's all for the fun of it and, though at times the humor slips into slap-stick, the skilled hand of director Stevenson (working on his 19th Disney film) keep the situations within bounds. Liam Dunn, who had an unbilled cameo appearance as a dogcatcher, died before completing his part.

p, Bill Anderson; d, Robert Stevenson; w, Don Tait (based on the novel *The Hound Of Florence* by Felix Salten); ph, Frank Phillips (Technicolor); m, Buddy Baker; ed, Bob Bring, Norman Palmer; art d, John B. Mansbridge, Perry Ferguson; set d, Robert Benton; cos, Chuck Keehne, Emily Sundby; m/l, title song, Shane Tatum, Richard McKinley (sung by Dean Jones).

Comedy/Fantasy   Cas.   (PR:AAA   MPAA:G)

SHAGGY DOG, THE**   (1959) 101m Walt Disney/BV bw

Fred MacMurray *(Wilson Daniels)*, Jean Hagen *(Frieda Daniels)*, Tommy Kirk *(Wilby Daniels)*, Annette Funicello *(Allison D'Alessio)*, Tim Considine *(Buzz Miller)*, Kevin Corcoran *(Moochie Daniels)*, Cecil Kellaway *(Prof. Plumcutt)*, Alexander Scourby *(Dr. Mikhail Andrassy)*, Roberta Shore *(Franceska Andrassy)*, James Westerfield *(Officer Hanson)*, Jacques Aubochon *(Stefano)*, Strother Martin *(Thurm)*, Forrest Lewis *(Officer Kelly)*, Ned Wever *(E.P. Hackett)*, Gordon Jones *(Capt. Scanlon)*, John Hart *(Police Broadcaster)*, Jack Albertson *(Reporter)*, Mack Williams *(Betz)*, Paul Frees *(Psychiatrist, Narrator)*, Shaggy.

This was the first so-called "live-action comedy" from the Disney studios, and was extremely successful at the box office, garnering $8 million in its first release. The film inspired many changes in Disney productions and signaled the return of MacMurray to comedy, where he got his start in the 1930s. After this film, Disney realized the combination of situation comedy and fantasy was an idea worth pursuing further, and that repetition – and the obvious – were assured of getting laughs. The performances of MacMurray, as the bumbling father, and Lewis, as a policeman in a series of running gags, were followed by future roles in other Disney comedies. The film also led to the highly successful sequel, THE SHAGGY D.A., which was made some 20 years later. THE SHAGGY DOG initially met criticism upon its release for having elements thought to be frightening to young children: The transformation of Kirk into a dog was likened to that in which humans change into werewolves in horror films. Here he plays the father to Kirk, a kid who turns into a dog when he becomes the possessor of an ancient Latin ring, which slips into his pants cuff as he leaves a museum. After reading the inscription on the back, Kirk finds himself transformed into a large sheep dog, identical to one owned by the next-door neighbors. This poses a problem for MacMurray, who happens to be allergic to dogs. The dog (Kirk) overhears a conversation by the next-door neighbor, who turns out to be a spy, and he ends up chasing the spies when they attempt escape. MacMurray and the neighbor's dog get all the credit, although Kirk actually performed the heroic deed. The best comic situations come in segments totally unrelated to the plot, and a number of them are overly predictable. But those that hit do so with an innocent charm, an example of this being a scene where the dog acts like a human.

p, Walt Disney, Bill Walsh; d, Charles Barton; w, Walsh, Lillie Hayward (based on the novel *The Hound of Florence* by Felix Salten); ph, Edward Coleman; m, Paul J. Smith; ed, James D. Ballas; art d, Carroll Clark; set d, Emile Kuri, Fred MacLean; cos, Chuck Keehne, Gertrude Casey.

Comedy/Fantasy   Cas.   (PR:AAA   MPAA:NR)

SHAKE HANDS WITH MURDER**

(1944) 63m American
Productions/PRC bw

Iris Adrian (Patsy Brent), Frank Jenks (Eddie Jones), Douglas Fowley (Steve Morgan), Jack Raymond (Joe Blake), Claire Rochelle (Secretary), Herbert Rawlinson (John Clark), Juan De La Cruz (Stanton), Forrest Taylor (Kennedy), George Kirby (Adams), Gene Stutenroth [Roth] (Howard), Anita Sparrow (Waitress), Buck Harrington (Sergeant), I. Stanford Jolley (Haskins).

A thinly plotted murder mystery serves as the background for the comic antics of Adrian, Jenks, and Fowley, of which there is good supply. Adrian and Jenks are partners in the business of bailing out criminals. In this case Fowley is the man accused of stealing bonds from his business partner. Things get a bit rough when the partner turns up dead, and Fowley is the main suspect. Fowley is proven innocent when the real culprit is discovered.

d, Albert Herman; w, John T. Neville (based on the story by Martin Mooney); ph, Robert Cline; ed, George Merrick; md, Lee Zahler; art d, Paul Palmentola.

Comedy/Mystery   (PR:A   MPAA:NR)

SHAKE HANDS WITH THE DEVIL***½

(1959, Ireland) 111m
Pennebaker/UA bw

James Cagney (Sean Lenihan), Don Murray (Kerry O'Shea), Dana Wynter (Jennifer Curtis), Glynis Johns (Kitty Brady), Michael Redgrave (The General), Sybil Thorndike (Lady Fitzhugh), Marianne Benet (Mary Madigan), John Breslin (McGrath), Harry Brogan (Cassidy), Robert Brown (Sergeant), Lewis Casson (The Judge), John Cairney (Mike O'Callaghan), Harry H. Corbett (Clancy), Eileen Crowe (Mrs. Madigan), Allan Cuthbertson (Captain), Donal Donnelly (Willie Cafferty), Wilfred Downing (Tommy Connor), Eithne Dunne (Eileen O'Leary), Paul Farrell (Doyle), Richard Harris (Terence O'Brien), William Hartnell (Sgt. Jenkins), John LeMesurier (British General), Niall MacGinnis (Michael O'Leary), Patrick McAlinney (Donovan), Ray McAnally (Paddy Nolan), Clive Morton (Sir Arnold Fielding), Noel Purcell (Liam O'Sullivan), Peter Reynolds (Captain), Christopher Rhodes (Col. Smithson), Ronald Walsh (Sergeant, Black and Tans), Alan White (Capt. Fleming).

There's an old Irish proverb that reads, "Those who shake hands with the devil often have trouble getting their hands back," and in this picture it's Cagney who has firmly gripped the devil's outstretched hand. A college medical professor at Dublin's Royal College of Surgeons, Cagney spends his days lecturing students but at night wears the hat of a militant member of the Irish Republican Army. The 1921 conflict between the freedom fighters and the British Black and Tans is apparent from the opening frames as a group of militiamen break up a seemingly innocent funeral service. It is innocent only in appearance, however. When the wooden casket is sent crashing to the ground it is a supply of guns that falls out, not a corpse. Cagney is a man driven, obsessed, with the idea of living in an Ireland which is free from British rule. As Cagney the doctor heals patients, so will Cagney the revolutionary heal his war-torn country. Cagney tries to influence some of his students, especially the innocent Irish-American Murray, to set down their stethoscopes and take up arms. Murray resists until he witnesses the murder of a friend by the Black and Tans. He takes refuge with the IRA and soon begins to understand what they are fighting for. He finds himself torn between his devotion to a cause and his growing love for Wynter, a member of the royal family who has been taken prisoner by Cagney. Though a peace treaty promises to put an end to the violence, Cagney refuses to give up his ideals. Acting to sabotage the passage of the treaty, Cagney tries to kill Wynter. Angered at Cagney's unflinching belief in violence, Murray guns him down just before Wynter is about to be shot. As Cagney lived by the violence which accompanied the devil's handshake, so did he die by it. Although somewhat uneven in its production values (nearly all critics unduly complained about the inconsistency of the actors' brogues), SHAKE HANDS WITH THE DEVIL provides Cagney with the finest role of his later period. Fortunately, Cagney is not left to carry the film by himself, being blessed with a splendid Dublin locale and a superb cast of supporting players from IRA commander-in-chief Redgrave down to the bits from the Abbey Theatre company. Reflecting on his role in SHAKE HANDS WITH THE DEVIL compared to his previous "tough guy" roles, Cagney has said, "In this film I'm not playing a gunman. I'm a revolutionary. I'm one of a band of hard men, dedicated men who fought the battle to bring peace and freedom to Ireland. It's not just a man with a gun. It's a man with a gun and a purpose. The gun is incidental to the purpose...I'm a revolutionary and the gun is part of my professional equipment, as much a part of it as the stethoscope I carry as a doctor. What is important to me is that the character has reality and validity; he's the prototype of the men who fought in 1921 to free Ireland."

p&d, Michael Anderson; w, Ivan Goff, Ben Roberts, Marian Thompson (based on the novel by Reardon Connor); ph, Erwin Hillier; m, William Alwyn (performed by the Sinfonia of London); ed, Gordon Pilkington; md, Muir Mathieson; prod d, Tom Morahan; set d, Josie Macavin; cos, Irene Gilbert; tech adv, Lt. Col. William O'Kelly.

Drama   (PR:C   MPAA:NR)

SHAKE, RATTLE, AND ROCK!**½

(1957) 74m AIP bw

Fats Domino, Joe Turner (Themselves), Lisa Gaye (June), Touch [Mike] Connors (Garry), Sterling Holloway (Axe), Raymond Hatton (Horace), Douglas Dumbrille (Eustace), Margaret Dumont (Georgianna), Tommy Charles (Himself), Annita Ray (Herself), Paul Dubov (Bugsy), Eddie Kafafian (Nick), Clarence Kolb (Judge), Percy Helton (Hiram), Choker Campbell (Himself), Charles Evans (Bentley), Frank Jenks (Director), Pierre Watkin (Armstrong), Joe Devlin (Police Captain), Jimmy Pickford (Eddie), Nancy Kilgas (Nancy), Giovanna Fiorino (Helen), Leon Tyler (Aloysius), Patricia Gregory (Pat).

Connors poses as a T.V. star who wants to open up a music club for the benefit of underprivileged kids, and meets with strong opposition from conservative parents who see 'rock' music as a menace to society. The case goes to court and the kids win; the evidence that tips the scale in their favor is footage of a young Dumont, now a stuck-up biddy, flapping the "charleston." Real fun comes in performances of the musical greats. Fats Domino sings "I'm In Love Again," "Ain't That A Shame" and "Honey Chile"; Joe Turner does "Feelin' Happy" and "Lipstick, Powder and Paint"; and Tommy Charles and Annita Ray team up on "Sweet Love On My Mind" and "Rockin' On Saturday Night".

p, James H. Nicholson; d, Edward L. Cahn; w, Lou Rusoff; ph, Frederick F. West; m, Alexander Courage; ed, Robert S. Eisen.

Comedy/Musical   (PR:A   MPAA:NR)

SHAKEDOWN, THE**

(1929) 70m UNIV bw

James Murray (Dave Hall), Barbara Kent (Marjorie), George Kotsonaros (Battling Roff), Wheeler Oakman (Manager), Jack Hanlon (Clem), Harry Gribbon (Bouncer).

Early talkie, produced and directed by Wyler was not one of his better efforts; it moves at a dreadfully slow pace, possibly the result of the mixing of half dialog and half silent episodes. Murray plays a crooked boxer who travels around with Oakman and Kotsonaros, as manager and rival boxer, respectively. Their racket is to plant Murray in various towns as a challenge to oaf Kotsonaros. It works pretty well until Murray meets up with a young orphan lad, Hanlon, and a pretty waitress, Kent. He gives up the racket and puts his rival down for the count.

p&d, William Wyler; w, Charles A. Logue, Albert De Mond, Clarence Marks (based on a story by Logue); ph, Charles Stumar, Jerome Ash; ed, Lloyd Nosler, Richard Cahoon.

Drama   (PR:A   MPAA:NR)

SHAKEDOWN, 1934   (SEE: BIG SHAKEDOWN, THE, 1934)

SHAKEDOWN*½

(1936) 55m COL bw

Lew Ayres (Bob Sanderson), Joan Perry (Edith Stuart), Thurston Hall (T. Gregory Stuart), Victor Killian (Caretaker), Henry Mollison (Ralph Gurney), John Gallaudet (Hawsley), George McKay (Spud), Gene Morgan (Presto Mullins, Reporter).

Flimsy story focuses on Ayres, who wants to marry Perry but won't until he proves himself in business first. So Ayres gets a job as a messenger in Perry's father's company, determined to make a good show of himself, and winds up stopping a scheme to kidnap his heartthrob. Direction, acting, and mounting did little to help the story along.

p, Harry Decker; d, David Selman; w, Grace Neville (based on the story by Harry Shipman); ph, Henry Freulich; ed, Gene Milford.

Crime/Drama   (PR:A   MPAA:NR)

SHAKEDOWN***½

(1950) 80m UNIV bw

Howard Duff (Jack Early), Brian Donlevy (Nick Palmer), Peggy Dow (Ellen Bennett), Lawrence Tierney (Colton), Bruce Bennett (David Glover), Anne Vernon (Nita Palmer), Stapleton Kent (City Editor), Peter Virgo (Roy), Charles Sherlock (Sam), Will Lee, Carl Sklover (Taxi Drivers), Josephine Whittell (Mrs. Worthington), Steve Roberts (Magazine Representative), John Miller (Brownie), Ken Patterson (Thurman), Leota Lorraine (Guest), Charles Flynn (Fireman), Jack Reitzen (Fat Man), Roy Engel (Captain), Jack Rice (Floorwalker), Bert Davidson, Ralph Brooks, Doug Carter (Photographers), Kay Riehl (Mrs. Spencer), Wendy Waldron (Information Clerk), Elsie Baker (Maid), Donald Kerr (Newsboy), Doretta Johnson (Nurse), Jack Chefe (Proprietor), Forbes Murray (Mr. Spencer), William Marks (Detective), Steve Wayne (Reporter), Joe Dougherty, Bill O'Brien, James Garwood, Chester Conklin (Men).

A disturbing, unrelentingly grim indictment of blind ambition starring Duff as a cynical, unscrupulous news photographer who will do anything to secure a position on a major San Francisco newspaper. Landing a probationary position with the paper, Duff tries to cement his chances of full-time work by starting an affair with his boss, Dow. He is given an assignment to photograph an elusive mobster, Donlevy, so Duff cleverly convinces the hood that it would be in his best interest to cooperate and allow only flattering photos to be printed in the papers. Donlevy agrees and even allows

Duff to photograph a robbery committed by one of his mob, Tierney. Duff then uses the photo to blackmail Tierney. Outraged, Tierney confronts Donlevy with the news. Feeling betrayed by his boss, Tierney plants a bomb in Donlevy's car and Duff takes pictures, including a sensational shot of the chief mobster being blown to bits. The picture makes Duff famous overnight and he takes a job with a national magazine. Hiding the pictures of Tierney planting the bomb in Dow's apartment for safekeeping, Duff sets out to romance Donlevy's widow, Vernon. Dow learns of Duff's duplicity and, fed up with his selfish ambition, she breaks off their relationship. Duff continues to blackmail Tierney and convinces the gangsters to rob a swanky high-society party that he has been assigned to photograph. Tierney tires of Duff, however, and tells Vernon that the photographer killed her husband. Desperate to clear himself with Vernon, Duff begs Dow to bring the photographs showing Tierney planting the bomb in Donlevy's car. Dow refuses to believe that the pictures even exist and declines. In the confusion, Vernon is accidentally shot and Tierney murders Duff. As Duff falls dying, he manages to snap one last picture of his killer. Ironically, the San Francisco newspaper that gave him his start publishes the sensational photo alongside Duff's favorable obituary–the world never learning what a cruel and vicious man the photographer really was. Duff is sensational as the ambitious photographer, creating the type of evil, wholly irredeemable character not seen on the screen since James Cagney in WHITE HEAT (1949). While Duff's character is a man to be reviled, SHAKEDOWN encourages understanding and analysis of what it is in the American psyche that drives a person to commit such foul deeds in pursuit of success.

p, Ted Richmond; d, Joseph Pevney; w, Alfred Lewis Levitt, Martin Goldsmith (based on a story by Nat Dallinger, Don Martin); ph, Irving Glassberg; ed, Milton Carruth; md, Joseph Gershenson; art d, Bernard Herzbrun, Robert Clatworthy; set d, Russell A. Gausman, Ruby R. Levitt; cos, Yvonne Wood; makeup, Bud Westmore, Del Armstrong.

Crime   **(PR:C   MPAA:NR)**

SHAKEDOWN, THE**½   (1960, Brit.) 92m Ethiro-Alliance/UNIV bw

Terence Morgan (Augie Cortona), Hazel Court (Mildred Hyde), Donald Pleasence (Jessel, Photographer), Bill Owen (Spettigue), Robert Beatty (Inspector Jarvis), Harry H. Corbett (Gollar), Gene Anderson (Zena), Eddie Byrne (George, Barman), John Salew (Arnold), Georgina Cookson (Miss Firbank), Joan Haythorne (Miss Ogilvie), Sheila Buxton (Nadia), Dorinda Stevens (Grace), Jack Lambert (Sgt. Kershaw), Larry Burns (1st Thug), Jack Taylor (3rd Thug), Charles Lamb (Dinza), Laurence Taylor (2nd Thug), Linda Castle (Sylvia), Patty Dalton (Photo Model), Arthur Lovegrove (Barman), Paul Whitsun-Jones (Fat Drinker), Timothy Bateson (Estate Agent), Edward Judd, Douglas Bradley-Smith, Lynn Curtis, Leila Williams, Pauline Dukes, Angela Douglas, Julia Rogers, Diana Chesney, Frank Hawkins, Robert Sansom, Neal Arden, Candy Scott, Wendy Peters.

Fast-paced and heavy-hitting crime drama has Morgan as a freshly released convict anxious to get back into action. But this is much easier said than done, so he opens up a photography studio that actually is a front for pornographic photography and blackmail activities. He runs into trouble with rival gangster Corbett, and bitter warfare erupts. Scotland Yard tracks down Morgan by having Court go undercover as a model, thus infiltrating his set-up. Pleasance plays the alcoholic photographer whose studio Morgan uses for his headquarters. Performances are all good and realistic, given a believable setting. Direction keeps the pace moving, which helps to smooth over the inadequacies in the predictable script.

p, Norman Williams; d, John Lemont; w, Lemont, Leigh Vance; ph, Brendan J. Stafford; m, Philip Green; ed, Bernard Gribble.

Crime   **(PR:C   MPAA:NR)**

SHAKESPEARE WALLAH***   (1966, India) 115m CD bw

Shashi Kapoor (Sanju), Felicity Kendall (Lizzie Buckingham), Madhur Jaffrey (Manjula), Geoffrey Kendal (Mr. Tony Buckingham), Laura Liddell (Mrs. Carla Buckingham), Utpal Dutt (Maharaja), Parveen Paul (Didi), Jim D. Tytler (Bobby), Prayag Raaj (Sharmaji), Pincho Kapoor (Guptaji), Partap Sharma (Aslam), Hamid Sayani (Headmaster's Brother), Sudershan (Director), Jennifer Kapoor (Mrs. Bowen).

An exploration into the changes in Indian culture after the country gains independence from Britain. A British Shakespeare troupe that travels through India meets with rejection at almost every performance. The daughter of the two troupe leads, Felicity Kendall, falls in love with a wealthy Indian, Pincho Kapoor. But Kapoor eventually realizes that he can not marry Kendall because of their vast cultural differences. They soon separate, and Kendall returns to England.

p, Ismail Merchant; d, James Ivory; w, Ruth Prawer Jhabvala, Ivory (based on a story by Jhabvala); ph, Subrata Mitra; m, Satyajit Ray; ed, Amit Bose.

Drama   **(PR:A   MPAA:NR)**

SHAKIEST GUN IN THE WEST, THE*½   (1968) 100m UNIV c

Don Knotts (Jesse W. Heywood), Barbara Rhoades (Penelope Cushings), Jackie Coogan (Matthew Basch), Donald "Red" Barry (Rev. Zachary Grant), Ruth McDevitt (Olive), Frank McGrath (Mr. Remington), Terry Wilson (Welsh), Carl Ballantine (Swanson), Pat Morita (Wong), Robert Yuro (Arnold the Kid), Herbert Voland (Dr. Friedlander), Fay DeWitt (Violet), Dub Taylor (Pop McGovern), Hope Summers (Celia), Dick Wilson (Indian Chief), Vaughan Taylor (Rev. Longbaugh), Ed Peck (Sheriff), Edward Faulkner (Huggins), Arthur Space (Sheriff Tolliver), Gregory Mullavy (Phelps), Benny Rubin, Dorothy Neumann, E.J. Andre.

Inferior remake of the 1948 Bob Hope vehicle PALEFACE, with Knotts trying to fill the shoes of Hope, and Rhoades those of Jane Russell. TV director Rafkin had the honors of making Knotts look stupid, which isn't very hard. The film is done in pure television style, the only difference being the Techniscope photography. Yarn has Knotts as a Philadelphia dentist making the long trek out West, where he meets up with lady bandit Rhoades when she robs the stagecoach he is on. To get a pardon, she agrees to round up a group of gun traffickers. She tricks Knotts into marriage so that she can join a wagon train that doesn't accept single women. When Indians attack, Rhoades kills several Indians but Knotts and everyone else thinks he did the fancy shooting. Knotts is elevated to the status of a hero, but meets with shame when the truth is revealed. However, he redeems himself when Rhoades is kidnaped by Indians, and he rescues her by dressing up as a squaw. Knotts is definitely no Hope, and Rhoades is far from Russell. The combination of 5-foot-11-inches Rhoades and the scrawny Knotts looks more ridiculous than funny, which pretty well sums up this movie.

p, Edward J. Montagne; d, Alan Rafkin; w, Jim Fritzell, Everett Greenbaum (based on the screenplay of THE PALEFACE by Frank Tashlin and Edmund Hartmann); ph, Andrew Jackson (Techniscope, Technicolor); m, Vic Mizzy; ed, Tony Martinelli; md, Joseph Gershenson; art d, Alexander Golitzen, Henry Larrecq; set d, John McCarthy, Perry Murdock; cos, Grady Hunt; m/l, title song, Jerry Keller, Dave Blume (sung by the Wilburn Brothers); makeup, Bud Westmore.

Comedy/Western   **(PR:A   MPAA:NR)**

SHALAKO**   (1968, Brit.) 113m Kingston-Palomar/Cinerama c

Sean Connery (Shalako), Brigitte Bardot (Countess Irini Lazaar), Stephen Boyd (Bosky Fulton), Jack Hawkins (Sir Charles Daggett), Peter Van Eyck (Frederick von Hallstatt), Honor Blackman (Lady Julia Daggett), Woody Strode (Chato), Eric Sykes (Mako), Alexander Knox (Henry Clarke), Valerie French (Elena Clarke), Julian Mateos (Rojas), Donald Barry (Buffalo), Rodd Redwing (Chato's Father), "Chief" Tug Smith (Loco), Hans De Vries (Adjutant), Walter Brown (Peter Wells), Charles Stalnaker (Marker), Bob Cunningham (Luther), John Clarke (Hockett), Bob Hall (Johnson).

The Bond-BB pairing that SHALAKO offers simply can't pump much life into this otherwise typical big-budget oater set in 19th-Century New Mexico. Connery is a wandering cowboy (his Indian name means "he who brings rain") who comes to the rescue of a snooty group of aristocrats after they run into trouble in Apache territory. It seems they were led there by appropriately dusty trail-boss Boyd in a scheme to make them an easy target for robbery. Connery makes a special effort to come to Bardot's aid, especially since she has two factors in her favor–her royal blood and her obligatory topless scene. The wealthy fools aren't so eager to leave Indian territory, and it takes a bloodletting ambush to change their minds. After putting his life on the line, Connery goes on his way, followed by BB, while the rest of her group returns to Britain. Photographed in Spain (looking much like the New Mexico locale, however), SHALAKO is clearly a money making venture rather than an attempt to contribute to the genre. Initially, Henry Fonda was cast as the lead, but upon realizing he wasn't a box-office name (at least in Connery's league), he pulled out. Connery, turning down the lead in ON HER MAJESTY'S SECRET SERVICE, was offered the role. Bardot also passed on the same Bond picture, missing her chance to play opposite George Lazenby's forgettable Bond. SHALAKO was Bardot's first picture in nearly two years, bringing her 350,000 pounds in salary plus 15 percent of the profits, enough to let her sunbathe on the Riviera for another year before getting in front of the camera again.

p, Euan Lloyd; d, Edward Dmytryk; w, J.J. Griffith, Hal Hopper, Scot Finch (based on a screen story by Clarke Reynolds, from Louis L'Amour's novel); ph, Ted Moore (Franscope, Technicolor); m, Robert Farnon; ed, Bill Blunden; md, Muir Mathieson; art d, Herbert Smith; cos, Cynthia Tingey; spec eff, Michael Collins; m/l, title song, Farnon Jim Dale; makeup; Trevor Cole-Rees; stunt, Bob Simmons.

Western   **Cas.**   **(PR:O   MPAA:M/PG)**

SHALL THE CHILDREN PAY?   (SEE: WHAT PRICE INNOCENCE, 1933)

SHALL WE DANCE***½   (1937) 101m RKO bw

Fred Astaire ("Petrov"/Pete Peters), Ginger Rogers (Linda Keene), Edward Everett Horton (Jeffrey Baird), Eric Blore (Cecil Flintridge), Jerome Cowan (Arthur Miller), Ketti Gallian (Lady Tarrington), William Brisbane (Jim Montgomery), Harriet Hoctor (Harriet Hoctor), Ann Shoemaker (Mrs.

Fitzgerald), Ben Alexander (*Bandleader*), Emma Young (*Tai*), Sherwood Bailey (*Newsboy*), Pete Theodore (*Dancing Partner*), Marek Windheim, Rolfe Sedan (*Ballet Masters*), George Magrill (*Room Steward*), Charles Coleman (*Cop in Park*), Frank Moran (*Charlie the Big Man*), Charles Irwin, Jean de Briac, Norman Ainsley, Sam Wren, Pauline Garon, Leonard Mudie, Vasey O'Davoren, Alphonse Martell, Helena Grant, William Burress, Matty Roubert, J. M. Kerrigan, Sam Hayes, Torben Meyer, Spencer Teakle, Mantan Moreland.

For the seventh time in four years, Astaire and Rogers teamed for another frolicsome romp, but this time the results were not so satisfying, neither critically nor financially. It was a rehash of all the films that preceded, replete with the usual mistakes in the love department, people pretending to be what they weren't, too few stylized dances, and a sensational Gershwin brothers score. Astaire is a Russian ballet dancer with Horton as his impresario. Rogers is a high-powered musical-comedy star. Both need a boost for their careers, so Rogers' manager, Cowan, cooks up a phony romance for the breathless press to report and you can guess what happens from there. The two of them don't want to do it, realize that they must, and once they are in each other's arms, love happens and the bogus love affair blossoms into reality. They secretly marry on the proviso that a divorce will follow shortly, once the brouhaha dies down. Naturally, the divorce doesn't work out. Astaire and Rogers had been turning out these films for RKO at a furious rate but this was their only effort for 1937. It was while this was being shot that the studio bosses gathered that the bloom may have been off the rose because their previous picture, SWING TIME, was not doing the box-office business everyone had supposed. George and Ira Gershwin were not accustomed to having so few songs in a movie. It was their second picture (their first film had been DELICIOUS for Fox in 1931), and their only one for Rogers and Astaire. Upon first hearing by the public, this was not a hit-laden score, but time proved the Gershwins right and a number of standards came out of this film. They included: "Slap That Bass" (sung by Astaire), "Beginner's Luck" (Astaire), "Let's Call the Whole Thing Off" (Astaire, Rogers), "Walking the Dog" (strictly instrumental), "They All Laughed" (Astaire, Rogers), "They Can't Take That Away from Me" (Astaire), "Shall We Dance" (Astaire, Harriet Hoctor). In "Slap That Bass," Astaire does his work in the engine room of a luxurious ocean liner as he dances in time with the rhythm of the machinery in the heart of the ship. "Beginner's Luck" is a brief snippet of Astaire dancing to music from a 78 rpm phonograph record. In "They All Laughed," Fred and Ginger have their best dance duet as they trip the light fantastic in a penthouse restaurant. "They Can't Take That Away from Me" is done by Astaire aboard the New Jersey ferry where the two have gone to be married (so they can get their immediate divorce). A mistake was made when Astaire did "Shall We Dance" with contortionist Hoctor. The best novelty in the film was a roller-skating sequence by Astaire and Rogers for "Let's Call the Whole Thing Off." When the film was nearing conclusion, Rogers and Alfred Vanderbilt, Jr., tossed a huge cast party at a Los Angeles roller rink and it was such a smash that very few people drank too much. "They Can't Take That Away from Me" was nominated for an Oscar but lost to the Harry Owens composition "Sweet Leilani" from WAIKIKI WEDDING. Good musical arrangements from Robert Russell Bennett, Joseph Livingston, and Hal Borne. Not as much dancing as audiences had expected and that may have been what cut down the profits to under a half-million dollars on the first release. The first time the audience hears "Slap That Bass" it's sung by a man who was unbilled in the film but continued his career and became a star in the CHARLIE CHAN movies as the redoubtable Hawaiian's Driver, Mantan Moreland. If the U.S. had not seen many better Astaire-Rogers pictures, SHALL WE DANCE might have made a deeper impression, but as it stood, it was more of the same old thing, albeit with the Gershwin score to send audiences out humming.

p, Pandro S. Berman; d, Mark Sandrich; w, Allan Scott, Ernest Pagano, P.J. Wolfson (based on the story "Watch Your Step" by Lee Loeb, Harold Buchman), ph, David Abel; m, George Gershwin; ed, William Hamilton; md, Nathaniel Shilkret; art d, Van Nest Polglase; set d, Darrell Silvera; cos, Irene; spec eff, Vernon Walker; ch, Hermes Pan, Harry Losee; m/l, George Gershwin, Ira Gershwin; makeup, mel Burns.

Musical/Comedy   Cas.   (PR:A MPAA:NR)

SHAME   (SEE: INTRUDER, THE, 1962)

SHAME* ½**   (1968, Swed.) 103m Svensk Filmindustri/Lopert bw
(SKAMMEN)

Liv Ullmann (*Eva Rosenberg*), Max von Sydow (*Jan Rosenberg*), Gunnar Bjornstrand (*Col. Jacobi*), Sigge Furst (*Filip*), Birgitta Valberg (*Mrs. Jacobi*), Hans Alfredson (*Lobelius*), Ingvar Kjellson (*Oswald*), Raymond Lundberg (*Jacobi's Son*), Frank Sundstrom (*Chief Interrogator*), Willy Peters (*Elder Officer*), Ulf Johansson (*Doctor*), Axel Duberg (*Pilot*), Rune Lindstrom (*Stout Man*), Bengt Eklund (*Guard*), Vilgot Sjoman (*Interviewer*), Lars Amble (*Officer*), Ake Jornfalk (*Condemned Man*), Bjorn Thambert (*Johan*), Karl-Axel Forssberg (*Secretary*), Gosta Pruzelius (*Rector*), Brita Oberg (*Woman in Interrogation Room*), Agda Helin (*Shopkeeper*), Ellika Mann (*Woman Guard*), Frej Lindqvist (*Stooping Man*), Barbro Hiort af Ornas (*Woman on Boat*), Gregor Dahlman, Nils Whiten, Borje Lundh, George Skarstadt, Per Berglund, Stig Lindberg, Jan Bergman, Nils Fogeby, Brian Wikstrom, Lilian Carlsson, Eivor Kullberg, Karl-Arne Bergman,

Monica Lindberg.

A stark, chilling film of incredible despair by Ingmar Bergman, taking place in an unnamed country during a civil war. Concert musicians Ullmannand von Sydow are a husband and wife who avoid the atrocities that have gripped the rest of their country by fleeing to a small isolated island. But their peace is short lived, as the island becomes a virtual battleground, forcing the pair to face directly horrors they had isolated themselves from. As the fighting intensifies and their situation worsens, the marriage between Ullmann and von Sydow also changes. Never having to really fend for themselves to remain alive, they find the new strains placed on them give them a different perspective. Ullmann sleeps with a friend of von Sydow to get out of jail. The jealous von Sydow, refusing to help the friend after he's arrested, allows the man to be killed. But this is just the beginning of the depths to which von Sydow sinks. He goes as far as to kill an innocent soldier just for his boots. Ullmann becomes more distressed and, upon leaving the island on a small boat, the two travel through a sea literally filled with floating dead bodies. This scene is almost dreamlike in its stark and vivid imagery. Though the subject can be viewed as unfitting for the cinema, SHAME effectively illustrates the bounds to which civilized humans can descend when their comfort is taken away. Both Ullmann and von Sydow do an excellent job of portraying personalities taken to the limits of emotional perseverance.

d&w, Ingmar Bergman; ph, Sven Nykvist; ed, Ulla Ryghe; art d, P.A. Lundgren, Lennart Blomkvist; cos, Mago; spec eff, Evald Andersson.

Drama   (PR:O MPAA:R)

SHAME OF MARY BOYLE, THE   (SEE: JUNO AND THE PAYCOCK, 1930, Brit.)

SHAME OF PATTY SMITH, THE   (SEE: CASE OF PATTY SMITH, THE, 1962)

SHAME OF THE SABINE WOMEN, THE*½   (1962, Mex.) 80m Constelacion/United Produce rs Releasing Organization c (EL RAPTO DE LAS SABINAS; AKA: THE MATING OF THE SABINE WOMEN; THE RAPE OF THE SABINES)

Lex Johnson (*Hostes*), Lorena Doude (*Hersilia*), Teresa Doude (*Rhea*), William Wolf (*Romulus*), Luis Induni (*Titus Tatius*), John Monfort (*Acron*), Joan Crespi (*Egea*), C. Jimerson (*Rebel Woman*), Leandro Vizcaino, Rubins-kis.

The early days of the Roman civilization serve as the setting for this tale in which Romulus (Wolf) kills his twin brother, giving him total control of the small empire. The empire is without women, so Wolf leads an army to capture some to become their brides. Though at first not very fond of their treatment, the Sabine women eventually grow to love their Roman captors.

p,d&w, Alberto Gout; ph, Alex Phillips (Eastman C.V. color); m, Gustavo Cesar Carrion; ed, Jorge Bustos, John F. Link; art d, John Albert.

Adventure   (PR:A MPAA:NR)

SHAME, SHAME, EVERYBODY KNOWS HER NAME*   (1969) 79m Distribpix-J.E.R. Pictures bw

Karen Carlson (*Susan Barton*), Getti Miller (*Diane Rogers*), Augustus Sultatos (*Vic Keller*), Tony Seville (*Tony Martinelli*), Rita Bennett (*Go-Go Dancer*), Dennis Johnson (*Roy Davenport*), Tyrus Chesney (*Gen. Motley*), John Harrison (*George Michaels*), Vic Vallaro (*Jim Norton*), Karil Daniels (*Carol Taggart*), John Cardoza (*Photographer*), Stuart Coffee (*Marvin Witherspoon*).

Carlson plays a naive Midwesterner who comes to the Big Apple to meet men and excitement. She gets more than she asked for when she moves in with Miller, a lesbian attracted to her. Through a number of disappointing and very disturbing affairs, Carlson decides she's had enough of men and goes to Miller for support.

p&d, Joseph Jacoby; w, William Dorsey Blake (based on the story by Jacoby); ph, Stephen R. Winsten; m, George Craig; ed, Kemper Peacock.

Drama   (PR:O MPAA:R)

SHAMELESS OLD LADY, THE*   (1966, Fr.) 95m S.P.A.C. Cinema/CD bw (LA VIEILLE DAME INDIGNE)

Sylvie (*Mme. Berthe*), Malka Ribovska (*Rosalie*), Victor Lanoux (*Pierre*), Etienne Bierry (*Albert*), Francois Maistre (*Gaston*), Pascale de Boysson (*Simone*), Lena Delanne (*Victoire*), Jeanne Hardeyn (*Rose*), Jean-Louis Lamande (*Charles*), Robert Bousquet (*Robert*), Andre Jourdan (*Lucien*), Armand Meffre (*Ernest*), Pierre Decazes (*Charlot*), Jean Bouise (*Alphonse*), Andre Thorent (*Dufour*), Max Amyl, Emmanuelle Drey.

A film adaptation of a Bertolt Brecht story gave French actress Sylvie something of an international reputation; she was 81 at the time and had been involved in films for almost half a century. Here she plays the recently widowed mother of five, who has devoted her entire life to her husband and family. To her children's surprise, she does a total about face and decides to seek adventure. She befriends a prostitute, buys a car with the last bit of her money, and goes on a vacation. Having lived her adventure, she dies happy.

p, Claude Nedjar; d&w, Rene Allio (based on the story "Die Unwurdige Greisin" by Bertolt Brecht); ph, Denys Clerval; ed, Sophie Coussein; art d, Hubert Monloup; m/l, "One Ne Voit Pas Le Temps Passer," "Loin," "Tu M'as Jamais Quitte," Jean Ferrat (sung by Ferrat); tech adv, Jean Ravel.

Comedy/Drama   (PR:A   MPAA:NR)

SHAMPOO***   (1975) 109m COL c

Warren Beatty (George Roundy), Julie Christie (Jackie Shawn), Goldie Hawn (Jill), Lee Grant (Felicia Carr), Jack Warden (Lester Carr), Tony Bill (Johnny Pope), Carrie Fisher (Lorna Carr), Jay Robinson (Norman), George Furth (Mr. Pettis), Ann Weldon (Mary), Randy Sheer (Dennis), Susanna Moore (Gloria), Mike Olton (Ricci), Luana Anders (Devra), Brad Dexter (Sen. Joe East), William Castle (Sid Roth), Jack Bernardi (Izzy), Doris Packer (Rosalind), Hal Buckley (Kenneth), Howard Hesseman (Red Dog), Cheri Latimer (Girl in Car), Richard E. Kalk (Younger Detective), Brunetta Bennett (Mona), Melinda Smith, Constance Smith (Twins), Susan McIver (Customer), Michele Phillips (Girl at Party), Kathleen Miller, Larry Bischof.

This satire is a wicked romp as Beatty mercilessly lampoons his own off-screen image. He plays a popular hairdresser for the wealthy women of Beverly Hills, who does more than cut hair for his clients. The film, which takes place on November 4, 1968 (the day Richard Nixon was elected President), opens as Beatty is engaged in an affair with Grant, an attractive older woman who is married to Warden. Their lovemaking is interrupted by a phone call from Hawn, another of Beatty's client-lovers. He rushes over to her home, and ends up spending the rest of the night with her. Later Beatty, who wants to escape from his nagging boss Robinson, talks to a bank loan officer, hoping to get the money to open his own hair salon. The loan officer thinks Beatty is a poor risk, and the angered hairdresser retaliates by screaming, "I've got the heads!" Grant suggests Beatty approach her husband and borrow the money from him. Warden is currently having an affair with Christie, an old lover (as well as customer) of Beatty's. Warden agrees to consider Beatty's request, assuming that Beatty is a homosexual because of his profession. Warden also asks Beatty to escort Christie to an election night party, since he must take his wife. Beatty reluctantly agrees, and the party proves to be a fiasco. Christie gets angry when Warden ignores her, and subsequently gets drunk. She makes a scene at a dinner table by virtually attacking Beatty in a lustful frenzy. Beatty is instructed to take her home, but instead Beatty and Christie head off to another Beverly Hills party. Warden gets drunk as well, and is separated from his wife when the building is evacuated because of a bomb threat. He gets a lift from Hawn and her escort, producer Bill, ending up at the same party Beatty and Christie have gone to. Warden, along with Hawn and Bill, surprises Beatty and Christie as they make love. Hawn is furious and Beatty goes chasing after her. The next morning, Beatty, who has been threatened by Warden who has learned of his indiscretions with both Grant and Christie, races his motorcycle to catch up with Christie. He wants to marry her, but she turns him down, explaining that Warden is leaving Grant to marry her. From a hilltop, Beatty watches as Grant and Warden drive off. SHAMPOO offended many with its amoral characters and frank sexual nature. However, it is these very things that are the target of its satire, showing the ugly foundations that lie beneath the beautiful people of Beverly Hills. These are shallow people, concerned only with gratifying themselves, caring not a whit for the consequences of their actions. Surface appearance is everything, and one of the funniest moments has Christie and Grant discovering to their mutual horror that Beatty has given them the exact same hairstyle. The lines of sexual entanglements turn into a weblike mess, and occasionally get out of hand, straying from the film's theme. Beatty, who produced SHAMPOO and cowrote the script (reportedly working for six years on it), is marvelous as the not-too-bright Romeo. Beatty's off-screen romances were well chronicled, and in SHAMPOO he attacks this public image with venom. His character is empty and juvenile, claiming he wants only to please his customers when all he wants is to satisfy his own libido. His proposal to Christie is more out of desperation for stability than for love. Hawn sums up his character nicely when she shouts at him: "You never stop moving! You never go anywhere!" Beatty's use of television election returns during the election night party is effective. Though history is changing before their very eyes, the party guests remain oblivious to it, instead caught up in the drama of their own sexual politics. Though SHAMPOO's pace is uneven, the satire works, and the cast is marvelous. Grant received an Oscar for Best Supporting Actress, while Beatty's skills as a screenwriter (along with Towne) earned a nomination for the script. Warden also received a nomination as Best Supporting Actor. Simon's music is one of the film's biggest detriments, an annoying guitar accompanied by the popular singer's humming. It intrudes on the action, injecting saccharine where the actors' talents are strong enough to carry the material. The best use of music comes over the closing credits. The Beach Boys' popular song "Wouldn't It Be Nice" plays as the credits roll, a final black-humored punch line to the film. Fisher made her film debut here as Grant's feisty daughter who seduces Beatty in record time. Reportedly Fisher's mother, Debbie Reynolds, was furious with her daughter for taking the part. SHAMPOO was an enormous success at the box office, taking in some $60 million during its initial release.

p, Warren Beatty; d, Hal Ashby; w, Robert Towne, Beatty; ph, Laszlo Kovacs (Panavision, Technicolor); m, Paul Simon; ed, Robert Jones; prod d, Richard Sylbert; art d, Stu Campbell; set d, George Gaines, Robert Resh, Charles Zacha; cos, Anthea Sylbert; makeup, Tom Case.

Comedy   **Cas.**   (PR:O   MPAA:R)

SHAMROCK HILL½**   (1949) 70m Vinson-Equity/EL bw

Peggy Ryan (Eileen Rogan), Ray McDonald (Larry Hadden), Trudy Marshall (Carol Judson), Rick Vallin (Oliver Mathews), John Litel (Ralph Judson), Mary Gordon (Grandma Rogan), Tim Ryan (Uncle), James Burke (Michael Rogan), Lanny Simpson (Joey Rogan), Douglas Wood (Judge Mayer), Patsy Bolton (Patsy), Barbara Brier (Doris), Tim Graham (Officer Merrick).

A pleasant enough picture that has Ryan a firm believer in the power of leprechauns, who has taken advantage of an abandoned hill as a setting to tell the local children fairy tales. Her little Utopia is almost destroyed when businessman Litel buys the property so he can build a television station. Ryan, with help from McDonald, takes Litel to court and wins. Ryan supplies the needed charm as well as a pleasant singing voice. Of the songs she sings, "Do You Believe" (Robert Bilder) is probably the best. "Madcap Mood" (Bilder, George O. Walbridge) also provides musical background for a dance number by Ryan and McDonald.

p&d, Arthur Dreifuss; w, Arthur Hoerl, McElbert Moore (based on the story by Hoerl); ph, Philip Tannura; ed, Arthur A. Brooks; md, Herschel Gilbert; art d, Danny Hall; set d, Murray Waite; cos, Barbara Brier; ch, Nick Castle.

Musical   (PR:AA   MPAA:NR)

SHAMUS****   (1959, Brit.) 54m Border/New Realm c

John Francis Rooney (Seamus Rooney), Tiny Littler (Leprechaun).

Enjoyable children's fantasy film which places the legend of the little green creatures from Ireland in a moral context. Littler is the leprechaun who makes life miserable for a young orphaned lad by giving him a tail. The only way the boy can lose the tail is to find a missing donkey.

p, O. Negus-Fancey; d&w, Eric Marquis.

Fantasy   (PR:AA   MPAA:NR)

SHAMUS****   (1973) 98m COL c

Burt Reynolds (Shamus McCoy), Dyan Cannon (Alexis Montaigne), John Ryan (Col. Hardcore), Joe Santos (Lt. Promuto), Georgio Tozzi (Il Dottore), Ron Weyand (E.J. Hume), Larry Block (Springy), Beeson Carroll (Bolton), Kevin Conway (The Kid), Kay Frye (Bookstore Girl), John Glover (Johnnie Bronston), Merwin Goldsmith (Schnook), Melody Santangelo (1st Woman), Irving Selbst (Heavy), Alex Wilson (Felix Montaigne), Tony Amato, Jr (Willie), Lou Martell (Rock), Marshall Anker (Dealer), Bert Bertram (Doorman), Jimmy Kelly (Grifter), Alisha Fontaine (Hatcheck Girl), Mickey Freeman (Pimp), Capt. Arthur Haggerty (Handler), Tommy Lane (Tait), Ric Mancini (Angie), Norman Marshall (Marvin), Fat Thomas Rand (Big Jake), Frank Silvero, Don Cost (Bookies), Alex Stevens (Knifer), Steven Vignari (Hardnose), Mark Weston (Detective), Glenn Wilder, Charles Picerni, Tony Amato, Sr (Thugs).

The original derivation of the word "shamus" comes from "shammes," which is the title given to the sexton who watches the synagog. The original derivation of this movie is from Raymond Chandler's THE BIG SLEEP, the initial screen version of which starred Humphrey Bogart, and it starts off as what appears to be a parody of that classic but then settles into being merely a copy. Reynolds plays it for laughs and manages to give the feeble comedy lines the right delivery (almost like Johnny Carson), which helps to lift this traditional picture to a height it doesn't deserve. Filmed on location all over New York City, it's the story of a Brooklyn private eye who sleeps on a pool table above a billiard parlor. He gets a phone call asking him to visit the estate of wealthy Weyand, a diamond merchant who keeps his house cooled to 40 degrees while he sips iced tea (In THE BIG SLEEP, Bogart had to perspire as he met his client in a hothouse). Weyand says that some diamonds have been stolen and Reynolds can pick up 10 grand if he finds them. Obviously, the thieves play for keeps, as the man who had the gems was murdered. Reynolds travels around a few pool halls, where he supplements his detective wages by playing like Fast Eddie Felsen (THE HUSTLER). He enlists the aid of Block, a bookmaker who doesn't ever write anything down because his mind is like a Xerox machine. Block will nose around and see if he can uncover any data on the killing and robbery. Reynolds goes back to his tacky quarters and is whacked soundly by hoodlums who warn him off the job. This only serves to pique Reynolds's interest, so he talks to Tozzi (known as "Il Dottore," which means "the Doctor"), a gangland chief who runs a restaurant as a front. (Tozzi does well in an unaccustomed role, considering his major experience is as a basso profundo in operatic productions.) Tozzi is busily making lunch for some of his police cronies and says he'll see what he can come up with. Later, Block tips Reynolds on a possible lead, and when Reynolds recognizes some thugs outside the restaurant where he and Block are, he quickly takes refuge in a bookstore where he toys with Frye, the plain-looking clerk who is an easy sexual mark. (This scene also appears, in a better form, in THE BIG SLEEP between Bogart and Dorothy Malone.) Following the information from Block, Reynolds arrives at a warehouse and finds a large cache of arms and ammo. When his presence is felt by the guards, he has to escape in an exciting sequence that sees him leaping over buildings. Reynolds does some more investigating and discovers that a multinational company owns the facility. He visits the penthouse aerie occupied by Wilson, a former football player and now one of the bosses of that company, and he encounters Cannon, Wilson's sister and a leading butterfly in the social set. He tells Cannon that Wilson may be a dupe of some powerful people and Cannon, who fears for her thick-headed sibling, puts Reynolds on her payroll so he can get to the bottom of things. Later that night, Cannon arrives at Reynolds's Brooklyn pad and the two consummate their relationship on the pool table-bed that dominates his office-apartment. Police officer Santos gets in touch with Reynolds and asks that he come to the warehouse where Block's body is found. Santos warns the grieving Reynolds to keep away from this situation, as it's bigger than he realizes. Reynolds is now getting angry and asks Cannon to help him nail Weyand, who he thinks must be an illegal arms dealer, not the diamond merchant he claims to be. With Cannon's help, Reynolds has a meeting in a Staten Island surplus depot with Ryan, a business associate of Weyand's. Cannon and Reynolds masquerade as possible buyers of serious military equipment and Ryan attempts to sell them a tank in much the same way that one of those late-night TV car salesmen do. While in the midst of his spiel, Ryan is shot by a hidden gunman. Reynolds and Cannon climb into the tank, fire up the engines, and crash out of the building by going through a wall. Later, Reynolds goes to Weyand's mansion and sees that Wilson is being tortured by Weyand and his cohorts. Reynolds sneaks into the house and Wilson is shot to death as he tries to get away. There is a battle that Reynolds wins, and when the cops arrive, led by Santos, Reynolds has the situation in hand and cedes Weyand to Santos in the hopes that the man will be tried and convicted for illegal weapons dealing and the murders of Wilson and Block. Reynolds bids them all farewell and starts back to see the woman he's now in love with, Cannon. Lots of twists and turns in the movie for no other reason than to distinguish it from the movie it took its best scenes from. Screenwriter Beckerman is the son of producer-packager Sidney Beckerman, the man who gave the world PORTNOY'S COMPLAINT. Reynolds makes the script sound better than it read, but they could never make up their mind if this was a hard-boiled drama, a comedy, or a send-up, so they tried to do it all. Kulik's direction is fast, the editing is sharp, and Goldsmith's music is excellent, although they can't make up for the lack of depth in the script or Cannon's shrill performance. If she could only learn to lower that voice four decibels or so. The major problem with SHAMUS is that it has more "red herrings" than a Moscow fish store.

p, Robert M. Weitman; d, Buzz Kulik; w, Barry Beckerman [Sam Pessin]; ph, Victor J. Kemper (Panavision, Eastmancolor); m, Jerry Goldsmith; ed, Walter Thompson; art d, Philip Rosenberg; set d, Edward Stewart; cos, Frank Thompson; stunts, Glenn Wilder; makeup, Vincent Callaghan.

Crime/Comedy **Cas.** **(PR:C MPAA:PG)**

SHANE***** (1953) 118m PAR c

Alan Ladd *(Shane)*, Jean Arthur *(Marion Starrett)*, Van Heflin *(Joe Starrett)*, Brandon de Wilde *(Joey)*, Jack Palance *(Wilson)*, Ben Johnson *(Chris)*, Edgar Buchanan *(Lewis)*, Emile Meyer *(Ryker)*, Elisha Cook, Jr. *(Torrey)*, Douglas Spencer *(Shipstead)*, John Dierkes *(Morgan)*, Ellen Corby *(Mrs. Torrey)*, Paul McVey *(Grafton)*, John Miller *(Atkey)*, Edith Evanson *(Mrs. Shipstead)*, Leonard Strong *(Wright)*, Ray Spiker *(Johnson)*, Janice Carroll *(Susan Lewis)*, Martin Mason *(Howell)*, Helen Brown *(Mrs. Lewis)*, Nancy Kulp *(Mrs. Howell)*, Howard J. Negley *(Pete)*, Beverly Washburn *(Ruth Lewis)*, Charles Quirk *(Clerk)*, George J. Lewis, Jack Sterling, Henry Wills, Rex Moore, Ewing Brown, Chester W. Hannan, Bill Cartledge, Steve Raines *(Ryker Men)*.

Few westerns, though the genre is durable and seemingly endless, can lay claim to being classic films, but this picture, brilliantly directed by Stevens and acted by Ladd, Heflin, Arthur, and de Wilde, certainly can and is. Heflin and Arthur are shown struggling on their small farm in the wide, stretching plains of the Grand Teton range in Wyoming, their adventurous young son, de Wilde, busying himself by pretending to shoot the deer and elk that roam freely through his parents' farm. One day, the boy spots a stranger riding toward the farm and calls to his father, Heflin, who takes the boy's gun and stands ready for anything. The horseman, Ladd, approaches and asks for water for himself and his horse. Heflin welcomes him. Then Meyer and his men come riding across the plain and Heflin orders Ladd from his place, thinking that Ladd is part of Meyer's gang, Meyer being a brutal old cattleman who covets all the land in the Teton range. Before Ladd leaves, he bristles at being ordered off Heflin's place and tells the farmer, "I'd like it to be my idea." Heflin nods and Ladd rides his horse behind the log cabin farmhouse. Meyer arrives with his men and tells Heflin that he and his family have to move out, that he wants his land back, that all the land on the range belongs to him. He begins to threaten Heflin, who holds his son's small rifle in his hands. Ladd reappears, stepping from around the corner of the house, startling Meyer who asks who he is. Ladd tells him that he's a friend of Heflin's and rests his hand on his gun butt. (Earlier, when arriving at the farm, Ladd was startled by a noise made by de Wilde and whirled about, drawing his gun with such lightning speed that Heflin, Arthur, and de Wilde had no doubt that he was a gunfighter. This, and Ladd's kind remarks to de Wilde when arriving, planted the seeds of hero-worship in the boy.) Meyer and his men, staring at Ladd, back off and leave Heflin's spread. When they are gone Heflin apologizes to Ladd for thinking him part of the Meyer bunch and asks him to stay to eat with his family. Ladd finishes his meal and tells Arthur that he can't remember when he has had such "an elegant dinner." Following the meal, Heflin is amazed to see Ladd swinging an axe against a gigantic tree stump that has been vexing the farmer and he joins the gunslinger, the two men working through the dusk of the day, battling against nature to chop away at a stubborn old stump, bonding themselves in friendship through their exhaustive efforts. The two men finally manage to uproot the stump in what is one of the great scenes of any western-frontier epic. Ladd stays on to work for Heflin, hanging up his guns and accepting the role of hired hand. When going to town with the farmers, Ladd walks from the general goods store through a door which interconnects with the saloon where Meyer's tough cowboys sit drinking and playing cards. Ladd asks the bartender for some soda pop for de Wilde, and Johnson, one of the biggest and most surly of the cowboys, tells him that he's not welcome in the bar, that "pig farmers" and "sod busters" like him cannot drink with real men. Ladd stands staring at Johnson as the cowboy orders a drink and tosses it on Ladd's shirt front. Ladd clenches his fists but does nothing, silently turning away and going back into the store and finally out of town. That night the farmers in the area, all of them being pressured by Meyer to abandon their farms, meet at Heflin's home and discuss what to do. Heflin is the driving force that keeps them together and he tells them that they must stay together, that there is strength in unity. Upstart Cook, an ex-Confederate soldier who had served with Stonewall Jackson during the Civil War, brags that he'll "get my Colt 'pistol' and go to town" any time he pleases without an escort. His fellow farmers make fun of his bragging ways, one of them frenetically playing "Dixie" on his harmonica. Ladd does not attend the meeting, excusing himself, and Buchanan, one of the farmers who saw him humiliated at the saloon earlier that day, tells the farmers they cannot count on the new hired man. Most of the men believe Ladd to be a coward and even de Wilde starts to have doubts about his hero, finally telling Ladd that "Pa doesn't want you to fight his battles for him, just help with the work." That's fine with Ladd. He wants desperately to hang up his guns. But when the farmers next go to town, Ladd once more goes into the saloon to get some soda pop for de Wilde and once again the hulking Johnson approaches him and tells him to get out. Ladd replies "the last time I was here you bought me a drink. Now I'm going to buy you one." He orders two drinks and while the startled Johnson stares at him, Ladd tosses the shots of liquor onto the cowboy's shirt front and follows this with a terrific punch that sends Johnson reeling. The two man battle the length of the saloon with Ladd finally smashing his antagonist down the bar, hitting him again and again until Johnson is on his knees. Then, with Johnson almost unconscious, and in front of a dozen gaping Meyer gunmen, Ladd yanks Johnson's head up by the hair and punches him one more time so hard that he is knocked cold. De Wilde witnesses this fight from the swinging doors of the food store and rushes to Ladd's side to beg him to leave when Meyer's men begin to move toward him. "There's too many, Shane," he pleads. "You wouldn't want to think I was a coward, would you, Joey?" Ladd says, fists clenched, waiting for the men to attack him. He orders the boy to go as the men jump in to beat him senseless. Before that can happen, Meyer steps behind the bar and tells Ladd that he will give him a job with top pay but Ladd refuses, telling the cattle baron that he likes working for Heflin. Then Meyer prophetically states that the reason why a man like Ladd is staying on at the Heflin farm is because of Heflin's pretty wife, Arthur. Ladd calls him a "filthy old man" and Meyer explodes, telling his men to attack Ladd. They close in on him but for a while Ladd manages to outfight the crowd as he moves quickly about the saloon. The cowboys finally pin back Ladd's arms and Meyer begins punching Ladd in the face. De Wilde runs to his father and tells Heflin "they're killing Shane!" Heflin grabs a pickaxe handle and rushes into the saloon, smashing the heavy handle over Meyer's head and using it to bash in the faces of several cowboys. The battle is on with Heflin and Ladd fighting the entire crowd fiercely, knocking their enemies backward, over the bar, through doors and across tables, until they stand back-to-back punching their exhausted enemies, smiling at each other briefly when they realize that they, for the first time, have the upper hand. They begin to slowly back out of the saloon while the owner, McVey, shouts for everyone to stop fighting and then to Heflin and Ladd, "It's beginning to make sense–you've won." Heflin yells with victory in his throat: "Ryker ain't paying for this, I am! No, by God, Shane and I will pay for the damage!" When the victorious farmers leave, the beaten Meyer crawls up from the floor and wipes the blood from his face, then tells his sleazy brother, Dierkes, to send a rider to Cheyenne. As is revealed later, Meyer has sent for a professional gunfighter, Palance, to break the backs of the farmers and kill them, if need be, to drive them off the range he covets. "Next time," Meyer vows, "the air will be filled with gunsmoke!" On the Fourth of July, which is also the 10th wedding anniversary for Heflin and Arthur, the entire farming community gathers at one of the farms to make merry, everyone enjoying an old-fashioned square dance. Ladd dances with Arthur and it is clear that he is emotionally involved with the gentle woman but he respectfully keeps his distance. Heflin notices the attraction his wife and Ladd have for each other but says nothing. During the festivities, a man dressed all in black, Palance, enters the distant town and goes into the saloon. His presence is so sinister that even the town dog cannot bear it and slinks from the place. Later, at Heflin's farm, Ladd shows de Wilde how to fire a six-gun, shooting a can dead center each time and sending it pinging through the air so that the boy stands in awe of the deadly accurate gunman. Arthur comes running at the sound of the gunfire and tells Ladd that she does not want her child growing up to use weapons like a gunfighter. Ladd tells her, "A gun is a tool, no better and no worse than the man using it." One of the worst men to use a gun is Palance and later he sees Cook come swaggering toward the saloon. He blocks the little man's path. He insults Cook's background as a Confederate soldier, telling him: "I'm saying that all them Southern scum was trash–Lee, Stonewall Jackson, you, too." Cook frowns and replies: "You're a low-down Yankee liar." Palance gives him a wide, evil grin and whispers: "Prove it." Cook hesitates, then slowly goes for his gun, not pulling it all the way out of his holster, staring at Palance and knowing then and there that he is a dead man. Palance mercilessly pulls his two guns and blasts Cook into the mud of the street, never losing his maniacal grin. He slowly turns in his high black boots and quietly steps back into the saloon, leaving Cook's body to be dragged back to the homesteaders by another farmer. The farmers sorrowfully gather at a little cemetery on the plains to bury Cook as the harmonica player renders a sweet version of "Dixie." This death marks the end of the farmers, most of them declaring, against Heflin's pleas, that they will leave the territory. Stevens, at this point, shows the keening women, Cook's widow, collapsing, then turns his cameras slowly to encompass the beautiful, purple, Grand Teton mountain range and then stops to focus on the distant town, the culprit. Heflin vows that he will go to town and face down this new gunman, but Arthur begs Ladd to intercede. He does, and he and Heflin have a terrific battle to see which one confronts Palance. Ladd barely wins, knocking out Heflin with a gun butt, an act de Wilde witnesses and labels "unfair." Ladd tells de Wilde to take care of his mother and father when he grows up and then saddles his horse and slowly rides toward town as the sun begins to set. De Wilde races after him, along with his dog, down hills, across streams, over the plains. Ladd arrives at the saloon at dusk, walking slowly inside, wearing his gun and the buckskin outfit he wore when first coming into the valley. He goes to the bar and orders a drink, then turns to see Palance sitting at a poker table, staring at him. After the two men eye each other for some moments Ladd says, "I've heard about you." "What have you heard," says Palance through the same sinister grin, standing up to square off against Ladd. "I've heard," says Ladd very slowly and with a deep voice,"that you're a low-down Yankee liar." Palance drops his hands to just above the gun butts of his two pistols and, still clinging to his icy grin, says in a lethal whisper, "Prove it!" Both men go for their guns. Ladd is faster, blasting the gunfighter across a table so that he crashes dead into a corner, a pile of barrels falling down on him, covering his body, except for his long black boots which protrude ignominiously from beneath the debris. De Wilde has seen the shoot-out, having come up to the saloon just as the two men faced each other, peering at them with his dog from beneath the saloon's swinging doors. He sees Ladd turn away from the dead man and then spots Dierkes coming forward on a balcony with a shotgun. He shouts a warning to Ladd who whirls about and shoots Dierkes just as the would-be killer lets loose both barrels, one of the blasts slightly wounding Ladd in the arm. Dierkes, shot dead, falls forward, breaks a wooden beam on his descent, and crashes to the main floor of the saloon. Ladd glances about at the carnage he has created, a look of sorrow on his handsome face. He steps outside and mounts his horse. De Wilde excitedly asks him: "Was that him, Shane? Was that Wilson?" Ladd replies: "Yes, that was Wilson. He was fast–fast on the draw." He is about to ride away when he reaches forward and pats de Wilde on the head, telling the boy that he must be moving on, even though de Wilde protests, begging him to stay, saying that his father has work for him to do and that his mother wants him to stay. "A man has to be what he is," Ladd tells him. "You can't break the mold. There's no living with a killing; it's a brand that sticks." He looks at de Wilde with a little smile of affection and says, finally: "Go home now, Joey, and tell your mother that there are no more guns in this valley." He begins to ride out of the valley with de Wilde running desperately after him, calling and calling for him to come back, the boy's voice echoing across the land as night falls: "Shane, come back! Come back! Shane!" But there is no turning back for Ladd and, head down, he rides over the hills, gone forever out of the lives of those he has enriched at the expense of his own desires. The poignant ending of this marvelous film packs an emotional wallop consistent with its entirety. Stevens, one of the most meticulous directors of the sound era, and one of the most conscientious, here creates a milestone western in the tradition of HIGH NOON. Each scene is well-planned and executed; Stevens paints his historic and powerful drama of an Old West dying as the new age, the era of the homesteader, the family, takes over the range, settles it, and, in the words of the new pioneer, Heflin, protects it "to build families on it." Ladd, who was never better as the doomed hero, and gives one of the greatest performances ever rendered in *any* western, knows he is a thing of the past and says so while confronting the cattle baron, Meyer. "Your days are over," Ladd tells Meyer decisively. "Mine?" says the surprised Meyer. "What about yours, gunslinger?" Ladd is silent for a moment and then replies just as firmly: "The difference is, I know it." Though he knows he cannot escape his reputation, Ladd willingly puts it to good use for once in his life, protecting the kind of life he cannot have. Unlike most westerns, the hero here is an outcast looking in on a society that has rejected him, one he still tries to embrace. After searching for just the right location for more than a year, Stevens selected a beautiful valley outside of Jackson Hole, Wyoming, and built a small town and several farms on the open plains there, his cameras later capturing some of the most eye-pleasing geography ever put on film. Of the six Academy Award nominations earned by this film (see Index) only one was awarded, an Oscar going to Griggs for his cinematography, ironic in that during the extensive 16-month post-production period, SHANE was converted to a widescreen process and lost much of its natural color. Palance, with his sharply chiseled features, was a sensation after the film was released, even though he spoke only 12 lines in the movie (and was nominated for an Oscar as Best Supporting Actor). He would never again have the impact he projected in SHANE but would essentially go on playing the gunfighter Wilson in film after film, usually winding up beneath the barrels somewhere. Heflin is magnificent in his role of the rock-ribbed farmer and Arthur is wonderful as his tender, devoted wife, she appearing to be more of a pioneer than the whole community. De Wilde is charming as the innocent boy whose goodness offsets Palance's evil incarnate. Ladd, who should have been nominated for a Best Actor Oscar, did not receive it. He was leaving Paramount for Warner Bros. following the completion of SHANE and it was later felt that his old studio ignored him for his desertion, refusing to enter him in the lists. Yet he leaves, with this film, a great legacy, for Alan Ladd was Shane, the very embodiment of the man. This was one of the most popular films of the 1950s and it earned Paramount more than $9 million from its initial release. SHANE remains to this day a classic western, one that only improves with age.

p&d, George Stevens; w, A.B. Guthrie, Jr., Jack Sher (based on the novel by Jack Schaefer); ph, Loyal Griggs (Technicolor); m, Victor Young; ed, William Hornbeck, Tom McAdoo; art d, Hal Pereira, Walter Tyler; set d, Emile Kuri; cos, Edith Head; spec eff, Gordon Jennings; tech adv, Joe De Young.

Western   Cas.   (PR:C MPAA:NR)

SHANGHAI**   (1935) 76m PAR bw

Loretta Young (*Barbara Howard*), Charles Boyer (*Dimitri Koslov*), Warner Oland (*Ambassador Lun Sing*), Fred Keating (*Tommy Sherwood*), Charles Grapewin (*Truesdale*), Alison Skipworth (*Aunt J.B.*), Libby Taylor (*Corena*), Josephine Whittell (*Mrs. Truesdale*), Walter Kingsford (*Hilton*), Olive Tell (*Mrs. Hilton*), Arnold Korff (*Van Hoeffer*), Willie Fung (*Wang*), Keye Luke (*Ambassador's Son*).

Three writers developed this story specifically for Young and Boyer. Unfortunately, however, the picture just drags along and is never able to take off. Young plays an American woman who meets and falls in love with Boyer, an industrialist of Chinese and Russian heritage. Unable to consider marriage because of their racial differences, Boyer leaves for the mountains of China. A determined Young follows, but despite their love the relationship ends. Young and Boyer are excellently cast, with the latter doing an outstanding job of expressing his inner turmoil.

p, Walter Wanger; d, James Flood; w, Gene Towne, Graham Baker, Lynn Starling; ph, James Van Trees; ed, Otho Lovering.

Drama   (PR:A MPAA:NR)

SHANGHAI CHEST, THE*½   (1948) 56m MON bw

Roland Winters (*Charlie Chan*), Mantan Moreland (*Birmingham Brown, Chan's Chauffeur*), Deannie Best (*Phyllis*), John Alvin (*Vic Armstrong*), Victor Sen Young (*Tommy Chan*), Tim Ryan (*Lt. Ruark*), Pierre Watkin (*Judge Armstrong*), Russell Hicks (*District Attorney Bronson*), Philip Van Zandt (*Tony Pindello*), George Eldredge (*Finley*), Willie Best (*Willie*), Tristam Coffin (*Ed Seward*), Milton Parsons (*Mr. Grail the Undertaker*), Edward Coke (*Cartwright*), Olaf Hytten (*Bates the Butler*), Erville Alderson (*Walter Somervale*), Charlie Sullivan (*Officer Murphy*), Paul Scardon (*Custodian*), William Ruhl (*Jailer*), Lois Austin (*Landlady*), Chabing (*Miss Lee*), John Shay (*Stacey*).

Winters, the least effective of the three Charlie Chans, is called upon to solve a triple-murder case. While doing so, he spouts off some Chinese proverb every third or fourth line, or so it seems. Fingerprints that belong to a dead man are left in obvious sight at all three murders, so Winters figures someone above suspicion has been using the false prints. Of course he's right. Director Beaudine was left helpless with the material given, and it shows. (See CHARLIE CHAN series, Index.)

p, James S. Burkett; d, William Beaudine; w, W. Scott Darling, Sam Newman (based on the story by Newman); ph, William Sickner; ed, Ace Herman, Otho Lovering; md, Edward Kay; art d, David Milton; set d, Raymond Boltz, Jr.

Mystery   (PR:A MPAA:NR)

SHANGHAI COBRA, THE*½   (1945) 64m MON bw

Sidney Toler (*Charlie Chan*), Benson Fong (*Tommy Chan*), Mantan Moreland (*Birmingham Brown, Chan's Chauffeur*), Walter Fenner (*Inspector Harry Davis*), James Cardwell (*Ned Stewart*), Joan Barclay (*Paula Webb*), James Flavin (*Jarvis*), Addison Richards (*John Adams/Jan Van Horn*), Arthur Loft (*Bradford Harris/Hume*), Gene Stutenroth [Roth] (*Morgan*), Joe Devlin (*Taylor*), Roy Gordon (*Walter Fletcher*), Janet Warren (*Lorraine*), George Chandler (*Short Order Cook*), Paul Newlan (*Bank Guard*).

This below par Charlie Chan outing is overly talky and lacks suspense. Sleuth Toler is hired by the government to solve the mysterious murders of people bitten by a cobra. It seems that someone is trying to steal a supply of radium being stored in a bank; the main suspect is a bank guard, who turns out to be innocent. (See CHARLIE CHAN series, Index.)

p, James S. Burkett; d, Phil Karlson; w, George Callahan, George Wallace Sayre (based on the story by Callahan); ph, Vince Farrar; ed, Ace Herman; art d, Vin Taylor.

Mystery   **(PR:A   MPAA:NR)**

SHANGHAI DRAMA, THE*   (1945, Fr.) 76m David Brill bw (LE
                                                  DRAME DE SHANGHAI)

Louis Jouvet (Ivan), Christiane Mardayne (Kay), Raymond Rouleau (Franchon), Dorville ("Big" Bill), Suzanne Despers (Vera), Elina Labourdette (Nana), Gabrielle Dorziat (Superintendent of School), Mila Parey (Dancing Girl), Linh-Nam (Cheng), V. Inkijinoff ("Black Dragon" Agent), Ky-Duyen, Hoang Dao ("Black Dragon" Henchmen).

Though originally made in 1938, THE SHANGHAI DRAMA did not make its way to the U.S. until after the war was over. The politically ambiguous Pabst was working in France at the time, having temporarily left Germany because of the Nazi takeover. He later returned to Germany and made two Nazi propaganda pictures. Yarn concerns White Russian refugees in Shanghai, prior to the Sino-Japanese War, working for the Japanese effort against the Chinese. One of them, Mardayne, a cabaret singer, wants out, mainly for the sake of her daughter's safety. She never makes it to freedom, but her daughter is saved through the help of a journalist. Fellow German Schufftan, who emigrated to the U.S. in 1940, photographed this drama for Pabst (Schufftan would later receive the Academy Award for his photography of THE HUSTLER), and through his highly stylized lighting created a unique atmosphere appropriate to the Chinese setting. Pabst directed in a subtle manner, concentrating on characters instead of action, and filling the background with numerous interesting faces. (In French; English subtitles.)

p, Marc Sorkin; d, G.W. Pabst; w, Leo Laniz, A. Arnoux (based on the novel Shangai Chambard et Cie by Oscar Paul Gilbert); ph, Eugen Schufftan (Eugene Shuftan); m, Ralph Erwin; English titles, Herman G. Weinberg.

Spy Drama   **(PR:A   MPAA:NR)**

SHANGHAI EXPRESS**   (1932) 80m PAR bw

Marlene Dietrich (Shanghai Lily), Clive Brook (Capt. Donald "Doc" Harvey), Anna Mae Wong (Hui Fei), Warner Oland (Henry Chang), Eugene Pallette (Sam Salt), Lawrence Grant (Rev. Carmichael), Louise Closser Hale (Mrs. Haggerty), Gustav von Seyffertitz (Eric Baum), Emile Chautard (Maj. Lenard), Claude King (Albright), Neshida Minoru (Chinese Spy), James Leong (Rebel), Willie Fung (Engineer), Leonard Carey (Minister), Forrester Harvey (Ticket Agent), Miki Morita (Officer).

The fourth of the Sternberg-Dietrich collaborations, following THE BLUE ANGEL, MOROCCO, and DISHONORED, and interrupted by AN AMERICAN TRAGEDY (which unsuccessfully replaced Dietrich with Sylvia Sydney), SHANGHAI EXPRESS is a remarkably mystical and exotic story of love and destruction-the kind of film for which both star and director became legends. The film begins at the Peking Railroad as China's great train, The Shanghai Express, is being boarded and loaded with baggage. En route to Shanghai is a mixed assortment of characters, including Dietrich, a lady of most objectionable reputation known as "the White Flower of the Chinese coast"; Brook, a British Medical Corps officer; Oland, a shady half-caste merchant with a penchant for carrying a cane; and Wong, an American-bred Chinese prostitute with plans of starting anew in marriage. The train trip is rounded out with less major characters: Salt, a gambling engineer; Grant, an obsessed missionary; von Seyffertitz, a drug-smuggling German businessman; Hale, an uppity boarding house proprietor; and Chautard, a disgraced French officer who speaks no English-all given to react very differently in a tense situation. The time of the journey is one of great political unrest, with the possibility of bands of rebels attacking the train looming large. Before the train even leaves the station, arrests are made. Brook is surprised to find that he is traveling with Dietrich, a past love of his who he deserted. Because of his constant work and busy schedule, he has never heard of her reputation as a glamorous prostitute and seductress. Inquiring of her last five years, Brook asks if she's married. Her response, one of the most famous lines to ever emerge from those sleek, tight lips, is: "It took more than one man to change my name to Shanghai Lily." Only then does Brook begin to understand Dietrich and the power she holds over men. In the meantime, it becomes clear to everyone on board that Oland is a rebel leader, desperate over the arrest of his aides. Along the way, Oland orders the train stopped at an old station which has been taken over for use as rebel headquarters, while he make plans to take hostages from among his fellow first-class passengers. Oland, like Brook, is strongly attracted to the elusive Dietrich, but when the rebel leader asks Dietrich to be his mistress he is flatly refused. Oland pressures Dietrich into giving in by threatening to torture Brook. Only then-in order to save Brook-does Dietrich give in. Brook, however, is unaware of what she has done, coming to her room after his release to find her dressed erotically in a black negligee, smoking a cigarette, and exuding a post-sex aura. Oland's fate is sealed, though not by Dietrich or Brook, but by Wong, the prostitute in search of redemption, who has earlier been raped by the insatiable rebel leader. As Oland returns to his room, Wong stabs him to death, thereby

freeing herself, the Shanghai Express, and the love between Dietrich and Brook. Though von Sternberg insists the film was based on a one-page treatment handed him by Harry Hervey, the story of THE SHANGHAI EXPRESS is clearly drawn from Guy de Maupassant's classic short story of a French prostitute during the Franco-Prussian war, "Boule de Suif." The final film, however, is all Sternberg, with his enigmatic creation Dietrich filling the screen with her stunning persona. It was that icy hot face and the ravishing body dressed in Travis Banton furs and feathers that brought in an eye-popping $3 million (a truly hefty sum for the time) to the box office and convinced Hollywood that von Sternberg had his finger on the right button. Dietrich, as always, gave von Sternberg the exact performance he had envisioned, but feuds and hard feelings ran rampant between the director and the remainder of the cast. Cameraman Lee Garmes, who erroneously claimed to have created the Dietrich face, remembers the director's antics on the set, acting out each character's roles in wild theatricality: "First he was Clive Brook kissing Marlene, and then Marlene kissing Clive Brook! You should've seen Clive Brook's face! His impersonation of Anna May Wong had us all in stitches. But we didn't dare show our amusement. Clive Brook wanted to be Clive Brook. Von Sternberg wanted him to be von Sternberg. For hours on end they would sit and battle." At one point during the film Brook complained to the director about the monotonous delivery of much of the dialog only to have him reply: "Exactly, I want that. This is 'The Shanghai Express.' Everyone must talk like a train." If Brook didn't always see eye to eye with von Sternberg, he, in his later years, shortly before his death, had nothing but praise for his costar Dietrich: "She was always such a beautiful, simple girl then. She used to cook delicious food and bring it to us each morning on the set. Now she's like a character from one of her own films. Seems to be playing Marlene Dietrich." Not surprisingly, von Sternberg was something of a tyrant on the set, and actors received the brunt of his wrath. Of Oland, von Sternberg wrote in his autobiography: "I had an actor who said to me when he was engaged 'to act in the film', 'They call me One-take Warner.' It took me hours in one of the scenes of SHANGHAI EXPRESS to get Mr. Oland to say no more than 'Good morning'-and this with the aid of a blackboard." Of Grant, the missionary of the film, Brook recalls how von Sternberg treated the struggling actor: "He 'von Sternberg' would go on indefinately taking shots. He was a great man to wear an actor down. Poor Lawrence Grant on SHANGHAI EXPRESS, was kept hard at it from nine until six one day until the poor man burst into tears. 'I don't think I can go on, Mr. von Sternberg.' 'You have done it,' he 'von Sternberg' said. 'The last take is good.'" Even further promoting his tyrannical image on the set, von Sternberg, who had nearly lost his voice from shouting, dismissed a suggestion from Sam Jaffe to use a megaphone, instead hooking up a public address system. Remembered Jesse Lasky in his memoirs, "As I entered the stage....I could hear the booming voice of the director reverberating through the enormous structure. Jo was staging an enormous closeup of Marlene and Clive Brook, almost breathing in their faces as he gave them directions, but still talking into the microphone!" This enthusiasm and complete control over the production paid off for von Sternberg and for SHANGHAI EXPRESS come Oscar time. The film was nominated for Best Picture (losing to GRAND HOTEL), von Sternberg received a nomination for Best Direction (his second in a row), and Garmes walked away with a statuette for his cinematography.

p, Josef von Sternberg; w, Jules Furthman (based on a story by Harry Hervey); ph, Lee Garmes; m, W. Franke Harling; prod d, Hans Dreier; cos, Travis Banton.

Drama   **(PR:O   MPAA:NR)**

SHANGHAI GESTURE, THE*½   (1941) 106m UA bw

Gene Tierney (Poppy Charteris), Walter Huston (Sir Guy Charteris), Victor Mature (Dr. Omar), Ona Munson (Mother Gin Sling), Phyllis Brooks (Dixie Pomeroy), Albert Basserman (Van Alst the Commissioner), Maria Ouspenskaya (Amah), Eric Blore (Caesar Hawkins the Bookkeeper), Ivan Lebedeff (Gambler), Mike Mazurki (Coolie), Clyde Fillmore (Comprador), Rex Evans (Counselor Brooks), Grayce Hampton (Lady Blessington, Social Leader), Michael Delmatoff (Bartender), Marcel Dalio (Croupier), Mikhail Rasumny (Cashier), John Abbott (Escort), Leland Hodgson (Ryerson, Charteris' Assistant).

The fascinating von Sternberg returns to the East of SHANGHAI EXPRESS with this trip into the underworld of a gambling den which stars Munson as its twisted, criminal proprietor who hides behind an impenetrable mask of makeup. Pressured by Huston, an English financier, Munson is threatened with the closing of her casino, despite the fact that she has adequately bribed the local authorities. Although Munson tries to come to an agreement with Huston, she is never able to contact him. Desperate to remain in business, Munson searches for information by which she can pressure Huston and discovers that he was forced to leave China, taking with him his wife's money, plotting to kill her, and leaving behind an infant daughter. The daughter, now grown, is Tierney, a favored and deeply indebted guest of Munson's casino. With this information, Munson is now ready to turn the tables on Huston. Meantime, Tierney refuses her father's wishes to leave town, falls in love with Mature, and grows to hate Munson. Huston finally accepts Munson's offer to come to some sort of agreement, knowing full well that he is being blackmailed. She not only tells him what she's learned, but also informs him that she is the wife he left behind in China. Shocked even more than Huston at the news is Tierney, who vehemently refuses to accept Munson, as contemptible as she believes she is, as her mother. One Chinese New Years, after a raging argument between mother and daughter, Munson shoots Tierney, though the sound of the gunshot is obliterated by the exploding of fireworks in celebration of the holiday. Based on a racy 1925 Broadway play by John Colton, THE SHANGHAI GESTURE was finally made after over 30 attempts by various producers, writers, and directors to pass a screenplay past the Hays Office censors. For von Sternberg to get the script through he had to make numerous changes in plot and characterization, though not in spirit. "Mother Goddam" of the play became "Mother Gin Sling" of the film, the original setting of a brothel became a gambling den, an erotic relationship became a broken marriage, and the daughter's drug addiction simply became a name, "Poppy," which only hinted at her dependency on drugs. What remained was the physical reality, in the form of Poppy, of a broken relationship, the *film noir* "dark side" of Poppy's mixing of real life and imagination, and the interest in vices–all favorite themes of von Sternberg's, and the qualities which make this a von Sternberg film rather than a Colton play. As with von Sternberg's finest films, THE SHANGHAI GESTURE is masterfully photographed and lit, bringing forth a poetic, stylized ballet of movements and gestures which envelop the erotic romanticism that von Sternberg is able to find in the normally seedy gambling casino. (The casino is baroquely decorated with huge wall murals painted by actor Keye Luke of "Charlie Chan" series fame.) Completed to help foreign producer Arnold Pressburger find a place in Hollywood, THE SHANGHAI GESTURE was von Sternberg's last great film, and anything but an easy assignment for the director. As he wrote in his autobiography *Confessions from a Chinese Laundry*: "Most of the film–though this does not show–I directed from a cot, while lying on my back. Despite this handicap, it launched Gene Tierney and Victor Mature as stellar attractions." The film, however, did not become a great attraction at the box office, turning in only a moderate showing, though it did receive a pair of Oscar nominations–Best Black-and-White Decoration, Leven, and Best Score, Hageman.

p, Arnold Pressburger; d, Josef von Sternberg; w, von Sternberg, Karl Vollmoeller, Geza Herczeg, Jules Furthman (based on the play by John Colton); ph, Paul Ivano; m, Richard Hageman; ed, Sam Winston; art d, Boris Leven; set d, Howard Bristol; cos, Oleg Cassini, Royer.

Crime Drama   (PR:C   MPAA:NR)

SHANGHAI LADY**   (1929) 66m UNIV bw (GB: THE GIRL FROM CHINA)

Mary Nolan (*Cassie Cook*), James Murray (*"Badlands" McKinney*), Lydia Yeamans Titus (*Polly Voo*), Wheeler Oakman (*Repen*), Anders Randolf (*Mandarin*), Yola D'Avril (*Lizzie*), Mona Rico (*Rose*), Jimmy Leong (*Counselor*), Irma Lowe (*Golden Almond*).

An exotic Chinese setting is the background for this early talkie about an offbeat relationship between Nolan, a former prostitute freshly fired from an opium den, and Murray, an ex-con. Each takes the other for being something respectable, and they keep the charade going.

d, John S. Robertson; w, Houston Branch, Winifred Reeve (based on the play "Drifting" by John Colton, Daisy H. Andrews); ph, Hal Mohr; ed, Milton Carruth.

Drama   (PR:A   MPAA:NR)

SHANGHAI MADNESS**   (1933) 63m FOX bw

Spencer Tracy (*Lt. Pat Jackson*), Fay Wray (*Wildeth Christie*), Ralph Morgan (*Li Po Chang*), Eugene Pallette (*Lobo Lonergan*), Herbert Mundin (*1st Officer Larsen*), Reginald Mason (*William Christie*), Arthur Hoyt (*Van Emery*), Albert Conti (*Rigaud*), Maude Eburne (*Mrs. Glissen*), William von Brincken (*Von Uhlenberg*).

Navy lieutenant Tracy receives a dishonorable discharge for firing at Communist ships in China. He is without a job and has trouble finding one. He meets society woman Wray, whose life is saved by Tracy. The girl takes a liking to him and, against her father's wishes, follows him across China by hiding on the boat he works on. While on the boat, which carries weapons for the Mandarin government, Tracy becomes a hero when he thwarts a Communist attack. The Navy reinstates him, and he and Wray are allowed by her father to marry. Well-paced direction gives the tired story a bit of zip.

d, John Blystone; w, Austin Parker, Gordon Wong Wellesley (based on the story by Frederick Hazlitt Brennan); ph, Lee Garmes; ed, Margaret Clancy; md, Samuel Kaylin.

War/Drama   (PR:A   MPAA:NR)

SHANGHAI STORY, THE**   (1954) 90m REP bw

Ruth Roman (*Rita King*), Edmond O'Brien (*Dr. Dan Maynard*), Richard Jaeckel (*"Knuckles" Greer*), Barry Kelley (*Ricki Dolmine*), Whit Bissell (*Paul Grant*), Basil Ruysdael (*Rev. Hollingsworth*), Marvin Miller (*Col. Zorek*), Yvette Dugay (*Mrs. De Verno*), Paul Picerni (*Mr. De Verno*), Isabel Randolph (*Mrs. Merryweather*), Philip Ahn (*Maj. Ling Wu*), Frances Rafferty (*Mrs. Warren*), Frank Ferguson (*Mr. Haljerson*), James Griffith (*Carl Hoyt*), John Alvin (*Mr. Warren*), Frank Puglia (*Mr. Chen*), Victor Sen

Yung (*Sun Lee*), Janine Ferreau (*Penny Warren*), Richard Loo (*Junior Officer*).

A rather obvious yarn that takes place in the oriental city shortly after the Communist takeover of China. Miller is the police chief who rounds up Americans and Europeans he fears may be spies. These include O'Brien as a dedicated doctor, a priest, an industrialist, and a sea captain. All along the real culprit is Roman, who has been using her affair with Miller to gain information. She later helps O'Brien and Jaeckel escape, and O'Brien returns to rescue Roman, his new-found love. Proper atmosphere is maintained through photography and setting, but the story starts to drag and performances are uneven.

p, Herbert J. Yates; d, Frank Lloyd; w, Seton I. Miller, Steve Fisher (based on the story by Lester Yard); ph, Jack Marta; m, R. Dale Butts; ed, Tony Martinelli.

Spy Drama   (PR:A   MPAA:NR)

SHANGHAIED LOVE**   (1931) 75m COL bw

Richard Cromwell, Noah Beery, Sr, Sally Blane, Willard Robertson, Sidney Bracey, Dick Alexander, Edwin J. Brady, Erville Alderson, Lionel Belmore, Jack Cheatham, Fred "Snowflake" Toones.

A fairly entertaining action film, with Beery as a rough and very mean sea captain who's abusive to his crew. Beery is so low that he steals the wife and child of another sailor. The woman dies after being subjected to harsh treatment from the captain, who raises the child himself. The husband gets his revenge, however, after he signs on aboard the captain's ship. Toomes and Alexander are around for much needed comic relief.

d, George B. Seitz; w, Roy Chanslor, Jack Cunningham (based on a story by Norman Springer); ph, Teddy Tetzlaff; ed, Gene Milford.

Drama   (PR:A   MPAA:NR)

SHANGRI-LA*   (1961) 63m Shangri-La/Joseph Brenner c

Sammy Petrillo, Pamela Perry, Harold Gary.

Silly exploitation film has a zoo keeper relating stories about his vacation to his friend. He follows two women to a resort, to Washington, D.C., and to Florida, and then ends up at a nature park called Camp Shangri-La. He serves as the master of ceremonies for a beauty contest, and eventually is expelled for violating camp rules. The vacation was so successful that the friend decides to take a similar trip.

p, Dick Randall; ph, Weegee (Eastmancolor).

Drama   (PR:O   MPAA:NR)

SHAN-KO LIEN   (SEE: SHEPHERD GIRL, THE, 1965, Hong Kong)

SHANKS**   (1974) 93m PAR c

Marcel Marceau (*Malcolm Shanks/Old Walker*), Tsilla Chelton (*Mrs. Barton*), Philippe Clay (*Mr. Barton*), Cindy Eilbacher (*Celia*), Helena Kallianiotes (*Mata Hari*), Larry Bishop (*Napoleon*), Don Calfa (*Einstein*), Biff Manard (*Goliath*), Mondo (*Genghis Khan*), Read Morgan (*Policeman*), William Castle (*Grocer*), Phil Adams (*Beethoven*), Lara Wing (*Little Girl*).

This was to be the last film directed by Castle, known mainly for the advertising gimmickry in some of his 1950s productions. Marceau was given the chance to display his mime talents in a rather weird tale about a puppeteer who, having been put down his entire life, finally has his revenge. In a double role in which he also plays an aging scientist who has learned to bring dead things back to life (a la FRANKENSTEIN), Marceau also lets it be known that he has a voice. When the scientist dies, the puppeteer uses the tricks he's learned to get even with heartless members of his family. A gang of nasty bikers who ride into town rape Eilbacher and cause general havoc, giving Marceau the perfect target to display his new-found talents. All along, Marceau never loses his innate charm, which makes this tale fascinating in a strange sort of way.

p, Steven North; d, William Castle; w, Ranald Graham; ph, Joseph Biroc (Movielab Color); m, Alex North; ed, David Berlatsky; prod d, Boris Leven; set d, John Austin; ch, Marcel Marceau; cos, Guy Verhille.

Fantasy/Drama   (PR:A   MPAA:PG)

SHANNONS OF BROADWAY, THE**   (1929) 65m UNIV bw

James Gleason (*Mickey Shannon*), Lucille Webster Gleason (*Emma Shannon*), Charles Grapewin (*Swanzey, Hotel Owner*), Mary Philbin (*Tessie Swanzey*), John Breeden (*Chuck*), Tom Santschi (*Bradford*), Harry Tyler (*Eddie Allen*), Gladys Crolius (*Alice Allen*), Helen Mehrmann (*Minerva*), Robert T. Haines (*Albee*), Slim Sumerville (*Newt the Lawyer*), Tom Kennedy (*Burt*), Walter Brennan (*Hez*).

The Gleasons, in the film rendition of their Broadway musical, are a couple of goodhearted country bumpkins trying to make a go of it on the vaudeville circuit. But they meet with rejection and settle down to life as hotel owners. They are quickly back on the stage, however, when they strike it big in real estate and are able to produce their own show. Sets and other aspects of production can't compare to Broadway staging, but the Gleasons managed enough laughs and musical routines to keep it hopping.

d, Emmett J. Flynn; w, Agnes Johnston, James Gleason (based on the Broadway play by Gleason); ph, Jerry Ash; ed, Byron Robinson; titles, Gleason; m/l, "Somebody to Love Me," Ray Kalges, Jesse Greer.

Musical/Comedy   **(PR:A MPAA:NR)**

SHANTY TRAMP*   (1967) 72m Trans-International bw

Lee Holland, Bill Rogers, Lawrence Tobin.

Another quickly made movie from the South (shot on location in Florida) designed for the drive-in crowd. This one involves a young woman of loose morals who tries to seduce an evangelist. She then gets involved with a motorcycle gang, which only leads to trouble. She is saved by a black youth who is accused by the girl's sharecropper father of raping his daughter and a sheriff's posse is sent out him. He's forced to steal a car (from a moonshiner no less) but dies after when the vehicle crashes. The daughter then has it out with her father, stabbing him to death, and heading off to her evangelist in hopes of leaving town.

p, K. Gordon Murray; d, Joseph Prieto; w, Reuben Guberman; ph, J.R. Remy.

Drama   **(PR:O MPAA:NR)**

SHANTYTOWN**   (1943) 65m REP bw

Mary Lee (Liz Gorty), John Archer (Bill Allen), Majorie Lord (Virginia Allen), Harry Davenport (Doc Herndon), Billy Gilbert (Papa Ferrell), Anne Revere (Mrs. Gorty), J. Frank Hamilton (Mr. Gorty), Frank Jenks (Whitey), Cliff Nazarro (Shortcake), Carl "Alfalfa" Switzer (Bindy), Robert E. Homans (Dugan), Noel Madison (Ace Landers), Matty Malneck and His Orchestra.

Lee plays the rough-and-tumble daughter of the proprietors of a rundown boarding house. She takes an immediate liking to the new mechanic in town, Archer, but the object of her desire is married and expecting a kid. Archer, in his naive way, is taken by the excitement of local hoods, who wind up asking the kid to drive a getaway car. When Archer is forced into hiding because of the holdup, Lee goes onto an amateur-hour show in an effort to reunite Archer with his wife, Lord. The picture moves along at a good pace, with Lee proving to have a diversity of talent.

p, Harry Grey; d, Joseph Santley; w, Olive Cooper (based on a play by Henry Moritz); ph, Ernest Miller; ed, Thomas Richards; md, Walter Scharf; art d, Russell Kimball.

Drama   **(PR:A MPAA:NR)**

SHAPE OF THINGS TO COME, THE*   (1979, Can.) 95m CFI
                                          Investments/Film Ventures International c

Jack Palance (Omus), Carol Lynley (Niki), John Ireland (Sen. Smedley), Barry Morse (Dr. John Caball), Nicholas Campbell (Jason Caball), Eddie Benton (Kim Smedley), Greg Swanson (Voice of Sparks), William Hutt (Voice of Lomax), Bill Lake (Astronaut), Arods Bess (Merrick), Lynn Green (Lunar Technician), Albert Humphries (Robot Technician), Michael Klinbell, Marc Parr, Wili Liberman, Rod McEwan, Jonathan Hartman, Angelo Pedari (Robots), Danny Gage, Jo-Anne Lang, Terry Martin, Lutz Brodie, Terry Spratt, Linda Carter, Bill Jay (Members of Niki's Army).

An unambitious and poorly made remake of the 1936 sci-fi classic THINGS TO COME, which was itself a popular and successful rendition of the H.G. Wells novel. Even with the advent of technological advances in special effects, this modern version comes nowhere close to being as convincing as its predecessor. The acting and script also leave much to be desired. Palance is the evil menace who vies to become dictator of the moon by taking over the planet where the drug is produced which combats radiation sickness caused by the nuclear holocaust on the Earth. His efforts are thwarted by the tactics of Lynely.

p, William Davidson; d, George McGowan; w, Martin Lager; ph, Reginald Morris; spec eff, Wally Gentleman, Bill Wood.

Fantasy   **(PR:A MPAA:PG)**

SHARE OUT, THE½**   (1966, Brit.) 61m Merton Park/Schoenfeld bw
                                                   (AKA: THE SHAREOUT)

Bernard Lee (Detective Supt. Meredith), Alexander Knox (Col. Calderwood), Moira Redmond (Diana Marsh), William Russell (Mike Stafford), Richard Vernon (John Crewe), Richard Warner (Mark Speller), John Gabriel (Monet), Jack Rodney (Gregory), Stanley Morgan (Detective Sgt. Anson), Robert Percival (Britton), Ann Harriman (Receptionist), Julie Shearing (Judy), Fanny Carby (Mrs. Wall), Ian Hamilton (Waiter), Walter Horsbrugh (Registrar).

This British crime thriller much in the vein of American film noir has Russell as a private dick who agrees to undertake an assignment for Scotland Yard to expose Knox. He poses as a spy for Knox, but falls in love with the object of his observation, namely, Redmond. Russell winds up

killing Knox and exposing his gang; he then tries to make it out of the country with Redmond and some diamonds that belonged to the gang. But Scotland Yard detective Lee puts him behind bars.

p, Jack Greenwood; d, Gerald Glaister; w, Philip Mackie (based on the novel Jack O' Judgment by Edgar Wallace); ph, Bert Mason; ed, Bernard Gribble; md, Bernard Ebbinghouse; art d, Peter Mullins; makeup, Aldo Manganaro.

Crime   **(PR:A MPAA:NR)**

SHARK**   (1970, U.S./Mex.) 92m Heritage-Cinematografica
Calderon/Excelsior c (UN ARMA DE DOS FILOS) (AKA: MANEATER)

Burt Reynolds (Caine), Barry Sullivan (Mallare), Arthur Kennedy (Doc), Silvia Pinal (Anna), Enrique Lucero (Barok), Carlos Berriochoa (Smoky-Smoky), Manuel Alvarado (Latalla), Emilia Stuart (Asha).

Sam Fuller was at home once again in the world he created for SHARK, one of viciousness and backstabbers, where the woman one slept with the night before is liable to kill him the next morning if it's to her profit. This cynical type of approach to the world is what made the French critics rave about Fuller, and is what made his masterpieces, SHOCK CORRIDOR and THE NAKED KISS, so biting. Reynolds, as a gun runner in Africa, fits into this world quite nicely; his rugged individuality makes him the perfect Fuller anti-hero. He also possesses a soft spot which leaves him prey to the more vicious members of the cast, particularly to Pinal, a femme fatale whose malicious intent knows no bounds. Reynolds takes refuge in a small Sudanese town after being pursued by soldiers for the truckload of guns he was trying to ditch. He is enlisted by Sullivan and Pinal to assist in an expedition to gather fish specimens in the ocean, but the excursion is really a hunt for treasure buried at the bottom of the sea. Reynolds and Sullivan successfully get the treasure to the boat Pinal is on; she then decides she wants all the take for herself and attracts some sharks to do in her cohorts. Sullivan meets a nasty end, but Reynolds survives to make it back to the boat and give Pinal a good knock on the head. Suspicious police chief Lucero then makes an appearance. He also wants, the gold, using Reynolds suspicious background as a type of blackmail. But Reynolds feeds the shiftless cop to the sharks and now must only contend with a reviving Pinal. She forces Reynolds off the boat and drives off into the sunset with her new-found riches. But Reynolds gets his last minute revenge when the boat sinks because he has opened the ballast valves. Shot in Mexico, the settings are not always reminiscent of Sudan, but enough interesting characters fill in the background to make up for this. The picture was originally shot in 1967, but took some time making its way to the screen in the U.S., mainly because the producers spent their time cutting a version that suited their fancy.

p, Skip Steloff, Marc Cooper, Jose Luis Calderon; d, Samuel Fuller; w, Fuller, John Kingsbridge (based on the novel His Bones Are Coral by Victor Canning); ph, Raul Martinez Solares (Eastmancolor); m, Carlos Moroyoqui; ed, Carlos Savage; art d, Manuel Fontanals.

Adventure   **Cas.**   **(Pr:C MPAA:PG)**

SHARK GOD, THE   (SEE: OMOO OMOO, THE SHARK GOD, 1949)

SHARK REEF   (SEE: SHE-GODS OF SHARK REEF, 1956)

SHARK RIVER**   (1953) 80m UA c

Steve Cochran (Dan Webley), Carole Mathews (Jane Daughterty), Warren Stevens (Clay Webley), Robert Cunningham (Curtis Parker), Spencer Fox (Johnny Daughterty), Ruth Foreman (Mrs. Daughterty), Bill Piper (Sheriff).

Nineteenth-Century Florida is the setting for this routinely acted and scripted story in which Cochran scourges through the Everglades in an attempt to get his convict brother, Stevens, to the safety of Cuba. They never make it there, even though Mathews gives them refuge while falling in love with Cochran. The bullheaded Stevens runs into a bunch of angry Seminoles, whom he decides to fight and is killed in the process. Some nifty footage of the wildlife of the swamps, given a nice color tint, is worth a watch.

p&d, John Rawlins; w, Joseph Carpenter, Lewis Meltzer; ph, Stanley Cortez (Cinecolor); m, Irving Gertz; ed, Hal B. Gordon; m/l, Meltzer.

Adventure/Drama   **(PR:A MPAA:NR)**

SHARK WOMAN, THE**   (1941) 59m World bw

Ahmang (The Pearl Diver), Sai-Yu (His Sweetheart), Ko-Hal (Little Brother), Mamounah (Mother), Chang-Fu (Captain of Pearling Schooner).

Paper-thin story centers on the pearl divers of a small Malaysian island. The underwater footage, especially the fight between a shark and an octopus, is great. The cast was comprised of Malaysian natives.

p, Charles Hunt; d, Ward Wing; w, Lori Bara; ph, John C. Cook; ed, Tom J. Geraghty; md, Abe Meyer; underwater ph, Stacy Woodward.

Adventure   **(PR:A MPAA:NR)**

SHARKFIGHTERS, THE*½   (1956) 73m Goldwyn/UA c

Victor Mature (*Lt. Comdr. Ben Staves*), Karen Steele (*Martha Staves*), James Olson (*Ens. Harold Duncan*), Philip Coolidge (*Lt. Comdr. Leonard Evans*), Claude Akins (*Chief "Gordy" Gordon*), Rafael Campos (*Carlos*), George Neise (*Comdr. George Zimmer*), Nathan Yates (*Capt. Ruiz*), Jesus Hernandez (*Vincente*), Lorin Johns, David Westlein (*Themselves*), Charles Collingwood (*Narrator*).

Mature plays the overseer of a Navy project to develop a shark repellent to be used by WW II pilots forced to land in the ocean. Because his only desire is to get the project completed as quickly as possible, he almost has an ineffective serum passed to the Navy. But the death of an innocent lad brings the scientist back to the research lab. Mature assigns himself the job of testing the final solution, which, luckily for Mature, actually works. Not much to get excited about. Filmed on location in Cuba.

p, Samuel Goldwyn, Jr.; d, Jerry Hopper; w, Lawrence Roman, John Robinson (based on the story by Jo and Art Napoleon); ph, Lee Garmes (CinemaScope, Technicolor); m, Jerome Moross; ed, Daniel Mandell; md, Emil Newman; m/l, Mercy Ferrer, Cesar Portillo (sung by The Aida Quartette).

Adventure   (PR:A   MPAA:NR)

SHARK'S TREASURE*½   (1975) 95m UA c

Cornel Wilde (*Jim*), Yaphet Kotto (*Ben*), John Neilson (*Ron*), Cliff Osmond (*Lobo*), David Canary (*Larry*), David Gilliam (*Johnny*), Caesar Cordova (*Pablo*), Gene Borkan (*Kook*), Dale Ishimoto (*Ishy*), Carmen Argenziano (*Lieutenant*), Roxanna Donilla (*Girl*), Marv Fisher (*Convict*), Clint Denn.

Another project by Cornel Wilde in which he tries to carry the whole load: he wrote, produced, directed, and starred in this simplistic tale that has a sea captain helping out in a treasure hunt. An aging fisherman, Wilde is willing to give up the boat he cherishes in order to go after the treasure. Of course, with this picture coming right on the tail of JAWS, there had to be a number of shark shots. That underwater photography is the best part of the film.

p,d&w, Cornel Wilde; ph, Jack Atcheler; m, Robert O. Ragland; ed, Bryon "Buzz" Brandt; underwater ph, Al Giddings.

Adventure   Cas.   (PR:A   MPAA:PG)

SHARKY'S MACHINE***   (1928) 122m Deliverance-Orion/WB c

Burt Reynolds (*Sharky*), Vittorio Gassman (*Victor*), Brian Keith (*Papa*), Charles Durning (*Friscoe*), Earl Holliman (*Hotchkins*), Bernie Casey (*Arch*), Henry Silva (*Billy Score*), Richard Libertini (*Nosh*), Darryl Hickman (*Smiley*), Rachel Ward (*Dominoe*), Joseph Mascolo (*Joe Tipps*), Carol Locatell (*Mabel*), Hari [Harry] Rhodes (*Highball Mary*), John Fiedler (*Barrett*), James O'Connell (*Twigs*), Val Avery (*Man with Siakwan*), Suzee Pai (*Siakwan*), Aarika Wells (*Tiffany*), Tony King (*Kitten*), William Diehl (*Percy*), Dan Inosanto (*Chin 1*), Weaver Levy (*Chin 2*), May Keller Pearce (*May*), Sheryl Kilby (*Lisa*), James Lewis, Scott Newell (*Police*), Glynn Ruben (*Pregnant Woman*), Bennie Moore (*Bus Driver*), Alveda King Beale, Gayle Davis, Atiim Kweli (*Bus Riders*), Brenda Bynum (*Aging Hooker*), Gus Mann (*Flasher*), Elaine Falone, Wanda Strange, Barbara Stokes (*Hookers*), John Greenwell (*Rachel*), John Arthur (*Pusher*), Terrayne Crawford, Mary Beth Busbee, J. Don Ferguson, Monica Kaufman, Dave Michaels, Wes Sarginson, Forrest Sawyer, Colonel Beach, Danny Nelson, Lamar Jackson, Sue Cockrell, Lisa Hall, Pam Newman, April Reed, Susan Williamson, Diana Szlosberg.

Reynolds proved himself a capable director with this effort in which he played a tough cop out to uncover gangster kingpin Gassman. Though first going undercover, a mishap reveals his identity and he is demoted to the vice squad. But Reynolds shows just how good a cop he is (not that his bosses think so) by shaping up his new coworkers into a force which is too hot for Gassman's gang. An interesting twist to a standard romantic theme has Reynolds falling in love with high-class hooker Ward, the woman he's been staking out around the clock. A scene where she appears to have her head blown off by one of Gassman's hitmen is particularly well conceived. The dead woman turns out to be someone else, something that Reynolds is grateful for in a sadistic sort of way. SHARKY'S MACHINE is loaded with violence and nonstop action. Reynolds was quite inventive in his direction, bringing in twists that added intrigue to the story. One of the most complex and dangerous stunts ever attempted took place in SHARKY'S MACHINE: one daring stuntman fell 16 floors through a broken window.

p, Hank Moonjean; d, Burt Reynolds; w, Gerald Di Pego (based on the novel by William Diehl); ph, William A. Fraker (Technicolor); m, Snuff Garrett, Al Capps; ed, William Gordean; prod d, Walter Scott Herndon; set d, Phil Abramson; cos, Norman Salling; m/l, "Let's Keep Dancing," Bobby Troup, Snuff Garrett (sung by Peggy Lee).

Crime   Cas.   (PR:O   MPAA:R)

SHARPSHOOTERS**½   (1938) 64m FOX bw

Brian Donlevy (*Steve Mitchell*), Lynn Bari (*Diane Woodward*), Wally Vernon (*Waldo*), John King (*Prince Alexis*), Douglas Dumbrille (*Count Maxim*), C. Henry Gordon (*Kolter*), Sidney Blackmer (*Baron Orloff*), Martin Joseph Spellman, Jr (*Prince Michael Martin*), Frank Puglia (*Ivan*), Hamilton MacFadden (*Bowman*), Romaine Callender (*Consul's Assistant*).

This was supposed to be the first in a series of adventures revolving around a newsreel cameraman. Donlevy plays the photographer who not only captures the news but makes it as well. Here he spoils the plot of a gang of revolutionaries who have assasinated the king of a mythical European monarchy and plan to do in the prince, whose coronation Donlevy has come to cover. This film was the only segment of the proposed series to make the theaters. It is filled with plenty of evenly paced action and the director also does a decent job in making the characters believable, even though the story has little to offer in itself. Vernon is the sidekick around for laughs.

p, Sol M. Wurtzel; d, James Tinling; w, Robert Ellis, Helen Logan (based on a story by Maurice Rapf, Lester Ziffren); ph, Barney McGill; ed, Nick De Maggio; md, Samuel Kaylin.

Adventure/Drama   (PR:A   MPAA:NR)

SHATTER   (SEE: CALL HIM MR. SHATTER, 1976, Brit.)

SHATTERHAND   (SEE: OLD SHATTERHAND, 1968, Ger./Yugo./Fr./Ital.)

SHE***   (1935) 95m RKO bw

Helen Gahagan (*She*), Randolph Scott (*Leo Vincey*), Helen Mack (*Tanya Dugmore*), Nigel Bruce (*Archibald Holly*), Gustav Von Seyffertitz (*Prime Minister Billali*), Samuel S. Hinds (*John Vincey*), Noble Johnson (*Amahagger Chief*), Lumsden Hare (*Dugmore*), Jim Thorpe (*Captain of the Guards*), Anatol Winogradoff.

H. Rider Haggard was a British civil servant who began writing to win a bet with his brother after they'd argued about what made good literature. Haggard's first book of many (58 works of fiction, seven non-fiction) was King Solomon's Mines. She was his second in 1887. When adapted for this screen version, the locale was altered from humid Africa to the frozen wastes of the near-Arctic. Producer Cooper, who had squired KING KONG to great success, gave it a first-rate treatment with a cast of 5,000, fantastic sets, and a script by one of KING KONG'S writers, Ruth Rose. To play the lead in this orgy of special effects, he chose a newcomer, Helen Gahagan, who was later to start a trend of actors turning to politics. Joel McCrea and his wife, Frances Dee, were originally asked to star in the film, but when they were unavailable, Scott and Mack got the jobs. Hinds is dying when he tells his nephew, Scott, to join British scientist Bruce on an expedition to find the secret of eternal life. There is a story in the family annals that one of their long-dead ancestors had done that and discovered a mysterious fire that burned with such intensity that it preserved, rather than destroyed. Scott and Bruce take off for the uncharted territory around northern Manchuria. Once there, they meet Hare, a traveling trader, and his daughter, Mack. The two parties team up, face weather problems, and eventually find the remains of a long-ago group of explorers. A body is inside a block of ice, and when Hare tries to dig it out, thousands of tons of snow are released and everyone in the group is killed, except Scott, Bruce, and Mack. They continue on and are captured by a strange group led by Seyffertitz, a priest of this tribe. Just as the trio is about to be killed, Seyffertitz calls it off and takes them below the frozen tundra into an underground world known as Kor where it's as hot as the Sudan. There they meet Gahagan, an immortal creature of great beauty who is known as "She-Who-Must-Be-Obeyed" (which is what Rumpole of the Bailey called his shrewish wife on the PBS TV series imported from England). The trio learn that Gahagan bathed her comely body in the Flame of Life and is now immortal and that she was once in love with Scott's ancestor and killed him when he wouldn't return that love. Since then, she's been down there waiting for Scott to show up. Gahagan is not thrilled about Mack's presence, so she commands her to be killed. Scott saves Mack, then Gahagan leads the trio to the Flame and walks into it so they can see it is life-giving. When she steps out of the Flame, a change comes over her and she ages before their eyes like Margo in LOST HORIZON and instantly becomes thousands of years old. It isn't seconds before she becomes a pile of bones and flesh as the movie ends. In the 1980's Steven Spielberg and George Lucas and many others would go back to this kind of picture for some of their derivative work. It was originally made in 1919, then again in 1926, in silent form. In 1965, Ursula Andress starred in an MGM version that never made much noise. Gahagan was a Brooklyn woman whose life was one of the most unusual stories of the era. A student at New York's Barnard College, she went on the stage and did many plays, then gave it up to study opera in Europe. After developing her voice, came home to the stage, met and married Melvyn Douglas in 1931, and bore him three children. In 1944, she ran for Congress as a liberal and was very popular with her voters, winning again in 1946 and 1948. After establishing her credentials with the California voters, she decided to try for the Senate and came up against Richard Nixon, who used unprecedented smear tactics against her by intimating that she was a Communist because hundreds of times she'd voted similarly to radical Vito Marcantonio of New York. What the "pink sheets" Nixon distributed did not say is that almost all members of Congress had voted the same way because most of the issues were not political and conservatives and leftists had agreed on them. Nixon convinced the gullible California voters that she was not to be trusted and he won by a huge plurality. The odd part of that was Nixon had used the same tactics to secure his Congressional seat when he ran against Jerry Voorhis after the war. Nobody thought that a U.S. politician would ever lie about such matters. This was Gahagan's only movie appearance and it was the U.S.'s loss that she never worked in films again. There do not seem to be any copies left of this picture.

p, Merian C. Cooper; d, Irving Pichel, Lansing C. Holden; w, Ruth Rose, Dudley Nichols (based on the novel by H. Rider Haggard); ph, J. Roy Hunt; m, Max Steiner; art d, Van Nest Polglase, Al Herman; spec eff, Vernon Walker; ch, Benjamin Zemach.

Adventure/Fantasy (PR:A MPAA:NR)

SHE½** (1965, Brit.) 104m Hammer-Seven Arts-ABF-Pathe/MGM c

Ursula Andress *(Ayesha)*, John Richardson *(Leo Vincey)*, Peter Cushing *(Maj. Horace Holly)*, Bernard Cribbins *(Job)*, Rosenda Monteros *(Ustane)*, Christopher Lee *(Billali)*, Andre Morell *(Haumeid)*, John Maxim *(Captain of the Guard)*.

Hammer Films, Seven Arts, and Associated British-Pathe got together to do this fourth version of Haggard's classic story. It's a mammoth spectacle and, in some ways, even larger than the 1935 version which starred Congress-woman Helen Gahagan Douglas in her only movie role. WW I is ending and Richardson is hoisting a drink in a Jerusalem night spot where he meets Monteros, a female slave who has a mission to bring Richardson to meet her mistress, Andress, a mysterious woman of indeterminate age who longs for the man that she murdered centuries before. When Richardson meets Andress, she offers him riches and power beyond his wildest dreams if he will accompany her to a mountain city. She gives Richardson a ring and a map. Richardson's friend, Cushing, recognizes the ring as a relic of Egypt from more than 2,000 years before. Further, Cushing knows about this lost city, and when he sees the map, he realizes that it is the way to that city, a fabulous place filled with untold riches, if one is to believe the legends. Monteros and the two men, accompanied by her aide, Cribbins, go off to find the city. Miles and miles of desert (much too long in the scheme of things) pass. By this time, Monteros wants Richardson for her own so she takes them to a village where Andress' slaves are ruled by Monteros' father, Morell. Richardson, Cushing, and Cribbins are captured and about to be sacrificed when Lee, the high priest, steps in and takes Richardson to meet Andress. It turns out that Richardson is the spitting image of her old beau. Andress stays young because she has been bathed in the Flame of Life, and when Richardson follows her into the Flame so he can stay young, she disintegrates into a pile of ashes, forgetting that it can only be used once for immortality. Cushing and Cribbins leave, saddened by the fact that this flame only flares every couple of thousand years and that Richardson is now doomed to immortality until the next time it erupts. Shot in Israel, this epic suffers from too much grandeur and not enough adventure. Andress was better than she'd ever been and showed that she could act, as well as fill out a bikini. The picture looks much bigger than the actual budget because the pound was strong against the Israeli currency and they were able to afford some tremendous production values. The sequel was THE VENGEANCE OF SHE, which suffered from the loss of Andress. Looking at the sets and some of the costumes, it's not hard to see where Steven Spielberg and some of the other younger directors of the 1970's and 1980's got their inspiration.

p, Michael Carreras; d, Robert Day; w, David T. Chantler (based on the novel by H. Rider Haggard); ph, Harry Waxman (CinemaScope, Technicolor); m, James Bernard; ed, James Needs, Eric Boyd-Perkins; art d, Robert Jones, Don Mingaye; cos, Carl Toms, Roy Ashton; spec eff, George Blackwell; ch, Christine Lawson.

Adventure (PR:A-C MPAA:NR)

SHE ALWAYS GETS THEIR MAN* (1962, Brit.) 61m Danziger/UA bw

Terence Alexander *(Bob Conley)*, Ann Sears *(Betty Tate)*, Sally Smith *(Sally)*, William Fox *(Waling)*, Avril Edgar *(Sylvia)*, Bernice Swanson *(May)*, Gale Sheridan *(Phyllis)*, Michael Balfour *(Runkle)*.

Inane farce revolving around the efforts of a group of girls staying at a youth hostel to keep another young lady from taking a wealthy man for a ride. To do so they get an actor to portray the rich man, thus diverting the schemes of the vamp. Lighter than air fare that adds up to a lot of nothing.

p, John Ingram; d, Godfrey Grayson; w, Mark Grantham.

Comedy (PR:A MPAA:NR)

SHE AND HE½** (1967, Jap.) 110m Iwanami-Eizo-Sha/Brandon bw
(KANOJO TO KARE)

Sachiko Hidari *(Naoko)*, Eiji Okada *(Eiichi)*, Kikuji Yamashita *(Ikona)*, Mariko Igarashi *(Hanako)*, Akio Hasegawa *(Laundry Boy)*, Takanobu Hobuzi *(Doctor)*, Kuma the Dog.

A social consciousness drama that concentrates on the inability of people from different classes to accept each other, resulting in the guilt which develops in an upper-class home. Hidari and Okada play a moderately well-off couple, who come in contact with Yamashita, an old classmate of Okada, now an impoverished ragpicker. Hidari's attempts to befriend Yamashita only result in castigation of them both and the sad realization that despite her efforts, there is little she can do to aid the poor man.

d, Susumu Hani; w, Hani, Kunio Shimizu; ph, Juichi Nagano; m, Toru Takemitsu.

Drama (PR:A MPAA:NR)

SHE AND HE* (1969, Ital.) 95m Cinecenta c

Laurence Harvey *(He)*, Sylva Koscina *(She)*, Isa Miranda *(Mother)*, Felicity Mason *(Aunt)*, Isabella Cini *(Grandmother)*, Nella Tessieri-Frediani *(Great-Grandmother)*, Amalia Carrara *(Great-Great-Grandmother)*, Vanni Castellani *(Veterinary Surgeon)*, Franca Sciuto *(Girl in Accident)*, Guido Mannari *(1st Mechanic)*, Giorgio Tavaroli *(2nd Mechanic)*.

"Heavy" would be the best way to describe this allegory of passion. Harvey plays a poet who is in love with Koscina. She is a fiery Italian who seems interested only in lovemaking; he is a bit more conventional when it comes to romance. Too many metaphors, cloud the emotional impact of this plain old love-hate relationship. The lush Italian scenery and a soundtrack by Morricone help to create the appropriate atmosphere.

p, Laurence Harvey; d, Mauro Bolognini; w, Ottavio Jemma, Vittorio Schiraldi, Bolognini (based on the play by Goffredo Parise); ph, Ennio Guarnieri (Technicolor); m, Ennio Morricone; ed, Giovanni Baragli; art d, Carlo Bini; set d&cos, Vanni Castellani.

Drama (PR:O MPAA:NR)

SHE ASKED FOR IT*½ (1937) 65m PAR bw

William Gargan *(Dwight Stanford)*, Orien Heyward *(Penelope Stanford)*, Vivienne Osborne *(Ceila Stettin)*, Richard Carle *(Ted Hoyt)*, Harry Beresford *(Randolph Stettin)*, Harry Beresford *(Mr. Switch, Lawyer)*, Alan Birmingham *(Conrad Norris)*, Harry Fleischmann *(Jenkins)*, Tully Marshall *(Old Man Stettin)*, Miki Morita *(Kaito)*.

This takeoff on THE THIN MAN has Gargan, a mystery writer, turn detective in order to solve the murder of Marshall. Heyward plays his sidekick wife, but their dialog lacks any zest, making for a feeble imitation.

p, B.P. Schulberg; d, Erle C. Kenton; w, Frederick Jackson, Theodore Reeves, Howard Irving Young; ph, Leon Shamroy; ed, Robert Bischoff; md, Boris Morros; art d, Albert D'Agostino.

Mystery (PR:A MPAA:NR)

SHE BEAST, THE½** (1966, Brit./Ital./Yugo.) 74m Leith/Europix c
(IL LAGO DI SATANA; LA SORELLA DI SATANA; GB: THE RE-
VENGE OF THE BLOOD BEAST)

Barbara Steele *(Veronica Vardella)*, Ian Ogilvy *(Philip)*, John Karlsen *(Count von Helsing)*, Mel Welles, Jay Riley, Richard Watson, Ed Randolph.

Honeymooning in some unspecified Soviet satellite country, Ogilvy and Steele, in their car, run off the road and plunge into a lake where, an opening flashback has shown, a witch was drowned in the 18th Century, cursing the villagers and shouting, "I'll be back." Ogilvy swims to safety, but Steele has vanished, her place taken by the hideous witch who goes on a murder spree against the descendants of her killers. Karlsen is a nobleman of an old witch-hunting, vampire-stalking family fallen on hard times under the new regime, who has stayed in Transylvania waiting for the witch to fulfill her curse. He convinces Ogilvy that witchcraft is behind his wife's disappearance and the two team up to capture the witch and properly exorcise her. They conduct the ritual by the lake while dunking the witch. She disappears from the dunking chair and for a moment the men panic, thinking she has escaped. Then Steele floats up, unable to recall anything of her ordeal. As the couple resume their honeymoon (with Karlsen, his work done, in the back seat), Ogilvy comments on what an awful place they've just left. Steele disagrees, saying she rather enjoyed it, and adding, "I'll be back" as a strange smile crosses her face. Director Reeves' first feature (he had previously taken over CASTLE OF THE LIVING DEAD halfway through production) shows some of the themes that would emerge in his two later films. Over the course of this film one can almost see Reeves growing as a director, and one standout sequence intercuts a brutal cockfight with the witch dispatching some of her victims in an equally brutal manner. Only when Reeves tries to inject some humor into the situation does he flop totally, and he learned his lesson well enough to avoid any light moments in his finest work, THE CONQUEROR WORM. THE SHE BEAST also begins Reeves' penchant for downbeat endings, found in all three of his films, and coming here after what appears to be a conventional happy ending: the witch is dead and Steele is restored, but her closing comment makes it terribly plain to the audience, if not to Ogilvy and Karlsen, that she is still possessed by the witch. The film continually shows the restraints of its low budget, but some of the performances are quite good, especially those of cult favorite Steele and Ogilvy, who star in all three of Reeves' films. By no means a great film, but one worth seeing, by a director who brought grim new vistas to the horror film before committing suicide at the age of 25.

p, Paul Maslansky; d, Michael Reeves; w, Michael Byron; ph, Amerigo Gengarelli; m, Ralph Ferraro; ed, Nira Omri.

Horror   **Cas.**   **(PR:C   MPAA:NR)**

SHE COULDN'T SAY NO**   (1930) 70m WB bw

Winnie Lightner (*Winnie Harper, Blues Singer*), Chester Morris (*Jerry Casey*), Sally Eilers (*Iris*), Johnny Arthur (*Tommy Blake*), Tully Marshall (*Big John*), Louise Beavers (*Cora*).

Conceived just to suit the talents of Lightner, which proved to be not as vast as the part called for. She plays a cabaret singer with a good friend in gangster Morris. The latter helps the singer find her way to success, receiving a number of bruises to get, her there. But all along Morris is in love with society dame Eilers, who has all the stylized charm Lightner lacks. The comedy and singing scored a hit, but the dramatics were far too sentimental. Songs include: "Darn Fool Woman Like Me," "Watching My Dreams Go By," and "Bouncing the Baby Around" (Al Dubin, Joe Burke, sung by Winnie Lightner).

d, Lloyd Bacon; w, Robert Lloyd, Arthur Caesar, Harvey Thew (based on the play by Benjamin M. Kaye); ph, James Van Trees.

Drama   **(PR:A   MPAA:NR)**

SHE COULDN'T SAY NO**   (1939, Brit.) 72m ABF bw

Tommy Trinder (*Dugsie Gibbs*), Fred Emney (*Herbert, Dugsie's Agent*), Googie Withers (*Dora*), Greta Gynt (*Frankie Barnes*), David Hutcheson (*Peter Thurston*), Bertha Belmore (*Dr. Grimstone*), Basil Radford (*Lord Pilton*), Cecil Parker (*Jimmy Reeves*), David Burns (*Chester*), Wylie Watson (*Thrumgood*), Doris Hare (*Amelia Reeves*), Geoffrey Sumner (*Announcer*).

Despite a plot that is nearly impossible to follow, this spicy piece of slapstick is fairly good fun; a result of well timed performances from a cast who didn't seem to care what the film was suppose to be about. Emney and friend Trinder attempt to retrieve Gynt's diary from the safe where it has been locked away by her cautious guardian, and in the process encounter a gang of thieves attempting to ransack the same safe.

p, Walter C. Mycroft; d, Godfrey Grayson; w, Clifford Grey, Elizabeth Meehan, Bert Lee (based on the play "Funny Face" by Paul Smith and Fred Thompson); ph, Claude Friese-Greene.

Comedy   **(PR:A   MPAA:NR)**

SHE COULDN'T SAY NO**   (1941) 63m WB bw

Roger Pryor (*Wallace Turnbull*), Eve Arden (*Alice Hinsdale*), Cliff Edwards (*Banjo Page*), Clem Bevans (*Eli Potter*), Vera Lewis (*Pansy Hawkins*), Spencer Charters (*Hank Woodcock*), Irving Bacon (*Abner*), Ferris Taylor (*Judge Josiah Jenkins*), Chester Clute (*Ezra Pine*), George Irving (*Henry Rockwell*), Zeffie Tilbury (*Ma Hawkins*), George Guhl (*Barber*), Frank Mayo (*Town Marshal*), Ann Edmunds (*Rockwell's Secretary*), Creighton Hale (*Jasper*), Al Lloyd (*Man*), Inez Gay (*Mathilda*), Drew Roddy, Sonny Bupp (*Boys*), Leo White, Paul Panzer, Glen Cavender (*Jurors*), Jessie Perry, Jean Maddox, Paulette Evans, Alexis Smith (*Gossips*).

Pryor plays a lawyer with Arden as his secretary. She, in fact, is well versed in legal aspects herself, but future hubby Pryor refuses to have her at the bar. Things take a drastic change, however, all because the ancient Bevans hasn't come around to marrying the woman he's dated for the past 15 years, Lewis. She decides to sue Bevans for breach of promise, with Arden defending the man and Pryor defending Lewis. The courtroom scenes make for the all too obvious jokes and the eventual reconciliations come as no surprise. The picture does have its moments, particularly in the performance of Bevans as the old bachelor. Based on a 1926 Broadway hit, SHE COULDN'T SAY NO was also a remake of an earlier Warners film of the same name, done in 1930.

p, William Jacobs; d, William Clemens; w, Earl Baldwin, Charles Grayson (based on the play by Benjamin M. Kaye); ph, Ted McCord; ed, Harold McLeron.

Comedy   **(PR:A   MPAA:NR)**

SHE COULDN'T SAY NO*½   (1954) 88m RKO bw (GB: BEAUTIFUL BUT DANGEROUS)

Robert Mitchum (*Doc*), Jean Simmons (*Corby Lane*), Arthur Hunnicut (*Otley*), Edgar Buchanan (*Ad Meeker*), Wallace Ford (*Joe*), Raymond Walburn (*Judge Holbert*), Jimmy Hunt (*Digger*), Ralph Dumke (*Sheriff*), Hope Landin (*Mrs. McMurtry*), Gus Schilling (*Ed Gruman*), Eleanor Todd (*Sally*), Pinky Tomlin (*Elmer Wooley*), Burt Mustin (*Amos*), Edith Leslie (*Nora*), Martha Wentworth (*Mrs. Holbert*), Gloria Winters (*Barbara*), Barry Brooks (*Clerk*), Wallis Clark (*Minister*), Florence Lake (*Mrs. Gruman*), Jonathan Hale (*Mr. Bentley*), Keith Harrington (*TV Announcer*), James Craven (*Plumber*), Tol Avery, Mary Bayliss, Joy Hallward, Morgan Brown, Clyde Courtwright, Coleman Francis, Mike Lally, Leo Sulky, Clarence

Muse, Maxie Thrower, Dabbs Greer, Dan White, Bob Hopkins, Charles Watts, Ruth Packard, Teddy Mangean, Sammy Shack, Carl Sklover, Charles Cane, Tony Merrill, Marjorie Holliday, Marilyn Gladstone.

Simmons and Mitchum found themselves together again after their successful outing in ANGEL FACE. However, they are sorely out of place in this offbeat comedy that has Simmons as a wealthy woman who decides to lend a hand to those people who helped her earlier in life. When she was a girl, the people of Progress, Arkansas, had helped to raise the money for a much needed operation for her. She now wishes to show her gratitude by bestowing monetary gifts upon the townspeople. However, her plan fails when these windfalls disrupt the lives of some of Progress' most prominent citizens: Judge Walburn decides to pack up and move; general storekeeper Buchanan closes shop; and postman Tomlin ceases his appointed rounds. In addition, all sorts of riffraff move into town in the hope of collecting some dough. Simmons reveals herself to be the source of all the new found wealth and makes ready to leave, but Mitchum, the town doctor, persuades her to stay and marry him. All of this was supposed to be funny, but the humor never really works. This was the last of three films Simmons made in rapid succession to complete her RKO contract obligations (ANGEL CITY and AFFAIR WITH A STRANGER were the others). She couldn't say no to the opportunity to escape from Howard Hughes' financially troubled studio and Hughes couldn't make up his mind what to call this film with which he had hoped to revive the screwball comedy tradition of the 1930's and 1940's. Although it was shot in 1952, Hughes and company fiddled with it for another 16 months before releasing it. In the process, he toyed with the idea of calling it BEAUTIFUL BUT DANGEROUS, ENOUGH FOR HAPPINESS, and SHE HAD TO SAY YES before deciding on the title as we know it.

p, Robert Sparks; d, Lloyd Bacon; w, D.D. Beauchamp, William Bowers, Richard Flournoy (based on the story "Enough for Happiness" by Beauchamp); ph, Harry J. Wild; m, Roy Webb; ed, George Amy; md, Constantin Bakaleinikoff; art d, Albert S. D'Agostino, Carroll Clark.

Comedy/Drama   **Cas.**   **(PR:A   MPAA:NR)**

SHE COULDN'T TAKE IT**   (1935) 89m COL bw (GB: WOMAN TAMER)

George Raft (*Spot Ricardi*), Joan Bennett (*Carol Van Dyke*), Walter Connolly (*Mr. Van Dyke*), Billie Burke (*Mrs. Van Dyke*), Lloyd Nolan (*Tex*), Wallace Ford (*"Finger" Boston*), James Blakeley (*Tony Van Dyke*), Alan Mowbray (*Alan Hamlin*), William Tannen (*Cesar*), Donald Meek (*Uncle Wyndersham*), Frank Conroy (*Raleigh*), Tom Kennedy (*Slugs*), Ivan Lebedeff (*Count*), Franklin Pangborn (*Secretary*), Thomas Jackson (*Spieler*), Huey White (*Eddie Gore*), Mack Gray (*Ike*), Peppino Dallalic (*Don*), Robert Middlemass (*Desk Sergeant*), Walter Walker (*Judge*), Stanley Andrews (*Wyndersham*), Wyrley Birch (*Dr. Schaeffer*), Maynard Holmes (*Edgar*), Maxine Lewis (*Crooner*), Irving Bacon (*Man at Toll Gate*), Ky Robinson, James Burtis, Ted Oliver (*Motorcycle Cops*), Eddie Gribbon (*Detective*), Loren Riebe (*Human Fly*), Olaf Hytten (*Butler*), George McKay (*Red*), Ed Dearing, Gene Morgan (*District Attorney's Men*), Frank Austin (*Railroad Attendant*), George Lloyd (*Turnkey*), Emmett Vogan (*Reporter*), John Quillian (*Bellboy*), Victor Potel, James B. "Pop" Kenton, Jack Duffy (*Farmers*), Jimmy Harrison, Stanley Mack, Tom Costello, Antrim Short, Jack Gardner, Billy West, Charles Sherlock, Joe Clive (*Reporters*), Arthur Rankin, Henry Roquemore, Lee Shumway, John Webb Dillon, Arthur Stuart Hull, Paul Power (*Men*), Lois Lindsey, Edith Kingden, Bess Flowers, Grace Goodall, Gladys Gale, Carrie Daumery (*Women*), Frank Rice (*Milkman*), Frank LaRue, Frank Marlowe, Robert Wilber, Walter Perry, Stark Bishop, Al Ferguson (*Prisoners*), Nadine Dore (*Girl*), John Ince (*Prison Official*), Donald Kerr (*Sailor*), Harrison Greene (*Spieler*), Lee Phelps (*Bailiff*), Jack Daley (*District Attorney's Man*), Henry Sylvester (*Stage Manager*), Lon Poff (*Judge*), George Webb (*Editor*), J. Merrill Holmes (*Prison Doctor*), Frank G. Fanning (*Warden*), Mike Lally, William E. Lawrence (*Photographers*), Joe North (*Butler*), Raymond Turner (*Janitor*), Oscar Rudolph (*Newsboy*), C.A. Beckman (*Traffic Cop*), Kernan Cripps (*Guard*), Phillip Ronalde (*Waiter*).

It was around this time that gangster movies and screwball comedies were tilting for the movie-goer's dollar, so Columbia decided to combine the two and do a screwball gangster comedy. Connolly is a rich banker who is nailed by the IRS for fiddling with his income tax and sent to the federal pen at Atlanta. His madcap family's spending is what got him in trouble and he welcomes the respite and a chance to sort things out in the confines of the prison. Once there, he meets Raft, a convicted bootlegger, who has taken the opportunity to invade the jail's library and educate himself. Raft, like many criminals, is a conservative type, and he plans to tread the straight and narrow once he gets out. Connolly is so taken by Raft that he names him trustee of his fortune and executor of his will; then Connolly promptly keels over with a coronary. Raft comes out of jail to meet his new responsibilities. Burke is Connolly's addle-pated widow and her daughter, Bennett, proves that the apple doesn't fall far from the tree. Both women are angered that they are now in the hands of Raft, a one-time criminal, and they take steps to make his life difficult. Bennett is dating Mowbray, a phony actor-type who is little more than a gigolo. She tries everything to annoy Raft but he stays cool and amused at her antics, eventually throwing her into the lake in Central Park and frightening Mowbray out of her life. As revenge, blonde

Bennett contacts Nolan, a hood, to stage a phony kidnaping. Then Nolan thinks it might be a good idea to actually nab the heiress and he does, forcing Raft to steal a car from the police, race after the kidnapers in a Keystone-Kops-like chase and save her. At the conclusion, Bennett comes to understand that Raft is a hell of a macho guy and probably the only man in New York who can make her toe the line. The picture could have been much funnier if they'd gone all the way and made it a full slapstick farce, but they were too timid and Raft's comedic ability had not yet been proven (actually, it never was), so they held back. It's a variation of Shakespeare's "Taming of the Shrew," except that Bennett is not shrewish enough. In a tiny role as a newsboy, note Oscar Rudolph, who grew up to become one of Hollywood's most successful TV directors in the 1950's and 1960's. Even though this was an original Garrett screenplay, it feels very much like a Damon Runyon story.

p, B.P. Schulberg; d, Tay Garnett; w, Oliver H.P. Garrett (based on a story by Gene Towne, Graham Baker); ph, Leon Shamroy; ed, Gene Havlick; art d, Stephen Goosson.

Comedy   (PR:A MPAA:NR)

SHE-CREATURE, THE*½   (1956) 76m Golden State/AIP bw

Chester Morris (*Dr. Carlo Lombardi*), Marla English (*Andrea*), Tom Conway (*Timothy Chappel*), Cathy Downs (*Dorothy*), Lance Fuller (*Ted Erickson*), Ron Randell (*Lt. Ed James*), Frieda Inescort (*Mrs. Chappel*), Frank Jenks (*Police Sergeant*), El Brendel (*Olaf, the Butler*), Paul Dubov (*Johnny*), Bill Hudson (*Bob*), Flo Bert (*Marta*), Jeanne Evans (*Mrs. Brown*), Kenneth MacDonald (*Prof. Anderson*), Paul Blaisdell (*Creature*).

Morris plays a hypnotist who puts English into a trance, then calls up her past self, a creature that has been lurking at the bottom of the sea since prehistoric times. Promoter Conway gets wind of the proceedings and thinks up a scheme to make a buck by having Morris predict the murders of the evil creature. But Fuller sees through the gimmick as his interest in English deepens, until English is eventually able to control her other self without the aid of Morris. She uses this skill to turn the creature on Morris and Conway, before allowing it a well-deserved rest in the ocean, in preparation for an appearance in VOODOO WOMAN. Some interesting concepts were touched on, but quickly pushed to the background in the name of plot development, which in this case is one cliche after another. Later remade as CREATURE OF DESTRUCTION.

p, Samuel Z. Arkoff, Alex Gordon; d, Edward L. Cahn; w, Lou Rusoff (based on the story by Rusoff); ph, Frederick E. West; m, Ronald Stein; ed, Ronald Sinclair.

Horror   (PR:A MPAA:NR)

SHE DANCES ALONE**½   (1981, Aust./U.S.) 87m D.H.D./CD c

Kyra Nijinsky (*Herself*), Bud Cort (*Director*), Patrick Dupond (*Dancer*), Sauncey LeSuer (*Kyra as a Child*), Walter Kent (*Doctor*), Rosine Bena (*Ballerina*), Jeanette Etheridge (*Girl Friend*), Franco DeAlto (*Patient in Hospital*), Laura Hoover (*Little Ballerina*), Max von Sydow (*Voice of Nijinsky*).

Picture concentrates on the efforts to make a documentary about the daughter of the famous Russian dancer Nijinsky. Along the way it sheds light on the woman, then 60 years old, who had tried to pursue her own career as a dancer, with the problems and profits of such a parentage. Kyra turns out to be quite a woman in her own right. Dornhelm does a decent job in combining seemingly unrelated parts into a finely tuned whole. Although this was primarily a U.S. independent production, Austrian television played an important role in the proceedings. (In English.)

p, Frederico DeLaurentiis, Earle Mack; d, Robert Dornhelm; w, Paul Davis, Jon Bradshaw (based on an idea by Dorhelm); ph, Karl Kofler; m, Gustavo Santolalla; ed, Tina Frese; m/l, "She Dances Alone," Bruce Roberts (sung by Bud Cort).

Drama   (PR:A MPAA:NR)

SHE DEMONS*   (1958) 76m Astor bw

Irish McCalla (*Jerrie Turner*), Tod Griffin (*Fred Maklin*), Victor Sen Yung (*Sammy Ching*), Charlie Opuni (*Kris Kamara*), Gene Roth (*Egore*), Rudolph Anders (*Herr Osler, Scientist*), Leni Tana (*Mona*), Billy Dix, Bill Coontz, The Diana Nellis Dancers.

The Nazis are still trying to create a perfect race in this poorly made feature in which Anders plays a Nazi scientist who turns the maiden beauties of a tropical island into near monsters. At the same time, he uses their fine skin to bring back the looks of his severly scarred wife. McCalla and Griffin wind up on the island via a crash, with the former interesting the doctor because of her shapely physique. But the little group is saved by what else but an active volcano.

p, Arthur A. Jacobs; d, Richard E. Cunha; w, Cunha, H.E. Barrie; ph, Meredith Nicholson; m, Nicolas Carras; ed, William Shea; spec eff, David Koehler.

Horror/Adventure   **Cas.**   (PR:A MPAA:NR)

SHE DEVIL*½   (1957) 77m FOX bw

Albert Dekker (*Dr. Rach*), Jack Kelly (*Dr. Scott*), Mari Blanchard (*Kyra*), Blossom Rock (*Hannah*), John Archer (*Kendall*), Fay Baker (*Mrs. Kendall*), Paul Cavanagh (*Sugar Daddy*), George Baxter (*Floor Manager*), Helen Jay (*Nurse*), Joan Bradshaw (*Redhead*), Tod Griffin (*Intern*).

Basically just a reworking of the old Jekyll-and-Hyde theme, SHE DEVIL puts a member of the distaff side through ghastly changes. Kelly is attempting to find a universal cure for disease, and Blanchard, who has tuberculosis, agrees to be a guinea pig for his experiments. The injections he gives her make her quite fit, but with the rather horrible side effect that she becomes a dangerous and knavish witch, immune to any form of injury. She first kills Baker, the wife of Archer, whom Blanchard marries and then does away with in a car crash. This leaves her with millions, but Kelly and Dekker decide that enough is enough, and transform the woman back to her sickly self. Little, if anything, new is offered in this poor effort by director Neumann (best known for his success with THE FLY), which fails to maintain suspense thoughout the picture. Karl Struss, who worked on the Fredric March version of DR. JEKYL AND MR. HYDE, handled the effects on this film, which weren't very exciting. The only visual indication of Blanchard's change in personality is the change in the color of her hair and people with graying hair can perform the same magic with dye.

p&d, Kurt Neumann; w, Neumann, Carrol Young (story by John Jessel); ph, Karl Struss (RegalScope); m, Paul Sawtell, Bert Shefter; ed, Carl Pierson; art d, Theobold Holsopple.

Horror   (PR:A MPAA:NR)

SHE-DEVIL ISLAND*½   (1936, Mex.) 65m FD bw (AKA: MARIA
                                                                        ELENA)

Carmen Guerrero (*Maria Elena*), J.J. Martinez Casado (*Rogelio*), Adolfo Giron (*Gonzalo Peralta*), Beatriz Ramon (*Carmen*), Lucy Delgado (*Charito*), Gmo. Calles (*Indalecio*), Pedro Armendariz (*Eudardo*), Carlos Baz (*Lopez*), Luz Carmona (*Aunt Ursula*), Emilio, Amparo (*Bamba Dancers*).

Film about a mysterious island inhabited only by women. They find their free lifestyle interrupted when it is discovered that the island is rich in pearls. Two rival groups fight it out for the pearls, with the warrior women inhabitants fleeing at the first sound of gunfire. Picturesque scenery of Mexico is visually pleasing, but the plot wears thin. (In English.)

p, Charles Kimball; d, Raphael J. Sevilla; w, Alfonso Liguori, Sevilla (based on the story by Ernesto Cortazar); ph, Lauron Draper, Lorenzo Barcelata.

Adventure   (PR:A MPAA:NR)

SHE-DEVILS ON WHEELS zero   (1968) 83m Creative Film
                                                          Enterprises/Mayflower c

Betty Connell (*Queen*), Pat Poston (*Whitey*), Nancy Lee Noble (*Honey-Pot*), Christie Wagner (*Karen*), Rodney Bedell (*Ted*), Ruby Tuesday (*Terry*), Joani Kramer (*Russian*), David Harris (*Bill*), Donna Testa (*Poodle*), Laura Platz (*Supergirl*), John Weymer (*Joe-Boy*), Steve White (*Doodie*), Roy Collodi (*Bartender*), Rick Williams (*Outlaw*), Donna Stelzer (*Mac*), John Shackleford, John Chaffin (*Police*).

Popular gory movie about a gang of women motorcyclists called the "Man-Eaters" who stage a weekly cycle race on an abandoned airport runway. Connell stars as the gang's leader who is used to winning the race and having her pick of the men who follow the gang, known as the "Stud-Line." When Wagner unexpectedly wins the race one week and picks Connell's favorite man, Harris, Connell gets angry and orders Wagner to either drag the tied and beaten Harris around the track behind her bike or be kicked out of the gang. Wagner regretfully chooses the former and kills Harris in carring out the order. Noble plays the new gang member who is initiated into the group by a massive orgy. When the Man-Eaters beat a rival male motorcycle gang in a fight, the male leader, Weymer, vows revenge and kidnaps Noble and beats her. She is returned to the Man-Eaters with a threatening note attached to her newly pierced nose. The women retaliate by decapitating Weymer. Throughout the movie, Wagner's boy friend, who wants no part of gangs, tries to talk her into leaving the gang, but to no avail. In the end, the Man-Eaters are arrested for murder, but are soon released for lack of evidence. Wagner, now a hard-core member, rides off with the gang in their quest for danger and excitement.

p&d, Herschell Gordon Lewis; w, Louise Downe; ph, Roy Collodi (Eastmancolor); m, Robert Lewis, Larry Wellington; ed, Richard Brinkman; set d, Robert Enrietto; m/l, "Get Off the Road," Sheldon Seymour.

Adventure   (PR:O MPAA:NR)

SHE DIDN'T SAY NO!***   (1962, Brit.) 96m GW/WB c

Eileen Herlie (*Bridget Monahan, Dressmaker*), Perlita Nielson (*Mary Monahan*), Wilfred Downing (*Tommy Monahan*), Ann Dickins (*Poppy Monahan*), Teresa and Lesley Scoble (*The Twins*), Raymond Manthorpe (*Toughy Monahan*), Niall MacGinnis (*Jamesy Casey*), Patrick McAlinney (*Matthew Hogan*), Jack MacGowran (*William Bates*), Joan O'Hara (*Mrs. Bates*), Ray McAnally (*Jim Power*), Betty McDowell (*Mrs. Power*), Ian Bannen (*Peter Howard*), Eithne Dunne (*Miss Hogan*), Hilton Edwards (*Film

Director), Maureen Halligan (*Miss Kelly*), Harry Hutchinson (*Judge*), Paul Farrell (*Darmody*), Shirley Joy (*Maybella Merton*), Viola Keats (*Mrs. Merton*), Anna Manahan (*Maggie Murphy*), Michael O'Brien (*Sergeant*), Liam Redmond (*Dr. Cassidy*), John Welsh (*Inspector*).

A pleasant, light-hearted yarn that treats the touchy subject of illegitimacy in a small Irish community with a sense-of-humor. Herlie plays an unwed mother of six whose fathers, except for one, are the village's most prominent citizens. Because she is a threat to other members of the village, particularly O'Hara, the wife of MacGowran, one of Herlie's former lovers, ways are thought up of removing the woman from the confines of the village. First they attempt to have Herlie declared an unfit mother in order to have the children taken from her. But she proves to be a more caring mother than the other women of the town. An old farm, far away from the village, is bought for the family to live on, but before this happens problems seem to work themselves out. One of the fathers asks to adopt his child, as his wife remains childless; one of Herlie's daughters becomes engaged; and another takes off for London with a movie contract. The happy ending has Herlie finally finding a husband in MacGinnis, father to one of the brood, and the whole family taking off for the newly acquired farm. The child actors who make up Herlie's family add the perfect charm to a story whose humor depends upon the ironic situation, rather than jokes and routines.

p, Sergei Nolbandov; d, Cyril Frankel; w, T.J. Morrison, Una Troy (based on the novel *We Are Seven* by Troy); ph, Gilbert Taylor (Technicolor); m, Tristam Carey; ed, Charles Hasse; prod d, William Kellner.

Comedy   **(PR:A MPAA:NR)**

SHE DONE HIM WRONG**   (1933) 66m PAR bw

Mae West (*Lady Lou*), Cary Grant (*Capt. Cummings, "The Hawk"*), Owen Moore (*Chick Clark*), Gilbert Roland (*Serge Stanieff*), Noah Beery, Sr (*Gus Jordan*), David Landau (*Dan Flynn*), Rafaela Ottiano (*Russian Rita*), Dewey Robinson (*Spider Kane*), Rochelle Hudson (*Sally Glynn*), Tammany Young (*Chuck Connors*), Fuzzy Knight (*Ragtime Kelly*), Grace LaRue (*Frances*), Robert E. Homans (*Officer Doheney*), Louise Beavers (*Pearl*), Wade Boteler (*Pat*), Aggie Herring (*Mrs. Flaherty*), Tom Kennedy (*Big Billy*), James C. Eagles (*Pete*), Tom McGuire (*Mike*), Al Hill, Arthur Housman (*Bar Flies*), Mary Gordon (*Cleaning Lady*), Michael Mark (*Janitor*), Mike Donlin (*Tout*), Harry Wallace (*Steak McGarry*), Lee Kohlmar (*Jacobson*), Frank Moran (*Framed Convict*), Heinie Conklin (*Street Cleaner*), Jack Carr (*Patron*), Ernie Adams (*Man in Audience*).

After beginning a lengthy stage career at the age of eight, Mae West reigned supreme on the Broadway stage for a while, then did a small role in NIGHT AFTER NIGHT at the age of 39. With SHE DONE HIM WRONG, West became an enormous star. She made 12 movies all told, 10 of which she wrote either alone or with collaborators. While still a teenager, she toured with several shows, and in 1912 was known as a "muscle dancer" who could manipulate her body in unique ways. Her first play "Sex" was a sensation, ran almost a year, offended all the blue-noses, and brought her to millions of dollars worth of publicity when she was tossed into jail for 10 days after losing a morals trial. She stayed in jail only eight days, came out, and donated 1000 books to the Welfare Island Workhouse Library. Her next show was "Diamond Lil," and it is that play which was the basis for this film. SHE DONE HIM WRONG was shot in the very brief schedule of 18 days, plus one week of rehearsal, as West fiddled with the lines to sanitize them for the prudish censors. Paramount was teetering on the brink of bankruptcy when they invested $200,000 in this movie. It returned more than 10 times that amount domestically and another million in foreign release, despite having been banned in Austria after the first night's showing. It began shooting on November 21, 1932, and finished before the New Year rang in. After 30 years of professional performing, West had her turn at bat and hit a home run, defying all predictions that her persona would never translate to the screen or that the Gay Nineties, during which this tale is set, were old hat and would never appeal to the Depression-era audience. West is a curvaceous, wise, and funny woman who must rank as one of the first truly liberated women ever seen on screen as she runs a Bowery saloon, fronting for owner Beery. Grant is a captain at the local mission, similar to a Salvation Army outpost, and he spends more than the usual amount of time in the bar, in what seems to be an attempt to save her immortal soul from going below decks where all wanton women wind up. It isn't long before the buxom West is in love with the youthful Grant (appearing in his eighth film before he was 30). West is the mistress of Beery and he plies her with her favorite item, diamonds, so when her heart begins to obscure the glow of the gems, she knows she's in trouble. Her ex-boy friend, Moore, is already in the slammer for having sought to drench her rounded form with jewels. Moore breaks out of jail and says he will murder West unless she accompanies him. Beery is discovered to have been running a counterfeiting ring and, as a sideline, is sending young women to San Francisco to be pick pockets. (Actually, this was toned down. In the play, they were sent to be prostitutes.) Hudson is a would-be suicide because she's made love to a man and now he won't marry her. West talks the young thing out of taking her own life. Hudson asks: "Who would want me after what's happened?" and West replies: "When women go wrong, men go right after them." Beery has Roland and Ottiano (a holdover from the stage show) passing the bogus money that he needs to pay for West's diamonds. On their first meeting, West says to Grant, "Why don't you come up sometime, and see me?" but

that line has since gone down in legend as "Why don't you come up and see me sometime?" (Another example of mistakenly remembered dialog is the Alfonso Bedoyline in TREASURE OF THE SIERRA MADRE when he tells Bogart and the others: "Badges? I don't have to show you any stinkin' bandges." That line has come to be known as "I don't have to show you no stinkin' badges," which was then mistakenly used as the title of a 1985 play.) In a battle, West bumps off Ottiano, and Grant drops his religious disguise to reveal that he is a cop who has been working undercover next door in the building owned by Kohlmar so he could get the goods on the various villains who frequent Beery's place. West is taken out with the others to be clapped into jail, but whereas they have to climb into the police van, Grant leads West to a waiting taxi and takes off all her rings so he can put a simple mini-diamond on her finger. She smiles and says, "Dark and handsome." He replies: "You bad girl," and as the picture closes she retorts, "You'll find out." Many of West's best one-liners pepper the dialog, including such favorites as (in a speech to Grant when he talks about the men he's attempting to rescue at his mission): "Ain't none of 'em worth saving. Hang around 'em long enough and you'll get that way yourself." When a lady says that she is a fine woman, West rolls her eyes and answers: "One of the finest women who ever walked the streets." In another scene, with her black maid Beavers, West claims, "Once I was so poor that I didn't know where my next husband was coming from." She was a clean-living woman in real life, didn't drink or smoke, as suggested by the line she tosses at Grant, "Smoking is gonna make a man look effeminate before long." Although only 5'3", she wore very high heels, and at 130 pounds was a bit overweight, but it mattered not. In between all the plot points and jokes, there was time for some music as Mae sang "Maizie," "A Guy what Takes His Time," "Haven't Got No Peace of Mind" (Leo Robin, Ralph Rainger), "I Wonder Where My Easy Rider's Gone" (Shelton Brooks), "Silver Threads Among the Gold" (Egbert Van Alstyne), "Frankie And Johnnie" (traditional). West spotted Grant on the Paramount lot and asked to have him in the picture, a request that pleased director Sherman who had worked with Grant while directing Marlene Dietrich in BLONDE VENUS, so it was a pleasurable association for all concerned. In the years to come, West played this "Diamond Lil" role in almost every movie she did, but with varying character names. It was always the bawdy, lusty woman who sailed through life with a quip and a smile and no guilt. To promote this picture, West appeared in person at New York's Paramount Theatre on Times Square, did several of the tunes, and played some of the funnier sequences "live" with George Metaxa. When one sees some of the fat movies of the 1980's, one appreciates the economy of this jam-packed film at a mere 66 minutes.

p, William LeBaron; d, Lowell Sherman; w, Mae West, Harvey Thew, John Bright (based on the play "Diamond Lil" by West); ph, Charles Lang; ed, Alexander Hall; art d, Bob Usher; cos, Edith Head; ch, Harold Hecht.

Comedy   **(PR:C MPAA:NR)**

SHE FREAK*½   (1967) Sonney c (AKA: ALLEY OF NIGHTMARES)

Claire Brennen (*Jade Cochran*), Lee Raymond (*Blackie Fleming*), Lynn Courtney (*Pat Mullins*), Bill McKinney (*Steve St. John*), Van Teen (*Mr. Babcock*), Felix Silla (*Shortie*), Marsha Drake (*Olga*), Claude Smith (*Greasy*), Bobby Mathews (*Max*), William Bagdad (*"Pretty Boy"*), Ben Moore (*Advance Man*), David Boudrot (*Customer in Cage*), Mme. Lee (*Snake Charmer*), Sandra Holcomb.

A ripoff of Tod Browning's illustrious FREAKS, this has Brennen as the hardened seductress who marries freak show owner McKinney while carrying on a masochistic affair with Ferris Wheel operator Raymond. A midget, Silla, tells McKinney about his bride's extra marital affair, which leads to a showdown between McKinney and Raymond in which Raymond is victorious. Her husband killed in the fracas, Brennen becomes the new owner of the show. Her first duty is to punish Silla for squealing on her. This action enrages the rest of the freaks, who attack Brennen, making her one of them and another weird attraction in the show. Friedman had previously produced the trashy BLOOD FEAST and 2000 MANIACS for Hirschel Gordon Lewis. With this feature he continues in the same vein of gore for gore's sake.

p, David F. Friedman; d, Byron Mabe; w, Friedman; ph, William Troiano; m, Billy Allen; ed, Mabe; makeup, Harry Thomas.

Horror   **(PR:O MPAA:NR)**

SHE GETS HER MAN*½   (1935) 65m UNIV bw

ZaSu Pitts (*Esmeralda*), Hugh O'Connell (*Windy*), Helen Twelvetrees (*Francine*), Edward Brophy (*Flash*), Warren Hymer (*Spike*), Bert Gordon (*Goofy*), Ward Bond (*Chick*), Louis Vincenot (*Chinese Merchant*), King Baggott (*Businessman*), Lou Seymour (*Theater Manager*), Jack Norton (*Drunk Reporter*), Stanley Andrews (*Kelly*), Philip Dunham (*Brown*), Ottola Nesmith, Virginia Grey, Isabelle Lamal (*Club Women*), Stanley Price, Emmett Vogan (*Reporters*), Georgia O'Dell (*Spinster*), George Cleveland (*Drunk in Lunch Room*), John Carradine, Anne O'Neal, Evelyn Miller (*Customers*), Laura Treadwell (*Mrs. Ginsberg*), Leo White (*Michael*), Mike Pat Donovan (*Guard*), Archie Robbins (*Reporter*), Lester Dorr (*Photographer*), Nell Craig (*Raid Leader*), Jane Kerr, Helen Dickson, Blanche Payson (*Raiders*), Dutch "O.G." Hendrian (*Butch*), Jack Kennedy (*Police Captain*), Constance Bergen, Bernadene Hayes (*Molls*), Huey White Johnny Indrisano, Richard Alexander, George Lloyd, Russ Clark, Sam Lufkin, Charles Sullivan (Gangsters), Richard Cramer (Bookkeeper), Monte Montague (Butler), Ray Brown (Barton), Al St. John (Teller), Frank Adams (Bumpkin), Dorothy McGowan (Stand-in for Pitts).

Pitts plays a lunch-counter waitress who spoils a bank robbery. O'Connell, an ambitious press agent, sees this as a chance to capitalize on Pitts' image, and goes about making the innocent gal a national hero. The really silly part of the already silly story comes when Pitts is kidnaped by gangsters because she is making them look bad. Pitts talks her way out of the mess, reforming the hoodlums in the process. It just wasn't funny.

p, David Diamond; d, William Nigh; w, Aben Kandel (based on a story by Diamond, Kandel); ph, Norbert Brodine; ed, Bernard W. Burton.

Comedy   **(PR:A MPAA:NR)**

SHE GETS HER MAN**   (1945) 74m UNIV bw

Joan Davis (Jane "Pilky" Pilkington), Leon Errol (Officer Mulligan), William Gargan (Breezy Barton), Vivian Austin (Maybelle Clarke), Milburn Stone (Tommy Tucker), Russell Hicks (Mayor), Donald MacBride (Henry Wright), Paul Stanton (Dr. Bleaker), Cy Kendall (Police Chief Brodie), Emmett Vogan (Hatch), Eddie Acuff (Boze, the Photographer), Virginia Sale (Phoebe), Ian Keith (Oliver McQuestion), Maurice Cass (Mr. Fudge), Chester Clute (Charlie, in Play), Arthur Loft (Waldron), Sidney Miller (Boy), Al Kikume (Joe, in Play), Leslie Denison (Barnsdale, in Play), Bob Allen (Song Specialty), Vernon Dent (Doorman), Charles Sherlock (Moe), Jerry Jerome (Bat), Nan Brinkley (Girl), Pierre Watkin (Johnson), George Lynn (Sinister Cameraman), Syd Saylor (Waiter, Tour Guide), William Hall (Bill the Policeman), Richard Hirbe (Newsboy), Ruth Roman (Glamor Girl), Sam Flint (Dignified Man), Howard Mitchell (Train Announcer), George Lloyd (Town Character), Hank Bell (Clem), William "Billy" Newell (Bettor), Claire Whitney (Landlady), Harold Goodwin (Winning Companion), Olin Howlin (Hank), Bobby Barber (Trombone Gag, Short Man), Sid Troy (Trombone Gag, Tall Man), Max Wagner (Mailman), Perc Launders (Hot Dog Man), Charles Sullivan (Cigar Gag Man), William J. O'Brien (Painted Suit Gag), Kit Guard (Bootblack Gag), Charles Hall (Painter Gag).

Basically a vehicle to capitilize on the comic talent of the popular Davis, here teamed with an aging Errol. A fair amount of laughs are managed, Davis goes through the usual body twists, and both she and Errol feed each other with a number of swift one-liners. But the plot is very weak and holds little if any interest. Davis plays the daughter of "Ma Pilkington," a small town heroine known for her great sleuthing abilities. (She also plays Ma in a brief, funny scene.) Thinking that the daughter will have the same finesse, the authorities call in Davis to solve several murders that have all been done with a blowgun. She is given Errol to help out, and the two fumble their way through a number of misleading clues until totally by accident, they discover the real killer. The unsatisfying ending, an easy way out for the writers, has the respected town doctor as the murderer : he first drugs his victims and then stabs them with poison darts, with no apparent motive. Ruth Roman, who was soon to become a major star, had a brief walk- on part as a chorus girl. When she is leaving a theater, a guard approaches her, to which she responds by opening her fur coat, revealing a very sexy gown underneath and saying, "I assure you officer, I'm not concealing anything." That's the type of line this film thrived on.

p, Warren Wilson; d, Erle C. Kenton; w, Wilson, Clyde Bruckman, Ray Singer, Dick Chevillat; ph, Jerome Ash; ed, Paul Landres; md, Frank Skinner; art d, John B. Goodman, Robert Clatworthy; cos, Vera West; m/l, "For All We Know," Sam M. Lewis, J. Fred Coots.

Comedy   **(PR:A MPAA:NR)**

SHE-GODS OF SHARK REEF*½   (1958) 63m AIP c (GB: SHARK REEF)

Don Durant (Lee), Bill Cord (Chris), Lisa Montell (Mahia), Jeanne Gerson (Dua), Carol Lindsay (Hula Dancer).

Not much of a story here, but lots of picturesque footage and beautiful native women, as Durant and Cord, the former an escaped convict, find themselves ship wrecked on an island with nothing but women who spend their time diving for pearls and going through strange rituals. Cord falls deeply in love with Montell, taking her back to civilization after saving her from being sacrificed in a ritual feeding to the sharks. Durant, on the other hand, tries to stretch his luck by making off with some pearls, and gets his just rewards when he's devoured by sharks. Title song "Nearer My Love to You" (Jack Lawrence, Frances Hall) received a moderate amount of air-play.

p, Ludwig H. Gerber; d, Roger Corman; w, Robert Hill, Victor Stoloff; ph, Floyd Crosby (Pathecolor); m, Ronald Stein; ed, Frank Sullivan.

Fantasy/Drama   **(PR:A MPAA:NR)**

SHE GOES TO WAR***   (1929) 87m Inspiration/UA bw

Eleanor Boardman (Joan Morant), John Holland (Tom Pike), Edmund Burns (Reggie), Alma Rubens (Rosie), Al St. John (Bill), Glen Walters (Katie), Margaret Seddon (Tom's Mother), Yola D'Avril (Yvette), Evelyn

Hall (Joan's Aunt), Dina Smirnova (Joan's Maid), Augustino Borgato (Major), Yvonne Starke (Major's Wife), Eulalie Jensen (Matron of Canteen), Capt. H.M. Zier (Major), Edward Chandler (Top Sergeant), Ann Warrington (Lady Hostess), Gretchen Hartman, Florence Wix (Knitting Ladies).

One of the many minor efforts by Director King, who managed to add life to an only fair script by injecting comedy, pathos, and romance in all the right spots. The yarn has to do with a spoiled rich kid, Boardman, who gets a yen to be of some use in WW I. She splits for France and meets up with the outfit of her fiance, a real coward who stays behind when the troops are called up to the front. Boardman gets her fill of action, as she is almost killed during an attack, but a fluke has her saving the rest of the outfit. Alma Rubens, in her last screen appearance, played a part as a canteen worker and gave the most solid performance of the entire cast. She is most memorable for the scene in which she pretends to be the mother of a young dying soldier, providing the most heartfelt moment of the whole film. Rubens was to die two years later at the age of 33, mainly because of the long battle she fought with drug abuse. Titles substitute for dialog for most of this early talkie.

p, Victor and Edward Halperin; d, Henry King; w, Mme. Fred De Gresac Howard Estabrook, John Monk Saunders (based on a story by Rupert Hughes); ph, Tony Gaudio, John Fulton; ed, Lloyd Nosler; art d, Albert S. D'Agostino, Robert M. Haas; m/l, "There's a Happy Land," Harry Akst.

War   **(PR:A MPAA:NR)**

SHE GOT HER MAN   (SEE: MAISIE GETS HER MAN, 1942)

SHE GOT WHAT SHE WANTED**   (1930) 81m Cruze/TIF bw

Betty Compson (Mahyna), Lee Tracy (Eddie), Alan Hale (Dave), Gaston Glass (Boris, Bookshop Owner), Dorothy Christy (Olga, the Happiness Girl), Fred Kelsey (Dugan).

Compson plays a Russian emigre to New York who dreams of a life better than that offered by her struggling writer husband, Glass. Finding her in this state, Tracy and Hale both woo her. She marries Hale, the owner of a casino who can keep her in a posh environment, while Glass continues hanging around working on his soon-to-be published book. When Hale becomes involved with some shady dealings that include murder, Compson returns to her former husband, the only man she really ever loved. Pleasant romantic drama adorned with bits of comedy.

p, Samuel Zierler; d, James Cruze; w, George Rosener; ph, C. Edgar Schoenbaum.

Drama/Comedy   **(PR:A MPAA:NR)**

SHE HAD TO CHOOSE*½   (1934) 65m Darmour/Majestic bw

Larry "Buster" Crabbe (Bill), Isabel Jewell (Sally), Sally Blane (Clara), Regis Toomey (Jack Berry), Maidel Turner (Mrs. Cutler), Fuzzy Knight (Wally), Wallis Clark, Arthur Stone, Edwin Gargan.

Crabbe is the love target of Jewell, a poor orphaned girl, and Blane, a rich society woman. Toomey, Blane's brother, is after Jewell, and following a number of unrealistic dramatics in which Jewell and Toomey marry, Crabbe kills the groom, Jewell and Crabbe finally have their go at it and Crabbe is exonerated by some legerdemain of the law. Crabbe and Blane at least attempt to act, which no one else seems to do. But the lack of plot is the real culprit.

d, Ralph Cedar; w, Houston Branch (based on a story by Mann Page, Izola Forrester); ph, James S. Brown, Jr.; ph, Charles Harris.

Drama   **(PR:A MPAA:NR)**

SHE HAD TO EAT*   (1937) 71m FOX bw

Jack Haley (Danny Decker), Rochelle Hudson (Ann Garrison), Arthur Treacher (Carter, Valet), Eugene Pallette (Raymond Q. Nash), Douglas Fowley (Duke Stacey), John Qualen (Sleepy), Maurice Cass (Fingerprint Expert), Wallis Clark (G Man), Lelah Tyler (Mrs. Cue), Tom Kennedy (Pete), Tom Dugan (Rusty), Franklin Pangborn (Mr. Phonecian-Wylie).

A weak attempt at comedy sputters along with few snickers as Haley plays an Arizona filling station operator adopted by a rich eccentric who travels around the country in his private train and drinks himself into oblivion. Spoofing starts with Haley being kidnaped by gangsters who are trying to worm some money out of the millionaire. Even Treacher, as the rich man's butler, is wasted in this unfortunate outing for comedian Haley.

p, Samuel G. Engel; d, Malcolm St. Clair; w, Engel (based on a short story by Morris Musselman, James Edward Grant); ph, Barney McGill; ed, Louis Loeffler; md, Samuel Kaylin; m/l, Sidney Clare, Harry Ault.

Comedy   **(PR:A MPAA:NR)**

SHE HAD TO SAY YES**   (1933) 64m FN-WB bw

Loretta Young (*Florence Denny*), Lyle Talbot (*Danny Drew*), Regis Toomey (*Tommy Nelson*), Suzanne Kilborn (*Birdie*), Winnie Lightner (*Maizie*), Helen Ware (*Mrs. Haines*), Ferdinand Gottschalk (*Sol Glass*), Hugh Herbert (*Luther Haines*), Harold Waldridge (*Office Boy*).

Berkeley's first solo effort as a director was hardly an indication of the popular successes he would create a few years later. Appearing in her 40th film at the age of 20, Young is a secretary who spends her time away from the office showing prospective buyers about town. This leads to romantic complications with fiance Toomey, whom she eventually drops for the more promising Talbot.

p, Henry Blanke; d, Busby Berkeley, George Amy; w, Rian James, Don Mullahy (based on the story "Customers' Girl" by John Francis Larkin); ph, Arthur Todd; ed, Ralph Dawson.

Comedy   (PR:A   MPAA:NR)

SHE HAD TO SAY YES, 1954   (SEE: SHE COULDN'T SAY NO,1954)

SHE HAS WHAT IT TAKES*½   (1943) 66m COL bw

Jinx Falkenburg (*Fay Weston*), Tom Neal (*Roger Rutledge*), Constance Worth (*June Leslie*), Douglas Leavitt (*Paul Miloff*), Joe King (*Lee Shuleman*), Mat Willis ("One Round" *Beasley*), Daniel Ocko (*Nick Partos*), George McKay (*Mike McManus*), George Lloyd ("Shocker" *Dodie*), Robert E. Homans (*Cap. Pat O'Neal*), Joseph Crehan (*George Clarke*), John H. Dilson (*Chamberlain Jones*), Barbara Brown (*Mrs. Walters*), Harry Hayden (*Mr. Jason*), Armand "Curly" Wright (*Tony*), Jack Rice (*Kimball*), Cy Ring (*Photographer*), Michael Owen, David McKim (*Call Boys*), Frank O'Connor (*Police Sergeant*), Tyler Brooke (*Stage Manager*), Ernie Adams (*Actor*), Jayne Hazard, Alma Carroll, Elizabeth Russell (*Chorus Girls*), Frank Hagney (*Trainer*), Eddie Dunn, Dave Willock (*Cab Drivers*), Eddie Chandler, Ray Teal, William Haade (*Cops*), Jack Gardner (*Clerk*), Harry Tyler (*Hotel Manager*), Richard Chandler (*Western Union Boy*), Netta Packer (*Receptionist*), Milt Kibbee, Wilbur Mack (*Men*), John Estes (*Elevator Boy*), Ann Evers (*Janesy*), Eddie Kane (*Dillway*), The Radio Rogues, The Vagabonds.

Little more than an excuse to display some minor musical talent, and long-stemmed ex-model Falkenberg's nice legs and "amateur" acting ability. Unfortunately titled yarn has Falkenberg pretending to be the daughter of a once prominent stage actress as a means of getting into a Broadway play. Neal is the Walter Winchell-like columnist bait she uses to get in to the show. But Neal's enemy columnist Worth learns of Falkenberg's true identity and sets off a bomb under the plan. A frothy, senseless thing today, it was little musical numbers like this one that gave war-weary production line workers a temporary escape from their numbing jobs. Songs include: "Let's March Together" (Saul Chaplin); "I Bumped My Head on a Star" (Cindy Walker); "Honk, Honk" (Roy Jacobs, Gene De Paul); "Timber Timber" (Don Reid, Henry Tobias); "Moon on My Pillow" (Charles, Henry, Elliot Tobias).

p, Colbert Clark; d, Charles Barton; w, Paul Yawitz (based on the story by Yawitz, Robert Lee Johnson); ph, Phillip Tannura; ed, Al Clark; md, M.W. Stoloff; art d, Lionel Banks.

Musical   (PR:A   MPAA:NR)

SHE KNEW ALL THE ANSWERS**   (1941) 85m COL bw

Joan Bennett (*Gloria Winters*), Franchot Tone (*Mark Willows*), John Hubbard (*Randy Bradford*), Eve Arden (*Sally Long*), William Tracy (*Benny*), Pierre Watkin (*George Wharton*), Almira Sessions (*Elaine Wingate*), Thurston Hall (*J.D. Sutton*), Grady Sutton (*Ogleby*), Luis Alberni (*Inventor*), Francis Compton (*Tompkins*), Dick Elliott, Selmer Jackson (*Brokers*), Roscoe Ates (*Gas Station Attendant*), Chester Clute (*Butter and Egg Man*), Frank Sully (*Cop*), Ed Conrad (*Waiter*), Patti McCarty (*Hatcheck Girl*), William Benedict (*Singing Telegraph Boy*), Fern Emmett (*Woman Applicant*), Pauline Starke (*Prim Woman*), Don Beddoe (*Barber*), Patricia Hill (*Manicurist*), Onest Conley (*Shine Boy*), George Hickman (*Elevator Operator*), Byron Foulger (*Man*), Alice Keating (*Telephone Operator*), George Beranger (*Head Waiter*), Tom Metletti (*Milkman*), Edward Earle (*Harassed Man*).

Tired story has impeccably bred Bennett in love with wealthy playboy Hubbard. They want to marry but can't because guardian and broker Tone says no. The fiery Bennett doesn't take this lightly and, deciding to show up Tone, gets a job on Wall Street and winds up falling for him, as Hubbard bows out gracefully. The only saving grace are some timely comic moments, for which Tone proves to have quite a flair, given his conservative demeanor.

p, Charles R. Rogers; d, Richard Wallace; w, Harry Segall, Kenneth Earl, Curtis Kenyon (based on the story by Jane Allen); ph, Henry Freulich; ed, Gene Havlick; md, M.W. Stoloff; art d, Lionel Banks.

Comedy   (PR:A   MPAA:NR)

SHE KNEW WHAT SHE WANTED*½   (1936, Brit.) 74m
                                                                Rialto/Wardour bw

Albert Burdon (*Dugsie*), Betty Ann Davies (*Frankie*), Claude Dampier (*Jimmy Reeves*), W.H. Berry (*Herbert*), Fred Conyngham (*Peter Thurston*), Ben Welden (*Chester*), Googie Withers (*Dora*), Hope Davy (*June*), Sybil Grove (*Mme. Piccard*), Albert le Fre (*Butler*), Murray Ashford, Edgar Sawyer, Judy Shirley, Sam Costa.

Lame tale about an obnoxious young woman [Davies! who can't seem to change her devious childish habits, despite being kicked out of a finishing school. Unlike other pictures dealing with this type of character, Davies' asocial behavior only benefits her, and eventually she winds up catching the man of her dreams.

p&d, Thomas Bentley; w, Tom Geraghty, Frank Miller (based on the play "Funny Face" by Paul Gerard Smith, Fred Thompson); ph, Curt Courant.

Comedy   (PR:A   MPAA:NR)

SHE KNOWS Y'KNOW**   (1962, Brit.) 72m Eternal/GN bw

Hylda Baker (*Hylda Worswick*), Cyril Smith (*Joe Worswick*), Joe Gibbons (*Charlie Todger*), Peter Myers (*Leslie Worswick*), Linda Castle (*Marilyn Smallhope*), Tim Connor (*Terry Roy*), Neil Wilson (*Clarence Smallhope*), Joan Sanderson (*Euphemia Smallhope*).

Mindless sex comedy which sees the desperate mother of a notorious flirt try to pin her daughter's pregnancy on her hapless lodger. Typical ribald British innuendoes abound.

p, Maurice J. Wilson; d, Montgomery Tully; w, Tully, Maurice J. Wilson (based on the play "The Reluctant Grandmother" by Kate Sullivan).

Comedy   (PR:C   MPAA:NR)

SHE LEARNED ABOUT SAILORS**   (1934) 78m FOX bw

Lew Ayres (*Larry Wilson*), Alice Faye (*Jean Legoi*), Harry Green (*Jose Pedro Alesandro Lopez Rubinstein, Impresario*), Frank Mitchell (*Peanuts*), Jack Durant (*Eddie*), Wilma Cox (*Brunette*), Paul McVey (*Hotel Clerk*), June Vlasek [Lang] (*Girl at Dance Hall*), Ray McClennan (*Recording Man*), Pete Rasch (*Russian Character*), Russ Clark (*Marine*), Gay Seabrook (*Stenographer*), James Conlin (*Irate Neighbor*), Edward LeSaint (*Justice of the Peace*), Al Hill (*Sailor*), Harry Tung (*Chinese Head Waiter*), Ernie Alexander (*Drunk*), Allen Jung, Ed Lee, Susan Fleming.

Rather obvious plot has contralto Faye as a nightclub singer in a sleazy Shanghai spot when ladies man Ayres arrives in town and sweeps her off her feet. The sailor is only in port for a short time, then returns to the U.S. with his ship. Because he doesn't feel he can support Faye on his meager wages, Ayres writes to tell her that they can't see each other again. But the letter never makes it to her; instead jokesters Mitchell and Durant send her another letter saying how much Ayres loves her, which sets the girl on the first boat to L.A. But Ayres refuses to have anything to do with Faye when she arrives, leaving Mitchell and Durant to think up a crafty scheme to get the two together. This was Rudy Vallee-discovery Faye's third film. Unfortunately she was given such poor material that she was unable to display much of her talent, though it did mark the development of some of her trademarks, such as the winking eye and quivering lip. Though Durant and Mitchell were to supply the comedy aspects, they were not very funny. Faye sings one song: "Here's the Key to My Heart" (Richard Whiting, Sidney Clare). Others include "She Learned About Sailors" (Clare, Whiting), "If I Were Adam and You Were Eve" (James Hanley).

p, John Stone; d, George Marshall; w, William Counselman, Henry Johnson (based on the story by Randall H. Faye); ph, Harry Jackson; md, Samuel Kaylin; set d, Duncan Cramer; cos, Royer.

Comedy/Drama   (PR:A   MPAA:NR)

SHE LET HIM CONTINUE   (SEE: PRETTY POISON, 1968)

SHE LOVED A FIREMAN**   (1937) 57m FN-WB bw

Dick Foran (*Red Tyler*), Ann Sheridan (*Margie Shannon*), Robert Armstrong (*Smokey Shannon*), Eddie Acuff (*Skillet*), Veda Ann Borg (*Betty*), May Beatty (*Mrs. Michaels*), Eddie Chandler (*Callaban*), Lane Chandler (*Patton*), Ted Oliver (*Lt. Grimes*), Pat Flaherty (*Duggan*), Leo White (*Barber*), Kathrin Clare Ward (*Mrs. Murphy*), Myrtle Stedman (*Mrs. Brown*), Brick Sullivan (*Man at Dance*), Janet Shaw (*Girl at Dance*), Fred "Snowflake" Toones (*Joe*), Minerva Urecal (*Nurse Purdy*), Huey White (*Turtle*), Allen Mathews (*Junior Officer*), Wilfred Lucas (*Captain*), Eddie Hart (*McDermott*).

Cowboy star Foran took off his spurs to join the fire department in this mostly-for-kiddies fare. He plays a smart aleck who winds up on the wrong side of fire captain Armstrong when he dates Armstrong's sister, Sheridan. A zestful fist fight ensues, but everything works out in the end when Foran rescues Armstrong from a blaze. Acuff is around to provide laughs, and there is enough action to keep the plot interesting.

p, Bryan Foy; d, John Farrow; w, Carlton C. Sand, Morton Grant (based on the story "Two Platoons" by Sand); ph, Lou O'Connell; ed, Thomas Pratt; m/l, M.K. Jerome, Jack Scholl.

Drama   (PR:A   MPAA:NR)

SHE LOVES ME NOT**½   (1934) 83m PAR bw

Bing Crosby (*Paul Lawton*), Miriam Hopkins (*Curly Flagg*), Kitty Carlisle (*Midge Mercer*), Edward Nugent (*Buzz Jones*), Henry Stephenson (*Dean Mercer*), Warren Hymer (*Mugg Schnitzel*), Lynne Overman (*Gus McNeal*), Judith Allen (*Frances Arbuthnot*), George Barbier (*J. Thorval Jones*), Henry Kolker (*Charles M. Lawton*), Maude Turner Gordon (*Mrs. Arbuthnot*), Margaret Armstrong (*Martha*), Ralf Harolde (*J.B.*), Matt McHugh (*Andy*), Franklyn Ardell (*Arkle*), Vince Barnett (*Baldy O'Mara*).

Better in terms of plot than the usual Crosby vehicle of the early 1930s. This film adaptation of the popular Broadway play, still running when the picture was released, has Bing and Nugent as roommates at Princeton. They take pity on Hopkins, a cabaret singer who witnessed a murder and fled for fear of involvement. They give her a place to stay but insist that she wear men's clothing to keep them from rousing suspicion. She in turn helps to wreck the engagement of Crosby to the dean's daughter, Carlisle. It's all light-spirited enough, handled briskly in both direction and writing. Bing is his usual relaxed self, with his voice doing its bit. Songs include: "Love in Bloom" (Ralph Rainger, Leo Robin), "After All, You're All I'm After" (Edward Heyman, Arthur Schwartz), "Straight from the Shoulder (Right from the Heart)," I'm Hummin (I'm Whistlin', I'm Singin'), "Put a Little Rhythm in Everything You Do" (Mack Gordon, Harry Revel), and "Cocktails for Two" (Arthur Johnston, Sam Coslow). Remade as TRUE TO THE ARMY and HOW TO BE VERY, VERY POPULAR.

p, Benjamin Glazer; d, Elliott Nugent; w, Glazer (based on the play by Howard Lindsay from the novel by Edward Hope); ph, Charles Lang; ed, Hugh Bennett; set d, A.E. Freudeman; cos, Edith Head.

Musical/Comedy   (PR:A   MPAA:NR)

SHE MADE HER BED*   (1934) 71m PAR bw

Richard Arlen (*Wild Bill Smith*), Sally Eilers (*Lura Gordon*), Robert Armstrong (*Duke Gordon*), Grace Bradley (*Eve Richards*), Roscoe Ates (*Santa Fe*), Charley Grapewin (*Joe Olsen*), Richard Arlen, Jr (*Ron*).

Inanely scripted story has Arlen in love with Eilers, and she with him, but Eilers is married to fairgrounds owner and cheat, Armstrong. A bizarre climax has the two making a show of it after a carnival tiger gets loose in the home of Eilers and Armstrong and makes a meal out of Armstrong when he attempts to rescue the baby. A fire then starts, and Eilers saves the child by putting it in the ice box as she runs out of the house. The baby is later saved, all right, and is found to have hidden itself among the vegetables, and it emerges with a chain of hot dogs around its neck, neither suffocated nor felled by pneumonia. Sound ridiculous? Armstrong's character is the only believable one in the film and he is thoroughly disliked.

d, Ralph Murphy; w, Casey Robinson, Frank R. Adams (based on the story "Baby in the Ice Box" by James M. Cain); ph, Milton Krasner.

Comedy/Drama   (PR:A   MPAA:NR)

SHE MAN, THE zero   (1967) 68m Southeastern bw

Dorian Wayne (*Dominique*), Wendy Roberts (*Secretary*), Crystal Hans, Diane O'Donnell, Jeff Gillen.

Unpleasant comedy from the man who would later go on to direct one of the most obnoxious-yet-successful comedies of all time, PORKY'S (1982), Bob Clark. THE SHE MAN details the efforts of an Army deserter to run an extortion scheme while disguised as a French maid. Totally ridiculous.

p, Charles W. Brown, Jr.; d, Bob Clark; w, Clark, Jeff Gillen (based on a story by Harris Anders); ph, Gerhard Maser; m, George Backahle; ed, Holt Gurnstein.

Comedy   (PR:C   MPAA:NR)

SHE MARRIED A COP**   (1939) 66m REP bw

Phil Regan (*Jimmy*), Jean Parker (*Linda*), Jerome Cowan (*Bob*), Dorothea Kent (*Mabel*), Benny Baker (*Sidney*), Barnett Parker (*Bekins the Butler*), Horace MacMahon (*Joe*), Oscar O'Shea (*Pa Duffy*), Mary Gordon (*Ma Duffy*), Muriel Campbell (*Minnie*), Peggy Ryan (*Trudy*), Richard Keene (*Pete*).

Regan plays a New York Irish cop with a charming singing voice. He is discovered by producers Cowan and Parker when they hear him sing at the Policeman's Ball. They need a voice for the cartoon feature they are working on – "Paddy the Pig" – and hire him. Regan thinks he is going to be a star, and tells one and all about it. As this is occurring, he and Parker marry, she never revealing to him what she has done. When the premiere comes and all his police buddies and friends are in the audience, Regan's pride takes a breathless plunge when he sees that his voice was recorded for a pig's and everybody is laughing at him. With that, he kisses off his bride and rejoins the force. But a happy reunion is quickly underway. Salkow's direction fails

to bring anybody in the script to life, and even breezy Parker acts without zest.

p, Sol C. Siegel; d, Sidney Salkow; w, Olive Cooper; ph, Ernest Miller; ed, Ernest Nims; md, Cy Feuer; art d, John Victor Mackay; m/l, "I Can't Imagine," "I'll Remember," Ralph Freed, Burton Lane (sung by Phil Regan); animation, Leon Schlesinger.

Comedy   (PR:A   MPAA:NR)

SHE MARRIED AN ARTIST*½   (1938) 78m COL bw

John Boles (*Lee Thornwood*), Luli Deste (*Toni Bonnet*), Frances Drake (*Sally Dennis*), Helen Westley (*Martha Moriarity*), Alexander D'Arcy (*Philip Corval*), Albert Van Dekker [Dekker] (*Whitney Holton*), Marek Windhelm (*Jacques*), Franklin Pangborn (*Paul*), Jacqueline Wells [Julie Bishop] (*Betty*).

Drab story about a half-crazed artist, Boles, who suddenly finds himself in demand by magazines. A model, Drake, who poses for Boles, is in love with him and he with her, but Boles first weds Deste, an old art school friend and a Paris fashion designer. A divorce, and the wise guidance of housekeeper Westley, gets the two lovers back together, with something still haunting Boles; which, apparently, the creators think to be a problem with all artists. Picture never manages to take off.

p, Sidney Buchman; d, Marion Gering; w, Delmer Daves, Gladys Lehman (based on the short story "I Married an Artist" by Avery Strakosch); ph, Merritt Gerstad; ed, Viola Lawrence; md, M.W. Stoloff; art d, Stephen Goosson.

Drama   (PR:A   MPAA:NR)

SHE MARRIED HER BOSS***   (1935) 85m COL bw

Claudette Colbert (*Julia Scott*), Michael Bartlett (*Lonnie Rogers*), Melvyn Douglas (*Richard Barclay*), Raymond Walburn (*Franklin*), Jean Dixon (*Martha*), Katherine Alexander (*Gertrude*), Edith Fellows (*Annabel*), Clara Kimball Young (*Parsons*), Grace Hayle (*Agnes*), Charles E. Arnt (*Manager of Department Store*), Schuyler Shaw, Buddy Roosevelt (*Chauffeurs*), Selmer Jackson (*Andrews*), John Hyams (*Hoyt*), Georgia Caine (*Fitzpatrick*), Edward Cooper (*Russell*), Geneva Mitchell (*Saleswoman*), Robert E. Homans, Richard J. Frank (*Detectives*), Arthur G. Wanzer, Sam Ash, David O'Brien, Louis Natheaux, Ernie Adams, John Ince, Oliver Eckhardt, Howard Chase, Harrison Greene (*Men*), William Jeffrey (*Hayden*), Grace Goodall, Arthur Stuart Hull, Dora Clement, Louis LaVoie, Corrinne William, Lillian Moore, Henry Sylvester, Billy Arnold (*Department Heads*), Adalyn Doyle, Lillian Rich (*Telephone Operators*), Lloyd Whitlock (*Department Store Manager*), Dewey Skipworth (*Stunt Driver*), Gladys Gale, Susan Lang, Ruth Clifford, Edna Lyall, Billie Van Every, Adda Gleason, Bess Flowers (*Women*), Edmund Burns, Jack Gardner (*Assistant Window Dressers*), Dorothy Short (*Girl*), Helen Woods, Ellen Clancy, Theo Holly (*Secretaries*), Hal Greene (*Office Boy*), Isabelle LaMal, Marie Wells, Billie Lee, Pat Patrick (*Saleswomen*), Lynton Brent (*News Photographer*), Rose Plummer (*Cook*), Arthur S. Byron (*Store Watchman*), Ruth Cherrington (*Old Maid Saleswoman*).

Snappy comedy in which director LaCava manages to turn what could have been a heavy, serious drama into a delightful farce that skims along with the lighthearted attitude that graces all his comedies. The plot is simple. Colbert falls in love with her boss, Douglas, and takes him to the altar. The new family she inherits is not very receptive to its latest member. This includes a prudish sister-in-law, Alexander, who is jealous of the attention Colbert receives, and a stepdaughter with a vile mouth. But Colbert soon proves who the boss is in her own calculating manner that combines experience with women's intuition. The entire cast does a grand job, making for a good time all around.

p, Everett Riskin; d, Gregory LaCava; w, Sidney Buchman (based on the story by Thyra Samter Winslow); ph, Leon Shamroy; ed, Richard Cahoon; art d, Stephen Goosson.

Comedy   (PR:A   MPAA:NR)

SHE MONSTER OF THE NIGHT
       (SEE: FRANKENSTEIN'S DAUGHTER, 1958)

SHE PLAYED WITH FIRE*½   (1957, Brit.) 95m COL bw (GB: FORTUNE IS A WOMAN)

Jack Hawkins (*Oliver Branwell*), Arlene Dahl (*Sarah Moreton*), Dennis Price (*Tracey Moreton*), Violet Farebrother (*Mrs. Moreton*), Ian Hunter (*Clive Fisher*), Malcolm Keen (*Old Abercrombie*), Geoffrey Keen (*Michael Abercrombie*), Patrick Holt (*Fred Connor*), John Robinson (*Berkeley Reckitt*), Michael Goodliffe (*Sgt. Barnes*), Martin Lane (*Watson*), Bernard Miles (*Mr. Jerome*), Christopher Lee (*Charles Highbury*), Greta Gynt (*Vere Litchen*), John Phillips (*Willis Croft*), Patricia Marmont (*Ambrosine*).

Convoluted and slow drama starring Hawkins as an insurance investigator who discovers that Price is selling valuable paintings to rich Americans and substituting forgeries that are mysteriously destroyed in fires, thus collecting twice for the same paintings. Hawkins reserves judgment, however, because Price happens to be married to his old flame Dahl, and he fears she may be implicated in the scheme. So Hawkins snoops around on his own time, and Price solves his dilemma by accidentally killing himself in one of his own fires. This opens the door for a rekindled romance between Hawkins and Dahl, and, after a decent interval, they marry. Unfortunately, there are those who surmise that Hawkins and Dahl had planned things to work out this way from the beginning. A subsequent police investigation brings a few aspects of paranoia and strain to the romance, but, as usual, all winds up for the best.

p, Frank Launder, Sidney Gilliat; d, Gilliat; w, Gilliat, Launder, Val Valentine (based on the book FORTUNE IS A WOMAN by Winston Graham); ph, Gerald Gibbs; m, William Alwyn; ed, Geoffrey Foot; md, Muir Mathieson; art d, Wilfred Shingleton.

Suspense/Drama   **(PR:C   MPAA:NR)**

SHE SHALL HAVE MURDER*   (1950, Brit.) 90m Concanen/IF bw

Rosamund John *(Jane Hamish)*, Derrick de Marney *(Dagobert Brown)*, Mary Jerrold *(Mrs. Robinson)*, Felix Aylmer *(Mr. Playfair)*, Joyce Heron *(Rosemary Proctor)*, Jack Allen *(Maj. Stewart)*, Henryetta Edwards *(Sarah Swinburne)*, Harry Fowler *(Albert Oates)*, John Bentley *(Douglas Robjohn)*, Beatrice Varley *(Mrs. Hawthorne)*, June Elvin *(Barbara Jennings)*, Jack McNaughton, Olaf Pooley, Leon Davey, Denys Val Norton, Francis de Wolff, Jonathan Field, Jimmy Rhodes, Anthony Hilton, Frances Leak, Wanda Rands, Duncan Lamont.

Slow as molasses murder mystery starring beautiful John as a law clerk and aspiring mystery writer who finds herself embroiled in a real-life killing when one of her company's clients turns up murdered. John becomes determined to discover the identity of the murderer, and after what seems to be weeks she does so.

p, Derrick de Marney, Guido Coen; d, Daniel Birt; w, Allan Mackinnon (based on the novel by Delano Ames); ph, Robert Navarro.

Crime   **(PR:A   MPAA:NR)**

SHE SHALL HAVE MUSIC** (1935, Brit.) 92m Imperial/Twickenham bw

June Clyde *(Dorothy Drew)*, Claude Dampier *(Eddie)*, Bryan Lawrence *(Brian Gates)*, Gwen Farrar *(Miss Peachum)*, Marjorie Brooks *(Mrs. Marlowe)*, Edmond Breon *(Freddie Gates)*, Felix Aylmer *(Black)*, Jack Hylton and His Band, Mathea Merryfield, Magda Neeld, Diana Ward, Two Mackeys, Carmona, Baby Terry, Freddie Schweitzer, Terry's Juveniles, Sonny Farrar, Billie Carlisle, Ernest Sefton, Leslie Carew, Langley Howard, Eddie Hooper, Billy Mann, Ken Smoothy, Leon Woizikowski Ballet, The Dalmora Can-Can Dancers.

Light entertainment is mainly an excuse to show off a number of musical talents, particularly those of Jack Hylton, a wildly popular British band leader of the time, who has been hired by a wealthy businessman to broadcast from aboard his cruiser. A business rival wrecks the scheme but the entertainment remains intact.

p, Julius Hagen; d, Leslie H. Hiscott; w, Arthur Macrae, H. Fowler Mear, Paul England, C. Denier Warren; ph, Sidney Blythe, William Luff; ch, Howard Deighton; m/l, Maurice Sigler, Al Goodhart, Al Hoffman, Jimmy Kennedy, Michael Carr.

Musical/Comedy   **(PR:A   MPAA:NR)**

SHE SHOULDA SAID NO   (SEE: WILD WEED, 1949)

SHE STEPS OUT   (SEE: HARMONY AT HOME, 1930)

SHE WANTED A MILLIONAIRE*½   (1932) 80m FOX bw

Joan Bennett *(Jane Miller)*, Spencer Tracy *(William Kelly)*, Una Merkel *(Mary Taylor)*, James Kirkwood *(Roger Norton)*, Dorothy Peterson *(Mrs. Miller)*, Douglas Cosgrove *(Mr. Miller)*, Donald Dillaway *(Humphrey)*, Tetsu Komai *(Charlie)*, Lucille LaVerne *(Mother Norton)*.

A millionaire is exactly what beauty contest winner Bennett got in Kirkwood, but this one is plagued with a jealous streak a mile long, interspersed with bouts of insanity. When Kirkwood winds up dead after attempting to kill his spouse by trying to feed her to a bunch of dogs, Bennett goes back to original sweetheart Tracy. The picture is scripted and directed in a very uneven manner. It starts out on a light enough key, but quickly gets lost in heavy dramatics which are taken far too seriously by the creators. Even the talents of Tracy, who can usually make anything look at least decent, and Bennett have trouble generating any enthusiasm.

p, John Considine, Jr.; d, John Blystone; w, William Anthony McGuire (based on the story by Sonya Levien); ph, John Seitz; ed, Ralph Dixon; md, George Lipschultz.

Drama   **(PR:A   MPAA:NR)**

SHE WAS A HIPPY VAMPIRE
              (SEE: WILD WORLD OF BATWOMAN, THE, 1966)

SHE WAS A LADY*½   (1934) 77m FOX bw

Helen Twelvetrees *(Sheila Vane)*, Donald Woods *(Tommy Traill)*, Ralph Morgan *(Stanley Vane)*, Monroe Owsley *(Jerry Couzins)*, Paul Harvey *(Jeff Dyer)*, Doris Lloyd *(Alice Vane)*, Harold Goodwin *(Yank)*, Barbara Weeks *(Moira)*, Jackie Searl *(Herbie Vane)*, Karol Kay *(Sheila, the Child)*, Ann Howard *(Iris Vane)*.

Slow-paced drama of class consciousness has Twelvetrees as the daughter of a disinherited English aristocrat, now making do in the U.S. Dad dies before Twelvetrees can make any claim to her aristocratic past which proves a problem when she romances a young man whose wealthy father doesn't approve of her background. But Twelvetrees turns out to be a lady and the father quickly agrees to the marriage. Plot and performances fail to generate any moments of excitement.

p, Al Rockett; d, Hamilton MacFadden; w, Gertrude Purcell (based on the novel by Elisabeth Cobb); ph, Bert Glennon; ed, Dorothy Spencer.

Drama   **(PR:A   MPAA:NR)**

SHE WAS ONLY A VILLAGE MAIDEN**   (1933, Brit.) 60m Sound City/MGM bw

Anne Grey *(Priscilla Protheroe)*, Lester Matthews *(Frampton)*, Carl Harbord *(Peter)*, Barbara Everest *(Agatha)*, Julian Royce *(Duke of Buckfast)*, Antony Holles *(Vicar)*, Gertrude Sterroll *(Lady Lodden)*, Daphne Scorer *(Emily)*, Ella Daincourt *(Mrs. Cruickshank)*.

Grey, romantically inclined and longing for a man at 30 years of age, is left a fortune by one of the two older sisters with whom she lives. The only condition of the will states that Grey must leave the other sister for six months. Once word of her inheritance leaks out, Grey finds herself deluged with suitors. To defuse their interest, Grey declares herself engaged to lawyer Matthews, and in the end it is he whom she actually marries.

p, Ivar Campbell; d, Arthur Maude; w, John Cousins, N.W. Baring-Pemberton (based on the play "Priscilla the Rake" by Fanny Bowker).

Comedy/Romance   **(PR:A   MPAA:NR)**

SHE WENT TO THE RACES*½   (1945) 86m MGM bw

James Craig *(Steve Canfield)*, Frances Gifford *(Dr. Ann Wotters)*, Ava Gardner *(Hilda Spotts)*, Edmund Gwenn *(Dr. Pecke)*, Sig Rumann *(Dr. Gurke)*, Reginald Owen *(Dr. Pembroke)*, J.M. Kerrigan *(Jeff Habbard)*, Charles Halton *(Dr. Collyer)*, Frank Orth *(Bartender)*, Chester Clute *(Mason)*, Buster Keaton *(Bellboy)*, Matt Moore *(Duffy)*, John Dehner *(Announcer)*, Johnny Forrest *(Usher)*.

Story line has Gifford as a professor who develops a scientific system for beating the horses. Troubles arise when she falls for Craig, a horse owner. In competition for Craig is Gardner, a high society debutante. Unfortunately, the humor is forced and the plot weak.

p, Frederick Stephani; d, Willis Goldbeck; w, Lawrence Hazard (based on the story by Alan Friedman, DeVallon Scott); ph, Charles Salerno; m, Nathaniel Shilkret; ed, Adrienne Fazan; art d, Cedric Gibbons, Preston Ames; set d, Edwin B. Willis.

Comedy   **(PR:A   MPAA:NR)**

SHE WHO DARES   (SEE: THREE RUSSIAN GIRLS, 1943)

SHE-WOLF, THE**   (1931) 90m UNIV bw (AKA: MOTHER'S MILLIONS)

May Robson *(Harriet Breen)*, James Hall *(David Talbot)*, Lawrence Gray *(Tom Breen)*, Frances Dade *(Faire Breen)*, Edmund Breese *(William Remington)*, Lillian Harmer *(Maria Peppy, Housekeeper)*, Leah Winslow *(Mrs. Talbot)*, Elinor Flynn *(Peggy)*, William L. Thorne *(Detective Burke)*.

Robson plays a Wall Street businesswoman who crushes anything that gets in her way. Her main goal is to destroy her late husband's business adversary, whom she hates with a vengeance. She neglects her family, but through her artful manipulation, she manages to keep them satisfied. Robson, a native of Australia, began acting to support her children after she was left a widow. She appeared in several stage productions and on Broadway. She developed into a respected character actress at the turn of the century and occasionally appeared in silent films. Her career peaked, however, in the 1930s, when she won roles in several major Hollywood productions. She typically portrayed domineering society matrons, but is remembered most for her role as Apple Annie in Frank Capra's LADY FOR A DAY, for which she received an Oscar nomination.

d, James Flood; w, Winifred Dunn, Gene Lewis (based on the play "Mother's Millions" by Howard McKent Barnes); ph, Ernest Hall.

Drama   **(PR:A   MPAA:NR)**

SHE-WOLF, THE** (1963, USSR) 50m Gorky Film Studio/Artkino bw
(U KRUTOGO YARA)

Valeriy Isakov (*Senya*), M. Chebotarenko (*Masha*), V. Markin (*Kostya*), G. Svetlani-Penkovskiy (*Gurey*), P. Lyubeshkin (*Aleksey Stepanovich*), V. Ivanov (*Korney Petrovich*), A. Titov, T. Savich, V. Nosik, L. Burkova.

A tale of Russian peasantry about a young man who outsmarts a couple of wolves he has been assigned by the villagers to hunt down. His method involves gaining the trust of the wolves by letting them adjust to his presence. This makes the local villagers distrustful and skeptical of the young man. But he proves to be the wiser by entering the lair, stealing a cub, and killing the adult wolves when they return.

d&w, Kira Muratov, A. Muratov (based on a story by G. Troye Polskiy); ph, A. Maslennikov; m, O. Karavaychuk; ed, R. Skoretskaya; art d, I. Zakharova, M. Khablenko; spec eff, A. Petukhov.

Adventure   **(PR:A   MPAA:NR)**

SHE-WOLF OF LONDON*½   (1946) 61m UNIV bw

Don Porter (*Harry Lanfield*), June Lockhart (*Phyllis Allenby*), Sara Haden (*Martha Winthrop*), Jan Wiley (*Carol Winthrop*), Dennis Hoey (*Inspector Pierce*), Lloyd Corrigan (*Latham*), Eily Malyon (*Hannah, Maid*), Martin Kosleck (*Dwight Severn*), Frederic Worlock (*Constable*), Clara Blandick (*Mrs. McBroom*).

Turn-of-the-century London is the setting for this unsuspenseful, low-budget horror film, starring Lockhart as the last descendant of a family under a werewolf curse. After a series of murders occur, the young girl, told by aunt Haden she's part werewolf, is convinced she is the culprit. She breaks off her engagement to Porter, who loves Lockhart enough to track down the real killer, and thus win her back.

p, Ben Pivar; d, Jean Yarbrough; w, George Bricker (based on the story by Dwight V. Babcock); ph, Maury Gertsman; ed, Paul Landres; md, William Lava; art d, Jack Otterson, Abraham Grossman; set d, Russell A. Gausman, Leigh Smith.

Crime/Mystery   **(PR:A   MPAA:NR)**

SHE WORE A YELLOW RIBBON****   (1949) 103m Argosy/RKO c

John Wayne (*Capt. Nathan Brittles*), Joanne Dru (*Olivia Dandridge*), John Agar (*Lt. Flint Cohill*), Ben Johnson (*Sgt. Tyree*), Harry Carey, Jr. (*Lt. Ross Pennell*), Victor McLaglen (*Sgt. Quincannon*), Mildred Natwick (*Mrs. Abby Allshard*), George O'Brien (*Maj. Mack Allshard*), Arthur Shields (*Dr. O'Laughlin*), Francis Ford (*Barman*), Harry Woods (*Karl Rynders*), Chief John Big Tree (*Pony That Walks*), Noble Johnson (*Red Shirt*), Cliff Lyons (*Trooper Cliff*), Tom Tyler (*Cpl. Mike Quayne*), Michael Dugan (*Sgt. Hochbauer*), Mickey Simpson (*Wagner*), Fred Graham (*Hench*), Frank McGrath (*Trumpeter/Indian*), Don Summers (*Jenkins*), Fred Libby (*Col. Krumrein*), Jack Pennick (*Sergeant Major*), Billy Jones (*Courier*), Bill Goettinger, , Post Parks (*Noncommissioned Officers*), Fred Kennedy (*Badger*), Rudy Bowman (*Pvt. John Smith/Gen. Rome Clay, C.S.A.*), Ray Hyke (*McCarthy*), Lee Bradley (*Interpreter*), Chief Sky Eagle (*Indian*), Paul Fix (*Gunrunner*), Irving Pichel (*Narrator*), Paul Fix.

The second of John Ford's "Cavalry Trilogy" has Wayne in one of the best performances of his life and Oscar-winning photography of a Technicolored Monument Valley. Wayne is a career officer in the U.S. Cavalry marking off on a calendar the final days before his retirement from the service. In the wake of the massacre of Custer and the Seventh Cavalry, the local Indians are becoming restless, and worse, confident. Wayne is assigned to escort two women (Dru and Natwick) from the fort to the stagecoach stop at Sudrow's Wells. Along the way they spot a large concentration of hostile Arapahos, but because of the women they must avoid a fight and make a long detour around the force, thereby missing a rendezvous with another patrol. When they finally arrive, late, they find the other party has been attacked and barely held out. A wounded soldier asks Wayne where he was, and Wayne can only answer that he wanted to be there. Seeing the danger this attack foretells, Wayne sends off a detachment to ride to Sudrow's Wells to warn the people there, but the troop arrives late again, and the Indians have attacked and burned the stage and killed a number of civilians and soldiers. One mortally wounded trooper, an old man, is revealed to be a former Confederate general, retreated now to the lowest level of service as a sort of monastic discipline. A number of men gather around him as he dies, all of them former comrades in the Confederate cavalry, including sergeant Johnson, whom the dying man calls "captain." Wayne allows him to be buried under an improvised Confederate Stars-and-Bars with the honors due a general. With no chance now to get the women evacuated from the area, Wayne heads back to the fort as quickly as possible. Along the way scout Johnson watches as the fort sutler tries to sell the Indians Winchester rifles. When he tries to demand his payment, they simply shoot him. Wayne and his force are pursued hard now, and at a river crossing he leaves a rear guard under the command of Agar. Returning to the fort, Wayne is upset because his entire mission has been a frustrating string of delays and too-late arrivals. He immediately makes preparations to go back out to relieve Agar, but fort commander O'Brien reminds him that his retirement is the next day and orders a troop under green lieutenant Carey to go out in the morning. O'Brien tells Wayne that Agar and Carey must learn to

make a river crossing under fire, just like they did when they were green. Wayne tries to go along as an advisor, but O'Brien tells him: "Every time Cohill 'Agar' gave an order, men would turn round and look at you–they'd wonder if he was doing the right thing." Before the troop moves out in the morning, they present Wayne with a pocket watch; he has to pull a pair of spectacles out of his blouse to read the inscription "Lest we forget." The men then ride out, leaving Wayne behind. Later he sadly rides out of the fort, but he rides straight to the troop, finding them on a ridge overlooking the main hostile encampment. With Johnson he rides boldly into the village and up to the old chief, a long-time friend of Wayne's (played by Seneca chief John Big Tree, this aging Indian's face may be familiar to numismatists–in 1912 he posed for the Indian head nickel). The Indian tells Wayne that the war is beyond his control, and that he has relinquished his leadership of the village to younger men, just as Wayne must. He tries to get Wayne to go away with him to go buffalo hunting and "smoke many peace pipes," but Wayne tells him he cannot. The two men ride out of the village unmolested, but Wayne has the information he wants–the location of the pony herd. Back on the ridge, he looks at his watch and announces it to be a few minutes before midnight, the official time of his retirement. He orders a charge into the village that scatters the ponies and makes the Indian threat empty. After the attack, pulled off with no casualties, Wayne again looks at his watch and pronounces the time as 12:02 and himself as officially retired. He tells Agar to follow at a distance so as not to hurt the Indian's pride as they walk back to the reservation, then again rides off. But soon a rider catches up to him, Johnson, bringing news that he has been appointed civilian chief of scouts. They ride back to the fort where a dance is being held in his honor, but Wayne stays only a moment before walking out to a hilltop to speak to the graves of his wife and daughters who died on the frontier. Wayne gives one of the finest performances of his career here, the first serious role Ford had ever given him. Wayne later said, "Jack 'Ford' never respected me as an actor until I made RED RIVER." As Capt. Brittles, a man a full generation older than the actor, Wayne is at his most human. He plays a man who has made the Army his whole life, even sacrificing the lives of his family to it, now having to watch his Army career disappear, and ending it on a note of failure. The passing of time is the recurring theme: Wayne arriving late with his troops, being forced to retire because of his age, leaving the dance to speak to his dead wife. Even the inscription on the watch plays on this theme of time lost and recalled. The Monument Valley location has never been used to such beautiful advantage. Ford had shot here before with STAGECOACH and FORT APACHE, and he knew his way around the landscapes and the roads leading to them. He shot the film in just 31 days and a half- million dollars under budget. On the set he clashed with cinematographer Hoch, a technical perfectionist who would endlessly fiddle with his camera while the cast baked in the sun. One day on the floor of the desert, a line of threatening clouds darkened the horizon, foretelling a thunderstorm. Hoch started to pack up his equipment but Ford ordered him to continue shooting. Hoch did as he was ordered, but filed an official protest with his union. The shot that emerged, a fantastic purple sky with jagged streaks of lightning arcing to earth in the distance, was breathtaking and helped Hoch win an Oscar for his work on the film. Ford's main inspiration for the scenic look of the film was the western paintings of Frederic Remington. He later told Peter Bogdanovich, "I tried to get his color and movement and I think I succeeded partly." The only thing that keeps this film from ranking as a masterpiece is Ford's eternal weakness for injecting physical comedy into his stories, especially comedy in an Irish vein, here carried off by McLaglen. The most striking feature of the film is its structure, heaping anticlimax on anticlimax for the entire last half of the film. From almost the halfway point of the picture scenes seem to build to a rousing end, only to trickle away as the next scene picks up: when the troop rides out after giving Wayne his watch; when Wayne himself leaves the fort, after running off the Indian pony herd, and again at the dance, where Wayne leaves everyone celebrating while he goes to look again at his past, the graves of his family. At the same time, Dru makes her choice between the two young lieutenants, opting for Agar, and Carey is last seen staring out into the darkness, destined to follow the same life as Wayne. But the film ends on a mythic note–as cavalrymen ride across the desert, a narrator intones: "So here they are, the dog-faced soldiers, the regulars, the 50 cents-a-day professionals, riding the outposts of a nation. From Fort Reno to Fort Apache, from Sheridan to Stark, they were all the same. Men in dirty shirt blue, and only a cold page in the history books to mark their passing. But wherever they rode, and whatever they fought for, that place became the United States."

p, John Ford, Merian C. Cooper; d, Ford; w, Frank Nugent, Laurence Stallings (based on the stories "War Party" and "The Big Hunt" by James Warner Bellah); ph, Winton C. Hoch, Charles P. Boyle (Technicolor); m, Richard Hageman; ed, Jack Murray; md, Constantin Bakaleinikoff; art d, James Basevi; set d, Joe Kish; cos, Michael Meyers, Ann Peck; spec eff, Jack Cosgrove, Jack Caffee.

Western   **Cas.**   **(PR:A   MPAA:NR)**

SHE WOULDN'T SAY YES**½   (1945) 87m COL bw

Rosalind Russell (*Susan Lane*), Lee Bowman (*Michael Kent*), Adele Jergens (*Allura*), Charles Winninger (*Dr. Lane*), Harry Davenport (*Albert*), Sara Haden (*Laura Pitts*), Percy Kilbride (*Judge Whittaker*), Lewis Russell (*Col. Brady*), Mary Green (*Passenger*), Mabel Paige (*Mrs. Whittaker*), George

Cleveland *(Ticket Seller)*, Charles Arnt *(Train Conductor)*, Almira Sessions *(Miss Downer)*, Mantan Moreland, Willie Best *(Porters)*, Ida Moore, Eily Malyon *(Spinsters)*, Arthur Q. Bryan *(Little Man)*, John Tyrrell *(Traveling Salesman)*, Ernest Whitman *(Bartender)*, Dudley Dickerson *(Waiter)*, Cora Witherspoon *(Patient)*, Marilyn Johnson, Doris Houck *(Girls)*, Darren McGavin *(The Kid)*, Sam McDaniel *(Steward)*, Clarence Muse, Jesse Graves, Nick Stewart *(Other Porters)*, Carl "Alfalfa" Switzer *(Delivery Boy)*, Ed Gargan, Tom Dugan *(Cab Drivers)*.

A mildly amusing Russell comedy which sees the statuesque star as a well-respected psychiatrist seeking to prove her theory that a person can maintain a healthy mental attitude if he retains strict control of his emotions. Into her life stumbles the perfect guinea pig, Bowman, a goofy cartoonist whose successful character "Nixie" is the antithesis of Russell's theory. In the funny papers "Nixie" advocates free emotions and immediate action on impulses as the road to happiness. The differences between Russell and Bowman lead to some predictable comedy situations, and they also manage to fall in love. Effective but uninspired.

p, Virginia Van Upp; d, Alexander Hall; w, Van Upp, John Jacoby, Sarett Tobias (based on a story by Láslo Gorog, William Thiele); ph, Joseph Walker; m, Marlin Skiles; ed, Viola Lawrence; md, Morris Stoloff; art d, Stephen Goosson, Van Nest Polglase; set d, Wilbur Menefee.

Comedy   **(PR:A MPAA:NR)**

SHE WROTE THE BOOK½   (1946) 74m UNIV bw

Joan Davis *(Jane Featherstone)*, Jack Oakie *(Jerry Marlowe)*, Mischa Auer *(Boris/Joe)*, Kirby Grant *(Eddie Caldwell)*, Jacqueline DeWit *(Millicent)*, John Litel *(Dean Fowler)*, Thurston Hall *(Van Cleve)*, Lewis L. Russell *(George Dixon)*, Raymond Largay *(Governor Kilgour)*, Verna Felton *(Mrs. Kilgour)*, Jack J. Ford *(Orchestra Leader)*, Phil Garris *(Elevator Boy)*, Edgar Dearing *(Motorcycle Cop)*, Selmer Jackson *(Fielding)*, Cora Witherspoon *(Carrothers)*, Olin Howlin *(Baggage Master)*, Walden Boyle, Frank Dae *(Professors)*, Marie Harmon *(Blonde)*, Milton Charleston, Pat Lane *(Reporters)*, Chester Conklin *(Man at Bar)*, George Bunny *(Gardner)*, Wilbur Mack *(Man on Train)*, Gloria Stuart *(Phyllis Fowler)*, Victoria Horne *(Maid)*.

Lighthearted tale has Davis as the conservative math teacher at a midwestern university. On the insistence of the dean's wife, she goes to New York to collect the royalties for a zesty romance novel. But a knock on the head has Davis believing she really is the author. Oakie is the publisher who has cooked up a nifty publicity scene that involves the posing authoress. After some torrid adventures with a phony Russian count, Auer, Davis regains her faculties and returns to her sedate life on campus. All for the laughs, which Davis delivers in her own unusual style, having Oakie as good support.

p, Warren Wilson; d, Charles Lamont; w, Wilson, Oscar Brodney; ph, George Robinson; ed, Fred R. Feitchans, Jr.; md, Edgar Fairchild; art d, Jack Otterson, Richard H. Reidel.

Comedy   **(PR:A MPAA:NR)**

SHEBA BABY*   (1975) 90m AIP c

Pam Grier *(Sheba)*, Austin Stoker *(Brick)*, D'Urville Martin *(Pilot)*, Rudy Challenger *(Andy)*, Dick Merrifield *(Shark)*, Christopher Joy *(Walker)*, Charles Kissinger *(Phil)*, Charles Broaddus *(Hammerhead)*, Maurice Downes *(Killer)*, Ernest Cooley *(Whale)*, Edward Reece, Jr *(Racker)*, William Foster, Jr *(Waldo)*, Bobby Cooley *(Tank)*, Sylvia Jacobson *(Tail)*, Paul Grayber *(Fin)*, Leroy Clark, Jr *(Customer)*, Mike Clifford *(Policeman No. 2)*, Rose Ann Deel *(Policewoman)*.

Black exploitation that mainly a vehicle to show off Grier's looks, as well as a tough black woman making a shambles of the crooked white folk. In this case she gains vengeance on her father's murder by exposing the wealthy white businessman responsible for the terrorism. Grier proves a match for the toughest hood, with a .44 to back her up. Audiences went to the theater in droves, but the phase died fairly quickly.

p, David Sheldon; d&w, William Girdler (based on a story by Sheldon, Girdler); ph, William Asman (Movielab Color); m, Monk Higgins, Alex Brown; ed, Henry Asman, Jack Davies; prod d, J. Patrick Kelly III; spec eff, Gene Grigg; m/l, Cleveland and Ranifere (sung by Barbara Mason).

Crime   **(PR:C MPAA:PG)**

SHED NO TEARS*½   (1948) 70m EL bw

Wallace Ford *(Sam Grover)*, June Vincent *(Edna Grover)*, Robert Scott *(Ray Belden)*, Johnstone White *(Huntington Stewart)*, Dick Hogan *(Tom Grover)*, Frank Albertson *(Hutton)*.

Poorly handled production has Ford feigning death at the urgings of his wife, Vincent, in order to cash in on an insurance policy. Hogan, Ford's son by a previous marriage, smells something fishy and hires detective Scott to do some investigating. But this twist in the plot is quickly brought to an end when the detective is bought off. Easy cop-out for the story has Ford jumping to his death when he discovers his wife has been carrying on with someone else with her new-found wealth. Story plods most of the way through; only the performance of Ford breathes some life into the stagnant

material.

p, Robert Frost; d, Jean Yarbrough; w, Brown Holmes, Virginia Cook (based on the novel by Don Martin); ph, Frank Redman; ed, Norman A. Cerf; md, Ralph Stanley; art d, Walter Koessler; set d, Fay Babcock; cos, Lon Anthony.

Crime/Drama   **(PR:A MPAA:NR)**

SHEEPDOG OF THE HILLS**   (1941, Brit.) 76m BUT bw

David Farrar *(Rev. Michael Verney)*, Philip Friend *(Dr. Peter Hammond)*, Helen Perry *(Francis Miller)*, Dennis Wyndham *(Riggy Teasdale)*, Len Sharp *(Geordie Scott)*, Jack Vyvyan *(Constable Scott)*, Arthur Denton *(Hawkins)*, Philip Godfrey *(Sam Worrow)*, Johnnie Schofield *(Tom Abbott)*, Moss the Dog.

Moss the Sheepdog steals the show in this touching drama from the Devon countryside, where preacher Farrar must battle his own desires as he marries the woman with whom he is in love to another man. While the preacher is contending with this problem, the farmers in the area have their own troubles; their sheep have been mysteriously disappearing. The only man who manages to keep his animals is Wyndham, because, or so the others think, he has a particularly good sheepdog. However, this dog has been trained to steal sheep and bring them to Wyndham. When this is discovered Wyndham is drowned trying to escape, and Moss makes the newlyweds a present of four sheep.

p, F.W. Baker; d, Germain Burger; w, Kathleen Butler, Vera Allinson; ph, Burger.

Drama   **(PR:A MPAA:NR)**

SHEEPMAN, THE***   (1958) 85m MGM c

Glenn Ford *(Jason Sweet)*, Shirley MacLaine *(Dell Payton)*, Leslie Nielsen *(Johnny Bledsoe, Col. Stephen Bedford)*, Mickey Shaughnessy *(Jumbo McCall)*, Edgar Buchanan *(Milt Masters)*, Willis Bouchey *(Mr. Payton)*, Pernell Roberts *(Choctaw)*, Slim Pickens *(Marshal)*, Buzz Henry *(Red)*, Pedro Gonzales Gonzales *(Angelo)*, Harry Woods, Roscoe Ates, Harry Harvey, Tom Greenway.

A pleasant, amusing western starring Ford as a sheep rancher who runs into trouble while driving his herds through cattle territory. In Powder Valley he is met with opposition from an entire town which is run by cattle baron Nielsen, whose will is enforced by gunslinger Shaughnessy. Fearing that his sheep will ruin the grazing land for the cattle, Nielsen dispatches Shaughnessy and his men to raid Ford's camp. In the battle, several of Ford's men are killed and the enraged sheep rancher sets out to destroy Nielsen. Ford learns that Nielsen has concealed his past as an infamous gunslinger known as Johnny Bledsoe and he enlists town windbag Buchanan to help him expose the cattle baron. While in town, Ford also learns that the spunky MacLaine is engaged to marry Nielsen, but she has second thoughts after meeting the noble Ford. Continuing his campaign against Nielsen, Ford confronts the hulking Shaughnessy in a bar, and after ordering a glass of milk for himself, humiliates the gunslinger and proves him to be a coward. There follows a showdown between Ford and Nielsen, despite MacLaine's attempts to point out the absurdity of the situation. Now in love with Ford, MacLaine gets the drop on the extra shooters that Nielsen brought along for help, thus allowing for a fair showdown. To no one's surprise, Ford wins the battle and MacLaine. Though most viewers familiar with the western have seen all this before, THE SHEEPMAN is successful because it pokes fun at the age-old cattlemen vs. sheepherders rivalry that has been dramatized in everything from Charles Starrett oaters to George Stevens' SHANE (1953). Under the skillful helm of veteran director Marshall, THE SHEEPMAN offers up a charming spoof of the genre, while remaining honest and respectful of its roots. The film doesn't make fun of westerns as Mel Brooks did in BLAZING SADDLES (1974), but instead has fun *with* them. MacLaine is relaxed, refreshing, and funny in this early phase of her career, as is veteran actor Ford, but it is Buchanan who steals the show as the mischievous loudmouth. Solid family entertainment.

p, Edmund Grainger; d, George Marshall; w, William Bowers, James Edward Grant (based on a story by Grant, adapted by William Roberts); ph, Robert Bronner (CinemaScope, Metrocolor); m, Jeff Alexander; ed, Ralph E. Winters; art d, William A. Horning, Malcolm Brown; set d, Henry Grace, Hugh Hunt; cos, Walter Plunkett; makeup, William Tuttle.

Western/Comedy   **(PR:A MPAA:NR)**

SHEHERAZADE   (SEE: SCHEHERAZADE 1965, Fr./Ital./Span.)

SHEIK STEPS OUT, THE*½   (1937) 65m REP bw

Ramon Novarro *(Ahmed Ben Nesib)*, Lola Lane *(Flip Murdock)*, Gene Lockhart *(Sam Murdock)*, Kathleen Burke *(Gloria Parker)*, Stanley Fields *(Abu Saal)*, Billy Bevan *(Munson)*, Charlotte Treadway *(Polly Parker)*, Robert Coote *(Lord Byington)*, Leonid Kinskey *(Allusi Ali)*, Georges Renavent *(Mario)*, Jamiel Hasson *(Kisub)*, C. Montague Shaw *(Minister)*, George Sorel *(Lt. Bordeaux)*.

Novarro, the once popular romantic lead of the silents with BEN HUR as his most famous leading role, tried his hand unsuccessfully in this talkie where he plays an Arab sheik. Lane is a spoiled rich American, whose father made his millions selling corkscrews. She wagers her English fiance that she can find a horse faster than any in his stable and goes off to Arabia with her insipid father, comical aunt, and bratty cousin. There the uncouth Americans mistake Novarro, a sheik who breeds some of the fastest horses in the world, for a baggage porter and travel guide. He decides to teach the ill-mannered Yanks a lesson by staging a fake kidnaping of Lane and then abandoning her in the desert. His final joke on her fiance is when he snatches her from the altar during their wedding ceremony and takes her for his own bride.

p, Herman Schlom; d, Irving Pichel; w, Adele Buffington, Gordon Khan (based on a story by Buffington); ph, Jack Marta; ed, Murray Seldeen, Ernest Nims; md, Alberto Colombo; m/l, Feliz Bernard, Winston Tharp, Elsie Janis, Colombo.

Drama/Musical (PR:A MPAA:NR)

SHEILA LEVINE IS DEAD AND LIVING IN NEW YORK**

(1975) 113m PAR c

Jeannie Berlin (*Sheila Levine*), Roy Scheider (*Sam Stoneman*), Rebecca Dianna Smith (*Kate*), Janet Brandt (*Bernice*), Sid Melton (*Manny*), Charles Woolf (*Wally*), Leda Rogers (*Agatha*), Jack Bernardi (*Uncle Herm*), Allen Secher (*Rabbi*), Talley Parker (*Rochelle*), Jon Miller (*Norman*), Noble Willingham (*Principal*), Richard Rasof (*Attendant*), Evelyn Russell (*Miss Burke*), Don Carrara (*Harold*), Sharon Martin Goldman (*Melissa*), Karen Anders (*Aunt Min*), Craig Littler (*Steve*), Sandy Helberg (*Artist*), John Morgan Evans (*Conductor*), Charles Walker (*Engineer*), Charles Arthur (*Clerk*), Cecilia McBride, Susan Waugh (*Typists*), Erin Fleming (*Girl*), Lyle Moraine (*Pianist*), Sandra Golden, Victor Raphael (*Performers*).

An attempt to portray the life of urbanites in their cosmic struggle falls flat most of the time as the actors grab for humor that isn't there. Still, there is enough recognizability to make for a few chuckles. Anyone who lives in a city where the buildings are taller than the pickup trucks will know someone like the protagonists. Berlin is a frumpy suburbanite who makes her way to the East Side of Manhattan. She brings with her all the neuroses and insecurities of generations, but she seems able to cope with her upbringing and the layers of guilt which have supposedly been lathered upon her head. She wanders into a singles bar one evening, meets Scheider, a doctor, and they have a one-night stand. To Scheider it's just an evening, but to Berlin, it's the love of her life, so, as is so often the case, one is the smitten and the other is the smittee. When Scheider snubs her, Berlin is in mental pain and she gets even more upset when the physician begins to date her swinging roommate, Smith. Nothing much happens to change anyone in the picture, but we are treated to at least a cursory examination of life in New York in the early 1970s. The movie makes points when it examines the life of the "struggler," the woman not so fair of face and with no talent or ambition who realizes that she has to get someone with those qualities or be left behind. Berlin is one of those many who are destined to be left on the side while the grand scheme of things continues. The picture might have been shot with a "banaloscope" as the details are those appreciated by ordinary folks, not the Hollywood or Fifth Avenue glitzers. Berlin is excellent and comes by her believable acting genetically, as she is the daughter of Elaine May. Scheider is also good and Melton and Brandt are convincing as Berlin's middle-class parents. Leda Rogers does an interesting, albeit extraneous, bit as the lesbian next door. The screenwriters were long-time TV sketch writers for Carol Burnett and other variety artists and, at times, some of this looks like a skit. To his credit, director Furie put aside his bag of cinematic tricks to attempt a more conventional telling of a story. A few sharp lines and comments, but most of the characters have been seen all too often before. Talsky's costume design is right on the money.

p, Harry Korshak; d, Sidney J. Furie; w, Kenny Solms, Gail Parent (based on the novel by Parent); ph, Donald M. Morgan (Panavision, Technicolor); m, Michel Legrand; ed, Argyle Nelson; prod d, Fernando Carrere; set d, Reg Allen; cos, Ronald Talsky; m/l, Leo Robin, Ralph Rainger, Hal David, Leon Carr.

Comedy Cas. (PR:A-C MPAA:PG)

SHE'LL HAVE TO GO (SEE: MAID FOR MURDER, 1963, Brit.)

SHELL SHOCK* (1964) 84m Canyon Productions/Parade Releasing Organization bw

Beach Dickerson (*Rance*), Carl Crow (*Johnny Wade*), Frank Leo (*Gil Evans*), Pamela Grey (*Maria*), Bill Guhl (*Wrigley*), Max Huber (*Major*), Dolores Faith (*American Girl*), Martin Brady, Roland Roberts, Bill Robin.

Dickerson plays a WW II sergeant stationed in Italy. Crow is one of his soldiers who is suffering from shell shock. Dickerson is jealous of Crow because of the medals he's received. He believes Crow is faking being shell shocked and encourages him to escape, then volunteers to go after him. He plans to kill Crow, but then falls for an Italian-American woman and has a change of heart. In the meantime, Crow has taken refuge with Grey, an Italian woman he's in love with. Grey mistakes Dickerson for a German and kills him. She and Crow are rescued by American soldiers, and soon after, Crow recovers from his shell shock.

p, Charles Beach Dickerson; d, John Hayes; w, Randy Fields, Hayes; ph, Vilis Lapenieks; m, Jaime Mendoza-Nava; ed, Thomas Conrad; art d, Mendoza-Nava; spec eff, Ross Hahn, Sam Altonian.

War (PR:C MPAA:NR)

SHENANDOAH***½ (1965) 105m UNIV c

James Stewart (*Charlie Anderson*), Doug McClure (*Sam*), Glenn Corbett (*Jacob Anderson*), Patrick Wayne (*James Anderson*), Rosemary Forsyth (*Jannie Anderson*), Philip Alford (*Boy Anderson*), Katharine Ross (*Ann Anderson*), Charles Robinson (*Nathan Anderson*), James McMullan (*John Anderson*), Tim McIntire (*Henry Anderson*), Paul Fix (*Dr. Tom Witherspoon*), Denver Pyle (*Pastor Bjoerling*), James Best (*Carter*), George Kennedy (*Col. Fairchild*), Warren Oates (*Billy Packer*), Strother Martin (*Engineer*), Dabbs Greer (*Abernathy*), Harry Carey, Jr (*Jenkins*), Kevin Hagen (*Mule*), Tom Simcox (*Lt. Johnson*), Berkeley Harris (*Capt. Richards*), Edward Faulkner (*Union Sergeant*), Peter Wayne (*Confederate Corporal*), Gregg Palmer (*Union Guard*), Bob Steele (*Union Guard with Beard*), James Heneghan, Jr (*1st Picket*), Eugene Jackson, Jr (*Gabriel*), Pae Miller (*Negro Woman*), Rayford Barnes (*Horace*), Dave Cass (*Ray*), Hoke Howell (*Crying Prisoner*), Kelly Thordsen (*Carroll*), Lane Bradford (*Tinkham*), Shug Fisher (*Confederate Soldier*), John Daheim (*Osborne*), Joe Yrigoyen (*Marshal*), Henry Wills, Buzz Henry, James Carter, Leroy Johnson (*Riders*).

James Stewart does one of his best roles in this fine Civil War drama that makes a few points about the futility of war as it entertains. The producers secured the services of many well-known western actors and each of them contributes to their roles, even in the smallest ones. Stewart is a wealthy Virginia farmer in 1863 who maintains a neutral stance during the Civil War. He's a widower who has raised six sons and a daughter after his wife died in childbirth. The war is taking place near their farm, but he remains steadfast in staying out of any conflict that involves slavery, a practice he morally opposes. Forsyth, his daughter, is to marry McClure, and when the son-in-law is called to serve in the Southern forces on the wedding day, the battle begins to take its toll on the Stewart family. Next, the youngest son, Alford, is captured by the North and suspected of being a Johnny Rebel It's only then that Stewart decides this has gone far enough. With a ubiquitous cigar butt in his clenched teeth and a molasses accent that makes every comedy line sound better than the dry words on paper, Stewart leaves the ranch and sets out to rescue Alford, while son Wayne and his pregnant wife, Ross, remain behind to keep an eye on the spread. Stewart takes some of his other children on the trip and they can't seem to come up with an answer to Alford's whereabouts. By this time, McClure is in a Union prison camp. Stewart, who has been angered by the North's order of the sale of some his horses, sets fire to a Union train that's taking Southern soldiers to prisons. When Stewart and his family return home, they are stunned to discover that Wayne and Ross have been murdered by looters. Next, Corbett is accidentally killed by a Confederate soldier who is about the same age as Alford. At the conclusion, Stewart and the remaining members of his family – Forsyth, McIntire, McMullan, and Robinson – are at church when Alford walks in and there is a joyful reunion. Director McGlaglen, who is known for some of his action epics, does well in his handling of the more touching scenes and bypasses the battle gore that might have been. The location scenes were done in Oregon, near Eugene, and served well to duplicate Virginia. In 1974, this story was used as the basis for a family musical on Broadway of the same name. Although it did not receive rave notices, there was enough interest to sustain the show through several months. MacMullan was a Universal contract player who would appear in many films at that studio as well as in the "Lawyers" segment of "The Bold Ones." In a small role, note veteran western actor Bob Steele as the bearded Union Guard. Steele will best be recalled for his role as "Curly" in OF MICE AND MEN. The Wayne-Ross death scene will be frightening to youngsters.

p, Robert Arthur; d, Andrew V. McLaglen; w, James Lee Barrett; ph, William H. Clothier (Technirama, Technicolor); m, Frank Skinner; ed, Otho Lovering; md, Joseph Gershenson; art d, Alexander Golitzen, Alfred Sweeney; set d, John McCarthy, Oliver Emert; cos, Rosemary Odell; makeup, Bud Westmore, Frank Westmore, Rolf Miller, Hank Edds.

War Drama Cas. (PR:C MPAA:NR)

SHENANIGANS (SEE: GREAT BANK HOAX, THE, 1977)

SHEP COMES HOME** (1949) 60m Lippert/Screen Guild bw

Robert Lowery (*Mark*), Billy Kimbley (*Larry*), Flame the Dog (*Shep*), Margia Dean (*Martha*), Martin Garralaga (*Manuel*), Sheldon Leonard (*Swifty*), Michael Whalen (*Chance*), J. Farrell MacDonald (*Cap*), Lyle Talbot (*Doctor*), Frank Jenks (*Iceman*), Edna Holland (*Mrs. Fleming*), Matt Willis (*George*), Ben Erway (*Mr. Gardner*).

Sequel to the successful MY DOG SHEP has Kimbley playing an orphaned boy who keeps out of the orphanage by turning to the wilderness with only his dog to keep him company. He still manages his amount of trouble, but the local sheriff soon overlooks this when the boy and his dog help foil a couple of bankrobbers.

p, Ron Ormond; d&w, Ford Beebe; ph, Ernest Miller; m, Walter Greene; ed, Hugh Winn; md, Greene; art d, Fred Preble.

Drama   (PR:AA MPAA:NR)

SHEPHERD GIRL, THE**½   (1965, Hong Kong) 105m Shaw
                                                     Brothers/Frank Lee International c

Julie Yeh Feng *(Hsiu Hsiu)*, Kwan Shan *(Liu Ta-lung)*, Yang Chi-ching
(Ku), Chu Mu *(Tiger Tseng)*, Chiang Kuang-chao *(Yao Teh-pao)*, Li Ting
(Hsiao Tsui), Ouyang Sh-fei *(Widow Chu)*, Lin Feng *(Wei)*.

Feng plays a young shepherdess whose father is a compulsive gambler
gravely in debt. She's in love with young boatman Shan but her hand is
sought by Mu who offers to pay off her father's debts if he agrees to the
marriage. Feng rejects him, however, until she mistakes Shan's helpfulness
towards another woman as romance. She then becomes friendly towards
Mu, until a friendly widow, Sh-fei, explains to her that Feng is Shan's
truelove. Shan then takes on a dangerous mission at sea as a way to pay off
her father's debts. But when he doesn't return after quite some time, she
agrees to marry Mu. At the wedding, Shan appears, battles with Mu, and
carries off Feng.

p, Run Run Shaw; d&w, Lo Chen; ph, Liu Chi (Eastmancolor); m, Wang
Fu-Ling; ed, Chiang Hsing-lung; m/l, Li Lo-Young.

Drama/Musical   (PR:A MPAA:NR)

SHEPHERD OF THE HILLS, THE***   (1941) 98m PAR c

John Wayne *(Young Matt Matthews)*, Betty Field *(Sammy Lane)*, James
Barton *(Old Matt Matthews)*, Harry Carey *(Daniel Howitt, the Shepherd)*,
Beulah Bondi *(Aunt Mollie Matthews)*, Samuel S. Hinds *(Andy Beeler)*,
Marjorie Main *(Granny Becky)*, Ward Bond *(Wash Gibbs)*, Marco Lawrence
(Pete Matthews), John Qualen *(Coot Royal)*, Fuzzy Knight *(Mr. Palestrom)*,
Tom Fadden *(Jim Lane)*, Olin Howland *(Corky)*, Dorothy Adams *(Elvy
Royal)*, Vivita Campbell *(Baby Royal)*, Fern Emmett *(Mrs. Palestrom)*, John
Harmon *(Charlie, Deputy)*, Selmer Jackson *(Doctor)*, Charles Middleton
(Blacksmith), Bob Kortman *(Hand)*, Hank Bell *(Man with Mustache)*,
William Haade, Henry Brandon, Jim Corey *(Bald Knobbers)*.

This was the third, and probably best, attempt to film Wright's popular
novel about life in the backwoods of Missouri. Wayne plays a young
moonshiner with a vengeance, whose father deserted him at an early age,
causing his mother's untimely death. He vows to someday find his father
and kill him, which keeps Field, the girl he loves, from marrying him
because she does not wish to contend with the hate he's possessed by. The
father, played by Carey, eventually comes back to the Ozarks, and quickly
makes friends with the entire community. He becomes known as "The
Shepherd," because of his many acts of kindness among the people living
there. Wayne hits it off with Carey until he discovers that the old man is
actually his father. He attempts to kill him in a duel, but is unable to do so
when he discovers that Carey did not desert his family, but rather has spent
all this time in jail for killing another man. Wayne and Carey resolve their
differences, leaving Field free to marry Wayne. Cast is strong, with minor
characters displaying realistic and touching performances of the backwoods
people. This film helped give Wayne's career a healthy boost, as it followed
his first major role in the successful movie STAGECOACH.

p, Jack Moss; d, Henry Hathaway; w, Grover Jones, Stuart Anthony (based
on the novel by Harold Bell Wright); ph, Charles Lang, Jr., W. Howard
Greene (Technicolor); m, Gerard Carbonara; ed, Ellsworth Hoagland; art d,
Hans Dreier, Roland Anderson.

Adventure/Drama   (PR:A MPAA:NR)

SHEPHERD OF THE HILLS, THE**   (1964) 110m Macco/Howco
                                                     International c (AKA: THUNDER MOUNTAIN)

Richard Arlen *(Old Matt)*, James W. Middleton *(Daniel Howitt)*, Sherry
Lynn *(Sammy Lane)*, James Collie *(Wash Gibbs)*, Lloyd Durre *(Doc
Coughlan)*, Hal Meadows *(Young Matt)*, James Bradford *(Sheriff)*, Joy N.
Houck, Jr *(Ollie Stewart)*, Gilbert Elmore *(Jess Lane)*, George Jackson *(Jed
Holland)*, Delores James *(Aunt Mollie)*, Danny Spurlock *(Pete)*, Reubin
Egan *(Howard)*, Tom Pope, Roy Idom, Jim Teague, Roger Nash, Jim Greene
(The Baldknobbers).

Remake of the 1941 film that starred Harry Carey and John Wayne, this
film has Middleton as an old man living in the Ozarks. He is known in the
Mountains as "The Shepherd," because of his kindness, and is especially
close to Meadows' family. It seems that years earlier his son, played by
Egan, deserted Meadows' mother, who died giving birth to him. Meadows
is in love with Lynn, but she is promised to Houck. When Houck overhears
Collie bragging about a bank robbery, Houck alerts the sheriff. A shootout
follows and Collie is killed. Middleton admits that Meadows is his grandson
and exposes the gold he has been mining for years. He gives this gold to
Meadows' family, instructing Meadows and Lynn that the only binding
contract is love. Lynn and Meadows marry shortly after and the gold is used
to help the community.

p, Jim McCullough; d&w, Ben Parker (based on the novel by Harold Bell
Wright); ph, Ted Saizis, Vincent Saizis (Eastmancolor); m, Marlin Skiles; ed,
Marcell Greco; art d, Sterling Merritt; cos, Don Mitchell; spec eff, Gene
Corso; m/l, "Fair is My Lover," (Skiles), "The Buggy Ride Song," (Skiles,
Gregg Hunter)

Drama   (PR:A MPAA:NR)

SHEPHERD OF THE OZARKS**½   (1942) 70m REP bw (GB:
                                                                            SUSSANA)

Leon Weaver *(Abner)*, Frank Weaver *(Cicero)*, June Weaver *(Elviry)*,
Marilyn Hare *(Susanna Weaver)*, Frank Albertson *(Jimmy Maloney)*,
Thurston Hall *(James Maloney)*, Johnny Arthur *(Doolittle)*, William Haade
(Dudd Hitt), Wade Crosby *(Kirk)*, Joe Devlin *(Louie)*, Fred Sherman
(Scully), Guy Usher *(Gen. Tobin)*.

Albertson plays an army lieutenant forced to bail out of a plane during
maneuvers. He lands in the middle of the Ozarks, and receives a warm
welcome from the inhabitants, especially the beautiful Hare. The lieutenant's father arrives with the objective of obtaining valuable mineral
deposits. To do so, he takes the Weavers to the city, but his plan is
unsuccessful, and it's back to the Ozarks where a mock battle is occurring.
The Weavers, however, think it's the real thing, and quickly come to the aid
of what they take to be the Americans. Fun in this picture comes from
watching the Weaver clan displaying their genuine backwood mannerisms,
which more than makes up for the flimsy plot. (See WEAVER FAMILY
series, Index).

p, Armand Schaefer; d, Frank McDonald; w, Dorrall McGowan, Stuart
McGowan; ph, Ernest Miller; m, Cy Feuer; ed, Charles Craft; md, Feuer; art
d, Russell Kimball.

Comedy   (PR:A MPAA:NR)

SHEPPER-NEWFOUNDER, THE   (SEE: PART-TIME WIFE, 1930)

SHERIFF OF CIMARRON**½   (1945) 56m REP bw

Sunset Carson *(Sunset Carson)*, Linda Stirling *(Helen Burton)*, Jack Kirk
(John Burton), Jack Ingram *(McCord)*, Riley Hill *(Ted Carson)*, Olin Howlin
(Pinkly Snyder), Bob Wilke *(Dobie)*, Edward Cassidy *(Sam Tucker)*, George
Chesebro *(Mine Owner)*, Dickie Dillon *(Little Boy)*, Tom London *(Frank
Holden)*, Jack O'Shea *(Shad)*, Sylvia Arslan *(Little Girl)*, Henry Wills
(Prisoner), Hal Price *(Stage Passenger)*, Carol Henry *(Townsman)*.

"Adventure as Big as the West!" screamed the ads for SHERIFF OF
CIMMARRON, and for once they were right. Famed stuntman Canutt
directed this exciting entry in the Sunset Carson series and the action is
virtually nonstop. The film opens as Carson rides into the town of
Cimmarron, having recently been released from prison after serving three
years on a rustling charge he was framed for. Searching for his brother, Hill,
in the hopes that his sibling can help him clear his name, Carson blunders
into a holdup of the local express office. The cowboy foils the robbery and
the grateful town asks him to be their sheriff. Unknown to Carson, his
brother, Hill, is actually a cold-blooded crook running with a vicious gang
of hoods led by Ingram. In fact, Hill is so mean he was the man responsible
for framing Carson on the rustling charge three years back. Eventually
Carson learns the truth about his brother and follows him back to the gang's
hideout. A blazing gunbattle ensues, resulting in Ingram's death and Hill's
capture. With Hill's confession, Carson clears his name and the townsfolk
of Cimmaron ask him to stay on as sheriff permanently.

p, Thomas Carr; d, Yakima Canutt; w, Bennett Cohen; ph, Bud Thackery;
ed, Tony Martinelli; md, Richard Cherwin; art d, Fred A. Ritter; set d, Earl
Wooden.

Western   (PR:A MPAA:NR)

SHERIFF OF FRACTURED JAW, THE***   (1958, Brit.) 103m FOX c

Kenneth More *(Jonathan Tibbs)*, Jayne Mansfield *(Kate)*, Henry Hull
(Mayor Masters), William Campbell *(Keno)*, Bruce Cabot *(Jack)*, Robert
Morley *(Uncle Lucius)*, Ronald Squire *(Toynbee)*, David Horne *(James)*,
Eynon Evans *(Mason)*, Reed de Rouen *(Clayborne)*, Charles Irwin *(Luke)*,
Gordon Tanner *(Wilkins)*, Tucker McGuire *(Luke's Wife)*, Nick Brady
(Slim), Nicholas Stuart *(Feeney)*, Sheldon Lawrence *(Johnny)*, Susan Denny
(Cora), Sidney James *(The Drunk)*, Donald Stewart *(The Drummer)*, Clancy
Cooper *(R Barber)*, Larry Taylor *(Gun Guard)*, Jack Lester *(Coach Driver)*,
Charles Farrell *(Bartender)*, Chief Jonas Applegarth *(Running Deer)*, Chief
Joe Buffalo *(Red Wolf)*, Connie Francis *(Voice)*.

After nearly forty years in films in which director Walsh made a career of
concentrating on strong, virile male images, he did a complete about-face in
this spoof on westerns. The result is strange, if not a bit fascinating. More
plays a Londoner and recent heir to a gun producing company, which leads
him out West in order to display his wares. He is hoodwinked into becoming
town sheriff, an unlikely job for the cowardly More. But he manages all
right, never losing control of his proper English mannerisms. In fact he
begins reforming the town into accepting some of these manners, such as
settling down to an afternoon tea instead of the usual whiskey. He also earns
the respect of local Indians, who perform the task of keeping the town under
control. In direct contrast to More, the femme lead is a toughened Jayne
Mansfield, who's a sure-fire shot, and the eventual wedding partner of More.
She even sings a few songs, though only lip-synching while Connie Frances
is responsible for the actual honors.

p, Daniel M. Angel; d, Raoul Walsh; w, Arthur Dales (based on the story by Jacob Hay); ph, Otto Heller (CinemaScope, DeLuxe Color); m, Robert Farnon; ed, John Shirley; md, Muir Mathieson; art d, Bernard Robinson; cos, Julie Harris; ch, George Carden; m/l, Harry Harris; makeup, George Partleton.

Western/Comedy   Cas.   (PR:A   MPAA:NR)

SHERIFF OF LAS VEGAS**   (1944) 55m REP bw

William "Wild Bill" Elliott, Bobby Blake, Alice Fleming, Peggy Stewart, Selmer Jackson, William Haade, Jay Kirby, John Hamilton, Keene Duncan, Bud Geary, Jack Kirk, Dickie Dillon, Frank McCarrol, Freddie Chapman.

"Red Ryder" Elliott and his pal Blake find the real killers of a local judge after the murdered man's estranged son is framed for the crime. Another solid entry in the popular series. (See RED RYDER series, Index).

p, Stephen Auer; d, Lesley Selander; w, Norman S. Hall.

Western   (PR:A   MPAA:NR)

SHERIFF OF REDWOOD VALLEY**   (1946) 54m REP bw

William "Wild Bill" Elliott, Bobby Blake, Alice Fleming, Bob Steele, Peggy Stewart, Arthur Loft, James Craven, Tom London, Kenne Duncan, Bud Geary, John Wayne Wright, Tom Chatterton, Budd Buster, Frank McCarroll, Frank Linn.

Another entry in the RED RYDER series sees Elliott and Blake clearing an innocent man of a crime he was framed for several years back, while bringing the true villains to justice. (See RED RYDER series, Index)

p, Sidney Picker; d, R.G. Springsteen; w, Earle Snell; ph, Reggie Lanning; ed, Ralph Dixon; md, Richard Cherwin; art d, Fred A. Ritter; set d, John McCarthy, Jr., Allan Alperin.

Western   (PR:A   MPAA:NR)

SHERIFF OF SAGE VALLEY**   (1942) 57m PRC bw (AKA: BILLY THE KID, SHERIFF OF SAGE VALLEY)

Buster Crabbe (Billy the Kid/Kansas Ed), Al St. John (Fuzzy Jones), Tex "Dave" O'Brien (Jeff), Maxine Leslie (Janet), Charles King (Sloane), John Merton (Nick), Kermit Maynard (Slim), Hal Price (Harrison), Curley Dresden, Jack Kirk, Lynton Brent.

The seventh of the BILLY THE KID westerns starring serial favorite Crabbe, who took over the role from Bob Steele in the previous year after scoring in his first film for PRC, JUNGLE MAN (1941). Crabbe, who became PRC's greatest box office draw, continued in the western series for some time, while simultaneously appearing in yet another jungle epic, JUNGLE SIREN (1942) which costarred ecdysiast/actress Ann Corio. Crabbe played many dual roles. In this one, he is two bandit brothers. One brother, Billy, is mistaken for a straight-shooter by the mayor of the title town and is appointed sheriff. He rises to the challenge of the job and attempts to clean up the town which, unbeknownst to him, is menaced by his casino-owning brother, who is in hiding, being wanted for murder. The bad brother traps the good one and changes clothes with him, being recognized as the legitimate sheriff, a perfect disguise for the furtherance of his nefarious deeds. With the assistance of sidekicks St. John and O'Brien, the good brother recovers and triumphs over the bad. However, in the process, his relationship is exposed; he must turn in his badge and move on. (See BILLY THE KID Series, Index)

p, Sigmund Neufield; d, Sherman Scott (Sam Newfield); w, Milton Raison, George W. Sayre; ph, Jack Greenhalgh; m, Johnny Lange, Lew Porter; ed, Hobrook N. Todd.

Western   (PR:A   MPAA:NR)

SHERIFF OF SUNDOWN**   (1944) 55m REP bw

Allan Lane (Tex Jordan), Linda Stirling (Lois Carpenter), Max Terhune (Third Grade Simms), Twinkle Watts (Little Jo), Duncan Renaldo (Chihuahua Ramirez), Roy Barcroft (Jack Hatfield), Herbert Rawlinson (Governor Brainerd), Bud Geary (Ward), Jack Kirk (Andy Craig), Tom London (Tom Carpenter), Bob Wilke (Bradley), Kenne Duncan (Albert Wilkes), Rex Lease (Murdock), Nolan Leary (Dineem), Jack O'Shea, Herman Hack, Carl Sepulveda, Cactus Mack, Horace B. Carpenter.

Standard western fare with Lane as a cattleman driving his herd to Sundown (a symbolic name for a town if there ever was one) where he plans to prepare for a long vacation away from the dusty, dangerous cattle trail. He quickly finds himself pitted against Barcroft, a swindling cattle baron whose monopolizing ways are infuriating the locals. Young Kirk gets himself killed by Barcroft, causing Lane to toughen his stance. He pays a visit to the governor and presents him with Sundown's dilemma, but in the meantime, the town sheriff, London, is killed. Barcroft's men come out in full force, trying to sway the townsfolk with their guns. Lane and his sidekicks Terhune and Renaldo take up the defense and manage to bring law and order to Sundown.

p, Stephen Auer; d, Lesley Selander; w, Norman S. Hall; ph, Bud Thackery;

m, Joseph Dubin; ed, Harry Keller; art d, Fred A Ritter.

Western   (PR:A   MPAA:NR)

SHERIFF OF TOMBSTONE**   (1941) 56m REP bw

Roy Rogers (Bret Starr), George "Gabby" Hayes ("Gabby"), Elyse Knox (Mary Carson), Addison Richards (Mayor Keeler), Sally Payne (Queenie), Harry Woods (Shotgun Cassidy), Zeffie Tilbury (Granny Carson), Hal Taliaferro (Slade), Jay Novello (Joe Martinez/John Anderson), Jack Ingram (Bill Starr), George Rosenor, Jack Kirk, Frank Ellis, Art Dillard, Herman Hack, Vester Pegg, Al Haskell, Ray Jones, Jess Cavan, Roy Barcroft, Jack Rockwell, Trigger the Horse.

Arriving in Tombstone with his sidekick Hayes, Rogers is mistaken for the gunslinger the mayor has sent for. Rogers goes along with the impersonation, becoming sheriff and discovering a plot by the crooked mayor to gain control of the town. The real gunslinger comes to town, but by this time Rogers is thoroughly onto the mayor, and manages to handle the hired gun in a manner that looks easy. Along the way Rogers spouts off two songs: "Ridin' on a Rocky Road" (Styne, Meyer), "Sky Bald Paint" (Nolan), and saloon girl Knox sings two more: "You Should Have Seen Pete" (Styne, Meyer), and "Don't Gamble with Romance" (Tinturin). (See ROY ROGERS Series, Index)

p&d, Joseph Kane; w, Olive Cooper (based on a story by James Webb); ph, William Nobles; ed, Tony Martinelli; md, Cy Feuer; m/l, Jule Styne, Sol Meyer, Peter Tinturin, Bob Nolan.

Western   Cas.   (PR:A   MPAA:NR)

SHERIFF OF WICHITA**½   (1949) 60m REP bw

Allan "Rocky" Lane (Allan "Rocky" Lane), Black Jack (His Stallion), Eddy Waller (Nugget Clark), Roy Barcroft (Sam Stark), Lyn Wilde (Nancy Bishop), Clayton Moore (Raymond D'Arcy), Eugene (Gene), Trevor Bardette (Ira Flanders), House Peters, Jr (Jack Thorne), Earle Hodgins (Jenkins), Edmund Cobb (James), John Hamilton (Warden), Steve Raines (Will), Jack O'Shea (Joe), Dick Curtis, Lane Bradford.

In an unusually complicated story line for a series western, a one-time army lieutenant who had been convicted of the theft of an army payroll five years earlier escapes from prison after receiving a mysterious missive. The note directs him to an old fort, where he discovers Lane, plus other escapees who had been convicted of the same crime, all of whom had received similar injunctions. Lane enlists the aid of the escapees in re-opening the case, and with their help he traps the true perpetrators, Barcroft and Bardette. Lane and Black Jack perform plenty of stunts in this one, including a jump straight at the camera (a feature which was to be repeated in even more spectacular ways in later outings).

p, Gordon Kay; d, R.G. Springsteen; w, Bob Williams; ph, John MacBurnie; ed, Tony Martinelli; art d, Frank Arrigo; set d, John McCarthy, Jr., Charles Thompson; spec eff, Howard Lydecker, Theodore Lydecker.

Western   (PR:A   MPAA:NR)

SHERLOCK HOLMES***   (1932) 65m FOX bw

Clive Brook (Sherlock Holmes), Ernest Torrence (Professor Moriarty), Reginald Owen (Dr. Watson), Miriam Jordan (Alice Faulkner), Howard Leeds (Little Billy), Alan Mowbray (Gore-King), Herbert Mundin (Pubkeeper), Montague Shaw (Judge), Arnold Lucy (Chaplain), Lucien Prival (Hans, the Hun), Roy D'Arcy (Manuel Lopez), Stanley Fields (Tony Ardetti), Eddie Dillon (Ardetti's Henchman), Robert Graves, Jr (Gaston Roux), Brandon Hurst (Secretary to Erskine), Claude King (Sir Albert Hastings).

Clive Brook's acting career lasted nearly a half century before he died in 1974 at the age of 87, and yet he is hardly remembered for his portrayals of Sherlock Holmes because most people think of Basil Rathbone as the definitive Baker Street detective. Brooks did his first Holmes part in THE RETURN OF SHERLOCK HOLMES in 1929, then this one, which was based on Gillette's stage play from the Conan Doyle stories. To anyone accustomed to the asexual Rathbone role, Brook's portrayal will come as a surprise as the script calls for a man who has an ongoing relationship with a woman that carries through the entire picture and results in the two of them being united at the conclusion. Brook had shown he could play drawing room antics with Dietrich in SHANGHAI EXPRESS and was again called upon to do that here with Jordan. Although the screenplay's derivation is credited to Gillette's stage drama, it was actually scenarist Milhauser, who would write many of the later Holmes films, who added his own wit and intelligence to the ancient play and made it come out the way it did, filled with humor and biting observations. The infamous professor Moriarty, Torrence, is on trial and sentenced to hang for his nefarious deeds. Torrence tells Scotland Yard inspector Mowbray and judge Shaw that they will die before he does. (Mowbray played in several of these films, appearing as Inspector Lestrade as well as Sebastian Moran.) Next, we are in Brook's apartment when Jordan arrives and their loving relationship is established with some sharp exchanges. Young Leeds arrives, a lad studying criminology (he grew up in a TV comedy writer-producer), to serve tea. Then Owen enters (as Dr. Watson) to say that Torrence is now out of the way. (Owen played Holmes in A STUDY IN SCARLET, thus making him the only actor to have played *both* leading roles in the Conan Doyle stories.) It isn't long before they get word that Torrence has escaped and means to get even with Mowbray, Brook and the prosecutor who handled the case. Brook and Mowbray clash after the prosecutor disappears. When his body is eventually discovered, the name of his killer is scrawled on the wall: "Moriarty." At a wax museum, four top criminals from Germany, Spain, France, and the U.S. are there to meet Torrence. Suddenly, in the eerie half-light, one of the wax figures comes to life. It's Torrence, who has been holding himself still and listening to the crooks. He tells them that he wants to bring organized crime techniques to London and reap the rewards. Torrence arranges to have Brook inadvertently kill Mowbray when he lets loose the information that an assassin is coming to kill him. Brook shoots and Mowbray falls to the floor. The newspapers have a field day as they know that Brook and Mowbray have been enemies over the years. But it's all a ruse cooked up by Brook and Mowbray to bring Torrence out into the open. The Torrence gang starts to extort money from businesses (there's a very funny scene with Mundin as a Cockney pub owner), beginning the British version of the "protection" game. One afternoon at Jordan's family's estate, Brook arrives dressed in drag and looking like Ray Bolger in CHARLEY'S AUNT. He tells Jordan's father, a banker, that the plot perpetrated by Torrence and his international goons, Prival, D'Arcy, Fields and Graves, is a ploy. Their real plot is to rob the old man's bank. Now Torrence calls at the estate to tell Jordan's father that Jordan is now his hostage and will be killed unless the old man helps the crooks rob his own bank; The denouement occurs underneath the savings institution with a shootout that kills Torrence and results in the others being captured. Back at Brook's apartment, a wedding is planned and Mowbray will stand in as Best Man because Owen has been called away due to his mother's illness (probably because the good doctor couldn't stand to see his roommate marry). Brook and Jordan will leave London and take up lives as, believe it or not, chicken farmers. Lots of fun, good comedy relief and an unaccustomed romantic Holmes make this worth seeing, despite some of the more dated aspects of the picture. (See: SHERLOCK HOLMES series, Index.)

d, William K. Howard; w, Bertram Milhauser (based on the stories by Sir Arthur Conan Doyle and the play by William Gillette); ph, George Barnes; art d, John Hughes; cos, Rita Kaufman.

Drama/Comedy   **(PR:A MPAA:NR)**

SHERLOCK HOLMES, 1939   (SEE: ADVENTURES OF SHERLOCK HOLMES, THE, 1939)

SHERLOCK HOLMES AND THE DEADLY NECKLACE½**
(1962, Ger.) 84m Constantin/Screen Gems bw (SHERLOCK HOLMES UND DAS HALSBAND DES TODES; AKA: VALLEY OF FEAR)

Christopher Lee (*Sherlock Holmes*), Senta Berger (*Ellen Blackburn*), Hans Sohnker (*Prof. Moriarty*), Hans Nielson (*Inspector Cooper*), Ivan Desny (*Paul King*), Leon Askin (*Chauffeur Charles*), Wolfgang Lukschy (*Peter Blackburn*), Edith Schultz-Westrum (*Mrs. Hudson*), Bernard Lajarrige (*French Police Inspector*), Linda Sini (*Light Girl*), Bruno W. Pantel (*Auctioneer*), Heinrich Gies (*American*), Roland Armontel (*Doctor*), Max Strassberg (*Johnny*), Danielle Argence (*Librarian*), Thorley Walters (*Dr. Watson*).

A German version of the tales of Sir Arthur Conan Doyle's famed detective, with a Hammer director in Fisher, and Hammer leads in Lee and Walters, as Holmes and Watson respectively. Both Fisher and Lee are more at home in horror films, which, combined with the mood created by the German set designers, helps to create a more than appropriately eerie atmosphere. Lee wore a phony nose (to make him look more like Basil Rathbone, presumably), but had his voice dubbed in both the English and German versions. Walters' rendition of Watson concentrated heavily upon the comic side, making the character look more ridiculous than customary. He even saves Lee's life in one instance by imitating the sound of a police siren. The culprit here is again Moriarty, played by Sohnker in a rendition that has him as an honored citizen, even trusted by Scotland Yard despite Lee's warnings. This allows for several public confrontations between Lee and Sohnker, where they match wits in cunning word games. The object of Sohnker's interest is a necklace stolen from the tomb of Cleopatra several years earlier. When the co-conspirators of Moriarty are uncovered they quickly turn up dead, leaving Lee the task of pinning the murders on Sohnker. He never succeeds in seeing his arch-enemy go to jail for either the murders or the theft of the necklace (this would hinder possibilities for a sequel), but the sleuth does manage to return the necklace to its proper place. In fact Lee recovers the necklace from Sohnker in two instances, the second when he dresses up as a sleazy sailor to infiltrate the gang. This was one of the more strange depictions of a Holmes mystery. (See SHERLOCK HOLMES Series, Index)

p, Arthur Brauner; d, Terence Fisher, Frank Winterstein; w, Curt Siodmak (based on the novels of Sir Arthur Conan Doyle).

Mystery   **(PR:A MPAA:NR)**

SHERLOCK HOLMES AND THE SECRET CODE
(SEE: DRESSED TO KILL, 1946)

SHERLOCK HOLMES AND THE SECRET WEAPON*\
(1942) 68m UNIV bw

Basil Rathbone (*Sherlock Holmes*), Nigel Bruce (*Dr. John H. Watson*), Kaaren Verne (*Charlotte Eberli*), Lionel Atwill (*Prof. Moriarty*), William Post, Jr (*Dr. Franz Tobel*), Dennis Hoey (*Inspector Lestrade*), Harry Woods (*Man*), George Burr MacAnnan (*Gottfried*), Paul Fix (*Mueller*), Holmes Herbert (*Sir Reginald Bailey*), Mary Gordon (*Mrs. Hudson*), Henry Victor (*Frederick Hoffner*), Harold de Becker (*Peg Leg*), Harry Cording (*Jack Brady, Hoodlum/Carpenter*), Leyland Hodgson (*R.A.F. Air Officer*), Robert O. Davis (*Braun*), Phillip Van Zandt (*Kurt*), Paul Bryar (*Waiter*), Vicki Campbell (*Aviatrix*), Gerard Cavin (*Scotland Yard Man*), Guy Kingsford (*London Bobby*), George Eldredge (*Policeman*), John Burton, Leslie Denison, James Craven (*Bits*).

Rathbone disguises himself as an old Swiss bookseller, a villainous waterfront lascar, and a bearded scientist in an attempt to keep his arch-enemy Professor Moriarty, played by Atwill, from the newly developed bombsight the English hope to use on Hitler. Atwill pops up just when everyone thought he to be long dead, and he's working for the Nazis, having little concern for his native country. In one confrontation between Rathbone and Atwill, the former is strapped to a table and tortured by having his blood taken from his veins, drop by drop. Bruce turns up in the knick of time to save his partner, with Atwill falling sixty feet to his presumed death. Undoubtedly he will turn up in another HOLMES adventure. This was the first of 11 in the series to be directed by Neill, who kept everything at a swift pace, including the dialog. Other items of the series which had their origins in this outing were Dennis Hoey as the Scotland Yard detective Lestrade, jealous of Holmes' exploits, and the fitting quote Rathbone retorts at the end of each film. When Bruce comes out with "Things are looking up, Holmes. This little island (England) is still on the map." Rathbone responds from Shakespeare: "Yes. This fortress – built by Nature for herself. This blessed plot, this earth, this realm, this England." (See SHERLOCK HOLMES series, Index)

p, Howard Benedict; d, Roy William Neill; w, Edward T. Lowe, W. Scott Darling, Edmund L. Hartmann (based on the Sir Arthur Conan Doyle story "The Dancing Men"); ph, Lester White; m, Frank Skinner; ed, Otto Ludwig; md, Charles Previn; art d, Jack Otterson.

Mystery   **Cas.**   **(PR:A MPAA:NR)**

SHERLOCK HOLMES AND THE SPIDER WOMAN**½**
(1944) 62m UNIV bw (AKA: SPIDER WOMAN)

Basil Rathbone (*Sherlock Holmes*), Nigel Bruce (*Dr. John H. Watson*), Gale Sondergaard (*Andrea Spedding*), Dennis Hoey (*Inspector Lestrade*), Vernon Downing (*Norman Locke*), Alec Craig (*Radlik*), Arthur Hohl (*Adam Gilflower, Spider Specialist*), Stanley Logan (*Colonel*), Donald Stuart (*Artie*), John Roche (*Croupier*), Mary Gordon (*Mrs. Hudson*), John Burton (*Announcer*), Lydia Bilbrook (*Colonel's Wife*), Belle Mitchell (*Fortune Teller*), Harry Cording (*Fred Garvin*), John Rogers (*Clerk*), Teddy Infuhr (*Larry, Boy*), Marie de Becker (*Charwoman*), Angelo Rossitto (*Pygmy*), Gene Stutenroth (*Taylor*).

One of the most entertaining of the Rathbone-Bruce Holmesian ventures, this one, like so many of the others, melds two different temporal periods; the fogbound settings are reminiscent of the London of the 1800s, but automobiles, airplanes, and Adolf Hitler are very much in evidence. The film also mixes sources, being an amalgam of several of Conan Doyle's stories, with fresh material thrown in. Rathbone fakes his own death by drowning in a Scottish mountain stream in order to throw the miscreants off his track. Sondergaard is their leader, responsible for a series of "Pajama Suicides"–actually murders–with the victims being well-to-do, heavily insured men, and herself the beneficiary of their policies (screenwriter Millhauser had apparently never scanned the suicide clauses of an insurance contract). The nature of the diabolical plot leads Rathbone to suspect a woman's touch; the misogynistic sleuth attests that not even his arch-enemy Professor Moriarty could be so fiendish as to have devised such a system. Rathbone dons the disguise of a wealthy East Indian officer and, noting that the pajama-clad victims were all fond of gambling, heads for a casino. There he simulates despondency over presumed heavy gambling losses, and is consoled by Sondergaard, who counsels him that he can borrow against his life insurance policy if he finds a new beneficiary. Rathbone pretends to go along with her and takes tea at her flat; when she spills tea on his arm, his dyed skin runs: the clever criminal has recognized him. That night, a deadly spider is released in his flat; Rathbone and police inspector Hoey discover a carrying case with air holes and the footprints of a "child" on the roof. Back at 221-B Baker Street, Rathbone–now known to be alive–and Bruce receive a visit from the spidery Sondergaard, accompanied by mute child Infuhr, a scene-stealing terror. Her purpose is ostensibly to engage the great detective to locate the missing Indian officer. As the deadly distaff departs, the mute lad throws some candy wrappers into the fire and the room fills with poisonous smoke. Rathbone manages to smash a window before the detective and his faithful physician friend faint from the fumes. Rathbone enlists the assistance of a celebrated arachnologist to trace the deadly spider that was released in his flat but finds an impostor, gang member Craig, in his place. Recognized, Craig releases some spiders as a diversion and escapes Rathbone's clutches. The detective discovers the body of the real scientist, as well as charred fragments of his African diary, which refer to some animal which is "doglike," "immune," and "faithful." The bumbling Bruce, who himself possesses at least two of those three qualities, finds a small skeleton in a closet. The skeleton, he avers, is *not* that of a child, despite its size. Rathbone makes the appropriate deduction: the skeleton is that of a pygmy, and such a pygmy has been the spider woman's agent of destruction, the bratty Infuhr having been merely a false scent. Rathbone traces the pygmy to a sideshow at a carnival, where he is trapped by Sondergaard's minions and tied to a shooting-gallery target, a cutout of Adolf Hitler. He frees himself in the nick of time just as Bruce is about to shoot and he and his friends round up Sondergaard and her mob, including pygmy Rossitto. The smoothly menacing Sondergaard was so fine in this film that she returned three years later, but without Rathbone, in THE SPIDER WOMAN STRIKES BACK. This was the first film in the SHERLOCK HOLMES series (see Index) in which exhibitors were offered the option of either using the Holmes name in the title of the picture or not, as they pleased; the studio felt that the series impact had been reduced with time and familiarity, and the same option was offered in succeeding releases. (See SHERLOCK HOLMES Series. Index)

p&d, Roy William Neill; w, Bertram Millhauser (based on the story "The Sign of the Four" by Sir Arthur Conan Doyle); ph, Charles Van Enger; ed, James Gibbon; art d, John B. Goodman.

Mystery   **(PR:A   MPAA:NR)**

SHERLOCK HOLMES AND THE VOICE OF TERROR**½
                                            (1942) 65m UNIV bw

Basil Rathbone *(Sherlock Holmes)*, Nigel Bruce *(Dr. John H. Watson)*, Evelyn Ankers *(Kitty)*, Reginald Denny *(Sir Evan Barham)*, Montagu Love *(General Jerome Lawford)*, Henry Daniell *(Anthony Lloyd)*, Thomas Gomez *(R.F. Meade)*, Olaf Hytten *(Fabian Prentiss)*, Leyland Hodgson *(Capt. Ronald Shore)*, Arthur Blake *(Crosbie)*, Harry Stubbs *(Taxi Driver)*, Mary Gordon *(Mrs. Hudson)*, Hillary Brooke *(Jill Grandis)*, Edgar Barrier *(Voice of Terror)*, Robert O. Davis *(Nazi)*, Harry Cording *(Ex-Convict)*, Lon Chaney, Jr *(Gavin, Murdered Man)*, Leslie Denison *(Air Raid Warden)*.

This was the first of Universal's SHERLOCK HOLMES series starring Rathbone and Bruce, a series which was updated to contemporary times, which offended many aficionados of the famed detective stories. The two had played the same roles in 20th Century-Fox's productions of THE HOUND OF THE BASKERVILLES and THE ADVENTURES OF SHERLOCK HOLMES (1939) in full period regalia, and the plots of those two films adhered much more closely to author Conan Doyle's original stories than did any of Universal's 11 releases in the series. The plot has Rathbone single-handedly saving Britain from a German invasion during WW II. Invited by suave diplomat Denny to a meeting of the "Intelligence Inner Council," Rathbone is invited to solve the riddle of the sabotage acts performed only moments after they are announced by "The Voice of Terror," pinpointed as broadcast from Nazi Germany. Rathbone is assigned a uniformed woman driver, Brooke – replacing the originally cast Marjorie Lord, Brooke was acquainted with the series, having played a bit in the second of the Fox releases – and chauffeured through the sandbagged streets of wartime London to his Baker Street flat. There, one of his informants bursts through his door and, mouthing the word "Christopher," expires, a knife protruding from his back. The informant's origins lead Rathbone and Bruce to explore the sinister docks of London's Limehouse district. In a waterfront dive, he finds the informant's sweetheart, Kitty (Ankers), an entertainer, and invites the distraught girl to avenge her lover's death by organizing an army of her friends – cutthroats, thieves, and prostitutes – to repel the German threat. She exhorts her acquaintances to form themselves into an invisible army to assist in the grim battle and they rally behind her. With Ankers' assistance, Rathbone locates the abandoned Christopher dock and, trailed by suspicious-acting Inner Council member Daniell, journeys there with Bruce at his side. Apparently trapped by Nazi agent Gomez, Rathbone has in reality ambushed the Nazis: his secret army of wharf rats overwhelms them. Daniell reproaches Rathbone for permitting their leader, Gomez, to escape through a hidden trap door, a purposeful act on the part of the sleuth. Ankers locates the evasive Nazi's hideout and befriends him, becoming his confidante (and, implicitly, his mistress). Through her, Rathbone discovers that some important event is to occur that very evening at Denny's country estate: perhaps his assassination. Joining Denny in a twilight stroll, Holmes hears sirens; an enemy aircraft lands on the adjacent park grounds. Denny fires a pistol at the plane, which takes off again. Looking about, Rathbone spots Gomez lurking in the bushes, but the Nazi again escapes. That very evening, the "Voice of Terror" broadcasts a message to the effect that England's defenseless Northern coast is to be invaded on the following day. Rathbone deduces that all the previous broadcasts have been diversions, leading up to this one: the attack, he reasons, is actually to occur on the *South* coast. A call to Downing Street convinces the reluctant Inner Council to accede to his plan to ambush the Nazis at their gathering place, an abandoned church on the South coast, where the waiting Nazi agents – including Gomez – are rounded up. But the mystery has not ended; Rathbone avers that the mastermind must be a member of the Inner Council, privy to its secrets. The man is Denny, who shot at the enemy plane to warn it away. Denny is an Agent In Place, a doppelganger who took the place of the real aristocrat many years ago. As the noise of aircraft is heard, Denny proudly admits the deception, stating, "Even now our Messerschmitts are roaring overhead." But the planes are

British ones, returning from their successful repulsion of the German invaders. In the ensuing confusion, Gomez produces a pistol and kills Ankers, whom he now realizes has betrayed him (girls who go to bed with bad guys had to pay the price according to production codes of the time). The film closes with its only bow to its nominal source, Conan Doyle's "His Last Bow," with Rathbone quoting it almost verbatim: "Good old Watson – the one fixed point in a changing age. There's an east wind coming all the same, such a wind as never blew on England yet. It will be cold and bitter, Watson, and a good many of us may wither before its blast. But it's God's own wind, nonetheless, and a greener, better, stronger land will lie in the sunshine when the storm has cleared." The Conan Doyle estate had originally insisted that the filmed Holmes stories must comply at least in part with the original stories. This closing quote was as near as Universal came to such compliance. The film was generally regarded to be among the weakest in the series from Universal. It was the only one of the 11 not directed by Roy William Neill. (See SHERLOCK HOLMES Series, Index)

p, Howard Benedict; d, John Rawlins; w, Lynn Riggs, Robert D. Andrews, John Bright (based on "His Last Bow" by Arthur Conan Doyle); ph, Woody Bredell; m, Frank Skinner; ed, Russell Schoengarth; md, Charles Previn; art d, Jack Otterson.

Mystery   **Cas.**   **(PR:A   MPAA:NR)**

SHERLOCK HOLMES FACES DEATH***   (1943) 68m UNIV bw

Basil Rathbone *(Sherlock Holmes)*, Nigel Bruce *(Dr. John H. Watson)*, Dennis Hoey *(Inspector Lestrade)*, Arthur Margetson *(Dr. Sexton)*, Hillary Brooke *(Sally Musgrave)*, Halliwell Hobbes *(Brunton, Butler)*, Minna Phillips *(Mrs. Howells)*, Milburn Stone *(Capt. Vickery)*, Gavin Muir *(Phillip Musgrave)*, Gerald Hamer *(Maj. Langford)*, Vernon Downing *(Lt. Clavering)*, Olaf Hytten *(Capt. MacIntosh)*, Heather Wilde *(Jenny)*, Frederick Worlock *(Geoffrey Musgrave)*, Peter Lawford *(2nd Sailor)*, Harold de Becker *(Pub Proprietor)*, Mary Gordon *(Mrs. Hudson)*, Holmes Herbert *(Man)*, Norma Varden *(Grace, Pub Proprietress)*, Ian Wolfe *(Antique Store Clerk)*.

The first in Universal's SHERLOCK HOLMES series to stick fairly close to a Conan Doyle story, this film – although updated to contemporary times, as with the others in Universal's series – lacked the wartime patriotic fervor of the others. As the *New York Herald Tribune* reviewer pointed out, "at least this one has practically nothing to do with the Nazis." The picture is basically a haunted-manor mystery thriller, albeit the war enters into it in the person of the manor's occupants, many of whom are convalescing military officers. The impoverished, aristocratic Musgraves (brothers Muir and Worlock and their sister, Brooke) have converted their ancestral home into a retreat for these disturbed, brooding men, employing Rathbone's long-time Boswell, Bruce, as its medical director. (In Conan Doyle's original, the character played by Bruce is conspicuously absent, the story being related by the sleuth himself.) When Bruce's medical assistant Margetson is stabbed and noncritically wounded, and the manor's tower clock strikes 13 times – according to legend, a portent of the death of a Musgrave – Bruce recruits his old friend Rathbone, who joins him at the manor. Once there, Rathbone discovers the body of Worlock under a pile of leaves, made into mulch by a murderer. In these eerie environs, all are suspect: the disturbed patients, the sinister-appearing housekeeper, the besotted butler. The death of a Musgrave demands a traditional ritual, performed by Brooke: the recitation of an ancient heraldic chant, seemingly meaningless. The bibulous butler, Hobbes, disappears after drinking heavily. At a public house in the nearby village, Rathbone and Bruce encounter Brooke, pursuing them to announce that her other brother, Muir, has disappeared. The pub's tame raven flies to the boot of her roadster and begins pecking furiously as Rathbone points out that such carrion eaters are excellent at locating dead things. Yes, Muir's corpse is discovered in the boot. While descending the main staircase at Musgrave manor, Rathbone discerns that the checkered marble floor of the main hall resembles a gigantic chessboard. Recalling the references to knaves, queens, and kings in the ancient litany of the Musgrave death ritual, he recruits the occupants of the grim manor as chess pieces, following the moves indicated in the rhyme. At the culmination of the recitation, a secret passage is discovered, one that leads to an ancient burial crypt (the same set used in DRACULA, 1931). There, the body of the butler, Hobbes, is discovered. Rathbone hastily isolates the area, explaining that the butler had scratched some incriminating marks on the stone floor of the death chamber prior to expiring, marks which may point to the murderer. The marks are merely a ruse, bait for murderer Margetson, who creeps to the crypt at night and is apprehended by the great detective. But Margetson struggles and gains possession of the sleuth's pistol. Holding Rathbone at bay, he confesses his crimes: he found the crypt early on, and with it a valuable land grant which would make the Musgrave legatee -- in this case the survivor, Brooke – among the wealthiest people in England. The demented doctor planned to wed Brooke before "discovering" her inheritance. To divert suspicion from himself, the felonious physician had deliberately wounded himself. Musgrave shoots Rathbone, and is quickly arrested by the waiting Lestrade–Hoey--who had, with Bruce, heard his confession. Rathbone rises; his pistol had been loaded with blank cartridges in a further scheme to trap the harried healer. In a stunningly unexpected development, heiress Brooke throws the ancient land grant into the blazing fireplace, explaining that she has no intention of denuding the long-term residents of the area of their property and possessions. She then presumably progresses to a life of continuing poverty with the young captain, Stone, who has been courting her. Stone, who went from such juvenile roles to become a fine character actor, felt himself sadly miscast. He was much shorter than the other players. When he walked with Rathbone, technicians had to build an elevated walkway for him. During a romantic scene with the taller Brooke, he felt that he looked "almost like a midget" seated next to her. The property department provided pillows to put their heads on an appropriate level. Peter Lawford played a bit part as a sailor in the pub scene. This visually effective film was the first to be produced as well as directed by Neill, who further demonstrated his penchant for the macabre by directing FRANKENSTEIN MEETS THE WOLFMAN in the same year. Rathbone's summary statement – a common thread in the Universal series – departed from the convention of previous films, since it was not a quote from Shakespeare, Winston Churchill, or Franklin Delano Roosevelt. Instead of patriotic wartime bombast, it reflected postwar social change. When Bruce avers that Brooke might regret having destroyed the document that would have made her wealthy, Rathbone muses, "There's a new spirit abroad in the land. The old days of grab and greed are on the way out. We're beginning to think of what we owe the other fellow, not just what we're compelled to give him...." This was not the last time Rathbone and Bruce were to appear as Holmes and Watson during 1943. They appeared in a short comic cameo as the famed duo in the Olsen and Johnson vehicle CRAZY HOUSE later that year. (See SHERLOCK HOLMES Series, Index)

p&d, Roy William Neill; w, Bertram Millhauser (based on the story "The Musgrave Ritual" by Sir Arthur Conan Doyle); ph, Charles Van Enger; ed, Fred Feitchans; md, H.J. Salter; art d, John B. Goodman, Harold MacArthur.

Mystery   **(PR:O   MPAA:NR)**

SHERLOCK HOLMES' FATAL HOUR**½   (1931, Brit.) 75m
                              WB-Twickenham/FD bw (GB: THE SLEEPING CARDINAL)

Arthur Wontner (*Sherlock Holmes*), Ian Fleming (*Dr. John H. Watson*), Minnie Rayner (*Mrs. Hudson*), Leslie Perrins (*Ronald Adair*), Jane Welsh (*Kathleen Adair*), Norman McKinnell (*Col. Henslowe/Robert Moriarty*), William Frazer (*Thomas Fisher*), Philip Hewland (*Inspector Lestrade*), Gordon Begg (*Marston*), Louis Goodrich (*Col. Sebastian Moran*), Sidney King (*Tony Rutherford*), Harry Terry (*No. 16*), Charles Paton (*J. J. Godfrey*).

Hoping to boost business in the United Kingdom, and fearful of the inroads made by Hollywood–with its generally superior features–the British established a quota system in 1928. Feature film exhibitors and distributors were required by law to devote a certain percentage of playing time to domestically made pictures, thereby supporting their local production facilities. Responding to the nationalistic trend in Blighty, Warner Bros. and other American film companies began financing movies across the water. This Twickenham Studios feature was made entirely with English talent, and proved to be equal to the best the U.S. could offer in its genre. Wontner's Sherlock Holmes was animated and excellent, giving life and character to the famed sleuth. Fleming (no relation to the author of the JAMES BOND series), whose name was misspelled as "Jan Fleming" in studio releases, was harshly criticized in the Dr. Watson role; nevertheless, he continued to play the character against Wontner's Holmes in four more films. Based on two of the Conan Doyle stories, the film covers a litany of crimes from counterfeiting to killing, with a little treason thrown in, all orchestrated by Holmes' evil nemesis, the mysterious Moriarty (played for the first and only time by McKinnell). A silent sequence in silhouette opens the film, with dim, scuffling figures robbing the Bank of England and committing a murder in the process. Despite the skepticism of the inept inspector, Hewland, the great detective suspects the involvement of that doyen of disguises, the prolific professor of crime, McKinnell, whom "none have ever seen..." Young Perrins, a Foreign Office bureaucrat, is blackmailed by the unseen McKinnell–who knows of the youth's card cheating–after transporting him to a secret room blindfolded. The professor speaks from behind a painting– significantly, a likeness of famed plotter Cardinal Richelieu–inveigling the imperiled Perrins to smuggle some contraband out of the country in his diplomat's pouch. Refusing, Perrins is left with a pistol and a little time to consider the only honorable out, suicide. The egocentric professor then visits Wontner in his Baker Street flat, swathed in a muffler and wearing dark glasses, to offer the detective a deal: you leave my enterprises alone and I'll leave you alone. The visit proves perilous to the professor, since the sleuth is able to identify the criminal's bootmaker from the cut of his footwear. The resulting raid reveals the rascal's lair, replete with printing press and counterfeit banknotes, but the professor and his minions have fled the premises. That same evening, Perrins' body is discovered with a bullet wound in the head; his sister Welsh is accused of his murder by the idiotic inspector. Exploring the dead youth's rooms, Wontner runs into a gambling acquaintance of Perrins, a trig retired colonel, who lost an arm to a ravenous tiger in India years before. The colonel, we later discover, is the professor in disguise. Realizing that an attempt is to be made on his own life, the sleuth enlists the services of his motherly housekeeper, Rayner, having the woman crawl on the floor moving a plaster bust before his windows. An impact shatters the bust; McKinnell has fired a powerful air rifle from across the street. He is apprehended, of course. Having taken the most dangerous criminal in Europe, Wontner settles back to his violin and his pipe, his happy housekeeper hovering, proud of her part in the case. Rayner was to continue to play Mrs. Hudson in the series. Wontner's portrayal of the detective makes an interesting contrast to that of Basil Rathbone; the latter, almost

neurotically incisive, is perhaps closer to Conan Doyle's character as written than is Wontner's glib, kindly banterer. (See SHERLOCK HOLMES Series, Index)

p, Julius Hagen; d, Leslie S. Hiscott; w, Cyril Twyford, H. Fowler Mear, Hiscott, Arthur Wontner (based on the stories "The Final Problem", "The Empty House", by Sir Arthur Conan Doyle and William Gillette's play [Uncredited]); ph, Sidney Blythe; ed, Jack Harris; art d, James Carter.

Mystery   **(PR:A   MPAA:NR)**

SHERLOCK HOLMES GROSSTER FALL
                     (SEE: STUDY IN TERROR, A, 1966, Brit./Ger)

SHERLOCK HOLMES IN WASHINGTON**   (1943) 71m UNIV bw

Basil Rathbone (*Sherlock Holmes*), Nigel Bruce (*Dr. John H. Watson*), Marjorie Lord (*Nancy Partridge*), Henry Daniell (*William Easter*), George Zucco (*Stanley*), John Archer (*Lt. Peter Merriam*), Gavin Muir (*Bart Lang*), Edmund MacDonald (*Detective Lt. Grogan*), Don Terry (*Howe*), Bradley Page (*Cady*), Holmes Herbert (*Mr. Ahrens*), Thurston Hall (*Senator Henry Babcock*), Gilbert Emery (*Sir Henry Marchmont*), Gerald Hamer (*John Grayson/Alfred Pettibone*), Clarence Muse (*George, Train Steward*), Ian Wolfe (*Antique Clerk*), Margaret Seddon (*Miss Pringle, Lady with Mouse*), Mary Forbes (*Alfred Pettibone's Mother*).

The master sleuth makes his first trip to America, just in order to pursue a match book cover. But these matches contain secret government documents. A British clerk is killed over them while transporting them from London to Washington. This simple plot device (having too much similarity to an Alfred Hitchcock "MacGuffin") is used to stretch this story out far beyond its real level of suspense. The matchbook goes from hand to hand, eventually winding up in those of the Nazi spy, posing as a respected Washington citizen, who doesn't even realize he has what he has been searching for all along. The American setting is played to the hilt, with the updated and highly scientific sleuthing of the FBI no match for Rathbone's mental deductions, and Bruce finding the game of baseball a sport almost as enjoyable as his beloved cricket. But these tidbits of interest and the usual fine performance of Rathbone were not enough to help the straining script, resulting in one of the less successful films in the Universal series. The detective's physical appearance was modified for this film to match its setting: he sported a raffish windblown hairdo and wore a checkered Norfolk jacket with a loosened shirt collar and necktie. This was the first of the Rathbone-Bruce Holmes films which made no pretense of being based on a story by Sir Arthur Conan Doyle (although few of the others in the Universal series had much to do with the plots of the famed tales). Villain Zucco had played Holmes' nemesis Professor Moriarty (who was *not* a character in this film) in THE ADVENTURES OF SHERLOCK HOLMES (1939); the equally sinister Daniell was to play the villain later in THE WOMAN IN GREEN (1945). (See SHERLOCK HOLMES Series, Index)

p, Howard Benedict; d, Roy William Neill; w, Bertram Millhauser, Lynn Riggs (based on a story by Millhauser and characters created by Arthur Conan Doyle); ph, Lester White; m, Frank Skinner; ed, Otto Ludwig; md, Charles Previn; art d, Jack Otterson.

Mystery   **(PR:A   MPAA:NR)**

SHE'S A SOLDIER TOO**   (1944) 67m COL bw

Beulah Bondi, Nina Foch, Jess Barker, Lloyd Bridges, Percy Kilbride, Ida Moore, Erik Rolf, Jeanne Bates, Shelley Winter [Winters], Marilyn Johnson.

Seeking the son he left behind years ago, a young soldier enlists the aid of a female cabbie in his search. One of the first films directed by William Castle, who by the 1950s would become the P.T. Barnum of horror movies with such releases as THE HOUSE ON HAUNTED HILL (1959), THE TINGLER (1959), and MR. SARDONICUS (1961).

p, Wallace McDonald; d, William Castle; w, Melvin Levy (based on a story by Hal Smith); ph, Benjamin Kline; ed, Aaron Stell; art d, Lionel Banks, George Brooks.

Drama   **(PR:A   MPAA:NR)**

SHE'S A SWEETHEART**   (1944) 69m COL bw

Jane Frazee (*Maxine Lecour*), Larry Parks (*Rocky Hill*), Jane Darwell (*Mom*), Nina Foch (*Jeanne*), Ross Hunter (*Paul*), Jimmy Lloyd (*Pete Ryan*), Loren Tindall (*Jimmy Loomis*), Carole Mathews (*Frances*), Eddie Bruce (*Fred Tilly*), Pat Lane (*Matt*), Danny Desmond (*Poker*), Ruth Warren (*Edith*), Dave Willock (*Wes*).

Easygoing fare in which Darwell converts her large house into a boarding house for soldiers on leave. Not only does she supply room and board, as well as a little bit of musical entertainment, she also helps out in getting the boys dates. One of these soldiers, Parks, hooks singer Frazee, with wedding bells chiming in the near future. Everyone involved just took this as light fun, except for Darwell, the screen's most recognized character actress who remains forced throughout. Parks played in minor films such as this one until he hit it big in THE JOLSON STORY (1946) and its sequel JOLSON SINGS AGAIN (1949). After he admitted to membership in the Communist

Party during the McCarthy era, Columbia dropped him as a contract player. Hunter, who played leads in a number of low budget musicals during a two year period in the 1940s, became a successful producer in the early 1950s, with such hits to his credit as IMITATION OF LIFE (1959) and AIRPORT (1970). Songs include: "Who Said Dreams Can't Come True" (Benny Davis, Al Jolson, Harry Akst), "I've Waited a Lifetime" (Edward Brandt), "I Can't Remember When" (Robert Schermann, Jack Krakeur), "What the Sergeant Said" (Jackie Camp), "My Other Love" (Bob Wright, Chet Forrest), "Mom" (Saul Chaplin), and "American Prayer" (Lawrence Stock, Vincent Rose, Al Stillman).

p, Ted Richmond; d, Del Lord; w, Muriel Roy Bolton; ph, Benjamin Kline; ed, Al Clark.

Musical (PR:A MPAA:NR)

SHE'S BACK ON BROADWAY** (1953) 95m WB c

Virginia Mayo (*Catherine Terris*), Gene Nelson (*Gordon Evans*), Frank Lovejoy (*John Webber*), Steve Cochran (*Rick Sommers*), Patrice Wymore (*Karen Keene*), Virginia Gibson (*Angela Korinna*), Larry Keating (*Mitchell Parks*), Paul Picerni (*Jud Kellogg*), Ned Young (*Rafferty*), Jacqueline de Wit (*Lisa Kramer*), Condos & Brandow (*Specialty Dance*), Douglas Spencer (*Lew Ludlow*), Mabel Albertson (*Velma Trumbull*), Lenny Sherman (*Ernest Tandey*), Cliff Ferre (*Lyn Humphreys*), Ray Kyle (*Mickey Zealand*), Sy Melano (*Baritone Singer*), Taylor Holmes (*Talbot*), Paul Bryar (*Ned Golby*), Harry Tyler (*Rhodes*), Phyllis Coates (*Blonde*), Caleen Calder (*Val*), Howard Price (*Sandy*), Ray Walker (*Guide Bus Driver*), Minerva Urecal (*Landlady*), Harlan Hoagland (*Waiter*), Jack Kenney (*Loader*), Kathleen Freeman (*Annie*), Percy Helton (*News Vendor*).

Mayo plays a failing movie star (at the ripe age of 27) who wants to get her career back in motion via a Broadway play. This sets the stage for the usual type of backstage happening. Cochran plays the director of the play; he's also Mayo's former lover from whom she took a walk several years earlier. By the end of the film the two are back in each other's arms, depite the efforts of dancer Wymore to make claim to Cochran. Wymore, the third–and final–wife of Errol Flynn, delivered the actor's youngest daughter, Arnella Roma Flynn, the year of this picture's release. She retired from the screen for six years following this picture to care for both her child and the aging, ill actor, resuming her career after his death in 1959. Although the characters are of interest, with the cast members doing their bits well, too many situations are left unexplained or unmotivated, making for shaky goings. Songs include: "I'll Take You as You Are", "One Step Ahead of Everybody," "The Ties that Bind," "Breakfast In Bed," "Behind the Mask" (Bob Hilliard, Carl Sigman), and the oldie, "I Think You're Wonderful."

p, Henry Blanke; d, Gordon Douglas; w, Orin Jannings; ph, Edwin DuPar (Warner Color); ed, Folmar Blangsted; art d, Edward Carrere; ch, LeRoy Prinz; m/l, Bob Hilliard, Carl Sigman.

Musical (PR:A MPAA:NR)

SHE'S DANGEROUS*½ (1937) 68m UNIV bw

Tala Birell (*Stephanie Duval*), Cesar Romero (*Nick Shelton/Al Shaw*), Walter Pidgeon (*Dr. Scott Logan*), Walter Brennan (*"Ote" O'Leary*), Warren Hymer (*Herman Valentz*), Samuel S. Hinds (*Warden*), Jonathan Hale (*Charles Fitzgerald*), Richard Carle (*Kegley*), Franklin Pangborn (*Renaud the Couturier*), Richard Tucker (*District Attorney*), June Brewster (*Betty Mason*), Stanley Andrews (*Franklin Webb*), Martha O'Driscoll (*Blonde Girl*), Reverend Neal Dodd (*Chaplain*), Georges Renavent (*Eduardo, the Headwaiter*), Grady Sutton (*Drunk*), Pierre Watkin (*H. J. Conrad*), Maidel Turner (*Dowager*), Barry Norton (*Joseph, the Gigolo*), Matty Fain (*Lon Lowry*), Claire Rochelle (*Jane Hope*), Tom McGuire (*Bartender*), Jack George (*Execution Witness*), Jim Farley (*Sheriff*), Edward LeSaint (*Judge*), Ray Turner (*Shoeshiner*), Stanley Blystone (*Cop*).

Birell as a lady cop poses as a jewel thief in order to infiltrate Romero's gang. The comic relief of Brennan and Hymer, the latter as a part of the gang, are the strongest points of this otherwise uninteresting story. Blonde beauty Birell, Vienna-born, had been hailed as "another (Greta) Garbo" but her career quickly declined to such low-budget thrillers as this one. Her proclivity for prison films was legendary; she appeared in SEVEN MILES FROM ALCATRAZ (1942), WOMEN IN BONDAGE (1943), and GIRLS OF THE BIG HOUSE (1945). Lovely child actress O'Driscoll, in a bit part, later grew up and, like Birell, starred in B pictures.

p, E.M. Asher; d, Lewis R. Foster, Milton Carruth; w, Lionel Hauser, Albert H. Perkin (based on the story "Blonde Dynamite" by Murray Roth, Ben Ryan); ph, Milton Krasner; ed, Frank Gross; md, Lou Forbes; art d, Jack Otterson, Loren Patrick; spec eff, John P. Fulton.

Crime (PR:A MPAA:NR)

SHE'S FOR ME** (1943) 60m UNIV bw

George Dolenz (*Phil Norwin*), David Bruce (*Michael Reed*), Grace McDonald (*Jan Lawton*), Lois Collier (*Eileen Crane*), Charles Dingle (*Bradford Crane*), Helen Brown (*Miss Carpenter*), Louis Da Pron (*The Kid*), Mantan Moreland (*Sam*), Douglas Wood (*Milbourne*), Leon Belasco (*Acton*), Charles Coleman (*Clark*), Frank Faylen (*Keys*), Charles Trowbridge (*Dr. Folsom*),

Ray "Crash" Corrigan (*Gorilla Man*), Grace Hayle (*Dowager*), Carol Hughes (*Maxine LaVerne*), Eddie Bruce (*Cab Driver*), Frank Penny (*Bartender*), Gerald Pierce (*Bellboy*), Teddy Infuhr (*Child*), Rogers Trio, Eddie Le Baron and his Rhumba Orchestra.

A strange love triangle has Dolenz and Bruce as buddies working for the same law firm. The former starts wooing the boss's niece, Collier, whom Bruce likes in a brotherly sort of fashion. To get Dolenz off Collier's track, Bruce hires singer McDonald, a former lover of Dolenz, to get his rival out of the way. His ploy is successful, but when Collier is finally in Bruce's arms, he decides that he's really in love with McDonald. Director Le Borg managed to squeeze a number of laughs out of the weak material. McDonald sings a few songs, which include: "Cae, Cae" (John Latouche, Pedro Barrios, Roberto Martins), "Do I Know What I'm Doing?", "Closer and Closer", and "Ain't You Got No Time for Love?".

p, Frank Gross; d, Reginald Le Borg; w, Henry Blankfort; ph, Paul Ivano; ed, Paul Landres; md, Charles Previn; art d, John B. Goodman; ch, Louis Da Pron; m/l, Joan Costello, Freddy Stewart, Mitchell Parish, Harry Woods.

Comedy (PR:A MPAA:NR)

SHE'S GOT EVERYTHING*½ (1938) 72m RKO bw

Gene Raymond (*Fuller Partridge*), Ann Sothern (*Carol Rogers*), Victor Moore (*Waldo Eddington, Bookie*), Helen Broderick (*Aunt Jane*), Parkyakarkus (*Nick*), Billy Gilbert (*Chaffee*), William Brisbane (*Roger*), Herbert Clifton (*Watkins*), Alan Bruce (*Courtland*), Solly Ward (*Corrio, Hypnotist*), Alec Craig (*Justice of the Peace*), Fred Santley (*Reporter*), Richard Tucker (*Dr. Bricker*), George Irving (*Doctor*), Jack Carson (*Ransome*), Paul Guilfoyle (*Hotel Manager*), Al Hill (*Cab Driver*), Pat Flaherty (*Van Driver*).

Except for one or two sequences this is a fairly dull vehicle in which Sothern finds herself terribly in debt when her father dies. She gets a job as secretary to rich Raymond and wedding bells soon pop up, which makes Sothern's creditors all very happy. This is what Raymond starts to believe, at least, forcing him to temporarily postpone the marriage. But Sothern is not to be denied, and manages to convince her boss that she is in love with him despite the monetary rewards. Even though the majority of the cast were fine comic actors, they were given little more than slapstick routines with which to prove their talents. The result was the absence of much humor. Look for second banana Carson in a small role during his first year in Hollywood.

p, Albert Lewis; d, Joseph Santley; w, Joseph Hoffman, Monroe Shaff (based on a story by Harry Segall, Maxwell Shane); ph, Jack McKenzie; ed, Frederic Knudtson; m/l, "It's Sleepy Time In Hawaii," Leon and Otis Rene.

Comedy (PR:A MPAA:NR)

SHE'S IN THE ARMY**½ (1942) 63m MON bw

Lucille Gleason (*Sgt. Hannah*), Veda Ann Borg (*Diane*), Marie Wilson (*Susie*), Lyle Talbot (*Steve*), Robert Lowerey (*Lt. Jim*), Maxine Leslie (*Rita*), Charlotte Henry (*Helen*), John Holland (*Lundigan*), Marcella Richards (*Lewis*), Warren Hymer (*Joe*).

The training camp for women ambulance drivers during WW II serves as the background for this well-crafted independent feature. Borg plays a former cabaret singer, now in the ambulance corps, who falls in love with Army captain Talbot. Gleason is the tough sergeant responsible for getting the women into shape. The situations make for quite a few laughs well planted through the direction of Yarbrough, who for a change was given some decent material in Sidney Sheldon's script. Sheldon, who won an Academy Award for his screenplay of THE BACHELOR AND THE BOBBY SOXER, went on to become a successful novelist in the 1970s. Two of his steamy works, THE OTHER SIDE OF MIDNIGHT and BLOODLINE, were made into movies.

p, T.H. Richmond; d, Jean Yarbrough; w, Sidney Sheldon; ph, Harry Neumann; ed, Jack Ogilvie; art d, Frank Sylos.

Comedy/Drama (PR:A MPAA:NR)

SHE'S MY LOVELY (SEE: GET HEP TO LOVE, 1942)

SHE'S MY WEAKNESS*½ (1930) 75m RKO bw

Sue Carol (*Marie Thurber*), Arthur Lake (*Tommy Mills*), William Collier, Sr (*David Duttle*), Lucien Littlefield (*Warren Thurber*), Alan Bunce (*Bernard Norton*), Walter Gilbert (*Wilson*), Emily Fitzroy (*Mrs. Oberlander*).

Lake desperately wants to wed his sweetheart, Carol, though to any discerning mind they are much too young to marry. This is what Carol's uncle thinks at least, and he does his best to keep the two from the altar. The only way Lake can get up the needed money is to sell a piece of land, which he eventually does successfully. Except for a laugh here and there, the story is hardly enough to keep most adults interested.

p, Henry Hobart; d, Melville Brown; w, J. Walter Ruben (based on the play "Tommy" by Howard Lindsay and Bertram Robinson); ph, Leo Tover; art d, Max Ree.

Comedy   (PR:A MPAA:NR)

SHE'S NO LADY*   (1937) 70m PAR bw

Ann Dvorak (*Jerry*), John Trent (*Carter*), Harry Beresford (*Uncle*), Guinn "Big Boy" Williams (*Jeff*), Aileen Pringle (*Mrs. Douglas*), Arthur Hoyt (*Mr. Douglas*), Paul Hurst (*Cop*).

The attempt to create a sophisticated comedy out of this weak story, in which an insurance investigator and detective help solve a jewel robbery, was a total failure. It's hard to pinpoint just what to call this, but it certainly doesn't deserve to be called comedy. Before joining Paramount in 1925, Schulberg, as an independent producer, discovered Clara Bow and made her famous as the "It Girl." He returned to independent filmmaking in 1932 and worked as a staff producer for various Hollywood companies, but was unable to get work after WW II.

p, B.P. Schulberg; d, Charles Vidor; w, George Bruce, Frank Partos (based on the story by James Edward Grant); ph, George Clemons.

Comedy/Crime   (PR:A MPAA:NR)

SHE'S WORKING HER WAY THROUGH COLLEGE***
                                                         (1952) 101m WB c

Virginia Mayo (*Angela Gardner, "Hot Garters Gertie"*), Ronald Reagan (*John Palmer*), Gene Nelson (*Don Weston*), Don DeFore (*Shep Slade*), Phyllis Thaxter (*Helen Palmer*), Patrice Wymore (*Ivy Williams*), Roland Winters (*Fred Copeland*), Raymond Greenleaf (*Dean Rogers*), Norman Bartold (*"Tiny" Gordon*), Amanda Randolph (*Maybelle*), Henrietta Taylor (*Mrs. Copeland*), Hope Sansbury (*Mrs. Rogers*), George Meader (*Professor*), Eve Miller (*Secretary*), The Blackburn Twins (*Themselves*), Dick Reeves (*Mike*), Donald Kerr (*Vendor*), Patricia Hawks (*Donna Ring*), Frances Zucco (*Coeds*), Frank Scannell, Jimmy Ames, Paul Maxey, Charles Watts (*Men*), John Perri, Glen Turnbull (*Tramps*), Betty Arlen, Valerie Vernon, Hazel Shaw, Barbara Ritchie (*Chorus Girls*), Mark Lowell, Jimmy Ogg (*Sailors*), Charles Marsh (*Stage Manager*), Jack Gargan (*Professor*), Ray Linn, Jr (*Senator*), Jessie Arnold (*Wardrobe Woman*), Rolland Morris, Malcolm Mealey (*Hep Boys*), Louis Cutelli (*"Square"*), Ginger Crowley, Larry Craig (*Students*).

A musical version of THE MALE ANIMAL (which starred Henry Fonda, Olivia de Havilland, and Jack Carson), this was an example of the way Warner Brothers recycled their earlier films with remakes and musicalizing. Mayo is "Hot Garters Gertie," a burlesque dancer who would like to improve her mind, as there is absolutely nothing lacking in her body. Her intention is to forsake the bangles and beads for literature and become a writer. To that end, she enrolls in a small college in the heartland and takes writing courses from quiet, conservative Reagan, who doubles as the school's resident director of theatrical shows. Mayo moves into Reagan's home as a boarder but it's all very innocent. The usual theatrical fare at the school is a revival of some classic and Mayo thinks that they might have more fun by mounting a musical. She writes a show and Nelson, the college football heart throb who is mad about her, takes a part in it. Nelson has been seeing Wymore, who is jealous of his attentions to Mayo, so she tells the school authorities about Mayo's burlesque background. Well! This prompts the college's chief, Winters, to tell Reagan that he must toss Mayo out of his class. It will never do to have *that* kind of woman at the school. Reagan is married to Thaxter and their domestic life has been disturbed by the return of her old beau DeFore, and Reagan wonders what's going on between the two. Reagan takes a stance and appeals to the students and explains why he will not allow the school to pressure him to get rid of Mayo. Once he does that, he is a hero with students and fellow teachers alike. Mayo then recognizes the prudish Winters as a man who once tried to bribe her for her loving favors with a fur coat. After Winters's balloon has been pricked, Mayo goes on in the show which is, of course, a big hit, and she will presumably finish her degree studies. The sequel to this picture, SHE'S BACK ON BROADWAY, starred Mayo and Nelson but Reagan stayed at home. DeFore had also appeared in the Fonda version in 1942 and played a small role as one of the football players. In this, he was doing the Carson role, and not doing it justice. DeFore is truly one of the least funny light comedians who ever trudged across a screen and was the subject of a scathing satire by Albert Brooks who made a short film about a mythical institution called "The Don DeFore School of Comedy." Director Humberstone, who was better known for pictures like CHARLIE CHAN AT THE OPERA, TARZAN'S FIGHT FOR LIFE, and I WAKE UP SCREAMING, shows that he knows his way around light comedy and musicals here and does a good job. They took the Al Dubin-Harry Warren tune from GOLD DIGGERS of 1937, "With Plenty Of Money And You," and plunked it in here for Mayo to sing. The remainder of the songs were by Sammy Cahn and Vernon Duke. They included: "She's Working Her Way Through College," "I'll Be Loving You," "The Stuff that Dreams Are Made Of," "Give 'Em What They Want," (sung by Mayo, Nelson) "Am I In Love?" (Nelson), and "Love Is Still for Free" (Wymore, the Blackburn Twins). Many of Milne's jokes fall flat, but the elan of the performers and Humberstone's knowledgeable handling keeps matters at a high level.

p, William Jacobs; d, H. Bruce Humberstone; w, Peter Milne (based on the play "The Male Animal" by James Thurber, Elliott Nugent); ph, Wilfred M. Cline (Technicolor); m, Vernon Duke; ed, Clarence Kolster; md, Ray

Heindorf; art d, Charles H. Clarke; ch, LeRoy Prinz; m/l, Sammy Cahn, Duke, Al Dubin, Harry Warren.

Musical/Comedy   (PR:A MPAA:NR)

SHICHININ NO SAMURAI   (SEE: SEVEN SAMURAI, THE, 1954, Jap.)

SHIELD FOR MURDER**½   (1954) 81m camden/UA bw

Edmond O'Brien (*Barney Nolan*), Marla English (*Patty Winters*), John Agar (*Mark Brewster*), Emile Meyer (*Capt. Gunnarson*), Carolyn Jones (*Girl at Bar*), Claude Akins (*Fat Michaels*), Larry Ryle (*Laddie O'Neil*), Herbert Butterfield (*Cabot*), Hugh Sanders (*Packy Reed*), William Schallert (*Assistant District Attorney*), David Hughes (*Ernest Sternmueller*), Richard Cutting (*Manning*).

O'Brien, in his first attempt at direction, also stars as a crooked cop who shoots a gangster, steals $25,000 and tells his superiors it was all in the line of duty. But there was one witness, who O'Brien also kills when he is assigned the job of investigating the murder he earlier committed. Detective Agar, a cop tramed by O'Brien, and gangster Sanders get wise to O'Brien's antics and track down the cop at his newly built suburban home, where the stolen money is hidden. O'Brien meets with his just rewards when the police gun him down. Though pacing is a bit off, O'Brien is convincing as the crooked cop, caught up in his own greed and the desire to maintain a middle-class existence in suburbia.

p, Aubrey Schenck; d, Edmond O'Brien, Howard W. Koch; w, Richard Alan Simmons, John C. Higgins (based on the novel by William P. McGivern); ph, Gordon Avil; m, Paul Dunlap; ed, John F. Schreyer; prod d, Charles D. Hall.

Crime   (PR:A MPAA:NR)

SHIELD OF FAITH, THE**   (1956, Brit.) 56m Gregory, Hake and Walker-Church and Chapel/RFD bw

Mervyn Jones, Adrienne Corri, Emrys Jones.

Basically a religious inspiration film, THE SHIELD OF FAITH shows how a group of airline passengers rediscover God after surviving a plane crash. Professionally produced Sunday-school theology with little entertainment value.

d, Norman Walker; w, Lawrence Barrett (based on a story by Joseph Arthur Rank, R.N.F. Evans).

Drama   (PR:A MPAA:NR)

SHILLINGBURY BLOWERS, THE**½ (1980, Brit.) 82m Inner Circle
                                                         c

Trevor Howard (*Dan "Saltie" Wicklow*), Robin Nedwell (*Peter*), Diane Keen (*Sally*), Jack Douglas (*Jake*), Sam Kydd (*Reggie*), Eric Francis (*Sam*), Joe Black (*Harvey*), Tony Sympson (*Basil*), John Le Mesurier (*Council Chairman*).

Charming story that has pop musician Nedwell and his wife, Keen, leaving the hectic city to live in the peaceful village of Shillingbury. But he is soon put to work as the leader of the town band, which is in bad need of some fine tuning. Howard plays the aging band leader who loses his job with the arrival of Nedwell. Unpretentious light entertainment.

p, Greg Smith; d, Val Guest; w, Francis Essex; ph, Frank Watts; m, Ed Welch; ed, Bill Lenny; art d, Albert Witherick.

Drama/Comedy   (PR:A MPAA:NR)

SHIN NO SHIKOTEI   (SEE: GREAT WALL, THE, 1965, Jap.)

SHINBONE ALLEY**   (1971) 83m FA/AA c

Voices: Carol Channing (*mehitabel*), Eddie Bracken (*archy*), Allen Reed (*Big Bill, Sr.*), John Carradine (*Tyrone T. Tattersall*), Jackie Ward Singers, Ken Sansom, Hal Smith, Joan Gerber, Sal Delano.

Popular comic strip that ran from 1916-1930 is brought to the screen and, with its theme of unrequited love, aimed more at adults than at children. Channing and Bracken are the voices of the main characters, which they did earlier on a record album, recreating roles played by Eartha Kitt and Bracken on Broadway. Main cartoon character is a cockroach, who is the reincarnation of a despondent poet who had committed suicide. He composes his poetry on the typewriter of a newspaper columnist and the main object of his verses and affection is a friendly female cat. These two characters seem to take on the personalities of the people behind the voices, namely Bracken and Channing. The roach writes letters and poems by hopping on typewriter keys, but he can't use the shift-lock key, so everything is in lower-case letters. The animation style of SHINBONE ALLEY was compared by some critics to YELLOW SUBMARINE (1968), which mixed visual forms in a montage-like fashion and shifted painting styles. Songs included "I Am Only a Poor Humble Cockroach," "Blow Wind Out of the North," "Cheerio My Deario (Toujours Gai)," "Ah, the Theater, the Theater," "What Do We Care If We're Down and Out?," "The Moth Song,"

"Lullaby for Mehitabel's Kittens," "The Shinbone Alley Song," "The Lightning Bug Song," "Here Pretty Pretty Pussy," "Ladybugs of the Evening," "Archy's Philosophies," "They Don't Have it Here," "Romeo and Juliet," "Come to Meeoww" (George Kleinsinger, Joe Darion).

p, Preston M. Fleet; d, John David Wilson; w, Joe Darion (based on the book for the musical play by Darion, Mel Brooks, from the "archy and mehitabel" stories by Don Marquis); ph, Wally Bullock, Gene Borghi, Ted Bemiller (Eastmancolor); ed, Warner Leighton; prod d, Gary Lund, Wilson, Cornelius Cole, James Bernardi, David Detiege, Jules Engel, Sam Cornell; animation, Frank Andrina, John Sparey, Amby Paliwoda, Gil Rugg, George Waiss, Bob Bransford, Jim Hiltz, Fred Grable, Brad Case, Frank Gonzales, Barrie Nelson, Ken Southworth, Russ Von Neida, Frank Onaitis, Bob Bemiller, Rudy Cataldi, Spencer Peel, Selby Daley.

Cartoon   **Cas.**   **(PR:A   MPAA:G)**

SHINE ON, HARVEST MOON*½   (1938) 55m REP bw

Roy Rogers (Roy), Mary Hart [Lynne Roberts] (Claire), Lulubelle and Scotty (Themselves), Stanley Andrews (Jackson), William Farnum (Brower), Frank Jacquet (Sheldon), Chester Gunnels (Chet), Matty Roubert (Ben), Pat Henning (Shag), Jack Rockwell (Jim), Joe Whitehead (Clay), David Sharpe, Trigger the Horse.

One of the weaker Rogers vehicles is about a range war that erupts when Andrews becomes a cattle rustler after his partnership with Farnum fizzles. Rogers, as the son to Farnum's former partner, does his bit to restore peace. Lulubelle and Scotty were imported from the WLS National Barn Dance radio show in Chicago to take up the comic end, but they fail miserably. In addition, the title of the film has nothing to do with the story.

p, Charles E. Ford; d, Joseph Kane; w, Jack Natteford; ph, William Nobles; ed, Lester Orlebeck; md, Cy Feuer.

Western   **Cas.**   **(PR:A   MPAA:NR)**

SHINE ON, HARVEST MOON**   (1944) 111m WB c/bw

Ann Sheridan (Nora Bayes), Dennis Morgan (Jack Norworth), Jack Carson (The Great Georgetti), Irene Manning (Blanche Mallory), S.Z. Sakall (Poppa Karl), Marie Wilson (Margie), Robert Shayne (Dan Costello), Bob Murphy (Police Sergeant), The Four Step Brothers (Dance Team), The Ashburns (Dance Team), William B. Davidson (Tim Donovan), Will Stanton (A Drunk), James Bush (William Fowler), Joseph Crehan (Harry Miller), Betty Bryson (Soubrette), Don Kramer, George Rogers (Dancers), Harry Charles Johnson (Juggler), Walter Pietila (Acrobat), Paul Panzer (Doorman), Al Hill (Captain of Waiters), Mike Mazurki, Frank Hagney (Bouncers), Jack Norton, Bert Roach (Drunks), Nestor Paiva (Romero the Chef), Charles Marsh, Tom Quinn, Jack Boyle, Duke Johnson, Billy Bletcher, Peggy Carson, Anita Pike, Doria Caron (Vaudevillians), Gino Corrado (Cook), Brandon Hurst (Watchman), Johnnie Berkes, Bill Young (Tramp Ambassadors in the "My Own United States" Number), Jack Daley, Mike Donovan, Frank McCarroll, Charles McAvoy, Kernan Cripps, Thomas Murray, George McDonald, Bob Reeves, Bill O'Leary, Charles McMurphy, Allen D. Sewell (Policemen in the "It Looks to Me Like a Big Night" Number).

A film adaptation of the the life of Broadway vaudevillian Nora Bayes, played by Sheridan, who becomes business partner to Jack Norworth (Morgan), and eventually marriage partner. Story veers a bit far from actual fact, but things had to be spiced up a bit to make the story entertaining. Most of the action takes place backstage, occurring between 1905 and 1910. The most memorable routine is a comedy bit called "So Dumb But So Beautiful" (M.K. Jerome, Kim Gannon). The last 10 minutes served as a sort of grand finale, with chorus girls and the whole shot. In the sequence, filmed in color, Sheridan and Morgan perform the title song (Jack Norworth, Nora Bayes). Other songs include: "When It's Apple Blossom Time In Normandy" (Harry Gifford, Huntley Trevor, Tom Mellor), "What's the Matter with Father?" (Harry Williams, Egbert Van Alstyne), "Pretty Baby" (Gus Kahn, Tony Jackson), "Time Waits for No One" (Cliff Friend, Charles Tobias), "I Go for You" (Jerome, Gannon), "Every Little Movement Has a Meaning of Its Own" (Otto Harbach, Karl Hoschna), "Just Like a Gypsy" (Seymour B. Simons, Bayes), "Take Me Out to the Ball Game" (Norworth, Albert von Tilzer), and "Along with the Breeze" (Haven Gillespie, Simons, Richard A. Whiting).

p, William Jacobs; d, David Butler; w, Sam Hellman, Richard Weil, Francis Swann, James Kern (based on the story by Weil); ph, Arthur Edeson (Technicolor); ed, Irene Morra; md, Leo F. Forbstein; art d, Charles Novi; set d, Jack McCanaghy; spec eff, Edwin A, Du Par; ch, LeRoy Prinz.

Musical   **(PR:A   MPAA:NR)**

SHINEL   (SEE: OVERCOAT, THE, 1965, USSR)

SHINING, THE***   (1980) 146m WB c

Jack Nicholson (Jack Torrance), Shelley Duvall (Wendy Torrance), Danny Lloyd (Danny), Scatman Crothers (Halloran), Barry Nelson (Ullman), Philip Stone (Grady), Joe Turkel (Lloyd), Anne Jackson (Doctor), Tony Burton (Durkin), Lia Beldam (Young Woman in Bathtub), Billie Gibson (Old

Woman in Bathtub), Barry Dennen (Watson), David Baxt, Manning Redwood (Forest Rangers), Lisa Burns, Louise Burns (Grady Girls), Robin Pappas (Nurse), Alison Coleridge (Secretary), Burnell Tucker (Policeman), Jana Sheldon (Stewardess), Kate Phelps (Receptionist), Norman Gay (Injured Guest).

THE SHINING is an odd movie, alternatively infuriating, gorgeous, dumb, frightening, funny, and boring. Kubrick is a master of the haunting visual, as seen in 2001: A SPACE ODYSSEY and BARRY LYNDON, but he sometimes allows his eye to get in front of his good sense. Here, he again demonstrates camera technique you may take home with you and replay over and over in your memory. As beautiful as the picture looks, it is brought down by the eccentricities of the players, mainly Duvall and Nicholson, who show more ham than the Hormel factory. Why Kubrick allowed them to play so broadly is a bewilderment because it serves to destroy any credibility. Duvall and Nicholson are a youngish couple with a gifted son. Nicholson is a former teacher who wants to write a novel. He and wife Duvall and son Lloyd move into a large mountain hotel called The Overlook which stays open only during the summer. In the winter, it's necessary to have someone there to make sure everything goes well but the snow makes it impossible to get in and out, so anyone who lives there must be able to withstand the silence that accompanies the job. Nelson interviews Nicholson and the job is his. Nicholson is thrilled as it will afford him the time to write and also give him a chance to get closer to his family. Nelson admits that the former winter caretaker of the well-kept behemoth of a hotel went insane, killed his wife and children and committed suicide, perhaps due to the isolation. Nicholson shrugs that off and they move into the hotel. They soon learn that Lloyd has a special power of extra sensory perception and that he talks to an invisible twin he calls "Tony". Crothers is the chief cook at the hotel and the last person to leave at the end of the season. He is also a clairvoyant and he senses a kinship in Lloyd and lets the child know that there is trouble in store but it will all be fine as long as the youngster stays out of room 237. Time passes and Nicholson is exhibiting signs of "mountain fever" as he neglects his work, drinks heavily and becomes increasingly irritable. He spends time in the hotel bar talking to an imaginary barkeeper, Turkel (who is a Kubrick veteran, having played in PATHS OF GLORY). Lloyd becomes very frightened by what he feels and Duvall does her best to mother him. One night, while in the hotel public bathroom, Nicholson meets Stone, who appears to be the ghost of the man who killed his wife and children, then himself. Stone is functioning as a washroom attendant and warns Nicholson to be sterner with Lloyd. After Lloyd somehow receives a wound on his neck, Nicholson begins to chase the child and Duvall around the hotel wielding various weapons but they manage to elude him. Crothers senses that the boy is in trouble and tries to call the hotel. When that doesn't work, he makes his way through the snowdrifts in a snowmobile. No sooner does Crothers arrive when he's killed by Nicholson who is in a frenzy of blood-lust by this time. Nicholson chases after Lloyd in the snow outside the hotel and can't quite catch the boy, finally ending up dead of exposure at the conclusion. Kubrick, who will always take great pains to achieve scenic perfection, seems to have given Nicholson free rein to do whatever he wanted to do in the role of the man possessed. This makes for a disturbing juxtaposition of styles as Kubrick mixes grand vistas with outlandish, almost cartoon characters running, hobbling and, in the case of Duvall, often whimpering. The last shot of Nicholson's frozen grimace is half-serious, half-comic and an indication of the movie in general. It's hard to know when to laugh or when to shudder and one wonders if this was Kubrick's intent or was it merely a mistake? There was precious little remaining from the King novel other than the setting and the title, and the script took huge liberties that were as ridiculous as they were beguiling. When Nicholson smashes through the door to his apartment with an axe, sticks his face through and maniacally yells (in a parody of Ed MacMahon)... "Heeeeeere's Johnny]" we think that it must be for a laugh. Then the blood begins to spurt. The picture looks better than it sounds and baffles better than it looks and yet, the images one recalls will be forever etched: Lloyd meets two little girls, Lisa and Louise Burns, in the hallway, a pair of Diane Arbus-like moppets who are a mixture of innocence and evil; Blood gushes through the area near the elevators, etc. The music is played by Wendy Carlos (who was once Walter Carlos before a sex change operation altered him to her but didn't seem to hurt his musical ability) and is from the works of Bela Bartok, which are eerie enough. Crothers is sensational as the cook and Lloyd is excellent as the child but Nicholson's mugging, shrieking, chortling performance discredits any real menace. Duvall doesn't have much to do and what she does with it is not much. It is, despite all the money lavished on it, a disappointing film that is neither terror nor camp but something somewhere in between that pleases no one. Carlos and Rachel Elkind composed "The Shining" and "Rocky Mountains"; "Lontano" was by Gyorgy Ligeti, and Krzysztof Penderecki wrote "Utrenja, The Awakening of Jacob" and "De Natura Sonoris N. 2." Bartok's pieces included "Music for Strings, Percussion and Celesta." Another song was "Home" (Henry Hall).

p&d, Stanley Kubrick; w, Kubrick, Diane Johnson (based on the novel by Stephen King); ph, John Alcott m, Bela Bartok, Wendy Carlos, Rachel Elkind, Gyorgy Ligeti, Krzysztof Penderecki; ed, Ray Lovejoy; prod d, Roy Walker; art d, Les Tomkins; cos, Milena Canonero; makeup, Tom Smith.

Horror   **Cas.**   **(PR:C-O   MPAA:R)**

SHINING HOUR, THE½   (1938) 76m MGM bw

Joan Crawford (*Olivia Riley*), Margaret Sullavan (*Judy Linden*), Melvyn Douglas (*Henry Linden*), Robert Young (*David Linden*), Fay Bainter (*Hannah Linden*), Allyn Joslyn (*Roger Franklin*), Hattie McDaniel (*Belvedere*), Frank Albertson (*Benny Collins*), Oscar O'Shea (*Charlie Collins*), Harry Barris (*Bertie*), Tony De Marco (*Olivia's Dance Partner*), Claire Owen (*Stewardess*), Jim Conlin, Granville Bates (*Men*), Roger Converse (*Clerk*), Francis X. Bushman, Jr (*Doorman*), Frank Puglia (*Headwaiter*), George Chandler (*Press Agent*), Sarah Edwards (*Woman*), Buddy Messinger (*Elevator Boy*), Charles C. Coleman (*Butler*), Edwin Stanley (*Minister*), E. Allyn Warren (*Leonard*), Grace Hayle (*Mrs. Briggs*), Jacques Vanaire (*Waiter*), Cyril Ring (*Candid Cameraman*), Bess Flowers (*Nurse*), Grace Goodall (*Mrs. Smart*), Jack Raymond (*Farmer*).

A typical 1930s picture with a plot as familiar as the palm of one's hand. Crawford is a New York night club terpsichorean who is wooed and won by Douglas, a well-to-do conservative type whose family is not thrilled about the marriage. Apparently, the chief objector is Douglas's brother, Young. Crawford and Douglas move on to the huge family estate/farm where Douglas's spinster sister, Bainter, runs the place like a prison camp. Friction erupts between Bainter and Crawford but the young wife finds a friend in Young's spouse, Sullavan, as they are of the same age and disposition, despite coming from different castes. As it turns out, Young wants to keep Crawford away from the family compound because he finds himself attracted to her and feels it would be safer if she were not allowed in his general proximity. Crawford feels the same way about Young so trouble is bubbling on the home front. Bainter is no fool and spots what's happening, then attempts to use it as a wedge against Crawford to get her to leave. Douglas is blissfully happy with Crawford and has no idea what's going on behind his back. Sullavan, once she is wise to the situation, plans to walk out, leaving Young and Crawford to each other. Her decision is based on sacrifice, not rancor. Young finds it difficult to handle the guilt and is at a loss to solve the problem when Bainter sets fire to the house. (It's a bit rash, one might think) Crawford saves Sullavan from the flames but the sister-in-law is burned critically. When Young visits his wife, who is covered in bandages and can't respond to his words, he realizes that she is, and always has been, the woman for him. Douglas and Crawford reconcile, despite Bainter's thrusts and parries, and will try to make a life with each other. Big names can do nothing to overcome the soapy and sappy script. With the witty Ogden Nash as a co-author, one might have expected more from the dialog.

p, Joseph L. Mankiewicz; d, Frank Borzage; w, Jane Murfin, Ogden Nash (based on the play by Keith Winters); ph, George Folsey; m, Franz Waxman; ed, Frank E. Hull; art d, Cedric Gibbons, Paul Groesse; set d, Edwin B. Willis; cos, Adrian; ch, Tony DeMarco.

Drama   (PR:A-C   MPAA:NR)

SHINING STAR   (SEE: THAT'S THE WAY OF THE WORLD, 1975)

SHINING VICTORY**   (1941) 80m WB bw

James Stephenson (*Dr. Paul Venner*), Geraldine Fitzgerald (*Dr. Mary Murray*), Donald Crisp (*Dr. Drewett*), Barbara O'Neil (*Miss Leeming*), Montagu Love (*Dr. Blake*), Sig Ruman[n] (*Prof. Herman Von Reiter*), George P. Huntley, Jr (*Dr. Thornton*), Richard Ainley (*Dr. Hale*), Bruce Lester (*Dr. Bentley*), Leonard Mudie (*Foster*), Doris Lloyd (*Mrs. Foster*), Frank Reicher (*Dr. Esternazy*), Hermine Sterler (*Miss Hoffman*), Billy Bevan (*Chivers*), Clare Verdera (*Miss Dennis*), Crauford Kent (*Dr. Corliss*), Alec Craig (*Jeweler*).

Overly sentimental drama has Stephenson as a devoted medical researcher forced to flee from Budapest when his boss discovers some of his findings. He goes to Scotland and quickly gets back to work. His stubborn character comes into play when he is provided with a woman, Fitzgerald, as an assistant. But the two fall in love anyway and make plan to marry once Stephenson's research is completed. However, Fitzgerald is killed in a fire in an attempt to save Stephenson's records. He then devotes the rest of his career to her memory and travels to China to continue her medical missionary work. Both Stephenson and Fitzgerald are convincing, but the material is heavy-handed and a bit hard to stomach. This was the first directorial job for Rapper, whose talents for tear-jerkers would be fulfilled in NOW VOYAGER the following year.

p, Robert Lord; d, Irving Rapper; w, Howard Koch, Anne Froelick (based on the play "Jupiter Laughs" by A.J. Cronin); ph, James Wong Howe; m, Max Steiner ed, Warren Low.

Drama   (PR:A   MPAA:NR)

SHINJU TEN NO AMIJIMA   (SEE: DOUBLE SUICIDE, 1970, Jap.)

SHIP AHOY**   (1942) 96m MGM bw

Eleanor Powell (*Tallulah Winters*), Red Skelton (*Merton K. Kibble*), Bert Lahr (*Skip Owens*), Virginia O'Brien (*Fran Evans*), William Post Jr (*H.U. Bennett*), James Cross (*Stump*), Eddie Hartman (*Stumpy*), Stuart Crawford (*Art Higgins*), John Emery (*Dr. Farno*), Bernard Nedell (*Pietro Polesi*),

Moroni Olsen (*Inspector Davis*), Ralph Dunn (*Grimes*), William Tannen (*Flammer*), Mary Treen (*Nurse*), Russell Hicks (*Capt. C.V. O'Brien*), Philip Ahn (*Koro Sumo*), Nestor Paiva (*Felix*), Bobby Larson (*Waldo*), Mariska Aldrich (*Waldo's Mother*), John Dilson (*Dr. Loring*), Barbara Bedford (*Mrs. Loring*), Carol Hughes, Gladys Blake, Mary Currier (*Secretaries*), Addison Richards (*Agent in Puerto Rico*), Grandon Rhodes (*Lt. Cmdr. Thurston*), Grant Withers, Otto Reichow (*Waiters*), Hillary Brooke, Natalie Thompson (*Girls*), Tommy Dorsey and His Orchestra (*Themselves*), Frank Sinatra, Connie Haynes, The Pied Pipers.

A jumble of songs, some comedy, silly patriotic cliches, and a spy spoof story all adds up to less than meets the eye. Powell had scored well aboard ships in BORN TO DANCE, HONOLULU, and BROADWAY MELODY OF 1940 so this time they really put her at sea with a dull script and a series of situations that bordered on sleep. The studio must have felt that spy tales were the thing to do because they also gave Jeanette MacDonald the unenviable task of appearing in CAIRO that same year. Powell is a tap dancer who works with Dorsey's band and they are all on their way to Puerto Rico by ocean liner. Also with the band are drummer Buddy Rich, trumpeter Ziggy Elman and a skinny singer named Sinatra who does most of the crooning in the film. Emery is an enemy agent and he masquerades as an an F.B.I. man when he hands Powell a package and asks her to deliver it, for her country, to some people in San Juan. She is nervous about the assignment but since it's for her government, she accepts the task. She doesn't know that the package contains a model and plans for a new mine that the bad guys are trying to sneak out of the country without having to go past U.S. Customs. Once aboard the ship, her luggage is misplaced and switched for that of Skelton, a daffy hack writer of pulp fiction. Powell's pal is deadpan O'Brien and she falls for Lahr, who works for Skelton. What none of them know is that this booking has all been arranged by the bad guys for the sole purpose of getting the plans and the model of the mine out of the U.S. and into the hands of the enemy. They are going to appear at a floating cafe which is operated by another foreign agent. When they get close to Puerto Rico, the baggage switch takes place and Skelton tries to leave the boat with the mine. Powell gets the mine back, innocently gives it to the bad guys and then, with the help of Skelton and Lahr, they manage to overturn the plot after Powell taps out a message in Morse code to undercover F.B.I. men in the audience at the San Juan club. In a huge leap of logic, a submarine surfaces near the floating night club which is commanded by a captain who is hip to lead the shenanigans. The villains are overplayed in the usual 1940s fashion. Skelton has only a few moments where he can shine as a comic, and it's hard to believe that this little script took seven writers. The best part of the movie was Powell's rat-a-tat dancing and some of the other musical numbers which included "Last Call for Love" (Burton Lane, E.Y. Harburg, Margery Cumming, sung by Sinatra), "Poor You" (Lane, Harburg, done by Skelton, O'Brien, Sinatra, and Dorsey Orchestra), "On Moonlight Bay" (by Percy Wenrich, Edward Madden, done by Sinatra, The Pied Pipers, Dorsey Orchestra), "Tampico" (by Walter Ruick, done by Powell), "I'll Take Tallulah" (Harburg, Lane, done by Powell), "Cape Dance" (by Ruick, done by Powell), "Ship Ahoy" (Lane, Harburg, done by Powell with James Cross, Eddie Hartman). Rich and Elman have stand-out solos and Dorsey gets in some of his smooth trombone licks. The picture looks as though it were shot over a weekend.

p, Jack Cummings; d, Edward N. Buzzell; w, Harry Clork, Harry Kurnitz, Irving Brecher (based on a story by Matt Brooks, Bradford Ropes, Bert Kalmar); ph, Leonard Smith, Robert Planck; m, Axel Stordahl, Sy Oliver, Leo Arnaud, George Bassman, Basil Adlam George Stoll, Henry Russell; ed, Blanche Sewell; md, George Stoll; art d, Cedric Gibbons, Harry McAfee; set d, Edwin B. Willis; cos, Robert Kalloch; ch, Bobby Connolly.

Musical/Comedy   (PR:A   MPAA:NR)

SHIP CAFE**½   (1935) 65m PAR bw

Carl Brisson (*Chris Anderson*), Arline Judge (*Ruby*), Mady Christians (*Countess Boranoff*), William Frawley (*Briney O'Brien*), Eddie Davis (*Himself*), Inez Courtney (*Molly*), Grant Withers (*Rocky Stone*), Harry Woods (*Donovan*), Irving Bacon (*Slim*), Fred Warren (*Harry*), Jack Norton (*Mr. Randall*).

Brisson plays a stoker aboard a ship whose singing voice is discovered one day while he's throwing coals into the fire. He's talked into pursuing a job at a cafe in a docked ship. This paves the way for some tunes, and the romances between Brisson and society dame Christians and fellow singer Judge. Songs include: "Fatal Fascination," "I won't Take No For An Answer," "It's a Great Life," "I Lost My Heart," "Lazybones Gotta Job Now" (Harlan Thompson, Lewis Gensler), "Change Your Mind" (Ray Noble) and "My Home Town" (Eddie Davis).

p, Harold Hurley; d, Robert Florey; w, Harlan Thompson, Herbert Fields; ph, Theodore Sparkuhl; ed, James Smith.

Musical   (PR:A   MPAA:NR)

SHIP FROM SHANGHAI, THE**   (1930) 72m MGM bw

Conrad Nagel (*Howard Vazey*), Kay Johnson (*Dorothy Daley*), Carmel Myers (*Viola Thorpe*), Holmes Herbert (*Paul Thorpe*), Zeffie Tilbury (*Lady Daley*), Louis Wolheim (*Ted, Yacht Steward*), Ivan Linow (*Pete the cook*), Jack McDonald (*Reid*).

Adventures on the high seas centers around a crazed ship's steward, compellingly portrayed by Wolheim, who takes charge of the ship after tossing the captain overboard. With his new position of power, Wolheim becomes a virtual tyrant, saved from his irate crew only because of the presence of the giant oafish cook Linow as his protector. The crew is eventually relieved of their oppressor when Wolheim loses total control of his mind and jumps to his death. Almost all of the action takes place aboard ship, a fact the director seemed at a loss to contend with.

d, Charles Brabin; w, John Howard Lawson (based on the novel *The Ordeal* by Dale Collins); ph, Ira Morgan; ed, Grant Whytock; art d, Cedric Gibbons.

Adventure/Drama   **(PR:A   MPAA:NR)**

SHIP OF CONDEMNED WOMEN, THE½**
(1963, ITAL.) 95m EX/Globe Pictures-President Films c (LA NAVE DELLE DONNE MALEDETTE)

Kerima *(Rosario)*, Giorgio Capecchi *(Police Captain)*, Ettore Manni *(Da Silva)*, Olga Solbelli *(Anita)*, May Britt *(Consuelo)*, Gualtiero Tumiati *(Pietro Silveris)*, Tania Weber *(Isabella)*, Elvy Lissiak *(Carmen)*, Luigi Tosi *(Fernandez, the Ship's Captain)*, Marcella Rovena *(Nora)*, Romolo Costa *(Manuel de Haviland)*, Eduardo Ciannelli *(Michele)*, Flo Sandons.

Interesting twist to "the ship of lost souls" has a ship of women convicts being taken to the colonies to be kept under control. One of these, Britt, has been framed in the killing of her child. Manni, the lawyer responsible for her conviction, sneaks on board after suffering remorse for his deeds. Also on board ship is Britt's cousin, Weber, the real murderer who has gained her passage through a marriage to a rich businessman. She allows her husband to die in order to inherit his riches, and then takes up with the captain. When Britt and Manni publically denounce her, the prisoners mutiny, killing Weber and the captain. A storm rises up, and despite the women's prayers, everyone drowns but Britt and Manni.

p, Alfredo De Laurentiis; d, Raffaello Matarazzo; w, Ennio De Concini, Matarazzo; ph, Aldo Tonti (Gevacolor); m/l, "Malasierra," Flo Sandons.

Drama   **(PR:A   MPAA:NR)**

SHIP OF FOOLS**
(1965) 148m COL bw

Vivien Leigh *(Mary Treadwell)*, Simone Signoret *(La Condesa)*, Jose Ferrer *(Rieber)*, Lee Marvin *(Tenny)*, Oskar Werner *(Dr. Schumann)*, Elizabeth Ashley *(Jenny)*, George Segal *(David)*, Jose Greco *(Pepe)*, Michael Dunn *(Glocken)*, Charles Korvin *(Capt. Thiele)*, Heinz Ruehmann *(Lowenthal)*, Lilia Skala *(Frau Hutten)*, Barbara Luna *(Amparo)*, Christiane Schmidtmer *(Lizzi)*, Alf Kjellin *(Freytag)*, Werner Klemperer *(Lt. Heebner)*, John Wengraf *(Graf)*, Olga Fabian *(Frau Schmitt)*, Gila Golan *(Elsa)*, Oscar Beregi *(Lutz)*, Stanley Adams *(Hutten)*, Karen Verne *(Frau Lutz)*, Charles de Vries *(Johann)*, Lydia Torea *(Pastora)*, Henry Calvin *(Fat Man)*, Paul Daniel *(Carlos)*, David Renard *(Woodcarver)*, Silvia Marino *(Ric)*, Rudy Carrella *(Ric)*, Anthony Brand *(Guitarist)*, Peter Mamakos *(Religious Man)*, Walter Friedel *(Waiter)*, Bert Rumsey *(2nd Officer)*, Jon Alvar *(Student)*, Charles H. Radilac *(Headwaiter)*, Steven Geray *(Steward)*, Justo Robles Quintero, Maribel DeCirez Garcia, Jose Santiago Martinez.

The movie, Signoret, Dunn, Mann, Werner and Laszlo were all nominated for Oscars in SHIP OF FOOLS but only Laszlo won for his cinematography. Dwarf Dunn later confided to friends that had he won, his acceptance speech would have been short and sweet and simply..."I'd like to thank the Academy for this award. You've made me feel four feet tall." Mann's adaptation of this "Grand Hotel" at sea was excellent as he managed to condense a hefty book into a palatable screen time, and his nomination was merited. It's the early 1930s and an oceanliner peopled with a cross-section of society is leaving Vera Cruz for Bremerhaven. In the high class section are several well-to-do people while below decks, are a horde of sugar field workers who are returning to Spain after a season of work in Cuba. There are several wealthy Germans on the ship and all are asked to sit at the captain's table, save two. Korvin is the captain of the ship and he thinks it might be best if Ruehmann, a Jew, and Dunn, a dwarf, not dine with the others in view of Hitler's theory of Aryan purity. Kjellin, another German, leaves the table and sits with Dunn and Ruehmann when it is learned that Kjellin's wife is Jewish. Werner is the ship's doctor, a man with a bad heart, and he spends a great deal of his time with Signoret, a Spaniard being shipped back to Europe for having engaged in political activities. She is facing prison and takes solace in drugs. Although unattractive, Werner finds her fascinating and the two fall in love. Marvin is a failed baseball player whose career went awry because he couldn't hit the outside curve ball (something that has been a bugaboo since Abner Doubleday invented the game). Marvin is a satyr, a drunk and has an hysterical scene when he attempts to explain his hitting problem to Dunn, who is as familiar with baseball as Marvin is with teetotaling. Also on the ship are Segal and Ashley. They are unmarried lovers and he resents the fact that he can't make a living as an artist but they are so sexually magnetized to each other that their arguments usually end up in a passionate embrace. Leigh is a divorcee who flirts with everyone and enjoys leading men on and then shunting them aside. (This was her final screen appearance before she died in 1967.) Wengraf is a religious evangelist who goes down into the hold and preaches to the sugar workers, stirring them into a free-for-all brawl. Wengraf is aboard the ship with his young nephew, de Vries, who has a roll in the hay

with a hooker traveling with Jose Greco's dance group. Greco not only runs the troupe, he is also a panderer. Golan is a young woman who despairs because she feels she's ugly and is only brought out of her self-doubt through the help of Ashley and the fact that Ruehmann thinks she's charming and beautiful. The ship stops and Signoret is taken off to jail; then it goes on to Bremerhaven where Werner dies of a heart attack and the others get off to face whatever is their future. All of the above stories are interwoven, soap opera style, so we never follow any single story for any lengthy period of time. It's an adult picture with graphic language and important themes, the main one being Nazism. Ferrer is the principle espouser of Hitler's words and a hated creature throughout the film. Superb acting in a script that seldom descends into bathos. Three tunes from Ernest Gold (who knew his way around ships with Jewish passengers, having written the score for EXODUS) and Jack Lloyd, a German-American lyricist who spent his last years doing charity work for many groups in Los Angeles. The tunes were: "Heute Abend," "Geh'n Wir Bummelin Auf Der Reeperbahn," and "Irgendwie, Irgendwo, Irgendwanh." Producer-director Kramer made many films focusing on Nazism and racism, including JUDGMENT AT NUREMBERG, THE JUGGLER, PRESSURE POINT, and THE DEFIANT ONES, and the themes crept into much of his other work.

p&d, Stanley Kramer; w, Abby Mann (based on the novel by Katherine Anne Porter); ph, Ernest Laszlo; m, Ernest Gold; ed, Robert C. Jones; prod d, Robert Clatworthy; set d, Joseph Kish; cos, Bill Thomas, Jean Louis; spec eff, Albert Whitlock, Farciot Edouart, John Burke; makeup, Ben Lane.

Drama   **(PR:C   MPAA:NR)**

SHIP OF WANTED MEN*   (1933) 63m Screencraft/Showmens bw

Dorothy Sebastian, Fred Kohler, Leon Waycoff [Ames], Gertrude Astor, Maurice Black, Jason Robards, Sr, James Flavin.

A boat filled with convict refugees head toward an island where they can obtain sanctuary. Along the way they come across Sebastian, who has just jumped a yacht after shooting a man. She is offered to stay at the island, but first must obtain $5000 in order to stay. The ways to obtain this amount are not very pleasant. At the last moment the captain decides that he doesn't want to subject Sebastian to this type of treatment, and turns the boat around. Sebastian didn't kill the man, so she's allowed to go free. But the rest of the passengers are a welcome sight to the U.S. government.

d, Lew Collins; w, Ethel Hill; ph, George Meehan; ed, Rose Smith.

Drama   **(PR:A   MPAA:NR)**

SHIP THAT DIED OF SHAME, THE*½**
(1956, Brit.) 91m Ealing/GFD, Continental bw (AKA: PT RAIDERS)

Richard Attenborough *(Hoskins)*, George Baker *(Bill)*, Bill Owen *(Birdie)*, Virginia McKenna *(Helen)*, Roland Culver *(Fordyce)*, Bernard Lee *(Customs Officer)*, Ralph Truman *(Sir Richard)*, John Chandos *(Raines)*, Harold Goodwin *(Second Customs Officer)*, John Longden *(Detective)*, Stratford Johns, David Langton.

With a highly original premise taken from the *Saturday Evening Post* story by Monsarrat, this movie starts in an exciting fashion and seldom slows down to take on more fuel. McKenna and Baker are married during WW II. When she dies in an air raid, Baker is heartbroken. He runs one of the fast gunboats that race in and out of German waters doing various bits of sabotage, blowing up airfields and engaging in exciting missions. Baker's ship, His Majesty's Motor Gun Boat 1087, is of little use when the war ends, and he, too, has nothing to do except mourn his late wife. Baker is contacted by Attenborough and Owen, two of his crew members, and they propose to get 1087 back and use it in a surreptitious fashion that won't hurt anyone, just bring some needed goods to the people who will pay for them. The men buy their old, trusty boat and engage in smuggling across the English Channel. At first, it's the usual stuff like nylons, booze and various other hard-to-get items. The money begins to pour in and Attenborough becomes avaricious and uses the boat to ferry counterfeit money and contraband weapons. Baker is against this new turn of events but is in too deep to get out. Greed takes over and a mutiny takes place aboard the ship. Their enemy, Culver, is killed and when Attenborough and Baker have a fight, the former falls overboard. The title is derived from the last sequence when the boat seems to rebel against all the illegal doings aboard ship. The engines misfire, the steering becomes difficult and the ship finally aims for the rocks where it commits suicide out of shame, rather than be put to any further illicit usage. Baker and Owen swim to safety and vow never to engage in such matters again as 1087 is pounded to shards and splinters in the angry sea. An unusual film from Ealing Studios, which had been known for comedy in that era. The Rank Organization released it in England and it came around in the U.S. out of two different distributors at different times.

p&d, Michael Relph, Basil Dearden; w, John Whiting, Relph, Dearden (based on the novel by Nicholas Monsarrat); ph, Gordon Dines; m, William Alwyn; ed, Peter Bezencenet; md, Dock Mathieson; art d, Bernard Robinson; cos, Anthony Mendleson.

Crime/Adventure   **(PR:A   MPAA:NR)**

SHIP WAS LOADED, THE (SEE: CARRY ON ADMIRAL, 1957, Brit.)

SHIPBUILDERS, THE**½   (1943, Brit.) 89m BN/Anglo American bw

Clive Brook (*Leslie Pagan*), Morland Graham (*Danny Shields*), Nell Ballantyne (*Mrs. Shields*), Finlay Currie (*McWain*), Maudie Edwards (*Lizzie*), Geoffrey Hibbert (*Peter Shields*), Allan Jeayes (*Ralph*), Moira Lister (*Rita*), Frederick Leister (*Mr. Villier*), Gus McNaughton (*Jim*), John Turnbull (*Baird*), Ian Sadler, Bertram Wallis (*Caven Watson*), James Woodburn, Beckett Bould, Patric Curwen, Michael Gainsborough, Emrys Jones, David Keir, Ian MacLean, Dudley Paul, Walter Roy, David Trickett, C. Denier Warren, Alec Faversham.

Well-made story about a shipbuilder (Brook) whose failing business is brought back to life with the opening of WW II. Troubling Graham is an errant son who narrowly escapes a prison term for murdering a man, and is straightened out by being pushed into the navy by Brook. The film ends on a sad note with Graham's son being killed while serving aboard a ship Brook had built years earlier.

p&d, John Baxter; w, Gordon Wellesley, Reginald Pound, Stephen Potter (based on a story by George Blake); ph, Jimmy Wilson.

Drama   (PR:A MPAA:NR)

SHIPMATES**   (1931) 73m MGM bw

Robert Montgomery (*Jonesy*), Ernest Torrence (*Scotty*), Dorothy Jordan (*Kit*), Hobart Bosworth (*Adm. Corbin*), Gavin Gordon (*Mike*), Cliff Edwards (*Bilge*), Joan Marsh (*Mary Lou*), Edward Nugent (*What-Ho*), E. Allyn Warren (*Wong*), George Irving (*Capt. Beatty*), Hedda Hopper (*Auntie*), William Worthington (*Adm. Schuyler*).

Montgomery plays a young sailor with an eye for the admiral's daughter, Jordan, but first he must contend with a petty officer, Torrence, who uses Montgomery as a whipping post to vent his anger. After the customary heroics, Montgomery takes up with the Naval Academy, which makes him a suitable match for the admiral's daughter. This was to be Montgomery's first production in which he received star status. Unfortunately, there was nothing memorable in his performance or the tired story.

d, Harry Pollard; w, Lou Edelman, Delmer Daves, Raymond L. Schrock, Lt. Commander Frank Wead, Malcolm Stuart Boylan (based on the story "Maskee" by Ernest Paynter); ph, Clyde DeVinna; ed, William Levanway.

Adventure/Drama   (PR:A MPAA:NR)

SHIPMATES FOREVER**½   (1935) 109m COS/WB bw

Dick Powell (*Richard John Melville III*), Ruby Keeler (*June Blackburn*), Lewis Stone (*Adm. Richard Melville*), Ross Alexander (*Sparks*), Eddie Acuff (*Cowboy*), Dick Foran (*Gifford*), John Arledge (*Coxswain Johnny Lawrence*), Robert Light (*Ted Sterling*), Joseph King (*Cmdr. Douglas*), Frederick Burton (*Adm. Fred Graves*), Henry Kolker (*The Doctor*), Joseph Crehan (*Spike*), Carlyle Moore, Jr (*Second Classman*), Mary Treen (*Cowboy's Girl*), Martha Merrill (*Spark's Girl*), Harry Seymour (*Harry*), Ernie Alexander, Victor Potel (*Radio Fans*), Emmett Vogan (*Officer*), James Flavin (*Instructor*), Guy Usher (*Captain*), Frank Marlowe (*Seaman*), Peter Potter (*Upper Classman*), Ed Keane (*Doctor*), Dennis O'Keefe (*Trainee*), Meglin Kiddies (*Children*).

Fresh from the success of FLIRTATION WALK, the writing-directing team of Daves and Borzage were given the same cast, with a story that differed little from its predecessor. The result was a sure-fire success at the box office. Powell plays the son of Admiral Stone. To please his father, Powell enlists in the Navy Academy, but all along would rather pursue a career as a singer. Spending little time with his fellow classmates, he's not very popular at the Academy. His only friend is dance instructor Keeler, with whom he plans on marrying. But she has reservations because of her long family tradition in the Navy. She wants a real sailor. When Powell saves the life of a fellow mate during a fire aboard a training cruise, he has a change of heart toward the Navy, to everyone's pleasure. Songs include: "Don't Give Up the Ship," "I'd Rather Listen to Your Eyes," "All Aboard the Navy," "I'd Love to Take Orders from You," and "Do I Love My Teacher" (Al Dubin, Harry Warren).

d, Frank Borzage; w, Delmar Daves (based on a story by Daves); ph, Sol Polito; ed, William Holmes; md, Leo F. Forbstein; art d, Robert M. Haas; cos, Orry-Kelly; ch, Bobby Connolly; tech adv, Comdr. M.S. Tisdale, U.S.N., Lt. W.J. Beecher, U.S.N., Edward L. Adams, former cadet.

Musical   (PR:A MPAA:NR)

SHIPMATES O' MINE**   (1936, Brit.) 87m BUT bw

John Garrick (*Jack Denton*), Jean Adrienne (*Lorna Denton*), Wallace Lupino (*Bill Webb*), Mark Daly (*Andrew McFee*), Frank Atkinson (*Oliver Bright*), Cynthia Stock (*Angela Bright*), Richard Hayward (*Mike Dooley*), Derek Blomfield (*Tony Denton*), John Turnbull (*Capt. Roberts*), Polly Ward, Guy Dixon, Patrick Colbert, Gordon Little, Navarre, Jack Hodges, Sherman Fisher Girls, Radio Male Voice Choir, Horace Sheldon and his Orchestra.

A strong dose of soppy seafaring sentiment spiced with lots of music. The story follows the career of a sailor as he moves up the ladder until he finally earns the command of a ship. Unfortunately, disaster strikes when his ship is rammed and he is forced to abandon ship to save the lives of his passengers. Stripped of his command, the captain retires to the country and spends time with his wife and son. Years later, the son gathers up the members of his father's old crew and the ship is put back into service with his father at the helm.

p, T.A. Welsh; d, Oswald Mitchell; w, Mitchell, George Pearson (based on a story by Ivor Bellas); ph, Robert Martin.

Musical   (PR:A MPAA:NR)

SHIPS OF HATE*   (1931) 63m MON bw

Lloyd Hughes (*Bart Wallace*), Dorothy Sebastian (*Grace Walsh*), Charles Middleton (*Capt. Lash*), Lloyd Whitlock (*Norman Walsh*), Ted Adams (*The Professor*), Constantine Romanoff (*Hans*), Gordon De Main (*First Mate*), Jean Mason (*Peg*).

Cheaply produced sea adventure about a ruthless captain and an equally ruthless crew. Their boat crashes into another boat and Sebastian is saved without even damaging her makeup.

p, Trem Carr; d, J.P. McCarthy; w, Wellyn Totman; ph, Archie Stout; ed, J.F. Harrington.

Adventure   (PR:A MPAA:NR)

SHIPS WITH WINGS**   (1942, Brit.) 89m EAL/UA bw

John Clements (*Lt. Dick Stacey*), Leslie Banks (*Adm. Wetherby*), Jane Baxter (*Celia Wetherby*), Ann Todd (*Kay Gordon*), Basil Sydney (*Capt. Fairfax*), Edward Chapman (*Papadopulous*), Hugh Williams (*Wagner*), Frank Pettingell (*Fields*), Michael Wilding (*Lt. Grant*), Michael Rennie (*Lt. Peter Maxwell*), Frank Cellier (*Gen. Scarappa*), Cecil Parker (*Air Marshal*), John Stuart (*Cmdr. Hood*), Morland Graham (*CPO Marsden*), Charles Victor (*MacDermott*), Hugh Burden (*Lt. Wetherby*), John Laurie (*Lt. Cmdr. Reid*), Betty Marsden, Graham Penley, Charles Russell, Elizabeth Pengally, George Merritt.

WW II action thriller stars Clements as an R.A.F. pilot, one of three men in love with an admiral's daughter, played by Baxter. When he takes a plane up without permission, he crashes, killing Baxter's brother in the process. Courtmartialed from the service, he takes a job with a Greek airline on an island crawling with Germans. His mistress, Todd, and best friend, Chapman, are killed, and in the process Clements discovers plans to sink an aircraft carrier. He manages to warn his ex-commander, during which he learns that Baxter has married one of her admirers. Feeling he has one last chance to display his loyalty to his country, he thwarts the Germans' plans by crashing his plane into a strategic dam, which in turn floods out the German post. Clements dies a hero. Superbly staged aerial battles more than make up for the slow-moving plot.

p, Michael Balcon; d, Sergei Nolbandov; w, Patrick Kirwan, Austin Melford, Diana Morgan, Nolbandov; ph, Mutz Greenbaum, Wilkie Cooper, Roy Kellino, Eric Cross; m, Geoffrey Wright; ed, Robert Hamer; art d, Wilfred Shingleton; m/l, Morgan; technical advisor, Lt. Cmdr. J. Reid, R.N.

War   (PR:A MPAA:NR)

SHIPWRECK   (SEE: SEA GYPSIES, THE, 1978)

SHIPYARD SALLY**   (1940, Brit.) 77m FOX bw

Gracie Fields (*Sally Fitzgerald*), Sydney Howard (*Maj. Fitzgerald*), Morton Selten (*Lord Randall*), Norma Varden (*Lady Patricia*), Oliver Wakefield (*Forsyth*), Tucker McGuire (*Linda Marsh*), MacDonald Parke (*Diggs*), Richard Cooper (*Sir John Treacher*), Joan Cowick, Monty Banks.

Pleasant comedy which is mainly a vehicle to display the talents of Fields. She plays the daughter of a well-meaning, but irresponsible, Howard, the new owner of a pub next to the shipyards. Fields takes over management for her father, doing a fairly good business until the shipyard is closed down. She rallies the workers to march to London, but meets with general disapproval. So the singer goes about getting the men's jobs back herself, allowing a mistake in identity to gain admission to the needed diplomat. One of the film's songs, "Wish Me Luck as You Wave Me Goodbye," later became a marching tune favorite of troops going off to WW II.

p, Robert T. Kane; d, Monty Banks; w, Karl Tunberg, Don Ettlinger (based on the story by Gracie Fields, Tom Geraghty, Val Valentine); ph, Otto Kanturek; md, Louis Levy.

Comedy/Musical   (PR:A MPAA:NR)

SHIRALEE, THE**½   (1957, Brit.) 99m EAL/MGM bw

Peter Finch (*Jim Macauley*), Elizabeth Sellars (*Marge Macauley*), Dana Wilson (*Buster Macauley*), Rosemary Harris (*Lily Parker*), Tessie O'Shea (*Bella*), Sidney James (*Luke*), George Rose (*Donny*), Russell Napier (*Parker*), Niall MacGinnis (*Beauty Kelly*), Reg Lye (*Desmond*), Charles Tingwell (*Jim Muldoon*), Barbara Archer (*Shopgirl*), Alec Mango (*Papadoulos*), John

Phillips (Doctor).

"Shiralee" is an Australian Aborigine word which means a burden. Finch plays an Australian laborer who drifts around the country looking for work. After a few years he returns to his wife, Sellars, only to find her living with another man. He takes Wilson, their five year old daughter away from this atmosphere and she becomes Finch's "shiralee". He cannot relate to the girl, unable to give her the love and affection she needs. Still the child prefers to be with her father and the mother instigates court action against her husband. Finch gets beaten up by some thugs and Wilson is almost killed by a truck, but THE SHIRALEE ends on a happy note for father and daughter. Their relationship is the heart of this film and ultimately the key factor in making the picture work. The episodic nature gets a bit wearysome at times, but the locational shooting in Australia is picturesque.

p, Jack Rix; d, Leslie Norman; w, Neil Paterson, Norman (based on the novel by D'Arcy Niland); ph, Paul Beeson; m, John Addison; ed, Gordon Stone; art d, Jim Morahan.

Drama   (PR:C   MPAA:NR)

SHIRIKURAE MAGOICHI   (SEE: MAGOICHI SAGA, THE, 1970, Jap.)

SHIRLEY THOMPSON VERSUS THE ALIENS*
                          (1968, Aus.) 104m Kolossal Films bw-c
Jane Harders (Shirley Thompson), John Likoxitch, Helmut Bakaitis, Tim Eliott, June Collins, Marion Johns, Ronn Haddrick.

While in a session with her psychiatrist, Harders relates a story (told in black and white flashbacks) about her encounters with visitors from outer space. The aliens have come to her in the form of a motorcycle gang during her visit to a local amusement park. Harders tries to tell people her story, but when no one will believe her, she goes mad. Haddrick plays a Duke of Edinburgh statue in a wax museum that the aliens bring to life to be their spokesperson between themselves and the earthlings. This off-the-wall comedy was made by the director of THE ROCKY HORROR PICTURE SHOW (1975). Like ROCKY HORROR, SHIRLEY THOMPSON VERSUS THE ALIENS was originally a stage production before hitting the screen. Sharman shows a good use of the cinematic tools he has available. There's varying uses of black and white (in flashback scenes), cleverly underexposed film in scenes from the asylum where Harders spends time, and wonderfully filmed fantasy scenes in color.

p&d, Jim Sharman; w, Sharman, Helmut Bakaitis; ph, David Sanderson.

Science Fiction/Fantasy   (PR:O   MPAA:NR)

SHIRO TO KURO   (SEE: PRESSURE OF GUILT, 1961, Jap.)

SHIVERS   (SEE: THEY CAME FROM WITHIN, 1976, Can.)

SHLOSHA YAMIN VE' YELED   (SEE: NOT MINE TO LOVE, 1969, Israel)

SHNEI KUNI LEMEL   (SEE: FLYING MATCHMAKER, THE, 1970, Israel)

SHOCK**   (1934) 70m MON bw
Ralph Forbes (Derek Marbury), Gwenllian Gill (Lucy Neville), Monroe Owsley (Bob Hayworth), Reginald Sharland (Capt. Peabody), David Jack Holt (Rickey Marbury), Billy Bevan (Meadows), Clyde Cook (Hawkins), Mary Forbes, Charles Coleman, Colin Campbell, David Dunbar, Montague Shaw, Eric Snowden, Olaf Hytten, Harry Holden.

A British officer in WW I marries a young girl. He's unexpectedly called back to the front. Later on a voluntary mission, the officer, Forbes, is shell-shocked. He finally returns home to discover that he is the father of a grown son. Fairly routine melodrama competently told but with nothing in it that's fresh, original or exciting. It's the same old war story in a new package. Acting and technical aspects are okay for this minor B film.

d, Roy J. Pomeroy; w, Madeline Ruthven (based on a story by Pomeroy); ed, Jack Ogilvie.

War Drama   (PR:C   MPAA:NR)

SHOCK**   (1946) 70m FOX bw
Vincent Price (Dr. Cross), Lynn Bari (Elaine Jordan), Frank Latimore (Lt. Paul Stewart), Anabel Shaw (Janet Stewart), Michael [Steve] Dunne (Stevens), Reed Hadley (O'Neill), Renee Carson (Mrs. Hatfield), Charles Trowbridge (Dr. Harvey), John Davidson (Mr. Edwards), Selmer Jackson (Dr. Blair), Pierre Watkin (Hotel Manager), Mary Young (Miss Penny), Charles Tannen (Hotel Clerk), Margaret Brayton, Claire Richards (Nurses), Bob Adler (Male Nurse), George E. Stone (Cabdriver), Cecil Weston.

In his first starring role, Price plays a prominent psychiatrist who along with his nurse Bari who is also his mistress, murders his wife. The slaying is witnessed by Shaw, a woman who is already teetering on the brink of a nervous breakdown due to the fact that her husband is being held in a Japanese P.O.W. camp. When the husband, Latimore, finally arrives home, Shaw attempts to tell him what she has seen while looking over at Price's office one day, but Price is able to convince Latimore that what his wife really needs is some good psychiatric care. Of course, Price and Bari plan to silence Shaw, and luckily Latimore has second thoughts before permitting her incarceration. Aided by district attorney Hadley, Price is apprehended in the end. At the time this film was released, this picture outraged serious critics and psychiatrists everywhere for its loathsome portrayal of the highly respected profession.

p, Aubrey Schenck; d, Alfred Werker; w, Eugene Ling, Martin Berkeley (based on the story by Albert DeMond); ph, Glen MacWilliams, Joe MacDonald; m, David Buttolph; ed, Harmon Jones; md, Emil Newman; art d, Lyle Wheeler, Boris Leven; set d, Thomas Little, O. Clement Halverson; spec eff, Fred Sersen.

Psycho-Drama/Suspense   **Cas.**   (PR:O   MPAA:NR)

SHOCK, 1979   (SEE: BEYOND THE DOOR II, 1979, Ital.)

SHOCK CORRIDOR½   (1963) 101m AA bw/c
Peter Breck (Johnny Barrett), Constance Towers (Cathy), Gene Evans (Boden), James Best (Stuart), Hari [Harry] Rhodes (Trent), Larry Tucker (Pagliacci), William Zuckert (Swanee), Philip Ahn (Dr. Fong), Neyle Morrow (Psycho), John Mathews (Dr. Cristo), Chuck Roberson (Wilkes), John Craig (Lloyd), Frank Gerstle (Police Lieutenant), Paul Dubov (Dr. Menkin), Rachel Romen (Singing Nymphomaniac), Linda Randolph (Dance Teacher), Barbara Perry, Marlene Manners, Lucille Curtis, Jeanette Dana, Marie Devereux, Karen Conrad, Allyson Daniell, Chuck Hicks, Wally Campo, Ray Baxter, Linda Barnett, Harry Fleer.

In his obsession to win a Pulitzer Price, Breck convinces his editor (Zuckert) to let him go undercover in a mental hospital. A patient named Sloane was knifed there and Breck thinks solving the murder will bring him the coveted prize. Zuckert introduces the reporter to Ahn, a psychiatrist who teaches Breck a few things about insanity. Towers, Breck's stripper girl friend, thinks the plan is ridiculous. But when Breck threatens to stop seeing her, she finally agrees to go along with him on it. She poses as his sister and runs to the police, claiming Breck has made sexual advances towards her. The reporter is arrested and questioned by Mathews. Thanks to Ahn's coaching, Breck anticipates the questions about insanity and incest, answering with replies that convince Mathews the man needs some hospitalization. Once inside Breck begins investigating Sloane's murder. There are two attendants in the men's ward he is staying at: Craig, a frustrated, mean-spirited man who thinks the men are incurable, and Roberson who appears to be an amiable sort. Breck seeks out the three patients he suspects witnessed the murder: Best, a Korean war veteran who became a traitor in the conflict and now thinks he's a Confederate general; Rhodes, a young black man who tried to enroll in an all-white Southern university and now thinks he's white and a member of the Klu Klux Klan; and Evans, a scientific genius who helped create the atom bomb, but now has deteriorated to a six year old emotional level. During one of Best's rare moments of sanity he tells Breck that an attendant is the murderer. Rhodes is too mad to be of any use for the reporter. Breck next wants to speak with Evans, but the surroundings are beginning to have their effect on his own mind. He begins having nightmares about Towers with other men and is often awakened by Tucker, a fat opera-singing patient who holds down Breck and shoves gum in his mouth. Nicknamed "Pagliacci", Tucker also forces Breck to listen to him sing. Later the reporter is attacked by some nymphomaniacs from the women's ward. The hospital has a riot and Breck is placed in a straitjacket. He's given shock therapy and slowly begins to believe Towers really is his sister. Towers finds out and demands Mathews give him more shock in hopes the treatment will return him to his normal frame of mind. But this doesn't work and Breck stops speaking for a period. After regaining his mind, Breck confronts Evans. He slowly works the former genius back to a sane state by letting the man paint a portrait of the reporter. Evans reveals that the seemingly nice guy Roberson was the actual murderer. Apparently the attendant was using women patients for his own sexual needs and killed Sloane to cover up his crime. Breck sees his portrait and his mind snaps. He beats up the scientist who reverts once more to his six year old state. Breck is now too insane to remember who the murderer was. But after imagining a terrible thunderstorm in the hallway, Breck recalls that Roberson was the killer. He beats up the attendant and takes him to Mathews for a confession. Breck is then released and writes his story. He wins the Pulitzer he so desperately wanted, but the whole experience has been overwhelming. He suffers a mental breakdown and ends up a complete catatonic. Towers comes to the hospital and hugs her boy friend, but he is too mad to respond. This film is a real mixture of quality. At points the story is nothing more than lurid melodrama and gratuitous in nature. The shock therapy sessions and scenes of Breck locked up with six nymphomaniacs seem to exist solely to satisfy the seamier elements of the audience. But Fuller, an intelligent B director, goes beyond the plot's more lurid moments to create some fine highly cinematic portrayals of madness. Using color sequences the director shot in Japan and Africa (as early as 1955), Fuller creates weird and unusual hallucinogenic scenes with Best and Rhodes. Best sees himself back in the war, while Rhodes recalls the terror of the Klan. It's not entirely successful but an interesting technique nonetheless. A good deal about the nature of success in America is implied in the film. Each one of the three key patients was a success story in one form or other (a war hero, a civil rights activist, a scientific pioneer) until each man's respective deeds began to haunt the mental interior. Breck himself suffers the most from the success syndrome Fuller puts forth. In his own drive "to be in the company of the journalistic greats" as the reporter puts it, Breck ends up in a worse state than the others catatonic and a victim of his own ambition. All in all though, SHOCK CORRIDOR never quite fulfills the artistic achievements of some other low-grade films. Its cheap budget hampers the film (the sets look like sets rather than a real hospital) and the lurid emphasis takes away from the deeper psychological implications. On its initial release SHOCK CORRIDOR was attacked by the critics, who felt the film was nothing more than vicious trash. While it's not that bad, this is not the high art some might believe. Fuller followed this piece with what was probably one of his best works, THE NAKED KISS.

p,d&w, Samuel Fuller (based on the scenario "Straitjacket" by Fuller); ph; Stanley Cortez, Fuller (Technicolor); m, Paul Dunlap; ed, Jerome Thoms; art d, Eugene Lourie; set d, Charles Thompson; cos, Einar H. Bourman; ch, John Gregory; spec eff, Charles Duncan, Lynn Dunn; makeup, Dan Greenway.

Drama   **(PR:O MPAA:NR)**

SHOCK TREATMENT**   (1964) 93m Arcola/FOX bw

Stuart Whitman (Dale Nelson), Carol Lynley (Cynthia), Roddy McDowall (Martin Ashly, Gardener), Lauren Bacall (Dr. Edwina Beighley), Olive Deering (Mrs. Mellon), Ossie Davis (Capshaw), Donald Buka (Psychologist), Pauline Myers (Dr. Walden), Evadne Baker (Interne), Robert J. Wilke (Technician Newton), Bert Freed (Josephson), Judith DeHart (Matron), Judson Laire (Harley Manning), Lili Clark (Alice), Douglas Dumbrille (Judge), Timothy Carey (Hulking Patient), Jack Braddock (Jim, the Technician), Roy Gordon (Butler), Olan Soule (Hugo Paige), Paul Denton (Uniformed Guard), Leonard Stone (Psychiatrist), John Lawrence (Nurse), Sheila Rogers (Miss Gould).

A psychotic gardener (McDowell) has recently beheaded his wealthy employer. He's tossed into an asylum, but is suspected of taking a million bucks from his late boss and either burning it or stowing it away in secret. Bacall, a long way from KEY LARGO, is a shrink at the hospital who just may be in cahoots with her psycho patient. Whitman plays a professional actor hired to fake madness so that he can investigate the mystery. Part of his job unfortunately includes submission to electro-shock therapy and a few injections here and there. He also compounds his problems by falling for a hospitalized manic-depressive (Lynley). Bacall finally goes insane herself and becomes a patient in the hospital, while Whitman discovers that she had nothing to do with McDowell's plot. In this laughable fare Whitman's okay, but Bacall is obviously capable of better than this inane role. Direction is flat and unexciting, though a surprisingly good music score does help the proceedings somewhat.

p, Aaron Rosenberg; d, Denis Sanders; w, Sydney Boehm (based on a novel by Winfred Van Atta); ph, Sam Leavitt (CinemaScope); m, Jerry Goldsmith; ed, Louis R. Loeffler; art d, Jack Martin Smith, Hilyard Brown; set d, Walter M. Scott, Paul S. Fox; cos, Moss Mabry; spec eff, L.B. Abbott, Emil Kosa, Jr.; makeup, Harry Maret, Ben Nye.

Drama/Suspense   **Cas.**   **(PR:O MPAA:NR)**

SHOCK TREATMENT**   (1973, Fr.) 90m
Lira-A.J.-Medusa/SNC-Imperia/New Line c (TRAITEMENT DE CHOC)

Alain Delon (Devilers), Annie Girardot (Helene), Robert Hirsch (Gerome), Michel Duchaussoy (Bernard), Jean-Francois Calve (Gassin).

Things are a bit strange at a sanatorium located on a small French coastal island. It caters exclusively to the wealthy and a few other types as well. Girardot is a made-it-herself rich woman who becomes depressed and begins feeling her age when a younger lover abandons her. She goes to the sanatorium to cheer up, but runs into a few unexpected problems. The head doctor (Delon) is a younger man and seems normal enough, but his patients are a different story. There's something odd about the lot that makes her wonder. Slowly the secret begins to unfold. A group of Portuguese boys arrive to do some work but they are quickly gone, apparently because the climate doesn't agree with them. In reality they are subjects of Delon's bizarre medical practices. He drugs the young people and slowly bleeds them to death so he can use the bodies to keep his older affluent clientele feeling younger. Girardot discovers this and catches the mad doctor in his lab. There, amid corpses of the Portuguese boys, she kills the good doctor, but only is arrested herself for murder by a police lieutenant staying on the island. SHOCK TREATMENT starts off with some clever and suspenseful moments in a relatively good looking setting. However the tension quickly degenerates into predictable fare that lacks the necessary suspense. Some attempts at satirizing the affluent classes pay off but aren't anything new or terribly witty. Delon gives some heart to his part and Girardot works, but it never quite comes together just right, resulting in a suspense film without much suspense.

d&w, Alain Jessua; ph, Jacques Robinson (Eastmancolor); ed, Helene Plemmianikov; art d, Yannis Kokos.

Horror/Suspense   **(PR:O MPAA:NR)**

SHOCK TREATMENT zero   (1981) 94m FOX c

Jessica Harper (Janet Majors), Cliff DeYoung (Brad Majors/Farley Flavors), Richard O'Brien (Cosmo McKinley), Patricia Quinn (Nation McKinley), Charles Gray (Judge Oliver Wright), Ruby Wax (Betty Hapschatt), Neil Campbell (Nurse Ansalong), Rik Mayall ("Rest Home" Ricky), Barry Humphries (Bert Schnick), Darlene Johnson (Emily Weiss), Manning Redwood (Harry Weiss), Wendy Raebeck (Macy Struthers), Jeremy Newson (Ralph Hapschatt), Chris Malcolm (Vance), Ray Charleson (Floor Manager), Eugene Lipinski (Kirk), Barry Dennen (Irwin), Imogen Claire (Wardrobe Mistress), Betsy Brantley, Perry Bedden, Rufus Collins (Neely and Her Crew), Gary Shail, Donald Waugh, Claire Toeman, Sinitta Renet, David John, Gary Martin.

Six years after the release of the successful sex musical THE ROCKY HORROR PICTURE SHOW, producers were amazed to discover the high camp, low grade flick had turned into a cult sensation on the midnight film circuit. Such popularity could only mean one thing to the minds behind the original–a sequel must be what the public wants! Maybe so, but certainly not this piece of junk, a witless uninspired bastard child of the original. Harper and DeYoung (taking over the roles originally played by Susan Sarandon and Barry Bostwick) are the naive young couple who accidentally stumble onto a night of musical debauchary. This time out they're married and contestants on the TV game show "Marriage Maze." DeYoung is taken away for some of the title amusements, while the show's sponsor (also played by DeYoung) takes Harper away to make her a new television star as well as his own little toy. ROCKY HORROR vets Quinn, Gray, Campbell and O'Brien (who co-wrote the screenplay with director Sharman, as he did on the original film) are on hand, though it really doesn't matter much. SHOCK TREATMENT is nothing more than a cheap attempt to cash in on the ROCKY HORROR craze sweeping America in the late 1970s. Harper, a vastly underrated actress, clearly shows more talent than this film deserves: she's the only real standout with some minor support by DeYoung. Considering the crude campy fun of the original, one might think that its creators might be able to maintain the sense of fun in successive films. Instead they give us this lame, unfunny tripe that will bore rather than amuse with its hit-you-over-the-head attempts at parody. Shock treatment is recommended–as the only device to keep you awake during this ninety minutes of tripe.

p, John Goldstone; d, Jim Sharman; w, Sharman, Richard O'Brien, Brian Thomson (based on a book by O'Brien); ph, Mike Molloy (Technicolor); m, Richard Hartley, O'Brien; ed, Richard Bedford; prod d, Thomson; art d, Andrew Sanders; cos, Sue Blane; ch, Gillian Gregory; m/l, O'Brien, Hartley.

Musical   **Cas.**   **(PR:O MPAA:PG)**

SHOCK TROOPS***   (1968, Ital./Fr.) 106m Terra-Les Productions
Artistes-Compagnia Cinematografica Montoro-Sol/UA c (UN HOMME DE TROP)

Jean-Claude Brialy (Jean), Bruno Cremer (Cazal), Jacques Perrin (Kerk), Gerard Blain (Thomas), Claude Brasseur (Groubac), Michel Piccoli (The Extra Man), Pierre Clementi (Lucien), Francois Perier (Moujon), Charles Vanel (Passevin), Paolo Fratini (Philippe), Michel Creton (Solin), Claude Brosset (Ouf), Nino Segurini (Paco), Med Hondo (Lecocq), Julie Dassin (Girl).

Twelve Frenchman are condemned to die in a German prison camp during WW II. Cremer plays the leader of the resistance fighters who go in to save their countrymen. Their mission is a success, but they discover that an extra man has been rescued as well. They cannot decide if he is an innocent party or a Nazi spy, but when he's discovered wearing German boots and carrying no identification some decisions must be made. Brialy, a more outspoken member of the group, leads other men in demanding this extra man's execution. They take the stranger along on a raid of a tax bureau. There the man risks his life in the fray to save a young child who accidentally gets in the line of fire. However Cremer is unmoved and orders Blain, a faithfull follower, to execute the man by the river. The two go and there the man finally opens up. He tells of his desertion from the army because of his pacifistic beliefs and Blain allows the man to get away. But that night the stranger (Piccoli) returns to warn that they are surrounded by the Nazis. Cremer leaves to warn other resistance fighters, but many of the group are eventually captured by German forces, including Piccoli. They are sentenced to be hanged, but Piccoli manages to escape as the others are killed.

p, Raymond Froment; d&w, Costa-Gavras (based on the novel Un Homme de Trop by Jean-Pierre Chabrol); ph, Jean Tournier (Techniscope, Technicolor); m, Michel Magne; ed, Christian Gaudin; art d, Maurice Colasson; spec eff, Rene Albouze, Georges Iaconelli.

War Drama   **(PR:O MPAA:NR)**

SHOCK WAVES½**   (1977) 86m Lawrence Friedricks
Enterprises/Cinema Shares c (AK A: DEATH CORPS; ALMOST HUMAN)

Peter Cushing (Scar, SS Commander), John Carradine (Capt. Ben), Brooke Adams (Rose), Fred Buch (Chuck), Jack Davidson (Norman), Luke Halpin

(Keith), D. J. Sidney *(Beverly)*, Don Stout *(Dobbs)*, Tony Moskal, Gary Levinson, Jay Maeder, Bob Miller, Talmadge Scott, Bob White *(Death Corps Members)*.

During WW II the Nazis decided to use the ultimate secret weapon: a troop consisting of super zombies. Predictably they didn't quite live up to the Fuehrer's needs and at the war's end, the battalion was sunk with their ship off the Caribbean coast. During a storm some 35 years later, a group of passengers aboard a luxury liner are stranded on a deserted island, where an underground explosion resurrects the squadron. This NIGHT OF THE LIVING DEAD-style horror flick is surprisingly well made considering its tiny budget. Adams, Buch, and ex-FLIPPER star Halpin are the nice people attacked by the zombies. The creatures rising from the water are interesting stuff and though this is nothing great as far as horror films go, SHOCK WAVES does have some moments of fun that nicely overcome its obvious flaws. Old time horror vet Cushing plays the squadron leader.

p, Reuben Trane; d, Ken Wiederhorn; w, Wiederhorn, John Harrison; ph, Trane (TVC Color); m, Richard Einhorn; ed, Norman Gay; prod d, Jessica Sack; art d, George Richmond; set d, Michael Matee; cos, Jacquie Kabelis; makeup, Alan Ormsby.

Horror   **Cas.**   **(PR:O   MPAA:PG)**

SHOCKER   (SEE: TOWN WITHOUT PITY, 1961, US/Swiss./Ger.)

SHOCKING MISS PILGRIM, THE**   (1947) 87m FOX c

Betty Grable *(Cynthia Pilgrim)*, Dick Haymes *(John Pritchard)*, Anne Revere *(Alice Pritchard)*, Allyn Joslyn *(Leander Woolsey)*, Gene Lockhart *(Saxon)*, Elizabeth Patterson *(Catherine Dennison)*, Elizabeth Risdon *(Mrs. Pritchard)*, Arthur Shields *(Michael Michael)*, Charles Kemper *(Herbert Jothan)*, Roy Roberts *(Mr. Foster)*, Tom Moore *(Office Clerk)*, Stanley Prager *(Lookout in Office)*, Edward Laughton *(Quincy)*, Hal K. Dawson *(Peabody)*, Lillian Bronson *(Viola Simmons)*, Raymond Largay *(Mr. Packard)*, Constance Purdy *(Sarah Glidden)*, Mildred Stone *(Miss Nixon)*, Pierre Watkin *(Wendell Paige)*, Junius Matthews *(Mr. Carter)*, Mary Field, Kay Riley *(Teachers)*, John Sheehan *(Vendor)*, Vic Potel *(Speaker)*, Frank Dawson *(Waiter)*.

In 1874 Boston Grable is a typist for a shipping company. Her boss is played by Haymes and the two fall in love. Their relationship becomes strained though by her "shocking" advocation of women's rights and participation in the early suffragette movement. Haymes predictably will not tolerate such improprieties, but a few tunes and overworked jokes later he comes around for the predictably happy ending. The studio thought they'd give something daring for Grable to do and thus put her in a period picture that actually dared to *cover* the legs, which broke many a sailor's heart. The screenplay is fairly ridiculous and un-funny with overemphasized "a woman's place is in the home" stuff. However, the film is redeemed somewhat by its music. Some unpublished songs of the late genius composer George Gershwin were collated and reworked by Kay Swift and Gershwin's brother (and lyricist) Ira. The latter wrote new lyrics for these undiscovered tunes, including "For You, For Me, For Evermore," "Aren't You Glad We Did?," "Stand Up and Fight," "Waltz Me No Waltzes." Other songs include: "Changing My Tune," "Back Bay Polka," "One, Two, Three," "But Not in Boston," "Sweet Packard," "Waltzing is Better Sitting Down," "Demon Rum."

p, William Perlberg; d&w, George Seaton (based on the story by Ernest Maas, Frederica Maas); ph, Leon Shamroy (Technicolor); ed, Robert Simpson; md, Alfred Newman, Charles Henderson; art d, James Basevi, Boris Leven; ch, Hermes Pan; m/l, George Gershwin, Ira Gershwin.

Musical   **(PR:A   MPAA:NR)**

SHOCKPROOF***   (1949) 79m COL bw

Cornel Wilde *(Griff Marat)*, Patricia Knight *(Jenny Marsh)*, John Baragrey *(Harry Wesson)*, Esther Minciotti *(Mrs. Marat)*, Howard St. John *(Sam Brooks, Parole Officer)*, Russell Collins *(Frederick Bauer)*, Charles Bates *(Tommy Marat)*, Gilbert Barnett *(Barry)*, Frank Jaquet *(Monte)*, Ann Shoemaker *(Dr. Daniels)*, King Donovan *(Joe Wilson)*, Claire Carleton *(Florie Kobiski)*, Al Eben *(Joe Kobiski)*, Fred Sears, Jimmy Lloyd *(Clerks)*, Isabel Withers *(Switchboard Operator)*, Virginia Farmer *(Mrs. Terrence)*, Charles Jordan *(Hot Dog Man)*, Buddy Swan *(Teenage Boy)*, Crane Whitley *(Foreman)*, Robert R. Stephenson *(Drunk)*, Richard Benedict *("Kid")*, Cliff Clark *(Police Lieutenant)*, Arthur Space *(Police Inspector)*, Charles Marsh *(Manager)*.

After serving only five years of her life sentence for murder, Knight is released from prison on parole. Her parole officer (Wilde) tries to help her by giving Knight a job caring for his blind mother (Minciotti). Wilde is popular with local political figures and is looking to move up in stature. He doesn't count on falling in love with Knight though. The two end up marrying, but trouble brews when her old lover, Baragrey, whom she is forbidden to see by a court order, turns up. Baragrey threatens Knight and she accidentally shoots her past amour. Knight and her husband run off and go into hiding, but eventually decide it would be best to give themselves up. It turns out, however, that Baragrey has only been slightly wounded and he isn't even going to press charges. Up until the contrived ending forced on

the director, this is a taut, well made example of *film noir*. The semi-documentary style shot in the Los Angeles streets works well and the pacing is uniformly excellent. The screenplay (co-written by future director Fuller) is excellent until its hokey finish, giving meaty roles to the players. Wilde and Knight are both strong in their roles and are well supported by a good cast of secondary players.

p, S. Sylvan Simon, Helen Deutsch; d, Douglas Sirk; w, Deutsch, Samuel Fuller; ph, Charles Lawton, Jr.; m, George Duning; ed, Gene Havlick; md, Morris Stoloff; art d, Carl Anderson; set d, Louis Diage; cos, Jean Louis; makeup, Clay Campbell.

Crime   **(PR:C   MPAA:NR)**

SHOE SHINE****½   (1947, Ital.) 93m Lopert bw (SCIUSCIA; AKA SHOESHINE; SHOE-SHI NE)

Rinaldo Smordoni *(Giuseppe)*, Franco Interlenghi *(Pasquale)*, Aniello Mele *(Raffaele)*, Bruno Ortensi *(Arcangeli)*, Pacifico Astrologo *(Vittorio)*, Francesco de Nicola *(Ciriola)*, Antonio Carlino *(L'Abruzzese)*, Enrico de Silva *(Giorgio)*, Antonio Lo Nigro *(Righetoo)*, Angelo D'Amico *(Siciliano)*, Emilio Cigoll *(Staffera)*, Giuseppe Spadaro *(Attorney Bonavino)*, Leo Garavaglia *(Commissario)*, Luigi Saltamerenda *(Il Panza)*, Maria Campi *(La Chiromante)*, Irene Smordoni *(Giuseppe's Mother)*, Anna Pedoni *(Nannarella)*.

Stories about two boys have always been part of folklore from Romulus and Remus to Damon and Pythias. In this, one of the first pictures to come out of Italy after WW II, a semidocumentary approach is given that almost justifies the jumpy editing and ragged camera work. Smordoni and Interlenghi are shoe shine boys, waifs who eke out existences by harassing American soldiers into spending a few lire to have their boots cleaned. They get involved in some benign black marketeering through Smordoni's brother. By doing so, they raise enough money to buy a horse for themselves, just as the youth of today yearn for Grand Ams or Corvettes. This soon leads them to a larger scheme. They are arrested and taken to a reformatory which is a mini-version of San Quentin, or the "hardest time" a crook can get. The moment the iron doors close on the two frightened boys, the picture gets extremely depressing. Neither one will confess to their deed (selling stolen army goods) and it's only when a beating of Smordoni is faked that Interlenghi, in order to save his pal from further pain, tells the authorities about their adult associates. Now that they are part of the prison population, they are prey for the older boys, one of whom, a bully, wants to separate the youths. When the bully tries an escape, he rings in Smordoni and they get away as a film projector being used by some priests catches on fire. They race to where the horse is stabled and take it. Interlenghi feels that he's been betrayed and leads the authorities to the stable. Now he finds the other two and the bully runs away as Interlenghi angrily confronts Smordoni. Interlenghi is so hurt by what he feels is Smordoni's abandonment of him that he takes off his belt, in an imitation of what the prison men have done, and begins beating his best friend to death. All he means to do is teach him a lesson but he applies the belt too zealously and the result is the final end to their friendship. It's an indictment of the Italian prison system for youngsters and bears a bit of a resemblance in its despair to THE 400 BLOWS. Dealing in friendship, betrayal and tragedy, SHOESHINE was a watermark in the Italian neorealistic school of cinema. (In Italian; English titles.)

p, Paolo W. Tamburella; d, Vittorio De Sica; w, Cesare Zavattini, Sergio Amidei, Adolfo Franci, Cesare Giulio Viola, De Sica (based on a story by Zavattini); ph, Anchise Brizzi; m, Alessandro Cicognini.

Drama   **(PR:C   MPAA:NR)**

SHOEMAKER AND THE ELVES, THE**½   (1967, Ger.) 75m Schongerfilm/K. Gordon Murray-Trans-International c (HEINZEL-MANNCHEN)

Nora Minor, Ado Reigler, Heini Gobel, Toni Strassmeir, Bobby Todd, Rudolf Reif, Elisabeth Gobel.

It's the age-old story of those mischievous little elves who befriend the impoverished shoemaker. One night every 100 years they come to a small village to help out the inhabitants. While helping the kindly shoemaker, they also manage to make some toys at a factory and capture a robber by holding him in a barrel of tar. In the morning, the tailor's wife tries to capture the little men, but they run off, gone for another 100 years.

p, Hubert Schonger; d, Erich Kobler; w, Schonger (based on "Die Wichtelmanner" by Jakob Grimm, Wilhelm Grimm); ph, Wolf Schwan (Colorscope, Eastmancolor); m, Carl Stueber.

Fantasy   **(PR:AAA   MPAA:NR)**

SHOES OF THE FISHERMAN, THE***   (1968) 162m MGM c

Anthony Quinn *(Kiril Lakota)*, Laurence Olivier *(Piotr Ilyich Kamenev)*, Oskar Werner *(Father David Telemond)*, David Janssen *(George Faber)*, Vittorio De Sica *(Cardinal Rinaldi)*, Leo McKern *(Cardinal Leone)*, John Gielgud *(Elder Pope)*, Barbara Jefford *(Dr. Ruth Faber)*, Rosemarie Dexter *(Chiara)*, Frank Finlay *(Igor Bounin)*, Burt Kwouk *(Peng)*, Arnoldo Foa *(Gelasio)*, Paul Rogers *(Augustinian)*, George Pravda *(Gorshenin)*, Clive Revill *(Vucovich)*, Niall MacGinnis *(Capuchin Monk)*, Marne Maitland

(Cardinal Rahamani), Isa Miranda *(The Marchesa)*, Gerald Harper *(Brian)*, Leopoldo Trieste *(Dying Man's Friend)*, Peter Copley, Arthur Howard *(English Cardinals)*, Jean Rougeul *(Dominica)*, Al Thomas *(Negro Cardinal)*, Dom Moore *(Polish Cardinal)*, John Frederick *(American Cardinal)*.

Morris West wrote the screenplay but was so disappointed by the results that he asked for, and was granted, the deletion of his name from that credit, while keeping his novel's source credit on screen. Casting Quinn in the lead as the man who became the leader of the Church occasioned some laughter among wags who dubbed this movie "Zorba, The Pope." Quinn is a Russian Catholic (not Russian Orthodox) priest who has been a political prisoner in a Siberian hard labor camp for 20 years. Olivier is the Soviet premier and he orders Quinn's release, but with a strange proviso. The Chinese communists, under the thumb of Kwouk (who was Peter Sellers' aide in the PINK PANTHER movies so how could he be taken seriously?), are getting more powerful and Olivier is allowing Quinn to go to Rome so the USSR will have a friend in the Vatican. There is a powerful famine taking place (this is supposed to be in the 1980s) and the world is close to atomic annihilation over lack of food. Quinn leaves for Rome with Werner, a priest who is vocal about his feelings about the Church and whose writings have put him in trouble with the hierarchy. They arrive at Rome and are immediately interviewed by American TV newsman Janssen. (In a silly subplot, Janssen is married to Jefford and fooling around with Dexter.) The current Pope is Gielgud, who quickly gives the Cardinal's red hat to Quinn, realizing that this might be a good move to establish relations between the Soviets and the Free World. Werner is called before the special commission that is investigating his writings. The group is headed by McKern, a tough old bird who is an arch-conservative. While this is going on, Gielgud dies unexpectedly and, at almost the same moment, word comes in that the starving Chinese have their armies ready to cross the borders into India and Mongolia. With no Holy Father to lead the people, the cardinals go into their conclave and electioneering begins to choose a new Pope. It winds up in a deadlock and Quinn, a reluctant candidate, is chosen. He is the first non-Italian Pope (West must have had ESP, because in 1978, a Pope from Poland was elected, life imitating art) in four centuries. Olivier contacts Quinn and asks him to intercede with the Chinese. Quinn has taken the name of "Kiril," the saint who spread the Word in Russia. Quinn is puzzled by his new duties and resents the fact that he is kept from the people so he dons standard cleric's garb and goes into the Roman streets. There, he meets Jefford, a physician. She tells him about her problems with Janssen and he offers some fatherly advice about love and marriage. Later, he goes to a meeting in the Far East with Olivier and Kwouk and promises that he will try to find some way that he can help feed the millions of Chinese who are on the brink of death. Back in the Vatican, Quinn consults with his friend, Werner, but Werner is felled by a cerebral hemorrhage and dies in Quinn's company. Quinn does some heavy thinking, talks with McKern and comes to a momentous decision. The time comes for his coronation in St. Peter's Square and Quinn accepts the office, then removes the crown and tells the waiting throngs that he intends to give all of the wealth of the Church to feed the hungry, even if it means bringing the Church to poverty. The picture ends after 162 minutes (at least 25 could have come out) and everyone leaves with a good feeling, though nobody believes it for a moment. They built a replica of the Sistine Chapel in California, then sent it to Rome because commercial movie companies are not allowed to get too close to the inner apses and naves of the Vatican. The entire Janssen/Jefford/Dexter triangle could easily have been lost from this story, which concerns much grander problems than a cheating husband. North's score was nominated by the Academy but that's all the notice that was taken. The picture cost nearly $9 million and failed at the box office. McKern, De Sica, Copley and Howard are terrific as men of the cloth and Finlay and Revill do well as Russian officials. Excellent lensing of Rome by Hillier and, at times, it looks more like a travelogue than a movie. It was at this time that Olivier told the press he was suffering from cancer and determined to beat it. Nearly 20 years later, in 1986, Olivier had made good his promise and was still acting.

p, George Englund; d, Michael Anderson; w, John Patrick, James Kennaway, (Morris L. West, uncredited), (based on the novel by West); ph, Erwin Hillier (Panavision, Metrocolor); m, Alex North; ed, Ernest Walter; md, North; art d, George W. Davis, Edward Carfagno; set d, Arrigo Breschi; cos, Orietta Nasalli-Rocca; makeup, Amato Garbini.

Religious Drama   **(PR:A   MPAA:G)**

SHOGUN ASSASSIN***   (1980, Jap.) 86m Toho-Katsu/New World c

Tomisaburo Wakayama *(Lone Wolf)*, Masahiro Tomikawa *(Daigoro the Son)*, Kayo Matsuo *(The Supreme Ninja)*, Minoru Okhi, Shoji Kobayashi, Shin Kishida *(The Masters of Death)*.

This really violent Japanese adventure is surprisingly good. It really doesn't have much of a plot and focuses on Wakayama, an "official decapitator" running around the country with his young son in tow (via a wooden cart!) seeking revenge on the men who killed his wife. Lots of spurting blood and dismembered parts are the movie's main feature, all done in a cartoon-like fashion that even makes the violence palatable. Sometimes the blood even fires onto the camera] The film is narrated by the man's child, making this a weird sort of near-comic adventure. Actually, SHOGUN ASSASSIN is edited down from two films in the popular Japanese series Lone Wolf: BABY CART AT RIVER STYX and SWORD OF VENGEANCE, both of which

were based on a Japanese comic book. The American dubbing is quite good, using a minimum of dialog for maximum effect. One of the voices is dubbed by Sandra Bernhard, who played the crazy "Sasha" in Martin Scorsese's THE KING OF COMEDY, and Mark Lindsay, formerly of the popular 1960s rock group Paul Revere and The Raiders. Other voices were dubbed by Gibran Evans (Daigaro), Lamont Johnson, Marshall Efron, Vic Davis, Lennie Weinrib, Lainie Cook, Sam Weisman, David Weisman, Robert Houston. An electronic musical soundtrack for the American release was created by Lindsay.

p, David Weisman; d, Robert Houston; w, Kazuo Koike, Houston, Weisman (based on a story by Koike, Goseki Kojima); ph, Chriski Makiura (Tohoscope, Metrocolor); m, Hideakira Sakurai, W. Michael Lewis, Mark Lindsay; ed, Lee Percy; art d, Akira Naito.

Martial Arts   **Cas.**   **(PR:O   MPAA:R)**

SHOGUN ISLAND   (SEE: RAW FORCE, 1982)

SHONEN SSARUTOBI SASUKE   (SEE: MAGIC BOY, 1961, Jap.)

SHOOT*   (1976, Can.) 92m Getty-Essex/AE c

Cliff Robertson *(Maj. Rex Jeanette)*, Ernest Borgnine *(Lou)*, Henry Silva *(Zeke Springer)*, James Blendick *(Pete)*, Larry Reynolds *(Bob Lissitzen)*, Les Carlson *(Jim Wales)*, Helen Shaver *(Paula Lissitzen)*, Gloria Carlin Chetwynd *(Ellen Jeanette)*, Kate Reid *(Mrs. Graham)*, Alan McRae *(Billy Platt)*, Ed MacNamara *(Sgt. Bellows)*, Peter Langley *(Marshall Flinn)*, Helena Hart *(Helen Newhouse)*, Sidney Brown *(Carl)*, Pam Leawood *(Receptionist)*, James Ince, George Markas, John Rutter, Robert Meneray, John Stoneham, Lloyd White *(Volunteers)*.

In a small town a group of National Guardsmen can't help scratching their itchy trigger fingers. A group of hunters fire at them from the woods and, of course, they fire back. One hunter is killed and the whole thing balloons to an all out war. Robertson, who deserved better roles than this, is the only good thing here, giving a decent performance despite the film's overwhelming stupidity. It's little more than a rip-off of DELIVERANCE, with faint echos of TAXI DRIVER tossed in as well. Wholly unoriginal, it seems to exist solely for the sake of allowing characters to fire some prop guns and of giving fascism pseudo-psychological insight. A real waste of celluloid.

p, Harve Sharman; d, Harvey Hart; w, Dick Berg (based on the novel by Douglas Fairbairn); ph, Zale Magder (Technicolor); m, Doug Riley; ed, Ron Wisman, Peter Shatalow; art d, Earl Preston; makeup, Bill Morgan.

Drama/Action   **(PR:O   MPAA:R)**

SHOOT FIRST***   (1953, Brit.) 88m Raymond Stross/UA bw (GB: ROUGH SHOOT)

Joel McCrea *(Lt. Col. Robert Taine)*, Evelyn Keyes *(Cecily Taine)*, Herbert Lom *(Peter Sandorski)*, Marius Goring *(Hiart)*, Roland Culver *(Randell)*, Frank Lawton *(Richard Hassingham)*, Patricia Laffan *(Magda Hassingham)*, Cyril Raymond *(Cartwright)*, Karel Stepanek *(Diss)*, Dennis Lehrer *(Reimann)*, Laurence Naismith *(Blossom)*, Megs Jenkins *(Mrs. Powell)*, Robert Dickens *(Tommy)*, Jack McNaughton *(Inspector Matthews)*, Arnold Bell *(Sgt. Baines)*, Ellis Irving *(P.C. Wharton)*, Clement McCallin *(Inspector Sullivan)*, David Hurst *(Lex)*, Arnold Bell *(Sgt. Bains)*, Joan Hickson *(Station Announcer)*, Powys Thomas *(Ambulance Driver)*.

McCrea is an American army colonel stationed in England, who gets involved with helping Culver and Lom of the British Secret Service. A plot is discovered to smuggle in foreign agents, and McCrea and Lom pose as his allies when they go to meet him. Other agents try to pin a murder charge on McCrea, and the action culminates in a chase through a wax museum. Spies, counterspies, murder and suspense are nicely woven together for an intriguing thriller. McCrea is excellent in the lead, with good support from Lom and Keyes as McCrea's wife. Direction is taut, with speedy pacing that helps the suspense immensely. Though not an outstanding espionage feature, it works well in the programmer format.

p, Raymond Stross; d, Robert Parrish; w, Eric Ambler (based on the novel *A Rough Shoot* by Geoffrey Household); ph, Stanley Pavey; m, Hans May; ed Russell Lloyd; art d, Ivan King.

Thriller   **(PR:C-O   MPAA:NR)**

SHOOT FIRST, LAUGH LAST**   (1967, Ital./Ger./U.S.) 90m Primex Italiana/Juventus/ Reverse c (UN UOMO, UN CAVALLO, UNA PISTOLA)

Tony Anthony, Dan Vadis, Marco Guglielmi, Daniele Vargas, Marina Berti, Jill Banner.

An outlaw is robbing stagecoaches and it's up to Anthony as the spaghetti western-type loner, to find the man who's behind it. The plot is confusing and highly complex in this otherwise routine fare. Anthony borders on self-parody with his machismo mocking, super-cowboy role.

p, Roberto Infascelli, Massimo Gualdi; d, Vance Lewis [Luigi Vanzi]; w, Jose Many [Giuseppe Mangione], Bob Enescelle, Jr.; ph, Marcello Masciocchi.

Western   (PR:O MPAA:NR)

SHOOT IT: BLACK, SHOOT IT: BLUE*   (1974) 93m Shoot
                                         It/Levitt-Pickman c

Michael Moriarty (*Herbert G. Rucker*), Eric Laneuville (*Lamont*), Paul Sorvino (*Ring*), Earl Hindman (*Garrity*), Linda Scruggs (*Stacy*), Bruce Kornbluth (*Buddy*), Anthony Charnota (*Sal*), Fred Burrell (*Teacher*), Lynda Wescott (*Hattie*), Val Pringle (*Wardell*), Buck Buchanan (*Mark S. Johnson*), George Dicenzo (*George*), Molly McGreevy (*Salesgirl*), Michael Shannon (*Purcell*), Joella Deffenbaugh (*Brenda*), John Quastler (*Karl*), Art Ellison (*Heon*), Gilbert Milton (*Pops*), Bob Phillips (*Dougie*), Cecil Burton (*Old Woman*), Linda McGuire (*Victim in Park*), Irene Ballinger (*Bernice*), LeRoy Vaughn (*Coach*), Don Peterson (*Sniper*), Tom Turner (*Hot Camera Dealer*), Ronnie Sellers (*Black Cop*).

Moriarty plays a not-too-bright policeman who is seen taking a bribe by a traffic violator and later kills a purse snatcher whom he has caught red-handed. The widow of the dead man, who was black, sues Moriarty for $1,000,000. He feels assured, however, that a white policeman won't be found guilty of killing a black man. The cop's problems begin to mount when it's discovered that a young black teenager with a passion for filmmaking has recorded the crime on camera and tape. He proceeds to tail Moriarty in an effort to make a documentary. In the end, Moriarty is killed in a car crash when another black man shoots out his automobile tire. This independent feature could have been an excellent study of black-white tensions common within big-city police departments. However SHOOT IT... only skims the surface of this sensitive issue, and the result is a meandering, boring police melodrama with stock (though very well-acted) characters. Too much detail is paid to Moriarty's lifestyle and not enough to the relationship between him and the black filmmaker. A real disappointment, particularly from an actor of Moriarty's caliber.

d&w, Dennis McGuire (based on the novel *Shoot It* by Paul Tyner); ph, Bob Bailin (Movielab Color); m, Terry Stockdale; ed, Bob Brady.

Crime   **Cas.**   (PR:O MPAA:R)

SHOOT LOUD, LOUDER... I DON'T UNDERSTAND**
        (1966, Ital.) 100m Master Film/EM c (SPARA FORTE, PIU
                               FORTE...NON CAPISCO)

Marcello Mastroianni (*Alberto Saporito*), Raquel Welch (*Tania Mottini*), Guido Alberti (*Pasquale Cimmaruta*), Leopoldo Trieste (*Carlo Saporito*), Tecla Scarano (*Aunt Rosa Cimmaruta*), Eduardo De Filippo (*Uncle Nicola*), Rosalba Grottesi (*Elvira Cimmaruta*), Paolo Ricci (*Aniello Amitrano*), Regina Bianchi (*Mrs. Amitrano*), Franco Parenti (*Chief Police Inspector*), Angela Luce (*Beautiful Woman*), Silvano Tranquilli (*Lt. Bertolucci*), Pina D'Amato (*Matilde Cimmaruta*), Carlo Bagno (*Marshal Bagnacavallo*), Pia Morra (*Maid*), Gino Minopoli (*Luigi Cimmaruta*), Alberto Bugli (*Deputy Police Inspector*), Ignazio Spalla (*Carmelo Vitiello*).

An Italian sculptor and antique dealer, played by Mastroianni, is a dreamer who has a hard time separating his fantasies from fact. Mastroianni lives with De Filippo, his eccentric uncle, and the two share a beat-up little residence. De Filippo, disgusted with the human race, hasn't spoken in 50 years. Instead he relies on firecrackers as a form of communication. Mastroianni meets the sexy Welch, then imagines that Ricci, his wealthy neighbor, has been murdered by relatives. The antique dealer heads for the police and reports the death, but later confesses that he may have been dreaming. The police are skeptical because Ricci is a noted gangster. Ricci's family is arrested, which leaves Mastroianni in a daze, unsure if he is awake or dreaming. Ricci confronts Mastroianni and demands that he hand over his passport so he can escape to South America. Mastroianni pretends to fetch his papers but instead goes back to the police. His efforts to disclose that the gangster is indeed alive are interrupted by an enormous explosion. De Filippo apparently has the last word when he sets off his biggest – and final – fireworks message. Mastroianni, fearing everyone is after him, takes the opportunity in the confusion to leave town, taking Welch with him. This attempted spoof of Fellini-style filmmaking never really quite makes it. The blurs between fantasy and reality are too jumbled and confusing, marring the film as a whole. However, Mastroianni is good in his role, giving his unusual part some fine moments. Welch, whose voice is dubbed into Italian, is okay in a minor role. Photography and the stagey art direction nicely capture the dream-like quality intended. (In Italian; English subtitles.)

p, Pietro Notarianni; d, Eduardo De Filippo; w, De Filippo, Suso Cecchi D'Amico (based on the play "Le Voci di Dentro" by De Filippo): ph, Aiace Parolin, Danilo Desideri (Eastmancolor); m, Nino Rota; ed, Ruggero Mastroianni; art d, Gianni Polidori; set d, Ennio Michettoni; cos, Enrico Job.

Drama/Fantasy   (PR:O MPAA:NR)

SHOOT OUT**   (1971) 94m UNIV c

Gregory Peck (*Clay Lomax*), Pat Quinn (*Juliana Farrell*), Robert F. Lyons (*Bobby Jay*), Susan Tyrrell (*Alma*), Jeff Corey (*Trooper*), James Gregory (*Sam Foley*), Rita Gam (*Emma*), Dawn Lyn (*Decky*), Pepe Serna (*Pepe*), John Chandler (*Skeeter*), Paul Fix (*Brakeman*), Arthur Hunnicutt (*Homer Page*), Nicolas Beauvy (*Dutch Farrell*).

After being released from prison, Western gunman Peck sets out to get revenge on the partners who double-crossed him after a bank robbery. He must also take care of Lyn, an abandoned orphan girl. Gregory plays the man's former partner, who hires psychotic gunman Lyons to kill Peck. Made by the same director, producer and screenwriter of the much better TRUE GRIT, SHOOT OUT suffers from lethargic direction and some unbelievably hammy performances. Peck merely walks through his role and is too nice to be believed as a vengeful man, and Lyons overacts with enormous zeal. The scenery is well used, however, with some beautiful mountain settings, but it's not enough to make the film work. The result is a boring, inconsequential western. This is a remake of the 1934 film THE LONE COWBOY.

p, Hal B. Wallis; d, Henry Hathaway; w, Marguerite Roberts (based on *The Lone Cowboy* by Will James); ph, Earl Rath (Technicolor); m, David Grusin; ed, Archie Marshek; art d, Alexander Golitzen, Walter Tyler; set d, John McCarthy; makeup, Bud Westmore, Frank Prehoda.

Western   (PR:C MPAA:GP)

SHOOT OUT AT BIG SAG**   (1962) 64m Brennan/Parallel bw (AKA:
                                        SHOOTOUT AT BIG SAG)

Walter Brennan (*Preacher Hawker*), Leif Erickson (*Sam Barbee*), Luana Patten (*Hannah Hawker*), Chris Robinson (*Lee Barbee*), Constance Ford (*Goldie Bartholomew*), Virginia Gregg (*Sarah Hawker*), Les Tremayne (*Chan Bartholomew, Saloon Owner*), Don O'Kelly (*Fargo*), Andy Brennan, William Foster, Robert Beecher, Lennie Geer.

Brennan is a self-appointed clergyman who wants the Big Sag area of Montana for himself and family. He tries to run newly arrived Texans Erickson and son Robinson off the land so he can have it for his own. Gregg, knowing her husband is a coward who will never follow through with his plan, sends her daughter (Patten) off to town with a note for Tremayne, owner of the First and Last Chance Saloon. En route Patten is delayed by a storm and meets Robinson. The two young people fall in love, but Patten continues to carry out her mother's orders. She delivers the note and Tremayne makes a pass at her. Ford, Tremayne's alcoholic wife, foils the seduction by shooting her husband dead. It turns out Tremayne also had hired a killer (O'Kelly), who is shot by Brennan. The preacher performs the marriage ceremony for his daughter and former rival's son, then vows never again to pick up a gun. This production was produced by Brennan's son and copywrited under the title "Barb Wire (The Rawhide Halo)." It was to be the pilot episode for a television series called "Barbed Wire," which was never produced. SHOOT OUT AT BIG SAG stayed on the shelf for two years before it finally was given a minor theatrical release in 1962.

p, Walter A. Brennan, Jr., Bud S. Issacs; d&w, Roger Kay (based on the novel *Barb Wire* by Walt Coburn); ph, Lothrop Worth; m, William Loose, Jack Cookerly; ed, Issacs; art d, Archie Bacon; cos, Ed Lossman; spec eff, Howard A. Anderson Co.; makeup, Lee Greenway.

Western   (PR:C MPAA:NR)

SHOOT-OUT AT MEDICINE BEND**½   (1957) 87m WB bw

Randolph Scott (*Cap Devlin*), James Craig (*Clark*), Angie Dickinson (*Priscilla*), Dani Crayne (*Nell*), James Garner (*Maitland*), Gordon Jones (*Clegg*), Trevor Bardette (*Sheriff*), Don Beddoe (*Mayor*), Myron Healey (*Sanders*), John Alderson (*Walters*), Harry Harvey, Sr (*King*), Robert Warwick (*Brother Abraham*), Howard Negley, Marshall Bradford, Ann Doran, Daryn Hinton, Dickie Bellis, Edward Hinton, Lane Bradford, Francis Morris, Robert Lynn, Sam Flint, Philip Van Zandt, Guy Wilkerson, Syd Saylor, Harry Rowland, Marjorie Bennett, Jesslyn Fax, Marjorie Stapp, Nancy Kulp, George Meader, Rory Mallinson, Dee Carroll, Gerald Charlebois, Dale Van Sickel, Gil Perkins, Harry Lauter, George Russ, Carol Henry, George Pembroke, Tom Monroe, John Roy, Buddy Roosevelt, George Bell.

Scott plays a Civil War vet from the Union Army. His clothes are stolen, along with those of some friends, so they don garb given to them by some friendly Quakers. The clothing comes in handy when Scott's brother and his troops are killed in an Indian attack and the soldier goes undercover to find out who sold the dead man faulty ammunition. The climax is an action-filled sequence in which Scott catches up with bad guy Craig. Garner, in one of his earliest roles, plays one of Scott's sidekicks. Dickinson also made one of her first appearances here as Scott's love interest. The film is routine fare, but lively enough entertainment. The well-paced direction and Scott's performance are the film's highlights. Unlike most of Scott's black and white films, SHOOT-OUT AT MEDICINE BEND was not color tinted. Watch for Kulp, Miss Jane on T.V.'s "Beverly Hillbillies" and 1984 congressional candidate (she lost) in a minor role.

p, Richard Whorf; d, Richard L. Bare; w, John Tucker Battle, D. D. Beauchamp; ph, Carl Guthrie; m, Roy Webb; ed, Clarence Kolster; cos, Marjorie Best; m/l, "Kiss Me Quick," Ray Heindorf, Wayne Shanklin (sung by Dani Crayne).

Western   (PR:A MPAA:NR)

SHOOT THE MOON**   (1982) 124m c

Albert Finney *(George Dunlap)*, Diane Keaton *(Faith Dunlap)*, Karen Allen *(Sandy)*, Peter Weller *(Frank Henderson)*, Dana Hill *(Sherry)*, Viveka Davis *(Jill)*, Tracey Gold *(Marianne)*, Tina Yothers *(Molly)*, George Murdock *(French DeVoe)*, Leora Dana *(Charlotte DeVoe)*, Irving Metzman *(Howard Katz)*, Kenneth Kimmins *(Maitre D')*, Michael Aldredge *(Officer Knudson)*, Robert Costanzo *(Leo Spinelli)*, David Landsberg *(Scott Gruber)*, Lou Cutell *(Willard)*, James Cranna *(Harold)*, Nancy Fish *(Joanne)*, Jeremy Schoenberg *(Timmy)*, Stephen Morrell *(Rick)*, Jim Lange *(Master of Ceremonies)*, Georgann Johnson *(Isabel)*, O-Lan Shepard *(Countergirl)*, Helen Slayton-Hughes *(Singer)*, Robert Ackerman *(Waiter)*, Eunice Suarez *(Mexican Woman)*, Hector M. Morales *(Mexican Man)*, Morgan Upton *(Photographer)*, Edwina Moore *(Reporter)*, Kathryn Trask *(Nurse)*, Bill Reddick *(Priest)*, Bonnie Carpenter, Margaret Clark, Jan Dunn, Rob Glover *(Mourners)*.

MGM, upon seeing the rushes of this movie, thought that they had a big hit on their hands. After all, it was a modern story of the disintegration of a modern marriage, it had two potent stars in the leads, and it was as timely as the seven o'clock news. They were wrong and the picture sank quickly under its own weight because it was such a patently phony attempt to cash in on the Yuppie generation. Finney is a successful writer married to Keaton. They have four young daughters and live in luxury in trendy Marin County, just north of San Francisco. They have been married 15 years and ennui has replaced passion, so it is no surprise when they split up and he takes Allen as his new lover. Keaton finds solace with the tennis court contractor, Weller, and the four kids do their best to try and get their parents together. In the end, it's as predictable as Ex-Lax. Finney and Keaton each have their heavy dramatic moments and get to run their emotional gamuts, but there is nothing new in Goldman's script that hadn't been seen and heard before in a thousand other, and often better, movies. Sexual situations and raw language mean this should be avoided by anyone who is about the age of the daughters in the movie.

p, Alan Marshall; d, Alan Parker; w, Bo Goldman; ph, Michael Seresin (Metrocolor); ed, Gerry Hambling; prod d, Geoffrey Kirkland; art d, Stu Campbell, cos, Kristi Zea.

Drama   **Cas.**   **(PR:C-O   MPAA:R)**

SHOOT THE PIANO PLAYER*****   (1962, Fr.) 80m Films de la Pleiade/Astor bw (TIREZ SUR LE PIANISTE; GB: SHOOT THE PIANIST)

Charles Aznavour *(Charlie Koller/Edouard Saroyan)*, Marie DuBois *(Lena)*, Nicole Berger *(Theresa)*, Michele Mercier *(Clarisse)*, Albert Remy *(Chico Saroyan)*, Jacques Aslanian *(Richard Saroyan)*, Richard Kanayan *(Fido Saroyan)*, Claude Mansard *(Momo)*, Daniel Boulanger *(Ernest)*, Serge Davri *(Plyne)*, Claude Heymann *(Lars Schmeel)*, Alex Joffe *(Passerby)*, Boby Lapointe *(Singer)*, Catherine Lutz *(Mammy)*.

For his followup to THE 400 BLOWS (1959) Truffaut chose not to deliver another episode of his autobiography nor to address childhood, but to pay homage to Hollywood's gangster films. He enlisted Charles Aznavour, one of France's most popular singers, to play the role of Charlie Koller, a honky-tonk cafe piano player who has given up his life as a famed concert pianist and changed his name. One evening at the club, Aznavour is visited by his gangster brother, Aslanian, who is on the run from a couple of thugs he and his other brother, Remy, double-crossed. He helps Aslanian get away, but in the process gets mixed up with the gangsters, Mansard and Boulanger. Aznavour now fears for his own safety and that of his younger brother Kanayan, with whom he lives. After his eventful night, Aznavour walks home with DuBois. He becomes infatuated with her, but cannot summon up the courage to hold her hand. He returns to his own apartment and spends the night with a friendly prostitute, Mercier, who lives across the hall and cares for Kanayan. Their apartment is being staked out by Mansard and Boulanger, who bungle an early morning attempt to kidnap Kanayan while he is on his way to school. The two hoodlums do, however, succeed in abducting Aznavour and DuBois. Although they carry guns and look threatening, they actually seem to be a friendly, jovial pair. They talk about their love for women and Mansard even admits that he once tried on a pair of his sister's silk panties. Aznavour and DuBois easily escape from their captors when Boulanger, the driver, gets pulled over for running a red light. DuBois offers to hide Aznavour in her apartment, one wall of which is covered by a poster for an Edouard Saroyan concert appearance. In a flashback, he explains why he left his other life behind: his happy marriage to Berger began to dissolve as he became a great success. He cared more for his piano than he did for Berger. One afternoon Berger admitted that she slept with the classical impressario, Heymann, to insure that Aznavour got his big break. Upon hearing this, Aznavour assumes the role of tough guy and walks out on Berger, against his better judgment. In his head he hears the words, "Take her in your arms, forgive her," but he doesn't. He suddenly decides to run back to her, only to find that she has just jumped to her death from a window. After reminiscing, Aznavour and DuBois sleep together. When Aznavour returns to his flat he learns that Kanayan has been kidnaped. On DuBois' urging, Aznavour accompanies her to their club where they both plan to quit. DuBois gets into a row with the owner, Davri, who sold Aznavour's address to Boulanger and Mansard. Aznavour ignores their argument and sits at the piano to play. Davri, jealous of the piano player, picks a fight. A struggle ensues and Aznavour accidentally (he tries

to nick his enemy's arm) stabs Davri in the back. DuBois drives Aznavour to his brothers' snow-covered mountain hideout in order to escape from the police. Mansard and Boulanger discover the hideout and bring Kanayan there with them. DuBois tries to warn Aznavour of their presence but gunfire breaks out and she gets caught in the crossfire. Her collapsing body slides down a snowy slope. While the gangsters finish their gunplay, Aznavour and Kanayan rush to DuBois' side and wipe the snow from her lifeless body. Soon afterwards, Aznavour is back behind his piano in the club, playing his honky-tonk rhythms while the owner breaks in DuBois' replacement. SHOOT THE PIANO PLAYER is a magnificent picture not because of its debt to America's gangster genre, but because of Truffaut's personal approach to that genre. Truffaut does not concern himself with plot mechanisms. Those have been provided for him countless times by Hollywood. The gangster story is simply a frame on which he can hang his own personal ideas (much in the same way the science-fiction genre served him in FAHRENHEIT 451, and the Republic gangster pictures served Jean-Luc Godard in BREATHLESS). As Truffaut said, "The idea behind SHOOT THE PIANO PLAYER was to make a film without a subject, to express all I wanted to say about glory, success, downfall, failure, women, and love by means of a detective story. It's a grab bag." The plot synopsis doesn't give an adequate picture of SHOOT THE PIANO PLAYER. More than anything it is a collection of beautifully scripted and photographed moments, many of which do nothing to further the narrative but instead add a humanistic "feel" to the film. One of the most memorable moments in SHOOT THE PIANO PLAYER lasts only a split second. Davri, the heartless club owner, swears to DuBois that he is telling her the truth about selling the address. "If I am lying, may my mother drop dead," he exclaims. At the very moment, Truffaut cuts to a shot of a decrepit old woman dropping to the floor. It is only one shot but it illustrates Truffaut's charming playfulness when it comes to film. As important as the visuals in SHOOT THE PIANO PLAYER is the superb score by Georges Delerue, who has consistently provided Truffaut with haunting melodies. (Some filmographies mistakenly credit Jean Constantine with the music. Constantine was contracted with by Truffaut but never delivered a score. Delerue was hired in his place.) His remarkable scores have had such a profound effect on so many Truffaut films from JULES AND JIM to DAY FOR NIGHT to THE WOMAN NEXT DOOR, THE LAST METRO, and CONFIDENTIALLY YOURS, as well as such non-Truffaut Films as A LITTLE ROMANCE and SILKWOOD. Truffaut's knack for including hummable songs continues with Boby Lapointe, a real-life Parisian club singer who delivers a vulgar, fast-paced tune that translates as "Vanilla and Raspberry." The importance of music in SHOOT THE PIANO PLAYER is obvious from Truffaut's casting of Aznavour. He combines the proper blend of cafe piano-man Charlie Koller and classic pianist Edouard Saroyan. He's a man alone amidst a world of love and gangsters. He gains our sympathy when Berger dies and again when DuBois dies. But the only love that he hasn't lost is music, his true love. Released in 1960 in France, SHOOT THE PIANO PLAYER followed Truffaut's debut masterpiece THE 400 BLOWS and paved the way for yet another in JULES AND JIM. (In French, English subtitles).

p, Pierre Braunberger; d, Francois Truffaut; w, Truffaut, Marcel Moussy (based on the novel *Down There* by David Goodis); ph, Raoul Coutard (Dyaliscope); m, Georges Delerue; ed, Cecile Decugis, Claudine Bouche; art d, Jacques Mely; m/l, "Dialogues Amoureux" Felix Leclerc, Lucienne Vernay, "Vanille et Framboise" Boby Lapointe.

Crime/Drama   **Cas.**   **(PR:C   MPAA:NR)**

SHOOT THE WORKS**   (1934) 64m PAR bw (GB: THANK YOUR STARS)

Jack Oakie *(Nicky)*, Ben Bernie *(Joe Davis)*, Dorothy Dell *(Lily Raquel)*, Arline Judge *(Jackie)*, Alison Skipworth *(The Countess)*, Roscoe Karns *(Sailor Burke)*, William Frawley *(Larry Hale)*, Paul Cavanagh *(Bill Ritchie)*, Lew Cody *(Axel Hanratty)*, Jill Dennett *(Wanda)*, Lee Kohlmar *(Prof. Jonas)*, Monte Vandergrift *(Man from Board of Health)*, Tony Merlo *(Headwaiter)*, Ben Taggart *(Detective)*, Charles McAvoy *(Cop)*, Frank Prince *(Crooner)*, Clara Lou [Ann] Sheridan *(Secretary)*.

Oakie is a lovable louse who's mad about Dell. She finally realizes the guy's okay just before she is about to marry another. Set against a carnival backdrop, this skimpily plotted film also had a sub-plot involving Frawley as a Broadway columnist engaged in a comic feud with Bernie, a radio maestro. The action takes place at Hubert's Museum, a cheesy joint which later became a starting point for 1960s media sensation Tiny Tim (Hubert's was also immortalized in a marvelous routine by comedian Lenny Bruce.) Unfortunately there's little to this piece other than the music. The songs -- including "Do I Love You?" (Ralph Rainger, Leo Robin), "Were Your Ears Burning?", "With My Eyes Wide Open I'm Dreaming," sung by Dell, and "In the Good Old Wintertime" (Mack Gordon, Harry Revel) – are catchy enough, but never elevate this to anything more than a minor musical. The film was based on a play by talented writers Fowler and Hecht (though they weren't credited), and the title was taken from a revue by Heywood Broun. Dell died shortly after completion of the film, as did fellow player Cody. The not-yet-famous Ann Sheridan, then known as Clara Lou Sheridan, has a bit part. Songs also included "Take a Lesson from the Larks" (Rainger, Robin), "A Bowl of Chop Suey," "You-ey" (Al Goering, Ben Bernie).

p, Albert Lewis; d, Wesley Ruggles; w, Howard J. Green, Claude Binyon (based on the play "The Great Magoo" by Ben Hecht, Gene Fowler); ph, Leo Tover; art d, Hans Dreier, Robert Usher.

Musical   (PR:A   MPAA:NR)

SHOOT TO KILL***   (1947) 64m Screen Guild bw

Russell Wade (*George Mitchell*), Susan Walters (*Marian Langdon*), Edmund MacDonald (*Lawrence Dale*), Douglas Blackley (*Dixie Logan*), Vince Barnett (*Charlie Gill*), Nestor Paiva (*Gus Miller*), Douglas Trowbridge (*John Forsythe*), Harry Brown (*Jim Forman*), Ted Hecht (*Al Collins*), Harry Cheshire (*Mike Blake*), Robert Riordan (*Ed Carter*), Joe Devlin (*Smokey*), Eddie Foster (*Bingo*), Frank O'Connor (*Clem*), Sammy Stein (*Blackie*), Gene Rodgers (*Piano Player*).

In this film, told in flashback, MacDonald is a crooked assistant district attorney who's in the pocket of local gangster Paiva. The pair works to control the town they live in, but encounter problems when another gangster tries to work his way into their operations. After they frame the man (Blackley), his wife, Walters, and reporter Wade team up to uncover the plot. This film boasts several strong performances; Walter's is a little less believable. Her flashback narration is occasionally a problem because she appears aware of events of which she has no knowledge. Still, SHOOT TO KILL features good direction that provides suspense and successfully weaves together several plot lines. An interesting minor B picture.

p&d, William Berke; w, Edwin V. Westrate; ph, Benjamin Kline; m, Darrell Calker; ed, Arthur A. Brooks; md, David Chudnow; art d, William Glasgow, set d, Thomas Thompson.

Crime   (PR:C   MPAA:NR)

SHOOT TO KILL**   (1961, Brit.) 64m Border/NR bw

Dermot Walsh (*Mike Roberts*), Joy Webster (*Lee Fisher*), John East (*Boris Altovitch*), Frank Hawkins (*Neale Patterson*), Zoreen Ismael (*Anna*), Theodore Wilhelm (*Nicholi*), Victor Beaumont (*Nauman*), Ronald Adam (*Wood*).

Routine espionage thriller set in Geneva which sees some intrepid reporters outwit Communist agents in pursuit of Western atomic secrets. Shots of Geneva, the diplomatic center of the East and West, lend some interest to the proceedings.

p, O. Negus Fancey; d&w, Michael Winner.

Spy Drama   (PR:A   MPAA:NR)

SHOOTIN' IRONS   (SEE: WEST OF TEXAS, 1943)

SHOOTING, THE****   (1971) 82m Proteus-Favorite Films/Jack H. Harris c

Jack Nicholson (*Billy Spear*), Millie Perkins (*Woman*), Warren Oates (*Willet Gashade*), Will Hutchins (*Coley*), B.J. Merholz (*Leland Drum*), Cuy El Tsosie (*Indian*), Charles Eastman (*Bearded Man*).

In the bleakness of a desert setting, a group of bounty hunters has made camp. When Oates returns to camp after being out on the desert, he finds out that his brother had gotten drunk in town and run down a little boy. His brother's partner also was shot in the back by an unknown gunman. After all periods throughout Hutchins, fearful of the goings-on, gives equally paranoid Oates his guns. The next day, the two hear a shot and see Perkins near her camp. Perkins, who has just killed her horse, offers Oates $1,000 to take her to the town of Kingsley. He agrees, even though he dislikes her. The trio heads off and constantly argue along the trail. After passing a small town, Oates learns his brother had been seen there. Upon reaching the desert, Perkins starts flirting with Hutchins, but is stopped by Oates, who realizes she is sending some sort of signal to an unknown person following them. Nicholson finally appears and joins up the trio. He and Hutchins don't get along and constantly threaten one another. Oates tells his partner to stop it. Given the chance, Nicholson would like nothing better than to kill the man. When Perkins' new horse dies on the trail, Hutchins gives up his and rides with Oates. Nicholson then orders his nemesis to dismount and forces him to remain in the desert. The others soon meet an acquaintance of Perkins, who is stranded in the desert with a broken leg. The stranger tells the three that they are close to Perkins' destination. She gives him some water and the party moves on. Later Hutchins gets the man's horse and uses it to charge on Nicholson. Nicholson kills the man, which angers Perkins and saddens Oates. He buries his friend and the tedious journey begins a catastrophic denouement. Water runs out and the horses all die. Then Oates and Nicholson get into a fight. Oates wins by crushing Nicholson's shooting hand with a large rock. Perkins runs up to some rocks and Oates follows her. She spots a man she believes killed her child. He turns around and they discover it is Oates' brother. Perkins and Oates engage in a gun battle with the man and they are killed. Nicholson, whose death is inevitable, is left to wander aimlessly in pain around the desert. This unusual, existential western is highly effective, playing with various levels of character and ideas. At times it approaches a sort of quasi-surrealism, particularly during the climactic battle between Oates and his look-alike brother. Only bits of information are revealed to the audience, leaving much left to mull over when the film is over. The sparse dialog and dramatic, disorienting use of

close-ups are highly effective. The bleak location shooting in the Utah desert is perhaps the best of all, allowing the audience to almost feel the heat and sense the impending doom projected by the barren land. Black comedy is found as well (at one point the man dying from his broken leg is offered some candy!) The ensemble is without a doubt uniformly excellent. Oates' character is fascinating; but is most expressive with simple facial gestures. Perkins (a minor starlet in the 1950s) and Nicholson are equally good in their unusual, esoteric roles. THE SHOOTING was filmed back-to-back with RIDE THE WHIRLWIND during a six-week period in 1965. Both films were produced on minuscule budgets by Nicholson and director Hellman, with an uncredited Roger Corman serving as executive producer. Nicholson also wrote the script for WHIRLWIND, whose sparse dialog and thematic material is strikingly similar to THE SHOOTING. (The script for THE SHOOTING was by Joyce, who later wrote Nicholson's classic FIVE EASY PIECES). No distributor would touch either film, despite excellent reviews at the Montreal Film Festival and an out-of-competition screening at Cannes. Nicholson finally sold the rights to a French producer, who soon went bankrupt. The two films gathered dust for a couple of years before being dumped on a few T.V. late, late shows. Through word of mouth, a few screenings took place and, with the success of EASY RIDER, THE SHOOTING was given a limited release. A real pity that this all had to be, because THE SHOOTING is a fine western stylization that should not be missed.

p, Monte Hellman, Jack Nicholson; d, Hellman; w, Adrien Joyce; ph, Gregory Sandor (DeLuxe Color); m, Richard Markowitz; ed, Hellman.

Western   **Cas.**   (PR:O   MPAA:R)

SHOOTING HIGH*½   (1940) 65m FOX bw

Jane Withers (*Jane Pritchard*), Gene Autry (*Will Carson*), Marjorie Weaver (*Marjorie Pritchard*), Robert Lowery (*Bob Merritt*), Katharine [Kay] Aldridge (*Evelyn Trent*), Hobart Cavanaugh (*Clem Perkie*), Frank M. Thomas (*Calvin Pritchard*), Jack Carson (*Gabby Cross*), Hamilton MacFadden (*J. Wallace Rutledge*), Charles Middleton (*Hod Carson*), Ed Brady (*Mort Carson*), Tom London (*Eph Carson*), Eddie Acuff (*Andy Carson*), Pat O'Malley (*Sam Pritchard*), George Chandler (*Charles Pritchard*), Champion the Horse.

"Mr. Autry has a unique way of projecting moods," wrote Bosley Crowther in a famous crack written about the singing cowboy in his New York Times review of SHOOTING HIGH. "He does not change expression; he just changes cowboy suits." Crowther's comments were right on the mark with this film, a boring, inane piece that marked Autry's first venture outside the Republic studio. Here he plays not himself, but an ordinary man set to be a stand-in for Lowery in a western about Autry's famous grandfather. Autry, however, proves to be a worthy heir to the role when he foils a bank robbery while the cameras are rolling. Withers plays a precocious brat who manages to scare Lowery into high tailing it from town, and Weaver is Autry's love interest. When Autry isn't playing his amiable self, his acting talents prove painfully useless and wooden. He just goes through the motions here. The self-parody by the studio of the filmmaking process is self-serving here.

p, John Stone; d, Alfred E. Green; w, Lou Breslow, Owen Francis; ph, Ernest Palmer; ed, Nick De Maggio; md, Samuel Kaylin; art d, Richard Day, Lewis Creber; m/l, Felix Bernard, Paul Francis Webster, Gene Autry, Johnnie Marvin, Harry Tobias, Charles Newman, Fred Glickman.

Western/Satire   (PR:A   MPAA:NR)

SHOOTING STRAIGHT**½   (1930) 72m RKO bw

Richard Dix ("*Lucky*" *Larry Sheldon*), Mary Lawlor (*Doris Powell*), James Neill (*Rev. Powell*), Matthew Betz (*Martin*), George Cooper (*Chick*), William Janney (*Tommy Powell*), Robert Emmett O'Connor (*Hagen*), Clarence Wurtz (*Stevens*), Eddie Sturgis (*Spike*), Richard Curtis (*Butch*).

A gambler, played by Dix, thinks he's committed a murder and hops aboard a train heading out of town. The train crashes and he ends up recovering at the home of Neill, a local minister who mistakes him for a traveling evangelist. Dix quickly assumes the new identity and falls for Lawlor, the reverend's daughter. All appears well with Dix's new life and romance, until the past catches up with him. But, he's proven innocent of the crime, and Lawlor forgives him. Though this is a moldy and thoroughly contrived story, it is redeemed through the good production values and well-paced action sequences. Dix also is good in the lead.

p, Louis Sarecky; d, George Archainbaud; w, J. Walter Ruben, Wallace Smith (based on a story by Barney Sarecky); ph, Edward Cronjager; ed, Otto Ludwig; art d, Max Ree.

Drama   (PR:A   MPAA:NR)

SHOOTIST, THE****   (1976) 100m DD/PAR

John Wayne (*John Bernard Books*), Lauren Bacall (*Bond Rogers*), Ron Howard (*Gillom Rogers*), James Stewart (*Dr. Hostetler*), Richard Boone (*Sweeney*), Hugh O'Brian (*Pulford*), Bill McKinney (*Cobb*), Harry Morgan (*Marshall Thibido*), John Carradine (*Beckum*), Sheree North (*Serepta*), Richard Lenz (*Dobkins*), Scatman Crothers (*Moses*), Gregg Palmer (*Burly*

Man), Alfred Dennis *(Barber)*, Dick Winslow *(Streetcar Driver)*, Melody Thomas *(Girl on Streetcar)*, Kathleen O'Malley *(School Teacher)*.

John Wayne's last film is a truly moving, dignified, and eloquent last hurrah for a man who had superseded mere movie star status and became a beloved icon of American culture. Appropriately, the film is a western. Opening with a black-and-white montage of scenes from Wayne's earlier westerns, the film traces the career of infamous gunfighter J.B. Books (Wayne) from 1871 to the contemporary year of 1901. As we move through scenes from RED RIVER, HONDO, RIO BRAVO, and EL DORADO, Wayne ages before our eyes until he rides up before the camera and the film turns to color. During this sequence a voice-over spoken by Howard tells us that Wayne had killed 30 men in 30 years, but he was never an outlaw. In fact, he was a lawman for a while. Wayne's credo: "I won't be wronged, I won't be insulted, and I won't be laid a hand on. I don't do these things to other people and I expect the same from them." The cold January winds bite into Wayne as he rides his old horse "Dolor" (Spanish for pain and sorrow) through the snowy plains. Wayne is halted by an unlikely bandit who brandishes a rifle and demands his wallet. Wayne looks a bit amused while reaching into his coat. Hidden in his wallet is a derringer and Wayne plugs the robber just under the belly. The man collapses and screams, "You done murdered me!" "No, but you're gonna have a long winter's belly ache, you boob," replies Wayne as he retrieves his wallet and rides off. The old gunslinger's skills are still very much in evidence. Wayne then rides into Carson City, Nevada. It is a bustling town of telephone poles, trolley cars, door bells, electric lights, running water, and dry-cleaning. While the stranger buys a newspaper announcing the recent death of Queen Victoria, he encounters a surly milk wagon master, McKinney, and his helper, Howard. McKinney calls Wayne an old man and commands him to get out of the way. Wayne goads McKinney a bit and sees the man glance at his guns. "Try it," is Wayne's calm challenge. McKinney backs off and goes on his way. The old man then rides up to Stewart's doctor's office. He brings with him a frilly red pillow he stole from a whorehouse to sit on. Stewart is glad to see Wayne and remarks how he hasn't been around since the gunfight at the Acme saloon. "Only time I was ever hit," states Wayne, who also remarks that it was some amateur who came out of nowhere that got him. Getting down to business, Wayne asks Stewart to examine him because another doctor had looked him over and he doesn't trust the conclusions. Telling Stewart that he has deep pains in his back that hurt "like sin," Wayne submits to the examination. Afterwards Stewart is visibly shaken by the results and Wayne demands a straight answer. He has terminal cancer and nothing can be done. He may have as little as two months to live. Wayne asks that the information be kept secret and Stewart complies. After the examination, Wayne goes to get a room at Bacall's boarding house. It turns out that Howard, the milk wagon delivery boy, is Bacall's son. While Bacall watches, Wayne unpacks several pistols and is evasive about his identity. He tells the widowed landlady that his name is William Hickock and that he's a marshal from Abilene. Meanwhile, Howard has taken Wayne's horse to the stables owned by Crothers, and they spot the name "J.B. Books" on Wayne's saddle. Excited that an infamous celebrity is staying in his house, Howard tells his mother the news. The next morning Bacall asks Wayne to leave and he refuses. She calls sheriff Morgan to come by and make him leave. Morgan arrives and is obviously scared witless of Wayne. His fear suddenly turns to joy when Wayne tells him that he is dying of cancer and plans to spend his last days at the boarding house. Whooping, hollering, and laughing, Morgan tells Wayne that "The day they lay you away what I do on your grave won't pass for flowers." After Morgan leaves, the gunslinger apologizes to Bacall for lying about his identity and tells her that he is dying. Feeling sorry for him, Bacall lets him stay. The next day Lenz, an obnoxious reporter, stops by and tries to persuade Wayne to let him write a sensational, authorized biography of his "life and bloody times." Wayne kicks him out. On another visit to Stewart, Wayne is given laudanum, a mixture of opium and alcohol, to drink for the pain. Urged to by the gunman, Stewart describes the horrible pain and agony that will soon set in because of the cancer. He concludes by saying, "I would not die a death like I just described. Not if I had your courage." While Howard practically worships Wayne, Bacall has grown to respect him as a man and she agrees to take a buggy ride with him because he'd like to see the trees, hills, lakes, and sky again. During the excursion, the two grow close and develop a real rapport and fondness for each other. Meanwhile, word has spread throughout the town that Wayne is dying. O'Brian, a faro dealer at the local saloon who happens to be a skilled gunman, regrets that he'll never get a chance to take Wayne on. When heckled by a customer, O'Brian has a shootout with the man from across the saloon and kills him with one shot through the heart at 84 feet. On the way back through town, Wayne and Bacall run into Boone, a local rancher who drives an automobile. Boone is a mean and surly man dripping with seedy charm. Wayne once killed Boone's brother and it is obvious the man in the automobile wants revenge. That night, two local boys try to kill Wayne in his bed, but the old gunfighter kills them both and, though winded, emerges without a scratch. The next morning, the rest of Bacall's boarders move out. Wanting to pay Bacall back for the damage and loss of business, Wayne decides to sell his horse and saddle to Crothers for $300, knowing the stable owner will turn around and sell them for much more. That afternoon Wayne gives Howard a shooting lesson, and although the youngster is very good with a pistol, he knows little about reality. "It isn't always being fast, or even accurate, that counts," Wayne states, "It's being willing. I found out early that most men, regardless of cause or need, aren't willing. They blink an eye or draw a breath before they pull the trigger. I won't." Later that day Wayne gets a surprise visit from North, a dance-hall girl the gunfighter once loved. She tells him that she would like to marry him so that she can write his authorized biography with Lenz, the local reporter. Wayne, who was at first overjoyed by North's arrival, suddenly becomes repulsed by her pettiness and asks her to leave. While getting a haircut the next day, Wayne is visited by Carradine, the local undertaker. Carradine offers to give the gunman a funeral with the best of everything for free. Wayne knows that Carradine will turn his funeral into a circus and charge a fee to view the body for as long as the public is interested. The gunslinger refuses and instead asks for a tombstone with a simple inscription and charges the undertaker $50 for the honor of doing it. When Wayne leaves the barber shop, the barber scoops up all his cut hair (and that from other heads) with plans to sell it. That night Wayne asks Howard to contact O'Brian, Boone, and McKinney, and ask them to meet him at the saloon on Monday morning. Since Wayne has finished reading the newspaper he bought when he first came to town, refuses to buy another bottle of laudanum, and asks to have his best suit dry cleaned, Bacall senses that Wayne is preparing to "do something." Wayne makes her promise that when he leaves the house on Monday morning there will be no questions and no tears. She promises. When Howard returns from his errand, Wayne tells him that he has bought his horse back from Crothers and presents the young man with the bill of sale. The next morning, Wayne's birthday, the gunslinger take the trolley to the saloon for his meeting with the men who want to kill him. Wayne takes a drink, and seeing McKinney nervously drawing his pistol reflected in the mirror, dives behind the bar. Wayne then kills McKinney easily. Boone fires next and wounds Wayne in the shoulder. Wayne returns fire and shoots Boone several times before the big man finally collapses and dies. O'Brian shoots and also wounds Wayne. Wayne stays behind the bar, lying down, and waits for O'Brian to peer around the edge. The old gunman then dispatches O'Brian with one shot to the head. Wounded, out of breath, and very much alive, Wayne gets on his feet and surveys the carnage. He seems disappointed that none of the men were able to do him in. Howard, who was standing across the street, enters the bar to see what has happened. Before he has a chance to yell a warning, the bartender appears from out of nowhere with a shotgun and blows two holes in Wayne's back. Howard rushes to Wayne, grabs the pistol from his hand, and shoots the bartender several times. Standing with Wayne dying beneath him, Howard stares at the bloody pistol in his hand, now fully aware of its horrible potential. He hesitates for a moment, and then throws it across the room. Wayne, who has worriedly watched this moment of decision, smiles approvingly at Howard and dies. Howard leaves the saloon as the gawkers file in. Bacall, dressed as if in mourning, silently waits for her son and they walk back home together. Wayne is magnificent in THE SHOOTIST and it is his picture all the way. Through much of the 1960s and 1970s, Wayne had begun to parody himself in his films and seemed to gently poke fun at his image. Here he manages to bring a disarming, very serious self-awareness to the role and uses it to his advantage. Despite all his proclamations to the contrary, it seems as if Wayne knew this would be his last performance and that he wished to go out on a film that was a summation of his career and image. In THE SHOOTIST, Wayne seems to carry the weight of a mighty reputation that has begun to wear him down. Quietly desperate to maintain his dignity in a changing world that has no place for him, Wayne bravely faces his fate and lives up to what everyone expects of him and what he expects of himself. During this private battle, he also manages to teach others. Howard is an immature braggart struggling to grow up by cussing, acting tough, and drinking whiskey. Wayne teaches him there is more to being a man than acting macho. THE SHOOTIST is most reminiscent of Sam Peckinpah's masterpiece RIDE THE HIGH COUNTRY, which was the swan song of two beloved cowboy stars, Randolph Scott and Joel McCrea. With its emphasis on dignity, self-respect, and living up to one's code of honor, Peckinpah's film was a moving elegy to these men as icons of the Old West, and as actors. Unfortunately, THE SHOOTIST falls short of masterpiece status for several nagging reasons. The film lacks subtlety of character and forces Wayne, Bacall, Morgan, et al, to make speeches on the nature of good, evil, heroism, bravery, dignity, and violence. Little is shown in THE SHOOTIST, most of it is talked about. Where long dialog sequences are also present in RIDE THE HIGH COUNTRY, they are spoken on the trail, outdoors, where the characters are busy doing other things. THE SHOOTIST is confined to a handful of rooms where the characters must sit and talk. Perhaps this is a visual demonstration of the effect progress has had on the once expansive West, but it has a frustratingly cheap feel to it that annoys. Another major problem with the film is the lack of development in the gunslingers Wayne faces at the end. Aside from O'Brian, who is allowed a rudimentary demonstration of prowess with a gun, Boone and McKinney are just verbalized threats. We are never shown that these men are even worth Wayne's time and reputation, negating any threat they could possibly pose to him. Boone, always an interesting actor, tries desperately to wring a memorable character out of his brief appearance, but the film just doesn't give him enough time. Problems aside, THE SHOOTIST is filled with precious moments. The relationship between Wayne and Bacall is well detailed and their moments together sparkle. Carradine as the undertaker wonderfully underplays his part and adds a wee bit more class to the proceedings (he played the gambler in STAGECOACH, the film that catapulted Wayne to stardom). But, in the end, THE SHOOTIST is all Wayne. He uses what we know about him personally (his battles with cancer, aging, failing health, being misunderstood by a new generation) to his advantage in the film and combines them with the characteristics of J.B. Books. This is a heartfelt performance that has depth, emotion, and dignity to it, and an old actor couldn't ask for a better farewell.

p, M.J. Frankovich, William Self; d, Don Siegel; w, Miles Hood Swarthout, Scott Hale (based on the novel by Glendon Swarthout); ph, Bruce Surtees (Panavision, Technicolor); m, Elmer Bernstein; ed, Douglas Stewart; prod d, Robert Boyle; set d, Arthur Parker; cos, Moss Mabry, Luster Bayless, Edna Taylor; spec eff, Augie Lohman.

Western   Cas.   (PR:O   MPAA:PG)

SHOOTOUT   (SEE: SHOOT OUT, 1971)

SHOOTOUT AT MEDICINE BEND
                    (SEE: SHOOT OUT AT MEDICINE BEND, 1957)

SHOP ANGEL**   (1932) 71m Tower bw

Marion Shilling, Holmes Herbert, Anthony Bushell, Walter Byron, Dorothy Christy, Creighton Hale.

Shilling is a store dress designer who, wanting to move up in status, goes after her boss. The two go out and there's a big car crash. The store employees try to quiet the fact that the boss was out with another worker. A scandal is averted, however, because the boss's daughter and her fiance were also in the car. The daughter takes Shilling's place in the auto and her fiance (Bushell) takes Shilling home. Bushell and Shilling fall in love. Meanwhile, an ad man tries to shake down the boss for money. The boss thinks that Shilling is in on the blackmail scheme, but of course she's not. She ends up marrying Bushell and all ends happily. Routine programmer from a long-gone independent studio. The story is well told, but it's not much to begin with. The production values are first-rate and the acting isn't bad.

d, E. Mason Hopper; w, Edward T. Lowe (based on a story by Izola Forrester); ph, William Hyer.

Drama   (PR:C   MPAA:NR)

SHOP AROUND THE CORNER, THE*****   (1940) 97m MGM bw

James Stewart (Alfred Kralik), Margaret Sullavan (Klara Novak), Frank Morgan (Hugo Matuschek), Joseph Schildkraut (Ferencz Vadas), Sara Haden (Flora), Felix Bressart (Perovitch), William Tracy (Pepi Katena), Inez Courtney (Ilona), Charles Halton (Detective), Charles Smith (Rudy), Sarah Edwards, Gertrude Simpson (Woman Customers), Grace Hayle (Plump Woman), Charles Arnt (Policeman), William Edmunds (Waiter), Mary Carr (Grandmother), Mabel Colcord (Aunt Anna), Renie Riano, Claire DuBrey, Ruth Warren, Joan Blair, Mira McKinney (Customers), Edwin Maxwell (Doctor).

It's been said that there are two kinds of films–those with grand themes and those with little themes. Grand themes are evident in such masterpieces as THE BIRTH OF A NATION, GREED, or ALL QUIET ON THE WESTERN FRONT, while the little theme has been most masterfully handled by Lubitsch in THE SHOP AROUND THE CORNER. It is in this film that the brilliant Lubitsch has come closest to bringing the lives of everyday people to the screen. In contrast to Lubitsch's other heroes–Jack Benny in TO BE OR NOT TO BE, Don Ameche in HEAVEN CAN WAIT, or Greta Garbo in NINOTCHKA–Jimmy Stewart's Alfred Kralik character is as common as they come. He does not fight the Nazis (like Benny), he is not a wealthy playboy (like Ameche), nor is he a bureaucrat (like Garbo). Stewart is just a sales clerk whose integrity and devotion touch a common chord in the hearts of all audiences. Working in a leather goods shop in Budapest, Stewart is the top clerk and a trusted friend of owner Morgan. Because Stewart's ideas are perceived as "genius" by Morgan, he is an invaluable commodity. Morgan even goes so far as to invite him to his house to meet the wife, who of course is duly charmed. Together Morgan and Stewart head a tightly knit work force, all eager to please. Among the workers is Stewart's closest ally, Bressart, an aging clerk who leads a simple life and avoids confrontation; Schildkraut, a braggart who flashes recently acquired wealth; and Tracy, an aspiring clerk who is constantly being bossed around. Trouble brews when the unemployed Sullavan enters the shop and makes a plea to Morgan to hire her as Christmas help. He impolitely refuses and tells the pouting girl to go away. Before she leaves, however, she manages to sell a musical cigar box (which Stewart has tried to deter Morgan from buying a large quantity of) to a rotund woman for use as a candy box. Convinced of her ability to sell, Morgan gives her a job, creating instant jealousy of her in Stewart. But Stewart also has his mind on something else, which he confides in Bressart. Through a "Lonely-Hearts" ad, Stewart has met a most wonderful girl whom he knows only through her box number–237. After exchanging a number of increasingly romantic letters, Stewart prepares to meet the girl at a cafe. He will be wearing a red carnation, while she will be using one as a bookmark in a copy of Anna Karenina. It is Stewart's plan to propose to the girl. Also expecting a proposal of marriage is Sullavan, who is carrying on a letter romance with a man she's never met. Unknown to Sullavan, that man is Stewart. While they may love each other in their letters, they grow increasingly spiteful toward each other at the shop. Stewart reprimands Sullavan about everything, including the way she dresses. On the night that they are both supposed to meet at the cafe, Morgan asks everyone to stay late and redecorate the windows. When

Stewart asks for the night off, Morgan's temper inexplicably flares. Unknown to Stewart, Morgan has discovered that his wife is having an affair with one of his employees. Although Morgan is unsure about which employee is guilty, he suspects Stewart since he is the only one to have met his wife. Before the night is over, Stewart is fired. Afterward, Morgan sends everyone home, allowing time for Sullavan to get to the cafe. Stewart, who has destroyed his carnation in anger, decides to enter the cafe at Bressart's urging, even though he feels unworthy of a wife now that he is unemployed. When he realizes that Sullavan is his lonely-hearts sweetheart, he makes conversation with her, but does not let on why he is there. Sullavan, however, is completely unresponsive, delivering insult after insult to Stewart. Sullavan brags about how she is waiting for her fiance-to-be, a man far superior to Stewart. Stewart threatens her with the thought that her man may not show (he is already late), but she will not listen. Dejected, Stewart decides to leave, thereby ensuring that Sullavan will be stood up. Meantime, Tracy has returned from an errand to find an empty shop. He enters the boss' office just as Morgan is about to kill himself, saving his life. Afterwards, in appreciation, Morgan promotes Tracy to sales clerk. Stewart comes to visit Morgan and is asked to temporarily manage the store at an increase in salary. He is also asked to fire Schildkraut, who is actually the one carrying on with his wife. As a thank-you, Stewart promises to make this coming Christmas the most profitable ever. The cash register doesn't stop ringing up the sales and, by the approach of night, the day has indeed proven profitable. Morgan passes out Christmas bonuses and, after unsuccessfully trying to find a dinner companion for the evening (having split from his wife), decides to take the store's new errand boy, Smith, to a ritzy restaurant. Extending his duties as a boss, Stewart pays a visit to Sullavan who has become bedridden by her depression over being jilted by her mysterious lover. Sullavan continues to brush off Stewart, and when she receives a long-awaited letter from her lonely-hearts lover her health miraculously returns. The following day at work, Sullavan fills Stewart in about her romance. Only then, after Sullavan goes on and on about her sweetheart, does Stewart admit that he is the one who has been writing the letters. After realizing that he indeed is the one she loves, she throws her arms around her no-longer-anonymous love. While THE SHOP AROUND THE CORNER does not come out and strike at the audience like the more spectacular TO BE OR NOT TO BE or HEAVEN CAN WAIT, this latter-period Lubitsch picture reaches out to the viewer's heart. It is a rare moment in film when the characters on the screen perfectly reflect those people who are sitting in the theater watching them. But such is the case with THE SHOP AROUND THE CORNER. In the characters who work at Matuschek's, one can see all human emotions–happiness, love, devotion, dishonesty, jealousy, and sorrow. In a letter to Herman G. Weinberg, author of the directorial study The Lubitsch Touch, Lubitsch listed what he felt were the best pictures of his career. After citing TROUBLE IN PARADISE as his best film stylistically and NINOTCHKA as his sharpest satire, he mentioned THE SHOP AROUND THE CORNER: "As for human comedy, I think I never was as good as in THE SHOP AROUND THE CORNER. Never did I make a picture in which the atmosphere and the characters were truer than in this picture."

p&d, Ernst Lubitsch; w, Samson Raphaelson (based on the play "Parfumerie" by Nikolaus Laszlo); ph, William Daniels; m, Werner R. Heymann; ed, Gene Ruggerio; art d, Cedric Gibbons, Wade Rubottom; set d, Edwin B. Willis.

Comedy/Romance   (PR:A   MPAA:NR)

SHOP AT SLY CORNER, THE   (SEE: CODE OF SCOTLAND YARD,
                                                    1948, Brit.)

SHOP ON HIGH STREET, THE   (SEE: SHOP ON MAIN STREET,
                                                   THE, 1965)

SHOP ON MAIN STREET, THE***½   (1966, Czech.) 128m
     Barrandov/Prominent bw (OBCH OD NA KORZE) (AKA: THE SHOP
                                              ON HIGH STREET)

Jozef Kroner (Tono Brtko), Ida Kaminska (Rosalie Lautmann), Hana Slivkova (Evelina Brtko), Frantisek Zvarik (Marcus Kolkotsky), Helena Zvarikov (Rose Kolkotsky), Martin Holly (Imro Kuchar), Martin Gregory (Katz, the Barber), Adam Matejka (Piti Baci), Mikulas Ladizinsky (Marian Peter), Eugen Senaj (Blau, the Printer), Frantisek Papp (Andoric), Gita Misurova (Andoricova), Luise Grossova (Eliasova), Alojz Kramar (Balko Baci), Tibor Vadas (Tobacconist).

It is WW II and the setting is Slovakia, a small Eastern European country. Kroner is an amiable carpenter with a nagging wife (Slivkova) who thinks they should be moving up in the world. Her brother (Zvarik), a fascist, agrees and tells Kroner to join forces with the occupying troops. To appease his wife and brother-in-law, Kroner takes a job as the "Aryan comptroller" for a Jewish-owned button shop on Main Street. To his dismay, he finds the owner (Kaminska) is a deaf old woman who has gone bankrupt, and there's not a button in the store. Kroner's dreams of prestige are quickly dashed and his frustration is compounded by Kaminska's deafness. Communicating with her is virtually impossible. Apparently it's been too much of an effort for those close to her, because she doesn't seem to realize there's a war on. Her Jewish friends talk Kroner into accepting some money if he'll pose as her new assistant. He agrees, and slowly the two build a close and loving friendship. But troubles arise when an edict is passed, demanding the deportation of the town's Jewish citizens. Somehow Kaminska's name has been left off the list and Kroner is wrought with mixed emotions: Does he protect his friend, thereby risking arrest for harboring a Jew, or should he obey the law and turn her in? The Jews are gathered for the deportation in front of the shop, and Kroner panics. He tries to get Kaminska to join them but she realizes what is happening and tries to get away. Kroner shoves her into a cupboard and locks it, and waits until the trouble is over before freeing her. But on opening the cupboard he finds Kaminska has died. Wrought with guilt, the carpenter hangs himself. This unusual story gives a horrifyingly realistic look at Czechoslovakia during the Nazi occupation. The first portion, told in comic style, is quite amusing. Kroner's relationship with Kaminska is genuine and quite touching. The film's sudden switch from comedy to tragedy is all too real and works well. The direction is, for the most part, excellent, despite a few slow moments. Kroner and Kaminska are excellent. They have effective chemistry and handle the drastic emotional switches with great sensitivity. The film was first shown in this country at the New York Film Festival, where it received a standing ovation; it was well-received by both the viewing public and critics. Later THE SHOP ON MAIN STREET received an Oscar as Best Foreign Film of 1965. Kaminska received a well-deserved nomination for best actress. A beautiful, touching work that should not be missed. (In Czechoslovakian; English subtitles.)

p, Ladislav Hanus, Jaromir Lukas, Jordan Balurov; d, Jan Kadar, Elmar Klos; w, Kadar, Klos, Ladislav Grossman (based on the story "Obchod No Korze" by Grossman); ph, Vladimir Novotny; m, Zdenek Liska; ed, Jaromir Janacek, Diana Heringova; art d, Karel Skvor; English subtitles, Lindsay Anderson.

Drama   **Cas.**   **(PR:C-O MPAA:NR)**

SHOPWORN**   (1932) 72m COL bw

Barbara Stanwyck (Kitty Lane), Regis Toomey (David Livingston), ZaSu Pitts (Dot), Lucien Littlefield (Fred), Clara Blandick (Mrs. Livingston), Robert Alden (Toby), Oscar Apfel (Judge Forbes), Maude Turner Gordon (Mrs. Thorne), Albert Conti (Andre), James Durkin (District Attorney), Wallis Clark (Mr. Dean), Edwin Maxwell (Bierbauer), Joseph Sauer [Sawyer], Joan Standing, Martha Mattox, Dorothea Wolbert.

Stanwyck is a waitress engaged to Toomey. His mother (Blandick) opposes her son's marriage to someone as common as Stanwyck. She goes to her friend Apfel, a judge, who gets Stanwyck sent to a prison workhouse for a three-month sentence. After her release, Stanwyck becomes an overnight musical sensation and renews her romance with Toomey. His mother finally consents to the marriage since Stanwyck's social status has been raised. Stanwyck, a replacement for the originally slated Lila Lee, does what she can with her role in this tired drama and the plot is riddled with holes. Stanwyck's switch from ex-con to singing star is anything but plausible.

p, Harry Cohn; d, Nicholas Grinde; w, Jo Swerling, Robert Riskin, Sarah Y. Mason (based on a story by Mason); ph, Joseph Walker; ed, Gene Havlick.

Drama   **(PR:A MPAA:NR)**

SHOPWORN ANGEL, THE**½   (1928) 82m PAR bw

Nancy Carroll (Daisy Heath), Gary Cooper (William Tyler), Paul Lukas (Bailey), Emmett King (The Chaplain), Mildred Washington (Daisy's Maid), Roscoe Karns, Bert Woodruff.

When happy-go-lucky showgirl Carroll witnesses a parade of soldiers marching off to WW I, she begins to awaken to the seriousness of America's participation in the fight. That night she is involved in a harmless automobile fender-bender with a young Texas soldier, Cooper. The two strike up a friendship and soon Cooper falls in love with Carroll. Carroll, however, is dating a rich man, Lukas, and views her relationship with Cooper as platonic only. Lukas, threatened by the presence of Cooper in Carroll's life, demands the showgirl stop seeing the soldier. Carroll reluctantly agrees. Soon after, Cooper's orders come in and he's to be shipped off to France. Still deeply in love with Carroll and also afraid of the war, Cooper, goes to the showgirl and tells her how he feels. Realizing that she loves him as well, Carroll agrees to marry him and they immediately make the arrangements. During the wedding ceremony Carroll is overcome by the thought that Cooper could be killed overseas and faints. The wedding is never completed and Cooper is shipped out on the next boat. Fortified by Carroll's love, Cooper informs his bride-to-be that he now feels he can face any obstacle without fear. Cooper also has had an effect on Carroll and she decides to shun all her frivolous friends and concentrate on her new chorus job. While rehearsing, she thinks of Cooper in the war and resolves to become a better person in time for his return. Almost entirely a silent film, THE SHOPWORN ANGEL was already in production when the studio decided to try out the new sound techniques on two of their most promising stars, Cooper and Carroll. Both passed the test with flying colors, thus ensuring their transition into a new era. The climax of the film suddenly bursts with sound, allowing Carroll to perform a musical number entitled "A Precious Little Thing Called Love" (Lou Davis, J. Fred Coots). This material was recycled by MGM in 1938 starring Jimmy Stewart and Margaret Sullavan and again in 1959 under the title THAT KIND OF WOMAN with

Sophia Loren and Tab Hunter.

p, Louis D. Lighton; d, Richard Wallace; w, Howard Estabrook, Albert Shelby Le Vino (based on the story Private Pettigrew's Girl by Dana Burnet); ph, Charles Lang; m, Max Bergunker; ed, Robert Bassler.

Romance   **(PR:A MPAA:NR)**

SHOPWORN ANGEL***½   (1938) 85m MGM bw

Margaret Sullavan (Daisy Heath), James Stewart (Bill Pettigrew), Walter Pidgeon (Sam Bailey), Nat Pendleton (Dice), Alan Curtis (Guy with Thin Lips), Sam Levene (Guy with Leer), Hattie McDaniel (Martha the Maid), Charley Grapewin (Wilson the Caretaker), Charles D. Brown (Mr. Gonigle the Stage Manager), Jimmy Butler (Elevator Boy), Eleanor Lynn (Sally the Waitress), William Stack (Minister), Hudson Shotwell (Jack the Soldier), John Merton (Speaker), Wesley Giraud (Bellboy), Harry Tyler (Eddy), Mary Howard, Virginia Grey (Chorus Girls), Wade Boteler (Irish Policeman), James Flavin (Guard), George Chandler (Soldier), Grace Hayle (Mistress of Ceremonies), Jack Murphy (Sailor), Frank McGlynn Jr (Motorcyclist), Edward Keane (Captain), Mary Dees, Joan Mitchell, Frances Millen (Babes), Eddy Chandler (Corporal), Paul Spiegel (Stage Manager), Don Brodie (Attendant), Roger Converse (Hotel Clerk), Francesco Maran (Headwaiter), Paul Kruger (Riveter), Dorothy Granger (Dancer).

Dana Burnet's 1918 Saturday Evening Post story was slim stuff but provided enough for a 1929 Gary Cooper-Nancy Carroll film. They decided to remake the semi-talkie in 1938 and see if Stewart and Sullavan could handle the chores. It's the middle of WW I and Stewart, a gangly, folksy Texan soldier, is in New York, prior to being shipped overseas to fight. The streets are chock-full of people who are excitedly celebrating the entry of the U.S. into the fracas overseas when Sullavan's car almost runs down Stewart. They meet and he falls in love with the actress-performer who comes from a totally different background. She thinks he's a yokel but doesn't tell him to buzz off, as she also finds something charming about his sweet, naive personality. Sullavan has a sort-of boy friend in Pidgeon and he is content to stand by and let her tour the town with Stewart, from Broadway to Brooklyn's Coney Island, where she accompanies him through the amusement area. Stewart's army buddies don't believe that he actually knows a real live actress and she helps him prove that by cuddling up close to him. Pidgeon finally gets jealous and puts his foot down. Sullavan insists that she loves Pidgeon and is just being motherly with this young soldier who is about to go off and fight for the country. Pidgeon won't accept that and answers that their relationship might be on shaky ground due to her palling around with Stewart. Nothing actually happens between Stewart and Sullavan, and when he learns that his unit is about to be shipped overseas right away, he pleads with her to marry him, with no sexual strings attached (they don't have time, as the boat is leaving that night). Even though Sullavan does not love Stewart, she understands how much this means to him and she agrees to the hastily done wedding at the Army camp. Afterwards, she explains the situation to Pidgeon who appreciates her deception and thinks that there will be time enough to tell Stewart the truth when he returns from service. In Europe, Stewart is killed in the front lines during an enemy onslaught. Sullavan is about to go on stage to do her act when she gets the news. She sighs, wipes away her tears, and walks on to the nightclub floor and sings "Pack up Your Troubles in Your Old Kit Bag and Smile, Smile, Smile" (Felix Powell, George Asaf) as she, and the movie audience, sniffle. Pidgeon and Sullavan realize the sacrifice that Stewart has made and are united in their love for each other at the conclusion. There were some major changes between this version and the earlier one; in that, Salt's screenplay softened some of the hard-bitten side of the chorine and made her a great deal more vulnerable. She is hardly the "Shopworn Angel" in this remake that she was previously, but they decided to keep the title, as the 1929 picture was a hit. Also, the Pidgeon character was more dangerous than when played by Paul Lukas in the first film. Stewart was appearing in his fifteenth picture at the age of 30 and in his second with Sullavan, the first also being a remake of SEVENTH HEAVEN, with considerable less success than this. Remade as THAT KIND OF WOMAN.

p, Joseph L. Mankiewicz; d, H.C. Potter; w, Waldo Salt (based on the story "Private Pettigrew's Girl" by Dana Burnet); ph, Joseph Ruttenberg; m, Edward Ward; ed, W. Donn Hayes; art d, Cedric Gibbons, Joseph C. Wright; set d, Edwin B. Willis; cos, Adrian; ch, Val Raset.

Drama   **(PR:A MPAA:NR)**

SHORT CUT TO HELL***   (1957) 87m PAR bw

Robert Ivers (Kyle), Georgann Johnson (Glory Hamilton), William Bishop (Stan), Jacques Aubuchon (Bahrwell), Peter Baldwin (Adams), Yvette Vickers (Daisy), Murvyn Vye (Nichols), Milton Frome (Los Angeles Police Captain), Jacqueline Beer (Waitress), Gail Land (Girl), Dennis McMullen (Los Angeles Policeman), William "Billy" Newell (Hotel Manager), Sarah Selby (Adam's Secretary), Mike Ross (Inspector Ross), Douglas Spencer (Conductor), Danny Lewis (Piano Player), Richard Hale (A.T.), Douglas Evans (Mr. Henry), Hugh Lawrence, Joe Bassett (Patrolmen), William Pullen (Used Car Lot Manager), Russell Trent (Trainman), Joe Forte (Ticket Seller), Roscoe Ates (Ext. Road Driver), John Halloran (Guard).

Ivers is a hired killer who knocks off two men for a friend. His friend pays him with stolen money and the cops know the serial numbers. He pursues the double-crossing friend, with the cops on his tail for the murders. The killer is forced to kidnap Johnson, the girl friend of the detective in charge of the investigation, to protect himself. In the end he's gunned down by the police. A remake of THIS GUN FOR HIRE in 1942, SHORT CUT TO HELL is a competent thriller that marks the directorial debut of star Cagney. He appears in a brief prologue and shows some real talent behind the camera. The film moves at a good pace and has some interesting visual moments. Ivers and Johnson work well as the leads. Cagney's deal with the producer stipulated that he would get the minimum salary allowable with a percentage of any profit the film might bring in.

p, A.C. Lyles; d, James Cagney; w, Ted Berkman, Raphael Blau (based on a screenplay by W.R. Burnett, from the novel *This Gun for Hire* by Graham Greene); ph, Haskell Boggs (VistaVision); m, Irvin Talbot; ed, Tom McAdoo; art d, Hal Pereira, Roland Anderson; set d, Sam Comer, Frank McKelvy; cos, Edith Head; spec eff, John P. Fulton; makeup, Wally Westmore.

Crime   **(PR:O MPAA:NR)**

SHORT EYES* ½   (1977) 104m PAR-Film League c (AKA: SLAMMER)

Bruce Davison (*Clark Davis*), Jose Perez (*Juan*), Nathan George (*Ice*), Don Blakely (*El Raheem*), Shawn Elliott (*Paco*), Tito Goya (*Cupcakes*), Joe Carberry (*Longshore*), Kenny Steward (*Omar*), Bob Maroff (*Mr. Nett*), Keith Davis (*Mr. Brown*), Miguel Pinero (*Go Go*), Willie Hernandez (*Cha Cha*), Tony De Benedetto (*Tony*), Bob O'Connell (*Mr. Allard*), Mark Margolis (*Mr. Morrison*), Richard Matamoros (*Gomez*), Curtis Mayfield (*Pappy*), Freddie Fender (*Johnny*).

Davison, the rat man of WILLARD, plays a child molester sent to prison. The prison slang for his crime is "short eyes," viewed by the other convicts as the lowliest offense one can commit. His fellow inmates, a rag-tag collection of rapists, murderers, junkies and pimps, make his life a living hell. This gritty, well-acted drama was filmed on location in the abandoned New York City Men's House of Detention, in pseudo-documentary style. SHORT EYES has a dark, claustrophobic feeling that heightens the drama. Former convicts and ex-junkies are cast, which adds to the realism. The ensemble is a tight one that places the audience right in the middle of the nightmare. This was adapted from a play by Pinero (an ex-con himself) that was originally produced on stage by Joseph Papp. At moments SHORT EYES acknowledges its theatrical beginnings with some slightly stagey speeches. But overall, the tense, taut drama speaks for itself. A fine film that unfortunately was overlooked upon release. Look for musicians Fender and Mayfield (the latter of whom scored the film) in minor parts as convicts.

p, Lewis Harris; d, Robert M. Young; w, Miguel Pinero (based on his play); ph, Peter Sova; m, Curtis Mayfield; ed, Edward Beyer; prod d, Joe Babas; set d, Pat Prather; cos, Paul Martino; m/l, "Do Do Wrap is Strong in Here," "Back Against the Wall," Mayfield, "Break it Down," H.P. Denenberg, Martin Hirsch.

Drama   **Cas.**   **(PR:O MPAA:R)**

SHORT GRASS*   (1950) 82m AA/MON bw

Rod Cameron (*Steve*), Cathy Downs (*Sharon*), Johnny Mack Brown (*Keown*), Raymond Walburn (*McKenna*), Alan Hale, Jr (*Chris*), Morris Ankrum (*Hal Fenton*), Jonathan Hale (*Bissell*), Harry Woods (*Dreen*), Mario Dwyer (*Jennie*), Riley Hill (*Randee*), Jeff York (*Curley*), Stanley Andrews (*Pete*), Jack Ingram (*Jack*), Myron Healey (*Les*), Tris [Tristram] Coffin (*John Devore*), Rory Mallinson (*Jim Westfall*), Felipe Turich (*Manuel*), George J. Lewis (*Diego*), Lee Tung Foo (*Lin*), Kermit Maynard.

Rancher Cameron returns to his spread five years after being forced off of it by greedy Ankrum. He finds that his girl friend has married Coffin, the local drunk. Brown is the marshal who comes to square things away. The story builds to an engrossing and climactic street fight, with Cameron winning back his land and his girl. Though late in time for a programmer western (a genre which by now had moved into TV), this is a fine outing. The script is excellent, and superior acting succeeds in carrying it off well.

p, Scott R. Dunlap; d, Lesley Selander; w, Tom W. Blackburn (based on the novel by Blackburn); ph, Harry Neumann; m, Edward J. Kay; ed, Otho Lovering; art d, David Milton.

Western   **(PR:C MPAA:NR)**

SHORT IS THE SUMMER ½   (1968, Swed.) 109m Sandrews/Shaw c (KORT AR SOMMAREN)

Jarl Kulle (*Thomas Glahn*), Bibi Andersson (*Edvarda Mack*), Claes Gill (*Merchant Mack*), Liv Ullmann (*Eva*), Allan Edwall (*Doctor*), Ingvar Kjellson (*Baron*), Jens Bolling (*Smith*), Marie Goranzon (*Vicar's Daughter*), Carl Johan Seth (*Jacob*), Britt-Marie Eklund (*Edvarda's Girl Friend*), Bjorg Vatle (*Henriette*).

Kulle plays a Swedish lieutenant who goes to an isolated isle off the Lapland coast for a summer to escape social pressures. There he meets Gill and rents a hunting lodge from him. Gill's daughter, Andersson, is attracted to the stranger but since she cannot trust men his advances are repelled. But soon he shows her how beautiful love is and she comes to trust him. But then she

becomes jealous of Ullmann, her father's mistress, who has also attracted Kulle. Gill notices that his mistress and daughter are becoming increasingly intolerant of his brutal nature and in retaliation he brings Kjellson, a baron who had previously tried to woo Andersson, to the island. Gill tells Andersson that her lover and Ullmann are having an affair. She won't believe him but when she catches the two locked in an embrace she is crushed and announces her engagement to the baron. Gill tries to seduce his former mistress but she runs off into the mountains. Kulle fires off some shots which are meant as a signal to Andersson and the noise triggers an avalanche that kills Ullmann. Gill becomes crazed with anger and sets fire to the hunting lodge as vengeance. Kulle realizes he must leave the island and tries to make peace with Andersson before going. However, she is still crushed by the course of events and rejects his attempts at reconciliation. A noble attempt to put author Hamsun's great paean to nature into film, which of course totally misses the mystical lyricism of his prose.

p, Rune Waldekranz; d, Bjarne Henning-Jensen; w, Henning-Jensen, Astrid Henning-Jensen (based on the novel *Pan* by Knut Hamsun); ph, Gunnar Fischer (AgaScope/Eastmancolor); m, Hilding Rosenberg; ed, Lennart Wallen; set d, Jan Boleslaw

Drama   **(PR:O MPAA:NR)**

SHOT AT DAWN, A*   (1934, Ger.) 73m UFA bw (SCHUSS IM MORGENGRAUEN)

Heinz Salfner (*Joachim Taft*), Ery Bos (*Irene Taft*), Karl Ludwig Diehl (*Petersen*), Theodor Loos (*Bachmann, Bookseller*), Fritz Odemar (*Dr. Sandegg*), Peter Lorre (*Klotz*), Gerhard Tandar (*Muller IV*), Kurt Vespermann (*Bobby*), Ernst Behmer (*Gas Station Attendant*), Curt Lucas (*Holzknecht*), Hermann Speelmans (*Schmitter*), Genia Nikolajeva (*Lola*).

After a robbery, shady jeweler Salfner is confronted by his cohorts (Odemar and Lorre) for a bigger share of the loot. Salfner claims to have already spent the money. As consolation, he arranges to leave a hotel key for the pair so they can enter the room of his ex-wife and steal her diamond ring. Odemar gets the stone but it's quickly taken from him by Diehl, a man previously caught snooping in Bos' room. She had been attracted to this handsome thief and did not have him prosecuted. When his partner returns empty-handed, Lorre finds they are joined by a third party, Diehl, who claims the ring was a phony and has a plan to get the real one. Odemar and Lorre introduce the man to their boss, Loos, a bookseller using his store as a front. They fool Bos into going to her husband's villa where they will interrogate her about the ring. This is foiled when everyone at the villa is surprised by Diehl's announcement that he is a police inspector. Before he can make any arrests, Lorre knocks him out with a beer bottle. Diehl's reinforcements come and a terrific gun battle between the cops and robbers ensues. At last the battle ends with the police capturing the gang. Diehl comes to and turns over the real diamond (which he had been keeping all along) to Bos. He also uses the moment to suggest to the woman that perhaps they can get better acquainted. This is a good gangster picture from Germany's famous UFA studios told with efficiency and excitement. It is one of Lorre's early films and while his part is small, he does a fine job. The American release was limited to theaters in German neighborhoods for a short run in 1934. In their attempt to achieve realism the Germans used real bullets in the final gun battle (a practice unknown in Hollywood). The first two days of shooting were limited to the destruction of the villa by bullets, with the third day reserved for close ups. All went according to plan until Lorre showed reluctance to have a beer bottle shot out of his hand by a live bullet. He explained he had every confidence in the off-camera sharpshooter but was fearful of the injury he might sustain if flying glass hit him. After much explanation by the director and the sharpshooter, Lorre finally agreed to do the take, accepting the sharpshooter's explanation that his face would be hit by glass only if the bullet was aimed that way. The moment was finally shot without any problems.

p&d, Alfred Zeisler; w, Rudolph Katscher, Otto and Egon Eis (based on the play "Die Frau Und Der Smaragd" by Harry Jenkins); ph, Konstantin Tschet, Werner Bohne; art d, W.A. Herrmann, Herbert Lippschitz.

Crime   **(PR:C MPAA:NR)**

SHOT GUN PASS   (SEE: SHOTGUN PASS, 1932)

SHOT IN THE DARK, A* ½   (1933, Brit.) 53m REA/RKO bw

Dorothy Boyd (*Alaris Browne*), O.B. Clarence (*Rev. John Malcolm*), Jack Hawkins (*Norman Paul*), Russell Thorndike (*Dr. Stuart*), Michael Shepley (*Vivian Waugh*), Davy Burnaby (*Col. Michael Browne*), A. Bromley Davenport (*Peter Browne*), Hugh E. Wright (*George Barrow*), Henrietta Watson (*Angela Browne*), Margaret Yarde.

When a hated old miser is found a suicide, Clarence, a reverend attending the reading of the will, suspects murder and decides to investigate the case himself. After the usual amount of routine sleuthing, wherein several people confess to the crime, Clarence proves that the dead man's nephew is responsible for the murder.

p, Julius Hagen; d, George Pearson; w, H. Fowler Mear (based on the novel by Gerard Fairlie).

Crime   (PR:A MPAA:NR)

SHOT IN THE DARK, A**   (1935) 69m CHES bw

Charles Starrett (*Ken Harris*), Robert Warwick (*Joseph Harris*), Edward Van Sloan (*Prof. Bostwick*), Marion Shilling (*Jean Coates*), Doris Lloyd (*Mrs. Coates*), Helen Jerome Eddy (*Miss Case*), James Bush (*Byron Coates/John Mesereux*), Julian Madison (*Charlie Penlon*), Ralph Brooks (*Sam Anderson*), Eddie Tamblyn (*Bill Smart*), Robert McKenzie (*Sheriff*), George Morell (*Deputy*), Herbert Bunston (*College President*), Broderick O'Farrell (*Dr. Howell*), John Davidson (*Prof. Brand*), Jane Keckley (*Housekeeper*).

Movie cowboy Starrett trades in his spurs for a magnifiying glass in this unexciting thriller. Three murders occur at a New England college. When one youth's roommate is killed, his father (whose hobby incidentally is sleuthing) sets out to discover the killer. It turns out that a professor and his son are the parties responsible, with the motive an inheritance. Some needless plot complications muddy matters until all clears up at the end. The production values are passable and acting is average for this boring programmer. A possible "first" was established in this film, the use of an air gun for a murder weapon, used many times afterward in crime stories and films. The device was simplicity itself: a cattle-killing instrument which, propelled by an air gun, inserted a sharp object under the animal's skull, killing it.

p, George R. Batcheller; d, Charles Lamont; w, Charles Belden (based on the novel *The Dartmouth Murders* by Clifford Orr); ph, M.A. Andersen; ed, Roland Reed; md, Abe Meyer; art d, Edward C. Jewell.

Mystery   **Cas.**   (PR:C MPAA:NR)

SHOT IN THE DARK, THE**½   (1941) 57m FN-WB bw

William Lundigan (*Peter Kennedy*), Nan Wynn (*Dixie Waye*), Ricardo Cortez (*Phil Richards*), Regis Toomey (*Bill Ryder*), Maris Wrixon (*Helen Armstrong*), Noel Madison (*Al Martin, Bodyguard*), John Gallaudet (*Schaffer*), Donald Douglas (*Roger Armstrong*), Noel Madison (*Al Martin*), Frank Wilcox (*Naval Officer*), Theodore Von Eltz (*George Kilpatrick*), Lee Phelps (*Blaney*), Frank M. Thomas (*Klein*), Emory Parnell (*Marsotti*), Garrett Craig (*Connors*), Jack Wise (*Photographer*), Lucia Carroll (*Clare Winters*).

A night club owner is murdered and everybody's a suspect. It's up to reporter Lundigan and cop Toomey to get to the bottom of things. Is the killer mob leader Cortez, who wants to get out of the club business so he can marry Writon and lead a normal life? Maybe it's the jealous sweetie Carroll, of the mobster who doesn't want him to leave her and the club. When she's killed, the mystery deepens. A nifty denouement makes this a better than average programmer mystery. Despite it's small budget, the actors make the screenplay work and the direction carries them through well.

p, William Jacobs; d, William McGann; w, M. Coates Webster (based on a story "No Hard Feelings" by Fred Nebel); ph, James Van Trees; ed, Harold McLernon

Mystery/Crime   (PR:C MPAA:NR)

SHOT IN THE DARK, A****   (1964) 103m Mirisch-Geoffrey/UA c

Peter Sellers (*Inspector Jacques Clouseau*), Elke Sommer (*Maria Gambrelli*), George Sanders (*Benjamin Ballon*), Herbert Lom (*Chief Inspector Charles Dreyfus*), Tracy Reed (*Dominique Ballon*), Graham Stark (*Hercule Lajoy*), Andre Maranne (*Francois, Dreyfus' Assistant*), Douglas Wilmer (*Henri Lafarge*), Vanda Godsell (*Mme. Lafarge*), Maurice Kaufman (*Pierre, 2nd Chauffeur*), Ann Lynn (*Dudu, 1st Maid*), David Lodge (*Georges, Gardener*), Moira Redmond (*Simone, 3rd Maid*), Martin Benson (*Maurice, 1st Butler*), Burt Kwouk (*Kato*), Reginald Beckwith (*Receptionist at Camp*), Turk Thrust [Bryan Forbes] (*Charlie, Locker Attendant*), John Herrington (*Doctor*), Jack Melford (*Psychoanalyst*).

This picture, the second in the Inspector Clouseau series starring Sellers, was drawn from a French play "L'idiote" by Marcel Achard which opened in Paris in the fall of 1960. About a year later, Kurnitz presented his adaptation on Broadway, "A Shot In The Dark", and it is from both these plays that the screenplay was fashioned. Sommer is a chambermaid in the Parisian residence of Sanders and Reed. Sommer has been accused of murdering her boy friend and Sellers is mistakenly assigned to the case. His superior, Lom, would like to get him off the case, as he knows the havoc the man can wreak when he states: "Give me 10 men like Clouseau and I could destroy the world." On the surface, it would seem that all the clues point to Sommer having done the Spaniard in, but Sellers believes she is innocent because there are just too many bits of evidence against her. Lom succeeds in pulling Sellers away from the case and has Sommer taken to jail. Then Lom is chagrined to learn that his superiors want Sellers back on the case and they overrule him. Sommer is released and is soon discovered with another dead body, which results in another arrest. Still sure of her innocence, Sellers has Sommer allowed to leave prison and he trails her to a nudist camp where still another body, this time the corpse of Sanders first maid, Lynn, is found. Again, the eye of the law is focused on Sommer. Now Wilmer, another employee at the Sanders' residence, is killed and Lom insists that Sommer is arrested once more and that Sellers be taken off the case, as Sommer is a modern-day Lucretia Borgia and death follows

wherever those lovely legs take her. Still under pressure from above, Lom is forced to put Sellers back on the case and allow Sommer to leave jail. Sellers squires Sommer for an evening of Parisian boite-hopping and there are a number of attempts on Sellers' life, none of which he notices. The result of these assassination tries is a quartet of innocent victims who drop like flies around the addled Sellers. In a THIN MAN-type conclusion, Sellers gets the suspects together in the Sanders' residence and lets things happen. All six of the potential murderers begin accusing each other of having done the deeds. The lights are suddenly doused and they all flee, leaving Sellers and Sommer alone. Now the whole group scrunch into one car, but a bomb has been placed in the automobile which was meant to disintegrate Sellers. While Sommer and Sellers watch open-mouthed, the car explodes and all of the suspects are killed, so Sellers has, in fact, put an end to the murders. Lom goes mad because he is, in fact, the real killer and had knocked off all of the people in order to heap shame upon Sellers and now he falls off the edge when Sellers is acclaimed a sleuthing genius. The picture is filled with one sight gag after another, many having been seen before by anyone old enough to remember the glory days of silent comedies. The funniest sustained sequence occurs when Sellers attempts to bed down Sommer and his aide, Kwouk, leaps into the room for the violent judo lesson that punctuated many of the later comedies. The original Achard-Kurnitz plays had the lead character as a nutty judge, but that was altered in this screenplay to fit the character Sellers played in the first PINK PANTHER film. In the movies that followed, Lom continued as the boss, despite having murdered all of the victims in this one.

p&d, Blake Edwards; w, Edwards, William Peter Blatty (based on plays by Harry Kurnitz, Marcel Achard); ph, Chris Challis (Panavision, De Luxe Color); m, Henry Mancini; ed, Bert Bates; prod d, Michael Stringer; cos, Margaret Furse; m/l, "Shadow of Paris", Mancini, Robert Wells.

Comedy   **Cas.**   (PR:A-C MPAA:NR)

SHOTGUN***   (1955) 81m AA c

Sterling Hayden (*Clay*), Yvonne De Carlo (*Abby*), Zachary Scott (*Reb*), Robert J. Wilke (*Bentley*), Guy Prescott (*Thompson*), Ralph Sanford (*Chris*), John Pickard (*Perez*), Ward Wood (*Ed*), Rory Mallinson (*Frank*), Paul Marion (*Delgadito*), Harry Harvey, Jr (*Davey*), Lane Chandler (*Fletcher*), Angela Greene (*Aletha*), Robert E. Griffin (*Doctor*), Al Wyatt (*Greybar*), Bob Morgan (*Sam*), Peter Coe (*Apache*), Charles Morton, James Parnell (*Cavalrymen*), Richard Cutting (*Holly*), Fiona Hale (*Midge*), Frances McDonald (*Dishwasher*).

Good western features Hayden, a deputy with a sawed-off shotgun, on the trail of killer Prescott, who blew the local marshal in half with his gun. Hayden is joined on the trail by De Carlo, whom he saves from a band of Apaches. Later the pair becomes a trio when bounty hunter Scott, who's also looking for Prescott, joins up. The film ends with an exciting shotgun battle between hero and protagonist. Directed with precision, the film is marvelously photographed, making splendid use of the scenery. The actors flesh out their characters, with style saving this from turning into a programmer western. The script was cowritten by Calhoun, who had hoped to have the starring role. However, this dream was shattered when Allied Artists picked up the property and Calhoun had to be satisfied with just the writing credit.

p, John Champion; d, Lesley Selander; w, Champion, Rory Calhoun, Clark E. Reynolds; ph, Ellsworth Fredericks (Technicolor); m, Carl Brandt; ed, John Fuller; md, Brandt.

Western   (PR:O MPAA:NR)

SHOTGUN PASS*   (1932) 59M COL bw

Tim McCoy, Virginia Lee Corbin, Frank Rice, Dick Stewart, Joe Marba Monte Vandergrift, Ben Corbett, Albert J. Smith, Archie Ricks.

A routine western action picture. McCoy is involved with some horses that have to be herded over a certain owner's land. Of course the man says, "Nothing doing", which leads to some two-fisted action, shoot 'em ups, and romance. A poor entry from Columbia, which normally had much higher standards than the assembly line air that seems to permeate the film. McCoy was not making a very good transition from silent to sound, as this film shows, but he went on to make the switch in a bravura manner.

d, J.P. McGowan; w, Robert Quigley; ph, Benjamin Kline; ed, S. Roy Luby

Western   (PR:A MPAA:NR)

SHOTGUN WEDDING, THE**   (1963) 64m Arkota c

Jenny Maxwell, Valerie Allen, Nan Peterson, J. Pat O'Malley, Peter Colt.

A family of hillbillies is stuck on a riverboat in the same muddy area for 30 years. When a woman carnival worker fleeing the police hides out with them, she agrees to marry the son, though she's really smitten with a fake preacher. The son, meanwhile, is in love with another hillbilly, the daughter of some moonshiners who have been feudin' with his kin for years. Of course, love conquers all and the couples all end up with their hoped-for beaus. Utter nonsense from the pen of Wood, who wrote such immortal classics as GLEN OR GLENDA (1953), and PLAN NINE FROM OUTER

SPACE (1959).

p&d, Boris L. Petroff; w, Edward D. Wood, Jr.

Comedy　　　　　　　　　　　　　　　　**(PR:A-C　MPAA:NR)**

SHOULD A DOCTOR TELL? zero　　　　(1931, Brit.) 52m BL/RF bw

Basil Gill (*Dr. Bruce Smith*), Norah Baring (*Joan Murray*), Maurice Evans (*Roger Smith*), Gladys Jennings (*The Wife*), Anna Neagle (*Muriel*), A.G. Poulton (*Judge*), Harvey Braban (*Prosecution*).

A doctor wins public plaudits when he refuses to give out information that would violate his oath of confidence during a divorce case. Then he discovers that his son is engaged to a woman who he knows has had a baby. Should he tell his son? The story dully winds its way to a finale with the father lecturing the son, the woman confessing her indiscretion, and the son and father happily reconciled. Bad in every department of filmmaking, this lot of nothing is particularly embarrassing for detective story writer Edgar Wallace, who penned it, and for the future illustrious Shakespearian and George Bernard Shaw actor Evans, who has never appeared as well in the movies as he has on the stage.

p, S.W. Smith; d, Manning Haynes; w, Edgar Wallace (based on a story by G.B. Samuelson); ph, Jack Mackenzie, Bob Martin.

Drama　　　　　　　　　　　　　　　　**(PR:C　MPAA:NR)**

SHOULD A GIRL MARRY?*½　　　　　　(1929) 65m RAY bw

Helen Foster (*Alice Dunn*), Donald Keith (*Jerry Blaine*), William V. Mong (*Andrew Blaine, Banker*), Andy Clyde (*Harry*), Dot Farley (*Mae Reynolds*), George Chesebro (*Jarvin*), Dorothy Vernon (*Aunt Ida*).

A very early talkie, mostly silent, which sees noble girl Foster murder an evil Don Juan type who has wronged her alcoholic sister. This, of course, leads to a big courtroom scene which contains most of the dialog. Foster is acquitted, but not until she is lectured by the judge about killing people just because she doesn't like them.

d, Scott Pembroke; w, Terry Turner (based on a story by Arthur Hoerl); ph, Hap Depew; ed, J.S. Harrington.

Crime　　　　　　　　　　　　　　　　**(PR:A　MPAA:NR)**

SHOULD A GIRL MARRY?*　　　　　　　(1939) 61m MON bw

Anna Nagel (*Margaret*), Warren Hull (*Dr. Robert Benson*), Mayo Methot (*Betty Gilbert*), Weldon Heyburn (*Harry Gilbert*), Aileen Pringle (*Mrs. White*), Lester Matthews (*Dr. White*), Helen Brown (*Mary Winters*), Sarah Padden (*Mrs. Wilson*), Gordon Hart (*Mr. Wilson*), Edmond Elton (*Dr. Turner*), Robert Elliott (*Warden*), Claire Rochelle (*Hysterical Patient*).

Hull is the stalwart, honest surgeon who is being double crossed by doctors Heyburn and Matthews. Nagel is the young innocent who plays the romantic interest as Hull upholds the honor of his profession no matter what the outcome. A stagey, sticky melodrama with stilted dialog to trip up some very fine acting performances by not only the principals but by the supporting players as well.

p, E.B. Derr; d, Lambert Hillyer; w, Gayl Newbury, David Silverstein; ph, Paul Ivano.

Drama　　　　　　　　　　　　　　　　**(PR:A　MPAA:NR)**

SHOULD HUSBANDS WORK?**　　　　　(1939) 71m REP bw

James Gleason (*Joe Higgins*), Lucille Gleason (*Lil Higgins*), Russell Gleason (*Sidney Higgins*), Harry Davenport (*Grandpa Higgins*), Berton Churchill (*Barnes*), Marie Wilson (*Myrtle*), Mary Hart (*Jean Higgins*), Tommy Ryan (*Tommy Higgins*), Henry Kolker (*Taylor*), Arthur Hoyt (*Roberts*), Barry Norton (*Ronald McDonald*), Mary Forbes (*Mrs. Barnes*), William Brisbane (*Williams*), Harry Bradley (*Snodgrass*).

A formula entry in Republic's "Higgins Family" series (which featured the real life Gleason family) is a good programmer. James Gleason, the father, is about to be promoted until his wife (Lucille Gleason) lets out a business secret that mars a merger. The wife ends up with the husband's job and he stays at home and does the housework. The jokes and gags are ancient but the essential goodness and loyalty of the family, an essential ingredient in all the films of the series, are there in abundance. (See HIGGINS FAMILY series, Index.)

p, Sol. C. Siegel; d, Gus Meins; w, Jack Townley, Taylor Caven; ph, Jack Marta; m, Cy Feuer; ed, William Morgan.

Comedy　　　　　　　　　　　　　　　**(PR:AAA　MPAA:NR)**

SHOULD LADIES BEHAVE?**　　　　　(1933) 78m MGM bw

Lionel Barrymore (*Augustus Merrick*), Alice Brady (*Laura Merrick*), Conway Tearle (*Max Lawrence, Artist*), Katharine Alexander (*Winifred Mansfield*), Mary Carlisle (*Leone Merrick*), William Janney (*Geoffrey Cole*), Halliwell Hobbes (*Butler*).

Middle-aged Brady is married to an older man. Seeking a bit of belated romance, she starts a flirtation with Tearle, a gigolo artist, who she believes was her childhood sweetheart. Trouble is, Tearle is in love with her daughter and with a many times married Alexander. Giddy Brady whams her way through these contretemps tiresomely to a minor surprise ending when, as easily guessed, the artist turns out to be not a former boy friend, but a man who happens to have the same name. Brady lost her contract at MGM after this mishmash, the studio mistakingly thinking the distinguished actress and future Oscar winner was on the skids with the public. Time told a different story.

p, Lawrence Weingarten; d, Harry Beaumont; w, Bella and Samuel Spewack (based on the play "The Vinegar Tree" by Paul Osborn); ph, Ted Tetzlaff; ed, Hugh Wynn; m/l, Nacio Herb Brown, Arthur Freed.

Comedy　　　　　　　　　　　　　　　**(PR:C-O　MPAA:NR)**

SHOUT, THE**　　　　(1978, Brit.) 87m Recorded Picture Company/Films, Inc. c

Alan Bates (*Crossley*), Susannah York (*Rachel*), John Hurt (*Anthony*), Robert Stephens (*Medical Man*), Tim Curry (*Robert*), Julian Hough (*Vicar*), Carol Drinkwater (*Wife*), Nick Stringer (*Cobbler*), John Rees (*Inspector*), Susan Woolridge (*Harriet*).

During a cricket match at an asylum, patient Bates relates his story to Hurt and wife York. It seems he once lived with Australian aborigines and learned the secret of "the shout," which has the power to kill. He moves in with Hurt, an experimental music composer and begins to seduce York. Hurt himself is having an affair with a local woman. One afternoon Bates demonstrates his power on a local shepherd and his flock. Amazed, Hurt saves himself by covering his ears. Gradually he takes control of Hurt and York, leading to an unusual solution. This is a weird, often difficult to understand film that could be easily dismissed as nonsense. However, there's a certain compelling element to it that involves the viewer as the unusual story is told with precision and skill. The cast is good and helps make the drama work. The electronic score is well used as counterpoint to Bates' power.

p, Jeremy Thomas; d, Jerzy Skolimowski; w, Michael Austin, Skolimowski (based on a story by Robert Graves); ph, Mike Molloy; m, Rupert Hine, Anthony Banks, Michael Rutherford; ed, Barrie Vince; art d, Simon Holland.

Drama/Horror　　　　　　　**Cas.**　　　　　**(PR:O　MPAA:R)**

SHOUT AT THE DEVIL½**　　　　　　　(1976, Brit.) 128m AIP c

Lee Marvin (*Flynn*), Roger Moore (*Sebastian*), Barbara Parkins (*Rosa*), Ian Holm (*Mohammed*), Rene Kolldehoff (*Commissioner Fleischer*), Horst Janson (*Kyller*), Karl Michael Vogler (*Von Kleine*), Gernot Endemann (*Braun*), Maurice Denham (*Mr. Smythe*), Jean Kent (*Mrs. Smythe*), Heather Wright (*Cynthia*), Bernard Horsfall (*Capt. Joyce*), Robert Lang (*Capt. Henry*), Peter Copley (*Adm. Howe*), Murray Melvin (*Lt. Phipps*), Geoff Davidson (*Mackintosh*), Gerard Paquis (*French Pilot*), George Coulouris (*El Keb*), Renu Setna (*Mr. Raji*).

A German warship is hidden away for repairs in East Africa, circa WW I. Moore is the witty Englishman and Marvin the hard drinking Irish-American who want to blow it up and show the Nazis a thing or two. Kolledehoff is a German officer who starts trouble in the first place by stopping the pair from poaching on his territory. Like many of the big star-big budget action flicks of the 1970s, SHOUT AT THE DEVIL does have its moments, but for the most part it's an overlong work with caricature performances. The action sequences are well handled, recalling the work of John Ford or John Huston, but the overall production is empty and meaningless. At 128 minutes for the American release, it's still too long despite losing about twenty minutes from the original British running time.

p, Michael Klinger; d, Peter Hunt; w, Wilber Smith, Stanley Price, Alastair Reid (based on the novel by Smith); ph, Mike Reed (Panavision, Technicolor); m, Maurice Jarre; ed, Michael Duthie; prod d, Sid Cain; art d, Ernie Archer, Bob Laing; spec eff, Derek Meddings.

War/Drama　　　　　　　**Cas.**　　　　　**(PR:C　MPAA:PG)**

SHOW BOAT**　　　　　　　　　　　　(1929) 130m UNIV bw

Prologue: Tess "Aunt Jemima" Gardella, Otis Harlan, Helen Morgan, Jules Bledsoe, The Jubilee Singers, The Plantation Singers, Carl Laemmle, Florenz Ziegfeld Story: Laura La Plante (*Magn olia*), Joseph Schildkraut (*Gaylord Ravenal*), Otis Harlan (*Capt. Andy Hawks*), Emily Fitz roy (*Parthenia Ann Hawks*), Alma Rubens (*Julie*), Elsie Bartlett (*Elly*), Jack McDonald (*Windy*), Jane La Verne (*Magnolia as a Child/Kim*), Neely Edwards (*Schultzy*), Theodore Lorch (*Fr ank*), Stepin Fetchit (*Joe*), Gertrude Howard (*Queenie*), Ralph Yearsley (*The Killer*), Ge orge Chesebro (*Steve*), Harry Holden (*Means*), Max Asher (*Utility Man*), Jim Coleman (*St age-hand*), Carl Herlinger (*Wheelsman*), voices of The Billbrew Chorus, Silverstone Quartet, The Four Emperors of Harmony, Claude Collins.

A disappointing first go-around for the stage classic, it was shot silent, then had songs and dialogue added for the sound version plus an endless prologue featuring Broadway producer Florenz Ziegfeld and film boss Laemmle with Jerome Kern-Oscar Hammerstein II numbers performed by the members of the original cast. Tess Gardella sings "C'Mon, Folks" and "Hey, Feller" with the Jubilee Singers; Jules Bledsoe does "Ol' Man River" (Joseph Cherniavsky, Kern, Hammerstein II) with the play's chorus; and Helen Morgan sings "Bill" (P.G. Wodehouse, Kern, Hammerstein II) and "Can't Help Lovin' Dat Man" (Cherniavsky, Kern, Hammerstein II). The plot hews to the stage play as Schildkraut, a gambler, plays the cad all through the picture and wakes up near the end to return to La Plante (whose vocals were looped by Eva Olivetti), an overplaying actress who wrings too many tears from the role. The story of the showboat that wends its way up and down the Mississippi is filled with several characters in a multifated epic that, at times, seems only there to give a reason for the songs. This was not the case in Ferber's novel but something had to be trimmed to make room for the music and much of that was motivation and characterization. All of the dialog was added later by director Pollard and titles-writer Tom Reed, so about half the movie has talking. Schildkraut, who was born in Austria, unsuccessfully attempts to bury his Viennese accent in favor of a Southern drawl. In order to do that, he is also guilty of overacting and, as a result, looks a great deal better than he sounds. On Broadway, the pivotal role of "Captain Andy" was played by Charles Winninger and it is here essayed by Otis Harlan but the screenplay calls for him to be killed early by drowning and Harlan doesn't get any chance to play the comedy inherent in the role. The best acting was done by Alma Rubens as Julie, in her tragic role. Rubens real life was equally tragic and she became a drug abuser, eventually dying of her addiction at an insane asylum at the age of 33, two years after this film was released. The score was glorious but not given long shrift by the singers or the production. Tunes included: "Look Down that Lonesome Road" (Gene Austin, Nathaniel Shilkret), "Here Comes that Show Boat" (Billy Rose, Maceo Pinkard), "Down South" (William H. Myddleton, and Sigmund Spaeth, who was later to become the "Tune Detective" who often testified at musical plagiarism trials), "Love Sings a Song in My Heart" (Joseph Cherniavsky, Clarence J. Marks), "Coon, Coon, Coon" (Leo Friedmann, Gene Jefferson), and traditional spirituals like "Deep River," and "I've Got Shoes." Unfortunately, most of the hits are done in the prologue so they aren't repeated in the picture, a truly dumb way of doing things. The film drags, the editing is atrocious, the actors hammy and the in-and-out nature of silent-to-sound technique jars the senses. The picture was not a hit and it's a tribute to the foresight of the people who produced the first remake that they were able to see through the lack of success and realize that it wasn't the fault of the material, just the execution. If you ever wondered where the character of "Aunt Jemima" came from, the heavy-set woman who adorns your pancake syrup bottle, look no further than this movie in which she plays herself, whatever that means.

p, Carl Laemmle; d, Harry Pollard; w, Charles Kenyon, Pollard, Tom Reed (based on the novel by Edna Ferber and the Flo Ziegfeld stage production); ph, Gilbert Warrenton; m, Joseph Cherniavsky; ed, Edward J. Montaigne, Maurice Pivar, Daniel Mandell.

Musical   **(PR:A   MPAA:NR)**

SHOW BOAT**   (1936) 110m UNIV bw

Irene Dunne (Magnolia Hawks), Allan Jones (Gaylord Ravenal), Charles Winninger (Capt. Andy Hawks), Helen Westley (Parthy Hawks), Paul Robeson (Joe), Helen Morgan (Julie), Donald Cook (Steve), Sammy White (Frank Schultz), Queenie Smith (Ellie), J. Farrell MacDonald (Windy), Arthur Hohl (Pete), Charles Middleton (Sheriff Vallon), Hattie McDaniel (Queenie Joe's Wife), Francis X. Mahoney (Rubberface), Sunnie O'Dea (Elder Kim), Marilyn Knowlden (Younger Kim), Patricia Barry (Baby Kim), Dorothy Granger, Barbara Pepper, Renee Whitney (Chorus Girls), Harry Barris (Jake), Charles Wilson (Jim Green), Clarence Muse (Sam the Janitor), Stanley Fields (Zebe), "Tiny" Stanley J. Sandford (Backwoodsman), May Beatty (Landlady), Bobby Watson (Lost Child), Jane Keckley (Mrs. Ewing), E.E. Clive (Englishman), Helen Jerome Eddy (Reporter), Donald Briggs (Press Agent), LeRoy Prinz (Dance Director), Eddie "Rochester" Anderson (Young Black Man), Patti Patterson (Banjo Player), Helen Hayward (Mrs. Brencenbridge), Flora Finch (Woman), Theodore Lorch (Simon Legree), Arthur Housman (Drunk), Elspeth Dudgeon (Mother Superior), Monte Montague (Old Man), Lois Verner (Small Girl), Grace Cunard (Mother), Marilyn Harris (Little Girl), Jimmy Jackson (Young Man), Eddy Chandler, Lee Phelps, Frank Mayo, Ed Peil Sr, Edmund Cobb, Al Ferguson (Gamblers), Maude Allen (Fat Woman), Artye Folz, Barbara Bletcher (Fat Girls), Forrest Stanley (Theater Manager), Curtis Wilson (Juvenile), George H. Reed (Old Black Man), Georgia O'Dell (Schoolteacher), Selmer Jackson (Hotel Clerk), George Hackathorne (YMCA Worker), Ernest Hilliard, Jack Mulhall, Brooks Benedict (Race Fans).

This time around, Universal Studios got it right. The 1929 part-silent movie had been produced by Carl Laemmle and his son, Carl Jr., took over the reins here and made it a splendid bow-out for the Laemmle faction at the studio. It's still the same romance between Southern belle Dunne and Jones, the Mississipi gambler who lives for the turn of the card and the roll of the dice. Dunne is the daughter of Winninger. The actor was repeating his successful Broadway stint as "Captain Andy," and almost every lead in the cast had, at one time or another, played in the show on a stage somewhere, with the exceptions of Queenie Smith and Helen Westley. That familiarity with the material is what sends this movie soaring to heights never dreamed

of by the makers of the original film, which was miscast on almost every level. Universal built an actual riverboat on their San Fernando Valley back lot and paged a British director, Whale, to helm the chores. Whale was considered an odd choice because his only previous hits had been in the horror genre, his masterpiece being FRANKENSTEIN. Their faith in Whale was well-founded and he turned in a corking good job as he kept the pace up and the songs moving without ever making it look rushed. Morgan had played the role of "Julie" on the stage, after having established herself as a nightery thrush famous for singing while seated on a piano. (She was played by Ann Blyth in her 1957 biography, THE HELEN MORGAN STORY.) She was born to play the part although she, and everyone else in the motion picture, was overlooked by the Academy. Dunne, a singer on her dad's boat, meets Jones. They marry, have a child, Barry, who grows up to be Knowlden while Jones is off somewhere plying his trade and too busy to check in with his family. He comes back as Knowlden is becoming a singing star in her own right. Jones and Dunne are happily reunited and all ends well. The many-tiered plot takes second place to the score, all of the tunes being interpolated seamlessly into the story, a forerunner of the many Rodgers and Hammerstein musicals which would integrate songs into the story. Tunes from the score by Jerome Kern and Oscar Hammerstein include: "O' Man River," "Ah Still Suits Me" (sung by Paul Robeson in a superlative fashion), "Bill," "Can't Help Lovin' Dat Man" (sung by Morgan), "Only Make Believe," "I Have the Room Above," "You Are Love" (sung by Dunne, Jones), "Gallivantin' Around," (sung by Dunne in embarrassing black face makeup), "Cotton Blossom," "Cap'n Andy's Ballyhoo," "Where's the Mate for Me?" and "Mis'ry's Comin' Around." The classic " Why Do "I Love You" was filmed, then edited from the picture, which they felt was too long at 110 minutes, so it only exists as background music. Other songs were "After the Ball" (Charles K. Harris), "Goodbye, My Lady Love" (Joe Howard), "At a Georgia Camp Meeting" (Kerry Mills), and John Phillip Sousa's "Washington Post March." Robeson is magnetic as he sings the classic paean to the Mississippi and Sammy White, reprising his stage role, is effective as the comic relief. The only drawback to the film is the many loose ends in the story which were glossed over and never totally resolved. Other than that, SHOW BOAT is one of the most pleasing musicals ever made.

p, Carl Laemmle Jr.; d, James Whale; w, Oscar Hammerstein II (based on the novel by Edna Ferber and the play by Hammerstein, Jerome Kern); ph, John Mescall; m, Jerome Kern; ed, Ted Kent, Bernard W. Burton; md, Victor Baravalle; art d, Charles D. Hall; cos, Doris Zinkeison; spec eff, John P. Fulton; ch, LeRoy Prinz;

Musical   **(PR:A   MPAA:NR)**

SHOW BOAT*½   (1951) 107m MGM c

Kathryn Grayson (Magnolia Hawks), Ava Gardner (Julie LaVerne), Howard Keel (Gaylord Ravenal), Joe E. Brown (Capt. Andy Hawks), Marge Champion (Ellie May Shipley), Gower Champion (Frank Schultz), Robert Sterling (Stephen Baker), Agnes Moorehead (Parthy Hawks), Adele Jergens (Cameo McQueen), William Warfield (Joe), Leif Erickson (Pete), Owen McGiveney (Windy McClain), Frances Williams (Queenie), Regis Toomey (Sheriff Ike Vallon), Frank Wilcox (Mark Hallson), Chick Chandler (Herman), Emory Parnell (Jake Green), Sheila Clark (Kim Ravenal), Ian MacDonald (Drunken Sport), Fuzzy Knight (Troc Piano Player), Norman Leavitt (George the Calliope Player), Anne Marie Dore, Christian Lind, Lyn Wilde, Marietta Elliott, Joyce Jameson, Bette Arlen, Helen Kimbell, Tac Porchon, Mitzie Uehlein, Judy Landon, Nova Dale, Mary Jane French, Marilyn Kinsley, Alice Markham (Showboat Cast Girls), Michael Dugan, Robert Fortier, George Ford, Cass Jaeger, Boyd Ackerman, Roy Damron, Joseph Roach (Showboat Cast Boys), George Lynn (Dealer), Louis Mercier (Dabney), Lisa Ferraday (Renee), Anna Q. Nilsson (Seamstress), Ida Moore (Little Old Lady), Alphonse Martell (Headwaiter), Edward Keane (Hotel Manager), Tom Irish (Bellboy), Jim Pierce (Doorman), William Tannen (Man with Julie), Bert Roach (Drunk), Earle Hodgins (Bartender).

This is the third time the redoubtable musical was filmed and it's almost as good as the second and much better than the first. The use of color greatly enhances the story that began as a Ferber novel, came to Broadway in 1927, was filmed in 1929, then again in 1936. It's one of those shows that has everything and seldom misses doing terrific business whenever it's revived. At a total cost of almost $2,000,000, the receipts quadrupled the outlay the first time it was released and it continues to be a popular picture in revival houses. The movie Academy barely acknowledged this production and only nominated Rosher's cinematography and the musical direction by Adolph Deutsch and Conrad Salinger. Salinger also did the excellent orchestrations while Robert Tucker handled the vocal arrangements. There were many changes from the second film, most notably the compression of the story to a much briefer time span. Brown (whom Ferber admired so much that she admitted she'd based the character of "Captain Andy" on him) is the captain of a Mississippi show boat that slowly wends its way up and down the river. He's married to Moorehead, a tough cookie. The star of their presentations is Gardner, a half-black married woman whom the public adores. Erickson is a deckhand on "The Cotton Blossom" and he has an eye on Gardner but she doesn't care much about him and stymies his advances whenever they are forwarded. Erickson is angered by her attitude so he tells the sheriff, Toomey, that Gardner is married to a white man and therefore guilty of miscegenation, a serious offense in those days. Gardner gets off the ship before Sheriff Toomey can arrest her. Now out of a job, she has no way to earn a living. Moorehead's daughter, Grayson, becomes enamored of Keel, a gambler. The two of them fall in love and get married. Once Keel turns over a new leaf, he forsakes his gambling ways and signs on as a performer aboard the boat. But old habits are hard to break and Keel is soon back at his gambling, causing a split between him and Grayson. Then, with the help of Gardner, the two are reconciled and find love in each other's arms once more. Gardner had attempted to sing her two songs and they went so far as to pre-record but, in the end, she was to mouth the words that were sung by Annette Warren, which ticked off Gardner no end. After Universal made the 1936 picture, the founders were pushed out and the new bosses sold the rights to MGM for a remake. Nelson Eddy and Jeanette MacDonald were considered as the leads but became too occupied with their own projects. The idea was shelved until Freed and his long-time aide, Roger Edens (who was an uncredited associate producer on this, along with credited Ben Feiner, Jr.) thought that they'd test the waters by talking MGM into financing a stage revival in 1946. When that proved successful, plans were made to shoot this version. Freed had thought of Judy Garland in the Grayson role but Garland was already causing trouble and had to be replaced twice in other films due to her behavior. The movie was to be shot on the Mississippi, until it was calculated that building sets on the back lot would be cheaper than moving the entire cast across country. A huge boat was constructed from scratch at a cost of more than $125,000. This boat was over 170 feet long, nearly 60 feet high and was seldom filmed after this movie so it eventually rotted on the lake in Culver City. It was seen in the 1952 film DESPERATE SEARCH, which also starred Keel, in a non-singing role. This was the second time that Grayson would play the role of "Captain Andy's" daughter. In the fanciful biography of Kern, TILL THE CLOUDS ROLL BY, she was seen in the SHOW BOAT segment five years before so it was a natural that she come back for the real thing. At one point, the boat caught fire and the cost of refinishing the charred ship was half of what it cost to build. It wasn't until after the first preview in a small Southern California theatre that Gardner's voice was deleted. No one in that Pacific Palisades audience seemed to like her singing, which they felt lacked the passion necessary to carry off the lyrics, so Warren's voice was looped to Gardner's lip movements, although her original singing can be heard on the cast album and she continues to share in the recording royalties, such as they are. So much of the story was changed from the 1936 version that these often seem like two different tales and both merit scrutiny. Musical numbers are almost entirely the original Jerome Kern and Oscar Hammerstein II collaborations, including a stirring rendition of "0' Man River" by Warfield, "Gambler's Song, "Where's the Mate for Me?" (sung by Keel), "You Are Love," "Make Believe," "Why Do I Love You?" (Keel, Grayson), "Can't Help Lovin' that Man" (Gardner, Grayson, reprised by Grayson), "Cotton Blossom," "Mis'-ry's Comin' Round" (chorus), "I Might Fall Back on You," "Life Upon the Wicked Stage," "Buck and Wing Dance" (performed by Marge and Gower Champion, towards the beginning of their long career as a dance team), "Ballyhoo," "Hey Fella." In the finale, curiously, after all those Kern-Hammerstein tunes, Grayson sings Charles K. Harris' "After the Ball," which was also in the 1936 version. In addition, P.G. Wodehouse and Guy Bolton wrote new lyrics for "Bill," performed by Gardner/Warren, and a new arrangement of "Auld Lang Syne" was made for the film by Deutsch. Marge Champion had actually been in films before her husband when, as a child, she appeared in THE STORY OF VERNON AND IRENE CASTLE while using her stage name, Marjorie Bell (she was born Marjorie Belcher). She married Gower in 1947, just after he'd made his first movie appearance in TILL THE CLOUDS ROLL BY. This was their first film together. Gardner auditioned for her role by making a screen test in which she mouthed the words from a Lena Horne record. Horne still carps about the fact that she didn't get the part whenever she does her concert act. Warfield had been found after the producers noted the reviews he'd received from a recital. His rendition of "0' Man River" was excellent but nowhere near as dynamic as Robeson's in 1936. Most of the other roles were small, almost cameos from Robert Sterling, Adele Jergens, and Erickson. There were three songs not used in the picture, "Ah Still Suits Me," "I Have The Room Above," and the haunting "Nobody Else But Me," which was written for the 1946 revival and is now seldom heard (except in hip piano bars). This 1951 picture was far more expensive, surely more colorful, and even somewhat more tuneful than the 1936 SHOW BOAT but it just missed having the elan and fire of that one.

p, Arthur Freed; d, George Sidney; w, John Lee Mahin (uncredited), George Wells, Jack McGowan (based on the musical by Jerome Kern and Oscar Hammerstein II based on the novel by Edna Ferber); ph, Charles Rosher (Technicolor); m, Kern, ed, John Dunning, md, Adolph Deutsch Conrad Salinger; art d, Cedric Gibbons, Jack Martin Smith; set d, Edwin B. Willis, Alfred Spencer, cos, Walter Plunkett; spec eff, Warren Newcombe, Peter Ballbusch; ch, Robert Alton; m/l, Hammerstein, Kern, Guy Bolton P.G. Wodehouse, Charles K. Harris; makeup, William J. Tuttle.

Musical   Cas.   (PR:A   MPAA:NR)

SHOW BUSINESS***   (1944) 92m RKO bw

Eddie Cantor (Eddie Martin), George Murphy (George Doane), Joan Davis (Joan Mason), Nancy Kelly (Nancy Gaye), Constance Moore (Constance Ford), Don Douglas (Charles Lucas, Agent), Bert Gordon, Gene Sheldon, Pat Rooney, Jesse and James, George Jessel (Themselves), Forbes Murray

(Director), Bert Moorhouse (Desk Clerk), Shirley O'Hara, Dorothy Malone, Daun Kennedy, Elaine Riley (Girls), Jerry Maren (Midget), Joseph Vitale (Caesar), Claire Carleton (Nurse), Russ Clark (Army Doctor), Chef Milani (Head Waiter), Ralph Dunn (Taxi Driver), Myrna Dell, Mary Meade, Ruth Valmy, Gloria Anderson, Dorothy Garner, Shelby Payne, Barbara Coleman, Kay Morley, Doris Sheehan, Alice Wallace (Show Girls), Stymie Beard (Harold), Harry Harvey, Jr (Page Boy), Billy Bester (Call Boy).

After 35 years in show business, Cantor decided to produce a film based on his early career. The result was a film where the title told all. SHOW BUSINESS looks at a troop of four performers (Cantor, Murphy, Davis, and Moore) as they begin in 1914 on the vaudeville circuit and work their way up to the creme de la creme: the Ziegfeld Follies. A number of vaudeville vets re-create their original acts in this fun, enjoyable musical. This vision of vaudeville may be somewhat romanticized, but it certainly serves as an excellent record of what that great American entertainment probably looked like. Some wonderful old tunes including "Alabamy Bound" (Ray Henderson, Buddy De Sylva, Bud Green), "I Want a Girl (Just Like the Girl Who Married Dear Old Dad)" (Harry von Tilzer, Will Dillon), the lovely "It Had to be You" (Gus Kahn, Isham Jones); and of course, Cantor's big hit "Making Whoopee" which Kahn and Donaldson wrote for the Ziegfeld production "Whoopee." This is a film that literally is fun for all, especially the performers who are clearly enjoying themselves. Look for Beard, a former OUR GANG kid, in a minor role. Murphy of course went on to become a U.S. Senator from California. Other songs include: "Why Am I Blue" (Kahn, Jones), "I Don't Want to Get Well" (Howard Johnson, Harry Pease, Harry Jentes), "They're Wearing 'Em Higher in Hawaii" (Joe Goodwin, Halsey K. Mohr), "The Curse of an Aching Heart" (Harry Fink, Al Rantadosi), "While Strolling in the Park One Day" (Robert A. King), "Dinah" (Sam M. Lewis, Joe Young, Harry Akst), "You May Not Remember" (George Jessel, Ben Oakland), "The Daughter of Rosie O'Grady" (Monte Brice, Donaldson). Followed by IF YOU KNEW SUSIE.

p, Eddie Cantor; d, Edwin L. Marin; w, Joseph Quillan, Dorothy Bennett, Irving Elinson (based on a story by Bert Granet); ph, Robert DeGrasse; ed, Theron Warth; md, C. Bakaleinikoff; art d, Albert S. D'Agostino, Jack Okey; ch, Nick Castle.

Musical   Cas.   (PR:AAA   MPAA:NR)

SHOW FLAT*   (1936, Brit.) 70m British and Dominions/PAR British
bw

Eileen Munro (Aunt Louisa), Anthony Hankey (Paul Collett), Clifford Heatherley (Ginnsberg), Max Faber (Ronnie Chubb), Polly Ward (Mary Blake), Vernon Harris (Tom Vernon), Miki Decima (Miss Jube), Billy Bray (Fox).

Shallow comedy starring Hankey as an aspiring author desperate to get financing for his new play. Seeking to impress his wealthy aunt so that she will invest in his show, Hankey tells her he lives in a swanky flat. In reality the apartment is just for show and had been decorated by one of his friends. The aunt is duly impressed, but reluctantly breaks the news to her nephew that her fortune has dwindled to nothing. Luckily, his friend's fiancee knows a rich investor and the show is saved. Unremarkable material with no spark of inspiration or originality.

p, Anthony Havelock-Allan; d, Bernard Mainwaring; w, Sherard Powell, George Barraud (based on the play by Cecil Maiden, Martha Robinson).

Comedy   (PR:A   MPAA:NR)

SHOW FOLKS**   (1928) 70m Pathe bw

Eddie Quillan (Eddie Kehoe, Vaudeville Hoofer), Lina Basquette (Rita Carey, Dancer), Carol [Carole] Lombard (Cleo), Dancer and Gold Digger, Robert Armstrong (Owens), Musical Revue Manager, Bessie Barriscale (Kitty), Crauford Kent (McNary, Theater Owner).

Quillan's a show biz performer who meets Basquette when she tries to sell him a prop duck in a theatrical supply store. Instead, he sells her half his act and the two become a dance team. Of course they become romantically involved as well. The pair are given their big chance at a Broadway revue but after arguing over some trivial point, Basquette takes a walk. Quillan has to hire a new partner who is terrible. The show flops and the new girl leaves. Quillan's left alone, until Basquette hears of his defeat, breaks her new Broadway contract, and comes back fully costumed and ready for a big finale. This early talkie has only about ten minutes of dialog, which comes at the film's end. The story is standard tripe and not well handled. It plays like a fairly connected set of interlocking cliches about show business without much effect. Quillan's comic performance is good though, probably better than the film deserved.

p, Ralph Block; d, Paul L. Stein; w, Jack Jungmeyer, George Drumgold, John Krafft (based on a story by Philip Dunning); ph, J. Peverell Marley, David Abel; ed, Doane Harrison; art d, Mitchell Leisen; m/l, "No One But Me," Al Koppel, Billy Stone, Charles Weinberg.

Comedy   (PR:A   MPAA:NR)

SHOW GIRL** (1928) 61m FN-WB bw

Alice White (*Dixie Dugan*), Donald Reed (*Alvarez Romano*), Lee Moran (*Denny*), Charles Delaney (*Jimmy Doyle, Tabloid Reporter*), Richard Tucker (*Jack Milton*), Gwen Lee (*Nita Dugan*), James Finlayson (*Mr. Dugan*), Kate Price (*Mrs. Dugan*), Hugh Roman (*Eppus, Theatrical Producer*), Bernard Randall (*Kibbitzer, his Partner*).

Average comedy about a portly wife (Price), her pencil thin hubbie (Finlayson, Laurel & Hardy's usual sidekick), and their daughters. One of the girls (White) wants to be in show biz and meets Delaney, a cub reporter. Using (and slightly abusing) various contacts, he gets his girl into a show, and of course the film ends happily. This is a mostly silent film (employing such witty titles as "Brooklyn. Like an elephant's rear end. Big, but unimposing"), but there are a few musical numbers at the wind up. Okay picture for its time, with plenty of laughs.

d, Alfred Santell; w, James T. O'Donohue, George Marion (based on the novel *Show Girl* by J. P. McEvoy); ph, Sol Polito; ed, LeRoy Stone; cos, Max Ree; m/l, "Show Girl," "Buy, Buy for Baby," Bernie Grossman, Ed Ward.

Comedy **(PR:A MPAA:NR)**

SHOW GIRL IN HOLLYWOOD** (1930) 80m FN-WB bw-c (GB: THE SHOWGIRL IN HOLLYWOOD)

Alice White (*Dixie Dugan*), Jack Mulhall (*Jimmy Doyle*), Blanche Sweet (*Donna Harris*), Ford Sterling (*Sam Otis, Film Producer*), John Miljan (*Frank Buelow, Film Director*), Virginia Sale (*Otis' Secretary*), Lee Shumway (*Kramer*), Herman Bing (*Bing*), Walter Pidgeon (*Guest Star*), Spec O'Donnell.

White plays a musical comedy star who's seen in a New York night club by a Hollywood producer. Before you can say "Lights, camera, action!" she's whisked off to the land of fruits and nuts to become a big star. This was supposed to be a parody of how movies were created, but was a poorly thought out comedy that played flatly. It does give an interesting and fairly accurate portrayal of how early silent pictures were made in some behind-the-scenes sequences, but otherwise SHOW GIRL IN HOLLYWOOD is inconsequential and forgettable. White was supposed to be First National's answer to Clara Bow, but was unsuccessful as a comedienne. The most memorable sequence is performed by Sweet as a fading movie star singing "There's a Tear for Every Smile in Hollywood." Other songs include: Hang On to the Rainbow," "I've Got My Eye On You." This picture featured a few color sequences in an otherwise all black and white production.

p, Robert North; d, Mervyn LeRoy; w, Harvey Thew, James A. Starr (based on the novel *Hollywood Girl* by J.P. McEvoy); ph, Sol Polito (Technicolor); ed, Peter Fritch; md, Leo F. Forbstein; art d, Jack Okey; ch, Jack Haskell; m/l, Bud Green, Sam H. Stept, Buddy De Sylva, Lew Brown, Ray Henderson.

Comedy **(PR:A MPAA:NR)**

SHOW GOES ON, THE**½ (1937, Brit.) 93m Associated Talking Pictures/ABF bw

Gracie Fields (*Sally Scowcroft*), Owen Nares (*Martin Fraser*), John Stuart (*Mack*), Horace Hodges (*Sam Bishop*), Edward Rigby (*Mr. Scowcroft*), Amy Veness (*Mrs. Scowcroft*), Arthur Sinclair (*Mike O'Hara*), Cyril Ritchard (*Jimmy*), Jack Hobbs (*Nicholson*), Dennis Arundell (*Felix Flack*), Billy Merson (*Manager*), Frederick Leister (*O.B. Dalton*), Patrick Barr (*Designer*), Nina Vanna (*Maniana*), Tom Payne, Lawrence Hanray, Aubrey Dexter, Carl Randall, Andrea Malandrinos, Fred Hutchings, Queenie Leonard, Isobel Scaife, Elsie Wagstaffe, Sybil Grove, Florence Harwood, Olsen's Sea Lions.

Popular comedienne Fields stars in this semi-autobiographical account of her rise from lowly mill girl to famed songstress. When a composer, Nares, hears Fields sing in an out-of-the-way dive, he realizes her potential and woos her away to sing the songs he has composed. Blessed with new, more popular material to croon, she soon finds herself booked into large music halls and becomes a huge success. Unfortunately, Nares has had tuberculosis for some time and the ailment finally kills him as Fields reaches the height of her popularity, a point in her real life when Fields was the world's highest paid star. This was a change of pace for Fields whose forte had always been in the comedic vein. Though she handles the serious material admirably, her public was not happy with the change of image and ignored the film at the box office, unhappily for the producer, Dean, who actually discovered her.

p&d, Basil Dean; w, Austin Melford, Anthony Kimmins, E.G. Valentine (based on a story by Dean); ph, Jan Stallich.

Musical **(PR:A MPAA:NR)**

SHOW GOES ON, THE** (1938, Brit.) 70m GAU bw (GB: THE THREE MAXIMS)

Anna Neagle (*Pat*), Tullio Carminati (*Toni*), Leslie Banks (*Mac*), Arthur Finn (*Hiram K. Winston*), Olive Blakeney (*Mrs. Winston*), Miki Hood (*Valentine*), Anthony Ireland (*Val*), Nicolas Koline (*Niki*), Gaston Palmer (*Juggler*), Leonard Snelling (*Prodigy*), Winifred Oughton (*His Mother*),

Beatrix Fielden-Kaye (*Madame Thomas*), Lawrence Hanray (*Thomas*), Tarva Penna (*The Doctor*), Vincent Holman (*Cafe Proprietor*), Henry Caine (*Stage Manager*), Horace Hodges (*Mike*), 12 Hippodrome Girls.

Story centers on Neagle, Carminati, and Banks, a trapeze act called The Three Maxims that is the main attraction of a French traveling circus. Banks is in love with Neagle, but when he declares his affections, she admits that she's in love with Carminati. Jealous, Banks narrowly misses catching Carminati during one of their acts. Neagle realizes what Banks is up to and afraid for Carminati's life, she faints in mid air and almost falls to her death, saved only by a daring feat of Carminati. Realizing that he has lost in the game of love, Banks tells the two to take time off for a honeymoon. He has hopes of the three resuming their act in the near future, but the audience is left wondering whether or not the trust needed for such daring feats can ever be replaced.

p&d, Herbert Wilcox; w, Herman Mankiewicz (based on a story by Nicolas Farkas); ph, F.A. Young, Jack Cox; md, Geraldo; cos, Cathleen Mann.

Drama **(PR:C MPAA:NR)**

SHOW-OFF, THE*** (1934) 79m MGM bw

Spencer Tracy (*Aubrey Piper*), Madge Evans (*Amy Fisher*), Lois Wilson (*Clara Harling*), Grant Mitchell (*Pa Fisher*), Clara Blandick (*Ma Fisher*), Claude Gillingwater (*J.B. Preston, Company President*), Henry Wadsworth (*Joe*), Alan Edward (*Frank Harling*), Richard Tucker (*Edwards*).

Even though he is only an office clerk, Tracy pretends to be an important railroad tycoon in order to win the heart of Evans. He may be able to fool her but he can't pull the wool over her mother's eyes (Blandick). He takes his charade too far and begins making impossible promises. This results in him losing his job and getting tossed out of Evans' house. The best job Tracy can get is walking around town wearing an advertising sandwich board. On his job he meets Wadsworth, an inventor. The man sells Tracy on his idea for a new device. With Tracy's help the device is sold to the railroad and wins back Evans. They are to be married, leaving her mother wondering what fool-hardy problems her new son-in-law shall bring. This is an amiable little comedy that gave Tracy a good forum for his comic talents. The story had been filmed twice before by Paramount studios, once in 1926 and again in 1929. Based on a popular Broadway show, it would be put on the screen once more in 1946 with Red Skelton in the lead. Tracy was working for Fox studios at the time of this film and wasn't happy with the situation. He hadn't had a good role since leaving Broadway for the pictures in 1930 and was traded on a one picture deal to MGM (in return for Robert Young's services). The property had been originally bought as a film for an actor named Lee Tracy, who was no relation to Spencer. The former actor was dropped from MGM for "riotous behavior" and the film given to the latter Tracy. Ironically, the next year he was dropped by Fox for the same reason and picked up by MGM. It marked the beginning of a happy and long collaboration between studio and actor.

p, Lucien Hubbard; d, Charles F. Riesner; w, Herman J. Mankiewicz (based on the play "The Show Off" by George Kelly); ph, James Wong Howe; ed, William S. Gray; art d, David Townsend; set d, Edwin B. Willis.

Comedy **(PR:A MPAA:NR)**

SHOW-OFF, THE** (1946) 84m MGM bw

Red Skelton (*Aubrey Piper*), Marilyn Maxwell (*Amy*), Marjorie Main (*Mrs. Fisher*), Virginia O'Brien (*Hortense*), Eddie "Rochester" Anderson (*Rochester*), George Cleveland (*Pop Fisher*), Leon Ames (*Frank Hyland*), Marshall Thompson (*Joe Fisher*), Jacqueline White (*Clara Hyland*), Wilson Wood (*Horace Adams*), Lila Leeds (*Flo*), Emory Parnell (*Appleton*), Charles Lane (*Quiz Master*), Grady Sutton (*Mr. Hotchkiss*), Frank Orth (*Kopec*), Francis Pierlot (*Judge Ederman*), Russell Hicks (*Thorbison*), Ida Moore (*Mrs. Ascot*), Pat McVey, Robert Williams (*Officers*), Byron Foulger (*Jenkins*), Kitty Murray (*Rochester's Girl Friend*), John Tyers (*Producer*), Jody Gilbert (*Woman*), Tim Hawkins (*Little Boy*), Robert Emmett O'Connor (*Motorman*).

Skelton is the n'er-do-well who will tell girl friend Maxwell just about anything to impress her, which gets him in big trouble. By now the story was pretty moldy considering the first version of this film had been filmed twenty years previously, following with versions made in 1929 and 1934. Audiences caught on as well for the film did lousy at the box office. Though Anderson (on loan apparently from Jack Benny) is given a featured billing, the talented man has surprisingly little to do. Production values are okay.

p, Albert Lewis; d, Harry Beaumont; w, George Wells (based on the play by George Kelly); ph, Robert Planck; m, David Snell; ed, Douglas Biggs; art d, Cedric Gibbons, Preston Ames; set d, Edwin B. Willis, Ralph S. Hurst.

Comedy **(PR:A MPAA:NR)**

SHOW THEM NO MERCY*** (1935) 76m FOX bw (GB: TAINTED MONEY)

Rochelle Hudson (*Loretta Martin*), Cesar Romero (*Tobey*), Bruce Cabot (*Pitch*), Edward Norris (*Joe Martin*), Edward Brophy (*Buzz*), Warren Hymer (*Gimp*), Herbert Rawlinson (*Kurt Hansen*), Robert Gleckler (*Gus Hansen*), Charles C. Wilson (*Clifford*), William B. Davidson (*Chief Haggerty*), Frank

Conroy (*Reed*), Edythe Elliott (*Mrs. Hansen*), William Benedict (*Willie*), Orrin Burke (*Judge Fry*), Boothe Howard (*Lester Mills*), Paul McVey (*Dr. Peterson*), Lester Dorr (*Milkman*), Georgie Cooper, Grace Goodall (*Women*), Stanley E. King, Larry Wheat, Philip Morris, Lee Shumway (*G-Men*), Gregg O'Brien, Stanley Blystone (*Announcers*), Wilfred Lucas (*Druggist*), Edward Keane (*Doctor*), Otto Hoffman (*Hick*).

Hudson and Norris play a young mechanic and his wife out for a drive. During a sudden storm the couple take their baby and rush into a seemingly abandoned home. Unfortunately, this is really the hideout of kidnappers led by Cabot. Cabot wants to kill the newcomers, but his henchman, Romero convinces him not to. The crooks have Norris go to town and spend some of their stolen money to see if they've been given marked bills. He returns and apparently the answer is no, though unbeknown to anyone, this is indeed marked cash. This is soon discovered and three gang members flee. Two are killed by the cops but one comes back. He's shot by Cabot who wants all the cash for himself. Cabot then shoots Norris, but is surprised by Hudson holding a machine gun. She kills him and the remaining gang members try to figure out how to split the money. At this point the police surround the house and save Norris, Hudson, and their baby. This is a well made crime thriller, carefully mixing humor with the rougher stuff. It's typical for the period, and a fun bit of entertainment. The film opens with a prologue featuring the parents of a kidnapped boy, with them explaining their anguish over the whole ordeal. What follows was supposed to be an example of how the FBI was attempting to crack down on the recent spree of kidnappings. Reworked as the western, RAWHIDE.

p, Darryl F. Zanuck; d, George Marshall; w, Kubec Glasmon, Henry Lehrman (based on a story by Glasmon); ph, Bert Glennon; ed, Jack Murray; md, David Buttolph.

Crime Thriller   (PR:C   MPAA:NR)

SHOWDOWN, THE½   (1940) 65m PAR bw

William Boyd (*Hopalong Cassidy*), Russell Hayden (*Lucky Jenkins*), Britt Wood (*Speedy*), Morris Ankrum (*Baron Rendor*), Jan Clayton (*Sue Willard*), Wright Kramer (*Col. White*), Donald Kirk (*Harry Cole*), Roy Barcroft (*Bowman*), Kermit Maynard (*Johnson*), Walter Shumway (*Snell*), The King's Men (*Riders*).

A better than average outing for Boyd features him, along with sidekick Hayden, on the trail of some horse thieves. A seemingly honest ranch turns out to be a bad egg and some city slickers (led by Ankrum as a European villain) are after some horses. Despite Cassidy's relatively modern-day dress, the film shows Civil War era locomotives] The best thing here is a drawn out poker match pitting Boyd against a crooked dealer. How he outwits the man is clever and well thought out. Maynard, in a minor role, was a former series star himself and brother of popular movie cowboy Ken. (See HOPALONG CASSIDY series, Index.)

p, Harry Sherman; d, Howard Bretherton; w, Harold Kusel, Daniel Kusel (based on the story by Jack Jungmeyer, based on the characters created by Clarence E. Mulford); ph, Russell Harlan; m, John Leopold; ed, Carroll Lewis; art d, Lewis J. Rachmil.

Western   (PR:A   MPAA:NR)

SHOWDOWN, THE, 1940   (SEE: WEST OF ABILENE, 1940)

SHOWDOWN, THE*   (1950) 86m REP bw

William Elliott (*Shadrach Jones*), Walter Brennan (*Capt. MacKellar*), Marie Windsor (*Adelaide*), [Henry Morgan] (*Rod Main*), Rhys Williams (*Cokecherry*), Jim Davis (*Cochran*), William Ching (*Mike Shattay*), Nacho Galindo (*Gonzales*), Leif Erickson (*Big Mart*), Henry Rowland (*Dutch*), Charles Stevens (*Indian Joe*), Victor Kilian (*Hemp*), Yakima Canutt (*Davis*), Guy Teague (*Pickney*), William Steele (*Terry*), Jack Sparks (*Bartender*).

Elliott, in his last film for Republic, is searching for the killer of his brother. He joins up with a wagon train, knowing that one of the men traveling with it is the guilty party. Through intimidation he pushes the men past their endurance levels, until he discovers Brennan, cast strikingly against type, is the guilty party. Brennan ends up being gored to death by a steer and Elliott has his revenge. Elliott gives a fine performance under an intelligent, suspenseful direction. By now location shooting was ending and Republic shot many features on back lots using rear projection. Though not the same as the wide open spaces, the technique was used here and worked nicely.

p, William J. O'Sullivan, William Elliott; d&w, Dorrell McGowan, Stuart McGowan (based on a story by Richard Wormser, Dan Gordon); ph, Reggie Lanning; m, Stanley Wilson; ed, Harry Keller; art d, Frank Arrigo.

Western   (PR:A   MPAA:NR)

SHOWDOWN**   (1963) 79m UNIV bw

Audie Murphy (*Chris Foster*), Kathleen Crowley (*Estelle*), Charles Drake (*Bert Pickett*), Harold J. Stone (*Lavalle*), Skip Homeier (*Caslon*), L.Q. Jones (*Foray*), Strother Martin (*Charlie Reeder*), John McKee (*Marshal Beaudine*), Henry Wills (*Chaca*), Joe Haworth (*Guard*), Kevin Brodie (*Buster*), Carol Thurston (*Smithy's Wife*), Dabbs Greer (*Express Man*), Charles

Horvath (*Hebron*), E.J. Andre.

After being involved in a fight along a Mexican border town, Murphy and Drake are chained to a post. They manage to escape along with some other prisoners led by outlaw Stone. After grabbing $12,000 worth of stolen securities, the pair flee but are soon caught by Stone. Murphy is held by the badman while his partner must go to town and try to cash in the securities. He gives the securities to his former girlfriend, dance hall girl Crowley, instead and comes back with nothing. Stone becomes furious and lets Murphy go after the woman to get the money. Crowley tells Murphy that Drake's gambling is the reason she must work at her lowly job and reluctantly gives the money to Murphy. However, she follows him to the hiding place. Drake tries to save both her and his pal from Stone, but is killed for his efforts. The two survivors escape and Stone follows. But Murphy kills him in the end and settles down with Crowley. Plenty of hard riding action here, all directed with effectiveness. But the results are pretty routine fare aimed at a generation raised on TV cowboys. Jones, who plays a small role as one of Stone's henchmen, later directed the science fiction cult film A BOY AND HIS DOG.

p, Gordon Kay; d, R.G. Springsteen; w, Bronson Howitzer; ph, Ellis W. Carter; m, Hans J. Salter; ed, Jerome Thoms; md, Joseph Gershenson; art d, Alexander Golitzen, Alfred Sweeney; set d, Oliver Emert; cos, Rosemary Odell; makeup, Bud Westmore.

Western   (PR:A   MPAA:NR)

SHOWDOWN**½   (1973) 99m UNIV c

Rock Hudson (*Chuck Jarvis*), Dean Martin (*Billy Massey*), Susan Clark (*Kate Jarvis*), Donald Moffat (*Art Williams*), John McLiam (*P. J. Wilson*), Charles Baca (*Martinez*), Jackson Kane (*Clem*), Ben Zeller (*Perry Williams*), John Richard Gill (*Earl Cole*), Philip L. Mead (*Jack Bonney*), Rita Rogers (*Girl*), Vic Mohica (*Big Eye*), Raleigh Gardenhire (*Deputy Joe Williams*), Ed Begley, Jr (*Pook*), Dan Boydston (*Rawls*).

This re-working of the Damon and Pythias theme features Martin and Hudson as best of pals in the old west. Martin's a train robber and his friend is the sheriff who must bring him in. To complicate matters, Hudson's married to Martin's former sweetheart, Clark, which is the bone of contention between the two. Their past relationship is somewhat muddled through a poor use of flashback, but this is an amiable enough comedy Western with a few decent laughs. It's nothing terribly special or new though, and probably would have ended up as a TV movie had it been made a few years later. Seaton's direction is okay (this was to be his final film), though not his best work. The photography, employing a process known as Todd-AO 35, gives the film a look of precise clarity, using the picturesque locations of New Mexico.

p&d, George Seaton; w, Theodore Taylor (based on a story by Hank Fine); ph, Ernest Laszlo (Todd-AO 35, Technicolor); m, David Shire; ed, John W. Holmes; md, Hal Mooney; art d, Alexander Golitzen, Henry Bumstead; set d, George Milo; cos, Edith Head; spec eff, Albert Whitlock.

Western   (PR:A   MPAA:PG)

SHOWDOWN AT ABILENE***   (1956) 80m UNIV c

Jock Mahoney (*Jim Trask*), Martha Hyer (*Peggy Bigelow*), Lyle Bettger (*Dave Mosely*), David Janssen (*Verne Ward*), Grant Williams (*Chip Tomlin*), Ted de Corsia (*Dan Claudius*), Harry Harvey, Sr (*Ross Bigelow*), Dayton Lummis (*Jack Bedford*), Richard H. Cutting (*Nelson*), Robert G. Anderson (*Sprague*), John Maxwell (*Frank Scovie*), Lane Bradford (*Loop*).

When the former sheriff of Abilene returns home from the Civil War, he brings with him a troubled mind and a reluctance towards guns. Mahoney plays the man who finds his troubles compounded because he's killed his old friend Bettger's brother accidentally during the war. On his return he finds Bettger has taken Mahoney's girl (Hyer) and has also been dealing in land grabbing from farmers. Mahoney must overcome his troubles and stop the former friend from his villainous activities. Though the plot is routine, the direction is well paced and creates some intelligent sequences, lifting this film to a better level than the typical B Western. The characters are nicely fleshed out and believable, with color photography used to the best advantage. Remade in 1967 as GUNFIGHT IN ABILENE.

p, Howard Christie; d, Charles Haas; w, Bernie Giler (based on the novel *Gun Shy* by Clarence Upson Young); ph, Irving Glassberg (Technicolor); ed, Ray Snyder; md, Joseph Gershenson; art d, Alexander Golitzen, Richard Riedel; cos, Rosemary Odell.

Western   (PR:A   MPAA:NR)

SHOWDOWN AT BOOT HILL***½   (1958) 71m RF/FOX bw

Charles Bronson (*Luke Welsh*), Robert Hutton (*Sloane*), John Carradine (*Doc Weber*), Carole Mathews (*Jill*), Fintan Meyler (*Sally*), Paul Maxey (*Judge*), Thomas Browne Henry (*Con Maynor*), William Stevens (*1st Cowhand*), Martin Smith (*2nd Cowhand*), Joseph McGuinn (*Mr. Creavy*), George Douglas (*Charles Maynor*), Michael Mason (*Patton*), George Pembroke (*Sheriff*), Argentina Brunetti (*Mrs. Bonaventure*), Ed Wright (*Brent*), Dan Simmons (*Bartender*), Barbara Woodell (*Mrs. Maynor*), Norman

Leavitt (*Photographer*), Stacey Marshall, Shirle Haven, Tony Douglas, Jose Gonzales-Gonzales.

After tracking down a wanted murderer and then killing him, U.S. Marshal Bronson finds that his victim was respected in the town of his death. None of the townspeople will identify the corpse which means that Bronson can't collect his bounty. This forces Bronson to look at his life and why he is what he is. This interesting psychological Western is a well scripted, nicely directed piece that goes well beyond it's programmer budget. Bronson gives one of his better performances as the tortured man, with fine support from Mathews as a madame and Carradine, the town barber/undertaker. Fowler was better known for directing such films as I WAS A TEENAGE WEREWOLF (1956) and I MARRIED A MONSTER FROM OUTER SPACE (1959), but shows that he had much more going for him than those films might have suggested. Despite some good critical reaction, the studio failed to realize Bronson's potential. SHOWDOWN AT BOOT HILL was dumped into action theaters as a double feature filler and was largely ignored. Though Bronson (sans his famous Fu Manchu moustache) shows some real talent, it would take him ten more years and a new career in European films before he would become a star. Perhaps audiences of the 1950s were not yet ready for as untraditional a leading man as Bronson.

p, Harold E. Knox; d, Gene Fowler, Jr.; w, Louis Vittes; ph, John M. Nickolaus, Jr. (RegalScope); m, Albert Harris; ed, Frank Sullivan; md, Harris; art d, John Mansbridge; set d, Walter M. Scott, Maurice Mulcahy.

Western　　　　　　　　　　　　　　　　　　　**(PR:A　MPAA:NR)**

SHOWDOWN FOR ZATOICHI**½　　　(1968, Jap.) 87m Daiei c (ZATO ICHI JIGOKUTABI)

Shintaro Katsu (*Zatoichi*), Mikio Narita (*Tadasu Jumonji*), Chizu Hayashi (*Enoshimeya*), Kaneko Iwasaki (*Otane*), Gaku Yamamoto (*Tomonoshin Sagawa*).

It is the Japanese New Year and Katsu, a blind master swordsman, is on his way to Mount Fuji for a huge celebration. He is attacked by five robbers but he defeats them easily despite his handicap. Katsu continues his trek via ship and on board wins a large sum of money while gambling. The gamblers are members of a gang led by Hayashi. Katsu also meets Narita, a fine chess player/swordsman and the two leave ship together when it reaches its destination. Hayashi is waiting for the blind man and leads him to a seeming doom. But the gang leader is no match for the swordsman and loses a battle, though a little girl nearby is accidentally wounded. Katsu is overcome with guilt and tries to gamble his winnings to earn money for the girl's medicine. This time he loses, but his friend Narita wins and pays for the needed medicine. It turns out that the girl's mother (Iwasaki) is the widow of a man that Katsu has previously slain in self-defense. Hayashi's gang wants her to spy on the man, but she falls for him instead. Katsu soon becomes troubled when he learns that his friend Narita enjoys killing others. A young samurai warrior and his sister come to town looking for the person responsible for their father's brutal murder. It dawns on Katsu that Narita is the one behind it and realizes he must kill his friend. Before they can engage in a showdown, however, Narita is killed by the brother and sister of his victim.

d, Kenji Misumi; w, Daisuke Ito (based on a story by Kan Shimozawa) ph, Chishi Makiura (Eastmancolor); m, Akira Ifukube.

Action　　　　　　　　　　　　　　　　　　　**(PR:C-O　MPAA:NR)**

SHOWGIRL IN HOLLYWOOD
　　　　　　　(SEE: SHOW GIRL IN HOLLYWOOD, 1930)

SHOWOFF　　　　　　　　　　　(SEE: SHOW-OFF, THE, 1946)

SHOWTIME**½　　　(1948, Brit.) 90m EM/WB-EFI bw (GB: GAIETY GEORGE)

Richard Greene (*George Howard*), Ann Todd (*Kathryn Davis*), Peter Graves (*Carter, Columnist*), Hazel Court (*Elizabeth Brown*), Leni Lynn (*Florence Stephens*), Ursula Jeans (*Isobel Forbes*), Morland Graham (*Morris*), Frank Pettingell (*Grindley*), Charles Victor (*Collier*), Daphne Barker (*Miss de Courtney*), Jack Train (*Hastings*), Maire O'Neill (*Mrs. Murphy*), Phyllis Robins (*Chubbs*), John Laurie (*McTavish*), Frederick Burtwell (*Jenkins*), Antony Holles (*Wade*), David Horne (*Lord Mountsby*), Patrick Waddington (*Lt. Travers*), Claud Allister (*Archie*), Wally Patch (*Commissionaire*), Graeme Muir (*Lord Elstown*), Evelyn Darvell, Paul Blake, John Miller, Richard Molinas, Gerhard Kempinski, Carl Jaffe, Maxwell Reed, Roger Moore.

A fitfully successful movie biography of famed British musical comedy producer George Edwardes (here called George Howard for some reason), starring Greene as the beloved impresario. The film follows Greene from the 1890s when he leaves Ireland and arrives in London full of ambition and bold ideas. He purchases a rundown music hall and soon turns it into the talk of the town by bringing musical comedy to the masses. In the process he meets a beautiful dance-hall girl, Todd, and makes her his wife. With her help, Greene becomes Britain's biggest musical producer. Unfortunately, tragedy strikes for Greene during WW I when he is captured and held in a German prisoner of war camp for much of the war. Upon release, with his

health severely impaired by the experience, he attempts a comeback. With the help of Todd and his former associates, Greene makes it back to the top, but his triumph is short lived and he soon dies from his ailments. Greene turns in a fine performance as Howard and Todd almost steals the film as his supportive wife, but the film fails during the badly staged, nearly lackadaisical musical numbers which demonstrate none of the brilliance possessed by the film's subject. Musical numbers include excerpts from the musical comedies "Tallo-ho Girl" and "Tomboy Princess."

p, George King; d, King, Freddie Carpenter, Leontine Sagan; w, Katherine Strueby, Basil Woon (based on a story by Richard Fisher, Peter Cresswell); ph, Otto Heller, Gus Drisse; ed, Hugh Stewart; md, Jack Beaver; art d, William C. Andrews; m/l, George Posford, Eric Maschwitz.

Musical/Biography　　　　　　　　　　　　　　**(PR:A　MPAA:NR)**

SHRIEK IN THE NIGHT, A*½　　　(1933) 65m Allied Pictures bw

Ginger Rogers (*Patricia Morgan*), Lyle Talbot (*Ted Rand, Reporter*), Purnell Pratt (*Inspector Russell*), Arthur Hoyt (*Wilfred, Russell's Assistant*), Harvey Clark (*"Petey" Peterson, Janitor*), Lillian Harmer (*Augusta, Maid*), Maurice Black (*Martini*), Louise Beavers (*Maid*), Clarence H. Wilson (*Perkins, Editor*).

Rogers and Talbot are a pair of rival newspaper reporters. They're always trying to out do each other for that "big scoop" and find themselves in real trouble when they stumble onto a string of murders being commited at an ultra-modern apartment complex. Rogers almost gets fried to a crisp in a blazing furnace, but is saved at the last minute and all ends well. This film, shot on the RKO lots for Allied Productions, marked Rogers' return to melodrama. It was not one of her better efforts, reminiscent of the previous Rogers-Talbot collaboration, THE THIRTEENTH GUEST. She does her job adequately, but is costumed in unflattering styles and hampered by strictly routine material.

p, M. H. Hoffman; d, Albert Ray; w, Frances Hyland (based on a story by Kurt Kempler); ph, Harry Neumann, Tom Galligan; ed, Leete R. Brown; md, Abe Meyer; art d, Gene Hornbostel; cos, Alfreda.

Drama　　　　　　　　　**Cas.**　　　　　　　　**(PR:A　MPAA:NR)**

SHRIEK OF THE MUTILATED zero　　　(1974) 92m AM Films/Film Brokers c

Alan Brock (*Ernst Prell*), Tawn Ellis (*Dr. Karl Werner*), Jennifer Stock (*Karen Hunter*), Michael Harris (*Keith Henshaw*), Morton Jacobs (*Laughing Crow*), Darcy Brown.

The ads claimed, "A Frenzied Hunt for a Hideous Beast Uncovers an Evil Cannibal Cult and Death is the Devil's Blessing]," and that pretty much sums it up. This is one of the all-time worst, but the unintentional laughs provided may just make it worth a look for those who can stomach inept filmmaking. Brock stars as a college professor who takes four of his students on an expedition to Boot Island to search for the Abominable Snowman. There they meet with Brock's associate, Ellis, and his native servant, Jacobs, a dangerous looking mute. Together the small group begin their exploration of the island and soon two of the students are ripped to pieces by a large, white beast who blow-dries its bushy mane. This leaves only two students and they begin to suspect things on this island aren't quite what they seem. The remaining girl, Stock, is cornered in the bathroom by two of the fuzzy brutes and is scared to death. Her boy friend, Harris, who was conveniently knocked out in the woods, comes to in time to witness the two professors and Jacobs cannibalizing one of the corpses with their fuzzy white costumes hanging in a nearby closet. Harris takes off and finds a cop, but when they arrive on the scene it is revealed that the cop is a member of this cannibal cult as well and the film ends with the cannibals carving up Stock's body with an electric knife. Wretched stuff and the credits read like a *Who's Who* of bad cinema. Lead actor Brock was a bit player in the 1930s who gave up the screen to become an agent, his cohort Ellis starred in CAT WOMEN OF THE MOON (1954), and writer-producer Adlum (a former rock critic for *Creem* magazine) was also responsible for the equally vile INVASION OF THE BLOOD FARMERS. For rabid horror aficionados only.

p, Ed Adlum; d, Michael Findlay; w, Adlum, Ed Kelleher; m/l, "Hot Butter."

Horror　　　　　　　　　　　　　　　　　　　**(PR:O　MPAA:R)**

SHRIKE, THE**　　　　　　　　　　　(1955) 88m UNIV bw

Jose Ferrer (*Jim Downs*), June Allyson (*Ann Downs*), Joy Page (*Charlotte Moore*), Kendall Clark (*Dr. Bellman*), Isabel Bonner (*Dr. Barrow*), Jay Barney (*Dr. Kramer*), Somer Alberg (*Dr. Schlesinger*), Ed Platt (*Harry Downs*), Dick Benedict (*Gregory*), Herbie Faye (*Tager*), Will Kuluva (*Ankoritis*), Martin Newman (*O'Brien*), Billy Greene (*Schloss*), Joe Comadore (*Major*), Leigh Whipper (*Carlisle*), Mary Bell (*Miss Wingate*), Adrienne Marden (*Miss Raymond*).

A gross miscasting of lovable June Allyson as a miserable woman is what sets this drama on its ear. A shrike is supposedly a soft, innocent bird which impales her victim on its long, thin beak. The hit play showed the woman to be a vicious person who manipulated her husband to such a degree that he winds up in an insane asylum and must cow-tow to his wife. They soft-pedal the situation here, so the husband, Ferrer, eventually does go into a mental ward but it's more a result of his own doing and, as the picture ends in a contrived happy conclusion, Ferrer and Allyson get together in the hopes of making their marriage work. Ferrer, who starred in the play and directed it, does the same here, making his debut in film as a director. The play won the Pulitzer Prize but you'd never know it from what's up there on screen. Gone is the tension and the unbearable woman. Instead, a non-psychotic Allyson is seen to have all sorts of saving graces. Ferrer tells the story in flashback to his psychiatrist, Clark. Ferrer likes Page, but there is no way that Allyson is going to allow a divorce, so that is unrequited. Some good scenes in the mental hospital, although they are lemonade compared to THE SNAKE PIT or some of the other, more superior psychological movies. The woman who plays the analyst is Bonner, who also did it in the play. She was married to playwright Kramm and the scuttlebutt has it that it was she who inspired the portrait of the terrible woman in THE SHRIKE. Whereas the shrike was a certified black widow spider on stage, here she is just a creepy crawler with her fatal stinger removed.

p, Aaron Rosenberg; d, Jose Ferrer; w, Ketti Frings (based on the play by Joseph Kramm); ph, William Daniels; m, Frank Skinner; ed, Frank Gross; md, Joseph Gershenson; art d, Alexander Golitzen, Richard H. Riedel.

Drama   (PR:C MPAA:NR)

SHUBIN   (SEE: SCANDAL, 1964, Jap.)

SHUT MY BIG MOUTH***   (1942) 71m COL bw

Joe E. Brown (*Wellington Holmes*), Adele Mara (*Conchita Montoya*), Victor Jory (*Buckskin Bill*), Fritz Feld (*Robert Oglethorpe*), Don Beddoe (*Hill*), Will Wright (*Long*), Russell Simpson (*Mayor Potter*), Pedro de Cordoba (*Don Carlos Montoya*), Joan Woodbury (*Maria*), Ralph Peters (*Butch*), Joe McGuinn (*Hank*), Lloyd Bridges (*Skinny*), Forrest Tucker (*Red*), Noble Johnson (*Chief Standing Bull*), Chief Thunder-Cloud (*Indian Interpreter*), Art Mix, Blackjack Ward (*Bandits*), Hank Bell (*Stage Coach Driver*), Earle Hodgins (*Stage Coach Guard*), Eddy Waller (*Happy*), Fern Emmett (*Maggie*), Lew Kelly (*Westerner*), Dick Curtis (*Joe*), Edmund Cobb (*Stage Agent*), Bob Folkerson (*Boy*), Clay De Roy (*Spanish Driver*), Ed Peil, Sr (*Hotel Proprietor*), Al Ferguson (*Pursuer*), John Tyrell (*Man*), Georgia Backus (*Woman*).

Enjoyable brown vehicle finds him as an Easterner out West. He unwittingly becomes the sheriff and must fight off the blackhearted villain, Jory. This is done in drag of all things, with marvelous comic effect. Lots of laughs and some good direction that never overplays its hand.

p, Robert Sparks; d, Charles Barton; w, Oliver Drake, Karen De Wolf, Francis Martin (based on a story by Drake); ph, Henry Freulich; ed, Gene Havlick; md, Morris W. Stoloff; ch, Eddie Prinz.

Comedy   (PR:AAA MPAA:NR)

SHUTTERED ROOM, THE***   (1968, Brit.) 100m
                                             SevenArts-Troy-Schenck/WB c

Gig Young (*Mike Kelton*), Carol Lynley (*Susannah Kelton/Sarah*), Oliver Reed (*Ethan*), Flora Robson (*Aunt Agatha*), William Devlin (*Zebulon Whateley*), Bernard Kay (*Tait*), Judith Arthy (*Emma*), Robert Cawdron (*Luther Whateley*), Celia Hewitt (*Aunt Sarah*), Ingrid Bower (*Village Girl*), Anita Anderson (*Susannah as a Child*), Charles Lloyd Pack (*Bargee*), Peter Porteous, Clifford Diggins.

A spine-chilling tale that's long on atmosphere and short on bright dialog, but the actors do well with what they are given and Greene's moody direction almost saves the day. Although supposedly set in New England, it was actually shot in *Olde* England at Cornwall, but only the most knowledgeable will note the sham. Lynley and her husband, Young, return to a bleak island where Lynley grew up. She's inherited an old mill and wants to see if it's worth anything. When her parents died, Lynley, still a child, went to New York, where she grew up. Not having been back to this desolate place (similar to Block Island, just off Providence in Rhode Island) for years, she is surprised at the manner in which the locals respond when she talks about using the mill house as a vacation retreat. It seems that the place has a frightening history. Reed is Lynley's cousin, a weird and evil type. He tells her to avoid the mill house. So does her aunt, the magnificently eccentric Robson. There's a room in the mill house that's tightly locked and she's warned to let it stay that way. (We've seen this in THE SHINING, THE PICTURE OF DORIAN GRAY, and many other "locked room" movies.) Lynley decides to see what's so secret. At the same time, Young has been beaten up by Reed and some of his sullen townspals. Before she gets to the room in question, Reed steps out of the darkness and, it would seem, is interested in having his way with her. She races into the shuttered room and Reed follows her inside, carrying a burning torch. In the darkness, someone or something causes Reed to fall out of the high window and die. Young has been talking to Robson, who has disclosed the secret of the room now that Reed's girl friend, Arthy, has been also murdered. It turns out that the shuttered room has been occupied for all these years by Lynley's sister (also played by Lynley), a demented creature who has a crippled body and a maniacal and murderous streak. She's been confined in the room and taken care of by Robson for decades. Young races to the mill house and the room is now on fire, due to Reed's torch having been dropped. Lynley and Young

get away but Robson arrives and locks herself in the room with the mad sister, thus allowing the flames to engulf them both. Lynley was excellent and Reed showed his customary brand of malevolence. The dialog is, at best, serviceable words to carry along the brooding, often frightening visuals.

p, Phillip Hazelton; d, David Greene; w, D.B. Ledrov, Nathaniel Tanchuck (based on the story by August Derleth, H.P. Lovecraft); ph, Kenneth Hodges (Technicolor); m, Basil Kirchin; ed, Brian Smedley-Aston; md, Jack Nathan; art d, Brian Eatwell; cos. Caroline Mott, Hylan Baker; makeup, Harry Frampton.

Horror   (PR:C-O MPAA:NR)

SI PARIS NOUS ETAIT CONTE   (SEE: IF PARIS WERE TOLD TO
                                             US, 1956, Fr.)

SI VERSAILLES M'ETAIT CONTE (SEE: ROYAL AFFAIRS IN
                                             VERSAILLES, 1957, Fr.)

SIAVASH IN PERSEPOLIS*½   (1966, Iran) 100m Djame
                                 Djam-Iran-Ashna bw (KHUN-E S IAAVASH)

Minou Farjad (*Siavash*), Marva Nabili (*Soudabeh*), Abbas Moayeri (*Kaous*), Nader Kouklani (*Garsivaz*), Amir Farid (*Afrasiab*), Ashgar Zolfaghari (*Rustam*).

Farjad is the son of the sovereign of Iran. His father's first wife (Nabili) makes advances towards him, but keeping his honor as a knight, Farjad refuses her. Angered at being refused, Nabili tells Moayeri that his son is her lover and that she has given birth to children for him, though the offspring were murdered. The prince is sentenced to a trial by fire, which he manages to get through alive. He takes command of the armies fighting the enemy Turan and forgives Nabili when she is officially pardoned for her lies. Meanwhile, Farid, the sovreign of Turan dreams that his country will be destroyed if he does battle with Iran. He makes a peace offering and gives up 100 hostages at Farjad's request. However, Moayeri is skeptical and orders his son to kill the 100. The prince refuses and ends up moving to a neutral country. He stops in Turan though, and ends up marrying Farid's daughter. Her uncle Kouklani opposes this union and ends up having Farjad killed as a traitor. An Iranian legend is then related which declares that from the blood of the prince grew the herb known as the "blood of Siavash." Based on the 11th-Century epic by Ferdowsi Shahnameh, this film was shot in 16 millimeter stock and probably released in Iran in 1965.

d, Ferydoun Rahnema; ph, Palan.

Historical Epic   (PR:C MPAA:NR)

SICILIAN CLAN, THE**½   (1970, Fr.) 121m FOX-Europa-Les Films
                                 du Siecle/FOX c (LE CLAN DES SICILIENS)

Jean Gabin (*Vittorio Manalese*), Alain Delon (*Roger Sartet*), Lino Ventura (*Inspector Le Goff*), Irina Demick (*Jeanne Manalese*), Amedeo Nazzari (*Tony Nicosia*), Sydney Chaplin (*Jack*), Elisa Cegani (*Maria Manalese*), Karen Blanguernon (*Theresa*), Marc Porel (*Sergio Manalese*), Yves Lefebvre (*Aldo Manalese*), Philippe Baronnet (*Luigi*), Leopoldo Trieste (*Stamp Expert*), Cesar Chauveau (*Roberto*), Danielle Volle (*Monique Sartet*), Edward Meeks (*Pilot*), Jacques Duby (*Rovel*), Yves Brainville, Gerard Buhr, Raoul Delfosse, Sally Nesbitt, Andre Pousse, Andre Thorent.

Delon is a condemned murderer who escapes from prison thanks to the help of Gabin, a Sicilian mobster. Delon and Gabin plan to steal a collection of jewels from an exhibition in Venice, but Gabin's American pal Nazzari suggests instead hijacking the airplane which is to transport the jewels from Venice to New York City. Gabin arranges for his family (the family that robs together ...) to carry out the job, which they do nicely. They all scamper back to Europe with the loot and go into hiding. But when Gabin finds Delon has been bedding down with his daughter-in-law Demick, he tries to lure the man to Paris to get what's coming to him. Delon arrives ahead of schedule and sees one of Gabin's sons, sent to kill Delon, arrested before he can carry out the job. But Gabin is a hardliner and sees that both Delon and Demick are finally rubbed out. After completing the job himself, Gabin returns home to find the police waiting for him. A nifty gangster picture, somewhat predictable in scripting, but still a great job. The ensemble acting is terrific and the direction tells the story well. This is hardly just another gangster picture. THE SICILIAN CLAN was one of the biggest box-office successes ever in France and its English-language version also did well, grossing over $2 million in the U.S.

p, Jacques E. Strauss; d, Henri Verneuil; w, Verneuil, Jose Giovanni, Pierre Pelegri (based on the novel *Le Clan Des Siciliens* by Auguste Le Breton); ph, Henri Decae (Panavision, DeLuxe Color); m, Ennio Morricone; ed, Albert Jurgenson, Pierre Gillette, Jean-Michel Gautier; md, Bruno Nicolai; art d, Jacques Saulnier; set d, Charles Merangel; cos, Helene Nourry; makeup, Michel Deruelle.

Crime   (PR:O MPAA:GP)

SICILIAN CONNECTION, THE*   (1977) 100m Joseph Green c

Ben Gazzara, Silvia Monti, Fausto Tozzi, Jess Hahn.

Worthless crime potboiler which chronicles the efforts of a narcotics agent to go undercover and pose as the manager of a nightclub to get the goods on an international drug smuggling operation. A yawner, despite Gazzara's presence.

d, Ferdinando Baldi (Technicolor).

Crime   **Cas.**   **(PR:O MPAA:NR)**

SICILIANS, THE**   (1964, Brit.) 69m BUT bw

Robert Hutton (*Calvin Adams*), Reginald Marsh (*Inspector Webb*), Ursula Howells (*Mme. Perrault*), Alex Scott (*Henri Perrault*), Susan Denny (*Carole Linden*), Robert Ayres (*Angela di Marco*), Eric Pohlmann (*Inspector Bressin*), Patricia Hayes (*Passenger*), Warren Mitchell (*O'Leary*), Murray Kash (*George Baxter*).

When a mobster turns state's evidence to save his neck, former associates kidnap the man's son to ensure his silence. With the help of a dancer, an American embassy employee, and Scotland Yard, the boy is recovered and the mob is dealt a death blow.

p, John I. Phillips, Ronald Liles; d, Ernest Morris; w, Liles, Reginald Hearne.

Crime   **(PR:A MPAA:NR)**

SIDDHARTHA***   (1972) 86m Lotus/COL c

Shashi Kapoor (*Siddhartha*), Simi Garewal (*Kamala*), Romesh Sharma (*Govinda*), Pinchoo Kapoor (*Kamaswami*), Zul Vellani (*Vasudeva*), Amrik Singh (*Siddhartha's Father*), Shanti Hiranand (*Siddhartha's Mother*), Kunai Kapoor (*Siddhartha's Son*).

A simple story about a young Indian Brahmin (Kapoor), based on Hesse's famed novel. Kapoor goes searching for the meaning of life, falling in with holy men, and eventually encountering someone who might be the Gautama Buddha. Kapoor becomes a wealthy merchant and finally finds peace on a river boat after being introduced to sensual pleasures by a courtesan. This is a film of frequent lyrical beauty, wonderfully filmed by Ingmar Bergman's regular cameraman Nykvist. However, the film fails to capture the essence of Hesse's book, try though it may. It is more a series of filmed events than an interpretation of the story. Shot on location in India by an American director, this picture came to the screen at a time when Hesse's book was still very much in vogue on U.S. college campuses. Originally published in 1922, but not given an English translation until the 1950s, Siddhartha, its search for meaning, and its spiritual journey East spoke directly to the concerns of 1960s youth.

p,d&w, Conrad Rooks (based on the novel by Herman Hesse); ph, Sven Nykvist (Panavision, Eastmancolor); m, Hemanta Kumar; ed, Willy Kemplen; art d, Malcolm Golding; cos, Bhanu.

Drama   **(PR:C MPAA:R)**

SIDE SHOW**   (1931) 68m WB bw

Winnie Lightner (*Pat*), Charles Butterworth (*Sidney*), Evalyn Knapp (*Irene*), Donald Cook (*Joe*), Guy Kibbee (*Col. "Pop" Gowdy*), Louise Carver (*Minn*), Matthew Betz (*Whalen*), Ann Magruder (*Jen*), Luis Alberni (*Santini*), Edward Morgan (*Jimmy*), Tom Ricketts (*Tom*), Otto Hoffman (*Otto*), Lucille Ward, Vince Barnett.

Lightner executes a host of jobs for a circus side show–everything from hula dancing to high diving. She delivers a fine performance in this role, even if the material isn't quite up to her talents, and Butterworth plays off her well as the eccentric, shy man who loves her. There are some interesting behind-the-scenes looks at the circus provided, but, for the most part, this is pretty routine fare.

d, Roy Del Ruth; w, William K. Wells, Arthur Caesar (based on a story by Wells); ph, Dev Jennings; ed, Jim Gibbons.

Comedy   **(PR:A MPAA:NR)**

SIDE STREET**½   (1929) 70m RKO bw

Tom Moore (*Jimmy O'Farrell*), Matt Moore (*John O'Farrell*), Owen Moore (*Dennis O'Farrell*), Kathryn Perry (*Kathleen Doyle*), Frank Sheridan (*Mr. O'Farrell*), Emma Dunn (*Mrs. O'Farrell*), Arthur Housman ("*Silk*" *Ruffo*), Mildred Harris (*Bunny*), Charles Byer (*Maxse*), Edwin August (*Mac*), Irving Bacon (*Slim*), Walter McNamara (*Patrick Doyle*), Al Hill ("*Blondie*"), Heinie Conklin ("*Drunk*"), Dan Wolheim ("*Pinkie*").

The epitome of Hollywood's Irish cliches, SIDE STREET is the tale of three brothers – Tom Moore, a kindly policeman; Matt Moore, a surgeon; and Owen Moore, a bootlegger known to his cronies by the alias Barney Muller, a name he uses to keep his illegal activities secret from his brothers. When Tom gets a promotion he is assigned to a murder case involving the Muller gang. In the meantime, Tom's fiancee, Perry, is invited to a party at Muller's Manhattan home and overhears information that implicates Muller. With Perry and Matt the doctor's help, Tom discovers that Muller is really an alias for his brother, Owen. Owen hires a hitman to kill Tom, unaware that he has just ordered his brother's death. A trap is set for Tom, but Owen interferes and tries to stop the killing. He, in turn, is shot and dies in his brother's arms. To save his parents from shame, Tom tells them that Owen went away on a long trip thereby preserving Owen's character. SIDE STREET is about as hokey as they come, but still a pleasant piece of entertainment.

p, William Le Baron; d, Mal St. Clair; w, John Russell, St. Clair, George O'Hara, Eugene Walter (based on a story by St. Clair); ph, William Marshall, Nick Musuraca; cos, Max Ree; m/l, Oscar Levant, Sidney Clare.

Drama   **(PR:A MPAA:NR)**

SIDE STREET**½   (1950) 83m MGM bw

Farley Granger (*Joe Norson*), Cathy O'Donnell (*Ellen Norson*), James Craig (*Georgie Garsell*), Paul Kelly (*Capt. Walter Anderson*), Edmon Ryan (*Victor Backett*), Paul Harvey (*Emil Lorrison*), Jean Hagen (*Harriet Sinton*), Charles McGraw (*Stanley Simon*), Ed Max (*Nick Drummon*), Adele Jergens (*Lucille "Lucky" Colner*), Harry Bellaver (*Larry Giff*), Whit Bissell (*Harold Simpsen*), John Gallaudet (*Gus Heldon*), Esther Somers (*Mrs. Malby*), Harry Antrim (*Mr. Malby*), George Tyne (*Detective Roffman*), Kathryn Givney (*Miss Carter*), King Donovan (*Gottschalk*), Norman Leavitt (*Pete Stanton*), Sid Tomack (*Louie*), Joe Verdi (*Vendor*), Don Terranove, James Westerfield (*Patrolmen*), Gail Bonney, Marjorie Liszt (*Women's voices*), Brett King (*Pigeon Man*), Peter Thompson (*Mickey*), John A. Butler (*Elevator Man*), Herbert Vigran (*Photographer*), Robert Malcolm (*Charlie*), Paul Marion (*Dave*), William Ruhl (*Manny*), Ransom Sherman (*Superintendent*), Ruth Warren (*Housekeeper*), Eula Guy (*Florence*), Ed Glover (*Fingerprint Expert*), William Hansen (*Dr. Harry Sternberg*), Tom McElhany (*Newsboy*), Jack Diamond (*Bum*), George David (*Syrian Proprietor*), Don Haggerty (*Rivers*), Mildred Wall (*Mrs. Glickburn*), Angi O. Poulos (*Ahmed*), Albert Morin (*Ismot Kimal*), W.P. McWatters, Peter DeBear (*Tommy Drummon, Jr.*), Bee Humphries (*Mrs. Farnol*), Sarah Selby (*Nurse Williams*), Margaret Brayton (*Woman Clerk*), Charles McAvoy (*Bank Guard*), George Lynn (*Frank, Technician*), John Maxwell (*Monitor's Voice*), Nolan Leary (*Doorman*), Ralph Riggs (*Proprietor*), Ben Cooper (*Young Man*), Marie Crisis (*Headwaitress*), Lynn Millan (*Hatcheck Girl*), David Wolfe (*Smitty*), Ralph Montgomery (*Milkman*), Minerva Urecal (*Landlady*), Ollie O'Toole (*Voice*), Walter Craig (*Radio Clerk*), Helen Eby-Rock (*Mother*), Frank Conlon (*Night Elevator Operator*), John Phillips (*Detective*), Ellen Lowe (*Mrs. Rivers*), James O'Neil (*Priest*).

Granger is a postman married to the pregnant O'Donnell. He wants to give her some of life's better things but doesn't have the means for it. In desperation he steals an envelope stuffed with cash that he finds lying in an office on his mail route. What Granger doesn't know is that this money is a blackmail payoff that is connected to some murders. Granger uses a portion of the money to build up his life style but eventually guilt catches up with him and he tries to return the money. He takes it back to where he stole it but no one seems to know anything about the loot. Granger gets frightened that this will lead to big trouble and tells O'Donnell that a sudden out-of-town job has cropped up and he must leave home temporarily. Granger checks into a flea-bag hotel for a hideout and gives the cash to a friend. The friend runs off with the money, though, and Granger is then confronted by some gangsters. They're part of the money's origin and want to know where the postman has hidden it. He escapes and takes refuge amid the underbelly of society, a lonely world of cheap nightclubs and gangster hangouts. Granger is accused of the original murders and is chased by both the cops and the gangsters. The gangsters finally catch up with him and decide to kill him. But the police are on to them and in a high-speed chase through the streets of New York City eventually catch up with Granger and the mobsters. In a shoot-out Granger is hit, though not fatally, and finally is reunited with O'Donnell. SIDE STREET is a film of mixed quality. Granger and O'Donnell had co-starred in the fine picture THEY LIVE BY NIGHT (1949) and MGM thought the same team would once more create an equally compelling film. However the unfolding of this story is often dragged out and boring, with some poorly written dialog. But what the film lacks in writing, it makes up in cinematic technique. Shot on the streets of New York City, the director has a good eye for location (the chase sequence denouement is terrific) with some interesting high-angle shots that create a trapped effect. The photography is probably the film's best point: unlike many *film noir* pieces this chooses natural lighting instead of the usual expressionistic flairs and the style works well. Craig, as the gangster leader, is particularly vicious, working well in his against-type role. The snowballing plot has some good moments (if only the dialog were better) and the cast handles the material with competence.

p, Sam Zimbalist; d, Anthony Mann; w, Sydney Boehm (based on a story by Boehm); ph, Joseph Ruttenberg; m, Lennie Hayton; ed, Conrad A. Nervig; art d, Cedric Gibbons, Daniel B. Cathcart; set d, Edwin B. Willis, Charles de Crof; spec eff, A. Arnold Gillespie; makeup, Jack Dawn.

Crime   **(PR:C MPAA:NR)**

SIDE STREET ANGEL**½   (1937, Brit.) 63m WB-FN bw

Hugh Williams (*Peter*), Lesley Brook (*Anne*), Henry Kendall (*Boscomb*), Reginald Purdell (*McGill*), Phyllis Stanley (*Laura*), Madeleine Seymour (*Mrs. Kane*), Edna Davies (*Loretta*).

Goofy comedy starring Williams as a rich society boy who, after being embarrassed by his fiancee at a party, runs off into the seedier areas of town where he meets an ex-convict. Thinking that Williams is a classy thief, the crook takes the society beau to a hostel for reformed crooks, run by Brook. There are romantic rumblings between Williams and Brook, but before anything can get started he finds himself being dragged off to do a job by the ex-con and his gang. Luckily, Williams is saved by Brook before things go too far and he gratefully buys the hostel so that she may continue her work without fear of financial ruin. The lead performances are engaging enough to sustain the silly material.

p, Irving Asher; d, Ralph Ince; ph, Basil Emmott.

Comedy   (PR:A   MPAA:NR)

SIDE STREETS**   (1934) 63M WB-FN bw (GB: A WOMAN IN HER
                                                                            THIRTIES)

Aline MacMahon (*Bertha Krasnoff*), Paul Kelly (*Tim O'Hara*), Ann Dvorak (*Marguerite Gilbert*), Helen Lowell (*Tillie*), Dorothy Tree (*Ilka*), Henry O'Neill (*George*), Marjorie Gateson (*Mrs. Thatcher*), Mayo Methot (*Maizie*), Renee Whitney (*Mabel*), Lynn Browning (*Madeline*), Lorena Layson (*Helen*), Dorothy Peterson (*Mrs. Richards*), Clay Clement (*Jack*), Paul Kaye (*Ray*).

MacMahon is a San Francisco businesswoman who meets Kelly, a derelict sailor. She gives him a job in her shop and finally ends up marrying him. But their life is disrupted when women from Kelly's past stop by the shop, one of whom brings along a child he fathered. MacMahon and Kelly adopt the kid and also have one of their own. If that's not enough, MacMahon's sister wants to run off with Kelly, but–redeemed by fatherhood–he decides to stay with his wife. Turgid little soaper with a poor script that was short in the believability department. The acting is all right considering what the actors have to deal with.

p, Sam Bischoff; d, Alfred E. Green; w, Manuel Seff (based on the story "Fur Coats" by Ann Garrick, Ethel Rill); ph, Byron Haskin; ed, Herbert Levy; art d, Anton Grot; cos, Orry-Kelly.

Drama   (PR:A   MPAA:NR)

SIDECAR RACERS*   (1975, Aus.) 100m UNIV c

Ben Murphy (*Jeff Rayburn*), Wendy Hughes (*Lynn Carson*), John Clayton (*Dave Ferguson*), John Derum (*Pete McAllister*), Peter Graves (*Carson*), John Meillon (*Ocker Harvey*), Peter Gwynne (*Rick Horton*), Serge Lazareff (*Bluey Wilson*), Paul Bertram (*Bob Horton*), Patrick Ward (*Tex Wilson*), Arna Maria Winchester (*Marlene*), Vicki Raymond (*Virginia*), Kevin Healy (*Store Manager*), Brian Anderson (*Store Detective*), Brenda Senders (*Mrs. Horton*), Liddy Clark (*Cashier*), Bryan Niland (*Ambulance Man*), Loretta Saul (*Girl Singer*).

Murphy is an American motorcyclist drifting around Australia who ends up sidecar racing with partner Clayton. The two vie for the attentions of Hughes amid the endless racing footage. Graves makes a brief cameo appearance as Murphy's wealthy pop. This is a ridiculous and boring piece, about ten years past its time. The characters are cardboard cutouts trapped in a dull, lifeless screenplay and routine, uninspired direction. It was aimed right at the heart of a teenage audience in what was supposed to be a new program designed to bring film production to Australia. In a few short years the dream would come to fruition with a myriad of fine films and directors while moldy, rip-off junk like SIDECAR RACERS was properly forgotten.

p, Richard Irving; d, Earl Bellamy; w, Jon Cleary; ph, Paul Onorato (Eastmancolor); m, Tom Scott; ed, Robert L. Kimble.

Sports Drama   (PR:A   MPAA:PG)

SIDEHACKERS, THE   (SEE: FIVE THE HARD WAY, 1969)

SIDELONG GLANCES OF A PIGEON KICKER, THE**
         (1970) 106m Saturn Pictures/MGM-Plaz a c (AKA: PIGEONS)

Jordan Christopher (*Jonathan*), Jill O'Hara (*Jennifer*), Robert Walden (*Winslow Smith*), Kate Reid (*Jonathan's Mother*), William Redfield (*Jonathan's Father*), Lois Nettleton (*Mildred*), Boni Enten (*Naomi*), Elaine Stritch (*Tough Lady*), Melba Moore (*Model at Party*), Peter Link [Riggs O'Hara] (*Oliver*), Kristoffer Tabori (*Oliver's Boy Friend*), Don Warfield (*Young Stutterer*), Jean Shevlin (*Mrs. Abelman*), Matt Warner (*Mr. Abelman*), Ethel Smith (*Blowsy Lady at Pinball Machine*), Mary Orr (*Saleslady*), Nancy Andrews (*Passenger with Crying Child*), Tony Capodilupo (*Van Man*), Christian Ericson (*Gordon*), Maria Cellario (*Pretty Girl in Laundromat*), Pat Ast (*Fat Lady at Party*), Sara Wilson (*Lesbian at Party*), Helen Ludlam (*Old Lady on Train*), Paul Norman (*Orderly*), Richard Clarke (*Englishman*), Janet Maria Burtis (*Cranky Lady Passenger*), Bert Bertram (*Doorman*), Ellis Richardson, Buddy Butler (*Negro Passersby*), Adam Reed (*Little Redhaired*

Boy), Sean Campbell (*Boy on Crutches*), Margaret Brewster (*Pigeon Lady*), Arthur Anderson (*Floorwalker*), Steve Dawson (*Desk Sergeant*), Bonnie Paul (*Crying Girl*), Bill Herndon (*Cop at the Pier*), Anne Shropshire (*Mother at Department Store*), Esther Bussler (*Christmas Shopper in Cab*), Salo Douday (*Sad Bum*), Frank Hamilton (*Gallstone Man in Hospital*), Wyman Pendleton (*Doctor*), David Doyle (*Mr. Seigbert*), Edward Dunne (*Skinny Fag*), Sean Bersell (*Little Boy in Cab*).

Though a Princeton graduate, Christopher finds himself disgusted with the rat race, so three years after graduation he's perfectly content driving a cab in Manhattan. He insults his obnoxious passengers and acts out his various frustrations by kicking pigeons in the park. Of course such a rebellious type naturally has an assortment of oddball friends. Christopher's cohorts include a leather-outfitted, twenty-four year old virgin motorcyclist (Walden); Link, a gay interior decorator who comes on to male guests at the parties he throws; and O'Hara, a middle-class girl who's out "finding herself". She's Christopher's neighbor, and her bold philosophical experiment is being financed by none other than her parents. While at one of Link's mad affairs Christopher is attacked by Enten, a former lover. She drags him into the bathroom (complete with a dada-style fur-lined tub) and removes her clothing, inviting Christopher to do the same. He declines the offer and goes home, stopping off to visit O'Hara. Though he likes her, Christopher tries to explain to his neighbor that their relationship should stay at some emotional distance–but the two are soon in bed. Christmas comes and he brings her to his parents' suburban home in Connecticut. His mother catches them in bed and after a fight at a Christmas party Christopher and O'Hara return to New York. Christopher finds himself becoming quite confused. He really is attached to O'Hara but isn't ready for marriage. He becomes distanced and uncaring towards his friends but is surprised by finding O'Hara in bed with Walden one night. Overcome with emotion he jumps in his cab and goes out driving aimlessly, eventually ending up driving into the river. He's rescued and put into the hospital where O'Hara comes to visit him. She claims to love him and wants another chance. But Christopher will have none of this. When the time is right he sneaks out of the hospital and heads out to Des Moines, Iowa where he intends to take up truck driving. This is one of those "lovable arrested adolescent" films, told in a stagy, pseudo-hipster style. It wanders around the aimless plot, occasionally showing moments of good biting wit, but mostly suffers from pretentiousness. Christopher does a fair job with the role but he's hardly an attractive character, giving the audience little with which to sympathize. The characters lean heavily towards stereotyped caricatures (Christopher could easily be a partly grown-up version of Holden Caulfield) but O'Hara comes through with some honesty as the girl friend. SIDELONG GLANCES...is not a bad film really; it doesn't know what it wants to say or how to say it, but somehow tries to get a message across anyway. After its initial release by MGM the studio sold the rights to Plaza Pictures which shortened both title and running time (to PIGEONS and 87 minutes respectively) for their release of the film. Songs include "Freedom Song" and "Faces of You" (sung by Warren Marley; played by Gasmask and Great Jones).

p, Richard Lewis; d, John Dexter; w, Ron Whyte (based on the novel *The Sidelong Glances of a Pigeon Kicker* by David Boyer); ph, Urs Furrer (Movielab Color); m, Pat Williams, Lee Holdridge, Edd Kaleroff, Chris Dedrick, Warren Marley; ed, John Oettinger; md, Phillip Ramone; art d, Manny Gerard; set d, Bob Drumheller; cos, Domingo Rodriguez; makeup, John Alese.

Comedy   (PR:O   MPAA:R)

SIDESHOW**   (1950) 67m MON bw

Don McGuire (*Steve Arthur*), Tracey Roberts (*Dolly Jordan*), John Abbott (*Pierre*), Eddie Quillan (*Big Top*), Ray Walker (*Sam Owen*), Richard Foote (*Deke*), Jimmy Conlin (*Johnny*), Iris Adrian (*Nellie*), Ted Hecht (*Willie*), Stephen Chase (*McGregor*), Donald Kerr (*Barker*), Frank Fenton (*Manson*), Kathy Johnson (*Child*), Jack Ingram (*Dave*), Dale Van Sickel (*Miller*).

Some gem thieves, led by Abbott and Walker, use a carnival sideshow as their front. McGuire is the Treasury man who goes undercover as a carny handyman in order to ferret out the thieves. Roberts is a cooch dancer who helps him out. The film ends with a climactic chase through a wax museum leading to the roller coaster, where Walker plunges to his death. The script is a confusing mess, hampered by some choppy editing. The direction does what it can but is ultimately hampered by the film's low budget. The performers are fine for the fare. Leading-man McGuire gave up his acting career the year following the release of this one to become a director/writer; his writing credits include BAD DAY AT BLACK ROCK (1954). This appears to be actress Roberts' first leading role; most research sources suggest that her screen career started two years after this film's release.

p, William F. Broidy; d, Jean Yarbrough; w, Sam Roeca (based on a story by Broidy); ph, William Sickner; ed, Ace Herman; md, Edward Kay; art d, Dave Milton.

Crime   (PR:C   MPAA:NR)

SIDEWALKS OF LONDON***   (1940, Brit.) 84m Mayflower/PAR bw
                                    (GB: ST. MARTIN'S LAN E)

Charles Laughton (*Charles Saggers*), Vivien Leigh (*Libby*), Rex Harrison (*Harley Prentiss*), Larry Adler (*Constantine*), Tyrone Guthrie (*Gentry*), Gus McNaughton (*Arthur Smith*), Bart Cormack (*Strang*), Edward Lexy (*Mr. Such*), Maire O'Neill (*Mrs. Such*), Basil Gill (*Magistrate*), Claire Greet (*Old Maud*), David Burns (*Hackett*), Cyril Smith (*Blackface*), Ronald Ward (*Temperley*), Romilly Lunge (*Duchesi*), Helen Haye (*Lady Selina*), Phyllis Stanley (*Della Fordingbridge*), Jerry Verno (*Drunk*), Polly Ward (*Frankie*), Alf Goddard (*Doggie*), Carroll Gibbons and His Orchestra, The Luna Boys.

Laughton plays a busker (a London street entertainer) who meets up with a gamin, Leigh. She engages in minor theft to keep herself alive but Laughton–after he catches her stealing from songwriter Harrison– takes pity on her and makes Leigh part of his act. She gets spotted performing by Harrison and is vaulted to fame in the British music hall. But she can't forget Laughton's help and seeks out the man who saved her. She wants to help him get into the big time as well but Laughton declines her offer. The busker's life is the life for him] (In his classical study *London Labour and the London Poor* of the mid-1900s, Henry Mayhew quoted one such street performer: "We can never stand being confined to hard work, after being used to the freedom of the streets. None of us saves money; it goes either in a lump, if we get a lump, or in dribs and drabs, which is the way it mostly comes to us. I've known several in my day who have died in St. Giles's workhouse. In old age or sickness we've nothing but the parish to look to.") Utter froth all whipped up in a sweet little comedy that plays quite nicely. Laughton is a delight, as is Leigh. Her love interest is played by the then minor actor Harrison, who is quite a stand-out. The film accurately captures the gaiety of London street life and the direction carries the story along nicely, carefully drawing out characters as well. This film was acquired by Paramount for American distribution in 1939. However with the success Leigh had with GONE WITH THE WIND in that year for MGM, the studio wisely held it back and then released THE SIDEWALKS OF LONDON on the crest of her new fame. Laughton was already well-known in the U.S., where he had starred in several films. The supporting cast is wonderful. Famed legitimate-stage producer/director Guthrie makes a rare film appearance as one of Laughton's busker partners.

p, Eric Pommer; d, Tim Whelan; w, Clemence Dane (based on her story "St. Martin's Lane"); ph, Jules Kruger; m, Arthur Johnson; ed, Hugh Stewart, Robert Hamer; md, Muir Mathieson; ch, Philip Buchel; m/l, Johnson, Eddie Pola.

Comedy   **Cas.**   **(PR:AA   MPAA:NR)**

SIDEWALKS OF NEW YORK**   (1931) 70m MGM bw

Buster Keaton (*Harmon*), Anita Page (*Margie*), Cliff Edwards (*Poggie*), Frank Rowan (*Butch*), Norman Phillips, Jr (*Clipper*), Frank LaRue (*Sergeant*), Oscar Apfel (*Judge*), Syd Saylor (*Mulvaney*), Clark Marshall (*Lefty*).

Simplistic comedy features Keaton as a wealthy apartment building owner. Though a rich playboy, Keaton falls for one of his tenement residents, played by Page. Keaton, a silent genius, muddles through this early talkie with little success. The story was cooked up by no less than four writers; the two directors had previously done short canine comedies. (White would go on to work with the vastly overrated Three Stooges.) Keaton's problem was creative frustration compounded by alcohol. He was a victim of the new technology of sound and of studio executives who didn't understand their star. Stripped of creative freedom and control, Keaton's downward spiral began here, a plunge from which he never completely recovered. Fortunately, his silent work was recognized for the art it was shortly before his death, and Keaton was able to see a revival of his comedy classics revered by an entire new generation of filmgoers. Had he been allowed to continue working silent–as Chaplin did–Keaton could have produced an astounding body of work in the 1930s.

p, Lawrence Weingarten; d, Jules White, Zion Myers; w, George Landy, Paul Gerard Smith, Eric Hatch, Robert E. Hopkins; ph, Leonard Smith; ed, Charles Hochberg.

Comedy   **(PR:AAA   MPAA:NR)**

SIDEWINDER ONE*   (1977) 96m Ibex/AE c

Marjoe Gortner (*Digger*), Michael Parks (*J.W. Wyatt*), Susan Howard (*Chris Gentry*), Alex Cord (*Packard Gentry*), Charlotte Rae (*Mrs. Holt*), Barry Livingston (*Willie Holt*), Bill Vint (*Jerry Fleming*), Byron Morrow (*Gentry Executive*), Sue Ann Carpenter.

Parks is a motorcycle cross-country racer who somehow gets romantically involved with rich, snooty motorcycle heiress Howard. Gortner is the man who helps smooth out the lumpy romance. That's it for plot in what is really just an excuse to film lots of motorcycle racing action. Lots of shots are used time and time again and the film never really goes anywhere. The acting is what you'd expect, though Gortner–the former baby evangelist and subject of a fascinating documentary–gives his part some real energy.

p, Elmo Williams; d, Earl Bellamy; w, Nancy Voyles Crawford, Thomas A. McMahon; ph, Dennis Dalzell (DeLuxe Color); m, Mundell Lowe; ed, Frank Bracht; md, Lowe; art d, Tracy, Liz Bousman; set d, Ray Paul; cos,

Bernadene Mann; spec eff, Cliff Wenger; stunts, Gary Davis; makeup, Wes Dawn.

Drama   **(PR:C   MPAA:PG)**

SIDNEY SHELDON'S BLOODLINE   (SEE: BLOODLINE, 1979)

SIEGE***   (1983, Can.) 83m Salter/Summa Vista c

Doug Lennox (*Cube*), Tom Nardini (*Horatio*), Brenda Bazinet (*Barbara*), Darel Haney (*Chester*), Terry-David (*Daniel*), Jeff Pustil (*Goose*), Jack Blum (*Patrick*), Keith Knight (*Steve*), Brad Wadden (*Ian*), Gary Dempster (*Lloyd*), Dennis O'Connor, Rick Collins, Dug Rotstein, Ted Germaine, Barbara Jones, Patricia Vroom, Alan MacGillivray, Kevin Jollimore, John D'Arte, Glen Wadman, Carolyn van Gurp, Blaine Hensaw.

A vigilante right-wing group called the "New Order" goes to a gay bar called The Crypt. After the group wreaks havoc on the patrons, Despres escapes and holes up in Nardini's apartment. The New Order follows after it executes several Crypt patrons, and tries to take over the building. But this time the victims are ready and a non-stop barrage begins. Set during a Nova Scotia police strike, this has echoes of ASSAULT ON PRECINCT 13, though it's not quite as effective. This is not to say, however, that SIEGE is a bad film. The direction takes a slightly far-fetched premise and works it into a powerful action film. Moments are stretched for the maximum amount of suspense possible, with some fine camera work highlighting the onslaught. Though the opening is slow, once SIEGE gets going it never stops. It is an effective and frightening piece of filmmaking.

p, Michael Donovan, John Walsch, Maura O'Connell, Paul Donovan; d, P. Donovan, O'Connell; w, P. Donovan (based on an idea by Marc Vautour); ph, Les Krizsan (Eastmancolor); m, Peter Jermyn, Drew King; ed, Ian McBride; prod d, Malachi Salter.

Crime   **(PR:O   MPAA:NR)**

SIEGE AT RED RIVER, THE***   (1954) 86m Panoramic/FOX c (AKA:
                                    THE SIEGE OF RED RIVER)

Van Johnson (*Jim Farraday*), Joanne Dru (*Nora Curtis*), Richard Boone (*Brett Manning*), Milburn Stone (*Benjy*), Jeff Morrow (*Frank Kelso*), Craig Hill (*Lt. Braden*), Rico Alaniz (*Chief Yellow Hawk*), Robert Burton (*Sheriff*), Pilar Del Rey (*Lukoa*), Ferris Taylor (*Anderson Smith*), John Cliff (*Sgt. Jenkins*).

It is close to the end of the Civil War, and Johnson and his partner Stone are Confederate officers who smuggle Union Army guns via a Medicine Show wagon. On the way back to camp they run across Dru, a Yankee nurse whose wagon has broken down. They offer her a lift and are confronted by Boone, who steals the guns and sells them to Shawnee Indians for their attack on a Union fort. Morrow, a Pinkerton detective, and Union man Hill arrest Johnson, who helps them defend the Shawnee and retrieve the guns. They decide to let him go since he did help and the war is nearly over as well. Johnson heads south but promises Dru he will return for her. Though the story is routine, this is a fairly good programmer western, punched up with some exciting direction. The color photography is used with good effect, especially at the climax, and interesting camera angles are used. The ending here is almost lifted directly from the 1944 film BUFFALO BILL, but works as an exciting finish anyway. Johnson and Stone provide funny moments in their rendition of "Tapioka."

p, Leonard Goldstein; d, Rudolph Mate; w, Sydney Boehm (based on a story by J. Robert Bren, Gladys Atwater); ph, Edward Cronjager (Technicolor); m, Lionel Newman; ed, Betty Steinberg; cos, Renie, Charles LeMaire.

Western   **(PR:C   MPAA:NR)**

SIEGE OF FORT BISMARK½**   (1968, Jap.) 98m Toho c (CHINTAO
                                    YOSAI BAKUGEKI MEIR EI)

Makoto Sato, Yosuke Natsuki, Yuzo Kayama, Ryo Ikebe, Mie Hama, Toru Ibuki.

German forces build a fort in Japan shortly before the beginning of WW I. Their aim is to protect their colonial interests in the Far East. When the Japanese join up with the Allied forces, one of their immediate goals is to capture the German fort. Two biplanes purchased from France, which constitute the entire Japanese air force, encounter a German aircraft. But in the ensuing confusion, no pictures are taken. After another flight, little damage is done, but a Japanese plane is shot down. The Japanese Navy conducts an all-out attack and the remaining biplane, equipped with a bomb, successfully destroys a train loaded with supplies for the fort.

p, Tamoyuki Tanaka; d, Kengo Furusawa; w, Katsuya Suzaki; ph, Fukuzo Koizumi (Tohoscope, Eastmancolor); m, Hachiro Matsui; spec eff, Eiji Tsuburaya.

War   **(PR:C-O   MPAA:NR)**

SIEGE OF HELL STREET, THE (SEE: SIEGE OF SIDNEY STREET, THE, 1960, Brit.)

SIEGE OF PINCHGUT (SEE: FOUR DESPERATE MEN, 1960, Aus.)

SIEGE OF RED RIVER, THE   (SEE: SIEGE AT RED RIVER THE, 1954)

SIEGE OF SIDNEY STREET, THE**½   (1960, Brit.) 93m Mid-Century/United Producers bw (AKA: THE SIEGE OF HELL STREET)

Donald Sinden (*Inspector John Mannering*), Nicole Berger (*Sara*), Kieron Moore (*Yoska*), Peter Wyngarde (*Peter the Painter*), Godfrey Quigley (*Blakey*), Angela Newman (*Nina*), T.P. McKenna (*Lapidos*), Maurice Good (*Gardstein*), James Caffrey (*Hefeld*), Harold Goldblatt (*Hersh*), Christopher Casson (*Police Commissioner*), Harry Brogan (*Old Harry*), Alan Simpson (*Police Inspector*), Robert Lepler (*Jeweler*), Margaret D'Arcy (*Nurse*), Joe Lynch (*Sgt. Todd*), Stanley Illsley (*Doctor*), Anne Sharpe (*Woman on Estate*), Bart Bastable (*Sgt. Tucker*), Paul Farrell (*Barman*), Bill Foley (*1st Detective*), Aiden Grennell (*2nd Detective*), Jimmy Sangster (*Winston Churchill*), Leonard Sachs (*Svaars*), Tutte Lemkow (*Dmiitrieff*), George Pastell (*Brodsky*).

A gang of Russian anarchists is holed up in London in 1911. They are headed by Wyngarde, a silent but utterly ruthless man who has the gang commit robbery and murder to finance its political activities. Berger is an orphaned young Russian girl, alone in the city. She sings at a club and meets Wyngarde there one night. Though attracted to him, she finds his murderous activities repugnant. Wyngarde justifies his gang's actions by claiming the group is fighting political oppression. Sinden is the police inspector after the gang. He goes underground and comes to understand Berger and why she is so drawn to the anarchist cause. The gang's savage acts continue and, on Jan. 3, 1911, the police surround its hideout on Sidney Street and stage a raid. Though based on true events, this is a heavily fictionalized story. The story is laid out matter-of-factly, making it too pedestrian and not very interesting. The politics are watered down heavily, making the anarchists resemble simple thieves. The acting isn't bad, however, and the final sequence makes up for the rather straightforward handling of the rest of the film.

p&d, Robert S. Baker, Monty Berman; w, Jimmy Sangster, Alexander Baron (based on a story by Sangster); ph, Baker, Berman (Dyaliscope); m, Stanley Black; ed, Baker, Berman, Peter Bezencenet; md, Black; art d, William Kellner; set d, Freda Pearson; spec eff, Cliff Richardson; m/l, "Ya Vas Lyu-Blyu," David Palmer, Robert Musel, Black (sung by Nicole Berger); makeup, Jill Carpenter.

Drama   **(PR:O MPAA:NR)**

SIEGE OF SYRACUSE** (1962, Fr./Ital.) 97m Glomer-Galatea-Societe Cinematographique Lyre/PAR c (L'ASSEDIO DI SIRACUSA; ARCHIMEDE; LE SIEGE DE SYRACUSE)

Rossano Brazzi (*Archimedes*), Tina Louise (*Diana*), Sylva Koscina (*Clio*), Enrico Maria Salerno (*Gorgia*), Gino Cervi (*Gerone*), Alberto Farnese, Luciano Marin, Alfredo Varelli.

Romans and Carthaginians are battling in the city of Syracuse and Brazzi has been given the defense strategies. When his lover, Louise, becomes pregnant, her evil stepbrother, Salerno takes the girl to a group of Roman soldiers. She goes into shock, loses her memory and ends up marrying a Roman consul. Meanwhile, Brazzi heeds his father's wishes and marries Koscina. A few years later Brazzi goes to Rome to arrange an alliance. He sees Louise, who regains her memory. For the sake of their son, they remain silent about their past. Once more the Romans attack Syracuse and, by using "burning glasses" to magnify the sun's rays, Brazzi deflects their fleets. Louise and Brazzi's spouses are killed, leaving the couple free to marry. They do so but agree to continue to keep their son's identity a secret.

p, Enzo Merolle; d, Pietro Francisci; w, Francisci, Giorgio Graziosi, Ennio De Concini; ph, Carlo Carlini (Dyaliscope, Eastmancolor); m, Angelo Francesco Lavagnino; art d, Ottavio Scotti.

Historical Drama   **(PR:C MPAA:NR)**

SIEGE OF THE SAXONS**½   (1963, Brit.) 85m Ameran/COL c

Ronald Lewis (*Robert Marshall*), Janette Scott (*Katherine*), Ronald Howard (*Edmund of Cornwall*), Mark Dignam (*King Arthur*), John Laurie (*Merlin*), Jerome Willis (*Limping Man*), Richard Clarke (*Saxon Prince*), Charles Lloyd Pack (*Doctor*), Francis De Wolff (*Blacksmith*), John Gabriel (*Earl of Chatham*), Peter Mason (*Young Monk*), Michael Mellinger (*Thief*), Gordon Boyd (*Captain*), Robert Gillespie, Kenneth Cowan (*Soldiers*).

Dignam, the noted King of Camelot, becomes ill during his 20th year on the throne and heads off to Howard's castle to recover. Unbeknown to Dignam, Howard is involved with the Saxons, a group that wants to overthrow the King and kill him. Lewis, a Robin Hood-type outlaw, stops them from killing Dignam but they eventually succeed. Howard tries to complete his takeover

by marrying the King's daughter, Scott, but she runs off with Lewis. Howard announces that Scott has died, and that he is now King. Meanwhile, Lewis and Scott seek out the ancient wizard Merlin, played by Laurie. Together they form a trio that interrupts Howard's coronation, after which Laurie challenges Howard to remove the King's sword Excalibur from its scabbard. He fails, but Scott succeeds and becomes the rightful heir to the throne. Howard runs off with the Saxons, but all of the English armies unite to crush the rebellion, leaving Scott free to rule in peace. She knights Lewis and all ends happily. SIEGE OF THE SAXONS freely mixes the legends of Arthur, Robin Hood, and comic book esthetics in this cliche-ridden but fun film version of an oft told story. The direction is effective, and the acting is well-done.

p, Jud Kinberg; d, Nathan Juran; w, Kinberg, John Kohn; ph, Wilkie Cooper, Jack Mills (Technicolor); m, Laurie Johnson; ed, Maurice Rootes; art d, Bill Constable.

Historical Adventure   **(PR:A MPAA:NR)**

SIERRA*½   (1950) 83m UNIV c

Wanda Hendrix (*Riley Martin*), Audie Murphy (*Ring Hassard*), Burl Ives (*Lonesome*), Dean Jagger (*Jeff Hassard*), Richard Rober (*Big Matt*), Anthony [Tony] Curtis (*Brent Coulter*), Houseley Stevenson (*Sam Coulter*), Elliott Reid (*Duke Lafferty*), Griff Barnett (*Dr. Robbins*), Elisabeth Risdon (*Aunt Susan*), Roy Roberts (*Sheriff Knudson*), Gregg Martell (*Hogan*), Sara Allgood (*Mrs. Jonas*), Erskine Sanford (*Judge Prentiss*), John Doucette (*Jed Coulter*), Jim Arness (*Little Sam*), Ted Jordan (*Jim Coulter*), I. Stanford Jolley (*Snake Willens*), Jack Ingram (*Al*).

After Jagger is wrongly accused of a crime, he heads for the hills with his son, Murphy. The two hole up in a secret lair, but are eventually proven innocent when Hendrix, Jagger's lawyer (and at one time off-screen wife), stumbles onto the hideout. She discloses that a member of the posse chasing Jagger confessed before he died. Despite some nice color photography, this routine western was lowered several notches thanks to the flat direction and endless string of cliches. Murphy's portrayal is uninspired. Watch for Curtis (then known as Anthony) in a minor role. A remake of FORBIDDEN VALLEY (1938).

p, Michel Kraike; d, Alfred E. Green; w, Edna Anhalt, Milton Gunzburg (based on the novel by Stuart Hardy); ph, Russell Metty (Technicolor); m, Walter Scharf; ed, Ted J. Kent; art d, Bernard Herzbrun, Robert F. Boyle; cos, Yvonne Wood; m/l, Frederick Herbert, Arnold Hughes, Burl Ives.

Western   **(PR:A MPAA:NR)**

SIERRA BARON**½   (1958) 80m FOX c

Brian Keith (*Jack McCracken*), Rick Jason (*Miguel Delmonte*), Rita Gam (*Felicia Delmonte*), Mala Powers (*Sue Russell*), Steve Brodie (*Rufus Bynum*), Carlos Muzquiz (*Andrews*), Lee Morgan (*Frank Goheen*), Allan Lewis (*Hank Moe*), Pedro Galvan (*Judson Jeffers*), Fernando Wagner (*Grandall*), Enrique Lucero (*Anselmo*), Alberto Mariscal (*Lopez*), Lynne Ehrlich (*Vicky Russell*), Michael Schmidt (*Ralph*), Tommy Riste (*Ralph's Father*), Reed Howes (*Sheriff*), Robin Glattley (*Baker*), Enrique Inigo (*Assayer*), Faith Ferry (*Young Sue*), Doris Contreras (*Young Felicia*), Marc Lambert (*Cart Driver*), Stillman Segar (*Butcher*), Alicia del Lago (*Juanita*), Jose Trowe (*Major-domo*), Lolla Davila (*Emmy*), Ricardo Adalid (*1st Playboy*), Roy Fletcher (*2nd Playboy*), John Courier (*Express Rider*), Mark Zachary (*1st Miner*), Paul Arnett (*2nd Miner*), Bob Janis (*Henchman*), Armando Saenz (*Eduardo*), Ferrusquilla [Jose Espinoza] (*Felipe*).

It is 1848 and the setting is the California territory. Jason owns a large parcel of land that is part of a Spanish land grant. Americans from the East, led by Brodie, try to take over. They bring in a gunslinger from Texas, Keith to scare Jason, and Keith ends up falling in love with Jason's sister, Gam. But a gun battle claims Keith's life and shatters Gam's dreams. This better-than-average western features marvelous color photography in Mexican settings. Though the story was set in California, the producers felt compelled to head south for the proper look, and the results were excellent. Despite good acting, this stood as a good-looking routine western of only programmer status.

p, Plato A. Skouras; d, James B. Clark; w, Houston Branch (based on the novel by Thomas Wakefield Blackburn); ph, Alex Phillips (Cinema Scope, Deluxe Color); m, Paul Sawtell, Bert Shefter; ed, Frank Baldridge; art d, John Mansbridge; cos, Georgette Somohano.

Western   **(PR:A MPAA:NR)**

SIERRA DE TERUEL   (SEE: MAN'S HOPE, 1947, Span.)

SIERRA PASSAGE**   (1951) 81m MON bw

Wayne Morris (*Johnny Yorke*), Lola Albright (*Ann*), Alan Hale, Jr (*Yance*), Roland Winters (*Sam*), Lloyd Corrigan (*Thad King*), Jim Bannon (*Jud Yorke*), Billy Grey (*Young Johnny Yorke*), Paul McGuire (*Andy*), Richard Karlan (*Bart*), George Eldredge (*Sheriff*).

Hale shoots a man, leaving the dead man's son an orphan. The boy is raised by Winters and Corrigan, owners of a minstrel show. Upon reaching adulthood, the boy, Morris, becomes a talented sharpshooter for the show. But he has only one thought in mind: revenge for his father's death. Okay western though the minstrel show reflected racism at its Hollywood worst. Direction is well-paced and the cast performs adequately.

p, Lindsley Parsons; d, Frank McDonald; w, Warren D. Wandberg, Sam Roeca, Tom W. Blackburn; ph, William Sickner; m, Edward J. Kay; ed, Leonard W. Herman; md, Kay; art d, David Milton; m/l, "Down the Lane," Bobby Burns, George Howe, "Love is Magic," Charles Dixon, Max Goodwin, "Let's Break the Ice," Hugo Peretti, Herb Pine (all sung by Lola Albright).

Western   (PR:A   MPAA:NR)

SIERRA STRANGER*   (1957) 74m Acirema/COL bw

Howard Duff (Jess Collins), Gloria McGhee (Meg Anderson), Dick Foran (Bert Gaines), John Hoyt (Sheriff), Barton MacLane (Lem Gotch), George E. Stone (Dan), Ed Kemmer (Sonny Grover), Robert Foulk (Tom Simmons), Eve McVeagh (Ruth Gaines), Henry "Bomber" Kulky (Matt), Byron Foulger (Claim Clerk).

When Kemmer is in trouble, Duff rescues him from a beating. Duff realizes he should have left well enough alone when the punk holds up a stagecoach and points his gun right at his rescuer. The direction is clumsy and takes the minor story nowhere. The script is convoluted and chock full of unneeded characters. The cast manages to do a fairly good job in spite of the script's many shortcomings. Look for Foran, a former singing cowboy star, in a secondary role.

p, Norman T. Herman; d, Lee Sholem; w, Richard J. Dorso; ph, Sam Leavitt; m, Alexander Courage; ed, Leon Barsha; md, Courage; art d, Ernst Fegte.

Western   (PR:C   MPAA:NR)

SIERRA SUE½   (1941) 64m REP bw

Gene Autry (Gene), Smiley Burnette (Frog), Fay McKenzie (Sue Larrabee), Frank M. Thomas (Stacy Bromfield), Robert E. Homans (Larabee), Earle Hodgins (Brandywine), Dorothy Christy (Verebel), Kermit Maynard (Jarvis), Jack Kirk (Sheriff), Eddie Dean (Jerry Willis), Budd Buster (Greg Travis), Rex Lease (Rancher), Hugh Prosser, Vince Barnett, Hal Price, Syd Saylor, Roy Butler, Sammy Stein, Eddie Cherkose, Bob McKenzie, Marin Sais, Bud Brown, Gene Eblen, Buel Bryant, Ray Davis, Art Dillard, Frankie Marvin, Champion the Horse.

In this modern-day western, Autry is cast as a government inspector investigating poisonous weed that's killing ranchers' cattle. The ranchers are upset and want to burn the area but Autry thinks a chemical spraying via airplane is in order. The head of the cattleman's association doesn't like the idea but finally gives in. He forgets about a hired gunman, who goes through with a plan to shoot the plane out of the sky. It explodes in a fiery crash, which sets off a cattle stampede. Somehow Autry works in the time for a couple of tunes as well. An okay outing for the cowpoke in one of his few modern-day story lines. Look for Dean, who later appeared in movies as a singing cowboy.

p, Harry Grey; d, William Morgan; w, Earl Felton, Julian Zimet; ph, Jack Marta; ed, Lester Orlebeck; m/l, J.B. Carey, Gene Autry, Fred Rose, Fleming Allan, Nelson Shawn.

Western   (PR:A   MPAA:NR)

SIETE HOMBRES DE ORO   (SEE: SEVEN GOLDEN MEN, 1966, Ital.)

SIGN OF AQUARIUS**   (1970) 95m Cinar c (AKA: LOVE COMMUNE; GHETTO FREAKS)

Paul Elliot, Gabe Lewis, Mickey Shiff, Jim Coursar, Nick Kleinholtz III, Toni Ceo, Virginia Morris.

After being arrested at a peace demonstration, a bunch of hippies go home to their communal apartment to plot their next course of action. At a club that night they watch as a mother comes to fetch her daughter away from the group, who she feels is an unhealthy influence. One of the hippies passes the girl a note with their address on it. After arriving home, one of the hippies has a bad LSD experience and hallucinates that she's giving birth to an enormous egg. The young girl arrives and tries some LSD herself. The next day the group goes to sell newspapers on the street. During the evening one hippie and the girl are accosted by a gangster who supplies drugs. His thugs beat the hippie when he refuses to become a dealer. After the next peace demonstration, the thugs wait in an alley for the hippies once more. They accidentally shoot the young girl. Solemnly the hippies take her body and parade it through the streets.

p, George B. Roberts, Paul Rubenstein; d, Robert J. Emery; w, Emery, John Pappas; ph, Rubenstein; md, Thomas Baker; ch, Jeff Kutash; m/l, "The Aquarians," "I'm Gonna Dodge the Draft," "Om Pax Om," Al Zbacnic, Baker.

Musical Drama   (PR:O   MPAA:R)

SIGN OF FOUR, THE½   (1932, Brit.) 63m Associated Talking Pictures/World Wide bw

Arthur Wontner (Sherlock Holmes), Isla Bevan (Mary Morstan), Ian Hunter (Dr. John H. Watson), Gilbert Davis (Athelney Jones), Graham [Ben] Soutten (Jonathan Small), Edgar Norfolk (Capt. Morstan), Herbert Lomas (Maj. John Sholto), Claire Greet (Mrs. Hudson), Miles Malleson (Thaddeus Sholto), Roy Emerton (Bailey), Togo (Tonga), Mr. Burnhett (Tattoo Artist), Kynaston Reeves (Bartholomew).

Hunter, as the famed sidekick of the equally famous detective, becomes enraptured with Bevan. She's a young girl, all alone in London after her father disappears. To compound her troubles a mysterious stranger has given her a lustrous pearl. Wontner first goes to the home of Lomas, "an oasis of art in the howling desert of South London" (supposedly a character in Conan Doyle's original story modeled after Oscar Wilde). Lomas is being given a hard time by a mysterious man as well, which leads Wontner on the trail of Soutten, a peg-legged crook with a Pygmy as an aide. The mystery wraps up in an exciting speedboat chase down the Thames River. Reaction to the second version of the popular Doyle story (there had also been a silent version) was mixed. At times the British accents were overpowering to American audiences, which caused the mystery to get more than a little confusing. But Wontner made up for that with his fine, witty performance as Holmes, his third time cast in the role probably his best. At the suggestion of producer Lee, Wontner picked up his pacing with excellent results. (Lee later went to Hollywood, where he became known for his dark, moody production techniques at Universal. He worked on SON OF FRANKENSTEIN and TOWER OF LONDON, both featuring Basil Rathbone, the best-known Sherlock Holmes.) Hunter was also a treat as Watson. He too joined up in the move to California, where he gained much acclaim as a character actor. (See SHERLOCK HOLMES series, Index.)

p, Rowland V. Lee; d, Graham Cutts; w, W.P. Lipscomb (based on the novel by Sir Arthur Conan Doyle); ph, Robert G. Martin, Robert De Grasse; ed, Otto Ludwig.

Mystery   (PR:C   MPAA:NR)

SIGN OF FOUR, THE*   (1983, Brit.) 100m Mapleton c

Ian Richardson (Sherlock Holmes), David Healy (Dr. Watson), Thorley Walters (Maj. John Sholto), Terence Rigby (Inspector Layton), Joe Melia (Jonathan Small), Cherie Lunghi (Mary Morstan), Michael O'Hogan (Mordecai Smith), John Pedrick (Tonga), Clive Merrison.

A boring, inept remake of the Holmes story. Richardson plays the famed sleuth without much heart, and Healy plays Watson as a buffoon. The two are after an ex-con with a wooden leg and cannibalistic midget. The production is amateurish and most of the acting is laughable. Surprisingly enough, the sets are quite detailed and have a good period look. It's a shame they were wasted on this nonsense. This premiered out of competition at the Cannes Film Festival as the first film in a new 13-part Holmes series. (See SHERLOCK HOLMES series, Index.)

p, Otto Plaschkes; d, Desmond Davis; w, Charles Pogue (based on the novel by Arthur Conan Doyle); m, Harry Rabinowitz; ph, Denis Lewiston; ed, Timothy Gee; art d, Eileen Diss, Fred Carter; cos, Julie Harris; spec eff, Alan Whibley; makeup, Tom Smith, John Webber.

Mystery   (PR:C   MPAA:NR)

SIGN OF THE CROSS, THE*½   (1932) 124m PAR bw

Frederic March (Marcus Superbus), Elissa Landi (Mercia), Claudette Colbert (Empress Poppaea), Charles Laughton (Emperor Nero), Ian Keith (Tigellinus, Head of the Praetorian Guard), Vivian Tobin (Dacia), Harry Beresford (Flavius), Ferdinand Gottschalk (Glabrio), Arthur Hohl (Titus), Joyzelle Joyner (Ancaria), Tommy Conlon (Stephan), Nat Pendleton (Strabo), Clarence Burton (Servillus), William V. Mong (Licinius), Harold Healy (Tibul), Richard Alexander (Viturius), Robert Manning (Philodemus), Charles Middleton (Tyros), Joe Bonomo (Mute Giant), Kent Taylor (A Lover), John Carradine (Leader of Gladiators/Christian), Lane Chandler (Christian in Chains), Ethel Wales (Complaining Wife), Lionel Belmore (Bettor), Angelo Rossitto (Pygmy), Lillian Leighton, Otto Lederer, Wilfred Lucas, Jerome Storm, Florence Turner, Gertrude Norman, Horace B. Carpenter, Carol Holloway, Ynez Seabury, Henry Kleinbach 'Brandon'.

This florid spectacle of ancient and decadent Rome was the meat upon which epic-maker DeMille could gnaw with wild delight. It had everything his flesh-pleasuring eye could behold: beautiful virgins panting after lusty Roman soldiers, a nutcase emperor, a sluttish empress, and endless Christians to feed to starving lions. The story is relatively simple. March, the handsome, dashing Prefect of Rome, spots the ravishingly beautiful Landi and desires her, but his carnal ambitions are dashed when he discovers she is a Christian and will have nothing to do with his pagan ways. To humiliate Landi, March orders her to live with Joyner, a notorious lesbian, but Joyner has no more luck in wooing Landi than had March. Colbert, the vampy, trampy wife of the certifiably insane Laughton, playing Nero, is enamored of March and, between taking baths in the milk of asses, the sultry, slinky empress busies herself trying to seduce the noble prefect who can only think of the virginal Landi. Meanwhile, Laughton decides he wants a new Rome and the fastest way to get it is to burn down the old city without bothering to tell its occupants. He sets fire to the city and then, when all Rome begins to turn against him, he blames the Christians for the deadly conflagration. The Christians, Landi included, are rounded up and all are condemned to horrible deaths in the arena; they are to be eaten by flesh-craving lions. When March learns that the pure-of-heart Landy has been captured and sentenced to death, he appeals to Laughton to free her. The cuckoo emperor wavers, but as he thinks it over his sexy wife Colbert begins to persuade him to hold back his reprieve from Landi. This she does to spite March, who has scorned her love, and Colbert is persuasive, convincing the girthsome Laughton that he should uphold his thumbs down on the pretty Christian. When March realizes that there is no hope for Landi he joins her in the dungeons where the Christians wait to be led into the arena and to death. There he vows his love for her and states that her faith is so strong and sincere that he is willing to follow her with eternal love into the regions of death. He and Landi go arm and arm into the arena as the final scene dissolves. THE SIGN OF THE CROSS saw DeMille at his best in managing enormous crowd scenes and engineering his superb cast through sumptuous sets that reeked of authenticity, DeMille personally selecting every prop on camera and certifying it acceptable for the period he was portraying. March, with his wonderful presence and clear articulation, is impressive as the Roman who loses his heart to Landi and his body to the lions, while Landi is perfect as the virginal and ethereal Christian whose faith is stronger than any emperor. As Nero, Laughton, overweight and crawling about with only a mini-toga to cover his flabby body, is a spectacle unto himself. DeMille apparently allowed Laughton a free hand in the film, for the British actor devours each scene and would have consumed the entire film had it been on his menu. Laughton was never hammier than in THE SIGN OF THE CROSS but he is so outrageous as a swishy Nero, whose lisping words drip from a limp wrist, that he is fascinating to watch in a repulsive sort of way. (In an interview following the completion of the film, Laughton told newsmen: "Nero was nuts! I played him straight.") Colbert is lusciously sinful in this film, the precursor to her famous CLEOPATRA, one which allows her to wear the skimpiest of costumes while displaying as much of her curvacious body as the censors would permit, and that was a lot more than usual since this was a DeMille film and the great showman, in the name of historic epic, was given a wider moral latitude than any other director-producer of his era. In fact, since the silent days, when DeMille produced such classics as THE TEN COMMANDMENTS and KING OF KINGS, he was considered the unofficial guardian of public morality, at least when it came to filming anything to do with the Bible or ancient epochs. When DeMille decided to make THE SIGN OF THE CROSS, he went back to his old studio, Paramount, having deserted that studio for greener pastures years earlier. But DeMille's track record had been spotty in recent years and he had not had a hit film since his silent days. His most recent films at MGM–DYNAMITE, MADAM SATAN, and THE SQUAW MAN–had bombed at the box office and only Jesse Lasky, who had helped build Paramount from the beginning with DeMille and Adolph Zukor, wanted the showman back at the studio. DeMille was humiliated repeatedly by Zukor who insisted that he give him several promissory memos that guaranteed he would not make THE SIGN OF THE CROSS with his usual unlimited budget concepts. Head of production at Paramount B.P. Schulberg (father of author Budd Schulberg) backed DeMille but Zukor held out for the director's promise and finally DeMille said he would make the film for no more than $650,000 and he said it in writing. DeMille even arranged to finance some of this budget, and to show the mogul Zukor that he meant what he said, he took only a $450 salary during the production. Then, when the film was approved, Lasky was ousted and later Schulberg was driven from the Paramount hierarchy, leaving only Zukor whose relationship with DeMille was tenuous at best. Zukor thought DeMille was floundering when the director actually proposed to resurrect silent film stars to play the leading ladies of his new talking picture. DeMille thought about having the role of Poppaea, Nero's wife, played by either Norma Talmdadge or Pola Negri, both of these women long having faded from the public popularity. When he found himself without a sexy leading lady, DeMille became desperate and actually picked an actress who happened to be walking past the sound stage where he was working, Colbert. She accepted the role of the empress and gave a wonderful serpentine interpretation of the manipulative vixen. Laughton was cast early by DeMille, as was March. Landi, who was tested for the empress role and rejected, was brought back to play the role of the Christian girl. The tall, attractive Landi had been with Fox since 1930 and had arrived with great pomp in Hollywood, the daughter of Countess Zenardi Landi who claimed to be the illegitimate child of Empress Elizabeth of Austria. Hollywood was then in a craze about any kind of royalty and Landi became a star mostly due to her regal connections. THE SIGN OF THE CROSS was actually her biggest film and she would fade through the 1930s after her appearance in this DeMille extravaganza. DeMille brilliantly organized his 4,000-plus extras into groups of 10 (as he had been doing since his silent days) with an assistant director to correct details for each group. He put together eye-popping epic scenes. A scaled-down Rome was constructed on the Paramount ranch by hundreds of workmen and this was burned down within a few hours when flame was put to caches of gasoline appropriately placed throughout the miniature city. At the signal from DeMille the whole two-acre area was put to the torch and thousands of extras went screaming through the wild flame-engulfed scenes (DeMille audaciously filmed the entire scene, and many others, with a red gauze over his cameras, while filming nighttime scenes illuminated only by torches). The director had 16 different cameras record the burning of Rome sequence but he limited his crews to four cameras while shooting an almost naked Colbert in her famous bathing scene, here using real milk from asses (spouting into a giant pool from a spigot shaped like a human mouth, a lascivious-looking ornament that, among dozens of scenes in this provocative movie, brought down the wrath of the censors). Struss photographed Colbert for two days as she endlessly bathed in the milk, directed by DeMille to float almost breast high in the exotic bath (which he claimed to have researched as a genuine bath taken by the empress, his information coming from recently excavated Roman baths which revealed charts and blueprints found on the walls to support his re-creation). The problem in shooting this scene was that the milk turned to cheese and the bath set gave out such a foul smell that Colbert nearly fainted from it several times and technicians plugged up their noses in order to work next to DeMille, who was just beyond the pool directing every movement of the creamy-skinned Colbert, his sense of smell oblivious to the stench. For the arena scenes the director went all out, having a Roman Circus set built that seated 7,500 extras, an arena that spread over 90,000 feet. He looted a dozen zoos of elephants, lions, tigers, and bears. From carnivals and fairs he hired every kind of strange-looking human freak, and he was especially interested in showing giants and dwarves battling to the death as bizarre-looking gladiators in the arena. Like many another film epic set in ancient Rome, DeMille had a hard time getting the lions to attack even dummies stuffed with recently slaughtered lambs passing for Christians. They lazily roamed about the arena, occasionally lapping up some of the lambs' blood and then did nothing at all fierce, causing DeMille to do what he never did, phony up some of his lion shots by having men in lion's suits, shot at a far distance, crawl angrily and unconvincingly about, chewing on dummies stuffed with dead lambs. Inside of eight weeks, DeMille closed down his cameras, and he shut them off so abruptly as to startle his cast and crew. An assistant raced up to the director while he was right in the middle of some retakes and whispered, "We've just spent the last dime of our budget." DeMille shouted "cut!" and, in the middle of that take, the great showman walked off the set, dismissing everyone. He told his editor, Bauchens, to have the film in the can in a week and later showed a print to Zukor who was very impressed with THE SIGN OF THE CROSS. Yet there was one more big hurdle to jump over, that of the censor. The Hays Office objected to just about every scene in THE SIGN OF THE CROSS, the lesbians trying to bed Landi, the homosexual attendants lick-spittling at Laughton's feet, Laughton's own outlandish and decidedly homosexual performance, an orgy and a dance of almost naked slave girls before March, the lesbian dance before Landi, Colbert's semi-nude bath sequence, the incredible violence of the film. Even during the fire, March is shown whipping his chariot through the streets of burning Rome, trampling and running over those in the mob who get in his desperate way to save Landi. The scenes showing the eating of humans in the arena, chiefly Christians, aroused the wrath of the Catholic Church and several prelates complained to Paramount. DeMille, however, remained unflappable. He received a call from Will Hays who specifically objected to the orgiastic dance performed by the slave girls and demanded to know from DeMille what he was going to do about the lascivious dance. "Listen carefully, Will," replied DeMille, "because you might want to quote me. Not a damned thing." "Not a damned thing?" repeated the stunned Hays, whose power was almost absolute in Hollywood. "Not a damned thing," said DeMille, closing the conversation. He later explained to Hays when he calmed down: "How are you going to resist temptation if there isn't any? That's what the dance was all about and the heroine's rejection was a triumph of virtue." The director had just summarized his philosophy of making films and the reason why he got away with much more than anybody else when making them. He showed the battle of good and evil, and spirit was always shown to be victorious over flesh but not until all the flesh DeMille could assemble was shown in its most quivering, undulating glory. THE SIGN OF THE CROSS was an enormous success, combining DeMille's fractured view of history, with sex, nudity, arson, homosexuality, lesbianism, mass murder, and orgies big and small. It made millions for Paramount and re-established DeMille as a major force in filmmaking. Further, the film was well made. The public flocked to see it, spending as much as $1.50 per ticket, even at the nadir of the Great Depression, and thousands offered IOUs when the Bank Holiday occurred, offering to redeem the notes when the banks reopened. The notes were taken and redeemed.

p&d, Cecil B. DeMille; w, Waldemar Young, Sidney Buchman (based on the play by Wilson Barrett); ph, Karl Struss; m, Rudolph Kopp; ed, Anne Bauchens.

Historical Epic **(PR:C-O MPAA:NR)**

SIGN OF THE GLADIATOR* (1959, Fr./Ger./Ital.) 84m Glomer/AIP c (NEL SEGNO DI ROMA)

Anita Ekberg *(Zenobia, Queen of Palmyra)*, George Marshall [Georges Marchell] *(Marcus Valerius, Roman General)*, Folco Lulli *(Semanzio, Zenobia's Prime Minister)*, Chelo Alonso *(Erica, Slave Dancer)*, Jacques Sernas *(Julian)*, Lorella De Luca *(Bathsheba)*, Alberto Farnese *(Marcel)*, Mimo Palarmo *(Lator)*, Alfredo Varelli *(Ito)*, Sergio Sauro *(Tullius)*, Paul Muller *(Head Boy)*, Gino Cerv *(Emperor Aurelian)*.

Ekberg is cast as Queen of Palmyra in 217 A.D. Marshall is a general who is taken prisoner and feigns hatred of Rome to gain Ekberg's confidence. His soldiers take her prisoner but Marshall, who has fallen in love with her, gets her released. He tells the Senate Ekberg's misdeeds toward Rome were perpetrated by a counsellor, and the Romans buy it. This poorly dubbed epic, which runs a long 84 minutes, throws logic gleefully to the wind. Lots of scantily clad virgins and men in bedsheets, and really poor color photography. Screenwriter Leone became known in the 1960s as director of several successful spaghetti westerns starring Clint Eastwood.

p, Guido Brignone; d, Vittorio Musy Glori; w, Francesco De Feo, Antonio Thellung, Roberti Sergio Leone, Giuseppe Mangione; ph, Luciano Trasatti (Colorscope, Eastmancolor); m, Angelo-Francesco Lavagnino; ed, Giovanni Baragli md, Lavagnino; art d, Ottavio Scotti; ch, Claude Marchant.

Historical Drama   **(PR:C MPAA:NR)**

SIGN OF THE PAGAN*½   (1954) 91m UNIV c

Jeff Chandler (*Marcian*), Jack Palance (*Attila the Hun*), Ludmilla Tcherina (*Princess Pulcheria*), Rita Gam (*Kubra*), Jeff Morrow (*Paulinus*), Allison Hayes (*Ildico*), Eduard Franz (*Astrologer*), George Dolenz (*Theodosius*), Sara Shane (*Myra*), Alexander Scourby (*Chrysaphius*), Walter Coy (*Valentinian*), Pat Hogan (*Sangiban*), Howard Petrie (*Gundahar*), Michael Ansara (*Edecon*), Leo Gordon (*Bleda*), Rusty Wescoatt (*Tula*), Moroni Olsen (*Pope Leo*), Chuck Roberson (*Mirrai*), Charles Horvath (*Olt*), Robo Bechi (*Chilothe*), Sim Iness (*Herculanus*).

The well-known conquerer Attila the Hun is given the glossed-over Hollywood treatment in this highly fictionalized big budget bust. Palance plays the noted Hun as a neurotic, not-so-bad guy who's obsessed with Christ (the actual Attila was a cruel midget who died while making love). The humanized Hun is out to pillage Rome (how's that for humanistic behavior?) and centurion Chandler just can't convince emperor Dolenz to fight back. SIGN OF THE PAGAN is an overacted, overblown waste that is too ludicrous to be taken seriously. Too bad the filmmakers didn't concentrate on the real character of Attila the Hun–it could have been an interesting film. While Sirks' direction does result in some energetic moments, he was capable of far better work.

p, Albert J. Cohen; d, Douglas Sirk; w, Oscar Brodney, Barre Lyndon; ph, Russell Metty (CinemaScope, Technicolor); m, Frank Skinner, Hans J. Salter; ed, Milton Carruth, Al Clark; md, Joseph Gershenson; art d, Alexander Golitzen, Emrich Nicholson; set d, Russell A. Gausman, Oliver Emert; cos, Bill Thomas; ch, Kenny Williams.

Adventure/Historical Drama   **(PR:C MPAA:NR)**

SIGN OF THE RAM, THE**   (1948) 88m COL bw

Susan Peters (*Leah St. Aubyn*), Alexander Knox (*Mallory St. Aubyn*), Phyllis Thaxter (*Sherida Binyon*), Peggy Ann Garner (*Christine St. Aubyn*), Ron Randell (*Dr. Simon Crowdy*), Dame May Whitty (*Clara Brastock*), Allene Roberts (*Jane St. Aubyn*), Ross Ford (*Logan St. Aubyn*), Diana Douglas (*Catherine Woolton*), Margaret Tracy (*Emily*), Paul Scardon (*Perowen*), Gerald Hamer (*Rev. Woolton*), Doris Lloyd (*Mrs. Woolton*).

In a seemingly quiet English home, Peters is the foster mother to the three grown children of her husband Knox. Confined to a wheelchair, Peters slowly becomes a dominating force over the entire family. She breaks up a romance for one daughter and nearly drives the son's fiancee to suicide. Descending further into madness, Peters finally ends it all by wheeling her chair off a cliff to certain death. The obscure title comes from Peters' character's birth sign, which is supposed to be a sign of trouble. Despite some good performances, THE SIGN OF THE RAM suffers from weak scripting and lackluster direction, and never really gets off the ground. Thus, it ends up a routine, below-average soaper. Peters' performance marked her film comeback, after a hunting accident a few years earlier caused her to lose the use of her legs.

p, Irving Cummings, Jr.; d, John Sturges; w, Charles Bennett (based on the novel by Margaret Ferguson); ph, Burnett Guffey; ed, Aaron Stell; md, M.W. Stoloff; art d, Stephen Goosson.

Drama   **(PR:A MPAA:NR)**

SIGN OF THE VIRGIN**½   (1969, Czech.) 83m Barrandov/Brandon
                                                  Films bw (SOUHVEZD I PANNY)

Josef Cap (*Standa*), Jaroslava Obermaierova (*Jana*), Vladimir Pucholt (*Velebra*), Jiri Wimmer (*Beiman*), Ilja Prachar (*Capt. Pazourek*), Jiri Adamira (*Lt. Brezina*), Rudolf Jelinek (*Lt. Toneiser*), Ivan Vyskocil (*Vyskocil*), Jan Kotva (*Samek*), Jaroslava Pokorna (*Chambermaid*), Jan Libicek (*Augustine*).

Cap is a member of the Czechoslovakian army. He's engaged to Obermaierova and the two don't want to wait for the wedding night to consummate their relationship. However, Army rules state no women are allowed on the base, but Obermaierova leaves her home in Prague and goes to the base anyway. Cap is afraid he'll be reprimanded if she's found; there also is no private place where the two can go. Finally they gain the sympathy of a medical officer, who allows them to use an infirmary bed.

d, Zbynek Brynych; w, Milan Uhde, Brynych (based on a story by Uhde); ph, Jan Kalis (CinemaScope); m, Jiri Sternwald; ed, Miroslav Hajek; art d, Milan Nejedly; m/l, "Stairway to Heaven," Karel Kopecky (sung by Kopecky).

Comedy   **(PR:O MPAA:NR)**

SIGN OF THE WOLF**   (1941) 69m MON bw

Michael Whalen (*Rod Freeman*), Grace Bradley (*Judy*), Darryl Hickman (*Billy*), Mantan Moreland (*Ben*), Louise Beavers (*Beulah*), Wade Crosby (*Gunning*), Tony Paton (*Red*), Joseph Bernard (*Hank*), Ed Brady (*Jules*), Eddie Kane (*Martin*), Brandon Hurst (*Dr. Morton*), Grey Shadow, Smoky the Dogs.

During a championship competition at Madison Square Garden, two canine contestants get into a fight. This disqualifies the pair and their young mistress decides to sell the one she likes the least. But her servant can't let the dog go, so he smuggles it aboard their plane back to Canada. The plane crashes and the dog runs for help. Okay kid fare for the time, but the portrayal of black servants, meant to be comedic, is stereotyping at its worst. Some of the photography is curiously dark, but the snowy outdoors scenery is convincing.

p, Paul Malvern; d, Howard Bretherton; w, Elizabeth Hopkins, Edmond Kelso (based on a story by Jack London); ph, Fred Jackman, Jr.; ed, Jack Ogilvie; md, Edward Kay.

Wilderness Drama   **(PR:AAA MPAA:NR)**

SIGN OF VENUS, THE* (1955, Ital.) 98m Gala-Titanus bw (IL SEGNO
                                                              DI VENERE)

Franca Valeri (*Cesira*), Sophia Loren (*Agnese*), Raf Vallone (*Ignazio*), Vittorio De Sica (*Alessio Spano*), Alberto Sordi (*Romolo Proietti*), Peppino de Filippo (*Mario*), Virgilio Riento (*Agnese's Father*), Tina Pica (*Agnese's Aunt*).

Another of the best-forgotten films Loren made in Italy before showing up unwanted on the doorstep of the world film industry. Here she plays second lead to Valeri, a young girl from the country who comes to Rome to stay with her uncle and his daughter, Loren. Loren is a gorgeous girl who attracts men constantly and without trying, to the point where it's quite a nuisance. Valeri has no such problems and badly wants them. She goes to a fortune teller who tells her that she was born under the sign of Venus and that she is therefore lucky in love. She is heartened by this news but her depression returns when she looks at the available men around her: bumbling car thief Sordi, selfish writer De Sica, aging photographer de Filippo, and her best hope, fireman Vallone. All of them manipulate her for their own ends as Sordi goes to jail, Vallone impregnates Loren, and De Sica runs off with the fortune teller. Disgusted by the whole thing, Valeri flees Rome for good. A film of little significance and less interest, and Loren's performance is minor enough to avoid damaging the whole film too much.

p, Marcello Girosi; d, Dino Risi; w, Luigi Comencini, Franca Valeri, Agenore Incrocci, Ennio Flaiano, Cesare Zavattini (based on a story by Anton Chekhov); ph, Carlo Montuori; m, Renzo Rossellini; ed, Mario Serandrei; art d, Gaston Medin.

Comedy   **(PR:C MPAA:NR)**

SIGN OF ZORRO, THE*½   (1960) 91m BV bw

Guy Williams (*Zorro, Don Diego*), George J. Lewis (*Don Alejandro*), Gene Sheldon (*Bernardo, Don Diego's Servant*), Britt Lomond (*Capt. Monastario*), Henry Calvin (*Sgt. Garcia, Monastario's Aide*), Tony Russo (*Martinez*), John Dehner (*Viceroy*), Lisa Gaye (*Viceroy's Daughter*), Jan Arvan (*Nacho Torres*), Eugenia Paul (*Elena Torres*), Romney Brent, Than Wyenn, Elvira Corona.

A retelling of the Zorro legend spliced from episodes of the 13-part Disney television series. Williams is cast as the masked avenger who's always one step ahead of the evil politicos, trying to find out his secret identity. Although they come close, Williams' servant, Sheldon helps him keep his mask in place. After achieving success with turning TV show "Davy Crockett" into a full-length movie, the Disney people decided to repeat the recipe with THE SIGN OF ZORRO. However, the film is too episodic, having been shot in a television style that translated poorly to the larger medium. Lewis, who plays Williams' father, was cast as Zorro in the Republic serials ZORRO'S BLACK WHIP in 1944. The music was composed by Lava, who had also created the score for the Republic series. After THE SIGN OF ZORRO was released, Republic tried to cash in by re-releasing their old features GHOST OF ZORRO and ZORRO RIDES AGAIN, as did 20th Century Fox, which re-released THE MARK OF ZORRO (1940). All of the films, including THE SIGN OF ZORRO, did poorly at the box office.

p, Walt Disney, William H. Anderson; d, Norman Foster, Lewis R. Foster; w, N. Foster, Lowell S. Hawley, Bob Wehling, John Meredyth Lucas (based on the "Zorro" stories by Johnston McCulley); ph, Gordon Avil; m, William Lava; ed, Roy Livingston, Stanley Johnson, Cotton Warburton, Hugh Chaloupka; art d, Marvin Aubrey Davis; set d, Emile Kuri, Hal Gausman; cos, Chuck Keehne; m/l, title song, Norman Foster, George Burns; makeup, Pat McNalley.

Adventure   **Cas.**   **(PR:AAA MPAA:NR)**

SIGNALS-AN ADVENTURE IN SPACE   (1970, E. Ger./Pol.) 91m
Defa/Zespoly Filmowe (Signale-ein Weltraumabenteuer)

Piotr Pavlikovsky, Yevgeny Sharikov, Gojko Mitic, Yuri Darie, Helmut
Schreiber, Alfred Mueller, Irena Karel, Soheir Morshedy, Karin Schroeder,
Wolfgang Kieling.

Sometime in the 21st Century, an outerspace craft gets lost and another
craft investigates the disappearance. The second spaceship is just on a
routine patrol or is it? The special effects in the film, s hot in 70mm, are
better than average, creating a good sense of outerspace environments and
the dimensions of the heavens. However, the story is little more than typical
adventure stuff aimed at younger audiences, with a simplistic plot and
characters that easily could have wandered over from a nearby western set.

d, Gottfried Kolditz; w, Kolditz, Claus-Ulrich Wiesner (based on the novel
Asteroidenjaeger by Carlos Rasch); ph, Otto Hainisch; spec eff, Hainisch,
Kurt Marks, Stanislaw Duelz.

Science Fiction   **(PR:A   MPAA:NR)**

SIGNED JUDGEMENT   (SEE: COWBOY FROM LONESOME RIVER,
1944)

SIGNORA SENZA CAMELIE   (SEE: LADY WITHOUT CAMELLIAS,
1953, Ital.)

SIGNORE E SIGNORI   (SEE: BIRDS, THE BEES, AND THE
ITALIANS, THE, 1967, Fr./Ital.

SIGNPOST TO MURDER   (1964) 75m Marten/MGM bw

Joanne Woodward (*Molly Thomas*), Stuart Whitman (*Alex Forrester*),
Edward Mulhare (*Dr. Mark Fleming*), Alan Napier (*The Vicar*), Joyce
Worsley (*Mrs. Barnes*), Leslie Denison (*Supt. Bickley*), Murray Matheson
(*Dr. Graham*), Hedley Mattingly (*Officer Rogers*), Carol Veazie (*Auntie*).

Whitman murders his wife and spends ten years in an asylum for the
criminally insane. Mulhare plays his doctor who tells the man of an obcure
law which will get Whitman a new trial if he can escape and remain free for
14 days. The prisoner breaks loose and holes up in the home of Woodward,
an unhappily married woman whose husband is away on business. The two
are attracted to one another, but Whitman wonders what's going on when
he discovers a dead man's body at a mill wheel next to the house. He falls
down a flight of stairs and is knocked unconscious; later the corpse is gone.
When the police find it, Woodward claims that Whitman is the killer. She
eventually breaks down however, admitting that she and Mulhare are
lovers and Whitman's entire escape was hatched by the pair so he could be
framed for the murder. Though somewhat stagy and with a contrived
ending, this thriller was well made in terms of production values. Shot on
location in England.

p, Lawrence Weingarten; d, George Englund; w, Sally Benson (based on the
play by Monte Doyle); ph, Paul C. Vogel (Panavision); m, Lyn Murray; ed,
John McSweeney; art d, George W. Davis, Edward Carfagno; set d, Henry
Grace, Frank McKelvy; cos, Travilla; spec eff, J. McMillian Johnson;
makeup, William Tuttle.

Mystery/Thriller   **(PR:O   MPAA:NR)**

SIGNS OF LIFE   (1981, Ger.) 91m Werner Herzog
Filmproduktion/New Yorker bw (L EBENSZEICHEN)

Peter Brogle (*Stroszek*), Wolfgang Reichmann (*Meinhard*), Athina Za-
charopoulou (*Nora*), Wolfgang von Ungern-Sternberg (*Becker*), Wolfgang
Stumpf (*Captain*), Henry van Lyck (*Lieutenant*), Julie Pinheiro (*Gypsy*),
Florian Fricke (*Pianist*), Heinz Usener (*Doctor*), Achmed Hafiz (*Greek
Resident*), Jannakis Frasakis, Katerinaki.

After being wounded in combat during WW II, Brogle and his wife
(Zacharopoulou) are sent to a Nazi-held Greek isle in order to guard a
fortress. Accompanied by Reichmann and Sternberg, they find themselves
with little to do and search for different ways to fill up their tedium. They
paint their quarters, raise goats, and make rockets from a discovered cache
of explosives. Sternberg begins translating some of the Greek writings
carved into the old castle and discovers it was once held by pirates.
Reichmann concocts a bizarre device for capturing and executing cockroaches in a military fashion. Pinherio, a mysterious gypsy, appears and gives
the group a wooden owl whose eyes are given life by the flies trapped inside.
Gradually the boredom catches up with Brogle, and he cracks after hearing
a pianist play Chopin. After an appeal to the commander, Brogle and
Reichmann are assigned to guard a ridge. There Brogle loses control and
fires upon some windmills. His comrade stops him and reports the incident.
Brogle feels betrayed by his island compatriots, and forces them to leave the
fortress. Brogle then begins a final assault, firing onto a local village and
threatening to blow it up. Eventually his rebellion is stopped. An interesting
early work from noted German director Herzog, inspired by an article
describing a true incident during the Seven Years' War. Released in
Germany in 1968. (In German; English subtitles.)

p,d&w, Werner Herzog; ph, Thomas Mauch; m, Stavros Xarhakos; ed, Beate

Mainka-Jellinghaus, Maxi Mainka.

Drama   **(PR:O   MPAA:NR)**

SILENCE½   (1931) 60m PAR bw

Clive Brook (*Jim Warren*), Marjorie Rambeau (*Mollie Burke*), Peggy
Shannon (*Norma, Jim's Daughter*), Charles Starrett (*Arthur Lawrence*),
Willard Robertson (*Phil Powers*), John Wray (*Harry Silvers*), Frank
Sheridan (*Joel Clarke*), Paul Nicholson (*Walter Pritchard*), J.M. Sullivan
(*Father Ryan*), Ben Taggart (*Alderman Conners*), John Craig (*Fake Chap-
lain*), Charles Trowbridge (*Mallory*), Wade Boteler, Robert E. Homans
(*Detectives*).

A story of blackmail and murder with lurid elements involving a "love
child," which was a risque topic for audiences in the early 1930s. The
complicated tale, told in flashback, stars Brook as a man imprisoned for
killing his partner, who was trying to double-cross him. It was actually
Shannon who shot his partner, but Brook takes the rap for Shannon, who
is his illegitimate daughter. Brook never reveals his true identity to
Shannon, allowing her to live out her life believing she is the daughter of
Robertson. Starrett, as Shannon's fiance, gives a good performance here,
and would soon become a highly successful movie cowboy.

d, Louis Gasnier, Max Marcin; w, Marcin (based on the play by Marcin); ph,
Charles Rosher.

Drama/Crime   **(PR:O   MPAA:NR)**

SILENCE, THE   (1964, Swed.) 95m Svensk/Janus bw
(TYSTNADEN)

Ingrid Thulin (*Ester*), Gunnel Lindblom (*Anna*), Jorgen Lindstrom (*Johan*),
Hakan Jahnberg (*Hotel Waiter*), Birger Malmsten (*Restaurant Waiter*), The
Eduardini (*The Seven Dwarfs*), Eduardo Gutierrez (*Dwarf Manager*), Lissi
Alandh (*Girl in Cabaret*), Leif Forstenberg (*Man in Cabaret*), Nils Waldt
(*Cashier in Cinema*), Birger Lensander (*Usher in Cinema*), Eskil Kalling,
Karl-Arne Bergman, Olof Widgren (*Shadows*).

Bergman's final film in his trilogy about faith (following THROUGH A
GLASS DARKLY and WINTER LIGHT) is typical of his filmic style: stark,
mystic, and loaded with hidden meanings and symbolism. Thulin is a lesbian
intellectual who is strongly attracted to her younger sister, Lindblom.
Lindblom is the sexually active mother of a ten-year-old boy. As Thulin
drinks herself into an alcoholic depression and slowly deteriorates from
tuberculosis, her carefree sister watches a couple make love at a movie
theater, then picks up a hotel waiter. Her son Lindstrom, meets a troupe of
midgets who dress the boy in women's clothing, then leave him to the tales
of Jahnberg, an elderly hotel waiter. After hearing the details of her sister's
affairs, Thulin is left alone in her hotel room to masturbate. After they
quarrel, Lindblom leaves the hotel with her son and Thulin is left alone with
the aging waiter as she approaches her death. The film ends with Lindstrom
contemplating a strange note from his sickly aunt. Like so many of
Bergman's films, this work wanders between the pretentious and the
profound. The miniscule dialog and absence of music leave much of the work
to the actors who do a fine job projecting the story's drama. Ultimately the
film is dependent on each individual viewer to decide its worth. Bergman
has dropped his obsession with God here and replaced it with an obsession
for physical passion, with the results often astounding. Though his confusing
style definitely makes Bergman a darling of cinephiles, he is a great artist
whose work must be viewed time and again to approach any real
understanding of the meaning.

p, Allan Ekelund; d&w, Ingmar Bergman; ph, Sven Nykvist; m, Bo Nilsson,
Johann Sebastian Bach; ed, Ulla Ryghe; art d, P.A. Lundgren; cos, Marik
Vos-Lundh; makeup, Borje Lundh.

Drama   **(PR:O   MPAA:NR)**

SILENCE½   (1974) 88m Cinema Financial of America c (AKA:
CRAZY JACK AND THE BOY)

Will Geer (*Crazy Jack*), Ellen Geer (*Barbara*), Richard Kelton (*Al*), Ian Geer
Flanders (*Eric*), Craig Kelly (*Sheriff*), Sam Robustelli (*Deputy*), Tad Geer,
Raleigh Geer (*Car Thieves*).

A real family film (in the literal sense of the word) as Geer, his daughter,
and grandsons star in this simple, occasionally charming story. Geer plays
a hermit in the mountainous California woodlands. His daughter Ellen is
foster mother to Flanders (her real-life son), an autistic boy who gets lost in
the forest. Geer finds him and teaches the supposedly unreachable lad a few
things before the rescue party finds the pair. Geer, a fine actor, gives a
sensitive performance and overcomes some of the film's inherent sentimentality. The story occasionally drags, needing some tighter editing. The script
was co-authored by Mackey, a woman noted for her educational filmwork.

p, James Polakof; d, John Korty; w, Mary Mackey, Ellen Geer; ph, Hiro
Morikawa (Eastmancolor); m, Ed Bogus, High Country; ed, Vivien Hill-
grove; prod d, Joe Guerena

Family Drama   **(PR:AAA   MPAA:G)**

SILENCE HAS NO WINGS**½ (1971, Jap.) 103m Nippon Eiga Shinsha/Toho bw (TOBENAI CHINMOKU)

Mariko Kaga, Fumio Watanabe, Hiroyuki Nagato, Toshie Kumura, Kunie Tanaka, Minoru Nakahira, Takeshi Kusaka, Yukoo Shirukaya, Katamasa Komatsu, Shoichi Ozawa.

This symbolic story about the lack of human values in contemporary society opens with a little boy capturing a rare butterfly. He eagerly brings it to his teacher but she thinks him to be a liar as this species is never found in their region. Since he doesn't wish to be known as a liar, the boy tearfully destroys the beautiful insect. Then the film takes a fanciful look at how the rare butterfly may have migrated from the south to northern Japan. Along the route we see the dehumanizing aspects of big city-life, as in Nagasaki, Hiroshima, Kyoto, and Hong Kong, portrayed through the butterfly's eyes.

p, Yasuo Matsukawa; d, Kazuo Kuroki; w, Matsukawa, Kuroki, Hisaya Iwasa; ph, Tatsuo Suzuki; m, Teizo Matsumura.

Drama (PR:A MPAA:NR)

SILENCE OF DEAN MAITLAND, THE**½ (1934, Aus.) 95m Cinesound/British Empire bw

John Longden (Dean Maitland), George Lloyd, John Warwick, Charlotte Francis, Jocelyn Howarth, Les Wharton.

A well-known Australian tale which played on the stage a number of times and was previously filmed as a silent. Longden (in one of his handful of Australian films between 1934-36 before returning to England to appear in more Hitchcock pictures) stars as a minister who molests the town tease, Francis. The girl becomes pregnant and her father plans action against Longden. A struggle ensues and the father is accidentally killed. Longden escapes blame because he was dressed in the local doctor's clothes, thereby throwing blame on the doctor. The doctor, who is engaged to the minister's sister, refuses to endanger Longden's reputation by implicating him. Longden cannot face the guilt that accompanies his silence so he prepares a confession. Before he can tell the truth, however, he is stricken with a heart attack and the doctor is sent to prison. Twenty years later, the doctor is released and vows to kill Longden, who has now become a dean. Meanwhile, Longden receives word that the girl he molested is dying and the messenger who brings him those sad tidings is his own child. After another heart attack, Longden learns that the doctor is willing to let him live. Eaten away by his silence, Longden confesses to his congregation from the pulpit and then collapses on the altar. THE SILENCE OF DEAN MAITLAND is excellently done melodrama.

d, Ken G. Hall; w, Gayne Dexter; ph, Frank Hurley.

Drama (PR:C-O MPAA:NR)

SILENCE OF DR. EVANS, THE**½ (1973, USSR) 90m Mosfilm bw (MOLCHANIYE DOKTORAIVENS)

Sergei Bondarchuk (Dr. Evans), Zhanna Bolotova, I. Kuznetsov, Leonid Obolenski, Irina Skobtseva.

Bondarchuk plays a scientist researching a process that will prolong life. His work is interrupted and he takes a second look at what he is doing after the arrival of three aliens from the planet Oraina. Oraina is a peaceful culture, and the aliens are shocked by the violent and unjust society they have found on Earth. Bondarchuk realizes that before he can prolong life, society must first be improved. He eventually dies, and the female alien is killed. Her fellow travelers leave Earth with the impression that their visit was premature because this planet is still a primitive civilization. This is an unusual theme from the normally dogmatic Soviet cinema, but that doesn't make this a good film. The message is too simplistic and the moral aspects are driven in with all the subtlety of a sledgehammer. Bondarchuk is better known to American audiences for his direction of two East-West co-productions WAR AND PEACE (1967) and WATERLOO (1969). Obolenski, in a lesser role, was a real Soviet film veteran. He had appeared in a 1924 film, THE EXTRAORDINARY ADVENTURES OF MR. WEST IN THE LAND OF THE BOLSHEVIKS, directed by the great film theorist Lev Kuleshov.

d&w, Budimir Metalnikov; ph, Yuri Sokol, Vladimir Bondarev.

Science Fiction (PR:C MPAA:NR)

SILENCE OF THE NORTH** (1981, Can.) 94m UNIV c

Ellen Burstyn (Olive Fredrickson), Tom Skerritt (Walter Reamer), Gordon Pinsent (John Fredrickson), Jennifer McKinney (Little Olive Reamer), Donna Dobrijevic (Vala Reamer), Jeff Banks (Lewis Reamer), Colin Fox (Arthur Herriott), David Fox (Lea Goodwin), Richard Farrell (John Goodwin), Larry Reynolds (Auctioneer), Frank Turner (Young Man), Ute Blunck (Young Woman), Thomas Hauff (Billy), Murray Westgate (Doctor), Ken James (Ralph), Booth Savage (Flier), Louis Banks (Louis), Sean McCann (Man on Soup Line), Frank Adamson (Trapper), Chappelle Jaffe (John's Girl Friend), Ken Pogue (Wild Man), Freddie Lang, Dennis Robinson, Robert Clothier, Brian Fustukian, Larry Musser, Leah Marie Hopkins, Ken James, Albert Angus, Kay Hawtrey, Lynn Mason Green, Graham McPherson, Chester Robertson, Paul Verden, Sean Sullivan, Tom McEwen, Tom

Harvey, Ken Babb, Anna Freidman, Janet Amos, Frank Gay, Peter Stefaniuk, George Myron.

Burstyn plays a plucky young woman married to Skerritt, a trapper, in the wilderness of 1919 Canada. They battle the various natural elements together, but Burstyn must finally cope alone after Skerritt drowns. It's up to her to raise the children, which she does nicely before remarrying, this time to Pinsent. The standard hardships and cliches abound in this corny film. The narration by Burstyn is redundant and hackneyed, giving it a curious period feeling as though it belonged to another era. The photography of the Canadian woodlands is marvelous however. Based on a true story.

p, Murray Shostak; d, Allan Winton King; w, Patricia Louisiana Knop (based on the book by Olive Fredrickson, Ben East); ph, Richard Leiterman (Panavision); m, Allan MacMillan; ed, Arla Saare; prod d, Bill Brodie; art d, Susan Longmire, Alice Keywan, Gavin Mitchell; cos, Olga Dimitrov.

Drama Cas. (PR:C MPAA:PG)

SILENCERS, THE** (1966) 103m Meadway-Claude /Col c

Dean Martin (Matt Helm), Stella Stevens (Gail, Big O's Girl), Daliah Lavi (Tina Batori), Victor Buono (Tung-Tze), Aruthur O'Connell (Wigman), Robert Webber (Sam Gunther), James Gregory (MacDonald), Nancy Kovack (Barbara), Roger C. Carmel (Andreyev), Cyd Charisse (Sarita), Bevery Adams (Lovey Kravezit), Richard Devon (Domino), David Bond (Dr. Naldi), John Reach (Traynor), Robert Phillips (1st Armed Man), John Willis (M.C.), Frank Gerstle (Frazer), Grant Woods (Radio Man), Patrick Waltz (Hotel Clerk), Dirk Evans, Bill Couch, Chuck Hicks, Gary Lasdun (Armed Men), Pamela Rodgers, Carolyn Neff, Rita Thiel, Barbara Burgess, Gigi Michel, Jan Watson, Gay MacGill, Marilyn Tindall, Susan Holloway, Victoria Lockwood, Margaret Teele (Slaymates), Mary Jane Mangler, Margie Nelson, Anna Lavelle, Larri Thomas (Specialty Dancers), Todd Armstrong, Tom Steele, Myron Cook, Scott Perry, Richard Tretter, Tom Sweet (Guards), Glenn Thompson, John Doheim (Student Guards), Tommy Horton, Bruce Ritchey (Hunters), Ray Montgomery (Agent C), Harry Holcombe (Agent X), Vincent Van Lynn (Agent Z), Ted Jordan, Robert Ward, Pat Renella (Men), Grace Lee (Oriental Girl), Carole Cole (Waitress), Inga Neilsen (Statue), Art Koulias (Engineer), Guy Wilkerson (Farmer), Saul Gross (Pilot), Pat Hawley (Eddie, the Bartender), Robert Glenn (FBI Agent), Frank Hagney (Drunk), Amedee Chabot (Girl), Cosmo Sardo (Bit).

Buono is the big cheese of Big O, an organization that wants to sabotage the American atomic missile system. It's up to secret agent Martin to save the day so pray he's stayed away from the vodka martinis. This silly, sexist nonsense was the first and probably best of Martin's four Matt Helm films, though that's not saying much. Filled with explosions, Martin-style sex jokes, and some good action sequences, THE SILENCERS was Columbia's attempt to cash in on the James Bond craze. However Martin's Matt Helm has none of the style or wit of Ian Flemming's legendary character and the results are painfully obvious. Charisse, who deserved a better fate than this, got to sing the title song–some compensation. Three sequels unfortunately followed; MURDERER'S ROW (1966), THE AMBUSHERS (1967), and THE WRECKING CREW (1968).

p, Irving Allen; d, Phil Karlson; w, Oscar Saul (based on the novels The Silencers and Death of a Citizen by Donald Hamilton); ph, Burnett Guffey (Pathe Color); m, Elmer Bernstein; ed, Charles Nelson; art d, Joe Wright; set d, George R. Nelson; cos, Moss Mabry; ch, Robert Sidney; m/l, Bernstein, Mack David (sung by Cyd Charisse, Dean Martin, Vicci Carr); makeup, Ben Lane.

Action/Comedy Cas. (PR:0 MPAA:NR)

SILENT BARRIERS** (1937, Brit.) 82m GAU bw (GB: THE GREAT BARRIER)

Richard Arlen (Hickey), Antoinette Cellier (Mary Moody), Barry Mackay (Steve), Lilli Palmer (Lou), J. Farrell MacDonald (Maj. Hell's Bells Rogers), Jock McKay (Bates), Roy Emerton (Moody), Ben Welden (Joe), Ernest Sefto, (Magistrate), Henry Victor (Bulldog Kelly), Reginald Barlow, Arthur Loft, Frank McGlynn, Sr.

An accurate recounting of the construction of the Canadian-Pacific railroad line between Montreal and Vancouver, insofar as the details of construction are concerned. Realistic rolling stock and the details ails of the tunnelers' battle with the gorgeous Canadian Rockies are interrupted by a conventional plot. Arlen and Mackay are gambler-drifters in a railroad boom town hoping to pick up some fast winnings. Arlen falls in love with Cellier, the daughter of construction chief Emerton; this induces him to divest himself of his deck and pick up a sledge hammer. Mackay, plundered by grasping bar girl Palmer, redeems himself by sacrificing his life in the interest of the railroad's progress.

p, Gunther Stapenhorst; d, Milton Rosmer, Geoffrey Barkas; w, Ralph p, Gunther Stapenhorst; d, Milton Rosmer, Geoffrey Barkas; w, Ralph Spence, Michael Barringer, Rosmer (based on the novel The Great Divide by Alan Sullivan); ph, Arthur Crabtree, Glen MacWilliams, Sepp Allgeir, Robert Martin; m, Hubert Bath; ed, Charles Frend, B.H. Hipkins.

Drama (PR:A MPAA:NR)

SILENT BATTLE, THE (SEE: CONTINENTAL EXPRESS, 1939, Brit.)

SILENT CALL, THE½   (1961) 62m AP/FOX bw

Gail Russell (Flore Brancato), David McLean (Joe Brancato), Roger Mobley (Guy Brancato), Roscoe Ates (Sid), Milton Parsons (Mohammed), Dal McKennon (Old Man), Sherwood Keith (Johnny), Jack Younger (Muscles), Rusty Wescoatt (Moose), Pete, the Dog of Flanders, Joe Besser (Art), H. Tom Hart.

A family must move from Elko, Nevada, to Los Angeles but, unfortunately, there's no room for the dog. It breaks the heart of Mobley, the overgrown dog's young master, when they have to give the dog to a not-so-nice neighbor until he can be sent for. Naturally, the pooch doesn't wait; he follows the car on the 1000-mile journey until he's reunited with the boy. The dog's journey contains the usual adventures with conventional slice-of-life episodes featuring truckers, hobos, and bad weather until the tearful reunion. Though nothing new, it is competently acted and directed with a child audience in mind. Watch for Besser, a member of The Three Stooges in the late 1950s, in a bit part.

p, Leonard A. Schwartz; d, John Bushelman; w, Tom Maruzzi; ph, Kay Norton (CinemaScope); m, Richard D. Aurandt; ed, Carl Pierson; md, Aurandt; art d, John Mansbridge; set d, Harry Reif; cos, Joseph Dimmitt; makeup, John Sylvester.

Drama   (PR:A MPAA:NR)

SILENT CONFLICT½   (1948) 61m UA bw

William Boyd (Hopalong Cassidy), Andy Clyde (California Carlson), Rand Brooks (Lucky Jenkins), Virginia Belmont (Rene Richards), Earle Hodgins (Doc Richards), James Harrison (Speed Blaney), Forbes Murray (Randall), John Butler (Clerk), Herbert Rawlinson (Yardman), Richard Alexander (1st Rancher), Don Haggerty (2nd Rancher).

One of Boyd's cowhand buddies is swayed into joining in some crooked activities after falling under the spell of a hypnotist. The title is misleading: there's too much talk and not enough conflict with only a minimum of gunplay and two-fisted action. This is one of the Hopalong Cassidy films tht Boyd produced himself after he took over the series from original producer Harry Sherman. The year SILENT CONFLICT was released, 1948, was the year the film series ended. (See HOPALONG CASSIDY series, Index.)

p, Lewis J. Rachmil; d, George Archainbaud; w, Charles Belden (based on characters created by Clarence E. Mulford); ph, Mack Stengler; m, Ralph Stanley; ed, Fred W. Berger; art d, Jerome Pycha, Jr; set d, George Sawley.

Western   (PR:A MPAA:NR)

SILENT DEATH   (SEE: VOODOO ISLAND, 1957)

SILENT DUST*½   (1949, Brit.) 82m Independent
                                               Sovereign/ABF-MON bw

Sally Gray (Angela Rawley), Stephen Murray (Robert Rawley), Derek Farr (Maxwell Oliver), Nigel Patrick (Simon Rawley), Beatrice Campbell (Joan Rawley), Seymour Hicks (Lord Clandon), Marie Lohr (Lady Clandon), Yvonne Owen (Nellie), James Hayter (Pringle), George Woodbridge (Foreman), Edgar Norfolk (Simpson), Irene Handl (Cook), Maria Var (Cafe Singer).

When his son is killed in battle, Murray, a blind man, becomes obsessed with his boy's memory and plans a memorial service for him. Shortly before the unveiling is to take place, the son (Patrick) returns. Instead of dying in battle, he had deserted the army and taken to blackmail and murder. He's returned home supposedly to make a new life for himself. Gray is Patrick's former wife, now frightened to tell him that she has remarried. The story builds to a climactic ending with Patrick and Murray fighting on a balcony. Patrick tries to kill his father, but falls to his death. Despite the small budget, this adaption of a popular English play is well told, with snappy direction and some excellent characterizations.

p, Nat A. Bronsten; d, Lance Comfort; w, Michael Pertwee (based on the play "The Paragon" by Michael Pertwee, Roland Pertwee); ph, Wilkie Cooper, Robert Day; m, Georges Auric; ed, Lito Carruthers; md, George Melachrino; art d, C.P. Norman.

Drama/Suspense   (PR:A MPAA:NR)

SILENT ENEMY, THE* (1930) 84m Burden-Chanler/PAR-Publix bw

Chief Yellow Robe (Chetoga the Tribal Leader), Chief Long Lance (Baluk the Mighty Hunter), Chief Akawanush (Dagwan the Medicine man), Spotted Elk (Neewa, Chetoga's Daughter), Cheeka (Cheeka, The Medicine Man's Son).

A fictional documentary about a tribe of Indians in northern Ontario, detailing their customs and rituals. The prologue by Chief Yellow Robe is the only part of the picture with dialog and consists of his explaining that "Everything you will see here is real, everything as it has always been." What little plot there is has rival tribesmen Chief Long Lance and Chief

Akawanush fighting for control of the tribe. Food is scarce and Chief Yellow Robe is near death. Chief Long Lance decides to lead the tribe south towards a herd of caribou, over the protests of Chief Akawanush who calls his rival a coward. After days without food or water, a tribal meeting is called. Chief Akawanush summons the gods and tells Chief Long Lance that they want him to be sacrificed. As Chief Long Lance is preparing to burn himself to death on a funeral pyre, a caribou stampede is spotted. Chief Long Lance is made tribal leader, and receives Spotted Elk as his bride, while Chief Akawanush is banished from the tribe. Interesting only from an anthropological standpoint, THE SILENT ENEMY came forth from an expedition sponsored by New York's Museum of Natural History.

p, W. Douglas Burden, William C. Chanler; d, H.P. Carver; w, Richard Carver; ph, Marcel Le Picard, Frank M. Broda, Horace D. Ashton, William Casel, Otto Durkoltz; m, Massard Kur Zhene; m/l, "Song of the Waters," Zhene; "Rain Flower" Sam Coslow, Newell Chase.

Drama   (PR:C MPAA:NR)

SILENT ENEMY, THE½   (1959, Brit.) 92m Romulus/UNIV bw

Laurence Harvey (Lt. Lionel Crabb), Dawn Addams (3rd Officer Jill Masters), Michael Craig (Leading Seaman Knowles), John Clements (The Admiral), Sidney James (Chief Petty Officer Thorpe), Alec McCowen (Able Seaman Morgan), Nigel Stock (Able Seaman Fraser), Ian Whittaker (Ordinary Seaman Thomas), Arnold Foa (Tomolino), Gianna Maria Canale (Conchita), Massimo Serato (Forzellini), Giacomo Rossi-Stuart (Rosati), Carlo Justini (Fellini), Raymond Young (Celloni), Howard Marion Crawford (Wing Commander), Cyril Shaps (Miguel), Lee Montague (Miguel's Mate), Terence Longdon (Lt. Bailey), Alan Webb (British Consul), John Moffatt (Driver Volunteer), Sydney King (Cruiser Captain), Peter Welch (Helmsman), Murray Kash (Tattooed Sailor), Yvonne Warren (Spanish Girl), Ewen Solon (Willowdale Captain), Brian Oulton (Holford), David Lodge, Ian McNaughton, John Lee, Harold Siddons, Michael Brill, Sydney King, Hugh Moxey, Jerome Willis, Desmond Jordan, Tom Watson, Jack May, Derren Nesbitt, Laurence Brooks, Peter Welsh, Yvonne Romain.

Harvey stars in the true-life exploits of a British frogman who won a British George Medal for his wartime activities. During WW II Harvey is a Royal Navy bomb-disposal officer who takes on both the Italian menace and the red tape of Navy bureaucracy. Slipping away from his commander, Harvey, along with Craig, discovers an Italian base operating out of Spain. Using diving equipment, they manage to infiltrate the operation and steal some valuable hidden documents before blowing up the Italian ship. Some good underwater footage and capital performances help raise this adventure beyond its stereotypical, gung ho plot line.

p, Bertram Ostrer; d&w, William Fairchild (based on the book Commander Crabb by Marshall Pugh); ph, Otto Heller; m, William Alwyn; ed, Alan Osbiston; md, Muir Mathieson; art d, Bill Andrews.

War   (PR:C MPAA:NR)

SILENT FLUTE, THE   (SEE: CIRCLE OF IRON, 1979)

SILENT INVASION, THE* (1962, Brit.) 70m Danziger/Planet bw

Eric Flynn (Erik von Strafen), Petra Davies (Maria), Francis de Wolff (Emile), Martin Benson (Borge), Jan Conrad (Sergeant- Major), Noel Dyson (Mme. Veroux), Andre Maranne (Argen), Melvyn Hayes (Jean), C. Denier Warren (Gillie).

WW II melodrama starring Davies as a Frenchwoman who falls in love with Nazi captain Flynn. Unfortunately, the romance comes to an abrupt end when her brother, a saboteur working for the Resistance, is killed and she is forced to face reality. Overwrought and too unrealistic to be taken seriously.

p, John Draper; d, Max Varnel; w, Brian Clemens.

War   (PR:A MPAA:NR)

SILENT MOVIE*½   (1976) 86m FOX c

Mel Brooks (Mel Funn), Marty Feldman (Marty Eggs), Dom DeLuise (Dom Bell), Bernadette Peters (Vilma Kaplan), Sid Caesar (Studio Chief), Harold Gould (Engulf), Ron Carey (Devour), Carol Arthur (Pregnant Lady), Liam Dunn (Newsvendor), Fritz Feld (Maitre d'), Chuck McCann (Studio Gate Guard), Valerie Curtin (Intensive Care Nurse), Yvonne Wilder (Studio Chief's Secretary), Arnold Soboloff (Acupuncture Man), Patrick Campbell (Hotel Bellhop), Harry Ritz (Man in Tailor Shop), Charlie Callas (Blind Man), Henny Youngman (Fly in Soup Man), Eddie Ryder (British Officer), Al Hopson, Rudy DeLuca, Barry Levinson, Howard Hesseman, Lee Delano, Jack Riley (Executives), Inga Nielsen, Sivi Aberg, Erica Hagen (Beautiful Blondes), Robert Lussier (Projectionist), Marcel Marceau, Paul Newman, Liza Minnelli, Burt Reynolds, Anne Bancroft, James Caan.

Technically, this should have been included in our silent volume because it is what it says it is, a silent movie. However, it does have John Morris' music, sound effects, and one word, uttered by that m an of no words, mime Marcel Marceau, who says "non" at one point (the French word for "no"). Writer Ron Clark conceived the film and thought that there would be only two directors who could make such a bold idea work, Brooks and Woody Allen. Since Brooks was local in Los Angeles, he took it to him at Fox and a deal was made on the spot. Brooks wanted some help with the script and Clark suggested two men he'd worked with in the past, DeLuca and Levinson. They were hired and all four contributed to the outcome. (Both Levinson and DeLuca would eventually become directors. DeLuca did TRANSYLVANIA 6-5000 in 1985 and Levinson scored with DINER. Clark got into the directing act after having been production consultant on this film. He returned to his native Canada tp helm his original, FUNNY FARM.) Brooks is a film director who has seen (and heard) better days. In an attempt to quell nagging doubts about his talents and his dubious future, Brooks turns to alcohol. Two of his pals, Feldman and DeLuise, rescue him from his despair and try to convince Brooks that there's more to life than a whisky bottle. Brooks is not convinced but decides to give it a try and make a silent movie (thus making the plot of the picture close to what actually happened when they attempted to convince the studio to do this). The trio, who seem to be a modern version of Curly, Larry, and Moe, go off to find some bankable stars who will agree to appear in the picture, then visit Caesar, the "current studio chief" (which is what it says on the sign on his desk), who is worried about the future of the studio because it is about to be bought by the huge conglomerate of Engulf & Devour (a swipe at Gulf & Western, who bought Paramount) which is helmed by Gould. Once Gould gets his talons into the studio, it spells the end and Caesar is desperate to keep that from happening. Brooks, Feldman, and DeLuise next visit a host of stars in their natural and unnatural habitats. They find Caan in his trailer, Bancroft doing her nightclub act (which leads to a tango routine by the three men and Bancroft), and Burt Reynolds is nailed in his shower. They manage to convince several actors to be in the movie, including Paul Newman, Marceau, and Liza Minnelli, and are about to commence production when Brooks begins to drink again. He is again saved by his cronies and his girl friend, Peters. The movie is made, turns out to be a huge smash (in real life, SILENT MOVIE grossed well over $20 million), and disaster is averted. Since there is no dialog, the sight gags take its place and they come with the rapidity of an Uzi machine gun. There are so many jokes that it's impossible to list them. Not all are wonderful, some are in the toilet humor category, but if you don't like one of the funnies, wait a few seconds and there will be several more that you will like. Anthony Goldschmidt designed titles, so one could say it is captioned for the humor-impaired. The list of superb comic actors is a who's who of mirth. There are more second bananas than on a 50-foot stalk. Chuck McCann is the perfect Studio Guard, a dictator in a uniform. Riley, who surely must be the radio voice of the 1980s because he seems to be on every radio commercial, joins writers Levinson and DeLuca, along with TV's Hesseman, Delano and Hopson, as executives. Henny Youngman does a brief bit with a fly and on and on. A very funny movie done with surprising restraint on the part of Brooks. It is that restraint which makes this funnier than many of his other films which seemed to stop at nothing to get a laugh. Author Clark said: "The whole idea came to me all at once, the set pieces, the plot, even the notion of the cameos from stars. I made a list of their names and we got every single one of them to appear. In order to secure the services of Marceau, I called upon Jacques Fabbri, a French actor who appeared for five years in the Gallic version of 'Norman, Is that You?' (which Clark wrote with Sam Bobrick) and he contacted Marceau for me, who immediately agreed to do the film, thereby breaking his vow of show business silence."

p, Michael Hertzberg; d, Mel Brooks; w, Brooks, Ron Clark, Rudy DeLuca, Barry Levinson (based on a story by Clark); ph, Paul Lohmann (DeLuxe Color); m, John Morris; ed, John C. Howard, Stanford C. Allen; prod d, Al Brenner; set d, Rick Simpson; cos, Pat Norris; spec eff, Ira Anderson, Jr.; ch, Rob Iscove; makeup, William Tuttle; stouts, Max Kleven; titles, Anthony Goldschmidt.

Comedy   Cas.   (PR:A-C MPAA:PG)

SILENT NIGHT, BLOODY NIGHT   (1974) 88m Cannon c (AKA: NIGHT OF THE DARK FULL MOON; DEATH HOUSE)

Patrick O'Neal (Carter), John Carradine (Towman), Walter Abel (Mayor), Mary Woronov (Diane), Astrid Heeren, James Patterson, Candy Darling, Ondine, Tally Brown, Jack Smith, Walter Klavun, Philip Burns, Fran Stevens.

A horror film featuring O'Neal as a lawyer who spends the night in a house he's trying to sell for owner Patterson. The place was once an insane asylum, and its history is told in unsettling flashbacks starring New York underground film actors Ondine, Smith, Darling, and Brown. The film's modern-day scenes feature O'Neal with a few problems of his own when seemingly nice, but mute, newspaper editor Carradine turns out to be the local ax murderer. Though it has its narrative problems, SILENT NIGHT, BLOODY NIGHT does have some moments of interest, and is better than most shockers of this ilk.

p, Ami Artzi, Jeffrey Konvitz; d, Theodore Gershuny; w, Gershuny, Konvitz, Artzi, Ira Teller.

Horror   Cas.   (PR:O MPAA:R)

SILENT NIGHT, EVIL NIGHT   (SEE: BLACK CHRISTMAS, 1974, Can.)

SILENT PARTNER**   (1944) 55m REP bw

William Henry (Jeffrey Swales), Beverly Lloyd (Mary Price), Grant Withers (Bob Ross), Ray Walker (The Drunk), Joan Blair (Lady Sylvia Marlowe), Roland Drew (Harry Keating), George Meeker (Desk Clerk), Wally Vernon (2nd Waiter), John Harmon (Blackie Barton), Dick Elliott (Pop), Eddie Fields (Tony), the Junk Man, Pat Knox (Dolly Darling).

Henry, a freelance player for MGM and Paramount, got a chance at a leading role in this programmer for Republic. He plays a newspaper reporter who finds a murder victim's address book. He attempts to make contact with five people listed in the book and eventually finds the killer, but only after several attempts on his life. Far-fetched, but competently acted considering its low-budget, programmer status.

p&d, George Blair; w, Gertrude Walker; ph, William Bradford; ed, Ralph Dixon; md, Morton Scott; art d, Russell Kimball.

Crime   (PR:C MPAA:NR)

SILENT PARTNER, THE**½   (1979, Can.) 103m EMC Film Corp. c

Elliott Gould (Miles Cullen), Susannah York (Julie Carver), Christopher Plummer (Harry Reikle), Celine Lomez (Elaine), Michael Kirby (Packard), Ken Pogue (Detective), John Candy (Simonson), Gail Dahms (Louise), Michael Donaghue (Berg), Jack Duffy (Fogelman), Nancy Simmonds (Girl in Sauna), Nuala Fitzgerald (Mrs. Skinner), Guy Sanvido (Locksmith), Aino Perkskanen (Mrs. Evanchuck), Michele Rosen (Young Woman in Bank), Ben Williams (Newsboy), Sandy Crawley (2nd Detective), Jan Campbell (Boy's Mother), Jimmy Davidson (Little Boy), Eve Norman (Girl at Party), John Kerr (3rd Detective), Sue Lumsden (TV Reporter), Candace O'Connor (Bank Assistant), Stephen Levy (Freddie).

An entertaining crime comedy filmed independently in Toronto and using Canadian and British actors and crew, presumably in order to take advantage of certain financial breaks which are given by the government for "Canadian Content." (It was this order that caused the cast of "Second City TV" to add the Canadian satire of "The McKenzie Brothers," which then led to movies starring the actors who played the roles, Rick Moranis and Dave Thomas. Another of the Canadian comedy contingent is John Candy, seen here in one of his earliest films.) Good plot finds Gould as a branch office bank teller in a shopping mall, who learns that Plummer, a bank robber in a Santa Claus suit, is about to rob the coffers. York knows about the deal and so does Lomez, an aide to Plummer. When the robbery begins, Gould hides $50,000 in cash and when the returns on the robbery are reported by the press, Plummer realizes he is being accused of having stolen more than he got. So where did the money go? Plummer figures it out and begins to besiege Gould, who has put the money in a safety deposit box at the bank but has somehow lost the key. In the end, it gets a bit brutal and bloody but Gould and York wind up as winners. Some very funny lines and the always-delightful Gould carries off his role with aplomb. Plummer, whom we've all come to know as a benign and heroic type, etches a sensational performance as an incredibly vicious villain. The battle of wits is peppered with funny lines and the suspense seldom flags. Made on a budget, although you'd never know it.

p, Joel B. Michaels, Stephen Young; d, Daryl Duke; w, Curtis Hanson (based on the novel Think of a Number by Anders Bodelson); ph, Billy Williams; m, Oscar Peterson; prod d, Trevor Williams; m/l, "C'mon Downtown," Nancy Simmonds (sung by Simmonds).

Crime/Comedy   Cas.   (PR:C-O MPAA:R)

SILENT PASSENGER, THE**½   (1935, Brit.) 75m Phoenix/ABF bw

John Loder (John Ryder), Peter Haddon (Lord Peter Wimsey), Mary Newland (Mollie Ryder), Austin Trevor (Inspector Parker), Donald Wolfit (Henry Camberley), Leslie Perrins (Maurice Windermere), Aubrey Mather (Bunter), Wimsey's Valet, Robb Wilton (Porter), Ralph Truman (Saunders), Percy Rhodes, Frederick Burtwell, Gordon McLeod, George de Warfaz, Vincent Holman, Ann Codrington, Dorice Fordred, Annie Esmond.

The first film featuring novelist Dorothy L. Sayer's popular Lord Peter Wimsey character, but unfortunately her fascinating amateur detective is portrayed as something of an eccentric twit who solves murders in spite of himself. The tale begins as railroad detective Wolfit decides to rid himself of an annoying blackmailer, played by Perrins. Wolfit kills Perrins and stuffs the body in a trunk owned by Loder which is on its way from London to the English Channel by train. By coincidence, the corpse just happens to be the former lover of Loder's wife, Newland (he blackmailed her as well), and when the body is finally discovered things look bad for Loder. Sensing the young man's innocence, another passenger on the train, Lord Peter Wimsey (Haddon), works to clear his fellow traveler's name. Using the accused as bait, Haddon flushes out the real killer, Wolfit, and all ends up well. THE SILENT PASSENGER is not based on one of Sayer's novels, but was inspired by a story written by her to fulfill a contractual agreement for the production company. An interesting character, Wimsey would have few screen appearances until the BBC resurrected him for a television series in

1973 that would later debut on American TV screens as part of PBS's "Masterpiece Theater" series.

p, Hugh Perceval; d, Reginald Denham; w, Basil Mason (based on a story by Dorothy L. Sayers); ph, Jan Stallich.

Crime (PR:A MPAA:NR)

SILENT PLAYGROUND, THE* (1964, Brit.) 75m Focus/BL bw

Roland Curram (Simon Lacey), Bernard Archard (Inspector Duffy), Jean Anderson (Mrs. Lacey), Ellen McIntosh (Mavis Nugent), John Ronane (Alan), Desmond Llewellyn (Dr. Green), Rowena Gregory (Jane Wilson), Basil Beale (Sgt. Clark).

After being released from a mental hospital, Curram takes some barbituates down to the local movie theater. There he passes out the colored tablets to some children, telling them it's candy. The kids become quite ill and are rushed to the hospital. Archard is the cop who leads the investigation while Anderson plays Curram's worried mother. The story never panders to its more sensationalistic elements, instead being an intelligent and sensitive thriller. Made as a first-time feature on a $75,000 budget (shot in only 24 days), director Goulder brings his experience from documentary filmmaking to THE SILENT PLAYGROUND with fine results. The dialog is natural and the story is well directed, a tight control over a sensitive topic.

p, George Mills, Esther Kiss; d&w, Stanley Goulder; ph, Martin Curtis; m, Tristram Carey; ed, Peter Musgrave.

Drama (PR:C-O MPAA:NR)

SILENT RAGE*½ (1982) 100m Topkick/COL c

Chuck Norris (Dan Stevens), Ron Silver (Dr. Tom Halman), Steven Keats (Dr. Philip Spires), Toni Kalem (Alison Halman), William Finley (Dr. Paul Vaughn), Brian Libby (John Kirby), Stephen Furst (Charlie), Stephanie Dunnam (Nancy Halman), Joyce Ingle (Mrs. Sims), Jay DePland (Bike Leader), Lillette Zoe Raley (Tatooed Mama), Mike Johnson, Linda Tatum, Kathy Lee, Desmond Dhooge, Joe Farago, John Barrett, Paula Selzer, Sandy Lang, Sonny Jones, Russel Higginbotham, Eddie Galt, David Andre Unger.

A crazed man kills a woman and her bratty brood with a handy ax. After doing the same to one other individual, the small town's sheriff, karate star Norris, arrests the man and tosses him in the back of a squad car. But this is no ordinary psycho, and he breaks the handcuffs and heads for the hills. Some deputies shoot him and the story would seem to be over–or is it? One of the surgeons who operate on him is a mad scientist, complete with the appropriate leers and smirks into the camera. He wants to test his new drug, which supposedly will hurry the human healing process. Filled with implausibilities and unintentionally funny moments, this early Norris feature was little more than an excuse for the actor to use his karate skills on the killer as well as a few bikers. Exploitative in nature, but popular with its audiences.

p, Anthony B. Unger; d, Michael Miller; w, Joseph Fraley; ph, Robert Jessup, Neil Roach (Metrocolor); m, Peter Bernstein, Mark Goldenberg; ed, Richard C. Meyer; art d, Jack Marty; spec eff, Jack Bennett, Randy Fife.

Action Cas. (PR:O MPAA:R)

SILENT RAIDERS ** (1954) 68m Enterprise Cinema/Lippert bw

Richard Bartlett, Earle Lyon, Jeanette Bordeaux, Earle Hansen, Robert Knapp, Fred Foote, Frank Stanlow, Carl Swanstrom.

Routine WW II actioner which sees a seven-man commando unit sent to the French coast to wipe out a Nazi communications center. Producer Lyon and director Bartlett also played the lead roles.

p, Earle Lyon; d, Richard Bartlett; w, Bartlett; m, Elmer Bernstein; m/l, Bernstein, Bartlett, J.A. Wenzel.

War (PR:C MPAA:NR)

SILENT RUNNING* (1972) 89m UNIV c

Bruce Dern (Freeman Lowell, Botanist), Cliff Potts (Wolf), Ron Rifkin (Barker), Jesse Vint (Keenan), Steven Brown, Mark Persons, Cheryl Sparks, Larry Whisenhunt (Drones).

In the year 2008 all of Earth's vegetation is dead and a space station orbiting Saturn is set up by the government to serve as an outer space greenhouse. The greenhouse is tended by Dern and three other men in hope that the nuclear devastated Earth may one day be ready for replanting. When the order comes to terminate the greenhouse, Dern kills his colleagues and, with the help of two robots (known as Huey and Dewey), he remains in his outerspace utopia. This was the directorial debut of Trumbull, who had previously worked with Stanley Kubrick on 2001: A SPACE ODDYSSEY's special effects. SILENT RUNNING also concentrates heavily on the special effects resulting in some stunning imagery. Dern gives a marvelous performance, utterly compelling in its intensity. SILENT RUNNING falters most in its script; there's simply not enough in it to justify feature length. The writing team of Washburn, Bochco, and Cimino would go on to make

the Viet Nam drama THE DEER HUNTER, where a problem in scripting was also evident. (Cimino, of course, would later direct the ultimate in film debacles, HEAVEN'S GATE.) The unusual score is by Schickele, better known for his classical music parodies under the name P.D.Q. Bach. The songs sung by Baez are dated and become annoying after a while. Over the years SILENT RUNNING has built up a respectable cult status.

p, Michael Gruskoff; d, Douglas Trumbull; w, Deric Washburn, Steve Bochco, Michael Cimino; ph, Charles F. Wheeler (Technicolor); m, Peter Schickele; ed, Aaron Stell; set d, Francisco Lombardo; spec eff, Trumbull, John Dykstra, Richard Yuricich, Richard O. Helmer, James Rugg, Marlin Jones, R.L. Helmer, Vernon Archer; m/l, "Silent Running," "Rejoice in the Sun," Schickele, Diane Lampert (sung by Joan Baez); makeup, Dick Dawson.

Science Fiction Cas. (PR:C MPAA:PG)

SILENT SCREAM*½ (1980) 87m American Cinema Releasing c

Rebecca Balding (Scotty Parker), Cameron Mitchell (Lt. McGiver), Avery Schreiber (Sgt. Rusin), Barbara Steele (Victoria Engles), Steve Doubet (Jack), Brad Reardon (Mason), John Widelock (Peter), Juli Andelman (Doris), Yvonne De Carlo (Mrs. Engels), Jack Stryker (Police Chief), Tina Taylor (Victoria at age 16), Jason Zahler (Mason at Age 3), Thelma Pelish, Joan Lemmo, Ina Gould, Virginia Rose, Ernie Potvin, Rachel Bard.

Balding, Doubet, Widelock, and Andelman are some college kids who can't get on-campus housing. They need to live somewhere so the coed quartet takes up residence with Reardon and his mother, De Carlo. De Carlo apparently brought over some old haunts from her days on "The Munsters" for this house is full of weird surprises and numerous murders. Mitchell and Schreiber are the honest, if unusual, pair of cops who investigate all the troubles. There are some good moments in this cheap shocker, but they are overwhelmed by scenes of utter tastelessness and cruelty.

p, Jim Wheat, Ken Wheat, d, Denny Harris; w, Jim Wheat, Ken Wheat, Wallace C. Bennett; ph, Michael D. Murphy, David Short (MGM Color); m, Roger Kellaway; ed, Edward Salier; prod d, Christopher Henry; spec eff, Steve Karkus; m/l, "I Love You Baby, Oh Baby, I Do," Roger Kellaway.

Horror Cas. (PR:O MPAA:R)

SILENT STAR (See: FIRST SPACESHIP ON VENUS, 1960, Ger./Pol.)

SILENT VOICE, THE (SEE: MAN WHO PLAYED GOD, THE, 1932)

SILENT VOICE, THE (SEE: PAULA, 1952)

SILENT WITNESS, THE* (1932) 73m FOX bw

Lionel Atwill (Sir Austin Howard), Greta Nissen (Nora Selmer), Weldon Heyburn (Carl Blake), Helen Mack (Sylvia Pierce), Bramwell Fletcher (Anthony Howard), Mary Forbes (Lady Howard), Herbert Mundin (Henry Hammer), Billy Bevan (Horace Ward), Montague Shaw (Inspector Robbins), Wyndham Standing (Sir John Lawson, Barrister), Alan Mowbray (Arthur Drinton, King's Counsel), Lowden Adams (Justice Bond), Lumsden Hare (Col. Grayson, Scotland Yard Commissioner), Eric Wilton (Clerk of the Court).

Better than average programmer features former matinee idol Atwill in a powerful performance as a father taking the blame for a murder his son is charged with. The son choked his lover and had fled the scene, not realizing she was still alive. It turns out all right for Atwill but not before a grueling courtroom sequence that nicely builds tension and results in a gripping finale. The film was based on a popular London play in which Atwill played the same role.

d, Marcel Varnel, R.L. Hough; w, Douglas Doty (based on the play by Jack DeLeon, Jack Celestin); ph, Joseph August; ed, Jack Murray.

Mystery/Drama (PR:C MPAA:NR)

SILENT WITNESS, 1942 (SEE: SECRETS OF A CO-ED, 1942)

SILENT WITNESS, THE ** (1962) 70m Emerson Film Enterprises bw

Tris Coffin (Lt. Williams), Marjorie Reynolds (Mary), George Kennedy (Gus Jordan), Andrea Lane (Lola), Billy Shanley (Danny), Dick Haynes, Dick Kruse, Ora Keller, George Salem, Teddy Keller, George Dunn, Steve Pavlisin, John Hill, Ben Avery, Jon Moxley, Vern Porter, R. James Straley, King Byrne, John Waschak, Stephanie Watts, Paul Moore, Patricia Lasky.

This independent feature shot on location in Denver features Reynolds as a police officer's widow. Her son (Shanley) delivers the local paper and is best friends with another policeman's son, whose father (Coffin) is in love with Reynolds, but she won't have anything to do with another policeman for a husband. A second plot line develops as Kennedy, playing a wrestler with a bad heart, steals a fur for his girl friend, Lane. She discovers the fur is stolen and is killed by Kennedy in an argument. Shanley sees the murder while delivering his papers. Kennedy tries to find the boy and ends up chasing him into an amusement park not yet opened for the day. The climactic chase ends atop a roller coaster where Kennedy suffers a heart seizure. Shanley tries to help the man but Kennedy realizes his weight will cause both of them to fall and lets go of the boy's hand, plunging to his death. Coffin rescues Shanley and Reynolds predictably marries him. Minor stuff and forgettable.

p&d, Ken Kennedy; w, Frank Jessy; ph, Richard E. Cunha; m, Gene Kauer, Douglas Lackey; ed, Herbert L. Strock.

Crime/Drama   **(PR:O   MPAA:NR)**

SILHOUETTES zero   (1982) 100m LaStrada-Claire/Primi Piani Enterprises c

George David Weiss (Paul), Susan Monts (Michele), Kathryn Cordes (Caroline), Michael A. Pappalardo (Don), Giuseppe Murolo (Angelo), David Chase (Sid), Luciano Crovato (Carlo), Tom Felleghy (Doctor), Fabrizio Guarducci (Street Artist), Anna Terminiello (Mama Luna), Natalia de Capua (Music Student), Mariella Russo (Sales Clerk), Female Soccer Team.

Weiss, an American lyricist and composer who made his cinematic acting and writing debut with this trash, plays a songwriter from the U.S. living in Sorrento, Italy. He meets Monts, a beautiful art student, and they fall in love. The drippy romance is backed by picture postcard scenery right out of films from 20 years before. Weiss' diatribes against rock groups like the Rolling Stones versus classical music is woefully outdated for a film released in 1982, and his acting is about as amateurish as the film is bland. Finally, the two break off their romance in a bittersweet conclusion where Monts makes references to an unspecified "career" that must take precedence over marriage.

p, Hayes G. Shimp; d, Giuseppe Murolo; w, George David Weiss, Murolo, Russell Firestone; ph, Roberto D'Ettore Piazzoli (Technicolor); ed, Eugenio Alabiso; art d, Amedeo Mellone; songs, Weiss, Renato Serio, Murolo, Nino Tassone, Pino Bologna.

Romance   **(PR:C   MPAA:NR)**

SILICATES   (SEE: ISLAND OF TERROR, 1967, Brit.)

SILK EXPRESS, THE**   (1933) 61m WB bw

Neal Hamilton (Kilgore, Importer), Sheila Terry (Paula Nyberg), Guy Kibbee (McDuff, Railway Detective), Arthur Byron (Clark, Train Conductor), Dudley Digges (Professor Nyberg), Allen Jenkins (Rusty), Harold Huber (Craft), Arthur Hohl (Wallace Myton), George Pat Collins (Burns), Robert Barrat (Calhoun), Vernon Steele (Dr. Ralph), Ivan Simpson (Johnson), Edward Van Sloan, Douglas Dumbrille, Tom Wilson.

Hamilton is a silk manufacturer on a Seattle-to-New York train to deliver an important shipment for his company. He's got to face Hohl, the leader of some unscrupulous businessmen who want to corner the silk market. On the train are the usual slice-of-life people including Kibbee, a railroad detective, Digges, an ailing professor going to New York's Rockefeller Institute, and Terry, his daughter. The elements for an effective programmer are all in place but the dialog and Hamilton, who is woefully miscast, leave much to be desired.

p, Henry Blanke; d, Ray Enright; w, Houston Branch, Ben Markson (based on a story by Branch); ph, Tony Gaudio.

Drama   **(PR:A   MPAA:NR)**

SILK HAT KID*   (1935) 65m FOX bw

Lew Ayres (Eddie Howard), Mae Clarke (Laura Grant), Paul Kelly (Tim Martin), Ralf Harolde (Lefty Phillips), William Harrigan ("Brother Joe" Campbell), Billy Lee (Tommy), John Qualen (Mr. Fossbender), Warren Hymer (Misty), Vince Barnett (Mr. Rabinowitz), William Benedict ("Uncle Sam").

Harrigan runs a settlement house for wayward youths who accepts some money from a shady nightclub dealer (Ayres). Ayres is out to impress Clarke, a teacher who works with the house. Problems arise when Ayres' bodyguard also falls for Clark in this hokey programmer. Though the direction is typical for a feature like this, the script is full of unbelievable situations and dialog that drowns the cast.

p, Joseph Engel; d, H. Bruce Humberstone; w, Edward Eliscu, Lou Breslow, Dore Schary (based on a story by Gerald Beaumont); ph, Daniel Clark; m, Samuel Kaylin.

Drama   **(PR:A   MPAA:NR)**

SILK NOOSE, THE**½   (1950, Brit.) 76m ABF/MON bw (GB: NOOSE)

Carole Landis (Linda Medbury), Joseph Calleia (Sugiani), Derek Farr (Capt. Jumbo Hoyle), Stanley Holloway (Inspector Rendall), Nigel Patrick (Bar Gorman), Ruth Nixon (Annie Foss), Carol Van Derman (Mercia Lane), John Slater (Pudd'n Bason), Leslie Bradley (Basher), Reginald Tate (Editor), Edward Rigby (Slush), John Salew (Greasy Anderson), Robert Adair (Sgt. Brooks), Hay Petrie (Barber), Uriel Porter (Coaly), Ella Retford (Nelly),

Brenda Hogan (Maffy), Michael Golden, Sydney Monckton, Howard Douglas, John Harvey, Michael Ripper, Michael Brennan, Arthur Lovegrove, Monte de Lyle, W. E. Hodge, Dennis Harkin, Diana Hope, Arthur Gomez, Kenneth Buckley, Ben Williams, Vi Kaley, John Martell, Ernest Metcalfe, Maria Berry. Ronald Boyer, Jeanne Ravel, Olive Lucius.

Calleia is a top London gangster who runs his black market operation from a Soho night club. He and his top henchman, Patrick, control underworld counterfeiting as well as being involved in a smuggling operation. They conduct the business with ruthless zeal, killing anyone who interferes with their plans. Landis (who died before the film's release) plays a newspaperwoman who investigates a murder and ends up exposing the gang. THE SILK NOOSE is really a character study that shows gangsters as only the movies can. Calleia and Patrick give fine performances though it's definitely stock characters they are playing. The direction is efficient, but workmanlike, attempting nothing out of the ordinary.

p, Edward Dryhurst; d, Edmond T. Greville; w, Richard Llewellyn, Dryhurst (based on the play by Llewellyn); ph, Hone Glending m, Charles Williams; ed, David Newhouse; art d, Bernard Robinson.

Crime   **(PR:A   MPAA:NR)**

SILK STOCKINGS****   (1957) 117m MGM c

Fred Astaire (Steve Canfield), Cyd Charisse (Ninotchka), Janis Paige (Peggy Dainton), Peter Lorre (Brankov), Jules Munshin (Bibinski), Joseph Buloff (Ivanov), George Tobias (Commissar Vassili Markovich), Wim Sonneveld (Peter Ilyitch Boroff), Belita (Dancer Vera), Ivan Triesault (Russian Embassy Official), Betty Barrie Chase (Dancer Gabrielle), Da Utti, Tybee Afra (Dancers).

There are 10, count 'em, 10 writers who worked on this script and the material that led to the screenplay and here was a case where too many cooks *improved* the delicate broth. Many years ago, a story was penned by Melchior Lengyel that served as the basis for the 1939 screenplay of NINOTCHKA, starring Greta Garbo, written by Billy Wilder, Charles Brackett and Walter Reisch. A musical based on the movie was presented, starring Hildegarde Neff and written by George S. Kaufman, his wife Leueen McGrath, and Abe Burrows, with a score by Cole Porter. When that played 478 performances, the adaptation chores were given to Leonard Spigelgass, Leonard Gershe and, uncredited, Harry Kurnitz, with a score by Porter that included two new songs written for the screen. The result of all this effort turned out to be light entertainment that paid off in heavy dividends at the ticket booths. Astaire, appearing in his last MGM picture until he co-hosted THAT'S ENTERTAINMENT 17 years later, is a producer who has come to Paris to make a movie. Once having arrived, he meets Sonneveld, a famous Russian composer and artiste who is due to return to the U.S.S.R. after having finished his concert engagements. Sonneveld was a Danish actor making his U.S. film debut. Astaire wants Sonneveld to write the score for the movie and the honored Soviet agrees. This enrages his superiors in Moscow who feel that their national treasure may, gasp, defect, so they send 3 underlings to Paris to bring the musician back. The trio are Lorre (who was very funny, but unable to keep up with the dance numbers so he was surreptitiously placed on the sidelines while the difficult terping took place. Matter of fact, since the film was shot in CinemaScope, the edges are cut off when the movie is shown on TV and Lorre is barely seen), Munshin and Buloff. Their boss is Tobias, who also appeared in the 1939 picture as well as the stage show. The moment they get to Paris, Astaire grabs them and charms them with all of the materialistic trappings of the West. Tobias realizes he must bring out the heavy ammunition so he sends one of his best communists, Charisse, a woman whom he feels certain will not be entranced by the capitalist system. The moment she arrives in Paris, Astaire begins his campaign. She has specific sites she wants to see, like the various municipal buildings, power plants, factories, and sewer system. Astaire takes her to those places but intersperses them with salons, couturiers, jewelry shops and like that. It's not too long before Astaire is totally enamored of Charisse and asks for her hand, but he is soon involved with the making of his film and they drift apart. Sonneveld does the score and the others feel he has sublimated his classical talents in favor of a dreadful commercial enterprise. The entire group goes home to Russia. Sometime later, Charisse is told by Tobias that she must fly to Paris where Lorre, Munshin and Buloff are now ensconced as the officials in charge of selling Soviet films to the West. At this point, they have yet to sell one and Charisse's job is to bring them back. The moment Charisse returns to Paris, she learns why the trio have refused to go back to Moscow; they are now owners of a successful night club with Astaire as the man who has lent them the backing. Charisse is is again united with Astaire and converted through love to capitalism. The picture began shooting the first week of November, 1956 and was completed on the last day of January, 1957, a short schedule when one considers all the spectacular dance numbers. Hermes Pan was in charge of Astaire's choregraphy while Eugene Loring handled the rest. The excellent orchestrations were done by veterans Al Woodbury and Skip Martin with Bob Tucker handling the vocal supervision. Buloff and Munshin both had some dancing ability and one needs to have it in order, believably, to dance badly. Lorre had, by this time, ballooned to epic proportions and could not keep up with the steps. The direction by Mamoulian was brisk and serviceable, though not outstanding. It was his last completed film in a movie career that began in 1929 with APPLAUSE.

Charisse, who is second to few in her dancing, was vocally looped by Carol Richards. The songs were witty, airy, and tuneful, though not as memorable as many of Porter's others. They include: "Too Bad" (sung and danced by Astaire, Munshin, Lorre, Buloff, with additional dancers Chase, Afra, Utti), "Paris Loves Lovers" (Charisse, Astaire), "Fated To Be Mated" (Astaire, Charisse – this was not in the stage score but was written specifically for the film), "The Ritz Roll'n Rock " (Astaire, also written for the film), "Silk Stockings (danced by Charisse), "Red Blues" (sung and danced by Charisse, Lorre, Buloff, Munshin, Sonneveld), "All Of You" (danced by Charisse, sung by Astaire, Charisse), "Stereophonic Sound" (sung and danced by Paige, Astaire), "Josephine," "Satin And Silk" (Paige), "Without Love," "Chemical Reaction" (Charisse), "Siberia" (sung and danced by Lorre, Munshin, Buloff), "Red Blues" (sung and danced by Charisse, Munchin, Lorre, Buloff, Sonneveld, et. al.) Note that one of the dancers is Barrie Chase, who was to star with Astaire on his Emmy-winning TV specials. Also dancing was Tybee Afra, who later teamed with John Brascia to become one of the best of the Nevada dance teams that opened for the starring acts at various Vegas, Reno and Tahoe hotels. SILK STOCKINGS did not have the same warmth or fire as NINOTCHKA because the chemistry between Charisse and Astaire was not as potent as Garbo and Douglas. It did, however, have some wonderful musical moments and it's the kind of picture that anyone of any age will enjoy.

p, Arthur Freed; d, Rouben Mamoulian; w, Leonard Gershe, (Harry Kurnitz, uncredited), Leonard Spigelgass (based on the musical play by George S. Kaufman, Leueen McGrath, Abe Burrows and the screenplay by Billy Wilder, Charles Brackett, Walter Reisch from Ninotchka, by Melchior Lengyel); ph, Robert Bronner (CinemaScope, Metrocolor); m, Cole Porter; ed, Harold F. Kress; md, Andre Previn; art d, William A. Horning, Randall Duell; set d, Edwin B. Willis, Hugh Hunt; cos, Helen Rose; ch, Hermes Pan, Eugene Loring; m/l, Porter; makeup, William Tuttle.

Musical/Comedy   Cas.   (PR:A MPAA:NR)

SILKEN AFFAIR, THE**   (1957, Brit.) 96m Dragon/RKO bw

David Niven (Roger Tweakham/New Accountant), Genevieve Page (Genevieve Gerard), Ronald Squire (Marberry), Beatrice Straight (Theora), Wilfrid Hyde White (Sir Horace Hogg), Howard Marion-Crawford (Baggott), Dorothy Allison (Mrs. Tweakham), Miles Malleson (Mr. Blucher), Richard Wattis (Worthington), Joan Sims (Lady Barber), Irene Handl (Receptionist), Charles Carson (Judge), Harry Locke (Tobacconist), Martin Boddey, Colin Morris (Detectives), Leonard Sharp (Elevator Operator), John Carroll (Henry), Anthony Shaw, Geoffrey Sumner, Ralph Truman, Leslie Weston, Shirley Ann Field.

Unable to fight an urge to increase his silk company's profits, Niven uses his position as company accountant to inflate the books and make his firm look better than a rival nylon manufacturer whose books he also doctors to put it on the skids. He uses the inflated receipts of the first company to live it up with a carefree French girl until he's caught and fined. This film tries to be a light, stylish British comedy in the sophisticated manner that is one of Britain's best exports; however, the plot is too implausible and the script doesn't give the actors much to work with. The direction compensates somewhat in a handsome looking production. The cast does give it their all with Niven in his usual witty performance and French and international leading lady Page as the love interest, winning kudos from the critics for her debut into English films.

p, Douglas Fairbanks, Jr., Fred Feldkamp; d, Roy Kellino; w, Robert Lewis Taylor (based on an idea by John McCarten); ph, Gilbert Taylor; m, Peggy Stuart; ed, Richard Best.

Comedy   (PR:A MPAA:NR)

SILKEN SKIN   (SEE: SOFT SKIN, THE, 1962, Fr.)

SILKEN TRAP, THE   (SEE: THE MONEY JUNGLE, 1968)

SILKWOOD****   (1983) 131m Fox c

Meryl Streep (Karen Silkwood), Kurt Russell (Drew Stephens), Cher (Dolly Pelliker), Craig T. Nelson (Winston), Diana Scarwid (Angela), Fred Ward (Morgan), Ron Silver (Paul Stone), Charles Hallahan (Earl Lapin), Josef Sommer (Max Richter), Sudie Bond (Thelma Rice), Henderson Forsythe (Quincy Bissell), E. Katherine Kerr (Gilda Schultz), David Strathairn (Wesley), Bruce McGill (Mace Hurley), J.C. Quinn (Curtis Schultz), Kent Broadhurst (Carl), Richard Hamilton (Georgie), Les Lannom (Jimmy), M. Emmet Walsh (Walt Yarborough), Graham Jarvis (Union Meeting Doctor), Ray Baker (Pete Dawson), Bill Cobbs (Man in Lunchroom), Norm Colvin (Zachary), Haskell Kraver (Ham), Kathie Dean (Stewardess), Gary Grubbs (Randy Fox), Susan McDaniel (Tana Hensley, Anthony Fernandez (Karen's Children), Betty Harper (May Bissell), Tess Harper (Linda Dawson), Anthony Heald (2nd Union Meeting Doctor), Nancy Hopton, Betty King (Nurses), Dan Lindsey (Man at Fence), John Martin (Man with Flashlight), Will Patton (Joe), Vern Porter (Bill Charlton), Christopher Saylors (Buddy), Don Slaton (Man in Moonsuit), James Rebhorn, Michael Bond, Tom Stovall (Los Alamos Doctors).

Karen Silkwood, a worker at the Kerr-McGee plant in Cimarron, Oklahoma,

died in 1974 as she was on her way to blow the whistle on some alleged improprieties at her factory. She was to meet a reporter from The New York Times and died in an auto accident that was, to say the least, suspect. The autopsy showed a bit of blood alcohol and a dose of a tranquilizer. An examination of the auto indicated that she may have been bumped from behind as she drove along the lonely and desolate road. Several years later, Silkwood's family successfully sued the Kerr-McGee Corporation and proved they were negligent in providing safeguards for the workers. Silkwood had been heavily contaminated by radiation and was suffering due to that when she died. Kerr-McGee paid her estate more than $10 million. In 1986, the proof of the danger of nuclear power unleashed was tragically witnessed by the world when the plant near Kiev, U.S.S.R., exploded and sent a death-dealing cloud over the entire Earth. This film, based on truth, takes a few liberties but does tone down some of the realities. Even so, it's a sensational expose of big business as seen through the eyes of average people who toil in silence. Streep, in another brilliant portrayal, is the title character, a hard-drinking, tough woman who works for Kerr-McGee in a job that is as dangerous as it is dull. She resides with her boy friend, Russell, and Cher, a lesbian pal. They smoke, drink, and live for the moment. Streep's three children are with her common law husband, whom she has left for Russell, so it's established quickly that she is not a bastion of ladylike morality. She has apparently spent a great deal of time with many men and enjoys their company, to the consternation of Cher. Scarwid, a lesbian beautician who specializes in grooming dead bodies so they'll be fit for viewing before burial, moves in with Cher. Her comment about the bodies of workers who are in the employ of the corporation is, "They all look as though they died before they died," which is an omen. Streep is briefly contaminated and has to be scrubbed down. She sees that her boss, Nelson, is retouching photographic negatives to hide something, a deficiency that is not only in the K-M products, but in the safety precautions as well. Streep and some of the other union members go to Washington, D.C., where she tells the chiefs of the union that something fishy is going on. At first, the union leaders don't pay much attention, but when Streep says that she can get proof, their ears perk up. The fuel rods at K-M are below par and the x-rays have been tampered to show they are in good order. Streep undertakes her own undercover work and gathers a pile of evidence that she intends to give to the reporter. Russell can't take her activities anymore, as she is totally consumed by her spying and paying no attention to him, so he briefly departs, then returns before her third contamination incident. Armed with a folder that contains all the material, Streep leaves for the meeting that never takes place. Although no one is accused of the death of Streep, it's clear that the screenwriters meant to indicate that she was silenced to save the plant from being closed. As it is, the plant was shuttered a scant year after Silkwood died. Nichols had done nothing in motion pictures since the unfortunate THE FORTUNE in 1975 and this marked his return. He seemed to have forgotten all the cute little tricks he used in other films and concentrated on extracting performances from the actors, and what performances they were. Streep did an Oscar calibre job, but she'd just won one for SOPHIE'S CHOICE the year before and there was no way the Academy would give her two in a row, even though she deserved it. So the statuette went to Shirley MacLaine for the overrated TERMS OF ENDEARMENT. Cher took a nomination but lost to Linda Hunt in THE YEAR OF LIVING DANGEROUSLY. Nichols, the script, and O'Steen's editing were also nominated. It's the kind of movie that Jane Fonda might have starred in and, for a while, her company did own the rights and the research material by Hirsch and Cano. Streep, who continues to amaze with her ability to imitate various accents, doesn't hit a false "y'awl" in her dialog, just as her Danish accent in OUT OF AFRICA was flawless and her Polish accent in SOPHIE'S CHOICE would have convinced Lech Walesa. They knew they were making a movie about an important subject when they began this and the care is evident in every frame. Questions are asked and not answered but that's as it should be when the truth will probably never be told. SILKWOOD makes a case against nuclear power and the inherent dangers to anyone who works closely with it, a fact brought sadly home by what happened at Three Mile Island and in the Ukraine. It will be frightening for any youngster and the language and sexuality are honest, but raw.

p, Mike Nichols, Michael Hausman; d, Nichols; w, Nora Ephron, Alice Arlen; ph, Miroslav Ondricek (Technicolor); m, Georges Delerue; ed, Sam O'Steen; prod d, Patrizia Von Brandenstein; art d, Richard James; set d, Derek Hill, Dennis Peeples; cos, Ann Roth.

Biography   Cas.   (PR:C-O MPAA:R)

SILLY BILLIES*   (1936) 63m RKO bw

Bert Wheeler (Roy Banks), Robert Woolsey ("Doc" Pennington), Dorothy Lee (Mary Blake), Harry Woods (Hank Bewley), Ethan Laidlaw (Trigger), Chief Thunderbird (Chief Cyclone), Delmar Watson (Morton), Richard Alexander (John Little).

The once popular team of Wheeler and Woolsey were clearly at a low ebb in this weak effort which came late in their partnership. They play a dentist and his faithful assistant, heading out West to cash in on the Gold Rush and the dental problems of miners. They really had some problems of their own in this tired comedy which tried to put some life into numerous moldy gags and routines. Frankenstein had more success raising the dead than the creators of this nonsense did in raising a laugh. Made on a minimul budget,

Wheeler and Woolsey didn't have much of a career left as SILLY BILLIES, like all of their films in this period, was a big money loser.

p, Lee Marcus; d, Fred Guiol; w, Al Boasberg, Jack Townley (based on a story by Guiol, Thomas Lennon); ph, Nick Musuraca; ed, John Lockert; md, Roy Webb; m/l, "Tumble On Tumbleweed," Dave Dryer, Jack Scholl.

Comedy   (PR:A   MPAA:NR)

SILVER BANDIT, THE zero   (1950) 54m Friedgen bw

Spade Cooley, Bob Gilbert, Virginia Jackson, Richard Elliott, Billy Dix, Jene Gray.

Cooley, a former vocalist for Charlie Starrett westerns and a country western band leader of the time, got a chance at his own series in this inept nonsense. The story has him playing a dude out to capture the title villain. His singing is okay but his thespian talents are wretched. The photography is uncredited, perhaps a blessing as it is often so blurry that cast members cannot be identified. The direction is horribly inept.

p, J. R. Camomile; d, Elmer Clifton; w, Elmer S. Pond (Elmer Clifton).

Western   (PR:A   MPAA:NR)

SILVER BEARS**   (1978) 113m COL c

Michael Caine (*Doc Fletcher*), Cybill Shepherd (*Debbie Luckman*), Louis Jourdan (*Prince di Siracusa*), Stephane Audran (*Shireen Firdausi*), David Warner (*Agha Firdausi*), Tom Smothers (*Donald Luckman*), Martin Balsam (*Joe Fiore*), Jay Leno (*Albert Fiore*), Tony Mascia (*Marvin Skinner*), Charles Gray (*Charles Cook*), Joss Ackland (*Henry Foreman*), Jeremy Clyde (*Nick Topping*), Moustache (*Signore Bendetti*), Mike Falco (*Boston*), Philip Mascellino (*St. Louis*), Leni Del-Genio (*New York*), Gus Guiffre (*Chicago*), Tommy Rundell (*Miami*), Max Starky (*Los Angeles*), Steve Plytas (*Clerk*), Victor Baring (*Accountant*), Joe Treggonino (*Chef*), Patricia Lecchi (*Maid*), Tom Andrew (*Dorso*), Phil Brown, Bruce Boa, Shane Rimmer, Robert Robinson (*Bankers*), Anthony Broad, David English, Phil Caton, Edward Duke, Mark Penfold, Nigel Nevinson (*Stockbrokers*).

A good idea goes awry here as Erdman's novel is given a hopelessly convoluted script whereas it would have benefited from an aligning of the story, rather than a twisting adaptation. There's not much to like about any of the protagonists. Each of the grasping, greedy characters, save for Smothers, ranks from crummy to despicable. Who winds up getting it in the end? You guessed it, the good guy. Caine is the character Filbert who travels to Switzerland to open a bank for Balsam, a gangster of the old-fashioned school. Caine is assisted by Jourdan, who has his own swindle in mind. The two meet Audran, who is partnered with Warner in an Iranian silver mine. At the same time, another banker, Ackland, sends Smothers and his wife, Shepherd, to Switzerland to buy a bank as a front for Gray, a billionaire metals mogul who would like a place to hide his gains. Shepherd is an ambitious, self-serving woman who is bored with her husband and sees this foray into high finance as a way she can improve her status. In the end, several schemes are put into operation and the man left holding the bag is Smothers, who winds up in jail while Shepherd is happily in the sack with Caine. The movie is well-paced but there is so much happening that it's not easy to recall who did what to whom. The sum of this movie was less than the total of the parts as each of the actors does well enough in their brief moments but it flashes by like a Nolan Ryan fastball in the Wrigley Field dusk. Director Passer added to his string of less-than-satisfactory films which include CRIME AND PASSION, BORN TO WIN, and LAW AND DISORDER. In a small role as Balsam's heir, note comedian Jay Leno, one of the funniest commentators on the U.S. scene. They should have let him write the script, or, at least, his own lines. With this many good performers, it's sad to see such a toss-away of a potentially funny movie.

p, Arlene Sellers, Alex Winitsky; d, Ivan Passer; w, Peter Stone (based on a novel by Paul E. Erdman); ph, Anthony Richmond (Technicolor); m, Claude Bolling; ed, Bernard Gribble; art d, Edward Marshall; cos, Ruth Myers.

Comedy   Cas.   (PR:C   MPAA:PG)

SILVER BLAZE   (SEE: MURDER AT THE BASKERVILLES, 1941, Brit.)

SILVER BULLET, THE*½**   (1942) 56m UNIV bw

Johnny Mack Brown (*"Silver Jim" Donovan*), Jennifer Holt (*Nancy Lee*), Fuzzy Knight (*Wild Bill Jones*), William Farnum (*Dr. Thad Morgan*), LeRoy Mason (*Walter Kincaid*), Rex Lease (*Rance Harris*), Grace Lenard (*Queenie Canfield*), Claire Whitney (*Emily Morgan*), Charles "Slim" Whitaker (*Buck Dawson*), Michael Vallon (*Nevada Norton*), Merrill McCormick (*Pete Sloan*), Harry Holman, Lloyd Ingraham, Hank Bell, William Desmond, James Farley, Pals of the Golden West, Nora Lou Martin.

When Brown is shot in the back and his father killed, the cowboy digs the silver bullet out of his hide and goes on the trail of the man who committed the crime. He finds the villain (Brown) and kills him in a climactic shootout, considered by many to be one of the best western shootouts of all time. The direction is taut and sharp and that final confrontation is unforgettable. Songs: "My Gal, She Works in the Laundry" (Oliver Drake, Milton Rosen,

Jimmy Wakely, sung by Fuzzy Knight), "Sweetheart of the Rio Grande" "Vote for Emily Morgan" (Drake, Rosen, Wakely, sung by the Pals of the Golden West), "Red River Valley" (sung by Pals of the Golden West).

p, Oliver Drake; d, Joseph H. Lewis; w, Elizabeth Beecher (based on a story by Drake); ph, Charles Van Enger; ed, Maurice Wright; md, Hans J. Salter; art d, Jack Otterson.

Western   (PR:C   MPAA:NR)

SILVER CANYON½**   (1951) 70m Gene Autry/COL bw

Gene Autry (*Gene Autry*), Pat Buttram (*"Cougar" Claggett*), Gail Davis (*Dell Middler*), Jim Davis (*Wade McQuarrie*), Bob Steele (*Walt Middler*), Edgar Dearing (*Col. Middler*), Richard Alexander (*Luke Anders*), Terry Frost (*Irving Wyatt*), Peter Mamakos (*Laughing Jack*), Steve Clark (*Dr. Seddon*), Stanley Andrews (*Maj. Weatherly*), Duke York (*Sgt. Laughlin*), Eugene Borden (*Gus Poppalardo*), Bobby Clark, Frankie Marvin, Boyd Stockman, Sandy Sanders, Kenne Duncan, Bill Hale, Jack O'Shea, Frank Matts, Stanley Blystone, John Merton, Jack Pepper, Pat O'Malley, Martin Wilkins, Jim Magill, John R. McKee, Champion, Jr.

Routine Autry series entry with a better-than-average supporting cast. Davis is the leader of some guerrilla raiders during the Civil War. Autry and pal Buttram (later to become the shady Mr. Haney on TV's "Green Acres") are some scouts for the Union forces at a military post in Utah. The two are jailed in a frame-up but break free and go through the usual number of fist fights and gun battles before the happy denouement. The direction is routine and photography above average. This was one of the 32 films starring himself that Autry's own production company made for release by Columbia between 1947 and 1953 after a contract dispute with Republic Studios, for the financial success of which his series had largely been responsible. During Autry's service in the Air Force during WW II, that studio had been grooming Roy Rogers as Autry's replacement, so it wasn't too badly injured by its top draw's departure. Oddly enough, Autry's usually good crooning just isn't up to par here in four numbers, including "Riding Down the Trail." (See Gene Autry series, Index.)

p, Armand Schaefer; d, John English; w, Gerald Geraghty (based on a story by Alan James); ph, William Bradford; ed, James Sweeney; md, Mischa Bakaleinikoff; art d, Charles Claque

Western   (PR:A   MPAA:NR)

SILVER CHAINS   (SEE: KID FROM AMARILLO, THE, 1951)

SILVER CHALICE, THE*   (1954) 143m WB c

Virginia Mayo (*Helena*), Jack Palance (*Simon*), Paul Newman (*Basil*), Pier Angeli (*Deborra*), Alexander Scourby (*Luke*), Joseph Wiseman (*Mijamin*), E.G. Marshall (*Ignatius*), Walter Hampden (*Joseph*), Jacques Aubuchon (*Nero*), Herbert Rudley (*Linus*), Albert Dekker (*Kester*), Michael Pate (*Aaron*), Lorne Greene (*Peter*), Terence De Marney (*Sosthene*), Don Randolph (*Selech*), David Stewart (*Adam*), Phillip Tonge (*Ohad*), Ian Wolfe (*Theron*), Robert Middleton (*Idbash*), Mort Marshall (*Benjie*), Larry Dobkin (*Ephraim*), Natalie Wood (*Helena as a Girl*), Peter Reynolds (*Basil as a Boy*), Mel Welles (*Marcos*), Jack Raine (*Magistrate*), Beryl Machin (*Eulalia*), John Sheffield, John Marlowe, Paul Power (*Witnesses to Adoption*), Frank Hagney, Harry Wilson (*Ruffians*), Charles Bewley (*Roman Commander*), David Bond (*Cameleer*), Allen Michaelson (*High Priest*), Lester Sharpe (*Oasis Keeper*), Laguna Festival of Art Players (*Tableau Performers*), Antony Eustral (*Maximus, the Ship's Master*).

A tedious religious epic that wasted the talents of many, THE SILVER CHALICE marked the movie debut of Paul Newman at the age of 29 and it's a tribute to his staying power that he managed to have such a huge career after the terrible basting he took from the critics and the ennui shown by audiences for this $4.5 million loser. Based on a best seller by Thomas Costain, it's a rambling tale that never gets into focus and the result is a lot of people running around with not enough motivation and nonexistent direction. Newman is a young, Greek sculptor with something of an inheritance to his name. His greedy relatives sell him into Roman slavery so they can get their hands on his drachmae. In the Eternal City he has several adventures and is eventually noted for his sculpting abilities. Newman marries Angeli, a shy young woman who adores him, but he is not above dallying with curvaceous Mayo, whom he's known since his earliest days in Greece. He winds up in Jerusalem where he accepts an assignment from the Christian leaders (Lorne Greene plays Peter) to design and sculpt a receptacle for the chalice Jesus used at the Last Supper. Everyone wants the chalice and it's coveted by a horde of characters so Newman is forced to engage in various feats of bravery, is captured, escapes and finally finds happiness with his life and his wife. Along the way, Newman meets Palance, a magician who thinks he can fly...and fails, Aubuchon, as the mad Nero, several of the Apostles, and what must have been the first of millions of Palestinian rebels. The chalice is eventually lost and Greene predicts that it will be found in the future to help lead a battling world back to the basics of Christ's teachings. Too many words, not enough drama and a poor debut for Newman. More interesting than any of the leads is a brief appearance by Natalie Wood, who is seen as the younger Mayo while Peter Reynolds plays Newman as a youth. One other notable item is the inclusion of the

Laguna Arts Festival Players, who appear as tableau performers. Every summer, residents of Laguna Beach volunteer to engage in a long-standing tradition. A large frame is placed on stage in a small outdoor theater that looks like a miniature of the Hollywood Bowl. The anonymous, often nude, performers, under cover of darkness, get into positions in the frame to simulate famous paintings or statues by old and young masters while the history of individual works of art are narrated. When the stage is lit, the effect is startling.

p&d, Victor Saville; w, Lesser Samuels (based on the novel by Thomas B. Costain); ph, William V. Skall (CinemaScope, WarnerColor); m, Franz Waxman; ed, George White; prod d, Rolf Gerard; art d, Boris Leven; cos, Rolf Gerard; ch, Stephen Papick.

Religious drama   **Cas.**   **(PR:A MPAA:NR)**

SILVER CITY, 1948   (SEE: ALBUQUERQUE, 1948)

SILVER CITY**½   (1951) 90m PAR c (GB: HIGH VERMILION)

Edmond O'Brien (*Larkin Moffatt*), Yvonne De Carlo (*Candace Surrency*), Barry Fitzgerald (*R.R. Jarboe*), Richard Arlen (*Charles Storrs*), Gladys George (*Mrs. Barber*), Laura Elliot (*Josephine*), Edgar Buchanan (*Dutch Surrency*), Michael Moore (*Taff*), John Dierkes (*Arnie*), Don Dunning, Warren Earl Fisk, James Van Horn, John Mansfield, Harvey Parry, Boyd "Red" Morgan, Frank Cordell, Leo J. McMahon (*Townsmen*), Howard Joslin (*Freed*), Robert G. Anderson (*Rucker*), Frank Fenton (*Creede*), Myron O. Healey (*Bleek*), James R. Scott (*Miner*), Paul E. Burns (*Paxton*), Cliff Clark (*Bartender*), Billy House (*Malone*), Howard Negley (*Spence Fuller*), Ray Hyke (*Dacy*), Slim Gaut (*Storekeeper*).

Buchanan and De Carlo are a father and daughter who lease a silver mine from Fitzgerald. They find a rich pocket of the metal and with it comes trouble in the form of Fitzgerald's hired gun Moore. O'Brien is a mining expert who's been disgraced and is trying to return to his former profession. Arlen is trying to stop him. When O'Brien comes to the aid of Buchanan and De Carlo he wins the daughter's heart. Of course there are the usual fights, gunplay, and a few explosions as well in this average western with an above average cast. The ensemble makes the film work nicely for what it is. Unlike most westerns, the romance is given almost as much development as the story's action.

p, Nat Holt; d, Byron Haskin; w, Frank Gruber (based on a story by Luke Short); ph, Ray Rennahan (Technicolor); m, Paul Sawtell; ed, Elmo Billings; art d, Hal Pereira, Franz Bachelin.

Western   **(PR:C MPAA:NR)**

SILVER CITY BONANZA**½   (1951) 67m REP bw

Rex Allen (*Himself*), Buddy Ebsen (*Gabriel Horne*), Mary Ellen Kay (*Katie McIntosh*), Billy Kimbley (*Jimmy McIntosh*), Alix Ebsen (*Susie McIntosh*), Bill Kennedy (*Monk Monroe*), Gregg Barton (*Hank*), Clem Bevans (*Townsman*), Frank Jenks (*Theater Owner*), Hank Patterson (*Postman*), Harry Lauter (*Peter*), Harry Harvey (*Groggins*), "Koko."

Knife-throwing Kennedy murders a blind man and tries to force Kay off of her ranch so he can get at the silver he knows is on the bottom of her land's lake. Allen and comedy sidekick Ebsen are the two heroic cowpokes who use the blind man's dog to track down Kennedy and stop his evil schemes once and for all. This is definitely one of the more outrageous programmer westerns, utilizing a haunted ranch and an underwater battle as plot devices! However, the film is just amiable enough to make the fantastic script (by the always imaginative Williams) work well in its own way. Roy Rogers and Republic parted company the year of this film's release; singing star Allen had been groomed by the company's clever head man, Herbert J. Yates, as the new "King of the Cowboys," just as Rogers had been groomed to replace Gene Autry in that sobriquet. By this time, though, the singing-cowboy craze had nearly run its course. Comic-relief Ebsen dances with little Alix Ebsen in one sequence. He does well; and why not? He and his sister Vilma had done a dance act in the Ziegfeld Follies and in vaudeville and early films for some years. The lovely Kay was given substantially more to do in this film than most heroines in most westerns; she made five others with Allen in 1951 and 1952, and also worked with western stars Allan "Rocky" Lane and Charles Starrett. Songs – sung by Allen, of course – include "Lollipop Lane," "Sweet Evalina," and the cowpoke classic "I Ride an Old Paint."

p, Melville Tucker; d, George Blair; w, Bob Williams; ph, John MacBurnie; m, Stanley Wilson; ed, Robert M. Leeds; art d, Frank Hotaling.

Western   **(PR:A MPAA:NR)**

SILVER CITY KID**   (1944) 55m REP bw

Allan "Rocky" Lane, Peggy Stewart, Wally Vernon, Twinkle Watts, Frank Jacquet, Harry Woods, Glenn Strange, Lane Chandler, Bud Geary, Tom London, Tom Steele, Jack Kirk, Sam Flint, Frank McCarroll, Hal Price, Edward Piel, Sr, Fred Graham, Frank O'Connor, Horace B. Carpenter.

Lane is the foreman of a silver mine working to expose a local banker who has been stealing the valuable ore for his own purposes. A Republic

programmer that stands up as a good action picture.

p, Stephen Auer; d, John English; w, Taylor Caven (based on a story by Bennett Cohen); ph, Reggie Lanning; m, Joseph Dubin; ed, Charles Craft; art d, Fred A. Ritter.

Western   **Cas.**   **(PR:A MPAA:NR)**

SILVER CITY RAIDERS***   (1943) 55m COL bw (GB: LEGAL LARCENY)

Russell Hayden (*Lucky Harlan*), Bob Wills (*Bob Wills*), Dub Taylor (*Cannonball*), Alma Carroll (*Dolores Alvarez*), Paul Sutton (*Dawson*), Luther Wills (*Steve*), Jack Ingram (*Dirk*), Edmund Cobb (*Ringo*), Art Mix (*Slim*), Jack Rockwell, John Tyrell, Merrill McCormack, George Morrell, Horace B. Carpenter, Tex Palmer.

Ingram is a nasty land grabber who uses all sorts of dirty tricks to stop Hayden and his rancher buddies from getting the land they rightfully deserve. Of course Hayden defeats the man with some good comedy support from Taylor. Well acted and nicely directed, this is a good entry in the eight films of the series Hayden made for Columbia. Wills and his Texas Playboys provide some of their "Western Swing," which darn near steals the show.

p, Leon Barsha; d, William Berke; w, Ed Earl Repp; ph, Benjamin Kline; ed, Jerome Thoms.

Western   **(PR:A MPAA:NR)**

SILVER CORD**½   (1933) 75m RKO bw

Irene Dunne (*Christina Phelps*), Joel McCrea (*David Phelps*), Frances Dee (*Hester Phelps*), Eric Linden (*Robert Phelps*), Laura Hope Crews (*Mrs. Phelps*), Helen Cromwell (*Delia*), Gustav von Seyffertitz, Reginald Pasch, Perry Ivins.

Crews, who was later to portray everybody's twittery, lightheaded aunt, is superb in this Oedipal film – adapted from a Theater Guild stage play – that anticipated the "momism" concept of Philip Wylie's famed book of 1942, *Generation of Vipers*. The mother of married son McCrea – who, at the instigation of wife Dunne, has left the nest – and of single son Linden – who is romantically involved with Dee – clings to her younger boy with the tenacity of an octopus. When scientist Dunne is transferred to New York from her native Germany, she and husband McCrea pay a courtesy call on mom, who expends every effort to get them to settle in with her. Crews uses every trick in the book to rejoin the severed umbilical cords, including simulated heart failure. Dunne's strength of character suffices to wrench husband McCrea away, but the younger Linden succumbs to mom's importunities and gives Dee up to remain at home. Audiences of the time found some of Crews' tricks funny. Dunne, who was an up-and-comer at the studio, got top billing over Crews. She did well with her role, but it was Crews' picture all the way.

p, Pandro S. Berman; d, John Cromwell; w, Jane Murfin (based on the play by Sidney Howard); ph, Charles Rosher; m, Max Steiner; ed, George Nicholls, Jr.

Drama   **(PR:A MPAA:NR)**

SILVER DARLINGS, THE**   (1947, Brit.) 93m Holyrood/Pathe bw

Clifford Evans (*Roddy*), Helen Shingler (*Catrine*), Carl Bernard (*Angus*), Norman Shelley (*Hendry*), Jean Shepheard (*Mrs. Hendry*), Simon Lack (*Don*), Norman Williams (*Tormad*), Phyllis Morris (*Tormad's Mother*), Murdo Morrison (*Finn*), Christopher Capon (*Finn as a Child*), Stanley Jay (*Bo'sun*), Harry Fine (*Lieutenant*), Josephine Stuart (*Una*), Carole Lesley [Lester] (*Una as a Child*), Iris Vandeleur (*Kirsty*), Jack Faint (*Skipper Bremner*), Hugh Griffith (*Packman*), Bennett O'Loghlin (*Callum*), Wilfred Caithness (*1st Crofter*), Michael Martin-Harvey (*2nd Crofter*), Anne Allan (*Meg*), Phema Clyne (*Marie*), Peter Illing (*Foreign Buyer*), Roddy Hughes (*Shoemaker*), Hamilton Deane (*Professor*), Kenneth Warrington (*Doctor*), Paula Clyne.

In the Hebrides Islands Williams, a dispossessed farmer, is a herring fisherman. His wife (Shingler) hates the life of the sea and when her husband is forced by a press gang to go into the Navy she goes to live with an aunt. In this new locale Shingler meets Evans, the skipper of a herring boat. She ignores the smell and falls for him but the romance is interrupted by a cholera outbreak, her son's will to become a fisherman, and a few storms. Of course the lovers end up together in a final embrace, but who could expect anything less from this routine, uninspired drama? The plot works against the remainder of the film, which otherwise is a John Grierson-inspired documentary about the hard lives of the Hebridean crofters forced by the hard conditions of their infertile isles to take to the sea. Grierson himself handled the subject much better in his first directorial effort, DRIFTERS (1929). (Documentary films are not included in *The Motion Picture Guide*.) Writer/codirector Elder had been the supervising art director of more than 250 pictures; this was his maiden directorial effort. Star and codirector Evans had been acting in films since 1936 and writing screenplays for Ealing Studios.

p, Karl Grune; d, Clarence Elder, Clifford Evans; w, Elder (based on the novel by Neil M. Gunn); ph, Francis Carver; m, Clifton Parker; ed, Max

Brenner; md, Muir Mathieson, John Hollingsworth, Robert King; art d, Ivan King; spec eff, Leslie Ostinelli; makeup, Robert Clark.

Drama   (PR:A MPAA:NR)

SILVER DEVIL   (SEE: WILD HORSE, 1931)

SILVER DOLLAR*½**   (1932) 83m FN bw

Edward G. Robinson (*Yates Martin*), Bebe Daniels (*Lily Owens*), Aline MacMahon (*Sarah Martin*), Jobyna Howland (*Poker Annie*), De Witt Jennings (*Mine Foreman*), Robert Warwick (*Col. Stanton*), Russell Simpson (*Hamlin*), Harry Holman (*Adams*), Charles Middleton (*Jenkins*), John Marston (*Gelsey*), Marjorie Gateson (*Mrs. Adams*), Emmett Corrigan (*President Chester A. Arthur*), Wade Boteler, William Le Maire, David Durand (*Miner*), Lee Kohlmar (*Rische*), Theresa Conover (*Mrs. Hamlin*), Leon Waycoff 'Ames' (*Secretary*), Virginia Edwards (*Emma Abbott*), Christian Rub (*Hook*), Walter Rogers (*Gen. Grant*), Niles Welch (*William Jennings Bryan*), Bonita Granville (*Little Girl in Store*), Wilfred Lukas, Alice Wetherfield, Herman Bing, Walter Long, Willard Robertson, Frederick Burton, Charles Coleman.

Robinson turns in one of his greatest performances in this little-seen fictionalized screen biography of H.A.W. "Silver Dollar" Tabor, a lowly farmer who struck it rich with a silver mine and gained political power only to lose everything when the nation switched to the gold standard. Renamed Yates Martin for the film because Tabor's widow (nicknamed "Baby Doe") was still alive during the production, Robinson is a Kansas farmer who packs up his belongings and his wife MacMahon and heads for Colorado to open a general store in the hope of getting rich off all the prospectors flooding the area. Unfortunately, Robinson begins extending credit to the miners and soon finds himself broke. Just as he and MacMahon are about to give up and return to Kansas, Robinson stumbles across a rich vein of silver and suddenly finds himself a millionaire. Because of his new-found wealth Robinson is able to enter politics, being elected to such important offices as mayor, postmaster, sheriff, and lieutenant governor. Robinson spends his money as if there is no tomorrow and gives liberally to every charity that crosses his path. Not only does he throw money at charitable causes, but he sinks a huge portion of his fortune into a mansion in Denver and an opera house. While living in the fast lane Robinson meets Daniels, a beautiful blonde who lives for luxury. Taken with this new woman, Robinson leaves his boring wife for the nightlife-loving Daniels. The relationship causes a scandal and threatens to destroy his bid for a seat in the U.S. Senate, but Robinson survives the crisis, gets elected, divorces MacMahon, and marries Daniels. During his stay in Washington, D.C., Robinson socializes with such luminaries as Presidents Grant (Rogers) and Arthur (Corrigan) and a young William Jennings Bryan (Welch). Back in Denver, Robinson continues his carefree spending habits which are now pushed to new heights by Daniels. Eventually disaster strikes when President Cleveland switches the country to a gold standard, demonetizing silver. Robinson's fortune is wiped out by the stroke of a pen. When the money vanishes so does Daniels and Robinson spends the rest of his days wandering the streets he helped build. The once wealthy and important man stumbles into the opera house he built and dies of a heart attack–alone. Though the film is directed in a straightforward, unimaginative manner by helmsman Green, SILVER DOLLAR is dominated by Robinson's superb and detailed performance which proved to Hollywood he could handle more than tough-guy gangster roles. The rather melodramatic life of H.A.W. Tabor was also turned into a popular opera in 1956 entitled "The Ballad of Baby Doe" by Douglas Moore and John Latouche. The real-life "Baby Doe" Tabor lived alone in a cabin near the silver mine that started it all. She was found in the cabin–well into her 80s–frozen to death in 1935.

d, Alfred E. Green; w, Carl Erickson, Harvey Thew (based on a biography by David Karsner); ph, James Van Trees; ed, George Marks; art d, Robert Haas; cos, Orry-Kelly.

Biographical Drama   (PR:A MPAA:NR)

SILVER DREAM RACER*   (1982, Brit.) 111m Wickes-RANK/Almi c

David Essex (*Nick Freeman*), Beau Bridges (*Bruce McBride*), Cristina Raines (*Julie Prince*), Clarke Peters (*Cider Jones*), Harry H. Corbett (*Wiggins*), Diane Keen (*Tina*), Lee Montague (*Jack Freeman*), Sheila White (*Carol*), David Baxt (*Ben Mendoza*), Ed Bishop (*Al Peters*), Nick Brimble (*Jack Davis*), Stephen Hoye (*Clarke Nichols*), T. P. McKenna (*Bank Manager*), Richard Parmentier (*Journalist*), Patrick Ryecart (*Benson*).

Someone influential in Britain's Rank Organization had been watching too many Yankee biker pictures. Minor cult rock star Essex stars as a garage mechanic with a sneer. He's also got the hot prototype motorcycle of his late elder brother and fully intends to enter it in a race against American punk Bridges. Bridges is known as one of the dirtiest racers since Professor Fate went up against The Great Leslie in THE GREAT RACE (1965) but you'd never guess that from the racing sequences here. The poor editor must have worked late into the night trying to piece the footage together in an exciting fashion, but it doesn't work in the least. The plot is a string of cliches leading up to some unispired racing. The direction is confusing as the script is bad, leaving the fairly good cast floundering about in a very bad movie. Essex wrote the music for the film though it's in no way up to regular caliber.

p, Rene Dupont; d&w, David Wickes; ph, Paul Beeson (Panavision, Eastmancolor) ; m, David Essex; ed, Peter Hollywood; md, John Cameron; art d, Malcolm Middleton; cos, Judy Moorcroft.

Drama   Cas.   (PR:C MPAA:PG)

SILVER DUST***   (1953, USSR) 102m Mosfilm bw (USSR: SIERIEBRISTAYA PYL)

M. Bolduman, Valentina Utchakova, Vladimir Larionov, A. Chanov, S. Pilyavskaya.

After 1949, the spate of anti-German, pro-ally films ceased in the Soviet Union, and many of the great directors were castigated as pro-Western revisionists. Director Room had made the picture IN THE MOUNTAINS OF YUGOSLAVIA in 1946. This film lauded the exploits of Marshal Tito, who became anathema to Russia's Josef Stalin, so Room was suspect and references to the film were expunged from Soviet history books. Like many other Soviet directors, Room hastened to do a film in which Cold-War America was depicted as a menace. This phase of Soviet filmmaking lasted until the death of Stalin in 1953., This film tells the story of an American scientist (Bolduman) who discovers a radioactive dust and then searches for some human subjects to test it on. He's got some competition for the atomic substance from a pair of businessmen, who with the aid of a war-minded general and an ex-Nazi scientist (apparently modeled on Werner von Braun) are after the dust for their own purposes. This is a clever and amusing little film, photographed by Tisse, the lensman for the great Soviet director Eisenstein. In an interesting Cold War parallel, SILVER DUST might be considered the Soviet counterpart to 1950s Hollywood films portraying Communists. However the film was viewed by a reporter from Life magazine, who angrily accused SILVER DUST of being "red propaganda." Considering that the American government did indeed use its military personnel and prison populations for tests similar to those portrayed here, SILVER DUST might better be considered as some astute thinking on the part of its creators.

d, Abram Room; w, August Jakobson, A. Filimonov; ph, Edouard Tisse; spec eff, P. Malaniksev.

Satire   (PR:C MPAA:NR)

SILVER FLEET, THE**½**   (1945, Brit.) 77m The Archers/PRC bw

Ralph Richardson (*Jaap van Leyden*), Googie Withers (*Helene van Leyden*), Esmond Knight (*Von Schiller*), Beresford Egan (*Krampf*), Frederick Burtwell (*Capt. Muller*), Willem Akkerman (*Willem van Leyden*), Dorothy Gordon (*Janni Peters*), Charles Victor (*Bastiaan Peters*), John Longden (*Jost Meertens*), Valentine Dyall (*Markgraf*), Philip Leaver (*Chief of Police*), Ivor Barnard (*Admiral von Rapp*), Margaret Emden (*Bertha*), Joss Ambler (*Cornelius Smit*), Kathleen Byron (*School-mistress*), George Schelderup (*Dirk*), Neville Mapp (*Joop*), John Carol (*Johann*), John Arnold (*U-Boat Navigator*), Laurence O'Madden (*Capt. Schneider*), Anthony Eustrel (*Lt. Wernicke*), Charles Minor (*Bohme*), Lt. Schouwenaar (*U-Boat Captain*), Lt. Van Dapperen (*U-Boat Lieutenant*), personnel of the Royal Netherlands Navy.

During WW II, Richardson is a Dutch shipyard engineer who helps the Nazis build two prototype submarines. His friends and his wife stop speaking to him since they think Richardson has allied himself with the enemy. It turns out that Richardson is a hero, though, for he convinces top Nazi officials to accompany him on the ship's trial voyage. Unbeknownst to the Germans, Richardson has rigged the U-boat with dynamite, killing both himself and the enemy in a fiery explosion. Simultaneously, he has arranged for the commando-raid capture of a sister submarine by partisans, who get it to England. Richardson gives his usual fine performance in this routine film – released in 1943 in England – in support of war effort.It's a little slow to start, but once the script knows where it's going, THE SILVER FLEET becomes a nifty little story packed into the propaganda formula. Actor Knight, a wartime hero – he was blinded during the British attack on the pocket battleship Bismarck — gives a stunningly menacing performance as the chief of the Gestapo at the occupied shipyard. Producers Powell and Pressburger proved to be one of Britain's best filmmaking teams in later years with such marvelous pieces as THE RED SHOES (1948). Richardson also served as a coproducer here.

p, Michael Powell, Emeric Pressburger, Ralph Richardson; d&w, Vernon Campbell Sewell, Gordon Wellesley; ph, Erwin Hillier, Cecil Cooney; m, Allan Gray; ed, Michael C. Chorlton; prod d, Alfred Junge.

War Drama   (PR:A MPAA:NR)

SILVER HORDE, THE**½**   (1930) 76m RKO bw

Evelyn Brent (*Cherry Malotte*), Louis Wolheim (*George Balt*), Joel McCrea (*Boyd Emerson*), Raymond Hatton (*Fraser*), Jean Arthur (*Mildred Wayland*), Gavin Gordon (*Fred Marsh*), Blanche Sweet (*Queenie*), Purnell Pratt (*Wayne Wayland*), William B. Davidson (*Thomas Hilliard*), Ivan Linow (*Svenson*).

It's rough-and-ready action set against the background of Alaskan salmon fishing. McCrea, in his first he-man part, is fighting both for control of a fishery as well as control of his love life. Dance-hall floozy Brent helps the macho man defeat villainous competitor Gordon, and proves to be the real lady for him, despite inroads on his heart by society-lady Arthur. Of course they defeat him in the end, but not without a few fist:cuffs. This worked well in parts, with some good action sequences and a newsreel style look at the processes of a salmon cannery. It had previously been produced as a silent film in 1920, taking its story from a popular novel by Beach. THE SILVER HORDE proved to be a pretty good part for McCrea and was one of his earliest breaks. This was veteran character actor Hatton's first "sidekick" role – that of McCrea's comic-relief companion – in a talking picture. He went on to play similar parts in a host of westerns. Sweet, a fine actress in many silent pictures, ended her film career here with a small, inconsequential part that was undeserving of her talents. Arthur would go on to work with Frank Capra on many films, though none of her real talents are evident in THE SILVER HORDE.

p, William Le Baron; d, George Archainbaud; w, Wallace Smith (based on the novel by Rex Beach); ph, Leo Tover; ed, Otto Ludwig; art d, Max Ree.

Adventure   **(PR:A MPAA:NR)**

SILVER KEY, THE   (SEE: GIRL IN THE CASE, 1944)

SILVER LINING** (1932) 75m Patrician/UA bw (AKA: THE SILVER LINING; THIRTY DAYS)

Maureen O'Sullivan (Joyce Moore), Betty Compson (Kate Flynn), John Warburton (Larry Clark), Montagu Love (Michael Moore), Mary Doran (Doris Lee), Cornelius Keefe (Jerry), Martha Mattox (Matron), Wally Albright (Bobby O'Brien), Grace Valentine (Mrs. O'Brien), John Holland.

A story of tenement life opens with a small boy falling down three flights of stairs. Warburton is a lawyer who goes to wealthy slum landlordO'Sullivan (giving one of her worst performances in an otherwise fine career) for damages. She won't pay and her uncle argues with her over this. O'Sullivan ends up walking out and is mugged for her troubles. The cops mistake her for a drunk and she gets thrown in jail for 30 days. There she meets Compson, a slumdweller who has taken the rap for the mother of the injured boy. Compson's in the pokey because the boy's mom, her neighbor, stole some food to feed her child. SILVER LINING does its best as O'Sullivan does an about-face and ends up marrying Clark. The story is full of implausible situations that haven't aged well. By contemporary standards this is pretty funny stuff. The direction is all right considering the material's inherent shortcomings and performances are fair to middling.

p, George Bertholon; d, Alan Crosland; w, Gertrude Orr, Clair Corvalho (based on a story by Hal Conklin); ph, Robert Planck h; m, Lee Zahler; ed, Doris Draught; art d, Jack Schultze.

Drama   **(PR:A MPAA:NR)**

SILVER LODE***   (1954) 80m RKO-Pinecrest/RKO c

John Payne (Dan Ballard), Dan Duryea (Ned McCarthy), Lizabeth Scott (Rose Evans), Dolores Moran (Dolly), Emile Meyer (Sheriff Wooley), Harry Carey, Jr (Johnson), Morris Ankrum (Zachary Evans), John Hudson (Michael "Mitch" Evans), Robert Warwick (Judge Cranston), Stuart Whitman (Wickers), Alan Hale, Jr (Kirk), Frank Sully (Paul Herbert), Paul Birch (Reverend Field), Florence Auer (Mrs. Elmwood), Roy Gordon (Dr. Elmwood), Edgar Barrier (Taylor), Al Hill, Gene Roth (Townsmen), Al Haskel (Deputy), William Haade, Frank Ellis, I. Stanford Jolley (Searchers), Barbara Wooddell, Sheila Bromley (Townswomen), Lane Chandler (Man at Fire), Joe Devlin (Walt Little), Burt Mustin (Spectator), John Dierkes (Blacksmith), Byron Foulger (Prescott, Banker), Ralph Sanford (Joe, the Bartender), Myron Healey (Rider).

On the day of his wedding to Scott, Payne is surprised by four strangers who ride into town. Their leader, Duryea, says that Payne is wanted for murder in California. Payne knows he's innocent and tries to convince his friends that these so-called marshals are wrong. However, he quickly discovers that his friends are a bunch of hypocrites who turn their back on him now that Payne is in trouble. He's forced to prove himself at the end in a climactic gunfight. Duryea is proved a fake and Payne knows who his friends are. This interesting little western was intended as a quick programmer with obvious debts to the classic HIGH NOON. However, Dwan's direction gives the film an interesting visual style that propels the material to a higher plane. Though some of the acting leaves a little to be desired there's a certain degree of realism to the film, nicely captured against the Technicolor scenery. Some thought SILVER LODE served as a fine allegory to the political climate of the time, conveying some definite anti-(Sen. Joseph) McCarthy values. The entire film takes place during a three-hour period on July 4, with an apparent debt to Akiro Kurosawa evident in recurrent scenes of the same happening seen through the memories and the prejudices of the different principals, as in RASHOMON (1951).

p, Benedict Bogeaus; d, Allan Dwan; w, Karen De Wolfe; ph, John Alton (Technicolor); m, Louis Forbes; ed, James Leicester; art d, Van Nest Polglase.

Western   **(PR:A MPAA:NR)**

SILVER ON THE SAGE**½   (1939) 66m PAR bw

William Boyd (Hopalong Cassidy), Russell Hayden (Lucky Jenkins), George!!gabby]iF. Hayes (Windy Halliday), Ruth Rogers (Barbara Hamilton), Stanley Ridges (Earl Brennan/Dave Talbot), Frederick Burton (Tom Hamilton), Jack Rockwell (City Marshal), Roy Barcroft (Ewing), Edward Cassidy (Pierce), Wen Wright (Lane), Jim Corey (Martin), Sherry Tansey (Baker), Bruce Mitchell (Bartender), Hank Bell, George Morrell, Frank O'Connor, Buzz Barton, Herman Hack, Dick Dickinson, Topper the Horse.

Having had a herd of Bar 20 cattle rustled away by unknown crooks, Boyd goes undercover as an eastern gambler and gets a job as a dealer in Ridges' gambling den in order to dig up information on the rustlers. He suspects that casino owner Ridges and a local ranch foreman are actually twin brothers who provide alibis for each other when committing crimes. When one is out rustling, the other dresses in his brother's clothes and makes himself conspicuous, thus providing witnesses that will swear they saw him on the night of the crime. Boyd's identity is revealed, however, when a gunslinger in town for a bit of gambling recognizes him. Ridges plans to trap Boyd and kill him, but Hoppy outwits them and a posse captures the Ridges brothers and their gang. A better than average "Hopalong Cassidy" adventure highlighted by Boyd's obvious relish with playing an eastern dandy for laughs. (See HOPALONG CASSIDY series, Index.)

p, Harry Sherman; d, Lesley Selander; w, Maurice Geraghty (based on the novel On The Trail of the Tumbling T by Clarence E. Mulford); ph, Russell Harlan; ed, Robert Warwick; md, Borris Morros; art d, Lewis J. Rachmil.

Western   **Cas.**   **(PR:A MPAA:NR)**

SILVER QUEEN**   (1942) 80m UA bw

George Brent (James Kincaid), Priscilla Lane (Coralie Adams), Bruce Cabot (Gerald Forsythe), Lynne Overman (Hector Bailey), Eugene Pallette (Steve Adams), Janet Beecher (Mrs. Forsythe), Guinn "Big Boy" Williams (Blackie), Roy Barcroft (Dan Carson), Eleanor Stewart (Millicent Bailey), Arthur Hunnicutt (Brett, Editor), Sam McDaniel (Toby), Spencer Charters (Doc Stonebraker), Cy Kendall (Sheriff), Georges Renavent (Andres, Maitre'D), Francis X. Bushman, Franklyn Farnum (Creditors), Marietta Canty (Ruby), Herbert Rawlinson (Judge), George Eldredge (Admirer), Earle Hodgins (Desk Clerk), Fred "Snowflake" Toones (Butler), Frederick Burton (Dr. Hartley), Ed Cassidy (Colonel), Jason Robards, Sr (Bank Teller).

Lane plays an aristocratic young woman of the 1870s who finds herself in trouble after her ne'er-do-well gambling father (Pallette) passes away. He leaves her numerous debts and has gambled away a rich silver mine. The deed for the mine is later won by Brent in a poker game and he falls for Lane when he discovers the origins of his prize. She's marrying Cabot, though, a man who can give her back the social standing she once held. Brent gives the deed to Cabot as a present for the bride, but she never sees it. Lane decides to run off to the West and open a saloon called the "Silver Queen." With the profits she is able to pay off the family debts with the money she sends back entrusted to Cabot. Cabot uses the money to look for more silver in the mine, though, and it's up to Brent to right all the wrongs. Typical western material with standard direction and a somewhat overblown budget for a B picture. Young received an Oscar nomination for his musical score.

p, Harry Sherman; d, Lloyd Bacon; w, Bernard Schubert, Cecile Kramer (based on original story by Forrest Halsey, William Allen Johnston); ph, Russell Harlan; m, Victor Young; ed, Sherman A. Rose; art d, Ralph Berger.

Western   **Cas.**   **(PR:A MPAA:NR)**

SILVER RAIDERS**   (1950) 55m MON bw

Whip Wilson (Larry), Andy Clyde (Quincy), Leonard Penn (Corbin), Dennis Moore (Boland), Virginia Herrick (Patricia), Patricia Rios (Dolores), Reed Howes (George), Riley Hill (Bill), Marshall Reed (Horn), George DeNormand (Clark), Kermit Maynard (Larkin).

Plenty of action and western cliches all packed into a little less than an hour. Wilson is an Arizona ranger who infiltrates a group of outlaws. The gang is smuggling silver from Mexico to the U.S. and Wilson puts a handy stop to the proceedings after they kidnap a young Mexican lady. Typical stuff.

p, Vincent M. Fennelly; d, Wallace W. Fox; w, Dan Ullman; ph, Harry Neumann; ed, Richard Heermance; md, Edward Kay; art d, Dave Milton.

Western   **(PR:A MPAA:NR)**

SILVER RIVER**   (1948) 108m WB bw

Errol Flynn (Capt. Mike McComb), Ann Sheridan (Georgia Moore), Thomas Mitchell (John Plato Beck), Bruce Bennett (Stanley Moore), Tom D'Andrea (Pistol Porter), Barton MacLane (Banjo Sweeney), Monte Blue (Buck Chevigee), Jonathan Hale (Maj. Spencer), Alan Bridge (Sam Slade), Arthur Space (Maj. Ross), Art Baker (Maj. Wilson), Joe Crehan (President Grant), Norman Jolley (Scout), Jack Davis (Judge Advocate), Harry Strang (Soldier), Norman Willis (Honest Harry), Ian Wolfe (Deputy), Jim Ames (Barker), Lois Austin, Gladys Turney (Ladies), Marjorie Bennett (Large Woman), Dorothy Christy, Grayce Hampton (Women), Joe Bernard (River Boat Captain), Harry Hayden (Schaefer, the Teller), Lester Dorr (Taylor), Russell

Hicks (*Edwards, the Architect*), Fred Kelsey (*Townsman*), Ben Corbett (*Henchman*), Leo White (*Barber*), Franklyn Farnum (*Officer*), Bud Osborne (*Posse Man*), Ed Parker (*Bugler*), Jerry Jerome, Harry Strang, Frank McCarroll, James H. Harrison, Bob Stephenson, Ross Ford (*Soldiers*), Henry "Harry" Morgan (*Tailor*), Harry Woods (*Card Player*), Dan White, Otto Reichow (*Miners*).

The seventh and final collaboration between director Walsh and star Flynn was a clunker and came nowhere near the excitement and verve of their previous works. The picture begins with lots of action then disintegrates into talkiness. It's quite unsatisfying for many reasons, the most important of which is that Flynn is seen as a power-hungry cad who will stop at nothing to gain his goals. Flynn is tossed out of the Union Army and takes up gambling for a living, then uses his strength to move in on the silver mining business and winds up as an important man in the area. He loves Sheridan but she's married to Bennett, who works for him, so he deliberately sends Bennett into a situation where the man is killed so Flynn can marry his widow. Mitchell is Flynn's boozy attorney and helps him expand his interests until Flynn is involved in banking, and other income producing businesses. When Sheridan sees what kind of a man Flynn really is, she leaves him and he suddenly realizes that he's been on the wrong path so he changes his ways and begins to fight on behalf of the poor and downtrodden. MacLane makes a fine villain and D'Andrea as Flynn's sidekick does a good portrayal of a pal who sticks by his friend through almost everything. Shot in the High Sierras, Calabasas and Hollywood, SILVER RIVER was based on an unpublished novel by Stephen Longstreet, who has had a long career in yet another field, art. Longstreet's sketches of Ghandi, Virginia Woolf and George Bernard Shaw are quite valuable and if he ever lost the power to write, he could make a fine living as a water colorist. The love story in this movie is a thinly-veiled 1860s version of the David and Bathsheba tale. Walsh and Flynn were long-time pals and made a pact that required Flynn to stay sober until after five in the afternoon, at which time Walsh would sit down and tipple with Flynn. Walsh was a stern taskmaster who could always control the mercurial Tasmanian but 3 years had passed since their last film and Flynn grew irate in Walsh's leash this time and seemed disinterested in the material.

p, Owen Crump; d, Raoul Walsh; w, Stephen Longstreet, Harriet Frank Jr. (based on an unpublished novel by Longstreet); ph, Sid Hickox; m, Max Steiner; ed, Alan Crosland, Jr.; art d, Ted Smith; set d, William G. Wallace; cos, William Travilla, Marjorie Best; spec eff, William McGann, Edwin DuPar; makeup, Perc Westmore; tech adv, J.G. Taylor.

Western   **(PR:A   MPAA:NR)**

SILVER SKATES★★½   (1943) 75m MON bw

Kenny Baker (*Danny*), Patricia Morison (*Claire*), Belita (*Belita*), Frick & Frack (*Themselves*), Danny Shaw (*Billie*), Irene Dare (*Katrina*), Eugene Turner (*Himself*), Joyce Compton (*Lucille*), Frank Faylen (*Eddie*), Paul McVey (*Hayes*), Ruth Lee (*Mrs. Martin*), John Maxwell (*Blake*), Henry Wadsworth (*Tom*), George Stewart (*Himself*), Jo Ann Dean (*Herself*), Ted Fio Rito and His Orchestra.

The minor story involving a romance between Baker and Morison as a singer and ice-skating impresario was little more than Monogram's excuse to sink more than their usual measure of production dollars into this not-so-bad film built around various skating talents. Some good camera work follows the skaters around the ice, and young Dare gets in three good routines. She had previously done a few skating pictures for producer Sol Lesser and shows her talents nicely in this film, as do Belita and champion Turner. The light musical numbers were tailored for Baker's tenor voice and include: "Dancing on Top of the World," "Cowboy Joe," "Can't You Hear Me Calling from the Mountain," "Lovely Lady," "Love is a Beautiful Song," "A Girl Like You – A Boy Like Me" (David Oppenheim, Roy Ingraham), "Sing a Song of the Sea" (Oppenheim, Archie Gottler).

p, Lindsley Parsons; d, Leslie Goodwins; w, Jerry Cady; ph, Mack Stengler; m, David Oppenheim, Roy Ingraham; ed, Richard Currier; md, Edward Kay.

Musical   **(PR:A   MPAA:NR)**

SILVER SPOON, THE★   (1934, Brit.) 64m WB-FN bw

Ian Hunter (*Capt. Watts-Winyard*), Garry Marsh (*Hon. Roland Stone*), Binnie Barnes (*Lady Perivale*), Cecil Parker (*Trevor*), Cecil Humphreys (*Lord Perivale*), Joan Playfair (*Denise*), O.B. Clarence (*Parker*), George Merritt (*Inspector Innes*).

Inane comedy starring Hunter and Marsh as two former society gents down on their luck and living as tramps. When the police announce that the woman they love, Barnes, has been accused of murdering her husband, Humphreys, the noble bums take the rap for her. Predictably, the real murderer is caught before Hunter and Marsh are executed, ensuring a happy ending to this insipid outing.

p, Irving Asher; d, George King; w, Brock Williams; ph, Basil Emmott.

Comedy   **(PR:A   MPAA:NR)**

SILVER SPURS★★   (1936) 61m UNIV bw

Charles "Buck" Jones (*Jim Fentriss*), Muriel Evans (*Janet Allison*), J. P. McGowan (*Webb Allison*), Robert Fraser (*Art Holden*), William Lawrence (*Snell*), George Hayes (*Drag Harlan*), Earl Askam (*Durango*), Bruce Lane (*Yuma Kid*), Denny Meadows (*Dude*), George French (*Station Agent*), Beth Marion (*Peggy Wyman*), Kerman Cripps (*Sheriff*).

Fairly good Jones western features him going after some rustlers. Fraser is the bad guy. It's low on two-fisted action, but not a bad effort from the actors.

d, Ray Taylor; w, Joseph Franklin Poland (based on a story by Charles Alden Seltzer); ph, Allan Thompson, H. Kirkpatrick.

Western   **(PR:A   MPAA:NR)**

SILVER SPURS★★★   (1943) 68m REP bw

Roy Rogers (*Roy*), Trigger (*The Smartest Horse in the Movies*), Smiley Burnette (*Frog Milhouse*), John Carradine (*Lucky Miller*), Phyllis Brooks (*Mary Hardigan*), Jerome Cowan (*Jerry Johnson*), Joyce Compton (*Mildred "Millie" Love*), Dick Wessel (*Buck Walters*), Hal Taliaferro (*Steve Corlan*), Forrest Taylor (*Judge Pebble*), Charles Wilson (*Mr. Hawkins*), Bryon Foulger (*Justice of the Peace*), Bob Nolan and the Sons of the Pioneers, Jack Kirk, Kermit Maynard, Pat Brady, Jack O'Shea, Slim Whitaker, Arthur Loft, Eddy Waller, Tom London, Bud Osborne, Fred Burns, Henry Wills.

There's oil on Cowan's ranch and Carradine wants it. The wily villain also wants the railroad right-of-way for himself and tries to trip up Cowan with liquor and a mail-order bride. Rogers is on hand as the ranch foreman who catches on to Carradine but not before his boss is murdered by some henchmen. In an action-packed climax Rogers saves the day with the help of Trigger (did the mighty steed cut a deal with Rogers to get his billing in this outing?) and sidekick Burnette. Yakima Canutt, who served as John Wayne's nemesis in numerous B Westerns, provided the stunts for Rogers, putting in nearly as much time as Rogers. The direction is sharp and the production reflects the bigger budgets the studio was now giving its popular cowboy in this first of his films to appear following his cover appearance as "King of the Cowboys" in the hugely popular *Life* magazine.

p, Harry Grey; d, Joseph Kane; w, John K. Butler, J. Benton Cheney; ph, Reggie Lanning; ed, Tony Martinelli; md, Morton Scott; art d, Russell Kimball; set d, Otto Siegel.

Western   **Cas.**   **(PR:A   MPAA:NR)**

SILVER STALLION★   (1941) 60m MON bw

David Sharpe (*Davey*), Janet Waldo (*Jan*), LeRoy Mason (*Pascal*), Chief Thundercloud (*Freshwater*), Thornton Edwards (*Tronco*), Walter Long (*Benson*), Fred Hoose (*Dad*), Thunder the Wonder Horse (*Silver Stallion*), Black Jack the Horse (*Black Stallion*), Captain Boots (*Boots the Police Dog*).

The title horse (actually white in color) fights off rattlesnakes, wild dogs, and other assorted creatures to protect his mare and foal. The story is confusing and utterly mindless, with an unconvincing additional plot line involving some horse stealing by bad guy Sharpe. A real mess.

p&d, Edward Finney; w, Robert Emmett (Tahsey); ph, Marcel A. LePicard; ed, Fred Bain.

Western   **(PR:A   MPAA:NR)**

SILVER STAR, THE★   (1955) 73m Lippert bw

Edgar Buchanan (*Bill Dowdy*), Marie Windsor (*Karen*), Lon Chaney, Jr (*John W. Harmon*), Earle Lyon (*Gregg*), Richard Bartlett (*King Daniels*), Barton MacLane (*Tiny*), Morris Ankrum (*Childress*), Edith Evanson (*Mrs. Dowdy*), Michael Whalen (*Brainey*), Steve Rowland (*Shakespeare*).

Lyon, who also served as producer, stars as a man elected sheriff of a western town. He doesn't want the job because he's a pacifist. His defeated opponent (Chaney) hires some killers (including director Bartlett) to take on Lyon. The new sheriff is forced to strap on his gun and take on the trio after Buchanan, a retired marshal, shames him into it. With heavy borrowing from HIGH NOON, THE SILVER STAR never builds the necessary moods or tension that would have made it work. The direction and performances are bland, causing the film to drag on until the final credits.

p, Earle Lyon; d, Richard Bartlett; w, Bartlett, Ian MacDonald; ph, Guy Roe; m, Leon Klatzken; ed, George Reid; m/l, Jimmy Wakely (sung by Wakely).

Western   **(PR:A   MPAA:NR)**

SILVER STREAK, THE★★   (1935) 85m RKO bw

Sally Blane (*Ruth Dexter*), Charles Starrett (*Tom Caldwell*), Hardie Albright (*Allan Dexter*), William Farnum (*B. J. Dexter*), Irving Pichel (*Bronte*), Arthur Lake (*Crawford*), Theodore von Eltz (*Ed Tyler*), Guinn "Big Boy" Williams (*Higgins*), Mechanic, Edgar Kennedy (*O'Brien*), Murray Kinnell (*Dr. Flynn*), Doris Dawson (*Molly*), Harry Allen (*McGregor*), James Bradbury (*Lowery*), Robert E. Homans (*Dam Engineer*), Dave O'Brien (*Dam Phone Operator*), John Dilson (*Doctor*).

Starrett, in his pre-cowboy days, is the engineer of a Chicago-to-Nevada train. On board are the usual cast of characters, including Farnum, the railroad president, and his daughter Blane – the apple of Starrett's eye. Pichel is a German mechanic in a hurry to leave Chicago after murdering an official from his native land at the Century of Progress exposition. Also aboard is a shipment of iron lungs which must reach their destination in just 19 hours in order to halt a deadly outbreak of infantile paralysis. It's all formula material, told at a lightning-fast pace which handily covers up the numerous holes and implausiblities. The Burlington Railroad's Zephyr gets plenty of plugs here, undoubtedly as compensation for RKO's use of their choo-choo. Audiences apparently enjoyed this train ride, for THE SILVER STREAK cleared over $107,000 in profits, a tidy sum for the day.

p, Glendon Allvine; d, Tommy Atkins, w, H. W. Hanemann, Jack O'Donnell, Roger Whately (based on a story by Whately); ph, Roy Hunt, Vernon Walker

Drama/Thriller   Cas.   **(PR:A MPAA:NR)**

SILVER STREAK**½   (1976) 113m FOX c

Gene Wilder (*George Caldwell*), Jill Clayburgh (*Hilly Burns*), Richard Pryor (*Grover Muldoon*), Patrick McGoohan (*Roger Devereau*), Ned Beatty (*Sweet*), Clifton James (*Sheriff Chauncey*), Ray Walston (*Mr. Whiney*), Stefan Gierasch (*Johnson/Prof. Schreiner*), Len Birman (*Chief*), Valerie Curtin (*Plain Jane*), Richard Kiel (*Reace/Goldtooth*), Lucille Benson (*Rita Babtree*), Scatman Crothers (*Ralston*), Fred Willard (*Jerry Jarvis*), Delos Smith (*Burt*), Matilda Calnan (*Blue-Haired Lady*), Nick Stewart (*Shoe Shiner*), Margarita Garcia (*Mexican Mama San*), Jack Mather (*Conductor*), Lloyd White (*Porter*), Ed McNamara (*Benny*), Ray Goth (*Night Watchman*), John Day (*Engineer*), Tom Erhart (*Cab Driver*), Gordon Hurst (*Moose*), Jack O'Leary, Lee McLaughlin (*Fat Men*), Henry Beckman, Steve Weston, Harvey Atkin (*Conventioneers*).

A derivative farce from one of the masters of derivation, Colin Higgins, who has made a career of studying Hitchcock, transforming some of the plots to comedies, and riding the crest of the wave to success. This picture earned well over $30 million due, in great part, to Pryor's brief but hysterical appearance. He and Wilder would team up again for STIR CRAZY. Wilder is a meek book executive who wants to take a leisurely train ride from Los Angeles to Chicago aboard the Silver Streak train but his trip turns out to be a nightmare. He meets and romances Clayburgh, an art professor's assistant who is traveling in an adjoining compartment. (Watching Wilder operate like Cary Grant just doesn't make any sense in this scene; it's something like seeing Douglas Fairbanks as Larry, Moe or Curly.) Clayburgh tells Wilder that her boss is about to expose a pack of art forgers. Wilder witnesses Clayburgh's boss falling off the speeding train. He races around the Silver Streak attempting to tell people what he's seen but nobody will believe him, with the exception of Beatty, an undercover agent masquerading as a traveling salesman. McGoohan is the leader of the villains and he is on to Beatty so he instructs his thugs to get rid of him, which they do. Meanwhile, McGoohan and Walston continue to attempt to kill Wilder, which results in a series of Harold Lloyd-type stunts as they keep throwing him off the train. Somehow, he manages to get back on each time in a comical fashion. About halfway into the story, Wilder is joined by Pryor and the movie takes a sudden turn to excellence. Wilder and Pryor have one funny scene where Pryor, in order to disguise him, blackens Wilder's face and teaches him how to walk like a hipster. The final scene has the train derailed and crashing through the Chicago station. This smash-up appears to have been tossed in for no other reason than to provide a spectacular ending. Clayburgh, who was coming off the disastrous GABLE AND LOMBARD and had since licked her critical wounds, delivers a believable performance but she is no Grace Kelly or Audrey Hepburn. Still, her work stands out as an oasis of characterization in a Sahara of madcap, antic, frenzied performances. It's almost as though she was acting in CHARADE while the others were in ABBOTT AND COSTELLO MEET THE MARX BROTHERS. Mancini's score is a bit too elegant and sophisticated for the goings-on. SILVER STREAK is a throwback to the screwball comedies of the 1930s but with none of the verve or the motivation needed to get an audience to swallow the shenanigans. What Higgins apparently did was to study STRANGERS ON A TRAIN, then THE LADY VANISHES, and figure a way to combine the two with a bit of laughter. (This is only supposition but appears to be well-founded. McGoohan, whom most believe is British because of his success on TV in "The Prisoner" and his many films in England, was actually born in the U.S.A. and acquired the accent later in his life. When director Hiller lays his hands on a good script, as in THE IN-LAWS and HOSPITAL, he does well but all his talents could not overcome all the cliches in ROMANTIC COMEDY or this. Wilder does his by now boring screaming act. He seems to have two speeds in his acting, frantic and manic. Some gory moments make this a bad selection for tots.

p, Thomas L. Miller, Edward K. Milkis; d, Arthur Hiller; w, Colin Higgins; ph, David M. Walsh, Ralph Woolsey (DeLuxe Color); m, Henry Mancini; ed, David Bretherton; prod d, Alfred Sweeney; set d, Marvin March; cos, Phyllis Garr, Michael Harte; spec eff, Fred Cramer; stunts, Mickey Gilbert; makeup, William Tuttle.

Comedy   Cas.   **(PR:C MPAA:PG)**

SILVER TOP*½   (1938, Brit.) 66m Triangle/PAR bw

Marie Wright (*Mrs. Deeping*), Betty Ann Davies (*Dushka Vernon*), Marjorie Taylor (*Hazel Summers*), David Farrar (*Babe*), Brian Buchel (*Flash Gerald*), Brian Herbert (*Jem Withers*), Polly Emery (*Martha Bains*), Isobel Scaife (*Aggie Murbles*), Alice Bolster, Fred Sinclair.

An unimaginative weepie starring Wright as a beloved old woman who owns the local confectionery. Recently she has inherited a small fortune which, of course, brings baddies to her door. Crooks force Farrar to pose as the woman's long-lost son in hopes of gaining access to the cash, but he falls in love with the vicar's daughter and undergoes a moral transformation, dropping out of the plan and confessing everything to Wright. Wright, of course, knew all along that Farrar wasn't really her son and forgives him. Pretty tedious.

p&d, George King; w, Gerald Elliott, Dorothy Greenhill (based on a story by Evadne Price); ph, Hone Glendinning.

Crime   **(PR:A MPAA:NR)**

SILVER TRAIL, THE*½   (1937) 58m Reliable/Principal bw

Rex Lease (*Bob Crandall*), Mary Russell (*Molly*), Ed Cassidy (*Sheridan*), Roger Williams (*Dunn*), Steve Clark (*Tom*), Slim Whittaker (*Slug*), Oscar Gahan (*Curt*), Sherry Tansey (*Tex*), Tom London (*Looney*), Rin-Tin-Tin, Jr (*Rinty*).

Stagey, dopey little melodrama features Lease as a miner whose partner is murdered. Claim grabbers have taken his mine and fooled around with the deed . The son of Rin-Tin-Tin runs around and barks a lot, but that's the extent of the realistic action and thespian talent in the film. The fights look like the fakes they are and the plot takes some boring, silly turns but never really goes anywhere. A real dog in every sense of the word.

p&d, Raymond Samuels [B. B. Ray] w, James Oliver Curwood, Forest Sheldon; ph, Pliny Goodfriend.

Western   **(PR:A MPAA:NR)**

SILVER TRAILS**½   (1948) 53m MON bw

Jimmy Wakely (*Jimmy*), "Cannonball"!!Dub]¡Taylor (*Cannonball*), Christine Larson (*Diane*), George J. Lewis (*Jose*), Whip Wilson (*Whip*), George Meeker (*Jackson*), Pierce Lyden (*Ramsay*), William Norton Bailey (*Chambers*), Connie Asnis (*Girl*), Fred L. Edwards (*Sturgis*), Robert Strange (*Esteban*), Bob Woodward (*Dirk*), Bud Osborne, Dan Tyler.

Some California land grabbers, headed by Meeker, try to stir up trouble between new arrivals and the long-time locals. Wakely rides in to save the day with Taylor along for comic relief. This unexceptional little western marked an end and a beginning for two minor cinema names. This was the last film for director Cabanne, who began his career in 1913. It also served as debut for Wilson, a whip-crackin' cowboy who would soon go on to some success with his own series.

p, Louis Gray; d, Christy Cabanne; w, J. Benton Cheney; ph, Harry Neumann; ed, John C. Fuller; md, Edward Kay; m/l, Jimmy Wakely, Don Weston, Jimmy Rogers.

Western   **(PR:A MPAA:NR)**

SILVER WHIP, THE**½   (1953) 73m FOX bw

Dale Robertson (*Race Crim*), Rory Calhoun (*Sheriff Tom Davisson*), Robert Wagner (*Jess Harker*), Kathleen Crowley (*Kathy*), James Millican (*Bowen*), Lola Albright (*Waco*), J. M. Kerrigan (*Riley*), John Kellogg (*Slater*), Ian MacDonald (*Hank*), Harry Carter (*Tex Rafferty*), Robert Adler (*Man in Tom's Posse*), Clancy Cooper (*Bert Foley*), Burt Mustin (*Uncle Ben*), Dan White (*Dodd Burdette*), Paul Wexler (*Homer*), Charles Watts (*Doc Summers*), Jack Rice (*Morrison*), Bobby Diamond (*Jody*), Cameron Grant (*Charles Hatt*).

New stagecoach driver Wagner is fired from the job after he's held up by Kellogg. Robertson is the guard aboard the coach and is wounded during the holdup. He swears revenge on the outlaw, which ultimately leads to his doom. Later in the story Wagner becomes a deputy for sheriff Calhoun. Kellogg is captured and held in the jail under Wagner's guard. When the townspeople descend on the jail demanding a lynching, Wagner discovers his old friend Robertson is the mob's leader. This forces the deputy to face some deep moral questions. Does he give in to mob justice or protect the rights of the accused? In the end he stays by the law and is forced to shoot Robertson. This film never really gets beyond a B western level, but it certainly poses some interesting questions. The treatment is routine and a little offbeat, telling its simplistic tale nicely. Wagner plays his stereotyped character with good effect.

p, Robert Bassler, Michael Abel; d, Harmon Jones; w, Jesse L. Lasky, Jr. (based on a novel by Jack Schaefer); ph, Lloyd Ahern; ed, George A. Gittens; md, Lionel Newman; art d, Lyle Wheeler, Chester Gore.

Western   **(PR:A MPAA:NR)**

SILVERSPURS　　　　　(SEE: SILVER SPURS, 1936)

SIMBA**½　　　　　(1955, Brit.) 99m Group/Lippert c

Dirk Bogarde (*Allan Howard*), Donald Sinden (*Tom Drummond*), Virginia McKenna (*Mary Crawford*), Basil Sydney (*Mr. Crawford*), Marie Ney (*Mrs. Crawford*), Joseph Tomelty (*Dr. Hughes*), Earl Cameron (*Karanja*), Orlando Martins (*Headman*), Ben Johnson (*Kimani*), Huntley Campbell (*Joshua*), Frank Singuineau (*Waweru*), Slim Harris (*Chege*), Glyn Lawson (*Mundati*), Harry Quashie (*Thakla*), John Chandos (*Settler at Meeting*), Desmond Roberts (*Col. Bridgeman*), Errol John (*African Inspector*), Willy Sholanke (*Witch Doctor*).

White farmers in Kenya come under siege from the Mau Maus. Some natives try to help them and it's later discovered that the father of a native doctor is the secret leader of the Mau Maus. SIMBA presents some fairly entertaining material with good direction and performances. However, there is an exploitative aspect to the film (as well as a timeliness) in that it capitalizes on the political upheaval taking place at the time of its filming in a Kenya anxious to attain its independence from British colonial rule. Beware of some fairly gruesome scenes.

p, Peter de Sarigny; d, Brian Desmond Hurst; w, John Baines, Robin Estridge (based on a novel by Anthony Perry); ph, Geoffrey Unsworth (Eastmancolor); m, Francis Chagrin; ed, Michael Gordon; art d, John Howell; spec eff, Bill Warrington, Charles Staffel.

Action/Drama　　　　　**(PR:O　MPAA:NR)**

SIMCHON FAMILY, THE**½　　　　　(1969, Israel) 88m Noy /Israel bw
(MISHPACHAT SIMCHON)

Meir Margalit (*Noah Simchon*), Shoshana Barnea (*Zfira*), Oded Kotler (*Gabi*), Rina Ganor (*Na'ava*), Tikva Mor (*Orna*), Zalman Leviush (*Zwirn*), Sharaga Friedman, Elisheva Michaeli, Eddie Calver and Band.

Maraglit is a befuddled Israeli diplomat who lives well beyond his income in hopes of impressing society bigwigs. He moves his family into a fancy condominium, which he proceeds to furnish lavishly. His daughter is a telephone junkie and the strange son of the family plans his own imagined wars. Margalit's wife, ever bemused by the goings-on of her family, somehow manages to put up with it all in this fairly cute little comedy based on a popular Israeli radio series.

p, Shlomo Nouman, Yair Pecker; d, Yoel Zilberg; w, Moshe Ben-Ephraim, Leo Filler, Zilberg (based on an Israeli radio series); ph, Marco Ya'acobi!!-Marco Yocovlevitz]! m, Dov Seltzer; ed, Helga Cranston; m/l, "Speak to Me with Flowers," Seltzer.

Comedy　　　　　**(PR:C　MPAA:NR)**

SIMON***　　　　　(1980) 97m Orion/WB c

Alan Arkin (*Simon Mendelssohn*), Madeline Kahn (*Cynthia*), Austin Pendleton (*Becker*), Judy Graubart (*Lisa*), William Finley (*Fichandler*), Jayant (*Barundi*), Wallace Shawn (*Van Dongen*), Max Wright (*Hundertwasser*), Fred Gwynne (*Korey*), Adolph Green (*Commune Head*), Keith Szarabajka (*Josh*), Ann Risley (*Pam*), Pierre Epstein (*Military Aide at Map*), Roy Cooper (*General's Aide*), Rex Robbins (*Army Doctor*), David Warrilow (*Blades*), Hetty Galen (*Voice of Mother*), David Gideon (*Security Guard*), David Susskind, Dick Cavett (*Themselves*), Remak Ramsay (*TV Newscaster*), Hansford Rowe (*TV Priest*), Yusef Bulos (*TV Philosopher*), Jerry Mayer (*TV Scientist*), Sol Frieder (*TV Rabbi*), William Griffis (*TV Senator*), Frank J. Lucas (*TV Psychologist*).

Director-writer Brickman co-authored ANNIE HALL with Woody Allen and won an Oscar. This was his directorial debut and he showed that he needed Allen (who is renowned as a sensational editor) to excise what didn't work. SIMON is a hit-and-miss picture that would have benefited by a few judicious snips in the script or the celluloid. Arkin, who is second only to Gene Wilder for screaming, screams again in this movie. He is a misguided professor at a New York college. His life is an olio of mad ideas and he seeks to prove them feasible while his girl friend, Graubart, is attempting to get Arkin to stop all this nonsense and arrange his life in a more orderly fashion. Right at the start, we see Arkin's mania by watching him put himself into a sensory deprivation tank (you've seen it before in THE IPCRESS FILE) where he happily spends a great deal of time, much to the ire of Graubart (whom you've seen before if you ever watched TV's PBS show "The Electric Company"). Cut to a squad of brains at a "think tank" led by Pendleton. Their job is to solve the weighty problems of the world, but they are bored by it all. The associates are Shawn (the playwright and actor from MY DINNER WITH ANDRE), Finley, Jayant, Wright, and Kahn, who does little more than a cameo in the picture, even though she gets high billing. Now they decide that they would like to create an alien. Well, not really an alien, just someone who thinks he's an alien. (If you can swallow that premise, go on. If it sticks in your craw, forget about the rest of this review or seeing the movie.) In order to make that happen, they must find someone who is capable of being brainwashed, someone who has never shown up on their computers, someone who has no traceable family lineage. (The same situation is the crux of the Jack Finney book *Time And Again*, which has served as the starting point for several movies, like SOMEWHERE IN

TIME, TIME AFTER TIME, and BACK TO THE FUTURE.) Need we tell you who they choose? Since Arkin is an orphan and a dreamer, he is the perfect fodder for their intellectual cannons. They contact him and bring him to their headquarters, where they lie and state that they are interested in some of his weird ideas. He is flattered by their attention. Once he is there, the scientists brainwash him and cause him to believe that he is an alien from a distant galaxy who has been sent to Earth to bring a celestial message from the other creatures inhabitating the universe. Arkin believes it, then escapes to a commune to spread his message. (Some of this is very funny and a satire of the communal life of the 1960s and 1970s, as Green plays the role of a guru who reads *TV Guide* to his flock and makes them sing commercial jingles in lieu of hymns or psalms. Green, the screen and stage author (with Betty Comden) of a host of hits, is very funny as he pretends to be a former network executive in charge of programming for ABC–an inside joke. Once the word gets out that Arkin has escaped, he is pursued by troops who have been given orders to shoot on sight by their leader, Gwynne. Eventually, it winds up happily, but before "The End" flashes on the screen, some heavy issues have been put on the scales, including the dehumanization of individuals and the oppression of the military, two themes Brickman interweaves. Too often, though, the author's message invades the story and the preachiness begins to resemble a liberal version of Jerry Falwell. Graubart is good, but Pendleton is the most outstanding of the secondary actors as the villainous boss of the smarties. Silverman's score is perky and keeps matters moving well. Although it seems to be farout, there remains a ring of reality to what Brickman has written, especially for anyone who has witnessed the cult phenomena of Elbert Hubbard, Bhagwan Rashneesh and Sun Myung Moon. When Arkin can be controlled, as in THE HEART IS A LONELY HUNTER or WAIT UNTIL DARK or HEARTS OF THE WEST, he can be brilliant. When he is allowed to rant, it's time to shut off the lights and call the law.

p, Martin Bregman; d&w, Marshall Brickman; ph, Adam Holender (Technicolor); m, Stanley Silverman; ed, Nina Feinberg; prod d, Stuart Wurtzel; set d, John Godfrey; cos, Santo Loquasto; spec eff, Ed Drohan.

Comedy　　　　　**Cas.**　　　　　**(PR:A-C　MPAA:PG)**

SIMON AND LAURA***　　　　　(1956, Brit.) 91m Group/UNIV c

Peter Finch (*Simon Foster*), Kay Kendall (*Laura Foster*), Muriel Pavlow (*Janet Honeyman*), Hubert Gregg (*Bertie Burton*), Maurice Denham (*Wilson*), Ian Carmichael (*David Prentice*), Richard Wattis (*Controller*), Thora Hird (*Jessie*), Terence Longdon (*Barney*), Clive Parritt (*Timothy*), Alan Wheatley (*Adrian Lee*), Joan Hickson (*Barmaid*), Cyril Chamberlain (*Bert*), Marianne Stone (*Elsie*), Muriel George (*Grandma*), Charles Hawtrey (*Porter*), Tom Gill, David Morrell, Nicholas Parsons (*TV producers*), Beverly Brooks (*Mabel*), Philip Gilbert (*Joe*), Julia Arnall (*Makeup Girl*), Gilbert Harding, Lady Barnet, John Ellison, George Cansdale, Peter Haigh, Barry Steele, Hal Osmond, Jill Ireland, Stuart Saunders, Susan Beaumont, Isobel Barnett, Shirley Ann Field.

After looking for the perfect television couple, a group of producers end their search with Finch and Kendall. They are the perfect married pair and ideal for a new domestic series broadcast from their home. The problem is Finch and Kendall can't stand each other. On camera it's all sweetness and light, but once the shooting stops it's one of the nastiest bouts since Dempsey met Tunney. Eventually the off-camera relationship catches up with them and with the help of some liquored refreshments everything comes to a head before the cameras on a Christmas special. Cleverly played by Finch and Kendall, SIMON AND LAURA takes a popular British play and turns it into an entertaining movie farce. The chemistry between the two stars is good and the premise is made believable by them. Some nice parodies of the show business life are also mixed in under competent direction.

p, Teddy Baird; d, Muriel Box; w, Peter Blackmore (based on the play by Alan Melville); ph, Ernest Steward (VistaVision, Technicolor); m, Benjamin Frankel; ed, Jean Barker; md, Frankel; art d, Carmen Dillon.

Comedy　　　　　**(PR:C-O　MPAA:NR)**

SIMON, KING OF THE WITCHES*　　　　　(1971) 91m Fanfare c

Andrew Prine (*Simon*), Brenda Scott (*Linda*), George Paulsin (*Turk*), Norman Burton (*Rackum*), Gerald York (*Hercules*), Ultra Violet (*Sarah*), Michael C. Ford (*Shay*), Lee J. Lambert (*Troy*), William Martel (*Commissioner Davies*), Angus Duncan (*Colin*), Richmond Shepard (*Stanley*), Richard Ford Grayling (*John Peter*), Allyson Ames (*Olivia Gebhart*), Harry Rose (*Landlord*), Mike Kopcha (*Lab Technician*), John Yates, Jerry Brooks (*Policemen*), Ray Galvin (*Chief Boyle*), Buck Holland (*Detective*), David Vaile (*TV Newscaster*), Art Hern (*Mayor*), Helen Jay (*Mrs. Carter*), John Hart (*Doctor*), Sharon Berryhill (*Secretary*), Earl Spainard, Frank Corsentino, Bob Carlson, John Copage, Bill McConnell (*Reporters*), Luanne Roberts, Jay Della, Stevi Freeman, Elizabeth Saxon, Avanell Irwin, Harri Sidonie, Jason Max, Eris Tillare.

Prine lives in the sewer with his good friend, a magic mirror. He's a warlock, you see, who, according to the advertising, "curses the Establishment." However, this invective is little more than an excuse to allow the film's pseudo-psychedelic confusion to masquerade as drug-oriented satanic thrills. The plot is hopelessly confusing, though Prine has a good time among the mess. He later went on to star in the Jaws ripoff GRIZZLY and in the innocuous garbage known as CENTERFOLD GIRLS.

p, David Hammond; d, Bruce Kessler; w, Robert Phippeny; ph, David Butler (Eastmancolor); m, Stu Phillips; ed, Renn Reynolds; md, Phillips; art d, Dale Hennesy; set d, Robert De Vestel; spec eff, Roger George; makeup, Maurice Stein.

Horror   **Cas.**   **(PR:O MPAA:R)**

SIMPLE CASE OF MONEY, A½**   (1952, Fr.) 82m
Pathe-Cinema/Discina International bw (MILLONAIRES D'UN JOUR)

Gaby Morlay (*Helene Berger*), Jean Brochard (*Pierre Berger*), Jacques Baumer (*The Judge*), Yves Deniaud (*The Tramp*), Max Revol (*The Sailor*), Pierre Larquey (*Pere Jules*), Gabriello (*The Mayor*), Bernard Lajarrige (*The Journalist*), Leon Bellieres (*The Publisher*), Jeanne Fusier-Gir (*Louise*).

When a young French newspaperman accidentally publishes the wrong numbers for the lottery, the lives of various people are affected. Bellieres, Lajarrige's publisher, brings his newshound to court and calls various would-be winners as witnesses. Among the courtroom parade are an inebriated bum, an unhappily married couple, a river barge captain, and the oldest man in France, feisty 107-year-old. It turns out that although none of them get the money they thought they had won, the group is still much better off than they had been before the error. This French production is charming in its own way, though it suffers from some unnecessary repetition of gags. The cast and direction are competent, making the offbeat premise work nicely.

p&d, Andre Hunebelle; w, Jean Halain (based on a story by Alex Joffe); ph, Marcel Grignon; m, Jean Marion; set d, Lucien Carre.

Comedy   **(PR:A MPAA:NR)**

SIMPLY TERRIFIC*½**   (1938, Brit.) 73m WB-FN bw

Claude Hulbert (*Rodney Cherridew*), Reginald Purdell (*Sam Todd*), Zoe Wynn (*Goldie Divine*), Patricia Medina (*Heather Carfax*), Aubrey Mallalieu (*Sir Walter Carfax*), Glen Alyn (*Stella Hemingway*), Hugh French (*Dickie*), Laura Wright (*Annie Hemingway*), Ian McLean (*Foster*), Frederick Burtwell.

SIMPLY TERRIFIC is the same old hackneyed comedy churned out regularly by the British. Hulbert stars as a rich heir out to impress Purdell, the wealthy father of his girl friend, Wynn. Hoping to prove his business acumen to Purdell, Hulbert tries to persuade his potential father-in-law to invest in a ruined businessman's new product, which is called "Socko." Unfortunately, there is no product to go along with the "Socko" name. Luckily, Hulbert discovers an old flower woman who has invented a cure for the hangover and he uses her formula for "Socko." Trouble looms, however, when the flower woman's evil daughter sees Hulbert as a potential gravy train and tries to seduce him, but the intrepid entrepreneur sidesteps her advances and all ends well.

p, Irving Asher; d, Roy William Neill; w, Anthony Hankey, Basil Dillon (based on a story by Basil Woon); ph, Robert Lapresle.

Comedy   **(PR:A MPAA:NR)**

SIN, THE   (SEE: GOOD LUCK MISS WYCOFF, 1979)

SIN FLOOD   (SEE: WAY OF ALL MEN, THE, 1930)

SIN NOW...PAY LATER (SEE: LOVE NOW...PAY LATER, 1966, Ital.)

SIN OF HAROLD DIDDLEBOCK, THE
                    (SEE: MAD WEDNESDAY, 1950)

SIN OF MADELON CLAUDET, THE**
                    (1931) 74m MGM bw (GB: THE LULLABY)

Helen Hayes (*Madelon Claudet*), Lewis Stone (*Carlo Boretti*), Neil Hamilton (*Larry*), Robert Young (*Dr. Claudet*), Cliff Edwards (*Victor*), Jean Hersholt (*Dr. Dulac*), Marie Prevost (*Rosalie*), Karen Morley (*Alice*), Charles Winninger (*Photographer*), Alan Hale (*Hubert*), Halliwell Hobbes (*Roget*), Lennox Pawle (*St. Jacques*), Russ Powell (*Claudet*), Otto Hoffman (*Official*), Frankie Darro (*Larry at Age 12*).

Hayes makes her sound film debut in this well-acted soaper, scripted by her husband MacArthur. Hersholt narrates the story in flashback. Hayes is a French girl who falls in love with Hamilton, an American artist. The two move in together without marrying, but their idyllic life is ruined when Hamilton must leave, and ends up marrying another woman. Hayes becomes involved with Stone, but he is arrested on jewel theft charges. Stone kills himself rather than face the law, and Hayes is sentenced to 10 years in prison on accomplice charges. To support her illegitimate son (Young), Hayes becomes a streetwalker on her release, then sends the money to Hersholt, a doctor tutoring Young in medicine. Young is suspicious about the money because of the irregular sums that arrive sporadically. Hayes lies, telling Young this money is from the estate of his late mother. Eventually Young becomes a successful doctor and sets Hayes

up in a Parisian apartment. The film ends as Hersholt finishes his narration. He has been telling the story to Young's wife, a woman upset by Young's devotion to his career. She had been considering leaving him, but after hearing Hayes' story, the woman reconsiders. All the while, Hersholt has never revealed Hayes' painful secret. Hayes won a well-deserved Oscar for this performance, taking her character from a young girl to old woman with astonishing believability. Makeup enhances her as she ages, but the character chiefly works thanks to Hayes' gifted talent. The story wrings emotional twist after twist, coming close to self-parody, but audiences of the day loved the picture. The story had been made numerous times under the title MADAME X. The two silent versions were in 1915 and 1920, while sound versions were made in 1929, 1937, 1948, 1960 (as THE TRIAL OF MADAME X), 1966, and a 1981 television film.

d, Edgar Selwyn; w, Charles MacArthur (based on the play "The Lullaby" by Edward Knoblock); ph, Oliver T. Marsh; ed, Tom Held; art d, Cedric Gibbons.

Drama   **(PR:C MPAA:NR)**

SIN OF MONA KENT, THE**   (1961) 75m Mermaid/Astor c (AKA:
                    THE SINS OF MONA KENT)

Johnny Olsen (*Himself*), Sandra Donat (*Elvira Kowalski/Mona Kent*), Vic Ramos (*Eddie Logan*), Gil Brandsen (*Jerry Roberts*), Joy Violette (*Janice Lane*), Allan Frank (*Stephan Gregory*), Sam Alfredo (*Bartender*).

Real-life New York radio and TV interviewer Olsen plays himself in this CITIZEN KANE-style film tracing the career of Broadway star Donat. She first arrives in New York after winning a faked beauty contest. This wakens her to life's realities, but she carries on. She takes up with Violette, an actress, and Ramos, a painter. The latter gets her a job as a hatcheck girl. Soon Donat meets Frank, an older gossip columnist who changes her name from the ethnic "Elvira Kowalski" to "Mona Kent." She goes to a party at his home and there takes a swim dressed only in her lingerie. This attracts some attention and Donat starts getting parts in summer stock. After she takes a nude swim along deserted beach, Brandsen, a young photographer, snaps some photos of her. He promises never to reveal the shots to anyone and the two become friends. When Donat suffers a career setback she returns to hatchecking while continuing to pose for Brandsen. When Frank proposes, Donat is absolutely flabbergasted. When she discovers that both her painter and photographer have sold nude portraits of her, she ends up dumping them and marrying the older man with the promise that he'll make her a star.

p&d, Charles J. Hundt; w, Dick Brighton; ph, James Lillis (DeLuxe Color); m, Corelli Jacobs; ed, Eric Albertson; m/l, "Mona," Michael Merlo, Patrick Welch.

Drama   **(PR:O MPAA:NR)**

SIN OF NORA MORAN*   (1933) 65m Majestic bw (AKA: VOICE
                    FROM THE GRAVE)

Zita Johann (*Nora Moran*), Alan Dinehart (*John Grant*), Paul Cavanagh (*Bill Crawford*), John Miljan (*Paulino*), Claire Dubrey (*Mrs. Crawford*), Sarah Padden (*Mrs. Watts*), Henry B. Walthall (*Father Ryan*), Otis Harlan (*Mr. Moran*), Cora Sue Collins, Aggie Herring.

Poorly made programmer about a circus girl who's manipulated into becoming the lover of a governor. When the governor kills the former circus boss, Johann takes the blame and faces the electric chair. The story is average, but is lost in a confusing series of flashbacks that lack the necessary drama. The acting and direction are well below programmer standards.

d, Phil Goldstone; w, Frances Hyland (based on the play "Burnt Offering" by William Maxwell Goodhue); ph, Ira Morgan; ed, Otis M. Garrett.

Drama/Crime   **Cas.**   **(PR:A MPAA:NR)**

SIN ON THE BEACH**   (1964, Fr.) 75m Les Films
                    Universal/American Film Distributing bw (LE CRI DE LA CHAIR;
                    AKA: ROMANCE ON THE BEACH)

Monique Just (*Maria*), Sylvia Sorrente (*Brigitte*), Michele Lemoine (*Jean-Marc*), Gisele Gallois (*Francoise*).

A French couple (Sorente and Lemoine) are unhappy with their life together. They go off to a remote seaside resort owned by Just, whose husband is sickly. She falls in love with Lemoine, but is blackmailed by him when her husband dies. He threatens to tell the police that Just helped hasten the man's death unless Sorente and Lemoine are allowed to stay on at the hotel's expense. Sorente becomes bored with life there and does a striptease for the bartender. Just discovers this and seduces the woman into a lesbian relationship. She hopes to make Lemoine jealous, but her efforts are to no avail. Sorente and Lemoine reunite, but she walks out after a quarrel. Lemoine takes up with Just once more and makes love with her on the beach. However, Sorente reappears with her own blackmail plans, and Just finally reveals that she was indeed responsible for her husband's death.

p&d, Jose Benazeraf; w, Grisha M. Dabat, Yves-Claude Denaux (based on the novel *L'Eternite Pour Nous* by G. J. Arnaud); ph, Marcel Combes (Dyaliscope); m, Louiguy; ed, Georges Marchalk; art d, Claude Bouxin.

Drama   (PR:O MPAA:NR)

SIN SHIP*½   (1931) 65m RKO bw

Louis Wolheim (*Capt. McVeigh*), Mary Astor (*Kitty*), Ian Keith (*Marsden*), Hugh Herbert (*Charlie*), Russell Powell (*Tourist/Detective*), Alan Roscoe (*Dave*), Bert Starkey (*Cook*).

A two-masted schooner run by captain Wolheim is the scene of some unhappy action for Astor. She is being chased by the captain as well as by Keith. Wolheim discovers the so-called minister and his wife (Keith and Astor) are really a pair of thieves, and they are arrested by undercover detective Powell in the end. Not much of a thriller, the film implausibly allows Astor to go free at the finale, never bothering to explain why. This was also Wolheim's first attempt at directing and, unfortunately, he died a few months before the film's release. Herbert, who plays the ship's first mate, wrote the screenplay.

p, Myles Connolly; d, Louis Wolheim, Lynn Shores; w, Hugh Herbert (based on a story by Keene Thompson, Brand Leahy); ph, Nicholas Musuraca.

Drama/Thriller   (PR:A MPAA:NR)

SIN TAKES A HOLIDAY**½   (1930) 81m Pathe/RKO bw

Constance Bennett (*Sylvia Brenner*), Kenneth MacKenna (*Gaylord Stanton*), Basil Rathbone (*Durant*), Rita LaRoy (*Grace Lanier*), Louis John Bartels (*Richards*), ZaSu Pitts (*Anna*), Kendall Lee (*Miss Munson*), Murrel Finley (*Ruth*), Fred Walton (*Butler*), Richard Carle (*Minister*), Helen Johnson (*Miss Graham*), Judith Wood.

Bennett plays a lowly stenographer who enters into a marriage of convenience with boss MacKenna so that he won't have to tie the knot with LaRoy, his divorcee girl friend. MacKenna tells LaRoy that his wife is an institutionalized invalid, and Bennett ventures to Paris, where she meets the cultured European Rathbone, who teaches her a thing or two. Rathbone implores her to seek a divorce, but when Bennett returns stateside she and her husband discover that they were meant for each other and end up back together at the film's conclusion. Though mild by today's standards, this was a fairly sophisticated programmer in its time. SIN TAKES A HOLIDAY was made at Pathe, but the rights reverted to RKO when the latter studio received it in a Hollywood business takeover.

p, E.B. Derr; d, Paul L. Stein; w, Horace Jackson (based on a story by Robert Milton, Dorothy Cairns); ph, John Mescall; ed, Daniel Mandell; art d, Carroll Clark; cos, Gwen Wakeling.

Drama   (PR:A MPAA:NR)

SIN TOWN**   (1942) 75m UNIV bw

Constance Bennett (*Kye Allen*), Broderick Crawford (*Dude McNair*), Anne Gwynne (*Laura Kirby*), Patric Knowles (*Wade Crowell*), Andy Devine (*Judge Eustace Vale*), Leo Carrillo (*Angelo Colina*), Ward Bond (*Rock Delaney*), Arthur Aylesworth (*Sheriff Bagby*), Ralf Harolde (*Kentucky Jones*), Charles Wagenheim (*Dry Hole*), Billy Wayne (*Hollister*), Hobart Bosworth (*Humiston*), Bryant Washburn (*Anderson*), Jack Mulhall (*Hanson*), Paul Bryar (*Grady*), Rebel Randall, Jean Trent (*Dance Hall Girls*), Oscar O'Shea (*Conductor*), Eddy Waller (*Forager*), Clarence Muse (*Porter*), Ben Erdway (*Dr. Prendergast*), Ed Peil, Sr (*Hedges*), Harry Strang (*Jessup*), Guy Usher (*Man on Train*), Victor Zimmerman George Lewis (*Oil Men*), Larry McGrath (*Stick Man*), Murray Parker (*Juggler*), Frank Hagney (*Bartender*), Neeley Edwards, Jack C. Smith (*Gamblers*), Kernan Cripps, Art Miles, Charles Marsh, Frank Coleman (*Men*).

In a frontier oil-boomtown in 1910, Crawford and Bennett are a pair of opportunists who save Bond from a hanging. They proceed to take over the saloon-gambling hall and aren't above a little dishonesty now and then. Gwynne is the local newspaper editor who doesn't take a liking to Crawford, to put it mildly. Little more than a string of western cliches in a new environment, SIN TOWN is directed with vigor and the result is an entertaining little package. Bond winds up dead with Crawford and Bennett riding off in search of greener pastures and bucks.

p, George Waggner; d, Ray Enright; w, W. Scott Darling, Gerald Geraghty, Richard Brooks; ph, George Robinson; ed, Edward Curtiss; md, H.J. Salter; art d, Jack Otterson.

Western   (PR:A MPAA:NR)

SIN YOU SINNERS* (1963) 73m Farno/Joseph Brenner Associates bw

June Colbourne (*Bobbi*), Dian Lloyd (*Jule*), Derek Murcott (*Dave*), Beverly Nazarow (*Gloria*), Charles Clements (*Ben*), Douglas Gregory.

With the power of an amulet worn around the neck, a middle-aged stripper manages to take psychic hold on anyone near her. The owner of the cabaret she dances in conspires with a hooker to steal the valuable amulet and with it the woman's powers; meanwhile, the stripper's daughter has similar ideas. However, the woman catches on and puts the cabaret owner under a hypnotic spell. Under the trance he murders the hooker and kills himself when he realizes what's happened. But the woman ends up losing the amulet and it's found by her daughter, who gains its power. Her mother's good looks

disappear with the amulet, along with her confidence. Crushed, she runs into the street and is hit by a truck.

d, Anthony Farrar; w, Joe Sarno.

Drama   (PR:O MPAA:NR)

SINAI COMMANDOS: THE STORY OF THE SIX DAY WAR**½
      (1968, Israel/Ger.) 99m Aero-Ran/Gillman c (HA'MATARAH TIRAN; SCHATTEN UBER TIRAN–KOMMANDO SINAI; DER 6-TAGE KRIEG; AKA: SINAI COMMANDOS)

Robert Fuller (*Capt. Uri Litman*), John Hudson (*Gen. Golan*), Esther Ullman (*Nira*), Avram Mor (*Lt. Moshe Kramer*), Eli Sinai (*Sgt. Zwi Neumann*), Gabi Amrani (*Nissim*), Avram Hefner (*Elihu Goldfarb*), Reuven Bar-Yotam (*Bulgaro*), Raffi Nathan (*Yigal*), Boris Rosenberg (*Nathan*), Ziona Tukterman (*Ellen Neumann*), Aviva Marks (*Sylvia Litman*), Joseph Shiloach (*Capt. Hallil*), Ammon Berenson (*Air Force Pilot*).

Made shortly after the Six-Day War, this film tells the story of Fuller, the leader of an Israeli task force that is assigned to knock out some important Arab radar installations. Ullman is the woman who uses her father's boat to land the squadron on the coastline along the Sinai Peninsula. In order to avoid capture by the Egyptians, she sinks the boat and joins the team. The mission is a success and the squad has made it safe for Israeli war planes to hit their Egyptian target. Though made in color, this film incorporates some black-and-white footage shot on the actual battlegrounds during the war.

p&d, Raphael Nussbaum; w, Jack Jacobs (based on a story by Nussbaum); ph, Benno Bellenbaum (Eastmancolor); m, Horst A. Haas, Rolf Bauer, Roy Etzel; ed, Ursula Mohrle, Erika Stegman; m/l, "Sharm Al-Sheikh," Ron Eliran.

War Drama   Cas.   (PR:C MPAA:GP)

SINAIA   (SEE: CLOUDS OVER ISRAEL, 1966, Israel)

SINBAD AND THE EYE OF THE TIGER**   (1977, U.S./Brit.) 112m
                                             Morningside/COL c

Patrick Wayne (*Sinbad*), Taryn Power (*Dione*), Margaret Whiting (*Zenobia*), Jane Seymour (*Princess Farah*), Patrick Troughton (*Melanthius, Magician*), Kurt Christian (*Rafi*), Nadim Sawaiha (*Hassan*), Damien Thomas (*Prince Kassim*), Bruno Barnabe (*Balsora*), Bernard Kay (*Zabid*), Salami Coker (*Maroof*), David Sterne (*Aboo-Seer*).

Wayne (son of John) plays the famed mythical sailor from *A Thousand and One Nights* in this childish adventure. He is enlisted by princess Seymour to help rid her brother, prince Thomas, of the spell cast upon him which is turning him by degrees into an ape. Thomas is about to ascend to the throne and Whiting, an evil sorceress, has cast the spell in the hope of seeing her own son (Rafi) become the ruler. Wayne and company set sail in search of the solution to Thomas' growing problem and Whiting and her evil entourage follow, attempting to sabotage the quest of the rightful heir to the thrown. The plot is aimed strictly at the younger set and the performances are pure hambone, but the film boasts terrific effects by master animator Harryhausen. It's a shame these truly special effects can't be seen by connoisseurs in a higher quality film. The beasties include a sabre-tooth tiger, a chess-playing baboon, a giant walrus, and three nasty ghouls. Power, the shapely co-star with little talent, is the daughter of Tyrone. This was the third film in Harryhausen and Schneer's "Sinbad" series (THE 7th VOYAGE OF SINBAD and THE GOLDEN VOYAGE OF SINBAD preceded it. See SINBAD series, Index.)

p, Charles H. Schneer, Ray Harryhausen; d, Sam Wanamaker; w, Beverley Cross (based on a story by Cross, Harryhausen from *A Thousand and One Nights*); ph, Ted Moore (Metrocolor); m, Roy Budd; ed, Roy Watts; prod d, Geoffrey Drake; art d, Fernando Gonzales, Fred Carter; cos, Cynthia Tingey; spec eff, Harryhausen; makeup, Colin Arthur.

Fantasy   Cas.   (PR:AAA MPAA:G)

SINBAD THE SAILOR***   (1947) 117m RKO c

Douglas Fairbanks, Jr. (*Sinbad*), Maureen O'Hara (*Shireen*), Walter Slezak (*Melik*), Anthony Quinn (*Emir*), George Tobias (*Abbu*), Jane Greer (*Pirouze*), Mike Mazurki (*Yusuf*), Sheldon Leonard (*Auctioneer*), Alan Napier (*Aga*), John Miljan (*Moga*), Barry Mitchell (*Muallin*), Glenn Strange (*Slave Master*), George Chandler (*Commoner*), Louis-Jean Heydt (*Mercenary*), Cy Kendall (*Kahn of Basra*), Hugh Prosser (*Captain of the Guard*), Harry Harvey (*Crier at Execution*), George Lloyd (*Lancer Guard*), Paul Guifoyle (*Camel Drover*), Jean Lind, Mary Bradley, Norma Creiger, Vonne Lester (*Dancing Girls*), Nick Thompson (*Beggar on Street*), Billy Bletcher (*Crier*), Max Wagner (*Assistant Overseer*), Norbert Schiller (*Timekeeper*), Wade Crosby (*Soldier*), Ben Welden (*Porter*), Charles Soldani, Mikandor Dooraff, Joe Garcio, Chuck Hamilton (*Merchants*), Phil Warren, Lida Durova, Dolores Costelli, Milly Reauclaire, Teri Toy, Joan Webster, Leslie Charles, Norma Brown, Ann Cameron, Jamiel Hasson, Al Murphy, Bill Shannon, Dave Kashner, Eddie Abdo, Charles Stevens, Gordon Clark.

A lengthy, purely escapist swashbuckling adventure with Fairbanks, Jr.

conjuring up images of double-cross heroic father in such films as THE THIEF OF BAGDAD (1924) and THE BLACK PIRATE (1926). An Arabian Nights tale, SINBAD THE SAILOR casts Fairbanks in the title role, sailing the seas in order to find a hidden treasure. With his first mate Tobias, Fairbanks makes a stop in Daibul where his ship is put up for auction. O'Hara, a wealthy and beautiful adventuress, makes a bid for the ship but Fairbanks, stealing money from the auctioneer's pocket, bids higher. Fairbanks becomes enamored of O'Hara, which angers the sword-wielding Quinn, the Emir of Daibul. Quinn prepares to kill Fairbanks but is stopped by the love-stricken O'Hara, who passes him off as a member of royalty. Fairbanks and O'Hara run off in the night, but are caught and again Quinn is driven to kill. Again he is stopped, this time by Slezak, a Mongolian sailor who concocts a scheme to hunt for the treasure with Fairbanks and Quinn–dividing the booty into three equal parts. With O'Hara in tow, the three men set sail for Deryabar, where the treasure is supposed to be buried under the ruins of Alexander the Great's palace. Fairbanks discovers that Slezak is planning to double- double-cross and keep the riches for himself. Quinn, however, doesn't believe Fairbanks. By the film's end, Slezak has poisoned himself and Quinn has died while trying to prevent Fairbanks and O'Hara from fleeing on his ship. A framing story has Fairbanks telling this story to a group of gullible friends who eagerly await a peek at the jewels. Fairbanks lets out a hearty laugh at the senseless audience who foolishly believed his tale. Displaying a mastery of ornate set design and a collection of spangly, glittering Arabian fashions, SINBAD THE SAILOR badly needs a cohesive plot, but somehow that just doesn't matter.

p, Stephen Ames; d, Richard Wallace; w, John Twist (based on a story by Twist, George Worthing Yates); ph, George Barnes (Technicolor); m, Roy Webb; ed, Sherman Todd, Frank Doyle; md, C. Bakaleinikoff; art d, Albert S. D'Agostino, Carroll Clark; set d, Darrell Silvera, Claude Carpenter; spec eff, Vernon L. Walker, Harold Wellman.

Adventure   **Cas.**   **(PR:A MPAA:NR)**

SINCE YOU WENT AWAY****   (1944) 172m UA bw

Claudette Colbert (*Anne Hilton*), Jennifer Jones (*Jane*), Shirley Temple (*Bridget "Brig" Hilton*), Joseph Cotten (*Lt. Anthony Willett*), Monty Woolley (*Col. Smollett*), Robert Walker (*Cpl. William G. Smollett II*), Lionel Barrymore (*Clergyman*), Hattie McDaniel (*Fidelia*), Agnes Moorehea (*Emily Hawkins*), Guy Madison (*Harold Smith*), Craig Stevens (*Danny Williams*), Keenan Wynn (*Lt. Solomon*), Albert Basserman (*Dr. Sigmund Gottlieb Golden*), Nazimova (*Zosia Koslowska*), Lloyd Corrigan (*Mr. Mahoney*), Jackie Moran (*Marine Officer*), Jane Devlin (*Gladys Brown*), Ann Gillis (*Becky Anderson*), Dorothy Garner (*Sugar*), Byron Foulger (*Principal*), Edwin Maxwell (*Businessman*), Florence Bates (*Hungry Woman*), Theodore von Eltz (*Desk Clerk*), Adeline de Walt, Doodles Weaver, Warren Hymer (*Convalescents*), Jonathan Hale (*Conductor*), Eilene Janssen (*Sergeant's Child*), Williams B. Davidson (*Taxpayer*), Ruth Roman (*Envious Girl*), Rhonda Fleming (*Girl*), Andrew McLaglen (*Former Plowboy*), Jill Warren (*Waitress*), Terry Moore (*Refugee Child*), Robert Johnson (*Black Officer*), Dorothy Dandridge (*Black Officer's Wife*), Johnny Bond (*AWOL*), Irving Bacon (*Bartender*), George Chandler (*Cabbie*), Addison Richards (*Maj. Atkins*), Barbara Pepper (*Pin Girl*), Harry Hayden (*Conductor*), Jimmy Clemons, Jr (*Boy Caroler*), Charles Williams, Neila Hart, Robert Anderson, Shelby Bacon, Aileen Pringle, Wallis Clark, James Carlisle, Leonide Mostovoy, Joyce Horn, John A. James, Mary Anne Durkin, Richard C. Wood, Ruth Valmy, Grady Sutton, Buddy Gorman, Tom Dawson, Patricia Peters, George Lloyd, Russell Hoyt, Loudde Claar, Helen Koford, Don Marjarian, Conrad Binyon, Jimmy Dodd, Christopher Adams, Martha Outlaw, Verna Knopf, Robert Cherry, Kirk Barron, Earl Jacobs, Cecil Ballerino, Jack Gardner, James Westerfield, Ralph Reed, Paul Esberg, William Jillson, Dorothy Mann, Peggy Maley, Dorothy Adams, Derek Harris, Eddie Hall, Warren Barr, Neyle Marx, Betsy Howard, Terry Revell, Stephen Wayne, Walter Baldwin, Marilyn Hare, Eric Sinclair, Lela Bliss, Harlan Miller, Mrs. Roy Feldman, Soda the Bulldog.

While THE BEST YEARS OF OUR LIVES examined the situation of Americans after WW II, this movie showed the plight of those who were left behind during the conflict and was a smash hit with critics and public alike, grossing well over $4 million, a large sum in the days when people could go to the movies for 25 cents. Margaret Buell Wilder wrote a regular column for the Dayton, Ohio, *Journal Herald*. She collected the letters she wrote to her husband in the column and put them into a book which she rewrote as a screen story. Then producer Selznick used the story to write a long, episodic, but always interesting screenplay that had no major plot, but endless minor ones which added up to a more than satisfying potpourri. Colbert is the noble mother, with Jones and Temple as her two daughters. Her husband, a man in his late 30s, has left a good job in the advertising business to go off and fight. He is never seen in the movie but is always such an important part of it that memory will play tricks and, recalling the story, one might think he was there on screen. A photo of Neil Hamilton (who was later to star on the "Batman" TV series as Commissioner Gordon) is seen to represent the absent husband and father. Woolley is an acerbic boarder at the Colbert house and gets in his digs, punctuating the drama with his inimitable comedic manner. Jones has a boy friend, Walker, who returns from the service and the relationship between the two is so true-to-life that, at times, we can't believe they are acting. Jones and Walker were married at the time and divorced a year or so later but when this was made, there

was starlight in their eyes. Cotten is a friend of the family, a Navy man who stops by to be a staunch supporter and never uses Colbert's loneliness in an unseemly manner. The battle scenes were realistic and when a soldier was hurt he really looked wounded and incapable of the phony battlefield heroics seen in many other films of the period. Selznick has mined gold from the Wilder stories, but what else can one expect from the producer who gave us GONE WITH THE WIND and REBECCA? SINCE YOU WENT AWAY was nominated as Best Picture, with other nominations going to Colbert, Jones, Woolley and Cortez. Steiner won the only Oscar for his music. Each scene is a little gem of its own, sometimes having nothing to do with the story and easily deleted but, when it is all over, the nearly three-hour length goes by very quickly because we are made to care about everyone who struts and frets across the screen. SINCE YOU WENT AWAY is a marvelous example of Hollywood filmmaking expertise at its best. Songs include "The Dipsy-Doodle" (Larry Clinton), "Together" (B.G. DeSylva, Lew Brown, Ray Henderson, who had a movie made about their lives, THE BEST THINGS IN LIFE ARE FREE, starring Dan Dailey, Gordon MacCrae, and Ernest Borgnine, and the title tune "Since You Went Away" (Ted Grouya, Kermit Goell.) In small roles, note Ruth Roman as "an envious girl" and Rhonda Fleming, who was just 21 and appearing in her second film. The scene-stealer was the family's English bulldog, Soda, who played himself. Temple was making her first screen appearance after a layoff of a couple of years while she got over that awkward stage, having last worked in MISS ANNIE ROONEY. Viewers should have at least one box of tissues at their side while watching this. If not sincerely moved by SINCE YOU WENT AWAY, they should have their pulse rate taken.

p, David O. Selznick; d, John Cromwell; w, Selznick (based on the novel *Together* by Margaret Buell Wilder, adaptation by Wilder); ph, Stanley Cortez, Lee Garmes, Jack Cosgrove, Clarence Silver; m, Max Steiner, Louis Forbes; ed, Hal C. Kern, James E. Newcom, Don DiFaure, Arthur Fellows, Wayland M. Hendrys; prod d, William L. Oereira; set d, Mark-Lee Kirk, Victory A. Gangelin; spec eff, Jack Cosgrove, Clarence Slifer; ch, Charles Walters; makeup, Robert Stephanott.

Drama   **(PR:A MPAA:NR)**

SINCERELY YOURS zero   (1955) 115m International Artists/WB c

Liberace (*Anthony Warrin*), Joanne Dru (*Marion Moore*), Dorothy Malone (*Linda Curtis*), Alex Nicol (*Howard Ferguson*), William Demarest (*Sam Dunne*), Lori Nelson (*Sarah Cosgrove*), Lurene Tuttle (*Mrs. McGinley*), Richard Eyer (*Alvie Hunt*), James Bell (*Grandfather Hunt*), Herbert Heyes (*J. R. Aldrich*), Edward Platt (*Dr. Eubank*), Guy Williams (*Dick Cosgrove*), Ian Wolfe (*Mr. Rojeck*), Otto Waldis (*Zwolinski*), Barbara Brown (*Mrs. Cosgrove*).

When a concert pianist (Liberace) loses his hearing, he becomes embittered and locks himself away in his plush Manhattan penthouse. He takes to spying on the people below with a telescope and, in one of the great movie implausibilities of all time, learns to read lips! He discovers that others have troubles worse than his and gets involved with helping them. Tuttle is an elderly lady whose daughter has married into high society and grown ashamed of her mother. Leave it to Liberace to fix things. He arranges for Tuttle to attend a high-class ball where she's an absolute hit with everyone including her daughter's in-law's! Of course, no schmaltzy film is complete without a crippled child, and Liberace gets his chance to help a sickly young boy who dreams of becoming a football player. Sadly, the pianist's new skill at lip-reading leads him to discover that his fiancee loves another, but it's all right in the end, and he winds up with Dru and miraculously regains his hearing! Liberace's sincere campy style may be okay for television and the smarmy world of Las Vegas, but it sure didn't translate well into film. This is horrendously awful, an unintentional self-parody that lovingly wallows in its unbelievable hokum. The studio heads at Warner Brothers were aptly rewarded for this poor remake of George Arliss's THE MAN WHO PLAYED GOD; SINCERELY YOURS was a box-office disaster, barely lasting two weeks (if that long) in many major markets. Today it plays as great camp if you're really hard up for some cheap laughs. Liberace, of course, was hardly done in by this disaster, returning to Las Vegas, where they swallowed up his flamboyant style like cotton candy. Considering that at the height of his TV popularity Liberace was drawing as many as 30 million viewers, it is not surprising that Warners thought they had a box-office gold mine on their hands when they set out to do SINCERELY YOURS. Sadder but wiser, the studio didn't exercise their option to make another film with Liberace, and he wouldn't make another film appearance until Tony Richardson's THE LOVED ONE (1965). Along with 29 costume changes, Liberace tickled the ivories on a host of musical numbers, including: "Minuet in G" (Ignacy Paderewski), "Sonata No. 9" (Wolfgang Amadeus Mozart), "Traumerei," "Liebestraum" (Franz Liszt), "Rhapsody in Blue," "Embraceable You," "The Man I Love," "I Got Rhythm," "Liza" (George Gershwin), "Cornish Rhapsody" (Hubert Bath), "Tea for Two" (Vincent Youmans, Irving Caesar), "Sincerely Yours" (Paul Francis Webster, Liberace), "The Notre Dame Fight Song," "Chopsticks," "The Beer Barrel Polka," and "When Irish Eyes Are Smiling."

p, Henry Blanke; d, Gordon Douglas; w, Irving Wallace (based on the play "The Man Who Played God" by Jules Eckert Goodman); ph, William H. Clothier (Warner Color); ed, Owen Marks; art d, Edward Carrere; set d, George James Hopkins; cos, Howard Shoup.

Drama (PR:A MPAA:NR)

SINFONIA PER DUE SPIE (SEE: SERENADE FOR TWO SPIES, 1966, Ital./Ger.)

SINFONIA PER UN MASSACRO (SEE: SYMPHONY FOR A MASSACRE, 1965, Fr./Ital.)

SINFUL DAVEY**½ (1969, Brit.) 95m Mirisch-Webb/UA c

John Hurt (*Davey Haggart*), Pamela Franklin (*Annie*), Nigel Davenport (*Constable Richardson*), Ronald Fraser (*MacNab*), Robert Morley (*Duke of Argyll*), Fidelma Murphy (*Jean Carlisle*), Maxine Audley (*Duchess of Argyll*), Fionnuala Flanagan (*Penelope*), Donal McCann (*Sir James Graham*), Allan Cuthbertson (*Capt. Douglas*), Eddie Byrne (*Yorkshire Bill*), Niall MacGinnis (*Boots Simpson*), Noel Purcell (*Jock*), Judith Furse (*Mary*), Francis De Wolff (*Andrew*), Paul Farrell (*Bailiff of Stirling*), Geoffrey Golden (*Warden McEwan*), Leon Collins (*Dr. Gersham*), Mickser Reid (*Billy the Goat*), Derek Young (*Bobby Rae*), John Franklyn (*George Bagrie*), Eileen Murphy (*Mary Kidd*).

A good cast overcomes the somewhat heavy hand of Huston's direction in this TOM JONES-inspired comedy. Hurt, excellent in one of his first leading roles, is a Scottish young man of the 1820s who vows to follow in his father's footsteps in the profession of a highwayman. He hopes to be a bit more successful than the old man, who was hanged at age 21 for a bungled robbery of Morley. Hurt deserts the army and joins up with slimy pickpocket Fraser, but only ends up in jail for his efforts. Hurt manages to slip into the women's prison, where he has a bit of fun with bawdy Murphy. His childhood friend from the orphanage he was raised in (Franklin, in a fun performance) bails out Hurt, who, in turn, helps Fraser escape. He then commits a stagecoach robbery, though news of the crime reaches constable Davenport. Franklin warns Hurt that he'll end up like his father, but helps him by foiling Davenport's pursuit. Hurt heads for the hills (literally), hiding out in the Scottish highlands where he has more adventures. He saves McCann from some robbers and pockets the money himself. McCann doesn't realize his rescuer is a thief and takes Hurt with him to the home of his uncle, who turns out to be Morley. Hurt is eager to meet the man who hanged his father and goes off with McCann. Hurt is being followed though by his old partner, Fraser, in the company of Murphy. They, in turn, are followed by Franklin and Davenport. The three bandits end up robbing everyone at a grand ball, but are foiled by Franklin, who wants to reform Hurt and return all the jewels. After a comical chase Hurt is arrested and sentenced to the gallows. Fraser and Franklin rig the noose, saving Hurt's life, and Hurt and Franklin ride off together in the end. The cast is just marvelous, giving this film the right amount of zest and daring do to make it work. However, Huston's direction is plodding, with no sense at all for comedy. It's merely a repetitive style of set up and punch line that goes on and on until the end. Shot on location in Ireland, this was based on the memoirs of an actual 19th-Century highwayman.

p, William N. Graf; d, John Huston; w, James R. Webb (based on the book *The Life of David Haggart* by David Haggart); ph, Freddie Young, Edward Scaife (Panavision, DeLuxe Color); m, Ken Thorne; ed, Russell Lloyd; prod d, Stephen Grimes; md, Thorne; art d, Carmen Dillon; set d, Josie MacAvin; cos, Margaret Furse; spec eff, Richard Parker; ch, Alice Dalgarno; m/l, "Sinful Davey" Thorne, Don Black (sung by Esther Ofarim); makeup, Neville Smallwood.

Historical Comedy (PR:O MPAA:M)

SING A JINGLE** (1943) 62m UNIV bw (GB: LUCKY DAYS)

Allan Jones (*Ray King*), June Vincent (*Muriel Crane*), Samuel S. Hinds (*J.P. Crane*), Gus Schilling (*Bucky*), Betty Kean (*Myrtle*), Jerome Cowan (*Andrews*), Edward Norris (*Abbott*), Joan Castle (*Vera Grant*), Richard Love (*Wilbur Crane*), Vivian Austin (*Ann*), Billy Newell (*Wiggins*), Dean Collins (*Benny*), Chester Clute (*Hendricks*), Jeanne Carroll (*Jane*), Mary O'Brien (*Marie*), Jean Davis (*Helen*), William Haade (*Announcer*), Edward Kean (*Philip Jonas*), Martin Ashe (*Timekeeper*), Jason Robards, Sr (*3rd Man*), the Kings Men.

When radio singing star Jones is turned down by the Army at his physical in WW II the tenor decides to do his part for Uncle Sam by working at a midwestern defense plant. There he meets the boss' daughter (Vincent) and falls in love. Finally he organizes a big show to help sell war bonds. Typical studio propaganda made to relieve the tedium of the "Rosie the Riveters," and entertaining for what it is with standard production values. The comedy team of Kean and Schilling have some slapstick love scenes together and there's plenty of singing and dancing. Songs include: "Sing a Jingle," "We're the Janes that Make the Planes," "Mademoiselle" (Inez James, Sidney Mitchell), "The Night We Called It a Day" (Tom Adair, Matt Dennis), "Beautiful Love" (Haven Gillespie, Wayne King, Victor Young, Egbert Van Alstyne), "Love, You are My Music" (Dan Twohig, Gustave Klemm).

p&d, Edward Lilley; w, John Grey, Eugene Conrad, Lee Sands, Fred Rath; ph, Jerome Ash; ed, Charles Maynard; md, Charles Previn; art d, John Goodman.

Musical (PR:A MPAA:NR)

SING ALONG WITH ME*½ (1952, Brit.) 78m HH Films-Challenge/BL bw

Donald Peers (*David Parry*), Dodo Watts (*Gwynneth Evans*), Dennis Vance (*Harry Humphries*), Jill Clifford (*Shelia*), Mercy Haystead (*Gloria*), Cyril Chamberlain (*Jack Bates*), Humphrey Morton (*Syd Maxton*), George Curzon (*Mr. Palmer*), Leonard Morris (*Uncle Ebeneezer*), Michael Bilton, Ben Williams, Bryan Royceston, Norah Gordon, Leonard Sharp, Sam Kydd, Elsie Monks, Helen Forrest, Dorothy King, Marian Edwards-Greene, Maureen Allen, Dennis Castle, Dennis Brian, Harold Huth.

Peers plays a Welsh grocer who suddenly realizes his dream of becoming a songwriter after winning a contest that lands him a contract with a major publishing company in London. Leaving his girl, Watts, behind, Peers moves to the city and soon suffers from bouts of loneliness that stifle his songwriting ability. He is able to provide the company with songs he had previously written, but he struggles to write something new. Eventually he comes up with one and it is almost stolen by an unscrupulous publisher. Luckily, Peers saves his music and renews his relationship with Watts. A pointless exercise in maudlin sentiment populated with selfish characters.

p, John Croydon, Harold Huth; d, Peter Graham Scott; w, Scott, Dennis Vance; ph, Gerald Gibbs.

Musical (PR:A MPAA:NR)

SING AND BE HAPPY** (1937) 67m FOX bw

Anthony [Tony] Martin (*Tony Mason*), Leah Ray (*Ann Lane*), Dixie Dunbar (*Della Dunn*), Joan Davis (*Myrtle*), Helen Westley (*Mrs. Henty*), Allan Lane (*Hamilton Howe*), Berton Churchill (*John Mason*), Andrew Tombes (*Thomas Lane*), Chick Chandler (*Mike*), Edward Cooper (*Mason's Butler*), Irving Bacon (*Palmer*), Luis Alberni (*Posini*), Bruce Warren (*Orchestra Leader*), Carroll Nye (*Announcer*), Cullen Morris (*Boy Dancer*), Lynn Bari, June Gale (*Secretaries*), Charles Tannen (*Clerk*), Arthur Rankin, Paul McVey (*Car Passengers*), Frank McGlynn, Sr (*Sheriff*).

Martin is the bane of his father, refusing to take a position at the family ad agency and instead flitting about the country. He returns home and goes to the office but just upsets the businesslike decorum. He complicates matters by trying to woo Ray, the daughter of his father's rival. The two agencies come head to head over a pickle account in this light-hearted (and headed) little musical. It was Martin's first starring role and was little more than a vehicle designed to give him a boost. The production is okay and the acting is passable, considering the featherweight story. Songs: "Sing and Be Happy," "Travelin' Light," "What a Beautiful Beginning" (Sidney Clare, Harry Akst).

p, Milton H. Feld; d, James Tinling; w, Ben Markson, Lou Breslow, John Patrick; ph, Daniel B. Clark; md, Samuel Kaylin.

Musical (PR:A MPAA:NR)

SING AND LIKE IT** (1934) 71m RKO bw

ZaSu Pitts (*Annie Snodgrass*), Pert Kelton (*Ruby*), Edward Everett Horton (*Adam Frink, Producer*), Nat Pendleton (*Fenny*), Ned Sparks (*Toots*), John M. Qualen (*Oswald*), Richard Carle (*Abercrombie*), Stanley Fields (*Butch*), Joseph Sauers [Sawyer], William M. Griffith, Grace Hayle, Roy D'Arcy, Florence Roberts.

While working their way into a bank vault, a gang of robbers, led by Pendleton, hear singing. It turns out to be Pitts, rehearsing a sentimental song about mothers for the Union Bank Little Theater group. Pendleton is reduced to tears by the tune and the hardened gangster with marshmallow insides sets up a show for Pitts to sing the song in. Of course it's the worst show imaginable, but he forces critics to like it unless they want to contend with him and the boys. Though clever in parts, this is a one joke film that continually repeats itself. Pitts is fairly good in the lead, a role she was getting with increasing frequency at this stage of her career. Production values are typical for the day.

p, Howard J. Green; d, William A. Seiter; w, Marion Dix, Laird Doyle (based on the story *So You Won't Sing, Eh?* by Aben Kandel); ph, Nick Musuraca; ed, George Crone; m/l, "Your Mother," Dave Dreyer, Roy Turk.

Comedy (PR:A MPAA:NR)

SING AND SWING** (1964, Brit.) 78m Three Kings/UNIV bw (GB: LIVE IT UP)

David Hemmings (*Dave Martin*), Jennifer Moss (*Jill*), John Pike (*Phil*), Heinz Burt (*Ron*), Steven Marriott (*Ricky*), Joan Newell (*Margaret Martin*), Ed Devereaux (*Herbert Martin*), Veronica Hurst (*Kay Miller*), Penny Lambirth (*Barbara*), Peter Glaze (*Mike Moss*), David Bauer (*Mark Watson*), Anthony Ashdown (*Bob*), Douglas Ives (*Bingo*), Paul Hansard (*Film Director*), Geoffrey L'Oise (*Assistant*), Nancy Spain (*Columnist*), Peter Haigh (*Announcer*), Peter Noble (*Interviewer*), Trevor Maskell (*Aldo*), John Mitchell (*Andrews*), Anthony Shepard (*Commissionaire*), David Clark (*Recording Man*), Pat Gilbert (*Housekeeper*), Kenny Ball and His Jazzmen, Gene Vincent, Patsy Ann Noble, Kim Roberts, The Outlaws, Sounds Incorporated, Andy Cavell and the Saints.

Hemmings is a post office messenger boy and leader of the rock group The Smart Alecs. His father won't have any of this teenaged nonsense and gives Hemmings a month to succeed or give it up. Hemmings loses an all-important audition tape on the way to delivering a package to a film studio, but as the contrived plot twist would have it, American producer Bauer finds the tape. He loves it and begins a search for the group. Finally, over a taxi intercom, Hemmings and his boys have their big audition, which they pass with resounding success. The group ends up in a musical rock film and Hemmings shows his father what rock is all about. Even THE WIZARD OF OZ had a more believable plot than this nonsense, though Hemmings, in a pre-BLOW UP outing, isn't bad. Watch for rock star Vincent in a cameo. "Rondo," "Hand Me Down My Walkin' Shoes," "Live It Up!" "Temptation Baby," "Please Let It Happen to Me," "Keep It Moving," "Law and Order," "Loving Me This Way," "Don't Take You from Me," "Don't You Understand," "Sometimes I Wish" (Joe Meek, Norrie Paramor, Kenny Ball), "Accidents Will Happen" (Paramor, Bob Barratt, sung by Patsy Ann Noble).

p&d, Lance Comfort; w, Lyn Fairhurst (based on a story by Fairhurst) from an idea by Harold Shampan]; ph, Basil Emmott; ed, John Trumper; art d, Jack Shampan; cos, John Stephen, Mary Quant; makeup, George Blackler.

Rock Comedy   (PR:C MPAA:NR)

SING ANOTHER CHORUS**   (1941) 64m UNIV bw

Johnny Downs (*Andy Peyton*), Jane Frazee (*Edna*), Mischa Auer (*Stanislaus*), George Barbier (*Mr. Peyton*), Iris Adrian (*Francine La Verne*), Sunnie O'Dea (*Peggy*), Joe Brown, Jr (*Ralph*), Walter Catlett (*Theodore Gateson*), Charles Lane (*Ryan*), Peter Peters (*Morris*), Ronald Peters (*Boris*), Rossario and Antonio (*Specialty*), Nell O'Day (*Girls*), Elaine Morley (*Girls*), Greta Grandstedt (*Soubrette*), Ann Doran (*Bronx Dame*), Pat Costello (*Actor*), Joe Recht (*Messenger Boy*), Ed Kane (*Maxwell*).

A starry-eyed college graduate, fresh from writing and producing his campus variety show, talks his father into letting him stage a production using the employees of his father's dress factory. A producer cons the heady graduate out of the money the father advances him, but thanks to the employees the show does indeed go on, with rousing success. Typical grinder musical from Universal with one of its bottom-of-the-barrel plots. The singing and dancing isn't bad, with the wonderful Spanish dance team of Rossario and Antonia stealing the show. Songs include: "Two Weeks Vacation with Pay," "Mister Yankee Doodle," "Rug-Cuttin' Romeo," "Boogie Woogie Man," "Dancing on the Air," "Walk With Me," "We Too Can Sing" (Milton Rosen, Everett Carter).

p, Ken Goldsmith; d, Charles Lamont; w, Marion Orth, Paul Gerard Smith, Brenda Weisberg (based on a story by Sam Robins); ph, Jerome Ash; m, Charles Previn; ed, Arthur Hilton; ch, Larry Ceballos.

Musical   (PR:A MPAA:NR)

SING AS WE GO***   (1934, Brit.) 80m Associated Talking
                                                     Pictures/ABF bw

Gracie Fields (*Gracie Platt*), John Loder (*Hugh Phillips*), Dorothy Hyson (*Phyllis Logan*), Stanley Holloway (*Policeman*), Frank Pettingell (*Murgatroyd Platt*), Lawrence Grossmith (*Sir William Upton*), Morris Harvey (*Cowboy*), Arthur Sinclair (*Maestro*), Maire O'Neil (*Mme. Osiris*), Ben Field (*Nobby*), Olive Sloane (*Violet*), Margaret Yarde (*Mrs. Clotty*), Evelyn Roberts (*Parkinson*), Norman Walker (*Hezekiah Crabtree*), James R. Gregson, Richard Gray, Margery Pickard, Florence Gregson, Muriel Pavlow.

An amusing star vehicle for popular comedienne Fields who sees her once again cast as a spunky mill girl. When the financially troubled mill is forced to close down during the summer, Fields makes do by going through a series of holiday-related jobs in Blackpool that lead to some clever comedic situations. One day Fields meets wealthy businessman Grossmith and she persuades him to invest in the ailing mill, thus saving the day. A better than average British comedy blessed with an appealing star and an equally fascinating look at industrial Britain before WW II.

p&d, Basil Dean; w, Gordon Wellesley (based on a story by J.B. Priestley); ph, Bob Martin.

Comedy   (PR:A MPAA:NR)

SING AS YOU SWING**   (1937, Brit.) 82m Rock/British Independent
                                          bw (AKA: LET THE PEOPLE LAUGH)

Evelyn Dall (*Cora Fane*), Claude Dampier (*Pomphrey Featherstone-Chaw*), Luanne Meredith (*Sally Bevan*), Brian Lawrance (*Jimmy King*), Clampham & Dwyer, Four Mills Brothers, Beryl Orde, Billie Carlisle, Mantovani and His Tipicas, Nat Gonella and His Georgians, Sherman Fisher Girls, Billie Carlisle, Edward Ashley, H.F. Maltby, Jimmy Godden, Chilton & Thomas.

Typical British song and dance revue with a radio background. To compete with commercial broadcasts from continental Europe, a national radio station has the team of Clampham & Dwyer host a variety show. A thin plot line and scattershot quality from the acts, showcasing various talents. A cut-down version of the film was released in 1941 and two shorts – SWING TEASE and THE MUSIC BOX – were also culled from the footage.

p, Joe Rock; d, Redd Davis; w, Syd Courtenay (based on a story by Clifford

Grey); ph, Jack Parker.

Musical/Comedy   (PR:A MPAA:NR)

SING, BABY, SING***   (1936) 90m FOX bw

Alice Faye (*Joan Warren*), Adolphe Menjou (*Bruce Farraday*), Gregory Ratoff (*Nicky*), Ted Healy (*Al Craven*), Patsy Kelly (*Fitz*), Michael Whalen (*Ted Blake*), Ritz Brothers (*Themselves*), Montagu Love (*Robert Wilson*), Dixie Dunbar (*Telephone Operator*), Douglas Fowley (*Mac*), Paul Stanton (*Brewster*), Tony Martin (*Tony Renaldo*), Virginia Field (*Farraday's Nurse*), Paul McVey (*Doctor*), Carol Tevis (*Tessie*), Cully Richards (*Joe*), Lynn Bari.

A fast-moving musical comedy that bore more than a passing resemblance to the true-life romance which was taking place between John Barrymore and Elaine Barrie at the time and filled the tabloids. A new-look Faye (she let her eyebrows grow in and had a more appealing hair style than ever before) is a singer at a New York night club. She loses her job and is disconsolate, but her agent, Ratoff, thinks he might have an idea. In the 1930s, debutante-singers were all the rages so Ratoff concocts a bogus background for Faye and offers her to a radio station manager, Stanton, who at first is pleased, but then spurns her when he learns that Ratoff's story is a sham. Faye is about to perform her last show at the club and in the audience is Menjou, a bombastic, tipsy Shakespearean actor in for a spell from Hollywood. Ratoff, his secretary, Kelly, and her brother, Healy, have a few drinks with Menjou, who becomes enamored with Faye before he passes out from too much alcohol and must be taken to the hospital. Before he is toted away, Menjou eyes Faye as though she were Juliet and he a mustached Romeo. Whalen, a newsman looking for a bit of gossip about the famed movie star, follows Ratoff and Healy to the hospital where he hears them promise to bring Faye to the woozy Menjou, who now wants another drink. There's no whisky in the hospital so Healy hands Menjou some barber's shave lotion (bay rum) which Ratoff claims is a special kind of South American brandy and stows it in the hot water bottle next to the bed. Later, Faye and Kelly arrive, with Whalen hot on their heels. Whalen shoots a few pictures and has his story in time for the early edition of his paper. Now Ratoff dangles Menjou's name in front of radio man Stanton and says he can produce the star if Faye gets a job on the air. The show is about to be broadcast when Menjou's cousin, Love, comes on the scene and puts an end to matters because he thinks Faye is a cheap woman seeking to trade off Menjou's name. Love drags Menjou away and the two men board a train going to California. Whalen and Faye go after Menjou in an airplane and catch up to him in Kansas City where a hastily put-together broadcast team made up of locals from the "show-me" state gather for a broadcast starring Menjou and Faye. (The singer with the band is Tony Martin, whom Faye was married to from 1936 through 1940.) Love tries to keep Menjou from going on the air while several others go through their turns and songs. Whalen snatches Menjou from Love's safekeeping, rushes him to the station, and Menjou appears on the show, which results in Faye getting a radio contract. The Ritz Brothers, Harry, Jimmy and Al, make their movie debut here as themselves and are hysterical. They use a few of their tried and true vaudeville routines in which they satirize Ted Lewis and Harry Richman as well as Dr. Jekyll and Mr. Hyde. Once Al died, the other brothers were at a loss and, with the passing of bug-eyed Harry in 1986, an era ended. Menjou was sensational as the drunken movie star and showed a comedy side that was to stand him in good stead as he bridged the gap between leading man and character actor. Faye had wanted Tyrone Power to play the Whalen role as she thought he had that elusive something that separates juveniles from stars but the studio bosses reckoned the role should be played by a name and Whalen was assigned. Later, Faye was to make several films with Power. Good songs from several composers included the Oscar-nominated "When Did You Leave Heaven?" (Walter Bullock, Richard A. Whiting, sung by Tony Martin), "You Turned the Tables on Me" (Sidney D. Mitchell, Louis Alter, sung by Faye), "Love Will Tell," "Sing, Baby Sing" (Lew Pollack, Jack Yellen, sung by Faye), "The Music Goes 'Round and 'Round" (Mike Riley, Red Hodgson, Ed Farley, sung by The Ritz Brothers), "Singing a Vagabond Song" (Harry Richman, Sam Messenheimer, Val Burton, sung by The Ritz Brothers), and "When My Baby Smiles At Me" (Andrew B. Sterling, Bill Munro, Ted Lewis, sung by The Ritz Brothers). Zanuck, who personally produced this film, was bound and determined to make Faye a star and he gave the slim story lots of gloss, heavy production values, and a supporting cast of outstanding comic actors to help her up the ladder.

p, Darryl F. Zanuck; d, Sidney Lanfield; w, Milton Sperling, Jack Yellen, Harry Tugend (based on a story by Sperling, Yellen); ph, Peverell Marley; ed, Barbara McLean; md, Louis Silvers; art d, Mark-Lee Kirk; set d, Thomas Little; cos, Royer.

Musical/Comedy   (PR:A MPAA:NR)

SING, BOY, SING**   (1958) 90m FOX bw

Tommy Sands (*Virgil Walker*), Lili Gentle (*Leora Easton*), Edmond O'Brien (*Joseph Sharkey*), John McIntire (*Rev. Walker*), Nick Adams (*C.K. Judd*), Diane Jergens (*Pat*), Josephine Hutchinson (*Caroline Walker*), Jerry Paris (*Fisher*), Tami Conner (*Ginnie*), Regis Toomey (*Rev. Easton*), Art Ford, Bill Randle, Biff Collie (*Disc Jockeys*), Marie Brown (*Mrs. Fitzgerald*), Madge Cleveland (*Miss Keyes*), Tom Greenway (*Haggarty*), Lloyd Harter (*Hillman*), Patrick Miller (*Fitzgerald*).

Minor pop star Sands makes a successful screen debut in this JAZZ SINGER-styled story which serves as a showcase for his talents. He's a successful rock star with a $300,000-a-year income and a pushy agent (O'Brien) and press agent (Paris). But his dying grandfather (McIntire) is an old-time preacher who tells the boy his life is full of sin. The old man dies and Sands, overwhelmed by guilt, takes to preaching. But his heart isn't in it and finally he returns to the rock life after his aunt (Hutchinson) convinces him that one should always use the gifts given to them by God. Originally this had been a Kraft TV Playhouse drama before being transferred to the big screen. Songs include: "Rock of Ages," "Sing, Boy, Sing," "Gonna Talk with My Lord," "Who Baby?" "Crazy 'Cause I Love You," "Bundle of Dreams," "Your Daddy Wants to Do Right," "Just a Little Bit More," "That's All I Want from You," "People In Love," "Soda-Pop Song," "Would I Love You."

p&d, Henry Ephron; w, Claude Binyon (from the story *The Singin' Idol* by Paul Monash); ph, William C. Mellor (CinemaScope); m, Lionel Newman; ed, William Mace; art d, Lyle R. Wheeler, Herman A. Blumenthal; ch, Nick Castle.

Drama/Musical   (PR:C MPAA:NR)

SING, COWBOY, SING***   (1937) 59m GN bw

Tex Ritter (*Tex Archer*), Louise Stanley (*Madge*), Al St. John (*Biff*), Karl Hackett (*Kalmus*), Charles King (*Red Holman*), Robert McKenzie (*Judge Dean*), Budd Buster (*Marshal Pinker*), Heber Snow [Hank Worden], Chick Hannon (*Henchmen*), Horace Murphy, Snub Pollard, Tex Palmer, Jack C. Smith, Oscar Gahan, Herman Hack, Chester Conklin.

A covered wagon train of supplies is heading West and some bad guys want the cargo for themselves. An enjoyable outing for Ritter, with more of an emphasis on comedy than standard western plot devices. Former silent Mack Sennett loonies St. John, Pollard, and Conklin are part of the fun. Ritter saves the day and gets the girl in an overall good western. Director Bradbury collaborated with Ritter on "Twilight Reverie," one of the songs in the film. Other songs include: "Sing, Cowboy, Sing" (Ted Choate), "Goodbye, Old Paint" (Ritter).

p, Edward Finney; d, Robert N. Bradbury; w, Robert Emmett [Tansey]; ph, Gus Peterson.

Western   Cas.   (PR:A MPAA:NR)

SING, DANCE, PLENTY HOT** (1940) 70m REP bw (GB: MELODY GIRL)

Ruth Terry (*Irene*), Johnny Downs (*Johnny*), Barbara Allen [Vera Vague] (*Susan*), Billy Gilbert (*Hector*), Claire Carleton (*Evelyn*), Mary Lee (*Judy*), Elisabeth Risdon (*Agatha*), Lester Matthews (*Scott*), Leonard Carey (*Henderson*).

After buying a story by Duane Decker from Collier's magazine for the grand sum of $500, Republic bosses promptly threw out the original plot and kept the title for what was to be one of their big musicals for 1940. The results are anything but big, though, it being a standard story with Matthews as a phony promoter of charity shows. He always runs off with the money he's gathered but now he finds himself bargaining with more than he hoped for when he gets involved with Allen, Risdon, and Terry. The three want to raise money for an orphanage, and Matthews' assistant, Downs, finally catches on to his boss' scams and turns him in to cop Gilbert (who manages to sneak in a few turns of his famous sneezing routine). Terry and Downs become romantically involved, which may have had something to do with Downs' turnabout. Strictly formula material. Songs include: "Tequila" (sung by Downs, Terry), "I'm Just a Weakie" (sung by Allen, Gilbert), "What Fools These Mortals Be," "When A Fella's Got a Girl," (Jule Styne, George R. Brown, Sol Meyer).

p, Robert North; d, Lew Landers; w, Gordon Rigby, Bradford Ropes (based on a story by Vera Caspary, Ropes); ph, Ernest Miller; ed, Edward Mann; md, Cy Feuer; art d, John Victor Mackay; ch, Larry Ceballos.

Musical   (PR:A MPAA:NR)

SING FOR YOUR SUPPER**   (1941) 66m COL bw

Jinx Falkenburg (*Evelyn Palmer*), Charles "Buddy" Rogers (*Larry Hays*), Bert Gordon ("*The Mad Russian*"), Eve Arden (*Barbara Stevens*), Don Beddoe (*Wing Boley*), Bernadene Hayes (*Kay Martin*), Henry Kolker (*Myron T. Hayworth*), Benny Baker (*William*), Dewey Robinson ("*Bonzo*"), Luise Squire (*Mildred*), Larry Parks (*Mickey*), Lloyd Bridges (*Doc*), Harry Barris (*Jimmy*), Walter Sande (*Irv*), Berni Gould (*Art*), Red Stanley, Perc Launders, Harry Lang (*Musicians*), Don Porter (*Tim*), Virginia Pherrin (*Helen*), Jessie May Jackson (*Mary*), Dona Dax (*Dorothy*), Patricia Knox (*Sue*), Sig Arno (*Raskalnikoff*), Eve Carlton, Franchon Estes, Valeri Gratton, Betty Brooks, Dorothy Trail (*Hostesses*), Earle Hodgins (*Yokel*), Judith Linden (*Ticket Girl*), Ed Bruce (*Jerk*), Glen Turnbull Dink Freeman (*Seamen*), Earl Bunn (*Counterman*), Mildred Gover (*Nancy*).

Minor B film has Rogers playing a struggling band leader. He's about to lose his dance hall when Falkenburg, a socialite, saves the day. Forgettable material with a weak script, though the cast isn't bad. Songs include: "Why

Is It So?" (sung by Falkenburg), "Booglie Wooglie Piggy" (sung by Falkenburg, Rogers, Gordon), "Sing for Your Supper" (Sammy Cahn, Saul Chaplin).

p, Leon Barsha; d, Charles Barton; w, Harry Rebuas [Sauber], (based on a story by Rebuas); ph, Franz F. Planer; ed, Arthur Seid; art d, Lionel Banks.

Musical   (PR:AA MPAA:NR)

SING ME A LOVE SONG   (SEE: MANHATTAN MOON, 1935)

SING ME A LOVE SONG*½ (1936) 78m COS/FN-WB bw (GB: COME UP SMILING)

James Melton (*Jerry Haines*), Patricia Ellis (*Jean Martin*), Hugh Herbert (*Siegfried Hammersblag*), ZaSu Pitts (*Gwen*), Allen Jenkins (*Chris Cross*), Nat Pendleton (*Red, the Chauffeur*), Ann Sheridan (*Lola Parker*), Walter Catlett (*Sprague*), Hobart Cavanaugh (*Mr. Barton*), Charles Halton (*Mr. Willard*), Charles Richman (*Mr. Malcolm*), Dennis Moore (*Ronald Blakeley*), Georgia Caine (*Mrs. Parker*), Granville Bates (*Goodrich*), Billy Arnold (*Waiter*), Lyle Moraine (*Bellboy*), George Guhl (*Cop*), Betty Farrington (*Customer*), George Sorel (*Headwaiter*), Adrian Rosley (*Waiter*), Linda Perry (*Miss Joyce, the Secretary*), Gordon Hart (*Caldwell*), Robert Emmett O'Connor, Harry Hollingsworth (*Detectives*), Emmett Vogan (*Floorwalker*).

Rich playboy Melton goes incognito and takes a job as a clerk for a store he owns. He wants to learn the insides of the business but he gets distracted in his aims by music counter clerk Ellis; a perfect contrivance to pepper this forgettable programmer with equally forgettable tunes sung by Melton. Herbert has some funny moments as a kleptomaniac, but this is mostly an inept musical that suffers from a silly screenplay and a lower than usual budget. Songs include: "Summer Night," "The Little House that Love Built," "That's the Least You Can Do for a Lady" (Al Dubin, Harry Warren), "Your Eyes Have Told Me So" (Gus Khan, Walter Blaufuss, Egbert Van Alstyne).

p, Sam Bischoff; d, Raymond Enright; w, Sig Herzig, Jerry Wald (based on a story by Harry Sauber); ph, Arthur Todd; ed, Terry Morse; md, Leo Forbstein; ch, Bobby Connolly.

Musical   (PR:A MPAA:NR)

SING, NEIGHBOR, SING*½   (1944) 70m REP bw

Brad Taylor (*Bob Reed*), Ruth Terry (*Virginia Blake*), Virginia Brissac (*Cornelia Blake*), Beverly Lloyd (*Beverly*), Charles Irwin (*Prof. Jasper Cartwright*), Olin Howlin (*Joe the Barber*), Maxine Doyle (*Maxine*), Mary Kenyon (*Ruth*), Roy Acuff and his Smoky Mountain Boys, with Rachel, Lulubelle and Scotty, Harry "Pappy" Cheshire, the Milo Twins, Carolina Cotton.

A lothario (Taylor) comes to a small college town in hopes of seducing various coeds. He poses as an older and quite distinguished English psychologist and does nicely for himself. However, his plans are destroyed when the real psychologist turns up, but all ends well when Taylor reforms. Grafted onto this minor fluff are a number of country radio singers who were popular at the time, each crooning their respective hillbilly tunes. It was made by the studio with country audiences in mind.

p, Donald H. Brown; d, Frank McDonald; w, Dorrell and Stuart McGowan; ph, Reggie Lanning; ed, Ralph Dixon; md, Morton Scott; art d, Gano Chittenden; ch, Jerry Jarrette; m/l, Fred Rose, Milo Brothers, John Marvin, Krumet and Kurtis, Scott Wiseman, J. Elliott, D. Butts.

Musical   (PR:A MPAA:NR)

SING SING NIGHTS*½   (1935) 60m MON bw (GB: REPRIEVED)

Conway Tearle (*Floyd Cooper*), Mary Doran (*Anne McCaigh*), Hardie Albright (*Howard Trude*), Boots Mallory (*Ellen Croft*), Ferdinand Gottschalk (*Prof. Varney*), Berton Churchill (*Gov. Duane*), Jameson Thomas (*Robert McCaigh*), Lotus Long (*Li Sung*), Henry Kolker (*Kurt Nordon*), Richard Tucker (*Attorney General*), George Baxter (*Sergei Krenwicz*).

When globetrotting newsman Tearle is killed with three bullets, Albright, Thomas, and Baxter are all accused of murder. Each confesses and each is sentenced to the electric chair. Gottschalk, a professor, brings in a lie detector of his own devising that eventually gets two men a pardon and one the death penalty. Though based on a popular novel, this production suffers from inept direction and some ridiculous performances. The script has some interesting twists, but these are tempered by the other dull production values.

d, Lew Collins; w, Marion North, Charles Logue (based on a novel by Harry Stephen Keeler); ph, Archie Stout; ed, Carl Pierson.

Drama   Cas.   (PR:C MPAA:NR)

SING SINNER, SING zero   (1933) 74m Majestic bw

Paul Lucas (*Phil Carida*), Leila Hyams (*Lela Larson*), Donald Dillaway (*Ted Rendon*), Ruth Donnelly (*Margaret Flannigan*), George E. Stone (*Spats*), Joyce Compton (*Gwen*), Jill Dennett (*Sadie*), Arthur Hoyt (*Uncle Homer*),

Walter McGrail (Louis), Gladys Blake (Cecily Gordon), Arthur Housman (Jerry), Edgar Norton, John St. Polis, Stella Adams, Pat O'Malley, Walter Brennan, Walter Humphry.

Poorly constructed B film deals with the problems of a torch singer and her millionaire husband. Packed with jazz and cabaret stock footage, some terrible miscasting, and a bad dubbing job on Hyams' singing voice, this programmer has little to recommend it. Lucas was capable of far better things.

p, Phil Goldstone; d, Howard Christy; w, Edward T. Lowe (based on a play by Wilson Collison); ph, Ira Morgan

Drama   (PR:C   MPAA:NR)

SING WHILE YOU DANCE**   (1946) 88m COL bw

Ellen Drew, Robert Stanton, Andrew Tombes, Edwin Cooper, Robert Stevens, Ethel Griffies, Amanda Lane, Eddy Waller, Paul E. Burns, Eddie Parks, Bert Roach, Mary Gordon, Walter Baldwin, Trevor Bardette, Jean Donahue, Crystal Reeves.

Drew is a would-be composer struggling to make it big along Tin Pan Alley. She meets Griffies, the widow of a noted composer, and induces the wealthy woman to let some minor changes be made in her late husband's music. The outcome is predictable bit of fluff. Songs include "Oh What a Lovely Dream" (Milton Drake, Ben Oakland), "It's a Blue World" (Bob Wright, Chet Forrest), "I Don't Know How You Did It" (Doris Fisher, Allan Roberts).

p, Leon Barsha; d, D. Ross Lederman; w, Robert Stephen Brode (based on a story by Lorraine Edwards); ph, Allen Siegler; ed, Alan Havlick; art d, Cary Odell; set d, George Montgomery.

Musical/Comedy   (PR:A   MPAA:NR)

SING WHILE YOU'RE ABLE*   (1937) 66m Melody/Modern bw

Pinky Tomlin (Whitey), Toby Wing (Joan), H.C. Bradley (Williams), Monte Collins (Adams), Sam Wren (Bennett), Suzanne Kaaren (Gloria), Bert Roach (Blodgett), "Prince" Michael Romanoff (Prince), Jimmy Newell (Himself), The Three Brian Sisters (Rita), Jane, and Dotty.

When a rich man and his daughter have car problems in the South they accidentally discover Tomlin, a hillbilly singer, and his constantly grinning sidekick, Wing. They sign up for radio, but the father's business manager fears Tomlin will get in the way of his romance with the daughter. Shortly before his first radio broadcast Tomlin is kidnaped by the blighter, but he manages to escape. He catches cold and loses his voice, but in the end he's back to singing and wins over the heart of his benefactor. Cardboard acting and weak production values sink this inept musical. The list of grating musical numbers includes "I'm Gonna Sing While I'm Able" (Paul Parks, Connie Lee), "Swing, Brother, Swing" (Al Heath, Buddy LeRoux), "Leave It Up to Uncle Jake" (Parks, Lee, Heath, LeRoux), "You're My Strongest Weakness" (Coy Poe, Heath, LeRoux), "One Girl In My Arms" (Harry Tobias, Roy Ingraham), "I'm Just a Country Boy at Heart" (Parks, Lee, Pinky Tomlin).

p, Maurice Conn; d, Marshall Neilan; w, Sherman Lowe, Charles Condon (based on a story by Condon, Stanley Lowenstein); ph, Jack Greenhalgh; ed, Martin G. Cohn; md, Edward L. Kaye; m/l, Connie Lee, Paul Perks, Buddy LeRoux, Al Heath, Harry Tobias, Roy Ingraham.

Musical   (PR:A   MPAA:NR)

SING YOU SINNERS***½   (1938) 88m PAR bw

Bing Crosby (Joe Beebe), Fred MacMurray (David Beebe), Donald O'Connor (Mike Beebe), Elizabeth Patterson (Mrs. Beebe), Ellen Drew (Martha), John Gallaudet (Harry Ringmer), William Haade (Pete), Paul White (Filter), Irving Bacon (Lecturer), Tom Dugan (Race Fan), Herbert Corthell (Nightclub Manager), drummer Earl Roach.

Until this picture, Crosby had been playing cliched light comedy roles that made him popular, but did nothing to show his acting talent as the parts were usually just an extension of what everyone thought Bing was: a happy-go-lucky guy with a mellow voice. In this film, he is able to present another side to his character and the results loudly rang the cash register. Crosby is a 35-year-old wastrel who spends most of his time trying to stay out of work and concocting plans to make money without toil. His mother, Patterson, wishes Crosby would be more like another son, MacMurray, a garage mechanic devoted to the work ethic who dreams of owning his own establishment. Patterson also wants Crosby to set a better example for her youngest son, O'Connor (who was 13 at the time and in his second film). They have very little money but they have great love for each other and an overpowering unity when it comes to music. The three brothers are musicians and make a few extra bucks working at a small night club (MacMurray was, in fact, a saxophonist before he became an actor). Not content with barely squeezing out an existence, Crosby leaves the others and travels to Los Angeles to widen his horizons. He pledges to the others that as soon as he gets a good job he'll send them enough money for fare. Time passes and Patterson hears from Crosby that he's now in a new business and doing well. That's enough for her to divest herself of all her household goods,

sell the family home and go to Los Angeles. Once she and O'Connor arrive, they learn that Crosby has sold his second-hand merchandise business and used the money to purchase a race horse with, at best, a hidden history. Crosby has squandered all of his ready cash on the steed and when he can't come up with his rent, he is given an eviction notice. Patterson is annoyed at his casual ways and he tries to convince her that he's done right and that the horse will make them wealthy when he can be trained and groomed and prepared for racing. That process takes many months and Crosby has only weeks before he has to vacate. MacMurray and his wife-to-be, Drew, show up in Los Angeles and the hard-headed and practical mechanic is angered to see that Crosby hasn't changed his ways. O'Connor is pressed into service as the animal's jockey after joining his brothers in their musical act to keep body and soul together. They barely hold on until the Big Race when the horse runs away and hides from the competition. After the race, there's a battle royal wherein the two brothers combine to thwack some hoods who wanted to fix the race. With their fortune assured, Patterson extracts a promise that Crosby will give up trying to make a buck in the Sport of Kings and concentrate on keeping the family's musical act going as the picture ends. Several neat tunes interweave with the Runyon-type script by Binyon (who worked with director Ruggles on many movies before becoming a director himself). They include: "Small Fry" (Hoagy Carmichael, Frank Loesser, sung by Crosby and MacMurray), "Don't Let that Moon Get Away" (James V. Monaco, Johnny Burke, sung by Crosby), "I've Got a Pocketful of Dreams," "Laugh And Call It Love," and "Where Is Central Park?" (Monaco, Burke, sung by Crosby, MacMurray, O'Connor). Director Ruggles does well with the subject matter and keeps matters moving at a good clip, jamming everything into the film in a brisk 88 minutes. He was the younger brother of Charles Ruggles and lived many years in Beverly Hills with his wife, Arline Judge.

p&d, Wesley Ruggles; w, Claude Binyon; ph, Karl Struss; ed, Alma Macrorie; md, Boris Morros; art d, Hans Dreier, Ernst Fegte; set d, A.E. Freudeman.

Musical Comedy   (PR:AA   MPAA:NR)

SING YOUR WAY HOME*   (1945) 72m RKO bw

Jack Haley (Steve), Marcy McGuire (Bridget), Glenn Vernon (Jimmy), Anne Jeffreys (Kay), Donna Lee (Terry), Pattie Brill (Dottie), Nancy Marlow (Patsy), James Jordan, Jr (Chuck), Emory Parnell (Captain), David Forrest (Windy), Ed Gargan (Jailer).

Unbelievably hokey film finds Haley as an egotistical war correspondent heading back to New York after WW II's end in Europe. He's in charge of a group of teenagers who had been trapped for four years in Europe while entertaining during the war. Apparently the kids can't get enough of show business life as they constantly put on production numbers that make one wonder what tortures they must have endured. There's also a plot twist involving a "love code" Haley had sent his editor to which a woman in love with him had added some closing lines of her own, violating censorship regulations, and he is thrown in jail. But all ends happily when Haley is freed without explanation. Haley does little more than go through the motions, though he shows an occasional glimmer of real talent. The music isn't the worst around but was nothing special. McGuire was the only standout in the teen cast. Songs include: "I'll Buy That Dream" (sung by Anne Jeffreys), "Heaven Is A Place Called Home," "Seven O'Clock in the Morning (Waking up Boogie)," "Somebody Stole My Poor Little Heart" (Herb Magidson, Allie Wrubel), "The Lord's Prayer" (arrang ed by Albert Hay Malotte).

p, Bert Granet; d, Anthony Mann; w, William Bowers (based on a story by Edmund Joseph, Bart Lytton); ph, Frank Redman; ed, Harry Marker; md, C. Bakaleinikoff; art d, Albert S. D'Agostino, Al Herman.

Musical   (PR:A   MPAA:NR)

SING YOUR WORRIES AWAY**   (1942) 71m RKO bw

Bert Lahr (Chow Brewster), June Havoc (Rocksey Rochelle), Buddy Ebsen (Tommy Jones), Patsy Kelly (Bebe), Dorothy Lovett (Carol), Sam Levene (Smiley Clark), Margaret Dumont (Flo Faulkner), Morgan Conway (Chesty Martin), Fortunio Bonanova (Gaston), Don Barclay (Luke Brown), Russ Clark (1st Henchman), Sammy Stein (2nd Henchman), Alvino Rey Orchestra with the King Sisters.

Designed specifically for Lahr's talents, this awkward comedy features the talented clown as a carefree songwriter whose world turns upside down when he inherits $3,000,000. Some gangsters want the loot which causes Lahr nothing but woe. Somewhere in the mess Ebsen gets a chance to show his dance talents. The comedy runs roughshod over everything else though, never giving the other performers a chance to show their real talents. The film proved to be a money loser for the studio, with a $255,000 loss charted. Songs include: "It Just Happened to Happen," "Sally, My Dear Sally," "Sing Your Worries Away," "Cindy Lou McWilliams," "How Do You Fall in Love?"

p, Cliff Reid; d, A. Edward Sutherland; w, Monte Brice (based on a story by Erwin Gelsey, Charles E. Roberts, based on an idea by Charles S. Belden); ph, Frank Redman; ed, Henry Berman; md, C. Bakaleinikoff; ch, Val Raset; m/l, Mort Greene, Harry Revel.

Comedy/Musical   Cas.   (PR:A   MPAA:NR)

SINGAPORE*   (1947) 79m UNIV bw

Fred MacMurray (Matt Gordon), Ava Gardner (Linda), Roland Culver (Michael Van Leyden), Richard Haydn (Chief Inspector Hewitt), Thomas Gomez (Mr. Mauribus), Spring Byington (Mrs. Bellows), Porter Hall (Mr. Bellows), George Lloyd (Sascha Barda), Maylia (Ming Ling), Lal Chand Mehra (Mr. Hussein), H.T. Tsiang (Sabar), Rudy Robles (Desk Clerk), Frederick Worlock (Cadum), Holmes Herbert (Reverend Barnes), Philip Ahn (Bartender), George Sorel (Maitre d'), Reginald Sheffield (Travel Agent), Pat Aherne, Leyland Hodgson (British Officers), Gerald Oliver Smith (Englishman), Edith Evanson (Miss Barnes), Dick Elliott (Passenger), Maxine Chevelier (Singer), David Ralston (Hewitt's Assistant), Luke Chan (Chinese Waiter), Curt Conway (Pepe), Arthur Gould Porter (Broadcaster), Monica Winckel, Cha-bing (Native Women), Norman Ainsley (Immigration Official), Don Escobar (Night Desk Clerk).

At the end of WW II former sailor MacMurray returns to Singapore where he takes up his old business of pearl smuggling. His life before this time is told in flashback: in the past he had romanced and wed Gardner. However, on their wedding night there was an attack by a Japanese air squadron and Gardner was presumed killed. It turns out she is quite alive, though suffering from amnesia and now married to Culver. Mixed in with this is a sub-plot involving some gangsters who want MacMurray to reveal the whereabouts of some pearls he hid in a hotel room during the war. Gardner is kidnaped but MacMurray saves her in this far-fetched and slow paced adventure. MacMurray is okay but Gardner doesn't work at all in her role. The direction is uninspiring and short on excitement. SINGAPORE was made on an "A" picture budget, but couldn't escape its "B" reputation. It was remade in 1957 with a new title and location: ISTANBUL.

p, Jerry Bresler; d, John Brahm; w, Seton I. Miller, Robert Thoeren (based on a story by Miller); ph, Maury Gertsman; m, Daniele Amfitheatrof; ed, William Hornbeck; md, David Tamkin; art d, Bernard Herzbrun, Gabriel Scognamillo; set d, Russell A. Gusman, Oliver Emert; spec eff, David Horsley.

Drama   (PR:A   MPAA:NR)

SINGAPORE, SINGAPORE**   (1969, Fr./Ital.) 95m Les Films
Number One-Poste Parisie n-Franco Riganti/Ben Barry and Associates c
(CINQ GARS POUR SINGAPOUR) (CINQUE MARINES PER SINGAPORE) (AKA: FIVE ASHORE IN SINGAPORE)

Sean Flynn (Capt. Art Smith), Marika Green (Monica), Terry Downes (Sgt. Gruber), Marc Michel (Capt. Kevin Grey), Peter Grayford (Mr. Brown), Denis Berry (Dan), Bernard Meusnier (Angel), Andrew Ray [Andrea Aureli] (Ta-tchouen), Jessy Greek (Ten-sin), Trudy Connor (Tchin-saw), William Brix (Captain).

After meeting with Grayford of the British Secret Service, CIA agent Flynn (the son of Errol) joins up with four Marines to search for 17 fellow soldiers reported missing. They discover that Ray, a mad scientist, is keeping the missing men alive through frozen hibernation and is preparing to perform experiments to brainwash his victims. He offers to turn over the Marines for cash and weapons, but his plans are foiled. Flynn and Downes, one of the Marines, sneak aboard his floating laboratory and rescue the men, and the British forces, along with the three other volunteer Marines, destroy the ship.

p, Pierre Kalfon; d, Bernard Toublanc-Michel; w, Kalfon, Toublanc-Michel, Sergio Amidei (based on the novel Cinq Gars Pour Singapour by Jean Bruce); ph, Jean Charvein (Eastmancolor); m, Antoine Duhamel, Ward Swingle; ed, Gabriel Rongier; art d, Gilbert Margerie.

Action Thriller   (PR:C   MPAA:NR)

SINGAPORE WOMAN**   (1941) 64m FN-WB bw

Brenda Marshall (Vicki Moore), David Bruce (David Ritchie), Virginia Field (Claire Weston), Jerome Cowan (Jim North), Rose Hobart (Alice North), Heather Angel (Frieda), Richard Ainley (John Wetherby), Dorothy Tree (Mrs. Bennett), Bruce Lester (Clyde), Connie Leon (Suwa), Douglas Walton (Roy Bennett), Gilbert Emery (Sir Stanley Moore), Stanley Logan (Commissioner), Abner Biberman (Signa), Eva Puig (Natasha).

Marshall is a woman who's convinced that she's under a curse. She's brought to Bruce's plantation to recuperate and of course finds love in the process. While there she undergoes a transformation from unhappy woman to radiant beauty. But a former husband, whom she's thought dead for years, turns up alive. He's conveniently killed in a car wreck in this plodding, dull remake of DANGEROUS. The locale switch from New York to Singapore is of no help, and Marshall is definitely no Bette Davis (the star of the original). The direction is a straightforward style, but the drama comes across as trite and the plot's implausiblities are evident.

p, Harlan Thompson; d, Jean Negulesco; w, M. Coates Webster, Allen Rivkin (based on the story Hard Luck Dame by Laird Doyle); ph, Ted McCord; ed, Everett Dodd; art d, Charles Novi.

Drama   (PR:A   MPAA:NR)

SINGER AND THE DANCER, THE** (1977, Aus.) 54m Australian
Council For Arts, Radio, Film, and TV Board/COL c

Ruth Cracknell (Old Mrs. Bilson), Elizabeth Crosby (Charlie), Jude Kuring (Mrs. Herbert), Russell Kiefel (Pete), Gerry Duggan (Doctor), Jane Buckland (Young Girl), Kate Sheil (Young Mrs. Bilson).

In this intelligent drama, an older woman, Cracknell, watches as a younger woman, Crosby, lives her life as she did. Cracknell tries to help the younger Crosby escape some of the patterns she wove, but ultimately both woman are caught up in webs of their own doings, unable to break free. The film works well, with sparing use of dialog that allows the situations to speak for themselves. The fine chemistry between Cracknell and Crosby gives the psychological and emotional aspects an added edge of honesty. Some interesting early work in this short film from the director of MY BRILLIANT CAREER and MRS. SOFFEL.

p&d, Gillian Armstrong; w, Armstrong, John Pfleffer; ph, Russell Boyd; m, Robert Murphy; ed, Nick Beauman; art d, Sue Armstrong.

Drama   (PR:C   MPAA:NR)

SINGER NOT THE SONG, THE**   (1961, Brit.) 132m RANK/WB c

Dirk Bogarde (Anacleto), John Mills (Father Keogh), Mylene Demongeot (Locha), Laurence Naismith (Old Uncle), John Bentley (Chief of Police), Leslie French (Father Gomez), Eric Pohlmann (Presidente), Nyall Florenz (Vito), Roger Delgado (De Cortinez), Philip Gilbert (Phil Brown), Selma Vaz Dias (Chela), Laurence Payne (Pablo), Jacqueline Evans (Dona Marian), Lee Montague (Pepe), Serafina Di Leo (Josefa).

Quantano is a small and isolated Mexican town run by the tyrannical, atheistic bandito, Bogarde. Mills arrives in Quantano as a dedicated Roman Catholic priest who ignores Bogarde's rules and invites people to attend church. His life is threatened, but Mills forges ahead and begins building a following, including Demongeot, a young girl who has a crush on the clergyman. Angered by this defiance, Bogarde begins killing peasants in alphabetical order, but stops after building a sort of reluctant admiration for the feisty priest. He even has one of his own men killed after another attempt on the priest's life. Bogarde confronts Mills and tells him that he will be allowed to live if he can determine which inspires good: the "singer" (priest) or the "song" (religion). Demongeot's family learns that she loves the priest and they try to force another on her in marriage. Consequently she heads off to hide in the mountains. Bogarde finds her and tells Mills he will let her live if he admits he's a failure as a priest from the pulpit. Mills agrees, but goes against his word when he sees that Demongeot is safe. Instead, he denounces evil and Bogarde, who is consequently arrested. His gang helps him escape and a gun fight ensues. Both Mills and Bogarde are mortally wounded and the two die side by side with Bogarde muttering "The Singer, not the Song." At times this is a plodding film, but more often than not the fine screenplay overcomes the sensationalistic direction. A strange love triangle is subtly built up between Demongeot and Mills and Bogarde. Though not overt, there are strong suggestions that Bogarde's obsession with the priest has homosexual overtones. Mills and Bogarde have a strong chemistry between them that makes this unusual relationship believable. Not a great film by any means, but certainly an interesting one.

p&d, Roy [Ward] Baker; w, Nigel Balchin (based on the novel The Singer, Not the Song by Audrey Erskine Lindop); ph, Otto Heller (CinemaScope, Technicolor); m, Philip Green; ed, Roger Cherrill; art d, Alex Vetchinsky; set d, Arthur Taksen; cos, Yvonne Caffin; makeup, George Blackler.

Western   **Cas.**   (PR:O   MPAA:NR)

SINGIN' IN THE CORN zero   (1946) 64m COL bw (GB: GIVE AND
TAKE)

Judy Canova (Judy McCoy), Allen Jenkins (Glen Cummings), Guinn "Big Boy" Williams (Hank), Charles Halton (Obediah Davis), Alan Bridge (Honest John Richards), Robert Dudley (Gramp McCoy), Nick Thompson (Indian Chief), Frances Rel (Ramona), George Chesebro (Texas), Ethan Laidlaw (Silk Stevens), Frank Lackteen (Medicine Man), The Singing Indian Braves (Themselves), Guy Beach (Judge), Jay Silverheels, Rodd Redwing (Braves), Dick Stanley, Charles Randolph (Indians), Si Jenks (Old Man), Pat O'Malley (O'Rourke), Chester Conklin (Austin Driver), Mary Gordon (Mrs. O'Rourke).

Canova plays a carnival mind reader who inherits her late uncle's estate under the condition that a ghost town be returned to the rightful owners, the Indians. Fortunately for Canova, her uncle's ghost makes an appearance and advises her on what to do. The film lacks the credibility and story line necessary to make it work. Instead, it's padded with stock footage and musical numbers, sung by The Singing Indian Braves. Canova was a popular radio singer of the time, but this film did nothing for her career. Watch for Silverheels, TV's "Tonto" of later years. Songs include: "I'm a Gal of Property," "Pepita Chequita," "An Old Love Is a True Love" (Doris Fisher, Allan Roberts), "Ma, He's Making Eyes at Me" (Sidney Clare, Con Conrad).

p, Ted Richmond; d, Del Lord; w, Isabel Dawn, Monte Brice (based on story by Richard Weil); ph, George B. Meehan; ed, Aaron Stell; art d, Sturges Carne.

Musical   (PR:A   MPAA:NR)

SINGIN' IN THE RAIN***** (1952) 103m MGM c

Gene Kelly *(Don Lockwood)*, Donald O'Connor *(Cosmo Brown)*, Debbie Reynolds *(Kathy Selden)*, Jean Hagen *(Lina Lamont)*, Millard Mitchell *(R.F. Simpson, Studio Head)*, Rita Moreno *(Zelda Zanders)*, Douglas Fowley *(Roscoe Dexter, Director)*, Cyd Charisse *(Dancer)*, Madge Blake *(Dora Bailey, Radio Gossip Columnist)*, King Donovan *(Rod)*, Kathleen Freeman *(Phoebe Dinsmore, Diction Coach)*, Bobby Watson *(Diction Coach)*, Jimmie Thompson *(Male Lead in "Beautiful Girls" Number)*, Dan Foster *(Assistant Director)*, Margaret Bert *(Wardrobe Woman)*, Mae Clarke *(Hairdresser)*, Judy Landon *(Olga Mara)*, John Dodsworth *(Baron de la May de la Toulon)*, Stuart Holmes *(J.C. Spendrill III)*, Dennis Ross *(Don as a Boy)*, Bill Lewin *(Bert, Villain in Western)*, Richard Emory *(Phil, Cowboy Hero)*, Julius Tannen *(Man on Screen)*, Dawn Addams, Elaine Stewart, *(Ladies in Waiting)*, Carl Milletaire *(Villain, "Dueling Cavalier" and "Broadway Rhythm")*, Jac George *(Orchestra Leader)*, Wilson Wood *(Vallee Impersonator)*, Dorothy Patrick, William Lester, Charles Evans, Joi Lansing *(Audience)*, Dave Sharpe, Russ Saunders *(Fencers)*, Patricia Denise, Jeanne Coyne *(Girl Dancers)*, Bill Chatham, Ernest Flatt, Don Hulbert, Robert Dayo *(Male Dancing Quartet)*, David Kasday *(Kid)*.

Beyond question and doubt, this film is the greatest musical MGM or anyone else ever produced, though there were many that came as close as a gnat's eyelash. The film has everything–great songs, great dances, a wonderful, nostalgic story, and a superb cast, all directed with a dazzling pace equal to the speed-crazy era it profiles, the Roaring Twenties. The film is multidimensional in that, beyond presenting a great musical, it subtly and sometimes not-too-subtly comments on the wild characters studio machinations of the day, often unfavorably but always accurately. The film opens in 1927 to show a movie ritual of pomp and little circumstance, the Hollywood premiere, with floodlights bathing a Los Angeles theater showing a new swashbuckling movie and cheering crowds with screaming teenagers being held back by police lines and long limousines arriving in front of the theater about to show for the first time a film starring Kelly and his blonde bombshell leading lady, Hagen. A Louella Parsons-type gossip columnist, Blake, greets the arriving stars, talking into a radio microphone to tell listeners across the land about the wonderful event. All the Hollywood types are present, including the cigar-smoking producers, the sex queens, and the Lotharios of the cinema. Song and dance man O'Connor arrives but gets a dying cheer when spectators realize he's no one of importance. Then the big names arrive, Kelly, dressed in a long white polo coat and white hat, and Hagen, wrapped in expensive furs, both smiling so wide their faces seem that they will crack, and waving frantically to their swooning, cheering fans. They march up the long red carpet to the microphone and Blake, who begins to ask inane questions of the grinning pair. Because Hagen possesses one of the world's worst voices, a screeching, shrieking voice that sounds like a rusty saw striking nails, Kelly is terrified of allowing her to answer any of Blake's fatuous questions. He prevents her from talking, monopolizing the conversation with Blake so as not to allow the public to hear Hagen's awful voice. This, of course, is the peak of the silent movie era, and the actress has never been heard to speak, not even in public, a dictate enforced by Mitchell, head of her studio, Monumental Pictures. Mitchell has rightly concluded that if Hagen's voice were to be heard the public would stay away from her films and he would lose a fortune. To occupy the time of Blake's gushy, posturing interview, Kelly recounts his career, but not in terms of reality, talking about how he worked hard at ballet classes and music conservatories with his friend O'Connor. In flashback, the viewer is shown how Kelly and O'Connor really came up the ladder, first playing in burlesque houses as comic musicians, wearing loud clothes and doing frenetic dance numbers, and here the two dancers perform their "Fit as a Fiddle and Ready for Love" number (Freed, Al Hoffman, Al Goodhart, the song originally appearing in the film COLLEGE COACH, 1933). As Kelly narrates his fabricated past, we see him in flashback, arriving with O'Connor in Hollywood where Kelly becomes a daredevil stuntman, taking punches in westerns, being blown out of airplanes, and even doing stunts around the already-established silent film star Hagen, an egomaniacal, idiotic, and empty-headed sexpot who likes to quote a reviewer of one of her films, who said she was "the brightest star in the firmament." Director Fowley, stereotyped with riding boots, jodhpurs, and beret, "discovers" Kelly while he is performing impossible stunts and makes a leading man out of him, teaming him with Hagen who expects Kelly to woo her now that he has joined her in the "firmament." He cannot hide the fact that he despises her, but–and by then we have a flash forward to the premiere–Kelly makes a point of adoring his leading lady in public. He ends the brief recital of his laborious rise to the top of the Hollywood heap stating that he was guided by his motto, "Dignity, always dignity." Later, to escape the clutches of the cloying Hagen, Kelly walks down a street, only to be attacked by a bevy of rabid teenage fans who tear his clothes and cause him to flee for his life. He jumps into a car driven by Reynolds who recognizes him but does not seem impressed. She drives him to a safe place and, en route, tells him that films have nothing to do with real art, that they are just cheap entertainment and that she is a *real* actress. Kelly gets the brush-off from the pretty young girl but is later startled to see her pop out of a cake and then dance as part of a chorus line, bumping and grinding, at a Hollywood party. He approaches her after she does her number and points out that what she has just done is not what he would call high art. Reynolds, furious at being exposed for the pretentious girl she is, picks up a cake and throws it at Kelly but he ducks and it hits Hagen square in the face, right in the middle of one of her screeching monologs (a scene which certainly pays tribute to the pie-throwing techniques of the silent comedians). Kelly races after Reynolds while Hagen explodes in one of her pyrotechnical displays of temper. Something else explodes at the party given by mogul Mitchell. He shows a talking picture, a revolutionary new technical concept which all present pooh-pooh as a novelty item and not worth much discussion. Mitchell thinks the same way, stating, "The Warner Brothers are making a whole talking picture with this gadget–THE JAZZ SINGER. They'll lose their shirts." But Mitchell soon changes his thinking when THE JAZZ SINGER becomes an overnight sensation, realizing that talking pictures are "here to stay." He stops production on the studio's most recent opus, THE DUELING CAVALIER, and orders that the film be made as a talkie, desperately conferring with Kelly and O'Connor, until they decide to make a musical out of the Kelly-Hagen film, retitling it THE DANCING CAVALIER, but there is one terrible snag: Hagen cannot sing, let along talk in a voice that would be acceptable to a mongoose. Kelly learns that Reynolds has a job at Monumental and he quickly falls in love with her and she with him, and he croons, "You Were Meant for Me" (Freed, Brown, originally sung in BROADWAY MELODY, 1929) on a sound stage, and they become lovers, although their liaison must be kept secret from the possessive Hagen who mistakenly believes that Kelly is her fiance. Meanwhile, the DANCING CAVALIER is completed but the primitive sound equipment causes it to be a technical disaster. When it is released, the audiences first seeing the film howl with laughter at the distorted voices, the wires on which the players trip, the out-of-synchronization sound of the entire film. Mitchell pulls it out of distribution, trying to figure a way to doctor it and save his studio, the chief problem being Hagen's miserable voice. Meanwhile, O'Connor and Kelly have some fun with the stuffy voice coach, Watson, the studio has hired, dancing about the perplexed Watson and singing a song that pokes fun of his exaggerated elocution lessons, "Moses Supposes" (specially written for this film by Edens, Comden, and Green). Later that night Kelly, O'Connor, and Reynolds try desperately to think of a way to save THE DANCING CAVALIER, staying up all night and, at dawn, singing "Good Morning" (originally done in BABES IN ARMS, 1939). By then they have come up with the perfect solution, or, at least, O'Connor has, mustache-twisting is to have Reynolds dub her voice for the screeching Hagen. At first Reynolds resists the idea but Kelly persuades her that in this way she will begin her film career and will later be given parts where she will be seen on screen. She agrees to lip-sync for the horrid Hagen and the film goes ahead. The film is released with Reynolds dubbing Hagen's speaking and singing voice (Reynolds' own voice was dubbed in her vocals by Betty Royce), and Kelly adds a spectacular singing and dancing number to the movie, "Broadway Ballet," a story within a story, about a young hoofer who arrives on Broadway and becomes, through hard work and talent, a big name along the Main Stem, with a long, near-adagio dance done by Kelly and a sexy, tall, and sultry Charisse, a vamp he meets in a nightclub, a gangster's moll who captivates him. (Charisse is terrific in this dance number, her hair cut short, with bangs, made up to look like silent screen star Louise Brooks. This dance gave Charisse an opportunity to perform dazzling movements with Kelly and display the most attractive long legs in show business, a little too long for Kelly who had to arrange some tricky steps so that he would not appear shorter than Charisse, which he was.) The new and revamped DANCING CAVALIER is an enormous success and Kelly plans to reveal that the sweet voice singing for the pathetic Hagen is his own true love, Reynolds. But at the premiere of the film, Hagen viciously stipulates that Reynolds must go on singing and talking for her, that she will remain behind the scenes and make the blonde bombshell look good to the public and that she will never be allowed to have a film career of her own. The audience cheers loudly for the stars of the film and shouts for Hagen to sing to them from the stage. A tearful Reynolds, knowing she will never have a career now, is ordered to go behind a curtain and begin singing while Hagen appears before the crowd and moves her lips as Reynolds lip-syncs for her. But Hagen is not to triumph in her evil plan. Kelly, O'Connor, and studio boss Mitchell, who has had enough of Hagen's high-handed ways, step up to a rope and begin to pull it so that the curtain behind Hagen goes up and Reynolds is seen standing behind the posturing Hagen, singing for her. This brings the audience to howls of laughter, ending Hagen's ridiculous career on the spot. She storms off the stage. Reynolds, embarrassed, is about to run off when Kelly stops her and introduces her to the audience as "the real star of the DANCING CAVALIER." United in real life, Kelly and Reynolds are shown on a billboard at the film's end, one which advertises their new film together, for now they are a successful celluloid love team. The camera pulls back to show Kelly and Reynolds standing before the billboard and going into an embrace for the fadeout. This superb musical, matchless in its story and music, was really a pastiche of numbers taken from the best of MGM's total musical output since the talkies began. And all of them, except a few, were Freed and Brown tunes. The tune Reynolds and other chorus girls dance wildly to at the Hollywood party, "All I Do Is Dream of You" first appeared in SADIE McKEE (1934). The song "Should I?" appeared in LORD BYRON OF BROADWAY (1930), the classic "Singin' in the Rain" (sung and danced to by Kelly, Reynolds, and O'Connor at the beginning of the film behind credits and, later, in one of the greatest dance numbers ever done for the screen, by Kelly) appeared in HOLLYWOOD REVUE OF 1929. "The Wedding of the Painted Doll" and "Broadway Melody" are from BROADWAY MELODY (1929), "Would You" from SAN FRANCISCO (1936), "I've Got a Feelin' You're Foolin' ", "You Are My Lucky Star" and "Broadway Rhythm" from BROADWAY MELODY (1936), and "Beautiful Girl" (which is sung with panache by Jimmie Thompson) was originally crooned by Bing Crosby in GOING HOLLYWOOD (1933). Just as Kelly and Donen looted the studio of every great tune it had presented in earlier musicals, especially those that captured the flavor of the 1920s, the codirectors also used every prop and vehicle in MGM warehouses. Reynolds, for instance, at the beginning of the film, is driving Andy Hardy's old jalopy when she rescues Kelly from his "adoring" fans. The mansion in which Kelly lives is decorated with tables, chairs, carpets, and chandeliers left over from the sets of a John Gilbert and Greta Garbo silent classic, FLESH AND THE DEVIL. But then everything about the film harkened back to the colorful Hollywood past. Comden and Green, whose names are forever brightly linked to this masterpiece, were given a writing assignment to put together a musical that would employ all the Freed-Brown numbers, but their research revealed that most of these excellent tunes were presented in films made during the transition from the silent era to the talkie period. The writers then brilliantly conceived of showing that time frame in the musical, with all its confusion about the new sound equipment and the new stars replacing the old ones, where bright and shiny faces took the places of heavily mascared vamps and mustache-twisting villains. They first thought about remaking BOMBSHELL (aka, BLONDE BOMBSHELL, 1933), a Jean Harlow vehicle, and the front office pushed Howard Keel, then one of the leading baritones on the screen, to star. But this notion was later abandoned and Kelly was brought in. The dancer really created the entire, delightful ambience of this spectacular musical, designing and dancing through the marvelous "Broadway Ballet" sequence with its imaginative sets and wonderful guest appearance by Charisse, and Charisse's astounding "Crazy Veil" ballet number where she worked with a 25-foot long piece of white China silk which streamed about her, kept floating in the air by three airplane motors whirring off-camera. Of course the *tour de force* dance number is Kelly's, when he does the spectacular title number, tapping and leaping through a rain-clogged street, swinging around a lamppost, splashing and jumping in joy over having fallen in love with Reynolds (who was only 19 when she got this, her first big break). It is a scene radiating sheer ebullience and energy. Kelly later commented about this scene: "The concept was so simple I shied away from explaining it to the brass at the studio in case I couldn't make it sound worth doing. The real work for this one was done by the technicians who had to pipe two city blocks on the backlot with overhead sprays, and the poor cameraman who had to shoot through all that water. All I had to do was dance....My concern for this piece was making the action logical and we arrived at that by setting it up as you would a short story, with a beginning, a middle, and an end. The reason for the dance is his happiness at winning the girl. The logic of his antics in the street is the expression of that happiness, and the conclusion is his being spotted by a policeman, snapping him out of his rapture. He then gives the umbrella to a passerby and walks away." Kelly simplified what he achieved in this unforgettable sequence, for in skirting about the upside-down umbrella, letting water from a gushing drainpipe cascade onto his smiling face, skipping and dancing along the sidewalk and gutter in the downpour, and displaying acrobatic dance moves no other hoofer, including Fred Astaire, could hope to achieve, he brought a lasting image of utter joy to the screen. This dance number alone is worth the whole film. And second to it is the hilarious, magnificent comic dance O'Connor (who never topped his performance in this film) performs with props and sets on a sound stage in a wild number, "Make 'Em Laugh" (a Freed-Brown tune which unabashedly lifts Cole Porter's number, "Be a Clown"). O'Connor is so frenetic, so energetic in this piece that he appears to be like a puppet being manipulated by unseen hands. He leaps against fake walls, jumps over couches, twirls with a cloth dummy like a dervish, and lands on the floor, where he performs sort of a running movement but is really turning himself on his side, before jumping up and crashing through a wall for a frantic finale. If O'Connor, a hoofer since childhood and a great one, had never made another film after SINGIN' IN THE RAIN, his reputation would have been secure with this single number. Reynolds was a concern at the front office but Kelly and Donen convinced executives that the pert young starlet could hold her own in the film and she did. She later stated about SINGIN' IN THE RAIN that she "learned a lot from Gene 'Kelly'. He is a perfectionist and a disciplinarian—the most exciting director I've ever worked for. And he has a good temper. Every so often he would yell at me and make me cry. But it took a lot of patience for him to work with someone who had never danced before. It's amazing that I could keep up with him and Donald O'Connor." The overwhelming "Broadway Ballet" number came into existence simply because, as Kelly later stated, "We had to have a number there. We never meant it to be that long, but since we were introducing a new character...we had to keep adding to it and adding to it. It went on for hours, it seems." This sequence took a month to rehearse, two weeks to shoot, and cost $600,000, almost a fifth of the overall budget. The fabulous costumes by Plunkett cost more than $157,000 and the entire film had a price tag of $2,540,800, going over the preproduction budget by $665,000. It was worth it, as MGM discovered only months later when the film earned back $7,665,000 from its initial release. Probably the most astounding dramatic performance in this film was rendered by villainous Hagen whose normal voice was well-pleasing but she distorted it into a piercing whine throughout the film and projected an utterly repulsive character that epitomized some of the unscrupulous and vanity-bound actresses of the silent era. She is another gem in this shining musical that is undoubtedly the most popular ever made, any time, anywhere.

p, Arthur Freed; d, Gene Kelly, Stanley Donen; w, Adolph Green, Betty Comden (suggested by the song "Singin' in the Rain"); ph, Harold Rosson

(Technicolor); m, Nacio Herb Brown; ed, Adrienne Fazan; md, Lennie Hayton; art d, Cedric Gibbons, Randall Duell; set d, Edwin B. Willis, Jacques Mapes; cos, Walter Plunkett; spec eff, Warren Newcombe, Irving G. Ries; m/l, Freed, Brown, Comden, Green, Roger Edens, Hoffman, Goodhart.

Musical   **Cas.**   **(PR:A MPAA:NR)**

SINGING BLACKSMITH*   (1938) 116m Collective/New Star bw

Moishe Oysher *(Yankel)*, Miriam Riselle *(Tamara)*, Florence Weiss *(Rivke)*, Anna Appel *(Chaya-Peshe)*, Ben-Zvi Baratoff *(Bendet)*, Michael Goldstein *(Baffuel)*, Lea Noemi *(Mariashe)*, Max Vodnoy *(Simche)*, Lube Wesely *(Fumeh)*, Yudel Dublinsky *(Reb Aaron)*, Luba Rymer *(Sprintze-Gnesye)*, Benjamin Fishbein *(Frolke)*, R. Wendroff *(Ella)*, Ray Schneir *(Rivke's Mother)*, Hershel Bernardi *(Young Yankel)*, Sophie Bressler *(Maid)*, Libby Charney *(1st Girl)*, Clara Deutschmann *(Chaike)*, Janet Deutschmann *(2nd Girl)*, R. Shanock *(Leah)*, Riesa Halpern *(Seamstress)*.

This film is a presentation of a 1909 Yiddish theater play that was quite popular with the immigrant Jewish community. Oysher is the blacksmith in love with life, and Riselle is his dutiful wife. Entering their happy marriage is Weiss, as the other woman, who is married to the weak-willed Goldstein. Members of the Yiddish Arts Players also participated, making this an important record of a fading American theater form. As a film it has its flaws with some of the direction and photography; however, Oysher has such presence that these factors are quickly forgotten. Watch for Bernardi in a sequence of Oysher's childhood. Bernardi would grow up to do some good work of his own, including a stint as Tevye in "Fiddler on the Roof." (In Yiddish; English subtitles.)

d, Edgar G. Ulmer; w, David Pinski (based on the play "Yankel Der Schmidt" by Pinski); ph, Bill Miller; md, Jacob Weinberg.

Drama   **(PR:C MPAA:NR)**

SINGING BUCKAROO, THE*   (1937) 56m Spectrum/Advance bw

Fred Scott, William Faversham, Victoria Vinton, Cliff Nazarro, Howard Hill, Charles Kaley, Roger Williams, Dick Curtis, Lawrence LeBaron, Rosa Caprino, Pinky Barnes, Carl Mathews, Slim Carey, Augie Gomez, The Singing Buckaroos, White King.

Cowgirl Vinton is riding the range with $25,000 in a satchel. A crook from the city is after the dough and will stop at nothing to get it. He uses a pair of hoodlums to help him kidnap Vinton's father. In rides Scott, complete with white hat, to save the day with the help of an arrow shooting Indian. Typical low budget independent western. Oddly enough the producers never gave the characters any names, but simply listed the cast as is.

p, Jed Buell, George H. Callaghan; d&w, Tom Gibson; ph, Robert Doran.

Western   **Cas.**   **(PR:AA MPAA:NR)**

SINGING COP, THE*   (1938, Brit.) 78m WB bw

Keith Falkner *(Jack Richards)*, Marta Labarr *(Maria Santova)*, Chili Bouchier *(Kit Fitzwillow)*, Ivy St. Helier *(Sonia Kassona)*, Glen Alyn *(Bunty Waring)*, Athole Stewart *(Sir Algernon Fitzwillow)*, George Galleon *(Drips Foster-Hanley)*, Ian Maclean *(Zabisti)*, Bobbie Comber *(Bombosa)*, Robert Rendel *(Sir Treves Hallam)*, Vera Bogetti *(Rosa)*, Brian Buchel *(Pemberton)*, Derek Gorst *(Capt. Farquhar)*, Frederick Burtwell, Chorus of The Royal Opera House Covent Garden.

If a prize could be awarded for the most outlandish premise to be filmed, this movie would be a leading contender. Someone is leaking valuable secrets to enemy agents and all guilt points toward opera prima donna Labarr. Falkner, a policeman who coincidentally possesses a great voice himself, is enlisted to watch her under cover, posing as a member of the opera chorus. Bouchier, another opera singer, falls for the cop, as does the suspect. Bouchier grows jealous over Labarr's affection towards her would-be beloved, so she helps prove the opera star really is a spy! This absurd story is somehow blessed with good opera sequences. Otherwise, it's just another so-bad-it's-good film.

p, Irving Asher; d, Arthur Woods; w, Brock Williams, Tom Phipps (based on a story by James Dyrenforth, Kenneth Leslie-Smith); ph, Basil Emmott.

Crime/Musical   **(PR:A MPAA:NR)**

SINGING COWBOY, THE½   (1936) 56m REP bw

Gene Autry *(Gene)*, Smiley Burnette *(Frog)*, Lois Wilde *(Helen)*, Creighton [Lon] Chaney, Jr *(Martin)*, Ann Gillis *(Lou Ann)*, Earle Hodgins *(Prof. Sandow)*, Harvey Clark *(Blake)*, John Van Pelt *(Stevens)*, Earl Eby *(Trenton)*, Ken Cooper *(Bill)*, Harrison Green *(Mayor)*, Wes Warner *(Jack)*, Jack Rockwell *(Sheriff)*, Tracy Layne *(Kirk)*, Oscar Gahan *(Tom)*, Frankie Marvin *(Shorty)*, Jack Kirk *(Lane)*, Audrey Davis *(Gene's Man)*, George Pearce *(Dr. Hill)*, Charles McAvoy *(Johnson)*, Alfred P. James *(Justice of Peace)*, Snowflake *(Entertainer)*, Pat Caron *(Miss Kane)*, Champion the horse.

In this Autry picture, a little girl needs an operation so that she won't be crippled for life. Autry takes off to the big city where he talks a coffee company into sponsoring a broadcast to raise some money. In order to attract a bigger audience, they decide to use the then infant medium of television. Audiences of the time must have wondered who would watch, since most people then didn't own a television. Despite the fact that the heroine gets locked in a runaway wagon forcing the entire ranch out after her, the broadcast is a success and the needed money for the operation is raised. Autry, then nicknamed "Public Cowboy No. 1," once worked on the night shift as a telegraph operator. Legend has it that he bought a guitar to fill in the time and one night was overheard by a stranger who suggested that he try to get on the radio. That stranger was Will Rogers. Autry took Rogers' advice and with the hit song "That Silver Haired Daddy Of Mine" (1929), the rest is history. Autry was known for his high moral standards in his pictures. He almost never kissed the girl and when he did, it was almost always by the nudging of his famous horse, Champion. This picture's songs include: "Rainbow Trail," "My Old Saddle Pal."

p, Nat Levine; d, Mack V. Wright; w, Dorrell McGowan, Stuart McGowan (based on a story by Tom Gibson); ph, William Nooles, Edgar Lyons; m, Harry Grey; ed, Lester Orlebeck; md, Grey; m/l, Smiley Burnette, Oliver Drake.

Western   **Cas.**   (PR:A MPAA:NR)

SINGING COWGIRL, THE*   (1939) 60m Coronado/GN bw

Dorothy Page (Dorothy Hendrick), David O'Brien (Dick Williams), Vince Barnett (Kewpie), Ed Piel (Tom Harkins), Dix Davis (Billy Harkins), Stanley Price (John Tolen), Warner Richmond ("Gunhand" Garrick), Dorothy Short (Nora Pryde), Paul Barrett (Rex Harkins), Lloyd Ingraham (Dr. Slocum), Ethan Allen (Sheriff Teasley), Ed Gordon ("Trigger" Wilkins), Merrill McCormick (Deputy Sheriff).

Poorly made western features Page as the heroine in the last of her ill-fated series. Price, a crooked lawyer, along with Richmond are a band of outlaws who want to take over a ranch they think has a gold mine. They murder the owner and his wife, leaving their eight-year-old son an orphan. The boy's neighbor happens to be Page, who with the help of O'Brien, rides in to save the day. The idea of a female hero was unusual for the 1930s and was never able to overcome the sexist stereotypes of the series westerns. Page and O'Brien are good in their roles, but the female heroine simply could not work under the constraints of western formulas.

p, George Hirliman; d, Samuel Diege; w, Arthur Hoerl; ph, Mack Stengler; ed, Guy V. Thayer, Jr.; m/l, Al Sherman, Walter Kent, Milton Drake.

Western   **Cas.**   (PR:A MPAA:NR)

SINGING FOOL, THE***   (1928) 105m WB-Vitaphone bw

Al Jolson (Al), Betty Bronson (Grace), Josephine Dunn (Molly), Reed Howes (John Perry), Edward Martindel (Marcus), Arthur Housman (Blackie Joe), David Lee (Sonny Boy), Robert Emmett O'Connor (Cafe Manager).

After the success of THE JAZZ SINGER (Jolson had faith in it as he took much of his salary in Warner Brothers stock), it was only natural to rush out another one starring the entertainer. This time it's a weeper with Jolie playing the part of a waiter-songwriter who tries to convince the singer (Dunn) at the club that he's the guy for her. At first, she is not convinced, then she succumbs to his entreaties when he writes a song for her and sings it on the night club floor. It just so happens that a big-time Broadway producer is in the place, Martindel, and he brings Jolson to Broadway. Jolson and Dunn marry, have a child, Lee, but after four years, she doesn't want to have anything more to do with him, so she takes Lee and travels to France. Jolson's career goes straight down and he is almost a case for welfare when he meets cigarette girl Bronson who helps him back up the ladder. Jolson goes on top again, then learns that his little son is dying. He rushes to the hospital, holds the lad and sings, you guessed, "Sonny Boy," just before Lee dies, then walks on stage to do his act for a crowd that doesn't know the pain he's in. THE SINGING FOOL is only a part-talkie and printed titles by dialoger Joe Jackson bridge the gap. Jolson was paid $150,000 for this film, which was more than the budget of some African countries at the time. "Sonny Boy" (Lew Brown, B.G. DeSylva, Ray Henderson) was penned as a gag and it eventually sold over three million copies of sheet music. The trio also wrote "It All Depends On You" and "I'm Sittin' On Top Of The World" (both sung by Jolson, who does every tune in the movie, as was his practice). Jolson, Billy Rose, and Dave Dreyer wrote "There's A Rainbow 'Round My Shoulder," and other tunes included "Golden Gate" (Rose, Dreyer, Jolson, Joseph Meyer), "Keep Smilin' At Trouble" (Jolson, DeSylva, Lewis E. Gensler), and "The Spaniard Who Blighted My Life" (Billy Merson). Little Lee was not yet 4 years of age and almost stole the movie from Jolson, a scene-stealer of no mean repute. The picture grossed more than $4 million.

d, Lloyd Bacon; w, Joseph Jackson, C. Graham Baker (based on the story by Leslie S. Barrows); ph, Byron Haskin; ed, Ralph Dawson, Harold McCord.

Musical/Drama   (PR:A MPAA:NR)

SINGING GUNS*   (1950) 91m Palomar/REP c

Vaughn Monroe (Rhiannon), Ella Raines (Nan Morgan), Walter Brennan (Dr. Mark), Ward Bond (Cardac), Jeff Corey (Richards), Barry Kelley (Mike), Harry Shannon (Judge Waller), Tom Fadden (Express Agent), Ralph Dunn (Traveler), Rex Lease (Stage Driver), George Chandler (Smitty), Billy Gray (Albert), Mary Bear (Mother), Jimmie Dodd (Stage Guard).

Popular bandleader Monroe made an unusual screen debut, switching from the ballroom to the prairie. When Monroe is denied a gold mine he believes rightfully belongs to him, the conductor becomes a Robin Hood style outlaw who plunders the mine. Corey is the bad guy, with Brennan as a doctor/preacher and Bond once more playing a sheriff. Raines is the saloon keeper and love interest for Monroe. SINGING GUNS is nothing more than a routine western that runs much longer than necessary. Monroe's hit of 1949, "Mule Train," is included in the soundtrack. Other songs include "Singing My Way Back Home," "Mexican Trail."

p, Abe Lyman; Melville Tucker; d, R. G. Springsteen; w, Dorrell McGowan, Stuart McGowan (based on a novel by Max Brand); ph, Reggie Lanning (Trucolor); m, Nathan Scott; ed, Richard L. Van Enger; m/l, Johnny Lange, Fred Glickman, Hy Heath, Wilton Moore, Al Vann, Sunny Skylar.

Western   (PR:A MPAA:NR)

SINGING HILL, THE**   (1941) 75m REP bw (AKA: THE SINGING HILLS)

Gene Autry, Smiley Burnette, Virginia Dale, Mary Lee, Spencer Charters, Gerald Oliver Smith, George Meeker, Wade Boteler, Harry Stubbs, Cactus Mack, Jack Kirk, Chuck Morrison, Monte Montague, Sam Flint, Hal Price, Fred Burns, Herman Hack, Jack O'Shea, Champion the horse.

Autry is back in the saddle again when a young woman wants to give up her rightful inheritance, which would mean a loss of free grazing land for local ranchers. Average oater outing. (See GENE AUTRY Series, Index)

p, Harry Grey; d, Lew Landers; w, Olive Cooper (based on a story by Jesse Lasky, Jr., Richard Murphy); ph, William Nobles; ed, Les Orlebeck.

Western   (PR:AA MPAA:NR)

SINGING IN THE DARK*   (1956) 84m A.N.O./Budsam bw

Moishe Oysher (Leo), Joey Adams (Joey Napoleon), Phyllis Hill (Ruth), Lawrence Tierney (Biff), Kay Medford (Luli), Mickey Knox (Barry), Dave Starr (Larry), Cindy Heller (Fran), Al Kelly (Mons. La Fontaine), Henry Sharpe (Dr. Neumann), Stan Hoffman (Stan), Paul Andor (Refugee), Abe Simon (Thug).

After WW II, a refugee of a Nazi concentration camp (Oysher) arrives in America. Suffering from amnesia, he gets a job as a hotel clerk and is then discovered by Broadway showman Adams. He takes Oysher on as a partner and the two become a successful burlesque-style song and comedy act. But eventually Oysher tires of show biz and finally becomes a cantor. The script is highly contrived, often on the verge of stupidity. This isn't helped much by uneven direction and too much use of stock footage. Oysher, a veteran of the Yiddish theater, isn't very impressive here until he starts singing. Adams is okay when he clowns around, but unfortunately, the film is mostly tripe. Adams also produced.

p, Joey Adams; d, Max Nosseck; w, Aben Kandel, Ann Hood, Stephen Kandel (based on a story by A. Kandel, from an idea by Moishe Oysher, Nosseck); ph, Boris Kaufman; ed, Leonard Anderson, Mare Sorkin.

Drama   (PR:A MPAA:NR)

SINGING KID, THE**   (1936) 85m WB-FN bw

Al Jolson (Al Jackson), Allen Jenkins (Joe Eddy), Lyle Talbot (Bob Carey), William Davidson (Barney Hammond), Frank Mitchell (Dope), Edward Keane (Potter), Sybil Jason (Sybil Haines), Tom Manning (Doorman), Winifred Shaw (Singer), Edward Everett Horton (Davenport Rogers), Beverly Roberts (Ruth Haines), Jack Durant (Babe), Joseph King (Dr. May), Joseph Crehan (Fulton), Claire Dodd (Dana Lawrence), Kay Hughes (Mary Lou), John Hale (Dr. Brown), Four Yacht Club Boys, Cab Calloway and His Band, with Eddie Barefield (tenor saxophone), Al Morgan (bass).

After THE SINGING FOOL was such a smash, they waited several years for Jolson to bring out this disappointment. Lightning did not strike twice and the picture coughed, wheezed and finally died. Jolson is a big-time musical star with a radio show. His secretary is Horton, his valet is Jenkins, and Mitchell and Durant are his gag writers (the jokes they do are so lame that one wonders how they could have kept their jobs). Jolson loses his voice and takes a vacation in the country to recover. He meets and falls for Roberts but it's her young niece, Jason, who brings life to the screen whenever she's on. In the end, Jolson is back on Broadway with his voice better than ever and a woman to love. Ray Heindorf gets one of his earliest film credits for his arrangements on the Harold Arlen-E.Y. "Yip" Harburg score which included "My, How This Country Has Changed," "I Love To Sing-a," "Here's Looking At You" (sung by Jolson), "You're The Cure For What Ails Me" (Jolson, Jason), "Save Me, Sister" (Jolson, Shaw, Calloway, Chorus). Cab Calloway and Irving Mills wrote "You Gotta Have That

Hi-Di-Ho In Your Soul." Robert Lord, who wrote the bearded story whence the equally hoary screenplay sprung, was the supervisor on the film, an old title that was in use before people became known as producers. He'd won an Oscar for writing the story for ONE WAY PASSAGE in 1932 and later teamed with Humphrey Bogart to form their own productioon company, Santana, named after Bogie's yacht. Director Keighley, who would later take the helm on several superior films like THE MAN WHO CAME TO DINNER, GEORGE WASHINGTON SLEPT HERE, THE PRINCE AND THE PAUPER, and EACH DAWN I DIE, could do little with this tired tale.

p, Robert Lord; d, William Keighley; w, Warren Duff, Pat C. Flick (based on a story by Lord; ph, George Barnes; ed, Tom Richards; md, Leo F. Forbstein; art d, Carl Weyl; cos, Orry-Kelly; ch, Bobby Connolly.

Musical   **(PR:A   MPAA:NR)**

SINGING MARINE, THE**   (1937) 105m WB bw

Dick Powell (*Robert Brent*), Doris Weston (*Peggy Randall*), Lee Dixon (*Slim Baxter*), Hugh Herbert (*Aeneas Phinney/Mrs. Fowler*), Jane Darwell (*Ma Marine*), Allen Jenkins (*Sgt. Mike Kelly*), George "Doc" Rockwell (*Doc Rockwell*), Larry Adler (*Himself*), Rose King (*Fanny Hatteras*), Marcia Ralston (*Helen Young*), Guinn "Big Boy" Williams (*Dopey*), Veda Ann Borg (*Diane*), Jane Wyman (*Joan*), Berton Churchill (*J. Montgomery Madison*), Addison Richards (*Fowler*), Eddie Acuff (*Sam*), James Robbins (*Sammy*), Henry O'Neill (*Capt. Skinner*), Tetsu Komai (*Chang*), Miki Morita (*Ah Ling*), Edward Price (*Travel Information Clerk*), Walter Miller, Ward Bond (*First Sergeants*), Lane Chandler, Hal Craig (*Squad Leaders*), John Hamilton (*Colonel*), Lucille Osborne (*Soubrette*), Sam McDaniel (*Black Man*), Murray Alper (*Marine*), Jane Weir, Trudy Marson, Frances Morris, Patsy "Babe" Kane (*Girls at Phone*), Eric Portman (*Derelict*), Valerie Bergere (*Chinese Madame*), Suzanne Kim (*Chinese Dancer*), Pierre Watkin, Ralph Dunn, Grace Hayle, Richard Loo.

Powell is the title character, a talented fighting marine who ends up with overnight fame after winning a radio contest. But with his new found fame comes an inflated ego which causes Powell to be one unpopular fellow with his old buddies in the corps, to say nothing of his girl friend, Weston. Eventually he sees the error of the ego trip and is once more the nice guy his friends know and love. Predictable and only mildly amusing, though Powell gives his usual amiable, squeaky clean performance. Musical numbers staged by Busby Berkeley are worth looking at. The songs are typical musical numbers of the period, but one piece-"The Song of the Marines" - was adopted as the official Marine Corps anthem. Other songs include: "I Know Now," "'Cause My Baby Says It's So," "Night Over Shanghai," "The Lady Who Couldn't Be Kissed," "You Can't Run Away From Love Tonight."

p, Lou Edelman; d, Ray Enright; w, Delmer Daves (based on the story by Daves); ph, Arthur L. Todd, Sid Hickox; ed, Thomas Pratt; cos, Orry-Kelly; ch, Busby Berkeley; m/l, Harry Warren, Al Dubin, Johnny Mercer.

Musical   **(PR:A   MPAA:NR)**

SINGING NUN, THE**   (1966) 98m MGM c

Debbie Reynolds (*Sister Ann*), Ricardo Montalban (*Father Clementi*), Greer Garson (*Mother Prioress*), Agnes Moorehead (*Sister Cluny*), Chad Everett (*Robert Gerarde*), Katharine Ross (*Nicole Arlien*), Juanita Moore (*Sister Mary*), Ricky Cordell (*Dominic Arlien*), Michael Pate (*Mr. Arlien*), Tom Drake (*Fitzpatrick*), Larry D. Mann (*Mr. Duvries*), Charles Robinson (*Marauder*), Monique Montaigne (*Sister Michele*), Joyce Vanderveen (*Sister Elise*), Ann Wakefield (*Sister Brigitte*), Pam Peterson (*Sister Gertrude*), Marina Koshetz (*Sister Marthe*), Nancy Walters (*Sister Therese*), Violent Rensing (*Sister Elizabeth*), Inez Pedroza (*Sister Consuella*), Ed Sullivan (*Himself*).

The sentimental true story of nun Soeur Sourire, who made it all the way to the Ed Sullivan Show, is faithfully retold. Reynolds plays the guitar-strumming Belgian nun who takes an interest in Cordell, a motherless boy whose father is alcoholic. The only one who loves the tyke is his 17-year-old sister, Ross. Reynolds writes the song "Dominique" for Cordell, and Montalban, a warmhearted priest, does his best to see the song gets somewhere. He talks to Everett, an old pal who is now a record producer. It turns out that he and Reynolds attended the Paris Conservatory of Music together. Reynolds is shocked when she discovers that Ross has posed for some risque photographs so she could support her family, and is admonished by Garson (in a cameo role as Mother Prioress) for letting Ross' father know about the photos. Meanwhile, Everett is pushing "Dominique" and taking a somewhat romantic interest in Reynolds. The song becomes an international hit and brings Ed Sullivan to Brussels with a camera crew, to film her for his popular TV show. Reynolds, understandably confused by all of this, goes to Montalban for advice. When Cordell is hurt in an accident, she promises to give up her music if she recovers. Naturally he does and Reynolds heads for a tiny African village, leaving her guitar with Ross. THE SINGING NUN was created in the style of MGM's popular family musicals of the 1940s, loaded with gloss and sugary sentimentality. The direction shamelessly panders to these elements, resulting in sluggish development. The story is somewhat fictionalized because the Catholic Church authorities objected to autobiographical films about members of its clergy. However, audiences had a real sweet tooth that year, and this ended up being a big

box-office success. Songs, sung by Reynolds, include "Dominique [The Nun's Song!]," "Sister Adele," "It's a Miracle," "Beyond the Stars," "A Pied Piper's Song" (Soeur Sourire, Randy Sparks) "Brother John," "Lovely" (Sparks) "Raindrops" (Sparks, inspired by Sourire's "Chante Riviere") "Je Voudrais," "Mets Ton Joli Jupon," "Avec Toi," "Alleluia" (Sourire).

p, John Beck Hayes Goetz; d, Henry Koster; w, Sally Benson, John Furia, Jr. (based on a story by Furia) ph, Milton Krasner (Panavision, Metrocolor); m, Harry Sukman; ed, Rita Roland; md, Harold Gelman; art d, George W. Davis, Urie McCleary; set d, Henry Grace, Jerry Wunderlich; ch, Robert Sidney; makeup, William Tuttle.

Drama   **(PR:A   MPAA:NR)**

SINGING OUTLAW**½   (1937) 57m T/C-Glenn Cook/UNIV bw

Bob Baker (*Scrap Gordon*), Joan Barclay (*Joan McClain*), Fuzzy Knight (*Longhorn*), Carl Stockdale (*Sheriff Haight*), Harry Woods (*Cueball Qualey*), LeRoy Mason (*Teton Joe*), Ralph Lewis (*Col. Bixer*), Glenn Strange (*Pete*), Jack Montgomery (*Marshal Sam Fairfax*), Georgia O'Dell (*Lucy Harris*), Jack Rockwell, Ed Piel, Jack Kirk, Bob McKenzie, Budd Buster, Lafe McKee, Hank Worden, Art Mix, Chick Hannon, Herman Hack, Curley Gibson.

After witnessing a "singing" outlaw and U.S. marshal kill each other, roving cowpoke Baker takes on the marshal's identity. This gets him into more than he bargained for; he manages to squelch a cattle-rustling scheme and win a rancher's daughter before it's all over. A routine plot that is helped somewhat by good direction and exceptional photography.

p, Paul Malvern; d, Joseph H. Lewis; w, Harry O. Hoyt; ph, Virgil Miller; ed, Charles Craft.

Western   **Cas.**   **(PR:A   MPAA:NR)**

SINGING PRINCESS, THE**½   (1967, Ital.) 76m Ima
                                            Film/Trans-National c (LA ROSA DI BAGDAD)

Voices: Julie Andrews (*Princess Zeila*), Howard Marion-Crawford (*Narrator*).

Originally released in Italy in 1949, with an English version produced in Britain in 1952, this animated film features the voice of Andrews as a princess being prepared for marriage by her uncle. One of her suitors, a cruel sheik with an evil wizard for an assistant, wants to marry the princess to gain her kingdom. A court minstrel catches on to the plot and is imprisoned by the wizard high on a mountain. He escapes and is given Aladdin's lamp by an old woman. With the help of the genie inside, the minstrel defeats the bad guys and marries the princess.

p&d, Anton Gino Domeneghini; w, Nina Maguire, Tony Maguire; ph, Cesare Pelizzari (Technicolor); m/l, "Song for the Bee," "Sunset Prayer," "The Flower Song," Riccardo Pick Mangiagalli, N. Maguire, T. Maguire (sung by Julie Andrews).

Animated Fantasy   **(PR:A   MPAA:NR)**

SINGING SHERIFF, THE**   (1944) 63m UNIV bw

Bob Crosby (*Bob Richards*), Fay McKenzie (*Caroline*), Fuzzy Knight (*Fuzzy*), Iris Adrian (*Lefty*), Samuel S. Hinds (*Seth*), Edward Norris (*Vance*), Andrew Tombes (*Jonas*), Joe Sawyer (*Squint*), Walter Sande (*Butch*), Doodles Weaver (*Ivory*), Pat Starling, Louis Da Pron, Spade Cooley and his Orchestra.

This unique western is unfortunately hampered by its completely routine treatment. Crosby, the star of a Broadway musical who goes west to help a pal in trouble, accidentally ends up as sheriff. Through a series of comic blunders Crosby ends up stopping a group of murderous outlaws. The film, intended as a western spoof, doesn't work at all on that level. As a straight comedy it has its moments, though Crosby's double takes grow weary after a while. The direction is good, but the script suffers from stiff dialog and a misfired premise. Songs sung by Crosby include "Beside the Rio Tonto" (Don Raye, Gene DePaul), "Reach for the Sky," "You Look Good to Me" (Inez James, Sidney Miller), "Another Night" (Don George, Irving Bibo), "Who's Next" (Virginia Wicks, Bill Lava), "When a Cowboy Sings" (Dave Franklin).

p, Bernard W. Burton; d, Leslie Goodwins; w, Henry Blankfort, Eugene Conrad (based on a story by John Grey); ph, Charles Van Enger; ed, Edward Curtiss; md, Sam Freed, Jr.; art d, John B. Goodman, Abraham Grossman.

Western   **(PR:A   MPAA:NR)**

SINGING TAXI DRIVER*½   (1953, Ital.) 88m Cines/IFE bw (TAXI
                                                             DI NOTTE)

Beniamino Gigli (*Nello Spadoni*), Danielle Godet (*Laura Morani*), Philippe LeMaire (*Alberto Franchi*), Virginia Belmont (*Luisa Forenti*), Carlo Ninchi (*Forenti l'Industriale*), William C. Tubbs (*Mr. William Simon*), Ione Morino (*Signora Forenti*), Aroldo Tieri (*Conte Tattini*), Giuseppe Varni (*Major Domo*).

Director Gallone combines his love for the flamboyant with his love of the opera, and comes up with this tale of a cabbie in Rome who loves to kick out an aria while behind the wheel. He is offered a shot at singing in the States but thinks it a hoax. He eventually agrees to try, but it's too late and he misses his chance. Likeable for a while, but overlong and thinly scripted. Released in Italy in 1950. (In Italian; English subtitles).

p&d, Carmine Gallone; w, Aldo de Benedetti (based on the story by Bruno D'Agostino); ph, Aldo Giordani; m/l, Kaslar Donato.

Comedy/Opera   **(PR:A   MPAA:NR)**

SINGING THROUGH**   (1935, Brit.) 50m Union/Apex bw (GB: BE CAREFUL MR. SMITH)

Bobbie Comber (Geoffrey Smith), Bertha Belmore (Jenny Smith), Frank Atkinson, Cecil Ramage, Bertha Ricardo, C. Denier Warren, Warren C. Jenkins.

After retiring from his clerical job, Atkinson must deal with his nagging wife. To escape her nasty tongue the henpecked husband gets involved with a bookmaking outfit. Some hustlers want to muscle in on the business but thanks to Atkinson's clever actions, all works out in the end. Minor and forgettable, this originally had been released in a 72-minute version but lost 22 minutes with no harm at all.

p&d, Max Mack; w, Frank Atkinson, Ernest Longstaffe.

Comedy   **(PR:A   MPAA:NR)**

SINGING VAGABOND, THE**   (1935) 55m REP bw

Gene Autry (Tex), Smiley Burnette (Frog), Ann Rutherford (Lettie), Barbara Pepper (Honey), Warner Richmond (Buck LaCrosse), Frank La Rue (Col. Seward), Grace Goodall (Hortense), Niles Welch (Judge Lane), Tom Brower (Old Scout), Robinson Neeman (Jerry Barton), Ray Bernard [Ray Corrigan] (Pvt. Hobbs), Henry Roquemore (Otto), Allan Sears (Utah Joe), Chief Big Tree (White Eagle), Robert Burns, Charles King, Chief Thunder Cloud, June Thompson, Janice Thompson, Marion O'Connell, Marie Quillan, Elaine Shepherd, Edmund Cobb, George Letz [Montgomery], Celia McCanon, Champion the Horse.

When outlaws, led by Richmond and Sears, take over a wagon train and kidnap Rutherford, it's up to Autry to save the day. Burnette's comedic bungling gets in the way of the heroics, but all turns out well in the end. Typical Autry entry that has a few problems in plot structure, but plenty of action. Songs by Autry and Burnette include "Friends of the Prairie, Farewell" and "Wagon Train."

p, Armand Schaefer; d, Carl Pierson; w, Oliver Drake, Betty Burbridge (based on a story by Drake); ph, William Nobles; ed, Lester Orlebeck.

Western   **Cas.**   **(PR:A   MPAA:NR)**

SINGLE-HANDED   (SEE: SAILOR OF THE KING, 1953, Brit.)

SINGLE-HANDED SANDERS*   (1932) 59m T/C/MON bw

Tom Tyler, Margaret Morris, Robert Manning, G. D. Woods, John Elliott, Hank Bell, Lois Bridge, Fred "Snowflake" Toones, Snowball the Horse.

Tyler is a frontier village blacksmith. His brother, who is involved in some political skullduggery with a senator, cheats Tyler's girl friend out of $5,000. The brother is caught and all ends happily in this poorly made western. Though the film looked like it wanted to be "important", any pretentions at that were quickly detonated by the muddled direction and photography. The script also was simplistic. The budget was fairly large for a film of this nature, but it didn't really show.

p, Trem Carr; d, Lloyd Nosler; w, Charles A. Post (based on a story by Adele Buffington); ph, Archie Stout.

Western   **(PR:A   MPAA:NR)**

SINGLE ROOM FURNISHED*   (1968) 93m Unifilm/Crown International c

Jayne Mansfield (Johnnie/Mae/Eilene), Dorothy Keller (Flo), Fabian Dean (Charley), Billy M. Greene (Pop), Terri Messina (Maria Adamo), Martin Horsey (Frankie), Walter Gregg (Billy), Bruno Ve Sota (Mr. Duck), Velia Del Greco (Mrs. Adamo), Isabelle Dwan (Grandmother), Jean London, Nancy Brock (Girls), Margie Duncan, Ava Sheara (Dancers), Michael Rich, Elisa Rich (Grandchildren), Erie MacGruder (Girl at Window), Robert Van Strawder (Grocery Boy).

Mansfield's last film is a real mess, both on screen and off. She's moved into a new apartment with her husband, Horsey, but he leaves once she announces a baby's on the way. After Mansfield loses the baby, she decides to start her life over. She dyes her hair and becomes a waitress, complete with a new name. She has an affair with Ve Sota, who also leaves her pregnant and alone. Her sympathetic neighbor Dean takes pity on her, and the two eventually get engaged. But he too leaves her and Mansfield gives the baby up for adoption. She changes her name once more and takes up life as a prostitute. The amateurish direction was by Mansfield's lover Ot-

taviano, who later went on to direct Pia Zadora in the equally awful BUTTERFLY. Mansfield had met him while performing in a production of "Bus Stop," and Ottaviano soon replaced husband Mickey Hargitay as the man in Mansfield's life. During the filming of SINGLE ROOM FURNISHED the star and director got into a fight and Mansfield headed off to Florida to calm down. The production was halted until her return, but tragedy intervened when Mansfield was killed in a car crash outside of New Orleans. Ottaviano was forced to pad out his film with a hopelessy awful subplot involving Keller and Dean as two parents who warn their daughter Messina about their floozy neighbor Mansfield. Even worse was a maudlin and lengthy "tribute" to Mansfield, narrated by Walter Winchell, which served as a prologue. One of the redeeming features of this film is some early work by noted cinematographer Kovacs, who toiled on cheapies like this until his career took off. Brianne Murphy, a cinematographer, had claimed that she directed this film, but her name does not turn up in the credits.

p, Hugo Grimaldi; d, Matteo Ottaviano (Matt Cimber); w, Michael Musto (based on a play by Gerald Sanford); ph, Leslie [Laszlo] Kovacs (Deluxe Color); m, James Sheldon; ed, Grimaldi; art d, Mike McCloskey.

Drama   **(PR:O   MPAA:GP)**

SINGLE SIN*½   (1931) 90m TIF bw

Kay Johnson (Kate Adams), Bert Lytell (Joe Strickland), Paul Hurst (Slug), Mathew Betz (Frank Bowman), Holmes Herbert (Roger Van Dorn), Geneva Mitchell (Marian), Sandra Ravel (French Maid), Charles McNaughton (Butler), Lillian Elliott (Cook), Robert Emmett O'Connor (Detective).

After spending 90 days in jail for her involvement in a bootlegging operation, Johnson is freed and becomes secretary to millionaire Herbert. The two fall in love and become man and wife. Their bliss is threatened by humorous turns, though, when Johnson's old bootlegging comrades turn up in Herbert's employ as well. When Johnson gets a touch potted, things look dark for her happy marriage but all works out neatly in the end. The treatment is anything but subtle in this comedy, with a script that's wholly unbelievable in any way, shape, or form. Johnson and Herbert give the film its only touch of quality.

d, William Nigh; w, Frances Hyland (based on a story by A.P. Younger); ph, Max Dupont; ed, Charles Harris.

Comedy   **(PR:A   MPAA:NR)**

SINISTER HANDS*   (1932) 65m CAP bw

Jack Mulhall (Detective Capt. Devlin), Phyllis Barrington (Ruth Frazer), Crauford Kent (Judge McLeod), Mischa Auer (Swami Yomurda), Jimmy Burtis (Watkins), Phillips Smalley (Richard Lang), Louis Natheaux (Nick Genna), Gertrude Messenger (Betty Lang), Lloyd Ingraham (John Frazer), Helen Foster (Vivian Rogers), Lillian West (Mrs. Lang), Fletcher Norton (Lefty Lewis, Butler), Bess Flowers (Mary Browne), Russell Collar (Tommy Lang).

Dumb little murder mystery features Mulhall as the police captain trying to get to the bottom of some nasty goings-on. When Smalley is killed during a seance, an Oriental dagger turns up as the murder weapon, and all present become suspects. Each had a reason for disliking the murdered man: His wife (West) hated her husband, and is having an affair with Auer, who also was present at the seance. Messenger was at odds with her father because of her involvement with a gangster. Smalley's butler, Norton, turns out to be an ex-convict. The script is poorly plotted, pitted with bad jokes and some awkwardly crafted moments, and the ending is unsuspenseful and anti-climactic. SINISTER HANDS was among a small number of "indoor pictures" made by Kent, who was known for his work in "quickie" westerns. Burtis, who has a small role in this film, was a top star and director for Universal during the silent film era.

p, Willis Kent; d, Armand Schaefer; w, Norton Parker, Oliver Drake (based on the novel The Seance Mystery by Parker); ph, William Nobles.

Mystery   **(PR:A   MPAA:NR)**

SINISTER HOUSE   (SEE: WHO KILLED "DOC" ROBBIN?, 1948)

SINISTER JOURNEY**   (1948) 60m UA bw

William Boyd (Hopalong Cassidy), Andy Clyde (California Carlson), Rand Brooks (Lucky Jenkins), Elaine Riley (Mrs. Garvin), John Kellogg (Lee Garvin), Don Haggerty, Stanley Andrews, Harry Strang, Herbert Rawlinson, John Butler, Will Orleans, Wayne Treadway.

Typical Cassidy western in which Boyd helps a young man framed for murder. The boy has eloped with the daughter of a railroad man who didn't approve of the union, but Boyd straightens everything out in just under an hour. Not as much action as usually found in Cassidy's films. The movie also is hampered by a weak script, but the direction makes up for the lost energy, and Clyde provides some good comic relief. (See HOPALONG CASSIDY series, Index)

p, Lewis J. Rachmil; d, George Archainbaud; w, Doris Schroeder; ph, Mack Stengler; ed, Fred W. Berger; md, Darrel Calker; art d, Jerome Pycha, Jr.

Western   **(PR:A   MPAA:NR)**

SINISTER MAN, THE½   (1965, Brit.) 61m Merton Park/Schoenfeld
                                                                           bw

John Bentley (*Superintendent Wills*), Patrick Allen (*Dr. Nelson Pollard*),
Jacqueline Ellis (*Elsa Marlowe*), Eric Young (*Johnny Choto*), Arnold Lee
(*Soyoki*), John Glyn-Jones (*Dr. Maurice Tarn*), Brian McDermott (*Detective
Sgt. Stillman*), Gerald Andersen (*Maj. Paul Amery*), Yvonne Buckingham
(*Miss Russell*), William Gaunt (*Mitch Hallam*), Michael Deacon (*Angus*),
Leslie Nunnerley (*Vera Martin*), Malcolm Russell (*Joe Martin*), Yvonne
Shima (*Tamaya*), Robert Lee (*Nam Lee*), Burt Kwouk (*Capt. Feng*), John
Horsley (*Pathologist*), Wilfrid Brambell (*LockKeeper*), Keith Faulkner (*His
Assistant*), Edward Atienza (*Clerk*).

An Oxford scholar investigating an archeological find known as the Kytang
Wafers is found murdered. When the Kytang Wafers disappear, an
investigation is conducted among his collegues at the Oriental Research
Institute. Bentley is an inspector from Scotland Yard who first suspects
Young, then learns from Ellis that Allen, a Korean war veteran, is secretly
commiserating with the Kytang ambassador. The ambassador is about to
kill Allen when Bentley arrives and arrests them both for murder. Based on
a novel by the popular mystery writer Edgar Wallace.

p, Jack Greenwood; d, Clive Donner; w, Robert Stewart (based on the novel
The Sinister Man by Edgar Wallace); ph, Bert Mason; ed, Derek Holding;
md, Charles Blackwell; art d, Peter Mullins.

Mystery   **(PR:C   MPAA:NR)**

SINISTER URGE, THE zero   (1961) 75m Headliner bw (AKA:
                                           HELLBORN; THE YOUNG AND THE IMMORAL)

Kenne Duncan (*Lt. Matt Carson*), James Moore (*Sgt. Randy Stone*), Jean
Fontaine (*Gloria Henderson*), Carl Anthony (*Johnny Ryde*), Dino Fantini
(*Dirk Williams*), Jeanne Willardson (*Mary Smith*), Harry Keatan (*Jaffe*),
Reed Howes (*Police Inspector*), Harvey Dunne (*Mr. Romaine*), Kenneth
Willardson (*Theatrical Agent*), Vic McGee (*Syndicate Man*), Judy Berares
(*Frances*), Vonnie Starr (*Secretary*), Oma Soffian (*Nurse*), Toni Costello,
Kathy Randall, Sylvia Marenco, April Lynn (*Models*), Fred Mason, Jean
Baree, Clayton Peca (*Policemen*).

Attention all camp fans! This film is a landmark in the "it's so bad, it's good"
category, marking the final work of veteran camp director Wood. The man
who took on transsexuals in GLEN OR GLENDA? now turns his attention
to the evils of pornography in this epic. After three pornographic models are
murdered, cops Duncan and Moore try to get to the bottom of things. The
trail leads them to Anthony, a failed legitimate filmmaker reduced to smut
flicks (posters of Wood's actual films decorate his walls). Meanwhile, nice
guy Fantini sees a naughty picture of Willardson, a wholesome girl (with the
name "Mary Smith" no less) who's been dragged into society's underbelly
by Anthony and his producer, Fontaine. As a result, Fantini goes insane and
proceeds to rape and murder poor Willardson. The cops find him and smash
the seamy world of pornography. Wood, as with all of his work, directs with
such sincere feeling that one can't help but enjoy. The message – pornography turns young men into wanton beasts - is wonderfully simplistic and
depicted with the deepest of convictions. Wood himself makes a cameo
appearance in a fight scene, and some of his other marvelous touches, such
as a cop in drag and an anti-porno speech by a judge, are well in place. Its
outrageous quality will hold the viewer's interest, and the film should be
considered a classic work in bad-film history.

p,d&w, Edward D. Wood, Jr.

Drama   **Cas.**   **(PR:O   MPAA:NR)**

SINK THE BISMARCK!   (1960, Brit.) 97m FOX bw

Kenneth More (*Capt. Jonathan Shepard*), Dana Wynter (*Anne Davis*), Carl
Mohner (*Capt. Lindemann*), Laurence Naismith (*First Sea Lord*), Geoffrey
Keen (*A.C.N.S.*), Karel Stepanek (*Adm. Lutjens*), Michael Hordern (*Com-
mander on King George*), Maurice Denham (*Cmdr. Richards*), Michael
Goodliffe (*Capt. Banister*), Edmund Knight (*Captain on Prince of Wales*),
Jack Watling (*Signals Officer*), Jack Gwillan (*Captain on King George*),
Mark Dignam (*Captain on Ark Royal*), Ernest Clark (*Captain on Suffolk*),
John Horsley (*Captain on Sheffield*), Peter Burton (*Captain on 1st Destroy-
er*), John Stuart (*Captain on Hood*), Walter Hudd (*Admiral on Hood*), Sidney
Tafler (*Workman*), Ed Morrow.

Screenwriter Edmund North knows how to write about war, as he proved
years later with his Oscar winning screenplay for PATTON. Here, he has
taken a true occurrence and fashioned it into a taut, tense war-time drama
based on the real story of how the Germans' most powerful naval fighting
machine was destroyed. It starts with actual newsreel footage as the
Bismarck is launched in Hamburg to the cheers of the Nazi chiefs in 1938.
Flash ahead to 1941 and the War Room of the British Admiralty where More
begins to conduct the campaign to blow the battleship out of the water.
German subs have been potshotting British shipping, Dunkirk has decimated the Army and if the Bismarck is let loose, it will spell the end of Britain's
chance to rule the sea. More, a tough bird, is still stunned by the death of
his wife in an air raid while he oversees the efforts to nail the battleship.

Wynter is a WREN, the British equivalent of a WAVE, and she is at his side
in the War Room. No sooner does More take over the job when word comes
in that the Bismarck has left its hiding place and is now steaming toward
the battle zone. More has to figure some way to use his sparse fleet, and the
news is bad as the Bismarck sinks the Hood, one of England's best, then
maims the cruiser Prince of Wales. Churchill realizes that the Bismarck
must be sunk at all costs and issues that order. More's son is a gunner on
the Ark Royal, a carrier More sends to fight the Bismarck. It rushes from
Gibraltar and goes after the Bismarck, damaging the behemoth enough to
cause it to seek shelter on the French coast. Once the Bismarck is slowed
down, the British ships King George V and Rodney are able to catch up with
it and finally destroy it in a huge sea battle. The film is a marvel of
intercutting as it goes from More and Wynter in the War Room, to action
aboard the German battleship, to all the other British ships as they begin
to tighten the noose. More is seen handling the models of his ships as he
tactically deploys them in the War Room, then we watch the ships make
their moves at sea to conform with his orders as he spends countless hours
in his work, grabbing a snatch of a nap here and there as he unburdens his
personal woes to the ubiquitous Wynter, who is always at his side. Actual
footage of the battle is used in conjunction with well-staged scenes executed
by Gilbert and his assistants so it all seems as real as this morning. Mohner
is the German Captain and, although there's a bit of caricature in the
portrayal of the Nazis, it is still evenhanded enough so that these villains
become flesh and blood rather than two-dimensional. The miniature work
is almost flawless and one must be an expert to realize when floating models
are used rather than real ships. Those effects by Howard Lydecker and Bill
Harrington are enough to merit special attention. It is a first-class British
sea drama which will rank with IN WHICH WE SERVE and COCKLE-
SHELL HEROES as examples of how to make excitement on a budget when
one is blessed with a great script. The most impressive part of what North
has written is that we are almost able to look inside More's head to see why
he does what he does, and once that's established, we are privy to a superior
military mind in action.

p, John Brabourne; d, Lewis Gilbert; w, Edmund H. North (based on the
book by C.S. Forester); ph, Christopher Challis (CinemaScope); m, Clifton
Parker; ed, Peter Hunt; md, Muir Mathieson; spec eff, Howard Lydecker,
Bill Harrington.

War Drama   **Cas.**   **(PR:A   MPAA:NR)**

SINNER, THE   (SEE: DESERT DESPERADOES, 1943)

SINNER TAKE ALL*   (1936) 74m MGM bw

Bruce Cabot (*Ernie, Reporter*), Margaret Lindsay (*Lorraine Lampier*),
Joseph Calleia (*Frank Penny*), Stanley Ridges (*Mackelvie, Editor*), Vivienne
Osborne (*Alicia Mackelvie, his Wife*), Charley Grapewin (*Aaron Lampier*),
Edward Pawley (*Royce, Chief of Homicide Squad*), George Lynn (*Stephen
Lampier*), Theodore Von Eltz (*David Lampier*), Eadie Adams (*Shirley*),
George Zucco (*Bascomb, Lawyer*), Dorothy Kilgallen (*Reporter*).

Simple but effective whodunit has reporter Cabot investigating the murders
of an entire family. He solves the crime with some help from love interest
Lindsay and policeman Pauley. The film is a standard, though nicely
handled production. The story is well scripted, and Cabot gives a good
performance. The direction is brisk, with a good feel for the material.

p, Lucien Hubbard, Samuel Marx; d, Errol Taggart; w, Leonard Lee, Walter
Wise (from the novel *Murder for a Wanton* by Whitman Chambers); ph,
Leonard Smith; m, Edward Ward; ed, William S. Gray; cos, Dolly Tree; m/l,
Walter Donaldson, Chet Forrest, Bob White.

Mystery/Crime   **(PR:C   MPAA:NR)**

SINNERS, THE   (SEE: FIVE SINNERS, 1961, Ger.)

SINNERS GO TO HELL   (SEE: NO EXIT, 1962, US/Arg.)

SINNER'S HOLIDAY*   (1930) 60m WB bw

Grant Withers (*Angel Harrigan*), Evalyn Knapp (*Jennie Delano*), James
Cagney (*Harry Delano*), Lucille La Verne (*Ma Delano*), Noel Madison
(*Buck*), Otto Hoffman (*George*), Warren Hymer (*Mitch McKane*), Ray
Gallagher (*Joe Delano*), Joan Blondell (*Myrtle*), Hank Mann (*Happy*),
Purnell B. Pratt (*Sykes*).

Significant as the film which started Cagney's career, SINNER'S HOLIDAY
tells the story of a penny arcade owner, La Verne, who lives with her two
sons, Cagney and Gallagher, and daughter, Knapp. Hymer, a sideshow
operator and bootlegger, incessantly flirts with Knapp until one of his
employees, Withers, intervenes. Also employed by Hymer is Cagney, a
cowardly punk who takes charge of the bootlegging operation when Hymer
is apprehended by police. Cagney, who has been skimming the profits, is
confronted by Hymer when he is released. Cagney then shoots Hymer,
confessing the murder to his possessive mother. In order to keep her son out
of trouble, La Verne stashes the gun in Withers' valise. Knapp, however,
witnessed the murder and turns Cagney over to the police, saving her
sweetheart Withers in the process. While only Cagney's first movie role,

SINNER'S HOLIDAY clearly defines the sort of character that he would later be associated with in such films as PUBLIC ENEMY and WHITE HEAT. As in the two later films, SINNER'S HOLIDAY has Cagney playing a murderous thug who is gentle as can be when it comes to "mom." Whether it be Beryl Mercer in PUBLIC ENEMY, Margaret Wycherly in WHITE HEAT, or Lucille La Verne in SINNER'S HOLIDAY, Cagney's mother always has a nearly psychotic, obsessive, unconditional love for her son. The finest moment in SINNER'S HOLIDAY shows Cagney at his most pathetically weak, clinging to his mother and burying his head in her breast. Lamenting over the murder he committed, he weeps: "I didn't mean to, Ma. I couldn't help it. Honest I couldn't. Don't leave me. You got to believe me. You've got to help me. I'm scared, Ma." The next logical extension is to have this Cagney character grow up into Cody Jarrett (his WHITE HEAT role) and give his apocalyptic yell "Made it, Ma, top of the world." Based on a stage play, "Penny Arcade," SINNER'S HOLIDAY became a film thanks to the enthusiasm of Al Jolson. Jolson, who saw the play on Broadway during its short three-week run, bought the rights for $20,000. He then sold the play to Warner Bros. with the stipulation that Cagney and Blondell be involved (the stage director, William Keighley, was replaced by Adolfi, but later directed Cagney in EACH DAWN I DIE, 1939, and THE FIGHTING 69TH, 1940, among others). Although Warner Bros. was not pleased that Jolson could dictate the cast, they agreed, signing Cagney and Blondell to play the same parts they played on stage. Both were signed to their first contracts--Cagney at $400 a week and Blondell at half that. While the reviews for the film were less than favorable, Cagney and Blondell received numerous raves. (Blondell actually made her second screen appearance in SINNER'S HOLIDAY, first hitting the theaters in THE OFFICE WIFE which was filmed after this picture but released first.) Strangely, Cagney, who owed this first break to Jolson, never managed to meet the "jazz singer."

d, John G. Adolfi; w, Harvey Thew, George Rosener (based on the play "Penny Arcade" by Marie Baumer); ph, Ira Morgan; ed, James Gibbons; md, Leo F. Forbstein; makeup, Perc Westmore.

Crime   (PR:A MPAA:NR)

SINNERS IN PARADISE*   (1938) 64m UNIV bw

Madge Evans (Anne Wesson), John Boles (Jim Taylor), Bruce Cabot (Robert Malone), Marion Martin (Iris Compton), Gene Lockhart (Sen. Corey), Charlotte Wynters (Thelma Chase), Nana Bryant (Mrs. Franklin Sydney), Milburn Stone (Harrison Brand), Donald Barry (Jessup), Morgan Conway (Honeyman), Willie Fung (Ping).

An airplane carrying the standard slice-of-life cast of characters crash-lands on a deserted island in the South Seas. They all have troubled pasts: the wife (Evans) is running away from her husband; Cabot is a gunman on the run; Lockhart is a corrupt politician; and Barry and Conway are nefarious salesmen. The island appears deserted until Boles, an escaped convict facing a murder rap, shows up. The plot is pretty lurid and takes the film's entire length to unfold. The message of the story--that one must face up to past mistakes--is driven home with all the subtlety of a jackhammer.

p, Ken Goldsmith; d, James Whale; w, Lester Cole, Harold Buckley, Louis Stevens (based on the story "Half Way to Shanghai" by Buckley); ph, George Robinson; ed, Maurice Wright; md, Charles Previn; art d, Jack Otterson.

Drama   **Cas.**   (PR:C MPAA:NR)

SINNERS IN THE SUN**   (1932) 70m PAR bw

Carole Lombard (Doris Blake), Chester Morris (Jimmie Martin), Adrienne Ames (Claire Kinkaid), Alison Skipworth (Mrs. Blake), Walter Byron (Eric Nelson), Reginald Barlow (Mr. Blake), Zita Moulton (Mrs. Florence Nelson), Cary Grant (Ridgeway), Luke Cosgrave (Grandfather Blake), Ida Lewis (Grandmother Blake), Russ Clark (Fred Blake), Frances Moffett (Mrs. Fred Blake), Pierre De Ramey (Louis), Veda Buckland (Emma), Rita La Roy (Lil), Maude Turner Gordon (Wife), Anderson Lawler (Gigolo).

A formula picture based on a Mildred Cram story, SINNERS IN THE SUN has little to recommend it beyond the slick gloss that the studio has chosen to lather upon this sow's ear. Lombard is a dress model in a small shop and madly in love with Morris, a hardworking and honest mechanic. He wants to marry her but she thinks it would be better to wait until he can gather enough cash to be able to go into his own business, as she has no desire to continue working after they are wed. Morris feels that she's being downright selfish and mercenary so he angrily departs and takes a chauffeur's job for socialite Ames. She's a rich, attractive young woman who sees that Morris, for all his rough-hewn ways, is a kindly man. It's not long before Ames falls in love with Morris and he, with no one else to love, agrees to marry her. Once Morris is plunged into the whirlwind of Long Island society, he is uncomfortable, not having been born to the manor, and he can't psychologically handle being a consort, so he departs and takes employment as a car salesman. At the same time, Lombard is at a fashion show where she meets wealthy Byron, a married man who is about to leave his wife, La Roy. Lombard becomes Byron's mistress, is installed in a plush apartment and showered with baubles. La Roy takes up with Grant and the two couples embark on a round of pleasure-seeking as they travel, drink and dance. But La Roy is only marking time in seeking fun to coat her depression and she eventually commits suicide by drinking poison. Morris and Lombard get together later, after he has left Ames and she has quit Byron to take a

menial job in the dress business. Both are still in love with each other but too proud to admit it at first. After they iron matters out, the two realize that they have far more to offer each other than do the idle rich. They may spend the rest of their lives together in poverty, but they'll always be happy. The comedy is non-existent and even Grant, appearing in only his second film, seems bored by the whole thing.

d, Alexander Hall; w, Vincent Lawrence, Waldemar Young, Samuel Hoffenstein (based on the story "Beach-Comber" by Mildred Cram); ph, Ray June; cos, Travis Banton.

Romantic Drama   (PR:C MPAA:NR)

SINS OF JEZEBEL**   (1953) 74m Lippert c

Paulette Goddard (Jezebel), George Nader (Jehu), John Hoyt (Elijah, Prophet), Eduard Franz (King Ahab), John Shelton (Loram), Margia Dean (Deborah), Joe Besser (Yonkel, Chariot Man), Ludwig Donath (Naboth), Carmen D'Antonio (Dancer).

Goddard, who'd come a long way from her heyday with Chaplin, is the title's Biblical princess. She worships the evil god Baal and then marries Franz, the king of Israel, bringing him and the kingdom nothing but grief. The powers of God eventually bring about Goddard's demise. The production credits and acting are quite good, but as Bible pictures go SINS OF JEZEBEL is minor fodder that incorporated salvation and sex in a tidy entertainment package. Watch for Besser, who played "Curly Joe" in the later Three Stooges episodes, in a minor role.

p, Sigmund Neufeld; d, Reginald LeBorg; w, Richard Landau; ph, Gilbert Warrenton (Ansco Color); m, Bert Shefter; ed, Carl Pierson; art d, F. Paul Sylos.

Biblical Drama   (PR:C MPAA:NR)

SINS OF LOLA MONTES, THE   (SEE: LOLA MONTES 1955, Fr.)

SINS OF MAN*   (1936) 77m FOX bw

Jean Hersholt (Christopher Freyman), Don Ameche (Karl Freyman/Mario Singarelli), Allen Jenkins (Crusty), J. Edward Bromberg (Anton Engel), Ann Shoemaker (Anna Engel), DeWitt Jennings (Twicheleska), Fritz Leiber (Father Prior), Francis Ford (Town Drunk), Christian Rub (Fritz), Adrian Rosley (Singarelli's Butler), Gene Reynolds (Karl Freyman as a boy), Mickey Rentschler (Gabriel Freyman as a Boy), John Miltern (Mr. Hall), Paul Stanton (Minister), Edward Van Sloan (Austrian Army Doctor), Egon Brecher (Doctor), Fred Kohler, Jr, Maxine Reiner, Ruth Robinson.

Ameche, formerly an obscure Chicago radio actor, makes his film debut playing the two sons of Austrian bell-ringer Hersholt. After Hersholt's wife dies in childbirth, he finds out the newborn is deaf. He becomes estranged from his older son, who heads to America to become an aeronautical engineer. He takes the deaf child to a monastery and, before long Hersholt is a resident of the Bowery. The deaf son grows up and somehow regains his hearing in a WW I accident. He becomes a musician and follows his brother to America. He becomes a great conductor and eventually is reunited with Hersholt, who always loved music. Hersholt becomes a bell ringer in his son's orchestra and the film ends. Overly long with tedious direction, this film also is hampered by the contrived plot. There are implausible moments, and some props lack authenticity. During the film's initial release, a short trailer was shown introducing Ameche as a newcomer at 20th Century-Fox.

p, Kenneth Macgowan; d, Gregory Ratoff, Otto Brower; w, Frederick Kohner, Ossip Dymow, Samuel G. Engel (based on the novel Job by Joseph Roth); ph, Sidney Wagner; ed, Barbara McLean; md, Louis Silver; cos, Royer.

Drama   (PR:A MPAA:NR)

SINS OF RACHEL CADE, THE**½**
                          (1960) 123m WB c (AKA: RACHEL CADE)

Angie Dickinson (Rachel Cade), Peter Finch (Col. Henri Derode), Roger Moore (Paul Wilton), Errol John (Kulu, Rachel's Assistant), Woody Strode (Muwango), Juano Hernandez (Kalanumu), Frederick O'Neal (Buderga), Mary Wickes (Marie Grieux), Scatman Crothers (Musinga), Rafer Johnson (Kosongo), Chuck Wood (Mzimba), Douglas Spencer (Dr. Bikel).

Dickinson is a nurse in the African Congo who works hard to win the trust of the locals. Finch, in a role similar to his role in A NUN'S STORY (1959), is the Belgian administrator who tries to seduce the nurse during a native fertility dance. She rejects him, and falls in love with Moore, a handsome RAF pilot who crashes in the area. Moore, an American volunteer for the RAF, is equally smitten with Dickinson's charms as she nurses him through his convalescence. The time comes for him to go, but not before the two consummate their love. Moore leaves and Dickinson discovers that she's pregnant. She tells Finch who telegraphs Moore in Boston. Moore leaves his thriving medical practice and offers to take Dickinson home with him, but she realizes that this offer is more out of duty than love. After Finch has requested to be sent to the battlefield, Dickinson realizes that he really was the man for her. Utter soap opera, with some good dialog and lush photography. Dickinson is adequate as the Christian woman forced to make some heavy decisions about her faith. Watch for Olympic decathlon winner Rafer Johnson in a minor role.

p, Henry Blanke; d, Gordon Douglas; w, Edward Anhalt (based on the novel *Rachel Cade* by Charles E. Mercer); ph, J. Peverell Marley (Technicolor); m, Max Steiner; ed, Owen Marks; art d, Leo K. Kuter; set d, Ralph S. Hurst; cos, Marjorie Best; ch, James Truitte; makeup, Gordon Bau.

Drama (PR:O MPAA:NR)

SINS OF ROSE BERND, THE** (1959, Ger.) 85m Bavaria/President c
(ROSE BERND)

Maria Schell (*Rose Bernd*), Raf Vallone (*Arthur Streckmann*), Kaethe Gold (*Henriette Flamm*), Leopold Biberti (*Christoph Flamm*), Hannes Messemer (*August Kell*), Arthur Wiesner (*Vater Bernd*), Christa Keller (*Maria Schubert*), Siegfried Lowitz (*Judge*).

Schell is a postwar German peasant girl who falls in love with three men – Vallone, Biberti, and Messemer – then learns that she is pregnant. The unborn baby's father is estate owner Biberti, but instead of enjoying a family life Schell is shunned by the community. She packs her things and flees, giving birth outdoors with tragic results. From a popular play by Gerhardt Hauptmann.

p, Hans Abich; d, Wolfgang Staudte; w, Walter Ulbrich (based on the play "Rose Bernd" by Gerhardt Hauptmann); ph, Klaus von Rautenfeld (Agfacolor); m, Herbert Windt; ed, Lilian Seng.

Drama (PR: MPAA:NR)

SINS OF THE BORGIAS (SEE: LUCRECE BORGIA 1953, Fr./Ital.)

SINS OF THE CHILDREN*** (1930) 86m Cosmopolitan/MGM bw
(GB: THE RICHEST MAN IN THE WORLD; AKA: FATHER'S DAY)

Louis Mann (*Adolf Wagenkampf, Barber*), Robert Montgomery (*Nick Higginson*), Elliott Nugent (*Johnnie*), Leila Hyams (*Alma*), Clara Blandick (*Martha Wagenkampf*), Mary Doran (*Laura*), Francis X. Bushman, Jr (*Ludwig, Adolf's Son*), Robert McWade (*Joe Higginson*), Dell Henderson (*Ted Baldwin*), Henry Armetta (*Tony*), Jane Reid (*Katherine*), James Donlan (*Bide Taylor*), Jeane Wood (*Muriel Stokes*), Lee Kohlmar (*Dr. Heinrich Schmidt*), Philippe de Lacey, Gordon Thorpe, Betsey Ann Hisle, Evelyn Mills, Edwin Mills (*The Children*).

Just when he is about to achieve some financial success with a building and loan proposition, Mann must take his son Bushman away for a two-year convalescence in a drier climate. This proves to be good for the boy but bad for his father as McWade, Mann's partner, writes him off as a failure in business. However, Mann learns that he is far from being a failure at home for his children have given him more riches than any business possibly could. Despite the simplistic nature of the plot, SINS OF THE CHILDREN is a good drama, helped greatly by the strong cast and professional direction from Wood. This was the second grouping of Mann, Montgomery, and Wood (the first was SO THIS IS COLLEGE), and the team is successful here. The humanity of the story is brought out, but does not pander to its more maudlin elements. The natural performances by the children are an added benefit.

d, Sam Wood; w, Elliott Nugent, Clara Lipman, Samuel Ornitz (based on the novel *Father's Day* by Elliott Nugent, J.C. Nugent); ph, Henry Sharp; ed, Frank Sullivan, Leslie F. Wilder; art d, Cedric Gibbons; cos, David Cox; titles, Wilder.

Drama (PR:A MPAA:NR)

SINS OF THE FATHERS**½ (1928) 87m PAR bw

Emil Jannings (*Wilhelm Spengler*), Ruth Chatterton (*Gretta*), Barry Norton (*Tom Spengler*), Jean Arthur (*Mary Spengler*), Jack Luden (*Otto*), ZaSu Pitts (*Mother Spengler*), Matthew Betz (*Gus*), Harry Cording (*The Hijacker*), Arthur Housman (*The Count*), Frank Reicher (*The Eye Specialist*), Douglas Haig (*Tom as a Boy*), Dawn O'Day (*Mary as a Girl*), "Speed" Webb and His Orchestra.

Jannings stars as a German waiter working in an American restaurant to support himself and Pitts, his pregnant wife. When the news comes that she has given birth, Jannings becomes so excited he spills gravy on a patron's dress. Surviving this mishap, Jannings becomes the owner of the restaurant some years later. He falls in love with adventuress Chatterton, a romance which devastates Pitts and leads to her death. Time passes and Prohibition cramps America's nightlife. To fatten his pocketbook, Jannings gets involved in bootlegging, selling poisonous mash to the unsuspecting. He lives life to the hilt, enjoying all the luxuries money can buy and spending his money on Chatterton, who has agreed to marry him. Tragedy strikes when his son, Norton, (who is now of drinking age) gets drunk on his father's brew and is blinded. Janning's problems worsen when he is arrested, prompting Chatterton to run off with another fellow. After serving a short prison term, Jannings is released. He takes a job as a waiter in a beer garden where he runs into his son who has since regained his sight. The upbeat ending has the two coming together for a cheerful reunion. Jannings, as usual, is superb in a taxing role which stretches over a 25-year span,

through sorrow and supreme happiness. Unfortunately; however, SINS OF THE FATHERS suffers from mediocre scripting and direction. Having worked with such greats as Von Sternberg, Lubitsch, and Fleming in 1927 and 1928, Jannings did not benefit from directorial genius in Ludwig Berger. Though a competent director, Berger was far more concerned with film's musical aspects, thereby accounting for the fact that SINS OF THE FATHERS contains an adroitly directed singing sequence (the only synchronized sequence – talking or otherwise – in the film) of Jannings delivering an aria from "Der Trompeter Von Saeckingham." The film did mark Chatterton's first film appearance, casting her off on a short but memorable career which ended only 10 years later. After appearing for a number of years on stage, the 34-year-old actress was spotted by Jannings during a staging of "The Devil's Plum Tree." He immediately recognized her appeal and insisted that she star opposite him. The following two years had Chatterton receiving Oscar nominations for her roles in MADAME X and SARAH AND SON.

d, Ludwig Berger; w, E. Lloyd Shelton (based on a story by Norman Burnstine); ph, Victor Milner; m, Hugo Riesenfeld; ed, Frances Marsh.

Drama (PR:A MPAA:NR)

SINS OF THE FATHERS**½ (1948, Can.) 96m Canadian Productions
bw

Austin Willis (*Dr. Ben Edwards*), Joy LaFleur (*Patsy Curran*), John Pratt (*Marty Williams*), Phyllis Carter (*Daphne*), Suzanne Avon (*Leona*), Frank Heron (*Charlie Mitchell*), Mary Barclay (*Ellen Carter*), Gerald Rowan (*Higgins*), Norman Taviss (*Shorty*).

This Canadian feature, shot in cooperation with the Federal Department of National Health and Welfare in just 11 days, is a documentary-style feature about the horror of veneral diseases. Willis is a health officer who is trying to clean up a town of both crooked politicians and the dread disease. LaFleur is a councilman's daughter who picks up VD, a fact that eventually causes her father to switch his crooked style to a more reformed position. Cromlen handles the cast well, getting them to deliver their performances with a brisk, realistic flavor. Though dated by today's standards and knowledge SINS OF THE FATHERS was commendable for its time by never playing to the more sensationalistic aspects of the subject. Rather, the message was nicely contained in a well-told story.

p, Larry Cromlen; d, Phil Rosen, Richard J. Jarvis; w, Gordon Burwash; ph, William Steiner; m, Morris C. Davis; ed, Jarvis; md, Samuel Hersenhoren.

Drama (PR:C MPAA:NR)

SIN'S PAYDAY* (1932) 61m Mayfair bw

Dorothy Revier, Forrest Stanley, Harry Semels, Alfred Cross, Hal Price, Lloyd Whitlock, Bess Flowers, Mickey McGuire [Rooney].

When her lawyer husband defends gangsters, Revier raises Cain. But business is booming and her husband will not give it up. She leaves him and the lawyer becomes despondent. McGuire, a young boy, enters his life and the lawyer's spirits pick up. However, this soon comes to an end when McGuire is killed in the crossfire of a gang war. The lawyer gives up his old clientele and successfully prosecutes the killers, causing Revier to return to him. McGuire is good in his small role but the rest of the film is pretty bad. Dialog suffers the double whammy of poor writing and a bad sound job. This is coupled with lackadaisical direction that never gives the film any sort of spirit. The film was shot on a low budget, which is reflected on screen.

p, Ralph M. Like; d, George B. Seitz; w, Gene Morton, Betty Burbridge; ph, Jules Cronjager; ed, Byron Robinson.

Drama (PR:A MPAA:NR)

SIOUX CITY SUE**½ (1946) 69m REP bw

Gene Autry (*Himself*), Lynne Roberts (*Sue Warner*), Sterling Holloway (*Nelson "Nellie" Bly*), Richard Lane (*Jefferson Lang*), Ralph Sanford (*Big Gulliver*), Ken Lundy (*Jody*), Helen Wallace (*Miss Price*), Pierre Watkin (*G.W. Rhodes*), Cass County Boys, Kenne Duncan, Edwin Wills, Minerva Urecal, Frank Marlowe, LeRoy Mason, Harry Cheshire, George Carleton, Sam Flint, Michael Hughes, Tex Terry, Tris [Tristram] Coffin, Frankie Marvin, Forrest Burns, Tommy Coats, Champion the Horse.

Autry's first postwar film features one of his more unusual plots. He is spotted by talent scout Roberts who whisks him off to Hollywood for a starring role in a new western musical. It turns out this new western musical is an animated cartoon and Autry's "starring role" is the voice of a singing donkey. Naturally the cattleman is more than a little upset at being tricked and he heads home for some real western action. Seems some bad guys want to blow up his dam and drown all his livestock. This is stopped thanks to Roberts, warning and all is righted between Autry and the film studio. How Roberts knew about the dam explosion is one of the film's more outrageous plot points but the film does have some good production values and plenty of songs including the title tune, which was quite popular. Other tunes by Jimmy Hodges, Dick Thomas, Gonzale Roig, Jack Sherr, A. Rodriguez, John Rex and Sosnik Adams include: "Ridin' Double," "Someday You'll Want Me to Want You," "Chisholm Trail," "Yours," and "You Stole My Heart." Autry warbles all the songs, some more than once.

p, Armand Schaefer; d, Frank McDonald; w, Olive Cooper; ph, Reggie Lanning; m, Dale Butts; ed, Fred Allen; md, Morton Scott; art d, Gano Chittenden; cos, Adele Palmer; spec eff, Howard Lydecker, Theodore Lydecker.

Western   **Cas.**   **(PR:A MPAA:NR)**

SIR GAWAIN AND THE GREEN KNIGHT
                        (SEE: GAWAIN AND THE GREEN KNIGHT

SIR HENRY AT RAWLINSON END***
                        (1980, Brit.) 72m Charisma bw

Trevor Howard (*Sir Henry Rawlinson*), Patrick Magee (*Rev. Slodden*), Denise Coffey (*Mrs. E.*), J.G. Devlin (*Old Scrotum*), Harry Fowler (*Buller Bullethead*), Sheila Reid (*Florrie*), Vivian Stanshall (*Hubert*), Suzanne Danielle (*Candice*), Daniel Gerroll (*Rafe*), Ben Aris (*Lord Tarquin of Staines*), Liz Smith (*Lady Philippa of Staines*), Jeremy Child (*Peregrine*), Susan Prorett (*Porcelain*).

An extremely British comedy features Howard lurking about a mansion in search of a ghost. It's the spirit of his brother, Stanshall, who had been accidentally shot by Howard. Stanshall had been wearing no pants when he was killed and must regain his trousers if his spirit is ever to rest. An utterly delightful example of stylish, bawdy British humor at its naughty best. Employing elements of Ealing Studio horror films with a good dash of Monty Python gags mixed in, the film is directed with style. The black and white cinematography adds to the atmosphere, feeling and the cast carries out its roles with restrained glee. Originally this had been a British radio show, then a popular recording before being transferred to film. The film's production company was a division of Charisma Records, the company that released the recorded version of the tale. Not for everyone but certainly a must for fans of this sort of humor.

p, Tony Stratton Smith; d, Steve Roberts; w, Roberts, Vivian Stanshall; ph, Martin Bell; m, Stanshall; ed, Chris Rose; art d, Jim Acheson

Comedy   **(PR:O MPAA:NR)**

SIR, YOU ARE A WIDOWER*½**   (1971, Czech.) 90m Studio
Barrandov bw (PANE VY JSTE VDOVA; AKA: MISTER, YOU ARE A
                                                    WIDOWER)

Iva Janzurova, Olga Shoberova, Jiri Sovak, Jiri Hrzan, Jan Libieck, Eduard Cupak, Frantisek Filipovsky, Milos Kopecky.

A richly black comedy features Janzurova in three roles, all neatly played. The extremely gory and terribly funny story involves transplants between real and artificial limbs and even brains by an oddball group of medical people. A king, an actress, and a murderer (the latter two played by Janzurova who also was featured as a completely artifical creation called Mrs. Stub) all receive their needed body parts. In the glorious finish, the army is completely disbanded and a wonderful fireworks display lights up the happy occasion. Very strange, and not for the weak stomached but definitely worth watching.

d, Vaclav Vorlicek; w, Vorlicek, Milos Makourek; ph, Vaclav Hanus.

Comedy   **(PR:O MPAA:NR)**

SIREN OF ATLANTIS*   (1948) 75m UA bw (AKA: ATLANTIS;
                                                    QUEEN OF ATLANTIS)

Maria Montez (*Queen Antinea*), Jean-Pierre Aumont (*Andre St. Avit*), Dennis O'Keefe (*Jean Morhange*), Henry Daniell (*Blades*), Morris Carnovsky (*Le Mesge*), Alexis Minotis (*Cortot*), Milada Mladova (*Tanit Zerga*), Allan Nixon (*Lindstrom*), Russ Conklin (*Eggali*), Herman Boden (*Cegheir*), Margaret Martin (*Handmaiden*), Pierre Watkin (*Colonel*), Charles Wagenheim (*Doctor*), Jim Nolan (*Major*), Joseph Granby (*Expert*), John Shelton.

Producer Nebenzal's remake of his 1932 film DIE HERRIN VON ATLANTIS is an unfortunately successful flirt with disaster. O'Keefe and Aumont are foreign legionnaires who find a secret passage in the middle of the desert which leads them to the "Lost "Continent. Montez is the queen of Atlantis, a ruthless woman with whom Aumont falls hopelessly in love. The film was a disaster from the word go. The original director was Arthur Ripley who was soon replaced by John Brahm. He proved no better, and finally Tallas, the film's editor, was brought in to clean up the mess as the third director. Footage from the original film (directed by the great G.W. Pabst) was also used to no avail. The result was a real campfest with lots of posturing and completely hambone performances. Good for some cheap laughs but not much else, though the film developed a minor cult following because it was one of Montez's final films.

p, Seymour Nebenzal; d, Gregg G. Tallas; w, Roland Leigh, Robert Lax, Thomas Job (based on the novel *L'Atlantide* by Pierre Benoit); ph, Karl Struss; m, Michel Michelet; ed, Tallas; prod d, Lionel Banks; md, Heinz Roemheld; set d, George Sawley; cos, Jean Schlumberger; spec eff, Rocky Cline; ch, Lester Horton; makeup, Lee Greenway

Drama   **(PR:A MPAA:NR)**

SIREN OF BAGDAD**½**   (1953) 77m COL c (AKA: SIREN OF
                                                    BAGHDAD)

Paul Henreid (*Kazah*), Patricia Medina (*Zendi*), Hans Conried (*Ben Ali*), Charlie Lung (*Sultan El Malid*), Laurette Luez (*Orena*), Anne Dore (*Leda*), George Keymas (*Soradin*), Vivian Mason (*Beautiful Girl*), Michael Fox (*Telar*), Karl Davis (*Morab*), Carl Milletaire.

Henreid and Conried do a lesser version of the Bob Hope-Bing Crosby road formula as they run around Bagdad. Henreid is a magician and womancher, helped by his cowardly assistant Conried (later the voice of Snidley Whiplash on "Dudley Do-Right" and other characters in Jay Ward cartoons). Henreid temporarily ends his numerous affairs when he meets Medina, but gets more than he had planned when he finds her father Fox is a deposed sultan. Lung is the current sultan who is so enamored of his harem that he does not notice his assistant Keymas is up to no good. Leave it to H and C to fix everything in this amiable, good looking comedy. The supporting players are admirable, providing a goodly amount of chuckles. Production values are fine with nice, colorful settings.

p, Sam Katzman; d, Richard Quine; w, Robert E. Kent, Larry Rhine (based on a story by Kent); ph, Henry Freulich (Technicolor); ed, Jerome Thoms; art d, Paul Palmentola.

Comedy   **(PR:A MPAA:NR)**

SIRENE DU MISSISSIPPI (SEE: MISSISSIPPI MERMAID, 1969, Fr.)

SIROCCO***   (1951) 98m Santana/COL bw

Humphrey Bogart (*Harry Smith*), Marta Toren (*Violette*), Lee J. Cobb (*Col. Feroud*), Everett Sloane (*Gen. LaSalle*), Gerald Mohr (*Maj. Leon*), Zero Mostel (*Balukjian*), Nick Dennis (*Nasir Aboud*), Onslow Stevens (*Emil Hassan*), Ludwig Donath (*Flophouse Proprietor*), David Bond (*Achmet*), Vincent Renno (*Arthur*), Martin Wilkins (*Omar*), Peter Ortiz (*Maj. Robbinet*), Edward Colmans (*Col. Corville*), Al Eben (*Sergeant*), Peter Brocco (*Barber*), Jay Novello (*Hamal*), Leonard Penn (*Rifat*), Harry Guardino (*Lt. Collet*).

A downbeat Middle East drama set in the milieu where Bogart had his greatest triumph in CASABLANCA. This time, he's far less complex and sympathetic and he also doesn't have Bergman as the object of his affection. It's 1925 in Syria where Stevens heads a rebel Syrian force battling against the French who are occupying Damascus and environs. Bogart is a black marketeer from the U.S. who makes his living running guns to Stevens and his troops, thus making him a target for Cobb, the chief of the French Intelligence Corps who knows that if Stevens can't get arms, he can't continue the rebellion. Cobb sends his aide, Guardino, to nab the local gun runners, including Bogart, and tells them that they must sell their weapons only to the French or face severe penalties. Bogart reluctantly agrees, is released and later meets Toren, who is Cobb's girl friend. Bogart romances her, but we're not sure if he really likes her or is doing this out of revenge. Toren tells Cobb she wants to go to Cairo and he must give her a pass. Cobb won't do it as he suspects the relationship between Toren and Bogart is growing. In a subterranean passage under the city, Bogart receives his last payment from Stevens and is told that his presence is no longer needed because he's been uncovered by Cobb. Bogart grabs Toren and they try to leave Damascus but Cobb's men stop them. Bogart gets away and Toren is arrested at the bus station although she's not taken to jail, just sent back to her residence because Cobb is still in love with her. Guardino is killed and when his corpse is sent to Cobb, the French officer would like to put an end to the killing so he arranges to meet with Stevens in an attempt to bring peace to the area. In order to effect that meeting, Cobb must enlist the aid of Bogart as a go-between and he offers Bogart a bribe, a pass to leave Damascus for Cairo (sort of a parallel to the "letters of transit" that everyone wanted in CASABLANCA). Bogart introduces Cobb to one of Stevens' men and leaves immediately to get his pass at the French headquarters. The moment he arrives, he is taken to see the General in charge, Sloane, who is annoyed that Cobb has taken it upon himself to try this peace move. There's no question in Sloane's mind that Cobb will never come back alive, so Sloane appeals to Bogart to help rescue Cobb. Bogart is adamant – a deal is a deal. His part of the agreement was to bring Cobb to Stevens. In return for that, he was to receive his pass. Now, what's it to be? Sloane gives Bogart the pass and one for Toren. Cobb, knowing that he might meet his death, had thoughtfully arranged for safe passage for Toren as well. Bogart has second thoughts and sees that Cobb was a good man in doing what he did and deserves a better fate than death at the hands of Stevens. Bogart suggests that the rebels need money and that Cobb might be able to go free if they buy off the Stevens group. Sloane agrees, gives Bogart the money and Bogart returns to the catacombs under the city which he has been specifically instructed to avoid by the Syrians. Bogart could have just taken the money and the pass and Toren and fled, but he has changed his way of thinking and, against his nature, will do this far far better thing. Once there, Stevens tells Cobb and thinks that the whole idea of a peace treaty is ludicrous but he admires Cobb for his heroism in walking into this lion's den. Bogart hands the money to Stevens who orders Cobb's release but, in a cruel joke, Stevens has Bogart blown up with a hand grenade as his services to them are now over. Zero Mostel appears briefly for a bit of comedy and Nick Dennis plays a Bogart aide. Even though many of the same elements as seen in CASABLANCA are here, it just doesn't jell, mainly because the ending is so hopeless and the love story between Bogart and Toren seems contrived.

p, Robert Lord; d, Curtis Bernhardt; w, A.I. Bezzerides, Hans Jacoby (based on the novel *Coup de Grace* by Joseph Kessel); ph, Burnett Guffey; m, George Antheil; ed, Viola Lawrence; md, M.W. Stoloff; art d, Robert Peterson; set d, Robert Priestley; makeup, Clay Campbell.

Drama   (PR:A MPAA:NR)

SIROCCO D'HIVER   (SEE: WINTER WIND, 1970, Fr./Hung.)

SIS HOPKINS**   (1941) 98m REP bw

Judy Canova (*Sis Hopkins*), Bob Crosby (*Jeff Farnsworth*), Charles Butterworth (*Horace Hopkins*), Jerry Colonna (*Professor*), Susan Hayward (*Carol Hopkins*), Katharine Alexander (*Clara Hopkins*), Elvia Allman (*Ripple*), Carol Adams (*Cynthia*), Lynn Merrick (*Phyllis*), Mary Ainslee (*Vera de Vere*), Charles Coleman (*Butler*), Andrew Tombes (*Mayor*), Charles Lane (*Rollo*), Byron Foulger (*Joe*), Betty Blythe (*Mrs. Farnsworth*), Frank Darien (*Jud*), Joe Devlin, Elliot Sullivan, Hal Price, Anne O'Neal (*Bits*), the Bob Crosby Orchestra with the Bobcats.

Republic tried its best to make hayseed Canova a star with this vehicle, and succeeded in launching a film that would be reissued four times. Canova mistakenly believes her uncle Butterworth is down on his luck (actually he is quite well-off and recently retired), so she invites him and family to her farm. But on their arrival Butterworth and family discover Canova's house has burned to the ground so the city cousins take in the country girl, much to the horror of Canova's snobby cousin Hayward. Butterworth compounds Hayward's furor by sending Canova to the same college she is attending. Canova's an instant hit and inadvertently bumps Hayward from a campus play. Crosby, Hayward's boy friend, thinks Canova is great in the play, which causes an argument and Hayward begins plotting revenge. She fools her cousin into appearing at a burlesque show under the ruse that this is part of a sorority initiation. Canova's dress is rigged to fall apart and Hayward has informed the local police, who raid the club. Though Canova escapes arrest she is expelled from school. But Hayward feels guilty about what she has done and explains everything to her father. Butterworth tells the dean the whole story and Canova is reinstated for a happy ending. The rural versus city humor appealed to the grass roots audience but was dated even in the big cities at the time of the film's release, resulting in a dumb, broad humored bore for some and a delight to others. Hayward was good as the nasty cousin in her first Republic outing, giving a glimmer of better things to come, but most of the cast coasts through the formula vehicle. This was one of Republic's more expensive ventures. It was filmed at a cost of $500,000 which was quite a sum for the small studio. The rights to the story, which had been a Broadway play and then a silent Mabel Normand comedy, cost $50,000 alone. Songs by Frank Loesser and Jule Styne include: "Cracker Barrel Country," "If You're in Love," "Well! Well!," "It Ain't Hay (It's the USA)," and "Look at You, Look at Me" (sung by Susan Hayward and Bob Crosby). Canova sings the traditional "Wait for the Wagon" and her own version of "Some of These Days." After only two films, Canova, on the strength of SIS HOPKINS, demanded and received script, cast, and director approval and the right to co-own her pictures. No one else in the entire Republic stable received such a contract except John Wayne, and that at a much later date.

p, Robert North; d, Joseph Santley; w, Jack Townley, Milt Gross, Edward Eliscu (based on the play by F. McGrew Willis); ph, Jack Marta; ed, Ernest Nims; md, Cy Feuer; art d, John Victor Mackay; ch, Ada Broadbent.

Comedy   (PR:A MPAA:NR)

SISSI   (SEE: FOREVER MY LOVE, 1962, Aus.)

SISTER-IN-LAW, THE**   (1975) 85m Crown International c

Anne Saxon, John Savage, W.G. McMillan, Meredith Baer, Frank Scioscia, Jon Oppenheim, Tom Mahoney.

Sporadically interesting drama has Savage singing several folk songs of his own composition as he becomes enmeshed in a drug-smuggling scheme concocted by his brother and his brother's wife. Depressing end leaves a bad taste in the mouth, but still worth checking out.

p, Jonathan Krivine, Joseph Ruben; d&w, Ruben; ph, Bruce G. Sparks (DeLuxe Color).

Crime   (PR:O MPAA:R)

SISTER KENNY***½   (1946) 116m RKO bw

Rosalind Russell (*Elizabeth Kenny*), Alexander Knox (*Dr. Aeneas McDonnell*), Dean Jagger (*Kevin Connors*), Philip Merivale (*Dr. Brack*), Beulah Bondi (*Mary Kenny*), Charles Dingle (*Michael Kenny*), John Litel (*Medical Director*), Doreen McCann (*Dorrie*), Fay Helm (*Mrs. McIntyre*), Charles Kemper (*Mr. McIntyre*), Dorothy Peterson (*Agnes*), Gloria Holden (*Mrs. McDonnell*), Virginia Brissac (*Mrs. Johnson*), Frank Reicher (*Chuter*), Paul Stanton (*Dr. Gideon*), Charles Halton (*Mr. Smith*), Alan Lee (*Farm Hand*), David Martinson (*Cobbler*), Lloyd Ingraham (*Farmer*), Ellen Corby, Nan

Leslie (*Nurses*), Doris Lloyd (*Matron*), Egon Brecher (*Frenchman*), Lumsden Hare (*Dr. Shadrack*), Regis Toomey, Leo Bonnell (*Reporters*), Daphne Moore (*Waitress*), Franklyn Farnum (*Doctor*), Gertrude Astor.

A very respectful, if slow, biography of a woman who fought her entire life to bring her own system of treating polio victims to international acceptance. Russell was nominated for an Oscar for her work as she limns a nearly 40-year period in the life of Australian Kenny, aging from her college days to 60. Working from the book by Kenny and Ostenso, the screenwriters (who included co-star Knox, a Canadian who played the President in WILSON) have toyed a bit with history in order to get a solid story on the screen, but their rearrangements were not major and didn't matter that much to the overall effect. Russell is the daughter of Bondi and Dingle, a newly graduated nurse who travels to the Aussie "Outback" where she first encounters the ravages of infantile paralysis. She has a relationship with Jagger but he soon realizes that she is so involved with her efforts to ease the pain of the polio sufferers that there is no room for romance. Russell evolves a theory for treatment and, like so many far-sighted creators, she is scorned by the medical establishment as her ideas do not conform to the norm. Knox is a Scot physician who believes in Russell's ideas and he is also in trouble with the other doctors, led by Merivale, who think it's a lot of hogwash. Her first patient is little McCann, and when good results are forthcoming, Russell knows she's right and carries on the battle until she arrives in the U.S. in 1940 and sets up her own institute at the University of Minnesota. The picture lost almost $700,000 when it was released, perhaps because the country thought the whole idea of polio rehabilitation was futile. It was years later when Dr. Jonas Salk made it a moot point for anyone who took his vaccine. The movie is a bit lethargic in spots but Russell's performance is luminous as the woman who would eventually be associated with "The March Of Dimes," an organization which began in 1938 and was headed by Roosevelt's former law partner.

p&d, Dudley Nichols; w, Nichols, Alexander Knox, Mary McCarthy, and (uncredited) Milton Gunzburg (based on the book *And They Shall Walk* by Elizabeth Kenny with Martha Ostenso); ph, George Barnes; m, Alexander Tansman; ed, Roland Gross; md, C. Bakaleinikoff; art d, Albert S. D'Agostino, William E. Flannery; set d, Darrell Silvera, Harley Miller; cos, Travis Banton; spec eff, Vernon L. Walker.

Biography   **Cas.**   (PR:A MPAA:NR)

SISTER TO ASSIST'ER, A*½   (1930, Brit.) 64m F.A. Thompson/GAU bw

Barbara Gott (*Mrs. May*), Pollie Emery (*Mrs. McNash*), Donald Stuart (*Alf*), Alec Hunter (*Mr. McNash*), Charles Paton (*Thistlethwaite*), Maud Gill (*Miss Pilbeam*), Johnny Butt (*Sailor*).

Creaky stage farce in its first talking film appearance. Gott is a poor but clever old woman who skips out on her rent, then impersonates her rich sister in order to get her bags back from landlady Emery. Hardly memorable.

p, H.B. Parkinson; d&w, George Dewhurst (based on the play by John le Breton).

Comedy   (PR:A MPAA:NR)

SISTER TO ASSIST'ER, A*½   (1938, Brit.) 72m Associated Industries/COL bw

Muriel George (*Mrs. May*), Pollie Emery (*Mrs. Getch*), Charles Paton (*Mr. Harris*), Billy Percy (*Alf*), Harry Herbert (*Mr. Getch*), Dorothy Vernon (*Mrs. Thistlethwaite*), Dora Levis (*Mrs. Hawkes*).

A later version of the popular play finds some of the character names changed, but the story remains intact as George pretends to be her own rich sister in order to recover a trunk being held by landlady Emery in lieu of back rent. No better than the rest of the films from this source.

p, Widgey Newman; d, Newman, George Dewhurst; w, Dewhurst (based on the play by John le Breton).

Comedy   (PR:A MPAA:NR)

SISTER TO ASSIST'ER, A*½   (1948, Brit.) 60m Bruton-Trytel/Premier bw

Muriel Aked (*Daisy Crawley*), Muriel George (*Gladys May*), Michael Howard (*Alf*).

The last of director Dewhurst's five film chestnuts of the same low stage comedy. The first two were silents, 1922 and 1927, then three talkies, 1930, 1938, and 1948, with Dewhurst writing and at least codirecting all of them. In addition, he used a virtual stock company on the pictures, with Pollie Emery playing the same part in four of them, and Mary Brough, Muriel Aked, Muriel George, and Charles Paton all making multiple appearances. The most fascinating thing of all is that with all these attempts at filming the same story, none is any good. The story of the conniving old lady who tricks her landlady out of her trunk that is being held for back rent is still here, and no more funny than it was the first four times.

p, W.L. Trytel; d&w, George Dewhurst (based on a play by John le Breton);

ph, Reggie Pilgrim.

Comedy (PR:A MPAA:NR)

SISTERS** (1930) 66m COL bw

Sally O'Neil (Sally Malone, Model), Molly O'Day (Molly Shannon), Russell Gleason (Eddie Collins), Jason Robards, Sr (John Shannon), Morgan Wallace (William Tully), John Fee (Johnson), Carl Stockdale (Jones).

A strained romantic melodrama starring O'Neil as a young Manhattan model who meets and falls for Gleason, a rural-born boy who has just landed a job as a census taker. Gleason's small town roots immediately sense trouble when he is introduced to O'Neil's acquaintance, Wallace, a dandy from Chicago. When O'Neil's sister, O'Day, finds herself forced to ask her sibling for a loan because her husband, Robards, has been out of work, Wallace moves in to take advantage of the vulnerable housewife and arranges a tryst. Meanwhile, Gleason learns that Wallace was indeed a crook in Chicago and exposes him to the police. All ends well when O'Day and Robards are reunited, leaving Gleason and O'Neil to marry and settle down out in the country using the reward money.

p, Harry Cohn; d, James Flood; w, Jo Swerling (based on a story by Ralph Graves); ph, Ted Tetzlaff; ed, Gene Havlick; art d, Harrison Wiley.

Drama (PR:A MPAA:NR)

SISTERS, THE**½ (1938) 98m WB bw

Bette Davis (Louise Elliott), Errol Flynn (Frank Medlin), Anita Louise (Helen Elliott), Jane Bryan (Grace Elliott), Ian Hunter (William Benson), Henry Travers (Ned Elliott), Beulah Bondi (Rose Elliott), Donald Crisp (Tim Hazleton), Dick Foran (Tom Knivel), Patric Knowles (Norman French), Alan Hale (Sam Johnson), Janet Shaw (Stella Johnson), Lee Patrick (Flora Gibbon), Laura Hope Crews (Flora's Mother), Harry Davenport (Doc Moore), Irving Bacon (Norman Forbes), Mayo Methot (Blonde), Paul Harvey (Caleb Ammon), Arthur Hoyt (Tom Selig), John Warburton (Lord Anthony Bittick), Stanley Fields (Ship's Captain), Ruth Garland (Lora Bennett), Larry Williams (Young Man, Announcer), Robert Homans (Editor), Stuart Holmes (Bartender), Constantine Romanoff (Spectator), Susan Hayward, Rosella Towne, Paulette Evans, Frances Morris (Telephone Operators), Richard Bond (Boy), Jack Mower (Ship's Officer), Vera Lewis, Lottie Williams, Bessie Wade, Mira McKinney, Georgie Cooper (Women), Lee Phelps, Granville Bates (Announcers), Bob Perry (Referee), Edgar Edwards (Soldier), Mildred Gover (Black Maid), Jang Lim (Chinese Man), Loia Cheaney (Maid), Peggy Moran (Girl).

A solid Krims screenplay based on the bestseller by Brinig makes for good drama in this three-way tale of a trio of sisters in a four-year period just after the new century came into being. Teddy Roosevelt has just been elected and there's a large party in a small Montana town where the three daughters of Bondi and Travers are the belles of the election-night ball. The oldest is Davis, next is Louise, and then Bryan. Louise becomes engaged to millionaire Hale, a kindly man whom she will marry for money, not love. She is really in love with Warburton, a handsome Englishman, but she opts for Hale and stays with him until he dies, after which she teams with Warburton. Davis had been seeing Foran, the son of the town's banker; when that's over, he takes up with Bryan, marries her and they remain in Montana and have a happy enough life, with the exception of one small fling Foran has with a local hat maker. Davis is the major focus of the tale. She runs off with Flynn, a sports reporter on a San Francisco newspaper. He's a handsome weakling who takes to drink when he can't earn enough of a living to support the woman he loves. Then he ships out to Singapore rather than face her and she is worried sick about his whereabouts as she's just learned she's expecting. The San Francisco earthquake hits (they used some stock footage from their 1927 film, IN OLD SAN FRANCISCO) and although it's not nearly as spectacular as the same tremor in MGM's SAN FRANCISCO, it is there more as a story point than for its own sake. After roaming the burning city, Davis is taken in by Crews, the mother of neighbor Patrick. She has a miscarriage and they help her through it. Later, she tries to find Flynn and fails, gains employment at a store owned by Hunter, who falls hard for her. She's on holiday in Montana when Flynn comes back to San Francisco after having been away three years. Davis, Bryan and Louise attend a celebration for new President Taft when Hunter arrives with Flynn in tow. Flynn now comes to the realization that he still loves Davis and asks her to reconcile. Hunter gentlemanly steps aside and the two are reunited. Note Susan Hayward in a bit, her second film. Also, watch for Bogart's battling wife, Mayo Methot, as a nameless blonde.

p, Hal B. Wallis, David Lewis; d, Anatole Litvak; w, Milton Krims (based on the novel by Myron Brinig); ph, Tony Gaudio; m, Max Steiner; ed, Warren Low; md, Leo F. Forbstein; art d, Carl Jules Weyl; cos, Orry-Kelly.

Drama (PR:A MPAA:NR)

SISTERS, THE** (1969, Gr.) 96m Damaskinos-Michaelides/Joseph Brenner bw (AKA: MAKE ME A WOMAN)

Petros Fissoun (Constantis), Elli Fotiou (Thalia), Nikos Rizos (Yorghis), Despo Diamantidou ("The Lady"), Vangelis Kazan (Yorghis' Mother), Niki Shellby (English Bar Girl).

Fissoun and Rizos are two sponge divers living in a small town on the Greek isle of Lesbos. Though Fissoun owns his own ships they are rendered useless when Diamantidou, the town's richest lady, impounds them until he can pay his debts. Fotiou is one of Diamantidou's three daughters who is being forced into a strange lesbian-incestual relationship with her two siblings. She does not care for Rizos but prefers him to her present company. The diving season begins and Fissoun and Rizos try to negotiate a fair price for boats from Diamantidou. Fotiou meets Fissoun and becomes interested. She seduces him then gives him the money to recover his boats from her mother. The loyalty to his friend comes first though and Fissoun breaks off the relationship. Diamantidou strongly disapproves of her daughter's involvement with any men but Fotiou becomes engaged to Rizos. However, her passion for Fissoun is too much to bear and she runs off with him during her engagement party. (In Greek; English Subtitles.)

p, Theophanis A. Damaskinos, Viktor G. Michaelides; d, Errikos Andreou; w, Panos Kontellis, Irene Vardoulaki; ph, Demetris Papakonstantis; m, Yannis Markopoulos; English subtitles, Peter Fernandez.

Drama (PR:C MPAA:NR)

SISTERS*** (1973) 92m Pressman-Williams/AIP c (GB: BLOOD SISTERS)

Margot Kidder (Danielle Breton), Jennifer Salt (Grace Collier), Charles Durning (Joseph Larch), Bill Finley (Emil Breton), Lisle Wilson (Phillip Woode), Barnard Hughes (Mr. McLennen, Editor), Mary Davenport (Mrs. Collier), Dolph Sweet (Detective Kelley).

Though De Palma may have gone overboard in remaking REAR WINDOW/ VERTIGO into BODY DOUBLE, this early Alfred Hitchcock hommage is a nifty suspense film that showed some real style and an oddball sense of humor. Salt is a nosy reporter who sees Kidder murder Wilson. She calls the police who do not believe her because Kidder and Finley have cleaned up the murder site. Salt continues to investigate on her own with private eye Durning's help. The trail leads her to a mental hospital/retreat where the story takes some really strange twists. Though clearly inspired by PSYCHO (the plot structure alone owes a good deal to this classic work) De Palma comes up with some great cinematic embellishments of his own. Using the splitscreen he builds up a great feeling of suspense and plays with the audiences loyalties. The dream sequences are highly imaginative with a really fine sense of the macabre. The score is by Hitchcock's great composer Bernard Herrmann. Reportedly De Palma cut an early murder sequence with Herrmann's shower scene music from PSYCHO, which enraged the great composer to no end. The score here is similar to PSYCHO's but with enough flair of its own to add to the fun. A fine early effort and some critics believe the beginning of unfulfilled promise.

p, Edward R. Pressman; d, Brian De Palma; w, De Palma, Louisa Rose (based on a story by De Palma); ph, Gregory Sandor (Movielab Color); m, Bernard Herrmann; ed, Paul Hirsch; prod d, Gary Weist.

Suspense/Horror Cas. (PR:O MPAA:R)

SISTERS, OR THE BALANCE OF HAPPINESS**½**
(1982, Ger.) 92m Bioskop Westdeutscher Rundfunk/Cinema 5 c
SCHWESTERN, ODER DIE BALANCE DES GLUECKS)

Jutta Lampe (Maria), Gudrun Gabriel (Anna), Jessica Frueh (Miriam), Konstantin Wecker (Robert), Rainer Delventhal (Maurice), Agnes Fink (Mother), Heinz Bennent (Muenzinger, Maria's Boss), Fritz Lichtenhahn (Fritz), Guenther Schuetz (Professor), Ilse Bahrs (Blind Woman), Barbara Sauerbaum (Maria as a Child), Marie-Helene Diekmann (Anna as a Child), Liselotte Arnold (Frau Eder), Editha Horn (Sister of Blind Woman), Ellen Esser (Nurse Fritz), Heinrich Marmann (Porter), Edith Garten (Language Teacher), Kathie Thomsen (Flutist), Volker Schwab (Robert's College), Dionysos Kawathas (Student).

Two sisters, played by Lampe and Gabriel, grow emotionally dependent upon each other in this controlled, detailed study of sibling relations. Lampe is the elder sister, a successful secretary whom university biology student Gabriel worships. When Gabriel commits suicide Lampe feels a need to fill the void left by her sister's death. She takes up with Frueh, a coworker, and soon develops the same emotional feelings that she shared with Gabriel. Lampe finds her late sister's diary and begins to read. She discovers that their great dependency may have caused the suicide so Lampe breaks off her new friendship and bravely faces the world alone. The message is somewhat heavy handed and blatantly obvious though the actresses carry off their roles with conviction. The directorial style takes things slowly with care for detail, paticularly, in moments of intimacy. Though this is not always successful SISTERS holds interest throughout. Von Trotta directed a much similar film two years later, THE GERMAN SISTERS, which shared many of the traits found in this picture.

p, Eberhard Junkersdorf; d, Margarethe von Trotta; w, von Trotta, Martje Grohmann, Luisa Francia (based on extracts from Traumprotokolle by Wolfgang Bachler); ph, Franz Raht, Thomas Schwan; m, Konstantin Wecker; ed, Annette Dorn; art d, Winifred Hennig; set d, Hennig; cos, Ingrid Zore.

Drama (PR:O MPAA:NR)

SISTERS UNDER THE SKIN**   (1934) 70m COL bw (GB: THE
                                                        ROMANTIC AGE)

Elissa Landi (*Blossom Bailey*), Frank Morgan (*John Hunter Yates*), Joseph Schildkraut (*Zukowski*), Doris Lloyd (*Elinor Yates*), Clara Blandick (*Miss Gower*), Shirley Grey (*Gilda Gordon*), Samuel S. Hinds (*Winters*), Henry Kolker (*Jones*), Arthur Stewart Hull (*Smith*), Montague Shaw (*Brown*), Howard Hickman (*Dutton*), Robert Graves (*Wiggins*), Selmer Jackson (*Mullen*).

A love triangle exists between Morgan, his wife Lloyd, and young actress Landi. Stripped to the bare bones of a story by its B picture status, this is a standard tale with standard characters. The direction is a little slow but the dialog is good.

d, David Burton; w, Jo Swerling (based on a story by S.K. Lauren); ph, Joseph Black; ed, Gene Milford; md, Louis Silvers; cos, Robert Kalloch.

Drama   (PR:C   MPAA:NR)

SIT TIGHT*½   (1931) 75m WB bw

Winnie Lightner (*Dr. Winnie O'Neil*), Joe E. Brown (*Jojo*), Claudia Dell (*Sally Dunlap*), Paul Gregory (*Tom Weston*), Lotti Loder (*French Girl*), Hobart Bosworth (*Walter Dunlap*), Frank Hagney (*Olaf*), Snitz Edwards (*Charley*).

A lesser vehicle for the usually funny Lightner and Brown. They run a health clinic and are training Gregory as a championship wrestler. Somehow Brown gets into the ring for a few laughs when he faces a monstrous masked opponet but the film never really goes anywhere. The fault lies with the weak script, full of contrived situations and tired jokes. Lightner, surprisingly, is not very good though Brown does give it his best shot.

d, Lloyd Bacon; w, Rex Taylor, William K. Wells (based on a story by Taylor); ph, William Rees; ed, Jimmy Gibbons; m/l, "Face It with a Smile" (sung by Winnie Lightner).

Comedy   (PR:A   MPAA:NR)

SITTING BULL**½   (1954) 105m Frank-Tele-Voz/UA c

Dale Robertson (*Parrish*), Mary Murphy (*Kathy*), J. Carrol Naish (*Chief Sitting Bull*), Iron Eyes Cody (*Chief Crazy Horse*), John Litel (*Gen. Howell*), Bill Hopper (*Wentworth*), Douglas Kennedy (*Col. G.A. Custer*), Bill Tannen (*O'Connor*), Joel Fluellen (*Sam*), John Hamilton (*President U.S. Grant*), Tom Brown Henry (*Webber*), Felix Gonzalez (*Young Buffalo*), Al Wyatt (*Swain*).

This version of the battle of Little Big Horn has both its bad and good points. The drama unfortunately is overlong and tediously directed in parts. However, SITTING BULL ranks as one of the more accurate accounts of the battle, with none of the racism found in so many programmer westerns. Robertson is the cavalry major who believes the Indians should receive just treatment under the law. He tries to prevent Kennedy from riding into disaster but to no avail. He is court-marshaled for befriending the enemy and sentenced to death. However Naish, as the great Indian leader Sitting Bull, intervenes by petitioning the President, Hamilton, who had been Robertson's commander during the Civil War. Robertson and Naish give good performances but are hampered by the spotty direction and some bad photography. Naish also played Sitting Bull in ANNIE GET YOUR GUN (1950). Cody, who does a good job as Crazy Horse, served as technical advisor which undoubtly contributed to the more favorable treatment of the native Americans in this film. The historical tale presented here is far closer to reality than the over-rated epic THEY DIED WITH THEIR BOOTS ON. Cody later achieved national recognition as the "crying Indian" for some TV commercials on environmental protection.

p, W.R. Frank, Alfred Strauss; d, Sidney Salkow; w, Salkow, Jack Dewitt; ph, Charles Van Enger (CinemaScope, Eastmancolor); ed, Richard Van Enger.

Western   (PR:C   MPAA:NR)

SITTING DUCKS***   (1979) 90m International Rainbow-Sunny Side
                                        Up/United Film Dis tribution c

Michael Emil (*Simon*), Zack Norman (*Sidney*), Patrice Townsend (*Jenny*), Irene Forrest (*Leona*), Richard Romanus (*Moose*), Henry Jaglom (*Jenny's Friend*).

Two small-timers decide to go for the big time by stealing money from gangsters. Once they have the money they intend to head to Central America and live it up. Emil and Norman have a marvelous chemistry in this great zany comedy. Along the way they meet Townsend and Forrest and the quartet play nicely off one another. Comedy is believable when the characters alone can carry a simple premise and that is what is done here. The result is a rollicking good time, directed with style and a sense of fun.

p, Meira Attia Dor; d&w, Henry Jaglom; ph, Paul Glickman (Metrocolor); m, Richard Romanus.

Comedy   **Cas.**   (PR:C   MPAA:R)

SITTING ON THE MOON***   (1936) 76m REP bw

Roger Pryor (*Danny West*), Grace Bradley (*Polly Blair*), William "Billy" Newell (*Mike*), Henry Kolker (*Worthington*), Pert Kelton (*Mattie*), Henry Wadsworth (*Charlie Lane*), Joyce Compton (*Blossom*), Pierre Watkin (*Tucker*), William Janney (*Young Husband*), June Martel (*Young Wife*), The Theodores (*Dance Team*), Jimmy Ray (*Feature Dancer*), Harvey Clark (*Hotel Manager*), George Cooper (*Taxi Driver*).

Enjoyable programmer features Pryor and Newell as a pair of songwriters who fall for former film queen Bradley and her friend Kelton. Problems arise for Pryor when Compton, a professional blackmailer, arrives and claims he married her while he was drunk. The radio background is used nicely with some terrific dance sequences thrown in also.

p, Nat Levine; d, Ralph Staub; w, Raymond L. Schrock, Rex Taylor, Sidney Sutherland (based on a story by Julian Field); ph, Ernest Miller; m/l, "Sitting on the Moon," "Lost in My Dreams," "How Am I Doin' with You?," Sam Stept, Sidney D. Mitchell.

Musical   (PR:A   MPAA:NR)

SITTING PRETTY***   (1933) 85m PAR bw

Jack Oakie (*Chick Parker*), Jack Haley (*Pete Pendleton*), Ginger Rogers (*Dorothy*), Thelma Todd (*Gloria Duval*), Gregory Ratoff (*Tannenbaum*), Lew Cody (*Jules Clark*), Harry Revel (*Pianist*), Jerry Tucker (*Buzz*), Mack Gordon (*Song Publisher*), Hale Hamilton (*Vinton*), Walter Walker (*George Wilson*), Kenneth Thomson (*Norman Lubin*), William B. Davidson (*Director*), Lee Moran (*Assistant Director*), Art Jarrett (*Singer*), Anne Nagel (*Girl at Window*), Joyce Matthews (*Blond Chorus Girl*), Irving Bacon, Stuart Holmes (*Dice Players*), Fuzzy Knight (*Stock Clerk*), Harvey Clark (*Motorist*), Wade Boteler (*Jackson*), Frank La Rue (*Studio Gateman*), Sidney Bracey (*Manager*), Jack Mower (*Clark's Aide*), Frank Hagney (*Bar Manager*), Larry Steers, Henry Hall (*Party Guests*), Russ Powell (*Counterman*), Charles Williams, George Brasno, Olive Brasno (*Neighbors*), Rollo Lloyd (*Director*), Lee Phelps (*Studio Aide*), Harry C. Bradley (*Set Designer*), Phil Tead (*Aide*), Dave O'Brien (*Assistant Cameraman*), Charles Coleman (*Butler*), James Burtis (*Mover Foreman*).

A pleasant little comedy with lots of music and proof again that Hollywood liked nothing better than making movies about Hollywood. The two Jacks, Oakie and Haley, are a songwriting team in New York. Their publisher, Gordon. and the rehearsal pianist, Revel, advise them to "Go West, Young Men". (Gordon and Revel also wrote the film's music and lyrics). They hitchhike to Hollywood, meet Rogers, who runs a lunch place, and she joins them. Once in Lotus Land, they meet agent Ratoff and movie producer Cody and their music makes them important. Oakie's head begins to swell to watermelon proportions but he's eventually brought back to earth. Sharp and satirical dialog from the writers plus a melodious score make this a fast-moving, happy film that is pleasant to the ears as well as to the eyes. Songs include: "There's a Bluebird at My Window," "Good Morning Glory," "Did You Ever See a Dream Walking?" (Rogers), "You're Such a Comfort to Me," (Rogers, Haley, Oakie), plus "I Wanna Meander With Miranda," "Ballad Of The South," "Lucky Little Extra," "Lights, Action, Camera, Love," "Many Moons Ago," "And Then We Wrote," "Lazy Louisiana Liza," and "Blonde, Blase and Beautiful." In a small role as a chorus girl is the beauteous Joyce Matthews, who was married to Billy Rose and Milton Berle, at different times, of course.

p, Charles R. Rogers; d, Harry Joe Brown; w, Jack McGowan, S.J. Perelman, Lou Breslow (based on a story by Nina Wilcox Putnam); ph, Milton Krasner; md, Howard Jackson; art d, David Garber; cos, Travis Banton; ch, Larry Ceballos; m/l, Mack Gordon, Harry Revel.

Musical/Comedy   (PR:A   MPAA:NR)

SITTING PRETTY****   (1948) 84m Fox bw

Robert Young (*Harry*), Maureen O'Hara (*Tacey*), Clifton Webb (*Lynn Belvedere*), Richard Haydn (*Mr. Appleton*), Louise Allbritton (*Edna Philby*), Randy Stuart (*Peggy*), Ed Begley (*Hammond*), Larry Olsen (*Larry*), John Russell (*Bill Philby*), Betty Ann Lynn (*Ginger*), Willard Robertson (*Mr. Ashcroft*), Anthony Sydes (*Tony*), Roddy McCaskill (*Roddy*), Grayce Hampton (*Mrs. Appleton*), Cara Williams, Marion Marshall (*Secretaries*), Charles Arnt (*Mr. Taylor*), Ken Christy (*Mr. McPherson*), Ann Shoemaker (*Mrs. Ashcroft*), Minerva Urecal (*Mrs. Maypole*), Mira McKinney (*Mrs. Phillips*), Sid Saylor (*Cab Driver*), Ruth Warren (*Matron*), Isabel Randolph (*Mrs. Frisbee*), Ellen Lowe (*Effie*), Dave Morris (*Mailman*), Anne O'Neal (*Mrs. Gibbs*), Albin Robeling (*Maitre d'*), Josephine Whittell (*Mrs. Hammond*), Mary Field (*Librarian*), Billy Wayne (*Newsreel Man*), Charles Owens, Iris James, Robert Tidwell, Barbara Blaine (*Jitterbugs*), Gertrude Astor (*Woman*), Jane Nigh (*Mable*), J. Farrell MacDonald (*Cop*), Charles Tannen (*Director*), Dorothy Adams (*Mrs. Goul*).

If ever an actor was born to play a part, it was Webb in this Oscar-nominated role as a prissy genius who takes a job as a babysitter. The scene is "Hummingbird Hill," a typical suburban community where McCaskill, Olsen and Sydes, the three sons of Young and O'Hara, are so bratty that the family has lost a trio of maids. The word is out on these kids and no one wants to work at their home, for fear of pain and madness. O'Hara advertises in the local paper and in walks Webb, a self-proclaimed genius with definite ideas as to how to raise children. He is stern but fair and it's not long before the boys knuckle under his discipline. When the baby tosses oatmeal at Webb, his response is to toss the goop right back at the baby, thereby establishing his superiority. The neighborhood is filled with gossips and busybodies led by Haydn (in a superb performance) and they are all shocked when the real reason for Webb's presence is unveiled: he's a writer (besides being a doctor, lawyer, philosopher, and everything else) who has been taking down all the facts about the area, and the town is exposed when Webb's book is published and becomes a bestseller. The two sequels to this successful film were not nearly as witty or biting, MR. BELVEDERE GOES TO COLLEGE and MR. BELVEDERE RINGS THE BELL. In 1985, a TV series was attempted based on the Webb character but failed to register much interest. Webb's comedy timing is impeccable and even the most minor lines in Herbert's script adaptation of the Davenport novel are delivered with such aplomb that they often sound better than they should. Webb, who began life in Indianapolis as Webb Parmallee Hollenbeck, started as a dancer, then moved to playing drama in London, appeared in some silent films while still in his 20s, then made his mark as the villain in LAURA, for which he was nominated for an Oscar. His other nomination came for THE RAZOR'S EDGE. From the moment he appeared in SITTING PRETTY, Webb's screen image was altered and he spent the rest of his life playing acerbic types whose every phrase was an epigram.

p, Samuel G. Engel; d, Walter Lang; w, F. Hugh Herbert (based on the novel *Belvedere* by Gwen Davenport); ph, Norbert Brodine; m, Alfred Newman; ed, Harmon Jones; md, Edward Powell; art d, Lyle Wheeler, Leland Fuller; set d, Thomas Little, Ernest Lansing; cos, Kay Nelson; spec eff, Fred Sersen; makeup, Ben Nye.

Comedy   (PR:AAA   MPAA:NR)

SITTING TARGET**   (1972, Brit.) 93m MGM c

Oliver Reed (*Harry Lomart*), Jill St. John (*Pat Lomart*), Ian McShane (*Birdy Williams*), Edward Woodward (*Inspector Milton*), Frank Finlay (*Marty Gold*), Freddie Jones (*MacNeil*), Jill Townsend (*Maureen*), Robert Beatty (*Gun Dealer*), Tony Beckley (*Soapy Tucker*), Mike Pratt (*Prison Warder Accomplice*), Robert Russell (*Prison Warder No. 1*), Joe Cahill (*Prison Warder No. 2*), Robert Ramsey (*Gun Dealer's Bodyguard*), Susan Shaw (*Girl in Truck*), June Brown (*Lomart Neighbor*), Maggy Maxwell (*Irate Mother*).

When convict Reed suspects his wife, St. John, is being unfaithful, he breaks out of prison with his friend McShane. They leave several bodies lying in their wake as they blast their way across the country to meet St. John and their inevitable violent deaths. Strictly for those who like their action hard and fast. The direction breaks the land speed record, maintaining a tense mood and keeping excitement running at a fevered pitch. The violence is sometimes quite brutal, made more believable by Reed and McShane in some good performances.

p, Barry Kulick; d, Douglas Hickox; w, Alexander Jacobs (based on the novel by Laurence Henderson); ph, Edward Scaife (Metrocolor); m, Stanley Myers; ed, John Glen; prod d, Jonathan Barry; cos, Emma Porteous; spec eff, John Stears; makeup, Paul Rabiger.

Action   (PR:O   MPAA:R)

SITUATION HOPELESS--BUT NOT SERIOUS½**
                                        (1965) 97m Castle/PAR bw

Alec Guinness (*Herr Frick*), Michael Connors (*Lucky*), Robert Redford (*Hank*), Anita Hoefer (*Edeltraud*), Mady Rahl (*Lissie*), Paul Dahlke (*Herr Neusel*), Frank Wolff (*Quartermaster Master Sergeant*), John Briley (*Sergeant*), Elisabeth Von Molo (*Wanda*), Carola Regnier (*Senta*).

During the closing days of WW II, American bombers are sent to destroy the German town of Altheim, though the only industrial target is a harmless sauerkraut factory. Surprisingly, one of the bombers is shot down and the two airmen aboard, Connors and Redford, parachute into enemy territory. Escaping from the Nazis, the two find refuge in the cellar of Guinness, a shy, quiet shop clerk who lives alone. Discovering the Americans, Guinness decides to capture them by locking the cellar door. Having finally found a way to keep from being lonely and purposeless, Guinness keeps the men captive and seeks their cooperation by explaining that if he released them the Nazis would surely put them in a prison much worse than his cellar. The men agree and settle down for the duration. Months later the war ends and American occupation forces arrive in Altheim. Not wanting to lose his "guests," Guinness keeps the Allied victory a secret and invents fictitious tales of brilliant Nazi military exploits. Seven years go by and the two prisoners grow depressed at the thought of a world run by the Nazis. Soon the Christmas season is once again upon Altheim and Guinness leaves his house to buy a Christmas goose for Redford and a prostitute for Connors. Guinness ventures into the Daffy-Dil Club and speaks with the madame, Rahl. The shy shopkeeper trys to explain that he wants a girl to come to his house where the man she is to "entertain" is chained to a bed in the cellar, but Rahl concludes he's a crazy man and has him thrown out. The unexpected excitement gives Guinness a heart attack and he is taken to the hospital and forced to convalesce for several days. Panicked that Connors and Redford are starving to death, Guinness escapes from the hospital, steals a bicycle, and pedles home with two policemen in hot pursuit. Fearing discovery, Guinness gives the men provisions and sends them on their way

without telling them that the war is over. While making their way through the streets of Germany, Connors and Redford notice all the rebuilding and conclude that Germany has indeed won the war. Finally the men make it to the German-Swiss border, but their path is blocked by Nazi soldiers, who in reality are just extras in a Hollywood movie being shot there. Determined to make their bid for freedom, the two flyers bravely fight their way through the "enemy" and make it to Switzerland. Of course the men soon learn the truth, and, back in America, Connors and Redford throw a party where they promise to tell of their bizzare imprisonment. Halting in mid-sentence, they explain that only one man can really relate the story properly and Redford calls in his happy butler, Guinness, to tell the tale. Based on a popular novel by Robert Shaw and directed by Reinhardt, SITUATION HOPELESS–BUT NOT SERIOUS was only the second screen appearance of Redford. The young star found the director unimaginative and the shooting tedious, though he used the opportunity to learn from Guinness, one of Britain's greatest actors. Despite the potential, the material had to be a truly funny and insightful movie, and the film suffers from a lackluster pace and heavy-handed direction which only makes the American flyers' 7-year imprisonment feel like it's going by in real time. Though SITUATION HOPELESS – BUT NOT SERIOUS contains a few bright moments, overall the situation is monotonous and not very funny.

p&d, Gottfried Reinhardt; w, Silvia Reinhardt, Jan Lustig (based on the novel *The Hiding Place* by Robert Shaw); ph, Kurt Hasse; m, Harold Byrns; ed, Walter Boos; art d, Rolf Zehetbauer; cos, Ilse Dubois; makeup, Arthur Schramm, Albert Nagel.

Comedy/War   (PR:A   MPAA:NR)

SIX BLACK HORSES**   (1962) 80m UNIV c

Audie Murphy (*Ben Lane*), Dan Duryea (*Frank Jesse*), Joan O'Brien (*Kelly*), George Wallace (*Boone*), Roy Barcroft (*Mustanger*), Bob Steele (*Puncher*), Henry Wills (*Indian Leader*), Phil Chambers (*Undertaker*), Charlita Regis (*Mexican Girl*), Dale Van Sickel (*Man*), Richard Pasco (*Charlie*).

Completely routine Murphy outing features the western hero as a man wrongly accused of horse thievery. He is saved from hanging by Duryea, and O'Brien hires them to escort her through hostile Indian territory so she can reunite with her husband. The party is attacked and hides out in an abandoned mission ruin. O'Brien is about to shoot Duryea in the back when she is hit by a spear. She confesses to Murphy that Duryea murdered her husband and she was about to have her revenge. Duryea wants some of her money that is being held in a bank. He punches Murphy and rides off with the wounded woman. Murphy catches up and kills Duryea in a showdown, and gets O'Brien in the end. The script is not much more than a compendium of 1950s western cliches though the direction gives the production some life. The photography is the real attraction with some gorgeous shots of the southern Utah locations. The players are adequate. Watch for former serial cowpokes Steele and Barcroft in lesser roles.

p, Gordon Kay; d, Harry Keller; w, Burt Kennedy; ph, Maury Gertsman (Eastmancolor); m, Joseph Gershenson; ed, Aaron Stell; art d, Alexander Golitzen, Robert Luthardt; set d, Oliver Emert; makeup, Bud Westmore.

Western   (PR:A   MPAA:NR)

SIX BRIDGES TO CROSS½**   (1955) 96m UNIV bw

Tony Curtis (*Jerry Florea*), Julie Adams (*Ellen Gallagher*), George Nader (*Edward Gallagher*), Jay C. Flippen (*Vincent Concannon*), Kendall Clark (*Sanborn*), Sal Mineo (*Jerry Florea as a Boy*), Jan Merlin (*Andy Norris*), Richard Castle (*Skids Radzievich*), William Murphy (*Red Flanagan*), Kenny Roberts (*Red Flanagan as a Boy*), Peter Avramo (*Hymie Weiner*), Hal Conklin (*Jerry's Attorney*), Don Keefer (*Special Prosecutor Sherman*), Harry Bartell (*Father Bonelli*), Tito Vuolo (*Angie*), Ken Patterson (*Inspector J.L. Walsh*), Paul Dubov (*Bandit Leader*), Peter Leeds (*Harris*), James F. Stone (*George Russell*), Howard Wright (*Judge*), Elizabeth Kerr (*Governess*), Charles Victor (*Clerk*), Carl Frank (*Judge Manning*), Grant Gordon (*Dr. Moreno*), Di Di Roberts, Doris Meade, Harold W. Miller (*Jail Visitors*), John J. Muldoon (*Radio Dispatcher*), Claudia Hall (*Maggie*), Anabel Shaw (*Virginia Stewart*), Cary Loftin (*Policeman*).

Purportedly based on a magazine article by Joseph F. Dinnen entitled "They Stole $2,500,000 and Got Away with It" which detailed the infamous Boston Brink's robbery, SIX BRIDGES TO CROSS bears only passing resemblance to that case or the men who were involved in it. Curtis stars in this traditional rise-and-fall of a hood story which was shot on location in and around Boston. The film opens with Mineo playing Curtis as a boy. The standard events which lead to the young Mineo turning to a life of crime occur in a predictable fashion with a documentary-style narrator filling in the gaps and giving a deadly serious air to the proceedings. Despite the concerned attentions of kindly cop Nader and his wife Adams, Mineo graduates from juvenile criminal pursuits to bigger escapades. Now played by Curtis, the young hoodlum decides to please his unoffically adopted parents and pretends to go straight, all the while planning the ultimate heist–Brink's. Finally the time is right and the plan is enacted. Curtis and his gang pull off the robbery without a hitch and make off with $2.5 million. After the flawless robbery Curtis has a change of heart and decides against leaving the country with the loot. Secretly, he decides to return the money to Brink's and remain in Boston, but one of the gang members learns of the plan and kills him. Aside from the magnificent location shooting and a few fine moments from Mineo in the early scenes, SIX BRIDGES TO CROSS offers nothing new or fresh to the viewer. Perhaps if they had stuck to the facts the film would have been more than a tired cliche. Tony Pino, the real mastermind behind the Brink's robbery, was indeed a small-time hood before planning the heist of his life. Researching the Brink's operation for six years, he uncovered all the company's flaws and devised a foolproof plan to rob the vaults. Using an amazingly large gang, Pino made off with exactly $2,775,395.12. The job took only 20 minutes. A more accurate version of this material was filmed in 1978 entitled THE BRINK'S JOB, starring Peter Falk. Directed by William Freidkin (THE FRENCH CONNECTION, THE EXORCIST) the film also has some flaws, but for those interested in the actual Brink's robbery it comes much closer to the truth.

p, Aaron Rosenberg; d, Joseph Pevney; w, Sidney Boehm (based on the article "They Stole $2,500,000–And Got Away with It" by Joseph Dineen); ph, William Daniels; ed, Russell Shoengarth, Verna MacCurran; md, Joseph Gershenson; art d, Alexander Golitzen, Robert Clatworthy; cos, Jay Morley, Jr.; m/l, Jeff Chandler, Henry Mancini. (vocals by Sammy Davis, Jr.)

Crime   **(PR:A   MPAA:NR)**

SIX CYLINDER LOVE**   (1931) 79m FOX bw

Spencer Tracy (William Donroy), Edward Everett Horton (Monty Winston), Sidney Fox (Marilyn Sterling), William Collier, Sr (Richard Burton), Una Merkel (Margaret Rogers), Lorin Raker (Gilbert Sterling), William Holden (Stapleton), Ruth Warren (Mrs. Burton), Bert Roach (Harold Rogers), El Brendel (Janitor).

When newlywed couple Fox and Raker get an expensive new car they become quite popular with their friends. Everyone hangs out for rides and parties. Fox smashes the car and Raker appropriates $5,000 from his boss to pay the damages. Finally their troubles end and the couple is out of debt when they sell the car to Brendel, a slightly confused janitor. Some amusing moments but really nothing more than a lesser comedy programmer. The only real interest is Tracy, in an early role, as the man who sells the couple their auto in the first place.

d, Thornton Freeland; w, William Conselman, Norman Houston (based on the play by William Anthony McGuire); ph, Ernest Palmer: ed, J. Edwin Robbins.

Comedy   **(PR:A   MPAA:NR)**

SIX-DAY BIKE RIDER*   (1934) 69m FN bw

Joe E. Brown (Wilfred Simpson), Maxine Doyle (Phyllis Jenkins), Frank McHugh (Clinton Hemmings), Gordon Westcott (Harry St. Clair), Arthur Aylesworth (Col. Jenkins), Lottie Williams (Mrs. Jenkins), Dorothy Christy (Mrs. St. Clair), Harry Seymour (Radio Announcer), Lloyd Neal (Uncle Ezra), William Granger (Pop O'Hara).

Unusually poor outing for Brown finds him entering a six-day bicycle race, which he naturally wins. There was some real opportunity within this thin framework for Brown to show his stuff; instead, the script is filled with gags left over from silent comedy shorts. As it is, the film is too long and as predictable as they come. Doyle is the romantic interest, though her part is dull and a mere time filler.

p, Sam Bischoff; d, Lloyd Bacon; w, Earl Baldwin; ph, Warren Lynch; ed, George Amy; art d, Anton Grot.

Comedy   **(PR:A   MPAA:NR)**

SIX DAYS A WEEK**   (1966, Fr./Ital./Span.) 91m Ultra
                Film-Consortium Pathe-Tecisa/Atlantic Pictures bw (LE PARTAGE DE
                CATHERINE, LA BUGIARDA, LA MENTIROSA).

Catherine Spaak (Maria/Silvana/Caterina), Enrico Maria Salerno (Count Adriano Silveri), Marc Michel (Arturo Santini), Manuel Miranda (Gianni Moraldi), Pepe Calvo, Riccardo Cucciolla, Nando Angelini, Didi Perego, Mara Fernandez, Janine Reynaud, Daina Saronni, Grazia Martini, Giuseppe Ranieri, Mario de Gual, Guadalupe Munoz Sampedro, Maria Fernanda Ladron de Guevara.

Spaak plays a female lothario who disguises as her French roommate so she can carry on with various lovers. Since her roommate is a stewardess, this makes things all the easier. Salerno is one lover, an official of the Vatican. Another lover is Michel, a Roman dentist. She meets with each man three days a week, reserving the final day for Miranda, a man who knew Spaak when they were both students. Naturally, the trio finds out what's going on, but somehow Spaak convinces each man that he's the only guy for her.

d, Luigi Comencini; w, Marcello Fondato, Comencini, Jose G. Maesso (based on the play "La Bugiarda" by Diego Fabbri); ph, Armando Nannuzzi; m, Benedetto Ghiglia; set d, Luigi Scaccianoce, Francisco Canet.

Comedy   **(PR:O   MPAA:NR)**

SIX FEMMES POUR L'ASSASSIN
                (SEE: BLOOD AND BLACK LACE, 1965, Fr./Ital./Ger.)

SIX GUN GOLD***   (1941) 57m RKO bw

Tim Holt (Don Cardigan), Ray Whitley (Smokey), Jan Clayton (Penny Blanchard), Lee "Lasses" White (Whopper), LeRoy Mason (Marshal), Eddy C. Walker (Ben Blanchard), Davison Clark (Robinson), Harry Harvey (Vander), Slim Whitaker (Miller), Lane Chandler (Brad Cardigan), Jim Corey (Chuck), Fern Emmett (Jenny Blanchard).

When Holt and sidekick White ride off to meet Holt's brother Chandler, they are confronted by Mason, a bad guy who's masquerading as the newly-appointed marshal. Seeing no sign of Chandler, the two run off, pretending to be scared out of their wits. Holt soon discovers that Mason and his cohorts have kidnaped Chandler and are stealing gold from miners. In an action-packed climax, Holt fires plenty of bullets and saves his brother, halting the outlaws nefarious schemes. This is a good entry in Holt's series for RKO, full of action and a few plot twists that differentiate it from most westerns. Direction and production values are good for the fare.

p, Bert Gilroy; d, David Howard; w, Norton S. Parker (based on a story by Tom Gibson); ph, Harry Wild; ed, Frederic Knudtson; md, Paul Sawtell; m/l, "Six Gun Gold," Fred Rose, Ray Whitley.

Western   **(PR:A   MPAA:NR)**

SIX GUN GOSPEL**   (1943) 59m MON bw

Johnny Mack Brown, Raymond Hatton, Inna Gest, Eddie Dew, Roy Barcroft, Kenneth MacDonald, Edmund Cobb, Milburn Morante, Artie Ortego, L.W. "Lynton" Brent, Bud Osborne, Kernan Cripps, Jack Daley, Mary MacLaren.

Standard Brown oater which sees his pal Hatton go undercover as a parson to get the goods on some crooks. While incognito, Hatton finds himself deluged with requests from the female members of his congregation to lead the choir in song, so the craggy-faced cowboy sits down at the piano and solemnly warbles a folk song about Jesse James, much to their surprise.

p, Scott R. Dunlap; d, Lambert Hillyer; w, Ed Earl Repp, Jess Bowers [Adele Buffington]; ph, Harry Neumann; ed, Carl Pierson; md, Edward Kay.

Western   **(PR:A   MPAA:NR)**

SIX-GUN LAW**½   .   (1948) 54m COL bw

Charles Starrett (Steve Norris), Smiley Burnette (Smiley Burnette), Nancy Saunders (June Wallace), Paul Campbell (Jim Wallace), Hugh Prosser (Boss Decker), George Chesebro (Bret Wallace), Billy Dix (Crowl), Bob Wilke (Larson), Bob Cason (Ben), Ethan Laidlaw (Sheriff Brackett), Pierce Lyden (Jack Reed), Bud Osborne (Barton), Budd Buster (Bank Clerk Duffy), Curly Clements and his Rodeo Rangers.

Okay "Durango Kid" series entry has Starrett framed by Prosser into thinking he's killed the town sheriff. Since Prosser runs the town, Starrett's forced to fill the vacant post and keep an eye closed to Prosser's evil schemes. Starrett goes undercover in his Durango Kid guise, stops a bank robbery by Prosser's outlaw gang and makes an arrest with the help of a U.S. Marshal. The film is at its best when there's action and gunplay. The script shows some wit and the direction isn't bad, though the plot development scenes aren't quite up to par. (See Durango Kid series, Index.)

p, Colbert Clark; d, Ray Nazarro; w, Barry Shipman; ph, George F. Kelley; ed, Henry DeMond.

Western   **Cas.**   **(PR:AA   MPAA:NR)**

SIX GUN MAN*½   (1946) 59m PRC bw

Bob Steele (Bob Storm), Syd Saylor (Syd McTavish), Jimmie Martin (Tim Hager), Jean Carlin (Laura Barton), I. Stanford Jolley (Matt Haley), Brooke Temple (Ed Slater), Bud Osborne (Sam Elkins), Budd Buster (Joe Turner), Stanley Blystone (Lon Kelly), Roy Brent (Slim Peters), Steve Clark (Sheriff Jennings), Dorothy Whitmore (Mrs. Barton), Ray Jones.

Simplistic Steele western finds him as a U.S. Marshal stopping a slew of cattle rustlers. The performances and direction are well below western standards. Plenty of meaningless action pads the film's meager plot.

p, Arthur Alexander; d&w, Harry Fraser; ph, Jack Greenhalgh; ed, Roy Livingston; md, Lee Zahler; art d, George Montgomery.

Western   **(PR:A   MPAA:NR)**

SIX-GUN RHYTHM**   (1939) 57m Arcadia/GN bw

Tex Fletcher (Tex), Joan Barclay (Jean), Ralph Peters (Spud), Reed Howes (Davis), Bud McTaggert (Harper), Ted Adams (Sheriff), Walter Shumway (Bart), Slim Hacker (Pete), Carl Mathews (Jake), Art Davis (Mike), Bob Fraser (Baker), Jack McHugh (Butch), Sherry Tansey (Pat), Kit Guard (Slim), Art Felix, Joe Pazen, Jack O'Shea, Cliff Parkinson, Frank Ellis, Wade Walker, Adrian Hughes.

Singing radio cowpoke Fletcher made his only western film with this minor piece. He's a professional football player, of all things, who goes to Texas after his father's killed by some outlaws. He brings the baddies to justice with little trouble and manages to play left-handed guitar every once in a while. Grand National released this film with much bluster, but its minor budget and routine treatment were hardly worth the effort. Barclay, who played the love interest for many a cowboy, takes the romantic honors.

p&d, Sam Newfield; w, Fred Myton (based on a story by Ted Richmond); ph, Art Reed; ed, Bob Crandall; m/l, "Cabin In the Valley," "They Won't Stretch My Neck If I Know It," "When I Go Back To The Range," "Serenade to a Lovely Senorita," Lew Porter, Johnny Lange.

Western (PR:A MPAA:NR)

SIX GUN SERENADE** (1947) 55m MON bw

Jimmy Wakely, Lee "Lasses" White, Jimmie Martin, Steve Clark, Pierce Lyden, Bud Osborne, Rivers Lewis, Arthur "Fiddlin" Smith, Stanley Ellison, Chick Hannon, Kay Morley, Cactus Mack, Artie Ortego, Jack Hendricks, Steve Clark.

Unjustly jailed cowpokes are bailed out of prison by a group of ranchers desperate to stop the rustlers who are ruining their business. Blazing six guns "serenade" the crooks and stop their monkeyshines.

p, Barney Sarecky; d, Ford Beebe; w, Ben Cohen; ph, Marcel LePicard; ed, Edward A. Biery, Jr; md, Frank Sanucci; set d, Vin Taylor; m/l, Lee "Lasses" White, Arthur Smith, Wanda Daniels.

Western (PR:A MPAA:NR)

SIX HOURS TO LIVE*½ (1932) 80m FOX bw

Warner Baxter (Capt. Paul Onslow), Miriam Jordan (Valerie von Sturm), John Boles (Karl Kranz), George Marion (Professor Otto Bauer), Beryl Mercer (the Widow), Halliwell Hobbes (Baron von Sturm), Edwin Maxwell (Police Commissioner), John Davidson (Kellner), Edward McWade (Ivan), Dewey Robinson (Blucher), Hans von Twardowski, William von Brincken.

Baxter plays a diplomat from a mythical country in this unusual story. He's assassinated at an international trade conference after expressing some controversial opinions. Marion is a scientist with a machine that can restore life for up to six hours, which is all the time Baxter needs to save his country from signing a bad treaty with an enemy. He also manages to set up his love interest, Jordan, with a new man, Boles. Though this was a bizarre subject for its time, the film has not aged well. The direction isn't bad, but the acting is overly dramatic and without a trace of humor.

d, William Dieterle; w, Bradley King (based on the story "Auf Wiedersehen" by Gordon Morris and Morton Barteaux); ph, John Seitz.

Science Fiction/Drama (PR:C MPAA:NR)

SIX IN PARIS*** (1968, Fr.) 96m Les Films du Losange-Barbet Schroeder/New Yorker c (PARIS VU PAR....)

"Saint-Germain-des-Pres": Barbara Wilkin (Katherine), Jean-Francois Chappey (Jean), Jean-Pierre Andreani (Raymond), "Gare du Nord": Nadine Ballot (Odile), Barbet Schroeder (Jean-Pierre), Gilles Queant (Stranger), "Rue Saint-Denis": Micheline Dax (Prostitute), Claude Melki (Leon), "Place de l'Etoile": Jean-Michel Rouziere (Jean-Marc), Marcel Gallon (Victim), "Montparnasse-Levallois": Joanna Shimkus (Monica), Philippe Hiquilly (Roger), Serge Davri (Ivan), "La Muette": Stephane Audran (Wife), Claude Chabrol (Husband), Gilles Chusseau (Boy), Dinah Saril (Maid).

This six-part compilation film, which opened in Paris in October of 1965, is notable for the talent that worked on some of the segments. In "Saint-Germain-des-Pres," Chappey brings American student Wilkin to his flat for the night. He rids himself of her the next day, announcing that he's flying to Mexico to join his father. Wilkin is later disillusioned when Chappey turns up as a model in her art class. She then allows Andreani to pick her up, only to discover that this boy had loaned his apartment to Chappey for the original affair. The photographer was Almendros, who became popular for his talents with a lens during the 1970s. In "Gare du Nord," Ballot runs out on her husband after a fight. She's almost run down by Queant, a handsome stranger in a fancy car. He says he's going to kill himself but will change his mind if Ballot goes away with him. She refuses, and he takes a plunge off a railway bridge. "Rue Saint-Denis" finds shy, young Melki bringing lady of the evening Dax back to his place for a night of fun. His incessant conversation leads to Dax's staying for dinner before they can get to bed. "Place de l'Etoile," directed by Rohmer, has salesman Rouziere bumping into Gallon, a street person, on his way to work. He hits the poor man with his umbrella during the confrontation and Gallon falls down. Rouziere is convinced he's killed the derelict and looks for news of his death in the papers. A few weeks later, he sees Gallon engaged in a similar argument with another person at the same place. "Montparnasse-Levallois" was directed by the bad boy of the Nouvelle Vogue, Godard, and photographed by noted American documentary filmmaker Maysles. This story has Shimkus serving as a lover for two men. She sends each a note telling the site of their respective rendezvous but panics when she thinks she mistakenly switched the mates. She goes to each lover to explain away her

mistake and is surprised when each man throws her out, then she realizes the mistake was all in her mind. The last segment, "La Muette," was written and directed by Chabrol. He also acts, playing a man who constantly fights with his wife about money and who flirts with the house maid. His son, tired of the noise, buys some earplugs for himself. The earplugs end up doing more harm than good when his mother falls down the stairs and the boy doesn't hear her cry out for help.

p, Barbet Schroeder; "Saint-Germain-des-Pres" d, Jean Douchet; w, Douchet, Georges Keller; ph, Nestor Almendros (Ektachrome); "Gare du Nord" d, w, Jean Rouch; ph, Etienne Becker (Ektachrome); "Rue Saint-Denis" d&w, Jean-Daniel Pollet; ph, Alain Levent (Ektachrome); "Place de l'Etoile" d&w, Eric Rohmer; ph, Almendros, Alain Levent (Ektachrome); "Montparnasse-Levallois" d&w, Jean-Luc Godard; ph, Albert Maysles (Ektachrome); "La Muette" d&w, Claude Chabrol; ph, Jean Rabier (Ektachrome); ed, Jackie Reynal; art d, Eliane Bonneau.

Comedy/Drama (PR:C-O MPAA:NR)

SIX INCHES TALL (SEE: ATTACK OF THE PUPPET PEOPLE, 1958)

SIX LESSONS FROM MADAME LA ZONGA*½ (1941) 62m UNIV bw

Lupe Velez (Madame La Zonga), Leon Errol (Senor Alvarez), Helen Parrish (Rosita Alvarez), Charles Lang (Steve), William Frawley (Beheegan), Eddie Quillan (Skat), Guinn "Big Boy" Williams (Alvin), Shemp Howard (Gabby), Frank Mitchell (Maxwell), Jimmy Wakely (Pony), Danny Beck (Danny), Lorin Raker (Brady), John Bond (Tex), Richard Reinhart (Jim), Rosa Turich (Maid), Wade Boteler (Captain), George Humbert (Carriage Driver), Eddie Acuff (Steward), Ken Christy (Employment Manager), Francisco Maran (Officer), Paco Moreno (Jailer), Lee Phelps (Anderson), Jack Clifford (McGuire), Minerva Urecal (Irate Woman), Paul Ellis (Dance Teacher), Jose Tortosa (Banker), James McNamara (Postman), Enrique Acosta (Excited Cuban), Rico de Montez (Bellboy), Demetrius Emanuel (Cuban Policeman).

Stupid comedy features Velez in the title role, as the singing sensation of a Cuban nightclub called La Zonga. Great name, boring place. Velez goes through a few rumba numbers (modified a bit to please the censors) while Lang attempts the unbelievable as he tries to get his Oklahoma jazz band booked at the club. Merely an excuse for some average production numbers, with poor direction and the meagerest of story lines. Watch for an appearance by Frawley, who would again run into Cuban nightclubs on television's "I Love Lucy."

p, Joseph G. Sandford; d, John Rawlins; w, Stanley C. Rubin, Marion Orth, Larry Rhine, Ben Chapman (based on a story by Rhine and Chapman); ph, John W. Boyle; ed, Edward Curtiss; md, Charles Previn; m/l, "Six Lessons," "Mister Moon," "Jitterhumba", Milton Rosen, Everett Carter.

Musical (PR:A MPAA:NR)

SIX MEN, THE*½ (1951, Brit.) 65m Planet/Eros bw

Harold Warrender (Supt. Holroyd), Olga Edwardes (Christina Frazer), Peter Bull (Walkeley), Avril Angers (Herself), Desmond Jeans (Colonel), Michael Evans (Hunter), Ivan Craig (Wainwright), Reed de Rouen (Lewis), Christopher Page (Johnny the Kid), Louis Weichart (The Mole).

Foolish crime drama starring Warrender and Evans as two Scotland Yard investigators trying to crack a gang of jewel thieves known as "The Six Men." Using a blind informer called "The Mole" (Weichart), the detectives locate an actress connected with the gang. By pitting one gang member against another, Warrender and Evans destroy the ruinous six.

p, Roger Proudlock; d, Michael Law; w, Reed de Rouen, Law, Richard Eastham (based on a story by E. and M.A. Radford); ph, S.D. Onions.

Crime (PR:A MPAA:NR)

SIX OF A KIND*** (1934) 62m PAR bw

Charlie Ruggles (J. Pinkham Whinney, Bank Clerk), Mary Boland (Flora Whinney), W. C. Fields (Sheriff "Honest John" Hoxley), George Burns (George Edwards), Gracie Allen (Gracie De Vore), Alison Skipworth (Mrs. "Duchess" K. Rumford, Innkeeper), Bradley Page (Ferguson), Grace Bradley (Trixie), William J. Kelly (A. B. Gillette, Bank President), James Burke (Sparks, Detective), Dick Rush (Steele), Walter Long (Butch, Robber), Leo Willis (Mike, Robber), Lew Kelly (Joe, Bank Guard), Alfred P. James (Tom), Tammany Young (Dr. Busby), Lee Phelps (Airline Official), Irving Bacon (Hotel Desk Clerk), Paul Tead (Newspaper Accountant), George Pearce (Tourist), Verna D. Hillie (Bank Safety Deposit Clerk), Florence Enright (Tourist's Wife), William Augustin (Cop), Kathleen Burke (Woman), Phil Dunham (Drunk), Marty Faust (Porter), Neal Burns (Bank President's Secretary), Harry Bernard (Eyeshade Man), Robert McKenzie (Good Time Charlie), Sam Lufkin (Hotel Clerk), Glen Falls.

A veritable smorgasbord of comedy was served up by Paramount in SIX OF A KIND which features not one, but six veteran comedy performers. Ruggles and his wife, Boland, decide to travel to California for their second honeymoon. To defray costs, Boland puts an ad in the paper asking for another couple to join them and share expenses. Much to the honeymooners' dismay, none other than Burns and Allen answer the ad, accompanied by a huge Great Dane. The couples pile their belongings, including the slobbering hound, into the car and speed off for California. Unbeknownst to Ruggles, however, a clerk in the bank where he works has stolen $50,000 and hidden it in one of the suitcases bound for California. The crooked clerk then intends to rob Ruggles out on the open road. Luckily, Allen insists on traveling a different route than planned and the evil clerk is left to wait in vain. Unfortunately, their luck is short-lived for highwaymen accost the travelers, causing the giant attack dog to flee in panic. Once again the travelers escape harm because the robbers overlook the $50,000 and depart. Meanwhile, detectives have discovered the theft and Ruggles becomes their main suspect. The detectives attempt to head off the vacationers and warn sheriff Fields in Nuggetville, Nevada. Determined to capture the scoundrels, Fields and innkeeper Skipworth team up to arrest the travelers. After much craziness Ruggles is cleared of any wrongdoing, leaving the obnoxious Burns and Allen to find another unsuspecting traveling couple to leech onto. Finally alone, Ruggles and Boland look forward to what is left of their second honeymoon. Directed by Leo McCarey, a man who knew how to let the cameras roll and not interfere with great comedians doing their stuff (see the Marx Brothers in DUCK SOUP), SIX OF A KIND offers up a variety of good laughs, but the highlight is definitely W.C. Fields and his billiards routine. Having developed and fine-honed the hilariously complicated act during his years in vaudeville, it became one of Fields' best-loved bits. In fact, Fields' very first movie, POOL SHARKS (1915), was supposed to capture the act on film, but in the end very little of the routine was actually used. Nearly 20 years later the classic act was faithfully recreated in SIX OF A KIND. While telling a stranger how he got the name "Honest John" (he returned a man's lost glass eye]), sheriff Fields attempts to play some pool. After fussing with several distorted pool cues, an elaborate chalking up procedure, and finding just the right spot to set his hat, Fields attempts to break. Unfortunately, while lining up the shot Fields loses control of his pool cue and struggles to grasp it as the chalked end floats away from his fingers as if weightless. After several attempts to recapture the business end of the pool cue, Fields finally succeeds and makes his shot. The cue ball misses the break, speeds to the opposite end of the table, ricochets off the bumper, flies through the air, and makes a beeline for Fields' forehead. The ball smacks him in the head, bounces straight up, and while Fields clutches his head in agony with one hand, he catches the cue ball in the air with the other and places it back on the pool table–all without any evidence of camera trickery. Grimacing in pain, Fields once again attempts a break, this time by employing a fancy trick shot which sees the pool cue held perpendicular to the cue ball. Fields makes the shot, misses the cue ball, and drives the entire pool cue through the table, making a large hole. While struggling to pull the long stick out of the expensive pool table, Fields glances furtively about, making sure that the owner hasn't seen him ruin the table. Finally freeing the cue stick, Fields places a flower basket over the gaping hole and makes a hasty escape. This hysterical scene has to be seen to be believed. Several viewings are required to catch every subtle nuance that Fields employs to make the brief routine such an amazing display of skilled comedic craftsmanship. The attention to little details and bits of business during the routine is pure genius, as is the endlessly interrupted story about the man with the glass eye. It is one of the most brilliant moments in Fields' undeniably brilliant career and moviegoers throughout the world should say a silent prayer of thanks to director Leo McCarey for having the intelligence and foresight to let his performers perform unhindered by a heavy directorial hand.

d, Leo McCarey; w, Walter DeLeon, Harry Ruskin (based on a story by Keene Thompson, Douglas MacLean); ph, Henry Sharp; m, Ralph Rainger; ed, LeRoy Stone; art d, Hans Dreier, Robert Odell.

Comedy   **(PR:A   MPAA:NR)**

SIX PACK**   (1982) 110m Lion Share/FOX c

Kenny Rogers *(Brewster Baker)*, Diane Lane *(Breezy)*, Erin Gray *(Lilah)*, Barry Corbin *(Sheriff)*, Terry Kiser *(Terk)*, Bob Hannah *(Diddler)*, Tom Abernathy *(Louis)*, Robbie Fleming *(Little Harry)*, Anthony Michael Hall *(Doc)*, Robby Still *(Swifty)*, Benji Wilhoite *(Steven)*, Buddy Baker *(Himself)*, Gary McGurrin *(Hank)*, Charles Kahlenberg *(Stan)*, Roy Tatum *(Harley)*, Terry L. Beaver *(Pensky)*, Bill Ash *(Old Man)*, Ernest Dixon *(Clarence)*, Jay McMillian, Tim Bays *(Hippies)*, Jo Ahl *(Deanna)*, Charlie Briggs, Warde Q. Butler, Jr *(Stewards)*, Allison Bigger *(Ludi)*, Tony Maniscalco, Bob Terhune, Ross Guerrero, Jerry Campbell *(Thugs)*, Barney Johnston *(Jake)*, Bill Gribble *(Mechanic)*, Chuck Woolery, Chris Economaki *(TV Commentators)*, Jon Hayden *(Rich Boy)*.

Rogers, the country-western singer and human teddy bear, makes his film debut in this oh-so-cute story about a stock car racer and six orphans. Rogers is a loner who's been away from racing for a few years. He finds six kids trying to strip his car and catches up with the brood, who prove to be no Brady Bunch. They've taken to stealing car parts to make some cash, but Rogers still takes a liking to them. They join forces and Rogers goes on to win the (inevitable) big race. For all its cute contrivances this really isn't a bad film, though it probably belonged on television rather than the big screen. The direction and script know the audience for this film, cueing in on points guaranteed to warm the hearts of Rogers' fans. Of all the kids,

Lane and Hall showed real promise, which they improved upon in their later film work like THE COTTON CLUB (Lane) and SIXTEEN CANDLES (Hall).

p, Michael Trikilis; d, Daniel Petrie; w, Mike Marvin, Alex Matter; ph, Mario Tosi (DeLuxe Color); m, Charles Fox; ed, Rita Roland; prod d, William J. Creber; set d, Bill Durrell.

Drama/Comedy   **Cas.**   **(PR:C   MPAA:PG)**

SIX PACK ANNIE***   (1975) 88m United Producers/AIP c

Lindsay Bloom *(Annie)*, Jana Bellan *(Mary Lou)*, Joe Higgins *(Sheriff Waters)*, Larry Mahan *(Bustis)*, Raymond Danton *(Mr. O'Meyer)*, Richard Kennedy *(Jack Whittlestone)*, Danna Hansen *(Aunt Tess)*, Pedro Gonzales-Gonzales *(Carmello)*, Bruce Boxleitner *(Bobby Joe)*, Sid Melton *(Angelo)*, Louisa Mortiz *(Flora)*, Doddles Weaver *(Hank)*, Stubby Kaye *(Bates)*.

This provocative character study was unfortunately dumped on the Southern drive-in market without seeing a more deserved distribution. Hansen is an old woman who's trying to keep her beloved diner from closing. Daughters Bloom and Bellan lend a needed hand, but Hansen's pride gets in the way of her asking for additional help. The diner is sort of a community gathering place where everyone comes to vent their problems. In an effort to save the diner, Hansen goes to Miami in search of a "sugar daddy." She runs into various types including a lunatic Napoleon and a married Texan, but she never gets the money she needs. In the end, the needed cash is somehow attained and the diner is saved. Though some moments pander to cheap sentiments, this film is for the most part a realistic look at a poor woman's struggle in the rural South. The direction is good, with a fine feeling for the characters and their problems. Hansen's performance is marvelous.

p, John C. Broderick; d, Graydon F. David; w, Norman Winski, David Kidd, Wil David; ph, Daniel Lacambre; m, Raoul Kraushaar; ed, J.H. Arrufat.

Drama   **(PR:O   MPAA:R)**

SIX P.M.**   (1946, USSR) 65m Mosfilm Studios/Artkino bw

Marina Ladynina *(Varya Pankova)*, Eugene Samoilov *(Lt. Kudriashev)*, Ivan Lubeznov *(Lt. Demidov)*, Anastasia Lysak *(Fenia)*, Elena Savitskaya *(Aunt Katia)*.

A Russian musical romance set in World War II and equivalent to its Hollywood counterparts. Ladynina is a Soviet lass who promises to meet her sweetheart Samoilov when the war is over. They arrange to rendezvous on a Moscow bridge at six p.m., hence the title. Both performers have strong voices and do well in their parts. This helps carry the film, as the story line is weak and the direction is often inept. (In Russian; English subtitles.)

d, Ivan Piriev; w, Victor Gusev; ph, Valentin Paulov; m, Tikhon Khrenikov; English subtitles, Charles Clement.

Musical   **(PR:A   MPAA:NR)**

6.5 SPECIAL**   (1958, Brit.) 85m Anglo-Amalgamated c

Lonnie Donegan, Dickie Valentine, Jim Dale, Petula Clark, Russ Hamilton, Joan Regan, The King Brothers, Don Lang, Johnny Dankworth, Cleo Laine, Jackie Dennis, The Kentones, Desmond Lane, John Barry Seven, Mike and Bernie Winters, Victor Soverall, Jimmy Lloyd, Paddy Stone, Leigh Madison, Avril Leslie, Finlay Currie, Diane Todd, Jo Douglas, Pete Murray, Freddie Mills, Diane Todd, Josephine Douglas, Pete Murray.

Okay teeny-bopper film based on a popular BBC television show of the day. Two kids want to make it big in the music business, and they head for London. They manage to get an audition with the "6-5 Special" producer and naturally, they make the grade. This leads to a television debut, with some British pop stars (in those oh-so-innocent pre-Beatle days) playing themselves. Lots of forgettable music and plenty of screaming teenies make this a film definitely rooted in its time. The direction shows an understanding of a specific audience, and the acting is acceptable for the film's intended viewing group. Songs include "King of Dixieland," "Come to My Arms" (sung by Dickie Valentine), "The Gypsy In My Soul" (sung by The Kentones), "Say Goodbye Now" (sung by Victor Soverall), "Ever Since I Met Lucy" (sung by Jimmy Lloyd), "Midgets" (sung by Joan Regan, The King Brothers, Desmond Lane).

p, Herbert Smith; d, Alfred Shaughnessy; w, Norman Hudis; ph, Leo Rogers; ed, Jocelyn Jackson; ch, Paddy Stone.

Musical   **(PR:A   MPAA:NR)**

SIX SHOOTIN' SHERIFF**½   (1938) 59m GN bw

Ken Maynard *(Trigger)*, Marjorie Reynolds *(Molly)*, Lafe McKee *(Zeke)*, Walter Long *(Chuck)*, Bob Terry *(Kid)*, Harry Harvey *(Todd)*, Tom London *(Furman)*, Dick Alexander *(Big Boy)*, Warner Richmond *(Kendall)*, Ben Corbett *(Kid)*, Earl Dwire *(Holman)*, Roger Williams *(Bart)*, Bud Osborne, Ed Piel, Milburn Morante, Carl Mathews, Glen Strange, Herb Holcombe, Tarzan the Horse.

Good Maynard outing features him as a cowboy framed for bank robbery. He's sentenced to work the rock pile but gets out and rights the wrongs he has been handed. Maynard was a little heavier than he usually was for his films, and the extra weight shows up uncomfortably.

p, Max and Arthur Alexander; d, Harry Fraser; w, Weston Edwards [Harry Fraser]; ph, William Hyer; ed, Charles Henkel.

Western **Cas.** **(PR:A MPAA:NR)**

633 SQUADRON**½ (1964) 94m UA c

Cliff Robertson (Wing Comdr. Roy Grant), George Chakiris (Lt. Erik Bergman), Maria Perschy (Hilde Bergman), Harry Andrews (Air Marshal Davis), Donald Houston (Wing Comdr. Tom Barrett), Michael Goodliffe (Squadron Leader Bill Adams), John Meillon (Flight Lt. Gillibrand), John Bonney (F/Lt. Scott), Angus Lennie (F/Lt. Hoppy Hopkinson), Scot Finch (F/Lt. Bissel), Barbara Archer (Barmaid), Julian Sherrier (F/Lt. Singh), Suzan Farmer (Sgt. Mary), John Church (F/Lt. Evans), Sean Kelly (F/Lt. Nigel), Geoffrey Frederick (F/Lt. Frank), Johnny Briggs (F/Lt. Jones), Jeremy Wagg (F/Lt. Reynolds), Edward Brayshaw (F/Lt. Guenier), Arnold Locke (Innkeeper), Peter Kriss (F/Lt. Maner), Drewe Henley (Thor), Richard Shaw (Johanson), Cavan Malone (Ericson), Chris Williams (Goth), Anne Ridley (S.S. Woman).

During WW II American aviator Robertson is given command of a British squadron on an important and dangerous mission into Norway to bomb a German V2 factory. Leaving nothing to chance, the Allies enlist the aid of Chakiris, a brave Norwegian freedom fighter who takes action to ensure that the mission will be a success. While preparations for the raid are being made, a romance develops between Robertson and Perschy, the Norwegian resistance leader's sister. Unfortunately, Chakiris is captured by the Nazis and brutally tortured until he reveals the RAF's plan of attack. Luckily, Robertson and his men are able to circumvent the Germans and during a vicious battle they destroy the factory. While the film is hampered by some frequently inept dialog and an unnecessary romance, the action scenes in 633 SQUADRON are impressively handled and quite stunning. War film aficionados will revel in the wide-screen air battle sequences, but the narrative weaknesses affect the whole film and lessen the impact of what could have been a truly epic war movie.

p, Cecil F. Ford; d, Walter E. Grauman; w, James Clavell, Howard Koch (based on the novel by Frederick E. Smith); ph, Edward Scaife, John Wilcox (DeLuxe Color); m, Ron Goodwin; ed, Bert Bates; prod d, Michael Stringer; spec eff, Tom Howard.

War **(PR:C MPAA:NR)**

6000 ENEMIES*** (1939) 60m MGM bw

Walter Pidgeon (Steve Donegan), Rita Johnson (Anne Barry), Paul Kelly (Dr. Malcolm Scott), Nat Pendleton ("Socks" Martin), Harold Huber (Joe Silenus), Grant Mitchell (Warden Parkhurst), John Arledge (Phil Donegan), J. M. Kerrigan (Dan Barrett), Adrian Morris ("Bull" Snyder), Guinn "Big Boy" Williams (Maxie), Arthur Aylesworth (Dawson), Raymond Hatton ("Wibbie" Yern), Lionel Royce ("Dutch" Myers), Tom Neal (Ransom), Willie Fung (Wang), Helena Phillips Evans ("Peachie"), Esther Dale (Matron), Selmer Jackson (Judge), Ernest Whitman (Willie Johnson), Frank Lackteen (Bolo), Robert Emmett Keane (Sam Todd), Horace MacMahon (Boxcar), Jack Mulhall (O'Toole), Ernie Adams, George Magrill, Drew Demarest (Henchmen).

When Pidgeon, a fighting prosecuting attorney, is framed for a crime, he's tossed into prison and immediately pegged by some of the men he sent there himself. After taking a severe beating in a prison boxing match, he is accepted by the inmates as one of their own and they let him in on their escape plans. Before he makes the break, Pidgeon gets involved with Johnson, a prisoner in the woman's ward who's also in on a frame. After successfully escaping, Pidgeon proves that he's innocent and sends Huber to the cooler for racketeering and murder. The script is tight, telling only what needs to be said and directed with a certain intensity that has a real feel for the surroundings. Pidgeon is fine as the lead, and he is given good support. Pidgeon and Johnson met under dangerous circumstances again that year in NICK CARTER, MASTER DETECTIVE.

p, Lucien Hubbard; d, George B. Seitz; w, Bertram Millhauser (based on a story by Wilmon Menard and Leo L. STanley); ph, John Seitz; ed, Conrad A. Nervig; art d, Cedric Gibbons, Daniel B. Cathcart; set d, Edwin B. Willis.

Prison Drama **(PR:C MPAA:NR)**

SIX WEEKS*½ (1982) 107M UNIV c

Dudley Moore (Patrick Dalton), Mary Tyler Moore (Charlotte Dreyfus), Katherine Healy (Nicole Dreyfus), Shannon Wilcox (Peg Dalton), Bill Calvert (Jeff Dalton), Joe Regalbuto (Bob Crowther), John Harkins (Arnold Stillman), Michael Ensign (Choreographer), Ann Ditchburn (Asstistant Choreographer), Chea Collette (Ballet Instructor), Clement St. George (TV Interviewer), Joan Yale Edmundson (Interviewer), Gary Nulsen (Doctor), Martin Casella (Volunteer/Campaign Office), Darwyn Carson (Girl in Office), Fausto Barajas (Man in Office), Darrell Larson (Art Teacher), Frank Adamo, Frank Patton (Subway Passengers), Barbara Bradish (Cashier), Lloyd Wilson (Foreman), Laurel Page (Interviewer), Jennifer Adams, Joseph Clark (Dancers of Ballet West).

"The Moore the Merrier" would seem to be the theme of this film that stars a pair of unrelated Moores in a story that can only be described as a "weeper." SIX WEEKS is sentimentally cloying, inadvertently funny (when it didn't want to be) and lasted about half the time of the title at the box office, thereby becoming one of the larger gobblers of 1982. The script had been tossed around since 1975 and many other actors were mentioned for the leads, all of whom should be happy they decided against it or were rejected for it. Considered to play the Dudley Moore role were Paul Newman, Burt Reynolds, George Segal, Nick Nolte and even Sylvester Stallone. The Mary Tyler Moore part was variously penciled in for Jacqueline Bisset, Faye Dunaway, and Audrey Hepburn. Even the young girl's part, played by Healy, had been offered to Quinn Cummings and Tatum O'Neal, according to Hollywood tongue-waggers. Finally, the two Moores were hired to be directed by one-time actor Bill (who had impressed with his direction of MY BODYGUARD.) This picture must have looked great on paper; a pair of familiar stars, a story that was a teenage version of LOVE STORY, two high-powered producers (Guber and Peters) and a director who was coming off a hit. Unfortunately, movies are not made on paper; they are made on 35 millimeter film. It begins with a long-winded speech by Dudley Moore as to why he is running for office in California (when he should be running for a seat in Parliament). Great lengths are gone to in order to explain Moore's accent (he came to the U.S. at the age of 20 and has long since become a citizen). That out of the way, the story begins. Healy, the daughter of wealthy businessperson M.T. Moore, is dying of leukemia. She's had everything a child could ever want, except a father. Her precociousness borders on outright obnoxiousness and never allows an audience to like her. We may feel sympathy for her plight but her attitude is such that we are dared to care. Dudley Moore meets Healy and she takes an immediate liking to him. She wants to work for his campaign and makes no bones about it. He would rather not have this brat doing anything for him but once he finds out about her disease, his heart cockles are warmed and he will do anything to make her last days brighter. Due to Healy, Moore and Moore get closer and closer (which is not too thrilling for Dudley Moore's wife, Wilcox, or his son, Calvert.) When Wilcox finds out about Moore and Moore, she fears the worst, a love affair. Her husband assures her that it won't happen but, needless to say, it does. Dudley goes off with M.T. Moore and Healy to a fantasy vacation of all the best things one can do in New York City. The three of them set Gotham agog and Moore (Dudley), knowing that Healy is an aspiring ballet dancer, manages to get her cast in a large production of "The Nutcracker." In the final sequence, the two Moores take Healy for a ride on the Lexington Avenue line of the New York subway system and she dies of her disease. This emotionally unsatisfying trifle was weak on several levels and will only satisfy the least difficult audiences. There's nothing real about the film and even the death of the child is given a gloss that makes it seem paltry. Mary Tyler Moore was appearing in her second movie in which she lost a child, something that happened to her in real life. Dudley Moore was on a downward ride in which he selected several poor scripts in which to star. His character in the film was poorly drawn, a fuzzy liberal who attracts the sophisticated set who might invite a token black to a cocktail party but would never dream of appearing in public with one. In a small role as the TV interviewer, note Clement St. George, speaking in an English accent. St. George's real name is Clement Von Frankenstein and he is a descendant of the family that inspired the Mary Shelley novel.

p, Peter Guber, Jon Peters; d, Tony Bill; w, David Seltzer (based on a novel by Fred Mustard Stewart); ph, Michael D. Margulies (Metrocolor); m, Dudley Moore; ed, Stu Linder; prod d, Sandy Veneziano; art d, Hilyard Brown; set d, Jerry Wunderlich, Ira Bates; ch, Ann Ditchburn.

Drama **Cas.** **(PR:C MPAA:PG)**

SIXTEEN (SEE: LIKE A CROW ON A JUNE BUG, 1972)

SIXTEEN FATHOMS DEEP** (1934) 57m MON/FD bw

Sally O'Neil (Rosie), Creighton Chaney [Lon Chaney, Jr.] (Joe), George Regas (Savanis), Maurice Black (Nick), Lloyd Ingraham (Old Athos), George Nash (Young Athos), Robert Kortman (Cimos), Si Jenks (Sculpin), Russell Simpson (Crockett), Jack Kennedy (Mike), Constantine Romanoff, Richard Alexander, Philip Kiefer, Jean Gehring, Raul Figarola.

It's danger and intrigue in the world of deep-sea sponge fishing with this unusual idea for an otherwise routine programmer. Chaney needs some cash to buy a boat, so he borrows money from a rival fisherman. Regas lends the money, plotting all the while to sabotage Chaney's operation and make it impossible for him to marry his girl, O'Neil. With O'Neil's help, the villain is defeated and ends up killing himself. The film boasts some interesting underwater footage as well as some nice location work on Catalina Island. The direction is okay for the fare, but some unnecessary comedy mars the story. The heavy is not as well developed as he could have been. Remade in 1948.

p, Paul Malvern; d, Armand Schaefer; w, Norman Houston (adaptation by B. B. Barringer based on the story "Sixteen Fathoms Under" by Eustace L. Adams); ph, Archie Stout.

Adventure **(PR:A MPAA:NR)**

SIXTEEN FATHOMS DEEP   (1948) 83m MON c

Lon Chaney, Jr *(Dimitri)*, Arthur Lake *(Pete)*, Lloyd Bridges *(Douglas)*, Eric Feldary *(Alex)*, Tanis Chandler *(Simi)*, John Qualen *(Athos)*, Ian MacDonald *(Nick)*, Dickie Moore *(George)*, Harry Cheshire *(Miki)*, John Bleifer *(Capt. Briaeos)*, Grant Means *(Joe)*, John Gonatos *(Johnny)*, Allen Mathews *(Bus Driver)*.

This re-make of the 1934 feature was about as entertaining as its predecessor. The story tells of some sponge hunters who run into trouble with Chaney, the heavy who wants to get the boat away from the protagonists. They have to fend off sharks at a slowpace that doesn't build excitement until the film's nearly over. Bridges, featured as an ex-Navy diver, ironically went on to star as an underwater diver for TV's "Sea Hunt." Lake took leave from his BLONDIE films to play a comic tourist. SIXTEEN FATHOMS DEEP is probably most notable as being the first film released in the Ansco color process.

p, James S. Burkett, Irving Allen; d, Allen; w, Max Trell, Forrest Judd (based on the story "Sixteen Fathoms Under" by Eustace L. Adams); ph, Jack Greenhalgh (Ansco); ed, Charles Craft; md, Lud Gluskin.

Adventure   (PR:A   MPAA:NR)

SIXTH AND MAIN½   (1977) 103m National Cinema c

Leslie Nielsen *(John Doe)*, Roddy McDowall *(Skateboard)*, Beverly Garland *(Monica)*, Leo Penn *(Doc)*, Joe Maross *(Peanut)*, Bard Stevens *(Carlsburg)*, Sharon Tomas *(Tina)*, Gammy Burdett.

Garland is a writer who decides to hang out in the Los Angeles slum areas so she can absorb the atmosphere for a book project. She meets Nielsen, a denizen of the area who lives in a beat-up trailer. Garland discovers that the man is also a writer who possesses a number of well-written manuscripts. She takes the manuscripts to Maross, a literary critic, and tries to promote Nielsen as a great new talent. It turns out that Nielsen was once a great screenwriter who became tired of what success had brought him. He had faked his own death to escape and when Garland's plans remind him of the old days Nielsen quietly disappears. The story is forced at times but overall, this is a good independent feature with nice looking production values. The direction hides the script weaknesses, overcoming some of the cliches and stereotypes. The strongest attraction is the wonderful cast of street characters. Burdett is a junkie prostitute about to have a child. She's supported by McDowall, a disabled character who refuses to judge her. Burdett's performance is particularly accomplished, taking her character through several emotional turns with some nice feeling.

p,d&w, Christopher Cain; ph, Hilyard John Brown (CFI Color); m, Bob Summers; ed, Ken Johnson; cos, Gwen Capetanos; m/l, Penny Askey; stunts, Sandy Gimpel.

Drama   (PR:C   MPAA:NR)

SIXTH MAN, THE   (SEE: OUTSIDER, THE, 1961)

SIXTH OF JUNE, THE   (SEE: D-DAY, THE SIXTH OF JUNE, 1956)

SIXTY GLORIOUS YEARS*   (1938, Brit.) 90m Imperator/RKO c
                                   (AKA: QUEEN OF DESTIN Y)

Anna Neagle *(Queen Victoria)*, Anton Walbrook *(Prince Albert)*, C. Aubrey Smith *(Duke of Wellington)*, Walter Rilla *(Prince Ernst)*, Charles Carson *(Sir Robert Peel)*, Felix Aylmer *(Lord Palmerston)*, Lewis Casson *(Lord John Russell)*, Pamela Standish *(Princess Royal)*, Gordon McLeod *(John Brown)*, Henry Hallatt *(Joseph Chamberlain)*, Wyndham Goldie *(A.J. Balfour)*, Malcolm Keen *(W.E. Gladstone)*, Frederick Leister *(H.H. Asquith)*, Derrick de Marney *(Benjamin Disraeli)*, Joyce Bland *(Florence Nightingale)*, Frank Cellier *(Lord Derby)*, Harvey Braban *(Lord Salisbury)*, Aubrey Dexter *(Prince of Wales)*, Stuart Robertson *(Mr. Anson)*, Olaf Olsen *(Prince Fredrick)*, Marie Wright *(Maggie)*, Laidman Browne *(Gen. Gordon)*, Harvey Braban, Jack Watling.

An unnecessary, but worthwhile, sequel to the epic screen biography VICTORIA THE GREAT (1937). Managing to return most of the original cast members to the screen for the sequel, SIXTY GLORIOUS YEARS opens as Neagle announces her engagement to Walbrook. Unfortunately the Parliament doesn't trust Walbrook (he's a foreigner) and neither do the masses. Walbrook's frustration by his lack of popularity and power strains the marriage and Neagle struggles to devise something that her husband can become involved in and make his own. She hits on the idea of the Crystal Palace Exhibition and Walbrook devotes himself to the massive event. Meanwhile, Neagle is visited by a bevy of dignitaries including Disraeli (de Marney), Florence Nightingale (Bland), Gladstone (Keen), and various lords, princes, and other officials who help shape policy. Such historical events as the Crimean War and the Charge of the Light Brigade are briefly illustrated, but it is the epic romance between Neagle and Walbrook that gives the narrative its drive. The film follows Victoria's reign to the very end, which climaxes with the Diamond Jubilee and Neagle's demise. As was the case in VICTORIA THE GREAT, Wilcox's production values are superlative, with the sets and costumes accurate reproductions of the actual items which are housed at the British Museum. The American public was

so interested in both the Queen Victoria films that RKO and Wilcox formed a contract that ensured distribution of British films in the U.S. and an exchange of American and British talent for various productions. This led to husband and wife Wilcox and Neagle's next project, NURSE EDITH CAVELL (1939), which was produced in Hollywood.

p&d, Herbert Wilcox; w, Charles de Grandcourt, Miles Malleson, Robert Vansittart; ph, F.A. Young (Technicolor).

Historical Drama   (PR:A   MPAA:NR)

SKAMMEN   (SEE: SHAME, 1968, Swed.)

SKATEBOARD*   (1978) 97m Blum Group/UNIV c

Allen Garfield [Goorwitz] *(Manny Bloom)*, Kathleen Lloyd *(Millicent Broderick)*, Leif Garrett *(Brad Harris)*, Richard Van Der Wyk *(Jason Maddox)*, Tony Alva *(Tony Bluetile)*, Steve Monahan *(Peter Steffens)*, David Hyde *(Dennis)*, Ellen Oneal *(Jenny Bradshaw)*, Pam Kenneally *(Randi)*, Anthony Carbone *(Sol)*, Sylvester Words *(Sol's Henchman)*, Gordon Jump *(Harris)*, Pat Hitchcock *(Mrs. Harris)*, Orson Bean *(Himself)*, Joe Bratcher *(Vito)*, Harvey Levine *(U.E.O. Clerk)*, Thelma Pelish *(Woman in Motel)*, John Fox *(Charlie)*, Damon Douglas *(Scott)*, Marilyn Roberts *(Waitress)*, David Carlile *(Palmdale Announcer)*, Chuck Niles *(Race Announcer)*, Raymond Kark *(Gas Station Attendant)*, Owen Bush *(Sign Painter)*, Eugene Elman *(Maitre d')*, Carol McGinnis *(Script Girl)*, Hubie Kerns, Reid Rondell, Tanya Russell, Randy Clark, Denise Dubarry, Jean Markell, Tom Padaca, Phil Settle, Sondra Theodore, Marylou York, Sabina Weber, Valerie Clark.

Poor Garfield is a down-on-his-luck agent who's got a bookie hot on his tail. He needs some big money, and fast. As luck would have it, Garfield runs into a group of skateboarding kids who would just love to help him out. They form a team and Garrett, a minor pop idol who went nowhere fast, enters a downhill race for a $20,000 prize. Just why someone would offer that much for a skateboard race is more than a little farfetched, as is the gangster who tries to get Garrett to throw the big event. Must have been a slow day at the track. This independent quickie was hastily thrown together to cash in on a skateboarding craze that was sweeping the country. Direction is pretty inept and the acting is what you'd expect for trash like this. The camera work is flawed through several boom-microphone-bordered shots, if any transducer trivia collectors are interested.

p, Harry N. Blum, Richard A. Wolf; d, George Gage; w, Wolf, Gage (based on a story by Wolf); ph, Ross Kelsay (Technicolor); m, Mark Snow; ed, Robert Angus; cos, Elizabeth Gage; m/l, Snow, Richard Sarstedt.

Children's   (PR:C   MPAA:PG)

SKATETOWN, U.S.A.*   (1979) 98m Rastar/COL c

Scott Baio *(Richie)*, Flip Wilson *(Harvey Ross)*, Ron Palillo *(Frankey)*, Ruth Buzzi *(Elvira)*, Dave Mason *(Himself)*, Greg Bradford *(Stan)*, Maureen McCormick *(Susan)*, Patrick Swayze *(Ace)*, Billy Barty *(Jimmy)*, Kelly Lang *(Allison)*, David Landsberg *(Irwin)*, Lenny Bari *(Alphonse)*, Murray Langston *(The Drunk)*, Bill Kirkchenbauer *(Skatetown Doctor)*, Denny Johnston *(Wizard)*, Vic Dunlop *(Ripple)*, Joe E. Ross *(Rent-a-Cop)*, Sydney Lassick *(Murray)*, Sandra Gould, Gary Mule Deer, Rick Edwards, Leonard Barr, Jonna Veitch, Deborah Chenoweth, Dorothy Stratten, Brigid Devlin, Kristi Kane, Connie Downing, Lou Mulford, Steve Bourne, Stanley Mieloch, Randall Brady, Mario Lieu, Richard Wygant, Ronald Kleyweg, Charles Pitt, Kenneth Wright, Garry Kluger, Sue Weicberg, Kurt Paul, Judy Landers, Gary Hudson, Harlene Winsten, Johnny Pool, Bob Minor, Maurice Cooke, April Allen, Gail Collier.

What happens to stars of bad TV shows like "The Brady Bunch," "Welcome Back Kotter," and "Happy Days"? They end up in bad movies like SKATETOWN, U.S.A. This nonsense had the dubious honor of being the first film to cash in on the minor roller-disco fad of the late 1970s and featured such great has-beens as Wilson, Buzzi, Palillo, and a host of talentless actors. The simplistic story has good-guy Bradford taking on bad-guy Swayze in a roller skating contest. You'll know Swayze's the heavy because he wears black leather. This dumb excuse for a feature film is heavily padded out with endless skating, dance, and comedy numbers as well as some really bad rock 'n' roll. Watch for an appearance by Dorothy Stratten, the Playboy Playmate whose tragic murder was the basis for STAR '80 (1983).

p, William A. Levey, Lorin Dreyfuss; d, Levey; w, Nick Castle (based on a story by Levey, Dreyfuss, Castle); ph, Donald M. Morgan (Metrocolor); m, Miles Goodman, Dave Mason; ed, Gene Fowler, Jr.; art d, Larry Wiemer; set d, George Gaines; cos, Betsy Heimann, Bob Labansat; ch, Bob Banas; stunts, Hank Hooker.

Comedy   (PR:A   MPAA:PG)

SKATING-RINK AND THE VIOLIN, THE
                   (SEE: VIOLIN AND ROLLER, 1962, USSR)

SKAZA O KONKE-GORBUNKE
(SEE: LITTLE HUMPBACKED HORSE, THE, 1962, USSR)

SKELETON ON HORSEBACK½** (1940, Czech.) 80m Moldavia/Carl Laemmle-Michael Min dlin bw (BILA NEMOC; AKA: THE WHITE SICKNESS; SKELETON ON HORSEBACK)

Hugo Haas (*Dr. Galen*), Bedrich Karen (*Prof. Sigelius*), Vaclav Vydra (*Baron Krog*), Ladislav Bohac (*Krog, Jr.*), Karla Olicova (*Marshal's Daughter*), Zdanek Stepanek (*The Marshal*), Jaroslav Prucha (*Dr. Martin*), Frantisek Smolik (*The Father*), Helena Frydlova (*The Mother*), Eva Svobodova (*The Daughter*), Vitezslav Bocek (*The Son*), Jaroslav Vojta (*A Patient*), Vladimir Smeral (*1st Assistant*), Miroslav Svoboda (*2nd Assistant*), Karel Dostal (*Propaganda Minister*), Otta Rubik (*Adjutant*), Rudolif Deyl (*1st Kommissar*), Karel Jicinsky (*2nd Kommissar*).

This allegory on fascism features Haas as a doctor who finds a cure for a leprous disease that represents this political theory. Both young and old are subject to the new fascist government and Haas will provide his cure only if the ruling dictator will promise peace. However the country goes off to war and is ultimately defeated. Haas is killed by a mob of angry citizens and the dictator succumbs to the disease. The doctor's assistant then saves humankind from the ravages of the ailment. The story packs a good deal of dramatic power. The more intimate moments are well handled, with skill and care. The crowd sequences are less accomplished, though, with some poor photography. SKELETON ON HORSEBACK was reportedly the last Czechoslovakian film made before the Nazi invasion. Its anti-fascist stance caused the banning of the film in much of Europe; it reached American screens only after being smuggled out of Czechoslovakia by producer-director-screenwriter Haas and being seen by American cinema mogul Carl Laemmle in Paris. Laemmle, founder of Universal Studios–which he lost in 1935 due to financial difficulties during the Great Depression–initially distributed the film through an independent company he set up himself. He died in 1939, before the film's U. S. release. Haas came to the U. S., where he wrote, produced, directed, and starred in a succession of brooding, musty melodramas dealing with a crude old man's–Haas'-relationship with a buxom young blonde woman, played by Cleo Moore. Photographer Heller also fled his native land just after the Nazi invasion; he went to England, where he worked on such successes as THE LADYKILLERS (1955) and THE IPCRESS FILE (1965). Prolific Czech writer Capek–best known for his futuristic play "R.U.R.", in which the word robot was first coined–strongly objected to the film's ending, which deviated from that of his play. In the play, there's a Mexican standoff; humankind destroys itself (as it had done in "R.U.R.", a play in which robots are the only characters). Capek died in 1938; this was a filmed adaptation of his last play. Famed author Fannie Hurst was sufficiently impressed by the picture to volunteer to edit it and write the subtitles. (In Czechoslavakian; English subtitles.)

p,d&w, Hugo Haas (based on the play "The White Disease" by Karel Capek); ph, Otto Heller; ed, Fannie Hurst; English subtitles, Hurst.

Drama   (PR:C MPAA:NR)

SKI BATTALION½** (1938, USSR) 73m Lenfilm/Amkino bw

Otto Zhakov (*Toivo Antikanien*), I. Chuvelev (*Artu*), I. Selianin (*Yalmar*), Aleinikov (*Elno*), P. Kirilov (*Riutta*), N. Kriuchkov (*Yukka*), F. Volkov (*Yuri*), A. Kartashova (*Old Woman*).

In 1921 the Soviet Bolshevists must defend their border from the Finnish army, among many other armies. The regiment marches and does its fighting while on skis, hence the title. This well-directed film has all the classic elements of the U.S.S.R.'s party-controlled propaganda filmmaking, complete with a nationalistic theme and the evilest of enemies. Unlike most films of this nature, though, the direction manages to overcome the dogma and present a reasonably entertaining package. Like many Soviet films intended for export, this one is best viewed in the historical context of the time of its release. Finland's Mannerheim line was being reinforced by German "advisors" with weapons that gave the Finns the capacity to raze Leningrad by shelling. In 1939, Soviet troops crossed the border and engaged the Finns in a bitter, costly war. This film was intended as a warning, just as ALEXANDER NEVSKY (1939) was intended to be a warning to the Germans. Oddly, the Soviets were no stars at ski touring at the time. The Finns were the accomplished skiers, as they demonstrated by soundly whipping the Red Army horse cavalry. That may be why this picture denoted the bulk of the Bolshevik troops as being expatriate Finns converted to the Leninist philosophy. The camerawork is creative, nicely capturing the battle and ski sequences with real vigor. The acting, though obviously constrained by the humorless material, is pretty good for what this is. (In Russian; English subtitles.)

d, R. and Y. Muzikant; w, G. Fish, R. and Y. Muzikant; ph, V. Velichko.

War Drama   (PR:C MPAA:NR)

SKI BUM, THE zero (1971) 94m Joseph E. Levine/AE c

Zalman King (*Johnny*), Charlotte Rampling (*Samantha*), Joseph Mell (*Burt Stone*), Lori Shelle (*Liza Stone*), Dimitra Arless (*Liz Stone*), Anna Karen (*Golda Lanning*), Tedd King (*Maxwell Enderby*), Dwight Marfield (*Dr. Walter Graham*), Freddie James (*Brad Stone*), Barbara Grover, Pierre

Jalbert, David Chow, Bruce Clark, Marc Siegler.

This is an utterly inept variation on a fairly good novel by noted writer Gary. The producers were trying to cash in on the youth market, which was quite lucrative after the success of EASY RIDER. Joseph E. Levine hired some youthful UCLA film school graduates to work on the project and the results are totally amateurish. King is a ski bum fooling around with married lady Rampling. She gets him a job working at a lodge owned by a stereotyped middle-class family who alienate him no end. The film drones on and on, looking for meaning and finding nothing. The entire structure and plot of Gary's novel was changed for the film, obviously a mistake. Reportedly Peter O'Toole was offered the lead but he nixed it after the wretched script was revealed.

p, David R. Dawdy; d, Bruce Clark; w, Clark, Marc Siegler (suggested by the novel *The Ski Bum* by Romain Gary); ph, Vilmos Zsigmond (Widescreen, Technicolor); m, Joseph Byrd; ed, Misha Norland, Clark.

Drama   (PR:O MPAA:R)

SKI FEVER* (1969, U.S./Aust./Czech.) 98m GAU-Parnass Ceskoslovensky/AA c (LIEBE SSPIELE IM SCHNEE)

Martin Milner (*Brian Davis*), Claudia Martin (*Susan Halsey*), Vivi Bach (*Karen Sloan*), Dietmar Schonherr (*Toni Brandt*), Toni Sailor (*Franz Gruber*), Dorith Dom (*Dominique Leseur*), Kurt Grosskurth (*Max*), Curt Bock (*MacDoodle*), Karla Chadimova, Lenka Fiserova, Jana Novakova, Rajmund Gabriel, Vladimir Pospisil, Milos Zavadil.

At an Austrian ski resort, American music student Milner works as a ski instructor. There's a stipulation in his contract that he must entertain female guests in the evening. Nice work if you can get it. This inevitably leads to a series of sophomoric hijinks, including wiring a pinball machine to one of the beds the instructors use to seduce the girls. They all bet to see when the machine will go tilt. Martin (daughter of Dean) comes to the lodge and is put off by the seduction games and Milner as well, though he's not a part of it. Of course, he ends up winning her heart after the obligatory ski-jumping contest. This film tries to be a sort of beach picture against a snowy setting and succeeds on that level; it's just as bad as the majority of beach pictures. The dialog is incredibly bad and of course the acting styles match. The ski jumping is obviously faked and dotted with stock footage in what ends up forgettable nonsense. Writer/director Siodmak, who wrote DONOVAN'S BRAIN (1953) can do much better.

p, Wolfgang Schmidt, Mark Cooper; d, Curt Siodmak; w, Siodmak, Robert L. Joseph (based on a story by Frank Agrama, Edward Zatlyn); ph, Jan Stallich (Eastmancolor); m, Hemric, Styner; ed, Antonin Zelenka; art d, Karel Cerny; m/l, "Ski Fever," Guy Hemric, Jerry Styner (sung by Styner).

Comedy/Drama   (PR:C MPAA:M)

SKI PARTY* (1965) 90m AIP c

Frankie Avalon (*Todd Armstrong/Jane*), Dwayne Hickman (*Craig Gamble/Nora*), Deborah Walley (*Linda Hughes*), Yvonne Craig (*Barbara Norris*), Robert Q. Lewis (*Donald Pevney*), Bobbi Shaw (*Nita*), Aron Kincaid (*Freddie Carter*), Steve Rogers (*Gene*), Mike Nader (*Bobby*), Jo Collins (*Jo*), Mickey Dora (*Mickey*), John Boyer, Ronnie Dayton (*Ski Boys*), Bill Sampson (*Arthur*), Patti-Chandler (*Janet*), Salli Sachse (*Indian*), Sigi Engl (*Ski Instructor*), Mikki Jamison, Mary Hughes, Luree Holmes (*Ski Girls*), The Hondells, James Brown and the Famous Flames, Lesley Gore (*Themselves*), Annette Funicello.

Take away the sand and replace it with snow, it's still the same old formula for Avalon. He and Hickman (far from his heyday as television's hipster "Dobie Gillis") are a couple of college guys who can't figure out why their girls (Walley and Craig) are attracted to the stodgy Kincaid. Everyone heads off to a ski lodge where Avalon and Hickman take up cross dressing to find out what Kincaid's appeal is. Of course Kincaid can't figure out the ruse and flirts away. But this is no SOME LIKE IT HOT. The humor is weak, but kind of fun. The direction is quickly paced, never making more out of the material than need be. Even Avalon's old beach bunny Funicello pops in for a few moments. Performances by Brown and Gore are the best things going in this film. Songs include "Lots, Lots More" (Ritchie Adams, Larry Kusik), "Paintin' the Town" (Bob Gaudio), "We'll Never Change Them" (Guy Hemric, Jerry Styner, sung by Deborah Walley, Styner), "Ski Party" (Gary Usher, Roger Christian), "I Got You (I Feel Good)" (performed by James Brown and the Famous Flames), and other songs by Howard Liebling, Ted Wright, Marvin Hamlisch.

p, Gene Corman; d, Alan Rafkin; w, Robert Kaufman; ph, Arthur E. Arling (Panavision, PatheColor); m, Gary Usher; ed, Morton Tubor; art d, Howard Campbell; set d, George R. Nelson; cos, Richard Bruno; makeup, Ted Coodley.

Musical Comedy   (PR:A MPAA:NR)

SKI PATROL* (1940) 64m UNIV bw

Philip Dorn (*Viktor Ryder*), Luli Deste (*Julia Engle*), Stanley Fields (*Birger Simberg*), Samuel S. Hinds (*Per Vallgren*), Edward Norris (*Paave Luuki*), John Qualen (*Gustaf Nerkuu*), Hardie Albright (*Tyko Galien*), John Arledge

(Dick Reynolds), John Ellis *(Knut Vallgren)*, Henry Brandon *(Jan Sikorsky)*, Kathryn Adams *(Lissa Ryder)*, Reed Hadley *(Ivan Dubroski)*.

At the 1936 Winter Olympics a Russian, a Finn and an American win the Gold, Silver and Bronze medals in a skiing competition. The officials proudly proclaim that war is a thing of the past but the film's audience knows better. From there the story goes to the Russian-Finnish border where troops on skis try to protect a hill from being overrun by the enemy. The film is simplistic and full of standard war cliches intercut with plenty of stock footage. The dialog is humdrum with an irrelevant romance thrown in to please more viewers. The film was made to capitalize on the Russo-Finnish war, but the war was over by the time the movie was released.

p, Warren Douglas; d, Lew Landers; w, Paul Huston; ph, Milton Krasner; ed, Ed Curtis.

War   **(PR:A   MPAA:NR)**

SKI RAIDERS, THE   (SEE: SNOW JOB, 1972)

SKI TROOP ATTACK**   (1960) 63m Filmgroup bw

Michael Forest *(Lt. Factor)*, Frank Wolff *(Sgt. Potter)*, Wally Campo *(Ed)*, Richard Sinatra *(Herman)*, Sheila Carol *(Ilse)*.

A group of American soldiers goes behind Nazi lines to blow up a German railway bridge. The familiar cliche army officers, hard-bitten sergeant and idealistic young lieutenant, travel on skis. They are offered shelter by German fraulein Carol who then tries to poison them. An early Corman feature, this is a crude but effective piece with some good action sequences. The film was shot in Deadwood, South Dakota which also served as the location for BEAST FROM THE HAUNTED CAVE. The ski teams from local high schools were used as extras.

p&d, Roger Corman; w, Charles Griffith; ph, Andy Costikyan; m, Fred Katz; ed, Anthony Carras.

War Drama   **(PR:C   MPAA:NR)**

SKID KIDS**   (1953, Brit.) 65m Bushey/ABF-Children's Film
                                                              Foundation bw

Barry McGregor *(Swankey Clarke)*, Anthony Lang *(Bobby Reynolds)*, Peter Neil *(Police Constable)*, Tom Walls *(Mr. Clarke)*, Angela Monk *(Sylvia Clarke)*, A.E. Matthews *(Man in Taxi)*, Frank Hawkins, Tom Macauley.

A gang of young bicycle enthusiasts are accused of stealing bikes from a factory and promptly barred from the track where they have been training for the big race. The youths capture the real hoods responsible for the thefts, and as a reward have their track repaved.

p, Gilbert Church; d, Don Chaffey; w, Jack Howells; ph, S.D. Onions.

Drama   **(PR:AAA   MPAA:NR)**

SKIDOO zero   (1968) 97m PAR c

Jackie Gleason *(Tony Banks)*, Carol Channing *(Flo Banks)*, Frankie Avalon *(Angie)*, Fred Clark *(Tower Guard)*, Michael Constantine *(Leech)*, Frank Gorshin *(Man)*, John Phillip Law *(Stash)*, Peter Lawford *(Senator)*, Burgess Meredith *(Warden)*, George Raft *(Capt. Garbaldo)*, Cesar Romero *(Hechy)*, Mickey Rooney *("Blue Chips" Packard)*, Groucho Marx *("God")*, Austin Pendleton *(Fred the Professor)*, Alexandra Hay *(Darlene Banks)*, Luna *("God's" Mistress)*, Arnold Stang *(Harry)*, Doro Merande *(Mayor)*, Phil Arnold *(Mayor's Husband)*, Slim Pickens, Robert Donner *(Switchboard Operators)*, Richard Kiel *(Beany)*, Tom Law *(Geronimo)*, Jaik Rosenstein *("Eggs" Benedict)*, Stacy King *(The Amazon)*, Renny Roker, Roman Gabriel *(Prison Guards)*, Harry Nilsson *(Tower Guard)*, William Cannon *(Convict)*, Stone Country *(Themselves)*, Orange County Ramblers *(Green Bay Packers)*.

It had been 15 years since Preminger's last comedy, THE MOON IS BLUE, and he seemed to have forgotten what was funny and what was in bad taste by the time he made this star-studded stinker. Preminger, who died in the spring of 1986, was one of the most inconsistent directors who ever lifted a rangefinder to his eye. When he was good, he was very, very good, and when he was bad, which was more often, he was .... This film is an example of the latter. He'd been looking for a writer for another project when Cannon's script came across his desk as a writing sample and he decided to shoot it. Great sums of money were lavished on this dull attempt at humor that failed on almost every level. Gleason is a one-time racketeer who now lives happily with his wife, Channing, in San Francisco where they own and operate a legitimate business, a car wash. Their daughter, Hay (who was billed as being "introduced" but who had actually been in GUESS WHO'S COMING TO DINNER), takes up with hippie Law, which does not delight the essentially conservative Gleason. Now Romero and his son, Avalon, arrive with an order from Gleason's former boss, syndicate chief Marx (who was appearing in his final film) and the request of their boss is that Gleason come out of his docile retirement and do one last hit, rub out Rooney, who is in prison and awaiting his day before a Senate investigations group probing organized crime. Gleason wants no part of it but when his old pal, Stang, is shot, Gleason realizes that Marx means business. It's arranged that Gleason be sent to the

same jail where Rooney resides in baronial splendor (he keeps track of the stock market via a ticker tape in his cell) and Gleason is to find the right moment, kill Rooney and then make a escape. With Gleason in jail (the exteriors were shot at Alcatraz in San Francisco Bay, the interiors at the abandoned Lincoln Heights jail in downtown Los Angeles), Channing allows Law and his long-haired pals to establish a flower-child commune on the property. Pendleton is a draft dodging professor in jail and he is also an LSD user. He has writing paper that has been surreptitiously dipped into the drug and when cell mate Gleason gets some of the drug into his bloodstream by handling the paper, he goes on an acid trip that alters his feelings about crime and he decides against killing Rooney. (In order to lend reality to this, Preminger admitted that he took LSD after first discussing the idea with a prominent New York physician.) Gleason and Pendleton arrange to pour LSD into the inmates' soup, then flee the prison in large trash containers which have been attached to plastic food bags filled with helium. They float out of the jail and descend on the yacht owned by Marx, where he lives with his young mistress, Luna. Hay is a hostage on Marx's yacht (captained by a dapper Raft) and it looks bad for all until Channing, Law and a crew of hippies attack. Marx sees that he is outnumbered so he dons mod clothes and leaves on a raft with Pendleton as Gleason is embraced by Channing, Hay and Law, his new son-in-law. It's an attempt at a Damon Runyon story with sympathetic criminals and humorous situations but there's barely anything to laugh at. Several writers were brought in to try to fix this while it was shooting, including Elliott Baker and Stanley Ralph Ross. By the time Ross was called in, the picture was nearly half done and the scenes Ross suggested be cut had already been shot and roughly edited. Preminger never stinted on wages and paid Ross, Baker and several other writers many thousands in a vain attempt to add jokes but he steadfastly refused to alter the structure of the story and that was its downfall. Talents such as Meredith (the warden), Clark (appearing in his last film as a prison guard), Gorshin and Constantine (inmates), are totally wasted. Only Nilsson's music and some sharp one-liners not found in the original screenplay merit any attention whatsoever. Preminger tyrannized his actors by yelling at them and in one prison scene, forced them to do 25 "takes" at a lunch table. In each "take," Constantine had to eat a meatball. After 4 takes (and this was right after lunch), he had to fake it or become ill. One of Preminger's assistant directors on this was Erich von Stroheim, Jr.

p&d, Otto Preminger; w, Doran William Cannon [uncredited, Elliott Baker, Stanley Ralph Ross] (based on a story by Erik Kirkland); ph, Leon Shamroy (Panavision, Technicolor); m, Harry Nilsson; ed, George Rohrs; md, George Tipton; art d, Robert E. Smith; set d, Fred Price; cos, Rudi Gernreich; spec eff, Charles Spurderson; ch, Tom Hansen; m/l, Nilsson; makeup, Web Overlander.

Comedy   **(PR:C   MPAA:M)**

SKIES ABOVE   (SEE: SKY ABOVE HEAVEN, 1964, Fr./Ital.)

SKIMPY IN THE NAVY*   (1949, Brit.) 84m Advance/Adelphi bw

Hal Monty *(Skimpy Carter)*, Max Bygraves *(Tommy Anderson)*, Avril Angers *(Sheila)*, Les Ritchie *(Lickett)*, Chris Sheen *(Joe)*, Vic Ford *(Spud)*, Terence Downing, Derrick Penley, Bart Allison, Ivan Craig, Billy Rhodes, Chick Lane, Arthur Mullard, Patricia Hayes.

Silly farce has Monty, Bygraves, and Ritchie quitting the army in order to join the navy and help a young woman search for buried treasure. Mainly an excuse for an overabundance of tasteless slapstick and some easily forgettable tunes.

p, David Dent; d, Stafford Dickens; w, Aileen Burke, Leone Stuart, Hal Monty; ph, Gerry Moss.

Comedy   **(PR:A   MPAA:NR)**

SKIN DEEP*   (1929) 64m WB bw

Monte Blue *(Joe Daley)*, Davey Lee *(Son of District Attorney)*, Betty Compson *(Sadie Rogers)*, Alice Day *(Elsa Langdon)*, John Davidson *(Blackie Culver)*, John Bowers *(District Attorney Carlson)*, Georgie Stone *(Dippy)*, Tully Marshall *(Dr. Bruce Langdon)*, Robert Perry *(Tim)*.

This low-budget melodrama twists and turns more than a roller coaster. Blue is a gangster framed by his cheating wife Compson. Next she takes up with a rival mobster, then gets her husband to escape in order to kill the district attorney. To further complicate matters Blue gets in a car crash that gives him a new face and even an educated accent. The direction is as much of a joke as the script, paying little attention to believability or continuity. A remake of the 1922 Associated First National film featuring Milton Sills and Florence Vidor, the 1929 SKIN DEEP was released in both silent and sound versions (titles for the silent by De Leon Anthony). Some of the plot elements can be seen again in the Humphrey Bogart thriller DARK PASSAGE (1947).

d, Ray Enright; w, Gordon Rigby (based on the story "Lucky Damage" by Mark Edmund Jones); ph, Barney McGill; ed, George Marks; m/l, "I Came to You," Sidney Mitchell, Archie Gottler, Con Conrad.

Crime/Drama   **(PR:C   MPAA:NR)**

SKIN DEEP***½ (1978, New Zealand) 103m Phase Three Films c

Jim Macfarlane (Boxing Manager), Ken Blackburn (Bob Warner), Alan Jervis (Vic Shaw), Grant Tilly (Phil Barrett), Bill Johnson (Mike Campbell), Arthur Wright (Les Simpson), Kevin J. Wilson (Policeman), Glenis Leverstam (Alice Barrett), Deryn Cooper (Sandra Ray), Wendy Macfarlane (Motel Manageress), Bob Harvey (Stephen Douglas).

A small town in New Zealand wants to attract a bigger share of the country's tourist trade. A local gym is turned into a massage parlor and soon the local gentlemen all go there for some sexual adventures. This thin plot is handled with sensitivity and care, never cheapening its characters. Cooper is the woman who runs the business, giving a fine performance as a woman disillusioned by her trade and the people she must deal with. This was shot on a relatively low budget and was one of the first films created by New Zealand's fledgling film industry.

p, John Maynard; d, Geoff Steven; w, Steven, Piers Davies, Roger Horrocks; ph, Leon Narby (Gevacolor).

Drama (PR:O MPAA:NR)

SKIN GAME, THE** (1931, Brit.) 85m BIP bw

Phyllis Konstam (Chloe Hornblower), Edmund Gwenn (Mr. Hornblower), John Longden (Charles Hornblower), Frank Lawton (Rolf Hornblower), C.V. France (Mr. Hillcrest), Jill Esmond (Jill Hillcrest), Edward Chapman (Dawker), Helen Haye (Mrs. Hillcrest), Ronald Frankau (Auctioneer), Herbert Ross (Mr. Jackman), Dora Gregory (Mrs. Jackman), R.E. Jeffrey (1st Stranger), George Bancroft (2nd Stranger).

This early Hitchcock talkie shows none of the mastery that would subsequently make the director an internationally recognized genius. The story involves two families, one old-fashioned and the other more modern in their ways. As they feud over land rights, the patriarch of the aristocrats threatens to blackmail the young wife of one of his foes. In the end she attempts suicide. Based on a popular play, the film is little more than a lesser programmer told in the typical stodgy British style. The acting isn't bad but even so there's little to hold interest. In his interviews with Francois Truffaut Hitchcock himself dismissed the film as a worthless entry in his body of work.

p, John Maxwell; d, Alfred Hitchcock; w, Hitchcock, Alma Reville (based on the play "The Skin Game" by John Galsworthy); ph, John J. Cox; ed, Rene Harrison A. Gobett.

Drama (PR:C MPAA:NR)

SKIN GAME, THE** (1965, Brit.) 71m Searchlight/William Mishkin bw (GB: KIL 1; AKA: SKIN GAMES)

Ronald Howard (Inspector Gordon), Jess Conrad (Ted-o), Melody O'Brian (Marlene), Peter Gray (Hon John Edgar), David Graham (Alvero Belda), Peter Hager (Sgt. Phelan), Lawrence Taylor (Sammy), Anne Martin (Mrs. Markham), Jane Wilde (Laura), John Scott (Supt. Train), Headley Colson (Sgt. Brown), Peter Evans (Mr. Lethbridge), Michael Lee (Q Car Driver), Ivor Phillips (Ian Lethbridge), Pauline Wingfield (Lucy).

Graham, Taylor and Gray run a car theft operation from a junkyard where they pass bum checks to people selling their autos. When young Phillips is killed Graham gets the wrecked car and takes the plates, which read KIL 1. He takes a same model auto and paints it to look exactly like the wrecked car, then puts it up for sale. Conrad is a gangster mechanic who gets caught with Graham's mistress. Beaten up, he retaliates by killing Graham, then takes the car and heads off with the girl friend. But the unusual license plate is spotted by Phillips' father, who believes this to be his son's car. He reports this to Howard, a Scotland Yard detective who's been investigating the bad check scam. Conrad tries to escape a police roadblock but he and his girl are killed when the car goes over a cliff.

p, Stanley A. Long, Arnold Louis Miller; d, Miller; w, Bob Kesten; ph, Long; m, De Wolfe; ed, John Dunsford.

Drama/Crime (PR:O MPAA:NR)

SKIN GAME***½ (1971) 102m Cherokee/WB c

James Garner (Quincy Drew), Lou Gossett (Jason O'Rourke), Susan Clark (Ginger), Brenda Sykes (Naomi), Edward Asner (Plunkett), Andrew Duggan (Calloway), Henry Jones (Sam), Neva Patterson (Mrs. Claggart), Parley Baer (Mr. Claggart), George Tyne (Bonner), Royal Dano (John Brown), Pat O'Malley (William), Joel Fluellen (Abram), Napoleon Whiting (Ned), Juanita Moore (Viney), Dort Clark (Pennypacker), Robert Foulk (Sheriff), Athena Lourde (Margaret), George Wallace (Auctioneer), James McCallion (Stanfil), Tracy Bogart (Lizabeth), Mary Rings (Emaline), Don Haggerty (Speaker), Jason Wingreen (2nd Speaker), Sam Chew (Courtney), Al Checco (Room Clerk), Jim Boles (Auction Clerk), Paris Nathan Earl, Edward Lee McClain, Eugene Smith, Bill Terrell (The Songhais), Forrest Lewis.

Shortly before the Civil War white man Garner and black man Gossett team up to form a business. Garner "sells" Gossett at an auction to the highest bidder, then rescues him so they can move on and hold another sale elsewhere. They make good money until Dano appears and "frees" Gossett.

Eventually the two con men reunite and start their skin game again until they meet someone they've pulled this con on before. Clark, a handy pickpocket who had previously lifted Garner's wallet, comes to their rescue. This is a funny, entertaining comedy that handles its touchy subject with great skill and sensitivity. What makes it work is the fine chemistry between the two leads. Garner is wonderfully roguish in his best role in quite some time while Gossett handles the various turns his character has to take with ease. The direction is amiable, with a light-hearted sense of humor. Gossett later appeared in a lesser made-for-TV version called Sidekicks, reprising his role with less success.

p, Harry Keller; d, Paul Bogart; w, [David Giller], Pierre Marton [Peter Stone] (based on a story by Richard Alan Simmons); ph, Fred Koenekamp (Panavision, Technicolor); m, David Shire; ed, Walter Thompson; art d, Herman Blumenthal; set d, James Payne; makeup, Gordon Bau.

Comedy Cas. (PR:C MPAA:GP)

SKINNER STEPS OUT*½ (1929) 70m UNIV bw

Glenn Tryon (William Henry Skinner), Merna Kennedy ("Honey" Skinner), E. J. Ratcliffe (Jackson), Burr McIntosh (McLaughlin), Lloyd Whitlock (Parking), William Welsh (Crosby), Katherine Kerrigan (Mrs. Crosby), Frederick Lee (Gates), Jack Lipson (Neighbor), Edna Marion (Neighbor's Wife).

Below-average comedy about a nagging wife who bullies her milquetoast husband into impressing a big businessman. His boisterous behavior nearly blows everything for his company but all is fixed by the end. There were several "Skinner" films made during the silent era, all following the same plot lines, and this sound version is no better than its predecessors.

d, William James Craft; w, Albert De Mond, Matt Taylor (based on a story by Henry Irving Dodge); ph, R. Allyn Jones; m, David Broekman; ed, Harry Lieb.

Comedy (PR:A MPAA:NR)

SKIP TRACER, THE*** (1979, Can.) 93m Highlights c

David Petersen.

A modest but well crafted story about a man who repossesses items for stores when buyers default in their payments. Some people are out to kill him so he's got to escape. The direction paces the story slowly, building suspense and a moody air with a sense of style. Petersen delivers a good performance.

p, Laara Dalen; d, Zale Dalen; ph, Ron Oreiux.

Drama (PR:C MPAA:NR)

SKIPALONG ROSENBLOOM*** (1951) 72m UA bw (AKA: THE SQUARE SHOOTER)

"Slapsie" Maxie Rosenbloom (Skipalong Rosenbloom), Max Baer (Butcher Baer), Jackie Coogan (Buck James), Fuzzy Knight (Sneaky Pete), Hillary Brooke (Square Deal Sal), Jacqueline Fontaine (Caroline), Raymond Hatton, Ray Walker, Sam Lee, Al Shaw, Joseph Greene, Dewey Robinson, Whitey Haupt, Carl Mathews, Artie Ortego.

Humorous parody begins with a typical postwar family arguing over what to watch on the tube. When the kid turns his cap gun on his parents everyone agrees to watch TV cowboy "Skipalong Rosenbloom." From there the film turns into a cute version of a cowboy show complete with commercials. Rosenbloom and Baer, both ex-fighters, do a variety of the "save the ranch" theme seen in countless Westerns. This is mild fun. Direction is well paced and the two fighters make a good cowboy team.

p, Wally Kline; d, Sam Newfield; w, Dean Reisner, Eddie Forman; ph, Ernie Miller; ed, Victor Lewis, J. R. Whittredge; m/l, Jack Kenney.

Western/Satire (PR:A MPAA:NR)

SKIPPER SURPRISED HIS WIFE, THE** (1950) 85m MGM bw

Robert Walker (Cmdr. William Lattimer), Joan Leslie (Daphne Lattimer), Edward Arnold (Adm. Homer Thorndyke), Spring Byington (Agnes Thorndyke), Leon Ames (Dr. Philip Abbott), Jan Sterling (Rita Rossini), Anthony Ross (Joe Rossini), Paul Harvey (Brendon Boyd), Kathryn Card (Thelma Boyd), Tommy Myers (Tommy Lattimer), Rudy Lee (Davey Lattimer), Finnegan Weatherwax, Muscles, the Dog.

Navy Cmdr. Walker tries to run his household in military fashion after wife Leslie breaks her leg. He goes door to door asking housewives how they do things then tries to apply their advice to his home. Of course their advice doesn't work that well in his house, and Leslie is grateful when she can return to her job and Walker goes back to sea. This unoriginal, one-joke comedy has some good moments, but not many. The direction is fair but the cast was clearly more talented than the material required.

p, William H. Wright; d, Elliott Nugent; w, Dorothy Kingsley (based on an article by W. J. Lederer); ph, Harold Lipstein; m, Bronislau Kaper; ed, Irvine Warburton; art d, Cedric Gibbons, Eddie Imazu.

Comedy   (PR:A MPAA:NR)

SKIPPY***½   (1931) 85m PAR bw

Jackie Cooper (*Skippy Skinner*), Robert Coogan (*Sooky Wayne*), Mitzie Green (*Eloise*), Jackie Searl (*Sidney*), Willard Robertson (*Dr. Herbert Skinner*), Enid Bennett (*Mrs. Ellen Skinner*), David Haines (*Harley Nubbins*), Helen Jerome Eddy (*Mrs. Wayne*), Jack Clifford (*Dogcatcher Nubbins*), Guy Oliver (*Dad Burkey*).

A charming children's picture that doesn't neglect adults and was good enough to secure Oscar nominations as Best Picture, Best Director, Best Story and for Cooper as Best Actor. Taurog's direction won the statuette. 1931 saw hundreds of movies released and this was but one of more than 60 from Paramount alone. It grossed a fortune and every penny was deserved. Based on a comic strip by Percy Crosby (who also co-adapted the story), it's a simple, heartwarming and adorable tale of boys and girls and their dogs. Cooper is the son of physician Robertson and his wife Bennett. His best friend is Coogan (younger brother of Jackie Coogan) and when Coogan's dog is captured by the local dogcatcher, Clifford, the boys have to raise money to buy a license for the animal. In order to get the necessary $3, they try everything. One of the plans is staging a show and they collect a dollar from Green when they promise her the lead in their musical. They attempt to sell tickets, lemonade, etc. Cooper has an unbreakable bank for his spare coins and they try to smash it by putting it under a truck's wheels but that doesn't work. Coogan's dog dies and Cooper trades his new bike to Green for her dog, which he intends to give to Coogan. But Coogan has already gotten a new pet. Coogan lives in a slum area where the other children are forbidden to trespass by their parents, who fear that the neighborhood is rife with disease. Skinner is in charge of the city's health and the slums are about to be razed when Cooper convinces his dad that the place can be saved if they eradicate the health problems. There are many wonderful childlike moments in the picture and watching Cooper cry is worth the price of admission. There were few child actors who could convince as well as he could. The sequel was SOOKY, which was made after Cooper did DONOVAN'S KID and THE CHAMP a few months later. He eventually became a successful TV and film director and occasionally makes acting appearances as in SUPERMAN (all of them) where he plays the Daily Planet's editor, Perry White. Jackie Searl is the villain, a mean little kid whom W.C. Fields would probably have throttled. He made 30 pictures from the ages of 9 through 28 after starting in radio in 1923 before he was 4. Green also began performing at 3, moving into movies at 9 and retiring at 14. Years later, she came back to play in a couple of movies while she was married to director Joe Pevney.

p, Louis D. Lighton; d, Norman Taurog; w, Joseph L. Mankiewicz, Norman McLeod, Don Marquis, Percy Crosby, Sam Mintz (based on the comic strip by Crosby); ph, Karl Struss.

Children's Drama/Comedy   (PR:AAA MPAA:NR)

SKIRTS AHOY!**   (1952) 109m MGM c

Esther Williams (*Whitney Young*), Joan Evans (*Mary Kate Yarbrough*), Vivian Blaine (*Una Yancy*), Barry Sullivan (*Lt. Comdr. Paul Elcott*), Keefe Brasselle (*Dick Hallson*), Billy Eckstine (*Himself*), Dean Miller (*Archie O'Conovan*), Margalo Gillmore (*Lt. Comdr. Stauton*), The De Marco Sisters (*The Williams Sisters*), Jeff Donnell (*Lt. Giff*), Thurston Hall (*Thatcher Kinston*), Russell "Bubba" Tongay (*Little Boy*), Kathy Tongay (*Little Girl*), Roy Roberts (*Capt. Graymont*), Emmett Lynn (*Plumber*), Hayden Rorke (*Doctor*), Debbie Reynolds, Bobby Van (*Themselves*), Paul Harvey (*Old Naval Officer*), Ruth Lee (*Mrs. Yarbrough*), Whit Bissell (*Mr. Yarbrough*), Rudy Lee (*Randy*), Madge Blake (*Mrs. Vance*), Mae Clarke (*Miss LaValle*), Byron Foulger (*Tearoom Manager*), Juanita Moore, Millie Bruce, Suzette Harbin (*Black Drill Team*), Henny Backus (*Nurse*), Robert Board (*Young Sailor*), Mary Foran (*Fat Girl*), William Haade (*Bosun's Mate*), Marimba Merrymakers (*Themselves*).

Three WAVES played by Williams, Evans, and Blaine set their respective amorous eyes on Sullivan, Brasselle, and Miller. Before they can get their men, the female trio has to go through a variety of song and dance numbers, as well as Williams' token water ballet. Female sailors chasing males make an interesting twist of the more common reverse story line, but the picture is still predictable formula fare. The cast gives it occasional spurts of energy and during a show-within-the-show, Debbie Reynolds and Bobby Van sing "Oh By Jingo" (Lew Brown, Albert Von Tilzer). Original but inconsequential musical numbers include "Hold Me Close to You" (Harry Warren, Ralph Blane, sung by Billy Eckstine), "What Makes a WAVE?" (Warren, Blane, sung by Williams and the DeMarco Sisters), "What Good Is a Gal Without a Guy?" (Warren, Blane, sung by Williams, Evans, Blaine), "Skirts Ahoy!," "Glad to Have You Aboard," "The Navy Waltz," "I Get a Funny Feeling," "We Will Fight," "Hilda Matilda" (Warren, Blane).

p, Joseph Pasternak; d, Sidney Lanfield; w, Isobel Lennart; ph, William Mellor (Technicolor); ed, Cotton Warburton; md, Georgie Stoll; art d, Cedric Gibbons, Daniel B. Cathcart; ch, Nick Castle.

Musical   (PR:A MPAA:NR)

SKULL, THE**½   (1965, Brit.) 83m Amicus/PAR c

Peter Cushing (*Prof. Christopher Maitland*), Patrick Wymark (*Marco*), Christopher Lee (*Sir Matthew Phillips*), Jill Bennett (*Jane Maitland*), Nigel Green (*Inspector Wilson*), Michael Gough (*Auctioneer*), George Coulouris (*Dr. Londe*), Patrick Magee (*Police Doctor*), Peter Woodthorpe (*Travers*), April Olrich (*French Girl*), Maurice Good (*Man in Cloak*), Frank Forsyth (*Judge*), Anna Palk (*Maid*), Paul Stockman, Geoffrey Cheshire (*Guards*), George Hilsdon (*Policeman*), Jack Silk (*Driver*).

This effective shocker features Cushing as a man drawn to the occult who buys a skull from Wymark, a strange man who deals in such unusual items. According to Wymark the skull was stolen from the grave of the Marquis de Sade. Cushing is warned by his friend Lee not to touch it and Lee should know. He had once owned it, but it had been stolen from him. Cushing ends up obsessed by the skull, which hovers about, takes control of him, and makes him commit murder. The film is surprisingly good for a low-budget horror flick, boasting some intriguing photography and special effects. The final sequence is quite cinematic, told without the benefit of dialog. The script has its problems, but the good cast and overall eeriness achieved overcome them.

p, Max J. Rosenberg, Milton Subotsky; d, Freddie Francis; w, Subotsky (based on "The Skull of the Marquis de Sade" by Robert Bloch); ph, John Wilcox (Technicolor); m, Elisabeth Lutyens; ed, Oswald Hafenrichter; md, Philip Martell; art d, Bill Constable; set d, Scott Slimon; cos, Jackie Cummins; spec eff, Ted Samuels; makeup, Jill Carpenter.

Horror   (PR:O MPAA:NR)

SKULL AND CROWN*   (1938) 58m Reliable bw

Regis Toomey (*Franklin*), Molly O'Day (*Ann*), Jack Mulhall (*Ed*), Jack Mower (*Zorro*), James Murray (*Brent*), Lois January (*Barbara*), Tom London (*Jennings*), John Elliott (*Norton*), Robert Walker (*Saunders*), Milburn Morante, Rin-Tin-Tin Jr (*Rin the Dog*).

So often in the movies, the child of a famous actor is never as good as the parent. Such is the case here as Rin-Tin-Tin, Jr. shows that the rule of thumb applies to animal stars as well. He's helping Toomey break up a group of smugglers led by Mower. The dialog is laughably awful and the whole film plays like an unintentional comedy. Though sound was sophisticated by 1938, this film woefully sticks to cinematic techniques of the silent era, adding to the laughter.

p, Bernard B. Ray; d, Elmer Clifton; w, Bennett Cohen, Carl Krusada (based on a story by James Oliver Curwood); ph, Pliny Goodfriend; ed, Fred Bain.

Adventure   (PR:AAA MPAA:NR)

SKULLDUGGERY**   (1970) 105m UNIV c

Burt Reynolds (*Douglas Temple*), Susan Clark (*Dr. Sybil Greame*), Roger C. Carmel (*Otto Kreps*), Paul Hubschmid [Christian] (*Vancruysen*), Chips Rafferty (*Father "Pop" Dillingham*), Alexander Knox (*Buffington*), Pat Suzuki (*Topazia*), Edward Fox (*Bruce Spofford*), Wilfrid Hyde-White (*Eaton*), William Marshall (*Attorney General*), Rhys Williams (*Judge Draper*), Mort Marshall (*Dr. Figgins*), Michael St. Clair (*Tee Hee Lawrence*), Booker Bradshaw (*Smoot*), John Kimberley (*Epstein*), James Henry Eldridge (*District Officer*), Totty Ames (*Motel Manager*), James Bacon (*Commentator*), Gilbert Senior (*Kauni*), Clarence Harris (*Siria*), Burnal "Custus" Smith (*Chief*), John Woodcock (*Spigget*), Newton D. Arnold (*Inspector Mimms*), Wendell Baggett (*Rev. Holzapple*), Michael Preece (*Naylor*), Charles Washburn (*Papuan*), Cliff Bell, Jr (*Worker*), Alex Gradussov (*Russian delegate*), Jim Alexander (*Reporter*), Saul David (*Berle Tanen*), Bernard Pike (*Associate Judge*), Eddie Fuchs (*Israeli delegate*), Students of University of Djakarta (*The Tropis*).

This early Reynolds outing is a pretty good camp comedy though that certainly wasn't the aim of the producers. In a plot right out of Johnny Weissmuller's Jungle Jim series Reynolds is an adventurer in New Guinea accompanied by archeologist Clark. They accidentally stumble on a tribe of missing link-type humanoids played by a bunch of Indonesian college kids and headed by Suzuki in long hair and a beard. Hubschmid, an evil Dutch scientist, wants to breed these creatures and sell them as slaves. Reynolds tries to put a stop to such evil and they all wind up in court pushing their different theories about exactly what the creatures are. The film tries hard to come off as social commentary but it's all too silly to be taken on that level. Reynolds is pretty good, giving a comic performance that communicates his feeling about the material nicely but only reinforces the story's lack of credibility. Who deserves the final credit or blame for the film is hard to say. One week into production director Gordon Douglas was fired and replaced by Richard Wilson. The script was based on a novel by the French writer Vercors, who was furious with what had been done to his work and had his name removed from the picture.

p, Saul David; d, Gordon Douglas, Richard Wilson; w, Nelson Gidding (based on *Les Animaux Denatures [You Shall Know Them]* by Vercors [Jean (Marcel) Brewer]) ph, Ruben Moreno (Panavision, Technicolor); m, Oliver Nelson; ed, John Woodcock; prod d, Hilyard M. Brown; set d, George Milo; cos, Edith Head; spec eff, Albert Whitlock; makeup, Bud Westmore, Jack Young.

Adventure   Cas.   (PR:C MPAA:M-PG)

SKUPLIJACI PERJA (SEE: I EVEN MET HAPPY GYPSIES, 1968, Yugo.)

SKY ABOVE HEAVEN**½ (1964, Fr./Ital.) 107m GAU/Galatea bw, (LE CIEL SUR LA TETE; STADE ZERO; IL CIELO SULLA TESTA; AKA: SKIES ABOVE; SKY BEYOND HEAVEN)

Andre Smagghe, Jacques Monod, Marcel Bozzufi, Yves Brainville, Guy Trejean, Henri Piegay, Yvonne Monlaur, Bernard Fresson, Beatrice Cenci, Jean Daste.

When a mysterious radioactive satellite appears over the U.S., the U.S. and U.S.S.R. governments take action. At first there is a lot of suspicion and errors on both sides that nearly cause WW III but eventually the two superpowers work together to stop the satellite, which then disappears as mysteriously as it arrived. The story is often engrossing, with good direction that achieves a sense of drama and urgency. However, rather than being an anti-military or pacifist film this glorifies the military and all its hardware. It was made with the assistance of the French navy and the carrier "Clemenceau" served as the main set.

p, Irenee Leriche; d, Yves Ciampi; w, Ciampi, Alain Satou, Jean p, Irenee Leriche; d, Yves Ciampi; w, Ciampi, Alain Satou, Jean Chapot; ph, Edmond Sechan, Guy Tabary.

War/Fantasy   (PR:C MPAA:NR)

SKY BANDITS, THE** (1940) 62m Criterion/MON bw

James Newill, Louise Stanley, Dave O'Brien, William Pawley, Ted Adams, Bob Terry, Dwight Frye, Joseph Stefani, Dewey Robinson, Jack Clifford, Kenne Duncan.

That singing hero of the Royal Canadian Mounted Police Newill is off to the Yukon, backed as always by his gal pal Stanley. He's searching for some hijacked airplanes that carried gold shipments as well as a death ray some gangsters have convinced an innocent inventor is part of a national defense program. It's not very exciting and the last of the "Renfrew of the Mounties" series.

p, Phil Goldstone; d, Ralph Staub; w, Edward Halperin (based on the story "Renfrew Rides the Sky" by Laurie York Erskine); ph, Eddie Linden.

Adventure   (PR:A MPAA:NR)

SKY BEYOND HEAVEN (SEE: SKY ABOVE HEAVEN, 1964, Fr./Ital.)

SKY BIKE, THE** (1967, Brit.) 62m Eveline/Children's Film Foundation c

Spencer Shires (Tom Smith), Liam Redmond (Mr. Lovejoy), Ian Ellis (Porker), William Lucas (Mr. Smith), Ellen McIntosh (Mrs. Smith), Della Rands (Daphne), John Howard (Jack), Bill Shine (Wingco), David Lodge (Guard), Harry Locke (Owner).

Imaginative children's adventure film about a slightly crazed inventor who creates a flying bicycle and then must depend on his young friend to fly it and win the reward for the first flying vehicle solely powered by man. Situations are not always believable, but this can easily be passed over given the high energy of this production.

p, Harold Orton; d&w, Charles Frend; ph, (Eastmancolor).

Drama/Adventure   (PR:AAA MPAA:NR)

SKY BRIDE** (1932) 78m PAR bw

Richard Arlen (Speed Condon), Jack Oakie (Alec Dugan), Virginia Bruce (Ruth Dunning), Robert Coogan (Willie), Charles Starrett (Jim Carmichael), Louise Closser Hale (Mrs. Smith), Tom Douglas (Eddie), Harold Goodwin (Bill Adams).

When his buddy is killed in a crash fly boy Arlen gives up piloting. He takes up a trade as an airplane mechanic but of course returns to the air when he's the only one who can rescue a young boy who sneaked aboard an airplane to try out a homemade parachute. Arlen renews his courage and wins Bruce in the process. Oakie has some funny comic moments that are about the best this routine programmer has to offer.

d, Stephen Roberts; w, Joseph L. Mankiewicz, Agnes Brand Leahy, Grover Jones (based on a story by Waldemar Young); ph, David Abel, Charles Marshall.

Drama   (PR:A MPAA:NR)

SKY CALLS, THE**½ (1959, USSR) 77m Dovzhenko Studio bw (NIEBO ZOWIET; AKA: THE HEAVENS CALL)

Ivan Perevertsev, Alexander Shvorin, Konstantin Bartashevich, Taisa Litvinenko, G. Tonunts, V. Cheriyak, V. Dobrovolski, A. Popova, L. Borisenko, S. Filimonov.

Two rockets manned by cosmonauts blast off to the moon and Mars. On their way the ships stop off at a space station which serves as an outer-space greenhouse and scientific research and living area. This film was the first major Soviet space movie since 1935, coming on the heels of the Sputniks. It was notable for its terrific special effects, which were later pirated for the American film BATTLE BEYOND THE SUN (1963).

d, Aleksander Kozyr, Mikhail Karyukov; w, A. Sazonov, Yevgeny Pomeshchikov; ph, Nikolai Kulchitsky; spec eff, F. Syemyannikov, N. Ilushin.

Science Fiction   (PR:A MPAA:NR)

SKY COMMANDO*½ (1953) 69m COL bw

Dan Duryea (Col. Ed Wyatt), Frances Gifford (Jo McWethy), Touch [Mike] Connors (Lt. Hobson Lee), Michael Fox (Maj. Scott), William R. Klein (Lt. John Willard), Freeman Morse (Danny Nelson), Dick Paxton (Capt. Frank Willard), Selmer Jackson (Gen. Carson), Dick Lerner (Jorgy), Morris Ankrum (Gen. Combs), Paul McGuire (Maj. Daly).

Weak, conventional story about some fighter pilots and the tribulations they go through during the WW II. Duryea is a squadron leader who's disliked by his men but later proves himself flying a dangerous mission in Rumania. The stereotyped characters merely go through the motions in this hackneyed piece heavily padded with stock footage. Direction is fair.

p, Sam Katzman; d, Fred F. Sears; w, Samuel Newman (based on a story by William Sackheim, Arthur Orloff, Newman); ph, Lester H. White; m, Ross Di Maggio; ed, Edwin Bryant; spec eff, Jack Erickson.

War Drama   (PR:A MPAA:NR)

SKY DEVILS** (1932) 90m UA bw

Spencer Tracy (Wilkie), William [Stage] Boyd (Sgt. Hogan), George Cooper (Mitchell), Ann Dvorak (Mary), Billy Bevan (The Colonel), Yola D'Avril (Fifi), Forrester Harvey (The Innkeeper), William B. Davidson (The Captain), Jerry Miley (The Lieutenant).

Silly comedy features an early Tracy as an ex-lifeguard who can't swim. He and friend Cooper try to desert the army after being drafted during WW I, but inadvertently end up in the war zone. Boyd is their tough-as-nails sergeant who tries to make their lives miserable. When the two go A.W.O.L. to win Dvorak's affections, they somehow end up destroying an enemy ammunitions site while fighting over the lady. They return as heroes but cause a row in their own troops when demonstrating how they surprised the Germans. The episodic structure works well for what this is and Tracy delivers a fairly good performance. A few of the production talents went on to much better things than this. Some of the airplane footage was leftover takes from HELL'S ANGELS, another Hughes produced film.

p, Howard Hughes; d, Edward Sutherland; w, Sutherland, Joseph Moncure March, Robert Benchley, James Starr, Carroll Graham, Garrett Graham (based on a story by March, Sutherland); ph, Gaetano Gaudio; m, Alfred Newman; md, Newman; ch, Busby Berkeley.

War/Comedy   (PR:A MPAA:NR)

SKY DRAGON**½ (1949) 64m MON bw

Roland Winters (Charlie Chan), Keye Luke (Lee Chan), Mantan Moreland (Birmingham Brown, Chan's Chauffeur), Tim Ryan (Lt. Ruark), Milburn Stone (Tim Norton), Noel Neill (Jane Marshall), Elena Verdugo (Marie Burke), Iris Adrian (Wanda LaFern), Lyle Talbot (Andy Barrett), Paul Maxey (John Anderson), John Eldredge (William French), Eddie Parks (Mr. Tibbetts), Lyle Latell (Ed Davidson), Gaylord [Steve] Pendleton (Ben Edwards), Emmett Vogan (Doctor), Edna Holland (Old Maid), Joe Whitehead (Doorman), Lee Phelps (Plainclothesman), Frank Cady (Clerk), Charlie Jordan (Assistant Stage Manager), Louise Franklin (Lena), Suzette Harbin (Strange Dark Girl), George Eldredge (Stacy), Bob Curtis (Watkins), Joe Whitehead.

The passengers and crew on a flight to San Francisco are drugged and a man guarding $250,000 is murdered. Winters and number one son Luke investigate in this fairly entertaining entry in Monogram's Charlie Chan series. The supporting cast is good and Winters gives an engaging performance. The script and direction are typical good genre material. Winters replaced Sidney Toler (who took over after the original Chan, played by Warner Oland) as the famous Chinese detective. He starred in six Charlie Chan movies, after which the series disappeared. (See CHARLIE CHAN series, Index.)

p, James S. Burkett; d, Lesley Selander; w, Oliver Drake, Clint Johnston (based on a story by Johnston); ph, William Sickner; ed, Roy Livingston; md, Edward Kay; art d, David Milton; set d, Ray Boltz; makeup, Webb Overlander.

Mystery   (PR:A MPAA:NR)

SKY FULL OF MOON½   (1952) 73m MGM bw

Carleton Carpenter (*Harley Williams*), Jan Sterling (*Dixie Delmar*), Keenan Wynn (*Al*), Robert Burton (*Customer*), Elaine Stewart (*Change Girl*), Emmett Lynn (*Otis*), Douglas Dumbrille (*Rodeo Official*), Sheb Wooley, Jonathan Cott (*Balladeers*).

Fun-filled little comedy has innocent cowboy Carpenter taking part in a Las Vegas rodeo. While there he meets Sterling, a change girl for casino slot machines. She takes a liking to him and a romance starts to blossom. When Carpenter wins some big cash, the two head off, but Sterling comes to realize that her cowboy is just a naive youth. She sends him back to the rodeo and she returns to her life in the casino. The direction gives this film real charm. Carpenter has a nice naive quality to his performance and Sterling is a good support.

p, Sidney Franklin, Jr.; d&w, Norman Foster; ph, Ray June; m, Paul Sawtell; ed, Frederick Y. Smith; art d, Cedric Gibbons, Leonid Vasian; set d, Edwin B. Willis, Ralph Hurst; m/1, Charles Wolcott, Harry Hamilton, Paul Campbell.

Comedy   (PR:A   MPAA:NR)

SKY GIANT***   (1938) 81m RKO bw

Richard Dix (*W. R. "Stag" Cahill*), Chester Morris (*Ken Stockton*), Joan Fontaine (*Meg*), Harry Carey (*Col. Stockton*), Paul Guilfoyle (*Fergie*), Robert Strange (*Weldon*), Max Hoffman, Jr (*Brown*), Vicki Lester (*Edna*), William Corson (*Claridge*), James Bush (*Thompson*), Edward Marr (*Austin*), Harry Campbell (*Goodwin*), Harry Hayden (*Justice of the Peace*), Donald Kerr, Gaylord [Steve] Pendleton, Frances Gifford, Bernice Pilot.

Robust, entertaining programmer features Dix, Morris, and Fontaine crash landing an airplane in the frozen Arctic wastelands. To complicate matters, both men are in love with the girl. The direction is fresh and straightforward and Dix delivers his machoness with good style. The photography features some terrific aerial footage as well. Carey tends to overact a bit as the leader of an army flying school, but otherwise this is a first class B film.

p, Robert Sisk; d, Lew Landers; w, Lionel Houser (based on the novel *Ground Crew* by Houser); ph, Nicholas Musuraca; ed, Harry Marker; spec eff, Vernon Walker.

Adventure/Romance   (PR:A   MPAA:NR)

SKY HAWK**½   (1929) 67m FOX bw

Helen Chandler (*Joan Allan*), John Garrick (*Jack Bardell*), Gilbert Emery (*Maj. Nelson*), Lennox Pawle (*Lord Bardell*), Lumsden Hare (*Judge Allan*), Billy Bevan (*Tom Berry, Mechanic*), Daphne Pollard (*Minnie, Bar Patron*), Joyce Compton (*Peggy*), Percy Challenger (*Butler*).

In London, Garrick is a young rich man who's injured when the plane he was flying has crashed. He had been on a mission, but was returning for a quick goodbye to his girl, Chandler, when the accident happened and now his character comes under question. Garrick is paralyzed from the waist down, but manages to recover and flies another mission when a German Zeppelin attacks London. The main feature of this programmer is the final sequences that featured the aerial battle over London. The fight between the plane and Zeppelin was created with miniatures that were quite accomplished for their time. Bevan nearly steals the picture with his comic relief character of an airline mechanic. Direction is good, with a nice feel for the material.

d, John Blystone; w, Llewellyn Hughes, Campbell Gullan (based on a magazine story by Hughes); ph, Conrad Wells; ed, Ralph Dietrich, m/l, "Song of Courage," Edward Lynn, Charles Wakefield Cadman.

Adventure   (PR:A   MPAA:NR)

SKY HIGH*   (1952) 60m Lippert bw

Sid Melton (*Herbert*), Mara Lynn (*Sally*), Sam Flint (*Col. Baker*), Doug Evans (*Maj. Talbot*), Fritz Feld (*Doctor Kapok*), Mark Krah (*The Boss*), Margia Dean (*Lily Gaylord*), Paul Bryar (*Kurt Petrov*), Thayer Roberts (*Maj. Catastrophe*), Don Frost (*Col. Baker's Clerk*), John Peletti (*George Grady*), Ernie Veneri (*Joe Bush*), John Phillips (*Lt. Col. Turbojet*), Will Orleans (*Examination Room Clerk*), Peter Damon (*Radio Operator*).

At a military air force base, Melton is a GI who isn't playing with a full deck. It seems this soldier looks very much like a spy who is trying to get hold of plans for a secret new plane. Melton is recruited to catch the man and bust up his ring, a task he accomplishes in spite of himself. The direction shows no comic sense and the story rolls along predictably, until it finally collapses and dies.

p, Sigmund Neufeld; d, Samuel Newfield; w, Orville Hampton; ph, Jack Greenhalgh; m, Bert Shefter; ed, Carl Pierson; art d, F. Paul Sylos.

Comedy   (PR:A   MPAA:NR)

SKY IS RED, THE*   (1952, Ital.) 99m Realart bw

Marina Berti (*Carla*), Jacques Sernas (*Tullio*), Mischa Auer, Jr (*Daniel*), Anna Maria Ferrero (*Giulia*), Liliana Pellini (*Nora*), Lauro Gazzolo (*Shoemaker*).

In post-war Italy two young couples try to carry on their torrid affairs amid life in a quarantined zone. The film is a confusing, incompetent work that's hardly spiced up with its numerous sex scenes.

d, Claudio Gora; w, Gora, Lamberto Santilli, Leopoldo Trieste, Cesare Zavattini; ph, Vaclav Vic; m, Valentino Bucchi; md, Willy Ferrero.

Drama   (PR:O   MPAA:NR)

SKY IS YOURS, THE   (SEE: LE CIEL EST A VOUS, 1957, Fr.)

SKY LINER**   (1949) 61m Lippert/Screen Guild bw

Richard Travis (*Steve Blair*), Pamela Blake (*Carol*), Rochelle Hudson (*Amy Winthrop*), Steven Geray (*Bokejian*), Greg McClure (*J.S. Conningsby*), Gaylord [Steve] Pendleton (*Smith*), Michael Whalen (*Ben Howard*), Anna May Slaughter (*Mary Ann*), Ralph Peters (*Joe Kirk*), Lisa Ferraday (*Mariette La Fare*), David Holt (*Buford*), Dodie Bauer (*Grace Ward*), Herbert Evans (*Sir Harry Finneston*), Roy Butler (*Mr. Jennings*), Jean Clark (*Mrs. Jennings*), Bess Flowers (*Mother*), John McGuire (*George Eakins*), Alan Hersholt (*Courier*), Jack Mulhall (*Col. Hanson*), George Meeker (*Financier*), William Lester (*Pilot*), Jean Sorel (*2nd Stewardess*), Burt Wenland (*Co-Pilot*).

Action aboard a commercial airliner as Travis plays an FBI agent on the trail of a spy who has lifted top secret government documents from a corpse and taken to the air. A taut thriller is developed through the interaction of the various characters upon the west bound airplane, including Slaughter who is seeking fame and fortune on the West Coast and is willing to display her lack of talent to anyone who asks.

p, William Stephens; d, William Berke; w, Maurice Tombragel (based on the story by John Wilste); ph, Carl Berger; m, Raoul Kraushaar; ed, Edward Mann; md, Kraushaar; art d, Martin Obzina; spec eff, Howard Weeks; makeup, Earl Young.

Spy Drama   (PR:A   MPAA:NR)

SKY MURDER*½   (1940) 71m MGM bw

Walter Pidgeon (*Nick Carter*), Donald Meek (*Bartholomew*), Karen Verne (*Pat Evens*), Edward Ashley (*Cortland Grand*), Joyce Compton (*Christina Cross*), Tom Conway (*Andrew Hendon*), George Lessey (*Sen. Monrose*), Dorothy Tree (*Kathe*), Frank Reicher (*Dr. Gratten*), Chill Wills (*Sheriff Beckwith*), George Watts (*Judge Whitmore*), Byron Foulger (*Kuse*), William Tannen (*Gus*), Milton Parsons (*Brock*), Tom Neal (*Steve Cossack*), Lucien Prival (*Brucker*), Grady Sutton (*Buster*), Kay Sutton (*"Texas" O'Keefe*), Anne Wigton (*Miss Shakespeare*), Judith Allen (*"Ruffles" Macklin*), Celia Travers (*Cissy Minch*), Virginia O'Brien (*Lucille La Vonne*), Warren McCollum (*Boy*), Edwin Parker, Ted Oliver (*Cops*), Cyrus [Cy] Kendall (*Harrigan*), Arthur Aylesworth (*Man*).

Dull attempt at a mystery-thriller has Pidgeon playing the detective from the popular novel. Here he is investigating a spy ring, bringing the culprits to justice without doing much sleuthing. (See NICK CARTER series, Index.)

p, Frederick Stephani; d, George B. Seitz; w, William R. Lipman; ph, Charles Lawton; m, David Snell; ed, Gene Ruggiero; art d, Cedric Gibbons, Howard Campbell; set d, Edwin B. Willis.

Spy Drama   (PR:A   MPAA:NR)

SKY PARADE*½   (1936) 70m PAR bw

Jimmie Allen (*Himself*), William Gargan (*Speed Robertson*), Katherine DeMille (*Geraldine Croft*), Kent Taylor (*Tommy Wade*), Grant Withers (*Casey Cameron*), Syd Saylor (*Flash Lewis*), Robert Fiske (*Scotty Allen*), Bennie Bartlett (*Jimmie Allen, age 9*), Billy Lee (*Jimmie Allen, age 4*), Edgar Dearing (*Gat Billings*), Georges Renevant (*Baron Ankrovith*), Keith Daniels (*Spike*), Colin Tapley (*Rigs*).

Gargan, Taylor, and Fiske play three WW I buddies who continue their escapades in the air via a commercial airline. When the special plane they have been developing is in danger of being stolen by enemy agents, Allen is called upon to wind up the culprits. He accomplishes this feat in the air just as if he were back in the war.

p, Harold Hurley; d, Otho Lovering; w, Brian Marlowe, Byron Morgan, Arthur Beckhard (based on material by Robert M. Burtt, Wilfred G. Moore); ph, William Mellor.

Spy Drama/Adventure/Aviation Drama   (PR:A   MPAA:NR)

SKY PATROL*½   (1939) 61m MON bw

John Trent (Tailspin), Marjorie Reynolds (Betty Lou), Milburn Stone (Skeeter), Jackie Coogan (Carter), Jason Robards, Sr (Smith), Bryant Washburn (Bainbridge), Boyd Irwin (Colonel), LeRoy Mason (Mitch), John Peters (Jackson), Johnny Day (Ryan), Dickie Jones (Bobby).

Another in the "Tailspin Tommy" series. This time Trent is in charge of training a group of young flyers for the government. He has them guard a border to gain some experience. One of the cadets, Coogan, is shot down and captured by a gang of smugglers. Trent tracks the lad to an amphibious airplane used by Mason and his gang. The former child star Coogan was attempting to forge a new career as an adult actor, but he was given little material here that would help his future. (See TAILSPIN TOMMY series, Index.)

p, Paul Malvern; d, Howard Bretherton; w, Joseph West, Norman S. Parker (based on the cartoon strip by Hal Forrest); ph, Fred Jackman, Jr.; ed, Carl Pierson.

Adventure/Aviation Drama   (PR:A MPAA:NR)

SKY PIRATE, THE**   (1970) 105m Filmmakers Distribution Center c

Michael McClanathan (Joe), Claudia Leacock (Charlie), Frank Meyer (Norman), Margaret Kramer (Shy Lady), Lorenzo Mans (Pepe), Zelda Keiser (Sarah), Francesca Annis (Uptight Girl), Rainy Michaelyan (Carmen), Joy Bang (Lynn Beasy).

Modestly budgeted independent feature that concentrates on what leads McClanathan to hijack a plane to Cuba. Apparently it is to recapture his stay there while in the Navy. This memory is given new life via a conversation McClanathan has with his niece's leftist boy friend, Meyer, who sees Cuba as the revolutionary ideal. But McClanathan only thinks about the prostitute with whom he had such a wonderful time. Told entirely in flashback from the time Leacock hears radio reports of her uncle's exploits. The filmmakers attempt to explore the various fantasies about Latin America.

p,d&w, Andrew Meyer; m, Brian Trentham; ed, Meyer, Suki Poor; spec eff, Trentham.

Drama   (PR:C MPAA:NR)

SKY RAIDERS*   (1931) 59m COL bw

Lloyd Hughes (Bob), Marceline Day (Grace), Wheeler Oakman (Willard), Walter Miller (Kelley), Kit Guard (Pete), Ashley Buck, Jerome J. Jerome, William H. O'Brien, Jay Eaton, Dick Rush.

A pilot crashes a plane and kills his girl friend's brother. He gets another chance when he helps capture a group of pirates responsible for hijacking money-laden planes. Never gets off the ground.

d, Christy Cabanne; w, Harvey Gates; ph, Al Zeigler; ed, Gene Havlick.

Adventure/Aviation Drama   (PR:A MPAA:NR)

SKY RAIDERS, THE*   (1938, Brit.) 57m Sovereign/FN bw

Nita Harvey (June Welwyn), Ambrose Day (Crealand Wake), Ronald Braden (David Welwyn), Michael Hogarth (Jack Weatherby), Beatrice Marsden (Miss Quarm), Harry Newman (Hawkins), David Keir (Dr. Martin), Stuart Christie, George de Brook, Rupert Mitford, Pat Keogh, Guy Waring.

Lifeless thriller has Harvey kidnaped by a gang of thieves in order to get her pilot brother to assist them in a skyjacking caper. Once the heist is pulled off, Harvey and her brother must then find a means of escaping the gang's grasp or meet with certain death. Neither performances nor plotting are believable for a moment.

p,d&w, Fraser Foulsham.

Crime/Aviation Drama   (PR:A MPAA:NR)

SKY RIDERS**   (1976, U.S./Gr.) 91m FOX c

James Coburn (Jim McCabe), Susannah York (Ellen Bracken), Robert Culp (Jonas Bracken), Charles Aznavour (Inspector Nikolidis), Werner Pochath (No. 1), Zou Zou (No. 6), Kenneth Griffith (Fred Wasserman, Art Expert), Harry Andrews (Carl Auerbach), John Beck (Ben Miller), Ernie Orsatti (Joe), Steven Keats (Rudy), Henry Brown (Martin), Cherie Latimer (Cora), Barbara Trentham (Della), Simon Harrison (Jimmy Bracken), Stephanie Matthews (Sue Bracken), Anthony Antypas (Dimitri), Telis Zottos (Orkin), Nikos Tsahiridas (Gatekeeper), Bob Wills, Chris Price, Dean Tanji, Roy Hooper, Chris Wills, Dix Roper, Kurt Keifer, Susie Wills, Carol Price (Glider Team).

A standard kidnaping plot is used as an excuse to display some dazzling hang gliding exploits and the scenic beauty of Greece. When the wealthy Culp's wife, York, and two children are kidnaped by a group of crazed political anarchists, Culp asks York's ex-husband, Coburn, for assistance. The latter develops a scheme using hang glider experts to raid the Greek mountain where York is being held captive, which is pulled off successfully

giving Coburn a chance to display some incredible heroics such as hanging from the wing of a glider. For a change, Coburn is actually called upon to do some acting, stemming from the emotional and sexual tensions between him and York. He also performed some dangerous stunts by himself. But the plot is little more than formula with any sympathy generated the result of the extremely thwarted depiction of the kidnapers. A minor scandal was created when a Greek electrician was killed while working on this feature.

p, Terry Morse, Jr.; d, Douglas Hickox; w, Jack DeWitt, Stanley Mann, Gary Michael White (based on a story by Hall T. Sprague, Bill McGaw); ph, Ousama Rawi, Greg McGillivray, Jim Freeman (Todd-AO, DeLuxe Color); m, Lalo Schifrin; ed, Malcolm Cooke; art d, Terry Ackland-Snow; set d, Ian Whittaker; cos, Emma Porteous; spec eff, John Stears; makeup, Richard Mills; stunts, Peter Brayham.

Adventure/Aviation Drama   Cas.   (PR:C MPAA:PG)

SKY SPIDER, THE**   (1931) 69m Action bw

Glenn Tryon, Pat O'Malley, John Trent, Beryl Mercer, Blanche Mehaffey, Joseph Girard, Philo McCullough, George Chesebro, Jay Hunt.

Tryon and his two older brothers become pilots for the mail service while remaining extremely devoted to their mother. When the eldest brother is shot down in the line of duty, investigations lead to McCullough as the man responsible. The latter, a good friend of Tryon, is considered above suspicion by everyone except the boy's mother. A secondary plot has Tryon and his eldest brother, who is eventually killed, both after Mehaffey. Concentration is more upon the family relationships than the flying action, though plenty of this is provided.

d, Richard Thorpe; w, Grace Keel Norton; ph, Jules Cronjager.

Aviation Drama   (PR:A MPAA:NR)

SKY TERROR   (SEE: SKYJACKED, 1972)

SKY WEST AND CROOKED   (SEE: GYPSY GIRL, 1966, Brit.)

SKYDIVERS, THE*   (1963) 75m Crown International bw

Kevin Casey (Beth Rowe), Marcia Knight (Suzy Belmont), Eric Tomlin (Joe), Tony Cardoza (Harry Rowe), Titus Moede (Frankie Bonner), Michael Rae (Red), Bob Carrano (Bob), Paul Francis (Peter), Jimmy Bryant and the Night Jumpers, Monty McRae, Marilyn McRae, Jack Kupp.

Cardoza and Casey play a husband and wife who own and operate a skydiving school with Cardoza's friend Tomlin. An attractive wealthy woman, Knight, is attracted to Cardoza but he spurns her advances. Tensions arise when Tomlin finds himself falling in love with Casey. As a result of Cardoza's rejections, Knight creates trouble, including sabotaging Casey's plane, nearly causing a crash. Knight loses control totally when she and an accomplice pour acid into Cardoza's parachute resulting in his falling to his death. Knight is then killed while being pursued by the authorities.

p, Anthony Cardoza; d&w, Coleman Francis; ph, Austin McKinney, Lee Strosnider; ed, Bob Lusby; md, John Bath; ch, Robert Banas; m/l, "Ha-So," "Tobacco Worm," "Stratosphere Boogie," Jimmy Bryant and the Night Jumpers; aerial ph, Jack Kupp.

Aviation Drama   (PR:C MPAA:NR)

SKYJACKED**   (1972) 100m MGM c (AKA: SKY TERROR)

Charlton Heston (Henry O'Hara), Yvette Mimieux (Angela Thacher), James Brolin (Jerome K. Weber), Claude Akins (Sgt. Ben Puzo), Jeanne Crain (Mrs. Clara Shaw), Susan Dey (Elly Brewster), Roosevelt Grier (Gary Brown), Mariette Hartley (Harriet Stevens), Walter Pidgeon (Sen. Arne Lindner), Ken Swofford (John Bimonte), Leslie Uggams (Lovejoy Wells), Ross Elliott (Harold Shaw), Nicholas Hammond (Peter Lindner), Mike Henry (Sam Allen), Jayson William Kane (William Reading), Toni Clayton (Jane Burke), John Hillerman (Walter Brandt), Kelley Miles (Hazel Martin), John Fiedler (Robert Grundig), Maureen Connell (Mrs. O'Hara), Ed Connelly, Forrest Wood (1st Class Passengers), Wesley Lau (Stanley Morris), Jenifer Shaw (Cosmetic Sales Girl), Jack Denbo (Thompson), Roy Engel (Bonanza Pilot), Joe Canutt (Hunter), Grahame Pratt (Bronson), Genadii Biegouloff (Russian Leader), Craig Shreeve (Airline Attendant), Lorna Thayer (Weber's Mother), Daniel White (Weber's Father), William Martel (General).

Heston plays the pilot of a commercial airplane that is hijacked by a maniacal Brolin, who orders, through a lipstick message on the bathroom mirror, that the plane be taken to Moscow. His reasons for picking that particular destination are never made clear, and once he makes it he's instantly killed by Russian soldiers. In addition to the suspense created by the main plot line, a number of developments occur in the personal lives of the passengers and staff. These include a pregnant woman, who just happens to go into labor during the incident; and tensions caused by memories of a former affair between Heston and hostess Mimieux, who is now seeing the co-pilot. Heston gives his usual authoritative performance, conveying a naive and shallow adherence to law and order that almost stifles the rest of the performances in the picture. Brolin (formerly of TV's

MARCUS WELBY, MD), is convincing as the soldier who is driven to perform the skyjacking.

p, Walter Saltzer; d, John Guillermin; w, Stanley R. Greenberg (based on the novel *Hijacked* by David Harper); ph, Harry Stradling, Jr. (Panavision, Metrocolor); m, Perry Botkin, Jr.; ed, Robert Swink; art d, Edward C. Carfagno; set d, Charles Pierce; cos, Jack Bear; spec eff, Ralph Swartz; makeup, Siegfried H. Geike.

Adventure/Aviation Drama (PR:A MPAA:PG)

SKYLARK**½ (1941) 94m PAR bw

Claudette Colbert (*Lydia Kenyon*), Ray Milland (*Tony Kenyon*), Brian Aherne (*Jim Blake*), Binnie Barnes (*Myrtle Vantine*), Walter Abel (*George Gore*), Grant Mitchell (*Frederick Vantine*), Mona Barrie (*Charlotte Gorell*), Ernest Cossart (*Theodore*), James Rennie (*Ned Franklin*), Fritz Feld (*Maitre d'Hotel*), Warren Hymer (*Beefy Individual in Subway Car*), Hobart Cavanaugh (*Little Individual in Subway Car*), Leon Belasco (*Long-Haired Man in Subway Car*), Edward Fielding (*Scholarly Individual in Subway Car*), Irving Bacon (*Ferryman*), Leonard Mudie (*Jewelry Clerk*), Patricia Farr (*Lil the Waitress in Hamburger Stand*), William "Billy" Newell (*Counterman at Hamburger Stand*), Margaret Hayes (*Receptionist*), Robert Dudley (*Pedestrian*), James Flavin (*Subway Guard*), Howard Mitchell (*Man in Front of Tony*), Edward Piel, Sr (*Man Behind Tony*), Frank Orth (*Subway Cashier*), May Boley (*Fat Woman in Subway Car*), Minerva Urecal, Virginia Sale (*Middle Aged Women in Subway Car*), Ella Neal (*Usherette*), Henry Roquemore (*Bartender*), Keith Richards (*Counterman at Second Hamburger Stand*), Francisco Maran (*Mr. Harrison, Travel Agency Man*), Armand Kaliz (*Jeweler*).

Colbert plays the neglected wife of businessman Milland, who would rather devote himself to an ad agency than to his loving wife. Their fifth wedding anniversary arrives and Milland promises to quit his job to be with his wife more often. But Colbert is wise to the ploy and quickly heads to the Reno divorce courts. She begins an affair with playboy Aherne, but ends it after the two take a cruise together, which winds up being anything but a smooth trip. Colbert then attempts to patch up her marriage with Milland. Played only for laughs, with a light-hearted atmosphere and a quick pace. Colbert adds her special charm, while Milland fits the mold as the man trying to win his wife back.

p&d, Mark Sandrich; w, Zion Myers, Allan Scott (based on the novel and play by Samson Raphaelson); ph, Charles Lang; ed, LeRoy Stone; art d, Hans Dreier, Roland Anderson.

Comedy (PR:A MPAA:NR)

SKYLARKS* (1936, Brit.) 73m Reunion bw

Jimmy Nervo (*Jimmy Doakes*), Teddy Knox (*Teddy Cook*), Nancy Burne (*Marion Hicks*), Queenie Leonard (*Maggie Hicks*), Eddie Gray, Amy Veness.

Nervo and Knox play a pair of RAF pilots who decide to go for a joyride during a drunken spree and wind up breaking the air endurance record. They certainly didn't break any records in audience laughter with this effort.

p, John Gossage; d, Thornton Freeland; w, Russell Medcraft.

Comedy (PR:A MPAA:NR)

SKYLINE** (1931) 68m FOX bw

Thomas Meighan (*James McClellan*), Hardie Albright (*John Breen*), Maureen O'Sullivan (*Kathleen Kearny*), Donald Dillaway (*Gerry Gaige*), Myrna Loy (*Paula Lambert*), Stanley Fields (*Capt. Breen*), Jack Kennedy (*Kearny*), Alice Ward (*Mrs. Kearny*), Dorothy Peterson (*Rose Breen*), Robert McWade (*Judge West*).

Meighan plays the engineer famous for creating the New York skyline, and known for being a real risk taker. He befriends a young orphan, Albright, who has left his foster father's barge in order to have a go at the big city, and, as it happens, Albright is really the long lost son of Meighan. Meighan meets his proper end by falling from one of his sky scrapers, but only from the third floor. The interesting camera angles and photography of the New York skyline leave the greatest impression in this story that otherwise stifles the actors with its contrived narrative.

d, Sam Taylor; w, Kenyon Nicholson, Dudley Nichols, William Anthony McGuire (based on the novel *East Side, West Side* by Felix Reisenberg; ph, John Mescall; ed, Harold Shuster.

Drama Cas. (PR:A MPAA:NR)

SKY'S THE LIMIT, THE**½ (1937, Brit.) 78m GFD bw

Jack Buchanan (*Dave Harber*), Mara Loseff (*Mme. Isobella*), William Kendall (*Thornwell Beamish*), David Hutcheson (*Teddy Carson*), H.F. Maltby (*Lord Beckley*), Athene Seyler (*Miss Prinney*), Sara Allgood (*Mrs. O'Reilly*), Antony Holles (*Marillo*), David Burns ("*Ballyhoo*" *Bangs*), C.M. Hallard (*Lord Morgan*), Charles Stone (*Orchestra Leader*), Andrea Malandrinos (*Headwaiter*), Morris Harvey (*Batavian Ambassador*), Barry Lupino

(*Drunk*), Wally Patch (*Commissionaire*), Leslie Mitchell, Sam Wilkinson, Rawicz and Landauer, The Four New Yorkers.

Pleasant, well-paced farce teams Buchanan with opera singer Loseff to find a designer who can help solve their woes. But the plot is just an excuse to display Buchanan's fine comic talents, a subtle combination of mime and wit. Loseff's singing abilities are a disappointment.

p, Jack Buchanan; d, Lee Garmes, Buchanan; w, Buchanan, Douglas Furber (based on a story by Ralph Spence); ph, Henry Harris, Roy Clark, Garmes.

Musical/Comedy (PR:A MPAA:NR)

SKY'S THE LIMIT, THE**½ (1943) 89m RKO bw

Fred Astaire (*Fred Atwell/Fred Burton*), Joan Leslie (*Joan Manion*), Robert Benchley (*Phil Harriman*), Robert Ryan (*Reg Fenton*), Elizabeth Patterson (*Mrs. Fisher*), Marjorie Gateson (*Canteen Hostess*), Richard Davies (*Lt. Dick Merlin*), Clarence Kolb (*Harvey J. Sloan*), Freddie Slack and His Orchestra (*Colonial Club Orchestra*), Eric Blore (*Jackson*), Henri DeSoto (*Headwaiter*), Dorothy Kelly (*Harriman's Secretary*), Norma Drury (*Mrs. Roskowski*), Jerry Mandy (*Italian Waiter*), Clarence Muse (*Doorman*), Ida Shoemaker (*Flower Woman*), Paul Hurst (*Stevedore Foreman*), Amelita Ward (*San Francisco Girl*), Rhoda Reese (*Powers Model*), Neil Hamilton (*Naval Commander*), Dick Rush (*Railway Conductor*), Georgia Caine (*Charwoman*), Ann Summers, Rita Maritt (*Bits*), Buck Bucko, Roy Bucko, Clint Sharp (*Cowboys*), Ed McNamara (*Barman*), Joe Bernard, Al Murphy (*Bartenders*), Jack Carr (*Customer*), Ferris Taylor (*Keifer the Chef*), Peter Lawford (*USAF Officer*), Olin Howland (*4-F Man*), Victor Potel (*Joe the Bartender*), Ella Mae Morse (*Singer*).

An ordinary musical comedy that gives Astaire a new dancing partner, Leslie, who surprised audiences with her terpsichore although her singing voice was looped by Sally Sweetland. Astaire didn't have to don the "soup and fish" for this, a rare movie that eschewed formal clothes. Perhaps he should have. He's a Flying Tiger hero back for a ten-day respite in between battles. He and his pals, Ryan and Davies, are supposed to tour the U.S. and raise money for the war effort, but he doesn't want to be lionized and make the rubber chicken circuit, so he doffs his uniform and pretends to be an ordinary Joe. Leslie works for Benchley, who runs a *Life* magazine type of publication. She is gung-ho to travel to the war zone and report on where the action is happening. She meets Astaire and thinks he's just another guy who has managed to stay out of the service. He is entranced by Leslie and begins a campaign to win her hand, without revealing the fact that he's a hero. His onslaught is, of course, musicalized, which gives the duo an opportunity to do a bit of lively footwork, but most of the routines are lackluster and not nearly up to the standards Astaire had established with Rogers in his prior RKO outings. Benchley gets a chance to be funny at a dinner for aircraft millionaire Kolb, where he rehashes the confusing, amusing routines he did in various short subjects. The picture ends with the two being united and swearing love that they hope will take them through the end of the war. Leslie was a contract player at Warner Bros. and when RKO asked for her to do this movie, and for John Garfield to appear in THE FALLEN SPARROW, the Hollywood lot had to give the Burbank lot their hold on the movie options for OF HUMAN BONDAGE and THE ANIMAL KINGDOM. Although technically a musical, there weren't many tunes in this. Harold Arlen and Johnny Mercer did have one hit from the score, and that was "One For My Baby," (sung and danced by Astaire). The other songs were "My Shining Hour," (sung by Leslie [Sweetland! then reprised by Leslie, Astaire) and "I've Got A Lot In Common With You." Harline's musical direction and "My Shining Hour" were nominated for Oscars, although "One For My Baby" was the song that became a standard. Press agent Sam Wall claims to have written the ultimate parody on that song for his one-time client, Dean Martin, in which Martin sang: "It's quarter to three, there's no one in the place except you and me. So stick 'em up, Joe! . . . ."

p, David Hempstead, Sherman Todd; d, Edward H. Griffith; w, Frank Fenton, Lynn Root (based on their story "A Handful of Heaven"); ph, Russell Metty; ed, Roland Gross; md, Leigh Harline; art d, Albert S. D'Agostino, Carroll Clark; set d, Darrell Silvera, Claude Carpenter; spec eff, Vernon L. Walker; ch, Fred Astaire; cos, Rene Hubert; m/l, Johnny Mercer, Harold Arlen.

Musical/Comedy Cas. (PR:A MPAA:NR)

SKYSCRAPER SOULS*½ (1932) 80m MGM bw

Warren William (*David Dwight*), Maureen O'Sullivan (*Lynn Harding*), Gregory Ratoff (*Vinmont*), Anita Page (*Jenny*), Verree Teasdale (*Sarah Dennet*), Norman Foster (*Tom Shepherd*), Jean Hersholt (*Jake*), Wallace Ford (*Slim*), Hedda Hopper (*Ella Dwight*), Helen Coburn (*Myra*), George Barbier (*Norton*), John Marston (*Bill*).

A hundred-story skyscraper is the setting for a number of personel dramatics that occur within its structure and are all forcibly intertwined. William plays the building's owner, a man as ruthless in his personal affairs as he is with his business deals. He gets his just rewards from a discarded lover. But his finale does not match the ending which features a fallen woman jumping to her death from the top of the building in a silly metaphoric climax. Foster and Ratoff both went on to direct films.

d, Edgar Selwyn; w, C. Gardner Sullivan, Elmer Harris (based on the novel *Skyscraper* by Faith Baldwin); ph, William Daniels; ed, Tom Held.

Drama   **(PR:A MPAA:NR)**

SKYSCRAPER WILDERNESS   (SEE: BIG CITY, 1937)

SKYWATCH   (SEE: LIGHT UP THE SKIES, 1960)

SKYWAY*   (1933) 70m MON bw

Kathryn Crawford, Ray Walker, Lucien Littlefield, Tom Dugan, Arthur Vinton, Claude Gillingwater, Jed Prouty, Alice Lake, Jack Pennick, George ["Gabby"] Hayes, Jack Kennedy.

Sluggish story has Walker as a former pilot who takes a job in a bank in order to please his girl. When money turns up missing, all hands point to Walker, who clears his name by catching the real culprit, vice-president Prouty, as he is trying to make his escape. A fast pace helps to gloss over a dull story.

d, Lew Collins; w, Albert E. DeMond (based on a story by Paul B. Franklin).

Drama   **(PR:A MPAA:NR)**

SLA FORST, FREDE!   (SEE: OPERATION LOVEBIRDS, 1968, Den.)

SLADE   (SEE: JACK SLADE, 1953)

SLAMMER   (SEE: SHORT EYES, 1977)

SLAMS, THE*   (1973) 91m Penelope/MGM c

Jim Brown *(Curtis Hook)*, Judy Pace *(Iris Daniels)*, Roland "Bob" Harris *(Stambell)*, Paul E. Harris *(Jackson Barney)*, Frank de Kova *(Capiello)*, Ted Cassidy *(Glover)*, Frenchia Guizon *(Macey)*, John Dennis *(Sgt. Flood)*, Jac Emel *(Zack)*, Quinn Redecker *(Warden)*, Betty Coles *(Mother)*, Robert Phillips *(Cohalt)*, Jan Merlin *(Saddler)*.

An excessively violent prison film has Brown put behind bars after having stashed megabucks he obtained by outwitting the mob. Everyone is willing to help cut Brown loose for a piece of the take. The plot is just an excuse to show a lot of people being blown to bits.

p, Gene Korman; d, Jonathan Kaplan; w, Richard L. Adams; ph, Andrew Davis (Metrocolor); m, Luther Henderson; ed, Morton Tubor; art d, Jack Fisk.

Crime   **(PR:O MPAA:R)**

SLANDER½   (1956) 81m MGM bw

Van Johnson *(Scott Ethan Martin)*, Ann Blyth *(Connie Martin)*, Steve Cochran *(H.R. Manley, Publisher)*, Marjorie Rambeau *(Mrs. Manley)*, Richard Eyer *(Joey Martin)*, Harold J. Stone *(Seth Jackson, Agent)*, Philip Coolidge *(Homer Crowley)*, Lurene Tuttle *(Mrs. Doyle)*, Lewis Martin *(Charles Orrin Sterling)*.

An attack against the gossip magazines that thrive on creating scandals while ruining people's lifes. In this case Johnson is the victim of a particularly ruthless publisher, Cochran, who exercises his egocentricities by printing slanderous items. He threatens to reveal that Johnson was convicted for armed robbery as a teenager unless Johnson supplies him with behind-the-scenes gossip about a Broadway star. Johnson refuses and is quickly fired from the television job he struggled so hard to obtain. Even sadder is the death of his son who is run over as he runs from teasing youths. But Cochran gets his when his mother, Rambeau, apearently guilt-ridden at the monster she brought into the world, shoots her son. Though the plot is contrived and too much of it depends on dialog, it makes its point.

p, Armand Deutsch; d, Roy Rowland; w, Jerome Weidman (based on the story by Harry W. Junkin); ph, Harold J. Marzerati; m, Jeff Alexander; ed, George Boemler; art d, William A. Horning, Hans Peters.

Drama   **(PR:A MPAA:NR)**

SLANDER HOUSE*½   (1938) 65m Progressive bw

Adrienne Ames *(Helene)*, Craig Reynolds *(Pat Fenton)*, Esther Ralston *(Ruth De Milo)*, George Meeker *(Dr. Stallings)*, Pert Kelton *(Mazie)*, William "Billy" Newell *(Terry Kent)*, Dorothy Vaughn *(Mrs. Horton)*, Edward Keane *(George Horton)*, Vivien Oakland *(Mrs. Conway)*, Ruth Gillette *(Mme. Renault)*.

Ames plays the young owner of a beauty salon that caters to wealthy society women, paving the way for interesting situations made by gossip the girls overhear and do their best to spread.

p, B.N. Judell; d, Charles Lamont; w, Gertrude Orr, John W. Krafft (based on the novel by Madeline Woods); ph, M.A. Andersen; ed, Roy Luby.

Comedy   **(PR:A MPAA:NR)**

SLAP SHOT**   (1977) 123m UNIV c

Paul Newman *(Reggie Dunlop)*, Strother Martin *(Joe McGrath)*, Michael Ontkean *(Ned Braden)*, Jennifer Warren *(Francine Dunlop)*, Lindsay Crouse *(Lily Braden)*, Jerry Houser *("Killer" Carlson)*, Andrew Duncan *(Jimm Carr)*, Jeff Carlson *(Jeff Hanson)*, Steve Carlson *(Steve Hanson)*, David Hanson *(Jack Hanson)*, Yvon Barrette *(Denis Le Mieux)*, Allan Nicholls *(Upton)*, Brad Sullivan *(Wanchuk)*, Stephen Mendillo *(Jim Ahern)*, Yvan Ponton *(Drouin)*, Matthew Cowles *(Charlie)*, Kathryn Walker *(Anita McCambridge)*, Melinda Dillon *(Suzanne Hanrahan)*, M. Emmet Walsh *(Dickie Dunn)*, Swoosie Kurtz *(Shirley)*, Paul D'Amato *(Tim McCracken)*, Ronald L. Docken *(Lebrun)*, Guido Tenesi *(Billy Charlebois)*, Myron Odegaard *(Final Game Referee)*, Christopher Murney *(Tommy Hanrahan)*, Jean Rosario Tetreault *(Bergeron)*, Ned Dowd *(Ogilthorpe)*, Gracie Head *(Pam)*, Nancy N. Dowd *(Andrea)*, Barbara L. Shorts *(Bluebird)*, Larry Block *(Peterboro Referee)*, Paul Dooley *(Hyannisport Announcer)*.

At 123 minutes, if every foul word were excised from the movie, it might have lost an hour. Never before have so many four-letter words been used in one film. If we are to believe screenwriter Dowd (who was working, she claims, from tape recordings made by her brother, who was a minor league hockey player), hockey men are a cross between cretins and sadists with vocabularies slimmer than their intelligence quotients. There have been hockey movies before (PAPERBACK HERO) out of Canada but none can compare with the garbage flowing out of the mouths of these skaters. And yet, all that aside, there is more than a bit of fun to be found in SLAP SHOT (which refers to the hardest thwack a player can give the puck with his stick). Newman, at age 52, is the player-coach for a raggedy minor-league club run by Martin. Nobody comes to the games anymore because his team stinks up the ice. Further, Newman's wife, Warren, has left him for a multitude of reasons. Martin tells Newman that he has employed Hanson, Carlson, and Carlson, a trio of astigmatic goons, to bring life to the team. Newman takes a look at the three and thinks that Martin must be mad; these guys are one step down from a tulip in the brains department. The team is about to play another club and Newman takes a respite by sleeping with the other team's goalie's (Murney) wife, Dillon, who admits to Newman that she swings both ways and enjoys the company of women. When the game is played, Newman needles Murney about Dillon's proclivities and Murney comes out of the crease; the winning goal is scored against him when he blows his cool. Newman thinks he may have the secret to success – play dirty – although his star scorer, Ontkean, thinks it's a bad move. Ontkean was a great college player at an Ivy League school and believes that the best man will win, a theory that is not subscribed to by Newman. He works on his players to adopt a more assertive attitude and the result is that the team begins winning, using every advantage it can in order to achieve success. Fans begin coming back to the arena. Meanwhile, Carlson, Carlson, and Hanson have been warming the bench as Newman doesn't want to tamper with the mild flurry of wins the team has been having. The team is decimated during one game and Newman is forced to call upon the trio who respond by showing that they are the most vicious players since the lions took the Christians. The team goes on a hot streak, led by the thick-lensed brothers, and now has become one of the most successful franchises in minor-league hockey, with busloads of fans to accompany them to their "away" games. Ontkean, who is married to wealthy Crouse, remains aloof from the tactics used by the others and continues to play aggressively, but cleanly. The team comes back to the small Pennsylvania mill town (it was shot in Johnstown, home of the great flood) and is accorded the kind of welcome Lindbergh got after his flight. Warren informs Newman that she is leaving the city and moving to New York, with a divorce decree in hand. At the same time, Crouse walks out on Ontkean and settles in with Newman, who is nonplussed at her appearance on his doorstep but he won't ever turn away an attractive woman. Nobody really knows who owns this team as Martin keeps it under wraps but when Newman threatens to expose Martin's homosexual leanings, the old man is pushed to reveal that the club is owned by Walker, a wealthy widow with 3 kids. Newman approaches Walker with some ideas as to how to put some profit into the club and she responds by telling him that she intends to dissolve the franchise, rather than sell it, because she has some income tax problems that can only be rectified in that manner. Newman's response is to hurl invective at the woman that would be too salty for a John Holmes videocassette. Meanwhile, Ontkean has resigned from the team and the big game is on the horizon. Newman appeals to the classy player to return and promises that there will be an end to the physical violence. Ontkean comes back and they keep winning. Now the final battle is about to take place against the same team seen earlier on which the cuckolded Murney is goalkeeper. This is a group that is second only to the Wehrmacht for bloodletting. The stands are packed with scouts from the National Hockey League who are there to pick up players as they know that the team is about to disband. The men charge out on the ice to fight to the death, with Ontkean laying back. Once the game starts, the gore begins and Ontkean is shocked to see his cold wife, Crouse, seated with the players' spouses and screaming just as loudly as they for the team to murder the other bums. Ontkean, disgusted by everything around him, skates on to the ice and begins an Ice Capades ballet dance that is soon a strip tease. The other players stand there startled and Murney, who can't believe what he's seeing, complains to the referee. When he gets no satisfaction, Murney punches the ref and Newman's team takes the game on a default as the crowd goes wild. There's a huge parade in their honor the next day and Newman sees ex-wife-to-be Warren, who is on her way to

New York. He's gotten the offer of a coaching job in Minnesota and swears he'll change, but her mind is made up, and she departs as the picture ends. Dowd's screenplay celebrates violence and then puts it down and so there is no real point-of-view to the goings-on. The picture made nearly $15 million in gross receipts but the TV runs have had to be drastically edited to conform to tasteful standards and so it didn't garner that much revenue from the tube. Dowd and her brother, Ned, do small cameos and Houser is excellent as the team's goalie. Most of the laughs come from the near-sighted trio of Carlson, Carlson, and Hanson, who must have been players at one time or another as their skating is realistic. Co-producer Wunsch had been an agent, then a network executive, segued into being a producer, and became bored with the time it took to get a movie project on the screen so he went back to agenting. This was Hill's 3rd collaboration with Newman. The previous two were THE STING and BUTCH CASSIDY AND THE SUNDANCE KID. The great hockey film has yet to be made. Keep the kids away from this because of language, sex, violence, and almost everything else. In many theaters, half the crowd walked out muttering at having seen Newman do such awful things and speak such awful words. The half who stayed in their seats wound up applauding.

p, Robert J. Wunsch, Stephen Friedman; d, George Roy Hill; w, Nancy Dowd; ph, Victor Kemper (Panavision, Technicolor); m, Elmer Bernstein; ed, Dede Allen; art d, Henry Bumstead; set d, James Payne; cos, Tom Bronson; stunts, Ned Dowd; m/l, "Right Back Where We Started From" (sung by Maxine Nightingale); makeup, Rick Sharp, Steve Abrams.

Sports Drama/Comedy   Cas.   (PR:O MPAA:R)

SLASHER, THE** (1953, Brit.) 75m Daniel Angel-Romulus/Lippert bw
(GB: COSH BOY)

James Kenney (*Roy Walsh*), Joan Collins (*Rene Collins*), Betty Ann Davies (*Elsie Walsh*), Robert Ayres (*Bob Stevens*), Hermione Baddeley (*Mrs. Collins*), Hermione Gingold (*Queenie*), Nancy Roberts (*Gran Walsh*), Stanley Escane (*Pete*), Sean Lynch (*Darky*), John Briggs (*Skinny*), Michael McKeag (*Brian*), Edward Evans (*Sgt. Woods*), Laurence Naismith (*Inspector Donaldson*), Frederick Piper (*Mr. Easter*), Walter Hudd (*Magistrate*), Sidney James (*Sergeant*), Cameron Hall, Arthur Howard, Peter Swanwick.

Unpleasant story of London street youth Kenney, who coshes old ladies and steals their purses (cosh is British slang for blackjack). Eventually he winds up in jail with an attempted murder charge against him. Joan Collins, even then, in her second year in films, looking too sophisticated for the role, plays a young girl he seduces, and Hermione Gingold stands out as an aging streetwalker. Overdose of cockney diction makes it hard for Americans to understand.

p, Daniel M. Angel; d, Lewis Gilbert; w, Gilbert, Vernon Harris (based on the play "Master Crook" by Bruce Walker); ph, Jack Asher; m, Lambert Williamson; ed, Charles Hasse; art d, Bernard Robinson.

Drama   (PR:O MPAA:NR)

SLASHER, THE* (1975) 88m William Mishkin c (AKA: BAD GIRLS)

Farley Granger, Sylva Koscina, Susan Scott, Chris Avram, Paul Oxon, Krista Nell.

Cheating wives meet messy ends as a mad killer acts out his anger toward women. Enter cop Granger to track down the psycho and rid society of the menace. Worthless splatter movie that predates most of the genre.

p, Eugene Florimont; d, Robert Montero; w, Montero, Lou Angelli, I. Fasant; ph, George Gaslini, F. Rossi (Eastmancolor).

Horror   Cas.   (PR:O MPAA:R)

SLATTERY'S HURRICANE**½ (1949) 83m FOX bw

Richard Widmark (*Will Slattery*), Linda Darnell (*Aggie Hobson*), Veronica Lake (*Dolores Greaves*), John Russell (*Lt. F.J. Hobson*), Gary Merrill (*Comdr. Kramer*), Walter Kingsford (*Milne*), Raymond Greenleaf (*Adm. William F. Olenby*), Stanley Waxman (*Frank*), Joseph 'Joe' De Santis (*Gregory*), Norman Leavitt (*Waiter*), Kenny Williams (*M.C.*), Morris Ankrum (*Doctor*), Amelita Ward (*Marie, B-Girl*), William Hawes (*Dispatcher*), Lee MacGregor (*Navigator*), John Davidson (*Maitre d'*), Don Hicks (*Tower Operator*), Frank Richards, Howard Negley (*Bartenders*), Ted Jordan (*Radarman*), David Wolfe (*Dr. Ross*), Grandon Rhodes (*Meteorologist*), John Wald (*Newscaster*), Gene Reynolds, Harry Lauter (*Control Tower Operators*), Howard Negley (*Bartender*), Joe Forte (*Waiter*), Ruth Clifford (*Nurse Bailey*), Maude Prickett (*Nurse Collins*), Dick Wessel.

After crossing up a pal, pilot Widmark attempts to make up for the wrongdoing by flying a dangerous assignment in rough weather for the wronged friend. As the winds bounce his craft through the air he begins thinking back over his life and the things he has done. Widmark's story is told in flashback. After serving in WW II as a pilot where he had singlehandedly sunk a Japanese ship, Widmark returns to civilian life. He takes a job as a pilot for a candy company with obvious mob connections. When he learns that his employers are also in on dope smuggling he decides to get a piece of the action himself. After engaging in an affair with Lake, a company secretary and girl friend of a mob leader, Widmark runs into

Russell, a buddy from the Navy. Russell is married to Darnell, an old flame of Widmark's. His passion for her still runs deep so he tries to wreck their marriage in hope of getting Darnell back. However, Darnell is not an easy victim for Widmark's schemes and makes the roguish man reform. As his own penance, Widmark takes Russell's place on a Weather Bureau hurricane flight and performs a heroic service. SLATTERY'S HURRICANE is an entertaining yarn that makes good use of the cast. Widmark gives the right amount of vileness to his character, an unsympathetic portrait with a moral turn that is honest and believable. Lake is solid support as his junkie lover. At this point both her professional and personal life were in disarray and this would be her last major film role. The cuts back and forth from Widmark in his plane to the events in his life occasionally bog things down, though, as the technique is relied on more than is necessary. The hurricane special effects are realistic, making Widmark's peril all the more suspenseful. Though essentially a routine melodrama, this is injected with plenty of enthusiasm by its cast to lift it above weaknesses in the script. At the time Lake was married to the film's director, de Toth, though this would end in divorce three years later.

p, William Perlberg; d, Andre de Toth; w, Herman Wouk, Richard Murphy (based on a book by Wouk); ph, Charles G. Clarke; ed, Robert Simpson; md, Lionel Newman; art d, Lyle Wheeler, Albert Hogsett; spec eff, Fred Sersen, Ray Kellogg.

Drama   (PR:C MPAA:NR)

SLAUGHTER*½ (1972) 91m AIP-Slaughter c

Jim Brown (*Slaughter*), Stella Stevens (*Ann Cooper*), Rip Torn (*Dominick Hoffo*), Don Gordon (*Harry Bastoli*), Cameron Mitchell (*A.W. Price*), Marlene Clark (*Kim Walker*), Robert Phillips (*Frank Morelli*), Marion Brash (*Jenny*), Norman Alfe (*Mario Felice*), Eddie LoRusso (*Little Al*), Buddy Garion (*Eddie*), Ronald C. Ross, Ricardo Adalid, B. Gerardo Zepeda (*Hoods*), Roger Cudney (*Gio*), Lance Winston (*Interne*), Juan Jose Laboriel (*Uncle*), Francisca Lopes de Laboriel (*Aunt*).

When ex-Green Beret Brown's parents are murdered, he undertakes the job of punishing the hoods responsible. Because he does such a "good" job, Mitchell forces him to help go after the kingpin down Mexico-way. Torn is oddly cast as a gangster, and seeming to realize how out of place he is, he adds a satirical quality, which is inappropriate but is more acting than the others do. There is actually a sequel, SLAUGHTER'S BIG RIP-OFF.

p, Monroe Sachson; d, Jack Starrett; w, Mark Hanna, Don Williams; ph, Rosalio Solano (DeLuxe Color); m, Luchi De Jesus; ed, Clarence C. "Renn" Reynolds; md, De Jesus; set d, Carlos Grandjean; spec eff, Herman Townsley, Leon Ortega; m/l, title song, Billy Preston (sung by Preston), "In Your Arms" De Jesus, Ric Marlow (sung by Ella Woods); makeup, Sara Mateos; stunts, Paul Knuckles.

Crime   (PR:O MPAA:R)

SLAUGHTER HOTEL* (1971, Ital.) 72m Hallmark c (LA BESTIA UCCIDE A SANGUE FREDDO ; AKA: ASYLUM EROTICA)

Klaus Kinski, Margaret Lee, Rosalba Neri.

Kinski's diabolical stare is put to good use as he plays the crazed head of an insane asylum, forms of treatments within which are not worth mentioning. The following year the talented Kinski would get relief from such trite roles in AGUIRRE: THE WRATH OF GOD.

p, Armando Novelli, Tizio Longo; d, Fernando Di Leo; w, Di Leo, Nino Latino; ph, (Eastmancolor).

Horror   (PR:O MPAA:R)

SLAUGHTER IN SAN FRANCISCO* (1981) 87m Golden Harvest/World Northal c

Don Wong, Chuck Norris, Sylvia Channing, Robert Jones, Dan Ivan, Bob Talbert, Robert J. Herguth, James Economides, Chuck Boyde.

Though originally shot in 1973, this film was not released in the U.S. until the 1980s, when Norris had a solid enough following to ensure some box office success. An oddity of this film is that Norris plays the bad guy, and in the climactic scene, he gets pounced on by the hero Wong. Otherwise just another martial arts film in which mean whites pick on Orientals and blacks. Set in Daly City near San Francisco.

p, Leonard K.C. Ho; d&w, William Lowe; ph, David Bailes; m, Joe Curtis; ed, Fred Cumings.

Martial Arts   Cas.   (PR:O MPAA:R)

SLAUGHTER OF THE VAMPIRES, THE
(SEE: CURSE OF THE BLOOD GHOULS, 1969, Ital.)

SLAUGHTER ON TENTH AVENUE*** (1957) 103m UNIV bw

Richard Egan (*William Keating*), Jan Sterling (*Madge Pitts*), Dan Duryea (*John Jacob Masters*), Julie Adams (*Dee*), Walter Matthau (*Al Dahlke*), Charles McGraw (*Lt. Anthony Vosnick*), Sam Levene (*Howard Rysdale*),

Mickey Shaughnessy *(Solly Pitts)*, Harry Bellaver *(Benjy Karp)*, Nick Dennis *(Midget)*, Ned Weaver *(Eddie "Cockeye" Cook)*, Billy M. Greene *("Monk" Mohler)*, John McNamara *(Judge)*, Amzie Stickland *(Mrs. Cavanagh)*, Mickey Hargitay *(Big John)*, George Becwar.

The title for this movie is drawn from the Richard Rodgers music he did for a ballet in the stage presentation "On Your Toes." It's a highlight of this semidocumentary as Joe Gershenson's musical direction and Herschel Burke Gilbert's magnificent orchestrations keep it humming in the background. This was made a few years after ON THE WATERFRONT and covers much the same territory, although not as well. Egan, playing the real-life Pennsylvania poor boy who came to New York to be the assistant district attorney, gets the task of discovering who shot Shaughnessy, a longshoreman who had been working on exposing the gangsters in and around the docks. Shaughnessy's widow is Sterling (a marvelous, sympathetic role) and she and two of the law-abiding dock workers, Bellaver and Dennis, reluctantly help Egan get to the bottom of things. Levene is Egan's boss and pushing his charge to keep going in the face of a "code of silence" put up by everyone else. The bad guys are led by Matthau, who had not yet become a major comedy actor and Duryea, who is the criminals' mouthpiece. Egan's wife, Adams, sticks by her man as he goes deeper into the underworld to uncover the truth. Shaughnessy lingers on the edge of death for a while and then, when he knows he is checking out, gives Egan the information that leads to the trial at the end of the picture. At one point, Egan thinks Levene may be part of the cabal because Duryea had once worked for him and continues to be a friend. In the end, the case is solved and the racketeers are run off the docks so the honest workers can go back to what they do. The killer is menacingly played by Weaver and Hargitay, once mainly known as being one of Mae West's night club act muscle men before he married Jayne Mansfield, is a tough guy. McGraw chips in with a solid performance as a cop and Shaughnessy, in an unaccustomed dramatic role, proves that he can play serious as well as funny with equal ability. Laven, who was later to become very successful in a TV partnership with Levy and Gardner ("The Rifleman," etc.) handles the directing well and gives it a gritty feeling of reality.

p, Albert Zugsmith; d, Arnold Laven; w, Lawrence Roman (based on *The Man Who Rocked The Boat* by William J. Keating, Richard Carter); ph, Fred Jackman; m, Richard Rodgers; ed, Russell F. Schoengarth; md, Joseph Gershenson; art d, Alexander Golitzen, Robert E. Smith; cos, Bill Thomas.

Crime Drama   (PR:A-C   MPAA:NR)

SLAUGHTER TRAIL*½   (1951) 78m RKO c

Brian Donlevy *(Capt. Dempster)*, Gig Young *(Vaughn)*, Virginia Grey *(Lorabelle Larkin)*, Andy Devine *(Sgt. McIntosh)*, Robert Hutton *(Lt. Morgan)*, Terry Gilkyson *(Singalong)*, Lew Bedell *(Hardsaddle)*, Myron Healey *(Heath)*, Ken Koutnik *(Levering)*, Eddie Parks *(Rufus Black)*, Ralph Peters *(Stage Driver)*, Rick Roman *(Chief Paako)*, Lois Hall *(Susan)*, Robin Fletcher *(Nancy)*, Ralph Volkie *(Sentry)*, Fenton Jones *(Caller)*.

The attempt to move the story along, by interjecting folksinger Gilkyson to warble out events, backfired, and only slowed the story. This formula western just wasn't the proper material for such a device. (CAT BALLOU would be a more fitting use of this idea). Donlevy plays a cavalry commander who has a lot of angry Indians on his hands for the senseless killing of two braves. The culprit is Young, a supposedly honest rancher who really robs stages; once he is killed peace is restored. Originally Howard Da Silva had Donlevy's role, but because of his allegedly Communist connections, when Howard Hughes bought the film all the scenes in which Da Silva appeared were reshot using Donlevy. Reworking had to be done, to say the least. Songs include: "Hoofbeat Serenade," "Ballad of Bandelier," Lyn Murray, Sid Kuller, "The Girl in the Wood," Terry Gilkyson, Neal Stuart, "Everyone's Crazy 'Ceptin' Me," Gilkyson, Kuller, "Jittery Deer-Foot Dan," Gilkyson.

p&d, Irving Allen; w, Sid Kuller; ph, Jack Greenhalgh (Cinecolor); ed, Fred Allen; md, Darrell Calker; art d, George Van Marta.

Western   (PR:A   MPAA:NR)

SLAUGHTERHOUSE-FIVE**½   (1972) 104m UNIV-Vandas/UNIV c

Michael Sacks *(Billy Pilgrim)*, Ron Leibman *(Paul Lazzaro)*, Eugene Roche *(Edgar Derby)*, Sharon Gans *(Valencia Marble Pilgrim)*, Valerie Perrine *(Montana Wildhack)*, Roberts Blossom *(Wild Bob Cody)*, Sorrell Brooke *(Lionel Merble)*, Kevin Conway *(Weary)*, Gary Waynesmith *(Stanley)*, John Dehner *(Rumford)*, Stan Gottlieb *(Hobo)*, Perry King *(Robert Pilgrim)*, Friedrich Ledebur *(German Leader)*, Nick Belle *(Young German Guard)*, Henry Bumstead *(Eliot Rosewater)*, Lucille Benson *(Billy's Mother)*, Gilmer McCormick *(Lily)*, Holly Near *(Barbara)*, Richard Schaal *(Campbell)*, Karl Otto Alberty *(German Guard, Group 2)*, Tom Wood *(Englishman)*.

A bold attempt at adapting Vonnegut's book fails, but there are enough moments in the film to make it worth a viewing. Sacks, in his movie debut, is a middle-aged optometrist living in a small New York town, married to rotund Gans, and the father of two children, King and Near. Sacks writes some letters to the local paper stating that he has been time-tripping, traveling around in different eras besides his own, and he doesn't know what to do about it. He relives his WW II experiences, his mental collapse before

coming home to the U.S., his marriage to Gans, and his current life. He is also transported to another future century and an uncharted planet where he spends most of his time making love to Perrine, a porno movie star, who has also been taken to this odd planet where they are viewed by the natives as they live in a clear, plastic dome. Sacks' wife, Gans, is a rich woman, totally devoted to him. His daughter, Near, is rapidly becoming a carbon copy of Gans, and King, who was a hippie, has now been transformed into a right-wing war lover. In his WW II life, Sacks meets Roche, an older GI, when they are captured by the Germans and placed in a slaughterhouse that has been converted to a prison in Dresden. Leibman is a pyschopathic GI who harasses Sacks and accuses him of having killed a pal. Dresden is bombed in February of 1945 and the city loses more than 130,000 citizens, who die when the fires sweep the area. The shame of the fire-storm is that Dresden is not an important target, has no military meaning, and is an area that is solely residential, with no defenses. The American prisoners are given the assignment of clearing the bodies. Roche, a sympathetic man who is both a friend and an inspiration to Sacks, picks up a small figure from the ashes and is shot immediately by a German soldier for looting. Flash to another time when Sacks survives a plane crash on his way to an optometry conclave. Gans hears of the accident and is on her way to see Sacks at the hospital when she is killed in a car crash. Sacks recovers, returns home to an empty house, as his kids are now on their own. Near is now married to gentle Waynesmith and they offer to take Sacks in so he won't be lonely. Sacks begs off, preferring to remain alone. He speaks at a local meeting hall to explain his letters about jumping across time and is there shot and killed by Leibman, who has harbored his grudge for decades. Instead of his life ending then and there, Sacks goes back to the distant planet where he is told that there is no life or death in a person's life, just moments in an infinite period. Perrine delivers a baby by Sacks and the planet's inhabitants, known as Tralfamadorians, cheer the birth of the child and send up fireworks in celebration. Geller's adaptation struggled to bring something to the book that wasn't there. Benson is Sacks' mother, a prime example of a cliche in action as she pulls his strings like a marionette. If this film had been shot in a strict time progression, it would not have been nearly as interesting and they were wise to stick with the inter-cutting. Harvard graduate Sacks makes an excellent lead but the promise he showed was never taken up by producers and he's done precious little since. The movie cost more than $3 million, not that much when one considers that it was shot in Prague, Minnesota, and California and that the sensational sets by Henry Bumstead (who also plays the part of Rosewater, a continuing character in Vonnegut's works) were very complex. Perrine made her picture debut here and was refreshing and untrammeled, a definite contrast to the sterile, stiff performances of some of the other players. It took almost eight months to edit, won an award at Cannes, and never made a dent at the box office. The music was by Bach, as interpreted by Canadian pianist Glenn Gould. Upon first viewing, SLAUGHTERHOUSE-FIVE is a disappointment but it is one of those rare pictures that seems to get better and make more sense with each screening. However, with so many wonderful movies to see, that should not have been the case. The sex, violence, and language make this a poor choice for children.

p, Paul Monash; d, George Roy Hill; w, Stephen Geller (based on the novel *Slaughterhouse-Five Or The Children's Crusade* by Kurt Vonnegut, Jr.); ph, Miroslav Ondricek (Technicolor); m, Glenn Gould (from the works of Johann Sebastian Bach); ed, Dede Allen; prod d, Henry Bumstead; art d, Alexander Golitzen, George Webb; set d, John McCarthy; makeup, John Chambers, Mark Reedall.

Science Fiction/War   Cas.   (PR:O   MPAA:R)

SLAUGHTER'S BIG RIP-OFF*½   (1973) 93m A]P c

Jim Brown *(Slaughter)*, Ed McMahon *(Duncan)*, Brock Peters *(Reynolds)*, Don Stroud *(Kirk)*, Gloria Hendry *(Marcia)*, Richard Williams *(Joe Creole)*, Art Metrano *(Burtoli)*, Judy Brown *(Norja)*, Eddie LoRusso *(Arnie)*, Jackie Giroux *(Mrs. Duncan)*, Russ Marin *(Crowder)*, Tony Brubaker *(Ed Pratt)*, Gene LeBell *(Leo)*, Fuji *(Chin)*, Russ McGinn *(Harvey)*, Hoke Howell, Chuck Hicks, Leu Camacho, Piper Alvez, Lisa Moore, Chuck G. Niles, Reg Parton.

The original SLAUGHTER did well enough at the box office to warrant a successor which differs little in content, theme, and overabundant violence. This time the syndicate, led by Ed McMahon, is out to do Brown in for his exploits in the original film. He manages to evade them with ingenious methods, but when his girl friend is killed, Brown goes on a killing rampage. Performances are a little better this time in that the performers are at least putting some effort forth.

p, Monroe Sachson; d, Gordon Douglas; w, Charles Johnson (based on the character created by Don Williams); ph, Charles Wheeler (Movielab Color); m, James Brown, Fred Wesley; ed, Christopher Holmes; art d, Alfeo Bocchicchio; set d, Tony Montenaro; spec eff, Logan Franzee; m/l, Brown, Wesley, Charles Bobbitt.

Crime   (PR:O   MPAA:R)

SLAVE, THE*½   (1963, Ital.) 90m Titanus-Arta/MGM c (IL FIGLIO DI SPARTACUS; AKA: SON OF SPARTACUS)

Steve Reeves *(Randus, the Son of Spartacus)*, Jacques Sernas *(Vezio)*, Gianna Maria Canale *(Clodia)*, Claudio Gora *(Cesare Grassus)*, Ivo Garrani

(Julius Caesar), Enzo Fiermonte *(Gular)*, Ombretta Colli *(Slave Girl)*, Roland Bartrop, Franco Balducci, Renato Baldini, Gloria Parri, Benito Stefanelli, Ahmed Ramzy.

Under the guise of working for Caesar, Reeves leads a slave revolt against a tyrannical Gora, carving an "S" into each of his victims. When the muscle-bound warrior is captured by Gora, his followers come to his rescue by pouring melted gold onto Gora's face. Ouch! Reeves is labeled a hero in the land he freed, where once his father, Spartacus, died defending against the Romans.

d, Sergio Corbucci; w, Adriano Bolzoni, Bruno Corbucci, Giovanni Grimaldi (based on a story by Bolzoni); ph, Enzo Barboni (CinemaScope, Eastmancolor); m, Piero Piccioni; ed, Ruggero Mastroianni; md, Pierluigi Urbini; art d, Ottavio Scotti; set d, Riccardo Domenici; cos, A. Antonelli, Mario Giorsi; makeup, Piero Mecacci, Franco Di Girolamo.

Adventure/Drama (PR:A MPAA:NR)

SLAVE GIRL*½ (1947) 80m UNIV c

Yvonne De Carlo *(Francesca)*, George Brent *(Matt Claibourne)*, Broderick Crawford *(Chips Jackson)*, Claibourne's Bodyguard, Albert Dekker *(Pasha)*, Lois Collier *(Aleta)*, Andy Devine *(Ben)*, Carl Esmond *(El Hamid)*, Arthur Treacher *(Liverpool)*, Philip Van Zandt *(Yusef)*, Dan Seymour *(Telek Taurog)*, Trevor Bardette *(Proprietor of "Sign of the Grapes")*, Eddie Dunn *(Captain)*, Mickey Simpson *(Head Guard)*, Rex Lease, George J. Lewis, Jack Ingram, Harold Goodwin, Don Turner, Phil Schumacher, Jack Shutta, Paul Bratti, Joseph Haworth *(Americans)*, Toni Raimondo *(Slave Girl)*, June Marlowe *(Mildred)*, Shimen Ruskin *(Rug Merchant)*, Nancy Brinckman *(Maid)*, Roseanne Murray *(Sally)*, Harry Cording *(Guard Captain)*, Noble Johnson *(Native Guard)*, Jack Reitzen *(Auctioneer)*, Raman Al Amar, Yussef Ali *(Guards)*, Jerome Groves, Rudolph Medina, Harry Lamont, Tony Del Rio *(Natives in Torture Chamber)*, Lloyd Ingraham *(Locksmith)*, Lacia Sonami *(Native Girl)*, Bert Richman, Eddie Abdo, Michael Gaddis *(Natives)*, Lumpy the Camel.

Spoof on swashbucklers stars Brent as a U.S. diplomat on his way to Tripoli to claim 10 American hostages held by Dekker. Along the way he is hijacked and loses the money he was to use to buy back the sailors. The rest of the film concentrates on his efforts to retrieve the stolen money, his encounters ranging from harems to torture chambers. He eventually gets the money and saves De Carlo at the same time, she being a mystery girl who keeps popping up at opportune moments. Film's saving grace is a talking camel named Lumpy that has a Brooklyn accent and comments on the action as it takes place. Otherwise the jokes aren't really funny; they are, for the most part, overused slapstick routines. De Carlo and Brent are both horribly out-of-place in this type of stuff.

p, Michael Fessier, Ernest Pagano; d, Charles Lamont; w, Fessier, Pagano; ph, George Robinson, W. Howard Greene (Technicolor); m, Milton Rosen; ed, Frank Gross; md, David Tamkin; art d, Abraham Grossman; set d, Russell A. Gausman, Edward R. Robinson; cos, Yvonne Wood; ch, Si-Lan Chen.

Comedy (PR:A MPAA:NR)

SLAVE GIRLS (SEE: PREHISTORIC WOMEN, 1967, Brit.)

SLAVE OF THE CANNIBAL GOD* (1979, Ital.) 85m New Line c (IL MONTAGNA DI DIO CANNIBALE; LA MONTAGNA DEL DIO CANNIBALE; AKA: MOUNTAIN OF CANNIBAL GODS)

Ursula Andress, Stacy Keach, Helmut Berger, Claudio Cassinelli, Franco Fantasia.

Keach and Andress search the jungles of New Guinea for Andress' lost husband, who is found to be dead and the object of worship to a tribe of headhunters. Scripters thought of every ploy possible to create suspense, but failed miserably.

p, Danio; d, Sergio Martino.

Adventure Cas. (PR:O MPAA:R)

SLAVE SHIP* (1937) 90m FOX bw

Warner Baxter *(Jim Lovett)*, Wallace Beery *(Jack Thompson)*, Elizabeth Allan *(Nancy Marlowe)*, Mickey Rooney *(Swifty)*, George Sanders *(Lefty)*, Jane Darwell *(Mrs. Marlowe)*, Joseph Schildkraut *(Danelo)*, Arthur Hohl *(Grimes)*, Minna Gombell *(Mabel)*, Billy Bevan *(Atkins)*, Francis Ford *(Scraps)*, J. Farrell MacDonald *(Proprietor)*, Miles Mander *(Corey)*, Douglas Scott *(Boy)*, Jane Jones *(Ma Belcher)*, J.P. McGowan *(Helmsman)*, Chester Gan, Bobby Dunn, Jack Low, John Bleifer, Sven Hugo Borg *(Crew Members)*, DeWitt Jennings *(Snodgrass)*, Stymie Beard *(Black Boy on Pier)*, Eddie Dunn *(Ostler)*, Lon Chaney, Jr, Russ Clark *(Laborers)*, Herbert Heywood *(Sea Captain)*, Holmes Herbert *(Judge)*, Landers Stevens *(Owner)*, Winter Hall *(Minister)*, Anita Brown *(Slave Woman)*, Dewey Robinson, Tom Kennedy *(Bartenders)*, Paul Hurst, Edwin Maxwell, Dorothy Christy, Charles Middleton, Marilyn Knowlden, Arthur Aylesworth.

Slave trader Baxter wants to go straight, deciding to replace his crew in order to start fresh. But his shipmen don't want to give up their ship so

easily and mutiny, paving the way for blazing sword fights and dazzling rescues. Rooney plays the cabin boy whose job it is to serve up a laugh or two.

p, Darryl F. Zanuck; d, Tay Garnett; w, Sam Hellman, Lamar Trotti, Gladys Lehman, William Faulkner (based on the novel *The Last Slaver* by Dr. George S. King); ph, Ernest Palmer; m, Alfred Newman; ed, Lloyd Nosler; art d, Hans Peters; cos, Royer.

Adventure (PR:A MPAA:NR)

SLAVERS* (1977, Ger.) 102m Lord Film/ITM c

Trevor Howard *(Alec Mackenzie)*, Ron Ely *(Steven Hamilton)*, Britt Ekland *(Anna von Erken)*, Jurgen Goslar *(Max von Erken)*, Ray Milland *(Hassan)*, Don Jack Rousseau *(Mazu)*, Helen Morgan *(Malika)*, Ken Gampu, Cameron Mitchell, Larry Taylor, Brian O'Shaughnessy, Art Brauss, Eric Schumann, Vera Jesse, Rinaldo Talamonti.

Highly authentic depiction, down to some of the most gruesome details, of the slave trade in the late 19th Century. Milland plays an Arab with a strict sense of moral responsibility but little regard for the lives of the slaves, whom he treats worse than animals (using them for target practice, to name just one of the atrocities). Intertwined are the attempts of a black couple and a white couple to carry on love affairs. Filmed on location in Rhodesia.

p&d, Jurgen Goslar; w, Henry Morrison, Nathaniel Kohn, Marcia MacDonald; ph, Igor Luther (Eastmancolor); m, Eberhard Schoener; ed, Fred Srp; art d, John Rosearne, Peter Roehrig; cos, Siegbert Kammerer; spec eff, Richard Richtsfeld, Helmut Klee.

Adventure/Drama Cas. (PR:O MPAA:R)

SLAVES (1969) 110m Theatre Guild–Walter Reade/Continental c

Stephen Boyd *(Nathan MacKay)*, Dionne Warwick *(Cassy)*, Ossie Davis *(Luke)*, Robert Kya-Hill *(Jericho)*, Barbara Ann Teer *(Esther)*, Marilyn Clark *(Mrs. Bennett)*, Gale Sondergaard *(New Orleans Lady)*, Nancy Coleman *(Mrs. Stillwell)*, Shepperd Strudwick *(Arthur Stillwell)*, Julius Harris *(Shadrach)*, David Huddleston *(Holland)*, Eva Jessye *(Julia)*, James Heath *(Luther)*, Aldine King *(Emmeline)*, Oscar Paul Jones *(Zacharious)*.

A sincere but ineptly handled and badly dated attempt to illustrate the evils of American slavery while showing sympathy and understanding for all involved. The result is a misfired mess that becomes frequently laughable because of the unfocused, pretentious, and overambitious nature of the screenplay. Davis stars as the favorite slave of a Kentucky rancher who is forced to sell his holdings circa 1850. Mississippi plantation owner Boyd buys Davis and two other slaves (Kya-Hill, King) from the rancher and transports them south. Boyd, a former slave ship captain, is an educated man with an appreciation for African culture which is demonstrated by the African art that adorns his home. Unfortunately he is a man with a cruel nature which he takes out on his slaves, especially his black mistress, Warwick. Though he generously provides nice clothing and jewelry for Warwick, he never hesitates to degrade and humiliate her privately or publicly. Davis' deep distrust of Boyd turns to outrage when the vicious plantation owner allows a slave woman to die during childbirth rather than call a doctor for her. Davis decides to raise the child as his own and vows that the infant girl will never grow into slavery. The complacent Warwick begins to see things through Davis' eyes and draws strength from him. One night when Boyd is drunk, Warwick defies the slave owner and threatens him with a knife. Davis interrupts the scene, disarms Warwick, and promises to help her escape before Boyd can enact revenge. Aided by Kya-Hill, Davis hides Warwick, King, and the baby girl in an attic. Boyd learns of the plan and tortures Kya-Hill to gain specific information on the whereabouts of the women. Failing to make the slave speak, Boyd cleverly offers Davis his freedom in exchange for the information. The noble black refuses and is killed. Davis' sacrifice serves to unite the other slaves on the plantation and they set fire to the cotton fields to divert attention from the women in the attic who manage to escape during the chaos. For all its good intentions, SLAVES is really no better than overwrought melodrama seeking to exploit the racial unrest of the 1960s. Davis is much too old for his virile character to be convincing, Boyd chews the scenery, and Warwick, in her movie debut, is a better singer than an actress. SLAVES was the first film to be directed by Herbert J. Biberman in 15 years due to the blacklisting he suffered in the 1950s. Finally able to return to the set, Biberman used the opportunity to return his wife Gale Sondergaard to the screen, for she, too, had been blacklisted. Unfortunately, her appearance in this slightly embarrassing effort is best forgotten.

p, Philip Langner; d, Herbert J. Biberman; w, Biberman, John O. Killens, Alida Sherman; ph, Joseph Brun (Eastmancolor); m, Bobby Scott; ed, Sidney Meyers; art d, Burr Smidt; cos, Robert Magahay, Laurence Gross; m/l, "Slaves," "Lullaby," "Another Mornin'," Scott (sung by Dionne Warwick).

Drama (PR:O MPAA:NR)

SLAVES OF BABYLON*½   (1953) 82m COL c

Richard Conte (*Nahum*), Linda Christian (*Princess Panthea*), Maurice Schwartz (*Daniel*), Terrance Kilburn (*Cyrus*), Michael Ansara (*Belshazzar*), Leslie Bradley (*Nebuchadnezzar*), Ruth Storey (*Rachel*), John Crawford (*General Avil*), Ric Roman (*Arrioch*), Robert Griffin (*King Astyages*), Beatrice Maude (*Cyrus' Mother*), Wheaton Chambers (*Cyrus' Father*), Paul Purcell (*Overseer*), Julie Newmeyer [Newman] (*Specialty Dancer*), Ernestine Barrier (*Princess Mandane*).

The classic Bible tale of the Israelites, rescue from Babylon was given a bit of reworking to fit the Hollywood story-telling mold. Schwartz is the Jew who uses his wit, helped along by a few miracles, to free his people. Movement of the story depends upon too much dialog, and Castle directs in his usual way.

p, Sam Katzman; d, William Castle; w, DeVallon Scott; ph, Henry Freulich (Technicolor); ed, William A. Lyon; md, Mischa Bakaleinikoff; art d, Paul Palmentola.

Religious Adventure   **(PR:A   MPAA:NR)**

SLAYER, THE*½   (1982) 80m International Picture Show/21st Century c (AKA: NIGHTMARE ISLAND)

Sarah Kendall (*Kay*), Frederick Flynn (*Eric*), Carol Kottenbrook (*Brooke*), Alan McRae (*David*), Michael Holmes (*Marsh*), Carl Kraines (*The Slayer*).

Four vacationers on a small island off the coast of Georgia run around the island looking for their companions before becoming dinner for an unseen monster. The only good thing about the nightmares of this picture is that the artist in the group, Kendall, develops a stronger surrealistic style, and could make some money with her paintings–if she gets off the island alive.

p, William R. Ewing; d, J.S. Cardone; w, Cardone, Ewing; ph, Karen Grossman (DeLuxe Color); M, Robert Folk; ed, Edward Salier; set d, Jerie Kelter; spec eff, Robert Babb; makeup, Robert Short; Stunts, Hill Farnsworth.

Horror   **Cas.**   **(PR:O   MPAA:R)**

SLEEP, MY LOVE***   (1948) 97m Triangle/UA bw

Claudette Colbert (*Alison Courtland*), Robert Cummings (*Bruce Elcott*), Don Ameche (*Richard Courtland*), Rita Johnson (*Barby*), George Coulouris (*Charles Vernay*), Hazel Brooks (*Daphne*), Anne Triola (*Waitress*), Queenie Smith (*Mrs. Vernay*), Keye Luke (*Jimmie*), Fred Nurney (*Haskins*), Maria San Marco (*Jeannie*), Raymond Burr (*Lt. Strake*), Lillian Bronson (*Helen*), Ralph Morgan (*Dr. Rhinehart*), Jimmy Dodd (*Elevator Boy*), Ralph Peters (*Mac*), Syd Saylor (*Milkman*), Murray Alper (*Drunk*), Eddie Dun (*Bartender*), Lillian Randolph (*Maid*).

After 12 years away from films, Mary Pickford was the backstage executive producer of this murder-mystery with her husband Buddy Rogers. Wealthy Colbert, a socialite married to Ameche, is found aboard a train chugging toward Boston. She has no idea what she's doing on the train or how she got there. Smith, a nice old lady, helps her get in touch with Ameche, who is at their residence with police, whom he's called after Colbert's disappearance. The phone conversation is heard by officer Burr, as Ameche reminds Colbert that she had earlier threatened his life with a revolver, a fact Colbert does not recall. Colbert hops the commuter flight back to New York and runs into charming Cummings, who shares an acquaintance with Colbert. Cummings is taken by Colbert and is rapidly moon-eyed. Back in Manhattan, Ameche suggests that Colbert see psychiatrist Coulouris. In their session, Coulouris browbeats Colbert who can't stand up to his aggressive attitude. Coulouris exits, leaving Colbert and Ameche together. Ameche leaves their residence where the session was taking place, telling his wife that he has an important business engagement. Camera follows Ameche to learn that his business is with Brooks, his voluptuous mistress. Now we discover that Ameche and Brooks have brought in Coulouris, a photographer, to masquerade as the psychiatrist and attempt to cause Colbert to take her own life, thus leaving Ameche her huge riches. Cummings arrives at the Colbert-Ameche residence and finds her sleepwalking on a high balcony, just inches from going over the side. Cummings smells a rat, does a bit of sleuthing, goes to Coulouris' photo studio and tells the man he needs a small passport picture. Colbert's description of her "psychiatrist" matches that of Coulouris and Cummings is now hip to what's happening. At their apartment, Ameche attempts to drug Colbert but she is wise and only pretends to be under the influence. Ameche, knowing that Coulouris can use his information to blackmail the illicit couple, plans to have Colbert kill Coulouris. When Coulouris arrives to have a "session" with his patient, he realizes what the plan is and tries to escape, but is shot by Ameche, who then turns his gun on Colbert and is about to shoot her when Cummings arrives and saves the day. The explanation is easy, once we learn that the nice old lady on the train was, in fact, the wife of Coulouris and the whole ploy was planned from the start. Some good suspense, a few shocking moments, but nowhere near many of the other *noir* classics for style, wit and cinematography. The paucity of sharp lines is odd to consider because one of the screenwriters was a very funny writer, Rosten, who also used the named "Leonard Q. Ross" when writing some of his very K*a*p*l*a*n funny books, like *The Education of H*y*m*a*n K*a*p*a*n*.

p, Charles "Buddy" Rogers, Ralph Cohn; d, Douglas Sirk; w, St. Clair McKelway, Leo Rosten [Cyril Endfield, Decla Dunning, uncredited] (based on the novel by Rosten); ph, Joseph Valentine; m, Rudy Schrager; ed, Lynn Harrison; md, Schrager; art d, William Ferrari; set d, Howard Bristol; cos, Margaret Jennings, Sophie; makeup, Burris Grimwood.

Mystery   **(PR:A   MPAA:NR)**

SLEEPAWAY CAMP*½   (1983) 85m American Eagle/United Film c

Mike Kellin (*Mel*), Felissa Rose (*Angela*), Jonathan Tierston (*Ricky*), Karen Fields (*Judy*), Christopher Collet (*Paul*), Paul De Angelo (*Ron*), Robert Earl Jones (*Ben*), Katherine Kamhi (*Meg*), John E. Dunn (*Kenny*).

A mad slasher stalks the boys and girls of Camp Arawak, slaughtering them in messy ways. A sense of humor lifts this one just slightly above the pack, but not far enough to attract anyone except fans of the genre. The director seems to go out of his way to show how cheesy the effects are.

p, Michele Tatosian, Jerry Silva; d&w, Robert Hiltzik; ph, Benjamin Davis (Technicolor); m, Edward Bilous; ed, Ron Kalish, Sharyn L. Ross; prod d, William Billowit; spec eff, Ed Fountain; m/l, Frankie Vinci; stunts, Cliff Cudney; makeup, Edward French.

Horror   **Cas.**   **(PR:O   MPAA:R)**

SLEEPER***½   (1973) 88m Rollins-Joffe/UA c

Woody Allen (*Miles Monroe*), Diane Keaton (*Luna Schlosser*), John Beck (*Erno Windt*), Marya Small (*Dr. Nero*), Bartlett Robinson (*Dr. Orva*), Mary Gregory (*Dr. Melik*), Chris Forbes (*Rainer Krebs*), Peter Hobbs (*Dr. Dean*), Spencer Milligan (*Jeb Hrmthmg*), Stanley Ralph Ross (*Sears Wiggles*), Whitney Rydbeck (*Janus*), Susan Miller (*Ellen Pogrebin*), Lou Picetti (*M.C.*), Brian Avery (*Herald Cohen*), Don McLiam (*Dr. Agon*), Don Keefer (*Dr. Tryon*), Jessica Rains (*Woman in the Mirror*).

Woody Allen owed a debt of gratitude to H.G. Wells for this idea, which is slightly similar to a tale by the master–"When the Sleeper Awakes"–that had, at one time, been a possible vehicle for AIP's major horror star, Vincent Price, around the time he was making DR. GOLDFOOT for the exploitation company. Like most of Allen's intelligent movies, this was better than the box-office receipts showed and still looks good and bright, many years after it was shot. Allen never lets his actors see a full script while they are shooting so no one, except Allen, knows what's happening in the film. Consequently, many of the performers were confused by their roles in the plot, something Allen prefers. He's a Greenwich Village health food store owner who dabbles in Dixieland jazz when he reluctantly goes to the hospital for an ulcer operation in 1973. The operation fails and the doctors quickly put him into the deep freeze. He awakens two hundred years later into a world beyond his ken. In this new world, the two doctors who revive him, Robinson and Gregory, want to enlist his help to overthrow the "Big Brother" leader who rules the world. The Leader is not a whole person, just a nose, and his aides propose to clone the tissue from that nose to build a new order. Allen gets out of the hospital in a disguise as a domestic robot and is brought to Keaton, a wealthy woman who has ordered a new robot for her home. Once she is aware that he's actually human, the two of them get to like each other and she reluctantly joins him, although she is so rich that there's no reason why she should become a revolutionary. The police begin to chase them and they wind up at the home of two gay men, Milligan and Ross, who have a swishy domestic robot, Rydbeck. Sex is a no-no in those years and people get their jollies by rubbing a metal ball known as "The Orgasmatron" which takes care of their sensuous needs. (At one point, Allen makes a comment that death is probably better than sex as one does not get nauseous after death.) Allen and Keaton flee again and are captured. Allen has his brain washed in a very funny scene and Keaton is allowed to leave. She contacts the underground and joins with their chief, Beck. The Leader has a new project in mind and the Revolutionaries send Keaton to get Allen out of the police clutches. She does so and they capture the Leader and hold the nostrils as hostage until they finally get out of the clutches of the bad guys. One sight gag after another, in a physical Buster Keaton-like fashion, and many, many literate throwaways, barbs that puncture contemporary rather than futuristic targets. When someone asks what happened to Norman Mailer, Allen says that he donated his ego to science. The MacDonald's signs show trillions of hamburgers sold, etc. One anachronistic note is that the music is all Dixie as played by Allen with the Preservation Hall Jazz Band and the New Orleans Funeral and Ragtime Orchestra. SLEEPER is a highly inventive science-fiction parody that is typical of Allen's tight, well-edited movies, which usually come in under 90 minutes. Costumes by Joel Schumacher were excellent; he later gave up sewing for writing (CAR WASH) and then directing. Both Milligan and Rydbeck eventually starred in their own Saturday morning TV shows. While shooting their scene, Allen consulted Ross,–whom he knew to be a writer, as Ross had written a TV movie for Allen's ex-wife, Louise Lasser, titled COFFEE, TEA OR ME. Allen asked, "Do you think this is funny?" and Ross shrugged as he replied, "I can't tell, Woody. I don't know what the movie is about, where this scene is in the picture or anything else." "Yes," replied Allen, "but is this scene you're in funny?" Ross answered, "Why do you ask?" Allen shook his head: "The producers don't think the movie is funny." Ross nodded, "Tell them it's funny, Woody. Tell them that if they knew what was funny, they'd be Woody Allen." "Do you do that?" wondered Allen? "All the time," smiled Ross. Allen frowned as he walked away muttering: "Gee, I wish I had your confidence." In the years to come, Allen would never again suffer from any lack of perception of his own talents as he got better and better, winning the Oscar for ANNIE HALL's direction and script and making one unique film after another, not all of them successful, but every one an attempt at broadening his own horizons.

p, Jack Grossberg; d, Woody Allen; w, Allen, Marshall Brickman; ph, David M. Walsh; m, Allen; ed, Ralph Rosenblum; md, Felix Giglio; prod d, Dale Hennesy; art d, Dianne Wager; set d, Gary Moreno; cos, Joel Schumacher; spec eff, A. D. Flowers, Gerald Endler; makeup, Del Acevedo.

Science Fiction/Comedy   Cas.   (PR:A-C MPAA:PG)

SLEEPERS EAST*½   (1934) 64m FOX bw

Wynne Gibson (Lena Karelson), Preston Foster (Jason Everett), Mona Barrie (Ada Robillard), Harvey Stephens (Martin Knox), J. Carrol Naish (Carl Izzard), Howard Lally (Jack Wentworth), Roger Imhof, Suzanne Kaaren.

A haphazard production and confusing script centered around the trial of a man who is wrongly accused of murdering a man, though he really had planned to but didn't get to his goal in time. Gibson plays the main witness who slips out of town, but is forced to appear at the trial, which accounts for the title about the train ride back.

p, Sol M. Wurtzel; d, Kenneth MacKenna; w, Lester Cole (based on the novel by Frederick Nebel); ph, Ernest Palmer; m, Samuel Kaylin; cos, Royer.

Crime   (PR:A MPAA:NR)

SLEEPERS WEST*½   (1941) 74m FOX bw

Lloyd Nolan (Michael Shayne), Lynn Bari (Kay Bentley), Mary Beth Hughes (Helen Carlson), Louis Jean Heydt (Everett Jason), Edward Brophy (George Trautwein), Don Costello (Carl Izzard), Ben Carter (Pullman Porter), Don Douglas (Tom Linscott), Oscar O'Shea (McGowan), Harry Hayden (Conductor Lyons), Hamilton MacFadden (Meyers), Ferike Boros (Old Lady).

Dull story starring Nolan as a private dick trying to bring a key witness (Hughes) from Denver to San Francisco via train so the girl can clear a man convicted of murder. Along the way Nolan must protect her from people who don't want her to reach the final destination. Based on some character names and the novel by Nebel, this seems to be a partial remake of SLEEPERS EAST (1934). (See MICHAEL SHAYNE series, Index.)

p, Sol M. Wurtzel; d, Eugene Forde; w, Lou Breslow, Stanley Rauh (based on a novel by Frederick Nebel and the character created by Brett Halliday); ph, Peverell Marley; ed, Fred Allen; md, Emil Newman.

Crime/Drama   (PR:A MPAA:NR)

SLEEPING BEAUTY***½   (1959) 75m Disney/BV c

Voices: Eleanor Audley (Maleficent), Verna Felton (Flora), Barbara Jo Allen [Vera Vague] (Fauna), Barbara Luddy (Merryweather), Taylor Holmes (King Stefan), Bill Thompson (King Hubert), Candy Candido (Goons), Mary Costa (Princess Aurora), Bill Shirley (Prince Phillip).

One of the most ambitious projects ever undertaken by Disney, SLEEPING BEAUTY opens as the King and Queen decide to throw a gala celebration to announce the birth of their daughter Aurora and her immediate betrothal to the infant Prince Phillip. Unfortunately, the overjoyed parents neglect to invite the evil fairy Maleficent, causing the rebuked and angry denizen of the forest to place a curse on the infant girl that ensures she will prick her finger on a spindle upon her 16th birthday and die. The curse is altered somewhat when a good fairy casts a counterspell that changes death to sleep. Hoping to prevent the black prophecy from coming to fruition, three good fairies named Flora, Fauna, and Merryweather take the baby into the forest where they can raise her away from the prying eyes of Maleficent. The fairies keep the girl's royal identity a secret from her and she grows up to be a normal young woman. One day she meets Prince Phillip in the forest, and though both are unaware that they have been betrothed since birth, they fall in love. Tragedy soon strikes despite the three good fairies precautions because on Aurora's 16th birthday the curse is enacted and she falls into a deep sleep which can only be broken by the kiss of a brave Prince. Knowing Prince Phillip will try to awaken Aurora, the evil Maleficent kidnaps him. The fairies cast a spell over the kingdom so that no one will know what transpires and then go to the rescue of the Prince and help him escape. Enraged, Maleficent transforms herself into a hideous fire-breathing dragon and tries to block their path. Phillip bravely battles the evil creature and defeats her. The threat removed, Phillip goes to Aurora and revives her with a kiss. The good fairies then remove the spell from the kingdom and a celebration is held to announce the marriage of Aurora and Phillip. SLEEPING BEAUTY was initiated by Walt Disney in 1950 with the declaration that it would be the pinacle of animated filmmaking. Work began on the film, but in 1954 the project was shelved for two years due to the Disney organization's concentration on their television series and, of course, Disneyland. Work finally resumed on the film with plans to shoot in 70mm wide-screen Technirama and stereo sound. Three years and $6 million later SLEEPING BEAUTY was ready for release. It was the most expensive

animated film ever made and every penny was on the screen. The attention to movement and detail is stunning, with multi-leveled layers of action filling the frame. The highlight of the film, the fight with the dragon, is terrifying, exciting, and brilliantly executed, though some may find it a bit too scary for youngsters. Unfortunately, for all its technical virtuosity SLEEPING BEAUTY is something of a disappointment in the script department. Aurora and Prince Phillip are cookie-cutter imitations of Snow White and her Prince and though the film runs a scant 75 minutes, there is little action. On its initial release the film grossed $5.3 million which made it neither a hit with the public, nor financially successful for the studio. Disney learned his lesson well and stayed away from fairy tales and instead concentrated on more contemporary fare like 101 DALMATIONS (1961) and innocuous live-action films like THE SHAGGY DOG (1959), THE ABSENT MINDED PROFESSOR (1961), and SON OF FLUBBER (1963). In addition to themes from Tchaikovsky's "Sleeping Beauty," songs include "Once Upon a Dream" (Sammy Fain, Jack Lawrence), "Hail the Princess Aurora" (Tom Adair, George Bruns), "I Wonder" (Winston Hibler, Ted Sears, Bruns), "The Skump Song" (Adair, Erdman Penner, Bruns), "The Sleeping Beauty Song" (Adair, Bruns).

p, Walt Disney; d, Clyde Geronimi, Eric Larson, Wolfgang Reitherman, Les Clark; ph, (Technirama, Technicolor); m, George Bruns from Petr Illich Tchaikovsky's "Sleeping Beauty Ballet";; ed, Roy M. Brewer, Jr., Donald Halliday; prod d, Donald Da Gradi, Ken Anderson; animation, Hal King, Hal Ambro, Don Lusk, Blaine Gibson, John Sibley, Bob Carson, Ken Hultgren, Harvey Toombs, Fred Kopietz, George Nicholas, Bob Youngquist, Eric Cleworth, Henry Tanous, John Kennedy, Ken O'Brien; backgrounds, Frank Armitage, Thelma Witmer, Albert Dempster, Walt Peregoy, Bill Layne, Ralph Hulett, Dick Anthony, Fil Mottola, Richard H. Thomas, Anthony Rizzo.

Fantasy/Animation   (PR:AAA MPAA:G)

SLEEPING BEAUTY**½   (1965, Ger.) 70m Fritz Genschow/Childhood (DORNROSCHEN)

Karin Hardt (The Queen), Fritz Genschow (The King), Angela von Leitner (Sleeping Beauty), Gert Reinholm (Prince Charming), Paul Tripp (Narrator), Renee Stobrawa, Gustav Bertram, Elfe Schneider, Wulf Rittscher, Gisela Schauroth, Rudolf Stor, Anni Marle, Theodor Vogeler, Walter Bluhm.

The Grimms' fairy tale about the young beauty who falls into a deep sleep as the result of an evil curse is set in the Bavarian forest to add impact. It was released, at 82 minutes, in West Germany in 1955, and dubbed and rescored for its U.S. release.

p&d, Fritz Genschow; w, Genschow, Renee Stobrawa, Helga Weichert (based on "Dornroschen" by Jakob and Wilhelm Grimm); ph, Gerhard Huttula (Agfacolor); m, Hans-Joachim Wunderlich; md (English version), Lehman Engel; art d, Otto Reysser, Waldemar Volkmer; m/l (English version), Anne Delugg, Milton Delugg; ch, Carola Krauskopf.

Adventure/Fantasy   (PR:AAA MPAA:NR)

SLEEPING BEAUTY, THE**½   (1966, USSR) 90m Lenfilm/Royal c (SPYASHCHAYA KRASAVITSA)

Alla Sizova (Princess Aurora), Yuri Soloviev (Prince Desire), Natalia Dudinskaya (The Wicked Fairy), Irina Bazhenova (The Lilac Fairy), Vsevolod Ukhov (The King), O. Zabotkina (The Queen), Natalia Makasova (Princess Florina), Valeri Panov (Blue Bird), V. Riazanov (Master of Ceremonies), E. Minchenok (Tenderness), I. Korneyeva (Playfulness), L. Kovalyova (Generosity), K. Fedicheva (Courage), N. Sakhnovskaya (Light-heartedness), G. Kekisheva (White Pussy), S. Kuznetsov (Puss in Boots), Sergei Vykulov, Kirov State Academic Theatre Corps de Ballet, Students of the Vaganova Dancing School.

A filmed version of the famous Tchaikovsky ballet in which a curse is placed upon an infant princess. On the girl's 16th birthday, the kingdom falls into a slumber that lasts for 100 years, at which time a handsome prince travels through the forest to the palace, kisses the sleeping girl, and awakens the entire kingdom.

d, Apollinariy Dudko, Konstantin Sergeyev; w, Sergeyev, Iosif Shapiro (based on "La Belle Au Bois Dormant" by Charles Perrault); ph, Anatoliy Nazartov (Techniscope, Technicolor); m, Peter Ilich Tchaikovsky; md, B. Khaykin, V. Gamaliya; art d, T. Vasilkovskaya, V. Ulitko; set d, Ye. Yakuba; spec eff, N. Pokoptsev, M. Krotkin; ch, Sergeyev (based on that of Marius Petipa).

Ballet   (PR:AAA MPAA:NR)

SLEEPING CAR**   (1933, Brit.) 82m GAU/Gaumont Ideal bw

Madeleine Carroll (Anne), Ivor Novello (Gaston), Laddie Cliff (Pierre), Kay Hammond (Simone), Claud Allister (Baron Delande), Stanley Holloway (Francois), Vera Bryer (Jenny), Ivor Barnard (Durande), Pat Fitzpatrick, Sam Keen, Richard Littledale, Peggy Simpson.

While traveling across the European continent, wealthy widow Carroll is taken in by her flirtatious conductor. She uses him as a way to stay in France, but eventually they fall in love.

p, Michael Balcon; d, Anatole Litvak; w, Franz Schultz.

Comedy   (PR:A   MPAA:NR)

SLEEPING CAR MURDER THE*½**   (1966, Fr.) 92m PECF-Seven
Arts/FOX bw (COMPARTIMENT TUEURS).

Yves Montand (*Inspector Grazzi*), Simone Signoret (*Eliane Darres*), Pierre
Mondy (*Commissioner*), Catherine Allegret (*Bambi*), Pascale Roberts (*Geor-
gette Thomas*), Jacques Perrin (*Daniel*), Michel Piccoli (*Cabourg*), Jean-
Louis Trintignant (*Eric*), Charles Denner (*Bob*), Claude Mann (*Jean-Lou*),
Nadine Alari (*Madame Grazzi*), Georges Geret, Claude Dauphin, Daniel
Gelin, Marcel Bozzufi, Tanya Lopert, Bernadette Lafont, Francoise Arnoul,
Andre Valmy, Maurice Chevit, Jacques Dynam, Jean Lefebvre, Jean-Pierre
Perier, Christian Marin, Serge Rausseau, Paul Pavel, Albert Michel, Jenny
Orleans, Clement Harari, B. Paul, R. Sabatier, J. Steiner.

Costa-Gavras (Z, STATE OF SIEGE, MISSING) made his directorial debut
with this tightly constructed suspense thriller which stars Montand as a
French police inspector investigating the murder of a woman who was
sleeping in a lower berth on a moving train. Aided by his assistant Mann,
Montand begins to track down all the passengers who were in the train
compartment where the murder took place. Piccoli, an office worker who
was on the train, volunteers information but is found murdered soon after.
At the same time two other passengers, Allegret and Perrin, attempt to
avoid the police because the latter is a runaway who will be taken back to
his parents if found. Perrin was hiding from the conductor in a berth and
was aided by Allegret, a young woman traveling to a new job in Paris. After
the murder the pair stumble across the wallet of Signoret, an aging actress
who also was a passenger on the train that night, and they then go to her
home to return it. Before knocking at her door, they notice she is being
interrogated by Montand. Perrin and Allegret hide nearby and watch as a
young man, Trintignant, slips out the back door of Signoret's house. During
the interrogation Signoret reveals that Perrin was hiding in an upper berth
of the compartment. Soon after Montand leaves, Signoret is murdered.
Eventually the police manage to determine that Trintignant was Signoret's
lover and when interrogated the young man provides an airtight alibi.
Meanwhile, Perrin overhears a plot by two men to kill Allegret and he tells
the girl to hide out in a hotel. The young runaway then goes to Montand and
spills everything he knows. When the police arrive they thwart the murder
attempt on Allegret and capture Trintignant. The suspect reveals that he
was only an accomplice and that the real killer is Montand's assistant Mann,
who masterminded the whole scheme in order to pilfer Signoret's large bank
account. Trintignant then goes on to state that Mann is out in the streets of
Paris now seeking to kill Perrin. Montand immediately sets out after Mann
and after a thrilling chase he saves Perrin and captures the killer. THE
SLEEPING CAR MURDERS was sort of a family affair for Montand and
Signoret who were married, and the beautiful Allegret is Signoret's
daughter by writer director Yves Allegret. While less political than the films
he would soon go on to make, Costa-Gavras' taut direction coupled with a
superior cast of foreign actors propels this somewhat impenetrable mystery
along at breakneck speed and makes for an intriguing, highly entertaining
thriller. (In French; English subtitles.)

p, Julien Derode; d, Constantin Costa-Gavras; w, Costa-Gavras, Sebastien
Japrisot (based on the novel *Compartiment Tueurs* by Japrisot); ph, Jean
Tournier; m, Michel Magne; ed, Christian Gaudin; art d, Rino Mondellini.

Crime   (PR:C-O   MPAA:NR)

SLEEPING CAR TO TRIESTE**   (1949, Brit.) 95m TC/EL bw

Jean Kent (*Valya*), Albert Lieven (*Zurta*), Derrick de Marney (*George
Grant*), Paul Dupuis (*Detective Inspector Jolif*), Rona Anderson (*Joan
Maxted*), David Tomlinson (*Tom Bishop*), Bonar Colleano (*Sgt. West*), Finlay
Currie (*Alastair MacBain*), Coco (*Gregoire*), Aslan (*Poirier*), Hugh Burden
(*Mills*), Alan Wheatley (*Poole*), David Hutcheson (*Denning*), Claude Larue
(*Andree*), Zena Marshall (*Suzanne*), Leslie Weston (*Randall*), Michael Ward
(*Elvin*), Gerard Heinz (*Ambassador*), Eugene Deckers (*Jules*), Gaston
Richer (*Henri*), George de Warfaz (*Chef du Train*), Toni de Lungo (*Beppo*),
Tony Etienne (*Benoit*), Michael Balfour (*Spiegel*), Marcel Poncin (*Charles*),
Michael Yannis (*Guido*), Henrik Jacobsen (*Embassy Butler*), Dino Galvani
(*Pierre*), Oscar Nation (*Luigi*), David Paltenghi (*Vincente*), Boris Ranevsky
(*Elderly Frenchman*), Sheila Martin (*Francois*), John Stevens (*Military
Young Man*), A.G. Guinle (*Lucien*), Andrea Malandrinos (*Italian Police
Inspector*), Norman Watson (*British Army Major*), John Serret (*Station
Master -- Dijon*), Christina Forbes (*Ilse*), Yves Chanteau (*French Station
Official*), Reginald Drummond (*Italian Policeman*), Primrose Milligan
(*Nursemaid*), Joy Harington (*Mother*), Victor Robinson (*Boy*), Mona Lilian
(*Italian Policewoman*), Merle Tottenham (*Miss Smith*), Anne Chambers,
Diana Chandler, Elaine Doran, Rose Ann Garland, Barbara Gay, Christine
Gelvard, Anne Gilchrist, Barbara Goalen, Pamela Grenville, Valerie Moss
(*Embassy Guests*).

Kent and Lieven play two thieves aboard a train, bound for the Orient, on
which is hidden a diplomat's diary containing valuable strategic information. A murder takes place aboard the train and is discovered during the
search for the diary. The plot takes the easy way out by having the last
remaining spy jump in front of a train to keep from having to work out a
more interesting ending. Based on Film ROME EXPRESS.

p, George H. Brown; d, John Paddy Carstairs; w, Allan Mackinnon, William
Douglas Home (based on the story "Rome Express" by Clifford Grey); ph,
Jack Hildyard; m, Benjamin Frankel; ed, Sidney Stone; md, Muir Mathie-
son; art d, Ralph Brinton.

Spy Drama   (PR:A   MPAA:NR)

SLEEPING CARDINAL, THE   (SEE: SHERLOCK HOLMES' FATAL
HOUR, 1931, Brit.)

SLEEPING CITY, THE**   (1950) 85m UNIV bw

Richard Conte (*Fred Rowan*), Coleen Gray (*Ann Sebastian*), Peggy Dow
(*Kathy Hall*), John Alexander (*Inspector Gordon*), Alex Nicol (*Dr. Bob
Anderson*), Richard Taber (*Pop Ware*), James J. Van Dyk (*Dr. Sharpley*),
Hugh Reilly (*Dr. Foster*), Michael Strong (*Dr. Connell*), Frank M. Thomas
(*Lt. Lally*), Richard Kendrick (*Dr. Druta*), Henry Hart (*Dr. Nester*), Robert
Strauss (*Lt. Marty Miller*), Herbert Ratner (*Detective Reese*), Mickey
Cochran (*Detective Diamond*), Ernest Sarracino (*Detective Abate*), Russell
Collins (*Medical Examiner*), Mrs. Priestly Morrison (*Miss Wardly*), James
O'Neill (*Engle*), Frank Tweddell (*Kingdon*), Victor Sutherland (*Holland*),
Jack Lescoulie (*Paulsen*), Carroll Ashburn (*Surgeon*), Tom Hoirer (*Gaye*),
William Martell (*Male Nurse*), James Little (*Travers*), Terry Denim, Harold
Bayne, Frank Baxter, James Daly, Dort Clark (*Interns*), Mimi Strongin
(*Little Girl*), Rod McLennan (*Detective*), Ralph Hertz (*Patient with Broken
Leg*).

A surprisingly intense and disturbing look at corruption in a big-city
hospital starring Conte as a police undercover agent who is assigned to pose
as a new intern to investigate the murder of a young physician and the
suicide of another. Conte learns that the dead interns were involved in
stealing and selling drugs in order to cover their gambling debts. The
reprehensible activity not only destroys the traditional trust enjoyed by
medical personnel, but endangers the lives of patients by depriving them of
needed medication. Upon further investigation Conte discovers that a nurse,
Gray, has also become involved in the drug trade, but only to aid a poor sick
child. In the end it is revealed that an elderly elevator operator, Taber, is
in fact the evil kingpin of the operation who has been blackmailing the
hospital staff to do his bidding. Though Conte has fallen in love with Gray
and has ambivalent feelings regarding her guilt, he turns her over to the
police at the end, having become deeply disturbed by the whole bleak
experience. The effect of THE SLEEPING CITY is particularly distressing
because rarely do crime films situate such a grim and sobering view of
society within a hospital, traditionally looked upon as a place of healing. The
neatly starched white gowns and general antiseptic atmosphere of the
hospital contrast sharply with the seedy goings-on. The film's view of urban
institutions (hospital, police) is one of total cynicism and corruption. Only
the Conte character demonstrates any sense of optimism or honor, but by
the end of the film he too is well on the road to hopelessness. When New
York City Mayor O'Dwyer voiced a strong protest about the film's portrayal
of the city, the studio agreed to insert a prolog in which Richard Conte
appears and states that THE SLEEPING CITY does not seek to condemn
any specific American city, but that the action about to unfold could happen
in any large city.

p, Leonard Goldstein; d, George Sherman; w, Jo Eisinger; ph, William
Miller; m, Frank Skinner; ed, Frank Gross; art d, Bernard Herzbrun, Emrich
Nicholson; set d, Fred Ballmeyer; cos, Rosemary Odell; makeup, Ira Senz.

Crime   (PR:C   MPAA:NR)

SLEEPING DOGS*½**   (1977, New Zealand) 107m Aardvark/Satori c

Sam Neill (*Smith*), Bernard Kearns (*Prime Minister*), Nevan Rowe (*Gloria*),
Ian Mune (*Bullen*), Ian Watkin (*Dudley*), Don Selwyn (*Taupiri*), Tommy
Tinirau (*Old Maori Man*), Bill Johnson (*Cousins*), Roger Oakley (*Assassin
Leader*), Clyde Scott (*Jesperson*), Dorothy McKegg (*Gloria's Mother*), Tony
Groser (*Gloria's Father*), Davina Whitehouse (*Elsie*), Bill Julliff (*Burton*),
Donna Akersten (*Mary*), Warren Oates (*Willoughby*), Melissa Donaldson
(*Melissa*), Raf Irving (*Reporter*), Cass Donaldson (*Cass*), Bernard Moody
(*Man at Wharf*).

This was director Donaldson's theatrical film debut and the first film from
New Zealand to gain international recognition. Yarn takes place in the near
future when New Zealand comes under extreme right-wing control due to
an assassination of democratic leaders. Neill joins a group of freedom
fighters trying to save democratic ideals, and Oates is a soldier of fortune
hired to do the rebels in. Direction is well paced and the New Zealand
backgrounds are used to the fullest, but too many plot points are left
unresolved, making the overall impact less powerful.

p&d, Roger Donaldson; w, Ian Mune, Arthur Baysting (based on the novel
Smith's Dream by Karl Stead); ph, Michael Sarasin; m, Murray Grindlay
David Calder, Mathew Brown; ed, Ian John; cos, Craig McLeod; spec eff,
Geoff Murphy.

Drama   Cas.   (PR:C   MPAA:NR)

SLEEPING PARTNER, 1961   (SEE: SECRET AFFAIR, THE, 1961, Brit.)

SLEEPING PARTNERS*½   (1930, Brit.) 71m Geneen/BIP bw

Seymour Hicks (He), Edna Best (She), Lyn Harding (It), Herbert Waring (Emile), Marguerite Allan (Elise), David Paget (Virtuoso).

Early British comedy – the producers hadn't yet discovered the use of various camera angles and settings to help tell a story, so it's little more than a filmed version of a play. Hicks, who also directed and scripted, plays the "other man" of married woman Best, whose husband has been busy pursuing his own affairs. Hicks takes Best to his apartment and accidentally gives her sleeping powder, and Best winds up staying the night. Harding, as the husband, shows up early the next morning, not to get his wife, but to get some advice from Hicks. This gives the latter the chance of bringing husband and wife back together. Picture has its moments but not enough to keep interest throughout.

p, Sascha Geneen, Maurice J. Wilson; d&w, Seymour Hicks (based on a play by Sascha Guitry); ph, Carl Freund; ed, Edward Jonsenn.

Comedy   (PR:A   MPAA:NR)

SLEEPING PARTNERS, 1964   (SEE: CARNIVAL OF CRIME, 1964)

SLEEPING TIGER, THE½**   (1954, Brit.) 89m Insignia/Anglo Amalgamated bw

Dirk Bogarde (Frank Clements), Alexis Smith (Glenda Esmond), Alexander Knox (Dr. Clive Esmond), Hugh Griffith (Inspector Simmons), Patricia McCarron (Sally), Maxine Audley (Carol), Glyn Houston (Bailey), Harry Towb (Harry), Russell Waters (Manager), Billie Whitelaw (Receptionist), Fred Griffiths (Taxi Driver), Esma Cannon (Window Cleaner).

A petty thief, Bogarde, gets more than he bargained for when he breaks into the home of a criminal psychiatrist, Knox. Knox manages to subdue the intruder, and has him agree to serve as a guinea pig in his psychological experiments in exchange for his freedom. If Knox's theories prove correct, he will be able to totally rehabilitate Bogarde after six months of intensive reconditioning. When Knox's wife Smith returns from a vacation she allows herself to be seduced by Bogarde and the two make plans to run off together. Bogarde plans to make one last robbery that will pay their way, but the police uncover the plot and try to arrest the thief. Surprisingly, Knox provides an alibi for Bogarde, frustrating the investigators' efforts to arrest him. Shocked by Knox's actions, Bogarde rejects Smith's advances and begins to respond to the psychiatrist's treatments. Seeking vengeance, the rebuffed Smith tells her husband that Bogarde attacked her. Knox suspects the truth, however, and pretends to shoot Bogarde dead. Bogarde then escapes the house, but he is picked up by Smith who drives frantically from the scene and crashes the car off a cliff. THE SLEEPING TIGER was American director Joseph Losey's first feature film after being blacklisted by Hollywood because he refused to testify for the House Un-American Activities Committee. Forced to flee to England, Losey was allowed to direct but he was credited under the pseudonym "Victor Hanbury" – a real director, turned producer – so as not to ruin the market for the film in the U.S. For his return to the screen, Losey turned in a competent, although unremarkable, crime melodrama which did little to enhance his reputation among the critics. Though Losey had little enthusiasm for the material he was given to direct and accepted the job just to keep working, he managed to expand upon his thematic concerns with morality, corruption, and the loss of spirituality. THE SLEEPING TIGER is also notable for the first-time collaboration of director Losey and actor Bogarde. Both men began fine-honing their respective skills together and would go on to make several fascinating, more mature films including THE SERVANT (1963), KING AND COUNTRY (1964), MODESTY BLAISE (1966), and ACCIDENT (1967).

p, Victor Hanbury; d, Hanbury (Joseph Losey); w, Derek Frye (Harold Buchman, Carl Foreman) (based on the novel by Maurice Moiseiwitsch); ph, Harry Waxman; m, Malcolm Arnold; ed, Reginald Mills; md, Muir Mathieson; art d, John Stoll.

Drama   (PR:C   MPAA:NR)

SLEEPLESS NIGHTS½**   (1933, Brit.) 66m BIP/Remington bw

Stanley Lupino (Guy Raynor), Polly Walker (Marjorie Drew), Gerald Rawlinson (Gerald Ventnor), Frederick Lloyd (Summers), Percy Parsons (Mr. Drew), Charlotte Parry (Mrs. Drew), David Miller (Captain), Hal Gordon (Gendarme).

Lupino plays a reporter on duty in the Riviera. The girl in the adjoining hotel suite (Walker) becomes locked out of her room, and she wanders through Lupino's room to get to her own but is spotted. Lupino quickly solves the problem by telling everyone they're married. The rest of the film concentrates upon the two continuing with their pretense of marriage, paving the way for hearty laughs. Lupino (father of Ida) offers a vivid display of his dancing, singing, and comic talents, and is given ample support by Walker. Songs include: "I Don't Want to Go to Bed" and "I'm Awfully Glad It's Happened to Me."

p, Walter C. Mycroft; d, Thomas Bentley; w, Victor Kendall (based on a story by Stanley Lupino); ph, John J. Cox; m, Noel Gay; ed, Walter Stokvis; ch, Ralph Reader.

Musical/Comedy   (PR:A   MPAA:NR)

SLEEPY LAGOON*½   (1943) 65m REP bw

Judy Canova (Judy Joyner), Dennis Day (Lancelot Hillie), Ruth Donnelly (Sarah Rogers), Joseph Sawyer (Lumpy), Ernest Truex (Dudley Joyner), Douglas Fowley (J "The Brain" Lucarno), Will Wright (Cyrus Coates), Herbert Corthell (Sheriff Bates), Forrest Taylor (Samuel), Eddy Chandler (Ticket Seller), Kitty McHugh (Mrs. Small), Ellen Lowe (Mrs. Simms), Margaret Reid (Mrs. Crumm), Chief of Police, Sammy Stein, Jack Kenney, Jay Novello, Eddie Gribbon (Lugs), Jack Raymond (Joe the Clown), Mike Riley and Band (Themselves), Larry Stewart (Man), Emil Van Horn (Gorilla), Rondo Hatton (Hunchback), Frank Austin (Wolf Man), Johnny Walsh (Boy), James Farley (Bailiff), Frank Graham (Narrator).

Canova is up to her usual antics again, this time running for office in a small town whose crooked politicos keep everything under their control. The lady wins the election and promptly undertakes the struggle to make the small town run smoothly and legally again. Songs include: "If You Are There," "You're the Fondest Thing I Am Of," "I'm Not Myself Anymore" (Ned Washington, Phil Ohman), "Sleepy Lagoon" (Jack Lawrence, Eric Coates), "I'm On My Way," "I Do" (Buddy Pepper, Inez James), "Take It And Git" (James T. Marshall, Johnny Green).

p, Albert J. Cohen; d, Joseph Santley; w, Frank Gill, Jr., George Carleton Brown (based on the story by Prescott Chaplin); ph, Bud Thackery; ed, Richard Van Enger; md, Walter Scharf; art d, Russell Kimball.

Musical/Comedy   (PR:A   MPAA:NR)

SLEEPYTIME GAL*½   (1942) 84m REP bw

Judy Canova (Bessie Cobb), Tom Brown (Chick Patterson), Ruth Terry (Sugar Caston), Mildred Coles (Connie), Billy Gilbert (Chef Acropolis), Harold Huber (Honest Joe), Fritz Feld (Chef Petrovich), Jay Novello (Chef Gonzales), Skinnay Ennis (Danny Marlowe), Jerry Lester (Downbeat), Jimmy Ames (Gus), Elisha Cook, Jr (Ernie), Frank Sully (Dimples), Thurston Hall (Mr. Adams), Paul Fix (Johnny Blake), Vicki Lester (Blonde), Lester Dorr, Walter Merrill, Pat Gleason, Fred Santley, Mady Laurence (Reporters), Edward Earle (Dr. Bell), Hillary Brooke (Railroad Station Blonde), Ric Vallin, Cyril Ring (Clerks), William Forrest (Hotel Manager), Carl Leviness (Husband), Gertrude Astor (Wife), Marguerite Whitten (Maid), Dwight Frye, Eddie Acuff (Mugs), Eugene Borden (Maitre D'Hotel), Skinnay Ennis' Orchestra.

Canova finds herself in a very touchy situation when she is mistaken for a nightclub singer on the mob's hit list. The lady comedian gives her usual overbearing performance, which even proves too much for the gangsters who are after her. Songs include: "I Don't Want Nobody At All," "Barrelhouse Bessie," "When the Cat's Away" (Jule Styne, Herb Magidson, sung by Canova), "Sleepytime Gal" (Richard A. Whiting, Ange Lorenzo, Joseph R. Alden, Ray Egan, sung by Canova).

p, Albert J. Cohen; d, Albert S. Rogell; w, Art Arthur, Albert Duffy, Max Lief (based on the story by Mauri Grashin, Robert T. Shannon); ph, Jack Marta; ed, Ernest Nims; md, Cy Feuer; art d, Russell Kimball.

Musical/Comedy   (PR:A   MPAA:NR)

SLENDER THREAD, THE*   (1965) 98m Athenes/PAR bw

Sidney Poitier (Alan Newell), Anne Bancroft (Inga Dyson), Telly Savalas (Dr. Coburn, Psychologist), Steven Hill (Mark Dyson), Indus Arthur (Marion), Greg Jarvis (Chris Dyson), Robert Hoy (Patrolman Steve Peters), John Benson (Patrolman Bert Enyard), Paul Newlan (Sgt. Harry Ward), Edward Asner (Det. Judd Ridley), Jason Wingreen (Medical Technician), Dabney Coleman (Charlie), Janet Dudley (Edna), Lane Bradford (Al McCardle), John Napier (Dr. Alden Van), Marjorie Nelson (Mrs. Thomas), H.M. Wynant (Doctor), Thomas Hill (Liquor Salesman), Steve Marlo (Arthur Foss), Stephen Pellegrini, Jerome R. Brand, Kay Doubleday, Jo Helton, Richard Doorish, Charlotte Stewart, Viola Harris, George Savalas, O.L. Haavik, Nicholas Prebezac, Drew Eskenazi, Erin Almond, Pam Bagby, William R. Rhodes, Charles C. Andrews, Melody Greer, Sons Of Adam, Walter Mazlow, Allen Emerson, Lou Clark, David Harris, Phillip Browne, Archie Smith, Joseph R. Denini.

Based on an actual incident, Poitier plays a volunteer at a medical clinic who receives a call from distraught Bancroft, a married woman driven to take an overdose of sleeping pills. While Bancroft relates the events leading to her attempted suicide (mainly the treatment she has received as a result of her husband's discovery that he is not the son's real father), an intensive search throughout Seattle is made to locate the woman. Several flashbacks are inserted depicting Bancroft's life, while a patient, yet equally tormented, Poitier struggles to hold the woman on the phone. Eventually, police sergeant Newlan is able to trace the call to the proper hotel room, and reaches Bancroft just as she collapses. This was director Pollack's directorial debut in filmmaking, from a background of extensive work in television productions. He managed to unwind a taut drama revolving around the phone call, and added much realism through the photography of Seattle and the workman like performances of the men in search of the dying woman. Poitier and Bancroft contribute to the suspense through their poignant performances. Bancroft conveys much of her inner turmoil through the sound of her voice.

p, Stephen Alexander; d, Sydney Pollack; w, Stirling Silliphant (based on the story "Decision To Die" by Shana Alexander); ph, Loyal Griggs; m, Quincy Jones; ed, Thomas Stanford; art d, Hal Pereira, Jack Poplin; set d, Robert R. Benton, Joseph Kish; cos, Edith Head; makeup, Wally Westmore.

Drama (PR:C MPAA:NR)

SLEPOY MUZYKANT (SEE: SOUND OF LIFE, 1962, USSR)

SLEUTH**** (1972, Brit.) 138m Palomar/FOX c

Laurence Olivier (*Andrew Wyke*), Michael Caine (*Milo Tindle*), Alec Cawthorne (*Inspector Doppler*), Margo Channing (*Marguerite*), John Matthews (*Detective Sgt. Tarrant*), Teddy Martin (*Police Constable Higgs*).

This intelligent and stylish mystery opens with Caine, a successful owner of a chain of hair salons, paying a call on Olivier. Olivier is a well-known detective novelist with a grand passion for elaborate games. He lives in a 16th Century home outfitted with intricate toys, mazes, and even robots. While Olivier and Caine chat, the writer reveals that he knows about Caine's affair with his wife. Instead of feeling cuckolded, Olivier claims he's glad to be rid of the woman. Now he has arranged a plan to have Caine steal his wife's jewels. Caine is to pawn the jewels in Amsterdam so he can support his lover, while Olivier collects insurance on the stolen items. Caine goes along with the scheme, despite Olivier's pointed insults about the younger man's background. Olivier is insistent that Caine commit the crime while dressed in a clown suit. Caine goes along with this, then, after completing the job, is horrified to learn this has all been a ruse. Olivier has no intention of leaving his wife. This elaborate game has all been staged so the novelist will have an excuse to shoot Caine as a home intruder. Olivier ignores Caine's pleas for mercy and shoots him with a handgun. Later, Olivier is surprised when a police inspector arrives. The inspector claims to be looking into Caine's sudden disappearance, and Olivier admits the gun had merely contained blanks. Caine had fainted from sheer terror, then left after coming to. The inspector conducts a routine search, and finds Caine's hidden clothes, as well as bloodstains and an apparently freshly dug grave. Olivier breaks down, but the inspector suddenly reveals himself to be Caine, hidden by makeup and an elaborate disguise. Olivier is relieved, but the game is far from over. Caine says he has murdered his mistress, Olivier's wife, and left telltale clues around the house. Olivier has just 15 minutes to find them before the police arrive to arrest him for the killing. He frantically begins a search and achieves some professional, as well as personal, satisfaction when he uncovers everything. Caine has the last laugh, though, explaining the wife's death was a hoax as well. Olivier is enraged at being deceived, and his normally rational psyche snaps. He grabs Caine's pistol and shoots the man just as the police arrive. Caine looks up at his adversary, and with his dying breath murmurs, "Tell him it was only a game." SLEUTH is a thoroughly engaging film, grabbing the audience with its premise, then twisting the plot time after time as the "game" grows more complicated. Shaffer (who had scripted Alfred Hitchcock's FRENZY) adapted the script from his own play, without sacrificing any of the original work's style or wit. Mankiewicz wisely avoids any overt stylization with his direction, instead letting the story unfold naturally. Some subtle touches, such as his macabre shots of Olivier's toys and robots, are often jarring, adding to the overall effect. The script is an actor's dream, and the two costars whip up their roles with relish. They play well off one another, constantly pulling the mystery back and forth in this deadly cat-and-mouse game. Caine, who replaced Albert Finney in the part, was at first intimidated by working with an actor of Olivier's stature. Olivier was the only British actor ever named to be a lord, and Caine was at a loss at how he should even refer to his costar. Shortly before production began, Caine received a letter from Olivier that read "...so happy we're working together. One minute after we meet, I shall call you Michael and you will call me Larry, and that's how it will remain forever" (quoted from *Raising Caine* by William Hall). At one point in rehearsal, Mankiewicz asked Olivier if he could possibly do anything to make himself a bit more attractive to fit the image of a respected literary figure. Olivier responded by donning a fake mustache, which achieved the desired effect with perfect subtlety. Mankiewicz was determined to keep the unusual nature of his mystery a secret to the audience throughout, and, following the play's example, used phony names in the cast list. Listed in the closing credits as playing Olivier's wife Marguerite is an actress named Margo Channing. Of course any film buff would easily recognize this as the name of Bette Davis' famed character in Mankiewicz's classic film ALL ABOUT EVE. Mankiewicz further complicates the matter by listing the actress as "Eve Channing" in the opening titles. In actuality, Marguerite only appears in the film as a portrait on Olivier's wall. Serving as a model for the portrait was actress Joanne Woodward.

p, Morton Gottlieb; d, Joseph L. Mankiewicz; w, Anthony Shaffer (based on his play); ph, Oswald Morris (DeLuxe Color); m, John Addison; ed, Richard Marden; prod d, Ken Adam; art d, Peter Lamont; set d, John Jarvis; cos, John Furniss; makeup, Tom Smith.

Mystery Cas. (PR:C-O MPAA:PG)

SLIGHT CASE OF LARCENY, A** (1953) 71m MGM bw

Mickey Rooney (*Augustus 'Geechy' Cheevers*), Eddie Bracken (*Frederick Winthrop Clopp*), Elaine Stewart (*Beverly Ambridge*), Marilyn Erskine (*Emily Clopp*), Douglas Fowley (*Mr. White*), Robert Burton (*Police Captain*), Charles Halton (*Willard Maibrunn*), Henry Slate (*Motor Cop*), Rudy Lee (*Tommy Clopp*), Mary Ellen Clopp), Joe Turkel, Al Jackson, Russ Saunders, Bob Meinhart, Walter Ridge.

Rooney and Bracken play old army buddies who decide to make it rich by opening a gas station. This is all on the insistence of Rooney, who basically takes over his buddy's life to see his plan through. Bracken does most of the leg work while his partner masterminds the operation. They become very successful with the station, but are faced with a problem when a large oil company opens a station across from theirs. This prompts the two partners to siphon gas from the pipeline leading to the competitor's hoses. Luckily, Rooney did not approach this role with his over exuberant energy, which made his performance bearable, and gave Bracken a well deserved chance to display his comic talent.

p, Henry Berman; d, Don Weis; w, Jerry Davis (based on the story by James Poe); ph, Ray June; ed, Ben Lewis; art d, Cedric Gibbons, William Ferrari.

Comedy (PR:A MPAA:NR)

SLIGHT CASE OF MURDER, A**** (1938) 85m WB bw

Edward G. Robinson (*Remy Marco*), Jane Bryan (*Mary Marco*), Willard Parker (*Dick Whitewood*), Ruth Donnelly (*Nora Marco*), Allen Jenkins (*Mike*), John Litel (*Post*), Eric Stanley (*Ritter*), Harold Huber (*Giuseppe*), Edward Brophy (*Lefty*), Paul Harvey (*Mr. Whitewood*), Bobby Jordan (*Douglas Fairbanks Rosenbloom*), Joseph Downing (*Innocence*), Margaret Hamilton (*Mrs. Cagle*), George E. Stone (*Ex-Jockey Kirk*), Bert Hamilton (*Sad Sam*), Jean Benedict (*Remy's Secretary*), Harry Seymour (*The Singer*), Betty Compson (*Loretta*), Joe Caites (*No Nose Cohen*), George Lloyd (*Little Butch*), John Harmon (*Blackhead Gallagher*), Harry Tenbrook (*A Stranger*), Duke York (*Champ*), Pat Daly (*Champ's Manager*), John Hiestand (*Radio Commentator*), Bert Roach (*Speakeasy Proprietor*), Harry Cody (*Pessimistic Patron*), Ben Hendricks (*1st Policeman*), Ralph Dunn (*2nd Policeman*), Wade Boteler (*3rd Policeman*), Myrtle Stedman, Loia Cheaney (*Nurses*).

In this marvelous parody of gangster films Robinson plays a beer baron who has made his fortune during Prohibition. He doesn't realize that his brew is wretched and only sold because alcohol was illegal. The 21st Amendment opens up the market and Robinson's booming business begins losing money. Undaunted, he decides to retire and attempts to make his way into high society. Robinson drives out to his new country estate and along the way he picks up Jordan, a street-wise kid the old gangster wants to tutor in business. Robinson's daughter Bryan falls for Parker, the unemployed son of a millionaire. Bryan refuses to marry Parker unless he finds a job so the eager young man hits the pavements. To his future father-in-law's horror, Parker is hired to be a motorcycle cop! Robinson's problems are compounded when he finds some corpses strewn around his new house. Some rival mobsters held up a racetrack, then went to Robinson's home in an effort to frame him for the crime. The gangsters ended up in an argument and consequently killed each other in a gun battle. One gangster (Downing) manages to survive the fray and hides out in Robinson's home with the $500,000 racetrack booty. Bryan and Parker arrive and the newly deputized lawman shoots all the dead gangsters. Jordan finds Downing, along with the loot. Since the bank has been threatening Robinson with foreclosure, this instant revenue couldn't come at a better time. Robinson takes the cash, while Parker takes credit for the arrest. In the end, Robinson finally samples his brew and realizes why its popularity has suddenly declined. He has the formula changed to save his business, while Parker is made a hero for his seemingly brave actions. Though Robinson will probably best be remembered for LITTLE CAESAR, this marvelous romp (along with the similar THE LITTLE GIANT '1935') was a perfect vehicle for his marvelous comic talents. Robinson successfully spoofs his own image, yet balances out the comic performance with enough serious touches to make the character believable. The film, adapted from a failed play by Runyon and Lindsay, is delightfully Runyonesque in character and plot development. The ensemble gives their characterizations some marvelous personal quirks, taking each crazy turn well in hand. The farce is nicely paced by Bacon's direction, giving the proceedings a genuine sense of fun. A SLIGHT CASE OF MURDER was popular with both critics and filmgoers and was later remade as STOP, YOU'RE KILLING ME in 1952, with Broderick Crawford in the Robinson role. Robinson, in his autobiography *All My Yesterdays*, said of the film "...I had absolutely no fault to find with the script because it was beautifully constructed and written and it was very funny." An admirer of Runyon's work, Robinson claimed that the writer "...was absolutely unlike the characters he invented; he was soft-spoken, reserved, and never once did he utter a Runyonism."

p, Hal B. Wallis; d, Lloyd Bacon; w, Earl Baldwin, Joseph Schrank (based on the play by Damon Runyon, Howard Lindsay); ph, Sid Hickox; ed, James Gibbons; md, Leo F. Forbstein; art d, Max Parker; m/l, M.K. Jerome, Jack Scholl.

Comedy/Crime (PR:A MPAA:NR)

SLIGHTLY DANGEROUS***   (1943) 94m MGM bw

Lana Turner (Peggy Evans/Carol Burden/Narrator), Robert Young (Bob Stuart), Walter Brennan (Cornelius Burden), Dame Mae Whitty (Baba), Eugene Pallette (Durstin), Alan Mowbray (English Gentleman), Florence Bates (Mrs. Roanoke-Brooke), Howard Freeman (Mr. Quill), Millard Mitchell (Baldwin), Ward Bond (Jimmy), Pamela Blake (Mitzi), Ray Collins (Snodgrass), Paul Stanton (Stanhope), Robin Raymond (Girl), Kay Medford (Girl Getting off Bus), Grace Hayle (Lady Customer), Ann Doran, Catherine Lewis (Salesgirls), Almira Sessions (Landlady), Edward Earle (Employee), Eddie Acuff (Sailor), Frank Faylen (Gateman), Norma Varden (Opera Singer), Mantan Moreland (Waiter), Cliff Clark (Detective), Harry Hayden (Doctor), Mimi Doyle (Miss Kingsway), Joe Devlin (Painter), Bobby Blake (Boy on Porch), Robert Emmett O'Connor (Reporter), Mary Elliott (Operator), Ray Teal (Pedestrian), Marjorie "Babe" Kane (Customer), Frances Rafferty (Girl Getting off Bus), Spencer Charters (Claudius, Owner of Swade Cafe), Murray Alper (Sailor), Pat West (Man Getting on Bus), James Ford (Reggie, Amanda's Escort).

Buster Keaton was under contract to MGM for many years as an uncredited comedy advisor and any physical humor in this film is a result of his collaboration with director Ruggles, himself a former "Keystone Kop." Turner appears as a blonde and a brunette as she assumes two identities. The picture opens as she's a soda jerkette in a small department store in a tiny town. She is so bored by this aimless job that, in order to vary her working hours, she makes sundaes blindfolded. Young is the store manager who doesn't appreciate her shenanigans and asks her to come to his office, where he bawls her out. Turner rushes from Young's office in tears and the other employees incorrectly reckon that he's been sexually harassing her. She leaves the tiny burg but no one knows that and when a suicide note is uncovered, Young is fired from his position. Turner arrives in New York and buys some new clothes with her last few bucks. At the front door of a newspaper, she's hit on the head by a bucket of paint and walks into the paper dripping red. Once inside, she manages to convince Pallette, the boss, that she's the long-lost daughter of wealthy Brennan, a millionaire manufacturer. Once she meets Brennan, even he is taken in by her charade. The newspapers across the country trumpet Brennan's daughter's reappearance and when Young sees Turner's photo, he hurries to New York hoping to get her to clear his name in their small town. Turner has been claiming amnesia and Young shows her a bogus marriage license which states they are married. Turner can do nothing about that lest she admit the amnesia is fraudulent. Brennan does some investigating and discovers the truth about Turner, but he's come to care so much for her that it doesn't matter that she's not his real daughter. And – as you must have expected – Turner and Young fall in love, which was a foregone conclusion from the first reel. A cute film helped enormously by some of the best character actors in the business at the time. Every role, no matter how small, has a gem of a performance in it by these veterans. In a tiny role, note Robert Blake (TV's "Baretta," et al) at the age of 9.

p, Pandro S. Berman; d, Wesley Ruggles; w, Charles Lederer, George Oppenheimer (based on a story by Ian McLellan Hunter, Aileen Hamilton); ph, Harold Rosson; m, Bronislau Kaper; ed, Frank E. Hull; art d, Cedric Gibbons, Malcolm Brown; set d, Edwin B. Willis, Mildred Griffiths; cos, Irene.

Comedy   **(PR:A MPAA:NR)**

SLIGHTLY FRENCH**   (1949) 81m COL bw

Dorothy Lamour (Mary O'Leary), Don Ameche (John Gayle), Janis Carter (Louisa Gayle), Willard Parker (Douglas Hyde), Adele Jergens (Yvonne La Tour), Jeanne Manet (Nicolette), Frank Ferguson (Marty Freeman), Myron Healey (Stevens), Leonard Carey (Wilson), Earle Hodgins (Barker), William Bishop (Voice of J.B., Producer), Patricia Barry (Hilda), Jimmy Lloyd, Michael Towne (Assistants), Fred Sears (Cameraman), Frank Mayo (Soundman), Fred Howard, Robert B. Williams (Newsmen), Charles Jordan (Studio Policeman), Hal K. Dawson (Director), Carol Hughes (Secretary), Frank Wilcox (Starr, Playwright), Will Stanton (Cockney Barber), Al Hill (Brazilian Barker), Pierre Watkin (Publicity Man).

A remake of Columbia's earlier LET'S FALL IN LOVE (1934), SLIGHTLY FRENCH casts Ameche as the hard-driving director who forces his leading lady to a near breakdown and is thus promptly fired from the production. He comes across Brooklyn lass Lamour, and creates the actress needed for the movie, via a Pygmalion-type transformation. The major talent this actress must possess is that of being French, and Lamour's convincing imitation soon gets Ameche his job back. And, of course, Lamour winds up falling in love with her egocentric coach. Director Sirk was far from home with light entertainment of this nature, but he still approached the project with an earnest professionalism, which would see its rewards in later masterpieces. Songs include: "Fifi from the Folies Bergere," "I Want to Learn about Love" (sung by Lamour), "Night," "I Keep Telling Myself" (Lester Lee, Allan Roberts), "Let's Fall in Love" (Harold Arlen, Ted Koehler, sung by Lamour).

p, Irving Starr; d, Douglas Sirk; w, Karen DeWolf (from the story by Herbert Fields); ph, Charles Lawton, Jr.; ed, Al Clark; md, George Duning, Morris Stoloff; art d, Carl Anderson; set d, James Crowe; cos, Jean Louis; ch, Robert Sidney.

Comedy/Musical   **(PR:A MPAA:NR)**

SLIGHTLY HONORABLE**½   (1940) 83m UA bw

Pat O'Brien (John Webb), Broderick Crawford (Russell Sampson), Edward Arnold (Vincent Cushing), Ruth Terry (Ann Seymour), Bernard Nedell (Pete Godena), Alan Dinehart (District Attorney Joyce), Claire Dodd (Alma Brehmer), Douglas Dumbrille (George Taylor), John Sheehan (Mike Deley), Addison Richards (Inspector Melvyn Fromm), Cliff Clark (Capt. Graves), Eve Arden (Miss Alter), Phyllis Brooks (Serilla Cushing), Ernest Truex (P. Hemingway Collins), Douglas Fowley (Charles Madder), Janet Beecher (Mrs. Cushing), Evelyn Keyes (Miss Vlissenger), Willie Best (Art the Elevator Operator), Eddie Chandler (O'Leary the Cop), Bud Jamison (Humboldt the Cop), Robert Middlemass (Sen. Barry), Frank Dae (President of Senate), George Magrill, Tay Garnett (Reporters), Charles K. French (Pallbearer), John Deering, Dale Armstrong, Art Baker (Radio Announcers), Howard Hickman (Sen. Sam Scott), Wheaton Chambers (Guest), Babe Kane (Switchboard Operator), Jack Greene, Dick Rush (Detectives), Vic Potel (Proprietor), Zack Williams (Black Preacher), Max Rose (Fingerprint Expert), Jack Wynn (Surveyor).

Two attorneys, played by O'Brien and Crawford, decide to take advantage of political scandals in the highway department to gain some business. Dodd, a pretty divorcee involved in the scandal, is found dead with a knife in her back, and gangster Arnold gets the blame pinned on O'Brien. Though innocent, O'Brien's problems are compounded when his secretary is killed in the same manner. O'Brien sets out to solve the crimes, but finds himself getting into deeper trouble with each step he takes. Also hampering his investigation is Terry, a feather-headed chorus girl with a yen for the attorney. Eventually the truth is bared, revealing Crawford as the man behind the crimes. This is an old-fashioned detective story, but not an entirely successful one. The film is pockmarked by too many cliches, such as knives with notes attached flying through the air. Garnett's direction never pulls the material together, consistently diverting from the main story for a variety of subplots. There are some good moments of comedy, but these brief flashes aren't enough to carry the film. O'Brien and Crawford suffice in the lead roles, though clearly they deserved better material. For a fight scene between the two, the set was cleared and the actors went at each other with no holds barred. "Fortunately," O'Brien later recalled, "Brod 'knew' every trick of pulling punches, and I had learned a few from 'James' Cagney. There were no serious injuries, just a few bruises and aches, discolorations, but the scene was worth it, 'executive producer Walter Wanger' said." Garnett had initially been pleased with the production, priding himself on finishing ahead of schedule and under budget. "I realized exactly how bad SLIGHTLY HONORABLE must be," he wrote in his autobiography, Light Your Torches and Pull Up Your Tights, "when the officer at the United Artists' gate (the man who had been parking my car) asked me for identification one morning."

p&d, Tay Garnett; w, John Hunter Lay, Robert Allman, Ken Englund (based on the story "Send Another Coffin" by E.G. Presnell); ph, Merritt Gerstad; m, Werner Janssen; ed, Otho Lovering; art d, Alexander Golitzen; m/l, George R. Brown, Jule Styne.

Crime   **Cas.**   **(PR:A MPAA:NR)**

SLIGHTLY MARRIED*½   (1933) 65m IN/CHES bw

Evalyn Knapp, Walter Byron, Marie Prevost, Jason Robards, Sr, Dorothy Christy, Robert Ellis, Clarissa Selwynne, Phillips Smalley, Herbert Evans, Lloyd Ingraham, Mary Foy.

Tired plot has Knapp forced to marry a total stranger when she learns she's pregnant. The spouse is Byron, a nice guy whose mother has different marrying plans for him. These are almost carried out, until he becomes attached to the baby, in which case he decides to stick it out with Knapp. Actually his attachment to the child consists of nothing more than a single glance.

d, Richard Thorpe; w, Mary McCarthy; ph, M. A. Anderson.

Drama   **(PR:A MPAA:NR)**

SLIGHTLY SCANDALOUS*½   (1946) 66m UNIV bw

Fred Brady (Jerry, John, James), Paula Drew (Trudy Price), Sheila Ryan (Christine Wright), Walter Catlett (Mr. Wright), Isabelita (Lola), Louis Da Pron (Rocky), Jack Marshall (Erwin), Nick Moro, Frank Yaconelli (Mexican Duet), Guadalajara Trio (Themselves), Dorese Midgley, Georgann Smith (Specialty Dancers), Harry Tyler (Hotel Desk Clerk), Dewey Robinson (Man), Anne O'Neal (Minerva).

In a dual role as twin brothers, one a TV producer and the other an insurance salesman, Brady proves unconvincing in both. As the first brother, he is forceful and pushy and has three girls, Drew, Ryan, and Isabelita. Naturally the other is shy and without a gal. As the TV man, Brady gets his brother to give him backing for a program, causing several romantic entanglements when the insurance salesman is mistaken for his brother by the latter's girlfriends. As if two of Brady weren't enough, another one had to be thrown in to clean up the plot. Songs include "I Couldn't Love You Anymore," "When I Fall in Love," "Negra Leona" (Sung by Isabelita), "Same Old Routine," "The Mad Hatter," "Baa Baa to You" (Jack Brooks).

p, Stanley Rubin; d, Will Jason; w, Erna Lazarus, David Mathews, Joel Malone, Jerry Warner; ph, George Robinson; m, Jack Brooks; ed, Fred R. Feitshans, Jr; md, Milton Rosen; art d, Jack Otterson, Harold H. MacArthur; cos, Vera West; spec eff, D. S. Hursley.

Musical   **(PR:A   MPAA:NR)**

SLIGHTLY SCARLET**   (1930) 70m PAR bw

Evelyn Brent (*Lucy Stavrin*), Clive Brook (*Hon. Courtenay Parkes*), Paul Lukas (*Malatroff*), Eugene Pallette (*Sylvester Corbett*), Helen Ware (*His Wife*), Virginia Bruce (*Enid Corbett*), Henry Wadsworth (*Sandy Weyman*), Claud Allister (*Albert Hawkins*), Christiane Yves (*Marie*), Morgan Farley (*Malatroff's Victim*).

A remake of BLACKBIRDS (1915), SLIGHTLY SCARLET is a diverting tale about two classy jewel thieves, Brent and Brook, who find true love despite the competitiveness of their field. After the two finally get together, they give up their underworld lives and attempt to go legit. Allister, Pallette and a few others supplied additional laughs, which they did quite successfully. A French version of the film appeared in the same year under the title, L'ENIGMATIQUE MONSIEUR PARKES.

D, Louis Gasnier, Edwin H. Knopf; w, Howard Estabrook, Joseph L. Mankiewicz (based on the play by Percy Heath); ph, Allan Siegler; ed, Eda Warren; m/l, "You Still Belong to Me," Elsie Janis, Jack King.

Comedy   **(PR:A   MPAA:NR)**

SLIGHTLY SCARLET***   (1956) 90m RKO c

John Payne (*Ben Grace*), Arlene Dahl (*Dorothy Lyons*), Rhonda Fleming (*June Lyons*), Kent Taylor (*Frank Jansen*), Ted de Corsia (*Sol Caspar*), Lance Fuller (*Gauss*), Frank Gerstle (*Dave Dietz*), Buddy Baer (*Lenhardt*), George E. Stone (*Roos*), Ellen Corby (*Martha*), Roy Gordon (*Norman Marlowe*).

Loosely based on James M. Cain's novel *Love's Lovely Counterfeit*, this fascinating low-budget *film noir* stars Payne as a small-time hoodlum who works for crime kingpin de Corsia. The latter's criminal empire is threatened when a law-and-order candidate decides to run for mayor and it looks as if he'll win. Seeking to short-circuit the candidate's campaign, de Corsia assigns Payne to begin smear tactics. Payne uncovers information regarding the candidate's redheaded secretary, Fleming, and her sister, Dahl, an immoral vixen who has served time in prison, who also happens to be a redhead. Digging for more incriminating information, Payne begins to date Fleming. He soon falls in love with the secretary and with a new-found sense of honor decides to work for the reform candidate by providing the information necessary to convict de Corsia. The information is turned over to a newspaperman, causing the enraged Corsia to kill the reporter. Faced with a long jail term, de Corsia flees the city vowing revenge on Payne. Payne takes over the mob, but his reign is plagued with confusion and self-doubt, especially since Fleming's sister Dahl is trying to seduce him. Eventually de Corsia returns, determined to kill Payne. In an effort to stall de Corsia until the police arrive, Payne allows the deposed mob chieftain to shoot him several times. By the time the police show up Payne has sustained several wounds, but de Corsia is caught with the smoking gun in his hand. De Corsia is captured and the badly wounded Payne is led off with Fleming and Dahl following behind. Unusual for its use of Technicolor in the traditionally black-and-white world of *film noir*, veteran director Dwan who, along with his cinematographer Alton, used the color to advantage by creating a shadowy world accentuated by lurid colors. The visual effect is unsettling at times, proving that *film noir* can be just as effective in a colorful environment as it is in black and white. Kurt Neumann had originally contracted to direct the film, but Dwan brought in his talented team of regulars (he'd helmed a string of westerns with the help of cinematographer Alton and art director Polglase), who proved to work as effectively in wide-screen color as they did in black-and-white.

p, Benedict Bogeaus; d, Allan Dwan; w, Robert Blees (based on the novel *Love's Lovely Counterfeit* by James M. Cain); ph, John Alton (Superscope, Technicolor); m, Louis Forbes; ed, James Leicester; art d, Van Nest Polglase; set d, Alfred Spencer; cos, Norma Koch.

Crime   **Cas.**   **(PR:C   MPAA:NR)**

SLIGHTLY TEMPTED*   (1940) 60m UNIV bw

Hugh Herbert (*Prof. Ross*), Peggy Moran (*Judy Ross*), Johnny Downs (*Jimmy Duncan*), Gertrude Michael (*Duchess*), George E. Stone (*Petey*), Elisabeth Risdon (*Ethelreda Knox*), Robert Emmett Keane (*Gentleman Jack*), Harry C. Bradley (*Cartwright*), Harry Holman (*Mayor Ammerson*), Walter Soderling (*Findiggle*), William "Billy" Newell (*Warcross*).

Herbert plays an aging kleptomaniac just released from jail, who is unable to go straight despite promises to his daughter. However, his thieving does some good for his daughter, when he winds up stealing the heart of a wealthy woman. This was supposed to be funny, but after the first couple of sequences it was hard to find anything to laugh about.

p, Ken Goldsmith; d, Lew Landers; w, Arthur T. Horman, Goldsmith (based on the story by Max Marcin, Manuel Seff); ph, Charles Van Enger.

Comedy   **(PR:A   MPAA:NR)**

SLIGHTLY TERRIFIC*½   (1944) 61m UNIV bw

Leon Errol (*Tuttle*), Anne Rooney (*Julie Bryant*), Eddie Quillan (*Charlie*), Richard Lane (*Mike Hamilton*), Betty Kean (*Marie Mason*), Lorraine Krueger (*Peggy*), Ray Malone (*Joe Bryant*), Lee Bennett, Lillian Cornell, Oyer Cornell, The Stardusters, Maritza Dancers, The Eight Rhythmeers, Donald Novis, Jayne Forrest.

A case of mistaken identity between Errol as a producer and his twin brother, a wealthy industrialist, serves as a paper thin plot about a group of theatrical youths who want to stage their own show. Although Errol promises to see their show through, it is only because he is mistaken for his brother that the production is allowed to take place. Songs include "Hold That Line," "A Dream Said Hello" (sung by Rooney and the Stardusters), "Me and My Whistle," "Come Back Erin," "Rhythm's What You Need," "The Happy Polka," "Stars and Violins" (Everett Carter, Milton Rosen), "The Blue Danube" (Johann Strauss, adapted by Katherine Bellamann), "Put your Arms Around Me Honey" (June McCree, Albert von Tilzer).

p, Alexis Thurn-Taxis; d, Edward F. Cline; w, Edward Dein, Stanley Davis (based on the story by Edith Watkins, Florence McEnany); ph, Paul Ivano; ed, Norman A. Cerf; md, Don George; art d, John B. Goodman; cos, Vera West.

Musical   **(PR:A   MPAA:NR)**

SLIM½**   (1937) 86m FN/WB bw

Pat O'Brien (*Red Blayd*), Henry Fonda (*Slim*), Margaret Lindsay (*Cally*), Stuart Erwin (*Stumpy*), J. Farrell MacDonald (*Pop Traver*), Craig Reynolds, Alonzo Price, Tom Wilson, George Lloyd, Douglas Williams (*Gamblers*), Joe Sawyer (*Wilcox*), Richard Purcell (*Tom*), Jane Wyman (*Stumpy's Girl Friend*), James Robbins (*Braithwaite*), John Litel (*Wyatt Ranstead*), Harland Tucker (*Garretson*), Joseph King (*Steve*), Carlyle Moore (*Grunt*), Maidel Turner (*Mrs. Johnson*), Max Wagner (*Griff*), Walter Miller (*Jim Vincent*), Ben Hendricks (*Kelly*), Dick Wessel (*Al*), Cliff Saum (*Reel Boss*), Herbert Heywood (*Timekeeper*), Edwin Maxwell (*Corton*), Ferdinand Schumann-Heink (*Waiter*), Brenda Fowler (*Miss Ferredice*), Davison Clark (*Sam*), Emmett Vogan (*Clerk*), Dorothy Vaughan (*Nurse*), John Harron, Henry Otho (*Workmen*), Wade Boteler (*Man*).

A solid if unremarkable action melodrama which teams up O'Brien and Fonda as rough-and-tumble power company employees who work the high-tension power lines. The film opens as Fonda, a young farmboy, spots a crew of men working on the power lines near his father's farm. Enthralled by the dangerous work and anxious to leave the rural life behind him, Fonda asks the crew's hard-boiled boss, O'Brien, for a job. O'Brien likes Fonda's manner and decides to give the kid a try. After some intensive training in the repair and maintenance of the dangerous high-voltage power lines, Fonda is assigned his first job. Swallowing his fears, the novice climbs up the steel tower and performs the task admirably. Meanwhile, Fonda has developed a liking for his buddy O'Brien's girl friend Lindsay, and she for him. Sensing that the two were meant for each other, O'Brien bows out of the relationship, preferring the danger of the high-voltage lines to romance. The decision puts little strain on the men's friendship, and Fonda proves his loyalty by suffering a stab wound in a bar fight to save O'Brien. The danger of his job combined with the drinking and carousing afterward begins to take its toll on Lindsay and she encourages Fonda to quit. Despite her worries, Fonda refuses to give up the lifestyle. Soon after, O'Brien and Fonda are sent out in a blizzard to repair a line knocked out during the storm. As O'Brien tries to climb the tower in the blinding storm, he accidentally touches a live power line and falls to his death. Regardless of the hazards, Fonda bravely completes the job and is more determined than ever to remain a lineman. Knowing that Fonda would be unhappy in another line of work, Lindsay resigns herself to the fact that she will always be in love with the danger-seeking Fonda and decides to remain by his side. While no great shakes as high drama, SLIM is a well-crafted buddy picture which offers a detailed look at an occupation little seen in movies. Warners was specializing in films devoted to the common working man, many of which starred O'Brien in a variety of occupations. Having usually teamed O'Brien with James Cagney, Warner Bros. decided to go with a new face that was younger and more idealistic than the diminutive tough guy. Relative newcomer Fonda was perfect for the part because he embodied all the engaging sincerity needed to make the part of the naive farm boy work. SLIM was Fonda's first film for Warner Bros. and his talents complemented O'Brien's perfectly. The plot device of having Lindsay coming between friends O'Brien and Fonda was lifted from TIGER SHARK (1932) and would be borrowed again for MANPOWER (1941), eventually becoming a Warner Bros. standard.

p, Hal B. Wallis, Sam Bischoff; d, Ray Enright; w, William Wister Haines, (based on his novel); ph, Sid Hickox; m, Max Steiner; ed, Owen Marks; md, Leo F. Forbstein; art d, Ted Smith; spec eff, Byron Haskin.

Drama   **(PR:A   MPAA:NR)**

SLIM CARTER**½   (1957) 82m UNIV c

Jock Mahoney (*Slim Carter/Hughie Mack*), Julie Adams (*Clover Doyle*),
Tim Hovey (*Leo Gallagher*), William Hopper (*Joe Brewster*), Ben Johnson
(*Montana Burriss*), Joanna Moore (*Charlene Carroll*), Walter Reed (*Richard L. Howard*), Maggie Mahoney (*Hat Check Girl*), Roxanne Arlen
(*Cigarette Girl*), Jim Healy (*M.C.*), Bill Williams (*Frank Hannemann*),
Barbara Hale (*Allie Hanneman*), Roxanne Arlen.

A satire on the old Hollywood oater stars, somewhat influenced by the life
of William "Bill" Boyd, has Mahoney playing an obnoxious and egotistical
movie star who takes full advantage of his catapult into fame. This is much
to the dismay of the many studio people who have to endure him, especially
Adams as the press agent assigned to watch over the rowdy cowboy. When
a young boy wins a contest with the reward of a month's stay in the home
of Mahoney, Adams has her hands full trying to hide the real cowboy from
the lad. But this proves a blessing in disguise as the kid sees through the
star, and helps him get back to earth. In the process the star develops a
strong attachment for Adams. Cast does a decent job with the material given
them, despite a direction which concentrated more heavily on getting laughs
than on developing story and characters.

p, Howie Horwitz; d, Richard H. Bartlett; w, Montgomery Pittman (based
on the story by David Bramson, Mary C. McCall, Jr.); ph, Ellis W. Carter
(Eastmancolor); m, Herman Stein; ed, Fred McDowell; md, Joseph Gershenson; art d, Alexander Golitzen, Eric Orbom; cos, Bill Thomas; m/l, Ralph
Freed, Beasley Smith, Jimmy Wakely, Gershenson.

Comedy/Western   (PR:A   MPAA:NR)

SLIME PEOPLE, THE*   (1963) 60m Hansen bw

Robert Hutton (*Tom Gregory the Aviator*), Robert Burton (*Professor*), Susan
Hart (*Lisa the Professor's Daughter*), William Boyce (*Marine*), Les Tremayne (*Norman Talliver*), Judee Morton, John Close.

Prehistoric monsters are awakened from a deep slumber because of nuclear
testing. They take over the city of Los Angeles, creating a foggy atmosphere
more appropriate for their living conditions and forcing the remainder of
the city's human population to flee for safety. But scientist Burton figures
out how the fog is created, and quickly puts an end to the monsters. This
cheapie feature was shot in a Los Angeles meat market.

p, Joseph F. Robertson; d, Robert Hutton; w, Vance Skarstedt; ph, William
Troiano; m, Lou Froman; ed, Donald Henderson, Lew Guinn; spec eff,
Charles Duncan.

Fantasy   Cas.   (PR:A MPAA:NR)

SLIPPER AND THE ROSE, THE***   (1976, Brit.) 146m
                              Paradine/UNIV c (AKA: THE STORY OF CINDERELLA)

Richard Chamberlain (*Prince Edward*), Gemma Craven (*Cinderella*), Annette Crosbie (*Fairy Godmother*), Edith Evans (*Dowager Queen*), Christopher Gable (*John*), Michael Hordern (*King*), Margaret Lockwood
(*Stepmother*), Kenneth More (*Lord Chamberlain*), Julian Orchard (*Montague*), Lally Bowers (*Queen*), Sherrie Hewson (*Palatine*), Rosalind Ayres
(*Isobella*), John Turner (*Major Domo*), Keith Skinner (*Willoughby*), Polly
Williams (*Lady Caroline*), Norman Bird (*Dress Shop Proprietor*), Peter
Graves (*General*), Gerald Sim (*First Lord of the Navy*), Elizabeth Mansfield,
Ludmilla Nova (*Ladies in Waiting*), Roy Barraclough (*Tailor*), Geoffrey
Bayldon (*Archbishop*), Valentine Dyall (*Second Major Domo*), Tim Barrett
(*Minister*), Vivienne McKee (*Bride*), Andre Morell (*Bride's Father*), Myrtle
Reed (*Bride's Mother*), Peter Leeming (*Singing Guard*), Marianne Broome,
Tessa Dahl, Lea Drehgorn, Eva Reuber-Staier, Ann Rutherford, Suzette St.
Claire (*Princesses*), Jenny Lee Wright (*Milk Maid*), Patrick Jordan, Rocky
Taylor (*Prince's Guards*), Paul Schmitzburger (*Cow Herd*), Bryan Forbes
(*Herald*).

Modernized version of the CINDERELLA fairy tale, with Chamberlain as
the suave prince and Craven as the young servant girl he falls in love with.
The dialog is also translated into more up-to-date language, with a tendency
toward wit as engaging to adults as youngsters. The scenic Austrian
background, for the outdoor sequences, adds the appropriate atmosphere.
Songs include "Why Can't I Be Two People?" (sung by Chamberlain), "Once
I Was Loved" (sung by Craven), "What a Comforting Thing to Know" (sung
by Chamberlain, Gable), "Protocoligorically Correct" (sung by Hordern,
More, Graves, Barrett, Chorus), "A Bride Finding Ball" (sung by Chamberlain, Orchard), "Suddenly It Happens" (sung by Crosbie, Craven), "Secretly
Kingdom" (Chamberlain, Craven), "He Danced With Me, She Danced With
Me" (sung by Craven, Chamberlain), "Position and Positioning" (sung by
Gable, Turner, Schmitzburger, Wright, Jordan, Taylor, Chorus), "Tell You
Anything (But Not that I Love Him)" (sung by Craven).

p, Stuart Lyons; d, Bryan Forbes; w, Forbes, Richard M. & Robert B.
Sherman; ph, Tony Imi (Panavision, Technicolor); m, Richard M. and Robert
B. Sherman; ed, Timothy Gee; pd, Raymond Simm; md, Angela Morely; art
d, Bert Davey; cos, Julie Harris; ch, Marc Breaux.

Musical   Cas.   (PR:AAA MPAA:G)

SLIPPER EPISODE, THE**   (1938, Fr). 80m Helgal/French Film
                                        Exchange bw (GB: RUNAWAY LADIES)

Betty Stockfield (*Beatrice*), Roger Treville (*Georges*), Raymond Cordy (*The
Angler*), Jean Tissier (*Jacques de Tourville*), Janine Guise (*Laurence de
Tourville*), Claude Dauphin (*Andre Chabrolles*), Jean Dax (*Hotel Director*).

A lot of fuss is made over a missing shoe, so much so that Stockfield drives
all the way from Paris to Locarno to return it to its proper owner. But she
doesn't get it there in time, causing a lot of marital strife for the friend she
was trying to keep out of a jam. During her trip a lot of pretty Swiss scenery
is displayed, but not enough laughs or story to maintain much interest. It
appears as though an English language version of this film was shot
simultaneously, using a slightly different cast, titled RUNAWAY LADIES,
and released in Britain in 1935. (In French; English subtitles.)

d, Jean de Limur; w, H. Rose, G. Lampin (based on the novel *Le Voyage
Imprevu* by Tristan Bernard); ph, F. Bourgas; m, Jean Wiener, Paul Segnitz.

Comedy   (PR:A   MPAA:NR)

SLIPPY MCGEE**   (1948) 65m REP bw

Donald Barry (*Slippy McGee*), Dale Evans (*Mary Hunter*), Tom Brown
(*Father Shanley*), Harry V. Cheshire (*Dr. Moore*), James Seay (*Thomas
Eustis*), Murray Alper (*Red*), Dick Elliott (*Fred Appelby*), Maude Eburne
(*Mrs. Dexter*), Raymond Largay (*John Hunter*), Eddie Acuff (*Charlie*),
Michael Carr (*Al*), George Nokes (*Tommy*).

When safecracker Barry breaks his leg trying to save a young child from a
speeding truck, he gains a new outlook on life, mainly through the efforts
of well-meaning priest, Brown. Barry even resorts to doing in his own gang
in order to get back the bank's money. An interesting approach to
bad-guy-turned-good theme.

p, Lou Brock; d, Albert Kelley; w, Norman S. Hall, Jerry Gruskin (based on
the novel by Marie Conway Oemler; ph, John MacBurnie; ed, Les Orlebeck;
md, Mort Glickman; art d, James Sullivan; set d, John McCarthy, Jr, Charles
Thompson; cos, Adele Palmer.

Drama   (PR:A   MPAA:NR)

SLIPSTREAM**½   (1974, Can.) 92m Pacific Rim c

Luke Askew (*Mike Mallard*), Patti Oatman (*Kathy*), Eli Rill (*Allec*), Scott
Hylands (*Terry*), Danny Friedman (*Hitch*).

Askew plays a lonely deejay, broadcasting from the backwoods of Alberta,
who gets involved with the very emotional Oatman. The girl leaves his life
as quickly as she enters it, forcing Askew to contend with isolation again.
This time he cracks, with the added push provided by radio producer Rill,
and resorts to burning his station down. There is little in any of these
characters worth liking, since they are portrayed as stereotypes. Combined
with an extremely isolating environment created through the photography
of Alberta and the manipulation of the soundtrack, the results are pretty
heavy going.

p, James Margellos; d, David Acomba; w, William Fruet (based on the story
by Acomba); ph, Marc Champion (Bellevue-Pathe Color); m, Brian Ahern,
Van Morrison, Eric Clapton; ed, Tony Lower.

Drama   Cas.   (PR:O   MPAA:NR)

SLITHER***   (1973) 97m MGM c

James Caan (*Dick Kanipsia*), Peter Boyle (*Barry Fenaka*), Sally Kellerman
(*Kitty Kopetzky*), Louise Lasser (*Mary Fenaka*), Allen Garfield (*Vincent J.
Palmer*), Richard B. Shull (*Harry Moss*), Alex Rocco (*Man With Ice Cream*),
Alex Henteloff (*Man at Phone Booth*), Garry Goodrow (*Man with Camera*),
Len Lesser (*Jogger*), Seamon Glass (*Farmer in Truck*), Wayne Storm
(*Highway Patrolman*), William Noland (*Conductor*), James Joseph (*Short
Order Cook*), Diana Darrin (*Band Singer*), Stuart Nisbet (*Buddy*), Edwina
Gough (*Bingo Nut*), Virginia Sale (*Bingo Caller*), Al Dunlap (*Man in Men's
Room*).

The feature film debut of director Zieff, a respected veteran of TV
commercials who'd won every major advertising award, and screenwriter/
associate producer Richter, who went on to become one of the most
expensive, though not necessarily commercial, writers in the movie world.
Caan is an ex-con just out of jail after a two-year stint for grand theft-auto.
He and fellow parolee Shull are happy to be free and go to Shull's tacky
California shed where the latter is gunned down by snipers. With his final
words, Shull tells Caan that he can have lots of money if he finds Boyle and
just mentions the name of Garfield. Caan is confused by this but there is no
time to explain. Using his last strength, Shull orders Caan into the basement
to hide, then lights explosives and blows the farmhouse to shards so that
anyone watching will believe both men are dead. Later, Caan thumbs a ride
with Kellerman, a speed freak. They arrive at a roadside luncheonette and
she pulls out a gun and fires it, then holds up the cashier. Caan doesn't want
any part of this woman and gets away. He eventually locates Boyle, who
admits that he and the late Shull had stolen over $300,000 from a show
business agency and gave the money to investment counselor Garfield to
keep safely. Neither man trusted the other so each had one half of the

information needed to get the cash. Shull knew Garfield's name and Boyle had the correct address. For the past seven years, Boyle has made his living peddling trailers and working as a comedian at meetings of the local Polish fraternal order. Boyle's wife is the daffy Lasser and she recalls Caan from the days when he was the football hero at her high school. The trio take off for Garfield's place in Boyle's expensive Airstream motor home of which he is justly proud. Once they get to their destination, they are told by Garfield (who is posing as someone else) that the man in question has divested himself of his holdings and moved north to Pismo Beach. Caan, Boyle and Lasser go back on the road and again encounter Kellerman, who becomes part of the entourage. The mobile home is being tracked by a big van with dark windows so they can't see who is after them. They arrive at Pismo Beach and note that another van has joined the chase. There is no information regarding Garfield at the coastal town and Caan, stretching his legs on the street, is suddenly surrounded by a quartet of business types, all dressed in conservative clothing. Caan escapes and gets into a trailer park bingo parlor where Sale is doing the calling. Kellerman sees that Caan is in danger and starts a fight among the players, under cover of which Caan flees. Lasser tells Caan that Boyle has vanished and she fears for his life and Caan thinks that his associate must be in one of the vans so he goes after them in the Airstream. What follows, is every possible type of car collision known, ending with the vans out of commission and the sleek trailer bubbling at the bottom of a lake. Caan sees someone running away from the vans and catches up to him. It's Garfield, and he soon tells the truth, that he is really the man they've been searching for. It seems that he lost all of the money from Shull and Boyle by putting it into what he thought was a good, solid investment scheme, a children's camp. The vans had been bought for the camp and the four men in suits weren't hoods at all, they were the accountants who'd been stung. Boyle shows up and says that he wasn't kidnaped at all, he'd just been out to get a tuna sandwich. Caan disgustedly eyes the wreckage and walks away, happy that he wasn't killed in the carnage. Some very funny moments and good editing by Bretherton, who once won an Oscar for snipping CABARET. Kovacs' cinematography was a plus and the picture looks better than it is for his achievement. It's sort of like a commercial as it promises a lot and delivers much less. Zieff later made THE MAIN EVENT, HOUSE CALLS and HEARTS OF THE WEST, his best film. In a small role, note young veteran character actor Henteloff, who co-starred with Louis Gossett in a short-lived TV series about the Revolutionary War. Henteloff, realizing that show business can be a transitory existence, wisely invested in the California vineyard, Acacia, where he became a vice-president. His acting is now more for fun than income as Acacia became one of the most popular wine producers in the U.S. and did splendid business when there was an Italian wine scare in 1986. The company behind this film was a consortium of industrialist Norton Simon and the Talent Associates firm begun by David Susskind. Too much violence makes this cautionary film of no use for young eyes. Several songs used in the background score include "Oklahoma Hills" (Woody and Jack Guthrie), "Blue Moon" (Richard Rodgers, Lorenz Hart), "Happy Days Are Here Again" (Jack Yellen, Milton Ager), "Stompin' at the Savoy" (Chick Webb, Andy Razaf, Benny Goodman, Edgar Sampson, clarinet soloist Abe Most), "One O'Clock Jump" (Count Basie), "Everything I Have Is Yours" (Burton Lane, Harold Adamson), "Once in a While" (Bud Green, Michael Edwards), "Easy To Love" (Cole Porter), "Deep Purple" (Peter De Rose, Mitchell Parish), "Just You, Just Me" (Raymond Klages, Jesse Greer).

p, Jack Sher; d, Howard Zieff; w, W.D. Richter; ph, Laszlo Kovacs (Metrocolor); m, Tom McIntosh; ed, David Bretherton; art d, Dale Hennessy; set d, Harry Gordon; cos, Lambert Marks, Janet Strong; spec eff, John Coles; stunts, Jimmy Nickerson; makeup, Monte Westmore.

Comedy   (PR:C   MPAA:PG)

SLITHIS*   (1978) 86m Fabtrak c (AKA: SPAWN OF THE SLITHIS)

Alan Blanchard, Judy Motulsky, Mello Alexandria, Dennis Lee Falt, Win Condict, Hy Pyke, Don Cummins.

The far-out inhabitants of Venice, California, have one more member with whom to cope, a creature whose birth is a result of nuclear pollution. Only this citizen isn't quite so harmless or friendly as the usual street people. It is a scaly monster and its antics help provide some very good entertainment.

p, Stephen Traxler, Paul Fabian; d&w, Traxler; ph, Robert Caramico; m, Steve Zuckerman.

Horror   Cas.   (PR:C   MPAA:PG)

SLOGAN*   (1970, Fr.) 90m Orphee-Hamster/Royal c

Serge Gainsbourg (Serge), Jane Birkin (Evelyne), Andrea Parisy (Wife), Daniel Gelin (Father), Juliette Berto (Secretary), James Mitchell (Hugh), Gilles Millinaire (Dado), Henri-Jacques Huet, Pierre Doris.

Gainsbourg plays a television producer facing middle-age and finding that his life is fulfilled, both professionally and personally. He turns to filmmaking and the companionship of young girls, bidding his hitherto successful life farewell.

d&w, Pierre Grimblat; ph, Jean-Louis Maligne, Claude Beausoleil (Eastmancolor); m, Serge Gainsbourg; ed, Francois Garnault; art d, Jean-Daniel Vignat.

Drama   (PR:C   MPAA:GP)

SLOW DANCING IN THE BIG CITY* **½**   (1978) 101m UA c

Paul Sorvino (Lou Friedlander), Anne Ditchburn (Sarah Gantz), Nicolas Coster (David), Anita Dangler (Franny), Hector Jaime Mercado (Roger), Thaao Penghlis (Christopher), Linda Selman (Barbara), G. Adam Gifford (Marty), Tara Mitton (Diana), Dick Carballo (George), Jack Ramage (Dr. Foster), Daniel Faraldo (T.C.).

A tearjerker from Avildsen (ROCKY) that almost loses itself through the abundance of sentimental material. Sorvino plays a New York columnist in love with the dancer, Ditchburn, who has just moved into his building after a recent break up with her boy friend. The girl is forced to continue dancing despite an illness. While working on a story about a ghetto boy trying to overcome his debilitating environment, Sorvino takes on a story about the dancer. In the process true love develops. Sorvino is quite good as the writer, giving a performance not overly bogged down in the material, as would perhaps be the case with a lesser actor.

p, Michael Levee, John G. Avildsen; d, Avildsen; w, Barra Grant; ph, Ralf Bode; m, Bill Conti; ed, Avildsen; art d, Henry Shrady; set d, Charlie Truhan; cos, Ruth Morley; ch, Robert North, Anne Ditchburn.

Drama   (PR:C   MPAA:PG)

SLOW MOTION   (SEE: EVERY MAN FOR HIMSELF, 1980, Fr.)

SLOW RUN*   (1968) 78m Film-Makers bw

Saul Rubinek (Narrator), Bruce Gordon, David Flower, Heather Sim, Jane Amsten, Pat Jones, Rita Stein, Melvyn Green.

A young Canadian fears that he is becoming too bourgeois after living the hip life in New York City, and is faced with the problem of whether or not to return to his old ways. His reveries about "the days that were" make up the major part of this nostalgic motion picture.

p,d,w,&ph, Larry Kardish; m, Saul Rubinek; ed, Kardish.

Drama   (PR:O   MPAA:NR)

SLUMBER PARTY '57 zero   (1977) 89m Movie Machine-Athena/Cannon-Happy c

Noelle North (Angie), Bridget Hollman (Bonnie May), Debra Winger (Debbie), Mary Ann Appleseth (Jo Ann), Rainbeaux Smith (Sherry), Janet Wood (Smitty), R.L. Armstrong (Silas), Rafael Campos (Dope Fiend), Larry Gelman (Cat Burglar), Will Hutchins (Harold Perkins), Joyce Jillson (Gladys), Victor Rogers (Movie Star), Joe E. Ross (Patrolman), Bill Thurman (Mr. Willis).

An attempt to cash in on the nostalgia rampant in the late 1970s results in this sexploitation piece in which six nasty girls relate their first sexual experiences during an overnight party. Other than unbelievably trite dialog, and little attention to the sequence of real events, none of these characters could possibly have existed. Even the music of The Platters, Jerry Lee Lewis, Patti Page, The Big Bopper, The Crew Cuts, The Danleers, Dinah Washington, and Paul and Paula could not improve this one.

p, John A. Ireland Jr., William A. Levey; d, Levey; w, Frank Farmer (based on a story by Levey); ph, Robert Caramico (Movielab Color); m, Miles Goodman; ed, Bill Casper; art d, Ed Bash; Set d, Bash; Cos, Francis Dennis.

Drama/Comedy   Cas.   (PR:O   MPAA:R)

SLUMBER PARTY IN A HAUNTED HOUSE
   (SEE: GHOST IN THE INVISIBLE BIKINI, THE, 1968

SLUMBER PARTY IN HORROR HOUSE
   (SEE: GHOST IN THE INVISIBLE BIKINI, THE, 1968)

SLUMBER PARTY MASSACRE, THE* **½** (1982) 84m Sante Fe/PFC c

Michele Michaels (Trish), Robin Stille (Valerie), Michael Villela (Russ), Andre Honore (Jackie), Debra Deliso (Kim), Gina Mari (Diane), David Millbern (Jeff), Joe Johnson (Neil), Pamela Roylance (Coach Jana), Brinke Stevens (Linda), Rigg Kennedy (David), Howard Furgeson (Devereaux), Ryan Kennedy, Jean Vargas, Anna Patton, Pam Cazano, Aaron Lipstadt, Francis Menedez, Joe Dante, Jim Boyce, Jennifer Meyers.

Mostly a cut as slasher films, this movie takes a familiar theme of a high school girls' slumber party being invaded by a mad killer, this time wielding a power drill. The result is contrived, though funny at times, with the characters even a little likable, particularly the heroine.

p, Amy Jones; d, Jones, Aaron Lipstadt; w, Rita Mae Brown; ph, Steve Posey (DeLuxe Color); m, Ralph Jones; ed, Wendy Green; art d, Francesca Bartoccini.

Horror   Cas.   (PR:O   MPAA:R)

SMALL BACK ROOM, THE   (SEE: HOUR OF GLORY, 1949, Brit.)

SMALL CHANGE**   (1976, Fr.) 105m Les Films du Carrosse-Les
Artistes Associes/New World c (L'ARGENT DE POCHE)

Geory Desmouceaux (*Patrick*), Philippe Goldman (*Julien*), Claudio Deluca
(*Mathieu Deluca*), Franck Deluca (*Franck*), Richard Golfier (*Richard*),
Laurent Devlaeminck (*Laurent Riffle*), Bruno Staab (*Bruno Rouillard*),
Sebastien Marc (*Oscar*), Sylvie Grezel (*Sylvie*), Pascale Bruchon (*Martine*),
Corinne Boucart (*Corinne*), Eva Truffaut (*Patricia*), Jean-Francois Stevenin
(*Jean-Francois Richet*), Chantal Mercier (*Chantal Petit*), Francis Devla-
eminck (*Mons. Riffle*), Tania Torrens (*Nadine Riffle*), Virginie Thevenet
(*Lydia Richel*), Laura Truffaut (*Madeleine Doinel*), Francois Truffaut
(*Martine's Father*), Le Petit Gregory (*Gregory*), Rene Barnerias, Katy
Carayon, Jean-Marie Carayon, Annie Chevaldonne, Michel Dissart, Michele
Heyraud, Paul Heyraud, Jane Lobre, Vincent Touly.

Francois Truffaut once said, "Whatever picture I choose to make will
inevitably contradict the one I have just made." SMALL CHANGE, which
follows the dark and obsessive THE STORY OF ADELE H., is a sentimental
homage to children and their innocent ways. Chiefly a collection of
vignettes, the film features two young boys–Desmouceaux and Goldman–
most prominently. Desmouceaux is a shy, slightly plump boy who takes care
of his paralyzed father and is infatuated with a schoolmate's mother. His
desire for romance is finally satisfied by the film's end when he gets his first
kiss from schoolgirl Bruchon. Goldman's life is the polar opposite of
Desmouceaux's. He is a long-haired, neglected boy–a present day "wild
child" (a reference to Truffaut's 1972, film THE WILD CHILD) who lives in
a hovel with his hateful mother and grandmother. During a school medical
checkup, welts and burns are found on the boy's body and his guardians are
hauled away by the police. In the center of the children's lives is
schoolteacher Stevenin, a thoughtful, fatherly man who during the course
of the film becomes a father himself. In a role that is drawn from Truffaut's
own personality, Stevenin explains to the youngsters that the things they
learn in childhood will shape them as adults. When Stevenin arrives in class
the morning after his child is born, he is unprepared for a lecture and simply
engages in an open discussion with his pupils. The film is filled with adorable
youngsters. There's Sylvie, a 7-year-old who has two pet fish (named "Plic"
and "Ploc") and a fuzzy elephant purse that her parents won't let her bring
to a restaurant. As punishment her parents leave her at home. In retaliation,
Sylvie grabs her father's bullhorn and begs her neighbors for food. There are
also the Deluca brothers, two youngsters who offer to play barber in order
to save a classmate some money. Not surprisingly, the haircut is horrendous, though they're convinced no one will be the wiser. Last, and most
definitely not least, is "Le Petit Gregory," a mischievous tyke who is too
charming to become angry with. In the film's most telling scene Gregory
frolics with his cat on the window ledge of a high-rise apartment, unaware
of the danger that awaits him should he fall. He does fall, but lands safely
on the grass. Onlookers faint, but a laughing Gregory jumps to his feet and
exclaims, "Gregory va boom" (Gregory goes boom). Admittedly unrealistic,
this scene illustrates a belief of Truffaut's that children are special–that they
"are in a state of grace." SMALL CHANGE has been wrongly criticized for
being too charming or too sweet. Truffaut, however, is not oversimplifying
childhood but portraying it on the screen exactly as it occurs in real life. The
key to SMALL CHANGE is that it stars real kids. Truffaut screen-tested a
number of children by having them read a speech of Moliere's which is used
in the film. From that point on, Truffaut worked his screenplay around the
children, using them as his inspiration instead of forcing his screenplay on
them. The result is a collection of the most natural sequences ever filmed.
An example of Truffaut's brilliant directorial hand is a sequence in which
one giggling boy tells a dirty joke to his friends. He and his friends laugh
hysterically at the punch line, though it is obvious that none of them
understands the joke. It is in a scene like this that Truffaut's insight and
thoughtfulness must be appreciated. It is easy to dismiss SMALL CHANGE
as a cute picture about kids, but to do so means to ignore the talent it takes
to capture people so naturally on film. The title SMALL CHANGE was
suggested by Steven Spielberg, who was asked by Truffaut what would be
a better translation for L'ARGENT DE POCHE–"Small Change" or "Loose
Change"–since the literal translation "Pocket Money" had already been
used for a 1972 Paul Newman film. (In French; English subtitles.)

d, Francois Truffaut; w, Truffaut, Suzanne Schiffmann; ph, Pierre-William
Glenn (Eastmancolor); m, Maurice Jaubert; ed, Yann Dedet; art d, Jean-
Pierre Kohut-Svelko; cos, Monique Dury; m/l, "Children Are Bored on
Sunday," Charles Trenet; makeup, Thi-Loan N'Guyen.

Drama/Comedy   Cas.   (PR:C MPAA:PG)

SMALL CIRCLE OF FRIENDS, A**   (1980) 113m UA c

Brad Davis (*Leo DaVinci*), Karen Allen (*Jessica*), Jameson Parker (*Nick
Baxter*), Shelley Long (*Alice*), John Friedrich (*Haddox*), Gary Springer
(*Greenblatt*), Craig Richard Nelson (*Harry*), Harry Caesar (*Jimmy the Cook*),
Nan Martin (*Mrs. Baxter*), Dan Stern (*Crazy Kid*), Jason Laskay (*Dorm
Proctor*), Jamie Squire (*Karate Student*), Mary Margaret Amato (*Girl in
Shower*), David Hollander (*Crimson Editor*), Frank Rich (*2nd Crimson
Editor*), Pamela Cresant (*Underground Woman*), Severn Darden (*Art
Professor*), Nick Kairis (*Army Doctor*), Jonathan Moore (*Dean*), Nancy
Penoyer (*Karate Instructor*), Deborah Offner (*Sarah*), John Peters (*Rizzo*),

Doug Llewelyn, Brett Smith, Jeannetta Arnette, Anita Sangiola, Michael
Shaunessy, Doree Sitterly, Navabeh, Joe La Creta, William N. Chamber-
lain, Samson X. Greiff, Don Bennett, Amy Leitman, Annie McGuire, Peter
Pollard, Lawrence Chevis Prince, William J. Sahlein, David Tomaras,
Robert Underwood.

Well-intentioned depiction of life on a college campus during the turbulent
1960s fails to gel, mainly due to the misdirection which forces the actors to
perform to lines instead of each other. Davis and Parker play best
friend-roommates who share a similar liking for the zesty Allen. Though the
more outgoing Davis first beds her, Parker and Allen later have their go at
it. They even move in together in a relationship of no commitment. The film
attempts to show how changing attitudes toward sex, politics, and women's
roles were taking place on the campus and affecting the lives of these three
friends. But in the end, the three still care more for each other than for
anything else. The attempt to keep everything low-key, as if the viewer were
just witnessing three lives passing, backfires with the performances of Davis
and Allen, which almost jump out of the screen. It is a relief that as little
time as possible was spent on campus revolutionaries.

p, Tim Zinnemann; d, Rob Cohen; w, Ezra Sacks; ph, Michael Butler
(Technicolor); m, Jim Steinman; ed, Randy Roberts; prod d, Joel Schiller;
md, Steven Morgoshes; set d, Al Kemper, Nicolas Laborczy, Rick Simpson;
spec eff, Larry Cavanaugh, Joe Lombardi, Rudy Liszcak.

Drama   Cas.   (PR:O MPAA:R)

SMALL HOTEL**   (1957, Brit.) 59m Welwyn/ABP-Pathe bw

Gordon Harker (*Albert*), Marie Lohr (*Mrs. Samson-Fox*), John Loder (*Mr.
Finch*), Irene Handl (*Mrs. Gammon*), Janet Munro (*Effie*), Billie Whitelaw
(*Caroline Mallet*), Ruth Trouncer (*Sheila*), Francis Matthews (*Alan Pryor*),
Frederick Schiller (*Foreigner*), Derek Blomfield (*Roland*), Dora Bryan,
Dorothy Bromily.

Average comedy has Harker as the long-time headwaiter at the title
establishment who discovers that he is to be replaced by a young woman.
He spies, blackmails, and cajoles his way into keeping his job. A popular
British play adapted as a star vehicle for Harker.

p, Robert Hall; d, David Macdonald; w, Wilfred Eades (based on a play by
Rex Frost); ph, Norman Warwick.

Comedy   (PR:A MPAA:NR)

SMALL HOURS, THE*   (1962) 95m Bell Film Exchange bw (AKA:
FLAMING DESIRE)

Michael Ryan (*Tom Anderson*), Lorraine Avins (*Laurie*), Henry Madden
(*Easton*), Bryce Holman (*Martin*), Tony Madden (*Gomez*), Marilyn Thorson
(*Kit Anderson*), Jewel Walker (*Preacher*), Lynn Norris (*Cindy*).

Depressed New York businessman Ryan reaches an even deeper low when
he learns of his partner's suicide. He attempts to shake it off through a night
of partying and the development of an affair with Avins. Still troubled the
next day, his depression becomes even greater when he discovers that his
wife has been cheating on him. To relieve the audience of any further
depression, Ryan is conveniently hit by a car when he thinks he sees his
dead partner walking down the street.

p,d&w, Norman C. Chaitin; ph, Sheldon Rochlin; m, Daniel Hart; ed, Chaitin.

Drama   (PR:O MPAA:NR)

SMALL MAN, THE½**   (1935, Brit.) 71m Baxter and Barter/UNIV
bw

George Carney (*Bill Edwards*), Minnie Rayner (*Alice Roberts*), Mary
Newland (*Mary Roberts*), Ernest Butcher (*Arthur*), Mark Daly (*Scotty*),
Edgar Driver (*Titch*), Charles Mortimer (*Director*), Ian Colin (*His Son*),
Roddy Hughes (*David*), C. Denier Warren (*Manager*), Haydn Wood, Thorpe
Bates, Walter Amner, Stanley Kirkby, Albert Sandler and His Orchestra,
The Gresham Singers, Foden's Brass Band.

Shopkeepers are threatened by the owners of a big department store who
want to buy up their stalls. The shopkeepers unite and organize a sale to
attract more business to their failing enterprises, but the sale flops and they
are forced to sell. By holding out so long, however, they get a lot more money
out of the store chain. Above-average drama has some excellent performances.

p, John Barter; d, John Baxter; w, Con West; ph, Desmond Dickinson.

Drama   (PR:A MPAA:NR)

SMALL MIRACLE, THE   (SEE: NEVER TAKE NO FOR AN
ANSWER, 1951, Brit.)

SMALL TOWN BOY*½   (1937) 61m GN bw

Stuart Erwin (*Henry*), Joyce Compton (*Molly*), Jed Prouty (*Mr. Armstrong*),
Clara Blandick (*Mrs. Armstrong*), James Blakely (*Eddie*), Dorothy Appleby
(*Sandra*), Clarence Wilson (*Mr. French*), Edward Waller (*Sloane*), Eddie

Kane (Tony), George Chandler (Clipper), Victor Potel (Towner), Paul Hurst (Lafferty), Erville Alderson (Skindle).

Erwin plays the Mr. Nobody who finds a $1,000 bill and is the object of quite a bit of attention from the locals. In the process, his personality changes from that of a humble boy to a ruthless businessman type. Concentration is on character and character changes, but the part is too shallow to begin with and given little help through Erwin's rendition to be of much consequence.

p, Zion Myers; d&w, Glenn Tryon (based on the play "The Thousand Dollar Bill" byManuel Komroff); ph, Edward Snyder; ed, James Morley; md, Abe Meyer.

Drama (PR:A MPAA:NR)

SMALL TOWN DEB** (1941) 72m FOX bw

Jane Withers (Patricia Randell), Jane Darwell (Katie), Bruce Edwards (Jack Richards), Cobina Wright, Jr (Helen Randall), Cecil Kellaway (Mr. Randall), Katharine Alexander (Mrs. Randall), Jack Searl (Tim Randall), Buddy Pepper (Chauncey Jones), Robert Cornell (Dave Barton), Margaret Early (Sue Morgan), Douglas Wood (Mr. Richards), John T. Murray (Mr. Anthony), Ruth Gillette (Clerk), Nora Lane (Customer), Daphne Ogden (Eloise), Marie Blake (Beauty Operator), Henry Roquemore (Barber), Jeff Corey (Hector), Edwin Stanley (Mr. Blakely), Isabel Randolph (Mrs. Jones).

Basically a vehicle for Withers in an attempt to nudge her toward a more adult role. She finds herself in the midst of domestic strife with a snob for a sister, an unsympathetic mother, and a brother who is too busy being cool to bother. Her only friend is her father, Kellaway, with housekeeper Darwell around to lend a hand. Yarn has big sis trying to marry Edwards, but Withers is always around to cause trouble. The good kid eventually makes sure the marriage takes place, at the same time helping her father square off a business deal. It's all in the family and should properly stay there.

d, Harold Schuster; w, Ethel Hill (based on a story by Jerrie Walters); ph, Virgil Miller; ed, Alexander Troffey; md, Emil Newman; cos, Herschel; m/l, "I Yi Yi Yi Yi (I Like You Very Much)," Harry Warren, Mack Gordon (sung by Jane Withers).

Comedy (PR:A MPAA:NR)

SMALL TOWN GIRL**½ (1936) 90m MGM bw (AKA: ONE HORSE TOWN)

Janet Gaynor (Kay Brannan), Robert Taylor (Bob Dakin), Binnie Barnes (Priscilla), James Stewart (Elmer), Lewis Stone (Dr. Dakin), Elizabeth Patterson (Ma Brannan), Frank Craven (Pa Brannan), Andy Devine (George), Isabel Jewell (Emily), Charley Grapewin (Dr. Fabre), Agnes Ayres (Catherine), Nella Walker (Mrs. Dakin), Robert Greig (Childers), Edgar Kennedy (Capt. Mack), Mary Forbes (Mrs. Hyde), Willie Fung (So So), John Harron (Pat), Nora Lane (Cissie), Walter Johnson (Jim), Drue Leyton (Felicia), Joan Breslau (Martin Girl), Joan Russell (June Brannan), Douglas Fowley (Chick), Adrian Rosley (Cafe Proprietor), Richard Carle (J.P.), James Donlan (Attendant), Frank Sully (Bill), Claire McDowell (Bit in Bed), Buster Phelps (Boy), Grace Hayle (Floor Nurse), Ethel Wales (Mrs. Johnson), Leonard Carey (Concierge), Helen Shipman, Ellen Lowe (Nurses), Robert Livingston (Man), Thelma "Pat" Ryan [Nixon] (Bit), George Breakston (Little Jimmy), Otto Fries (Cook), Jack Hatfield, William Wayne, Franklyn Parker (Reporters), Ivan Simpson (Hyde Butler), Edna Bennett (Nurse), Eddie Kane (Proprietor), Charles Wilson (Chief Engineer).

A leading lady of Hollywood, Gaynor played opposite the up-and-coming Taylor in this offbeat love story. She is a dreamy New England girl and he is a wealthy young doctor. They meet when Taylor stops Gaynor for directions on his way to a local college football game. He asks if she would like to go with him to the game, a night of drunken festivities follows, and the two wake up married to each other the next morning. Although Taylor is already engaged to the snooty Barnes and Gaynor has her own hometown honey in Stewart, they give married life a try. When Gaynor realizes that Barnes won't let Taylor out of her clutches, she makes her way back to the small town. Taylor eventually has second thoughts about spending his life with Barnes, deciding that Gaynor is his true love. This picture was given a highly polished look by MGM but little shines beyond that polish, including the standard performances. Only Stewart adds a bit of integrity as the home town bumpkin. Director Wellman was out of character with these types of romances, but he managed to put the laughs in the right places and make the stars look as pleasing as possible. The title song became quite popular after the film's release.

p, Hunt Stromberg; d, William Wellman; w, John Lee Mahin, Edith Fitzgerald (based on the novel Small Town Girl by Ben Ames Williams); ph, Charles Rosher; ed, Blanche Sewell; art d, Cedric Gibbons.

Drama (PR:A MPAA:NR)

SMALL TOWN GIRL**½ (1953) 93m MGM c

Jane Powell (Cindy Kimbell), Farley Granger (Rick Belrow Livingston), Ann Miller (Lisa Bellmount), S.Z. Sakall (Eric Schlemmer, Druggist), Robert Keith (Judge Gordon Kimbell), Bobby Van (Ludwig Schlemmer), Billie

Burke (Mrs. Livingston), Fay Wray (Mrs. Gordon Kimbell), Chill Wills (Happy, Jailer), Nat "King" Cole (Himself), Dean Miller (Mac), William Campbell (Ted), Philip Tonge (Hemmingway), Jonathan Cott (Jim the Cop), Bobby Hyatt (Dennis), Rudy Lee (Jimmy), Beverly Wills (Deidre), Gloria Noble (Patsy), Jane Liddell (Betty), Nancy Valentine (Mary), Janet Stewart (Sandra), Pegi McIntire (Susie), Virginia Hall (Girl Friend), Marie Blake.

When millionaire playboy Granger speeds through a small town, he gets more than he bargained for with a 30-day stay in the slammer. This causes problems with his engagement to Miller, the show gal he had hoped to elope with. Instead, Granger finds love in the arms of the judge's daughter, Powell, who acts as guardian for Granger during his one night on the town. Many well-performed song and dance numbers are interspersed throughout, including several numbers staged by Busby Berkeley, who added his usual ingenious touches. Most notable among these are "Take Me to Broadway," performed by Van, and Ann Miller's "I've Got to Hear That Beat." For the latter, 50 hands wielding instruments came popping out of the floor. Other songs include: "My Flaming Heart" (Nicholas Brodszky, Leo Robin, sung by Nat "King" Cole), "Fine, Fine, Fine," "The Fellow I'd Follow," Lullaby of the Lord," "Small Towns Are Smile Towns, "My Gaucho" (Brodszky, Robin).

p, Joe Pasternak; d, Leslie Kardos; w, Dorothy Cooper, Dorothy Kingsley (based on the story by Cooper); ph, Joseph Ruttenberg (Technicolor); ed, Albert Akst, Andre Previn; art d, Cedric Gibbons, Hans Peters; ch, Busby Berkeley; makeup, William Tuttle.

Musical (PR:A MPAA:NR)

SMALL TOWN IN TEXAS, A**½ (1976) 95m CoCaCo Service/AIP c

Timothy Bottoms (Poke), Susan George (Mary Lee), Bo Hopkins (Duke), Art Hindle (Boogie), John Karlen (Lenny), Morgan Woodward (C.J. Crane), Patrice Rohmer (Trudy), Hank Rolike (Cleotus), Buck Fowler (Bull Parker), Clay Tanner (Junior).

Bottoms plays a recently released convict who makes his way back home to his girl friend, George, and their illegitimate son. Tensions flare when he finds the woman involved with Hopkins, the close-minded sheriff who busted Bottoms in the first place. This sets the stage for Bottoms' plot of vengeance against his enemy, reaching the finale with a slam-bam car chase. Though strife-filled relationships are well conveyed, the action turns toward a formula-type vengeance theme. Bottoms' performance is similar to that of a moody, picked-upon youth. George has little more to do than look cute, while the rugged portrayal of a cop by Hopkins offers the only real acting.

p, Joe Solomon; d, Jack Starrett; w, William Norton; ph, Bob Jessup (Movielab Color); m, Charles Bernstein; ed, John C. Horger, Larry L. Mills; Jodie Copelan; art d, Elayne Ceder; stunts, Paul Knuckles.

Adventure/Drama Cas. (PR:C MPAA:PG)

SMALL TOWN LAWYER (SEE: MAIN STREET LAWYER, 1939)

SMALL TOWN STORY* (1953, Brit.) 69m Almanack/GFD bw

Donald Houston (Tony Warren), Susan Shaw (Patricia Lane), Alan Wheatley (Nick Hammond), Kent Walton (Bob Regan), George Merritt (Michael Collins), Margaret Harrison (Jackie Collins), Norman Williams (Elton), Arthur Rigby (Alf Benson), Denis Compton, Raymond Glendenning, Billy Milne, Richard Wattis, Michael Balfour, Johnnie Schofield, Middlesex Cricket Club, Arsenal, Millwall, Hayes Football Clubs.

Walton is a Canadian soldier who remains in Britain after WW II to play soccer. His team stands to win a great deal of money if it does well enough to be promoted to another division. Shaw, Walton's former girl friend, is paid by a rival team to lure Walton away to another team, but he remains loyal to his teammates. Fast-paced game scenes don't help this tedious picture.

p, Otto Kreisler, Ken Bennett; d, Montgomery Tully; w, George Fisher (based on a story by Franz Marischka and Maurice Weissberger); ph, Jo Jago, Peter Hamilton.

Drama (PR:A MPAA:NR)

SMALL VOICE, THE (SEE: HIDEOUT, 1948, Brit.)

SMALL WORLD OF SAMMY LEE, THE*** (1963, Brit.) 107m Bryanston-Seven Arts-Elgin- BL/Seven Arts bw

Anthony Newley (Sammy Lee), Julia Foster (Patsy), Robert Stephens (Gerry), Wilfrid Brambell (Harry), Warren Mitchell (Lou), Miriam Karlin (Milly), Kenneth J. Warren (Fred), Clive Colin Bowler (Johnny), Toni Palmer (Joan), Harry Locke (Stage Manager), Al Mulock (Dealer), Cyril Shaps (Morrie), Roy Kinnear (Lucky Dave), Harry Baird (Buddy Shine), Alfred Burke (Big Eddie), June Cunningham (Rita), Ronald Radd (Big Alf), Elmer, Lynda Baron, Ken Wayne.

Newley's up-and-down career got a boost in this well-made picture based on a TV drama in England named "Sammy." It was later done on U.S. TV as "Eddie" but Hughes went back to the original name of the protagonist for this film version. Newley is a fast-talking master of ceremonies in a tawdry

Soho strip joint where tired businessmen rest their eyes by ogling voluptuous dancers in the afternoon. Oily Stephens owns the club and keeps Newley in check. Newley is a gambler and owes about $800 to Warren, a tough bookie. He has to come up with the pounds or the gangster's musclemen, will rearrange his face for him. The time limit to find the cash is about five hours. Newley tries to extract the money from his brother, Mitchell, a hard-working delicatessen owner, but Mitchell's wife, Karlin, won't allow it as Newley has been in trouble before and always turns to Mitchell to bail him out. (Mitchell was to become one of the most beloved TV stars in England when he played in the hit show "Till Death Us Do Part," which became the basis for the smash "All In The Family.") Newley is desperate and tries to get some money in a fast series of shady schemes but none of them seem to work out and, as the time grows short, he begins to fear for his existence. Foster is a naive girl from the north of England who comes to London because Newley had promised to help her with a show business career some time before. It was an idle promise at best but she believed him and has arrived. In order to help Newley, she will do a striptease for the boss, Stephens. Newley has some semblance of morality so he tells her to forget it and sees her to a bus station, with the vague pledge that he'll get in touch with her sometime down the line. Newley's plots begin to pay off, but all he has is a check and no cash, and when Warren's men arrive–Brambell, Locke, and Bowler–he accepts his beating, then learns that he still has most of the money and that the beating, which he survived, was not as bad as he thought and now he has enough money to start all over again. Newley doesn't sing at all and his desire to direct is not seen as he accepts Hughes' suggestions and turns in one of his best acting jobs, with little of the mugging and eyebrow twisting which have served him poorly in other movies. When Newley can be properly handled (no easy task), he can be superior. But once he is allowed to overplay and go into his patented, mannered tricks, he becomes a parody of himself. Hughes did well by Newley and vice versa and the result is an interesting, sometimes funny look at the underbelly of Soho.

p, Frank Godwin; d&w, Ken Hughes; ph, Wolfgang Suschitzky; m, Kenny Graham; ed, Henry Richardson; md, Philip Martell; art d, Seamus Flannery; ch, Lili Berde; makeup, Jimmy Evans.

Drama   (PR:C   MPAA:NR)

SMALLEST SHOW ON EARTH, THE***

(1957, Brit.) 80m Times Films bw (AKA: BIG TIME OPERATORS)

Bill Travers (Matt Spenser), Virginia McKenna (Jean Spenser), Leslie Phillips (Robin Carter), Peter Sellers (Percy Quill), Margaret Rutherford (Mrs. Fazackalee), Bernard Miles (Old Tom), Francis De Wolff (Hardcastle), June Cunningham (Marlene Hogg), Sidney James (Mr. Hogg), George Cross (Commissioner), George Cormack (Bell), Stringer Davis (Emmett), Michael Corcoran (Taxi Driver), Sam Kydd.

Delightful comedy has Travers and McKenna inheriting a run-down theater. Sellers is the drunken projectionist, Rutherford is the ticket seller, an organ player during the silent era, and Miles is the aging doorman. In addition to these three eccentrics that come with the theater, a nearby train track causes the entire building to vibrate with the passing of each train. Travers and McKenna initially plan to sell the place, only to discover that they could never meet the bills they have inherited. They devise a plan to jack up the asking price, but this is foiled, leaving a shutdown as the only alternative. Fearful of losing his beloved position, Miles decides to torch the opposing theater, thus forcing a hefty offer to come from the competitors. Highlighting the many comic situations are those in which Sellers attempts to project films while in a plastered state, resulting in the picture taking on a number of odd shapes. For this latter sequence, audience members attempt to compensate by standing on their heads.

p, Frank Launder, Sidney Gilliat, Michael Relph; d, Basil Dearden; w, William Rose, John Eldridge (based on a story by Rose); ph, Douglas Slocombe; m, William Alwyn; ed, Oswald Hafenrichter; md, Muir Mathieson; art d, Allan Harris.

Comedy   (PR:A   MPAA:NR)

SMART ALEC*

(1951, Brit.) 58m Vandyke/GN bw

Peter Reynolds (Alec Albion), Mercy Haystead (Judith), Leslie Dwyer (Gossage), Edward Lexy (Inspector), Kynaston Reeves (Uncle Edward), Charles Hawtrey, John Harvey.

Reynolds murders his rich uncle with an ice bullet that melts away, leaving no evidence, after he predicts the old man's death to the police commissioner. He is acquitted at a trial, but fate sees that justice is done nonetheless. A few nice ideas, but weak overall.

p, Roger Proudlock; d, John Guillermin; w, Alec Coppel; ph, Ray Elton.

Crime   (PR:A   MPAA:NR)

SMART ALECKS*½

(1942) 88m MON bw

Leo Gorcey (Ethelbert "Muggs" McGinnis), Bobby Jordan (Danny Stevens), Huntz Hall (Glimpy), Gabriel Dell (Henry "Hank" Salko), Stanley Clements (Stash), "Sunshine Sammy" Morrison (Scruno), David Gorcey (Peewee), Bobby Stone (Skinny), Maxie Rosenbloom (Butch Brocalli), Gale Storm

(Ruth Stevens), Roger Pryor, Jr (Officer Joe Reagan), Walter Woolf King (Dr. Ornsby), Herbert Rawlinson (Capt. Bronson), Joe Kirk (Mike), Sam Bernard (Dr. Thomas), Dick Ryan (Prison Warden), Marie Windsor (Nurse), Betty Sinclair (Receptionist).

An uneven story starts with Gorcey and gang attempting to buy uniforms for their baseball team and winding up with Gorcey actually praying for the life of his friend Jordan. In between Jordan gets a hefty reward for helping in the capture of gangster Rosenbloom, who repays the boy with a vicious beating when he escapes from jail. Dell, in a familiar role, plays the neighborhood kid who takes up with gangsters, only to return to his pals after seeing the light. The usual wisecracks are mouthed off, mainly through Hall and Gorcey, one of the few things that makes many of the "Bowery Boys" entries bearable. (See BOWERY BOYS, Index.)

p, Sam Katzman, Jack Dietz; d, Wallace Fox; w, Dietz, Harvey H. Gates; ph, Mack Stengler; ed, Robert Golden; md, Edward Kay; art d, David Milton.

Drama   (PR:A   MPAA:NR)

SMART BLONDE*½

(1937) 65m WB bw

Glenda Farrell (Torchy Blane), Barton MacLane (Steve McBride), Winifred Shaw (Dolly Ireland), Craig Reynolds (Tom Carney), Addison Richards (Fitz Mularkey), Charlotte Winters (Marcia Friel), Jane Wyman (Dixie), David Carlyle [Robert Paige] (Lewis Friel), Joseph Crehan (Tiny Torgensen), Tom Kennedy (Gahagan), John Sheehan (Blyfuss), Max Wagner (Chuck Cannon), George Lloyd (Pickney Sax), Allen Pomeroy, Al Hill (Taxi Drivers), Cliff Saum (Conductor), Paul Panzer (Blind Beggar), Joseph Cunningham (City Editor), Jack H. Richardson (Murphy), Chic Bruno (Bozo), Frank Faylen (Ambulance Driver), Wayne Morris (Information Clerk), Dennis Moore (Intern), Milton Kibbee (Harms), the Ballistics Expert, Fred "Snowflake" Toones, Martin Turner (Red Caps).

This was to be the first of a series in which Farrell played Torchy Blane, the determined newspaper reporter who gets involved in numerous crime adventures. In this case, she is mainly around to give detective MacLane a hard time. He is busy trying to crack the murder of Crehan. Farrell's snooping helps to prove that an ex-gangster who poses as a changed man really isn't as honest as the cops take him to be. Performances could do little to make the sluggish story and burdensome lines presentable. (See TORCHY BLANE series, Index.)

d, Frank McDonald; w, Don Ryan, Kenneth Gamet (based on the story by Frederick Nebel); ph, Warren Lynch; ed, Frank Magee; m/l, M.K. Jerome, Jack Scholl.

Crime   (PR:A   MPAA:NR)

SMART GIRL**

(1935) 69m PAR bw

Ida Lupino (Pat Reynolds), Kent Taylor (Nick Graham), Gail Patrick (Kay Reynolds), Joseph Cawthorn (Karl Krausemeyer), Pinky Tomlin (Hans Krausemeyer), Sidney Blackmer (Harry Courtland), Greta Meyers (Mrs. Krausemeyer), Claude King (James Reynolds), Fern Emmett (Miss Brown), Perry Ivins (Auctioneer), Harold Minjir (Nelson), Charles Wilson (Morgan), Boothe Howard (Donovan), Kernan Cripps (O'Brien), Louise Brien (Helen Barton), Theodore Von Eltz (Fred Barton), Monte Vandegrift (Smith), Ernest Hilliard (Waiter), Broderick O'Farrell (Minister), Otto Hoffman, Stanley Blystone.

Lupino and Patrick play two sisters left to fend for themselves when their wealthy father dies and leaves them without any money. The more resourceful of the two, Lupino, gets involved in the hat business to make a buck, at which she becomes quite successful. Patrick winds up marrying the man Lupino originally had an eye for, bringing the latter's spirit down until she meets and falls in love with Taylor. Though she is not given much in terms of original material, Lupino is able to give her role a degree of charm, leaving the few laughs provided in the hands of Cawthorn.

p, Walter Wanger; d, Aubrey Scotto; w, Frances Hyland, Wilson Collison (based on a story by Hyland); ph, John Mescall; ed, Tom Persons.

Drama   (PR:A   MPAA:NR)

SMART GIRLS DON'T TALK*½

(1948) 81m WB bw

Virginia Mayo (Linda Vickers), Bruce Bennett (Marty Fain), Robert Hutton ("Doc" Vickers), Tom D'Andrea (Sparky Lynch), Robert Rober (Lt. McReady), Helen Westcott (Toni Peters), Richard Benedict (Cliff Saunders), Ben Welden (Nelson Clark), Richard Walsh (Johnny Warjak), Phyllis Coates (Cigarette Girl), Creighton Hale (Apartment House Clerk), Leo White (Headwaiter), Edna Harris (Miss Frey), Philo McCullough (Roulette Croupier), Jack Mower (Houseman), Ted Stanhope (Bert), Eddie Foster, George Hoagland, Bud Cokes (Gunmen).

Overly talky gangster yarn has Mayo playing a society woman who gets mixed up with some gangsters, including Bennett, the kingpin. The two begin an affair, even though members of Bennett's gang are thinking up a way to do in Mayo's brother, Hutton. Although the goal here was to shed some light on the way gangsters operate, the filmmakers were not successful. The portrayals are not very realistic, and the characters get bogged down in dialog.

p, Saul Elkins; d, Richard Bare; w, William Sackheim (based on his story "Dames Don't Talk"); ph, Ted McCord; m, David Buttolph; ed, Clarence Kolster; art d, Stanley Fleischer; set d, William Wallace; spec eff, Robert Burks; makeup, Perc Westmore.

Crime   (PR:A   MPAA:NR)

SMART GUY*½   (1943) 63m MON bw (GB: YOU CAN'T BEAT THE LAW)

Rick Vallin (*Johnny*), Bobby Larson (*Bobby*), Veda Ann Borg (*Lee*), Wanda McKay (*Jean*), Jack La Rue (*Taylor*), Mary Gordon (*Maggie*), Paul McVey (*Kilbourne*), Addison Richards (*District Attorney*), Roy Darmour (*Kearns*), John Dawson (*Evans*).

Tired story in which gambler Vallin adopts a newspaper boy so he can look good before those trying him on manslaughter charges. When Vallin thinks there's no chance he can win the case, he splits for the country with the boy in tow. He meets up with country lass Borg, who teaches him a thing or two about ethics. He reforms, of course. There is nothing about this picture to make it the least bit memorable.

p, John T. Coyle; d, Lambert Hillyer; w, Charles R. Marion, John W. Krafft (based on the story by Harrison Jacobs); ph, Mack Stengler; ed, Carl Pierson; md, Edward Kay.

Drama   (PR:A   MPAA:NR)

SMART MONEY***½   (1931) 90m WB bw

Edward G. Robinson (*Nick "The Barber" Venizelos*), James Cagney (*Jack*), Evalyn Knapp (*Irene Graham*), Ralf Harolde (*Sleepy Sam*), Noel Francis (*Marie*), Margaret Livingston (*District Attorney's Girl*), Maurice Black (*The Greek Barber*), Boris Karloff (*Sport Williams*), Morgan Wallace (*District Attorney Black*), Billy House (*Salesman-Gambler*), Paul Porcasi (*Alexander Amenoppopolus*), Polly Walters (*Lola*), Ben Taggart (*Hickory Short*), Gladys Lloyd, Wallace MacDonald (*Cigar Stand Clerks*), Clark Burroughs (*Back-to-Back Schultz*), Edwin Argus (*Two-Time Phil*), John Larkin (*Snake Eyes*), Walter Percival (*Dealer Barnes*), Mae Madison (*Small Town Girl*), Allan Lane (*A Suicide*), Eulalie Jensen (*Matron*), Charles Lane (*Desk Clerk*), Edward Hearn (*Reporter*), Eddie Kane (*Tom, Customer*), Clinton Rosemond (*George, Porter*), Charles O'Malley (*Machine-Gunner*), Gus Leonard (*Joe, Barber Customer*), Wallace MacDonald (*Cigar Stand Clerk*), John George (*Dwarf on Train*), Harry Semels (*Gambler*), Charlotte Merriam (*Girl at Gaming Table*), Larry McGrath, Spencer Bell.

After the smashing success of LITTLE CAESAR, the studio decided to team its two hottest stars, Robinson and Cagney, in a crime picture guaranteed to do big business--it would be the only time the two "tough guys" would ever appear on film together. Robinson plays a barber shop owner in a small town. He has a penchant for gambling, booze, and women, and he exercises his vices by running a gambling den in the back room. Cagney is a barber in Robinson's shop who also serves as his enthusiastic right-hand man. One day, a seedy gambler, Karloff, shows up to try his luck at Robinson's poker table. Despite the fact that Karloff cheats, Robinson wins anyway and then kicks the bum out. The barber's friends marvel at his luck and skill in games of chance and with Cagney's encouragement, they raise $10,000 to stake Robinson in a big-time syndicate poker game in the city. Robinson decides to try his hand against the big boys, and on his way to the train station he is met by Karloff who gives him an additonal $1,000 to gamble with. In the city, Robinson is wooed by a pretty girl, Francis, who steers him to a game run by Taggart. The game is a disaster and Robinson loses everything. Realizing the whole thing was a setup engineered by Francis, Taggart, and one of the gamblers, Harolde, Robinson vows revenge. He sends for Cagney and they both get barbering jobs in the city and work out their scheme. When they have enough money, Robinson tries his luck at the racetrack and begins winning big. Porcasi, a wealthy Greek, notes Robinson's luck and offers to stake the gambler with big money. Soon the money pours in and Robinson begins his revenge. He ensnares Francis and forces her to live with him. He then bankrupts both Taggart and Harolde and sets up his own massive gambling den using the familiar barber shop as a front. This attracts the attention of District Attorney Wallace, and he sets out to destroy Robinson by hitting his main weakness--women. One day Robinson sees a beautiful blonde, Knapp, about to commit suicide. He saves the girl and the two begin a romance. Cagney, ever wary, suspects Knapp is an informant and keeps an eye on her. Knapp eventually plants some incriminating evidence in Robinson's coat pocket and when the police raid the gambling den he is caught red-handed. The frame means a six-month jail term for Robinson. Cagney, who saw Knapp plant the incriminating evidence, slaps her across the face and calls her a stool pigeon. Robinson comes to her defense and accidentally kills Cagney. Knapp confesses that she indeed framed Robinson, but that the District Attorney forced her to because she was facing a blackmail charge. Robinson takes pity on the girl and she promises to wait for him. Sentenced to 10 years for the killing, Robinson tells reporters, "Two to one I'm out in five." SMART MONEY was written by the same team who had penned THE PUBLIC ENEMY, and the script provided Robinson and Cagney with a fast-paced story a bit different from the ones they had previously starred in (more humor and much less violence--the original story was nominated for an Oscar). Warner Bros. gave the film "A" production values and the supporting cast is solid, including an appearance

by Karloff who would soon go on to do FRANKENSTEIN for Universal and reach superstardom of his own. Robinson was a proven star by the time SMART MONEY went before the cameras, and Warner Bros. knew Cagney would score big with moviegoers just by watching the rushes from THE PUBLIC ENEMY. Cagney worked on both films at the same time, running from one soundstage to the other. This isn't to say that Warner Bros. wasn't hedging their bets on the young actor. His role in SMART MONEY is relatively small when compared with Robinson's, and he is totally absent from the center of the film. Luckily, THE PUBLIC ENEMY proved to be a smash when released and it is a shame that Cagney's part isn't bigger in SMART MONEY. Meanwhile, Robinson, who still hadn't fully comprehended his popularity in the wake of LITTLE CAESAR, was called by the studio to come to New York to attend the premiere of SMART MONEY at the Winter Garden theater. Robinson recalls the event in his autobiography: "After forty plays and a couple of movies I had always been able to walk into an A&P or Macy's or stroll the art galleries on Fifty-seventh Street with no one bothering me, no one looking at me, no one having the faintest notion who I was. But today was different. I was surrounded by autograph hunters, redcaps, crowds, people shoving me, pushing me, stealing my handkerchief, and tearing off my shirt buttons. I'd never known anything like it; I was frightened and, deep inside, a little excited...I felt as if I were in a lunatic asylum...In order to get into the Winter Garden, I hid on the floor of the car...I said to myself: "Face it, Manny. You're a movie star!"

d, Alfred E. Green; w, Kubec Glasmon, John Bright, Lucien Hubbard, Joseph Jackson (based on the story "The Idol" by Hubbard, Jackson); ph, Robert Kurrle; ed, Jack Killifer; md, Leo F. Forbstein; makeup, Perc Westmore.

Crime   (PR:A   MPAA:NR)

SMART POLITICS**½   (1948) 65m MON bw

Freddie Stewart (*Freddie*), June Preisser (*Dodie*), Frankie Darro (*Roy*), Warren Mills (*Lee*), Noel Neill (*Betty*), Donald MacBride (*Phineas Wharton, Sr./Phineas Wharton, Jr.*), Martha Davis (*Martha*), Butch Stone (*Butch*), Don Ripps (*Joe*), Candy Candido (*Alvin*), Harry Tyler (*Peabody*), Monte F. Collins (*Dean McKinley*), George Offerman, Jr (*Breezie*), George Fields (*Eddie*), Dick Paxton (*Johnny*), Tommy Mack (*Murphy*), Billy Snyder (*Policeman*), Gene Krupa Orchestra, Cappy Barra Harmonica Boys.

Thinly plotted story in which Stewart and Preisser lead a group of teenagers in their efforts to transform an old warehouse into a youth center. Their biggest problem is the mayor, who has his own ideas for the space the kids wish to convert. Winning the mayor over allows for a number of laughs and some pretty nifty musical numbers, including appearances by Gene Krupa's Orchestra. Musical numbers include: "Young Man with a Beat" (performed by the Gene Krupa Orchestra), "Sincerely Yours" (sung by Stewart), "Isn't This a Night for Love?" (sung by Stewart), "Household Blues" (sung by Davis), "Young Man" (sung by Davis, Stewart). A light and unpretentious film whose only aim (outside of the box office) is to be fun.

p&d, Will Jason; w, Hal Collins (based on the story by Hal Collins and Monte F. Collins); ph, Mack Stengler; ed, Will Austin; md, Edward Kay; m/l, Freddie Stewart, Hal Collins, Bobby Troup, Val Burton, Sid Robin, Jason.

Musical/Comedy   (PR:A   MPAA:NR)

SMART WOMAN**   (1931) 68m RKO bw

Mary Astor (*Nancy Gibson*), Robert Ames (*Donald Gibson*), Edward Everett Horton (*Billy Ross*), Noel Francis (*Peggy Preston*), John Halliday (*Sir Guy Harrington*), Gladys Gale (*Mrs. Preston*), Ruth Weston (*Sally Ross*), Alfred Cross (*Brooks*), Pearl Varvelle (*Ellen*), Lillian Harmer (*Mrs. Windleweaver*).

Astor returns from a trip abroad to discover that her no-good husband, Ames, has found a new woman to share his affection, a pretty but dumb Francis. Astor devises a plan to make her husband jealous in order to separate her husband from his new love. She enlists the aid of Halliday to carry out their plan, which succeeds. She falls in love with Halliday and decides she wants to marry him. She heads to Reno for a divorce, only to decide once and for all to stay married to Ames. Although the script was filled with enough witty wordplay to carry it along, director La Cava got lost in attempting to sort things out. The cast also didn't have the energy needed to make the material work.

p, Bertram Millhauser; d, Gregory La Cava; w, Salisbury Fields (based on the play "Nancy's Private Affair" by Myron C. Fagan); ph, Nick Musuraca; ed, Ann McKnight.

Comedy/Drama   (PR:A   MPAA:NR)

SMART WOMAN**   (1948) 93m MON-AA bw

Brian Aherne (*Robert Larrimore*), Constance Bennett (*Paula Rogers*), Barry Sullivan (*Frank McCoy*), Michael O'Shea (*Johnny Simons, Reporter*), James Gleason (*Sam, Larrimore's Aide*), Otto Kruger (*District Attorney Bradley Wayne*), Isobel Elsom (*Mrs. Rogers*), Richard Lyon (*Rusty*), Selena Royle (*Mrs. Wayne*), Taylor Holmes (*Dr. Jasper*), John Litel (*Clark*), Nita Hunter (*Patty Wayne*), Lee Bonnell (*Joe the Secretary*), Willie Best (*Porter*), Horace McMahon (*Lefty*), Benny Baker (*Fat Photographer*), Al Bridge (*Hotel Clerk*), Larry Gaze (*Bellboy*), Robert Riordan (*Burkette*), Phyllis Kennedy (*Tele-*

phone Operator), Netta Packer (Woman), Wally Walker (Man), John Phillips (Fred Johnson), Jimmy Ames (Bellhop), George Carleton (Elderly Judge), Paul Bryar (Bartender), Phil Arnold (Elevator Operator), Jack Mower (Bailiff), Ralph Sanford (Petitioner/Man's Voice), Doris Kemper (Woman Driver), Milton Parsons (Conrad the Witness), Margaret Tracy (Anna the Maid), Eddie Gribbon (Man in Bar), Iris Adrian (Sob-Sister Newspaper Columnist), Houseley Stevenson (Joe Smith), Joseph Fields (Paula's Assistant), Gladys Blake (Elsie), John Eldredge (Lester Flynn the Reporter), Lesley Farley (Woman in Bar), Charles Lane, Wallace Scott, Peter Virgo (Reporters), Douglas Aylesworth (Court Clerk), Lois Austin (Woman Juror), Frank Mayo (Uniformed Guard), Paul Maxey (Wise), Jimmy Conlin (Miller the Printer), John H. Elliott (Harker), Edward Gargan (Interrogator), Harry Strang, Michael Gaddis, Stanley Blystone (Cops), Cliff Clark (Police Captain).

Bennett and Aherne play lawyers who, though at each other's throats in the courtroom, carry on an off-duty romance when court's not in session. Sullivan plays the racketeer Bennett is defending, who turns out to be her former husband. This fact is finally revealed despite problems it may cause for Bennett with lover Aherne, as well as for her son. Old story is told in a unique way. Direction and script are first-rate, and the story is given an odd twist to add a bit of interest.

p, Hal E. Chester; d, Edward A. Blatt; w, Alvah Bessie, Louis Morheim, Herbert Margolis, Adela Rogers St. John (based on the story by Leon Gutterman, Edwin V. Westrate); ph, Stanley Cortez; m, Louis Gruenberg; ed, Frank Gross; md, Constantine Bakaleinikoff; art d, F. Paul Sylos; set d, Ray Boltz, Jr.; cos, Adrian; makeup, Dave Grayson.

Drama   **(PR:A MPAA:NR)**

SMARTEST GIRL IN TOWN**   (1936) 58m RKO bw

Gene Raymond (Dick Smith), Ann Sothern (Francis Cooke), Helen Broderick (Gwen), Eric Blore (Philbean, Dick's Valet), Erik Rhodes (Torine), Harry Jans (Terry), Frank Jenks, Alan Curtis, Edward Price, Rolfe Sedan.

Raymond plays a millionaire who pretends to be a model in order to win the affection of model Sothern. Meanwhile, she searches for a wealthy suitor upon the insistence of her sister, Broderick, who married a bum. When all seems lost for Raymond, he fakes a suicide, attracting Sothern's attention and winning her love. (A similar theme would be handled with much more taste in HOW TO MARRY A MILLIONAIRE, the famous Marilyn Monroe vehicle.)

p, Edward Kaufman; d, Joseph Santley; w, Viola Brothers Shore (based on the story by Muriel Scheck, H.S. Kraft); ph, J. Roy Hunt; ed, Jack Hively.; m/l, "Will You?" Gene Raymond.

Comedy   **(PR:A MPAA:NR)**

SMARTY**   (1934) 64m WB bw (GB: HIT ME AGAIN)

Joan Blondell (Vicki Wallace Thorpe), Warren William (Tony Wallace), Edward Everett Horton (Vernon Thorpe), Frank McHugh (George Lancaster), Claire Dodd (Anita), Joan Wheeler (Bonnie), Virginia Sale (Edna), Leonard Carey (Tilford), Dennis O'Keefe (Dancing Extra), Lester Dorr (Court Recorder), Bert Moorehouse (Clerk), Frederick Burton (Judge), Camille Rovelle (Mrs. Crosby), Frank Darien (Court Spectator), Sarah Edwards (Mrs. Crosby's Mother).

When a slugfest develops between married couple Blondell and William, lawyer Horton suggests a visit to divorce court. Horton first represents Blondell, and then marries her. And, although saying he despises anyone who would hit a woman, he is not beyond giving Blondell a slap or two. But Blondell has been in love with her first husband all along, and this paves the way for an eventual reconciliation. Horton's performance as the straight-laced, jealous husband is a show-stealer., Frank McDonald, who served as dialog director, became a director in his own right after 1935. He directed some 100 B movies for various studios, turning out light romances, musicals, mysteries, and westerns starring Gene Autry and Roy Rogers.

p, Robert Presnell; d, Robert Florey; w, F. Hugh Herbert, Carl Erickson (based on the story by Herbert); ph, George Barnes; ed, Jack Killifer; md, Leo F. Forbstein; art d, John Hughes.

Comedy   **(PR:A MPAA:NR)**

SMASH AND GRAB   (SEE: LARCENY STREET, 1941, Brit.)

SMASH PALACE***   (1982, New Zealand) 100m Aadvark Films-New
                                Zealand Film Commision/Atlantic c

Bruno Lawrence (Al Shaw), Anna Jemison (Jacqui Shaw), Greer Robson (Georgie Shaw), Keith Aberdein (Ray Foley), Desmond Kelly (Tiny), Margaret Umbers, Sean Duffy, Bryan Johnson, Terence Donovan, Dick Rollo, Ian Barber, Mike Beytagh, Brian Chase, Ross Davies, Colin Fredricksen, Thomas King, Chris Pasco, Evan Sommerville, Frank Taylor, Mike Wiggins, Ray Littlewood, Doug McKenzie, Don Lee, Lynne Robson.

Former racing champ Lawrence returns home to his native New Zealand to take over his father's old auto junk shop. Accompanying him is his pregnant

European wife, Jemison, who through the years becomes bored with her life. She eventually grows tired of her husband and leaves him to live with Lawrence's best friend, police officer Aberdein. A maniacal Lawrence attempts one last reconciliation by kidnaping his daughter and running off into the bush, forcing a widespread hunt for the missing child. Although the plot is fairly thin, the concentration is on the characters, and on the growing tension between the married couple. The result is a pointed look into the formation and dissolution of a relationship where neither person is to blame. Lawrence is outstanding as the self-absorbed man, whose personality undergoes massive changes throughout the course of the film.

p&d, Roger Donaldson; w, Peter Hanson, Donaldson, Bruno Lawrence; ph, Graeme Cowley (Eastmancolor); m, Sharon O'Neill; ed, Mike Horton; art d, Reston Griffiths; cos, Annabel Blackett.

Drama   **Cas.**   **(PR:O MPAA:R)**

SMASHING BIRD I USED TO KNOW, THE
                    (SEE: SCHOOL FOR UNCLAIMED GIRLS, 1973, Brit.

SMASHING THE CRIME SYNDICATE
                    (SEE: HELL'S BLOODY DEVILS, 1970)

SMASHING THE MONEY RING**½   (1939) 57m FN-WB bw

Ronald Reagan (Lt. Brass Bancroft), Margot Stevenson (Peggy), Eddie Foy, Jr (Gabby Watters), Joe Downing (Dice Mathews), Charles D. Brown (Parker), Elliott Sullivan (Danny), Don Douglas (Gordon), Charles Wilson (Kilrane), Joe King (Saxby), William B. Davidson (Warden), Dick Rich (Guard Davis), Max Hoffman, Jr (Guard Shelden), John Hamilton (Night Captain), Ralph Sanford (Night Clerk), Sidney Bracey (Pop), Jack Mower (Night Guard), Nat Carr (Prison Doctor), Don Turner (Joe), Frank Mayo (Van Doctor), George Chesebro (Convict), Tom Wilson (Convict 18701), Jack Wise (Runner), Al Herman (Convict 15222), Dutch Hendrian (Fats), Lee Phelps (Gate Guard), John Ridgely (Policeman), Monte Vandegrift, Bob Perry (Guards), Ralph Dunn, Pat O'Malley (Custodians), Milton Frome (Bailiff).

In the third film that casts Reagan as an agent for the Secret Service, he goes undercover to find the hoods responsible for widespread counterfeiting. He poses as a convicted counterfeiter and goes to prison to infiltrate the mob. He tracks the bills to the prison printing press, and leads the government agents to the operation. Reagan gives a standard performance as the All-American boy turned cop, with sidekick Foy around to provide comic relief. Foy is the film's most memorable facet.

p, Bryan Foy; d, Terry Morse; w, Anthony Coldeway, Raymond Schrock (based on the story "Murder in Sing Sing" by Jonathan Finn); ph, James Van Trees; ed, Frank Magee.

Crime   **(PR:A MPAA:NR)**

SMASHING THE RACKETS**   (1938) 65M RKO bw

Chester Morris (Jim Conway), Frances Mercer (Susan Lane), Bruce Cabot (Steve Lawrence), Rita Johnson (Letty Lane), Donald Douglas (Spaulding), Ben Welden (Whitey Clark), Edward Pawley (Chin Martin), Frank M. Thomas (Judge Wend), Walter Miller (Mac), George Irving (Greer), Kay Sutton (Peggy), Theodore Von Eltz (Ellis), Edith Craig (Flo), George Lloyd (Leonard), Paul Fix (Maxie), Edward "Eddie" Acuff, Joseph de Stefani, Frank O'Connor.

Loosely based on the career of Thomas E. Dewey, the district attorney responsible for cleaning up the New York rackets, who went on to become governor and an unsuccessful presidential candidate. A lot of heroics are offered, none of which seems very realistic, but the pace is built up to gloss over these inadequacies. Morris is miscast in the lead, lacking the ruggedness needed for such a part. Other performances are little more than caricatures of inarticulate hoodlums.

p, B.F. Fineman; d, Lew Landers; w, Lionel Houser (based on the story by Forrest Davis); ph, Nicholas Musuraca; ed, Harry Marker.

Crime   **(PR:A MPAA:NR)**

SMASHING THE SPY RING*½   (1939) 59m COL bw

Ralph Bellamy (John Baxter), Fay Wray (Eleanor Dunlap), Regis Toomey (Ted Hall), Walter Kingsford (Dr. Carter), Ann Doran (Madelon Martin), Warren Hull (Phil Dunlap), Forbes Murray (Col. Scully), Lorna Gray (Miss Loring), Paul Whitney (Mason), John Tyrrell (Johnson), May Wallace (Mrs. Baxter).

Pre-WW II spy drama in which FBI agent Bellamy thwarts Kingsford's plan to steal government military equipment plans. Along the way he meets and falls in love with Wray, whose G-man brother is killed by the enemy. Bellamy tries to infiltrate headquarters by faking amnesia, posing as a famous scientist who developed a poison-gas formula, and having himself committed to the hospital that the spies are using as a front. Material rarely rises above mediocrity.

p, Jack Fier; d, Christy Cabanne; w, Arthur T. Horman, Dorrell McGowan,

Stuart E. McGowan (based on the story by D. and S. McGowan); ph, Allen G. Siegler; m, M.W. Stoloff; ed, James Sweeney.

Spy Drama (PR:A MPAA:NR)

SMASHING THROUGH (SEE: CHEYENNE CYCLONE, 1932)

SMASHING TIME** (1967 Brit.) 96m Partisan/PAR c

Rita Tushingham (*Brenda*), Lynn Redgrave (*Yvonne*), Michael York (*Tom Wabe*), Anna Quayle (*Charlotte Brilling*), Irene Handl (*Mrs. Gimble*), Ian Carmichael (*Bobbi Mome-Rath*), Toni Palmer (*Toni*), Jeremy Lloyd (*Jeremy Tove*), Arthur Mullard (*Cafe Boss*), Sydney Bromley (*Tramp*), Howard Marion-Crawford (*Hall Porter*), Murray Melvin (*1st Exquisite*), Paul Danquah (*2nd Exquisite*), Valery Leon (*Tove's Secretary*), Adele Strong (*Gossiping Customer*), Jerold Wells (*Man in Cafe No. 6*), Peter Jones (*Dominic*), George A. Cooper (*Irishman*), Ronnie Stevens (*1st Waiter*), John Clive (*Sweenie Todd Manager*), Mike Lennox (*Disc Jockey*), Bruce Lacey (*Clive Sword*), Cardew Robinson (*Custard-Pie Vicar*), David Lodge (*The Caretaker*), Ray Mackin (*2nd Waiter*), Amy Dalby (*Demolished Old Lady*), The Tomorrow (*The Snarks*), Bart Allison, Gabor Baraker, Eve Belton, Kate Binchy, Yuri Borienko, Teresa Buckingham, Veronica Carlson, Golda Casimir, Richard Coe, Julian Curry, Desmond Davies, Jonathon Elsom, Olivia Farjeon, Tom Gill, Danny Green, Luanshiya Greer, Geoffrey Hughes, Brenda Kempner, Leigh Kostelanetz, Sam Kydd, Valerie Leon, Arthur Lovegrove, George O'Gorman, Stuart Saunders, Frank Sieman, Will Stampe, Bernard Stone, Michael Ward, Susan Whitman.

Tushingham and Redgrave play two women from England's North Country who go to London's "mod" Carnaby Street in search of excitement and success. The girls stick together throughout their misadventures, which include washing dishes to pay for food, and working as cocktail hostesses. Redgrave manages a to get her picture taken by famous photographer York (a la BLOW UP), as an example of the way not to dress. She later becomes a successful recording star, but her fame dies quickly. Tushingham, on the other hand, is promoted by York as "the face of the 1970s" (this still being 1967), and her career takes off. Having gone their separate ways, Tushingham and Redgrave meet up again at a party given in Tushingham's honor, where they both decide that they've had enough of the "hip" life style and head back home together. SMASHING TIME attempted to satirize the London scene of the late 1960s, using a system of direction and editing that owes much to Richard Lester. Unfortunately, the material is nothing more than slapstick, and worn-out slapstick at that. Songs include: "Day Out," "While I'm Still Young," "Baby Don't Go," "It's Always Your Fault," "Smashing Time," "Trouble," "Waiting for My Friend" (John Addison, George Melly), "New Clothes" (Addison, Melly, sung by Rita Tushingham).

p, Carlo Ponti, Roy Millichip; d, Desmond Davis; w, George Melly; ph, Manny Wynn (Eastmancolor); m, John Addison, Victor Smith; ed, Barry Vince; art d, Ken Bridgeman; cos, Ruth Meyers; makeup, Richard Mills.

Comedy (PR:C MPAA:NR)

SMASH-UP, THE STORY OF A WOMAN*
(1947) 103m UNIV bw (GB:A WOMAN DESTROYED)

Susan Hayward (*Angie Evans*), Lee Bowman (*Ken Conway*), Marsha Hunt (*Martha Gray*), Eddie Albert (*Steve*), Carl Esmond (*Dr. Lorenz*), Carleton Young (*Mr. Elliott*), Charles D. Brown (*Mike Dawson*), Janet Murdoch (*Miss Kirk*), Tom Chatterton (*Edwards*), Sharyn Payne (*Angelica*), Robert Shayne (*Mr. Gordon*), Larry Blake (*Emcee*), George Meeker (*Wolf*), Erville Alderson (*Farmer*), George Meader (*Attorney*), Ruth Sanderson (*Maggie*), Steve Olsen, Fred Browne (*Bartenders*), Virginia Carroll, Nanette Vallon, Dorothy Christy (*Women*), Al Hill, Richard Kipling, Clarence Straight (*Men*), William Gould (*Judge*), Connie Leon (*Mary*), Vivien Oakland (*Woman at Bar*), Robert Verdaine (*Maitre d'*), Laurie Douglas (*Singer*), Ernie Adams (*Waiter*), Ethel Wales (*Farmer's Wife*), Ralph Montgomery (*Doorman*), Noel Neill (*Girl at Party*), Lee Shumway (*Benson*), Joan Shawlee (*Fulton*), Peg LaCentra, Matt Dennis (*Offstage Voices*), Bess Flowers, Barbara Woodell, Alice Fleming, Jan Cravan, Frances Morris, Hal Derwin.

In Hayward's first major role, she portrays the character that was to become her trademark: the fallen woman struggling to come back. She was nominated for an Academy Award for her vivid performance as a successful nightclub singer who sacrifices her career when she marries Bowman, also a singer and songwriter. Using her connections to get him started, Bowman's popularity quickly grows. Meanwhile, Hayward gives birth to a baby daughter and is spending time in their newly acquired country home. Bowman's career continues to flourish which keeps him away from home more often. Depressed, Hayward takes greater and greater solace in alcohol. Eventually becoming too wapped up in jealousy and alcohol to think clearly, she physically attacks Bowman's secretary, Hunt, at a party. Bowman sues for divorce and demands custody of their daughter. A desperate Hayward makes one last attempt to keep her family together by kidnaping her daughter, only to almost lose the child when she carelessly starts a fire. This occurrence shocks Hayward into taking steps to get back on her feet. Hayward was magnificent in her role in the film, which combined elements of THE LOST WEEKEND and A STAR IS BORN. Unfortunately, Bowman was miscast in the role of her husband.

p, Walter Wanger; d, Stuart Heisler; w, John Howard Lawson, Lionel Wiggam (based on the story by Dorothy Parker and Frank Cavett); ph, Stanley Cortez; m, Daniele Amfitheatrof; ed, Milton Carruth; art d, Alexander Golitzen; set d, Russell Gausman, Ruby R. Levitt; m/l, "I Miss the Feeling," "Hush-a-Bye Island," Jimmy McHugh, Harold Adamson (sung by Susan Hayward, dubbed by Peg LaCentra), "Life Can Be Beautiful," McHugh, Adamson (sung by Lee Bowman, dubbed by Hal Derwin); Jack Brooks, Edgar Fairchild.

Drama Cas. (PR:C MPAA:NR)

SMELL OF HONEY! THE (SEE: SMELL OF HONEY, A SWALLOW OF BRINE, A, 1966)

SMELL OF HONEY, A SWALLOW OF BRINE! A*
(1966) 71m Essaneff/Sonney Amusement bw (AKA: THE SMELL OF HONEY!; A TASTE OF HONEY, A SWALLOW OF BRINE!)

Stacey Walker (*Sharon Winters*), Neville Coward (*Lowell Carter*), Sharon Carr (*Paula*), Bob Todd (*Tony*), Michael Wright (*Mr. Gordon*), Michael O'Kelly (*Roy*), Tom Hughes (*Dick Owens*).

Walker plays a pretty young woman who likes to tease men and then accuse them of rape. She ruins three men's lives, but she doesn't seem to care. She eventually meets up with Todd, who won't stand for her games; he gives her a nasty beating and then forces her into a life of prostitution. Music in the film is performed by "et cetera."

p, David F. Friedman; d, B. Ron Elliott; w, Friedman; ph, Art Radford; m, Mark Wayne; ed, Byron Mabe.

Drama (PR:O MPAA:NR)

SMILE*½ (1975) 113m UA c

Bruce Dern ("*Big Bob*" *Freelander*), Barbara Feldon (*Brenda DiCarlo*), Michael Kidd (*Tommy French*), Geoffrey Lewis (*Wilson Shears*), Nicholas Pryor (*Andy DiCarlo*), Colleen Camp (*Connie Thompson/"Miss Imperial County"*), Joan Prather (*Robin Gibson/"Miss Antelope Valley"*), Denise Nickerson (*Shirley Tolstoy/"Miss San Diego"*), Annette O'Toole (*Doria Houston/"Miss Anaheim"*), Maria O'Brien (*Maria Gonzales/"Miss Salinas"*), Melanie Griffith (*Karen Love/"Miss Simi Valley"*), Kate Sarchel (*Judy Wagner/"Miss Modesto"*), Titos Vandis (*Emil Eidleman*), Dennis Dugan (*Logan*), William Traylor (*Ray Brandy*), Eric Shea ("*Little Bob*" *Freelander*), Adam Reed (*Freddy*), Brad Thompson (*Chuck*), Paul Benedict (*Orren Brooks*), Dick McGarvin (*Ted Farley*), Helene Nelson (*Jo Ann Marshall*), Caroline Williams (*Helga*), George Skaff (*Dr. Malvert*), Shawn Christianson ("*Miss Fountain Valley*").

A huge cast, with many first-timers, is well handled by director Ritchie in this satirical glimpse of a real beauty pageant staged in Santa Rosa, California. Working from an original script by TV veteran Belson, the laughs are heavy but there are so many people in the picture that we never have the chance to truly know any of them and the result, while often hilarious, is ultimately skin-deep, just as the beauty contestants are. Dern is a mobile home dealer in the town and the chief judge of the contest. His son, Shea, is a pre-teener with an eye toward female flesh and money so he takes some surreptitious shots of the nude beauties and means to sell them to his pals. When that's discovered, father and son have to see a court-ordered psychiatrist, Skaff, in order to allow the boy to go back to school. Kidd is a tired choreographer who has received this second-rate assignment and hopes it might lead to a rekindling of his flagging career. The president of the beauty pageant is Lewis and the prudish female chief of the proceedings is Feldon, who is married to Pryor and is as cold as an Arctic night to him. Cutting between all of these people and the many contestants, Ritchie tries to give us a picture like NASHVILLE with multiple stories going at the same time. The final scenes were staged at the actual pageant and no one, except Belson and Ritchie, knew the winner so there was a sense of reality at the conclusion. The best of the beauty contestants is Prather, who has to alter her character from naive waif to win-at-any-cost contestant. Feldon's husband, Pryor, eventually shoots her out of frustration, thus reducing the film's level to something near Tom and Jerry. Before that, however, there is enough laughter to make this picture superior in many ways. In 1986, a stage musical based on the movie was being financed, with music by Marvin Hamlisch. The music for SMILE was based on Charles Chaplin's original song "Smile," which became a hit for Nat "King" Cole. Osborn's incidental music was appropriate and some pop tunes by Neil Sedaka, Shirley and Lee, and The Beach Boys were also used. Like many of Ritchie's films, it was sharp but not good-natured and people stayed away from it in droves. Most of the beauty contest participants were exactly that and it's a tribute to Ritchie's ability with actors that he manages to get them to seem like they are nonactors, which is one of the most difficult things an actor can do.

p&d, Michael Ritchie; w, Jerry Belson; ph, Conrad Hall (DeLuxe Color); m, Daniel Osborn, Leroy Holmes, Charles Chaplin; ed, Richard Harris; cos, Patricia Norris; ch, JimBates; m/l, Osborne, Ritchie, Neil Sedaka, The Beach Boys, Shirley and Lee.

Comedy Cas. (PR:C-O MPAA:PG)

SMILE ORANGE** (1976, Jamaican) 86m Knuts c

Carl Bradshaw (Ringo), Glenn Morrison (Bus Boy), Stanley Irons (Joe), Vaughn Crosskill (Assistant Manager).

Somewhat of a followup to the very successful THE HARDER THEY COME (1973), Bradshaw is a resort hotel worker who has developed a system to take advantage of naive white tourists. The gritty film techniques that gave THE HARDER THEY COME a sense of immediacy get a bit irritating in SMILE ORANGE, making the viewer want to cry out for an audible soundtrack and focused images.

p, Edward Knight; d, Trevor D. Rhone; w, Rhone, David Ogden (based on the play by Rhone); ph, David McDonald; m, Melba Liston; ed, Mike Gilligan.

Drama　　　　　　**(PR:C　MPAA:PG)**

SMILES OF A SUMMER NIGHT*** (1957, Swed.) 108m Svensk Filmindustri/Rank bw (SOMMARNATTENS LEENDE)

Ulla Jacobsson (Anne Egerman), Eva Dahlbeck (Desiree Armfeldt), Margit Carlquist (Charlotte Malcolm), Harriet Andersson (Petra the Maid), Gunnar Bjornstrand (Fredrik Egerman), Jarl Kulle (Count Malcolm), Ake Fridell (Frid the Groom), Bjorn Bjelvenstam (Henrik Egerman), Naima Wifstrand (Mrs. Armfeldt), Gull Natrop (Malla, Desiree's Maid), Birgitta Valberg, Bibi Andersson (Actresses), Anders Wulff (Footman), Svea Holst (Dresser), Hans Straat (Almgren the Photographer), Lisa Lundholm (Mrs. Almgren), Sigge Furst (Policeman), Gunnar Nielsen (Niklas), Gosta Pruzelius (Footman), Lena Soderblom, Mona Malm, Joseph Norrman, John Melin, Sten Gester.

It is the Swedish countryside in the year 1900 and the summer air is permeated with the power of love. Visiting an old country estate are a married couple, Bjornstrand, a lawyer, and his still-virgin wife of two years, Jacobsson. Also in attendance are Bjornstrand's son, Bjelvenstam; Dahlbeck, an actress who is also the former mistress of the lawyer; and Kulle and Carlquist, a count and countess. In the course of this midsummer's eve, Jacobsson will run off with her stepson, Bjornstrand will rekindle his romance with Dahlbeck, and Kulle and Carlquist will come to a reconciliation of their marriage. SMILES OF A SUMMER NIGHT is a delightful comedy, full of blithe feelings within the varied love affairs. "It was an attempt to be witty," claimed Bergman. "People were always bawling me out for being such a gloomy guy." Indeed, of the few comedies within the director's body of work, it is this one that is the best known. Bergman approached the film as a sort of mathematical love problem, taking various couples and through addition, subtraction, and multiplication created entanglements among the characters. The ensemble handles the task with delight and verve, making the romantic complications a true-to-life comedy without ever dipping to farcical levels. But this is a far from perfect film. At times the action is slowed down by a theatrical-like presentation. The director often relies too much on situation for humor rather than the natural qualities within the well-drawn characters. Ultimately it is these characters who come shining through, creating a memorable comedy. Influenced by Shakespeare's "A Midsummer Night's Dream," this proved to be an inspiration for other artists as well. The Broadway musical (and subsequent film) "A Little Night Music" successfully transplanted the story to stage. Woody Allen, a self-admitted Bergman follower, attempted, with lesser results, to rework some of the ideas (along with similar settings) in his own A MIDSUMMER NIGHT'S SEX COMEDY. (In Swedish; English subtitles.)

p, Allan Ekelund; d&w, Ingmar Bergman; ph, Gunnar Fischer; m, Erik Nordgren; ed, Oscar Rosander; art d, P.A. Lundgren; cos, Mago.

Comedy　　　　　　**(PR:A　MPAA:NR)**

SMILEY***½ (1957, Brit.) 97m LFP/FOX c

Ralph Richardson (Rev. Lambeth), John McCallum (Rankin), Chips Rafferty (Sgt. Flaxman), Colin Petersen (Smiley Greevins), Jocelyn Hernfield (Miss Workman), Bruce Archer (Joey), Margaret Christensen (Ma Greevins), Reg Lye (Pa Greevins), Charles Tingwell (Mr. Stevens), Marion Johns (Mrs. Stevens), Guy Doleman (Boundary Rider), William Rees (Johnson), Gavin Davies (Fred Stevens), Chow Sing (Ah Foo), Bob Simm (King Billy), Reggie Weigand (Jackie).

High-spirited young Peterson has his eyes set on a new bicycle and, with the aid of pal Archer, he undertakes several jobs to earn money. He earns the money only to have it taken away by his low-life father, Lye, who must pay gambling debts. Though the plot is rather sketchy, the characters are realistic and touching. The audience also is given insight into the world Peterson inhabits: the tough backwoods of Australia. Peterson is energetic in his role, without being overly cute. He becomes involved in realistic situations with people out to take advantage of a poor kid, such as the drug dealer who tricks him into delivering drugs. Richardson is superb as the country preacher who lends advice to the young achiever. SMILEY did well enough at the box office to inspire the sequel SMILEY GETS A GUN.

p&d, Anthony Kimmins; w, Moore Raymond, Kimmins (based on the novel by Raymond); ph, Ted Scaife (CinemaScope, DeLuxe Color); m, William Alwyn; ed, md, Muir Mathieson; art d, Stan Wollveridge.

Drama　　　　　　**(PR:A　MPAA:NR)**

SMILEY GETS A GUN**½ (1959, Brit.) 89m Canberra/FOX c

Sybil Thorndike (Granny McKinley), Chips Rafferty (Sgt. Flaxman), Keith Calvert (Smiley Greevins), Bruce Archer (Joey), Margaret Christensen (Ma Greevins), Reg Lye (Pa Greevins), Grant Taylor (Stiffy), Verena Kimmins (Miss McCowan), Leonard Teale (Mr. Stevens), Jannice Dinnen (Jean Holt), Brian Farley (Fred Jackson), Richard Pusey (Jimmy Goodwin), Barbara Eather (Elsie), Guy Dolman (Quirk), Ruth Cracknell (Mrs. Gaspen), Bruce Beeby (Dr. Gaspen), Charles Tasman (Vicar), Frank Ransom (Mick Mooney), John Fegan (Tom Graham), John Tate (Dave Rudge), Val Cooney (Nurse), William Rees (Mr. Protheroe), Gordon Chater (Rev. Galbraith).

Set in the backlands of the Australian wilderness, Calvert plays the young lad whose yen for mischief motivates local policeman Rafferty to come up with a solution. He promises the boy a new gun if he can keep out of trouble and learn to show respect for the other members of the community. Calvert undertakes his assignment with the utmost sincerity, but people start to chide him and bet on whether he will accomplish his goal. Real problems erupt when old lady Thorndike is robbed, and she points her finger at Calvert. The films highlights include first-rate photography and an effective performance by Calvert. Thorndike adds some flavor in her part as the old eccentric. (Sequel to SMILEY)

p&d, Anthony Kimmins; w, Kimmins, Rex Rienits (based on the novel by Moore Raymond); ph, Ted Scaife (CinemaScope, DeLuxe Color); m, Wilbur Sampson; ed, G. Turney-Smith; m/l, "A Little Boy Called Smiley," Clyde Collins.

Drama/Comedy　　　　　　**(PR:A　MPAA:NR)**

SMILIN' THROUGH***½ (1932) 96m MGM bw

Norma Shearer (Moonyean Clare/Kathleen), Frederic March (Kenneth Wayne/Jeremy Wayne), Leslie Howard (John Carteret), O.P. Heggie (Dr. Owen), Ralph Forbes (Willie Ainley), Beryl Mercer (Mrs. Crouch), Margaret Seddon (Ellen), Cora Sue Collins (Kathleen as a Child), Forrester Harvey (Orderly), David Torrence (Gardener).

First sound version of the beloved epic romance with a touch of the supernatural which was first a stage play, then a silent film in 1922 starring Norma Talmadge. The film begins in 1868 England on the day of Shearer's wedding to country squire Howard. Tragedy strikes during the ceremony however, when Shearer's jealous suitor, March, shows up drunk and crazed. He pulls a pistol and fires at his rival, but the bullet misses its intended target and hits Shearer. As Shearer lay dying in her fiancee's arms, she promises him that she will always be near and that someday they will be reunited. March manages to escape and disappears. Howard spends the rest of his days as a lonely recluse grieving over his loss. Fifty years go by and Howard's loneliness is interrupted by the arrival of his beautiful young niece–the spitting image of her dead aunt (also played by Shearer)--who comes to live with the old man after her parents are drowned in an accident. Howard grows quite fond of the girl and enjoys having her around because she is a living legacy of his departed beloved. One day Shearer and her boyfriend Forbes are caught in a violent rainstorm and seek shelter in an old empty house. The house turns out to be the very one March had fled 50 years before. While exploring the place, Shearer meets March's son (also played by March), and there is an instant romantic attraction between the two. Shearer excitedly tells Howard of her discovery, but the old man turns angry and tells her never to see young March again. Sympathetic to Howard's feelings, Shearer agrees to try and forget March. Soon after, WW I begins and March goes off to war. He is wounded in battle and returns home. Shearer, whose love for March has grown despote their seperation, is desperate to see him but she continues to heed Howard's wishes. Guilty for holding Shearer back, Howard summons the spirit of his dead wife, and she implores him to let the past go and allow Shearer to see March for she is now feeling the same pain that he has felt for 50 years. Chastened by his wife's spirit, Howard relents and gives Shearer permission to marry March. During a chess game with his friend Heggie, Howard quietly dies. His spirit rises from the body–young again–and joins Shearer as they enter the wedding coach and ride off into eternity together. SMILIN' THROUGH is an excellent example of sentimental melodrama at its best. Given a superb production, the film boasts a strong cast and all handle their roles with aplomb. Shearer, who was at the height of her stardom, was married to super-producer Irving Thalberg and they both gave the film their all. The romantic pairing of March and Shearer (both in dual roles) was a stroke of brilliance since both were rapidly becoming two of the best known and most respected actors of the era. Shearer recieved the Oscar for Best Actress of 1930 for THE DIVORCEE, and March would share Best Actor of 1932 for his tour de force in DR. JEKYLL AND MR. HYDE (Wallace Beery also won for THE CHAMP). The film proved popular at the box office, but sensing that her husband badly needed rest from the strain of battling Louis Mayer, Shearer took a year off and accompanied Thalberg on a trip to Europe. SMILIN' THROUGH was made again as a musical in 1941.

d, Sidney Franklin; w, Ernest Vajda, Claudine West, Donald Ogden, Stewart James, Bernard Fagan (based on the play by Jane Cowl, Jane Murfin, Langdon McCormick); ph, Lee Garmes; ed, Margaret Booth, art d, Cedric Gibbons; cos, Adrian.

Drama　　　　　　**(PR:A　MPAA:NR)**

SMILIN' THROUGH***   (1941) 100m MGM c

Jeanette MacDonald (*Kathleen Clare/Moonyean Clare*), Brian Aherne (*Sir John Carteret*), Gene Raymond (*Kenneth Wayne/Jeremy Wayne*), Ian Hunter (*Rev. Owen Harding*), Jackie Horner (*Kathleen as a Child*), Frances Robinson (*Ellen*), Patrick O'Moore (*Willie*), Eric Lonsdale (*Charles*), Frances Carson (*Dowager*), Ruth Rickaby (*Woman*), David Clyde (*Sexton*), Wyndham Standing (*Doctor*), Emily West (*Chorus Singer, "Land of Milk and Honey."*).

The third film version of the popular melodrama SMILIN' THROUGH was turned into a musical to showcase the vocal talents of its star, MacDonald, and was the only version to be filmed in color. MacDonald buffs will also note that this is the only film the star ever made with her husband, Raymond. The film opens in 1897 England on the Queen Victoria's 50th jubilee. An old man, Aherne, visits the cemetery where his departed wife lies. Her spirit, MacDonald, appears and she tells him that they soon will be reunited. Aherne's old friend Hunter arrives and sadly informs him that his wife's sister and her husband have been killed in a tragic accident leaving their 5-year-old girl an orphan. Aherne agrees to adopt the child and soon the little girl, Horner, and the old man are as close as father and daughter. As the years pass, Aherne's niece (now played by MacDonald) grows to be ·the spitting image of his dear, departed wife. The resemblance takes its toll on Aherne and he is constantly reminded of his loss. One day while MacDonald and her boy friend O'Moore are out for a walk, they are caught in a thunderstorm and forced to seek shelter in an old house. The house has not been lived in since 1864 (an old newspaper on the floor confirms the date) and an air of mystery surrounds the place. Footsteps are heard and Raymond, an American, appears. He is the son of the man who owned the house and he invites MacDonald and O'Moore to have a drink with him. MacDonald is immediately taken with the handsome American and the next day they enjoy a picnic together. When Aherne learns that MacDonald is seeing Raymond, he flies into a rage and demands she never see the young man again. MacDonald wants an explanation, and Aherne, his voice full of emotion, tells her of his tragic wedding day back in 1864. In flashback we see that Aherne and Raymond (he plays both father and son) were rivals for MacDonald's affections. MacDonald finally agreed to marry Aherne, and immediately after the ceremony, a drunken and crazed Raymond arrived and drew a pistol on Aherne. MacDonald threw herself in front of her new husband as Raymond fired and was killed. Raymond fled the country, leaving a grief-stricken Aherne to bury his bride. Back in the present, MacDonald tells her uncle that she now understands and will abide by his wishes. Raymond enlists and goes off to war (WW I), while MacDonald does her part by singing for the troops. MacDonald becomes quite bitter towards her uncle, but despite her growing hatred he remains firm. Aherne's friend Hunter is also dismayed by his stand and breaks off their friendship. Alone again, Aherne is visited by the spirit of his wife who tells him that they will never be together unless he forgives and allows MacDonald to marry Raymond. Four years later the war is over and Raymond returns on a pair of crutches– crippled in battle. When MacDonald learns that he is back, she immediately rushes to him, but he conceals his injury from her. MacDonald wants to elope with Raymond, but he lies and tells her he no longer loves her and that he's returning to America alone. Hunter learns of this and goes to Aherne with the sad tale, begging him to allow the couple to marry. Aherne still refuses and Hunter declares that if he insists on keeping the youngsters apart, then he hopes Aherne and his wife will never be together. MacDonald returns home, very upset about Raymond. Aherne finally softens and tells her that her soldier has come back a cripple and refused to reveal the truth because he did not want her to feel obligated to take care of him. Aherne urges MacDonald to rush to the train station and bring Raymond back. A joyous MacDonald passes Hunter on the road to the station and tells her uncle's friend what Aherne has done. Hunter goes back to the house and thanks Aherne for making the girl so happy. The two men settle down to a game of chess, and during the match, Aherne quietly dies. The spirit of MacDonald returns and is joined by Aherne's spirit, which rises from his body again a young man. The ghostly couple enter their wedding carriage and ride off into the great beyond. While this version of SMILIN' THROUGH has its advantages (color and music), it fails to top its 1932 predecessor, which boasted a top-notch cast in all three lead roles. The plot is virtually the same, with room made for the pleasant musical interludes (perhaps a few too many). MacDonald was a bit too old to successfully essay the role of a teenager, while Raymond is stiff and uninteresting as the dashing young suitor. Ironically, the real-life husband and wife made a rather dull screen love duo. Songs include: "The Kerry Dance" (L.J. Molloy, sung by MacDonald, Horner), "Drink to Me Only with Thine Eyes" (Ben Johnson, sung by MacDonald), "A Little Love, a Little Kiss" (Leo Silesu, Adrian Ross, sung by MacDonald), "Ouvre ton Coeur" (Georges Bizet, sung by MacDonald), "Smilin' Through" (Arthur Penn, sung by MacDonald), "There's a Long, Long Trail A-winding" (Alonzo Elliott, Stoddard King, sung by MacDonald, Chorus), "Smiles" (Lee S. Roberts, J. Will Callahan), "Land of Hope and Glory" (based on "Pomp and Circumstance, Sir Edward Elgar, A.C. Benson, sung by MacDonald), "Recessional" (Reginald de Koven, Rudyard Kipling).

p, Victor Saville; d, Frank Borzage; w, Donald Ogden Stewart, John Balderston (based on the play by Jane Cowl, Jane Murfin); ph, Leonard Smith (Technicolor); ed, Frank Sullivan; md, Herbert Stothart; art d, Cedric Gibbons; set d, Edwin B. Willis; cos, Adrian, Gile Steele; spec eff, Warren Newcombe; makeup, Jack Dawn.

Musical Drama   Cas.   (PR:A MPAA:NR)

SMILING ALONG**½   (1938, Brit.) 83m FOX bw (GB: KEEP SMILING)

Gracie Fields (*Gracie Gray*), Roger Livesey (*Bert*), Mary Maguire (*Avis*), Peter Coke (*Rene Sigani*), Jack Donohue (*Denis*), Hay Petrie (*Jack*), Mike Johnson (*Charlie*), Eddie Gray (*Silvo*), Tommy Fields, Gladys Dehl, Nino Rossini (*The Three Bolas*), Edward Rigby (*Silas Gray*), Joe Mott (*Bill Sneed*), Gus McNaughton (*Eddie Perkins*), Phillip Leaver (*De Courcy*), Skippy the Dog (*Mr. Skip*).

Basically a vehicle to promote popular British entertainer Fields in the States, given a story and comic routines tailored to American tastes. Fields plays an entertainer who has had it with the antics of her crooked manager. She walks out on him and takes the rest of the troupe along. They wind up on her uncle's farm, where popular musician Livesy takes a liking to the group and lends it a helping hand. This paves the way for a long engagement at a Brighton theater. Though much of the humor is slapstick, some fairly clever routines using the farm background are created for maximum effect. Maguire, as the dancing ingenue, was the only American player in the supporting cast. Skippy the dog also became known as "Asta" in the "Thin Man" series. Songs include "Swing Your Way to Happiness," "The Holy City" (both sung by Fields) "Giddy Up," "Mrs. Binns' Twins."

p, Robert T. Kane; d, Monty Banks; w, William Conselman, Val Valentine, Rodney Ackland; ph, Mutz Greenbaum; ed, James B. Clark; md, Bretton Byrd.

Musical/Comedy   (PR:A MPAA:NR)

SMILING GHOST, THE*½   (1941) 71m WB bw

Wayne Morris (*Lucky Downing*), Brenda Marshall (*Lil Barstow*), Alexis Smith (*Elinor B. Fairchild*), Alan Hale (*Norton*), Lee Patrick (*Rose Fairchild*), David Bruce (*Paul Myron*), Helen Westley (*Grandmother Bentley*), Willie Best [Sleep 'n Eat] (*Clarence*), Charles Halton (*Great-Uncle*), Roland Drew (*Uncle*), Richard Ainley (*Cousin*), George Mender (*Mr. Dinwiddie*), Clem Bevans (*Sexton*), Arthur Aylesworth (*Justice of the Peace*).

Morris plays the fiance to Smith, an heiress whose three previous betrotheds have mysteriously died mysterious deaths. The setting is Smith's mansion which is reportedly haunted and complete with sliding panels, creaking footsteps, and dimming lights. Good performances by Hale, Patrick, Westley and other cast members, and well-paced direction by Seiler are among the highlights in this suspenseful comedy/mystery.

p, Edmund Grainger; d, Lewis Seiler; w, Kenneth Gamet, Stuart Palmer (based on a story by Palmer); ph, Arthur Todd; ed, Jack Killifer.

Mystery/Comedy   (PR:A MPAA:NR)

SMILING IRISH EYES**½   (1929) 90m FN/WB bw

Colleen Moore (*Kathleen O'Connor*), James Hall (*Rory O'More*), Claude Gillingwater (*Michael O'Connor*), Robert E. Homans (*Shamus O'Connor*), Aggie Herring (*Granny O'More*), Betty Francisco (*Frankie West*), Julanne Johnston (*Goldie DeVere*), Robert Emmett O'Connor (*Sir Timothy Tyrone*), Edward Earle (*George Prescott*), Tom O'Brien (*"Black Barney" O'Toole*), Fred Kelsey (*County Fair Manager*), Mme. Bosocki (*Fortune Teller*), George "Gabby" Hayes (*Taxi Driver*), Anne Schaefer (*Landlady*), John Beck (*Sir Timothy's Butler*), Oscar Apfel (*Max North*), Otto Lederer (*Izzy Levi*), William Strauss (*Moe Levi*), Dave Thursby (*Scotch Barker*), Dan Crimmins (*Tho II Trouble-Maker*), Barney Gilmore, Charles McHugh (*County Fair Assistants*).

This early musical, which suffers from poor, haphazard direction, features Moore in her first all-singing, all-dancing role. Hall plays an Irish songster who decides to try pushing his talent on Broadway. He takes off for the bright lights, leaving his sweet lass Moore behind. She follows him to America, where she eventually becomes disillusioned. This was Moore's first real chance to prove her vocal abilities, and she shines through. McCormick, Moore's husband, served as producer.

p, John McCormick; d, William A. Seiter; w, Tom J. Geraghty; ph, Sid Hickox, Henry Freulich; ed, Al Hall; md, Louis Silvers; set d, Anthony Grot; cos, Edward Stevenson; ch, Walter Wills, Larry Ceballos, Carl McBride; m/l, "A Wee Bit of Love," "Then I'll Ride Home with You," "Old Killarney Fair," Ray Perkins, Norman Spencer, Herman Ruby.

Musical/Drama   (PR:A MPAA:NR)

SMILING LIEUTENANT, THE****   (1931) 102m PAR bw

Maurice Chevalier (*Niki*), Claudette Colbert (*Franzi*), Miriam Hopkins (*Princess Anna*), George Barbier (*King Adolf*), Charles Ruggles (*Max*), Hugh O'Connell (*Orderly*), Robert Strange (*Adjutant von Rockoff*), Janet Reade (*Lily*), Lon MacSunday (*Emperor*), Elizabeth Patterson (*Baroness von Schwedel*), Harry Bradley (*Count von Halden*), Werner Saxtorph (*Josef*), Karl Stall (*Master of Ceremonies*), Granville Bates (*Bill Collector*), Maude Allen (*Woman*), Charles Wagenheim (*Arresting Officer*).

Hans Muller's 1907 novel *Nux der Prinzgemahl* (Nux, The Prince Consort) was adapted by Leopold Jacobson and Felix Doermann into the libretto for the operetta "Ein Walzertraum" (A Waltz Dream) with music by Oscar Strauss. UFA, the famed German film studio, assigned Ernst Lubitsch to make it into a silent movie with Mady Christians and Willy Fritsch, but he left for the U.S. and the directing job was handed to Ludwig Berger, who did a fine job as the picture was a hit in the U.S. as well as wherever else it was shown. Whether or not the inspiration for the tale came from the situation of prince consort Albert to his beloved Queen Victoria has never been determined, but anyone who knew that true story will see parallels. Six years after the silent was released, Lubitsch decided that the advent of sound would help the tuneful story greatly, so he gathered Chevalier, Colbert and Hopkins, moved them into Paramount's Astoria, Long Island, studios and made this movie as well as a French-language version, LE LIEUTENANT SOURIANT, with the same cast doing a new French script by Jacques Bataille-Henri, who also adapted Grey's lyrics Gallically. It was a charming movie that featured a reunion between Lubitsch and Chevalier after their successful movie THE LOVE PARADE two years before. Colbert is a violinist who has been seeing Ruggles. She dumps him for Chevalier, an officer of the guards, and the two share a Viennese apartment where they are blissfully happy. Barbier is a king visiting Austria with his plain daughter, Hopkins, who despairs of ever finding a husband. At an official function, Chevalier flashes his famous grin at Colbert but Hopkins thinks the smile is meant for her and she resents it because she thinks the handsome guardsman is just being kind due to her unattractiveness. Chevalier, ever the gentleman, protests her feelings and is so lovable that Hopkins immediately falls in love with him, thus complicating his life to no end. Barbier is thrilled that such a good-looking man should take an interest in his dowdy daughter and announces that the two are to be wed. Chevalier doesn't know how to handle this and, for the sake of his country, marries Hopkins, but will have nothing to do with her in the boudoir. She despairs of losing her virginity due to his disinterest and he returns to his affair with Colbert. When Hopkins finds out about Colbert, she insists the violinist come to the castle. A wonderful confrontation scene occurs during which Colbert sees that Hopkins is actually a pretty woman, but she doesn't know what to do with what God has given her. Colbert sets out to transform Hopkins into a silk purse, rearranges her appearance, and the plain princess is suddenly ravishing. Colbert returns to her apartment and writes a good-bye letter to Chevalier, then disappears from the center of Austrian culture. Chevalier learns of her departure, races back to the castle to berate his wife, then is stunned by her beauty and changes his mind, realizing that he is wed to a gorgeous and adoring wife and that life inside a castle isn't so bad after all. It's an operetta plot all right, with hardly any resemblance to reality, but the players are so good and the dialog so witty and the direction so delicious that no one much cares about this, especially not during the early 1930s when the world was reeling under economic woes and wanted to forget, even for as brief a time as 102 minutes. Hopkins was appearing in her second film and already showing her mettle. Colbert was only 26 and in her ninth film. The French language version of the movie was no problem for Colbert, as she was born in Paris. While shooting the film, Chevalier's wife, Yvonne, sued for divorce and his mother died, though you'd never know any of that from his bouyant screen presence. Songs by Oscar Strauss and Clifford Grey were: "Toujours L'Amour in the Army," "Breakfast Table Love" (sung by Chevalier), "Jazz Up Your Lingerie" (sung by Colbert, Hopkins), "Live For Today" (sung by Chevalier, Colbert), "One More Hour Of Love" (sung by Chevalier), "While Hearts Are Singing." A box office success that was also nominated for an Oscar as Best Picture but lost to GRAND HOTEL. Because sound was still new there wasn't much dialogue but what was there was choice. Since this was made before censors began hacking away at Lubitsch, it may be too racy for youngsters.

p&d, Ernst Lubitsch; w, Ernest Vajda, Samson Raphaelson, Lubitsch (based on the operetta "A Waltz Dream" by Leopold Jacobson, Felix Doermann, and the novel *Nux der Prinzgemahl* by Hans Muller); ph, George Folsey; m, Oscar Strauss; ed, MerrillWhite; md, Adolph Deutsch; art d, Hans Dreier; m/l, Strauss, Clifford Grey.

Musical/Comedy   (PR:A-C MPAA:NR)

SMITH**½**   (1969) 102m Walt Disney/BV c

Glenn Ford (*Smith*), Nancy Olsen (*Norah Smith*), Dean Jagger (*Judge*), Keenan Wynn (*Vince Heber*), Warren Oates (*Walter Charlie*), Chief Dan George (*Ol' Antoine*), Frank Ramirez (*Gabriel Jimmyboy*), John Randolph (*Mr. Edwards*), Christopher Shea (*Albie Smith*), Roger Ewing (*Donald Maxwell*), Jay Silverheels (*McDonald Lasheway*), James Westerfield (*Sheriff*), Indian Actors Workshop of Hollywood.

A well-meaning but but overly naive depiction of the unfair treatment of modern-day Indians. Ford plays the rancher whose pal, George, has hidden a young Indian, Ramirez, accused of murdering a storekeeper. With the sadistic sheriff, Wynn, trailing the fugitive, George decides to turn him into the police and use the reward to obtain the services of a lawyer. But George is placed in jail as well, forcing Ford to become more deeply involved in the case. He frees his buddy and takes over at the trial as interpreter. He replaces Oates, a double-crossing Indian willing to stick a knife in his people's back if the price is right. George's speech about the misdeeds against the Indians sways the jury to release Ramirez, ending the film on the note that justice may yet be had for the Indians. Ford gives a compelling performance, but most memorable is Oates as the back-stabbing Indian. Jay

Silverheels (Tonto of THE LONE RANGER series) has a bit part and directs the Indian Actors Workshop in their roles.

p, Bill Anderson; d, Michael O'Herlihy; w, Louis Pelletier (based on the novel *Breaking Smith's Quarter Horse* by Paul St. Pierre); ph, Robert Moreno (Technicolor); m, Robert F. Brunner; ed, Robert Stafford; art d, John B. Mansbridge, Robert E. Smith; set d, Emile Kuri, Hal Gausman; cos, Chuck Keehne, Emily Sundby; m/l, "The Ballad of Smith and Gabriel Jimmyboy," Bob Russell (sung by Russell); makeup, Otis Malcolm.

Western/Drama   (PR:A MPAA:G)

SMITH'S WIVES*   (1935, Brit.) 59m FOX bw

Ernie Lotinga (*Jimmy Smith*), Beryl de Querton (*Norah Smith*), Tyrell Davies (*Dick Desmond*), Richard Ritchie (*Rev. James Smith*), Kay Walsh (*Mabel Smith*), Jean Gillie (*Anne*), Vashti Taylor (*Dierdre Fotheringay*), Gilbert Davis, Wilfrid Hyde-White, Harold Wilkinson, Daisy Brindley, Fred Gretton.

Forced comedy revolving around the mishaps which occur as the result of two couples, each with the last name Smith, having apartments directly across from the other. Like most early British comedies, this was based on a play and should have remained in that form.

p, Ernest Garside; d, Manning Hayes; w, Con West, Herbert Sargent (based on the play "Facing the Music" by James Darnley).

Comedy   (PR:A MPAA:NR)

SMITHY**   (1933, Brit.) 53m WB/FN bw

Edmund Gwenn (*John Smith*), Peggy Novak (*Jane*), D.A. Clarke-Smith (*Boyd*), Eve Gray, Clifford Heatherley, Viola Compton, Charles Hickman.

Gwenn (MIRACLE ON 34TH STREET, THE TROUBLE WITH HARRY) starred in this early British programmer as a daydreaming clerk whose fantasies are fulfilled when he wins a large sum of money in a competition. He shares his winnings on a carefree spree with a caberet singer, the only friend he seems to have. Warm drama, made more so by Gwenn's charismatic personality.

p, Irving Asher; d, George King.

Comedy/Drama   (PR:A MPAA:NR)

SMITHY**½**   (1946, Aus.) 118m COL bw

Ron Randell (*Sir Charles Kingsford-Smith*), Muriel Steinbeck (*Lady Kingsford-Smith*), John Tate (*Charles Ulm*), Joy Nicholls (*Kay Suttor*), Nan Taylor (*Nan Kingsford-Smith*), Alec Kellaway (*Capt. Allan Hancock*), John Dease (*Sir Hubert Wilkins*), Joe Valli (*Stringer*), Marshall Crosby (*Arthur Powell*), Right Hon. W.M. Hughes, Capt. P.G. Taylor, John Stannage (*Themselves*).

Good Australian-made biography of native air hero Charles Kingsford-Smith, fighter ace and early transpacific pioneer. Well-acted and directed, the film unfortunately marked the end of the prolific and interesting early period of Australian film. Director Hall retired after this effort, Randell went abroad to become a leading man in British second features, and Australian audiences would have to wait until the early 1970s to see any significant product from their own shores.

p, Nick Perry; d, Ken G. Hall; w, Alec Coppel, Max Afford; ph, George Heath; ed, Terry Banks.

Biography   (PR:A MPAA:NR)

SMITHEREENS**½**   (1982) 90m Domestic/New Line c

Susan Berman (*Wren*), Brad Rinn (*Paul*), Richard Hell (*Eric*), Nada Despotovich (*Cecile*), Roger Jett (*Billy*), Kitty Summerall (*Blonde*), Robynne White (*Landlady*), D.J. O'Neill (*Ed*), Joel Rooks (*Xerox Boss*), Pamela Speed (*Terry*), Tom Cherwin (*Mike*), Edie Schecter (*Christine*), Katherine Riley (*Hooker No. 1*), Amos Poe (*Hustler in Bar*), Ade McSpade (*Rasta*), Cookie Mueller, Edward E. French (*Horror Show Sequence*), Wolf Alan (*Pimp*), The Nightcaps X-sessive (*Leader Singer*), Paul Dunlap (*Bouncer*), Sara Sassin (*Tough Woman in Cafe*), Chel Chenier (*Cecile's Roommate*), Diana Hayes (*Nightclub Singer*), Marilyn Rall (*Woman at Bar*), Shawn Adams (*3-Card Monte Boy*), Geretta Giancarlo, Phylis Kay, Celia Maurice, Roma Maffia, Chris Noth (*Prostitutes*).

The first feature from Susan Seidelman (DESPERATELY SEEKING SUSAN), a graduate of New York University's film school, was a retelling of the old theme girl-comes-to-big-city-to-make-it-big, only given a much more gritty and realistic perspective. Basically a comment on how hyped media images control human values, more pointedly the effects of pop music and culture on modern youth, the film traces the journey of Berman through the depths of the lower East Side, latching on to rocker Hell in the hopes of getting her own chance on the music scene. Packed with the energy that is Berman's motivating force, SMITHEREENS effectively recreates an atmosphere that is destructive that its inhabitants want to break with the old mold of empty ideals. Yet a firm distrust remains in trying to provide direct answers and in creating new patterns. This picture was the first low-budget American independent to gain a showing at Cannes. Made on a budget of $80,000, shooting had to be halted for nearly a year after its star, Berman, broke her leg during a rehearsal. This gave Seidelman a chance to gain a firmer grasp of her material and figure out what messages she wanted to convey. Though SMITHEREENS is not without its problems – much of the material seems to be cliched, and already dated–it is a good display of what a persistent creative drive can achieve. The film was shot in 16mm and, blown up to 35mm.

p&d, Susan Seidelman; w, Ron Nyswaner, Peter Askin (based on a story by Nyswaner, Seidelman); ph, Chririne El Khadem; m, Glenn Mercer, Bill Million; ed, Seidelman; art d, Franz Harland; cos, Alison Lances.

Drama   **Cas.**   **(PR:O MPAA:R)**

SMOKE IN THE WIND*   (1975) 94m Gamalex c

John Ashley (*Whipple*), John Russell (*Cagle*), Myron Healey (*Mort*), Walter Brennan (*H.B. Kingman*), Susan Houston (*Laries*), Linda Weld (*Sarah*), Henry Kingi (*Smoky*), Adair Jameson (*Hannah*), Daniel White (*Col. Cullen*), Lorna Thayer (*Ma Mondier*), Billy Hughes, Jr (*Till*), Bill Foster (*Stapp*), Jack Horton (*Jebb*), Bill McKenzie (*Bartender*).

A disappointing independent western that was finished in 1971, but not released until four years later. It tells the tale of a family of Arkansas mountain men accused by the Confederacy after the Civil War of taking up with the Union forces. Brennan's storekeeper role is dismally minor in this film, his last. It was also the final outing for veteran director Kane.

p, Robert "Whitey" Hughes, Bill Hughes; d, Joseph Kane; w, Eric Allen; ph, Mario Tosi.

Western   **Cas.**   **(PR:C MPAA:PG)**

SMOKE JUMPERS   (SEE: RED SKIES OF MONTANA, 1952)

SMOKE SIGNAL**   (1955) 88m UNIV c

Dana Andrews (*Brett Halliday*), Piper Laurie (*Laura Evans*), Rex Reason (*Lt. Wayne Ford*), William Talman (*Capt. Harper*), Gordon Jones (*Cpl. Rogers*), Milburn Stone (*Sgt. Miles*), Douglas Spencer (*Garode*), William Schallert (*Pvt. Livingston*), Bill Phipps (*Pvt. Porter*), Bob Wilkie (*1st Sgt. Daly*), Pat Hogan (*Delche*), Peter Coe (*Ute Prisoner*).

Filmed in the Colorado River's Grand Canyon, the real star here is the glorious setting, which serves as a backdrop for a story about a cavalry troop headed by Talman. He is trying to escape Indian raids while bringing Andrews back to the post for a court-martial. It seems Andrews sympathized with the Indians when a commanding officer okayed the mistreatment of a tribe. Laurie does what she can with her role as the woman (the only one in the cast) who devotes herself to Andrews.

p, Howard Christie; d, Jerry Hopper; w, George Slavin, George W. George; ph, Clifford Stine (Technicolor); ed, Milton Carruth; md, Joseph Gershenson; art d, Alexander Golitzen, Richard H. Riedel; cos, Bill Thomas.

Western   **(PR:A MPAA:NR)**

SMOKE TREE RANGE½**   (1937) 62m UNIV bw

Buck Jones (*Lee Cary*), Muriel Evans (*Nan Page*), John Elliott (*Jim Cary*), Donald Kirke (*Wirt Stoner*), Ted Adams (*Gil Hawkins*), Dickie Jones (*Teddy Page*), Ben Hall (*Pete*), Earle Hodgins (*Sheriff Day*), Mabel Concord (*Ma Kelly*), Bob Kortman (*Paso Wells*), Eddie Cobb (*Sandy*), Lee Phelps, Charles King, Eddie Phillips, Bob McKenzie, Slim Whitaker, Silver the Horse.

Jones is fighting mad when a gang of rustlers make trouble for Evans and her son by threatening to evict them from their ranch. Jones does all that's expected of him, setting the crooks straight with some fine two-fisted action.

p, Buck Jones; d, Lesley Selander; w, Frances Guihan (based on a story by ArthurHenry Gooden); ph, Allen Thompson.

Western   **(PR:A MPAA:NR)**

SMOKESCREEN*½   (1964, Brit.) 66m BUT bw

Peter Vaughan (*Ropey Roper*), John Carson (*Trevor Baylis*), Yvonne Romain (*Janet Dexter*), Gerald Flood (*Graham Turner*), Glynn Edwards (*Inspector Wright*), John Glyn Jones (*Player*), Sam Kydd (*Waiter*), Deryck Guyler (*Porter*).

Unexciting thriller about an insurance investigator who is able to uncover an auto accident as being a deception to swindle the insurance company. Unimaginative premise has been dealt with far too much to enable this effort to hold any suspense.

p, John I. Phillips; d&w, Jim O'Connolly.

Crime   **(PR:A MPAA:NR)**

SMOKEY AND THE BANDIT*½   (1977) 96m Rastar/UNIV c

Burt Reynolds (*Bandit*), Jackie Gleason (*Sheriff Buford T. Justice*), Sally Field (*Carrie*), Jerry Reed (*Cledus Snow*), Mike Henry (*Junior Justice*), Paul Williams (*Little Enos Burdette*), Pat McCormick (*Big Enos Burdette*), Alfie Wise (*Traffic Jam Patrolman*), George Reynolds (*Sheriff Branford*), Macon McCalman (*Mr. B*), Linda McClure (*Waynette Snow*), Susan McIver (*Hot Pants*), Michael Mann (*Branford's Deputy*), Lamar Jackson (*Sugar Bear*), Ronnie Gay (*Georgia Trooper*), Quinnon Sheffield (*Alabama Trooper*), Ingeborg Kjeldsen ("*Foxy Lady*"), Mel Pape (*Nude Smokey*), Hank Worden (*Trucker*), Laura Lizer.

This was the first in the series and the best of a lousy lot. Depending on whom you want to believe, the movie grossed anywhere between $40 million and $70 million and that must be some sort of new record for fooling the public. It was the first picture directed by one of the highest-paid stunt men in movies, Hal Needham, and is one long, stupid car chase punctuated by four-letter words in a live-action version of the "Roadrunner" cartoons. The premise is based on the fact that it once was illegal for Coors to sell their Colorado beer east of Texas unless a special permit was secured. McCormick and Williams are a father-son team of filthy-rich Texans who have a car entered in an Atlanta stock race which they fully expect to win. In order to celebrate, they'd like to have enough Coors around for themselves and their guests but the race is the following day and there doesn't seem to be any means to get the beer there in time. Reynolds makes an $80,000 wager that he can drive to Texas and back in the needed 28 hours. Since that's a distance of about 1800 miles, McCormick and Williams figure they have a safe bet. Reynolds ask that they supply him with a new Pontiac Trans Am, which they do, and he enlists his erstwhile partner Reed as part of the plot. Reynolds will drive ahead of the beer-laden truck and make sure there are no "smokies" in the vicinity and if there are, he'll lead them on a merry chase in order to help Reed and the truck through the speed traps. They race across to Texas, pick up the beer and are on their ways back when Reynolds picks up Field, who is thumbing a ride while wearing a wedding gown. She explains that she was due to marry Henry (the ex-Rams football player) but has changed her mind and now just wants to get out of the neighborhood. She's a New York chorine and feels out of place among so many rednecks. Henry is the son of Gleason, a sheriff in the area, and the chase is now on. It wends across Arkansas, through Mississippi, and several smash-ups occur. In one, Gleason's pride and joy, his high-powered police vehicle, has the top cut away (in a scene similar to the chase in THE SEVEN UPS) and the door sliced off. Using the citizens band radio to keep in touch, Reynolds and Reed soon have a convoy of good ol' boy truckers following along and doing their best to help thwart Gleason in his quest for him. Reed stops at a roadside stand to stretch and use the facility and is soon in a squabble with a bunch of Hell's Angels motorcyclists. He takes revenge by squashing their bikes with his truck, then hits the road again. In the Trans Am, Field and Reynolds are discovering love in a hurry (there's hardly any time for characterization in a picture of this speed). While racing down the highway, various CBers help out, including Kjeldsen, a hooker who works out of a mobile brothel, and McIver, a waitress who talks the patrons at her restaurant into using their vehicles to block the road once Reynolds has driven by. They approach the Georgia race track and Reed passes Reynolds, arriving at the stock car race in plenty of time to win the bet. Reynolds doesn't take the money from McCormick, but instead doubles the bet to $160,000 if he can get from Georgia to Boston and back within 18 hours. The object is a container of fresh Massachusetts clam chowder. Reynolds, Reed, and Field (with Reed's long-faced basset hound along) dig out in McCormick's Cadillac (one of a dozen or so) just as Gleason and Henry show up in their shattered police car. Gleason and Reynolds talk briefly via the CB and then Gleason goes out after Reynolds again, swearing that he will not rest easily until he's captured the elusive Bandit. Naturally, with that kind of an ending, it was a foregone conclusion there would be sequels. The stunts are excellent, the comedy is numbing, and the acting is on a par with the most inept ever seen at a junior high school version of "Our Town." Even Gleason is lousy in the movie, and that's not easy. A few songs are tossed in to keep boot-toes tapping. Reed sings all of them. They are "East Bound And Down" (Reed, Dick Feller), "Bandit" (Feller), "The Legend" (Reed). The movie was filmed in Georgia and one wonders how a talented actress like Field ever got involved with this. Hollywood gossips say she and Reynolds were an item at the time and wanted to work together. The role could have been played by a robot. Adolph Coors and Sons must have been very happy because it's a 97-minute commercial for their brew.

p, Mort Engleberg; d, Hal Needham; w, James Lee Barrett, Charles Shyer, Alan Mandel (based on a story by Needham, Robert L. Levy); ph, Bobby Byrne (Panavision, Technicolor); m, Bill Justis, Jerry Reed; ed, Walter Hannemann, Angelo Ross; art d, Mark Mansbridge; set d, Anthony C. Montenaro; spec eff, Art Brewer; m/l, Reed, Dick Feller; stunts, Alan Gibbs; makeup, Tom Ellingwood, Guy Del Russo.

Comedy   **Cas.**   **(PR:C-O MPAA:PG)**

SMOKEY AND THE BANDIT II*   (1980) 95m Rastar-Mort Engelberg/UNIV c (GB: SMOKEY AND THE BANDIT RIDE AGAIN)

Burt Reynolds (*Bandit*), Jackie Gleason (*Sheriff Buford T. Justice/Reginald Van Justice/Gaylord Van Justice*), Jerry Reed (*Cledus*), Dom DeLuise (*Doc*), Sally Field (*Carrie*), Paul Williams (*Little Enos*), David Huddleston

(John Conn), Mike Henry *(Junior)*, Pat McCormick *(Big Enos)*, John Anderson *(Governor)*, Brenda Lee *(Nice Lady)*, Phil Balsley, Lew DeWitt, Don Reid, Harold Reid *(Statler Brothers)*, Mel Tillis *(Fairground Owner)*, Don Williams, Terry Bradshaw, "Mean Joe" Greene, Joe Klecko, Charlotte the Elephant *(Themselves)*, Jeffrey Bryan King *(Football Player)*, Nancy Lenehan *(Ramona)*, John Megna *(P.T.)*, Dudley Remus *(Everglades Attendant)*, Hal Carter *(Gas Station Attendant)*, Jerry Lester *(Warehouse Guard)*, Rick Allen *(Safari Park Attendant)*, Patrick Moody *(Ambulance Driver)*, Charles Yeager *(Party Guest)*, John Robert Nicholson *(Patient)*, Ritchey Brown *(Young Man)*, Anthony T. Townes *(Young Black Boy)*, Nancy Lee Johnson *(Young Girl)*, Gayle Davis *(Older Girl)*, James L. Buchanan II.

Infantile remake of the 1977 SMOKEY AND THE BANDIT which was infantile to begin with, not to mention moronic, gratuitously violent, and monotonous--your basic sneering Hollywood remake which panders to the lowest common denominator of the audience. The "plot" sees Reynolds as a washed-up drunk who has fallen hard from the folk hero heights he obtained during the first film. His girl friend Fields has left him due to his egotistical posturing, leaving the crushed Reynolds alone with the bottle and little purpose. Rescuing Reynolds from his pathetic state are McCormick and Williams who once again hire the "good ol' boy" and his buddy Reed to make a cross-country haul for a fee of $400,000. Instead of Coors beer, this time it's a pregnant elephant which is to be delivered to a Republican convention in Dallas. To care for the giant beast, the pair kidnap an Italian gynecologist, DeLuise, whose appearance is just an excuse for some obnoxious ethnic and toilet humor. Meanwhile, Fields has decided to go back home and marry Gleason's dull son Henry. From this point on the film is practically a copy of the original. Gleason returns as the foul-mouthed sheriff determined to nail Reynolds and Reed, and this time a pair of his brothers (both played by Gleason) make an appearance. Not even Gleason can pull this dreary, unfunny mess out of the doldrums and the whole thing plays like a bad inside joke for Reynolds and his buddies. A helpful rule of thumb: when the funniest moments in a comedy are the outtakes run under the closing credits, you're in for trouble. Believe it or not this mess made $40,002,000 at the box office and was followed by SMOKEY AND THE BANDIT PART 3 which is totally useless.

p, Hank Moonjean; d, Hal Needham; w, Jerry Belson, Brock Yates (based on a story by Michael Kane and characters created by Needham, Robert L. Levy); ph, Michael Butler (Technicolor); m, Snuff Garrett; ed, Donn Cambern, William Gordean; prod d, Henry Bumstead; art d, Bernie Cutler; set d, Richard De Cines; spec eff Cliff Wenger; stunts, Richard Ziker.

Comedy   Cas.   (PR:C-O   MPAA:PG)

SMOKEY AND THE BANDIT--PART 3 zero   (1983) 88m UNIV C

Jackie Gleason *(Buford T. Justice)*, Jerry Reed *(Cletus/Bandit)*, Paul Williams *(Little Enos)*, Pat McCormick *(Big Enos)*, Mike Henry *(Junior)*, Colleen Camp *(Dusty Trails)*, Faith Minton *(Tina)*, Burt Reynolds *(The Real Bandit)*, Sharon Anderson *(Policewoman)*, Silvia Arana *(Latin Woman)*, Alan Berger *(Hippie)*, Ray Bouchard *(Purvis R. Beethoven)*, Connie Brighton *(Girl)*, Earl Houston Bullock *(Flagman)*, Ava Cadell *(Blond)*, Cathy Cahill *(Mother Trucker)*, Dave Cass *(Tough Guy)*, Leon Cheatom *(Guide)*, Candace Collins *(Maid)*, Peter Conrad *(Midget)*, Janis Cummins *(Nudist Female)*, Jackie Davis *(Blackman No. 1)*, DeeDee Deering *(Mrs. Fernbush)*, Al DeLuca *(Flower Vendor)*, Ray Forchion *(Tar Worker)*, Veronica Gamba *(Girl at Picnic)*, Jorge Gil *(Gas Station Attendant)*, Marilyn Gleason *(Lady Ticket)*, Charles P. Harris *(Hot Dog Vendor)*, Timothy Hawkins *(Man in Truck)*, Craig Horwich *(Crash Guy)*, Pirty Lee Jackson *(Blackman No. 2)*, Austin Kelly *(Painter)*, William L. Kingsley *(Announcer)*, Will Knickerbocker *(Hotel Clerk)*, Kim Kondziola *(Baby Enos)*, Dick Lowry *(Sand Dumper)*, Sandy Mielke *(Driving Instructor)*, Toni Moon *(Girl No. 2)*, Alejandro Moreno *(Street Latin)*, Gloria Nichols *(Latin Woman)*, Mel Pape *(Police Officer)*, Dan Rambo *(TV Director)*, Richard Walsh *(Nudist Male)*, Curry Worsham *(Skip Town)*.

A reprehensible ripoff, this third in the series of SMOKEY AND THE BANDIT films doesn't even boast the dubious talents of star Reynolds or director Hal Needham. Reynolds, who only appears in a brief cameo, must have finally wised up to the overall effect these moronic car chase movies had been having on his career and bowed out of this one. Once again the so-called plot sees McCormick and Williams hiring Reed to haul an item at high speeds across the nation's highways. The first time it was Coors beer, the second a pregnant elephant, this time it's an imitation of the shark from JAWS that the brothers want to install at their new seafood chain restaurant. For company, Reed brings along former Playboy playmate, Camp, and, of course, Gleason and his moronic son, Henry, are in hot pursuit. Incredibly, this film doesn't even have the basic narrative coherence of the first two movies, and it rambles about aimlessly with little humor or action. Not only is it insulting, but it also cheats the very people who made the first two films such massive hits.

p, Mort Engelberg; d, Dick Lowry; w, Stuart Birnbaum, David Dashev; (based on characters created by Hal Needham, Robert L. Levy); ph, James Pergola (Panavision, Technicolor); m, Larry Cansler; ed, Byron "Buzz" Brandt, David Blewitt, Christopher Greenbury; art d, Ron Hobbs; set d, Don K. Ivey; cos, Andre Lavery, Linda Benedict; stunts, David Cass.

Comedy   Cas.   (PR:C-O   MPAA:PG)

SMOKEY BITES THE DUST zero   (1981) 85m New World c

Jimmy McNichol *(Roscoe Wilton)*, Janet Julian *(Peggy Sue Turner)*, Walter Barnes *(Sheriff Turner)*, Patrick Campbell *(Lester)*, Kari Lizer *(Cindy)*, John Blyth Barrymore *(Harold)*, Kedric Wolfe *(Deputy Bentley)*, Bill Forsythe *(Kenny)*.

Very rarely does a film come along that can aptly be described by its title, but this is definitely one – SMOKEY BITES THE DUST bites the dust. Clean-cut delinquent, McNichol, tears up a small town, smashing stolen car after stolen car, with the town's homecoming queen (also the sheriff's daughter) in the passenger seat. The minimal plot is reminiscent of those found on television. Includes borrowed footage from other New World features, such as MOVING VIOLATIONS, EAT MY DUST, GRAND THEFT AUTO, and THUNDER AND LIGHTING.

p, Roger Corman, Gale Hurd; d, Charles B. Griffith; w, Max Apple (based on a story by Brian Williams); ph, Gary Graver (Metrocolor); m, Bent Myggen; ed, Larry Bock; stunts, Gene Hartline, Chris Howell.

Adventure   (PR:C   MPAA:PG)

SMOKEY SMITH*½   (1935) 58m Supreme/Steiner bw

Bob Steele, Mary Kornman, George "Gabby" Hayes, Warner Richmond, Earl Dwire, Horace B. Carpenter, Tex Phelps, Archie Ricks.

Hawk-faced Steele is teamed with Gabby Hayes in this routine oater in which the duo search for the killers of an elderly couple, innocently gunned down while traveling. Another western in which Steele is directed by his father, the prolific Robert Bradbury.

p, A.W. Hackel; d&w, Robert N. Bradbury; ph, William Nobles; ed, S. Roy Luby.

Western   Cas.   (PR:A   MPAA:NR)

SMOKING GUNS zero   (1934) 62m UNIV bw

Ken Maynard *(Ken Masters)*, Gloria Shea *(Alice)*, Walter Miller *(Dick)*, Harold Goodwin *(Hank)*, Bob Kortman *(Biff)*, Jack Rockwell *(Adams)*, Ed Coxen *(Masters)*, Martin Turner *(Cinders)*, William Gould, Etta McDaniels, Slim Whitaker, Hank Bell, Horace B. Carpenter, Blue Washington, Wally Wales, Edmund Cobb, Bob Reeves, Fred McKaye, Jim Corey, Roy Bucko, Buck Bucko, Ben Corbett, Jack Ward, Bud McClure, Tarzan the Horse.

A truly awful film based on a story written by B-western star, Ken Maynard, who also appears in this fiasco. Supposedly intended as a parody, SMOKING GUNS features Maynard assuming the identity of a Ranger who was chomped to death by a crocodile, even though he looks nothing like the dead man. He then proceeds to save his father from a gang of outlaws who have held the father captive for years. One sequence depicts Maynard preparing to amputate a fellow's leg, but the patient shoots himself in the head rather than become a victim of his "doctor's" hot poker. Universal seemed to catch on to the fact that Maynard just used this picture as an excuse to write off a hunting trip, and demanded that he reshoot the footage. Maynard, instead, quit the studio and turned to independent productions.

p, Ken Maynard; d, Alan James; w, Nate Gatzert (based on a story by Maynard); ph, Ted McCord; ed, Charles Harris.

Western   (PR:A   MPAA:NR)

SMOKY**   (1933) 70m FOX bw

Victor Jory *(Clint)*, Irene Bentley *(Betty Jarvis)*, Frank Campeau *(Jeff Nicks)*, Hank Mann *(Buck)*, LeRoy Mason *(Lefty)*, Leonid Snegoff *(Junkman)*, Will James *(Narrator)*, Smoky the Horse.

Jory is a rodeo star who grows attached to the title horse, but eventually the two part company. Smoky ends up pulling a junk cart and is faced with the slaughterhouse when Jory comes along and saves his four-legged pal. An enjoyable and charming picture with James, who wrote the novel on which the film is based, serving as narrator.

d, Eugene Forde; w, Stuart Anthony, Paul Perez (based on the novel *Smoky, the Cowhorse* by Will James); ph, Daniel B. Clark; cos, Royer.

Western   (PR:A   MPAA:NR)

SMOKY***   (1946) 86m FOX c

Fred MacMurray *(Clint Barkley)*, Anne Baxter *(Julie Richards)*, Burl Ives *(Bill)*, Bruce Cabot *(Frank)*, Esther Dale *(Gram)*, Roy Roberts *(Jeff)*, J. Farrell MacDonald *(Jim, the Cook)*, Max Wagner *(Bart)*, Guy Beach *(Sheriff)*, Howard Negley *(Nelson)*, Bud Geary *(Peters)*, Harry Carter *(Bud)*, Bob Alder *(Scrubby)*, Victor Kilian *(Junk Man)*, Herbert Heywood *(Livery Stable Proprietor)*, Doug Spencer *(Gambler)*, Stanley Andrews *(Rancher)*.

MacMurray portrays the Utah cowboy whose bond with his horse, Smoky, was immortalized in Will James' classic tale. The cowboy captures and trains the wild horse, but during a cattle raid is separated from it. It's not until years later, after the horse has been mistreated by others that the two are reunited. The best of the three versions of the story, which also made it to the screen in 1933 and 1966. Musical numbers include well-known folk and cowboy songs such as "The Foggy, Foggy Dew," "Blue Tail Fly," "Woolly Boogie Bee."

p, Robert Bassler; d, Louis King; w, Lillie Hayward, Dwight Cummins, Dorothy Yost (based on the novel *Smoky, the Cowhorse* by Will James); ph, Charles Clarke (Technicolor); m, David Raksin; ed, Nick Di Maggio; md, Emil Newman; art d, Lyle Wheeler, Chester Gore; set d, Thomas Little, Harold Cramp; spec eff, Fred Sersen.

Western (PR:A MPAA:NR)

SMOKY**** (1966) 102m Arcola Pictures/FOX c

Fess Parker (*Clint*), Diana Hyland (*Julie*), Katy Jurado (*Maria*), Hoyt Axton (*Fred*), Robert J. Wilke (*Jeff*), Armando Silvestre (*Gordon*), Jose Hector Galindo (*Manuel*), Jorge Martinez de Hoyos (*Pepe*), Ted White (*Abbott*), Chuck Roberson, Robert Terhune, Jack Williams (*Cowboys*), Diamond Jet (*Smoky the Horse*).

An overlong remake of the Will James tale, which was first produced in 1933 at only 66 minutes. The original story was not eventful enough to stretch out into another 40 minutes so new plot elements were added. Parker plays an old cowboy and rodeo star who grows attached to a wild horse which he eventually tames. Parker's evil brother attempts to exchange the horse, Smoky, for some I.O.U. debts, but allows the horse to escape when trying to steal him from the corral. The brother is trampled to death in the process, and Parker and his horse are separated. Parker enlists in the armed services. Mean while the horse is ruined on the rodeo circuit, eventually ending up pulling a junk wagon. After many years, Parker and Smoky are brought together again. Includes the songs: "Smoky" (Ernie Sheldon, Leith Stevens – sung by Hank Thompson), "Five Dollar Bill," "Smile as You Go By," "Trouble and Misery," "Queen of the Rockin' R" (Hoyt Axton – sung by Axton).

p, Aaron Rosenberg; d, George Sherman; w, Harold Medford (based on the screenplay by Lillie Hayward, Dwight Cummins, Dorothy Yost from the novel *Smoky, the Cowhorse* by Will James); ph, Jack Swain (DeLuxe Color); m, Leith Stevens; ed, Joseph Silver; art d, Jack Martin Smith, John M. Elliott; makeup, Ben Nye; horse trainer, Les Hilton.

Western (PR:A MPAA:NR)

SMOKY CANYON** (1952) 55m COL bw

Charles Starrett (*Steve Brent*), The Durango Kid, Smiley Burnette (*Himself*), Jack [Jock] Mahoney (*Himself*), Dani Sue Nolan (*Roberta Woodstock*), Tristram Coffin (*Buckley*), Larry Hudson (*Sheriff Bogart*), Cris Alcaide (*Lars*), Sandy Sanders (*Spade*), Forrest Taylor (*Wyler*), Charles Stevens (*Johnny Big Foot*), Boyd "Red" Morgan (*Joe*), Leroy Johnson (*Ace*).

The Durango Kid comes to the rescue of some Montana cattle owners and sheepherders after a feud breaks out between the two. He uncovers a plot by Coffin to keep the cattle from making it to the market, thereby raising the price of beef. When one of Coffin's gang kills a decent rancher, the dead man's daughter and her fiance get in trouble with the law, that is, until Starrett clears their name and puts an end to the range war. (See DURANGO KID series, Index.)

p, Colbert Clark; d, Fred F. Sears; w, Barry Shipman; ph, Fayte Browne; m, Mischa Bakaleinikoff; ed, Paul Borofsky; art d, Charles Clague.

Western (PR:A MPAA:NR)

SMOKY MOUNTAIN MELODY** (1949) 61m COL bw

Roy Acuff (*Himself*), Guinn "Big Boy" Williams (*Saddle Grease*), Russell Arms (*Kid [Bruce] Corby*), Sybil Merritt (*Mary Files*), Jason Robards, Sr (*Josh Corby*), Harry V. "Pappy" Cheshire (*Dr. Moffett*), Fred Sears (*Mr. Crump*), Carolina Cotten (*Parky Darkin*), Tommy Ivo (*Tommy Darkin*), Trevor Bardette, Jock Mahoney, Lonnie Wilson, John Elliott, Ralph Littlefield, Sam Flint, Eddie Acuff, Jack Ellis, Heinie Conklin, Olin Howlin, Peter Kirby, Jimmy Riddle, Joe Zinkan, Tommy Magness, The Smoky Mountain Boys.

Roy Acuff and his Smoky Mountain Boys inherit a ranch and are allowed to manage it on a three-month trial basis, much to the chagrin of the former owner's sons. They try to frame kindly old Roy, but he teaches them a thing or two while still finding time to turn out a couple of tunes with the boys in the band. Roy Acuff was, and still is, a legend in the country music field both for his music and as one of the original performers on Nashville's famed live radio show, the Grand Ole Opry. This film represents Hollywood's attempt to cash in on a rise in popularity of country western music after WW II.

p, Colbert Clark; d, Ray Nazarro; w, Barry Shipman; ph, Rex Wimpy; ed, Paul Borofsky.

Western (PR:A MPAA:NR)

SMOKY TRAILS* (1939) 57m Metropolitan bw

Bob Steele (*Archer*), Jean Carmen (*Marie*), Murdock MacQuarrie (*Mr. Archer*), Bruce Dane (*Cooksy*), Carleton Young (*Mort*), Ted Adams (*Chief*), Frank LaRue (*Sheriff*), Jim Aubrey (*Deputy*), Bob Terry (*Burke*), Frank Wayne (*Sloan*), George Chesebro.

Steele's father is gunned down by an outlaw gang led by Adams and Young, causing the tough hero to go on the hunt for the culprits. He eventually finds them with the help of Sheriff LaRue, and deals them the vengeance he deems necessary. A less than entertaining B-western.

p, Harry S. Webb; d, Bernard B. Ray; w, George Plympton; ph, Edward Kull; ed, Fred Bain; m/l, Dercas Cochran, Charles Rosoff.

Western (PR:A MPAA:NR)

SMOOTH AS SILK*½ (1946) 64m UNIV bw

Kent Taylor (*Mark Fenton*), Virginia Grey (*Paula*), Jane Adams (*Susan*), Milburn Stone (*John Kimble*), John Litel (*Stephen Elliott*), Danny Morton (*Dick Elliott*), Charles Trowbridge (*Fletcher Holliday*), Theresa Harris (*Louise*), Harry Cheshire (*Wolcott*), Bert Moorhouse, Ralph Brooks (*Detectives*), Joe Kirk (*Joe*), Regina Wallace (*Middle-Aged Woman*), Boyd Davis (*Eddie*), Helen Chapman (*Daughter*), Stuart Holmes (*Old Friend*), Chester Conklin (*Doorman*), Jack Davidson (*Sam*), Jack Frack, Frank Marlowe (*Reporters*), William O'Brien (*Headwaiter*), Claire Whitney (*Woman*).

A better-than-average programmer that features respected attorney, Taylor, concocting a plot of murder and revenge after his sweetheart jilts him for a wealthy producer. Complete with engrossing performances, a carefully plotted script, and some inventive twists.

p, Jack Bernhard; d, Charles Barton; w, Dane Lussier, Kerry Shaw (based on the story *Notorious Gentleman* by Florence Ryerson, Colin Clements); ph, Woody Bredell; m, Ernest Gold; ed, Ray Snyder; art d, Jack Otterson, Robert Clatworthy; set d, Russell A. Gausman, Ted Von Hemert; Cos, Vera West.

Crime/Drama (PR:A MPAA:NR)

SMORGASBORD*½ (1983) 83m WB c (AKA: CRACKING UP)

Jerry Lewis (*Warren Nefron/Dr. Perks*), Herb Edelman (*Dr. Jonas Pletchick*), Zane Busby (*Waitress*), Foster Brooks (*Pilot*), Buddy Lester (*Passenger*), Milton Berle (*Female Patient*), Dick Butkus, Francine York, Bill Richmond, Robin Bach, Paul Davidson.

Lewis, in his usual persona, grinds out slapstick routines as a suicidal goofball who visits his psychiatrist. The situation allows Lewis to relate via flashback failed attempts at maintaining a job. It's all very stagy and disjointed with the gags running on long past the point of humor and into the realm of annoyance. As usual, Jerry has 'em rollin' in the aisles in France-- one of the great mysteries in cinema.

p, Peter Nelson, Arnold Orgolini; d, Jerry Lewis; w, Lewis, Bill Richmond; ph, Gerald Perry Finnerman; m, Morton Stevens; ed, Gene Fowler, Jr.; art d, Terry Bousman.

Comedy (PR:C MPAA:PG)

SMUGGLED CARGO** (1939) 62m REP bw

Barry Mackay (*Gerry*), Rochelle Hudson (*Marian*), George Barbier (*Franklin*), Ralph Morgan (*Clayton*), Cliff Edwards (*Professor*), John Wray (*Chris*), Arthur Loft (*Masterson*), Wallis Clark (*Dr. Hamilton*), Robert E. Homans (*Kincaid*).

An engaging programmer set in California and centering on a conflict between orange growers and Loft, who is trying to cheat the farmers into having to sell at below cost. Britisher Mackay and Hudson, the daughter of a millionaire fruit financier, get to the bottom of the plot and save the crop from going under.

p&d, John H. Auer; w, Michael Jacoby, Earl Felton; ph, Jack Marta; ed, Ernest Nims; md, Cy Feuer.

Drama (PR:A MPAA:NR)

SMUGGLERS, THE½ (1948, Brit.) 86m Production Film Services/EL c (GB: THE MAN WITHIN)

Michael Redgrave (*Richard Carlyon*), Jean Kent (*Lucy*), Joan Greenwood (*Elizabeth*), Richard Attenborough (*Francis Andrews*), Francis L. Sullivan (*Mr. Braddock*), Felix Aylmer (*Priest*), Ronald Shiner (*Cockney Harry*), Basil Sydney (*Sir Henry Merriman*), Ernest Thesiger (*Farne*), Allan Jeayes (*Judge*), Ralph Truman (*Prison Interrogator*), David Horne (*Dr. Stanton*), George Merritt (*Hilliard*), Charles Rolfe (*Court Usher*), Lyn Evans (*Warder*), Herbert Lomas (*Farmer*), John Olson (*Junior Counsel*), Danny Green, Maurice Denham (*Smugglers*), Torin Thatcher (*Jailer*), Andrew Crawford, Allan McClelland.

It is the early 1820s and Attenborough is being tortured in a jail by interrogators, so he begins a story which unreels in flashback. As a young orphan, Attenborough became the ward of Redgrave, a smuggler, and went to sea with Redgrave and his group of brigands. Attenborough is not a good seaman and is soundly chastized by the others for his inability to take the rigors of the ocean. As his life progresses, Attenborough grows to hate his existence and particularly Redgrave when he is punished for an offense he did not commit. To get himself out of this terrible situation, Attenborough informs on the smugglers to the customs officials and a battle ensues during which a customs man dies and Attenborough's shipmates are captured. Attenborough hides at the home of the dead customs official where he meets the man's stepdaughter, Greenwood, who encourages him to testify against the others. Attenborough goes to the court where Kent, the mistress of the Crown's attorney, promises that she will have an affair with him if he testifies against the smugglers, thereby putting a feather in her boyfriend's cap. Attenborough is brought to the witness box and gives evidence against the others but refuses to name Redgrave as the leader of the pack, a repayment for when the man took him in as a child. Too much talk in this early Technicolor outing from England, one of the first since the Gainsborough Studios were turning out their period romances during the mid-1940s. Greenwood's Sussex accent is a bit unwieldy to the American ear (and to many in England as well), but she showed her talents early and went on to co-star with Guinness in THE MAN IN THE WHITE SUIT. Attenborough was only 24 at the time and already was appearing in his ninth movie.

p, Sydney Box; d, Bernard Knowles; w, Muriel and Sydney Box (based on the novel by Graham Greene) ph, Geoffrey Unsworth (Technicolor); m, Clifton Parker; ed, Alfred Roome; md, Muir Mathieson; art d, Andrew Mazzei; cos, Elizabeth Haffenden; makeup, W.T. Partleton.

Historical Adventure   **(PR:A   MPAA:NR)**

SMUGGLERS, THE*   (1969, Fr.) 80m New Yorker bw (LES
                                             CONTREBANDIERES)

Francoise Vatel (Brigitte), Monique Thiriet (Francesca), Johnny Monteilhet (Customs Officer), Albert Juross (Poacher), Paul Martin (Official), Bernard Cazassus (Nomad), Luc Moullet ("Connard"), Gerard Tanguy, Patrick Huber (Syndicate Members).

A customs officer gets involved with two female smugglers separated by a border during wartime. When the fighting ends, however, the women meet and decide to share the customs agent. They live together for a while, but tensions flare and a gun is drawn. Eventually the two women are forced to escape from the authorities and, during the pursuit, become inseparable friends. After an attempt to return to city life and real jobs, they continue their life of smuggling.

p,d&w, Luc Moullet; ph, Philippe Theaudiere; ed, Cecile Decugis.

Drama   **(PR:C   MPAA:NR)**

SMUGGLERS' COVE*   (1948) 66m MON bw

Leo Gorcey (Terrence "Slip" Mahoney), Huntz Hall (Horace Debussy "Sach" Jones), Gabriel Dell (Gabe Moreno, Private Eye), Billy Benedict (Whitey), David Gorcey (Chuck), Benny Bartlett (Butch), Martin Kosleck (Count Petrov Bons), Paul Harvey (Terrence Mahoney, Esquire), Amelita Ward (Teresa Mahoney), Jacqueline Dalya (Sandra Hasso), Eddie Gribbon (Digger), Gene Stutenroth [Roth] (Capt. Drum), Leonid Snegoff (Dr. Latka), John Bleifer (Franz Leiber), Andre Pola (Karl), William Ruhl (Ryan), Building Foreman, Emmett Vogan (Attorney Williams), Buddy Gorman (Messenger), George Meader (Building Manager).

A topnotch BOWERY BOYS entry featuring Gorcey who mistakenly believes he has inherited an old mansion, which actually belongs to Harvey. The boys pack their things and head for the house, but soon discover that the house is a cover for a smuggling operation led by Kosleck. The house is filled with secret panels, hidden passageways, and paintings equipped with spy holes, all of which add to the slapstick adventures of the gang's pursuit of the boys, and vice versa. Harvey is so distraught because of the excitement and his high blood pressure that he lets the boy keep the house after the crooks are finally hauled in. Surprisingly, Gorcey, Hall, and the other Bower Boys are given less screen time than usual, but the remainder of the cast is so good they are hardly missed. (See BOWERY BOYS series, Index.)

p, Jan Grippo; d, William Beaudine; w, Edmond Seward, Tim Ryan (based on the story by Talbert Josselyn); ph, Marcel Le Picard; ed, Otho Lovering, William Austin; md, Edward J. Kay; art d, David Milton; set d, Raymond Boltz, Jr.

Comedy/Crime   **(PR:A   MPAA:NR)**

SMUGGLER'S GOLD**   (1951) 64m COL bw

Cameron Mitchell (Mike Sloan), Amanda Blake (Susan Clarke), Carl Benton Reid (Pop Hodges), Peter Thompson (Frank Warren), Bill Phillips (Chet Blake), William Forrest (Arthur Rayburn), Robert Williams (Hank Peters), Harlan Warde (George Brewster), Al Hill (Walt), Paul Campbell (Ensign Davis).

Reid is a well-respected ship's captain and owner of a boat dealership who gets involved with a scheme to smuggle gold out of the U.S. Mitchell and his fiancee, Blake, Reid's niece, catch on to the dealings, but are almost killed

in the process. Blake manages to contact the Coast Guard, while Mitchell is forced to dive for some gold on a threat by the captain. Average entertainment.

p, Milton Feldman; d, William Berke; w, Daniel Ullman (based on the story by Al Martin); ph, Allen Siegler; m, Mischa Bakaleinikoff; ed, Al Clark; art d, Victor Greene.

Crime Drama   **(PR:A   MPAA:NR)**

SMUGGLER'S ISLAND**   (1951) 75m UNIV c

Jeff Chandler (Steve Kent), Evelyn Keyes (Vivian Craig), Philip Friend (Allan Craig), Marvin Miller (Bok-Ying), Ducky Louie (Kai Lun), David Wolfe (Lorca), Jay Novello (Espinosa), H.T. Tsiang (Chang).

A harmless programmer featuring Chandler as an independent diver and Navy veteran who falls in love with Keyes. She is married to smuggler Friend, though this is unknown to Chandler at first. She hooks him on a scheme to dive for $200,000 in illegal gold, and he reluctantly agrees. He nearly winds up dead when Friend is anything but friendly and tries to frame Chandler. The smash finale has Chandler's boat, using fireworks as its disguised cargo, being blown to smithereens by Friend, killing the crook, and leaving Chandler to continue his romance with Keyes.

p, Ted Richmond; d, Edward Ludwig; w, Leonard Lee, Herbert Margolis, Louis Morheim (based on a story by Margolis and Morheim); ph, Maury Gertsman (Technicolor); ed, Ted J. Kent; md, Joseph Gershenson; art d, David Herzbrun, Alexander Golitzen; cos, Bill Thomas.

Adventure   **(PR:A   MPAA:NR)**

SNAFU**   (1945) 82m COL bw (GB: WELCOME HOME)

Robert Benchley (Ben Stevens), Vera Vague [Barbara Jo Allen] (Madge Stevens), Conrad Janis (Ronald Stevens), Nanette Parks (Laura Jessup), Janis Wilson (Kate Hereford), Jimmy Lloyd (Danny Baker), Enid Markey (Aunt Emily), Eva Puig (Josephina), Ray Mayer (Detective), Marcia Mae Jones (Martha), Winfield Smith (Col. West), John Souther (Taylor), Byron Foulger (Phil Ford), Kathleen Howard (Dean Garrett).

The Army phrase "Situation Normal, All Fouled Up," from which the film's title is taken, serves as the description of a soldier's life (Janis) when it is discovered that he is too young to be in the service. His parents get him an honorable discharge and bring him back home, which is just where the youngster doesn't want to be. An amusing but poorly paced comedy that involves Janis' attempts to get used to nonmilitary life.

p&d, Jack Moss; w, Louis Solomon, Harold Buchman (based on the play by Solomon and Buchman); ph, Frank F. [Franz] Planer; m, Paul Sawtell; ed, Aaron Stell; md, M. W. Stoloff; art d, Stephen Goosson, Walter Holscher; set d, Frank Kramer.

Comedy   **(PR:A   MPAA:NR)**

SNAKE PEOPLE, THE*   (1968, Mex./U.S.) 90m Azteca-COL/Horror
International c (ISLA DE LOS MUERTOS; LA MUERTE VIVIENTE;
AKA: ISLE OF THE SNAKE PEOPLE; THE ISL E OF THE DEAD;
THE LIVING DEATH)

Boris Karloff (Dr. Carl Van Boulder/Damballah), Julissa (Deirdre), Charles East (Lt. William), Ralph [Rafael] Bertrand (Capt. Laresh), Judy Carmichael (Mary Ann Vanderberg), Tongolee (Bondemo), Quentin Miller (Gomez), Santanon, Quinton Bulnes.

One of Karloff's final four films, partly shot in Mexico. Karloff's scenes were filmed in Los Angeles, back-to-back with his scenes from the other three films, all made by the same company during a five-week stretch. Karloff plays a wealthy landowner who is shocked by the disappearance of his niece, Julissa. She and a number of other natives of Coaibai Island have become victims of a strange voodoo ritual involving snake poison and sacrifices. Police captain Bertrand investigates and learns that Karloff is the tribal leader, then destroys him and the ritual site with a charge of dynamite. A bad film, even for Karloff fans.

p, Luis Enrique Vergara [Henry Verg], Juan Ibanez; d, Ibanez, Jack Hill; w, Hill; ph, Austin McKinney, Raul Dominguez (Eastmancolor); m, Alice Uretta.

Horror   **(PR:O   MPAA:NR)**

SNAKE PIT, THE**½   (1948) 108m FOX bw

Olivia de Havilland (Virginia Stuart Cunningham), Mark Stevens (Robert Cunningham), Leo Genn (Dr. Mark Kirk), Celeste Holm (Grace), Glenn Langan (Dr. Terry), Helen Craig (Miss Davis), Leif Erickson (Gordon), Beulah Bondi (Mrs. Greer), Lee Patrick, Isabel Jewell, Victoria Horne, Tamara Shayne, Grace Poggi (Asylum Inmates), Howard Freeman (Dr. Curtis), Natalie Schafer (Mrs. Stuart), Ruth Donnelly (Ruth), Katherine Locke (Margaret), Frank Conroy (Dr. Jonathan Gifford), Minna Gombell (Miss Hart), June Storey (Miss Bixby the Ward Nurse), Ann Doran (Valerie), Damian O'Flynn (Mr. Stuart), Lora Lee Michel (Virginia at Age 6), Esther Somers (Nurse Vance), Jacqueline de Wit (Celia Sommerville), Betsy Blair

(Hester), Lela Bliss (Miss Greene), Virginia Brissac (Miss Seiffert), Queenie Smith (Lola), Mae Marsh (Tommy's Mother), Ashley Cowan (Young Man), Sally Shepherd (Nurse), Geraldine Garrick, Theresa Lyon, Sylvia Andrew, Jeri Jordan, Marie Blake, Ellen Lowe, , , Minerva Urecal, Barbara Pepper (Patients), Jan Clayton (Singing Inmate), Helen Servis (Miss Servis), Celia Lovsky (Gertrude), Lester Sharpe (Doctor Somer), Mary Treen (Nurse), Victoria Albright (Virginia at Age 2), Dorothy Newmann (Miss Neumann), Grayce Hampton (Countess), Syd Saylor (Visor).

Another in the series of serious social examinations produced under the helm of 20th Century Fox studio head Darryl F. Zanuck. Where GENTLE-MAN'S AGREEMENT (1947) attacked anti-Semitism, and racial prejudice would be the subject of PINKY in 1949, THE SNAKE PIT explored mental illness and its treatment. In a tour de force performance, de Havilland plays a disturbed young woman who is put into a mental institution by her husband, Stevens. Stevens loves his wife, but he sees that she needs more help than he can give her. Luckily, de Havilland's case comes to the attention of Genn, a patient, thoughtful, and deeply caring doctor who devotes much of his time to her. Though the hospital is overcrowded and understaffed, Genn manages to concentrate on her case while desperately trying to keep his hospital from becoming the "snake pit" most people regard mental instituions as. Stevens provides Genn with some backround on his wife and it is learned that de Havilland became deeply depressed soon after their marriage and began behaving erratically. This was followed by the breakdown that moved Stevens to have her committed. Through kindness and understanding, Genn is able to coax de Havilland into trusting him, but her problem is so severe that he is forced to subject her to hydrotherapy, electric shock, and drugs accompanied by intense sessions of psychoanalysis. The success of her treatment fluctuates between making progress and taking two steps back. During his probing, Genn learns that de Havilland had an unhappy childhood and was dominated by her mother. Because of her mother's overbearing demeanor and her father's early death, de Havilland grew up clinging to her father's memory. When she was old enough to date, de Havilland became fond of a young man, Erickson. Tragically, Erickson was killed in a car wreck in which she was a passenger. With another man she loved abruptly taken from her, de Havilland began to subconsciously believe that she was a jinx on men and that her love could prove fatal. After her marriage to Stevens, she became depressed because she felt she was signing his death warrant. The process of uncovering all this is quite painful and slow, and now Genn is faced with the task of restructuring de Havilland's fears and presenting them to her in a form she can understand and accept in her conscious mind. This also proves to be a slow and delicate process, but eventually de Havilland is cured and she goes off with Stevens to start a new life. Though the portrayal of the causes of mental illness and its cures is a bit too simplistic in THE SNAKE PIT (a completely cured de Havilland is overly optimistic), the film was one of the first to seriously examine the subject and treat it with dignity and respect. Producer-director Litvak saw the galley pages to Mary Jane Ward's fictionalized autobiography and immediately paid $75,000 for the film rights. After trying to sell the idea to every studio in town, Litvak went to Fox and his friend Zanuck as a last resort (Fox rarely took on independent productions). Zanuck was a bit leery about the subject matter, but he felt that films should deal with important subjects so he agreed to finance the project. Zanuck worked closely with Litvak and together they fine-honed the script so that a degree of "suspense and urgency" would compel viewers to accept the more unpleasant passages of the film while driving home the basic message. Litvak spent three months in preproduction researching mental facilities and procedures, and he required his cast and crew to accompany him. Author Ward had envisioned de Havilland in the role, and Litvak concurred. During preproduction the actress exposed herself to every aspect of mental illness and its treatment, and returned full of compassion for the mentally ill, discovering that they could be charming and appealing despite their illness. De Havilland gave a detailed, subtle, passionate performance and was deservedly nominated for a Best Actress Oscar (she lost to Jane Wyman for JOHNNY BELINDA). THE SNAKE PIT turned out to be a critical and financial success for Zanuck, and he was quite proud of the fact that the film called such attention to the treatment of mental illness that 26 states passed new legislation pertaining to procedures in state institutions.

p, Anatole Litvak, Robert Bassler; d, Litvak; w, Frank Partos, Millen Brand (based on the novel by Mary Jane Ward); ph, Leo Tover; m, Alfred Newman; ed, Dorothy Spencer; md, Newman; art d, Lyle Wheeler, Joseph C. Wright; set d, Thomas Little, Ernest Lansing; cos, Bonnie Cashin; makeup, Ben Nye.

Drama   **Cas.**   **(PR:C MPAA:NR)**

SNAKE RIVER DESPERADOES   (1951) 54m COL bw

Charles Starrett (Steve Reynolds/The Durango Kid), Smiley Burnette (Himself), Don Reynolds (Little Hawk), Tommy Ivo (Billy), Monte Blue (Jim Haverly), Boyd "Red" Morgan (Brandt), George Chesebro (Josh [Dad] Haverly), John Pickard (Dodds), Charles Horvath (Black Eagle), Sam Flint (Jason Fox), Duke York (Pete).

Starrett gets some help from a couple of youngsters in this B western, which features Starrett trying to prevent a range war between the whites and the Indians. Blue and his fellow scoundrels think they could profit from the bloodshed, but the Durango Kid, an Indian boy, Reynolds, and Reynolds'

white friend, Ivo, put an end to Blue's terrorism. Starrett sings the tune "Brass Band Polka" to keep his buddies entertained. (See DURANGO KID series, Index.)

p, Colbert Clark; d, Fred F. Sears; w, Barry Shipman; ph, Fayte Browne; ed, Paul Borofsky; md, Ross Di Maggio; art d, Charles Clague.

Western   **(PR:A MPAA:NR)**

SNAKE WOMAN, THE*   (1961, Brit.) 68m Caralan & Dador/UA bw

John McCarthy (Inspector Charles Prentice), Susan Travers (Atheris Adderson), Geoffrey Danton (Col. Wynborn), Arnold Marle (Dr. Murton), Elsie Wagstaff (Aggie, Midwife), John Cazabon (Dr. Adderson), Frances Bennett (Polly), Jack Cunningham (Constable), Hugh Moxey (Inspector), Michael Logan (Barkis), Dorothy Frere (Martha Adderson), Stevenson Lang (Shepherd).

A chilling atmosphere can't save this lame horror picture set in England just after the turn of the century. A herpetologist cures his insane wife of her madness using snake venom. A short while later, they produce a daughter who can turn into a snake at will. The curvy Travers takes advantage of her metamorphosis skills and begins to wreak havoc on the town's male population. Nothing worthwhile.

p, George Fowler; d, Sidney J. Furie; w, Orville H. Hampton; ph, Stephen Dade; m, Buxton Orr; ed, Anthony Gibbs; md, Philip Martell; art d, John G. Earl; makeup, Freddie Williamson.

Horror   **(PR:C MPAA:NR)**

SNAPSHOT   (SEE: DAY AFTER HALLOWEEN, THE, 1981, Aus.)

SNIPER, THE*   (1952) 87m Kramer/COL bw

Adolphe Menjou (Lt. Kafka), Arthur Franz (Eddie Miller), Gerald Mohr (Sgt. Ferris), Marie Windsor (Jean Darr), Frank Faylen (Inspector Anderson), Richard Kiley (Dr. James G. Kent), Mabel Paige (Landlady), Marlo Dwyer (May Nelson), Geraldine Carr (Checker), Jay Novello (Pete), Ralph Peters (Police Interlocutor), Max Palmer (Chadwick), Sidney Miller (Intern), Hurb Latimer (Sam), Dani Sue Nolan (Sandy), Harry Cheshire (Mayor), Cliff Clark (Chief of Police), Robert Foulk, Vern Martell, Fred Hartman, Don Michaelian, Renaldo Viri, Kernan Cripps, Rory Mallinson, J. Anthony Hughes (Policemen), John Bradley (Rookie Policeman), Danny Mummert (Boy), George Dockstader (Mapes), Les Sketchley (Flaherty), Carl Benton Reid (Liddell), Bryon Foulger (Pete Eureka), Roy Maypole (TV Announcer), Paul Marion (Al), Grandon Rhodes (Mr. Fitzpatrick), Kay Sharpe (Millie), Harland Warde (Harper), John Brown (Wise), John Eldredge (Stonecroft), Patricia Toun, Helen Linstrom, Wanda Wirth, Luanna Scott, Kathleen O'Rielly, Elsa Weber, Helen Eliot, Aline Watson, Mary Holly, Alice Bartlett, Betty Shute, Gail Bonney, Sarah Selby, Robin Raymond, Marlene Lyden, Jean Willes, Kathleen O'Mally, Adrienne Marden, Jessie Arnold (Women), Elizabeth Whitney (Nurse), John H. Algate, Thomas Heidt, Richard Freye, Harry Bechtel, Wilis West, Norman Nazarr, Robert Day, Nolan Leary, Billy Wayne, Paul Du Bov, Charles Lane, Harry Harvey, John A. Butler, Frank Sully, Donald Kerr (Men), Ralph Smiley (Tony Debiaci, Suspect), John Pickard (Allen Martin, Suspect), Ralph Volkie (Suspect), Joe Miksak, Richard Glyer, Howard Negley, David McMahon, Robert Malcolm, Charles Watts, Steve Darrell (Detectives), Frank Shaw (Anna Potch), Frank Kreig (Jailer), Victor Sen Young (Waiter), Gaylord Pendleton (Ambulance Man), Clark Howat (Police Photographer), Dudler Dickerson (Cleaner), Edgar Novack, Mike Lally, George Chesebro (Concessionaires), Charles Marsh (Manager), Lillian Bon (Mrs. Fitzpatrick), Donald Kerr, Joe Palma (Men), Barry Brooks (Attendant), Bruce Cameron (Motorcycle Policeman), Tommy Hawkins (Outfielder), Lucas Farara (Child), Al Hill (Bartender), Ralph O. Clark (Man Who Falls from Smokestack).

A taut psychological police drama has Franz playing a loner who knows that his mental condition makes him a dangerous man. His hostile feelings toward women drive him to kill, but Franz tries to overcome his compulsions by seeking help. He deliberately burns his hand in order to be admitted to a psychiatric hospital. There he finds doctors to be indifferent to his inner turmoil so Franz finally gives in to his compulsions. He takes to the rooftops of San Francisco with a rifle, picking off various women with whom he has come in contact. Menjou is a slovenly policeman assigned to find the killer. As he probes into the case Menjou comes to realize these random murders are the work of a mentally disturbed individual with no criminal intent. Fighting against both political and media pressures, Menjou eventually closes in on Franz. He captures the sniper in a room, stocked with guns. Franz experiences a feeling of relief knowing that his internal tortures are finally recognized. The film operates at several levels of tension as it meshes the psychological aspects and the police hunt without detracting from either element. Dmytryk's *mise en scene* is a fine example of this combination, using the San Francisco setting to its fullest extent. Darkened settings and unusual camera angles give this the gritty, tense feel of a good *film noir* police drama while at the same time matching the stylized settings of silent German Expressionism films. Franz' feelings are fully entrenched within the darkened streets he inhabits, as dangerous and unclear as his own mind. Director Dmytryk took great care to maintain a consistently interesting visual style throughout his film, employing the use of a sketch artist to visualize sequences before the actual shooting. Deciding to incorporate a clothesline amidst a rooftop chase, the director gave the idea to an accomplished sketch artist to fill in what he believed to be missing. The results were striking and Dmytryk was impressed. "If the artist can come up with just one original, usable conception of a film, he has earned his salary," he wrote in his biography *It's a Hell of a Life But Not a Bad Living*. The entire production was shot in a remarkably short period of just 18 days, including location and studio work. The choice of actors for the leads is another enhancement. Franz has the stereotypical look of the all-American boy of the 1950s with his short haircut and quiet demeanor, yet beneath it lurks something truly disturbed, shown in his constantly darting eyes. Franz's face is remarkably expressive as well, showing the torture he is undergoing in the film's early moments contrasted with the look of relief he shows at his capture. Menjou is well cast against his image of the dapper gentleman with the mustache–as a clean-shaven, badly dressed character. His is a sympathetic portrait; he knows he must bring in his man and yet he feels something for the killer as well. THE SNIPER raises several important and uncomfortable issues about the treatment of the mentally ill and how modern society should deal with the psychologically bent criminal. Questions are raised but not always answered, giving the audience more to think about than an ordinary police story. Dmytryk had been one of the infamous Hollywood Ten and had gone to England after being blacklisted in order to work. There he made a few films before eventually coming back to America. After Dmytryk served some time in jail Kramer bucked popular sentiment by offering him a chance to direct in Hollywood again with this film. Thus it came as a surprise to many on both sides of the political spectrum when the politically conservative Menjou was cast to work with Dmytryk. The Communist newspaper The Daily Worker lashed out at Dymtryk, calling him "palsy-walsy with his erstwhile foe–the rabid witch-hunter and haberdasher's gentleman–Adolphe Menjou. Now Dmytryk and Menjou are together again–this time as friends. Menjou has a leading role in THE SNIPER, which Dmytryk, gone over to warmongering and restored to favor of the Big Money, is now directing..." In his defense, Dmytryk argued that he had simply cast Menjou against type and as far as he could tell no warmongering occurred on the set. Menjou also came under criticism from his own political circle for working with the formerly blacklisted director and with liberal producer Kramer. When confronted with this by fellow conservatives, the angered Menjou gave less honorable reasons for taking the part. "Because I'm a whore!" he reportedly retorted to detractors. The story had a semi-factual basis. Screenwriter Brown, along with original story writers Edna and Edward Anhalt, explained they had fashioned Franz' character from a variety of men they had researched who were convicted of violent crimes against women. Unexpected publicity for the film came shortly before the film's opening when a real-life sniper named Evan Charles Thomas was arrested on charges of a shooting spree similar to the one portrayed in the film.

p, Stanley Kramer; d, Edward Dmytryk; w, Harry Brown (based on a story by Edna Anhalt, Edward Anhalt); ph, Burnett Guffey; m, George Antheil; ed, Harry Gerstad, Aaron Stell; md, Morris Stoloff; prod d, Rudolph Sternad; art d, Walter Holscher; set d, James Crowe.

Crime   **(PR:O   MPAA:NR)**

SNIPER'S RIDGE**½   (1961) 61m AP/FOX bw

Jack Ging *(Pvt. Scharack)*, Stanley Clements *(Cpl. Pumphrey)*, John Goddard *(Capt. Tombolo)*, Douglas Henderson *(Sgt. Sweatish)*, Gabe Castle *(Lt. Peer)*, Allan Marvin *(Wardy)*, Anton Van Stralen *(Bear)*, Mason Curry *(David)*, Mark Douglas *(Bo-Bo)*, Scott Randall *(Soldier)*, George Yoshinaga *(Mongolian)*, Albert C. Freeman, Jr *(Gwathney)*, Henry Delgado *(Tonto)*, Joe Cawthon *(Young Soldier)*, Richard Jeffries *(Soldier)*, Thomas A. Sweet.

A decent war picture set in Korea just hours before the cease-fire, featuring a psychotic captain, Goddard, planning one final attack in the hopes of achieving a moment of glory. While doing so, however, he steps on a land mine and cannot step off without being blown up. Private Ging offers his assistance by wrapping Goddard in flak jackets for protection, but gets himself wounded in the process. The cease-fire is signed and Goddard apologizes to his men who refuse to accept his feeble, nearly fatal, excuse.

p&d, John Bushelman; w, Tom Maruzzi; ph, Kenneth Peach (CinemaScope); m, Richard La Salle; ed, Carl Pierson; art d, John Mansbridge; set d, Harry Reif; cos, Robert Olivas; makeup, Ernie Park.

War   **(PR:A   MPAA:NR)**

SNOOPY, COME HOME***½   (1972) 80m Cinema Center/NG c

Voices: Chad Webber *(Charlie Brown)*, Robin Kohn *(Lucy Van Pelt)*, Stephen Shea *(Linus Van Pelt)*, David Carey *(Schroeder)*, Johanna Baer *(Lila)*, Hilary Momberger *(Sally)*, Chris De Faria *(Peppermint Patty)*, Linda Ercoli *(Clara)*, Linda Mendelson *(Frieda)*, Bill Melendez *(Snoopy)*.

The adventures of America's favorite beagle are brought to the big screen for the second time (A BOY NAMED CHARLIE BROWN was his premier film) under the creative skill of Charles M. Schulz. Snoopy packs his bowl and faithful bird Woodstock and heads for the hospital where his original owner is calling for him. Where this film towers above the first one, however, is in the music, boasting Disney folks Richard M. and Robert B. Sherman as the writers, while A BOY NAMED CHARLIE BROWN tried

the audiences' patience with Rod McKuen tunes. Thoroughly enjoyable for kids and adults alike. Songs include: "Snoopy, Come Home," "Lila's Tune," "Fun on the Beach," "Best of Buddies," "Changes," "Partners," "Getting It Together," "No Dogs Allowed" (Richard M. Sherman, Robert B. Sherman).

p, Lee Mendelson, Bill Melendez; d, Melendez; w, Charles M. Schulz (based on the cartoon characters created by Schulz); ph, Nick Vasu (Technicolor); m, Donald Ralke; ed, Robert T. Gillis, Charles McCann, Rudy Zamora, Jr.

Animated Feature   **Cas.**   **(PR:AAA   MPAA:G)**

SNORKEL, THE***   (1958, Brit.) 74m Hammer-Clarion/COL bw

Peter Van Eyck *(Jacques Duval)*, Betta St. John *(Jean Duval)*, Mandy Miller *(Candy Duval)*, Gregan Aslan *(Inspector)*, William Franklyn *(Wilson)*, Marie Burke *(Daily Woman)*, Irene Prador *(French Woman)*, Henry Vidon *(Italian Gardener)*, Robert Rietty, Armando Guinle, David Ritch, Flush *(Toto)*.

Van Eyck tries his hand at committing the perfect crime in this ingenious murder mystery. In order for his wife's murder to appear a suicide, he gives her a dose of tranquilizers, locks the doors and windows from the inside, turns on all the gas, and hides in a cubbyhole underneath the floor. From there he breathes through a snorkel tube and waits until the police arrive, remove the body, and declare it a suicide before he comes out. His plan is foiled when the dead woman's daughter from a previous marriage catches on to Van Eyck's scheme. A gimmick that works.

p, Michael Carreras; d, Guy Green; w, Jimmy Sangster, Peter Myers (based on the novel by Anthony Dawson); ph, Jack Asher; m, Francis Chagrin; ed, James Needs; md, John Hollingsworth; art d, John Stoll; cos, Molly Arbuthnot.

Crime   **(PR:A   MPAA:NR)**

SNOUT, THE   (SEE: UNDERWORLD INFORMERS, 1965, Brit.)

SNOW**½   (1983, Fr.) 90m Babylone/Papp-Public c (NEIGE)

Juliet Berto *(Anita)*, Jean-Francois Stevenin *(Willy)*, Robert Liensol *(Jocko)*, Paul le Person *(Bruno)*, Patrick Chenais, Jean Francois Balmer *(Policeman)*, Nini Crepon *(Betty)*, Res Paul Nephtali, Anna Prucnal.

Berto, who was superb as Celine in CELINE AND JULIE GO BOATING, acted in and directed this visually alive picture set in Paris' decadent Pigalle. She plays a waitress at a bar frequented by drug pushers and addicts. Berto is aided in her attempts to help her strung-out friends by a priest who is believed to perform miracles. An admirable, but minor first film released in France two years earlier. (In French; English subtitles.)

p, Ken Legarguant, Romaine Legarguant; d, Juliet Berto, Jean-Henri Roger; w, Marc Villard (based on an idea by Berto); ph, William Lubtchansky (Eastmancolor); m, Bernard Lavilliers, Francois Breant; ed, Yann Dedet.

Drama   **(PR:O   MPAA:NR)**

SNOW COUNTRY**   (1969, Jap.) 115m Shochiku/Shochiku Films of
                                                          America c (YUKIGUNI)

Shima Iwashita *(Komako)*, Isao Kimura *(Shimamura)*, Mariko Kaga *(Yoko)*, Tamotsu Hayakawa *(Yukio)*, Chieko Naniwa *(The Masseuse)*, Sadako Sawamura *(The Dance Teacher)*, Mineko Bandai *(The Landlady)*, Shinichi Yanagisawa *(The Banto)*, Mutsuko Sakura *(The Maid)*, Kakuko Chino *(Kikuyu)*, Kyomi Sakura *(Kintaro)*, Takanobu Hozumi *(The Drunk Guest)*, Ushio Akashi *(The Stationmaster)*, Kaneko Iwasaki *(Mrs. Shimamura)*, Taketoshi Naito *(Koizumi)*, Michisumi Sugawara *(Komako's Patron)*, Nijiko Kiyokawa *(Mistress of Geisha House)*.

The tale of a Japanese writer who falls in love with a geisha while visiting a hot springs resort. He soon returns to his wife and child in Tokyo, but visits the geisha again the following winter. Unable to commit himself to her and her devotion, he decides to continue his marriage and never see the geisha again. Released in Japan in 1965, and previously filmed in 1957 by Shiro Toyoda.

p, Shizuo Yamanouchi; d, Hideo Oba; w, Ryosuke Saito, Oba (based on the work *Yukiguni* By Yasunari Kawabata); ph, Toichiro Narushima (Shochiko GrandScope, Fuji Color); m, Naozumi Yamamoto; prod d, Ryotaro Kuwata; art d, Inko Yoshino.

Drama   **(PR:O   MPAA:NR)**

SNOW CREATURE, THE, zero   (1954) 80m Planet Filmways/UA bw

Paul Langton *(Dr. Frank Parrish)*, Leslie Denison *(Peter Welles)*, Teru Shimada *(Subra)*, Rollin Moriyama *(Leva)*, Robert Kino *(Inspector Karma)*, Robert Hinton *(Airline Manager)*, Darlene Fields *(Joyce Parrish)*, George Douglas *(Corey, Jr.)*, Robert Bice *(Fleet)*, Rudolph Anders *(Dr. Dupont)*, Bill Phipps *(Lt. Dunbar)*, Jack Daly *(Edwards)*, Rusty Westcott *(Guard in Warehouse)*, Dick Sands *(The Snow Creature)*, Keith Richard *(Harry Bennett)*.

Billy Wilder's talentless brother put together this fourth-rate abominable snowman film (the first and the worst), with a poorly costumed monster roaming the streets of Los Angeles. Langton, the scientist who brought him back from Tibet, wants him for scientific purposes, but a full-scale manhunt catches up to the fur-faced fright in the city's sewer system. Frequently the phony appearance of a man in a monster suit is obscured by the manner in which the monster is shot--covered by shadows, through glass or a snowstorm, etc.

p&d, W. Lee Wilder; w, Myles Wilder; ph, Floyd D. Crosby; m, Manuel Compinsky; ed, Jodie Copelan; md, Compinsky; art d, Frank Sylos; spec eff, Lee Zavitz.

| Science Fiction | Cas. | (PR:A MPAA:NR) |

SNOW DEMONS (SEE: SNOW DEVILS, THE, 1965, Ital.)

SNOW DEVILS, THE zero (1965, Ital.) 78m Mercury-Southern Cross/MGM bw (I DIAVOLI DELLO SPAZIO; AKA: SPACE DEVILS; SNOW DEMONS; THE DEVILS FROM SPACE; THE DEVIL MEN FROM SPACE)

Giacomo Rossi-Stuart, Ombretta Colli, Renato Baldini, Archie Savage, Wilbert Bradley, Halina Zalewska, Furio Meniconi, Peter Martell, Iscaro Ravaioli, Enzo Fiermonti, Freddy Hagar.

The occasional flashes of visual interest aren't nearly enough to make this Italian science-fiction film worth sitting through. Abominable snowmen survivors from the distant planet Aytia plan to upset the meteorological balance of Earth, but the heroics of a couple of explorers prevent this doomsday from occuring.

p, Joseph Fryd, Antonio Margheriti; d, Margheriti; w, Charles Sinclair, William Finger, Ivan Reiner, Moretti (based on a story by Audrey Wisberg); ph, Riccardo Pallotini; m, A. Francesco Lavagnino; ed, Otello Colangeli; set d, R. Perron; spec eff, Victor Sontolda.

| Science Fiction | | (PR:A MPAA:G) |

SNOW DOG** (1950) 63m MON bw

Kirby Grant (Rod), Elena Verdugo (Andree), Rick Vallin (Louis), Milburn Stone (Dr. McKenzie), Richard Karlan (Biroff), Jane Adrian (Red Feather), Hal Gerard (Antoine), Richard Avonde (Phillippe), Duke York (Duprez), Guy Zanette (Baptiste), Chinook the Wonder Dog.

Grant and his trusty dog, Chinook, uncover a plot in the snowy north woods to steal an ore-rich mine. What appears to be death at the jaws of a wild, snow-white wolf is really murder at the hands of Stone, a supposedly friendly doctor. Chinook gets in trouble with the locals when it is revealed that he is a dead ringer for the killer wolf. A decent programmer made with children in mind.

p, Lindsley Parsons; d, Frank McDonald; w, William Raynor (based on the story "Tentacles of the North" by James Oliver Curwood); ph, William Sickner; ed, Ace Herman; md, Edward Kay; art d, David Milton.

| Adventure | | (PR:AA MPAA:NR) |

SNOW IN THE SOUTH SEAS** (1963, Jap.) 103m Toho c (MINAMI NO SHIMA NI YUKI GA FURA)

Daisuke Kato, Hisaya Morishige, Tatsuya Mihashi, Franky Sakai, Junzaburo Ban.

A war drama about a Japanese army troop stationed in New Guinea during WW II suffering from low morale. Kato, a writer and actor turned soldier, is asked to stage a play and supervise construction of a theater. The final performance of the play, which contains a symbolic snowfall, is staged as the Allied forces prepare to invade.

d, Seiji Hisamatsu; w, Ryozo Kasahara (based on the story by Daisuke Kato); ph, Tokuzo Kuroda (Eastmancolor); m, Kenjiro Hirose.

| War Drama | | (PR:C MPAA:NR) |

SNOW JOB** (1972) 90m Englund-Rissien/WB c (GB: THE SKI RAIDERS)

Jean-Claude Killy (Christian Biton), Daniele Gaubert (Monica Scotti), Cliff Potts (Bob Skinner), Vittorio De Sica (Enrico Dolphi), Lelio Luttazzi (Bank Manager), Delia Boccardo (Lorraine Borman).

An odd crime film with Olympic ski champion Killy heading downhill on skis, with his acting talent (or lack thereof) sloping alongside him. Killy plays a ski instructor in the Alpine Mountains who teams with Gaubert and Potts to rob the bank at the mountain resort where he works. They successfully pull off the daring robbery, but insurance investigator De Sica discovers the three to be the thieving culprits and threatens them with arrest. They return the money to De Sica only to figure out that he was a fraud and that they have been tricked out of their ill-gotten gains. They break up the team, deciding to go their separate ways. The plot twists again when Killy catches a train with De Sica, his partner from the beginning. Though Killy cannot act, he can ski, while, on the other hand, famed Italian

director De Sica cannot ski, but his performance is the best in the film.

p, Edward L. Rissien; d, George Englund; w, Ken Kolb, Jeffrey Bloom (based on the story "$125,000 Ski Bum Holdup" by Richard Gallagher); ph, Gabor Pogany (Panavision, Technicolor); m, Jacques Loussier; ed, Gary Griffen; art d, Aurelio Crugnola; cos, Bona Nassalli-Rocca; ski ph, Willy Bogner.

| Crime | | (PR:A MPAA:GP) |

SNOW QUEEN, THE**½ (1959, USSR) 70m Soyuzmultfilm/UNIV c

Voices: Sandra Dee (Gerda), Tommy Kirk (Kay), Patty McCormack (Angel), Louise Arthur (The Snow Queen), Paul Frees (Ol' Dreamy/The Raven), June Foray (Court Raven), Joyce Terry (The Princess), Richard Beals (The Prince), Lillian Buyeff (Granny), Art Linkletter, Tammy Marihugh, Jennie Lynn, Billy Booth, Rickey Busch.

An excellently animated Soviet version of Hans Christian Andersen's fairy tale about two youngsters in search of a friend held captive in the palace of the evil Snow Queen. For its release in America, the feature was dubbed with English voices and show n with a six-minute, live-action prologue featuring Linkletter and some enthusiastic children.

p, Robert Faber; prologue d, Phil Patton; w, (based on the fairy tale by Hans Christian Andersen); prologue w, Alan Lipscott, Bob Fisher; ph, (Eastmancolor); m, Frank Skinner; ed, Hugo Grimaldi; md, Joseph Gershenson; m/l, "The Snow Queen," "The Jolly Robbers," Diane Lampert, Richard Loring, "Do It While You're Young," Lampert, Loring (sung by Sandra Dee).

| Animated Children's | | (PR:AAA MPAA:NR) |

SNOW TREASURE** (1968) 95m Sagittarius/AA c

James Franciscus (Lt. Kalasch), Ilona Rodgers (Bente Nielsen), Paul Austad (Peter Lundstrom), Raoul Oyen (Victor Lundstrom), Randi Borch (Inger Lundstrom), Tor Stokke (Lars Lundstrom), Wilfred Breistrand (Capt. Kantzeler), Bente Nielsen.

An embarrassingly stilted and unexciting WW II adventure tale about Norwegian youngsters who secretly smuggle some gold in their backpacks to a boat manned by the Norwegian underground. Franciscus is cast in a relatively small part as a Nazi soldier who discovers the Norwegians' game, but offers his assistance instead of bringing it to the attention of the authorities.

p&d, Irving Jacoby; w, Jacoby, Peter Hansen (based on the novel by Marie McSwigan); ph, Sverre Bergli (Eastmancolor); m, Egil Monn-Iversen; ed, Ralph Sheldon; art d, Grethe Hejil.

| Adventure | Cas. | (PR:A MPAA:NR) |

SNOW WHITE** (1965, Ger.) 74m Schongerfilm/Childhood c (SCHNEEWITTCHEN UND DIE SIEBEN ZWERGE)

Paul Tripp (Narrator), Elke Arendt (Snow White), Addi Adametz (Evil Queen), Renate Eichholz (Good Queen), Nils Clausnitzer (Prince), Dietrich Thomas (Huntsman), Zita Hitz (Chambermaid), Erwin Platzer, Susi Bohm Dance School.

Arendt plays the beautiful Snow White in this version of the classic Grimm fairy tale, which has her the victim of evil queen Adametz and her poison apple. The proverbial Prince Charming comes along and, with a little kiss on the lips, saves the day. Originally released in Germany in 1956.

p, Hubert Schonger; d, Erich Kobler; w, Konrad Lustig, Walter Oehmichen (based on the fairy tale by Jakob Grimm, Wilhelm Grimm); ph, Wolf Schwan (Eastmancolor); m, Carl Steuber, Franz Miller; ed, Horst Rossgerber; md, Lehman Engel; art d, Gunther Strupp; cos, W. Pechanz; m/l, Anne Delugg, Milton Delugg.

| Fantasy | | (PR:AAA MPAA:NR) |

SNOW WHITE AND ROSE RED** (1966, Ger.) 55m Schongerfilm/Childhood c (SCHNEEWEISSCHEN UND ROSENROT)

Paul Tripp (Narrator), Rosemarie Seehofer (Snow White), Ursula Herion (Rose Red), Heini Gobel (Prince), Ruth von Zerboni, Nils Clausnitzer, Dieter Wieland, Richard Kruger.

Seehofer plays the familiar Snow White, and Herion her younger sister Miss Red, who live in the woods with their dear mother. When a local prince gets turned into a brown bear by a malicious magical dwarf, the girls help to destroy the wicked man and break the spell he cast on the prince. Released in Germany in 1955.

d, Erich Kobler; w, Walter Oemichen, Konrad Lustig (based on the fairy tale by Jakob Grimm, Wilhelm Grimm); ph, Wolf Schwan (Eastmancolor); m, Oskar Sala.

| Fantasy | | (PR:AAA MPAA:NR) |

SNOW WHITE AND THE SEVEN DWARFS***
(1937) 83m Disney/RKO c

Voices: Adriana Caselotti (*Snow White*), Harry Stockwell (*Prince Charming*), Lucille LaVerne (*The Queen*), Moroni Olsen (*Magic Mirror*), Billy Gilbert (*Sneezy*), Pinto Colvig (*Sleepy/Grumpy*), Otis Harlan (*Happy*), Scotty Mattraw (*Bashful*), Roy Atwell (*Doc*), Stuart Buchanan (*Humbert, the Queen's Huntsman*), Marion Darlington (*Bird Sounds and Warbling*), The Fraunfelder Family, Jim Macdonald (*Yodeling*).

Dubbed by his detractors "Disney's Folly," SNOW WHITE AND THE SEVEN DWARFS was for Walt Disney an artistic masterpiece, as well as a personal success; the end result of a dream to pioneer animation in a scope beyond anyone's imaginings. The film opens (as Disney was to begin many of his future films) on a storybook. As the theme "Some Day My Prince Will Come" wafts in the background, the turning pages explain how the orphaned Snow White has been brought up working as a servant for a wicked queen. The queen, an icily beautiful woman with eyes that pierce, stands before her Magic Mirror, and poses her vain, oft-asked question: "Mirror, mirror, on the wall, who is the fairest of them all?" The queen is shocked when the Mirror gives the unexpected answer: "Snow White." Snow White, a happy young girl despite her misfortunes, is working in the garden, singing–with the birds that flock around her–the song "I'm Wishing." It is her dream to have a handsome young man take her from these toils so she can live in happiness. Prince Charming, the man of her dreams, hears her singing and surprises the girl as she finishes her song. Meanwhile, the queen, enraged at the Mirror's revelation, orders her huntsman to take the girl to the forest and kill her. She presents him with a small casket, in which the huntsman is to place the dead girl's heart as proof he has carried out his task. Snow White and the huntsman go into the forest and, as she is picking flowers, the would-be assassin raises his knife. Before he can follow through, Snow White turns around and sees what is about to happen. The huntsman cannot bear to kill her, and tells Snow White she should run into the forest to escape from the queen's wrath. As Snow White flees, her mind conjures up unknown horrors as frightening pairs of eyes flash all around her. Snow White collapses in fear, but it turns out her imagination has gone wild: these eyes belong to the friendly forest animals. The animals take her to a small cottage, which is covered with dust. Snow White merrily cleans up, singing "Whistle While You Work," as the animals help her with her chores. In another part of the forest, the day is quickly coming to an end. In a diamond mine, seven dwarfs are finishing their daily dig. They begin the trek home, singing "Heigh Ho" along the way. Meanwhile, Snow White has grown tired from the day's events. She goes to the second floor of the cottage where she finds seven beds, each marked with the name of its occupant. When the dwarfs enter their home, they are surprised to find it neat as a pin. When they find Snow White on the second floor, she suprises Doc, Happy, Sleepy, Sneezy, Bashful, Grumpy, and Dopey by already knowing their names, courtesy of the beds. She explains why she is there and the dwarfs agree to let her stay. The next day, as the dwarfs go off to work, they warn Snow White to be careful of the wicked queen. The queen, through her Magic Mirror, learns that Snow White has not been killed and decides to do the girl in herself. She prepares a magical potion that turns her into an ugly old hag, then ventures to the dwarfs' cottage. Once there, she encounters Snow White and offers the unsuspecting girl a bright red apple. The apple is poisoned and Snow White falls to the ground, locked in a deep sleep only a kiss of love can break. Snow White's animal friends see what has happened and fetch the dwarfs. They chase the queen to the top of a mountain, where she dies when the rocky ledge she is cornered on gives way. The dwarfs are heartbroken, and place the beautiful Snow White on a bier where all her friends of the forest might view her. Their sadness comes to an end when Prince Charming arrives. He gently kisses Snow White, and the spell is broken. The dwarfs and animals are overjoyed, while Snow White and her prince ride off for a happy ending. With SNOW WHITE AND THE SEVEN DWARFS Disney created what many were convinced could not be done. The familiar story, adapted from the Grimm brothers' tale, pulls in the audience with its imaginative development. This was animation as never before experienced, with images both engaging and terrifying. Disney wisely realized the film could only work if it was full of believable characters. Each personality is distinct, from the purity of Snow White to the absolute evil of the queen. The seven dwarfs are aptly named, with characteristics that match their demeanors, and even the animals display anthropomorphized traits. Disney realized the importance of the forest inhabitants to their human counterparts, and his standards for the animals were rigid. Each sequence is a gem, carefully created, reflecting the enormous work that went behind the film. Disney had been working towards the artistry in SNOW WHITE with his studio's short cartoons. After encountering a Parisian theater manager who made quite a profit showing a program of only cartoon shorts, Disney began to toy with the idea of creating a feature-length animation. He was interested in exploring character development within a cartoon, and saw feature length as the only logical forum. In the fall of 1934, Disney brought together his animation staff and explained his idea, insistent that the studio would bring the Grimms' "Snow White" to the screen. (Disney openly admitted that one of his first filmgoing experiences was a silent version of the fairy tale.) He spent the next hour performing the entire story for the assemblage, playing each part with perfection. His enthusiasm was contagious and the staff eagerly began work on the project. Disney projected a budget of $500,000, which sent his money-conscious brother Roy into a frenzy. "You're going to

ruin us," Roy exclaimed. "Half a million dollars for a single film? Why can't we just stay with Mickey Mouse?" Considering that an average release of the time cost no more than $250,000 to make, Roy Disney's qualms were not without merit. However, Disney pressed on, determined to make his dream come true. Wanting to make Snow White look realistic, Disney had the wife of animator Art Babbit, dancer Margery Belcher (who later married Gower Champion and had a fine screen career of her own) photographed, then used this footage to create Snow White. Louis Hightower modeled Prince Charming. The witch side of the wicked queen was handled by character actress Lucille LaVerne, who specialized in such roles, having portrayed old hags in films such as ORPHANS OF THE STORM and A TALE OF TWO CITIES. LaVerne served as both voice and visual model for the transformed queen. Voices were tested, and at one point Disney considered using 13-year-old Durbin. Though impressed with her audition, Disney felt recordings of Durbin's voice sounded too mature, and decided against her. He took to listening to actresses over a loudspeaker system so their voices could be judged non-visually on their own merit. Eventually 20-year-old Caselotti was chosen, as Disney felt her thin soprano was best for the character. Production problems mounted as the film took shape. Because so much detail was going into each animation cel, the studio had to devise a new method of photographing the work. The cels used in short cartoons proved to be too small to accommodate SNOW WHITE, so the size had to be increased. Next, in order to create depth of field, Disney employed the multiplane camera, an animation camera first used on the highly acclaimed short THE OLD MILL. This camera had seven tiers and was capable of photographing numerous cels simultaneously. Each cel could be moved at a different rate of speed to create realistic parallax differences between "near" and "far" objects, lending a feeling of depth to the picture. The result was a clear image capable of holding an incredible amount of information. With this camera, the Disney animators were able to conjure up some amazing moments. As Snow White runs through the forest, trees leap out, the eyes dance in horror, and logs change into alligators with frightening ease. The climactic chase of the dwarfs and the queen, a confrontation between good and evil, also benefits with the marvelous coloring of the sky, the shadows, the falling rocks, and the two ominous vultures that lurk above, swooping downward after the queen takes her plunge to doom. Some of the subtler character details were developed in less extravagant ways. Frank Thomas, a Disney animator, recalled (in the Christopher Finch book *The Art of Walt Disney*) the struggle to give Snow White's face a little color. Tinting only made her face red, but one woman in the inking department hit on a novel idea. "One of the girls said, 'Walt, can we try putting a little rouge on her cheeks?' He said, 'What do you mean?' So she took out her makeup kit and put some rouge on the cel and it looked keen. Walt said, 'Yeah, but how the hell are you going to get it in the same place every day? And on each drawing?' And the girl said, 'What do you think we've been doing all our lives?'....They just knew where it ought to go and, without any kind of guide, they made Snow White up on each cel..." As the production wore on, problems grew with funding. "We considered changing the name of the picture from SNOW WHITE to FRANKENSTEIN," Disney later remarked. With the film still incomplete, the production found itself in need of another $500,000 to finish. Roy contacted the Bank of America in hopes of getting a loan. Joseph Rosenberg, an official with that institution, contacted other movie officials on the project's potential. Most felt a feature-length cartoon was a foolhardy idea, and Louis Mayer, the callous head of MGM, told Rosenberg: "Who'd pay to see a drawing of a fairy princess when they can watch Joan Crawford's boobs for the same price at the box office?" Though Disney was protective of the yet unseen footage, he finally acquiesced to Roy's pleadings when Bank of America executives wanted to see what Rosenberg was so eager to sink half a million dollars into. An extremely rough cut was shown, while Disney ad libbed a narration to link the sequences. For moments where the footage was still unfinished, Disney himself substituted, once more playing out the SNOW WHITE story for a highly responsive audience. Fred Moore, an animator sitting in on the session, later recalled: "It was just too brilliant for words! Walt had never been so good, so eloquent. He played every single role in the movie, and each one was worth an Oscar. Even Roy, who was a tough nut to crack, had tears running down his cheeks." (Quoted from *Disney's World* by Leonard Mosley.) The loan was approved and the film neared completion. Confidence was high, and in an unprecedented move, Radio City Music Hall booked the film a year in advance, boldly taking out a *Variety* ad to announce their move. Shortly before the opening Disney cut some of the film's sequences, including one depicting the death of Snow White's mother (pictures of which had already appeared in *Look* magazine), and another in which the dwarfs indulge in some soup. Disney felt these sequences, though good, slowed the plot development. Ward Kimball, who had worked on the soup-eating sequence, later recalled: "...That was one of the early tragedies of my life....As much as he hated to do it–he even called me up on the phone and apologized–he had to take it out of the picture. Disney premiered his film December 21, 1937 at the Cathay Circle Theater in Hollywood, determined to show the filmmaking community that feature animation had triumphantly come to stay. Speaking before the star-studded crowd, Disney exclaimed: "I always dreamed that one day I would attend a gala premiere in Hollywood of one of my cartoons. Tonight you've made it come true. You make me feel like one of you." Later in the evening, he told his wife Lilly, "They no longer think I smell bad. It's wonderful!" Public reception was equally enthusiastic. The final budget, coming in at $1.5 million, was made back and then some as SNOW WHITE AND THE SEVEN DWARFS grossed over $8 million in its first release. Re-releases added to the profit, making this Disney's single most popular film. SNOW WHITE-related items were also big business, with "Dopey" toys making over $100,000 for their manufacturer. A Snow White Cafe even opened on Hollywood Boulevard, complete with the title characters' footprints memorialized in cement. Disney's vision proved to be a powerful one in its depictions of good versus evil, and some of the sequences were so frightening that the film was initially banned in England for anyone under age 16. (Because of some genuinely terrifying moments, parents should be cautious in bringing the youngest family members to see SNOW WHITE.) Disney received special recognition at the Oscar ceremonies for his work, accepting (from presenter Shirley Temple) one large statuette accompanied by seven smaller Oscars. SNOW WHITE AND THE SEVEN DWARFS remains a classic film, a shining example of the wonderment and brilliance that is Disney animation. The other songs by Frank Churchill, Larry Morey, Paul J. Smith, and Leigh Harline include: "One Song," "With a Smile and a Song," the immortal "Whistle While You Work," "Bluddle-Uddle-Um-Dum," "The Dwarfs' Yodel Song."

p, Walt Disney; d, 'supervising d' David Hand, 'sequence d' Perce Pearce, Larry Morey, William Cottrell, Wilfred Jackson, Ben Sharpsteen; w, Ted Sears, Otto Englander, Earl Hurd, Dorothy Ann Blank, Richard Creedon, Dick Richard, Merrill De Maris, Webb Smith (based on the fairy tale "Sneewittchen" in the collection *Kinder-und Hausmarchen* by Jacob Grimm, Wilhelm Grimm); m, Frank Churchill, Leigh Harline, Paul Smith, Morey; art d, Charles Phillippi, Hugh Hennesy, Terrell Stapp, McLaren Stewart, Harold Miles, Tom Codrick, Gustaf Tenggren, Kenneth Anderson, Kendall O'Connor, Hazel Sewell; character d, Albert Hunter, Joe Grant; supervising animators, Hamilton Luske, Vladimir Tytla, Fred Moore, Norman Ferguson; animators, Frank Thomas, Dick Lundy, Arthur Babbitt, Eric Larson, Milton Kahl, Robert Stokes, James Algar, Al Eugster, Cy Young, Joshua Meador, Ugo D'Orsi, George Rowley, Les Clark, Fred Spencer, Bill Roberts, Bernard Garbutt, Grim Natwick, Jack Campbell, Marvin Woodward, James Culhane, Stan Quackenbush, Ward Kimball, Wolfgang Reitherman, Robert Martsch; backgrounds, Samuel Armstrong, Mique Nelson, Merle Cox, Claude Coats, Phil Dike, Ray Lockrem, Maurice Noble.

Animated Feature　　　　　　　　**(PR:AAA　MPAA:G)**

SNOW WHITE AND THE THREE CLOWNS
　　　(SEE: SNOW WHITE AND THE THREE STOOGES)

SNOW WHITE AND THE THREE STOOGES*
(1961) 107m Chanford/FOX c (GB: SNOW WHITE AND THE THREE CLOWNS)

Carol Heiss (*Snow White*), The Three Stooges [Moe Howard, Larry Fine, "Curly" Joe DeRita] (*Themselves*), Edson Stroll (*Prince Charming*), Patricia Medina (*The Queen*), Guy Rolfe (*Count Oga*), Michael David (*Rolf*), Buddy Baer (*Hordred*), Edgar Barrier (*King Augustus*), Lisa Mitchell (*Linda*), Chuck Lacy (*Frederick*), Owen McGiveney (*Physician*), Sam Flint (*Chamberlain*), Blossom Rock (*Servant*), Robbi LaLonde (*Snow White as a Child*).

"Ye Stooges Three" take to the screen again in this sour adaptation of the Grimm brothers' fairy tale, which casts 1960 Olympic figure-skating champion Heiss in the role of Snow White. Set in the 17th Century, Heiss runs away from her evil stepmother and winds up at the cottage run by the seven dwarfs. The regular residents are working out in King Solomon's mines, however, and Heiss is aided by Moe, Larry, and "Curly" Joe, who just happen to be around. Heiss soon winds up fast asleep, and it takes Prince Charming's lips to bring her around. The Stooges simply are not funny this time out, failing to get laughs from even the most easily pleased youngsters. It could have been worse, however, maybe Snow White and the Seven Stooges. Songs include: "A Place Called Happiness," "I Said It Then, I Say It Now," and "Because I'm in Love" (Harry Harris), "Once in a Million Years" (Earl Brent), and "We're Looking for People."

p, Charles Wick; d, Walter Lang; w, Noel Langley, Elwood Ullman (based on a story by Wick and the fairy tale by Jakob Grimm, Wilhelm Grimm); ph, Leon Shamroy (CinemaScope, DeLuxe Color); ed, Jack W. Holmes; md, Lyn Murray; art d, Jack Martin Smith, Maurice Ransford; set d, Walter M. Scott, Paul S. Fox; cos, Renie; spec eff, L. B. Abbott, Emil Kosa, Jr.; ice ch, Ron Fletcher; makeup, Helen Turpin.

Fantasy/Comedy　　　　**Cas.**　　　　**(PR:A　MPAA:NR)**

SNOWBALL* 　　　　(1960, Brit.) 69m Independent Artists/Rank bw

Gordon Jackson (*Bill Donovan*), Kenneth Griffith (*Phil Hart*), Zena Walker (*Mary Donovan*), Daphne Anderson (*Nora Hart*), Denis Waterman (*Mickey Donovan*), John Welsh (*Ted Wylie*), Myrtle Reed (*Betty Martin*), Wensley Pithey (*Jim Adams*), Eric Pohlmann (*Editor*), Ronald Adam (*Mr. King*).

An 11-year-old boy tells one lie too many, sparking events which develop into intrigue and the eventual death of another villager, a former POW suffering from amnesia. Modest thriller is a decent effort considering its low budget, though it suffers from an inconsistent script and uneven direction.

p, Julian Wintle, Leslie Parkyn; d, Pat Jackson; w, Anne Francis (based on the novel by James Lake).

Crime/Drama　　　　　　　　**(PR:A　MPAA:NR)**

SNOWBALL EXPRESS* 　　　　(1972) 99m Disney/BV c

Dean Jones (*Johnny Baxter*), Nancy Olson (*Sue Baxter*), Harry Morgan (*Jesse McCord*), Keenan Wynn (*Martin Ridgeway*), Johnnie Whitaker (*Richard Baxter*), Michael McGreevey (*Wally Perkins*), George Lindsey (*Double L. Dingman*), Kathleen Cody (*Chris Baxter*), Mary Wickes (*Miss Wigginton*), David White (*Mr. Fowler*), Dick Van Patten (*Mr. Carruthers*), Alice Backes (*Miss Obelvie*), Joanna Phillips (*Naomi Voight*), John Myhers (*Mr. Manescue*), George Kirkpatrick (*Mr. Wainwright*).

Disney follows its usual formula in this slapstick comedy featuring Jones, a New York executive, who inherits a dilapidated Colorado ski resort. He packs up the family and tries to make a go of it, running into more problems than he can handle. Eventually the property turns a profit and the ski trade begins to climb. Remembered mainly for an outrageous ski snowmobile chase which colors the film's finale.

p, Ron Miller; d, Norman Tokar; w, Don Tait, Jim Parker, Arnold Margolin (based on the novel *Chateau Bon Vivant* by Frankie O'Rear, John O'Rear); ph, Frank Phillips (Technicolor); m, Robert F. Brunner; ed, Robert Stafford; art d, John B. Mansbridge, Walter Tyler; set d, Emile Kuri, Frank R. McKelvy; cos, Emily Sundby, Chuck Keehne; spec eff, Eustace Lycett, Art Cruickshank, Danny Lee; makeup, Robert J. Schiffer.

Comedy　　　　**Cas.**　　　　**(PR:AAA　MPAA:G)**

SNOWBOUND* 　　　　(1949, Brit.) 85m Gainsborough/UNIV bw

Robert Newton (*Derek Engles*), Dennis Price (*Neil Blair*), Herbert Lom (*Keramikos*), Marcel Dalio (*Stefan Valdini*), Stanley Holloway (*Joe Wesson*), Guy Middleton (*Gilbert Mayne*), Mila Parely (*Carla Rometta*), Willy Fueter (*Aldo*), Richard Molinas (*Mancini*), Catherine Ferraz (*Emilia*), Massimo Coen (*Auctioneer*), William Price (*Stelben*), Zena Marshall (*Italian Girl*), Gilbert Davis (*Commissionaire*), S. Rossiter-Shepherd (*Italian Lawyer*), Lionel Grose (*Cpl. Holtz*).

A standard adventure tale which has an expedition searching for hidden Nazi gold in the Alps. They are snowed in but eventually rescued by a heroic scriptwriter, who tempers the raging emotions that have arisen between the cabin-bound group.

p, Aubrey Baring; d, David MacDonald; w, David Evans, Keith Campbell (based on the novel *The Lonely Skier* by Hammond Innes); ph, Stephan Dade; m, Cedric Thorpe Davie; ed, Charles Knott; art d, George Provis, Maurice Carter; cos, Joan Ellacott; makeup, W. Partleton.

Adventure　　　　　　　　**(PR:A　MPAA:NR)**

SNOWED UNDER*½ 　　　　(1936) 63m FN/WB bw

George Brent (*Alan Tanner*), Genevieve Tobin (*Alice Merritt*), Glenda Farrell (*Daisy Lowell*), Patricia Ellis (*Pat Quinn*), Frank McHugh (*Orlando Rowe*), John Eldredge (*Robert McBride*), Porter Hall (*Arthur Layton*), Helen Lowell (*Mrs. Canterbury*), Olin Howland (*Sheriff*), Joseph King (*Jean*), John Elliott, Stuart Holmes (*Actors*), Richard Purcell (*Bert*), Kay Hughes (*Dumb Stenographer*), George Sorel (*Milkeimer*), Eddie Shubert (*Taxi Driver*), Iris March, Naomi Judge (*Girls*), Shirley Lloyd (*Blonde*), Mary Treen, Alma Lloyd (*Secretaries*), George Andre Beranger (*Maza*), Lester Dorr, Edward Peil, Sr (*Men in Producer's Office*).

A poorly scripted comedy about a scriptwriter who heads for the solitude of his country cottage in the hopes of finishing the last act of his play. His quiet life does not last long when he is visited by his first wife, Tobin, then his second wife, Farrell, and then his new flame, Ellis. A forgettable comedy.

p, Harry Joe Brown; d, Raymond Enright; w, F. Hugh Herbert, Brown Holmes (based on a story by Lawrence Saunders); ph, Arthur Todd; ed, Harold McLernon; md, Leo F. Forbstein; art d, Robert Haas; cos, Orry-Kelly.

Comedy　　　　　　　　**(PR:A　MPAA:NR)**

SNOWFIRE* 　　　　(1958) 73m AA c

Molly McGowan (*Herself*), Don Megowan (*Mike McGowan*), John Cason (*Buff Stoner*), Claire Kelly (*Carol Hampton*), Melody McGowan (*Herself*), Mike Vallon (*Poco*), Rusty Westcoatt (*Luke Stoner*), Bill Hale (*Skip Stoner*), Paul Keast, Snowfire the Horse.

Youngster Molly McGowan befriends the title horse, who was captured as part of a wild herd by her dad. While some villainous fellows try to get their hands on the horse, she helps the animal stay one step ahead of captivity. She turns on the charm and persuades her dad to let her keep the horse under the condition that it will not be branded and can roam free. A charming, independent family effort from the McGowan clan.

p,d&w, Dorrell McGowan, Stuart McGowan; ph, Brydon Baker (Eastmancolor); m, Albert Glasser; ed, Arthur M. Nadel, Jerry Young; art d, Alfeo Bocchicchio; cos, Muriel Pool, Bob Richards.

Drama　　　　　　　　**(PR:AAA　MPAA:NR)**

SNOWMAN (SEE: LAND OF NO RETURN, THE, 1981)

SNOWS OF KILIMANJARO, THE*½** (1952) 117m FOX c

Gregory Peck *(Harry)*, Susan Hayward *(Helen)*, Ava Gardner *(Cynthia)*, Hildegarde Neff *(Countess Liz)*, Leo G. Carroll *(Uncle Bill)*, Torin Thatcher *(Johnson)*, Ava Norring *(Beatrice)*, Helene Stanley *(Connie)*, Marcel Dalio *(Emile)*, Vincente Gomez *(Guitarist)*, Richard Allan *(Spanish Dancer)*, Leonard Carey *(Dr. Simmons)*, Paul Thompson *(Witch Doctor)*, Emmett Smith *(Molo)*, Victor Wood *(Charles)*, Bert Freed *(American Soldier)*, Agnes Laury *(Margot)*, Monique Chantel *(Georgette)*, Janine Grandel *(Annette)*, John Dodsworth *(Compton)*, Charles Bates *(Harry at Age 17)*, Lisa Ferraday *(Vendeuse)*, Maya Van Horn *(Princess)*, Ivan Lebedeff *(Marquis)*, Martin Garralaga *(Spanish Officer)*, Salvador Baguez, George Navarro, *(Stretcher Bearers)*, George Davis *(Servant)*, Julian Rivero *(Old Waiter)*, Edward Colmans *(Clerk)*, Ernest Brunner, Arthur Brunner *(Accordian Players)*.

Hemingway's stories and novels have not always been brought to full fruition when put on film. This one, the story of a writer who loses his intellectual and emotional way after having early commercial success, works splendidly under King's sure directorial hand and is enacted with power and conviction by Peck. Scriptwriter Robinson took the original story beyond its printed bounds and extended his script by incorporating many more tales of the Hemingway persona but it all works beautifully and, despite some carping from Hemingway purists, the film was an immense box-office success. Peck is shown half delirious with fever, lying on a cot in an African campsite. Before him, rising from the Kenyan plain, is the majestic mountain, Kilimanjaro, with its snowcapped peak glistening in the brilliant sun. A rich and popular author, Peck finds himself with nothing really to live for. He languishes on the cot with his wealthy wife Hayward at his side. As he drifts in and out of consciousness, he thinks back on his colorful life, first at his teenage years, seeing himself at age 17 (Peck is doubled by a youth standing in shadows, but his own voice is heard). He is shown making his first girl friend, Stanley, unhappy since he's decided to leave the Midwest and search for adventure. His uncle, Carroll, a guiding light throughout Peck's spectacular literary career, encourages him to see the world and discover the people in it. As a young writer living in Montparnasse in Paris, Peck is shown wandering around the bistros and finally, one night, listening to some black musicians play soulful jazz at a private party. He finds Gardner sitting next to him and when he lights her cigarette she says, looking at a musician playing a saxophone, "Hasn't that African got any piety?" Peck, utterly charmed by her dark beauty, tells her: "Why don't you and I just 'piety' right out of here?" They leave together and soon fall in love, Gardner inspiring Peck to finish his first novel, which he calls *The Lost Generation*, and one in which she is the heroine. He sells his book and is delighted when he receives his first advance, telling Gardner that "now we can go to Africa!" She smiles wanly and accepts Peck's ambitions, although it is clear that she would rather settle down and have a family. In Africa Peck is obsessed with the wild country and with hunting fierce beasts, but he still looks for a reason in life, a purpose. Gardner is there only to please him and when she questions their white hunting guide, Thatcher, about the meaning in all the hunting, he cuts her off and refuses to get in between what he knows is an impending family squabble. Once back in Nairobi, Gardner, who has hidden the fact that she is pregnant from Peck, realizes that she will lose him if she insists that they settle down. She either falls or purposely throws herself down some stairs and has a miscarriage. An attending doctor, Carey, leaves her room later to tell a surprised Peck that she has lost the child but that she will be all right. Peck mumbles something about not even knowing Gardner was pregnant and Carey stares at him incredulously, saying, "Don't you people talk to each other?" Peck and Gardner, through this tragedy, vow their love for each other but Peck is still full of wanderlust, and feels it's his job as a writer "to buzz around." The pair go to Spain to see the bullfights but here Gardner, realizing that Peck is hoping to go to the distant French-Syrian war and write about it, is afraid of losing the only man she'll ever love. She cannot go on trooping after him like a camp follower, however, and, almost close to a nervous breakdown, Gardner leaves him sitting in a Madrid cafe, departing with a guitarist. (This was a role Gardner was to repeat often; she would be forever going off with bullfighters and the like in such films as THE SUN ALSO RISES and THE BAREFOOT CONTESSA.) Peck goes off to cover the war, then returns to write more popular novels on the French Riviera where he meets wealthy Neff who more or less keeps him. Carroll visits Peck and disapproves of the female company he is keeping, a countess with no emotional makeup whatsoever, a frigid and manipulative female whose only ambition is to hold on to Peck as a showpiece writer. A letter arrives from Spain addressed to Peck but Neff intercepts it and, at a small gathering, she asks who the letter writer is, mentioning Gardner's name. Peck, eager to read the letter but not wishing to reveal his true emotions, tells Neff that the letter is not important. She smugly tears it up and throws it away and Peck explodes, smashing his drink on the floor and going to his room to pack. As he is packing, Neff comes to him, begging him to stay with her. He ignores her, grabbing his bags and heading for the door. "Oh, Harry," she tells him, "you look so ridiculous–like a knight questing for the Holy Grail." He gives her a stern look and replies, "Maybe I'll just have a good looksee for that grail." He leaves for Madrid but gets caught up in the Spanish Civil War, fighting on the Loyalist side. During one battle, he sees an ambulance hit by gunfire and turned on its side. Gardner is the driver and he pulls her from the wreckage, seeing that she is seriously injured, holding on to her and calling for stretcher bearers to carry her back to a field hospital. "God should spit on me," Peck tells her, apologizing for mistreating her, telling her he loves her. Finally, stretcher bearers pick up Gardner and begin running to the rear lines with her, Peck running after them. One of the Loyalist commanders, thinking Peck is deserting, orders him to halt and when he doesn't, shoots him in the leg. Peck looks after the stretcher bearers and sees Gardner's arm fall limp. He believes she has died, but is never really sure. Following the war he looks for her but she is nowhere to be found. Drunk one night in Paris, he mistakes Hayward for Gardner and they later begin an affair and get married. Hayward is a wealthy woman who only wants Peck to reciprocate her love for him. He is lost in the memory of Gardner, however, and even another safari to Africa cannot dim the memory of his one great love. He is injured while hunting and his leg becomes infected. Peck is now back in the present; he has drifted in and out of the past and present while slipping back and forth between unconsciousness and consciousness, while all the while Hayward has stayed at his side, praying that the gangrene spreading through his leg will not kill him. He abuses and makes fun of her, sneaking booze when he can to deaden the pain. It is clear to Hayward that the doctor she expects to arrive by plane will be too late unless she does something. That night she cleans the bloated leg, heats a knife to white heat, and lances the infected limb, causing Peck to pass out. Through the night Hayward stays with Peck, awakened at the darkest hour by a foul smelling beast, a hyena, which smells the blood from Peck's wound and is about to enter the tent until Hayward drives off the beast. (Director King actually imitated the sound of the hyena laughing). Peck awakens miraculously to see with Hayward that the rescue plane is landing on the savannah and that his life will not only be saved but that in his cathartic memories, he has found some meaning in living it, and in being able to love the woman who has sacrificed herself for him. More importantly, he now wants to write the things "that are truly important," and follow the noble literary course his uncle Carroll had urged him to take years earlier, even when giving him a riddle to solve, one that asked a question about a dead leopard that had been found close to the summit of Mt. Kilimanjaro, its carcass frozen and no one knowing what the beast was seeking at that altitude. The riddle is solved at the end of this film, one which clearly states that Peck is the leopard and what he is seeking is the truth of his own life and ambitions, a dangerous truth that comes close to killing him. This beautifully photographed film, King's favorite, combines many Hemingway tales to make its point and it features a magnificent score by Herrmann, one that captures all the exotic locales profiled. Gardner is excellent as the star-crossed lover but Hayward has a part that is mostly lost inside the flashbacks featuring Gardner. Peck had played a Hemingway hero in THE MACOMBER AFFAIR five years earlier, essaying a great white hunter in Africa, and that film had also been written by Robinson. The script for SNOWS OF KILIMANJARO was so well written by Robinson that director King proudly stated later: "You couldn't tell where Hemingway's quit and Robinson's began. He developed a Hemingway style, drew a little bit on everything Hemingway had written." The film would remain one of Gardner's favorites and she would later say of it: "I really felt comfortable in that part. I could understand the girl I played so well. She was a good, average gal with normal impulses. I didn't have to pretend." Hemingway didn't like the film, or said he didn't, calling Fox mogul Zanuck personally to say that it was a compilation of his stories and that it should have been called "the Snows of Zanuck." The mogul checked later and discovered that Hemingway had never even bothered to see the film. Anne Francis had been originally slated to play the Gardner role but was dropped when King thought she was not sexy enough. Although a second unit shot marvelous footage for the film in Africa, the top stars never left the Fox lot where all the major scenes were filmed. Some theater owners expressed fears to Fox that the public would stay away from a film having the word "Kilimanjaro" in it, because they could not pronounce it. Zanuck laughed at that and released the film, which became one of 1952's biggest box-office winners.

p, Darryl F. Zanuck; d, Henry King; w, Casey Robinson (based on the short story by Ernest Hemingway); ph, Leon Shamroy (Technicolor); m, Bernard Herrmann; ed, Barbara McLean; art d, Lyle Wheeler, John De Cuir; set d, Thomas Little, Paul S. Fox; cos, Charles LeMaire; spec eff, Ray Kellogg; ch, Antonio Triana; m/l, "Love is Cynthia," Alfred Newman; makeup, Ben Nye.

Drama/Adventure **Cas.** **(PR:C MPAA:NR)**

SNUFFY SMITH (SEE: SNUFFY SMITH, YARD BIRD, 1942)

SNUFFY SMITH, YARD BIRD*½
(1942) 67m MON bw (GB: SNUFFY SMITH; AKA: PRIVATE SNUFFY SMITH)

Bud Duncan *(Snuffy Smith)*, Edgar Kennedy *(Sgt. Cooper)*, Sarah Padden *(Loweezie)*, Doris Linden *(Cindy)*, Andria Palmer *(Janie)*, J. Farrell MacDonald *(General)*, Pat McVeigh *(Lloyd)*, Frank Austin *(Saul)*, Jimmie Dodd *(Don)*.

Based on the famous comic strip, Duncan plays the small moonshiner who finds himself in the Army, with his commanding sergeant, Kennedy, the "revenooer" who is always on his tail. The clash between the two enemies makes for some good laughs. A sequel, HILLBILLY BLITZKREIG, followed later in the same year. This was a comeback film for the bulb-nosed Duncan (whose acne rosacea rivaled that of W.C. Fields); his last picture had been a silent, THE HAUNTED SHIP (1927). Perfect for the part on the basis of physical appearance alone, the short comedian had worked in vaudeville and films for years with lumbering Lloyd Hamilton; the duo was billed as "Ham and Bud." Kennedy, the master of the slow burn, makes a fine foil for Duncan.

p, Edward Gross; d, Edward F. Cline; w, John Gray, Jack Henley, Lloyd French, Doncho Hall (based on the comic strip by Billy De Beck); ph, Marcel Le Picard; ed, Robert Crandall; md, Rudy Schrager; art d, Richard IRvine.

Comedy (PR:A MPAA:NR)

SO BIG** (1932) 90m WB bw

Barbara Stanwyck (Selina Peake Dejong), George Brent (Roelf Pool), Dickie Moore (Dirk Dejong as a Boy), Bette Davis (Dallas O'Mara), Guy Kibbee (August Hemple), Mae Madison (Julie Hemple), Hardie Albright (Dirk Dejong as a Man), Robert Warwick (Simeon Peake), Arthur Stone (Jan Steen), Earle Foxe (Pervus Dejong), Alan Hale (Klaas Pool), Dorothy Peterson (Maartje), Dawn O'Day [Anne Shirley] (Selina Peake as a Girl), Dick Winslow (Roelf, Age 14), Elizabeth Patterson (Mrs. Tebbits), Rita LaRoy (Paula Storm), Blanche Frederici (Widow Paarlenburg), Lionel Belmore (Rev. Dekker), Noel Francis (Fancy Woman), Harry Beresford (Adam Ooms), Eulalie Jensen (Mrs. Hemple), Willard Robertson (The Doctor), Harry Holman (Country Doctor), Lon Poff (Fat Man), Olin Howland (Jacob), Andre Charon (The General), Martha Mattox, Emma Ray (The Maiden Aunts).

This, the third version of Edna Ferber's Pulitzer Prize novel, was not so big at all, either at the box office or with the critics. First filmed as a silent in 1925, starring Colleen Moore, it was done as a short in 1930, as directed by Bryan Foy, starring Helen Jerome Eddy, John Litel, Gardner James, and Marian Marsh. This very short picture seems long as they attempt to portray many years in the life of Stanwyck, et al, and fail. O'Day is the young daughter of gambler Warwick, who sends her to a fancy school. She grows up to be Stanwyck and when Warwick dies without a cent in his trousers, she is out in the cold. Madison's father, Kibbee, is enlisted to help and he finds Stanwyck a job teaching school in a community of Dutch farmers in Illinois just after the turn of the century. She tutors Winslow (who grew up to be a popular entertainer in Los Angeles and, in the 1980s, was still performing as a one-man band) while living as a boarder in Hale's family home. Eventually, she marries older farmer Foxe, who spends much of his time tilling the old-fashioned way, refusing to make any adjustment to modern methods. Foxe's hard work kills him (thus putting the lie to the statement that hard work never killed anybody) and she is left with a young son, Moore, whom she loves and measures daily as the boy grows "so big." Moore grows into Albright and Winslow matures into Brent. Stanwyck wants Albright to study to be an architect but he disappoints her by preferring to hawk stocks and bonds, after quitting a job as an architect in training. Albright's boss's wife, LaRoy, arranges the job for him as she is fascinated by the youth. Meanwhile, Brent becomes a well known artist-sculptor and when he comes back to the small town after setting Europe on its ear with his creations, he tells Stanwyck that it is all due to her tutoring, as she exerted the greatest influence on him while he was growing up, and that he couldn't have done any of this without her as his mentor. Stanwyck is thrilled at this and even happier when her son, Albright, comes to her house with a new amour in tow, Davis. She is an artist and doesn't much respect Albright at first but when she meets Stanwyck, she sees that Albright comes from good stock and that he may eventually come to his senses and return to the world of architecture. Stanwyck and Brent become very affectionate toward each other, even though she's older. This was the only film in which Stanwyck and Davis appeared in the same scenes, although they did play in another movie together, HOLLYWOOD CANTEEN, but were never on screen at the same time. Irish-born Brent, a one-time IRA member, had been playing on the stage for years and was now appearing in his seventh film. In just two years, Davis had made eight films and did well in this, one of her larger roles since her first movie, BAD SISTER. The major trouble with this version of SO BIG was that so much action and material was jammed into the brief running time that there was no opportunity to flesh out the characters. A somewhat more successful version was attempted in 1953 with Jane Wyman and Nancy Olson in the Stanwyck and Davis roles.

p, Jack L. Warner; d, William A. Wellman; w, J. Grubb Alexander, Robert Lord (based on the novel by Edna Ferber); ph, Sid Hickox; m, W. Franke Harling; ed, William Holmes; art d, Jack Okey; cos, Orry-Kelly.

Historical Drama (PR:A MPAA:NR)

SO BIG*** (1953) 101m WB bw

Jane Wyman (Selina DeJong), Sterling Hayden (Pervus DeJong), Nancy Olson (Dallas O'Mara), Steve Forrest (Dirk DeJong), Elisabeth Fraser (Julie Hempel), Martha Hyer (Paula Hempel), Walter Coy (Roelf Pool), Richard Beymer (Roelf, Age 12-16), Tommy Rettig (Dirk), Age 8, Roland Winters (Klaas Pool), Jacques Aubuchon (August Hempel), Ruth Swanson (Maartje Pool), Dorothy Christy (Widow Paarlenberg), Oliver Blake (Adam Ooms), Lily Kemble Cooper (Miss Fister), Noralee Norman (Geertje Pool), Jill Janssen (Jozina Pool), Kerry Donnelly (Paul, Age 8), Kenneth Osmond (Eugene, Age 9), Lotte Stein (Meena), Vera Miles, Evan Loew, Frances Osborne, Jean Garvin, Carol Grel (Girls), Grandon Rhodes (Bainbridge),

Bud Osborne (Wagon Driver), Dorothy Granger, Elizabeth Russell (Ladies), Dick Alexander (Bidder), David McMahon (Cop), Kenner G. Kemp (Hempel's Chauffeur), Paul Brinegar (Farmer), Marjorie Bennett (Housekeeper), Frank Ferguson (Draftsman), Douglas Evans (Mr. Hollis).

This is the fourth go-around for Edna Ferber's sprawling novel. The first was a silent, then there was a short, then the 1932 Stanwyck version, and finally this one, which was the best of the lot. It encompasses 25 years in Wyman's life and it is a tribute to the makeup crew that they were able to pull it off. Wyman is from a well-to-do family and, when she is suddenly poor, she takes a job in a Dutch community in Illinois as a teacher, meets and marries Hayden and lives him with the arduous farm labors, tasks that she was hardly raised to do. They have a son, Rettig (who would go on to become famous as "Lassie's" best pal), who eventually grows up to be Forrest. Meanwhile, she makes friends with Beymer, a gifted young lad who aspires to be a pianist. He matures into Coy. Forrest has an eye for architecture but a penchant for money so he eschews the creative art for a position with a merchandise company where he works as a sales promotion executive, over and above the protestations of Wyman, who knows that her son is artistically talented and feels that he is wasting his time pursuing money. Coy (in a role that was originally an artist) is Wyman's best friend, a man true to his calling, and she finds in him a surrogate child who understands that money isn't everything and that "ars gratia artis" should triumph. Forrest meets Olson, an artist trained in Paris, and she helps the floundering youth make his decision in favor of the far more rewarding, though not as commercial, world of Frank Lloyd Wright breakthrough architecture. A good production, but a bit inflated, SO BIG commits the same error as the 1932 picture in that it stuffs a quarter of a century and many characters into not enough time. This was Beymer's second film, after INDISCRETION OF AN AMERICAN WIFE, in a spotty acting career that he eventually gave up to become an independent filmmaker and cinematographer. In a small role as a disciplinarian farmer, note Roland Winters, who, well into his eighties was still working in between stints at his favorite haunt, the Players Club, at New York's Gramercy Park. He was the third "Charlie Chan."

p, Henry Blanke; d, Robert Wise; w, John Twist (based on the novel by Edna Ferber); ph, Ellsworth Fredericks; m, Max Steiner; ed, Thomas Reilly; art d, John Beckman; cos, Milo Anderson, Howard Shoup.

Historical Drama (PR:A MPAA:NR)

SO BRIGHT THE FLAME (SEE: GIRL IN WHITE, THE, 1952)

SO DARK THE NIGHT***½ (1946) 70m COL bw

Steven Geray (Henri Cassin), Micheline Cheirel (Nanette Michaud), Eugene Borden (Pierre Michaud), Ann Codee (Mama Michaud), Egon Brecher (Dr. Boncourt), Helen Freeman (Widow Bridelle), Theodore Gottlieb (Georges), Gregory Gay (Commissionaire Grande), Jean Del Val (Dr. Manet), Paul Marion (Leon Achard), Emil Ramu (Pere Cortot), Louis Mercier (Jean Duval), Billy Snyder (Chauffeur), Frank Arnold (Antoine), Adrienne d'Ambricourt (Newspaper Woman), Marcelle Corday (Proprietor), Alphonse Martel (Bank President), Andre Marsaudon (Postmaster), Francine Bordeaux (Flower Girl), Esther Zeitlin (Peasant Woman), Cynthia Gaylord (Bootblack).

An outstanding film noir programmer, SO DARK THE NIGHT is set in a small provincial village in France and stars Geray as a respected super sleuth from the Paris Surete. Taking his first vacation in 11 years, Geray travels to a family-run inn out in the country. There he meets and falls in love with the beautiful young Cheirel, the daughter of inn owners Borden and Codee. Encouraged by her mercenary mother, Cheirel responds to Geray's romantic advances despite the fact she is engaged to local farmer Marion. The middle-aged detective soon proposes to the pretty young girl and she accepts. Not to be denied, an angry Marion informs Geray that if the wedding takes place he will hound Cheirel and never give their marriage a moment's peace. Realizing that she truly loves Marion, Cheirel deserts Geray and runs off with the farmer. The next day the couple is found murdered. Outraged that killers would dare test his investigative powers by murdering his bride-to-be, Geray becomes obsessed with solving the crimes. With only a muddy footprint as a clue, he helps the local police with the investigation. Soon after, Cheirel's mother, Codee, is found murdered as well. Frustrated by his lack of progress, Geray goes back to Paris to give the experienced police artist a try at identifying the killer from the footprint. What the artist comes up with is deeply disturbing to Geray–the killer greatly resembles him. Shaken, Geray tries writing with his left hand and is horrified when the handwriting exactly matches the notes the killer has left. Convinced he has a split personality, Geray turns himself in. Unfortunately, the strain of custody causes Geray's evil side to become dominant and he escapes the prison. Returning to the inn, he is caught by police and fatally shot just as he is about to kill the owner, Borden. As he lies dying, Geray sees his face as it was when he first arrived on holiday in the inn's window. The good and evil images merge into one and, with the last of his strength, Geray smashes the reflections, thus "catching" the killer. Despite the failure of this low-budget Hollywood production to convincingly portray its French setting, SO DARK THE NIGHT is an engrossing crime drama that succeeds on many levels. As a character study it is amazingly complex and draws a detailed portrait of the tortured detective played by Geray. The age-old conflict of a lawman becoming so embroiled in catching criminals that he begins to think like one is taken to its extreme here by having the master detective actually becoming the hunter and the hunted. On a visual level the film is extremely effective, making brilliant use of light, shadow, rain, and a motif of frames within frames that trap the characters in their environment. SO DARK THE NIGHT is a bit obscure but well worth uncovering.

p, Ted Richmond; d, Joseph H. Lewis; w, Martin Berkeley, Dwight Babcock (based on a story by Aubrey Wisberg); ph, Burnett Guffey; m, Morris W. Stoloff, Hugo Friedhofer; ed, Jerome Thoms; art d, Carl Anderson; set d, William Kiernan.

Crime   (PR:C   MPAA:NR)

SO DEAR TO MY HEART****   (1949) 82m Disney/RKO

Burl Ives (Uncle Hiram), Beulah Bondi (Granny Kincaid), Harry Carey (Judge), Luana Patten (Tildy), Bobby Driscoll (Jeremiah Kincaid), Raymond Bond (Storekeeper), Daniel Haight (Storekeeper's Son), Walter Soderling (Villager), Matt Willis (Horse Trainer), Spelman B. Collins, Voices of John Beal, Ken Carson, Bob Stanton, The Rhythmaires.

A lovely, heartwarming live-action film with several superb animation sequences that blend perfectly and never intrude. Set around the turn of the century in Indiana, it tells the story of young Driscoll, a boy who yearns to own a horse like the great trotter "Dan Patch" and who names his pet lamb "Danny" after the famous horse. Driscoll lives with his grandmother, Bondi, and raises his lamb with love and affection, even though the animal is adventuresome and sometimes a problem. Uncle Hiram is Ives, the local blacksmith, and he supports Driscoll's love for the animal. Ives thinks that the lamb just might be championship calibre and encourages Driscoll to enter it in the county fair, but Bondi doesn't want Driscoll's mind filled with such ideas. It will cost a few bucks to get to the fair and pay the entry fee and Driscoll is determined to do it, so he takes a job gathering honey when storekeeper Bond tells him that honey is scarce. With his young companion, Patten, to help him, Driscoll amasses enough honey (at 10 cents the ounce) to raise $17. The fair is fast approaching but Driscoll's hopes are dashed when the lamb escapes. He chases after it during a thunderous storm and Bondi has to bring the shattered boy home, saying that his only reason for feeling so hurt is not the love for the animal, rather it is a desire to win a blue ribbon for himself. Driscoll makes a deal with his Maker and says that if he can find the lamb alive, he won't take it to the fair but merely be content in loving and caring for the animal. Next day, Driscoll finds the lamb and brings it home, announcing to Bondi what his deal with God was. Bondi is sincerely touched by Driscoll and counters that she has made a deal with God that if He allowed the lamb to live through the storm, she'd make certain that he would be taken to the fair. Since she has known God a good deal longer than Driscoll, she reckons that her agreement with the Lord supercedes Driscoll's. Driscoll takes the lamb to the fair where Carey is the judge of the livestock. The black animal has no pedigree, which is against him, and when the little creature pushes Carey, that also stands him in bad stead. Driscoll figures he can't win the blue ribbon but is happy to have been there and to have entered his pet. Another sheep wins the prize and Driscoll is taking his home when he hears that he's been awarded a Special Prize, the first time in four decades that this has been given, for having taken an animal without a lineage and making it into a prize sheep by dint of affection only. Driscoll and the others return to their Brown County area and get off the railroad train where the entire town greets them as though he were a national hero as the picture ends. A simple tale, often funny, always intelligent and never overly sentimental, SO DEAR TO MY HEART's animated sequences were used as part of Driscoll's fantasies as he pored over his scrapbook and a wise owl came to life to illustrate the importance of staying with one's dream, then in a scene where a souvenir program from the fair erupts into life, plus others. The director, Schuster, had been under contract at Fox and when Disney saw his MY FRIEND FLICKA, he arranged to have Schuster come to the Burbank lot to helm this movie. Driscoll and Patten were under contract at Disney and couldn't have been better in their roles, especially Driscoll, who was as natural as grass growing. This was Carey's last screen appearance after a distinguished career. He died in 1947 before the movie was released and never did see his excellent work. Atmospherically correct, SO DEAR TO MY HEART was an indication of Disney's yearning for the uncomplicated days of his own youth, something he brought to fruition when he built Disneyland, with its Main Street that evokes memories of a time when America was young. Tunes from a corps of writers included: "Sourwood Mountain," "Billy Boy" (sung by Ives, traditional), "So Dear To My Heart" (Ticker Freeman, Irving Taylor (who would later go on to make a hysterical album of his own entitled "The Garbage Collector Of Beverly Hills")), "County Fair" (Mel Torme and Robert Wells, who also wrote "The Christmas Song"), "Stick-To-It-Ivity," "Ol' Dan Patch" (by Eliot Daniel, Larry Morey), "It's Watcha Do With Watcha Got" (Don Raye, Gene De Paul), and "Lavender Blue (Dilly Dilly)" (a traditional tune that was adapted by Morey and Daniel well enough to merit an Oscar nomination). SO DEAR TO MY HEART is highly recommended for children. Special kudos to Ken Darby's vocal direction, Edward H. Plumb's orchestrations and the superb cartoon story work from William Peet, Ken Anderson, and Marc Davis.

p, Walt Disney, Perce Pearce; d, Harold Schuster; cartoon d, Hamilton Luske; w, John Tucker Battle, Maurice Rapf, Ted Sears (based on the book

Midnight and Jeremiah by Sterling North); ph, Winton C. Hoch; m, Paul J. Smith; ed, Thomas Scott, Lloyd L. Richardson; art d, John Ewing; set d, Mac Alper; animated, Eric Larson, John Lounsbery, Hal King, Milt Kahl, Les Clark, Don Lusk, Marvin Woodward; spec eff (anim), George Rowley, Joshua Meador, Dan McManus.

Historical Drama/Musical   (PR:AAA   MPAA:NR)

SO ENDS OUR NIGHT***   (1941) 120m Loew-Lewin/UA bw

Fredric March (Joseph Steiner), Margaret Sullavan (Ruth Holland), Frances Dee (Marie Steiner), Glenn Ford (Ludwig Kern), Anna Sten (Lilo), Erich von Stroheim (Brenner), Allan Brett (Merrill), Joseph Cawthorn (Potzloch), Leonid Kinskey (The Chicken), Alexander Granach (The Pole), Roman Bohnen (Mr. Kern), Sig Rumann (Ammers), William Stack (Prof. Meyer), Lionel Royce (Barnekrogg), Ernst Deutsch (Dr. Behr), Spencer Charters (Swiss Policeman), Hans Schumm (Kobel), Walter Stahl (Police Captain), Philip Van Zandt (Bachman), Fredrik Vogeding (Gestapo Colonel), Joe Marks (The Bird), Greta Rozan (Elvira), James Bush (Herbert), Emory Parnell (Weiss), Kate MacKenna (Mrs. Ammers), Edith Angold (Ammer's Sister-in-Law), Edward Fielding (Durant), William von Brincken (German Official), Gisela Werbiseck (The Harpy), Lisa Golm (The Pale Woman), Adolf Milar (Black Pig Proprietor).

A wartime drama dealing with the struggles of three Europeans trying to escape persecution by the Nazis. March, a strong-willed German outspoken in his disapproval of the new regime, leaves his wife behind just as Hitler overtakes Austria. While on the run he meets a young Jewish pair–Ford and Sullavan–also seeking asylum. With falsified passports and identification papers, the trio make their way across Europe–sometimes together, sometimes splitting up. They travel through Prague, Zurich, and Geneva, each time fearing that the officials will discover their game. March learns that his wife, Dee, has been taken ill and is dying in Austria. Risking his life, he goes to see her before she passes away, and then, after a fight, he carries Nazi von Stroheim with him to his death. Meanwhile, Ford and Sullavan find safety and romance in Paris. While lengthy at 120 minutes and somewhat repetitive in its telling of the trio's exploits, SO ENDS OUR NIGHT offers some virtuoso performances. March, as usual, is effective, as is Dee in her role as his wife. Von Stroheim fills the screen with his foreboding "man you love to hate" image. Receiving the most favorable raves, however, were a 24-year-old baby-faced Ford and Sullavan (on loan for a one-picture deal from Universal), whose on screen romance proved to be thoroughly convincing and touching.

p, David L. Loew, Albert Lewin; d, John Cromwell; w, Talbot Jennings (based on the novel Flotsam by Erich Maria Remarque); ph, William Daniels; m, Louis Gruenberg; ed, William Reynolds; art d, Jack Otterson; spec eff, Jack Cosgrove.

Drama   (PR:A   MPAA:NR)

SO EVIL MY LOVE***½   (1948, Brit.) 112m PAR bw

Ray Milland (Mark Bellis), Ann Todd (Olivia Harwood), Geraldine Fitzgerald (Susan Courtney), Moira Lister (Kitty Feathers), Raymond Lovell (Edgar), Roderick Lovell (Sir John Curle), Muriel Aked (Miss Shoebridge), Finlay Currie (Dr. Krylie), Ivor Barnard (Mr. Watson), Hugh Griffith (Coroner), Gus Le Fuevre (Dr. Pound), Clarence Bigge (Dr. Cunningham), Leonie Lamartine (Proprietress), Leo G. Carroll (Jarvis), Raymond Huntley (Henry Courtney), Martita Hunt (Mrs. Courtney), Zena Marshall.

Novelist Joseph Shearing specialized in using real cases which took place in Victorian England, altering them for fictional purposes and writing bestsellers, many later used as the basis for films, including MOSS ROSE and MARK OF CAIN. British-born director Allen and Milland returned home to make this mean-spirited suspense drama that was a little longer on verbiage than was absolutely necessary. Todd is the recently widowed wife of a missionary in Jamaica. She returns to England to begin a new life and meets Milland on the trip. Milland is a charming snake sought by police for several nefarious deeds and Todd is vulnerable to his winning ways. When there's a disease outbreak on their ship, Todd helps Milland through his malaria fever crisis. They arrive in London and Todd settles into her suburban home where she must now take in boarders to make ends meet. Milland arrives, moves in, and proclaims his love for her, though anyone can see through his sham. He's marking time and living there free as he plans his next schemes. Todd's old friend is Fitzgerald, an alcoholic who is married to a man she doesn't love, Huntley. Before marrying Huntley, Fitzgerald had written some letters revealing indiscretions to Todd. Milland sees that as an opportunity to make a few bucks as Fitzgerald's husband is quite wealthy and she has access to some of that. Todd is quickly enlisted in the scheme because of her love for Milland, for whom she'll do anything. Huntley finds out about matters and, through his legal pals, uncovers Milland's seedy history. Todd puts some poison in Huntley's tonic and keeps mum when Fitzgerald is arrested for the man's murder. Milland has now fallen in love with Todd and they are planning to leave England. Milland's ex-girl friend arrives, not knowing about Todd, and blurts out that she and he were to have one last tryst. Todd is angered, meets Milland later, and drives a knife into his worthless body as they ride in a taxi. Then she orders the driver to take her to the police station where, it is to be assumed, the beans will be spilled. Leo G. Carroll is seen in a small role. He alternated between his native England and the U.S., eventually starring in two TV series, "Topper" and as "Mr. Waverly," chief of spy operations on "The Man From UNCLE." England specializes in superb actors who are willing to take small parts and fashion them into gems. This film is filled with those actors and each role sparkles.

p, Hal B. Wallis; d, Lewis Allen; w, Leonard Spigelgass, Ronald Millar (based on the novel by Joseph Shearing); ph, Max Greene; m, Victor Young, William Alwyn; ed, Vera Campbell, Leonard Trumm; md, Muir Mathieson; art d, Thomas H. Morahan; cos, Edith Head.

Mystery   **(PR:C   MPAA:NR)**

SO EVIL SO YOUNG**   (1961, Brit.) 77m Danziger/UA c

Jill Ireland (*Ann*), Ellen Pollock (*Miss Smith*), John Charlesworth (*Tom*), Jocelyn Britton (*Lucy*), Joan Haythorne (*Matron*), John Longden (*Turner*), Sheila Whittingham (*Mary*), Bernice Swanson (*Claire*), Colin Tapley (*Inspector*).

The cruelties of reform school are realistically exposed in this story about a girl wrongly accused of a robbery. Placed in a reformatory that is run like a prisoner-of-war camp, she attempts to escape to prove her innocence, but first must contend with the practices of an evil headmistress. This film has never been shown theatrically in the U.S., but it should be.

p, Brian Taylor; d, Godfrey Grayson; w, Mark Grantham.

Crime/Drama   **(PR:A   MPAA:NR)**

SO FINE***   (1981) 91m WB c

Ryan O'Neal (*Bobby*), Jack Warden (*Jack*), Mariangela Melato (*Lira*), Richard Kiel (*Eddie*), Fred Gwynne (*Chairman Lincoln*), Mike Kellin (*Sam Schlotzman*), David Rounds (*Prof. McCarthy*), Joel Stedman (*Prof. Yarnell*), Angela Pietro Pinto (*Sylvia*), Michael Lombard (*Jay Augustine*), Jessica James (*Vicki*), Bruce Millholland (*Sir Alec*), Merwin Goldsmith (*Dave*), Irving Metzman (*Accountant*), Lois DeBanzie (*Waitress in House of Pancakes*), Rick Lieberman (*Rick*), Anthony Siricco, Jr, Michael LaGuardia (*Mr. Eddie's Associates*), Chip Zien (*Wise Guy in Disco*), Bill Luhrs (*Gas Station Attendant*), Dick Boccelli (*Lino*), Lydia Laurens (*Manicurist*), Margaret Hall (*Saleslady*), Sally Jane Heit (*Shopper*), Henry Lawrence (*Security Guard*), James Hong, Danny Kwan (*Orientals*), Paul Price (*Man in Towel*), Tyra Farrell (*Receptionist*), Joseph Montabo, Jose Machado (*Shipping Clerks*), Sophie Schwab (*Sophie*), Jerome Binder (*Sy*), Hy Mencher (*Hy*), Maria Tai, Beda Elliot (*Seamstresses*), Joseph Ilardi (*Gus*), John Bentley (*Elevator Starter*), Herb Schlein (*Delivery Boy*), Alma Cuervo (*Prof. Adler*), John Stockwell (*Jim*), Beverly May (*Mrs. Lincoln*), P.K. Fields (*Coed in Office*), Webster Whinery, Kathie Flusk (*Couple in Volkswagon*), Randy Jones, Christopher Loomis (*Campus Cops*), Hyla Marrow, Gail Lawrence (*Nuns*), Martha Gaylord (*Texas Buyer*), Bernie McInerny (*St. Paul Buyer*), Alan Leach, Pamela Lewis (*Buyers*), Jim Jansen (*Conductor*), Pierre Epstein (*Prompter*), Tony Aylward, Todd Isaacson (*Stage Managers*), Adam Stolarsky (*Enzo*), Judith Cohen (*Renata*).

SO FINE runs the comedy gamut from high camp to low farce, from satirical satiation to sophisticated shenanigans often bordering on the screwball. Writer/director Andrew Bergman was involved in co-writing BLAZING SADDLES as well as having a solo credit on THE BROTHERS-IN-LAW. He is also a good novelist and produced a pair of funny hard-boiled detective comedies "Hollywood And LeVine" and "The Big Kiss-Off Of 1944." His first directorial job is not as successful as his writing, perhaps because he tried to jam every possible style and genre into this piece for fear that he might never have the opportunity again. O'Neal is a professor of English who often quotes Shakespeare when he can't think of anything to say. His father, Warden, is a clothing manufacturer who is being menaced by Kiel, the seven-footer who will always be remembered as "Jaws," the gargantuan villain who chased after James Bond. Kiel wants to see Warden out of business and planted beneath the sod because Warden can't pay off the debt he accumulated at a usurious interest rate. Warden pleads with O'Neal to come to work for the firm and help save the business before it goes bankrupt. O'Neal has been protected from the shark-infested world of garment manufacturing, but must now exit the groves of academe in order to aid the family firm. No sooner is O'Neal in operation when Melato, hot-to-trot a woman if there ever was one, falls hard for him and chases him as avidly as Keil is chasing Warden. One major difference and problem, Melato is married to Kiel, a jealous type indeed: so now there are two members of the family on Kiel's hit list. After O'Neal and Melato have a tryst, he puts on a pair of her jeans, which are too tight. The rear splits, exposing O'Neal's behind. O'Neal puts a plastic piece in to replace the split rear and has now discovered a new fashion, bare-bottom jeans. As it turns out, it's a fortuitous error. Warden sees it and thinks it's a good idea. He begins manufacturing the design and business booms. The company is saved and O'Neal thinks he can go back to his old job at the university. The pneumatic Melato follows him to school and is, in turn, tailed by Kiel, making for a new old-fashioned sex farce. Somehow, the four lead actors wind up on stage during an amateur production of Verdi's opera "Otello," and the result is a forced farce that attempts to resemble A NIGHT AT THE OPERA, but instead looks more like a "Tom And Jerry" cartoon. O'Neal shows that he can play comedy as he did before in PAPER MOON and WHAT'S UP, DOC? He's often overlooked as a light comedian, perhaps

because he's just too pretty. Kiel, who is, in real life, one of the gentlest human beings in show business, proves he's not just another ugly face as he keeps the threat of mayhem going. Melato goes a trifle too far as a woman whose brain and body seem to be there only as a life-support system for her genitalia. The person who must receive the most applause is Warden, who does his usual bang-up job as a second banana with customary finesse. He is the quint essential supporting player and even though we always know we're watching Warden, everything he does is on the money. Morricone's score helps the pace and bounces along as frantically as the visuals. It's a near-miss for everyone concerned and not the best choice for Bergman's debut although it might serve for a tired businessman coming home on a Friday night after a hard day at the plant or office, who wants to just sit there with a brew and not have to think. Rough language and some flashes of flesh make this a no-no for children.

p, Mike Lobell; d&w, Andrew Bergman; ph, James A. Contner (Technicolor); m, Ennio Morricone; ed, Alan Heim; prod d, Santo Loquasto; art d, Paul Eads; set d, Les Bloom; cos, Rose Trimarco, Bill Christians; ch, Grover Dale.

Comedy   **Cas.**   **(PR:C-O   MPAA:R)**

SO GOES MY LOVE**½   (1946) 88m UNIV bw (GB: A GENIUS IN
                                                                THE FAMILY)

Myrna Loy (*Jane*), Don Ameche (*Hiram Stephen Maxim*), Rhys Williams (*Magel*), Bobby Driscoll (*Percy Maxim*), Richard Gaines (*Mr. Josephus*), Molly Lamont (*Anty Gannet*), Sarah Haden (*Bridget*), Renie Riano (*Emily*), Clara Blandick (*Mrs. Meade*), John Gallaudet (*Theodore*), John Phillips (*Raymond*), Bruce Edwards (*Weldon*), Howard Freeman (*Willis*), Wheaton Chambers (*Committee Man*), Pierre Watkin (*Committee Man*).

Hiram Stephen Maxim was an inventor in the 1800s and his son, Hiram Percy Maxim, wrote a book about his late father which served, as the basis for this romantic comedy. Once again, Ameche is an inventor (after having played Bell in THE STORY OF ALEXANDER GRAHAM BELL, his name became a slangy synonym for the telephone) who is struggling. Loy is a Bostonian who seeks a wealthy husband but winds up with Ameche. The movie depicts their travails, struggles, hopes, joys, and domestic squabbles. Ameche is extremely eccentric (like many geniuses) and Loy is the stability he needs. They have a son, Driscoll, and the relationship between he and Ameche is a stand-out in the story. It's quite episodic and there seems to have been too judicious an editor because certain motivating scenes appear to have been snipped. The nostalgic settings contribute to the pleasure of the film which is as light as a gauze banner wafting in the wind. Gaines does a small role as the rich man to whom Loy is engaged when she falls for the much more exciting Ameche. Williams does a short but telling cameo as a nutty artist whom Loy hires to paint a portrait of Ameche. Loy was 3 years older than Ameche when this picture was made (she was 41, he was 38) but you'd never know it as her beauty continued long after others' had faded. She'd recently married writer Gene Markey, a man who knew his way around attractive women, having previously been the husband of Joan Bennett and Hedy Lamarr. Markey was her third mate (of four) with the prior two being producer Arthur Hornblow, Jr. (RUGGLES OF RED GAP, GASLIGHT, THE ASPHALT JUNGLE, many more), and John Hertz, Jr., the man who put us all in the driver's seat. Good music from Hans Salter, who used his initials H.J. in the credits because the German name of Hans was not very popular in the days immediately following WW II.

p, Bruce Manning, Jack H. Skirball; d, Frank Ryan; w, Manning, James Clifden (based on the book *A Genius in the Family* by Hiram Percy Maxim); ph, Joseph Valentine; m, Hans J. Salter; ed, Ted J. Kent; md, Salter; art d, Lionel Banks; cos, Travis Banton, Vera West.

Biography/Comedy   **(PR:A   MPAA:NR)**

SO IT'S SUNDAY**½   (1932) 69m SONO bw

Jess Devorska (*Isodore Levine*), Charles Hill Mailes (*Sean O'Brien*), Sharon Lynn (*Leah Levine*), Dolores Brinkman (*Rachel Levine*), Vester Pegg (*Patrick O'Brien*), Rosa Rosanova (*Mrs. Cohen*), J. Farrell MacDonald (*James O'Brien*).

MacDonald and Devorska play competing clothiers in this big-city Irish/ Jewish conflict comedy that has Lynn, Devorska's daughter, falling in love with Mailes, scion of the house of MacDonald. The ethnic conflict is resolved through the good offices of matchmaker and busybody Rosanova, who fakes a heart attack to bring the families together for a happy ending in this clone of the hit play "Abie's Irish Rose."

d, Edward I. Luddy; w, Abel Ingram (based on his story); ph, Edward Kull.

Comedy   **(PR:A   MPAA:NR)**

SO LITTLE TIME**½   (1953, Brit.) 88m Mayflower/MacDonald bw

John Bailey (*Phillipe de Malvines*), Maria Schell (*Nicole de Malvines*), Gabrielle Dorziat (*Mme. de Malvines*), Stanley van Beers (*Prof. Perronet*), Oscar Quitak (*Gerard*), Barbara Mullen (*Anna*), Harold Lang (*Lt. Seger*), David Hurst (*Blumel*), Marius Goring (*Col. Hohensee*), Andree Melly (*Paulette*), Olga Lowe (*Florine*), Wolf Frees (*German Doctor*), Lucie Mannheim (*Lotte Schonberg*), Alison Peline (*Vivianne*), Jeremy Geidt (*Gilles*).

When German troops commandeer the house of a Belgian aristocrat, one of the officers, Goring, falls in love with Schell, the aristocrat's daughter. Goring, a concert pianist in civilian life, spends time with Schell, teaching her how to play the piano, but because of her family's hatred for the Germans she must betray her love or die. A familiar war story which is handled with a fair amount of insight. Shura Cherkassky performs the piano solos.

p, Maxwell Setton, Aubrey Baring; d, Compton Bennett; w, John Cresswell (based on the novel *Je Ne Suis Pas Une Heroine* by Noelle Henry); ph, Oswald Morris; m, Louis Levy, Robert Gill; ed, V. Sagovsky; cos, Julie Harris.

War Drama   **(PR:A   MPAA:NR)**

SO LONG AT THE FAIR***½   (1951, Brit.) 90m
                                                   Gainsborough/EL-Rank bw

Jean Simmons *(Vicky Barton)*, Dirk Bogarde *(George Hathaway)*, David Tomlinson *(Johnny Barton)*, Marcel Poncin *(Narcisse)*, Cathleen Nesbitt *(Mme. Herve)*, Honor Blackman *(Rhoda O'Donovan)*, Betty Warren *(Mrs. O'Donovan)*, Eugene Deckers *(Day Porter)*, Zena Marshall *(Nina)*, Felix Aylmer *(British Consul)*, Andre Morell *(Dr. Hart)*, Austin Trevor *(Police Commissaire)*, Nelly Arno *(Mme. Verni)*, Natasha Sokolova *(Charlotte)*.

A highly inventive and original plot makes up for the lack of deep characterization in this movie that keeps audiences guessing. It's 1889 in Paris where the Great Exhibition is taking place. (This was sort of a Worlds Fair, but since another one had been done in the U.S., they had to call it something different.) The city is packed with people and enjoying good weather when Simmons and her brother, Tomlinson, arrive from England to partake of the pleasure of Paris. They have separate rooms and when she wakes up one morning after a night on the town, she can't find him. Further, there is no evidence of his having been there at all. His name doesn't appear on the hotel's register; even his room no longer exists! She appeals to all of the hotel's staff to no avail; everyone denies even seeing him. She goes to the British consul, Aylmer, and to the local police chief, Trevor, but neither of them find any merit in her story, especially since no one at the hotel will back it up. Simmons is beside herself with grief and anguish and doesn't know where to turn. Then she meets Bogarde, a British artist on a short trip to Paris, and he helps her unravel the mystery of the missing Tomlinson. Their investigation leads them all around the city and they finally find Tomlinson in an isolation ward of a local hospital where they ultimately learn the truth: Tomlinson had come down with the deadly bubonic plague. If the word ever got out that the plague was in Paris, the city would have emptied in an instant. The medical authorities felt that they had successfully isolated all the cases when Tomlinson awakened, complained of being ill to the hotel management, and was whisked away. Rather than expose the truth, the hotel, with the nod of the city authorities, concocted this plot to erase Tomlinson from existence until such time as he was cured or dead. Good suspense from start to finish, with Simmons and Bogarde making a fine pair of inadvertent sleuths set against the glories of The City Of Light. In a small role, note the beauteous Honor Blackman (about 24) before she achieved international fame in the role of "Pussy Galore" in GOLDFINGER.

p, Betty E. Box; d, Terence Fisher, Antony Darnborough; w, Hugh Mills, Anthony Thorne (based on the novel by Thorne); ph, Reginald Wyer; m, Benjamin Frankel; ed, Gordon Hales; md, Frankel; art d, George Provis; cos, Elizabeth Haffenden; spec eff, Bill Warrington, Leslie Bowie.

Mystery   **(PR:A   MPAA:NR)**

SO LONG, BLUE BOY**   (1973) 100m Maryon/Dakota c

Arthur Franz *(Ed Rilke)*, Rick Gates *(Isaiah Jenkinson)*, Neile Adams McQueen *(Julie Stevens)*, Richard Rowley *(Dean)*, Pamela Collins *(Cathy)*, Anne Seymour *(Martha)*, Richard McMurray *(Eli)*, Henry Brandon *(Buck)*.

Without attempting to make gay themes more accessible to a general audience, this feature realistically portrays the problems a homosexual has in finding and maintaining a fulfilling relationship in a straight world. Gates plays a young sculptor having an affair with aging professor Franz, which tragically ends when Franz is accidentally killed by his lover. The sculptor then has a heated affair with one of his male models, but this also ends when the model (Rowley) decides he likes women more than men. Straight audiences will find SO LONG, BLUE BOY hard to empathize with; perhaps the greatest reason why they should make an attempt to see it.

p, Kenneth Sprague; d, Gerald Gordon; w, David Long, Chris Long; ph, James A. Larson (CFI Color); m, Bruce Buckingham; ed, Al Street; art d, Robinson Royce, Barren Rouche.

Drama   **(PR:O   MPAA:R)**

SO LONG LETTY**   (1929) 64m WB bw

Charlotte Greenwood *(Letty Robbins)*, Grant Withers *(Harry Miller)*, Bert Roach *(Tommy Robbins)*, Claude Gillingwater *(Uncle Claude Davis)*, Helen Foster *(Sally Davis)*, Marion Byron *(Ruth Davis)*, Patsy Ruth Miller *(Grace Miller)*, Hallam Cooley *(Clarence De Brie, Composer)*, Harry Gribbon *(Joe Casey)*, Lloyd Ingraham *(Judge)*, Jack Grey *(Police Sergeant)*.

Greenwood stars as the title character, the eccentric wife of Roach, who allows a substitute wife to sit in for a while when her husband's wealthy uncle pays them a visit. Her hope is that the uncle will give them his fortune when he dies, but she fears her personality will be too much for him. Includes the songs: "One Sweet Little Yes," "Clowning," "Beauty Shop," "Am I Blue?," "Let Me Have My Dreams," "My Strongest Weakness is You," (by Grant Clarke, Harry Akst), "Down Among the Sugar Cane" (by Clarke, Charles Tobias), and "So Long Letty" (Earl Carroll).

d, Lloyd Bacon; w, Arthur Caesar, Robert Lord (based on the play by Oliver Morosco, Earl Carroll, Elmer Harris); ph, James Van Trees; ed, Jack Killifer.

Musical/Comedy   **(PR:A   MPAA:NR)**

SO LONG PHILIPPINE   (SEE: ADIEU PHILIPPINE, 1963, Fr.)

SO PROUDLY WE HAIL****   (1943) 126m PAR bw

Claudette Colbert *(Lt. Janet Davidson)*, Paulette Goddard *(Lt. Joan O'Doul)*, Veronica Lake *(Lt. Olivia D'Arcy)*, George Reeves *(Lt. John Summers)*, Barbara Britton *(Lt. Rosemary Larson)*, Walter Abel *(Chaplain)*, Sonny Tufts *(Kansas)*, Mary Servoss *(Capt. "Ma" McGregor)*, Ted Hecht *(Dr. Jose Bardia)*, John Litel *(Dr. Harrison)*, Dr. Hugh Ho Chang *(Ling Chee)*, Mary Treen *(Lt. Sadie Schwartz)*, Kitty Kelly *(Lt. Ethel Armstrong)*, Helen Lynd *(Lt. Elsie Bollenbacher)*, Lorna Gray *(Lt. Tony Dacolli)*, Dorothy Adams *(Lt. Irma Emerson)*, Ann Doran *(Lt. Betty Peterson)*, Jean Willes *(Lt. Carol Johnson)*, Lynn Walker *(Lt. Fay Leonard)*, Joan Tours *(Lt. Margaret Stevenson)*, Jan Wiley *(Lt. Lynne Hopkins)*, Mimi Doyle, Julia Faye, Hazel Keener, Frances Morris *(Nurses)*, James Bell *(Col. White)*, Dick Hogan *(Flight Lt. Archie McGregor)*, Bill Goodwin *(Capt. O'Rourke)*, James Flavin *(Capt. O'Brien)*, Byron Foulger *(Mr. Larson)*, Elsa Janssen *(Mrs. Larson)*, Richard Crane *(Georgie Larson)*, Boyd Davis *(Col. Mason)*, Will Wright *(Col. Clark)*, James Millican *(Young Ensign)*, Damian O'Flynn *(1st Young Doctor)*, Roy Gordon *(Ship's Captain)*, Jack Luden *(Steward)*, Harry Strang *(Maj. Arthur)*, Edward Dew *(Capt. Lawrence)*, Yvonne De Carlo *(Girl)*, William Forrest *(Major, San Francisco Dock)*, Isabel Cooper, Amparo Antenercruz, Linda Brent *(Filipino Nurses)*, Victor Kilian, Jr. *(Corporal)*, Edward Earle, Byron Shores *(Doctors)*, Hugh Prosser *(Captain)*, Charles Lester *(Soldier)*.

A surprisingly unglamorous Hollywood depiction of the lives of three nurses--Goddard, Lake, and Colbert--who survive the battles at Bataan and Corregidor in WW II. The film begins with a group of Army nurses arriving by ship in the U.S. They then relate their story in flashback, beginning in December of 1941. After the attack on Pearl Harbor, the Hawaii-bound ship the trio is on is diverted to Bataan, and finally to Corregidor. Along the way, the girls witness war at its most brutal, but also find time for relaxation and romance. Never, however, does SO PROUDLY WE HAIL fall victim to the glamour usually associated with its pin-up stars. Sandrich's direction from Scott's screenplay instead concentrates on the ugly realities of war and such painful scenes as a mother standing by as her son has both legs amputated. All three leads are superbly cast--Colbert shines as the mother-hen nurse who avoids romance and eventually winds up married to Reeves; the angry Lake fights a private battle against the Japanese, who killed her boy friend at Pearl Harbor; and the showy Goddard evenly divides her time between the war and her romance with happy-go-lucky Kansas lad Tufts. Because of the popularity of the stars, the patriotic spirit of the film, and the novelty of women combat nurses, SO PROUDLY WE HAIL made a sizable dent in the box office. The critics praised its authenticity, which Sandrich went to great lengths to achieve. Having read a news item about 10 nurses who escaped the fall of Corregidor in May 1942, Sandrich, together with Scott, tracked them down. He hired one of them, Lt. Eunice Hatchitt, as a technical advisor and, after receiving permission from the government to tell their story, went ahead with the film. Although he was certain to hit box-office gold with the big Paramount names of Colbert, Lake, and Goddard, Sandrich was also guaranteed to have a battle of egos on his hands. The feuding began when Goddard told a reporter that she preferred working with Lake because "after all, we are closer in age." Colbert was naturally upset at the reference to her elder status among the three. (Goddard, in fact, was wrong. She was born in 1911, making her seven years younger than Colbert, while eight years older than Lake.) There were also arguments over how they were photographed by Lang and over their professional abilities (Goddard and Lake were seen as personalities, while only Colbert was viewed as an actress). Often Sandrich would have to retake scenes countless times to accommodate Lake and Goddard, while it rarely took Colbert more than a couple of takes. When Oscar time came around, however, it was Goddard who received acclaim with a Best Supporting Actress nomination. Also nominated was Scott for Best Original Screenplay, Lang for Best Black-and-White Cinematography, and Edouart, Jennings, and Dutton for Best Special Effects. Fans of Lake and her famous peek-a-boo hair style should be forewarned that she dons a short hairdo in this picture. Reportedly, the government asked that she not appear as a servicewoman with that hair style because of the number of female factory workers whose long, Lake-inspired hair was getting tangled in the machinery. As bitter as the feuds were on SO PROUDLY WE HAIL, Colbert, Lake, Goddard, and Tufts (having quickly become hot properties) each re-created their roles for a "Lux Radio Theatre" performance on November 1, 1943.

p&d, Mark Sandrich; w, Allan Scott; ph, Charles Lang; m, Miklos Rozsa; ed, Ellsworth Hoagland; art d, Hans Dreier, Earl Hedrick; set d, Stephen

Seymour; spec eff, Gordon Jennings, Farciot Edouart, George Dutton; m/l, "Loved One" Edward Hayman, Rozsa; tech adv, Lt. Eunice Hatchitt, Col. Thomas Doyle.

War Drama   **Cas.**   **(PR:A   MPAA:NR)**

SO RED THE ROSE**½   (1935) 82m PAR bw

Margaret Sullavan (*Vallette Bedford*), Walter Connolly (*Malcolm Bedford*), Janet Beecher (*Sally Bedford*), Harry Ellerbe (*Edward Bedford*), Robert Cummings (*George Pendleton*), Charles Starrett (*George McGehee*), Johnny Downs (*Yankee Boy*), Daniel Haynes (*William Veal*), Randolph Scott (*Duncan Bedford*), Elizabeth Patterson (*Mary Cherry*), Dickie Moore (*Middleton Bedford*), Clarence Muse (*Cato*), James Burke (*Maj. Rushton*), Warner Richmond (*Confederate Sergeant*), Alfred Delcambre (*Charles Tolliver*).

This was the first major sound film to deal with the Civil War's effects on the Southern family. It preceded GONE WITH THE WIND by four years, and Margaret Mitchell's novel by a year. Sullavan plays the daughter of Connolly and Beecher, the heads of the Bedfords, wealthy plantation-owning family, whose sons and cousins fought the North. Southern belle Sullavan falls in love with her cousin Scott, who is opposed to the bloodshed occurring on both sides of the Mason-Dixon line. While the picture is occasionally on target, it is more often uneventful and downright absurd in its treatment of the slavery issue.

p, Douglas McLean; d, King Vidor; w, Laurence Stallings, Edwin Justus Mayer, Maxwell Anderson (based on the novel by Stark Young); ph, Victor Milner; m, W. Frank Harling; ed, Eda Warren; art d, Hans Dreier, Ernst Fegte; cos, Travis Banton.

Drama/Romance   **(PR:A   MPAA:NR)**

SO SAD ABOUT GLORIAzero   (1973) 90m Centronics/Libert Films
                                                             International c

Lori Saunders, Dean Jagger, Bob Ginnaven, Seymour Treitman, Lou Hoffman, Linda Wyse.

A schlocky, low-budget piece of nonsense which has Saunders driven even crazier than she already is by Jagger and her haunting visions of a ghost. Another slice 'n' dice quickie that plays on people's inbred fear of axe murderers, but rarely offers anything frightful.

p&d, Harry Thomason; w, Marshal Riggan; ph, Jim Roberson; m/l, Jerald Reed, Terry Trent.

Horror   **(PR:C-O   MPAA:PG)**

SO THIS IS AFRICA*   (1933) 68m COL bw

Robert Woolsey (*Alexander*), Bert Wheeler (*Wilbur*), Raquel Torres (*Leader of Amazon Women*), Esther Muir (*Mrs. Johnson-Martini*), Berton Churchill (*President*), Henry Armetta (*Street Cleaner*), Spencer Charters (*Doctor*), Clarence Moorehouse.

Wheeler and Woolsey take their comedy efforts to the dark continent in this jumbled outing which originally ran 90 minutes, but even 68 minutes is too long. The pair head for Africa to make a picture, but instead try to avoid the amorous native women by dressing in drag. Disjointed and as far from laughs as they are from civilization.

d, Eddie Cline; w, Norman Krasna; ph, Leonard Smith; ed, Wheeler Wright.

Comedy/Adventure   **(PR:A   MPAA:NR)**

SO THIS IS COLLEGE**   (1929) 97m MGM bw

Elliot Nugent (*Eddie*), Robert Armstrong (*Biff*), Cliff Edwards (*Windy*), Sally Starr (*Babs*), Phyllis Crane (*Betty*), Polly Moran (*Polly*), Lee Shumway (*Coach*), Dorothy Dehn (*Jane*), Max Davidson (*Moe*), Ann Brody (*Momma*), Oscar Rudolph (*Freshie*), Gene Stone (*Stupid*), Delmer Daves.

College life is again used as a backdrop and an excuse to show footage from a football game. This time it's USC against Stanford from 1928 (the game was, in reality, won by USC 10-0, but through the magic of cinema, Stanford comes out on top 9-7. Nugent and Armstrong are players who share the same room and the same girl, Starr. It is a well-kept secret until half time of the big game, causing an argument between the roommates. Their coach gives them a "Gipper" speech, persuading them that winning is more important than Starr, and their team goes on to score in the nick of time. Songs include: "Sophomore Prom" (by Jesse Greer), "College Days," "Campus Capers" (by Martin Broones), and "I Don't Want Your Kisses" (by Fred Fisher, Broones; sung by Nugent). This marked Broadway actress Sally Starr's film debut.

d, Sam Wood; w, Al Boasberg, Delmer Daves, Joe Farnham; ph, Leonard Smith; m, Martin Broones; ed, Frank Sullivan, Leslie F. Wilder; md, Arthur Lange; art d, Cedric Gibbons; cos, Henrietta Frazer.

Musical/Comedy   **(PR:A   MPAA:NR)**

SO THIS IS LONDON**½   (1930) 92m FOX bw

Will Rogers (*Hiram Draper*), Irene Rich (*Mrs. Hiram Draper*), Frank Albertson (*Junior Draper*), Maureen O'Sullivan (*Elinor Worthing*), Lumsden Hare (*Lord Percy Worthing*), Mary Forbes (*Lady Worthing*), Bramwell Fletcher (*Alfred Honeycutt*), Dorothy Christy (*Lady Amy Ducksworth*), Martha Lee Sparks (*Martha*), Ellen Woodston (*Nurse*).

Rogers is in top form as an American businessman who takes his family with him on a trip to the British Isles for a meeting with Hare, an English lord. Rogers does not like the Brits any more than Hare likes the Yanks, but eventually they come to terms, especially when their children fall for each other. The finale sequence has Rogers and Hare singing a duet of "My Country Tis Of Thee" and "God Save The King"–in unity. Based on the play by George M. Cohan, and remade on the other side of the Atlantic in 1939.

d, John G. Blystone; w, Owen Davis, Sr., Sonya Levien (based on Arthur Frederick Goodrich's adaptation of George M. Cohan's play); ph, Charles G. Clarke; ed, Jack Dennis; art d, Jack Schultze; cos, Sophie Wachner; m/l, James F. Hanley, Joseph McCarthy.

Comedy   **(PR:A   MPAA:NR)**

SO THIS IS LONDON**½   (1940, Brit.) 84m FOX bw

Alfred Drayton (*Lord Worthing*), Robertson Hare (*Henry Honeycutt*), Ethel Revnell (*Dodie*), Gracie West (*Liz*), Berton Churchill (*Hiram Draper*), Lily Cahill (*Mrs. Draper*), Carla Lehmann (*Elinor Draper*), Fay Compton (*Lady Worthing*), Stewart Granger (*Lawrence*), George Sanders (*Dr. de Reseke*), Mavis Clair (*Mrs. Honeycutt*), Aubrey Mallalieu (*Butler*), David Burns (*Drunk*).

Based on George M. Cohan's stageplay, this comedy has Churchill, a U.S. businessman, venturing to London to strike a deal with Drayton, a British lord. The negotiations are progressing sourly until Churchill's daughter is attracted to Drayton's son. Clair, in a minor role, gets in a few laughs as a sleepwalker.

p, Robert T. Kane; d, Thornton Freeland; w, William Counselman, Ben Travers, Tom Phipps, Douglas Furber (based on Arthur Goodrich's adaptation of a play by George M. Cohan); ph, Otto Kanturek; ed, James B. Clark.

Comedy   **(PR:A   MPAA:NR)**

SO THIS IS LOVE**½   (1953) 101m WB c (GB: THE GRACE MOORE
                                                             STORY)

Kathryn Grayson (*Grace Moore*), Merv Griffin (*Buddy Nash*), Joan Weldon (*Ruth Obre*), Walter Abel (*Col. Moore*), Rosemary De Camp (*Aunt Laura Stokley*), Jeff Donnell (*Henrietta Van Dyke*), Douglas Dick (*Bryan Curtis*), Ann Doran (*Mrs. Moore*), Margaret Field (*Edna Wallace*), Mabel Albertson (*Mary Garden*), Fortunio Bonanova (*Dr. Marafioti*), Marie Windsor (*Marilyn Montgomery*), Noreen Corcoran (*Grace Moore at 8*), The Szonys (*Dance Specialty*), Lillian Bronson (*Mrs. Wilson Green*), Ray Kellogg (*John McCormack*), Roy Gordon (*Otto Kahn*), Moroni Olsen (*Arnold Reuben*), Mario Siletti (*Gatti Casazza*), Charles Meredith (*Arthur Bodansky*), William Boyett (*George Gershwin*).

The all-too-short life of beloved soprano Grace Moore is given the full screen biography treatment here complete with Technicolor and the usual factual errors. The saga begins with Moore at the age of eight (played by Corcoran), stuck in Tennessee, but already demonstrating the talent and determination that would soon serve her well. Desperate to become a singer, the youngster convinces her father to let her pursue her dream and study music. When she reaches adolescence (she is now played by Grayson) she runs away from home and heads for New York in search of fame and fortune. It's a long road to stardom and Grayson is forced to sing for her supper in a nightclub before a roller coaster ride of events finally catapult her to the stage of the Metropolitan Opera House. There she brings down the house with her performance of Mimi in "La Boheme," which garnered an incredible 28 curtain calls. The film ends with Grayson on top, but it never deals with the soprano's tragic death in a Copenhagen plane crash in 1947 at age 46. Making his film debut is a very young Merv Griffin, who provides an early romantic interest for Grayson, but she rejects him (and later Dick) to pursue her dream. In retrospect it seems the talk-show host route was a smart career move for Griffin. Songs include, "The Kiss Waltz," "Time On My Hands" (Harold Adamson, Mark Gordon, Vincent Youmans), "Remember" (Irving Berlin), "I Wish I Could Shimmy Like My Sister Kate" (Armand J. Piron, Peter Bocage), "Ciribiribin" (Harry James, Jack Lawrence, A. Pestalozza), excerpts from "The Marriage of Figaro" (Wolfgang Amadeus Mozart), "Faust" (Charles Francis Gounod) and "La Boheme" (Giacomo Puccini).

p, Henry Blanke; d, Gordon Douglas; w, John Monk, Jr. (based on Grace Moore's autobiography *You're Only Human Once*); ph, Robert Burks (Technicolor); m, Max Steiner; ed, Folmar Blangsted; md, Ray Heindorf; art d, Edward Carrere; cos, Leah Rhodes; ch, LeRoy Prinz.

Musical/Biography   **(PR:A   MPAA:NR)**

SO THIS IS NEW YORK***   (1948) 79m Enterprise/UA bw

Henry Morgan (*Ernie Finch*), Rudy Vallee (*Herbert Daley*), Bill Goodwin (*Jimmy Ralston*), Hugh Herbert (*Mr. Trumbull*), Leo Gorcey (*Sid Mercer*), Virginia Grey (*Ella Finch*), Dona Drake (*Kate Goff*), Jerome Cowan (*Francis Griffin*), Dave Willock (*Willis Gilbey*), Frank Orth (*A.J. Gluskoter*), Arnold Stang (*Western Union Clerk*), William Bakewell (*Hotel Clerk*).

A side-splitting look at the events that occur when country folk, Morgan, Grey, and Drake, visit bustling New York City. They encounter all types of city slickers, especially cabbies whose lines are translated with sub-titles. Morgan takes his radio act to the big screen for the time, rarely failing to score with his humor. Dead Ender Gorcey is in top form as a drunken jockey.

p, Stanley Kramer; d, Richard O. Fleischer; w, Carl Foreman, Herbert Baker (based on the novel *The Big Town* by Ring Lardner); ph, Jack Russell; m, Dimitri Tiomkin; ed, Walter Thompson; art d, F. Frank Sylos; set d, Edward G. Boyle; cos, Elois Jenssen.

Comedy   (PR:A   MPAA:NR)

SO THIS IS PARIS**½   (1954) 96m UNIV c

Tony Curtis (*Joe Maxwell*), Gloria De Haven (*Colette D'Avril/Jane Mitchell*), Gene Nelson (*Al Howard*), Corinne Calvet (*Suzanne Sorel*), Paul Gilbert (*Davey Jones*), Mara Corday (*Yvonne*), Allison Hayes (*Carmen*), Myrna Hansen (*Ingrid*), Christiane Martel (*Christiane*), Ann Codee (*Grand'mere Marie*), Arthur Gould-Porter (*Albert*), Roger Etienne (*Pierre Deshons*), Lizette Guy (*Jeannine*), Michelle Ducasse (*Simone*), Maithe Iragui (*Cecile*), Lucien Plauzoles (*Eugene*), Numa Lapeyre (*Charlot*), Pat Horn (*Dancer*), Regina Dombek (*Miss Photo Flash*), Jean De Briac (*Mr. Sorel*), Rolfe Sedan (*Cab Driver*), Andre Villon (*Gendarme*), Marcel De La Brosse (*Headwaiter*), Carlos Albert (*Mailman*).

Colorful, energetic musical numbers set against the glorious backdrop of Paris can barely cover for an empty, unimaginative script. SO THIS IS PARIS follows the escapades of three sailors on leave who meet and fall for three Parisian girls. They all have a good time, sing and dance, and finally stage a benefit for a few orphans. You've seen it all before, but with different songs. This one includes: "So This is Paris," "Two Of Us," "A Dame's a Dame," "Three Bon Vivants," "If You Want to Be Famous," "Looking for Someone to Love," "If You Were There," "Wait Till Paris Sees Us" (by Pony Sherrell, Phil Moody), and "I Can't Give You Anything But Love" (by Jimmy McHugh, Dorothy Fields; sung by De Haven in French).

p, Albert J. Cohen; d, Richard Quine; w, Charles Hoffman (based on a story by Ray Buffum); ph, Maury Gertsman (Technicolor); ed, Virgil Vogel; md, Joseph Gershenson; art d, Alexander Golitzen, Eugene Lourie; cos, Rosemary Odell; ch, Gene Nelson, Lee Scott.

Musical   (PR:A   MPAA:NR)

SO THIS IS WASHINGTON**½   (1943) 64m Jack William
                                       Votion/RKO bw

Chester Lauck (*Lum*), Norris Goff (*Abner*), Alan Mowbray (*Mr. Marshall*), Roger Clark (*Robert Blevins*), Mildred Coles (*Jane Nestor*), Sarah Padden (*Aunt Charity*), Minerva Urecal (*Mrs. Pomeroy*), Dan Duncan (*Grandpappy*), Matt McHugh (*Stranger*), Barbara Pepper (*Taxi Driver*).

Radio personalities Lum 'n' Abner (Lauck and Goff) try to help the war effort by inventing synthetic rubber. They take their idea to Washington for some governmental advice, but before long they are the ones giving advice. They offer their commodity of common sense to senators and representatives who are completely bogged down in the bureaucracy. Likeable wartime fluff.

p, Ben Hersh; d, Ray McCarey; w, Leonard Praskins, Roswell Rogers (based on the story by Rogers, Edward James); ph, Harry Wild; ed, Duncan Mansfield; md, Lud Gluskin; art d, Hans Peters.

Comedy   (PR:A   MPAA:NR)

SO THIS WAS PARIS   (SEE: THIS WAS PARIS, 1942, Brit.)

SO WELL REMEMBERED**½   (1947, Brit.) 114m Alliance/RKO bw

John Mills (*George Boswell*), Martha Scott (*Olivia*), Patricia Roc (*Julie*), Trevor Howard (*Whiteside*), Richard Carlson (*Charles*), Reginald Tate (*Mangin*), Beatrice Verley (*Annie*), Frederick Leister (*Channing*), Ivor Barnard (*Spivey*), Julian D'Albie (*Wetherall*), Juliet Mills (*Baby Julie*), John Turnbull (*Morris*), Kathleen Boutall (*Woman*), Lyonel Watts (*Mayor*), Roddy Hughes (*Librarian*), James Hilton (*Narrator*), Sydney Benson, Rhona Sykes.

A British and American cast struggle to make this long, slow movie into something more than the soap opera it is. Told in flashback on the eve of the victory in Europe in WW II, it's a multi-layered story of several people in the small Lancashire town of Browdley, England. Scott is a vicious, greedy woman whose father was sent to jail as an extortionist. She's now married to Mills, a newspaper editor/publisher who has taken the side of the local mill workers in a labor squabble. Mills is a popular man due to his stance and Scott pushes him into running for Parliament. A diphtheria

epidemic breaks out; Mills finds that more important than his campaign so he uses his time to help the local doctor, Howard, in combating the disease. Howard is a drunk who is overworked and underpaid but zealous in his attentions to the populace. Mills' and Scott's son dies in the epidemic and Howard adopts the orphan Juliet Mills (who was the actor's daughter and later a U.S. TV star). Scott can't stand Mills' selfless manner and leaves him when he decides to spend his time rectifying social injustices. Time passes; Scott remarries, is widowed, and returns to the area with her son, Carlson, by her second marriage. Carlson meets and falls in love with Roc (the grown-up Juliet Mills). He is a flying officer and when his face is mangled in a crash, it looks as though interfering Scott is going to put an end to his budding romance with Roc, but Mills steps in to bring the young lovers together and Scott leaves town. Since Mills is depicted as a fine human being and ex-wife Scott is shown to be ambitious and predatory, the audience is left with a good feeling when the harridan is outfoxed. James Hilton, who wrote the novel as well as "Lost Horizon" is the wordy narrator. The movie looks good and was shot in an 11-week schedule at Denham studios near London as well as in the English countryside where it was set. Producer Scott, director Dmytryk, and composer Eisler were all being scrutinized by the red-baiters at this time and the result was that nuances were read into this movie that never existed. Several of the more right-wing critics found this to be a communist-inspired movie when it was, in fact, a drama and little else. Hilton's novel would have never been deemed pink, but the addition of the aforementioned trio caused the paranoids to come out of the woodwork and attack the humanity of the story as being Marxist/Leninist. Nonsense.

p, Adrian Scott; d, Edward Dmytryk; w, John Paxton (based on the novel by James Hilton); ph, Frederick A. Young; m, Hanns Eisler; ed, Harry Gerstad; md, C. Bakaleinikoff; art d, L. P. Williams; cos, Renie.

Drama   (PR:A-C MPAA:NR)

SO YOU WON'T TALK?**   (1935, Brit.) 84m WB-FN/FN bw

Monty Banks (*Tony Cazari*), Vera Pearce (*Edith*), Bertha Belmore (*Harriet*), Enid Stamp-Taylor (*Pauline*), Muriel Angelus (*Katrina*), Ralph Ince (*Ralph Younger*), Claude Dampier (*Wilbur Whistle*), Julian Royce (*Peebles*), A. Bromley Davenport (*Mr. Fielding*), Peter Bernard, Jack Harley.

Banks stars as a fellow who, in order to inherit his uncle's fortune, must not talk or write for 30 days. A witty comedy which owes all the laughs to Banks' superb performance which relies solely on facial expressions.

p, Irving Asher; d, Monty Banks; w, Russell Medcraft, Frank Launder (based on a story by Tom Geraghty); ph, Basil Emmott.

Comedy   (PR:A   MPAA:NR)

SO YOU WON'T TALK**   (1940) 69m COL bw

Joe E. Brown (*Whiskers/Brute Hanson*), Frances Robinson (*Lucy Walters*), Vivienne Osborne (*Maxie Carewe*), Bernard Nedell (*Bugs Linaker*), Tom Dugan (*Dude*), Dick Wessel (*Dopey*), Anthony Warde (*Dolf*).

Developing along standard lines is this mistaken identity comedy with Brown taking on a dual role. After girl friend Robinson begs him to shave off his mustache, he is assumed to be a gangster who was released from prison that same day. Expectedly, he is carted off by awaiting mobsters and the gangster's moll, eventually fulfilling the Brown-meets-Brown obligatory scene.

d, Edward Sedgwick; w, Richard Flournoy; ph, Allen G. Siegler; ed, James Sweeney; md, M.W. Stoloff; art d, Lionel Banks.

Crime/Comedy   (PR:A   MPAA:NR)

SO YOUNG, SO BAD**½   (1950) 91m UA bw

Paul Henreid (*Dr. Jason*), Catherine McLeod (*Ruth Levering*), Grace Coppin (*Mrs. Beuhler*), Cecil Clovelly (*Mr. Riggs*), Anne Jackson (*Jackie*), Enid Pulver (*Jane*), Anne Francis (*Loretta*), Rosita [Rita] Moreno (*Dolores*).

Henreid succeeds in bringing reform to a women's prison through psychiatric means and understanding, but some of his coworkers would rather bully the girls into their way of thinking. When a state board investigates, Henreid comes out on top thanks to the testimony of two courageous inmates. A well-meaning indictment of those who misuse their authority. Shooting in New York City, Henreid was allowed by the Danziger brothers, novice movie producers, to interview more than 300 women for the leads of this film, and he selected Francis, Moreno and Jackson, who all went on to spectacular film careers. For risking his career with this independent production, Henreid was promised fifty percent of the profits of the film, later stating in his autobiography, *Ladies Man*: "The picture did well and I made more money out of it than out of anything I've ever been connected with."

p, Edward J. Danziger, Harry Lee Danziger; d, Bernard Vorhaus; w, Jean Rouverol, Vorhaus; ph, Don Malkames; m, Robert W. Stringer; ed, Carl Lerner.

Drama   (PR:A   MPAA:NR)

SOAK THE RICH**   (1936) 86m PAR bw

Walter Connolly (*Humphrey Craig*), Mary Taylor (*Belinda Craig*), John Howard (*Buzz Jones*), Alice Duer Miller (*Miss Beasely*), Ilka Chase (*Mabel*), Edwin Philips (*"Blackeye" Lockwood*), Lionel Stander (*Joe Muglia*), Robert Wallsten (*Tommy Hutchins*), John W. Call (*Sandwich Man*), George Watts (*Rockwell*), Francis Compton (*Tullio*), Joseph Sweeney (*Capt. Pettijohn*), Allan Ross MacDougall (*Dr. Keats*), Isabelle Foster (*Jenny*).

One of four MacArthur-Hecht productions, this collegiate comedy has Taylor returning from Europe to attend her father's school. She soon is involved with radicals who are opposed to the ways of the rich, such as her father. She falls in love with Howard, the campus' top radical, who has begun a movement to keep a controversial professor from being fired. Taylor's dad is intent on firing the professor, whose book, *Soak The Rich*, certainly isn't on the faculty's best seller list. Eventually the daughter and the radical marry and dad's actions become less extreme; the film finishes with a happy finale. One of a few social consciousness films of the period along with RED SALUTE (1935), FIGHTING YOUTH (1935), and SPRING MADNESS (1938), which popped up when it was hip to be Red.

p,d&w, Ben Hecht, Charles MacArthur; ph, Leon Shamroy, Charles Hansen; ed, Leo Zockling.

Comedy/Drama   **(PR:A   MPAA:NR)**

SOAPBOX DERBY**½   (1958, Brit.) Rayant/Children's Film
                                              Foundation bw

Michael Crawford (*Peter Toms*), Keith Davis (*Legs Johnson*), Roy Townsend (*Foureyes Fulton*), Alan Coleshill (*Lew Lender*), Malcolm Kirby (*John*), Carla Challoner (*Betty*), Mark Daly (*Grandpa*), Denis Shaw (*Lender*), Harry Fowler (*Barrow Boy*), Raymond Dudley, Jean Ireland, David Williams.

Two rival London youth groups, the Battersea Bats and the Victoria Victors, are involved in heated preparation for the upcoming "Soapbox Derby." When the Bats come up with a design that seems unbeatable, the Victors steal the car and make it appear as though Townsend, the designer, is responsible for the theft. The hoax is uncovered just in the of time; the Bats then go on to win the race. Energetic efforts by the children actors make this picture well worth watching.

p, Anthony Gilkison; d&w, Darcy Conyers (based on the story by Robert Martin); ph, Douglas Ransom.

Drama   **(PR:AAA   MPAA:NR)**

SOB SISTER**   (1931) 67m FOX bw (GB: THE BLONDE REPORTER)

James Dunn (*Garry Webster*), Linda Watkins (*Jane Ray*), Minna Gombell (*Vonnie*), Howard Phillips (*Ned*), George E. Stone (*Johnnie the Sheik*), Molly O'Day (*Daisy*), Charles Middleton (*City Editor Baker*), Ernest Wood (*Dave*), Sarah Padden (*Ma Stevens*), Wallie Albright (*Billy Stotesley*), Eddie Dillon (*Pat*), Harold Waldridge (*Johnny*), Neal Burns (*Freddie*), Harry Beresford (*Pa Stevens*), George Byron (*Dutch*), Maurice Black (*Gimp Peters*), Clifford Dempsey (*Uncle Henry*), Lex Lindsay (*Slim*), Alan Dinehart, Edwin Sturgis, Joe Brown.

An inconsistent romancer about a pair of newspaper reporters, Dunn and Watkins, who fall in love after constantly writing about the same news events. The love story is spotty, but the newsroom scenes are more authentic than most films made at the time.

d, Alfred Santell; w, Edwin Burke (based on the novel by Mildred Gilman); ph, Glenn Mac Williams; ed, Ralph Dietrich.

Romance/Drama   **(PR:A   MPAA:NR)**

SOCIAL ENEMY NO. 1   (SEE: NO GREATER SIN, 1941)

SOCIAL LION, THE*½   (1930) 72m PAR-Publix bw

Jack Oakie (*Marco Perkins*), Mary Brian (*Cynthia Brown*), Richard "Skeets" Gallagher (*"Chick" Hathaway*), Olive Borden (*Gloria Staunton*), Charles Sellon (*Jim Perkins*), Cyril Ring (*Ralph Williams*), E.H. Calvert (*Henderson*), James Gibson (*Howard*), Henry Roquemore (*Smith*), William Bechtel (*Schultz*), Richard Cummings (*McGinnis*), Jack Byron (*"Knockout" Johnson*).

Oakie stars in this weak social comedy which satirizes everything from prize fighting to polo as he gives up the boxing ring for the polo court and then returns to fighting and the girl he left behind to become a "social lion." An Oakie formula story with that special touch of pathos in his comedy that is his trademark.

d, A. Edward Sutherland; w, Joseph L. Mankiewicz, Agnes Brand Leahy (based on the story "Marco Himself" by Octavus Roy Cohen); ph, Allen Siegler; ed, Otho Lovering.

Comedy   **(PR:A   MPAA:NR)**

SOCIAL REGISTER*½   (1934) 72m COL bw

Colleen Moore (*Patsy Shaw*), Charles Winninger (*"Jonesie"*), Pauline Frederick (*Mrs. Breene*), Alexander Kirkland (*Charlie*), Robert Benchley (*Himself*), Ross Alexander (*Lester Trout*), Margaret Livingston (*Gloria*), Roberta Robinson (*Kay*), Olive Olsen (*Ruth*), John Miltern (*Mr. Breene*), Edward Garvie (*Wiggins*), Georgette Harvey (*Lulu*), Hans Hansen (*Chris*), Frey and Braggioti (*Piano Duo*), Ramona (*Herself*).

Chorus girl Moore falls in love with a society fellow, but has to deal with his family before she can be accepted. Her main opposition comes at a party in which wealthy mom Frederick tries to make Moore look like a fool. She fails, however, and Moore is taken under the family's wing. Frederick played the same part in a surprisingly similar movie from 1932 entitled WAYWARD.

d, Marshall Neilan; w, Grace Perkins, Clara Beranger, James Ashmore Creelman (based on a story by John Emerson, Anita Loos); ph, Merritt Gerstad; ed, Robert Snody; m/l, Con Conrad, Ford Dabney.

Drama   **(PR:A   MPAA:NR)**

SOCIETY DOCTOR**   (1935) 67m MGM bw (GB: AFTER EIGHT
                                     HOURS; AKA: ONLY EIGHT HOURS)

Chester Morris (*Dr. Morgan*), Virginia Bruce (*Madge*), Robert Taylor (*Dr. Ellis*), Billie Burke (*Mrs. Crane*), Raymond Walburn (*Dr. Waverly*), Henry Kolker (*Dr. Harvey*), William Henry (*Frank Snowden*), Mary Jo Matthews (*Mary*), Robert McWade (*Harris Snowden*), Donald Meek (*Moxley*), Dorothy Peterson (*Mrs. Harrigan*), Louise Henry (*Telephone Operator*), Johnny Hines (*Hardy*), Addison Richards (*Harrigan*), Bobby Watson (*Albright*).

The usual events occur when rising young medic Morris proves his worth to his hospital coworkers. They are jealous of his success and self-assured ways, however, and kick him out on his own. He is befriended by Burke, who sets him up in his own practice, but deserted by Bruce, who chooses to give her love to Taylor. When Morris gets shot by a gangster patient, he has Taylor perform the surgery, but under his own guidance. Morris recovers completely, with Bruce returning to the patient's side for the finale. SOCIETY DOCTOR is of filmic historical importance because of three statements it had to make on the human condition of movie stars. First, it was supposed to be a vehicle to promote Morris, but Taylor won all the attention. Second, it also was supposed to be a film that would accelerate the career of Bruce, John Gilbert's recent ex-wife. Instead, Burke far outshown her and almost, in fact, stole the show. Lastly, never again would Taylor play bit parts in the movies. Louis B. Mayer reportedly stated after viewing a screening of the picture that he saw the potential promise of Taylor for the first time. So did moviegoers, for when WEST POINT OF THE AIR, in which Taylor appeared and which was made before SOCIETY DOCTOR, came out the next month, fans wrote the studio asking why there was not more Taylor in it.

p, Lucien Hubbard; d, George B. Seitz; w, Michael Fessier, Samuel Marx (based on the novel *The Harbor* by Theodore Reeves); ph, Lester White; m, Oscar Radin; ed, Ben Lewis; art d, Cedric Gibbons, Howard Campbell; set d, Edwin B. Willis.

Drama   **(PR:A   MPAA:NR)**

SOCIETY FEVER*½   (1935) 66m IN/CHES bw

Lois Wilson (*Portia Prouty*), Lloyd Hughes (*Graham Smith*), Hedda Hopper (*Mrs. Vandergriff*), Guinn "Big Boy" Williams (*Edgar Prouty*), Grant Withers (*Ronald Dawson*), Marion Shilling (*Victoria Vandergriff*), George Irving (*Mr. Vandergriff*), Sheila Terry (*Lucy Prouty*), Maidel Turner (*Mrs. Prouty*), Lois January (*Julie Prouty*), Erville Alderson (*Uncle Andy*), Katherine Sheldon (*Minnie*), Reginald Sheffield (*Lord Michael*), Shirley Hilf (*Marjorie Vandergriff*), Lew Kelly (*Hanly*), Anthony Marsh (*Allan Prouty*), Richard Hemingway (*Bob Miller*), Robert McKenzie, Roland Reed.

Wilson lives with her wacky family which was once prosperous but now is penniless, trying to win over anyone rich who sets foot on their property. One son is a lawyer who has contrived to snare what's left of the family fortune, while another son collects bugs, none of the clan paying any attention to Wilson's sane attempts to survive. Her efforts prove fruitful, however, when she hooks Hughes, a businessman with enough cash to get the family mansion back in shape. The film boasts a large collection of rambunctious characters and none of them very impressive.

p, Maury Cohen; d, Frank Strayer; w, Karen De Wolfe; ph, M.A. Anderson; ed, Roland Reed.

Comedy   **(PR:A   MPAA:NR)**

SOCIETY GIRL**   (1932) 67m FOX bw

James Dunn (*Johnny Malone*), Peggy Shannon (*Judy Gelett*), Spencer Tracy (*Briscoe*), Walter Byron (*Warburton*), Bert Hanlon (*Curly*), Marjorie Gateson (*Alice Converse*), Eula Guy Todd (*Miss Halloway*).

Dunn, while preparing for a championship boxing match, meets and falls in love with society woman Shannon, much to the disappointment of his trainer, Tracy. Instead of concentrating on training for the fight, he devotes all his energies to Shannon. Before the match, however, she packs her bags, leaving Dunn to take the 10 count. He loses the fight but winds up marrying Shannon, with every hope of making a comeback. Tracy steals every scene he's in, making one wonder why he wasn't playing the lead, especially since he looked more the part of a prize fighter than Dunn.

d, Sidney Lanfield; w, Elmer Harris (based on the play by John Larkin, Jr.); ph, George Barnes; ed, Margaret Clancy; md, George Lipschultz; art d, Gordon Wiles; cos, David Cox.

Drama/Romance   **(PR:A MPAA:NR)**

SOCIETY LAWYER**   (1939) 78m MGM bw

Walter Pidgeon (*Christopher Durant*), Virginia Bruce (*Pat Abbott*), Leo Carrillo (*Tony Gazotti*), Eduardo Ciannelli (*Jim Crelliman*), Lee Bowman (*Phil Siddall*), Frances Mercer (*Sue Leonard*), Ann Morriss (*Judy Barton*), Herbert Mundin (*Layton Valet*), Frank M. Thomas (*Lt. Stevens*), Edward S. Brophy (*Max*), Tom Kennedy (*Alf*), Clarence Kolb (*Mr. Leonard*), Pierre Watkin (*Henry V. Adams*), Ian Wolfe (*Schmidt*), Paul Guilfoyle (*Murtock*), Joseph Crehan (*City Editor*), Lillian Yarbo (*Sadie*), Selmer Jackson (*Inspector*), James Millican (*Reporter*), Ferris Taylor (*Foreman*), Bess Flowers (*Mary the Secretary*), Frank Orth (*Man*), Lester Dorr (*Photographer*), Harry Strang, Harry Fleischmann, Howard Mitchell (*Plainsclothesmen*), Sharon Lewis (*Gangster's Moll*).

Pidgeon is an honest, hard-working lawyer who runs into corruptible times when he wins a court case for gangster Ciannelli. The mobster's girl friend, Bruce, impressed with Pidgeon, clings to him, pushing Ciannelli to fight dirty. The gangster plans to kill his ex-girl friend and frame Pidgeon. But the deed backfires, and the gangster is sent to jail. A remake of PENT-HOUSE.

p, John Considine, Jr.; d, Edwin L. Marin; w, Frances Goodrich, Albert Hackett, Leon Gordon, Hugo Butler (based on the story by Arthur Somers Roche and the screenplay "Penthouse" by Goodrich, Hackett); ph, George Folsey; m, Edward Ward; ed, Howard O'Neill; md, Georgie Stoll, Roger Edens; art d, Cedric Gibbons, Howard Campbell; set d, Edwin B. Willis; cos, Dolly Tree; m/l, "I'm in Love with the Honorable Mr. So-and-So," Sam Coslow (sung by Virginia Bruce).

Drama   **(PR:A MPAA:NR)**

SOCIETY SMUGGLERS*   (1939) 65m UNIV bw

Preston Foster (*Sully*), Irene Hervey (*Joan Martin*), Walter Woolf King (*Massey*), Frank Jenks (*Emery*), Fred Keating (*Larry Kearns*), Regis Toomey (*Johnny Beebe*), Frances Robinson (*Mary Larson*), Raymond Parker (*Ames*), Clay Clement (*Harrison*), Doris Rankin (*Miss Wexley*), Harry Hayden (*Dr. Lee*), Kernan Cripps (*Detective*), Frank Reicher (*Jones*), Milburn Stone (*Peter Garfield*), Jack Norton (*Prentis*), Michael Mark (*Rug Merchant*), Peter George Lynn (*Austin*), Eddie Acuff (*Radio Expert*), Mary Field (*Secretary*).

Only in the minds of Hollywood screenwriters would this implausible plot turn up. Foster is hired by the U.S. Treasury Department to crack a smuggling ring headed by King, who uses a luggage shop as a front. He concocts a hare-brained scheme to send five winners of a slogan contest overseas and fill their luggage with valuable gems. Foster ends up as one of the five and smashes the ring.

p, Ken Goldsmith; d, Joe May; w, Arthur T. Horman, Earl Felton (based on the novel *Key Woman* by Joseph Steele); ph, John W. Boyle; ed, Philip Cahn; md, Charles Previn; art d, Jack Otterson.

Crime   **(PR:A MPAA:NR)**

SOD SISTERS zero   (1969) 74m Popular Prod. bw (AKA: HEAD FOR THE HILLS)

Genie Palmer (*Jeannie*), Breege McCoy (*Lil*), Hank Harrigan (*Zeb*), Tim E. Lane (*Tom*), James Schacht (*Hood*), Glen Stannel (*Moose*), Joseph Mikel, Lou Tu, Pat McLamry.

A worthless moonshine picture has Lane playing a bootlegging crook who gets amnesia and cannot remember where he hid the stolen money. One of a pair of oversexed sisters finds the money and throws it into a nearby river, while the other gang members try to recover it. Sounds exciting, doesn't it?

p, J.T. Urishin, Rod Witmer; d, Lester Williams; w, Stan Potosky; ph, Witmer; ed, Urishin.

Crime   **(PR:O MPAA:NR)**

SODOM AND GOMORRAH**½**   (1962, U.S./Fr./Ital.) 154m Titanus-Pathe Cinema-S.G.C. /FOX c (SODOME ET GOMORRHE: SODOMA E GOMORRA; THE LAST DAYS OF SODOM AND GOMOR-RAH)

Stewart Granger (*Lot*), Pier Angeli (*Ildith*), Stanley Baker (*Astaroth*), Rossana Podesta (*Shuah*), Anouk Aimee (*Queen Bera*), Claudia Mori (*Maleb*), Rik Battaglia (*Melchir*), Giacomo Rossi Stuart (*Ishmael*), Feodor Chaliapin (*Alabias*), Aldo Silvani (*Nacor*), Enzo Fiermonte (*Eber*), Scilla Gabel (*Tamar*), Antonio De Teffe (*Captain*), Gabriele Tinti (*Lieutenant*), Daniele Vargas (*Segur*), Massimo Pietrobon (*Isaac*), Andrea Tagliabue

(*Eber's Son*), Francesco Tensi (*1st Old Man*), Mitsuko Takara (*Orpha, the Dancer*), Liana Del Balzo (*Hebrew Woman*), Mimmo Palmara (*Arno*), Ellen Kessler, Alice Kessler (*The Dancers*), Giovanna Galletti (*Malik*), Vittorio Artesi (*Eber's Other Son*), Primo Moroni (*2nd Old Man*).

A biblical epic from Robert Aldrich which casts Granger as Lot, leading his people to the Valley of Jordan and making a pit stop in the twin pits of decadence, Sodom and Gomorrah. Aimee is the gorgeous, vice-happy ruler who tries to strike a deal with Granger, but eventually he leads his people away in God's name. Granger's wife, Angeli, does not heed the Lord's warnings, turns back to take a final look at the cities, and is transformed into a pillar of salt. An interesting addition to the Aldrich filmography, which is laden with moral cynicism. Sergio Leone is credited with directing the Italian version and some action scenes.

p, Goffredo Lombardo; d, Robert Aldrich, Sergio Leone; w, Hugo Butler, Giorgio Prosperi; ph, Silvano Ippoliti, Mario Montuori, Cyril Knowles (DeLuxe Color); m, Miklos Rozsa; ed, Peter Tanner; art d, Ken Adam; set d, Gino Brosio, Emilio D'Andria; cos, Giancarlo Bartolini Salimbeni; spec eff, Lee Zavitz, Serse Urbisaglia, Wally Veevers; ch, Archie Savage; makeup, Euclide Santoli.

Biblical Epic   **(PR:C MPAA:NR)**

SODOMA E GOMORRA   (SEE: SODOM AND GOMORRAH, 1962, Fr./Ital.)

SOFI**   (1967) 96m Golden Bear Films bw

Tom Troupe (*The Clerk*).

Essentially a one-man show, SOFI stars Troupe as a 19th Century Russian clerk who becomes so obsessed with his boss' daughter that he begins to lose his mind. He first talks to a wooden puppet, then writes imaginary letters that Sofi's dog supposedly has written to him. The final straw is his belief that he is King Ferdinand VIII of Spain. Needless to say, the clerk is then admitted to an insane asylum.

p&d, Robert Carlisle; w, Tom Troupe, Don Eitner (based on the story "Zapiski Sumasshedshego" by Nikolay Vasilyevich Gogol, and the play "Diary Of A Madman" by Eitner, Troupe); ph, Alfred Taylor; m, Allyn Ferguson; ed, Robert Grant; art d, Michael Haller; makeup, Harry Thomas.

Drama   **(PR:A MPAA:NR)**

SOFIA**   (1948) 83m ARPI/FC c

Gene Raymond (*Steve Roark*), Sigrid Gurie (*Linda Carlsen*), Patricia Morison (*Magda Onescu*), Mischa Auer (*Ali Imagu*), John Wengraf (*Peter Goltzen*), George Baxter (*James Braden*), Charles Rooner (*Dr. Stoyan*), Fernando Wagner (*Dr. Viertel*), Luz Alba (*Ana Sokolova*), Egon Zappert (*Marow*), Hamil Petroff (*Bell Captain*), Peter O'Crotty (*Brother Johannes*), John Kelly (*Lt. Cmdr. Stark*), Chel Lopez (*Chodorov*), Jose Torvay (*Warden*).

A completely implausible Soviet-bad-guy picture which cashed in on the communist scare of the era by casting Raymond as part of an operation to rescue some kidnapped atomic scientists. In Hollywood, one cannot have espionage without romance, so Raymond's former love, Gurie, happens to be one of the scientists. Lots of people talking with bad accents and passing secret messages in cakes, but it is all done in the name of mindless entertainment.

p, Robert S. Presnell, Sr., John Reinhardt; d, Reinhardt; w, Frederick Stephani; ph, William Clothier (Cinecolor); ed, Charles L. Kimball; md, Raul Lavista; art d, Alfred Ybarra, Jorge Fernandez; cos, Don Loper; m/l, Serge and Karen Walter.

Spy Drama   **(PR:A MPAA:NR)**

SOFT BEDS AND HARD BATTLES
                    (SEE: UNDERCOVERS HERO 1975, Brit.)

SOFT BODY OF DEBORAH, THE
                    (SEE: SWEET BODY OF DEBORAH, THE, 1969, Ital./Fr.)

SOFT SKIN, THE**½**   (1964, Fr.) 120m Films du Carrosse-S.E.D.I.F./Cinema V Dist. bw (LA PEAU DOUCE); (GB: SILK-EN SKIN)

Jean Desailly (*Pierre Lachenay*), Francoise Dorleac (*Nicole Chomette*), Nelly Benedetti (*Franca Lachenay*), Daniel Ceccaldi (*Clement*), Laurence Badie (*Ingrid*), Jean Lanier (*Michel*), Paule Emanuele (*Odile*), Philippe Dumat (*Reims Cinema Manager*), Pierre Risch (*Canon*), Dominique Lacarriere (*Pierre's Secretary*), Sabine Haudepin (*Sabine*), Maurice Garrel (*Bookseller*), Gerard Poirot (*Franck*), Georges de Givray (*Nicole's Father*), Charles Lavialle (*Night Porter at Hotel Michelet*), Carnero (*Lisbon Organizer*), Catherine Duport (*Young Girl at Reims Dinner*), Maximilienne Harlaut (*Mme. Leloix*), Olivia Poli (*Mme. Bontemps*), Theresa Renouard (*Cashier*), Brigitte Zhendre-Laforest (*Linen Deliverywoman*), Jean-Louis Richard (*Man in Street*).

One of Truffaut's least successful films, THE SOFT SKIN came as a reaction to the resounding impact of JULES AND JIM, the former concentrating on love in the city, while the latter concentrates on love in the country. Truffaut's idea with this picture was, as he put it: "a violent answer to JULES AND JIM. It's as though someone else had made JULES AND JIM ... it is a truly modern love; it takes place in planes, in elevators; it has all the harassments of modern life." From the opening, with its quick, short shots, THE SOFT SKIN surely does not seem like a Truffaut film. It is distant, restrained, and like the title implies, a surface film in which emotions run only skin-deep. It tells the story of Desailly (named after a young friend of Truffaut's, Robert Lechenay), a literary critic and lecturer who specializes in Honore de Balzac (a personal favorite of Truffaut's, having also known in THE 400 BLOWS), who falls in love with stewardess Dorleac after a trip to Lisbon. Since Desailly is married to Benedetti, his meetings with his mistress are few and awkward. His domestic life blows up in an argument with Benedetti, sending him off to Dorleac with a proposal of marriage, who unsympathetically turns him down. The jilted husband calls his wife in the hope of reconciliation, but is unable to reach her. Benedetti finds him in a restaurant, presents him with some incriminating photos, and kills him with a shotgun. The controversial ending, based on a newspaper clipping Truffaut had read, added an unsettling, but effective finish to a film which had concentrated on the generic qualities of the romantic triangle for the previous hour and a half. Jean-Pierre Leaud, Truffaut's Antoine Doinel and star of THE 400 BLOWS, served as a directorial apprentice on this picture and a number of others for New Wave directors.

d, Francois Truffaut; w, Truffaut, Jean-Louis Richard; ph, Raoul Coutard; m, Georges Delerue; ed, Claudine Bouche; cos, Renee Rouzot; makeup, Nicole Felix.

Drama   **(PR:C-O MPAA:NR)**

SOFT SKIN AND BLACK LACE
       (SEE: SOFT SKIN ON BLACK SILK, 1964, Fr./Span.)

SOFT SKIN ON BLACK SILK*   (1964, Fr./Span.) 90m Pecsa-Contact Organisation-Sopadec-P.I.P.-Petrus/Audubon bw (TENTATIONS; UN MUNDO PARA MI; AKA: SOFT SKIN AND BLACK LACE)

Agnes Laurent (Theresa), Armand Mestral (Don), Barbara Laage (Isabelle), Vincent Parra (Andre), Edie Burke (Nicole), Ira Lewis (Roger), Sandrine, Jose Marco Davo, Queti Clavijo, Maria Valence, Marujita Bustos.

A combination of footage – old, new, borrowed, and simply bad – this poorly constructed melodrama has Burke and Lewis in about 40 minutes of newly-shot beach scenes. Lewis tells Burke about a plan to kill an adulterous neighbor, when Burke relates a story to him in an effort to keep the peace. Previously released footage is a jumble about a priest-to-be, adultery, cabarets, and murder, none of which calms the murderous Lewis down. It's not until Burke seduces the disgruntled Lewis that he settles down and realizes that life is not so bad after all. Released in Spain in 1959, it was recut by Metzger who lopped out 42 minutes of footage and replaced it with 40 minutes of Burke and Lewis. The only thing that is even partially worthwhile is the middle 50 minutes with which Metzger was not involved.

p, Rene Thevenet; d, Jose Antonio de la Loma, Louis Duchesne, Radley H. Metzger; w, de la Loma, L.S. Poveda, LaVerne Owens; ph, Alfredo Fraile; m, Daniel White, Federico Martinez Tudo; ed, Louis Devaivre, Teresa Alcocer; art d, Alfonso de Lucas.

Drama   **(PR:O MPAA:NR)**

SOFT WARM EXPERIENCE, A   (SEE: SATIN MUSHROOM, THE, 1969)

SOGEKI   (SEE: SUN ABOVE, DEATH BELOW, 1969, Jap.)

SOGGY BOTTOM U.S.A.**   (1982) 90m Gaylord c

Ben Johnson, Anne Wedgeworth, Lois Nettleton, Dub Taylor, Anthony Zerbe, Jack Elam, P.J. Soles, Lane Smith, Don Johnson.

A weak comedy about a sheriff who tries to keep law and order in his southern community, but gains little of the support he needs. The script is as weak as they come, but a knockout cast makes it worthwhile. Everyone from Ben Johnson and Elam (THE WILD BUNCH) to P.J. Soles (ROCK 'N' ROLL HIGH SCHOOL) to Don Johnson (television's "Miami Vice") shows style in this one.

p, Elmo Williams; d, Ted Flicker; w, Eric Edson, Stephen C. Burnham, Joy N. Houck, Jr. (based on a story by Hal L. Harrison, Jr); m/l, Larry Cansler, John Stewart, Gary White.

Comedy   **Cas.**   **(PR:C MPAA:PG)**

SOHO CONSPIRACY*   (1951, Brit.) 85m Do-U-Know Film bw

Zena Marshall (Dora), Jacques Labreque (Carlo Scala), Peter Gawthorne (Father Shaney), Syd, Max Harrison (Gondotti Brothers), John Witty (Guy), Tito Gobbi, Tito Schipa, Beniamino Gigli, Gino Becchi (Themselves).

Bargain basement musical about a number of Soho residents who band together to put on a show to raise money for the restoration of a local church. All musical number footage was borrowed from other films.

p, E.J. Fancey; d, Cecil H. Williamson; w, Williamson, Ralph Dawson (based on the story by S. and M. Monicelli); ph, Jeff Davis, R. Densham.

Musical   **(PR:A MPAA:NR)**

SOHO INCIDENT   (SEE: SPIN A DARK WEB, 1956, Brit.)

SOL MADRID**½**   (1968) 90m MGM c (AKA: THE HEROIN GANG)

David McCallum (Sol Madrid), Stella Stevens (Stacey Woodward), Telly Savalas (Emil Dietrich), Ricardo Montalban (Jalisco), Rip Torn (Dano Villanova), Pat Hingle (Harry Mitchell), Paul Lukas (Capo Riccione), Michael Ansara (Capt. Ortega), Perry Lopez (Hood), Michael Conrad (Scarpi), Robert Rockwell (Chief Danvers), Merritt Bohn (Refinery Engineer), Madge Cameron (Woman in Cantina), Shepherd Sanders (Cantina Operator), Henry Escalante, George Sawaya (Dietrich's Gunmen), Ken Del Conte (Joe Brighton), Robert McNamara (Oilfield Foreman), Tony Barbario (Stacey's Dance Partner).

McCallum stars as a narcotics agent traveling south of the border in this neatly plotted thriller. His only clue to the whereabouts of a former mafia kingpin is Stevens, the mobster's one-time girl friend. When McCallum goes undercover as a pusher, he learns that the man he is looking for has been murdered. A barrage of action and gunplay follows when McCallum enlists the aid of the local police force, chasing a gang of smugglers through a Mexican forest and eventually killing all the lawbreakers. Savalas and Montalban both perform in an admirably campy fashion.

p, Hall Bartlett; d, Brian G. Hutton; w, David Karp (based on the novel Fruit of the Poppy by Robert Wilder); ph, Fred Koenekamp (Panavision, Metrocolor); m, Lalo Schifrin; ed, John McSweeney; art d, George W. Davis, Carl Anderson; set d, Henry Grace, Hugh Hunt; cos, Moss Mabry; makeup, William Tuttle.

Crime/Adventure   **(PR:C MPAA:NR)**

SOLANGE DU DA BIST   (SEE: AS LONG AS YOU'RE NEAR ME, 1956, Ger.)

SOLARIS**½**   (1972, USSR) 165m Mosfilm-Magna/Sovexport c

Nathalie Bondarchuk (Harey), Youri Yarvet (Snaut), Donatas Banionys (Kris), Anatoli Sonlinitsin (Sartorius), Vladislav Dvorjetzki (Burton), Nikolai Grinko (Father), Sos Sarkissian (Gibarian).

A superb science fiction film directed by Andrei Tarkovsky, very possibly the finest director to come out of the Soviet Union since the earliest days of their cinematic history. It concerns a cosmonaut who travels to the distant space station of Solaris, a super-intelligent being who materializes into human form for communication purposes. He is there to investigate a phenomenon in which his fellow space travelers have recurring visions of quiet home lives back on Earth. Tarkovsky, who eventually would leave the U.S.S.R. in search of cinematic freedom, went on to explore the concept of nostalgia and history in his NOSTALGHIA (1983) and ANDREI ROUBLOV (1973).

d, Andrei Tarkovsky; w, Tarkovsky, Friedrich Gorenstein (based on the novel by Stanislas Lem); ph, Vadim Jusov (Sovcolor); m, Eduard Artemyer; art d, Mikhail Romadin.

Science Fiction   **Cas.**   **(PR:C MPAA:PG)**

SOLDATERKAMMERATER PA VAGT   (SEE: OPERATION CAMEL, 1961, Den.)

SOLDIER, THE*   (1982) 96m Embassy c (GB: CODENAME: THE SOLDIER)

Ken Wahl (The Soldier), Klaus Kinski (Dracha), William Prince (U.S. President), Alberta Watson (Susan Goodman), Jeremiah Sullivan, Joaquim DeAlmeida, Peter Hooten, Steve James, Alexander Spencer, William Anagos, Bob Andrews, Lisa Cain, Gerald Cantor, Tony Cecere, Al Cerullo, Jr, Shirley Cina, David Cooper, Roy Milton Davis, William De Niro, Daniel Dod, Taylor E. Duncan, Allen Duzak, Ned Eisenberg, Gary D. Fisher, Manfred Gschneider, Ron Harper, Eivind Harum, Jery Hewitt, Martin Honer, Al Israel, Zeljko Ivanck, Audrey Johnston, Jeffrey Jones, Eugene Key, Tim Klein, David Lipman.

Lacking even the imagination to give its title character a name, THE SOLDIER is a preposterous CIA world espionage thriller packed with enough gore to shame most makers of this trash. A couple of Russian terrorists hijack a truck loaded with plutonium from a U.S. highway (are you with us so far?), then threaten to put the big bang theory into action unless Israeli troops vacate the West Bank of Jordan. Of course the president's hands are tied and the only answer is superagenttootought-odieonemanarmy Wahl, a carbon copy of all those other one-man armies. Blood, guts, exploding things, fast cars, tough looks, and slow-motion deaths fill up the screen time that is not cluttered with plot. Just a hair better than Glickenhaus' earlier fiasco THE EXTERMINATOR.

p,d&w, James Glickenhaus; ph, Robert M. Baldwin, Jr., (Eastmancolor); m, Tangerine Dream; ed, Paul Fried; prod d; William DeSeta; art d, Jam Schlubach; spec eff, W.H. "Candy" Flanagin; stunts, Baldwin.

Adventure   Cas.   (PR:O MPAA:R)

SOLDIER AND THE LADY, THE**½
(1937) 83m RKO bw (GB: MICHAEL STROGOFF)

Anton Walbrook (Strogoff), Elizabeth Allan (Nadia), Margot Grahame (Zangarra), Akim Tamiroff (Ogareff), Fay Bainter (Mother), Eric Blore (Blount), Edward Brophy (Packer), Paul Guilfoyle (Vasiloff), William Stack (Vladimir), Michael Visaroff (Innkeeper), Paul Harvey (Tsar).

Nonstop action marks this unusual screen adaptation of Jules Verne's oft-filmed novel Michael Strogoff. European actor Walbrook, who had starred in both French and German productions of the same material, was hired by producer Berman to once again play the loyal courier of the Tzar Alexander II who is entrusted to deliver a new military strategy to the army in Siberia, which is busy fending off a vicious horde of Tartars led by Tamiroff. After successfully avoiding a trap set by a seductive spy (Grahame) and nearly being blinded by one of the Tartars (Strogoff was blinded in Verne's novel), Walbrook finally makes it to the front and delivers the message. The strategy proves successful and the villains are crushed for mother Russia. This production of THE SOLDIER AND THE LADY is a strange amalgamation of different screen versions of Verne's novel. RKO producer Berman was approached by French producer Joseph Ermolieff, who had secured the rights to both the French and German versions of MICHAEL STROGOFF, starring Walbrook. Impressed by the epic battle sequences, Berman bought the rights to the French picture, hired Walbrook, and intercut newly-filmed U.S. footage with the spectacular action scenes from the foreign version. The trick worked, but the overall effect is weakened somewhat by the unnecessary forays into broad comic relief provided by Blore and Brophy, who play two wise-cracking journalists sent to cover the war. Considering the film was a cut-and-paste job, it was surprisingly successful.

p, Pandro S. Berman; d, George Nicholls; w, Mortimer Offner, Anthony Veiller, Anne Morrison Chapin (based on the novel Michael Strogoff by Jules Verne); ph, Joseph H. August; ed, Frederic Knudtson.

Drama   (PR:C MPAA:NR)

SOLDIER BLUE*
(1970) 112m (AE) c

Candice Bergen (Cresta Marybelle Lee), Peter Strauss (Pvt. Honus Gant), Donald Pleasence (Isaac Q. Cumber), Bob Carraway (Lt. John McNair), Jorge Rivero (Spotted Wolf), Dana Elcar (Capt. Battles), John Anderson (Col. Iverson), Martin West (Lt. Spingarn), Jorge Russek (Running Fox), Marco Antonio Arzate (Kiowa Brave), Ron Fletcher (Lt. Mitchell), Barbara Turner (Mrs. Long), James Hampton (Pvt. Menzies), Mort Mills (Sgt. O'Hearn), Ralph Nelson (Indian Agent), Aurora Clavel (Indian Woman).

Disguising a Vietnam allegory as a calvary versus Indians picture seems to be more the intention here than any great concern for Indian rights. SOLDIER BLUE is an excessive, tastelessly violent picture illustrating the atrocities enacted by the oh-so-bad calvary men on the oh-so-good Cheyennes. Bergen and Strauss are the only survivors of an Indian slaughter by the cavalry after Bergen had been kidnaped and living in the Cheyenne's company for two years. They try to make their way back to the safety of an army outpost and enroute experience a maximum of violent encounters. A typical picture of the era, which blindly resorts to a narrow view of good and bad without making room for some middle shade of gray. This one gets worse as time passes.

p, Gabriel Katzka, Harold Loeb; d, Ralph Nelson; w, John Gay (based on the novel Arrow in the Sun by Theodore V. Olsen); ph, Robert Hauser, Arthur J. Ornitz (Panavision, Technicolor); m, Roy Budd; ed, Alex Beaton; art d, Frank Arrigo; set d, Carlos Grandjean; cos, Ted Parvin; spec eff, Herman Townsley; m/l, "Soldier Blue," "No One Told Me," "Buffy Sainte-Marie" (sung by Sainte-Marie); makeup, Del Armstrong; tech adv, Eddie Little Sky.

Western   Cas.   (PR:O MPAA:PG)

SOLDIER IN LOVE   (SEE: FANFAN THE TULIP 1952, Fr.)

SOLDIER IN SKIRTS   (SEE: TRIPLE ECHO, 1973, Brit.)

SOLDIER IN THE RAIN**½
(1963) 87m AA-Cedar-Solar/AA bw

Jackie Gleason (M/Sgt. Maxwell Slaughter), Steve McQueen (Supply Sgt. Eustis Clay), Tuesday Weld (Bobby Jo Pepperdine), Tony Bill (Pfc. Jerry Meltzner), Tom Poston (Lt. Magee), Chris Noel (Frances McCoy), Ed Nelson (MP Sgt. Priest), Lew Gallo (MP Sgt. Lenahan), Rockne Tarkington (1st Sgt. William Booth), Lewis Charles (Sgt. Tozzi), Sam Flint (Old Man), Paul Hartman (Chief of Police), Adam West (Capt. Blekeley), John Hubbard (Battalion Major).

A curious comedy-drama with Gleason providing both and McQueen providing neither. Gleason is a marvel to watch and can say more with no words than most actors can with pages of dialog. He's a career top sergeant in the army and very happy with his service life. Fellow sergeant McQueen idolizes Gleason and is looking forward to leaving the army and getting involved in busines. enterprises. He tries to convince Gleason that there's a fortune to be made outside the army but Gleason is quite content: he has his room and board paid for, he has an air-conditioned room. in their Southern camp, and he even has a free soft drink machine that he can tap at any time – what could be better? Gleason is a lifelong bachelor and carries his copious weight around with him as a shield against getting involved in male-female relationships. McQueen introduces Gleason to Weld, a teenage blonde, and they go out together even though he is old enough to be her father. They have a good time with each other and Gleason takes a paternal attitude toward her. She is to date Gallo and stands him up. Later, Gallo dresses her down and Gleason steps in and forces Gallo to apologize to the girl, which impresses Weld. Gallo and Nelson hate McQueen (this is never explained fully) for some old slight and, being tough MPs who wield their clubs with abandon, beat McQueen to a bloody pulp. Gleason arrives before they kill McQueen and stops the beating, but he is so exhausted by his efforts that he suffers a collapse. On the following day, Gleason tells McQueen that when he retires, his goal is to find some quiet tropical island, kick back and let the rest of the world go by. It never happens. Gleason dies and McQueen, touched by what's happened, re-enlists in the service, perhaps as a tribute to his late friend. Gleason's acting is fluid and realistic, and McQueen, perhaps thinking that Gleason was stealing the movie, overplayed and is second only to Paul Newman in his vain attempts at comedy. The situation between Gleason and Weld never comes to fruition but the by-play between the two is charming to watch and Weld acquits herself well. Gallo later gave up acting to become a successful TV producer, along with his wife Lillian. Nelson went from this small role to a leading part on TV's "Peyton Place." Director-producer Tony Bill is seen in one of his early roles, and Adam West, who was to burst upon America's screen two years later as "Batman," does a neat job as a superior officer. Not enough comedy to put it into the NO TIME FOR SERGEANTS category and not enough interesting drama either.

p, Martin Jurow; d, Ralph Nelson; w, Maurice Richlin, Blake Edwards (based on the novel by William Goldman); ph, Philip Lathrop; m, Henry Mancini; ed, Ralph Winters; md, Mancini; art d, Phil Barber, James W. Payne; cos, Jerry Alpert, Shirlee Strahm; spec eff, Lawrence A. Hampton; makeup, Bud Bashaw.

Drama/Comedy   Cas.   (PR:C MPAA:NR)

SOLDIER OF FORTUNE**½
(1955) 96m FOX

Clark Gable (Hank Lee), Susan Hayward (Jane Hoyt), Michael Rennie (Inspector Merryweather), Gene Barry (Louis Hoyt), Tom Tully (Tweedie), Alex D'Arcy (Rene), Anna Sten (Mme. Dupree), Russell Collins (Icky), Leo Gordon (Big Matt), Richard Loo (Po-Lin), Soo Yong (Dak Lai), Frank Tang (Ying Fai), Jack Kruschen (Austin Stoker), Mel Welles (Rocha), Jack Raine (Maj. Leith-Phipps), George Wallace (Gunner), Alex Finlayson (Australian Airman), Noel Toy (Luan), Beal Wong (Chinese Clerk), Robert Burton (Father Xavier), Robert Quarry (Frank Stewart), Charles Davis (Hotel Desk Clerk), Victor Sen Yung (Goldie), Frances Fong (Maxine), Ivis Goulding, Barry Bernard (English People), Kam Tong (Needle), George Chan (Cheap Hotel Clerk), William Yip (Bartender), Danny Chang (Billy Lee).

When her photographer husband Barry is missing in the Far East Hayward goes to Hong Kong in search of him. She gets no help from either American or British authorities but she remains undaunted. After checking into a somewhat seedy hotel, populated by various rogues from different lands, Hayward contacts Rennie, a local police captain. His hands are tied by department regulations but he attempts to do some work on his own time to help her. After Hayward identifies two cameras found by authorities as possessions of Barry's, Rennie suggests she go to a local hangout for some help. There she meets D'Arcy, who manages to keep her from being tossed out. He claims to have known Barry, telling Hayward that her husband hung out with Rocha and Fong. Though the information is paltry, Hayward looks up Fong, who takes her to Gable, an American soldier of fortune. He runs a smuggling operation out of Communist China and is immediately taken with Hayward, whom he offers to help if it means he can get anywhere with her. Hayward is put off by his obvious attempts at seduction but eventually agrees to let him help. After a drunken celebration Gable forces Tully, the local bar's owner, into finding out where Barry is. It's learned Barry is in Canton and Gable prepares to take his boat for a rescue try. However, Rennie is waiting on board and Gable is forced to take him hostage. Gable's crew deserts before the ship reaches the Communist shores and Rennie then realizes that this is not just another smuggling run. He offers assistance and Barry is eventually rescued. They are chased, but Gable eludes the pursuers by sailing his boat into a bay full of hundreds of fishing junks. Barry and Hayward are reunited but the photographer realizes that his life will always be a haphazard one full of wanderings. He persuades his wife to go with Gable, who truly loves her and is willing to give up his dangerous life for her. Though just a potboiler drama, SOLDIER OF FORTUNE is an entertaining little adventure that makes good use of the Hong Kong setting. Gable was a little too old for the part but he still has some fun with his rugged he-man characterization. Everyone involved with the production understood that this was a quickie production but that didn't prevent them from making it entertaining. Ironically directed by Dmytryck, one of the Hollywood Ten, the film waltzes around the sensitive issue of communism by never actually specifying that Barry must be rescued out of Red China. Dymtryk was very impressed with the organizational abilities of the Hong Kong locals in helping shoot the film. In order to shoot the escape sequence into the harbor, he had to count on the help of numerous fishermen, all cooperating against various elements such as wind changes and camera setups. The shooting was a success, he recalled in his autobiography, It's a Hell of a Life but Not a Bad Living, thanks to the skilled extras. "I have worked in almost every country of the so-called technically superior Western world, but I have never seen planning, organization, or execution anywhere near that shown by this group of fishermen, lightermen, and smugglers," he wrote. Hayward, because of legal difficulties involving her bitter divorce from Jess Barker the year before, was not allowed to bring her children to Hong Kong. She chose not to go along on the location shooting and in an act of generosity by the studio (undoubtedly fueled by Hayward's box office appeal) the script was rewritten to accommodate her. Her scenes were all shot in the studio and the mockup Hong Kong was indistinguishable from the real thing. Gable had originally wanted Grace Kelly as a costar and didn't even know who Hayward was. This came as a surprise to many, for at a party some 10 years earlier he had spent the better part of his time eyeing the red-haired beauty. She had also been one of many who tried unsuccessfyully to be Gable's costar in GONE WITH THE WIND.

p, Buddy Adler; d, Edward Dmytryk; w, Ernest K. Gann (based on his novel); ph, Leo Tover (CinemaScope, DeLuxe Color); m, Hugo Friedhofer; ed, Dorothy Spencer; md, Lionel Newman; art d, Lyle Wheeler, Jack Martin Smith; set d, Walter M. Scott, Stuart A. Reiss; cos, Charles LeMaire; spec eff, Ray Kellogg.

Drama/Adventure   **Cas.**   **(PR:C MPAA:NR)**

SOLDIER OF LOVE   (SEE: FANFAN THE TULIP, 1951, Fr.)

SOLDIER OF ORANGE*½   (1979, Dutch) 165m RANK/International Picture Show c

Rutger Hauer (Erik), Jeroen Krabbe (Gus), Peter Faber (Will), Derek De Lint (Alex), Eddy Habbema (Robby), Lex Van Delden (Nico), Edward Fox (Col. Rafelli), Belinda Meuldijk (Esther), Susan Penhaligon (Susan), Andrea Domburh (Queen Wilhelmina), Huib Rooymans (John), Dolf De Vries (Jacques), Rijk De Gooyer (Breitner), Guus Hermus (Van Der Zanden), Rene Koldehoff (Geisman), Del Henney (Sergeant).

An expertly directed war drama which details the effects of Nazi occupation on a group of Dutch students. Hauer takes top acting honors as a half-hearted member of the resistance effort who gets more involved when he escapes to England. After the war has ended, Hauer returns to his homeland to find that most of his fellow students and resistance fighters have been killed by Nazis, while others have come through the war barely affected. An exceptional character study from Verhoeven, who would again work with screenwriter Soeteman and actors Krabbe and DeVries in his haunting THE FOURTH MAN. (In Dutch; English Subtitles.)

p, Rob Houwer; d, Paul Verhoeven; w, Verhoeven, Gerard Soeteman, Kees Holierhoek (based on the autobiography of Erik Hazelhoff Roelfzema); ph, Peter De Bont, Jost Vacano (Eastmancolor); m, Rogier Van Otterloo; ed, Jane Speer; art d, Roland De Groot; cos, Elly Claus.

War Drama   **Cas.**   **(PR:O MPAA:R)**

SOLDIER, SAILOR**   (1944, Brit.) 61m Realist/UA bw

Sgt. Ted Holliday, Gun Slayer Al Beresford, Engineer David Sime, Rosamund John, Jean Kent, Charles Victor, George Carney, Jean Cadell, Jimmy Knight, Bill Elliot, John Rae, Neville Mapp, Jimmy Plant, Esme Lee, Men of the New Zealand Expeditionary Force.

Well-made WW II propaganda film has an unsuspecting merchant vessel becoming the target of a Nazi air attack. Though the boat is badly damaged in the scuffle, it is able to stay afloat long enough for those aboard to be rescued by a passing convoy. This places the civilians in the middle of more heated action against the Nazis, in which they do their best to assist in the fighting. Includes actual war footage, giving the drama a realistic look.

p, John Taylor; d, Alexander Shaw; w, Frank Launder, St. John L. Clowes, Al Lloyd; ph, A.E. Jeakins, Raymond Elton.

War   **(PR:A MPAA:NR)**

SOLDIERS, THE   (SEE: LES CARABINIERS, 1968 Fr.)

SOLDIERS AND WOMEN**   (1930) 69m COL bw

Aileen Pringle (Brenda Ritchie), Grant Withers (Capt. Clive Branch), Helen Johnson (Helen Arnold), Walter McGrail (Capt. Arnold), Emmett Corrigan (Gen. Mitchell), Blanche Frederici (Martha), Wade Boteler (Sgt. Conlon), Raymond Largay (Col. Ritchie), William Colvin (Doctor), Sam Nelson (Pvt. Delehanty).

Mystery shrouds an Army post when the husband of one of two women having an affair with a soldier is killed. The daughter of the commanding officer who actually did the killing tries to implicate her lover, but upon being presented with proof of her guilt, she kills herself.

p, Harry Cohn; d, Edward Sloman; w, Dorothy Howell (based on a play "The Soul Kiss" by Paul Hervey Fox, George Tilton); ph, Ted Tetzlaff; ed, Leonard Wheeler art d, Harrison Wiley.

Mystery   **(PR:A MPAA:NR)**

SOLDIERS OF FORTUNE   (SEE: WAR CORRESPONDENT 1932)

SOLDIERS OF PANCHO VILLA, THE   (SEE: LA CUCARACHA, 1961 Mex.)

SOLDIERS OF THE KING   (SEE: WOMAN IN COMMAND, 1934, Brit.)

SOLDIERS OF THE STORM*½   (1933) 69m COL bw

Regis Toomey (Brad Allerton), Anita Page (Natalie), Barbara Weeks (Spanish Waitress), Robert Ellis (Moran), Wheeler Oakman (George), Barbara Barondess (Sonia), Dewey Robinson (Chuck Bailey), George Cooper (Red), Arthur Wanzer (Adams), Henry Wadsworth (Dodie).

A below par programmer which places Toomey in an airplane for most of the picture, fighting a ring of smugglers. Page, Toomey's sweetheart, joins the gang for a while, but is safely on the side of the law when the gang is turned over to the government. Loaded with stock aerial stunts that you have probably seen countless times before.

d, D. Ross Lederman; w, Charles Condon, Horace McCoy (based on the story by Thomson Burtis); ph, Ted Tetzlaff; ed, Maurice Wright.

Crime   **(PR:A MPAA:NR)**

SOLDIER'S PLAYTHING, A*½   (1931) 71m WB bw (GB: A SOLDIER'S PAY)

Lotti Loder (Gretchen Rittner), Harry Langdon (Tim), Ben Lyon (Georgie Wilson), Jean Hersholt (Grandfather Rittner), Noah Beery, Sr (Capt. Plover), Fred Kohler, Sr (Hank), Otto Matieson (Herman), Marie Astaire (Lola), Frank Campeau (Dave).

Undistinguished farce set at the beginning of WW I centering on a few young men as they enter the army, each with a separate reason for becoming a soldier. Well-meaning effort handled in a flat manner by Curtiz (CASABLANCA, MILDRED PIERCE). Songs include: "Forever," "Qui, Qui," "Honey Boy," "Ja, Ja, Ja," "Side By Side."

d, Michael Curtiz; w, Perry Vekroff, Arthur Caesar (based on the story "Come Easy" by Vina Delmar); ph, J.O. Taylor; ed, Jack Killifer.

Drama/Comedy   **(PR:A MPAA:NR)**

SOLDIER'S PRAYER, A*   (1970, Jap.) 190m Ninjin Club-Shochiku Co./Shochiku Films of America bw (NINGEN NO JOKEN III)

Tatsuya Nakadai (Kaji), Michiyo Aratama (Michiko), Taketoshi Naito (Pvt. Tange), Keijiro Morozumi (Cpl. Hironaka), Yusuke Kawazu (Pvt. Terada), Kyoko Kishida (Ryuko), Reiko Hitomi (Umeko), Fijio Suga (Capt. Nagata), Nobuo Kaneko (Cpl. Kirahara), Tamao Nakamura (Female Refugee), Hideko Takamine (Woman in Settler's Village), Chishu Ryu (Village Elder).

The third and final part of Kobayashi's massive undertaking known collectively as THE HUMAN CONDITION, a critical look at Japanese society and the horrors of prison camps during wartime. With WW II drawing to a close and Manchuria falling to Russian troops, Nakadai surrenders in the hope that his captors will be more humane than the Japanese. His hopes are soon shattered, leading him to murder and then escape. While trying to trek across the snowy, empty Manchurian landscape he collapses and dies in a blizzard. A stark and depressing picture that follows the model set by the previous two films, THE HUMAN CONDITION (1959) and ROAD TO ETERNITY (1961). Originally released in Japan in 1961.

p, Shigeru Wakatsuki, Masaki Kobayashi; d, Kobayashi; w, Kobayashi, Zenzo Matsuyama, Koichi Inagaki (based on Volumes 5 and 6 of Jumpei Gomigawa's novel); ph, Yoshio Miyajima (Shochiku Grandscope); m, Chuji Kinoshita; ed, Keiichi Uraoka; art d, Kazue Hirataka.

War Drama   **(PR:C MPAA:NR)**

SOLDIER'S TALE, THE   (1964, Brit.) 52m British Home Entertainment c

Robert Helpmann (The Devil), Brian Phelan (The Soldier), Svetlana Beriosova (The Princess).

The age old tale of a man who sells his soul (in this case a violin) to the devil in return for the promise of good fortune. When Phelan, the greedy soldier, falls in love with ballerina Beriosova he finds that the Devil is not such a generous fellow after all. The Melos Ensemble conducted by Derek Hudson Performs the music.

p, Leonard Cassini, Dennis Miller; d&w, Michael Birkett (based on the opera by Igor Stravinsky, C.F. Ramuz); ph, Miller (Technicolor); m, Stravinsky; ed, Richard Marden.

Ballet   (PR:A MPAA:NR)

SOLDIERS THREE**½   (1951) 87m MGM bw

Stewart Granger (*Pvt. Archibald Ackroyd*), Walter Pidgeon (*Col. Brunswick*), David Niven (*Capt. Pindenny*), Robert Newton (*Pvt. Jock Sykes*), Cyril Cusack (*Pvt. Dennis Malloy*), Greta Gynt (*Crenshaw*), Frank Allenby (*Col. Groat*), Robert Coote (*Maj. Mercer*), Dan O'Herlihy (*Sgt. Murphy*), Michael Ansara (*Manik Rao*), Richard Hale (*Govind-Lal*), Walter Kingsford (*Fairfax*), Charles Cane (*Boggs*), Patrick Whyte (*Maj. Harrow*), Movita Castenada (*Proprietress*), Charles Lang (*Merchant*), Cyril McLaglen (*Scot*), Harry Martin, Pat O'Moore, Dave Dunbar (*Cavalrymen*), Stuart Hall (*Lieutenant*), John Sheehan (*Drunk*), Clive Morgan, Pat Aherne, Wilson Wood (*Soldiers*).

In 1890s India Pidgeon is a British officer trying to capture Hale, an Indian leader who wants his people to rise against the queen's rule. Pidgeon is recalled from this duty, though, and sent to a base at Hyderalipore. There he meets Allenby, who takes command over Pidgeon. In addition to this new worry from above Pidgeon must constantly monitor the behavior of three men in his command: Granger, Newton, and Cusack, who are consistently disobedient and often drunk. Pidgeon gets Niven, an adjutant officer, to promote Granger from the rank of private to sergeant, hoping to break up the threesome and stop the shenanigans. However, one battle later and the unholy trio is back together. In another attempt to stop them from their hell-raising, Newton and Cusack are sent to accompany an ammunition convoy without their pal. Granger manages to desert the army and catch up with his friends. He finds they are under attack from Ansara, a former ally who has turned from Hale now that it seems his ideas are more in line with the Britons'. Pidgeon ignores his superior's orders and leads an attack to save the convoy. He is successful and Granger kills Ansara in the onslaught. Though he should be court-martialed for disobedience, Pidgeon receives a promotion to brigadier-general, while Granger is demoted for desertion, which of course reunites him with his two comrades. This is a slight but enjoyable romp. The story line is thin but the antics of Granger, Newton, and Cusack, playing their roles as broadly as can be, make up for this. This was the second Kipling-based picture for producer Berman, who had done GUNGA DIN in 1939. Many considered this film a disappointment considering the quality of that picture. Portions of the Kipling-based adventure, CAPTAINS COURAGEOUS, were used as backgrounds for this film as well. SOLDIERS THREE had the honor of being awarded by the British *Daily Express* before production was even begun. MGM studios was given a special medal by the nationally conscious newspaper for casting Englishmen in the film, and also for having the intelligence to import other Britons to fill out the production's minor roles.

p, Pandro S. Berman; d, Tay Garnett; w, Marguerite Roberts, Tom Reed, Malcolm Stuart Boylan (based on the book of short stories by Rudyard Kipling); ph, William Mellor; m, Adolph Deutsch; ed, Robert J. Kern; art d, Cedric Gibbons, Malcolm Brown.

Adventure   (PR:A MPAA:NR)

SOLDIERS 3   (SEE: SERGEANTS 3, 1962)

SOLID GOLD CADILLAC, THE****   (1956) 99m COL bw

Judy Holliday (*Laura Partridge*), Paul Douglas (*Edward L. McKeever*), Fred Clark (*Clifford Snell*), John Williams (*John T. Blessington*), Hiram Sherman (*Harry Harkness*), Neva Patterson (*Amelia Shotgraven*), Ralph Dumke (*Warren Gillie*), Ray Collins (*Alfred Metcalfe*), Arthur O'Connell (*Jenkins*), Richard Deacon (*Williams*), Marilyn Hanold (*Miss L'Arriere*), Anne Loos (*Blessington's Secretary*), Audrey Swanson (*Snell's Secretary*), Larry Hudson (*Chauffeur*), Sandra White (*Receptionist*), Harry Antrim (*Sen. Simpkins*), Paul Weber (*Elevator Man*), Emily Getchell (*Elderly Lady*), Maurice Manson (*1st Lawyer*), Suzanne Alexander (*Model*), Oliver Cliff (*Advertising Man*), Voltaire Perkins (*Judge*), Joe Hamilton (*2nd Lawyer*), Jean G. Harvey (*Farm Woman*), Bud Osborne (*Spanish-American War Veteran*), Lulu Mae Bohrman (*Dowager*), Madge Blake (*Lady Commentator*), Jack Latham (*Bill Parker*), George Burns (*Narrator*).

A charming, often hysterically funny poke at big business, government and the plight of the underdog who nips at the heels of the rat pack that runs a huge conglomerate. The script was by Abe Burrows, based on the hit Broadway play starring a much older Josephine Hull, written by Kaufman and Teichmann. Burrows would later be involved with another successful comedy on the same general subject entitled HOW TO SUCCEED IN BUSINESS WITHOUT REALLY TRYING. The original play was to have had a younger woman but when Hull, who was so delicious in ARSENIC AND OLD LACE, became available, she was paged for the part. In the film, Holliday has the role, and a love story was added to fill the romantic gaps. She plays her patented daffy blonde with a heart of gold who owns 10 shares in a massive company. The board of directors of the organization are a panel

of stern-visaged prigs including Clark, Williams, Sherman, Collins, and Dumke. Holliday shows up at a stockholders meeting and protests some of the shenanigans of the board. At first, she is a mere fly in their gargantuan ointment but her presence is duly noted by the press and things begin to happen. The former head of the company is Douglas, a hard-driving tycoon who has given up his role as top man on that totem pole in order to donate his services to the government, for which he is functioning as a a "dollar-a-year" man. (Note: This was not uncommon back then. Now, however, since the government raised salaries to livable standards, even the wealthiest of political appointees takes a pay check home, although it's hardly enough to pay for their broken stemware.) Holliday meets the bombastic Douglas and enlists him in her quest to secure representation for the small stockholders. When Douglas learns that his former aides have stabbed him in the back in their running of the company he started and nurtured, he joins with Holliday to get proxy votes from all the little people and to regain his position with the firm. O'Connell is the "don't rock the boat" office manager who is over Holliday in her job and Patterson is her secretary who aids and abets Holliday's mischief. George Burns handles the narrating chores in the same way Fred Allen did it (pre-recorded) on Broadway. The narration provides a few funny lines and bridges some of the gaps. The title stems from Holliday's fervent wish to own a solid gold cadillac. At the film's conclusion, with Douglas and Holliday united and running the company, she gets her desire. The humor in the screenplay seldom derives from one-liners. Rather, it is in the situations, the types it shoots darts into, and the unflagging energy of Holliday and Douglas as these two disparate people find love with each other and blend to defeat the pompous executives who think that they can pull the string of the ordinary people. Kaufman, who was known as "The Great Collaborator" wrote with more people than the average sit-com scribe. His partners included Moss Hart (YOU CAN'T TAKE IT WITH YOU, among others), Edna Ferber (THE ROYAL FAMILY OF BROADWAY), Marc Connelly (MERTON OF THE MOVIES), Morrie Ryskind (A NIGHT AT THE OPERA), Ring Lardner, Sr. and many more. His sole effort for the stage was "The Butter And Egg Man."

p, Fred Kohlmar; d, Richard Quine; w, Abe Burrows (based on the play by George S. Kaufman, Howard Teichmann); ph, Charles Lang; m, Cyril J. Mockridge; ed, Charles Nelson; md, Lionel Newman; art d, Ross Bellah; set d, William Kiernan, Louis Diage; cos, Jean Louis; makeup, Clay Campbell.

Comedy   (PR:A MPAA:NR)

SOLIMANO IL CONQUISTATORE
            (SEE: SULEIMAN THE CONQUEROR, 1963, Ital.)

SOLITAIRE MAN, THE**   (1933) 68m MGM bw

Herbert Marshall (*Oliver Lane*), May Robson (*Mrs. Vail*), Elizabeth Allan (*Helen*), Ralph Forbes (*Bascom*), Mary Boland (*Mrs. Hopkins*), Lionel Atwill (*Wallace*), Lucille Gleason (*Mrs. Peabody*), Robert McWade (*Mr. Peabody*), Harry Holman (*Mr. Hopkins*).

Marshall is the top dog in a diamond smuggling ring who, while in flight from Paris to London, finds dissension among his gang and that there has been some double dealing. The honor among thieves code is put into action in the claustrophobic quarters of the plane's cabin, with the disloyal crooks getting killed.

d, Jack Conway; w, James K. McGuinness (based on a story by Bella Spewack, Samuel Spewack); ph, Ray Overbaugh; ed, Frank Sullivan.

Crime   (PR:A MPAA:NR)

SOLITARY CHILD, THE**½   (1958, Brit.) 64m Beaconsfield/BL bw

Philip Friend (*James Random*), Barbara Shelley (*Harriet*), Sarah Lawson (*Ann*), Rona Anderson (*Jean*), Julia Lockwood (*Maggie*), Catherine Lacey (*Mrs. Evans*), Jack Watling (*Cyril*), Violet Farebrother (*Mrs. Dennison*), John Fabian (*Archie*), Frank Forsyth (*Doctor*).

Friend marries a farmer who was previously acquitted for the murder of his first wife, but the question arises in her mind that he may actually have been guilty, especially when her own life is threatened. The mystery is finally solved but not before everyone involved including the man's daughter, his first wife's lover, and the local veterinarian are all suspected of guilt. Unfortunately hampered by its short running time.

p, Peter Rogers; d, Gerald Thomas; w, Robert Dunbar (based on the novel by Nina Bawden); ph, Peter Hennessy; ed, Peter Boita.

Mystery   (PR:A MPAA:NR)

SOLNTSE SVETIT VSEM   (SEE: SUN SHINES FOR ALL, THE, 1961, USSR)

SOLO**   (1970, Fr.) 90m Balzac Eclair-Cinevog/CCFC-DIFEX c

Jean-Pierre Mocky (*Vincent*), Denis Le Guillou (*Virgile*), Anne Deleuze (*Annabel*), Eric Burnelli (*Marc*), Alain Fourez (*Eric*), Sylvie Breal (*Micheline*), R. J. Chauffard (*Rouquin*), Henri Poirier (*Inspector*), Christian Duvaleix (*Larrighi*).

Mocky, an actor turned director, puts himself in front of and behind the camera in this violent and angry look at the results of the events in France during May of 1968. Mocky casts himself as the violin-playing brother of the anarchist Le Guillou, who with his girl friend turns to mass murder as an extension of the student May Day riots. Mocky is trying to get in contact with his younger brother, but never does, instead falling victim to a police trap, while his brother gets away. Mocky tosses in some interesting touches but ultimately a revolution is a revolution is a revolution.

d, Jean-Pierre Mocky; w, Mocky, Alain Moury; ph, Marcel Weiss (Eastman-color); m, Georges Moustaki; ed, Marguerite Renoir; art d, Jacques Flamand, Francoise Hardy.

Drama/Crime (PR:O MPAA:NR)

SOLO** (1978, New Zealand/Aus.) 97m Hannay-Williams c

Martyn Sanderson (*Jules*), Lisa Peers (*Judy*), Jock Spence (*Radio Operator*), Vincent Gil (*Paul*), Perry Armstrong (*Billy*), Frances Edmund (*Schoolteacher*), Davina Whitehouse (*Rohana Beaulieu*), Maxwell Fernie (*Crispin Beaulieu*), Gillian Hope (*Woman on Train*), Veronica Lawrence (*Sue*), Val Murphy (*Anita*).

A "road movie" which takes place for the most part in the air as flier Gil meets up with wanderer Peers. They pal around for a while before she finally decides to move on, but not until she brings Gil and his teenaged son closer together. The aerial views of the New Zealand scenery provide a stunning visual treat, while the acting and script fall short.

p, David Hannay, Tony Williams; d, Williams; w, Williams, Martyn Sanderson; ph, John Blick.

Drama Cas. (PR:O MPAA:NR)

SOLO CONTRO ROMA (SEE: ALONE AGAINST ROME, 1963, Ital.)

SOLO FOR SPARROW** (1966, Brit.) 56m Merton Park/Schoenfeld bw

Anthony Newlands (*Mr. Reynolds*), Glyn Houston (*Inspector Sparrow*), Nadja Regin (*Mrs. Reynolds*), Michael Coles (*Pin Norman*), Allan Cuthbertson (*Chief Supt. Symington*), Ken Wayne (*Baker*), Jerry Stovin (*Lewis*), Jack May (*Inspector Hudson*), Murray Melvin (*Larkin*), Peter Thomas (*Bell*), Michael Caine (*Mooney*), Neil McCarthy (*Dusty*), Susan Maryott (*Sue Warren*), Nancy O'Neil (*Miss Martin*).

An average crime investigation picture which has Houston, a local detective, taking a leave of absence to sleuth in his own right when Scotland Yard interferes with his jurisdiction. He successfully discovers that Coles and storekeeper Newlands were behind a jewel store robbery which resulted in the death of Norman's wife, the store cashier. Houston nearly experiences the same fate, but after exchanging gunfire with the culprits, he turns them over to Scotland Yard. Released in Britain in 1962, the film's U. S. release was held up for four years, by which time ZULU - Michael Caine's first real success - had given him sufficient exposure so that his name on a marquee meant something.

p, Jack Greenwood; d, Gordon Flemyng; w, Roger Marshall (based on the novel *The Gunner* by Edgar Wallace); ph, Bert Mason; ed, Derek Holding; md, Bernard Ebbinghouse; art d, Peter Mullins; makeup, Michael Morris.

Crime (PR:A MPAA:NR)

SOLOMON AND SHEBA** (1959) 139m Edward Small/UA

Yul Brynner (*Solomon*), Gina Lollobrigida (*Magda, Queen of Sheba*), George Sanders (*Adonijah*), David Farrar (*Pharaoh*), Marisa Pavan (*Abishag*), John Crawford (*Joab*), Laurence Naismith (*Herzrai*), Jose Nieto (*Ahab*), Alejandro Rey (*Sittar*), Harry Andrews (*Baltor*), Julio Pena (*Zadok*), Maruchi Fresno (*Bathsheba*), William Devlin (*Nathan*), Felix De Pomes (*Egyptian General*), Jean Anderson (*Takyan*), Jack Gwillim (*Josiah*), Finlay Currie (*King David*).

For last feature film, King Vidor unfortunately helmed this overblown and rather silly biblical epic. It also carries an unhappy legacy as being the film that killed Tyrone Power. Adapting freely from the Old Testament story of Solomon and Sheba, this opens with Brynner (as Solomon) and his brother Adonijah (Sanders) preparing for an attack by the Egyptian army. After the Israelites handily defeat their enemy in an enormous battle sequence, the Queen of Sheba (Lollobrigida) enters the scene. She insults Sanders, then rides off to join her people. Back in Jerusalem, Currie (as King David) is on his deathbed. He tells of a dream where the Lord revealed Brynner would be the next king, a move that naturally upsets the power-hungry Sanders. In homage to Currie, Brynner builds the Great Temple. Farrar, the Egyptian Pharaoh, fears Brynner will send the Israelites to attack his land. He enlists Lollobrigida's help to stop Brynner, using her sensuality to stop the Jewish king. Bearing a plethora of expensive gifts, Lollobrigida manages to get Brynner to fall for her, which upsets prophet Devlin and his cronies known as "The Elders." They demand Lollobrigida be cast out of Israel, but Brynner does not comply. Sanders is angered by this and arranges for some men to kill Brynner. Brynner outwits the would-be assassins, then forces Sanders to leave the country. Lollobrigida holds an enormous feast, then

goes to a palace orgy. She seduces Brynner, which incurs the wrath of the Lord. Lightning bolts destroy the temple, but this is only the beginning of Brynner's new troubles. The Egyptians attack, nearly wiping out Brynner's troops. Lollobrigida learns she is pregnant, but makes a pact with the Lord. At the ruins of the Temple, she promises to renounce her own faith and return to Sheba if Brynner's turmoils will end. The Israelites return from battle, then polish their shields on Brynner's command. The high-gloss shields catch sunlight, temporarily blinding the Egyptians, which causes the enemy troops to fall over a ledge. Back in Jerusalem, the people are convinced Brynner has lost the war. Sanders takes over as king and commands Lollobrigida be stoned to death. These plans are thwarted when Brynner returns victorious, then kills Sanders in a sword fight. He takes Lollobrigida's body to the temple, where amid a background chorus and fancy lighting, her life is restored. Lollobrigida returns to Sheba, while Brynner begins reconstruction of the temple. Packed into this slam-bang history lesson are most of the famous stories associated with Solomon, including the famed debate between two mothers over the ownership of a baby. Following the two acclaimed biblical epics of the 1950s–THE TEN COMMANDMENTS and BEN HUR–SOLOMON AND SHEBA sticks to the unwritten Hollywood code that big spending equals great filmmaking. This is packed with colorful (if historically inaccurate) costumes and sets and mammoth battle sequences, but these elements don't cover up the stiff dialog. Every utterance is packed with sophistries, with such typical lines as "Abjure this woman and her idolatries. Tear down the obscene abomination she has erected!" The screenplay was credited to three writers and "based on a story by Crane Wilbur," though the Lord was given no credit for the original concept. Considering this takes place in the Holy Land, such unusual contrasts as Lollobrigida's thick Italian accent working in tandem with Sanders' crisp British pronunciations gives the film a slightly absurd feeling. The battle sequences are adequately staged, though nothing outstanding. Despite the historical inaccuracies in the set design (the predominant Stars of David that adorn nearly everything weren't commonly used until the 17th Century A.D.), the producers knew one thing for certain: sex sells. To this end, they employed the services of Granville Heathway, an Englishman who claimed to have extensive knowledge of orgies throughout history. Heathway helped re-create the poorly staged sex fest in the film, for which he received one of the most unusual production credits in cinema history: "Orgy-Sequence Adviser." The production was shot in Spain, where the government happily cooperated with the filmmakers. The Spanish army was incorporated to serve as extras for battle sequences, but problems arose when the English-speaking cast and crew had difficulty communicating with the soldiers. To solve this problem, American and British tourists were rounded up from vacation hot spots and used in addition to the soldiers. The military extras were paid what amounted to one dollar a day, working under often life- threatening conditions. Many ended up in the hospital but were shown little sympathy by their superior officers. In a letter to his friend Brian Aherne, Sanders wrote of one soldier who was trampled on by some horses, then run over by a chariot: "A Spanish officer yelled to him to get up and keep running so as not to spoil the shot. He staggered to his feet, ran a few paces, and then dropped in his tracks and passed out. The ambulance took him away. It is possible that, if he recovers, the officers will be lenient with him but generally speaking when this happens the officers beat them with their whips until they get up again. There is, of course, no doubt whatsoever that this is the proper way to treat extras." For his part, Sanders was decked out in a costume made of fiberglas and papier mache, and the inside of his chariot was padded with sponge rubber to protect him against the slightest bruise. This was shot in a new wide-screen technique called Super Technirama-70, a 70-millimeter film stock that also claimed would turn the film- going experience to real life. Six million dollars were poured into the production budget, and surprisingly the film made a respectable profit. The American box office came in at $5.5 million, while the European take was an even better $10 million. Power was originally cast in the lead, starring against his ofttime screen opponent Sanders. Filming commenced in the fall of 1958, and nearly 75 percent of the shooting (including crowd sequences) was completed when, on November 15, Power collapsed from a heart attack while shooting a sword fight with Sanders. Vidor later said: "...I felt he was giving his best performance; I also thought that the completed picture would have been his best." Production was temporarily halted while the filmmakers sorted out their options. It was finally decided to reshoot all of Power's sequences with a new actor, while collecting the $1,229,172 insurance policy on Power's death. In the interim, Sanders left Spain to shoot another film, but then returned to SOLOMON AND SHEBA, where he received $65,000 over his original salary. Brynner, an experienced biblical-epic thespian (THE TEN COMMANDMENTS), was hired to play Solomon. Perhaps the best-known bald man to come out of Hollywood, this is one of the few performances for which Brynner wore hair. His performance is adequate, but Vidor was convinced Brynner misunderstood the part. The director saw King Solomon as a man fighting dual emotions, but claimed Brynner "...fought the idea of a troubled monarch and wanted to dominate each situation without conflict. It was an attitude that affected the depth of his performance and probably the integrity of the film." Despite this necessary replacement, many long shots and rear views of Power were used in the final cut. p, Ted Richmond; d, King Vidor; w, Anthony Veillier, Paul Dudley, George Bruce (based on a story by Crane Wilbur); ph, Freddie Young (Super Technirama-70, Technicolor); m, Mario Nascimbene; ed, John Ludwig; art d, Richard Day, Alfred Sweeney; spec eff, Alex Weldon; ch, Jaroslav Berger

Biblical Epic   **Cas.**   **(PR:C MPAA:NR)**

SOLOMON KING zero   (1974) 110m Sal-Wa-Stage Struck c

Sal Watts *(Solomon King)*, "Little Jamie" Watts *(Maney King)*, Claudia
Russo *(Princess Onceba)*, Felice Kinchelow *(Albert)*, Samaki Bennett *(Sama-
ki Miller)*, Louis Zito *(O'Malley)*, Bernard B. Burton *(Abdulla)*, Richard
Scarso *(Hassan)*, Tito Fuentes *(Himself)*, C. B. Lyars *(Preacher)*.

An insulting black exploitation picture which is solely the fault of producer,
co-director, writer, co-editor, and star Sal Watts. He avenges the death of
princess Russo, a past flame, and organizes a commando squad to wreak
havoc in an Arab sheikdom. Overlong, painfully overstuffed with exposition
scenes, and far from exciting. A cameo from former baseball player Tito
Fuentes is its only claim to fame.

p, Sal Watts; d, Watts, Jack Bomay; w, Watts (based on a story by Jim
Alston); ph, Chuck Colwell, Phil Caplan (CFI Color); m, Jimmy Lewis; ed,
Watts, Colwell; art d, Al Brown.

Adventure   **(PR:O MPAA:R)**

SOLUTION BY PHONE*½   (1954, Brit.) 60m Pan/ABF bw

Clifford Evans *(Richard Hanborough)*, Thea Gregory *(Ann Selby)*, John
Witty *(Peter Wayne)*, Georgina Cookson *(Frances Hanborough)*, Enid Hewitt
(Mrs. Garner), Geoffrey Goodhart *(Inspector Kirby)*, Max Brimmell *(Sgt.
Woods)*, Charles Lamb, Diana Payan, Johnnie Schofield, Jessica Cairns.

A writer, Evans, is wrongly convicted of murdering his wife after the real
killer solicits knowledge from Evans, who specializes in crime novels, on
how to get rid of a corpse. Could have been much better with a tighter script
and more discrete direction.

p, Geoffrey Goodhart, Brandon Fleming; d, Alfred Travers; w, Fleming; ph,
Hilton Craig.

Crime   **(PR:A MPAA:NR)**

SOMBRERO*½   (1953) 103m MGM c

Ricardo Montalban *(Pepe Gonzales)*, Pier Angeli *(Eufemia Calderon)*,
Vittorio Gassman *(Alejandro Castillo)*, Cyd Charisse *(Lola de Torrano)*,
Yvonne De Carlo *(Maria)*, Rick Jason *(Ruben)*, Nina Foch *(Elena Cantu)*,
Kurt Kasznar *(Father Zacaya)*, Walter Hampden *(Don Carlos Castillo)*,
Thomas Gomez *(Don Homero Calderon)*, Jose Greco *(Gintanillo de Tor-
rano)*, John Abbott *(Don Daniel)*, Andres Soler *(Little Doctor)*, Fanny
Schiller *(Dona Fela)*, Luz Alba *(Rosaura)*, Rosaura Revueltas *(Tia Mag-
dalena)*, Alfonso Bedoya *(Don Inocente)*, Jorge Trevino *(Don Nacho)*, Tito
Novaro *(Napoleon Lopez)*, Manuel Arvide *(Manager)*, Felipe De Flores
(Tomas), Beatriz Ramos *(Senora Inocente)*, Florencio Castello *(Mozo)*,
Arturo Rangel *(Professor)*, Salvador Baquez *(Bartender)*, Juan Duval
(Bellhop), Rita Conde *(Silveria)*, Pascual Pena *(Drunk)*, Louise De Carlo,
Gabrielle Roussellon *(Girls in Cafe)*, Tom Hernandez, Orlando Beltran,
George Derrick, Carlos Barbee, Eduardo Cansino, Miguel Contreras *(Men
in Cafe)*, Alma Beltran, Amapola Del Vando, Pilar Del Rey, Dorita Pallais,
Delmar Costello *(Party Guests)*.

Producer Jack Cummings never stopped attempting to do different kinds of
films. His work ranged from six wet and wonderful Esther Williams movies
to intriguing biographies like THE STRATTON STORY to well-tailored
comedies such as THE TEAHOUSE OF THE AUGUST MOON. In SOM-
BRERO, he tried to do a truthful musical about the way life was in Mexico
and used, as the basis, three tales from Niggli's book. Three sets of lovers
are depicted. The tale of Montalban (whom Cummings "discovered") and
Angeli provides the humor, as both come from feuding villages and the
towns must be calmed before the two can marry (a south of the border
ROMEO AND JULIET type story). Gassman, whom MGM had just
imported from Italy, is an heir to a large fortune and in love with dirt-poor
De Carlo. His family is totally against his affections for her and when he
learns he is dying of a tumor, he pleads with her to marry him but she
declines and arranges a loveless match between him and Foch. After
Gassman's death, his father, Hampden, finds De Carlo and brings her into
his home where she can have a place to stay. Charisse is the sister of Greco,
a matador, and in love with street peddler Jason. Greco doesn't like Jason
and tries to break them up, going so far as to lure Jason into the bull ring,
but it backfires and the raging toro gores Greco to death. After Jason and
Charisse marry, it soon disintegrates and she realizes her brother was right
about Jason. Into all of this, there are several songs, including: "Cartas a
Ufemia" (sung by Montalban, written by Ruben Fuentes, Ruben Mendez,
with English lyrics by Saul Chaplin), "Gypsy Dance" (danced by Charisse,
written by Chaplin and Leo Arnaud). Despite a mild response from the U.S.,
SOMBRERO did quite well in Spanish speaking countries and, surprisingly,
in the Philippines, Japan, and Ireland.

p, Jack Cummings; d, Norman Foster; w, Josefina Niggli, Foster (based on
the novel *A Mexican Village* by Niggli); ph, Ray June (Technicolor); ed,
Cotton Warburton; md, Leo Arnaud; art d, Cedric Gibbons, Daniel R.
Cathcart; set d, Edwin B. Willis, Fred MacLean; cos, Helen Rose; spec eff,
Warren Newcombe; ch, Hermes Pan, Jose Greco; m/l, Ruben Fuentes,
Ruben Mendez, Saul Chaplin, Augustin Lara, Ray Gilbert, Alfonso Esparza
Oteo, A. Fernandez Bustamente, Geronimo Villavino, Arnaud.

Drama/Musical   **(PR:A-C MPAA:NR)**

SOMBRERO KID, THE*   (1942) 56m REP bw

Don "Red" Barry *(Jerry Holden)*, Lynn Merrick *(Dorothy Russell)*, John
James *(Tommy Holden)*, Joel Friedkin *(Uriah Martin)*, Rand Brooks
(Phillip Martin), Robert E. Homans *(Tom Holden, Sr.)*, Stuart Hamblen
(Smoke Denton), Bob McKenzie *(Judge Tater)*, Lloyd "Slim" Andrews
(Panamint), I. Stanford Jolley *(Taggart)*, Frank Brownlee *(Barnett)*, Anne
O'Neal *(Mrs. Barnett)*, Kenne Duncan, Bud Geary, William Nestell, Hank
Bell, Curley Dresden, Jack O'Shea, Pascale Perry, Griff Barnett, Chick
Hannon, Merrill McCormack, Edward Cassidy.

A standard, entertaining oater which has Barry innocently getting involved
in a murder when a gang of thieves led by banker Friedkin infringe upon
Barry's father's mine. He is arrested, however, by his own brother and
nearly hanged before his buddies help him put the real culprits behind bars.
Filled with all the action you could want from this sort of film.

p&d, George Sherman; w, Norman S. Hall (based on a story by Doris
Schroeder, Eddy White); ph, William Bradford; ed, William Thompson; md,
Cy Feuer; art d, Russell Kimball.

Western   **Cas.**   **(PR:A MPAA:NR)**

SOME BLONDES ARE DANGEROUS*   (1937) 65m UNIV bw

Noah Beery, Jr *(Bud Mason)*, William Gargan *(George Regan)*, Dorothea
Kent *(Rose Whitney)*, Nan Grey *(Judy Williams)*, Roland Drew *(Paul Lewis)*,
Polly Rowles *(Mrs. Lewis)*, John Butler *(McNeil)*, Lew Kelly *(Jeff)*, Eddie
Roberts *(Battle O'Keefe)*, Joe Smallwood *(Spike)*, Edward Stanley *(Reilly)*,
Walter Friedman *(Dink Pappas)*.

Boxer Beery, Jr., dumps his manager and devoted girl friend Grey when he
becomes champion, knowing that he can do better by himself. He marries
empty-headed Kent for her glamorous status and sets up a match with an
up-and-comer who's after the title. On the night of the big fight, Beery, Jr.,
learns of Kent's unfaithfulness and this, combined with his lack of training,
causes him to lose the fight. Grey returns and consoles the big lug. Typical
boxing picture with a few exciting fight scenes. A remake of the same
studio's IRON MAN (1931); remade again with that title in 1951.

p, E.M. Asher; d, Milton Carruth; w, Lester Cole (based on the novel and
screenplay *Iron Man* by W.R. Burnett); ph, George Robinson; ed, Frank
Gross.

Sports Drama   **(PR:A MPAA:NR)**

SOME CALL IT LOVING*½   (1973) 103m CineGlobe c

Zalman King *(Robert)*, Carol White *(Scarlett)*, Tisa Farrow *(Jennifer)*,
Richard Pryor *(Jeff)*, Veronica Anderson *(Angelika)*, Logan Ramsey *(Doc-
tor)*, Brandy Herred *(Cheerleader)*, Ed Rue *(Mortician)*, Pat Priest *(Nurse)*,
Joseph DeMeo *(Bartender)*.

A strange fable of love, reminiscent of the classical fairy tale "Sleeping
Beauty," which has King buying the snoozing Farrow from a carnival side
show. His idealistic view of love is never realized and eventually he returns
her to her sleeping state. Pryor plays King's drug-crazed friend. White is
charismatic as the apparently bisexual mistress of the manor where King
takes his newly awakened beauty. Farrow is the younger sister of actress
Mia Farrow. This was writer-producer-director Harris' second directorial
stint; he directed THE BEDFORD INCIDENT in 1965.

p,d&w, James B. Harris (based on the short story "Sleeping Beauty" by
John Collier); ph, Mario Tossi (Technicolor); m, Richard Hazard; ed, Paul
Jasiukonis; md, Hazard; cos, Jax; song, "The Very Thought of You,"
performed by Nat "King" Cole.

Fantasy   **Cas.**   **(PR:O MPAA:R)**

SOME CAME RUNNING*½   (1959) 137m MGM c

Frank Sinatra *(Dave Hirsh)*, Dean Martin *(Bama Dillert)*, Shirley MacLaine
(Ginny Moorhead), Martha Hyer *(Gwen French)*, Arthur Kennedy *(Frank
Hirsh)*, Nancy Gates *(Edith Barclay)*, Leora Dana *(Agnes Hirsh)*, Betty Lou
Keim *(Dawn Hirsh)*, Larry Gates *(Prof Robert Haven French)*, Steven Peck
(Raymond Lanchak), Connie Gilchrist *(Jane Barclay)*, Ned Wever *(Smitty)*,
Carmen Phillips *(Rosalie)*, John Brennan *(Wally Dennis)*, William Schallert
(Al), Roy Engel *(Sheriff)*, Marion Ross *(Sister Mary Joseph)*, Denny Miller
(Dewey Cole), Chuck Courtney *(Hotel Clerk)*, Paul Jones *(George Huff)*,
Geraldine Wall *(Mrs. Stevens)*, Janelle Richards *(Virginia Stevens)*, George
Brengel *(Ned Deacon)*, George Cisar *(Hubie Nelson)*, Donald Kerr *(Doc
Henderson)*, Jan Arvan *(Club Manager)*, Don Haggerty *(Ted Harperspoon)*,
Frank Mitchell *(Waiter)*, Dave White *(Bus Driver)*, Len Lesser *(Dealer)*, Ric
Roman *(Joe)*, George E. Stone *(Slim)*, Anthony Jochim *(Judge Baskin)*,
Guitarist Al Viola.

Author James Jones wrote one of the definitive books about the war, *From
Here To Eternity*, which benefited greatly from the brilliant editing of
Maxwell Perkins. Sinatra won an Oscar for his part in that 1953 epic and
came back to appear in Jones' next book's movie adaptation, a postwar tale
that rambled on and on. The novel took Jones seven years and ran better

than 1,200 pages, so trimming it to filmable length was a difficult task. The screenwriters succeeded partially. Sinatra is a veteran who comes back to his home town of Parkman, Illinois, after trying his luck and failing as a writer after WW II. (The actual town they used was Madison, Indiana, and the peccadilloes of the cast are still spoken of in whispers by the populace.) Sinatra carries with him a new manuscript he's just completed under one arm, and a funny floozy, MacLaine, draped over the other. She is in love with him and the appearance of the two creates a minor sensation in the small town. Sinatra's brother is Kennedy, a rigid businessman married to Dana but having an affair with his assistant, Nancy Gates. Dana doesn't much like Sinatra and turns her nose up at him. Hyer teaches at the local college and finds Sinatra intriguing as she's never been out of that tiny burg and not accustomed to this kind of spirited person. She reads Sinatra's work and thinks that it has merit. The one local "character" is Martin, a loose gambler who finds in Sinatra a kindred spirit and the two men enjoy reveling with each other, running after women, drinking too much, and playing endless games of cards. Martin is suffering from diabetes and on his last legs. Since he is superstitious, he never removes his hat to keep his luck going well. Sinatra hates Kennedy because the older brother sent him to an orphanage when their parents died. He also hates Kennedy for his disdain for MacLaine, despite the fact that Kennedy's affair with Gates is an open secret. Sinatra finds himself falling for Hyer, who remains aloof to his entreaties. MacLaine remains on the scene and makes herself available whenever Sinatra wants her. Sinatra finally proposes to Hyer and still she refuses him. He is depressed by this rejection, grabs hold of MacLaine and Martin, and they drive off to have a wild time. They arrive in Terre Haute, meet Kennedy's teenage daughter, Keim, who fled the town with her young boy friend, Brennan, when she found out about her father's dalliance with Gates. Sinatra brings Keim back to the Kennedy-Dana home and tells them off for the lying lives they lead, and exits. Later, he informs a disbelieving Martin that he intends to marry MacLaine. Martin doesn't know why anyone would want to marry such a trollop. After the wedding, Peck, one of MacLaine's many ex-lovers, enters. He tries to kill Sinatra for taking her away and MacLaine takes the bullet meant for Sinatra. At her funeral, Martin is so moved that he lifts the hat he never would lift for anyone else. The title is from the Gospel According to St. Mark and the picture is from the novel according to Minnelli. He made many concessions to Sinatra, who is notorious for disliking more than one take and who refuses to work regular hours, preferring a noon to 8 p.m. schedule over the usual start at 7. It was a large grosser for MGM, perhaps due to the Oscar nominations accorded MacLaine, Hyer, Kennedy, and the tune "To Love and Be Loved" by Sammy Cahn and Jimmy Van Heusen. Though MacLaine remembers this as her favorite role, it was Hyer who stole the picture as the frosty teacher. She lost to Wendy Hiller for SEPARATE TABLES and Kennedy lost out on his fifth nomination to Burl Ives for THE BIG COUNTRY. While on location in Madison, MacLaine palled around with Sinatra and Martin and became part of the "Clan" which included Peter Lawford, Sammy Davis, Jr., and, occasionally, Joey Bishop. Martin's easy-going gambler was also effective and he proved here, as he did in THE YOUNG LIONS, that he was more than able to function without Jerry Lewis.

p, Sol C. Siegel; d, Vincente Minnelli; w, John Patrick, Arthur Sheekman (based on the novel by James Jones); ph, William H. Daniels (CinemaScope, Metrocolor); m, Elmer Bernstein; ed, Adrienne Fazan; md, Bernstein; art d, William A. Horning, Urie McCleary; set d, Henry Grace, Robert Priestley; cos, Walter Plunkett; m/l, "To Love and Be Loved" Sammy Cahn, James Van Heusen; makeup, William Tuttle.

Drama (PR:C MPAA:NR)

SOME DAY** (1935, Brit.) 68m WB bw

Esmond Knight (Curly Blake), Margaret Lockwood (Emily), Henry Mollison (Canley), Sunday Wilshin (Betty), Raymond Lovell (Carr), Ivor Barnard (Hope), George Pughe (Milkman), Jane Cornell (Nurse).

Simple romance about lovers Knight and Lockwood who attempt to make use of an apartment that is suppose to be temporarily vacated, but isn't. Lockwood's employer comes to the pair's rescue, enabling them to eventually marry. Lightweight material has enough promising moments to make it worthwhile.

p, Irving Asher; d, Michael Powell; w, Brock Williams (based on the novel Young Nowheres by I.A.R. Wylie); ph, Basil Emmott, Monty Berman; ed, Bert Bates; art d, Ian Campbell-Gray.

Drama (PR:A MPAA:NR)

SOME GIRLS DO** (1969, Brit.) 93m RANK-Ashdown/UA c

Richard Johnson (Hugh Drummond), Daliah Lavi (Baroness Helga Hagen), Beba Loncar (Pandora), James Villiers (Carl Petersen), Vanessa Howard (Robot No. 7), Maurice Denham (Mr. Mortimer), Robert Morley (Miss Mary), Sydne Rome (Flicky), Adrienne Posta (Angela, Drummond's Daily), Florence Desmond (Lady Manderley), Ronnie Stevens (Peregrine Carruthers), Virginia North (Robot No. 9), Nicholas Phipps (Lord Dunberry, Air Minister), George Belbin n (Maj. Newman), Yutte Stensgaard (Number One), Richard Hurndall (Aircraft Company President), Marga Roche (Birgit), Douglas Sheldon (Kruger).

An uninspired James Bond clone (see Index) which casts the barely debonair

Johnson as Bulldog Drummond, pitting him against the barely malevolent Villiers. Johnson is trying to prevent his archenemy from sabotaging the British government's testing of its first supersonic jet. Villiers organizes an army of mini-skirted female robots to do away with Johnson, but he renders them inactive, thereby saving the world from being overrun. Morley's performance as a cooking instructor is one of the picture's high points. A sequel to DEADLIER THAN THE MALE. (See BULLDOG DRUMMOND series, Index.)

p, Betty E. Box; d, Ralph Thomas; w, David Osborn, Liz Charles-Williams (based on "Sapper's" [H.C. McNeile] Bulldog Drummond character); ph, Ernest Steward (Eastmancolor); m, Charles Blackwell; ed, Ernest Hosler; art d, Edward Marshall; set d, Martin Atkinson; cos, Yvonne Caffin; spec eff, Kit West; m/l, Blackwell, Don Black; makeup, Basil Newall, Eddie Knight.

Crime/Comedy (PR:C MPAA:NR)

SOME KIND OF A NUT, 1959 (SEE: DOWN AMONG THE Z-MEN, 1959, Brit.)

SOME KIND OF A NUT zero (1969) 90m Mirisch-DFI-T.F.T./UA c

Dick Van Dyke (Fred Amidon), Angie Dickinson (Rachel Amidon), Rosemary Forsyth (Pamela Anders), Zohra Lampert (Bunny Erickson), Elliott Reid (Gardner Anders), Steve Roland (Baxter Anders), Dennis King (Otis Havemeyer), Pippa Scott (Dr. Sara), Peter Brocco (Mr. Suzumi), Robert Ito (George Toyota), Peter Turgeon (Mr. Defoe), Harry Davis (Dr. Ball), Benny Baker (Cab Driver), Lucy Saroyan (Samantha), Roy Roberts (1st Vice-President), Jonathan Hole (2nd Vice-president), Ned Wertimer (Larry), Danny Crystal (Dr. Abrams), Connie Gilchrist (Mrs. Boland), Heywood Hale Broun (Himself), Milo Boulton (Bank Guard), David Doyle, Carole Shelley.

An unfunny comedy which may have been an amusing five-minute student project, but falls short of filling up its 90-minute time slot. Kanin produced, acted as executive producer, director, and writer of this Dick Van Dyke vehicle, casting him as a bank teller involved with Forsyth while awaiting a divorce from Dickinson. He gets stung by a bee one afternoon and comes to work with a bandage on his face. He then decides to grow a beard over the wound, refusing to shave it off when the bank executives ask. Forsyth has her two brothers try to forcibly defuzz his face, but he evades them in his underwear and the men in white suits show up and haul the "crazy" Van Dyke off to the loony bin. What? They really made a feature length movie out of this? Why?

p, Walter Mirisch; d&w, Garson Kanin; ph, Burnett Guffey, Gerald Hirschfeld (DeLuxe Color); m, Johnny Mandel; ed, Richard Farrell; art d, Albert Brenner; set d, Ward Preston; cos, Anthea Sylbert; spec eff, Jerome Rosenfeld, Justus Gibbs; makeup, Tom Tuttle.

Comedy (PR:C MPAA:M/PG)

SOME KIND OF HERO*** (1982) 97m PAR c

Richard Pryor (Eddie Keller), Margot Kidder (Toni), Ray Sharkey (Vinnie), Ronny Cox (Col. Powers), Lynne Moody (Lisa), Olivia Cole (Jesse), Paul Benjamin (Leon), David Adams (The Kid), Martin Azarow (Tank), Shelly Batt (Olivia), Susan Berlin (Jeanette), Tim Thomerson (Cal), Mary Betten (Teller), Herb Braha, Peter Jason (Honchos), Anthony R. Charnota (Commander), Matt Clark (Mickey), Jude Farese (Bandit), Elizabeth Farley (Secretary), John Fujioka (Captain), Raymond Guth (Motel Clerk), Anne Haney (Monica), Mary Jackson (Frances), Caren Kaye (Sheila), Enid Kent (Reporter), Nan Martin (Hilda), Bill Morey (Major), Warren Munson (Bank President), Kenneth O'Brien (Bartender), Antony Ponzini (Sal), Kario Salem (Young Soldier), Pearl Shear (Customer), Sara Simmons (Nurse), Jon Van Ness (Aide), Sandy Ward (Colonel), Aka, Danny Wong (Guards), David Banks (Disc Jockey), David Byrd (Doorman), Mathew Clark (Bandit), Kenneth S. Eiland, Alberto Isaac, Leigh Kim (V.C. Guards), Stephen Kurumada (Dentist), Richard McKenzie (Psychiatrist), Nicholas Mele (Officer), Harvey Parry (Old Drunk), Bill M. Ryusaki (Basketball Player), William Schoneberger (Technician), Hayward Soo Hoo (Soldier).

Richard Pryor is a joy to behold. Even in the most dismal movies (like THE TOY or SUPERMAN III), Pryor manages to rise above the material and etch his persona on the memory. In this uneven picture, Pryor again succeeds in convincing audiences. This time he's a Vietnam veteran who returns home from the Far East to find that his life has been changed and can never be the same. The film begins with Pryor fighting in Vietnam (which looks a great deal like California), being captured by the enemy, and placed in a cell with a friendly mouse and fellow prisoner Sharkey. When Sharkey becomes violently ill, he is denied medical attention unless Pryor agrees to sign a document denouncing U.S. involvement in Indochina. Pryor returns to the U.S., is acclaimed a hero, and the plaudits last only momentarily when the document he signed surfaces. Because of this, Pryor is told by the authorities that he will not receive his back pay, a considerable amount, as he was incarcerated for about five years. To further complicate his life, Pryor learns that his wife has taken a new lover and that his daughter thinks of the new man as "Daddy." His mother is recovering from a stroke and his life is a general shambles. Through all of this, Cox is trying to help Pryor's adjustment to civilian life in his capacity as an Army colonel. The bookstore Pryor had owned before he went to war has gone bankrupt and, due to the publicity accorded him, he can't get a loan. Pryor is now so down in the dumps that there is no way to go but up and that happens when he meets Kidder, the cliche hooker with a heart of gold. The two of them begin a serious relationship that is the only bright spot in his bleak existence. Pryor's attitude turns cheery once he begins seeing Kidder, although he hasn't a penny and thinks about committing an illegal act to raise a few bucks. Pryor is torn between good and evil and, of course, makes the right decision. The script was based on a book by James Kirkwood, son of actor James Kirkwood and actress Lila Lee, and was cowritten by Kirkwood and associate producer Robert B oris. It's a mixture of sentiment and slapstick that might have been better if one or the other were featured. In a small role, comedian Tim Thomerson stands out as Cal. Thomerson was a nightclub performer who successfully switched to acting and has had some success since. Editing on this movie leaves much to be desired and any scenes with more than three people seem to have a "stagey" feeling about them. When director Pressman moves in close for one-on-one scenes, he is at his best. Sharkey is a believable actor and it's a shame that his role is limited to the first quarter of the movie. Kidder's character is too familiar to warrant much mention. Softhearted prostitutes have been a staple of literature since the Bible and this one is no different, although Kidder's talents make the words seem better than they are. Foul language and a very explicit sexual scene with Pryor and Kidder make this a film that should not be seen by anyone under 18.

p, Howard W. Koch; d, Michael Pressman; w, James Kirkwood, Robert Boris (based on the novel by Kirkwood); ph, King Baggot (Movielab Color); m, Patrick Williams; ed, Christopher Greenbury; art d, James L. Schoppe; set d, John Anderson.

War Drama/Comedy   **Cas.**   **(PR:O   MPAA:R)**

SOME LIKE IT COOL*   (1979, Ger./Aust./Ital./Fr.) 100m Neue Delta-Pan-Panther-COFCI-TV 13/PRO International c (AKA: CASANO-VA AND CO.)

Tony Curtis, Marisa Berenson, Hugh Griffith, Marisa Mell, Britt Ekland, Jean Lefebvre, Andrea Ferreol, Umberto Orsini, Sylva Koscina, Victor Spinetti, Lillian Meuller, Werner Pochath, Olivia Pascal.

A dismal waste of energy for Tony Curtis who appeared in the similarly titled SOME LIKE IT HOT 20 years earlier. This time, however, Curtis (in a dual role) has a worthless script to work from, and an even less impressive director. The feeble story line – an impotent Giacomo Casanova who has stand-ins do his "dirty" work – is merely an excuse to show off some topless actresses. Released in Vienna in 1977 as CASANOVA AND CO.

p, Franz Antel, Carl Szokoll; d, Francois Legrand [Franz Antel]; w, Joshua Sinclair, Tom Priman; ph, Hans Matula; m, Riz Ortolani; ed, Michel Lewin.

Comedy   **(PR:O   MPAA:R)**

SOME LIKE IT HOT½**   (1939) 63m PAR bw (AKA: RHYTHM ROMANCE)

Bob Hope (*Nicky Nelson*), Shirley Ross (*Lily Racquel*), Una Merkel (*Flo Saunders*), Gene Krupa (*Himself*), Rufe Davis (*Stoney*), Bernard Nedell (*Stephen Hanratty*), Frank Sully (*Sailor Burke*), Bernadene Hayes (*Miss Marble*), Richard Denning (*Mr. Weems*), Clarence H. Wilson (*Mr. Ives*), Dudley Dickerson (*Sam*), Harry Barris (*Harry*), Wayne "Tiny" Whitt (*Bass Fiddler*), Edgar Dearing (*MacCrady*), Jack Smart (*Joe*).

Bob Hope averred that he would prefer not to be reminded of this phase of his comic career. Not to be confused with the 1959 Billy Wilder-directed transvestite farce with Marilyn Monroe, Jack Lemmon, and Tony Curtis. The syncopated style of drummer Gene Krupa overshadows the negligible performance of Hope as a carnival barker who tries to make a buck off the swing craze. He tries to secure Krupa's band a gig in a respectable dance hall, but can't convince the owners to take a chance until Krupa and his band draw a crowd at a boardwalk concert. Worth it mostly for the music, which includes "The Lady's in Love with You" (Frank Loesser, Burton Lane), "Some Like it Hot" (Loesser, Krupa, Remo Biondi), "Heart and Soul" (Loesser, Hoagy Carmichael). From a play by Ben Hecht and Gene Fowler, which was previously filmed as SHOOT THE WORKS (1934).

p, William C. Thomas; d, George Archainbaud; w, Lewis R. Foster, Wilkie Mahoney (based on the play "The Great Magoo" by Ben Hecht, Gene Fowler); ph, Karl Struss; ed, Edward Dmytryk.

Musical/Comedy   **(PR:A   MPAA:NR)**

SOME LIKE IT HOT***   (1959) 120m Ashton-Mirisch/UA bw

Marilyn Monroe (*Sugar Kane Kowa*), Tony Curtis (*Joe/Josephine*), Jack Lemmon (*Jerry/Daphne*), George Raft (*Spats Columbo*), Pat O'Brien (*Mulligan*), Joe E. Brown (*Osgood E. Fielding III*), Nehemiah Persoff (*Little Bonaparte*), Joan Shawlee (*Sweet Sue*), Billy Gray (*Sig Poliakoff*), George E. Stone (*Toothpick Charlie*), Dave Barry (*Beinstock*), Mike Mazurki, Harry Wilson (*Spats' Henchmen*), Beverly Wills (*Dolores*), Barbara Drew (*Nellie*), Edward G. Robinson, Jr. (*Johnny Paradise*), Tom Kennedy (*Bouncer*), John Indrisano (*Waiter*).

SOME LIKE IT HOT is one of the greatest of all film comedies, a masterful spoof of gangster films and gender roles that revels in inventive effervescence. It is February, 1929 and Curtis and Lemmon are two out-of-work musicians desperate for work. The pair accidentally witness the St. Valentine's Day Massacre, as they watch mobster Raft and his henchmen wipe out Stone and his gang. Forced to leave town in a hurry, Curtis and Lemmon take the first job they can: playing in Shawlee's all-girl band. Dressing up as women, the two join the rest of the band on their train ride to Florida. Both Curtis and Lemmon are thrown for a loop when they see Shawlee's lead singer, Monroe. Lemmon feels like a little boy let loose in a pastry shop, but Curtis reminds him there is to be no sampling. On the train, the band members throw a little party, where Curtis learns Monroe is searching for a millionaire husband. Curtis listens sympathetically, while a plot takes seed in his mind. Upon arrival at their hotel in Florida, the band is greeted by some flirtatious millionaires. Brown is among them and he immediately falls for Lemmon, not realizing this woman is no lady. While the band goes out to frolic on the beach, Curtis doffs his dress and wig, and decks himself out in yachtsman's clothes. He goes to the beach and there begins flirting with Monroe. Curtis speaks to her in a perfect Cary Grant voice, telling Monroe that his family owns Shell Oil. Monroe doesn't recognize Curtis outside of his feminine garb, and immediately falls in love. When the smitten Brown invites Lemmon for a night on his yacht, Curtis demands the two go out dancing so he can woo Monroe on the yacht himself. Once on board, Curtis claims he can't warm up to the kiss of a woman and Monroe, falling for the ruse, decides to cure the affliction. Later, when Curtis returns to his hotel room, he finds Lemmon happily dancing the tango by himself. It seems Brown has proposed to Lemmon, sealing the engagment with an expensive bracelet. Curtis tries to talk Lemmon out of this crazy marriage, but Lemmon will not listen. At the same hotel, a convention is being held for the "Friends of Italian Opera." This turns out to be none other than a gathering of mobsters, including Robinson. Curtis, in his Cary Grant voice, calls Monroe, telling her he must leave for good. In trying to flee, Curtis and Lemmon end up witnessing another mob slaying. Raft is killed by Persoff, a friend of Stone's seeking revenge. The two "women" manage to escape, but before going, Curtis says goodbye to Monroe on the bandstand. He kisses her and Monroe realizes that this woman is the man she loves. Monroe pursues the two down to the boat docks. They get into Brown's speedboat, where Monroe tells Curtis she doesn't care if he's not a millionaire. Lemmon frantically tries to explain to Brown that they can't marry because they are both men. Brown simply shrugs his shoulders, and fires off one of the cinema's greatest punchlines: "Well, nobody's perfect." SOME LIKE IT HOT takes a simple one-joke idea, then expands on it with hysterical results. This is a near-perfect ensemble, with each of the major characters shining like a perfect jewel. Lemmon and Curtis are marvelous as the men-turned-women, creating believable characters, never camping up their parts in the least. Monroe (whom Lemmon describes early on as "jello on springs!") is at her best as well, a delightful spoof of her dizzy blonde image. Raft enjoys some self-parody as well, and at one point asks a thug flipping a coin where he picked up such a stupid trick. Wilder and Diamond's script is witty and full of clever twists, throwing in unexpected turns at a frenetic, but totally controlled pace. The script was written with Lemmon in mind, but at one point Frank Sinatra was considered as a possible replacement. Fortunately, this fell through when Monroe expressed interest in doing the film. Though her presence was welcomed to the film, both cast and crew lived to regret this. Monroe's bad reputation on set proved to be a well earned one, as she consistently showed up late, forgot her lines, and would spend endless amounts of time in her dressing room. Wilder took to writing her lines on furniture in hopes of helping Monroe get her scenes done right, but even this drastic effort failed. The other actors resented Monroe's antics, and Curtis compared kissing her to kissing Hitler. Ironically, her constant absences led to creation of Brown's classic exit line. Knowing Monroe was too unreliable, Wilder took to shooting around her. It was decided that they would finish the film on a close-up of Brown and Lemmon as Lemmon explains why they cannot marry. "We wrote it the night before we had to shoot it," Diamond told an interviewer, "and I mentioned a line I'd considered using at some earlier point....Billy said, 'Do you think it's strong enough for the tag of the picture?' And I said 'I don't know.' But it was getting to be 11 o'clock at night, so we wrote it that way, and he said, 'Well, maybe we'll think of something better on the set.' Fortunately, we didn't think of anything better on the set." (Quoted from *The Screenwriter Looks at the Screenwriter* by William Froug.) Wilder and Diamond based their script on an old German film called FANFARES OF LOVE. This film involved two musicians who would do anything to work, donning a variety of disguises to get jobs in different bands. Diamond was convinced they needed a better reason to motivate Curtis and Lemmon to take such drastic steps and kicked the idea around with Wilder. One morning Wilder came into a script conference and told Diamond, "Driving home last night, I was thinking about what you said, and I think I have the solution...Chicago, 1929, St. Valentine's Day Massacre..." "And suddenly," Diamond recalled, "we were in business." Key to the film's success was the believability of Curtis and Lemmon as men passing for women. To this end, Wilder deliberately shot in black and white (infuriating Monroe who preferred to be filmed in color) so that their makeup wouldn't look gaudy and ridiculous to filmgoers. While creating female costumes, Lemmon had a wonderful time, while Curtis was a bit more reluctant to leave the dressing room. "...Jack came out of his room floating ten feet high, completely normal and natural," Wilder recalled. "Tony didn't dare come out, he was so embarrassed by the whole thing. Lemmon had to take him by the hand and drag him out." Wilder even had a famous European female impersonator come to Hollywood to teach his boys how to be girls. In Lemmon's biography, written by Don Widener, the actor said, "...the impersonator gave up in disgust and went back to Europe in three days. He told Wilder that Curtis was fine but Lemmon was totally impossible." Eventually both actors were able to convincingly pass as women, and on a daring jaunt, they went, dressed in their costumes and makeup, into the ladies' room of the studio commissary. There they primped their faces, and fixed their lipstick with no one the wiser. Lemmon and Curtis did have a difficult time adjusting to wearing high heels, and would often plunge their aching feet into ice water at the end of a take. For the scene in which Raft shoots Stone, Wilder insisted that the famous movie gangster kick the trademark toothpick from the mouth of his murdered rival. Raft, fearing he would kick Stone in the head, continually missed the toothpick take after take. Finally, after ten tries, Wilder was furious. He tried to show Raft just how to do it right without kicking the actor, but ending up putting the toe of his shoe into Stone's face. Stone was taken to the hospital, and Raft suggested that perhaps the toothpick should be replaced with something else to avoid accidents. A nail, painted as a toothpick, served as substitute, and with a bigger target to aim at, Raft was able to complete the shot in just one take. (It was no small irony that Raft is killed in SOME LIKE IT HOT by Edward G. Robinson, Jr., the son of one of his greatest rivals from Hollywood's era of classic gangster films.) When the shooting finally wrapped up, a party was held for cast and crew though Monroe, in what undoubtedly was a response to her troublesome behavior on the set, was not invited. Monroe may have had the last laugh, for she received 10 percent of the film's gross, and, considering the instant popularity of this great comedy, that came to a tidy sum. The film made over $8 million in its initial release, and would make several million more over the next few years. "You have to be orderly to shoot disorder; this was the best disorder we ever had," Wilder jokingly remarked after the often difficult shooting was completed. SOME LIKE IT HOT inspired a Broadway musical, "Sugar," and remains a popular film with both audiences and critics, an unsurpassed gathering of comic talent in an unsurpassed comedy film. Monroe, in addition to showing her marvelous comic and physical gifts, sings three songs: "I Wanna Be Loved By You" (Herbert Stothart, Bert Kalmar), "Running Wild" (A.H. Gibbs, Leo Wood), "I'm Through with Love" (Matty Malneck, Gus Kahn).

p&d, Billy Wilder; w, Wilder, I.A.L. Diamond (based on Robert Thoeren and M. Logan's screenplay for the film FANFARES OF LOVE); ph, Charles Lang, Jr.; m, Adolph Deutsch; ed, Arthur Schmidt; art d, Ted Haworth; set d, Edward G. Boyle; cos, Orry Kelly; spec eff, Milt Rice.

Comedy   Cas.   (PR:C   MPAA:NR)

SOME MAY LIVE*½   (1967, Brit.) 89m RKO-Krasne/BUT c (AKA: In SAIGON, SOME MAY LIVE)

Joseph Cotten (Col. Woodward), Martha Hyer (Kate Meredith), Peter Cushing (John Meredith), John Ronane (Capt. Elliott Thomas), David Spenser (Inspector Sung), Alec Mango (Ducrai), Walter Brown (Maj. Matthews), Kim Smith (Allan Meredith), Burnell Tucker (Lawrence), Edwina Carroll, Paula Li Shiu, Keith Bonnard, Lee Peters, Carol Cleveland.

A good cast is wasted in this poorly conceived war drama in which Cotten plays an Army intelligence officer stationed in Vietnam who is faced with the problem of discovering who has been spying for the Communists. Important topics are trivialized for expediency's sake.

p, Philip Krasne, Clive Sharp; d, Vernon Sewell; w, David T. Chantler; ph, Ray Parslow (Technicolor); m, Cyril Ornadel; ed, Gordon Pilkington; prod d, George Lack; m/l, Ornadel, Peter Callander.

War   (PR:A   MPAA:NR)

SOME OF MY BEST FRIENDS ARE...*½
        (1971) 109m Bluebird-Cutler Griffin/AIP c (AKA: THE BAR)

Alan Dellay (Pete Thomas), Nick Denoia (Phil), Tom Bade (Tanny), David Baker (Clint), Paul Blake (Kenny), Gary Campbell (Terry), Carleton Carpenter (Miss Untouchable), Robert Christian (Eric), Candy Darling (Karen/Harry), Jeff David (Leo), Dan Drake (Lloyd), David Drew (Howard), Jim Enzel (Gable), Tommy Fiorello (Ernie), Fannie Flagg (Helen), Joe George (Al), Gil Gerard (Scott), Uva Harden (Michel), Rue McClanahan (Lita Joyce), Hector Martinez (Jose), Peg Murray (Mrs. Nabour), Dick O'Neil (Tim Holland), Larry Reed (Louis Barone), Gary Sandy (Jim Paine), Lou Steele (Barrett Hartman), Clifton Steere (Giggling Gertie), Sylvia Sims (Sadie), Joe Taylor (Nebraska), Ben Yaffee (Marvin Hocker).

A dramatic expose of the lives of a group of gays who meet on Christmas Eve in a New York bar (a disguised version of Gotham's Zodiac Bar). A wide array of curiosities (including the actually pretty female impersonator Candy Darling, an Andy Warhol "superstar") fill the bar, but on the whole the picture is just as annoying as most "understanding the basis of a relationship" films. Even for the audience this is geared to, it's not much of a film. There's nothing here that Fassbinder hasn't done a hundred times better. Highly derivative of the 1970 homosexual hit THE BOYS IN THE BAND, but more morose and less witty.

p, Marty Richards, John Lauricella; d&w, Mervyn Nelson; ph, Tony Mitchell (Movielab Color); m, Gordon Rose, Phil Moore; ed, Angelo Ross, Richard

Cadenas; art d, Ray Menard.; set d, Nino Nocellino, Frank Schoen; cos, Andy Greenhut; makeup, Gudron Holt.

Drama   (PR:O   MPAA:R)

SOME PEOPLE*   (1964, Brit.) 93m Vic/AIP c

Kenneth More (Mr. Smith), Ray Brooks (Johnnie), Annika Wills (Anne Smith), David Andrews (Bill), Angela Douglas (Terry), David Hemmings (Bert), Timothy Nightingale (Tim), Frankie Dymon, Jr (Jimmy), Harry H. Corbett (Johnnie's Father), Fanny Carby (Johnnie's Mother), Michael Gwynn (Vicar), Cyril Luckham (Magistrate), Fred Ferris (Clerk of the Court), Richard Davis (Harper), Dean Webb (Mike).

A propagandistic piece of youth trash which has three members of a Bristol, England motorcycle gang – Brooks, Andrews, and Hemmings – losing their licenses after being clocked at over 100 mph and winding up in an accident. They decide to form a rock 'n' roll band and take interest in the Duke of Edinburgh's Award Scheme. They receive a push from choir leader/organist More to take part, causing some dissension amongst the teens. Everyone is accepting of the one-time delinquents by the picture's finale, with the adults' common sense working a miracle cure on the wild ones. That's not quite the way it works in real life. Here the scriptwriters are more concerned with giving their youth program a pat on the back than actually confronting the issues. Released in Britain in 1962. Hemmings was the only one of the young actors to make it big in later films, following his role in Michelangelo Antonioni's BLOWUP (1966).

p, James Archibald; d, Clive Donner; w, John Eldridge; ph, John Wilcox (Eastmancolor); m, Ron Grainer; ed, Fergus McDonnell; m/l, Grainer, Johnny Worth.

Drama   (PR:A   MPAA:NR)

SOME WILL, SOME WON'T*½   (1970, Brit.) 90m Transocean/Williams and Pritchard c

Ronnie Corbett (Herbert Russell), Thora Hird (Agnes Russell), Michael Hordern (Denniston Russell), Leslie Phillips (Simon Russell), Barbara Murray (Lucille), Wilfrid Brambell (Henry Russell), Dennis Price (Benson), James Robertson Justice (Sir Charles Robson), Sheila Steafel (Sheila Wilcott), Eleanor Summerfield (Elizabeth Robson), Arthur Lowe (Sergeant).

Forced farce revolving around the extreme efforts of four individuals to alter their normal personalities in order to inherit their part of an immense fortune. Remake of Mario Zampi's LAUGHTER IN PARADISE (1951, Brit.) just isn't funny.

p, Giulio Zampi; d, Duncan Wood; w, Lew Schwartz (based on the screenplay LAUGHTER IN PARADISE by Jack Davies, Michael Pertwee); ph, Harry Waxman (Technicolor); m, Howard Blake.

Comedy   (PR:A   MPAA:NR)

SOMEBODY ELSE'S CHILDREN   (SEE: STEPCHILDREN, 1962, USSR)

SOMEBODY KILLED HER HUSBAND*   (1978) 96m COL c

Farrah Fawcett-Majors (Jenny Moore), Jeff Bridges (Jerry Green), John Wood (Ernest Van Santen), Tammy Grimes (Audrey Van Santen), John Glover (Hubert Little), Patricia Elliott (Helene), Mary McCarty (Flora), Laurence Guittard (Preston Moore), Beeson Carroll (Frank Danziger), Vincent Robert Santa Lucia (Benjamin), Eddie Lawrence (Other Neighbor), Arthur Rhytis (Customer), Jean-Pierre Stewart (Man in Beret), Sands Hall (Girl Typist), Joseph Culliton (Night Doorman), Dave Johnson (Day Doorman), Melissa Ferris (Employee), Jeremiah Sullivan (Odd Couple Husband), Sloan Shelton (Odd Couple Wife), Mary Alan Hokanson (Indignant Woman), John Corcoran (Macy's Night Watchman), Mark Haber (Elf), Terry DuHaime (Lulu's Mother), Tony Farentino, Jim Lovelett, Liz Kallimeyer, Bill Anagnos, John Gibson.

Contrary to popular belief, it's not Farrah's performance that killed this picture, but a poorly conceived script and equally lifeless direction. Bridges again shows his versatility as a Macy's clerk with aspirations of writing children's books, who is carrying on an affair with Farrah, a store customer. When they discover that her husband has been murdered, as well as a couple of neighbors and a fake detective, they decide to play amateur sleuths. Their search for the real killer is filled with outrageous comic antics that culminate in a Macy's Thanksgiving Day Parade.

p, Martin Poll; d, Lamont Johnson; w, Reginald Rose; ph, Andrew Laszlo, Ralf D. Bode; (Panavision, Movielab Color); m, Alex North; ed, Barry Malkin; prod d, Ted Haworth; art d, David Chapman; set d, Leslie Bloom; cos, Joseph G. Aulisi; m/l, "Love Keeps Getting Stronger Every Day" (sung by Sedaka) Neil Sedaka, Howard Greenfield.

Comedy/Crime   (PR:A   MPAA:PG)

SOMEBODY LOVES ME*** (1952) 97m PAR c

Betty Hutton (Blossom Seeley), Ralph Meeker (Benny Fields), Robert Keith (Sam Doyle), Adele Jergens (Nola Beach), Billie Bird (Essie), Henry Slate (Forrest), Sid Tomack (Lake), Ludwig Stossel (Mr. Grauman), Sydney Mason (Mike Fritzol), Virginia Hall (Jean), Bea Allen, Les Clark (Specialty Dancers), Howard Joslin, Jimmie Dundee (Dealers), George Chandler (Stage Hand), Lester Dorr, Franklyn Farnum (Waiters), Herbert Vigran (Booker), Kenneth R. MacDonald, Milton Parsons (Doctors), Charles O'Curran (French Soldier), Nick Adams (Western Union Boy), Jack Benny (Himself), James Cross (M.C.), Richard H. Gordon, Charles Quirk (Men in Audience), The Chez Paree Adorables.

This typical, but entertaining, rags-to-riches musical biography has Hutton playing famed vaudeville entertainer Blossom Seeley. The film opens in 1906, on San Francisco's Barbary Coast. After the city is struck by a devastating earthquake, Hutton takes a try at the vaudeville stage. She achieves some success, then quits show biz during WW I to do some volunteer work. She decides to go back to vaudeville, then meets Benny Fields (Meeker). At first Meeker manipulates Hutton to the altar, but then falls in love with her after they marry. Despite this, Meeker tries to be a solo act. Hutton's own career comes to a halt, and eventually the couple reunites. She helps Meeker develop his talents, and he is at last a success. Having tasted the glory of the stage, Hutton is finally content at being a helpmate to her husband. The story, though highly fictionalized, is enjoyable, and Hutton's performance is delightful. The tale is presented simply, and a surprise cameo by Jack Benny adds to the fun. Shortly before production began, Hutton had a growth removed from her vocal cords and happily this had no effect on her performance. However, this was Hutton's last major film, due to arguments she had with Paramount studio executives. She demanded that her second husband, Charles O'Curran (who choreographed SOMEBODY LOVES ME), be allowed to direct her subsequent pictures. When the request was denied, Hutton walked out on her contract, and her career consequently fell apart. The songs include:"Rose Room" (Harry Williams, Art Hickman), "Way Down Yonder in New Orleans" (Henry Creamer, J. Turner Layton), "Teasing Rag" (Joe Jordan), "Dixie Dreams" (Arthur Johnston, George W. Meyer, Grant Clarke, Roy Turk), "On San Francisco Bay" (Vincent Bryan, Gertrude Hoffman), "Somebody Loves Me" (Buddy De Sylva, George Gershwin), "Jealous" (Jack Little, Tommy Malie, Dick Finch), "June Night" (Cliff Friend, Abel Baer), "I Cried for You" (Gus Arnheim, Arthur Freed, Abe Lyman), "I'm Sorry I Made You Cry" (N.J. Clesi, Theodore Morse), "Toddling the Todalo" (E. Ray Goetz, A. Baldwin Sloane), "Smiles" (J. Will Callahan, Lee S. Roberts), "Wang Wang Blues" (Gus Mueller, Buster Johnson, Henry Busse), "I Can't Tell You Why I Love You" (Will J. Cobb, Gus Edwards), "Love Him," "Thanks to You," "Honey, Oh My Honey" (Ray Evans, Jay Livingston).

p, William Perlberg, George Seaton; d&w, Irving Brecher (suggested by the careers of Blossom Seeley and Benny Fields); ph, George Barnes (Technicolor); ed, Frank Bracht; md, Emil Newman; art d, Hal Pereira, Earl Hedrick; set d, Sam Comer, Russ Dowd; ch, Charles O'Curran.

Musical Biography (PR:A MPAA:NR)

SOMEBODY UP THERE LIKES ME***½ (1956) 113m MGM bw

Paul Newman (Rocky Graziano), Pier Angeli (Norma), Everett Sloane (Irving Cohen), Eileen Heckart (Ma Barbella), Sal Mineo (Romolo), Harold J. Stone (Nick Barbella), Joseph Buloff (Benny), Sammy White (Whitey Bimstein), Arch Johnson (Heldon), Robert Lieb (Questioner), Theodore Newton (Commissioner Eddie Eagan), Steve McQueen (Fidel), Robert Easton (Cpl. Quinburg), Ray Walker (Ring Announcer), Billy Nelson (Commissioner), Robert Loggia (Frankie Peppo), Matt Crowley (Lou Stillman), Judson Pratt (Johnny Hyland), Donna Jo Gribble (Yolanda Barbella), James Todd (Colonel), Jack Kelk (George), Russ Conway (Capt. Grifton), Harry Wismer (Himself), Tony Zale (Himself), Sam Taub (Radio Announcer), Terry Rangno (Rocky at Age 8), Jan Gillum (Yolanda at Age 12), Ralph Vitti 'Michael Dante' (Shorty), Walter Cartier (Polack), John Eldredge (Warden Niles), Clancy Cooper (Capt. Lancheck), Dean Jones (Private), Ray Stricklyn (Bryson), Caswell Adams (Sam), Charles Green (Curtis Hughtower), Angela Cartwright (Audrey at Age 3), David Leonard (Mr. Mueller), John Rosser, Frank Campanella (Detectives), Courtland Shepard.

After a disastrous film debut in THE SILVER CHALICE and an unremarkable second try in THE RACK, touted Actors Studio graduate Newman finally hit the big numbers on his third try. SOMEBODY UP THERE LIKES ME is the screen biography of boxer Rocky Graziano adapted by Lehman from Graziano's autobiography. The film follows Newman as Graziano from his unhappy, poverty- stricken childhood to his triumph as middleweight champion of the world. Having grown up with a father whose own dreams of a boxing championship were drowned in a sea of cheap wine, young Newman takes to the streets with his buddy Mineo where they commit petty crimes. From there he graduates to reform school, and then to the Army where he is dishonorably discharged. Newman eventually lands in Leavenworth Prison and it appears that he will be nothing other than an ex-con and petty criminal for the rest of his life. Luckily the physical instructor at the prison, Pratt, sees potential in Newman and encourages him to use the rage and fury bubbling inside him to get somewhere in life–legally. Newman takes up boxing, and when he is released from prison he hits the circuit with a fury. He hooks up with a small-time manager, Sloane, and Newman soon

learns that the world of boxing is just as corrupt and diseased as the environment that spawned him. Newman finds himself being manipulated and pushed by characters looking to make big bucks. Though he's out on the streets and making money without stealing, Newman is still something of a thug–until he meets and falls in love with Angeli. His attempts at romance are clumsy, but the effort endears him to her. The relationship with Angeli brings new meaning and direction to Newman's life. Now given something and someone to care about, Newman begins to strive for self-respect and takes more control over his destiny. Newman works his way to the top slot in boxing and eventually faces Tony Zale (playing himself) in the bout for the championship. It is a lengthy, brutal contest but Newman attains his glory and uses his new position of fame and respect to serve as a beacon for youngsters, proving that they too can live through adversity and make something of themselves. Whereas director Wise's previous boxing film, THE SET-UP, condemned boxing as a brutal, cruel, and grim fate for those trapped within the ring, SOMEBODY UP THERE LIKES ME–which stills sees boxing in an unsavory light–is a much more optimistic tale, even sentimental, chronicling one man's rise from the gutter to the top (in THE SET-UP, Robert Ryan never comes close to the top, but achieves dignity by never giving up). Newman is superb as Graziano. The actor spent time with the boxer in New York City and observed his speech patterns, mannerisms, movements, and boxing style. Newman and Graziano had long talks and the actor absorbed every tiny aspect of the boxer's character he could uncover. He then lifted weights and worked his body into that of a professional fighter, including sparring with some of the game's top boxers. Though Newman's performance dominates the film, the supporting cast is superior. Angeli, Sloane, and Mineo register memorably, with Heckart and Stone real standouts as the boxer's parents (a very young Steve McQueen has a bit part as well). As is the case with most of Wise's work, the technical aspect is flawless. Cinematographer Ruttenberg and art director Gibbons each won an Oscar for their work.

p, Charles Schnee; d, Robert Wise; w, Ernest Lehman (based on the autobiography of Rocky Graziano written with Rowland Barber); ph, Joseph Ruttenberg; m, Bronislau Kaper; ed, Albert Akst; art d, Cedric Gibbons, Malcolm Brown; m/l, "Somebody Up There Likes Me," Sammy Cahn, Kaper (sung by Perry Como).

Biography Cas. (PR:C MPAA:NR)

SOMEONE*½ (1968) 80m Bizarre/Continental Theaters c

Joe Adair (The Model), Bambi Allen (Young Girl), David Russell (Hustler), Joe Caruso (Photographer), Kay Hall (Pianist).

An honest attempt to portray Adair, a young male model who is searching for his sexual identity. After being propositioned by photographer Caruso, he turns to Allen, only to realize he's not attracted to the opposite sex. He pursues a stint as a male prostitute, but is left unfulfilled and in the end, returns to Caruso. Concentrating more on the relationship than the physical side of homosexuality, this ultra-low budgeter (shot in 8 days for a miraculous $1,200) has a solid plot; but uneven color tones, mismatched shots, and poorly written dialog reveal its low production costs and take away from its attempt to honestly portray many young men's lack of a strong sexual identity.

p&d, Pat Rocco; w, Edward Middleton; ph&ed, Rocco.

Drama (PR:O MPAA:NR)

SOMEONE AT THE DOOR* (1936, Brit.) 74m BIP/Wardour bw

Billy Milton (Ronald Martin), Aileen Marson (Sally Martin), Noah Beery, Sr (Harry Kapel), Edward Chapman (Price), John Irwin (Bill Reid), Hermione Gingold (Mrs. Appleby), Charles Mortimer (Sgt. Spedding), Edward Dignon (Soames), Lawrence Hanray (Poole), Jimmy Godden (Police Constable O'Brien), Eliot Makeham.

Far-fetched early British farce in which Milton goes to the outrageous extreme of making it appear as though he has murdered his sister to get a newspaper scoop. He unsuspectingly stumbles on a couple of actual murders committed by a gang of jewel thieves, which leads to his hoped-for story.

p, Walter C. Mycroft; d, Herbert Brenon; w, Jack Davies, Marjorie Deans (based on the play by Dorothy and Campbell Christie); ph, Brian Langley.

Crime/Comedy (PR:A MPAA:NR)

SOMEONE AT THE DOOR** (1950, Brit.) 65m Hammer/Exclusive bw

Michael Medwin (Ronnie Martin), Garry Marsh (Kapel), Yvonne Owen (Sally Martin), Hugh Latimer (Bill Reid), Danny Green (Price), Campbell Singer (Inspector Spedding), John Kelly (Police Constable O'Brien).

A remake of the 1936 film of the same title has Medwin plotting to make it appear as though he has murdered his sister (Owen) to advance his own reputation as a reporter. However, things do not go exactly according to plan and Medwin narrowly escapes hanging for the supposed crime.

p, Anthony Hinds; d, Francis Searle; w, A.R. Rawlinson (based on the play by Dorothy and Maj. Campbell Christie); ph, Walter Harvey; m, Frank Spencer; ed, John Ferris; art d, Denis Wreford.

Comedy   (PR:A MPAA:NR)

SOMEONE BEHIND THE DOOR*   (1971, Fr./Brit.) 97m Lira/GSF c
(QUELQU' UN DERRIERE LA PORTE, (AKA: TWO MINDS FOR MUR-
DER)

Charles Bronson *(The Stranger)*, Anthony Perkins *(Laurence Jeffries)*, Jill
Ireland *(Frances Jeffries)*, Henri Garcin *(Paul Damien)*, Adriano Magestret-
ti *(Andrew)*, Agathe Natanson *(Lucy)*, Viviane Everly *(Young Girl On
Beach)*, Andre Penvern *(Intern)*.

A lame Bronson vehicle which seems to have been pressed out of the foreign
coproduction cookie cutter. Bronson is an amnesiac who has his brain and
memory altered into that of a crazed killer by neuro-psychiatrist Perkins.
He is programmed to kill Ireland, Perkins' wife, and her lover Garcin. The
latter is killed by the catatonic Bronson, but before he can kill Ireland,
Perkins intervenes and confesses his whole scheme.

p, Raymond Danon; d, Nicolas Gessner; w, Jacques Robert, Marc Behm,
Gessner, Lorenzo Ventavoli (based on the novel by Robert); ph, Pierre
Lhomme (Eastmancolor); m, Georges Garvarentz; ed, Victoria Mercanton;
art d, Marc Frederix; makeup, Anatole Paris.

Drama/Crime   (PR:C MPAA:GP)

SOMEONE TO REMEMBER*   (1943) 80m REP bw

Mabel Paige *(Mrs. Freeman)*, Harry Shannon *(Tom Gibbons)*, John Craven
(Dan Freeman), Dorothy Morris *(Lucia Stanton)*, Charles Dingle *(Jim
Parsonss)*, David Bacon *(Ike Dale)*, Peter Lawford *(Joe Downes)*, Tom Seidel
(Bill Hedge), Richard Crane *(Paul Parker)*, Chester Clute *(Mr. Roseby)*,
Elizabeth Dunne *(Timid Miss Green)*, Vera Lewis *(Aggressive Miss Green)*,
John Good *(Charlie Horne)*, Susan Levine *(Patricia)*, Buz Buckley *(Roger)*,
Harry Bradley, Edward Keane, George Lessey *(College Trustees)*, Flo Buzby
(Mrs. Marston), James Carlisle *(Mr. Marston)*, Wilbur Mack *(Mr. Thurber)*,
George Reed *(John)*, Jesse Graves *(Elevator Operator)*, Virginia Brissac
(Mrs. Parson), Jimmy Butler *(Bob Edgar)*, Michael Owen *(Peter Myrick)*,
Selmer Jackson *(Mr. Freeman)*, Irene Shirley *(Mrs. Freeman)*, Frank Jaquet
(Man in Store), Ann Evers *(Girl)*, Lynette Bryant *(Mary Ann Mayberry)*, Ada
Ellis *(Governess)*, Russell Hicks *(Mr. Stanton)*, Madeline Grey *(Mrs. Stan-
ton)*, Edward Earle *(Mr. Fielding)*, Leona Maricle *(Mrs. Fielding)*, Henri De
Soto *(Head Waiter)*, Georgia Davis *(Girl in Cafe)*, Leo White *(Waiter)*,
Broderick O'Farrell *(Gentleman)*.

A charming programmer which stars Paige as a sweet old white-haired
woman who lives in an apartment building that has been purchased by a
neighboring university in order to construct dorms for the boys. When the
school officials realize they can't break Paige's lease, they go ahead and
begin renovating. Paige is enthusiastic about the project, especially since
her husband is long dead, and her son is a college flunkie who disappeared
years ago. The students fall in love with her, arranging every conceivable
convenience. She takes a liking to Craven, a student who shares the same
name as her son, helping him with his studies and even playing a part in his
romance with Morris. She is secretly convinced that Craven is her grandson,
fathered by her missing son. Before she is able to learn if her hunch is
correct, she dies a peaceful, content death during the night. It turns out that
her son died in prison some 20 years earlier, news that killed her husband.
Paige saves the picture from the ranks of obscurity (where most of
Republic's programmers wound up) by her heartwarming, tear-jerking
performance which, due to the film's status, was unjustly overlooked by the
Academy. Remade in 1957 with Ethel Barrymore as JOHNNY TROUBLE.

p, Robert North; d, Robert Siodmak; w, Frances Hyland (based on the story
by Ben Ames Williams); ph, Jack Marta; ed, Ernest Nims; md, Walter
Scharf.

Drama   (PR:A MPAA:NR)

SOMETHING ALWAYS HAPPENS**   (1934, Brit.) 69m WB bw

Ian Hunter *(Peter Middleton)*, Nancy O'Neil *(Cynthia Hatch)*, Peter Gaw-
thorne *(Mr. Hatch)*, Johnny Singer *(Billy)*, Muriel George *(Mrs. Badger)*,
Barry Livesey *(George Hamlin)*, Millicent Wolf *(Glenda)*, Louie Emery *(Mrs.
Tremlett)*, Reg Marcus *("Coster")*.

Charming comedy in which Hunter plays an unemployed car salesman
pushed by his wealthy girl friend to try and sell the idea of commercializing
gas stations. His original pleas with Gawthorne, who is actually his girl's
father, prove fruitless. But Hunter persists with another company which
takes to the idea much better. Enjoyable picture with good performances
and capable direction.

p, Irving Asher; d, Michael Powell; w, Brock Williams; ph, Percy Strong,
Basil Emmott; ed, Bert Bates; art d, Peter Proud.

Comedy   (PR:A MPAA:NR)

SOMETHING BIG½**   (1971) 107m Stanmore-Penbar/NG c

Dean Martin *(Joe Baker)*, Brian Keith *(Col. Morgan)*, Honor Blackman
(Mary Anna Morgan), Carol White *(Dover MacBride)*, Ben Johnson *(Jesse
Bookbinder)*, Albert Salmi *(Johnny Cobb)*, Don Knight *(Tommy MacBride)*,

Joyce Van Patten *(Polly Standall)*, Denver Pyle *(Junior Frisbee)*, Merlin
Olsen *(Sgt. Fitzsimmons)*, Robert Donner *(Angel Moon)*, Harry Carey, Jr
(Joe Pickens), Judi Meredith *(Carrie Standall)*, Ed Faulkner *(Capt. Tyler)*,
Armand Alzamora *(Luis Munos)*, David Huddleston *(Malachi Morton)*, Bob
Steele *(Teamster)*, Shirleena Manchur *(Stagecoach Lady)*, Jose Angel
Espinosa *(Emilio Estevez)*, Juan Garcia *(Himself)*, Robert Gravage *(Sam)*,
Chuck Hicks *(Cpl. James)*, John Kelly *(Barkeeper)*, Enrique Lucero *(Indian
Spy)*, Lupe Amador *(Woman in Village)*, Scruffy *(Tuffy)*.

In this picture, Martin stars as a renegade waiting for the arrival of his
fiancee, White. He was supposed to have acquired a fortune while out west
and now she's on her way to set the marriage in motion. The problem is that
Martin is as broke as when he first headed west, so in desperation, he
decides to rob the stolen treasure of a Mexican bandit. He needs a gatling
gun to pursue his efforts, however, and Salmi is the man who owns one, but
won't part with it unless Martin first gets him a woman. So Martin kidnaps
Blackman from a passing stagecoach, unbeknownst to him that she's the
wife of a Colonel (Keith). While trying to transport the gatling gun, Martin
is apprehended by Keith, out on a search for his kidnaped wife. Story ends
with the predictable shootout, with Blackman persuading her husband
Keith that since he's retiring anyway, he should allow Martin to pull off his
one last attempt at acquiring "something big."

p&d, Andrew V. McLaglen; w, James Lee Barrett; ph, Harry Stradling, Jr.
(Technicolor); m, Marvin Hamlisch; ed, Robert Simpson; art d, Alfred
Sweeney; cos, Ray Summers, Richard Bruno; spec eff, Logan Frazee; m/l,
"Something Big," Burt Bacharach, Hal David (sung byMark Lindsay;
makeup Don Schoenfeld, Hank Edds.

Western   (PR:A MPAA:GP)

SOMETHING FOR EVERYONE*   (1970) 111m Media-Cinema
Center/NGP c (AKA: THE ROOK; GB: BLACK FLOWERS FOR THE
BRIDE)

Angela Lansbury *(Countess Herthe von Ornstein)*, Michael York *(Conrad
Ludwig)*, Anthony Corlan *(Helmuth von Ornstein)*, Heidelinde Weis *(An-
naliese Pleschke)*, Eva-Maria Meineke *(Mrs. Pleschke)*, John Gill *(Mr.
Pleschke)*, Jane Carr *(Lotte von Ornstein)*, Despo *(Bobby)*, Wolfried Lier
(Klaus), Walter Janssen *(Father Georg)*, Klaus Havenstein *(Rudolph)*, Enzi
Fuchs *(Waitress)*, Erland Erlandson *(Schoenfeld)*, Hans Possenbacher *(Carl)*,
Hilde Weisner *(Princess Palamir)*, Hela Gruel *(Cook)*, Marius Aicher
(Scullery Boy), Mogens von Gadow *(Station Master)*, James F. Hurley
(General), Ernst Zeigler *(Elderly Man)*, Erik Jelde.

Satirical attempt at black comedy stars York as a man who will do anything
to get ahead. He sees the estate of Countess Lansbury as ripe for the taking.
He gets himself hired as a footman and gradually works his way up using
every trick in the book, including murder and sex (both hetero and homo).
Everything goes according to his evil plans until he gets Lansbury to agree
to marry him. Then the axe falls when Carr, as the Countess' fat ugly
daughter, reveals that she's been keeping tabs on York and has written
down every last detail of his ambitious acts. She threatens to tell unless York
marries her, thus blocking the final move in his so-far successful attempt to
take over Lansbury's estate. Songs include "Weil du so schon tanzen
kannst" (Hans Otter), "Das Kleine Rendezvous" (Karl Shachinger, Max
Schachinger), "Geh alte Schau mi net so teppart an" (Friedl Szalat, Bert Ull,
Ernst Geiger).

p, John P. Flaxman; d, Harold Prince; w, Hugh Wheeler (based on the novel
The Cook by Harry Kressing); ph, Walter Lassally (Eastmancolor); m, John
Kander; ed, Ra lph Rosenblum; md, Harold Hastings; art d, Otto Pischinger;
set d, Herta Pischinger; cos, Florence Klotz; makeup, Raimund Stangl.

Horror   (PR:O MPAA:R)

SOMETHING FOR THE BIRDS½**   (1952) 81m FOX bw

Victor Mature *(Steve Bennett)*, Patricia Neal *(Anne Richards)*, Edmund
Gwenn *(Johnnie Adams)*, Larry Keating *(Patterson)*, Gladys Hurlbut *(Mrs.
Rice)*, Hugh Sanders *(Grady)*, Christian Rub *(Leo)*, Wilton Graff *(Taylor)*,
Archer MacDonald *(Lemmer)*, Richard Garrick *(Chandler)*, Ian Wolfe
(Foster), Russell Gaige *(Winthrop)*, John Brown *(Mr. Lund)*, Camillo Guercio
(Duncan), Joan Miller *(Mac)*, Madge Blake *(Mrs. Chadwick)*, Norman Field
(Judge), Gordon Nelson *(O'Malley)*, Emmett Vogan *(Beecham)*, John Ayres
(Congressman Walker), Charles Watts *(Jessup)*, Rodney Bell *(Announcer)*,
Norma Varden *(Congresswoman Bates)*, Elizabeth Flournoy *(Receptionist)*,
Herbert Lytton *(Captain)*, Fred Datig, Jr *(Bellhop)*, Paul Power *(Court
Clerk)*, Robert Livingston *(General)*, Edmund Cobb *(Reporter)*, Joan Shawl-
ee *(Woman in Station)*, Walter Baldwin *(Bigelow)*, Louise Lorimer *(Mrs.
Winthrop)*, Leo Curley *(Congressman Macy)*, John Maxwell *(Congressman
Craig)*, Sam McDaniel.

A determined Neal descends upon Washington, lobbying for the dying
condors in California. She comes across Washington party-crasher Gwenn
(he forges his own invitations to social functions) which enables her to meet
Mature. Mature is working for an oil company that wants the land the birds
are on. She woos her way into his heart and gets him to change his way and
help her cause. Gwenn adds some light touches along with some heavy
moments as he is investigated for bribery.

p, Samuel G. Engel; d, Robert Wise; w, I.A.L. Diamond, Boris Ingster (based on stories by Alvin M. Josephy, Joseph Petracca, Ingster); ph, Joseph La Shelle; m, Sol Kaplan; ed, Hugh S. Fowler; md, Lionel Newman; art d, Lyle Wheeler, George Patrick; set d, Thomas Little, Bruce MacDonald.

Comedy   **(PR:A   MPAA:NR)**

SOMETHING FOR THE BOYS½**   (1944) 87m FOX c

Carmen Miranda *(Chiquita Hart)*, Michael O'Shea *(Staff Sgt. Rocky Fulton)*, Vivian Blaine *(Blossom Hart)*, Phil Silvers *(Harry Hart)*, Sheila Ryan *(Melanie Walker)*, Perry Como *(Sgt. Laddie Green)*, Glenn Langan *(Lt. Ashley Crothers)*, Roger Clark *(Lieutenant)*, Cara Williams *(Secretary)*, Thurston Hall *(Col. Jefferson L. Calhoun)*, Clarence Kolb *(Col. Grubbs)*, Paul Hurst *(Supervisor)*, Andrew Tombes *(Southern Colonel)*, Roger Clark *(Lieutenant)*, Judy Holliday *(1st Girl/Defense Plant)*, Murray Alper *(Sergeant)*, Eddie Acuff *(Operator)*.

Loosely based on Cole Porter's musical play, this fluffy musical picture was the screen debut for Como. Plot involves Miranda, Blaine, and Silvers as distant cousins who inherit a broken down plantation. They decide to turn it into a home for Army wives, but in order to raise the necessary cash for much needed repairs, they put on a big production. Songs include: "In the Middle of Nowhere," "I Wish We Didn't Have to Say Goodnight" (sung by Como), "Boom Brachee," "Samba Boogie" (sung by Miranda), "Wouldn't It Be Nice" (sung by Como, Blaine).

p, Irving Starr; d, Lewis Seiler; w, Robert Ellis, Helen Logan, Frank Gabrielson (based on a musical comedy by Herbert Fields, Dorothy Fields, Cole Porter); ph, Ernest Palmer, (Technicolor); ed, Robert Simpson; md, Emil Newman, Charles Henderson; art d, Lyle Wheeler, Albert Hogsett; ch, Nick Castle; m/l, Porter, Jimmy McHugh, Harold Adamson.

Musical   **(PR:A   MPAA:NR)**

SOMETHING IN THE CITY**   (1950, Brit.) 76m Nettlefold/BUT bw

Richard Hearne *(Mr. Ningle)*, Garry Marsh *(Mr. Holley)*, Ellen Pollock *(Mrs. Holley)*, Betty Sinclair *(Mrs. Ningle)*, Tom Gill *(Richard Holley)*, Diana Calderwood *(Beryl Ningle)*, Bill Shine *(Reporter)*, Dora Bryan *(Waitress)*, George Merritt *(Inspector)*, Horace Kenney *(Squeaker Man)*, Molly Weir, Stanley Vilven, Gerald Rex, Vi Kaley, Ben Williams, Esme Beringer, Kenneth Henry, Mackenzie Ward.

Hearne plays a pavement artist who has managed to deceive his wife and daughter into thinking he is actually a successful businessman. Keeping his true professional identity a secret for a number of years, he has to blow his cover when his "other" self is thought to have been murdered, and Hearne is the most likely suspect. Lighthearted comedy is a remake of THE STRANGE ADVENTURES OF MR. SMITH, from the same team of Rogers and Maltby.

p, Ernest G. Roy; d, Maclean Rogers; w, H.F. Maltby; ph, Brendan J. Stafford.

Comedy   **(PR:A   MPAA:NR)**

SOMETHING IN THE WIND**½   (1947) 89m UNIV bw

Deanna Durbin *(Mary Collins)*, Donald O'Connor *(Charlie Read)*, John Dall *(Donald Read)*, Charles Winninger *(Uncle Chester)*, Helena Carter *(Clarissa Prentice)*, Margaret Wycherly *(Grandma Read)*, Jan Peerce *(Tony)*, Jean Adair *(Aunt Mary Collins)*, The Four Williams Brothers *(Singing Quartet)*, Jacqueline de Wit *(Saleslady)*, William Ching *(Master of Ceremonies)*, Patricia Alphin *(Model)*, Chester Clute *(Beamis)*, Frank Wilcox *(Masterson)*.

Dancer O'Connor steals the film from star Durbin in a story that sings about and deals with mistaken identity. Weak story has Durbin as a disc jockey with an antagonistic romance with Dall. O'Connor is more or less the third wheel in the whole affair until the end. Dall thinks the woman is a former mistress of his wealthy uncle, so he kidnaps her and she falls in love with him. O'Connor finally dances in to the rescue. Some of the songs performed are: "Something in the Wind," "Turntable Song," "It's Only Love," "You Wanna Keep Your Baby Lookin' Right," "Happy Go Lucky and Free." Most were sung by Durbin but in the long run, O'Connor's energetic performance took all the credit.

p, Joseph Sistrom; d, Irving Pichel; w, Harry Kurnitz, William Bowers (based on a story by Fritz Rotter, Charles O'Neal); ph, Milton Krasner; m, Johnny Green; ed, Otto Ludwig; md, Green; m/l, Green, Leo Robin.

Musical   **(PR:A   MPAA:NR)**

SOMETHING IS OUT THERE (SEE: DAY OF THE ANIMALS, 1977)

SOMETHING MONEY CAN'T BUY**   (1952, Brit.) 83m Vic
                                                             British/UNIV bw

Patricia Roc *(Anne Wilding)*, Anthony Steele *(Harry Wilding)*, Moira Lister *(Diana Haverstock)*, A.E. Matthews *(Lord Haverstock)*, David Hutcheson *(Buster)*, Michael Trubshawe *(Willy)*, Diane Hart *(Joan)*, Charles Victor *(Borough Treasurer)*, Henry Edwards *(Gerald Forbes)*, Mary Hinton *(Mrs. Forbes)*, Joss Ambler *(Mr. Burton)*, D.A. Clarke-Smith *(Critic)*, Mara Lane

(Film Star), John Barry *(Film Star)*, Dennis Arundell *(Director)*, Michael Brennan, Helen Goss, Joe Linnane, Oscar Quitak, Irene Prador, Johnnie Schofeld, Olwen Brookes, Margaret Vyner.

A comedy that deals with an officer's attempt to lead a normal life after the war is over. Struggling to make ends meet, his wife starts a successful secretarial agency, while Steele plays housewife at home. Depressed, he talks two fellow servicemen into helping him start a catering business. After some initial setbacks, the catering business takes off, and Roc is forced to give up her agency and return to being a housewife.

p, Joseph Janni; d, Pat Jackson; w, Jackson, James Lansdale Hodson; ph, C. Pennington Richards; m, Nino Rota; ed, Sidney Hayers; art d, Alex Vetchinsky.

Comedy/Drama   **(PR:A   MPAA:NR)**

SOMETHING OF VALUE***½   (1957) ll3m MGM bw

Rock Hudson *(Peter McKenzie)*, Dana Wynter *(Holly Keith)*, Wendy Hiller *(Elizabeth)*, Sidney Poitier *(Kimani)*, Juano Hernandez *(Njogu)*, William Marshall *(Leader)*, Robert Beatty *(Jeff Newton)*, Walter Fitzgerald *(Henry McKenzie)*, Michael Pate *(Joe Matson)*, Ivan Dixon *(Lathela)*, Ken Renard *(Karanja)*, Samadu Jackson *(Witch Doctor)*, Frederick O'Neal *(Adam Marenga)*, Paul Thompson *(Kipi)*, Lester Matthews *(Game Warden)*, Garry Stafford *(Little Henry)*, Duncan Richardson *(Little Jeff)*, Mme. Sul-te-wan *(Midwife)*, Leslie Denison *(Crown Consul)*, Barbara Foley *(Wanjiru)*, Carl Christian *(Cook)*, Bob Anderson *(Mr. Barker the Client)*, Bruce Lester *(Doctor)*, Wesly Bly *(Night Clerk)*, Pauline Myers *(Kikuyu Woman)*, Kim Hamilton *(Kipi's Wife)*, Barry Bernard *(Superintendent)*, Morgan Roberts *(Chief Hings)*, Ottola Nesmith *(Nurse)*, Naaman Brown *(Hand Clerk)*, Ike Jones *(Askari)*.

Hudson and Poitier play boyhood friends who grow up with opposite loyalties towards the colonization of Kenya, East Africa. Hudson is on the side of English farmers who want to harvest the land, but understands that this is an issue with varying shades of gray. He realizes that harmony will prevail only if the white settlers come to an understanding with the local tribes. The differences between the two cultures are not so easily settled, though, as the downtrodden tribesmen begin staging violent raids on the English settlers. Settlers are ruthlessly killed while Poitier battles his own emotions as he finds himself caught between his white friends and his people. Eventually the tensions build into an explosive and bloody climax as Poitier struggles for the Mau Mau cause before finally giving in to authority. This is a film brimming with strong performances by its ensemble. At the heart of the story is Poitier, a native African caught between the English settlers and his tribesmen. His performance is well controlled and deeply moving. Brooks' direction weaves together some very difficult elements with skill and care. Beginning with a filmed prolog with Winston Churchill discussing the real-life Mau Mau raids, Brooks roots the film in reality. The location shooting in East Africa lends a great deal to this as do the gruesomely detailed scenes of Mau Mau rituals. Marshall's character of a tribal chieftain reportedly takes some basis from Jomo Kenyatta, an African Kikuyu leader. Though the story is fiction, the film rings true, with a fair portrait of both sides of the conflict.

p, Pandro S. Berman; d&w, Richard Brooks (based on the novel by Robert C. Ruark); ph, Russell Harlan; m, Miklos Rosza; ed, Ferris Webster; art d, William A. Horning, Edward Carfagno; cos, Helen Rose.

Drama   **(PR:O   MPAA:R)**

**SOMETHING SHORT OF PARADISE*½   (1979) 91m AIP c

Susan Sarandon *(Madeleine Ross)*, David Steinberg *(Harris Soane)*, Jean-Pierre Aumont *(Jean-Fidel Mileau)*, Marilyn Sokol *(Ruthie Miller)*, Joe Grifasi *(Barney Collins)*, Robert Hitt *(Edgar Kent)*, David Rasche *(David)*, Bob Kaliban *(George)*, Ted Pugh *(Frank)*, Ann Robey *(Gail)*, William Francis *(Hotel Manager)*, Adrienne Jalbert *(Fru-Fru)*, Terrence O'Hara *(Donny)*, Fred Nassif *(Desk Clerk)*, Sonya Jennings *(Beth)*, Ellen March *(Lisa)*, Loretta Tupper *(Alice)*, Martha Sherrill *(Mrs. Peel)*.

Lack of character development hurts this adaption of Fred Barron's screenplay. Boring comedy has Sarandon as a journalist who gets involved with a theater manager, Steinberg. She asks stupid questions during press conferences, in an attempt to copy Woody Allen's studies of intellectuals. They do plenty of talking, trying to make this a thinking man's film, but it comes off more as a shallow picture befitting its title.

p, James C. Gutman, Lester Berman; d, David Helpern, Jr.; w, Fred Barron; ph, Walter Lassally (Panavision, TVC Color); m, Mark Snow; ed, Frank Bracht; art d, William De Seta.

Comedy   **Cas.**   **(PR:C-O   MPAA:PG)**

SOMETHING TO HIDE**   (1972, Brit.) 100m Atlantic c

Peter Finch *(Harry Field)*, Shelley Winters *(Gabriella)*, Colin Blakely *(Biagdon)*, John Stride *(Tom Washington)*, Linda Hayden *(Lorelei)*, Harold Goldblatt *(Didbick)*, Rosemarie Dunham *(Elsie)*, Helen Fraser *(Miss Bunyan)*, Graham Crowden *(Lay Preacher)*, Jack Shepherd *(Joe Pepper)*.

An obscure British psychodrama starring Finch as a spineless, lowly bureaucrat who is married to Winters, a shrewish woman who harps on his inadequacies. After an intense fight with her husband, Winters declares she's had enough and flies back home to the U.S. The loneliness suits Finch fine and he goes about listening to classical music and tinkering in his garden. Finally Winters has a change of heart and announces her return. Finch goes to meet her at the airport, but she is not on the plane. On the way back Finch picks up a pregnant hitchhiker, Hayden, and he reluctantly takes her in for the night when she tells him she has no place to go. One night's stay turns into days, leaving Finch helpless because the girl threatens to make up a sensational story for the police if thrown out. Hayden soon goes into labor and Finch delivers the baby himself. One day Finch returns home from work to find the baby dead and the girl gone. Not knowing what to do, he puts the tiny corpse in a cardboard box and takes it with him to the office. After a day of indecision, Finch brings his morbid package home and finally decides to burn the body on the beach in broad daylight. All goes well until a Jewish survivor of Auschwitz recognizes the smell and calls the police. When the cops arrive the now-demented Finch greets them with a shotgun blast and then kills himself. Upon investigation, detectives discover that Finch had killed his wife months ago and buried the body on the beach. Aside from good performances from Finch and Winters (whose role could almost be considered a cameo), SOMETHING TO HIDE is a confused, manipulative, and revolting thriller with gaping plot holes. The film plods along at a deliberate pace until the bizarre events of the climax, which explodes in some gratuitous bloodletting. The vague ending, where the viewer is left to wonder whether Finch was crazy from the beginning, is cheap and unsatisfying.

p, Michael Klinger; d&w, Alistair Reid (based on a novel by Nicholas Monsarrat); ph, Wolfgang Suschitzky (EastmanColor); m, Roy Budd; ed, Reggie Beck; art d, Anthony Pratt.

Drama   **(PR:C-O   MPAA:NR)**

SOMETHING TO LIVE FOR**½   (1952) 89m PAR bw

Joan Fontaine (*Jenny Carey*), Ray Milland (*Alan Miller*), Teresa Wright (*Edna Miller*), Richard Derr (*Tony Collins*), Douglas Dick (*Baker*), Herbert Heyes (*Mr. Crawley*), Paul Valentine (*Albert*), Frank Orth (*Waiter*), Bob Cornthwaite (*Young Man*), Helen Spring (*Mrs. Crawley*), Rudy Lee (*Chris Miller*), Patric Mitchell (*Johnny Miller*), Richard Barron (*Headwaiter*), Paul Newlan (*Bartender*), John Indrisano (*Party Guest*), Jessie Proctor, Lillian Clayes, Genevieve Bell, Patsy O'Byrne, Helen Dickson, Cora Shannon (*Old Ladies*), Mari Blanchard (*Hat Check Girl*), Ida Moore, Mary Field, Judith Allen (*Women*), Kerry Vaughn (*Cocktail Waitress*), Jean Acker Valentino (*Wife*), Sue Carlton (*Intellectual*), Alex Akimoff (*Waiter*), Eric Alden (*Pharoah*), Jody Gilbert (*Woman in Telephone Booth*), Norman Field (*Man*), Maurice Cass, Erville Alderson (*Critics*), Paul Maxey (*Hoffstater*), Douglas Spencer (*Joey*), Donald Dillaway, Al Kunde, George M. Lynn (*Executives*), Arthur Tovey (*Desk Clerk*), James E. Moss, Lee Aaker (*Alternate Boys*), Slim Gaut (*Derelict*), Anne M. Kunde (*Cleaning Woman*), Raymond Bond (*Box Office Man*), Peter Hanson, Laura Elliot, Charles Dayton (*Stage Cast*), Susan Freeman, Sherry Jackson, Gerald Courtemarch (*Little Children*), Helen Brown (*Miss Purdy*), Rolfe Sedan, Marcel De La Brosse, Charles Andre (*Frenchmen*), Jeanne Lafayette (*Frenchwoman*), Harold Miller (*European*), Dulce Daye (*Actress*), Korla Pandit (*Hindu Man*), King Donovan (*Stage Manager*), Gloria Dea, Josette Deegan, Lavonne Battle (*Slave Girls*).

A film that gave Alcoholics Anonymous a boost in the public's eye. Fontaine and Milland are two people with a fondness for the bottle. He gets a call on the AA hotline to help Fontaine and a romance is born as they struggle to help each other. He is married, though unsatisfied with his career at the time, while she uses the bottle to hide her fear from appearing on a Broadway stage. They come to grips with their emotions and that makes them deal with their problem successfully, as Wright, Milland's faithful wife, watches patiently from the sidelines. All win in the end and Milland and Fontaine go their different paths but are now happy that they have control over their own lives and the bottle doesn't.

p&d, George Stevens; w, Dwight Taylor; ph, George Barnes; m, Victor Young; ed, William Hornbeck; art d, Hal Pereira, Walter Tyler; cos, Edith Head.

Drama   **(PR:A   MPAA:NR)**

SOMETHING TO SHOUT ABOUT*½   (1943) 88m COL bw

Don Ameche (*Ken Douglas*), Janet Blair (*Jeanie Maxwell*), Jack Oakie (*Larry Martin*), William Gaxton (*Willard Samson*), Cobina Wright, Jr (*Donna Davis*), Veda Ann Borg (*Flo*), Hazel Scott (*Herself*), Jaye Martin (*Dan Howard*), Lily Norwood [Cyd Charisse] (*Lily*), James "Chuckles" Walker (*Chuckles*), The Bricklayers, Teddy Wilson and His Band.

Mediocre attempt to revive vaudeville shows the backstage workings of a show and how much fun everyone has in its production. Predictable story is about a woman who has won a big alimony settlement, so she decides to put on a vaudeville show. Wright is the untalented star and backer of the show, whom Blair replaces at the last minute. Only highlights of this cliched script are the musical numbers by Cole Porter. Songs include: "You'd Be So Nice to Come Home To," "I Always Knew," "Hasta Luego," "Lotus Bloom," "Something to Shout About," "Through Thick and Thin."

p&d, Gregory Ratoff; w, Lou Breslow, Edward Eliscu, George Owen (based on a story by Fred Schiller); ph, Franz F. Planer; m, David Raksin, Gil Grau; ed, Otto Meyer; prod d, Nicolai Remisoff; md, M.W. Stoloff; art d, Lionel Banks; ch, David Lichine.

Musical   **(PR:A   MPAA:NR)**

SOMETHING TO SING ABOUT***½   (1937) 90m GN bw (AKA: BATTLING HOOFER)

James Cagney (*Terry Rooney*), Evelyn Daw (*Rita Wyatt*), William Frawley (*Hank Meyers*), Mona Barrie (*Stephanie Hajos*), Gene Lockhart (*Bennett O. Regan*), James Newill (*Orchestra Soloist*), Harry Barris (*Pinky*), Candy Candido (*Candy*), Cully Richards (*Soloist*), William B. Davidson (*Cafe Manager*), Richard Tucker (*Blaine*), Marek Windheim (*Farney*), Dwight Frye (*Easton*), John Arthur (*Daviani*), Philip Ahn (*Ito*), Kathleen Lockhart (*Miss Robbins*), Kenneth Harlan (*Transportation Manager*), Herbert Rawlinson (*Studio Attorney*), Ernest Wood (*Edward Burns*), Chick Collins (*The Man Terry Fights*), Duke Green (*Other Man*), Harland Dixon, Johnny Boyle, Johnny "Skins" Miller, Pat Moran, Joe Bennett, Buck Mack, Eddie Allen (*Dancers*), Bill Carey (*Singer*), The Vagabonds (*Specialty*), Elinore Welz, Eleanor Prentiss (*Girls*), Pinkie and Pal (*Arthur Nelson's Fighting Cats*), Frank Mills (*Cabby*), Duke Green (*Stuntman*), Larry Steers (*Studio Official*), John "Skins" Miller (*Sailor in Drag*), Eddie Kane (*San Francisco Theater Manager*), Edward Hearn (*Studio Guard*), Dottie Messmer, Virginia Lee Irwin, Dolly Waldorf (*Three Shades of Blue*), Robert McKenzie (*Ship's Captain*), Bo Peep Karlin, Paul McLarand.

Cagney shows his dance ability in this, the second of his independent films for Grand National. Director Schertzinger wrote the story and the tunes for this lightweight work which delighted audiences and even got an Oscar nomination for Bakaleinikoff's musical score. He was helped a great deal by the first rate orchestrations by Myrl Alderman. The simple story tells of successful Manhattan band leader Cagney who gets his chance at a movie contract and wends his way west. There are excellent pot shots at the studio system (Cagney must have been taking personal revenge against Warner Brothers) and when Cagney thinks he's a bust, becoming convinced of that by Lockhart, an unscrupulous producer, he goes back to New York to marry a woman who has been a soloist with his orchestra. This is Daw, a young Dakotan who got the plumb acting job after a single audition with the director. They take off for a lovely honeymoon in a tropical paradise and when they come back to New York, Cagney is surprised to learn that he's been asked to sign a long-term contract by the film studio. There's a catch, though. The studio and its press boss, Frawley, think that Cagney would be a much more interesting star if he were single so the contract calls for him to remain a bachelor for the duration of his stay in Hollywood. Cagney and Daw are very much in love with each other and attempt to carry off the masquerade but find that neither can live without the other and that their marriage means more than his career. After the usual twists and turns and complications, they're off to New York to take up life as a couple and do what they've always wanted to do–make music. Schertzinger shot the film in continuity, a rare decision that didn't seem to make much sense, as the story didn't have all that much going for it. Score includes: "Any Old Love" (sung by Cagney and Three Shades Of Blue), Daw sang "Right or Wrong," "Loving You," "Out of the Blue," and "Something to Sing About," while Cagney showed he hadn't lost a step when it came to tap dancing. The wit in Parker's screenplay would be especially appreciated by anyone who has ever been around a film studio. The movie was released again 10 years later as BATTLING HOOFER. Daw's career never again reached this height.

p, Zion Myers; d, Victor Schertzinger; w, Austin Parker (based on a story by Schertzinger); ph, John Stumar; m, C. Bakaleinikoff; ed, Gene Milford; md, Bakaleinikoff; art d, Robert Lee, Paul Murphy; ch, Harland Dixon.

Musical/Comedy   **Cas.**   **(PR:A   MPAA:NR)**

SOMETHING WAITS IN THE DARK

(SEE: SCREAMERS, 1978, Ital.)

SOMETHING WEIRD*   (1967) 83m Hur-Lew/Mayflower c

Tony McCabe, Elizabeth Lee, William Brooker, Mudite Arums, Ted Heil, Lawrence J. Aberwood, Stan Dale, Ione.

A horror-love story that revolves around McCabe as an electrical engineer whose face is disfigured in a high-tension wire accident. As a result of the accident, he discovers that he has acquired ESP and telekinetic powers, enabling him to see into the future and move objects. Depressed about his scarred face, he pays a visit to a witch, played by Lee, who agrees to fix his face if he will be her lover. Lee appears beautiful to the rest of the world, but because of his powers, McCabe is able to see her as she really is, horribly ugly. Together, they travel around the country, and McCabe becomes famous for his powers. He is called to a small town to help solve a murder case, where he is also being watched by a doctor who is actually an ESP expert from the government. After Lee warns McCabe about the doctor, he uses his powers and attempts to kill the man with his own bedclothes, but the doctor escapes. McCabe then predicts an attempt on his own life by the town cop, who is also the murderer. McCabe is killed anyway, when the ESP expert delays the cops. After killing the cop, the doctor is able to see Lee as she really is and he flees. Angry, Lee causes the doctor to fall and burn his face. She then makes a pact with him: a beautiful face in exchange for love.

p, James F. Hurley; d, Herschell Gordon Lewis; w, Hurley; ph, Lewis, Andy Romanoff.

Horror   **Cas.**   **(PR:O MPAA:NR)**

SOMETHING WICKED THIS WAY COMES**½
                                    (1983) 94m WB-Bryna/BV c

Jason Robards, Jr (*Charles Halloway*), Jonathan Pryce (*Mr. Dark*), Diane Ladd (*Mrs. Nightshade*), Pam Grier (*Dust Witch*), Royal Dano (*Tom Fury*), Vidal Peterson (*Will Halloway*), Shawn Carson (*Jim Nightshade*), Angelo Rossitto (*Little Person No. 1*), Peter D. Risch (*Little Person No. 2*), Tim T. Clark, Jill Carroll (*Teenage Couple*), Tony Christopher (*Young Ed*), Sharan Lea (*Young Miss Foley*), Scott DeRoy (*Cooger as a Young Man*), Sharon Ashe (*Townswoman*), Arthur Hill (*Narrator*), Mary Grace Canfield (*Miss Foley*), Richard Davalos (*Mr. Crosetti*), Jake Dengel (*Mr. Tetley*), Jack Dodson (*Dr. Douglas*), Bruce M. Fischer (*Mr. Cooger*), Ellen Geer (*Mrs. Halloway*), Brendan Klinger (*Cooger as a Child*), James Stacy (*Ed*), the Bartender.

Ray Bradbury has thrilled millions of readers with his tales of fantasy and the supernatural. So when it was announced that *Something Wicked This Way Comes* would be made into a movie, the anticipation was much greater than the end result. Disney sunk $20 million into this picture and lost a bundle on it. Story revolves around Pryce and his traveling carnival who come into a small Illinois town in the early 20th Century and immediately enthrall the townsfolk. Most of the people in this small town have unfulfilled dreams or wishes for a better life and Pryce can give that to them, but only if they join his dark circus as freaks. Top-line special effects lift the ending, but the picture is never quite as scary as was promised. Director Clayton achieved major success early in his career with THE GREAT GATSBY, but this time around failed in his attempt to capture the frightening theme of Bradbury's novel.

p, Peter Vincent Douglas; d, Jack Clayton; w, Ray Bradbury (based on the novel by Bradbury); ph, Stephen H. Burum (Technicolor); m, James Horner; ed, Argyle Nelson, Barry Mark Gordon; prod d, Richard MacDonald; art d, John B. Mansbridge, Richard James Lawrence; set d, Rick Simpson; cos, Ruth Myers; spec eff, Lee Dyer.

Horror   **Cas.**   **(PR:C MPAA:PG)**

SOMETHING WILD**   (1961) 112m Prometheus Enterprises/UA bw

Carroll Baker (*Mary Ann*), Ralph Meeker (*Mike*), Mildred Dunnock (*Mrs. Gates*), Charles Watts (*Warren Gates*), Jean Stapleton (*Shirley Johnson*), Martin Kosleck (*Landlord*), Ken Chapin (*Manager of 5 & 10*), Clifton James (*Detective Bogarde*), George L. Smith (*Policeman*), Warren Lyons (*College Student*), Duke Howard (*Young Boy*), Tanya Lopert, Peg Shirley, Virginia Baker, Doris Roberts, Anita Cooper (*Girls in 5 & 10*), Jane MacArthur, Roger Dekoven, Logan Ramsey, William Hickey, Nancy Baker, Diane Ladd, Reid Cruickshanks, Evelyn Wall.

Drama about a rape and its repercussions has Baker playing a school girl who is brutally raped one evening in a Brooklyn park. She is unable to tell her prudish mother, Dunnock, and so she leaves home and takes an apartment on the edge of Harlem. She gets a job at a run down five and dime and procedes to carry on her life as if nothing happened. But the hostility from the girls she works with, plus the depressive after effects of the rape, lead her to attempt suicide one night. She is rescuedby Meeker, a garage mechanic who takes her back to live with him at his apartment. He appears to be a compassionate man, until he gets drunk one night and tries to rape her. Baker flees, only to return a few days later with the offer to marry her. Story ends with Baker getting in touch with her mother to tell her she is going to have a baby.

p, George Justin; d, Jack Garfein; w, Garfein, Alex Karmel (based on the novel *Mary Ann* by Karmel); ph, Eugen Shuftan; m, Aaron Copland; ed, Carl Lerner; art d, Richard Day

Drama   **(PR:A MPAA:NR)**

SOMETHING'S ROTTEN*
                                    (1979, Can.) 90m Hazelton Motion
                                              Pictures/Dabara c

Charlotte Blunt (*The Queen*), Geoffrey Bowes (*Prince Calvin*), Trudy Weiss (*Marina Falk*), Christopher Barry (*Prince George*), Cec Linder (*Alexis Alexander*), Jean-Peter Linton (*Dr. Burns*).

For almost everyone involved, from the director on down, this picture was their first effort, and it shows all the way through. Story centers on a set of twins, both rivals for succession to the throne in central Europe. One twin is good, the other bad, but the bad twin wins in the end. Acting, editing, and production are poor, with a badly written script that fails in its attempt at humor.

p, David F. Eustace, Nancy E. Stewart; d, F. Harvey Frost; w, Norman Fox; ph, Brian R.R. Hebb; m, John Kuipers; ed, Brian Ravok.

Mystery   **(PR:C MPAA:NR)**

SOMETIMES A GREAT NOTION***½   (1971) 113m
Newman-Foreman/UNIV c (AKA: NEVER GIVE AN INCH)

Paul Newman (*Hank Stamper*), Henry Fonda (*Henry Stamper*), Lee Remick (*Viv Stamper*), Michael Sarrazin (*Leeland Stamper*), Richard Jaeckel (*Joe Ben Stamper*), Linda Lawson (*Jan Stamper*), Cliff Potts (*Andy Stamper*), Sam Gilman (*John Stamper*), Lee De Broux (*Willard Eggleston*), Jim Burk (*Biggy Newton*), Jim Jenson (*Elwood*), Joe Maross (*Floyd Evenwrite*), Roy Poole (*Jonathan Draeger*), Charles Tyner (*Les Gibbons*), Bennie Dobbins, Alan Gibbs, Mickey Gilbert, Dick Hudkins, Terry Leonard, Fred Lerner, Gary McLarty, Hal Needham, J. N. Roberts, Dean Smith, Fred Waugh, Fred Zendar.

Paul Newman's second directing job is quite a bit different from the intimacy of his first, RACHEL, RACHEL. The original director assigned to the film was Richard Colla but when Newman broke his ankle while riding a motorcycle in June, 1970, the production had to shut down while the bones healed. When he came back, there were problems between Newman and Colla and guess who lost? Right. Fonda, playing an old man for the first time at the age of 65, is the stern but benevolent father of Newman and Jaeckel. They own their own logging company in Oregon (where the film was shot) and Fonda rules the roost with a firm hand. Newman's wife is Remick (totally miscast and far too chi-chi for the part of a logger's wife) and Jaeckel's wife is Lawson, who was perfect in her role. The other loggers in the town go on strike against the bosses but Fonda, who has a contract, will honor it, thus facing the enmity of his neighbors. Fonda has a broken arm and leg from an accident but that doesn't daunt his iconoclastic attitude. The union wants everyone on strike but since Fonda and family are independent contractors, they decide to fulfill their obligations to the mill they serve. Sarrazin arrives. He's another Fonda son by his second marriage. Sarrazin's mother left Oregon a decade before when she could not take the harsh life. Since then, Sarrazin became involved with drugs while attending college, and his mother took her own life. Sarrazin comes back to the family home, not so much out of love for his crusty father, but because he doesn't have a home anywhere else. Sarrazin shows his mettle and is soon accepted by the others as he demonstrates what must be genetic ability with lumber. Remick and Sarrazin become attracted to each other and he sees in her a copy of his late mother in that she is also finding fault with the life she leads and thinking that there must be a better way to spend one's years. The local people have gone from resentment of the Fonda family to outright violence in their anger about the refusal to adhere to the strike. Sarrazin is almost killed when an unseen hand cuts a cable and he narrowly misses a downhill rolling log. Fonda's dog is shot by a sniper and the annual touch football game between the lumber workers almost erupts into murder as a fight breaks out when one of the townspeople intimates that Newman and Fonda's second wife had a fling years before. One of their trucks is destroyed and there seems to be only one way to get their logs to the mill, by floating them downstream. The family begins to cut the logs to the proper length for shipping by water and an accident happens. Fonda's arm is cut off and Jaeckel is pinned under logs as the tide comes in. Newman does everything short of Herculean efforts to save his brother but Jaeckel drowns (in the best scene in the picture and surely the reason Jaeckel received an Oscar nomination). Fonda is in the hospital and Newman is with him as the old man, whose credo is "Never give an inch," dies. Newman goes home and learns that Remick has departed. He takes to the bottle, then gets up, determined to be what his father would have wanted him to be. Newman and Sarrazin double-handedly take the logs down the twisting river pulling them with a tug. On the tug, there sits Fonda's severed hand, with all the fingers bent down save the middle one, in the universal symbol of "I ain't down yet." It's a tawdry joke to end what was, until then, a good enough movie in the 1930s Warner Bros. genre of working men's stories. Kesey's 600-plus-page novel would have made a fine six-hour mini-series, and it's a tribute to scenarist Gay that he managed to condense that much material into under two hours. The picture barely returned what it cost to make, which was a shame as it was a good movie with excellent work on the part of most of the actors. The tune "All His Children" (Henry Mancini, Marilyn and Alan Bergman; sung by Charlie Pride) won a nomination from the movie academy. Joe Maross stands out in a small role and if you look fast, you'll see stuntman Hal Needham—who went on to direct many of Burt Reynolds' movies–in a bit part. The cinematography is extraordinary but it's hard to determine if it was the work of Moore, who photographed the breathtaking Oregon panoramas, or God, who created them. Several scenes were cut from the final print, including one sexual liaison between Sarrazin and Remick, while Newman is at Fonda's deathbed-side. It's this which causes Remick to leave. Without that motivation, her departure is oddly abrupt.

p, John C. Foreman; d, Paul Newman; w, John Gay (based on the novel by Ken Kesey); ph, Richard Moore (Panavision, Technicolor); m, Henry Mancini; ed, Bob Wyman; md, Mancini; art d, Philip Jefferies; set d, William Kiernan; cos, Edith Head; stunts, Jim Arnett; (sung by makeup, Monte Westmore.

Wilderness Drama   **Cas.**   **(PR:O MPAA:PG)**

SOMETIMES GOOD*   (1934, Brit.) 68m BIP/PAR bw

Henry Kendall (Paul Everard), Nancy O'Neil (Millie Tarrant), Minnie Rayner (Jessica Mallory), Hal Gordon (Michael Trout), Charles Mortimar (John Everard), Madeleine Seymour (Mrs. Everard), Jimmy Godden (Col. Mortimer), Edna Davies (Ella Tyfield), Gladys Jennings (Mrs. Smyth-Jenkins), Millicent Wolf.

O'Neil leaves her menial job and decides to stay with her aunt, a housemaid to a missing explorer. She then poses as the explorer's niece in order to snare Kendall, her former employer's son. Her folly ends when the explorer returns and blows her cover. All ends well as the two are granted approval to marry.

p, Fred Browett; d, W.P. Kellino; w, Michael Barringer (based on a story by Emily Rushforth); ph, James Wilson.

Comedy   (PR:A   MPAA:NR)

SOMEWHERE I'LL FIND YOU***   (1942) 108m MGM bw

Clark Gable (Jonathan Davis), Lana Turner (Paula Lane), Robert Sterling (Kirk Davis), Reginald Owen (Willie Manning), Lee Patrick (Eve Manning), Charles Dingle (George L. Stafford), Tamara Shayne (Mama Lugovska), Leonid Kinskey (Dorloff), Diana Lewis (Penny), Molly Lamont (Nurse Winifred), Patricia Dane (Crystal Jones), Sara Haden (Miss Coulter), Richard Kean (Prof. Anatole), Francis Sayles (Pearcley), Tom O'Grady (Bartender), Donald Kerr (Waiter), Gayne Whitman (Penny's Companion), Grady Sutton (Boy), Dorothy Morris (Girl), Keye Luke (Thomas Chang), Miles Mander (Fred Kirsten), Eleanor Soohoo (Ming), Allen Jung (Sam Porto), Douglas Fowley (Captain), Benny Inocencio (Felipe Morel), Van Johnson (Lt. Wayne Halls), Angel Cruz (Manuel Ortega), Keenan Wynn (Sgt. Tom Purdy), Frank Faylen (Slim), J. Lewis Smith (Pete Brady), Lee Tung Foo (Chinese Doctor), Rags Ragland (Charlie), Diana Lewis (Penny), Luke Chan (Japanese Soldier).

Notable mainly because this was the film Gable was working on when his beloved wife, actress Carole Lombard, was killed in a plane crash, SOMEWHERE I'LL FIND YOU is a standard war-torn romance which saw the second screen teaming of Gable and Turner (the first was HONKY TONK). Gable and his younger brother, Sterling, are a pair of American correspondents in Germany who suddenly find themselves without work when their editor calls them back to New York because he refuses to believe their predictions regarding a world war. Gable returns to the home of old friends where he runs into Turner. He quickly introduces himself and kisses her. She reminds him that they had met before–when she was a cub reporter–and tells him that she had a crush on him. Gable is bemused by this revelation, but then learns that Turner is now his brother's steady girl. Gable doesn't quite trust Turner so he sets out to prove to his brother that she is no good for him because of her capriciousness. This causes tension between Sterling and Gable, especially when Turner breaks off the romance because she thinks Gable wants to marry her. Her illusions are soon shattered, however, when she is assigned to cover the fighting in Indochina and Gable makes no attempt to stop her. Weeks later, the brothers find themselves rehired by their old editor, who has finally come to see that their predictions are coming true. They are also sent to Indochina and there they happen to meet up with Turner, who is now involved in smuggling refugee Chinese babies out of danger. Seeing Turner's obvious dedication to the children, Gable begins to soften his attitude toward her. Meanwhile, the Japanese have bombed Pearl Harbor and the patriotic Sterling joins the armed forces. Turner decides to become a nurse and all three end up on Bataan. Sterling is killed during the bloody struggle, Turner goes missing, and Gable covers the story for the folks back home. Gable eventually finds Turner alive and admits his love for her. Three days into production of SOMEWHERE I'LL FIND YOU, on January 16, 1942, Carole Lombard was killed returning from a war bonds drive when the TWA twin-engine DC-3 she was flying in crashed into the side of a cliff 13 minutes after takeoff from Las Vegas. MGM was about to close the set permanently when Gable returned to complete the picture less than a month after the tragedy. Gable, who was normally open and quite friendly to cast and crew, requested that the set remain closed to all visitors and that he be left alone in his dressing room. Police were hired to guard his privacy. To the amazement of all, Gable forced himself to finish the film. Critics of the time, while applauding his show- must-go-on determination, noted that Gable's performance seemed subdued and strained. The old Gable sparkle was missing. Perhaps because of the tragedy, or perhaps because of his teaming with Turner, the curious public turned out in droves to see SOMEWHERE I'LL FIND YOU and the film became one of the studio's biggest hits.

p, Pandro S. Berman; d, Wesley Ruggles; w, Marguerite Roberts, Walter Reisch (based on a story by Charles Hoffman); ph, Harold Rosson; m, Bronislau Kaper; ed, Frank E. Hull; art d, Cedric Gibbons, Malcolm Brown; set d, Edwin B. Willis, Hugh Hunt; cos, Robert Kalloch.

Romance/Drama   (PR:A   MPAA:NR)

SOMEWHERE IN BERLIN**   (1949, E. Ger.) 77m DEFA/Central
                                                        Cinema bw

Charles Knetchke (Gustav Iller), Hans Trinkaus (Willi), Siegfried Utecht (Captain), Harry Hindemith (Herr Iller), Hedda Sarnow (Frau Iller), Hans

Leibelt (Herr Eckmann), Paul Bildt (Herr Birke), Fritz Raup (Uncle Kalle), Walter Bluhm (Waldemar), Magdalene von Nussbaum (Willi's Mother).

Documentary-type story on how a family copes in postwar Berlin and the struggles they encounter. Supposedly fiction, this story has very real touches to it. Many shots entail kids playing among ruined buildings or people dealing with black marketeers to emphasize the shortage of goods. The depressing film has a worn-out soldier returning from a prisoner-of-war camp to his family, trying to put the pieces of his life back together amidst the rubble. Good symbolic shots, but too many left-open questions don't help this half-powerful film, one of the earliest post-WW II pictures made at the new state-owned DEFA studio with Soviet help (MURDERERS AMONG US, 1948, was the first). (In German; English subtitles).

p, Georg Klaup; d&w, Gerhard Lamprecht; ph, Werner Krien; m, Erich Einegg; ed, Lena Naumann; set d, Otto Erdmann.

Drama   (PR:A   MPAA:NR)

SOMEWHERE IN CAMP*½**   (1942, Brit.) 88m Mancunian/Bit bw

Harry Korris (Sgt. Korris), Frank Randle (Pvt. Randle), Robbie Vincent (Pvt. Enoch), Dan Young (Pvt. Young), John Singer (Pvt. Jack Trevor), Toni Lupino (Jean Rivers), Peggy Novak (Mrs. Rivers), Clifford Buckton (Col. Rivers), Gus Aubrey (Pvt. Lofty), Betty Wheatley (Mrs. Randle), Evie Carcroft (Mrs. Korris).

A lively music-hall adventure about three army privates and their sergeant who concoct a plot to help private Singer win over the commanding officer's daughter. Their plan is a success only after the sergeant poses as a love-stricken housekeeper. Eighty eight-minutes of episodic silliness and tolerable musical numbers. (See SOMEWHERE series, Index)

p&d, John E. Blakeley; w, Roney Parsons, Anthony Toner, Frank Randle; ph, Stephen Dade.

Comedy/Musical   (PR:A   MPAA:NR)

SOMEWHERE IN CIVVIES*   (1943, Brit.) 87m But bw

Frank Randle (Pvt. Randle), George Donnan (Sgt. Doonan), Suzette Tarri (Mrs. Spam), Joss Ambler (Matthews), H.F. Maltby (Col. Tyldesley), Nancy O'Neil (Mary Randle), Grey Blake (Ralph Tyldesley), Gus Aubrey.

Randle is an army private who will receive a healthy inheritance from his uncle if he can prove he is of sound mind. His malicious cousin tries to get the money for himself by committing Randle to a mental home. His wrongdoing is soon exposed and Randle is paid his money. Another weak entry in the series of British SOMEWHERE pictures. (See SOMEWHERE series, Index.)

p, T.A. Welsh; d, Maclean Rogers; w, Con West; ph, Geoffrey Faithfull.

Comedy   (PR:A   MPAA:NR)

SOMEWHERE IN ENGLAND**   (1940, Brit.) 79m Mancunian/But bw

Harry Korris (Sgt. Korris), Frank Randle (Pvt. Randle), Winki Turner (Irene Morant), Dan Young (Pvt. Young), Robbie Vincent (Pvt. Enoch), Harry Kemble (Cpl. Jack Vernon), John Singer (Bert Smith), Sidney Monkton (Adjutant), Stanley King, Eight Master Singers, Percival Mackey's Orchestra.

The first of many British SOMEWHERE comedies, this one starring Korris, Randle, Vincent, and Young. Corporal Kemble is demoted in the ranks after being framed by a rival serviceman who shares an interest with Kemble in the adjutant's daughter. The outrageous quartet saves the corporal from further punishment and wins him back his girl. (See SOMEWHERE series, Index.)

p&d, John E. Blakeley; w, Arthur Mertz, Roney Parsons; ph, Geoffrey Faithfull.

Comedy   (PR:A   MPAA:NR)

SOMEWHERE IN FRANCE**   (1943, Brit.) 89m Michael
      Balcon-EAL/UA bw (GB: THE FOREM AN WENT TO FRANCE)

Tommy Trinder (Tommy), Constance Cummings (Anne), Clifford Evans (Fred Carrick), Robert Morley (French Mayor), Gordon Jackson (Jock), Ernest Milton (Stationmaster), Francois [Francis L. Sullivan] Sully (French Skipper), Owen Reynolds (Collins), Ronald Adams (Sir Charles Fawcett), Paul Bonifas (Prefect), John Williams ("English" Captain), Mervyn Johns (Official, Passport Office), John Boxer (Official, Ministry of Home Security), Anita Palacine, Thora Hird (Barmaids), Charles Victor, Bill Blewett (Spotters), Mrs. Blewett, Eric Maturin, Tony Ainley, Michele Forbes-Fraser, Edward Lisle, Robert Bendall, Nora Herman, Irone Kiriloff, Madeleine Rive.

Evans plays an English factory foreman (the film is dedicated to his real-life counterpart, Melbourne Johns, the subject of author Priestley's story) who journeys to newly-occupied France at the outset of WW II, charged with recovering three machine parts which are important to the Allied war effort. Trinder, a popular British comedian of the time (executive producer Sir

Michael Balcon called him "the only comedian I know who is as light-hearted off the stage as on") and Jackson (in his screen debut) are the two lorry-driving British Army tommies assigned to accompany Evans on his dangerous quest. Cummings is effective as the American girl who assists and accompanies them; Morley is disarming as a secret collaborator who misdirects the Parsifal-like Evans and his cohorts, who finally reach their coastal rendezvous at La Rogette with the machinery. Made at a time when France was off limits to Britons, the simulations of the French towns and countryside are surprisingly effective. Expatriate French peasants and children were pressed into service for the documentary-seeming sequences of mass flight from threatened communities (producer Cavalcanti had been head of the G.P.O. film unit, making documentary films in 1939 and 1940). The technical talent was excellent for this interesting blend of comedy and pathos. Co-scripter Arliss is the son of George Arliss, famed for his portrayals of great historical figures; Arliss the younger had made his co-directorial debut two years before the release of this film. Editor Hamer later became a producer and director, with a classic comedy to his credit: KIND HEARTS AND CORONETS (1949), featuring Alec Guinness in eight roles as murder victims belonging to one family. Evans did a creditable job as the peripatetic foreman; after the completion of the shooting schedule, he served in the armed forces for four years. Upon his return, he appeared in only two more films, turning his attention instead to screenwriting. Jackson, a fine character actor, appeared in many postwar films, but achieved real prominence as an actor with the BBC Masterpiece Theatre TV series "Upstairs, Downstairs" as the butler, the connective thread of the series' segments. SOMEWHERE IN FRANCE, which some consider one of the best war films of all time, was released in England in 1942.

p, Alberto Cavalcanti; d, Charles Frend; w, John Dighton, Angus McPhail, Leslie Arliss (based on a story by J. B. Priestley, and the experiences of Melbourne Johns); ph, Wilkie Cooper; m, William Walton; ed, Robert Hamer; art d, Tom Morahan.

War/Comedy   **(PR:A   MPAA:NR)**

SOMEWHERE IN POLITICS**   (1949, Brit.) 110m Mancunian bw

Frank Randle (*Joe Smart*), Tessie O'Shea (*Daisy Smart*), Josef Locke (*Willoughby*), Sally Barnes (*Marjorie Willoughby*), Syd Harrison (*Tommy Parker*), Max Harrison (*Arthur Parker*), Bunty Meadows (*Pat Parker*), Jimmy Clitheroe (*Sonny*), Sonny Burke (*Reggie Smart*).

A standard programmer which stars Randle as a radio repairman who enters the political arena against his own boss. Randle wins the election but runs into mounds of problems in the process. Nothing here that you haven't seen done better before. (See SOMEWHERE series, Index.)

p&d, John E. Blakeley; w, Harry Jackson, Arthur Mertz, Frank Randle; ph, Ernest Palmer, Ben Hart.

Comedy   **(PR:A   MPAA:NR)**

SOMEWHERE IN SONORA**   (1933) 59m WB bw

John Wayne (*John Bishop*), Henry B. Walthall (*Bob Leadly*), Shirley Palmer (*Mary Burton*), J. P. McGowan (*Monte Black*), Ann Fay (*Patsy Ellis*), Frank Rice (*Riley*), Billy Franey (*Shorty*), Paul Fix (*Bart Leadly*), Ralph Lewis (*Burton*), Slim Whitaker, Blackie Whiteford, Jim Corey, Duke the Miracle Horse.

The fifth of the six westerns in the series Wayne made for Warner Bros. which established him as a western star (he had appeared in a few westerns previously, but his roles were a mixed bag until this time; the studio brought him out of poverty row, where he had landed after an altercation with Harry Cohn, boss of Columbia Pictures–said to be over a woman both were interested in–where he had been a contract player). Wayne plays a rodeo performer who, accused of fixing a stagecoach race, is forced to travel to Mexico. Once there, he makes like an outlaw and joins the gang which has shanghaied the son, (Fix) his first picture with Wayne, and the start of a long association) of his old rodeo boss, Walthall. Wayne foils the felons in their effort to rob Lewis' silver mine, thereby clearing his name and winning the love of the mine owner's daughter, Fay. Like some of the other pictures of the series, this was a remake of a Ken Maynard silent. The studio used many of the expensive outdoor silent sequences from the 1927 Maynard film in this later version, cleverly costuming Wayne and the heroine sufficiently like their earlier counterparts to be indistinguishable in long shots. As in all the other films in this series, the hero's front handle was *John*, a trick often used by the studios to establish continuity and identification with a specific actor.

p, Leon Schlesinger; d, Mack V. Wright; w, Joe Roach (based on a story and the novel *Somewhere South in Sonora* by Wsll Levington Comfort); ph, Ted McCord; m, Leo F. Forbstein; ed, William Clemens.

Western   **(PR:A   MPAA:NR)**

SOMEWHERE IN THE NIGHT***   (1946) 100m FOX bw

John Hodiak (*George Taylor*), Nancy Guild (*Christy*), Lloyd Nolan (*Lt. Donald Kendall*), Richard Conte (*Mel Phillips*), Josephine Hutchinson (*Elizabeth Conroy*), Fritz Kortner (*Anzelmo*), Margo Woode (*Phyllis*), Sheldon Leonard (*Sam*), Lou Nova (*Hubert*), John Russell (*Marine Captain*),

Houseley Stevenson (*Conroy*), Charles Arndt (*Little Man*), Al Sparlis (*Cab Driver*), Richard Benedict (*Technical Sergeant*), John Kellogg (*Medical Attendant*), Phil Van Zandt (*Navy Doctor*), Whitner Bissell (*Bartender*), Forbes Murray (*Executive*), Jeff Corey (*Bank Teller*), Paula Reid (*Nurse*), Mary Currier (*Miss Jones*), Sam Flint (*Bank Guard*), Henry Morgan (*Swede*), Charles Marsh (*Hotel Clerk*), Clancy Cooper (*Attendant*), Jack Davis (*Dr. Grant*), Louis Mason (*Brother Williams*), Henri De Soto (*Headwaiter*), Harry Tyler (*Baggage Room Attendant*), Maynard Holmes (*Police Stenographer*), Edward Kelly, Jr., Cy Schindel (*Men at Bar*), Elaine Langan (*Hat Check Girl*), Milt Kibbee (*Proprietor*).

An engrossing crime thriller about a Marine, Hodiak, who suffers from amnesia and is discharged from the service. His only clue to his real identity is a Los Angeles address. Once there he unearths an angry letter from a girl unknown to him, and a letter from one "Larry Cravat" His search for Cravat leads him to a nightclub and its singer, Guild. Before he can get much information he gets knocked around by two thugs–Kortner (an aging veteran of German silents) and Nova (a real-life boxer with a short career in the movies). Hodiak hides out with Guild in her apartment and receives some help in his search from nightclub owner Conte and police detective Nolan. Hodiak's investigating leads him to Stevenson, a witness to a murder that Cravat committed. Stevenson tells him that a briefcase is hidden under a dock in San Pedro. Hodiak and Guild locate the money but in the process Hodiak realizes that he is really Cravat. Conte helps the pair escape when gunfire begins to fill the air. Hodiak's confusion begins to clear as he remembers that he was once partners with Conte and that Conte is really the killer. Hodiak lures Conte into a trap and in a final battle Nolan shoots and kills Conte. Having found his true identity, Hodiak is left to start anew with sweetheart Guild. Although the plot is convoluted, Mankiewicz's direction moves it all along at a feverish pace, adding some bizarre stylistic touches, such as the military doctors and nurses speaking directly into the camera as if the audience shares a point of view with Hodiak. The film's most glaring minus, however, is the wooden Guild in a standard performance that could have been handled by any of a hundred mediocre Hollywood starlets. This was her debut role and Fox gave her a big push, informing the anxious millions that "Guild rhymes with Wild." She even sings, delivering the forgettable "Middle of Nowhere," which is just where her career was headed.

p, Anderson Lawler; d, Joseph L. Mankiewicz; w, Howard Dimsdale, Mankiewicz, Lee Strasberg (based on the story "The Lonely Journey" by Marvin Borowsky); ph, Norbert Brodine; m, David Buttolph; ed, James B. Clark; md, Emil Newman; art d, James Basevi, Maurice Ransford; set d, Thomas Little, Ernest Lansing; cos, Kay Nelson; spec eff, Fred Sersen; makeup, Ben Nye.

Crime   **(PR:C   MPAA:NR)**

SOMEWHERE IN TIME**½   (1980) 103m Rastar/UNIV c

Christopher Reeve (*Richard Collier*), Jane Seymour (*Elise McKenna*), Christopher Plummer (*W. F. Robinson*), Teresa Wright (*Laura Roberts*), Bill Erwin (*Arthur*), George Voskovec (*Dr. Gerald Finney*), Susan French (*Older Elise*), John Alvin (*Arthur's Father*), Eddra Gale (*Genevieve*), Sean Hayden (*Young Arthur*), Audrey Bennett (*Richard's Date*), Richard Matheson (*Astonished Man*), W. H. Macy, Laurence Coven (*Critics*), Susan Bugg (*Penelope*), Christy Michaels (*Beverly*), Ali Matheson, George Wendt (*Students*), Steve Boomer (*Hippie*), Patrick Billingsley (*Professor*), Ted Liss (*Agent*), Francis X. Keefe (*Desk Clerk*), Taylor Williams (*Maitre d'*), Noreen Walker (*Librarian*), Evans Ghiselli (*Coin Shop Operator*), David Hull (*Hotel Manager*), Paul M. Cook (*Doctor*), Barbara Giovannini, Don Franklin, Victoria Michaels, William P. O'Hagen, Maud Strand, Bo Clausen, James P. Dunnigan, Sean Hayden, Hal Frank, Hayden Jones, Val Bettin.

Anyone who ever read Jack Finney's brilliant novel *Time and Again* will recognize a disturbing similarity between it and the screenplay for this sentimental love story that never comes close to Finney's original work in conception or excitement. Set in the Grand Hotel on Mackinac Island in Michigan, it's the story of a young Chicago playwright, Reeve (in his first role away from "The Man of Steel"–Superman– although he plays this as if he had a ramrod for a spine), who comes to the hotel and sees a photo of a 1912 actress who once played there. Her face looks familiar because he'd met an old lady who told him "Come back to me", and she could have been this woman. After the old lady passes away, Reeve realizes that he did meet the actress, Seymour, a long time ago and they were in love in 1912, when he led another life. In order to go back in time, he checks into the same room he thinks he occupied back then, dons the clothes of the period, and tries to recreate what happened then, using the theory that everything that was ever spoken or done in that room is still there, we just don't have the proper retrieval equipment to bring it back. (This is the exact same premise as in Finney's novel, with the locale switched from the Dakota apartment building in New York, the same building outside which John Lennon was killed.) Reeve, able to effect the change, finds himself back in 1912 where Seymour is under the influence of Plummer, a man who rules her life like a master puppeteer. So it is a love story that transcends time and the studio thought it would attract the romantic crowd. They were wrong. The picture sank in the U.S. but was, surprisingly, a hit in Japan, where they probably hadn't yet seen the "Twilight Zone" episodes that often used the same sort of ideas. Szwarc does well in his best directing job to date after having had two bombs with BUG and JAWS II. A special note to Dorleac for his costumes. If that name sounds familiar, he is the brother of the late Françoise Dorleac, a promising actress (THAT MAN FROM RIO) whose life was cut short in an auto accident. Seymour is gorgeous to look at but was not given enough to do. Reeve, on the other hand, is given too much to do. Barry's music was evocative of romance, especially when he used Rachmaninov's "Variations on a Theme by Paganini."

p, Stephen Deutsch; d, Jeannot Szwarc; w, Richard Matheson (based on his novel *Bid Time Return*); m, John Barry (Sergei Rachmaninov); ed, Jeff Gourson; prod d, Seymour Klate; set d, Mary Ann Biddle; cos, Jean-Pierre Dorleac; spec eff, Jack Faggard.

Science Fiction/Romance   Cas.   (PR:C MPAA:PG)

SOMEWHERE ON LEAVE*½   (1942, Brit.) 96m Mancunian/But bw

Frank Randle (*Pvt. Randle*), Harry Korris (*Sgt. Korris*), Robbie Vincent (*Pvt. Enoch*), Dan Young (*Pvt. Young*), Toni Lupino (*Toni Beaumont*), Pat McGrath (*Pvt. Roy Desmond*), Noel Dainton (*Capt. Delvaine*), Tonie Edgar Bruce (*Mrs. Delvaine*), Percival Mackey and His Orchestra.

The four outrageous army men of the SOMEWHERE series get involved in some wildly amusing adventures while on leave at a wealthy army buddy's ritzy home. A splendid time is had by all, especially the rich host, McGrath, who is lucky enough to snare the girl of his dreams. Inexplicably this picture (and others in the series) smashed box office records in northern England, but fizzled without notice in the southern parts. (See SOMEWHERE series, Index.)

p&d, John E. Blakeley; w, Roney Parsons, Anthony Toner, Frank Randle; ph, Geoffrey Faithfull.

Comedy   (PR:A MPAA:NR)

SOMMARLEK   (SEE: ILLICIT INTERLUDE, 1954, Swed.)

SON COMES HOME, A**   (1936) 75m PAR bw

Mary Boland (*Mary Grady*), Julie Haydon (*Jo*), Donald Woods (*Denny*), Wallace Ford (*Steve*), Roger Imhof (*Detective Kennedy*), Anthony Nace (*Brennan*), Gertrude W. Hoffman (*Effie Wimple*), Eleanor Wesselhoeft (*Essie Wimple*), Charles Middleton (*Prosecutor*), Thomas Jackson (*District Attorney*), John Wray (*Gasoline Station Owner*), Robert Middlemass (*Sheriff*), Lee Kohlmar (*Proprietor*), Herbert Rawlinson (*Bladen*), Defense Attorney, Ann Evers (*Nurse*).

Groomed for Paramount as a successor to Marie Dressler (who died in 1934), Boland–who had, for the most part, played fluttery scatterbrains as in RUGGLES OF RED GAP (1935)–was here shifted to a Dressler-style role as the tough but soft-hearted owner of Mary Grady's Chowder House in San Francisco. Reporter Ford, a chowder-hound, writes a newspaper story about gruff widow Boland's prodigal son, Nace, missing for some 15 years. The story is scanned by Woods, a drifter on the lam for a murder he tried to prevent. Woods sees a chance to adopt a new persona, so he presents himself as the prodigal. Boland and her adopted daughter, Haydon, are skeptical at first, but when detective Imhof nears his quarry, the two women leap to the lad's defense. Woods spots a picture of Boland's late husband, and the resemblance convinces him that the murder was committed by the true missing son. With Boland and Ford hot on the trail of the latter, warm-hearted Woods bends every effort to frustrate their finding Nace, despite the danger to himself. All to no avail: the seafood-serving sleuth snares her son, who is butchered by police bullets after acknowledging his parentage. Well directed by the celebrated German, Dupont (VARIETY, 1928) who, after an unsuccessful Hollywood career, dropped out of films for a 10-year period to become a talent agent, then returned to direct a number of low-budget films.

p, Albert Lewis; d, E. A. Dupont; w, Sylvia Thalberg (based on a story by Harry Hervey); ph, William C. Mellor.

Drama   (PR:A MPAA:NR)

SON-DAUGHTER, THE*½   (1932) 79m MGM bw

Ramon Novarro (*Tom Lee*), Helen Hayes (*Lien Wha*), Lewis Stone (*Dr. Dong Tong*), Warner Oland (*Fen Sha*), Ralph Morgan (*Fang Fou Hy*), Louise Closser Hale (*Toy Yah*), H. B. Warner (*Sin Kai*).

No, not a tale of a transsexual. This story has to do with antiquated customs and historic male-female roles in a changing world. A name director (Clarence Brown), a fine performance by Hayes, and a cast of great actors can't save this tale about love affairs and protocol in San Francisco's Chinatown. The cast is about as Oriental as the Harlem Globetrotters; Novarro can't hide his Latin accent while attempting to add an Oriental lilt. Hayes does well, but shouldn't be proud of this. The story takes place in 1911, with the start of the revolution that will bring an end to the 267-year domination of the Ch'ing dynasty of China and bring Sun Yat-Sen to the presidency of the new republic. Oland (no stranger to oriental makeup; he'd been playing Charlie Chan - see Index - for some time) is the royalist villain to whom heroine Hayes, true to tradition, barters herself in order to raise money for arms for the republican revolutionists, led by her father, Stone. Novarro is the lad she truly loves. After Oland's tong toughies butcher her

family and friends, Hayes exacts revenge by strangling him with his own pigtail (ironically, a hair style held to be humiliating by the revolutionists, and one outlawed subsequent to the successful revolt).

d, Clarence Brown; w, John Goodrich, Claudine West, Leon Gordon (based on a play by David Belasco, George M. Scarborough); ph, Oliver T. Marsh; m, Herbert Stothart; ed, Margaret Booth; m/l, Stothart, Anselm Goetzl.

Drama   (PR:A MPAA:NR)

SON OF A BADMAN**½   (1949) 64m Western Adventure/Screen Guild bw

Lash La Rue (*Lash*), Al "Fuzzy" St. John (*Fuzzy Q. Jones*), Noel Neill (*Vicki*), Michael Whalen (*Dr. Jarvis/El Sombre*), Zon Murray (*Horn*), Jack Ingram (*Rocky*), Steve Raines (*Larson*), Chuck [Bob] Cason (*Bart*), Don Harvey (*Sheriff Ragel*), Edna Holland (*Mrs. Burley*), Bill Bailey (*Brad Burley*), Francis McDonald (*Joe Christ*), Frank Lackteen (*Piute*), Sandy Sanders (*Pete*), Doyle O'Dell (*Tex James*).

Special U.S. Marshal La Rue and his comical sidekick St. John ride into Star City, assigned to clear the town of a group of bandits headed by "El Sombre", a mystery man. Ambushed by the bandits, the two fight them off. Once in town, St. John heads for the office of dentist Whalen to have an aching tooth pulled; La Rue meets the sheriff, Harvey, of whom he quickly becomes suspicious. Harvey proves to be the minion of land-grabber McDonald, who is also in league with "El Sombre". The gang is after the property of widow Holland, whose murdered husband had sent for the marshal. Holland's daughter Neill, following La Rue's plan, transfers the deed to the land to McDonald, who immediately charges an outrageous toll to the local cattlemen for the right to traverse the territory to cattle-feeding land. Surprise! Neill was underage, and not competent to peddle the property. Angered, McDonald gets physical with the two women, but is killed by "El Sombre", who smells a double-cross. La Rue goes to dentist Whalen to get his teeth repaired, and is given some pills by the doctor, who then discloses that *he* is "El Sombre", and that the marshal will soon die from the poisonous pellets. But the lawman has only palmed the pills and whales Whalen with his whip, delivering him to justice. This was one of a series of films made after La Rue's long-time production company, the "Poverty Row" Producers Releasing Corporation, went out of business. Film historian Les Adams said of these films, "Those who consider PRC's offerings as coming from the bottom of the pit have evidently never been exposed to Ron Ormond productions circa anytime. Compared to those, PRC was an uptown dude in high-yeller shoes". Indeed, sidekick St. John became so disgruntled about the diminishing quality of these productions that he retired from the screen for good in 1951. La Rue, whose own personal life bottomed out shortly afterward, said of St. John, "his personal life was sad....Fuzzy was an alcoholic."

p, Ron Ormond; d, Ray Taylor; w, Ormond, Ira Webb; ph, Ernest Miller; m, Walter Greene; ed, Hugh Winn; art d, Fred Preble; set d, Ted Offenbecker.

Western   (PR:A MPAA:NR)

SON OF A GUNFIGHTER**   (1966, U.S./Span.) 92m Zurbano/MGM c
(EL HIJO DEL PISTOLERO)

Russ [Rusty] Tamblyn (*Johnny*), Kieron Moore (*Deputy Fenton*), James Philbrook (*Ketchum*), Fernando Rey (*Don Fortuna*), Maria Granada (*Pilar*), Aldo Sambrell (*Morales*), Antonio Casas (*Pecos*), Barta Barri (*Esteban*), Ralph Browne (*Sheriff*), Andy Anza (*Fuentes*), Fernando Hilbeck (*Joaquin*), Hector Quiroga (*Stagecoach Guard*), Carmen Tarrazo (*Maria*), Maria Jose Collado (*Sarita*), Julio Perez Tabernero.

Philbrook and Sambrell are a couple of crooks, creating havoc along the Mexican-American border in 1877. A stagecoach coming into town is attacked by Philbrook's gang of outlaws, but they are turned away by the fast gun work of Tamblyn, who absolutely despises the bad guys. Quick-draw Tamblyn is wounded by Sambrell during an attack on local rancher Rey, whose daughter falls for Tamblyn. Tamblyn and Moore set out after Philbrook, Moore hoping to collect some reward money, but Philbrook declines to fight because Tamblyn is his son. Moore has no such qualms and wounds the outlaw. The kid saves his old man and rides back to the ranch to stop Sambrell's Mexican bandits. They finally get rid of them as Sambrell and Philbrook gun each other down. Tamblyn settles down on the ranch with Granada and hangs up his six-shooters. Former child star Tamblyn doesn't quite cut it as a gunslinger.

p, Lester Welch; d, Paul Landres; w, Clarke Reynolds; ph, Manuel Berenguer (CinemaScope, Metrocolor); m, Robert Mellin; ed, Sherman Rose; md, Frank Barber; art d, Julio Molina; set d, Jose Maria Tapiador; makeup, Carmen Martin.

Western   (PR:A MPAA:NR)

SON OF A SAILOR*½   (1933) 70m FN bw

Joe E. Brown (*Handsome Callahan*), Jean Muir (*Helen Farnsworth*), Thelma Todd [Alison Loyd] (*The Baroness*), Johnny Mack Brown (*Duke*), Frank McHugh (*Gaga*), Garry Owen (*Sailor Johnson*), Sheila Terry (*Genevieve*), George Blackwood (*Armstrong*), Samuel S. Hinds (*Adm. Farnsworth*), Arthur Vinton (*Vincent*), George Irving (*Rear Adm. Lee*), Walter

Miller *(Kramer)*, Kenneth Thomson *(Williams)*, John Marston *(Lt. Reed)*, Joe Sauers [Sawyer] *(Slug)*, Clay Clement *(Blanding)*, Purnell Pratt *(Capt. Briggs)*, Merna Kennedy.

Brown mugs his way through another comedy. This time he is an offbeat sailor who has an aversion to battle. He somehow gets promoted when he accidentally foils an espionage ring that's after some important Navy documents. He gets himself on a target ship set out to sink, and hooks up with the admiral's daughter, who decides to take him home to meet daddy. Much of the film was shot on the aircraft carrier USS Saratoga to add excellent realism. This was lovely actress Muir's first leading role. Known as "The Studio Pest" because of her proclivity for questioning every phase of the movie-making business, she played in many other low-budget films until she was unfairly smeared by the vicious, anonymously published "anti-Communist" pamphlet *Red Channels* in the early 1950s. Blacklisted by industry executives for years, she became a teacher, her earlier curiosity standing her in good stead. Actress Todd was to die under mysterious circumstances at the age of 30 two years later; this comedy was made during her stormy 20-month marriage to talent agent "Pat" DiCicco. This was a relatively rare comedy appearance for Johnny Mack Brown at the time; after some years playing opposite Greta Garbo and other leading actresses in big-budget films, he had already segued into B westerns.

P, James Seymour; d, Lloyd Bacon; w, Al Cohn, Paul Gerard Smith, Ernest Pagano, H.M. Walker; ph, Ira Morgan; ed, James Gibbons; art d, Anton Grot.

Comedy (PR:A MPAA:NR)

SON OF A STRANGER* (1957, Brit.) 68m Danziger/UA bw

James Kenney *(Tom Adams)*, Ann Stephens *(Joannie)*, Victor Maddern *(Lenny)*, Basil Dignam *(Dr. Delaney)*, Catharine Finn *(Mrs. Adams)*, Diana Chesney *(Mrs. Peck)*, Mona Washbourne.

Incredibly antisocial little film has Kenney, a slum youth, supporting himself by mugging old women. He dreams his missing father is rich, so when he gets a lead on his whereabouts, he leaves his hated mother and goes off to find him. In a small town he murders a woman, then finds that his father is the town doctor. When the doctor discovers that the killer is his own son, he gets his gun but accidentally is shot himself. Kenney is arrested for his killing and hangs. Kenney basically repeats his role from THE SLASHER (1953, Brit.).

p, Edward J. and Harry Lee Danziger; d, Ernest Morris; w, Stanley Miller; ph, Jimmy Wilson.

Crime (PR:O MPAA:NR)

SON OF ALI BABA** (1952) 75m UNIV c

Tony Curtis *(Kashma Baba)*, Piper Laurie *(Kiki)*, Susan Cabot *(Tala)*, William Reynolds *(Mustafa)*, Hugh O'Brian *(Hussein)*, Victor Jory *(Caliph)*, Morris Ankrum *(Ali Baba)*, Philip Van Zandt *(Kareeb)*, Leon Belasco *(Babu)*, Palmer Lee [Gregg Palmer] *(Farouk)*, Barbara Knudson *(Theda)*, Alice Kelley *(Calu)*, Gerald Mohr *(Capt. Youssef)*, Milada Mladova *(Zaza)*, Katherine Warren *(Princess Karma)*, Robert Barrat *(Commandant)*.

Can a streetwise kid from New York make it big in far-off Araby? A satire on the Arabian Nights theme. Jory wants the wealth of ex-thief Ankrum and forces kidnaped princess Laurie to pretend to be a slave girl and go to the home of Ankrum's son Curtis. She takes up with Curtis, even though she had been promised to the Shah. By "rescuing" her, Jory will not only gain favor with the Shah, but also secure the treasure without much trouble. He just hadn't planned on Curtis and his boys giving him so much trouble. Plenty of sword-banging as Curtis keeps the treasure and the girl. The movie almost wants to play it straight, but the leading roles can't carry it off without a smirk. The picture abounds with topical gags which contemporary audiences may miss entirely (Farouk–the character played by Lee, who in 1954 changed his name to Gregg Palmer and continued his career–was the name of the recently deposed monarch of Egypt, a fat, disgusting playboy who had been much in the news). Producer Goldstein parted company with Universal prior to the film's release. The associate producer was Ross Hunter, who just returned to the industry after a stint as a teacher; he had been a leading man in musicals of the mid-1940s.

p, Leonard Goldstein; d, Kurt Neumann; w, Gerald Drayson Adams; ph, Maury Gertsman (Technicolor), ed, Virgil Vogel; md, Joseph Gershenson; art d, Bernard Herzbrun, Emrich Nicholson; set d, Russell A. Gausman, John Austin; ch, Harold Belfer.

Adventure (PR:A MPAA:NR)

SON OF BELLE STARR*½ (1953) 70m AA c

Keith Larsen *(The Kid)*, Dona Drake *(Dolores)*, Peggie Castle *(Clara Wren)*, Regis Toomey *(Tom Wren, Editor)*, James Seay *(Clark)*, Myron Healey *(Sheriff)*, Frank Puglia *(Manuel)*, Robert Keys *(Bart Wren)*, I. Stanford Jolley *(Rocky)*, Paul McGuire *(Pinkly)*, Lane Bradford *(Beacher)*, Mike Ragan [Holly Bane] *(Earl)*, Joe Dominguez *(Pablo)*, Alex Montoya *(Mexican)*.

A heavy and almost unnecessary ending hurts this decent no-name western. Larsen is a young man who has to turn to crime, almost forced to do so

because of his mother's outlaw reputation. (The real-life Belle Starr actually did have a son, Ed Reed, who was suspected of shooting his mother in the back; she also had a daughter, Pearl, believed to have been fathered by outlaw Cole Younger–see BELLE STARR'S DAUGHTER, 1947.) He is recruited by underhanded sheriff Healey to help in a robbery. Larsen goes along with the plan because he wants to find out who set him up the year before. During the robbery, the sheriff's cronies turn on him and try to put him away. But Larsen guns them down and stashes the loot, hoping to find out the real mind behind the plan. He gets his man, but his reputation as an outlaw gets Larsen in the end too, as a posse shows up and kills him right when he's proving his innocence.

p, Peter Scully; d, Frank McDonald; w, D. D. Beauchamp, William Raynor (based on a story by Jack DeWitt); ph, Harry Neumann (Cinecolor); m, Marlin Skiles; ed, Bruce Schoengarth; art d, David Milton.

Western (PR:A MPAA:NR)

SON OF BILLY THE KID** (1949) 65m Western Adventure/Screen Guild bw

Lash La Rue *(Jack Garrett)*, Al St. John *(Fuzzy Q. Jones)*, June Carr *(Betty Raines)*, George Baxter *(Jim Thorn)*, Marion Colby *(Norma)*, Terry Frost *(Cy Shaeffer)*, John James *(Colt)*, House Peters, Jr *(1st Outlaw)*, Clarke Stevens *(2nd Outlaw)*, Bob Duncan *(Yantis)*, Cliff Taylor *(Jake)*, William Perrott *(Billy the Kid)*, Felipe Turich *(Jose Gonzales)*, Rosa Turich *(Rosa Gonzales)*, Jerry Riggio *(Sanchos)*, Eileen Dixon *(Dance Hall Girl)*, I. Stanford Jolley *(Fergus)*, Bud Osborne *(Guard)*, Fraser McMinn *(Joe)*.

Another in the series of Ron Ormond productions starring La Rue made following the demise of Producers Releasing Company, this quickie (another in the series was released exactly two weeks later) has it that sheriff Pat Garrett never actually killed Billy the Kid in 1881; the Kid survived, straightened out, and became a respectable, honest banker. St. John–much plagued by the matrimonial guest of dance-hall girl Carr in the comedy-relief scenes–drives a stagecoach carrying gold shipments to meet the payroll for the coming railroad's construction workers. The coach is attacked by bandits, including handsome young James, but the bandits are repelled with the help of a lone rider, La Rue, who happens along. The bandits are under the dominion of the supposedly respectable Frost, who hopes to bankrupt Baxter's bank so he can grab the land and mortgages and squeeze the railroad out of cash. The bandits, thwarted in their attempts on the stagecoach, rob the bank, but are double-crossed by James, who grabs the gold and runs. Attempting again to hold up a shipment, the bandits are killed or captured through a ruse devised by La Rue; rather than gold, the wagon holds armed deputies. Later, Baxter's secretary-niece, Colby, pulls a gun on the banker and reveals that she has been in league with Frost all along. Attempting to steal the contents of the bank's vault, she is disarmed by the mysterious James. Baxter reveals himself as the one-time outlaw, and James is the SON OF BILLY THE KID, who joined the outlaw gang in order to save his father from their ravages. One unanswered question remains: is La Rue– as Jack Garrett–*the son of Pat Garrett*? We'll never know. The picture's poster reads, "Dead or alive...he rode the plains of the untamed west!" When he rides, the film comes alive. When he talks, the film dies.

p, Ron Ormond; d, Ray Taylor; w, Ormond, Ira Webb; ph, Ernest Miller; m, Walter Greene; ed, Hugh Winn; art d, Fred Preble; set d, Ted Offenbecker.

Western (PR:A MPAA:NR)

SON OF BLOB (SEE: BEWARE THE BLOB, 1972)

SON OF CAPTAIN BLOOD, THE*½ (1964, U.S./Ital./Span.) 88m C.C.M.-Producciones Benito Perojo/PAR c (IL FIGLIO DEL CAPITANO BLOOD; EL HIJO DEL CAPITAN BLOOD)

Sean Flynn *(Robert Blood)*, Alessandra Panaro *(Abbigail)*, Jose Nieto *(De Malagon)*, Ann Todd *(Arabella Blood)*, John Kitzmiller *(Moses)*, Raffaele Baldassarre *(Bruno)*, Fernando Sancho *(Timothy)*, Roberto Camardiel *(Orguelthorpe)*, Carlos Casaravilla, Luisa De Cordoba, Ray Martino, Simonetta Simeoni, Ettore Ribotta, Angeles Macua.

Errol Flynn swung across the screen in CAPTAIN BLOOD 30 years earlier and Paramount, in the ultimate publicity gimmick, released his son Sean Flynn in THE SON OF CAPTAIN BLOOD. However, his son can't swing as well as the old man in this sea story riddled with cliches. Flynn is growing up with his mother Todd but wants to become a pirate like the old man; she'd rather have him be a doctor. She finally relents and he joins a ship's company, where he romances passenger Panaro. The ship is taken over by bad pirate Nieto, who happened to be an old enemy of Flynn's father; when Nieto discovers the kid's bloodlines, he has a field day. The young couple are rescued by the old man's cronies and Flynn leads them on to some action-packed adventures. They head back to the mainland in time to save everyone from a tidal wave and become heroes. With enough of the pirate life in him, Flynn opts for the simple life of a doctor with Panaro. Handsome young Flynn (his mother was actress Lili Damita) handles his action scenes with adequate bravura. One critic averred that when he learned to act he might do quite well in pictures. This was his second film as a star. The far-ranging Flynn made a number of others in different parts of the world; his last acting job was in Singapore. He then became a photographer correspondent, covering the war in southeast Asia. He was reported missing and presumed dead in 1970, an apparent victim of the conflict in Cambodia. British actress Todd came out of near-retirement for this one.

p, Harry Joe Brown; d, Tulio Demicheli; w, Casey Robinson (based on characters created by Rafael Sabatini); ph, Alejandro Ulloa (CinemaScope, Technicolor); m, Gregorio Garcia Segura, Angelo Francesco Lavagnino; ed, Renato Cinquini, Antonio Ramirez; art d, Piero Filippone, Enrique Alarcon.

Adventure   (PR:A   MPAA:NR)

SON OF DAVY CROCKETT, THE*½

                                     (1941) 59m COL bw (GB: BLUE CLAY)

Bill Elliott (*Dave Crockett*), Iris Meredith (*Doris Mathews*), Dub Taylor (*Cannonball*), Kenneth MacDonald (*King Canfield*), Richard Fiske (*Jesse Gordon*), Eddy Waller (*Grandpa Mathews*), Don Curtis (*Jack Ringe*), Paul Scardon (*Zeke*), Edmund Cobb (*Lance*), Steve Clark (*Curly*), Harrison Greene (*President U.S. Grant*), Lloyd Bridges, Curley Dresden, Frank Ellis, Dick Botiller, Ray Jones, Tom London, John Tyrell, Nick Thompson, Merrill McCormack, Martin Garralaga, Lew Meehan, Francis Sayles, Jack Ingram, Frank LaRue, Chuck Hamilton.

Not enough action and too much talking; this one has Elliott playing a young Crockett progeny helping out President Grant right after the Civil War. His job is to get Texas' vote to join the Union, but MacDonald and his evil crew want to stay with the confederacy. Crockett arrives, fools the gang into thinking he is with them, but gets Texas of them in the finale and gets the people in the Union. Elliott, usually billed as "Wild Bill"–a result of his long-time connection with the character of Wild Bill Hickok–played another historical figure in the same year in THE RETURN OF DANIEL BOONE. This was one of 10 films in which the star was teamed with comic sidekick Taylor.

p, Leon Barsha; d&w, Lambert Hillyer; ph, Benjamin H. Kline; ed, Mel Thorsen.

Western   (PR:A   MPAA:NR)

SON OF DR. JEKYLL, THE*½

                                                   (1951) 77m COL bw

Louis Hayward (*Edward Jekyll*), Jody Lawrence (*Lynn*), Alexander Knox (*Dr. Curtis Lanyon*), Lester Matthews (*John Utterson*), Gavin Muir (*Richard Daniels*), Paul Cavanagh (*Inspector Stoddard*), Rhys Williams (*Michaels*), Doris Lloyd (*Lottie Sarelle*), Claire Carleton (*Hazel Sarelle*), Patrick O'Moore (*Joe Sarelle*), James Logan, Leslie Denison (*Constables*), Robin Camp (*Willie Bennett*), Bruce Lester (*Reporter*), Holmes Herbert (*Local Constable*), Matthew Boulton (*Inspector Grey*), Pat Aherne (*Landlord*), Wheaton Chambers (*Magistrate*), Vesey O'Davoren (*Butler*), Harry Martin (*Plainclothesman*), Olaf Hytten (*Plainclothesman*), Stapleton Kent (*Proprietor*), Joyce Jameson (*Barmaid*), Betty Fairfax (*Woman in Window*), Keith Hitchcock (*Bobby*), Ottola Nesmith (*Nurse*), Carol Savage (*Young Woman*), Robin Hughes (*Alec*), Dave Dunbar, Frank Hagney (*Men in Pub*), Guy Kingsford (*Male Nurse*), Benita Booth, Ida McGill, Ola Lorraine (*Women*), Leonard Mudie (*Pharmacist*), Phyllis Morris (*Tea Woman*), Alec Harford (*Clerk*), David Cole (*Copy Boy*), Jimmie Long, Robert Reeves.

Hayward grows up and wants to set the record straight–his father was not the madman everyone made him to be. But this film moves so slowly, the audience wants them both dead and buried. It begins with the original Mr. Hyde being killed and his son being hidden away by a couple of the doctor's friends. It catches up to Hayward 30 years later as he is getting ready to marry Lawrence. The two old-timers then tell him about his father. He puts off the wedding to clear his dad's name but Knox, who had helped take care of Hayward, wants the money for himself and tries to get the son to follow in his father's path. With the whole town against him, Hayward finally proves his innocence. But in the finale he dies in a fire, like his father did 30 years before.

d, Seymour Friedman; w, Mortimer Braus, Jack Pollexfen; ph, Henry Freulich; m, Paul Sawtell; ed, Gene Havlick; md, Morris Stoloff; art d, Walter Holscher.

Horror   (PR:A   MPAA:NR)

SON OF DRACULA**½

                                                   (1943) 78m UNIV bw

Lon Chaney, Jr (*Count Alucard*), Robert Paige (*Frank Stanley*), Louise Allbritton (*Katherine Caldwell*), Evelyn Ankers (*Claire Caldwell*), Frank Craven (*Dr. Harry Brewster*), J. Edward Bromberg (*Prof. Lazlo*), Samuel S. Hinds (*Judge Simmons*), Adeline DeWalt Reynolds (*Mme. Zimba*), Patrick Moriarity (*Sheriff Dawes*), Etta McDaniel (*Sarah*), George Irving (*Col. Caldwell*), Walter Sande (*The Jailor*), Cyril Delevanti (*The Coroner*), Jack Rockwell (*Deputy Sheriff*), Jess Lee Brooks (*Steven*), Joan Blair (*Mrs. Land*), Sam McDaniel (*Andy*), Charles Moore (*Mathew*), Robert Dudley (*Kirby*), Charles Bates (*Tommy Land*), Emmett Smith (*Servant*).

Chaney and Universal cranked out this film to cash in on the younger Chaney's box-office popularity as the man with the famous dental problem (he played the Wolf Man in several horror films, most of which were made in the 1940s). This time he heads to Louisiana to take occult worshipper Allbritton as his new bride. She thinks he is a member of Hungary's high

society. Her former boy friend, Paige, notices some strange things going on with the couple and decides to investigate. Chaney avoids trouble by turning either into a bat or mist. But in the end, Paige kills Chaney and Allbritton, who has gone over to the dark side. Chaney's character name is Count Alucard, or Dracula spelled backwards. This spelling was to be used again in many bad movies. (See DRACULA series, Index)

p, Ford Beebe; d, Robert Siodmak; w, Eric Taylor (based on a story by Curtis Siodmak); ph, George Robinson; ed, Saul Goodkind; art d, John Goodman.

Horror   (PR:C   MPAA:NR)

SON OF DRACULA*

                              (1974, Brit.) 90m Cinemation/Apple c (AKA: YOUNG DRACULA)

Harry Nilsson (*Count Down*), Ringo Starr (*Merlin the Magician*), Dennis Price (*Van Helsing*), Freddie Jones (*Dr. Frankenstein*), Suzanna Leigh (*Girl*), Peter Frampton, Keith Moon, John Bonham (*Musicians*), Rosanna Lee (*Amber*).

Ringo was better off playing drums and enjoying royalties from his Beatle days than producing and acting in this horror-comedy that is neither frightening nor funny. Nilsson is the sorry son of Dracula and Starr plays Merlin the Magician. This movie also featured the late Keith Moon and the late John Bonham, drummers for The Who and Led Zeppelin. Musician Peter Frampton also makes an appearance. (See DRACULA series, Index)

p, Ringo Starr; d, Freddie Francis; w, Jay Fairbanks; ph, Norman Warwick; m, Harry Nilsson.

Comedy   (PR:C   MPAA:PG)

SON OF FLUBBER**½

                                             (1963) 102m Disney/BV bw

Fred MacMurray (*Prof. Ned Brainard*), Nancy Olson (*Betsy Brainard*), Keenan Wynn (*Alonzo Hawk*), Tommy Kirk (*Biff Hawk*), Elliott Reid (*Shelby Ashton*), Joanna Moore (*Desiree de la Roche*), Leon Ames (*President Rufus Daggett*), Ed Wynn (*A.J. Allen*), Ken Murray (*Mr. Hurley*), Charlie Ruggles (*Judge Murdock*), William Demarest (*Mr. Hummel*), Bob Sweeney (*Mr. Harker*), Paul Lynde (*Sportscaster*), Stuart Erwin (*Coach Wilson*), Edward Andrews (*Defense Secretary*), Alan Hewitt (*Prosecutor*), Leon Tyler (*Humphrey Harker*), Forrest Lewis (*Officer Kelly*), James Westerfield (*Officer Hanson*), Alan Carney (*1st Referee*), Lee Giroux (*Newscaster*), Jack Albertson (*Mr. Barley*), Eddie Ryder (*Mr. Osborne*), Harriet MacGibbon (*Edna Daggett*), Beverly Wills (*Mother*), Wally Boag (*Father*), Walter Elias Miller (*Baby Walter in TV Commercial*), Robert Shayne (*Assistant to Defense Secretary*), Henry Hunter (*Admiral*), Hal Smith (*Bartender*), J. Pat O'Malley (*Sign Painter*), Norman Grabowski (*Rutland Football Player No. 33*), Gordon Jones (*Rutland Coach*), Lindy Davis (*Newsboy Joey Marriano/ 1st Hobgoblin*), Hope Sansberry (*Secretary*), Byron Foulger (*Proprietor*), Jack Rice, Dal McKennon (*Jurors*), Burt Mustin (*1st Bailiff*), Ned Wynn (*Rutland Student Manager*), Joe Flynn (*Announcer in TV Commercial*), Harvey Korman (*Husband in Commercial*), Mari Lynn (*Wife in Commercial*), Belle Montrose (*Mother in Commercial*), John Olsewski (*Rutland Football Player No. 15*), Darby Hinton (*2nd Hobgoblin*), Brad Morrow (*1st Football Player*), William H. O'Brien (*Attendant*).

This is the first sequel Disney ever produced. The possibilities for fun with new inventions and the success of THE ABSENT-MINDED PROFESSOR were too great, so two years later SON OF FLUBBER was released. Fred MacMurray reprises his role and gets help from almost the same cast as was in the first film. MacMurray becomes entangled in red tape so that his newest invention, anti-gravity gop, goes unsold. He heads back to the lab and invents "dry rain." But the shotgun apparatus that produces the rain causes all the glass within a certain area to break. Meanwhile, Kirk uses MacMurray's tools and helps to create a flubber gas to infalte suits to help football players. Then MacMurray's wife, Olson, leaves him and he must stand trial for the damage caused by the "dry rain." But a county extension agent appears at the trial and says that this "dry rain" has improved agricultural production and MacMurray is free and gets Olson back. The flubber gas helps the local football team win the big game and the professor is a hero. He and Olson fly through the air in their Model T once again.

p, Bill Walsh, Ron Miller; d, Robert Stevenson; w, Walsh, Don DaGradi (based on the story "A Situation of Gravity" by Samuel W. Taylor and the Danny Dunn books by Jay Williams, Raymond Abrashkin); ph, Edward Colman; m, George Bruns; ed, Cotton Warburton; art d, Carroll Clark, Bill Tuntke; set d, Emile Kuri, Hal Gausman; cos, Bill Thomas; spec eff, Peter Ellenshaw, Eustace Lycett, Robert A. Mattey; makeup, Pat McNalley.

Comedy   **Cas.**   (PR:AAA   MPAA:G)

SON OF FRANKENSTEIN****

                                                   (1939) 95m UNIV bw

Basil Rathbone (*Baron Wolf von Frankenstein*), Boris Karloff (*The Monster*), Bela Lugosi (*Ygor*), Lionel Atwill (*Inspector Krogh*), Josephine Hutchinson (*Elsa von Frankenstein*), Donnie Dunagan (*Peter von Frankenstein*), Emma Dunn (*Amelia*), Edgar Norton (*Thomas Benson*), Perry Ivins (*Fritz*), Lawrence Grant (*Burgomaster*), Lionel Belmore (*Emil Lang*), Michael Mark (*Ewald Neumuller*), Caroline Cook (*Frau Neumuller*), Gustav von Seyffertitz (*Councilor*), Edward Cassidy (*Dr. Berger*), Tom Ricketts, Lorimer Johnson (*Burghers*), Jack Harris, Betty Chay, Harry

Cording, Ward Bond, Dwight Frye, Bud Wolfe, Eddie Parker.

The third film in the Universal FRANKENSTEIN series and the last feature film appearance by Karloff as the monster. The film boasts some stunning set design, a good script, and a magnificent cast which is topped by Lugosi, who gives the performance of his career as Ygor. Not only was SON OF FRANKENSTEIN a critical and commercial success, but it spawned the second wave of well- crafted Hollywood horror films that would last until after WW II. Set 25 years after the end of THE BRIDE OF FRANKENSTEIN, the film begins as the late Baron von Frankenstein's son, Rathbone, returns to his homeland from America. Accompanied by his wife, Hutchinson, and their young son, Dunagen, Rathbone receives a weak welcome from the Burgomaster, who presents him with a box containing his father's papers. Once safe in their castle, Rathbone and his family are visited by Atwill, a very military police inspector who has a false arm which he must position by using his good arm. Atwill warns Rathbone that he is not welcomed by the villagers, who fear that he will continue his father's experiments. Rathbone laughs off their suspicions, but Atwill relates that the fears are very real. When Atwill was a child, the Monster had ripped out his arm by the roots, thus destroying his ambition to be an army officer. The next day, Rathbone wanders the ruins of his father's laboratory and glances warily into a nearby pit which is boiling with sulfur. There he meets Lugosi, a grotesque former shepherd with a broken neck. Lugosi explains he was hanged for stealing bodies for Rathbone's father and left for dead. He somehow survived his execution and now hides among the ruins guarding his "friend." Lugosi shows Rathbone that his "friend," Karloff, was struck by lightning and was revived enough to survive all these years. The comatose monster is laid out on a slab, immobile, but very much alive. Rathbone becomes obsessed with the idea of bringing Karloff back to full power and then vindicating his father by teaching the monster to behave. New equipment is installed in the laboratory with only Lugosi and the butler, Norton, allowed inside. Rathbone's experiments prove disappointing, until his young son informs him that a giant man had visited him in his bedroom. Realizing that the monster is loose, Rathbone learns that Lugosi has gained Karloff's confidence and is ordering him to kill the jurors who had sentenced him to death. Soon after, Norton is killed by Karloff and Atwill learns that the monster has returned. Rathbone, seeking to stop the killings, confronts Lugosi in the laboratory. The broken-necked shepherd attacks Rathbone, but the scientist shoots him dead and leaves. When Karloff finds Lugosi's body, he screams in anguish at the death of his only friend and goes on the rampage, wrecking the lab. Wanting revenge, Karloff kidnaps Rathbone's son and threatens to throw him into the bubbling sulfur pit. Atwill and Rathbone race to the lab to stop the monster. Atwill fires several shots into Karloff who stands with one large foot holding down the child, but the monster simply reaches out and rips off the inspector's artificial limb and waves it like a club. Desperate to save his son, Rathbone grabs a chain dangling overhead and swings into Karloff with all his might. The impact sends the monster tumbling backward into the sulfur pit where he disappears beneath the bubbling ooze. Realizing that he really doesn't belong at the castle, Rathbone and family bid farewell to the villagers and go back home to America. SON OF FRANKENSTEIN is a rousing, memorable addition to the series that almost never got made. In 1936, the original founders of Universal Studios, Carl Laemmle and his son, found themselves in severe financial straits that required desperate measures. Forced to sell an option to buy the studio for a loan of $750,000, the Laemmles were faced with a buyout. Standard Capital Corporation bought Universal for $5.5 million and booted the father-and-son team out, including all their patronage employees. The new management was much more conservative and hated the very horror films that had built the studio. In 1937, the British banned all horror films from distribution, thus stripping the American studios of a lucrative overseas market. Hollywood stopped making horror films. In 1938, there was a purge of Universal's new management with more creative, open-minded men replacing the stodgy money-grubbing types. Meanwhile, the owner of the Los Angeles Regina Theatre was desperately trying to improve his dwindling box-office receipts. Finding a distributor offering a triple bill of DRACULA, FRANKENSTEIN, and SON OF KONG for only $99 a week, the man booked the films and played them up big in the papers. To everyone's surprise, lines formed around the block for the horror show and screenings were held from 10 a.m. to 3 a.m. in order to accommodate the crowds. The public obviously wanted to see horror films. This was not lost on Universal's new management, which immediately struck 500 new prints of DRACULA and FRANKENSTEIN and booked them as a double feature nationwide. The films proved to be a big hit and the studio decided to make a new horror film, a second sequel to FRANKENSTEIN. Hoping to get it out cheap and quick, Universal budgeted the new film at $250,000, significantly less than the original 1931 film had cost. Director Lee, who had helmed such hits as THE COUNT OF MONTE CRISTO (1934) and THE THREE MUSKETEERS (1935) demanded the studio double the budget and shoot it in color. This was agreed to, but shooting in color was abandoned after tests showed Karloff's makeup to be unsuitable for color. The studio originally wanted Peter Lorre to play Wolf von Frankenstein, but this was changed for the prestige of Basil Rathbone. Lugosi, who had fallen on very hard times during the horror film drought, jumped at the chance to play Ygor and even relished the heavy makeup he usually disdained. The studio, however, tried to take advantage of the vulnerable Lugosi by cutting his salary from $1,000 a week to $500, and then scheduling his performance to be shot in only one week. Outraged, director Lee expanded Lugosi's part and kept the actor working through the whole shoot. It was a brilliant move on Lee's part because Lugosi steals the entire show. Through his gruff voice, bizarre appearance, and cackling laugh, Lugosi created one of the most memorable characters in classic horror films and he would make a return appearance in THE GHOST OF FRANKENSTEIN (1942). Atwill also creates a distinct character in Inspector Krogh. The actor milked his false arm for all it was worth, and even stuck a handful of darts in it while playing against Rathbone in one gripping interrogation scene. Mel Brooks resurrected the scene in hilarious fashion for his parody of the series, YOUNG FRANKENSTEIN. A bit of a disappointment is Karloff. Somewhere between the two films, his beloved monster lost the ability to speak, and for SON OF FRANKENSTEIN he was turned into little more than a robot. Karloff is allowed a few memorable scenes in the film, especially when he finds Lugosi's dead body, sees himself in a mirror, and shows a genuine curiosity for children's books. The actor was sadly dismayed at what he considered a reversal of progress for the monster and decided never to play him again. Karloff celebrated his 51st birthday during filming and the crew threw him a surprise birthday party which the cast participated in while still in their monster makeup and costumes. Some major cuts were made in the film with Dwight Frye, who had been Frankenstein's assistant in the first two films, having his entire role as one of the villagers cut out. A part that did survive sees a young Ward Bond playing a policeman who utters one line. While the offbeat vision and humor of James Whale (the director of the first two Frankenstein films) are missing, Lee managed to create a memorable world all his own and was helped immensely by his superior cast and big-budget production. The series would go downhill from here and end with a rousing parody of the whole genre in ABBOTT AND COSTELLO MEET FRANKENSTEIN (1948). (See FRANKENSTEIN series, Index.)

p&d, Rowland V. Lee; w, Willis Cooper (based on characters created by Mary Shelley); ph, George Robinson; m, Frank Skinner; ed, Ted Kent; md, Lionel Newman; art d, Jack Otterson; set d, Russell Gausman; cos, Vera West; spec eff, John P. Fulton; makeup, Jack P. Pierce.

Horror **(PR:C MPAA:NR)**

SON OF FURY*** (1942) 98m FOX bw

Tyrone Power *(Benjamin Blake)*, Gene Tierney *(Eve)*, George Sanders *(Sir Arthur Blake)*, Frances Farmer *(Isabel Blake)*, Roddy McDowall *(Benjamin as a Boy)*, John Carradine *(Caleb Green)*, Elsa Lanchester *(Bristol Isabel)*, Harry Davenport *(Amos Kidder)*, Kay Johnson *(Helen Blake)*, Dudley Digges *(Bartholomew Pratt)*, Halliwell Hobbes *(Purdy)*, Marten Lamont *(Kenneth Hobart)*, Arthur Hohl *(Capt. Greenwood)*, Pedro De Cordoba *(Fennou)*, Dennis Hoey *(Lord Tarrant)*, Heather Thatcher *(Maggie Martin)*, Lester Mathews *(Prosecutor)*, Robert Grieg *(Judge)*, Ray Mala *(Mornoa)*, Ethel Griffies *(Matron)*, Clifford Severn *(Paddy)*, Mae Marsh *(Mrs. Purdy)*, Marilyn Knowlden *(Isabel as a Girl)*, Cyril McLaglen *(Gimes)*, Harry Cording *(Turnkey)*, James Craven *(Guard)*, Olaf Hytten *(Court Clerk)*, Leonard Carey *(Pale Tom)*, Ignacio Saenz *(Native Boy)*, Clive Morgan *(Lord St. George)*, Charles Irwin *(Captain)*, Virginia Gilmore, Cobrina Wright, Jr.

Cast in another adventurous role is Power as the title character of Marshall's swashbuckling period novel *Benjamin Blake*. Set in England during the days of King George III, SON OF FURY begins with a young heir to a dukedom (McDowall) who is being raised by his dastardly uncle, Sanders. The youngster has been snatched, legally, from his grandfather, Davenport, after the death of the boy's nobleman father. Sanders makes the young heir a bonded servant. Time passes and the boy grows into Power, a stablehand who is incessantly badgered and humiliated by Sanders. Power soon finds himself attracted to Sanders' beautiful daughter, Farmer. Sanders mercilessly beats Power one day after finding him and Farmer together in each other's arms. Power escapes via a cargo ship bound for India. Although living conditions on board are worse than in the stables, Power receives some hope from Carradine, a raggedy sailor who befriends him. In search of a better life, the two jump overboard and swim to the safety of a Polynesian island. Their good will is accepted by the initially hostile islanders, especially native girl Tierney, who falls in love with Power. Spending their time as pearl divers, Power and Carradine amass a small fortune. When a ship bound for England makes a stop on the island, Power accepts a ride back in order to settle his score with Sanders. Power hires a lawyer, Digges, to prove that the dukedom belongs to Power and not to Sanders. Power then travels to his estate where he has been betrayed by Farmer. He handily defeats Sanders in a furious fist fight, and then victoriously orders Sanders and Farmer to leave. After handing over control of the estate to his loyal friends and servants, Power returns to Tierney, his island love. Employing all the usual island romance cliches (an excess of tropic vegetation, clear serene pools of water, and revealing bathing suits, the island sequences sepia toned), SON OF FURY is a solid escapist adventure yarn. Guided by the adroit direction of Cromwell, the all-star cast never fails to hold one's attention. The casting, however, did not come easily for Cromwell and company. Originally Virginia Gilmore had been cast in the role of Sanders' wife, only to be replaced by the more regal looking Johnson (who not-so-coincidentally was director Cromwell's wife). Another role switch occurred with Cobina Wright, Jr., who was first cast as Sanders' daughter. The part was given to Farmer and, as it turns out, it was her final role until THE PARTY CRASHERS in 1958. SON OF FURY was remade in 1952 as THE TREASURE OF THE GOLDEN CONDOR, filmed in glorious Technicolor, starring Cornel Wilde. Actresses Wright and Gilmore, though cut from their feature-player roles, can still be observed in long shots in SON OF FURY if one looks closely.

p, Darryl F. Zanuck; d, John Cromwell; w, Philip Dunne (based on the novel *Benjamin Blake* by Edison Marshall); ph, Arthur Miller; m, Alfred Newman; ed, Walter Thompson; md, Newman; art d, Richard Day, James Basevi; set d, Thomas Little; cos, Gwen Wakeling.

| Adventure | Cas. | (PR:A   MPAA:NR) |

SON OF GOD'S COUNTRY*½   (1948) 60m REP bw

Monte Hale *(Himself)*, Pamela Blake *(Cathy Thornton)*, Paul Hurst *(Eli Walker)*, Jim Nolan *(Bill Sanger)*, Jay Kirby *(Frank Thornton)*, Steve Darrell *(Bigelow)*, Francis McDonald *(Tom Ford)*, Jason Robards, Sr *(John Thornton)*, Fred Graham *(Hagen)*, Herman Hack.

Cliches, drag down this western, almost making it a comedy on horses. Story line involves land, as always, with Hale the good guy on the scene to break up the bad guys' scheme. Story is set after the Civil War and so the bad guy starts to blame all the Southern ranchers for the troubles.

p, Melville Tucker; d, R.G. Springsteen; w, Paul Gangelin, Bob Williams; ph, John MacBurnie; m, Dale Butts; ed, Harry Keller; art d, Frank Arrigo; m/l, "Railroad Corral" (sung by Monte Hale).

| Western | Cas. | (PR:A   MPAA:NR) |

SON OF GODZILLA*   (1967, Jap.) 86m TOHO bw (GOJIRA NO MUSUKO)

Tadao Takashima *(Dr. Kuzumi)*, Akira Kubo *(Goro)*, Beverly Maeda, Akihiko Hirata, Yoshio Tsuchiya, Kenji Sahara, Susumu Kurobe.

Godzilla comes back to the screen for the eighth time, this time in child form (in Godzilla's way). This movie was made mostly to compete in a market that had emerged for baby monsters and the fad that followed. A scientist's experiments on an island go haywire, causing the temperature to rise dramatically making things grow to giant sizes. An egg on the island hatches and out comes little Godzilla while dad watches over as the kid blows smoke rings like the old man. The little one takes a liking to Maeda, who is attacked by a giant spider. She is rescued by the father-son duo. The scientist starts dropping the temperatures to freeze everything, forcing the Godzilla clan into hibernation and the humans to leave. This Godzilla film had some of the better special effects of the eight films.

p, Tomoyuki Tanaka; d, Jun Fukuda; w, Shinichi Sekizawa, Kazue Shiba; ph, Kazuo Yamada; spec eff, Eiji Tsuburaya, Sadamasa Arikawa.

| Science Fiction | Cas. | (PR:C   MPAA:NR) |

SON OF GREETINGS   (SEE: HI, MOM!, 1970)

SON OF INDIA**   (1931) 75m MGM bw

Ramon Novarro *(Karim)*, Conrad Nagel *(William Darsay)*, Marjorie Rambeau *(Mrs. Darsay)*, Madge Evans *(Janice)*, C. Aubrey Smith *(Dr. Wallace)*, Mitchell Lewis *(Hamid)*, John Miljan *(Juggat)*, Nigel de Brulier *(Rao Rama)*.

Too typical of a racially conscious film, this time an Indian boy in love with an American. Film starts quickly enough, with scenes showing Novarro as a young boy with his father on a trip to Bombay. His wealthy father is killed by a gang and the boy is left for dead. All he has is a diamond from his father. He finally makes it to Bombay, looking all ragged and is framed by a greedy merchant for thievery. A kindly white man sticks up for him and he is released. He meets Evans, who had made the successful jump from child actress to adult actress with no faltering, and falls in love. But her brother tells Novarro to forget her. Everyone is sad and the tale ends with him kissing her dress while consulting a holy man about his decision. He is reassured that he did the right thing, even though he becomes a wealthy young man. This was also Novarro's first talking film.

d, Jacques Feyder; w, Ernest Vadja, John Meehan, Claudine West (based on the novel *Mr. Isaacs* by F. Marion Crawford); ph, Harold Rosson; ed, Conrad A. Nervig.

| Drama | | (PR:A   MPAA:NR) |

SON OF INGAGI   (1940) 70m Sack Amusement/Hollywood Productions bw

Zack Williams *(Ingeena)*, Laura Bowman, Alfred Grant, Spencer Williams, Jr, The Four Toppers, Daisy Bufford, Arthur Ray, Earl J. Morris, Jesse Graves.

INGAGI came out in 1930, supposedly as an African documentary. That one had a gorilla carrying around topless women. This has nothing to do with the original. It features a lonely apeman and an all black ensemble. Williams is the apeman and he goes off to steal a bride and whisks her off to his lab. Williams went on to fame as Andy on the "Amos 'n' Andy Show."

p&d, Richard C. Kahn; w, Spencer Williams, Jr. (based on a story by Williams); ph, Roland Price, Herman Shopp; ed, Dan Milner.

| Mystery | | (PR:A   MPAA:NR) |

SON OF KONG***   (1933) 70m RKO bw

Robert Armstrong *(Carl Denham)*, Helen Mack *(Hilda Peterson)*, Frank Reicher *(Capt. Englehorn)*, John Marston *(Helstrom)*, Victor Wong *(Chinese Cook)*, Ed Brady *(Red)*, Lee Kohlmar *(Mickey)*, Clarence Wilson *(Peterson)*, Katherine Ward *(Mrs. Hudson)*, Gertrude Short *(Girl Reporter)*, Gertrude Sutton *(Servant Girl)*, James B. Leong *(Chinese Trader)*, Noble Johnson *(Native Chief)*, Steve Clemento *(Witch King)*, Frank O'Connor *(Process Server)*, Constantine Romanoff *(Bell)*, Harry Tenbrook *(Tommy)*, Leo "Dutch" Hendrian *(Dutch)*.

Hot to capitalize on the massive success of KING KONG, RKO Studios, now under the direction of Merian C. Cooper, decided to rush a sequel before the cameras. The result is a funny, entertaining little film that pales in comparison with the original, but has enough value in its own right. Picking up where KING KONG left off, the irrepressible Carl Denham (Armstrong) finds nearly every lawyer in New York City ready to sue him for the damage done by the late Eighth Wonder of the World. In an effort to avoid these lawsuits, Armstrong and Captain Englehorn (Reicher) set off for the China Seas on the trusty *Venture* with Wong still working as the cook. Making money by transporting freight among the tiny islands, the adventurous pair learn of a hidden treasure stashed on Skull Island, the very place that spawned King Kong. Determined to find the valuables, Armstrong and Reicher decide to return to Skull Island. During the voyage it is discovered that a circus girl they met in Java, Mack, has stowed away on the *Venture*. Armstrong and Mack are attracted to each other and begin a romance. Meanwhile, the crew learns where the ship is headed and they mutiny. Tossing Armstrong, Mack, Reicher, and Wong into a lifeboat, the crew dumps them overboard and leaves them to their fate. Marston, an evil former sea captain who had murdered Mack's father and taken refuge on the ship, is also tossed overboard when he gets too pushy for the crew's liking. Reicher, against his better judgment, saves the evil man. The tiny boat and its inhabitants finally make it to Skull Island and when Reicher, Wong, and Marston go looking for food, Armstrong and Mack meet the son of Kong. Standing a mere 25 feet tall (his dad towered over 50 feet), this new gorilla's most striking feature is his white fur. Armstrong and Mack find this big white beast trapped up to his chest in quicksand. Having been friendly with the little guy's father, Armstrong rescues the gorilla by pushing a dead tree into the bog so that the beast can climb out. Kong's son has a much more pleasant disposition than his father, and, grateful for the help, tags alongside the humans, offering his large helping hands. Of course there are several giant beasts roaming the island to threaten the humans (including a brontosaurus, a stegosaurus, a lizard-like creature, and a sea monster), and the friendly Kong Jr. even battles a cave bear in a rather comical fight. When Kong wounds his finger, Armstrong bandages it. With the white gorilla's help, the explorers find the hidden treasure in an old temple. Reicher, Wong, and Marston return to the group, and when Marston sees the giant gorilla, he runs back to the rowboat. Suddenly, there is a catastrophic earthquake and the island starts to sink. Armstrong and Kong Jr. try to pack up the treasure while Reicher, Wong, and Mack go after Marston to make sure he doesn't steal the rowboat. As Marston tries to escape, a giant sea monster rises from the depths and eats him. With the waters rushing up to his neck, Kong Jr. finds his foot pinned in the rocks. Knowing he will not survive, the noble gorilla grabs his friend Armstrong and holds him above the water until Reicher can reach him with the rowboat. With only his hand above water, Kong Jr. waves goodbye to his friends and disappears beneath the waves. Where KING KONG was heavy and dramatic, filled with excitement and action, SON OF KONG relies on comedy and cuteness. Kong Jr. is a comical creature who is very friendly to the humans and has an extremely expressive face. In keeping with the behavior of real gorillas, Kong Jr. is shown to mimic the behavior of those around him. This approach to the material was probably budgetary. Once Cooper (who served as executive producer) had sold the idea of a quick sequel to RKO executives, they in turn told him to make it even bigger and better, then handed him a budget of merely $250,000, more than $400,000 *less* than they spent on KING KONG. Seeking to defray costs, Cooper hired most of the key players and crew by paying them with percentage points of the profits and no cash up front (Johnson and Clemento, who played the native chief and witch doctor, respectively, also returned for the sequel, but much of their footage wound up on the editing room floor). Knowing there was no time or money to make an elaborate adventure filled with animated monsters, Cooper and his wife, screenwriter Rose, went to work on a story that emphasized and developed the human characters with the special effects kept to a minimum. Anticipating overwhelming press and public interest in a sequel to KING KONG, Cooper announced that RKO's next big production was entitled "Jamboree" and it would be filmed under tight security. This film was actually SON OF KONG, and the lie was told to keep prying eyes from uncovering secrets. Willis O'Brien, who did the marvelous effects for KING KONG, reluctantly returned for SON OF KONG. Unhappy with the emphasis on humor in the script, and the limited money and screen time he was getting, O'Brien still did some of his best work. Three white-haired Kong Jr. models were constructed by stripping some of the armatures of the original Kong and then rebuilding. White fur was added and between the two pictures O'Brien and his assistant, Marcel Delgado, had figured out how to minimize the unwanted movement of the hair during the animation process. The large hand from the first film was also reconstructed and fitted with white fur. With the exception of the brontosaurus, all the creatures in SON OF KONG were newly devised and built exclusively for the sequel. Another technical improvement on the original was the matte work which is more detailed and finely integrated. Composer Max Steiner turned in another outstanding score, this time evoking a single musical theme with different variations, with a specific theme for Kong Jr. and quotes from the score of the original film. Songs and musical numbers include "Runaway Blues"(Steiner, Edward Eliscu), "Maple Leaf Rag" (Scott Joplin), "Glow Worm" (Paul Lincke), "Dill Pickles" (Charles Johnson, Alfred Bryan), "Fit as a Fiddle" (Hoffman and Goodhart), "Billboard March" (John N. Klohr). Amazingly, SON OF KONG was released in late December, 1933, the same year the original KING KONG was released. Considering the low budget and hurried nature of the production, the sequel is a fine, though minor, effort and provides enough laughs and thrills to be of interest.

p, Archie S. Marshek; d, Ernest B. Schoedsack; w, Ruth Rose; ph, Eddie Linden, Vernon Walker, J. O. Taylor; m, Max Steiner; ed, Ted Cheesman; art d, Van Nest Polglase, Al Herman; set d, Thomas Little; cos, Walter Plunkett; spec eff, Willis O'Brien, Marcel Delgado, E. B. Gibson, Carroll Shepphird, Fred Reefe, W.G. White, Mario Larrinaga, Byron L. Crabbe.

Adventure   Cas.   (PR:A   MPAA:NR)

SON OF LASSIE½   (1945) 102m MGM c

Peter Lawford (*Joe Carraclough*), Donald Crisp (*Sam Carraclough*), June Lockhart (*Priscilla*), Nigel Bruce (*Duke of Rudling*), William "Billy" Severn (*Henrik*), Leon Ames (*Anton*), Donald Curtis (*Sgt. Eddie Brown*), Nils Asther (*Olav*), Robert Lewis (*Sgt. Schmidt*), Fay Helm (*Joanna*), Peter Helmers (*Willi*), Otto Reichow (*Karl, German Guard*), Patricia Prest (*Hedda*), Helen Koford [George Moore] (*Thea*), Leon Tyler (*Arne*), Lotta Palfi (*Old Woman*), Eily Malyon (*Washwoman*), Lester Matthews (*Major*), Pedro de Cordoba (*Village Priest*), Hans Schumm (*German Command Officer*), Lassie the Dog, Laddie the Dog.

Sequel to the classic LASSIE COME HOME. This time Lassie's son, Laddie, follows his master all over Europe as he fights the Nazis during WW II. The real story begins when Laddie sneaks on to Lawford's plane and Lawford is shot down over Norway and parachutes with Laddie in his arms. Lawford is hurt and Laddie takes off to get help. Laddie unwittingly comes back with two Nazis. Couldn't the dog tell the bad guys from the good guys?) Lawford escapes. He tries to reach safe territory through the underground and Laddie keeps coming after his master with the Nazis in pursuit. Everytime Lawford and the dog get together, the dog lets the Nazis in on the secret. Finally, the pair escapes to freedom. (See LASSIE series, Index.)

p, Samuel Marx; d, S. Sylvan Simon; w, Jeanne Bartlett (based on characters by Eric Knight); ph, Charles Schoenbaum; m, Herbert Stothart; ed, Ben Lewis; art d, Cedric Gibbons, Hubert B. Hobson; cos, Irene; spec eff, A. Arnold Gillespie, Warren Newcombe, Danny Hall.

Drama   (PR:AAA   MPAA:NR)

SON OF MINE   (SEE: POLICE COURT, 1932)

SON OF MONGOLIA** (1936, USSR) 105m Lenfilm/Amkino bw (SYN MONGOLII)

Tseven Rabdan (*Tseven*), Igin-Khorlo (*Dulma*), Sosor-Rarma (*Chauffeur*), Gombo (*Innkeeper*), Bato-Ochir (*Prince*), Ir-Kan (*Prince's Foreign Advisor*), Zigmit (*The Monk*).

Early Russian propaganda film shot in Mongolia. Rabdan is simple shepherd who is competing with two others for the heart of Igin-Khorlo. One of his competitors cons a monk to send Rabdan into Manchuria. He learns of the plot, but while in Manchuria discovers that his country is about to be attacked. He gets back to the country and warns his people so they can prepare. For his efforts, Rabdan gets to marry the girl. (In Mongolian; English subtitles.)

d, Illya Trauberg; w, B. Lapin, Lev Slavin, Z. Khazrevin; ph, M. Kaplan, V. Levitin, E. Shtirtskober; m, Isaac Rabinovich, E. Grikurov; art d, I. Vuskovich.

Drama   (PR:A   MPAA:NR)

SON OF MONTE CRISTO**   (1940) 102m UA bw

Louis Hayward (*Count of Monte Cristo*), Joan Bennett (*Grand Duchess Zona*), George Sanders (*Gurko Lanen*), Florence Bates (*Mathilde*), Lionel Royce (*Col. Zimmerman*), Montagu Love (*Baron Von Neuhoff*), Ian MacWolfe (*Conrad Stadt*), Clayton Moore (*Fritz Dorner*), Ralph Byrd (*Gluck*), Georges Renevant (*French Ambassador*), Michael Visaroff (*Pavlov*), Rand Brooks (*Hans Mirbach*), Theodor von Eltz (*Captain*), James Seay (*Lieutenant*), Henry Brandon (*Schultz*), Jack Mulhall (*Schmidt*), Edward Keane, Stanley Andrews (*Turnkeys*), Lawrence Grant (*Baron*), Charles Trowbridge (*Priest*), Leyland Hodgson (*Officer*), Maurice Cass (*Tailor*), Charles Waldron, Ernie Adams, Ted Oliver Wyndham Standing, Lionel Belmore.

Not even close to the original, this is the unwanted son. Instead of the fast-paced action enjoyed in THE COUNT OF MONTE CRISTO, the slow-paced son cannot live up to his father's name. The story begins with

Bennett, a grand duchess, heading to Paris to get help from Napoleon. Sanders is trying to take over her country and has sent troops after her. His troops also are after Hayward. Hayward rescues her and eventually loses her. He finally gets her back again by fooling Sanders into thinking that he is a banker wanting a loan. Just as Sanders forces Bennett to the altar, Hayward swoops in to kill Sanders then completes the marriage ceremony with Bennett.

p, Edward Small; d, Rowland V. Lee; w, George Bruce; ph, George Robinson; m, Edward Ward; ed, Arthur E. Roberts.

Adventure   Cas.   (PR:A   MPAA:NR)

SON OF OKLAHOMA**   (1932) 63m Sono Art/World Wide bw

Bob Steele (*Dan Clayton*), Josie Sedgwick (*Mary Clayton*), Robert E. Homans (*John Clayton*), Julian Rivero (*Manuel*), Carmen La Roux (*Anita*), Earl Dwire (*Brent*), Henry Rocquemore.

A western that starts showing the principal characters as kids so we know why they turned out the way they did. A bad guy breaks up a family and everyone is separated. Years pass and the mother, father, and little boy meet again. Now mom is a saloon keeper with a heart of gold, still longing to see her son. Dad has become the local sheriff and when the boy (now a man) shows up in search of a gold mine, they all come together as a happy family once again.

p, Trem Carr; d, Robert N. Bradbury; w, Burl Tuttle, George Hull (based on a story by Wellyn Totman); ph, Archie Stout.

Western   (PR:A   MPAA:NR)

SON OF PALEFACE***½   (1952) 95m PAR c

Bob Hope (*Junior*), Jane Russell (*Mike*), Roy Rogers (*Himself*), Bill Williams (*Kirk*), Lloyd Corrigan (*Doc Lovejoy*), Paul E. Burns (*Ebenezer Hawkins*), Douglas Dumbrille (*Sheriff McIntyre*), Harry Von Zell (*Stoner*), Iron Eyes Cody (*Indian Chief*), Wee Willie Davis (*Blacksmith*), Charley Cooley (*Charley*), Robert L. Welch, Cecil B. DeMille, Bing Crosby (*Guest Spots*), Charles Morton (*Ned*), Don Dunning (*Wally*), Leo J. McMahon (*Crag*), Felice Richmond (*Genevieve*), Charmienne Harker (*Bessie*), Isabel Cushin (*Isabel*), Jane Easton (*Clara*), Homer Dickinson (*Townsman*), Lyle Moraine (*Bank Clerk Weaverly*), Hank Mann (*Bartender*), Michael A. Cirillo (*Micky*), the Bartender, Isabel Cushin (*Becky*), Chester Conklin (*Townsman*), Flo Stanton (*Flo*), John George (*Johnny*), Joseph Epper, George Russell, Lewis H. Morphy, Danny H. Sands, James Van Horn (*Posse*), Charles Quirk (*Zeke*), Frank Cordell (*Dade*), Willard Willingham (*Jeb*), Warren Fiske (*Trav*), Carl Andre (*Pedra*), Anne Dore (*She-Devil*), Gordon Carveth (*Indian*), Freddie Zendar (*Ollie*), Al Ferguson (*Man*), Rudy Lee (*Boy*), Hazel Boyne (*Old Lady*), Wally Boyle (*Perkins*), Rus Conklin (*Indian*), Oliver Blake (*Telegrapher*), Bob St. Angelo (*Lem*), Howard Joslin (*Sam*), Rose Plummer (*Townswoman*), Art Cameron (*Art*), Geraldine Farnum (*Cigarette Girl*), Louise Lane, Joanne Arnold, Marie Shaw, Blanche Renze (*Dance-Hall Cuties*), Sue Carlton, Valerie Vernon (*Girls in Bedroom Scene*), Marie Shaw (*Matron*), Jonathan Hale (*Governor*), Jean Willes (*Penelope*), Jack Pepper (*Customer in Restaurant*).

A very funny sequel to THE PALEFACE that took four years to put on the screen while Hope made a few other pictures. This time, Hope plays his own son. The original character of the pioneer dentist was done by Hope and now he comes back, again with Russell, as the Harvard graduate who goes West to claim the inheritance left by his father. Russell is a bandit who sings in a saloon known as "The Dirty Shame." Hope teams with Rogers and Trigger (playing themselves) to nab a crook who has been robbing various gold shipments. They suspect that the criminal may be Russell. She thinks Rogers is a handsome guy and has the warms for him, but he would rather kiss his horse so, for one of the few pictures Hope's ever done, he gets the girl. SON OF PALEFACE is a satire of every cowboy cliche and it seems that not one of them is overlooked in the merry-making. Hope gets the chance to rattle off one-liners while the action goes through Indian uprisings, lynch mobs, posses, ghost towns, mirages, deserts, quick-draws, saloon brawls – in other words, everything that John Wayne ever did for real. Tashlin was receiving his first directorial credit, although he had co-directed THE LEMON DROP KID with Sid Lanfield but was not credited. He'd written THE PALEFACE with Ed Hartmann and was rewarded with this assignment, a job he didn't muff. It's fast, witty and all the rootin' tootin' shootin' cannot be taken seriously for a moment. Tashlin was a one-time cartoonist and it shows, as he sets up the scenes like animated sequences, much to the picture's benefit. In the original, Ray Evans and Jay Livingston wrote the Oscar tune "Buttons and Bows," and they wisely bring it back for another go-around with new lyrics, as sung by Hope, Rogers and Russell. "There's a Cloud In My Valley of Sunshine" was written by Lyle Moraine, Jack Brooks, and Hope's brother, Jack, sung by Rogers. They also collaborated to write another tune for Rogers, "Four-Legged Friend." Livingston and Evans chipped in again with "What a Dirty Shame" (sung by a chorus), "Wing Ding Tonight" (sung by Hope, Russell), and "California Rose" (sung by Rogers). Brooks wrote "Am I in Love?" for Hope and Russell to sing. Crosby stops by for a guest spot, as does Cecil B. DeMille. Rogers had been the king of the small western movies for over a decade, but after this movie, began to limit his appearances. He did a small guest bit in ALIAS JESSE JAMES, then a role in MACKINTOSH AND T.J. Other than those, he spent most of his time tending his huge real estate investments which are worth over $100 million.

p, Robert L. Welch; d, Frank Tashlin; w, Tashlin, Welch, Joseph Quillan; ph, Harry J. Wild (Technicolor); m, Lyn Murray; ed, Eda Warren; art d, Hal Pereira, Roland Anderson; spec eff, Gordon Jennings, Paul Lerpae, Farciot Edouart; ch, Josephine Earl.

Comedy (PR:A MPAA:NR)

SON OF ROARING DAN½** (1940) 63m UNIV bw

Johnny Mack Brown (*Jim Reardon*), Fuzzy Knight (*Tick Belden*), Nell O'Day (*Jane Belden*), Jeanne Kelly (*Eris Brooks*), Robert E. Homans (*Dan McPhail*), Tom Chatterton (*Stuart Manning*), John Eldredge (*Thorndyke*), Ethan Laidlaw (*Matt Gregg*), Lafe McKee (*Brooks*), Dick Alexander (*Big Taylor*), Eddie Polo (*Charlie Gregg*), Bob Reeves, Chuck Morrison, Frank McCarroll, Lloyd Ingraham, Jack Shannon, Ben Taggert, Ralph Peters, Ralph Dunn, Jack Montgomery, The Texas Rangers (*Musicians*).

Roaring Dan (Homans) snarls and growls at everybody as the phony father of Brown, a charade they set up between them to catch the killers of Brown's real father, in this refreshing Johnny Mack Brown outing. Two women are involved for a change, and Brown ends up with Kelly as the story moves along very well to a stunning fist fight finish between Brown and crook Eldredge.

p, Joseph G. Sanford; d, Ford Beebe; w, Clarence Upson Young; ph, William Sickner; ed, Paul Landres; md, Charles Previn; m/l, "I Worry All the Time," "Powder River," "Yippee" (Milton Rosen, Everett Carter, sung by The Texas Rangers).

Western (PR:A MPAA:NR)

SON OF ROBIN HOOD* (1959, Brit.) 81m Argo/FOX c

Al Hedison (*Jamie*), June Laverick (*Deering Hood*), David Farrar (*Des Roches*), Marius Goring (*Chester*), Philip Friend (*Dorchester*), Delphi Lawrence (*Sylvia*), George Coulouris (*Alan A. Dale*), George Woodbridge (*Little John*), Humphrey Lestocq (*Blunt*), Noel Hood (*Prioress*), Shelagh Fraser (*Constance*), Jack Lambert (*Will Scarlet*), Maya Koumani (*Lady in Waiting*), Oliver Johnston, Russell Napier, Alastair Hunter, Robert Bruce, Jack Taylor, Chkristine Halward, Richard Walters, Doreen Dawne.

Farrar is a nobleman bent on controling England. Crusader Hedison comes on the scene and poses as son of Robin Hood to help save everyone from Farrar's evil ways. But Robin Hood's followers need a leader and send for his son, Deering Hood,' only to find out that she is a girl, as talented as her father, but the followers would rather be led by Hedison. The two do join forces along the way and get rid of Farrar, as Laverick more than holds her own in the hand-to-hand combat, to win everyone's hearts and save England as well.

p&d, George Sherman; w, George W. George, George Slavin; ph, Arthur Grant; (CinemaScope, DeLuxe Color); m, Leighton Lucas; ed, Alan Osbiston; art d, Norman Arnold.

Adventure (PR:A MPAA:NR)

SON OF SAMSON*½ (1962, Fr./Ital./Yugo.) 89m Jolly Film-Gallus-C.I. C.C.-Dubrava Film/Medallion c (LE GEANT DE LA VALLEE DES ROIS; MACISTE NELLA VALLE DEI RE)

Mark Forest (*Maciste*), Chelo Alonso (*Queen Smedes*), Angelo Zanolli (*Kenamun*), Vira Silenti (*Tekaet*), Frederica Ranchi (*Nofret*), Carlo Tamberlani (*Armitee*), Petar Dorric (*Vizier*), Nino Musco (*Nenneka*), Ignazio Dolce, Zvonimir Rogoz, Andrea Fantasia, Mario Girotti, Ada Ruggeri.

Alonso, the queen of Egypt, has begun a reign of terror across the land. She plans to eventually turn everything over to the Persians and has kidnaped her stepson, Zanolli, to make him marry her. Forest comes into town looking for his buddy Zanolli and with his great strength defeats the queen's troops. He finds Zanolli and Alonso tries to use her beauty to win Forest over but she fails. So, she tosses him into the dungeon, but he escapes and leads the slaves against her. She gets hers when she falls into a crocodile pit and Zanolli takes the crown. Peace now reigns and Forest, the son of Samson, heads to the hills from whence he came.

p, Ermanno Donati, Luigi Carpentieri; d, Carlo Campogalliani; w, Oreste Biancoli, Ennio De Concini; ph, Riccardo Pallottini (Totalscope, Technicolor); m, Carlo Innocenzi; ed, Roberto Cinquini; art d, Oscar D'Amico; cos, Maria De Matteis; ch, Tito LeDuc.

Adventure (PR:A MPAA:NR)

SON OF SINBAD*½ (1955) 88m RKO c (AKA: NIGHTS IN A HAREM)

Dale Robertson (*Sinbad*), Sally Forrest (*Ameer*), Lili St. Cyr (*Nerissa*), Vincent Price (*Omar Khayham the poet*), Mari Blanchard (*Kristina*), Leon Askin (*Khalif*), Jay Novello (*Jiddah*), Raymond Greenleaf (*Simon*), Nejla Ates (*Dancer in Market*), Kalantan (*Dancer in Desert*), Ian MacDonald (*Murad*), Donald Randolph (*Councillor*), Larry Blake (*Samit*), Edwina

Hazard (*Lota*), Fred Aldrich (*Torturer*), John Merton, George Sherwood, M.U. Smith, Woody Strode (*Guards*), George Barrows (*Khalif Officer*), Marilyn Bonney (*Veronica*), Janet Comerford (*Latisse*), Alyce Cronin (*Helena*), Mary Ann Edwards (*Rosine*), Dawn Oney (*Alicia*), Marvleen Prentice (*Zaza*), Joan Pastin (*Camilla*), Judy Ulian (*Dalya*), Suzanne Alexander, Randy Allen, Jane Easton, Jeanne Evans, Helene Hayden (*Harem Girls*), Joanne Jordan (*Ghenia*), Wayne Berk (*Gondra*), James Griffith (*Arab Guide*), Bette Arlen, Joann Arnold, Gwen Caldwell, Anne Carroll, Carolea Cole, Claire De Witt, Nancy Dunn, Marjorie Holliday, Judy Jorell, Joi Lansing, Diane Mumby, Jonni Paris, Jeanne Shores, Maureen Stephenson, Libby Vernon, Doreen Woodbury, Betty Onge, Dee Gee Sparks, DeDe Moore, Sue Casey, Carol Brewster, Chris Fortune, Helen Chapman, Barbara Drake, Bobette Bentley, Joan Whitney, Dolores Michaels, Barbara Lohrman, Zanne Shaw, Gloria Watson, Ann Ford, Donna Hall, Pat D'Arcy, Charlotte Alpert, Roxanne Arlen, Eleanor Bender, Evelyn Bernard, Shirley Buchanan, Roxanne Delman, Mary Ellen Gleason, Diane James, Keith Kerrigan, Mary Langan, Gloria Laughlin, Vonne Lester, Nancy Neal, Gloria Pall, Lynne Forrester, Audrey Allen, Nancy Moore, Phyllis St. Pierre, Evelyn Lovequist, Gerri Patterson, Kim Novak, Rosemary Webster, Laura Carroll, Penny Sweeney, Trudy Wroe, Joyce Johnson (*Raiders*), Bob Wilke (*Musa*), Tom Monroe, Peter Ortiz (*Cutthroats*), Virginia Bates, Katherine Cassidy, Honey King, Sally Musik (*Trumpeters*), Leonteen Danies, Elaine Dupont, Gilda Fontana, Joy Lee, La Rue Malouf, Anna Navarro, Paula Vernay (*Slave Girls*), Michael Ross (*Palace Guard*), Michael Mark (*Caravan Merchant*), Bob Hopkins (*Slave Auctioneer*), Gus Schilling (*Jaffir*), Max Wagner (*Merchant at Market Place*), Nancy Westbrook (*Wench*), Elizabeth Smith, Wanda Barbour, Irene Bolton, Joy Langstaff, Betty Sabor, Eileen Maxwell, Louise Von Kories, Annabelle Thiele, Arlene Hunter (*Tartar Girls*), Naji Gabby, Laura Carroll (*Arabs*).

Howard Hughes oversaw this Sinbad adventure that had parents screaming and covering their children's eyes. Robertson as Sinbad and Price as his right-hand man again sail off to more adventures. But this time all the evil ones were women and scantily-dressed to incur the outrage. Hughes, known for promising young women a chance to be a star, gave about 40 of them a chance in this one. In a publicity ploy, he did not release the film for two years, letting it build a "hot" reputation. Sinbad just cavorts with the beauties in a story that has no plot, no anything really except for skin.

p, Robert Sparks; d, Ted Tetzlaff; w, Aubrey Wisberg, Jack Pollexfen; ph, William Snyder (Superscope, Technicolor); m, Victor Young; ed, Roland Gross, Frederic Knudtson; md, C. Bakaleinikoff; art d, Albert S. D'Agostino, Walter E. Keller; set d, Darrell Silvera; cos, Michael Woulfe; ch, Olga Lunick.

Adventure Cas, (PR:A MPAA:NR)

SON OF SPARTACUS (SEE: SLAVE, THE, 1963, Ital.)

SON OF THE BLOB (SEE: BEWARE THE BLOB, 1972)

SON OF THE BORDER*½ (1933) 55m RKO bw

Tom Keene, Edgar Kennedy, Julie Haydon, David Durand, Creighton Chaney [Lon Chaney, Jr.], Charles King, Al Bridge, Claudia Coleman.

A gang of outlaws is terrorizing stagecoaches that carry gold. Keene is the local official assigned to stop them. In one battle, he kills a good friend, Chaney, who gets mixed up with the bad guys. To avenge his buddy's death, he adopts Chaney's son and teaches him right from wrong. Action scenes are rather sparse.

p, David Lewis; d, Lloyd Nosler; w, Wellyn Totman, Harold Shumate (based on a story by Totman); ph, Nick Musuraca; ed, Frederic Knudtson.

Western (PR:A MPAA:NR)

SON OF THE GODS* (1930) 92m FN-WB bw/c

Richard Barthelmess (*Sam Lee*), Constance Bennett (*Allana*), Dorothy Mathews (*Alice Hart*), Barbara Leonard (*Mabel*), James Eagles (*Spud*), Frank Albertson (*Kicker*), Mildred Van Dorn (*Eileen*), King Hoo Chang (*Moy*), Geneva Mitchell (*Connie*), E. Alyn Warren (*Lee Ying*), Ivan Christie (*Cafe Manager*), Anders Randolf (*Wagner*), George Irving (*Attorney*), Claude King (*Bathurst*), Dickie Moore (*Boy*), Robert E. Homans (*Dugan*).

A touchy subject at the time suffers from a poor plot that had some promise. Too many ripe situations that could have occurred (prejudice, as one example) were never considered, leaving this film unfulfilled. Barthelmess has grown up and thinking he is Chinese all his life and has handled the racism that accompanies being different. He and Bennett fall in love and of course, encounter many obstacles that only bring them closer together. It turns out after all the trouble he has run into that he is Caucasian. To explain the twist in fate, the film flashes back to when he was born to a Nordic couple. Too much fluff and not enough realism on what could have been a powerful film.

d, Frank Lloyd; w, Bradley King (based on a novel by Rex Beach); ph, Ernest Haller (Technicolor); m/l, "Pretty Little You," Ben Ryan, Sol Vidinsky.

Drama (PR:A MPAA:NR)

SON OF THE NAVY**   (1940) 72m MON bw

James Dunn (Malone), Jean Parker (Steve Moore), Martin Spellman (Tommy), William Royle (Capt. Moore), Selmer Jackson (Capt. Parker), Dave O'Brien (Nelson), Sarah Padden (Mrs. Baker), Craig Reynolds (Brad Wheeler), Charles King (Johnson), Gene Morgan (Burns).

Well-constructed Navy film brought James Dunn back to the fold after a time away from films. Dunn plays a Navy man with marriage far from his mind. A little orphan boy spots him and decides Dunn will be his father no matter what. A few laughs, a few tears as Dunn first tries to shake the kid, then eventually learns to love him and adopts him as his son. Parker comes on to the scene to provide some romance and finally makes the family one, happy unit. The story was done on radio by the Silver Theatre and written by True Boardman and Grover Jones.

p, Grant Withers; d, William Nigh; w, Marion Orth, Joseph West (based on a radio Silver Theatre playlet by True Boardman, Grover Jones); ph, Harry Neumann; ed, Russell Schoengarth.

Drama   (PR:A   MPAA:NR)

SON OF THE PLAINS**½   (1931) 59m SYN bw (GB: VULTURES OF THE LAW)

Bob Custer, Doris Phillips, Al St. John, J.P. McGowan, Edward Hearn, Gordon DeMain.

Early talkie western and not half-bad. Plenty of action, fist-fights, and fancy riding help take the place of the overdone and sometimes wooden dialog. Hearn is a bandit known as the Polka Dot Kid. He grabs the father of Custer's girl friend. Custer, playing the deputy sheriff, not only has to bring Hearn to justice because it's his job, but his love life also rides on it. And of course, he wins on all counts.

p, W. Ray Johnson; d&w, R.N. Bradbury; ph, Archie Stout.

Western   (PR:A   MPAA:NR)

SON OF THE RED CORSAIR**   (1963, Ital.) 97m Panda/Medallion c (IL FIGLIO DEL CORSARO ROSSO)

Lex Barker (Enrico di Ventimiglia), Sylvia Lopez (Carmen di Montelimar), Vira Silenti (Neala), Luciano Marin, Luigi Visconti, Saro Urzi, Antonio Crast, Vicki Lagos, Elio Pandolfi, Franco Fantasia, Diego Michelotti, Livio Lorenzon, Nietta Zocchi.

Barker is the exiled son of the "Red Corsair" and comes back to avenge his father's death. He and his pirates take over a galleon searching for the man who betrayed his father. To save his skin, the man tells Barker his sister, who was thought to be dead, was working for the governor's sister-in-law. Barker rushes off to save her and is charged with kidnaping. The countess, Lopez, has a soft spot for him, but when he spurns her she betrays him. Silenti was not working for Lopez but actually was a prisoner of the governor, who was going to make her his wife, against her will. The governor is going to kill Silenti's boy friend and tortures his wife to get Silenti to wed him. But Barker arrives on the scene, kills him in a duel, and rescues the two women he loves.

p, Ermanno Donati, Luigi Carpentieri; d, Primo Zeglio; w, Alberto Liberati, Fede Arnaud, Zeglio (based on a story by Emilio Salgari); ph, Carlo Carlini (Totalscope, Eastmancolor); m, Roman Vlad; art d, Mario Chiari, Alfredo Montori; cos, Maria Da Matteis.

Adventure   (PR:A   MPAA:NR)

SON OF THE REGIMENT*½   (1948, USSR) 73m Soyuzdetfilm Studio/Artkino bw

Yura Yankin (Vanya Sointsev), Alexander Morosov (Capt. Yenakiev), Gregory Pluzhnik (Bidenko), Nikolai Parfenov (Gorbunov), Nikolai Yakhontov (Yegorov/Soboliev), Vova Sinev (Cpl. Vosnesensky), Pavel Volkov (Vasily Ivanovich).

Russia suffered some heavy losses in WW II and its movies studios were no exception. This was supposed to whip the natives to a patriotic pitch, but instead made them turn away from the screen because of the laughable production. In a typical, heart-tugging war story, a young orphan is adopted by an army regiment and the gruff commander. The Germans are taken prisoner and they display their evilness. In the heat of battle the kid finally becomes part of the army. The fitting climax features the kid in the grand march in front of the Soviet leader in a Moscow parade before screaming crowds. And everyone is proud to be a Russian. (In Russian; English subtitles)

d, Vassili Pronin; w, Valentin Katayev; ph, Gregory Garibyan.

War Drama   (PR:A   MPAA:NR)

SON OF THE RENEGADE*½   (1953) 57m Schwarz/UA bw

John Carpenter (Red River Johnny), Lori Irving (Lori), John McKellen (Valley), Valley Keene (Dusty), Jack Ingram (Three Fingers), Verne Teters (Sheriff Masters), Bill Goonz (Wild Bill), Ted Smile (Cherokee), Bill Ward (Baby Face Bill), Roy Canada (The Gun Slinger), Whitey Hughes (The Long-Haired Kid), Lennie Smith (Deputy Sheriff), Ewing Brown (Wild Bill Hickock), Freddie Carson (Big Fred), Percy Lennon (The Australian Kid), Jack Wilson (The Texas Kid), Pat McGeehan (Narrator).

Low-budget western of standard fare and it shows all the way through. Carpenter not only had the lead role, but he also got the credit for producing and writing (maybe he should also get the blame). Carpenter is a good guy who inherits a large ranch owned by his father who happened to be a bad guy in town. Irving, McKellen, and Keene give Carpenter not just one love interest, but three to keep him busy. Ingram wants the land and the women, so he tries to frame Carpenter for a series of robberies. Of course, Carpenter and his buddies expose Ingram just as his group is planning a bank robbery.

p, John Carpenter; d, Reg Brown; w, Carpenter; ph, William Thomson; m, Daryl Caulker.

Western   (PR:A   MPAA:NR)

SONG AND DANCE MAN, THE**   (1936) 70m FOX bw

Claire Trevor (Julia Carroll), Paul Kelly (Hap Farrell), Michael Whalen (Alan Davis), Ruth Donnelly (Patsy O'Madigan), James Burke (Lt. Mike Boyle), Helen Troy (Sally), Lester Matthews (C.B. Nelson), Ralf Harolde (Crosby), Gloria Roy (Dolores), Margaret Dumont (Mrs. Whitney), Billy Bevan (Curtis), Irene Franklin (Goldie McGuffy).

The legendary George M. Cohan wrote the original Broadway show in 1924 but would have yanked it out of Hollywood had he known how the film would turn out. Simple dance-team story that features Trevor and Kelly as the hoofers on Broadway. While the carefree Kelly enjoys such pleasures as drinking and gambling, he still has a heart of gold making sure his partner is always happy. And she is happiest in Whalen's arms. When it looks bad on the horizon for her and Whalen, Kelly changes his bad habits and not only saves the show, he gets Trevor and Whalen together for good. Kelly should have stayed at the gambling tables. Songs by Sidney Clare and Lew Pollack include: "You're My Favorite One," "On Holiday in My Playroom," "Join the Party," "Let's Get Going," "Ain't He Good Looking?" and "Dancing in the Open."

p, Sol M. Wurtzel; d, Allan Dwan; w, Maude Fulton (based on the play by George M. Cohan); ph, Barney McGill; m, Samuel Kaylin; ed, Al De Gaetano; cos, William Lambert; ch, Fancon.

Musical   (PR:A   MPAA:NR)

SONG AND THE SILENCE, THE*½   (1969) 80m Cloverhouse bw

Annita Koutsouveli (Rivkeh Shlomo), Harry Rubin (Rabbi Shlomo), Jim Murphy (Fievel), Nana Austin (Mrs. Shlomo), Mary Antoianette (Channaleh), Jonathan Scott (David Shlomo), Harry Leshner (Principal), Felix Fiebich (Matchmaker).

Poor handling of a very intense subject, genocide, not dealt with much at the time, sinks Nathan Cohen's first attempt at a feature film. The former NBC television cameraman has to take most of the blame, however, because he wrote the original story and screenplay, produced, directed and even handled the camerawork for the film. The movie's major statement focuses on the treatment of Polish Jews in 1939, and the view that non-Jewish Poles just stood by and permitted the senseless killing of their countrymen. Cohen leads into his subject with a story about a rabbi's attempt to convince one of his students that he should marry the rabbi's daughter. Though he would rather finish school first, the couple fall in love. The two marry but are broken up when the Germans invade the village and send them off to concentration camps. After the Jews are rounded up and taken away, the non-Jews are seen going back to their normal, day-to-day tasks, seemingly indifferent to the tragedy. Flashforwards were inserted within the surface narrative at a pace that increases as the film progresses, showing the impending massacre. The entire film was shot in the Catskills, and the cast was supplemented with Hasidic Jews from Brooklyn.

p,d,w,ph&m, Nathan Cohen.

Drama   (PR:A   MPAA:NR)

SONG AT EVENTIDE**   (1934, Brit.) 83m BUT bw

Fay Compton (Helen d'Alaste), Lester Matthews (Lord Belsize), Nancy Burne (Patricia Belsize), Leslie Perrins (Ricardo), Tom Helmore (Michael Law), Minnie Rayner (Blondie), O.B. Clarence (Registrar), Alfred Wellesley (Rosenbaum), Tully Comber (Jim), Barbara Gott (Anna), Charles Paton (Director), Frank Titterton (Singer), Marie Daine, Eve Chipman, Barbara Everest, Ian Wilson, Marie Ault, Basil Atherton.

Compton sings in cabarets until she is blackmailed. To protect her daughter, Burne, from the scandal, she fakes her own death, then enters a convent as a nun. Bizarre melodrama includes a number of songs.

p, John Argyle; d, Harry Hughes; w, John Hastings Turner; ph, Desmond Dickinson.

Crime   (PR:C   MPAA:NR)

SONG FOR MISS JULIE, A*½   (1945) 69m REP bw

Shirley Ross (Valerie), Barton Hepburn (George Kimbro), Jane Farrar (Julie), Roger Clark (Steve), Cheryl Walker (Marcelle), Elisabeth Risdon (Mrs. Charteris), Lillian Randolph (Eliza), Peter Garey (Pete), Rene Riano (Mrs. Calhoun), Harry Crocker (John Firbank), The Robertos, Vivian Fay, Alicia Markova, Anton Dolin (Themselves).

A big-time production and an expensive set couldn't lift this directionless musical. Hepburn and Clark are writers who are working on an operetta and look for a clinching story to win some notice. They decide on doing a story about a Southern gentleman in the 1850s, who has something hidden in his past. While the two search for the missing piece, the man's only living relative surfaces and tries to block the production. Finally, she relents and even lets them use her old, stately Louisiana home for the operetta, which eventually ends up on Broadway. Songs done in a big way to hide the weak script are: "It All Could Have Happened Before," "What I Like About You," "The Country Ain't the Country Anymore" and "I Love to Remember" (Marla Shelton, Louis Herscher). Also included is "Bayou Calls."

p, William Rowland, Carley Harriman; d, Rowland; w, Rowland Leigh, Leighton Brill (based on a story by Michael Foster); ph, Mack Stengler; ed, James Smith; md, David Chudnow; art d, John Datu; set d, Maurice Yates; ch, Larry Ceballos.

Musical   (PR:A   MPAA:NR)

SONG FOR TOMORROW, A*   (1948, Brit.) 62m Production Facilities/GFD bw

Evelyn McCabe (Helen Maxwell), Ralph Michael (Roger Stanton), Shaun Noble (Derek Wardwell), Valentine Dunn (Mrs. Wardwell), James Hayter (Klausemann), Christopher Lee (Auguste), Conrad Phillips (Lt. Fenton), Sam Kydd, Yvonne Forster, Carleen Lord, Ethel Coleridge, Martin Boddey, Lockwood West.

Noble is a hapless amnesiac, a WW II casualty whose last memory before unconsciousness is of the contralto voice of diva McCabe. When recovers his health he falls in love with her as his only link to his past. But then when his memory also is restored he returns to his fiancee and his doctor takes up with the diva. A touch of amnesia on the audience's part would help them forget this insipid mash.

p, Ralph Nunn-May; d, Terence Fisher; w, William Fairchild; ph, Walter Harvey.

Drama   (PR:A   MPAA:NR)

SONG FROM MY HEART, THE**½   (1970, Jap.) 99m Shochiku/Shochiku Films of America c (WAGA KOI WAGA UTA)

Kanzaburo Nakamura (Hideo Yoshino), Shima Iwashita (Tomiko), Kaoru Yachigusa (Hatsuko), Katsuo Nakamura (Koichi), Muga Takewaki (Kenji), Sanae Kitabayashi (Motoko), Ken Ogata (Hitomi Yamaguchi), Mitsuyo Kamei (Mitsuyo), Sadako Sawamura (Hitomi's Mother), Norihei Miki (Kasui Wakabayashi), Anna Losen, Hideko Okiyama, Kankuro Nakamura, Seitaro Okamura, Ushio Akashi, Jun Kojima, Nobuo Takagi, Reijiro Osugi, Kosaku Mizuno, Keiko Sawai, Kosaku Yamayoshi, Yoji Toki, Hideaki Komori, Sanzaemon Nakamura, Koyu Tsuruta, Takashi Suga, Noriyuki Watanabe, Eriko Wada, Nobuko Suzuki, Naoki Izumi, Reiko Mizuki.

Based on the life of famed Japanese poet Hideo Yoshino, the subject shares his memories during an interview with a Swedish student, which begins when she asks him if his poetry deals with sex. Yoshino (Nakamura) recalls his happy marriage to Yachigusa, during which time he wrote his best poetry. When his wife dies, he spends time raising his family and neglects his work. Nakamura eventually marries his housekeeper, Iwashita, upsetting his daughter, Kitabayashi. He then is shunned by his two sons, who feel inadequate compared with their father's talent. Right before his death, Nakamura reconciles with one of his sons, inspiring him to write one final poem. Yoshino himself is believed to have possibly collaborated on the original story or written an autobiographical novel. However, this has not been confirmed, leaving the extent of his involvement in the film unclear.

p, Koichi Enatsu; d, Norboru Nakamura; w, Sakae Hirosawa, Nakamura (based on a story by Hitomi Yamaguchi, Soji Yoshino); ph, Hiroshi Takemura (Shochiko GrandScope, Eastmancolor); m, Masaru Sato; art d, Chiyoo Umeda.

Drama   (PR:A   MPAA:NR)

SONG IS BORN, A***½   (1948) 113m RKO c

Danny Kaye (Prof. Hobart Frisbee), Virginia Mayo (Honey Swanson), Benny Goodman (Prof. Magenbruch), Hugh Herbert (Prof. Twingle), Steve Cochran (Tony Crow), J. Edward Bromberg (Dr. Elfini), Felix Bressart (Prof. Gerkikoff), Ludwig Stossel (Prof. Traumer), O.Z. Whitehead (Prof. Oddly), Esther Dale (Miss Bragg), Mary Field (Miss Totten), Howland Chamberlain (Mr. Setter), Paul Langton (Joe), Sidney Blackmer (Adams), Ben Welden (Monte), Ben Chasen (Ben), Peter Virgo (Louis), Joseph Crehan (District Attorney), Jill Meredith, Janie New, Barbara Hamilton, Jeffrey Sayre, Gene Morgan (People at Dorsey Club), Pat Walker (Photographer at Dorsey Club), Lane Chandler (Policeman at Inn), Joe Devlin (Gangster), Robert Dudley

(Justice of the Peace), Jack Gargan (Stenotypist), Muni Seroff, Will Lee (Waiters), Norma Gentner (Girl with Samba King), Susan George (Cigarette Girl), Tommy Dorsey and Orchestra, Louis Armstrong and Orchestra, Charlie Barnet and Orchestra, Mel Powell and Orchestra, Louis Bellson (Drums), Harry Babasin (Bass), Alton Hendrickson (Guitar), Buck and Bubbles, The Page Cavanaugh Trio, The Golden Gate Quartet, Russo and The Samba Kings, John Impolito, Alice Wallace, William Haade, Karen X. Gaylord, Irene Vernon, Diana Mumby, Martha Montgomery, Marjorie Jackson, Shirley Ballard, Donald Wilmot.

Danny Kaye was making his last film for Goldwyn, the man who discovered him and made him a star. Goldwyn was stunned by Kaye's departure for Warners as well as Mayo's leaving in favor of the same studio. So much for gratefulness. This was a direct remake of BALL OF FIRE with the same director, editor, cinematographer, art director, and most of the same crew. It was only seven years after the first picture and a bit too soon. Oddly, there was no screenplay credit on the screen, only the original writers of BALL OF FIRE are mentioned. The writer for this film was Harry Tugend, the talented scribe who also wrote screenplays for POCKETFUL OF MIRACLES, WHO'S MINDING THE STORE? and countless others. A corps of professors have united to trace the history of music. Kaye is in charge of the U.S. division of the Totten Foundation and the other monastic intellectuals include Herbert, Bressart, Whitehead, and Stossel. Kaye's work has taken him up to ragtime, then he meets a pair of hip window washers, Buck and Bubbles, who tell him all about jazz, jive, and boogie woogie. Mayo enters the scene. She's a singer on the run from her menacing boyfriend, Cochran, a gangster. She is also trying to keep away from the district attorney, Crehan, who wants her to testify against Cochran. (In the original, Barbara Stanwyck was a stripper.) In order to become aware of the new music, Kaye is thrust into the world of night spots, dives, jazz joints, etc. Kaye falls in love with Mayo and she pretends to like him to be able to stay at the Foundation and hide out from Cochran. She's nabbed by Cochran, then he comes back to the Foundation to show her what kind of a sissy Kaye is, but Kaye and his aged fellow musicologists manage to overcome the gangster and all ends well. It's a happy movie with non-stop music but not enough of the madcap, free-wheeling comedy for which Kaye had become famous. Members of Music's Hall Of Fame appear as themselves and anyone with an ear for the big band sound will love this picture. The songs and the performers include: "A Song Is Born" (Gene De Paul, Don Raye, performed by Mayo, Louis Armstrong, Benny Goodman, Tommy Dorsey, Lionel Hampton, Charlie Barnet, Mel Powell, Louis Bellson), "Bach Boogie" (J.S. Bach, interpolated by Buck on piano), "Anitra's Dance" (Edvard Grieg, performed by Goodman on clarinet, Buck on piano), "I'm Getting Sentimental Over You" (Ned Washington, George Bassman, performed by Tommy Dorsey and Orchestra), "Blind Barnabas" (Willie Johnson, performed by Golden Gate Quartet), "Mockin' Bird" (traditional, performed by Golden Gate Quartet), "Redskin Rhumba" (Dale Bennet, performed by Charlie Barnet and Orchestra), "The Goldwyn Stomp" (Louis Armstrong, performed by Armstrong with Hampton and Orchestra), "Daddy-O" (Don Raye, Gene De Paul, performed by Mayo with Page Cavanaugh Trio), "Stealin' Apples" (Fats Waller, Andy Razaf, performed by Mel Powell, Goodman, Hampton, Harry Babsin, Alton Hendrickson), "Longhair Jam Session" (Giuseppe Verdi, Rossini, done by Mayo, Bubbles, the Professors), "Oh, Genevieve" (George Cooper, Henry Tucker, done by Kaye, Professors), "Guadeamas Igitur" (traditional, performed by Professors), "Joshua Fit De Battle O' Jericho" (traditional, performed by Golden Gate Quartet), "Anvil Chorus" (Verdi, performed by chorus), "Flyin' Home" (Goodman, Hampton, Sid Robin, performed by Armstrong, Goodman, Dorsey, Barnet, Powell), and "Muskrat Ramble," (Willis Ramsey, performed by Mel Powell Septet). Missing from all this music was any of the brilliant special material that Kaye's wife, Sylvia Fine, used to write for him. The loss was noted. Mayo's voice was looped by Jeri Sullivan. A SONG IS BORN was not one of Kaye's best, and marks a disappointing bow-out to his Goldwyn contract.

p, Samuel Goldwyn; d, Howard Hawks; w, Harry Tugend [uncredited] (based on the story "From A to Z" by Thomas Monroe and Billy Wilder); ph, Gregg Toland (Technicolor); ed, Daniel Mandell; md, Emil Newman, Hugo Friedhofer; art d, George Jenkins, Perry Ferguson; cos, Irene Sharaff; spec eff, John P. Fulton; makeup, Robert Stephanoff.

Musical/Comedy   (PR:A   MPAA:NR)

SONG O' MY HEART***   (1930) 85m FOX bw

John McCormack (Sean O'Callaghan), Maureen O'Sullivan (Eileen O'Brien), John Garrick (Fergus O'Donnell), J.M. Kerrigan (Peter Conlon), Tommy Clifford (Tad O'Brien), Alice Joyce (Mary O'Brien), J. Farrell MacDonald (Joe Rafferty), Effie Ellsler (Mona), Emily Fitzroy (Aunt Elizabeth), Andre DeSegurola (Guido), Edwin Schneider (Vincent Glennon), Edward Martindel (Fullerton).

Irish tenor McCormack, whose film debut won him rave reviews and audiences, plays a singer in love with Joyce, who is forced to marry someone else. Completely devastated, he abandons his singing career. Her husband eventually deserts her and her two children, and McCormack helps support the family because Joyce is the only woman he has ever loved. This early talkie was filmed in 70mm and recorded using Movietone, a sound-on-film process developed in the late 1920s for the Fox film company. Use of the process enhanced McCormack's performance of 11 songs, including: "Little

Boy Blue" (Ethelbert Nevin), "Paddy Me Lad" (Albert Hay Malotte), "I Hear You Calling Me" (Harold Herford, Charles Marshall), "A Fair Story by the Fireside," "Just for a Day," "Kitty My Love," "The Rose of Tralee" (Charles Glover, C. Mordaunt Spencer), "A Pair of Blue Eyes," "I Feel You Near Me," "Song O' My Heart" (Glover, William Kernell, James Hanley), "Then You'll Remember Me" (Alfred Burns, William Michael Balfe). Other songs were "Loughi Sereni E Cari" and "Ireland, Mother Ireland."

p, William Fox; d, Frank Borzage; w, Sonya Levien, Tom Barry; ph, Chester Lyons, Al Brick, J.O. Taylor (Grandeur); ed, Margaret V. Clancy; art d, Harry Oliver; cos, Sophie Wachner.

Musical   **(PR:A   MPAA:NR)**

SONG OF ARIZONA**   (1946) 68m REP bw

Roy Rogers (Himself), George "Gabby" Hayes (Gabby Whittaker), Dale Evans (Clare Summers), Lyle Talbot (King Blaine), Tommy Cook (Chip), Johnny Calkins (Clarence), Sarah Edwards (Dolly Finnocin), Tommy Ivo (Jimmy), Michael Chapin (Cyclops), Dick Curtis (Bart), Edmund Cobb (Sheriff), Tom Quinn (Tom), Kid Chissell (Jim), Robert Mitchell Boy Choir, Bob Nolan and The Sons of the Pioneers, Trigger the Horse.

In this modern-day western, Rogers' pal Hayes is proprietor of a ranch for homeless youths. One boy's father is a bank robber who, before being killed, leaves stolen loot with his son. Other robbers learn the boy has the money and show up to take it. Hayes contacts Rogers, who arrives with a group called the Son of the Pioneers to hit the trail and chase the bad guys. Along the way, Rogers, Evans and the Sons of the Pioneers have time to sing eight songs, including "Will Ya Be my Darling", "Way Out There", "Round and Round-the Lariat Song", "Song of Arizona," "Did You Ever Get the Feeling in the Moonlight?," "Michael O' Leary, O'Brien, O'Toole," "Half-a-Chance Ranch," "Mr. Spook Steps Out."

p, Edward J. White; d, Frank McDonald; w, M. Coates Webster (based on a story by Bradford Ropes); ph, Reggie Lanning; ed, Arthur Roberts; m/l, Jack Elliott, Ira Schuster, Larry Stock, J. Cavanaugh, Mary Ann Owens, Bob Nolan, Gordon Forster.

Western   **Cas.**   **(PR:A   MPAA:NR)**

SONG OF BERNADETTE, THE**   (1943) 156m FOX bw

Jennifer Jones (Bernadette Soubirous), William Eythe (Antoine), Charles Bickford (Peyremaie), Vincent Price (Dutour), Lee Cobb (Dr. Dozous), Gladys Cooper (Sister Vauzous), Anne Revere (Louise Soubirous), Roman Bohnen (Francois Soubirous), Mary Anderson (Jeanne Abadie), Patricia Morison (Empress Eugenie), Aubrey Mather (Lacade), Charles Dingle (Jacomet), Edith Barrett (Croisine), Sig Rumann (Louis Bouriette), Blanche Yurka (Bernarde Casterot), Ermadean Walters (Marie Soubirous), Marcel Dalio (Callet), Pedro de Cordoba (Le Crampe), Jerome Cowan (Emperor Napoleon), Charles Waldron (Bishop of Tarbes), Moroni Olsen (Chaplain), Nana Bryant (Convent Mother Superior), Manart Kippen (Charles Bouhouhorts), Merrill Rodin (Jean Soubirous), Nino Pipitone, Jr (Justin Soubirous), John Maxwell Hayes (Father Pomian), Jean Del Val (Estrade), Tala Birell (Mme. Bruat), Eula Morgan (Mme. Nicolau), Frank Reicher (Dr. St. Cyr), Charles La Torre (Duran), Linda Darnell (Blessed Virgin), Nestor Paiva (Baker), Dorothy Shearer (Mother Superior), Nino Pipitone, Sr (Mayor's Secretary), Edwin Stanley (Mr. Jones), Lionel Braham (Baron Massey), Ian Wolfe (Minister of the Interior), Andre Charlot (Bishop), Irina Semochenko, Marie Carrozza, Joyce Miller, Alicia Diaz (Bernadette's Schoolmates), Ruth Robinson (Nun), Alan Napier (Psychiatrist), Eugene Borden (Gendarme), Edward Clark (Hospital Attendant), Frank Leigh (Cleric), Charles Bates (Bouhouhorts' Boy, Age 7), Claudine LeDuc, Margaret Hoffman, Connie Leon, Edythe Elliott, Elvira Curci, Adrienne d'Ambricourt, Belle Mitchell, Mae Marsh, Fernanda Eliscu, Ruth Warren, Lucille Ward, Minerva Urecal, Cecil Weston, Marie Pope, Marjorie Copley (Women), Alex Papana, Alphonse Martell, Muni Seroff, Frank Lackteen, Stephen Roberts, Frank Dae, Louis Pacigalupi (Men), Harry Denny (Priest), Curt Furberg, Armand Cortez, Louis Arco, George Sorel (Franciscan Monks), Jean De Briac, Davison Clark, Antonio Filauri, Julian Rivero (Dominican Monks), Charles Wagenheim (Peasant), Edward Keane, Hooper Atchley (Policemen), Edward Van Sloan, Edward Fielding, John Dilson, Tom Stevenson (Doctors), Fred Essler (Minister of Justice), Harry Cording (Stone Mason), Pat Dillon (Bouhouhorts' Boy), Louis Mercier (Huckster), Dickie Moore (Adolar), Fritz Leiber, Arthur Hohl (Monks), Geraldine Wall (Nun).

This film depicts the true story of the woman who saw the Virgin Mary in a grotto at Lourdes in 1858. Jones won an Oscar for this role, her first major part after showing her stuff in various supporting tasks. She is the not-too-bright (by her own admission) asthmatic daughter of Revere and Bohnen, a very poor couple with no money and no prospects for any. The family lives in the town jail because they have no place of their own. One morning, Jones is out gathering sticks of wood near the grotto when she sees Darnell as Virgin Mary. She's been directed to dig at the grotto for water, a fluid that will have healing ability for the lame and the halt. Everyone scoffs and sneers at her except her devout mother and, eventually, Bickford, who is the priest at the small Lourdes church. He helps her get into a convent where she becomes a Sister although she never fully convinces Cooper, a frosty nun who is jealous because this simple girl is receiving messages from on high. Price is one of the scoffers, the prosecutor in the

town who attempts to have Jones clapped away in a mental home but, in the end, when he learns he has cancer, he says "Bernadette, pray for me," so we know that he has converted to believing. Despite all of the opposition, Jones, like Joan of Arc, never wavers in her faith and it is that consistency which wins everyone over. The years pass, Jones becomes ill, then dies, and is ultimately canonized. Since that time, millions have flocked to Lourdes to bathe in the Holy Water. Lest you scoff as well, it often works. Cripples have tossed away crutches, mutes have spoken, blind people have seen...and it continues to this day. Bickford puts it perfectly when he says: "For those who believe in God, no explanation is necessary. For those who do not believe in God, no explanation is possible." Every single role, no matter how small, has been exquisitely cast, the script was sensitive and literate, the direction was gentle and spiritual, and the cinematography was flawless. All of this resulted in a smash hit at the box office at a time when the U.S. was besieged by the war in movies and in the news and needed to renew faith. Newman's music and Miller's photography won Oscars while the movie itself, Seaton's script, King's direction, and the acting of Bickford, Cooper, and Revere were accorded Academy nominations. No matter what religion someone may be, including devout atheist, there is no doubting that this was a first-rate movie made with love and care and ranks as one of the best dramas of the era.

p, William Perlberg; d, Henry King; w, George Seaton (based on the novel by Franz Werfel); ph, Arthur Miller; m, Alfred Newman; ed, Barbara McLean; md, Newman; art d, James Basevi, William Darling; set d, Thomas Little, Frank E. Hughes; spec eff, Fred Sersen; cos, Rene Hubert.

Biography   **Cas.**   **(PR:AAA   MPAA:NR)**

SONG OF FREEDOM***   (1938, Brit.) 66m Hammer/Treo Exchange
                                                                          bw

Paul Robeson (John Zinga), Elizabeth Welch (Ruth Zinga), George Mozart (Bert Puddick), Esme Percy (Donizetti), Joan Fred Emney (Nell), Arthur Williams (Witch Doctor), Ronald Simpson (Blane), Jenny Dean (Marian), Bernard Ansell (Pyrie), Robert Adams (Monty), Cornelia Smith (Queen Zinga), Sydney Benson (Gate-Keeper), Will Hammer (Potman), Alf Goddard (Alf), Ambrose Manning (Trader), Ronald Adam.

Robeson's powerful persona helps carry this film, in which he plays Zinga, a British dockhand-turned-singer and descendant of an African queen. Though happily married to Welch, he decides to go to Africa and trace his ancestry. All he has to go on in finding his forebears is a medallion, which leads to the discovery that he is heir to the throne of Cazanga. The film then centers on Robeson's efforts to help the islanders rid their land of disease through modern medicine and of domination by witch doctors. The plot of the film is believed to be based on an African legend. Robeson performs "Song of Freedom," "Sleepy River," "Stepping Stones," "Lonely Road."

p, H. Fraser Passmore; d, J. Elder Wills; w, Fenn Sherie, Ingram d'Abbes, Michael Barringer, Philip Lindsay (based on a story by Maj. Claude Wallace and Dorothy Holloway); ph, Eric Cross, T.A. Glover, Harry Rose; ed, Arthur Tavares.

Drama   **Cas.**   **(PR:A   MPAA:NR)**

SONG OF IDAHO**   (1948) 66m COL bw

Kirby Grant (King Russell), June Vincent (Eve Allen), Tommy Ivo (Junior), Dorothy Vaughn (Sara Mom), Emory Parnell (J. Chester Nottingham), Eddie Acuff (Hash Brown), Maudie Prickett (Millie), The Hoosier Hot Shots, The Sunshine Boys, The Sunshine Girls, The Starlighters.

Lots of singing pads out simple story with Grant as a hillbilly singer whose radio show is yanked off the airwaves. To get his sponsor to renew the show, he must first win over the sponsor's bratty son. The Hoosier Hot Shots and Grant try to please the kid, who decides to blackmail the group. Grant's baritone is well-suited to such tunes as "Idaho," "Driftin'" and "Nobody Else But You." Musical assistance is lent by The Hot Shots, the Sunshine Boys, the Sunshine Girls and the Starlighters.

p, Colbert Clark; d, Ray Nazarro; w, Barry Shipman; ph, Vincent Farrar; ed, Aaron Stell; md, Mischa Bakaleinikoff; art d, Charles Clague.

Comedy   **(PR:A   MPAA:NR)**

SONG OF INDIA**   (1949) 77m COL bw

Sabu (Ramdar), Gail Russell (Princess Tara), Turhan Bey (Gopal), Maharajah of Hakwar, Anthony Caruso (Maj. Doraj), Aminta Dyne (Aunt Shayla), Fritz Leiber (Nanaram), Trevor Bardette (Rewa), Robert H. Barrat (Maharajah of Ranjat), David Bond (Ranjit Singh), Rodric [Rodd] Redwing (Kumari), Ted Hecht (Numtai).

India is the setting for this jungle adventure, featuring Sabu. Bey, an Indian prince who captures big-game animals for zoos, heads into a sacred jungle where hunting is forbidden. Animals and humans have lived there peacefully, and legend has it if an animal is killed, a villager must die also. Bey and his love Russell chuckle at the natives' ignorance and continue with the hunt. Sabu, prince of the jungle, frees the animals from their cages and holds Russell captive. Sabu and Bey fight it out with knives, and a wounded tiger rescues Sabu by forcing Bey down a mountainside. Alexander Lazlo's score was based on Nicolai Rimsky-Korsakov's "Song of India."

p&d, Albert S. Rogell; w, Art Arthur, Kenneth Perkins (based on a story by Jerome Odlum); ph, Henry Freulich; m, Alexander Lazlo; ed, Charles Nelson; md, M.W. Stoloff; art d, Sturges Carne.

Adventure　　　　　　　　　　　　　　**(PR:A　MPAA:NR)**

SONG OF KENTUCKY*½　　　　　(1929) 79m FOX bw

Joseph Wagstaff (Jerry Reavis), Lois Moran (Lee Coleman), Dorothy Burgess (Nancy Morgan), Douglas Gilmore (Kane Pitcairn), Herman Bing (Jake Kleinschmidt), Hedda Hopper (Mrs. Coleman), Edwards Davis (Mr. Coleman), Bert Woodruff (Steve).

Creaky early talkie has Moran falling in love with songwriter Reavis, although she is engaged to cad Gilmore. When Gilmore discovers her romance, he arranges to have Reavis framed for a crime. Moran believes the charges and agrees to marry Gilmore, but only if her horse loses the Kentucky Derby. It does lose and just before the ceremony she goes to a concert where Reavis is conducting. The charges against him are proven false and the lovers live happily ever after. Sources conflict on the basis for the film: some credit a book by Conrad, Mitchell, and Gottler, and others cite a story by Brennan.

p, Chandler Sprague; d, Lewis Seiler; w, Frederick Hazlitt Brennan (based on a book by Con Conrad, Sidney Mitchell, Archie Gottler); ph, Charles G. Clarke; ed, Carl Carruth; art d, William Darling; cos, Sophie Wachner; m/l, "Sitting by the Window," "A Night of Happiness," Conrad, Mitchell, Gottler.

Drama　　　　　　　　　　　　　　　**(PR:A　MPAA:NR)**

SONG OF LIFE, THE**　(1931, Ger.) 54m Filmkunst/Tobis Forenfilms
　　　　　　　　　　　　bw (DAS LIED VOM LEBEN)

Margot Ferra (Erika), Albert Mog (Igor).

Early German film heavy with symbolism caused controversy with its graphic depiction of the birth of a child. The film was banned in Germany, though American censors apparently found nothing objectionable. The film, a mix of science and fantasy, opens with the engagement party of a young girl and her elderly fiance. Gripped by the realization of what she is doing, she flees in horror from the party, later meeting with a young sailor. They fall in love, and she sails away with him. When they return home, she enters a hospital and gives birth to a child, who will later follow in his sailor father's footsteps. Film contains minimal dialog and four songs. Actors do a capable job.

d, Alexis Granowsky; w, Victor Trivas and Dr. H. Lechner; ph, Victor Trinkler, Heinrich Belasch; ed, Mark Asarow; m/l, Friedrich Hollander, H. Adams.

Science Fiction/Fantasy　　　　　　　**(PR:A　MPAA:NR)**

SONG OF LOVE, THE**　　　　　(1929) 76m COL bw

Belle Baker (Anna Gibson), Ralph Graves (Tom Gibson), David Durand (Buddy Gibson), Eunice Quedens [Eve Arden] (Mazie), Arthur Housman (Joe, Acrobat), Charles Wilson (Traveling Salesman).

Baker, a member of a vaudeville family, finally realizes that she is not giving son Durand a normal childhood. When she quits the stage act, her husband, Graves, teams up with Quedens, with whom he becomes romantically involved, but she leaves him and he starts drinking heavily. Meanwhile, Baker resumes singing after her son goes to military school and a friend of Graves takes the boy to see his dad in the hope of straightening him out. They decide to catch Baker's new act and join her in the finale to seal their reunion. Songs include: "I'm Somebody's Baby Now" (Mack Gordon, Max Rich), "I'll Still Go on Wanting You" (Bernie Grossman), "Take Everything but You," "I'm Walking on Moonbeams (Talking to the Stars)" (Gordon, Rich, Maurice Abrahams), "White Way Blues" (Gordon, Rich, George Weist).

p, Harry Cohn; d, Erle C. Kenton; w, Howard Green, Henry McCarthy, Dorothy Howell, Norman Houston; ph, Joseph Walker; ed, Gene Havelick.

Musical　　　　　　　　　　　　　　　**(PR:A　MPAA:NR)**

SONG OF LOVE**½　　　　　　(1947) 119m MGM bw

Katharine Hepburn (Clara Wieck Schumann), Paul Henreid (Robert Schumann), Robert Walker (Johannes Brahms), Henry Daniell (Franz Liszt), Leo G. Carroll (Prof. Wieck), Else Janssen (Bertha), Gigi Perreau (Julie), "Tinker" Furlong (Felix), Ann Carter (Marie), Janine Perreau (Eugenie), Jimmie Hunt (Ludwig), Anthony Sydes (Ferdinand), Eilene Janssen (Elsie), Roman Bohnen (Dr. Hoffman), Kurt Katch (Judge), Ludwig Stossel (Haslinger), Tala Birell (Princess Valerie Hohenfels), Henry Stephenson (King Albert), Konstantin Shayne (Reinecke), Byron Foulger (Court Officer), Josephine Whittell (Lady in Box), Betty Blythe (Lady with Opera Glasses), Clinton Sundberg (Dr. Richarz), Andre Charlot (Pompous Gent), Mary Forbes, Winifred Harris (Women at Party), Lela Bliss (Mrs. Heller).

It's hard to believe that they missed with this story, a love tale with some

of the greatest music of the ages by Brahms, Liszt and Schumann. Hepburn was wonderful and submerged most of her mannerisms in the role of a popular pianist who gives up her career to marry struggling composer Henreid. In no time at all, seven children are born, including sisters Gigi and Janine Perreau. Hepburn's father is Carroll and he would have wished that all of her training might have been put to use. Walker enters, a young student of Henreid's, and thinks Hepburn is a doozy, despite her being the mother of a septet. Henried applies himself to teaching and composing and eventually goes mad from the strain, is taken to a mental hospital where he eventually passes away. Walker has now become a famous composer and makes a proposal of marriage to Hepburn. She turns him down and decides to devote the remainder of her life to her children and to playing the music of her late husband on the concert stage in an attempt to popularize it. History was altered here, though not with the same disdain shown by the writers of the Chopin movie, A SONG TO REMEMBER. Hepburn studied with piano teacher Laura Dubman, a pupil of Artur Rubenstein, so it would seem she was actually playing when, in fact, the music was provided by Rubenstein. Daniell is excellent as Liszt, Henreid's friend, who tries to help bring Henreid's compositions the merit they deserve. Singing was done by the St. Luke's Boys Choir, and William Steinberg conducted MGM's Symphony Orchestra. Musical pieces included Schumann's "Traumerei, Opus 15, No. 7," "Arabeske, Opus 18," "Dedication, Opus 25, No. 1," plus Liszt's "Mephisto Waltz" (which was the title for an award-winning foreign film in the 1980s), and Brahms contributed his "Lullaby" and "Rhapsody No. 2 in G Minor." Good acting from all save Walker, who seemed too moon-eyed and flighty to convince anyone he may have been Brahms. Unfortunately, there were many inadvertent laughs in the script to counterpoint the heavy dramatic scenes, such as the one where Henreid announces to Hepburn (while he's residing in the mental institution) that he's composed a new piece, and he plays her a work he wrote many years before. It was a good-looking movie, with opulent sets and costumes to give it a fine production, but there was much more that could have been said about these monumental geniuses.

p&d, Clarence Brown; w, Ivan Tors, Irmgard Von Cube, Allen Vincent, Robert Ardrey (based on the play by Bernard Schubert, Mario Silva); ph, Harry Stradling; m, Johannes Brahms, Franz Liszt, Robert Schumann; ed, Robert J. Kern; md, Bronislau Kaper; art d, Cedric Gibbons, Hans Peters; set d, Edwin B. Willis; cos, Irene, Walter Plunkett, Valles; spec eff, Warren Newcombe; musical adviser, Laura Dubman; makeup, Jack Dawn.

Musical/Biography　　　　　　　　　**(PR:A　MPAA:NR)**

SONG OF MEXICO*　　　　　　(1945) 57m REP bw

Adela Mara, Edgar Barrier, George Lewis, Jacqueline Dalya, Jose Pulido, Raquel de Alva, Margaret Falkenberg, Elizabeth Waldo, Carmen Molina, Tipica Orchestra.

South-of-the-border musical features Mara as a bride-to-be who calls a halt to the proceedings when she decides her man is more interested in his career than in her. Lightweight enough to avoid being annoying, but no more.

p,d&w, James A. Fitzpatrick; ph, John Alton, George Stahl; m, Lecuona; ed, Harry Keller; md, Manuel Esperson, Richard Cherwin; art d, Jesus Bracho; m/l, Esperson, Alfredo Nunez de Borbon, Anita Lopez, Pedro Galindo, Pablo Marin.

Musical　　　　　　　　　　　　　　　**(PR:A　MPAA:NR)**

SONG OF MY HEART**　　　(1947) 85m Symphony Films/AA bw

Frank Sundstrom (Peter Ilich Tchaikovsky), Audrey Long (Amalya), Sir Cedric Hardwicke (Grand Duke), Mikhail Rasumny (Sergei/Stephan), Gale Sherwood (Sophia), Serge Krizman (Ivan), Charles Trowbridge (Jurgesen), Kate Lawson (Nurse), Lester Sharpe (Lubenstein), Drew Allen (Kolya), Scott Elliott (Lt. Sanderson), Gordon Clark (Lt. Julian), Jimmie Dodd (Pvt. Murphy), David Leonard (Nikolai Rimsky-Korsakoff), John Hamilton (Czar), William Ruhl (Cesar Cui), Steve Darrell (Aide in Uniform), Robert Barron (Aleksandr Borodin), Elvira Curci (Housekeeper), Maurice Cass (Ballet Master), Grandon Rhodes (Doctor), William "Billy" Newell (Doorman), Leonard Mudie (Conductor), Lane Chandler (Policeman), Leonid Snegoff (Manager), Lewis Howard (Modest Moussorgsky), Stan Johnson (Capt. Weatherly), Leo Kaye (Mess Sergeant), Jack George (Priest), Vernon Cansino (Evans), Nina Hansen (Sophia's Mother).

The life of Russian composer Peter Ilich Tchaikovsky is presented on the big screen for the first time, against a background of excerpts from several of his songs and symphonies. However, the filmmakers apparently felt they could take dramatic license with much of the biographical material, and chose to offer the audience a highly fictionalized account of the composer's life. The story concentrates on his love affair with his sponsor, a princess whose father prevents them from marrying. Tchaikovsky was, in fact, a homosexual whose marriage ended only after a few days. The story is told in flashbacks by a Russian lieutenant whose father had been the composer's valet. Sherwood, as the composer's wife, sings "I Looked for Love." Excerpts from Tchaikovsky's 4th, 5th, and 6th symphonies are heard, as well as portions of the B-Flat Piano Concerto, the Nutcracker Suite, Swan Lake, the Romeo and Juliet Fantasy, the 1812 Overture, Marche Slave, and Caprice Italien. Pianist Jose Iturbi dubbed Sundstrom's performance of piano works, but was uncredited because of other contractual commitments. The most sparkling performance is given by Rasumny who, in a dual role as the valet and lieutenant, provides comic relief.

p, Nathaniel Finston, J. Theodore Reed; d, Benjamin Glazer; w, Glazer, Bernard Schubert; ph, Roland Totheroh; m, Peter Ilich Tchaikovsky; ed, Richard Heermance; md, Finston, Edward J. Kay; art d, Arthur Lonergan; set d, Raymond Boltz, Jr.; ch, Paul Oscard; m/l, Janice Torre, Fred Spielman.

Musical　　　　　　　　　　　　　　　　　　**(PR:A　MPAA:NR)**

SONG OF NEVADA**½　　　　　　　　　　　　(1944) 75m REP bw

Roy Rogers (*Roy*), Dale Evans (*Joan Barrabee*), Mary Lee (*Kitty Hanley*), Lloyd Corrigan (*Prof. Jeremiah Hanley*), Thurston Hall (*John Barrabee*), John Eldredge (*Rollo Bingham*), Forrest Taylor (*Col. Jack Thompson*), George Meeker (*Calahan*), Emmett Vogan (*Master of Ceremonies*), LeRoy Mason (*Ferguson*), William B. Davidson (*Worthington*), Bob Nolan and the Sons of the Pioneers, Kenne Duncan, Si Jenks, Frank McCarroll, Henry Wills, Jack O'Shea, Helen Talbot, Trigger the Horse.

Rogers sets Evans straight this time around in this musical western. Rogers meets Hall, a rich ranch owner who is believed to be dead after his plane crashes. While he is in hiding, he hires Rogers to straighten out Evans, his high society daughter, who has taken on Eastern ways. She has come west to sell Hall's ranch to make money for herself and her sharp, big-city boy friend, but is wooed by Rogers who sings his way into her heart and convinces her that she belongs with her father in Nevada. Songs include: "It's Love, Love, Love" (sung by Dale Evans), "New Moon Over Nevada," "Hi Ho Little Dogies," "The Harum Scarum Baron of the Harmonium," "What Are We Going to Do?" "A Cowboy Has to Yodel in the Morning."

p, Harry Grey; d, Joseph Kane; w, Gordon Kahn, Olive Cooper; ph, Jack Marta; m, Morton Scott; ed, Tony Martinelli; md, Fred A. Ritter; ch, Larry Ceballos.

Musical/Western　　　　　**Cas.**　　　　　　**(PR:A　MPAA:NR)**

SONG OF NORWAY**½　　　　　　　　　　　(1970) 138m Cinerama c

Toralv Maurstad (*Edvard Grieg*), Florence Henderson (*Nina Grieg*), Christina Schollin (*Therese Berg*), Frank Porretta (*Rikard Nordraak*), Harry Secombe (*Bjornsterne Bjornson*), Robert Morley (*Berg*), Edward G. Robinson (*Krogstad*), Elizabeth Larner (*Mrs. Bjornson*), Oscar Homolka (*Engstrand*), Frederick Jaeger (*Henrik Ibsen*), Henry Gilbert (*Franz Liszt*), Richard Wordsworth (*Hans Christian Andersen*), Bernard Archard (*George Nordraak*), Susan Richards Chitty (*Aunt Aline*), John Barrie (*Hagerup*), Wenke Foss (*Mrs. Hagerup*), Ronald Adam (*Gade*), Carl Rigg (*Capt. Hansen*), Aline Towne (*Mrs. Thoresen*), Nan Munro (*Irate Woman*), James Hayter (*Berg's Butler*), Avind Harum (*Freddie*), Rolf Berntzen (*Doctor*), Tordis Maurstad (*Mrs. Schmidt*), Erik Chitty (*Helsted*), Charles Lloyd Pack (*Chevalier*), Robert Rietty (*Winding*), Rosalind Speight, Ros Drinkwater (*Liszt's Friends*), Tracey Crisp (*Receptionist*), Cyril Renison (*Rome Butler*), Manoug Parikian (*Violinist*), Richard Vernon (*1st Councilman*), Eli Lindtner (*Bjornson's Secretary*), Ilse Tromm (*Girl's Mother*), Jeffrey Taylor, Peter Salmon, Roy Jones, Gordon Coster, Paddy McIntyre, Barrie Wilkinson, Rupert Lupone, Stephen Reinhardt, Jane Darling, Barbara von der Heyde, Hermione Farthingale, Jennie Walton, Michele Hardy, Susan Claire, Denise O'Brien, Jane Kells (*Dancers*), Ernest Clark (*2nd Councilman*).

"The road to Hell is paved with good intentions" and the intentions here were splendid but the road was paved with potholes. After the phenomenal success of THE SOUND OF MUSIC, they searched about for something in the same genre and came up with this 1944 play that was a success with wartime audiences. Wright and Forrest, who did the same thing for Borodin when they adapted his music for KISMET, took Grieg's tunes and wrote lyrics in English which served as the score for Grieg's biography. It was shot on location in Europe at a cost of $4 million and did not return much more than that at the box office. The corn in this screenplay is as high as anything found in OKLAHOMA! as they take liberties with the rather dull life of Grieg in order to put some dramatic punch into it. One could immerse oneself in that bathos on the screen and any similarity to human beings is totally accidental. Maurstad, a popular Norwegian actor, is Grieg. He's just come out of the conservatory at Leipzig and needs money in order to keep studying music in Italy. Schollin is a classmate who thinks that Maurstad is a genius so she tries to get her father, Morley, to give Maurstad the money. Morley is not so sure but Schollin makes a deal with him; he's been trying to convince her to marry the son of a wealthy family. It's a business arrangement at best and she's been against it, but if Morley will give Maurstad the money he needs, she'll acquiesce. Morley, who doesn't trust his own taste, arranges a recital at which Maurstad will play for some of Sweden's top music critics and Schollin promises to stay away from Maurstad as her part of the bargain. He plays to great huzzahs and when he can't find Schollin, he wonders what's happened to her. Maurstad goes to Copenhagen and encounters Porretta, another Norwegian composer. The two men become close friends. Porretta introduces Maurstad to Wordsworth (as Hans Christian Anderson, although everyone will always think of Danny Kaye as the fairy-tale writer) who is happy when Maurstad's first cousin, Henderson, sings some songs which Maurstad has written, using Wordsworth's poetry. Henderson and Maurstad fall in love but since they are first cousins, that creates a bit of a scandal in the family, particularly with their parents, Foss and Barrie. Nevertheless, they plan to wed and on the day they

are to tie the knot, Maurstad hears from the missing Schollin. She sends a letter saying that her engagement has been cancelled and that she would like nothing better than to see him once more. He chooses to toss the letter aside and marry Henderson. Maurstad is desirous of becoming the conductor at the National Theatre and enlists the aid of Porretta and Secombe, a noted Norwegian playwright who is related to Porretta. He can't get the job due to circumstances beyond his control and must now give music lessons in order to keep body and soul together. Everywhere he turns, there doesn't seem to be any way for him to raise his level of living. Meanwhile, Schollin has been following the travails of Maurstad and puts up her own money to rent a local auditorium for one night, then contacts Secombe and says that the rent on the hall has been lowered. Secombe is against the sham but tells Maurstad about it on Christmas Eve, when the men and their families get together for a fine night of wassail. Then Secombe and Maurstad agree to work together on an opera based on the trolls, the leprechauns of Norway. The concert takes place but it's a bust. Schollin explains to Maurstad that Norwegians are only impressed when a composer has first made his name elsewhere, in Germany or Italy. Henderson is frightened by Schollin and worries that Maurstad may leave her for the rich woman, especially after Schollin sends them a gift of a huge piano. Henderson had sold her ancient family cottage in order to buy a small piano for Maurstad from Robinson, the local music shop owner. Maurstad gets an effusive letter from Franz Liszt (Gilbert) which overflows with laudatory comments and he takes the letter and uses it to secure a grant to travel to Rome. There's not enough money for both of them so Henderson is to move in with her mother while Maurstad travels to Berlin, where he learns that Porretta is sick, then to Italy where he meets Jaeger (as Ibsen) who asks him to write the music for his play "Peer Gynt." Jaeger and Secombe are great enemies in the theatrical world and Maurstad owes a great deal to Secombe but he tosses aside loyalty and agrees to write the music for Jaeger's work. Maurstad goes further south to Rome where Schollin follows him and introduces him to all the right people so Maurstad stays longer than expected in the Eternal City. He plays several concerts and is a smash. Gilbert (Liszt) is a great booster and his life is finally going well when he meets Robinson, who is on a brief trip to Rome. Robinson informs Maurstad that Henderson did not go home to mother. Instead, she remained in their house and is living on a pittance. Maurstad is stunned to hear that, and then learns that Porretta has died. He comes to his senses, realizing he has been greedy and selfish and that it is time to give up this social whirl, return to Henderson in Norway, and start composing seriously without further training. He has the music of Norway in his genes and it is time he shared it. There was animation, puppetry, and everything else they could muster for this family-oriented picture that they prayed would bring in the youngsters. (The Stones later made an equally tiresome musical biography, THE GREAT WALTZ, about Johann Strauss, Jr.) The London Symphony Orchestra performed the score based on Grieg's music (as adapted by Wright and Forrest) with John Ogden and Brenda Lucas, pianists, and violin soloist Manoug Parikian. Songs include: "Strange Music" (sung by Maurstad), "The Song of Norway," "The Little House," "Be a Boy Again," "Three There Were" (Porretta), "A Rhyme and a Reason," "Wrong to Dream," "I Love You," "The Solitary Wanderer" (Henderson), "Hill of Dreams" (Porretta, Maurstad, Henderson), "Opening Concerto–The Life of the Wife of the Sailor," "Solvejg's Song–Norwegian National Anthem," "Betrothal Hymn," "Midsummer's Eve" (Chorus), "A Welcome Toast" (Secombe), "Freddie and His Fiddle" (Children, Chorus), "In The Hall Of The Mountain King," "At Christmas Time," "Ribbons And Wrappings," "When We Wed," "John Heggerstrom." Ogden was soloist for Grieg's Piano Concerto. The cinematography of the spectacular landscape looked, as Billy Crystal said in his impression of Fernando Lamas, "mah-velous," but that was the best element of the film. Maurstad and Porretta were hardly heard from again.

p, Andrew L. Stone, Virginia Stone; d, w, Andrew L. Stone (based on the musical *Song of Norway* by Milton Lazarus, Robert Wright, George Forrest, based on a play by Homer Curran); ph, Davis Boulton (Super Panavision DeLuxe Color); m, Robert Wright, Forrest; ed, Virginia Lively Stone; md, Roland Shaw; art d. William Albert Havemeyer; cos, David Walker, Fiorella Mariani; ch, Lee Theodore; animation, Jack Kinney.

Musical/Biography　　　　　　　　　　　　**(PR:A　MPAA:G)**

SONG OF OLD WYOMING*½　　　　　　　　(1945) 65m PRC c

Eddie Dean (*Eddie Reed*), Sarah Padden (*Ma Conway*), Al "Lash" La Rue (*Cheyenne Kid*), Jennifer Holt (*Vickey*), Emmett Lynn (*Uncle Ezra*), Ray Elder (*Slim*), John Carpenter (*Buck*), Ian Keith (*Landow*), Lee Bennett (*Waco*), Bob Barron (*Dixon*), Horace Murphy (*Meeks*), Pete Katchenaro (*Ling*), Rocky Camron (*Ringo*), Bill Lovett (*Tex*), Richard Cramer (*Hodges*), Steve Clark (*Bank Clerk*), Don Williams.

A well-worn western with no new twists or exciting action to make it special. Dean plays the likable cowboy who fights only when he absolutely has to, and Padden is the do-gooder who wants Wyoming to be part of the Union despite the efforts of the evil La Rue. Dean is brought in by the villains to halt Padden's efforts, but turns out to be her long lost son. La Rue is classic as the black-clad scoundrel who reforms at the end. La Rue, with his trademark whip, would go on to become Lash La Rue in a series of B-westerns of his own. The film was shot in Cinecolor, a cheap color process which was not very effective.

p&d, Robert Emmett [Tansey]; w, Frances Kavanaugh; ph, Marcel Le Picard (Cinecolor); ed, Hugh Winn; md, Carl Hoeffle; art d, Edward C. Jewell; m/l, Ralph Rainer, Leo Robin, Eddie Dean, Milt Mabie, Hoeffle.

Western   **(PR:A   MPAA:NR)**

SONG OF PARIS   (SEE: BACHELOR IN PARIS, 1953, Brit.)

SONG OF RUSSIA**   (1943) 107m MGM bw

Robert Taylor *(John Meredith)*, Susan Peters *(Nadya Stepanova)*, John Hodiak *(Boris)*, Robert Benchley *(Hank Higgins)*, Felix Bressart *(Petrov)*, Michael Chekhov *(Stepanov)*, Darryl Hickman *(Peter)*, Jacqueline White *(Anna)*, Vladimir Sokoloff, Leo Bulgakov, Peter Meremblum's California Junior Symphony Orchestra.

Once upon a time, Russia was an ally and Germany was the enemy. Taylor, a long-time anti-communist, was against making this film and argued with Mayer about it but finally agreed when he was told that President Roosevelt wanted the picture done to strengthen U.S. sentiment toward the Soviets. He paid the price later by being called to testify in front of an investigating committee after the war which was searching for communist sympathizers in the movie business. It was Taylor's final film before entering the service and he regretted it all his life. MGM had made two anti-Russian comedies NINOTCHKA and COMRADE X, and both were successful but that was before WW II and so they were called upon to right the ship by doing something pro. At best, SONG OF RUSSIA was a yawner. Taylor is a famed U.S. symphony conductor on tour with his manager, Benchley. They go to the town where Tchaikovsky was born (it's called Tchaikovskoye) and are trapped there when the Nazis unleash their attack on Russia at the start of the war. He meets Peters, a sweet peasant girl with an ear for classical music, and they marry. War breaks out and he is all for leaving in a hurry but she wants to remain and fight the Germans alongside her fellow villagers. He departs but the pair swear their undying love for each other and promise they will meet again after the war. Taylor is unbelievable as the conductor and anyone with any knowledge of what a conductor does will laugh as Taylor's baton is totally out of synchronization with the music played by Peter Meremblum's California Junior Symphony Orchestra. Former actor Ratoff laid a directorial layer of borscht over the whole thing and the outcome was boiled potatoes. If one removed all of the pro-Soviet propaganda about their bravery against Nazi tyranny, the picture would have been much shorter, and much better.

p, Joseph Pasternak; d, Gregory Ratoff; w, Paul Jarrico, Richard Collins (based on a story by Leo Mittler, Victor Trivas, Guy Endore); ph, Harry Stradling; m, Herbert Stothart (Peter Ilich Tchaikovsky's and modern Russian compositions adapted by Stothart); ed, George Hively; md, Albert Coates; art d, Cedric Gibbons; spec eff, Arnold Gillespie; ch, David Lichine; m/l, "And Russia Is Her Name," E.Y. Harburg, Jerome Kern.

Drama   **(PR:A   MPAA:NR)**

SONG OF SCHEHERAZADE**   (1947) 105m UNIV c

Yvonne De Carlo *(Cara de Talavera)*, Brian Donlevy *(Captain)*, Jean Pierre Aumont *(Nikolai Rimsky-Korsakov)*, Eve Arden *(Mme. de Talavera)*, Philip Reed *(Prince Mischetsky)*, Charles Kullman *(Dr. Lin)*, John Qualen *(Lorenzo)*, Richard Lane *(Lieutenant)*, Terry Kilburn *(Lorin)*, George Dolenz *(Pierre)*, Elena Verdugo *(Fioretta)*, Robert Kendall *(Hassan)*, Rex Ravelle *(Sultan)*, Mickey Simpson *(Orderly)*, Sol Haines *(Giant)*, Florene Rozen *(Little Sister)*, William Brooks, William Ching, Leonard East, Edward Kelly, Russ Vincent, Peter Varney, Charles "Chuck" Roberson, Tom Skinner, Warren W. McCollum, Ernie Mishens, Marvin Press, Fred K. Hartsook, Gordon Arnold, Bill Cabanne, Don Garner, George Holmes *(Students)*, Milio Sheron *(Basso)*, Audrey Young, Karen Randle *(Native Girls)*, Joan Fulton [Shawlee] *(French Girl)*, Theodora Lynch *(Soprano)*, Dick Alexander *(Attendant)*, Beverlee Mitchell, Matia Antar *(European Girls)*, Mary Moore *(Spanish Girl)*, Duke Johnson *(Juggler)*, Chester Conklin *(Sailor)*, Ralph Brooks *(Junior Officer)*, Bob Barron *(Ice Cream Vendor)*, Yussuf Ali *(Cop)*, Emmett Vogan, Jr *(Coachman)*.

Scattered direction doesn't help this empty-headed, but superficially entertaining, musical, which is supposedly a biography of Russian composer Rimsky-Korsakov, played by Aumont. Aumont meets the sultry De Carlo after a world cruise, and she inspires him to write his great composition, "Song of Scheherazade." They fall in love but circumstances keep them apart. When the song is to be premiered in a ballet at the St. Petersburg Opera House, De Carlo shows up to dance the leading role. The events that transpired in order for De Carlo to get to that point are typical Hollywood contrivances. Arden, only a decade older than De Carlo, is, ridiculously enough, cast as her mother. Songs include: "Gypsy Song," "Navy March," "Song of India," "Arabesque," "Hymn to the Sun," "Flight of the Bumble Bee," "Capriccio Espagnole," "Opus 35 (Fandango)," "Song of Scheherazade," "Dance of the Tumblers" (Nikolai A. Rimsky-Korsakov, some lyrics by Jack Brooks).

p, Edward Kaufman; d&w, Walter Reisch; ph, Hal Mohr, William V. Skall (Technicolor); ed, Frank Gross; md, Miklos Rozsa; art d, Jack Otterson; ch, Tilly Losch.

Musical   **(PR:A   MPAA:NR)**

SONG OF SOHO*   (1930, Brit.) 96m BIP/FN-Pathe bw

Carl Brisson *(Carl)*, Edna Davies *(Camille)*, Donald Calthrop *(Nobby)*, Henry Victor *(Henry)*, Lucienne Herval *(Lucienne)*, Antonia Brough *(Antonia)*, Charles Farrell *(Legionnaire)*, Andrea Nijinsky *(Dancer)*.

Brisson is a French Foreign Legionnaire who becomes a singer to help friend Davies get her restaurant off the ground in London. Things go well and the restaurant is a success, then Brisson is accused of the murder of a prostitute. A blind man recognizes a song Brisson sings and provides an alibi. Ridiculous musical drama has a few good songs, sung by Brisson but little else.

p, John Maxwell; d, Harry Lachman; w, Arthur Wimperis, Randall Faye, Frank Launder (based on a story by Lachman, Val Valentine); ph, Claude Friese-Greene.

Musical   **(PR:A   MPAA:NR)**

SONG OF SONGS**½   (1933) 90m PAR bw

Marlene Dietrich *(Lily Czepanek)*, Brian Aherne *(Richard Waldow)*, Lionel Atwill *(Baron von Merzbach)*, Alison Skipworth *(Frau Rasmussen)*, Hardie Albright *(Walter von Prell)*, Helen Freeman *(Fraulein von Schwartzfegger)*, Morgan Wallace *("Admirer")*, Wilson Benge *(Butler)*, Hans Schumm, Eric Wilton *(Butler)*, Richard Bennett, James Marcus.

Dietrich's first U.S. film not made with Josef von Sternberg was, Paramount thought, a can't-miss project. It was based on a successful novel by Hermann Sudermann, made into a successful play by Edward Sheldon, filmed silently starring Elsie Ferguson, then again, as LILY OF THE DUST with Pola Negri. Despite all of the prior incarnations, this did have a slightly different feel about it, probably due to the direction of newcomer Mamoulian, who was just coming off his hit DR. JEKYLL AND MR. HYDE, starring Fredric March. Dietrich is a farm girl who has just lost her father. She goes to the big city of Berlin and moves in with an aunt, Skipworth, who owns a bookshop. Dietrich is employed in the shop and meets Aherne, a handsome sculptor who lives nearby. While Dietrich is on a ladder attending to business, Aherne's keen eyes spot the legs for which she was so famous and he wonders if she would like to pose for a statue. She turns him down but not totally. Late that night, while Skipworth is off in dreamland, Dietrich leaves the flat above the store and goes across the road to see Aherne. She agrees to pose in the altogether for a statue which will represent the Song of Solomon. They fall madly in love and spend as much time as they can with each other. The statue is done and Atwill, a rich patron of the arts, is stunned by its beauty when he sees it in Aherne's studio. He is even more taken when Dietrich, the model for the work, steps out. Aherne's and Dietrich's love deepens and Dietrich makes no bones about wanting to be Aherne's wife and the mother of his children but he finds it difficult to accept, as the acquisition of such responsibility might cause his art to suffer. At the same time, Atwill has been insidiously making friends with Skipworth, slipping her cash and gifts in an attempt to enlist her help for his ultimate goal–marriage to Dietrich. Atwill also works on Aherne and convinces him that it would be best for all concerned if Aherne and Dietrich called an end to their affair as Aherne could then go on with his sculpting and have no yoke around his neck. When Dietrich pads out of the apartment one night, Skipworth, who has set this up with Atwill, feigns anger and tells Dietrich that she is no longer welcome in the apartment or at her job. She runs to the studio but Aherne is not there. Instead, Atwill awaits her with an offer. Aherne has gone away and Atwill is willing to marry Dietrich, thus making her a baroness, with all the accoutrements that come with great wealth and social position. She agrees, having nowhere else to go, and now begins a "Pygmalion" sequence whereby Atwill's job is to make Dietrich over so she can step into her new stratum. Freeman is Atwill's housekeeper and envious of the interlopping woman in the house, feeling that her stature is about to be usurped. Freeman tells Atwill that any woman of position should be able to ride a horse and he agrees. Then Freeman tells handsome Albright to teach Dietrich, but also gives the youth the order to make a pass at Dietrich in order to discredit her with Atwill if she is amenable to the amour. Dietrich pays no heed to Albright's obvious intentions and stays true to Atwill. Her social education complete, Atwill plans a dinner with Dietrich and Aherne, to show off his wife. Atwill gets blind drunk and Dietrich attempts to demonstrate to Aherne that she's only married the old man because Aherne left her in the lurch. In order to show that she has no obligations to Atwill, she decides to visit Albright's small cottage on the property and to make certain the disbelieving Aherne sees it, thereby proving she cares not for Atwill. Once inside the cottage, Dietrich intends stopping short of an assignation, but Albright sweeps her up in his arms and is taking her to the bedroom when he knocks over a lighted lamp and it's not long before the cottage is aflame. Albright gets Dietrich out but Freeman, spotting this, tells her to leave before Atwill learns of the scandalous matter. Dietrich disappears and a distraught Aherne searches for her all over Berlin. He finally locates her, now singing in a night club. After her risque song, Aherne meets her again, rekindles their love and asks for her hand and she agrees. Schubert wrote Dietrich's tune "Heidenroslein," and Friedrich Hollander and Edward Hayman wrote "Johnny." Another song, "You Are My Song Of Songs," by Ralph Rainger and Leo Robin was shot and cut from the movie. After several stage successes and a few films in England, this was Aherne's U.S. debut, as well as the first picture for Freeman, who was cofounder of the Theatre Guild in New York and a well-known Broadway actress.

p&d, Rouben Mamoulian; w, Leo Birinski, Samuel Hoffenstein (based on the novel *Das Hohe Lied* by Hermann Sudermann and the play by Edward Sheldon); ph, Victor Milner; m, Karl Hajos, Milan Rodern; md, Nathaniel W. Finston; art d, Hans Dreier; cos, Travis Banton; sculptures, S.C. Scarpitta; m/l, "Heidenroslein," Franz Schubert, "Johnny," Friedrich Hollander, Edward Hayman, the "Pathetique," Tchaikovsky's Symphony No. 6.

Drama/Comedy   **(PR:A-C   MPAA:NR)**

SONG OF SURRENDER**   (1949) 93m PAR bw

Wanda Hendrix (*Abigail Hunt*), Claude Rains (*Elisha Hunt*), MacDonald Carey (*Bruce Eldridge*), Andrea King (*Phyllis Cantwell*), Henry Hull (*Deacon Parry*), Elizabeth Patterson (*Mrs. Beecham*), Art Smith (*Mr. Willis*), John Beal (*Dubois*), Eva Gabor (*Countess Marina*), Dan Tobin (*Clyde Atherton*), Nicholas Joy (*Gen. Seckle*), Peter Miles (*Simon Beecham*), Ray Walker (*Auctioneer*), Gigi Perreau (*Faith Beecham*), Ray [Raphael] Bennett (*Mr. Beecham*), Clancy Cooper (*Mr. Toorance*), Georgia Backus (*Mrs. Parry*).

A wandering story of romance that gets some help from the great voice of Enrico Caruso. Set in the early 1900s, the plot involves Hendrix as the young wife of a man in charge of the local museum. Theirs is a simple life until playboy Carey arrives and buys a house with King. He falls for Hendrix, who reciprocates his love while Caruso sings in the background. Village tradition states that Rains must renounce his wife and her adulterous ways from the church pulpit. After being banned from the town, she eventually returns when Rains has taken ill. Rains dies and the lovers are reunited.

p, Richard Maibaum; d, Mitchell Leisen; w, Maibaum (based on a story by Ruth McKenney, Richard Bransten); ph, Daniel L. Fapp; m, Victor Young; ed, Alma Macrorie; art d, Hans Dreier, Henry Bumstead; m/l, Young, Jay Livingston, Ray Evans.

Drama   **(PR:A   MPAA:NR)**

SONG OF TEXAS**½   (1943) 69m REP bw

Roy Rogers (*Roy*), Sheila Ryan (*Sue Bennett*), Barton MacLane (*Jim Calvert*), Harry Shannon (*Sam Bennett*), Arline Judge (*Hildegarde*), William Haade (*Fred Calvert*), Eve March (*Miss Murray*), Hal Taliaferro (*Pete*), Alex Nahera Dancers, Bob Nolan and the Sons of the Pioneers, Pat Brady, Yakima Canutt, Tom London, Forrest Taylor, Trigger the Horse.

An expensive production, with an emphasis on the music rather than the action, features Ryan coming from the East to visit her father, Shannon, out West. The problem is she thinks daddy owns the ranch when he actually is just another hired man. To help Shannon, Rogers and his buddies go along with the charade, but the girl accidentally causes half of the ranch to be sold to villain MacLane. To save the ranch, Rogers has to win a chuck wagon race, an exciting highlight in the film. Rogers lets loose with 10 songs, including "Mexicali Rose" and "Moonlight and Roses." The Alex Nahera Dancers add an authentic touch to the fiesta dance scene.

p, Harry Grey; d, Joseph Kane; w, Winston Miller; ph, Reggie Lanning; ed, Tony Martinelli; md, Morton Scott; art d, Russell Kimball.

Western   **Cas.**   **(PR:A   MPAA:NR)**

SONG OF THE BUCKAROO***   (1939) 58m MON bw

Tex Ritter (*Texas Dan*), Jinx Falkenberg (*Evelyn*), Mary Ruth (*Mary, Pianist*), Tom London (*Wade*), Frank LaRue (*Bayliss*), Charles King (*Groat*), Bob Terry (*Neal*), Horace Murphy (*Cashaway*), Snub Pollard (*Perky*), Dave O'Brien (*Alden*), Dorothy Fay (*Anna*), George Chesebro, Ernie Adams, White Flash the Horse.

One of Ritter's best films while under contract to Monogram Films. Cowboy Ritter, when not singing, is campaigning for mayor. But first, he must rout out a group of outlaws who want to steer the election their way. Falkenberg, a model, plays his love interest as Ritter cleans up the town for its folks. The main drawback is that songs are tossed in at random for no real reason and interrupt the flow. Musical numbers include: "Little Tenderfoot" (Johnny Lange, Fred Stryker–sung by Tex Ritter), "I Promise You" (Ritter, Frank Harford, sung by Ritter), "Texas Dan" (Carson Robison, sung by Ritter), "Buckaroo" (performed by Mary Ruth).

p, Edward Finney; d, Al Herman; w, John Rathmell; ph, Francis Corby; ed, Fred Bain; md, Frank Sanucci.

Western   **(PR:A   MPAA:NR)**

SONG OF THE CABELLERO**   (1930) 70m UNIV bw

Ken Maynard (*Juan*), Doris Hill (*Anita*), Francis Ford (*Don Pedro Madera*), Gino Corrado (*Don Jose*), Evelyn Sherman (*Dona Louisa*), Josef Swickard (*Manuel*), Frank Rice (*Andrea*), William Irving (*Bernardo*), Joyzelle (*Conchita*), Tarzan the Horse.

Maynard this time takes his gun and fists to Southern California. He is battling a Spanish rancher, who tossed his sister out because he didn't like her boy friend. Her son shows up to wreak vengeance and clear his mother's name. Maynard fought this time with swords. His films were always known for great horse stunts and this is no exception, with help from a fast-paced

story. Best part has Maynard wiping out 10 sword-wielding bad guys.

p, Ken Maynard; d, Harry Joe Brown; w, Bennett R. Cohen, Lesley Mason (based on the story by Kenneth Beaton, Norman Sper); ph, Ted McCord; ed, Fred Allen.

Western   **(PR:A   MPAA:NR)**

SONG OF THE CITY*½   (1937) 73m MGM bw

Margaret Lindsay (*Angelina*), Jeffrey Dean [Dean Jagger] (*Paul Herrick*), J. Carrol Naish (*Mario*), Nat Pendleton (*Benvenuto*), Stanley Morner [Dennis Morgan] (*Tommy*), Marla Shelton (*Jane Lansing*), Inez Palange (*Mrs. Ramandi*), Charles Judels (*Mr. Ramandi*), Edward Norris (*Guido*), Fay Helm (*Marge*), Frank Puglia (*Tony*).

Too many loose ends within an implausible story burden this film about a wimpy high society boy pulled out of the bay in San Francisco by a kind Italian fisherman. The man takes the kid under his wing and tries to show him how to be a real man. Dean falls in love with the daughter, Lindsay, who is a nurse by day and studying to be an opera singer at night. They get involved with a minor mob scam, but he grows up and she finds him in the weak ending. One decent scene is the fire on the bay at the end as the two clinch.

p, Lucien Hubbard, Michael Fessier; d, Errol Taggert; w, Fessier; ph, Leonard Smith; m, Dr. William Axt; ed, John B. Rogers; m/l, Gus Kahn.

Drama   **(PR:A   MPAA:NR)**

SONG OF THE DRIFTER**   (1948) 53m MON bw

Jimmy Wakely, Dub "Cannonball" Taylor, Mildred Coles, Patsy Moran, Bud Osborne, William Ruhl, Marshall Reed, Frank LaRue, Carl Mathews, Steve Clark, Wheaton Chambers, Bob Woodward, Dick Reinhart, Cliffie Stone, Arthur "Fiddlin'" Smith, Wayne Burson, Homer Bill Callahan.

Wakely manages to squeeze in several songs as he saves the town's water supply from the nefarious types out to poison it. Average singing oater too short to get very irritating.

p, Louis Gray; d, Lambert Hillyer; w, Frank H. Young; ph, Harry Neumann; ed, Fred Maguire; md, Eddie Kay; art d, Vin Taylor.

Western   **(PR:A   MPAA:NR)**

SONG OF THE EAGLE**   (1933) 70m PAR bw

Charles Bickford (*Nails Anderson*), Richard Arlen (*Bill Hoffman*), Jean Hersholt (*Otto Hoffman*), Mary Brian (*Elsa Krenzmeyer*), Louise Dresser (*Emma Hoffman*), Andy Devine (*Mud*), George E. Stone (*Gus*), Gene Morgan (*Charlie*), Bert Sprotte (*Emil Krenzmeyer*), George Hoffman (*August Hoffman*), Julie Haydon (*Gretchen*), Harry Walker (*Nolly*).

Story is about beer, not animals, nor is it a musical, so the title is a complete misnomer. It focuses on the efforts of how certain groups wanted complete control after liquor was made legal again after Prohibition. It shows the time when it was illegal, the closing of bars, and the battles for the illegal liquor territory that followed. To give the plot an anchor, story centers around a family and the brewery they run. It shows how making it legal almost wiped out first the father, then the son because they wouldn't join forces with the racketeers. There is a minor flaw in the film when it shows the Jess Willard-Jack Dempsey fight from Toledo being broadcast on radio into a speakeasy. The pair fought before the Prohibition era.

p, Charles R. Rogers; d, Ralph Murphy; w, Casey Robinson, Willard Mack (based on a story by Gene Towne, Graham Baker); ph, Henry Sharp; ed, Joseph Kane.

Drama   **(PR:A   MPAA:NR)**

SONG OF THE FLAME*½   .   (1930) 72m FN-WB bw

Alexander Gray (*Prince Volodya*), Bernice Claire (*Aniuta, the Flame*), Noah Beery, Sr (*Konstantin*), Alice Gentle (*Natasha*), Bert Roach (*Count Boris*), Inez Courtney (*Grusha*), Shep Camp (*Officer*), Ivan Linow (*Konstantin's Pal*), Janina Smolinska (*Dancer*).

Expensively produced. Gordon Rigby did an injustice to the play by Oscar Hammerstein II. It's a boring story of how a simple peasant girl causes a revolution just by singing "Song of the Flame." She then falls in love with a Russian prince who is taken by the mob. To save him, she must give up her virtue to the lecherous Noah Beery. Songs include: "The Cossack Love Song," "Song of the Flame" (Oscar Hammerstein II, Herbert Stothart), "Petrograd," "Liberty Song," "The Goose Hangs High," "Passing Fancy," "One Little Drink" (Grant Clarke, Harry Akst, Ed Ward), "When Love Calls" (Ward).

d, Alan Crosland; w, Gordon Rigby (based on the musical play by Oscar Hammerstein II, Otto Harbach, Herbert Stothart, George Gershwin); ph, Lee Garmes (Technicolor); m, Hammerstein; ed, Al Hall; md, Leo F. Forbstein; set d, Anton Grot; cos, Edward Stevenson; ch, Jack Haskell.

Musical   **(PR:A   MPAA:NR)**

SONG OF THE FOREST** (1963, USSR) 95m Dovzhenko/Artkino c
(LESNAYA PESNYA)

Raisa Nedashkovskaya *(Mavka)*, V. Sidorchuk *(Lukash)*, P. Vesklyarov *(Uncle Lev)*, V. Rudin *(Spirit of the Forest)*, V. Kvitka *(Forest Fire)*, V. Gubenko *(Lukash's Mother)*, R. Pirozhenko *(Kilina)*, R. Doroshenko, A. Rogovtseva *(Nymphs)*, Lyudmila Marchenko *(Kuts)*, N. Tayenko *(Water Sprite)*, Ye. Kharchenko *("Fever")*, V. Maksimenko *("One Who Sits on the Rocks")*, Borya Voblyy, Yura Barantsev *(Kilina's Children)*, Ira Semko, Seryozha Shiman.

A fantasy film has a water nymph in love with a simple country fellow, Sidorchuk, who is forced to wed the nasty Pirozhenko. To punish the boy for turning away from the nymph, the Spirit of the Forest changes him into a wolf. However, the nymph's love for him returns him to human form, but she in turn gets the wrath of Pirozhenko who turns her into a weeping willow tree. Sidorchuk is ordered to chop down the tree, but the Forest Fire who also loves the nymph embraces her, turning her into a bright ball of fire.

d&w, Viktor Ivchenko; ph, A. Prokopenko; m, I. Shamo; ed, L. Mkhitary-ants; md, I. Klyucharyov; art d, V. Agranov; cos, Ya. Dobrovolskaya; spec eff, V. Kurach, V. Deminskiy; ch, Ye. Vislotskaya.

Fantasy   (PR:A   MPAA:NR)

SONG OF THE FORGE** (1937, Brit.) 82m BUT bw

Stanley Holloway *(Joe/Sir William Barrett)*, Lawrence Grossmith *(Ben Dalton)*, Eleanor Fayre *(Sylvia Brent)*, Davy Burnaby *(Auctioneer)*, C. Denier Warren *(Farmer George)*, Arthur Chesney *(Huckleberry)*, Aubrey Fitzgerald *(Oldest Inhabitant)*, Hal Walters *(Sam Tucker)*, Charles Hayes *(Mayor)*, Ian Wilson *(Albert Meek)*, Hay Plumb *(Assistant)*, Bruce Gordon *(Ted Salter)*, Edward Hodge, Mervyn Johns, Bert Weston, Frank Tilton, L. MacArthur Gordon, Stanley Radcliffe, Colin Kent, Wensley Russell, Shaun Desmond, Jack Morris, Ailsa Buchanan, Ambrose Day, Stanley Vine, Patrick Barry, The Rodney Hudson Dancing Girls.

Holloway plays a dual role here, the village blacksmith and also his son who is disowned by his father when he wants to go off to become an engineer. Years later, when the son has become an automobile baron, he keeps his father from going to the poor farm and the two are reconciled. Holloway's performance is the best thing here.

p, Wilfred Noy, Norman Hope-Bell; d, Henry Edwards; w, H. Fowler Mear (based on a story by J.D. Lewin); ph, Desmond Dickinson.

Musical   (PR:A   MPAA:NR)

SONG OF THE GRINGO** (1936) 62m GN bw (GB: THE OLD CORRAL)

Tex Ritter, Joan Woodbury, Fuzzy Knight, Monte Blue, Richard Adams, Warner Richmond, Martin Garralaga, Al Jennings, William Desmond, Glenn Strange, Budd Buster, Murdock McQuarrie, Ethan Laidlaw, Slim Whitaker, Edward Cassidy, Earl Dwire, Jack Kirk, Bob Burns, Forrest Taylor, Robert Fiske, White Flash the Horse.

This was the first western for Ritter, whom many feel looked most like a real cowboy compared to the other two singing cowboys, Roy Rogers and Gene Autry. His first starring role has him as a sheriff on the trail of a gang of claim jumpers. He gets help from an ex-train robber, Jennings, who teaches him all about shooting a gun to make sure he gets the bad guys.

p, Edward F. Finney; d, John P. McCarthy; w, McCarthy, Robert Emmett [Tansey], Al Jennings; ph, Gus Peterson, ed, Fred Bain.

Western   **Cas.**   (PR:A   MPAA:NR)

SONG OF THE ISLANDS** (1942) 73m FOX bw

Betty Grable *(Eileen O'Brien)*, Victor Mature *(Jefferson Harper)*, Jack Oakie *(Rusty Smith)*, Thomas Mitchell *(Dennis O'Brien)*, George Barbier *(Harper)*, Billy Gilbert *(Palola's Father)*, Hilo Hattie *(Palola)*, Lillian Porter *(Palola's Cousin)*, Hal K. Dawson *(John Rodney)*, Harry Owens and His Royal Hawaiians *(Themselves)*, Amy Cordone *(Specialty)*, Bruce Wong *(House Boy)*, Bobby Stone, Rudy Robles *(Native Boys)*, Alex Pollard *(Valet)*, Harold Lishman *(Old Native)*.

Plenty of laughs, songs, and dancing to show off Grable's best assets, her legs. Story has a Hawaiian cattle owner fighting with an Irish farmer for a strip of beach the rich man needs. While the two heads of the households battle, Grable and the land baron's son, Mature, get romantic. Both fathers vehemently object but finally realize they can't stop true love and bury the hatchet themselves. The men in the audience get to see plenty of Grable, while the woman get a chance to ogle at Mature. Songs include: "Blue Shadows and White Gardenias," "O'Brien Has Gone Hawaiian" (ack Gordon, Harry Owens)," "Sing Me a Song of the Islands" (Gordon, Harry Warren), "Down on Ami Ami Oni Oni Isle," "Maluna Malolo Mawaena," "What's Buzzin' Cousin" (Gordon, Owens), "Hawaiian War Chant" (Ralph Freed, Johnny Noble, Prince Leleiohaku of Hawaii), "Cockeyed Mayor of Kaunakakai" (R. Alex Anderson, Al Stillman), "Home on the Range" (standard).

p, William LeBaron; d, Walter Lang; w, Joseph Schrank, Robert Pirosh,

Robert Ellis, Helen Logan; ph, Ernest Palmer (Technicolor); ed, Robert Simpson; md, Alfred Newman; ch, Hermes Pan.

Musical   (PR:A   MPAA:NR)

SONG OF THE LITTLE ROAD (SEE: PATHER PANCHALI, 1956, India)

SONG OF THE LOON** (1970) 79m Sawyer/Hollywood Cinema c

John Iverson *(Cyrus Wheelwright)*, Morgan Royce *(Ephraim MacIver)*, Lancer Ward *(John)*, Jon Evans *(Montgomery)*, Brad Fredericks *(Mr. Calvin)*, John Kalfas *(Singing Heron)*, Martin Valez *(Acomas)*, Michael Traxon *(Tiasholah)*, Lucky Manning *(Bear-Who-Dreams)*, Brad Della Valle *(Tsi-Nokha)*, John Drake *(Luke)*, Robert Vilardi *(Plum-of-the-Night)*.

A story about homosexuality in the mountains of California set in the 1870's. Story is told in a flashback style as an old mountain man, Calvin, tells how he lost his lover, Royce, because he was upset about how other homosexuals kept changing partners. Finally the young man went to see an Indian medicine man who counseled him that it was all right to have more than one lover. His mind now at ease, Royce moved on to find others to share his love with, leaving the old man alone in the mountains.

p, Richard Amory; d, Andrew Herbert; w, Amory (based on the story SONG OF THE LOOM by Amory), ph, Robert Maxwell (Eastmancolor); ed, Andrew Herbert.

Drama   (PR:O   MPAA:NR)

SONG OF THE OPEN ROAD** (1944) 93m UA bw

Charlie McCarthy, Edgar Bergen, Jane Powell, W.C. Fields *(Themselves)*, Bonita Granville *(Bonnie)*, Peggy O'Neill *(Peggy)*, Jackie Moran *(Jack)*, Bill Christy *(Bill)*, Reginald Denny *(Director Curtis)*, Regis Toomey *(Connors)*, Rose Hobart *(Mrs. Powell)*, Sig Arno *(Spolo)*, Irene Tedrow *(Miss Casper)*, Pat Starling *(Herself)*, Charlotte Treadway, Sammy Kaye and His Orchestra, The Condos Brothers, The Hollywood Canteen Kids, The Lipham Four, Chuck Faulkner Band, Catron and Pop.

A sweet young 14-year-old named Jane Powell made her debut in this film, and they surrounded her with several cameos to help the project along although she didn't need anyone but herself. In a slight parody of Shirley Temple-Judy Garland, Powell is an immensely successful and popular child movie actress who is lonely. She makes a movie about the CCC fruit pickers (this was an actual group begun by Roosevelt to help youngsters have employment during the Depression), and grows to love the life. So when her next acting job is offered, she takes off, leaves her mother, Hobart, a note, jumps aboard her bike and pedals out to where the young people are doing their best to harvest a crop before it dies on the vine. Powell changes her hair color, rearranges her tresses, alters her name and goes unspotted by the youngsters, who include Granville, Moran, O'Neill and Christy. Powell is happier than she's been in years to be just one of the guys. However, she bites off more than she can chew in her attempt at being a bicycle repair person and ruins several of them. She also thinks she's a matchmaker and almost puts an end to a pair of romances due to her meddling. All the while, Hollywood is up in arms about where Powell has gone, wondering if she was the victim of foul play. There's a problem with the crop and they need help so Powell goes back to Hollywood, rounds up a bunch of members of the movie crowd (hence the cameos) and they all pitch in and help save the crop on the ranch. In between the details of this simple story, Fields does a monologue, Bergen and McCarthy do some special material, Kaye leads his band and the Condos Brothers dance. McCarthy and Fields had already established their radio feud on several shows and it continues here, although the insults are not nearly as good as the ones that played on the air. Powell sings four of the tunes–beautifully. Songs include: "Here It Is Monday," "Rollin' Down The Road," "Delightfully Dangerous," "Too Much In Love" (Walter Kent, Kim Gannon), "Hawaiian War Chant" (Johnny Noble, Prince Leleiohaku of Hawaii, Ralph Freed), "Carmona," "Notre Dame," and Schubert's "Marche Militaire." Good dance direction from George Dobbs.

p, Charles R. Rogers; d, S. Sylvan Simon; w, Albert Mannheimer (based on a story by Irving Phillips, Edward Verdier); ph, John W. Boyle; m, Walter Kent; ed, Truman K. Wood; md, Charles Previn; art d, Bernard Herzbrun; ch, George Dobbs.

Musical/Comedy   (PR:A   MPAA:NR)

SONG OF THE PLOUGH (SEE: COUNTY FAIR, 1933, Brit.)

SONG OF THE ROAD, 1940 (SEE: END OF THE ROAD, 1936, Brit.)

SONG OF THE ROAD*½ (1937, Brit.) 71m UK Films/Sound City bw

Bransby Williams *(Old Bill)*, Ernest Butcher *(Foreman)*, Muriel George *(Mrs. Trelawney)*, Davy Burnaby *(Mr. Keppel)*, Tod Slaughter *(Showman)*, John Turnbull *(Bristow)*, Edgar Driver *(Titch)*, Fred Schwartz *(Solomon)*, Percy Parsons *(Showman)*, Peggy Novak *(Wife)*, H.F. Maltby *(Proprietor)*, Johnnie Schofield, Ernest Jay, Robert English, F.B.J. Sharp, Phil Thomas, Polly the Horse.

The inexorable march of technology makes Williams and his horse, Polly, jobless, so they take to the road looking for work. Eventually they find security and happiness living in the country. Sentimental drama has its absorbing moments.

p, John Barter; d&w, John Baxter (based on a story by Michael Kent); ph, John Stumar.

Drama   (PR:A   MPAA:NR)

SONG OF THE ROAD, THE, 1958 (SEE: PATHER PANCHALI, 1958, India)

SONG OF THE SADDLE**   (1936) 58m FN-WB bw

Dick Foran (*Frank Wilson, Jr.*), Alma Lloyd (*Jen Coburn*), Charles Middleton (*Phineas P. Hook*), Addison Richards (*Frank Wilson, Sr.*), Eddie Shubert (*Jake Bannion*), Monte Montague (*Simon Bannion*), Victor Potel (*Little Cassino*), Kenneth Harlan (*Marshal*), Myrtle Stedman (*Mrs. Coburn*), George Ernest (*Frank Wilson*), Pat West (*Curley*), James Farley (*Tom Coburn*), Bud Osborne (*Porter*), Julian Rivero (*Jose*), Bonita Granville (*Little Jen*), William Desmond (*Tim*), Bob Kortman, Roy Rogers, Bob Nolan, Tim Spencer, Hugh Farr, Carl Farr (*Sons of the Pioneers*).

Warner Bros. decided to take advantage of Foran's voice this time. In his second western, he is billed as the "Singing Kid." Although his voice is nice and new, the plot line isn't. When not pushing his vocal chords, Foran is on the trail of a band of murderers. They killed their father 10 years earlier and he wants revenge on all of them. Not only does Foran handle such songs as "Underneath a Western Sky" and "Vengeance" (by M.K. Jerome, Jack Scholl, Ted Fiorito) with ease, he's not too bad on his horse, either.

p, Bryan Foy; d, Louis King; w, William Jacobs; ph, Dan Clark; ed, Harold McLernon; md, Leo F. Forbstein; art d, Esdras Hartley; m/l, M.K. Jerome, Jack Scholl, Ted Fiorito.

Western   (PR:A   MPAA:NR)

SONG OF THE SARONG*½   (1945) 65m UNIV bw

Nancy Kelly (*Sharon*), William Gargan (*Drew*), Eddie Quillan (*Tony*), Fuzzy Knight (*Pete*), George Dolenz (*Kalo*), George Cleveland (*Reemis*), Mariska Aldrich (*Mahu*), Morgan Wallace (*Adams*), Larry Keating (*Potter*), Robert Barron (*Jolo*), Pete Katchenaro (*Servant*), Jack Slattery (*Announcer*), Silverheels Smith [Jay Silverheels] (*Spearman*), Al Kikume (*Guard*), George Bruggeman (*Native*), Clarence Lung (*Leader*), William Desmond, Pete Sosso, Jack Curtis (*Councillors*).

It's part comedy, part adventure, part musical, but all the parts don't add up to much. Gargan is a happy-go-lucky fellow, always looking for a quick buck. He takes an assignment of trekking to a distant island to snatch some pearls for $1,000,000. Problem is, they are under heavy guard by ruthless savages. The natives are ruled by Kelly, who shimmies through some dances, including one to save Gargan from burning at the stake. Songs include: "Pied Pipers from Swingtown" (Jack Brooks, sung by Eddie Quillan, Fuzzy Knight), "Ridin, on the Crest of a Cloud" (Brooks), "Lovely Luana" (Don Raye, Gene DePaul, sung by Nancy Kelly, The Native Girls), "Island of the Moon" (Raye, DePaul), "Camptown Races" (Stephen Foster, sung by Kelly, William Gargan).

p, Gene Lewis; d, Harold Young; w, Lewis; ph, Maury Gertsman; m, Edward Ward; ed, Fred R. Feitshan, Jr.; md, Edgar Fairchild; art d, John B. Goodman, Harold McArthur; ch, Carlos Romero.

Musical   (PR:A   MPAA:NR)

SONG OF THE SIERRAS*½   (1946) 55m MON bw

Jimmy Wakely, Lee "Lasses" White, Jean Carlin, Jack Baxley, Iris Clive, Jonathan Black, Bob Docking, Jasper Palmer, Zon Murray, Ray Jones, Budd Buster, Billy Dix, Robert Gilbert, Horace Mathews, Brad Slavin, Jack Rivers, Wesley Tuttle and His Texas Stars, Carl Sepulveda, Jesse Ashlock, Artie Ortego.

Wakely catches and breaks wild broncs for the races, finding time to croon some songs along the way. For fans of singing cowboys only.

p&d, Oliver Drake; w, Elmer Clifton (based on a story by Drake); ph, Marcel LePicard; ed, Ralph Dixon; md, Frank Sanucci.

Western   (PR:A   MPAA:NR)

SONG OF THE SIERRAS, 1947   (SEE: SPRINGTIME IN THE SIERRAS, 1947)

SONG OF THE SOUTH****   (1946) 94m Disney/RKO c

Ruth Warrick (*Sally*), James Baskett (*Uncle Remus/Voice of Brer Fox*), Bobby Driscoll (*Johnny*), Luana Patten (*Ginny*), Lucile Watson (*Grandmother*), Hattie McDaniel (*Aunt Tempy*), Glenn Leedy (*Toby*), George Nokes, Gene Holland (*The Favers Boys*), Erik Rolf (*John*), Mary Field (*Mrs. Favers*), Anita Brown (*Maid*), Nicodemus Stewart (*Voice of Brer Bear*), Johnny Lee (*Voice of Brer Rabbit*).

This Disney film, which broke new ground in animation techniques, is paradoxically a genuine charmer, and the studio's most controversial production. The story opens on the Reconstruction-era South. Driscoll is a little boy who goes with his mother (Warrick) to live on his grandmother's plantation after his parents separate. Driscoll is upset by things he cannot understand and decides to run away. Not far into his journey, Driscoll happens upon Baskett, a former slave, telling some folk tales to a group of black children. After learning Driscoll is running away, Baskett decides to trick the lad into returning home. He tells the boy he would like to run away as well, but first must stop home for a few things. As Baskett starts packing, he tells Driscoll a story. This segues into a marvelous combination of live action and animation, as Baskett appears in a brightly colored cartoon setting, singing "Zip-a-dee Doo-Dah" (penned by Allie Wruble and Ray Gilbert, this lively tune won an Oscar for Best Song). After Baskett encounters Brer Rabbit (voiced by Lee), the animation takes over completely. Brer Rabbit is also running away from home, but he's caught in a trap left for him by Brer Fox (voiced by Baskett). The clever rabbit catches the attention of Brer Bear (voiced by Stewart), convincing the slow-witted creature he's making money working as a scarecrow. Brer Bear eagerly takes Brer Rabbit's place, much to Brer Fox's chagrin. Switching back to live action, Baskett winds up the story by telling Driscoll one can't run away from troubles. Driscoll returns to Warrick, but continues to visit his new friend. Later Driscoll saves Patten, a girl his age, from two nasty boys. He asks Baskett for advice on how to deal with the bullies, and, once again, the film switches to an animated tale. Brer Fox and Brer Bear have made a tar figure, hoping to catch Brer Rabbit. When the figure ignores Brer Rabbit's friendly greetings, the gregarious bunny punches its tar nose. Soon he's trapped in the tar, just where Brers Fox and Bear want him. Thinking quickly, Brer Rabbit pleads for his life, begging not to be tossed in the briar patch. Of course, his two captors ignore this wish, and again Brer Rabbit is free. Later Driscoll uses this lesson when he's confronted by the bullies. They threaten to tell his mother about a dog Driscoll has saved from the two boys' hands. Driscoll begs them to do anything but tell their own mother. Like their cartoon counterparts, the bullies fall for this and end up being spanked. Warrick gives Driscoll a birthday party, and the boy invites Patten. When she is late, Driscoll finds the two bullies have pushed her in the mud, ruining her new dress. Patten is crushed, but Baskett happens on the children and tells them another story. Brer Rabbit is once more in the clutches of his two foes. As they prepare him for dinner, Brer Rabbit tells them of his secret "Laughing Place." Brers Fox and Bear demand to be taken there, but Brer Rabbit fools them once again. He takes them to a giant beehive, and as Brers Fox and Bear are attacked by the tiny winged creatures, Brer Rabbit breaks out in laughter. After all this is *his* laughing place. Driscoll and Patten enjoy the story, but Warrick arrives in anger. She doesn't like all the time her son is spending with Baskett and demands the old storyteller never see Driscoll again. Baskett is hurt by this, so he decides to leave the area. Driscoll sees his friend going and tries to stop him. He runs after Baskett's horse and buggy, but attracts the attention of a grazing bull. The bull tosses Driscoll, knocking the boy out. Warrick sends for Driscoll's father, but only Baskett's return is able to cure the lad. Driscoll's parents decide to stay together, while Baskett becomes less of a surrogate father and more of a friend to the youngster. The film closes with Baskett, Driscoll, and Patten walking down the road singing as the cartoon characters happily join them. SONG OF THE SOUTH's cartoon sequences are as fine as anything produced by the Disney animators. The live action projected into a cartoon setting was more than a gimmick, as the actors and caricatures were carefully matched within the frame. Baskett's performance (for which he was awarded an honorary Oscar) makes the technique work all the better, as he interacts in a genuine manner with the cartoon characters. The live-action sequences are less successful than the animation. Though Driscoll and Patten are natural actors, these sections are a bit treacly, particularly the scenes at Driscoll's sickbed. This was not the first live-action film from Disney, but was the studio's biggest foray into the form at that time. Driscoll became their first official contract player, and the boy's natural charm even bowled over Walt Disney himself. Both studio executives and animators were astonished at how fond the normally bad-tempered man became of Driscoll. However, SONG OF THE SOUTH stirred up a good deal of controversy with its idyllic portrait of the Reconstruction, particularly with black Americans. Such groups as the NAACP and the National Urban League protested over the stereotypes presented in the film. Disney officials reacted to such criticism by stating their film was "...a sincere effort to depict American folklore, to put the Uncle Remus stories into pictures." Despite the controversy, SONG OF THE SOUTH proved to be a popular film and was one of the biggest box-office attractions in 1946. Aside from Baskett's honorary Oscar and the Best Song, there was also an Academy Award nomination for the musical score. The other songs include: "How Do You Do" (Robert McGimsey), "Song of the South" (Sam Coslow, Arthur Johnston), "Uncle Remus Said" (Elliot Daniel, Hy Heath, Johnny Lange), "Sooner or Later" (Charles Wolcott, Ray Gilbert), "Everybody Has a Laughing Place" (Allie Wrubel, Gilbert), "You'll Always Be the One I Love" (Sunny Skylar, Ticker Freeman), "Let the Rain Pour Down," "Who Wants to Live Like That?" (Foster Carling). In 1956 the film was rereleased, and again was a hit. However, in light of the collective mood of the country during the 1960s, the Disney studio decided to withdraw the film permanently for public screenings in 1970. Fortunately this was rescinded later the next year, and in 1972 Disney released SONG OF THE SOUTH to an overwhelming response. With new attitudes towards the dignity of black actors who played stereotyped roles, the film was seen by its critics in a proper historical context. Sadly, Driscoll's life was plagued by drugs and in 1968 he died from an overdose. Shortly before the 1972 rerelease his mother was quoted as saying: "It will be painful to see him on the screen, but it will be nice, all the same. He was a fine boy."

p, Walt Disney; d, Harve Foster (live action), Wilfred Jackson (cartoons); w, Dalton Raymond, Morton Grant, Maurice Rapf (based on *Tales of Uncle Remus* by Joel Chandler Harris, original story by Raymond, cartoon story, William Peet, Ralph Wright, George Stallings); ph, Gregg Toland (Technicolor); m, Daniele Amfitheatrof, Paul J. Smith; ed, William M. Morgan; md, Charles Wolcott; art d, Perry Ferguson; cos, Mary Wills; spec eff, Up Iwerks; animation, Milt Kahl, Erick Larson, Oliver M. Johnston, Jr., Les Clark, Marc Davis, John Lounsberry, Don Lusk, Tom Massey, Murray McClellan, Jack Campbell, Hal King, Harvey Toombs, Ken O'Brien, Al Coe, Hal Ambro, Cliff Nordberg, Rudy Larriva.

Animated Feature/Children's   **(PR:AAA   MPAA:NR)**

SONG OF THE THIN MAN***   (1947) 86m MGM bw

William Powell (*Nick Charles*), Myrna Loy (*Nora Charles*), Keenan Wynn (*Clarence "Clinker" Krause*), Dean Stockwell (*Nick Charles, Jr.*), Phillip Reed (*Tommy Drake*), Patricia Morison (*Phyllis Talbin*), Gloria Grahame (*Fran Page*), Jayne Meadows (*Janet Thayar*), Don Taylor (*Buddy Hollis*), Leon Ames (*Mitchell Talbin*), Ralph Morgan (*David I. Thayar*), Warner Anderson (*Dr. Monolaw*), William Bishop (*Al Amboy*), Bruce Cowling (*Phil Brant*), Bess Flowers (*Jessica Thayar*), Connie Gilchrist (*Bertha*), James Burke (*Callahan*), Tom Trout (*Lewie the Shiv*), Henry Nemo (*The Neem*), Marie Windsor (*Helen Amboy*), Asta, Jr. (*Asta*), Tom Dugan (*Davis the Cop*), John Sheehan (*Manager*), Lennie Bremen, Lyle Latell (*Mugs*), Eddie Simms, Jimmy O'Gatty (*Hoods*), James Flavin (*Reardon the Cop*), Bill Harbach (*Whitley*), George Anderson (*Dunne*), Donald Kerr (*News Photographer*), Alan Bridge (*Nagle the Policeman*), Esther Howard (*Counterwoman*), Harry Burns (*Italian*), William Roberts (*Pete*), Clarke Hardwicke (*Bert*), Henry Sylvester (*Butler*), Matt McHugh (*Taxi Driver*), Clinton Sundburg (*Desk Clerk*), Gregg Barton (*Nurse*), Earl Hodgins (*Baggage Man*), Howard Negley (*Kramer*), George Sorel (*Headwaiter*), Charles Sullivan (*Sergeant*), Robert Strickland (*Musician*), Jeffrey Sayre (*Croupier*), Morris Ankrum (*Inspector*), Maria San Marco (*Oriental Girl*), George Chan (*Young Chinese*), Jerry Fragnol (*Young Nick at Age 5*).

The last and least of the long-lived series has Powell and Loy attending a party on board a gambling ship. When the bandleader is murdered Powell at first doesn't want to take the case, even when the owner of the ship, Cowling, who had argued with the bandleader beforehand and who is now the chief suspect, asks him to help clear his name. But when someone takes a shot at the ship owner, Powell's curiosity is piqued and he throws himself into the investigation. He enlists the help of musician Wynn and soon has put together an interesting list of suspects, including gambler Bishop, who owed the dead man $12,000; clarinet player Taylor; Morgan, the father of Cowling's fiancee; and Grahame, a singer the victim had jilted. Grahame is herself murdered and the obligatory call goes out to gather all the suspects in one room for Powell to expose the murderer. It turns out to be Ames, the dead man's business manager, with whom he had quarreled over the bandleader's attentions toward his wife, Morison. The formula had definitely gone stale by this time, the sixth THIN MAN film and the 13th and last Powell-Loy teaming in as many years. As always with the two stars, the film is well worth watching, but it had come down a long way from the first series entry more than a decade before. The writing doesn't crackle and spark like the earlier films, and the reliance on characters like Wynn to provide some of the laughs only points up how flat the lead duo had become with familiarity. Wynn does do a tolerable job here, and Grahame is always fun to watch, and here she sings a sultry song for good measure. The last entries of series are, as a rule, bad. This one breaks the mold and, while hardly in a league with the earlier films, it can hold its own against any B movie mystery of the period. (See THIN MAN series, Index.)

p, Nat Perrin; d, Eddie Buzzell; w, Perrin, Steve Fisher, James O'Hanlon, Harry Crane (based on a story by Stanley Roberts from characters created by Dashiell Hammett); ph, Charles Rosher; m, David Snell; ed, Gene Ruggiero; art d, Cedric Gibbons, Randall Duell; set d, Edwin B. Willis, Alfred E. Spencer; m/l, "You're Not so Easy to Forget," Herb Magidson, Ben Oakland (sung by Gloria Grahame).

Crime   **(PR:A   MPAA:NR)**

SONG OF THE TRAIL*½   (1936) 68m Ambassador bw

Kermit Maynard (*Jim*), Evelyn Brent (*Myra*), George Hayes (*Hobson*), Fuzzy Knight (*Pudge*), Wheeler Oakman (*Arnold*), Antoinette Lees [Andrea Leeds] (*Betty*), Lee Shumway (*Stone*), Roger Williams (*Miller*), Ray Gallagher (*Blore*), Charles McMurphy (*Curtis*), Horace Murphy (*Sheriff*), Lynette London (*Marie*), Bob McKenzie, Frank McCarroll, Artie Ortego, Rocky the Horse.

In the beginning of this western, some rodeo clips show off Maynard's past cowboy skills. Story has Lees' father swindled in a crooked card game and it's up to Maynard and Knight to save the old man. They not only have to save him from the outlaws, but also from the local authorities. Lots of killing and chases, but nothing new to spur or warrant any real interest.

p, Maurice Conn; d, Russell Hopton; w, George Sayre, Barry Barringer (based on the story "Playing With Fire" by James Oliver Curwood); ph, Arthur Reed; ed, Richard G. Wray.

Western   **Cas.**   **(PR:A   MPAA:NR)**

SONG OF THE WASTELAND*   (1947) 58m MON bw

Jimmy Wakely, Lee "Lasses" White, Dottye Brown, John James, Henry Hall, Marshall Reed, Holly Bane, Pierce Lyden, Chester Conklin, Ted Adams, John Carpenter, George Chesebro, Jack Rivers, Milburn Morante, The Saddle Pals [Johnny Bond, Dick Rinehart, Rivers Lewis], Jesse Ashlock, Cotton Thompson, Ray Jones, Gary Garrett.

Vigilantes give Wakely and his pals a hard time but Wakely sees that law and order are restored, singing all the while. Indistinguishable from countless other singing oaters.

p, Barney A. Sarecky; d, Thomas Carr; w, J. Benton Cheney; ph, Harry Neumann; ed, Fred Maguire; md, Edward Kay.

Western   **(PR:A   MPAA:NR)**

SONG OF THE WEST**   (1930) 78m WB c

John Boles (*Stanton*), Vivienne Segal (*Virginia*), Marie Wells (*Lotta*), Joe E. Brown (*Hasty*), Sam Hardy (*Davolo*), Marion Byron (*Penny*), Edward Martindel (*Colonel*), Eddie Gribbon (*Sgt. Major*), Rudolph Cameron (*Lt. Singleton*).

Slow moving drama of Oscar Hammerstein II and Laurence Stalling's operetta did not make a smooth transition to film. Boles and Segal were also victimized by poor sound recording and there was minimal character development. The operetta, set in the West during the 1849 Gold Rush era, tells of a couple's travels across the U.S. and how they arrive at San Francisco. Set in gambling saloons of the time, to give plenty of chances for singing and dancing. Songs include: "The Bride Was Dressed in White," "Hay Straw," "West Wind," "The One Girl" (Vincent Youmans, Oscar Hammerstein II), "Come Back to Me" (Grant Clarke, Harry Akst).

d, Ray Enright; w, Harvey Thew (based on the operetta "Rainbow" by Laurence Stallings, Oscar Hammerstein II); ph, Dev Jennings; ed, George Marks.

Musical   **(PR:A   MPAA:NR)**

SONG OVER MOSCOW**   (1964, USSR) 92m Lenfilm/Artkino c
                                                      (CHERYOMUSHKI)

Olga Zabotkina (*Lida*), Vladimir Vasilyev (*Boris*), M. Khotuntseva (*Masha*), Grigoriy Bortnikov (*Sasha*), Svetlana Zhivankova (*Lyusya*), V. Zemlyanikin (*Sergey*), Vasiliy Merkuryev (*Drebednev*), Marya Polbentseva (*Vava*), Ye. Leonov (*Barabashkin*), Fyodor Nikitin (*Baburov*), Konstantin Sorokin (*Kurochkin*), R. Zelyonaya (*Kurochkina*), S. Filippov (*Mylkin*), E. Treyvas (*Mylkina*), M. Pugovkin (*Kovalyov*), A. Aleksandrovich, A. Zilbert, Z. Rogozikova, T. Glinkina, G. Mnatsakanova, E. Khil (*Vocalists*).

Russian operetta has Zabotkina, a woman professor, who lives with her father in a typically small apartment. Happiness hits their household as they get to move to a bigger living quarter. Also there is Zhivankova, who has Vasilyev chasing her and newly married Khotuntseva and Bortnikov. Their happiness quickly fades when it turns out their superintendent will not give them the keys to the apartments. After some digging, Zabotkina finds out that a minor official has been permitted to expand his apartment to include theirs. With help from friends, they right the wrong that has befallen them. Now everyone can enjoy a peaceful existence in the new building.

d, Gerbert Rappaport; w, I. Glikman (based on the operetta "Moskva. Cheryomushki" by Dmitriy Dmitriyevich Shostakovich, Vladimir Zakharovich Mass, Mikhail Abramovich Chervinskiy); ph, Anatoliy Nazarov; m, Shostakovich; ed, K. Kozyreva; art d, M. Gaukhman-Sverdlov; cos, L. Shildknekht; spec eff, M. Shamkovich, M. Krotkin; makeup, M. Matusova, N. Elenbogen.

Musical   **(PR:A   MPAA:NR)**

SONG TO REMEMBER, A***½   (1945) 113m COL c

Paul Muni (*Professor Joseph Elsner*), Merle Oberon (*George Sand*), Cornel Wilde (*Frederic Chopin*), Stephen Bekassy (*Franz Liszt*), Nina Foch (*Constantia*), George Coulouris (*Louis Pleyel*), Sig Arno (*Henri Dupont*), Howard Freeman (*Kalbrenner*), George Macready (*Alfred DeMusset*), Claire Dubrey (*Mme. Mercier*), Frank Puglia (*Mons. Jollet*), Fern Emmett (*Mme. Lambert*), Sybil Merritt (*Isabelle Chopin*), Ivan Triesault (*Mons. Chopin*), Fay Helm (*Mme. Chopin*), Dawn Bender (*Isabelle Chopin, age 9*), Maurice Tauzin (*Chopin, age 10*), Roxy Roth (*Paganini*), Peter Cusanelli (*Balzac*), William Challee (*Titus*), William Richardson (*Jan*), Alfred Paix (*Headwaiter*), Charles Wagenheim, Paul Zaeremba (*Waiters*), Charles LaTorre (*Postman*), Earl Easton (*Albert*), Gregory Gaye (*Young Russian*), Walter Bonn (*Major Domo*), Henry Sharp (*Russian Count*), Zoia Karabanova (*Countess*), Michael Visaroff (*Russian Governor*), John George (*Servant*), Ian Wolfe (*Pleyel's Clerk*), Lucy Von Boden (*Window Washer*), Norma Drury

(Duchess of Orleans), Alfred Allegro, Cosmo Sardo *(Lackeys)*, Al Luttringer *(De La Croux)*, Darren McGavin *(Man)*, Eugene Bordon *(Duc of Orleans)*.

As a fictional tale of a Polish composer who gives his all for his music, this is a good picture. As a biography, it bears as much resemblance to the truth as NIGHT AND DAY did for the life of Cole Porter. Miklos Rozsa adapted Chopin's music and Jose Iturbi played it so well that Wilde was offered several concert engagements after the film came out and did enormous business. Muni was billed over everyone else in this, his first and only Technicolor movie. Muni gave an over-the-top performance that seemed to have no direction from Vidor and that made the whole thing slightly out of whack. The decor of the film was exquisite but the facts were so mangled by the screenwriters that it can only be taken as entertainment, not reality. Chopin was only 39 when he died, a frail man. Wilde is far too healthy-looking to make anyone believe he was suffering from the ravages of tuberculosis but he did it well enough to receive an Oscar nomination, one of several accorded the film. The others were to Marischka for his story, to Rozsa's musical adaptation of Chopin's works, to Stoloff's musical direction and to Gaudio's rich, opulent cinematography. If one is to believe the screenplay, Wilde is a patriotic Pole who spends his off-hours fighting the Czarist forces that control the country. He tosses in his lot with the revolutionary groups and encounters the disappointment of his teacher, Muni, who wishes Wilde would forget about all the political nonsense and just concentrate on making beautiful music. Muni's role is based on a real teacher-composer who wrote "Sabat Mater" and was well respected during his life. Muni is only peripherally involved with the undercurrent against the Russians, but Wilde incurs the wrath of a Russian by refusing to play a request during a concert, and his days are numbered. Wilde and Muni flee Poland and race to Paris. Muni knows that his student is a genius and feels he must be introduced to the people who matter in France so he arranges to have Wilde play for Bekassy (Liszt) and his genius is instantly recognized. With the help of Bekassy, Wilde meets Coulouris, a big-time publisher-manager, and an agreement is made for Coulouris to handle the young composer. Wilde also meets Oberon, a famous novelist who has taken to writing under the male pseudonym of "George Sand" and to wearing pants. Oberon is a cold, selfish woman who dominates everyone around her and Wilde is no exception. A brief trip to her country house on the isle of Majorca turns into a long-time affair (it actually lasted 10 years). He would like to get back to Europe and raise money through his concert tours for his compatriots but she encourages him to stay on and continue writing. He pens many gorgeous pieces but his one glorious work, "Polonaise," remains unfinished. Foch is one of the chiefs in the Polish revolutionary group and she calls upon Muni to say that some of the bosses in the organization have been tossed into jail by the Russians and money is needed to secure their release. Muni tells Wilde that it is up to him to help with the fund-raising, so Coulouris is contacted to set up an exhaustive tour for Wilde; the money realized will be donated to the cause. When Oberon hears that Wilde has agreed to do this, she pulls away from him and he goes off on the tour and plays what he's written of the "Polonaise" at each performance. In the end, his health becomes weak and finally falls apart altogether and he dies. The best thing that happened as a result of this movie is that the public had an opportunity to hear many of Chopin's works and the record sales were enormous with Iturbi's version of the "Polonaise" making a few record charts. Chopin was not a revolutionary, and when he and Sand ended their affair, she wanted to rekindle the flame but he was against it. Wilde looked forward to working with Muni and was surprised when the older actor did not give him any aid in the role. This may have been because Muni's first choice for the part was his pal, Glenn Ford, who had volunteered for the Marines and was not available. Wilde was just 30 years old and appearing in his 10th film. He was under contract to Fox and loaned out to Columbia for this part which was to make him a star. The Muni character was totally altered to fit the needs of the screenplay. He did not go to Paris with Chopin, nor did he battle with Sand for control of the composer. In real life, Chopin never embarked on that tour which took his life and the only place he played, outside of Paris and Majorca, was London. There are so many historical inaccuracies that it would take pages to list them. There are also many inadvertent cringing lines in the script that audiences bypassed in the 1940s, perhaps due to the desire to see movies other than war films. Chopin's music included: "Valse In D Flat (Minute Waltz)," "Mazurka In B Flat, Opus 7, No.1," "Fantasie Impromptu, Opus 66," "Etude In A Flat, Opus 25, No.1 (partial)," "Polonaise In A Flat, Opus 53 (partial)," "Scherzo In B Flat Minor," "Etude In C Minor, Opus 10, No.12," "Nocturne In C Minor, Opus 48, No.1," "Nocturne In E Flat, Opus 9, No.2," "Valse In A Flat, Opus 34, No.1," "Ballade In A Flat, Opus 47," "Waltz In C Sharp Minor, Opus 64, No.2," "Berceuse In D Flat, Opus 57," and "Etude In E, Opus 10, No.3" (this served as the movie's theme)..) The music supervisor was Mario Silva and no one could fault him for any of the music. In a small role, note Darren McGavin, who also made the movie FEAR in 1945, his first year in films.

p, Louis F. Edelman; d, Charles Vidor; w, Sidney Buchman (based on the story by Ernst Marischka); ph, Tony Gaudio, Allen M. Davey (Technicolor); m, adapted by Miklos Rozsa (performed by Jose Iturbi); ed, Charles Nelson; md, M.W. Stoloff; art d, Lionel Banks, Van Nest Polglase; set d, Frank Tuttle; cos, Walter Plunkett, Travis Banton; makeup, Clay Campbell.

Musical/Biography   **(PR:A MPAA:NR)**

SONG WITHOUT END*½   (1960) 145m COL c

Dirk Bogarde *(Franz Liszt)*, Capucine *(Princess Carolyne)*, Genevieve Page *(Countess Marie)*, Patricia Morison *(George Sand)*, Ivan Desny *(Prince Nicholas)*, Martita Hunt *(Grand Duchess)*, Lou Jacobi *(Potin)*, Albert Rueprecht *(Prince Felix Lichnowsky)*, Marcel Dalio *(Chelard)*, Lyndon Brook *(Richard Wagner)*, Walter Rilla *(Archbishop)*, Hans Unterkirchner *(Czar)*, E. Erlandsen *(Thalberg)*, Alex Davion *(Chopin)*, Katherine Squire *(Anna Liszt)*.

Here is yet another musical biography that toys with truth and dispenses with it entirely in places in order to make dramatic points. Charles Vidor began directing the film and when he fell ill (and eventually died), the chores were taken up by George Cukor. Liszt had been seen often on screen and will, no doubt, be seen again. Stephen Bekassy played him in Columbia's fraudulent biography of Chopin, A SONG TO REMEMBER, and Fritz Leiber played the genius in the 1943 version of PHANTOM OF THE OPERA. The story, as written by Millard, tells of Bogarde, a sensational success in his 20's as a pianist. He lives to the hilt, taking women with abandon and being as profligate as any human being can be. At the same time, he is deeply troubled by his decision to turn to a career in music because his mother, Squire, wishes he would have entered a seminary. Bogarde is tired of performing other writers' works and yearns to clef his own music. At the same time, he is feeling equal ennui in his relationship with his current amour, Page, a Countess. Bogarde is the toast of the continent and accolades are hurled at him from every corner. Capucine, a Russian princess (in her first movie after a successful modeling career in Paris), recognizes that Bogarde has talents beyond what he is showing. Page had left a husband and children in order to be wth Bogarde, and Capucine, also in love with him, can't secure a divorce for her mate. Bogarde's manager is the excitable Jacobi and he arrives at Bogarde's place with Davion (Chopin) and George Sand (Morison) and tells Bogarde that there's a new pianist in Europe who is getting rave reviews. This is Erlandsen and unless Bogarde quits resting on his laurels, he will soon fall from critical favor. That is the spur that gets Bogarde back to performing. When Bogarde and Capucine fall in love, they appeal to the Czar to arrange a divorce for her so they can be wed in a church. That the Catholic Church would not put up with this kind of plea is overlooked by the script. The Czar says okay but a local prelate tells them nix, even though Capucine had petitioned for an annullment on the grounds that she was coerced into her first marriage. The annullment is eventually granted and they are about to be married when the whole thing falls apart due to her husband and it doesn't work out. Liszt ultimately loses her, takes Holy Orders and enters the church where he becomes an abbe. The truth of the matter is that Liszt broke up with Page four years before meeting the Capucine character and those two lived together for more than a decade before they were to marry around his 50th birthday. Capucine's husband died before Liszt went into the church so it would have been fine for them to wed but they didn't and...oh, well, there are just so many errors they go on for days. While there is much to fault in the story, there's no criticizing the music. Sukman's adaptations, with consultant Abram Chasins and coordinator Victor Aller were excellent. The music was played by the Los Angeles Philharmonic and the Roger Wagner Chorale provided the throats, with Jorge Bolet doing the actual piano playing as Bogarde faked the finger movements. There was great luster to the production and lackluster in the music. Music from several composers included: "Mephisto Waltz," "Spozalizio," "Sonata In B Minor," "Un Sospiro," "Fantasy on Themes From 'Rigoletto,'" "Consolation In D Flat," "Liebestraum," "Les Preludes," "Piano Concerto No.1," "Hungarian Fantasy," "Venezia e Napoli," "Valse Oubliee," all by Liszt. Wagner contributed the "Pilgrim's Chorus" from "Tannhauser." Mendelssohn's "Rondo Capriccioso" was heard as well as Handel's "Largo," and Paganini's "La Campanella." "Rakoczy March" was arranged by Liszt and Beethoven's "Pathetique Symphony" and Bach's "Passacaglia In C Minor" were also heard. There were many bits and pieces in the score, including Schumann's "Carnaval" and Chopin's "Scherzo In B Flat Minor." Actually, only Liszt's version of Paganini's "Campanella" and his work on the "Rigoletto" quartet are heard in toto. Vidor died in early June, 1959, after having done about 10 to 15 percent of the movie so there is a definite style change from scene to scene and although Cukor did the lion's share, he took a smaller credit on screen. Bogarde himself disliked the picture. Sukman and Stoloff received Oscar nominations.

p, William Goetz; d, Charles Vidor, George Cukor; w, Oscar Millard; ph, James Wong Howe (CinemaScope, Technicolor); m, Franz Liszt, others, adaptation, Harry Sukman, performed by Jorge Boyet; ed, William A. Lyon; md, Morris Stoloff; art d, Walter Holscher; cos, Jean Louis.

Musical/Biography   **(PR:A MPAA:NR)**

SONG YOU GAVE ME, THE*½   (1934, Brit.) 86m BIP/Wardour bw

Bebe Daniels *(Mitzi Hansen)*, Victor Varconi *(Karl Linden)*, Claude Hulbert *(Tony Brandt)*, Lester Matthews *(Max Winter)*, Frederick Lloyd *(Baron Bobo)*, Eva Moore *(Grandmother)*, Iris Ashley *(Emmy)*, Walter Widdop *(Singer)*.

British International wanted some of that Hollywood glitter for its own films, so Daniels was cast in the lead role. She is a secretary, who has singer Varconi after her. His singing wins her in the end.

p, John Maxwell; d, Paul Stein; w, Clifford Grey (based on the play "The Song Is Ended" by Walter Reisch); ph, Claude Friese-Greene; ed, L.A. Appelbaum.

Musical   **(PR:A   MPAA:NR)**

SONGS AND BULLETS*½   (1938) 57m Spectrum/Stan Laurel bw

Fred Scott (*Melody Hardy*), Al St. John (*Fuzzy*), Alice Ardell (*Jeanette Du Mont*), Charles King (*Sheriff*), Karl Hackett (*Skelton*), Frank LaRue (*Morgan*), Budd Buster (*Zeke*), Dick Cramer (*Henchman*), Carl Mathews.

This was Stan Laurel's second effort as executive producer and he suffered the sophomoric jinx. Director Sam Newfield took Laurel's essay and made it into nothing. Scott sings in this typical western that has him break up a gang of cattle rustlers. Scott sings the five songs much better than he fights. Al St. John went on to become sidekick of the master of the whip, Lash LaRue in later films in the 1940s.

p, Jed Buell; d, Sam Newfield; w, Joseph O'Donnell, George Plympton (based on a story by Plympton); ph, Mack Stengler; ed, Helen Gurley, Robert Johns; m/l, Lew Porter.

Western   **Cas.**   **(PR:A   MPAA:NR)**

SONNY AND JED*   (1974, Ital.) 91m Loyola Cinematography-Terra K-Tel c (LA BANDA J.&S. CRONACA CRIMINALE DEL FAR WEST)

Tomas Milian (*Jed*), Susan George (*Sonny*), Telly Savalas (*Franciscus*), Rossana Yanny (*Linda*), Franco Giacobini (*Aparicito*), Eduardo Fajardo (*Garcia*), Herbert Fux (*Merril*), Laura Betti (*Donna Aparacito*), Arcuri Francesco, Alvaro De Luna, Werner Pochat, Luis Aller, Pilar Climent, Talleri Mario, Fedozzi Ruggero.

K-Tel should have stuck to putting out all those compilations of music hits instead of trying to pass off this spaghetti western as entertainment. The film works on the lovers as criminals bit, a la Bonnie and Clyde. Milian is a ruthless clod who robs rich Americans and Mexicans to help the poor peasants when not womanizing at night. George has led a sedate life and wants to experience life on the wild side. He takes her along, beats her incessantly, falls in love with her, and the two start terrorizing the rich of the countryside. She gains confidence and then starts beating him up. Savalas is the town marshal who wants to capture the pair but he is unsuccessful. The criminals always seem to face impossible odds when robbing, but manage to destroy whole armies to carry away their booty. Carry this one away forever.

p, Roberto Loyola; d, Sergio Corbucci; w, Sabatino Ciuffini, Mario Amendola, Adriano Bolzoni, Jose Maria Forque, Corbucci (based on a story by Corbucci); ph, Luis Cuadrado (Technicolor); m, Ennio Morricone; ed, Eugenio Alabiso; art d, Pietro Filippone.

Drama   **(PR:O   MPAA:R)**

SONNY BOY**   (1929) 70m WB bw

Davey Lee (*Sonny Boy*), Betty Bronson (*Aunt Winifred Canfield*), Edward Everett Horton (*Crandall Thorpe, Attorney*), Gertrude Olmstead (*Mary, Sonny Boy's Mother*), T. Murray (*Hamilton, Sonny Boy's Father*), Tommy "Tom" Dugan (*Mulcahy*), Jed Prouty (*Phil*), Edmund Breese (*Thorpe, Sr.*), Lucy Beaumont (*Mother Thorpe*), Al Jolson (*performer in film*).

Little Davey Lee steals the film with his cute smile while his parents wage a custody battle. After the film came out, everyone expected big things for the budding child star, but all the fame never materialized. Lee is the center of the story, caught in the middle of his parents' impending divorce. His mother cons her sister into stealing him because she is scared her husband will take him out of the country after the divorce is final. Bronson hides in the apartment of the husband's lawyer, who she thinks will be away for a while. But he shows up along with his folks so she has to pose as his wife and the comedy starts rolling. Finally, she decides to run again, but little Davey is missing, seems a theater marquee catches his young eye and he wanders toward it. He uses the fire escape, heads into the theater which is playing THE SINGING FOOL with Al Jolson, and gives everyone a rendition of "Sonny Boy." This was an early talkie, so the film interchanged from dialog to title cards throughout.

d, Archie Mayo; w, C. Graham Baker (based on a story by Robert Lord); ph, Ben Reynolds; m, Louis Silvers; ed, Owen Marks; m/l, "Sonny Boy," Ray Henderson, Buddy DeSylva, Lew Brown, Al Jolson; titles, J.A. Starr.

Drama   **(PR:A   MPAA:NR)**

SONORA STAGECOACH**   (1944) 61m MON bw

Hoot Gibson (*Hoot*), Bob Steele (*Bob*), Chief Thunder Cloud (*Thunder Cloud*), Rocky Camron (*Rocky*), Betty Miles (*Betty*), Glenn Strange (*Paul Kenton*), George Eldridge (*Larry Payne*), Karl Hackett (*Joe Kenton*), Henry Hall (*Sheriff Hampton*), Charles King (*Blackie Reed*), Bud Osborne (*Steve Martin*), Charlie Murray, Jr (*Weasel*), John Bridges (*Pop Carson*), Al Ferguson (*Red*), Forrest Taylor (*Judge Crandall*), Frank Ellis, Hal Price, Rodd Redwing, John Cason, Horace B. Carpenter.

The trio of Gibson, Steele, and Thunder Cloud provide nonstop action in this excellent western that never lets up. Not only can the three work the horses and fight with the best, but the women in this film can also do the job. The group has to stop an innocent man from hanging and are in charge of taking him to Sonora for a fair trial. Numerous times they fight bad guys who want to stop the stage but the three complete their mission and even squeeze a confession out of the real murderers. Interesting element of an offscreen narrator adds to the plot. (See TRAIL BLAZERS series, Index)

p&d, Robert Tansey; w, Frances Kavanaugh (based on a story by Robert Emmett [Tansey]; ph, Edward Kull; ed, John C. Fuller; md, Frank Sanucci.

Western   **(PR:A   MPAA:NR)**

SONS AND LOVERS***½   (1960, Brit.) 99m FOX bw

Trevor Howard (*Walter Morel*), Dean Stockwell (*Paul Morel*), Wendy Hiller (*Mrs. Morel*), Mary Ure (*Clara Dawes*), Heather Sears (*Miriam Lievers*), William Lucas (*William*), Conrad Phillips (*Baxter Dawes*), Donald Pleasance (*Pappleworth*), Ernest Thesiger (*Henry Hadlock*), Rosalie Crutchley (*Miriam's Mother*), Ruth Dunning (*Mrs. Leivers*), Elizabeth Begley (*Mrs. Radford*), Edna Morris (*Mrs. Anthony*), Ruth Kettlewell (*Mrs. Bonner*), Ann Sheppard (*Rose*), Sean Barrett (*Arthur*), Philip Ray (*Dr. Ansell*), Susan Travers (*Betty S*), Dorothy Gordon (*Fanny*), Sheila Bernette (*Polly*), Vilma Ann Leslie (*Collie*).

They might well have titled this SON AND MOTHER for that is the focus of the story, a respectful adaptation of Lawrence's autobiographical novel with very few punches pulled. A few characters were altered and one was dropped from the story (a minor sister) but they were hardly noticed. The picture was Britain's official entry at Cannes, won an Oscar for Francis' cinematography, and nailed nominations from the Academy for Best Picture, the script, Cardiff's direction, Trevor Howard, and Mary Ure. The only actor in the cast who was not British was former child actor Stockwell but only Henry Higgins would have noticed any lapses in his accent. Published in 1913, the story is set in the Nottingham area of Great Britain where Hiller and Howard have raised three sons on this miner's wages. She is a forceful woman who manipulates her men like a puppet mistress. Stockwell is the sensitive son who would like to follow an art career in London. He is seeing naive Sears for a while, then takes up with an older woman, Ure, who is married to Phillips. This artistic bent is attractive to women in the area because most of the men are either in the pits or in the pubs. Hiller puts an end to his relationship with Sears, and when Ure leaves her husband and has an affair with Stockwell, Hiller is livid. It's an Oedipus-Hamlet situation as Stockwell listens to his mother when he knows he should follow his heart, and he appears powerless to free himself of her grasp. No matter what he does, and even if she is not near, Hiller's presence is felt by Stockwell. He is totally emasculated by Hiller and the love that she should be giving her husband is, instead, showered upon Stockwell. When one of the sons dies in a mining accident and the other goes off to London, Stockwell is forced to abandon his dreams of art in order to be near his bereaved mother. In one scene, he bids her "good night, my love," and the relationship is firmly established. Hiller eventually dies and Stockwell leaves the area for London. Ure has gone back to Phillips and he has spurned Sears and now looks forward to a life away from the claustrophobic town, but we know that the specter of his dear mother will always be with him and influence everything he does, as witnessed by the book from whence this movie sprung. Many works have been written about the domination of sons by mothers but Lawrence was early in the game and his insights were many. Much of the dialogue comes right from the novel, which is a definite plus. The technical work in making the period seem authentic is superb and Cardiff's direction is first-rate. Cardiff had been a well-known cinematographer (THE RED SHOES, LEAVE HER TO HEAVEN, THE AFRICAN QUEEN, among many) but his directorial jobs were not as successful. All of the actors acquit themselves well, even in the most menial roles. Crutchley is exquisite as Sears' mother and veteran Thesiger is memorable. He was 81 at the time and had been acting in movies since 1918. This was his penultimate film, his last being THE ROMAN SPRING OF MRS. STONE. Cardiff's assistant on the film was Peter Yates, who later became a director on his own and scored with BULLITT, THE HOT ROCK, THE DEEP, and BREAKING AWAY.

p, Jerry Wald; d, Jack Cardiff; w, Gavin Lambert, T.E.B. Clarke (based on the novel by D.H. Lawrence); ph, Freddie Francis (CinemaScope); m, Mario Nascimbene; art d, Lionel Couch; cos, Margaret Furse.

Biography   **Cas.**   **(PR:C   MPAA:NR)**

SONS AND MOTHERS***   (1967, USSR) 95m Gorky Film Studio/Brandon-Artkino bw (SERDTSE MATERI)

Yelena Fadeyeva (*The Mother*), Mariya Aleksandrovna Ulyanova, Daniil Sagal (*The Father*), Ilya Nikolayevich Ulyanov, Nina Menshikova (*Anna*), Gennadiy Chertov (*Aleksandr*), Rodion Nakhapetov (*Vladimir Ilich [Lenin]*), Nina Vilvovskaya (*Olga*), Andrey Bogoslovskiy, Yuriy Solomin (*Dmitriy*), Olya Izgorodina (*Mariya*), Svetlana Balashova (*Mariya*), Georgiy Yepifantsev (*Yelizarov*), V. Safonov (*Ishcherskiy*), Fyodor Nikitin (*Neklyudov*), V. Mizin (*Gorchilin*), N. Ashikhmyan (*Pashka*), V. Churkin (*Fedka*), V. Salin (*Lenka*).

This Russian drama is set in a small town in 1886 and concerns a widowed woman with six children—four at home and two away at the university. Their father was involved with the peasants' rights and so are the couple's children. The two eldest are arrested for planning to assassinate the Czar, and the son is executed because he will not renounce his actions despite his mother's desperate pleas. The daughter is sent into exile and the family moves near her. The youngest boy, who admired his brother, follows in his footsteps and takes up law. He practices law where the family lives, but wants to be in Moscow where all the social action is and where he can have a greater impact. Finally, the mother relents, sends her other children to Moscow and takes off with her son as he crusades across Russia and becomes one of its most famous leaders—Nikolai Lenin.

d, Mark Donskoy; w, Zoya Voskresenskaya, Irina Donskaya; ph, Mikhail Yakovich (Sovscope); m, R. Khozak; art d, Boris Dulenkov.

Drama   (PR:A   MPAA:NR)

SONS O' GUNS*½   (1936) 82m WB bw

Joe E. Brown (*Jimmy Canfield*), Joan Blondell (*Yvonne*), Beverly Roberts (*Mary Harper*), Winifred Shaw (*Bernice Pearce*), Eric Blore (*Hobson, Canfield's Butler*), G.P. Huntley, Jr (*Capt. Archibald Ponsonby-Falcke*), Joseph King (*Col. Harper*), David Worth (*Arthur Travers*), Craig Reynolds (*Lt. Burton*), Robert Barrat (*Pierre*), Michael Mark (*Carl*), Frank Mitchell (*Ritter*), Bert Roach (*Vogel*), Hans Joby (*Fritz*), Mischa Auer, Otto Fries (*German Spies*), Max Wagner, Don Turner, Leo Sulky, Bill Dagwell (*Soldiers*), James Eagles (*Young Soldier*), Milton Kibbee, Allen Matthews (*Military Policemen*), Robert A'Dair, Olaf Hytten (*Sentries*), Pat Flaherty, Sol Gorss, Henry Otho (*Apaches*).

Joe E. Brown is terribly miscast in a role more suited to the talents of Al Jolson. He is a peace-loving singer and dancer, who for his stage show at the time, must wear a uniform. Next thing you know, he is in a military parade and in Germany. He is thrown in jail, but escapes, captures Hill 23 in a daring act, and is awarded the Croix de Guerre for his efforts while he is still trying to figure out what he is doing there in the first place.

p, Harry Joe Bown; d, Lloyd Bacon; w, Jerry Wald, Julius J. Epstein (based on a play by Fred Thompson, Jack Donahue); ph, Sol Polito; ed, James Gibbons; md, Leo F. Forbstein; ch, Bobby Connolly; m/l, "In the Arms of an Army Man," "For a Brick and a Quarter a Day," Al Dubin, Harry Warren (sung by Joe E. Brown).

Musical   (PR:A   MPAA:NR)

SONS OF ADVENTURE**½   (1948) 60m REP bw

Lynne Roberts (*Jean*), Russell Hayden (*Steve*), Gordon Jones (*Andy*), Grant Withers (*Sterling*), George Chandler (*Billy Wilkes*), Roy Barcroft (*Bennett*), John Newland (*Peter Winslow*), Stephanie Bachelor (*Laura*), John Holland (*Paul Kenyon*), Gilbert Frye (*Sam Hodges*), Richard Irving (*Eddie*), Joan Blair (*Glenda*), John Crawford (*Norton*), Keith Richards (*Harry*), James Dale (*Whitey*).

Directed by ex-stuntman Yakima Canutt, this picture gives a fleeting glimpse of behind-the-scenes Hollywood. A western star is killed on the set and Hayden starts snooping around to find the killer. He is interested in saving Jones, whom everyone believes did the deed. This puts him in danger time and time again but he escapes to finally track down the killer and bring him to justice.

p, Franklin Adreon; d, Yakima Canutt; w, Adreon, Sol Shur; ph, John MacBurnie; ed, Harold Minter; md, Morton Scott, art d, James Sullivan; set d, John McCarthy, Jr., James Redd; spec eff, Howard Lydecker, Theodore Lydecker.

Western   (PR:A   MPAA:NR)

SONS OF GOOD EARTH*½   (1967, Hong Kong) 120m
                                    Brothers/Frank Lee International bw

Peter Chen Ho (*Yu Jui*), Betty Loh Tih (*Lotus*), King Chuan (*Tiger Ting*), Julia Hsia (*Mrs. Li Meng-shih*), Chen Yen Yen (*Mrs. Tien*).

Slightly interesting Hong Kong-made war picture depicts the Japanese occupation of a village in Manchuria in 1931 and the guerrilla war fought against them, climaxing with a peasant uprising that savages the Japanese pitilessly. Beware of tiny English subtitles in some prints. (In Mandarin; English subtitles.)

p, Run Run Shaw; d&w, Hu Chin-chuan.

War   (PR:A-C MPAA:NR)

SONS OF KATIE ELDER, THE***   (1965) 122m PAR c

John Wayne (*John Elder*), Dean Martin (*Tom Elder*), Martha Hyer (*Mary Gordon*), Michael Anderson, Jr. (*Bud Elder*), Earl Holliman (*Matt Elder*), Jeremy Slate (*Deputy Sheriff Ben Latta*), James Gregory (*Morgan Hastings*), Paul Fix (*Sheriff Billy Wilson*), George Kennedy (*Curley*), Dennis Hopper (*Dave Hastings*), Sheldon Allman (*Judge Harry Eyers*), John Litel (*Minister*), John Doucette (*Undertaker Hyselman*), James Westerfield (*Banker Vannar*), Rhys Williams (*Charlie Bob Striker*), John Qualen

(*Charlie Biller*), Rodolfo Acosta (*Blondie Adams*), Strother Martin (*Jeb Ross*), Percy Helton (*Storekeeper Peevey*), Karl Swenson (*Doc Isdel/Bartender*), Harvey Grant (*Jeb*), Jerry Gatlin (*Amboy*), Loren James (*Ned Reese*), Red Morgan (*Burr Sandeman*), Chuck Robertson (*Townsman*), Ralph Volkie (*Bit Man*), Jack Williams (*Andy Sharp*), Henry Wills (*Gus Dolly*), Joseph Yrigoyen (*Buck Mason*).

When Katie Elder passes away her four sons return to their hometown of Clearwater, Texas, to pay their last respects to the woman who bore them. The eldest is Wayne, a tough gunfighter whose reputation precedes him. Next in line is Martin, a roguish gambler, followed by Holliman, the quiet one in the family who no man has ever called yellow more than once. Finally there is Anderson, the only family member to attend college and the hope of the clan. It's learned that their father was a drunk and gambled away the family ranch on the night he was killed, leaving their mother broke. The brothers begin to look into the killing despite warnings to lay off by sheriff Fix. Gregory and his son Hopper were the only witnesses to the father's murder, and fthey decide to cover their tracks by murdering the sheriff, then throwing the blame on Wayne and his brothers. Slate, the deputy sheriff, swears-in a posse, not knowing the men he enlists are allied with Gregory and Hopper. In an attempt to take the brothers to Laredo a gunfight breaks out, and Slate and Holliman are killed. Some of Gregory's hired guns escape and ride back to Clearwater, claiming Wayne's "gang" staged an ambush. Anderson himself had been wounded in the shooting and is now brought back to town by his siblings. They are greeted by an angry mob, who are held off by Wayne and Martin. Finally Wayne is able to let judge Allman know the truth and the jurist agrees to bring in a U.S. marshal. But while the older brother is trying to fix things legally, Martin decides to fix things his own way. He kidnaps Hopper in an effort to get a confession. Gregory tries to save his son but mistakenly shoots Hopper instead. In a deathbed confession Hopper divulges that Gregory was the gunman behind the deaths of Fix, Slate, and the father, a statement overheard by the judge. Martin has also been mortally wounded by Gregory, and tells Wayne he is now responsible for Anderson. Wayne challenges Gregory in a final battle, killing the man who has caused his family all their troubles. His family and friends revenged, Wayne returns to the rooming house run by Hyer, the late deputy's girl friend. She tells him Anderson will recover. Going indoors, her skirt grazes the old rocker of Wayne's mother, setting it in motion as though the mother is sitting in it. This was Wayne's first film after his battle with "the Big C" and one would never guess the Duke had undergone cancer surgery shortly before this was made. Following surgery Wayne wanted to prove he was still physically fit and his role here certainly goes to great lengths to show it. Wayne rides, shoots, and fights as though the worst that had happened to him was a mere hangnail. On the set he required an occasional lift from a portable oxygen machine but this was due to the thin air of the Mexican location sites more than to any physical problems. The Duke was commended for his public acknowledgement of the disease and for becoming a larger than life example of the ability to come back after cancer surgery. Hathaway was also swayed by Wayne's stand and admitted for the first time that he, too, had undergone cancer surgery some 12 years before at the Mayo Clinic. The film was a big success with the public, proving to be one of Wayne's most popular films of the 1960s. Hyer married producer Wallis the following year.

p, Hal B. Wallis; d, Henry Hathaway; w, William H. Wright, Allan Weiss, Harry Essex (based on a story by Talbot Jennings); ph, Lucien Ballard (Panavision, Technicolor); m, Elmer Bernstein; ed, Warren Low; art d, Hal Pereira, Walter Tyler; set d, Sam Comer, Ray Moyer; cos, Edith Head; spec eff, Bob Peterson.

Western   Cas.   (PR:A   MPAA:NR)

SONS OF MATTHEW   (SEE: RUGGED O'RIORDANS, THE, 1949,
                                                              Aus.)

SONS OF NEW MEXICO**   (1949) 71m COL bw (AKA: THE BRAT)

Gene Autry (*Himself*), Gail Davis (*Eileen MacDonald*), Robert Armstrong (*Pat Feeney*), Dick Jones (*Randy Pryor*), Frankie Darro (*Gig Jackson*), Irving Bacon (*Chris Dobbs*), Russell Arms (*Chuck Brunton*), Marie Blake (*Hannah Dobbs*), Clayton Moore (*Rufe Burns*), Sandy Sanders (*Walt*), Roy Gordon (*Maj. Hynes*), Frank Marvin (*Joe*), Paul Raymond (*Brad*), Pierce Lyden (*Watson*), Kenne Duncan (*Ed*), Harry Mackin, Bobby Clark, Gaylord [Steve] Pendleton, Billy Lechner, Champion, Jr. the Horse.

Autry becomes the executor of a friend's wealthy estate and gets a juvenile delinquent tossed in to the deal. He has to try like the devil to keep the kid away from flashy gambler Armstrong, who keeps trying to snare the kid so he can get the money. Autry sends the boy to military school, but the boy runs to Armstrong. Finally, the kid realizes he is in pretty deep and it is Autry and the military cadets to the rescue. Autry has his hands full with the boy and only stops to sing two songs. The film also marks Davis' first screen appearance in an Autry film. She would go on to co-star with him in many features for Columbia and became TV's "Annie Oakley."

p, Armand Schaefer; d, John English; w, Paul Gangelin; ph, William Bradford (Sepiatone); ed, Henry Batista; md, Mischa Bakaleinikoff; art d, Harold MacArthur.

Western   (PR:A   MPAA:NR)

SONS OF SATAN*   (1969, Ital./Fr./Ger.) 102m Ultra-PECF-Rhein
Main/WB c (I BASTARDI)

Rita Hayworth (Martha), Giuliano Gemma (Jason), Klaus Kinski (Adam), Margaret Lee (Karen), Serge Marquand (Jimmy), Claudine Auger (Barbara), Umberto Raho (Doctor), Hans Thorner, Karl Cik (Policemen), Paola Natalie, Mireilla Pompili (Dancers), Detlef Ule (TV Announcer).

This film, which was made in 1969, was not shown in the United States until 1973 when CBS aired it on late-night television. Hayworth is a former Ziegfeld Follies star, now an alcoholic. Adding to her misery are her two sons with whom she cannot cope. The two boys are so nasty, they pull off a jewel store heist in Arizona but die because they double-crossed each other. The film was criticized by CBS executives, who thought it was just blood with no plot and a terrible dubbing job. Hayworth did all her own dialog in each version of the film: Italian, French, and English.

p, Turi Vasile; d, Duccio Tessari; w, Ennio De Concini, Mario Di Nardo, Tessari (based on a story by Di Nardo); ph, Carlo Carlini (Technicolor); m, Carlo Rustichelli; ed, Mario Morra; md, Michel Magne; art d, Luigi Scaccianoce; set d, Dante Feretti; cos, Danda Ortone; makeup, Nilo Iacoponi.

Drama   (PR:C   MPAA:NR)

SONS OF STEEL**   (1935) 65m CHES bw

Charles Starrett (Phillip Mason), Polly Ann Young (Rose Mason), William Bakewell (Ronald Chadburne), Walter Walker (John Chadburne), Aileen Pringle (Enid Chadburne), Holmes Herbert (Curtis Chadburne), Richard Carlyle (Tom Mason), Florence Roberts (Sarah Mason), Adolf Millar, Jack Shutta, Lloyd Ingraham, Edward LeSaint, Tom Ricketts, Edgar Norton, Barbara Bedford, Harry Semels, Al Thompson.

Steel mills provide the background for this rough drama. Two brothers own a steel mill but lead decidedly different lives. One tries to join high society, while the other just works hard for his money. The social climber raises his boy in his own image, but the working father hides his social position from his son. The second man's son eventually leads the workers in a strike against his father. He discovers dad is the owner and makes peace with his dad and the other workers. Too much easy loving for a steel strike.

d, Charles Lamont; w, Charles Belden; ph, M.A. Anderson; ed, Ronald Reed.

Drama   (PR:A   MPAA:NR)

SONS OF THE DESERT**½   (1933) 68m MGM bw (AKA: SONS OF THE LEGION, CONVENTION CITY, FRATERNALLY YOURS)

Stan Laurel (Himself), Oliver Hardy (Himself), Charley Chase (Himself), Mae Busch (Mrs. Lottie Chase Hardy), Dorothy Christy (Mrs. Betty Laurel), Lucien Littlefield (Dr. Horace Meddick, Veterinary), John Elliott (Exalted Exhausted Ruler), Charley Young, John Merton, William Gillespie, Charles McAvoy, Robert Burns, Al Thompson, Eddie Baker, Jimmy Aubrey, Chet Brandenberg, Don Brodie (Sons of the Desert Coterie), Philo McCullough (Assistant Exhausted Ruler), Charita (Lead Hula Dancer), Harry Bernard (Bartender/Police Officer), Sam Lufkin, Ernie Alexander, Charlie Hall (Waiters), Baldwin Cooke (Man Who Introduces Steamship Official/Extra at the Sons Convention), Max Wagner, Stanley Blystone (Brawny Speakeasy Managers), Pat Harmon (Doorman), Ty Parvis (Singer at Sons Convention), Blade Stanhope Conway [Bob Cummings] (Crowd Extra During Steamship Radiogram Scene), The Hollywood American Legion Post (Sons Oasis "13" Crowd Dress Extras), The Santa Monica Lodge of Elks (People Parading in the Newsreel Footage), Billy Gilbert (Voice-Over as Mr. Ruttledge).

One of Laurel and Hardy's best feature-length films, SONS OF THE DESERT is a comedic send-up of lodge conventions. Based on the team's silent two-reeler WE FAW DOWN, the story involves Laurel and Hardy's trip to a convention of the Sons of the Desert. Because their wives do not want them to attend, Hardy makes up a lie about his needing a sea cruise for health reasons, and he and Laurel pretend to take an ocean voyage to Honolulu. Instead, they attend their convention in grand style and are even filmed by a newsreel crew covering the festivities. Upon their return home, they discover that not only did the ship sink that they supposedly sailed on, but their wives saw the newsreel that they were featured in. Thus, their ruse is exposed. Songs include "Honolulu Baby" and "Sons of the Desert." The national Laurel and Hardy fan club, still in existence, took their name, The Sons of the Desert, from the title of this film. (See LAUREL AND HARDY series, Index.)

p, Hal Roach; d, William A. Seiter; w, Frank Craven, Byron Morgan; ph, Kenneth Peach; ed, Bert Jordan; ch, Dave Bennett.

Comedy   Cas.   (PR:A   MPAA:NR)

SONS OF THE LEGION, 1933   (SEE: SONS OF THE DESERT, 1933)

SONS OF THE LEGION*½   (1938) 60m PAR bw

Donald O'Connor (Butch Baker), Billy Lee (Himself), Billy Cook (David Lee), Evelyn Keyes (Linda Lee), Elizabeth Patterson (Grandmother Lee), Tim Holt (Steven Scott), Lynne Overman (Charles Lee), William Frawley (Uncle Willie Lee), Richard Tucker (State Commander), Johnnie Morris (Mickey),

Wally Albright (Harold), Benny Bartlett (Red O'Flaherty), Edward Pawley (Gunman Baker), Lucille Ward (Margaret), Ronnie Paige (Boy), Tom Dugan, Keith MacKenzie.

The film tells the story of the formation of the Sons of the American Legion, an organization in conjunction with the Legion that is specifically geared to teaching the Legion's values to younger boys. One father is reluctant to help in the organizing because he received a dishonorable discharge from the army. He is still a hero in the eyes of his two sons however, after he chases down an escaped convict and pulls a former tough guy out of the gutter and reforms him. The father's name is cleared, and a parade is thrown, emphasizing patriotism and Legion ideals. A dated story line and premise.

p, Stuart Walker; d, James Hogan; w, Lillie Hayward, Lewis Foster, Robert F. McGowan; ph, Charles Schoenbaum; ed, Anne Bauchens; md, Boris Morros; art d, Hans Dreier, William Flannery.

Drama   (PR:A   MPAA:NR)

SONS OF THE MUSKETEERS   (SEE: AT SWORD'S POINT, 1951)

SONS OF THE PIONEERS**   (1942) 61m REP bw

Roy Rogers (Roy), George "Gabby" Hayes (Gabby Whittaker), The Sons of the Pioneers (Themselves), Maris Wrixon (Louis Harper), Forrest Taylor (Bixby), Minerva Urecal (Mrs. Bixby), Bradley Page (Frank Bennett), Hal Taliaferro (Briggs), Chester Conklin (Old Timer), Fred Burns (Rancher), Jack O'Shea, Frank Ellis, Tom London, Bob Woodward, Fern Emmett, Ken Cooper, Karl Hackett, Trigger the Horse.

Hayes is the sheriff of a town where a gang of outlaws have been wreaking havoc on the local farms at night. The townspeople are fed up with Hayes' inability to stop them and start rumbling about getting a new man for the badge. He travels back East to enlist the help of Rogers, who comes from a long line of famous sheriffs. But the latest Rogers would rather study insects than fire his six-shooter. After much pleading by Hayes, he agrees to help. He pretends to be a wimp to fool the scoundrels, and uses his microscope to find out why the cattle have been dying. Of course, he finally figures the problem out, obtains evidence to jail the outlaws, employed. Rogers, when not looking at insects, sings "Things Are Never What They Seem," "The West Is in My Soul," and "He's Gone Up the Trail" (Bob Nolan, Tim Spencer). Other songs include "Come and Get It" (Nolan, Spencer–sung by Pat Brady).

p&d, Joseph Kane; w, M. Coates Webster, Mauri Grashin, Robert T. Shannon (based on a story by Grashin, Shannon); ph, Bud Thackery; ed, Edward Schroeder; md, Cy Feuer; art d, Russell Kimball.

Western   (PR:A   MPAA:NR)

SONS OF THE SADDLE**   (1930) 70m UNIV bw

Ken Maynard (Jim Brandon, Foreman), Doris Hill (Ronnie Stavnow), Francis Ford (Red Slade), Carroll Nye (Harvey, Cowhand), Harry Todd (Pop Higgins), Joseph Girard (Martin Stavnow), Frank Rice, Tarzan the Horse.

During the time this film was made, cowboy star Maynard was intent on becoming a singer and incorporating that skill into his film career. He even signed a recording contract with Columbia Records. Universal, however, was less enthusiastic and dropped Maynard's B-western series when they discovered that the enormous expense of sound recording made their series films in general unprofitable. They quickly closed their series department and Maynard moved to the smaller Tiffany Studios. This film is the last one in Maynard's Universal series and does contain a couple of songs by the hopeful cowboy singer. Maynard plays the foreman of a ranch, who is the object of affection of the boss's daughter, though Maynard's friend, in turn, is in love with her. Trouble mounts when the ranch owner runs afoul of Ford and his outlaw gang. Maynard and his pal team up against Ford. SONS OF THE SADDLE also marks the split between Maynard and long-time friend and producer Harry Joe Brown, who moved to RKO.

d, Harry Joe Brown; w, Bennett Cohen, Lesley Mason; ph, Ted McCord; ed, Fred Allen; m/l, "Down the Home Trail With You," Bernie Grossman, Lou Handman, "Trail Herd Song."

Western   (PR:A   MPAA:NR)

SONS OF THE SEA**   (1939, Brit.) 82m British Consolidated/GN c

Leslie Banks (Capt. Hyde), Mackenzie Ward (Newton Hulls), Kay Walsh (Alison Devar), Simon Lack (Philip Hyde), Cecil Parker (Commander Herbert), Ellen Pollock (Margaret Hulls), Peter Shaw (Lt. John Strepte), Nigel Stock (Rudd), Charles Eaton (Commander-in-Chief), Kynaston Reeves (Prof. Devar), Gordon Begg, Robert Field.

The film details life at the Royal Naval College at Dartmouth, the training ground for British Naval officers. The story involves the commander's boy who accidentally helps an enemy espionage ring, but eventually his classmates bail him out and break open the spies' activity.

p, K.C. Alexander; d, Maurice Elveyf; w, D. William Woolf, Gerald Eliott, Elvey (based on a story by Woolf, George Barraud); ph, Eric Cross (Dufaycolour).

War Drama   (PR:A MPAA:NR)

SONS OF THE SEA, 1941   (SEE: ATLANTIC FERRY, 1941, Brit.)

SOOKY**   (1931) 85m PAR bw

Jackie Searl (*Sidney Saunders*), Willard Robertson (*Mr. Skinner*), Enid Bennett (*Mrs. Skinner*), Helen Jerome Eddy (*Mrs. Wayne*), Leigh Allen (*Mr. Saunders*), Harry Beresford (*Mr. Willoughby*), Jackie Cooper (*Skippy Skinner*), Robert Coogan (*Sooky Wayne*), Oscar Apfel (*Krausmyer*), Guy Oliver (*Mr. Moggs*), Gertrude Sutton (*Hilda*), Tom Wilson.

Second film in a series and the sequel to SKIPPY. A small-town boy would give anything to become a soldier and wear a uniform, as he takes real delight in blowing bubbles out of a bugle. The film takes a somber note, however, when the boy asks his father why people have to be sent to the poorhouse. His pal's mother is soon to be sent there and, eventually, the woman dies. All the attention focuses on the actions and reactions of the small boys, and they quickly win the audience's hearts.

d, Norman Taurog; w, Sam Mintz, Joseph L. Mankiewicz, Norman McLeod (based on the story "Dear Sooky" by Percy Crosby); ph, Arthur Todd.

Drama   (PR:A MPAA:NR)

SOPHIE LANG   (SEE: NOTORIOUS SOPHIE LANG, THE, 1934)

SOPHIE LANG GOES WEST*   (1937) 62m PAR bw

Gertrude Michael (*Sophie Lang*), Lee Bowman (*Eddie Rollyn*), Sandra Storme (*Helga Roma*), Larry [Buster] Crabbe (*Steve Clayson*), Barlowe Borland (*Archie Banks*), Jed Prouty (*J.H. Blaine*), C. Henry Gordon (*Sultan of Padaya*), Rafael Corio (*Laj*), Fred Miller, Herbert Ransom (*Policemen*), Nick Lukats (*Taxi Driver*), Guy Usher (*Inspector Parr*), Archie Twitchell (*Clerk*), Robert Cummings (*Curley*).

one of the more confusing entries from the SOPHIE LANG Series, with the confusion stemming more from a loss of what to do with the heroine than from weaving any form of suspense. The results are disastrous to say the least, with neither direction nor actors quite sure what to make of the script. As the girl who can't stay on the good side of the coppers no matter how hard she tries, Michael is once again trying to keep out of the hands of the law. Somehow she bumps into a scriptwriter (where was he when really needed) and helps him to come up with material to finish the idea he's been working on. In the process they solve the theft of a priceless necklace.

d, Charles Riesner; w, Doris Anderson, Brian Marlowe, Robert Wyler (based on the stories of Frederick Irving Anderson); ph, Ted Tetzlaff; ed, Chandler House; cos, Travis Banton, Edith Head.

Comedy/Crime   (PR:A MPAA:NR)

SOPHIE'S CHOICE***½   (1982) 157m ITC/UNIV c

Meryl Streep (*Sophie Zawistowska*), Kevin Kline (*Nathan Landau*), Peter MacNicol (*Stingo*), Josef Sommer (*Narrator*), Rita Karin (*Yetta Zimmerman*), Stephen D. Newman (*Larry*), Greta Turken (*Leslie Lapidus*), Josh Mostel (*Morris Fink*), Marcell Rosenblatt (*Astrid Weinstein*), Moishe Rosenfeld (*Moishe Rosenblum*), Robin Bartlett (*Lillian Grossman*), Eugene Lipinski (*Polish Professor*), John Rothman (*Librarian*), Joseph Leon (*Dr. Blackstock*), David Wohl (*English Teacher*), Nina Polan, Alexander Sirotin, Armand Dahan (*English Students*), Joseph Tobin (*Reporter*), Cortez Nance (*Bellboy*), Gunther Maria Halmer (*Rudolf Hoess*), Karlheinz Hackl (*SS Doctor*), Ulli Fessl (*Frau Hoess*), Melanie Pianka (*Emmi Hoess*), Krystyna Karkowska (*Prisoner Housekeeper*), Katharina Thalbach (*Wanda*), Neddim Prohic (*Josef*), Jennifer Lawn, Adrian Kalitka (*Sophie's Children*), Peter Wegenbreth (*Hoess' Aide*), Vida Jerman (*Female SS Guard*), Ivo Pajer (*Sophie's Father*), Michaela Karacic (*Sophie as a Child*), Eugeniusz Priwieziencew, Sandra Markota, Hrvoje Sostaric, Marko Zec, Irena Hampel.

Styron's best-selling novel is supposedly based on his real experiences as a southerner living in a Brooklyn boarding house in 1947. Pakula's screenplay was too respectful of the novel and could have been at least 30 minutes shorter. Streep continues to astound audiences as she manages to make characters her own. In this case, she actually learned German and Polish in order to speak them authentically and her Polish accent while speaking English is flawless. She did the same with British-accented English in THE FRENCH LIEUTENANT'S WOMAN and again with Danish in OUT OF AFRICA. Her performance here won an Oscar and she is, by far, the most outstanding element in what might have otherwise been a tedious movie. MacNichol is the cornpone author who has come from below the Mason-Dixon line to pursue a career of letters. He moves into the Brooklyn boarding house and meets Streep and Kline (in his debut after several successful stage shows in New York). Kline works as a research chemist in a nearby facility and Streep is a Polish refugee who has newly arrived from Europe where she suffered terrible degradation. She talks about her late father and reveres him as a freedom-loving man. Later, it is learned that he was one of the most virulent anti-Semites in that country. Streep's tales of her life in Europe have a strange and often unbelievable tint to them but this is, at first, overlooked. Kline is Jewish, Streep is Catholic, and

MacNichol is Southern Baptist, but they find much to like about each other and become a non-sexual menage a trois, sort of like the way it was in JULES AND JIM at the start. Kline is actively nuts and his personality changes happen often and violently. He becomes jealous of Streep and MacNichol, who are enjoying an innocent friendship. There is too much use of narration and another actor was employed to speak the words purportedly written by MacNichols. This was Sommer, but that may have been a bad choice as the story could have been told more cinematically without that. Much of the action takes place in the Brooklyn house, therefore giving it the look of a play that has been opened up, on occasion, by taking the trio on outings to parks and Coney Island. One wonders what her "choice" is for most of the picture and the obvious conclusion is that she will have to choose between Kline and MacNichols. That's not it at all as, near the 3/4 mark, the picture flashes back to monochrome sepia for Streep's remembrances of horrors past. She had two children and was ushered into a concentration camp where the SS chief forced her to make a chilling selection. One of her children was to live, the other to die, and the choice was hers! After that, she was little more than a receptacle for the bestial sexuality of the Nazi boss. Then it's back to the present and another twist that reveals ... but no. See this movie, if only to watch one of the world's best actresses in action. Hamlisch wrote the score but he mainly used the works of Johann Strauss, Mozart, Beethoven, Handel, Schumann, and Mendelssohn to augment his own work, something he did before when he adapted the brilliance of Scott Joplin for THE STING and took an Oscar for himself with nary a word for the originator of the music. Locations were filmed in Yugoslavia. The language is often raw and the Nazi scenes are far too frightening for anyone under 18.

p, Alan J. Pakula, Keith Barish; d&w, Pakula (based on the novel by William Styron); ph, Nestor Almendros (Technicolor); m, Marvin Hamlisch; ed, Evan Lottman; prod d, George Jenkins; art d, John J. Moore; set d, Carol Jaffe; cos, Albert Wolsky.

Historical Drama   **Cas.**   (PR:O MPAA:R)

SOPHIE'S PLACE**½   (1970) 106m WB-Seven Arts c (GB: CROOKS AND CORONETS)

Telly Savalas (*Herbie Hassler*), Edith Evans (*Lady Sophie Fitzmore*), Warren Oates (*Marty Miller*), Cesar Romero (*Nick Marco*), Harry H. Corbett (*Frank Finley*), Nicky Henson (*Lord Freddie Fitzmore*), Hattie Jacques (*Mabel*), Vickery Turner (*Annie*), Arthur Mullard (*Perce*), Frank Thornton (*Cyril*), Thorley Walters (*Hubbard*), Jeremy Young (*Reilly*), Leslie Dwyer (*Henry*), Will Leighton (*Bowers*), Clive Dunn (*Basil*), David Lodge (*Policeman*), David Bauer (*Jack*), Ivor Dean (*Bellows*), Joan Crane (*Sally*), Herman Cohen, Jim O'Connolly.

An odd coupling of Savalas and Oates works in this jovial portrayal of two kindly crooks. Working with crime boss Romero, the comic burglar duo plan to liquidate the belongings of one of Britain's stately mansions. They hook up with Tory mobster Corbett to pull off the heist. Tavalas and Oates con their way into the rich madam's household and are warmly treated as her guests. Guilt overwhelms them and they confess their plot, turning their energies instead to foiling Corbett's gang. Evans, in the meantime, turns her mansion into a successful casino. The snails-pace cutting forbids this one from building the momentum it so sorely needs.

p, Herman Cohen; d&w, Jim O'Connolly; ph, Desmond Dickinson (Technicolor); m, Patrick John Scott; ed, Martin Charles; art d, Alex Vetchinsky; set d, Freda Pearson.

Comedy   (PR:C MPAA:M/PG)

SOPHIE'S WAYS**½   (1970, Fr.) 97m Saroy-Films De La Licorne c (LES STANCES A SOPHIE)

Bernadette Lafont (*Celine*), Michel Duchaussoy (*Philippe*), Bulle Ogier (*Julia*), Serge Marquand (*Jean-Pierre*), Virginie Thevenet (*Stephanie*), Philippe Desprats (*Bruno*), Vigny Wowor (*Thomas*).

A movie that attempted to look at modern day marriage at a time when the Women's Liberation Movement was just starting to gain momentum. Lafont plays a free-thinking woman who falls in love with conservative Duchaussoy. Forsaking her liberated ideals, she agrees to marriage, only to find that married life is filled with double sta ndards and that she is merely an object of display to her husband. She becomes friends with Ogier who shows her the ropes in being a decorative spouse by teaching her to cheat on the bills to get the material things she wants. Lafont, in turn, convinces Ogier that they should try to preserve their dignity. She begins to paint as a means of escape from her unstimulating marriage. When Ogier is killed in a car accident, Lafont realizes that life is too short to waste, and she leaves Duchaussoy intent on living her own life. Although the men in this picture are not developed as clearly as the women, they successfully escape stereotyping, and the film succeeds in revealing the illusions people often have when going into marriage, and how the breakdown of these illusions can often break up a marriage.

p, Sam Roy; d, Moshe Mizrahi; w, Mizrahi, Christiane Rochefort (based on the book by Rochefort); ph, Jean-Marc Ripert (Eastmancolor); m, Art Ensemble of Chicago; ed, Dov Hoenig.

Drama/Comedy   (PR:O MPAA:NR)

SOPHOMORE, THE** (1929) 73m Pathe bw

Eddie Quillan *(Joe Collins)*, Sally O'Neil *(Margie Callahan)*, Stanley Smith *(Tom Weck)*, Jeanette Loff *(Barbara Lange)*, Russell Gleason *(Dutch)*, Sarah Padden *(Mrs. Collins)*, Brooks Benedict *(Armstrong)*, Spec O'Donnell *(Nephew)*, Walter O'Keefe *(Radio Announcer)*.

Well done comedy stars Quillan as a sophomore who on the first day of school loses his tuition money in a game of dice. He's forced to get a job at the local soda fountain where he meets and falls for O'Neil. The problem is that the boss also has a crush on her, and fires Quillan. Out of work and money, Quillan decides to leave school, but before he can withdraw, he receives the necessary funds in the mail. Thinking his mom sent it, he prepares for the big college football game to be held the next day. He spends most of the game on the bench until the last three minutes when the scores are tied. The coach puts him in the game, but he fumbles the ball and is knocked out cold in the scramble. As Quillan is carried away on a stretcher, he learns that O'Neill is the one who sent him the money. He jumps off the stretcher and proceeds to run across the field in an attempt to catch her at the train station. As he does so, the ball is thrown his way, and he makes the winning touchdown.

p, William Counselman; d, Leo McCarey; w, Earl Baldwin, Walter DeLeon, Joseph Franklin Poland, Anthony Brown (based on a story by Corey Ford, T.H. Wenning); ph, John J. Mescall; ed, Doane Harrison; m/l, "Little by Little," Bobby Dolan, Walter O'Keefe.

Comedy (PR:A MPAA:NR)

SORCERER***½ (1977) 121m Film Properties International/UNIV-PAR c (GB: WAGES OF FEAR)

Roy Scheider *(Jackie Scanlon/"Juan Dominguez")*, Bruno Cremer *(Victor Manzon/"Serrano")*, Francisco Rabal *(Nilo)*, Amidou *(Kassem/"Martinez")*, Ramon Bieri *(Corlette)*, Peter Capell *(Lartigue)*, Karl John *(Angerman/"Marquez")*, Frederick Ledebur *(Carlos)*, Chico Martinez *(Bobby Del Rios)*, Joe Spinell *(Spider)*, Rosario Almontes *(Agrippa)*, Richard Holley *(Billy White, Helicopter Pilot)*, Anne Marie Descott *(Blanche)*, Jean-Luc Bideau *(Pascal)*, Jacques Francois *(Lefevre)*, Andre Falcon *(Guillot)*, Gerard E. Murphy *(Donnelly)*, Desmond Crofton *(Boyle)*, Henry Diamond *(Murray)*, Ray Dittrich *(Ben)*, Frank Gio *(Marty)*, Randy Jurgensen *(Vinnie)*, Gus Allegretti *(Carlo Ricci)*, Nick Discenza *(Father Ricci)*.

William Friedkin's loose remake of Henri-Georges Clouzot's 1955 French thriller THE WAGES OF FEAR was needlessly savaged by critics who were either out to get the hot (in 1977) young director of THE FRENCH CONNECTION and THE EXORCIST, or eager to impress their readers by demonstrating a superior appreciation of foreign cinema. Instead of making a sacred cow of the original film (WAGES OF FEAR is a superior adventure film–but no masterpiece), Friedkin took the same highly charged situation and expanded upon it. Thus, SORCERER fits more into the realm of "inspired by" than "remake of." The film opens as we watch a cold-blooded professional assassin, Rabal, kill a man in a South American hotel. The action then shifts to Jerusalem where a group of Arab terrorists bombs an Israeli bank. Only one of the Arabs, Amidou, escapes police. We then go to Paris where we see a wealthy investment banker, Cremer, leave his wife and family to escape prosecution for a fraud scheme he was involved in. In the U.S. small-time hood Scheider is the getaway driver for a gang that decides to rob a wealthy Catholic church. During the robbery a priest is killed. The gang's escape is botched and Scheider is the only survivor. Much to his horror, Scheider learns that the murdered priest was the brother of a powerful New York Mafia don who is certain to seek revenge. Scheider flees the country. All four men turn up in the seedy South American town of Porvenir where they scrape to make a meager living and must turn a large portion of their earnings over to the police as hush money. One day a representative of an American oil company arrives and offers $10,000 and legal citizenship to any four men willing to drive a shipment of highly volatile nitroglycerin over 200 miles of dangerous terrain to an oil well that has been exploded by anti-American guerrillas. The fire spewing from the oil well is so intense that nitro has to be used to blow the fire out. After testing several men, the oil company picks Scheider, Cremer, Amidou, and a German, John. Before they leave, however, John is killed by assassin Rabal, who takes the dead man's place on the truck. The nitroglycerin is distributed on two monstrous old trucks–one called "Sorcerer," the other "Lazaro"–and the men begin their journey, Scheider partnered with Rabal, and Cremer teamed with Amidou. The tiny convoy immediately runs into trouble on the dangerous and crumbling mountain roads. They are then hit with a torrential tropical downpour while trying to cross a rope bridge where the wood planks have long been rotting. The trucks sway violently back and forth on the suspension bridge, lashed by the wind and rain. The sound of the storm is deafening. Both trucks eventually make the crossing, only to be blocked by a huge tree trunk that has fallen onto the narrow trail. Using a tiny bit of the nitro, Amidou fashions a crude detonator that barely allows him time to escape the blast when the tree is blown into splinters. Amidou and Cremer relax a bit as they steer the huge truck down a mountain road. But their relief is short-lived. One of the tires on the truck blows sending the vehicle out of control and over the edge. Scheider and Rabal, who were following far behind, see the explosion and realize what has happened. When they finally arrive on the scene, the men are waylaid by a small group of guerrillas (they had shot the tire on the first truck). The

guerrillas want to know what is in the truck and Scheider tells them it is supplies. When the bandits lead Scheider to the back of the truck, Rabal whips out his pistol and kills three of them. During the confusion Scheider manages to grab a shovel and kill the fourth man. Unfortunately, one of the bandits manages to get a few bursts of machine gun fire off and severely wounds Rabal. Scheider gathers the dying man into the truck and continues on. As Rabal lies bleeding, Scheider maneuvers the truck through the dark, cold, lunar terrain that leads to the oil well. Two miles from the encampment Rabal dies and the truck overheats and breaks down. Determined to deliver the nitro, Scheider unpacks the protective covering and carries the case of nitro on foot. The bright blaze of the oil well fire finally cuts through the darkness and an exhausted Scheider hands over the nitro and collapses. After a brief rest, Scheider awakens to discover that he is now a rich man. The oil company gives him all four $10,000 shares for completing the job. Scheider returns to Porvenir and tells his chartered plane to wait while he enters the local dive and dances one slow dance with Descott, the haggard barmaid–the only woman in town. As he moves to the music, Scheider fails to notice the hitmen from New York who have just entered the bar. Friedkin's SORCERER is just as gripping and spine-tingling an adventure film as THE WAGES OF FEAR and, at times, surpasses the original film with breathtaking photography and a superb use of sound (the scene on the bridge is truly amazing). The musical score by German electronic experimental band Tangerine Dream is brilliant and haunting. The eerie electronic music adds immeasurably to the overall effect of the film, complementing the exotic imagery perfectly. Tangerine Dream has since done dozens of superior scores for films as diverse as RISKY BUSINESS and THIEF (Friedkin once stated that if he had heard the band's music before he finished THE EXORCIST he would have hired it to do the music for that film as well). While critics bemoaned Friedkin and screenwriter Green's changes in the story line and lengthy expository passage (the film runs 70 minutes before the men actually board the trucks), they forgot that THE WAGES OF FEAR also had a long first half. Both films develop their characters fully and while the French film was more subtle and took some jabs at the American exploitation of foreign resources, SORCERER retains the French film's social concerns and goes one step further by introducing a revolutionary movement intent on removing the oil company. In addition to the overt changes, Friedkin and Green use the basic plot situation as a metaphor for world tensions. Four men from different countries and backgrounds who should hate each other pull together and cooperate because they are riding atop deadly explosives that can annihilate them all. While each man has his own set of problems, needs, and desires they all share the same instinct–survival. These seemingly self-absorbed, amoral characters adjust and adapt to each other and in the end develop a camaraderie and understanding that none previously possessed. This social, political, and humanistic content combined with thrilling action sequences makes for a highly entertaining, intelligent film. Unfortunately, SORCERER bombed at the box office. Blame fell on the confusing title which may have led some to believe that Friedkin was once again dealing with the bizarre supernatural world of THE EXORCIST. At a cost of over $22 million the film grossed a paltry $5.9 million and was deemed a financial disaster. Friedkin's career as a director has yet to recover. Though he bounced back slightly with the likable THE BRINK'S JOB in 1979, his subsequent films (CRUISING, DEAL OF THE CENTURY, and TO LIVE AND DIE IN L.A.) have been wretched efforts artistically and for the most part financial flops.

p&d, William Friedkin; w, Walon Green (based on the novel *The Wages of Fear* by Georges Arnaud); ph, John M. Stephens, Dick Bush (Panavision, Technicolor); m, Tangerine Dream; ed, Robert K. Lambert, Bud Smith; prod d, John Box; art d, Roy Walker; set d, Bob Laing; cos, Anthony Powell; m/l, "I'll Remember April," Don Raye, Gene De Paul, Patricia Johnston (performed by Charlie Parker), "Spheres (Movement 3)," (performed by Keith Jarrett), "So What" (performed by Miles Davis); stunts, Bud Ekins; makeup, Ben Nye, Jr., Bob Norin, John Norin.

Drama Cas. (PR:O MPAA:PG)

SORCERERS, THE*** (1967, Brit.) 85m Tigon-Curtwel-Global/AA c

Boris Karloff *(Professor Monserrat)*, Catherine Lacey *(Estelle Monserrat)*, Ian Ogilvy *(Mike)*, Elizabeth Ercy *(Nicole)*, Victor Henry *(Alan)*, Susan George *(Audrey)*, Dani Sheridan *(Laura)*, Ivor Dean *(Inspector Matalon)*, Peter Fraser *(Detective)*, Meier Tzelniker *(Snack Bar Owner)*, Bill Barnsley *(Constable)*, Martin Terry *(Tobacconist)*, Gerald Campion *(Customer)*, Alf Joint *(Ron)*.

A likable old experimenter and former stage hypnotist, Karloff has finally developed a device whereby one person can totally control the mental facilities of another. All he needs to find is a person willing to act as a guinea pig, which he discovers in Ogilvy as he notes the young man leaving the sight of a fight he just had with a friend. Karloff's intentions are only oriented toward providing good, but his aging wife, Lacey, has developed a cynically selfish attitude after years of poverty spent helping in her husband's experiments. When she sees the newly attained power at her disposal, which includes feeling the sensations of Ogilvy as he undertakes their commands, Lacey's desires become more sadistic and self-gratifying. This is a total reversal of Karloff's intentions, which he can do nothing about, as Lacey proves more powerful in controlling Ogilvy than does he. In a last ditch effort to destroy the monster he has created, Karloff has him crash the car he is driving; in this way he also kills himself and his wife, who also experience the impact and flames of the crash. A subtly menacing film given the proper atmosphere by the mere appearance of Karloff.

p, Patrick Curtis, Tony Tenser; d, Michael Reeves; w, Reeves, Tom Baker (based on the idea by John Burke); ph, Stanley Long (Eastmancolor); m, Paul Ferris; ed, David Woodward, Ralph Sheldon; md, Ferris; art d, Tony Curtis.

Horror   Cas.   (PR:C MPAA:NR)

SORCERESS*   (1983) 75m New World Pictures c

Leigh Harris (Mira), Lynette Harris (Mara), Bob Nelson (Erlick), David Milbern (Pando), Bruno Rey (Baldar), Ana De Sade (Dellisia), Robert Ballesteros (Traigon), Douglas Sanders (Hunnu), Tony Stevens (Khrakannon), Martin LaSalle (Krona), Silvia Masters (Kanti), William Arnold (Dargon), Teresa Conway (Amaya), Lucy Jensen (Dancer), Michael Fountain (Player), Peter Farmer (Armorer), Charles Rogers (Servant), Phillip Garrigan (Soldier), Mark Arevan (Gambler), Gloria Meister (Nursemaid), Randy Rothman (Peasant), Marla Hill (Rich Lady), Ginger Baum (Sister), Gerald Hood (Executioner).

Beefcake fantasy on swords and sorcerers type pictures, this one taking full advantage of the scantily clothed twins, Leigh and Lynette Harris, for sexual exploitation purposes. Forced story line has the Harris sisters playing twins who have been raised as boys in order to be kept secret from their father, Ballesteros. Ballesteros killed their mother years before, and would sacrifice the twins for power if he knew of their existence. Using the gimmick that twins think as one, picture has Leigh experiencing an orgasm when Lynette is raped by Nelson. This film was just an excuse to promote the beautiful bodies of the Harris twins, but they instead are upstaged by De Sade as the evil princess who is in cohorts with their father.

p, Jack Hill; d, Brian Stuart; w, Jim Wynorski; ph, Alex Phillips, Jr. (DeLuxe Color); ed, Larry Bock, Barry Zetlin; prod d, Charles Grodin; art d, Joe Greenman; cos, Kleomenes Stamatiades; spec eff, New World Effects, Marcus Patchet; makeup, Carol Palomino; special d, John Buechler; animal d, Deborah Gaydos.

Adventure/Fantasy   Cas.   (PR:O MPAA:R)

SORORITY GIRL*½ (1957) 60m AIP bw (GB: THE BAD ONE; AKA: CONFESSIONS OF A SORORITY GIRL)

Susan Cabot (Sabra Tanner), Dick Miller (Mort), Barboura O'Neill (Rita Joyce), June Kenney (Tina), Barbara Crane (Ellie Marshall), Fay Baker (Mrs. Tanner), Jeane Wood (Mrs. Fessenden).

A darker side of sorority life is displayed as malicious rich kid Cabot is refused acceptance into the Greek system, motivating her own devious form of revenge ranging from petty fights to blackmail. Cheap production is hampered by poor production techniques.

p&d, Roger Corman; w, Ed Waters, Lou Lieberman; ph, Monroe P. Askins; m, Ronald Stein; ed, Charles Gross, Jr.

Drama   (PR:C MPAA:NR)

SORORITY HOUSE½**   (1939) 64m RKO bw (GB: THAT GIRL FROM COLLEGE)

Anne Shirley (Alice Fisher), James Ellison (Bill Loomis), Barbara Read (Dotty Spencer), Helen Wood (Mme. President), J.M. Kerrigan (Lew Fisher), Doris Jordan (Neva Simpson), June Storey (Norma Hancock), Elisabeth Risdon (Mme. Scott), Margaret Armstrong (Mrs. Dawson), Selmer Jackson (Mr. Grant), Constance Keane [Veronica Lake] (Sorority Girl), Marge Champion (Coed), Chill Wills (Mr. Johnson), Adele Pearce, Pamela Blake, Dick Hogan.

Overly sentimental college film that focuses on the snobbish attitudes of the sorority system. Shirley plays a girl from a working-class family whose dream is to be accepted into a top sorority. She lies about her father's business to make it sound more impressive. When her father, Kerrigan, sells his food store and moves to be near his daughter, she ignores him when he shows up at a sorority function because she's embarrassed. Realizing how shallow she's become, she apologizes to her father and leaves the sorority system she held so dear. The film concentrates on the sorority angle, ignoring other facets of college life. Veronica Lake, who then was known as Constance Keane, played a bit role.

p, Robert Sisk; d, John Farrow; w, Dalton Trumbo (based on the three-act comedy "Chi House" by Mary Coyle Chase); ph, Nicholas Muscuraca; ed, Harry Marker; md, Roy Webb; cos, Edward Stevenson.

Drama   (PR:A MPAA:NR)

SORRELL AND SON   (1934, Brit.) 84m British and Dominion/UA bw

H.B. Warner (Capt. Stephen Sorrell), Peter Penrose (Kit Sorrell as a Child), Hugh Williams (Kit Sorrell as an Adult), Winifred Shotter (Molly Pentreath), Margot Grahame (Mrs. Dora Sorrell), Donald Calthrop (Dr. Richard Orange), Wally Patch (Buck), Evelyn Roberts (Mr. Roland), Hope Davy (Ethel), Louis Hayward (Duncan), Ruby Miller (Mrs. Palfrey), Arthur

Chesney (Mr. Porteous).

Repeating the role he performed in the silent version, Warner plays a captain whose wife walks out on him and leaves him with a young son to care for. Though down on his luck, Warner devotes every last bit of his energy to the boy's welfare. The son eventually becomes a successful doctor, and Warner lives long enough to see him marry his true love. Warner is nearly perfect in his portrayal of the broken man who refuses to give in, although choppy editing hinders the overall effort.

p, Herbert Wilcox; d, Jack Raymond; w, Lydia Hayward (based on the novel by Warwick Deeping); ph, Cyril Bristow.

Drama   (PR:A MPAA:NR)

SORROWFUL JONES*   (1949) 88m PAR bw

Bob Hope (Sorrowful Jones), Lucille Ball (Gladys O'Neill), William Demarest (Regret), Bruce Cabot (Big Steve Holloway), Thomas Gomez (Reardon), Tom Pedi (Once-Over Sam), Paul Lees (Orville Smith), Houseley Stevenson (Doc Chesley), Ben Welden (Big Steve's Bodyguard), Emmett Vogan (Psychiatrist), Mary Jane Saunders (Martha Jane Smith), Claire Carleton (Agnes "Happy Hips" Noonan), Harry Tyler (Blinky), John "Skins" Miller (Head Phone Man), Charley Cooley (Shorty), Marc Krah (Barber), Sid Tomack (Waiter at Steve's Place), Patsy O'Byrne (Charwoman), Ralph Peters (Cab Driver), Ed Dearing (Police Lt. Mitchell), Arthur Space (Plainclothesman), John Mallon, Frank Mills, Tony Cirillo, Allen Ray, Sam Finn, Bob Kortman, James Davies, James Cornell, Jack Roberts, Douglas Carter, Michael A. Cirillo (Horseplayers), Pat Lane, Billy Snyder, Kid Chissell, Eddie Rio (Bookies), William Yip, George Chan (Chinamen), Sally Rawlinson, Louise Lorimer (Nurses), Emmett Vogan, Maurice Cass (Psychiatrists), John Shay, Selmer Jackson (Doctors).

In his first semi-serious role, an unusually subdued Hope plays a New York bookie left with a gambler's daughter as a form of collateral. When the father doesn't return, the comedian attempts to cope with his new acquisition. Basically a remake of the Shirley Temple vehicle LITTLE MISS MARKER (1934), though Saunders proves every bit as capable as the famous child star. Much of the humor in this version is delivered by the various street characters the child meets while under Hope's care. This includes Ball as a Broadway singer who takes an interest in the kid. Hope is a pleasure to watch in a role that doesn't derive laughs solely from his hamming, but from witty dialog and peculiar situations. A forward narrated by Walter Winchell pays homage to Runyon and the characters he created.

p, Robert L. Welch; d, Sidney Lanfield; w, Melville Shavelson, Edmund Hartmann, Jack Rose (based on the story "Little Miss Marker" by Damon Runyon and a screenplay by William R. Lipman, Sam Hellman, and Gladys Lehman); ph, Daniel L. Fapp; m, Robert Emmett Dolan; ed, Arthur Schmidt; art d, Hans Dreier, Albert Nozaki; set d, Sam Comer, Bertram Granger; cos, Mary Kay Dodson; spec eff, Gordon Jennings; m/l, "Rock-A-Bye Bangtail (lyrics only)," "Havin' a Wonderful Wish," Jay Livingston, Ray Evans (sung by Lucille Ball); makeup, Wally Westmore.

Comedy   (PR:A MPAA:NR)

SORRY, WRONG NUMBER**   (1948) 89m PAR bw

Barbara Stanwyck (Leona Stevenson), Burt Lancaster (Henry Stevenson), Ann Richards (Sally Lord Dodge), Wendell Corey (Dr. Alexander), Harold Vermilyea (Waldo Evans), Ed Begley (James Cotterell), Leif Erickson (Fred Lord), William Conrad (Morano), John Bromfield (Joe, Detective), Jimmy Hunt (Jimmy Lord), Dorothy Neumann (Miss Jennings), Paul Fierro (Harpootlian), Kristine Miller (Dolly, Dr. Alexander's Girl Friend), Suzanne Dalbert (Cigarette Girl), Joyce Compton (Blonde), Tito Vuolo (Albert, Waiter), Ashley Cowan (Clam Digger), Cliff Clark (Sergeant Duffy), Igor Dega, Grace Poggi (Dancers).

A gripping film version of the classic 22 minute radio play which was made famous by Agnes Moorehead in a tour-de-force performance in 1943. Because Moorehead was not a "star" in Hollywood (despite her wonderful performances in Orson Welles' CITIZEN KANE and THE MAGNIFICENT AMBERSONS), Barbara Stanwyck was given the role in the movie version and she made it her own. Stanwyck plays a whining, domineering, paranoid, hypochondriac New York heiress who has developed a psychosomatic illness that has made her a bed-ridden invalid. She lives in a fancy apartment with her milquetoast husband, Lancaster, and her only contact with the outside world is the telephone. One evening an annoyed Stanwyck impatiently works the phone to find her husband who is late for dinner. Somehow her lines get crossed and she is patched into another conversation. Before hanging up, she becomes intrigued by what she hears and it slowly dawns on her that she is listening to two men plotting the murder of a woman. When the conversation ends, she immediately calls the police. Because she has proved herself to be an annoyance with the department before, the cops humor her somewhat and state that she doesn't have enough evidence to go on. Unsatisfied, she makes a flurry of phone calls--all to no avail--and eventually pieces together, from the little that she's been unable to uncover, that she is the intended victim. Meanwhile we learn that Lancaster, who had married Stanwyck for her inheritance, has gambled away a small fortune and is now being blackmailed. His back to the wall, he has decided to have his wife murdered so that he can collect the insurance and the inheritance, thereby paying off his debts and becoming a wealthy man. Lancaster has been pushed into this drastic decision by a mysterious hood, Conrad, and though it will solve all his problems, Lancaster is a bit ambivalent. When the frantic Stanwyck finally makes phone contact with Lancaster and begs for help, the conversation serves to confuse his conscience even further. Conrad forces Lancaster to leave town so that the murder will look like it occurred during a burglary attempt. At the last minute, Lancaster has a change of heart and calls to warn Stanwyck, but at that moment she sees the shadow of the killer coming up the stairs. All Lancaster hears is her horrified screams and then silence. A man's voice comes on the line and says, "Wrong number." Lancaster has called too late. The police, who have finally pieced the puzzle together, have traced the call and arrived at the phone booth to arrest Lancaster. SORRY, WRONG NUMBER is a taut, fast-paced chiller and director Litvak's handling of actors and flair for visuals are used to stunning affect. Visually, he and cinematographer Polito turn Stanwyck's lush apartment into a virtual prison from which there is no escape. The use of sound is quite effective here as well and serves to heighten the tension. The sense of claustrophobia is stifling and the situation made even more tragic with the knowledge that Stanwyck's invalid condition is all in her head– she can escape at any time. Stanwyck is superb in a role that requires her to maintain a sense of dread and hysteria throughout the entire picture. To help her essay her difficult performance, director Litvak shot all Stanwyck's scenes in sequence over a span of twelve days. The day-to-day calling up of fear and emotion proved difficult for the actress and she had trouble "coming down" at the end of a day's shooting. The performance won her a fourth Best Actress nomination, but she lost again– this time to Jane Wyman for JOHNNY BELINDA. Though the film is totally dominated by Stanwyck, Lancaster turns in an impressive performance that was quite against type. Originally thought too strong and rugged for the role of the henpecked husband driven to murder, Lancaster convinced producer Wallis that he would be perfect for the part because the audience would feel that this once strong, confident man had allowed himself to be bought by a rich woman and then had been destroyed by her shrewish behavior. Lancaster won the role and made the part much more human and memorable because of it. Lucille Fletcher, who had written the radio play, adapted the material for the screen herself and did a superior job fleshing out the characters and situations to fill a feature-length film. SORRY, WRONG NUMBER is another great example of how good films can be when all the right elements are put into place and executed with skill.

p, Hal B. Wallis, Anatole Litvak; d, Litvak; w, Lucille Fletcher (based on her radio play); ph, Sol Polito; m, Franz Waxman; ed, Warren Low; md, Waxman; art d, Hans Dreier, Earl Hedrick; set d, Sam Comer, Bertram Granger; cos, Edith Head; spec eff, Gordon Jennings.

Drama   **Cas.**   **(PR:C   MPAA:NR)**

SORRY YOU'VE BEEN TROUBLED   (SEE: LIFE GOES ON, 1932, Brit.)

SORYU HIKEN   (SEE: SECRET SCROLLS, PART II, 1968, Jap.)

SO'S YOUR AUNT EMMA   (SEE: MEET THE MOB, 1942)

SO'S YOUR UNCLE**   (1943) 64m UNIV bw

Billie Burke (Minerva), Donald Woods (Steve Curtis), Elyse Knox (Pat Williams), Frank Jenks (Joe Elliott), Robert Lowery (Roger Bright), Irving Bacon (Dempster), Chester Clute (Dinwiddle), Paul Stanton (John L. Curtis), Jack Norton (Drunk), Tom Kennedy (Cop), John Dilson (Stevens), Claire Whitney (Marta), William Ruhl (Crell), Jack Rice (Designer), Rita Gould (Mrs. Buffington), Syd Saylor (Meek Character), John Hamilton (Mr. Craig), Dick Elliott (Police Sergeant), Eddie Dunn (Proprietor), Emmett Vogan (Headwaiter), Gladys Gale (Elastic Woman), Anthony Warde (Stagehand), Lew Kelly (Doorman), Rex Lease (Hotel Clerk), Donald Kerr (Chauffeur), Warren Jackson (Policeman), Phil Warren (Vandini), Charles Hall (Waiter), Jacqueline Dalya (Garter Girl), Isabelle Lamal (Mrs. Van Cleave), Harry Harvey (Man), Edna Harris (2nd Woman), Jack Gardner (Stagehand), Barbara Fleming (Chorus Girl), Alice Draper (Pidgeon Girl), Genevieve Bell (1st Woman), Frank O'Connor (Burly Character), Mary O'Brien, Tailor Maids, Delta Rhythm Boys, Jan Garber and Jack Teagarden Orchestras.

Struggling actor-playwright Woods tries to avoid his creditors by impersonating his elderly uncle, only to get into a bigger jam when he's hit by a limo carrying Knox. The wealthy woman takes Woods home to her aunt, Burke, who is looking for another spouse. Woods, in his phony garb, fits the bill. He convinces the old woman to back "his nephew's" play, continuing his masquerade. Suddenly the real uncle shows up, and the film ends with a double wedding between him and Burke, and Woods and Knox. Songs include "St. Louis Blues" (W.C. Handy, sung by the Delta Rhythm Boys), "Don't Get Around Much Anymore" (Duke Ellington, Bob Russell, sung by the Delta Rhythm Boys), "Liza" (George Gershwin, sung by the Tailor Maids), "That's the Way It Goes" (Milton Rosen, Everett Carter, sung by Mary O'Brien), "You're Driving Me Crazy" (sung by Jan Garber and his Orchestra), "Dark Eyes" (sung by Mary O'Brien, with Jack Teagarden and His Orchestra). Other songs were penned by Walter Donaldson and W.C. Handy.

p&d, Jean Yarbrough; w, Maurice Leo, Clyde Bruckman (based on the story "Let Yourself Go" by Leonard Lee); ph, Elwood Bredell, Milton Krasner; ed, Paul Landres; md, Charles Previn; cos, Vera West.

Comedy   **(PR:A   MPAA:NR)**

SOTTO IL TALLONE   (SEE: CLOPORTES, 1966, Fr./Ital.)

SOUFFLE AU COUER, LE   (SEE: MURMUR OF THE HEART, 1971, Fr.)

SOUHVEZDI PANNY   (SEE: SIGN OF THE VIRGIN, 1969, Czech.)

SOUL KISS   (SEE: LADY'S MORALS, A, 1930)

SOUL OF A MONSTER, THE*½   (1944) 61m COL bw

Rose Hobart (Lilyan Gregg), George Macready (Dr. George Winson), Jim Bannon (Dr. Roger Vance), Jeanne Bates (Ann Winson), Erik Rolf (Fred Stevens), Ernest Hilliard (Wayne).

Hobart plays a demonic woman with supernatural powers, which she uses to save Macready's life. Now under her hypnotic spell, he carries out her evil deeds until Rolf and company are able to free their friend from Hobart's powers.

p, Ted Richmond; d, Will Jason; w, Edward Dein; ph, Burnett Guffey; ed, Paul Borofsky; md, Mischa Bakaleinikoff; art d, Lionel Banks, George Brooks.

Mystery/Horror   **(PR:A   MPAA:NR)**

SOUL OF NIGGER CHARLEY, THE**   (1973) 110m PAR c

Fred Williamson (Charley), D'Urville Martin (Toby), Denise Nicholas (Elena), Pedro Armendariz, Jr (Sandoval), Kirk Calloway (Marcellus), George Allen (Ode), Kevin Hagen (Col. Blanchard), Michael Cameron (Sgt. Foss), Johnny Greenwood (Roy), James Garbo (Collins), Nai Bonet (Anita), Robert Minor (Fred), Joe Henderson (Lee), Dick [Richard] Farnsworth (Walker), Tony Brubaker (Aben), Boyd "Red" Morgan (Donovan), Al Hassan (Vet), Ed Hice, Henry Wills (Mexicans), Phil Avenetti (Pedro), Fred Lerner (Woods).

Williamson and Martin take up where they left off in the popular LEGEND OF NIGGER CHARLIE: This time their goal is to free a number of slaves kept captive by a former Confederate general in Mexico. They enlist the aid of Mexican bandit Armendariz by offering him $100,000 stolen from the general, and an excessively bloody battle follows. Adaquate performances by Williamson, Martin, and the rest of the cast are marred by choppy editing. Spangler, who produced the original film, serves as director, and Lou Rawls sings two songs off-screen.

p&d, Larry Spangler; w, Harold Stone (based on a story by Spangler); ph, Richard C. Glouner (Movielab Color); m, Don Costa; ed, Howard Kuperman; art d, Gene Rudolph.

Western   **(PR:O   MPAA:R)**

SOUL OF THE SLUMS*   (1931) 64m Ralph M. Like-Actions bw (GB: THE SAMARITAN)

William Collier, Jr, Blanche Mehaffey, Murray Smith, James Bradbury, Jr, Walter Long, Paul Weigel, Max Asher.

Haphazardly constructed story has convict Collier leaving jail to seek revenge against the man who framed him However, Collier falls for the man's ex-girl friend Mehaffey, and vows to change his course in life. Collier, the son of actor William Collier, Sr., began appearing with his father as a child, making his screen debut at age 14. He developed into a popular leading man in silent films during the 1920s and made a successful transition to the sound era, but retired in the mid-1930s.

p, Ralph M. Like; d, Frank Strayer; w, W. Scott Darling; ph, Jules Cronjager; ed, Byron Robinson.

Crime/Drama   **(PR:A   MPAA:NR)**

SOUL SOLDIERS   (SEE: RED, WHITE, AND BLACK, THE, 1970)

SOULS AT SEA**½   (1937) 90m PAR bw

Gary Cooper (Michael "Nuggin" Taylor), George Raft (Powdah), Frances Dee (Margaret Tarryton), Henry Wilcoxon (Lt. Stanley Tarryton), Harry Carey (Captain of the "William Brown"), Olympe Bradna (Babsie), Robert Cummings (George Martin), Porter Hall (Court Prosecutor), George Zucco (Barton Woodley), Virginia Weidler (Tina), Joseph Schildkraut (Gaston de Bastonet), Gilbert Emery (Capt. Martisel), Lucien Littlefield (Tina's Father the Toymaker), Paul Fix (Violinist), Tully Marshall (Pecora), Monte Blue (Mate of the "William Brown"), Stanley Fields (Capt. Paul M. Granley), Fay Holden (Mrs. Martin), Clyde Cook (Hendry the Coachman), Rollo Lloyd (Parchy, Mate on Slaver), Wilson Benge (Doctor), Rolfe Sedan, Eugene

Borden *(Friends of de Bastonet)*, Lee Shumway *(Mate)*, Ethel Clayton *(Passenger)*, Harvey Clark *(Court Clerk)*, Forbes Murray *(Associate Justice)*, Davison Clark *(Bailiff)*, William Stack *(Judge)*, Charles Middleton *(Jury Foreman)*, Olaf Hytten *(Proprietor)*, Forrester Harvey *(Proprietor of Pub)*, Jane Weir *(Barmaid)*, Lina Basquette *(Brunette in Saloon)*, Pauline Haddon *(Blonde)*, Lowell Drew *(Jury Foreman)*, Paul Stanton *(Defense Attorney for "Nuggin" Taylor)*, Leslie Francis *(Woodley's Secretary)*, Robert Barrat *(The Reverend)*, Constantine Romanoff *(Pub Drinker)*, Henry Mowbray *(Bus Man)*, George Andre Beranger *(Henri)*, Lillian Dean, Betty Lorraine, Agnes Ayres, Alan Ladd, Lon McAllister, Luana Walters, Margaret Daggett, Galan Galt, Marty Faust, Beth Hartman, Fritzi Brunette, Francis Sayles, Bob McKenzie, Jane Keckley.

Cooper is first mate on a slave ship who assumes command when the captain is killed during an abortive mutiny. An abolitionist himself, Cooper sets the cargo free and subsequently allows the ship to be boarded by a British naval vessel. Cooper and his shipmate and friend Raft are brought to Liverpool to be tried for mutiny. The case is dismissed for lack of evidence but shortly thereafter Cooper is approached by agents of a naval intelligence agency and asked to help gather information that could put a stop to the slave trade once and for all. Cooper and Raft set sail on another ship, bound for America, and each falls in love: Cooper with Dee, whose officer brother is one of the slavers, and Raft with Bradna. Dee's brother, Wilcoxon, suspects Cooper's mission and ransacks his cabin. Cooper comes in and the two fight, the sound frightening the little girl in the next cabin, Weidler, who knocks over a lantern that soon has the whole ship ablaze. Only one lifeboat makes it into the water and Cooper tries to stop the passengers and crew from overcrowding the boat and swamping it. Wilcoxon turns up again and the two fight some more until Cooper throws him overboard. After seeing Dee safely into the boat, Cooper prepares to go down with the ship, but Raft comes up behind him and knocks him out, then tosses him into the dinghy. Raft, however, will not leave without Bradna, and when he finds her trapped and badly injured below deck, he stays with her while they both go to their watery grave. Cooper regains consciousness in the lifeboat and decides it is too crowded, so he chucks a couple more passengers overboard. This callous act horrifies Dee, and after they are rescued she presses charges. Another trial convenes, and Cooper is saved when the intelligence agent who had originally recruited him for the mission tells the court that Cooper had to save himself in order to successfully complete his important assignment. Dee promptly forgives him. This largely undistinguished Cooper vehicle was intended by Paramount to compete head to head with MGM's MUTINY ON THE BOUNTY and the studio was planning to release the film as a roadshow until somebody apparently pointed out that the film simply wasn't that good. It was recut to a more moderate length, losing a whole scene in Queen Victoria's court and a number of cast members, including Ward Bond, Edward Van Sloan, and many others. Raft was offered his role, but turned it down, refusing to die on screen for the umpteenth time. Then he proposed a compromise: if Cooper would die in the picture, so would he. This was totally unacceptable to the studio and they refused his offer, hiring Lloyd Nolan for the part. The studio people were not happy about having to go with Nolan, who they felt looked too much like Cooper (???), and when Nolan became ill, they hired Anthony Quinn for the role. Finally Raft relented and agreed to die for the camera again, and he earned a nomination for a Best Supporting Actor Oscar for his performance. Raft still gave the producers trouble, though, initially refusing to throw a rock at Dee as called for in the script, telling Hathaway, "I'd look like a real rat." The studio threatened to tear up his contract and he told them to go ahead. Finally he and Cooper went for a long walk over what were then the dirt roads of Beverly Hills and Raft explained his position. Cooper agreed with him and refused to do the picture without Raft, so the scene was cut. On location out on Catalina Island for seven months, Raft and Cooper became close friends, and director Hathaway, notorious for bullying his actors, was informed by the two stars' agents that if they were yelled at, they would walk off the picture. Hathaway never once raised his voice to them.

p, Henry Hathaway, Grover Jones; d, Hathaway; w, Jones, Dale Van Every, Richard Talmadge (based on a story by Ted Lesser); ph, Charles Lang, Jr.; m, W. Franke Harling, Milan Roder, Bernhard 'Bernard' Kaun, John Leipold; ed, Ellsworth Hoagland; md, Boris Morros; art d, Hans Dreier, Roland Anderson; set d, A.E. Freudemann; cos, Edith Head; spec eff, Gordon Jennings; m/l, "Susie Sapple," "Hang Boys Hang," Ralph Rainger, Leo Robin.

Drama   **(PR:A   MPAA:NR)**

SOULS FOR SABLES   (SEE: LOVEBOUND, 1932)

SOULS FOR SALE   (SEE: CONFESSIONS OF AN OPIUM EATER, 1962)

SOULS IN CONFLICT*½   (1955, Brit.) 75m Anglo-Scottish c

Joan Winmill *(Ann Woodbridge)*, Eric Micklewood *(Geoff Bradley)*, Charles Leno *(Tom Stock)*, Hilda Fenemore *(Ruth Stock)*, Frederick Leister *(Rev. Alan Woodbridge)*, Neal Arden *(Frank)*, Billy Graham, Colleen Townsend Evans, Don Moomaw.

Some religious-themed films reveal their ideas and messages in subtle forms. This one etches its message on a lead pipe and proceeds to bash the

audience soundly over the head with it. Three down-and-outers, a vicar's daughter turned actress, a test pilot, and a factory worker/failed gambler, all live their lives with little meaning. Enter the Billy Graham crusade, complete with the famed evangelist playing himself, and their once empty souls are rejuvenated. The film isn't helped any by its saccharine presentation. Among the cast only Graham comes across as sincere, but that's to no one's surprise. He also served as producer.

p, Billy Graham, Dick Ross; d&w, Ross, Leonard Reeve (based on a story by Ross); ph, Guy Green (Eastmancolor).

Religious Drama   **(PR:A   MPAA:NR)**

SOULS OF SIN   (SEE: MALE AND FEMALE SINCE ADAM AND EVE, 1961, Arg.)

SOUND AND THE FURY, THE***½   (1959) 115m FOX c

Yul Brynner *(Jason)*, Joanne Woodward *(Quentin)*, Margaret Leighton *(Caddy)*, Stuart Whitman *(Charles Busch)*, Ethel Waters *(Dilsey)*, Jack Warden *(Ben Compson)*, Francoise Rosay *(Mrs. Compson)*, John Beal *(Howard)*, Albert Dekker *(Earl)*, Stephen Perry *(Luster)*, William Gunn *(T.P.)*, Roy Glenn *(Job)*.

After watching Jerry Wald's production of Faulkner's novel, you won't wish you were in the land of cotton where old times are not forgotten. Decadence rules in Faulkner's world and this is no exception. Beal and Warden are brothers to Leighton, an alcoholic nymphomaniac. Warden is an imbecile who doesn't say a word and Beal's character is underwritten to a point where no one is quite sure about his place in matters. The focus is on Leighton, who had to alter her British accent to fit the role of a fallen Dixie woman. The father of this unlikely trio had remarried after the death of his first wife and acquired a stepson, Brynner, who now rules the family roost by dint of having taken on the name of his stepfather. Woodward is Leighton's illegitimate daughter and all of them are under the benevolent thumb of Brynner. Leighton had abandoned Woodward at her birth and gone off to play in the outside world. She returns now, ostensibly to reawaken her love for her daughter, but the truth is that she is so washed out that men won't play with her any longer and she needs a place to live. Woodward is starved for affection and finds it in the strong arms of circus roustabout Whitman. He has an affair with her, then exits and Woodward must now face the world alone. Woodward finds Brynner attractive, despite his being her uncle, although incest is never fully plumbed as it was in the book. In the end, the teenaged Woodward (who was actually 29 at the time) demonstrates that she is not willing to give up her uncle Brynner just because there's a little incest law that forbids it. Brynner wears a wig and tries to subvert his foreign accent in favor of chitlins in his speech and sometimes succeeds, though not often. Waters is the family retainer who heads a group of black servants, with Perry being the standout as the youngster who takes care of the mute Warden. Brynner's role was the most intriguing in that he was seen to be the head of this family, desperately attempting to keep them together. In one sequence, he offers Whitman money to leave Woodward be and when the circus man takes the cash, Woodward sees that Brynner was right in his assumption of Whitman's basic dishonesty. There are several stories going simultaneously, and credit must be given to the way the screenwriters handled the multi-layered tale. New Yorker Ritt, who had already looked south in THE LONG HOT SUMMER, was to make several movies about the area, including NORMA RAE and SOUNDER. The sexuality, no matter how subtly it was depicted, will not be lost on youngsters.

p, Jerry Wald; d, Martin Ritt; w, Irving Ravetch, Harriet Frank, Jr. (based on the novel by William Faulkner); ph, Charles G. Clarke (CinemaScope, DeLuxe Color); m, Alex North; ed, Stuart Gilmore; md, Lionel Newman; art d, Lyle R. Wheeler, Maurice Ransford; cos, Adele Palmer.

Drama   **Cas.**   **(PR:C-O   MPAA:NR)**

SOUND BARRIER, THE (SEE: BREAKING THE SOUND BARRIER, 1952)

SOUND OF FURY, THE*   (1950) 90m UA bw (AKA: TRY AND GET ME)

Frank Lovejoy *(Howard Taylor)*, Kathleen Ryan *(Judy Tyler)*, Richard Carlson *(Gil Stanton)*, Lloyd Bridges *(Jerry Slocum)*, Katherine Locke *(Hazel)*, Adele Jergens *(Velma)*, Art Smith *(Hal Clendenning)*, Renzo Cesana *(Dr. Simone)*, Irene Vernon *(Helen Stanton)*, Cliff Clark *(Sheriff Demig)*, Carl Kent *(Donald Miller)*, Donald Smelick *(Tommy Tyler)*, Dabbs Greer *(Mike)*, Mack Williams *(Prof. Martin)*, Jane Easton *(Barbara Colson)*, John Pelletti *(Herb Colson)*, Mary Lawrence *(Kathy)*, Lynn Gray *(Vi Clendenning)*.

Down-on-his-luck family man Lovejoy meets up with pretty thief Bridges, and the two stage a series of holdups. They graduate to kidnaping, and Bridges murders the victim, causing public outcry. Lovejoy decides to implicate Bridges, and both are jailed. A mob of townspeople attacks the jail and kills the two men. The tightly woven screenplay builds to the traumatic conclusion. The combining of scenes depicting Lovejoy's life before and after his turn to crime makes the outcome particularly hard-hitting. Entire cast is effective in their portrayals, particularly Bridges, as the heartless crook.

p, Robert Stillman; d, Cyril (Cy) Endfield; w, Jo Pagano (based on his novel *The Condemned*); ph, Guy Roe; m, Hugo Friedhofer; ed, George Amy; art d, Perry Ferguson.

Crime/Drama (PR:C MPAA:NR)

SOUND OF HORROR* (1966, Span.) 85m
Zurbano/Europix-Consolidated bw (EL SONIDO D E LA MUERTE; EL SONIDO PREHISTORICO; AKA: SOUND FROM A MILLION YEARS AGO; THE PR EHISTORIC SOUND)

James Philbrook *(Pete)*, Arturo Fernandez *(Prof. Andre)*, Soledad Miranda *(Maria)*, Ingrid Pitt *(Sofia)*, Antonio Casas, Jose Bodalo, Lola Gaos, Francisco Piquer.

An expedition into the Greek Isles to search for treasure turns only up two ancient dinosaur eggs. One cracks open and unleashes a deadly, brontosaurus-like monster that is invisible but makes noise when in motion. Expedition member Fernandez is killed by the creature, as are several other members of the group. Philbrook succeeds only in maiming it, after which an assistant sacrifices his life by setting himself and the monster on fire.

p, Gregorio Sacristan; d, Jose Antonio Nieves-Conde; w, Sacristan, Sam X. Abarbanel; ph, Manuel Berenguer; m, Luis de Pablo; ed, Margarita Ochoa; art d, Luis Perez Espinosa, Gil Parrondo; set d, Julio Molina.

Horror **Cas.** (PR:C MPAA:NR)

SOUND OF LIFE, THE*** (1962, USSR) 78m Mosfilm-Gorky Film Studio/Artkino c (SLE POY MUZYKANT)

Boris Livanov *(Uncle Maxim Yatsenko)*, Vasily Livanov *(Pyotr)*, M. Strizhenova *(Anna Mikhaylovna)*, L. Kurdyumova *(Evelina)*, Yu Puziyov *(Joachim)*, Aleksey Gribov *(Fyodor Kaniba)*, S. Blinnikov *(Stavruchenko)*, V. Nurganov *(Ilya)*, V. Grachyov *(Andrey)*, N. Kondratyev *(Kuzma)*, N. Kozinin *(Bell-Ringer)*, A. Smirnov *(Popelskiy)*, Sergei Shestopalov *(Pyotr as a Child)*, Marina Kurakova *(Evelina as a Child)*, Leonid Zolotukhin, N. Valandina, V. Yakovlev.

In pre-revolutionary Russia, Livanov plays the blind son of a wealthy noble family who, upon the advice of his wise uncle, forgoes enrollment into a music conservatory and instead travels across the country dressed as a peasant. Though he misses out on formal training, his many encounters fill him with the desire to create music motivated from his heart. He returns to give a spectacular premiere. Musical selections from works by Felix Mendelssohn and Frederic Chopin are performed.

d, Tatyana Lukashevitch; w, Iosif Manevich, A. Repina (based on the novel *The Blind Musician* by Vladimir Korolenko) ph, V. Masevich (Sovcolor); m, Yuriy Levitin; ed, A. Medvedeva; md, V. Dudarova; art d, B. Tsaryov; cos, V. Kiselyova; makeup, M. Agafonova.

Drama (PR:A MPAA:NR)

SOUND OF MUSIC, THE**** (1965) 174m FOX c

Julie Andrews *(Maria)*, Christopher Plummer *(Capt. Von Trapp)*, Eleanor Parker *(The Baroness)*, Richard Haydn *(Max Detweiler)*, Peggy Wood *(Mother Abbess)*, Charmian Carr *(Liesl)*, Heather Menzies *(Louisa)*, Nicholas Hammond *(Friedrich)*, Duane Chase *(Kurt)*, Angela Cartwright *(Brigitta)*, Debbie Turner *(Marta)*, Kym Karath *(Gretl)*, Anna Lee *(Sister Margaretta)*, Portia Nelson *(Sister Berthe)*, Ben Wright *(Herr Zeller)*, Daniel Truhitte *(Rolfe)*, Norma Varden *(Frau Schmidt)*, Gil Stuart *(Franz)*, Marni Nixon *(Sister Sophia)*, Evadne Baker *(Sister Bernice)*, Doris Lloyd *(Baroness Ebberfeld)*.

THE SOUND OF MUSIC is one of the most loved movie musicals ever made, but not necessarily one of the best. As a play, it was not ranked close to several of Rodgers and Hammerstein's classics, such as OKLAHOMA, CAROUSEL, or SOUTH PACIFIC. Even THE KING AND I had more respect from the Broadway wise guys. Despite that, the film came to life under the firm hand of director Wise and his minions, most of whom had worked together before on WEST SIDE STORY. If one discounts SATURDAY NIGHT FEVER, this would have to be called the most successful musical in history. Julie Andrews had won an Oscar in her motion picture debut with MARY POPPINS, but this is the one that made her an enduring star for the next few decades. Although Wise is credited with being the producer, many of those labors were turned over to his knowledgeable associate, Saul Chaplin, himself a songwriter of note, who oversaw many of the musical chores including auditioning many male singers before he chose Bill Lee to loop the vocals for Plummer. The idea was not to get the best voice, but to find someone who could sing the way Plummer would sing, *if* he could sing. Andrews is a young postulant at the nunnery run by Wood, a stern but caring taskmistress who is at odds with the fun-loving Andrews from the start. It isn't long before Andrews realizes that the cloister is not for her. And yet, she still believes in the values espoused by the other sisters, so she goes out into the world as a human ray of sunshine and attempts to bring the humanity she's learned to the lay world. Soon enough, Andrews is hired as a governess in the family of Plummer, a man who had forsworn warmth when his wife died and left him with a septet of children. He is the

typical autocrat-aristocrat and won't bend an inch. Andrews notes that the children appear to be cowed by their disciplinarian father and she strives to open their lives to the joy that's abundant around them. They live in one of the most beautiful sections of the Alps and yet do not appreciate the surrounding vistas until Andrews shows them, with her fresh outlook, what they have. The family sings and Haydn is a man who would like to ink them to a pact that would require them to work a great deal. At the same time, Plummer is lonely and considering a new mate in Parker, a rich peeress who makes no bones about her attraction to the man. Haydn wants the family to enter the Salzburg music festival and Plummer is totally against it. Andrews finds her affection growing for Plummer and doesn't quite know how to handle it so she goes back to the abbey. The children follow her and plead for her to return to their home. When Wood learns of the predicament, she encourages Andrews to go back to the children she loves so much. Once there, Andrews hears that Plummer and Parker are to be wed. But Parker, an understanding woman, becomes aware that Plummer truly loves Andrews and so she steps aside in favor of their happiness and Plummer marries Andrews. They go off on a blissful honeymoon but there is a storm over the horizon as the Nazis begin their *anschluss* and march into Austria, where Hitler was born. Haydn enters the children in the singing festival at Salzburg, knowing full well what Plummer's response will be upon his return, but hoping that the man will relent in the face of his new marital situation. Haydn is incorrect because when Plummer and Andrews come home, still aglow, his face darkens and he stops the idea of the children performing. Plummer is a proud Austrian of exceptional lineage and he despises the Nazis who now rule. They have given him orders to leave immediately and take over a ship as its captain. Plummer's response is to gather his wife and children and attempt to flee Austria but they are caught by the Nazis. Some fast-talking takes place and Plummer says that they are not leaving Austria, just making the trip to Salzburg where the children are to sing. As soon as that's done, he'll be happy to assume command of the vessel. The Nazis are not so sure so they accompany the family to the theater where the festival is taking place. The family sings and wins the first prize; then they utilize their encore number to make their escape through a tunnel to the mountains close by. The family gets away and the picture ends on a great note of hope. Filmed on location for 11 weeks in Salzburg (with interiors at the Fox lot in West Los Angeles), it's a visual treat and probably did more for the Austrian tourist business than any other single event. That was more than negated in 1986 when it was discovered that the former head of the UN was suffering from "Waldheimer's Disease," a unique ailment that causes men in their 60s and 70s to forget that they'd once been Nazis. Rodgers and Hammerstein's score included two new songs in place of three others which had been excised. The new tunes are "I Have Confidence in Me" (sung by Andrews) and "Something Good" (sung by Andrews, Plummer [Lee!). Neither of them were as melodious as those in the original score but were placed in the script for story purposes. The other songs were "The Sound of Music" (sung by Andrews), "Preludium," "Morning Hymn," "Alleluia," "Maria" (nun's chorus), "Sixteen, Going on Seventeen" (Carr, Truhitte), "My Favorite Things" (Andrews), "Climb Every Mountain" (Wood), "The Lonely Goatherd," "Do Re Mi" (Andrews, Carr, Truhitte, Menzies, Cartwright, Chase, Hammond, Karath, Turner), "Edelweiss" (Plummer [Lee!, Andrews, children – see above), "So Long, Farewell" (children). In her screen debut, note the woman who sang so often for other actresses, Marni Nixon, as one of the sisters. The score was not as good as that of many of the R&H plays but this movie was stunningly done, with such a slick patina and so calculated to tug the heart that it touched a chord in every audience and many saw it again and again. Another film was made on the same subject, THE TRAPP FAMILY, but it didn't hurt this at the box office. THE SOUND OF MUSIC was voted Oscars for Best Picture, Wise's direction, and Kostal's musical direction. Andrews, Wood, and the brilliant cinematography of McCord were nominated. Andrews became the top box-office attraction after this and stayed there for two years. The picture gets sticky at times and a little too cute for its own good and it could have used some cutting of the script and surely a bit more humor, but that's niggling if you can stand the sweetness. Diabetics beware.

p&d, Robert Wise; w, Ernest Lehman (based on the musical play by Richard Rodgers, Oscar Hammerstein II, Howard Lindsay, Russel Crouse); ph, Ted McCord (Todd-AO, DeLuxe Color); m, Rodgers; ed, William Reynolds; md, Irwin Kostal; prod d, Boris Leven; set d, Walter M. Scott, Ruby Levitt; cos, Dorothy Jeakins; spec eff, L.B. Abbott, Emil Kosa, Jr.; ch, Marc Breaux, Dee Dee Wood; m/l, Rodgers, Hammerstein II; puppeteers, Bill and Cora Baird.

Musical/Biography **Cas.** (PR:AAA MPAA:G)

SOUND OF TRUMPETS, THE*** (1963, Ital.) 90m Twenty-Four Horses-Titanus/Janus bw (IL POSTO)

Sandro Panzeri *(Domenico Cantoni)*, Loredana Detto *(Antonietta Masetti)*, Tullio Kezich *(Psychologist)*, Mara Revel *(Old Woman)*.

The films of Ermanno Olmi received notice from only a handful of Americans until THE TREE OF WOODEN CLOGS won the Gold Palm Award at the 1978 Cannes Film festival. His films are strongly influenced by the Neorealist movement, and like TREES concentrate on the seemingly minor events in a person's lifetime that are often the most significant. In SOUND OF THE TRUMPETS, Panzeri is an office boy who has a pleasant meeting with a young girl who works in his office. He dreams of starting a romance with her but sees her too rarely to ask for a date. With the company's New Year's Eve party soon to arrive, Panzeri anxiously awaits his chance to meet her, but she never shows. At the end, Panzeri receives a promotion after a co-worker dies. In a totally unconcerned manner, the people make room for the new worker and go about their business. In keeping with the Neorealist tradition, none of the actors used were professionals, enhancing the realistic tone emphasized through the photography.

p, Alberto Soffientini; d&w, Ermanno Olmi; ph, Lamberto Caimi; m, Pier Emilio Bassi; ed, Carla Colombo; art d, Ettore Lombardi.

Drama   **(PR:A   MPAA:NR)**

SOUND OFF**½   (1952) 83m COL bw

Mickey Rooney (*Mike Donnelly*), Anne James (*Lt. Colleen Rafferty*), Sammy White (*Joe Kirby*), John Archer (*Maj. Paul Whiteside*), Gordon Jones (*Sgt. Crockett*), Wally Cassell (*Tony Baccigalupi*), Arthur Space (*Barney Fisher*), Pat Williams (*Vonnie Vanderveer*), Marshall Reed (*Capt. Karger*), Helen Ford (*Mrs. Rafferty*), Mary Lou Geer (*Evelyn Ames*), Boyd "Red" Morgan (*M.P.*).

Director-producer-screenwriter Blake Edwards shared scripting honors in this lighthearted picture featuring Rooney as a hard-nosed entertainer who, to his surprise, is inducted into the Army. He gets involved in a series of mishaps, but all turns out well in the end, with Rooney becoming a troop entertainer. Pace is lively, and material is tailored to Rooney's special talents. Edwards scripted several films for director Quines, including RAINBOW ROUND MY SHOULDER, MY SISTER EILEEN, and OPERATION MADBALL. Since his debut as a film director in 1955, he has directed and produced several successful movies, including DAYS OF WINE AND ROSES, A SHOT IN THE DARK, BREAKFAST AT TIFFANY'S, 10, and a series of Pink Panther films.

p, Jonie Taps; d, Richard Quine; w, Quine, Blake Edwards; ph, Ellis W. Carter (Super CineColor); ed, Charles Nelson; md, Morris Stoloff; art d, Carl Anderson; m/l, "My Lady Love," Lester Lee, Bob Russell, "Blow Your Horn," Mickey Rooney; Freddy Karger, Paul Mertz, George Duning.

Comedy   **(PR:A   MPAA:NR)**

SOUNDER***½   (1972) 105m Radnitz-Mattel/FOX c

Cicely Tyson (*Rebecca Morgan*), Paul Winfield (*Nathan Lee Morgan*), Kevin Hooks (*David Lee Morgan*), Carmen Mathews (*Mrs. Boatwright*), Taj Mahal (*Ike*), James Best (*Sheriff Young*), Yvonne Jarrell (*Josie Mae Morgan*), Eric Hooks (*Earl Morgan*), Sylvia "Kuumba" Williams (*Harriet*), Janet MacLachlan (*Camille Johnson*), Teddy Airhart (*Mr. Perkins*), Rev. Thomas N. Phillips (*Preacher*), Judge William Thomas Bennett (*Judge*), Inez Durham (*Court Clerk*), Spencer Bradford (*Clarence*), Myrl Sharkey (*Mrs. Clay*).

This was the first teaming of producer Radnitz with the mammoth Mattel Toy company and the result was a hit, not only with the public, but most of the critics. The movie was nominated for Best Picture, Best Script from another source, for Tyson's work as Best Actress and for Winfield as Best Actor. Coming on the heels of several black exploitation films such as SHAFT, SUPER FLY, and MELINDA, it was truly a breath of spring by comparison to those. Heartwarming, heart-tugging, heartbreaking...you can apply all of those words to this touching movie, a story that celebrates the bond of a family dedicated to each other through whatever travails befall them. It's the 1930s in Louisiana where Winfield and Tyson are raising their three children, E. Hooks, Jarrell, and K. Hooks, as best they can under the poverty circumstances of the Depression. Winfield farms the land and supplements their meals by hunting for game, Tyson takes in washing, and the trio of children have an equal hand in doing the other tasks. Kevin Hooks, Winfield, and the family dog, Sounder, go out hunting for their dinner one night. (Note: In the book, the dog had a much larger role, hence the title.) There is no game to be had (they can actually nail a raccoon but the darn thing is so cute they don't shoot it; also, if they had, it wouldn't have motivated the rest of the story), so the family goes without food that night. The following morning, a ham is found in the kitchen and Winfield won't tell Tyson where he got it, only giving her the explanation that he wasn't about to allow the kids to go without eating. Kevin Hooks goes to school that morning. It's a white school and there could be a problem but Winfield and Tyson are determined to get their oldest son an education. That afternoon, Winfield is playing in a baseball game and afterward, he is arrested by the local lawman, Best, for having stolen the breakfast ham. Winfield is taken in handcuffs to the local jail as the dog chases after the pickup truck. The deputy shoots the dog with his shotgun and the animal yips, then limps away. Winfield comes before judge Bennett, is quickly tried and convicted and sentenced to one year at hard labor. Kevin Hooks comes to see him with the gift of a freshly baked cake still warm from Tyson's oven. The reason why Tyson didn't bring the cake herself is explained harshly and we learn that black women are precluded from visiting their men. Winfield is taken away, and Tyson and the children now begin a backbreaking schedule as they strive to work the land, make their quota and keep body and soul together. Kevin Hooks adores his father and appreciates what the man went through to bring food to his family so he asks Mathews, a kindly white woman who likes him, to intervene and find out where Winfield is being held, information the boy could not get without her help. He learns the location and sets off, by foot, with the dog, to find Winfield. It takes a long

time and the trip is dangerous and by the time he gets to the work camp, he is crushed to learn that Winfield has been transferred to another location, and no one seems to know where that is. The youth now begins on the road back and becomes lost, eventually winding up at a black school run by MacLachan, who sees how tired the boy is and has him stay the night with her. The next day, she brings him to her school where he sees a different kind of education being taught, a premise that blacks are entitled to enjoy their culture, and instillation of a desire for more schooling. After a while, the boy bids MacLachan farewell and returns to the small house where his mother and siblings had been worried for his safety. He joins them in the farm chores as they work the sugar cane fields. Suddenly, the dog's happy bark causes them to look up and see Winfield coming toward them, walking with a cane. He has a smile that would light up a coal mine and they surround him and shower him with affection. Winfield explains that he's been released early due to an accident in which he was innocently maimed by a TNT explosion. With Winfield home, albeit crippled, the family is whole once more and starts to live again the way they did before. MacLachan sends Kevin Hooks a note asking if he would like to be part of her class when the next semester begins. This puts the boy into a serious moral dilemma. If he leaves, that will be one less person to work the farm. If he stays, he may never get the opportunity MacLachan is offering. He runs into the dense woods to think matters through as his eyes well with tears. Winfield limps after him, finds his son and tells him that making the decision to go to MacLachan's school won't obliterate their love for him. A person's got to do what's best for himself and this would be the best course of action for Hooks. With that assurance, the boy dries his tears and goes off in a wagon with Winfield, after having kissed Tyson, Eric Hooks and Jarrell goodbye. Filmed on location in Louisiana's St. Helena Parish and East Feliciana Parish, the story comes from a slim book that was the 1970 Newberry Award winner for children's literature. Radnitz often went to that source for his earlier films, including ISLAND OF THE BLUE DOLPHINS. This is a true "family film," much more so than many of the others which purport to be that. When a "G" rating is seen, most adults feel that it must be strictly for the tots. Not so in this case. Anyone from the age of seven on up will be moved by the story and appreciate the nuances of the superb actors. Taj Mahal, who repeated his musical and acting chores in the sequel, makes an impressive debut here and should have had a promising acting career but he appears to have forsworn that in favor of his music. Soreheads will say that the family is just a little too polite, too sweet, too nice, but they are in the minority and probably lily-white. Anyone who has ever been in a black home, where respect is the cornerstone of the family, will recognize the truth of the characters. A triumph for all concerned.

p, Robert B. Radnitz; d, Martin Ritt; w, Lonne Elder III (based on a novel by William H. Armstrong); ph, John Alonzo (Panavision, DeLuxe Color); m, Taj Mahal; ed, Sid Levin; prod d, Walter Herndon; cos, Nedra Watt; m/l, "Needed Time," Taj Mahal (sung by Lightnin' Hopkins).

Drama   **Cas.**   **(PR:AAA   MPAA:G)**

SOUNDER, PART 2***   (1976) 98m Radnitz-Mattel-ABC/Gamma III c

Harold Sylvester (*Nathan Lee Morgan*), Ebony Wright (*Rebecca Lee Morgan*), Taj Mahal (*Ike Phillips*), Annazette Chase (*Camille Johnson*), Darryl Young (*David Lee Morgan*), Erica Young (*Josie Mae Morgan*), Ronald Bolden (*Earl Morgan*), Barbara Chaney (*Mrs. Boatwright*), Kuumba (*Harriet*), Ted Airhart (*Mr. Perkins*), Walter Breaux (*Stranger*), Harry Franklin, Sr (*Rev. Josephs*), Irene Nofles (*Mrs. Roberts*), Carol Sutton, Warren Kenner, Emanual Jarrell, Don Bynum, Earl Billings, Raymond Armelino.

Elder, who wrote the screenplay for SOUNDER, comes back to do it again on this sequel which uses the Armstrong novel as the basis, although much of what is on the screen is from Elder's fertile brain. The low-budget original did surprisingly well at the theaters (just under $10 million), so the American Broadcasting Company financed this as a TV movie. When they saw what turned out, they decided to release it theatrically first. It's 1933 in a black farming community of Louisiana where a family of sharecroppers, headed by Sylvester and Wright (replacing Paul Winfield and Cicely Tyson) maintain their tightness and dignity in the face of the treatment they receive from the surrounding whites (who are only spoken of). Chase is a schoolteacher (the part was played by Janet MacLachan in the first film) who espouses some firm ideas which frighten outside people and the school at which she teaches is shut down for fear of an uprising. The local people want their children to go to school so they won't have to face the same deprivation of living on other folks' property and the story basically concerns the efforts of the sharecroppers to build a school in which Chase can educate the kids. Taj Mahal, who also wrote the excellent score (he did the first one as well) plays a lovely role as a friendly neighbor given to singing folk tunes. The warmth and closeness of the family is beautiful to see and there is enough laughter, in spite of their plight, to witness how the human condition can be uplifted by humor. Very few of the actors had been seen on screen before and that was a plus, as it seemed that they were real people in a real situation. Swiss-born cinematographer Furrer died at 41 just prior to the film's release, after a brief career that included superb work on DESPERATE CHARACTERS, SHAFT, and THE SEVEN UPS.

p, Terry Nelson; d, William A. Graham; w, Lonne Elder III (based on the novel by William H. Armstrong); ph, Urs B. Furrer (Movielab Color); m, Taj

Mahal; ed, Sid Levin; prod d, Walter Scott Herndon; set d, Cheryal Kearney.

Drama   **(PR:AA MPAA:G)**

SOUP FOR ONE**   (1982) 87m WB c

Saul Rubinek (Allan), Marcia Strassman (Maria), Gerrit Graham (Brian), Teddy Pendergrass (Nightclub Singer), Richard Libertini (Angelo), Andrea Martin (Concord Seductress), Mordecai Lawner (Furniture Salesman), Lewis J. Stadlen (Allan's Father), Joanna Merlin (Allan's Mother), Christine Baranski, Ellen March, Maury Chaykin, Deborah Offner, Michael Jeter, Anna Deavere Smith, Laura Dean, Marley Friedman, Andrew Friedman, Jessica James, Kate Lynch, Suzzy Roche, Claudia Cron, Cheri Jamison, Hilary Shapiro, Libby Boone, Catherine Lee Smith, Marisa Smith, Jamie Tirelli, Christina San Juan, James Rebhorn, Ron Faber, Gloria Cromwell, Thomas Quinn, Rick Lieberman, Ellie Covan, Bo Rucker, Jack Chandler, Michael Pearlman, Lauren Sautner, Karen Werner, Maggie Jakobson, Max Gulack, William Cuellar, Mitchell Jason, Sherrie Bender, Kim Chan, Linda Ray, Lisa Parker, Merwin Goldsmith, Olivia K. Le'Aauanae.

Debut film for writer-director Kaufer is a humorous and somewhat bitter look at a young, conservative, Jewish New Yorker's (Rubinek) quest to find true love in an increasingly alienating world. Rubinek's character serves as off-screen narrator, allowing the story to move along in a cohesive manner. The film's self-deprecating tone can be compared to that often taken by Woody Allen. However, Kaufer lacks a distancing objectivity, making his humor more bitter. Rubinek eventually finds the woman of his dreams but, as these things predictably go, she finds Rubinek repulsive. However, he is persistent and a romance eventually develops. Meanwhile, Rubinek wonders if the relationship is really what he wants. Although this Woody Allen-type humor is nothing new, Kaufer brings a type of energy rare in the cinema to this film. Rubinek also is the perfect actor to convey the neurotic tendencies of the protagonist.

p, Marvin Worth; d&w, Jonathan Kaufer; ph, Fred Schuler (Technicolor); m, Nile Rodgers, Bernard Edwards, Johnny Mandel; ed, David Rawlins; prod d, Philip Rosenberg; set d, Ed Stewart, Gary Brink; cos, Robert DeMora.

Comedy   **Cas.**   **(PR:O MPAA:R)**

SOUP TO NUTS*   (1930) 65m FOX bw

Ted Healy (Ted), Frances McCoy (Queenie), Stanley Smith (Carlson), Lucille Browne (Louise), Charles Winninger (Schmidt), Hallam Cooley (Throckmorton), George Bickel (Klein), William H. Tooker (Ferguson).

Burdensome film that depends almost entirely on old slapstick routines which went out with the Keystone Kops. The producers, apparently unaware of this, went and sunk a lot of money into it for nothing. Vaudevillian Healy, playing a straight-man role, heads a group of Mexican revolutionaries in this alleged comedy. Cartoonist-inventor Rube Goldberg had the dubious honor of scripting this disappointing film, his first screenwriting effort.

d, Benjamin Stoloff; w, Rube Goldberg, Howard J. Green; ph, Joseph Valentine; ed, Clyde Carruth.

Comedy   **(PR:A MPAA:NR)**

SOUP TO NUTS, 1982   (SEE: WAITRESS, 1982)

SOURDOUGH*½   (1977) 94m Film Saturation c

Gil Perry (Fur Trapper), Gene Evans (Narrator).

An outdoors frontier film about an old fur trapper, Perry, who ventures through the wilderness while trying to escape the advances of modern civilization. The plot comes second to the picturesque photography of the crystalline expanses of Alaska – photography which is more suited for travelogs, which is essentially what this picture is. Intercut into the film are antique stills and old black-and-white footage, while the entire picture is narrated by Gene Evans. Like so many of the nature films of the 1970s (the best known being THE ADVENTURES OF THE WILDERNESS FAMILY, 1975, which also spawned a pair of sequels), SOURDOUGH was distributed by a method called four-walling, which consisted of the filmmakers renting theaters throughout the country, at one time, and saturating the market with commercials in order to recoup their investment at once.

p, George E. Lukens, Jr., Robert B. Pendleton; d, Martin J. Spinelli; w, Spinelli, Lewis M. Turner (based on a story by Rod Perry); ph, Perry (Eastmancolor); m, Jerrold Immel; ed, George Folsey, Jr.

Adventure   **(PR:AA MPAA:G)**

SOUS LES TOITS DE PARIS   (SEE: UNDER THE ROOFS OF PARIS, 1930, Fr.)

SOUTH AMERICAN GEORGE**   (1941, Brit.) 92m COL British bw

George Formby (George Butters/Gilli Vanetti), Linden Travers (Carole Dean), Enid Stamp-Taylor (Frances Martinique), Jacques Brown (Enrico Richardo), Felix Aylmer (Mr. Appleby), Ronald Shiner (Swifty), Alf Goddard (Slappy), Gus McNaughton (George White), Mavis Villiers (Mrs. Durrant), Eric Clavering (Mr. Durrant), Beatrice Varley (Mrs. Butters), Herbert Lomas (Mr. Butters), Muriel George, Cameron Hall, Charles Paton, Rita Grant, Norman Pierce.

To help out his exact double, Formby (in a dual role) takes the place of a noted South American tenor. This way he can help the opera star fulfill contract obligations and also win the heart of the man's lovely press agent, Travers. Formby ends up being chased by some hitmen hired to kill the opera singer, but all works out for a typically happy conclusion. Formby's comic talents give the unlikely story a few fun moments though the film is for the most part a hit-and-miss effort.

p, Ben Henry; d, Marcel Varnel; w, Leslie Arliss, Norman Lee, Austin Melford; ph, Arthur Crabtree.

Comedy   **(PR:A MPAA:NR)**

SOUTH OF ALGIERS   (SEE: GOLDEN MASK, THE, 1954, Brit.)

SOUTH OF ARIZONA*½   (1938) 55m COL bw

Charles Starrett (Clay Travers), Iris Meredith (Ann Madison), Bob Nolan (Bob), Dick Curtis (Ed Martin), Robert Fiske (Mark Kenyon), Edmund Cobb (Dorn), Art Mix (Santos), Richard [Dick] Botiller (Latigo), Lafe McKee (Lafe Brown), Ed Coxen (Jed), Hank Bell (Hank), Sons of the Pioneers [Nolan, Pat Brady, Hugh Farr, Carl Farr, Lloyd Perryman], Hal Taliaferro, George Morrell, Steve Clark, John Tyrrell.

The murder of an innocent youth forces the people of a peaceful town to keep silent for fear of angering killers Fiske and Curtis. In an effort to help out the victim's kid sister, Meredith, Starrett breaks the town's vow of silence to see that justice is done. In the process, a very trite romance between Starrett and Meredith takes root.

p, Harry Decker; d, Sam Nelson; w, Bennett Cohen; ph, Benjamin Kline; ed, William Lyon; m/l, Bob Nolan.

Western   **(PR:A MPAA:NR)**

SOUTH OF CALIENTE*   (1951) 67m REP bw

Roy Rogers (Himself), Dale Evans (Doris Stewart), Pinky Lee (Himself), Douglas Fowley (Dave Norris), Rick Roman (Josef), Leonard Penn (Commandante), Willie Best (Willie), Lillian Molieri (Gypsy Dancer), Charlita (Rosina), Pat Brady (Pat), Frank Richards (Studsy), Marguerite McGill, Roy Rogers Riders, Trigger the Horse.

A below-par outing for Rogers that lacks action and quick pacing. This time Rogers is out to nab the thieves who steal Evans' prize horse and try to sell it in Mexico. The villains turn out to be headed by Evans' trainer, Fowley. But before he is brought to justice, Rogers, Evans and Lee find time to sing four songs. They include: "Gypsy Trail," "My Home Is Over Yonder," and "Won'tcha Be a Friend of Mine?" (Jack Elliott), and "Yascha the Gypsy" (Lee Wainer).

p, Edward J. White; d, William Witney; w, Eric Taylor; ph, Jack Marta; ed, Harold Minter; md, Dale Butts; art d, Frank Hotaling.

Western   **(PR:A MPAA:NR)**

SOUTH OF DEATH VALLEY*½   (1949) 54m COL bw (GB: RIVER OF POISON)

Charles Starrett (Steve Downey/Durango Kid), Smiley Burnette (Himself), Gail Davis (Molly Tavish), Fred Sears (Ashton), Lee Roberts (Scotty Tavish), Richard Emory (Tommy Tavish), Clayton Moore (Bead), Jason Robards, Sr (Mullen), Tommy Duncan and his Western All Stars.

When a battle between local ranchers and a mining company erupts over pollution of the water source they share, Starrett is called upon to do some investigating. But the real heroics are carried out by his masked double, the DURANGO KID, who finds a way to bring peace to the valley. Burnette supplies the laughs. (See DURANGO KID series, Index.)

p, Colbert Clark; d, Ray Nazarro; w, Earle Snell (based on a story by James Gruen); ph, Fayte Browne; ed, Paul Borofsky; art d, Charles Clague; set d, George Montgomery.

Western   **(PR:A MPAA:NR)**

SOUTH OF DIXIE*½   (1944) 61m UNIV bw

Anne Gwynne (Dixie), David Bruce (Danny), Jerome Cowan (Brains), Ella Mae Morse (Barbara Ann), Joe Sawyer (Ernest), Samuel S. Hinds (Col. Morgan), Eddie Acuff (Jay), Marie Harmon (Annabelle), Oscar O'Shea (Col. Hatcher), Louise Beavers (Chloe), Pierre Watkin (Dean Williamson), Billy Bevan (Announcer), Marie Blake (Ruby), Rita Gould (Woman), Edward Keane (Mr. Platt), Manton Moreland (Porter), Ray Walker (Reporter), Eddie

Bruce *(Clerk)*, Jack Mulhall *(Photographer)*, Iris Clive [Eden] *(Girl Kibitzer)*, Joyce Miller *(Girl Piano Player)*, Donald Kerr, Joseph Haworth *(Reporters)*, Charles Stantz, Sherrill Luke, Bobby Brooks and Quartet, Lester Cole and the Debutantes, The Charmers.

Film is basically an excuse to perform a few fair tunes. Bruce is a famous writer of Southern ballads who actually hails from the North. When his partner promotes him as the subject for a biography, Bruce heads south to create a phony family background. Gwynne escorts him and tutors him on his accent. During the trip, the two fall in love, but their romance is temporarily interrupted when southern belle Morse, a colonel's daughter, takes a liking to Bruce. Songs include: "Shoo Shoo Baby" (Phil Moore; sung by Ellamae Morse), "I'm A-Headin' South," "Never Again," (sung by Morse) "Loo-Loo-Louisiana," "Cross My Heart" (Everett Carter, Milton Rosen), "When It's Darkness on the Delta" (Marty Symes, A.J. Neiberg, Jerry Livingston), and "Weep No More My Lady" (Joan Whitney, Alex Cramer).

p&d, Jean Yarbrough; w, Clyde Bruckman (based on a story by Sam Coslow); ph, Jerome Ash; ed, Paul Landres; md, Sam Freed, Jr.; art d, John B. Goodman, Harold H. MacArthur; Cos, Vera West.

Musical   **(PR:A   MPAA:NR)**

SOUTH OF PAGO PAGO**½   (1940) 96m UA bw

Victor McLaglen *(Bucko Larson)*, Jon Hall *(Kehane)*, Frances Farmer *(Ruby Taylor)*, Olympe Bradna *(Malla)*, Gene Lockhart *(Lindsay)*, Douglas Dumbrille *(Williams)*, Francis Ford *(Foster)*, Ben Welden *(Grimes)*, Abner Biberman *(Ferro)*, Pedro de Cordoba *(Chief)*, Rudy Robles *(Luna)*, Robert Stone *(Hono)*, Nellie Duran *(Laulau)*, James Flavin *(Cafe Customer)*, Nina Campana *(Hono's Mother)*, James Leong *(Waiter)*, Harry Woods *(Black Mike Rafferty)*.

McLaglen heads an expedition to the South Seas in search of pearls, but meets with resistance from a tribal chief who is protecting his people's wealth from the fortune hunters. McLaglen uses Farmer as a ploy to attract the chief, Hall. His plan works and the pair marries. But, the pearl hunt is thwarted when natives lead a bloody siege against the ship in which everyone dies, including Farmer. Hard-hitting action and first-rate photography make this story stand out from routine adventure films. Farmer, who made her screen debut in 1936, began what was expected to be a promising career in films and on stage. Though talented and beautiful, her alcoholism forced her into retirement in 1942; she also spent several years in mental institutions during the 1940s. She made one more film in the 1950s and hosted a local television show in Indianapolis. She died in 1970 at the age of 57. A movie about her life, FRANCES, was released in 1982.

p, Edward Small; d, Alfred E. Green; w, George Bruce; ph, John Mescall; ed, Ray Curtis; md, Edward Ward; art d, John DuCasse Schulze; ch, Jack Crosby; m/l, Bob Wright, Chet Forrest, Lew Pollack.

Adventure   Cas.   **(PR:A   MPAA:NR)**

SOUTH OF PANAMA*   (1941) 68m PRC bw

Roger Pryor *(Mike Lawrence)*, Virginia Vale *(Jan Martin)*, Lionel Royce *(Burns)*, Lucien Prival *(Raynor)*, Duncan Renaldo *(Police Chief)*, Lester Dorr *(Joe)*, Jack Ingram *(Wilton)*, Hugh Beaumont *(Paul)*, Warren Jackson *(Lake)*, Sam McDaniel *(Rod)*.

Shoddy attempt at an espionage thriller has Pryor as a U.S. agent fighting off spies after secret invisible paint plans. Plot is implausible, and film contains scenes that are irrelevant to the story line. Hugh Beaumont, who went on to become father Ward Cleaver in the "Leave it to Beaver" television series, plays a small role.

p, T.H. Richmond; d, Jean Yarbrough; w, Ben Roberts, Sidney Sheldon; ph, Mack Stengler; ed, Guy Thayer, Jr.; md, Alberto Columbo; art d, Frank Sylos.

Spy Drama   **(PR:A   MPAA:NR)**

SOUTH OF RIO*½   (1949) 60m REP bw

Monte Hale *(Jeff Lanning)*, Kay Christopher *(Carol Waterman)*, Paul Hurst *(Andrew Jackson Weems)*, Roy Barcroft *(Lon Bryson)*, Douglas Kennedy *(Bob Mitchell)*, Don Haggerty *(Chuck Bowers)*, Rory Mallinson *(Dan Brennan)*, Lane Bradford *(Tex)*, Emmett Vogan *(Henry Waterman)*, Myron Healey *(Travis)*, Tom London *(Weston)*.

Kicked out of the Texas Rangers because of his brother, Hale is allowed to pursu e Barcroft and gang without any red tape to hold him back. This enables him to get his brother, Kennedy, out of a jam and make the territory safe in its attempt to gain statehood. For his efforts the Rangers take him back and in the process, he wins the affection of Christopher.

p, Melville Tucker; d, Philip Ford; w, Norman S. Hall; ph, John MacBurnie; m, Stanley Wilson; ed, Harold Minter; art d, Frank Hotaling; set d, John McCarthy, Jr., James Redd; spec eff, Howard Lydecker, Theodore Lydecker.

Western   **(PR:A   MPAA:NR)**

SOUTH OF ST. LOUIS***½   (1949) 88m U.S. Pictures/WB c

Joel McCrea *(Kip Davis)*, Alexis Smith *(Rouge de Lisle)*, Zachary Scott *(Charlie Burns)*, Dorothy Malone *(Deborah Miller)*, Douglas Kennedy *(Lee Price)*, Alan Hale *(Jake Evarts)*, Victor Jory *(Luke Cottrell)*, Bob Steele *(Slim Hansen)*, Art Smith *(Bronco)*, Monte Blue *(Capt. Jeffrey)*, Nacho Galindo *(Manuel)*.

A colorful western tale about a trio of Texans–McCrea, Scott, and Kennedy–who jointly own a ranch which gets torched by Jory and his band of Union partisans at the start of the Civil War. Kennedy signs on with the Confederate army, while McCrea and Scott get tangled up in a gun-running scheme. They meet Smith, a lovely dancehall queen (who looks strangely out of place in her dancehall costumes), and have a number of run-ins with Jory and his henchman, Steele, their competition in the gun-running racket. After much table-smashing, fist swinging, and gun slinging, McCrea, Scott, and Kennedy are reunited, toppling Jory's band by the finale. Smith, who appears throughout the film in a variety of splendiferous costumes, takes McCrea for a final clinch, while McCrea's former sweetheart, Malone, pairs off with Kennedy. Bogged down in some unnecessarily complex plot twists, SOUTH OF ST. LOUIS (which oddly takes place almost exclusively in parts west of St. Louis) provides some solid, hard-hitting action. A fine supporting cast helps pull this one off–Jory and Steele are especially malicious as the bloodthirsty southern guerrillas, and Hale (in one of his final roles) excels as the saloon bartender.

p, Milton Sperling; c, Ray Enright; w, Zachary Gold, James R. Webb; ph, Karl Freund (Technicolor); m, Max Steiner; art d, Leo K. Kuter; ed, Clarence Kolster; cos, Milo Anderson; m/l, "Too Much Love," Ray Heinsdorf, Ralph Blane (sung by Alexis Smith).

Western   **(PR:A   MPAA:NR)**

SOUTH OF SANTA FE**   (1932) 60m Sono Art/World Wide bw

Bob Steele, Janis Elliott, Chris-Pin Martin, Jack Clifford, Eddie Dunn, Robert Burns, Hank Bell, Allan Garcia.

Cowboy Steele rides along the Mexican border where he finds trouble stirring amidst a group of renegades. Typical oater outing for this virile Saturday matinee idol.

p, Trem Carr; d, Bert Glennon; w, G.A. Durlam.

Western   Cas.   **(PR:A   MPAA:NR)**

SOUTH OF SANTA FE**   (1942) 55m REP bw

Roy Rogers *(Roy)*, George "Gabby" Hayes *(Mayor Whittaker)*, Linda Hayes *(Carol Stevens)*, Paul Fix *(Joe)*, Judy Clark *(Judy)*, Bobby Beers *(Bobby)*, Arthur Loft *(Moreland)*, Charles Miller *(McMahon)*, Sam Flint *(Prentiss)*, Jack Kirk *(Benton)*, Sons of the Pioneers, Jack Ingram, Hank Bell, Carleton Young, Lynton Brent, Robert Strange, Henry Wills, Jack O'Shea, Merrill McCormack, Trigger.

A novel idea has a bunch of cowpokes, armed with only six-shooters, battling big city mobsters, complete with machine guns, airplanes, high-powered cars, and other tools of their trade. This fight is brought about when Rogers is showing three big-shot investors some land and gangster Fix concocts a scheme for kidnaping the three gents, the blame falling on Rogers. Between all the shooting, Rogers manages to spin off three songs: "We're Headin' for the Home Corral," "Down the Trail," "Open Range Ahead."

p&d, Joseph Kane; w, James R. Webb; ph, Harry Neumann; ed, William Thompson; md, Cy Feuer.

Western   Cas.   **(PR:A   MPAA:NR)**

SOUTH OF SONORA*   (1930) 55m West Coast/Industrial bw

Buffalo Bill, Jr *(Bill Tracy)*, Betty Joy *(Betty)*, Fred Church, Lew Meehan, Horace B. Carpenter, Gene Schuler, Jack Walker, Frank Allen, James Merrill.

Buffalo Bill, Jr. helps out Joy with some problems before heading off to Sonra to clean up the town. However Joy's father mistakenly believes that the good guy is actually a rustler and forbids his daughter from seeing him again. But when a ranch hand is proven by Bill to be the true outlaw, all is forgiven. Joy even gets rescued by this man's man! Typical western outing from one of the lower-class production companies.

d, none listed, and no other credits specified.

Western   **(PR:A   MPAA:NR)**

SOUTH OF SUEZ**½   (1940) 86m FN/WB bw

George Brent *(John Gamble/Bradley)*, Brenda Marshall *(Katherine Sheffield)*, George Tobias *(Eli Snedeker)*, Lee Patrick *(Delia Snedeker)*, James Stephenson *(Inspector Thornton)*, Eric Blore *(Limey, Butler)*, Miles Mander *(Roger Smythe)*, Cecil Kellaway *(Henry Putnam)*, Mary Forbes *(Mrs. Putnam)*, Stanley Logan *(Prosecutor)*, Frederic Worlock *(Defense Counsel)*, Edward Fielding *(Judge)*, Leonard Mudie *(Registrar)*, Holmes Herbert *(Simpson)*, Craufurd Kent *(Sedley)*, Alec Harford *(Pidgeon)*, James Robinson

(Boy), Hassan Said *(Mechanic)*, James Levis *(Mako)*, Nathan Curry, Frank Baker *(Guards)*, Frank Hagney *(Miner)*, Ernie Stanton *(Private Detective)*, Leyland Hodgson *(Man)*, Sidney Bracey *(Butler)*, Fern Emmett *(Mrs. Wemsley)*, Gilbert Emery *(Manders)*, Charles Irwin *(Gervia)*, Prince Madupe *(Lano)*.

Settings change from the jungles of South Africa to the streets of London as Brent attempts to clear himself of the murder he didn't commit. He plays the foreman of a mining company whose boss, Mander, turns up dead. All evidence points to Brent, while the real murderer is Tobias. A steamy romance between Brent and the boss's daughter, Marshall, develops as the real culprit is sought. Fine performances by Brent and Marshall add the needed life to the slow-moving story.

p, William Jacobs; d, Lewis Seiler; w, Barry Trivers (based on the story "Gentleman From Kimberley" by Sheridan Gibney); ph, Arthur Todd; m, Leo F. Forbstein; ed, Clarence Kolster.

Drama   **(PR:A   MPAA:NR)**

SOUTH OF TAHITI**½   (1941) 75m UNIV bw (GB: WHITE SAVAGE)

Brian Donlevy *(Bob)*, Broderick Crawford *(Chuck)*, Andy Devine *(Moose)*, Maria Montez *(Melahi)*, Henry Wilcoxon *(Capt. Larkin)*, Abner Biberman *(Tahawa)*, Frank Lackteen *(Besar)*, Ignacio Saenz *(Kuana)*, Armida *(Putara)*, John Merton, Dave Wengren *(Sailors)*, H.B. Warner *(High Chief)*, Barbara Pepper *(Julie)*, Belle Mitchell *(Taupa)*, Al Kikume *(Policeman)*, Frank Brownlee *(Harbor Master)*, Mayta Palmera *(Dancer)*, Victor Groves, Jerry Seri Groves *(Sword Dancers)*, Tom Steele, George Magrill *(Sailors in Brawl)*.

Donlevy, Crawford, and Devine play three pearl hunters who become shipwrecked on a South Sea island where local beauty Montez is quick to steal Donlevy's heart. Story goes adrift in a number of ill-fitting slapstick routines, with the out-of-the ordinary ending that the three decide to stay on the island when Montez and Donlevy marry. A fascinating rendition of an initiation ceremony, given western choreography, gives this picture a little spark, though not enough to pull it out of its unbelievable storyline.

p&d, George Waggner; w, Gerald Geraghty (based on a story by Ainsworth Morgan); ph, Elwood Bredell; ed, Frank Gross; md, Charles Previn; art d, Jack Otterson; m/l, "Melahi," (sung by Maria Montez, dubbed by Martha Tilton) Frank Skinner, Waggner.

Comedy   **(PR:A   MPAA:NR)**

SOUTH OF THE BORDER*   (1939) 71m REP bw

Gene Autry *(Gene)*, Smiley Burnette *(Frog Millhouse)*, June Storey *(Lola)*, Lupita Tovar *(Dolores)*, Mary Lee *(Patsy)*, Duncan Renaldo *(Andreo)*, Frank Reicher *(Don Diego)*, Alan Edwards *(Saunders)*, Claire DuBrey *(Duenna)*, Dick Botiller *(Pablo)*, William Farnum *(Padre)*, Selmer Jackson *(Consul)*, Sheila Darcy *(Rosita)*, Rex Lease *(Flint)*, Charles King, Reed Howes, Jack O'Shea, Slim Whitaker, Hal Price, Julian Rivero, Curley Dresden, The Checkerboard Band, Art Wenzel, Champion the Horse.

Based on the title song, which soon became a standard, the film stars Autry and Burnette, who journey down to Mexico as agents of the U.S. government. Their assignment is to end a possible revolution instigated by foreign agents (Germans). The film served as a propaganda piece and was exhibited prior to America's and Autry's actual involvement in the war effort. The success of this picture gave Autry's career a boost, and paved the way for larger budgets for his later films. Eventually, the musical aspects of his films overcame the action, which was reduced significantly.

p, William Berke; d, George Sherman; w, Betty Burbridge, Gerald Geraghty (based on a story by Dorrell McGowan, Stuart McGowan); ph, William Nobles, ed, Lester Orlebeck; m/l, "South of the Border," Michael Carr, Jimmy Kennedy (sung by Gene Autry), Art Wenzel, Johnny Marvin, Autry, Fred Rose, E.G. Nelson.

Western   **Cas.**   **(PR:A   MPAA:NR)**

SOUTH OF THE RIO GRANDE**   (1932) 61m COL bw

Buck Jones, Mona Maris, Philo McCullough, Doris Hill, George J. Lewis, Paul Fix, Charles Requa, James Durkin, Harry Semels, Charles Stevens, Silver the Horse.

It's nonstop action in this early western with Jones south of the border as a Mexican Army captain. His prey is McCullough and Maris, a pair who have been stirring up quite a bit of trouble. Fix, as Jones' weaker brother, reprises his role from the earlier THE AVENGER (1931). SOUTH OF THE RIO GRANDE incorporates footage from another Jones' western, MEN WITHOUT LAW (1930).

p, Irving Briskin; d, Lambert Hillyer; w, Milton Krims (based on the story by Harold Shumate); ph, Benjamin Kline, ed, Maurice Wright.

Western   **(PR:A   MPAA:NR)**

SOUTH OF THE RIO GRANDE*   (1945) 62m Glenn Cook/MON bw

Duncan Renaldo *(Cisco)*, Martin Garralaga *(Pancho)*, Armida *(Pepita)*, George J. Lewis *(Sanchez)*, Lillian Molieri *(Dolores)*, Francis McDonald *(Torres)*, Charles Stevens *(Sebastian)*, Pedro Regas *(Luis)*, Soledad Jiminez *(Mama Maria)*, Tito Renaldo *(Manuel)*, The Guadalajara Trio.

Unexciting CISCO KID outing has Renaldo posing as a cattle inspector in order to expose the self-seeking Lewis, who, under the guise of a district officer, has been shooting local Mexican ranchers and than "impounding" their cattle. His excuse is that the ranchers are actually cattle rustlers, but Renaldo soon puts a stop to these deeds, organizing the rest of the ranchers to assist him. (See CISCO KID series, Index)

p, Philip N. Krasne; d, Lambert Hillyer; w, Victor Hammond, Ralph Bettinson (based on the character created by Johnston McCulley); ph, William Sickner; ed, William Austin; md, Edward J. Kay.

Western   **Cas.**   **(PR:A   MPAA:NR)**

SOUTH PACIFIC****   (1958) 171m South Pacific-Magna/FOX c

Rossano Brazzi *(Emile De Becque)*, Mitzi Gaynor *(Nellie Forbush)*, John Kerr *(Lt. Cable)*, Ray Walston *(Luther Billis)*, Juanita Hall *(Bloody Mary)*, France Nuyen *(Liat)*, Russ Brown *(Capt. Brackett)*, Jack Mullaney *(Professor)*, Ken Clark *(Stewpot)*, Floyd Simmons *(Harbison)*, Candace Lee *(Ngana, Emile's Daughter)*, Warren Hsieh *(Jerome, His Son)*, Tom Laughlin *(Buzz Adams)*, Beverly Aadland *(Dancer)*, Galvan De Leon *(Sub Chief)*, Ron Ely *(Co-Pilot)*, Archie Savage *(Native Chief)*, Robert Jacobs *(Communications Man)*, Richard Cutting *(Adm. Kester)*, John Gabriel *(Radio Man)*, Darleen Engle, Evelyn Ford *(Nurses)*, Doug McClure, Stephen Ferry *(Pilots)*, Joe Bailey *(U.S. Commander)*, Joan Fontaine.

SOUTH PACIFIC is a wonderful movie that should have been a screen classic, but wasn't. The play ran five years and it was nine years from the New York opening in April of 1949 until the movie was shown publicly in March of 1958. The much-beloved musical won every literary award and deserved them. The movie was nominated for Shamroy's cinematography, as well as Newman and Darby's musical direction, and that was it. How could such a popular play receive such disdain from the Academy as well as the critics? The same director handled both and that may have been a mistake, as Logan used stage techniques to hammer away at the audience, perhaps not realizing that the close-up camera requires subtler acting because there is no need to "play to the back of the house." An odd choice of color filters was used during the musical numbers that jarred the eyes and made us feel we were watching a movie, not life in the wartime tropics. Michener based many of the characters on real people he'd met while serving in that area and in 1986 went back to the South Pacific and found that the woman upon whom he patterned Bloody Mary was still alive. The trip was shown on CBS' "60 Minutes" and anyone who saw it was moved. Two stories travel side by side in the movie. Gaynor is a midwestern nurse who falls in love with a local widowed planter, Brazzi, who is much older, has children, and is very set in his ways (there is a parallel here with THE KING AND I). At the same time, Kerr is a young Marine who falls for Nuyen, a local native girl. Walston, in a role he played in the London version of the stage show, steals every scene in which he appears as a SeaBee conniver not unlike Phil Silvers, TV character Sergeant Bilko, or the James Garner part in THE AMERICANIZATION OF EMILY. Kerr goes off to war and is killed, thus ending any thoughts of miscegenation, and Gaynor and Brazzi, after the usual turmoil, do find love in each other's arms. Juanita Hall, who played Bloody Mary on the stage, is the only person to make it to the screen from Broadway. She is most effective in her role as Nuyen's mother, although Rodgers was not pleased with her voice when she did the pre-recording so he had Muriel Smith, who did the role in London, come in and loop the singing for Hall. Brazzi's voice work was sung by Giorgio Tozzi and the thought of using the original star, Ezio Pinza, never entered anyone's mind because he had already passed away in 1957 after an all-too-brief film career. Kerr's singing was done by Bill Lee, and Gaynor did her own. More than $5 million was spent on the movie and it all showed on the screen as they opened it up considerably and shot on location in Hawaii with a large cast that included such soon-to-be stars as Tom Laughlin (BILLY JACK, etc.), Ron Ely ("Tarzan" on TV), Doug McClure, and, just for fun, a non-speaking cameo by Joan Fontaine. Osborn's script was serviceable enough, but it is the glorious Rodgers and Hammerstein songs that make this movie a must-see. They include all of the tunes from the show plus one that had been cut from the stage production for time purposes and was herein utilized, the beautiful "My Girl Back Home," sung by Gaynor and Kerr. Other songs in the remarkable score were: "Dites-Moi" (sung by Gaynor, Brazzi, Children), "Bali Ha'i" (Hall), "Happy Talk" (Hall), "A Cockeyed Optimist" (Gaynor), "Soliloquies" (Gaynor, Brazzi), "Some Enchanted Evening" (Brazzi, Gaynor), "Bloody Mary" (Sailors), "I'm Gonna Wash That Man Right Out of My Hair" (Gaynor), "There Is Nothing Like a Dame" (Sailors), "Younger Than Springtime" (Kerr), "Honey Bun" (Walston, Gaynor), "You've Got to Be Carefully Taught" (Kerr), "I'm in Love with a Wonderful Guy" (Gaynor), "This Nearly Was Mine" (Brazzi). The movie was made by a consortium that included companies owned by Rodgers and Hammerstein, Logan, Leland Hayward, and George Skouras and large profits were realized. To anyone who saw Mary Martin and Pinza on the stage, this was a pale comparison, but on its own, with no foreknowledge of the Broadway show, it stands up even today as terrific entertainment. Special mention to the men who did the excellent orchestrations: Robert Russell Bennett, Pete King, Edward B. Powell, and Bernard Mayers.

p, Buddy Adler; d, Joshua Logan; w, Paul Osborn (based on the play by Oscar Hammerstein II, Richard Rodgers, Logan, from the book *Tales of the South Pacific* by James A. Michener); ph, Leon Shamroy (Todd-AO, Technicolor); ed, Robert Simpson; md, Alfred Newman, Ken Darby; art d, Lyle R. Wheeler, John DeCuir, Walter M. Scott, Paul S. Fox; cos, Dorothy Jeakins; spec eff, L.B. Abbott; ch, LeRoy Prinz.

Musical   **Cas.**   (PR:A MPAA:NR)

SOUTH PACIFIC TRAIL**   (1952) 60m REP bw

Rex Allen (*Himself*), Estelita Rodriguez (*Lita Alvarez*), Slim Pickens (*Himself*), Nestor Paiva (*Carlos Alvarez*), Roy Barcroft (*Link Felton*), Douglas Evans (*Rodney Brewster*), Joe McGuinn (*Ace*), Forrest Taylor (*Conductor*), Michael Barton, Darol Rice, George Bamby, Slim Duncan, Buddy (*The Republic Rhythm Riders*), Koko the horse.

In this western oater, Barcroft plays the foreman on a ranch owned by Rodriguez' grandfather, Paiva. He plots the crash of a train carrying $1 million in gold, causing it to disappear down an old mine shaft located on the ranch. Paiva is believed to be one of the passengers who died in the crash, but in reality he escapes death by stepping off the train at a depot and is left behind. He takes off on a three-week drive with Allen, and Evans, believing Paiva dead, moves onto the ranch and tries to take over its assets. Allen returns and attempts to stop the scam. Evans then teams up with Barcroft and together they try to drown Allen. But in the predictable ending, the good guys (Allen and Paiva) triumph over the outlaws. Songs include: "Ride Away Your Troubles," "The Railroad Corral," "I'll Sing a Love Song."

p, Edward J. White; d, William Witney; w, Arthur Orloff; ph, John MacBurnie; m, Stanley Wilson; ed, Harold Minter; art d, Frank Hotaling; set d, John McCarthy, Jr., James Redd; cos, Adele Palmer; m/l, Jack Elliott, Aaron Gonzales, Rex Allen.

Western   (PR:A MPAA:NR)

SOUTH RIDING***   (1938, Brit.) 85m LFP/UA bw

Edna Best (*Sarah Burton*), Ralph Richardson (*Robert Carne*), Edmund Gwenn (*Alfred Huggins*), Ann Todd (*Madge Carne*), John Clements (*Joe Astell*), Marie Lohr (*Mrs. Beddows*), Milton Rosmer (*Alderman Snaith*), Glynis Johns (*Midge Carne*), Joan Ellum (*Lydia Holly*), Herbert Lomas (*Castle*), Peggy Novak (*Bessie Warbuckle*), Gus McNaughton (*Tadman*), Lewis Casson (*Lord Sedgmire*), Felix Aylmer (*Chairman of Council*), Jean Cadell (*Miss Dry*), Skelton Knaggs (*Reg Aythorne*), Edward Lexy (*Mr. Holly*), Josephine Wilson (*Mrs. Holly*), Laura Smithson (*Mrs. Brimsley*), Florence Grosson (*Mrs. Malton*), Arthur Hambling, Davina Craig, Ralph Truman.

As a chronicle of England on the brink of WW II, this is worthless because there is virtually no mention of the troubles in Europe, so it is sort of an "if we don't talk about it, maybe it'll go away" setting. Instead, it's a glimpse at an England that was soon to cease, and never return. Based on a best seller by Holtby (who was to die before the picture came out), SOUTH RIDING is set in a fictitious area in Yorkshire, which has a West, a North, and an East Riding, but no South. There are similarities in structure to another book by a Yorkshirewoman, *Jane Eyre* by Charlotte Bronte, and this is an update of the tale as placed in modern times. Richardson is a once-wealthy estate owner whose wife, Todd, is in a mental hospital and he is rapidly going broke keeping her there. His daughter, Johns, is neurotic and strung tighter than a cheap mandolin. He has lived on this property since childhood and his family has owned the land since the early kings ruled England. Clements is a socialist who wants to clear away the slums in the town and build decent housing for the lower classes. He is supported in his desire by a few of the other local council members who are being manipulated by some real estate sharks. The idea is to get the town to buy a worthless piece of land that will net a large profit for the realtors. Richardson meets Best, a headmistress for a local school, and the two fall in love, but there is no way for them to get together permanently as long as Todd keeps raving in her asylum. Richardson uncovers the real-estate scam and Clements pulls out his support when he learns what's transpired. Richardson now comes to the aid of the people and offers his huge manor house, as well as his neighboring property, at a reasonable fee, for the city to use for building. But the proviso is that the main house be used for the school which Best will oversee. There were about five minutes worth of Depression-era scenes which were cut from the 90-minute version shown in England. These included seeing families living in abandoned double-decker buses. Richardson and Todd appeared together as lovers in THE RETURN OF BULLDOG DRUMMOND, then he aged and she didn't, so she played his daughter in BREAKING THE SOUND BARRIER. Listening to a Yorkshire accent is usually impossible for anyone outside Yorkshire, so the harsh, thick words were muted and Richardson and Best were able to make the point of their origin without belaboring it. Not an altogether satisfying love story, it is more interesting as a fairly accurate portrait of life in the country. Excellent sets by Meerson and well shot by Stradling, who was born in England but made his name in the U.S.

p&d, Victor Saville; w, Ian Dalrymple, Donald Bull (based on the novel by

Winifred Holtby); ph, Harry Stradling; m, Richard Addinsell; ed, Jack Dennis, Hugh Stewart; prod d, Lazare Meerson; md, Muir Mathieson; spec eff; Lawrence Butler, Edward Cohen.

Drama   (PR:A MPAA:NR)

SOUTH SEA ROSE**   (1929) 69m FOX bw

Lenore Ulric (*Rosalie Dumay*), Charles Bickford (*Capt. Briggs*), Kenneth MacKenna (*Dr. Tom Winston*), J. Farrell MacDonald (*Hackett*), Elizabeth Patterson (*Sarah*), Tom Patricola (*Willie Gump*), Ilka Chase (*Maid*), George MacFarlane (*Tavern Keeper*), Ben Hall (*Cabin Boy*), Daphne Pollard (*Mrs. Nott*), Roscoe Ates (*Ship's Cook*), Charlotte Walker (*Mother Superior*), Emile Chautard (*Rosalie's Uncle*).

In one of her few sound appearances, Ulric plays a French girl living in the South Seas whose charms soon become the object of sea captain Bickford. He marries her and takes her back home to New England, where the locals are shocked by Ulric's free-spirited lifestyle. Problems arise between Ulric and Bickford when she accuses him of caring for his ship more than for her. In the end, Bickford travels to France to discover that his wife has inherited a lot of money. Songs include: "Raymond," "Bric-a-Brac," "Sidewalks of New York," "An Idyll of the South Seas," "If You Believed in Me," and the title song.

p&d, Allan Dwan; w, Elliot Lester, Sonya Levien (based on the play "La Gringa" by Tom Cushing); ph, Harold Rosson; set d, William S. Darling; cos, Sophie Wachner; m/l, L. Wolfe Gilbert, Abel Baer.

Drama/Comedy   (PR:A MPAA:NR)

SOUTH SEA SINNER*½   (1950) 88m UNIV bw

MacDonald Carey ("*Jake*" *Davis*), Shelley Winters (*Coral*), Helena Carter (*Margaret Landis*), Luther Adler (*Cognac*), Frank Lovejoy (*Doc*), Art Smith (*Grayson*), John Ridgely (*Williams*), James Flavin (*Andrews*), Molly Lamont (*Kay Williams*), Silan Chen (*Lee*), Henry Kulky (*Bartender*), Fred Nurney (*Captain*), Phil Nazir (*Lieutenant*), Liberace (*Maestro*).

In this tropic picture, Carey finds that the rest and relaxation he is seeking on a small South Sea island is interrupted when he comes in contact with cabret singer Winters. This sparks some jealousy in her boss Adler, who makes things as rough as possible for the easy-going Carey. Neither the settings nor Winters' persona manage to evoke the type of exotic island atmosphere that was intended. Liberace makes his screen debut as the accompanying pianist for Winters' vocal numbers. Songs include: "I'm the Lonesomest Gal In Town" (Lew Brown, Albert Von Tilzer); "It Had To Be You" (Gus Kahn, Isham Jones), "Blue Lagoon" (Frederic Herbert, Arnold Hughes), "One Man Woman" (Jack Brooks, Milton Schwarzwald). Remake of SEVEN SINNERS, 1940.

p, Michel Kraike; d, Bruce Humberstone; w, Joel Malone, Oscar Brodney, Laslo Vadnay (based on the story "East of Java" by Ladislas Fodor, Vadnay); ph, Maury Gertsman; m, Walter Scharf; ed, Ted J. Kent; art d, Bernard Herzbraun, Richard E. Riedel, cos, Orry-Kelly.

Drama   (PR:A MPAA:NR)

SOUTH SEA WOMAN**½   (1953) 99m WB bw (AKA: PEARL OF
                                                  THE SOUTH PACIFIC)

Burt Lancaster (*Sgt. James O'Hearn*), Virginia Mayo (*Ginger Martin*), Chuck Connors (*Davey White*), Barry Kelley (*Col. Hickman*), Hayden Rorke (*Lt. Fears*), Leon Askin (*Marchand*), Veola Vonn (*Mme. Duval*), Raymond Greenleaf (*Capt. Peabody*), Robert Sweeney (*Lt. Miller*), Paul Burke (*Ensign Hoyt*), Cliff Clark (*Lt. Col. Parker*), John Alderson (*Fitzroy*), Rudolph Andres (*Van Dorck*), Henri Letondal (*Alphonse*), Georges Saurel (*Jacques*), Arthur Shields (*Jimmylegs Donovan*), William O'Leary (*Mr. Smith*), John Damler (*Lt. Kellogg*), Alena Awes (*Mimi*), Jacqueline Duval (*Julie*), Violet Daniels (*Suzette*), Paul Bryar (*Captain of the Gendarmes*), Anthony Radecki (*Military Policeman*), Keye Luke, Frank Kumagai, Edo Mito, Robert Kino, Rollin Moriyama (*Japanese Officers*), Tony Garsen (*Orderly*), Guy de Vestal, Gregory Gay (*Free French*), Strother Martin (*Young Marine*), Jim Hayward (*Masterson*), Peter Chong (*Woo Ching*), Grace Lem (*Mama Ching*), Danny Chang (*Wong*), Paul Liu (*Ho*), Noel Cravat (*Fatso*), Gisele Verlaine (*Olga*), Al Hill, Jack Kenney (*Bartenders*), Peter Chong, Sam Harris, Joe Connor.

A silly but likeable WW II comedy which opens as a young Marine, Lancaster, faces a court martial. Through testimony we learn the strange series of events that have catapulted Lancaster into his predicament. Two weeks before the Japanese bombing of Pearl Harbor, Lancaster went AWOL in an effort to stop his buddy Connors from marrying Mayo, a girl who works in a nightclub. Lancaster manages to snatch Connors away from the altar in time, and the two GIs try to catch up to their unit with Mayo in tow. The trio wind up on a remote South Sea island and are forced to pose as deserters to avoid capture by the Vichy Frenchman, Askin, who rules the territory. While Lancaster tries to dream up a plan so they can rejoin their unit, Connors remains determined to marry Mayo. Unfortunately for Connors and Mayo, Lancaster doesn't give the lovebirds a chance because he soon begins wreaking havoc on the island. Lancaster frees some French prisoners, steals a yacht from a German agent, grabs the romantic duo, and sets sail. On the high seas they manage to engage a Japanese destroyer and sink it, thus ruining an important enemy invasion. During the battle Conners is killed, leaving only Lancaster and Mayo to be rescued by the Allied forces. After hearing the testimony and examining the evidence, Lancaster is cleared, leaving him and Mayo to begin a romance. SOUTH SEA WOMAN is a fast paced adventure comedy that exploits Lancaster's athletic derring-do as well as his ability to handle romance and light comedy. Though not particularly memorable as a milestone in his career, SOUTH SEA WOMAN is an enjoyable addition to Lancaster's filmography.

p, Sam Bischoff; d, Arthur Lubin; w, Edwin Blum, Earl Baldwin, Stanley Shapiro (based on a play by William M. Rankin); ph, Ted McCord; m, David Buttolph; ed, Clarence Kolster; art d, Edward Carrere; set d, William L. Keuhl; cos, Moss Mabry; spec eff, H.F. Koenekamp; ch, Lester Horton; makeup, Gordon Bau.

Comedy/Adventure   **(PR:A MPAA:NR)**

SOUTH SEAS FURY   (SEE: HELL'S ISLAND 1955)

SOUTH TO KARANGA*   (1940) 59m UNIV bw

Charles Bickford (*Jeff Worthing*), James Craig (*Steve Hawley*), Luli Deste (*Julia Garrett*), John Sutton (*David Wallace*), Maurice Moscovitch (*Paul Stacco*), Paul Hurst (*Slats*), Abner Biberman (*Manek Sen*), Ben Carter (*Higgins*), Frank Reicher (*Dr. Greenleaf*), Addison Richards (*Edmund Daniels*).

Cliched story about gun-runners in South Africa who must get the ammunition to a mine in order to ward off attacks from the natives. Full of predictables including the speeding foreign train, fights on board, a murder, restless natives, and cliched character types. Uneven photography and cheap production do nothing to lift this unoriginal storyline.

p, Marshall Grant; d, Harold Schuster; w, Edmund L. Hartmann, Stanley Rubin; ph, Jerry Ash; ed, W. Donn Hayes; cos, Vera West.

Adventure   **(PR:A MPAA:NR)**

SOUTHERN COMFORT***½   (1981) 100m Phoenix-Cinema Group
                                                    FOX c

Keith Carradine (*Spencer*), Powers Boothe (*Hardin*), Fred Ward (*Reece*), Franklyn Seales (*Simms*), T.K. Carter (*Cribbs*), Lewis Smith (*Stuckey*), Les Lannom (*Casper*), Peter Coyote (*Poole*), Carlos Brown (*Bowden*), Brion James (*Trapper*), Sonny Landham, Allan Graf, Ned Dowd, Rob Ryder (*Hunters*), Greg Guirard, June Borel (*Cajun Couple*), Jeanne Louise Bulliard, Orel Borle, Jeannie Spector (*Cajun Dancers*), Marc Savoy, Frank Savoy, Dewey Balfa, John Stelly (*Cajun Musicians*).

A well-made, well-shot, and frightening story that resembles DELIVER-ANCE, as well as THE LONG RIDERS, which was directed by the same person, Hill. A group of National Guardsmen go out on a weekend's maneuvers in the boggy swamps of Louisiana. They are truly part-time warriors and ill-equipped for their work, but they look forward to the regular camaraderie they share. While out in the country, they take some canoes which belong to that unique group of backwoods people, the Cajuns, who live in the area, and they are soon chased for having stolen the boats. Smith makes the mistake of firing at the Cajuns with blanks, but the locals don't know that and return the fire with real bullets, killing one of the men. Now it becomes a life and death battle as the Guardsmen attempt to get out of the area before more blood is shed. They have no idea of the territory and are easy marks for their predatory pursuers. One by one, the men are killed, either by the chasers or within their own ranks, in one way or another. The manners of their deaths are grotesque and blood flows freely until Boothe and Carradine manage to make their ways to a Cajun festival thrown by what they think is a friendly group. The look at the Cajun way of life is authentic and fascinating as the men attempt to fit into the gala happenings in the small village and are never certain if the natives are being hospitable or if this is the prelude to a lynching. Putting fish out of water is always a prime mover in drama and seldom better demonstrated than in this film. There are marvelous touches, a few laughs, and lots of action. The Cajuns have seldom been explored in films, and if we are to believe this portrayal of the people, it's better to steer clear of them, although the motivations for their revenge are honestly shown. Boothe had just won an Emmy for his role as Jim Jones in the story of the Guyana massacre and proves here that it wasn't a flash in the pan. His career never quite took off the way it might have, perhaps due to his choice of roles, which included an HBO series as "Phillip Marlow" shot in England to masquerade as the U.S. and again in THE EMERALD FOREST, which was as visually exciting as this, but also failed to make much at the box office. Special kudos to Ry Cooder's music, which was interspersed with real Cajun songs. The picture was made in Louisiana and Texas over the winter and the sun seldom shone, thereby adding an overlay of gray depression to an already downbeat story. The title is misleading and probably meant to be a joke because there is virtually no comfort in watching this disturbing film, as the men in the audience will probably respond by wondering how they would react if placed in the same dangerous situation.

p, David Giler; d, Walter Hill; w, Michael Kane, Hill, Giler; ph, Andrew Laszlo (DeLuxe Color); m, Ry Cooder; ed, Freeman Davies; prod d, John Vallone; set d, Robert Gould.

Drama   **Cas.**   **(PR:O MPAA:R)**

SOUTHERN MAID, A**   (1933, Brit.) 85m BIP/Wardour bw

Bebe Daniels (*Dolores/Juanita*), Clifford Mollison (*Jack Rawden/Willough-by*), Harry Welchman (*Francisco del Fuego*), Lupino Lane (*Antonio Lopez*), Hal Gordon (*Pedro*), Morris Harvey (*Vasco*), Amy Veness (*Donna Rosa*), Nancy Brown (*Carola*), Basil Radford (*Tom*), James Stewart [Stewart Granger], John Beresford Cordwell, Sydney Monckton.

An uneventful musical romp with Daniels and Mollison each carrying the weight of two roles. In both cases they are lovers in Spain (20 years apart) with Welchman trying to get Daniels away from Mollison. Unfortunately for Welchman, in both cases he fails. A SOUTHERN MAID marked the first screen appearance for Stewart Granger, who was then going under his real name, James Stewart. The emergence of *the* James Stewart in the latter 1930s caused Granger to take on his new name.

p, Walter C. Mycroft; d, Harry Hughes; w, Austin Melford, Arthur Woods, Frank Miller, Frank Launder (based on the musical play by Dion Clayton Calthrop, Harry Graham); ph, Claude Friese-Greene, Philip Grindrod; m, Harold Franzer-Simson; ed, E.B. Jarvis; art d, David Rawnsley; cos, Norman Hartnell; Harry Graham, Adrian Ross, Holt Harvel.

Musical   **(PR:A MPAA:NR)**

SOUTHERN ROSES*½   (1936, Brit.) 79m CAP-Grafton/GFD bw

George Robey (*Mr. Higgins*), Neil Hamilton (*Reggie*), Gin Malo (*Mary Rowland*), Chili Bouchier (*Estrella Estrello*), Vera Pearce (*Carrie*), Richard Dolman (*Bill Higgins*), Athene Seyler (*Mrs. Rowland*), D.A. Clarke-Smith (*Senor Estrello*), Sara Allgood (*Miss Florence*), Leslie Perrins (*Don Ramon*), Hal Gordon (*Mr. Mountford*), Gus McNaughton (*Parker*).

Clumsily produced and confusingly scripted effort in which a troupe of English actors make their way to Spain while playing games in order to hide the fact from one of the actor's father that his son has married a girl he wasn't supposed to. Robey plays the man who must watch his true sweetheart pretend to be married to his best friend. But he really didn't seem to mind as much as the audience at the time who tried to figure what was happening.

p, Isidore Goldschmidt, Max Schach; d, Fred Zelnik; w, Ronald Gow (based on the play by Rudolph Bernauer); ph, Phil Tannura; m, Johann Strauss, Hans May.

Musical/Comedy   **(PR:A MPAA:NR)**

SOUTHERN STAR, THE**   (1969, Fr./Brit.) 104m
                  EuroFrance-Capitole-COL/COL c (L'ETOILE DU SUD)

George Segal (*Dan Rockland*), Ursula Andress (*Erica Kramer*), Orson Welles (*Plankett*), Ian Hendry (*Capt. Karl Ludwig*), Johnny Sekka (*Mata-kit*), Michel Constantin (*Jose*), Georges Geret (*Andre*), Sylvain (*Louis*), Charles Lamb (*Todd*), Guy Delorme (*Michel*), Harry Andrews (*Kramer*), Van Dooren (*Man in Bar*), National Ballet of Senegal.

Business entrepreneur Andrews pays Segal, a penniless American geologist, and several other experts and fortune hunters to uncover a large diamond, titled the "Southern Star." Segal, along with his companion, Sekka, finds the diamond and travels back to Andrews, where a party is held to celebrate the find. During the party, the lights go out and when they come back on, the diamond and Sekka have disappeared. Accused of being a partner in the theft, Segal takes off after Sekka, intent on securing the diamond, and his engagement to Andress, Andrews' daughter, in the process. Segal is followed by Hendry and his men who plan to secure the diamond for themselves, but Segal is able to rescue the diamond and Andrews gives his approval on the engagement of Segal and Andress.

p, Roger Duchet; d, Sidney Hayers; w, David Pursall, Jack Seddon, Jean Giono (based on the novel L'Etoile Du Sud, Le Pays Des Diamants by Jules Verne); Raoul Coutard (Techniscope, Technicolor); m, George Garvarentz; ed, Tristam Cones; set d, Pierre Thevenet; cos, Yvonne Caffin; spec eff, F. Sune, A. Trielli; m/l, (title song sung by Matt Monro) Don Black; makeup, Hugh Richards.

Adventure/Comedy   **(PR:C MPAA:M/PG)**

SOUTHERN YANKEE, A***   (1948) 90m MGM bw (AKA: MY
                                                     HERO!)

Red Skelton (*Aubrey Filmore*), Brian Donlevy (*Curt Devlynn*), Arlene Dahl (*Sallyann Weatharby*), George Coulouris (*Maj. Jack Drumman*), Lloyd Gough (*Capt. Steve Lorford*), John Ireland (*Capt. Jed Calbern*), Minor Watson (*Gen. Watkins*), Charles Dingle (*Col. Weatharby*), Art Baker (*Col. Clifford M. Baker*), Reed Hadley (*Fred Munsey*), Arthur Space (*Mark Haskins*), Addison Richards (*Dr. Clayton*), Joyce Compton (*Hortense Dob-son*), Paul Harvey (*Mr. Twitchell*), Jeff Corey (*Union Cavalry Sergeant*), Cliff Clark (*Dr. Cooper*), Dick Wessel, Ian MacDonald, John Hilton (*Orderl-ies*), Ed Gargan (*Male Nurse*), David Sharp (*Confederate Officer*), Frank McGrath (*Dispatch Rider*), David Newell (*Sentry*), William Tannen, Stanley Andrews, Roger Moore, Dick Simmons (*S.S. Men*), Susan Simon (*Jenny*),

Byron Foulger (*Mr. Duncan*), Paul Newlan (*Man with Saber*), Howard Mitchell, Paul Krueger, Vic Zimmerman, Chris Frank, James Logan (*Men*), Marcus Turk, Ralph Montgomery, Walter Merrill (*Confederate Soldiers*), Ralph Volkie, Steve Bennett, Allen Mathews, William "Bill" Phillips (*Soldiers*), Ann Staunton (*Nurse*), Henry Hall (*Thadeus Drumman*), Lane Chandler, Carl Saxe (*Sentries*), Weldon Heyburn, Sam Flint, Jack Lee, Forbes Murray (*Officers*), Harry Cording, Kermit Maynard, John Merton, Frank Hagney (*Horsemen*), Shelly Bacon, Drexle Bobbie Haywood (*Boys*), Dick Alexander (*Bartender*), Rod O'Connor (*Maj. Kingsby*), Pierre Watkin (*Major*), Bert Moorehouse (*Capt. Jeffrys*), Bill Kennedy (*Lt. Sheve*).

A comedy that works because of its star and the unheralded contributions of silent comic genius Buster Keaton. Skelton plays a not-so-bright bellboy of a St. Louis hotel during the Civil War. He ends up becoming a spy for Union forces when the infamous Confederate agent "The Gray Spider" is captured. Skelton fills in for the Southerner and is sent behind enemy lines to capture some important information that will help the Union cause. While squirreling about below the Mason-Dixon line he meets Dahl, a refined Southern belle, and tries to romance her and still keep his cover. Though not a shining example of screen comedy the film has its moments, chiefly because of the genuine earnestness Skelton gives to his character. This was a quality Keaton saw in Skelton's previous work and was convinced would shine with the right material. At this point in his career Keaton was working as a gag man for MGM, supplying material as needed for various comedies. He went to studio chief Louis Mayer and made an offer to work exclusively with Skelton. According to the Rudi Blesh biography *Keaton*, The Great Stone Face implored Mayer to let them do a series of films just as Keaton created his classic silent films in the 1920s. "...do it our way–the way I did my best pictures....I won't take a cent of salary until they have proved themselves at the box office," Keaton beseeched Mayer. Though Keaton was denied this, he was assigned as gag man for A SOUTHERN YANKEE and came up with the film's funniest moments. Most memorable is a sequence in which Skelton must walk a direct line between fighting Yankee and Confederate forces. In order to fool both sides into letting him pass, Skelton wears a uniform that is half blue and half gray, letting the appropriate side face each army. He also carries a flag that is one side Union, the other Confederate. Skelton seemingly makes it safely across when an unexpected wind whips the flag around, exposing the ruse. Keaton also made a key suggestion after watching a rough cut of the production. Convinced that Skelton's character was initially too idiotic to gain audience sympathy, he suggested eliminating much of the idiotic behavior in the film's opening sequences. This, Keaton felt, would gain Skelton more audience sympathy and make for a better comedy. These suggestions were well taken and the result was a much better comedy structure. Serving as director was Sedgwick, who came out of retirement for the film. He and Keaton had worked together in the late 1920s and early 1930s when Keaton's career as a screen comic was fading.

p, Paul Jones; d, Edward Sedgwick; w, Harry Tugend (based on a story by Melvin Frank, Norman Panama); ph, Ray June; m, David Snell; ed, Ben Lewis; art d, Cedric Gibbons, Randall Duell; set d, Edwin B. Willis, Arthur Krams; cos, Valles; spec eff, Warren Newcombe; makeup, Jack Dawn.

Comedy   **(PR:AAA MPAA:NR)**

SOUTHERNER, THE, 1931   (SEE: PRODIGAL, THE, 1931)

SOUTHERNER, THE****   (1945) 91m UA bw

Zachary Scott (*Sam Tucker*), Betty Field (*Nona Tucker*), Beulah Bondi (*Granny Tucker*), Jean Vanderwilt 'Bunny Sunshine' (*Daisy Tucker*), Jay Gilpin (*Jot Tucker*), Percy Kilbride (*Harmie Jenkins*), Blanche Yurka (*Ma Tucker*), Charles Kemper (*Tim the Narrator*), J. Carrol Naish (*Henry Devers*), Norman Lloyd (*Finlay Hewitt*), Jack Norworth (*Doc White*), Nestor Paiva (*Bartender*), Estelle Taylor (*Lizzie*), Dorothy Granger (*Party Girl*), Noreen Roth 'Nash' (*Becky*), Paul Harvey (*Ruston*), Paul E. Burns (*Uncle Pete Tucker*), Earle Hodgins (*Wedding Guest*), Almira Sessions (*Customer at Store*), Florence Bates (*Rose*), Rex (*Zoonie the Dog*).

A remarkably naturalistic portrayal of one family's struggle to start a farm in the South. With the coming of autumn, Scott, a man hardened by his years of working fields for other people, decides to work his own land on the advice of his dying uncle, Burns. He is given a plot of unused, out-of-the-way land, and packs his wife Field, children Vanderwilt and Gilpin, grandmother Bondi, a dog, and all of their possessions onto a beatup truck. What they find is a plot of unkempt, though workable, land and a dilapidated shanty that isn't fit for animals. Though they decide to stay and make a go of it, Bondi complains incessantly and even refuses to step foot inside their new "home." She prefers to sit in her rocking chair, which is still on the truck, protecting herself from the elements with her battered shawl. They get settled in, fix the front porch, put a fire in the stove, and do their best to make the space livable. When Scott realizes the well doesn't work, he pays a visit to a neighboring farm, one which, after years of toiling, has become what Scott hopes his will be. The farm belongs to Devers, an embittered man who cannot appreciate the success of his hard work without thinking about how it caused the deaths of his wife and child. Devers is less than hospitable, and reluctantly agrees to let Scott use his well on the condition that Scott supply a new rope when the old one wears thin. Also working Devers' farm are his friendly and lonely daughter, Roth, and the displaced and jittery Lloyd. As

time passes and winter arrives, Scott and his family plow the land and ready it for a cotton crop. To keep his daughter warm on her walks to school, Scott makes her a coat from Bondi's blanket, over the old woman's loud objections. For days, the family goes without any decent food, surviving on mash, until Scott successfully smokes a possum out of a hollow tree. Meal time brings the family together and gives Scott reason to thank the Lord with a simple prayer. Come spring, Gilpin gets stricken with pellagra or "spring sickness," forcing Scott to plant vegetables and find milk for the boy's nourishment. The vegetables begin to grow, but Scott has no money left for milk. Out of desperation, he appeals again to Naish, who, in front of Scott, proceeds to use an entire bucket of fresh milk for pig slop while refusing to spare even a drop for a sick child. When Roth tries to sneak Scott a small amount, Lloyd interferes and maliciously spills the milk rather than give it away. Kemper, a friend of Scott's from the city who has offered the farmer a factory job, does all he can to help by buying the family a cow, thereby saving the boy's life. Meantime, Scott's rivalry with Naish grows stronger when Naish's livestock are found in Scott's vegetable garden. Scott goes angrily to Naish's farm and a brawl begins between them with Naish finally ending up thrown in the pig pen. In retaliation, Naish grabs his rifle and heads for the river, where Scott is washing up. Before Naish can fire off a shot, he sees Scott's fishing line pull taut. Both he and Scott know that the fish that has been hooked is "Lead Pencil," a legendary giant catfish with whiskers as thick as lead pencils. It's been Naish's dream to catch the fish, so rather than shoot Scott, he helps him pull in the catch. The pair strike a deal– Naish will let Scott farm his vegetable garden and use his well, and in exchange Scott will let Naish have the glory of catching "Lead Pencil." Summer comes, the cotton crop shows promise, and Scott has hopes of life improving for him and the family. While they are in town at a wedding, a terrible rainstorm rages for hours. When the family arrives back at the farm, they find their crop completely destroyed, their house battered by the storm's high winds, and the river rising high onto Scott's property. With Kemper's help, Scott wades and swims through the river in search of his cow. Back at the house, Field, Bondi, and the children have come together to clean and repair. After getting the cow to safety, Kemper nearly gets carried off by the current, but is rescued before any harm comes. Soaking wet and spiritually beaten, Scott rests at the river's edge with Kemper. Scott decides to give up, leave his land behind, and take Kemper up on his offer of factory work. When he arrives back at the house, however, and finds that everyone has pitched in to make the place livable, he is convinced that he should stay and fight even harder. With the arrival of autumn, having completed the cycle of seasons, Scott and his family prepare for another year of farming.

THE SOUTHERNER, Renoir's most critically respected American film, is a superb depiction, in spirit if not in historical authenticity, of the plight of the farmer. The southerner of the title is not only the heroic Scott, but also the angry Devers (who like all Renoir's "evil" characters, has his reasons for being so), the obstinate grandmother, and the unbreakable Field. To Renoir, as he wrote in his autobiography *My Life and My Films*, "What I saw was a story in which all the characters were heroic, in which every element would brilliantly play its part, in which things and men, animals and Nature, all would come together in an immense act of homage to the divinity." As with such great pictures as OUR DAILY BREAD (1934), THE GRAPES OF WRATH (1940), and the brilliant government documentaries of Pare Lorentz (to which THE SOUTHERNER is most similar)–PLOW THAT BROKE THE PLAINS (1936) and THE RIVER (1937)–this picture makes characters of the land, the cotton, the plow, and the water, granting them the same importance as the actors. In THE SOUTHERNER, man is just another part which makes up the whole of this land, he is not in control of the divine elements but subject to their wrath. With the original Hugo Butler script of the Perry novel *Hold Autumn in Your Hand*, Renoir and his producers, Loew and Hakim, were able to convince Hollywood to make their film. When Butler dropped out of the production (in reverence to Renoir who, Butler felt, could rework the script however he pleased), Renoir feared financing would not come and even offered to resign as director in favor of "a more orthodox director." After casting Joel McCrea in the lead, THE SOUTHERNER was hit with another setback when he was not pleased with the final script and left. Scott, a Texan by birth, was finally chosen and was felt perfect for the part since the novel was set in Texas. Shooting was also to have taken place in Texas, but instead was moved to the equally arid looking part of Southern California. Not surprisingly, Renoir, a native of France who had only been in the U.S. since 1940, found it difficult to fully capture the dialog and dialect of the southern people. Nunnally Johnson, who had scripted THE GRAPES OF WRATH, was first brought in, followed by William Faulkner (both received no screen credit), who that year also had a hand in THE MALTESE FALCON and TO HAVE AND HAVE NOT. Faulkner, who had known Renoir since the director's first American film, SWAMP WATER (1941), and felt he was the greatest contemporary director, would later remark that working on THE SOUTHERNER had given him more pleasure than any other Hollywood production. Strangely, THE SOUTHERNER didn't make it to Paris, where Renoir's most avid admirers were, until 1950– a distribution move of such mind-boggling stupidity by United Artists that it is almost impossible to comprehend, especially in light of the film receiving the prestigious International Prize of the Venice Film Festival. When the film played at the 1949 Biarritz Film Festival it received next to no help from some members of the press. Renoir, in his autobiography, recalls a story told to him by Francois Truffaut about one film critic, Henri Magnan, who mangled a review: "Henri Magnan reported on it over the telephone. It was a bad connection, and the sub-editor who took down his review called it 'Le Souteneur (The Pimp)' instead of THE SOUTHERNER and described it as 'un film de genre noir (a sombre film)' instead of 'un film de Jean Renoir.' Oscar nominations went to Renoir for Best Director, Jack Whitney for Best Sound, and Werner Janssen for Best Score.

p, David L. Loew, Robert Hakim; d, Jean Renoir; w, Renoir, Hugo Butler, (uncredited) William Faulkner, Nunnally Johnson, (based on the novel *Hold Autumn in Your Hand* by George Sessions Perry); ph, Lucien Andriot; m, Werner Janssen (performed by the Janssen Symphony Orchestra); ed, Gregg Tallas; set d, Eugene Lourie.

Drama   **Cas.**   **(PR:A   MPAA:NR)**

SOUTHSIDE 1-1000**½   (1950) 73m AA/MON bw

Don Defore (*John Riggs/Nick Starns*), Andrea King (*Nora Craig*), George Tobias (*Reggie*), Barry Kelley (*Evans*), Morris Ankrum (*Eugene Deane*), Robert Osterloh (*Albert*), Charles Cane (*Harris*), Kippee Valez (*Singer*).

This film presents director Ingster's expertise in film noir, with realistic settings through footage of L.A.'s backstreets and San Quentin's penitentiary. Defore plays an agent investigating a counterfeit ring run by prison convict Ankrum. Although sick and aging, Ankrum pretends to be a convict-turned-religious who spends much of his time reading the Bible. He uses the Bible, however, as a guise to hide counterfeit plates, which he smuggles to the outside via a "priest." Assuming the identity of an Eastern king-pin, Defore makes a deal to purchase a large amount of the fake bills, therefore enabling him to infiltrate the gang. The mind behind the scheme turns out to be King the girl Defore is romancing. She figures out Defore's true identity as a government agent and attempts to do him in by setting fire to his hotel. But Defore manages to escape and pursues King down backstreets to the edge of a cliff. King tries to throw Defore off the cliff, but slips and falls to her death. Playing a role similar to that in RIDE THE PINK HORSE, King is superb as the romantic interest with a heart of ice.

p, Maurice King, Frank King; d, Boris Ingster; w, Leo Townsend, Ingster (based on a story by Milton M. Raison, Bert C. Brown); ph, Russell Harlan; m, Paul Sawtell, Stuart Frye; ed, Christian Nyby; prod d, Edward S. Haworth; art d, David Milton; set d, Raymond Boltz, Jr.; cos, Norma; m/l, "Je T'aime" (sung by Kippee Valez, Fritz Rotter, Harold Stern.

Crime/Drama   **(PR:A   MPAA:NR)**

SOUTHWARD HO!**   (1939) 57m REP bw

Roy Rogers (*Roy*), Mary Hart [Lynne Roberts] (*Ellen*), George "Gabby" Hayes (*Gabby*), Wade Boteler (*Denbigh*), Arthur Loft (*Jeffries*), Lane Chandler (*Crawford*), Tom London (*Hadley*), Charles Moore (*Skeeter*), Edwin Brady (*Mears*), Fred Burns, Frank Ellis, Jack Ingram, Frank McCarroll, Curley Dresden, Jim Corey, Rudy Bowman, George Chesebro, Trigger the Horse.

The first oater in which Rogers was teamed with his happy-go-lucky sidekick, Gabby Hayes. He and Rogers make claim to partial ownership of a ranch, after bidding farewell to the Confederate army. The other half of the ranch is owned by a former colonel in the Union army, whom the pair have had a run-in with before. This same Colonel is made the commanding officer of a cavalry unit sent in to enforce the law in the area that has been victimized by a high amount of bloodshed. The person responsible for the crime wave is the officer directly under the Colonel. Rogers figures out the culprit and rallies the rest of the ranchers to make the valley safe. Well paced with Rogers inserting four songs between the action.

p&d, Joseph Kane; w, Gerald Geraghty (based on a story by Jack Natteford, John Rathmell); ph, Jack Marta; ed, Lester Orlebeck; md, Cy Feuer.

Western   **Cas.**   **(PR:A   MPAA:NR)**

SOUTHWEST PASSAGE**   (1954) 75m UA c

Joanne Dru (*Lilly*), Rod Cameron (*Edward Beale*), John Ireland (*Clint McDonald*), Guinn "Big Boy" Williams (*Tall Tale*), Mary Hanna (*Hi Jolly*), Darryl Hickman (*Jeb*), Stuart Randall (*Lt. Owens*), Morris Ankrum (*Doc Stanton*), Kenneth MacDonald (*Sheriff Morgan*), Stanley Andrews (*Constable Bartlett*), John Dehner (*Matt Carrol*).

Familiar western tale with Cameron as an explorer with a desire to try new things. In this case, he pursues a new trail by way of the desert, promoting camels as the ideal beasts of burden. Posing as a doctor for the group, Ireland and his girl, Dru, become part of the team in an attempt to avoid a posse that is after him for robbing a bank. One of Cameron's men, Dehner, is wise to Ireland's true identity, and threatens exposure unless a price is paid. But attacking Indians and the search for water quickly place, his concern in the background. This picture was give 3-D perspective, a gimmick used to help promote its standard B western fare.

p, Edward Small; d, Ray Nazarro; w, Harry Essex, Geoffrey Homes (based on a story by Essex); ph, Sam Leavitt (PatheColor, 3-D); ed, Grant Whytock.

Western   **(PR:A   MPAA:NR)**

SOUTHWEST TO SONORA   (SEE: APPALOOSA, THE, 1966)

SOYLENT GREEN**½   (1973) 97m MGM c

Charlton Heston (*Detective Thorn*), Leigh Taylor-Young (*Shirl*), Chuck Connors (*Tab Fielding*), Joseph Cotten (*William Simonson*), Brock Peters (*Hatcher*), Paula Kelly (*Martha*), Edward G. Robinson (*Sol Roth*), Stephen Young (*Gilbert*), Mike Henry (*Kulozik*), Lincoln Kilpatrick (*Priest*), Roy Jenson (*Donovan*), Leonard Stone (*Charles*), Whit Bissell (*Santini*), Celia Lovsky (*Exchange Leader*), Jane Dulo (*Mrs. Santini*), Dick Van Patten (*Usher*), Tim Herbert (*Brady*), John Dennis (*Wagner*), Jan Bradley (*Bandana Woman*), Carlos Romero (*New Tenant*), Pat Houtchens (*Fat Guard*), Morgan Farley (*Book 1*), John Barclay (*Book 2*), Belle Mitchell (*Book 3*), Cyril Delevanti (*Book 4*), Forrest Wood, Faith Quabius (*Attendants*), Joyce Williams, Beverly Gill, Cheri Howell, Jennifer King, Erica Hagen, Suesie Eejima, Kathy Silva, Marion Charles (*Furniture Girls*).

It was a bit of a disappointment that Edward G. Robinson's long and satisfying career should have ended with this short and unsatisfying film. He knew he was dying when it was shot and his final scene was a suicide by a man who was tired of the modern world and wanted to go home peacefully. His career had spanned five decades and yet, through all his performances, he'd never once been nominated for an Oscar in more than 100 movies. Before his death in late January, 1973, Robinson was told that he would be receiving a special award at the March Oscar awards and he composed a "thank you" which his wife read. After his death, she married longtime friend George Sidney. This look at the future stinted somewhat on the sets and direction as the filmmakers attempted to portray what life and death would be like in the 21st Century. It's about 2020 and the Big Apple is rotten to the core. Smog is everywhere, the humidity is pervasively oppressive 12 months a year, space is at a premium, and the population explosion has placed more than 40 million people in the greater New York area, many of whom live on the streets, in subways, in abandoned vehicles and burnt-out buildings. Real food costs so much that no one can afford it and the government is taking care of the people by offering a synthetic comestible which they claim is made from the plankton of the sea. This food resembles communion wafers, is said to have all the vitamins and nutrients needed to maintain life, and is manufactured by a huge conglomerate known as the Soylent company. The starving people line up for their quota of the wafers. When there appears to be a temporary lack of food, riots begin and the cops have to gather in the crazed crowds by scooping them up with huge garbage gear that's usually used to clear debris. Heston is a New York detective who lives in a seedy apartment with Robinson, an aged research man who is a walking data bank of everything that's ever happened. Robinson is so old that he can recall the way things were back then, when people knew what bananas tasted like and had the pleasure of real soap against their skins. Cotten, an executive with the Soylent company, is killed and Heston gets the job of investigating the murder. He talks to Taylor-Young, who was Cotten's mistress, and finds out that Cotten had been depressed for a few weeks before his death and she could never fathom why. After all, he was one of the elite of this civilization, had a decent apartment that came equipped with "furniture" (which is the euphemism used for the willing women who take care of the heavyweight men) and seemed to have it all. Heston thinks that Cotten may have been killed by his bodyguard, Connors, in order to keep some sort of secret that Cotten may have been ready to divulge. Heston continues prying but then is told by his boss, Peters, that the governor, Bissell, has ordered that all detection cease. Heston is an honest cop who is dogged in his quest and he refuses to stop his work. When an attempt is made on his life by Young, Heston overcomes the wound and is ready to arrest the assassin but Young himself is killed by an unseen hand before Heston can nail him. Robinson begins investigating and winds up in the underground repository of books and records where nobody goes anymore. He uncovers the truth about the company that makes the food and understands what drove Cotten to such despair that he more-or-less condoned his own death. Once he knows the truth (which will be revealed in a moment, so read on), Robinson thinks that there is no longer a reason for him to live either so he asks to go to "Home," which is a suicidetorium. Taking one's own life is encouraged in the future and Robinson knows what he is to face. The elderly, the lame, the ill are given 20 minutes of their favorite music and films of the verdant vistas of yesteryear as they are administered painless narcotics which sap their lives away. Robinson has left a note for Heston and the cop races to the death clinic just before Robinson's life ebbs. Robinson tells him what he's discovered but Heston is still not sure he's right. Heston hides aboard a truck filled with people who've elected to die at the clinic and can't believe his eyes as he watches the dead being shipped along a belt and sent into a large manufacturing device at one end, only to emerge at the other end as the ubiquitous wafers of Soylent Green. Now that he knows the secret, his life is worthless. Connors and his thugs chase Heston and Heston eventually knocks off the left-handed ex-first baseman who went on to be "The Rifleman" on TV. Heston returns to the teeming city and is waylaid by more henchmen. As he is being beaten and kicked by the agents of the company (who, we presume, are also working for the government which is trying to suppress the truth), Heston shouts out what he's learned..."Soylent Green is people!" This is heard by a wide-eyed Peters as Heston is taken away, probably to become another batch of the food that feeds the world. The picture won the Nebula Award as best Science Fiction film of that year. It must have been a quiet year for the genre. Heston and Connors, who have two of the most stoical faces in films, looked as though they should have been on Mount Rushmore in their scenes together. Robinson is outstanding and seems to be the only person with any true humanity in the picture. In this role, as in every role he ever played, he gave it all he had. SOYLENT GREEN was a message picture and they even hired a technical consultant, Frank Bowerman, a professor and futurist. If this is the way Bowerman sees it, he has lost his faith in humankind's intelligence. Then again, he may be right. Avoid taking children to see this as it may cause bad dreams.

p, Walter Seltzer, Russell Thacher; d, Richard Fleischer; w, Stanley R. Greenberg (based on the novel *Make Room! Make Room!* by Harry Harrison); ph, Richard H. Kline (Panavision, Metrocolor); m, Fred Myrow; ed, Samuel E. Beetley; md, Gerald Fried; art d, Edward C. Carfagno; set d, Robert Benton; cos, Pat Barto; spec eff, A. J. Lohman, Robert R. Hoag, Matthew Yuricich; stunts; Joe Canutt; makeup, Bud Westmore.

Science Fiction/Crime   **Cas.**   **(PR:C MPAA:PG)**

SPACE AMOEBA, THE*   (1970, Jap.) 84m Toho (KESSEN NANKAI NO DAIKAIJU; NANKAI NO DAIKAIJU); (AKA: YOG-MONSTER FROM SPACE)

Akira Kubo, Atsuko Takahashi, Toshio Tsuchiya, Kenji Sahara, Noritake Saito, Yukihiko Kobayashi, Satoshi Nakamura, Yuko Sugihara.

The director of numerous GODZILLA movies, Honda was retreading old and tired ground in this story. Giant sea animals, a result of some alien force, lay seige to a small island. Poor technical work and a plot that is too predictable make for an unsuspenseful outing.

p, Tomoyuki Tanaka, Fumio Tanaka; d, Inoshiro Honda; w, El Ogawa; ph, Taiichi Kankura (TohoScope); spec eff, Sadamasa Arikawa, Yoichi Manoda.

Fantasy   **(PR:A MPAA:NR)**

SPACE CHILDREN, THE½**   (1958) 69m PAR bw

Adam Williams (*Dave Brewster*), Peggy Webber (*Anne Brewster*), Michel Ray (*Bud Brewster*), John Crawford (*Ken Brewster*), Jackie Coogan (*Hank Johnson*), Sandy Descher (*Eadie Johnson*), Richard Shannon (*Lt. Col. Manley*), John Washbrook (*Tim Gamble*), Russell Johnson (*Joe Gamble*), Raymond Bailey (*Dr. Wahrman*).

A surprisingly pacifist 1950's sci-fi film featuring a big alien brain that hides in a cave and telephathically controls the children of American nuclear missile scientists. The brain wants the children to sabotage their parents' project (the shipping of a hydrogen bomb into outer space), so it compels them to spout anti-nuclear proliferation messages to their folks in the hopes that the adults will wise up and stop messing around with dangerous atoms. The parents don't pay much attention, so the kids are forced to take more severe action and physically stop the launch with the help of the giant brain.

p, William Alland; d, Jack Arnold; w, Bernard C. Schoenfeld (based on a story by Tom Filer); ph, Ernest Laszlo; m, Van Cleave; ed, Terry Morse; art d, Hal Pereira, Roland Anderson; set d, Sam Comer, Frank McKelvy; spec eff, John P. Fulton; makeup, Wally Westmore.

Science Fiction   **(PR:A MPAA:NR)**

SPACE CRUISER**   (1977 Jap.) 101m Academy c (UCHUSENKAN YAMATO; AKA: SPACE CRUISER YAMATO)

Voice talent uncredited.

A Japanese animated sci-fi spectacular which borrows heavily from STAR WARS. The year is 2199 and Earth is suffering from the effects brought on by a lengthy and continuing war with the evil planet Gorgon. The Gorgons have used radical nuclear weapons and the Earth is in the throes of radiation poisoning. In order to search for an antidote, an old WW II battle ship is brought up from the bottom of the sea, fitted with ultramodern equipment, and then sent into space to find a cure for the fallout. The STAR WARS influence is felt through innumerable visual rip-offs and quite a few character borrowings, including a cute little robot who proves himself a hero. There is a cult of fans for this Japanese film, but while colorful and flashy, the films invariably suffer from an almost ridiculous amount of violence, purloined story lines, and bad dubbing into English. The film spawned two sequels, SARABA UCHU SENKAN YAMATO (1978) and YAMATO YO TOWANO (1979).

p&d, Yoshinobu Nishizaki; w, Nishizaki, Keisuke Fujikawa, Eiichi Yamamoto; m, Hiroshi Miyagawa; spec eff, Mitsuru Kashiwabara; animation, Noboru Ishiguro.

Science Fiction   **(PR:A MPAA:G)**

SPACE DEVILS   (SEE: SNOW DEVILS, THE, 1965, Ital.)

SPACE FIREBIRD 2772**   (1979, Jap.) 122m Tezuka/Toho c (HI NO TORI-2772, AKA: PHOENIX 2772)

Voice talent uncredited.

In this typical animated Japanese science fiction epic, a giant space ship flies

through the stars chasing a fiery bird-like monster which is causing problems for several planets. The astronauts want to capture it and convert its energy to help a rapidly dying Earth.

p, Kiichi Akitagawa; d&w, Osamu Tezuku, Suguru Sugiyama; ph, Iwao Yamaki.

Science Fiction   **(PR:A MPAA:NR)**

SPACE HUNTER: ADVENTURES IN THE FORBIDDEN ZONE
      (SEE: SPACEHUNTER: ADVENTURES IN THE FORBIDDEN ZONE, 1983)

SPACE INVASION FROM LAPLAND
      (SEE: INVASION OF THE SPACE PEOPLE 1962, U.S./Swed.)

SPACE MASTER X-7**   (1958) 71m Regal/FOX bw (AKA: MUTINY IN OUTER SPACE)

Bill Williams (*John Hand*), Lyn Thomas (*Lora Greeling*), Robert Ellis (*Radigan*), Paul Frees (*Charles Palmer*), Joan Nixon Barry (*Miss Meyers*), Thomas Browne Henry (*Prof. West*), Fred Sherman (*Morse*), Jesse Kirkpatrick (*Captain*), Moe Howard (*Cab Driver*), Rhoda Williams (*Miss Archer*), Carol Varga (*Elaine Frohman*), Thomas Wilde (*Collins*), Gregg Martell (*Engineer*), Court Shepard (*Chief Hendry*), Al Baffert (*Passenger*), Bob [Robert] Bice, Don Lamond, Judd Holdren, Ellen Shaw, Nesdon Booth, John Ward, Lane Chandler, Helen Jay, Edward McNally, Joseph Becker.

Once again thoughtless scientists send out a space probe and it returns to Earth with a nasty fungus that threatens to destroy life as we know it. When this insidious substance is mixed with blood, it becomes "blood rust" and kills Frees, the hapless scientist assigned to examine it. The fungus then spreads to Frees' fiancee, Thomas, and she goes a bit daft and begins spreading the awful stuff all over the country. Government agents Williams and Ellis are shipped out to track Thomas down and stop the rust from eating its way throughout the world. Armed with an antidote, the intrepid agents catch up to Thomas on a flight to Hawaii and manage to ditch the plane just before the fungus/rust eats the fuselage away in midflight. Eventually the heroes dispatch the world-threatening "blood rust."

p, Bernard Glasser; d, Edward Bernds; w, George Worthing Yates, Daniel Mainwaring; ph, Brydon Baker (Regalscope); m, Josef Zimanich; ed, John F. Link; cos, Clark Ross.

Science Fiction   **(PR:A MPAA:NR)**

SPACE MEN   (SEE: ASSIGNMENT-OUTER SPACE, 1961, Ital.)

SPACE MEN APPEAR IN TOKYO
      (SEE: MYSTERIOUS SATELLITE, THE, 1956, Jap.)

SPACE MISSION OF THE LOST PLANET
      (SEE: HORROR OF THE BLOOD MONSTERS, 1970)

SPACE MONSTER*   (1965) 80m AIP c (AKA: FIRST WOMAN INTO SPACE; VOYAGE BEYOND THE SUN)

Russ Bender (*John Andros*), Francine York (*Lisa*), James B. Brown (*Hanks*), Baynes Barron (*Paul*).

An unimaginative AIP outing which sees an American space ship splash down on a watery planet where they are forced to fight off badly costumed sea monsters. York, the first female astronaut, screams a lot, while the men, in turn, grunt a lot. In the end the crew meets a midget alien who is hiding in his mini-spaceship and eventually they return to Earth.

p, Burt Topper; d&w, Leonard Katzman; ph, Robert Tobey; m, Marlin Skiles; makeup, Don Post Studios.

Science Fiction   **(PR:A MPAA:NR)**

SPACE RAIDERS zero   (1983) 82m New World c (AKA: STAR CHILD)

Vince Edwards (*Hawk*), David Mendenhall (*Peter*), Patsy Pease (*Amanda*), Thom Christopher (*Flightplan*), Luca Bercovici (*Ace*), Drew Snyder (*Alderbarian*), Ray Stewart (*Zariatin*), George Dickerson (*Tracton*), Dick Miller (*Crazy Mel*), Virginia Kiser (*Janeris*), Don Washburn (*Jessup*), Michael Miller (*Lou*), Bill Boyett (*Taggert*), Howard Dayton (*Elmer*), Elizabeth Charlton (*Cookie*).

This should be called "stock-footage raiders" because producer Corman forced director/writer Cohen to dredge a new science fiction feature out of special effects used in New World's own, surprisingly successful low-budget space adventure BATTLE BEYOND THE STARS. Not only are the special effects lifted from another film (and shown over and over again), but the story is also a thinly disguised rip-off of STAR WARS. It features a mercenary band of space fighters led by Edwards battling an evil empire known as the "company" who are stationed in a giant, floating, impenetrable command ship in space. Even the musical score is lifted from BATTLE

BEYOND THE STARS. Trash.

p, Roger Corman; d&w, Howard R. Cohen; ph, Alec Hirschfeld (DeLuxe Color); m, James Horner; ed, Anthony Randel, Robert J. Kizer; art d, Wayne Springfield; spec eff, Tom Campbell; m/l, Murphy Dunne; makeup, Mike Jones; stunts, Rick Barker.

Science Fiction   **Cas.**   **(PR:C   MPAA:PG)**

SPACE SHIP, THE****½**   (1935, USSR) 70m Mosfilm bw
                    (KOSMITCHESKY REIS; AKA: THE COSMIC VOYAGE)

Sergey Komarov, V. Kovrigin, Nicolai Feokistov, Vassili Gaponenko, K. Maskalenko.

A rebellious Soviet scientist becomes fed up with the conservative Moscow Institute for Interplanetary Travel, so he builds his own spaceship, grabs his lady assistant, and zips off to the moon. The first Russian science fiction film since 1924's silent opus AELITA.

d, Vasili Zhuravlev; w, A. Filimonov; ph, A. Galperin.

Science Fiction   **(PR:A   MPAA:NR)**

SPACE STATION X   (SEE: MUTINY IN OUTER SPACE, 1965)

SPACE STATION X-14   (SEE: MUTINY IN OUTER SPACE, 1965)

SPACED OUT zero   (1981, Brit.) 90m Miramax c (AKA: OUTER TOUCH)

Barry Stokes (Oliver), Tony Maiden (Willy), Glory Annen (Cosia), Michael Rowlatt (Cliff), Ava Cadell (Partha), Kate Ferguson (Skipper), Lynne Ross (Prudence).

An amateurish British sex comedy about a group of female space invaders from the star system Betelgeuse who take male prisoners from Earth. There are spoofs of STAR WARS and 2001: A SPACE ODYSSEY, as well as some teenage gutter humor, none of which amounts to anything remotely funny.

p, David Speechley; d, Norman J. Warren; w, Andrew Payne, Bob Saget, Jeff de Hart; ph, John Metclafe, Peter Sinclair (Technicolor); m, Alan Brawer, Anna Pepper; ed, Edward Glass; song performed by The Chance.

Science-Fiction/Comedy   **Cas.**   **(PR:O   MPAA:R)**

SPACEFLIGHT IC-1**   (1965, Brit.) 63m Lippert/FOX bw

Bill Williams (Capt. Mead Ralston), Kathleen Breck (Kate Saunders), John Cairney (Steven "Doc" Thomas), Donald Churchill (Carl Walcott), Jeremy Longhurst (John Saunders), Linda Marlowe (Helen Thomas), Margo Mayne (Joyce Walcott), Norma West (Jan Ralston), Tony Doonan (Griffith), Andrew Downie (Capt. Burnett), John Lee (Dr. Garth), Chuck Julian (Webster), Max Kirby (Clown), Mark Lester (Don), Stewart Middleton (Michael), Anthony Honour (Robert).

Set in the near future, SPACEFLIGHT IC-1 sees a world controlled by one, powerful and computerized government which handpicks passengers for a planet-colonizing mission on the basis of age, health, and intelligence. The crew is then sent into space with loyal party member Williams at the helm. After a few weeks, the crew begins to rebel against the cold, heartless, autocratic rule and eventually mutinies, reestablishing a humanistic, democratic, albeit small, society in search of a planet. Good idea, but an indifferent script and dull direction weigh the action and ideas down.

p, Robert L. Lippert, Jack Parsons; d, Bernard Knowles; w, Harry Spalding; ph, Geoffrey Faithfull; m, Elisabeth Lutyens; ed, Robert Winter; md, Philip Martell; art d, Harry White; cos, Jean Fairlie; makeup, Harold Fletcher.

Science Fiction   **(PR:A   MPAA:NR)**

SPACEHUNTER: ADVENTURES IN THE FORBIDDEN ZONE**
          (1983) 90m COL c (AKA: ROAD GANGS, ADVENTURES IN THE CREEP ZONE)

Peter Strauss (Wolff), Molly Ringwald (Niki), Ernie Hudson (Washington), Andrea Marcovicci (Chalmers), Michael Ironside (Overdog McNabb), Beeson Carroll (Grandma Patterson), Hrant Alianak (Chemist), Deborah Pratt (Meagan), Aleisa Shirley (Reena), Cali Timmins (Nova), Paul Boretski (Jarrett), Patrick Rowe (Duster), Reggie Bennett (Barracuda Leader).

The last gasp of the second round of 3-D films spewed forth this uneven effort which presents Strauss as a mercenary salvage ship captain who hooks up with a pre-John Hughes (SIXTEEN CANDLES, THE BREAKFAST CLUB) Molly Ringwald and other misfits in a search for three stranded girls whose ship crashed on a planet called Terra Eleven. After battling a variety of threats including savages, mutants and monsters, he finds the girls in the evil clutches of demi-god Ironside, who is a cyborg. In the end he wipes out Ironside and his evil city. The special effects are well done, the set design is creative, and the performances OK (although Ringwald's affected dialect grates on the nerves). However, the film is filled with borrowings from every science fiction film from STAR WARS to THE ROAD WARRIOR which becomes a frustrating hindrance after awhile. It

is not surprising the film turned out as it did because of the revolving door of creative talent (director Jean Lafleur was replaced by Johnson and six writers wrestled with the screenplay), but with a bigger dose of originality, SPACEHUNTER could have become a popular and lasting sci-fi adventure despite the 3-D gimmicks and heavy inspiration from other, better, films.

p, Don Carmody, Andre Link, John Dunning; d, Lamont Johnson; w, David Preston, Edith Rey, Dan Goldberg, Len Blum (based on a story by Stewart Harding, Jean LaFleur); ph, Frank Tidy (3-D, Twin Panavision, Metrocolor); m, Elmer Bernstein; ed, Scott Conrad; prod d, Jackson DeGovia; art d, John R. Jenson, Brent Swift, Michael Nemirsky, Michael Minor; cos, Julie Weiss; spec eff, Dale Martin, Gene Warren, Jr., Peter Kleinow, Image 3; makeup, Thomas R. Burman; stunts, Walter Scott; effects animation, Ernest D. Farino.

Science Fiction   **Cas.**   **(PR:C   MPAA:PG)**

SPACEMAN AND KING ARTHUR, THE
          (SEE: UNIDENTIFIED FLYING ODDBALL, 1979, Brit.)

SPACEMEN SATURDAY NIGHT
          (SEE: INVASION OF THE SAUCER MEN, 1957)

SPACESHIP   (SEE: DAY MARS INVADED THE EARTH, THE, 1963)

SPACESHIP   (SEE: CREATURE WASN'T NICE, 1981)

SPACESHIP TO VENUS   (SEE: FIRST SPACESHIP ON VENUS, 1962, Ger./Pol.)

SPACEWAYS**   (1953, Brit.) 76m Hammer/Lippert bw

Howard Duff (Stephen Mitchell), Eva Bartok (Lisa Frank), Alan Wheatley (Smith), Philip Leaver (Dr. Keppler), Michael Medwin (Toby Andrews), Andrew Osborn (Philip Crenshaw), Cecile Chevreau (Vanessa Mitchell), Anthony Ireland (Gen. Hays), Hugh Moxey (Col. Daniels), David Horne (Minister), Jean Webster-Brough (Mrs. Daniels), Leo Phillips (Sgt. Peterson), Marianne Stone (Mrs. Rogers).

A weak British science fiction effort based on a radio play and starring American actor Duff as a rocket scientist helping the British with their space program. All his hard work is interrupted, however, when he discovers that his wife, Chevreau, is having an affair with a fellow scientist, Osborn, who also is a Soviet spy. When the sly pair disappear at about the same time Duff launches England's first satellite, inspector Wheatley assumes that the angry scientist killed them and shipped their bodies into outer space. Not wanting to be convicted for a crime he did not commit, Duff, along with his assistant Bartok, decide to be the first couple in space and hurriedly builds another rocket to blast off into space and retrieves the satellite to prove his innocence. Back on Earth, Wheatley is shocked to discover Chevreau and Osborn turn up very much alive, until Osborn kills Chevreau in a spat. Eventually Duff and Bartok are contacted and return to Earth. An early effort from Hammer horror director Fisher, who struggles mightily with the material and manages to bring some flair to the visuals. Many of the rocket effects are borrowed from ROCKETSHIP X-M (1950).

p, Michael Carreras; d, Terence Fisher; w, Paul Tabori, Richard Landau (based on a radio play by Charles Eric Maine); ph, Reginald Wyer; m, Ivor Slaney; ed, Maurice Rootes.

Science Fiction   **(PR:A   MPAA:NR)**

SPANIARD'S CURSE, THE**½   (1958, Brit.) 80m Wentworth/IF-BL bw

Tony Wright (Charlie Manton), Lee Patterson (Mark Brett), Michael Hordern (Judge Manton), Ralph Truman (Sir Robert Wyvern), Henry Oscar (Mr. Fredericks), Susan Beaumont (Margaret Manton), Brian Oulton (Frank Porter), Olga Dickie (Hannah), Roddy Hughes (Jody), Basil Dignam (Guy Stevenson), John Watson.

An interesting murder mystery but one which never really delivers what it promises. Dignam, an innocent man convicted of murder, places a curse on his judge and jury. Two of the cursed men mysteriously die and suspicion is placed on the condemned man. However, when Dignam dies the mystery deepens. The judge, Hordern, and his daughter, Beaumont, dig up some clues and uncover the identity of the real killer.

p, Roger Proudlock; d, Ralph Kemplen; w, Kenneth Hyde (based on the novel The Assize of the Dying by Edith Pargiter); ph, Arthur Grant; m, Lambert Williamson; ed, Stanley Hawkes; art d, Tony Masters.

Crime   **(PR:A   MPAA:NR)**

SPANISH AFFAIR½   (1958, Span.) 95m Nomad/PAR c

Richard Kiley (*Merritt Blake*), Carmen Sevilla (*Mari Zarubia*), Jose Guardiola (*Antonio*), Jesus Tordesillas (*Sotelo*), Jose Manuel Martin (*Fernando*), Francisco Bernal (*Waiter*), Rafael Farina (*Flamenco Singer*), Jose Marco Davo (*Father*), Purita Vargas (*Purita*), Antonio S. Amaya (*Miguel*).

Director Don Siegel (INVASION OF THE BODY SNATCHERS, DIRTY HARRY) seems a bit miscast for this assignment which is basically a romantic travelog of Spain with some fairly suspenseful thriller aspects thrown in. Kiley stars as an American architect on a business trip in Spain who hires a beautiful interpreter, Sevilla. Sevilla's fiance, Guardiola, becomes insanely jealous of the pairing and suspects that his woman and the handsome American are doing more than business. He decides to kill Kiley and follows them throughout Spain, waiting for his chance to strike. Meanwhile, as expected, Kiley and Sevilla fall in love, giving Guardiola a real reason for murder. A lengthy chase then ensues throughout the more scenic areas of Spain including Madrid, El Escorial, Toledo, Segovia, Barcelona, Tossa de Mars, and the Costa Brava.

p, Bruce Odlum; d, Donald Siegel; w, Richard Collins; ph, Sam Leavitt (VistaVision, Technicolor); m, Daniele Amfitheatrof; ed, Tom McAdoo; art d, Hal Pereira, Tambi Larsen; cos, Pedro Rodriquez; m/l, "The Flaming Rose," Amfitheatrof, Mack David (sung by Carmen Sevilla).

Drama   (PR:A MPAA:NR)

SPANISH CAPE MYSTERY**   (1935) 65m Liberty bw

Helen Twelvetrees (*Stella Godfrey*), Donald Cook (*Ellery Queen*), Berton Churchill (*Judge Macklin*), Frank Sheridan (*Godfrey*), Harry Stubbs (*Sheriff Moley*), Guy Usher (*Inspector Queen*), Huntley Gordon (*Kummer*), Betty Blythe (*Mrs. Godfrey*), Olaf Hytten (*DuPre*), Ruth Gillette (*Mrs. Constable*), Jack LaRue (*Gardner*), Frank Leigh (*Tiller*), Barbara Bedford (*Mrs. Munn*), Donald Kerr (*Hendricks*), George Cleveland (*Jorum*), George Baxter, Katherine Morrow, Arnold Gray, Lee Prather.

The first of only two appearances by sleuth Ellery Queen in the films of the 1930s and they were both programmers (the other was THE MANDARIN MYSTERY [1937!]). Cook plays Queen in this murder mystery which places the detective on vacation near the Spanish Cape when a string of killings happens in the area. Aided by an obnoxious local sheriff, Stubbs, Cook figures out who the killer is and allows Stubbs the honor of capturing him.

p, M.H. Hoffman; d, Lewis D. Collins; w, Albert DeMond (based on a novel by Ellery Queen); ph, Gilbert Warrenton; ed, Jack Ogilvie.

Mystery   (PR:A MPAA:NR)

SPANISH EYES*   (1930, Brit.) 71m Julian Wylie-Ulargui/MGM bw

Edna Davies (*Estrella*), Dennis Noble (*Amalio*), Donald Calthrop (*Mascoso*), Anthony Ireland (*Chechester*), Antonia Brough (*Landlady*).

A kind-hearted street musician adopts a blind youngster and arranges for him to be cured. A well-intentioned picture which drowns in its own syrupy goodness.

d, G.B. Samuelson.

Musical   (PR:A MPAA:NR)

SPANISH FLY zero   (1975, Brit.) 86m Winkle/EMI c

Terry-Thomas, Leslie Phillips, Graham Armitage, Frank Thornton, Sue Lloyd.

A vulgar British comedy about an enterprising chap in Majorca who boosts his wine sales by adding a special ingredient to the beverage–an aphrodisiac. Profits increase at an astronomical rate, but so does the sexual appetite of everyone in town. The performances of some veteran comics can't save this poor vintage from its foul aftertaste.

d, Bob Kellett; w, Robert Ryerson.

Comedy   (PR:O MPAA:R)

SPANISH GARDENER, THE**   (1957, Span.) 95m RANK c

Dirk Bogarde (*Jose*), Jon Whiteley (*Nicholas Brande*), Michael Hordern (*Harrington Brande*), Cyril Cusack (*Garcia*), Maureen Swanson (*Maria*), Lyndon Brook (*Robert Burton*), Josephine Griffin (*Carol Burton*), Bernard Lee (*Leighton Bailey*), Rosalie Crutchley (*Magdalena*), Ina De La Haye (*Jose's Mother*), Geoffrey Keen (*Dr. Harvey*), Harold Scott (*Pedro*), Jack Stewart, Richard Molinas (*Police Escorts*), Susan Lyall Grant (*Maid*), John Adderley (*Taxi Driver*), David Lander (*Policeman*).

Set against the picturesque background of Costa Brava, Spain, THE SPANISH GARDENER stars the anglo Bogarde as the gentle title character. He is employed by Hordern, a failed diplomat who is tortured by his own inadequacies. The diplomat's son, Whiteley, is an impressionable boy who is smothered by his father's overbearing possessiveness. When Whiteley takes a liking to Bogarde, Hordern feels rejected and objects. Hordern engineers a scheme to get rid of Bogarde by having the family valet, Cusack, plant a stolen watch him. Bogarde is arrested and carted off to prison on a

train. He manages to escape, however, and is left wounded in the hills. Whiteley, disgusted with his father's manipulating, runs away and hooks up with Bogarde. The gardener, genuinely concerned about the boy's relationship with his father, impresses upon on him the importance of returning home and forgiving his father. Hordern, having followed his son into the hills, overhears the conversation and reassesses his opinion of Bogarde. Whiteley and his father soon settle their differences and start anew with a stronger bond. This was Bogarde's second film with child star Whiteley, they having previously appeared together in THE STRANGER IN BETWEEN (1952). Whiteley's biggest claim to fame, however, is winning an honorary Oscar in 1954. Considering the fact that Whiteley was a child star he was given a miniature statuette for his performance in THE LITTLE KIDNAPPERS.

p, John Bryan; d, Philip Leacock; w, Lesley Storm, John Bryan (based on the novel by A.J. Cronin); ph, Christopher Challis (VistaVision, Technicolor); m, John Veale; ed, Reginald Mills; prod d, Maurice Carter; cos, Margaret Furse.

Drama   (PR:A MPAA:NR)

SPANISH MAIN, THE**½   (1945) 100m RKO c

Paul Henreid (*Laurent Van Horn*), Maureen O'Hara (*Francisca*), Walter Slezak (*Don Alvarado*), Binnie Barnes (*Anne Bonney*), John Emery (*Du Billar*), Barton MacLane (*Capt. Black*), J.M. Kerrigan (*Pillery*), Fritz Leiber (*Bishop*), Nancy Gates (*Lupita*), Jack LaRue (*Lt. Escobar*), Mike Mazurki (*Swaine*), Ian Keith (*Capt. Lussan*), Victor Kilian (*Santa Madre Captain*), Curt Bois (*Paree*), Antonio Moreno (*Commandante*), Alfredo Sabato (*Sailing Master*), Brandon Hurst (*Capt. Salter*), Bob O'Connor (*Master at Arms*), Tom Kennedy (*Capt. McLeon*), Marcelle Corday (*Senora Perez*), Norma Drury (*Senora Montalvo*), Abe Dinovich (*Singer*), Max Wagner, Ray Spiker (*Bullies*), Juan De La Cruz (*Major-Domo*), Leo White (*Hairdresser*), Cosmo Sardo, Leo Schlessinger (*Spanish Guards*), Jack Wise (*Manicurist*), Dan Seymour (*Jailer*), Ray Cooper, Jamiel Hasson, Alf Haugan, Al Haskell, George Bruggeman, Chuck Hamilton, Jean Valjean, Demetrius Alexis, Carl Deloro (*Officers*), Don Avalier (*Pirate*).

The first in a series of Technicolor films contracted by RKO, THE SPANISH MAIN is a typical pirate movie helped immensely by the energetic performances of Henreid, O'Hara, and Slezak. Slezak plays a villainous Spanish governor who orders a shipwrecked crew of Dutch sailors to be enslaved and their captain, Henreid, hung. The Dutchmen escape however, and form a pirate gang which concentrates its raids on the Spanish. Seeking revenge on Slezak, Henreid and his men kidnap his bride-to-be, O'Hara, off the ship from Mexico she was to arrive on. Henreid forces O'Hara to marry him, much to the chagrin of his crew who fear the whole Spanish Armada on their heads in retaliation. Henreid's crew steal O'Hara and take her to Slezak to prevent a slaughter. Unfortunately for Slezak, O'Hara has fallen in love with Henreid and she assists the pirate captain in his efforts to get her back.

p, Stephen Ames; d, Frank Borzage; w, George Worthing Yates, Herman J. Mankiewicz (based on a story by Aeneas MacKenzie); ph, George Barnes (Technicolor); m, Hanns Eisler; ed, Ralph Dawson; md, C. Bakaleinikoff; art d, Albert S. D'Agostino, Carroll Clark; set d, Darrell Silvera, Claude Carpenter; spec eff, Vernon L. Walker.

Adventure   **Cas.**   (PR:A MPAA:NR)

SPANISH SWORD, THE*½   (1962, Brit.) 62m Danziger/UA bw

Ronald Howard (*Sir Richard Clovell*), June Thorburn (*Lady Eleanor*), Nigel Green (*Baron Breaute*), Trader Faulkner (*Philip*), Derrick Sherwin (*Edmund*), Robin Hunter (*Thomas of Exeter*), Sheila Whittingham (*Frances*), Barry Shawzin (*Redbeard*).

Set in 11th Century England, this costumer has a brave knight undermining a baron's attempt to steal a treasure from King Henry III. A weak script is saved by some impressive battle scenes and authentic-looking costuming.

p, Brian Taylor; d, Ernest Morris; w, Brian Clemens.

Adventure   (PR:A MPAA:NR)

SPARA FORTE, PIU FORTE...NON CAPISCO
(SEE: SHOOT LOUD, LOUDER...I DON'T UNDERSTAND, 1966, Ital.)

SPARE A COPPER**   (1940, Brit.) 77m EAL-Associated Talking
                                                               Pictures/ABF bw

George Formby (*George Carter*), Dorothy Hyson (*Jane Grey*), Bernard Lee (*Jake*), John Warwick (*Shaw*), Warburton Gamble (*Sir Robert Dyer*), John Turnbull (*Inspector Richards*), George Merritt (*Edward Brewster*), Eliot Makeham (*Fuller*), Ellen Pollock (*Lady Hardstaff*), Edward Lexy (*Night Watchman*), Jack Melford (*Dame*), Hal Gordon (*Sergeant*), Jimmy Godden (*Manager*), Grace Arnold (*Music Shop Customer*), Charles Carson (*Admiral*).

A mediocre WW II comedy set in Merseyside and starring Formby as a member of the police War Reserve. He uncovers a plot to blow up a battleship, "The Hercules," on its maiden voyage. The police, however, think Formby is one of the saboteurs and chase him up and down the docks.

Formby manages to get the ship launched before the explosion occurs–destroying the slipway, but leaving "The Hercules" untouched.

p, Basil Dearden; d, John Paddy Carstairs; w, Roger Macdougall, Dearden, Austin Melford; ph, Bryan Langley; m, Louis Levy; ed, Ray Pitt; art d, Wilfred Shingleton.

Comedy   **(PR:A   MPAA:NR)**

SPARE THE ROD**   (1961, Brit.) 93m Weyland/BL bw

Max Bygraves *(John Saunders)*, Donald Pleasence *(Mr. Jenkins)*, Geoffrey Keen *(Arthur Gregory)*, Betty McDowall *(Ann Collins)*, Peter Reynolds *(Alec Murray)*, Jean Anderson *(Mrs. Pond)*, Eleanor Summerfield *(Mrs. Harkness)*, Mary Merrall *(Miss Fogg)*, Aubrey Woods *(Mr. Bickerstaff)*, Rory McDermott *(Mr. Richards)*, Richard O'Sullivan *(Fred Harkness)*, Claire Marshall *(Margaret)*, Jeremy Bulloch *(Angell)*, Annette Robertson *(Doris)*, Brian Lown *(Hoole)*.

Brave, idealistic, and young schoolteacher Bygraves overcomes the apathy of his fellow instructors and tries to teach the unruly East London school students in a meaningful manner. To do this, Bygraves plays on the youngsters sympathies and eventually wins their trust and respect after many harrowing episodes, including a riot. You have seen it all before.

p, Victor Lyndon, Jock Jacobson; d, Leslie Norman; w, John Cresswell (based on the novel by Michael Croft); ph, Paul Beeson; m, Laurie Johnson; ed, Gordon Stone.

Drama   **(PR:A   MPAA:NR)**

SPARKLE**   (1976) 98m WB c

Philip M. Thomas *(Stix)*, Irene Cara *(Sparkle)*, Lonette McKee *(Sister)*, Dwan Smith *(Dolores)*, Mary Alice *(Effie)*, Dorian Harewood *(Levi)*, Tony King *(Satin)*, Beatrice Winde *(Mrs. Waters)*, Paul Lambert *(Moe Gerber)*, Joyce Easton *(Lee)*, DeWayne Jessie *(Ham)*, Norma Miller *(Doreen)*, Talya Ferro, Robert W. Delegall, Armelia McQueen, Don Bexley, Timmie Rogers, Ken Renard, John Hawker.

A routine musical drama starring Cara, McKee, and Smith as three singing sisters striving to get out of their harrowing Harlem existence with the help of Thomas, who tries to transform them into rock 'n' roll sensations in the 1950s. Unfortunately the film wallows in the usual contrivances, i.e. alcohol, drug-abuse, and gangsters, which take their toll on the sisters until only Cara is left to make it big under Thomas' guidance. Good performances from the principals nearly pull the film out of the realm of sameness.

p, Howard Rosenman; d, Sam O'Steen; w, Joel Schumacher (based on a story by Schumacher, Rosenman); ph, Bruce Surtees (Technicolor); m, Curtis Mayfield; ed, Gordon Scott; art d, Peter Wooley; set d, Cheryal Kearney; ch, Lester Wilson.

Musical/Drama   **Cas.**   **(PR:C-O   MPAA:PG)**

SPARROWS CAN'T SING**   (1963, Brit.) 94m Carthage/Janus bw

James Booth *(Charlie Gooding)*, Barbara Windsor *(Maggie Gooding)*, Roy Kinnear *(Fred Gooding)*, Avis Bunnage *(Bridgie Gooding)*, Brian Murphy *(Jack)*, George Sewell *(Bert)*, Barbara Ferris *(Nellie Gooding)*, Griffith Davies *(Chunky)*, Murray Melvin *(Georgie)*, Arthur Mullard *(Ted)*, Peggy Ann Clifford *(Ted's Wife)*, Wally Patch *(Watchman)*, Bob Grant *(Perce)*, Stephen Lewis *(Caretaker)*, Victor Spinetti *(Arnold)*, Jenny Sontag *(Momma)*, May Scagnelli *(Gran)*, Fanny Carby *(Lil)*, Yootha Joyce *(Paddy the Barman)*, Janet Howse *(Janet)*, Queenie Watts *(Queenie)*, Harry H. Corbett *(Greengrocer)*, Marjie Lawrence *(Girl)*, Glynn Edwards *(Charlie's Friend)*, Gerry Raffles *(Lorry-Driver)*.

A Cockney melodrama starring Booth as a merchant marine who returns home after a two-year hitch to find his home replaced and his wife missing. Booth's mother knows the whereabouts of his wife (she's living with a bus driver), but won't let on because she fears his violent temper. Frustrated by this code of silence, Booth takes his brother Kinnear hostage in a pub and refuses to let him go until his wife arrives. Eventually his wife, Windsor, agrees to meet him in a park and she arrives wheeling a baby carriage. After learning that she is now living with Sewell, Booth is skeptical about the parentage of the child, but the couple decides to forgive each other. Booth prepares for his wife and child to move into his mother's house. That night, during a family celebration, Sewell arrives to reassert his claim on Windsor. After a knock-down drag-out, Sewell departs, leaving Booth and Windsor to continue their interrupted marriage. Some American release prints are subtitled due to the hard-to-understand Cockney dialect.

p, Donald Taylor; d, Joan Littlewood; w, Stephen Lewis, Littlewood (based on the play "Sparrers Can't Sing" by Lewis); ph, Max Greene, Desmond Dickinson; m, James Stevens; ed, Oswald Hafenrichter; md, Stanley Black; art d, Bernard Sarron; m/l, Title song, Lionel Bart (sung by Barbara Windsor); makeup, Bill Lodge.

Drama   **(PR:A   MPAA:NR)**

SPARTACUS****   (1960) 196m Bryna/UNIV c

Kirk Douglas *(Spartacus)*, Laurence Olivier *(Marcus Licinius Crassus)*, Tony Curtis *(Antoninus)*, Jean Simmons *(Varinia)*, Charles Laughton *(Gracchus)*, Peter Ustinov *(Lentulus Batiatus)*, John Gavin *(Julius Caesar)*, Nina Foch *(Helena Glabrus)*, Herbert Lom *(Tigranes)*, John Ireland *(Crixus)*, John Dall *(Glabrus)*, Charles McGraw *(Marcellus)*, Joanna Barnes *(Claudia Marius)*, Woody Strode *(Draba)*, Harold J. Stone *(David)*, Peter Brocco *(Ramon)*, Paul Lambert *(Gannicus)*, Bob Wilke *(Guard Captain)*, Nick Dennis *(Dionysius)*, John Hoyt *(Caius, Roman Officer)*, Frederick Worlock *(Laelius)*, Dayton Lummis *(Symmachus)*, Lili Valenty *(Old Crone)*, Jill Jarmyn *(Julia)*, Jo Summers, Autumn Russell, Kay Stewart, Lynda Williams, Louise Vincent *(Slave Girls)*, James Griffith *(Otho)*, Joe Haworth *(Marius)*, Dale Van Sickel *(Trainer)*, Vinton Haworth *(Metallius)*, Carleton Young *(Herald)*, Hallene Hill *(Beggar Woman)*, Paul Burns *(Fimbria)*, Leonard Penn *(Garrison Officer)*, Harry Harvey, Jr., Eddie Parker, Herold Goodwin, Chuck Roberson *(Slaves)*, Saul Gorss, Charles Horvath, Gil Perkins *(Slave Leaders)*, Dick Crockett, Harvey Parry, Rod Normond, Larry Perron, Carey Loftin *(Guards)*, Bob Morgan, Reg Parton, Tom Steele, Aaron Saxon, Wally Rose *(Gladiators)*, Ken Terrell, Boyd "Red" Morgan *(Ad Libs)*, Otto Malde *(Roman General)*, Bob Burns, Seamon Glass, George Robotham, Stubby Kruger *(Pirates)*, Chuck Courtney, Russ Saunders, Valley Keene, Tap Canutt, Joe Canutt, Wayne Van Horn, Brad Harris, Jerry Brown, Chuck Hayward, Buff Brady, Cliff Lyons, Rube Schaffer *(Soldiers)*, Ted de Corsia, Arthur Batanides, Robert Stevenson *(Legionaires)*, Terence de Marney *(Major Domo)*.

Probably the best epic about the ancient world ever produced for the screen, SPARTACUS tells the true story of a slave rebellion that panicked Rome for more than two years around 73 B.C. The film opens with Douglas, the son and grandson of slaves, working in a mine in Libya. There he is purchased by Ustinov, the proprietor of a school for gladiators. The conditions there are brutal, and the chief goal is to quickly give the men enough training to put up a little show before dying. As a reward, the men are sometimes given a woman, thrown into their cells. Under these circumstances Douglas meets and falls in love with Simmons, a slave from Britain. When wealthy senator Olivier comes to visit, along with his entourage, he asks that a match be set up for his amusement. Olivier's female companions choose the combatants, Douglas and Strode, an Ethiopian expert with the trident and net and Douglas' friend. The two men fight reluctantly and eventually Strode forces Douglas to the ground. With his spear at Douglas' neck, he looks up at the spectators for the signal. They give him a thumbs down, ordering him to kill Douglas, but he cannot. Instead he leaps up onto the balcony from which they watch, only to have his throat quickly and neatly slit by Olivier, blood splattering in his face. Later, Simmons is bought by Olivier and taken away, and when Douglas is taunted about this by a guard, he kills the man and leads a revolt by some 78 gladiators, who quickly overrun the school and take to the countryside, growing in numbers and strength as they pillage estates and attract escaped slaves to their ranks. He defeats several Roman forces sent out against him. Eventually he is joined by Simmons and another escaped slave from Olivier's household, Curtis (in a scene cut out of the final film, the motive for Curtis' escape is made clear when the effeminate Olivier makes a sexual pass at him). Douglas tries to make a deal with some pirates to carry him and his army away from Italy to freedom, but when he arrives on the coast to meet the ships, he finds the pirates have been bribed by Olivier to keep away, and three full legions have Douglas trapped with his back to the sea. An enormous battle ensues in which the slave army is destroyed. Six thousand men, Douglas among them, are captured and brought back to Rome in chains. Olivier, whose political ambitions against senator Laughton have been well-served by his victory, finds Simmons and her infant son–by Douglas–and tries to seduce her. When she spurns him he orders that Douglas and Curtis fight each other to the death, the winner to be crucified. Douglas uses his skills to save Curtis from that slow death, and finishes him off quickly. Laughton takes Simmons and her son away from Olivier and frees them, and as she leaves Rome she passes the thousands of rebels crucified along the Appian Way. She finds Douglas, almost dead now, and shows him his free son. More than $12 million, two years, and two directors went into this magnificent achievement. Douglas also served as the executive producer and was responsible for the firing of Anthony Mann from the picture after he shot the opening scenes set in Libya and at the gladiator school. Douglas then brought in Kubrick, whom Douglas had worked with on PATHS OF GLORY three years before. Kubrick was not happy with the project, mostly because he had not been in on the original writing of the script. Still, he rewrote extensively during the shooting, and the film that emerged shows his imprint. The performances are all superb, and although Douglas suffers in comparison to the skillful British cast (Olivier, Ustinov, Simmons, Laughton), he brings a vitality and intensity to the title role that none of these others could have. The script by Dalton Trumbo, his first screen credit since being blacklisted more than 10 years before, is literate and restrained, avoiding the obvious speeches about freedom and the like. Kubrick's handling of the camera reflects the same restraint, not showing the obvious, but rather what is more interesting behind it. The battle scene is one of the most spectacular ever filmed, with over 8,000 Spanish soldiers filling out the ranks of the slaves and the Roman army, in sharp contrast to those all-too-common ancient battle scenes in which fast cutting and close shots fail to create the illusion that the couple of dozen men fighting are two clashing armies. The film was a great success and allowed Kubrick to chuck the Hollywood rat race once and for all. After this he would work on his own projects, only six of which have appeared in the last quarter century.

p, Edward Lewis; d, Stanley Kubrick, (uncredited) Anthony Mann; w, Dalton Trumbo (based on the novel by Howard Fast); ph, Russell Metty, Clifford Stine (Super Technirama-70, Technicolor); m, Alex North; ed, Robert Lawrence, Robert Schulte, Fred Chulack; prod d, Alexander Golitzen; md, North, Joseph Gershenson; art d, Eric Orbom; set d, Russell A. Gausman; Julia Heron; cos, Bill Thomas, J. Arlington Valles; makeup, Bud Westmore; tech adv, Vittorio Nino Novarese.

Historical Epic   Cas.   (PR:C MPAA:NR)

SPASMS zero   (1983, Can.) 89m Cinequity-NTC-CFDC-Famous Players/PDC c (AKA: DEAT H BITE)

Peter Fonda (*Dr. Brasilian*), Oliver Reed (*Jason*), Kerrie Keane (*Susanne*), Al Waxman (*Crowley*), Miguel Fernandes (*Mendes*), Marilyn Lightstone (*Dr. Rothman*), Angus MacInnes (*Duncan*), Laurie Brown (*Allison*), Gerard Parkes (*Capt. Noveck*), George Bloomfield (*Rev. Thomas*).

A brainless picture about a killer devil-snake which surfaces every seven years to claim the souls of the dead. The snake is captured but soon escapes, leading Fonda and Reed on a ridiculous search. Reed has an edge in the search because he was bitten by the snake seven years earlier and now possesses the ability to "see through the snake's eyes." The only worthwhile aspect is the theme music by Tangerine Dream, who also supplied the music for THIEF (1981), THE SORCERER (1977), and RISKY BUSINESS (1983).

p, John G. Pozhke, Maurice Smith; d, William Fruet; w, Don Enright (based on the novel *Death Bite* by Michael Maryk, Brent Monahan); ph, Mark Irwin (Medallion Color); m, Eric N. Robertson, Tangerine Dream; ed, Ralph Brunjes; art d, Gavin Mitchell; spec eff, Brian Warner; makeup, Jim Hopkins, Dick Smith, Carl Fullerton, Stephen Dupuis.

Science-fiction/Horror   Cas.   (PR:O MPAA:R)

SPATS TO SPURS   (SEE: HENRY GOES TO ARIZONA, 1939)

SPAWN OF THE NORTH*½**   (1938) 110m PAR bw

George Raft (*Tyler Dawson*), Henry Fonda (*Jim Kimmerlee*), Dorothy Lamour (*Nicky Duval*), Akim Tamiroff (*Red Skain*), John Barrymore (*Windy*), Louise Platt (*Diane*), Lynne Overman (*Jackson*), Fuzzy Knight (*Lefty Jones*), Vladimir Sokoloff (*Dimitri*), Duncan Renaldo (*Ivan*), John Wray (*Dr. Sparks*), Michio Ito (*Indian Dancer*), Stanley Andrews (*Partridge*), Richard Ung (*Tom*), Slicker the Seal (*Himself*), Alex Woloshin (*Gregory*), Archie Twitchell, Lee Shumway, Wade Boteler, Galan Galt, Arthur Aylesworth, Rollo Lloyd (*Fishermen*), Guy Usher (*Grant*), Henry Brandon (*Davis*), Egon Brecher (*Erickson*), Harvey Clark (*Purser*), Monte Blue, Irving Bacon (*Cannam/Officials*), Robert Middlemass (*Davis*), Aida Kutzenoff (*Vashia*), Eddie Marr, Frank Puglia, Leonid Snegoff (*Red's Gang*), Edmund Elton (*Minister*).

The danger and romance of the salmon season in Alaska comes to the Paramount backlot in this adequate adventure yarn. Fonda and Raft are old friends who eventually end up on different sides of the law. While Fonda tries to pull an honest living out of the sea by putting out traps and nets for the spawning fish, Raft joins the gang of nefarious Russian Tamiroff in pillaging the nets of others. Meanwhile, Fonda is romancing Platt, the daughter of drunken newspaper editor Barrymore. Raft and Fonda finally come into direct conflict one night on the water, and in the ensuing gun battle Fonda shoots Raft. Dying, Raft pretends to be angry with Fonda and refuses to forgive him, but later, Raft takes the helm of his boat, and with all the Russian's gang aboard, he gives a familiar signal of friendship to Fonda with his horn, then crashes the boat against the base of a glacier, triggering a huge fall of ice that crushes the craft. The plot here is no great shakes, and the dialog is mostly laughable, but the film is exceedingly well crafted by Hathaway and his ace crew. Raft once again agreed to die on screen and accepted the script sight unseen just to have the chance to work with director Hathaway again (Raft had been nominated for a Best Supporting Actor Oscar for his performance in Hathaway's SOULS AT SEA the year before.) Fonda took his role only because Randolph Scott, originally announced for the role, had a prior commitment. Both of their performances, as well as the supporting cast, Barrymore, Lamour, and Tamiroff, especially, are solid and professional, if somewhat limited by script deficiencies. The most fascinating thing about this film, though, is its smooth mixing of studio shooting and location footage brought back by a second unit dispatched to Alaska. On the backlot technicians built a wharf and a number of shacks to create a small settlement from the early days of the century. Remade in 1954 as ALASKA SEAS.

p, Albert Lewin; d, Henry Hathaway; w, Jules Furthman, Talbot Jennings, (uncredited) Dale Van Every (based on the novel by Barrett Willoughby); ph, Charles Lang, Jr.; m, Dimitri Tiomkin; ed, Ellsworth Hoagland; art d, Hans Dreier; spec eff, Gordon Jennings, Farciot Edouart.

Drama   (PR:A MPAA:NR)

SPEAK EASILY½**   (1932) 80m MGM bw

Buster Keaton (*Prof. Post*), Jimmy Durante (*James*), Ruth Selwyn (*Pansy Peets*), Thelma Todd (*Eleanor Espere*), Hedda Hopper (*Mrs. Peets*), William Pawley (*Griffo*), Sidney Toler (*Stage Director*), Lawrence Grant (*Dr. Bolton*), Henry Armetta (*Tony*), Edward Brophy (*Reno*).

A disappointing Keaton vehicle which sees costar Durante dominate the best comedy moments. Keaton plays a dull college professor who is bored with his sedentary lifestyle. Durante is Keaton's loyal butler who decides to spruce up his boss' life by handing him a bogus inheritance letter which states that $750,000 is now his to spend. Keaton excitedly takes to the night life and runs into a troupe of frustrated, and untalented, actors trying to put on a show. Keaton falls in love with Todd, a fiesty, hard-drinking gal, but nice-girl Selwyn waits in the wings. The professor funds the troupe's show, but the premiere is a disaster until Keaton accidentally winds up on stage and becomes a star.

d, Edgar Sedgwick; w, Ralph Spence, Laurence E. Johnson (from the novel *Footlights* by Clarence Buddington Kelland); ph, Harold Wenstrom; fd, William Levanway.

Comedy   (PR:A MPAA:NR)

SPEAKEASY*½   (1929) 62m FOX bw

Paul Page (*Paul Martin*), Lola Lane (*Alice Woods*), Henry B. Walthall (*Fuzzy*), Helen Ware (*Min*), Warren Hymer (*Cannon Delmont, Paul's Fight Manager*), Stuart Erwin (*Cy Williams*), Sharon Lynn (*Mazie*), Erville Alderson (*City Editor*), James Guilfoyle (*Davey*), Joseph Cawthorn (*Yokel*), Ivan Linow (*Wrestler*), Marjorie Beebe, Sailor Vincent, Helen Lynch (*Speakeasy Hangers-on*).

An early talkie that intercuts Movietone newsreel footage with a dull drama starring Page as a down-and-out fighter who's being conned by his untrustworthy manager. Gal reporter Lane falls in love with the big dummy and helps his ego enough to get him back in the ring. The hackneyed climax is Page being beaten senseless in the championship match, his attention riveted to the empty seat where Lane is supposed to be. Just as it looks as if Page is down for the count, Lane arrives and he bounces back to win the fight. All the footage of Madison Square Garden, Times Square, Grand Central Station, the subway, the pressroom, and most of the street scenes are culled from the vaults of Movietone news.

d, Benjamin Stoloff; w, Frederick Hazlitt Brennan, Edwin Burke (based on the play by Edward Knoblock, George Rosener); ph, Joseph A. Valentine; ed, J. Edwin Robbins; cos, Sophie Wachner.

Drama   (PR:A MPAA:NR)

SPECIAL AGENT*   (1935) 78m COS/WB bw

Bette Davis (*Julie Carston*), George Brent (*Bill Bradford*), Ricardo Cortez (*Nick Carston*), Joseph Sawyer (*Rich*), Joseph Crehan (*Chief of Police*), Henry O'Neill (*District Attorney*), Irving Pichel (*U.S. District Attorney*), Jack La Rue (*Andrews*), Robert Strange (*Armitage*), Joseph King (*Wilson*), William B. Davidson (*Young*), J. Carroll Naish (*Durrell*), Paul Guilfoyle (*Secretary to District Attorney*), Robert Barrat (*Head of Internal Revenue Department*), Charles Middleton, Thomas E. Jackson, Jack Mower, Eddy Chandler, Ed Hart (*Cops*), Jack McHugh, Billy Naylor (*Newsboys*), Garry Owen, John Dilson (*Men*), Milton Kibbee (*Player*), Edwin Argus (*Looker-on*), John Alexander (*Manager*), Jerry Fletcher (*Young Man*), Lucille Ward (*Matron*), Herbert Skinner (*Henry*), Allan Cavaen (*Starter*), Bob Montgomery, Huey White, Dutch Hendrian (*Gangsters*), Louis Natheaux (*Clerk*), John Kelly (*Capper*), Emmett Vogan (*Police Announcer*), Frank G. Fanning (*Driver*), Douglas Wood (*Judge*), Lee Phelps (*Court Clerk*), Martha Tibbetts (*Operator*).

Rat-tat-tat-tat, arrgh. That's what you hear often in this fast-moving gangster picture typical of the Warner Bros. releases of the 1930s. Lots of shooting, action, and romance, all crammed into a brief 78 minutes as overseen by supervisor Sam Bischoff who went on to be the producer of such epics as THE CHARGE OF THE LIGHT BRIGADE, THE PHENIX CITY STORY, and many, many more. Cortez is a well-known racketeer with affectations such as wearing gloves when he plays solitaire. He's been a top dog in crime, and the IRS, knowing that they can't nail him for the misdeeds, seeks to get him on income tax evasion (which, as you know, is the manner in which Al Capone was finally jailed). Barrat is the chief IRS person and he deputizes newspaperman Brent as an agent to help amass evidence against Cortez preparatory to a trial in front of the Grand Jury. Brent is a popular newsman with lots of charm and he uses it on Davis, who keeps the books for Cortez. Cortez takes a liking to Brent, totally unaware that he's wearing the two hats of newsman and cop, and even gives him inside dope on some gangster doings so Brent's credibility is heightened with his newspaper. Naturally, there is an attraction between Brent and Davis, and he eventually reveals why he's nosing about the gangland group. He asks Davis if she will help him get Cortez. At first she is reluctant, but she is won over when Brent informs her that Cortez is, in fact, a murderer. Davis makes copies of the account ledgers and Cortez is taken in by the authorities. Guilfoyle, an employee of Cortez, is also working inside the government; he tells Cortez that Brent and Davis have been responsible for all this. Cortez orders his aides to kidnap Davis in order to keep her from testifying. Before that can happen, Brent reckons Cortez has something up his elegant sleeve so he calls for police to cordon Davis off and she is successfully shielded until the moment when she is being led up the steps to the courthouse. At that time, Cortez's men nab Davis. Brent manages to follow them to their lair and call for the cops and the men are arrested, with Davis being saved. Later, Cortez is tried and convicted and sent off to spend the next three decades on Alcatraz. In point of fact, Davis had been a conspirator, but she gets immunity for testifying and all charges against her disappear. Brent and Davis are deeply in love by now and plan to marry as the picture fades. One oddity about the film happens when Cortez is seen to move his lips but nothing comes out. It's not your TV set on the fritz, folks. The Hays Office, which was the censorship arbiter in those days, demanded a dialog cut after the picture had been edited and there was no way to excise the entire scene because many story points had been made. In order to make it work, they erased the offending line from the sound track and the scene kept going. It was easier doing that than calling in Brent, who was busy acting in IN PERSON, or Davis, who was working in DANGEROUS.

p, Martin Mooney; d, William Keighley; w, Laird Doyle, Abem Finkel (based on an idea by Martin Mooney); ph, Sid Hickox; ed, Clarence Kolster; md, Leo F. Forbstein; art d, Esdras Hartley.

Crime   (PR:A-C MPAA:NR)

SPECIAL AGENT**   (1949) 71m PAR bw

William Eythe (Johnny Douglas), George Reeves (Paul Devereaux), Laura Elliot (Lucille Peters), Paul Valentine (Edmond Devereaux), Tom Powers (Special Agent Wilcox), Carole Mathews (Rose McCreary), Frank Puglia (Grandfather Devereaux), Jeff York (Jake Rumpler), Virginia Christine (Mabel Rumpler), Walter Baldwin (Pop Peters), Robert Williams (Supt. Olmstead), Raymond Bond (Sheriff Babcock), Joseph Granby (Sheriff Dodson), Morgan Farley (Dr. Bowen), John Hilton (Frank Kent), Peter Miles (Jake Rumpler, Jr.), Jimmy Hunt (Tim Rumpler), Arthur Stone (Tad Miller), Truman Bradley (Narrator).

The heroic escapades of brave railroad special agent Eythe are detailed as he tries to solve the robbery of $100,000 in payroll receipts from a train. In the robbery an engineer was gunned down, and the dead man's daughter, Elliot, latches on to Eythe for support and romance. Eythe finds that the crime was committed by first-time robbers Reeves and Valentine, who are brothers, and he brings them to justice. Supposedly based on an actual special agent case.

p, William Pine, William C. Thomas; d, Thomas; w, Lewis R. Foster, Whitman Chambers (based on material by Milton Raison); ph, Ellis W. Carter; m, Lucien Caillett; ed, Howard Smith; art d, Lewis H. Creber.

Crime   (PR:A MPAA:NR)

SPECIAL AGENT K-7*   (1937) 66m SYN bw

Walter McGrail (Lanny), Queenie Smith (Ollie), Irving Pichel (Owens), Donald Reed (Billy), Willy Castello (Geller), Duncan Renaldo (Tony), Joy Hodges (Peppy), Richard Tucker (Adams), Malcolm MacGregor (Silky), Capt. John (Schmidt), George Eldredge (Prosecutor), Henry Menjou (Smaltz), David MacDonald (Goodwin), William Royle (Capt. Hall), Harry Harvey (Speedy), James Guilfoyle (Kennedy), Snub Pollard (Waiter).

McGrail plays a nosey FBI agent who takes over a local murder investigation to find that the boy friend of a female buddy of his is the main suspect. The standard mystery devices are all present, including false clues, courtroom histrionics, and surprise "twists" that can be predicted long before officially revealed.

p, C.C. Burr; d, Raymond K. Johnson; w, Phil Dunham (based on a story by George F. Zimmer); ph, Elmer Dyer; m/l, "Actions Speak Louder Than Words," Russ Magnus, Billy Rice.

Mystery   (PR:A MPAA:NR)

SPECIAL DAY, A* (1977, Ital./Can.) 105m CHAM-Canafox/Cinema 5 c
(UNA GIORNATA SPECIALE; AKA: THE GREAT DAY)

Sophia Loren (Antonietta), Marcello Mastroianni (Gabriele), John Vernon (Emanuele), Francoise Berd (Caretaker), Nicole Magny (Figlia Del Cavaliere), Patrizia Basso (Romana), Tiziano De Persio (Arnaldo), Maurizio Di Paolantonio (Fabio), Antonio Garibaldi (Littorio), Vittorio Guerrieri (Umberto), Allessandra Mussolini (Maria Luisa).

Poor, depressing film starring Loren and Mastroianni as the only two residents left in their seedy apartment building on the day that Hitler has come to Italy to visit Mussolini. All the other citizens have run out to the streets to view the spectacle, including Loren's macho, fascistic husband, and her six children, leaving her alone. Across the courtyard lives outcast homosexual Mastroianni and, over the course of the day, the two lonely people draw close to each other, seeking the love and companionship that they have been denied. Mastroianni temporarily abandons his homosexuality and makes love to Loren. But soon the day is over and her brutish husband returns, invigorated with the image of "Il Duce"; he has his way with her, returning her to the prison of her existence.

p, Carlo Ponti; d, Ettore Scola; w, Ruggero Maccari, Scola, Maurizio

Costanzo; ph, Pasqualino De Santis (Technicolor); m, Armando Trovaioli; ed, Raimondo Crociani; prod d, Luciano Ricceri; art d, Luciano Ricceri; cos, Enrico Sabbatini.

Drama   (PR:C MPAA:NR)

SPECIAL DELIVERY**½ (1955, Ger.) 86m Trans-Rhein/COL bw
(VOM HIMMEL GEFALLEN)

Joseph Cotten (Johnathan Adams), Eva Bartok (Sonja), Joerg Becker (Baby Sam), Rene Deltgen (Kovak), Bruni Loebel (Lila), Niall MacGinnis (Sidney), Lexford Richards (Wayne), Don Hanmer (Sgt. Coppenbarger), Robert Cunningham (Capt. Heinikan), Gert Froebe (Olaf), Ursula Herking (Mme. Debrov), Little Sam.

A comedy starring Cotten as a U.S. diplomat stationed behind the Iron Curtain who is saddled with the responsibility of caring for a baby left in the embassy garden by one of the locals. The all-male staff of the embassy struggle mightily, and amusingly, with trying to tend to the baby, but eventually they are forced to hire a nurse, Bartok, whom Cotten soon takes a liking to. Trouble brews when the communist government wants the kid back and Cotten refuses to turn it over. A fairly funny cold war comedy.

p, Stuart Schulberg, Gilbert de Goldschmidt; d, John Brahm; w, Phil Reisman, Jr., Dwight Taylor (based on an idea by Geva Radvanyi); ph, Joseph Brun; m, Bernhard Kaun; ed, George Klotz; md, Kaun; art d, Alf Buetow.

Comedy   (PR:A MPAA:NR)

SPECIAL DELIVERY**½   (1976) 98m Bing Crosby/AIP c

Bo Svenson (Jack Murdock), Cybill Shepherd (Mary Jane), Tom Atkins (Zabelski), Sorrell Booke (Bank Manager Hubert Zane), Gerrit Graham (Swivot), Michael C. Gwynne (Carl Graff), Jeff Goldblum (Snake), Robert Ito (Mr. Chu), Lynnette Mettey (Marj), Richard Drout Miller (Artie), John Quade (Barney), Vic Tayback (Wyatt), Edward Winter (Lorenzo Pierce), Kim Richards (Juliette), Mel Scott (Anderson), Alex Colon (Lopez), Phillip R. Allen (Browne), Marla Adams (Mrs. Zane), Timothy Blake (Mother), Lawrie Driscoll (Policeman), Joe Di Reda (Torgan), Charles Lampkin (Mailman), Deirdre Hall (Gloria).

Svenson stars as the leader of a group of unemployed Vietnam vets who execute a daring bank robbery due to financial desperation. The robbery is a success, but the getaway is loused up, and Svenson is the only one who escapes. Desperate to get rid of the evidence, Svenson dumps the loot in a mailbox. Unfortunately for Svenson, artist Shepherd and crooked barkeep Gwynne see the robber's deposit. Gwynne tries to get the dough for himself to pay off mafia drug dealers Ito and Tayback. Shepherd, however, is drawn to Svenson and helps him get the money back. They succeed and run off together on an ocean cruise, but are shocked to discover the president of the bank on the same ship. A fine, if unspectacular, romantic comedy.

p, Richard Berg; d, Paul Wendkos; w, Don Gazzaniga, Gil Ralston (based on a story by Gazzaniga); ph, Harry Stradling, Jr. (DeLuxe Color); m, Lalo Schifrin; ed, Houseley Stevenson; art d, Jack Poplin; set d, Don Sullivan; cos, Bruce Walkup, Betsy Cox; spec eff, Howard Jensen; makeup, Mike Moschella; stunts, Carey Loftin.

Comedy/Crime   **Cas.**   (PR:C MPAA:PG)

SPECIAL EDITION**   (1938, Brit.) PAR bw

Lucille Lisle (Sheila Pearson), John Garrick (Frank Warde), Norman Pierce (Aiken), Johnny Schofield (Horatio Adams), Frederick Culley (Dr. Pearson), Vera Bogetti (Mrs. Howard), Mabel Twemlow (Mrs. Cavendish), Vincent Holman (Inspector Bourne), Dino Galvani (Toni Lang), Fewlass Llewellyn (Coroner).

An average suspenser about a photographer, Pierce, who kills in retaliation for his wife's death on the operating table. Pierce works with news reporter Garrick on the case without revealing his true identity. Clues point to surgeon Culley, though his daughter, Lisle, insists that he is dead. Pierce's charade is up by the finale, however, and Culley and his daughter escape danger.

p&d, Redd Davies; w, Katherine Strueby (based on a story by Derek Neame); ph, Roy Fogwell.

Crime   (PR:A MPAA:NR)

SPECIAL INSPECTOR*   (1939) 53m Warwick/SYN bw

Charles Quigley (Tom Evans), Rita Hayworth (Patricia Lane), George McKay (Silver), Edgar Edwards (Bill), John Spacey (David Foster), Eddie Laughton (Tim), Bob Rideout (Dapper), Grant MacDonald (Skip), Bill Irving (Pete), Vivian Coombs (Mother Jones), Fred Bass (Ralph Collins), Vincent McKenna (Henricks), Don Douglas (Williams).

A very-low-budget crime film starring Quigley as a T-man trying to stop a ring of fur smugglers who stop truckers, kill them, and then reroute the furs across the border. Hayworth plays the sister of one of the murdered truckers, and teams up with Quigley to smash the crooked scheme.

Considered a turkey by the studio, distributors, and exhibitors, SPECIAL INSPECTOR was originally released in England only, and eventually found its way to American screens on a double bill with another early Hayworth film OLD LOUISIANA (which was retitled LOUISIANA GAL) which were re-released at the height of her popularity and sold as two Hayworth blockbusters despite the fact that she played minor roles.

p, Kenneth J. Bishop; d, Leon Barsha; w, Edgar Edwards; ph, George Meehan; ed, William Austin; md, Morris Stoloff; art d, Lionel Banks.

Crime   **(PR:A   MPAA:NR)**

SPECIAL INVESTIGATOR½**   (1936) 61m RKO bw

Richard Dix (Bill Fenwick), Margaret Callahan (Virginia Selton), Erik Rhodes (Denny Gray), Owen Davis, Jr (George Fenwick), Ray Mayer (Dutchman), Harry Jans (Cy Adams), Joseph Sawyer (Plummer), J. Carroll Naish (Selton), Sheila Terry (Judy Taylor), J.M. Kerrigan (Judge Plumgate), Jed Prouty (Dr. Reynolds), Russell Hicks (Perkett), Ethan Laidlaw (Larring), Si Jenks (Hiram).

Dix plays a successful criminal attorney who has made a bundle keeping rotten members of the mob from being tossed in the cooler. Dix is forced to reconsider his questionable ethics when his brother, who was an FBI agent, is killed by the same criminals he has made a career of defending. The lawyer joins the Department of Justice and becomes a special agent out to get mobboss Naish and his goons. The climax is a massive shootout at the gangster's hideout during which everyone is killed except Naish's sister, Callahan, who decides to give up a flirtation with crime for a romance with Dix.

p, Cliff Reid; d, Louis King; w, Louis Stevens, Thomas Lennon, Ferdinand Reyher (based on the novel by Erle Stanley Gardner); ph, Edward Cronjager; ed, George Hively.

Crime   **(PR:A   MPAA:NR)**

SPECIALIST, THE*½   (1975) 93m Crown c

Adam West (Jerry), John Anderson (Pike), Ahna Capri (Londa), Alvy Moore (Bailiff), Marlene Schmidt (Elizabeth), Harvey Jason (Hardin), Russell Schmidt (Sharkey), Charles Knapp (Judge).

Lawyer West seduces the beautiful Capri, unaware that she is a hit woman trying to fulfill a contract out on him. West, who is best remembered as the pinnacle of moral crime fighters as television's "Batman," never again equaled the success of that mid-1960s hit as this low-level camp outing proves. Also making an appearance is fellow television veteran Moore, best remembered as Mr. Kimball in the much underrated absurdist sitcom "Green Acres." Schmidt, who plays West's wife, was the film's executive producer and wife of director Avedis.

p&d, Hikmet Avedis; w, Avedis, Marlene Schmidt, Ralph B. Potts (based on the novel Come Now the Lawyers by Potts); ph, Masoud Joseph (DeLuxe Color); m, Shorty Rogers; m/l, "The Specialist," Sammy Fain, Paul Francis Webster (sung by Lou Rawls).

Crime/Satire   **Cas.**   **(PR:O   MPAA:R)**

SPECKLED BAND, THE*   (1931, Brit.) 66m British and
                                                       Dominions/FD bw

Raymond Massey (Sherlock Holmes), Athole Stewart (Dr. John Watson), Lyn Harding (Dr. Grimesby Rylott), Angela Baddeley (Helen Stoner), Nancy Price (Mrs. Staunton), Marie Ault (Mrs. Hudson), Stanley Lathbury (Rodgers), Charles Paton (Builder), Joyce Moore (Violet).

Raymond Massey made his screen debut playing Sherlock Holmes in this offbeat entry in the Arthur Conan Doyle series of adaptations. Set in modern-day 1930, Massey's Holmes has his office outfitted with the latest computerized detective tools. Automated filing systems, stenographers, secretaries, intercoms, recording devices, beakers, flasks, bunsen burners, and chemicals crowd Massey's house. Enter Stewart as Dr. Watson who asks his friend to investigate the strange death of his friend Baddeley's sister Moore. Moore was found dead in the large, dark, and mysterious manor of Harding, the girls' stepfather, but no cause of death could be determined. Harding is immediately under suspicion, but he points to the nomadic gypsies, who were camped nearby, as being the most likely suspects. Baddeley, who has decided to marry, might be eliminated by Harding next because when she leaves her inheritance would go with her. Harding decides to have some construction done on the house, so Baddeley is forced to sleep in her dead sister's room. That night the gypsies return to camp near the manor, and Massey disguises himself as a workman in order to gain entry into the house. Harding releases a giant poisonous snake into the air vent connected to the room where Baddeley sleeps. Holmes spots the snake and forces it back down the shaft, and it kills Harding instead. The visual style of THE SPECKLED BAND, heavily influenced by the German expressionists, is made up of harsh angles, contrasts of dark and light (especially in the scenes at the manor), and strange sets. Massey brings a different reading to the role of Sherlock Holmes and transforms him into a more cynical, cerebral, and rueful character than had been seen previously. (See SHERLOCK HOLMES series, Index.)

p, Herbert Wilcox; d, Jack Raymond; w, W.P. Lipscomb (based on the story by Sir Arthur Conan Doyle); ph, F.A. Young; ed, P.M. Rogers.

Mystery   **(PR:A   MPAA:NR)**

SPECTER OF FREEDOM, THE   (SEE: PHANTOM OF LIBERTY,
                                                       1974, Fr.)

SPECTER OF THE ROSE*   (1946) 90m REP bw

Judith Anderson (La Belle Sylph), Michael Chekhov (Max Polikoff), Ivan Kirov (Andre Sanine), Viola Essen (Heidi), Lionel Stander (Lionel Gans), Charles "Red" Marshall (Specs McFarlan), George Shadnoff (Kropotkin), Billy Gray (Jack James), Juan Panalle (Jibby), Lou Hearn (Mr. Lyons), Ferike Boros (Mamochka), Constantine (Alexis), Ferdinand Pollina (Giovanni), Polly Rose (Olga), Jim Moran (Jimmy), Frieda Filer, Miriam Schiller, Miriam Golden, Grace Mann, Allan Cooke, Alice Cavers, Nina Haven, John Stanley, Arleen Claire, Celene Radding (Dancers).

Over-the-hill ballerina Anderson is the doyenne of a dance troupe in this backstage suspense film filled with famed cinema scribe Hecht's acerbic barbs and ripostes. Chekhov is the company's somewhat effeminate impresario whose tendency to petulance is fostered by the strange doings on and off the stage. Kirov—a talented dancer, making his screen debut—is somewhat deranged; the ballet "Spectre de la Rose" invokes strange images in his mind: "The rose has a thorn," he whispers to himself, wielding a wicked-looking knife. Kirov has already "thorned" a former wife, prior to the picture's opening. Young dancer Essen, believing Kirov to be cured of his affliction, falls in love with the dancer and marries him. Stander, a balletomanic hanger-on, is a rough-hewn would-be poet, whose quips and aphorisms reflect the screenwriter's reflections. During a performance, Kirov's hallucinations recur and he is only barely prevented from killing his ballet-partner bride. Loyal to the last, she takes him to a hotel room, hoping to nurse him free of his strange affliction. After several days of constant nurturing care, the exhausted Essen falls asleep. The music sounds in Kirov's mind; he rises and begins his fateful solo, hovering near Essen with his blade. At the very last moment, he makes a virtuoso ballet leap, crashing through the window of the small room to be dasahed to his death on the pavement far below. One of high-paid scripter Hecht's several ventures into Orson Welles-like total control over product, THE SPECTER OF THE ROSE, like the others, was the result of Hecht's disaffection with his treatment by major studios. In his autobiography, A Child of the Century, the writer vented his spleen against producers: "$e3a movie is never any better than the stupidest man connected with it. There are times when this distinction may be given to the writer or director. Most often it belongs to the producer." With a free hand, except for financial restraints–the film's cost, reportedly, was a mere $160,000–Hecht wrote, directed, and produced an entertaining mixed bag here part drama, part comedy, part suspense film, with an unusual background. Republic, a studio more accustomed to westerns, picked up the product for release, probably on the strength of the writer's reputation. Campily entertaining, and with some surprises, the picture received mixed reviews, some critics finding it pretentious and arty. Author Saul Bellow said he would rather eat ground glass than sit through it a second time, but many other people enjoyed its arch humor and its cinematic inventiveness.

p,d&w, Ben Hecht (based in part on the ballet Spectre de la Rose); ph, Lee Garmes; m, George Antheil; ed, Harry Keller; md, Morton Scott; ch, Tamara Geva.

Suspense/Comedy   **(PR:C   MPAA:NR)**

SPECTRE OF EDGAR ALLAN POE, THE*½

                                                       (1974) 87m Cintel/Cinerama c

Robert Walker, Jr (Edgar Allan Poe), Cesar Romero (Dr. Grimaldi), Tom Drake (Dr. Forrest), Carol Ohmart (Lisa Grimaldi), Mary Grover (Lenore), Mario Milano (Joseph, Dr. Grimaldi's Assistant), Karen Hartford (Night Nurse), Dennis Fimple (Farron), Lisa's Brother, Paul Bryar (White, Poe's Publisher), Frank Packard (Jonah), Marsha Mae Jones (Sarah).

A lame, low-budget horror outing which purportedly details Edgar Allan Poe's traumatic romance with his great love, Lenore. Grover plays Lenore, who, after almost being buried alive, goes insane and must be put in a mental institution run by the mysterious Romero. Poe, played by Walker, has misgivings about leaving his love in the institution after a series of bloody killings. Walker discovers a basement torture chamber complete with a snake pit and other charming devices. It is revealed that Romero's wife, Ohmart, is homicidally insane and it is she who is hacking up inmates and visitors alike. In the end, Walker, too, goes insane.

p&d, Mohy Quandour; w, Quandour, Kenneth Hartford; ph, Robert Birchall (Eastmancolor); m, Allen D. Allen; ed, Abbas Amin; art d, Michael Milgrom; m/l, love theme (sung by Tom Bahlor).

Horror/Mystery   **Cas.**   **(PR:O   MPAA:PG)**

SPECTOR OF FREEDOM　　(SEE: PHANTOM LIBERTY, THE, 1974, Fr.)

SPEED**　　　　　　　　　　　　　(1936) 65m MGM bw

James Stewart (Terry Martin), Wendy Barrie (Jane Mitchell), Ted Healy (Gadget), Una Merkel (Josephine Sanderson), Weldon Heyburn (Frank Lawson), Patricia Wilder (Fanny Lane), Ralph Morgan (Mr. Dean), Robert Livingston (George Saunders), Charles Trowbridge, William Tannen (Doctors), Walter Kingsford (Uncle), Claudelle Kaye (Nurse), George Chandler (Rustic Bystander), Jack Clifford (Master of Ceremonies), Don Brodie (Track Official).

Stewart stars as a test driver for a large auto plant who is determined to perfect a new high-speed carburetor he and his crew have invented in time for the big race at the Indianapolis Speedway. While trying to work out the bugs in his new system, Stewart is encouraged by the daughter of the owner, Barrie, to allow her engineer friend, Heyburn, to have a look. Heyburn helps out, but soon tension develops between the two men who both have amorous eyes for Barrie. The day comes to test the new carburetor, but the experiment nearly ends in disaster when the car crashes, injuring driver Healy and nearly asphyxiating Stewart with carbon monoxide fumes. Heyburn saves the pair and they take the carburetor back to the drawing board. The pair finally perfect the invention which wins Stewart plaudits and Barrie. Despite a strong performance from Stewart, SPEED fails to live up to the promise of its title. The film is badly paced, relies heavily on stock footage of auto races, and practically stops dead in its tracks for a lengthy guided tour of the automobile assembly line. This makes the film heavy going at times, but the footage shot through the windshield of the test car at high speeds is quite effective.

p, Lucien Hubbard; d, Edwin L. Marin; w, Michael Fessier (based on a story by Milton Krims, Larry Bachman); ph, Lester White; ed, Harry Poppe.

Drama　　　　　　　　　　　　　**(PR:A　MPAA:NR)**

SPEED BRENT WINS　　(SEE: BREED OF THE BORDER, 1933)

SPEED CRAZY zero　　　　　　　　　(1959) 75m Viscount/AA bw

Brent Halsey (Nick), Yvonne Lime (Peggy), Charles Willcox (Hap), Slick Slavin (Smiley), Jacquelle Ravell (Gina), Keith Byron (Jim Brand), Charlotte Fletcher (Dee), Jackie Joseph (Laura), Vic Marlo (Charlie Dale), Robert Swan (Tommy), Mark Sheeler (Tolliver), Troy Patterson (Leather Jacket No. 1), Lucita (Ella), Eddie Durkin (Leather Jacket No. 2), Baynes Barron (Ace), Regina Gleason (Linda).

Wandering murderer and hot-rodder Halsey gets a job as a mechanic in a small town and soon alienates the whole racetrack scene by winning races and making passes at other guys' girls. The cops, meanwhile, have traced the tire tracks left at the sight of a murder and are hot on his trail. Halsey decides to kill again and goes after his boss Willcox, but the cops show up in the nick of time and the evildoer is killed in a wreck. Really awful.

p, Richard Bernstein; d, William Hole, Jr.; w, Bernstein, George Waters; ph, Ernest Haller; m, Dick LaSalle; ed, Irving Berlin; m/l, Slick Slavin (sung by Slavin).

Crime　　　　　　　　　　　　　**(PR:C　MPAA:NR)**

SPEED DEVILS*　　　　　　　　　　(1935) 61m Huffman/SYN bw

Paul Kelly, Marguerite Churchill, Russell Hardie, Leo Curley, Walter Fenner, Earl Mitchell.

Kelly plays an auto racer who quits the business when he and his friend Hardie crash and nearly get killed. The two open an auto shop together, but trouble stirs when local crooked politicos want them to be the city's garage. The mechanics know that there will be problems if they accept, so they decline the offer. This angers the power-brokers, so they arrange for Kelly and his sweetheart Churchill to be trapped in a burning house. Luckily, Kelly's partner arrives and rescues them. The crooks are brought to justice, the boys get the city contract with no strings attached, and Kelly and Churchill are married.

d, Ralph Henabery.

Drama　　　　　　　　　　　　　**(PR:A　MPAA:NR)**

SPEED LIMIT 65　　　　　　　(SEE: LIMIT, THE, 1972)

SPEED LIMITED zero　　　　　　　　(1940) 52m Regent bw

Ralph Graves (Jerry Paley), Evelyn Brent (Natalie), Claudia Dell (Marjorie), Andy Rice, Jr (Smitty), Walter Worden (G-Man), Vance Carroll (Tommy), Fred "Snow Flake" Toomes (Porter), Gordon Griffith (G-Man).

A dreary picture about a brave FBI agent hot on the trail of some kidnapers while romancing a dim-witted, flaky, divorced socialite. The story is bad enough but the film shows no sign of having been made by anyone with an inkling of technical knowledge.

p, George P. Reagan, Jr.; d, Al Herman; w, Ralph Graves; ph, William Hyer;

---

ed, Dan Milnere.

Crime　　　　　　　　　　　　　**(PR:A　MPAA:NR)**

SPEED LOVERS zero　　　(1968) 102m Associates and Wilmac/Jemco c

Fred Lorenzen (Himself), William McGaha, Peggy O'Hara, David Marcus, Carol Street, Glenda Brunson.

Real-life stock car racer Lorenzen inspires the son of a mechanic to become a professional stock car racer. Shot in Atlanta and features auto-racing footage from tracks all over the country. This is more a public relations film for the stock-car racing industry than a human drama meant to enlighten and entertain.

p&d, William McGaha; w, Elaine Wilkerson, McGaha, Fred Tuch; ph, Joe Shelton (Eastmancolor); m, Carleton Palmer; ed, John Fitzstephens, David Moscovitz, William Freda; prod d, Tuch; m/l, title song (sung by Billy Lee Riley).

Sports Drama　　　　　　　　　　**(PR:A　MPAA:NR)**

SPEED MADNESS*½　　　　　　　　(1932) 63m CAP bw

Richard Talmadge, Lucien Littlefield, Charles Sellon, Nancy Drexel, Pat O'Malley, Huntley Gordon, Matthew Betz, Wade Boteler, Donald Keith.

Talmadge plays the son of a shipping magnate who decides to do something constructive with his life after his best gal walks out on him. The kid sets about designing a boat that will pull his father's shipyard out of the financial abyss. On the day of the big race, evil gamblers sabotage the boat and it explodes during the competition, but Talmadge learns who the culprits are and vindicates his right to the big contract.

p, Richard Talmadge; d, George Crone; w, Charles R. Condon.

Drama　　　　　　　　　　　　　**(PR:A　MPAA:NR)**

SPEED REPORTER, THE 1931　　(SEE: SCAREHEADS, 1931)

SPEED REPORTER zero　　　　　　　(1936) 58m Reliable bw

Richard Talmadge (Dick Lawrence), Luana Walters (May), Richard Cramer (Brad Franklin), Bob Walker (Stanley), Frank Crane (Roger Renfrew), Earle Dwire (John Parker), John Ince (Madison), George Chesebro (Blackie Smith), Edward Cassidy (Edwards).

Another in the seemingly endless series of bad pictures devoted to the newspaper business. Talmadge stars as an energetic reporter out to smash a bogus reform league. Badly written, directed, photographed, and performed.

p&d, Bernard B. Ray; w, Rose Gordon (based on a story by Henri Samuels); ph, William Hyer; ed, Carl Himm.

Crime　　　　　　　　　　　　　**(PR:A　MPAA:NR)**

SPEED TO BURN**　　　　　　　　(1938) 60m FOX bw

Michael Whalen (Matt Kerry), Lynn Bari (Marion Clark), Marvin Stephens (Tim Turner), Henry Armetta (Papa Gambini), Chick Chandler (Sport Fields), Sidney Blackmer (Hastings), Johnnie Pirrone (Tony Gambini), Charles D. Brown (Pop Williams), Inez Palange (Mrs. Gambini).

Ambitious race track waif Stephens raises a pony for a horse trainer, and it looks like a winner, but the boy is shocked when the horse is sold to the local police department. Whalen plays the friendly policeman drafted by Stephens to find out why his horse was not allowed to compete. Eventually it is revealed that Stephen's horse was deemed too fast by crooked gamblers and, therefore, taken out of competition so as not to screw up the carefully planned odds. Whalen and Stephens get the horse back and enter it in a race with all of Whalen's fellow cops betting heavily on the horse. It wins of course.

p, Jerry Hoffman; d, Otto Brower; w, Robert Ellis, Helen Logan (based on a story by Edwin Dial Torgerson); ph, Edward Snyder; ed, Fred Allen; md, Samuel Kaylin; art d, Bernard Herzbrun, Chester Gore.

Drama　　　　　　　　　　　　　**(PR:A　MPAA:NR)**

SPEED TO SPARE*　　　　　　　　(1937) 60m COL bw

Charles Quigley (Tommy Morton), Dorothy Wilson (Eileen Hart), Eddie Nugent (Skids Brannigan), Patricia Farr (Peaches O'Brien), Gene Morgan (Breakaway Wilson), John Gallaudet (Dan Kelly), Gordon William ["Wild Bill"] Elliott (Steve Fellows), Jack Gardner (Ralph Bennett).

A tale of two brothers, Quigley and Nugent, separated at birth, who grow up to become professional auto racers and are unaware of each other until fate throws them together. Quigley is the good brother who has always followed the straight and narrow and is engaged to Wilson. When not-as-good sibling Nugent comes into the picture, Quigley sets out to show his brother the advantages of a clean life style and decent morals. Nugent does not pay much attention, however, because his libido is riveted to his brother's fiancee. Eventually Nugent wises up when he kills a buddy and almost destroys his brother during a big race.

d, Lambert Hillyer; w, Bert Granet, Hillyer; ph, Benjamin Kline; ed, Viola Lawrence.

Drama   (PR:A   MPAA:NR)

SPEED TO SPARE*½   (1948) 57m PAR bw

Richard Arlen (*Cliff Jordan*), Jean Rogers (*Mary*), Richard Traveis (*Jerry*), Pat Phelan (*Pete Simmons*), Nanette Parks (*Jane Chandler*), Roscue Karns (*Kangaroo*), Ian McDonald (*Pusher*), Paul Harvey (*Al Simmons*).

Arlen plays a race-car driver who has had one brush with death too many, so he retires and gets into the trucking business with a buddy. While the film emphasizes the noble safety record of the much maligned truckers, Arlen does not hesitate to zoom off after some crooks for a series of dangerous and thrilling chase scenes.

p, William Pine, William Thomas; d, William Berke; w, Milton Raison; ph, Ellis W. Carter; ed, Monty Pearce; art d, Lewis H. Creber.

Drama   (PR:A   MPAA:NR)

SPEED WINGS**   (1934) 60m COL bw

Tim McCoy (*Tim*), Evalyn Knapp (*Mary*), Billy [William] Bakewell (*Jerry*), Vincent Sherman (*Mickey*), Hooper Atchley (*Crandall*), Ben Hewlett (*Gregory*), Jack Long (*Haley*).

An offbeat McCoy western which sees most of the action taking place in airplanes. McCoy tries to foil a kidnaping with some lively aerial stunts, including a chase between a plane and a train.

d, Otto Brower; w, Horace McCoy; ph, Al Siegler; ed, Jack Rawlins.

Western   (PR:A   MPAA:NR)

SPEEDTRAP**   (1978) 113m First Artists-Intertamar c

Joe Don Baker (*Pete*), Tyne Daly (*Nifty*), Richard Jaeckel (*Billy*), Robert Loggia (*Spillano*), Morgan Woodward (*Capt. Hogan*), Lana Wood (*New Blosom*), Timothy Carey (*Loomis*), James Griffith (*Wino*).

When an automobile thief consistently outwits the police, private eye Baker is called in to help solve the case. He's teamed with lady cop Daly (who would later play "Lacey" on the highly acclaimed television cop show "Cagney and Lacey") and together they stop the thefts. Despite good performances from the cast, one can't deny that this is merely a poorly scripted action film with the usual plethora of car chases.

p, Howard Pine, Fred Mintz; d, Earl Bellamy; w, Stuart A. Segal, Walter M. Spear (based on the story by Mintz, Henry C. Parke); ph, Dennis Dalzell; ed, Michael Vejar.

Crime/Action   **Cas.**   (PR:A   MPAA:PG)

SPEEDWAY**   (1968) 92m MGM c

Elvis Presley (*Steve Grayson*), Nancy Sinatra (*Susan Jacks*), Bill Bixby (*Kenny Donford*), Gale Gordon (*R.W. Hepworth*), William Schallert (*Abel Esterlake*), Victoria Meyerink (*Ellie Esterlake*), Ross Hagen (*Paul Dado*), Carl Ballantine (*Birdie Kebner*), Poncie Ponce (*Juan Medala*), Harry Hickox (*The Cook*), Christopher West (*Billie Jo*), Beverly Hills (*Mary Ann*), Harper Carter (*Ted Simmons*), Bob Harris (*Lloyd Meadows*), Michele Newman (*Debbie Esterlake*), Courtney Brown (*Carrie Esterlake*), Dana Brown (*Billie Esterlake*), Patti Jean Keith (*Annie Esterlake*), Carl Reindel (*Mike*), Gari Hardy (*Dumb Blonde*), Charlotte Considine (*Lori*), Sandy Reed (*Race Announcer*), Ward Ramsey, Robert James, Garry LittleJohn, Ralph Adano, Tom McCauley (*Dado's Crew*).

Elvis Presley's 27th film outing sees him once again playing a successful race-car driver. He is an honorable chap who gives most of his money to charity, while still managing to live an opulent, swinging life style. Unfortunately, Elvis' business manager, Bixby, has mismanaged the racer's funds (seems he lost a lot betting on horse races) and Elvis is flat broke. If that is not enough, Bixby also bungled Elvis' taxes which sends IRS agent Sinatra to their door. Luckily Elvis and Sinatra fall in love and she helps him raise the necessary money to bail himself out. Songs include: "Your Groovy Self" (Lee Hazelwood, sung by Sinatra), "Speedway," "He's Your Uncle, Not Your Dad," "Who Are You? (Who Am I?)," "Let Yourself Go," "Your Time Hasn't Come Yet, Baby," "There Ain't Nothing Like a Song," "Five Sleepy Heads," "Western Union," "Mine," "Goin' Home," and "Suppose" (Mel Glazer, Stephen Schlaks, sung by Presley).

p, Douglas Laurence; d, Norman Taurog; w, Phillip Shuken; ph, Joseph Ruttenberg (Panavision, Metrocolor); m, Jeff Alexander; ed, Richard Farrell; art d, George W. Davis, Leroy Coleman; set d, Henry Grace, Don Greenwood, Jr.; spec eff, Carroll L. Shepphird; makeup, William Tuttle

Musical   **Cas.**   (PR:A   MPAA:G)

SPELL OF AMY NUGENT, THE**   (1945, Brit.) 75m Pyramid Amalgamated/PRC bw (GB: SPELLBOUND; AKA: PASSING CLOUDS)

Derek Farr (*Laurie Baxter*), Vera Lindsay (*Diana Hilton*), Frederick Leister (*Mr. Vincent*), Hay Petrie (*Mr. Cathcart*), Felix Aylmer (*Mr. Morton*), Marion Spencer (*Mrs. Stapleton*), Diana King (*Amy Nugent*), W.G. Fay (*Johnnie*), Winifred Davis (*Mrs. Baxter*), Enid Hewit (*Lady Laura Bethel*), Gibb McLaughlin (*Gibb*), Cameron Hall (*Mr. Nugent*), Irene Handl (*Mrs. Nugent*), Hannen Swaffer, Joyce Redman, Stafford Hilliard.

A limp attack on spiritualists starring Farr as a young college student obsessed with the memory of his dead girl friend. Desperate to contact her in the great beyond, Farr dabbles in the occult and manages to conjure his girl up during a seance. This little bite of the supernatural gives Farr a nervous breakdown. He is nursed back to health by Lindsay, who has been waiting in the wings for her chance at romance with Farr since childhood. Eventually her love conquers his obsession with the dead. Perhaps the most interesting aspect of SPELL is that the censors banned the film because they feared it would offend spiritualists (obviously a special interest group much more powerful back in 1941 than today). Luckily (depending on how you look at it), noted spiritualist Hannen Swaffer approved the film and agreed to appear in a prolog saying so.

p, R. Murray-Leslie; d, John Harlow; w, Miles Malleson (based on the novel The *Necromancers* by Hugh Benson); ph, Walter Harvey, Guy Green; ed, F.C. Wilson.

Drama   (PR:A   MPAA:NR)

SPELL OF THE HYPNOTIST*   (1956) Exploitation bw (AKA: FRIGHT)

Nancy Malone (*Ann Summers*), Eric Fleming (*Dr. Hamilton*), Frank Marth (*Morley*), Humphrey Davis (*Prof. Gore*), Dean L. Almquist (*Cullen*), Elizabeth Watts (*Lady Olive*), Amelia Conley (*Miss Ames*), Walter Klaven (*Warden*), Ned Glass (*Taxi Driver*), Norman Burton (*Reporter*), Tom Reynolds (*City Editor*), Robert Gardett (*Managing Editor*), Norman MacKaye (*City Editor*), Don Douglas (*Inspectors*), Philip Kenneally (*Policeman*), Sid Raymond (*Van Driver*), Chris Bohn (*TV Announcer*), Alney Alba (*Lady in Restaurant*).

Bizarre exploitation drama starring Malone as a young woman with delusions that she was the lover of Austria's Crown Prince Rudolph who died with him in a suicide pact in 1889. Her psychiatrist, Fleming, falls in love with his patient, but she withdraws when a trance takes over. Eventually Malone is brought back when criminal psychopath Marth is persuaded to impersonate the long-dead crown prince. Fleming played Gil Favor on TV's popular "Rawhide."

p&d, W. Lee Wilder; w, Myles Wilder.

Drama   (PR:A   MPAA:NR)

SPELLBINDER, THE*½   (1939) 69m RKO bw

Lee Tracy (*Jed Marlowe*), Barbara Read (*Janet Marlowe*), Patric Knowles (*Tom Dixon*), Allan Lane (*Steve Kendall, Reporter*), Linda Hayes (*Miss Simpson*), Morgan Conway (*Carrington*), Robert Emmett Keane (*Judge Butler*), Roy Gordon (*3rd Judge*), Robert Strange (*1st Judge*), Elliott Sullivan (*Ice Box Swinnerty*), Leonid Kinskey (*Harry Beldon, Horn Player*), Byron Foulger (*Henkins*), Emory Parnell (*Doorman*), Ed Gargan (*Taxi Driver*), Chester Clute (*Dr. H. Schunk*), Robert E. Homans (*Court Bailiff*), Paul E. Burns (*Hotel Clerk*).

One of the last lawyer movies of the 1930s, THE SPELLBINDER, stars Tracy as a unscrupulous attorney who takes a perverse pride in freeing guilty men until his daughter, Read, decides to marry one of his clients, Knowles. Doing a quick ethical turnaround, Tracy tries to persuade Knowles that he is not worthy of his daughter's hand. But Knowles refuses to disappear which forces the distraught Tracy to kill him. Soon Tracy is facing murder charges and offers no defense, and his daughter bursts in and announces that she and Knowles were secretly married. Tracy gets a brief prison sentence.

p, Cliff Reid; d, Jack Hively; w, Thomas Lennon, Joseph A. Fields (based on a story by Joseph Anthony); ph, Russell Metty; ed, Theron Warth.

Crime   (PR:A   MPAA:NR)

SPELLBOUND   (SEE: SPELL OF AMY NUGENT, THE, 1941, Brit.)

SPELLBOUND****   (1945) 111m SELZ-Vanguard/UA bw

Ingrid Bergman (*Dr. Constance Peterson*), Gregory Peck (*John "J.B." Ballantine*), Jean Acker (*Matron*), Donald Curtis (*Harry*), Rhonda Fleming (*Mary Carmichael*), John Emery (*Dr. Fleurot*), Leo G. Carroll (*Dr. Murchison*), Norman Lloyd (*Garmes*), Steven Geray (*Dr. Graff*), Paul Harvey (*Dr. Hanish*), Erskine Sanford (*Dr. Galt*), Janet Scott (*Norma*), Victor Kilian (*Sheriff*), Wallace Ford (*Stranger in Hotel Lobby*), Bill Goodwin (*House Detective*), Dave Willock (*Bellboy*), George Meader (*Railroad Clerk*), Matt Moore (*Policeman at Railroad Station*), Irving Bacon (*Gateman*), Art Baker (*Lt. Cooley*), Regis Toomey (*Sgt. Gillespie*), Michael Chekhov (*Dr. Alex Brulov*), Clarence Straight (*Secretary at Police Station*), Joel Davis (*J.B. as a Boy)*, Teddy Infuhr *(J.B.'s Brother)*, Addison Richards *(Police Captain)*, Richard Bartell *(Ticket Taker)*, Edward Fielding *(Dr. Edwardes)*, Harry Brown *(Gateman)*, Alfred Hitchcock *(Man Carrying Violin)*.

An intriguing Hitchcock thriller which probes the dark recesses of the mind through psychoanalytic treatment and the love of a woman. Peck, a young psychiatrist, begins a new assignment at a modern mental asylum as the center's new director. His behavior, however, is rather strange and eccentric. During a meal with the rest of the staff, Peck stares at the white tablecloth and the impressions left on it by a fork, becoming inexplicably anxious and disturbed. Bergman, a highly intelligent and emotionally icy doctor, grows suspicious of Peck. When she discovers that his real initials are J.B., she doubts that he is really the doctor– Dr. Edwardes–that the center had expected. She wonders not only what happened to Edwardes, but who Peck really is, thinking Peck is suffering from amnesia, or possibly an escaped patient who murdered Edwardes and then assumed his identity to cover up the crime. Bergman finds that her desires as a woman are stronger than those as a doctor, falling deeply in love with Peck, determined to help him remember his past and the meaning of the letters "J.B." Learning that his real name is John Ballantine and not Edwardes, Bergman fears for Peck's safety, urging him to leave the asylum with her and take refuge in the upstate home of her mentor and friend, Chekhov, a leader in psychoanalysis. Although Chekhov warns Bergman that she may be dealing with a deranged murderer, she is convinced that he is innocent and desperately in need of help. Her confidence, however, seems premature as Peck, himself, is unsure of his own innocence, at one point even standing over Bergman with a frightening grip on a knife. By now Peck realizes that he has fallen in love with Bergman and the two lovers fight Peck's memory block in order to discover what he is subconsciously trying to forget. During a ski outing, Peck's memory is jarred by the sloping white snow drifts and the impressed lines of the skis (the visual counterpart to the tablecloth and fork lines that earlier disturbed him). He recalls that he went skiing with Edwardes and the doctor disappeared over a cliff. Peck thinks he was to blame, but remembers that someone standing behind him with a gun shot Edwardes. This, however, is connected to a childhood memory of Peck's when he playfully slid down a cement porch into his brother, thereby causing him to fall and be impaled on a spiked iron fence. By interpreting a heavily symbolic dream of Peck's, Chekhov and Bergman are able to piece together enough clues to find out who really killed Edwardes. Bergman then returns to the asylum and accuses Carroll, a power-hungry doctor who admits to killing Edwardes in order to secure his own position at the center. Rather than let Bergman live to tell her story, Carroll pulls a gun from his drawer and aims it at her. She bravely calls his bluff and walks out of his office, as Carroll turns the gun on himself. Bergman, having cleared Peck of the murder, is now free to let herself love him. Based on a bizarre novel about a psychopath who assumes charge of an insane asylum (a plot line explored in the classic silent THE CABINET OF DR. CALIGARI), SPELLBOUND was an idea generated by Selznick, who purchased the rights because of his keen interest in psychoanalysis, which he was undergoing at the time. After selling Hitchcock on the story, MacPhail–who had just finished working with Hitchcock on one of the director's two propaganda shorts for the British Mininstry of Information, BON VOYAGE–was picked by Hitchcock to help him write the script. An early idea was to shoot the film in both black and white and color, depending on whether the scenes were about the sane or the insane. They even had the insane director of the asylum as "a high-priest of black masses, who had the cross of Christ tattooed on the soles of his feet so that he could tread it underfoot with every step." Not surprisingly, this idea never left the planning stages and Hitchcock brought in screenwriter Hecht, an advocate of psychoanalysis, to replace MacPhail. While the film often gets bogged down in psychiatric and psychoanalytic jargon, it is counterbalanced by the love story that develops between Peck and Bergman. Depending on preference, the breakthrough to Peck's guilt complex can be seen in one of two ways–the success of modern psychiatry or the power that love has to break through such walls. When Bergman was originally contacted for the role, she was hesitant, citing that "she didn't believe the love story." The story was strengthened, making SPELLBOUND more of a, as Hitchcock desribes it, "manhunt story wrapped up in pseudo-psychoanalysis" than a case study of a disturbed man. The psychoanalysis, although it appears to be the central idea that the plot revolves around, is actually more of a device, or McGuffin, for Hitchcock to use to tell a love story. Hitchcock's interest is with the Bergman eroticism that lies beneath her icy, professional exterior ready to burst out (a fact attested to in Hitchcock's next film, NOTORIOUS, in which Bergman is a caged tiger liberated of any inhibitions). SPELLBOUND is a film about a man whose problems are overcome by love, an idea which, to a Hollywood audience, is somehow less plausible than being cured by pyschoanalysis. Although heavy on dialog, SPELLBOUND is not without some brilliant visual touches. Most memorable is the first kiss between Peck and Bergman, over which is superimposed a number of opening doors–doors to Peck's past which are opened, not through a session on the couch, but through the warmth and love of Bergman's lips. Hitchcock's love of technical tricks and problems is again made clear in Bergman's confrontation with Carroll. As Bergman walks slowly to exit his office, the audience is treated to Carroll's point of view. In the foreground are his hand and his gun (as if we ourselves are holding it), pointed at Bergman and following her as she heads for the door. When she leaves and Carroll turns the gun on himself, we see the gun, still looming large in the foreground, make a 180 degree turn, pointing directly into the camera (and at the viewer). The finger pulls the trigger, the barrel spins into position, a shot is heard, and the screen goes black. (Some original prints had a split second of red inserted, which reportedly achieved its goal of disturbing the audience whose senses were assaulted with the simulated blood burst after becoming accustomed to the black and white.) In order to get both the gun and Bergman in focus without sacrificing clarity, Hitchcock had a model of a gun and hand built, which was four times larger than life. To retain some of the twisted tone of the original story, Hitchcock insisted to Selznick that a dream sequence be included. Hitchcock had in mind the famed avant-garde artist Salvador Dali, whose previous foray into film was as codirector, with Luis Bunuel, of two brilliant surrealist films, UN CHIEN ANDALOU (1928) and L'AGE D'OR (1930). Although it has since been revealed by Bunuel biographers (and Bunuel himself in his autobiography *My Last Sigh*) that Dali had almost no input in the actual filming of the two pictures, thereby erasing his alleged talent as a filmmaker, Dali was, at the time of SPELLBOUND, seen as an *artiste*. According to Hitchcock: "Selznick thought I wanted Dali only for publicity purposes. That wasn't true. I felt that if I was going to have dream sequences, they should be vivid. I didn't think we should resort to the old-fashioned blurry effect they got by putting vaseline on a lens. What I really wanted to do, and they wouldn't do it because of expense, was to have the dream sequences shot on the back lot in the bright sunshine....But I used Dali for his draftmanship. I wanted to convey the dreams with great visual sharpness and clarity, sharper than the film itself." The dream sequence, in its original conception, was far longer and more complex than the two-minute sequence that finally appeared. It was to have run 22 minutes (much of which was actually shot but edited out) and included a disturbing sequence described by Hitchcock: "he 'Dali' wanted a statue to crack like a shell falling apart, with ants crawling all over it, and underneath, there would be Ingrid Bergman, covered by the ants! It just wasn't possible." According to Bergman, the dream sequence "was really something to put in a museum. The final film did not include this complicated footage, in which I became a plaster statue in the man's dream (which meant we shot the film backward, with me breaking out of it 'note: minus the ants')....It was such a pity. It could have been really sensational." Hitchcock, however, did not shoot the dream sequence, returning instead to London. The brilliant visual stylist Josef von Sternberg was first considered, but William Cameron Menzies (director of the visually breathtaking science-fiction film THINGS TO COME, 1936) was finally chosen, with special effects cinematographer Rex Wimpy behind the camera. Displeased with his assignment and his results, Menzies asked that his name be removed from the credits. The film became a sensational box office success, bringing in nearly $8 million on a $1.7 million investment ($150,000 of which Hitchcock received), prompting Selznick to begin work on a new project, NOTORIOUS, which reunited Hitchcock with Bergman and Hecht. SPELLBOUND was nominated as Best Picture, Chekhov was nominated for Best Supporting Actor, Hitchcock for Best Director, Barnes for Best Cinematography, Jack Cosgrove for Best Special Effects, and Rozsa for Best Score, the only category which the film won.

p, David O. Selznick; d, Alfred Hitchcock; w, Ben Hecht, Angus MacPhail (based on the novel *The House of Dr. Edwardes* by Francis Beeding 'Hilary St. George Saunders, John Palmer'); ph, George Barnes, (uncredited) Rex Wimpy; m, Miklos Rozsa; ed, William Ziegler, Hal C. Kern; prod d, James Basevi; art d, John Ewing; cos, Howard Greer; spec eff, Jack Cosgrove; dream sequence, Salvador Dali, (uncredited) William Cameron Menzies.

Suspense/Drama **Cas.** **(PR:A-C MPAA:NR)**

SPENCER'S MOUNTAIN*** (1963) 121m WB c

Henry Fonda *(Clay Spencer)*, Maureen O'Hara *(Olivia Spencer)*, James MacArthur *(Clayboy Spencer)*, Donald Crisp *(Grandpa Spencer)*, Wally Cox *(Preacher Goodman)*, Mimsy Farmer *(Claris Coleman)*, Virginia Gregg *(Miss Parker)*, Lillian Bronson *(Grandma Spencer)*, Whit Bissell *(Dr. Campbell)*, Hayden Rorke *(Col. Coleman)*, Kathy Bennett *(Minnie-Cora Cook)*, Dub Taylor *(Percy Cook)*, Hope Summers *(Mother Ida)*, Ken Mayer *(Mr. John)*, Bronwyn Fitzsimmons *(College Secretary)*, Barbara McNair *(Graduation Singer)*, Larry Mann, Buzz Henry, Jim O'Hara, Victor French, Michael Greene, Med Flory, Ray Savage, Mike Henry *(Spencer Brothers)*, Gary Young *(Mat Spencer)*, Michael Young *(Mark Spencer)*, Veronica Cartwright *(Becky Spencer)*, Ricky Young *(Luke Spencer)*, Susan Young *(Shirley Spencer)*, Rocky Young *(John Spencer)*, Kym Karath *(Pattie-Cake Spencer)*, Michelle Daves *(Donnie Spencer)*, William Breen *(Mountain Man)*.

Earl Hamner, Jr., wrote a novel set in the Blue Ridge Mountains and the producers thought that the Grand Tetons might be more photogenic so they set the picture in Wyoming, rather than Virginia. Hamner eventually got his wish when his TV series "The Waltons" hewed more closely to what he knew about. The movie was successful, although Fonda purportedly hated every minute of it. Fonda is one of nine children of Crisp, a man who claimed a mountain and left it to his heirs. The only one left in the area is Fonda, who has nine children of his own by O'Hara (who doesn't have a hair out of place and looks scrumptious, albeit wrong to convince us she's borne that many kids) and who works a quarry nearby. Fonda is a larger-than-life type who drinks, gambles, and has a great passion for O'Hara's flesh, as witnessed by their brood. He is God-fearing but hates organized religion and makes no secret of his contempt for it. He feels that too many restrictions are placed upon man on earth by the church and he's against any group that would limit drinking, smoking, gambling, dancing, swearing, and healthy lust. Also living in the house are his parents, Crisp and Bronson, with whom he has an honest relationship. Fonda's dream is to build a good house for the family, something large enough so they aren't always stepping on each other. They save every penny they can for that goal. Fonda hates the church but likes the new minister, Cox, and gets him drunk on the first day Cox arrives in the small town. The oldest son, MacArthur, is a bright young lad about to graduate from high school, a feat heretofore unrealized by anyone in the family. His teacher, Gregg, suggests that MacArthur go to college, which would put a considerable strain on the Fonda-O'Hara finances. Gregg puts MacArthur up for a scholarship at the state college but when the only opening available is a scholarship in the name of divinity, Fonda can't bear to abjure his beliefs. MacArthur realizes that this may be the only way he'll get a higher education but his Latin is non-existent. Cox makes a deal with the young student; if MacArthur comes to services religiously every Sunday, he will give the boy lessons in Latin that may help him achieve the scholarship. MacArthur spends time at the local library and meets Farmer, the rich, attractive daughter of Rorke, who is Fonda's boss. Farmer (in her movie debut) and MacArthur have an instant passion for each other and the sexual scenes between them may be a trifle raw for youngsters. Crisp dies in an accident, crushed to death by a falling tree, and when MacArthur's application to college is accepted, it's learned that there is no more money available for students. Fonda sighs, nods; there's only one thing he can do. The heck with the dream house they've planned for two decades. He sells the plot of land and uses the money to finance MacArthur's education. As summer ends and fall begins, the family waves goodbye to MacArthur and he goes off to college. Lots of charm, some laughs, down-homespun philosophy and something of a forerunner for Fonda, who played a similar character years later in SOMETIMES A GREAT NOTION. Fonda always preferred the stage to the screen and when his agents disbanded under federal edict (MCA could not represent as well as produce, so they chose the latter and took over Universal Studios), his new agency wanted him to concentrate on films and recommended this one, after a play in which he appeared, "The Gift of Time," failed. What particularly galled him was that his new agency turned down a play without ever letting him read it. It had been written with him in mind but he never got to see the script. The play turned out to be "Who's Afraid of Virginia Woolf?" and Arthur Hill got the part. Later, there was some talk about him doing the film with Bette Davis under the helm of Fred Zinnemann. When Zinnemann became unavailable, Elizabeth Taylor and Mike Nichols entered the picture and she opted for Richard Burton. Fonda's brothers in the picture included stunt man Buzz Henry (the former child star), Florey (who has a secondary life as the leader of "Super Sax," a musical group), former footballer Mike Henry and French, who costarred with Michael Landon on TV in the 1980s.

p,d&w, Delmer Daves (based on the novel by Earl Hamner, Jr.); ph, Charles Lawton; r. (Panavision, Technicolor); m, Max Steiner; ed, David Wages; art d, Carl Anderson; set d, Ralph S. Hurst; cos, Marjorie Best; spec eff, Wellington Honn; makeup, Gordon Bau, James Barker.

Drama/Comedy　　　　　　　　　　　(PR:C　MPAA:NR)

SPENDTHRIFT**½**　　　　　　　　　　(1936) 70m PAR bw

Henry Fonda (*Townsend Middleton*), Pat Paterson (*Valerie "Boots" O'Connell*), Mary Brian (*Sally Barnaby*), George Barbier (*Uncle Morton Middleton*), Edward Brophy (*Bill McGuire*), Richard Carle (*Popsy*), J.M. Kerrigan (*O'Connell*), Spencer Charters (*Col. Barnaby*), June Brewster (*Topsy Martin*), Halliwell Hobbes (*Buel the Butler*), Jerry Mandy (*Enrico*), Greta Meyer (*Hilda the Maid*), Miki Morita (*Valet*), Jonathan Hale, Russell Hicks (*Attorneys*), Don Brodie, Lester Dorr (*Reporters*), William Ruhl (*Radio Operator*), Guy Usher (*Sheriff*), Clarence Muse (*Table Captain*), Charles Irwin (*Carlton the Polo Player*).

For the first film in which he was top billed, Fonda plays a millionaire playboy who enjoys spending money on a whim. This costly habit takes an inevitable toll and before long Fonda has frittered away some $23 million. This puts him in something of a quandary, but knowing no other course of action, Fonda continues his merry habits. Brian is a gold digger from the South who sees Fonda as her ticket to a higher social status. She marries Fonda but after discovering his fortune is no more, Brian dumps him faster than Dracula dissolves in sunlight. Fonda must now face up to reality and is forced to hit the streets in search of a job. In no time at all he's hired as a radio sports announcer for $1,000 a week–a 1936 salary that could only be found in the movies. With his new life comes a new love in the form of Paterson, a working-class daughter of an Irish stableman. This comedy is delivered in a light, frothy package that has all the staying power of a soap bubble. It's very typical for the period, yet another Hollywood product that makes some good-natured fun of America's upper classes. Without any of the wit and style that Preston Sturges or Ernst Lubitsch might have injected into the simplistic plot, SPENDTHRIFT was an instantly forgettable comedy that saw little popularity at the box office. Fonda's performance is amiable but unremarkable, and in his later years he claimed he couldn't even remember making this film. Both he and director Walsh would go on to far better things, but Brian, a minor actress known as "the sweetest girl in pictures," ruined her endearing image with this film by playing such a radical change from her usual type.

p, Walter Wanger; d, Raoul Walsh; w, Walsh, Bert Hanlon (based on a story by Eric Hatch); ph, Leon Shamroy; m, Boris Morros; ed, Robert Simpson; art d, Alexander Toluboff.

Comedy　　　　　　　　　　　　　　(PR:A　MPAA:NR)

SPERMULA**　　　　　　　(1976, Fr.) 105m Film and Co./PF c

Dayle Haddon (*Spermula*), Udo Kier (*Werner*), Georges Geret (*Grop*), Ginette Leclerc (*Gromama*), Jocelyn Boisseau (*Cascade*), Francois Dunoyer (*Tristan*), Isabelle Mercanton (*Blanche*).

If you can get past the title and the premise, you are in for a bizarre, erotic horror/sci-fi/soft-core porn film. Female vampires from outer space, who dress in the fashion of the 1930s, land on Earth in search of their life-giving fluid, sperm, which they ingest by performing fellatio on unsuspecting, albeit sexually active, Earthmen. The women invade a large, almost surreal art deco mansion and begin to take over the community (on their way to conquering the Earth), until their leader, Haddon, falls in love with Andy Warhol star Kier, putting the whole evil project in jeopardy. While moral indignation may move some to reject the whole film outright, it is directed with flair and atmosphere and should be judged on its own terms.

p, Bernard Lenteric; d&w, Charles Matton; ph, Jean-Jacques Flori (Eastmancolor); ed, Isabelle Rathery, Sarah Matton; art d, Matton.

Horror　　　　　　　　　　　　　　(PR:O　MPAA:R)

SPESSART INN, THE**　　　　　　(1961, Ger.) 99m Casino/United Film Enterprises c (DAS WIRTSHAUS IM SPESSART)

Liselotte Pulver (*Countess Franziska*), Carlos Thompson (*Robber Captain*), Gunther Lueders (*Baron Sperling*), Rudolf Vogel (*Buffon Parucchio*), Ina Peters (*Maid Barbara*), Veronika Fitz (*Maid Luise*), Herbert Huebner (*Count Sandau*), Hubert von Meyerinck (*Police Major*), Helmut Lohner (*Felix*), Hans Clarin (*Peter*), Paul Esser (*Corporal*), Otto Storr (*Reverend*), Karl Hanft (*Farmhand Jacob*), Vera Complojer (*Landlady*), Ernst Braasch (*Servant Anton*), Annette Karman (*Kitchen Maid Adele*), Wolfgang Neuss (*Robber Knoll*), Wolfgang Muller (*Robber Funzel*), Kai Fischer.

Pulver plays a countess who is kidnaped by bandits from her coach while en route to Wurzburg. She and the other passengers are held hostage in the Spessart Inn until a ransom for Pulver can be arranged. Changing clothes with a male passenger, Pulver escapes and makes her way back to her father's castle. Her father is glad to see her safe, but he refuses to pay for the release of the others. Disgusted, Pulver returns to the Inn, dressed as a man, to save the others. All of the kidnapers recognize her except for Thompson, their leader, and he refuses to believe them because he has fallen in love with the countess. A rebellion begins, but it is interrupted by the arrival of troops who capture all the kidnapers but Thompson, who Pulver hides. Pulver brings the robber back to her father's castle and hides him until the soldiers leave. Though she is betrothed to a man she does not love, Pulver prepares for her wedding. Thompson, however, arrives at the ceremony, announces he is really an Italian nobleman, and sweeps Pulver off her feet.

p, Georg Witt; d, Kurt Hoffmann; w, Heinz Pauck, Liselotte Enderle (based on the story by (Wilhelm Hauff); ph, Richard Angst (AgfaColor); m, Franz Grothe; ed, Claus von Boro; art d, Robert Herlth, Kurt Herlth; cos, Elisabeth Urbanic; m/l, Gunter Neumann; makeup, Georg Jauss, Charlotte Muller.

Drama/Romance　　　　　　　　　　(PR:A　MPAA:NR)

SPETTERS***　　　　　　　(1983, Holland) 109m VSE/EM c

Toon Agterberg (*Eve*), Maarten Spanjer (*Hans*), Hans Van Tongeren (*Reen*), Marianne Boyer (*Maya*), Renee Soutendijk (*Fientje*), Jeroen Krabbe (*Henkhof*), Rutger Hauer (*Witkamp*), Peter Tuinman, Saskia Ten Batenburg, Yvonne Valkenberg, Rudi Falkenhagen, Albert Abspoel, Hans Veerman, Ben Aerden, Margot Keune, Jonna Koster, Gees Linnebank, Hugo Metsers, Peter Oosthoek.

A flashy, fast-paced drama about three teenage motorcycle enthusiasts, Agterberg, Spanjer, and Van Tongeren, who dream of being as tough and successful as motorcycle champ Hauer. Soutendijk plays a conniving greasy-spoon cook who seduces the trio to get what she wants. One of the boys is beaten to death by a group of violent homosexuals, another is killed in a motorcycle accident, and the survivor is the one Soutendijk finally grabs. Director Verhoeven (SOLDIER OF ORANGE, THE 4TH MAN) once again demonstrates his penchant for startling visuals, explicit sex, and graphic violence, but all handled with humanity and insight.

p, Joop Van Den Ende; d, Paul Verhoeven; w, Gerard Soeteman; ph, Jost Vacano (Eastmancolor); m, Ton Scherpenzeel; ed, Ine Schenkkan; art d, Dick Schillemans, Peter Jasuai; cos, Yan Tax.

Drama　　　　　　　　Cas.　　　　　(PR:O　MPAA:R)

SPHINX, THE**½　　　　　　　　　(1933) 64m MON bw

Lionel Atwill (*Jerome Breen*), Sheila Terry (*Jerry Crane, Society Editor*), Theodore Newton (*Jack Burton, Reporter*), Paul Hurst (*Terrence Hogan*), Luis Alberni (*Bacigalupi, Janitor*), Robert Ellis (*Inspector Riley*), Lucien Prival (*Jenks*), Paul Fix (*Dave Werner*), Lillian Leighton (*Mrs. Werner*), Hooper Atchley (*Curran*), Wilfred Lucas (*Prosecutor*), George "Gabby" Hayes (*Casey*).

Deaf-mute Atwill is accused of murder by an immigrant janitor. After being found innocent by a jury Atwill is freed though reporter Newton still thinks he is guilty. Newton's girlfriend, Terry, his paper's society editor, begins looking into Atwill's charitable doings in order to investigate his background. After a series of more mysterious killings, Newton becomes suspicious that Atwill is not deaf-mute, using the disability only as a cover. A medical examination proves this theory wrong. Meanwhile, Terry goes to Atwill's home where she discovers a secret panel. Behind this door is Atwill's twin brother, the real deaf-mute. He tries to kill Terry but the cops break in at the last moment to rescue her. It is only then learned that rich guy Atwill has been using his brother to cover up his nefarious deeds. For a Poverty Row thriller this one isn't too bad. There's some wonderfully suspense-filled moments and Atwill handles this dual role with skill. Monogram remade this film some 10 years later under the title THE PHANTOM KILLER.

p, Trem Carr; d, Phil Rosen; w, Albert DeMond; ph, Gilbert Warrenton; md, Abe Meyer.

Mystery   Cas.   **(PR:A MPAA:NR)**

SPHINX zero   (1981) 117m Orion/WB c

Lesley-Anne Down (Erica Baron), Frank Langella (Ahmed Khazzan), Maurice Ronet (Yvon), Sir John Gielgud (Abdu Hamdi), Vic Tablian (Khalifa), Martin Benson (Muhammed), John Rhys-Davies (Stephanos Markoulis), Nadim Sawalha (Gamal), Tutte Lemkow (Tewfik), Saeed Jaffrey (Selim), Eileen Way (Aida), William Hootkins (Don), James Cossins (Carter).

A foolish Egyptian adventure tale starring Down as a tough female archaeologist who travels to the ancient tombs in search of riches. Along the way she is shot, beaten, nearly raped, grabbed at, threatened with a knife, forced to face some rotting corpses, and, of course, almost entombed alive. Laughable dialog and a silly script ruin what was only a pretty travelog to begin with. SPHINX cost $14 million to produce and grossed a pathetic $800,000.

p, Stanley O'Toole; d, Franklin J. Schaffner; w, John Byrum (based on the novel by Robin Cook); ph, Ernest Day (Panavision, Technicolor); m, Michael J. Lewis; ed, Robert E. Swink, Michael F. Anderson; prod d, Terence Marsh; art d, Peter Lamont, Gil Parrondo; cos, Judy Moorcraft; m/l, "Just for a Day," Lewis; Wendy Waldman.

Mystery/Adventure   Cas.   **(PR:C MPAA:PG)**

SPICE OF LIFE**   (1954, Fr.) 72m Gaumont Cinemaphonic bw

Noel-Noel, Bernard Blier, Jean Tissier, Marguerite Deval.

An interesting comedy that features popular French comic Noel-Noel giving a lecture on the different types of human bores –both public and private. Noel-Noel encounters women drivers, practical jokers, a man who swears he remembers him but cannot remember from where, people who gesture too much when they talk, gabby friends who talk forever on the phone, etc. As the film progresses, it becomes obvious that Noel-Noel himself is soon to be put in the same category. (In French; English subtitles.)

p, Arthur Mayer, Edward Kingsley; d, Jean Dreville, w, Noel-Noel; ph, Louis Burel; ed, Jean Featy.

Comedy   **(PR:A MPAA:NR)**

SPIDER, THE*½   (1931) 59m FOX bw

Edmund Lowe (Chartrand), Howard Phillips (Alexander), Lois Moran (Beverly Lane), Earle Fox (John Carrington), Manya Roberti (Estelle), George E. Stone (Dr. Blackstone), Purnell Pratt (Inspector Riley), El Brendel (Ole), Kendall McComas (The Kid), Warren Hymer (Schmidt), Ruth Donnelly (Mrs. Wimbledon), John Arledge (Tommy), William Pawley (Butch), Jesse de Vorska (Goldberg).

Some killer had the nerve to kill an audience member during stage magician Lowe's act and now it's up to him to figure out who did it. Of course there is the skeptical police investigator who thinks Lowe is nuts, but he lets the magician stage a spooky seance which eventually reveals the killer.

d, William Cameron Menzies, Kenneth MacKenna; w, Barry Conners, Philip Klein (based on the play by Fulton Oursler, Lowell Brentano); ph, James Wong Howe; ed, Al DeGaetano.

Mystery   **(PR:A MPAA:NR)**

SPIDER, THE*½   (1940, Brit.) 81m Admiral-Wembley/GFD bw

Derrick De Marney (Gilbert Silver), Diana Churchill (Sally Silver), Jean Gillie (Clare Morley), Cecil Parker (Lawrence Bruce), Frank Cellier (Julian Ismay), Allen Jeayes (George Hackett), Edward Lexy (Inspector Horridge), Jack Melford (Duke), Jack Lambert (Smith), Antony Holles (Baths Manager), Moira Lynd (Nurse), Ronald Shiner, William Byron.

Parker plays a crooked talent agent who kills his partner on a moving train after the man discovers Parker's shady dealings. The pair's star client, Gillie, witnesses the murder. Parker tries to kill her but fails. Gillie is left

stunned and an amnesiac. The girl is sent home to recuperate, giving Parker another chance to make sure she never regains her memory. Enter detective De Marney and his wife, Churchill, who solve the mystery.

p, Victor M. Greene; d, Maurice Elvey; w, Greene, Kenneth Horne, Reginald Long (based on the novel Night Mail by Henry Holt); ph, Ernest Palmer; ch, Buddy Bradley.

Crime   **(PR:A MPAA:NR)**

SPIDER, THE**   (1945) 61m FOX bw

Richard Conte (Chris Conlon), Faye Marlowe (Lila Neilson), Kurt Kreuger (Garonne), John Harvey (Burns), Martin Kosleck (Barak), Mantan Moreland (Henry), Walter Sande (Lt. Castle), Cara Williams (Wanda), Charles Tannen (Lt. Tonti), Margaret Brayton (Jean), Harry Seymour (Bartender), Ann Savage (Florence Cain), Jenn Del Val (Dutrelle), Odette Vigne (Mrs. Dutrelle), James Flavin (Johnny), Roy Gordon (Picket), William Halligan (Police Inspector), Lane Chandler, Eddie Hart (Radio Cops), Margo Woode (Pretty Girl).

Private eye Conte is hired by carnival mindreader Marlowe to locate her sister who has been missing for several years. Conte and his partner, Savage, dig for clues. Savage finds the answers, but she is killed before the information can change hands. The local police arrest Conte for the killing, but he weasels his way out of jail. When another body turns up after Conte had been seen with the victim, the cops are determined to throw him in jail. Luckily Conte finds the real murderer and reveals that he had also killed Marlowe's sister years ago and committed the recent killings in order to hush up the original murder.

p, Ben Silvey; d, Robert Webb; w, Jo Eisinger, W. Scott Darling (based on a play by Charles Fulton Oursler, Lowell Brentano); ph, Glen MacWilliams; m, David Buttolph; ed, Norman Colbert; md, Emil Newman; art d, Lyle Wheeler, Richard Irvine; spec eff, Fred Sersen.

Mystery   **(PR:A MPAA:NR)**

SPIDER, THE*½   (1958) 72m AIP bw (AKA: EARTH VS. THE SPIDER)

Ed Kemmer (Mr. Kingman), June Kenny (Carol Flynn), Gene Persson (Mike Simpson), Gene Roth (Sheriff Cagle), Hal Torey (Mr. Simpson), June Jocelyn (Mrs. Flynn), Mickey Finn (Mr. Haskel), Sally Fraser (Helen Kingman), Troy Patterson (Joe), Skip Young (Sam), Howard Wright (Jake), Bill Giorgio (Sheriff Sanders), Hank Patterson (Hugo, Janitor), Jack Kosslyn (Mr. Fraser), Bob Garnet (Pest Control Man), Shirley Falls (Switchboard Operator), Bob Tetrick (Dave, Second Day Sheriff), Nancy Kilgas (Dancer), George Stanley (Man in Cavern), David Tomack (Line Foreman), Merritt Stone (Mr. Flynn).

Another wacky AIP science fiction offering that stars Kemmer as a highschool biology teacher who takes a giant spider supposedly killed by the police and brings it to school to display in the gymnasium. When the rock 'n' roll band practicing for the prom cranks up their amplifiers, the loud music wakes the spider up and it begins terrorizing the small town, stepping on numerous miniature houses and cars. After sucking the life out of many teenagers, the spider is eventually killed when the enterprising Kemmer attaches a live power line to its web and fries it. This stunning climax was borrowed by THE BRAIN EATERS and both films turned up together on a double-bill upon release.

p&d, Bert I. Gordon; w, Laszlo Gorog, George Worthing Yates (based on a story by Gordon); ph, Jack Marta; m, Albert Glasser; ed, Ronald Sinclair.

Horror/Science Fiction   **(PR:A MPAA:NR)**

SPIDER AND THE FLY, THE½**   (1952, Brit.) 73m MayFlower-Pinewood/GFD bw

Guy Rolfe (Philippe de Ledocq), Nadia Gray (Madeleine Saincaize), Eric Portman (Fernand Maubert, Chief of Police), Edward Chapman (Minister of War), Maurice Denham (Col. de le Roche), George Cole (Marc), John Carol (Jean/Alfred Louis), Harold Lang (Belfort), May Hallatt (Monique), James Hayter (Mayor), Jeremy Spenser (Jacques), Sebastian Cabot (Inspector), Natasha Sokolova (Nicole Porter), John Salew (Minister's Secretary), Madge Brindley (Jacques' Grandmother), Patrick Young (Capt. Le Maitre), Arthur Lowe, Hal Osmond, Philip Stainton, Alistair Hunter, Frederic Steger, Wallace Douglas, Keith Pyott, Ann Gunning, Andrea Malandrinos, Howard Douglas, Hattie Jacques.

A friendly rivalry between clever safecracker Rolfe and French police inspector Portman comes to a head when the policeman offers to get the crook out of a five-year jail sentence in order to crack an enemy safe during WW I. Rolfe agrees and risks his life to get the list of enemy spies operating in France, only to find that the name of his own girl friend is on the list. Nicely done.

p, Maxwell Setton, Aubrey Baring; d, Robert Hamer; w, Robert Westerby; ph, Geoffrey Unsworth; m, Georges Auric; ed, Seth Holt; art d, Edward Carrick.

Crime   **(PR:A MPAA:NR)**

SPIDER BABY zero (1968) 80m Lasky-Monka/American General
Pictures, Distributors International bw (AKA: THE LIVER EATERS;
SPIDER BABY, OR THE MADDEST STORY EVER TOLD; CANNIBAL
ORGY, OR THE MADDEST STORY EVER TOLD)

Lon Chaney, Jr, Carol Ohmart, Quinn Redeker, Mantan Moreland, Beverly
Washburn, Mary Mitchell, Karl Schanzer, Sid Haig, Jill Banner, Carolyn
Cooper, Joan Keller.

Pathetic appearance by Lon Chaney, Jr. in the twilight of his long and
uneven career. Chaney plays one of the members of a family of demented,
cannibalistic adults who are cared for by a household employee after the
death of their father. A telegram arrives stating that unknown relatives are
coming to look over the estate, so the caretaker kills himself and his charges
in an explosion rather than see his "family" put in an asylum. Chaney also
sings the film's theme song. Really depressing.

p, Gil Lasky, Paul Monka; d&w, Jack Hill; ph, Alfred Taylor; m, Ronald
Stein; ed, Elliot Fayad; art d, Ray Storey.

Horror   **Cas.**   **(PR:O MPAA:NR)**

SPIDER BABY, OR THE MADDEST STORY EVER TOLD
(SEE: SPIDER BABY, 1968)

SPIDER WOMAN (SEE: SHERLOCK HOLMES AND THE SPIDER
WOMAN, 1944)

SPIDER WOMAN STRIKES BACK, THE** (1946) 59m UNIV bw

Brenda Joyce (Jean Kingsley), Gale Sondergaard (Zenobia Dollard), Kirby
Grant (Hal Witney), Rondo Hatton (Mario), Milburn Stone (Moore), Hobart
Cavanaugh (Mr. Stapleton), Norman Leavitt (Tom), Eula Guy (Molly
Corvin), Tom Daly (Sam Julian), Lois Austin (Jinnie Hawks), Ruth
Robinson (Mrs. Wentley), Adda Gleason (Martha).

A cheap but effective creeper starring Sondergaard (who also played the
Spider Woman in SHERLOCK HOLMES AND THE SPIDER WOMAN) as
an evil scientist who feigns blindness in order to entice nubile young women
with fresh blood into her home under the false impression that they will be
working as nurses. With the help of her brutish assistant Hatton, Sondergaard drains their blood and uses it in her unholy experiments with plants
and insects. The premise sounds absurd, but it works due to good
performances from Sondergaard and Hatton combined with some nice
atmospheric direction from Lubin.

p, Howard Welsch; d, Arthur Lubin; w, Eric Taylor; ph, Paul Ivano; ed, Ray
Snyder; md, Milton Rosen; art d, John B. Goodman, Abraham Grossman; set
d, Russell A. Gausman, Ralph Warrington.

Horror   **(PR:A MPAA:NR)**

SPIDER'S WEB, THE** (1960, Brit.) 89m UA c

Glynis Johns (Clarissa Hailsham-Brown), John Justin (Henry Hailsham-
Brown), Jack Hulbert (Sir Rowland Delahaye), Cicely Courtneidge (Miss
Peake), Ronald Howard (Jeremy), David Nixon (Elgin), Wendy Turner
(Pippa), Basil Dignam (Hugo), Joan Sterndale-Bennett (Mrs. Elgin), Ferdy
Mayne (Oliver), Peter Butterworth (Inspector Lord).

An entertaining film version of Agatha Christie's 1954 stage play about a
diplomat's wife who hides the corpse of her stepdaughter's father. Though
there is no Miss Marple or Hercule Poirot to push this programmer along,
it still moves at a lively pace. Christie's previous play, "Witness For The
Prosecution," had won the New York Drama Critics Circle Award for Best
Foreign Play of 1954-55, and fortunately was made into a fine film by Billy
Wilder in 1957.

p, Edward J.Danziger, Harry Lee Danziger; d, Godfrey Grayson; w, Albert
G. Miller, Eldon Howard (based on the play by Agatha Christie); m, Tony
Crombie.

Mystery   **(PR:A MPAA:NR)**

SPIDER'S WEB, THE, 1962 (SEE: IT'S HOT IN PARADISE, 1962,
Ger./Yugo.)

SPIELER, THE*½ (1929) 62m Pathe bw

Alan Hale (Flash), Renee Adoree (Cleo), Clyde Cook (Luke), Fred Kohler
(Red Moon), Fred Warren (The Barker), Jimmy Quinn (The Rabbit), Kewpie
Morgan (Butch), Billy Latimer (Bearded Lady).

Early talkie that features Adoree struggling to run an honest carnival
despite the fact that crooks have infiltrated her operation and are fleecing
the general public as fast as they can sell tickets to the freak show. The ring
leader of the con men is Kohler and he even commits murder on the midway.
Basically a criticism against carnivals. THE SPIELER does have some
interesting moments illustrating the various crooked techniques employed
by the hucksters to swindle the customers.

d, Tay Garnett; w, Hal Conklin, Garnett (based on a story by Conklin); ph,
Arthur Miller; ed, Doane Harrison; md, Josiah Zuro; set d, Walter Bradford.

Drama   **(PR:A MPAA:NR)**

SPIES A GO-GO (SEE: NASTY RABBIT, THE, 1964)

SPIES AT WORK (SEE: SABOTAGE, 1939)

SPIES OF THE AIR**½ (1940, Brit.) 62m BN/ABF bw (AKA: SPIES
IN THE AIR, LAW AND DISORDER)

Barry K. Barnes (Jim Thurloe), Roger Livesey (Houghton, Plane Designer),
Joan Marion (Dorothy Houghton), Basil Radford (Madison), Felix Aylmer
(Col. Cairns), John Turnbull (Sir Andrew Hamilton), Henry Oscar (Porter),
Edward Ashley (Stuart), Wallace Douglas (Hooper), Everley Gregg (Mrs.
Madison), Santos Casani (Foreigner).

Routine aviation thriller about a sympathetic test pilot who kills a
blackmailer attempting to ruin the company. The pilot then falls victim
himself to the temptation of selling plans for a secret aircraft to the enemy.
He is stopped by Scotland Yard before the sale is completed. Producer
Corfield had intended to call the film FIFTH COLUMN SQUAD for its U.S.
release but was sued by Ernest Hemingway who felt that the title had
infringed on his work The Fifth Column published a year earlier.
Hemingway, with his powerful literary standing, easily won the case.
Originally released in Britain at 77 minutes, but cut down for its stateside
release.

p, John Corfield; d, David Macdonald; w, A.R. Rawlinson, Bridget Boland
(from the play Official Secrets by Jeffrey Dell); ph, Bryan Langley.

Crime/Aviation Drama   **(PR:A MPAA:NR)**

SPIKES GANG, THE**½ (1974) 96m UA c

Lee Marvin (Harry Spikes), Gary Grimes (Will Young), Ron Howard (Les
Richter), Charlie Martin Smith (Tod Hayhew), Arthur Hunnicutt (Kid
White), Noah Beery, Jr (Jack Bassett), Marc Smith (Will's Father, Abel),
Don Fellows (Cowboy), Elliott Sullivan (Billy), Robert Beatty (Sheriff),
Ralph Brown (Posse Leader), Bill Curran (Gillis), Ricardo Palacios (Doctor),
David Thomson (Sheriff), Bert Conway (Teller), Adolpho Thous (Pawnbr-
oker), Allen E. Russell (Morton), Frances O'Flynn (Mrs. Young).

Lee Marvin is the only reason to watch this weak, unofficial follow-up to
BAD COMPANY (1972). Marvin plays a wounded outlaw who stumbles into
the good graces of youngsters Howard and Grimes. The youths nurse
Marvin back to health, and are thrilled by his tales of violence and
adventure. Seeing that the two boys are fresh and eager to form an outlaw
gang, Marvin enlists the duo in his robberies. Things turn grim when
Marvin double-crosses the pair and turns to bounty hunting, and it is up to
Grimes to settle the score. Fairly routine material, but Marvin is always
fascinating to watch.

p, Walter Mirisch; d, Richard Fleischer; w, Irving Ravetch, Harriet Frank,
Jr.; ph, Brian West (DeLuxe Color); m, Fred Karlin; ed, Ralph Winters,
Frank J. Urioste; art d, Julio Molino; set d, Antonios Mateos.

Western   **(PR:C MPAA:PG)**

SPIN A DARK WEB** (1956, Brit.) 76m Film Locations/COL bw (GB:
SOHO INCIDENT)

Faith Domergue (Bella Francesi), Lee Patterson (Jim Bankley), Rona
Anderson (Betty Walker), Martin Benson (Rico Francesi), Robert Arden
(Buddy), Joss Ambler (Tom Walker), Peter Hammond (Bill Walker), Peter
Burton (Inspector Collis), Sam Kydd (Sam), Russell Westwood (Mick),
Patricia Ryan (Audrey), Bernard Fox (McLeod), Peter Benson.

British crime melodrama starring Domergue as the sister of a powerful
London mobster who slowly seduces her lover, Patterson, into a life of crime.
He goes along reluctantly, but when things turn homicidal he tries to back
out. She won't let him. A slight change of pace for Domergue who usually
spent most of her cinematic time screaming at the sight of giant octopi (IT
CAME FROM BENEATH THE SEA, 1955), or alien creatures (THIS
ISLAND EARTH, 1954).

p, M.J. Frankovich, George Maynard; d, Vernon Sewell; w, Ian Stuart Black
(based on the novel Wide Boys Never Work by Robert Westerby); ph, Basil
Emmott; m, Richard Taylor; ed, Peter Rolfe Johnson; art d, Ken Adam; m/l,
"Love Me, Love Me Now," Mark Paul, Paddy Roberts (sung by Julie Dawn).

CRIME   **(PR:A MPAA:NR)**

SPIN OF A COIN (SEE: GEORGE RAFT STORY, THE 1969)

SPINOUT** (1966) 93m Euterpe/MGM c (GB: CALIFORNIA
HOLIDAY)

Elvis Presley (Mike McCoy), Shelley Fabares (Cynthia Foxhugh), Diane
McBain (Diana St. Clair), Deborah Walley (Les), Dodie Marshall (Susan),
Jack Mullaney (Curly), Will Hutchins (Lt. Tracy Richards), Warren Berlin-
ger (Philip Short), Jimmy Hawkins (Larry), Carl Betz (Howard Foxhugh),
Cecil Kellaway (Bernard Ranley), Una Merkel (Violet Ranley), Frederic

Worklock *(Blodgett)*, Dave Barry *(Harry)*.

Once again the king of rock 'n' roll, Elvis Presley, plays a successful race car driver/rock singer who has more women than he can handle. This time out Elvis must fend off the unwanted advances of spoiled millionnairess Fabares, author of a how-to-get-a-man-book, McBain, and even his own drummer (female), Walley. Between songs Elvis manages to outrun the femmes in his race cars, and eventually he hits upon a way to rid himself of their pesky attentions by marrying them off to various male members of the supporting cast. This one's okay if you like Elvis movies, but they all tend to blend together to the untrained eye. Songs by Elvis backed by The Jordanaires include: "Adam and Evil" (Fred Wise, Randy Starr), "Stop, Look, Listen" (Joy Byers), "All That I Am," "Am I Ready," "Smorgasbord" (Sid Tepper, Roy C. Bennett), "Never Say Yes" (Doc Pomus, Mort Shuman), "Beach Shack" (Bill Giant, Florence Kaye, Bernie Baum), "I'll Be Back" (Sid Wayne, Ben Weisman), "Spinout" (Wayne, Weisman, Darrell Fuller).

p, Joe Pasternak; d, Norman Taurog; w, Theodore J. Flicker, George Kirgo; ph, Daniel L. Fapp (Panavision, Metrocolor); m, George Stoll; ed, Rita Roland; art d, George W. Davis, Edward Carfagno; set d, Henry Grace, Hugh Hunt; spec eff, J. McMillan Johnson; ch, Jack Baker; makeup, William Tuttle; tech adv, Col. Tom Parker.

Musical   **(PR:A MPAA:NR)**

SPIONE UNTER SICHE   (SEE: DIRTY GAME, THE, 1966, Fr./Ital./Ger.)

SPIRAL ROAD, THE*   (1962) 145m UNIV c

Rock Hudson *(Dr. Anton Drager)*, Burl Ives *(Dr. Brits Jansen)*, Gena Rowlands *(Els)*, Geoffrey Keen *(Willem Wattereus)*, Neva Patterson *(Louise Kramer)*, Will Kuluva *(Dr. Sordjano)*, Philip Abbott *(Frolick)*, Larry Gates *(Dr. Kramer)*, Karl Swenson *(Inspector Bevers)*, Edgar Stehli *(The Sultan)*, Judy Dan *(Laja)*, Robert F. Simon *(Dr. Martens)*, Ibrahim Bin Hassan *(Stegomyia)*, Reggie Nalder *(Burubi)*, Leon Lontok *(Dr. Hatta)*, David Lewis *(Maj. Vlormans)*, Parley Baer *(Mr. Boosmans)*, Fredd Wayne *(Van Bloor)*, Leslie Bradley *(Krasser)*, Barbara Morrison *(Mrs. Boosmans)*, Martin Brandt *(Dr. Sander)*, Lang Yun *(Barmaid)*, Paul Keast *(Minister)*, David Frankham *(Drager's Replacement)*, Anna Shin, Lang Yun *(Hotel Girls)*, Dave Sharpe, Tom Steele *(Planters)*, Glen Walters, Sally Cleaves, James Gonzalez *(Bits)*.

Overlong, tedious drama starring Hudson as an atheistic, cynical young doctor who travels into the wilds of Java in 1936 seeking to use the research culled by fabled doctor Ives, who has been in the brush for many years. Hudson's uncaring, self-serving attitude catches up to him when he is faced with a dangerous dilemma at the hands of a vicious witch doctor, who has driven an alcoholic white man, Abbott, insane, forcing Hudson to kill him. Fueled by a hatred of the voodoo priest, Hudson vows vengeance and nearly loses his life in the struggle, but finds a spiritual faith he had never felt before. While the material is potentially interesting, Mulligan's direction is lackadaisical and stiff, allowing Hudson to sleepwalk through the lengthy film.

p, Robert Arthur; d, Robert Mulligan; w, John Lee Mahin, Neil Paterson (based on the novel by Jan De Hartog); ph, Russell Harlan (Eastmancolor); m, Jerry Goldsmith; ed, Russell F. Schoengarth; art d, Alexander Golitzen, Henry Bumstead; set d, Oliver Emert; cos, Rosemary Odell; makeup, Bud Westmore; tech adv, John Datu Arensma.

Drama   **(PR:A MPAA:NR)**

SPIRAL STAIRCASE, THE**** (1946) 83m RKO-Vanguard/RKO bw

Dorothy McGuire *(Helen Capel)*, George Brent *(Prof. Warren)*, Ethel Barrymore *(Mrs. Warren)*, Kent Smith *(Dr. Parry)*, Rhonda Fleming *(Blanche)*, Gordon Oliver *(Steve Warren)*, Elsa Lanchester *(Mrs. Oates)*, James Bell *(Constable)*, Charles Wagenheim *(Desk Clerk)*, Ellen Corby *(Neighbor)*, Richard Tyler *(Freddie)*, Erville Alderson *(Dr. Harvey)*, Sara Allgood *(Nurse Barker)*, Rhys Williams *(Mr. Oates)*, Myrna Dell *(Murder Victim)*.

The setting is an old, dark Gothic mansion located in New England at the turn of the century in this suspense-filled film. Young innocent McGuire, long ago made mute due to a childhood trauma, is a servant with a sunny disposition which lends a little light to the somber setting. Her employer is the bedridden Barrymore, a cantankerous, widowed invalid. The wealthy widow has a wild, hell-raising son, Oliver–a cad and ne'er-do-well who relies on his mother's money and maternal feelings to save him from his endless scrapes–and a stepson, Brent. The latter lavishes attention and care upon his stepmother, and seems an altogether decent sort. The gentle Brent is a scholar, a professor at a nearby college, and McGuire worships him, as we see in a dream sequence which depicts–in a diffusely photographed, elegant, time-altered manner–their imagined nuptials as visualized by the love-smitten maidservant. Smith, a local doctor, takes more than a passing interest in McGuire during his visits to treat the ailing matriarch, visits which increase in frequency in direct proportion to his growing ardor for the girl. Smith suggests that McGuire's condition might be reversible, and offers to see that she gets appropriate therapy. Suddenly, the quiet, peaceful town is struck by terror. A eugenics-minded madman murders a young crippled

woman; two more murders of deformed girls follow closely. The members of the household come to realize that the afflicted McGuire may be proper prey for the cripple-killer, who apparently has embarked on a Hitler-like campaign to stamp out human imperfection. The old house that McGuire has viewed as a sanctuary now becomes a place of terror, its every dark cranny a potential threat. Both Barrymore and the enamored Kent suggest to McGuire that she leave for her own safety: leave not only the house, but the community. Before McGuire is able to seek a safe haven and respite from her growing fear, another murder is committed, this time in the old mansion itself. Young rakehell Oliver is the obvious culprit; in the mandatory thunderstorm, McGuire flees from the threat he poses through the corridors and staircases of the sinister mansion. At last she succeeds in locking up the suspect, and breathes a sigh of relief, only to discover that the real maniac–whose eyes, seen in extreme closeup only, have long been on her–is the apparent gentleman, Brent, the compassionate professor. As the terrified girl cowers from the menacing Brent, the shock of the experience invigorates her vocal cords, and she cries out in terror. Barrymore, hearing, drags herself from her entombing bedclothes and painfully ventures to the hallway, pistol in hand, where she guns down her twisted stepson. McGuire gives a touching and totally convincing pantomime performance as the victimized mute in this prototype old-dark-house thriller, a role resembling the one that brought fame, fortune, and an Academy Award to another actress, Jane Wyman, two years later for the film JOHNNY BELINDA. Not one stereotype has been neglected in a picture that is virtually guaranteed to suffuse audiences with gooseflesh; creaking doors, wind-gusted curtains, flickering candles, lengthy transits through shaded places where evil seems to lurk, cutaways to the menacing eyes of the unseen, unknown murdering maniac, every element of terror is in place. McGuire's metamorphosis from a sunny-dispositioned servant girl with a support system of loving friends to a terrified victim is built with wonderful skill; we see her layers of trust peeling away one by one, as an onion might be unlayered. German-expatriate director Siodmak, noted for his expressionistic style, had made a number of atmospheric suspense films for Universal before joining with producer Schary and RKO for this one. RKO's leading suspense-film director at the time was Val Lewton, who turned out a number of smaller-budget pictures; Siodmak had the advantage here of producer Schary's personal interest, resulting in better production values and better-known players than the Lewton films were accorded. Barrymore is perfect as the cranky but caring invalid, and the revelation that the self-contained Brent is the maniac is a stunning shocker. Lanchester is a delight as McGuire's frightened fellow servant. Author White's novel was substantially modified for the film; in the book, the menaced serving girl had been a cripple rather than a mute, and the setting was contemporary England. The novel had been made into a radio play–hardly an appropriate medium for a mute performance–prior to the film's production; Helen Hayes had starred in that audio-only version. The picture was the first in a planned series of coproductions between RKO–which handled the actual filming–and David O. Selznick's Vanguard Films, which supplied the services of Schary, Siodmak, McGuire, and Barrymore, as well as the book and the screenplay. The picture brought in more than $1.6 million– profits split evenly between the co-production companies. Remade in Britain in 1975 under the direction of Peter Collinson in a far inferior version.

p, Dore Schary; d, Robert Siodmak; w, Mel Dinelli (based on the novel *Some Must Watch* by Ethel Lina White); ph, Nicholas Musuraca; m, Roy Webb; ed, Harry Marker, Harry Gerstad; md, C. Bakaleinikoff; art d, Albert S. D'Agostino, Jack Okey; set d, Darrell Silvera; spec eff, Vernon L. Walker.

Suspense Drama   **Cas.**   **(PR:C MPAA:NR)**

SPIRAL STAIRCASE, THE*   (1975, Brit.) 89m Raven/WB c

Jacqueline Bisset *(Helen)*, Christopher Plummer *(Dr. Sherman)*, John Philip Law *(Steven)*, Mildred Dunnock *(Mrs. Sherman)*, Gayle Hunnicutt *(Blanche)*, Sam Wanamaker *(Lt. Fields)*, John Ronane *(Dr. Rawley)*, Ronald Radd *(Oates)*, Sheila Brennan *(Mrs. Oates)*, Elaine Stritch *(Nurse)*, Christopher Malcolm *(Policeman)*, Heather Lowe *(Blind Girl)*.

An anemic remake of the 1946 thriller which wastes the talents of Bisset and Plummer. Bisset is a mute nurse (luckily saving her from mumbling the inane dialog) who is caring for an old invalid. Lurking in the house, however, is a crazed killer. None of it is at all scary, especially since it is set in the densely populated suburbs instead of the isolated house of the original version. Yet another remake which had no reason to have been remade.

p, Peter Shaw; d, Peter Collinson; w, Allan Scott, Chris Bryant; ph, Ken Hodges (Technicolor); m, David Lindup.

Horror/Suspense   **(PR:C-O MPAA:NR)**

SPIRIT AND THE FLESH, THE**   (1948, Ital.) 105m LUX/Variety bw

Gino Cervi *(Renzo)*, Dina Sassoli *(Lucia)*, Ruggero Ruggeri *(Il Cardinale)*, Armando Falcone *(Don Abbondie)*, Enrico Glori *(Don Rodrigo)*, Carlo Ninchi *(L'Innominalo)*, Luis Hurtado *(Padre Christoforo)*, Ines Zacconi *(Perpetua)*, Franco Scandurra *(Il Conie Attilio)*, Gilda Marchio *(Agnese)*, Dino Di Lucca *(Il Griso)*, Enze Biliotti *(Ferrier)*.

A romantic period piece from Italy starring Sassoli as the dashing young hero determined to marry his beloved fiancee Cervi, even though he must outfox the villainous Glori to do so. Based on a classic romantic novel by Italian writer Manzoni. (In Italian; English subtitles.)

p, Mario Canerini; d, Valentino Brosio; w, Canerini (based on the novel by Alessandro Manzoni); ph, Anchiso Brizzi; m, Ildebrando Pizzeti; ed, Gino Brosio, Nathan Cy Braunstein, Clement Douneias; English subtitles, John Erskine.

Romance **(PR:A MPAA:NR)**

SPIRIT IS WILLING, THE** (1967) 94m PAR c

Sid Caesar (*Ben Powell*), Vera Miles (*Kate Powell*), Barry Gordon (*Steve Powell*), John McGiver (*Uncle George*), Cass Daley (*Felicity Twitchell*), Ricky Cordell (*Miles Thorpe*), Mary Wickes (*Gloria Tritt*), Jesse White (*Fess Dorple*), Bob [Robert] Donner (*Ebenezer Twitchell*), Nestor Paiva (*Felicity's Father*), Doodles Weaver (*Booper Mellish*), J.C. Flippen ("*Mother*"), Jill Townsend (*Jenny/Priscilla Weems/Carol Weems*), John Astin (*Dr. Frieden*), Harvey Lembeck (*Capt. Pederson*), Mickey Deems (*Rabbit Warren*), Ricky Cordell (*Miles Thorpe*).

A witty haunted house comedy starring Caesar and Miles as a married couple who drag their precocious son Gordon along with them to a New England summer home that happens to be infested with ghosts. Soon after their arrival dozens of strange and malicious things occur (things breaking, moving, etc.) and everyone immediately assumes that Gordon is to blame. Gordon is the only one in the family who can see the spirits, and he learns that the three of them were condemned to haunt the establishment when the newlywed bride, Daley, caught her husband Donner in a compromising situation with servant girl Townsend and killed both of them and herself (by accident). Upset that their home has been disturbed, the ghostly trio set about driving the guests out. After the spirits sink not one, but two of Gordon's wealthy uncle McGiver's yachts, his parents think the boy has gone totally insane. Unfortunately for McGiver, ghost Daley takes a shine to him and scares him to death so that he may join her in the nether world. In the end the family packs up and heads for less bizarre surroundings, leaving McGiver, Daley, Donner, and Townsend in ghostly bliss. Produced and directed by horror vet William Castle who knew how to scare the pants off of moviegoers when he was feeling more serious.

p&d, William Castle; w, Ben Starr (based on the novel The Visitors by Nathaniel Benchley); ph, Hal Stine (Technicolor); m, Vic Mizzy; ed, Edwin H. Bryant; md, Mizzy; art d, Hal Pereira, Walter Tyler; set d, Robert R. Benton, Don Greenwood; spec eff, Paul K. Lerpae, Farciot Edouart, Lee Vasque; makeup, Wally Westmore, Monte Westmore.

Comedy/Horror **(PR:A MPAA:NR)**

SPIRIT OF CULVER, THE*½ (1939) 89m UNIV bw (GB: MAN'S HERITAGE)

Jackie Cooper (*Tom Allen*), Freddie Bartholomew (*Bob Randolph*), Tim Holt (*Capt. Wilson*), Henry Hull (*Doc Allen*), Andy Devine (*Tubby*), Gene Reynolds (*Carruthers*), Kathryn Kane (*June Macy*), Jackie Moran (*Perkins*), Walter Tetley (*Hank*), Pierre Watkin (*Capt. Wharton*), John Hamilton (*Maj. White*), Ed Brendel, Robert Keith, Milburn Stone.

Another in the seemingly endless string of "Spirit of...(name your favorite alma mater)" movies that were ground out with alarming regularity in the 1930s, THE SPIRIT OF CULVER is basically a remake of 1932's TOM BROWN OF CULVER. Cooper stars as an orphaned youngster who wins a cadet scholarship to Culver military academy. Entering with a chip on his shoulder (his father, Hull, was a decorated war hero who died in action), Cooper rebels against the academy's strict discipline and only survives the training due to the help from his roommate, Bartholomew. As it turns out, Cooper's dad isn't dead at all, but is very much alive and suffering from shell shock in a nearby V.A. hospital. Eventually Cooper becomes a man and Hull recovers his nerve and self-respect.

p, Burt Kelly; d, Joseph Santley; w, Nathanael West, Whitney Bolton (based on a story by George Green, Tom Buckingham, Clarence Marks); ph, Elwood Bredell; ed, Frank Gross; md, Charles Previn; art d, Jack Otterson; m/l, "You Are the Words to a Song," Frank Skinner, Charles Henderson (sung by Kathryn Kane).

Drama **(PR:A MPAA:NR)**

SPIRIT OF NOTRE DAME, THE** (1931) 80m UNIV bw (GB: Vigour of Youth)

Lew Ayres (*Bucky O'Brien*), William Bakewell (*Jim Stewart*), Andy Devine (*Truck McCall*), Harry Barris (*Wasp*), Sally Blane (*Peggy*), J. Farrell McDonald (*Coach*), Frank Carideo, Don Miller, Elmer Layden, Jim Crowley, Harry Stuhldreher, Adam Walsh, Paul "Bucky" O'Connor, John Law, Moon Mullins, Art McManmon, Al Howard, John O'Brien (*Themselves*), Nat Pendleton.

Released only months after Knute Rockne's tragic death and, therefore, dedicated to him, THE SPIRIT OF NOTRE DAME is virtually interchangable with all the other college football epics on the screens at the time, dedication notwithstanding. McDonald plays the coach to whom the whole team, including the real-life Four Horsemen of Notre Dame, owe their skills

and honor. Unfortunately, hot-headed egomaniac Ayres causes a rift between himself and the coach due to a misunderstanding over another player. McDonald's cooler head prevails and he forces the over-eager Ayres to warm the bench on the day of the big game until he is called in and allowed to make the winning touchdown in the proverbial final moments. There's even a "Gipper" character–no it's not Ronald Reagan, but Andy Devine–who is in the hospital recuperating from some broken ribs that were pushed close to his heart while he bravely played with the pain.

p, Carl Laemmle, Jr.; d, Russell Mack; w, Christy Walsh, Walter DeLeon (based on the story by E. Richard Schayer, Dale Van Every); ph, George Robinson; ed, Robert Carlisle.

Drama **(PR:A MPAA:NR)**

SPIRIT OF ST. LOUIS, THE**** (1957) 135m WB c

James Stewart (*Charles A. Lindbergh*), Murray Hamilton (*Bud Gurney*), Patricia Smith (*Mirror Girl*), Bartlett Robinson (*B.F. Mahoney*), Robert Cornthwaite (*Knight*), Sheila Bond (*Model/Dancer*), Marc Connelly (*Father Hussman*), Arthur Space (*Donald Hall*), Harlan Warde (*Boedecker*), Dabbs Greer (*Goldsborough*), Paul Birch (*Blythe*), David Orrick (*Harold Bixby*), Robert Burton (*Maj. Lambert*), James L. Robertson, Jr. (*William Robertson*), Maurice Manson (*E. Lansing Ray*), James O'Rear (*Earl Thompson*), David McMahon (*Lane*), Griff Barnett (*Old Farmer*), John Lee (*Jess the Cook*), Herb Lytton (*Casey Jones*), Roy Gordon (*Associate Producer*), Aaron Spelling (*Mr. Pearless*), Charles Watts (*O.W. Schultz*), Virginia Christine (*Secretary*), Syd Saylor, Lee Roberts (*Photographers*), Richard Deacon (*Levine*), Ann Morrison (*Mrs. Pearless*), William Neff, William White (*Cadets*), Nelson Leigh (*Director*), Jack Daly (*Louie*), Carleton Young (*Captain*), Eugene Borden (*French Gendarme*), Erville Alderson (*Burt*), Olin Howlin 'Howland' (*Surplus Dealer*), Robert B. Williams (*Editor, San Diego*), Percival Vivian (*Professor*), George Selk 'Budd Buster' (*Mechanic*), Paul Brinegar (*Okie*), Chief Yowlachie (*Indian*), Ray Walker (*Barker*).

Wilder's recreation of Charles A. Lindbergh's solo flight from New York to Paris in May of 1927 is an intelligent piece, marked by Stewart's strong performance as the brave pilot. The story, based on Lindbergh's autobiography, opens with Stewart working as an airmail pilot. His goals for flight go well beyond his mail route, and Stewart begins to think about a solo voyage across the Atlantic, something no single pilot has ever accomplished. Stewart tries to find people willing to back up his dream with the needed financial support, and, after much struggle, finds a willing group in St. Louis, Missouri. Stewart has a special plane built for the trip, and, in honor of his backers, dubs the single-engine monoplane *The Spirit of St. Louis*. On the day he is to take off from a New York airfield, Stewart is forced to spend some time in the plane while waiting for the rain to stop. In flashback, he thinks back on his career as a pilot. He begins flying with aerial circuses, stunt flying dangerous moves to the thrill of breathless crowds below. Later he becomes an airmail pilot, flying through dangerous weather to get his job done. At last, bearing only ham sandwiches, 450 gallons of fuel, and without a radio, Stewart takes off under less than ideal conditions. He continues to daydream during the flight in order to relieve the tedium. A fly, which has someway found its way into the cockpit, also becomes a source of diversion as Stewart engages the insect in conversation. Stewart, fighting physical and mental exhaustion throughout his tedious journey, must resort to navigation by the stars when his compass disappears. Problems develop when ice on the plane's wings nearly cause disaster, but Stewart perseveres and finally spots land. He lands just outside of Paris, where the heroic aviator is greeted by a mob of enthusiastic people. Though dazed by what he has just gone through, Stewart realizes he has achieved what no man before him ever has. The film closes as he is welcomed back in New York by a monumental ticker tape parade. This is a well-told story, accurately capturing the thoughts and feelings of a man alone under the most extraordinary of conditions. Stewart plays the part with understanding, sincere and thoughtful in his depiction of the 1920's greatest hero. Wilder's direction depicts the monotony of the flight without making his story tedious. By alternating present time with flashbacks, a more complete picture of Lindbergh emerges, one that shows this dangerous journey to be the fulfilment of a devotion and love for flying. Waxman's background score is fitting, a fine musical accomplishment that compliments the visuals without overwhelming their own inherent strength. Lindbergh's original *Spirit of St. Louis* cost some $13,000 to build, but the three replicas built for the film cost 10 times that amount. Wilder also had a 4,000-foot runway built at the Santa Monica airport specifically for the *Spirit of St. Louis'* New York takeoff. Shooting took place on location in both New York and France, as well as the Great Circle flight line, a route that extends along Long Island, Boston, Nova Scotia, Newfoundland, Ireland's Dingle Bay, the Cornish coast, the English Channel, and finally just outside Paris. Lindbergh had been a boyhood idol of Stewart's, and the actor was eager to play his hero. However, Stewart was 47-years-old when casting began while Lindbergh was only 25-years-old at the time of his historic flight. Producer Hayward felt Stewart was simply too old, and John Ericson, who was closer to Lindbergh's age, expressed interest in the role. Not wanting to hurt Stewart's feelings, Hayward put off the actor by telling he was too old to play Lindbergh. In the biography *Everybody's Man* by Jhan Robbins, Stewart recalled: "Now I've been called many things in my time, but never too fat....I was so determined to play Lindbergh that I went on a really tough diet. It paid off. After three weeks, they told me that I had the part, but at the same time they asked me to stop dieting because I was beginning to look terribly ill." Stewart actually had a chance to meet Lindbergh before production began. As a child he had hoped to get Lindbergh's autograph at a public appearance the flyer was making near Stewart's home. Because of the huge throngs, Stewart was unable to get more than a quick glimpse of the man. Now meeting his hero face to face, Stewart was overwhelmed. "...I still felt the same hero worship....I still wanted Lindy's autograph, but I was too shy to ask for it," he later said. Unfortunately, THE SPIRIT OF ST. LOUIS never captured the public's imagination. Budgeted at $6 million, its poor showing at the box office made this film one of the biggest flops in Warner Bros. history. Jack L. Warner, in his autobiography *My First Hundred Years in Hollywood*, expressed his own disappointment in the picture's failure, writing, "The exhibitors are still moaning about it, and I have never been able to figure out why it flopped."

p, Leland Hayward; d, Billy Wilder; w, Wilder, Wendell Mayes, Charles Lederer (based on the book by Charles A. Lindbergh); ph, Robert Burks, J. Peverell Marley (CinemaScope, Warner Color); m, Franz Waxman; ed, Arthur P. Schmidt; md, Waxman; art d, Art Loel; set d, William L. Kuehl; spec eff, H.F. Koenekamp, Louis Lichtenfield; tech adv, Maj. Gen. Victor Bertrandias, USAF (ret.), Harlan A. Gurney

Biography   **Cas.**   **(PR:AAA MPAA:NR)**

SPIRIT OF STANFORD, THE*   (1942) 74m COL bw

Frankie Albert (*Himself*), Marguerite Chapman (*Fay Edwards*), Matt Willis (*Link Wyman*), Shirley Patterson (*June Rogers*), Kay Harris (*Edna*), Robert Stevens (*Cliff Bonnard*), Lloyd Bridges (*Don Farrell*), Forrest Tucker (*Buzz Costello*), Billy Lechner (*Butch*), Harold Landon (*Skeats*), Volta Boyer (*Mrs. Bixby*), Ernie Nevers (*Himself*), Dale Van Sickel (*Frosh Backfield Coach*), John Gallaudet (*Frosh Coach*), Arthur Loft (*Varsity Coach*), Jim [James] Westerfield (*Man*), Stanley Brown (*Kenny*), Ed Laughton (*Assistant Coach*), John Tyrell (*Reporter*), Ray Walker (*Duke Connors*), Sheffield, Doodles Weaver, Richard Hogan (*Men*), Frank Ferguson (*Psychology Professor*), Ralph Brooks (*Sports Reporter*), Ken Carpenter (*Sports Announcer*), Lester Dorr (*Reporter*), Jack Gardner (*Photographer*), Knox Manning (*Sports Announcer -- Himself*), Thomas Quinn (*Sports Reporter*).

Tedious football drama starring real-life gridiron champ Albert as himself. Albert plays an egotistical football player who goes for the dough and quits school before the big game to play pro ball. But, like all good guys who have gone temporarily bad, Albert gets a bad case of guilt feelings and returns to the amateur field when word arrives that his roommate falls ill and cannot play. Of course Albert wins the game in the ever-suspenseful final moments.

p, Sam White; d, Charles Barton; w, Howard J. Green, William Brent, Nick Lucats (based on a story by Brent, Lucats); ph, Franz F. Planer, Charles Stumar; ed, James Sweeney; md, M.W. Stoloff; art d, Lionel Banks.

Drama   **(PR:A MPAA:NR)**

SPIRIT OF THE BEEHIVE, THE***½   (1976, Span.) 98m Ellas
                              Querejeta/Kino-Janus c (EL ESPIRITU DE LA COLMENA)

Ana Torrent (*Ana*), Isabel Telleria (*Isabel*), Fernando Fernan Gomez (*Fernando*), Teresa Gimpera (*Teresa*), Jose Villasante (*The Monster*), Lally Soldavilla (*Milagros*), Juan Margallo (*The Fugitive*), Miguel Picazo (*The Doctor*).

Praised by some as the greatest movie ever to come out of Spain, THE SPIRIT OF THE BEEHIVE (released there in 1973) is a haunting, atmospheric piece about two young girls who become obsessed with finding the Frankenstein monster. Torrent, a charming 8-year-old, and her 10-year-old sister Telleria live in a Castillian village in 1940, just after the end of the Spanish Civil War. Although their village was spared the destruction of battle, the after-effects of war are still felt. The villagers have buckled under the tyranny which has reigned for so long. The girls' parents have resorted to the most menial ways of passing time, displaying barely any life at all. The mother, Gimpera, lives in a dream world which is shared by an imaginary lover to whom she writes letters. The father, Gomez, is a dreary intellectual who tends a beehive and then retreats to a diary which he fills with metaphoric treatises on existence. The two girls pay a visit to a traveling theater which is passing through town and sit through a showing of FRANKENSTEIN. Afterwards Telleria convinces Torrent that a Frankenstein monster actually does exist. Torrent then devotes herself to finding the monster, positive that its spirit still exists. At one point, Torrent is convinced that she has found the spirit in the form of an escaped convict who is hiding out in an abandoned farmhouse. The torment that Torrent experiences adds an intriguing level to this slow-moving but lyrical picture. While the post-Civil War period is faithfully recreated, the most compelling facet of the picture is the young Torrent, whose eyes of wonderment and desire for the imagined fills the picture with memorable images. A stunning directorial feature-film debut from Erice who, for this film alone, will forever hold a place in the history of Spanish film.

p, Ellas Querejeta; d, Victor Erice; w, Francisco J. Querejeta (based on an idea by Erice, Angel Fernandez Santos); ph, Luis Cuadrado (Eastmancolor); m, Luis de Pablo; ed, Pablo G. del Amo; art d, Adolfo Cofino.

Drama   **Cas.**   **(PR:C MPAA:NR)**

SPIRIT OF THE DEAD   (SEE: ASPHYX, THE, 1972, Brit.)

SPIRIT OF THE PEOPLE (SEE: ABE LINCOLN IN ILLINOIS, 1940)

SPIRIT OF THE WEST*½   (1932) 62m Allied bw

Hoot Gibson, Doris Hill, Lafe McKee, Hooper Atchley, George Mendoza, Walter Perry, Tiny Sanford, Charles Brinley, Al Bridge.

Gibson, a retired sheriff turned rodeo star, joins his brother, a ranch foreman, in an effort to save heroine Hill's land from a gang of rustlers. Gibson goes under cover as a ranch dishwasher to get the lowdown. Some laughs, but just the usual fare.

p, M.H. Hoffman, Jr.; d, Otto Brower; w, Philip Graham White (based on a story by Jack Natteford); ph, Harry Neumann, Tom Galligan; ed, Mildred Johnston; set d, Jean Hornbustel.

Western   **Cas.**   **(PR:A MPAA:NR)**

SPIRIT OF THE WIND**   (1979) 98m Doyon Ltd./Raven c

Pius Savage (*George*), Chief Dan George (*Moses*), Slim Pickens (*Obie*), George Clutesi (*Father*).

Picturesque but dull tale about the father of an Alaskan wilderness family who struggles mightily with a bad leg while doing all the requisite "wilderness" things such as fishing, trapping, hunting, picking berries, training sled-dogs, etc. Very routine stuff, but it's always fun to hear the late, great Chief Dan George tell a few rustic tales. Story is based on a real-life character.

d, Ralph Liddle; w, Liddle, John Logue; ph, Logue; m, Buffy Sainte-Marie; ed, Mark Goldblatt.

Drama   **(PR:C MPAA:PG)**

SPIRIT OF WEST POINT, THE*½   (1947) 77m FC bw

Felix "Doc" Blanchard (*Himself*), Glenn Davis (*Himself*), Robert Shayne (*Col. Red Blaik*), Anne Nagel (*Mrs. Blaik*), Alan Hale, Jr (*Oklahoma Cutter*), George O'Hanlon (*Joe Wilson*), Michael Browne (*Mileaway McCarty*), Tanis Chandler (*Mildred*), Mary Newton (*Mrs. Blanchard*), William Forrest (*Dr. Blanchard*), Lee Bennett (*Cabot*), Mickey McCardle (*Quarterback*), John Gallaudet (*Ferriss*), Rudy Wissler (*Young Dr. Blanchard*), Tom Harmon (*Himself*), Bill Stern, Harry Wismer (*Sportscasters*), Margaret Wells (*Mrs. Davis*), Franklin Parker (*Ralph Davis, Sr.*).

West Point football stars Blanchard and Davis play themselves (they were on a 60-day leave between graduation and active duty when they shot this) in yet another typical tale of life in collegiate sports. Brief bios of the two are thrown in among the usual maybe-we-will-go-pro, maybe-we-won't histrionics but, of course, the Army wins out and the boys stay honorable.

p, John W. Rogers, Harry Joe Brown; d, Ralph Murphy; w, Tom Reed (based on a story by Mary Howard); ph, Lester White; ed, Harvey Manger; art d, George C. Van Marter; set d, Edward Ray Robinson.

Drama   **(PR:A MPAA:NR)**

SPIRIT OF YOUTH*   (1937) 65m GN bw

Joe Louis, Clarence Muse, Edna Mae Harris, Mae Turner, Mantan Moreland, Cleo Desmond.

A pretty lousy sports drama starring an all-black cast that includes heavyweight champ Joe Louis as himself (whom he doesn't play too convincingly unless it's fight footage). The film purportedly illustrates Louis' rise from the streets to the Golden Gloves competition and eventually the bigtime. Unfortunately just as he's about to break through, he falls for nightclub singer Harris and breaks his all-important training. During the big fight, Louis gets knocked out and hits the mat. Realizing what a fool he's been, Louis bears down and makes a comeback. During the championship fight, he finds himself once again being brutally beaten until his childhood sweetheart appears ringside and gives him enough incentive to win the bout.

p, Lew Golder; d, Harry Fraser; w, Arthur Hoerl; m/l, Clarence Muse, Clarence Carpenter.

Drama   **(PR:A MPAA:NR)**

SPIRITISM** (1965, Mex.) 85m Cinematografica Calderon/K. Gordon
                              Murray bw (ESPIRITISMO)

Nora Veyran, Jose Luis Jiminez, Jorge Mondragon, Rene Cardona, Jr, Maria Eugenia San Martin, Miguel Manzano, Rita Macedo, Antonio Bravo, Beatriz Aguirre, Carmel Gonzalez.

Mexican adaptation of "The Monkey's Paw" is about a distraught mother who uses one of her three wishes to bring her dead son to life. Unfortunately she does not like what comes knocking at the door.

p, Guillermo Calderon; d, Benito Alazraki; w, Rafael Garcia Travesi (based on a story by Travesi, Calderon, from the magazine story "The Monkey's

Paw" by W.W. Jacobs); ph, Enrique Wallace; m, Antonio Diaz Conde; ed, Jorge Bustos; art d, Jose Rodriguez Granada.

Horror   **(PR:C MPAA:NR)**

SPIRITS OF THE DEAD***   (1969, Fr./Ital.) 117m Les Films
Marceau-Cocinor-P.E.A. AIP c (HISTOIRES EXTRAORDINAIRES; TRE PASSI NEL DELIRIO)

Vincent Price, Clement Biddle Wood (*Narrators*), "Metzengerstein": Jane Fonda (*Countess Frederica*), Peter Fonda (*Baron Wilhelm*), Carla Marlier (*Claude*), Francoise Prevost (*Friend of Countess*), James Robertson-Justice (*Countess' Advisor*), Anny Duperey (*1st Guest*), Philippe Lemaire (*Philippe*), Serge Marquand (*Hugues*), Andreas Voutsinas (*2nd Guest*), Audoin de Bardot (*Page*), Douking (*du Lissier*), "William Wilson": Brigitte Bardot (*Giuseppina*), Alain Delon (*Wilson*), Katia Christina (*Young Girl*), Unberto D'Orsi (*Hans*), Daniele Vargas (*Professor*), Renzo Palmer (*Priest*), "Never Bet the Devil Your Head" or "Toby Dammit": Terence Stamp (*Toby Dammit*), Salvo Randone (*Priest*), Fabrizio Angeli (*1st Director*), Ernesto Colli (*2nd Director*), Marina Yaru (*Child*), Anne Tonietti (*Television Commentator*), Alcardo Ward (*1st Interviewer*), Paul Cooper (*2nd Interviewer*), Antonia Pietrosi, Rick Boyd, Polidor.

The idea of taking three separate short stories by Poe and handing them to a trio of famed European directors was far better in concept than execution. The movie was released in France as HISTOIRES EXTRAORDINAIRES and in Italy as TRE PASSI NEL DELIRIO and the Fellini portion was released as a short on its own. The first, *Metzengerstein*, was originally published in January, 1832, by the *Saturday Courier*. Vadim uses his wife, Fonda, as a medieval woman who likes her cousin, Peter Fonda, but when he shows no return of the affection, she takes her woman-scorned revenge by setting fire to his stable of horses. Peter Fonda runs into the blaze to save his pet horse but he is consumed by the flames. Somehow, the horse manages to get out of the inferno and Jane, the surviving Fonda, is suddenly fascinated by the animal and thinks it may have taken on the soul of her late cousin. Dressed in revealing clothing (Vadim always liked to show off his wive's bodies), she climbs aboard the horse which takes her headlong into a fire and she dies. Fonda had just finished BARBARELLA for Vadim and this role was outside her ken at the time. She was supposed to be dissolute, an orgiast, and not opposed to a bit of incest. Fonda's wholesome appearance went against the casting. A bit was made in the press about the brother and sister playing cousins with sexual overtones. The cinematography by Renoir was excellent but the whole thing was a trifle. In *William Wilson*, Delon is a mean-spirited Austrian officer who tells priest Palmer that he has murdered a man who is his doppelganger. Based on Poe's story in "The Gift; A Christmas And New Year's Present For 1840" (published in 1839), it's an eerie tale as Delon tells of his life, incidents which include a bunch of young boys lowering one of their compatriots into a vat filled with vicious rats, unanesthetized surgery on Christina, and whipping Bardot, the woman with whom he plays cards. Palmer is appalled by Delon's confession and can not offer him any balm so Delon commits suicide when he jumps off the top of the church. Bardot had earlier been married to Vadim and it is presumed that they had little to say to each other while this film was being made as it was done in different areas and the chances are they didn't even meet. In the final segment, based on Poe's "Never Bet Your Head" (published in 1841 by *Graham's Magazine*), the picture comes to life under the hand of Fellini. Stamp is a famous British movie star who steeps himself in Scotland's most plentiful product. When he is promised a brand new Italian sports car for making a movie in Rome, he agrees to the assignment, a Catholic western. With Angeli and Colli directing him, he finishes the movie but is haunted by a sweet-looking young girl who seems to be hanging around, bouncing a ball and looking a bit like a preteen Lolita. The Italian photographers and his producers shower him with affection at the wrap party for the film and he gets his Maserati during the wild proceedings (peopled with the usual Fellini "grotesques"). Stamp becomes drunker and drunker and can barely walk as he gets into the gleaming automobile. There's a crumbling bridge in his path and he is going to try to pull an Evel Knievel by jumping it. As he approaches the bridge at top speed, he says "Let the Devil take my head if I don't make it." He is so boozed that he fails to notice a low-strung wire in the road and his head is separated from his body as he goes past the metal guillotine. The little girl, Yaru, suddenly appears and picks up Stamp's head with the innocence she'd shown earlier when playing with her ball. The Devil must have been listening. Fellini's segment is far and away the best of the lot as it shows style, attention to detail, and, of course, Fellini's continuing love/hate relationship with Rome. If the other two stories had also been done by Fellini, this might have been much better. It is only when comparing Fellini with Malle and Vadim that we see how good he actually is.

"Metzengerstein": d, Roger Vadim; w, Vadim, Pascal Cousin, Clement Biddle Wood (based on a story by Edgar Allan Poe); ph, Claude Renoir (PatheColor); m, Jean Prodromides; ed, Helene Plemiannikov; art d, Jean Forestier; set d, Jean Andre; cos, Jacques Fonteray; "William Wilson": d, Louis Malle; w, Malle, Daniel Boulanger, Wood (based on a story by Poe); ph, Tonino Delli Colli (PatheColor); m, Diego Masson; ed, Franco Arcalli, Suzanne Garon; art d, Ghislain Uhry, Carlo Leva; cos, Uhry, Leva; "Never Bet the Devil Your Head" or "Toby Dammit": d, Federico Fellini; w, Fellini, Bernardino Zapponi, Wood (based on the story "Never Bet Your Head" by Poe); ph, Giuseppe Rotunno (PatheColor); m, Nino Rota; ed, Ruggero

Mastroianni; art d, Piero Tosi; cos, Tosi; spec eff, Joseph Natanson; m/l, "Ruby," sung by Ray Charles.

Horror   **(PR:O MPAA:R)**

SPIRITUALIST, THE**½   (1948) 79m EL bw (AKA: THE AMAZING MR. X)

Turhan Bey (*Alexis*), Lynn Bari (*Christine Faber*), Cathy O'Donnell (*Janet Burke*), Richard Carlson (*Martin Abbott*), Donald Curtis (*Paul Faber*), Virginia Gregg (*Emily*), Harry Mendoza (*Hoffman*).

Distraught but rich young widow Bari seeks the help of bogus spiritualist Bey to contact husband Curtis, who supposedly died in a car crash. Surprise! Curtis, who isn't dead at all, is in cahoots with Bey to grab Bari's dough. Routine material, but Bey makes a convincing conman.

p, Ben Stoloff; d, Bernard Vorhaus; w, Muriel Ross Bolton, Ian McLellan Hunter (based on an original story by Crane Wilbur); ph, John Alton; m, Alexander Laszlo; ed, Norman Colbert; md, Irving Friedman; art d, Frank Durlauf; set d, Armor Marlowe, Clarence Steensen; cos, Frances Ehren; makeup, Ern Westmore, Frank Westmore.

Mystery   **Cas.**   **(PR:A MPAA:NR)**

SPITFIRE***   (1934) 88m RKO bw

Katharine Hepburn (*Trigger Hicks*), Robert Young (*John Stafford*), Ralph Bellamy (*George Fleetwood*), Martha Sleeper (*Eleanor Stafford*), Louis Mason (*Bill Grayson*), Sara Haden (*Etta Dawson*), Virginia Howell (*Granny Raines*), Sidney Toler (*Mr. Sawyer*), High Ghere [Bob Burns] (*West Fry*), Therese Wittler (*Mrs. Sawyer*), John Beck (*Jake Hawkins*), Bob Kortman (*Mountaineer*).

If you can stretch your credulity and accept sophisticated Hepburn as an ill-educated backwoods mountain type, you might enjoy this film. Based on a play entitled "Trigger," they wisely changed the name to SPITFIRE because it sounded too much like a western. Hepburn is a lean, tough faith healer from the Ozarks and she truly believes that she has the gift in her hands to help the lame and the halt. The locals are frightened of her because she is such a zealot, as well as for her hair-trigger temper. There doesn't seem to be a handle anywhere that she won't fly off. Young is an engineer building a dam in the area. He works for Bellamy and the two men find Hepburn attractive and begin to make their feelings known. Young, on loan from MGM, is discovered to be married to Sleeper and Hepburn feels betrayed because he never told her. Hepburn finds a local baby dying and she sees that the parents will do nothing for the child so she kidnaps it and nurses the child to reasonable health. After she returns the tot, it again falls ill and eventually dies. Hepburn is scorned by everyone, beaten, and almost hanged for what's happened. Bellamy saves her life and Hepburn decides that it might be better if she left the area, just for a while; she will eventually come back to the Ozarks and, if he is still there, to Bellamy. In many movies, Bellamy lost the girl to the star. Here, while he doesn't actually get Hepburn, there is the hope that he might. Lots of religion mixes in with the dull love triangle and if they had taken a deeper look at faith healing, as in ANGEL BABY or ELMER GANTRY, this might have had something to say. Comedian Bob Burns must have been so embarrassed by his part that he took his name off the screen and used the nom de junque of "High Ghere" as his credit. The play was originally acquired for the talents of Dorothy Jordan but Hepburn wanted to expand herself and get away from those high-cheekboned Eastern types she'd been playing and try something new. She asked Berman for the part and got it, a bad decision as the film died at the box office. Hepburn had made a string of low-grossers and producers were wondering if she had any real appeal to the audience. Right after this, she returned to New York, where she always maintained a residence, and went into "The Lake," a play that never made it either. SPITFIRE was shot near Mexico, in the San Jacinto mountains. There's no question that it was a unique turn for Hepburn but, just as in later years audiences could only accept Sylvester Stallone with a machine gun in his hands or boxing gloves on his fists, they could not accept Hepburn in very many places outside of a drawing room.

p, Pandro S. Bermand, John Cromwell; w, Jane Murfin, Lula Vollmer (based on the play "Trigger" by Vollmer); ph, Edward Cronjager; m, Max Steiner; ed, William H. Morgan; art d, Van Nest Polglase, Carroll Clark; cos, Walter Plunkett; makeup, Mel Burns.

Drama   **(PR:A MPAA:NR)**

SPITFIRE***½   (1943, Brit.) 90m Misbourne-British Aviation/RKO bw
(GB: THE FIRST OF THE FEW)

Leslie Howard (*R.J. Mitchell*), David Niven (*Geoffrey Crisp*), Rosamund John (*Diana Mitchell*), Roland Culver (*Comdr. Bride*), Annie Firth (*Miss Harper*), David Horne (*Higgins*), John H. Roberts (*Sir Robert MacLean*), Derrick de Marney (*S/L Jefferson*), Rosalyn Boulter (*Mabel Livesey*), Tonie Edgar Bruce (*Lady Houston*), Gordon MacLeod (*Maj. Buchan*), Erik Freund (*Willi Messerschmidt*), Filippo del Guidice (*Bertorelli*), Brefni O'Rourke (*Specialist*), John Chandos (*Kranz*), Gerry Wilmott, Jack Peach (*Announcers*), Victor Beaumont, Suzanne Clair, Miles Malleson, George Skillan, Patricia Medina, F.R. Wendhausen, Robert Beatty, Bernard Miles, Herbert

Cameron.

Howard made his last screen appearance in this above-average biography with a strong propaganda message. Howard plays R.J. Mitchell, the designer of the Spitfire fighter that was to be the weapon that would foil Hitler's plans to invade England after gaining air superiority. The film opens as a squadron of fighter pilots sit at their base awaiting the next wave of German planes. The squadron leader, Niven, begins to tell the men about the designer of their craft. Flashback to 1922, as Howard picnics on the cliffs of Dover with wife John. As he watches the gulls swoop and soar, he becomes obsessed with a vision of a streamlined monoplane that would fly faster and with more maneuverability than anything else in the sky. His motives for this are purely patriotic, planning to give the design to the government for a fighter. Official interest in his mad dream could hardly be less, and he constantly has to scrape up money to build another prototype. He is joined by Niven, a flier from WW I who works as a test pilot. Howard's designs are fairly successful and win some assorted race trophies, but the coveted Schneider Cup, for fastest seaplane, eludes him. Vacationing with John and Niven in Germany in the middle 1930s, he watches the glider clubs fly but can scarcely hide his shock when one of his hosts mentions that they are developing new fighters in violation of the Versailles Treaty. With the threat of German rearmament in his mind, Howard goes back to his drawing board even more obsessed. His financial concerns are lifted when the head of Rolls-Royce Motors gives him the fiscal and physical means to work on his designs. Finally he wins the Schneider Cup for three years in a row, ending the competition and giving the trophy permanently to England. Still he works on honing his racer into a fighter, even after a doctor tells him his health is failing and that he has perhaps only a year to live if he doesn't take it easy. Howard can't, though, and works more furiously than ever. It is from a wheelchair on his lawn that he watches the first Spitfire fly overhead before dying. Flash forward back to the RAF base, and Niven winds up his speech to the pilots talking about dedication and patriotism and how they've got the best plane in the world thanks to Howard's dream and sacrifice. The siren goes off and the men scramble to their planes to stop another attack by the Luftwaffe. This was Howard's last film appearance before he was shot out of the sky by the Luftwaffe as he returned from a semi-secret diplomatic mission in Lisbon. There are rumors that the Germans knew Churchill was to be attending a meeting in Casablanca and Howard's plane was used as a decoy. Niven was actually detached from the service to appear in SPITFIRE and his smooth performance is probably the best in the film. The direction by Howard is assured and while avoiding any subplots, it keeps the story from getting bogged down in its own message. The score, by classical composer William Walton, is superb.

p, Leslie Howard, George King, John Stafford, Adrian Brunel; d, Howard; w, Anatole de Grunwald, Miles Malleson (based on a story by Henry C. James, Kay Strueby); ph, Georges Perinal; m, William Walton; ed, Douglas Myers; md, Muir Mathieson; art d, Paul Sheriff.

Biography   **Cas.**   **(PR:A MPAA:NR)**

SPLENDID FELLOWS*½   (1934, Aus.) 85m British Empire bw

Eric Colman, Frank Leighton, Leo Franklyn, Isabelle Mahon, Frank Bradley, Charles Zoll.

Ronald Colman's less popular (and less talented) brother Eric stars in this Australian drama as a young and unruly Englishman who is kicked out of the family estate and shipped down under (accompanied by his valet, of course) by his father. There Colman falls in love with Mahon, and hooks up with an eccentric priest whose hobby is aviation. He joins the priest in his efforts to build a speedy aircraft to enter in the Centenary air race. Colman has the lead in the race and could win easily, but news that the priest's plane has gone down causes him to drop out of the race to find his friend and mentor.

p, J.C. Williamson, Beaumont Smith; d, Smith; w, Ken Brampton (based on a story by Smith); ph, George Malcolm.

Drama   **(PR:A MPAA:NR)**

SPLENDOR**   (1935) 77m UA bw

Miriam Hopkins (Phyllis Manning Lorrimore), Joel McCrea (Brighton Lorrimore), Paul Cavanagh (Martin Deering), Helen Westley (Mrs. Lorrimore), Billie Burke (Clarissa), Katharine Alexander (Martha Lorrimore), Ruth Weston (Edith Gilbert), David Niven (Clancey Lorrimore), Ivan Simpson (Fletcher, Butler), Arthur Treacher (Capt. Ballinger), Torben Meyer (Baron von Hoffstatter), Reginald Sheffield (Billy Grimes), William R. [Billy] Arnold (Jake), Maidel Turner (Mrs. Hicks), Clarence H. Wilson (Process Server), Violet Axelle (Brighton Maid), Eddie Craven (Elevator Man), Lois January (Lena Limering), Cosmo Kyrle Bellew, Connie Howard (Guests at Dinner), Betty Blair (Fitter), Clinton Lyle (Chauffeur), Jeanie Roberts (Gertie), Frederick Lee (Track Attendant), Nina Penn (Woman Opera Attendant), William O'Brien (Theater Usher), Bob Beasley (Western Union Messenger), William Cartledge, John Van Eyck, Frank H. Hammond, George Bruggeman, Henry Hall, Dick Allen, Phyllis Crane, Mildred Booth, Georgette Rhodes.

Standard melodrama starring Hopkins as a poor girl who marries rich-kid McCrea, much to the dismay of his haughty parents. McCrea's folks are a

bit hypocritical because the family fortune is going to the dogs, so they decide to make some use of this unwanted, but attractive addition to the dynasty by pushing her into an affair with Cavanagh, a powerful broker who can do wonders for the family's finances. Scandal hits, Hopkins flees and becomes a dressmaker. McCrea finally gets a decent job and the couple reunites after mutual apologies. Good cast, routine handling. Niven appears here in his first featured player part. Crothers' story, which she had written 15 years earlier but was unable to develop for the Broadway stage, was sold to Goldwyn, whose films during the 1930s regularly depicted the elegant lifestyles, activities, and values of upperclass Americans. Amid this luxury, the film still managed to lecture the Depression-era masses on the values of marital fidelity and genteel poverty.

p, Samuel Goldwyn; d, Elliott Nugent; w, Rachel Crothers; ph, Gregg Toland; ed, Margaret Clancey; md, Alfred Newman; art d, Richard Day; cos, Omar Kiam.

Drama   **(PR:A MPAA:NR)**

SPLENDOR IN THE GRASS***   (1961) 124m NBI-Newton/WB c

Natalie Wood (Wilma Dean Loomis), Warren Beatty (Bud Stamper), Pat Hingle (Ace Stamper), Audrey Christie (Mrs. Loomis), Barbara Loden (Ginny Stamper), Zohra Lampert (Angelina), Fred Stewart (Del Loomis), Joanna Roos (Mrs. Stamper), Jan Norris (Juanita Howard), Gary Lockwood (Toots), Sandy Dennis (Kay), Crystal Field (Hazel), Marla Adams (June), Lynn Loring (Carolyn), John McGovern (Doc Smiley), Martine Bartlett (Miss Metcalf), Sean Garrison (Glenn), William Inge (Minister), Charles Robinson (Johnny Masterson), Phyllis Diller (Texas Guinan), Phoebe MacKay (Maid).

SPLENDOR IN THE GRASS had a few firsts attached to it. It was Beatty's debut in the movies; it was Inge's first work done specifically for the screen; and it was Kazan's first picture that failed to ultimately satisfy. The title is taken from a William Wordsworth poem which reads: "There's nothing can bring back the hour/Of splendor in the grass, of glory in the flower/We will grieve not, but rather find strength in what remains behind." Beatty was in his early twenties and had just appeared in Inge's play "A Loss Of Roses" in 1959, after having been discovered by Josh Logan and Inge while working in a small playhouse in New Jersey. Despite that play's failure, Inge was mesmerized by Beatty and wrote this screenplay for him. Later, he would adapt James Leo Herlihy's novel All Fall Down into a screenplay for Beatty, after Beatty himself had impressed another epicene playwright, Tennessee Williams, sufficiently to get the plum role in THE ROMAN SPRING OF MRS. STONE. While making this film, Beatty began his off-screen amours that have since become legendary. Wood was married to Robert Wagner (the first time around) and she was the first of many who would fall for Beatty, thus ending the union with Wagner that was to begin again and remain steadfast until Wood's accidental death. A steamy story of repressed sexuality, this takes place in 1925, in Kansas, where Inge grew up. Beatty and Wood are high schoolers who fall in love and attempt to keep their affection on an intellectual level, for they fear it would be wrong to express their physical needs. Wood is the daughter of shrew Christie, a domineering woman who pushes her husband, Stewart, around and who continuously warns Wood of having relations with men. Since she has absolutely no feelings below the waist, Christie attempts to instill the same frigidity into her nubile daughter. Beatty's father is wealthy Hingle, a blustering Midwest businessman who is stupid, despite his money. (Hingle had suffered from back problems when this was made and so his scenes were shot with a minimum of movement on his part.) Hingle discourages Beatty's love for Wood and suggests that the boy go back east, attend Yale, and if he still wants Wood after four years in New Haven, they can talk about it then. Wood and Beatty try to keep their love pristine and unsullied and the frustration takes its toll. Since they can't get married and since both feel they have gone about as far as they can go groping and grappling in the back seat of a car, they stop seeing each other. Beatty develops pneumonia, then begins squiring the local slut, Norris, who has slept with just about everyone in the county. Wood attempts to take her own life, then has a total nervous collapse and goes to an institution for mental rehabilitation. Time passes and several calamities befall Beatty. His amoral sister, Loden, dies in an auto accident (Loden is Kazan's second wife), and Hingle's vast fortune is obliterated by the stock market debacle in October, 1929, so he kills himself. Beatty quits Yale and marries Lampert, an Italian waitress from New Haven (the best acting in the movie) who is a refreshing change from the constrained types of Kansas. Wood gets out of the mental hospital and one of her pals from the sanitarium, Robinson, proposes marriage. Wood thinks about it for a while, then decides that she can't make that kind of move until she sees Beatty again. Wood travels to see Beatty, notes that Lampert is pregnant, and sees that while she has matured, Beatty is still a high school boy—just slightly older—who doesn't seem to have gotten wiser, just older. Wood leaves to begin a new life and the picture closes. In small bits, note Phyllis Diller as Texas Guinan, Sandy Dennis in her first film, and Gary Lockwood in his third. The holes in the story are vast. Beatty leaves Wood because he doesn't seem to be able to be with Wood without wanting her body and Wood goes mad because he gets involved with a more willing partner. Youth exploitation pictures were all the rage at the time, and while this is considerably above the others in execution and intent, it's still exactly that. A smash success, it also gave audiences a chance to see what the author looked like. Inge plays a minister. At the time they shot this, Kansas was evidently not in bloom, so Staten Island and a town in upstate New York were used to substitute for the Jayhawker state.

p&d, Elia Kazan; w, William Inge; ph, Boris Kaufman (Technicolor); m, David Amram; ed, Gene Milford; md, Amram; art d, Richard Sylbert; set d, Gene Callahan; cos, Anna Hill Johnstone; ch, George Tapps; makeup, Robert Jiras.

Drama   Cas.   (PR:C MPAA:NR)

SPLINTERS*½   (1929, Brit.) 100m British and Dominions/W&F bw

Hal Jones, Reg Stone, Lew Lake, Nelson Keys, Sydney Howard, George Baker, Wilfred Temple, Sidney Grantham, Walter Glynne.

Bored British army personnel in France during WW I stage a vaudeville show with songs, comedy and, of course, soldiers in drag. Climax sees the boys run off to battle, many still dressed as women. This is the film version of the famous concert party "Les Rouges et Noirs" organized by comic Jones and female impersonator Stone during WW I. Stone sings "I'll Be on My Way" and "Encore," while Jones performs "Lanky Carrie Fra' Lancasheer." Stone and Jones are the only members of the original troupe to appear in the film.

p, Herbert Wilcox; d, Jack Raymond; w, W.P. Lipscomb, Archie Ross; ph, Dave Kesson.

Comedy   (PR:A MPAA:NR)

SPLINTERS IN THE AIR*½   (1937, Brit.) 71 GFD bw

Sydney Howard (George/Sydney Metcalfe), Richard Hearne (Sgt. Hearne), Stuart Robertson (Sgt. Robertson), Ralph Reader (Sgt. Reader), Ellen Pollock (CO's Wife), D.A. Clarke-Smith (Warrant Officer), Franklyn Bellamy (Commanding Officer), Ronald Ward (Richards), Binkie Stuart (Mary), Lew Lake (Stage Manager), Geraldine Hislop, George Ellisha.

The final entry in the short-lived SPLINTERS series, SPLINTERS IN THE AIR tells the lame tale of an inventor of a prototype helicopter who accidently gets sent into the RAF in place of his twin brother. Things look grim for the inventor until he safely rescues the commanding officer's wife with his copter. The film still bears the trademark of servicemen in drag, but original troupe members Hal Jones and Reg Stone are nowhere to be seen.

p, Herbert Wilcox; d, Alfred Goulding; w, R.P. Weston, Bert Lee, Jack Marks (based on a story by K.R.G. Browne, Ralph Reader); ph, Eric Cross.

Comedy   (PR:A MPAA:NR)

SPLINTERS IN THE NAVY   (1931, Brit.) 76m Twickenham/Woolf
                                                  and Freedman bw

Sydney Howard (Joe Crabbs), Frederick Bentley (Bill Miffins), Helena Pickard (Lottie), Paddy Browne (Mabel), Alf Goddard (Spike Higgins), Rupert Lister (Admiral), Harold Heath (Master-at-Arms), Ian Wilson (Call Boy), Lew Lake, Hal Jones, Reg Stone, Wilfred Temple, Laurie Lawrence, Thomas Thurban.

A vigorous comedy loaded with servicemen in drag and starring Howard as a rough 'n' ready seaman. When the navy's boxing champion steals Howard's girl, the seaman decides to enter the ring and let his fists do the talking. The charged finale has the pair battling it out until only Howard is standing–the winner of both the match and the girl.

p, Julius Hagen; d, Walter Forde; w, R.P. Weston, Bert Lee, Jack Marks (based on the story by H. Fowler Mear).

Comedy   (PR:A MPAA:NR)

SPLIT, THE, 1962   (SEE: MANSTER, THE, 1962, Jap.)

SPLIT, THE½   (1968) 90m Spectrum/MGM c

Jim Brown (McClain), Diahann Carroll (Ellie), Julie Harris (Gladys), Ernest Borgnine (Bert Clinger), Gene Hackman (Lt. Walter Brill), Jack Klugman (Harry Kifka), Warren Oates (Marty Gough), James Whitmore (Herb Sutro), Donald Sutherland (Dave Negli), Jackie Joseph (Jackie), Harry Hickox (Detective), Joyce Jameson (Jenifer), Warren Vanders (Mason), George Cisar (Doorman), Karen Norris (Proprietress), Duane Grey, Reg Parton, Cal Brown, Jon Kowal, John Orchard (Guards), Barry Russo (Maccione, Top Guard), Ron Stokes (Detective), Anne Randall (Negli's Girl), Beverly Hills (Receptionist), Robert Foulk (Sergeant), Howard Curtis, Chuck Kicks, Bill Couch, Carl Saxe, Gene LeBell, George Robotham (Physical Instructors), Fabian Dean, Thordis Brandt (Clerks), Dee Carroll, Edith Evanson (Women), Lou Whitehill, Ron McCavour (Policemen), Orriel Smith, Cherie Lamour (Teenagers), Chance Gentry (Policeman), Jose Gallegos (Father), Tina Menard (Mother), Priscilla Ann (Daughter), Anthony Carbone (Man), Vanessa Lee (Little Girl), Jonathan Hole (Ticket Seller), Geneva Pacheco (Concessionaire).

Richard Stark, aka Donald Westlake, wrote many crime novels that were made into some pretty good pictures. Among them were POINT BLANK, THE HOT ROCK, and THE OUTFIT. This one is awash in blood, with a

great deal of gratuitous violence, and has little of the sharpness of the others. Especially missing is the wit and characterization so often found in the author's works. A good cast is wasted by the mindlessness of this film's execution although it did well in theaters where switchblades are sold next to the popcorn machine. Brown is a thief who has just come back to Los Angeles after having been away for several years. He teams up with one-time pal Harris, herself a criminal, and they plan a bold caper: the robbery of the proceeds from a sold-out football game at the Los Angeles Coliseum while the game is going on. (The lie here is that most of the tickets are purchased away from the stadium's box office, either by mail, through season ticket holders, or at the various ticket agencies that dot the city.) In order to assemble the proper gang for the robbery, Brown has to find people with the right mettle, so there's a 12-minute montage as he physically fights Borgnine, a gym instructor who is a strong-arm man; then he has a gun battle with sharpshooter Sutherland; next, he races with driver Klugman–who will be the "wheel man" on the job – and, finally, he uses a hooker to test the abilities of Oates, a safe-cracker/escape artist. The job is carefully planned and goes off like clockwork. Brown hides the money with his ex-wife, Carroll, who agrees to watch the cash with the provision that Brown cease and desist from his crimes so that they might be able to spend a happy life together after a reconciliation. Brown swears that this is the final job. Next day, Carroll's landlord, Whitmore, walks into the apartment and shows that he is a psychotic as he tries to have his way with her. When she resists, Whitmore kills Carroll, then steals the money. Hackman is a sleazy cop who is always looking to supplement his income. When he investigates Carroll's death, he recalls that Carroll and Brown were married and he makes the connection between her demise and the robbery at the Coliseum. The other gang members think they've been betrayed by Brown so they begin to work him over. A battle ensues and Klugman and Harris are killed while Brown gets away. Hackman tracks down Whitmore and shoots him for resisting arrest, then takes the half-million dollars for himself. Brown figures that Hackman must now have the cash and threatens to blow the whistle, then suggests that things can be worked out amicably if Hackman will share the money with him. Together, Hackman and Brown have a shoot-out with the other gang members, kill them off, and divide the cash. Hackman decides to give some of the money to his police bosses, keep some for himself, and make it appear as through Brown has left with the rest. Brown goes to the airport to leave for safety in Mexico with his part of the money but the promise he made to his late love, Carroll, sticks in his craw. He hears her voice in his mind and there's a final freeze frame so we don't know if he left for south of the border or decided to go straight. This was one of the earliest films that used two black stars as the romantic leads. The supporting cast was made up of multi-award winners. Borgnine had been Oscared for MARTY, Harris won the Tony and the Emmy, Klugman was to win an Emmy and Hackman won an Oscar later for THE FRENCH CONNECTION after having been nominated for BONNIE AND CLYDE and I NEVER SANG FOR MY FATHER. None of them could help this essentially exploitative picture that was a lame attempt at replicating the classic film noir pieces of the 1930s and 1940s. Just another twist on RIFIFI, it did benefit from Jones' driving score as well as three tunes, "The Split" (Quincy Jones, Ernie Shelby, sung by Billy Preston), "It's Just a Game, Love" (Jones, Shelby, sung by Arthur Prysock), and "A Good Woman's Love" (Jones, Sheb Wooley, sung by Wooley).

p, Irwin Winkler, Robert Chartoff; d, Gordon Flemyng; w, Robert Sabaroff (based on the novel The Seventh by Richard Stark [Donald Westlake]); ph, Burnett Guffey (Panavision, Metrocolor); m, Quincy Jones; ed, Rita Roland; art d, Urie McCleary, George W. Davis; set d, Keogh Gleason, Henry Grace; spec eff, Virgil Beck; makeup, William Tuttle.

Crime   (PR:O MPAA:R)

SPLIT IMAGE*   (1982) 111m Polygram/ORION c

Michael O'Keefe (Danny), Karen Allen (Rebecca), Peter Fonda (Kirklander), James Woods (Pratt), Elizabeth Ashley (Diana), Brian Dennehy (Kevin), Ronnie Scribner (Sean), Pamela Ludwig (Jane), John Dukakis (Aaron), Lee Montgomery (Walter), Michael Sacks (Gabriel), Deborah Rush (Judith), Peter Horton (Jacob), Ken Farmer (Collins), Cliff Stephens (Hall), Brian Hinson (Jerry), David Wallace (Gymnast), Kenneth Barry (Big Wig), Robert A. Cowan, Herbert Kirkpatrick (Coaches), Christopher McCarty, Lee Ritchey (Sentries), Lynette Walden (Sexy Girl), Robert Hibbard (Cop), Scott Campbell (Barry), Melanie Strange (Debbie), David Tanner (Guitarist), Tom Rayhall (Sargent), Jeanne Evans (Newsboy's Mother), Irma Hall (Maid), Bill Engvall (Student), Peter Hans Sprague (Person), John Carroll, Haley McLane, Kelly Wimberly (Homelanders).

Taken right from the headlines, this resembles TICKET TO HEAVEN which covered much of the same territory the year before. Dennehy and Ashley are a middle-aged couple who still like the rock'n'roll music that they grew up with. Their son is O'Keefe, an athlete and a possible Olympian in gymnastics. Their younger son is Scribner; the two boys have a good relationship while O'Keefe attends college and strives to improve his abilities. Allen is a convert to a cult run by Fonda. In outsiders' minds, it's not unlike the one run by Jim Jones or the Moonies and when Allen takes her new friend, O'Keefe, to the cult meeting, he is at first tickled by what he sees. How these apparently intelligent young people can fall under the influence of a man like Fonda is beyond his ken. So it's sort of jarring when O'Keefe is suddenly part of the organization, even though life in the cult is seen to be good and the kids in the group are leading clean, drug-free lives and devoting themselves to worthwhile activities. Ashley and Dennehy can't believe that their son has fallen into such a situation and when he won't come home of his own accord, they hire Woods, an expert in deprogramming, to kidnap the boy and get his mind in order. Woods is particularly good as the tacky deprogrammer and the questions in the film reflect his performance because we are asked to answer which is worse, the illness or the cure? That O'Keefe, an adult, has every right to determine his own life's path for himself is guaranteed by the law. And yet, the anguish of his parents is clearly indicated and anyone who has children will recognize their pain. The drama stems from both sides being presented with equal honesty. Fonda's cult does not espouse anything untoward, just a unity of spirit, so there is no chance of this being like the Bhagwan Rashneesh, who advocated free love and all the supplicant's money earned turned over to him. But parents want the best for their children, at any cost, and if that includes having to deal with a sleazeball like Woods, so be it. A good enough movie that benefits from Kotcheff's direction, SPLIT IMAGE disappeared quickly from the movie houses, despite good word-of-mouth from the very few people who got to see it. Far too rough for children.

p&d, Ted Kotcheff; w, Scott Spencer, Robert Kaufman, Robert Mark Kamen (based on a story by Spencer); ph, Robert Jessup (Panavision, DeLuxe Color); m, Bill Conti; ed, Jay Kamen; prod d, Wolf Kroeger; art d, Jack Marty; spec eff, Jack Bennett; m/l, Conti, Will Jennings; makeup, Jimi White.

Drama   **Cas.**   **(PR:O MPAA:R)**

SPLIT SECOND***   (1953) 85m RKO bw

Stephen McNally (*Sam Hurley*), Alexis Smith (*Kay Garven*), Jan Sterling (*Dottie*), Keith Andes (*Larry Fleming*), Arthur Hunnicutt (*Asa*), Paul Kelly (*Bart Moore*), Robert Paige (*Arthur Ashton*), Richard Egan (*Dr. Garven*), Frank de Kova (*Dummy*).

Song and dance manturned tough-guy private detective Dick Powell makes his directorial debut with this taut, intense thriller. McNally stars as the leader of a gang of escaped convicts holding a group of people hostage in a ghost town in Nevada. The other cons are Kelly and de Kova. The hostages are Smith, Sterling, Andes, Hunnicutt, Paige and Egan. The hostage situation begins to unravel when it is learned that the ghost town is actually a government nuclear test site upon which a new bomb is about to be dropped. Hunnicutt eventually helps outfox the kidnapers and leads all the hostages, with the exception of Smith, who tries to flee with Kelly, to an old mine shaft where they'll be safe from the blast. Well cast, with some amazingly detailed performances, especially McNally's (quite possibly his best).

p, Edmund Grainger; d, Dick Powell; w, William Bowers, Irving Wallace (based on a story by Chester Erskine, Wallace); ph, Nicholas Musuraca; m, Roy Webb; ed, Robert Ford; art d, Albert D'Agostino, Jack Okey; Cos, Michael Woulfe.

Drama   **Cas.**   **(PR:A MPAA:NR)**

SPLITFACE   (SEE: DICK TRACY, 1945)

SPLITTING UP**   (1981, Neth.) 92m Harlekijn Holland c (UIT ELKAAR)

Herman van Veen (*Herman*), Monique van de Ven (*Linda*), Frits de Rek (*Eric*), Merlous Fluitsma (*Evelein*).

Dutch director-writer-actor-singer Van Veen is the force behind this drama, which details via flashbacks the rift between a couple breaking up. Struck with the wanderlust, Van Veen has affairs and ruins his marriage. The split was hard enough, but the longing for his young son is too much to bear, so he writes and sings a series of songs illustrating his mixed emotions. A few powerful moments do surface, but the film seems more like a self-conscious one-man show than an insightful drama. This picture supposedly was the first European production to utilize Dolby sound. (In Dutch; English subtitles.)

p, Joost Taverne; d&w, Herman van Veen; ph, Ralf Boumans; m, Erik van der Wurff; ed, Edgar Burcksen, Hans van Beek.

Drama   **(PR:C MPAA:NR)**

SPOILED ROTTEN zero   (1968, Gr.) 89m Finos/Chancellor bw (AKA: PRIZED AS A MATE])

Zoe Laskari (*Rhea*), Nikos Kourkoulos (*Costas*).

Kourkoulos plays an insanely jealous and frequently violent adolescent who goes on a rampage when he learns his girl friend Laskari is having a fling with another man to make him jealous. Kourkoulos takes her out during an alleged reconciliation, strips her naked on a country road and leaves her there. He then goes back to town and beds Laskari's younger sister. Laskari comes home, catches the pair in bed and kills him.

d, Yannis Dalianidis.

Drama   **(PR:C-O MPAA:NR)**

SPOILERS, THE***   (1930) 85m PAR bw

Gary Cooper (*Roy Glenister*), Kay Johnson (*Helen Chester*), Betty Compson (*Cherry Malotte*), William "Stage" Boyd (*Alec McNamara*), Harry Green (*Herman*), Slim Summerville (*Slapjack Simms*), James Kirkwood (*Joe Dextry*), Lloyd Ingraham (*Judge Stillman*), Oscar Apfel (*Struve*), George Irving (*William Wheaton*), Edward Coxen (*Lawyer*), Jack Trent (*Bronco Kid*), Edward Hearn (*Lieutenant*), Knute Erickson (*Capt. Stevens*), John Beck (*Hansen*), Jack N. Holmes (*Voorhees*), Merrill McCormick (*Miner*), Charles K. French (*Man in Bar*).

The first sound version of the Rex Beach novel which was twice filmed silently–in 1914, with Tom Santschi, William Farnum, and Kathlyn Williams, and again in 1923 with Milton Sills, Noah Beery, and Anna Q. Nilsson. This time the story was brought to the screen as a vehicle for Cooper, who was hot off the success of THE VIRGINIAN (1929). The setting is once again an Alaskan boom town and Cooper is defending his Midas gold mine against the scheming ways of Boyd, who is determined to make the town his own. With assistance from a crooked judge, Ingraham, and a seemingly innocent niece, Johnson, Boyd manages to take control of Cooper's mine and put a freeze on his money. With the help of Compson, a gutsy card dealer who is the object of Boyd's unrequited love, Cooper regains control of the mine, and organizes a rebellion of fellow miners who have grown tired of Boyd's despoiling ways. Cooper is then given his chance to beat some sense into Boyd. In what has become the highlight of all five screen adaptations of the novel, Cooper and Boyd engage in a furious fistfight which splinters and smashes nearly everthing that isn't nailed down in the local saloon. In the end, Cooper triumphs and wins the affections of Compson. While this version provides an ample amount of excitement and a pair of fine performances from Cooper and Boyd, it lacks the electricity of the 1942 version. Another weak point here is the lack of a solid female character–a weakness which was easily overcome by Marlene Dietrich's sensational persona in the 1942 film. The stars of the 1914 original, Santschi and Farnum, made a comeback of sorts in this version working as technical advisors on the climactic fight scene.

p&d, Edwin Carewe; w, Bartlett Cormack, Agnes Brand Leahy (based on the novel by Rex Beach); ph, Harry Fischbeck; ed, William Shea; tech adv, Tom Santschi, William Farnum.

Western   **(PR:A MPAA:NR)**

SPOILERS, THE***½   (1942) 87m Charles K. Feldman Group/UNIV bw

Marlene Dietrich (*Cherry Malotte*), Randolph Scott (*Alexander McNamara*), John Wayne (*Roy Glennister*), Margaret Lindsay (*Helen Chester*), Harry Carey, Sr. (*Al Dextry*), Richard Barthelmess (*Bronco Kid Farrell*), George Cleveland (*Banty*), Samuel S. Hinds (*Judge Stillman*), Russell Simpson (*Flapjack Simms*), William Farnum (*Wheaton*), Marietta Canty (*Idabelle*), Jack Norton (*Mr. Skinner*), Ray Bennett (*Clark*), Forrest Taylor (*Bennett*), Charles McMurphy, Art Miles, William Haade (*Deputies*), Charles Halton (*Jonathan Struve*), Bud Osborne (*Marshall*), Drew Demarest (*Galloway*), Robert W. Service (*The Poet*), Robert Homans (*Sea Captain*), Irving Bacon (*Hotel Proprietor*), Robert McKenzie (*Restaurateur*), Chester Clute (*Montrose*), Harry Woods (*Complaining Miner*), William Gould (*Marshal Thompson*), Willie Fung (*Jailed Chinaman*), Lloyd Ingraham (*Kelly*).

Boasting three of Hollywood's biggest names and one of the most brutal fight scenes ever to hit the screen, THE SPOILERS manages to elevate itself above the B-western status it might otherwise have been relegated to. The story is a simple one, consisting of the sterotypical good guy (Wayne), bad guy (Scott), bad good-girl (Lindsay), and good bad-girl (Dietrich). It's the turn of the century and Wayne and partner Carey are miners in Nome, Alaska. They become the victims of a scam organized by gold commissioner Scott, who is intent on "spoiling" that region's gold-mining boom. The ownership of the mine is called into question by Scott, and Wayne's case is brought before judge Hinds, who, unknown to Wayne, is in cahoots with the gold commissioner. Also helping Scott is the seemingly proper Lindsay, Hinds' niece, whose womanly ways have convinced Wayne to abide by the court's decision. Carey, however, wants to bear arms and fight for his gold mine. The feud boils and their partnership is dissolved. In the meantime, Dietrich, a gin-joint proprietor, has taken a fancy to Wayne, while spurning Scott's advances. When Wayne's case is postponed for 90 days and his assets are frozen, he begins to think along Carey's lines. With help from Barthelmess, a card dealer employed by Dietrich, Wayne decides to steal his frozen assets from the bank's safe. Barthelmess, however, is planning to kill Wayne and keep Dietrich for himself. Wayne survives but is thrown into jail by Scott, who plans to let him escape and then gun him down. The thought of murder offends Hinds and Lindsay, causing them to split from Scott. Because of information that Dietrich lured out of Scott, Wayne successfully escapes with help from the reformed Barthelmess. Wayne organizes his fellow miners, who rise up and defeat Scott's henchmen. Wayne then gets his chance to even the score when he meets Scott in Dietrich's saloon. Scott tries to avoid the confrontation by telling Wayne that he is not armed. Wayne then proceeds to inform Scott that "we'll do it the hard way!" What follows is perhaps the most exciting, hard-hitting, furniture-smashing, two-fisted showdown in movies. Not surprisingly, Wayne emerges victorious, winning Dietrich's love as well. The fact that the fistfight is wholly unrealistic and unsurvivable is what makes it all the more exciting. This is Hollywood movie star indestructability at its finest. (While much of the fighting was done by Wayne and Scott, many of the more dangerous stunts were performed by doubles Eddie Parker and Alan Pomeroy.) It has also become the trademark of all five versions of THE SPOILERS from the 1914 and 1923 silents to the one previous talkie in 1930 and the subsequent 1955 remake. An interesting footnote is the inclusion in the cast of William Farnum, who starred in the 1914 version as Wayne's character, Roy Glennister, and Lloyd Ingraham, who appeared in the 1930 version as Hinds' character, Judge Stillman. In addition to the film's star quality and its spectacular brawl, THE SPOILERS also has some detailed art decoration and set design which earned an Oscar nomination for the four men responsible. Although songstress Dietrich, unfortunately, doesn't get a chance to sing in this picture, an old tune of hers from DESTRY RIDES AGAIN, "Little Joe the Wrangler" (Frederick Hollander, Frank Loesser), does sneak in as background music. Note famed gold-rush poet Service as (what else?) a poet.

p, Frank Lloyd; d, Ray Enright; w, Lawrence Hazard, Tom Reed (based on the novel by Rex Beach); ph, Milton Krasner; m, Hans J. Salter; ed, Clarence Kolster; md, Charles Previn; art d, Jack Otterson, John B. Goodman; set d, Russell A. Gausman, Edward R. Robinson; cos, Vera West; stunts, Eddie Parker, Alan Pomeroy.

Western   **Cas.**   **(PR:A MPAA:NR)**

SPOILERS, THE**½   (1955) 84m UNIV c

Anne Baxter (Cherry Malotte), Jeff Chandler (Roy Glennister), Rory Calhoun (Alex McNamara), Ray Danton ("Bronco" Blackie), Barbara Britton (Helen Chester), John McIntire (Dextry), Wallace Ford (Flapjack Simms), Carl Benton Reid (Judge Stillman), Raymond Walburn (Mr. Skinner), Ruth Donnelly (Duchess), Willis Bouchey (Jonathan Struve), Forrest Lewis (Banty Jones), Roy Barcroft (The Marshal), Dayton Lummis (Wheaton), John Harmon (Kelly), Paul McGuire (Thompson), Frank Sully, Bob Steele (Miners), Byron Foulger (Montrose), Arthur Space (Bank Manager), Lane Bradford (Sourdough), Terry Frost (Deputy).

The third sound version and first in color of Rex Beach's well- worn novel replaces Marlene Dietrich with Anne Baxter, John Wayne with Jeff Chandler, and Randolph Scott with Rory Calhoun. Needless to say, it loses their charisma and spark, though it still manages to entertain. Like the 1942 version, this one prominently features the female lead, Baxter, as a wealthy saloon owner in an Alaskan boom town who falls in love with Chandler, the co-owner of the region's most profitable gold mine. Chandler, however, falls victim to a scheme engineered by Calhoun, who pretends to be an upstanding gold commissioner. In cahoots with Calhoun is a corrupt judge, Reid, and his attractive niece, Britton, with whom Chandler falls in love. A helpless pawn in Calhoun's game, Chandler is jailed on a murder charge, but he manages to break out when he learns the extent of the corruption. Together with his partner, McIntire, Chandler reopens his mine and confronts Calhoun. This all leads up to the patented "Spoiler's fistfight" which has appeared in all five versions of the film (including two silents). Following the precedent set in 1914 by William Farnum and Tom Santschi, Chandler and Calhoun go after each other in a long drawn-out battle. Fists fly, furniture splinters, boots kick, glass shatters, and, in a new twist, the battle is waged in the mud-smothered streets of Nome. Considering the amount of mileage the studios had gotten out of the Beach novel from 1914 to 1955, one would think that a sixth reworking would have followed right along.

p, Ross Hunter; d, Jesse Hibbs; w, Oscar Brodney, Charles Hoffman (based on the novel by Rex Beach and the play by Beach, James MacArthur); ph, Maury Gertsman (Technicolor); ed, Paul Weatherwax; md, Joseph Gershenson; art d, Alexander Golitzen, Alfred Sweeney; cos, Bill Thomas.

Western   **(PR:C MPAA:NR)**

SPOILERS OF THE FOREST*½   (1957) 68m REP c

Rod Cameron (Boyd Caldwell), Vera Ralston (Joan Milna), Ray Collins (Eric Warren), Hillary Brooke (Phyllis Warren), Edgar Buchanan (Tom Duncan), Carl Benton Reid (John Mitchell), Sheila Bromley (Linda Mitchell), Hank Worden (Casey), John Compton (Billy Mitchell), John Alderson (Big Jack Milna), Angela Greene (Camille), Paul Stader (Dan), Mary Alan Hokanson (Marie Milna), Raymond Greenleaf (Clyde Walters), Eleanor Audley (Mrs. Walters), Don Haggerty (Williams the Ranger), William Haade (Loader), Jo Ann Lilliquist (Joan Milna as a Child), Bucko Stafford (Billy Mitchell as a Child), Robert Karnes, Ken Dibbs (Drivers), Rory Mallinson (Timber Cruiser), Virginia Carroll (Sarah the Maid), John Patrick (Bartender), Bob Swan (Secretary), Mack Williams (Minister), Theresa Harris (Nancy the Maid), Helen Wallace (Fainting Woman), Pauline Moore (Hysterical Woman), Judd Holdren (Mr. Peyton).

Woodsy drama, set in Montana, starring Ralston as owner of 64,000 acres of rich timberland who battles the efforts of lumbermen Collins and Cameron to cut down the trees. Cameron woos Ralston in hope of getting shot at the timber, but true love soon develops. This was one of the last movies to be made by the Republic studio, which abandoned film production in the 1950s for television fare.

p, Herbert J. Yates; d, Joe Kane; w, Bruce Manning; ph, Jack Marta (Trucolor); ed, Richard L. Van Enger; md, Gerald Roberts; art d, Frank

Arrigo; cos, Alexis Davidoff.

Drama   **(PR:A MPAA:NR)**

SPOILERS OF THE NORTH*½   (1947) 66m REP bw

Paul Kelly (Matt Garraway), Adrian Booth (Jane Koster), Evelyn Ankers (Laura Reed), James A. Millican (Bill Garraway), Roy Barcroft (Moose McGovern), Louis Jean Heydt (Inspector Winters), Ted Hecht (Joe Taku), Harlan Briggs (Salty), Francis McDonald (Pete Koster), Maurice Cass (Doctor), Neyle Morrow (Johnny).

Evil salmon fisher Kelly plots to seduce Ankers in hopes she will loan him the money to start a new fish cannery. When that's done, he charms Booth into drafting illegal Indian labor to work at his salmon-canning plant. All this double-dealing catches up with him when Booth's brother, McDonald, blows the whistle on his schemes.

p, Donald H. Brown; d, Richard Sale; w, Milton M. Raison; ph, Alfred Keller; ed, William Thompson; md, Mort Glickman; art d, Paul Youngblood; spec eff, Howard Lydecker, Theodore Lydecker.

Drama   **(PR:A MPAA:NR)**

SPOILERS OF THE PLAINS**   (1951) 68m REP bw

Roy Rogers (Himself), Penny Edwards (Frankie Manning), Gordon Jones (Splinters), Grant Withers (Gregory Camwell), William Forrest (Dr. J.D. Manning), Don Haggerty (Ben Rix), Fred Kohler, Jr (Brooks), House Peters, Jr (Scheller), George Meeker (Scientist), Keith Richards (Guard), Foy Willing and The Riders of the Purple Sage, Trigger the Horse, Bullet the Dog.

Slightly offbeat Rogers western features him battling an evil gang of foreign spies, led by Withers, who are intent on stealing a government weather satellite from a top-secret missile base. With the help of Trigger and Rogers' new dog, Bullet, the hero foils the rotten spies and battles to the death with Withers on top of an oil derrick. Nonstop action. (See ROY ROGERS Series, Index.)

p, Edward J. White; d, William Witney; w, Sloan Nibley; ph, Jack Marta; m, R. Dale Butts; ed, Tony Martinelli; spec eff, Howard Lydecker, Theodore Lydecker; m/l, Jack Elliott, Aaron Go nzales, Foy Willing.

Western   **(PR:A MPAA:NR)**

SPOILERS OF THE RANGE*   (1939) 57m COL bw

Charles Starrett (Jeff Strong), Iris Meredith (Madge Patterson), Dick Curtis (Lobo Savage), Kenneth MacDonald (Cash Fenton), Hank Bell (Sheriff), Bob Nolan (Bob), Edward LeSaint (Dan Patterson), Forbes Murray (David Rowland), Art Mix (Santos), Edmund Cobb (Kendall), Edward Peil, Sr (Harper), Ethan Laidlaw, Charles Brinley, Joe Weaver, Horace B. Carpenter, Sons of the Pioneers.

Dull Starrett western in which a crooked gambler fleeces the local ranchers by conning them into a $50,000 debt over a dam they've just built. The ranchers go along with the con man's terms and agree to pay off the dough on the due date to avoid stiff penalties, but the crook doesn't want the money on time so he hires some guns to prevent the cattlemen from getting their beef to market on time, thus rendering them broke. Of course, Starrett rides to the rescue.

p, Harry L. Decker; d, C.C. Coleman, Jr.; w, Paul Franklin; ph, Allen Siegler; ed, William Lyon; md, Morris Stoloff; m/l, Bob Nolan, Tim Spencer.

Western   **(PR:A MPAA:NR)**

SPOILS OF THE NIGHT**½   (1969, Jap.) 84m Toho/William Mishkin
                                                                          bw (IRO)

Tatsuo Umemiya (Toru Matoba), Mako Midori (Kazuko Uehara), Reiko Ohara (Hatsue Uehara), Akiyo Kubo (Older Woman).

Bartender/pimp/gigolo Umemiya snares naive sisters Midori and Ohara, forcing Midori to become a prostitute. When rival pimps get word of this, they give him a savage beating for which he is hospitalized. Soon after, Midori is arrested for solicitation and Umemiya refuses responsibility. Ohara, seeking revenge for what he has done to her sister, kills Umemiya. (In Japanese; English subtitles.)

d, Shinji Murayama; w, Masashige Narusawa; ph, Hanjiro Nakazawa; English titles, Lewis Mishkin.

Drama   **(PR:C-O MPAA:NR)**

SPOOK BUSTERS**½   (1946) 68m MON bw

Leo Gorcey (Terence "Slip" Mahoney), Huntz Hall (Sach), Douglas Dumbrille (Dr. Coslow), Bobby Jordan (Bobby), Gabriel Dell (Gabe), Billy Benedict (Whitey), David Gorcey (Chuck), Tanis Chandler (Mignon), Maurice Cass (Dr. Bender), Vera Lewis (Mrs. Grimm), Charles Middleton (Stiles), Chester Clute (Brown), Richard Alexander (Ivan), Bernard Gorcey (Louis Xavier Dumbrowski), Charles Millsfield (Dean Pettyboff), Arthur Miles (Herman),

Tom Coleman (Police Capt. Ryan).

Dan Ackroyd and Harold Ramis didn't come up with the idea for their inexplicably popular mega-hit GHOSTBUSTERS (1984) on their own–they borrowed it from the Bowery Boys. Gorcey, Hall and company go to school to learn how to be exterminators and their first assignment brings them to a haunted mansion filled with ghosts that must be eliminated. Not only are there ghosts in the house, but also mad scientist Dumbrille, who wants to transplant Hall's brain into the skull of a large, hairy gorilla. Eventually the boys manage to anesthetize the doc and his helpers, allowing them to get away. Pretty funny as Bowery Boys movies go. The first directed by William "One Shot" Beaudine, who would end up with a staggering 25 BOWERY BOYS films to his credit. (See BOWERY BOYS series, Index.)

p, Jan Grippo; d, William Beaudine; w, Edmond Seward, Tim Ryan; ph, Harry Neumann; ed, Richard Currier, William Austin; md, Edward J. Kay; makeup, Harry Ross.

Comedy   (PR:A   MPAA:NR)

SPOOK CHASERS*½   (1957) 62m AA bw

Huntz Hall (Horace Debussy), "Sach" Jones, Stanley Clements (Stanislaus 'Duke' Coreleski), David Gorcey (Chuck), Jimmy Murphy (Myron), Percy Helton (Mike Clancy), Darlene Fields (Dolly Owens), Eddie LeRoy (Blinky), Bill Henry (Harry Shelby), Peter Mamakos (Snap Sizzolo), Ben Welden (Ziggie), Robert Shayne (Lt. Harris), Robert Christopher (Ernie), Pierre Watkin (Dr. Moss), Audrey Conti (1st Doll), Anne Fleming (2nd Doll), Bill Cassidy (Photographer).

Once again the Bowery Boys find themselves in a haunted house, this one owned by local cafe owner Helton, who buys a dilapidated farmhouse, sight unseen, in which to relax. Of course everyone is disappointed when they see the condition of the place, but it really doesn't matter because Hall and the gang find a small cash fortune stashed inside. Shady realtor Henry becomes suspicious when the boys pay off the mortgage with a big wad of cash, and he decides he wants his property back. Local hoods also take an interest and soon all converge at the farmhouse. The boys, meanwhile, are fighting off some unfriendly ghosts, but the spooks turn out to be Henry and his equally evil secretary Fields, who are trying to scare the gang off the property. In the end all the crooks get turned over to the cops. (See BOWERY BOYS Series, Index.)

p, Ben Schwalb; d, George Blair; w, Elwood Ullman; ph, Harry Neumann; ed, Neil Brunnenkant; md, Marlin Skiles; art d, David Milton; spec eff, Augie Lohman; makeup, Emile LaVigne.

Comedy   (PR:A   MPAA:NR)

SPOOK TOWN*   (1944) 59m PRC bw

Dave O'Brien, James Newill, Guy Wilkerson, Mady Lawrence, Dick Curtis, Harry Harvey, Edward Cassidy, Charles King, Jr, Robert Barron, Richard Alexander, John Cason.

Ranchers turn their savings over to the Rangers for safekeeping, but a thief makes off with the loot. Angry ranchers blame the Ranger captain, but his men locate the money and the man who killed the thief who took it. Average entry in the series, still good fun. (See TEXAS RANGERS series, Index.)

p, Arthur Alexander; d&w, Elmer Clifton; ph, Robert C. Cline; ed, Charles Henkel, Jr.; md, Lee Zahler.

Western   (PR:A   MPAA:NR)

SPOOK WHO SAT BY THE DOOR, THE zero   (1973) 102m UA c

Lawrence Cook (Dan Freeman), Paula Kelly (Dahomey Queen), Janet League (Joy), J.A. Preston (Dawson), Paul Butler (Do-Daddy Dean), Don Blakely (Stud Davis), David Lemieux (Pretty Willie), Byron Morrow (General), Jack Aaron (Carstairs), Joseph Mascolo (Senator), Beverly Gill (Willa), Bob Hill (Calhoun), Jeff Hamilton (Policeman), Margaret Kromgols (Old Woman), Tom Alderman (Security Officer), Stephen Ferry (Colonel), Kathy Berk (Doris), Stephen Ferry II (Boy Guardsman), Frank Lesley (Commentator), Harold Johnson (Jackson), Anthony Ray (Shorty), Audrey Stevenson (Mrs. Duncan), John Charles (Stew), Ponciano Olayta, Jr (Soo), Sidney Eden (Inspector), Colostine Boatwright (Dancer), Johnny Williams (Waiter), Cora Williams, Bobbie Gene Williams, Ernie Robinson, Doug Johnson, Mark Williams, Robert Franklia, Jim Heard, Lenard Norris, Walter Lowe, Harold Harris, Kenneth Lee Orme, Don Greenlee, Johnnie Johnson, Maurice Wicks, Clinton Malcome, Larry Lawrence, Tyrone Livingston, James Mitchell, Frank E. Ford, Perry Thomas, Orlanders Thomas, Rodney McGrader, Ramon Livingston, Virgie Johnson.

Disturbing, violent, reverse-racist blaxploitation drama directed by "Hogan's Heroes" alumnus Ivan Dixon. Cook stars as the token black employee of the CIA. He eventually gets fed up with being shown off as a set piece during guided tours and quits to form an army of black "freedom fighters" in order to overthrow the country. His cadre recruits young, disorganized and unskilled black urban hoodlums and then trains them in the fine art of terrorism. The bunch then steals advanced weaponry from a National Guard armory and launches a bloody campaign, slaughtering scores of

"white devils." Offensive, mindless action, badly handled and conceived.

p, Ivan Dixon, Sam Greenlee; d, Dixon; w, Greenlee, Melvin Clay (based on the novel The Spook Who Sat By The Door by Greenlee); ph, Michel Hugo; m, Herbie Hancock; ed, Michael Kahn; art d, Leslie Thomas; set d, Sheryl Kearney; cos, Henry Salley.

Drama   (PR:O   MPAA:PG)

SPOOKS RUN WILD½**   (1941) 65m MON bw (GB: GHOSTS ON
                                                              THE LOOSE)

Bela Lugosi (Nardo the Monster), Leo Gorcey (Muggsy), Huntz Hall (Glimpy), Bobby Jordan (Danny), David Gorcey (Pee Wee), Sammy Morrison (Scruno), Dave O'Brien (Skinny), Dave O'Brien (Jeff Dixon), Dorothy Short (Linda Mason), Rosemary Portia (Margie), Dennis Moore ("Dr. Von Grogh"), Guy Wilkerson (Constable), Angelo Rossitto (Luigi, the Dwarf), P.J. Kelley (Len Harvey), Joe Kirk, Jack Carr, George Pembroke (Von Grosch).

Pretty good East Side Kids effort has the boys seeking refuge in a spooky old mansion after David Gorcey has suffered a gunshot wound from the pistol of a cemetery caretaker who got fed up with their shenanigans. Unfortunately, the creepy house is owned by the mysterious Lugosi, who (answering the door in full DRACULA regalia) sends chills down the boys' respective spines. After giving Gorcey something to ease his pain, Lugosi makes the boys spend the night. Soon the gang sees Gorcey wandering through the house like a zombie, and his pals assume that Lugosi has turned him into a monster. Help arrives in the form of Short, who has been looking for the missing kids. Accompanying her is Moore, a man claiming to be out to get Lugosi and to bring him to justice. After a series of comedic mishaps in the mansion, Moore is revealed to be the real menace and Lugosi turns out to be a famous magician. The silliness works due to Lugosi's straightforward, totally deadpan performance, which becomes a springboard for the goofiness of the East Side Kids. The boys and Lugosi respected one another on the set, both being intimidated by the other's reputation (East Side Kids known for their on-set pranks and rowdiness, Lugosi for his menacing "Dracula" stare and mysterious manner). Screenwriter Foreman, who was under contract to Huntz Hall early in his writing career, would later go on to co-author HIGH NOON (1952), THE BRIDGE ON THE RIVER KWAI (1957), THE GUNS OF NAVARONE (1961). (See BOWERY BOYS Series, Index.)

p, Sam Katzman; d, Phil Rosen; w, Carl Foreman, Charles Marion, Jack Henley; ph, Marcel Le Picard; ed, Robert Golden; prod d, Ed W. Rote; md, Johnny Lange, Lew Porter.

Comedy   **Cas.**   (PR:A   MPAA:NR)

SPORT OF A NATION   (SEE: ALL AMERICAN, THE, 1932)

SPORT OF KINGS, THE*½   (1931, Brit.) 90m Gainsborough/ID bw

Leslie Henson (Amos Purdie), Hugh Wakefield (Alfie Sprigge), Gordon Harker (Bates), Dorothy Boyd (Dulcie), Renee Clama (Jane), Jack Melford (Sir Reginald Toothill), Mary Jerrold (Mrs. Purdie), Barbara Gott (Cook), Wally Patch (Panama Pete), Daphne Scorer, Willie Graham.

A pair of gamblers find themselves staying at the home of a rabid anti-gambler, and they eventually convert him to the cause. The former non-better wins big at the horse track and soon sets up his own bookmaking business, but then loses his shirt on the big race and welshes. Luckily, his wife had bet on the winning horse and she wins enough money to bail him out.

p, Michael Balcon; d, Victor Saville; w, Angus Macphail (based on the play "The Sport of Kings" by Ian Hay); ph, Alex Bryce.

Comedy   (PR:A   MPAA:NR)

SPORT OF KINGS*½   (1947) 68m COL bw

Paul Campbell (Tom Cloud), Gloria Henry (Doc Richardson), Harry Davenport (Maj. Denning), Mark Dennis (Biff Cloud), Harry Cheshire (Theodore McKeogh), Clinton Rosemond (Josiah), Louis Mason (Bertie), Oscar O'Shea (Judge Sellers), Ernest Anderson (Alf).

Campbell and Dennis play two brothers from the North. They find themselves in possession of a Kentucky plantation that their father had won in a bet with the previous owner, a noted old horse racer (Davenport). Life isn't easy for the Yankee boys down South when the locals treat them as if they have the plague. To save face, the brothers bring back Davenport on a flimsy pretense, but the old man soon sees through it all. He threatens to walk until his horse, which they entered in the big race, wins the purse.

p, William Bloom; d, Robert Gordon; w, Edward Huebsch (based on a story by Gordon Grand); ph, Henry Freulich; ed, Aaron Stell; md, Mischa Bakaleinikoff; art d, Charles Clague; set d, Wilbur Menefee, William Kiernan.

Drama   (PR:A   MPAA:NR)

SPORT PARADE, THE**   (1932) 67m RKO bw

Joel McCrea (Sandy Baker), William Gargan (Johnny Brown), Marian Marsh (Irene Stewart), Walter Catlett (Promoter Morrison), Skeets Gallagher (Dizzy), Robert Benchley, Clarence H. Wilson, Ivan Linow.

McCrea plays a Cornell football star who ends up in the sportswriting biz, giving the filmmakers a dozen excuses to cut to seemingly endless stock footage of various sporting events. In the end, he manages to get himself into (and win) a wrestling match. Benchley is the highlight of the film, playing a goofy radio announcer.

d, Dudley Murphy; w, Corey Ford, Tom Wenning, Francis Cockrell (based on a story by Jerry Horwin, additional dialog by Robert Benchley); ph, J. Roy Hunt.

Drama   (PR:A MPAA:NR)

SPORTING BLOOD***   (1931) 82m MGM bw

Clark Gable (Rid Riddell), Ernest Torrence (Jim Relience), Madge Evans (Ruby), Lew Cody (Tip Scanlon), Marie Prevost (Angela), Harry Holman (Hartwick), Hallam Cooley (Ludeking), J. Farrell MacDonald (MacGuire), John Larkin (Uncle Ben), Eugene Jackson (Sammy), Tommy Boy the Horse.

Torrence is a horse breeder who sells a steed named Tommy Boy to MacDonald, a rich man interested in horses. MacDonald wins money with Tommy Boy but ends up selling the horse as well. The new owners are Prevost along with Holman, a gambler. The two make Tommy Boy work harder than he should and enter him in a race he cannot win. This angers Prevost since they end up losing a good chunk of cash. Holman goes to Gable, who runs a gambling house, and places a bet with him, hoping to win back the money he has lost. Instead he ends up losing Tommy Boy to Gable, who starts running the horse himself. At first he is honest about it, then he deliberately has Tommy Boy lose in order to win a heavy bet. Evans and Cody are two dealers who work for Gable and object to their employer using drugs on Tommy Boy. Tommy Boy then loses a big race, which puts Gable in serious trouble with some gangsters. Gable transfers ownership of the horse to Evans, who returns Tommy Boy to his original owner, Torrence. Torrence works with the horse and restores him to prime condition for the Kentucky Derby, which he wins despite pressure on Torrence from mobsters who want Tommy Boy to lose. Evans, who had previously been romantically linked with Gable, changes her mind and marries her coworker, Cody. Gable, sans mustache, took a step up from supporting cast member to featured player with this and proved that he could handle it smoothly. He is well supported by Cody and Evans, though it is Torrence who is the real standout in the cast. As the well-intentioned horse breeder, he steals scene after scene with little effort. Though the script is slight, this ensemble is talented enough to give some meat to what would have been an otherwise insignificant production. Brabin's direction is realistic, combining track footage and studio work faithfully for an honest feel to the drama. A cameo appearance is made by then-Vice President of the U.S. Charles Curtis (under President Herbert Hoover) in the racetrack footage, a fact dutifully pointed out for filmgoers by the on-screen track announcer.

d, Charles Brabin; w, Willard Mack, Wanda Tuchock (based on the novel Horseflesh by Frederick Hazlitt Brennan); ph, Harold Rossen; ed, William Gray.

Drama/Crime   (PR:A MPAA:NR)

SPORTING BLOOD**   (1940) 82m MGM bw

Robert Young (Myles Vanders), Maureen O'Sullivan (Linda Lockwood), Lewis Stone (Davis Lockwood), William Gargan (Duffy, Trainer), Lynne Carver (Joan Lockwood), Clarence Muse (Jeff), Lloyd Corrigan (Otis Winfield), George H. Reed (Stonewall), Tom Kennedy (Grantly), Russell Hicks ("Sneak" O'Brien), George Lessey (Banker Cobb), William Tannen (Ted Milner), Helene Millard (Martha Winfield), Allen Wood (Jockey), Eugene Jackson (Sam), Dora Clement, Richard Tucker (Guests), Etta McDaniel (Chloe), Claude King, Charles Wagenheim (Men At Race Track).

Young plays a struggling stable owner who returns to his run-down family homestead in Virginia and rekindles a long-standing family feud with rival Stone. Despite the danger, Young begins romancing one of Stone's daughters. After he is dumped by daughter no. 1, he immediately starts up with daughter no. 2, O'Sullivan, just to get the old man's goat. When Young's prize pony is injured in a stable fire just before an important race, he uses O'Sullivan's horse, which goes on to beat her daddy's best steed. Eventually everybody begrudgingly accepts one another at the fade.

p, Albert E. Levoy; d, S. Sylvan Simon; w, Lawrence Hazard, Albert Mannheimer, Dorothy Yost (based on a story by Grace Norton); ph, Sidney Wagner; m, Franz Waxman; ed, Frank Sullivan; art d, Cedric Gibbons, Stan Rogers; set d, Edwin B. Willis; cos, Dolly Tree.

Drama   (PR:A MPAA:NR)

SPORTING CHANCE*½   (1931) 63m Peerless bw

Buster Collier, Jr (Terry Nolan), Claudia Dell (Mary Bascom), James Hall (Phillip Lawrence, Jr.), Eugene Jackson (Horseshoes), Joseph Levering (Phillip Lawrence, Sr.), Henry Roquemore (Mullins), Hedwiga Reicher (Aunt Hetty), Mahlon Hamilton (Buddy).

Romance blossoms on the steeplechase track as suspiciously tall jockey Collier in turn sings a favorite of the day, "Old Playmat," twice and narrowly avoids the attentions of a sinister-looking man in a checkered suit. Jackson provides comic relief as a wide-eyed black stableboy. Mostly the film is an excuse for its race sequences, allegedly the first steeplechases ever staged for the talking screen, but fast-motion photography makes this very minor landmark look faked.

p&d, Albert Herman; w, King Baggott.

Drama   (PR:A MPAA:NR)

SPORTING CHANCE, A**   (1945) 55m REP bw

Jane Randolph, John O'Malley, Stephen Barclay, Edward Gargan, Isabel Withers, Janet Martin, Maxine Semon, Selmer Jackson, Robert Middlemass, Kenne Duncan.

Uninspired low-budget comedy has Randolph as a spoiled young woman who must find a job and support herself before she can inherit the family fortune. This was one of four films made in 1945 by prolific programmer director Blair.

p, Rudolph E. Abel; d, George Blair; w, Dane Lussier (based on a story by Paul Gangelin); ph, Marcel Le Picard; ed, Ralph Dixon; md, Richard Cherwin); art d, Russell Kimball; set d, Charles Thompson.

Comedy   (PR:A MPAA:NR)

SPORTING CLUB, THE zero   (1971) 107m AE c

Robert Fields (Vernor Stanton), Nicolas Coster (James Quinn), Maggie Blye (Janey), Jack Warden (Earl Olive), Richard Dysart (Spengler), William Roerick (Fortesque), Logan Ramsey (Scott), Leon B. Stevens (Olds), John Seymour (Newcombe), Helen Craig (Mrs. Olds), Diane Rousseau (Barbara), Lois Markle (Sheilah), James Noble (Canon Pritchard), Ralph Purdum (Murray), Ralph Waite (Olson), Jo Ann Harris (Lu), Linda Blair (Barby), Claibane Cary.

Obnoxious, bloody attempt at exploitative social relevancy which sees a group of rich folk traveling to a getaway in Northern Michigan. Here, all the sick decadence of the group surfaces in the space of a weekend. Orgies, killings and other gross happenings are paraded before the camera in what appears to be an extremely ignorant, modern American updating of Jean Renoir's THE RULES OF THE GAME. For a brilliant, subtle, perceptive and genuinely socially relevant masterpiece, stick to Renoir.

p, Lee M. Rich; d, Larry Peerce; w, Lorenzo Semple, Jr. (based on the novel The Sporting Club by Thomas McGuane); ph, John Courtland; m, Michael Small; ed, Lawrence Silk; art d, Joel Schiller; set d, Philip Abramson; cos, Ronald Talsky; makeup, Emile Lavigne.

Drama   (PR:O MPAA:R)

SPORTING LIFE   (SEE: NIGHT PARADE, 1929)

SPORTING LOVE**   (1936, Brit.) 70m Hammer/BL bw

Stanley Lupino (Percy Brace), Laddie Cliff (Peter Brace), Henry Carlisle (Lord Dimsdale), Eda Peel (Maud Dane), Bobbie Comber (Gerald Dane), Clarissa Selwyne (Aunty Fanny), Lu Ann Meredith (Nellie Gray), Wyn Weaver (Wilfred Wimple).

Lupino and Cliff play two young racehorse owners swimming in debts. They try to talk their rich aunt into giving them money in order to get back in the black. Consequently, they must pretend they've gotten married in order to please their aunt and release the money. The usual complications occur. Funny enough.

p, H. Fraser Passmore; d, J. Elder Wills; w, Fenn Sherie, Ingram D'Abbes (based on the play by Stanley Lupino); ph, Eric Cross.

Comedy   (PR:A MPAA:NR)

SPORTING WIDOW, THE   (SEE: MADAME RACKETEER, 1932)

SPOT   (SEE: DOGPOUND SHUFFLE, 1975, Can.)

SPOT OF BOTHER, A**   (1938, Brit.) 70m Pinebrook/GFD bw

Robertson Hare (Mr. Rudd), Alfred Drayton (Mr. Watney), Sandra Storme (Sadie), Kathleen Joyce (Margaret Watney), Ruth Maitland (Mrs. Watney), Gordon James (Joe), Robert Hale (Col. Pigge), Fewlass Llewellyn (Bishop of Barchester), Drusilla Wills (Miss Hagworthy), Julien Vedey (Scheipman), Edie Martin.

The cathedral restoration fund is short of its goal by 1,000 pounds, so bishop

Llewellyn turns the money over to Drayton, who promises to use it to raise the extra thousand within 24 hours. Drayton uses the money to buy smuggled goods, including silk lingerie and brandy. Selling the brandy at the church sale raises the needed money. Decent comedy with some good character performances.

p, Anthony Havelock-Allan; d, David MacDonald; w, John Cousins, Stephen Clarkson, A.B. Rawlinson (based on a play by Vernon Sylvaine); ph, Francis Carver.

Comedy   **(PR:A   MPAA:NR)**

SPOTLIGHT SCANDALS½**   (1943) 79m MON bw

Billy Gilbert, Frank Fay, Bonnie Baker (Themselves), Billy Lenhardt (Butch), Charles K. Brown (Buddy), Harry Langdon (Oscar), Iris Adrian (Bernice), Jimmy Hollywood, Eddie Burtell, Syd Chalton (Radio Rogues), James Bush (Jerry), Claudia Dell (Betty), Betty Blythe (Mrs. Baker), Eddie Parks, Henry King, Herb Miller (Themselves), Lottie Harrison (Suzy), Jim Hope (Blondel), Jack Boyle (Dance Director).

Gilbert stars as a small-town barber who hooks up with vaudeville comedian Fay when the latter needs a partner for his new act. The duo becomes a hit, but Gilbert nobly bows out when he learns that Fay has the chance to find fame as a radio star–if he goes solo. The two are reunited, however, when Fay finds himself in a tight spot and Gilbert dashes to his rescue. Songs include: "The Restless Age" (Ed Rose, Abe Olman), "Goodnight Now," "The Lilac Tree," "Tempo of The Trail," "Oh Johnny."

p, Sam Katzman, Jack Dietz; d, William Beaudine; w, William X. Crowley, Biryl Sachs; ph, Mack Stengler; ed, Carl Pierson; md, Edward Kay; ch, Jack Boyle.

Comedy/Musical   **(PR:A   MPAA:NR)**

SPOTS ON MY LEOPARD, THE½**   (1974, S. Africa) 97m Kavalier/Falcon American c

Mark Hopley (Robbie), Karen de Kock (Kati), Dale Cutts (Robbie's Father), Erica Rogers (Robbie's Mother), Bess Finney (Miss Baker), Denis Smith (Mr. Mantz), Van Dunlop (Liz), Delia Sheppard (Lulu), Johan Swanepoet (Philip).

South Africa's equivalent of a Disney boy-and-his-dog film sees two lonely children, Hopley and de Kock, adopting a wild cheetah. They turn it into a loving pet, only to have it taken from them and put in a travelling circus. Not wanting to see their pet locked up, the children make their way to the circus, steal the cat back, and eventually release it into the wild. Beautiful photography of South Africa combined with a heart-warming, albeit typical, story form, a film that will please undiscriminating family audiences.

p, Ben Vlok; d & ed, Tim Spring; w, Beyer Boshoff; ph, Ivo Pellegrini; m, Ina & Inno Leuvennink.

Drama   **(PR:A   MPAA:NR)**

SPRING½**   (1948, USSR) 105m Mosfilm/Artkino bw

Lubov Orlova (Irina Nikitina/Vera Shayrova Shatrova), Nikolai Cherkassov (Arkady Gromov), Nikolai Konovalov (Mukhin), Mikhail Sidorkin (Nikolai Roschin), Fenya Ranyevskaya (Nikitina's Housekeeper), Rostislav Pinaff (Rubenstov), Boris Petker (Operetta Director), Corps de Ballet of the Bolshoi Theater.

The Soviets attempted to make a musical and wound up with a very sorry resemblance to a Hollywood effort. Plot has a dancer who looks like a famous scientist getting to actually portray the scientist when a film studio decides to make a film about her. The film would probably be a lot better if one understood Russian, but as is, it's not very good nor very funny. (In Russian; English subtitles.)

d, Gregory Alexandrov; w, Alexandrov, A. Raskin, M. Slobodsky; ph, Yuri Yekelchik; m, Issac Dunayevsky, Vasyll Lebedyev-Kumach.

Musical/Comedy   **(PR:A   MPAA:NR)**

SPRING AFFAIR   (1960) 79m George Bagnall Associates bw

Lindsay Workman (Wilbur Crane), Merry Anders (Dorothy), Yvonne White (Martha), Don Kennedy (Dan), Albert Carrier (Arthur), Ron Kennedy (Ted), Coleman Francis (Smith), Oween Cameron (Elsie), Shawn Mallory (Model), Ellen Marty (Waitress), Cecile Rogers (Registrar), Brad Olson (Instructor), Charles Calvert (Tailor), Terry Loomis (Imaginary Blonde), Pat Wiles (Counter Blonde).

Workman plays a browbeaten husband who takes to carrying on with a prostitute. He becomes involved beyond the point of control, only to wake up and find it had all been a dream. Good technical credits for having to work on a very low budget. Producer Ray promised to donate half the profits received from this picture to the cancer fund, his wife having recently died from the dread disease.

p, d&w, Bernard "B.B." Ray; ph, Elmer Dyer, Roland Price; m, Manuel Francisco; ed, George Merrick.

Drama   **(PR:A   MPAA:NR)**

SPRING AND PORT WINE½**   (1970, Brit.) 101m Memorial/E.M.I. Anglo-Warner Pathe c

James Mason (Rafe Crompton), Susan George (Hilda Crompton), Diana Coupland (Daisy Crompton), Rodney Bewes (Harold Crompton), Hannah Gordon (Florence Crompton), Len Jones (Wilfred Crompton), Keith Buckley (Arthur Gasket), Adrienne Posta (Betty Duckworth), Avril Elgar (Betsy Jane Duckworth), Frank Windsor (Ned Duckworth), Ken Parry (Pawnbroker), Bernard Bresslaw (Lorry Driver), Arthur Lowe (Mr. Aspinall), Marjorie Rhodes (Mrs. Gasket), Joe Greig (Allan, TV Man), Christopher Timothy (Joe, TV Man), Eddie Robertson, Sandra Downes (Pay Clerks), Maria Mantella, George Nutkins, Reg Green, Jack Howarth (Weavers), Brian Mosley, Bryan Pringle, John Sharp (Bowlers).

The orderly existence of the Crompton family almost falls apart when strict father, Mason, takes things too far by demanding that his daughter, George, eat a piece of herring. Not wishing to be disobeyed, he serves the same herring everyday at tea time, waiting for George to change her mind. This simple catalyst nearly results in the mother's (Coupland) suicide, after she sells his new jacket to obtain money for George to escape to London, then is afraid to face Mason's wrath. A simple and effective look at the tensions within a family, concentrating not only on differences in age but on individual selfishness and closed-mindedness as well. Mason is wonderful as always, but the character he portrays is not always believable, especially in the explanation for his tyrannical behavior.

p, Michael Medwin; d, Peter Hammond; w, Bill Naughton (based on the play by Naughton); ph, Norman Warwick (Technicolor); m, Douglas Gamley; ed, Fergus McDonell.

Drama   **(PR:C-O   MPAA:NR)**

SPRING BREAK   (1983) 101m COL c

David Onell (Nelson), Steve Bassett (O.T.), Perry Lang (Adam), Paul Land (Stu), Richard B. Shull (Eddie), Corinne Alphen (Joan), Jayne Modean (Susie), Donald Symington (Ernest Dalby), Mimi Cozzens (May Dalby), Jessica James (Geri), Daniel Faraldo (Eesh), John Archie, Robert Small (Henchman), Fred Buch (Ames), Mark Pellicori (Biker), Bobbi Fritz, Rhonda Flynn (Girls in Corvette), Bert Sheldon (Detective), Alex Panas (Dope Dealer), Barry Hober (Man in Elevator), Ronn Carroll (Arresting Officer), Roger Minami (Dancing Officer), Paul Lorenzo (Candy Store M.C.), John Terry (Button M.C.), Marilyn Max, Lois Chamberlain, Laura J. Galgozy, Johanna Mileschikowsky (Hot Date Band Member), Elenore Raabe, Sheila Kennedy, Kathy Ryan, Maria Sedano, Christine Georgopulo (Girls).

Another worthless sex comedy which litters movie screens just on time for spring break. This one has four college guys being tossed into a hotel room together while trying to find romance on the beach. What passes for a plot is Knell's attempts to avoid his stepfather, Symington, a wealthy political candidate who wants his son's support. Symington sends his henchmen down to Ft. Lauderdale to track down Knell, but he manages to outwit them. Otherwise it's just an average beach movie complete with a token centerfold–1982 Penthouse Playmate of the Year, Alphen. Directed by Sean Cunningham of FRIDAY THE 13TH fame. Includes a second-rate rock 'n' roll soundtrack with Cheap Trick performing "Spring Break" (Rick Nielson) and .38 Special doing their hit tune "Caught Up In You." Harry Manfredini performs "Lauderdale Ladies," "Have Some Fun Tonight," "Do It to You" (Manfredini). Hot Date performs "Friends" (Marilyn Max). Big Spender delivers "Here Comes Trouble," "Hit the Beach" (Stephan Sasloe, Tommy McCulloh); NRBQ plays "Me and the Boys;" The Dreamers perform "Kids These Days;" Jack Mack and the Heart Attack perform "True Lovin' Woman," "Heart of the City."

p&d, Sean S. Cunningham; w, David Smilow; ph, Stephen Poster (Metrocolor); m, Harry Manfredi; ed, Susan Cunningham, Angie Ross; prod d, Virginia Field; art d, Nicholas Romanac; set d, Tom Coll; cos, Susan Denison, Sara Denning; ch, Roger Minami; stunts, Alexander Edlin, Mike Kirton, Arti Malesci, Jeff Moldovan, Peter Tors, Jay Amor, James Bates, Courtney Brown, Charles Buie, Bob Kenaston, March Mercury; makeup, Elizabeth Lambert.

Comedy   **Cas.**   **(PR:O   MPAA:R)**

SPRING FEVER½**   (1983, Can.) 100m Amulet/Comworld c

Susan Anton (Stevie Castle), Frank Converse (Louis Corman), Jessica Walter (Celia Berryman), Stephen Young (Neil Berryman), Carling Bassett (Karen Castle), David Mall (Beechman), Lisa Brady (Rhoda), Barbara Cook (Chris), Maria Hontzas (Bunny), Alan Fawcett (Roger), Derrick Jones (Scotty), Lisa Foster (Lena), Brian Crabb (Ralph), Martin Schecter (Umpire), Stephen Shellin (Andy), Shawn Foltz (Melissa Berryman), Sheldon Rybowski (Mike), Tina Basle, Stacey Schefflin, Katie Lawrence, Heidi Bassett, Ed Montgomery, Dale Houlihan, Briane Nasimok, Ray Bouchard, Diana Goad, Ron Jackson, Joe Rujas, Danielle Bollettieri, Cayce Connell, John Maschino, Gaston Forest, Bill Ciaccia, Michael Doby, Earl Summerline, Craig Thomas, Don Fontana, Michael Lara, Doug Manley, Al Orzechowski, David Richardson, Michael Allen Willis.

Boring flick about a group of young girls competing in a junior tennis championship. One of the girls (Carling Bassett) has a tough time making any friends because her mom, Anton, is just too good looking. She eventually establishes a friendship with another player, making for the little bit of plot that exists. When tennis balls aren't flying across the screen, some very poor acting is in evidence.

p, John F. Bassett; d, Joseph L. Scanlan; w, Fred Stefan, Stuart Gillard; ph, Donald Wilder (Film House Color); m, Fred Mollin; ed, Kirk Jones, Tony Lower ; art d, Bruno Rubeo, Carmi Gallo; set d, Richard D. Allen.

Drama   **Cas.**   **(PR:C   MPAA:PG)**

SPRING HANDICAP*   (1937, Brit.) 68m ABF bw

Will Fyffe (*Jack Clayton*), Maire O'Neill (*Meg Clayton*), Billy Milton (*Len Redpath*), Aileen Marson (*Barbara Clayton*), Frank Pettingell (*Scullion*), David Burns (*Amos*), Hugh Miller (*Selby*), Beatrice Barley (*Mrs. Tulip*).

Fyffe is a miner who inherits a fortune and then proceeds to lose a big piece of it at the racetrack. After he proves to be failure at betting, bookmaking, and owning, his wife finally talks some sense into him and Fyffe forgets about the horses. Not one of the sly comedian's more noteworthy efforts.

p, Walter C. Mycroft; d, Herbert Brenon; w, Elizabeth Meehan, William Freshman (based on the play "The Last Coupon" by Ernest E. Bryan).

Comedy   **(PR:A   MPAA:NR)**

SPRING IN PARK LANE***½   (1949, Brit.) 91m Imperadio/EL bw

Anna Neagle (*Judy Howard*), Michael Wilding (*Richard*), Tom Walls (*Uncle Joshua Howard*), Peter Graves (*Basil Maitland*), Marjorie Fielding (*Mildred Howard*), Nicholas Phipps (*Marquis of Borechester*), G.H. Mulcaster (*Perkins*), Catherine Paul (*Lady Borechester*), Josephine Fitzgerald (*Kate O'Malley*), Nigel Patrick (*Mr. Bacon*), Lana Morris (*Rosie*), H.R. Hignett (*Higgins*), Cyril Conway (*Antique Dealer*), Tom Walls, Jr (*Bates*).

A charming, light-hearted romp that is the essence of British drawing-room comedy. As in most good movies, it's the characters that take precedence over the plot and this one is as thin as the slices on a one-dollar turkey sandwich. Neagle works as the secretary for her uncle, the very rich Walls, who is a well-known collector of objets d'art. Into the mansion comes a new footman, Wilding, but Neagle questions his background as he appears far too sophisticated and reeking of class to have spent his early years in service. It turns out that Wilding is the son of a very rich family and in temporary need of money to get him to New York. Right now, he's lying low because he sold his family's art collection and took a bum check for the goods and he fears that his mistake will put him in bad stead with them. So until he can straighten matters out, he's posing as a domestic servant. While at the house, we are introduced to a multitude of types including satiric barbs at ego-inflated movie people, Colonel Blimp-type bores and the majoress domo who runs the house as though she owned it. It goes without saying that it works out in the end as Wilding and Neagle fall madly for each other and the check he'd taken turns out to be good after all. Wilding is wonderful in his role and rolls out the excellent script quips with perfection. Walls' son, Tom Jr., also makes an appearance and lest you confuse the Peter Graves listed in the cast with the one who spent so many years on TV's "Mission Impossible," be aware that they are two different blokes and this one is 14 years older. After a tiny role in MRS. PYM OF SCOTLAND YARD in 1939, Nigel Patrick had to wait almost a decade until he was cast in this movie, which began a career that saw him appear in many movies, notably SAPPHIRE, THE LEAGUE OF GENTLEMEN, THE PICKWICK PAPERS, and THE BROWNING VERSION. The joy of this movie is in the uproarious situations and the gleaming-bright witticisms in the Phipps screenplay. The one song's music was written by American Manning Sherwin, who went to England before the war because he couldn't sell his tunes in the U.S. and stayed there for years, writing many songs, including the most-British "A Nightingale Sang In Berkeley Square," and music for several reviews in London. Neagle, Britain's top star, was married to producer-director Wilcox and their production company made the film at the Amalgamated studios in England. Generally regarded as the best of the many light comedies stemming from their collaborative efforts, the picture was the top money-maker in Britain in 1948, the year of its release there.

p&d, Herbert Wilcox; w, Nicholas Phipps (based on the play "Come Out of the Kitchen" by Alice Duer Miller); ph, Max Greene [Mutz Greenbaum]; m, Robert Farnon; ed, F. Clarke, R. Poulton; md, Farnon; art d, W.C. Andrews; m/l, "The Moment I Saw You," Manning Sherwin, Harold Purcell; makeup, Harold Fletcher.

Comedy   **(PR:A   MPAA:NR)**

SPRING IN THE AIR*   (1934, Brit.) 74m Stafford/Pathe bw

Edmund Gwenn (*Franz*), Zelma O'Neal (*Ilona*), Theo Shall (*Paul*), Lydia Sherwood (*Vilma*), Gus McNaughton (*Max*), Mary Jerrold (*Albertina*), Winifred Oughton (*Minna*), Jane Welsh (*Rosa*).

O'Neal pretends to be the maid of Budapest friends Sherwood and McNaughton so that she can be near Shall, a frog expert who lives upstairs. McNaughton tries to seduce her, and concierge Gwenn Believes she is his

long-lost daughter. Complications abound until she ends up in the arms of Shall. An unfunny comedy that is best forgotten.

p, John Stafford; d&w, Victor Hanbury, Norman Lee.

Musical/Comedy   **(PR:A   MPAA:NR)**

SPRING IS HERE**   (1930) 65m FN bw

Lawrence Gray (*Steve Alden*), Alexander Gray (*Terry Clayton*), Bernice Claire (*Betty Braley*), Ford Sterling (*Peter Braley*), Louise Fazenda (*Emily Braley*), Inez Courtney (*Mary Jane Braley*), Natalie Moorhead (*Rita Clayton*), Frank Albertson (*Stacy Hayden*), Gretchen Thomas (*Maude Osgood*), Wilbur Mack, The Brox Sisters.

Silly musical has Claire courted by two men, Lawrence Gray and Alexander Gray, only one of whom is approved of by father Sterling. When the no-good Alexander Gray tries to elope with Claire, the other Gray arrives and carries her off. Songs include, "Spring Is Here in Person," "I Married an Angel," "Yours Sincerely," "Rich Man, Poor Man," "Baby's Awake Now," "With a Song in My Heart" (Richard Rodgers, Lorenz Hart), "Cryin' for the Carolines," "Have a Little Faith In Me," "Bad Baby," and "How Shall I Tell?" (Sam Lewis, Joe Young, Harry Warren).

d, John Francis Dillon; w, James A. Starr (based on the stage musical by Owen Davis, Lorenz Hart, Richard Rodgers); ph, Lee Garmes.

Musical   **(PR:A   MPAA:NR)**

SPRING MADNESS**   (1938) 80m MGM bw

Maureen O'Sullivan (*Alexandra Benson*), Lew Ayres (*Sam Thatcher*), Ruth Hussey (*Kate McKim*), Burgess Meredith (*The Lippencott*), Ann Morriss (*Frances*), Joyce Compton (*Sally*), Jacqueline Wells [Julie Bishop] (*Mady Platt*), Frank Albertson (*Hat*), Truman Bradley (*Walter Beckett*), Marjorie Gateson (*Miss Ritchie*), Renie Riano (*Mildred*), Sterling Holloway (*Buck*), Dick Baldwin (*Doc*).

Frivolous story has O'Sullivan and Ayres as a pair of college lovers about ready to face graduation, with Ayres planning to take a two-year excursion to Europe with roomy Meredith. By the time O'Sullivan gets through with him though, he decides to stay behind. Performers look a bit old to be playing college kids, but otherwise do a satisfactory job.

p, Edward Chodorov; d, S. Sylvan Simon; w, Chodorov, Eleanor Golden, Eloise Barrangon (based on the play "Spring Dance" by Phillip Barry); ph, Joseph Ruttenberg; m, Dr. William Axt; ed, Conrad A. Nervig.

Drama/Comedy   **(PR:A   MPAA:NR)**

SPRING MEETING**½   (1941, Brit.) 93m Pathe Pictures bw

Enid Stamp-Taylor (*Tiny Fox-Collier*), Michael Wilding (*Tony Fox-Collier*), Basil Sydney (*James, Butler*), Sarah Churchill (*Joan Furze*), Nova Pilbeam (*Baby Furze*), W.G. Fay (*Johnny*), Margaret Rutherford (*Aunt Bijou*), Henry Edwards (*Sir Richard Furze*), Hugh McDermott (*Michael Byrne*), Kieran Turney.

Stamp-Taylor plays a widow who is down on her luck and trying to get back on her feet. She attempts to arrange a marriage between her son, Wilding, and Churchill, daughter of a former flame. To everyone's surprise, Wilding falls for the charming younger sister, who is absent of the distasteful qualities shared by her sister and father. Highlights come in the characterizations of Rutherford as an eccentric aunt and Sydney as the family butler. The performances of these two make for some very delightful moments.

p&d, Walter C. Mycroft; w, Mycroft, Norman Lee (based on the play by M.J. Farrell, John Percy); ph, Walter Harvey.

Comedy   **(PR:A   MPAA:NR)**

SPRING NIGHT, SUMMER NIGHT   (SEE: MISS JESSICA IS
                                         PREGNANT, 1970)

SPRING PARADE***   (1940) 89m UNIV bw

Deanna Durbin (*Ilonka Tolnay*), Robert Cummings (*Harry Marten*), Mischa Auer (*The Peasant*), Henry Stephenson (*The Emperor*), S.Z. Sakall (*The Baker*), Butch and Buddy (*The Kids*), Walter Catlett (*Headwaiter*), Anne Gwynne (*Jenny*), Allyn Joslyn (*Count Zorndof*), Peggy Moran (*Irene*), Reginald Denny (*Captain*), Franklin Pangborn (*Wiedelmeyer*), Ed Gargan (*Fortune-Teller*), Samuel S. Hinds (*Von Zibberl*).

Universal was in deep trouble until Durbin came along. Her popularity is what saved the studio as she made one picture after another and became one of the biggest stars of her era. From 1936, when she made THREE SMART GIRLS, until 1947–when she retired after appearing in 21 pictures–she was the undisputed queen of the San Fernando Valley lot. In SPRING PARADE, producer Pasternak altered her all-American image to remake a movie he'd done in Hungary in 1934, a sweet Viennese story that was as close to being an operetta as a movie could get without Nelson Eddy or Jeanette MacDonald. Durbin is seen at a fair in Austria where Gargan, a fortune teller, sells her a card that says she will meet an important person and have a happy marriage. The young Hungarian gets a job as a baker's assistant to Sakall (who had just come to the U.S. and was in his second film, after IT'S A DATE). She next meets Cummings, a drummer corporal with the army who yearns to compose and conduct his own music. He is not allowed to write music due to certain military restrictions but Durbin takes one of his waltzes and sends it to the Emperor, Stephenson, along with the standing royal order of baked goods. Stephenson is a benevolent monarch and when he learns what she's done, he orders a command performance with Durbin singing while Cummings conducts. The picture ends happily as the young lovers are united and Cummings is acknowledged as a brilliant composer. It's a throwback to days of yore, long before Hitler marched back into Austria to take it over on behalf of Germany. There is not a shred of reality to the story but it's so light, engaging, and tuneful that audiences were willing to forget the newspaper headlines and settle back to watch the way it used to be in Vienna. Although technically a musical, there weren't that many songs. The score featured "Blue Danube Dream" (music by Johann Strauss, words by Gus Kahn), "When April Sings," "Waltzing In The Clouds," "It's Foolish But It's Fun" (Robert Stolz, Gus Kahn), "In a Spring Parade" (Charles Previn, Kahn), and "The Dawn Of Love" (Previn, Ralph Freed), all sung by Durbin. Lyricist Kahn was the subject of a movie about his life, I'LL SEE YOU IN MY DREAMS, which starred Danny Thomas as Kahn.

p, Joe Pasternak; d, Henry Koster; w, Bruce Manning, Felix Jackson (based on a story by Ernst Marischka); ph, Joseph Valentine; m, Robert Stolz, Hans Salter; ed, Bernard Burton; md, Charles Previn; art d, Richard H. Riedel; ch, Larry Ceballos; cos, Vera West.

Musical (PR:A MPAA:NR)

SPRING REUNION*½ (1957) 79m UA bw

Dana Andrews (Fred Davis), Betty Hutton (Maggie Brewster), Jean Hagen (Barna Forrest), Sara Berner (Paula Kratz), Robert Simon (Harry Brewster), Laura LaPlante (May Brewster), Gordon Jones (Jack Frazer), James Gleason (Mr. Collyer, Lighthouse Keeper), Irene Ryan (Miss Stapleton, Schoolteacher), Richard Shannon (Nick), Ken Curtis (Al), Herbert Anderson (Edward), Richard Benedict (Jim), Vivi Janiss (Grace), Florence Sundstrom (Mary), Mimi Doyle (Alice), Sid Tomack (Caterer), Shirley Mitchell (Receptionist), George Chandler (Zimmie), Dorothy Neumann (Roseanne), Barbara Drew (Verna), Richard Deacon (Sidney), Don Haggerty (Pete), Leon Tyler (Teenager in Car).

A class reunion allows for Andrews and Hutton to have a go at romance after being separated for many years. Very dull, leaving one believing that the only reason for class reunions is to dig up old loves. Hutton sings one number, which is below average in presentation.

p, Jerry Bresler; d, Robert Pirosh; w, Pirosh, Elick Moll (based on a story by Robert Alan Aurthur); ph, Harold Lipstein; m, Herbert Spencer, Earle Hagen; ed, Leon Barsha; art d, Paul Groesse; cos, Don Loper; ch, Sylvia Lewis; m/l, Johnny Mercer, Harry Warren (sung by Mary Kaye Irio).

Drama (PR:A MPAA:NR)

SPRING SHOWER*** (1932, Hung.) Hunnia/Adolphe Osso bw (TAVASZI ZAPOR)

Annabella (Mari).

A tragic, but uplifting, story about a poor maid who becomes pregnant when seduced by a young man. Forced to leave her place of employment, she finds temporary sanctuary in a squalid nightclub. With the birth of her child, the young woman finds short-lived happiness until the authorities take her baby away. In despair she returns to her village, only to be met with ridicule. As she kneels before a statue of the Madonna, the woman dies and her spirit goes to heaven, where it is kept busy scrubbing floors. An anecdote has the woman spying on her young daughter, who is about to enter into the same fate as her own. By creating a rain shower, the mother saves her daughter. Told mainly through visuals at a slow pace with very little dialog, this film might leave some people crying for action. Others, however, will be mesmerized by the beauty of the atmosphere and the charming performance by Annabella.

d, Paul Fejos; w, Ilona Fulop; ph, Peverell Marley, Istvan Eiben; m, Laszlo Angyal; ed, George Feld.

Drama (PR:A MPAA:NR)

SPRING SONG (SEE: SPRINGTIME, 1946, Brit.)

SPRING TONIC* (1935) 58m FOX bw

Lew Ayres (Caleb Enix), Claire Trevor (Betty Ingals), Walter King (Jose), ZaSu Pitts (Maggie), Jack Haley (Sykes), Tala Birell (Lola), Siegfried [Sig] Rumann (Matt), Frank Mitchell (Griffen Nasher), Jack Durant (Cambridge Nasher).

Total mayhem erupts when Trevor walks out on her fiance, Ayres, and winds up at a lodge where moonshiners, circus people, and eventually Ayres come to conglomerate. Not much of a plot here, with laughs coming in very sparse intervals.

p, Robert T. Kane; d, Clyde Bruckman; w, Patterson McNutt, H.W. Hanemann, Howard I. Young (based on the play "Man Eating Tiger" by Ben Hecht, Rose Caylor); ph, L.W. O'Connell; md, Arthur Lange; m/l, Jay Gorney.

Comedy (PR:A MPAA:NR)

SPRINGFIELD RIFLE*** (1952) 93m WB c

Gary Cooper (Maj. Lex Kearney), Phyllis Thaxter (Erin Kearney), David Brian (Austin McCool), Paul Kelly (Lt. Col. Hudson), Philip Carey (Capt. Tennick), Lon Chaney, Jr. (Elm), James Millican (Matthew Quint), Martin Milner (Olie Larsen), Guinn "Big Boy" Williams (Sgt. Snow), Jerry O'Sullivan (Lt. Evans), James Brown (Pvt. Ferguson), Jack Woody (Sims), Alan Hale, Jr. (Mizzell), Vince Barnett (Cook), Fess Parker (Jim Randolph), Richard Lightner (Lt. Johnson), Ewing Mitchell (Spencer), Poodles Hanneford (Cpl. Hamel), George Ross (Riley), Eric Hoeg (Southerner), Wilton Graff (Col. Sharpe), Ned Young (Sgt. Poole), William Fawcett (Cpl. Ramsey), Richard Hale (Gen. Henry W. Halleck), Ben Corbett (Sergeant Major), Guy E. Hearn (Calhoun), George Eldredge (Judge Advocate), Rory Mallinson, Ralph Sanford (Barflys), Paula Sowl (Woman), Ric Roman, Jack Mower (Guards), Holly Bane (Red), Ray Bennett (Commissioner), Michael Chapin (Jamie).

Following a standard western blueprint which has the hero going undercover to crack an outlaw gang, SPRINGFIELD RIFLE casts an aging Cooper (on the heels of his phenomenally successful HIGH NOON) as a Union officer during the Civil War. He gets himself booted out of the Army on charges of cowardice in order to infiltrate a Confederate gang and put his counterespionage scheme into effect. A rash of attacks on cavalry horse outposts leads Cooper to believe that an insider is supplying the raiders with information on the cavalry's operations. He joins up with Brian, the head of the raiders, and soon becomes a trusted member of the gang. Meantime, Union officials appeal to Cooper's wife, Thaxter, for information, but she is as confused about Cooper's mysterious loyalty shift as the others. The finale has Cooper breaking open the gang and, in the process, testing the Union's new weapon–the Springfield rifle. Although the plot seems ludicrously elementary (it's based on a story by Nibley, who for years supplied Roy Rogers with the same plot), SPRINGFIELD RIFLE is carried by Cooper's fine performance, as well as those of his exemplary supporting cast–Chaney, Jr., Milner, Williams, Hale, Jr., and Parker.

p, Louis F. Edelman; d, Andre De Toth; w, Charles Marquis Warren, Frank Davis (based on a story by Sloan Nibley); ph, Edwin Du Par (Warner Color); m, Max Steiner; ed, Robert L. Swanson; md, Murray Cutter; art d, John Beckman; set d, G. W. Berntsen; tech adv, Ben Corbett; makeup, Gordon Bau.

Western (PR:A MPAA:NR)

SPRINGTIME** (1948, Brit.) 80m BN/Anglo-American bw (GB: SPRING SONG)

Peter Graves (Tony Winster), Carol Raye (Janet Hill/Janet Ware), Lawrence O'Madden (Johnnie Ware), Leni Lynn (Vera Dale), Netta Westcott (Lady Norchester), David Horne (Sir Anthony), Diana Calderwood (Mary Norchester), Alan Wheatley (Menelli), Peter Penn (Carrington), Maire O'Neill (Dresser), Gerald Kempinski (Hotel Manager), Finlay Currie (Cobb), Jack Billings (Dancer).

Two lovers' stories, one in 1911 and the other in 1946, are connected by a valuable brooch. In both instances Graves plays the leading male character while Raye is the female partner, representing a mother and her daughter. The younger couple learn of the previous affair after Graves attempts to romance Raye and is forced to stay away by her father.

p, Louis H. Jackson; d, Montgomery Tully; w, Tully, James Seymour (based on a story by Lore and Maurice Cowan); ph, Ernest Palmer, Moray Grant; m/l, Hans Mau, Alan Shanks.

Drama (PR:A MPAA:NR)

SPRINGTIME FOR HENRY*½ (1934) 73m FOX bw

Otto Kruger (Henry Dewlip), Nancy Carroll (Julia Jelliwell), Nigel Bruce (Johnny Jelliwell), Heather Angel (Miss Smith), Herbert Mundin (Trivers), Arthur Hoyt (Alfred Ordway), Geneva Mitchell (Young Lady).

Kruger stars as a playboy who finds himself involved with the married Carroll, whom he almost decides to drop when his secretary shows him the possibility of a more stable life style. But he decides that the girl is not quite his cup of tea, so he goes back to Carroll, whose husband Bruce is glad to let him have her, while he goes for the secretary. Performances are very strained, while what comedy that does exist comes from tired slapstick routines. Carroll was at the peak of her popularity when this film was made.

p, Jesse L. Lasky; d, Frank Tuttle; w, Keene Thompson, Tuttle, Benn Wolf Levy (based on the play by Levy); ph, John Seitz; m, Louis deFrancesco; set d, Max Parker; cos, Rita Kaufman.

Comedy (PR:A MPAA:NR)

SPRINGTIME IN THE ROCKIES*½ (1937) 60m REP bw

Gene Autry (*Gene*), Smiley Burnette (*Frog*), Polly Rowles (*Sandra*), Ula Love (*Silly Sylvia*), Ruth Bacon (*Peggy*), Jane Hunt (*Jane*), George Chesebro (*Morgan*), Alan Bridge (*Briggs*), Tom London (*Tracy*), Edward Hearn (*Thorpe*), Frankie Marvin (*Frankie*), William Hole (*Bub*), Edmund Cobb (*Sheriff*), Fred Burns (*Harris*), Jimmy LeFuer's Saddle Pals (*Orchestra*), Art Davis, Lew Meehan, Jack Kirk, Frank Ellis, George Letz (*Montgomery*), Robert Dudley, Jack Rockwell, Oscar Gahan, Victor Cox, Jim Corey, Champion the Horse.

Below-par effort for Autry has him as the foreman on a cattle-country ranch, whose owner, Rowles, a recent grad from animal husbandry school, decides to bring in a flock of sheep. The local cattlemen don't take too kindly to the new inhabitants and trouble erupts despite Autry's attempts to keep things peaceful. Not surprisingly, Autry adds some songs to the accompaniment of Jimmy LeFuer's Saddle Pals.

p, Sol C. Siegel; d, Joseph Kane; w, Gilbert Wright, Betty Burbridge; ph, Ernest Miller; ed, Lester Orlebeck; song, "Springtime in the Rockies" (sung by Gene Autry).

Western   **Cas**   (PR:A MPAA:NR)

SPRINGTIME IN THE ROCKIES**½ (1942) 91m FOX c

Betty Grable (*Vicky*), John Payne (*Dan*), Carmen Miranda (*Rosita, Dan's Secretary*), Cesar Romero (*Victor*), Charlotte Greenwood (*Phoebe Gray*), Edward Everett Horton (*McTavish, Dan's Valet*), Frank Orth (*Bickle*), Harry Hayden (*Brown*), Jackie Gleason (*Dan's Agent*), Chick Chandler (*Stage Manager*), Iron Eyes Cody (*Indian*), Trudy Marshall (*Marilyn*), Bess Flowers (*Mrs. Jeepers*), Banda da Lua (*Themselves*), Billy Wayne (*Assistant Stage Manager*), Harry James and his Orchestra (*Themselves*).

Grable and Payne are a pair of Broadway performers and lovers who prove the truth of the old saying that those who love together also fight together. The biggest problem seems to be that Payne can't keep his mind off other women, which piques Grable to no end. To get even, she hooks up with Romero, as though she intends to marry him. Payne retaliates by romancing his Brazilian secretary, Miranda. Though the premise is slight, a good blend of music, dance, comedy, and even some drama, is combined in a very astute manner. Much of the action is played out against the backdrop of Lake Louise, Alberta, and Palmer's Technicolor cinematography fills the screen with the beauty of the Canadian Rockies. The story sets up Grable and Romero as dancing partners and they do a little hoofing to the accompaniment of Harry James and His Music Makers. This was the first film to give Grable top billing. Songs include "I Had the Craziest Dream" (Mack Gordon, Harry Warren, sung by Harry James, Helen Forrest), "Run Little Raindrop Run" (Gordon, Warren, sung by Betty Grable, John Payne), "A Poem Set to Music," "Pan American Jubilee" (Gordon, Warren, sung by Cesar Romero), "I Like to Be Loved by You," "Chattanooga Choo Choo," (Gordon, Warren, sung by Carmen Miranda), "Tic Tac Do Meu Coracao" (Vermelho, Silva, sung by Miranda).

p, William LeBaron; d, Irving Cummings; w, Walter Bullock, Ken Englund, Jacques Thery (based on a story by Philip Wylie); ph, Ernest Palmer (Technicolor); ed, Robert Simpson; md, Alfred Newman; art d, Richard Day, Joseph C. Wright; ch, Hermes Pan.

Musical   **Cas.**   (PR:A MPAA:NR)

SPRINGTIME IN THE SIERRAS**½ (1947) 75m REP bw (AKA: SONG OF THE SIERRA)

Roy Rogers (*Himself*), Jane Frazee (*Taffy Baker*), Andy Devine (*Cookie Bullfincher*), Stephanie Bachelor (*Jean Loring*), Hal Landon (*Bert Baker*), Harry V. Cheshire (*Capt. Foster*), Roy Barcroft (*Matt Wilkes*), Chester Conklin, Hank Patterson (*Old Timers*), Whitey Christy, Pascale Perry (*Henchmen*), Bob Nolan and the Sons of The Pioneers, Bob Woodward, Trigger the Horse.

A gang headed by Bachelor and lorded over by Barcroft has been illegally shooting game out of season, something that Rogers puts a stop to when he traces the murder of his buddy the game warden to Bachelor's ranch. He almost gets frozen to death in a meat freezer for his efforts, but escapes with plenty of time to see that justice is done. The usual stereotypes are offered, with Barcroft in one of his more villainous roles and Devine, a wonder as the comic relief. Songs include "Oh, What a Picture" (sung by Roy Rogers, Andy Devine), "Springtime in the Sierras," "The Quilting Party," "A Cowboy Has to Sing" (performed by Rogers, The Sons of the Pioneers), "Pedro from Acapulco" (sung by Rogers, Jane Frazee), "What Are We Gonna' Do Then?" (performed by The Sons of the Pioneers).

p, Edward J. White; d, William Witney; w, A. Sloan Nibley; ph, Jack Marta (Trucolor); ed, Tony Martinelli; md, Morton Scott; art d, Frank Arrigo; m/l, Jack Elliott, Bob Nolan, Tim Spencer.

Western   **Cas.**   (PR:A MPAA:NR)

SPRINGTIME ON THE VOLGA** (1961, USSR) 75m Gorky/Artkino c (DEVICHYA VESNA)

Mira Koltsava (*Galya*), D. Agafonova (*Vera*), G. Petrova (*Lena*), Garen Zhukovskaya (*Lugovaya*), Lyudmila Ovchinnikova (*Nastya*), E. Treyvas (*Angelina*), Anna Bogdanova (*Grandmother*), Lev Barashkov (*Volodya*), Vladimir Lepko (*Gamba*), Georgiy Tusuzov (*Cook*), Aleksandr Denisov (*Mechanic*), Georgiy Slabinyak (*Captain*), Vladimir Dorofeyev (*Grandfather*), A. Vanin (*Lyosha*), I. Ryzhov (*Porter*), L. Krauzova, M. Kutakhova, M. Grigoryeva (*Girls on Deck*), the Beryozka Dance Ensemble.

A boat down the Volga river acts as the setting for the budding romance between an optician and a dancer. The optician has kissed his normal job good-bye in order to follow the dancer as she travels down the famous Russian waterway, making for a humorous trip as the optician adapts to life in the kitchen, as well as to some of the other employees.

d, Veniamin Dorman, Genrikh Oganisyan; w, Mikhail Dolgopolov, Iosif Prut, Nadya Nadezhdina; ph, Vyacheslav Shumskiy (Sovcolor); m, Aleksandr Flyarkovskiy; ed, R. Shor; md, D. Shtilman, A. Ilin; art d, Mark Gorelik, Sergey Serebrenikov; cos, L. Silich; ch, Nadezhdina; m/l, "Devichya Vesna," Ye. Kuznetsov.

Comedy/Drama   (PR:A MPAA:NR)

SPURS** (1930) 60m UNIV bw

Hoot Gibson (*Bob Merrill*), Helen Wright (*Peggy Bradley*), Robert E. Homans (*Pop Merrill*), Frank Clark (*Charles Bradley*), Buddy Hunter (*Buddy Hazlet*), Gilbert "Pee Wee" Holmes (*Shorty*), William Bertram (*Indian Joe*), Philo McCullough (*Tom Marsden*), Cap Anderson (*Pecos*), Pete Morrison (*Blackie*), Artie Ortego [Art Ardigan] (*Eagle-Claw*).

A decent oater with Gibson as a rodeo star who also takes to taming a gang of cattle rustlers by infiltrating their secret hideout. And what a hideout it is! All sorts of gadgets must be manipulated to gain entrance and a bullet-spitting machine gun provides an imposing obstacle. The title refers to the pair of silver spurs Gibson wins for his exploits in the rodeo. This film was shot in both silent and sound versions.

p, Hoot Gibson; d&w, B. Reeves Eason; ph, Harry Neumann.

Western   (PR:A MPAA:NR)

SPUTNIK*½ (1960, Fr.) 94m Films Around The World bw (A PIED, A CHEVAL ET EN SPOUTNIK; AKA: A DOG, A MOUSE AND A SPUTNIK)

Noel-Noel (*Leon Martin*), Denise Grey (*Marguerite Martin*), Mischa Auer (*Professor*), Noel Roquevert (*Mayor*), Darry Cowl (*Sub-Attache*), Robert Lombard (*Chief of Police*), Natalie Nerval (*Dina*).

An offbeat French comedy with Noel-Noel taking a mouse and a dog into his home, unaware that both animals came from a Russian satellite that landed in the French countryside. Russian and French scientists plead with Noel to give up the animals, but he won't. He's invited to Moscow in hopes of changing his mind and ends up being launched in a rocket by accident. He saves the day when he lands the spacecraft safely after the cosmonaut on board falls sick. He goes back to France, a happy hero, with the dog.

p, Louis De Masure; d, Jean Dreville; w, Jean-Jacques Vital; ph, Andre Bac.

Comedy   (PR:A MPAA:NR)

SPY BUSTERS (SEE: GUNS IN THE HEATHER, 1968, Brit.)

SPY CHASERS** (1956) 61m AA bw

Leo Gorcey (*Terrence Aloysius "Slip" Mahoney*), Huntz Hall (*Horace Debussy "Sach" Jones*), Bernard Gorcey (*Louie Dumbrowski*), David (*Gorcey*), Condon (*Chuck*), Bennie Bartlett (*Butch*), Leon Askin (*Col. Alex Baxis*), Sig Rumann (*King Rako*), Veola Vonn (*Lady Zelda*), Lisa Davis (*Princess Ann*), Linda Bennett (*Little Girl*), Frank Richards (*George*), Paul Burke (*Michael*), Richard Benedict (*Boris*), Mel Welles (*Nick*), John Bleifer (*Phony Courier*).

The fortieth "Bowery Boys" entry has the boys aiding the King of Truania, who has temporarily been forced into exile because of political problems in his kingdom. Given the job of securing half a coin, with the receipt of the other part indicating that it is alright for the king to return to his country, Gorcey uncovers a plot by a trusted adviser to have the king return before it is safe. Gorcey and Hall are up to their usual antics of battling each other while trying to battle the culprits at the same time. (See BOWERY BOYS Series, Index.)

p, Ben Schwalb; d, Edward Bernds; w, Bert Lawrence, Jerome S. Gottler; ph, Harry Neumann; ed, Lester A. Sansom; John C. Fuller; md, Marlin Skiles; art d, David Milton; set d, Joseph Kish; spec eff, Ray Mercer; makeup, Bob Dawn.

Comedy   (PR:A MPAA:NR)

SPY FOR A DAY½   (1939, Brit.) 71m TC/PAR bw

Duggie Wakefield (*Sam Gates*), Paddy Browne (*Martha Clowes*), Jack Allen (*Capt. Bradshaw*), Albert Lieven (*Capt. Hausemann*), Nicholas Hannen (*Col. Pemberton*), Gibb McLaughlin (*Col. Ludwig*), Allan Jeayes (*Col. Roberts*), Alf Goddard (*Sgt. Bryan*), George Hayes (*Cpl. Boehme*), Eliot Makeham (*Mr. Trufit*), Hay Petrie (*Mr. Britt.*), O.B. Clarence (*Medical Officer*).

Farmhand Wakefield is kidnaped by Germans who mistake him for one of their own spies. He escapes, then is almost shot as a spy by the British, who make the same mistake. He convinces them of his identity and tells them where to find the real spy, then returns home a hero. Above average comedy has some very good moments.

p&d, Mario Zampi; w, Anatole de Grunwald, Hans Wilhelm, Emeric Pressburger, Ralph Block, Tommy Thompson (based on the story "Source of Irritation" by Stacy Aumonier).

Comedy   (PR:A   MPAA:NR)

SPY HUNT**   (1950) 75m UNIV bw (GB: PANTHER'S MOON)

Howard Duff (*Roger Quain*), Marta Toren (*Catherine Ullven*), Philip Friend (*Chris Denson*), Robert Douglas (*Stephen Paradou*), Philip Dorn (*Paul Kopel*), Walter Slezak (*Dr. Stahl*), Kurt Kreuger (*Capt. Halmer*), Aram Katcher (*Georg*), Otto Waldis (*Gormand*), Ivan Triesault (*Debron*), Jay Barney (*Fusek*), Carl Milletaire (*Ticket Clerk*), Antonio Filauri (*Telegraph Clerk*), Peter Ortiz, Peter Applequist (*Soldiers*), Carlo Tricoli (*Italian Man*), Betty Greco (*Italian Girl*), Carmela Restivo (*Italian Woman*), Jack Chefe (*Waiter*), Rudy Silva (*Young Italian Man*).

Fast-moving thriller in which a black panther is given the duties of getting valuable microfilm out of Europe. Toren and Duff team up to keep the photographed plans for a political assassination out of the hands of enemy agents Friend, Dorn, and Douglas. Efficient-pacing and capable direction hide the fact that this plot really had nothing new or very exciting to offer. Glassberg's camerawork and the fine special photography by Horsley merit mention.

p, Ralph Dietrich; d, George Sherman; w, George Zuckerman, Leonard Lee (from the novel *Panther's Moon* by Victor Canning); ph, Irving Glassberg; ed, Ted J. Kent; md, Joseph Gershenson; art d, Bernard Herzbrun, Alexander Golitzen; set d, Russell A. Gausman, John Austin; cos, Bill Thomas; spec eff, David S. Horsley; makeup, Bud Westmore.

Spy Drama   (PR:A   MPAA:NR)

SPY IN BLACK, THE   (SEE: U-BOAT 29, 1939, Brit.)

SPY IN THE GREEN HAT, THE*½   (1966) 92m MGM c

Robert Vaughn (*Napoleon Solo*), David McCallum (*Illya Kuryakin*), Jack Palance (*Louis Strago*), Janet Leigh (*Miss Diketon*), Leticia Roman (*Pia Monteri*), Eduardo Ciannelli (*Arturo "Fingers" Stilletto*), Allen Jenkins (*Enzo "Pretty" Stilletto*), Jack La Rue (*Federico "Feet" Stilletto*), Leo G. Carroll (*Alexander Waverly*), Ludwig Donath (*Dr. Heinrich von Kronen*), Joan Blondell (*Mrs. "Fingers" Stilletto*), Will Kuluva (*Mr. Thaler*), Penny Santon (*Grandma Monteri*), Vincent Beck (*Benjamin Luger*), Frank Puglia (*Padre*), Maxie Rosenbloom (*"Crunch" Battaglia*), Vince Barnett (*"Scissors"*), Elisha Cook (*Arnold*).

U.N.C.L.E. agents Vaughn and McCallum try to put a stop to Palance's plan to shift the course of the Gulf Stream in this rehash of episodes from the "Man From U.N.C.L.E." TV series, edited together to form a feature for theatrical release. Leigh plays one of Palance's accomplices and is nearly successful in doing McCallum in for good. Apparently fans couldn't get enough of the series on TV, as this proved to be quite a successful venture. The makers of the popular TV program had been sending up James Bond-style spy adventures for some time, but in this film they also poked some satirical fun at the gangster films of the past, and featured performances by a number of veterans of 1930s Warner Brothers' gangster films, including Ciannelli, Jenkins, La Rue, Blondell, Rosenbloom, Barnett, and Cook.

p, Boris Ingster; d, Joseph Sargent; w, Peter Allan Fields; ph, Fred Koenekamp; m, Nelson Riddle; ed, Ray Williford, Joseph Dervin; art d, George W. Davis, James W. Sullivan; set d, Henry Grace, Dick Pefferle, Francisco Lombardo; m/l, Jerry Goldsmith.

Spy Drama/Adventure   (PR:A   MPAA:NR)

SPY IN THE PANTRY   (SEE: MISSING TEN DAYS, 1941, Brit.)

SPY IN THE SKY*½   (1958) 75m AA bw

Steve Brodie (*Victor Cabot*), Sandra Francis (*Eva Brindisi*), Andrea Domburg (*Alexandrine Duvivier*), George Coulouris (*Col. Benedict*), Bob De Lange (*Sidney Jardine*), Hans Tiemeyer (*Dr. Keller*), Herbert Curiel (*Pepi*), Dity Oorthuis (*Fritzi*), Leon Dorian, A. E. Collin, E. F. Beavis, Alex Sweers, Harold Horsten, Rob Milton.

Vienna is the setting for a competition between Russian and American spies

who are trying track down Tiemeyer, a German scientist who had been working on the Soviet space program before making a dash for freedom. The American agent Brodie wins out, which comes as a surprise because he is presented more as a bungler than as a highly efficient secret agent. His biggest problem seems to be in overcoming his amorous affairs. The camerawork, with its preponderance of close-ups, seems to indicate that this film was made with television distribution in mind. Locations in Holland stand in for the Austrian capital and a number of Dutch personnel were used in the production.

p&d, W. Lee Wilder; w, Myles Wilder (based on the novel *Counterspy Express* by A. S. Fleischman); ph, Jim Harvey; m, Hugo de Groot; ed, Lien d'Oliveyra; md, de Groot; art d, Nico van Baarle; cos, Max Heymans.

Spy Drama   (PR:A   MPAA:NR)

SPY IN WHITE, THE   (SEE: SECRET OF STAMBOUL, THE, 1936, Brit.)

SPY IN YOUR EYE**   (1966, Ital.) 88m Italian International-Publi Italia/AIP c (BERLINO, APPUNTAMENTO PER LE SPIE); AKA: BERLIN, APPOINTMENT FOR THE SPIES)

Brett Halsey (*Bert Morris*), Pier Angeli (*Paula Krauss*), Dana Andrews (*Col. Lancaster*), Gastone Moschin (*Boris*), Tania Beryl, Alessandro Sperli, Mario Valdemarin, Tino Bianchi, Aldo De Francesco, Renato Baldini, Marco Guglielmi, Luciana Angiolillo, George Wang, Luciano Pigozzi, Massimo Righi, Franco Baltimor, Giulio Mecale, Aghul Rain Bozan.

Confusing plot has Andrews unknowingly becoming a spy for the Russians when a small camera is implanted in his eye during an operation. But, even as the head of U.S. intelligence operations he knows as little as the Russians about the secret in question, a death ray that has been developed by a noted scientist, now dead. The secret is implanted in the scientist's daughter's skull (something the girl and the spies are unaware of), and an agent, Halsey, is sent to tail her. While the Russians and Americans are busy trying to discover secrets, Halsey and the girl steal away to devote their time to romance. Though the picture is effectively mounted and some interesting concepts are developed, it gets bogged down by the confusion of the script and performances that are very sad to watch.

p, Fulvio Lucisano, Lucio Marcuzzo; d, Vittorio Sala; w, Romano Ferrara, Adriano Baracco, Adriano Bolzoni (based on a story by Marcuzzo); ph, Fausto Zuccoli (Pathe Color); m, Riz Ortolani; ed, Renato Cinquini, Roberto Cinquini; art d, Luciano Del Greco.

Spy Drama/Fantasy   (PR:A   MPAA:NR)

SPY OF NAPOLEON**   (1939, Brit.) 98m JH/Syndicate bw

Richard Barthelmess (*Gerard de Lancy*), Dolly Haas (*Eloise*), Frank Vosper (*Louis Napoleon III*), Francis L. Sullivan (*Chief of Police Toulon*), Joyce Bland (*Empress Eugenie*), C. Denier Warren (*Nicolet*), Henry Oscar (*Hugo Biot*), Marjorie Mars (*Anna*), Brian Buschel (*Philippe St. Paul*), Lyn Harding (*Prince Otto Von Bismarck*), Wilfred Caithness (*Count Helmuth Von Moltke*), George Merritt (*The Prussian Consul*), Stafford Hilliard (*Newsvendor*).

Barthelmess, an aristocrat who faces a death sentence for his role in a plot against Louis Napoleon, is spared when he agrees to marry the French ruler's illegitimate daughter (Haas), lending her his good name so that she can keep an eye on the aristocracy for the emperor. Later, Barthelmess even finds himself working undercover in the service of his country. Barthelmess is pretty bland in his performance, but Vosper, as Napoleon III, gives a realistic and effective portrayal. This costume drama, set in 1870, is based on a book by Baroness Orzy. It was filmed in Britain in 1936, but did not reach U.S. screens until 1939.

p, Julius Hagen; d, Maurice Elvey; w, L. du Garde Peach, Frederick Merrick, Harold Simpson (based on the novel by Baroness Orczy); ph, Curt Courant.

Historical Drama   **Cas.**   (PR:A   MPAA:NR)

SPY RING, THE*½   (1938) 61m T/C/UNIV bw (AKA: INTERNATIONAL SPY)

William Hall (*Capt. Todd Hayden*), Jane Wyman (*Elaine Burdette*), Leon Ames (*Frank Denton*), Ben Alexander (*Capt. Don Mayhew*), Don Barclay (*Timothy O'Reilly*), Robert Warwick (*Col. Burdette*), Paul Sutton (*Charley the Chauffeur*), Jack Mulhall (*Capt. Tex Randolph*), Philip Trent (*Capt. Scott*), LeRoy Mason (*Paul Douglas*), Jane Carleton (*Esther Ralston*), Egon Brecher (*Brig. Gen. A.R. Bowen*), Harry Woods (*Capt. Holden*), Glenn Strange (*The Champ*), Lester Dorr (*Radio Operator*), Harry Harvey, Eddie Parker, Pat Gleason, (*Reporters*), Eddie Gribbon, Forrest Taylor (*Sergeants*).

A polo match is used to trap a gang of spies who have developed a secret anti-aircraft gun. Hall is the captain at an army base where boring parties and polo matches are the only items to pass the time of day. Somehow spies get into the picture and interrupt Hall's usual star performance in the polo match. Pretty forced and hard to swallow, this film, nonetheless, features an early performance by Wyman.

p, Trem Carr; d, Joseph H. Lewis; w, George Waggner (based on the short story "International Spy" by Frank Van Wyck Mason); ph, Harry Neumann; ed, Charles Craft; md, Charles Previn.

Spy Drama   **(PR:A   MPAA:NR)**

SPY 77   (SEE: SECRET AGENT, 1936, Brit.)

SPY SHIP*½   (1942) 62m WB bw

Craig Stevens *(Ward Prescott)*, Irene Manning *(Pamela Mitchell)*, Maris Wrixon *(Sue Mitchell)*, Michael Ames *(Gordon Morrell)*, Peter Whitney *(Zinner)*, John Maxwell *(Ernie Haskell)*, William Forrest *(Martin Oster)*, Roland Drew *(Nils Thorson)*, George Meeker *(Paul)*, George Irving *(Harry Mitchell)*, Frank Ferguson *(Burns)*, Olaf Hytten *(Drake)*, Jack Mower *(Inspector Bond)*, Keye Luke *(Haru)*.

Uninspired and haphazard production that stars Manning as an heiress who hides secret information in her lectures against war, and it's not Uncle Sam who is intended to decipher it. Originally made in 1934 as FOG OVER FRISCO, in which Bette Davis played the role given here to Manning. It's hard to find any similarities between the two versions.

d, B. Reeves Eason; w, Robert E. Kent (based on the story "The Five Fragments" by George Dyer); ph, Harry Newmann (Neumann); ed, James Gibbon; art d, Ted Smith; cos, Milo Anderson.

Spy Drama   **(PR:A   MPAA:NR)**

SPY 13   (SEE: OPERATION 13, 1934)

SPY TRAIN**   (1943) 61m MON bw

Richard Travis *(Bruce)*, Catherine Craig *(Jane)*, Chick Chandler *(Stu)*, Thelma White *(Millie)*, Evelyn Brent *(Frieda)*, Gerald Brock *(Italian)*, Fred "Snowflakes" Toones *(Porter)*, Bill Hunter *(Detective)*, Steve Roberts *(Chief Nazi)*, Warren Hymer *(Herman)*, John Hamilton.

A travel bag containing a bomb causes a lot of back-stabbing and strange happenings when passengers aboard a train try to get their hands on it because they believe it to contain important government secrets. But the Nazi spies who placed it on the train made a mistake which isn't well received by other spies, who carry the luggage off the train and are blown sky-high.

p, Max King; d, Harold Young; w, Leslie Schwabacher, Wallace Sullivan, Bart Lytton (based on a story by Scott Littlefield); ph, Mack Stengler; ed, Martin G. Cohn.

Spy Drama   **(PR:A   MPAA:NR)**

SPY WHO CAME IN FROM THE COLD, THE****
                               (1965, Brit.) 112m Salem/PAR bw

Richard Burton *(Alec Leamas)*, Claire Bloom *(Nan Perry)*, Oskar Werner *(Fiedler)*, Peter Van Eyck *(Hans-Dieter Mundt)*, Sam Wanamaker *(Peters)*, George Voskovec *(East German Defense Attorney)*, Rupert Davies *(Smiley)*, Cyril Cusack *(Control)*, Michael Hordern *(Ashe)*, Robert Hardy *(Carlton)*, Bernard Lee *(Patmore)*, Beatrix Lehmann *(President of Tribunal)*, Esmond Knight *(Old Judge)*, Walter Gotell *(Holten)*, Tom Stern *(CIA Agent)*, Niall MacGinnis, George Mikell *(German Checkpoint Guards)*, Scott Finch *(German Guide)*, Katherine Keeton *(Stripper)*, Richard Caldicot *(Mr. Pitt)*, Marianne Deeming *(Frau Floerdke)*, Michael Ripper *(Lofthouse)*, Henk Mobenberg *(Passport Officer)*, Richard Marner *(Vopo Captain)*, David Bauer *(Young Judge)*, Steve Plytas *(East German Judge)*, Anne Blake *(Miss Crail)*, Michael Ritterman *(Security Officer)*, Edward Harvey *(Man in the Shop)*, Nancy Nevinson *(Mrs. Zanfrello)*, Warren Mitchell *(Mr. Zanfrello)*, Philip Badoc *(Young German Officer)*.

Spying is not James Bond or Michael Caine as Harry Palmer. Spying is a grim, desperate business that is, at once, boring and exciting, with dirty work behind the scenes and hardly any derring-do. In this superb adaptation of Le Carre's novel, all of that is felt and anyone who'd considered a career with the CIA must have had second thoughts. Audiences much preferred to see their spies wearing Cardin suits and Rolex watches and grabbing off one comely vixen after another because this film, which was one of the best ever made on the subject, failed to gather much interest at the box office. Produced and directed by Martin Ritt (who had an association with Paul Newman at the time although Newman took no credit) in Ireland and England, with some second-unit lensing in Europe, here at last is a movie that is an accurate depiction of the way it is among the trenchcoats. But since there is virtually no glamor and very little action, pea-brains could not follow the complex plot and began to yawn. Burton is a burnt-out case, a man who is looking forward to getting out of the spy game and retiring from British Intelligence. Just before he is to leave, Burton is called back to London and put on the carpet. It seems that several of his sub-agents have been caught by Van Eyck, who is Burton's counterpart on the East Berlin side. Van Eyck is a former Nazi who has taken over as chief of operations for the Communists and his handiwork is putting a crimp in the British operations. Since it is well known that Burton is tired of what he's doing, Burton's boss, Cusack, gives him his final assignment. He is to masquerade

as a drunk who wants to defect to the East Germans. If it works and Burton gets inside the Communist operations, he can find out if there is a "mole" in their own organization as well as get the goods on what's happening inside the East German operation. Burton meets Bloom. She is a librarian and he takes a job as her assistant, knowing all the while that she is a Communist. He has now retired and appears to be a drunk. Burton has a fight and is sent to jail for brawling. When he's let out, he is contacted by people in the employ of Werner, Van Eyck's assistant. Werner wants Van Eyck's job and will stop at nothing to get it. Burton will be given a great deal of money if he agrees to testify at a secret trial where Van Eyck is being accused of being a double agent. It's all going well and Burton feels that he has done his job and that Van Eyck will be eliminated. Suddenly, Bloom is called to testify. What she says makes Burton aware of what the *real* plot is, all carefully orchestrated by his bosses in England. Werner is the one they want taken out because Van Eyck is an agent for the West] Since the brilliant Werner had been secretly mustering power, the chiefs at British Intelligence could not afford to have their top double agent erased, so they concocted this convoluted plot to discredit Werner and keep Van Eyck in his lofty position. Once the trial is over, Van Eyck arranges to have Burton and Bloom – who is a meek and unwitting woman not part of the cabal – taken to the Berlin Wall where they are to be shown to safety. Burton feels betrayed because he was not let in on the operation. He and Bloom approach the wall, two pawns who have been used and tossed away in an international chess game that goes on to this day. Burton was nominated for an Oscar, one of several times up at bat for the actor, and he never did hit a home run with the Academy, losing out this year to Lee Marvin in CAT BALLOU. There are no gimmicks, no fast cars that turn into airplanes, no weapons that fire lasers, just a tense battle of wits where the suspense can get excruciating. The title refers to the time when an outside spy has to "come in from the cold" and take a sedentary job as another spy's control or even some menial desk assignment until the mandatory age limit forces retirement. Only Graham Greene has come close to Le Carre in detailing the painstaking way of life of these faceless men and women who fight a daily war with the forces of the KGB, et al. The semi-documentary fashion in which Morris shot the film added to the stark believability of the story and won him the British Film Academy's award as Best Black-and-White Cinematographer. It also won awards from the BFA as Best British Film, for Burton as Best Actor, and to the art direction team for Best Black-and-White Art Direction. Much of the shooting was done at the Ardmore Studios in Bray, Ireland, with other scenes at Shepperton in England. Parts of Dublin were utilized to serve as Berlin. Bernard Lee, who played Bond's boss, "M," for so many years, finally got a look at what spying really is. In the role of a stripper, note Kathy Keeton, long-time associate of *Penthouse* magazine topper Bob Guccione and for years the second highest-ra nking officer in his publishing empire. Penthouse began as a British company with offices in London's Bramber Road. It wasn't until years later that the magazine came to the U.S. to try to topple Hugh Hefner's Playboy.

p&d, Martin Ritt; w, Paul Dehn, Guy Trosper (based on the novel by John Le Carre); ph, Oswald Morris; m, Sol Kaplan; ed, Anthony Harvey; prod d, Hal Pereira, Tambi Larsen; art d, Edward Marshall; set d, Josie MacAvin; cos, Motley; makeup, George Frost.

Spy Drama   **(PR:A-C   MPAA:NR)**

SPY WHO LOVED ME, THE**   (1977, Brit.) 125m Eon/UA c

Roger Moore *(James Bond)*, Barbara Bach *(Maj. Anya Amasova)*, Curt Jurgens *(Karl Stromberg)*, Richard Kiel *(Jaws)*, Caroline Munro *(Naomi)*, Walter Gotell *(Gen. Gogol)*, Geoffrey Keen *(Minister of Defense)*, Bernard Lee *("M")*, Shane Rimmer *(Capt. Carter, U.S.S. Wayne)*, Bryan Marshall *(Commander Talbot, H.M.S. Ranger)*, Michael Billington *(Sergei)*, Olga Bisera *(Felica)*, Desmond Llewelyn *("Q" Maj. Boothroyd)*, Edward de Souza *(Sheik Hosein)*, Vernon Dobtcheff *(Max Kalba)*, Valerie Leon *(Hotel Receptionist)*, Lois Maxwell *(Miss Moneypenny)*, Sidney Tafler *(Liparus Captain)*, Nadim Sawalha *(Fekkesh)*, Sue Vanner *(The Log Cabin Girl)*, Eva Reuber-Staier *(Rubelvitch)*, Robert Brown *(Adm. Hargreaves)*, Marilyn Galsworthy *(Stromberg's Assistant)*, Milton Reid *(Sandor)*, Cyril Shaps *(Bechmann)*, Milo Sperber *(Markovitz)*, Albert Moses *(Barman)*, Rafiq Anwar *(Cairo Club Waiter)*, Felicity York, Dawn Rodrigues, Anika Pavel, Jill Goodall *(Arab Beauties)*, Yasher Adem, George Roubicek, Kim Fortune, Ray Hassett, Bob Sherman, Christopher Muncke, Doyle Richmond, Murray Salem, John Truscott, Peter Whitman, Vincent Marzello, Nicholas Campbell, Ray Evans, Anthony Forrest, Garrick Hagon, Ray Jewers, George Malaby, Anthony Pullen, Robert Sheedy, Don Staiton, Eric Stine, Stephen Temperley, Dean Warwick, Michael Howarth, Barry Andrews, Kevin McNally, Jeremy Bulloch, Sean Bury, John Sarbutt, David Auker, Dennis Blanch, Keith Buckley, Jonathan Bury, Nick Ellsworth, Tom Gerrard, Kazol Michalski, Keith Morris, John Salthouse, Lenny Rabin, Irvin Allen, Peter Ensor, The Egyptian Folklore Group.

As the BOND series moved deeper into the 1970s, emphasis was placed heavily on providing feats of daring and visual spectacle; budgets grew astronomically to provide such handicraft. This was done at the expense of an inventive script, the element that had made the Connery films masterpieces of the spy genre. If it was spectacle that the viewer wanted, that was just what he got. The Super Spy makes a daring jump off a 90-foot cliff to open the film, a feat that ski jumper Rick Sylvester was paid $30,000 to accomplish. That figure does not account for the helicopter and crew required to wait around for skiing conditions to be perfect: after waiting ten days they were lucky to get just one such daredevil shot. The largest studio set until that time was built to provide space for atomic submarines to be used in the story, as well as the menacing headquarters of Jurgens, the man intent on destroying the world with nuclear bombs pointed at both Moscow and New York. Shooting required taking film crews to such places as Egypt, Sardinia, Baffin Island (Canada), Malta, Scotland, Okinawa, Switzerland, and Nassau, the Bahamas. But the best spectacle of all was surprisingly a human one, this being the presence of 7'2" Richard Kiel, the henchman of Jurgens sent to do Moore in. It is refreshing to see that impact can still be made using a human being, and not just scantily dressed femmes, of which THE SPY WHO LOVED ME has its fair share (notably a helicopter operator who wears incredibly gawdy and revealing gowns). There is a plot beneath all this. It's not a very good one, and neither is the dialog which appears to have been thought up at the last minute when it was remembered that the characters had to say something. It would have been better if they hadn't. (And no less than 15 scriptwriters submitted material for this thing.) Yarn centers around the teaming of Moore (in his third Bond film) with Russia's top spy Bach to thwart the evil intentions of Jurgens. The latter has been stealing both Western and Soviet submarines to show that he means business. At first the two spies meet and fight a bit before realizing that another party is responsible for all the trouble. But then they band together and effectively combat Jurgens, although Kiel provides quite an obstacle before being pushed to the side. Only the title is borrowed from the Ian Fleming book – the author probably never even dreamed of such a tale. (See: JAMES BOND series Index.)

p, Albert R. Broccoli; d, Lewis Gilbert; w, Christopher Wood, Richard Maibaum (based on the novel by Ian Fleming); ph, Claude Renoir (Panavision, Eastmancolor); underwater ph, Lamar Boren; m, Marvin Hamlisch; ed, John Glen; prod d, Ken Adam; art d, Peter Lamont; set d, Hugh Scaife; cos, Ronald Paterson; spec eff, Derek Meddings (visual), Alan Maley (optical), John Evans (studio); m/l, James Bond theme, Monty Norman, "Nobody Does It Better," Hamlisch, Carole Bayer Sager (sung by Carly Simon); makeup, Paul Engelen.

Spy/Adventure   Cas.   (PR:C MPAA:PG)

SPY WITH A COLD NOSE, THE**½   (1966, Brit.) 93m Associated London-PAR-EM/EM c

Laurence Harvey (Dr. Francis Trevellyan), Daliah Lavi (Princess Natasha Romanova), Lionel Jeffries (Stanley Farquhar), Eric Sykes (Wrigley), Eric Portman (British Ambassador), Denholm Elliott (Pond-Jones), Colin Blakely (Russian Premier), June Whitfield (Elsie Farquhar), Nai Bonet (Belly Dancer), Paul Ford (American General), Peter Bayliss (Professor), Robert Flemyng (Chief of M.I. 5), Genevieve (Nightclub Hostess), Norma Foster ("Ark" Nurse), Renee Houston (Lady Blanchflower), Robin Bailey (M.I. 5 Commander), Michael Trubshawe (Braithwaite), Amy Dalby (Miss Marchbanks), Bernard Archard (Russian Intelligence Officer), Ronald Brittain (Commissionaire), Bruce Carstairs (Butler), Glen Mason ("Ark" Assistant), Perry Brooks, Trevor Delaney, Steven Morley (Farquhar's Children), Gillian Lewis (Lady Warburton), Tricia De Dulin (Air Hostess), Virginia Lyon (Lift Attendant), Julian Orchard (Policeman), John Forbes-Robertson (M.I. 5 Workshop Director), Arnold Diamond (Agent in Water Wagon), Wanda Ventham (Mrs. Winters), Marianne Stone, Sally Low, Disraeli the English Bulldog.

Entertaining spy spoof stars Harvey as a playboy veterinarian called upon by the British government to implant a transmitter inside the stomach of an English bulldog, to be presented to the Soviet Prime Minister as a gift. The plan works, but Harvey and agent Jeffries are forced to go to Russia when the dog becomes sick, for fear the transmitter would be discovered if a Russian veterinarian were to inspect him. Played for laughs, with numerous jokes made about JAMES BOND-type spy pictures.

p, Leonard Lightstone; d, Daniel Petrie; w, Ray Galton, Alan Simpson; ph, Ken Higgins (Pathe Color); m, Riz Ortolani; ed, Jack Slade; md, Ortolani; art d, Peter Mullins; cos, Yvonne Blake; makeup, Philip Leakey.

Comedy   (PR:A MPAA:NR)

SPY WITH MY FACE, THE*½   (1966) 86m Arena/MGM c

Robert Vaughn (Napoleon Solo), Senta Berger (Serena), David McCallum (Illya Kuryakin), Leo G. Carroll (Alexander Waverly), Michael Evans (Darius Two), Sharon Farrell (Sandy Wister), Fabrizio Mioni (Arsene Coria), Donald Harron (Kitt Kittridge), Bill Gunn (Namana), Jennifer Billingsley (Taffy), Paula Raymond (Director), Donna Michelle (Nina), Harold Gould (Doctor), Nancy Hsueh (Wanda), Michele Carey (Maggie), Paul Siemion (Clerk), Jan Arvan (Waiter).

A 60-minute episode from the television series "The Man From U.N.C.L.E." called "The Double Affair" had some extra footage added in order to release it at movie houses. Vaughn and McCallum are the two agents sent to Switzerland to install the combination of a safe that holds a top-secret nuclear weapon. In order to get at the weapon THRUSH agents use Berger to entice Vaughan while a double is put in his place who eludes even McCallum's suspicion. But an overlooked situation clues McCallum and he is able to take care of the enemy agents. Extra footage looks haphazard to go along with the forced direction and incredible script.

p, Sam Rolfe; d, John Newland; w, Clyde Ware, Joseph Caivelli (based on a story by Ware); ph, Fred Koenekamp (Metrocolor); m, Morton Stevens; ed, Joseph Dervin; art d, George W. Davis, Merrill Pye; set d, Henry Grace, Robert R. Benton; m/l, Title theme, Jerry Goldsmith.

Spy Drama   (PR:A MPAA:NR)

SPYASHCHAYA KRASAVITSA   (SEE: SLEEPING BEAUTY, 1966, USSR)

SPYLARKS**   (1965, Brit.) 104m RANK c (GB: THE INTELLIGENCE MEN)

Eric Morecambe (Eric Morecambe), Ernie Wise (Ernie Sage), William Franklyn (Col. Grant, M.I. 5), April Olrich (Mme. Petrovna), Gloria Paul (Gina Carlotti), Richard Vernon (Sir Edward Seabrook), David Lodge (Stage Manager), Jacqueline Jones (Karin), Terence Alexander (Reed), Francis Matthews (Thomas), Warren Mitchell (Prozoroff), Brian Oulton (Laundry Basket Man), Michael Peake (Sinister Stranger), Peter Bull (Phillipe), Tutte Lemkow (Seedy Schlect Agent), Rene Sartoris ("Siegfried" Dancer), Graham Smith ("Evil Owl" Dancer), Dilys Rosser (Girl in Cinema), Johnny Briggs (Boy in Cinema), Elizabeth Counsell (Girl in Cucaracha), Gerald Hely (Carlos), Joe Melia (Conductor), Marianne Stone (Woman in Lift), Jill Curzon (French Girl), Alexis Checnakov (Rostov), Laurence Herder (Ivan).

Morecambe and Wise are a pair caught up in foreign intrigue. The thin, yet complicated plot has them getting mixed up with Lemkow, a mysterious agent involved with an English-Russian trade pact. Unfortunately, the script is too muddled to figure out what's going on. Supposed humor falls flat and the story is occasionally overwhelmed by its complications. But Morecambe and Wise are the film's saving graces. They were popular with British television audiences at the time and three of their best loved routines are included in the story.

p, Hugh Stewart; d, Robert Asher; w, S.C. Green, R.M. Hills (based on a story by Peter Blackmore); ph, Jack Asher (Eastmancolor); m, Philip Green; ed, Gerry Hambling.

Comedy   (PR:A MPAA:NR)

SPYS   (SEE: S.P.Y.S., 1974)

SQUAD CAR**   (1961) 62m Key/FOX bw

Vici Raaf (Cameo Kincaid), Paul Bryar (Lt. Beck), Don Marlow (Jay Reinhart), Lynn Moore (Jeanne Haggerty), James Cross (Harry), Jack Harris (Manfred Stahl), Blu Wright (Robert Scalise), Jim Hurley (Bartender), Jimmy Dale (Bank Official), Norman MacDonald (Dell Taylor).

Standard crime melodrama starring Bryar as the Phoenix cop trying to uncover a counterfeiting ring that includes singer Raaf. Marlow becomes innocently involved when one of his employees is found murdered and Marlow is the chief suspect. With his girl friend's help, Marlow clears his name and assists Bryar in breaking the counterfeiting organization.

p&d, Ed Leftwich; w, E. M. Parsons, Scott Flohr; ph, Henry Cronjager.

Crime   (PR:A MPAA:NR)

SQUADRON LEADER X**   (1943, Brit.) 99m RKO bw

Eric Portman (Erich Kohler), Ann Dvorak (Barbara Lucas), Walter Fitzgerald (Inspector Milne), Martin Miller (Mr. Krohn), Beatrice Varley (Mrs. Krohn), Henry Oscar (Dr. Schultz), Barry Jones (Bruce Fenwick), Charles Victor (Marks), Mary Merrall (Miss Thorndike), Carl Jaffe (Luftwaffe Colonel), Marjorie Rhodes (Mrs. Agnew), Frederick Richter (Inspector Siegel), David Peel (Michael Bertholt), John Salew, Aubrey Mallalieu.

WW II drama about Nazi espionage efforts in Britain starring Portman and Miller as German soldiers who are forced to do undercover work for their country. Portman disguises himself as a member of the RAF and then attempts to bomb a Belgian town to make it look as though the Allies are bombing civilian targets. He is captured by the underground, who want to send him to England. As he is marked for death by the Gestapo, this puts him in the position of being hunted by the British and the Germans. The film is wartime propaganda, furthering the image of the Nazis as a deadly and inhumane force.

p, Victor Hanbury; d, Lance Comfort; w, Wolfgang Wilhelm, Miles Malleson (based on the story "Four Days in a Hero's Life" by Emeric Pressburger); ph, Mutz Greenbaum; m, William Alwyn; ed, Michael C. Chorlton; art d, W. C. Andrews; spec eff, Harry Miller.

War   (PR:A MPAA:NR)

SQUADRON OF HONOR*½   (1938) 62m COL bw

Don Terry (Blane), Mary Russell (Eve), Thurston Hall (Metcalf), Arthur Loft (Tanner), Robert Warwick (Kimball), Marc Lawrence (Lawlor), Dick Curtis (Craig), George McKay (Todd), Eddie Fetherston (Denton), Edward LeSaint (Forsythe), Ivan Miller, Harry Strang, Jimmy Hollywood.

An American Legion convention serves as the backdrop for a rather drab story starring Hall as the commander of the Legion who has a murder planted on him by Warwick. Warwick wants to use the Legion to back his resistance to the arms control bill as he just happens to work in the armament business. This gives other Legionnaires the chance to be heroic and get their fellow member out of trouble.

d, C. C. Coleman, Jr.; w, Michael Simmons (based on a story by Martin Mooney); ph, Lucien Ballard; ed, Al Clark; Cos, Robert Kalloch.

Crime   **(PR:A   MPAA:NR)**

SQUADRON 633*½**   (1964, U.S./Brit.) 94m Mirisch/UA c

Cliff Robertson (Wing Cmdr. Roy Grant), George Chakiris (Lt. Erik Bergman), Maria Perschy (Hilde Bergman), Harry Andrews (Air Marshal Davis), Donald Houston (Wing Cmdr. Tom Barrett), Michael Goodliffe (Squadron Leader Bill Adams), John Meillon (Flight Lt. Gillibrand), John Bonney (Flight Lt. Scott), Angus Lennie (Flight Lt. Hoppy Hopkinson), Scot Finch (Flight Lt. Bissel), Barbara Archer (Rosie the Barmaid), Julian Sherrier (Flight Lt. Singh), Suzan Farmer (Mary, WAF Sergeant), John Church (Flight Lt. Evans), Jeremy Wagg (Flight Lt. Reynolds), Johnny Briggs (Flight Lt. Jones), Sean Kelly (Flight Lt. Nigel), Edward Brayshaw (Flight Lt. Greiner), Arnold Locke (Kearns), Peter Kriss (Flight Lt. Milner), Geoffrey Frederick (Flight Lt. Frank), Richard Shaw (Johansen), Anne Ridley (SS Woman), Cavan Malone (Ericsen), Drewe Henley (Thor), John Dray (Henrik), Chris Williams (Goth).

Cliff Robertson is a pilot in real life and loves making movies about airplanes, so this was a perfect opportunity for him to exercise his penchant for flying. It's the dark days of WW II and Chakiris, a Norwegian patriot, tells the British that the occupying Nazis are making the dreaded V-2 rockets at a secret location in Norway, far away from the city. The plant is built under an overhang and set on a fjord. The only way to destroy the factory is to come in low and attempt to destroy the overhanging cliff, thus causing it to fall on the plant and crush it. Robertson is a wing commander with the RAF and he gets the assignment of knocking the plant out of commission. At the same time, Chakiris will muster his Norwegian underground and they will attack by land and mop up the mission. Before the bombing is to begin, Chakiris is captured by the Nazis and tortured so brutally that he reveals everything. Armed with that knowledge, the Nazis knock off all the patriots and the Robertson-led squadron flies into a trap prepared by the waiting Germans. The flight of light Mosquitoes hit a covey of pigeons and all the planes, save one (the one with Robertson in it, naturally), are destroyed. In the finale, the last bomb hits the cliff in the exact right spot, the tons of earth collapse on the V-2 factory, and the mission, despite all of the deaths, is a success. Chakiris's wife is played by Austrian Maria Perschy, a sexpot of the 1950s and 1960s in Europe. Robertson was so involved with his plane collection that he insisted on doing his own flying for the TV movie "The Sunshine Patriot," in which he co-starred with wife Dina Merrill. Due to an eye problem, he had a minor mishap on that picture and wound up in a slight accident. Since then, he has limited his flying somewhat.

p, Cecil F. Ford; d, Walter E. Grauman; w, James Clavell, Howard Koch (based on the novel by Frederick E. Smith); ph, Edward Scaife (Panavision, DeLuxe Color); m, Ron Goodwin; ed, Bert Bates; prod d, Michael Stringer; spec eff, Tom Howard; stunts, John Crewdson.

War Drama   **(PR:A-C   MPAA:NR)**

SQUALL, THE*   (1929) 104m FN-WB bw

Myrna Loy (Nubi), Richard Tucker (Josef Lajos, Farmer), Alice Joyce (Maria Lajos, his Wife), Carroll Nye (Paul Lajos, Their Son), Loretta Young (Irma), Harry Cording (Peter, Servant), ZaSu Pitts (Lena, Servant), Nicholas Soussanin (El Moro), Knute Erickson (Uncle Dani), George Hackathorne (Niki).

This picture has the honor of being the first talking effort of the great filmmaker Alexander Korda. Loy plays a Hungarian gypsy who takes refuge in a farm house after a terrible storm. She then continues to use her sex appeal to drive the men wild and the entire household upside down. The inadequate sound techniques was one variable that affected this picture, but the script is shallow and the performances are totally stilted by the material given them. Even Loy seems overpowered in a role that was just up her alley.

p, Richard A. Rowland; d, Alexander Korda; w, Bradley King (based on the play by Jean Bart); ph, John Seitz; m, Leo F. Forbstein; ed, Edward Schroeder; m/l, "Gypsy Charmer," Grant Clarke, Harry Akst.

Drama   **(PR:A   MPAA:NR)**

SQUARE DANCE JUBILEE*½   (1949) 78m Lippert bw

Don Barry (Don), Mary Beth Hughes (Barbara), Wally Vernon (Seldom), Spade Cooley (Spade), John Eldredge (Stratton), Thurston Hall (G.K.), Britt Wood (Grubby), Chester Clute (Yes-Man), Tom Kennedy (Bartender), Max Terhune (Sheriff), Tom Tyler (Buck), Clark Stevens (Bert), Lee Roberts (Smokey), Marshall Reed (Charlie), Slim Gault (Tall Comic), Cliff Taylor (Short Comic), Hazel Nilsen (Secretary), Ralph Moody (Indian Chief), Alex Montoya (Second Indian), Hal King (Television Operator), Cowboy Copas,

Broome Bros, Smiley & Kitty, Herman the Hermit, Ray Vaughn, Tumbleweed Tumblers, Elder Lovelies, Claude Casey, Buddy McDowell, Johnny Downs, Dana Gibson, Charlie Cirillo, Dot Remey, Les Gotcher.

A total of 21 country-western tunes are delivered with animal imitations hemmed around the thin plot of two television producers traveling out west to search for backup talent for a television show. There's even a subplot about cattle rustlers, with the New York boys caught in the middle.

p, Ron Ormand; d, Paul Landres; w, Ormond, Dan B. Ullman (based on a story by William L. Nolte); ph, Ernest W. Miller; m, Walter Greene; ed, Hugh Winn; md, Greene; art d, Fred Preble; set d, Fred Offenbecker.

Western/Musical   **(PR:A   MPAA:NR)**

SQUARE DANCE KATY*½   (1950) 76m MON bw

Vera Vague [Barbara Jo Allen], Phil Brito, Virginia Welles, Warren Douglas, Sheila Ryan, Dorothy Vaughan, Harry Cheshire, Fenton Jones, Jon Riffel, Warren Jackson, Donald Kerr, Paul Bryar, Earle Hodgins, Frank Sully, Russell Hicks, Stanley Blystone, Lee Phelps, Tristram Coffin, Edward Gargan, Joseph Crehan, Ray Walker, William Forrest, Jimmie Davis and His Sunshine Band.

Tired low-budget musical with the standard small-town-kids-make-good-in-the-big-city plot. Vague plays an aspiring singer from the backwoods who drags her bandleader boy friend off to New York City in search of fame and fortune. Pretty lifeless.

p, Lindsley Parsons; d, Jean Yarbrough; w, Warren Wilson; ph, William Sickner; ed, Ace Herman; md, Edward Kay; art d, Dave Milton.

Musical   **(PR:A   MPAA:NR)**

SQUARE JUNGLE, THE½**   (1955) 86m UNIV bw

Tony Curtis (Eddie Quaid/Packy Glennon), Pat Crowley (Julie Walsh), Ernest Borgnine (Bernie Browne), Paul Kelly (Jim McBride), Jim Backus (Pat Quaid), Leigh Snowden (Lorraine Evans), John Day (Al Gorski), David Janssen (Jack Lindsay), John Marley (Tommy Dillon), Barney Phillips (Dan Selby), Joseph Vitale (Tony Anderson), Wendell Niles (Chicago Ring Announcer), Kay Stewart (Mrs. Gorski), Frank Marlowe (Rip Kane), Frankie Van, Walter J. Ekwert (Seconds), Joe Louis (Himself), Carmen McRae (Singer), Clancy Cooper (Mike Walsh), Jesse Kirkpatrick (The Boss), Frank Moran (Referee), Dennis Moore (Bit), Barry Regan (Bartender), Jimmy Cross (Hawker).

Curtis plays a young man who turns to the ring to get his old man, Backus, out of jail. Though he originally only wanted the money to help his dad, he ends up winning the middleweight crown. Borgnine plays the gentle and reserved trainer who guides Curtis' fighting career. In the final title bout, Curtis badly beats his opponent and then is overcome with guilt. Although there is little to make this different from the usual ring yarn, good performances, especially by Borgnine, help to provide some freshness. A bit of lightening on the sentiment is in order too.

p, Albert Zugsmith; d, Jerry Hopper; w, George Zuckerman (based on a story by Zuckerman; ph, George Robinson; m, Heinz Roemheld; ed, Paul Weatherwax; md, Joseph Gershenson; art d, Alexander Golitzen, Alfred Sweeney; cos, Rosemary Odell.

Drama   **(PR:A   MPAA:NR)**

SQUARE OF VIOLENCE**   (1963, U.S./Yugo.) 98m Lovcen/MGM bw
                                          (NASILJE NA TRGU)

Broderick Crawford (Dr. Stefan Bernardi), Valentina Cortese (Erica Bernardi), Branko Plesa (Maj. Kohler), Bibi Andersson (Maria), Anita Bjork (Sophia), Bert Sotlar (Partisan Leader), Dragomir Felba (Serafin), Viktor Starcic (German Commandant), Nikola Simic (Radio Operator).

In one of Crawford's most demanding roles he plays a doctor and member of the resistance in a town occupied by Nazis. The underground movement plans an attack against the Germans, but is called off at the last minute without Crawford's knowledge. He goes through with his part anyway, tossing a bomb which kills 30 German soldiers. The enraged German officer, Plesa, demands to know the identity of the man responsible for the bombings; otherwise he threatens to kill 900 hostages held in the town square. Crawford is thus put in the trying position of whether or not to confess. If he does he will be subject to torture that may jeopordize the entire movement, and the hostages may not be released, or to hide and be killed with the hostages. He decides on the latter, but in an ironic ending, he is killed by another resistance member. Before he dies, however, he tells Plesa that he was responsible for the bombings. But the general kills the hostages anyway. A poignant look at the atrocities of war as they affect an individual. Crawford is brilliant in what may very well be the best performance of his career. He effectively transmits the inner turmoil his character is going through. At times the script depends too heavily upon dialog, and the dubbed voices of Yugoslav actors is annoying, but these minor flaws do not hurt the overall power of this picture.

p, Aleksandar Sekulovic, Leonardo Bercovici; d, Bercovici; w, Eric Bercovici, Leonardo Bercovici; ph, Sekulovic; m, Dusan Radic; ed, Roberto

Cinquini, Olga Skrigin; md, Franco Ferrera; art d, Zoran Zorcic.

War/Drama   (PR:A   MPAA:NR)

SQUARE PEG, THE**   (1958, Brit.) 89m RANK bw

Norman Wisdom (*Norman Pitkin/Gen. Schreiber*), Honor Blackman (*Lesley Cartland*), Edward Chapman (*Wilfred Grimsdale*), Campbell Singer (*Sgt. Loder*), Hattie Jacques (*Gretchen von Schmetterling*), Brian Worth (*Henri Le Blanc*), Terence Alexander (*Capt. Wharton*), John Warwick (*Col. Layton*), Arnold Bell (*Gen. Hunt*), Andre Maranne (*Jean-Claude*), Victor Beaumont (*Jogenkraut*), Frank Williams (*Capt. Ford*), Eddie Leslie (*Medical Officer*), Oliver Reed, Martin Boddey, Harold Goodwin.

Popular British comic Wisdom is given a dual role as a happy-go-lucky street repairer and strict Nazi officer in this farce. Wisdom's harassment of soldiers gets him inducted into a British army labor regiment. The purpose is to use his road mending skills, but in a miscalculation he parachutes behind enemy lines. Captured by the Nazis, Wisdom uses his resemblance to the German general to perform some goofy heroics and save himself and the other captives. Direction is slack, but the concentration is on Wisdom's antics.

p, Hugh Stewart; d, John Paddy Carstairs; w, Jack Davies, Henry E. Blyth, Norman Wisdom, Eddie Leslie; ph, Jack Cox; m, Philip Green; ed, Roger Cherrill.

Comedy   (PR:A   MPAA:NR)

SQUARE RING, THE**½   (1955, Brit.) 73m EAL/REP bw

Jack Warner (*Danny Felton*), Robert Beatty (*Kid Curtis*), Bill Owen (*Happy Burns*), Maxwell Reed (*Rick Martell*), George Rose (*Whitey Johnson*), Bill Travers (*Rowdie Rawlings*), Alfie Bass (*Frank Forbes*), Ronald Lewis (*Eddie Lloyd*), Sidney James (*Adams*), Joan Collins (*Frankie*), Kay Kendall (*Eve Lewis*), Bernadette O'Farrell (*Peg Curtis*), Eddie Byrne (*Lou Lewis*), Vic Wise (*Joe*), Michael Golden (*Warren*), Joan Sims (*Bunty*), Sidney Tafler, Alexander Gauge (*Wiseacres*), Kid Berg (*Referee*), Madoline Thomas (*Mrs. Lloyd*), Ben Williams (*Mr. Lloyd*), Harry Herbert (*de Grazos*), C.H. Nichols (*Timekeeper*), Ivan Staff, Alf Hines, Joe Bloom, Michael Ingrams, Vernon Kelso.

A boxing saga that involves five different stories taking place mainly in the dressing room prior to and after the various bouts. Concentration is on the characters who have taken to the ring for one reason or another, and what the fights they have that night mean to them. One boxer, estranged from his wife, dies after taking a savage beating. Though their is little plot development, interest is maintained through the development of the various characters. A good cast helps to pull it off.

p&d, Michael Relph, Basil Dearden; w, Robert Westerby, Peter Myers, Alec Grahame (based on the play by Ralph W. Peterson); ph, Otto Heller, Gordon Dines; m, Dock Mathieson; ed, Peter Bezencenet; md, Mathieson; art d, Jim Morahan; cos, Anthony Mendleson.

Drama   (PR:A   MPAA:NR)

SQUARE ROOT OF ZERO, THE*½   (1964) 80m Mark-L
Enterprises/Groovie-movies-Pat Patterson Productions bw (AKA: THIS IMMORAL AGE)

Michael Egan (*Zero*), Jimmy Gavin (*Alan*), Leslie Davis (*Jane Liggett*), Don Woodbury (*Arch Liggett*), Mary Bauer (*May Liggett*), Jeri Archer (*Nell*), George Quinn (*Garfield, the Chauffeur*), Roberta Longhi (*Agnes, the Housemaid*), Bob Spivak (*Hank*), Barbara Krauthamer (*Dorrie*), Dan Broyles (*The Indian*), K. T. Daggott (*Mrs. Harrison*).

Potshot at rich folks melodrama has Egan and Gavin as two New York Beatniks who go off on a camping trip to Maine. Egan is a potential writer of true-confession stories, but he's too lazy to ever write any of them down. They encounter a family also vacationing with a young daughter who spends all her time with Gavin, while Egan attempts to make conversation with her mother, a writer of soap-opera plays. When Gavin thinks that the daughter may be pregnant, the two youths decide to split, but not before staging a drowning that will get Gavin off the hook.

p, d&w, William Cannon; ph, Sheldon Rochlin; m, Elliott Kaplan; ed, Rochlin, Cannon, Otis Maclay; md, Kaplan; cos, Vincent Loscalzo; spec eff, Al Stahl, Maclay; makeup, Loscalzo.

Comedy   (PR:C   MPAA:NR)

SQUARE SHOOTER, THE (SEE: SKIPALONG ROSENBLOOM, 1951)

SQUARE SHOULDERS**½   (1929) 60m Pathe bw

Junior Coghlan (*Tad*), Louis Wolheim (*Slag*), Philippe De Lacy (*Eddie*), Anita Louise (*Mary Jane*), Montague Shaw (*Cartwright*), Johnny Morris (*Hook*), Kewpie Morgan (*Delicate Don*), Clarence Geldert (*Commandant*), Erich von Stroheim, Jr, Chuck Reisner, Jr.

An early partial talkie which stars Wolheim as a man who left his family behind to become a tramp. But his guilt creeps up on him and he is

determined to help his boy get ahead in life. He pulls off a robbery that requires doublecrossing his crooked pals. With the money, Wolheim anonymously enlists the boy, Coghlan, in a military school, with the father getting a job at the same school as a stable worker. But the tramps who had the wool pulled over their eyes come looking for Wolheim, with the latter winding up dead in an attempt to protect the school from his old friends. Coghlan never learns the true identity of his father. A bit heavy on the sentiment, but an otherwise good human interest story.

d, E. Mason Hopper; w, George Dromgold, Houston Branch, Peggy Prior; ph, Dave Abel; ed, Barbara Hunter; titles, John Kraft.

Drama   (PR:A   MPAA:NR)

SQUARED CIRCLE, THE (SEE: JOE PALOOKA IN THE SQUARED CIRCLE, 1950)

SQUARES**½   (1972) 92m Plateau International c (AKA: RIDING TALL)

Andrew Prine (*Austin Roth*), Gilmer McCormick (*Chase Lawrence*), Harriet Medin, Jack Mather (*Ruth's Parents*), William Wintersole (*State Policeman*), Sam Christopher (*Woman in Restaurant*), Dean Smith, Tom Hennessy, Tom Basham, Patricia Sauers.

A modern day western has drifter Prine being picked up by rich kid McCormick, who is running away from her stifling New York existence. The two start up a lofty affair, that is kept intense through each of their volatile and argumentative natures. When Prine meets with failure in his attempts at the rodeo, McCormick splits to an uncertain future, while Prine's own self-esteem grows. The emphasis here is on the relationship, how the two youths are coming to terms with approaching adulthood and how each one develops through their experiences, at least in Prine's case.

p&d, Patrick J. Murphy; w, Mary Ann Saxon; ph, John Koester (Metrocolor); m, Donald Vincent; ed, Grant Hoag; art d, Mike Minor.

Western/Drama   (PR:A   MPAA:GP)

SQUATTER'S DAUGHTER**   (1933, Aus.) 107m Cinesound
Productions/British Empire Films bw

Grant Lindsay, Jocelyn Howarth, George Cross, Fred McDonald, Lane-Balliff, Dorothy Dunkley, Katie Towers, Owen Ainley.

Though few feature length productions were undertaken in Australia prior to WW II, and even fewer shown outside of the island continent at that time, occasionally one did sneak out. This is one that did, and the photography is special in its depiction of Australian scenery. Story deals with the efforts of a young woman to prevent a feud between two ranchers, one of whom is trying to take over the other's land. The girl puts up a tremendous struggle in her efforts to restore peace to the area. In Australia, ranches are called stations, and their owners, squatters.

p&d, Ken G. Hall; ph, Capt. Frank Hurley.

Drama   (PR:A   MPAA:NR)

SQUAW MAN, THE**   (1931) 106m MGM bw (GB: THE WHITE MAN)

Warner Baxter (*Capt. James Wynnegate/Jim Carsten*), Lupe Velez (*Naturich*), Eleanor Boardman (*Diana Kerhill*), Charles Bickford (*Cash Hawkins*), Roland Young (*Sir John Applegate*), Paul Cavanagh (*Henry, Earl of Kerhill*), Raymond Hatton (*Shorty*), Julia Faye (*Mrs. Chichester Jones*), DeWitt Jennings (*Sheriff Bud Handy*), J. Farrell MacDonald (*Big Bill*), Dickie Moore (*Little Hal*), Mitchell Lewis (*Tabywanna*), Victor Potel (*Andy*), Frank Rice (*Grouchy*), Eva Dennison (*Lady Phoebe Kerhill*), Lillian Bond (*Babs*), Luke Cosgrave (*Shanks*), Frank Hagney (*Clark, Deputy*), Lawrence Grant (*Gen. Stafford*), Harry Northrup (*Butler*), Ed Brady (*McSorley*), Chris-Pin Martin (*Zeke*), Desmond Roberts (*Hardwick*), Artie Ortego (*Naturich's Brother*), Herbert Evans (*Conductor*), Pat Somerset (*Officer*), C. Aubrey Smith, Winifred Kingston.

Cecil B. DeMille, never a man to refrain from beating a good thing into the ground, filmed this old stage play for the third time here. The film tells the story of Baxter, an English captain who assumes the guilt for his embezzling aristocrat cousin, Cavanagh, whose wife (Boardman) he loves, and flees to the American West. He soon makes an enemy of rustler Bickford, from whose clutches he rescues Indian maiden Velez. He marries the Spanish-accented Indian woman and soon she bears him a child, Moore. Later, Velez kills Bickford as a sort of favor to her new husband. Boardman, Baxter's true love and wife of Cavanagh, shows up out West to tell Baxter that Cavanagh has died after confessing his guilt and that Baxter has inherited his title and estate. The sheriff comes around to arrest Velez for Bickford's murder and the squaw conveniently commits suicide, leaving Baxter free to return to England with Boardman and little Moore. DeMille, despite telling a Baltimore reporter, "I love this story so much that as long as I live I will make it every ten years," was not at all happy to remake his debut feature. He was anxious to get out of a three-picture contract with MGM and this seemed like the least painful way to complete his obligation to the company. In the first two versions (1914, 1918) he used real Indians to play Indians but now he was restrained by Hollywood standards and had to hire Velez as the title maiden. On the set she was a terror, foul-mouthed and unreliable. DeMille was so depressed and devoid of ideas that he asked for a copy of his 1914 version to be sent out to the location. He became even more depressed when he learned that all the copies were destroyed in a Philadelphia laboratory fire (although a print did later surface). Certainly the weakest of the three versions, overlong and dull, although it does have a lively performance by Velez. After the shoot, DeMille retreated to his yacht to indulge his hobby of deep-sea diving. He never got around to making a fourth or fifth SQUAW MAN. The 1913 movie version of the play (which opened on Broadway in 1907 with famed cowboy star William S. Hart as the villainous Cash Hawkins) ran for only half the time of this sound version. It had been the director's first feature (this was his 57th), and the first feature-length picture ever to be made in Hollywood. Its leading lady, Winifred Kingston, has a bit part in the sound version, which features dialog by the former Broadway musical star Elsie Janis.

p&d, Cecil B. DeMille; w, Lucien Hubbard, Lenore Coffee, Elsie Janis (based on the play by Edwin Milton Royle); ph, Harold Rosson; m, Herbert Stothart; ed, Anne Bauchens; art d, Mitchell Leisen.

Western   **(PR:A MPAA:NR)**

SQUEAKER, THE**   (1930, Brit.) 88m BL bw

Percy Marmont *(Capt. Leslie)*, Anne Grey *(Beryl Stedman)*, Gordon Harker *(Bill Annerley)*, Trilby Clark *(Millie Trent)*, Alfred Drayton *(Lew Fried-man)*, Eric Maturin *(Frank Sutton)*, Nigel Bruce *(Collie)*, W. Cronin Wilson *(Inspector)*.

The first all-talkie film based on an Edgar Wallace novel, and the author directed it himself. Marmont stars as a Scotland Yard detective posing as an ex-convict in order to trap a powerful fence known as the "Squeaker" who masquerades as the chairman of a philanthropic society.

p, S. W. Smith; d&w, Edgar Wallace (based on the play by Wallace); ph, Horace Wheddon.

Crime   **(PR:A MPAA:NR)**

SQUEAKER, THE, 1937 (SEE: MURDER ON DIAMOND ROW, 1937, Brit.)

SQUEALER, THE**   (1930) 67m COL bw

Jack Holt *(Charles Hart)*, Dorothy Revier *(Margaret Hart)*, Davey Lee *(Bunny Hart)*, Matt Moore *(John Sheridan, Hart's Lawyer)*, ZaSu Pitts *(Bella, Maid)*, Robert Ellis *(Valleti)*, Matthew Betz *(Red Majors)*, Arthur Housman *(Mitter Davis)*, Louis Natheaux *("Ratface" Edwards)*, Eddie Kane *(Whisper)*, Eddie Sturgis *(The Killer)*, Elmer Ballard *(Pimply-Face)*.

Holt stars as a bootleg gangster who has his rival killed. His wife, Revier, is having an affair with his best friend, Moore. After the murder of his rival, played by Ellis, Holt is arrested. He believes Moore has squealed on him and he breaks out of jail to get revenge, only to learn that the squealer is really his wife. Seems she tipped the police off to save Holt from a worse fate from the rival mob. Once he learns the truth, Holt decides his son is better off with Moore, and knowingly walks into a police trap where he is killed. Parts of the script were later used in MGM's THE LAST GANGSTER (1937). This film was also known for its unique character names, such as Ratface Edwards, Mitter Davis, and Pimply-Face.

p, Harry Cohn; d, Harry Joe Brown; w, Dorothy Howell, J. Casey Robinson, Jo Swerling (based on the novel by Mark Linder); ph, Ted Tetzlaff; ed, Leonard Wheeler; art d, Edward Jewell.

Crime/Drama   **(PR:A MPAA:NR)**

SQUEEZE, THE**   (1977, Brit.) 106m WB c

Stacy Keach *(Naboth)*, Freddie Starr *(Teddy)*, Edward Fox *(Foreman)*, Stephen Boyd *(Vic)*, David Hemmings *(Keith)*, Carol White *(Jill)*, Alan Ford *(Taff)*, Roy Marsden *(Barry)*, Stuart Harwood *(Des)*, Hilary Gasson *(Barbara)*, Alison Portes *(Christine)*, Keith Miles *(Jack)*, Lee Strand *(Dave)*, Lucinda Duckett *(Sharon)*, Lucita Lijertwood *(Mrs. Delgado)*.

Ex-cop Keach is called upon to assist with the kidnaping case of his former wife, White, now married to a hot-shot executive. While trying to perform heroics, Keach is also trying to control his drinking, with which he is helped by his pal Starr, an ex-hood Keach took an affectionate interest in. Performers are given little in the way of material to bring their characters above stereotypes, making pretty predictable going. The exceptional asset is the seedy atmosphere.

p, Stanley O'Toole; d, Michael Apted; w, Leon Griffiths (based on the novel *Whose Little Girl Are You?* by David Craig); ph, Dennis Lewiston (Technicolor); m, David Hentschel; ed, John Shirley; art d, William McGrow.

Crime   **(PR:O MPAA:NR)**

SQUEEZE, THE*½   (1980, Ital.) 100m Dritte Centama/Maverick c

Lee Van Cleef *(Chris)*, Karen Black *(Clarisse)*, Edward Albert *(Jeff)*, Lionel Stander *(Sam Epstein)*, Robert Alda *(Donati)*, Angelo Infanti *(Inspector)*, Antonella Murgia *(Jessica)*, Peter Carsten *(Von Stratten)*.

A lukewarm picture whose saving grace is the presence of Van Cleef (not his acting, just his taut expressions) as an aging safecracker given a final job to do. Albert hires Van Cleef to assist some Germans in a heist; but Van Cleef learns that his associates plan to kill him when the caper is completed. So he takes care of the opponents instead, and walks away with a wound that keeps him in bed for awhile – the duration of the film, in fact. His reward is Black, as a Brooklyn native believe it or not, who acts as his all-fulfilling servant.

p, Turi Vasile; d, Anthony M. Dawson [Antonio Margheriti]; w, Simon O'Neil, Marc Princi, Paul Costello; ph, Sergio D'Offizi (Technicolor); m, Paolo Vasile; ed, Robert Sterbini; art d, Francesco Bronzi, Hans Zillman; cos, Adrianna Berselli.

Crime Drama   **Cas.**   **(PR:O MPAA:R)**

SQUEEZE A FLOWER**   (1970, Aus.) 102m NLT Group W c

Walter Chiari *(Brother George)*, Jack Albertson *(Alfredo Brazzi)*, Dave Allen *(Tim O'Mahoney)*, Rowena Wallace *(June Phillips)*, Kirrily Nolan *(Maria)*, Alec Kellaway *(The Abbot)*, Michael Laurence *(Brother James)*, Alan Tobin *(Brother Peter)*, Charles McCallum *(Brother Sebastian)*, Harry Lawrence *(Signore Vequis)*, Franz Zavier Zach *(Father of Boy)*, Ricky Cilona *(Boy)*, Roger Ward *(Bosun)*, Alex Mozart *(Truck Driver)*, Sandy Harbutt *(Man Worker)*, Amanda Irving *(Girl Worker)*, Jeff Ashby *(Bert Andrews)*, Penny Sugg *(Stewardess)*, Sue Lloyd *(Receptionist)*, Barry Crocker *(Waiter)*, Lea Denfield *(Flower Seller)*, Pat Sullivan *(Laboratory Assistant)*, Beryl Cheers *(Housewife)*.

Chiari plays a monk who is the only person knowing the secret ingredients to a valuable and exotic liquor. When he is unable to get enough money out of the local wine merchant, Chiari leaves for Australia, where he forms a partnership with Albertson. Chiari sends the earnings back to the Italian monastery, and never forsakes his vows, not even when Albertson tries to get the formula from him by using the sexy publicity girl, Wallace. Scripting and direction are on the weak side, but the comic talents of Albertson and Chiari do a decent job of carrying the film.

p, George Willoughby; d, Marc Daniels; w, Charles Isaacs; ph, Brian West; m, Tommy Leonetti; ed, Stanley Moore; art d, Dennis Gentle; m/l, Title song, Leonetti (sung by Leonetti).

Comedy   **(PR:A MPAA:NR)**

SQUEEZE PLAY*   (1981) 92m Troma c

Jim Harris *(Wes)*, Jenni Hetrick *(Samantha)*, Rick Gitlin *(Fred)*, Helen Campitelli *(Jamie)*, Rick Kahn *(Tom)*, Diana Valentien *(Maureen)*, Alford Corley *(Buddy)*, Melissa Michaels *(Mary Lou)*, Melissa P. Morgan *(Bozo)*, Sonya Jennings *(Max)*, Sharon Kyle Bramblett *(Midge)*, Zachary *(Pop)*, Tony Hoty *(Koch)*, Lisa Beth Wolf *(Rose)*, Brenda Kaplan *(Brenda)*, Steven W. Kaman *(Russ)*, Kenneth Raskin *(Beasley)*, Edward D. Phillips *(Chester)*, Rosemary Joyce *(Wanda)*, Peter Van Norden *(Beauty Parlor Manager)*, William Kirksey *(Game Announcer, Narrator)*.

An offensive film that uses softball as an excuse to display body parts and tell dirty jokes. Thin plot is about a group of girls, abandoned by their baseball-loving boyfriends, forming their own team to get even. All the problems between the sexes are worked out on the playing field.

p, Lloyd Kaufman, Michael Herz; d, Samuel Weil; w, Haim Pekelis, Charles Kaufman; ph, Lloyd Kaufman; ed, George T. Norris.

Comedy   **Cas.**   **(PR:O MPAA:R)**

SQUIBS*½   (1935, Brit.) 77m Twickenham/GAU bw

Betty Balfour *(Squibs Hopkins)*, Gordon Harker *(Sam Hopkins)*, Stanley Holloway *(Police Constable Charley Lee)*, Margaret Yarde *(Mrs. Lee)*, Morris Harvey *(Inspector Lee)*, Michael Shepley *(Colin Barrett)*, Drusilla Wills *(Mrs. Parker)*, O.B. Clarence *(Sir John Barrett)*, Ronald Shiner *(Bill)*, Thomas Weguelin *(Alf)*.

Balfour repeats the role that made her a star in 1921, a Cockney flower girl who wants to marry policeman Holloway. Her father (Harker) puts a damper on her plans when he loses a bundle of money he was investing for someone else. Everything comes out for the best, though, when Balfour wins the sweepstakes and is able to marry the patrolman of her dreams. The silent was better.

p, Julius Hagen; d, Henry Edwards; w, Michael Hogan, H. Fowler Mear (based on a play by Clifford Seyler, George Pearson); ph, Sydney Blythe.

Musical   **(PR:A MPAA:NR)**

SQUIRM*   (1976) 93m AIP c

Don Scardino (Mick), Patricia Pearcy (Geri), R.A. Dow (Roger), Jean
Sullivan (Naomi), Peter MacLean (Sheriff), Fran Higgins (Alma), William
Newman (Quigley), Barbara Quinn (Sheriff's Girl), Carl Dagenhart (Willie
Grimes), Angel Sande (Millie), Carol Jean Owens (Bonnie), Kim Iocouvozzi
(Hank), Walter Dimmick (Danny), Julia Klopp (Mrs. Klopp).

Man-eating worms are created from the regular variety when an electrical
storm downs wires and fills the ground in which they harbor with high
voltage. A Georgia farm community is victim to the slimy creatures, which
have a way of drawing on underlying tensions of the townspeople. It is
claimed in the opening titles that this story issues from an actual occurrence
in Georgia in 1975.

p, George Manasse; d&w, Jeff Lieberman; ph, Joseph Mangine (Movielab
Color); m, Robert Prince; ed, Brian Smedley-Aston; art d, Henry Shrady; cos,
Dianne Finn Chapman; spec eff, Bill Milling, Don Farnsworth, Lee Howard;
makeup, Rick Baker.

Horror   **Cas.**   **(PR:C MPAA:PG)**

SSSSNAKE   (SEE: SSSSSSSS, 1973)

SSSSSSSS½   (1973) 99m Serena-Zanuck-Brown/UNIV c (AKA:
                                                             SSSSNAKE)

Strother Martin (Dr. Carl Stoner), Dirk Benedict (David Blake), Heather
Menzies (Kristine Stoner), Richard B. Shull (Dr. Ken Daniels), Tim
O'Connor (Kogen), Jack Ging (Sheriff Dale Hardison), Kathleen King (Kitty
Stewart), Reb Brown (Steve Randall), Ted Grossman (Deputy), Charles Seel
(Old Man), Ray Ballard (Tourist), Brendan Burns (Jock No.1), Rick Beckner
(Jock No.2), James Drum, Ed McCready, Frank Kowalski, Ralph Montgom-
ery, Michael Masters (Hawkers), Charlie Fox (Arvin Ley Doux), Felix Silla
(Seal Boy), Nobel Craig (Tim, Snake Man), Bobbi Kiger (Kootch Dancer),
J.R. Clark (Station Attendant), Chip Potter (Postal Clerk).

Martin plays a self-righteous scientist who has made a serum, derived from
the venom of a cobra, that can turn a man into a snake. His first victim,
Craig, didn't quite make it to being a snake and wound up on display in a
freak show. Benedict plays the lab assistant who is coaxed along to further
Martin's experiments. His first taste of the mind-expanding serum leaves
him wanting more, and Martin is able to transform him completely into a
snake. But the cobra he becomes is no match for the mongoose which gets
loose in his cage. Martin did a reputable job in the first film in which he was
called upon to take lead honors; he doesn't perform as a menacing or insane
scientist, but as someone too involved in his research to make moral
decisions. A lightness is maintained throughout, which leads one to believe
the makers were not too concerned about taking their material seriously.
The result is an unpretentious, sometimes funny, and not quite scary effort.

p, Dan Striepeke; d, Bernard L. Kowalski; w, Hal Dresner (based on a story
by Striepeke); ph, Gerald Perry Finnerman (Technicolor); m, Pat Williams;
ed, Robert Watts; art d, John T. McCormack; set d, Claire P. Brown; spec eff,
Elkin/Universal; makeup, John Chambers, Nick Marcellino.

Fantasy/Drama   **(PR:C MPAA:PG)**

STABLEMATES***   (1938) 89m MGM bw

Wallace Beery (Tom Terry), Mickey Rooney (Mickey), Arthur Hohl (Mr.
Gale), Margaret Hamilton (Beulah Flanders), Minor Watson (Barney
Donovan), Marjorie Gateson (Mrs. Shepherd), Oscar O'Shea (Pete Whalen),
Frank Hagney (Pool Room Owner), Cliff Nazarro (Himself), Johnnie Morris
(Dwarfish Ex-Jockey), James Morton (Bartender), Pat West, Kenneth Nolan
(Railbirds), Sam McDaniel (Black Bookie), Charles Dunbar (Stable Hand),
Scoop Martin (Groom), Stanley Andrews (Track Steward), Spencer Charters
(Choir Master).

In one of the eight roles Rooney performed in 1938, far too much for any
person with normal amounts of energy, he starred as a stableboy whose
favorite horse meets with ill health and just misses the glue factory. A
broken-down veterinarian, Beery, performs a miraculous operation on the
horse, cementing a relationship between him and Rooney, and providing the
doctor, whose main pursuit had been his next drink, with a bit of self-respect.
Although this theme could easily fall victim to over-sentimentality, it's
played pretty much at a low key, allowing for both Beery and Rooney to do
their bits.

p, Harry Rapf; d, Sam Wood; w, Leonard Praskins, Richard Maibaum (based
on a story by William Thiele, Reginald Owen); ph, John Seitz; m, Edward
Ward; ed, W. Donn Hayes; art d, Cedric Gibbons, Urie McCleary; set d,
Edwin B. Willis.

Drama   **(PR:A MPAA:G)**

STACEY!*½   (1973) 82m Penn-Pacific/New World c (AKA: STACEY
                                             AND HER GANGBUSTERS)

Anne Randall (Stacey Hansen), Marjorie Bennett, Anitra Ford, Alan
Landers, James Westmoreland, Cristina Raines, Nicholas Georgiade, Richard LePore, John Alderman, Eddie Ryder, Madeline Peterson, Michael

Keep, Miki Garcia.

Occasionally interesting exploitation item has Randall (a one-time Playboy
Playmate) as a super-detective cracking a tangled case involving a strange
cult. The requisite sex and violence are much in evidence here, detracting
from what could have been an intriguing plot.

p, Leon Mirell; d, Andy Sidaris; w, William Edgar (based on a story by
Sidaris, Mirell); ph, Mark Zavad (Metrocolor); m, Don Randi; ed, Craig
Stewart.

Crime   **Cas.**   **(PR:O MPAA:R)**

STACEY AND HER GANGBUSTERS   (SEE: STACEY, 1973)

STACY'S KNIGHTS*   (1983) 100m American Twist/Crown c (AKA:
                                                         DOUBLE DOWN)

Andra Millian (Stacy), Kevin Costner (Will), Eve Lilith (Jean), Mike
Reynolds (Shecky), Ed Semenza (Kid), Don Hackstaff (Lawyer), Gary Tilles
(Rudy), Garth Howard (Mr. C.), Cheryl Ferris (Marion), Roge Roush
(Rollin'), John Brevick (Floor Boss), Shawshanee Hall, Bobby Condor,
Frederick Hughes, Peter Farnum, Steve Noonan, Robin Landis, David
Brevick, Steve Kopanke, Jim Kosub, Ray Whittey, Roy Reeves, Teresa
Knox, JoAnn Lisosky, Theresa Thompson, Mark Conrad, Pete Borsz, Dennis
Pflederer, Jay Conder.

An inordinate amount of unbelievable scenes and characters fill this weak
picture about an innocent young girl, Millian, whose inexplicable talent at
the blackjack table leads her to high stakes. She hooks up with a group of
gambling aides, her "Knights," who guide her in the right direction. Before
long they are planning an unlikely "sting." Nothing here that separates
STACY'S KNIGHTS from a below average intelligence TV movie.

p, JoAnn Locktov, Freddy Sweet; d, Jim Wilson; w, Michael Blake; ph, Raoul
Lomas (DeLuxe Color); m, Norton Buffalo; ed, Bonnie Koehler; art d,
Florence Fellman; set d, Fellman; cos, Jill Ohannison.

Drama   **Cas.**   **(PR:C MPAA:PG)**

STADIUM MURDERS, THE*   (SEE: HOLLYWOOD STADIUM
                                                     MYSTERY, 1938)

STAGE DOOR***   (1937) 83m RKO bw

Katharine Hepburn (Terry Randall), Ginger Rogers (Joan Maitland),
Adolphe Menjou (Anthony Powell), Gail Patrick (Linda Shaw), Constance
Collier (Catherine Luther), Andrea Leeds (Kaye Hamilton), Samuel S. Hinds
(Henry Sims), Lucille Ball (Judy Canfield), Pierre Watkin (Richard Carmi-
chael), Franklin Pangborn (Harcourt), Elizabeth Dunne (Mrs. Orcutt),
Phyllis Kennedy (Hattie), Grady Sutton (Butcher), Jack Carson (Milbank),
Fred Santley (Dukenfield), William Corson (Bill), Frank Reicher (Stage
Director), Eve Arden (Eve), Ann Miller (Annie), Jane Rhodes (Ann Brad-
dock), Margaret Early (Mary), Jean Rouverol (Dizzy), Norma Drury (Olga
Brent), Peggy O'Donnell (Susan), Harriet Brandon (Madeline), Katherine
Alexander, Ralph Forbes, Mary Forbes, Huntley Gordon (Cast of Play),
Lynton Brent (Aide), Theodore Von Eltz (Elsworth the Critic), Jack Rice
(Playwright), Harry Strang (Chauffeur), Bob Perry (Baggageman), Larry
Steers (Theater Patron), Mary Bovard, Frances Gifford, Josephine Whittell,
Ada Leonard, Mary Jane Shower, Diana Gibson, Linda Gray, Alison Craig,
Lynn Gabriel (Actresses), Adele Pearce (Pamela Blake), Jack Gardner
(Script Clerk), Whitey the Cat (Eve's Cat), Ben Hendricks, Jr (Waiter), Jack
Gargan, Theodore Kosloff, Gerda Mora, Julie Kingdon (Dancing Instruc-
tors), Al Hill (Taxi Driver), Byron Stevens, D'Arcy Corrigan, Philip Morris.

A stellar cast, superb direction, and a screenplay that was even better than
the stage play upon which it was based all add up to one of the best movies
about show business ever made. Hepburn had been in several costume epics
and was beginning to be looked upon in that niche when she prevailed upon
La Cava for this role and the result was a look at a new Hepburn, a woman
who could play comedy and pathos in modern dress and convince audiences
that there was a vulnerability under those patrician cheekbones. She'd done
a similar role in MORNING GLORY, for which she won an Oscar, but this
was truly an ensemble film, not a star vehicle, and she had to play off some
heavyweight performers, each of whom was striving to stand out in the
large assemblage. Hepburn is a wealthy debutante from an important
family. She has come to New York to seek a career on the stage and, rather
than take a Park Avenue apartment, far removed from the mainstream, she
checks into a theatrical boarding house for young, aspiring actresses. The
luck of the draw puts her in a room with Rogers, a sarcastic tough cookie
who heckles everyone. The two of them are like flint and steel and are close
to hair-pulling on a few occasions. The "hen party" atmosphere is quickly
introduced as the actresses spend most of their time discussing work, food,
and potential husbands. Ball, who was in her twenty-seventh movie at the
age of 27, has been invited to dinner by some lumber barons from the
Northwest and she asks Rogers to double date with her. Rogers has a short
fuse and there is no mistaking her likes and dislikes. Among the latter is
Patrick, who is more of a mistress to Broadway producer Menjou than she
is an actual working actress. Leeds (on loan from Goldwyn) hasn't worked
for more than 12 months and she is trying to save some money so she often

forgoes meals at the boarding house, despite the fact that they are reasonable. Menjou is planning a new play, "Enchanted April," and Leeds thinks she may have a chance for the ingenue lead. (The actual play shown was a rewrite of "The Lake," a failed Hepburn vehicle that she starred in after making SPITFIRE.) Rogers and Miller audition for Menjou with the Hal Borne-Mort Greene song "Put Your Heart Into Your Feet and Dance," and he is taken by them, especially by Rogers. He gets them a job at a nightspot in which he has a financial stake. (The addition of this song and dance was probably insurance on the part of the studio. Having Rogers and Miller in a movie and not showing them in a musical number would have been a disappointment to audiences.) Menjou asks Rogers for a date and Rogers accepts – not that she finds the old lecher attractive, she just wants to make sure she and Miller get the dance job and she also wants to give the needle to Patrick. It's not long before Patrick is replaced by Rogers and fumes about it. Leeds is ready to audition for Menjou's play and goes there with Hepburn. When the reading is cancelled, Leeds faints from hunger in the reception area and Hepburn promptly tells Menjou off for the cavalier fashion in which he treats actors. Although he's in his office and apparently not busy with anything else, he has chosen to send the actors away, more out of a power play than anything else. Attorney Watkin goes to see Menjou and says that a wealthy client of his, Hinds (who is Hepburn's father), will back Menjou's show if Hepburn is hired for the lead. Hepburn is unaware of this and is using a different name. There's a sharp scene at Menjou's luxurious penthouse as Hepburn tells Rogers that Menjou is a blowhard who would sell his soul if the price was right, but Rogers pooh-poohs Hepburn's feelings as jealousy and the fact that the two women are always at each other's throats. Hepburn gets the job and does not do well during rehearsals. (This made the role even more interesting for Hepburn, as she had to convincingly play an amateur actress while in rehearsals.) Menjou would like to dump her, but since it's her father's money that's behind the project, his manicured hands are tied. Opening night rolls around and Leeds, who is seen to be a better actress than Hepburn, comes to wish Hepburn well and lend some advice as to the playing of a tricky scene. Later, Leeds is depressed and kills herself by leaping from a high window. Just before the play's curtain is to raise, Rogers tells Hepburn about Leeds and sincerely believes that Hepburn is responsible for Leeds's suicide. Hepburn's acting coach, Collier, says that the show must go on. Hepburn swallows her tears, pushes aside her personal feelings of guilt, and does a smashing job in the play. After the curtain falls, Hepburn walks on the theater's stage to pay tribute to her late friend, Leeds. Rogers is in the audience and is touched by Hepburn's words. Later, the two women make up and become what will be lifelong friends. Months pass; Hepburn is now the toast of Broadway and the goings-on at the boarding house remain the same. Just as they showed in ALL ABOUT EVE, a fresh, young actress arrives with stars in her eyes and hope in her heart and the cycle will begin again. La Cava was directing his first film since MY MAN GODFREY and showed that he could handle a bevy of women as well as he could do a straight two-lead comedy. The original cast starred Margaret Sullavan in the Hepburn role, Phyllis Brooks in the Rogers part, and Frances Fuller as the young suicide. For years, impressionists have done their version of Hepburn with the line, "the calla lillies are in bloom again." It was in the play-within-the-picture that Hepburn spoke those words. STAGE DOOR was nominated as Best Picture, for Best Screenplay, Best Director, and Leeds, for Best Supporting Actress. It was an expensive picture for its day, about $900,000, and while it did make some money, it was never the box-office bonanza everyone predicted. There was so much work done on the script that co-author of the play George S. Kaufman suggested waggishly that it should have been called "Screen Door." Legend has it that La Cava ordered the actresses to the studio for two weeks of rehearsal and just getting used to the boarding house set. Then he had a stenographer take their dialog down as they sat around in between rehearsals and their words were incorporated into the script. A large cast that was chosen with exquisite care included Eve Arden (in her fourth film and already taking out a patent on her particular form of comedy), Franklin Pangborn, Grady Sutton, and Jean Rouverol, who later became a well-known screenwriter with her husband, Hugo Butler. A brilliant script, realistic acting, a treat to the eyes and ears, especially seeing all those later stars like Ball and Carson and Miller and Arden in their early days. It's amazing how many ideas, laughs, tears, and genuine "moments" can be packed into just 83 minutes when it is left to the talents of giants.

p, Pandro S. Berman; d, Gregory La Cava; w, Morrie Ryskind, Anthony Veiller, (uncredited) La Cara (based on the play by Edna Ferber, George S. Kaufman); ph, Robert de Grasse; m, Roy Webb; ed, William Hamilton; md, Webb; art d, Van Nest Polglase, Carroll Clark; set d, Darrell Silvera; cos, Muriel King; makeup, Mel Burns; m/l, Hal Borne, Mort Greene.

Comedy/Drama   Cas.   (PR:A-C MPAA:NR)

STAGE DOOR CANTEEN**   (1943) 132m UA bw

Cheryl Walker (Eileen), William Terry (Ed "Dakota" Smith), Marjorie Riordan (Jean Rule), Lon McCallister ("California"), Margaret Early (Ella Sue), Michael Harrison [Sunset Carson] ("Texas"), Dorothea Kent (Mamie), Fred Brady ("Jersey" Wallace), Marion Shockley (Lillian), Patrick O'Moore (Australian), Ruth Roman (Girl), Judith Anderson, Henry Armetta, Kenny Baker, Tallulah Bankhead, Ralph Bellamy, Edgar Bergen and Charlie McCarthy, Ray Bolger, Helen Broderick, Ina Claire, Katharine Cornell, Lloyd Corrigan, Jane Cowl, Jane Darwell, William Demarest, Virginia

Field, Dorothy Fields, Gracie Fields, Lynn Fontanne, Arlene Francis, Vinton Freedley, Billy Gilbert, Lucile Gleason, Vera Gordon, Virginia Grey, Helen Hayes, Katharine Hepburn, Hugh Herbert, Jean Hersholt, Sam Jaffe, Allen Jenkins, George Jessel, Roscoe Karns, Virginia Kaye, Tom Kennedy, Otto Kruger, June Lang, Betty Lawford, Gertrude Lawrence, Gypsy Rose Lee, Alfred Lunt, Bert Lytell, Harpo Marx, Aline MacMahon, Elsa Maxwell, Helen Menken, Yehudi Menuhin, Ethel Merman, Ralph Morgan, Alan Mowbray, Paul Muni, Elliott Nugent, Merle Oberon, Franklin Pangborn, Helen Parrish, Brock Pemberton, George Raft, Lanny Ross, Selena Royle, Martha Scott, Cornelia Otis Skinner, Ned Sparks, Bill Stern, Ethel Waters, Johnny Weissmuller, Arleen Whelan, Dame May Whitty, Ed Wynn (Stage Door Canteen Stars), Count Basie and His Band, Xavier Cugat and His Orchestra with Lina Romay, Bennie Goodman and His Orchestra with Peggy Lee, Kay Kyser and His Band, Freddy Martin and His Orchestra, Guy Lombardo and His Orchestra (Themselves), Mack Gray (Waiter), Francis Pierlot.

You must see this movie. Not that the story is terrific, because it's a trifle, but you have to spend the requisite 132 minutes to revel in the 65 stars who play themselves and seem to be having more fun than they had when playing roles. The American Theatre Wing operated Stage Door Canteens in several cities with the flagship location on West 44th street in Manhattan. The stars all worked on a "favored nations" clause and 90 percent of the profits from this hit movie went back to the Theatre Wing to help defray the expenses for the Canteens, which were an oasis in the cities for young service people on brief leave from WW II duty. If you were an officer, you could go to your clubs, where dogfaces and gobs were not allowed. At the Stage Door Canteen, you had to be ranked below officer status to be allowed in and anyone old enough to recall the fun that was had at these sites will laugh and cry at the memories. It's jammed from start to finish with stars, music, laughs, tears, and pure entertainment. Walker is a young hostess at the Canteen and falls for soldier Terry. Riordan falls in love with McCallister and Kent goes ga-ga for Harrison. The three men have a one-day pass in New York and visit the Canteen where they meet the three women. When their ship is delayed, they are given a reprieve and can spend another day in New York. Then there's yet another day and, by that time, the romances have been fulfilled, despite the edict that the hostesses are not supposed to see the servicemen outside of the Canteen. Marriages are planned and the boys go off to war knowing that their girls will be waiting for them upon their return. That's about the size of the story and this could have been a short subject for all the actual story dialog but Daves and Borzage intersperse the love tale between the cavalcade of musical and comedy numbers and the many cameo appearances of the stars. Katherine Cornell makes her only film appearance and does a snippet from her stage version of "Romeo And Juliet," George Jessel reprises his famous phone call to "Mama," Harpo Marx runs around like a nut, George Raft is seen as a diswasher, Lunt and Fontanne have an argument, Paul Muni does a rehearsal of his new play and congratulates actress Walker on getting a role in his play, and on and on. Walker had been an extra and a stand-in for Claudette Colbert and Veronica Lake when she was tapped for this role. Two Oscar nominations were given for Fred Rich's scoring of a musical and to Al Dubin and Jimmy Monaco for their song "We Mustn't Say Goodbye," which was sung by Lanny Ross. Other tunes by Monaco and Dubin included: "Bombshell From Brooklyn" (Lesser also received writing credit on this, performed by Xavier Cugat and His Orchestra), "The Machine Gun Song" (sung by Gracie Fields), "Sleep, Baby, Sleep in Your Jeep" (performed by Guy Lombardo and His Orchestra), "Quick Sands" (sung by Ethel Waters), plus "You're Pretty Terrific Yourself," "Don't Worry Island," "We Meet in the Funniest Places," "A Rookie and His Rhythm," "American Boy." Richard Rodgers and Lorenz Hart wrote "The Girl I Love to Leave Behind" (sung by Ray Bolger), Ethel Merman sang "Marching Through Berlin" (an adaptation of "Deutschland Uber Alles," Belford Hendricks) and Benny Goodman played "Why Don't You Do Right?", (Joe McCoy). Other musical numbers include: "The Lord's Prayer" (Albert Hay Malotte, sung by Fields), "Bugle Call Rag" (Elmer Schoebel, Billy Meyers, Jack Pettie), "Ave Maria" (Franz Schubert, performed Yehudi Menuhin), and "Flight of the Bumble Bee" (Rimsky-Korsakov). When this was shown in theaters, patrons kept nudging each other as one star after another marched across the screen in the briefest bits. It was a patriotic moment for the players and the viewers and the box office rang happily with receipts. In addition to all the merriment, there were tributes paid to the Australians, the Chinese, and The Russians. Six of the most popular bands in the land are seen in Cugat, Goodman, Kyser, Martin, Lombardo and Basie. Peggy Lee, who was not billed, sings "Why Don't You Do Right?" which became a huge hit for her. In 1949, a fresh narration was added to the film and it was slightly edited and re-released. None of the six young leads went on to do much, except for McCallister, which was a shame, as they all showed some acting talent in this film.

p, Sol Lesser; d, Frank Borzage; w, Delmer Daves; ph, Harry Wild; p, Sol Lesser; d, Frank Borzage; w, Delmer Daves; ph, Harry Wild; m, Freddie Rich; ed, Hal Kern; prod d, Harry Horner, Clem Beauchamps; md, Constantin Bakaleinikoff; art d, Hans Peters; set d, Victor Gangelin; cos, Albert Dano.

Musical   Cas.   (PR:A MPAA:NR)

STAGE FRIGHT***   (1950, Brit.) 111m WB-FN/WB bw

Jane Wyman *(Eve Gill/Doris Tinsdale)*, Marlene Dietrich *(Charlotte Inwood)*, Michael Wilding *(Wilfrid O. "Ordinary" Smith)*, Richard Todd *(Jonathan Cooper)*, Alastair Sim *(Commodore Gill)*, Kay Walsh *(Nellie Goode)*, Dame Sybil Thorndike *(Mrs. Gill)*, Miles Malleson *(Mr. Fortesque)*, Hector MacGregor *(Freddie Williams)*, Joyce Grenfell *("Lovely Ducks' the Shooting Gallery Attendant)*, Andre Morell *(Inspector Byard)*, Ballard Berkeley *(Sergeant Mellish)*, Patricia Hitchcock *(Chubby Bannister)*, Alfred Hitchcock *(Passerby on Street as Wyman Talks to Herself)*, Irene Handl, Arthur Howard, Everley Gregg, Cyril Chamberlain, Helen Goss.

A standard British murder mystery is raised to a higher plateau by Hitchcock in STAGE FRIGHT, but still falters in comparison to the best of the master's works. Over the opening credits a theatrical safety curtain rises, revealing not a stage but London street life–the actual stage for Hitchcock's mystery. Wyman is an acting student at the Royal Academy of Dramatic Art when she runs into a past boy friend, Todd, who comes looking for help and shelter from the police. He explains, and we see in flashback, how his mistress, stage and singing star Dietrich, came to him wearing a dress bloodied when she killed her husband. Because of his involvement with Dietrich, Todd is suspected. Todd hides him aboard a boat and brings him to her father, Sim. When Sim and Wyman suggest that Todd may be being set up, the fugitive flies into a rage and throws the bloodstained dress, his only piece of evidence, into the fireplace. Wyman then decides to play detective and save Todd, whom she has grown to love again. She strikes a deal with Dietrich's dresser-maid, Walsh, who witnessed Todd's getaway, to work temporarily in her place, pretending to be a journalist in search of facts for a story. She also meets Wilding, a detective assigned to the case, to whom she soon becomes attracted. Wilding, however, is unaware of any of the roles she is playing–detective, reporter, or maid. When she finally goes to work for Dietrich, Wyman, dressed frumpily behind a pair of granny glasses and using the name Doris Tinsdale, becomes convinced that the glamorous star is the murderer, especially because of her reluctance to dress in black for mourning. Returning to her father, Wyman discovers that Todd has left for the city to see Dietrich, who is performing that evening. Wyman spots Todd hiding in the wings, but he fails to notice her in her disguise. As Dietrich prepares for her next number, "The Laziest Gal in Town" (Cole Porter), Wyman tries to coax incriminating information out of her, without much success. After Dietrich's performance, Todd hides out in her dressing room and barely escapes, thanks to Wyman's warning, though he doesn't recognize her "maid" voice. The following day, at a fairgrounds garden party, Sim concocts a plan which will force a confession out of Dietrich. He gets a doll from a shooting gallery (he cannot buy the doll and must skillfully shoot for it) and stains the doll's dress with blood, replicating the dress she wore during the murder. During a performance of "La Vie en Rose" (Louiguy, Edith Piaf), Sim gives the doll to a Boy Scout who carries it to Dietrich on the stage. Upon receiving the doll and seeing the ominous stain, Dietrich is unable to continue her performance while in the audience, detective Wilding watches the entire scene. Wyman is then summoned from the audience to help Dietrich, since she is her maid. Wyman, however, tries to play dumb, realizing that by going to the stage she reveals herself to With with whom she has since fallen in love. Later that evening after a Dietrich performance, the theater is empty except for the star and her maid. Sim and Wyman, however, have engineered another plan. They have rigged a hidden microphone in Dietrich's dressing room which broadcasts into the theater itself, where Sim has called Wilding and his police force. Dietrich realizes the ruse, and in the meantime Todd arrives at the theater and the police give chase. Todd retreats into the prop room to hide, where he is joined by the still-faithful though romantically torn Wyman. It is only then that she discovers that Todd is actually the murderer and that the story he told her (and the flashback we saw) was a lie. Todd makes his getaway but is crushed by the iron "safety curtain" that is lowered down upon him on the stage. STAGE FRIGHT was far from being one of Hitchcock's most memorable or successful films, drawing criticism for both his false flashback and the absence of any real threat of danger. Of the latter complaint, Hitchcock said in his interview with Francois Truffaut: "I became aware of that before the shooting was completed, but by then it was too late to do anything about it. Why are none of the people ever in danger? Because we're telling a story in which the villains themselves are afraid. The great weakness of the picture is that it breaks an unwritten law: The more successful the villain, the more successful the picture. That's a cardinal rule, and in this picture the villain was a flop!" Not only was the villain a flop, but the audience didn't even know who the villain was–because of the false flashback (an interesting technique which fails in this case) Dietrich is seen as the murderer, and Todd as the victim. A villain certainly cannot be successful if the audience doesn't even know the villain's identity. Hitchcock's main interest in the film, and its only truly interesting aspect, is the concentration on acting and deception. Like MURDER in 1930, the heroine is an actress. Here Wyman gets her finest training not from the Royal Academy of Dramatic Arts (where Hitchcock's daughter Patricia was enrolled, and where some of the film was photographed) but from real life. Her character's performance is not a simple one, forcing her to appear as something different to everyone–to Wilding she is an actress he has fallen in love with, to Dietrich she is a maid, to Todd and Sim she is the Nancy Drew-type detective, and to Walsh she is a newspaper reporter. All of her deceptions come to a boiling point at the garden party when she is forced into playing two roles at once, thereby revealing herself to Wilding. Her stage is London (as the opening

points out) and her fright is a real one which could end, not in sour grapes, but in death. The final irony of real-life and theater occurs as Todd is crushed beneath the safety curtain–the point where both of Wyman's worlds come together on one stage. Wyman, whom Hitchcock chose after her Oscar-winning performance in JOHNNY BELINDA, did not please the director once on the set. "I ran into great difficulties with Jane," Hitchcock told Truffaut. "In her disguise as a lady's maid, she should have been rather unglamorous; after all she was supposed to be impersonating an unattractive maid. But every time she saw the rushes and how she looked alongside Marlene Dietrich, she would burst into tears. She couldn't accept the idea of her face being in character, while Dietrich looked so glamorous, so she kept improving her appearance every day and that's how she failed to maintain character." Dietrich, on the other hand, completely charmed Hitchcock, calming that wild beast persona that so many actresses were submitted to over his career. Her shining, charismatic performance prompted Hitchcock to describe her as "a professional star." Referring to the complete understanding of filmmaking that she had acquired over her career, mainly through her association with Josef von Sternberg, Hitchcock added, "She was also a professional cameraman, art director, editor, costume designer, hairdresser, makeup woman, composer, producer, and *director*." Illustrating his confidence in Dietrich, Hitchcock allowed her complete control over her personal wardrobe–reins he always held obsessively tight over other actresses such as Grace Kelly, especially in REAR WINDOW– allowing her to hire Christian Dior. STAGE FRIGHT was one of four pictures that Jack Warner contracted Hitchcock for–STRANGERS ON A TRAIN, I CONFESS, and DIAL M FOR MURDER followed–over a six- and-a-half year period at a whopping $999,000. Shot at Elstree Studios, it was the last film he shot in his home country of England until 1971 when he returned to film FRENZY.

p&d, Alfred Hitchcock; w, Whitfield Cook, Alma Reville, James Bridie, (uncredited) Ranald MacDougall (based on the stories "Man Running" and "Outrun the Constable" by Selwyn Jepson); ph, Wilkie Cooper; m, Leighton Lucas; ed, Edward Jarvis; md, Louis Levy; set d, Terence Verity; cos, Christian Dior, Milo Anderson; makeup, Colin Guarde; m/l, Cole Porter, Louiguy, Edith Piaf.

Mystery   Cas.   (PR:A-c   MPAA:NR)

STAGE FROM BLUE RIVER (SEE: STAGE TO BLUE RIVER, 1952)

STAGE MOTHER**   (1933) 85m MGM bw

Alice Brady *(Kitty Lorraine)*, Maureen O'Sullivan *(Shirley Lorraine)*, Franchot Tone *(Warren Foster)*, Phillips Holmes *(Lord Aylesworth)*, Ted Healy *(Ralph Martin)*, Russell Hardie *(Fred Lorraine)*, C. Henry Gordon *(Ricco)*, Alan Edwards *(Dexter)*, Ben Alexander *(Francis Nolan)*.

Realistic rendition of the conflicts which arise when a mother (Brady) devotes herself to seeing that her daughter (O'Sullivan) makes it on the stage. Picture starts with Brady's husband falling to his death while doing a highwire act. From this point on the woman tries to fill her emptiness by focusing on her child. She interferes with a romance between O'Sullivan and Tone, but Brady gives in in the end after O'Sullivan has almost gotten rid of her mother for good by marrying into a British aristocratic family. Brady is convincing in an unflattering role, and is able to display some heart behind her blinding drive. Songs include "Dancing on the Rainbow" and "Right Little Girl."

p, Hunt Stromberg; d, Charles R. Brabin; w, John Meehan, Bradford Ropes (based on the novel by Ropes); ph, George Folsey; ed, Frank Hull; cos, Adrian; ch, Albertina Rasch; m/l, Nacio Herb Brown, Arthur Freed.

Drama   (PR:A   MPAA:NR)

STAGE STRUCK**   (1936) 86m WB-FN bw

Dick Powell *(George Randall)*, Joan Blondell *(Peggy Revere)*, Warren William *(Harris)*, Jean Madden *(Ruth Williams)*, Frank McHugh *(Sid)*, Carol Hughes *(Grace Randall)*, Hobart Cavanaugh *(Wayne)*, Spring Byington *(Mrs. Randall)*, Johnny Arthur *(Oscar Freud)*, Craig Reynolds *(Gilmore Frost)*, Andrew Tombes *(Burns Haywood)*, Lulu McConnell *(Toots O'Connor)*, Ed Gargan *(Riordan)*, Eddy Chandler *(Heney)*, Thomas Pogue *(Dr. Stanley)*, Libby Taylor *(Yvonne)*, George Offerman, Jr *(Wilbur)*, Irene Coleman *(Brunette)*, Henry Martin *(Chauffeur)*, Herbert Ashley *(Bartender)*, George Riley *(Drunk)*, Leo White *(Waiter)*, Mary Treen *(Clerk)*, Kathrin Clare Ward *(Landlady)*, Iris Adrian *(Miss DeRue)*, Rosalind Marquis *(Miss LaHenc)*, Jane Wyman *(Bessie Funfnick)*, Val and Ernie Stanton *(Marley and Cooper)*, John Alexander *(Red Cap)*, Mary Gordon *(Mrs. Cassidy)*, Glen Cavender, Walter Clyde *(Stagehands)*, Baldy Belmont *(Doorman)*, Sarah Edwards *(Spinster School Teacher at Aquarium)*, Charles Croker King *(Alexander the Critic)*, Yacht Club Boys.

A disappointing musical on most levels that managed to eke out a few dollars profit, probably due to the fact that Blondell and Powell became husband and wife immediately prior to the the movie's release and fans wanted to see the electricity between them that caused the union. Blondell is a musical performer with a minimum of talent. She puts up the money for a stage show which Powell is to direct. They immediately bang heads, as she has specific ideas of what she wants done that are in direct contrast to his thoughts. McHugh is Powell's right-hand man and provides the comedy as the couple battle, fall out, then fall in again when she backs yet another show. William is the savvy producer who smoothes matters over between the couple. Not even the usually flawless Busby Berkeley can overcome the basically cliched material in the script. The Yacht Club Boys do some funny special material that's of the time, in that it ribs Franklin Roosevelt, but anyone younger than 50 won't appreciate the satirical barbs. In small roles, note Jane Wyman in her fifth movie and radio star Lulu McConnell, one of the hysterical panel of "It Pays to bBe Ignorant." Songs from the team of Harold Arlen and "Yip" Harburg include "Fancy Meeting You," "The New Parade," "You're Kinda Grandish," and the one hit that came from the film, "In Your Own Quiet Way."

p, Robert Lord; d, Busby Berkeley; w, Tom Buckingham, Pat C. Flick (based on a story by Lord, Warren Duff); ph, Byron Haskin; ed, Tom Richards; md, Leo F. Forbstein; cos, Orry-Kelly.

Musical/Comedy   (PR:A MPAA:NR)

STAGE STRUCK*½   (1948) 71m MON bw

Kane Richmond (*Nick Mantee*), Audrey Long (*Nancy Howard*), Conrad Nagel (*Lt. Williams*), Ralph Byrd (*Sgt. Tom Rainey*), John Gallaudet (*Benny Nordick*), Anthony Warde (*Mr. Barda*), Pamela Blake (*Janet Winters*), Charles Trowbridge (*Capt. Webb*), Nana Bryant (*Mrs. Howard*), Selmer Jackson (*Mr. Howard*), Evelyn Brent (*Miss Lloyd*), Wanda McKay (*Helen Howard*), Jacqueline Thomas (*Ruth Ames*), Wilbur Mack (*Professor Corella*).

An interesting idea – girls trying to get to the Broadway stage but winding up as entertainment pieces at seedy nightclubs – fails to gel because of poor handling in the scripting and directing departments. The dead body of a young girl leads to police investigation and the uncovering of a "talent agency" which thrives on naive girls coming to the big city to try to get into show business. The girls are given jobs at a nightclub whose real purpose is not to display the girls' singing and dancing abilities. Plot takes a dreadfully long time to unfold, and the characters talk more than you would think these type of people would.

p, Jeffrey Bernerd; d, William Nigh; w, George Wallace Sayre, Agnes Christine Johnson (based on a story by Sayre); ph, Harry Neumann; ed, William Austin; md, Edward J. Kay; art d, Dave Milton; set d, Raymond Boltz, Jr.

Crime   (PR:C MPAA:NR)

STAGE STRUCK½**   (1958) 95m RKO/BV c

Henry Fonda (*Lewis Easton*), Susan Strasberg (*Eva Lovelace*), Joan Greenwood (*Rita Vernon*), Herbert Marshall (*Robert Harley Hedges*), Christopher Plummer (*Joe Sheridan*), Daniel Ocko (*Constantine*), Pat Harrington (*Benny*), Frank Campanella (*Benny*), John Fiedler (*Adrian*), Patricia Englund (*Gwen Hall*), Jack Weston (*Frank*), Sally Gracie (*Elizabeth*), Nina Hansen (*Regina*), Harold Grau (*Stage Doorman*), Leon Bibb (*Guitar Player*), Estelle Richie (*Nebraska Woman*), Clint Young (*Tom the Chauffeur*), Hilda Haynes (*Easton's Maid*), Roger C. Carmel (*Stagehand*).

The adaptation of Zoe Akins' play "Morning Glory" served to win Katharine Hepburn an Oscar in 1933. This was the second time around for the tale, which was already an old story when it was done the first time. We'd seen the same yarn in 42ND STREET, ALL ABOUT EVE, and many other movies. Lumet was doing his second film after 12 ANGRY MEN and he cast 20-year-old Strasberg in the Hepburn role after her successful outing in Broadway's "The Diary Of Anne Frank" and a bit part in PICNIC three years before. Twenty nine-year-old producer Millar assembled a New York cast and shot it entirely in Manhattan and environs with interiors done at the West 26th street Production Center studio. New England actress Strasberg comes to New York from a small town and is determined to make her name on the stage. She meets Fonda, a successful producer, and he shares her belief in herself, perhaps because he falls in love with her. For no apparent reason, Strasberg also attracts playwright Plummer and veteran actor Marshall, all of whom see something in her that movie audiences didn't. Plummer, in his film debut, doesn't show much of what he was to demonstrate later, as he spends most of his time reacting and wearing a silly grin. Strasberg attends a party with the men, drinks too much, and then does the entire balcony scene from "Romeo And Juliet" for the assemblage. She is tense about it but does it well enough to convince everyone in the group that she has some acting talent. Strasberg then falls asleep in the bedroom, and when she wakes up, Fonda alone is there. She tells him that she loves him but he says that nepotism is not in his makeup, and if she is going to triumph on the stage, she'll have to do it on talent only and perhaps it would be better if they only saw each other professionally. Fonda is producing Plummer's latest play, which stars Greenwood (in her second U.S. film). Plummer moves in to "manage" Strasberg's career and, at the same time, finds much fault in the temperamental Greenwood, in a thinly disguised mimicry of Tallulah Bankhead. When Greenwood throws a fit and strolls out on the production, Strasberg, who has been carefully coached in the role all along by Plummer, is ready to go on in Greenwood's stead. Plummer talks Fonda into allowing Strasberg to play the part. She does and the result is a smashing performance (did you think for one millisecond that it wouldn't be?). Everyone loves Strasberg and she is

suddenly transformed from a sweet young ingenue to a woman of the theater. Fonda, Plummer, and Marshall see that alteration and know that there is nary an inch of room in her life for any man. She is devoted to her work now and, perhaps in a few years when she realizes that the applause of the crowd is fleeting, she might find a moment for romance, but for the present, her goal is fame and fame only. Fonda preferred living in New York and the idea about making a movie about theater, his first love, appealed to him, but this picture did virtually nothing for his career. Strasberg is the daughter of Lee Strasberg, head of the Actors Studio and sometime actor himself before his death. It came as a bit of a surprise that she did a few lines about the Actors Studio in the film which were almost a commercial for the facility. Lots of inside material about the New York stage and a good look at what actually happens backstage, in the producer's office, in the dressing room, et cetera. It was not generally interesting enough to a non-show-biz audience, however, and didn't do sparkling business. Note Jack Weston, Pat Harrington, and Roger C. Carmel in small roles. All three went on to make their marks in later years. There's one wonderful snow-filled scene in the park that Planer photographed in a most intriguing fashion after both Lumet and Dozier questioned the possibility of working in such a pelting storm. It's a highlight. Strasberg went on to show that she had more acting ability than she demonstrated in this film. Her problem may have been that her mother, Paula, was on the set almost constantly and Strasberg was unable to let go in front of her.

p, Stuart Millar; d, Sidney Lumet; w, Ruth and Augustus Goetz (based on the play "Morning Glory" by Zoe Akins); ph, Franz F. Planer, Maurice Hartzband (Technicolor); m, Alex North; ed, Stuart Gilmore; art d, Kim Edgar Swados; cos, Moss Mabry.

Drama   (PR:A-C MPAA:NR)

STAGE TO BLUE RIVER*½   (1951) 55m MON bw (AKA: STAGE
                                                  FROM BLUE RIVER)

Whip Wilson (*Whip*), Fuzzy Knight (*Texas*), Lee Roberts (*Ted*), Phyllis Coates (*Joyce*), John Hart (*Kingsley*), Lane Bradford (*Reardon*), Pierce Lyden (*Preston*), Terry Frost (*Yarrow*), I. Stanford Jolley (*Westbrook*), William Fawcett (*Perkins*), Stanley Price (*Martin*), Steve Clark (*Clark*), Bud Osborne.

Coates' stage line is in danger of falling into the hands of sheriff Lyden, actually an unscrupulous villain who uses his badge to hide his true composition. But Wilson, flaunting a U.S. Marshal's badge, arrives in time to see that Coates remains prosperous and Lyden gets his just rewards.

p, Vincent M. Fennelly; d, Lewis Collins; w, Joseph F. Poland; ph, Ernest Miller; ed, Sam Fields; md, Raoul Kraushaar.

Western   (PR:A MPAA:NR)

STAGE TO CHINO**   (1940) 59m RKO bw

George O'Brien (*Dan Clark*), Virginia Vale (*Crinnie*), Hobart Cavanaugh (*Rogge*), Roy Barcroft (*Dude Elliott*), William Haade (*Slim*), Carl Stockdale (*Charles Lait*), Glenn Strange (*Bill Hoagland*), Harry Cording (*Pete Branagan*), Martin Garralaga (*Pedro*), Ethan Laidlaw (*Wheeler*), Tom London (*Dolan*), Elmo Lincoln, Billy Franey, Bruce Mitchell, Pals of the Golden West.

A decent western about O'Brien, as a U.S. postal inspector, working undercover as a stage driver to uncover a plot by Stockdale to force his niece (Vale) out of business. Barcroft is the bad guy under Stockdale's employ who is making things rough for the femme's stage line in order for his own stage line to prosper. It doesn't take long for the high-minded O'Brien to sort things out and get Vale's stagecoaches on wheels again. Before the final showdown, action from barn burning to barroom brawling is thrown in to spice up the story. For laughs there's Cavanaugh as the Eastern salesman who isn't accustomed to all the rough-housing.

p, Bert Gilroy; d, Edward Killy; w, Morton Grant, Arthur V. Jones (based on a story by Norton S. Parker); ph, J. Roy Hunt; ed, Frederic Knudtson; m/l, "Riding on the Stage to Chino," Fleming Allen.

Western   (PR:A MPAA:NR)

STAGE TO MESA CITY*½   (1947) 58m EL bw

"Lash" LaRue (*Cheyenne*), Al "Fuzzy" St. John (*Fuzzy*), Jennifer Holt (*Margie*), George Chesebro (*Padgett*), Brad Slaven (*Bob*), Marshall Reed (*Baxter*), Terry Frost (*Ed*), Carl Mathews (*Jim*), Bob Woodward (*Pete*), Steve Clark (*Watson*), Frank Ellis (*Stocker*), Lee Morgan (*Sheriff*), Dee Cooper, Wally West, Russell Arms.

A stage line to Mesa City has been heavily attacked, which leads to an investigation by Marshal LaRue. LaRue finds the brains behind the attacks to be Chesebro, in a usual villainous role. Between punches and gunshots, St. John supplies a few laughs.

p, Jerry Thomas; d, Ray Taylor; w, Joseph F. Poland; ph, James Brown, Sr.; m, Walter Greene; ed, Hugh Winn.

Western   (PR:A MPAA:NR)

STAGE TO THUNDER ROCK**½   (1964) 82m PAR c

Barry Sullivan (*Sheriff Horne*), Marilyn Maxwell (*Leah Parker*), Keenan Wynn (*Ross Sawyer*), Scott Brady (*Sam Swope*), Lon Chaney, Jr (*Henry Parker*), John Agar (*Dan Carrouthers*), Wanda Handrix (*Mrs. Swope*), Anne Seymour (*Myra Parker*), Allan Jones (*Mayor Ted Dollar*), Ralph Taeger (*Reese Sawyer*), Laurel Goodwin (*Julie Parker*), Robert Strauss (*Judge Bates*), Robert Lowery (*Seth Harrington*), Argentina Brunetti (*Sarita*), Rex Bell, Jr (*"Shotgun"*), Suzanne Cupito (*Sandy Swope*), Wayne Peters (*Toby Sawyer*), Paul E. Burns, Roy Jenson.

Sullivan plays a retiring lawman whose last job brings "ghosts" from his past. He is assigned to bring to justice the sons of the man who raised him when he was orphaned as a child. He kills one and takes the other to await the stage into town at a station being run by the parents of Maxwell, Sullivan's old sweetheart. Brady gets into the act as the gunman hired to make sure Sullivan doesn't have second thoughts; he's an old friend of Sullivan's but takes the job to help his daughter. These angles fit together to make an interesting western that is more concerned with character development than with nonstop action, but there is enough of that, too, to keep things jumping. An excellent role for Sullivan, who has an opportunity to show that there is a heart somewhere beneath his hardened exterior.

p, A. C. Lyles; d, William F. Claxton; w, Charles A. Wallace; ph, W. Wallace Kelley (Techniscope, Technicolor); m, Paul Dunlap; ed, Jodie Copelan; art d, Hal Pereira, Robert Smith; set d, Sam Comer, James Roach; makeup, Wally Westmore.

Western   (PR:A   MPAA:NR)

STAGE TO TUCSON**   (1950) 81m COL c (GB: LOST STAGE VALLEY)

Rod Cameron (*Grif Holbrook*), Wayne Morris (*Barney Broderick*), Kay Buckley (*Kate Crocker*), Carl Benton Reid (*"Doc" Benteen*), Roy Roberts (*Jim Maroon*), Harry Bellaver (*Gus Heyden*), Sally Eilers (*Annie Benson*), Douglas Fowley (*Ira Prentiss*), John Pickard (*Sam Granger*), Olin Howlin (*Chantry*), Charles Evans (*John Butterfield*), Boyd Stockman (*Juan Lopez*), Reed Howes (*Eddie*), James Kirkwood (*Sheriff Pete Deuce*), John Sheehan (*Bartender*).

The theft of several stagecoaches which end up in Atlanta from Arizona leads to an investigation by Cameron and Morris. Heavy Roberts is using the argument that the missing coaches will upset the Union's line of communication, as a means to line his own pocket. Though premise is far-fetched, enough action and good caricatures are supplied to mend the wounds. At one point Cameron and Morris are brought to blows over a girl, Buckley.

p, Harry Joe Brown; d, Ralph Murphy; w, Bob Williams, Frank Burt, Robert Libott (based on the novel by Frank Bonham); ph, Charles Lawton, Jr. (Technicolor); m, Paul Sawtell; ed, Charles Nelson; md, Morris Stoloff; art d, George Brooks.

Western   (PR:A   MPAA:NR)

STAGE WHISPERS   (SEE: GRIEF STREET, 1931)

STAGECOACH*****   (1939) 97m UA bw

Claire Trevor (*Dallas*), John Wayne (*The Ringo Kid*), John Carradine (*Hatfield*), Thomas Mitchell (*Dr. Josiah Boone*), Andy Devine (*Buck Rickabaugh the Stagecoach Driver*), Donald Meek (*Mr. Samuel Peacock*), Louise Platt (*Lucy Mallory*), George Bancroft (*Sheriff Curly Wilcox*), Berton Churchill (*Henry Gatewood*), Tim Holt (*Lt. Blanchard*), Tom Tyler (*Luke Plummer*), Chris Pin Martin (*Chris*), Elvira Rios (*Yakima, Chris's Wife*), Francis Ford (*Billy Pickett*), Marga Daighton (*Mrs. Pickett*), Cornelius Keefe (*Capt. Whitney*), Kent Odell (*Billy Pickett, Jr.*), Walter McGrail (*Capt. Sickels*), Chief Big Tree (*Indian Scout*), Brenda Fowler (*Mrs. Gatewood*), Louis Mason (*Sheriff*), Florence Lake (*Mrs. Nancy Whitney*), Joseph Rickson (*Ike Plummer*), Vester Pegg (*Hank Plummer*), Yakima Canutt (*Cavalry Scout*), Harry Tenbrook (*Telegraph Operator*), Paul McVey (*Express Agent*), Jack Pennick (*Jerry the Bartender*), William Hoffer (*Sergeant*), Bryant Washburn (*Capt. Simmons*), Nora Cecil (*Dr. Boone's Housekeeper*), Helen Gibson, Dorothy Appleby (*Dancing Girls*), Buddy Roosevelt, Bill Cody (*Cowboys*), Chief White Horse (*Geronimo*), Duke Lee (*Sheriff of Lordsburg*), Mary Kathleen Walker (*Lucy's Baby*), Ed Brady (*Saloon Keeper*), Robert E. Homans (*Editor in Lordsburg*), Franklyn Farnum (*Deputy*), Jim Mason (*Jim, Expressman*), Merrill McCormick (*Ogler*), Artie Ortega (*Barfly, Lordsburg*), Steve Clemente, Theodore Lorch, Fritzi Brunette, Leonard Trainor, Chris Phillips, Tex Driscoll, Pat Wayne, Teddy Billings, Al Lee, John Eckert, Jack Mohr, Patsy Doyle, Wiggie Blowne, Margaret Smith, Si Jenks, Many Mules.

The classic western, unequalled and without peers, STAGECOACH is John Ford's greatest epic of the frontier. This western eclipsed all films in the genre that had gone before it, and so vastly influenced those that followed that its stamp can be found in most superior westerns made since Ford stepped into Monument Valley for the first time. Wayne, other than his abortive leap into leading man status in THE BIG TRAIL, had been languishing on the tiny backlots of Poverty Row studios, riding nondescript-

ly through a host of forgettable B westerns until being summoned to fame, fortune, and stardom by Ford for this film. STAGECOACH, set in a landscape with endless horizons, is still a wonderful portrait of pioneer life in the untamed and uncivilized Great Southwest, but is really a microscopic view of eight characters, all diversified in pursuits and all traveling to separate fates in a journey packed with danger. High peril is evident from the first scenes which depict Geronimo on the warpath and the telegraph wires cut by raiding Apaches. Leaving the town of Tonto, New Mexico, are a bunch of social misfits with a few decent souls accompanying them. Mitchell, who would win a Supporting Actor Oscar for this role, is a conniving, drunken doctor who has long ago been kicked out of the medical profession for malpractice. But he still carries with him his doctor's bag full of medical instruments and is ready for any emergency, or so he says when cadging drinks at the local saloon. Leaving also on the stage is Trevor, a fallen lady whose sexual exploits have so unnerved the local women that they have banded together to oust her from their scandal-mongering society. Carradine, a shady gambler with the manners of a southern gentleman, has his own mysterious reasons for leaving Tonto and he pretends that the real reason is to offer Platt, who is married to a cavalry officer and is pregnant, his "protection" as she travels to be with her husband. Churchill, a pompous and demanding banker, with a shrewish wife, gets aboard the stagecoach carrying a small valise which is locked and which he will not let go of, whereas Meek carries a sample case which contains no mysterious contents, at least to Mitchell. He is a whiskey salesman and Mitchell considers him the finest traveling companion a drunk could ever have. These six strangers make up the passenger list and, riding on top on the driver's seat is driver Devine, a gregarious, garrulous type with a happy disposition and an aversion to Indians, and tough, gruff but fair-minded Bancroft, a lawman who is riding "shotgun" on this trip, on the alert for a cowboy who has just broken out of the state penitentiary. The stage moves off, heading for distant Lordsburg, but it travels only a few miles when, turning a bend, the travelers hear a rifle shot. The camera, in a sudden departure from the standard shots Ford has employed up to that time, shows, in a marvelous tracking shot that jars the viewer, Wayne, larger than life, legs spread apart, stoically facing the stagecoach rushing at him, twirling his rifle in one hand as he ejects an empty cartridge, his other hand holding, slung over his shoulder, his saddle. The camera assumes the form of the stagecoach being brought to a halt before the cowboy, the tracking shot moving in fast on Wayne, losing focus for a moment, to stop in a closeup of Wayne, looking up at U.S. Marshal Bancroft--who holds a shotgun leveled at him--and saying that his horse came up lame and he is going to Lordsburg, adding, "...looks like you got another passenger." He surrenders his rifle to Bancroft who tells him he is under arrest as an escaped convict. Holt, the officer in charge of the cavalry escort, rides up and asks Bancroft if everything is all right and Bancroft tells him that it is. Wayne gets into the coach after throwing his saddle on top of the stage. Devine drives the horses onward, nervously asking Bancroft about the possibility of Apaches raiding the area. Wayne had mentioned that he saw "a ranch house burning last night" before getting into the stage. Inside the stage, Wayne sits on the floor and Churchill looks down on him with a sneer, saying, "So, you're the notorious Ringo Kid." Wayne replies: "My friends just call me Ringo. Nickname I had as a kid. Right name's Henry." Mitchell believes he knows him, asking Wayne if he "didn't fix your arm once when you were bucked off a horse." Wayne tells Mitchell that he fixed his younger brother's arm, not his, and that "you did a good job, Doc, even if you was drunk." Mitchell asks what happened to Wayne's brother and the cowboy's face darkens as he replies, "He was murdered." The stage rolls on, through the great tracts of Monument Valley, huge, towering buttes jutting along the path of the scurrying coach. The coach comes to a way station and the passengers alight to have a meal while the horses are changed on the stage. The proper Platt refuses to sit next to prostitute Trevor and only Wayne sits with her to eat, noticing that no one is sitting next to *him*. "Looks like I got the plague, don't it?" he asks Trevor. "No," she replies tiredly, "it's not you." "Well, I guess you can't break out of prison and into society in the same week," says Wayne, not hearing her. Platt asks Carradine if he's ever been in Virginia and he tells her that he served in her father's regiment (in the Confederate Army during the Civil War). Wayne tells Trevor at the other end of the table that he wishes he had met her earlier and that he used to be a good cowhand but he won't go back to prison until he does a job in Lordsburg. The passengers are called to the stagecoach for the continuing journey and all climb aboard. Some miles across the open desert, the cavalry escort under Holt's command leaves the coach, going on its patrol in a different direction. Now the stage and its passengers are unprotected, racing along through the wild territory. Bancroft and Devine talk while driving the horses forward, discussing how Tyler, and his two brothers, Rickson and Pegg, have killed Wayne's father and brother, and are waiting in Lordsburg to kill Wayne. Bancroft tells Devine that Wayne doesn't stand a chance against them, "and the only safe place for Ringo is in the pen and I aim to get him there all in one piece." Wayne's purpose for breaking out of prison and going to Lordsburg is to settle accounts but Bancroft vows not to let the shootout happen. Bancroft looks about him and notices snow on the ground and asks why Devine is taking the mountain road. The heavyset driver grins and says: "I'm using my head. Those breach-clout Apaches don't like snow." Trevor sees the pregnant Platt looking tired and ill and offers to let her sit next to her so that she can put her head on her shoulder. Platt gives her a look of disgust and refuses the offer. Platt asks if there is any water and Carradine pours a drink from a canteen, offering Platt a little silver cup full of water. She looks at the cup and recognizes a crest, one from a famous southern plantation. When she asks Carradine about it he tells her "I wouldn't know....I won this cup on a wager." Wayne asks if Trevor can have a drink. The canteen is handed over but Carradine folds up the little cup and tucks it away. Wayne smiles and hands Trevor the canteen, saying, "Sorry, no silver cups." She smiles back and happily drinks from the canteen. Meanwhile, Churchill complains about the cavalry escort leaving them to the mercy of the savages and Mitchell continues to vex liquor salesman Meek by drinking one sample after another from his liquor case. The coach races onward, coming through a gap in the mountains to another rest station where armed Mexicans open the gates apprehensively to let the stage inside the compound. Martin, the proprietor of the station, tells Bancroft and the others that the Apaches raided the station the night before and then slowly tells Platt that her husband, a captain of the cavalry troop that had been stationed there, had been wounded in the skirmish and was taken to Lordsburg. Once inside the station, Platt feels faint and collapses. Bancroft carries her to a back room and Mitchell, who is sodden drunk from sampling Meek's wares, looks glumly down the hall toward the back room. Wayne shoves him in that direction and Mitchell goes down the hall and into the room on wobbly legs. Trevor rushes out of the room to tell Wayne to make plenty of hot water and he yells in Spanish for the hot water to Martin. Mitchell comes out of the room and goes to the bar, staring at a bottle of liquor. Carradine sneers at him, saying: "A fine member of the medical profession! Drunken beast!" Mitchell tears off his coat and shouts for hot coffee. He is shown gulping down the near-scalding brew, shouting to Bancroft and Wayne to: "give me coffee–black coffee–lots of it–more, more!" He finally turns to throw up, Wayne holding him. Carradine steps into the room where they are working on Mitchell to shout, "Isn't that drunken swine sober yet?" Mitchell, with water dashed in his face, finally walks somberly out of the back room and into another where Platt is waiting to deliver her baby. Outside, Martin's Indian wife gathers the Mexican hands and encourages them to flee. They saddle horses quietly and then open the gates, riding madly away as Bancroft and Wayne come running out of the station house. The Mexicans have fled with all the spare horses. Later, as a coyote is shown to howl in the distance, Wayne and the others sit impatiently about and finally there is the sound of a new-born baby crying. Trevor, beaming, steps out of the back room, holding the child and showing it to the men. Trevor tells them it's a little girl and that Platt is going to be all right. Mitchell steps out of the back room, triumphant, to be congratulated by everyone. When Trevor goes outside to get some air, Wayne follows her and she tries to talk him out of facing the Plummer gang in Lordsburg. He tells her he watched her with the baby and then begins to speak in broken sentences, his words all meaning the same thing, that he wants her for himself, adding that "I still got a ranch across the border, a real nice place...trees, grass, water...there's a cabin half-built. A man could live there–and a woman. Will you go?" She gives him a look of anguish and says, "But you don't know me, you don't know who I am." He replies, "I know all I want to know." She shakes her head and walks away toward the station house. Bancroft appears, as if to tell Wayne he will never be far from him. The next morning, Martin runs frantically about, shouting that his wife, an Apache woman, has run away. Bancroft instinctively reaches for his pistol when awakened and jerks upward into a sitting position so that he yanks the shackles he wears on his leg, the other end of which is locked around Wayne's foot. He unlocks the shackles as the passengers prepare to leave. When Churchill sees Devine helping him with his black case, he shouts for him to "keep your hands off my things!" Mitchell refuses a drink, now feeling proud to be a physician, and looks in on Platt to find that Trevor has been sitting with her all night, staying awake to watch over her and the child. Platt vows that she and her baby will get to Lordsburg and be reunited with her husband. Trevor goes into the hall for a private conversation with Mitchell and tells him that Wayne has asked her to marry him, almost pleading for assurance when she asks "Is that wrong–for a girl like me? If a man and woman love each other. It's all right, ain't it, Doc?" Mitchell gives her a severe look and responds: "You're going to be hurt, child, worse than you've ever been hurt. Don't you know the boy's headed back for prison? Besides, if you two go into Lordsburg together, he's going to know all about you." Trevor only wants one answer and tells Mitchell that Wayne isn't going to Lordsburg, saying, "All I want is for you to tell me that it's all right." Mitchell gives her a little smile and says, "Gosh, child, who am I to tell you what's right or wrong? All right, go ahead, do it if you can. Good–good luck." Later Trevor tells Wayne that if he leaves the station and heads for his ranch and stays away from Lordsburg she'll join him later and he makes a break for it. But by the time Bancroft runs after him to put the cuffs on him, he finds Wayne motionless, staring at the distant hills and telling him that the smoke rising from the hills are Indian war signals. The passengers hastily prepare to leave the station, carrying Platt and her baby on board the stagecoach. The stage races out into the open country, getting to the ferry to find that it has been burned out by raiding Apaches. Everyone gets out so that two logs can be tied to the sides of the coach to make it float while the horses pull it across. Meanwhile, Carradine removes his cloak and covers a woman who has been killed by the Apaches. The coach is pulled across the river and the passengers get in, the stage racing forward on its last leg of the trip toward Lordsburg. As it passes a ridge overlooking the barely visible roadway, the camera pulls back to reveal a horde of Indians on horseback, holding rifles and staring down wolf-like at the stage in the distance. Inside the stage the passengers begin to talk about the journey, as if it is over, and right in the middle of a word, Meek is suddenly struck in the chest with a quivering arrow. Mitchell grabs the little man as he pitches forward (he will survive). Down the ridge next to the racing stage come the attacking savages, firing at the coach as they ride. Bancroft returns fire as Devine whips the horses to a furious pace. The stage rolls down out of the foothills and onto the salt flats of the desert, a seemingly endless stretch of hardened sand, baked almost to concrete by the blistering sun. (Here Ford positioned one camera behind Bancroft, on top of the stagecoach, showing the hats worn by Devine and Bancroft, and Bancroft pitching large stones at the horses to make them go faster.) The Indians are gaining ground on the coach. Bancroft hands out weapons to the passengers reaching for guns from the open windows and Wayne climbs on top of the stage to get his rifle from Bancroft and fire at the Apaches now almost riding alongside the stage. Arrows plow into the stage as it rockets along. Inside the coach, Churchill panics and tries to get out but is stopped by Mitchell. The Indians on their fast ponies are almost engulfing the coach and the camera cuts to a low-level shot to show the coach approaching, the horses thundering forward, their legs galloping frantically, hooves thundering, the coach passing over the camera, an Indian right behind it, riding straight into the camera and then a cut to the top of the coach where Bancroft and Wayne are firing their rifles and a cut to the charging Indians, two of them hit and spilling forward in death dives from their horses, which roll and pitch after them. One brave races ahead of the others and tries to grab the reins of the lead horse and Wayne shoots him and he falls in front of the stage, its horses and carriage rolling over him. (This stunt was performed by the greatest Hollywood stuntman who ever lived, Yakima Canutt, one that he had perfected as a personal trademark over the years.) Firing carefully at the Indians who are now abreast of the coach are Mitchell and a wild-eyed Carradine. Devine is suddenly hit in the arm so that he loses his grasp of one rein and the stage begins to slow down. Wayne leaps from the coach to the first pair of horses, then the next and then the leading horses, finally mounting one of them and spurring the team onward. Mitchell calls up to Bancroft for more ammunition and the lawman can only open the breach of his rifle to show Mitchell his empty chamber. In the coach Trevor holds the baby close, looking down at the child, then buries her head in its blanket-wrapped body, believing the end is near. Carradine looks into the cylinder of his pistol to see only one bullet left. He turns to Platt who is praying with a look of desperation on her face. She does not see Carradine's hand reach forward and point the gun at her head, an act of mercy by the gambler to prevent her from falling into the hands of the savages. But, before he can pull the trigger, Carradine is himself shot. Faintly, with the camera closeup on Platt's hopeful face, there is the sound of a distant bugle, as if she is imagining the call of the cavalry, her husband's cavalry. Then she says, in a daze: "Do you hear it? Do you hear it? It's the bugle! They're blowing the charge!" And, miraculously, she is right. The camera cuts to a line of charging troopers, their horses at a full gallop, dashing forward, the bugler blaring his horn, the guidons of the cavalry rippling in the wind as the soldiers ride furiously to the rescue. A long shot behind the charging line of cavalrymen shows them racing away from the camera and toward the fast-approaching stagecoach, surrounded by the Indians, in the distance appearing to be bees hovering about a moving hive. The stage races forward as the cavalrymen meet it, go around it, and keep going after the Indians who have turned tail and are now fleeing pell-mell across the salt flats. The coach is brought to a halt, Wayne jumping off the lead horse and running to the carriage and throwing open the door. He sees Carradine, held by Mitchell and telling Platt with his dying words: "If you see Judge Greenfield...tell him his son..." The fallen aristocrat of the Old South slumps forward, dead. The cavalry escorts the battered stagecoach into Lordsburg. It is night and the baby and Platt are taken off the coach, Platt haltingly giving Trevor her thanks. Some friends of the Plummer boys see that Wayne is on the stage and run to tell Tyler who is playing cards in a saloon, just having received a hand of cards which the dealer prophetically announces when seeing it, "Aces and eights–dead man's hand, Luke." (This was the poker hand that Wild Bill Hickok was holding on August 2, 1876, when he was shot in the back and killed by Black Jack McCall in Deadwood, Colorado, and aces and eights has been known as "The Dead Man's Hand" ever since.) Tyler, the worst of the Plummer gang and killer of Wayne's father and brother, stands up with a grim look on his face and cashes in his chips, throwing down his cards. The camera, in closeup, shows the pair of aces and pair of eights. Tyler goes to the bar, belts down a shot of liquor, and looks around warily as other drinkers leave the bar quickly, knowing a shooting is about to occur. A sheriff shows up, not to arrest Wayne but to put the cuffs on an indignant Churchill, the banker who has looted his own vaults and has been carrying the money in his little black bag. As he struggles with the cuffs, the sheriff smugly states, "You didn't think they'd get the telegraph wire fixed, did you?" In gratitude for his life-saving action against the Apaches, Bancroft allows Wayne 10 minutes to face the Plummer gang. Wayne takes some bullets out of his hat while Bancroft hands him his rifle. He shows the lawman the bullets and says: "I lied to you, Curly. Got three left." Wayne finds Trevor outside of a brothel and asks her if that is where she lives and she says: "No, don't come any farther. It's all been a crazy dream! I been out of my mind–just hoping. Say goodbye, here Kid." "We ain't never gonna say goodbye," Wayne tells her, obviously knowing her scarlet past all along. In the saloon Tyler and his brothers Rickson and Pegg drink heavily, bolstering their nerves. Mitchell walks into the bar calmly, stands at the end of the bar, and then tells Tyler, who is about to step outside with a shotgun "I'll take that shotgun, Luke." Tyler gives him a lunatic grin and replies, "You'll take it in the belly if you don't get out of my way!"Nervelessly, Mitchell stares back at the dark-eyed gunman and says, "I'll have you indicted for murder if you step outside with that shotgun." Tyler pauses for a moment, then tosses the shotgun onto the bar, shoves Mitchell out of the way, and steps to the street with his two brothers. Outside, Tyler stops beneath a balcony and one of his saloon girls throws down a rifle to him. The Plummers saunter down the duckboard walkway but tense up when they hear a noise, one of them nervously pulling his pistol and shooting at a black cat that darts across their path. Pegg says to Rickson: "Missed 'em by four feet" and grins like the idiot he is. The Plummers step into the street and move forward cautiously, turning and looking in all directions at shadows. They are seen by the camera at a long distance down the street and, close up, Wayne steps into the scene and begins to walk toward them. The Plummers are shown marching forward. Wayne, shown advancing toward his lethal enemies, walks into the camera. The camera cuts back and forth quickly showing Wayne and the Plummers advancing toward one another and then only Wayne, shown from low level, walking resolutely forward, forward, forward, until he is almost on top of the camera before flopping to the ground, firing his three rounds rapidly as he falls. Trevor, outside the bordello, hears many shots and runs forward a little, then begins to weep. Tyler is shown walking back into the saloon, past a crowd of silent, staring men, and then, just as he is about to take a drink, falling down dead on the floor. Trevor hears boot heels on the wooden sidewalk coming toward her. She turns and looks anxiously into the dark, out of which steps Wayne. They embrace as Bancroft brings up a buckboard and asks Wayne if he's ready. Wayne gets into the buckboard and tells Trevor that Bancroft will take her to his place as the lawman has promised the outlaw. Says Bancroft, getting off the buckboard, "Maybe you'd like to ride aways with the Kid." She nods and gets in. Suddenly Bancroft and Mitchell begin throwing pebbles at the horses and shouting, driving the horses down the street wildly. Wayne and Trevor are surprised but delighted at being allowed to have a free life together. When they are gone Mitchell says to Bancroft, "Well, they're saved from the blessings of civilization." Bancroft offers to buy the liquor-loving Mitchell a drink and Mitchell holds up a finger and says, jokingly, "Just one!" The lawman and doctor go arm-and-arm grinning down the street toward the saloon and the camera cuts to the buckboard going slowly across the great expanse of the desert as the sun begins to rise with the credits at the finish.

Ford had not directed a western in 13 years before making STAGECOACH, his last film in the genre being THREE BAD MEN (1926). This film came as a shock to the movie community in that Ford was no longer thought of as a western director and now he had, out of the blue, so to speak, produced the greatest western ever seen. He would later state that "STAGECOACH blazed the trail for the 'adult' western," but this discounted too many great silent films of the genre, including his own and those of William S. Hart, who made many "adult" westerns such as HELL'S HINGES and TUMBLEWEEDS. But STAGECOACH was the first western to portray in-depth characters with allegorical themes running just beneath the surface plot of their life and death struggles. Moveover, Ford employs a dazzling array of technical skills in presenting this film as a major work, as well as framing each breathtaking scene as if it were a painting and essentially they are, with the landscape of the awesome Monument Valley serving both as a backdrop and a constant reminder of the freedom offered by the frontier and the dangers of enjoying that splendor and freedom. There is a constant sense of history running throughout the film as Ford's characters endure every hazard, undergo every indignity, survive most of the inherent deadfalls of the land they inhabit, some by trade, some by choice. There are many elements at work in STAGECOACH, the finest being Ford's conception of good triumphing over evil, with help along the way from basically weak but well-intentioned people, who, in the end, prove much stronger than they themselves envisioned. After reading a story by Haycox in *Collier's* Magazine in 1937, one entitled, "The Stage to Lordsburg," Ford contacted the author and bought the film rights for $4,000. (He would later say that he thought Haycox had gotten his idea for his story from Guy de Maupassant's *Boule de Suif*, a tale about an esteemed citizen and a prostitute traveling by coach through France during the war.) Ford was not above using good scenes done by others. The closeup of Carradine's hand holding the gun to Platt's head to show a mercy killing was almost a duplicate of a scene shot by D.W. Griffith in THE BATTLE OF ELDERBUSH GULCH (1913), when Lillian Gish is almost exterminated before falling into the hands of brutal savages. Ford's long-time scriptwriter, Nichols, deserves much of the credit for the literate and often humorous dialog, as well as the penetrating characters he created, many of these parts, though original at the time, going on to become stereotypes as the film was endlessly copied. The first person Ford thought of as the outlaw in STAGECOACH was an overgrown prop boy he had met 10 years earlier and had promoted into B westerns, Wayne. He called his favorite actor to his yacht in 1937 and asked him to read the script. Wayne read the script and then Ford asked him whom Wayne thought should play the outlaw. Wayne shocked the director by telling him that Lloyd Nolan would be a good bet. Ford shook his head and said; "Damn you, Duke, can't *you* do it?" When Wayne did decide to perform in the film, Ford had a hard time trying to sell Wayne and the story, as a major film, to any of the Hollywood studios. He finally convinced independent producer Wanger to put up $250,000 (one-tenth of the budget for THE BIG TRAIL, Wayne's only other major film to that time, although STAGECOACH would go into the can for a cost of $392,000.) Wanger at first wanted Gary Cooper to play the outlaw but Ford talked him out of it and promised the producer that he would give Trevor top billing since she had a more established name at the time. When finally getting the go-ahead from Wanger, Ford took his entire cast and crew, numbering 85 people, into primitive Monument Valley (location sites also included Utah-Colorado towns, Kernville, Victorville, Fremont Pass, Dry Lake, Calabasas, and Chatsworth, California.) No film had ever been made in the remote Monument Valley and its arid plains, 4,000 feet above sea level, and jutting buttes, some reaching 1,500 feet, startled audiences when it was first seen, a landscape that was both awesome and majestic. During the 1880s, stagecoaches had actually crossed this enormous valley and Ford made prompt use of the old coach trails which are seen running through the broad expanses like old scars. Canutt, who performs most of the incredible stunts in the film–although Ford allowed Wayne to do most of his own, including the jumping from horse to horse when the coach is about to go out of control–roomed with Wayne in a small cabin during the on-location shooting, teaching him stunts. The attack on the stagecoach was made by more than 300 Navajo Indians from the Arizona reservation and they, and the stagecoach during the running film battle, averaged 46 miles per hour on horseback across the flat plains of Monument Valley that were free of boulders and rocks and therefore allowed a magnificent, accident- free run. Some of Ford's shots of the stagecoach, shot on clear days, were taken as far as 40 miles away from the moving coach. When producer Wanger learned that Wayne was performing his own stunts, he went to Arizona and arrived just as Wayne was about to leap onto a horse. Wanger yelled at him to stop, that he was now an important actor and could get hurt (thereby damaging Wanger's valuable investment). Wayne snorted and said, "I'm not an actor! I don't act! I react! I'm a stuntman!" The cast and crew labored for 10 weeks in the Utah-Colorado wilds before Ford was satisfied with what he shot. But it was another three months before he had the film edited and scored (the composers winning Oscars for their score which was dotted with old western ballads and saloon songs such as "Lily Dale," "Bury Me on the Lone Prairie," "I Dream of Jeannie," "Joe the Wrangler," "She May Have Seen Better Days," "Careless Love," and Ford's own favorite, "Shall We Gather at the River?"). Wanger later made claims that STAGECOACH was all his idea and that he even discovered Wayne in the B films. Ford angrily issued statements to the contrary and Wanger backed away from his claims, admitting that "while I am proud to be the producer of STAGECOACH,...the picture 'should be' known as John Ford's achievement." The film, which would glean as much as $1 million after its initial release, established Wayne as a major talent and thrust Ford into the western-making limelight as its premiere helmsman where he remained to his death. STAGECOACH saw many successful reissues, mostly billed with LONG VOYAGE HOME, but its original negative prints over the years were either destroyed or lost. Wayne finally came to the rescue, as he did in so many celluloid tales, and provided his own copy of the film to be reproduced and preserved in 1970. The film suffered an abysmal remake in 1966 with Alex Cord and Ann-Margret in the lead roles and Bing Crosby in the role of the drunken doctor. The original STAGECOACH film was released in 1939, a stellar year for westerns, with such blockbusters as DESTRY RIDES AGAIN and JESSE JAMES in the lists but it was STAGECOACH that captured all the honors and rightly so, with Ford winning the New York Critic's Award for his spectacular film. Footage from this film classic surfaced in some B westerns later, notably I KILLED GERONIMO (1950) and LARAMIE MOUNTAINS (1952).

p, Walter Wanger; d, John Ford; w, Dudley Nichols (based on the short story "Stage to Lordsburg" by Ernest Haycox); ph, Bert Glennon; m, Richard Hageman, W. Franke Harling, Louis Gruenberg, Leo Shuken, John Leipold (adapted from 17 American folk tunes of the early 1880s); ed, Dorothy Spencer, Walter Reynolds; md, Boris Morros; art d, Alexander Toluboff; set d, Wiard B. Ihnen; cos, Walter Plunkett; spec eff, Ray Binger.

Western **Cas.** **(PR:C MPAA:NR)**

STAGECOACH** (1966) 114m FOX c

Ann-Margaret *(Dallas)*, Red Buttons *(Mr. Peacock)*, Michael Connors *(Hatfield)*, Alex Cord *(Ringo)*, Bing Crosby *(Doc Josiah Boone)*, Bob Cummings *(Mr. Gatewood)*, Van Heflin *(Curly)*, Slim Pickens *(Buck)*, Stefanie Powers *(Mrs. Lucy Mallory)*, Keenan Wynn *(Luke Plummer)*, Brad Weston *(Matt Plummer)*, Joseph Hoover *(Lt. Blanchard)*, Oliver McGowan *(Mr. Haines)*, David Humphreys Miller *(Billy Picket)*, Bruce Mars *(Trooper)*, Brett Pearson *(Sergeant)*, Muriel Davidson *(Woman)*, Ned Wynn *(Ike Plummer)*, Norman Rockwell *(Townsman)*, Edwin Mills *(Sergeant Major)*, Hal Lynch *(Bartender)*, Walker Edmiston *(Wells Fargo Agent)*, Barbara Wilkin *(Susan)*, John Gabriel *(Capt. Mallory)*.

Why Hollywood insists on remaking classics will always be a puzzle. John Ford's 1939 version of the Haycox story was a genuine western classic and this is a genuine western omelette. The presence of Crosby, in his last acting job in movies, saves the movie from being a total mess. In 1986, a TV version of the picture was done with several country music stars in the leads, as well as Liz Ashley and Anthony Newley. It was so awful, it made this movie look good by comparison. The original was made for about a half million and ranks as one of Ford's best pictures. Everyone who participated in this is wan by comparison. After a two-minute Indian rampage to show how cruel the redskins were, a stagecoach takes off from a small town. Aboard are Ann-Margaret, a dance hall "hostess" who has been asked to leave town by the local Army officer, Gabriel; Crosby, a drunken doctor whose face hasn't seen a razor for a spell and who hasn't drawn a sober breath in years; a southern card shark played by Connors; a meek bank clerk who is absconding with a payroll, Cummings; Buttons, a shy liquor salesman; and Powers, the pregnant wife of Army man Gabriel. The driver of the coach is Pickens and Heflin is aboard as a crusty police-type. It's GRAND HOTEL on wheels as the stories of all are revealed in between several incidents. Cord is a chased criminal who joins up with the coach and is arrested by Heflin. When Powers is about to deliver her child, Crosby gets sober for the first time and helps give birth to the baby. Indians come after the group and there's a pitched battle. Cord has been falsely accused of the murder of his father and brother, who were actually killed by Keenan Wynn and his sons Weston and Ned Wynn, and he is out for revenge. At the end, Cord manages to get through to cynical Ann-Margaret and they become lovers. The stagecoach arrives in Cheyenne and the journey is complete, but the action isn't. Cord is handcuffed to the stagecoach wheel to keep him from going after Keenan Wynn and family. Cummings enters the local bar run by Lynch, and when Heflin learns that Cummings has robbed a bank, he goes in after him but is wounded by Wynn's sons. Then Keenan Wynn shoots and kills Cummings to nab the ten grand Cummings had eloped with. Cord is set free to fight these nefarious people and nails Wynn, Wynn, and Weston as a fire sets the saloon ablaze. Although there's been a reward out for Cord, Heflin realizes that Cord is a good man and has, in fact, saved everyone's life, so he allows Cord and Ann-Margaret to leave while the rest of the town is trying to put out the fire. Whereas the original had engaging characters and not all that much violence, this one concentrates on bloodletting, the dialog is a failed attempt to be "adult," and the performances are generally substandard. Norman Rockwell appears briefly. He'd done the excellent portraits of the actors used with the end credit and they rewarded him with a role in the picture, his first and only. Wayne Newton sings "Stagecoach to Cheyenne" (Lee Pockriss and Paul Vance). It's the kind of song one dislikes upon first hearing and hates upon the second. Cord had the hardest shadow to play, as he was doing the John Wayne role and, even though the former stunt man did show some good underplaying, there was no way he could replace "the Duke" in anyone's memories. Ann-Margaret was better than anyone expected she could be and showed early that she was a talent to reckon with. But the big surprise was Crosby, who chose to find some humor in his part as the drunken medical man. Crosby, who was known to do some heavy tippling, had won an Oscar nomination as an alcoholic singer in THE COUNTRY GIRL 12 years before and showed that he wasn't just another pretty voice. He retired from the screen following STAGECOACH and only came back to host and narrate the Jack Haley, Jr. documentary of THAT'S ENTERTAINMENT eight years after this. Filmed on location in Colorado.

p, Martin Rackin; d, Gordon Douglas; w, Joseph Landon (based on the screenplay by Dudley Nichols from the story "Stage to Lordsburg" by Ernest Haycox); ph, William H. Clothier (CinemaScope, DeLuxe Color); m, Jerry Goldsmith; ed, Hugh S. Fowler; art d, Jack Martin Smith, Herman A. Blumenthal; set d, Walter M. Scott, Stuart A. Reiss; spec eff, L.B. Abbott, Emil Kosa, Jr.; makeup, Ben Nye; stunts, Dick Hudkins.

Western   (PR:A-C   MPAA:NR)

STAGECOACH BUCKAROO**½   (1942) 58m UNIV bw

Johnny Mack Brown (Steve), Fuzzy Knight (Clem), Neil O'Day (Molly), Anne Nagel (Nina), Herbert Rawlinson (Kincaid), Glenn Strange (Braddock), Ernie Adams (Blinky), Henry Hall (Denton), Lloyd Ingraham (Simpson), Kermit Maynard, Frank Brownlee, Jack C. Smith, Harry Tenbrook, Frank Ellis, Blackie Whiteford, Hank Bell, Ray Jones, Jim Corey, William Nestell, Carl Sepulveda, The Guardsmen.

Well-paced action picture is about Brown and sidekick Knight thwarting the attempts of Rawlinson and company to take advantage of the stagecoach run by O'Day's father. The hero tactics go as far as Knight dressing in women's clothing to prevent a holdup. A few songs are fit nicely into the action: "Don't Ever Be a Cowboy," "Just Too Gosh Darn Bashful," Wyomin' Will Be a New Home," and "Put It There."

p, Will Cowan; d, Ray Taylor; w, Al Martin (based on the story "Shotgun Messenger" by Arthur St. Clair); ph, Jerome Ash; md, H.J. Salter; m/l, Milton Rosen, Everett Carter.

Western   (PR:A   MPAA:NR)

STAGECOACH DAYS*   (1938) 56m COL bw

Jack Luden (Breezy Larkin), Eleanor Stewart (Mary Martin), Harry Woods (Moose Ringo), Hal Taliaferro (Milt Dodds), Lafe McKee (Tom Larkin), Jack Ingram (Virg), Charles "Slim" Whitaker (Butch Flint), Dick Botiller, Bob Kortman, Blackjack Ward, Tuffy the Dog.

Dull western in which a couple of stagecoaches race to reach their final destination with the hope of being bestowed with an honorary prize. Best thing in this picture is the dog Tuffy as he goes racing under the actors' feet, showing them what real entertainment is suppose to be. But no one seems to be watching.

p, Larry Darmour; d, Joseph Levering; w, Nate Gatzert; ph, James S. Brown, Jr.; ed, Dwight Caldwell.

Western   (PR:A   MPAA:NR)

STAGECOACH EXPRESS*½   (1942) 57m REP bw

Don "Red" Barry (Dave Gregory), Lynn Merrick (Ellen Bristol), Al St. John (Dusty Jenkins), Robert Kent (Griff Williams), Emmett Lynn (Charles Haney), Guy Kingsford (Sam Elkins), Ethan Laidlaw (Lou Hawkins), Eddie Dean.

Mail Clerk Lynn is involved in double dealing as he helps a gang of crooks get the proper information about stagecoach shipments, while trying to get his own stage line with the help of his boss Merrick. But Barry and his sidekick St. John ride into town and quickly put an end to Lynn's antics. One quirk in the plot is that Merrick is capable of running her own stage line, yet she is still portrayed as the helpless femme.

p&d, George Sherman; w, Arthur V. Jones (based on a story by Doris Schroeder); ph, John MacBurnie; ed, William Thompson; md, Cy Feuer.

Western   (PR:A   MPAA:NR)

STAGECOACH KID*   (1949) 60m RKO bw

Tim Holt (Dave), Richard Martin (Chito), Jeff Donnell (Jessie), Joe Sawyer (Thatcher), Thurston Hall (Arnold), Carol Hughes (Birdie), Robert Bray (Clint), Robert B. Williams (Parnell), Kenneth MacDonald (Sheriff), Harry Harvey (Dabney).

Holt and Martin as owners of a stagecoach try to save the ranch of Hall from several crooks under his employment. The two heroes are looking for gold stolen from one of their stagecoaches, which leads them to the ranch, where they also find the warm affection of Donnell to push them forward in their pursuit. A poor script, even for a "B" Western, and slack direction make this one of the worst Holt entries.

p, Herman Schlom; d, Lew Landers; w, Norman Houston; ph, Nicholas Musuraca; m, Paul Sawtell; ed, Les Millbrook; md, C. Bakaleinikoff; art d, Albert S. D'Agostino, Feild Gray; set d, Darrell Silvera, Jack Mills; makeup, Jack Barron.

Western   (PR:A   MPAA:NR)

STAGECOACH LINE   (SEE: OLD TEXAS TRAIL, THE, 1944)

STAGECOACH OUTLAWS*½   (1945) 58m PRC bw

Buster Crabbe (Billy Carson), Al "Fuzzy" St. John (Fuzzy Jones), Frances Gladwin (Linda), Ed Cassidy (Jed), I. Stanford Jolley (Steve), Kermit Maynard (Vic), Bob Cason (Joe), Robert Kortman (Matt), Steve Clark (Sheriff), George Chesebro, Hank Bell.

Cowpoke Crabbe and his sidekick St. John are up against a gambler trying to take over a stagecoach line run by the father of Gladwin, Crabbe's sweetheart. After the usual number of fistfights and chases, the hero comes out on top, as usual. (See BILLY CARSON series, Index.)

p, Sigmund Neufeld; d, Sam Newfield; w, Fred Myton; ph, Jack Greenhalgh; ed, Holbrook N. Todd.

Western   (PR:A   MPAA:NR)

STAGECOACH TO DANCER'S PARK**½   (1962) 72m Gray-Mac/UNIV bw

Warren Stevens (Jess Dollard), Martin Landau (Dade Coleman), Jody Lawrence (Dr. Ann Thompson), Judy Dan (Loi Yan Wu), Del Moore (Hiram Best), Don Wilbanks (Maj. John Southern), Bob Anderson (Carl "Whip" Mott), Rand Brooks (Quint Rucker), Gene Roth (Jude), Charles Tannen (Sheriff), Mike Ragan (Ben Wade), Mauritz Hugo (Roy), Tim Bolton (1st Holster), Milan Smith (2nd Holster), Alicia Li (Mai Lei), Cherrylene Lee (Ah Ling).

While riding in a stagecoach across the desert, one of the passengers, Dan, is accused of having smallpox. She and the others are kicked off the stage to fend for themselves on the desert. They come across the coach and find the driver and guard to be dead because of an Indian attack. Greed or some form of fluke accident leave the remaining members, except Dan and Stevens, dead. The low budget takes full advantage of the desert setting and the good performances to create a taut and ironic thriller.

p&d, Earl Bellamy; w, Kenneth Darling; ph, Ed Fitzgerald; m, Franz Steininger.

Western   (PR:A   MPAA:NR)

STAGECOACH TO DENVER*½   (1946) 56m REP bw

Allan Lane (Red Ryder), Bobby Blake (Little Beaver), Martha Wentworth (The Duchess), Roy Barcroft (Big Bill Lambert), Peggy Stewart (Beautiful), Emmett Lynn (Coon-Skin), Ted Adams (Sheriff), Edmund Cobb (Duke), Tom Chatterton (Doc Kimball), Bobby Hyatt (Dickie Ray), George Chesebro (Blackie), Edward Cassidy (Felton), Wheaton Chambers (Braydon), Forrest Taylor (Matt Disher), Britt Wood, Tom London, Stanley Price.

While investigating a stagecoach wreck which leaves a commissioner dead, Lane uncovers a land-grabbing plot supervised by Barcroft, of course, who is firmly planted as the town's leading citizen. Tight direction keeps the action going while interweaving a variety of plot angles. (See RED RYDER series, Index.)

p. Sidney Picker; d, R.G. Springsteen; w, Earle Snell (based on the cartoon strip "Red Ryder" by Fred Harmon); ph, Edgar Lyons; ed, Les Orlebeck; md, Mort Glickman; art d, Paul Youngblood; set d, John McCarthy, Jr., Earl Wooden.

Western   Cas.   (PR:A   MPAA:NR)

STAGECOACH TO FURY   (1956) 75m RF/FOX bw

Forrest Tucker (*Frank Townsend*), Mari Blanchard (*Barbara Duval*), Wallace Ford (*Lester Farrell*), Margia Dean (*Ruth*), Rodolfo Hoyos (*Lorenzo Gracia*), Paul Fix (*Tim O'Connors*), Rico Alaniz (*Miquel Torres*), Wright King (*Ralph Slader*), Ian MacDonald (*Sheriff Ross*), William Phillips (*Bartender*), Ellen Corby (*Sarah*), Alex Montoya (*Oro*), Rayford Barnes (*Zick*), Norman Leavitt (*Customer*), Leslie Banning (*Ann Stewart*), Steven Geray (*Nichols*), Paul Fierro (*Pedro*), Robert Karnes (*Talbot*).

Several stagecoach passengers are held captive by Mexican bandits, led by Hoyos, as the bandits wait for the arrival of a shipment of gold. Slowly the passengers and their pasts are unveiled, via flashback, as they face certain death. But ex-Cavalry officer Tucker gets a spark of courage to organize his fellow passengers and outwit the bandits. Although the plot takes a long time to develop, the performances and the focus on characterizations hold enough interest to make for worthy entertainment.

p, Earle Lyon; d, William Claxton; w, Eric Norden (based on a story by Norden and Lyon); ph, Walter Strenge (RegalScope); m, Paul Dunlap; ed, Carl Pierson; art d, Ernest Fegte.

Western   (PR:A   MPAA:NR)

STAGECOACH TO HELL (SEE: STAGE TO THUNDER ROCK, 1964)

STAGECOACH TO MONTEREY   (1944) 55m REP bw

Allan Lane, Peggy Stewart, Wally Vernon, Twinkle Watts, Tom London, Roy Barcroft, LeRoy Mason, Kenne Duncan, Bud Geary, Carl Sepulveda, Jack O'Shea, Jack Kirk, Fred Graham, Henry Wills, Cactus Mack.

When a group of sharpies from the East attempt to forge some certificates, Treasury men go undercover in an effort to stop the gang. Average western effort for Lane, who later became the voice for television's talking horse "Mr. Ed."

p, Stephen Auer; d, Lesley Selander; w, Norman S. Hall; ph, William Bradford; m, Joseph Dubin; ed, Harry Keller; art d, Gano Chittenden.

Western   (PR:A   MPAA:NR)

STAGECOACH WAR   (1940) 63m PAR bw

William Boyd (*Hopalong Cassidy*), Russell Hayden (*Lucky Jenkins*), Julie Carter (*Shirley Chapman*), Harvey Stephans (*Neal Holt*), J. Farrell MacDonald (*Jeff Chapman*), Britt Wood (*Speedy*), Rad Robinson (*Smiley*), Eddy Waller (*Quince Cobalt*), Frank Lackteen (*Twister Maxwell*), Jack Rockwell (*Mart Gunther*), Eddie Dean (*Tom*), Bob Kortman, The King's Men.

Inferior CASSIDY outing stars Boyd as the famous Western hero, chasing bandits who rob stagecoaches. These villains are not very menacing: they sing as they rob. In some ways the villains as portrayed by The King's Men are more likable than the hero. (See HOPALONG CASSIDY series, Index.)

p, Harry Sherman; d, Lesley Selander; w, Norman Houston, Harry F. Olmstead (based on characters created by Clarence E. Mulford); ph, Russell Harlan; ed, Sherman A. Rose; m/l, Phil Ohman, Foster Carling.

Western   (PR:A   MPAA:NR)

STAIRCASE½   (1969 U.S./Brit./Fr.) 96m FOX c

Richard Burton (*Harry Leeds*), Rex Harrison (*Charlie Dyer*), Cathleen Nesbitt (*Harry's Mother*), Beatrix Lehmann (*Charlie's Mother*), Stephen Lewis (*Jack*), Neil Wilson (*Policeman*), Gordon Heath (*Postman*), Avril Angers (*Miss Ricard*), Shelagh Fraser (*Cub Mistress*), Gwen Nelson (*Matron*), Pat Heywood (*Nurse*), Dermot Kelly (*Gravedigger*), Jake Kavanagh (*Choirboy*), Rogers and Starr (*Drag Singers*).

Actors, no matter how talented they are, can only stretch so far before they break. In this adaptation of a fairly successful stage play, Burton and Harrison have been cast as two older homosexuals and it just doesn't convince, despite the talents of both men. Harrison and Burton have been lovers for three decades. They live above the barber shop where they work and use the "staircase" in the title to walk from their flat to their place of business. Burton is losing his hair and is so vain about this condition that he keeps his head swathed in a turban. Harrison, the more flamboyant of the two, is on edge because he was out in public in full drag and was cited by the police. When the picture opens, he is anxious about his upcoming court appearance. The men are established as being snide and sharp with each other and it would seem that there is unusual tension between the two,

but it's soon understood that this is their relationship. Harrison is the more acerbic of the two and sends darts into Burton's psyche with regularity. Harrison had once been heterosexual and he receives a letter from his former mate explaining that their daughter is coming to town to visit and could he spend a day with her? Burton's mother is Nesbitt, an invalid who requires constant attention. She lives with them and Harrison asks if Burton would take her out for a drive while the father and daughter have a few hours together. Burton is livid at the suggestion because Nesbitt can barely be moved due to her arthritis. The summons to appear in court on the charge cited earlier arrives and Harrison has no money to hire a barrister so he prevails upon Burton for a loan and is refused. Harrison goes off to visit his aged mother, Lehmann, who resides in an old persons' home and she tongue-lashes him for being homosexual, so he exits before asking her for any money. Later, Harrison returns to the residence with Lewis, a gay he's met, and he tries to seduce the young man. Burton is hurt by Harrison's perfidy and locks himself in the bathroom. When Harrison can't get into the room, he breaks the door and finds Burton unconscious and fears that his lover has attempted suicide. Harrison pleads with the comatose Burton to never leave him, and when Burton awakens, he explains that the faint was not due to an overdose of anything; it was the result of having high blood pressure due to seeing Harrison with Lewis. Harrison is about to go to court for his case and Burton walks in wearing a terrible black toupee to hide his baldness. Harrison pokes fun at the wig and Burton pays no attention to it and remains steadfast in wanting to go to court with Harrison to lend some moral support. Harrison thinks that the specter of Burton in the wig would go against him in the eyes of the judge. Harrison walks out alone and is on his way to the court when he realizes that, despite all the abuse he's heaped on Burton and despite Burton's weird looks, he still loves him and needs him and wants him to be his partner forever. He calls for Burton to join him in court and the two men walk down the street, happy in their 30-year love for each other. There is no real conclusion to the picture and that might have been solved had they shown the actual trial. There is also no actual homosexual activity. It almost seems as though the two men were friends and roommates rather than lovers, so the absence of sensationalism works both for and against the picture. The music was by Dudley Moore and the single song was "Life's Staircase," as sung by Ray Charles. A downbeat, depressing movie that was opened up for the screen by the author of the play, STAIRCASE was filmed in Paris, which failed to simulate London. The reason for this Gallic lensing was that Burton had some tax problems and needed to be out of England for a while. He was then married to Elizabeth Taylor and they couldn't bear to be apart, so she had Fox build a Las Vegas set in Paris while she was making THE ONLY GAME IN TOWN with Warren Beatty. Nesbitt was stunning as Burton's mother and should have gotten at least an Oscar nomination but the picture was such a bomb that it was overlooked. Lehmann was also wonderful and the two women, in brief appearances, stole the film's thunder, what little there was. Producer-director Donen, who had specialized in gay musicals (in the old-fashioned sense of the word), seemed to let these two giants get out of hand at times and hardly an inch of scenery was spared by their molars.

p&d, Stanley Donen; w, Charles Dyer (based on the play by Dyer); ph, Christopher Challis, Philippe Brun (Panavision, DeLuxe Color); m, Dudley Moore; ed, Richard Marden; art d, Willy Holt; makeup, Alberto De Rossi, Ron Berkeley.

Drama/Comedy   Cas.   (PR:C-O   MPAA:R)

STAIRWAY TO HEAVEN**   (1946, Brit.) 104m Archers-Independent Producers/UNIV c-bw (GB: A MATTER OF LIFE AND DEATH)

David Niven, (*Squadron Leader Peter D. Carter*), Kim Hunter (*June*), Roger Livesey (*Dr. Reeves*), Robert Coote (*Bob Trubshawe*), Marius Goring (*Conductor 71*), Raymond Massey (*Abraham Farlan*), Kathleen Byron (*An Angel*), Richard Attenborough (*English Pilot*), Bonar Colleano (*American Pilot*), Joan Maude (*Chief Recorder*), Abraham Sofaer (*The Judge*), Robert Atkins (*The Vicar*), Bob Roberts (*Dr. Gaertler*), Edwin Max (*Mr. McEwan*), Betty Potter (*Mrs. Rucker*).

A delightful and exquisitely photographed fantasy about an RAF pilot, Niven, who is forced to bail out of his flaming plane as it is dropping out of the sky. With all his fellow crew members either dead or having parachuted to safety, and his own chute riddled with bullet holes, Niven gets on the radio and shares what he believes to be his last words with an American WAC, Hunter. Niven, a poet, has a romantic conversation with Hunter and falls hopelessly in love with her voice. When he finally jumps for his life, he lands in the ocean and is washed safely ashore. By some fateful coincidence he meets Hunter and the pair fall in love. Although Niven appears to be healthy, he actually is suffering from brain damage and must undergo an operation. Meanwhile, in heaven (photographed in dye-monochrome, while the real world is in Technicolor), it is realized that a terrible mistake has been made--that Niven who was scheduled to die has somehow lived. This discovery is made by Heavenly Conductor Number 71, Goring, a Frenchman who was beheaded in his country's revolution. While Goring and his superiors debate Niven's fate, Niven argues that because of their mistake and because he has fallen in love with Hunter, he should be allowed to remain on Earth. While Niven lies on the operating table, his appeal is heard by a group of heavenly judges led by prosecutor Massey, an American with strong anti-British sentiments, since he was the first colonial fighter killed in the American Revolution. Niven finally wins his case, emerges from a successful operation, and is reunited with sweetheart Hunter. A fantastic accomplishment which shines with surrealistic cinematic bravura, STAIRWAY TO HEAVEN is a marvel of technique and imagination created by the collective minds of Powell and Pressburger, with a notable contribution from production designer Junge. Most remarkable is his monumental stairway which reaches majestically into the heavens and is peopled with a cast of history's dead. Chosen as the first of the Royal Command Film Performances, STAIRWAY TO HEAVEN garnered some critical acclaim in Britain, but was generally attacked by stuffy detractors who felt it was anti-British. Once again proving that the greatest harm inflicted on the always unstable British Cinema is done by British critics themselves, who prefer to cut down their finest directors (namely Powell and Pressburger) instead of building them up. In America, it was met with great enthusiasm and compared, somewhat unfairly, to the 1941 Robert Montgomery vehicle HERE COMES MR. JORDAN, which was remade in 1978 as HEAVEN CAN WAIT. An enjoyable piece of escapist entertainment, though not without important underlying themes (the love and death of a poet, the strength of overcoming impossible barriers of love), which only improves with age.

p,d&w, Michael Powell, Emeric Pressburger; ph, Jack Cardiff (Technicolor); m, Allan Gray; ed, Reginald Mills; prod d, Alfred Junge; art d, Arthur Lawson; cos, Hein Heckroth; spec eff, Douglas Woolsey, Henry Harris; m/l, "Shoo Shoo Baby," Phil Moore.

Fantasy/Romance   **Cas.**   **(PR:A   MPAA:NR)**

STAKEOUT!**   (1962) 81m Crown International bw

Bing Russell (Joe), Billy Hughes (Joey), Bill Hale (Stoddard), Jack Harris (Gus), Bernie Thomas (Greer), William Foster (Benny), Eve Brent (Susie), Chris Wayne (Jimmy), Whitey Hughes (Sautu).

A familiar story about a convict who is released from jail and prevented from leading a decent life because his past keeps catching up with him. There is little new here in terms of plot, but a heart-felt performance by Russell adds a needed spark. Accompanied by his 10-year-old son, Russell wanders around the country in search of a job. In two cases he finds himself well-situated, only to have his prison record discovered and to be fired. In desperation he contacts an old prison friend to accompany him on a scheme to kidnap an oilman's son. The story ends tragically, with Russell dying while trying to save his own son's life.

p, Robert Hughes, William Hughes, Joe R. Gentile; d&w, James Landis; ph, Jack Specht; m, Tom Downing; art d, Emogene Chapman.

Drama/Crime   **(PR:A   MPAA:NR)**

STAKEOUT ON DOPE STREET**½   (1958) 83m WB bw

Yale Wesler (Jim), Jonathan Haze (Ves), Morris Miller (Nick), Abby Dalton (Kathy), Allen Kramer (Danny), Herman Rudin (Mitch), Philip Mansour (Lennie), Frank Harding (Capt. Allen), Bill Shaw (Chuck), A.J. Fenady (Stan), Slate Harlow (Lt. Donahue), Herschel Bernardi (Mr. Fennel), Carol Nelson (Nick's Girl), Ed Schaff (Mr. Alber), Matt Resnick (Officer Matthews), Charles Guasti (Mr. Lake), Ida Morgan (Girl Bowling), Wendy Wilde (Ves' Girl), John Savage (Doctor), Barbara O'Bannon (Nurse), Larry Raimond (Mr. Vespuchi), Byrd Holland (Suspect), Hal Saunders (Informant), Miles Stephens (Man), Geri Willis (Street Girl), Jim Giles (Detective), Colman Francis (2nd Detective), Ginny Roberts (Girl in the Hall), Mike Stoycoff (3rd Detective), Ernie Kaufman (Man at Table), Lillian Kay (Girl at Table), Lester Miller (2nd Doctor), Larry Frost (Dump Keeper), Hollywood Chamber Jazz Group (Bob Drasnin, Ollie Mitchell, Dick Houlgate, Phil Gray), Gene Estes, Mel Pollan, Ritchie Frost, Rubin Leon.

The first feature production directed by Kershner (THE EMPIRE STRIKES BACK, THE FLIM-FLAM MAN) is a tightly woven, documentary-like expose of three teenagers, Wexler, Haze, and Miller, who find two pounds of uncut heroine. Instead of turning it in to the police, they give in to their greed and try peddling it on the street. But they come up against obstacles they hadn't anticipated.

p, Andrew J. Fenady; d, Irvin Kershner; w, Kershner, Irwin Schwartz, Fenady; ph, Mark Jeffrey; m, Richard Markowitz; ed, Melvin Sloan; md, Markowitz.

Drama   **(PR:C   MPAA:NR)**

STALAG 17*****   (1953) 120m PAR bw

William Holden (Sefton), Don Taylor (Lt. Dunbar), Otto Preminger (Oberst Von Scherbach), Robert Strauss ("Animal" Stosh), Harvey Lembeck (Harry), Richard Erdman (Hoffy), Peter Graves (Price), Neville Brand (Duke), Sig Rumann (Schultz), Michael Moore (Manfredi), Peter Baldwin (Johnson), Robinson Stone (Joey), Robert Shawley (Blondie), William Pierson (Marko), Gil Stratton, Jr. (Cookie/Narrator), Jay Lawrence (Bagradian), Erwin Kalser (Geneva Man), Edmund Trzcinski (Triz), Harold D. Maresch, Carl Forcht (German Lieutenants), Alex J. Wells, Bob Templeton, Paul T. Salata (Prisoners with Beards), Jerry Singer (The Crutch), Bill Sheehan, Richard Porter Beedle, Warren Sortomme, Robin Morse, Ralph Jarvis Caston, James R. Scott, Harry Reardon, Ross Bagdasarian [David Seville] Seville', John P. Veitch, Wesley Ling, John Mitchum, William McLean, Tommy Cook (Prisoners of War), Janice Carroll, Yvette Eaton, Alla

Gursky, Olga Lebedeff, Mara Sondakoff (Russian Women Prisoners), Ross Gould (German Orderly), Mike Bush (Dancer), Joe Ploski (German Guard Volley), Max Willenz (German Lieutenant Supervisor), Peter Leeds (Barracks 1 POW), Herbert Street, Rodric Beckham, Jerry Gerber, William Mulcany, Russell Grower, Donald Cameron, James Dabney, Jr., Ralph Gaston, Svetlana McLee, Lyda Vashkulat, Audrey Strauss.

Holden, under the skillful hand of his "good luck" director Wilder, gives an unforgettable bravura performance in one of the best films produced during the 1950s. The film also offered a romp for a dozen character actors, notably Rumann, Lembeck, Strauss, Brand, not to exclude director-actor Preminger--who presents a portrait of sheer sadistic evil as the vicious, arrogant camp commandant--who is ultimately outwitted by the prisoners. All the inmates of Preminger's unruly camp are sergeants from the U.S. Army or Air Corps (then a division of the Army). As such, they prove to be a scheming, brawling, tough lot who can only plan escapes or provide constant vexation of their German captors. Among them is a cocky loner who is out for himself, Holden. To him, all the patriotic notions spouted by his fellow prisoners are gibberish. He is only interested in bettering his life and promotes games by which he can win money, cigarettes, and important boodle, such as booze and silk stockings, which he trades with female prisoners in adjoining compounds for sexual favors after properly bribing guards to look the other way. Almost at the opening of the film, two of the sergeants in Stalag 17 attempt an escape but their riddled bodies are shown to the assembled prisoners the next morning with Preminger lecturing the Americans on the foolishness of escape attempts. It is slowly concluded that the unthinkable has happened, that there is a spy somewhere in the camp who is informing the Germans on all the plans and plots created by the Americans. Holden is unconcerned and goes on trading with the enemy and bilking his fellow prisoners out of their cigarettes and Red Cross rations. He eats like a field marshal and tantalizes the men by cooking eggs on the stove. Strauss and Lembeck, the barracks clowns, watch him with wide eyes as he cooks an egg and Strauss asks dumbly, "What is it?" Holden smirks and replies, "An egg, bugwit." Lembeck asks Holden if he can have the broken shells of the egg and Strauss magnanimously gives him the shells. Lembeck hands one piece of shell to Strauss who asks him what he's supposed to do with it. "We're gonna plant 'em, animal," says Lembeck, "and grow us a chicken." When not planning escapes, the sergeants busy themselves with pulling pranks on their guards, especially Rumann. At one point, Rumann leaves a copy of Hitler's Mein Kampf in the barracks, telling the prisoners that commandant Preminger has ordered them to read the book and learn the Fuhrer's philosophy. When Rumann next enters the barracks, one of the prisoners is standing before the others, whose backs are turned to Rumann. The prisoner standing on the table, holding Mein Kampf in front of his face, is screaming in a wild imitation of Hitler's ranting voice and then drops the book and shouts "Sieg Heil!" His hair is combed over his forehead and a small black mustache is painted on his upper lip so that he looks like a carbon-copy Hitler. He orders the other prisoners to turn around and give the Nazi salute to Rumann and with that the whole population of the barracks spins around to display dozens of phony Hitlers, all with combed-down hair and little mustaches. Rumann is at first shocked and tells the sergeants to stop "foolin' around...one Fuhrer is enough." Meanwhile, Holden conducts races between mice, rents out a makeshift telescope so the sergeants can peer into the compound holding Russian female prisoners going through a bathhouse, and even creates a still and serves his homemade liquor to his fellow prisoners, all at a price, of course. He is hated by some of the more dedicated noncommissioned officers, especially Brand. Then an American pilot, Taylor, is brought into the barracks after being captured. He and one of his crew members are being temporarily housed at Stalag 17 until the insidious Preminger can discover how Taylor--who was being escorted to another prisoner-of-war camp via train--managed to blow up a German ammunition train going in the opposite direction. Preminger has Taylor brought into his offices and grills the sleepless Taylor ceaselessly, but he is unable to break him. By then, Brand and some others come to believe that Holden is the spy in their midst and they beat him mercilessly, injuring him so badly that he is bedridden for some time. Holden, however, fails to leave the barracks when Rumann orders it cleared one day and he overhears Rumann and the real spy, Graves, conferring, with Graves telling Rumann exactly how Taylor managed to sabotage the ammunition train, having learned this information from Taylor's crew member. After Graves demonstrates the use of a matchbook and a cigarette to create a "time bomb," Rumann says in amazement: "Ach, sooo?" Rumann and Graves leave the barracks and the battered Holden steps from behind a bunk bed, lighting his cigar, and saying knowingly: "Ach, sooo?" When the time comes for the Germans to move Taylor from the camp to be tried as a saboteur, however, the prisoners create a diversion with a homemade smoke bomb and spirit the pilot to a hiding place, keeping him in a water tower. That night everyone draws lots to see who is going to take Taylor out of the camp, but Graves steps forward and insists that he take Taylor to safety. When he is accepted for the role, he is told where Taylor can be found. Then Holden steps forward and tells the barracks chief, Erdman, that he has just told the Germans where the pilot is hiding. Erdman thinks he's crazy and Brand threatens to beat Holden up again. But before he can be interrupted, Holden confronts the real spy in the barracks, Graves, asking him, "Sprechen sie Deutsch?" Graves sneers at him and says, "No, I don't sprechen sie Deutsch." "Maybe just one word?" says Holden. "Kaput? Because you're kaput, Price!" Graves turns to Erdman and tells him to get Holden out of his hair "so I can go." Holden smiles and says: "Go where? To the commandant's office and tell him where Dunbar (Taylor) is?" Graves takes a step toward Holden menacingly and shouts: "I'll kill you for that!" Holden slaps his face with authority, as the other GIs stand transfixed, and tells Graves to "shut up! Security officer, huh? Screening everybody, only who screened you? Great American hero. From Cleveland, Ohio, enlisted right after Pearl Harbor? When was Pearl Harbor, Price, or don't you know?" Graves spits out: "December seventh, forty-one." "What time?" asks Holden. Graves smugly answers: "Six o'clock. I was having dinner." Holden grins triumphantly: "Six o'clock in *Berlin*. They were having lunch in Cleveland." He turns to his fellow prisoners and says: "Am I boring you boys?" Erdman tells him to go on. "He's a Nazi, Price is," concludes Holdne. "For all I know his name is Preishofer or Preissinger. Sure, he liked Cleveland, but when the war broke out he came back to the fatherland like a good little Bundist. He spoke our lingo, so they put him through spy school, gave him phony dogtags..." Just then Graves tries to make a break for it by slipping down through a hole the GIs have cut in the floor, an escape trapdoor, but he is caught and bound and gagged. Cans and other noisemaking devices are tied about his arms and legs and, when Holden is ready to take Taylor out of the camp himself, the spy is let loose in the yard as a diversion to draw the fire of the tower guards. Just before this happens, the GIs apologize to Holden and he blithely accepts their remarks but strikes a match on the side of Brand's face to let him know what he really thinks of him. He takes the wire cutters the GIs have been hiding, and some supplies, telling one and all that Taylor, who comes from a rich family, will bring a big reward if returned to the States in one piece, indicating his mercenary streak to the end. He dons a civilian hat and says, "I'll look pretty silly wearing this while yodeling my way through the Alps." Then he slips down into the hole in the floor and says bitterly to all present: "If I ever run into any of you bums on a street corner, just let's pretend we never met before. Understand?" and slips through the hole. (This departure was later thought too spiteful and not in keeping with the American spirit, so Wilder later had Holden pop back up through the hole for a moment and smile, while giving the sergeants a salute, and then disappearing again.) Holden works Taylor out of the water tower, massages his frozen legs, and then waits for Graves to cause the diversion. Graves is thrown out of the barracks and into the open compound, making a wild racket as he calls in German for help, but he draws machine gun fire from the towers and is killed in front of Preminger's office. Meanwhile, Holden drags Taylor along with him to the wire fence, cuts the wire, and slips through with Taylor following him on wobbly legs, Holden telling his blue-blood friend, "Let's blow, Chauncey." Inside the barracks, Erdman, Brand, and the others lie back in their bunks. Preminger steps from his office and expects to see another American GI dead at his feet but when he kicks over the body with his polished boot, he whips his bald head back in shock to see his own spy lying dead before him, a death he cannot seek vengeance for without admitting Graves' real identity. It is almost pitch black in the barracks, except for the tower lights playing upon the windows. "I wonder why he did it?" Lembeck says aloud, thinking about Holden. "Maybe he just wanted to steal our wire cutters," says the mindless Strauss. "Ever think of that?" Brand smiles in the dark, saying, "The crud did it." Stratton, who had been Holden's gopher throughout the film, begins to whistle "When Johnnie Comes Marching Home," which a full orchestra picks up and thunders triumphantly at the finish. Wilder's STALAG 17 is a stirring WW II film, released only eight years after the war had ended, so it packed plenty of memories for the adult male audience watching it. The director helmed this classic film with an iron hand and kept faith with the script he had prepared with Blum, maintaining a thrilling pace and making each scene come alive through his colorful characters–not the least of whom was the brilliant Holden, who won an Oscar for his startling performance of heel turned hero. The film was an enormous success with the public as it was with the critics, making $10 million within six months of release. Holden was surprised when he learned he had won the coveted Oscar, saying that Burt Lancaster–who had been nominated for his role in FROM HERE TO ETERNITY–should have won the golden statuette. He was told that he had really won the Oscar for his electrifying performance in SUNSET BOULEVARD and this may have been true to some extent, but Holden's performance in STALAG 17 is nothing short of magnificent. At first he declined the role when Wilder offered it to him, seeing the original Broadway play and walking out on it during the first act, but when he read Wilder's clever and often moving script–where his part was considerably altered and beefed up from the stage version–he accepted but he kept after Wilder to soften the heel's image a little bit, asking the director, "Couldn't I have a line or two that shows that I really hate the Germans?" Wilder refused and specifically told the entire cast that not one word of his stellar script could be changed. When he made his statement he purposely looked at Preminger, whom he had specifically asked to play the vicious commandant, and at Holden. Both complied. Holden went at his part full tilt and–according to costar Taylor–he was a different William Holden from the time they made SUBMARINE COMMAND together, now acting "wide-open," and holding nothing back. He became so serious about the role that he could not tolerate the pranks and wisecracks constantly coming from the stage actors who had appeared in the original play–professional clowns such as Lembeck and Strauss–and, on one occasion when their horseplay seemed to get out of hand, Holden yelled to the entire cast: "Goddammit! Can't you guys shut up for a minute? Some of us are trying to get some work done!" Preminger was outstanding as the pompous and cruel commandant whose entire character was summed up in one scene when he has his orderly help him slip on his highly glossed boots just so he can click his heels when calling a high-ranking superior in Berlin!

Wilder benefited by some splendid camerawork from Laszlo and a superb score from Waxman. In addition to the players taken right out of the smash Broadway production, Wilder gave a small part to one of the play's original authors, Trzcinski.

p&d, Billy Wilder; w, Wilder, Edwin Blum (based on the play by Donald Bevan, Edmund Trzcinski); ph, Ernest Laszlo; m, Franz Waxman; ed, Doane Harrison, George Tomasini; art d, Hal Pereira, Franz Bachelin; set d, Sam Comer, Ray Mayer; spec eff, Gordon Jennings; makeup, Wally Westmore.

War Drama   Cas.   **(PR:C MPAA:NR)**

STALKER*½   (1982, USSR) 160m Mosfilm/Media Transactions bw-c

Aleksandr Kaidanovsky (*Stalker*), Nikolai Grinko (*Scientist*), Anatoli Solonitsin (*Writer*), Alice Friendlich (*Stalker's Wife*), Natasha Abramova, F. Yurma, E. Kostin, R. Rendi.

The director of SOLARIS, Tarkovsky continued with many of the same themes he pursued in his earlier film, namely the quest to fulfill one's fantasy. This film is also given a sci-fi type framework. But this time the characters remain on Earth as they journey through a forbidden area called the Zone in order to reach its center. The center is a room which holds many answers and unveils fantasies. But when the three explorers get there, after going through many dangerous experiences, they refrain from entering, preferring that the truth they might find remain a secret. Settings and camera work to create an atmosphere that is suspenseful enough even without the excellent story it enhances. (In Russian; English subtitles.)

p, Alexandra Demidova; d, Andrei Tarkovsky; w, Boris Strugatsky, Arkady Strugatsky (based on their novel *Roadside Picnic*); ph, Aleksandr Knyazhinsky; prod d, Tarkovsky.

Fantasy   **(PR:C MPAA:NR)**

STALKING MOON, THE*½   (1969) 109m NG c

Gregory Peck (*Sam Varner*), Eva Marie Saint (*Sarah Carver*), Robert Forster (*Nick Tana*), Noland Clay (*Boy*), Russell Thorson (*Ned*), Frank Silvera (*Major*), Lonny Chapman (*Purdue*), Lou Frizzell (*Stationmaster*), Henry Beckman (*Sgt. Rudabaugh*), Charles Tyner (*Dace*), Richard Bull (*Doctor*), Sandy Wyeth (*Rachel*), Joaquin Martinez (*Julio*), Red Morgan (*Shelby, the Stage Driver*), Nathaniel Narcisco (*Salvaje*), Rolf the Dog.

Poorly conceived western that offers little action and an overabundance of talk has Peck as an Indian scout ready to retire to his New Mexico ranch when Saint pops into his life. The woman had been held captive by Apaches for the past 10 years, and has given birth to a half-breed son now 9 years old. Peck agrees to escort them to safety, but soon finds himself the prey of Narcisco, the Apache who is the boy's father and who wants him back. The Indian goes on a killing spree until Peck finally overpowers him in a cunning battle. There is little Peck or Saint can do with their roles since they are given material which sheds little light on the characters they are supposed to portray. Camera work fails to take advantage of the outdoor scenery.

p, Alan J. Pakula; d, Robert Mulligan; w, Alvin Sargent, Wendell Mayes (based on the novel by Theodore V. Olsen); ph, Charles Lang (Panavision, Technicolor); m, Fred Karlin; ed, Aaron Stell; art d, Roland Anderson, Jack Poplin; set d, Frank Tuttle; cos, Dorothy Jeakins, Seth Banks, Grace Harris; makeup, Del Armstrong, Frank Prehoda.

Western   **(PR:A MPAA:G)**

STALLION CANYON**   (1949) 72m Kanab/Astor c

Ken Curtis (*Curt Benson*), Carolina Cotton (*Ellen*), Shug Fisher (*Red*), Forrest Taylor (*Larsen*), Ted Adams (*Wolf*), Billy Hammond (*Little Bear*), Roy Butler (*Breezy, the Sheriff*), Alice Richy (*Aunt Millie*), L.H. Larsen (*Steve*), E.N. "Dick" Hammer (*Luke*), Clark Veater (*Dobie*), D.C. Swapp (*Judge*), Gail Bailey (*Laramie*), Bud Gates (*Idaho*), Bob Brandon (*Johnny Adams*).

Scenic Utah was used as the setting for this oater in which Curtis tries to get his Indian pal Hammond off a murder charge and save the ranch he works for from bankruptcy by winning a race. His wild stallion Thundercloud helps provide some of the more striking footage.

d, Harry Fraser; w, Hy Heath; ph, Jack McCluskey (Trucolor); md, Emil Velazco; art d, H.R. Brandon; m/l, "Hills of Utah," Heath.

Western   **(PR:A MPAA:NR)**

STALLION ROAD**   (1947) 97m WB bw

Ronald Reagan (*Larry Hanrahan*), Alexis Smith (*Rory Teller*), Zachary Scott (*Stephen Purcell*), Peggy Knudsen (*Daisy Otis*), Patti Brady (*Chris Teller*), Harry Davenport (*Dr. Stevens*), Angela Green (*Lana Rock*), Frank Puglia (*Pelon*), Ralph Byrd (*Richmond Mallard*), Lloyd Corrigan (*Ben Otis*), Fernando Alvarado (*Chico*), Matthew Boulton (*Joe Beasley*), Mary Gordon (*Mrs. Ford*), Nina Campana (*Maria*), Dewey Robinson (*Moxie*), Paul Panzer (*Tommy*), Bobby Valentine (*Beasley, Jr.*), Ralph Littlefield (*Cowhand*), Tom Wilson (*Sam*), Oscar O'Shea (*Doc Brady*), Leon Lenoir (*Bruno, the Headwaiter*), Monte Blue, Fred Kelsey (*Ranchers*), Maj. Sam Harris (*Dining*

Extra), Joan Winfield (*Nurse*), Danny Dowling (*Auto Park Attendant*), Douglas Kennedy (*Announcer*), Creighton Hale (*Mr. Byron*), Elaine Lange (*Mrs. Calhoun*), Roxanne Stark (*Miss Cooper*), Vera Lewis (*Guest*).

Reagan's first film appearance after his military duty has him as a veterinarian in Southern California where he treats Smith's prize nag and winds up falling in love with the owner. But the horse gets sick again, and when Smith calls Reagan he is too busy treating an outbreak of anthrax among a herd of cattle. Smith doesn't like this and neither do the rest of the horsebreeders, giving Reagan's writer buddy Scott a chance to ask for Smith's hand in marriage. Reagan has contracted a case of anthrax himself, and is all but given up for dead until Smith gives him an injection of the serum he used on the cattle. The doctor is saved and is able to continue pursuing his romance with Smith with Scott gracefully bowing out. Originally, Humphrey Bogart and Lauren Bacall were to have the roles assigned Smith and Scott, but backed out a week before shooting. Perhaps they could have had some success in making these characters come alive. But this is also the screenwriter's fault because he relied too heavily upon dialog to move the plot along.

p, Alex Gottlieb; d, James V. Kern, Raoul Walsh, (Uncredited); w, Stephen Longstreet (based on his novel); ph, Arthur Edeson; m, Frederick Hollander; d, David Weisbart; md, Leo F. Forbstein; art d, Stanley Fleischer; set d, Clarence Steensen; song, "Flusie," performed by the Ray Bauduc Quintet.

Drama   (PR:A   MPAA:NR)

STAMBOUL**   (1931, Brit.) 75m PAR bw

Warwick Ward (*Col. Andre de Sevigne*), Rosita Moreno (*Baroness von Strick*), Margot Grahame (*Countess Elsa Talven*), Henry Hewitt (*Baron von Strick*), Garry Marsh (*Prince Cernuwitz*), Alan Napier (*Bouchier*), Abraham Sofaer (*Mahmed Pasha*), Stella Arbenina (*Mme. Bouchier*), Annie Esmond (*Nurse*), Eric Pavitt (*Franz*).

One could probably benefit from a scorecard in order to keep up with all the romantic intrigues in this story. Against a Middle East background a baroness from Germany falls in love with an officer of the French military. Meanwhile, her husband also loves another and tries to catch his wife in a compromising position to gain custody of their child in a divorce. The Frenchman kills him before the plan can be carried out, taking with him evidence which could harm his beloved. But no one ends up happy, as the surviving lovers are apart at the finale. Complicated plot twists, but these are only covering up the fact that little is going on in the turgid drama. Versions are available in English and French.

p, Walt Morosco; d, Dmitri Buchowetzki; w, Reginald Denham (based on the play "L'Homme Qui Assassina" by Pierre Frondale).

Drama   (PR:A   MPAA:NR)

STAMBOUL QUEST***½   (1934) 88m MGM bw

Myrna Loy (*Annemarie*), George Brent (*Beall*), Lionel Atwill (*Von Strum*), C. Henry Gordon (*Ali Bey*), Douglas Dumbrille (*General*), Rudolf Amendt (*Karl*), Mischa Auer (*Roberts*), Robert Gleckler (*Naval Officer*), Reginald Barlow, Joseph Sawyer (*German Officers*), Christian Rub (*Dentist*), Judith Vosselli (*Mata Hari*), Belle Mitchell (*Maid*), Harry Schultz (*Doorman*), Edward Keane (*Companion*), Barlow Borland, Adrian Rosley (*Waiters*), Theodore Lodi (*Officer*), Otto H. Fries, Anders Von Haden (*Conductors*), Perry Ivins (*Steward*), Georges Renavent (*Manager*), Lal Chand Mehra (*Turkish Officer*), Tito H. Davison (*Bellhop*), Russ Powell (*Fat German*), Hans Joby, Frank Puglia (*German Aides*), Ralph Fitzsimmons (*General*), Hooper Atchley (*German Colonel*), Helen Freeman (*Nun*), Max Barwyn, Jamiel Hasson (*Aides*).

Loy was appearing in her first solo starring role in this unfortunately titled movie that was much better than the business it did. She was playing a German heroine, which was unusual at the time, because WW I was fresh in the memory and there was already a rumbling from behind the German border that would presage the establishment of the Third Reich. Loy essays the part of a real woman who was known as "Fraulein Doktor" and who, it is said, was the person who ordered the death of the redoubtable Mata Hari when she learned that the other female spy had fallen in love. There is no room for sentiment in the spying business. It's 1915 and the chief of operations for the Kaiser's intelligence office is Atwill, a no-nonsense pedant who is worried that information about his country's military operations in the Dardanelles is being discovered by the Allies. In order to stem the flow of data, he sends his top operative, Loy, to Turkey. The No. 1 suspect is Gordon, who runs the Turkish military units and they think that he might be trading the information for money. While in Berlin, Loy meets American med student Brent and he falls head over heels for her, never knowing that she is an undercover agent. When she goes off to Constantinople, Brent chases after her like a young swain in love, and Loy has to keep him at arm's length in order to get her work done. She manages to solve the puzzle and then Atwill tells her that Brent has been shot for being in the wrong place at the wrong time. By now she's fallen in love with him and the news of his death sends her over the edge and she repairs to a monastery to regain her mental health. But Atwill has been lying, and when Brent finds her, they are united. Sounds melodramatic but Mankiewicz's script sparkles with sharp insights (what else from the man who co-wrote CITIZEN KANE?) and the

nature of the assertive woman and the naive man is a switch on many other situations that plays well. In 1937, a French film about the same woman was made which starred Erich Von Stroheim, Clare Luce, and Dita Parlo. It was MADEMOISELLE DOCTEUR. The next time around, Suzy Kendall played the part in the 1969 Paramount release of FRAULEIN DOKTOR. Good romance with an overlay of suspense and many bright lines make this worth seeing. Howe's cinematography is particularly noteworthy.

d, Sam M. Wood; w, Herman Mankiewicz (based on a story by Leo Birinski); ph, James Wong Howe; ed, Hugh Wynn; art d, Cedric Gibbons, Stan Rogers; cos, Dorothy Tree.

Spy Drama/Romance   (PR:A   MPAA:NR)

STAMPEDE*½   (1936) 58m COL bw

Charles Starrett (*Larry*), Finis Barton (*Dale*), J.P. McGowan (*Stevens*), LeStrange Millman (*Milford*), Reginald Hincks (*Sheriff*), James McGrath (*Brooks*), Arthur Kerr (*Gans*), Jack Atkinson (*Hodge*), Michael Heppell (*Kyle*), Ted Mapes.

This was Charles Starrett's first appearance as an oater star and it wasn't long before he would become one of the hottest stars in the DURANGO KID series. Here he is only a rancher who wants to buy some cattle, but the heavies make this a hard task to accomplish, and push Starrett a bit too far when they kill his brother.

d, Ford Beebe; w, Robert Watson (based on a story by Peter B. Kyne); ph, George Meehan, William Beckway; ed, William Austin.

Western   (PR:A   MPAA:NR)

STAMPEDE**   (1949) 78m AA/MON bw

Rod Cameron (*Mike*), Gale Storm (*Connie*), Don Castle (*Tim*), Johnny Mack Brown (*Sheriff Ball*), Donald Curtis (*Stanton*), John Eldredge (*Cox*), John Miljan (*Furman*), Jonathan Hale (*Varick*), James Harrison (*Roper*), Wes C. Christensen (*Slim*), Duke York (*Maxie*), Bob Woodward (*Whiskey*), Steve Clark (*Dawson*), Boyd Stockman (*Fred*), Ted Elliott (*Pete*), Jack Parker (*Jake*), Chuck Roberson (*Sandy*), Tim Ryan (*Drunk*), Kenne Duncan (*Steve*), Carol Henry (*Ben*), Artie Ortego, Neal Hart, I. Stanford Jolley (*Link Spain*), Marshall Reed (*Shires*), Philo McCollough (*Charlie*), Adrian Wood (*Sanderson*).

One of Blake Edwards earliest scripts, (teamed here with Champion) it is uncharacteristic of the lighthearted comedies which would become his main-stay. Cameron and Castle play cattle baron brothers who find their territory impinged upon when the government opens up surrounding lands to homesteaders. But all the water is on the brothers' land, which leads crooks Curtis and Eldredge to come up with a plan to swindle the settlers and cause problems for Cameron. Plenty of action and good characterizations help in cases where inadequate pacing lets the plot down.

p, Scott R. Dunlap, John C. Champion, Blake Edwards; d, Lesley Selander; w, Champion, Edwards (based on novel by Edward Beverly Mann); ph, Harry Neumann; m, Edward Kay; ed, Richard Heermance; art d, Ernest Hickson; set d, Vin Taylor; makeup, Fred Phillips.

Western   (PR:A   MPAA:NR)

STAMPEDE, 1960   (SEE: GUNS OF THE TIMBERLAND, 1960)

STAMPEDED   (SEE: BIG LAND, THE, 1957)

STAND AND DELIVER   (SEE: BOWERY BLITZKRIEG, 1941)

STAND AT APACHE RIVER, THE*½   (1953) 77m UNIV c

Stephen McNally (*Sheriff Lane Dakota*), Julia [Julie] Adams (*Valerie Kendrick*), Hugh Marlowe (*Col. Morsby*), Jaclynne Greene (*Ann Kenyon*), Hugh O'Brian (*Tom Kenyon*), Russell Johnson (*Greiner*), Jack Kelly (*Hatcher*), Edgar Barrier (*Cara Blanca*), Forrest Lewis (*Deadhorse*).

Uninteresting saga in which eight people are held up at a stage coach station by a band of restless Apaches. McNally plays a sheriff who is transferring a prisoner, and finds himself charged with keeping peace in the small group and taking care of the Indians. To everyone's greatest pleasure he eventually succeeds with both tasks.

p, William Alland; d, Lee Sholem; w, Arthur Ross (based on the novel *Apache Landing* by Robert J. Hogan); ph, Charles P. Boyle (Technicolor); m, Frank Skinner; ed, Leonard Weiner; art d, Bernard Herzbrun, Hilyard Brown; cos, Bill Thomas.

Western   (PR:A   MPAA:NR)

STAND BY FOR ACTION***   (1942) 109M MGM bw (GB: CARGO OF INNOCENTS)

Robert Taylor (*Lt. Gregg Masterson*), Charles Laughton (*Rear Adm. Stephen Thomas*), Brian Donlevy (*Lt. Comdr. Martin J. Roberts*), Walter Brennan (*Chief Yeoman Henry Johnson*), Marilyn Maxwell (*Audrey Carr*), Henry

O'Neill *(Comdr. Stone, M.C.)*, Marta Linden *(Mary Collins)*, Chill Wills *(Chief Boatswain's Mate Jenks)*, Douglas Dumbrille *(Capt. Ludlow)*, Richard Quine *(Ens. Lindsay)*, William Tannen *(Flag Lt. Dudley)*, Douglas Fowley *(Ens. Martin)*, Tim Ryan *(Lt. Tim Ryan)*, Dick Simmons *(Lt. Royce)*, Byron Foulger *(Pharmacist Mate "Doc" Miller)*, Hobart Cavanaugh *(Carpenter's Mate "Chips")*, Inez Cooper *(Susan Garrison)*, Ben Welden *(Chief Quartermaster Rankin)*, Harry Fleischman *(Chief Signalman)*.

This flag-waving slap in the face to the Japanese was released about a year to the day after the attack on Pearl Harbor. By this time, all of the studios were making war movies and rushing them out to a waiting U.S. Many of them had the same plots, or variations, and this was no exception, although the special effects and the stellar cast raised the level of the proceedings considerably over many of the competitors. The lead role had been offered to Robert Donat after his huge success in GOODBYE, MR. CHIPS, but he declined and it was given to Taylor, who did well in the part of a Harvard-educated snob who is called into the service and has his cockiness whacked out of him when he faces real war. He's a Naval Reservist with a high-nose attitude and his patrician background causes him to be instantly unpopular with his fellows. His job is to be the aide to admiral Laughton, a crusty type who commands the base at San Francisco. Taylor can't stand a desk job but he'd rather be safe and sound in San Francisco than facing the guns of the enemy. This is in contrast to Laughton who is yearning to be at sea again. Donlevy is a one-time enlisted man who is a career Navy person. He's come up from swabbie to lieutenant commander by proving himself and his abilities on several occasions. Donlevy gets command of a rusty gutbucket from the last war. It's a creaky destroyer, but until the defense plants begin delivering new ships, the Navy is forced to put these old ones into commission. Taylor is assigned to be Donlevy's second in command and they take the vessel out for a shakedown cruise. While out at sea and discovering the many things wrong with the destroyer, they get orders to join a convoy and race across the roiling ocean to arrive there in time. The seas are heavy and the destroyer comes upon a lifeboat filled with women and infants who have been drifting since their ship was torpedoed. They bring the kids and the women on the destroyer and the men begin acting as nannies to the babies while the women, Linden and Maxwell, watch amusedly. The destroyer catches up to the convoy, which is being led by Laughton, happily on the brine again. Trouble lies ahead, as they are attacked by Japanese planes and a huge battleship steams toward them on the horizon. The small convoy will be no match for the gargantuan Japanese ship, so Donlevy shoots his ship at the trailing behemoth and lays down a smoke screen so the other ships can escape. Next, the small four-stack destroyer goes after the Japanese ship, like a David versus Goliath. Just as the little guy won in the Bible, it happens again as the U.S. ship uses stealth and speed to nail the big boat and send it down to meet Davey Jones. Donlevy has been wounded and Taylor takes over the command, covering himself with glory in the process and showing his inherent bravery. At the conclusion, Taylor, Donlevy, and their Chief Yeoman Brennan are given medals and go off to win the war for God and country. Terrific battle sequences and excellent special effects make this a cut above many of the films that used cheap miniatures in their water tanks at the time. Laughton is wasted in his attempt at a latter-day Captain Bligh. Actor Tim Ryan's name in the cast was the same as his own.

p, Robert Z. Leonard, Orville O. Dull; d, Leonard; w, George Bruce, John L. Balderston, Herman J. Mankiewicz (based on a story by Capt. Harvey Haislip, U.S.N., R.C. Sheriff, suggested by the story "A Cargo of Innocence" by Laurence Kirk); ph, Charles Rosher; m, Lennie Hayton; ed, George Boemler; art d, Cedric Gibbons; spec eff, Arnold Gillespie, Don Jahraus.

War Drama   **(PR:A   MPAA:NR)**

STAND EASY   (SEE: DOWN AMONG THE Z-MEN, 1959, Brit.)

STAND-IN*½   (1937) 90m UA bw

Leslie Howard *(Atterbury Dodd)*, Joan Blondell *(Lester Plum)*, Humphrey Bogart *(Douglas Quintain)*, Alan Mowbray *(Koslofski)*, Marla Shelton *(Thelma Cheri)*, C. Henry Gordon *(Ivor Nassau)*, Jack Carson *(Potts)*, Tully Marshall *(Pennypacker, Sr.)*, J.C. Nugent *(Pennypacker, Jr.)*, William V. Mong *(Pennypacker)*.

An entertaining comedy about Hollywood filmmakers which, underneath its humor, offers a scathing indictment of studio policies and priorities. Howard, a bank employee with a genius level intelligence of mathematical equations and financial dealings, gets sent to Hollywood to decide whether Colossal Studios should continue to get financing. When he arrives he discovers that he knows much about banking but very little about the motion picture business. Luckily, he meets Blondell, who teaches him about movie people–the technicians, laborers, and "stand-ins"–and how they keep the studios alive, while the producers, directors, and stars take all the credit. Howard hires Blondell as his secretary (instead of shorthand, she memorizes his dictation as if it's dialog from a script) before realizing that she is a "stand-in" for the vampish Shelton, the egotistical star of a new picture entitled "Sex and Satan." The film is to be a big-budget epic, directed by an extravagant foreigner, Mowbray (clearly an Erich von Stroheim characterization), who wastefully spends all the money he is given. All of this waste goes on under the nose of producer Bogart, who spends his time in a drunken depression over his unrequited love for Shelton. Howard then discovers that

Colossal's financial troubles are being engineered by a competing studio official, Gordon, who is in league with Shelton and Mowbray to run the budget of "Sex and Satan" far over its limit. Gordon nearly has the bank foreclose on the studio and then proceeds to declare the just-completed Shelton epic is a disastrous bomb. Howard and Blondell try to prevent the ruination of the studio by rallying the workers for a 48-hour period during which Bogart agrees to re-edit the picture. By whittling Shelton's role to a minor one, Bogart emerges from the editing room with a box-office smash and Colossal is saved. Not surprisingly, Hollywood executives were a bit upset and embarrassed by seeing themselves portrayed in such an unflattering light. Considering the film's negativism, it is even surprising that a major studio agreed to release the film (it was not produced by a major studio, but by Wanger's independent company). The most successful aspect of STAND-IN is the chemistry among the leads and the fine support they receive from the rest of the cast. Howard had requested that his costar be Blondell, and was happy to be working once again with his long time pal Bogart. It is the casting of Bogart that is the film's biggest surprise and, perhaps, one of his least typical roles. It was his first chance at comedy after a seemingly endless streak of tough-guy roles. However, director Garnett had to fight to get Bogart in the role. In his autobiography Garnett recalls: "I had decided, before rolling a camera, that STAND-IN could be spiced by using, in a sympathetic role, a man who usually played meanies." The perfect choice, of course, was Bogart, but after screening the "rushes" for his assistant Paul Schwegler he was under fire: "Have you lost your cottonpickin' mind?" Schwegler asked Garnett. "What makes you think you can turn that guy into a leading man? The S.O.B. lisps!"

p, Walter Wanger; d, Tay Garnett; w, Gene Towne, Graham Baker (based on the *Saturday Evening Post* story by Clarence Budington Kelland); ph, Charles Clarke; m, Heinz Roemheld; ed, Otho Lovering, Dorothy Spencer; md, Rox Rommel; art d, Alexander Toluboff, Wade Rubottom; cos, Helen Taylor.

Comedy   **(PR:A   MPAA:NR)**

STAND UP AND BE COUNTED*½   (1972) 99m COL c

Jacqueline Bisset *(Sheila Hammond)*, Stella Stevens *(Yvonne Kellerman)*, Steve Lawrence *(Gary McBride)*, Gary Lockwood *(Eliot Travis)*, Lee Purcell *(Karen Hammond)*, Loretta Swit *(Hilary McBride)*, Hector Elizondo *(Lou Kellerman)*, Anne Francine *(Mrs. Mabel Hammond)*, Madlyn Rhue *(Gloria Seagar)*, Alex Wilson *(Jerry Kamanski)*, Michael Ansara *(Playboy Representative)*, Dr. Joyce Brothers *(Herself)*, Jessica Rains *(Sadie)*, Meredith Baxter [Birney] *(Tracy)*, Greg Mullavey *(Harley Burton)*, Nancy Walker *(Agnes)*, Edith Atwater *(Sophie)*, Jeff Donnell *(Ruth)*, Kathleen Freeman *(Sarah)*, Shelley Morrison, Marsha Metrinko.

An awkward presentation of the Women's Liberation movement and its effect upon various relationships in the Denver area. Among those involved are Bisset as a journalist for a fashion magazine, her kid sister Purcell as an ultra-feminist who draws up a contract to have a baby, Stevens as the sex-starved wife of a wealthy manufacturer, and Swit as a typical wife and mother. All these women gain something from the movement, but you wouldn't think so by the way the material is handled. Several of the performances are quite good, but it's really all for naught. However, as the first Hollywood film to examine the Women's Movement, STAND UP AND BE COUNTED has some historical significance. Obviously, by 1972 there was enough awareness about this social trend to encourage filmmakers to make a movie about it. The fact that the screenwriter assigned to the job also wrote the scripts for such TV series as "The Flying Nun" and "The Partridge Family" tells you how seriously the Movement was taken at this time. The line between serious statement and comic relief is fuzzy at best, and what might pass for an illuminating examination of an important issue is negated by traditional gags thrown in at the expense of women. An insider's joke of interest to true connoisseurs is the face on the mock dollar bill used during the demonstration scenes. It belongs to veteran actress Binnie Barnes, wife of producer Frankovich.

p, M.J. Frankovich d, Jackie Cooper; w, Bernard Slade; ph, Fred Koenekamp (Eastmancolor); m, Ernie Wilkins; ed, Harold Kress; prod d, Lyle R. Wheeler; d, Morrie Hoffman; cos, Moss Mabry; makeup, Leo Lotito

Comedy/Drama   **(PR:C   MPAA:PG)**

STAND UP AND CHEER*½   (1934 80m FOX bw

Warner Baxter *(Lawrence Cromwell)*, Madge Evans *(Mary Adams)*, Nigel Bruce *(Eustace Dinwiddie)*, Stepin Fetchit *(George Bernard Shaw)*, Frank Melton *(Fosdick)*, Lila Lee *(Zelda)*, Ralph Morgan *(President's Secretary)*, Frank Mitchell *(Senator Danforth)*, Jack Durant *(Senator Short)*, Arthur Byron *(Harley)*, James Dunn *(Dugan)*, Skins Miller *(Hillbilly)*, Theresa Gardella *(Aunt Jemima)*, Nick [Dick] Foran, Shirley Temple, John Boles, Sylvia Froos, Jimmy Dallas *(Specialty Numbers)*, Frances Morris, Lurene Tuttle, Dorothy Gulliver, Bess Flowers, Lillian West *(Stenographers)*, Selmer Jackson, Clyde Dilson *(Correspondents)*, Edward Earle *(Secret Service Man)*, Gayne Whitman *(Voice for President)*, Frank Sheridan, Paul Stanton, Wallis Clark, Arthur Stuart Hull *(Senators)*, Si Jenks *(Rube Farmer)*, Aggie Herring *(Irish Washerwoman)*, Phil Tead *(Vaudevillian)*, Randall Sisters *(Trio)*, George K. Arthur *(Dance Director)*, Baby Alice Raetz

(*Child Bit*), Ruth Beckett (*Child's Mother*), Bobby Caldwell (*Gen. Lee*), Wilbur Mack (*Beamish*), Elspeth Dudgeon, Jessie Perry, Harry Northrup (*Reformers*), John Davidson (*Sour Radio Announcer*), Harry Dunkinson, Gilbert Clayton, Herbert Prior, Carlton Stockdale (*Quartette*), Lucien Littlefield (*Prof. Hi De Ho*), Arthur Loft, Jack Richardson, Dagmar Oakland, Vivian Winston (*Bits*), Joe Smith Marba (*Elephant Trainer*), Carleton E. Griffin, Paul McVey, Rolin Ray, Reginald Simpson (*Male Secretaries*), Arthur Vinton (*Turner*), Sam Hayes (*Radio Announcer*), Tina Marshall (*Boy's Mother*), Dora Clemant, Peggy Watt, Dorothy Dehn, Ruth Clifford (*Female Secretaries*), Glen Walters (*Hillbilly's Wife*), Lew Brown, Patricia Lee, Guy Usher, Lynn Bari, Morris Ankrum, Scotty Beckett.

This Depression era escapist entertainment has Baxter as a Broadway producer who is the newly appointed "Secretary of Entertainment." The simple premise succeeds by allowing an entourage of musical entertainment, including Shirtley Temple before she became the biggest money-maker in Hollywood, Aunt Jemima (Theresa Gardella), and a penguin posing as Jimmy Durante that serves to baffle Stepin Fetchit. Humorist Will Rogers is generally credited with the basic idea for this hodgepodge of movie, theater, and vaudeville stars and second bananas. Its aim was to give America a boost out of the Depression and into a land of happiness where a winsome tot like the 4-year-old Temple could reign supreme. Naturally plenty of musical numbers helped things along. Songs include: "I'm Laughing" (Jay Gorney, Lew Brown; sung by Nick Foran, Theresa Gardella), "We're Out of the Red" (Gorney, Brown; sung by John Boles, Gardella), "Broadway's Gone Hillbilly" (Gorney, Brown; sung by Sylvia Froos), "Baby Take a Bow" (Gorney, Brown; sung by Shirley Temple, James Dunn, Patricia Lee), "This is Our Last Night Together" (Gorney, Brown; sung by Boles, Froos), "She's Way Up Thar" (Brown), "Stand Up and Cheer" (Brown, Harry Akst).

p, Winfield Sheehan; d, Hamilton MacFadden; w, Ralph Spence, Lew Brown, (based on an idea by Will Rogers, Philip Klein); ph, Ernest Palmer, L.W. O'Connell; m, Lew Brown, Jay Gorney; ed, Margaret Clancy; md, Arthur Lange; art d, Gordon Wiles, Russell Patterson; ch, Sammy Lee.

Musical (PR:A MPAA:NR)

STAND UP AND FIGHT* (1939) 105m MGM bw

Robert Taylor (*Blake Cantrell*), Wallace Beery (*Capt. Boss Starkey*), Florence Rice (*Susan Griffith*), Helen Broderick (*Amanda Griffith*), Charles Bickford (*Arnold*), Barton MacLane (*Crowder*), Charley Grapewin (*Old Puff*), John Qualen (*Davey*), Clinton Rosemond (*Enoch*), Jonathan Hale (*Col. Webb*), Claudia Morgan (*Carolyn Talbot*), Robert Gleckler (*Sheriff Barney*), Cy Kendall (*Foreman Ross*), Paul Everton (*Allan*), Selmer Jackson (*Whittingham Talbot*), Minor Watson (*Marshal Cole*), Frank Darien (*Daniels*), William Tannen (*Lewis*), Edward Hearn (*Joe*), Edward Keane (*Donnelly*), Robert Middlemass (*Harkrider*), John Dilson (*Auctioneer*), Ben Welden (*Foreman*), Louise Springer (*Violet*), Eddy Waller (*Conductor*), Victor Potel (*Coach Driver*), Harry Allen (*Engineer*), Walter Soderling (*Passenger*), Syd Saylor (*Stooge*), Clem Bevans (*Bum*), James Kilgannon (*Fireman*), George Ovey (*Conductor*), Sam Ash (*Teamsters*), Trevor Bardette (*Mob Leader*), Claire McDowell (*Woman*).

There are more fisticuffs in this western than the average heavyweight title match and audiences loved the action. Taylor had been a "pretty-boy" actor at MGM and they did everything they could to crack that mold and make him a man of action. The battles Taylor had in the picture were, in some ways, the very best scenes because there was little else to fill out the time. Taylor is a Maryland plantation owner who has gone bankrupt and he's turned briefly to the bottle for solace. Beery runs a stagecoach line for Rice and is aiding slave traders, albeit not knowing he is. The two men clash often and hand each other merciless beatings. Taylor joins forces with the railroad people who want to force the stagecoach company out of business and take over their "right of way" for the high iron. In Taylor's first battle, he reacts when he is being cheated at cards in a saloon and bloodies several noses. Next, he has a bout with Beery and practically has his head handed to him. In the third skirmish, Taylor takes Beery's measure in a driving snowstorm. The villain of the picture is Bickford and Beery kills him after he learns that Bickford is in the slave business. When it looks as though ex-con Beery will be arrested for Bickford's death, Taylor gets him off the hook by not coming forward. In the end, Beery and Taylor become buddies and Taylor wins Rice's hand. It was only four years before that Taylor played a walk-on in the Beery-starred WEST POINT OF THE AIR. Times had changed and Beery, although still top-billed, now had to share the plaudits with Taylor on an almost equal footing. An enjoyable, rousing western that served to put Taylor in the highest ranks at the studio. Broderick Crawford's mother, Helen Broderick, does a small bit as Rice's aunt, the former girl friend of Beery. Van Dyke directed it with his customary alacrity, moving matters along at such a quick pace that you hardly have any time to notice the fact that there's almost no characterization to speak of. The fights are realistic and children may have a problem understanding it's all make-believe.

p, Mervyn LeRoy; d, W.S. Van Dyke II; w, James M. Cain, Jane Murfin, Harvey Ferguson (based on a story by Forbes Parkhill); ph, Leonard Smith; m, Dr. William Axt; ed, Frank Sullivan; art d, Cedric Gibbons, Urie McCleary; set d, Edwin B. Willis; cos, Dolly Tree, Valles.

Western (PR:A-C MPAA:NR)

STAND UP VIRGIN SOLDIERS*½ (1977, Brit.) 91m WB c

Robin Askwith (*Brigg*), Nigel Davenport (*Sgt. Driscoll*), George Layton (*Jacobs*), John Le Mesurier (*Col. Bromley-Pickering*), Warren Mitchell (*Morris-Morris*), Robin Nedwell (*Lt. Grainger*), Edward Woodward (*Sgt. Wellbeloved*), Irene Handl (*Mrs. Phillimore*), Fiesta Mei Lang (*Juicy Lucy*), Pamela Stephenson (*Bernice*), Lynda Bellingham (*Valerie*), David Auker (*Lantry*), Robert Booth (*Field*), Peter Bourke (*Villiers*), Leo Dolan (*Tasker*), Brian Godfrey (*Foster*), Paul Rattee (*Browning*), Patrick Newell (*Capt. Billings*), Miriam Margoyles (*Elephant Ethel*).

Inferior spoof which has Askwith and Davenport as soldiers in Singapore who are more concerned with finding sex than in finding Communists. Their first experiences are in one of the local cathouses before meeting a couple of nurses who appear to have the same thing on their mind. Most of the jokes and comic routines are old hat and don't provide the needed spark to make this lackluster venture come to life.

p, Greg Smith; d, Norman Cohen; w, Leslie Thomas (based on his novel); ph, Ken Hodges (Technicolor); m, Ed Welch; ed, Geoffrey Foot; prod d, Harry Pottle.

Comedy (PR:O MPAA:NR)

STANDING ROOM ONLY* (1944) 83m PAR bw

Paulette Goddard (*Jane Rogers*), Fred MacMurray (*Les Stevens*), Edward Arnold (*T.J. Todd*), Roland Young (*Ira Cromwell*), Hillary Brooke (*Alice Todd*), Porter Hall (*Hugo Farenhall*), Clarence Kolb (*Glen Ritchie*), Anne Revere (*Maj. Cromwell*), Isabel Randolph (*Mrs. Ritchie*), Marie McDonald (*Opal*), Veda Ann Borg (*Peggy Fuller*), Josephine Whittell (*Miss Becker*), Sig Arno (*Waiter*), Robin Raymond (*Girl*), John Hamilton (*General*), Regina Wallace (*General's Wife*), Boyd Davis (*Admiral*), Winifred Harris (*Admiral's Wife*), Roy Gordon (*Commander*), Mary Newton (*Commander's Wife*), Herbert Heyes (*Colonel*), Mira McKinney (*Colonel's Wife*), Eddie Dunn, Arthur Loft (*Foremen*), Lorin Raker (*Hotel Clerk*), Ralph Peters (*Counterman*), Marilynn Harris, Noel Neill, Yvonne De Carlo (*Secretaries*), Lal Chand Mehra (*Bey*), Elvira Curci (*Bey's Wife*), Judith Gibson, Marcella Phillips (*Office Girls*), Gayne Whitman (*Voice over Dictograph*), Rita Gould, Grayce Hampton, Ethel May Halls, Georgia Backus, Harry Hays Morgan, Forbes Murray, Edwin Stanley (*Guests at Ritchie Home*), Mary Currier (*Additional Guest*), Howard Mitchell (*Conductor*), Frank Faylen (*Cab Driver*).

Another madcap comedy which plays on the then-popular joke of over-crowding in Washington, D.C., during WW II (1943's THE MORE THE MERRIER being the most successful). MacMurray is a young executive who travels to the nation's capital in representation of Arnold's midwest toy manufacturing plant, hoping to secure a war production contract. With secretary Goddard in tow, he soon discovers that lodging is an impossibility. Goddard comes up with the ingenious idea of working as servants in the posh home of Young in order to secure a place to stay. When it comes to MacMurray actually working as a servant all confusion breaks loose. Not only does he teeter on the brink of disaster, he finds that all the dinner guests are Washington big-wigs, one of whom is the official in charge of war production contracts. A fast-paced comedy which is sure to hold interest, as well as evoke a few belly laughs. 1944 was a fine year for MacMurray and showed his versatility as an actor. STANDING ROOM ONLY was a fine comic performance, AND THE ANGELS SING displayed his musical talents (he began his career as a saxophone player) and the classic DOUBLE INDEMNITY allowed him to show off his powerful dramatic capability.

p, Paul Jones; d, Sidney Lanfield; w, Darrell Ware, Karl Tunberg (based on a story by Al Martin); ph, Charles Lang; m, Robert Emmett Dolan; ed, William Shea; art d, Hans Dreier, Earl Hedrick; set d, Ray Moyer; cos, Edith Head.

Comedy (PR:A MPAA:NR)

STANLEY zero (1973) 108m Crown c

Chris Robinson (*Tim Ochopee*), Alex Rocco (*Richard Thomkins*), Steve Alaimo (*Crail Denning*), Susan Carroll (*Susie Thomkins*), Mark Harris (*Bob Wilson*), Marcie Knight (*Gloria Calvin*), Rey Baumel (*Sidney Calvin*), Paul Avery (*Psycho Simpson*), Gary Crutcher (*Dr. Everett*), Mel Pape (*Medical Center Guard*), Butterball Smith (*Nightclub Stage Manager*), Pamela Talus (*Thomkins' Girl Friend*), Bill Marquez (*Wauchula*).

Hot on the heels of the phenomenally successful boy-and-his-killer-rat movie WILLARD (1972) and its sequel BEN (1972) came this stomach-churning epic about a crazed Vietnam vet of Seminole Indian descent, Robinson, and his pet rattlesnake named Stanley. His experiences in Southeast Asia having left his mental load shy one brick, Robinson finds solace in the company of snakes and soon breeds a whole shack full of them. Soon he sets up a snake empire with Stanley and his mate Hazel as king and queen. Robinson makes some money by selling snakes to a local scientist, Crutcher, who extracts their venom for experiments, without hurting the creatures. The only other human Robinson trusts not to hurt his snakes is Knight, a stripper who uses live snakes in her sleazy nightclub act. Trouble looms on the horizon when a rich snakeskin apparel manufacturer, Rocco (who played Moe Green in THE GODFATHER), offers to buy Robinson's shack o' snakes. Nature lover Robinson refuses because he would never consider selling his friends to a man who would slaughter them for wallets, purses, and shoes. In fact, the goofy vet frees a truckload of snakes that Rocco and his men had captured on their own. Outraged, Rocco swears vengence on Robinson and hires a psychopathic hitman appropriately named "Psycho" (Avery) to do the dirty work. Luckily, Stanley the snake and his minions know a bad guy when they see one and they slither off to Robinson's rescue. A few bites later most of the bad guys are done for, but Robinson's world begins to collapse when he learns that kindly doctor Crutcher has been reselling his snakes to Rocco. If that isn't enough to disgust a snake lover, Robinson is also horrified to discover that his friendly stripper friend has been biting the heads off her snakes (in close up) for the big finish of her act] These shocking revelations push Robinson over the edge and he decides to eliminate all the snake exploiters. For starters he gets rid of Knight and her scum-bag husband, Baumel, by filling their bed with poisonous snakes. He then gets rid of Rocco by infesting the snake-king's swimming pool with water moccasins just in time for his daily dip. Rocco's daughter Carroll witnesses the whole thing, but she didn't like her dad much anyway and runs off with Robinson. The pair have sex in his snake shack and he dreams of a running a snake kingdom with her at his side. Unfortunately, Carroll announces that she would rather join a commune, but thanks, anyway. Totally out of his gourd by now, Robinson orders Stanley and his slithering buddies to kill her, but the snakes rebel and kill their master. During the titanic struggle of man versus snakes the shack is set ablaze. Stanley and his army escape into the swamp, leaving a horribly bitten and swollen Robinson to crawl off into the grass to die. Wretched in every respect, STANLEY would be an entirely laughable affair if it wasn't so disturbingly gross. Not only does the very concept of this film insult Vietnam vets, Seminole Indians, snake aficionados, strippers, and wallet manufacturers, but the human performers are so awful that after five minutes the viewer hopes the snakes would be embarrassed enough to kill the entire cast quickly and slither off.

p&d, William Grefe; w, Gary Crutcher (based on a story by Grefe); ph, Cliff Poland (DeLuxe Color); m, Post Production Associates; ed, Julio Chavez; art d, Don Ivey; set d, Ivey; m/l, "Sparrow," "Start a New World," Jack Vino (sung by Vino); makeup, Marie Del Russo.

Horror Cas. (PR:O MPAA:PG)

STANLEY AND LIVINGSTONE*** (1939) 101m FOX bw

Spencer Tracy *(Henry M. Stanley)*, Nancy Kelly *(Eve Kingsley)*, Richard Greene *(Gareth Tyce)*, Walter Brennan *(Jeff Slocum)*, Charles Coburn *(Lord Tyce)*, Sir Cedric Hardwicke *(Dr. David Livingstone)*, Henry Hull *(James Gordon Bennett, Jr.)*, Henry Travers *(John Kingsley)*, Miles Mander *(Sir John Gresham)*, David Torrence *(Mr. Cranston)*, Holmes Herbert *(Frederick Holcomb)*, Montague Shaw *(Sir Oliver French)*, Paul Stanton *(Capt. Webb)*, Brandon Hurst *(Sir Henry Forrester)*, Hassan Said *(Hassan)*, Paul Harvey *(Col. Grimes)*, Russell Hicks, Frank Dae *(Commissioners)*, Clarence Derwent *(Sir Francis Vane)*, Joseph Crehan *(Morebhead)*, Robert Middlemass *(Carmichael)*, Frank Jaquet *(Senator)*, William Williams *(Mace)*, Ernest Baskett *(Zucco)*, Emmett Vogan *(Bennett's Secretary)*, James McNamara *(Committeeman)*, William Dunn *(Chuma)*, Emmett Smith *(Susi)*, Jack Clisby *(Mombay)*, Dick Stanley *(Lieutenant)*, Thomas A. Coleman *(Corporal)*, William E. "Red" Blair *(Sergeant)*, Frank Orth *(Man with Pills)*, Billy Watson *(Copy Boy)*, Harry Harvey *(Man)*, Vernon Dent *(Newspaperman)*, Everett Brown *(Bongo)*.

An intelligent if not entirely truthful telling of the Stanley and Livingstone legend, this hardy adventure succeeds largely because of the fine subdued performance of Tracy as the American journalist in search of the missing Hardwicke. The film opens with Tracy returning to New York after filing exclusive reports on the American Indian wars in the western states. He is accompanied by Brennan, an Indian scout whose expertise allowed Tracy to report on tribal affairs more deeply than any journalist before him. Hull, Tracy's editor, next wants his reporter to head into the jungles of Africa to find Hardwicke, a Scottish missionary who seemingly has disappeared. Tracy accepts the assignment, realizing the story's importance, and takes along Brennan to accompany him on the searching party. The trip proves to be a dangerous one, fraught with peril hidden within the jungle. Tracy comes down with jungle fever, yet will not let this stop the mission. Finally he encounters Hardwicke in a remote jungle settlement and utters the famous line, "Dr. Livingstone, I presume?" Hardwicke is living a contented life as a missionary in this isolated village, helping the natives with medical problems as well as giving them religious training. He is dedicated to these tasks and believes Tracy has come to help him. After spending time with the doctor, Tracy returns to civilization with his story, which creates an international furor. However, word reaches the British Geographers Society that Hardwicke has died of jungle fever and Tracy is disbelieved until a letter arrives from Hardwicke asking Tracy to carry on his work in the jungle. Tracy, thoroughly enraptured with Hardwicke's ideals, returns to continue the work his mentor began. Tracy had been loaned out to 20th Century-Fox for the film (he missed the chance to be in DARK VICTORY as a result) and gives a dignified portrait of a man who undergoes profound changes as a result of his experience. The drama is well constructed, combining the adventure of the story with the humanistic life Hardwicke espouses quite well. The film falters in some jungle sequences which are marred by poor technical qualities; footage shot in Africa and incorporated into the production through rear-screen projection unfortunately was poorly done. Another problem comes in the romantic notions of the story, adding fictional characters to suit Hollywood conventions as well as changing the truth about Stanley's life after his encounter with Livingstone. Kelly was added to the story to serve as Tracy's love interest, creating a jealous rift between him and party member Greene, though there is no factual basis for the character. And while Tracy spending the rest of his days working as a missionary might seem inspirational, the real Stanley did nothing of the sort. Rather, he continued his career as an explorer, helping to open up the African continent to the outside world. Be that as it may, STANLEY AND LIVINGSTONE still holds up as strong drama, a good example of a story structure and an actor's ability to create a most human character from the stuff of history.

p, Darryl F. Zanuck; d, Henry King; w, Philip Dunne, Julien Josephson (based on historical research and story outline by Hal Long, Sam Hellman); ph, George Barnes, Otto Brower; m, Robert R. Bennett, David Buttolph, Louis Silvers, R.H. Bassett, Cyril Mockridge, Rudy Schrager; ed, Barbara McLean; md, Silvers; art d, William Darling, George Dudley; set d, Thomas Little; cos, Royer.

Drama/Adventure Cas. (PR:AA MPAA:NR)

STAR, THE*** (1953) 89m FOX bw

Bette Davis *(Margaret Elliot)*, Sterling Hayden *(Jim Johannson)*, Natalie Wood *(Gretchen)*, Warner Anderson *(Harry Stone)*, Minor Watson *(Joe Morrison)*, June Travis *(Phyllis Stone)*, Katherine Warren *(Mrs. Morrison)*, Kay Riehl *(Mrs. Adams)*, Barbara Woodel *(Peggy Morgan)*, Fay Baker *(Faith)*, Barbara Lawrence *(Herself)*, David Alpert *(Keith Barkley)*, Paul Frees *(Richard Stanley)*.

A tough and relentless indictment of Hollywood that served Davis well in that she received an Oscar nomination. However, it was far too "inside" to get much appreciation from anyone outside the movie business and so this independently made picture did meagerly with general audiences. Davis is a fading star who has won an Oscar but has now fallen from favor. She is out of money and desperate as she has not worked for many years. Anderson is her long-time agent. When she approaches him for a loan to keep from going personally bankrupt, he refuses. (Agents are seldom seen in a good light by Hollywood scripters. A good example of that is William Holden's literary rep in SUNSET BOULEVARD.) Davis is forced to watch her personal belongings sold at a public auction to pay off her debts. The unemployment and a succession of bad investments have brought her to this and she is understandably depressed. For the last few years, Davis has helped support her sister, Baker, and the latter's husband, Alpert. They are greedy relatives who really don't like Davis, probably because they are taking her money. When they discover that Davis has no cash for them, they exit quickly, like rats deserting her sinking ship. Davis is living in a rented residence and can't pay her monthly fee so her landlady, a shrew (Riehl), tells her that she must leave if she doesn't come up with the cash in a hurry. Davis has a few bucks in her purse, buys a bottle of hooch, grabs for her Oscar, and gets into her car. she's hauled in for drunk driving and the news hits the local press. No one comes to her aid at first, then Hayden shows up. He's a former actor and once a costar to Davis. In the past few years, he's given up the silver screen in favor of the blue sea and now owns a successful boatyard. Hayden has loved Davis for years but she was such a huge star in her day that he never had the guts to state his love. Davis' daughter is Wood, who is now with her exhusband and his wife. Davis can't raise a penny from them although she tells Wood that she's close to getting another acting job. With the money from that assignment, she and Wood can be united. Wood is thrilled as she dislikes being separated from her mother. At Hayden's apartment, he finally musters up the courage to declare himself and to suggest that it's time for her to stop thinking she's a star and to get down to earth and live life like a real person, not some fabricated actress who has been molded by a studio publicity department. Davis is not ready to make that commitment and takes a job as a sales clerk in a department store. She intends to wait out the bad publicity she's received due to her drunk driving arrest and make her "comeback." Two customers in the store immediately recognize who she is and begin making comments. Davis responds by telling them off and she is sacked for her outburst. She returns to Anderson and pleads for him to do her one favor. There's a movie being produced by Watson and she knows that she would be right for the role. Can Anderson arrange a screen test for her? Anderson broaches the subject to Watson, who knows that Davis is far too old for the part she wants, but he recalls all of her great work and asks her to test for a small supporting role. Davis is overjoyed and has plans in mind. She will test for the older woman's role but will play it sexily and thus impress Watson enough to give her the role of the ingenue. Her screen test is a fiasco and when she sees the posturing and the almost grotesque way she looks, she finally realizes that her salad days have wilted. Tears well up in her mascaraed eyes and she races out of the screening room to Anderson's home where his wife, Travis, gives her solace. She sleeps for a while, then awakens when she hears the revelry of a party taking place. Joining the group, she begins talking with a young producer who tells her that he has a new project that she might be right for. It's the story of a fading actress and closely resembles her own life. It brings Davis up short because she now understands that she may be an actress, but she is first a woman and must be true to that. She exits the festivities and goes to where Wood has been staying. Gathering the youngster in tow, she drives to Hayden's at the marina where he welcomes her when she tells him that she is finished being a star, now all she wants is the love of a good man and the right to live her life in peace. The ending is too curt and too convenient to lend a ring of truth to the story. All the loose ends should not have been gathered. The young woman who gets the starring role in Watson's movie is Barbara Lawrence, who plays herself, and to whom the studio had given a huge hype. Much of the film is spent talking about Lawrence, seeing her photo, etc. She has as much effect as "Godot" or "Lefty" – both of whom were waited for in their respective plays and neither of whom ever arrived. In real life, Hayden had a great love for the sea and eventually grew enough of a beard to look like a Norwegian sea captain before he took off for a long trip around the world on his sea-going sailboat. In a small role, note Paul Frees, who later became one of advertising's most successful "voices" and whose narration can still be heard on many rides at Disneyland in Anaheim, California. Wood was 15 at the time this was made and already in her 19th picture.

p, Bert E. Friedlob; d, Stuart Heisler; w, Katherine Albert, Dale Eunson; ph, Ernest Laszlo; m, Victor Young; ed, Otto Ludwig; md, Young; art d, Boris Levin; cos, Orry-Kelly, Bill Edwards, Ann Peck; makeup, Del Armstrong.

Drama   (PR:A MPAA:NR)

STAR!* ½**   (1968) 175m (later 120m) FOX c (AKA: THOSE WERE
                     THE HAPPY TIMES)

Julie Andrews (Gertrude Lawrence), Richard Crenna (Richard Aldrich), Michael Craig (Sir Anthony Spencer), Daniel Massey (Noel Coward), Robert Reed (Charles Fraser), Bruce Forsyth (Arthur Lawrence), Beryl Reid (Rose), John Collin (Jack Roper), Alan Oppenheimer (Andre Charlot), Richard Karlan (David Holtzman), Lynley Laurence (Billie Carleton), Garrett Lewis (Jack Buchanan), Elizabeth St. Clair (Jeannie Banks), Jenny Agutter (Pamela), Anthony Eisley (Ben Mitchell), Jock Livingston (Alexander Woollcott), J. Pat O'Malley (Dan), Harvey Jason (Bert), Damian London (Jerry Paul), Richard Angarola (Cesare), Matilda Calnan (Dorothy), Lester Matthews (Lord Chamberlain), Bernard Fox (Assistant to Lord Chamberlain), Murray Matheson (Bankruptcy Judge), Robin Hughes (Hyde Park Speaker), Anna Lee (Hostess), Don Crichton (Gertrude's "Limehouse Blues" Dance Partner), Peter Church (Newsreel Narrator), Jan Gernat (Stage Manager), Conrad Bain (Salesman at Cartier's), The Daffodil Girls: Jeanette Landis (Eph), Dinah Anne Rogers (Molly), Barbara Sandland (Mavis), Ellen Plasschaert (Moo), Ann Hubbell (Beryl).

There's no doubt that Gertrude Lawrence was a huge star in England and on Broadway, but this was 16 years after her death and she never achieved motion picture fame so audiences wondered what all the hoopla was about when Fox spent about $14 million to do her biography (almost $350,000 of that just for the gowns). Andrews was not physically right for the part and, as a matter of fact, she was actually a better singer, dancer and, perhaps, even a better actress than the woman she portrayed. She was also a huge draw after MARY POPPINS and THE SOUND OF MUSIC, and when director Wise again teamed with long-time associate Chaplin, they agreed that Andrews would make a smashing Lawrence. On paper, it looked like a can't-miss proposition. However, movies are done on film, not paper, and the picture plummeted from the opening day. The following year, it was re-released as THOSE WERE THE HAPPY TIMES with 50 minutes or so deleted but that wasn't the answer either and the movie soon went bye-bye. It begins as Andrews is starring in the stage musical "Lady In The Dark," during the war. She watches a 1940s newsreel about her own life and is taken back in memory to 1915, Clapham, England. Andrews, now 25 years younger, leaves the home she shares with her mother to join her vaudevillian father, Forsyth, who is working in a run-down Brixton music hall with his partner, Reid. Despite the tackiness of it all, stars appear in Andrew's eyes and she decides to embrace a life upon the wicked stage. After a while, she gets a chorus job in one of the famous Charlot's Revues. The man who runs the shows, Oppenheimer, is not thrilled when Andrews exhibits scene-stealing tendencies which throw the carefully rehearsed sketches out of balance. She almost gets the sack but the stage manager, Collin, steps in on her behalf and Andrews manages to hang on. This kind gesture brings the two closer and they marry. He would like her to sit home and bear children but she still has grand ideas about performing and, after their daughter is born (played by Agutter when she grows up), Andrews leaves Collin to seek her destiny. Andrews is great friends with Massey (as Noel Coward) and since he is already a success, he uses his influence to pry her into Oppenheimer's new revue which is opening in New York. She is instantly acclaimed as a new find and her career goes soaring. With all these accolades come several romantics who would like to make her a wife again. These include stockbroker Eisley, actor Reed and British peer of the realm, Craig. She keeps them all at bay, but interested. Since her life is so devoted to making others happy and entertaining, Andrews finds that she has ignored Agutter and the two have drifted apart. At the same time, Andrews is earning oodles of money but she's spending oodles and oodles, thus putting her into a financial problem. It's a treadmill to oblivion as she overtaxes her frail self to pay her outsize debts. At the same time, she is still spending like a sailor on Saturday night and can't seem to catch up. She scores with Massey in his original play "Tonight at 8:30" (the writing in this, from Coward's pen, shows why he was so popular). After that, she appears in the dramatic "Susan and God" (by Rachel Crothers) and shows that she can handle other things besides comedy and music. It is a huge hit and while it's running, she meets banker Crenna, a New Englander who enjoys dabbling

in theatrical productions. Sparks fly between the two but that is a cover-up because there is a strong sexual attraction underneath. Crenna is presenting the play "Skylark" at his Massachusetts play house and she decides to do the show. The two get together and she moves right into "Lady In The Dark," then marries Crenna and is, at last, happy and fulfilled. The picture ends there. In real life, she lived about eight more years and died at the age of 54, after a tumultuous career in which she was far more noteworthy on the stage than on the screen. Her movies included THE BATTLE OF PARIS, AREN'T WE ALL?, LORD CAMBER'S LADIES, NO FUNNY BUSINESS, MIMI, REMBRANDT, and MEN ARE NOT GODS in England. Her two U.S. films were THE GLASS MENAGERIE and a cameo in STAGE DOOR CANTEEN. The movie lost more than $10 million, despite an enormous score which included: "Down at the Old Bull and Bush" (Harry Von Tilzer, P. Krone, Andrew B. Sterling, Russell Hunting, performed by the Chorus), "Piccadilly" (Paul Morande, Walter Williams, Bruce Seiver, performed by Andrews, Forsyth, Reid), "Star]" (Sammy Cahn, James Van Heusen, sung by Andrews), "Oh, It's a Lovely War" (Maurice Scott, J.P. Long, performed by Andrews, The Daffodil Girls), "In My Garden of Joy" (Saul Chaplin, performed by Andrews, The Daffodil Girls), "Forbidden Fruit" (Noel Coward, performed by Massey), "Parisian Pierrot" (written by Coward, performed by Andrews, Dancers), "Someday I'll Find You" (Coward, performed by Massey, Andrews), "Has Anybody Seen Our Ship?" (Coward, performed by Andrews, Massey), "N' Everything" (Bud G. De Sylva, Gus Kahn, Al Jolson, performed by Andrews, Garrett Lewis, Lynley Laurence, Charlot's Ensemble), "Burlington Bertie From Bow" (William Hargreaves, performed by Andrews), "Someone To Watch Over Me" (George and Ira Gershwin, performed by Andrews), "Do, Do, Do" (the Gershwins, performed by Andrews), "Dear Little Boy" (the Gershwins, performed by Massey and Andrews), "Limehouse Blues" (Douglas Furber, Philip Brahm, performed by Andrews and Dancers), "My Ship" (Kurt Weill, Ira Gershwin, performed by Andrews), "Jenny" (Weill, Ira Gershwin, performed by Andrews, Circus People, Ensemble), "The Physician" (Cole Porter, performed by Andrews, Dancers). The production was very slick, the dances by Kidd were excellent, nothing to fault in the acting, and the Academy nominated Massey as Best Supporting Actor, Laszlo for his cinematography, Hayton's musical direction, and the title song by Cahn and Van Heusen. So what was at fault? Well, it was far too big for the subject matter. Not that Lawrence didn't live an exciting life fraught with incident. It's merely that nobody in the great ticket-buying public knew who she was, so why would they have been intrigued by seeing a film about her? Shot at Fox with locations in London, Cape Cod, New York, and the South Of France, it was a lulu of a loser although it deserved a better fate. The shorter version moves quickly and is worthwhile watching, although many of the numbers listed above have been excised. As Charlot, note Oppenheimer, one of the most serviceable actors in the business who plays comedy or drama with equal facility and, in 1986, was earning large sums as a cartoon voice on the TV show "Rambo." Massey was superb as Coward, who was his actual godfather. He deserved the nomination and was nosed out by Jack Albertson for THE SUBJECT WAS ROSES that year. It was a tough race. Former English Music Hall "Chairman" Bernard Fox does a bit as assistant to Lord Chamberlain, Matthews. Fox spent years running revues in England and brought his expertise to Santa Monica in the 1970s and 1980s when he front-lined a recreation of those shows at the Mayfair Music Hall, the exquisite building seen in YOUNG FRANKENSTEIN when Peter Boyle sings "Puttin' on the Ritz."

p, Saul Chaplin; d, Robert Wise; w, William Fairchild; ph, Ernest Laszlo (Todd-AO, DeLuxe Color); ed, William Reynolds; md, Lennie Hayton; prod d, Boris Leven; set d, Walter M. Scott, Howard Bristol; cos, Donald Brooks; spec eff, L.B. Abbott, Art Cruickshank, Emil Kosa, Jr.; ch, Michael Kidd; m/l, dance music, Jay Thompson; makeup, Willard Buell, William Turner.

Musical/Biography   Cas.   (PR:A-C MPAA:G)

STAR CHAMBER, THE*   (1983) 109m FOX c

Michael Douglas (Steven Hardin), Hal Holbrook (Benjamin Caulfield), Yaphet Kotto (Detective Harry Lowes), Sharon Gless (Emily Hardin), James B. Sikking (Dr. Harold Lewin), Joe Regalbuto (Arthur Cooms), Don Calfa (Lawrence Monk), John DiSanti (Detective James Wickman), DeWayne Jessie (Stanley Flowers), Jack Kehoe (Hingle), Larry Hankin (Detective Kenneth Wiggen), Dick Anthony Williams (Detective Paul MacKay), Margie Impert (Louise Rachmil), Dana Gladstone (Martin Hyatt), Fred McCarren (Robert Karras), James Margolin (Albert Beamer), Hexin E. McPhee (Dawson), Diana Douglas (Adrian Caulfield), Keith Buckley (Assassin), Domingo Ambriz (Hector Andujar), Frances Bergen (Mrs. Cummins), Charlie Stavola (Detective Serkin), Robert Costanzo (Sgt. Spota), Paul Brennan (Garreth), David Proval (Officer Nelson), Robin Gammell (Judge Archer), Matthew Faison (Judge Stoner), Michael Ensign (Judge Kirkland), Jason Bernard (Judge Bocho), Jerry Taft (Judge Fogelson), Mike Austin (Judge Lang), Sheldon Feldner (Judge Culhane), Kate Zentall (Janet), George Cooper (State Senator Walden), Gary Rebstock (Newscaster), David Faustino (Tony Hardin), Jason Tomarken (Max Hardin), George Dickerson (George Tillis), Eddy C. Dyer (Garbage Man), John Garrett (Chuck Hurley), Danna Hyams (Caroline), Alan Oliney (Ladd), Don Pulford (Bailiff), Ron Cummins (Man No. 1), Jack Slate (Man No. 2).

An interesting idea goes awry when director/co-author Hyams bangs the audience over the head with a message instead of just letting us discover matters ourselves. The other problem was in casting Michael Douglas as a criminal courts judge when he barely looked old enough to be an attorney. Douglas was actually about 38 when he did the role but his face did not reflect that and it never rang true. He's a good man, caring about his judgemanship, married to Gless, and deeply concerned about justice. Two hoods, Regalbuto and Calfa, are picked up by the police and it seems that they may be the men responsible for kidnaping a child and torturing him to death. The men are brought to court and, due to a technicality about the manner in which they were arrested, they are released. The late child's father, knowing Douglas' adherence to the law and that many criminals have been let go in his jurisdiction, has a gun in his pocket and fires it in the courtroom, inadvertently wounding a cop. The grieving father, Sikking, is taken to jail where he will be held until his trial, and that he will do some time while the hoods are out free is a foregone conclusion. Douglas pals with Holbrook, a baseball-loving older judge married to Diana Douglas. When Douglas talks about how sorry he is for the way the laws are written, Holbrook decides it's time to bring the younger judge into the "Star Chamber." Based on a 15th Century judicial group who had already decided on the guilt of a prisoner before the case even began, this modern-day cabal consists of several judges who have had it with the law and have decided to take it into their own hands. In essence, they are a vigilante group who function as a tribunal. Each of the nine judges brings up a case in which a criminal has been allowed to get out of jail for some dumb reason. The judge presents the case and the other judges vote thumbs up or down. Once it's decided that the criminal should no longer walk this earth, a professional killer is contacted, through a web of intrigue that keeps the judges far enough away so they won't be able to be traced, and the hit is arranged. Douglas is admitted into the group and tells of the two who got away with murder. The others listen and decide that Regalbuto and Calfa must die. Douglas talks with Kotto, a hard-working detective who has no other life but his job. He wonders if Kotto has an opinion on the subject of the two hoods and Kotto reckons that it's up to the courts, he just catches them. When Douglas learns that the two men are innocent of the crime of killing Sikking's child, he tries to call off the hit and asks for a meeting with the others. It's too late to do it and the others feel that those two deserve to die anyhow as they've committed many other crimes. Douglas doesn't see it that way and races to the warehouse where Regalbuto and Calfa are making illicit drugs with synthetic ingredients. He tries to tell them that their lives are in danger and they respond by beating him up viciously because they fear he will inform on their drug business. There's a very exciting chase and it looks as though Douglas will be killed, but he manages to escape downstairs and faces a police officer with a shotgun. He thinks it's help but it turns out to be the killer. Just as Douglas is to be shot, the killer is laid low from a bullet out of Kotto's revolver. Kotto had suspected something and tailed Douglas. The last scene of the film shows Kotto and Douglas outside the house where the judges are meeting, listening to the conversation via a "bug" that picks up all the conversation. The action is fast and the acting is good but there are some long dialog stretches that should have been halved. Note Frances Bergen (Edgar's widow) in a bit. DeWayne Jessie provides what little humor is in the film, and improvisational comic Larry Hankin, who was so good in ESCAPE FROM ALCATRAZ, is briefly seen as one of the detectives.

p, Frank Yablans; d, Peter Hyams; w, Roderick Taylor, Hyams (based on a story by Taylor); ph, Richard Hannah (Panavision, DeLuxe Color); m, Michael Small; ed, Jim Mitchell, Charles Tetoni; prod d, Bill Malley; art d, Robert "Bo" Welch; set d, Rick Simpson; cos, Patricia Norris.

Crime Drama   **Cas.**   **(PR:C-O   MPAA:R)**

STAR CHILD   (SEE: SPACE RAIDERS, 1983)

STAR CRASH   (SEE: STARCRASH, 1979)

STAR DUST***   (1940) 85m FOX bw

Linda Darnell (Carolyn Sayres), John Payne (Bud Borden), Roland Young (Thomas Brooke), Charlotte Greenwood (Lola Langdon), William Gargan (Dane Wharton), Mary Beth Hughes (June Lawrence), Mary Healy (Mary Andrews), Donald Meek (Sam Wellman), Harry Green (Bird Man), Jessie Ralph (Miss Parker), Walter Kingsford (Napoleon), George Montgomery (Ronnie), Robert Lowery (Bell Boy), Hal K. Dawson (Wellman's Assistant), Jody Gilbert (Swedish Maid), Gary Breckner (Announcer), Paul Hurst (Lab Man), Irving Bacon (Clerk), Billy Wayne (Cameraman), Fern Emmett (Secretary), Tom Dugan (Bus Driver), Lynne Roberts (Girl), Manton Moreland (Waiter), Robert Shaw (Boy Leaving), Joan Leslie (College Girl), Frank Coghlan, Jr (Telegraph Boy), Philip Morris (Coach), Sid Grauman (Himself), Elyse Knox (Bit Girl), Kay Griffith (Stenographer).

A somewhat realistic–though not without the usual Hollywood gloss– treatment of a young girl's attempt to make it as a star in the motion picture industry. Darnell, in a portrayal not too dissimilar from her own experiences, is given a chance at a contract by talent scout Young. But she gets to Hollywood only to be turned down by studio boss Gargan (in an obvious impersonation of Darryl Zanuck), under the pretense of being too young. Instead of heading back home, she meets and falls in love with Payne, who pushes her along until she eventually lands a spot. Darnell injected her assignment with the needed charm to pull it off. An ironic note has Darnell

being caught in a blaze while watching STAR DUST on TV in 1965. She never recovered from her burns.

p, Kenneth Macgowan; d, Walter Lang; w, Robert Ellis, Helen Logan (based on a story by Jesse Malo, Kenneth Earl, Ivan Kahn); ph, Peverell Marley; ed, Robert Simpson; md, David Buttolph; cos, Gwen Wakeling; m/l, "Don't Let It Get You Down," Mack Gordon (sung by Charlotte Greenwood, Mary Healy), "Secret in Moonlight," Gordon (sung by John Payne), "Star Dust," Hoagy Carmichael (sung by Healy).

Drama   **(PR:A   MPAA:NR)**

STAR 80***   (1983) 102m Ladd-WB c

Mariel Hemingway (Dorothy Stratten), Eric Roberts (Paul Snider), Cliff Robertson (Hugh Hefner), Carroll Baker (Dorothy's Mother), Roger Rees (Aram Nicholas), David Clennon (Geb), Josh Mostel (Private Detective), Lisa Gordon (Eileen), Sidney Miller (Nightclub Owner), Keith Hefner (Photographer), Tina Willson (Bobo Weller), Shelly Ingram (Betty), Sheila Anderson (Exotic Dancer), Cis Rundle (Meg Davis), Kathryn Witt (Robin), Jordan Christopher (Peter Rose), James Luisi (Roy), Neva Patterson (Playboy Executive), Robert Fields (Director), Keenan Ivory Wayans (Comic), Sandy Wolshin (Woman M.C.), Robert Perault (Actor), James Blendick (Gunseller), Jacqueline Coleman (Nightclub Dancer), Don Granbery (Bartender), Stuart Damon (Vince Roberts), Ernest Thompson (Phil Wass), Budd Friedman (M.C.), Deborah Geffner (Billie), Norman Browning, Hagen Beggs (Detectives), Bobby Bass, Gilbert B. Combs (Hoods), Terence Kelly (Charlie), Tabitha Herrington (Blonde), Dean Hajum (George), Dan Zaleski (The Jock), Paul Ryan (Radio Announcer), Michael Joel Shapiro (Playboy Assistant), Fred Pierce (Head Butler), John Horn (Nightclub Owner, L.A.), David W. Rose (Assistant Director), Stanley Kamel (Nick), Liz Sheridan (Makeup Woman), Robert Picardo, Erica Yohn (Interviewers), Marilyn Madderom (Editor), Liis Kailey (Aram's Assistant), John Sala.

Based on the short life and gory death of Playboy "Playmate of the Year" Dorothy Stratten, this brutal picture might have been much better had Fosse concentrated on the young woman instead of the men who surrounded her. Since it is a true story, certain legalities had to be observed for fear of lawsuits. The Svengali-like influence that Peter Bogdanovich had over Stratten is altered to make the filmmaker into an Englishman who is reserved and shy, the opposite of the real director. The Teresa Carpenter article in "The Village Voice" won the young author a Pulitzer Prize and also served as the basis for the TV movie "Death of a Centerfold," which starred Jamie Lee Curtis in a monumental error of miscasting. Fosse takes great pains making his films and the TV people were able to rush theirs out long before this film was released. Hemingway had breast surgery for the role so she could better duplicate the curvaceousness of the Canadian who came to the big city of Vancouver to live and die in the fast lane. She's a sweet young thing and easy prey for the hustling Roberts, a sleazeball promoter with no ability of his own, only the talent to persuade other people to do what he says. Hemingway's mother, Baker, spots him for what he is but she can't control her daughter and the two are soon married. Roberts thinks he has a winner in his naive wife and he becomes her manager. They come south to Los Angeles and she at first resists his pleas to pose in the nude, then finally agrees to take it off for Roberts after first checking some centerfolds to see what the girls do in the shots. Roberts is perceived as being a man with gigantic complexes about his wife. He's insanely jealous, but doesn't mind that her naked pictures are seen by millions. He's violent and just as often gentle. He's bitter and he's sweet. Roberts makes the most of the portrayal and is by far the best actor in the film. Hemingway meets Robertson (as the pipe-smoking, Pepsi-drinking Hefner) and finds him to be a lovely man, more interested in her welfare than her body. Robertson can't stomach Roberts but keeps his annoyance in check. Hemingway next meets Rees (in the Bogdanovich role) and allows herself to be entranced by him. With all of these sophisticated types around her, she soon sees Roberts for what he is, a boorish lout who is earning a living by being her husband. She moves out of their residence and in with Rees. Roberts is in a frenzy and almost apoplectic. When Hemingway comes back to gather some of her gear, Roberts tries to make love to her but she is cold and unwilling. He picks up a shotgun and blasts that gorgeous face to a pulp, then turns the gun on himself. It's a cruel and unremitting story and the coldest part of it is that it's true. Hemingway is good enough in the role but the limelight is shone on Roberts and Robertson more than it is on her. An expensive exploitation picture is what it turned out to be, though the goal set was much higher. Zero Mostel's son, Josh, is seen as a private detective, and genial nightclub M.C. Budd Friedman plays a genial nightclub M.C. Friedman is co-owner of "The Improv," a popular Hollywood comedy club that gave the start to acts like Robin Williams, Billy Crystal, Andy Kaufman, Jay Leno, and the list goes on. Stratten made a few movies, including THEY ALL LAUGHED (directed by Bogdanovich) and the dismal sci-fi spoof GALAXINA, which opened on the day she was murdered. The blood, the language, and the sex make this a poor selection for anyone not old enough to read "Playboy" legitimately. Hefner's brother, Keith, a sometime actor, plays a small part as a photographer and we presume it was with Hef's approval.

p, Wolfgang Glattes, Kenneth Utt; d&w, Bob Fosse (based on "Death of a Playmate" by Teresa Carpenter); ph, Sven Nykvist (Technicolor); m, Ralph Burns; ed, Alan Heim; art d, Jack G. Taylor, Jr., Michael Bolton; set d, Ann McCulley, Kimberley Richardson; cos, Albert Wolsky; m/l, "Overkill,"

"Funky," Ralph Burns, "Off Ramp," "Improvise," Burns, Michael Tronick, "Just the Way You Are," Billy Joel.

Biography   **Cas.**   **(PR:O MPAA:R)**

STAR FELL FROM HEAVEN, A**   (1936, Brit.) 70m BIP/Wardour
                                                                    bw

Joseph Schmidt *(Josef)*, Florine McKinney *(Anne Heinmeyer)*, Billy Milton *(Douglas Lincoln)*, W.H. Berry *(Tomson)*, George Graves *(Fischer)*, Steven Geray *(Willi Wass)*, Judy Kelly *(Flora)*, C. Denier Warren *(Starfel)*, Iris Hoey *(Frau Heinmeyer)*, Bruce Lister *(Winkler)*, Eliot Makeham *(Professor)*, Hindle Edgar, Aubrey Mallalieu.

When Schmidt is called in to dub the singing for a film star who's lost his voice, he finds himself in a rather unusual position. The deception is discovered at the film's premiere, making the voice student an overnight star. The new-found fame is not without its pitfalls, though, for Schmidt loses his girl to the man whose voice he filled in. Okay comedy but it doesn't rise much beyond the intended programmer status. This one also employs one of filmdom's oldest jokes by naming the studio within the story Miracle Studios. "If it's good, it's a Miracle!"

p, Walter C. Mycroft; d, Paul Merzbach; w, Marjorie Deans, Dudley Leslie, Jack Davies, Gerald Elloitt, Val Guest, Geoffrey Kerr; ph, Ronald Neame.

Comedy   **(PR:AAA MPAA:NR)**

STAR FOR A NIGHT**½   (1936) 76m FOX bw

Claire Trevor *(Nina Lind)*, Jane Darwell *(Mrs. Lind)*, Arline Judge *(Mamie)*, Evelyn Venable *(Anna Lind)*, J. Edward Bromberg *(Dr. Spellmeyer)*, Dean Jagger *(Fritz Lind)*, Alan Dinehart *(James Dunning)*, Joyce Compton *(Ellen)*, Susan Fleming *(Mildred)*, Adrienne Marden *(Katharine Lind)*, Frank Reicher *(Dr. Helmkin)*, Dickie Walters *(Paul Lind)*, Chick Chandler *(Eddie)*, Astrid Allwyn *(Josephine Lang)*, Hattie McDaniel *(Hattie)*.

Touching story that has Darwell as a blind woman living in Europe thinking that her three children have all been leading successful careers in America. In reality they have all been pulling the wool over their mother's eyes, exaggerating their menial jobs to make it appear as though they are really hotshots. When Darwell decides to come to the U.S. to have an operation that will cure her blindness, the three offspring must think quickly about how to explain their true predicament. But this isn't necessary as the understanding Darwell is fully aware of her children's purpose. A bit heavy on the sentiment, but a well-meaning and entertaining project.

p, Sol M. Wurtzel; d, Lewis Seiler; w, Frances Hyland, Saul Elkins (based on a story by Michaelis Stangeland); ph, Ernest Palmer; ed, Alex Troffey; md, Samuel Kaylin; art d, Duncan Cramer; ch, Sammy Lee; m/l, "Way Down Around Malibu," Harry Akst, Sidney Claire.

Drama   **(PR:A MPAA:NR)**

STAR IN THE DUST**½   (1956) 80m UNIV c

John Agar *(Sheriff Bill Jorden)*, Mamie Van Doren *(Ellen Ballard)*, Richard Boone *(Sam Hall)*, Coleen Gray *(Nellie Mason)*, Leif Erickson *(George Ballard)*, James Gleason *(Orval Jones)*, Randy Stuart *(Nan Hogan)*, Terry Gilkyson *(The Music Man)*, Paul Fix *(Mike MacNamara)*, Harry Morgan *(Lew Hogan)*, Stuart Randall *(Jess Ryman)*, Robert Osterloh *(Rigdon)*, John Day *(Jiggs Larribee)*, Stanley Andrews *(Ben Smith)*, Stafford Repp *(Leo Roos)*, Lewis Martin *(Pastor Harris)*, Renny McEvoy *(Timothy Brown)*, Jesse Kirkpatrick *(Ed Pardee)*, James Parnell *(Marv Tremain)*, Anthony Jochim *(Doc Quinn)*, Clint Eastwood.

Agar is the town sheriff in the middle of a battle between ranchers and farmers about whether or not hired killer Boone should hang. The ranchers have hired him and want him to go free, while the farmers, stirred up by schoolteacher Osterloh, are anxious to see him dead. The real culprit is Erickson, the town banker who hired Boone to commit three murders; he is all for watching the gunman hang. The entire cast, which includes Clint Eastwood in a bit part, are all satisfactory portraying characters with escalating emotions.

p, Albert Zugsmith; d, Charles Haas; w, Oscar Brodney (based on the novel *Law Man* by Lee Leighton); ph, John L. Russell, Jr. (Technicolor); m, Frank Skinner; ed, Ray Snyder; md, Joseph Gershenson; art d, Alexander Golitzen, Alfred Sweeney; cos, Jay A. Morley, Jr.

Western   **(PR:A MPAA:NR)**

STAR IN THE WEST   (SEE: SECOND TIME AROUND, 1961)

STAR INSPECTOR, THE*½   (1980, USSR) 81m Mosfilm c
                                                        (ZVYOZDNYI INSPECTOR)

Vladimir Ivashov, Yuri Gusev, Timofei Spivak, Valentina Titova, Emmanuil Vitorgan.

A fairly crude rendition of a sci-fi theme that reverts to Cold War stereotypes (Russians good, Westerners bad) in order to establish its plot. Ivashov plays the commander of the Russian intergalactic police trying to track down independant companies responsible for space piracy. The villains all bear western names, underscoring what might happen if capitalism is allowed to continue and extend into outer space.

d, Vladimir Polin, Mark Kovalyov; w, Kovalyov, Vladislav Smirnov; ph, Vladimir Fastenko.

Fantasy   **(PR:A MPAA:NR)**

STAR IS BORN, A*****   (1937) 111m SELZ/UA c

Janet Gaynor *(Esther Blodgett/Vicki Lester)*, Fredric March *(Norman Maine)*, Adolphe Menjou *(Oliver Niles)*, Andy Devine *(Danny McGuire)*, May Robson *(Lettie)*, Lionel Stander *(Libby)*, Owen Moore *(Casey Burke)*, Elizabeth Jenns *(Anita Regis)*, J.C. Nugent *(Theodore Smythe)*, Clara Blandick *(Aunt Mattie)*, A.W. Sweatt *(Alex)*, Peggy Wood *(Central Casting Receptionist)*, Franklin Pangborn *(Billy Moon)*, Edgar Kennedy *(Pop Randall)*, Adrian Rosley, Arthur Hoyt *(Makeup Men)*, Edwin Maxwell *(Voice Coach)*, Guinn "Big Boy" Williams *(Posture Coach)*, Vince Barnett *(Photographer)*, Paul Stanton *(Academy Awards Speaker)*, Robert Emmett O'Connor *(Bartender at Santa Anita)*, Olin Howland 'Howlin' *(Rustic)*, Irving Bacon *(Station Agent)*, Clarence Wilson *(Justice of the Peace)*, Jonathan Hale *(Night Court Judge)*, Francis Ford, Kenneth Howell, Chris-Pin Martin *(Prisoners)*, Robert E. Homans, Lee Phelps *(Bailiffs)*, Wade Boteler *(Cop)*, Marshall Neilan *(Bert)*, Dr. Leonard Walker *(Orchestra Leader at Hollywood Bowl)*, Fred "Snowflake" Toones *(Black Prisoner)*, Gayne Whitman *(Announcer at Chinese Theater)*, Dennis O'Keefe, Claude King, David Newell, Eddie Kane *(People at Burke's Party)*, Carole Landis, Lana Turner *(Extras at Santa Anita)*, Jed Prouty *(Artie Carver)*, George Chandler *(Delivery Boy)*, Trixie Friganza, Jane Barnes *(Waitresses)*, Pat Flaherty *(Cuddles)*, Charles Williams *(Assistant Cameraman)*, Carleton Griffin *(Cameraman)*, Billy Dooley *(Painter)*, Helene Chadwick.

March and Gaynor are outstanding in this acerbic profile of Hollywood in the 1930s, he as a fading star and she as one shooting heavenward. March is a movie superstar whose heyday has slipped by, although he is still held in high esteem by his producer and studio head, Menjou. Everyone, except March, seems to know that he is losing popularity with the public and his films have seen less and less box-office success. At a Hollywood party where he drinks too much as usual, March meets and is attracted to Gaynor, who is serving sandwiches and, in his cups, he proposes to make her a star. She has been longing to become an actress and has been starving while waiting for Central Casting to call her for her big break, a call that never comes, which annoys her boarding house owner Kennedy no end. (Kennedy is earlier shown making out polite bills to give to Gaynor but he winds up tearing them to pieces before delivering them to her, not having the heart to make her feel more depressed than she already is.) March winds up breaking the dishes Gaynor is responsible for and he charms her into leaving the party with him, later painting a life of splendor and happiness as a movie star, encouraging her to follow his lead. March persuades a reluctant Menjou to give Gaynor a screen test and she proves herself. Menjou is about to make her a star and calls in his tough, conniving publicity director, Stander. Together they rechristen Gaynor Vicki Lester and they put her into March's next film, THE ENCHANTED HOUR, which is a success, but mostly due to Gaynor, not March. Gaynor becomes one of the nation's leading ladies of the screen but she loves March no less, marrying him in a small town under her own name, Esther Victoria Blodgett, and he under his own name, Alfred Henkel. They move into a beautiful new home replete with majestic weeping willows and a lagoon where graceful swans swim. While Gaynor's career accelerates, March's takes a complete nosedive and soon he is the most unemployable actor in Hollywood, shamelessly getting drunk in public and embarrassing a wife who loves him in spite of himself. When Gaynor wins an Academy Award, March accompanies her to the Biltmore Hotel in downtown Los Angeles (the actual site where the Awards ceremonies were traditionally held). March is again drunk and when Gaynor stands up to receive her Oscar, he jumps up to interrupt the ceremonies to tell the movie community that he is unemployed and needs to work and asks if anyone will give him a job. Gesticulating wildly, March accidentally strikes Gaynor in the face which brings hisses and boos from the audience; the gracious actress-wife calms her husband down and leads him away. March realizes that he must do something to save his life and marriage and puts himself into a sanitarium to "dry out." There he is guarded by musclebound male nurses, lest he should fall off the wagon. Menjou visits him in the sanitarium and is distressed to see him in such a place, telling him that he must put his life in order. "I hate to see you going the way of so many others," Menjou tells him. But March is now resolved to live a sober life and make the best of what he's got. He runs into Stander at the Santa Anita racetrack where he goes to the bar and orders only a soft drink. Stander, no longer bound to play the slavish publicity man for March, viciously insults him, taking out all the frustrations that have been pent up over the years due to March's outlandish behavior. He then tells March that he deserves no sympathy since he doesn't have a care in the world and that "you can live off your wife." March, infuriated, takes a swing at Stander, who promptly knocks him down. The commotion is observed by a lot of Hollywood types who merely conclude that March is on another bender. He doesn't disappoint them. To cover his humiliation, March stands up and orders a double Scotch. He vanishes for several days after that and a frantic Gaynor finally finds him in a drunk tank at a police station. March is brought before a judge who tells him that he will show no mercy to him, that he, March, has had all the advantages in life and has no excuse for turning into a drunken beast and going on destructive rampages. He is about to give March a stiff sentence when Gaynor arrives and begs the judge to release him to her custody. He does so reluctantly and now March is put to bed at the couple's Malibu home which is right on the ocean. He later overhears Gaynor and Menjou talking about him and Menjou saying that Gaynor is throwing away her career on a hopeless alcoholic, that March is "a shell of what he once was." Gaynor refuses to believe what she hears and tells the producer that she will give up films and acting and take care of the man she loves–that comes first. March now realizes for the first time that he is burdening his wife mercilessly by his presence, or so his boozy mind rationalizes, and he decides she will be better off without him. After Menjou leaves, he joins his wife, faking high spirits, telling Gaynor that he is going on a physical fitness program to put his body and mind back in shape. Then he announces to her that he is going for a swim as part of his new regimen. She smiles at him and begins to leave the room. He stops her and says, "Do you mind if I take just one more look?" Then he steps outside, walks across the beach to the water's edge, and takes off his bathrobe and slippers, walking into the gentle waves, going out steadily. The camera slowly rises after showing March's bare feet to encompass an ocean of water where March is nowhere to be seen. Later, at his funeral, the world believing that March died in an accidental drowning, Gaynor is attacked by a mob of screeching fans, her veil yanked from her face, causing her to scream in terror. (This scene is similar to the frantic, uncaring movie fans depicted in the brutal but incisive THE DAY OF THE LOCUST.) Gaynor retires from public appearances but is persuaded to attend a premiere some months later. She is asked at the premiere to say a few words to her millions of fans everywhere. Gaynor steps hesitantly to the radio microphone and announces, not her film name of Vicki Lester, but saying: "This is Mrs. Norman Maine..." A STAR IS BORN captures wonderfully the hustle of Hollywood, especially in scenes which show Gaynor being physically (and painfully) prepared for stardom by having her perfectly acceptable face redone by cosmetic experts, facial experts, eyebrow experts, hair stylists, and makeup magicians. It profiles the behind-the-scenes machinations of stars and producers, and it shows that, however accidental, a person of talent and sincerity and good-heartedness, sometimes slips through the corrosive Hollywood system to become a star. The film is marvelously constructed by Wellman who illicited from his stars, chiefly March, performances nothing short of great. Oddly, the stars of this film in real life have much in common with the roles they played, except in reverse. Gaynor, at age 31, was a real fading star when Selznick produced this film, having made her biggest hit in a silent, SEVENTH HEAVEN (1927), 10 years earlier, a film for which she won an Oscar in the first year of the Academy Awards, while March still had many great roles before him. Gaynor's career had been on the decline for years and there was some hesitancy in casting her for this role, one in which Gaynor is marvelous, somehow managing to go back to her origins and convincingly appear to be the innocent and aspiring actress whose charming naivete makes her all the more appealing. Producer Selznick tested several actresses for the role Gaynor subsequently got, not the least of whom was silent screen star Mary Brian. But Brian, who had appeared in such earlier day film blockbusters as BEAU GESTE (1926) and THE VIRGINIAN (1929), lost out to Gaynor, later saying: "It was almost a disappointment. I say 'almost' because when I saw Janet Gaynor in the picture I realized at once that she was the one who was meant to get it. She was absolutely wonderful!" Selznick had originally intended to call this film IT HAPPENED IN HOLLYWOOD but changed the title to A STAR IS BORN after he heard that Columbia was making a film with that title starring Richard Dix. The idea for the film began with director Wellman, although Selznick later tried to take complete credit for the film. The truth was that Wellman had always wanted to make a film on Hollywood and some of its more extravagant and flamboyant people and for years tried to interest producers in such a film, preparing an outline for a script on the subject with Robert Carson and submitting it to Selznick who was unenthusiastic about making the film. Then Irene Selznick, daughter of MGM mogul Louis B. Mayer, told her husband that the film would be a good idea and would probably make money. Selznick decided to make the film even more alluring to the public and to show off Hollywood in all its many-hued glories by making the film in color, albeit three-color Technicolor, the process then being in an experimental stage. (The colors in the film are not as rich as the process later became, but are more washed out and look similar to the awful colorization process to which Ted Turner and others subjected classic black and white films in recent years.) Selznick would later state that the entire project was exclusively his own making, "We started without anything more than a vague idea of where we were going, and it was really a relatively easy script to write." In addition to Wellman and Carson, Selznick, once underway with the production, brought in the acerbic Dorothy Parker and her husband Alan Campbell to handle the dialog. Moreover, since he was a man never satisfied with a so-called final draft, Selznick insisted that Carson touch up sections of the script and, secretly, had Budd Schulberg and Ring Lardner, Jr., two new young writers he had under contract, begin preparing a whole new version of the script. Wellman found out about the double-dealing and threatened to bring suit through his agent, Myron Selznick, the producer's own brother. Myron vigorously represented his clients and showed no favor to his sibling. When David O. Selznick heard Myron angrily threaten him with a lawsuit if he changed the STAR IS BORN script again, he backed off. The dialog created for this film is tough and most of the words Stander is given to growl present him and many Hollywood types like his character as vindictive and ruthless, people without pity, charisma, or compassion. Even after March dies of drowning, Stander can only spit out vicious quips: "First drink of water he's had in 20 years, and then he had to get it by accident. How do you wire congratulations to the Pacific Ocean?" Producer Menjou is no less cynical when evaluating the movie-going public: "Fans will write to anyone for a picture. It only takes a three-cent stamp and that makes pictures cheaper than wall paper." Of course, much of this acid- dripping dialog stemmed from the black humor for which Parker was famous. Wellman and Carson wound up receiving Oscars for the original story of the film and when Wellman was walking back to his seat at the Awards ceremonies that night, he stopped at Selznick's table and told him, "You ought to get this–you wrote more of it than I did." The character enacted by March is the most controversial profiled. His role, captured with consummate understanding by March, is based on several personalities who had ignited films and shocked Hollywood, notably John Barrymore and John Gilbert, both heavy drinkers who saw their careers fade before they reached middle age, although Barrymore managed to hang on, appearing in films almost up to the time of his death in 1942, even though these were minor productions. The scenes showing March in the sanitarium, drying out from his overwhelming drunken sprees, are all based on Barrymore, who had become such a heavy drinker that MGM could not trust him to remain sober during the production of ROMEO AND JULIET (1936), and insisted that he go to a sanitarium, which he did, one located close to the studio. Though he was watched night and day, Barrymore still managed to sneak bottles of booze into his room, usually by pulling them up at the ends of bedsheets lowered from the window of his room, bottles tied to same by his friends Gene Fowler and Charles MacArthur. Gilbert simply drank himself to death in 1936, after his career collapsed and he lost the love of *both* Greta Garbo and Marlene Dietrich. He had been one of the great screen personalities during the silent era, appearing in such smash hits as THE BIG PARADE and FLESH AND THE DEVIL. At the advent of the sound era, Gilbert's enemies, chiefly Louis B. Mayer of MGM, wrongly spread the word that Gilbert's voice was high-pitched and effeminate-sounding (as his talkies proved, this was never the case; he had a healthy baritone). Gilbert was used less and less and finally was reduced to begging for work much the same way March does in A STAR IS BORN. March's selfless suicide at the end of the film was a shocker during the 1930s and brought down criticism from the Hollywood censor board and many church leaders but Selznick managed to keep the scenes of March's demise in the film by *suggesting* his suicide and not actually showing it. This, too, was drawn from real life, based on the tragic end of film actor John Bowers, who, at age 45, had appeared in dozens of silent films but was washed by the sound era and, more frustrating to him, had recently lost his wife. Bowers told a friend one day that he had been thinking of sailing a boat "into the sunset" and never again returning. He rented a small sailboat on November 15, 1936, and started sailing toward the sunset. The boat was found empty the next day, drifting off Santa Monica, and Bowers' body was washed up on the beach the following day. Gossip columnist and sometime screenwriter, Adela Rogers St. Johns, thought the suicide was based on an incident involving John McCormick, a film producer who was separated from his wife, perky silent film star Colleen Moore, and who tried to drown himself over losing his famous spouse by swimming as far out into the ocean as he could. The smash ending of A STAR IS BORN comes from another source entirely and even a greater tragedy, that of silent screen star Wallace Reid. Since 1915 when Reid appeared in D.W. Griffith's BIRTH OF A NATION (as the intrepid blacksmith), the handsome leading man had been a rage with female moviegoers. But privately he was insecure and, to assuage his many fears, became hopelessly addicted to morphine; the deadly drug was actually supplied to him by his producers to keep him going on a frantic schedule where he appeared in several movies a week. He finally collapsed from an overdose and was taken to a Los Angeles sanitarium where he died a raving lunatic on January 18, 1923, begging for morphine with his last breath. He was 31. His wife, Dorothy Davenport, had been a popular silent screen actress and had appeared in many of her husband's films, including an ironic movie entitled THE SQUAW MAN'S SON, one where she marries Reid on camera and later turns into a drug addict and dies of an overdose! It was Mrs. Davenport who was responsible for the famous line Gaynor, and later Judy Garland, and still later Barbra Streisand (in the third remake of this film, the most abysmal), delivers at the end of A STAR IS BORN. Just after Reid's heavily attended funeral, Davenport appeared at a radio station to tell a nationwide listenership about her husband. She began her speech by saying: "This is Mrs. Wallace Reid..."

p, David O. Selznick; d, William A. Wellman; w, Dorothy Parker, Alan Campbell, Robert Carson, (uncredited) Selznick, Wellman, Ring Lardner, Jr., Bud Schulberg, John Le Mahin (based on the story by Wellman, Carson); ph, W. Howard Greene (Technicolor); m, Max Steiner; ed, James E. Newcom; art d, Lyle Wheeler; set d, Edward Boyle; cos, Omar Kiam; spec eff, Jack Cosgrove.

Drama **Cas.** **(PR:C MPAA:NR)**

STAR IS BORN, A**** (1954) 176m Transcona/WB c

Judy Garland *(Esther Blodgett/Vicki Lester)*, James Mason *(Norman Maine)*, Jack Carson *(Matt Libby)*, Charles Bickford *(Oliver Niles)*, Tommy Noonan *(Danny McGuire)*, Lucy Marlow *(Lola Lavery)*, Amanda Blake *(Susan Ettinger)*, Irving Bacon *(Graves)*, Hazel Shermet *(Libby's Secretary)*,

James Brown *(Glenn Williams)*, Lotus Robb *(Miss Markham)*, Joan Shawlee *(Announcer)*, Dub Taylor *(Driver)*, Louis Jean Heydt, Leonard Penn, Tristram Coffin *(Directors)*, Olin Howland *(Charley)*, Willis Bouchey *(Director McBride)*, Kathryn Card *(Landlady)*, Rex Evans *(M.C.)*, Emerson Treacy *(Justice of the Peace)*, Bob Jellison *(Eddie)*, Chick Chandler *(Man in Car)*, Blythe Daly *(Miss Fusselow)*, Mae Marsh *(Party Guest)*, Frank Ferguson *(Judge)*, Nadene Ashdown *(Esther at age 6)*, Heidi Meadows *(Esther at age 3)*, Henry Kulky *(Cuddles)*, Jack Harmon *(1st Dancer)*, Don McCabe *(2nd Dancer)*, Eric Wilton *(Valet)*, Grady Sutton *(Carver)*, Henry Russell *(Orchestra Leader)*, Robert Dumas *(Drummer)*, Laurindo Almeida *(Guitarist)*, Bobby Sailes *(Dancer)*, Percy Helton *(Drunk)*, Charles Watts *(Harrison)*, Pat O'Malley, Samuel Barrymore Colt *(Men at Race Track)*, Charles Halton, Joseph Mell *(Studio Employees)*, Stuart Holmes *(Spectator)*, Grandon Rhodes *(Producer)*, Frank Puglia *(Bruno)*, Wilton Graff *(Master of Ceremonies-- Last Scene)*, Phil Arnold, Rudolph Anders, Bess Flowers, Allen Kramer.

A STAR IS BORN was an artistic and personal triumph for Judy Garland. It was the finest work of her career as she took her character through an emotional gamut without displaying a single false note, a fascinating and often heart-rendering performance. This is a highly personal achievement, coming from the depths of the actress' tortured psyche. Garland never displayed such force in any of her films before or after this, showing a dramatic range of intense abilities, coupled with her magnificent singing voice that she pushed further than anyone could imagine. She takes on standards, ballads, and bouncy production numbers with zest, her voice sounding joyous with the energy she brings to the music. The story essentially follows the plot of the original 1936 film. Garland is a young singer (rather than the struggling actress Janet Gaynor played) who saves Mason, a famous star, from making a fool of himself on stage. Later, a sober Mason listens to Garland sing, and decides to help this incredible talent get started in pictures. After Garland joins the studio, Mason manages to get her the lead in a big musical. She is a smash success, but Mason's own career is begining to fall. The two elope, but Mason is later cut by the studio. His drinking increases, though Garland does what she can to cheer her husband. Finally, frustrated by the short memory of both his public and "friends," he drunkenly interrupts the Oscar ceremonies where Garland has won the award for Best Actress. He humbly pleads for a job, and accidentally slaps Garland in the face before the shocked gathering and nationwide television audience. Mason is hospitalized, and Garland begs studio chief Bickford to give her husband a part, any part. Bickford pays a call on Mason, who rebuffs the offer. Later, after his release, Mason gets into a fight with Carson, a powerful studio publicist. Shamed by the fistcuffs, Mason goes off on a drinking binge. He's arrested for drunken driving, but is released into Garland's custody. Realizing that his own disintigration is destroying Garland as well, Mason walks off into the ocean and drowns himself. In the wake of his death, Garland goes into seclusion, but Noonan, a member of her old band, angrily tells her this is no testament to her late husband's belief in her talents. Garland realizes Noonan is right, and, in her first public appearance after Mason's death, tells a hushed crowd gathered at a Hollywood benefit: "Hello, everybody. This is Mrs. Norman Maine." Cukor had filmed the story once before, as WHAT PRICE HOLLYWOOD? in 1932. Here he improves on that work, a much better effort of dramatic intensity. Cukor's use of light is effective, often relying on a single spot to highlight a face surrounded by darkness, varying this use with stunning results. Garland's face is singled out this way at the close of her first triumph, while Mason conversely has a similar lighting scheme when he realizes he is choking Garland's career. Cukor uses the long take to further the film's emotional impact, allowing events to unfold with natural rhythms, further accentuating the dramatic strengths of his cast. By allowing moments and characters to speak for themselves, Cukor draws heartfelt strokes that give A STAR IS BORN all the more power. Garland's excellent performance is well matched by Mason. His hellish descent is never without a deeply rooted sense of self-dignity, understanding completely what is happening and ultimately accepting his fate. There is no little irony that Mason's character in A STAR IS BORN closely parallels Garland's tumultuous off screen life. Like the character of Norman Maine, she had well-known troubles with alcohol and pills, a troublesome reputation in Hollywood, and was fired by MGM, the studio which discovered and nurtured her enormous talents. In 1950, after leaving MGM Garland's personal life turned into disaster. She divorced her husband, director Vincente Minnelli the following year, and soon attempted suicide. Her subsequent marriage to Sid Luft, however, marked a major turning point for her. Luft arranged for Garland to play New York's Palace Theater (it was to be a stunning comeback that broke box office records), then learned that Eddie Alperson, a producer friend, had bought the remake rights to A STAR IS BORN. Garland was ecstatic, for the Esther Blodgett-Vicki Lester role was one she longed to play on screen. She had essayed the part before, on December 28, 1942, for the Lux Radio Theater, in a production directed by no less than Cecil B. DeMille. Garland asked MGM chief Louis B. Mayer if the property could be developed as a film project for her, but Mayer dismissed Garland's notion, claiming the studio powers- that-be felt the story was too depressing, and, furthermore, Garland's fans would never accept her in such a screen role. Garland and Luft formed their own production company, dubbed Transcona, and set out to bring their dream to life. Warner Bros. expressed interest in the project, but it developed that David O. Selznick, in giving up A STAR IS BORN, had retained rights for the film's foreign distribution. This potential problem was averted when Warner Bros. sold Selznick the rights to Ernest Hemingway's *The Old Man and the Sea*, a property of theirs he desperately wanted. Full rights for A STAR IS BORN were retained, and the project was ready to begin. Hart was hired to write a new screenplay, receiving a flat $100,000, plus expenses. These included *two* houses, one in Los Angeles and one in Palm Springs. Both Garland and Luft wanted Cary Grant to play Norman Maine (Garland always admitted to having a crush on the debonair actor, one of the reasons she wanted him for the film). Other stars, including Humphrey Bogart and Frank Sinatra, expressed interest, but Grant remained the first choice. After much agonizing, Grant decided against taking the part, convinced that his well-known comic style might make Norman Maine's drinking habits seem humorous rather than sympathetic. After declining the role, Garland, though disappointed, told Luft that they should go with their second choice, James Mason. "Get Mason tomorrow," she told her husband after Grant turned Garland down. "He'll be a better drunk than Cary anyway." Arlen and Gershwin had been hired to write the songs, and their work was superb. They provided Garland with songs that would become standards in her concert repetoire, and her singing in the film was some of the finest in her career. "The Man that Got Away," which received an Oscar nomination for Best Song, is a classic, a number that Garland renders with incredible emotional power. Shooting began in October of 1953, and Cukor, knowing Garland's bad on-set reputation, took every step he could to accommodate his star. He shot many of her scenes at night, knowing that was when she worked best, but this didn't prevent her from causing some troubles during production. Early on in the shooting, she refused to come out of her dressing room (the same one once occupied by Bette Davis). Cukor, who normally refused to deal with such temperament from his actors, personally went to Garland and found her sitting hopelessly depressed in front of several mirrors that reflected her image around the room. Cukor asked his star if anything was wrong and then, realizing the stupidity of such a question, broke out in laughter. The laughter was infectuous, and Garland's spirit quickly changed. "This is the story of my life," she told Cukor. "I'm about to shoot myself and I'm asked if there's anything wrong..." Cukor was amazed at how far Garland pushed herself in her performance. After one particularly emotional scene, Cukor told Garland: "...that was just glorious! My blood froze." Garland, drained and in tears, looked at her director, then cracked, "You should come out to the house, George. I do that every afternoon." Garland's temperament was not the only problem that contributed to the film's slowly increasing budget and production schedule. Warner Bros. had wanted to shoot in CinemaScope, but because this process was owned by 20th Century-Fox, Warners decided to develop their own wide-screen process, dubbed WarnerScope. The process proved to be unsatisfactory, and Warners finally gave in, paying Fox for the CinemaScope, and reshooting many important scenes. The production finally wrapped up in March of 1954, but studio executives remained unsatisfied, claiming the film still needed a scene to show just why Garland became a star. This led to the creation of the classic "Born in a Trunk" sequence by Leonard Gershe. It is one of Garland's finest moments, a near autobiographical musical sequence that shows the rise of star, incorporating the songs "I'll Get By" (Roy Turk, Fred Ahlert), "You Took Advantage of Me" (Richard Rodgers, Lorenz Hart), "Black Bottom" (De Sylva, Brown, Henderson), "Peanut Vendor" (L. Wolfe Gilbert, Marion Sunshine, Moises Simon), "My Melancholy Baby" (George A. Norton, Ernie Burnett) and "Swanee" (Irving Ceasar, George Gershwin) into the number. Garland convincingly goes from playing a 16-year-old in the number to a woman twice that age in a bravura performance. Warners' even brought in Garland's old costumer from MGM, Irene Sharaff, to work on the number. The completed film cost close to $6 million dollars, and opened at Pantages Theater in Hollywood in the fall of 1954. Over 20,000 people showed up for the premiere, which was the first ever broadcast live to a nationwide office. Garland was nominated for an Oscar for her unsurpassed performance, but lost that year to Grace Kelly in THE COUNTRY GIRL. Garland, who had delivered her third child only days before the ceremony, watched the Oscar ceremony from her hospital bed, cameras trained on her should she win. When Kelly's name was announced, the crew simply packed up and left. Many in Hollywood felt Garland was being punished by her peers for her past troubles, and Groucho Marx, in a telegram to Garland, claimed her loss "was the biggest robbery since Brink's." A STAR IS BORN premiered at 182 minutes, but Warners, in response to theater owner complaints, decided to remove about 30 minutes of footage, including two of the Arlen-Gershwin songs ("Lose that Long Face," and "Here's What I'm Here For") as well as some key expository scenes between Garland and Mason. Another trimming gave the film a running time of 135 minutes, and while the power was never diminished, Cukor was furious. He felt the "Born in a Trunk" sequence (which he did not shoot) was wholly unnecessary to the plot, while what was removed was essential to character development. "If they thought it was too long," he later stated, "there were other ways of shortening it besides chopping and hacking out vital bits." Cukor, while not disowning the film, never considered Warner Bros. final cut to be the film he intended, and therefore never saw the film in this form. "Judy Garland and I felt like the English queen who had 'Calais' engraved on her heart...neither of us could ever bear to see that final version," he told writer Gavin Lambert. In 1973, in a booklet prepared for a Cukor retrospective, stills and script excerpts from the missing footage were published. This stirred up interest in a possible restoration of the complete version of A STAR IS BORN, and an intensive effort was made by film historian Ronald Haver to find the missing elements. He conducted an intensive search of the Warner Bros. studio vaults, and amid the musty, long forgotten cans, he found a gold mine.

Several important scenes, such as Mason's marriage proposal to Garland, and the missing musical numbers were found intact. Other finds including missing soundtrack sequences. These contained some crucial moments, including Mason's attempts to find Garland for a screen test after he is whisked off to a location shooting. Though the footage had been destroyed, Haver coupled the soundtrack with production stills and some alternate takes which had somehow survived. The effect was marvelous, giving the film a continuity that unfeeling hands had removed. The old footage fit right into place, and the still and soundtrack sequences worked well, though they served as painful reminders to the beauty that had been lost. Sadly Cukor passed away the night before he was to see his restored film. However, the film reopened in 1983 to enthusiastic crowds, a 29-year-old child that retained every ounce of its magnificence. Other songs in the Arlen-Gershwin score include: "It's a New World," "Gotta Have Me Go With You," and "Somewhere There's a Someone."

p, Sidney Luft; d, George Cukor; w, Moss Hart (based on the Dorothy Parker, Alan Campbell, Robert Carson screenplay from a story by William A. Wellman, Carson, based on the film WHAT PRICE HOLLYWOOD); ph, Sam Leavitt (CinemaScope, Technicolor); m, Harold Arlen; ed, Folmar Blangsted, (reconstruction ed) Craig Holt; md, Ray Heindorf; prod d, Gene Allen; art d, Malcolm Bert; set d, George James Hopkins; cos, Jean Louis, Mary Ann Nyberg, Irene Sharaff; spec eff, H.F. Koenekamp; ch, Richard Barstow; still photo sequences in reconstructed version, Lize Bechtold Blyth, Eric Durst.

Drama/Musical   **Cas.**   **(PR:A-C   MPAA:PG)**

STAR IS BORN, A***   (1976) 140m WB c

Barbra Streisand (*Esther Hoffman*), Kris Kristofferson (*John Norman Howard*), Gary Busey (*Bobby Ritchie*), Oliver Clark (*Gary Danziger*), Vanetta Fields, Clydie King (*The Oreos*), Marta Heflin (*Quentin*), M.G. Kelly (*Bebe Jesus*), Sally Kirkland (*Photographer*), Joanne Linville (*Freddie*), Uncle Rudy (*Mo*), Paul Mazursky (*Brian*), Tony Orlando (*Himself*), Robert Englund (*Patron*).

The fourth time around for this tale turns out to be a fairly good, though not great, remake. The first version was WHAT PRICE HOLLYWOOD, directed by George Cukor for RKO in 1932. Then William Wellman's look at the same subect in 1937 with Janet Gaynor, followed by the 1954 Judy Garland starrer, also directed by Cukor. Streisand was executive producer and her then boy friend, former hairdresser Jon Peters, was the producer. With the two of them as live-in creative people, there was nobody around to tell them that enough was enough so the picture went on for 140 minutes when it might have been told shorter and better if someone pointed out to the empress that she wasn't wearing clothes. The movie grossed nearly $40 million, mostly due to word of mouth as it was lanced repeatedly by the wise guy critics who can't stand anyone's success. True, the picture did have many faults but it was nowhere nearly as bad as the smart-mouthing and the proof was in the profits. Jerry Schatzberg had been the original directorial choice but that was short-lived and Pierson came in right away to take over the chores. Kristofferson is a highly paid rock star but his career is now in the descendancy and he has taken solace with booze to help. He fills his gullet to capacity and the resultant drunkeness causes him to appear blotto on several concert stages. There's a "tom-tom" in the music business and the drums begin to beat out the news that Kristofferson is over, done, history. He gives one particular show and is deep in his cups. When the audience doesn't respond, he lets his spleen vent, then walks off the stage. Later, in an attempt to calm down and get his senses back, he goes to a nightclub where he sees a trio of singers, two black women and one white. They are known as "The Oreos," (cute, huh?) with the white one in the center. The two blacks are Vanetta Fields and Clydie King. Can you guess who the one in the middle is? We thought you could. Kristofferson is mightily impressed by Streisand and tells her so when she comes to his table after the show. He offers to be her sort-of manager and will help her secure a recording contract. She can't believe such a famous person is actually talking to her, much less offering such a deal. Kristofferson is as good as his word and gets her an audition that leads to a recording contract. An album is released, Streisand becomes a star and can't believe her good fortune. She and Kristofferson marry but there is trouble in paradise. Her career soars as his plummets. She does her best to make him feel part of her success but he is resentful and doesn't want to be known as her husband. The public is fickle and they are soon forgetting Kristofferson. Streisand's latest record wins a "Grammy" and as she is accepting her award graciously, her staggering husband lurches on stage and ruins a highlight in her life. She still loves him and decides that they need time together, so they purchase a large estate in the outskirts and settle in to what is apparently a tranquil existence. But Kristofferson still can't handle what's happened to him and eventually leaves, then dies in a car crash. The picture should have ended there, but no, Streisand, who was to sing every song in her movie YENTL, felt she hadn't sung enough in this one so there is a 10-minute coda, a Streisand concert she dedicates to her late husband. Fans of the singer will love the extra footage. Others will yawn. Paul Mazursky does a good turn as Kristofferson's manager and all the acting is well done, except for Streisand, who has a tendency to become shrill. Surtees was academy-nominated for his cinematography and Kellaway was also named for his scoring. The songs, from several sources, were mostly by Paul Williams and Kenny Ascher. They were "Watch Closely Now" (a dreadful interminable

tune sung too often by Kristofferson), "Spanish Lies," "Hellacious Acres," "With One More Look at You," "Woman in the Moon." Rupert Holmes wrote "Queen Bee," and co-wrote "Everything" with Williams. "Crippled Cow" was written by Donna Weiss, and Kenny Loggins wrote the music for "I Believe in Love" with lyrics by Marilyn and Alan Bergman. Streisand herself teamed with Leon Russell to write "Lost Inside of You" and with Williams for their Academy Award-winning "Evergreen." Streisand took credit for "Musical Concepts" (whatever that means) and the tunes were produced by Phil Ramone. Ace assistant director Stu Fleming was on his third film with Streisand (he'd done FOR PETE'S SAKE and FUNNY LADY) and may have been the only person she got along with. There were screaming matches with Kristofferson and Pierson, and she wasn't even talking to Williams by the time the movie ended. The concert was shot in Phoenix and is one long sequence, with no cuts, due to the use of a special magazine that would take the extra film. Pierson later wrote a publicized article blasting his star for her megalomania.

p, Jon Peters; d, Frank Pierson; w, John Gregory Dunne, Joan Didion, Pierson (based on a story by William Wellman, Robert Carson); ph, Robert Surtees (Panavision, Metrocolor); m, Roger Kellaway; ed, Peter Zinner; md, Paul Williams; prod d, Polly Platt; art d, William Hiney; set d, Ruby Levitt; cos, Shirley Strahm, Seth Banks; spec eff, Chuck Gasper; ch, David Winters; makeup, Allan Snyder, Marvin C. Thompson.

Musical/Drama   **Cas.**   **(PR:C-O   MPAA:R)**

STAR MAKER, THE***   (1939) 85m PAR bw

Bing Crosby (*Larry Earl*), Linda Ware (*Jane Gray*), Louise Campbell (*Mary*), Ned Sparks ("*Speed*" *King*), Laura Hope Crews (*Carlotta Salvini*), Walter Damrosch (*Himself*), Janet Waldo (*Stella*), Thurston Hall (*Mr. Proctor*), Billy Gilbert (*Steel Worker*), Clara Blandick (*Miss Esther Jones*), Oscar O'Shea (*Mr. Flannigan*), John Gallaudet (*Duke*), Ben Welden (*Joe Gimlick*), Emory Parnell (*Mr. Olson*), Dorothy Vaughan (*Mrs. Riley*), Bodil Rosing (*Mrs. Swanson*), Paul Stanton (*Mr. Coyle*), Morgan Wallace (*Lou Morris*), Richard Denning, Joseph Crehan, Ethel Griffies, Frank Faylen, Grace Hayle, Johnny Morris, Selmer Jackson, Siegfried [Sig] Arno, Ralph Faulkner, Earl Dwire, Harry Bradley, Wally Maher, George Eldredge, Stanley Price, George Guhl, Jim Dundee, Max Wagner, Ralph Sanford, A.S. "Pop" Byron, Daisy Bufford, Allex Rox, Fritzi Brunette, Ed Stanley, Ottola Nesmith, Jack Pennick, George C. Pearce, Doro Merande, Frances Raymond, Philharmonic Orchestra of Los Angeles.

The life of Gus Edwards served as the inspiration for this movie but great liberties were taken and the result was an uneven picture that could have been terrific. Edwards discovered such talents as Eddie Cantor, Eleanor Powell, Mae Murray, George Jessel, Walter Winchell, Sally Rand, Bert Wheeler, Georgie Price, The Lane Sisters, The Duncan Sisters, The Menken Sisters, Ray Bolger, Jack Pearl, and many more. If someone made the true story of this man, it might have made sense. As it was, THE STAR MAKER is just a contrived tale that bears little resemblance to Edwards' career, so little that the names were changed. Crosby is a singer-songwriter who has yet to find his metier. After several problems, he says the heck with it and marries Campbell, then settles down to work in a department store. It isn't long before he is dissatisfied with his floor-walking position and decides to opt for the bright lights and glamor once more. He wants to do an act but can't decide what it should be, then hits upon the idea of assembling a troupe of kids, all teenagers or less. He finds a sextet of local newsboys, rehearses them into a finely tuned act, and manages to persuade impresario Hall to give them a spot in one of his revues. They open and are instantly successful. The next months find them enjoying great popularity. Crosby sees he has a gold mine and hires many more children and has several shows operating. Then the Bureau Of Child Welfare steps in and tells him that these kids cannot work those hours in those places. Crosby's fortunes are dim as he has no choice but to accept the law. Then he realizes that he can do the same thing in radio and not run afoul of the "after 8" rule that forbids the kids from working evenings. That's about the size of the plot. The songs are many. Johnny Burke and James Monaco wrote "Go Fly a Kite," "A Man and His Dream," "Still the Bluebird Sings," and "An Apple for the Teacher." "School Days" and "If I Were a Millionaire" came from the pens of Gus Edwards and Will Cobb. Edwards collaborated with Edward Madden on "Jimmy Valentine" and with Robert H. Smith on "Sunbonnet Sue." The classic commercial "In My Merry Oldsmobile" was also heard. Of the child actors, the best was Linda Ware. Famed conductor Walter Damrosch plays himself as he conducts the Los Angeles Philharmonic. Comedy was provided by Sparks in his usual long-faced role.

p, Charles R. Rogers; d, Roy Del Ruth; w, Frank Butler, Don Hartman, Art Caesar (based on a story by Caesar, William Pierce, suggested by the career of Gus Edwards); ph, Karl Struss; ed, Alma Macrorie; md, Alfred Newman; art d, Hans Dreier, Robert Usher; set d, A.E. Freudeman; cos, Edith Head.

Musical/Biography   **(PR:AA   MPAA:NR)**

STAR OF HONG KONG**   (1962, Jap.) 109m Cathay/ Toho c
(HONKON NO HOSHI)

Yu Ming, Wang Ing, Reiko Dan, Akira Takarada, Rin Tsuong, Mitsuko Kusabue, Wong Yen, So Yamamura, Sadako Sawamura, Lin Chong, Hiroshi Koizumi, Yu Fujiki, Daisuke Kato, Asami Kuji.

A young girl from Hong Kong studying in Japan continually resists the advances of a young man out of the respect she has toward another girl she believes is in love with the same man. But the man is persistent and follows the girl to Hong Kong where the two eventually decide to marry, but are separated when the man takes up residence in San Francisco and the girl remains in Hong Kong to pursue her work.

d, Yasuki Chiba; w, Ryozo Kasahara; ph, Rokuro Nishigaki (Tohoscope, Eastmancolor); m, Hachiro Matsui.

Drama   **(PR:A MPAA:NR)**

STAR OF INDIA*½   (1956, Brit.) 92m UA c

Cornel Wilde (*Pierre St. Laurent*), Jean Wallace (*Katrina*), Herbert Lom (*Narbonne*), Yvonne Sanson (*Mme. de Montespan*), John Slater (*Emile*), Walter Rilla (*Van Horst*), Basil Sydney (*King Louis XIV*), Arnold Bell (*Captain*), Leslie Linder (*Moulai*).

Wilde plays a nobleman in the France of Louis XIV who loses all his possessions and status while away serving his country. With the assistance of Wallace, who turns out to be a spy for Holland, Wilde gains possession of a famed jewel and re-establishes his fortune. Only the atmosphere of a decadent France and the crazed performance of heavy Lom add any elan to an otherwise silly yarn.

p, Raymond Stross; d, Arthur Lubin; w, Herbert Dalmas, Denis Freeman; ph, C. Pennington-Richards (Technicolor); m, Nino Rota; ed, Russell Lloyd; md, Muir Mathieson; art d, Cedric Dawe.

Adventure   **(PR:A MPAA:NR)**

STAR OF MIDNIGHT***   (1935) 90m RKO bw

William Powell (*Clay Dalzell*), Ginger Rogers (*Donna Mantin*), Paul Kelly (*Jim Kinland*), Gene Lockhart (*Horatio Swayne*), Ralph Morgan (*Roger Classen*), Leslie Fenton (*Tim Winthrop*), J. Farrell MacDonald (*Inspector Doremus*), Russell Hopton (*Tommy Tennant*), Vivien Oakland (*Gerry Classon*), Frank Reicher (*Abe Ohlman*), Robert Emmet O'Connor (*Sgt. Cleary*), Francis McDonald (*Kinland Gangster*), Paul Hurst (*Corbett*), Spencer Charters (*Doorman*), George Chandler (*Witness*), Syd Saylor (*Deliveryman*), Charles McMurphy (*Officer Lewis*), John Ince (*Doctor*), Hooper Atchley (*Hotel Manager*).

A good mystery-comedy with Powell playing another "Nick Charles" by another name, and without Myrna Loy as "Nora." Rogers was his new foil and in between ROBERTA and TOP HAT, both with Fred Astaire. Wit, sophistication, and gunshots all meld to make a fine entertainment as Powell is seen as a suave attorney who doubles as a detective. The leading lady of a Broadway show vanishes and when Powell is asked to look into matters, he is reluctant. Then a gossip columnist arrives with news of the disappearance. But before the goods can be spilled, the columnist is killed and Powell is now a suspect. He has to solve the crimes to clear himself. Rogers is his love, always there with a quip and a martini when he needs one and looking smashing in a series of super dresses. While they are unspooling the mystery, there is plenty of time for Rogers and Powell to be trading sharp lines. In the end, the villain is unmasked as Morgan but at no time is that ever presaged so it's a total shock. Herrings of a rosy hue have been distributed liberally in the screenplay and, until the denouement, we are never sure who the baddie is. The modestly budgeted picture made a tidy profit and continues to delight audiences on late-night TV. There's a glaring hole in the story at film's end but by that time you've laughed so hard at the dialog spoken by Rogers and Powell and the antics of Lockhart as the butler and O'Connor as the cop that it doesn't much matter.

p, Pandro S. Berman; d, Stephen Roberts; w, Howard J. Green, Anthony Veiller, Edward Kaufman (based on the novel by Arthur Somers Roche); ph, J. Roy Hunt; m, Max Steiner; ed, Arthur Roberts; md, Steiner; art d, Van Nest Polglase, Charles Kirk; cos, Bernard Newman; makeup, Mel Burns.

Crime Comedy   **Cas.**   **(PR:A MPAA:NR)**

STAR OF MY NIGHT**   (1954, Brit.) 71m Kenilworth/GFD bw

Griffith Jones (*Michael Donovan*), Kathleen Byron (*Eve Malone*), Hugh Williams (*Arnold Whitman*), Pauline Olsen (*Iris*), Harold Lang (*Carl*), Andre Mikhelson (*Papa Condor*), Ilona Ference (*Daisy*), Malcolm Mitchell Trio, Kenneth Edwards, Mona Washbourne.

Strange, dark, and not entirely successful drama has sculptor Jones dropping his cynical outlook after meeting ballerina Olsen. He becomes obsessed by the woman and begins building a life-sized statue of her. This makes her boy friend jealous and he beats up the artist. Jones begins to lose his sight as a result, but rather than have an operation to save this all-important sense, the sculptor works against time to finish the statue. He tries to convince Olsen that he no longer loves her, but the dancer discovers the truth and leaves her boy friend for Jones. This has its moments but is too deliberate in "artistic" feelings for its own good.

p, Edward J. Danziger, Harry Lee Danziger; d, Paul Dickson; w, Paul Tabori; ph, Jack Cox.

Drama   **(PR:C MPAA:NR)**

STAR OF TEXAS**   (1953) 68m Westwood/AA bw

Wayne Morris (*Ed Ryan*), Paul Fix (*Luke Andrews*), Frank Ferguson (*Marshal Bullock*), Rick Vallin (*William Vance*), Jack Larson (*John Jenkins*), James Flavin (*Captain of Rangers*), William Fawcett (*Soapy*), Robert Bice (*Al Slade*), Mickey Simpson (*Tom Traynor*), George Wallace (*Clampett*), John Crawford (*Ranger Stockton*), Stanley Price (*Hank Caldwell*), Lyle Talbot (*Telegraph Operator*).

Decent oater entry has Texas Ranger Morris posing as a wanted criminal to infiltrate a gang whose members all have concocted personalities as respectable townspeople, including Ferguson as the local sheriff. A semi-documentary flavor is added via offscreen narration (a la DRAGNET) which comments on the action.

p, Vincent M. Fennelly; d, Thomas Carr; w, Dan Ullman; ph, Ernest Miller; m, Raoul Kraushaar; ed, Sam Fields.

Western   **(PR:A MPAA:NR)**

STAR OF THE CIRCUS   (SEE: HIDDEN MENACE, 1940, Brit.)

STAR PACKER, THE*   (1934) 54m Lone Star/MON bw

John Wayne (*U.S. Marshal John Travers*), Verna Hillie (*Anita Matlock*), George ["Gabby"] Hayes (*Matt Matlock/"The Shadow"*), Yakima Canutt (*Yak, John's Indian Partner*), Ed Dwire (*Mason*), Ed Parker (*Parker*), George Cleveland (*Old Jake, the Matlock Cook*), William Franey (*Pete, Town Bum*), Tom Lingham (*Sheriff Davis*), Art Ortega (*Henchman*), Tex Palmer (*Stagecoach Driver*), Davie Aldrich (*Boy*), Glen Strange.

An early Wayne series entry that pushes plausibility to the limit, without providing much in the way of action. Wayne plays the U.S. Marshal who rides into a town victimized by a gang headed by a mysterious figure. While romancing Hillie, Wayne appoints the locals deputies, then identifies Hayes as the one responsible for all the shenanigans.

p, Paul Malvern; d&w, Robert N. Bradbury (based on a story by Bradbury); ph, Archie Stout, ed, Carl Pierson; md, Abe Meyer.

Western   **Cas.**   **(PR:A MPAA:NR)**

STAR PILOT*   (1977, Ital.) 95m Monarch c (AKA: 2 + 5 MISSIONE
                                                                      HYDRA)

Kirk Morris, Gordon Mitchell, Leonora Ruff.

Poorly produced science fiction film has an alien spacecraft landing in Rome where a bunch of crazy Italians try to figure out what's going on. Musclebound Morris and Mitchell are the heroes of the picture, originally released in 1966 but given another shot in 1977 to try to cash in on the STAR WARS craze.

p, Aldo Calamara, Ermanno Curti; d, Pietro Francisci; w, Francisci, Curti, Girolami, Michael Elder.

Fantasy   **(PR:A MPAA:PG)**

STAR REPORTER*½   (1939) 62m MON bw

Warren Hull (*John*), Marsha Hunt (*Barbara*), Morgan Wallace (*Draper*), Clay Clement (*Whittaker*), Wallis Clark (*Burnette*), Virginia Howell (*Mrs. Randolph*), Paul Fix (*Clipper*), Joseph Crehan (*Gordon*), Eddie Kane (*Sam Grey*).

Far-fetched story has Hull inheriting a newspaper when his father is murdered by notorious hoods. Hull uses the newspaper to wage war against the criminal element and avenge the death of his father. But the plot gets out of hand when Hull discovers that one of the men responsible for his father's murder is actually his real father. This man suddenly turns honest and provides all the evidence needed to clean up the town. Parallel pacing of various plot elements works well in moving the plot along, but this is not enough to overcome characters which have no resemblance to real human beings, not to mention the implausibility of the story itself.

p, E.B. Derr; d, Howard Bretherton; w, John T. Neville (based on a story by Neville); ph, Arthur Martinelli; ed, Russell Schoengarth.

Crime/Drama   **Cas.**   **(PR:A MPAA:NR)**

STAR SAID NO, THE (SEE: CALLAWAY WENT THATAWAY, 1951)

STAR SPANGLED GIRL*   (1971) 92m PAR c

Sandy Duncan (*Amy Cooper*), Tony Roberts (*Andy Hobart*), Todd Susman (*Norman Cornell*), Elizabeth Allen (*Mrs. MacKaninee, the Landlady*), Artie Lewis Mr. Karlson, Allen Jung (*Hip Woo, the Laundryman*), Helen Kleeb (*YWCA Receptionist*), Harry Northup (*Cowboy on Bus*), Gordon Bosserman, Jim Connors (*Karlson's Boys*), Peter Hobbs (*Man in Car*).

Poorly realized project in which Duncan plays the all-American girl up against the phony leftist ideals of newspaper people Roberts and Susman. The little bit of a story that does exist is given no aid by a direction more appropriate to TV and performances the caliber of Saturday morning cartoons.

p, Howard W. Koch; d, Jerry Paris; w, Arnold Margolin, Jim Parker (based on the play by Neil Simon); ph, Sam Leavitt (Movielab Color); m, Charles Fox; ed, Frank Bracht; prod d, Lawrence G. Paull; set d, Reg Allen; m/l, Fox, Norman Gimble; makeup, Lee Harmon.

Comedy   **(PR:A   MPAA:G)**

STAR SPANGLED RHYTHM*½**   (1942) 99m PAR bw

Betty Hutton (*Polly Judson*), Eddie Bracken (*Jimmy Webster*), Victor Moore (*Pop Webster*), Anne Revere (*Sarah*), Walter Abel (*Frisbee*), Cass Daley (*Mimi*), Macdonald Carey (*Louie the Lug*), Gil Lamb (*Hi-Pockets*), William Haade (*Duffy*), Bob Hope (*Master of Ceremonies*), Fred MacMurray, Franchot Tone, Ray Milland, Lynne Overman (*Men Playing Cards Skit*), Dorothy Lamour, Veronica Lake, Paulette Goddard, Arthur Treacher, Walter Catlett, Sterling Holloway (*Sweater, Sarong, and Peekaboo Bang Number*), Tom Dugan (*Hitler*), Paul Porcasi (*Mussolini*), Richard Loo (*Hirohito*), Alan Ladd (*Scarface*), Mary Martin, Dick Powell, Golden Gate Quartette (*Dreamland Number*), William Bendix, Jerry Colonna, Maxine Ardell, Marjorie Deanne, Lorraine Miller, Marion Martin, Chester Clute (*Bob Hope Skit*), Vera Zorina, Johnnie Johnston, Frank Faylen (*Black Magic Number*), Eddie "Rochester" Anderson, Katherine Dunham, Slim and Sam, Woodrow [Woody] Strode (*Smart as a Tack Number*), Susan Hayward (*Genevieve -- Priorities Number*), Ernest Truex (*Murgatroyd -- Priorities Number*), Marjorie Reynolds, Betty Rhodes, Dona Drake, Louise La Planche, Lorraine Miller, Donivee Lee, Don Castle, Frederic Henry, Sherman Sanders (*Swing Shift Number*), Bing Crosby (*Old Glory Number*), Virginia Brissac (*Lady from Iowa -- Old Glory Number*), Irving Bacon (*New Hampshire Farmer -- Old Glory Number*), Matt McHugh (*Man from Brooklyn -- Old Glory Number*), Peter Potter (*Georgia Boy -- Old Glory Number*), Edward M. Marr (*Heavy -- Old Glory Number*), Gary Crosby (*Himself*), Albert Dekker, Cecil Kellaway, Ellen Drew, Jimmy Lydon, Charles Smith, Frances Gifford, Susanna Foster, Robert Preston, Christopher King, Alice Kirby, Marcella Phillips (*Finale*), Walter Dare Wahl and Company (*Specialty Act*), Cecil B. DeMille, Preston Sturges, Ralph Murphy (*Themselves*), Maynard Holmes, James Millican (*Sailors*), Eddie Johnson (*Tommy*), Arthur Loft (*Casey*), Dorothy Granger, Barbara Pepper, Jean Phillips, Lynda Grey (*Girls*), Boyd Davis (*Capt. Kingsley*), Frank Moran (*Man with Sturges*), Eddie Dew, Rod Cameron (*Petty Officers*), Barney Dean, Jack Hope (*Themselves*), John Shay (*Sentry*), Keith Richards (*Officer*), Jack Roberts (*Assistant Director*), Karin Booth (*Kate*), Gladys Blake (*Liz*).

This array of Paramount's brightest stars was at once funny, tuneful, and joyous. More importantly, it is an historical cinematic document that freezes all these great stars in a moment in time in one picture. The cast list should be perused carefully for it not only includes 16 "above the title" actors, it also has two score of the best character people in the business as well as many directors playing themselves. The bare-bones plot has sailor Bracken getting off his ship and coming to Hollywood to visit his dad, Moore, a one-time silent western actor who has been reduced to working as Paramount's gate guard at the main entrance on Melrose Place. Bracken has been carrying on a correspondence with Hutton and she has bolstered the charade Moore has been playing. She's a switchboard operator and she and Moore have Bracken convinced that Moore runs the studio as its' top executive. Bracken and some his tar pals are due to arrive and Moore can't bear the thought of having his lie exposed. Since he is so beloved by everyone on the lot, the entire population of the Paramount company is pressed into service. The studio head leaves for a short while and Moore is placed in the posh office where he greets Bracken and the other sailors. The phones keep ringing with calls from heavyweights in the business and Moore takes the calls as the studio chief and hurls insults at the callers. When the boss gets back, everyone at the studio sneers at him and he can't understand why, never knowing that Moore has been acting in his stead. Moore and Hutton lead Bracken and his friends around the lot (and we see scores of actors as themselves or working in imaginary films) and then Hutton squires Bracken back to his ship and vows to marry him the following day if he can get some more leave on shore. Bracken appeals to Davis, his captain, for the extended leave and it is granted when Bracken says that he can get all of the famous stars he's met to do a special variety show for the sailors docked in the harbor. The following day, Moore sneaks into the boss' office and uses his phony power to order all of the stars to perform in the huge gala. When the boss, Abel, finds out what's happening, he fires Moore and bars him from the lot. Hutton personally appeals to the actors and actresses and tells them what's happened and that they must keep the truth from Bracken or he'll lose face with his crewmates. They all agree to perform. Abel tries to countermand Hutton's handiwork but the stars will do the show anyhow and when the event is a huge success, Moore is rehired by the studio in a better job. Lots of good music by Johnny Mercer and Harold Arlen. The songs include "A Sweater, a Sarong and a Peek-a-Boo Bang" (sung by Paulette Goddard, Dorothy Lamour, Veronica Lake – who was looped by Martha Mears, then parodized by Sterling Holloway, Arthur Treacher, Walter Catlett), "That Old Black Magic" (sung by Johnny Johnston, danced by Vera Zorina, Oscar nominated as Best Song), "Hit the Road to Dreamland" (sung by Dick Powell, Mary Martin, then again by the Golden Gate Quartet), "Old Glory" (Bing Crosby and the company against a studio set of Mount Rushmore and lots of waving flags). Other songs include "On the Swing Shift," "Doing It for Defense," "Sharp as a Tack,"

"He Loved Me Till the All-Clear Came." Many funny bits including Bendix and Hope in a shower as Hope tries to hide behind Bendix's body. A number of specialty bits, most notably the sticky-finger routine by Walter Dare Wahl (this was also seen in the musical "High Button Shoes") and a stand-out comedy spot with Alan Ladd and MacDonald Carey. Carey is pleading for his life in a pool hall and Ladd reaches into his trenchcoat and shoots him, with a bow and arrow. Crosby's 8 year-old son, Gary, makes his film debut. Many of the jokes will be lost on modern audiences because they are of the time but it's still very worth seeing, if only to watch so many stars at one time. Dolan was also nominated for his work.

p, Joseph Sistrom; d, George Marshall; w, Harry Tugend, Arthur Phillips (uncredited), sketches by George Kaufman, Arthur Ross, Fred Saidy Norman Panama, Melvin Frank; ph, Leo Tover, Theodore Sparkuhl; m, Robert Emmett Dolan; ed, Paul Weatherwax; md, Dolan; art d, Hans Dreier, Ernst Fegte; set d, Steve Seymour; cos, Edith Head; ch, Danny Dare, George Balanchine; m/l, Harold Arlen, Johnny Mercer; makeup, Wally Westmore.

Musical/Comedy   **(PR:A   MPAA:NR)**

STAR TREK: THE MOTION PICTURE½**   (1979) 132m PAR c

William Shatner (*Capt. James T. Kirk*), Leonard Nimoy (*Mr. Spock, Science Officer*), DeForest Kelley (*Dr. Leonard "Bones" McCoy*), James Doohan (*Chief Engineer Montgomery "Scotty" Scott*), George Takei (*Sulu*), Majel Barrett (*Dr. Christine Chapel*), Walter Koenig (*Chekov*), Nichelle Nichols (*Uhura*), Persis Khambatta (*Ilia*), Stephen Collins (*Cmdr. Willard Decker*), Mark Lenard (*Klingon Captain*), Billy Van Zandt (*Alien Boy*), Grace Lee Whitney (*Janice Rand*), Roger Aaron Brown (*Epsilon Technician*), Gary Faga (*Airlock Technician*), David Gautreaux (*Cmdr. Branch*), John D. Gowans (*Assistant to Rand*), Jon Rashad Kamal (*Ltd. Cmdr. Sonak*), Howard Itzkowitz (*Cargo Deck Ensign*), Marcy Lafferty (*Chief DiFalco*), Jeri McBride (*Technician*), Michele Ameen Billy (*Lieutenant*), Terrence O'Conner (*Chief Ross*), Michael Rougas (*Lt. Cleary*).

It finally happened. The characters loved by millions, never faltering even though the series had been off the air for nearly ten years, were born again. And this was the most exciting aspect of a film for which $40 million was spent to produce a story that becomes lost amid technical gadgetry. But a generation of young adults who had grown up watching one of the most successful television programs ever, really did find it fascinating to see what had become of the crew members of the U.S.S. Enterprise. Shatner is now an admiral called upon one last time to take over the command of his old ship in order to halt a strange alien craft that is gobbling up everything in its path and is headed directly for Earth. To undertake this mission he calls upon the assistance of all the old crew members, and some new ones as well. Spock (Nimoy) is interrupted while performing ardent Vulcan rituals and urged to use his superior intellect and cool logic to aid his old pal. The most interesting character of the bunch is Kelley as the crotchety doctor who must be tricked away from his life of hedonism to serve on a voyage he wants no part of. With Sulu (Takei) at the controls, the U.S.S. Enterprise takes on one more mission "to boldly go where no man has never gone before." This imposing craft proves to be nothing more than a 300-year-old NASA ship that has been programmed to continuously collect information and send it back to its creator. It has gotten out of control, but Shatner comes up with a plan to release the information the craft has been gathering. The method he uses is not nearly as intriguing as any single episode of the television series. Playing up the sentimental aspects, the script desperately tries to inject the sort of sophisticated plot twist the series was known for. But here it seems forced proving perhaps that it is not money as much as a good story that makes for an entertaining film. THE WRATH OF KHAN, Star Trek's sequel, would prove to be much more successful. The third episode in the movie series would be directed by Nimoy himself. It was called STAR TREK III, and it was a total flop.

p, Gene Roddenberry; d, Robert Wise; w, Harold Livingston, Roddenberry (based on a story by Alan Dean Foster, based on the TV program "Star Trek"); ph, Richard H. Kline (Panavision, Metrocolor); m, Jerry Goldsmith; ed, Todd Ramsey; prod d, Harold Michelson; art d, Michelson, Leon Harris, Joe Jennings, John Vallone; set d, Linda De Scenna; cos, Robert Fletcher; spec eff, Douglas Trumbull, John Dykstra, Dave Stewart, Don Baker, Robert Swarthe, Harry Moreau, Richard Yuricich; makeup, Fred Phillips.

Science Fiction   **Cas.**   **(PR:A   MPAA:G)**

STAR TREK II: THE WRATH OF KHAN*   (1982) 113m PAR c

William Shatner (*Adm. James T. Kirk*), Leonard Nimoy (*Mr. Spock*), DeForest Kelley (*Dr. Leonard "Bones" McCoy*), James Doohan (*Chief Engineer Montgomery "Scotty" Scott*), Walter Koenig (*Chekov*), George Takei (*Sulu*), Nichelle Nichols (*Cmdr. Uhura*), Bibi Besch (*Dr. Carol Marcus*), Merritt Butrick (*David*), Paul Winfield (*Starship Reliant Captain Terrell*), Kirstie Alley (*Saavik*), Ricardo Montalban (*Khan*), Ike Eisenmann, John Vargas, John Winston, Paul Kent, Nicholas Guest, Russell Takaki, Kevin Sullivan, Joel Marstan, Teresa E. Victor, Dianne Harper, David Ruprecht, Marcy Vosburgh.

Of the three Star Trek films, this second entry comes closest to attaining the vitality and ingenuity that made the television series such great fun. Unfortunately, it also has an overabundance of schmaltziness and blatant sentimentalism, particularly in the ending, which has Spock sacrificing his life so that the crew of the Enterprise will be able to continue on their flight across space. Shatner is still an admiral in the space fleet, but his desk job doesn't allow him to do the kind of work that is deep inside his blood. Cajoled by Nimoy and Kelley, the admiral agrees to take command of a mission that seems basically harmless; but the sudden appearance of Montalban makes for a very sticky situation. Actually a follow-up to the television episode in which Montalban starred as a ship commander gone bad and placed on a prison colony, the film gives him an opportunity to avenge himself against the man responsible for his incarceration. His opportunity comes in the form of a craft commanded by Winfield, which mistakenly lands on the planet where Montalban and his old crew have been passing their time. The crew are little more than savages. It appears that their isolation has developed the more instinctual and survivalist aspects of their personalities. Montalban appears as an almost superhuman being unstoppable and with a sadistic bent. His favorite form of torture is to put a tiny insect inside a person's ear; the bug slowly eats its way to the brain. Winfield is disposed of in this manner, as is Chekov (Koenig), and the forewarning presence of the little creature remains in the viewer's mind throughout the entire movie. Assisting on a project (appropriately named "Genesis") that is attempting to reintroduce living organisms in decaying areas, Montalban gets wind of Shatner's presence and gains a rudimentary understanding of the project. He quickly devises a plan to use this knowledge to his best advantage, and the result is a battle that puts the two sides in a virtual stalemate. Only when Spock sacrifices his life are Kirk and crew allowed to survive. Ending is a bit too forced when it shows Nimoy laying down his cold exterior for his moment of supreme sacrifice, and the intended sequel is telegraphed much too strongly. An interesting aspect of this film that was never brought into the television series was Shatner's family life back on Earth. The woman who heads the Genesis project is his old lover, with whom he had a son who is also part of the project. The tension between Shatner and his son (Butrick) emphasizes what the captain gave up in order to pursue his desire to shuttle across space. This feature was made for under $11 million, while the original cost in excess of $40 million, was not nearly as interesting or as good the film.

p, Robert Sallin; d, Nicholas Meyer; w, Jack B. Sowards (based on a story by Harve Bennett, Sowards and on the TV program "Star Trek" created by Gene Roddenberry); ph, Gayne Rescher (Panavision, Movielab Color); m, James Horner; ed, William P. Dornisch; prod d, Joseph R. Jennings; art d, Michael Minor; set d, Charles M. Graffeo; spec eff, Bob Dawson, Ken Ralston, Jim Veillieux, Alan Howarth; makeup, Werner Keppler, J.L. McCoy.

Fantasy **Cas.** **(PR:A MPAA:PG)**

STAR WARS***** (1977) 121m FOX c

Mark Hamill *(Luke Skywalker)*, Harrison Ford *(Han Solo)*, Carrie Fisher *(Princess Leia Organa)*, Peter Cushing *(Grand Moff Tarkin)*, Alec Guinness *(Ben [Obi-Wan] Kenobi)*, Anthony Daniels *(See Threepio [C3P0])*, Kenny Baker *(Artoo-Detoo [R2D2])*, Peter Mayhew *(Chewbacca)*, David Prowse *(Lord Darth Vader)*, Phil Brown *(Uncle Owen Lars)*, Shelagh Fraser *(Aunt Beru Lars)*, Jack Purvis *(Chief Jawa)*, Alex McCrindle *(Gen. Dodonna)*, Eddie Byrne *(Gen. Willard)*, Drewe Henley *(Red Leader)*, Dennis Lawson *(Red Two [Wedge])*, Garrick Hagon *(Red Three [Biggs])*, Jack Klaff *(Red Four [John D])*, William Hootkins Red Six *([Porkins])*, Angus McInnis *(Gold Leader)*, Jeremy Sinden *(Gold Two)*, Graham Ashley *(Gold Five)*, Don Henderson *(Gen. Taggi)*, Richard LeParmentier *(Gen. Motti)*, Leslie Schofield *(Commander No.1)*.

One of the best science-fiction movies ever made, STAR WARS was shot for a pittance when one thinks about what was up there on screen. It looked as though it cost at least three times the $9.5 million it took to make the movie and while one can find some fault with the simplistic dialog and the Zen overtones of the attitudes, it remains a rollicking good time from the first fade-in to the final lengthy credits. Lucas owes a debt to the years he must have spent watching "Flash Gordon" and "Buck Rogers" serials and anyone with even a smattering of knowledge about old films will see from whence much of this sprang. The difference is that Lucas did it better than some originals and thus created his own original, which has since been aped by many lesser filmmakers. Shot in Guatemala, Tunisia, Death Valley, and with interiors done at Elstree Studios in Borehamwood, England, STAR WARS was the next logical step for Lucas, who began his career with the experimental THX-1138, a futuristic fantasy that received acclaim from sci-fi fans but did sparse business. Between that and this, he directed the successful AMERICAN GRAFFITI, which inspired Fox to give him the money for this movie after Universal and United Artists turned their thumbs down. STAR WARS begins with a title card that tells about this happening "a long, long, time ago, in a galaxy far away" and quickly prints the "back story" so we know that this is not the beginning, but is actually the middle. (There was a planned total of nine movies in the series with sequels and prequels on the boards.) This particular galaxy is being ruled by the vicious and uncompromising Cushing and his cruel aide, Prowse (whose deep, evil voice is from the throat of James Earl Jones). They live and work aboard a leviathan space station known as Death Star, whose size is roughly that of Rhode Island. Fisher is a princess from one of the smaller worlds and she has stolen plans to the Death Star which she managed to get to a computer-robot, Baker. Fisher has now been captured and the small robot and its golden pal, Daniels, covertly steal aboard a small spaceship and flee the Death Star for a trip to a nearby world. (Baker and Daniels are marvelous comedy relief, a metal Abbott and Costello with engaging personalities.) Daniels and Baker arrive on the dry planet and are instantly captured by junk dealers and placed on the auction block to be sold to the highest bidder. They are bought by Hamill, a young agriculturist trying to scrape a living from the arid ground, and his uncle, Brown. Baker's mechanisms are bollixed so they get the robots for a low price. Hamill sets to work repairing the innards and is stunned to see a hologram of Fisher that pleads for aid from the famous Guinness, who is the last member of a planetary round table of Knights known as "The Jedis." The hologram is on a loop (like a tape) and repeats itself often until Hamill decides to take action. Hamill has vaguely heard of "The Jedis" and knows that they were, for years, the vigilantes who kept order in the universe in a benevolent, though forceful, fashion. Baker is the robotic equivalent of delirious and he is talking in circles as he leaves Hamill's farmhouse and walks into the torrid desert. Hamill and Daniels go out after him and are immediately set upon by nomads who pillage the area. These creatures are known as "The Sand People" and a battle takes place during which the metal arm of Daniels is torn from the socket and it appears that Hamill's life is about to be snuffed out. Suddenly, Guinness appears, a mysterious figure who seems to have come from the air. The bandits race away upon seeing him. Guinness has been searching for Hamill to tell him the following: his father was a one-time "Jedi" who was killed by turncoat Prowse, a formerly honest Knight who went over to the other side. Guinness gives Hamill a sword and explains that the power of Good comes from a higher source, an unexplainable strength known as "The Force" which can always be counted upon if one knows how to tap into it. Hamill tells Guinness about Fisher's plight and is invited to join in the rescue. He is not so sure he wants to risk his life for this woman he's never met and for a cause he knows nothing about. Later, he discovers that Cushing's men, who have been scouring the planets looking for Baker and Daniels, scorched his farm and killed his uncle and his aunt, Fraser. That's enough for Hamill to change his mind. Now he has a personal score to settle with Cushing and the others of his ilk. Hamill decides to follow in his father's footsteps. But the Death Star is way up there and they are down here and the problem is that they need a spaceship to get them off this planet. They go into town and enter a local bar filled with the oddest creatures anyone has ever seen. (The actors in this memorable scene were cast from a London office that specializes in ugly people. With those weird faces as a start, the makeup team made them even uglier. In one very funny bit, the camera pans these creatures, most of whom look as though they are straight out of THE ISLAND OF DR. MOREAU, and then the bartender refuses service to a robot, saying, "We don't serve their kind here]") Inside the bar, they locate Ford, a professional spaceship charter pilot who is for hire by anyone. Ford's sidekick is Mayhew, a "Wookie" that is a combination of a gorilla, a human, and several other species. A deal is struck and they get to Ford's ancient but souped-up space ship. Once in the stratosphere, they learn that Fisher's planet has been wiped out by Cushing because the hostage, Fisher, would not inform him where the space rebels are hiding. Cushing has long wanted to eradicate this last stronghold of resistance and Fisher knows which of the many planets is their hideout. Since she cared naught for her own life and refused to be intimidated by torture or death, Cushing exacted revenge by destroying her home and everyone on it. Ford's spaceship comes too close to the Death Star and is drawn into the huge Satellite by a powerful magnet. Inside the Death Star, they manage to get away, then knock out some of the guards and change clothes with them so they look as though they belong there. While this is going on, Guinness finds the central controls for the ship and pulls out some of the semi-conductors and doohickeys, thus crippling it somewhat. Baker and Daniels search the Death Star until they locate where Fisher is being held captive. Hamill, Ford, and the hairy Mayhew now rescue her and are being chased by the soldiers. They all fall into the central garbage dump where a "being" lives. It's a mammoth monster that eats everything sent its way. The walls of the dump begin to move in (in a bit right out of Edgar Allan Poe's "The Pit And The Pendulum") and they are doomed to be pressed flat. Daniels and Baker arrive in the nick of time to stop the mechanical compressor and all race for Ford's spaceship, which is still aboard the Death Star. Prowse, as a one-time Knight, is possessed of extra-sensory perception and he senses the fact that Guinness is nearby so he goes around the station looking for him, knowing full well that a fight to the death is in the offing. The two mortal enemies meet and duel each other with laser-beam swords. (The first time this was ever seen was on a Saturday morning TV show, which starred Chuck McCann and Bob Denver, known as "Far-Out Space Nuts" and McCann recalls seeing Lucas on the set, years before this movie was shot.) With one eye on Prowse and one eye on the escaping group, who are stealthily moving toward Ford's spaceship and safety, Guinness lets Prowse thwack him with the laser, then vanishes as he's hit. His death releases "The Force" from his body and, so we are told, it now moves into the bodies of the fleeing Hamill, Fisher, and Ford. They board the ship and make an exciting departure from the Death Star and head for the small planet where the rebels are hiding and waiting. Cushing orders his ship after Ford's but Ford turns on a special after-burner and leaves the other in his wake. Eventually, they know they will be caught up with but this superior speed has given them some extra time. They land on the secret planet, the fourth moon of a larger world. Safely there, they are able to extract the remainder of the information from Baker's data banks. There is one place only that a fighter ship could use to immobilize the Death Star. It requires superior flying down a long, slim rut in the Death Star's surface. Once the ship got to the end of the groove, a well-placed missile could send an explosive into a tiny pore in the skin of the Death Star and cause an explosion. That blast would totally destroy the Death Star due to an intricate chain reaction. Volunteers are called for the mission and Hamill joins them but Ford wants no part of it. He made a deal to save Fisher and his job is over. Now, pay him off and let him go somewhere else to ply his trade. The Death Star is coming closer to the small planet and decisions must be made right now. A squadron of fighters goes up after the Death Star and the larger firepower of the battle station soon takes a toll. One by one, the other fighters are knocked out of the sky or disabled. Hamill is in his ship with Baker and fears he cannot complete the task when he hears the voice of the dead Guinness telling him to stop thinking and just let it happen (a Zen practice) and allow the "Force" to take over. Hamill does that, then notes that Ford must have changed his mind because he is up there as well with Mayhew and the two are pot-shotting the enemy ships which have been shooting down the rebels. Hamill trusts his inner being and rides his ship down the long groove while he is being pursued. At the precise correct instant, his hand automatically hits the trigger, the missile is shot, and he flies off to see the Death Star begin to explode. Cushing and all the others are killed but Prowse barely manages to flee in a fighter. Back on the rebel planet, Ford and Hamill accept the accolades of the others and are given medals. Awards are also handed out to Mayhew, Baker, and Daniels and the picture ends as it must, with the forces of evil having been dispelled by the "Force" of Good. Lest you fear that this is a kiddie picture, and if you are one of the very few who never saw this movie which grossed near $200 million when it was first released, be aware that it can be enjoyed by anyone of any age, although some of the action and the language may be a trifle rough for really young children. Fisher had only appeared in "Shampoo" before this while Hamill was making his on-camera debut, after doing the voice only in WIZARDS and some TV shows. Ford had a much richer background with acting roles for 11 years prior to STAR WARS. He'd already done DEAD HEAT ON A MERRY-GO-ROUND, A TIME FOR KILLING, JOURNEY TO SHILOH, GETTING STRAIGHT, AMERICAN GRAFFITI, and THE CONVERSATION. Lucas and his producer had wanted to remake "Flash Gordon" but the asking price was out of their range so Lucas wrote an original, thereby making himself a multi-millionaire because he was able to reap the huge profits from the merchandising ventures, which included lunch buckets, models, T-shirts, dolls, every possible kind of toy, and several other items, all of which would have enriched the coffers of the people who owned "Flash Gordon" if they had had any sense. Prowse had worked before with ultimate villain Cushing in FRANKENSTEIN AND THE MONSTER FROM HELL so they already had a relationship. Baker is a "little person" under three feet tall and reputed to be one of the smallest men on earth. Mayhew is over seven feet tall and was found working at a hospital in London. They added special boots to his feet which made him large enough to qualify for the NBA draft. Despite all the good acting, it is the special effects that set this above the crowd. Wizard John Dykstra used a computer-assisted camera to help in his work and the result was three effects per minute (363 all told in a 121-minute picture) which is many more than Kubrick used in 2001, A SPACE ODYSSEY. There is no mistaking the good guys from the bad, a plus because there is no time for heavy analysis from anyone in the audience as events are happening with such speed that we can only marvel at them, not think about them. Two more films were made, THE RETURN OF THE JEDI and THE EMPIRE STRIKES BACK and both were also marvels of effects but had nowhere near the pow that this one had. All told, the three movies made more than $700 million and continue to rake it in. With re-releases and cassettes and TV showings, Lucas' company will probably recognize about a billion from the movies. If you saw Fritz Lang's METROPOLIS (recently re-released with a new score), you'll recognize where the gold-plated Daniels came from. And the idea of having only a small area to bomb was previously seen in several movies, notably SQUADRON 633 and THE DAM BUSTERS. Despite all of the financial rewards, the movie did not impress the Academy's final outcome. It was nominated for Best Picture, Best Direction, Best original Screenplay, Best Supporting Actor, Best Score, Best Art Direction, Best Costumes, Best Set Decoration, Best Film Editing, Best Sound, and Best Visual Effects. The winners were Barry, Reynolds, and Dilley for their Art Direction; Christian for his Set Decoration; Hirsch, Lucas, and Chew for their Editing; Mollo's costumes; John Williams for his score; John Stears, John Dykstra, Grant McCune, Robert Blalack, Richard Edlund for their Visual Effects; and the sound team of Bob Minkler, Derek Ball, Ray West, and Don MacDougall. A special Oscar was given to Benjamin Burt, Jr., for having created the robot voices. If you like science fiction, you'll love STAR WARS. If you hate science fiction, you'll probably love it even more because you'll have nothing to compare it with. President Reagan used the term to describe a defense system planned by the U.S. and Lucas objected to that because he is not a supporter of militaristic moves. He sued to cease and desist, and lost. Lucas is very bright, very rich, and very influential, but when it comes to fighting City Hall (or, in this case, the White House), you can't win.

p, Gary Kurtz; d&w, George Lucas; ph, Gilbert Taylor (Panavision, Technicolor); m, John T. Williams; ed, Paul Hirsch, Marcia Lucas, Richard Chew; prod d, John Barry; art d, Norman Reynolds, Leslie Dilley; set d, Roger Christian; cos, John Mollo, Ron Beck; spec eff, John Dykstra; anim, Adam Beckett; makeup, Stuart Freeborn, Rick Baker, Douglas Beswick; stunts, Peter Diamond; spec ph eff, John Dykstra; spec mech eff, John Stears; spec dialog, sound eff, Ben Burtt; sound ed, Sam Shaw, Robert R. Rutledge, Gordon Davidson, Gene Corso; anim, Rotoscope, Adam Beckett;

stop-motion anim, Jon Berg, Philip Tippet; spec visual eff, John Dykstra, Grant McCune, Robert Blalack, Richard Edlund; sound, Bob Minkler, Derek Ball, Ray West, Don MacDougall.

Science Fiction/Adventure   Cas.   (PR:A-C MPAA:PG)

STAR WITNESS***   (1931) 68m WB bw

Walter Huston (*Dist. Atty. Whitlock*), Charles "Chic" Sale (*Grandad Summerville*), Frances Starr (*Ma Leeds*), Grant Mitchell (*Pa Leeds*), Sally Blane (*Sue Leeds*), Edward J. Nugent (*Jackie Leeds*), Ralph Ince (*Maxey Campo*), Dickie Moore (*Donny Leeds*), George Ernest (*Ned Leeds*), Russell Hopton (*Deputy Thorpe*), Tom Dugan (*Brown*), Robert Elliott (*Williams*), Fletcher Norton (*Dopey*), Guy d'Ennery (*Jack Short*), Noel Madison (*Horan*), Mike Donlin (*Mickey*), Ed Dearing (*Sackett*), Nat Pendleton (*Big Jack*), George Irving (*Judge*), Allan Lane (*Clerk*), William A. Wellman (*Company Workman*).

A film that takes all the romanticism out of gangsterdom, something unusual but badly needed during this period of cinematic history. After a vicious mob battle during which the Leeds family has witnessed enough of the action to put the kingpin of one of the gangs behind bars for good, the family is terrorized endlessly. The gangsters' tactics include a severe beating of the father and the kidnaping of one of the sons, all to insure that no one from the family will testify. But the aging Sale, a crochety old war veteran, doesn't allow the hoods to scare him in the least; he rescues his grandson, then appears before the court with evidence sending the mob boss to the chair. Sale adds humor, sentiment, and charm to his role of the grandfather of a family he sees innocently victimized. Wellman's direction meshes Sales' performance with the movement of the story making for a powerful denouncement of gangsterdom.

d, William Wellman; w, Lucien Hubbard (based on a story by Hubbard); ph, James Van Trees; ed, Hal McLernon.

Crime/Drama   (PR:A MPAA:NR)

STARCRASH*½   (1979) 92m New World c (AKA: STELLA STAR, STAR CRASH)

Marjoe Gortner (*Akton*), Caroline Munro (*Stella Star*), Christopher Plummer (*The Emperor*), David Hasselhoff (*Simon*), Robert Tessier (*Thor*), Joe Spinnell (*Count Zarth Arn*), Nadia Cassini (*Queen of the Amazon*), Judd Hamilton (*Elle*), Hamilton Camp (*Voice of Elle*).

Cheaply made science-fiction film in which Munro plays an expert pilot called upon by the Master of the Universe to stop the evildoings of Spinnell. Aided only by a humanoid robot, Hamilton, and an alien, Gortner, with some special skills, the fiery woman saves the universe. Although dialog is extremely stilted and special effects are cheesy, STARCRASH possesses a naive charm reminiscent of some of the classic science-fiction films of the fifties.

p, Nat Wachsberger, Patrick Wachsberger; d, Lewis Coates [Luigi Cozzi]; w, Coates, Nat Wachsberger; ph, Paul Beeson, Roberto D'Ettore (Metrocolor); m, John Barry; ed, Sergio Montanari; prod d, Aurelio Crugnolla; spec eff, Armando Valcauda, Germano Natali, Matteo Verzini.

Fantasy   Cas.   (PR:C MPAA:PG)

STARDUST, 1938   (SEE: HE LOVED AN ACTRESS, 1938, Brit.)

STARDUST½**   (1974, Brit.) 113m Goodtimes Enterprises/COL c

David Essex (*Jim Maclaine*), Adam Faith (*Mike*), Larry Hagman (*Porter Lee Austin*), Ines Des Longchamps (*Danielle*), Rosalind Ayres (*Jeanette*), Marty Wilde (*Colin Day*), Edd Byrnes (*TV Interviewer*), Keith Moon (*J.D. Clover*), Dave Edmunds (*Alex*), Paul Nicholas (*Johnny*), Karl Howman (*Stevie*), Rick Lee Parmentier (*Felix Hoffman*), Peter Duncan (*Kevin*), John Normington (*Harrap*), Dave Daker (*Ralph Woods*), James Hazeldine (*Brian*), Anthony Naylor (*Keith Nolan*), Charlotte Cornwall (*Sally Potter*), Rose Marie Klespitz (*Lucille*), Michael Elphick, Claire Russell, Bobby Sparrow.

A sequel to THAT'LL BE THE DAY which takes up the rise to fame of a pop star at the point where the earlier picture ended. Essex is again the singer who suddenly finds himself the center of vast attention and the possessor of enough money to buy himself a castle in Spain. But as he immerses himself in casual sex and the heavy drug scene, his ego is warped by the ever-increasing adulation of his fans. The core of his personality seems to get burned away, and by the end of the film he is little more than a vacuum. A realistic and biting portrayal which stresses how important sincere human relations are for everyone, regardless of prestige or power. Essex, a pop star himself, was portraying an experience very close to his own life. Other members of the cast include Dave Edmunds and Keith Moon, whose real-life excesses led to his early death.

p, David Puttnam, Sanford Lieberson; d, Michael Apted; w, Ray Connolly; ph, Tony Richmond (Technicolor); m, Dave Edmunds, Puttnam; ed, Mike Bradsell.

Drama   (PR:O MPAA:R)

STARDUST MEMORIES**½   (1980) 90m UA bw

Woody Allen (*Sandy Bates*), Charlotte Rampling (*Dorrie*), Jessica Harper (*Daisy*), Marie-Christine Barrault (*Isobel*), Tony Roberts (*Tony*), Daniel Stern (*Actor*), Amy Wright (*Shelley*), Helen Hanft (*Vivian Orkin*), John Rothman (*Jack Abel*), Ann DeSalvo (*Sandy's Sister*), Joan Neuman (*Sandy's Mother*), Ken Chapin (*Sandy's Father*), Leonardo Cimino (*Sandy's Analyst*), Eli Mintz (*Old Man*), Bob Maroff (*Jerry Abraham*).

This is Woody Allen's slap in the face to his fans. Or is it? After a few films in which Allen flirted with bits and pieces of his own life in the screenplays, this time it seems that he's gone directly to personal experience to fashion a movie that pokes fun at those who admire his work. He's a comedian turned director who has achieved prominence in the cinematic world and is now surrounded by hordes of adoring critics who find allegory in his every word, maniacal fans who hang on his burps, thinking they are some sort of pronunciamento from on high, film experts who analyze everything to discover hidden meanings in his body of work. There are times when someone cuts through the pretentiousness to say, "I liked him when he made funny movies, not all this other stuff." That had been a criticism of Allen after his early movies which made no allusions, just wanted to make us laugh. As he matured, he expanded to attempt other things. Sometimes he failed, sometimes he partly succeeded, but he always had to be lauded for the try. This is an episodic picture with the usual neuroses, the problems with women (Rampling, Barrault, Harper) and a number of jokes along the way. But there is a mean spirit underneath it all, as though he'd gotten up on the wrong side of his psychiatrist's couch one day and decided to get even. (A book of Allen's short stories was named "Getting Even.") There are ways to have fun with the pompous persons who surround a celebrity. In the old days, Allen might have been content with being funny. This time, he goes beyond funny and into the land of anger, and it shows. STARDUST MEMORIES, with many laughs and many "inside jokes" (such as the head of United Artists, Andy Albeck, playing a film chief who is worried that the new movie has no laughs), is still a disappointing outing. In a small role note Daniel Stern, who was one of the leads in DINER, then came back as the millionaire rock star in HANNAH AND HER SISTERS and played the lead in the 1986 film THE BOSS'S WIFE. Allen's good friend, Roberts (who has been in many of Allen's movies), does his usual good work. The old man was played by Eli Mintz, who spent years on the TV show "The Goldbergs" as the aged uncle. Songs include: "I'll See You In My Dreams" (Isham Jones, Gus Kahn), "Body and Soul" (John Green, Edward Heyman, Robert Sour, Frank Eyton), "Tropical Mood Meringue" (Sidney Bechet, performed by Bechet), "Tickletoe" (Lester Young, performed by Young and Count Basie and His Orchestra), "Three Little Words," "One O'Clock Jump" (Basie, performed by the Jazz Heaven Orchestra), "Brazil" (Ary Barroso, English words by S.K. Russell, performed by the ODJB), "Night on Bare Mountain," "If Dreams Come True," (Irving Mills, Edgar Sampson, Benny Goodman, played by Chick Webb), "Hebrew School Rag" (Dick Hyman), "Just One of Those Things," "Easy to Love" (Cole Porter, performed by Hyman), "Sugar," "Sweet Georgia Brown," "Moonlight Serenade" (Glenn Miller, Mitchell Parish, performed by Louis Armstrong).

p, Robert Greenhut; d&w, Woody Allen; ph, Gordon Willis; ed, Susan E. Morse; prod d, Santo Loquasto; art d, Michael Molly.

Comedy   Cas.   (PR:C   MPAA:PG)

STARDUST ON THE SAGE*½   (1942) 65m REP bw

Gene Autry (*Gene*), Smiley Burnette (*Frog*), Bill Henry (*Jeff Drew*), Edith Fellows (*Judy Drew*), Louise Currie (*Nancy Drew*), Emmett Vogan (*Pearson*), George Ernest (*Curly*), Vince Barnett (*Haskins*), Betty Farrington (*Mrs. Haskins*), Roy Barcroft (*Murphy*), Tom London (*MacGowan*), Rex Lease, Frank Ellis, Edward Cassidy, Fred Burns, Frank LaRue, Franklyn Farnum, Edmund Cobb, Jerry Jerome, Merrill McCormack, Bert LeBaron, Monte Montague, George DeNormand, Bill Jamison, Jimmy Fox, George Sherwood, William Nestell, Frank O'Connor, Griff Barnett, Frankie Marvin, Lee Shumway, Champion the Horse.

It's one song after another with Autry taking time out from exercising his vocal chords to stop the shiftless foreman of a mining company from going through with his plan to steal the mine from its rightful owners. Autry also performs in the required number of fistfights and horse chases and romances the young heroine, adding up to standard oater entertainment. Songs include: "I'll Never Let You Go Again," "Goodnight, Sweetheart," "When Roses Bloom Again," "Wouldn't You Like to Know," "Home on the Range," "Deep in the Heart of Texas," "Roll on Little Doggies," and "You Are My Sunshine."

p, Harry Grey; d, William Morgan; w, Betty Burbridge (based on a story by Dorrell and Stuart McGowan); ph, Bud Thackery; ed, Edward Mann.

Western   (PR:A   MPAA:NR)

STARFIGHTERS, THE*½   (1964) 78m Riviera/Parade c

Robert Dornan (*Lt. John Witkowski*), Richard Jordahl (*Maj. Stevens*), Shirley Olmstead (*Mary Davidson*), Richard Masters (*Col. Hunt*), Steve Early (*Lt. York*), Robert Winston (*Lt. Lyons*), Carl Rogers (*Congressman Witkowski*), Ralph Thomas (*Capt. O'Brien*), Joan Lougee (*Betty Lyon*).

Silly war yarn has Dornan as the son of former Air Force hero and present congressman Rogers who is trying to prove himself a worthy pilot in a squadron his father disapproves of. Dornan eventually gets a chance to display his skill by flying a mission through a deadly storm. He wins the admiration of both his father and his squadron leader, earning a chance to prove himself in combat.

p,d&w, Will Zens; ph, Leif Rise (Technicolor); m, Stephen Paul; ed, Michael David.

War   (PR:A   MPAA:NR)

STARHOPS**   (1978) 82m Roseworld/First American c

Dorothy Buhrman (*Danielle*), Sterling Frazier (*Cupcake*), Jillian Kesner (*Angel*), Peter Paul Liapis (*Ron*), Anthony Mannino (*Kong*), Paul Ryan (*Norman*), Al Hobson (*Carter Axe*), Dick Miller (*Jerry*).

A harmless exploitationer which is as lacking in sex, violence, and vulgarity as it is in creativity. Frazier and Kesner, tagged Cupcake and Angel, take over an unprofitable drive-in and with the addition of short-skirted, chesty carhops on roller skates, business begins to boom. Hobson causes trouble when his oil company make plans to buy the property and turn it into a prototype for a line of futuristic gas stations. The film was originally rated PG, but the distributers opted for a different audience by tossing in a few vulgarities to secure an R rating.

p, John B. Kelley, Robert D. Krintzman; d, Barbara Peeters; w, Stephanie Rothman; ph, Eric Saarinen (CFI Color); ed, Steve Zaillian.

Comedy   Cas.   (PR:O   MPAA:R)

STARK FEAR*   (1963) 86m B.H.S./Ellis bw

Beverly Garland (*Ellen Winslow*), Skip Homeier (*Gerald Winslow*), Kenneth Tobey (*Cliff Kane*), Hannah Stone, Paul Scovil, Edna Neuman, Bruce Palmer, Cortez Ewing, Barbara Freeman, George Clow, Darlene Dana Reno, John Arville, Carey Mount, Bob Stone, Joseph Benton.

Garland stars as a down-and-out housewife who takes a job to help her unemployed husband pay the bills. He doesn't like the idea and leaves her, she follows, and they eventually divorce. She succeeds in breaking the emotional ties she had with him, and runs off to Mexico with her boss. Filmed independently in Oklahoma and Arkansas.

p, Joe E. Burke, Ned Hockman, Dwight V. Swain; d, Hockman; w, Swain; ph, Robert E. Bethard; m, Lawrence V. Fisher (performed by the Oklahoma City Symphony Orchestra); art & set d, Marcus Fuller; makeup, Melvin Parlow.

Drama   (PR:C   MPAA:NR)

STARK MAD*½   (1929) 70m WB bw

H. B. Warner (*Prof. Dangerfield*), Jacqueline Logan (*Irene*), Henry B. Walthall (*Capt. Rhodes, Yacht Commander*), Claude Gillingwater (*James Rutherford, Expedition Leader*), Warner Richmond (*1st Mate*), Lionel Belmore (*Amos Sewald*), Floyd Shackelford (*Sam the Cook*), Andre Beranger (*Simpson the Guide*), John Miljan (*Dr. Milo*), Louise Fazenda (*Mrs. Fleming*).

The captain of a yacht docked in South America is a wanted criminal, a fact unknown to his passengers, who are trying to locate the yacht owner's missing son. The fate of those on the yacht is placed in question when they find themselves up against natives and an ape, not to mention an overly dramatic script.

d, Lloyd Bacon; w, Harvey Gates (based on a story by Jerome Kingston); ph, Bernard McGill; ed, Ralph Dawson.

Adventure   (PR:A   MPAA:NR)

STARLIFT**½   (1951) 103m WB bw

Doris Day, Gordon MacRae, Virginia Mayo, Gene Nelson, Ruth Roman (*Themselves*), James Cagney, Gary Cooper, Virginia Gibson, Phil Harris, Frank Lovejoy, Lucille Norman, Louella Parsons, Randolph Scott, Jane Wyman, Patrice Wymore (*Guest Stars*), Janice Rule (*Nell Wayne*), Dick Wesson (*Sgt. Mike Nolan*), Ron Hagerty (*Cpl. Rick Williams*), Richard Webb (*Col. Callan*), Hayden Rorke (*Chaplain*), Howard St. John (*Steve Rogers*), Ann Doran (*Mrs. Callan*), Tommy Farrell (*Turner*), John Maxwell (*George Norris*), Don Beddoe (*Bob Wayne*), Mary Adams (*Sue Wayne*), Bigelowe Sayre (*Dr. Williams*), Eleanor Audley (*Mrs. Williams*), Pat Henry (*Theater Manager*), Gordon Polk (*Chief Usher*), Robert Hammack (*Piano Player*), Ray Montgomery (*Capt. Nelson*), Bill Neff (*Co-Pilot*), Stan Holbrook (*Ground Officer*), Jill Richards (*Flight Nurse*), Joe Turkel (*Litter Case*), Rush Williams (*Virginia Boy*), Brian McKay (*Pete*), Jack Larson (*Will*), Lyle Clark (*Nebraska Boy*), Dorothy Kennedy, Jean Dean, Dolores Castle (*Nurses*), William Hunt (*Boy with Cane*), Elizabeth Flournoy (*Army Nurse*), Walter Brennan, Jr. (*Driver*), Dick Ryan (*Doctor*), James Brown (*Non-Com*), Steve Gregory (*Boy with Camera*), Bill Hudson (*Crew Chief*), Sarah Spencer (*Miss Parsons' Assistant*), Eddie Coonz (*Reporter*), Robert Karnes, John Hedloe (*Lieutenants*), Richard Monohan (*Morgan*), Joe Recht, Herb Latimer (*Soldiers in Bed*), Ezelle Poule (*Waitress*).

A patriotic salute to the boys who went off to fight in Korea in 1951. Essentially an excuse to parade Warner Bros. stars across the screen, STARLIFT does have a paper-thin plot that rears its head every now and then. Hagerthy and Wesson are a pair of Air Force personnel who pretend to be heroes in order to impress starlet Rule who is visiting the troops at San Francisco's Travis Air Force base with Day and MacRae. Wesson talks Hagerthy into chasing after Rule and eventually the pair fall in love. The relationship takes a turn for the worse when Rule discovers Hagerthy's deception. They reconcile, however, when Hagerthy actually gets called up for duty. Produced in conjunction with a short-lived Hollywood project called "Operation Starlift" which was created to boost the morale of Korean War G.I.s. As a film, STARLIFT isn't very effective, but as a historical document of Hollywood it serves a purpose. Some of the biggest names of the day appeared including Cagney, who delivered a few of his usual tough guy lines, and Cooper, who was one-fourth of a singing quartet (Phil Harris, Virginia Gibson, and Frank Lovejoy rounded out the group) which delivered "Look Out Stranger, I'm a Texas Ranger" (Ruby Ralesin, Phil Harris). Day and MacRae teamed up for "You're Gonna Lose Your Gal" (Joe Young, James V. Monaco), while Day solos on "S'Wonderful" (George Gershwin, Ira Gershwin), and a medley of "You Ought to Be in Pictures" (Edward Heyman, Dana Suesse) and "You Do Something to Me" (Cole Porter). Another Porter tune, "What Is This Thing Called Love?" is performed by MacRae who, this time, teams with Lucille Norman. MacRae also teams with a male chorus for a rendition of "Good Green Acres of Home" (Irving Kahal, Sammy Fain). Others include "I May Be Wrong, but I Think You're Wonderful" (Harry Ruskin, Henry Sullivan, performed by Jane Wyman), George and Ira Gershwin's "Liza" delivered by Patrice Wymore who also adds some dance steps, Rule and Nelson dance to "It's Magic" (Sammy Cahn, Jule Styne), and Virginia Mayo offers up a rather sorry rendition of "Noche Carib" (Percy Faith). This obligatory effort by Warner Bros.' stable of stars has a few pleasing turns, but it isn't up to its WW II counterpart, STAGE DOOR CANTEEN (1943). The million-dollar production effort was excoriated in a press report for opening in theaters across the U.S. a month after the real "Operation Starlift"–funded by the studios only to the tune of $5,000–had to shut down for lack of money. Patriotism was no match for Hollywood hyperbole and parsimony.

p, Robert Arthur; d, Roy Del Ruth; w, John Klorer, Karl Lamb (based on a story by Klorer); ph, Ted McCord; ed, William Ziegler; md, Ray Heindorf; art d, Charles H. Clarke; set d, G. W. Berntsen; cos, Leah Rhodes; ch, LeRoy Prinz; makeup, Gordon Bau.

Musical   (PR:A   MPAA:NR)

STARLIGHT OVER TEXAS**   (1938) 55m MON bw

Tex Ritter (*Tex Newman*), Salvatore Damino (*Ramon*), Carmen LaRoux (*Rosita*), Rosa Turich (*Maria*), Snub Pollard (*PeeWee*), Horace Murphy (*Ananias*), Karl Hackett (*Kildare*), Charles King, Jr (*Hank Boston*), George Chesebro (*Ashley Hill*), Carlos Villarias (*Gov. Ruiz*), Edward Cassidy (*Capt. Brooks*), Martin Garralaga (*Capt. Gomez*), Jerry Gomez, Sherry Tansey, Bob Terry, Horace B. Carpenter, Dave O'Brien, Denver Dixon, Chick Hannon, Tex Palmer, Fred Velasco, Stelita, Carmen Alvarez, Eduardo Chaves, The Northwesterners [Mark and Ray Scobee], Shorty Brier, Budd Rasch, Chuck Davis], White Flash the Horse.

A maladroitly directed oater which has Ritter as the local marshal putting an end to raids on a U.S. arsenal. Engineered by a gang of outlaws, the raids have been yielding guns and ammunition which are then smuggled across the border.

p, Edward F. Finney; d, Al Herman; w, John Rathmell (based on a story by Harry MacPherson); ph, Francis Corby; ed, Fred Bain.

Western   **Cas.**   (PR:A   MPAA:NR)

STARLIGHT SLAUGHTER   (SEE: EATEN ALIVE, 1976)

STARS AND STRIPES FOREVER***
                                    (1952) 89m FOX c (GB: MARCHING ALONG)

Clifton Webb (*John Philip Sousa*), Debra Paget (*Lily*), Robert Wagner (*Willie*), Ruth Hussey (*Jennie*), Finlay Currie (*Col. Randolph*), Benay Venuta (*Mme. Bernsdorff-Mueller*), Roy Roberts (*Maj. Houston*), Tom Browne Henry (*David Blakely*), Lester Matthews (*Mr. Pickering*), Maude Prickett (*Maid*), Erno Verebes (*Organ Grinder*), Richard Garrick (*Secretary of the Navy*), Romo Vincent (*Music Professor*), Roy Gordon (*President Harrison*), Florence Shirley (*Navy Nurse*), Delos Jewkes (*Bass Singer*), Norman Leavitt (*Purvis*), Hellen Van Tuyl (*Mrs. Harrison*), Walter Woolf King, Roger Moore (*President's Aides*), Thomas E. Jackson (*Senator*), Maude Wallace (*Nora*), Lenee Martin (*Priscilla*), Sharon Jan Altman (*Helen*), Nicholas Koster (*Sousa, Jr.*), William Vedder (*Prof. Estaban*), Olan Soule (*Glove Salesman*), Aileen Carlyle (*Mme. Liebling*), Paul Maxey (*Mr. McCaull*), Frank Ferguson, Jack Rice, The Atlanta Stone Mountain Choir.

A lively and colorful biography of John Philip Sousa that preserves the spirit of the man's music with entertaining verve. The film opens with Webb as leader of the Marine Corps band. He leaves the military to form his own band, taking the group all over the country and around the world to entertain. Wagner is a member of the band who devises a giant horn which

he dubs the "Sousaphone" after his mentor. Webb has strict rules about wives going on tour with the band, which causes trouble for Wagner after he marries burlesque singer Paget. Eventually Webb relents and Paget becomes a singer for his band, traveling with the company on their tours. It's a thin plot packed into a quick 89 minutes, full of energy, music, and color. The 1890s are faithfully re-created including some wonderful period costumes. The cast gives the story everything it needs to work, with Webb giving an engaging, eccentric performance. Hussey, as his stoical wife, makes a good counterpoint to this, while Wagner and Paget carry the love story well. The attention to the real facts in Sousa's life is only slight, for the story of the young lovers is almost entirely fictional. Based on Sousa's autobiography *Marching Along*, the film does point out some little known facts about the composer's life, such as his secret dream to write ballads rather than marches. But it was the marches he was most famous for and the film is packed with them, along with other tunes of the era. They include: "Stars and Stripes Forever," "El Capitan," "Washington Post," "King Cotton" (John Philip Sousa), "The Battle Hymn of the Republic" (Julia Ward Howe, William Steffe), "Dixie" (Daniel Decatur Emmett), "Light Cavalry" (Von Suppe), "Turkey in the Straw" (traditional), "Hail to the Chief" (John Sanderson), and "The Bowery" (Percy Gaunt, Charles Hoyt).

p, Lamar Trotti; d, Henry Koster; w, Trotti, Ernest Vajda (based on *Marching Along* by John Philip Sousa); ph, Charles G. Clarke (Technicolor); ed, James B. Clark; md, Alfred Newman; art d, Lyle Wheeler, Joseph C. Wright; set d, Thomas Little, Claude Carpenter; ch, Al White, Jr., Nick Castle.

Musical/Biography   **Cas.**   (PR:AAA   MPAA:NR)

STARS ARE SINGING, THE**½**   (1953) 99m PAR c

Rosemary Clooney (*Terry Brennan*), Anna Maria Alberghetti (*Katri Walenska*), Lauritz Melchior (*Poldi*), Bob Williams (*Homer*), Fred Clark (*McDougall*), Tom Morton (*Buddy Fraser*), John Archer (*Dave*), Mikhail Rasumny (*Ladowski*), Lloyd Corrigan (*Miller*), Don Wilson (*Himself*), Red Dust the Dog.

A showcase for the talents of singing star Clooney, in her first film role, and Alberghetti, this musical had barely a thread of plot tying it together. Clooney is one of three vaudevillians who helps hide illegal alien Alberghetti from the immigration officers. Their neighbor, Melchior, a former opera singer, is the old family friend to whom Alberghetti turns after jumping ship. The Jay Livingston-Ray Evans tunes include: "I Do I Do I Do," "Haven't Got a Worry to My Name," "My Heart Is Home," "My Kind of Day," "Feed Fido Some Rruff," "New Father," "Lovely Weather for Ducks." Also: "Come-on-a-My-House" (Ross Bagdasarian, William Saroyan), "Voices of Spring" (Johann Strauss), "Una Voce Poco Fa" (Rossini, from "The Barber of Seville"), "Because" (Edward Teschemacher, Guy d'Hardelot), "Ah] Fors E Lui Che L'Anima" (Verdi, from "La Traviata"), "Vesti La Giubba" (Leoncavallo, from "Pagliacci"). "Come-on-a-My-House," penned by writer Saroyan and his sometime-actor cousin Bagdasarian, was the hit that had launched Clooney on her astronomical singing career in 1951.

p, Irving Asher; d, Norman Taurog; w, Liam O'Brien (based on a story by Paul Hervey Fox); ph, Lionel Lindon (Technicolor); m, Victor Young; ed, Arthur Schmidt; art d, Hal Pereira, Henry Bumstead; cos, Edith Head; ch, Jack Baker.

Musical   (PR:A   MPAA:NR)

STARS IN MY CROWN**½**   (1950) 89m MGM bw

Joel McCrea (*Josiah Doziah Gray*), Ellen Drew (*Harriet Gray*), Dean Stockwell (*John Kenyon*), Alan Hale (*Jed Isbell*), Lewis Stone (*Dr. D.K. Harris, Sr.*), James Mitchell (*Dr. D.K. Harris, Jr.*), Amanda Blake (*Faith Radmore Samuels*), Juano Hernandez (*Uncle Famous Prill*), Charles Kemper (*Prof. Sam Houston Jones*), Connie Gilchrist (*Sarah Isbell*), Jack Lambert (*Perry Lokey*), Arthur Hunnicutt (*Chloroform Wiggins*), Marshall Thompson (*Narrator*).

A mediocre but well-crafted film which focuses on the events that occur in a small Southern community in one year's time. McCrea is the preacher who, clenching a Bible in one hand and a pistol in the other, moves into the town and helps the locals solve their problems, which include a disastrous typhoid epidemic, KKK terrorism, and resistance to a new doctor. Western fans will recognize the new doctor's love interest as a young, young Amanda Blake, who would later go on to fame and fortune as Miss Kitty on TV's "Gunsmoke."

p, William H. Wright; d, Jacques Tourneur; w, Margaret Fitts (based on the novel by Joe David Brown); ph, Charles Schoenbaum; m, Adolph Deutsch (vocal arrangements, Robert Tucker); ed, Gene Ruggiero; art d, Ruggiero, Cedric Gibbons.

Drama   (PR:A   MPAA:NR/G)

STARS IN YOUR BACKYARD   (SEE: PARADISE ALLEY, 1962)

STARS IN YOUR EYES*½   (1956, Brit.) 96m Grand Alliance/BL c

Nat Jackley *(Jimmy Knowles)*, Pat Kirkwood *(Sally Bishop)*, Bonar Colleano *(David Laws)*, Dorothy Squires *(Ann Hart)*, Jack Jackson *(Rigby)*, Vera Day *(Maureen Temple)*, Hubert Gregg *(Crawley Walters)*, Joan Sims *(Walter's Secretary)*, Ernest Clark *(Ronnie)*, Gerald Harper *(Dicky)*, Meier Tzelniker *(Maxie Jago)*, Gabrielle Brune *(Effie)*, Aubrey Dexter *(Farrow)*, Roger Avon *(Grimes)*, Sammy Curtis *(1st Recruit)*, Dennis Murray *(2nd Recruit)*, Sonny Willis *(Sergeant)*, Michael Mellinger *(Night Club Proprietor)*, Jimmy Clitheroe *(Joey)*, Freddie Frinton *(Publican)*, Reginald Forsythe *(Pianist)*.

A group of washed-up vaudevillians decide to put on a show when a friend of theirs inherits a run-down theater, but on the opening night a spiteful group of hoods sabotage the performance. The BBC eventually gets word of their efforts, however, and agrees to broadcast the entire show live from the theater. Nothing more than an opportunity for a bunch of stage performers to try out the big screen, the skits are fine, but that's all there is to it.

p, David Dent; d, Maurice Elvey; w, Talbot Rothwell, Hubert Gregg (based on a story by Francis Miller); ph, S.D. Onions (CameraScope, Eastmancolor); ed, Robert Jordan Hill; m/l, Jack Jackson, Gregg, C.W. Murphy, Will Letters, Hilda Lynn, David Lee, Edwin Astley, Hazel Astley, Bert Elms, Malcolm Harvey, Don Pelosi, Leo Towers.

Musical   **(PR:A   MPAA:NR)**

STARS LOOK DOWN, THE****   (1940, Brit.) 104m GN bw

Michael Redgrave *(David Fenwick)*, Margaret Lockwood *(Jenny Sunley)*, Emlyn Williams *(Joe Gowan)*, Nancy Price *(Martha Fenwick)*, Allan Jeayes *(Richard Barras)*, Edward Rigby *(Robert Fenwick)*, Cecil Parker *(Stanley Millington)*, Linden Travers *(Laura Millington)*, Milton Rosmer *(Harry Nugent)*, George Carney *(Slogger Gowan)*, Ivor Barnard *(Wept)*, Olga Lindo *(Mrs. Sunley)*, Desmond Tester *(Hughie Fenwick)*, David Markham *(Arthur Barras)*.

This superb look at the plight of the British miner came out at around the same time as HOW GREEN WAS MY VALLEY and unfortunately ran into a problem at the box office due to that. The subject matter was quite similar and this one was far more realistically grim, with little of the warmth of the John Ford classic, so it was bypassed by theater owners even though it was made first in 1939 but not released in the U.S. until later. Reed had made a couple of films before this but THE STARS LOOK DOWN is what placed him in the forefront of the British movie world. A.J. Cronin's novel served as the basis for the screenplay which is set in a bleak coal mining town in the northern area of England and is one of the best looks at the honest lives of the men who go into the pits to mine the mineral that keeps the country perking. Redgrave is the son of miner Rigby and his wife, Price. The parents have struggled to give their boy a better life and he is sent to the university to get an education. Rigby works in the mine with his younger son, Tester, and attempts to organize the others because they are working in a pit with a faulty seam, one that could give way at any moment. While away at school, Redgrave meets Lockwood, a vain, grasping young woman who had been seeing Williams. When he dumped her, she set her sights on Redgrave and trapped him into marriage. The attempted strike fails and the men are forced back to work. Williams, an oily villain, comes back into the picture to renew his affair with Lockwood and she is perfidious to Redgrave. When he learns about it, he leaves her and turns his attention to helping the miners who have reluctantly gone into the pits. Redgrave tries to convince the heads of the union in the country about what's happening but they pay him no heed. There's a break in the seam and a catastrophe occurs. Rigby and Tester are killed with many others. Rescuers try to save the men but the only person who has a map of the mine is the owner and he dies of a heart attack (brought on by guilt) before they can locate the map. At the conclusion, Redgrave has decided to stay in the small town and devote his life to improving the lots of the miners. This was one of the first social dramas made in England and is as timely today as it was then. Shot at a colliery in Cumberland for a week's location, it then moved to Twickenham and Shepperton Studios for interiors. Lockwood took the place of Phyllis Calvert and convinced mightily that she was a greedy woman with no other interest than herself. Redgrave, Lockwood, and Reed had been contracted to Gainsborough Pictures and lent to Grafton Films for this unrelentingly serious semi-documentary. Williams is as known for his writing as his acting, having written NIGHT MUST FALL and THE CORN IS GREEN. Well into his 70s, Williams was touring the world doing his one-man show as Charles Dickens.

p, Sadore Goldschmidt; d, Carol Reed; w, J.B. Williams (based on the novel by A.J. Cronin); ph, Mutz Greenbaum (Ernest Palmer, Henry Harris, uncredited) m, Hans May; ed, Reginald Beck; art d, James Carter.

Drama   **Cas.**   **(PR:A-C   MPAA:NR)**

STARS ON PARADE**   (1944) 63m COL bw

Larry Parks *(Danny Davis)*, Lynn Merrick *(Dorothy Dean)*, Ray Walker *(Billy Blake)*, Jeff Donnell *(Mary Brooks)*, Robert Williams *(Jerry Browne)*, Selmer Jackson *(J.L. Carson)*, Edythe Elliott *(Mrs. Dean)*, Mary Currier *(Nan McNair)*, Danny O'Neil, Frank and Jean Hubert, The Chords, King Cole Trio, The Ben Carter Choir.

Contrary to the title's boast, there are no stars in STARS ON PARADE, just the usual struggling group of entertainers who want to prove to the L.A. producers that there's more than enough talent in their own town. While everyone in Hollywood is scouting all over the country for new names, Parks and Merrick put on a show which convinces the talent scouts. Numbers include: "My Heart Isn't In It" (Jack Lawrence), "It's Love Love Love" (Mack David, Joan Whitney, Alex Kramer), "When They Ask about You" (Sammy Stept), "Jumpin' at the Jubilee (Ben Carter, Mayes Marshall), "Taking Care of You" (Lou Brown, Harry Akst), "Where Am I without You?" (Don Raye, Gene De Paul), "Two Hearts in the Dark" (Dave Franklin), "Somewhere this Side of Heaven," Ezekial Saw the Wheel."

p, Wallace MacDonald; d, Lew Landers; w, Monte Brice; ph, L.W. O'Connell; ed, Jerome Thoms; art d, Lionel Banks, Walter Holscher.

Musical   **(PR:A   MPAA:NR)**

STARS OVER ARIZONA**   (1937) 62m MON bw

Jack Randall *(Jack)*, Kathleen Elliot *(Jane)*, Horace Murphy *(Grizzly)*, Warner Richmond *(Ace)*, Tom Herbert *(Doc)*, Hal Price *(Hashknife)*, Earl Dwire *(Sidewinder)*, Chick Hannon *(Yucca Bill)*, Charles Romas *(Chuckawalla)*, Shuma Shermatova, Jack Rockwell, Forrest Taylor, Bob McKenzie, Tex Palmer, Sherry Tansey.

Randall and Murphy are assigned to flush the outlaws out of Yuba City, and in the process learn what happened to the governor's missing son, who previously embarked on the same assignment. A standard oater which is weak when it comes to dubbing Randall's tunes.

p&d, R.N. Bradbury; w, Robert Emmett (Tansey), Ernie Adams; ph, Bert Longenecker.

Western   **(PR:A   MPAA:NR)**

STARS OVER BROADWAY**   (1935) 90m WB bw

Pat O'Brien *(Al McGillevray)*, James Melton *(Jan King)*, Jane Froman *(Joan Garrett)*, Frank McHugh *(Bugs Cramer)*, Marie Willson *(Molly)*, Frank Fay *(Announcer at Amateur Program)*, William Ricciardi *(Minotti)*, Craig Reynolds *(Announcer)*, E.E. Clive *(Butler)*, Maurice Black *(Jim Flugel)*, Eddie Conrad *(Freddie)*, Emmett Vogan *(Archie McNeish)*, George Chandler *(Charlie)*, Paul Porcasi *(Luigi)*, Gordon "Bill" Elliott *(Young Man)*, Frank Moran *(Champ)*, Ferdinand Munier, Bob Montgomery, Pat West, Larry McGrath, Sam Ash *(Men)*, Mr. Marlowe *(Milkman)*, Sarah Edwards *(Woman)*, Esther Howard *(Amateur Singer)*, Moran Family *(Entertainers)*, Lillian Worth *(Buxom Singer)*, Harry Seymour, Phil Regan, Patsy Flick.

A mediocre vehicle for the questionable acting talents of radio stars Froman and Melton, which has the latter playing a bellboy who gets discovered by agent O'Brien. Melton makes it to the pop charts, but really would rather be singing opera. O'Brien refuses, sending the disenchanted singer to the bottle, but finally gives in. When the studio realized how weak their two stars would be at the box office, they cut the budget to a safer amount. Unfortunately, instead of reducing Froman and Melton's screen time, a Busby Berkeley number was cut. He had planned a major production to "September in the Rain," which was to feature a forest full of swaying, dancing silver trees. The musical numbers that made it to the screen were: "Broadway Cinderella," "Where Am I?," "At Your Service Madam," "You Let Me Down," "Over Yonder Moon," "September in the Rain" (Al Dubin, Harry Warren), "Carry Me Back to the Lone Prairie" (Carson J. Robison), and selections from "Aida" (Giuseppe Verdi), and "Martha" (Friedrich von Flotow).

p, Sam Bischoff; d, William Keighley; w, Jerry Wald, Julius J. Epstein, Patsy Flick (based on the story by Mildred Ram); ph, George Barnes; ed, Bert L'Orle; md, Leo F. Forbstein; art d, Carl Weyl; cos, Orry-Kelly; ch, Busby Berkeley, Bobby Connolly.

Musical   **(PR:A   MPAA:NR)**

STARS OVER TEXAS**   (1946) 59m PRC bw

Eddie Dean *(Himself)*, Roscoe Ates *(Soapy)*, Shirley Patterson *(Terry Lawrence)*, Lee Bennett *(Waco-Bert)*, Lee Roberts *(Hank Lawrence)*, Kermit Maynard *(Knuckles)*, Jack O'Shea *(Ringo Evans)*, Hal Smith *(Tucker)*, Carl Mathews *(Two Horn)*, Matty Roubert *(Buggsy)*, Bill *(William)* Fawcett *(Judge Smith)*, The Sunshine Boys *(Themselves)*, Flash the Horse.

Dean and his boys lead a herd of cattle to Roberts' ranch only to discover that it's O'Shea that has taken over. Knowing something is wrong Dean digs up proof of O'Shea's shady dealings and puts him behind bars.

p&d, Robert Emmett Tansey; w, Frances Kavanaugh; ph, Ernest Miller; ed, Hugh Winn; md, Karl Hajos; art d, Edward C. Jewell; m/l, "Stars over Texas," "Sands of the Old Rio Grande," "Fifteen Hundred and One Miles of Heaven," Eddie Dean, Hal Blair, Glenn Strange.

Western   **(PR:A   MPAA:NR)**

STARSHIP INVASIONS** (1978, Can.) 89m HR/WB c (AKA: ALIEN ENCOUNTER; WAR OF THE ALIENS; WINGED SERPENT.)

Robert Vaughn (*Prof. Duncan*), Christopher Lee (*Capt. Rameses*), Daniel Pilon (*Anaxi*), Tiiu Leek (*Phi*), Helen Shaver (*Betty*), Henry Ramer (*Malcolm*), Victoria Johnson (*Gezeth*), Doreen Lipson (*Dorothy*).

The same year STAR WARS was released, this low-budget sci-fi hit the screens, minus the technical proficiency of George Lucas but with much of the spirit. The lack of funds coincided with the filmmaker's desire to pay homage to the 1940s serials produced by Republic–there is little synchronous dialog, a great deal of head nodding and facial expression, and vintage flying saucers. The familiar plot has a group of aliens led by Lee hovering above the Earth with the intention of finding a settlement. UFO scientist Vaughn is kidnaped and forced to help with the invasion. An unspectacular space battle occurs as the good guys (dressed in white) beat the bad guys (dressed in black), and restore harmony.

p, Norman Glick, Ed Hunt, Ken Gord; d&w, Hunt; ph, Mark Irwin; m, Gil Melle; ed, Millie Moore, Ruth Hope; art d, Karen Bromley; spec eff, Warren Keillor.

ScienceFiction   **(PR:AA   MPAA:PG)**

STARSTRUCK**½   (1982, Aus.) 102m Palm Beach/Cinecom c

Jo Kennedy (*Jackie Mullens*), Ross O'Donovan (*Angus Mullens*), Pat Evison (*Nana*), Margo Lee (*Pearl*), Max Cullen (*Reg*), Melissa Jaffer (*Mrs. Booth*), Ned Lander (*Robbie*), John O'May (*Terry Lambert*), Dennis Miller (*Lou*), Norman Erskine (*Hazza*), Philip Judd, Dwayne Hillman, Ian Gilroy, Buster Stiggs (*The Swingers*), Ian Spence (*Spider*), Kerry McKay (*Phil*), Mark Little (*Carl*), Peter Davies (*Timpany*).

A throwback to the star-studded musical vehicles of the 30s and 40s in which a couple of talented performers put on a big show, filled to the gills with glamorous and charming numbers. In this case it's 14-year-old O'Donovan who decides to make his new-wave, punkish cousin, Kennedy, a singing sensation. He gives her exposure through a televised New York talent contest which brings her a $25,000 prize, enough to keep her parents' hotel/bar from financial ruin. Not much better or worse than the films it emulates, STARSTRUCK differs only in its outlandish 80s tunes, which unfortunately aren't even that catchy. A change of pace for director Armstrong, who made her mark with MY BRILLIANT CAREER.

p, David Elfick, Richard Brennan; d, Gillian Armstrong; w, Stephen Maclean; ph, Russell Boyd; ed, Nicholas Beauman; md, Mark Moffatt; prod d, Brian Thomson; art d, Kim Hilder; set d, Lissa Coote, Sally Campbell; cos, Luciana Arrighi; ch, David Atkins.

Musical   **(PR:C   MPAA:PG)**

START CHEERING**½   (1938) 78m COL bw

Jimmy Durante (*Willie Gumbatz*), Walter Connolly (*Sam Lewis*), Joan Perry (*Jean Worthington*), Charles Starrett (*Ted Crosley*), Raymond Walburn (*Dean Worthington*), Broderick Crawford (*Biff Gordon*), Hal LeRoy (*Tarzan Biddle*), Ernest Truex (*Blodgett*), Dr. Craig E. Earle (*Professor Quiz*), Gertrude Niesen (*Sarah*), Arthur Loft (*Librarian*), Virginia Dale (*Mabel*), Romo Vincent (*Fatso*), Gene Morgan (*Coach Burns*), Louise Stanley (*Flo*), Howard Hickman (*Dr. Fosdick*), Minerva Urecal (*Miss Grimley*), Chaz. Chase (*Shorty*), Jimmy Wallington (*Announcer*), Nick Lukats, The Three Stooges, Louis Prima with His Band, Johnny Green and His Orchestra (*Themselves*), Arthur Hoyt.

A genuinely funny collegiate picture which blends music and comedy in the usual way. Starrett plays a Hollywood idol who makes a switch and enrolls in college classes, thinking that campus life will be more subdued than the spotlight. Manager Connolly and his sidekick Durante think differently, however, and try to get him back in front of the movie cameras. Songs include: "My Heaven on Earth" (Charles Tobias, Phil Baker, Samuel Pokrass, sung by Niesen); "You Walked into My Life," "Start Cheering" (Milton Drake, Ben Oakland), "Rockin' the Town," "Hail Sigma PSI" (Ted Koehler, Jimmy Green), "When I Strut Away in My Cutaway" (Jimmy Durante).

d, Albert S. Rogell; w, Eugene Solow, Richard E. Wormser, Philip Rapp (based on the story by Corey Ford); ph, Joseph Walker; ed, Gene Havlick; md, Morris Stoloff; spec eff, Ganahl Carson; cos, Robert Kalloch; ch, Danny Dare.

Musical/Comedy   **(PR:A   MPAA:NR)**

START THE REVOLUTION WITHOUT ME***

(1970) 90m Norbud/WB c

Gene Wilder (*Claude Coupe/Philippe DeSisi*), Donald Sutherland (*Charles Coupe/Pierre DeSisi*), Hugh Griffith (*King Louis XVI*), Jack MacGowran (*Jacques Cabriolet*), Billie Whitelaw (*Queen Marie Atoinette*), Victor Spinetti (*Duke d'Escargot*), Orson Welles (*Narrator*), Helen Fraser (*Mimi Montage*), Ewa Aulin (*Christina*), Harry Fowler (*Marcel*), Rosalind Knight (*Helen DeSisi*), Murray Melvin (*Blind Man*), Ken Parry (*Dr. Boileau*), Jacques Maury (*Lt. Sorel*), Maxwell Shaw (*Duke DeSisi*), Graham Stark (*Andre Coupe*), Barry Lowe (*Sergeant*), George A. Cooper (*Dr. Duval*), Michael

Rothwell (*Paul Duval*), Denise Coffey (*Anne Duval*).

This often hysterical farce starts like a house on fire, then burns down. Mel Brooks mined similar comedy ore with THE HISTORY OF THE WORLD, PART ONE but not as well. With some more attention paid to the vapid finish, this might have been a comedy classic. It alternates between the intellectual and the inane, with stops along the way for satire and silliness as it goes over the "Corsican Brothers" story with a new look, although Alexander Dumas is not credited. It's France in the 1700s when two sets of twin boys are born to two different families. One is a wealthy Corsican peer, Shaw, and the other is a peasant, Stark. The physician Dooper doesn't recall which children belong to whom so he takes one baby and replaces it with another, thus making certain that at least one of the children will be in the right family. Time passes and the boys grow up. The wealthy boys, Sutherland and Wilder, are now feared for their arrogant attitudes and their willingness to run their rapiers through anyone who opposes them. There is a revolution in the offing and the French King, Griffith, needs their epee expertise to help quell the rebels. Since they are so well-known and recognized, the two men go to Paris in the disguise of ordinary citizens. At the same time, the other set of brothers (whom we'll dub Gene and Donald to avoid confusion) are doltish peasants who have signed up with the rebelious forces under the leadership of MacGowran. Sutherland and Wilder hold no love for the king, and although he thinks they are coming to his assistance, the truth is that they are part of the cabal against him, led by the villainous duke, Spinetti, and Griffith's wife, queen Whitelaw (as Marie Antoinette). The brothers feel that they can get a huge share of the country since they know that Griffith is an added man and that France would prosper under the greedy supervision of Whitelaw and Spinetti. The barge carrying Wilder and Sutherland comes up the Seine and MacGowran's men go after it. Sutherland and Wilder are taken back to the rebel's headquarters where their snobbish actions cause them to be clapped into chains, as everyone thinks they are nuts. Simultaneously, Gene and Donald are mistakenly brought to the palace. Once there, Griffith confesses to the confused men that he knows Spinetti is after his wife and his throne and he assigns them the job of assassinating the conspirators. Spinetti is due to wed Aulin, the princess of Belgium. If he does that, he will have enough power to rule France, so the murder must take place immediately. Whitelaw is annoyed at Spinetti and would like him out of the way so she approaches Gene, thinking that he is Wilder, and suggests that he slay Spinetti. Then she and he can get rid of Griffith and wind up running France. Spinetti senses the machinations and thinks that the only way to work things out is to kill Gene and Donald (who they think are Wilder and Sutherland), so he and several of his personal guards go after the two peasants in the garb of monks, who have free reign in the palace. They make a number of funny attempts on the lives of Gene and Donald and fail. Meanwhile, Sutherland and Wilder get away from their captors and race for the palace. But when they arrive, everyone is uncertain as to who are the right Corsicans. While MacGowran and his minions are approaching the palace with an eye to placing the royal heads in guillotines, Gene and Donald have been working on Griffith to issue an edict with several social reforms. He finally signs the writ, but by this time, the revolution is in full force. All the while, the whole affair has been narrated by the mellifluous voice of Welles (and there have been some funny title cards to set scenes). We flash forward to modern times where Welles has been reading the tale from a book, but before he can tell us how the story turned out, descendants of Sutherland and Wilder appear and shoot Welles, then they are shot in turn by descendants of Gene and Don. (Or is it the other way around? No matter.) Wilder-Gene then shoots Sutherland-Don and he is then shot by "The Man in the Iron Mask" (who was freed earlier in the film from his long incarceration). The picture disintegrates into a "how the heck are we going to end this?" problem, not unlike the cop-out conclusion in BLAZING SADDLES. The locations were done in France at the Notre Dame Cathedral and the gorgeous Chateau de Rochefort. Welles' narration seems like an added attraction and lends nothing to the film and the ending is letting all the air out of a wonderful balloon. Griffith was very funny as the whacky king, and when there is a large palace ball and he comes dressed as a chicken, the result is hilarious. Much of the humor is derived from the names of the characters, a slightly sophomoric touch. When translated from French, Spinetti's name is "The Duke of Snails," while the other French words are "carbiolet," "coupe," and "montage." What's funniest in the picture are many of the sight gags, the best of which is the picture of "The Man in the Iron Mask" who is on a ledge in front of the palace as the rebels are firing. When his armored suit is hit by a bullet, he turns and runs in the opposite direction like one of those penny arcade shooting-gallery figures that were popular in the 1940s, 1950s and 1960s before video games took over the arcade business. This was the next to last film done by Yorkin and Lear before they began to concentrate on TV and hit gold with "All In The Family." Their final movie was COLD TURKEY.

p&d, Bud Yorkin; w, Fred Freeman, Lawrence J. Cohen (based on the story "Two Times Two" by Freeman); ph, Jean Tournier (Technicolor); m, John Addison; ed, Ferris Webster; md, Addison; art d, Francois de Lamothe; set d, Gabriel Bechir; cos, Alan Barrett.

Historical Comedy   **Cas.**   **(PR:C-O   MPAA:PG)**

STARTING OVER***½   (1979) 106m PAR c

Burt Reynolds (*Phil Potter*), Jill Clayburgh (*Marilyn Homberg*), Candice Bergen (*Jessica Potter*), Charles Durning (*Michael "Mickey" Potter*), Frances Sternhagen (*Marva Potter*), Austin Pendleton (*Paul*), Mary Kay Place (*Marie*), MacIntyre Dixon (*Dan Ryan*), Jay Sanders (*Larry*), Charles Kimbrough (*Salesman*), Alvie Wise, Wallace Shawn (*Workshop Members*), Sturgis Warner (*John Morganson*), Mary C. Wright, Daniel Stern, George Hirsch (*Students*), Ian Martin (*Doorman*), Aerin Asher (*Lord and Taylor Lady*), Ben Pesner (*Victor*), Mort Marshall (*Room Service Waiter*), Gilmer McCormick (*Stephanie*), Helen Stenborg (*Older Woman*), Michael Kaufman, Marvin Lichterman, Anne De Salvo, Connie Fleming, Alison Stevens, Michael McDermott, Russell Horton, Harold Lamson, Michael Belleran, Deborah Reagan, Kevin Bacon, Tara King, A.C. Weary, Cass Self, Lisa Sloan, Gabby Glatzer, Ed Murphy, Harriet Rawlings, Simon McQueen, Stacy Holiday, Nadine Darling, Kitty Muldoon, John Murray, Eric Geiger, Sol Schwade, Trudy Clemes, Anthony Romano.

This was perhaps the best performance ever given by Burt Reynolds. Casting against type, they chose him to star in this realistic movie about a lonely man whose wife has left him because she wants to spread her wings and "discover who I am." After being the ultimate macho man in many pictures, Reynolds showed he has a sensitive side to him but audiences didn't much care and the picture was not nearly the hit it was predicted to be, although it took in about $20 million. Reynolds is a writer, a kind, decent man who is coping with the world around him and, most closely, with the needs and desires of his wife, Bergen. She fancies herself a songwriter-singer and is just awful. Bergen is a liberated woman who wants to be liberated from the shackles of Reynolds, although he does his best to be a good husband. When she announces her desire for freedom, he is stunned and needs some time to himself, so he goes to Boston where he is consoled by Durning and Sternhagen, a duo of relatives. Reynolds, at first, has no idea that Bergen's yearning for single bliss also has an added fillip; she is having an affair with her boss. Struck by this new situation, Reynolds soon meets Clayburgh, a blowsy spinster schoolteacher who has managed to stay single by looking dowdy. She is not averse to short affairs but fears any entanglement past breakfast. Reynolds meets a group of men in the same boat and joins their "Divorced Men's Workshop." They include Shawn, Pendleton, Wise, Sanders, Dixon, and Whiting and the bonding scenes between these men are totally honest and touchingly funny. Psychiatrists Sternhagen and Durning both have suggestions as to how Reynolds can start over, none of which is practical. When Durning is in dire need of a Valium in a department store, every customer seems to have one, a comedy highlight. Reynolds shaved off his moustache for the film and with it went his hairshirt image. Here was a new Reynolds, a man able to be hurt, to worry, to show emotions. The story is not the key. Rather it is the attention to detail that makes it so rewarding. Bergen's character is funny, but never silly. There is a definite reason why she is the way that she is and so all of the motivation is laid in for the very funny sequence when she sings her dreadful autobiographical songs in a caterwauling screech. Clayburgh is again, "an unmarried woman" (the title of her Oscar-nominated role from the previous year) but with a different slant. All of the acting is superior but it is Reynolds who steals every scene with his underplaying and understanding of the role. He has been quoted as saying, "It was very close to the story of my life" and that is evident from the start. Audiences, however, like to see their heroes in familiar roles. Sylvester Stallone has not been a hit in any part other than the muscle man with either boxing gloves or machine guns in his hands. The same holds true for Clint Eastwood, who is capable of much more than Dirty Harry or "No-Name" in his "spaghetti westerns." And so it is with Reynolds. He's admirably tried to expand himself with this, THE END, and BEST FRIENDS, but none of them has induced audiences the way his dumb car-chase films have. Brooks, the producer-screenwriter who came from the "Mary Tyler Moore" TV show, later went on to make a name for himself as a director-writer-producer with TERMS OF ENDEARMENT. Shawn is the actor-playwright who was responsible for MY DINNER WITH ANDRE and Mary Kay Place scores as a predatory divorcee who thinks that any man under 90 is a potential husband. Good special material by Hamlisch and Carole Bayer Sager.

p, Alan J. Pakula, James L. Brooks; d, Pakula; w, Brooks (based on the novel by Dan Wakefield); ph, Sven Nykvist (Movielab Color); m, Marvin Hamlisch; ed, Marion Rothman; prod d, George Jenkins; set d, Phil Smith; cos, John Boxer; m/l, Hamlisch, Carole Bayer Sager.

Romance/Comedy   **Cas.**   **(PR:C-O   MPAA:R)**

STASTNY KONEC   (SEE: HAPPY END, 1968, Czech.)

STATE DEPARTMENT--FILE 649**   (1949) 87m FC c

Virginia Bruce (*Marge*), William Lundigan (*Ken*), Jonathan Hale (*Director-General*), Frank Ferguson (*Consul Reither*), Richard Loo (*Marshal Yun Usu*), Philip Ahn (*Col. Aram*), Raymond Bond (*Consul Brown*), Milton Kibbee (*Bill Sneed*), Victor Sen Yung (*Johnny Han*), Lora Lee Michel (*Jessica*), John Holland (*Ballinger*), Harlan Warde (*Rev. Morse*), Carole Donne (*Mrs. Morse*), Barbara Woodell (*Carrie*), Robert Stephenson (*Mongolian Spy*), Lee Bennett (*Don Logan*), H.T. Tsiang (*Wonto*), Joseph Crehan (*Government Official*), Ray Bennett (*Fur Trader*), Nana Bryant (*Peggy Brown*), Fred Coby (*Vice-Consul*), John Halloran, Jean Arden, John

Holland, Spencer Chan.

An uninspired espionage picture set against the backdrop of northern China. Lundigan is a consul from the U.S. Foreign Service held captive when Mongolian rebels, led by Loo, capture the small village where he lives. Loo tries to make a deal with the Chinese government and U.S. authorities, but in the end dies in an explosion which also kills the heroic Lundigan.

p, Sigmund Neufeld; d, Peter Stewart; w, Milton Raison; ph, Jack Greenhalgh (Cinecolor); m, Lucien Cailliet; ed, Holbrook N. Todd; art d, Edward Jewell.

Drama   **(PR:A   MPAA:NR)**

STATE FAIR***   (1933) 80m FOX bw

Will Rogers (*Abel Frake, Farmer and Hog Raiser*), Janet Gaynor (*Margy Frake, His Daughter*), Lew Ayres (*Reporter Pat Gilbert*), Sally Eilers (*Emily Joyce, Girl at the Fair*), Norman Foster (*Wayne Frake*), Louise Dresser (*Melissa Frake*), Frank Craven (*The Storekeeper*), Victor Jory (*The Barker at the Hoopla Stand*), Frank Melton (*Harry Ware, Farmer Neighbor*), John Sheehan (*Barker at Aerial Act*), Doro Merande (*Lady at Food Contest*), Erville Alderson (*Hog Owner*), Harry Holman, Hobart Cavanaugh (*Hog Judges*), Ruth Warren (*Mrs. Edwin Metcalfe*), Blue Boy the Hog.

This was the first time around for the screen adaptations of Stong's lovely story of Americana. Since it was so rooted in small-town life, the wise choice as the lead was Rogers, who represented country people well with his sharp, down-home wit. In Iowa, it's time for the annual State Fair, and Rogers, wife Dresser, son Foster, and daughter Gaynor eagerly await their trip to the city for the event. Rogers owns a huge hog known as Blue Boy, a Hampshire Boar, that he thinks has a shot for the blue ribbon as Best In Show. Dresser is an expert cook and is entering her pickles and mince in the contest and Gaynor and Foster (who later became one of the best B movie directors around) are along for the ride. The State Fair takes place on a camping ground and lasts a full week, so they have plenty of time to see everything. The problems begin immediately as Dresser frets while the judges taste her wares and Rogers can't seem to get his prized boar in the proper mood. Foster encounters Eilers, a trapeze artist working at the fair and the two are immediately attracted to each other. Gaynor meets newsman Ayres and they fall instantly in love (don't forget, the whole movie only takes eighty minutes so there is little time for development of relationships). Foster proposes to Eilers after one evening together but she is far more experienced than the farm boy and knows it's puppy love. She sagely talks him out of his ardor and suggests that he consider marrying his childhood sweetheart. The reverse occurs with Ayres and Gaynor. He has a history of being a trifler with women and when he proposes, Gaynor says she cannot accept right now but will take the matter under consideration. Meanwhile, Rogers can't seem to put any spark in his lazy boar and fears losing the prize. Then a seductive sow is put in the next pen and Blue Boy suddenly begins to act lively and the judges are suitably impressed. Blue Boy wins the prize. Now Dresser's foods are under scrutiny. She doesn't know that he put a dose of brandy into the mincemeat and he doesn't know that she did the same thing so the judges are struck by the alcohol and love it, awarding her the first prize in her division. The family goes home triumphant. Foster ruminates on his brief, torrid night with Eilers and Gaynor is saddened by her putting Ayres off when she wanted to say "Yes" all along. Once home, Ayres calls to say that he must have her and is on his way to their rural residence to propose again. A nice, pleasant tale, light enough to be a musical (which it eventually became, twice). The producers suggested Rogers buy Blue Boy but Rogers declined, saying "I can't do it. I just wouldn't feel right eating a fellow actor." The picture was such a hit that when Blue Boy died, his demise was noted in a January, 1934, edition of *Time* Magazine right next to the passing of various notables.

p, Winfield R. Sheehan; d, Henry King; w, Paul Green, Sonya Levien (based on the novel by Philip Stong); ph, Hal Mohr; ed, R.W. Bischoff; md, Louis DeFrancesco; art d, Duncan Cramer; cos, Rita Kaufman; m/l, Val Burton, Will Jason.

Comedy   **(PR:A   MPAA:NR)**

STATE FAIR****   (1945) 100m FOX c (AKA: IT HAPPENED ONE SUMMER)

Jeanne Crain (*Margy Frake*), Dana Andrews (*Pat Gilbert*), Dick Haymes (*Wayne Frake*), Vivian Blaine (*Emily Joyce*), Charles Winninger (*Abel Frake*), Fay Bainter (*Melissa Frake*), Donald Meek (*Hippenstahl*), Frank McHugh (*McGee*), Percy Kilbride (*Miller*), Henry [Harry] Morgan (*Barker*), Jane Nigh (*Eleanor*), William Marshall (*Marty*), Phil Brown (*Harry Ware*), Paul E. Burns (*Hank*), Tom Fadden (*Eph*), William Frambes (*Pappy*), Steve Olson (*Barker*), Josephine Whittell (*Mrs. Metcalfe*), Paul Harvey (*Simpson*), John Dehner (*Announcer*), Harlan Briggs, Will Wright, Alice Fleming (*Judges*), Walter Baldwin (*Farmer*), Ralph Sanford (*Police Chief*), Frank Mayo (*Man*), Minerva Urecal (*Woman*), Almira Sessions, Virginia Brissac (*Farmer's Wives*), Earl S. Dewey, Wheaton Chambers (*Assistant Judges*), Harry Depp (*Secretary to Judge*), Francis Ford (*Mr. Martin, Whirlwind's Owner*), Margo Wood, Jo-Carroll Dennison (*Girls*), Neal Hart (*Farmer*), Coleen Gray (*Girl*), Emory Parnell (*Senator*).

This, the second version of STATE FAIR, is a rare commodity as it's better than the original, which was pretty good in its own day and time, 12 years before. Hammerstein wrote the screenplay, based on the earlier screen version of Stong's bucolic novel. Rodgers and Hammerstein had just explored the hinterlands with "Oklahoma" and "Carousel" on the Broadway stage and they were a wise choice to write the words and music for this charming film. The story is virtually the same but the addition of the marvelous songs made this a smash. It's still Iowa in the middle of a pleasant summer. Winninger and Bainter are the parents of Crain and Haymes. The old man has a pig he wants to enter at the Fair and he treats the animal like a rich relative, lavishing affection upon the beast that his wife wishes he'd show to her. Bainter is preparing her locally noted pickles and mincemeat which she hopes will also cop the nod from the judges. Crain and Haymes are youngsters coming out of puberty but not yet adult enough to realize the sexual stirrings inside them. At the fair, Haymes falls for Blaine, the singer who fronts the dance band (in the first film that role was a trapeze artist but since this was a musical and since Blaine can really belt, they smartly altered her background but not her character). Blaine has some problems in her life (she's married to a man she doesn't love) but they are easy enough to iron out and once she does, she and Haymes are united. (The first picture had the wise woman sending the yokel boy back to his sweetheart). Crain meets Andrews, a newspaper reporter, and the same story as in the first takes place; e.g., he's a ladies man, she is a shy young woman who fears her heart being taken by this lothario and the ultimate outcome is that the two get together. Winninger's pig hogs the show, Bainter's mincemeat is spiked with brandy and gets the judges tipsy enough to award her the prize, and everyone winds up happy. Yes, it's simple and sappy and as heavy as a handful of cotton candy but everyone has such a good time and the sweetness of the rural life seems so appealing that big city people began to flock to various state fairs after this movie was released. The songs are beautiful and include "It Might as Well Be Spring" (performed by Jeanne Crain with her vocal being looped by Louanne Hogan), which won the Oscar as Best Song of the year. "It's a Grand Night for Singing" (performed by the entire company), "That's For Me" (Blaine, then Haymes), "Isn't It Kinda Fun?" (Haymes), "All I Owe Iowa" (the company), and "our State Fair." Alfred Newman's musical direction was nominated for an Oscar but lost to Georgie Stoll for ANCHORS AWEIGH. Newman and partner Charles Henderson owed a debt of gratitude to the excellent orchestrations by Edward Powell. All the technical credits were topnotch. If there is one little bit of nostalgia or a yearning for the simpler way of life in your heart, see this version of STATE FAIR. It's a celebration of the homespun, rustic ways of the past that will never come back again. This was Crain's fifth movie at the age of 20 and although she had impressed in her other roles, it was this one that made her an enduring star.

p, William Perlberg; d, Walter Lang; w, Oscar Hammerstein II, Sonya Levien, Paul Green (based on the novel by Phil Stong); ph, Leon Shamr Shamroy (Technicolor); ed, J. Watson Webb; md, Alfred Newman, Charles Henderson; art d, Lyle Wheeler, Lewis Creber; set d, Thomas Little, Al Orenbach; spec eff, Fred Sersen; m/l, Richard Rodgers, Hammerstein.

Musical Cas. (PR:A MPAA:NR)

STATE FAIR**½ (1962) 118m FOX c

Pat Boone (*Wayne Frake*), Bobby Darin (*Jerry Dundee*), Pamela Tiffin (*Margie Frake*), Ann-Margret (*Emily Porter*), Tom Ewell (*Able Frake*), Alice Faye (*Melissa Frake*), Wally Cox (*Hipplewaite*), David Brandon (*Harry*), Clem Harvey (*Doc Cramer*), Robert Foulk (*Squat Judge*), Linda Henrich (*Betty Jean*), Edward "Tap" Canutt (*Red Hoerter*), Margaret Deramee (*Lilya*), Albert Harris (*Jim*), Bebe Allan (*Usherette*), George Russell (*George Hoffer*), Edwin McClure (*Announcer*), Walter Beilbey (*Swine Judge*), Tom Loughney (*Dick Burdick*), Claude Hall (*Sime*), Tony Zoppi (*The Masher*), Mary Durant (*Woman Judge*), Sheila Mathews (*Hipplewaite's Girl*), Kay Sutton, Ken Hudgins, Dan Terrell, Louis Roussel, Milton Stolz, Bob Larkin, Tommy Allen, Carl Princi, Jack Carr, Mamie Harris, Paul Rhone, Freeman Morse.

The third, and, it is assumed, the last remake of STATE FAIR failed on many accounts, despite having many of the songs by Rodgers and Hammerstein which enlivened the prior version. Ferrer may have been the wrong director for this uniquely American story. It may have also been that the switching of the tale from rural Iowa to urban Texas took a toll on the rustic quality. Surely the players were not up to the previous actors, with the one exception being Faye as the mother, although Ann-Margret did show some early spunk. Ewell and Faye are husband and wife with their two children, Tiffin and Boone. They are off to Dallas for the State Fair and local pal, Harvey, makes a bet with Ewell that a catastrophe will occur while they are out of the area in the big city. Boone expects to drive in the Fair's sports car race and doesn't much care if he wins, only if he can beat his local enemy, Canutt. Tiffin is hoping she'll meet someone interesting in Dallas as all of the neighborhood boys are dull to her way of thinking. Ewell's hog, Blueboy, is to be entered in the livestock contest and Faye's brandied mincemeat will be tasted in the food division. At the Fair, Tiffin meets Darin, a fast-talking television announcer-interviewer and Boone falls hard for Ann-Margret, a showgirl working at the Fair. The two young couples become enamored of each other while Ewell's pig wins the livestock show and Faye's mincemeat gets judge Cox so drunk that he hands her the prize right away. Boone loses the race, and Ann-Margret, who dearly loves Boone, leaves him because she fears that this rural family will think she is a loose woman. Darin departs

in a hurry and Tiffin feels betrayed. The family returns to their farm but Boone manages to get his head on the right track when he decides to go back to his former sweetie. Tiffin is heartbroken but the shards of her ego are swept up again when Darin calls to say that he didn't mean to go away but he had to be in another town for a short spell and couldn't find her to tell her. He declares his love and proposes as the movie ends. What worked in the 1945 version was the sweetness of the story and apparent naivete of the actors. Here, Darin is not nearly guileless enough and is seen as a smarmy wise guy and one wonders what Tiffin sees in him. She, on the other hand, is so blanched and listless and empty of passion that it's hard to believe Darin would go for her. Ewell could not compete with the earlier actors, Rogers and Winninger, who had played the part. Faye had wanted Don Ameche to come back, thereby reuniting a popular screen duo, but that was impossible for various reasons. She was making a comeback after more than 16 years in retirement and showed she still had what it took to delight an audience. Many of the earlier Rodgers and Hammerstein songs were used as well as five new ones that Rodgers wrote music and lyrics for solo. One of the best in the 1945 picture had to be dropped because it referred to Iowa and since this one was set in Texas, it just didn't pertain. The held-over tunes by R&H were "Our State Fair" (performed by Ewell, Faye, Tiffin, Boone), "It's a Grand Night for Singing" (the company), "That's for Me" (Boone), "It Might As Well Be Spring" (Tiffin), "Isn't It Kind of Fun?" (Ann-Margret, chorus). The songs written by Rodgers alone were "More Than Just a Friend" (Ewell), "It's the Little Things in Texas (Ewell, Faye), "Willing and Eager" (Boone, Ann-Margret), "This Isn't Heaven" (Darin). The locations were shot in Dallas with some second unit work in Oklahoma City. Making the movie bigger did not make it better. Anita Gordon looped Tiffin's singing. This was the first time that anyone close to resembling a "heavy" appeared in this story. The role was played by Canutt but it hardly entered into the activities.

p, Charles Brackett; d, Jose Ferrer; w, Richard Breen, Oscar Hammerstein II, Sonya Levien, Paul Green (based on the novel by Philip Stong); ph, William C. Mellor (CinemaScope, DeLuxe Color); m, Alfred Newman; ed, David Bretherton; art d, Jack Martin Smith, Walter M. Simonds; set d, Walter M. Scott, Lou Hafley; cos, Marjorie Best; spec eff, L. B. Abbott; ch, Nick Castle; makeup, Ben Nye.

Musical Cas. (PR:A MPAA:NR)

STATE OF SIEGE***½ (1973, Fr./U.S./Ital./Ger.) 120m Reggana-Cinema 10-Unidis- Euro International-Dieter Geissler/Cinema 5 (ETAT DE SIEGE)

Yves Montand (*Philip Michael Santore*), Renato Salvatori (*Capt. Lopez*), O.E. Hasse (*Carlos Ducas*), Jacques Weber (*Hugo*), Jean Luc Bideau (*Este*), Evangeline Peterson (*Mrs. Santore*), Maurice Teynac (*Minister of Internal Security*), Yvette Etievant (*Woman Senator*), Harald Wolff (*Minister of Foreign Affairs*), Nemesio Antunes (*President of the Republic*), Andre Falcon (*Deputy Fabbri*), Mario Montilles (*Assistant Commissioner Fontant*), Jerry Brouer (*Anthony Lee*), Jean-Francois Boggi (*Journalist*), Eugenio Guzman (*Spokesman for Internal Security*), Maurice Jacquemont (*Dean of the Law School*), Roberto Navarette (*Commissioner Romero*), Gloria Lass (*Tortured Student*), Alejandro Cohen (*Manuel*), Martha Contreras (*Alicia*), Jacques Perrin (*Telephonist*), Gerard Manneveau (*Bardes*), Aldo Francia (*Dr. Francia*), Gilbert Brandini (*Journalist*), Douglas Harris (*Aid Director*), Robert Holmes (*Papal Nuncio*), Alejandro Sieverina (*Enrique Macchi*), Alejandro Misle (*President of the Assembly*), Julio Zarata (*Instructor at the Police Academy*).

Political rhetoric aside, this is a good film. Costa-Gavras and Montand had teamed before when Montand played a liberal slated for assassination in dictatorial Greece in Z (although the name of the country is not cited) and a communist in Czechoslovakia (which is also not mentioned) in THE CONFESSION. This time, there's no doubt the story is taking place where it happened, in Uruguay (although it was shot in Chile and France). Based on a true occurrence, it makes many fanciful assertions about the real life and death of Daniel Mitrione, a man who worked for the U.S. Agency for International Development (AID). His task was to work with the local cops to help in traffic control but the information released after his death alleged that he was an anti-guerrilla expert and had functioned with the government of Uruguay in the torture and murder of many revolutionary Tupamaros, the group who were fighting the right-wing regime that still rules Uruguay and has been known to give safe haven to Nazis on the run. It's 1970 in the capital of the South American country and there's a search in progress for Montand. He's been kidnapped by the rebels and the town is being turned upside down to find him. When his dead body is located in the rear of a car, the search ends. After the funeral sequence, the rest of the movie flashes back to how and why it happened. Montand is an Italian-born man now working for AID. He says goodbye to his family of seven children and his wife, Peterson; climbs into his limousine; and starts for his office. Along the road, the long car is waylaid by the Tupamaros, a league of guerrillas. Montand is wounded in the crossfire, then taken to their hideout and given dressings for his wounds, which are minor. A hooded interrogator wants to know what he's really doing in the country. The idea of a man teaching traffic control is ludicrous to them and they think he must be up to something else. They want to know if he was the man who taught methods of interrogation to reps from several pro-U.S. governments, all of whom were worried about thunder from the Left. They have what they believe is proof that Montand worked closely with the factions who overthrew legitimately elected governments in Santo Domingo and Brazil. The questions are many and Montand does his best to field them all and keep his cool. It's a battle of wits not unlike the Alec Guinness-Jack Hawkins confrontation in THE PRISONER. Meanwhile, feverish negotiations for Montand's release are being made and a deal is finally offered. The Tupamaros will free Montand in exchange for 150 political prisoners. The Uruguayan government won't hear of it and says that there are no such people as political prisoners in their country, only crooks and killers. The noose is tightening around Montand's neck as his captors continue to harangue him with evidence that proves his complicity in the charges they have leveled against him. At last, he admits that he has done some of the things they have accused him of but he feels that his actions were done for the benefit of mankind. The rebels see it in a different way and think that he is an international criminal who must pay the price. Knowing that they cannot free their 150 brethren from jail, the Tupamaros vote on whether or not to allow Montand to live. If he is let go, they will have shown weakness in their cause. If they kill him, the Uruguayan government will have all the more reason to become even stricter, perhaps declare martial law, and arrest anyone who breathes even a syllable against the men who run the country. Days pass and Montand's body is found. Then the new AID man is assigned to the embassy and his arrival is closely watched by the various Tupamaros who monitor every move. STATE OF SIEGE was so controversial that it was refused a screen at the American Film Institute theater in Washington, igniting a blaze of anger from film people who resented this obvious censorship. The main objection voiced to the film was that it glorified political assassination and that the material was so anti-American that it did not merit viewing. Costa-Gavras felt that it was not anti-American, that it was anti-government, and that he, personally, did not blame the American people for what their elected government did–just as he didn't blame the Greeks for what their fascist regime did a couple of movies ago. There is no question that Costa-Gavras stacked the deck in his film as he showed the right-wingers to be ugly, dumb, and boorish, while the left-wingers were seen to be handsome, honest, and filled with passion, as well as armed with proof positive of U.S. meddling in South American domestic affairs. If one is to believe the statements made by this movie, the U.S. government is like an infestation of cockroaches, rubbing their eight legs together and waiting to attack. The film's style is in keeping with the work Costa-Gavras did on his other films: quick cuts, sharp angles, etc. This is not as good as Z for a few reasons. There is far too much dialog and continuous pounding of points made earlier. A good movie, not a great one, and intensely disturbing to anyone who believes what they say in the script.

p, Jacques Perrin; d, Constantin Costa-Gavras; w, Franco Solinas, Costa-Gavras; ph, Pierre William Glenn (Eastmancolor); m, Mikis Theodorakis; ed, Francoise Bonnot; prod d, Jacques D'Ovidio; art d, D. Ovidio.

Drama   **Cas.**   **(PR:C   MPAA:PG)**

STATE OF THE UNION******** (1948) 124m Liberty/MGM bw (GB: THE WORLD AND HIS WIFE)

Spencer Tracy (Grant Matthews), Katharine Hepburn (Mary Matthews), Van Johnson (Spike McManus), Angela Lansbury (Kay Thorndyke), Adolphe Menjou (Jim Conover), Lewis Stone (Sam Thorndyke), Howard Smith (Sam Parrish), Maidel Turner (Lulubelle Alexander), Raymond Walburn (Judge Alexander), Charles Dingle (Bill Hardy), Florence Auer (Grace Orval Draper), Pierre Watkin (Sen. Lauterback), Margaret Hamilton (Norah), Irving Bacon (Buck), Patti Brady (Joyce), George Nokes (Grant, Jr.), Carl Alfalfa Switzer (Bellboy), Tom Pedi (Barber), Tom Fadden (Waiter), Charles Lane (Blink Moran), Art Baker (Leith), Rhea Mitchell (Jenny), Arthur O'Connell (1st Reporter), Marion Martin (Blonde Girl), Tor Johnson (Wrestler), Stanley Andrews (Senator), Dave Willock (Pilot), Russell Meeker (Politician), Frank I. Clarke (Joe Crandall), David Clarke (Rusty Miller), Del Henderson (Broder), Edwin Cooper (Bradbury), Davison Clark (Crump), Francis Pierlot (Josephs), Brandon Beach (Editor), Eddie Phillips (Television Man), Roger Moore, Lew Smith, Gene Coogan, Douglas Carter, Charles Sherlock, Wilson Wood, George Barton, Harry Anderson, Charles Coleman, Stanley Price, Fred Zendar, Jack Boyle (Photographers), Maurice Cass (Little Man), Eve Whitney (Secretary), Bert Moorhouse, Thornton Edwards, Marshall Ruth (Men).

One of the joys of the Broadway hit from whence this sprung was that the authors changed the dialog almost weekly to reflect what was happening in the news. The politically oriented script kept a freshness about it that caused audiences to return again to the play that opened in November 1945 and played 765 shows before going out on tour and doing land-office business. It starred Ralph Bellamy and Ruth Hussey (a former MGM actress) and delighted everyone who saw it. By making a movie of the last script, they had to freeze the dialog in time, although anyone old enough to recall the election year of 1948 will appreciate the jokes. Capra, George Stevens, William Wyler, and producer Sam Briskin organized the firm of Liberty Pictures which was to make a series of movies to be released through RKO. The first was IT'S A WONDERFUL LIFE and they had hopes this would be the second but the price was too high for RKO and the idea of using Gary Cooper and Claudette Colbert was abandoned when Colbert insisted that she would not work past five in the afternoon on the orders of her doctor and her agent. The fact that her doctor was her husband and her agent was her brother didn't faze her and she exited. MGM arrived and suggested Tracy,

but with Colbert's departure, a new feminine lead was needed. Despite the fact that Hepburn had turned down the play when it was offered on the stage (so did Helen Hayes and Margaret Sullavan), she wanted to do it with her lover, Tracy, and a deal was struck. This was all taking place during the onset of the Hollywood Communist witch hunts, a practice Hepburn deplored and costar Menjou embraced. The two had played well together in STAGE DOOR and MORNING GLORY (Hepburn's first Oscar role) but the camaraderie was gone over the diverse sides of the political spectrum that each had. Tracy is an aircraft multimillionaire who is seeking the Republican nomination in the election. He is a liberal type and thus close to the President in many ways but he sincerely feels there is enough of a difference in their philosophies to offer Americans a choice. At the start, he is an outsider from the party and given only the slimmest hopes of securing the nomination against ensconced politicians with "machines" behind them. To further complicate matters, Tracy is living apart from his wife, Hepburn, and they haven't gotten along for years. He has been having an affair with tough Lansbury, a wealthy newspaper publisher with great media power. Lansbury can throw her newspapers behind Tracy and help him gather support. (Lansbury, as always, was playing a part far older than her actual age, which was only in her mid-twenties at the time.) In order to show the U.S. that he is a solid citizen, Hepburn is asked to return and masquerade as Tracy's loving wife while he crosses the country stumping for votes and popularity. Hepburn makes it clear that she's doing this on a temporary basis and that she won't stay beyond his election, if he ever gets the nomination. With this charade as the backdrop, we begin to meet the powers behind the potential throne. Menjou is a long-time political boss who has thrown his weight behind Tracy knowing that he will benefit by it in the long run and Johnson is seen as a savvy newspaperman who has given up his column for the nonce in order to function as the publicist for Tracy. Tracy is a decent man with strong convictions, but as the tour continues, his morals begin to erode as he gets into the madness of elections. Little by little, the tenets of his political beliefs are chipped at and he is becoming the very person he used to decry. Hepburn watches him alter his values and finally can take it no longer and speaks up. She points out that the people Tracy has chosen to throw in his lot with are greedy, grasping, and basically corrupt. This happens at a dinner party and Hepburn's speech is a last-ditch attempt to make him see the light, as well as to break up his alliance with Lansbury. In the time it's taken to make the tour, Hepburn has fallen in love again with Tracy and she can't bear the thought of him winding up with the ambitious Lansbury who she feels doesn't love Tracy, just wants a ticket to the Inaugural Ball as First Lady. Tracy listens to Hepburn and understands what he has done. On a radio broadcast, he announces to the listening audience that he is taking his name off the nominating slate because he feels he is not worthy of consideration on the voters' part. With that done, Tracy feels as though a giant yoke has been removed from around his neck. He also realizes that Lansbury was not for him at all and that Hepburn was the one person who had the spunk to speak up and show him the right way. The picture ends and the audience cheers and sadly notes that it would be wonderful if real politicians had that kind of honesty. All of the acting was first-rate, as were the script, direction, and technical credits. And yet, it was totally bypassed by the Motion Picture Academy for any nominations. There were many changes from the play and the main one was the toning down of the Tracy-Lansbury liason, perhaps to concentrate on the politics rather than the sex. Please note in various roles Oscar-winner Arthur O'Connell, the beloved Margaret Hamilton, the host of TV's "You Asked For It," Art Baker, and Carl "Alfalfa" Switzer, without his cowlick hair standing up. Due to the nature of timely material becoming dated very soon, much of the power of the script is lost on 1980s audiences, but it remains a delight to see so many superb actors playing their trade and stealing scene after scene from each other. From the way they play together, you'd never know that Hepburn and Menjou were looking daggers at each other. They left their personal rancor at the sound-stage door. Now that's acting.

p&d, Frank Capra; w, Anthony Veiller, Myles Connolly (based on the play by Howard Lindsay, Russel Crouse); ph, George J. Folsey; m, Victor Young; ed, William Hornbeck; art d, Cedric Gibbons, Urie McCleary; set d, Emile Kuri; cos, Irene; spec eff, A. Arnold Gillespie.

Comedy/Drama   **Cas.**   **(PR:A   MPAA:NR)**

STATE OF THINGS, THE*****½** (1983) 121m Gray City/Artificial Eye bw

Isabelle Weingarten (Anna), Rebecca Pauly (Joan), Jeffrey Kime (Mark), Geoffrey Carey (Robert), Camilla Mora (Julia), Alexandra Auder (Jane), Patrick Bauchau (Friedrich, Director), Paul Getty III (Dennis, Writer), Viva Auder (Kate, Script-girl), Sam Fuller (Joe, Cameraman), Artur Samedo (Production Manager), Francisco Baiao (Soundman), Robert Kramer (Camera Operator), Allen Goorwitz [Garfield] (Gordon), Roger Corman (Lawyer), Martine Getty (Secretary), Monty Bane (Herbert), Janet Rasak (Karen), Judy Mooradian (Waitress).

An innovative and exciting saga of a filmmaker and his crew shooting a movie (a remake of Hollywood B-movie, THE MOST DANGEROUS MAN ON EARTH) on the outer edges of Spain. They are stranded with no money, and worse, no film. The adventure begins as the director searches to find an elusive American producer. More interesting than the film itself is the real life situation of director Wim Wenders. After spending a couple of years on HAMMETT, Wenders turned to Francis Ford Coppola to lend him the necessary funds to keep the production afloat. After a struggle in filmmaking limbo HAMMETT finally emerged, but bearing little resemblance to Wender's original conception. Wender's debt to Hollywood movies is once again repaid (his first payment was the Nick Ray documentary LIGHTNING OVER WATER in 1978) by casting Sam Fuller as a cameraman and Roger Corman as a lawyer.

p, Chris Sievernich; d, Wim Wenders; w, Wenders, Robert Kramer; ph, Henri Alekan, Fred Murphy; m, Jurgen Knieper; ed, Barbara von Weitershausen; art d, Ze Branco; cos, Maria Gonzaga.

Drama   (PR:A   MPAA:NR)

STATE PENITENTIARY**   (1950) 66m COL bw

Warner Baxter (*Roger Manners*), Onslow Stevens (*Jim Evans*), Karin Booth (*Shirley Manners*), Robert Shayne (*Stanley Brown*), Richard Benedict (*Tony Gavin*), Brett King (*Kid Beaumont*), John Bleifer (*Jailbreak Jimmy*), Leo T. Cleary (*Warden*), Rick Vallin (*Guard*), Rusty Wescoatt ("*Flash*" *Russell*), William Fawcett (*Bill Costello*), John Hart ("*Sandy*" *O'Hara*).

A cliched melodrama actually photographed in the Nevada State Penitentiary has Baxter serving time for an embezzlement scheme of which he is innocent. He escapes with the intention of capturing the real culprit, Shayne, the subject of Baxter's wife's (Booth) investigation. The police, in pursuit of the fugitive, are led to Shayne, bringing him back to prison in place of Baxter. This was Warner Baxter's last film. He died the next year from medical complications following a voluntary prefrontal lobotomy (at the time, the operation was widely regarded as a panacea for all sorts of problems, including the arthritis that plagued Baxter; for a more realistic view of this medical malpractice situation, see SUDDENLY, LAST SUMMER, released in 1959).

p, Sam Katzman; d, Lew Landers; w, Howard J. Green, Robert Libott, Frank Burt (based on the story by Henry E. Helseth); ph, Ira H. Morgan; ed, James Sweeney; md, Mischa Bakaleinikoff; and, Paul Palmentola.

Drama/Crime   (PR:A   MPAA:NR)

STATE POLICE*½   (1938) 60m T/C/UNIV bw

John King (*Sgt. Dan Prescott*), William Lundigan (*Pvt. Smith*), Constance Moore (*Helen Evans*), Larry Blake (*Trigger Magee*), J. Farrell MacDonald (*Charlie*), David Oliver (*Capt. Duffy*), Ted Osborn (*Evans*), Pierre Watkin (*Col. Clark*), Guy Usher (*Hughes*), Charles Wilson (*Capt. Halstead*), Eddy Waller (*Constable Higgins*), Sam Flint (*Palmer*).

Lundigan plays the swank, playboyish son of a police chief bent on preventing a coal mining racket in a small town. The gangsters try to pressure him, but eventually they and their bootlegging ring are squelched. Heavy on action but weakly constructed.

p, Trem Carr; d, John Rawlins; w, George Waggner (based on "State Trooper," a story by Waggner); ph, Harry Neumann; ed, Charles Craft; md, Charles Previn.

Crime   (PR:A   MPAA:NR)

STATE POLICE 1948   (SEE: WHIRLWIND RAIDERS, 1948)

STATE SECRET   (SEE: GREAT MANHUNT, THE, 1951, Brit.)

STATE STREET SADIE**   (1928) 75m WB bw (GB: THE GIRL
                                                          FROM STATE STREET)

Conrad Nagel (*Ralph Blake*), Myrna Loy (*Isobel*), William Russell (*The Bat*), George Stone (*Slinkey*), Pat Hartigan ("*The Bull*" *Hawkins*).

A partial-talkie delves into the fascination with the Underworld by casting Nagel as the honest brother of a dead gangster, who happens to be his twin. To avenge his brother's death he sets his sights on a gang boss known only as "The Chief," (no one seems to know his identity), dealing through Russell, his mouthpiece. A blazing gun battle reveals that Russell is, in fact, "The Chief," outwitted by Nagel's trickery and police pursuit.

d, Archie Mayo; w, E. T. Lowe, Jr. (based on a story by Melville Crossman [Darryl F. Zanuck]; ph, Barney McGill; m, Louis Silvers; ed, George Marks.

Crime   (PR:C   MPAA:NR)

STATE TROOPER**   (1933) 68m COL bw

Regis Toomey (*Michael Rolph*), Evalyn Knapp (*June Brady*), Raymond Hatton (*Carter*), Matthew Betz (*Jarvis*), Edwin Maxwell (*W. J. Brady*), Walter McGrail (*Burman*), Lew Kelley (*Graber*), Don Chapman (*Jimmy*), Eddie Chandler (*Morgan*).

Toomey plays a motorcycle cop who tickets oil tycoon Maxwell, but eventually sheds his badge to work for the oil company. With a price war under way and the possibility of sabotage looming, Toomey is hired to keep a protective eye on the refinery. The finale has him putting down a gangster attack and falling in love with Maxwell's daughter Knapp.

d, D. Ross Lederman; w, Stuart Anthony (based on the story by Lambert

Hillyer); ph, Benjamin Kline.

Crime/Drama   (PR:A   MPAA:NR)

STATELESS   (SEE: NO EXIT, 1962)

STATELINE MOTEL*   (1976, Ital.) 86m Fral/International
                Cinefilm-NMD c (AKA: LAST CHANCE FOR A BORN LOSER)

Ursula Andress, Eli Wallach, Fabio Testi, Massimo Girotti, Barbara Bach, Howard Ross, Carlo De Mejo.

The plot line from THE POSTMAN ALWAYS RINGS TWICE gets reworked with little imagination in this Italian production shot on location in Canada. Testi comes to the "Motel Last Chance" where he meets the passionate and sexy Andress. He conspires a plot to take the woman away from her less than virile husband Girotti, who ironically played the young stud in OSSESSIONE, which carried a similar story line. However, this film doesn't match that earlier effort. Its lurid detailing comes off cheaply, with little redeeming qualities.

p, Nicholas Demetroules; d, Maurizio Lucidi; ph, (Eastmancolor).

Crime/Drama   (PR:O   MPAA: R)

STATE'S ATTORNEY****   (1932) 73m RKO bw (GB: CARDIGAN'S
                                                                  LAST CASE)

John Barrymore (*Tom Cardigan*), Helen Twelvetrees (*June Perry*), William "Stage" Boyd (*Vanny Powers*), Jill Esmond (*Lillian Ulrich*), Raoul Roulien (*Senor Alvarado*), Ralph Ince (*Defense Attorney*), Frederick Burton (*Judge*), Leon Waycoff 'Ames' (*Prosecutor*), C. Henry Gordon, Ethel Sutherland.

In this entertaining though improbable courtroom drama, Barrymore plays a young man who becomes a lawyer after leaving reform school. He becomes attorney for Boyd, a powerful underworld figure and a former classmate of Barrymore's from reform school. Barrymore eventually turns over a new leaf, then works his way up to the state's attorney offices, where he becomes an assistant D.A. He is assigned to go after Boyd on gambling and murder charges, and in the course of the investigation Barrymore meets Twelvetrees. She is on trial through a misunderstanding of her presence at one of Boyd's gambling joints. Eventually Barrymore convicts Boyd, getting him the death penalty, but the attorney's past is exposed in the process. Barrymore graciously resigns from office, but with Twelvetrees by his side the future looks bright. Barrymore, in his first film at RKO, fairly chews up the scenery, then spits it out with his lively histronics. Though the script (written especially for the actor by Barrymore's good friend Fowler) is pure fabrication, Archainbaud's direction, coupled with his star's performance weaves an interesting tale. This originally was to be directed by cowriter Brown, but he was replaced twice: first by Irving Pichel, then by Archainbaud. According to Barrymore's biographer John Kobler (in his book *Damned In Paradise, The Life of John Barrymore*), the film's screenplay contains a line often attributed to the actor's father, Maurice. At one point Barrymore glances at a snowy landscape offered by an artist, then comments: "Winter is not as bad as it's painted." In 1937, this film was remade as CRIMINAL LAWYER with Lee Tracy in the Barrymore role.

p, David O. Selznick; d, George Archainbaud; w, Gene Fowler, Rowland Brown (based on a story by Louis Stevens); ph, Leo Tover; ed, Charles Kimball, William Hamilton; art d, Carroll Clark.

Drama   (PR:A   MPAA:NR)

STATION SIX-SAHARA**   (1964, Brit./Ger.) 99m CCC-Filmkunst/AA
                                                  bw (ENDSTATION 13 SAHARA)

Carroll Baker (*Catherine*), Peter Van Eyck (*Kramer*), Ian Bannen (*Fletcher*), Denholm Elliott (*Macey*), Hansjorg Felmy (*Martin*), Mario Adorf (*Santos*), Biff McGuire (*Jimmy*), Harry Baird (*Sailor*).

The tensions of a group of isolated oil workers are released when they rescue Baker and McGuire from an auto accident. However, instead of satisfying the men's desire, she only acts as catalyst to an explosive situation by sleeping first with Van Eyck, and then with Felmy. McGuire, her jealous ex-husband, watching from his sick bed as his love is taken from him, eventually stabs her to death and then takes his own life. With the visitors gone, the oil workers return to their previous existence. BABY DOLL star Baker, who raised sexual awareness in her 1956 film, here did the same by appearing in a nude sequence which, much to the chagrin of American audiences, was cut from the U.S. release print.

p, Victor Lyndon; d, Seth Holt; w, Bryan Forbes, Brian Clemens (based on the play "Men Without A Past" by Jacques Maret); ph, Gerald Gibbs; m, Ron Grainer; ed, Alastair McIntyre; art d, Jack Stephens; makeup, Gerry Fletcher.

Drama   (PR:C   MPAA:NR)

STATION WEST*** (1948) 92m RKO bw

Dick Powell (Haven), Jane Greer (Charlie), Agnes Moorehead (Mrs. Caslon), Burl Ives (Hotel Clerk), Tom Powers (Capt. Iles), Gordon Oliver (Prince), Steve Brodie (Stallman), Guinn "Big Boy" Williams (Mick), Raymond Burr (Mark Bristow), Regis Toomey (Goddard), Olin Howlin (Cook), John Berkes (Pianist), Michael Steele (Jerry), Dan White (Pete), John Kellogg (Ben), John Doucette (Bartender), Charles Middleton (Sheriff), Suzi Crandall (Girl), Al Hill (Croupier), Jack Stoney, Stanley Blystone (Bouncers), Joey Ray (Stickman), Marie Thomas (Dance-Hall Girl), Robert Gates (Sam), Robert Jefferson (Boy), Leo McMahon (Rider), William Phipps (Sergeant), Bud Osborne, Ethan Laidlaw, Monte Montague, Lomax Study (Men).

Powell is hired to locate the outlaws who murdered a pair of soldiers in charge of guarding a fort's gold shipment. He follows his clues to a gambling den operated by Greer, the beautiful but tough lady responsible for the crime. Powell gets himself hired as a bouncer in her establishment by displaying some fancy fist work, eventually gathering all the proof he needs to bring Greer down. Well directed and full of witty, intelligent dialog.

p, Robert Sparks; d, Sidney Lanfield; w, Frank Fenton, Winston Miller (based on the novel by Luke Short); ph, Harry J. Wild; m, Heinz Roemheld; ed, Frederic Knudtson; md, C. Bakaleinikoff; art d, Albert S. D'Agostino, Feild Gray; set d, Darrell Silvera, James Altwies; cos, Renie; spec eff, Russell A. Cully; m/l, "The Sun Shining Warm," "Sometime Remind Me to Tell You," Mort Greene, Leigh Harline; makeup, Gordon Bau

Western **Cas.** **(PR:A MPAA:NR)**

STATUE, THE Zero (1971, Brit.) 89m CINERAMA c

David Niven (Alex), Virna Lisi (Rhonda), Robert Vaughn (Ray), Ann Bell (Pat), Mircha Carven (Joachim), John Cleese (Harry), Bettine Milne (Dunhill), Derek Francis (Sanders), Tim Brooke-Taylor (Hillcrest), Desmond Walter-Ellis (Mr. Southwick), Susan Travers (Mrs. Southwick), David Mills (Mr. Euston), Zoe Sallis (Mrs. Euston), David Allister (Mr. Westbury), Maureen Lane (Mrs. Westbury), Granville Van Dusen (Chuck), Tony Gardner (Hunter), Hugh Burden (Sir Geoffrey), Eric Chitty (Mouser), Gianni Musi (Jacques), Katarina Lidfeldt (Melinda), Troy Patterson (Larry Patten), Tolis Karachalios (Greek Guide), Hazel Hoskins (Chief of CIA), Aldo De Carellis (Martinello), Sergio Silverio (1st Marine), Antonino D'Acquisto (2nd Marine), Lorenzo Fineschi (Mike), F.L. Greaves (Herbert Parker), Edward Danko (Harold Brodie), Dough Parish (Philip Muir), Julian Jenkins (1st Detective), Mike Atkinson (2nd Detective), Ron Hepher (3rd Detective), John Frederick (Military Advisor), Bill Vanders (Lawyer), Jack Repp (Air Force Officer), Robert Pomeroy (Navy Officer), Marine Maitland (UNO Secretary General), John Stacy (Commentator), Pistillo Antonio (Piet Bruder), Graham Chapman (News Reader), John Wregg (Policeman), Marco Gobbi (Hank Wills), Kiko Goncalves (Consul of Corteguay), Maria Comberti (Little Old Woman), Fortunato Arena (Custom Officer), Mario Guizzardi (George French), Amato Garbini (Italian Inspector), Pino Ferrara (Guide, Florence), Pamela Le Pelley (Schoolmistress), Nicolette Le Pelley (Caroline), Julie Fair (Ray's Secretary), Marco Tulli (Deaf Taylor), Brune Erba (Maurice Debois), Mike Harvey (U.S. Embassy Official), Roberto Lande (Young Italian Male), Christopher Cruize (1st Interview), Luigi Scavran (Senior Meteroa Monk).

Smarmy, sniggering, stupid and senseless, THE STATUE takes a one-joke premise not even suitable for an eight-minute segment of the old TV version of "Love, American Style" and blows it up into a full movie that is only made barely palatable by Niven's expert farcemanship, although one wonders if he actually read the script before accepting the role. Niven is a busy linguist in England who has just been awarded the Nobel Prize for having devised a universal language. (Evidently, the producers and writers must have forgotten that "Esperanto" had been invented decades before and failed.) Vaughn is the U.S. Ambassador in England (and looking far too young at 38 to convince us he is) and asks Niven's young, succulent wife, Lisi, to sculpt a statue of Niven as she is a renowned pounder of marble in her own right. The statue is to be placed in Grosvenor Square, in front of the Unispeak Foundation and the U.S. Embassy. Niven travels a great deal and has been home less than three weeks in three years so this May-December marriage is hardly filled with companionship. She presents, at a cost of $50,000, an 18-foot high statute of Niven, in the nude. There's no question that the face is his but Niven soon realizes that there is one part of the statue that bears no resemblance to him at all. This makes him think that Lisi must have been having an affair with someone as that section of the sculpture is quite different from Niven's personal parts. He secures a list of several men Lisi knows and goes off to find which one of them lent his likeness to that section of the 750-pound statue. He finds himself in a Turkish bath, at a nude stage play called "Skin," in a monastery, etc. When a man goes around looking at other men's you-know-whats, there is only one way to label him. In a rush to find out who is the poser, the entire resources of the U.S. are put into play and we see a tourist have his pants pulled down in Brazil, Army doctors snapping photos of inductees at a southern draft office, and lots of other "hilarious" stuff like that. The statue is yet to be unveiled and when Vaughn comes to see it in Lisi's studio he is shocked and pleads with her to add a fig leaf. She won't do it and says that would compromise her work. Vaughn's best moments in the film are when he's attempting to explain the entire situation to his boss, Nixon, on the long distance phone, as a photo of the former president hangs smiling on the wall. Vaughn has the statue taken

apart for fear of his job. At the same time, Niven is off in Florence, talking to Lisi's teacher. He then learns that the model for the statue's questionable area was Michelangelo's "David." The twist at the end has Lisi presenting a huge nude sculpture of Vaughn. Filmed in Italy, THE STATUE is a new low in tastelessness, made all the more cringing by the nature of the players. The name of the statue, for no reason, is "Charlie," which is the name of the song by Ortolani and Norman Newell, sung by The Statuettes. The other unmemorable tune was "Skin" by Audrey Nohra, Luis Enriquez Bacalov. In one of his earliest films, note John Cleese of the "Monty Python" group. THE STATUE is soft porn for soft heads.

p, Anis Nohra; d, Rod Amateau; w, Alec Coppel, Denis Norden (based on the play "Chip Chip Chip" by Coppel); ph, Piero Portalupi (Humphries Color); m, Riz Ortolani; ed, Ernest Hosler, Fergus McDonell; md, Ortolani; art d, Bruno Avesani; set d, Franco Fumagalli; cos, Orietta Nasalli Rocca; ch, Gino Landi; m/l, Ortolani, Norman Newell, Luis Enriquez Bacalov, Audrey Nohra; makeup, Amato Garbine.

Comedy **(PR:O MPAA:R)**

STAVISKY***½ (1974, Fr.) 115m Ariane-Cerita-Euro International/CINEMATION c

Jean-Paul Belmondo (Serge Alexandre Stavisky), Charles Boyer (Raoul), Francois Perier (Borelli), Anny Duperey (Arlette), Michel Lonsdale (Mezy), Claude Rich (Bonny), Marcel Cuvillier (Bosseaud), Jacques Spiesser (Granville), Gigi Balista (Henriet), Roberto Bisacca (Montalvo).

A fascinating true story of the man who almost brought down the French government. Serge Stavisky committed suicide on January 3, 1934. The Russian-born promoter had been involved with the issuance of phony bonds and several other crimes but he had evidently been protected by officials in high places (he supposedly distributed millions of francs in bribes). When one of the officials was murdered, there were accusations that this man in the public prosecutor's office was silenced to keep from spilling the beans. Factions from all of the parties began stirring up trouble and claiming that it was due to the basic corruption in the elected government. Riots began on February 6-8 and a general strike was called. The government teetered and fell, then a new coalition was formed by people who had been outside of the Stavisky influence and France went on. That's how it ended. How it all happened is the subject of the movie by Resnais, a different kind of film from the director who helmed LAST YEAR AT MARIENBAD and HIROSHIMA, MON AMOUR. The screenplay was by the man who wrote Z so it was literate and had more than a bit of politics attached. Belmondo plays the title role, a small-time hustler who migrates to France, becomes an embezzler, and uses his personal charm and diabolical tactics to quickly rise to a place of economic importance with a rash of bold moves. Belmondo's wife is Duperey, who goes along with his machinations, and Boyer is a poor Spanish nobleman who dreams of stirring up a civil war in Spain and taking over after the current regime has been destroyed. The picture belongs to Belmondo, who oozes confidence as he makes his way up through the eddies and whirlpools of politics and emerges as the most powerful man in the country. Then, when it seems as though he's gone too far, all of his associates desert him and he is left with only one recourse, the taking of his own life. With that, he duplicates what his dentist father did upon hearing that his son had been clapped in jail. The picture is technically brilliant, visually stunning, and ceaselessly interesting, but the hero is a villain without much to like and audiences want someone to root for so this movie did not make a great deal at the box office. The music by Stephen Sondheim was a bit too intellectual for the emotions seen on screen.

d, Alain Resnais; w, Jorge Semprun; ph, Sacha Vierny (Eastmancolor); m, Stephen Sondheim; ed, Albert Jurgenson.

Biography **Cas.** **(PR:C MPAA:PG)**

STAY AWAY, JOE* (1968) 101m MGM c

Elvis Presley (Joe Lightcloud), Burgess Meredith (Charlie Lightcloud), Joan Blondell (Glenda Callahan), Katy Jurado (Annie Lightcloud), Thomas Gomez (Grandpa), Henry Jones (Hy Slager), L.Q. Jones (Bronc Hoverty), Quentin Dean (Mamie Callahan), Anne Seymour (Mrs. Hawkins), Douglas Henderson (Congressman Morrissey), Angus Duncan (Lorne Hawkins), Michael Lane (Frank Hawk), Susan Trustman (Mary Lightcloud), Warren Vanders (Hike Bowers), Buck Kartalian (Bull Shortgun), Maurishka (Connie Shortgun), Caitlin Wyles (Marlene Standing Rattle), Marya Christen (Billie-Jo Hump), Del "Sonny" West (Jackson He-Crow), Jennifer Peak (Little Dear), Brett Parker (Deputy Sheriff Hank Matson), Michael Keller (Orville Witt).

Even die-hard Elvis fans will have a tough time accepting "The King" as a half-breed Indian with Meredith as his redskin dad. Elvis convinces a congressman to permit them to raise a herd of cattle in exchange for U.S. government assistance on their Arizona reservation. Elvis has some trouble distinguishing the bulls from the cows, but eventually gets the job done. When not rustling, he's running around with dopey Dean, the daughter of strict tavern owner Blondell, and singing tunes.

p, Douglas Laurence; d, Peter Tewksbury; w, Burt Kennedy, Michael A. Hoey (based on the novel by Dan Cushman); ph, Fred Koenekamp (Panavision, Metrocolor); m, Jack Marshall; ed, George W. Brooks; art d,

George W. Davis, Carl Anderson; set d, Henry Grace, Don Greenwood, Jr.; m/l, "Dominique," "Stay Away, Joe," Sid Tepper, Roy C. Bennett (sung by Elvis Presley), "U.S. Male," Jerry Reed (vocal backgrounds, The Jordanaires); makeup, William Tuttle.

Comedy/Drama (PR:A MPAA:M/PG)

STAY HUNGRY** (1976) 102m UA c

Jeff Bridges (*Craig Blake*), Sally Field (*Mary Tate Farnsworth*), Arnold Schwarzenegger (*Joe Santo*), R.G. Armstrong (*Thor Erickson*), Robert Englund (*Franklin*), Helena Kallianiotes (*Anita*), Robert E. Mosley (*Newton*), Woodrow Parfrey (*Craig's Uncle*), Scatman Crothers (*Butler*), Kathleen Miller (*Dorothy Stephens*), Fannie Flagg (*Amy Walterson*), Joanna Cassidy (*Joe Mason*), Richard Gilliland (*Hal Foss*), Ed Begley, Jr (*Lester*), Joe Spinell (*Jabo*), John David Carson (*Halsey*), Cliff Pellow (*Walter Jr.*), Dennis Fimple (*Bubba*), Mayf Nutter (*Packman*).

Jeff Bridges takes on Jack Nicholson's FIVE EASY PIECES character in this interesting but cliched film from Bob Rafelson. Bridges is a rich Southerner who involves himself in a real estate deal which depends on the sale of Armstrong's body building gym. The owner is not selling, but meanwhile Bridges gets immersed in the musclebound world he is exposed to and very different from that of his snobbish upbringing. He falls in love with Field, a tough working-class girl with a sexual aura that brings out an earthier side of Bridges. The usual Rafelson themes emerge – an amalgam of classes and backgrounds, an attraction to the raw, physical side of people – but aren't developed any further than in his FIVE EASY PIECES. The cast is superb with Schwarzenegger appearing in his first role, long before finding his niche as THE TERMINATOR. The script is well-crafted but the direction haphazard, never rising above the expected.

p, Harold Schneider, Bob Rafelson; d, Rafelson; w, Rafelson, Charles Gaines (based on the novel by Gaines); ph, Victor J. Kemper (DeLuxe Color); m, Bruce Langehorne, Byron Berline; ed, John F. Link II; prod d, Toby Carr Rafelson; set d, Bob Gould.

Drama Cas. (PR:O MPAA:R)

STAYING ALIVE zero (1983) 96m PAR c

John Travolta (*Tony Manero*), Cynthia Rhodes (*Jackie*), Finola Hughes (*Laura*), Steve Inwood (*Jesse*), Julie Bovasso (*Mrs. Manero*), Charles Ward (*Butler*), Steve Bickford (*Sound Technician*), Patrick Brady (*Derelict*), Norma Donaldson (*Fatima*), Jesse Doran (*Mark*), Joyce Hyser (*Linda*), Deborah Jensen (*Margaret*), Robert Martini (*Fred*), Sarah Miles (*Joy*), Tony Munafo (*Doorman*), Susan Olar (*Model*), Cindy Perlman (*Cathy*), Ross St. Phillip (*Sound Man*), Kurtwood Smith (*Choreographer*), Frank Stallone (*Carl*).

The curse of the sequel rears it's ugly head again, this time in a pathetic follow-up to SATURDAY NIGHT FEVER. Six years after Travolta laid down his dancin' shoes and left Brooklyn, he's re-emerged on Broadway with a minor role in an extravagant musical that stars Hughes. The animosity between him and the lead is deepened when he is elevated to the costar spot. Meanwhile, his true love Rhodes remains loyal to him. The show, "Satan's Alley," a poor man's Bob Fosse, is a hit and Travolta is a success. The film's main concern is Travolta's body—he sweats, dances, shows off his physique and sweats some more. This attention to physique is the work of none other than Sylvester Stallone who puts in a cameo appearance a la Hitchcock. Stallone's love of his own body is transposed to that of Travolta, whom he put through an intense physical training program. What it all amounts to is an embarrassing show of ego that can't even boast a soundtrack that approaches the original. STAYING ALIVE makes FLASH-DANCE look like a classic. It even won the Turkey of the Year award from Film Year Book. Songs include "The Woman In You," "I Love You Too Much," "Breakout," "Someone Belonging to Someone," "Life Goes On" (The Bee Gees), "Far From Over" (Frank Stallone, Vince DiCola), "Devils and Seducers" (Gary Wright), "(We Dance) So Close to the Fire" (Randy Bishop, Tommy Faragher), "Hope We Never Change," "Moody Girl," "I'm Never Gonna Give You Up," "The Winning End" (Stallone, DiCola, Joe Bean Esposito), "Waking Up" (Stallone, DiCola, Arthur Colatrella).

p, Robert Stigwood, Sylvester Stallone; d, Stallone; w, Stallone, Norman Wexler (based on characters created by Nik Cohn); ph, Nick McLean (Metrocolor); m, The Bee Gees, Frank Stallone, Johnny Mandel; ed, Don Zimmerman, Mark Warner; md, Robin Garb; prod d, Robert F. Boyle; art d, Norman Newberry; set d, Arthur Jeph Parker; cos, Thomas M. Bronson, Bob Mackie; ch, Dennon Rawles, Sayhber Rawles.

Musical Drama Cas. (PR:C MPAA:PG)

STEADY COMPANY** (1932) 65m UNIV bw

Norman Foster, June Clyde, ZaSu Pitts, Henry Armetta, Maurice Black, J. Farrell MacDonald, Morgan Wallace, Jack Perry, Morry Cohan, Willard Robertson.

Love and boxing mix in this minor programmer from Universal Studios. After getting badly beaten in a match, an up and coming pugster takes the advice of a promoter and accepts safer bouts. This pleases everyone involved, including the girl who holds the key to the fighter's heart. Typical

sappy nonsense done over and over again throughout film history!

d, Edward Ludwig; w, Earle Snell (based on a story by Edward I. Luddy); ph, Charles Stumar.

Sports Drama/Romance (PR:A MPAA:NR)

STEAGLE, THE*½ (1971) 90m AE c

Richard Benjamin (*Dr. Harold Weiss*), Chill Wills (*Tall-Guy McCoy*), Cloris Leachman (*Rita Weiss*), Jean Allison (*Florence Maguire*), Suzanne Charny (*Marcy*), Ivor Francis (*Clergyman*), Susan Tyrrell (*Louise*), Jack Bernardi (*Marty Panesh*), Susan Kussman (*Joan*), Peter Hobbs (*Dr. Worthington Payne*), Joe Bernard (*Max Levine*), Anita Alberts (*Loretta*), Frank Christi (*Mr. Forbes*), Diane Ladd (*Mrs. Forbes*), Harold Reynolds (*Dr. Plymile*), John Hiestand (*Matt Mayhew*), Lew Palter (*Older Man*), Alice Nunn (*Mrs. Furst*), Linnard Lane (*Sandy Weiss*), Lisa Cantor (*Lily Weiss*), Minta Durfee Arbuckle (*Old Lady*).

A confused satire has college prof. Benjamin living out his wildest fantasies when news of the 1962 Cuban missile crisis hits. Apparently thinking the end is near he sets out on a cross-country trek on which he meets an odd collection of people. It may have been funny as they were shooting it, but by the time it hit the screen it was nearly void of laughs. The attempted parallel between the international crisis and Benjamin's personal affairs does not come off.

p, Jim Di Gangi; d, Paul Sylbert; w, Sylbert (based on the novel *The Steagle* by Irvin Faust); ph, Burnett Guffey (Movielab Color); m, Fred Myrow; ed, Thomas Stanford; art d, Bill Malley, William Campbell; set d, William Kuehl; cos, Anthea Sylbert; makeup, Allen Snyder.

Comedy (PR:O MPAA:R)

STEAMBOAT ROUND THE BEND** (1935) 96m FOX bw

Will Rogers (*Dr. John Pearly*), Anne Shirley (*Fleety Belle*), Eugene Pallette (*Sheriff Rufe Jeffers*), John McGuire (*Duke*), Berton Churchill (*New Moses*), Stepin Fetchit (*Jonah*), Francis Ford (*Efe*), Irvin S. Cobb (*Capt. Eli*), Roger Imhof (*Pappy*), Raymond Hatton (*Matt Abel*), Hobart Bosworth (*Chaplain*), Louis Mason (*Boat Race Organizer*), Charles B. Middleton (*Fleety Belle's Father*), Si Jenks (*Drunk Farmer*), Jack Pennick (*Ringleader of the Boat Attack*), William Benedict (*Breck*), Lois Verner (*Addie May*), Fred Kohler Jr (*Popkins*), Fleety Belle's Suitor, Hobart Cavanaugh (*A Listener*), John Lester Johnson (*Uncle Jeff*), Pardner Jones (*New Elijah*), Ben Hall (*Fleety Belle's Brother*), Robert E. Homans (*Race Official*), Del Henderson (*Salesman*), Otto Richards (*Prisoner*), Captain Anderson (*Jailer*), Grace Goodall (*Sheriff's Wife*), Ferdinand Munier (*Governor*), D'Arcy Corrigan (*Hangman*), James Marcus (*Warden*), Luke Cosgrave (*Labor Boss*), Heinie Conklin (*Tattoo Artist*), John Wallace, Vester Pegg, John Tyke, Wingate Smith, Sam Baker.

One of three pictures John Ford made with Rogers (after DR. BULL, 1933, and JUDGE PRIEST, 1934), this audience-pleaser starred the famed humorist in his final film role (though IN OLD KENTUCKY had yet to be released). Rogers plays a steamboat captain intent on proving the innocence of McGuire, soon to be hanged for murder. With McGuire's sweetheart Shirley, Rogers sets out in search for the only witness who can save McGuire. It turns into a race against time as Rogers and Shirley burn everything on board, including a wax figure collection, to make it down the river before the hanging. While not a favorite of Ford's, STEAMBOAT ROUND THE BEND opened to some rave reviews. Ford, however, objected to Fox's show of power which resulted in their getting the final cut of the film and, in his opinion, "ruining" the picture.

p, Sol M. Wurtzel; d, John Ford; w, Dudley Nichols, Lamar Trotti (based on the novel *Steamboat Round The Bend* by Ben Lucian Burman); ph, George Schneiderman; ed, Alfred De Gaetano; md, Samuel Kaylin; art d, William Darling; set d, Albert Hogsett.

Drama (PR:A MPAA:NR)

STEEL**½ (1980) 99m World-Northal c (AKA: LOOK DOWN AND DIE, MEN OF STEEL)

Lee Majors (*Mike Catton*), Jennifer O'Neil (*Cass Cassidy*), Art Carney (*Pignose Moran*), George Kennedy (*Lew Cassidy*), Harris Yulin (*Eddie Cassidy*), Redmond Cleason (*Harry*), Terry Kiser (*Valentino*), Richard Lynch (*Dancer*), Ben Marley (*The Kid*), Roger Mosley (*Lionel*), Albert Salmi (*Tank*), Robert Tessier (*Cherokee*), Hunter Von Leer (*Surfer*), R.G. Armstrong (*Kellin*), Joseph DeNicola (*Tom*).

A harmless drama about a construction crew fighting to finish nine floors of a skyscraper before the bank interferes. Kennedy is the company's owner, who pitches in and helps the boys get the job done. An act of courage saves a young worker's life, but sends Kennedy to the pavement in the process, leaving the construction crew without a boss. O'Neil, Kennedy's daughter, takes over and hires Majors and his hand-picked crew of the top in the field. The crew completes the nearly impossible task, with Majors even finding time to court O'Neil. The danger present on the screen also creeped into real-life when stuntman A.J. Bakunis jumped to his death during production in Lexington, Kentucky. He had previously held the record for a stunt fall, leaping 232 feet from a helicopter during the filming of HOOPER. A fellow stuntman, Dar Robinson, decided to top Bakunis and took a 311-foot fall. Not to be outdone, however, Bakunis prepared a 323-foot fall from the 23-story Kincaid Towers. Instead of bouncing off the 12 ft. airbag, he broke through it, landing on the pavement.

p, Peter S. Davis, William N. Panzer; d, Steven Carver; w, Leigh Chapman (based on a story by Rob Ewing, Davis, Panzer). ph, Roger Shearman (Panavision, Movielab Color); m, Michael Colombier; ed, David Blewitt; prod d, Ward & Preston; set d, Lloyd Linean; cos, Doris Lynch, Sydney Gilbert; spec eff, Roger George; stunts, James Arnett.

Drama   **Cas.**   **(PR:C   MPAA:PG)**

STEEL AGAINST THE SKY*½   (1941) 68m WB bw

Lloyd Nolan (*Rocky Evans*), Alexis Smith (*Helen*), Craig Stevens (*Chuck Evans*), Gene Lockhart (*John Powers*), Edward Ellis (*Pop Evans*), Walter Catlett (*Prof. Sampson*), Howard da Silva (*Bugs*), Edward Brophy (*Pete Evans*), Julie Bishop (*Myrt*).

Romance causes dissension among three bridge-building brothers when Smith falls for Nolan, and then his sibling Stevens. The rivalry is forgotten, however, when Stevens saves Nolan's life. The film is a typical love triangle but set against an interesting backdrop, the mechanics of erecting a bridge, including the dangers facing the builders.

p, Edmund Grainger; d, A. Edward Sutherland; w, Paul Gerard Smith (based on the story "Bridge Built at Night" by Maurice Hanline, Jesse Lasky, Jr.); ph, James Van Trees; ed, Doug Gould.

Drama   **(PR:A   MPAA:NR)**

STEEL ARENA*½   (1973) 98m L-T Films c

Dusty Russell, Gene Drew, Buddy Love, Dutch Schnitzer (*Themselves*), Bruce Mackey (*Crash Chambers*), Laura Brooks (*Jo-Ann*), Speed Sterns, Ed "Chromedome" Ryan, Nancy Walton, Eric Nord.

If it's car crashes you're looking for, STEEL ARENA has a ton of them, all photographed for maximum effect. The story and characterization, however, fall into a void as Russell (playing himself, as do the other drivers) competes for the top spot in a travelling auto show. He finds himself pitted against the jealous Mackey who tries to maneuver him into a fatal stunt.

p, Mark L. Lester, Peter S. Traynor; d&w, Lester; ph, John A. Morrill (Technicolor); m, Don Tweedy; ed, Dave Peoples.

Action   **(PR:C   MPAA:PG)**

STEEL BAYONET, THE*   (1958, Brit.) 84m Hammer/UA bw

Leo Genn (*Maj. Gerrard*), Kieron Moore (*Capt. Mead*), Michael Medwin (*Lt. Vernon*), Robert Brown (*Sgt. Maj. Gill*), Michael Ripper (*Pvt. Middleditch*), John Paul (*Lt. Col. Derry*), Shay Gorman (*Sgt. Gates*), Tom Bowman (*Sgt. Nicholls*), Bernard Horsfall (*Pvt. Livingstone*), John Watson (*Cpl. Bean*), Arthur Lovegrove (*Jarvis*), Percy Herbert (*Clark*), Paddy Joyce (*Ames*), Jack Stewart (*Wentworth*), David Crowley (*Harris*), Barry Lowe (*Ferguson*), Michael Dear (*"Tweedie"*), Ian Whittaker (*Wilson*), Michael Balfour (*Thomas*), Raymond Francis (*General*), Anthony Warren (*Wounded German*), Rolf Carston (*German NCO*), Gerard Green (*German Company Commander*), Wolf Frees (*German Staff Officer*), Jeremy Longhurst (*German Sniper*), David Ritch (*Mahomet*), Abdul Noor (*Arab*), Victor Platt (*Sentry*), John Trevor (*Captain*).

This weak British war tale has Genn leading his men on a mission to hold an African post until the Allies arrive. Filmed almost entirely on a single set, STEEL BAYONET rarely rises above a cliched treatment of the effects of war. The all-male cast means well, but the British actors, whether they play Englishmen, Germans or Arabs, are no more convincing than the English scenery in this story supposedly taking place in North Africa.

p&d, Michael Carreras; w, Howard Clewes; ph, John Asher; m, Leonard Salzedo; ed, Bill Lenny; md, John Hollingsworth; art d, Ted Marshall.

War   **(PR:A   MPAA:NR)**

STEEL CAGE, THE*   (1954) 80m UA bw

Paul Kelly (*Warden Clinton T. Duffy*), Maureen O'Sullivan (*Mrs. Duffy*), Walter Slezak (*The Chef*), John Ireland, Lawrence Tierney (*The Ringleaders*), Arthur Franz, Kenneth Tobey, George Cooper, Alan Mowbray, George E. Stone, Lyle Talbot, Elizabeth Fraser, Stanley Andrews, Morris Ankrum, Don Beddoe, Robert Bice, George Chandler, Ned Glass, Herb Jacobs, Henry Kulky, Charles Nolte, Gene Roth, James Seay, Charles Tannen, Ben Welden.

A trio of prison dramas, the best being "The Chef," with Slezak as a discontented prison cook who gets framed by a fellow inmate with a taste for fine cuisine. Ireland, Tierney, and Talbot are cast in "The Hostages," a tale about a failed prison break and the bloodshed that follows. The final tale, "The Face," stars Tobey as a painter who finds God through his encounters with priest Franz. Sequel: DUFFY OF SAN QUENTIN, 1954.

p, Berman Swartz, Walter Doniger; d, Doniger; w, "The Hostages," Oliver Crawford (based on the story by Doniger, Swartz), "The Chef," Swartz, Doniger, "The Face," Guy Trosper (based on the story by Scott Littleton), all three based on the book *The San Quentin Story* by Clinton T. Duffy; Dean Jennings; ph, John Alton, Joseph Biroc; ed, Chester Schaeffer, Everett Dodd.

Drama   **(PR:A   MPAA:NR)**

STEEL CLAW, THE*   (1961) 96m Ponderey/WB c

George Montgomery (*Capt. John Larsen*), Charito Luna (*Lolita*), Mario Barri (*Santana*), Paul Sorensen (*Frank Powers*), Amelia De La Rama (*Christina*), Carmen Austin (*Rosa*), Ben Perez (*Dolph Rodriguez*), John MacGloan (*Commander*), Joe Sison (*Himself*), Pedro Faustino (*Father*), Oscar Keesee, Jr (*Child*), Al Wyatt (*Sergeant*).

Montgomery produced, directed, co-wrote, and starred in this lame war drama about a one-handed captain awaiting his discharge. Before he goes, however, he stages a Filipino attack on the invading Japanese forces. The totally unconvincing plot is further handicapped by inane dialog. Filmed on location in the Philippines, the scenery is as interesting as anything in the movie.

p&d, George Montgomery; w, Montgomery, Ferde Grofe, Jr., Malvin Wald; ph, Manuel Rojas (Technicolor); m, Harry Zimmerman; ed, Jack Murray; md, Zimmerman.

War   **(PR:A   MPAA:NR)**

STEEL FIST, THE**   (1952) 73m MON bw

Roddy McDowall (*Erik*), Kristine Miller (*Marlina*), Harry Lauter (*Franz*), Rand Brooks (*Capt. Giorg*), Byron Foulger (*Prof. Kardin*), Kate Lawson (*Mrs. Kreechow*), Bob Peoples (*1st Lieutenant*), Gil Perkins (*1st Organizer*), Fred Krone (*1st Student*), Murray Alper (*Nicholas*).

Young McDowall is the subject of a Communist manhunt when he starts a riot in protest against new labor rules. He is harbored by a tough young girl, Miller, and her brother, Lauter, who eventually help McDowall cross the border into safer territory. Little suspense is generated.

p&d, Wesley Barry; w, C.K. Kivari (based on the story "Flight into Freedom" by Phyllis Parker); ph, William Sickner; m, Edward J. Kay; ed, Ace Herman; art d, David Milton.

Drama   **(PR:A   MPAA:NR)**

STEEL HELMET, THE**   (1951) 84m Deputy/Lippert bw

Gene Evans (*Sgt. Zack*), Robert Hutton (*Pvt. "Conchie" Bronte*), Richard Loo (*Sgt. "Buddhahead" Tanaka*), Steve Brodie (*Lt. Driscoll*), James Edwards (*Cpl. "Medic" Thompson*), Sid Melton (*Joe, 2nd GI*), Richard Monahan (*Pvt. Baldy*), William Chun (*"Short Round"*), Harold Fong (*The Red, a North Korean Major*), Neyle Morrow (*1st GI*), Lynn Stallmaster (*2nd Lieutenant*).

Scripted in a week, shot in 10 days, and released only six months after the start of the Korean War, Sam Fuller's THE STEEL HELMET stands as one of the best films about that war, or, in fact, any war. Dark, violent, and disturbing, this film does not celebrate duty, honor, and heroism; instead it shows men simply trying to survive the madness of war. The film opens as Evans, a tough veteran sergeant, crawls through a smoky battlefield littered with corpses. Wounded in the leg, his arms tied behind him, Evans slithers painfully along the ground, trying to avoid the sniper that has slaughtered his whole company. Evans is saved by Chun, a South Korean orphan whose nickname is "Short Round" (a name stolen by Steven Spielberg for his cute oriental kid in INDIANA JONES AND THE TEMPLE OF DOOM in 1984), who cuts the soldier's binding. With scarcely a "thank you," Evans tends to his wound and packs up his belongings. Looking to settle his debt to the boy by giving him a chocolate bar, Evans discovers he has no candy and Chun tags along. Evans soon meets up with a black medic, Edwards, he, too, the only survivor of his unit. Evans asks the medic for a chocolate bar so that he can get rid of the kid, but the kid refuses to abandon Evans. Eventually the two soldiers and the boy meet up with a group of new recruits who have fallen into an ambush. Evans manages to extricate the soldiers from their predicament, but only agrees to lead them on their mission if one of the soldiers will give up his box of cigars. The tiny group then proceeds to an ancient Buddhist temple which is to be used as an observation post to aid the artillery. Also in the temple is a North Korean major, Fong, who is to be captured and brought back for questioning. At the temple, the cynical, somewhat racist soldiers are awestruck by the giant statue of Buddha that resides there and are moved to take their helmets off in its presence. Soon after their arrival, one of the GIs, Melton, is killed by Fong. Evans finds the Korean Communist and wounds him. Once subdued, Fong makes it clear to the Americans he is not a pawn of the Russians by asserting his nationalism: "I am not a Russian! I am a North Korean Communist." The defiant prisoner eventually pushes Evans too far when he ridicules Chun after the boy prays that Sgt. Zack will like him. When the boy is hit and killed by a stray bullet, Evans' repressed affection for the child surfaces and he shoots Fong for making light of the boy's prayer. After this momentary burst of emotion, Evans once agains assumes the cold, brutal barrier that has meant survival. When one of his men is killed, he tells the others not to retrieve the dog tags because "...a dead man is a dead man and nobody cares." When a soldier shocked at Evans' cynicism tries to remove the dead man's dog tags, a booby trap planted on the corpse explodes, killing the GI. Meanwhile, Fong, who is being tended to by medic Edwards, realizes he is about to die and rejects communist ideology by embracing his Buddhist roots. The dying man asks Edwards for a prayer and the medic gently tells him, "Buddha blesses you." Soon the Americans find themselves under siege by the North Koreans. After an intense battle, the GIs manage to defeat the Communists, but the film ends with the soldiers staring ahead, on the verge of madness with many battles yet ahead. THE STEEL HELMET is a gripping war film that does not glamorize conflict, but shows the men who fight trying to survive in an environment that is contradictory to the point of insanity. A veteran of WW II, Evans knows that if he allows himself emotion, he makes himself more vulnerable to pain. Theoretically a soldier is supposed to feel a passion for what and who he is fighting for. In Fuller's reality, emotional attachments and deeply felt passions can mean death. This is a film made for an audience tired of war. Five short years before, the world had welcomed home its battle-weary soldiers who had just fought the most violent and deadly conflict of all, WW II. Before Americans had time to put their lives back in order, families were again ripped apart when the men were called off to another war, one that proved not to be as clearcut. This time the public wondered whether the bloodshed was necessary. THE STEEL HELMET reflects these doubts. Those soldiers who are not confused and scared are cold and cynical. The rules of this war are different from the last. The enemy looks exactly like the people the soldiers are supposed to be defending. A confused soldier asks Evans, "How do you tell a North Korean from a South Korean?" Evans replies, "If he's running with you he's a South Korean. If he's running after you he's a North Korean." Director Fuller emphasizes this confusion visually. The film is very claustrophobic (most of the action takes place on a single set) and the characters nearly always seem to be immersed in smoke and fog. Things are never what they seem. GI Monahan's snoring is mistaken for the whistle of incoming shells, Buddhist priests turn out to be North Korean soldiers in disguise, and Loo, the intelligent and brave South Korean soldier, isn't trusted by the American lieutenant. By the end of the film, the American soldiers who have survived are on the brink of madness. Fuller's final comment on the situation comes with the closing credit which reads, "There is no end to this story."

p,d&w, Samuel Fuller; ph, Ernest W. Miller; m, Paul Dunlap; ed, Philip Cahn; art d, Theobald Holsopple; set d, Clarence Steenson; cos, Alfred Berke; spec eff, Ben Southland, Ray Mercer.

War   (PR:C   MPAA:NR)

STEEL HIGHWAY, THE   (SEE: OTHER MEN'S WOMEN, 1931)

STEEL JUNGLE, THE*½   (1956) 86m WB bw

Perry Lopez (*Ed Novak*), Beverly Garland (*Frances Novak*), Walter Abel (*Warden Keller*), Ted de Corsia (*Steve Marlin*), Kenneth Tobey (*Dr. Lewy*), Allison Hayes (*Mrs. Archer*), Gregory Walcott (*Guard Weaver*), Leo Gordon (*Lupo*), Kay Kuter (*Stringbean*), Bob Steele (*Dan Bucci*), Ralph Moody (*Andy Macklin*), Stafford Repp (*Beakeley*), Billy Vincent (*Harry*), Charles Cane, Fred Graham (*Detectives*), Carey Loftin (*Truck Driver*), Jack Kruschen (*Helper*), Edward Platt (*Judge Wahller*), Lyle Latell (*Bailiff*), Richard Karlan (*C.O.D.*), Frank Gerstle (*Kadinski*), Tom McKee (*Sgt. Hayes*), Eddie Baker (*Schiller*), Joel Smith (*Newspaperman*), Lane Bradford (*Guard*), Malcolm Atterbury (*Mailman*), Mack Williams (*Lt. Bryant*), Robert Bray (*Lt. Soberman*), Peter Gray (*Lt. Murray*).

Mob bookie Lopez chooses jail over informing on his syndicate ties, or remaining with his expectant wife Garland. He conducts business as usual from his cell, but eventually learns that his wife's loyalties are stronger than the mob's. Both Lopez and Garland were applauded as fresh faces deserving a crack at stardom when the film was released. Little else could be found, then or now, to be said for it.

p, David Weisbart; d&w, Walter Doniger; ph, J. Peverell Marley; m, David Buttolph; ed, Folmar Blangsted; art d, Leo K. Kuter.

Crime Drama   (PR:A   MPAA:NR)

STEEL KEY, THE**   (1953, Brit.) 69m Tempean/Eros bw

Terence Morgan (*Johnny O'Flynn*), Joan Rice (*Doreen Wilson*), Raymond Lovell (*Inspector Forsythe*), Dianne Foster (*Sylvia Newman*), Hector Ross (*Beroni*), Colin Tapley (*Dr. Crabtree*), Esmond Knight (*Prof. Crabtree*), Arthur Lovegrove (*Gilchrist*), Mark Baker, Mary Jones, Roger Maxwell, Sam Kydd, Esma Cannon.

Silly spy drama has Morgan looking for the inventor of a special formula for hardening steel who is being held captive by enemy agents. The complicated plot doesn't quite work, but audiences should enjoy it anyway. Not to be confused with TURN THE KEY SOFTLY, in which leading man Morgan also appeared in 1953.

p, Robert S. Baker, Monty Berman; d, Baker; w, John Gilling (based on a story by Roy Chanslor); ph, Gerald Gibbs.

Spy Drama   (PR:A   MPAA:NR)

STEEL LADY, THE*½   (1953) 84m UA bw (GB: TREASURE OF KALIFA)

Rod Cameron (*Mike Monohan*), Tab Hunter (*Billy Larsen*), John Dehner (*Syd Barlow*), Richard Erdman (*Jim Evans*), John Abbott (*Mustapha El Melek*), Frank Puglia (*Sheik Taras*), Anthony Caruso (*Zagora*), Christopher Dark (*Ibrahim*), Dick Rich (*Sanderson*), Charles Victor (*Radio Operator*), Carmen d'Antonio (*Dancer*).

This far-fetched WW II drama has a group of oil scouts downed in the Sahara using a German tank to travel to safety. It turns out that the tank is full of gems, and there's a band of Arabs after it. The movie is a prime example of German director E.A. Dupont's (VARIETY, 1925) later efforts, after his downfall relegated him to a series of forgettable programmers until his death in 1956.

p, Grant Whytock; d, E.A. Dupont; w, Richard Schayer (based on the story by Aubrey Wisberg); ph, Floyd Crosby; m, Emil Newman, Arthur Lange; ed, Whytock; art d, Frank Sylos.

War/Action   (PR:A   MPAA:NR)

STEEL TOWN**   (1952) 85m UNIV c

Ann Sheridan (*"Red" McNamara*), John Lund (*Steve Kostane*), Howard Duff (*Jim Denko*), William Harrigan (*John McNamara*), Eileen Crowe (*Millie McNamara*), Chick Chandler (*Ernie*), James Best (*Joe Rakich*), Nancy Kulp (*Dolores*), Elaine Riley (*Valerie*), Tudor Owen (*McIntosh*), Frank Marlowe (*Taxi Driver*), Robert Karnes (*Intern*), Herbert Lytton (*Doctor*), Lorin Raker (*Milquetoasty Man*), Lois Wilde (*Nurse*), James McLaughlin (*Helper*).

Steel company heir Lund and mill worker Duff become bitter enemies when they both share a love for the same woman, Sheridan. Lund causes dissention among the workers after he is responsible for their losing a tonnage contest, but regains their respect, and Sheridan's, when he saves her dad from certain death by molten steel.

p, Leonard Goldstein; d, George Sherman; w, Gerald Drayson Adams, Lou Breslow (based on the story by Leonard Freeman); ph, Charles P. Boyle (Technicolor); ed, Ted J. Kent; art d, Bernard Herzbrun, Robert Clatworthy; cos, Bill Thomas.

Drama   (PR:A   MPAA:NR)

STEEL TRAP, THE***½   (1952) 85m FOX bw

Joseph Cotten (*Jim Osborne*), Teresa Wright (*Laurie Osborne*), Eddie Marr (*Ken*), Aline Towne (*Gail*), Bill Hudson (*Raglin*), Benny Burt, Joey Ray, Sam Flint, Charlie Collins, Kurt Martell (*Bank Tellers*), Jonathan Hale (*Bowers*), Stephanie King (*Susan*), Carleton Young (*Chi. & So. Clerk*), Katherine Warren (*Grandmother*), Walter Sande9 (*Customs Inspector*), Tom Powers (*Valcourt*).

In this suspenseful comedy, Cotten plays an assistant manager for a Los Angeles bank, who realizes how easy it would be to remove $1 million from the bank's safe. One Friday afternoon he gives in to temptation and puts the cash in his briefcase. Though nearly caught in the vault, Cotten manages to get home safely, then tells his wife (Wright) the family is going to take a trip. The couple and their child head down to New Orleans, where they intend to catch a flight to Brazil. Cotten wants to go there because Brazil has no extradition laws, but a variety of problems causes the family to miss their plane. Cotten finally reveals the source of the money to Wright, who wants nothing to do with his plan. She returns to California with their child, leaving Cotten to think about his actions. He then realizes how wrong the theft is, and returns the money to the bank on Monday morning. Cotten handles his part well in an amusing performance, with Wright providing some good support. Stone's direction gives this equal amounts of humor and suspense, aligning audience sympathies with Cotten, while having some fun at his expense. An entertaining feature, though not a memorable one.

p, Bert E. Friedlob; d&w, Andrew Stone; ph, Ernest Laszlo; m, Dimitri Tiomkin; ed, Otto Ludwig; md, Tiomkin; m/l, "So Much to Me," Tiomkin, Stan Jones (sung by Helen Humes).

Crime/Comedy   (PR:A   MPAA:NR)

STEELYARD BLUES**   (1973) 92m WB c (AKA: THE FINAL CRASH)

Jane Fonda (*Iris Caine*), Donald Sutherland (*Jesse Veldini*), Peter Boyle (*Eagle Throneberry*), Garry Goodrow (*Duval Jacks*), Howard Hesseman (*Frank Veldin*), John Savage (*The Kid*), Richard Schaal (*Zoo Official*), Melvin Stewart (*Black Man in Jail*), Morgan Upton (*Police Captain*), Roger Bowen (*Fire Commissioner*), Howard Storm (*Health Inspector*), Jessica Myerson (*Savage Rose*), Dan Barrows (*Rocky*), Nancy Fish (*Pool Hall Waitress*), Lynn Bernay (*Bar Waitress*), Edward Greenberg (*Rookie Cop*), Jim Cranna (*Luncheonette Man*), Ruth Silveira (*Lady Electrician*), Larry Hankin (*Garbage Man*), David Moody (*Boxer*), John Brent (*Tattoo Parlor Man*), The Committee.

STEELYARD BLUES is a terrific 1960s movie. Unfortunately, it was made in the 1970s and therein lies the problem. Screenwriter David S. Ward had two of his scripts filmed in 1973, both by the same producers. One was THE STING and the other was this, something totally different and nowhere near as satisfying. Sutherland, who was also the executive producer, is a man who loves demolition derbies and his passion for them has caused him to have to steal cars. That, in turn, has put him up the river a few times, much to the dismay of Hesseman, his ambitious brother who seeks elected office higher than the district attorney's slot he now holds. Sutherland exits the slammer for his latest offense and gets in touch with Fonda, again playing a hooker– the same thing she did with Sutherland in KLUTE. Fonda's in a frizzy hairdo and while she likes Sutherland and wouldn't mind reawakening the love they once had for each other, she won't be part of his ultimate dream: the wrecking of school buses, campers, and mobile homes in a demolition derby to end all such derbies. Hesseman is acting as his own brother's parole officer and gets Sutherland a job at the local zoo, cleaning out the animals' cages. (There is a funny scene with Sutherland inside the cage of a yawning lion.) In his off hours, Sutherland hangs out with Savage and Boyle, a refugee from the funny farm. Boyle dresses up in a wild array of wigs and costumes, depending on what he has to do that day, and his wardrobe closet must be larger than Imelda Marcos', if one can believe he actually owns all this gear. Boyle and Savage take Sutherland in to meet Goodrow, who is spending all of his time attempting to rebuild a WW II plane. All agree that where they are is no place and that there must be a better world out there, a land where they don't have to worry about cops, where there are no rules, an Eden where they can be free to do as they wish. Sutherland agrees with Goodrow that this plane may be their ticket out of the conventional world and into the wherever. Boyle and Savage are quickly part of the group and Sutherland celebrates his soon-to-be freedom by quitting his job at the zoo, which immediately results in a call to Hesseman to announce that Sutherland has cracked the terms of his parole. Hesseman calls the cops to tell them what Sutherland's done and the parolee gets whacked around by the men in blue. Hesseman, for all his morality, is a regular patron of Fonda's and when she hears what the man has done to his own brother, she refuses to sleep with him and is also worked over. Goodrow announces that the plane will never get up in the air unless they can secure certain parts which are unavailable through regular sources. The only place where they can be found is in the parts department at the local naval air base. The gang dons all-black outfits with matching hoods and executes a raid on the Navy station and secures the goods, but Boyle somehow gets lost. They work all night on the plane and it's ready to fly at dawn. Here comes Hesseman leading a fleet of police cars and they block the runway so the plane can't get away. Now Boyle, dressed like Marlon Brando in VIVA ZAPATA, rides in leading a herd of horses. Sutherland sets off bombs that explode the plane. Fire and smoke cover the area and the cops can't move in, nor do they see that Boyle has a large helicopter waiting. Fonda, Sutherland, Boyle, Savage, and Goodrow board the chopper and whirl into the air as the picture closes. It was a mixture of KLUTE and M*A*S*H* but without the intelligence of the former or the wit of the latter. Badly directed by first-timer Myerson, who helped found San Francisco's "The Committee," an excellent improvisational troupe many of whom are in this film. Nick Gravenites and Michael Bloomfield wrote several songs for the film, none of which meant anything. The tunes were used primarily as background and included: "Woman's Love," Poachin'," "Being Different," "There She Goes," "Brand New Family," Headlines," "Common Ground," "Here I Come," "Swing with It," "They're Lettin' Me Drive Again." The songs were variously performed by the authors plus Merl Saunders, John Kahn, Maria Muhler, Chris Parker, and Paul Butterfield. In a small role, note Howard Storm, the former standup comic who has since become a sought-after comedy director for sit-coms. Myerson's direction was haphazard, technically inept, failed to mine any humor in potentially hilarious situations, and showed a distinct lack of knowledge of editing or camera placement. Other than that, his work was splendid.

p, Tony Bill, Michael Phillips, Julia Phillips; d, Alan Myerson; w, David S. Ward; ph, Laszlo Kovacs, Stevan Larner (Technicolor); m, Nick Gravenites, Paul Butterfield, David Shire; ed, Donn Cambern, Robert Grovenor; art d, Vincent Cresciman; m/l, Gravenites, Butterfield, Shire, Michael Bloomfield.

Comedy   Cas.   (PR:C   MPAA:PG)

STEFANIA**   (1968, Gr.) 92m Finos/Chancellor bw

Zoe Laskari (Stefania), Spiros Focas (Dr. Georges), Spyros Kalogyrou (Guard), Tasso Kavadia (Directress), Viron Pallis (Stepfather), Nora Valsami (Esther), Despo Diamantidou (Woman Guard), Kakia Panayotou (Stefania's Mother), Lefteris Vournas (Delivery Boy), Dimitrios Bislanis (Student).

A depressing prison film which has prostitute Laskari sent to a reform house where she is horrified at the living conditions. She soon discovers that the prison doctor is one of her past loves. He promises to get her out by marrying her. As she is about to be released, a perverted guard rapes and strangles her, ending the picture on a disheartening note, to say the least. In Greek; English subtitles.)

p, Filopimin Finos; d, Yannis Dalianidis; w, Dalianidis, Nelle Theodorou (from Theodorou's novel); ph, Nikos Kavoudikis; m, Mimis Plessas; set d, Markos Zervas; English subtitles, Herman G. Weinberg.

Drama   (PR:O   MPAA:NR)

STELLA**½   (1950) 83m FOX bw

Ann Sheridan (Stella), Victor Mature (Jeff De Marco), David Wayne (Carl Granger), Randy Stuart (Claire), Marion Marshall (Mary), Frank Fontaine (Don), Leif Erickson (Fred), Evelyn Varden (Flora), Lea Penman (Mrs. Calhoun), Joyce MacKenzie (Peggy Denny), Hobart Cavanaugh (Tim Gross), Charles Halton (Mr. Beeker), Walter Baldwin (Farmer), Larry Keating (Gil Wright), Mary Bear (Myra), Paul Harvey (Ralph Denny), Chill Wills (Officer), Lorelie Witek (Cigarette Girl).

A witty black comedy which has a family driven to wild extremes when an uncle dies an accidental death. Thinking that no one will believe their story, cousin Wayne buries the corpse in a remote spot. A $20,000 policy brings insurance agent Mature snooping around, and soon falling in love with Sheridan, the only normal member of the clan. When the truth leaks out, nobody can seem to remember just where they buried "Uncle Joe."

p, Sol C. Siegel; d&w, Claude Binyon (based on the novel Family Skeleton by Doris Miles Disney); ph, Joe MacDonald; m, Cyril Mockridge; ed, Harmon Jones; md, Lionel Newman; art d, Lyle Wheeler, Mark-Lee Kirk; cos, Edward Stevenson.

Comedy   (PR:A   MPAA:NR)

STELLA DALLAS****   (1937) 104m UA bw

Barbara Stanwyck (Stella Martin Dallas), John Boles (Stephen Dallas), Anne Shirley (Laurel Dallas), Barbara O'Neil (Helen Morrison), Alan Hale (Ed Munn), Marjorie Main (Mrs. Martin), Edmund Elton (Mr. Martin), George Walcott (Charlie Martin), Gertrude Short (Carrie Jenkins), Tim Holt (Richard), Nella Walker (Mrs. Grosvenor), Bruce Satterlee (Con), Jimmy Butler (Con, Grown Up), Jack Egger (Lee), Dickie Jones (John), Ann Shoemaker (Miss Phillibrown), Jessie Arnold (Landlady), Lon McAllister (Bit), Laraine Day (Girl at Soda Fountain), Lillian Yarbo (Gladys), Winifred Harris, Al Shean, Etta McDaniel, Lillian West, Mildred Gover, George Meeker, Ann Doran, Harry Bowen, Hazel Langton, Mabel Colcord, Dorothy Vaughan, Edythe Elliott, Paul Stanton, Frank Dickson, Francis Sayles, Michael Owen, Linda Gray, Frank Filban, Vesey O'Davoren, Harlan Briggs.

There is a fine line between drama and soap opera. STELLA DALLAS manages to walk that tightrope flawlessly. The expression "soap opera" came from the housewifely habit of listening to radio dramas in the 1930s and 1940s, most of which were sponsored by Procter and Gamble or Lever Brothers, both famed for their washday products. This story became the basis for one of the longest running soaps in radio history (more than 18 years), and had actors as diverse as Eg Begley, Joan Lorring, Luis Van Rooten, Frank Lovejoy, Tom Tully, and MacDonald Carey appear on it at one time or another. The star was Ann Elstner. Prouty's book came out and was a sensation in 1923, becoming a play in 1924 starring Mrs. Leslie Carter, and then a silent, also produced by Goldwyn, which featured Belle Bennett, Ronald Colman, Lois Moran, Jean Hersholt, Alice Joyce, and a very young Doug Fairbanks, Jr. It was directed by Henry King and made a fortune. More than a decade passed and the advent of sound gave Goldwyn the thought that the time was ripe for a remake. He auditioned more than 40 actresses and offered the part of Stella to Gladys George and Ruth Chatterton but both declined. Stanwyck already had 29 films behind her but Goldwyn made her test for it anyhow. Stanwyck has been quoted as saying that this was the best acting she'd ever done in her life and it remains this favorite role. Fans usually agree, despite some of her other memorable work in films like DOUBLE INDEMNITY, BALL OF FIRE, and SORRY, WRONG NUMBER. Goldwyn hired another King, King Vidor, and set off to make a tasteful picture that is distinguished by fine acting, superb photography, and excellent Alfred Newman music. Stanwyck is a tough cookie, a bit of a shrew and a grasping woman who snares Boles, a well-born young man whose family lost its old money when his father committed suicide. Boles has moved to a tiny New England town where he meets Stanwyck. He had been engaged to O'Neil, a woman of the same social stratum, but when he suddenly was without wherewithal, he left and she took up with another. Stanwyck is well aware of Boles' background as she is an avid reader of the tabloids that served as the 1930s' equivalent of The National Enquirer. They have a daughter but that does not make the difference in their classes any closer. Boles is offered a job in New York and asks Stanwyck to come with him but she won't as she fears being laughed at by all of his hoity-toity pals, so he goes south and she stays in the mill town. Stanwyck begins running around with the rough-hewn, hard-drinking friends of her youth but she remains a good mother, almost too good, as she lavishes love and affection on the child who grows up to be Shirley. Hale would like to marry Stanwyck but she lets him know that her life is devoted to Shirley and there is no way anyone else can get inside her heart at this time. Boles comes back to the small town every so often. On one of these trips, he intends to take Shirley to New York for Christmas and waits in the parlor. Stanwyck knows how conservative he is so she goes into her bedroom and removes some of the frills and cheap gew-gaws she's been wearing so she can look "right" for him, on the off-chance that they might get back together. All that is ruined when a drunken Hale enters and whatever warmth Boles was evidently feeling is now as cold as the Massachusetts weather outside. One day, while riding a train, Hale gets abusive and his behavior is noted by many of the townspeople, so when Shirley invites her friends to a birthday party, she and Stanwyck are snubbed in a particularly touching scene. Mother and daughter have arranged a table full of plates for the ice cream and birthday cake and as the messages are delivered to the effect that a child won't be there, they remove a plate, rearrange the table for the smaller group, and wait some more. In the end, there are only the plates for Stanwyck and Shirley and the two sit down and have a sad party for themselves. Shirley meets O'Neil, who is now a widow, and her sons. Boles would like a divorce so he can wed O'Neil but Stanwyck will not give her consent. Shirley and Stanwyck visit a posh resort, with Boles' cash, and on this trip Stanwyck learns that her coarse behavior and garish clothing stand in the way of Shirley's happiness. It seems that Shirley and Holt are in love and he is of a fine family who might not like Stanwyck as their son's mother-in-law. Stanwyck realizes that something must be done so she visits O'Neil and says that she will grant Boles the divorce if O'Neil would take Shirley in and raise her as her own daughter. O'Neil understands the depth of Stanwyck's love for her daughter and agrees. Once Shirley finds out what her mother has done, she can't believe it and doesn't want the arrangement but Stanwyck masquerades as a cold woman and insists that she is sick and tired of having to look after Shirley. She's reached an age where she wants some fun on her own and that does not include having to take care of a grown daughter who can now take care of herself. Later, Stanwyck sends a letter saying that she has left the country with Hale. Shirley goes to O'Neil and Boles and her wedding is planned. It's in the library of a fashionable New York townhouse and there is a crowd outside who will watch the ceremony. It's raining as the people stand near the window. Among them is Stanwyck. The bride and groom kiss, the service is over, and a cop tells them to move along. Stanwyck turns away from the window and the smile on her tear-strewn face says everything as she walks down the street. She always wanted the best for her daughter and she's done it. Stanwyck, who never won an Oscar until a special award was given her in 1985, should have won for this. She was only 30 years old at the time and had to age considerably to make her look right as the mother of a fully-matured daughter. The range of emotion was vast and she wrung every last smile and tear out of every speech. Even when she was simply reacting, Stanwyck glowed so strongly that all eyes were upon her. Hale gets whatever humor there is in the script and makes the most of it, Boles is a stick-although that's about right for the role. Stanwyck and Shirley were both nominated by the Academy. Stanwyck lost, and no one can explain why, to Luise Rainer in THE GOOD EARTH and Shirley was eclipsed as Best Supporting Actress by Alice Brady for IN OLD CHICAGO.

p, Samuel Goldwyn; d, King Vidor; w, Sarah Y. Mason, Victor Heerman (based on the novel by Olive Higgins Prouty and the play by Harry Wagstaff Gribble, Gertrude Purcell); ph, Rudolph Mate; ed, Sherman Todd; md, Alfred Newman; art d, Richard Day; cos, Omar Kiam.

Drama   **Cas.**   **(PR:A   MPAA:NR)**

STELLA PARISH   (SEE: I FOUND STELLA PARISH, 1935)

STELLA STAR   (SEE: STARCRASH, 1979)

STEP BY STEP**   (1946) 62m RKO bw

Lawrence Tierney (Johnny Christopher), Anne Jeffreys (Evelyn Smith), Lowell Gilmore (Von Dorn), George Cleveland (Simpson), Jason Robards, Sr (Bruckner), Myrna Dell (Gretchen), Harry Harvey (Senator Remmy), Addison Richards (James Blackton), Ray Walker (Jorgenson, F.B.I. Agent), John Hamilton (Capt. Edmunds), James Flavin, Pat Flaherty (Motorcycle Cops), Ralph Dunn (Patrol Car Cop), Bazooka the Dog.

Ex-Marine Tierney and government secretary Jeffreys are wanted for the murder of a federal agent, as well as being hunted by a gang of Nazis who want the dead man's secret documents. It turns out that the pair is innocent when their adventurous ordeal finally comes to an end.

p, Sid Rogell; d, Phil Rosen; w, Stuart Palmer (based on the story by George Callahan); ph, Frank Redman; m, Paul Sawtell; ed, Robert Swink; md, Constantin Bakaleinikoff; art d, Albert S. D'Agostino, Walter E. Keller; cos, Renie; spec eff, Russell A. Cully, Clifford Stine.

Crime   **(PR:A   MPAA:NR)**

STEP DOWN TO TERROR**   (1958) 75m UNIV bw (GB: THE SILENT STRANGER)

Colleen Miller (Helen Walters), Charles Drake (Johnny Williams), Rod Taylor (Mike Randall), Josephine Hutchinson (Mrs. Walters), Jocelyn Brando (Lily), Alan Dexter (Roy), Rickey Kelman (Doug), Ann Doran.

An uninspired remake of Hitchcock's SHADOW OF A DOUBT which casts Drake as a psychotic killer who returns home to his joyful mom, widowed sister-in-law, and orphaned nephew. They are unaware of his past, or his whereabouts during the last six years, but eventually begin to suspect that something's not right about Drake. Sister-in-law Miller's life is placed in danger, but she and the entire family are saved when Taylor, who has been on Drake's trail, shows up.

p, Joseph Gershenson; d, Harry Keller; w, Mel Dinelli, Czenzi Ormonde, Chris Cooper (based on the story by Gordon McDonell); ph, Russell Metty; m, Buddy Bregman; ed, Frank Gross; art d, Alexander Golitzen; spec eff, Clifford Stine.

Drama   **(PR:A   MPAA:NR)**

STEP LIVELY**   (1944) 88m RKO bw

Frank Sinatra (Glen), George Murphy (Miller), Adolphe Menjou (Wagner), Gloria DeHaven (Christine), Walter Slezak (Gribble), Eugene Pallette (Jenkins), Wally Brown (Binion), Alan Carney (Harry), Grant Mitchell (Dr. Glass), Anne Jeffreys (Miss Abbott), Frances King (Mother), Harry Noble (Father), George Chandler (Country Yokel), Rosemary La Planche (Louella), Shirley O'Hara (Louise), Elaine Riley (Lois), Dorothy Malone (Telephone Operator), Frank Mayo (Doorman).

In 1944, Sinatra was a combination of Elvis Presley, Michael Jackson, and Kenny Rogers in that he was the biggest vocal star in show business and packed houses wherever he sang. He'd appeared as a band vocalist with Tommy Dorsey in LAS VEGAS NIGHTS and SHIP AHOY, then as a singer in REVEILLE WITH BEVERLY before his first acting role in HIGHER AND HIGHER. Here, he gets top billing and does quite well in this re-tailored musical version of the old play "Room Service" which served as the springboard for one of the Marx Brothers' less memorable films. He's a yokel from upstate New York who has written a play and sent his savings, a matter of $1,500, with the play to fast-talking producer Murphy. When Sinatra gets to Murphy's hotel, he learns that the promoter has 22 actors holed up in the hotel because he can't pay the large bill and that Sinatra's money has been used for production of another show that's in rehearsal. Attorney Pallette enters. He is representing a client who wishes to give Murphy $50,000 toward his production on the proviso that Murphy uses his "protege," Jeffreys. DeHaven is one of the showgirls and there's an instant attraction between the two. Sinatra and DeHaven soon find much to enjoy about each other and it looks as though everything is jake when the check bounces higher than a pink tennis ball when dropped from the Empire State Building. Murphy knows that it will take a full five days for the check to come back from the San Francisco bank on which it was drawn so he and his assistants, Brown and Carney, rush to mount the new show, a musical. At the same time, Murphy has to avoid dumb hotel manager Slezak as well as his boss, Menjou, an angry efficiency expert who runs the chain of hotels. Sinatra keeps trying to find out about his play but Murphy continues to evade him, mumbling vague promises to keep him at bay while he frantically arranges the new show's production. They have a script, they have a great score, but they don't have anyone who can play the male lead. Then Murphy hears Sinatra sing and asks him to take the starring role. Sinatra is reluctant but Murphy uses all of his slickness to convince the crooner that he would he doing a great service for mankind if he did, to say nothing of the 22 actors who are desperate. Sinatra steps in, sings his lungs out, the show is a hit, and he winds up with DeHaven, who gives him his first screen kisses, thereby sending thousands of Frankophiles into swoons. Sinatra sings several tunes by Sammy Cahn and Jule Styne including "Some Other Time," "As Long As There's Music," "Where Does Love Begin?," and "Come Out, Come Out, Wherever You Are." Other songs were: "Why Must There Be an Opening Song?," "And Then You Kissed Me," and "Ask the Madame." This movie was somewhat better than the original and the tunes added a great deal to the slim story although there may have been a few too many as they sometimes interrupted the comedy flow. Axel Stordahl did Sinatra's arrangements and Ken Darby did the vocal arrangements.

p, Robert Fellows; d, Tim Whelan; w, Warren Duff, Peter Milne (based on the play "Room Service" by John Murray, Allen Boretz); ph, Robert DeGrasse; ed, Gene Milford; md, Constantin Bakaleinikoff; art d, Albert S. D'Agostino, Carroll Clark; set d, Darrell Silvera, Claude Carpenter; cos, Edward Stevenson; ch, Ernest Matray.

Musical/Comedy   **Cas.**   **(PR:A   MPAA:NR)**

STEP LIVELY, JEEVES**½   (1937) 67m FOX bw

Arthur Treacher (Jeeves), Patricia Ellis (Patricia Westley, Reporter), Robert Kent (Gerry Townsend), Alan Dinehart (Hon. Cedric B. Cromwell), George Givot (Prince Boris Caminov), Helen Flint (Babe Ross), John Harrington (Barney Ross), George Cooper (Slug), Arthur Housman (Max, Drunk), Max Wagner (Joey), Franklin Pangborn (Gaston).

Treacher is wonderfully cast as an English butler who is conned into coming to the U.S. under the impression that he is heir to the treasures of Sir Frances Drake. He actually is a stooge for a swindle organized by cons Givot and Dinehart, in which they plan to soak millionaire crime boss Harrington of his wealth. Unfortunately, not enough attention is paid to Treacher's fine characterization.

p, John Stone; d, Eugene Forde; w, Frank Fenton, Lynn Root (based on a story by Frances Hyland and the character created by P.G. Wodehouse); ph, Daniel B. Clark; ed, Fred Allen; md, Samuel Kaylin; cos, Herschel.

Comedy   **(PR:A   MPAA:NR)**

STEPCHILD*   (1947) 70m PRC bw

Brenda Joyce (Dale Bullock), Donald Woods (Ken Bullock), Terry Austin (Millie Lynne), Tommy Ivo (Jim Bullock), Gregory Marshall (Tommy Bullock), Griff Barnett (Burns), James Millican (Brian Reed), Selmer Jackson (Judge), Ruth Robinson (Miss Brighton).

A tired job of direction and scripting is displayed in this marital drama which has Woods remarrying in hopes of finding a home and a mother for his two children. The new wife, however, mistreats the kids in the worst way, and eventually sends Woods running back to his first wife for a reunion. Full of every cliche in the book.

p, Leonard S. Picker; d, James Flood; w, Karen De Wolfe (based on the story by Jules Levine); ph, Jackson Rose; m, Mario Silva; ed, Alfred DeGaetano; md, Irving Friedman; art d, Perry Smith; set d, Armor Marlowe.

Drama   **(PR:A   MPAA:NR)**

STEPCHILDREN***   (1962, USSR) 75m Gruziya/Artkino bw
(CHUZHIYE DETI; AKA: SOMEBODY ELSE'S CHILDREN)

Tsitsino Tsitsishvili *(Nato)*, Otar Koberidze *(Data)*, Asmat Kandaurishvili *(Teo)*, Nani Chikvinidze *(Liya)*, Mikho Borashvili *(Giya)*, S. Takayshvili *(Elisabed)*.

When a train engineer is widowed and left to care for his two children by himself, he searches for a wife to help him. He first asks his girl friend, but she refuses to take care of another woman's offspring. He eventually finds a woman and marries her, creating a happy home life for the children. However, this is disrupted when his girl friend returns and the engineer decides to run off with her. The wife decides to leave, but before her train can pull away, she returns to "her" children, who are running after her in hopes that she'll stay. Released in 1959 in the USSR, and expertly directed by Abuladze.

d, Tengiz Abuladze; w, Revas Dzhaparidze, Abuladze (based on a sketch by N. Aleksandrova); ph, Levan Paatashvili; m, Archil Kereselidze; ed, Vasiliy Dolenko; art d, Givi Gigauri, Kakhi Khutsishvili.

Drama   **(PR:A   MPAA:NR)**

STEPFORD WIVES, THE**½   (1975) 114m Palomar-Fadsin/COL c

Katharine Ross *(Joanna)*, Paula Prentiss *(Bobby)*, Peter Masterson *(Walter)*, Nanette Newman *(Carol)*, Patrick O'Neal *(Dale Coba)*, Tina Louise *(Charmaine)*, Carol Rosson *(Dr. Fancher)*, William Prince *(Artist)*, Paula Trueman *(Welcome Wagon Lady)*, Remak Ramsay *(Atkinson)*, John Aprea *(Policeman)*, Carole Mallory *(Kit Sunderson)*, Judit h Baldwin *(Mrs. Cornell)*, Toni Reid *(Marie Axhelm)*, Barbara Rucker *(Marie Ann Stavros)*, George Coe *(Claude Axhelm)*, Michael Higgins *(Mr. Cornell)*, Josef Somer *(Ted Van Sant)*, Simon Deckard *(Dave Markowe)*, Martha Greenhouse *(Mrs. Kirgassa)*, Joanna Cassidy.

Ira Levin is an eclectic writer who can do comedy-drama (SLEUTH), adventure (THE BOYS FROM BRAZIL), thrillers (ROSEMARY'S BABY), and science fiction like THE STEPFORD WIVES. His exciting novel is slowed to a laborious pace by Goldman's screenplay and Forbes' ponderous direction. Goldman is an often excellent writer who did BUTCH CASSIDY AND THE SUNDANCE KID and Forbes proved himself with SEANCE ON A WET AFTERNOON as well as many other films. So what happened here? The first hour takes what feels like two, and the last 44 minutes goes like an Indy car so the pace is alternately snail's and Lamborghini's. Ross and her husband, Masterson, leave the hectic world of Manhattan and settle in the small, quite tranquil town of Stepford, Connecticut (actually shot in Westport). She meets the local wives and they seem weird to her, talking about dumb things and sounding like Procter and Gamble commercials. The two women who perplex her most are Louise and Newman (Forbes' wife in real life). They are perfect, devoted to their husbands, to keeping their homes squeaky clean, to having every hair in place, etc. This odd contentment gnaws at Ross. Her only normal friend is also a newcomer, Prentiss. O'Neal is the important man in the town and runs a men's club that Ross and Prentiss would like to know more about. After much palaver, the truth comes out. These women are not women at all, just flawlessly executed robot replicas of the real wives who came to Stepford and who knows what's happened to the originals? The only difference is that these women never argue with their husbands, do everything that's asked of them, and fulfill every male chauvinist fantasy ever imagined. Ross would like to expose the truth once she learns it but by that time it's too late and she and Prentiss are seen at the conclusion as two of a gaggle of Stepford Wives, happily exchanging recipes in the supermarket as they shop for their hubbies' favorite dishes. There is more than a passing similarity to THE INVASION OF THE BODY SNATCHERS, although that was played totally serious and this has more than a number of laughs, particularly when the wives are acting in their "whatever you want, darling" mode. With 15 minutes cut out of the opening 60, this would have been a whizzer.

p, Edgar J. Scherick; d, Bryan Forbes; w, William Goldman (based on the novel by Ira Levin); ph, Owen Roizman (TVC Color); m, Michael Small; ed, Timothy Gee; prod d,Gene Callahan; set d, Robert Drumheller; makeup, Dick Smith.

Science Fiction/Comedy   **Cas.**   **(PR:A-C   MPAA:PG)**

STEPHANIA   (SEE: STEFANIA, 1968, Greece)

STEPPE, THE**   (1963, Fr./Ital.) 100m Zebra-Aera/Royal c (LA STEPPA; LA STEPPE)

Daniele Spallone *(Jegoruska)*, Pavle Vujisic *(Kuzmiciov)*, Charles Vanel *(Father Christopher)*, Milan Bosiljcic *(Dimov)*, Marina Vlady *(Countess Dranitsky)*, Pero Kvrgic *(Mossei)*, Hermina Pipinic *(Olga Ivanovna)*, Marianna Leibl *(Grandmother)*, Cristina Gajoni *(Girl of the River)*, Milan Djurdjevic *(Daniska)*, Ljuba Tadic *(Jamelian)*, Michele Bally *(Gypsy)*, Milorad Majic *(Pantalei)*, Fernando Cicero, Nastasia Petrovna.

The experiences of growing into adulthood are featured in this allegorical journey of a young man, Spallone, traveling with his uncle and father from the Russian countryside to the city where he will enroll in school. His adventures along the way, including love and death, pave the way for his becoming a man.

p, Moris Ergas; d, Alberto Lattuada; w, Lattuada, Enzo Currelli, Tullio Pinelli (based on the novel by Anton Chekhov); ph, Enzo Serafin (Totalscope, Eastmancolor); m, Guido Turchi; ed, Leo Catozzo; art d, Luigi Scaccianoce; makeup, Goffredo Rocchetti.

Drama   **(PR:A   MPAA:NR)**

STEPPENWOLF**   (1974) 105m Peter J. Sprague/D-R c

Max von Sydow *(Harry Haller)*, Dominique Sanda *(Hermine)*, Pierre Clementi *(Pablo)*, Carla Romanelli *(Maria)*, Roy Bosier *(Aztec)*, Alfred Baillou *(Goethe)*, Niels-Peter Rudolph *(Gustav)*, Helmut Furnbacher *(Franz)*, Charles Regnier *(Loering)*, Eduard Linkers *(Mr. Hefte)*, Sylvia Reize *(Dora)*, Helen Hesse *(Frau Hefte)*, Judith Mellics *(Rosa)*.

An abstract film version of Hermann Hesse's abstract novel which had a cult following among the college age crowd. The movie, however, was less well received simply because the images chosen don't match the visual description provided by Hesse. While the film is nearly plotless, it does concern von Sydow attempt to find a new meaning to life before reaching the age of 50, at which time he plans to commit suicide. There's an excessive use of video images, as well as surrealist paintings by Mati Klarwein, to illustrate the journey that von Sydow undertakes. Distributed on a four-wall basis, independently, by electronics magnate Peter J. Sprague.

p, Melvin Fishman, Richard Herland; d&w, Fred Haines (based on novel by Hermann Hesse); ph, Tomaslav Pinter; m, George Gruntz; ed, Irving Lerner; art d, Leo Karen; cos, Else Heckman; ch, Ray Bosier; anim, Jaroslav Bradac; video techniques, Klaus Dieter Stoltenberg.

Drama   **(PR:O   MPAA:R)**

STEPPIN' IN SOCIETY*½   (1945) 72m REP bw

Edward Everett Horton *(Judge Avery Webster)*, Gladys George *(Penelope Webster)*, Ruth Terry *(Lola Forrest)*, Robert Livingston *(Montana)*, Jack LaRue *(Bow Tie)*, Lola Lane *(The Duchess)*, Isabel Jewell *(Jenny the Juke)*, Frank Jenks *(George)*, Paul Hurst *(Cookie)*, Harry Barris *(Ivory)*, Iris Adrian *(Shirley)*, Tom Herbert *(Hilliard)*.

Judge Horton takes a vacation, but ends up stuck in an underworld club during a nasty storm. The mobsters mistakenly believe him to be a fellow racketeer, but eventually a moll with a memory blows his cover. It seems the judge ruined her love life by sending her beau up the river some time ago. Things turn out okay for Horton when he converts the entire gang to law-abiding citizens by the finale. Slow paced and desperately in need of a lively script.

p, Joseph Bercholtz; d, Alexander Esway; w, Bradford Ropes (based on the novel by Marcel Arnac); ph, Reggie Lanning; ed, Harry Keller; md, Morton Scott; art d, Gano Chittenden; set d, Otto Siegel; cos, Adele Palmer.

Crime/Comedy   **(PR:A   MPAA:NR)**

STEPPING INTO SOCIETY   (SEE: DOUGHNUTS AND SOCIETY, 1936)

STEPPING SISTERS*   (1932) 70m FOX bw

Louise Dresser *(Mrs. Ramsey)*, Minna Gombell *(Rosie La Marr)*, Jobyna Howland *(Lady Chetworth-Lynde)*, William Collier, Sr *(Herbert Ramsey)*, Howard Phillips *(Warren Tremaine)*, Stanley Smith *(Jack Carleton)*, Mary Forbes *(Mrs. Tremaine)*, Ferdinand Munier *(Ambassador Leonard)*, Barbara Weeks *(Norma Ramsey)*, Robert Greig *(Jepson, Butler)*.

Three lively gals–Dresser, Gombell, and Howland–try to pump life into this bloodless comedy by turning a society gathering upside down with their wild antics. None of the ladies is quite the socialite she appears to be since each has a past in burlesque. Thus, when they begin drinking and reminiscing, all sense of control is lost. Unfortunately, nothing that happens is very funny, due mainly to the fact that it's a one-joke movie stretched out to more than an hour.

d, Seymour Felix; w, William Conselman, William Collier, Sr. (based on the play by Howard Warren Comstock); ph, George Schneiderman; ed, Jack

Murray; cos, Dolly Tree.

Comedy　　　　　　　　　　　　　　　**(PR:A MPAA:NR)**

STEPPING TOES*½　(1938, Brit.) 85m UK-TC/British Independent bw

Hazel Ascot (*Hazel Warrington*), Enid Stamp-Taylor (*Mrs. Warrington*), Jack Barty (*Joe*), Edgar Driver (*Tich*), Ernest Butcher (*Stringer*), Richard Cooper (*Kenneth Warrington*), Ivan Samson (*Mr. Warrington*), Wilson Coleman (*Bob Burnham*), John Turnbull (*Representative*), Gerry Fitzgerald, Billy Thorburn, Alfredo Campoli, Duggie Ascot, Freddie Watts, Wee Georgie, Marjorie Battis, Henry Latimer, Charles Sewell, Rita Linden, The Sanders Twins, The Three Dots, Cone School Girls, Duke of York's School Boys.

Child tap-dancing prodigy Ascot enters a talent contest put together by her grandfather at a seaside resort and wins. In the process, she helps patch up differences between her estranged parents. Some good moments, but mostly unbearable. Director Baxter is best know in the U.S. for LOVE ON THE DOLE (1945).

p, John Barter; d, John Baxter; w, H. Fowler Mear (based on a story by Jack Francis, Barbara K. Emary).

Musical　　　　　　　　　　　　　　　**(PR:A MPAA:NR)**

STEPS TO THE MOON½**　(1963, Rum.) 60m Bucuresti bw (PASI SPRE LUNA)

Radu Beligan, Grigori Vasiliu-Birlic, Emil Botta, George Demetru, Ovidiu Teodorescu, Irina Petrescu.

An enjoyable children's film which stars Beligan as an astronaut preparing for his spaceship's blast-off, when the entire region experiences a blackout after he plugs in his electric razor. While sitting in the darkness, he fantasizes about meeting all those characters in history who have advanced space travel – from Prometheus and Artemis to Galileo and Jules Verne. A simplistic, but well-conceived comedy.

d&w, Ion Popescu-Gopo; ph, Stefan Horvath; spec eff, Alexandru Popescu.

Children's　　　　　　　　　　　　　　**(PR:A MPAA:NR)**

STEPTOE AND SON*　(1972, Brit.) 98m Associated London/EMI c

Wilfrid Brambell, Harry H. Corbett, Carolyn Seymour, Arthur Howard, Victor Maddern.

The popular British television series that inspired the American television series "Sanford and Son" goes for the big screen audience but falls short of the mark. TV stars don't work well on the screen and the writing is bad throughout.

p, Aida Young; d, Cliff Owen; w, Ray Galton, Alan Simpson (based on a television series "Steptoe and Son"); ph, John Wilcox (Technicolor); m, Roy Budd, Jack Fishman, Ron Grainer.

Comedy　　　　　　　　　　　　　　　**(PR:A-C MPAA:NR)**

STEREO*　(1969, Can.) 65m Emergent bw

Ronald Mlodzik, Iain Ewing, Jack Messinger, Clara Meyer, Paul Mulholland, Arlene Mlodzik, Glenn McCauley.

The first film from cult favorite David Cronenberg, Canada's top horror director (which admittedly isn't saying all that much), has many of the themes that would later pop up in his work. These include repressed sexuality and controlled telepathy. Here he has a group of youngsters involved in a scientific experiment for the Canadian Academy of Erotic Inquiry, in which an operation is performed that removes their ability to speak and increases their power of telepathic communication. Short, and therefore confused, STEREO does display some interesting concepts not usually found in the genre. Cronenberg was only 26 when he shot STEREO with a budget of only $3,500 and without the benefit of synchronized sound. He has since gone on to Hollywood to make THE DEAD ZONE (1983), a film with a bigger budget but not much to show for it. Re-released in 1984.

p,d&w, ph&ed, David Cronenberg.

Science-Fiction　　　　　　　　　　　**(PR:O MPAA:NR)**

STERILE CUCKOO, THE*½**　(1969) 108m Boardwalk/PAR c (GB: POOKIE)

Liza Minnelli (*Pookie*), Wendell Burton (*Jerry*), Tim McIntire (*Charlie Schumacher*), Elizabeth Harrower (*Landlady*), Austin Green (*Pookie's Father*), Sandra Faison (*Nancy Putnam*), Chris Bugbee (*Roe*), Jawn McKinley (*Helen Upshaw*), Fred M. Lerner, A. Frederick Gooseen, Mark P. Fish, Philip S. Derfler, John A. Hussey, Toni Shorrock, Eric Best, Becky Davis, Towyna Thomas, Frances Tobin, Tim Laurie, Margaret Markov, Anita Alberts, Warren Peterson, Paul McConnell, Adele Wynn, Cynthia Hull.

Alan Pakula's directorial debut, after having produced pictures that his partner, Robert Mulligan, directed, was a smasher. Unlike many first-time helmers, Pakula was understated, avoided cinematic tricks, and spent his time dealing with the actors and extracting superb performances from Minnelli (who was nominated for an Oscar), and Burton who was making his debut as well, after having been on Broadway for three years in the title role of "You're A Good Man, Charlie Brown." Shot primarily at the Hamilton College campus in upstate New York (where Alec Woollcott loved to tell people he attended), it's a tender story that concentrates on youth but cannot be classified as a youth picture because it transcends any age. Minnelli and Burton meet on a bus going up to school. They are at different colleges and he's glad of that as her quirky behavior embarrasses him while they ride. Burton is a quiet young man studying etymology and she is a motherless waif whose father has never understood her and who has sent her to a series of sleep-away camps and boarding schools, anything to keep her from him. It's not that her dad, Green, doesn't care about her, it's just that she is such a weirdo (which is the word she calls everyone else). Burton departs from the bus and settles into his dorm room with slob McIntire, a beer-drinking boor who talks endlessly of his sexual conquests. Burton is just about getting used to his new surroundings when Minnelli arrives, in a car that looks as though it should have been junked years before. She tells Burton that she intends to spend the weekend with him. He is hard-pressed to send her away after she's made a dangerous trip in that old automobile so he puts her in a local boardinghouse. They have a marvelous time over the weekend and find something wonderful in each other as she prates on and on about her background and confesses that her mother died giving birth to her. "My first victim," is how she puts it. Their schools are about 90 minutes apart but that doesn't stop them from spending as much time with each other as they can and the two diverse people begin to fall in love. Burton is sexually naive and Minnelli takes this opportunity to have them check into a motel and make love. While he stands there stiffly, with his heavy coat buttoned up to his neck, she takes off all her clothes and then says "Okay, Valentino. Hit it." It's a nervous moment for Burton but he makes it through and a new dimension has been added to their friendship. McIntire invites Burton to come with him for the Christmas break. His parents have a cabin in the mountains and the two boys can ski to their hearts' content. Minnelli has nowhere to go during the holidays and is hurt by Burton's decision to leave with McIntire so she lashes out by saying that she is carrying Burton's child. He is paled by this news but does the decent thing and asks her to get married, an offer she promptly declines. After returning to school, Minnelli tells Burton that she's no longer pregnant (and one wonders if she ever was). Later, he takes her to a party at his school and she drinks too much, becomes vicious, and smart-mouths all of his pals. When she calls him later to apologize, Burton says that he won't be going home for the Easter break but will remain at school to get in some much-needed studying. She asks if she can stay with him as she has nowhere to go during that holiday, either. At first, he is against this but she prevails on him with tears and swears she won't ever get in his way. Burton says okay and she moves in for the week. Although they both try their best, it's not working and when the week is over and McIntire is due to return, Burton suggests they take a respite from each other. Weeks pass and he calls her school to learn that she's left college. He locates her at the boardinghouse near his school and, in a scene that will tear your heart out, tells her that it might be better if she went home and ironed things out with her father. She understands the secondary meaning of the conversation, that this is the end of their romance, and she bids him goodbye. Both have grown from the experience of being with each other, especially Burton, who has a new confidence, a spring in his step that wasn't there at the start. A lovely movie that sometimes gets a bit too arch but usually remains touching and funny. Minnelli's performance is a tour de force and Burton, who seemed to disappear after his next picture, FORTUNE AND MEN'S EYES, is excellent as well. The song "Come Saturday Morning" (Fred Karlin, Dory Previn, performed by The Sandpipers) was nominated for an Oscar. Nudity, male and female, plus rough language. Upgraded from its original R rating by the MPAA in 1972.

p&d, Alan J. Pakula; w, Alvin Sargent; ph, Milton Krasner (Technicolor); m, Fred Karlin; ed, Sam O'Steen, John W. Wheeler; art d, Roland Anderson; set d, Chuck Pierce; cos, Jennifer Parsons, John A. Anderson; spec eff, Charles Spurgeon; makeup, Mike Moschella.

Drama/Comedy　　　　　　　　　　　**(PR:C MPAA:PG)**

STEVIE*½　(1978, Brit.) 102m Bowden/First Artists c

Glenda Jackson (*Stevie Smith*), Mona Washbourne (*Aunt*), Alec McCowen (*Freddy*), Trevor Howard (*The Man*).

A lifeless transposition of a London stage play to the screen, this film is claustrophobic and especially stiff. Based on the life and poetry of British poet Stevie Smith, the film can boast some admirable performances but is otherwise lifeless. Jackson is cast as the poet, who lives in a mundane apartment, the sole setting for the action, with Washbourne, who serves almost entirely as a sounding board for her niece's expository dialog.

p&d, Robert Enders; w, Hugh Whitemore (based on Whitemore's play and the works of Stevie Smith); ph, Freddie Young (Technicolor); m, Patrick Gowers; ed, Peter Tanner; art d, Bob Jones.

Biography　　　　　　　　　**Cas.**　　　　　**(PR:A MPAA:NR)**

STICK 'EM UP**   (1950, Brit.) 95m Film Studios
Manchester/Mancunian bw (GB: LET'S HAVE A MURDER)

Jimmy Jewel (*Jimmy Jewsbury*), Ben Warriss (*Ben Warren*), Lesley Osmond (*Marjorie Gordon*), Stewart Rome (*Col. Gordon*), Anthony Pendrell, Eva Eacott, Claude Dampier, Kitty Blewett [Bluett].

Jewel and Warriss, a popular British radio comedy team, attempt to extend their talents to the movies in this second feature of their careers. They play a pair of bumbling detectives afraid of their collective shadows, to say nothing of real-life crooks. While investigating a singer's murder the duo learn that a seemingly respectable psychiatrist is the culprit and notorious jewel thief as well. The humor was minor and basic to a plot that had been hashed over countless times in comedy detective films. As a result the film didn't do very well at the box office and was the last such venture for Jewel and Warriss.

p&d, John E. Blakeley; w, Anthony Toner; ph, Ernest Palmer.

Comedy   **(PR:A   MPAA:NR)**

STICK TO YOUR GUNS**   (1941) 63m PAR bw

William Boyd (*Hopalong Cassidy*), Brad King (*Johnny Nelson*), Andy Clyde (*California*), Jacqueline Holt (*June Winters*), Henry Hall (*Winters*), Joe Whitehead (*Buck*), Bob Card (*Frenchy*), Jimmy Wakely (*Pete*), Johnny Bond (*Skinny*), Dick Rinehart (*Bow Wow*), Jack Trent (*Red*), Homer Holcomb (*Lanky*), Tom London (*Waffles*), Mickey Eissa (*Ed*), Jack Smith (*Tex*), Johnny Bond, Dick Rinehart, Weldon Heyburn, Kermit Maynard, Frank Ellis, Jack Rockwell.

When a former Bar 20 boy now a feisty rancher, has trouble with a gang of rustlers, Boyd and the boys ride in and surround the bad guys until they either give up or get shot. Holt gets herself into the posse and ends up in the arms of King, who with Boyd leads the attack. (See HOPALONG CASSIDY series, Index.)

p, Harry Sherman; d, Lesley Selander; w, J. Benton Cheney (based on characters created by Clarence E. Mulford); ph, Russell Harlan; ed, Earl Moser.

Western   **(PR:A   MPAA:NR)**

STICK UP, THE*   (1978, Brit.) 101m Trident-Barber c (AKA: MUD)

David Soul (*Duke Turnbeau*), Pamela McMyler (*Rosie McCratchit*), Johnny Wade (*Smiley*), Tony Melody (*Tall Cop*), Norman Jones (*Short Cop*), Glynn Edwards (*Older Cop*), Robert Longden (*Younger Cop*), Pat Durkin (*George*), Alan Tilern (*Ritchie*), Cyd Child (*Amazon Lady*), Michael Balfour (*Sam*).

This uninteresting romantic comedy relies on the name of David Soul, from TV's "Starsky and Hutch" for its box office draw. That's about all it has going for it, centering on the stock robbery of an armoured truck with Irish lass McMyler as Soul's sidekick and romantic interest. Supposedly taking place in England in the 1930s, the sets look more like the late 1970s than any other decade.

p, George Pappas; d&w, Jeffrey Bloom; ph, Michael Reed; m, Michael J. Lewis; cos, Mike Jarvis.

Romance/Comedy   **(PR:A   MPAA:NR)**

STIGMA zero   (1972) 93m Cinerama c

Philip M. Thomas (*Dr. Calvin Crosse*), Harlan Cary Poe (*Bill Waco*), Josie Johnson (*D.D. Whitehead*), Peter H. Clune (*Sheriff Whitehead*), William Magerman (*Jeremy*), Connie Van Ess (*Tassie*), "Cousin" Bruce Morrow (*Himself*), Richard Geisman (*Joe*), Raina Barrett (*"B" Girl*), Carter Courtney (*Homosexual*), Rhonda Fuller (*Rhoda*), Kathy Joyce (*Kathleen*), Jean Parker (*Jeanie*), Edwin Mills (*Choir Leader*), Jim Grace (*Ed*).

This low-budget sexploitationer is about a neurotic young woman who spreads venereal disease to everyone possible in a small New England town. Black doctor Thomas and Vietnam veteran Poe help the bigoted community out of their epidemic by convincing the locals to stop their orgies until the culprit is found. Movie's heavy-handed treatment of promising premise results only in boredom, despite the highly improbable twists and turns of the plot.

p, Charles B. Moss, Jr.; d&w, David E. Durston; ph, Robert M. Baldwin; ed, Murray Solomon; makeup, Irvin Carlton.

Drama   **(PR:O   MPAA:R)**

STILETTO*   (1969) 98m AE c

Alex Cord (*Count Cesare Cardinali*), Britt Ekland (*Illeana*), Patrick O'Neal (*Asst. D.A.*), Joseph Wiseman (*Emilio Matteo*), Barbara McNair (*Ahn Dessje*), John Dehner (*D.A. Frank Simpson*), Titos Vandis (*Tonio*), Eduardo Ciannelli (*Don Andrea*), Roy Scheider (*Bennett*), Lincoln Kilpatrick (*Hannibal Smith*), Louis Elias (*Mann*), Luke Andreas (*Macy*), Dominic T. Barto (*Franchini*), James Tolkan (*Edwards*), Amaru (*Rosa*), Michaelina Martel (*Blonde at Casino*), Fat Thomas (*Dutch Wehrman*), Leonardo Cimino (*Allie Fargo*), Luis Antonio Martinez (*John Vanicola*).

Cord stars in this lame adaptation of a lame Harold Robbins novel as a contracted mob assassin, or stiletto, who wants a new job. Living the life of a jet-setter, Cord originally does the hits as a favor to Wiseman, a Mafia boss who once saved his life, but soon becomes indispensable in the mob's eyes. Lacking in suspense, STILETTO amounts to little more than a confusing soap opera-like tale of the underworld.

p, Norman Rosemont; d, Bernard Kowalski; w, A.J. Russell (based on the novel by Harold Robbins); ph, Jack Priestley (Berkey-PatheColor); m, Sid Ramin; ed, Frank Mazzola, Stuart Chasmar; art d, Jan Scott; set d, Bob Drumheller; cos, Alvin Colt; m/l, "Sugar in the Rain," Marilyn Bergman, Alan Bergman; makeup, John Alese.

Crime Drama   **Cas.**   **(PR:O   MPAA:R)**

STILL OF THE NIGHT**   (1982) 91m MGM-UA c

Roy Scheider (*Sam Rice*), Meryl Streep (*Brooke Reynolds*), Jessica Tandy (*Grace Rice*), Joe Grifasi (*Joseph Vitucci*), Sara Botsford (*Gail Phillips*), Josef Sommer (*George Bynum*), Rikke Borge (*Heather Wilson*), Irving Metzman (*Murray Gordon*), Larry Joshua (*Mugger*), Tom Norton (*Auctioneer*), Richmond Hoxie (*Mr. Harris*), Hyon Cho (*Mr. Chang*), Danielle Cusson (*Girl*), John Bentley (*Night Watchman*), George A. Tooks (*Elevator Operator*), Sigrunn Omark (*Receptionist*), Randy Jurgenson (*Car Thief*), Palmer Deane, William Major, Joseph Priestly, Will Rose (*Auction Spotters*), Arnold Glimcher, Jeffrey Hoffeld, Linda LeRoy Janklow, Elinor Klein, Susan Patricof (*Auction Bidders*).

Director-writer Benton's last film was the multi-award-winning KRAMER VS. KRAMER and this was a radical departure from the domesticity of that, perhaps too radical. Benton had wanted to make a movie on the order of Hitchcock (who doesn't? De Palma and Colin Higgins make a fine living doing it) and did so here, with moments recognizable from NORTH BY NORTHWEST, PSYCHO, VERTIGO, and SABOTEUR. Scheider is a Manhattan psychiatrist who is suspected of having killed one of his patients. The cops are not sure if he did it or not but they are sure he knows something and he will not divulge it to them, claiming the doctor-patient relationship as immunity. Streep is the mistress of the dead man and Scheider wonders if she is the killer. He lives a quiet, bachelor's life and she manages to use her wiles to get inside his tranquil existence until he begins to wonder why she is doing this. Streep is a chain-smoking frosty blonde, a combination of Bette Davis and Grace Kelly, who is bubbling at all times and looks as though she will explode with no provocation. Lots of psychiatric talk as Scheider begins having nightmares, seeing flashing knives, going through the same kind of hell Stewart went through in VERTIGO. He is determined to get to the bottom of things and must find out if Streep is the killer so he carefully plans his moves and gets closer and closer to her until.... aha! Let's leave the denouement to your imagination but be aware that it's exactly what you thought it would be. That's the major problem with this talky picture. There's suspense but no mystery. Legend has it that Benton wanted to do a funny "slasher" kind of movie with Lily Tomlin in the lead. The tentative title was "Stab" and that sounds a lot better than this. The knife scenes were out of PSYCHO, the dreams you already know, an art gallery auction is from NORTH BY NORTHWEST, and the finish is the hanging-by-a-sleeve scene between Norman Lloyd and Robert Cummings on the Statue of Liberty in SABOTEUR. Enough already with the *homages*!

p, Arlene Donovan; d&w, Robert Benton (based on a story by David Newman, Benton); ph, Nestor Almendros (Technicolor); m, John Kander; ed, Jerry Greenberg; prod d, Mel Bourne; art d, Michael Molly; set d, Steve Jordan; cos, Albert Wolsky.

Thriller   **Cas.**   **(PR:O   MPAA:PG)**

STILL ROOM IN HELL   (SEE: THERE IS STILL ROOM IN HELL, 1963, Ger.)

STILL SMOKIN'*   (1983) 91m PAR c (CHEECH AND CHONG'S STILL SMOKIN')

Cheech Marin, Tommy Chong (*Themselves*), Hans Van In't Veld (*Promoter*), Carol Van Herwijen (*Hotel Manager*), Shireen Strooker (*Assistant Manager*), Susan Hahn (*Maid*), Arjan Ederveen, Kees Prins (*Bellboys*), Mariette Bout (*Waitress*), Fabiola (*Barge Lady*), Carla Van Amstel (*Queen Beatrix*).

Even the most ardent Cheech and Chong fans will have a hard time finding much to enjoy in this pathetic showing from the drug-oriented comedy duo. Composed almost entirely of concert footage, there is a minimum of plot thrown in that has something to do with the Amsterdam Film Festival. Mild-mannered vulgarity ties the scenes together.

p, Peter MacGregor-Scott; d, Thomas Chong; w, Chong, Cheech Marin; ph, Harvey Harrison; m, George S. Clinton; ed, David Ramirez, James Coblentz; art d, Ruud Van Dijk.

Comedy   **Cas.**   **(PR:O   MPAA:R)**

STING, THE***** (1973) 129m Richard D. Zanuck-David Brown/UNIV
c

Paul Newman (*Henry Gondorff/Mr. Shaw*), Robert Redford (*Johnny Hooker/Kelly*), Robert Shaw (*Doyle Lonnegan*), Charles Durning (*Lt. William Snyder*), Ray Walston (*J.J. Singleton*), Eileen Brennan (*Billie*), Harold Gould (*Kid Twist*), John Heffernan (*Eddie Niles*), Dana Elcar (*FBI Agent Polk*), Jack Kehoe ("*Erie Kid", Joe Erie*), Dimitra Arliss (*Loretta Salino*), Robert Earl Jones (*Luther Coleman*), James J. Sloyan (*Mottola*), Charles Dierkop (*Floyd*), Sally Kirkland (*Crystal*), John Quade (*Riley*), Paulene Myers (*Alva Coleman*), William Benedict (*Roulette Dealer*), Avon Long (*Benny Garfield*), Arch Johnson (*Combs*), Lee Paul (*Bodyguard*), Ed Bakey (*Granger*), Brad Sullivan (*Cole*), Larry D. Mann (*Train Conductor*), Leonard Barr (*Burlesque Comedian*), Joe Tornatore (*Black-Gloved Gunman*), Jack Collins (*Duke Boudreau*), Tom Spratley (*Curly Jackson*), Ken O'Brien (*Greer*), Ken Samson (*Western Union Executive*), Ta-Tanisha (*Louise Coleman*).

By reuniting three of the most successful elements of the 1969 blockbuster BUTCH CASSIDY AND THE SUNDANCE KID–director George Roy Hill and actors Robert Redford and Paul Newman–THE STING emerged from the pack as an equally successful entertainment, masterfully told and played, outgrossing every other picture of the year. Set in a past era which seems more like a pleasant memory of Hollywood days gone by than an authentically detailed period piece, the story begins in September, 1936, in Joliet, Illinois. The city is run by corrupt officials, namely cop Durning, and is a hotbed for the numbers racket. When two-bit drifter Redford and his veteran partner Jones, the mentor of every con in the area, con one of the racketeers out of a $5,000 delivery, they find themselves mixed up with the big boys in Chicago and their head man, Shaw, a sleazy gangster who would gladly kill a drifter like Redford to retain control of his operation. Durning shakes down Redford, who has already gambled away or spent most of the money, threatening to kill him if he doesn't pay back the money he made in the con. Jones, who has decided to retire from the con game and get into a legitimate business, is not so lucky, and is killed by two of Shaw's thugs. On the run from Joliet police and Shaw's goons, Redford heads for Chicago to meet up with a friend of Jones', a man described as "the greatest con artist of them all," Newman. Determined to avenge the murder of Jones, Redford makes plans to "sting" Shaw out of a fortune in what Redford and Newman refer to as "the big con." Newman, a slobish drunk who lives in backroom squalor in a joint run by Brennan, is wary of hooking up with the green Redford and having to teach him how to perfect the con trade. When Newman suggests that Redford simply kill Shaw, he gets a simple response: "I don't know enough about killin' to kill him." Newman is convinced and they set the gears into motion. In the basement of an abandoned Chicago storefront, Redford and Newman set up a fake off-track betting parlor, renting all the necessary furnishings from a local supplier. To people the extravagant operation, Redford asks Newman if he can find enough cons for the job. "After what happened to Luther 'Jones'," Newman responds with a smile, "I don't know if I can get more than two...three hundred guys." Countless cons, all of whom want to pay a debt to the memory of Jones, lend a hand, with Walston taking a pivotal role as a race announcer. After the "set up," Redford and Newman get to work on "the hook," boarding a New York-to-Chicago train on which Shaw consistently stages games of high-stakes straight poker. In the film's finest scene, Newman buys his way into the game and masquerades as a cocky, gin- drinking sap, who seems to be more of a big talker than a big player. Fully aware of Shaw's predilection for cheating, Newman comes prepared. To Shaw's surprise, Newman starts winning, first small stakes, then big ones. Some players drop out, leaving only Shaw, Newman, and one other. It has now become a game not of who plays best, but of who cheats best. The stakes get higher as Shaw holds four "nines" to Newman's four "threes". The pot becomes enormous, bulging with $15,000 in chips, when the hands are finally called. Shaw proudly lays down his "four" nines. Newman, however, through some miracle of cheating, lays down four jacks. When Shaw discovers that his billfold is gone (it had earlier been swiped by the sure-handed Brennan), he is unable to pay his debt and further gets entangled in "the big con." Redford then plays his role, that of Newman's power-hungry right- hand man with his sight set on taking control of Newman's entire Chicago operation. Once in Chicago, Redford explains that he has a system for playing the horses which involves a friend at the wire service who gives results before the race is actually announced. Shaw begins placing bets for Redford at the phony parlor, and after thoroughly testing for any setups and traps, comes to trust Redford's system. In the meantime, Redford is being hounded by Durning, who, like a pit bull, will not let him out of his grip. Durning finally captures Redford and turns him over to FBI agent, Elcar, who turns the screws into the con man. Redford is forced to comply with Durning and Elcar, supplying them with information on the Shaw "sting." When the big day finally arrives, Shaw is told to "place it on Lucky Dan," and promptly heads for the betting parlor where he bets $500,000 on a horse named Lucky Dan to win. After getting an okay from Newman, and exchanging glances with the nervous Redford, Shaw confidently awaits the words of race announcer Walston, planning to collect the $2 million that the 4-to-1 odds will net him. Shaw is then informed than he was to bet to "place," not win. He panics and charges to the betting cage, claiming that a mistake has been made, but to no avail. Before anything can be done, FBI agents, led by Elcar, rush in and bust the operation. When Newman realizes that Redford was the informer, he shoots him, and is then shot himself by Elcar. Durning quickly rushes Shaw out of

the parlor in order to avoid any involvement, forcing him to leave his $500,000 behind. After both Shaw and Durning are gone, the ruse is made clear. Redford and Newman are both alive, having faked the gunfire, and Elcar is actually just a friend pretending to be an FBI agent. The betting parlor is dismantled, everyone gets their cut of Shaw's money, and Redford and Newman are left smiling about their ultimate "sting." A marvelous celebration of the golden age of Hollywood gangster pictures, THE STING provides superlative entertainment and a filling portion of comedy. The charisma of Redford and Newman, two of the top box- office stars of the era, is unequaled in recent memory, evoking the classic buddy team of Clark Gable and Spencer Tracy of the mid-1930s. Unlike most star packages of this caliber, THE STING began rather unexpectedly. While finishing up THE WAY WE WERE and awaiting the beginning of THE GREAT WALDO PEPPER (which was delayed due to THE WAY WE WERE), Redford began talking with Hill about the prospects of filming THE STING as a star vehicle solely for Redford. The film was originally slated with screenwriter David Ward to direct, but wary of working with a first-timer, Redford did not commit himself, until Hill announced plans to direct. When Newman heard the news he barked, "You're making another movie with Redford and there's no part for me?" With that seed planted in the director's head, he began to rethink the part of Henry Gondorff, originally, in Hill's words, "a burly, oafish slob of a man." After some rewriting, the roles of Gondorff and Hooker were molded to fit, respectively, Newman and Redford, both men receiving a $500,000 salary with Newman also getting a percentage of the gross. The gross for 1974, as it turned out, was a whopping $68,450,000 (a figure that, though spectacular at the time, is easily dwarfed by the Steven Spielberg and George Lucas blockbuster factory). THE STING was also big news come Oscar time, raking in 10 nominations and winning seven–Best Picture, Best Director (Hill), Best Screenplay (Ward), Best Art Direction-Set Decoration (Bumstead, Payne), Best Editing (Reynolds), Best Musical Adaptation (Hamlisch), Best Costume Design (Head). It lost out to the competition in only three categories–Best Actor (Redford), Best Cinematography (Surtees), and Best Sound (Ronald K. Pierce, Robert Bertrand). Much of the film's success, in obvious addition to the superb storytelling capabilities of Hill and the teaming of Redford and Newman, belongs to its visual brilliance–the aged look of Surtees photography which evokes a feeling of antiquity as if the film is being watched through nostalgic eyes, and the equally effective art direction, set decoration, and costuming. Marvin Hamlisch does a fine job of evoking the musical flavor of the era in adapting Scott Joplin's classic rags, especially "The Entertainer," which was soon heard all over the airwaves and sparked a renewed interest in the composer. Also included from Joplin's works are, "Easy Winners," "Pineapple Rag," "The Ragtime Dance," and "Gladiolus Rag."

p, Tony Bill, Julia Phillips, Michael Phillips; d, George Roy Hill; w, David S. Ward; ph, Robert Surtees (Technicolor); m, Scott Joplin, John Philip Sousa,; ed, William Reynolds; art d, Henry Bumstead; set d, James Payne; cos, Edith Head; spec eff, Bob Warner, Albert Whitlock.

Crime/Comedy   Cas.   (PR:C MPAA:PG)

STING OF DEATH zero   (1966) 81m Essen/Thunderbird c

Joe Morrison (*John Hoyt*), Valerie Hawkins (*Karen Richardson*), John Vella (*Egon*), Jack Nagle (*Dr. Richardson*), Sandy Lee Kane (*Louise*), Deanna Lund (*Jessica*), Barbara Paridon (*1st Girl*), Lois Etelman (*Donna*), Judy Lee (*Ruth*), Blanche Devreaux (*Susan*), Doug Hobart (*The Monster*), Robert Stanton (*Sheriff*), Tony Gulliver (*1st Boy*), Ron Pinchbeck (*2nd Boy*), John Castle (*3rd Boy*), Neil Sedaka (*Singer*).

A painfully mindless science fiction film has three marine biologists, Morrison, Nagle and Vella carrying out desperate experiments in the Florida Everglades. Vella, badly disfigured from a previous accident, is secretly testing jellyfish in his underground lab, using Hawkin's collegiate daughter's friends for his tests. He, of course, falls in love with the girl, but has transformed himself into a half-man, half-fish monster. Neil Sedaka, for some bizarre reason, appears singing a tune.

p, Joseph Fink, Richard S. Fink, Juan Hidalgo-Gato; d, William Grefe; w, Al Dempsey; ph, Julio C. Chavez, Julio Roldan (Eastmancolor); m, Al Jacobs, Lon Norman; ed, Chavez; makeup, Harry Kerwin.

Science Fiction   (PR:C MPAA:NR)

STING II, THE*   (1983) 102m UNIV c

Jackie Gleason (*Condorff*), Mac Davis (*Hooker*), Teri Garr (*Veronica*), Karl Malden (*Macalinski*), Oliver Reed (*Lonnegan*), Bert Remsen (*Kid Colors*), Kathalina Veniero (*Blonde with Kid Colors*), Jose Perez (*Carlos*), Larry Bishop (*Gallecher*), Frank McCarthy, Richard C. Adams (*Lonnegan's Thugs*), Ron Rifkin (*Eddie*), Harry James (*Bandleader*), Frances Bergen (*Lady Dorsett*), Monica Lewis (*Band Singer*), Danie-Wade Dalton (*Messenger*), Val Avery (*O'Malley*), Jill Jaress (*Gertie*), Paul Willson (*Man in Ticket Line*), Sidney Clute (*Ticket Clerk*), Al Robertson (*Redcap*), Hank Garrett (*Cab Driver*), Bob O'Connell (*Clancy*), John Hancock (*Doc Brown*), Larry Hankin (*Handicap*), Jerry Whitney (*Page Boy*), Michael D. Alldredge (*Big Ohio*), Danny Dayton (*Ring Announcer*), Tim Rossovich (*Typhoon Taylor*), Fred Dennis (*Card Player*), Sam Theard (*Old Second*), Marty Denkin (*Referee*), Rex Pierson (*Healy*), Angela Robinson (*Doc Brown's Girl*), Joe Monte (*Band Leader*), Carl Gottlieb (*Maitre d'*), David Ankrum (*Waiter*),

Tony Giorgio (*Macalinski's Man*), T. Max Graham (*Tom, Bartender*), Ron Stein (*Macalinski's Guard*), Max Wright (*Floor Manager*), Corey Eubanks, Mike Raden (*Fighters*), Melodie Bovee, Cynthia Cypert (*Girls in Club*), Elaine Goren, Iva Rifkin, Lise Kristen Gerard, Lenetta Kidd (*Macalinski's Girls*), Woody Parfrey (*Georgie*), Cassandra Peterson (*O'Malley's Girl*), Carolyn Carradine, Terry Berland.

This repulsive sequel to George Roy Hill's THE STING is harmed irreparably by the performances of Gleason and Davis as a couple of cons, neither of whom come anywhere near the expected Newman and Redford comparisons. The pair scheme to strike it rich with a boxing scam involving nightclub owner Malden, and Garr (the only bright piece of acting in sight). The usual twists and turns follow, without any wit or humor. It was scripted by David S. Ward, who also scripted the original and added nothing new or special to this sequel.

p, Jennings Lang; d, Jeremy Paul Kagan; w, David S. Ward; ph, Bill Butler (Technicolor); m, Lalo Schifrin; ed, David Garfield; prod d, Edward C. Carfagno; cos, Burton Miller; ch, Alton Ruff; m/l, Scott Joplin.

Comedy   **Cas.**   **(PR:C MPAA:PG)**

STINGAREE**   (1934) 76m Berman/RKO bw

Irene Dunne (*Hilda Bouverie*), Richard Dix (*Stingaree*), Mary Boland (*Mrs. Clarkson*), Conway Tearle (*Sir Julian Kent*), Andy Devine (*Howie*), Henry Stephenson (*Mr. Clarkson*), Una O'Connor (*Annie*), George Barraud (*Inspector Radford*), Reginald Owen (*Governor General*), Snub Pollard (*Victor*), Billy Bevan, Robert Greig.

A far-fetched but entertaining romance has Dix, a thief known as "Stingaree," falling in love with Australian opera singer Dunne. Dix isn't your normal bandit, however. He steals just for the sake of stealing. His climactic scam is snatching the uniform of general Owen and masquerading as him during a concert of Dunne's, after which he kidnaps the singer. Includes the songs "Stingaree Ballad," "Tonight Is Mine" (Gus Kahn, W. Franke Harling), "I Wish I Were a Fisherman," "Once You're Mine" (Edward Eliscu, Max Steiner), and excerpts from Gounod's "Faust" and Flotow's "Martha." The story was first filmed by the Kalem Company as a 12-part silent serial entitled THE ADVENTURES OF STINGAREE.

p, Pandro S. Berman; d, William A. Wellman; w, Becky Gardiner, Lynn Riggs, Leonard Spielgass (based on the stories by E.W. Hornung); ph, James Van Tress; ed, James B. Morley; md, Max Steiner; cos, Walter Plunkett; spec eff, Vernon L. Walker.

Musical   **(PR:A MPAA:NR)**

STINGRAY**   (1978) 99m AE c

Christopher Mitchum, Les Lannom, Sherry Jackson, Bill Watson, Bert Hinchman, Cliff Emmich, Sondra Theodore, Richard Cosentino, Russell Bender.

Mildly appealing car movie has Mitchum and Lannom buying a 1962 Corvette, then discovering that the trunk is full of cash and heroin that gangsters, led by Jackson, are quite anxious to get back. Lots of chases and violence, but whenever Mitchum or Lannom open their mouths, the movie stops dead in its tracks. Only Jackson, a foul-mouthed, two-fisted broad keeping her men in line as she tries to recover her property, is very interesting, and she's not seen nearly enough.

p, Donald Ham, Bill Bruce; d&w, Richard Taylor; ph, (Technicolor).

Crime   **Cas.**   **(PR:C MPAA:PG)**

STIR***   (1980, Aus.) 100m Smiley/Hoyts c

Bryan Brown (*China*), Max Phipps (*Norton*), Dennis Miller (*Redford*), Michael Gow (*Andrew*), Phil Motherwell (*Alby*), Gary Waddell (*Dave*), Ray Marshall (*Chalmers*), Ted Robshaw (*Partridge*), James Marsh (*Webster*), Paul Sonkkila (*McIntosh*), Keith Gallasch (*Tony*), Syd Heylen (*Old Bob*), Peter Kowitz (*Lewis*), Robert "Tex" Morton (*Governor*), Tony Wager (*Visiting Judge*), Les Newcombe (*Hogan*), Morris Saidi (*Chickenman*), Dave Taylor (*Prisoner's Spokesman No. 1*), Margaret Throsby (*TV Interviewer*), Robert Noble (*Riley*), Christ Smith, Ian Gray, Peter Barton, James Cameron, Greg Smith, Dennis Hunt.

A hard-edged prison drama that illustrates the intense differences between life on opposite sides of the bars. The story centers on Brown and his role in a violent prison riot, but each and every one of the supporting cast members carries the weight equally, many of the minor players having a prison background. Shot in a vacated Australian prison, the photography also contributes to the atmospheric harshness as does the script, which was penned by ex-con Jewson.

p, Richard Brennan; d, Stephen Wallace; w, Bob Jewson; ph, Geoffrey Burton (Eastmancolor); m, Cameron Allan; ed, Henry Dangar; spec eff, Chris Murray.

Drama   **(PR:O MPAA:NR)**

STIR CRAZY***   (1980) 111m COL c

Gene Wilder (*Skip Donahue*), Richard Pryor (*Harry Monroe*), Georg Stanford Brown (*Rory Schultebrand*), Jobeth Williams (*Meredith*), Miguellangel Suarez (*Jesus Ramirez*), Craig T. Nelson (*Deputy Ward Wilson*), Barry Corbin (*Warden Walter Beatty*), Charles Weldon (*Blade*), Nicolas Coster (*Warden Henry Sampson*), Joel Brooks (*Len Garber*), Jonathan Banks (*Jack Graham*), Erland Van Lidth De Jeude (*Grossberger*), Lee Purcell (*Susan*), Karmin Murcelo (*Theresa Ramirez*), Franklyn Ajaye (*Young Man in Hospital*), Estelle Omens (*Mrs. R.H. Broache*), Cedrick Hardman (*Big Mean*), Henry Kingi (*Ramon*), Pamela Poitier (*Cook's Helper*), Alvin Ing (*Korean Doctor*), Joseph Massengale (*Ceasar Geronimo*), Herman Poppe (*Alex*), Luis Avalos (*Chico*), Esther Sutherland (*Sissie*).

An essentially empty script is made palatable by Pryor's ability to be funnier than his material. Wilder and Pryor are two losers who are just barely managing in the frantic city of New York. They decide that things have to be better somewhere else so they drive cross-country on their way to California, where they hope their fortunes will pick up. Stopping in a small tank town, they are in need of a few dollars so they take a job wearing huge woodpecker suits in order to publicize a local event. After that's over, two crooks don the outfits and walk into the local bank where they lift many thousands from the till. The last persons seen in the ridiculous costumes were Pryor and Wilder, so they are immediately arrested and convicted and given 120-year terms. Pryor winces at the thought and says something to the effect of: "120 years? I'll be 155 by the time I get out!" The men are clapped in a tough jail filled with the usual types: the crazed killer whom everyone fears (De Jeude); the gay prisoner who lisps so much his dialog sounds like a room full of asps (Brown); et al. They have been assigned an attorney by the state, Williams, and she believes their story and will work hard to get them out; but that might take years and there is no guarantee unless the real culprits are found. Not wishing to spend their lives in jail, there is only one other way out: a jail break. The warden of the prison, Nelson, has a running battle with Coster, the warden of a rival facility. There's an annual rodeo between the two institutions and Wilder thinks they might be able to use that as a cover to escape as the men will be taken to an arena where there is a possibility of getting away. Now, there's a great leap of credibility as Wilder is discovered to have bronco riding ability (how a New Yorker developed that is never explained). The rodeo takes place and, with the help of De Jeude, whom Wilder has befriended and apparently tamed, and a few of the others, the escape is successful and Wilder winds up with Williams. Wilder is his usual strident self, yelling at the top of his lungs, popping his eyes like a minor league Marty Feldman and, in general, giving the same performance he usually gives, almost to a T. Poitier's direction gets as much as it can out of the surprisingly witless script (surprising because it was written by one of the country's better humorists). The language is rough and the sight gags are telegraphed, but Pryor is worth the price of admission. In a small role, note Franklyn Ajaye, one of the funniest black (or white) comics operating on a nightclub floor.

p, Hannah Weinstein; d, Sidney Poitier; w, Bruce Jay Friedman; ph, Fred Schuler (Metrocolor); m, Tom Scott; ed, Harry Keller; prod d, Alfred Sweeney; cos, Patricia Edwards; ch, Scott Salmon.

Comedy   **Cas.**   **(PR:C-O MPAA:R)**

STITCH IN TIME, A***   (1967, Brit.) 94m RANK/ZENITH
                                                            INTERNATIONAL bw

Norman Wisdom (*Norman Pitkin*), Edward Chapman (*Grimsdale*), Jeannette Sterke (*Janet Haskell*), Jerry Desmonde (*Sir Hector Hardcastle*), Jill Melford (*Lady Brinkley*), Glyn Houston (*Welsh*), Hazel Hughes (*Matron*), Patsy Rowlands (*Amy*), Peter Jones (*Russell*), Ernest Clark (*Professor Cranshaw*), Lucy Appleby (*Lindy*), Vera Day (*Betty*), Frank Williams (*Nuttall*), Penny Morell (*Nurse Rudkin*), Patrick Cargill (*Dr. Meadows*), Francis Matthews (*Benson*), Pamela Conway (*Woman Patient*), Danny Green (*Ticehurst*), Johnny Briggs (*Teddy Boy*), John Blythe (*Dale*).

Wisdom stars as a simple butcher's assistant who raises a ruckus in a hospital where his boss is undergoing surgery to remove a watch he swallowed. While getting kicked out Wisdom puts a smile on the face of an injured, recently orphaned young girl, and vows to come back and see her. He tries every way he can to regain entry—catching pneumonia, getting hit by a car, and finally showing up on TV for a charity ball, knowing that the young girl will be watching. A charming and sentimental piece of characterization from Wisdom.

p, Hugh Stewart; d, Robert Asher; w, Jack Davies, Norman Wisdom, Henry Blyth, Eddie Leslie; ph, Jack Asher; m, Philip Green; ed, Gerry Hambling; art d, Bert Davey; set d, Arthur Taksen; cos, Joan Ellacott; makeup, George Blackler.

Comedy   **(PR:A MPAA:NR)**

STOCK CAR**   (1955, Brit.) 68m Balblair/BUT bw

Paul Carpenter (*Larry Duke*), Rona Anderson (*Katie Glebe*), Susan Shaw (*Gina*), Harry Fowler (*Monty Albright*), Robert Rietty (*Roberto*), Paul Whitsun-Jones (*Turk McNeil*), Sabrina (*Trixie*), Alma Taylor (*Nurse Sprott*), Lorrae Desmond (*Singer*), Eve Raymond, Frank Thornton, Doreen Locke, Kim Parker, Fraser Hines, Reginald Barrett, Ann Croft.

A stock-car movie, as the title implies, this one runs in low gear and runs out of gas before the opening credits finish rolling by. The standard tale has Anderson battling to keep her father's garage open after he is killed in a race. She gets some help from Carpenter, but runs into a roadblock in Whitsun-Jones, an unsympathetic creditor who wants to foreclose on the garage. Whitsun-Jones gets even angrier when his girl, Shaw, takes a liking to Carpenter. In an attempt to get rid of the competition, Whitsun-Jones gets beaten up and nearly dies in a rigged race. As movie heroes are known to do, Carpenter makes a comeback, wins the big race, and walks off with the girl.

p, A.R. Rawlinson; d, Wolf Rilla; w, Rawlinson, Victor Lyndon; ph, Geoffrey Faithfull.

Action/Sports Drama   **(PR:A   MPAA:NR)**

STOKER, THE**   (1932) 70m Hoffman-Allied bw

Monte Blue (*Dick*), Dorothy Burgess (*Margarita*), Noah Beery, Sr (*Santino*), Natalie Moorhead (*Vera*), Richard Tucker, Charles Stevens, Clarence Gelder, Harry Vejar, Chris Martin.

Blue finds himself working in a ship's boiler room after his wife sends him to the poorhouse. From there, he takes a plantation job and defends the land (and Burgess) from an outlaw attack. Standard entertainment from a standard programmer.

d, Chester M. Franklin; w, F. Hugh Herbert (based on a story by Peter B. Kyne); ph, Harry Neumann, Tom Galligan.

Drama   **(PR:A   MPAA:NR)**

STOKER, THE**   (1935, Brit.) 70m Leslie Fuller/GAU bw (AKA: SHOVEL UP A BIT MORE COAL)

Leslie Fuller (*Bill*), George Harris (*Oswald*), Phyllis Clare (*Nita*), Leslie Bradley (*Frank Munro*), Olive Melville (*Alice*), Pat Aherne (*Russell Gilham*), Gibson Gowland (*Steve*), Robert English (*Sir Richard Munro*), Syd Courtenay, W.G. O'Neill.

A lightweight comedy which stars Fuller as a stoker for a railroad and his pal Harris as the train's steward. They befriend a young apprentice, Bradley, who also happens to be the railway chairman's son. When Bradley falls for a gold-digging adventuress, Fuller and Harris shake some sense into him and reveal the woman's true nature. Reissued in 1940 as SHOVEL UP A BIT MORE COAL.

p, Joe Rock; d, Leslie Pearce; w, Syd Courtenay, George Harris (based on a story by Wallace Geoffrey); ph, Charles Van Enger.

Comedy   **(PR:A   MPAA:NR)**

STOLEN AIRLINER, THE**   (1962, Brit.) 59m Associated British
                              Pathe-Children's Film Foundation/CD bw

Fella Edmunds (*Fred*), Diana Day (*Anne*), Peter Dyneley (*Uncle George*), Michael MacGuire (*John*), Nicola Braithwaite (*Kitty*), Ballard Berkeley (*Mr. Head*), Iris Russell (*Mrs. Head*), David King-Wood (*Controller*).

An international gang of crooks kidnaps a delegation interested in purchasing a plane from the British. The gang impersonates the buyers and commandeers the plane, which was being guarded by a group of youngsters. The crooks are overpowered in mid-air and the RAF eventually comes to the rescue. Released in Britain in 1955.

p, Howard Thomas; d&w, Don Sharp (based on the novel *Thursday Adventure* by John Pudney) ph, Jo Jago; m, Philip Green; ed, Eily Boland; art d, Bertram Tyrer.

Children's   **(PR:AA   MPAA:NR)**

STOLEN ASSIGNMENT*   (1955, Brit.) 62m ACT/BL bw

John Bentley (*Mike Billings*), Hy Hazell (*Jenny Drew*), Eddie Byrne (*Inspector Corcoran*), Patrick Holt (*Henry Crossley*), Joyce Carey (*Ida Garnett*), Kay Callard (*Stella Watson*), Jessica Cairns (*Marilyn Dawn*), Charles Farrell (*Percy Simpson*), Violet Gould, Michael Ellison, Desmond Rayner, Graham Stuart, Frank Forsyth, Raymond Rollett.

An inept crime story with a dash of comedy about two rival reporters--Bentley and Hazell--who battle each other to get the scoop on a recent murder. After aggravating the chief police inspector to no end, Hazell manages to find the necessary clues. Together they prove that the accused woman is innocent and that blame should be laid on her husband.

p, Francis Searle; d, Terence Fisher; w, Kenneth R. Hayles (based on a story by Sidney Nelson, Maurice Harrison); ph, James Harvey.

Crime/Comedy   **(PR:A   MPAA:NR)**

STOLEN DIRIGIBLE, THE*   (1966, Czech.) 88m Studio Barrandov
        bw (UKRADENA VZDUCHOLOD; AKA: TWO YEARS HOLIDAY)

Cestmir Randa (*Prof. Findejs*), Michal Pospisil, Hanus Bor, Jan Malat, Jitka Zelenohorska, Josef Hauvic, Josef Vetrovec.

An engrossing children's tale that has a group of five youngsters hijacking a dirigible from the 1889 World's Fair in Paris. They fly it to a deserted island and wind up in the middle of a Jules Verne-esque odyssey. A well-crafted adventure from Czechoslovakia's Verne-influenced Zeman.

d, Karel Zeman; w, Zeman, Radovan Kraty; ph, Josef Novotny, Bohuslav Pikhart.

Children's   **(PR:AAA   MPAA:NR)**

STOLEN FACE*½   (1952, Brit.) 72m Hammer/Lippert bw

Paul Henreid (*Dr. Philip Ritter*), Lizabeth Scott (*Alice Brent/Lilly*), Andre Morell (*David*), Mary MacKenzie (*Lilly*), John Wood (*Dr. Jack Wilson*), Susan Stephen (*Betty*), Arnold Ridley (*Dr. Russell*), Everley Gregg (*Lady Harringay*), Cyril Smith (*Alf*), Janey Burnell (*Maggie*), Grace Gavin (*Nurse*), Terence O'Reagan (*Pete Snipe*), Diana Beaumont (*May*), Alexis France (*Mrs. Emmett*), John Bull (*Charles Emmett*), Dorothy Bramhall (*Miss Simpson*), Ambrosine Philpotts (*Miss Patten*), Richard Wattis (*Wentworth*), Russell Napier (*Cutler*), Hal Osmond, William Murray, Howard Douglas, Brookes Turner, Bartlett Mullins, Philip Viccars, James Valentine, John Warren, Frank Hawkins, Ben Williams.

An interesting drama from Fisher in the days before Hammer was known for its horror entries. Henreid stars as a plastic surgeon who falls in love with concert pianist Scott, but loses her after a week of romance to her manager, Morell. To compensate for her absence Henreid transforms a prison inmate (MacKenzie) into his lost love (Scott, again), but cannot keep the girl under his thumb. She runs off with her own friends and leads a life of shoplifting. Eventually, pianist Scott returns to him with the promise of a future together.

p, Anthony Hinds; d, Terence Fisher; w, Martin Berkeley, Richard Landau; ph, Walter Harvey; m, Malcolm Arnold; ed, Maurice Rootes.

Drama   **(PR:A   MPAA:NR)**

STOLEN HARMONY½   (1935) 74m PAR bw

George Raft (*Ray Angelo/Ray Ferraro*), Ben Bernie (*Jack Conrad*), Grace Bradley (*Jean Loring*), Goodee Montgomery (*Lil Davis*), Lloyd Nolan (*Chesty Burrage*), Ralf Harolde (*Dude Williams*), William Cagney (*Schoolboy Howe*), William Pawley (*Turk Connors*), Charles E. Arnt (*Clem Walters*), Cully Richards (*Pete The Cabby*), Jack Norton (*Dick Phillips*), Christian Rub (*Mathew Huxley*), Leslie Fenton (*Joe Harris*), Fred "Snowflake" Toones (*Henry, Bus Bartender*), Ruth Clifford (*Nurse*), Carol Holloway (*Mother Of Six Kids*), Eddie Dunn (*Hotel Clerk*), Jack Judge (*Photographer*), Robert Emmett O'Connor (*Warden Clark*), Eddie McGill, Jack Perry, Jack Herrick (*Prison Trio*), John Kelly (*Bates, Prison Bandleader*), Jack Burnette (*Pianist*), Constantine Romanoff (*Piccolo Player*), Eddie Sturgis (*Musician*), James Mack (*Pop, Doorman*), Ed Dearing (*Motorcycle Cop*), Jack Hill, Ted Oliver (*Cops*), Stanley Andrews (*Patrol Chief*), Arthur Millet (*Deputy Sheriff*), Ernest Shield (*Elevator Operator*), Lois January, Ada Ince, Margaret Nearing, Adele Jerome (*Girls In Sextet*), Ben Taggart (*Sergeant, Cop at Motel*), Harry Bernard (*Peanut Vendor*), Oscar Smith (*Chimes Player in Prison*), Kit Guard (*Convict in Orchestra*), Earl Askam (*State Trooper*), Duke York (*Duke, Bus Driver*), John King (*Fagin*), Frank Prince (*Hero*), Purv Pullen (*Little Nell*), Billy Wilson (*Sheriff*), Mickey Garlock (*The Working Girl*), Dick Stabile (*Minister*), Colonel Manny Prager (*Nell's Father*), Al Goering (*Lady*), Paul Gerrits (*Ted Webb*), Sarah Jane Fulks [Jane Wyman] (*Girl*).

A lively gangster musical which sees Raft as an ex-con who joins up with Bernie's swing band by blowing a mean saxophone. During a cross-country tour Raft is approached by an old buddy who tries to lure the musician back into the crime arena. Raft refuses, but the heist is pulled off without him and he receives the blame. He clears his name when the band is kidnaped by Nolan, who longs for a private concert. Raft informs on Nolan, saves the band from an unscheduled performance, and regains his seat in the band. Includes the songs: "Would There Be Love," "Let's Spill the Beans," "I Never Had a Man to Cry Over," "Fagin Youse is a Viper" (Mack Gordon, Harry Revel).

p, Albert Lewis; d, Alfred Werker; w, Leon Gordon, Harry Ruskin, Claude Binyon, Lewis Foster (based on the story by Gordon); ph, Harry Fischbeck; m/l, Harry Revel, Mack Gordon; ed, Otho Lovering; art d, Hans Dreier, Bernard Herzbrun; ch, LeRoy J. Prinz.

Crime/Musical   **(PR:A   MPAA:NR)**

STOLEN HEAVEN*½   (1931) 73m PAR bw

Nancy Carroll (*Mary*), Phillips Holmes (*Joe*), Louis Calhern (*Steve Perry*), Edward Keane (*Morgan*), Joan Carr, G. Albert Smith, Dagmar Oakland, Joseph Crehan, Buford Armitage, Joan Kenyon, Guy Kibbee, Elmer Cornell.

An unconvincing tale about Carroll and Holmes, a pair of lovers who take off together after pulling a $200,000 heist. They intend to spend the cash frivolously and then commit suicide together. They eventually decide to live, but Holmes gets hauled off to the slammer while Carroll promises to wait for his return.

d, George Abbott; w, Abbott, George Hill (based on a story by Dana Burnet); ph, George Folsey; ed, Emma Hill; m, Leo Reisman Orchestra.

Romance/Crime   (PR:A MPAA:NR)

STOLEN HEAVEN½**   (1938) 88m PAR bw

Gene Raymond (*Carl*), Olympe Bradna (*Steffi*), Glenda Farrell (*Rita*), Lewis Stone (*Langauer*), Porter Hall (*Von*), Douglas Dumbrille (*Klingman*), Joseph Sawyer (*Bako*), Esther Dale (*Lieschen*), Charles Judels (*Hubert*), Ferdinand Gottschalk (*Lubert*), Charles Halton (*Polesie*), Bert Roach (*Wenzel*), Rolfe Sedan (*Gottlieb*), Horace Murphy (*Burgomaster*).

Jewel thieves Raymond and Bradna hole up in the house of a once-great concert pianist, Stone. They become friendly with the old man and eventually convince him to stage a comeback. Their future, however, is less stable when the police catch on to their hideout and haul them into jail. Includes a tune by Frank Loesser and Manning Sherwin, "Boys in the Band," plus a number of classical selections from the likes of Wagner, Liszt, Chopin, Grieg, Moskowski, and Strauss.

d, Andrew L. Stone; w, Eve Greene, Frederick Jackson (based on a story by Stone); ph, William C. Mellor; ed, Doane Harrison; art d, Hans Dreier, Franz Bachelin; m/l, Frank Loesser, Manning Sherwin.

Crime/Musical   (PR:A MPAA:NR)

STOLEN HOLIDAY½**   (1937) 84m FN-WB bw

Kay Francis (*Nicole Picot*), Claude Rains (*Stefan Orloff*), Ian Hunter (*Anthony Wayne*), Alison Skipworth (*Suzanne*), Alexander D'Arcy (*Anatole*), Betty Lawford (*Helen Tuttle*), Walter Kingsford (*Francis Chalon*), Charles Halton (*LeGrande*), Frank Reicher (*Ranier*), Frank Conroy (*Dupont*), Kathleen Howard (*Madame Delphine*), Wedgewood Nowell (*Borel*), Robert Strange (*Prefect of Police*), Egon Brecher (*Deputy Bergery*).

Based on the real-life Alexandre Stavisky affair, STOLEN HOLIDAY stars Francis as a rising model who weds Rains. Although exposed to his swindling, corrupt life style, she is protected by the French authorities. After Rains meets his end, Hunter becomes the object of Francis' affection, carrying on an idyllic romance. The Stavisky name again made it to the screen in 1974's STAVISKY by Alain Resnais.

p, Hal B. Wallis; d, Michael Curtiz; w, Casey Robinson (based on the story by Virginia Kellogg, Warren Duff); ph, Sid Hickox; ed, Terry Morse; md, Leo F. Forbstein; art d, Anton Grot; cos, Orry-Kelly; spec eff, Fred Jackman.

Drama   (PR:A MPAA:NR)

STOLEN HOURS*   (1963) 100m UA c

Susan Hayward (*Laura Pember*), Michael Craig (*Dr. John Carmody*), Diane Baker (*Ellen Pember*), Edward Judd (*Mike Bannerman*), Paul Rogers (*Dr. Eric McKenzie*), Robert Bacon (*Peter*), Paul Stassino (*Dalporto*), Jerry Desmonde (*Colonel*), Ellen McIntosh (*Miss Kendall*), Gwen Nelson (*Hospital Sister*), Peter Madden (*Reynolds*), Joan Newell (*Mrs. Hewitt*), Chet Baker (*Himself*).

A sudsy remake of Bette Davis' DARK VICTORY, this was shot in England and had a largely British supporting cast. Hayward is the rich, twice married (and divorced) socialite who is driving to London airport to meet her sister, Baker, when she has a dizzy spell and almost crashes. (In the original, the "sister" was a secretary played by Geraldine Fitzgerald.) She gathers her senses about her and continues to the airport. She has just left a soiree at her country place and Baker is concerned about Hayward's call to come to England. They drive back to her estate where the party continues and she introduces Baker to her latest amour, Judd, a handsome race car driver. While Baker and Judd have a conversation, Hayward goes to her sumptuous bedroom with a blinding headache and takes some pills to ease the pain. Down in the main room, Judd tells Baker that he suspects Hayward may be quite sick and he has hired a doctor, Craig, to examine her. Hayward comes down to talk to the other guests and seems fine. She meets Craig and she deftly does some tricks with him, almost in the form of a parlor game. But these tricks have an underlying reason. Craig has performed them to learn what he can about Hayward's condition. Hayward is angered when she finds out what he's been up to and lets him know that, but there is already a sexual stirring between the two and she heeds his advice for her to see a brain physician in London. Later, the specialist, Rogers, tells Craig that his worst fears have been realized. Hayward must have an operation immediately. Hayward is almost flighty about going in for surgery, but Craig sees right through her "la-dee-da" attitude and knows that it's only a cover up and that she is truly frightened by what's going on inside her head. The operation takes place and Rogers thinks that he's gotten all of the tumor out, or so he tells Judd and Baker. But he's not being honest. Craig now tells them the truth, that Hayward has, at most, a year left to live. Judd and Baker make a pact to keep the news from Hayward because they feel she just might give up if she knew and why not let her have some fun while she can. At first, Craig is all for telling Hayward, but when he sees her he can't bring himself to do it as he's fallen in love with her. They begin to date and are both crazy about each other. There is talk about getting married, then Hayward discovers the reality of her situation. She is irate at Craig for not being truthful and she accuses him of being her doctor, not her lover.

Hayward walks out on Craig and flies to Italy to be with Judd, who is busily following the racing circuit. Craig can't bear being without Hayward and he flies to Italy to bring her back. They are married in a Cornish village near the sea and Craig has decided to give up his London practice and spend the rest of Hayward's days in this charming town. Craig opens up a medical office and the two are happy. She knows now how good life can be and how much the love of a fine man can enrich a woman, especially after her two failed unions. Time is a precious commodity to both and they use it well to get to know each other; sharing every waking moment. There's no time for them to have children, but since she loves them, Hayward finds a friend in little Bacon, a young lad with a mother who doesn't appreciate him. Days go by all too quickly and the clock ticks down. Hayward begins to go blind and her last moments are spent with Bacon after she's told Craig to go off and deliver the baby of a villager. She knows her moment is near but she doesn't want him to be there so Craig goes off to do his medical work and Hayward dies next to the young Bacon as the movie ends. A good enough remake, it was well-mounted, but it might be that the production was too expensive. Hayward changed clothes about 30 times and wore a fortune in baubles. The movie took more than three months to shoot and would have been welcomed had it not been for the shadow of Davis' performance in DARK VICTORY hanging over the actress' shoulder. Jazz trumpeter Chet Baker is seen as himself and a scene showing Hayward being taught "The Twist" by 1960s idol Chubby Checker, was edited out of the film. Too bad. It could have used some fun to relieve the oppressive sadness. The lyrics for the movie's song were by Alan Bergman and Marilyn Keith, before she decided to use her husband's name. Bring two boxes of tissues.

p, Denis Holt; d, Daniel Petrie; w, Jessamyn West, Joseph Hayes (based on the play "Dark Victory" by George Emerson Brewer, Jr., Bertram Block); ph, Harry Waxman (DeLuxe Color); m, Mort Lindsey; ed, Graham Shipham; prod d, Wilfred Shingleton; art d, Tony Woollard; set d, John Hoesli; cos, Fabiani; m/l, Lindsey, Marilyn Keith, Alan Bergman; makeup, George Partleton, Tony Sforzini.

Drama   (PR:A-C MPAA:NR)

STOLEN IDENTITY**   (1953) 81m Helen Ainsworth bw

Francis Lederer (*Claude Manelli*), Donald Buka (*Toni Sponer*), Joan Camden (*Karen Manelli*), Adrienne Gessner (*Mrs. Fraser*), Inge Konrads (*Marie*), Gisele Wilke (*Old Doll*), Herman Erhard (*Inspector*), Egon Von Jordan (*Kruger*), Manfred Inger (*Heinth*).

Buka stars as a Viennese cab driver who is trying to get to America, but lacks the proper papers and identification. He gets his chance when Lederer kills an American businessman waiting to get into Buka's cab. Buka assumes the dead man identity and soon finds himself involved with Camden, a friend of the dead man's and the wife of Lederer. Camden first believes that Buka is the murderer, but when she realizes the truth she makes plans for both of them to escape to the States. Lederer won't let them get away without a chase, but he is soon apprehended. Buka is also caught, but he receives only a minor sentence. The faithful Camden decides after all that she'll wait for Buka to be released.

p, Turhan Bey; d, Gunther Fritsch; w, Robert Hill (based on the novel *Stolen Identity* by Alexander Lernet-Holenia); ph, Helmut Ashley; m, Richard Hageman; art d, Fritz Jupther Jonsdorff.

Drama   (PR:A MPAA:NR)

STOLEN KISSES**   (1929) 70m WB bw

May McAvoy (*May Lambert*), Hallam Cooley (*Hal Lambert*), Reed Howes (*Jack Harding, Divorce Lawyer*), Claude Gillingwater (*H. A. Lambert, Sr., Newspaper Publisher*), Edna Murphy (*Fanchon La Vere*), Arthur Hoyt (*Hoyt*), Agnes Franey (*Nanette*), Phyllis Crane (*Margot*).

Crotchety publisher Gillingwater nearly causes a divorce when he insists that his son, Cooley, produce a few grandchildren and stop taking a back seat to wife McAvoy's affections for her poodle. The romance goes on the rocks during an escapade in Paris, and it takes an appearance before the divorce judge for the pair to realize their mutual love. Gillingwater has a smile on his face when he learns that twins are on the way. An enjoyable but unmemorable comedy that is carried by Gillingwater.

d, Ray Enright; w, Edward T. Lowe, Jr., James A. Starr (based on a story by Franz Suppe); ph, Ben Reynolds; ed, George Marks.

Comedy   (PR:A MPAA:NR)

STOLEN KISSES***   (1969, Fr.) 90m Films Du Carrosse-Les Productions Artistes Associes/Lopert c (BAISERS VOLES)

Jean-Pierre Leaud (*Antoine Doinel*), Delphine Seyrig (*Fabienne Tabard*), Michel Lonsdale (*Mons. Tabard*), Claude Jade (*Christine Darbon*), Harry-Max (*Mons. Henri Tabard*), Daniel Ceccaldi (*Mons. Darbon*), Claire Duhamel (*Mme. Darbon*), Catherine Lutz (*Mme. Catherine*), Andrew Falcon (*Mons. Blady*), Paul Pavel (*Julien*), Serge Rousseau (*Stranger*), Marie-France Pisier (*Colette Tazzi*), Jean-Francois Adam (*Albert Tazzi, Her Husband*), Jacques Robiolles (*Writer*), Martine Ferriere (*Manager of Show Shop*), Simono (*Conjurer's Friend*), Roger Trapp (*Hotel Manager*), Jacques Delord (*Conjurer*), Jacques Rispal (*Deceived Husband*), Martine Brochard (*Unfaithful*

Wife), Robert Cambourakis *(Lover)*, Karine Jeantet, Francois Darbon.

The third look at the life of Antoine Doinel (Leaud), which began in THE 400 BLOWS, continued through an episode in LOVE AT TWENTY, entitled "Antoine And Colette." The story picks up with Leaud being discharged from the Army at age 20. He firsts pays a visit to a prostitute and then calls on Jade, his latest love, only to find her out on a date. Instead of leaving, however, he stays for dinner with her parents (a la LOVE AT TWENTY) and is offered a job. He begins working as a night clerk in a seedy hotel, but gets fired when he inadvertently lets a private eye (Harry-Max) into the room of a guest who turns out to be an unfaithful wife. Harry-Max finds Leaud a job with the Blady Detective Agency, where the rookie Sherlock Holmes bungles every case he investigates. He finally gets a simple case in a shoe store by displaying his "technical proficiency" in wrapping a shoe box. He is supposed to discover why the store's owner, Lonsdale, feels hated by everyone and whether there is some conspiracy against him. While working late one night in the stock room, he meets Seyrig, the owner's wife, and has lunch with her the following day. His awkward love for her causes him to flee, but she later follows him to his apartment, where they make love under the condition that they will never see each other again. He returns to Jade (he now is employed as a television repairman) and proposes to her. They walk through a nearby park, where they are approached by a stranger who, paralleling Leaud's devotion, proposes to marry Jade and be faithful to her forever. The lovers shrug off the stranger and walk away together. Dismissed by many critics as being too charming and too simplistic, Truffaut's STOLEN KISSES was oddly enough made during an extremely intense political crisis in Paris. The film is dedicated to Henri Langlois and the Cinematheque Francaise, which clearly illustrates Truffaut's indebtedness to Langlois's work and the films that the director grew up on. Four days after shooting began on STOLEN KISSES, Truffaut became involved with a Defense Committee that fought for the reinstatement of the Cinematheque's director, who was ordered removed by Minister of Culture Andre Malraux. Truffaut's shooting schedule often conflicted with his commitment to Langlois's supporters (everyone in cinema from Chaplin to Welles threatened to pull their films from the Cinematheque, as did S. Frederick Gronich of the MPAA, who planned to pull all major American films). Truffaut stated, "If STOLEN KISSES is good, it will be thanks to Langlois." As violence erupted in the streets of Paris (with such happenings as student revolts and university takeovers), Truffaut continued work on his most personal and charming film to that date. Instead of making a great impact on the film world, Truffaut chose only to affirm his beliefs in cinema and the thought that, as Seyrig states in the film, "people are wonderful." Followed by BED AND BOARD.

p, Marcel Berbert; d, Francois Truffaut; w, Truffaut, Bernard Revon, Claude de Givray; ph, Denys Clerval (Eastmancolor); m, Antoine Duhamel; ed, Agnes Guillemot; art d, Claude Pignot; m/l, "Que Reste T'Il de Nos Amours?", Charles Trenet (Sung by Trenet).

Romance/Comedy   **Cas.**   **(PR:O MPAA:R)**

STOLEN LIFE**   (1939, Brit.) 90m Orion/PAR bw

Wilfrid Lawson *(Thomas E. Lawrence)*, Elisabeth Bergner *(Sylvina/Martina Lawrence)*, Mabel Terry-Lewis *(Aunt Helen)*, Michael Redgrave *(Alan McKenzie)*, Richard Ainley *(Morgan)*, Kenneth Buckley *(Garrett)*, Pierre Jouvenet *(Doctor)*, Stella Arbenina *(Nurse)*, Ernest Ferney *(Police Superintendent)*, Dorice Fordred *(Eileen)*, Oliver Johnson *(Prof. Bardesley)*, Annie Esmond *(Cook)*, Clement McCallin *(Karl Anderson)*, Cyril Horrocks, O.B. Clarence, John Lloyd, Roy Russell, Homer Regus, Davina Carid, Dorothy Dewhurst, Fewlass Llewellyn, Paulette Preney, Kaye Seeley, Cot d'Ordan, D.J. Williams, Gayenne Michaeldze, Cyril Chamberlain, Danielle Mendaille, Boomsie the Dog.

An entertaining but highly implausible film tells the familiar story of a man mistaking one twin for the other and marrying the wrong one. Bergner plays both the fun-loving, carefree sister and the more serious one who passes her time climbing mountains. The latter falls in love with a fellow climber, who mistakenly proposes to her sister. The marriage somehow takes place, but the bridedrowns in a boating accident. The remaining sister takes the dead wife's place and secures her husband.

p, Anthony Havelock-Allan; d, Paul Czinner; w, Margaret Kennedy, George Barraud (based on the novel by Karel J. Benes); ph, Phillip Tannura.

Romance   **(PR:A MPAA:NR)**

STOLEN LIFE, A***   (1946) 107m WB bw

Bette Davis *(Kate Bosworth/Pat Bosworth)*, Glenn Ford *(Bill Emerson)*, Dane Clark *(Karnock)*, Walter Brennan *(Eben Folgor)*, Charles Ruggles *(Freddie Lindley)*, Bruce Bennett *(Jack Talbot)*, Peggy Knudsen *(Diedra)*, Esther Dale *(Mrs. Johnson)*, Clara Blandick *(Martha)*, Joan Winfield *(Lucy)*, Robert Dudley *(Old Fisherman)*, Jack Mower, Harlan Briggs, Tom Fadden *(Fishermen)*, Dale Van Sickel *(Man in Launch)*, Creighton Hale *(Attendant)*, James Flavin *(Investigator)*, Monte Blue *(Mr. Lippencott)*, Sherman Sanders *(Patricia's Dancing Partner)*, Leo White, Paul Panzer *(Waiters)*, Mary Forbes *(Woman Art Patron)*, Rosalie Rey *(Bridesmaid)*, Ruth Cherrington *(Large Woman)*, Philo McCullough *(Male Art Patron)*.

It was only six years before that Elizabeth Bergner made this same story

for Paramount, so it was a surprise that Davis chose it to be the first, and only, film she ever produced. She plays twins for the first time (she did it again in DEAD RINGER) and, as you can imagine, one is very good and one is not. (Well, of course. That's the way it has to be, otherwise there would be no story, si?) To avoid confusion, we'll name the good twin Bette and the evil one Davis, until one is out of the way. Bette is a sweet, shy artist. She and her sister, Davis, are wealthy orphans who have a guardian, Ruggles. She soon meets Ford, a lighthouse inspector (and when was the last time you met someone with that job?). They find each other when she misses the ferry to the island and Ford offers her a lift. On the two-hour ride, she sketches his face and it isn't long before the two start seeing each other. Ford is actually an engineer who wants to get away from the hustle of the city and thinks that a summer on Martha's Vineyard will be just the tonic. Brennan is the lighthouse keeper and Bette gets closer to Ford by arranging to do Brennan's portrait. Everything is lovely; then Davis arrives. She is, of course, the opposite of her sister. Noisy, flamboyant, and man-hungry, Davis makes a move on Ford and it isn't long before he has fallen for her. Bette is hurt, but she moves aside and lets the two get married, thus making herself a sister-in-law, not the wife she yearns to be. Bette now begins to study art with a passion and takes lessons from Clark, a good artist but a boorish lout. She sees Ford one day and he tells her that he and Davis are going to South America where he's just gotten a job as an engineer. She'll be sad to see them both go but that's the way it is. Ford has been very pleasant to Bette and she wonders if that's not an indication of his desire for her, then she realizes it's just his way and nothing more. Bette tells Clark that she is going to cease her painting studies as she is not very good and will never be. She goes back to the island and is surprised to see Davis, who didn't want to go to South America on the trip right now but will probably join Ford later. The two sisters go out sailing and Davis is washed overboard when a freakish squall hits the small boat. Bette tries to save Davis and the boat turns upside down. In attempting to save Davis, Bette winds up with the wedding ring from her doomed sister and when she is found by Brennan, he just assumes that Bette is Davis. She realizes that this may be her opportunity to get the man she wants, especially after Brennan informs her that Ford is coming home from South America and is due to arrive at any moment. When he gets back, Ford thinks that Bette is Davis and she is shocked to learn that their marriage was on thin ice as she had been cavorting with other men and Ford was about to ask for a divorce. Bette hears about all of this from the maid, Winfield. She pleads with Ford for another opportunity to make the marriage work and Ford grants it. Then more evidence of her sister's machinations are uncovered and Bette can take it no longer so she leaves. Ford follows her and now admits that he suspected it was Bette the moment he came home. He understands that he was infatuated with Davis but it was Bette he truly loved and he allowed himself to be sucked into a situation that is now over. They can begin their love again. A popular movie and one of the best examples of the "twin technique" that saw the same person play two roles. Of course, it was Davis' superb abilities that allowed her to put such a good division between the two characterizations. Ford had been borrowed from Columbia after a sensational performance opposite Rita Hayworth in GILDA.

p, Bette Davis; d, Curtis Bernhardt; w, Catherine Turney, Margaret Buell Wilder (based on the novel by Karel J. Benes); ph, Sol Polito, Ernest Haller; m, Max Steiner; ed, Rudi Fehr; md, LeoF. Forbstein; art d, Robert Haas; set d, Fred M. MacLean; cos, Orry-Kelly; spec eff, William McGann, E. Roy Davidson, Willard Van Enger, Russell Collings.

Drama   **(PR:A-C MPAA:NR)**

STOLEN PLANS, THE**   (1962, Brit.) 57m GAU/CD bw

Mavis Sage *(Nicolette Renaud)*, Lance Secretan *(Michael Foster)*, Peter Neil *(Tony Burton)*, Pamela Edmunds *(Mrs. Foster)*, Peter Burton *(Dr. Foster)*, Patrick Boxill *(Mr. Palmer)*, Len Sharp *(Tod)*, Geoffrey Goodheart *(The Boss)*, Larry Burns *(Alf)*, Ludmilla Tchakalova *(Meg)*.

A children's adventure tale which has Secretan and his French pen pal, Sage, trailing a crook who has stolen some valuable airplane designs. They bravely smash the thief's plans and arrange for the arrest of his gang. Released in Britain in 1952.

p, Frank Wells; d&w, James Hill (based on a story by Michael Poole); ph, Frank North, Gerry Massy-Collier; m, Jack Beaver; ed, Arthur Stevens; art d, Don Chaffey.

Children's   **(PR:AA MPAA:NR)**

STOLEN SWEETS*½   (1934) 75m CHES bw

Sally Blane *(Patricia Belmont)*, Charles Starrett *(Bill Smith)*, Jameson Thomas *(Barrington Thorne)*, Claude King *(Mr. Belmont)*, Johnny Harron *(Sam)*, Polly Ann Young *(Betty)*, Tom Ricketts *(Stoner)*, Aggie Herring *(Cook)*, Jane Keckley *(Priscilla Prattleigh)*, Phillips Smalley *(Mr. Thorne)*, Goodee Montgomery *(Rose)*, Maynard Holmes *(Phil)*.

A weak programmer whose only purpose was to fill the bottom half of a double bill. It's the familiar story of a society girl who falls in love with an insurance man and leaves her wealthy fiance behind.

d, Richard Thorpe; w, Karl Brown (based on a story by Brown); ph, M.A.

Anderson; ed, Roland Reed.

Romance   **(PR:A MPAA:NR)**

STOLEN TIME   (SEE: BLONDE BLACKMAILER, 1955, Brit.)

STOLEN WEALTH   (SEE: BLAZING SIX SHOOTERS, 1940)

STONE**½   (1974, Aus.) 140m Hedon/BEF Australia c

Ken Shorter (Stone), Sandy Harbutt (Undertaker), Keryck Barnes (Dr.
Townes), Hugh Keays-Byrne (Toad), Roger Ward (Hooks), Vincent Gil (Dr.
Death), Dewey Hungerford (Septic), James H. Bowles (Stinkfinger), Bindi
Williams (Captain Midnight), John Ifkovitch (Zonk), Lex Mitchell (Ballini),
Rhod Walker (Chairman), Owen Weingott (Adler), Slim deGrey (Hanni-
gan), Ray Bennett (Larsen), Bill Hunter (Barman), Helen Morse (Amanda),
Rebecca Gilling (Vanessa), Sue Lloyd (Tart), Ros Talamini (Sunshine),
Victoria Anoux (Flossie), Jane Gilling (Euridyce), Eva Ifkovitch (Tiger),
Billy Green, Julie Edwards, Michael Robinson, Peter King, Karyn Love,
Barry Butler, Jude Matthews, Neville Overall, Deborah Foreman, Jim
Walsh, Margaret Ure, Bruce McPherson, David Bracks, Ros Spiers, Harry
Lawrence, Leonora Cornall, Ron Ross, Patrick Ward, Michael Kent, Charles
Stringer, Garry McDonald, Terry Bader, Lachlan Jamieson, Drew Forsyth-
er, Fred Shaw, Tony Allyn, Reg Evabs.

A box office smash Down Under, this poorly scripted biker movie has
enough action to keep one's interest even if there are plot holes big enough
to drive a semi through. After a political assassination and a rash of biker
deaths, Shorter, a narcotics cop, is assigned to the investigation. He
befriends the gang members and soon discovers that another gang is
responsible. He grows to respect the bikers, but in the end is beaten to a
bloody pulp by them. The film's main fault is that it doesn't explain much.
It postulates the existence of a sort of biker moral code which the audience
is asked to accept as an article of faith. Fast-paced direction and expertly
photographed motorcycle scenes are a plus. Acting is good, and many of the
characters are played by real-life Australian bikers.

p&d, Sandy Harbutt; w, Harbutt, Michael Robinson; ph, Graham Lind; m,
Billy Green; ed, Ian Barry; art d, Tim Storrier; stunts, Peter Armstrong.

Action   **(PR:O MPAA:NR)**

STONE COLD DEAD*½   (1980, Can.) 97m Ko-Zak/Dimension c

Richard Crenna (Sgt. Boyd), Paul Williams (Julius Kurtz), Linda Sorenson
(Monica Page), Belinda J. Montgomery (Sandy MacAuley), Charles Shamata
(Sgt. Tony Colabre), Alberta Watson (Olivia Page), Monique Mercure (Dr.
Bouvier), Andree Cousineau (Bernice Carnival), Frank Moore (Teddy
Mann), George Chuvalo (Rosie), George Touliatos (Inspector Webb), Dennis
Strong (Danny De Lion), Jennifer Dale (Claudia Grissom), Nicky Fylan,
Carol Forte, Wendy Thatcher, Marie Clark, Sylvia Llewelyn, Miles Potter,
Yanci Bukovec, Mary Long, Donna Lee, Alexis Radlin, Booth Savage, Diane
Bigelow, Herb Pacheko, Elias Zarou, Robert McKuen, Gail Damms,
Jefferson Mappan.

Typical crime thriller with Crenna playing the tough cop and Williams (yes,
The Paul Williams) putting a fright into the audience as a maniacal mob boss
with his fingers in a prostitution racket. When a sniper starts picking off the
local hookers, Crenna comes out fighting and doesn't let up until he
uncovers the culprit. Stone cold boring.

p, George Mendeluk, John Ryan; d&w, Mendeluk (based on the novel The
Sin Sniper by Hugh Garner); ph, Dennis Miller; ed, Martin Pepler; art d, Ted
Watkins; set d, Jac Bradette.

Crime   **Cas.**   **(PR:0 MPAA:R)**

STONE KILLER, THE**½   (1973) 95m DD/COL c

Charles Bronson (Detective Lou Torrey), Martin Balsam (Vescari), David
Sheiner (Detective Guido Lorenz), Norman Fell (Detective Les Daniels),
Ralph Waite (Detective Mathews), Eddie Firestone (George Armitage the
Junkie), Walter Burke (J.D.), David Moody (Gus Lipper), Charles Tyner
(Psychiatrist), Paul Koslo (Al Langley, the Jazz Musician), Stuart Margolin
(Lawrence), John Ritter (Hart), Byron Morrow (L.A. Police Chief), Jack
Colvin (Lionel Jumper), Frank Campanella (Calabriese), Alfred Ryder (Tony
Champion), Gene Woodbury (Paul Long), Harry Basch (Mossman), Jan
Arvan (Vechetti), Lisabeth Hush (Helen), Mary Cross (Waitress), Kelly Miles
(Gerry Wexton, the Stewardess Dropout), Robert Emhardt (Fussy Man),
Cristina Raines (Mathews' Daughter), Tom Falk (Sergeant), Frenchia
Guizon (Drug Pusher).

A standard crime drama which is only distinguishable from the rest by its
star, Bronson, and its interesting though confused plot. Bronson is a former
New York cop working in L.A. to prevent a Mafia-organized murder plot
masterminded by Balsam. It seems Balsam is trying to settle a 40-year-old
score against the non-Sicilian faction of the mob. To do so he is recruiting
Vietnam vets to handle a mass hit since they have the necessary training,
but no ties at all to the crime world. Bronson shows everyone that he can
be a rock-solid killing machine when he has to be, just like in the rest of his
films. Tolerable as far as this genre goes.

p&d, Michael Winner; w, Gerald Wilson (based on the novel A Complete
State of Death by John Gardner); ph, Richard Moore (Technicolor); m, Roy
Budd; ed, Frederick Wilson; art d, Ward Preston; set d, Norman Rockett.

Crime/Action   **Cas.**   **(PR:O MPAA:R)**

STONE OF SILVER CREEK**½   (1935) 61m UNIV bw

Buck Jones (T. William Stone), Niles Welch (Timothy Tucker), Murdock
MacQuarrie (George J. Mason), Noel Francis (Lola), Marion Shilling
(Martha Mason), Peggy Campbell (Nancy Raymond), Rodney Hildebrand
(Graves), Harry Semels (Simmons), Grady Sutton (Jimmy), Kernan Cripps
(Ben), Frank Rice (Tom Lucas), Bob McKenzie, Lew Meehan, Silver the
Horse.

Jones is the proprietor of a respectable dance/gambling hall who strength-
ens his ties with the local pastor by pitching in every Sunday in church and
by helping the padre with his love life. When the preacher uncovers a plot
to rob Jones, he comes to the aid of the dance hall in return. Cleverly written
and quickly paced.

p, Irving Starr; d, Nick Grinde; w, Earle Snell (based on a story by R.R.
Harris); ph, Ted McCord; ed, B.T. Loftus.

Western   **Cas.**   **(PR:A MPAA:NR)**

STONY ISLAND***   (1978) 97m World-Northal c (AKA: MY MAIN
                                    MAN FROM STONY ISLAND)

Richard Davis (Richie Bloom), Edward Stoney Robinson (Kevin Tucker),
George Englund (Harold Tate), Gene Barge (Percy Price), Ronnie Barron
(Ronnie Roosevelt), Tennyson Stephens (Tennyson), Larry Ball (Larry),
Windy Barnes (Windy), Rae Dawn Chong (Janetta), Donnell Hagen (Don-
nell), Criss Johnson (Criss), Kenneth Brass (Kenny), Edwin William (Ed),
Steele L. Seals (Steele), Susanna Hoffs (Lucie), Nathan Davis (Lewis Moss),
Tom Mula (Raymond Popitch), Carmi Simon (Barry Cowan), Dennis Franz
(Jerry Domino).

An ambitious low-budget ($400,000) project shot on Chicago's South Side,
with Davis and Robinson starring as a couple of ghetto kids who form a
band. They sign up a few more musicians and receive advice from old blues
man, Barge. The characterizations are weak, but the love of music, and the
music itself, takes over and elevates the film to a higher plane. The actors,
only a few of whom were professionals, successfully portray the difficulties
in getting a band off the ground and surviving in the music business. Rae
Dawn Chong appears some three years before her role in QUEST FOR FIRE
and character actor Dennis Franz, a favorite of Brian DiPalma and member
of TV's "Hill Street Blues" cast, plays a minor role.

p, Andrew Davis, Tamar Hoffs; d, Davis; w, Davis, Hoffs; ph, Tak Fujimoto;
m, David Matthews (performed by The Stony Island Band, supervised by
Gene Barge); ed, Dov Hoenig.

Drama   **(PR:C MPAA:PG)**

STOOGE, THE**   (1952) 100m PAR bw

Dean Martin (Bill Miller), Jerry Lewis (Ted Rogers), Polly Bergen (Mary
Turner), Marion Marshall (Frecklehead Tait), Eddie Mayehoff (Leo Lyman),
Richard Erdman (Ben Bailey), Francis Bavier (Mrs. Rogers).

Martin and Lewis team up again, but in a venture that's less slapstick than
usual. Martin is cast as a vaudevillian accordion player who asks the
sheepish Lewis to join him on stage. The duo rises to fame on the strength
of Lewis' antics, but Martin soon decides to go it alone, failing miserably in
his attempt. It takes his newlywed wife Bergen and money-minded agent
Mayehoff to convince Martin that without Lewis he has no act. Moderately
amusing, and more than a little autobiographical. Martin's songs include: "A
Girl Named Mary and a Boy Named Bill" (Mack David, Jerry Livingston,
sung by Martin and Bergen), "Who's Your Little Whozis?" (Al Goering, Ben
Bernie, Walter Hirsch), "Just One More Chance" (Arthur Johnston, Sam
Coslow), "With My Eyes Wide Open I'm Dreaming" (Mack Gordon, Harry
Revel), "Louise" (Leo Robin, Richard A. Whiting), "I'm Yours" (E.Y.
Harburg, Johnny Green).

p, Hal B. Wallis; d, Norman Taurog; w, Fred Finklehoff, Martin Rackin,
Elwood Ullman (based on a story by Finklehoff, Sid Silvers); ph, Daniel L.
Fapp; ed, Warren Low; md, Joseph J. Lilley; art d, Hal Pereira, Franz
Bachelin; set d, Sam Comer, Bertram Granger; spec eff, Gordon Jennings.

Comedy   **(PR:A MPAA:NR)**

STOOGES GO WEST   (SEE: GOLD RAIDERS, 1952)

STOOLIE, THE**½   (1972) 90m Jama/Continental c

Jackie Mason (Roger Pitman), Marcia Jean Kurtz (Sheila Morrison), Dan
Frazer (Alex Brogan), Richard Carballo (Marco Ruiz), Gigi Gaus (Weehawk-
en Police Chief), William McCutcheon (Gas Station Proprietor), Anne Marie
(Nightclub Singer), Burt Harris (Climpton County Sheriff), Jerome Rudolph
(Cousin Ralphie), Leonard York (Maxie), Babette New (Sylvia), Josip Elic
(1st Hijacker), Reid Cruikshank (2nd Hijacker), Mary McKennedy, Sean

Walch, Thayer David, Ronnie Mellen, Marcie Knight, Jack Kagel, Sonny Sands, Lee Meredith, Robert Knapp, Poppy Fields, Phil Philbin, Frank Goldstein, Mildred Smith, Richard McKenzie, Hope Pomerance.

Mason stars as an employee of the Weehawken, N.J. police department who skips town with $7,500 in police money in an effort to make Frazer, a high-ranking official, look bad. He heads for Miami with the cash and spends it lavishly, eventually meeting the suicidal Kurtz. Mason is soon caught, but cannot produce the money he squandered. By the finale, Frazer has returned to Jersey with a package of heroin, and Mason and Kurtz are beginning a future together. An offbeat crime comedy from Avildsen, who also doubled on camera.

p, Chase Mellen III; d, John G. Avildsen (additional scenes directed by George Silano); w, Eugene Price, Larry Alexander, Marc B. Ray; ph, Avildsen, Charles Clifton (TVC Color); m, William Golstein; ed, Gerald Greenberg, Stanley Bochner.

Crime/Comedy (PR:C MPAA:PG)

STOP, LOOK, AND LOVE** (1939) 57m FOX bw

Jean Rogers (*Louise Haller*), William Frawley (*Joe Haller*), Robert Kellard (*Dick Grant*), Eddie Collins (*Dinty*), Minna Gombell (*Emma Haller*), Cora Sue Collins (*Dora Haller*), Jay Ward (*Willie Haller*), Roger McGee (*Harry Neville*), Lillian Porter (*Rita*).

A pleasant domestic comedy with Rogers as the daughter of Frawley and Gombell who can never seem to hang on to a boy friend. Mom Gombell has a tendency to be overly critical and scare the boys away until one comes along that Rogers really takes a liking to (Kellard). Dad Frawley comes to her aid and restrains Gombell so that she can't cause any problems. In keeping with the genre, marriage seems the next step for Rogers and Kellard.

p, Sol M. Wurtzel; d, Otto Brower; w, Harold Tarshis, Sada Cowan (based on the play "The Family Upstairs" by Harry Delf); ph, Lucien Andriot; ed, Nick DeMaggio; md, Samuel Kaylin; m/l, Sidney Clare, Jule Styne.

Comedy (PR:A MPAA:NR)

STOP ME BEFORE I KILL!**½ (1961, Brit.) 93m
Hammer-Falcon-Hilary/COL bw (GB: THE FULL TREATMENT)

Claude Dauphin (*Dr. David Prade*), Diane Cilento (*Denise Colby*), Ronald Lewis (*Alan Colby*), Francoise Rosay (*Mme. Prade*), Bernard Braden (*Harry Stonehouse*), Katya Douglas (*Connie Stonehouse*), Barbara Chilcott (*Baroness de la Vaillon*), Ann Tirard (*Nicole*), Edwin Styles (*Dr. Roberts*), George Merritt (*Dr. Manfield*).

A tortuous but interesting plot has Lewis as a race car driver injured on his wedding day in an accident that leaves him mentally unstable. His honeymoon with Cilento is postponed while he undergoes treatment with psychiatrist Dauphin. Lewis finds himself trying to strangle his wife every time they make love, but soon realizes that his feelings of anger aren't so misguided when he sees Dauphin and Cilento together. He confronts the psychiatrist, who nearly convinces his patient that he is suffering from hallucinations. Lewis chases Dauphin, who falls to his death while trying to escape in a cable car. Cilento and Lewis are then left to carry on with their honeymoon. Suspenseful direction and a beautiful Riviera location.

p&d, Val Guest; w, Guest, Ronald Scott Thorn (based on Thorn's novel *The Full Treatment*); ph, Gilbert Taylor (MegaScope); m, Stanley Black; ed, Bill Lenny; art d, Tony Masters; set d, Scott Slimon; cos, Beatrice Dawson; makeup, Tony Sforzini.

Mystery/Drama (PR:C MPAA:NR)

STOP PRESS GIRL* (1949, Brit.) 78m Aquila/GFD bw

Sally Ann Howes (*Jennifer Peters*), Gordon Jackson (*Jock Melville*), Basil Radford (*Engine Driver/Bus Driver/Fred/Projectionist/Copilot*), Naunton Wayne (*Fireman/Conductor/Fred's Boy/Projectionist/Copilot*), James Robertson Justice (*Mr. Peters*), Sonia Holm (*Angela*), Nigel Buchanan (*Roy Fairfax*), Joyce Barbour (*Miss Peters*), Julia Lang (*Carole Saunders*), Cyril Chamberlain (*Johnnie*), Campbell Cotts (*Mr. Fairfax*), Michael Goodliffe (*McPherson*), Humphrey Lestocq (*Commentator*), Kenneth More (*Sergeant*), Vincent Ball (*Hero*), Ann Valery (*Heroine*), Betty Cooper, Fred Griffiths, Oliver Burt, Arthur Lowe, Olive Walter, Alex Field, Stanley Rose, Olwen Brookes, Percy Walsh, Sam Kydd, Michael Balfour, Desmond Keith, Patti Morgan, Christine Silver, Patrick Waddington, Denys Val Norton, William Mervyn, Michael Ward, Frederick Owen, John Boxer, Jimmy Rhodes, Richard Vernon.

A British comedy with a premise that promises but never delivers. Howes is a girl with an inexplicable power to stop machinery within 15 minutes any time she gets near it. She falls for a newspaperman and then gets mixed up in a plot to put a rival paper's presses on hold.

p, Donald B. Wilson; d, Michael Barry; w, T.J. Morrison (based on a story by Morrison, Basil Thomas); ph, Bill Allan, Arthur Ibbetson, Cyril Bristow; m, Walter Goehr; ed, Sidney Hayers.

Comedy (PR:A MPAA:NR)

STOP THAT CAB*½ (1951) 58m Lippert bw

Sid Melton, Iris Adrian, Marjorie Lord, Tom Neal, William Haade, Greg McClure, Carla Martin, Chester Clute, Minerva Urecal, Glenn Denning, Diane Garrett, Mario Siletti, Renata Vanni, Jack Roper, Ed East, Jesse B. Kirkpatrick, Vito Scotti, Michael McHale, Joe Devlin.

A gang of careless jewel thieves is sent into a tailspin when they leave their stolen loot in a cab. Comic complications arise and a manic chase for the cab follows. Predictable gibberish which is mercifully short.

p, Abrasha Haimson; d, Eugenio De Liguoro; w, Louella McFarlane, Walter Abbott; ph, Carl Berger; m, Joe Sentesi; ed, Michael Luciano.

Comedy (PR:A MPAA:NR)

STOP THE WORLD--I WANT TO GET OFF**
(1966, Brit.) 100m WB c

Tony Tanner (*Littlechap*), Millicent Martin (*Evie/Anya/Ara/Ginnie*), Leila Croft (*Susan*), Valerie Croft (*Jane*), Neil Hawley (*Little Littlechap*), Graham Lyons (*Father-in-Law*), Georgina Allen, Natasha Ashton, Sandra Burville, Carlotta Barrow, Vivyen Dunbar, Katerina Holden, Margaret Frost, Ann Holloway, Liz Gold, Derina House, Marion Horton, Carolyn Irving, Pamela Hart, Pam Jones, Sarah Hardenburg, Kay Korda, Rosemary Philips, Judith McGilligan, Jo Anna Short, Julie Pitcher, Liz White, Heather Simms, Christy Carroll (*Dancers, Singers*).

A filmed stage play which successfully captured what the theatrical version had to offer, but lacked the spark provided by original stars Anthony Newley and Anna Quayle. Set in a circus ring (a heavy-handed symbol of the world), the story follows the rise to fame of Littlechap Tanner until he finally gets to the top, when he realizes that he succeeded at the expense of everyone around him. Remade in 1979 as SAMMY STOPS THE WORLD. Includes the tunes: "I Believed It All," "The New York Scene" (Al Ham; performed by t he Al Ham Orchestra), "A,B,C Song," "I Wanna Be Rich," "Gonna Build a Mountain," "Mumbo Jumbo," "Once in a Lifetime," "What Kind of Fool Am I?" (Anthony Newley, Leslie Bricusse; sung by Tony Tanner), "Glorious Russian," "Typically Japanese," "All American" (Newley, Bricusse; sung by Millicent Martin), "Typically English," "Lumbered," "Malinki Meilchick," "Family Fugue," "Nag, Nag, Nag," "Someone Nice Like You" (Newley, Bricusse; sung by Tanner, Martin).

p, Bill Sargent; d, Philip Saville; w, Anthony Newley, Leslie Bricusse, David Donable, Al Ham, Marilyn Bergman, Alan Bergman (based on the play by Newley, Bricusse); ph, Oswald Morris (Mitchell Camera System 35, Technicolor); ed, Jim Sibley; md, Al Ham; prod d, Sean Kenny; cos, Gina Fratini, Kiki Byrne; makeup, George Claff.

Musical (PR:A MPAA:NR)

STOP THE WORLD I WANT TO GET OFF
(SEE: SAMMY STOPS THE WORLD, 1978)

STOP TRAIN 349** (1964, Fr./Ital./Ger.) 95m Da. Ma.
Film-Hoche-Hans Oppenheimer-P.C.M./AA bw (LE TRAIN DE BERLIN EST ARRETE; UN TRENO E FERMO A BERLINO; VERSPATUNG IN MARIENBORN; DELAY IN MARIENBORN)

Jose Ferrer (*Cowan the Reporter*), Sean Flynn (*Lt. Novak*), Nicole Courcel (*Nurse Kathy*), Jess Hahn (*Sgt. Torre*), Joseph Yadin (*Maj. Menschikov*), Hans Joachim Schmiedel (*Banner*), Christiane Schmidtmer (*Karin*), Joy Aston (*Mrs. Abramson*), Art Brauss (*IMP*), Fred Durr (*Maj. Finnegan*), Wolfgang Georgi (*Russian Officer Gorski*), Annie Gorassini (*Abramson's Daughter*), Charles Hickman (*Cpl. Williams*), Carlo Hintermann (*Russian Officer*), Hjordis Hume (*Mrs. Watts*), Margaret Jahnen (*Mrs. Stein*), Maria Pia Luzi (*Teenager*), Lothar Mann (*East German Conductor*), Edward Meeks (*U.S. Capt. Kolski*), Antonella Murgia (*Teenager*), Robert Shankland (*U.S. Diplomat*), Narziss Sokatscheff (*Russian Officer*), Ted Turner (*Col. Abramson*), Konrad Thoms, Egon Vogel (*East German Conductors*), Len Monroe (*U.S. Soldier*).

An East German refugee sneaks aboard an American train bound for Frankfurt in hopes of reaching safety. The Germans discover that he is on the train and demand that he be handed over, an order that commanding officer Flynn has no intention of following. The issue begins to become an international one, and eventually at the urging of both the American and the Russian authorities, Flynn gives the prisoner up. An interesting character study which falters primarily because of its painfully slow pace.

p, Hans Oppenheimer, Ray Ventura; d, Rolf Haedrich; w, Victor Vicas, Jim Henaghan, Norman Borisoff (based on a story by Will Tremper); ph, Roger Fellous; m, Peter Thomas; ed, Georges Arnstam, Margot Jahn; set d, Dieter Bartels, Albrecht Hennings; makeup, Ruth Mohr.

Drama (PR:A MPAA:NR)

STOP, YOU'RE KILLING ME** (1952) 86m WB c

Broderick Crawford (*Remy Marko*), Claire Trevor (*Nora Marko*), Virginia Gibson (*Mary Marko*), Bill Hayes (*Chance Whitelaw*), Margaret Dumont (*Mrs. Whitelaw*), Howard St. John (*Mahoney*), Charles Cantor (*Mike*),

Sheldon Leonard *(Lefty)*, Joe Vitale *(Guiseppe)*, Louis Lettieri *(Donnie Reynolds)*, Henry [Harry] Morgan *(Innocence)*, Stephen Chase *(Cal Ritter)*, Don Beddoe *(Clyde Post)*, Henry Slate *(Ryan)*, Ned Glass *(Sad Sam)*, Jack Pepper *(The Singer)*, Joe McTurk *(Ex-Jockey Kirk)*, Ralph Sanford *(Cop)*, John Crawford *(State Trooper)*, Phil Arnold *(Little Dutch)*, Frank Richards *(Black Hat)*, Mushy Callahan *(No Nose)*, Phyllis Kirk *(Nurse)*, Sherry Moreland, Joann Arnold *(Party Girls)*, Dolly Jarvis *(Secretary)*.

An inferior remake of the 1938 A SLIGHT CASE OF MURDER with color and songs added. The Damon Runyon-Howard Lindsay play gave birth to O'Hanlon's script but all of the satire of the original became overdone farce in this. Crawford is an ex-hood who has been put out of the bootlegging business by the repeal of the Volstead Act. He's married to Trevor and she's delighted that he's out of the rackets. They have enough money and can now enjoy themselves without fear of a Tommy gun rat-tat-tatting at their front door. Crawford is going to turn his illegal beer operation into a legitimate business but he finds that it's not as easy as he'd thought it would be. Crawford's and Trevor's decide to take a brief vacation in Saratoga, where the horses run. With three of his ex-hoods in tow, Cantor, Vitale, and Leonard (who was so expert at interpreting Damon Runyon that he became the ultimate Runyon character and was seen in GUYS AND DOLLS, then gave up acting to become one of the richest producer-directors in TV), and a little orphan, Lettieri, they take up residence in a house and find that trouble is all around them. There are four slain gangland mobsters, there is a cache of cash belonging to a dead bookmaker, there are threats on their lives. All the while, Crawford and Trevor's daughter, Gibson, is falling for Hayes, the local young cop who comes from a very social family headed by his mother, Dumont. Just as in the later movie THE BUSY BODY, the corpses get switched around and the humor becomes grisly. A few laughs and a couple of songs by Bob Hilliard and Carl Sigman: "You're My Everloving," (Crawford, Trevor, reprised by Hayes, Gibson) and "Stop, You're Killing Me." Also a few chestnuts like "Baby Face" and "With Someone Like You." Not much else to recommend this low comedy. Hayes later went to Broadway, then spent almost 20 years as a soap opera star. The Henry Morgan listed in the cast is now Harry Morgan of "M*A*S*H" and about 10 other TV series. Dancer Henry Slate later teamed with his brother to open a famed Hollywood nightclub known as "The Slate Brothers" where Don Rickles and many other comedians got their first breaks.

p, Louis F. Edelman; d, Roy Del Ruth; w, James O'Hanlon (based on the play by Damon Runyon, Howard Lindsay); ph, Ted McCord (Warner Color); ed, Owen Marks; md, Ray Heindorf; art d, Charles H. Clarke; ch, LeRoy Prinz; m/l, Bob Hilliard, Carl Sigman.

Comedy   **(PR:A   MPAA:NR)**

STOPOVER FOREVER**   (1964, Brit.) 59m Pathe/WPD bw

Ann Bell *(Sue Chambers)*, Anthony Bate *(Trevor Graham)*, Conrad Phillips *(Eric Cunningham)*, Bruce Boa *(Freddie)*, Julian Sherrier *(Capt. Carlos Mordente)*, Britta von Krogh *(Jane Watson)*.

A standard murder mystery in which an airline stewardess realizes her life is in danger after one of her coworkers is killed when mistaken for her. Determined to learn why someone wants to kill her, the stewardess sets out to discover the identity of the murderer.

p, Terry Ashwood; d, Frederic Goode; w, David Osborne.

Crime   **(PR:A   MPAA:NR)**

STOPOVER TOKYO½   (1957) 100m FOX c

Robert Wagner *(Mark Fannon)*, Joan Collins *(Tina)*, Edmond O'Brien *(George Underwood)*, Ken Scott *(Tony Barrett)*, Reiko Oyama *(Koko)*, Larry Keating *(High Commissioner)*, Sarah Selby *(His Wife)*, Solly Nakamura *(Nobika)*, H. Okhawa *(Lt. Afumi)*, K.J. Seijto *(Katsura)*, Demmei Susuki *(Capt. Masao)*, Yuki Kaneko, Michei Miura.

A well-crafted espionage thriller set in Japan which stars Wagner as a U.S. Intelligence agent hired to protect an American ambassador from assassination. The problem is that the ambassador doesn't believe that anyone is really trying to kill him. Wagner proves his point when he discovers and disposes of a bomb meant for the ambassador, which had been planted by a crazed American Communist. Wagner is luckier at exposing criminals than at love, however, and Collins walks out on him after accusing him of being too dedicated to his job.

p, Walter Reisch; d, Richard L. Breen; w, Reisch, Breen (based on the novel by John P. Marquand); ph, Charles G. Clarke (CinemaScope, DeLuxe Color); m, Paul Sawtell; ed, Marjorie Fowler; art d, Lyle R. Wheeler, Eddie Imazu; md, (Japanese music) Tak Shindo.

Spy Drama   **Cas.**   **(PR:A   MPAA:NR)**

STORIA DI UNA DONNA   (SEE: STORY OF A WOMAN, 1970, U.S./Ital.)

STORIES FROM A FLYING TRUNK**   (1979, Brit.) 88m EMI c

Murray Melvin *(Hans Christian Andersen)*, Ann Firbank *(The Mother)*, Tasneem Maqsood *(The Little Match Girl)*, John Tordoff *(The Tramp)*, John Dalby *(Queen Victoria)*, Johanna Sonnex *(Little Ida)*, Gerd Larsen *(Ballet Mistress)*, Patricia Napier *(The Lettuce)*, Graham Fletcher *(Prince Potato)*, Lesley Collier *(The Princess)*, Dancers of the Royal Ballet, London *(Vegetables)*.

A moderately successful attempt at bringing three classic Hans Christian Andersen tales–"The Kitchen," "The Little Match Girl," and "Litte Ida"–to the big screen. Updated to a modern London locale, the three stories seem a bit too confused for most youngsters to follow, but they will thrill at the imaginative use of stopframe animation, which allows kitchenware and vegetables to jump around and dance.

p, John Brabourne, Richard Goodwin; d&w, Christine Edzard (based on the stories of Hans Christian Andersen); ph, Robin Browne, Brian West; m, Gioacchino Rossini; ed, Rex Pyke, M.J. Knatchbull; spec eff, Ken Worringham; ballet settings, Irene Groudinsky.

Children's   **(PR:AA   MPAA:NR)**

STORK½   (1971, Aus.) 95m Bilcock & Copping c

Bruce Spence, Jacki Weaver, Helmut Bakaitis, Graeme Blundell, Sean McEuen, George Whaley, Dennis Miller, Terry Norris.

An odd little comedy from down under which stars Bruce Spence (ROAD WARRIOR'S Gyro Captain) as a tall, gangly sort who can't seem to hold a job or find a girl to lose his virginity to. He moves in with three of his mates and a girl, whom he (and the three others) wind is up in bed with. With those kind of odds it isn't surprising that the girl gets pregnant, but nobody seems to know which one is dad. A wedding follows, but Spence ruins the ceremony with his slapstick antics and a malevolent fire hose. One's acceptance of the picture goes hand in hand with one's affections for Spence and his character.

d, Tom Burstall; w, David Williamson; ph, Robin Copping (Eastmancolor).

Comedy/Drama   **(PR:O   MPAA:NR)**

STORK BITES MAN**   (1947) 67m Comet/UA bw

Jackie Cooper *(Ernie)*, Gene Roberts *(Peg)*, Gus Schilling *(Butterfield)*, Emory Parnell *(Kimberly)*, Stanley Prager *(Voice of the Stork)*, Sarah Selby *(Mrs. Greene)*, Majorie Beckett *(Mabel)*.

An innocuous comedy which stars Cooper as an apartment manager who gets fired and evicted when his boss, who hates kids more than W.C. Fields, learns that Cooper's wife has one on the way. Taking advice from a mysterious stork (which is invisible to everyone), Cooper organizes an apartment workers strike, which eventually makes his leathery boss soften up.

p, Buddy Rogers, Ralph Cohn; d, Cyril [cy] Endfield; w, Endfield, Fred Freiburger (based on the story by Louis Pollock); ph, Vincent J. Farrar, Robert W. Pittack; m, Raoul Kraushaar; ed, Lynn Harrison; md, David Chudnow; set d, William Stevens.

Comedy   **(PR:A   MPAA:NR)**

STORK CLUB, THE½   (1945) 98m PAR bw

Betty Hutton *(Judy Peabody)*, Barry Fitzgerald *(Jerry B. Bates)*, Don Defore *(Danny Wilton)*, Robert Benchley *(Tom Curtis)*, Bill Goodwin *(Sherman Billingsley)*, Iris Adrian *(Gwen)*, Mikhail Rasumny *(Coretti)*, Mary Young *(Mrs. Edith Bates)*, Andy Russell *(Jim)*, Perc Launders *(Tom, Band Member)*, Mary Currier *(Hazel Billingsley)*, Noel Neill *(Jacqueline Billingsley)*, Gloria Donovan *(Barbara Billingsley)*, Mae Busch *(Vera)*, Pierre Watkin *(Hotel Manager)*, Charles Coleman *(Bates' Butler)*, Dorothy Garrett *(Cashier)*, Cosmo Sardo *(Rocco, Stork Club Waiter)*, Grady Sutton *(Peter, Salesman)*, Audrey Young *(Jenny, Check Girl)*, Roberta Jonay *(Molly the Check Girl)*, Anthony Caruso *(Joe the Fisherman)*, Jimmy Dundee *(Fred the Fisherman)*, Darrell Huntley *(Fred, Fisherman)*, Franklyn Farnum *(Diner)*, Sam Ash *(Ringsider)*, Reed Howes *(Patron)*.

Hutton is a struggling hatcheck girl at the Stork Club who saves Fitzgerald from a drowning accident. When she pulls him from the water, she learns that he is really a multi-millionaire. As a reward, Fitzgerald sets her up in a life of luxury in her own penthouse apartment. Defore, her bandleader beau, returns from the service and mistakenly thinks that his gal gave something to Fitzgerald in exchange for the goodies. He soon learns he is wrong, and the pair live happily ever after. This lighthearted chronicle of life and times at this legendary New York eatery and nightclub is an occasion to showcase the musical comedy talents of Hutton whose peppy charm and singing style were becoming more and more popular. Songs include: "Doctor, Lawyer, Indian Chief" (Hoagy Carmichael, Paul Francis Webster, sung by Betty Hutton), "Baltimore Oriole" (Carmichael, Webster), "I'm a Square in the Social Circle" (Jay Livingston, Ray Evans, sung by Hutton), "If I Had a Dozen Hearts" (Webster, Harry Revel, sung by Hutton, Andy Russell), "Love Me" (Sammy Cahn, Jule Styne), "China Boy" (Dick Winfree, Phil Boutelje), "In the Shade of the Old Apple Tree" (Harry H. Williams, Egbert Van Alstyne).

p, Buddy De Sylva; d, Hal Walker; w, De Sylva, John McGowan; ph, Charles Lang, Jr., Farciot Edouart; ed, Gladys Carley; md, Robert Emmett Dolan; art d, Hans Dreier, Earl Hedrick; ch, Billy Daniels.

Musical/Comedy   Cas.   (PR:A MPAA:NR)

STORK PAYS OFF, THE**   (1941) 68m COL bw

Victor Jory (Deak Foster), Rochelle Hudson (Irene Perry), Maxie Rosenbloom (Brains Moran), Horace MacMahon (Hinkle), George McKay (Photofinish Farris), Ralf Harolds (Stud Rocco), Danny Mummert (Herkemer), Bonnie Irma Dane (Bonnie), Arthur Loft (Barney).

A humorous little number which features a group of gangsters who are inadvertantly put in charge of a daycare center. Mob leader Jory soon takes a liking to the idea and sends his henchmen to night school in hopes of better educating them. His nursery efforts involve him in politics, which then leads to an aldermanic seat. Full of cute kids and delightful situations.

p, Jack Fier; d, Lew Landers; w, Fanya Foss, Aleen Leslie; ph, L.W. O'Connell; ed, Gene Milford; md, Morris W. Stoloff.

Comedy   (PR:A MPAA:NR)

STORK TALK**   (1964, Brit.) 85m Unifilms/Parade bw

Tony Britton (Dr. Paul Vernon), Anne Heywood (Lisa Vernon), John Turner (Dr. Robert Sterne), Nicole Perrault (Tina Monet), Daphne Anderson (Dr. Mary Willis), Marie Kean (Mrs. Webster, Housekeeper), Gladys Henson (Matron), John Sharp (Papa Pierre), John Malloy (Pram Salesman), Gerry Sullivan (Dr. Sefton), Pamela Mant (Mrs. Stanton), Genevieve Lyons, Ann Mulvey (Receptionists), Jimmy Gaffrey (Booking Office Clerk), Denise Hirst, Annest Williams (Sisters), Marie Conmee (Mrs. Jeffries), George Hill (Henry).

An ineffective sex comedy about a gynecologist who finds himself a little French mistress when he gets pregnant. After a reconciliaton with his wife, he learns that she, too, is expecting. His wife tries to work a scam with her husband's colleagues to register both her child and the French girl's as her own, making it seem as if she's had twins. Her plan backfires when both women give birth to a pair apiece. The problems are settled when the husband and wife reunite, while the partner and the French girl marry. Nothing memorable.

p, Charles Bruce Newberry; d, Michael Forlong; w, Donald Ford, Peter Rosser, William Hepper (based on the play "The Night Life of a Virile Potato" by Gloria Russell); ph, Norman Warwick; m, Tony Hatch; ed, John Jympson; art d, Norman Arnold; set d, Andrew Low; makeup, Gerry Fletcher.

Comedy   (PR:O MPAA:NR)

STORM, THE**½   (1930) 80m UNIV bw

Lupe Velez (Manette Fachard), Paul Cavanagh (Dave Stewart), William "Stage" Boyd (Burr Winton), Alphonse Ethier (Jacques Fachard), Ernie S. Adams (Johnny), Tom London, Nick Thompson, Erin La Bissoniere.

An energetic love triangle filmed against the special effects-laden backdrop of a destructive, blinding winter storm. Velez is cast as a French Canadian (doing her best to hide her Spanish accent) trapped in a log cabin with Boyd and Cavanagh, a situation which strains the men's friendship. This is a remake of two silent versions, one for Paramount in 1916, the other for Universal in 1922.

d, William Wyler; w, Wells Root, Charles A. Logue (based on the play "Men Without Skirts" by Langdon McCormick); ph, Alvin Wycoff.

Drama   (PR:A MPAA:NR)

STORM, THE**½   (1938) 75m UNIV bw

Charles Bickford (Bob Roberts), Barton MacKane (Capt. Cogswell), Preston Foster (Jack Stacey), Tom Brown (Jim Roberts), Nan Grey (Peggy Phillips), Andy Devine (Hansen), Frank Jenks (Peter Carey), Samuel S. Hinds (Capt. Kenny), Florence Roberts (Mrs. Roberts), Jack Mulhall (Blake), Helen Gilliland (Hungry), Stanley Hughes (Cadet), Joseph Sawyer (Kelly), Marion Martin (Jane), Dorothy Arnold (Nora), Milburn Stone (Man).

Packed with adventures at sea, THE STORM mainly centers on brothers Bickford and Brown, with the former trying to convince the latter to find a job on land. Brown ignores the advice of his hard-drinking brother, but soon winds up in trouble when he needs an emergency operation at sea. Grey bravely performs the surgery, acting only on radio instructions that are sent to her from a doctor on land. Brown and Grey eventually marry and return to solid ground, but not without Brown getting in some final licks with captain MacLane, who was responsible for a friend's death. Enough action to hold just about anyone's attention.

p, Ken Goldsmith; d, Harold Young; w, Daniel Moore, Hugh King, Theodore Reeves (based on the story by Moore, King); ph, Milton Krasner; ed, Frank Gross; md, Charles Previn; art d, Charles Previn.

Drama/Action   (PR:A MPAA:NR)

STORM AT DAYBREAK*½   (1933) 68m MGM bw

Kay Francis (Irina Dushan), Nils Asther (Geza), Walter Huston (Mayor Dushan), Phillips Holmes (Csaholyi), Eugene Pallette (Janos), C. Henry Gordon (Panto), Louise Closser Hale (Militza), Jean Parker (Danitza), Charles Halton, Leonid Kinskey (Villagers), Akim Tamiroff (Gypsy Fiddler), Mischa Auer (Assassin), Frank Conroy (Archduke Franz Ferdinand).

A weak love triangle which relies on the traditional conflict between Serbs and Hungarians for some added life. The film opens with a re-creation of the assassination of Archduke Ferdinand at Sarajevo and moves on to a friendship between Huston, a Serbian mayor, and his best friend, Asther, an Hungarian officer. When the latter steals Huston's wife, conflicts arise, but in the end the jilted husband sacrifices his life for the pair. Overlong even at 68 minutes, with not nearly enough plot to pass the time.

p, Lucien Hubbard; d, Richard Boleslavsky; w, Bertram Millhauser (based on the play "Black-Stemmed Cherries" by Sandor Hunyady); ph, George Folsey; m, Dr. William Axt; ed, Margaret Booth; m/l, Axt, Gus Kahn.

Drama   (PR:A MPAA:NR)

STORM BOY***   (1976, Aus.) 88m South Australian Film c

Greg Rowe (Storm Boy), Peter Cummins (Hide-Away Tom), David Gulpilil (Fingerbone Bill), Judy Dick (Miss Walker), Tony Allison (Ranger), Michael Moody (Boat Master), Graham Dow (Edwards), Frank Foster-Brown (Lynch), Eric Mack (Jones), Michael Caulfield, Paul Smith (Hunters), Hedley Cullen (Marina Manager), Schoolchildren from the Port Elliot Primary School.

A heartwarming tale of a young Australian boy (Rowe) who lives along the coast in an uninhabited area with his father, learning all he can about life just from living it. When he one day befriends an old aborigine and finds a nest of orphan pelicans, he begins to care for them at the old man's urging. As the picture progresses, the boy's relationships with his father and with the aborigine strengthen, adding a beautiful depth to the boy's personality. Filled with many a tearful moment.

p, Matt Carroll; d, Henri Safran; w, Sonia Berg (based on the novel by Colin Thiele); ph, Geoff Burton; m, Michael Carlos; ed, G. Turney-Smith; prod d, David Copping; pelican trainer, Gordon Noble.

Children's   Cas.   (PR:AAA MPAA:NR)

STORM CENTER**   (1956) 85m COL bw

Bette Davis (Alicia Hull), Brian Keith (Paul Duncan), Kim Hunter (Martha Lockridge), Paul Kelly (Judge Robert Ellerbe), Kevin Coughlin (Freddie Slater), Joe Mantell (George Slater), Sallie Brophy (Laura Slater), Howard Wierum (Mayor Levering), Curtis Cooksey (Stacey Martin), Michael Raffetto (Edgar Greenbaum), Edward Platt (Rev. Wilson), Kathryn Grant (Hazel), Howard Wendell (Sen. Bascomb), Burt Mustin (Carl), Edith Evanson (Mrs. Simmons), Joseph Kearns (Mr. Morrisey), Ted Marc (Bert), Rudy Lee (Charlie), Phillip Crampton (Joe), Dora Dee Stansauk, Lora Lee Stansauk (Paswolski Twins), Bucko Stafford (Jack), Malcolm Atterbury (Frank), Edwin Parker (Fireman), Paul Ryan (Mr. Fisher), George Selk (Bill), Mildred Hays (Mrs. Field), Emlen Davies (Miss Layton), Alexander Campbell (Jones).

A good idea that is always timely goes awry under the heavy direction of the implausible script. Davis is a widowed librarian in a small town. She's worked so long at the library that she feels she is the proprietor, rather than the custodian, of the books. Since her husband died in WW I, she's devoted herself to shaping the minds of her small town's children. A staunch Yankee (as she is in real life), she firmly believes in the Constitution. The children in the town adore her and will ask her questions they might not even ask their parents. One of her pets is Coughlin, a boy who spends every waking moment at the library, eagerly devouring everything he can. The town council gets together and asks her to take a communistic book off the shelves. She feels that their decision is stupid, almost like what the Nazis did in Germany, because the book is patently garbage. Despite her disagreement, they prevail upon her and she does what they ask. Later, she has second thoughts and decides that what they've requested is against her principles so she puts the book back on the shelves. The very fact that it's there is an affirmation of the American Way of Life. This adherence to her moral tenets results in her losing her beloved job and being replaced by Hunter, her assistant and longtime pal. The town's judge, Kelly, thinks she has been unfairly sacked and wants to get her job back so he calls for a town meeting and is opposed by Mantell. Hardly anyone shows up at the meeting as nobody much cares. Hunter's boy friend, Keith, is there and uses this as a springboard. He wants to run for office in the town and jumps on the bandwagon against Davis, calling her a Red and questioning her patriotism because she is a member of a few groups that some might call subversive. Davis defends herself by saying that she feels it's important to learn whatever she can but the others don't believe her and she is soon shunned by everyone in the small town. The only friend she still has is Coughlin. The other kids show typical cruelty and chastise him for being Davis' pet. This causes Coughlin to have several nightmares and winds up when the disturbed boy pads into the old library and sets it ablaze. While the library burns, the townspeople have a sudden change of heart and, led by their mayor, Wierum, ask Davis to come back to work for the town and supervise the building of a brand new library. Davis agrees to take the task and says that she is just as much at fault as they were because she did not stand up and fight for what she believed, that literature must stand above politics and no elected or appointed person should ever be able to tell people what they can or cannot read. Although this movie was made many years ago, the same battle still goes on and hardly a month goes by that some library doesn't remove "The Catcher In the Rye" or "The Joy of Sex" from circulation due to the proddings of conservatives (or liberals) who think that they know what people should or should not read. The idea of the film was forthright but the execution was dismal. And the sudden alteration in the town's beliefs is just too nonsensical to accept. In a small role, note Kathryn Grant who gave up acting soon afterward to become Mrs. Bing Crosby.

p, Julian Blaustein; d, Daniel Taradash; w, Taradash, Elick Moll; ph, Burnett Guffey; m, George Duning; ed, William A. Lyon; art d, Cary Odell; set d, Frank Tuttle; makeup, Clay Campbell.

Drama (PR:A MPAA:NR)

STORM FEAR½** (1956) 88m Theodora/UA bw

Cornel Wilde (*Charlie*), Jean Wallace (*Elizabeth*), Dan Duryea (*Fred*), Lee Grant (*Edna*), David Stollery (*David*), Dennis Weaver (*Hank*), Steven Hill (*Benjie*), Keith Britton (*Doctor*).

An engrossing film noir set mostly in the New England farmhouse of Duryea, the brother of bank robber Wilde who arrives with fellow gang members Grant and Hill in search of a hideout. Duryea is less than hospitable, while Grant and Hill are edgy and want to continue on. Wilde, however, is injured and in no hurry to move ahead, especially since it is revealed that he has a past with Duryea's wife, Wallace, and that Stollery is really his son and not Duryea's. Weaver, a hired farmhand, escapes in an attempt to notify the police, forcing the gang to leave quickly. Wilde brings Stollery along as a guide, shattering the kid's illusions that his uncle-father is a decent man when he shoots Duryea. Battles and gunfights occur until only Wilde and his son are left. Stollery helps him get away, but before he is in the clear, he is gunned down by Duryea, who has been following them. Horton Foote (TO KILL A MOCKINGBIRD, TENDER MERCIES) delivers characters with keen personality traits and bizarre idiosyncracies, such as the use of the collar of the dead family dog to decorate the Christmas tree.

p&d, Cornel Wilde; w, Horton Foote (based on the novel by Clinton Seeley); ph, Joseph La Shelle; m, Elmer Bernstein; ed, Otto Ludwig; prod d, Rudi Feld.

Crime Drama (PR:A MPAA:NR)

STORM IN A TEACUP** (1937, Brit.) 88m LFP/UA bw

Vivien Leigh (*Victoria Gow*), Rex Harrison (*Frank Burdon*), Sara Allgood (*Mrs. Hegarty*), Cecil Parker (*Provost Gow*), Ursula Jeans (*Lisbete Skirving*), Gus McNaughton (*Horace Skirving*), Arthur Wontner (*Fiscal*), Edgar K. Bruce (*McKellar*), Robert Hale (*Lord Skerryvore*), Quinton McPherson (*Baillie Callender*), Eliot Makeham (*Sheriff*), Ivor Barnard (*Watkins*), W.G. Fay (*Cassidy*), George Pughe (*Menzies*), Arthur Seaton (*Police Sergeant*), Cecil Mannering (*Police Constable*), Cyril Smith (*Councillor*), Scruffy the Dog.

An amusing comedy of manners, morals, and romance based on a German play and Anglicized well by James Bridie for the stage. The action takes place is a tiny provincial Scottish town. Harrison is a newspaper reporter from England and he comes north to take a job on the local publication. Once there, he reconnoiters the area and meets Leigh, daughter of the wealthy and dictatorial Parker, who is the town's leading legal light (they call him the Provost). Parker is attempting to establish himself in a further position of strength so he misuses his power. Allgood is a poor woman who has only one pleasure in life, the companionship of her dog, Scruffy. When she can't come up with the pittance for the annual license fee, Parker harumphs and says that Scruffy will have to be destroyed. Harrison is looking for a good story and when he hears what Parker has decreed, he decides to take it all the way and begins printing the story and constant updates as though this were the invasion of Scotland. The story is picked up by the national newspapers and becomes a *cause celebre* across the country and Parker's dreams of standing for Parliament are destroyed. He retaliates by suing Harrison for slander and there is a funny courtroom scene in which Leigh, who has fallen madly in love with Harrison, happily lies on the stand to save Harrison from jail. Before the trial, Harrison thinks he's lost Leigh so he goes ahead full bore with his campaign and winds up amazed by her testimony and, at the fade, the two are united. The picture was reissued in 1943 and again in 1946. It's a trifle dated by today's comedy standards but remains a good example of what was funny in the late 30s.

p, Victor Saville; d, Saville, Ian Dalrymple; w, Dalrymple, Donald Bull (based on James Bridic's adaptation of the play "Sturm im Wasserglas" by Bruno Frank); ph,Mutz Greenbaum (Max Greene); m, Frederic Lewis; ed, Hugh Stewart, Cyril Randell; prod d, Andre Andrejew; md, Muir Mathieson; spec eff, Ned Mann, Edward Cohen.

Comedy **Cas.** (PR:A MPAA:NR)

STORM IN A WATER GLASS** (1931, Aust.) 70m Sascha-Felsom bw
(STURM IM WASSERGLAS; DIE BLUMENFRAU VON LINDENAU;
AKA: THE FLOWER WOMAN OF LINDENAU)

Hansi Niese (*Frau Vogel, Flower Seller*), Renate Muller (*Victoria*), Paul Otto (*Dr. Thoss, the Alderman*), Harald Paulsen (*Burdach, Newspaperman*), Herbert Huebner (*Quilling*), Grete Maren (*Lisa*), Oscar Szabo (*Dog Catcher*), Otto Tressler (*Judge*), Franz Schafheitlin (*Prosecutor*), Hedy Kiesler [Lamarr] (*Burdach's Secretary*), Alfred Neugebauer (*Waiter*), Eugen Gunther, Karl Kneidinger (*Men in Courtroom*).

An amusing tale about a penniless flower seller, Niese, who has her dog taken away because she cannot afford the tax on the animal. She takes her case to the home of an alderman preparing his reelection campaign, and while waiting ends up talking with a newspaper reporter about the incident. The alderman throws her out of his house, an act of such inhumane proportions that the reporter feels compelled to write about the incident. Public sentiment is soon in Niese's favor, while voting the alderman out of office. Hedy Lamarr, billed here as Hedy Kiesler, appears in her second film role in a bit as the newsman's secretary. Remade in 1937 as STORM IN A TEACUP.

d, Georg Jacoby; w, Walter Wassermann, W. Schlee, Felix Salten (based on the play by Bruno Frank); ph, Guido Seeber, Bruno Timm.

Comedy (PR:A MPAA:NR)

STORM OVER AFRICA (SEE: ROYAL AFRICAN RIFLES, 1953)

STORM OVER BENGAL** (1938) 65m REP bw

Patric Knowles (*Jeffrey Allison*), Richard Cromwell (*Neil Allison*), Rochelle Hudson (*Joan*), Douglas Dumbrille (*Khan*), Colin Tapley (*Hallett*), Gilbert Emery (*Col. Torrance*), Douglas Walton (*Terry*), Halliwell Hobbes (*Sir John Galt*), John Burton (*Carter*), Clyde Cook (*Alf*), Claude Allister (*Redding*), Pedro De Cordoba (*Mir*), Edward Van Sloan (*Maharajah*).

A pair of brothers get involved in the heat of battle when the British troops clash with Indians in Bengal. Younger brother Cromwell is more trouble than he's worth early on, but by the picture's finish he has proven himself and saved the entire regiment. Star Knowles, usually consider ed to be the poor man (or poor woman's) Errol Flynn, got a chance to take center stage in this second rate Republic swashbuckler. At least it allowed him an opportunity to shine as he never had at Warner's where the genuine article, Flynn, was always on hand for the heroics.

p, Armand Schaefer; d, Sidney Salkow; w, Garret Fort; ph, Ernest Miller; ed, William Morgan.

War (PR:A MPAA:NR)

STORM OVER LISBON½** (1944) 86m REP bw

Vera Hruba Ralston (*Maritza*), Richard Arlen (*John Craig*), Erich von Stroheim (*Deresco*), Robert Livingston (*Bill Flanagan*), Otto Kruger (*Alexis Vanderlyn*), Eduardo Ciannelli (*Blanco*), Mona Barrie (*Evelyn*), Frank Orth (*Murgatroyd*), Sarah Edwards (*Maude*), Alice Fleming (*Agatha*), Leon Belasco, Vincent Girondo (*Fado Singers*), Bud Geary, Kenne Duncan, Roy Barcroft (*Henchmen*), Ruth Roman, Karen Randle, Annyse Sherman (*Checkroom Girls*), The Aida Broadbent Girls (*Dancers*), Marie Day (*Maid*), Lucien Prival, Muni Seroff (*Men in Tails*), Lester Sharpe (*Overfelder*), Kirk Alyn (*Bandleader*), Gino Corrado (*Headwaiter*), Jac George (*Waiter*), Will Kaufman (*The Baron*), Almeda Fowler (*Woman*), Alphonse Martell (*Maitre d'Hotel*), Louis Ludwig Lowy (*Croupier*), Manuel Paris (*Roulette Dealer*), Georgia Davis (*Canteen Girl*), Charles Wagenheim (*Frustrated Man*), Eula Guy (*Hysterical Wife*), George Derrick (*Gigolo*), Victor Travers (*Man with Newspaper*), Fred Rapport (*Claim Check Man*), Dick Alexander (*Doorman*), George Humbert (*Italian Waiter*), Georges Renavent (*Secret Service Official*), Jack Kirk (*Driver*).

Taking place mostly in a ritzy Portuguese cafe-gambling den, this average programmer is given life by the performance of von Stroheim as the club's unscrupulous owner. He runs up against Arlen and Ralston when he tries to sell the former's secrets to enemy spies, a common pastime for von Stroheim. Unfortunately, the picture isn't helped by Ralston's weak performance. The former ice skater turned actress proved she was better on the ice than on the set.

p&d, George Sherman; w, Doris Gilbert, Dane Lussier (based on the story by Elizabeth Meehan); ph, John Alton; m, Walter Scharf, Maurice de Packh; ed, Arthur Roberts; md, Morton Scott; art d, Gano Chittenden, Russell Kimball; spec eff, Theodore Lydecker.

Mystery (PR:A MPAA:NR)

STORM OVER THE ANDES½** (1935) 82m UNIV bw

Jack Holt (*Bob Kent*), Antonio Moreno (*Maj. Tovar*), Mona Barrie (*Theresa*), Gene Lockhart (*Cracker*), Juanita Garfias (*Pepita*), Grant Withers (*Mitchell*), Barry Norton (*Diaz*), George Lewis (*Garcia*), June Gittelson (*Big Woman*), Alma Rea l, Lucio Villegas Spanish Version: Jose Crespo (*Kent*), Lupita Tovar (*Theresa*), Romualdo Tirado (*Cracker*), Julio Pena (*Mitchell*).

Holt is a brash American flyer living and working in Bolivia who is caught up in battles between Bolivian and Paraguayan fliers. He also gets himself in a bind with the wife of a high-ranking officer, without realizing who she is. An average plot which is saved by some keenly staged action sequences and fine aerial stunts.

p, Maurice Pivar; d, Christy Cabanne; w, Al DeMond, Lt. Comdr. Frank Wead, Eva Greene (based on the story by Eliot Gibbons, Laclede Christy); ph, Charles Stumar, Harry Forbes; ed, Maurice E. Wright.

Action (PR:A MPAA:NR)

STORM OVER THE NILE** (1955, Brit.) 107m LFP/COL c

Laurence Harvey (*John Durrance*), Anthony Steel (*Harry Faversham*), James Robertson Justice (*Gen. Burroughs*), Geoffrey Keen (*Dr. Sutton*), Ronald Lewis (*Peter Burroughs*), Ian Carmichael (*Tom Willoughby*), Michael Hordern (*Gen. Faversham*), Jack Lambert (*Colonel*), Mary Ure (*Mary Burroughs*), Christopher Lee (*Karaga Pasha*), Ferdy Mayne (*Dr. Harraz*), John Wynne (*Sergeant*), Avis Scott (*Sergeant's Wife*), Roger Delgardo (*Native Spy*), Frank Singuineau (*Native Servant*), Ben Williams (*Faversham's Butler*), Vincent Holman (*Burroughs's Butler*), Paul Streather (*Harry as a Boy*), Raymond Francis (*Colonel's Aide*), Sam Kydd (*Joe the Instructor*).

Zoltan Korda resurrected his 1939 classic THE FOUR FEATHERS, adapting the lusty story for the new CinemaScope technologies of the 1950s. Unfortunately the results are a disappointment, pale in comparison to the original. Steel is the son of a military family who resigns his commission as an officer shortly before his unit is to leave for the Sudan. Harvey, Lewis, and Carmichael are three fellow officers who despise Steel's action, branding their former comrade a coward. Steel's fiancee Ure shares similar feelings, no longer able to look at her intended in the light she once saw him. To show their feelings each gives him a single feather, a symbol of Steel's cowardice. Gradually Steel's resignation has repercussions on his psyche. He decides to return to prove his bravery, taking up the guise of a native of the Sudan. Once arriving in the Sudan, Steel meets up once more with Harvey, who is now wandering blindly through the desert suffering from the effects of the sun. Steel helps out his old associate, then sets out to rescue Lewis and Carmichael. He frees them after the two have been captured by the enemy, finally proving to his former allies that he has the courage of any stalwart British officer. Alexander Korda had produced the 1939 film and his influence is sorely missed here. Instead, Zoltan Korda took over the producing, sharing his directorial credit with Young. Though the essentials of story are the same, the acting does not project the power so needed for the story. Steel is unable to sustain his character throughout the film, starting off well but eventually wearing thin. Lewis and Carmichael are tolerable in support but Harvey is completely miscast. The nature of the story makes this a natural for the epic screen of CinemaScope. Korda and Young do make effective use of the process, filling the eye with spectacular battle sequences that brim with colorful excitement and verve. Footage from THE FOUR FEATHERS of 1939 was also incorporated, but this was done with lesser success. The clips used had to be blown up to fit the CinemaScope process, which stretched the original images to some obvious ill proportions. One moment in particular contains a shot of the moon, stretched - to an oddly distorted body. Considering the possibilities of the story, as well as Korda's proven ability with the material, STORM OVER THE NILE ranks as a disappointment, reducing a heroic and epic story to a simple adventure tale of some very proper British soldiers. This film marked the cinematic debut of Ure, who here has little to do in an essentially masculine story.

p, Zoltan Korda; d, Korda, Terence Young; w, R.C. Sheriff, Lajos Biro, Arthur Wimperis (based on the novel *The Four Feathers* by A.E.W. Mason); ph, Ted Scaife (CinemaScope, Technicolor); m, Benjamin Frankel; ed, Raymond Poulton; prod d, Wilfred Shingleton; md, Frankel; art d, Shingleton; cos, Bridget Sellers.

Adventure (PR:A MPAA:NR)

STORM OVER THE PACIFIC (SEE: I BOMBED PEARL HARBOR, 1961, Jap.)

STORM OVER TIBET*½ (1952) 87m Summit/COL bw

Rex Reason (*David*), Diana Douglas (*Elaine*), Myron Healey (*Bill March*), Robert Ka rnes (*Radio Operator*), Strother Martin (*Co-Pilot*), Harold Fong (*Sgt. Lee*), Harald Dyrenforth (*Prof. Faber*), Jarmila Marton (*Mrs. Faber*), William Schallert (*Aylen*), John Dodsworth (*Malloy*), M. Concepcion (*High Lama*).

An excess of travel footage mars this weak programmer about a pilot, Reason, who snatches a sacred mask from a Tibetan temple and pays the price when he discovers that it's cursed. An evil spell is apparently responsible for the death of fellow flier Healey. Reason, out of guilt, returns to the U.S. to wed the flier's widow, Douglas, and then later joins up with a UNESCO Himalayan expedition. Heavy on authenticity, but weak on drama.

p, Ivan Tors, Laslo Benedek; d, Andrew Marton; w, Tors, Sam Meyer; ph, George E. Diskant, Richard Angst; m, Arthur Honegger, Leith Stevens; ed, John Hoffman.

Action (PR:A MPAA:NR)

STORM OVER WYOMING** (1950) 60m RKO bw

Tim Holt (*Dave*), Noreen Nash (*Chris*), Richard Powers [Tom Keene] (*Tug Caldwell*), Betty Underwood (*Ruby*), Bill Kennedy (*Rawlins*), Kenneth MacDonald (*Dawson*), Holly Bane (*Scott*), Leo McMahon (*Zeke*), Richard Kean (*Watson*), Don Haggerty (*Marshal*), Richard Martin (*Chito Rafferty*).

A formula oater which has Holt and Martin inadvertently getting in the middle of a cattlemen vs. sheepmen feud after they save the life of a cowhand. The only change of pace this one has to offer is an unusual amount of attention paid to dancehall gal Underwood, who helps out Holt on more than one occasion. Lots of action, but lacking in the writing department.

p, Herman Schlom; d, Lesley Selander; w, Ed Earl Repp; ph, J. Roy Hunt; ed, Robert Swink; md, Constantin Bakaleinikoff; art d, Albert S. D'Agostino, Feild Gray.

Western **Cas.** (PR:A MPAA:NR)

STORM PLANET*** (1962, USSR) 74m Leningrad Studio of Popular Science Films bw (PLANETA BURG; AKA: COSMONAUTS ON VENUS; PLANET OF STORMS)

Gennadi Vernov, Vladimir Temelianov, Yuri Sarantsev, Georgi Zhonov, Kyunna Ignatova.

One of the better Soviet space travel films, STORM PLANET takes a trio of spaceships on an exploration of Venus, led by captain Ignatova. Only one lands on the planet, scouting the surface and eventually meeting a Venusian, who is remarkably humanlike. Where this picture excels is in its attention to atmosphere and set design. However, it's less pretentious than many similar films. There's also a fair amount of humor, mostly from a robot tagged "John" who has a penchant for losing control and playing old swing tunes. Roger Corman bought the U.S. rights to this film, which then showed up in a scissored version as VOYAGE TO A PREHISTORIC PLANET with Basil Rathbone and Faith Domergue, a TV release from Peter Bogdanovich and Curtis Harrington. Bogdanovich again chopped the film into oblivion (under the name Derek Thomas) in 1966 under the tag VOYAGE TO A PLANET OF PREHISTORIC WOMEN. Poor Mister Klushantsev.

d, Pavel Klushantsev; w, Klushantsev, Alexander Kazantsev; ph, Arkady Klimov.

Science Fiction (PR:A MPAA:NR)

STORM RIDER, THE** (1957) 70m FOX bw

Scott Brady (*Jones*), Mala Powers (*Tay Rorick*), Bill Williams (*Coulton*), Olin Howlin (*Collins*), William Fawcett (*Cruikshank*), John Goddard (*Rorick*), Hank Patterson (*Milstead*), James Dobson (*Cooper*), John Close (*Forrest*), Jim Hayward (*Emery*), Cortland Shepard (*Flood*), Rocky Shahan (*Fred Feylan*), Frank Richards (*Will Feylan*), Rick Vallin (*Jack Feylan*), Ronald Foster (*Burns*), Tom London (*Todd*), Britt Wood (*Jake*), Al Baffert (*Blackie*), Rocky Lundy (*Bud Cooper*), John Cason (*Jasper*), Bud Osborne (*Toby*), Roy Engel (*Bonnard*), George Keymas (*Apache Kid*), Lane Chandler (*Doctor*), Jean Ann Lewis (*Mrs. Cooper*), Wayne Mallory (*Hanks*).

Brady stars as a hired gunman who is called upon by a small group of ranchers to protect them from the evils of a powerful rancher. He does so, but in the meantime falls in love with widow Powers, whose husband, Brady, was killed earlier, a fact she is unaware of. After his show of gunplay the ranchers can rest easy, and he moves on, leaving Powers and the memory of her husband behind.

p, Bernard Glasser; d, Edward Bernds; w, Bernds, Don Martin (based on a novel by L.L. Foreman); ph, Brydon Baker (Regalscope); m, Les Baxter; ed, John F. Link; art d, John Ushler.

Western (PR:A MPAA:NR)

STORM WARNING*** (1950) 93m WB bw

Ginger Rogers (*Marsha Mitchell*), Ronald Reagan (*Burt Rainey*), Doris Day (*Lucy Rice*), Steve Cochran (*Hank Rice*), Hugh Sanders (*Charlie Barr*), Lloyd Gough (*Cliff Rummel*), Raymond Greenleaf (*Faulkner*), Ned Glass (*George Athens*), Walter Baldwin (*Bledsoe*), Lynne Whitney (*Cora Athens*), Stuart Randall (*Walters*), Sean McClory (*Shore*), Paul E. Burns (*Hauser*), Dave McMahon (*Hollis*), Robert Williams (*Jaeger*), Charles Watts (*Wally*), Charles Phillips (*Bus Driver*), Dale Van Sickel (*Walter Adams*), Anthony Ward (*Juke Box Collector*), Paul Brinegar, Tom Wells (*Cameramen*), King Donovan (*Ambulance Driver*), Len Hendry, Ned Davenport (*Cops*), Frank Marlowe (*Al the Bus Driver*), Charles Marsh (*Fowler*), Lillian Albertson (*Mrs. Rainey*), Eddie Hearn (*Mr. Rainey*), Harry Harvey (*Mr. Louden*), Janet Barrett (*Mrs. Adams*), Walter Bacon (*Jury Foreman*), Norman Field, Don Dillaway, Michael McHale (*Converts*), Dewey Robinson, Gene Evans (*Klansmen*), Dick Anderson, Lloyd Jenkins, (*Interns*), Mary Alan Hokanson (*Secretary*), Fern Berry (*Wife*), Dabbs Greer (*Attendant*), Grandon Rhodes (*Pike*), Charles Conrad (*Jordan*), Alex Gerry (*Basset*), Leo Cleary (*Barnet*), Tommy Walker (*Bob*).

Rogers is a high fashion model from New York City who decides to pay a visit to her sister, Day, in a small southern town. Upon arrival, Rogers accidentally witnesses a group of Klansmen as they raid the local jail, spring a prisoner, then kill the man. Two men, Cochran and Sanders, remove their pointed hoods and Rogers gets a clear view of their faces. She finally arrives at Day's home, where to her horror Rogers discovers Cochran is her sister's husband. Day, who is expecting a child, pleads with her sister, telling Rogers to forget about what she has seen. She reluctantly acquiesces, but Reagan, the local district attorney, learns he has a witness to the crime. He subpoenas Rogers, counting on her testimony to destroy local Klan activity. Rogers, however, keeps her promise to Day and refuses to identify any of the men brought before the court. The Klansmen are jubilant, and after a booze-filled victory party, Cochran makes a pass at his sister-in-law as she prepares to return to New York. Day tries to stop him, and Cochran responds by striking both women. Rogers, who knows Cochran is the killer, realizes she cannot let this go on. After deciding to turn in Cochran, Rogers is kidnaped and taken to a Klan meeting. Sanders pronounces that Rogers will be whipped, then thrown out of the community, with promises of further beatings should she talk. Before the Klan members carry out the flogging, Day arrives bringing with her Reagan and a horde of policemen. Though the men are all cloaked in their Ku Klux Klan robes, Reagan is able to identify many of them. Sanders suddenly spills his story to the district attorney, telling Reagan that Cochran killed the man Rogers saw murdered by the KKK. Cochran fires at the traitorous Sanders, but misses him, shooting Day instead. The police fire back, killing Cochran, while Sanders is taken into custody. STORM WARNING is an intelligent film, marked by the strong performances of the ensemble. Day, in her first non-musical, proves to be a fine dramatic actress, showing a range many thought she was incapable of. She is well matched by Cochran, as her bigoted, sick-minded spouse, and Rogers as Day's sister. Rogers' part originally was intended for Lauren Bacall, who declined the role when she decided to join her husband, Humphrey Bogart, on the African location of his film THE AFRICAN QUEEN. Reagan is effective as the public defender concerned with the common good. He is earnest without being self-righteous, determined to see the Klan wiped out in his community. This was shot on location in Corona, California, which the producers felt embodied everything expected of a quintessential small American town. Corona's layout was ideal for the filmmakers, with several important buildings–such as the library and a church–centered in the city's downtown area. Filming took place shortly after Christmas and the producers insisted Corona's officials keep up the holiday decorations. This added to the all-American ambiance the producers wanted, making the darker side all the more frightening. Ironically, the mythical town depicted here was not that far removed from the truth. Located near a major prison, Corona was long rumored to be a hotbed for Ku Klux Klan activity. At one point, the future President of the United States was approached by one of Corona's townsmen, who claimed to be a member of the local Klan chapter. He told Reagan his group had plenty of available robes should the production company need to rent extra costumes. Though the drama is well built and sincerely acted, STORM WARNING has one particularly glaring omission. Despite the film's subject matter and setting, there is not a single black character in the story. Filming a story about the Ku Klux Klan while ignoring blacks was akin to shooting THE DIARY OF ANNE FRANK without any Jewish characters. Audiences noticed considerable stylistic similarities to another picture made by Warner Bros., and released to much acclaim during the same year, A STREETCAR NAMED DESIRE.

p, Jerry Wald; d, Stuart Heisler; w, Daniel Fuchs, Richard Brooks (based on their story "Storm Center"); ph, Carl Guthrie; m, Daniele Amfitheatrof; ed, Clarence Kolster; md, Ray Heindorf; art d, Leo K. Kuter; set d, G.W. Berntsen; cos, Milo Anderson; makeup, Perc Westmore, Frank Westmore.

Drama   **(PR:C-O MPAA:NR)**

STORM WITHIN, THE (SEE: LES PARENTS TERRIBLES, 1950, Fr.)

STORMBOUND* (1951, Ital.) 60m REP bw

Constance Dowling (Barbara), Andrea Checchi (Rol), Aldo Silvani (Marco), Blanca Doria (Maria), Mirko Ellis (Stefano), Tino Buazzelli (Sergeant), Paola Quattrini (Nina).

An inconsequential Italian import which has Dowling in the role of a news reporter who gets stuck in a shack during a storm with an infamous bandit who grants her an interview. A claustrophobic and overly talky entry. Dubbed into English.

p, Aldo Raciti; d, Luigi Capuano; w, Comenico Meccoli, Fulvio Palmieri, Corrado Pavolini (based on the story by Capuano); ph, Gabor Pogany; m, Alessandro Cicognini; ed, Robert M. Leeds.

Drama   **(PR:A MPAA:NR)**

STORMY* (1935) 68m UNIV bw

Noah Beery, Jr, (Stormy), Jean Rogers (Kerry Dorn), J. Farrell MacDonald (Trinidad Dorn), Fred Kohler, Sr, Walter Miller (Craig), James P. Burtis (Greasy), Charles Hunter, L.F. Costello, Curtis McPeters, Cal Short, John Jackson, Glenn Strange, John Luther (The Arizona Wranglers), Bud Osborne, Kenny Cooper, James Phillips, Jack Sanders, Jack Leonard, Monte Montague, Jack Shannon (Cowboys), Cecil Kellogg (Lark), Robert E.

Homans (Conductor), Wilfred Lucas (Horse Trainer), Samuel R. McDaniel (Hostler), Eddie Cobb (Brakeman), Charles Murphy (Bartender), James Welch (Boy), Shirley Marks (Girl), Chester Gan (Chinaman), William Welsh (Old Miner), W.H. Davis (Dear Man), Jack Kirk, Chuck Baldra, Rex the Wonder Horse.

The young Beery gets thrown from a train carrying a race horse and its colt, only to discover later that the train was wrecked. He befriends the young colt and becomes the only person who can even get near it. Beery finds himself in the middle of a conflict between two brothers--one who wants to save the colt and its pack of wild horses, the other who wants to make money from them. Eventually the kid charms the brothers into seeing things the right way.

p, Henry MacRae; d, Louis Friedlander [Lew Landers]; w, George H. Plympton, Ben G. Kohn (based on the story by Cherry Wilson); ph, Dick Fryer, William Sickner, John Hixon; ed, Saul Goodkind.

Drama   **(PR:A MPAA:NR)**

STORMY CROSSING* (1958, Brit.) 72m Tempean/Eros bw (AKA: BLACK TIDE)

John Ireland (Griff Parker), Derek Bond (Paul Seymour), Leslie Dwyer (Bill Harris), Maureen Connell (Shelley Baxter), Sheldon Lawrence (Danny Parker), Sam Rockett (Himself), Jack Taylor (Navigator), Joy Webster (Kitty Tyndall), Cameron Hall (Doctor), Arthur Lowe, John Horsley (Inspector Parry).

Substandard crime drama has Webster a model and cross-channel swimmer drowned by her oily manager (Bond) during her swim as he tries to keep their affair from his wife. Webster's other lover, fellow channel swimmer Lawrence, is suspicious and Bond tries the same scheme. It fails this time and the police close in. Silly plot in spite of the novel background, and badly pulled off.

p, Monty Berman; d, C. Pennington-Richards; w, Brock Williams (based on a story by Sid Harris, Lou Dyer); ph, Geoffrey Faithfull; m, Stanley Black; ed, Doug Myers.

Crime   **(PR:A-C MPAA:NR)**

STORMY TRAILS* (1936) 58m Colony-GN bw

Rex Bell (Tom Storm), Bob Hodges (Billy Storm), Lois Wilde (Connie Curlew), Lane Chandler (Dunn), Earl Dwire (Stephen Varick), Lloyd Ingraham (Curlew), Karl Hackett (Durante), Earl Ross (Thurman), Murdock McQuarrie (Sheriff), Roger Williams (Daniels), Jimmy Aubrey (Shives), Chuck Morrison, George Morrell.

Bell has to fight off a malevolent gang who will try anything to get their hands on his property. When they attempt to pin a murder rap on him, he fights back and brings the bandits to justice. Chock full o' gunslingin' and fistfightin'.

p, Arthur Alexander, Max Alexander; d, Sam Newfield; w, Phil Dunham (based on the story "Stampede" by E.B. Mann); ed, Charles Henkel.

Western   **(PR:A MPAA:NR)**

STORMY WATERS** (1946, Fr.) 77m Sedis/MGM bw (REMORQUES)

Jean Gabin (Laurent), Michele Morgan (Catherine), Madeleine Renaud (Yvonne), Blavette (Tanguy), Jean Marchat (Captain of Mirva), Fernand Ledoux (Bosco).

An insightful look at passion and fidelity set at sea with Gabin masterfully playing a tugboat captain. He carries on with Morgan after rescuing her from the stormy waters, but soon learns that his wife is near death. He stays at his wife's bedside until she dies, thinking that he was eternally faithful to her. Released in Paris in 1941, the picture was begun in 1939, but because of Gremillon's insistence on documentary storm footage and the restrictions of the Nazi Occupation, production had to be held up. The film was eventually completed in the studio, with Gremillon getting only a few of the realistic scenes he had hoped for. (In French; English subtitles.)

d, Jean Gremillon; w, Jacques Prevert, Andre Cayatte (based on the novel by Roger Vercel); ph, Armand Thirard, Louis Nee; m, Roland-Manuel; ed, Louisette Hautecoeur; art d, Alexander Trauner.

Romance   **(PR:A MPAA:NR)**

STORMY WEATHER** (1935, Brit.) 74m Gainsborough/GAU bw

Tom Walls (Sir Duncan Craggs), Ralph Lynn (Mr. Penny), Yvonne Arnaud (Louise Craggs), Robertson Hare (Mr. Bullock), Andrews Engelmann (Polotsky), Stella Moya (Moya), Gordon James (Salt Jasper), Louis Bradfield (Lacey), Fewlass Llewellyn (Pullman), Peter Gawthorne (Inspector), Graham Mofatt (Office Boy).

Surprisingly funny comedy starring Walls as a wealthy businessman who, accompanied by employees Lynn and Hare, travels to Chinatown in search of new business ventures. There he discovers that his wife's ex-husband,

Engelmann, is a notorious crook who intends to blackmail him. Determined to fight back, Walls sets out to destroy Engelmann and his evil empire, all done for laughs of course.

p, Michael Balcon; d, Tom Walls; w, Ben Travers (based on his play); ph, Philip Tannura; cos, Joe Strassner.

Comedy   **(PR:A MPAA:NR)**

STORMY WEATHER*½   (1943) 77m FOX bw

Lena Horne (*Selina Rogers*), Bill Robinson (*Corky*), Cab Calloway and Band (*Themselves*), Katherine Dunham and Her Troupe (*Themselves*), Fats Waller (*Fats*), Nicholas Bros (*Themselves*), Ada Brown (*Ada*), Dooley Wilson (*Gabe*), The Tramp Band (*Themselves*), Net Stanfield, Johnny Horace (*The Shadracks*), Babe Wallace (*Chick Bailey*), Ernest Whitman (*Jim Europe*), Zuttie Singleton (*Zuttie*), Mae E. Johnson (*Mae*), Flournoy E. Miller (*Miller*), Johnnie Lee (*Lyles*), Robert Felder (*Cab Calloway, Jr.*), Nicodemus Stewart (*Chauffeur*).

An amazing and important movie with an all-black cast, STORMY WEATH-ER is a cinematic document that has just about every living black musical star in it so it will be studied by movie buffs for years. The slim story is about Robinson, who is celebrating his career in show business that began in 1911. The action takes place between that year and 1936 and a magazine called Theatre World is used in flashback. Robinson sees the various ads and tributes to him and each one jolts his memory to the people who took the ads. He turns the pages and there are a number of small scenes, unrelated to each other, all of which are neat musical bits on their own and a few were later released as short subjects in black theaters. Robinson is seen in his struggles, his rise, his relationship with wife Horne, and their split and eventual reconciliation. In between this thin outline are a cavalcade of musical numbers from many writers. About the only person who doesn't sing is Dooley Wilson, and that was a mistake as his singing was so important in CASABLANCA and audiences just expected to hear him. Tunes include: "There's No Two Ways About Love" (Ted Koehler, Irving Mills, James P. Johnson, performed by Cab Calloway, Bill Robinson, Lena Horne), "Stormy Weather" (Harold Arlen, Koehler, sung by Horne, danced by Katherine Dunham and Her Troupe), "Ain't Misbehavin'" (Fats Waller, Andy Razaf, Harry Brooks, sung by Waller), "Rhythm Cocktail," (Calloway, performed by Robinson and Calloway), "Rang Tang Tang" (Cyril Mockridge, sung by Robinson, children), "Dat, Dot, Dah" (Mockridge, performed by Babe Wallace, The Tramp Band), "That Ain't Right" (Irving Mills, Nat "King" Cole, sung by Waller, Ada Brown), "I Can't Give You Anything But Love, Baby" (Dorothy Fields, Jimmy McHugh, performed by Horne, Robinson), "Digga Digga Doo" (Fields, McHugh, sung by Horne, chorus), "I Lost My Sugar in Salt Lake City" (Leon Rene, Johnny Lange, sung by Mae Johnson), "Geechy Joe" (Andy Gibson, Jack Palmer, sung by Calloway), "Jumpin' Jive" (Palmer, Calloway, Frank Froeba, performed by the Nicholas Brothers), "My, My, Ain't That Somethin'?" (Harry Tobias, Pinky Tomlin, performed by Robinson, reprised by Horne, Calloway, Nicholas Brothers). Some old classics as well, including "De Camptown Races" (Stephen Foster), "At a Georgia Camp Meeting" (Kerry Mills), "Linda Brown" (Al Cowans), "Nobody's Sweetheart" (Billy Meyers, Elmer Schoebel, Ernie Erdman, Gus Kahn), "Beale Street Blues" and "Basin Street Blues" (both sung by Wallace). Horne was a youngster, just 26. She had recently finished CABIN IN THE SKY and her star was already well in the heavens. Robinson was 65 and had been a legend for years. The fact that he was old enough to be her grandfather never entered into things and was conveniently overlooked. Publisher-writer Irving Mills had been at the forefront of handling music by black composers and he is listed as "production advisor" so it can be assumed that he had a great deal to do with the behind-the-scenes movements that must be done to assemble such a huge and stellar cast of talents. Jazz fans will recognize Zutty Singleton at the drums, Coleman Hawkins playing sax, Taps Miller on trumpet, and several others.

p, William LeBaron; d, Andrew Stone; w, Frederick Jackson, Ted Koehler, H.S. Kraft (based on a story by Jerry Horwin, Seymour B. Robinson); ph, Leon Shamroy; ed, James B. Clark; md, Emil Newman; art d, James Basevi, Joseph C. Wright; cos, Helen Rose; spec eff, Fred Sersen; ch, Clarence Robinson.

Musical   **Cas.**   **(PR:A MPAA:NR)**

STORY OF A CHEAT, THE**   (1938, Fr.) 83m Cineas/Gallic bw (LE
                                                       ROMAN D'UN TRICHEUR)

Sacha Guitry (*The Cheat*), Jacqueline Delubac (*Young Woman*), Rosine Derean (*The Jewel Thief*), Marguerite Moreno (*The Countess*), Pauline Carton (*Mme. Morlot, the Cousin*), Gaston Dupray (*Waiter*), Serge Grave (*The Cheat, as a Child*), Pierre Assy (*The Cheat, as a Young Man*), Frehel (*Singer*), Henri Pfeifer (*M. Charbonnier*), Pierre Labry (*M. Morlot*), Elmire Vautier (*Vautier*).

An exciting, funny, innovative, and brilliant effort from one of France's most prolific playwrights and filmmakers, Sacha Guitry. Correctly considered to be Guitry's masterpiece, THE STORY OF A CHEAT is just that–a story about a cheat, told to the audience by the cheat (Guitry, as usual, playing the role). He tells us the story while he is writing his memoirs at a Parisian cafe, while on the screen we see the events he is speaking of, acted out

without dialog. All we get to hear is Guitry's witty commentary. His life story begins with the first time he is caught being a cheat, an act which gets him sent to his room without supper. In a stroke of luck, however, his entire family eats poison mushrooms that evening and dies. Thus begins a long string of events in which Guitry benefits from his cheating instead of paying for it. Not only is the film itself unique, with its cutting back and forth between past and present, and its use of reverse motion and wipes, but its title sequence is also exceptional. Like Francois Truffaut's FAHRENHEIT 451, the credits are spoken by the director, but here we see the characters and filmmakers involved. Not surprisingly, his experimentation and humor have gone on to influence greatly those who've seen the picture, especially the filmmakers of the New Wave. It was chiefly the favorable criticism of filmmakers such as Truffaut, Jean-Luc Godard, and Alain Resnais (who cited THE STORY OF A CHEAT as one of the primary influences of HIROSHIMA MON AMOUR) that have brought about the reassessment of Guitry. An outstanding contribution to cinematic and narrative technique which Guitry never quite equaled again. Released in Paris in 1936.

d&w, Sacha Guitry (based on his novel *Memoires D'un Tricheur*); ph, Marcel Lucien; m, Adolph Borchard; ed, Myriam.

Drama   **(PR:O MPAA:NR)**

STORY OF A CITIZEN ABOVE ALL SUSPICION
    (SEE: INVESTIGATION OF A CITIZEN ABOVE SUSPICION, 1970,
                                                                        Ital.)

STORY OF A DRAFT DODGER
    (SEE: WINDFLOWERS, THE STORY OF A DRAFT DODGER, 1968)

STORY OF A LOVE STORY (SEE: IMPOSSIBLE OBJECT, 1973, Fr.)

STORY OF A TEENAGER   (SEE: JIM, THE WORLD'S GREATEST,
                                                                        1976)

STORY OF A THREE DAY PASS, THE*½   (1968, Fr.) 87m
                                  O.P.E.R.A./Sigma III bw (FR: LA PERMISSION)

Harry Baird (*Turner*), Nicole Berger (*Miriam*), Christian Marin (*Hotelman*), Pierre Doris (*Peasant*), Hal Brav, Tria French.

An impressive first feature from Melvin Van Peebles has a black American soldier, Baird, stationed in France and visiting Paris on a three-day pass. He meets and falls for a French girl, Berger, and together they spend his last two days living a poetically romantic existence. Upon his return, he is demoted by his captain for having dated a white girl. The film is a moving and brutally honest achievement from Van Peebles, who moved to Paris after living in San Francisco, Mexico, and Holland. He started in Paris (without speaking the language) as an author, eventually writing in French and becoming eligible for admission to the French Cinema Center as a director. He then applied for a grant and unexpectedly received $70,000 after expecting no more than $10,000. With a completed film, Van Peebles went back to the U.S. as a French filmmaker, confusing and surprising everyone when they learned he was actually a black American. Actress Berger, who also appeared in Francois Truffaut's SHOOT THE PIANO PLAYER, was killed just a short time after completing this picture.

p, Guy Belfond; d&w, Melvin Van Peebles; ph, Michael Kelber; m, Mickey Baker, Van Peebles; ed, Liliane Korb; set d, Yves Decaux.

Drama   **(PR:O MPAA:NR)**

STORY OF A WOMAN*   (1970, U.S./Ital.) 90m Westward/UNIV c
                                                      (STORIA DI UNA DONNA)

Bibi Andersson (*Karin Ullman*), Robert Stack (*David Frasier*), James Farentino (*Bruno Cardini*), Annie Girardot (*Liliana Cardini*), Frank Sundstrom (*Karin's Father*), Didi Perego (*Bruno's Girlfriend*), Francesco Mule (*Manzetti*), Birgitta Valberg (*Karin's Mother*), Cathy Riney (*Cathy*), Beppe Wolgers (*Mr. Fahlen*), Ingella Rossell (*Mrs. Fahlen*), Toiwo Pawlo (*Mr. Rushenkov*), Elsa Vazzoler (*Luisa*), Pippo Starnazza (*Mario*), Gisella Sofio (*Mrs. Curtis*), Diana Lante (*Ambassador's Wife*), Anna Liotti (*Nadia*), Mario Nascimbene (*Prof. Ferrara*), Erika Rosell (*Sissi*), Marco Raviart (*TV Announcer*).

A mindless love triangle has Andersson as a piano student who falls for Farentino, then Stack, then Farentino again, but in the meantime has wed Stack. By the time we make it to the teary finale Andersson is telling Farentino she plans to return to her husband, causing the jilted fellow to drive his car off a cliff. Andersson, who has demonstrated so often with Bergman that she is an actress of great gifts, is simply led through this one as if any one could have played the part, but she just happened to be there.

p,d&w, Leonardo Bercovici; ph, Piero Portalupi (Technicolor); m, Johnny Williams; ed, Milton Shifman; art d, Alexander Golitzen, Aurelio Crugnola; set d, John McCarthy, Franco Fumagalli; cos, Edith Head; m/l, "Uno di Qua, L'Altra di La," Williams, A. Amurri (sung by Ornella Vanoni); makeup, Bud Westmore, Guiseppe Banchelli, Cesare Gambarelli.

Drama   **(PR:O MPAA:R)**

STORY OF ADELE H., THE****　　　(1975, Fr.) 97m Les Films du Carrosse-Artistes Associates/New World c (L'HISTOIRE D'ADELE H.)

Isabelle Adjani (Adele Hugo), Bruce Robinson (Lt. Albert Pinson), Sylvia Marriott (Mrs. Saunders), Reubin Dorey (Mr. Saunders), Joseph Blatchley (Mr. Whistler), M. White (Col. White), Carl Hathwell (Lt. Pinson's Batman), Ivry Gitlis (The Hypnotist), Sir Cecil De Sausmarez (Mr. Lenoir), Sir Raymond Falla (Judge Johnstone), Roger Martin (Dr. Murdock), Madame Louise (Mme. Baa), Jean-Pierre Leursse (The Scribe), Francois Truffaut (Officer On Ramparts).

A hauntingly poetic tale of obsession which stars Adjani as the daughter of Victor Hugo, France's most beloved author. The picture opens in Halifax, Nova Scotia in 1863 after Adjani has left her father's Guernsey home in order to seek out her fiance Robinson, a young English lieutenant. She boards in a house owned by Marriott, but keeps her Hugo heritage a secret. When she finally tracks down Robinson she is shocked to learn that he has no intention of marrying her and, in fact, wants nothing to do with her. Her obsession for him grows. She writes to her father asking for more money. The money is sent, and along with it is a plea for her to return home. She only focuses more deeply on her beloved lieutenant – spying on him while he makes love to another woman, following him (or people she believes to be him) in the streets, and even printing a marriage notice in the French papers. Hugo is pleased to learn of her wedding plans, but is soon informed by Robinson that they are completely fabricated. Adjani is not only obsessed with Robinson, but with writing letters and journals. She pays frequent visits to a local bookstore where she buys reams of paper, and romantic interest sparks in a well-meaning book clerk. She retreats to her room and scrawls, indecipherably, in her journal, pouring her ideals of love onto the page. Before long Marriott discovers that Adjani is the daughter of Victor Hugo, but this recognition offends Adjani, who is trying to separate herself from her father. She feels that she cannot live up to his expectations – that she cannot fill the void that was left when her sister Leopoldine drowned tragically at the age of nineteen. She goes even further off the deep end when the book clerk presents her with a copy of Hugo's latest work Les Miserables. When Robinson is transferred to Barbados, Adjani follows, consumed by her desire. Her physical and mental condition deteriorating, she lives in the streets and with the vagrants in shelters. Detached from the real world, she wanders around in the distance dressed in a morbid black cape. When she finally stumbles upon Robinson, she fails to notice him, passing by in a trance. With the help of an illiterate and motherly native woman, Madame Louise, Adjani is returned home to Guernsey. Shortly thereafter, Hugo returns to Paris from exile with his daughter who would live there for 40 years, "playing the piano and writing her diary in code." One of Truffaut's most complex films, THE STORY OF ADELE H. combines the obsessive women that fill his films (Catherine from JULES AND JIM, Julie Kohler from THE BRIDE WORE BLACK, and Camille Bliss from SUCH A GORGEOUS KID LIKE ME) with his love of books, diaries, and the process of writing (FAHRENHEIT 451 and THE WILD CHILD). Based on a book by Frances V. Guille, who discovered Adele Hugo's diaries in 1955, THE STORY OF ADELE H. caught Truffaut's interest for the same reason that Dr. Jean Itard's memoirs were turned into THE WILD CHILD (1969). Truffaut wrote: "I had been fascinated by the creative process of using real-life events as the basis for a fiction story that would not distort the authenticity of the source material." After setting his sights on this project, Truffaut contacted Victor Hugo's estate. Permission was finally granted, but only under the condition that Hugo not be physically represented on the screen. Adjani earned herself a Best Actress nomination from the Motion Picture Academy in 1975, but lost to Louise Fletcher for her role in ONE FLEW OVER THE CUCKOO'S NEST. (In French and English; English subtitles).

p, Marcel Berbert; d, Francois Truffaut; w, Truffaut, Jean Gruault, Suzanne Schiffman, Jan Dawson (English adaptation) (based on the book Le Journal d'Adele Hugo by Frances V. Guille); ph, Nestor Almendros (Eastmancolor); m, Maurice Jaubert; ed, Yann Dedet; md, Patrice Mestral; art d, Jean-Pierre Kohut-Svelko; cos, Jacqueline Guyot; English trans, Helen G. Scott.

Drama　　　　　　　Cas.　　　　(PR:C-O MPAA:PG)

STORY OF ALEXANDER GRAHAM BELL, THE***½
　　　(1939) 97m FOX bw (GB: THE MODERN MIRACLE RACLE)

Don Ameche (Alexander Graham Bell), Loretta Young (Mrs. Bell), Henry Fonda (Tom Watson), Charles Coburn (Gardner Hubbard), Spring Byington (Mrs. Hubbard), Gene Lockhart (Thomas Sanders), Sally Blane (Gertrude Hubbard), Polly Ann Young (Grace Hubbard), Georgiana Young (Berta Hubbard), Bobs Watson (George Sanders, Jr.), Russell Hicks (Barrows), Paul Stanton (Chauncey Smith), Jonathan Hale (President of Western Union), Harry Davenport (Judge), Beryl Mercer (Queen Victoria), Elizabeth Patterson (Mrs. McGregor), Charles Trowbridge (George Pollard), Claire DuBrey (Landlady), Ralph Remley (D'Arcy), Zeffie Tilbury (Mrs. Sanders), Jan Duggan (Mrs. Winthrop), Harry Tyler (Doc Elliott), Lillian West (Nurse), Warren Jackson, Tyler Brooke (Singers), George Guhl (Mr. Winthrop), Mary Field (Piano Player), William Wagner (Bit), Dave Morris (Telegrapher), Jack Kelly (Banker's Son), Edmund Elton (Banker), Jarold Clifford Lyons (Infant), Landers Stevens (Manager of North Eastern Telephone Exchange), John Spacey (Sir John Cowell), Dick Elliott (Man Who Laughs), Jack Walsh (James J. Starrow), Charles Tannen (Court Clerk), Otto Hoffman (Pawnbroker).

It was only a fair movie but it's the one that Don Ameche will be most remembered for, despite having won an Oscar for COCOON more than 40 years later. It became so popular that his name became synonymous with the telephone and more than once scenes were shown in movies where someone said "Answer the Ameche" when the phone rang. A straightforward biography with some alterations to enhance the dramatic value, the movie was helped a good deal by Fonda, in a third-billed role. Fonda added some levity to Ameche's serious portrayal of the Scotsman who came to Boston to teach speech to deaf people, thus following in the footsteps of his father, who had pioneered the technique. It opens in 1873 as Ameche is trying to earn his living with mutes while spending his off-hours inventing. Wealthy Bostonite Coburn comes to Ameche and asks if the Scot could help teach his daughter how to speak. Ameche agrees, then meets the young woman and is happy to discover that she is the comely Young. (There are four sisters in Loretta's family and the other three were all in this movie. Georgianna and Polly Ann used their own names while Sally Blane didn't.) Young and Ameche fall in love and she asks her father to unbuckle his copious money belt to back one of her lover's inventions. Ameche hopes to perfect a process whereby he can use the same kind of wires Western Union uses for transmitting dots and dashes and, with any luck, send the sound of a human voice through them. With a few bucks on which to operate, Ameche hires the boyish Fonda as his aide and the two men work feverishly in the attic above Ameche's classroom. In between the long days and nights of inventing, Ameche asks Coburn for Young's hand but the old man is against it. Ameche is discouraged as his invention doesn't seem to be functioning. He decides to give it all up and devote himself fully to teaching. He writes Young a note to this effect on the back side of the dated plans he's drawn for his invention. When she reads it, Young is furious that he would give up without fighting to the finish. She convinces him that it's worth continuing. Ameche sighs, calls for Fonda, and the two men resume their labors. One day, Fonda is in another room when Ameche accidentally spills some acid on the transmitter. When a bit of the searing stuff also hits his leg, Ameche shouts "Mr. Watson] Come here, I want you." Fonda races in from the next room where the receiver is. He tells Ameche that he didn't hear him shout as the door was closed, but he did hear him over the receiver. The two men are startled and get to work again on the invention that was to become the telephone. Coburn now gives his okay for the couple to wed and advances Ameche more money to continue his inventing and the perfecting of the telephone. Western Union, which had a patent on the wires, sues Ameche and claims that they invented the phone. It looks bad for Ameche in court until Young arrives with the note he wrote on the telephone designs. Since the paper was dated, the court finds for Ameche. And that's how monopolies are born. The real story is that Bell was visiting his parents in Ontario when he got the idea. Later, he heard the sound of a plucked string 60 feet long in the workshop of Charles Williams. Watson pulled the string while trying to activate a harmonic telegraph transmitter. That was June, 1875. In June 1876, Bell showed it at the Philadelphia Exposition to Brazilian Emperor Dom Pedro, who leaped out of his seat yelling "I hear, I hear." By mid-October, Bell and Watson, using a borrowed telegraph line between Boston and Cambridge, had a three-hour conversation. Bell offered to sell his phone to Western Union but the company's president, William Orton, thought it was a "toy" and turned down the $100,000 price. Later, Western Union hired Thomas Edison to make improvements on the device. The first telephones were sold to the public in May, 1877, and by August there were more than 750 in homes and businesses. The company was owned by Bell, his father-in-law (30 percent each) with 30 percent to investor Tom Sanders who put up some of the early money. Watson received 10 percent and the company was on its way to becoming the largest in the world.

p, Darryl F. Zanuck; Kenneth MacGowan; d, Irving Cummings; w, Lamar Trotti (based on a story by Ray Harris); ph, Leon Shamroy; ed, Walter Thompson; md, Louis Silvers; cos, Royer.

Biography　　　　　　Cas.　　　　(PR:AA MPAA:NR)

STORY OF ARNOLD ROTHSTEIN
　(SEE: KING OF THE ROARING 20'S, THE STORY OF ARNOLD ROTHSTEIN, 1961)

STORY OF CINDERELLA, THE　　(SEE: SLIPPER AND THE ROSE, THE, 1976, Brit.)

STORY OF DAVID, A**　　　(1960, Brit.) 104m Scoton-Mardeb/BL c

Jeff Chandler (David), Basil Sydney (Saul), Peter Arne (Doeg), David Knight (Johnathan), Barbara Shelley (Abigail), Donald Pleasence (Nabal), Robert Brown (Jashobeam), Richard O'Sullivan (Abiathar), David Davies (Abner), Martin Wyldeck (Hezro), John van Eyssen (Joab), Angela Browne (Michal), Zena Marshall (Naomi), Charles Carson (Ahimelech).

A rather dull religious epic starring Chandler as the legendary title character whose famed trials and tribulations are detailed here without much flair or excitement. Originally shot for television, the film was released theatrically instead. Though far from being a memorable examination of David, it's better than the 1985 flop KING DAVID starring Richard Gere.

p, George Pitcher; d, Bob McNaught; w, Gerry Day, Terence Maple.

Drama **(PR:A MPAA:NR)**

STORY OF DR. EHRLICH'S MAGIC BULLET, THE
(SEE: DR. EHRLICH'S MAGIC BULLET, 1940)

STORY OF DR. WASSELL, THE*** (1944) 140m PAR c

Gary Cooper *(Dr. Corydon M. Wassell)*, Laraine Day *(Madeline)*, Signe Hasso *(Bettina)*, Dennis O'Keefe *("Hoppy" Hopkins)*, Carol Thurston *(Tremartini)*, Carl Esmond *(Lt. Dirk van Daal)*, Paul Kelly *(Murdock)*, Elliott Reid *("Andy" Anderson)*, Stanley Ridges *(Comdr. Bill Goggins)*, Renny McEvoy *(Johnny)*, Oliver Thorndike *(Alabam)*, Philip Ahn *(Ping)*, Barbara Britton *(Ruth)*, Melvin Francis *(Francis)*, Joel Allen *(Kraus)*, James Millican *(Whaley)*, Mike Kilian *(Boranetti)*, Doodles Weaver *(Hunter)*, Lester Mathews *(Dr. Ralph Wayne)*, Ludwig Donath *(Dr. Vranken)*, Richard Loo *(Dr. Wei)*, Davison Clark *(Dr. Holmes)*, Richard Nugent *(Capt. Carruthers)*, Morton Lowry *(Lt. Bainbridge)*, George Macready *(Capt. Blaen)*, Victor Varconi *(Capt. Ryk)*, Edward Fielding *(Adm. Hart)*, Harvey Stephens *(Captain in Charge of Evacuation)*, Frank Wilcox *(Captain's Aide for Evacuation)*, Minor Watson *(Rear Admiral-Australian)*, Edmund MacDonald *(Rear Admiral's Aide)*, William Severn *(Little English Boy)*, Edith Barrett *(Mother of Little English Boy)*, Catherine Craig *(Mrs. Wayne)*, Frank Puglia *(Javanese Temple Guide)*, Si Jenks *(Arkansas Mail Carrier)*, Irving Bacon *(Missionary)*, Ottola Nesmith *(Missionary's Wife)*, Sybil Merritt *(Javanese Girl)*, Maria Loredo *(Fat Javanese Girl)*, Loretta Luiz *(Pretty Javanese Girl)*, Luke Chan *(Chinese Coolie-Boatman)*, Oie Chan *(Chinese Coolie's Wife)*, Yu Feng Sung *(Chinese Priest)*, Moy Ming *(Chinese Tea Vendor)*, Hugh Beaumont *(Adm. Hart's Aide)*, Roy Gordon *(Commander, U.S. Navy)*, Ferdinand Schumann *(Ensign Watch Officer, U.S. Navy)*, Charles Trowbridge, Gus Glassmire *(Captains, U.S. Navy, Surabaya)*, Edward Earle, Allan Ray *(Officers, U.S. Navy, Surabaya)*, Anthony Caruso *(Pharmacist's Mate)*, Sven Hugo Borg *(Dutch Guard)*, Frank Lackteen *(Javanese Conductor)*, Fred Kohler, Jr. *(Bosun's Mate--Evacuation)*, Jack Luden *(Capt. Carruther's Driver)*, George Eldredge *(Damage Control Officer, U.S. Navy)*, Forbes Murray *(Captain, U.S. Navy--Australia)*, Mary Currier *(English Woman)*, John Mylong *(Joyful Passenger)*, Ann Doran *(Praying Woman)*, Stanley Price *(Sobbing Man)*, Maxine Fife, Ameda Lambert, Carla Boehm, Phyllis Perry, Marion de Sydow *(Women Evacuees)*, Gloria Dea, Forrest Dickson, Geraldine Fisette *(Javanese Nurses)*, Eric Alden, Richard Barrett, John Benson, Carlyle Blackwell, John Bogden, George Bronson, Edgar Caldwell, Tony Cirillo, James Cornell, James Courtney, Clint Dorrington, Reynold DuPont, Edward Howard, Henry Kraft, Buddy Messinger, Robert Wilbur *(U.S. Sailors)*, Yvonne De Carlo *(Native Girl)*, Jack Norton *(Man Passenger-- Companionway)*, Mike Lally *(Civilian)*, Sam Flint, Milton Kibbee, Hazel Keener, Cecil Weston, Frances Morris, *(Passengers--Janssens)*, Frank Elliott *(English Doctor)*, Rodric Redwing, Roque Espiritu, Joe Dominguez, Joe Bautista *(Javanese Orderlies)*, Russ Clark *(Chief Petty Officer--Marblehead)*, Douglas Fowley, Miles Mander, Isabel Cooper, Griff Barnett, Lane Chandler, Isabel Lamal *(Bits)*, Julia Faye *(Anne, Dutch Nurse)*, Sarah Edwards, Ron Randell *(Passengers)*, Elmo Lincoln.

Cooper plays a real-life hero in this Cecil B. DeMille contribution to the war effort. Cooper is Dr. Corydon M. Wassell, a missionary doctor in China, and after the outbreak of hostilities, a naval doctor stationed in Java. In the Japanese overrun of that island, he is placed in charge of evacuating the wounded. In the end, as the front is collapsing on all sides, he is told to leave the stretcher cases behind. He disobeys and takes nine badly wounded men across the island by train, fighting most of the way, then forces his way aboard one of the last ships out, which then barely escapes a Japanese blockade that claims a Dutch passenger ship filled with refugees who are also rescued. When he arrives with the wounded in Australia, Cooper fully expects to be court-martialed, but instead he is awarded with the Navy Cross. DeMille was listening to the radio on May 26, 1942, during one of then-President Franklin D. Roosevelt's "Fireside Chats," when the President told the story of Dr. Wassell and his heroic act. As soon as Roosevelt finished DeMille got a phone call from his own publicity man, who asked if DeMille had heard, and told him it would be a great subject for a film. DeMille agreed and set to work. His men tracked down Wassell and got his cooperation in return for $50,000 against ten percent of the gross, all of it to go to the Navy Relief Fund. Then they ran down all the men whom Wassell had saved and got their testimony (one of the men, Melvin Francis, was actually signed to play himself in the film). Novelist James Hilton (*Lost Horizon*) then was given the raw material to make a fictional narrative from which a script was then adapted, Hilton's narrative later emerging itself in book form. The jungle scenes were shot largely in Mexico, with the Mexican army filling in for the Japanese. (DeMille had also demanded the services of the U.S. Navy, as well as those of Dr. Wassell, but Secretary of the Navy Frank Knox told the imperious director "You can have Dr. Wassell, but the navy is rather busy nowadays.") While shooting some background footage in Mexico, second unit director Hal Rosson heard of a peasant who dislodged a rock with a plow. Steam started to erupt from the ground and within a couple of weeks there was a volcanic cone some two hundred feet high spewing lava and rocks. DeMille immediately dispatched the crew to the scene, and hastily wrote a volcanic eruption into the script, writing in his notebook "It's an ill volcano that never does anybody any good." Rosson took his crew to within a half mile of the crater, rocks crashing all around them, to get the spectacular, if utterly extraneous, shots. Most of the criticism of the picture centered on the way DeMille had loaded the stirring, true story with every Hollywood cliche he could find, from a romance with a nurse to Javanese dancing girls. Cooper is as strong and laconic as ever, but he simply has too much to do, proving his heroism and sheer perfection more than any real person could. Dr. Wassell called the film 98 percent documentary, but no doubt he was being kind. In fact he fought against the Hollywoodization of his life, but to no avail. The film was fairly successful at the box office and DeMille and Wassell went on tour across the country drumming up support for the movie and the war effort.

p&d, Cecil B. DeMille; w, Alan LeMay, Charles Bennett, James Hilton (based on the story by Dr. Corydon M. Wassell and the original story by Hilton); ph, Victor Milner (Technicolor); m, Victor Young; ed, Anne Bauchens; art d, Hans Dreier, Roland Anderson; set d, George Sawley; cos, Natalie Visart; spec eff, Farciot Edouart, W. Wallace Kelley, Gordon Jennings.

Biography/War **(PR:A-C MPAA:NR)**

STORY OF ESTHER COSTELLO, THE**** (1957, Brit.) 103m Romulus-Valiant/COL bw (AKA: GOLDEN VIRGIN)

Joan Crawford *(Margaret Landi)*, Rossano Brazzi *(Carlo Landi)*, Heather Sears *(Esther Costello)*, Lee Patterson *(Harry Grant)*, Ron Randell *(Frank Wenzel)*, Fay Compton *(Mother Superior)*, John Loder *(Paul Marchant)*, Denis O'Dea *(Father Devlin)*, Sidney James *(Ryan)*, Bessie Love *(Matron in Art Gallery)*, Robert Ayres *(Mr. Wilson)*, Maureen Delaney *(Jennie Costello)*, Estelle Brody *(Tammy)*, June Clyde *(Mrs. Forbes)*, Sally Smith *(Susan North)*, Megs Jenkins *(Nurse Evans)*, Andrew Cruickshank *(Dr. Stein)*, Diana Day *(Christine Brown)*, Victor Rietti *(Signor Gatti)*, Sheila Manahan *(Mary Costello)*, Tony Quinn *(Irish Pub Customer)*, Janina Faye *(Esther as a Child)*, Harry Hutchinson *(Irish Publican)*.

A powerful if sometimes seamy look at a problem that was later covered in William Gibson's "The Miracle Worker" when he took the true tale of Helen Keller and made it into a play, then a movie, then a sequel play, "Monday After The Miracle," which failed. Crawford is a wealthy Irish woman who went to the United States when she was very young, married Brazzi, and is now estranged from him due to his passion for women other than his wife. She is visiting the scenes of her childhood on the Emerald Isle when she meets Sears, a young girl who is deaf, blind, and mute as a result of an accident when she was quite small. Since she was born normal, there is no doubt that these ailments are mentally induced, not physical. Even so, they are real to Sears and she can do nothing about them. Sears is living like an animal; no one pays any attention to her as they have no idea how to help. Sears had been hurt in an explosion and since there is no medical service beyond the usual in the small town, she has been left to spend her life in a sightless, soundless, and wordless existence. In most Irish villages of this size, the priest is an important person so O'Dea, who sees that Crawford has exhibited interest in Sears, tries to get her to commit to something more than that. Crawford is having her own woes due to her failing marriage and tries hard not to care, but she is a good woman and O'Dea's appeals touch her so Crawford–who has no children by Brazzi–decides to take Sears into her life as a surrogate daughter. The two commence trying various sources of help but nothing seems to work apart from Crawford's patience with Sears. Crawford learns to read Braille so she can teach it to Sears. She also learns how to communicate with "hand talk" in order to break through. Time passes and Sears begins to respond. The press catches wind of the story and it isn't long before their story is known across the world. They are called upon to speak at many charitable dinners and fund drives and are enjoying their new status when Brazzi returns to Crawford's life. He is a slick, fast-talking promoter who knows the way back inside Crawford's heart and soon uses his Latin charm to talk her into reconciling. But Brazzi has something else in mind, a profit motive for wanting Crawford. Because Crawford and Sears are inseparable, Brazzi means to use this international story to make a lot of money for himself, with the full intent of collecting all that cash, then going off to some place like Monaco to spend it. Brazzi hires Randell to arrange a back-breaking series of tours that will increase his coffers. Since Sears is such an important story with the media, many reporters have been covering her progress and one of them is Patterson. He falls in love with the 21-year-old Sears and she feels the same about him. Brazzi is such a satyr that he can't resist the naive loveliness of Sears as one day, while Crawford is out of their residence on a short errand, Brazzi forces his attentions on Sears and brutally rapes the helpless girl. The shock of the act rectifies the results of the early explosion that took her faculties and Sears miraculously regains her sight, hearing, and speech. Later, Crawford is shocked by what happened, as well as by the cheap, conniving ideas that Brazzi has been employing to get rich. She doesn't let on that she knows, though. Now that Sears is back to normal, Crawford bids the young girl and Patterson farewell, then drives to meet Brazzi, who is coming back from a short business trip. He gets into the car unaware of what Crawford has in mind and she promptly drives them both to their deaths, shooting him, then herself. Sears and Patterson go off to spend the rest of their lives together and the film ends. It's more melodramatic than THE MIRACLE WORKER and the focus is as much on the people around the girl as the girl herself. Crawford showed all of her range of acting and the result was a Best Actress Award from the British Film Academy. A strong story, good acting, and a most literate script from the man who should know about the inner workings of the mind, Charles Kaufman, who also wrote the screenplay for FREUD.

p, Jack Clayton, David Miller; d, Miller; w, Charles Kaufman (based on the novel by Nicholas Monsarrat); ph, Robert Krasker; m, Georges Auric; ed, Ralph Kemplen; md, Lambert Williamson; art d, George Provis, Tony Masters; cos, Jean Louis.

Drama   (PR:C   MPAA:NR)

STORY OF G.I. JOE, THE**   (1945) 109m UA bw (AKA: WAR CORRESPONDENT)

Burgess Meredith (*Ernie Pyle*), Robert Mitchum (*Lt. Walker*), Freddie Steele (*Sgt. Warnicki*), Wally Cassell (*Pvt. Dondaro*), Jimmy Lloyd (*Pvt. Spencer*), Jack Reilly (*Pvt. Murphy*), Bill Murphy (*Pvt. Mew*), William Self (*Cookie Henderson*), Dick Rich (*Sergeant at Showers*), Billy Benedict (*Whitey*), Tito Renaldo (*Lopez*), Michael Browne (*Sergeant*), Yolanda Lacca (*Amelia*), Dorothy Coonan (*Nurse*), Don Whitehead, George Lait, Chris Cunningham, Hal Boyle, Sgt. Jack Foisie, Bob Landry, Lucien Hubbard, Clete Roberts, Robert Reuben (*Themselves, Correspondents*).

The story of the greatest of America's combat correspondents of WW II, THE STORY OF G.I. JOE immortalizes Ernie Pyle, who himself immortalized the common soldier in his dispatches and books, *Brave Men* and *Here Is Your War*. The film opens as Meredith, playing Pyle, catches up to a tired platoon of infantrymen in Italy, He observes, comments, and comforts as the men fight through town after town, enduring death, misery, boredom, fear, and a gamut of other emotions as they unhappily but determinedly do their job. The platoon is under the command of Mitchum, for whom the men have an awesome respect and admiration. One man carries a phonograph record of his wife and child they have sent him, and scours battlefields looking for a record player. When he finally finds one and plays the record, the emotion proves too much for him and he cracks, being taken out of the line by medics. Eventually, during an assault on a mountaintop along the German lines south of Rome, strings of casualties are brought down the mountain, among them Mitchum. (One of the most resounding lines in Pyle's works sets this scene: "Dead men have been coming down the mountain all night.") The men are angry and sad, but they know this is war, and while they bury Mitchum, other units enter Rome. Later, they move out again, Meredith still tagging along. Possibly the best film yet to emerge about WW II, it had the full cooperation of Pyle, who only got to see some rough cuts before being killed in the South Pacific by a Japanese machine gun. The film has no real story, only the consistent wearing down of the men through combat and fatigue. Meredith is superb, conveying the humanity and caring of Pyle, but it is Mitchum who steals the show (he received an Academy Award nomination as Best Supporting Actor), slowly growing into the most important person in the lives of all his men, tormented as he leads them to possible death again and again, and eventually dying himself. The scene where he is seen slung over a mule is one of the most moving in any war film ever. Mitchum was literally grabbed off the street to play the role, director Wellman spotting him one day and asking him to test for the role. "Everyone's after that role," Mitchum told the director, "Gary Cooper and all the rest. Why me?" Wellman later said of the test: "I very foolishly made the test of one of the most important scenes in the picture, the scene where he was the tired officer writing letters to the mothers of the kids who'd been killed. It was my big mistake, really, for I saw something so wonderful, so completely compelling, that I was mad at myself for not having built the set before so that I could have made the test the *actual* scene that came out in the picture. He was fantastic." A number of veteran soldiers on their way from Italy to the Pacific war were enlisted for the film, and Wellman recalled that whenever they were off the set, they'd be back behind the ruined village that had been built throwing knives endlessly. He adds that those men later went off to the Pacific and most didn't come back, and further adds that "It's the one picture of mine that I refuse to look at."

p, Lester Cowan; d, William A. Wellman; w, Leopold Atlas, Guy Endore, Philip Stevenson (based on the book by Ernie Pyle); ph, Russell Metty; m, Ann Ronell, Louise Applebaum; ed, Otho Lovering, Albrecht Joseph; md, Louis Forbes; art d, James Sullivan, David Hall; set d, Edward G. Boyle; m/l, "Linda," Jack Lawrence, Ronell, "I'm Coming Back," "Infantry March," Ronell; tech adv, Lt. Col. Roy A. Murray, Jr., Lt. Col. Edward H. Coffey, Lt. Col. Robert Miller, Maj. Walter Nye, Capt. Milton M. Thornton, Capt. Charles Shunstrom.

War   **Cas.**   (PR:A-C   MPAA:NR)

STORY OF GILBERT AND SULLIVAN, THE
          (SEE: GREAT GILBERT AND SULLIVAN, THE, 1953, Brit.)

STORY OF JOSEPH AND HIS BRETHREN THE*½
(1962, Ital.) 103m Cosmopolis Jolly/Colorama-CAP c (GIUSEPPE VEN-DUTO DAI FRATELLI; AKA: JOSEPH AND HIS BRETHREN; JO-SEPH SOLD BY HIS BROTHERS)

Geoffrey Horne (*Joseph*), Robert Morley (*Potiphar*), Belinda Lee (*Henet*), Vira Silenti (*Asenath*), Mario Girotti (*Benjamin*), Carlo Giustini (*Reuben*), Finlay Currie (*Jacob*), Arturo Dominici (*Rekmira*), Robert Rietty (*Pharoah*), Julian Brooks (*Chief Baker*), Mimo Billi (*Chief Butler*), Marietto (*Benjamin*

as a Child), Marco Guglielmi (*Judah*), Dante Di Paolo (*Simeon*), Charles Borromel (*Dan*), Helmut Schneider (*Zebulun*), Loris Bazzocchi (*Issachar*), Marin Marija (*Asher*), Antonio Segurini (*Gad*), Tonko Sarcevic (*Levi*).

This biblical spectacle is based on the familiar story of Joseph and his 11 brothers. The favorite son is sold into Egyptian slavery by his jealous siblings. He becomes the prophet and advisor to Pharoah and during a famine has the chance to reveal himself to his brothers and reunite the family. Typical religious epic offers nothing new or special.

p, Ermanno Donati, Luigi Carpentieri; d, English version, Irving Rapper, Italian version, Luciano Ricci; w, Italian version, Guglielmo Santangelo, Oreste Biancoli, Ennio De Concini, English version, Guy Elmes (based on a story by Santangelo); ph, Riccardo Pallottini (CineScope Eastmancolor); m, Mario Nascimbene; ed, Mario Serandrei; art d, Oscar D'Amico; cos, Maria De Matteis.

Religious Drama   (PR:A   MPAA:NR)

STORY OF LOUIS PASTEUR, THE**   (1936) 85m WB bw

Paul Muni (*Louis Pasteur*), Josephine Hutchinson (*Mme. Pasteur*), Anita Louise (*Annette Pasteur*), Donald Woods (*Jean Martel*), Fritz Leiber, Sr. (*Dr. Charbonnet*), Henry O'Neill (*Roux*), Porter Hall (*Dr. Rosignol*), Ray Brown (*Dr. Radisse*), Akim Tamiroff (*Dr. Zaranoff*), Walter Kingsford (*Napoleon III*), Iphigenie Castiglioni (*Empress Eugenie*), Herbert Heywood (*Boncourt*), Frank Reicher (*Dr. Pheiffer*), Halliwell Hobbes (*Dr. Joseph Lister*), Dickie Moore (*Phillip Meister*), Herbert Corthell (*President Louis-Adolphe Thiers*), Frank Mayo (*President Sadi Carnot*), William Burress (*Doctor*), Robert Strange (*Magistrate*), Mabel Colcord (*A Lady*), Niles Welch (*Courier*), Leonard Mudie (*Coachman*), Brenda Fowler (*Midwife*), Eric Mayne (*Lord Chamberlain*), Alphonze Ethier (*Finance Minister*), Edward Van Sloan (*Chairman*), George Andre Beranger (*Assistant*), Montague Shaw (*British Reporter*), Otto Hoffman (*Farmer*), Tempe Pigott (*Woman*), Richard Alexander (*Burly Farmer*), Lottie Williams (*Cecile*), Baron Hesse (*Fat Doctor*), Wheaton Chambers (*Alsatian*), Leonid Snegoff (*Russian Ambassador*), Fred Walton (*Government Inspector*), Wilfred Lucas, Gordon Elliott, Jack Santoro, Ferdinand Schumann-Heink (*Reporters*).

The film biography was a popular genre in the 1930s, and THE STORY OF LOUIS PASTEUR was one of the best despite Warner Bros. efforts to minimize the quality of the project. Muni (as Louis Pasteur) is working to find a cure for anthrax and hydrophobia. His colleagues at the Medical Academy are convinced his experiments are a waste of time, and Muni is ridiculed. He and his wife Hutchinson, along with their daughter Louise, decide to move into the French countryside, where Muni's experiments with sheep will be more readily accepted. Authorities learn that the sheep in Muni's area are disease-free, which causes some stir in the Medical Academy. Leiber, who has always been Muni's harshest critic, decides to rigidly test Muni's theory about microbes causing disease. Twenty-five sheep are given the anthrax vaccination while another 25 are left alone. Of course all the animals receiving the serum survive, and Muni is praised for his ground breaking work. Leiber remains obstinate, refusing to believe Muni's theories on microbes. Having found the cure for anthrax, Muni turns his attention toward the dread hydrophobia. He creates a vaccine he believes will work, though the drug needs to be tested. Moore is a local child who is bitten by a mad dog. Muni takes his cure and vaccinates Moore. Meanwhile, Muni's daughter Louise is about to have her first child. Married to Muni's assistant Woods, Louise is in desperate need of a doctor to deliver her child. The only one available is Leiber, who still remains at odds with Muni. He will only agree to sterilize the tools needed to deliver Louise's baby if Muni will repudiate his rabies vaccination. Realizing this means life or death for his grandchild, Muni reluctantly gives in. Leiber appears to have had the last word with his blackmail, but much to his surprise Moore recovers after receiving Muni's vaccination. Leiber finally realizes that Muni's theories are correct, and joins the Medical Academy in praising the doctor. THE STORY OF LOUIS PASTEUR is well told, complemented by an intelligent script and excellent performances. Careful attention is paid to scientific accuracy in the film, with enough interesting characters to avoid becoming a preachy educational film. Muni's performance won him an Oscar for Best Actor, a fine characterization that shows the famed scientist as a human being faced with extraordinary blockades. Muni, who would also star in the film biographies THE LIFE OF EMILE ZOLA (1937) and JUAREZ (1939) prepared for his part by reading books about Pasteur and his colleagues, as well as visiting the Pasteur Institute near Paris. Warner Bros. executives were against the film from the start, and getting this feature made proved to be as difficult a struggle as the one it portrays. Muni, along with director Dieterle and producer Blanke, fought studio pressures and eventually executives allowed the film to be made, though Hal B. Wallis claimed: "The public won't accept Muni with a beard. He'll look like a rabbi." Jack Warner agreed, claiming no one would want to see a film about bugs, and allowed the film only a $330,000 budget, relatively small in comparison to other important pictures of the time. Rather than construct new sets, leftover pieces from other films were incorporated into THE STORY OF LOUIS PASTEUR. The amphitheater of the Medical Academy had formally been used as a nightclub in a Busby Berkeley musical. When the film was finally completed, Warner Bros. released it with little fanfare, allowing it to be dumped as a second feature for double bills. Eventually the film's quality proved itself, and after much critical and public acceptance, the studio gave the film a better promotion. Both Muni and Leiber recreated their roles for a radio adaptation of the film, which was directed by Cecil B. DeMille for the Lux Radio Theater.

p, Henry Blanke; d, William Dieterle; w, Sheridan Gibney, Pierre Collins (based on the story by Gibney); ph, Tony Gaudio; ed, Ralph Dawson; md, Leo F. Forbstein; art d, Robert H. Haas; cos, Milo Anderson.

Biography   **Cas.**   **(PR:AA MPAA:NR)**

STORY OF MANDY, THE   (SEE: CRASH OF SILENCE, 1953)

STORY OF MANKIND, THE zero   (1957) 100m Cambridge WB c

Ronald Colman *(Spirit of Man)*, Hedy Lamarr *(Joan of Arc)*, Groucho Marx *(Peter Minuit)*, Harpo Marx *(Isaac Newton)*, Chico Marx *(Monk)*, Virginia Mayo *(Cleopatra)*, Vincent Price *(Devil)*, Agnes Moorehead *(Queen Elizabeth)*, Peter Lorre *(Nero)*, Charles Coburn *(Hippocrates)*, Sir Cedric Hardwicke *(High Judge)*, Cesar Romero *(Spanish Envoy)*, John Carradine *(Khufu)*, Dennis Hopper *(Napoleon)*, Marie Wilson *(Marie Antoinette)*, Helmut Dantine *(Anthony)*, Edward Everett Horton *(Sir Walter Raleigh)*, Reginald Gardiner *(Shakespeare)*, Marie Windsor *(Josephine)*, Cathy O'Donnell *(Early Christian Woman)*, Franklin Pangborn *(Marquis de Varennes)*, Melville Cooper *(Major Domo)*, Francis X. Bushman *(Moses)*, Henry Daniell *(Bishop of Beauvais)*, Jim Ameche *(Alexander Graham Bell)*, Dani Crayne *(Helen of Troy)*, Anthony Dexter *(Columbus)*, Austin Green *(Lincoln)*, Bobby Watson *(Hitler)*, Reginald Sheffield *(Caesar)*, Nick Cravat *(Apprentice)*, Alexander Lockwood *(Promoter)*, Melinda Marx *(Early Christian Child)*, Bart Mattson *(Cleopatra's Brother)*, Don Megowan *(Early Man)*, Marvin Miller *(Armana)*, Nancy Miller *(Early Woman)*, Leonard Mudie *(Chief Inquisitor)*, Major Sam Harris *(Noble in Queen Elizabeth's Court)*, Abraham Sofaer *(Indian Chief)*, Tudor Owen *(Court Clerk)*, Toni Gerry *(Wife)*, George E. Stone *(Waiter)*, Richard Cutting *(Court Attendant)*, William Schallert *(Earl of Warwick)*, Ziva Rodann *(Concubine)*, David Bond *(Early Christian)*, Eden Hartford *(Laughing Water)*, Harry Ruby *(Indian Brave)*, Angelo Rossitto *(Dwarf)*.

Irwin Allen, who has made some of the worst movies in history (and some of the most successful) began his talent for trash early with this awful tripe that used and abused the talents of some of the best actors in the business at that time. It's a name dropping comic-book version of history that was loosely adapted from the best-seller by Van Loon which was published in 1921 and stayed just below the Bible in sales for decades. Tedious, dreary, and poorly put together, it was the last movie for Ronald Colman, a rotten way to say Sayonara to motion pictures. The disaster begins as about a minute's worth of credits are shown. All the big stars get their own cards, with a large, noisy fanfare. Next, we discover that humanity has the secret of the hydrogen bomb about 60 years too soon, according to the celestial powers who rule the universe. There's a Supreme Tribunal in space and Hardwicke is the high judge. They are trying to determine whether or not to blow our paltry planet out of the skies or give us another chance (which is similar to the opening of THE MAN WHO COULD WORK MIRACLES). To that end, evidence is presented by Price, as the Devil, who lists all of the terrible inhuman things Man has done to Man. On the other end is Colman, as the Spirit Of Man, who cites the good things done on Earth and asks for leniency. The rest of the movie is a series of unrelated incidents, using name stars, showing half-a-million years of history in 100 minutes (less the opening scenes). We get to see Groucho Marx, with his ubiquitous cigar, as Peter Minuit buying Manhattan from the naive Indians, led by Abraham Sofaer, with songwriter Harry Ruby as a Brave; Chico Marx is a monk and Harpo is Isaac Newton, who has not one, but a hundred apples fall on his head. (Casting the 3 Marx Brothers was the only real humor in the picture but Allen unwisely chose to put them in different scenes); Hedy Lamarr is Joan of Arc (perhaps the most ridiculous miscasting. When she said "Attack" to her minions, audiences screamed with laughter at what was supposed to be an important historical moment); Peter Lorre is a maniacal Nero (second only to the Marxes for humor); Virginia Mayo is Cleopatra; Marie Wilson as Marie Antoinette, shouting "Let 'em eat cake" in her Anaheim accent; Dennis Hopper is a brooding Napoleon, looking like a man who has lost his motorcycle; Francis X. Bushman is Moses, and on and on. In order to shoot this on a reasonable schedule and budget, stock footage from old Warner Bros. pictures was used, including LAND OF THE PHARAOHS and HELEN OF TROY. Allen and Groucho were long-time pals so he cast Groucho's young daughter, Melinda, in a cameo, perhaps to get her a Screen Actor's Guild card. The stars were paid $2,500 each (excluding Colman, Price, and Hardwicke, who were in most of the scenes) and may have worked one day or less. Also jammed into the picture were the discovery of fire (they should have burned the negative of this movie), the wheel, moments at the Battle of Troy (with Dani Crayne as Helen. She later gave up acting to marry Buddy Greco, then David Janssen), moments with Hippocrates (Charles Coburn, who must have taken his own oath to never again appear in an Irwin Allen movie), Shakespeare, Da Vinci, Columbus, and, well, you know your history. Just think of any person whom you would have thought should be in this stinker and you'll be right. Allen had been an agent and columnist before directing two excellent documentaries, THE SEA AROUND US and THE ANIMAL WORLD. Perhaps he should have stuck with fish and beasts because he lost his touch when it came to working with real people. Colman, Hardwicke, and Price come out somewhat unscathed because each has a handle on the character. Colman is sagacious,

compassionate, and honest in his role and states his case well on behalf of Mankind. Price is properly evil as "Mr. Scratch," but not nearly as twinkly as Walter Huston was in the same role in THE DEVIL AND DANIEL WEBSTER (which had similarities to this film, as Huston and Edward Arnold called on witnesses in the trial of James Craig, who had sold his soul to Huston and was now trying to renege on the deal). Colman and Price had been on opposite sides before in CHAMPAGNE FOR CAESAR, a much funnier, better and more satisfying performance for each. This movie opened in Pennsylvania, did scant business the first week, worse business the second week, and by the third week, it was gone. No amount of advertising, discount tickets to students, and other lures could get the public to come in to see the movie as the stench permeated the theater. Since they were unable to get Don Ameche to recreate his role as Alexander Graham Bell, they did the next best thing and got his brother, Jim, a radio announcer. Undaunted by his failure, Allen went on and made many movies, most of which used all-star casts, like THE POSEIDON ADVENTURE, THE TOWERING INFERNO, THE SWARM, and VOYAGE TO THE BOTTOM OF THE SEA, which he later adapted as a TV series. At the end of the picture, the world is given another chance when Hardwicke decrees that there is much to say about man's goodness and his evil so he's taking the whole matter under advisement and will let the people on Earth decide their own fate. Phew, and we were worried there for a minute.

p&d, Irwin Allen; w, Allen, Charles Bennett (based on the book by Hendrik Willem Van Loon); ph, Nick Musuraca (Technicolor); m, Paul Sawtell; ed, Roland Gross, Gene Palmer; md, Sawtell; art d, Art Loel; cos, Marjorie Best.

Historical Drama/Fantasy   **Cas.**   **(PR:A MPAA:NR)**

STORY OF MOLLY X, THE**   (1949) 82m UNIV bw

June Havoc *(Molly X)*, John Russell *(Cash Brady)*, Dorothy Hart *(Anne)*, Connie Gilchrist *(Dawn)*, Cathy Lewis *(Molly's Roommate)*, Elliott Lewis *(Rod Markale)*, Charles McGraw *(Capt. Breen)*, Sara Berner, Sandra Gould, Katherine Warren, Wally Maher, Isabel Jewell.

Havoc is cast as the title character, a gang moll who seeks vengeance on the man who offed her husband. The police are on her trail, however, and put her in the lockup for a while, where she soon learns the meaning of the word reform. Havoc tries but can't do much with the weak script.

p, Aaron Rosenberg; d&w, Crane Wilbur; ph, Irving Glassberg; m, Milton Schwartzwald; ed, Edward Curtiss; art d, Bernard Herzbrun, Emrich Nicholson; set d, Russell A. Gausman, A. Roland Fields; cos, Rosemary Odell; makeup, Bud Westmore.

Crime Drama   **(PR:A MPAA:NR)**

STORY OF MONTE CRISTO, THE
(SEE: STORY OF THE COUNT OF MONTE CRISTO, THE, 1962, Fr./Ital.)

STORY OF ROBIN HOOD, THE*½**   (1952, Brit.) 84m
RKO-Disney/RKO c (GB: THE STORY OF ROBIN HOOD AND HIS MERRIE MEN)

Richard Todd *(Robin Hood)*, Joan Rice *(Maid Marian)*, Peter Finch *(Sheriff of Nottingham)*, James Hayter *(Friar Tuck)*, James Robertson Justice *(Little John)*, Martita Hunt *(Queen Eleanor)*, Hubert Gregg *(Prince John)*, Bill Owen *(Stutely)*, Reginald Tate *(Hugh Fitzooth)*, Elton Haytes *(Allan-a-Dale)*, Antony Eustrel *(Archbishop of Canterbury)*, Patrick Barr *(King Richard)*, Anthony Forwood *(Will Scarlett)*, Hal Osmond *(Midge the Miller)*, Michael Hordern *(Scathelock)*, Clement McCallin *(Earl of Huntingdon)*, Louise Hampton *(Tyb)*, Archie Duncan *(Red Gill)*, Julian Somers *(Posse Leader)*, Bill Travers *(Posse Man)*, David Davies *(Forester)*, Ivan Craig, Ewen Solon, John Stamp, John Brooking, John Martin, Geoffrey Lumsden, Larry Mooney, John French, Nigel Neilson, Charles Perry, Richard Graydon, Jack Taylor *(The Merrie Men)*.

After the success of Disney's first live-action feature TREASURE ISLAND the studio decided to make another, again in Britain, based on the familiar legend of Robin Hood. Unfairly dismissed today as merely a Disney adventure, this version holds up nearly as well as Michael Curtiz's THE ADVENTURES OF ROBIN HOOD (1938), but doesn't offer a cast that can compare to Flynn, de Havilland, Rathbone, and Rains. Director Annakin acknowledges the debt to Curtiz, but doubts that Disney had ever seen the picture – sure that his version was "bound to be different than anything else made on the subject before."

p, Perce Pearce; d, Ken Annakin; w, Lawrence E. Watkin; ph, Guy Green (Technicolor); m, Clifton Parker; ed, Gordon Pilkington; md, Muir Mathieson; art d, Carmen Dillon, Arthur Lawson; makeup, Geoffrey Rodway.

Adventure   **(PR:AAA MPAA:NR)**

STORY OF ROBIN HOOD AND HIS MERRIE MEN, THE
(SEE: STORY OF ROBIN HOOD, THE, 1952, Brit.)

STORY OF RUTH, THE★★   (1960) 132m Fox c

Stuart Whitman (*Boaz*), Tom Tryon (*Mahlon*), Peggy Wood (*Naomi*), Viveca Lindfors (*Eleilat*), Jeff Morrow (*Tob*), Elana Eden (*Ruth*), Thayer David (*Hedak*), Les Tremayne (*Elimelech*), Eduard Franz (*Jehoam*), Leo Fuchs (*Sochin*), Lili Valenty (*Kera*), John Gabriel (*Chilion*), Ziva Rodann (*Orpah*), Basil Ruysdael (*Shammah*), John Banner (*King of Moab*), Adelina Pedroza (*Iduma*), Daphna Einhorn (*Tebah*), Sara Taft (*Eska*), Jean Inness (*Hagah*), Berry Kroeger (*Huphim*), Jon Silo (*Tacher*), Don Diamond (*Yomar*), Chrystine Jordan, Kelton Garwood, Charles Wagenheim, Ralph Moody, Ben Astar, Charles Horvath, Robert Adler, Anthony Jochim, Inez Pedroza, Stassa Damacus, Doris Wiss.

This long biblical spectacle tells the tale of Ruth but not exactly as it is taught in Sunday School. The script has Ruth, played by Eden, as a priestess who denounces idols after finding Judaism and belief in the one God. Upon her visit to Bethlehem she encounters religious persecution, but the courts uphold her rights and allow her to wed Whitman. The usual religious epic ingredients are tossed in – mysticism and faith, lavish flowing robes, overly-dignified performances and even an evil high priestess who tries to upset Eden's marriage. It's interesting in some spots as it is boring in others.

p, Samuel G. Engel; d, Henry Koster; w, Norman Corwin; ph, Arthur E. Arling (Cinemascope, DeLuxe Color); m, Franz Waxman; ed, Jack W. Holmes; art d, Lyle R. Wheeler, Franz Bachelin; cos, Nino Novarese; ch, Danni Dassa.

Religious Drama   (PR:A MPAA:NR)

STORY OF SEABISCUIT, THE★★½
                    (1949) 93m WB c (GB: PRIDE OF KENTUCKY)

Shirley Temple (*Margaret O'Hara*), Barry Fitzgerald (*Shawn O'Hara*), Lon McCallister (*Ted Knowles*), Rosemary De Camp (*Mrs. Charles S. Howard*), Donald MacBride (*George Carson*), Pierre Watkin (*Charles S. Howard*), William Forrest (*Thomas Millford*), "Sugarfoot" Anderson (*Murphy*), William J. Cartledge (*Jockey George Woolf*), Forbes Murray, Edward Keane, Lou Harvey, Herman Kantor (*Buyers*), Gertrude Astor (*Wife*), Creighton Hale (*Husband*), Ral Erlenborn (*Cameraman*), Gil Warren (*Radio Announcer*), Jack Loman, Alan Foster (*Spectators*), James Simmons (*Swipe*).

A pleasantly harmless film which brings to the screen the legendary horse Seabiscuit in a fictionalized account of California owner C.S. Howard. Temple plays the niece of trainer Fitzgerald, who roots the champion to victory, and finds spare time for romancing jockey McCallister. The film includes three segments of actual race footage, showing Seabiscuit on the track at Pimlico against War Admiral, and in the 1940s Santa Anna Handicap.

p, William Jacobs; d, David Butler; w, John Tainter Foote (based on the story by Foote); ph, Wilfrid M. Cline (Technicolor); m, David Buttolph; ed, Irene Morra; md, Buttolph; art d, Douglas Bacon; set d, Lyle B. Reifsnider; cos, Leah Rhodes.

Drama   (PR:A MPAA:NR)

STORY OF SHIRLEY YORKE, THE★★   (1948, Brit.) 92m
                    Nettlefold/BUT bw

Derek Farr (*Gerald Ryton*), Dinah Sheridan (*Shirley Yorke*), Margaretta Scott (*Alison Gwynne*), John Robinson (*Dr. Bruce Napier*), Barbara Couper (*Muriel Peach*), Beatrix Thomson (*Lady Camber*), Ian Maclean (*Dr. Harris*), Jack Raine (*Stansfield Yorke*), Lesley Osmond (*Jennifer Ware*), Valentine Dyall (*Edward Holt*), Eleanor Summerfield (*Doris*), Bruce Seton (*Capt. Sharp*), Hugh Pryse, Charles Hawtrey.

When the invalid wife of a lord dies after receiving a special treatment developed by doctor Robinson and administered by nurse Sheridan, the nurse immediately comes under suspicion for murder because the lord had once been romantically involved with her. She is soon arrested and tried for murder based on evidence provided by Scott's friend Couper. Eventually Robinson is able to prove that it was Couper who killed the Lord's wife and clears his nurse's name. Released in 1952 with 16 minutes cut, some prints may still circulate.

p, Ernest G. Roy; d, Maclean Rogers; w, A.R. Rawlinson, Kathleen Butler Rogers, (based on the play "The Case of Lady Camber" by H.A. Vachell); ph, Geoffrey Faithfull.

Crime   (PR:A MPAA:NR)

STORY OF TEMPLE DRAKE, THE★★★½   (1933) 70m PAR bw

Miriam Hopkins (*Temple Drake*), Jack LaRue (*Trigger*), William Gargan (*Stephen Benbow*), William Collier, Jr. (*Toddy Gowan*), Irving Pichel (*Lee Goodwin*), Sir Guy Standing (*Judge Drake*), Elizabeth Patterson (*Aunt Jennie*), Florence Eldridge (*Ruby Lemar*), James Eagles (*Tommy*), Harlan E. Knight (*Pap*), James Mason (*Van*), Jobyna Howland (*Miss Reba*), Henry Hall (*Judge*), John Carradine (*Courtroom Extra*), Frank Darien (*Gas Station Proprietor*), Clarence Sherwood (*Lunch Wagon Proprietor*), Oscar Apfel (*District Attorney*), Kent Taylor, Clem Beauchamp (*Jellybeans*), Arthur Belasco (*Wharton*), Grady Sutton (*Bob*), George Pearce (*Doctor*), Hattie McDaniel (*Minnie*).

During Prohibition days, Hopkins, the wildly hedonistic daughter of a well-to-do judge, Standing, rejects the marriage proposal of an upstanding young attorney, Gargan. Hopkins prefers to continue partying with her retinue of admirers, which includes "Virginia gentleman" Collier, drinking bootleg hooch, and shimmying through the wee small hours of the morning. The teasing, vampish-but- virginal Hopkins is the center of attention for all the college boys in the area, h⌐ denish southern decadence personified. Driving in an open roadster with drunken Collier, Hopkins finds herself forced by circumstance into an alien world; a minor auto accident causes the two scions of southern wealth to seek assistance in a shack which serves as temporary headquarters for a mob of degenerate hooch-running hoodlums, led by the sinister LaRue. Others in the group are the toadying Eagles, muscleman Pichel, and the latter's mistress-slave, Eldridge. The terrorized Collier is quickly sent on his way, but Hopkins is forced to stay. The imperious girl gets her comeuppance from the taciturn gunman, (LaRue) who rapes her (implicity, in the picture). Later, LaRue guns down the cringing Eagles, arranging things so that Pichel will appear to be the culprit. LaRue carries Hopkins off to the big city and installs her as a feature attraction in his bordello. Initially outraged and resistant, Hopkins gradually finds herself enjoying her role, which appears to suit her temperament. When she and LaRue finally have a falling-out, Hopkins kills him with his own gun. Since the gangster's demise is mourned by nobody, this killing goes unpunished. However, the moronic bootlegger, Pichel, is brought to trial for the murder of the unfortunate Eagles. Freed from her life of degradation in the brothel, Hopkins realizes that her silence will sustain her former southern-belle reputation. A spark of decency shines in her eyes and she elects to testify–in the presence of her one- time sweetheart, attorney Gargan–to the sordid elements of her rape and subsequent captivity in order to save the unfortunate Pichel from execution. Author Faulkner's shocking, splenetic symphony of scorn toward southern aristocracy was a bombshell in its day. The Hays Office–Hollywood's self-censorship society of the time–had specifically warned the studios against attempting to film the story. When Paramount elected to defile the notorious novel, despite the negative injunction, the Hays Office advised the studio that no reference to the novel in the film's credits or publicity would be tolerated. Despite everything, screenwriter Garrett's script stays reasonably close to the novel in most respects. (In the novel, the gangster is impotent; the unnatural rape occurs with the hoodlum deflowering the girl using a corncob.) Hopkins gives an excellent performance, and LaRue is all evil. Many of the supporting players over-emote in silent- screen style in what is otherwise a well-mounted production. THE STORY OF TEMPLE DRAKE bears the dubious distinction of being the chief reason for the establishment of the Roman Catholic Church's Legion of Decency, formed the following year, which prohibited Catholics from viewing proscribed pictures. Such prospects of boycott were to be even more influential with theater exhibitors and production companies than even the Hays Code. Remade in a far inferior version, though more explicit, in 1961, under the title SANCTUARY, starring Lee Remick and Yves Montand.

p, Benjamin Glazer; d, Stephen Roberts; w, Oliver H.P. Garrett (based on the 'uncredited' novel *Sanctuary* by William Faulkner); ph, Karl Struss.

Drama   (PR:O MPAA:NR)

STORY OF THE COUNT OF MONTE CRISTO, THE★
(1962, Fr./Ital.) 132m S.N.E. Gau-Cineriz-Royal/WB c (LE COMTE DE MONTE CRISTO; IL CONTE DI MONTECRISTO; AKA: THE COUNT OF MONTE CRISTO; THE STORY OF MONTE CRISTO)

Louis Jourdan (*Edmond Dantes*), Yvonne Furneaux (*Mercedes*), Pierre Mondy (*Caderousse*), Franco Silva (*Mario*), Bernard Dheran (*Villefort*), Jean-Claude Michel (*Fernand de Mortcerf*), Jean Martinelli (*Vidocq*), Claudine Coster (*Haydee*), Henri Guisol (*Abbe Faria*), Marie Mergey (*Madame Caderousse*), Yves Renier (*Albert de Mortcerf*), Alain Ferral (*Benedetto*), Lupi Roldano (*Morel*), Henri Vilbert (*Dantes' Father*), Jean-Jacques Delbo.

An uninspired, old-fashioned rehash of the classic Dumas tale which casts Jourdan in the title role. Wrongly imprisoned for aiding Napoleon in a return from Elba, Jourdan sets out to find the men who put him away. Although nice to look at, it bears little resemblance to the original and falls victim to a poor dubbing job.

p, Jean-Jacques Vital, Rene Modiano; d, Claude Autant-Lara; w, Jean Halain (based on the novel by Alexander Dumas); ph, Jacques Natteau, Jean Isnard (Dyaliscope, Technicolor); m, Rene Cloerec; ed, Madeleine Gug; art d, Max Douy; cos, Rosine Delamare.

Adventure   (PR:A MPAA:NR)

STORY OF THE CRUELTIES OF YOUTH, A
                    (SEE: NAKED YOUTH, 1961, Jap.)

STORY OF THREE LOVES, THE★★★   (1953) 122m MGM c

"The Jealous Lover": Moira Shearer (*Paula Woodward*), James Mason (*Charles Coudray*), Agnes Moorehead (*Aunt Lydia*), Jacob Gimpel (*Pianist*), Miklos Rozsa (*Conductor*), John Lupton (*Studious Young Man*), Jack Raine (*Doctor*), Lysa Baugher (*Ballerina*), Flo Wix, Towyna Dally, Colin Kenny, Major Sam Harris (*Ad Libs*), Ottola Nesmith (*Usher*), Bruce Lansbury,

Bruce Edwards, Ivan Hayes *(Chorus Boys)*, Anne Howard, Paula Allen *(Chorus Girls)*, Reginald Sheffield *(Production Manager)*, "Mademoiselle": Ethel Barrymore *(Mrs. Pennicott)*, Leslie Caron *(Mademoiselle)*, Farley Granger *(Thomas Campbell, Jr.)*, Ricky Nelson *(Tommy, Age 12)*, Zsa Zsa Gabor *(Flirt at Bar)*, Paula Raymond *(Mrs. Campbell)*, Hayden Rorke *(Mr. Rorke)*, Larry Olsen *(Terry)*, Robert Horton *(Young Man on Boat)*, Manuel Paris *(Mr. Carlos)*, Alberto Morin *(Mr. Sandes)*, Andre Simeon *(Waiter)*, Z. Yacconelli *(Bellhop)*, Peter Brocco *(Bartender)*, Phyllis Graffeo *(Italian Girl)*, Argentina Brunetti *(Saleswoman)*, Nick Thompson *(Coachman)*, Tom Quinn *(American Man in Bar)*, Rudy Lee *(Little Boy)*, Noreen Corcoran *(Little Girl)*, Ernesto Morelli *(Railway Porter)*, Ed Agresti *(Railway Conductor)*, Victory Desni *(Italian Air Force officer)*, "Equilibrium": Pier Angeli *(Nina)*, Kirk Douglas *(Pierre Narval)*, Richard Anderson *(Marcel)*, Steven Geray *(Legay)*, Alix Talton *(Rose)*, Karen Verne *(Madame Legay)*, Torben Meyer *(Man)*, Ken Anderson *(Jacques)*, Peter Norman *(Rudolph Kramer)*, Jack Tesler *(Bartender)*, Joan Miller *(Woman on Bridge)*, Paul Bryar *(River Policeman)*, Kay English *(Nurse)*, Elizabeth Slifer *(Concierge)*, Christofer Appel *(Boy)*, Bertha Feducha *(Woman Vendor)*, Frank Scannell *(Master of Ceremonies)*, Paul Maxey *(Bill Cyrus)*, Leo Mostovoy *(Stranger in Cafe)*, Frank Wilcox, John Pickard *(Ship's Officers)*.

Three separate stories linked together aboard an ocean liner, with each having nothing to do with the others and the three of varying interest and quality. The first is "The Jealous Lover," with an original screenplay by ace short-story writer Collier and direction by Reinhardt. Mason is a brilliant ballet impresario, not unlike the Anton Walbrook role in THE RED SHOES. He is traveling on the liner and two balletomanes ask why Mason only staged his ballet "Astarte" once, and then never again. This jogs him into a flashback as he remembers how it came to be. Late one night, he walked into his theater and found Shearer on stage working out. (Shearer, you recall, was the ballerina in THE RED SHOES). He stood in the shadows and watched for quite a while and her elegance and beauty enraptured him. When she discovered he was there, she stopped, and he pleaded with her to continue her improvisation as he wished to note her moves on his drawing pad so he could fully stage a ballet for her. Mason didn't know that Shearer had been forbidden to dance strenuously because of a heart condition. He prevailed upon her to return with him to his studio so he could note her moves. With the music of Rachmaninoff's "Rhapsody on a theme by Paganini" in the background, she danced for him and he feverishly marked down her actions. After she left Mason's studio, she went home and died. Mason explains that he only presented the ballet that one time so Shearer, wherever she is, would have an opportunity to see the creation she inspired. The "jealous lover" referred to in the title was based on Mason's misconception that Shearer did not want to dance any further in the theater because, he thought, she might have a lover who wished her to cease her labors. The choreography is by Frederick Ashton of the Sadler's Wells ballet company. The second segment was directed by Minnelli from a screenplay by Lustig and Froeschel, based on a story by Phillips. Caron is a devoted Gallic governess who is nanny to wealthy Nelson (who took some time out from the TV show with his family to make this film). Caron is lonely and finds her charge to be a drag. Enter Barrymore, a witch. The 12-year-old Nelson wants to get out of strict Caron's clutches and Barrymore grants his wish to become a full-grown man. Thus, Nelson becomes Granger and when Granger and Caron meet, the inevitable happens and they fall in love. But the wish is only good for four hours and the time flies by all too quickly. When the spell ends, Granger disappears and Nelson is back in his pre-teen place. Caron is distraught but Barrymore whimsically assures her that he will return. (Note Gabor as the woman at the ship's bar, one of the few acting jobs she had in movies. Gabor has become famous over the years for being famous, but that's about it.) The third story, and perhaps the best, was again directed by Reinhardt and written by Collier from a story by Vajda and Maret. Also on this ship of fools is Douglas, a retired French circus performer who came down to earth because his partner died in a trapeze accident and he feels that it was his fault. For a while, he did consider doing it again when he saved Angeli. She was drowning herself in the Seine out of guilt, as she thought she may have been responsible for sending her late husband to a Nazi concentration camp where he was murdered. Douglas took Angeli under his wing and began to show her the tricks of his trade. Since she had already committed herself to death, she feared nothing and Douglas thought that lack of fear would make her a perfect partner for his daring stunts. They rehearsed for weeks and did their highly dangerous act at an audition for a large circus. The job was theirs if they wished but Douglas realizes that he has fallen in love with her and makes the decision to quit the high life and marry Angeli instead. This is the most realized of the trio and, with some fleshing out, could have been a movie by itself. Business was sparse at the box office.

p, Sidney Franklin; "The Jealous Lover": d, Gottfried Reinhardt; w, John Collier; ph, Charles Rosher (Technicolor); m, Miklos Rozsa, Sergey Rachmaninoff; ed, Ralph E. Winters; art d, Cedric Gibbons, Preston Ames, Edward Carfagno, Gabriel Scognamillo; cos, Helen Rose; ch, Frederick Ashton; "Mademoiselle": d, Vincente Minnelli; w, Jan Lustig, George Froeschel (based on a story by Arnold Phillips); ph, Harold Rosson (Technicolor); m, Rozsa; ed, Winters; art d, Gibbons, Ames, Carfagno, Scognamillo; cos, Rose; ch, Ashton; "Equilibrium": d, Reinhardt; w, Collier, Lustig, Froeschel (based on a story by Ladislas Vajda, Jacques Maret; ph, Rosher (Technicolor); m, Rozsa; ed, Winters; art d, Gibbons, Ames, Carfagno, Scognamillo; cos, Rose; ch, Ashton.

Drama **(PR:A MPAA:NR)**

STORY OF VERNON AND IRENE CASTLE, THE***½

(1939) 90m RKO bw

Fred Astaire *(Vernon Castle)*, Ginger Rogers *(Irene Castle)*, Edna May Oliver *(Maggie Sutton)*, Walter Brennan *(Walter)*, Lew Fields *(Himself)*, Etienne Girardot *(Papa Aubel)*, Janet Beecher *(Mrs. Foote)*, Rolfe Sedan *(Emile Aubel)*, Leonid Kinskey *(Artist)*, Robert Strange *(Dr. Foote)*, Douglas Walton *(Student Pilot)*, Clarence Derwent *(Papa Louis)*, Sonny Lamont *(Charlie)*, Frances Mercer *(Claire Ford)*, Victor Varconi *(Grand Duke)*, Donald MacBride *(Hotel Manager)*, Dick Elliott *(Conductor)*, David McDonald, John Meredith *(Army Pilots)*, Tiny Jones *(Lady in Revolving Door)*, Majorie Belcher [Marge Champion] *(Irene's Girl Friend)*, Roy D'Arcy, Don Brodie, Bill Franey, Joe Bordeaux, Neil Burns, Jack Perrin, Bill Paton, "Buzz" Barton, Neal Hart, Frank O'Connor, D.H. Turner, Bruce Mitchell, Max Darwyn, Leonard Mudie, Hugh McArthur, Esther Muir, Theodore Von Eltz, George Irving, Willis Clare, Russell Hicks, Hal K. Dawson, Adrienne d'Ambricourt, Ethyl Haworth, Kay Sutton, Allen Wood, Armand Cortez, Eugene Borden, Elspeth Dudgeon, Dorothy Lovett.

A very good film biography of the most beloved dance team in the early years of the 20th Century. Irene Castle was technical adviser on the film and created some problems by her insistence that Rogers be a brunette, that things didn't really happen the way they were being shown, etc. Castle's husband had died more than 20 years before (she was only 46 when this was made) but her remembrances were fresh so she began to exert strong influence until executive producer Berman and his millions came up with an ingenious way to get her off the set. She was violently pro-animal rights and when a ballot proposal against vivisection came up on the election slate, she was told about it again and again until she decided to throw her considerable influence behind it and exited the studio to work on the campaign. This was Astaire's and Rogers' final film for RKO after a score of hits. They teamed once more for MGM on THE BARKLEYS OF BROADWAY a decade later but the magic appeared to have fled. Rogers is the daughter of Beecher and Strange, a well-known New Rochelle physician, when she meets vaudeville performer Astaire. They marry, go to Paris, and are soon a famous ballroom dancing duo. They are so popular that the world wants to copy them. Her hair is duplicated in wigs, cigars are named after him, they invent several dance steps, they have their own line of cosmetics, they are, arguably, the first media stars. Astaire becomes a pilot in the World War with the Canadian Royal Flying Corps and when he returns, she is making the silent film PATRIA by herself. He sends for her to join him in Texas where he has a huge romantic reunion planned, including a private orchestra to play for them alone. Just before they are to unite, he's called back – in his job as flying instructor – to do a few apparently simple aerial exercises for the benefit of a visiting officer and he is killed in a crash at the age of 26. The fact that Vernon was British didn't enter into matters; there was no need for Astaire to attempt mimicking the accent because hardly anyone had ever heard the famed dancer speak. The details of the team's meteoric rise to stardom are sketchily intertwined with the many songs in the score. Edna May Oliver is their agent and does well as the woman who had faith in the happily-married couple as she pushed hard to get them good dates for their act. At the height of their success, the couple owned a nightclub in New York after having established themselves in Europe in a blaze of performances. Astaire was only 14 when he saw the Castles dance in the silent movie, THE SUNSHINE GIRL, and he fondly recalled their talents so he was thrilled to portray one of his terpsichorean idols. The dancing in the picture is more Castle than Astaire and Rogers. With Irene Castle around for a good part of the time, the movements were re-creations of the original steps, with little room for Astaire and choreographer Pan to make any alterations. In the final scene, Astaire returns as a ghost and dances off with Rogers for a tug at the heart. There are so many songs in the score that it would be impossible to list them all. They include: "Only When You're in My Arms" (the only tune written especially for the film. Written by Con Conrad, Harry Ruby, Bert Kalmar, done by Astaire, Rogers), "Missouri Waltz" (John Eppell, Frederick Logan, J.R. Shannon), "Oh, You Beautiful Doll" (Nat Ayer, A. Seymour Brown), "Nights of Gladness" (Charles Ancliffe), "By the Beautiful Sea" (Harry Carroll, Harold Atteridge), "Glow, Little Glow Worm" (Paul Lincke, Lillia Cayley Robinson), "Destiny Waltz" (Sidney Baynes), "Row, Row, Row" (James V. Monaco, William Jerome), "The Yama Yama Man" (Karl Hoschna, Collin Davis, done by Rogers in a terrific impersonation of Bessie McCoy), "Hello, Hello, Who's Your Lady Friend?" (Bert Lee, Harry Fragson, Worton David), "Take Me Back to New York Town" (Harry von Tilzer, Andrew B. Sterling), "It's a Long Way to Tipperary" (Harry Williams, Jack Judge), "Come, Josephine in My Flying Machine" (Fred Fisher, Alfred Bryan), "By the Light of the Silvery Moon" (Gus Edwards, Ed Madden), "Cuddle Up a Little Closer" (Karl Hoschna, Otto Harbach), "Way Down Yonder in New Orleans" (Henry Creamer, Turner Layton), "Texas Tommy" ("King Chanticleer" by Ayer), "The Darktown Strutters' Ball" (Shelton Brooks, with a French lyric by Elsie Janis), "While They Were Dancing Around" (Monaco, Joseph McCarthy), "Rose Room" (Art Hickman, Harry Williams), "Hello, Frisco, Hello" (Louis Hirsch, Gene Buck) "Tres Jolie Waltz" (Emil Waldteufel), "You're Here and I'm Here" (Jerome Kern, Harry B. Smith), "Syncopated Walk" (Irving Berlin), "Maxixe Dengozo" (Ernesto Nazareth), "Little Brown Jug" (Joseph E. Winter), "Too Much Mustard" (Cecil Macklin), and "Waitin' for the Robert E. Lee" (Abel Baer, L. Wolfe Gilbert). There were even more songs in the background score, just bits and pieces and snatches and it's a tribute to the talents of musical director Baravalle, who died before the film was released, that they felt "right" and never seemed crammed in for their own sake. The movie lost money. It might have been that too much time had passed since the Castles were stars or it could have been caused by the sad ending, marking the only time one of the costars died in a Rogers-Astaire film. Liberties taken by the screenplay include the casting of white Brennan in a part that was a black man in real life. An omission that did not please Mrs. Castle was the fact that she and Vernon danced to the arrangements of two black musical directors (Ford Dabney and Jim Europe, who is portrayed in the Bill Robinson/Lena Horne movie STORMY WEATHER of 1943) Mrs. Castle was not in love with the idea of blonde Rogers playing her and since she had a huge amount of creative control, the deal almost fell through but, lucky for audiences, it eventually was made. In a tiny role as Rogers's friend, note teenage Marjorie Belcher in her debut. If that name doesn't seem familiar, just know that she later married dancer Gower Champion and you can figure out whom she grew up to be. Lew Fields, who gave Vernon Castle his first job in a revue, plays himself with a dark wig that fails to convince. Fields was part of the famous comedy team of Weber and Fields and the father of Dorothy, the lyricist.

p, George Haight, Pandro S. Berman; d, H.C. Potter; w, Richard Sherman, Oscar Hammerstein, Dorothy Yost (based on the books *My Husband* and *My Memories of Vernon Castle* by Irene Castle); ph, Robert DeGrasse, ed, William Hamilton; md, Victor Baravalle; art d, Van Nest Polglase, Perry Ferguson; set d, Darrell Silvera; cos, Walter Plunkett, Edward Stevenson, Castle; spec eff, Vernon L. Walker, Douglas Travers; ch, Hermes Pan; makeup, Mel Burns.

Musical/Biography   **Cas.**   **(PR:A MPAA:NR)**

STORY OF VICKIE, THE**½   (1958, Aust.) 108m Marischka/BV c

Romy Schneider *(Victoria)*, Adrian Hoven *(Prince Albert)*, Magda Schneider *(Baroness Lehzen)*, Karl Ludwig Diehl *(Lord Melbourne, Prime Minister)*, Christl Mardayn *(Duchess of Kent)*, Paul Horbiger *(Prof. Landmann)*, Rudolf Vogel *(George, Palace Valet)*, Fred Liewehr *(Leopold, King of the Belgians)*, Alfred Neugebauer *(Lord Conyngham)*, Otto Tressler *(Archbishop of Canterbury)*, Stefan Skodler *(Sir John Conroy)*, Peter Weck *(Prince Henry of Orange)*, Rudolf Lenz *(Archduke Alexander of Russia)*, Hans Thimig *(The Dean)*, Peter Gerhard *(Taglione, Dance Master)*, Elisabeth Epf *(Lady Flora Hastings)*, Hilde Wagener *(Lady Littleton)*, Helene Lauterbock *(Lady Lansdowne)*, Eduard Strauss *(Johann Strauss, Sr.)*, Viktor Braun.

The story of Queen Victoria's rise to power is given an aura of charm by the casting of Schneider in the royal role. The film follows her from her days as a young princess about to assume the throne to her marriage to Prince Albert (Hoven). One particularly delightful scene has Schneider, knowing that she is soon to be married off to an unknown prince, falling in love with Hoven, only to discover that he has been chosen as her husband.

p,d&w, Ernst Marischka (based on letters and diaries of Queen Victoria and a comedy by Sil-Vara); ph, Bruno Mondi (Technicolor); m, Anton Profes; ed, Hermann Leitner, A. Wayne Smith, Manuel San Fernando; art d, Fritz Juptner-Joustorff.

Biography/Romance   **(PR:A MPAA:NR)**

STORY OF WILL ROGERS, THE***   (1952) 109m WB c

Will Rogers, Jr *(Will Rogers)*, Jane Wyman *(Mrs. Will Rogers)*, Carl Benton Reid *(Clem Rogers)*, Eve Miller *(Cora Marshall)*, James Gleason *(Bert Lynn)*, Slim Pickens *(Dusty Donovan)*, Noah Beery, Jr *(Wiley Post)*, Mary Wickes *(Mrs. Foster)*, Steve Brodie *(Dave Marshall)*, Pinky Tomlin *(Orville James)*, Margaret Field *(Sally Rogers)*, Virgil S. Taylor *(Art Frazer)*, Richard Kean *(Mr. Cavendish)*, Jay Silverheels *(Joe Arrow)*, William Forrest *(Flo Ziegfeld)*, Earl Lee *(Pres. Wilson)*, Brian Daly *(Tom McSpadden)*, Eddie Cantor *(Himself)*, Robert Scott Correll *(Younger Will, Jr.)*, Carol Ann Gainey *(Younger Mary)*, Michael Gainey *(Younger Jimmy/Young Will)*, Carol Nugent *(Young Mary)*, Jack Burnette *(Young Jimmy)*, Paul McWilliam *(Dead-Eye Dick)*, Dub Taylor *(Actor)*, Olan Soule *(Secretary)*, Madge Journeay *(Honey Girl Kate)*, Denver Dixon, Bob Rose *(Bits)*, Monte Blue *(Delegate)*.

A charming tribute to America's great humorist Will Rogers which offers a simple, reverent tale of his life. Cast in his father's role is Will, Jr., who accurately captures the man's wit, though more out of imitation than originality. The story follows Roger's life from his birth in 1879 in Oologah, Oklahoma to his marriage and experiences with a Wild West show, until his final fateful Alaska-bound plane crash in 1935.

p, Robert Arthur; d, Michael Curtiz; w, Frank Davis, Stanley Roberts, John C. Moffitt (based on "Uncle Clem's Boy," a story by Betty Blake Rogers) ph, Wilfrid M. Cline (Technicolor); m, Victor Young; ed, Folmar Blangsted; art d, Edward Carrere; cos, Milo Anderson.

Biography   **(PR:A MPAA:NR)**

STORY ON PAGE ONE, THE**   (1959) 123m FOX bw

Rita Hayworth *(Jo Morris)*, Anthony Franciosa *(Victor Santini)*, Gig Young *(Larry Ellis)*, Mildred Dunnock *(Mrs. Ellis)*, Hugh Griffith *(Judge Nielsen)*, Sanford Meisner *(Phil Stanley)*, Robert Burton *(Nordau)*, Alfred Ryder *(Lt. Mike Morris)*, Katherine Squire *(Mrs. Brown)*, Raymond Greenleaf *(Judge Carey)*, Myrna Fahey *(Alice)*, Leo Penn *(Morrie Goetz)*, Sheridan Comerate *(Francis Morris)*, Jay Adler *(Lauber)*, Biff Elliot *(Eddie Ritter)*, Carol Seflinger *(Avis Morris)*, Theodore Newton *(Dr. Kemper)*, James O'Rear *(Hauser)*, Richard Le Pore *(Calvin Lewis)*, Dan Riss *(Court Clerk)*, Joe Besser *(Gallagher)*, Joseph McGuinn *(Lt. Morris)*, Leonard George *(Jury Foreman)*, Miranda Jones *(Miss Monroe, the Secretary)*, George Turley *(Court Stenographer)*, Jerry Sheldon *(Quiet Man at Bar)*, Art Salter *(Bartender)*, Bru Danger *(Cook)*, Valerie French *(Liz, the Waitress)*, William Challee *(Lemke)*, Virginia Carroll *(Police Matron)*, Tom Greenway *(Capt. Kelly)*.

A potentially explosive courtroom drama is ruined by inept direction, a wordy script, and gross miscasting, except for Hayworth, Dunnock, Squire, and Ryder. Odets hadn't directed a film since his first, NONE BUT THE LONELY HEART, many years ago, and his rustiness behind the megaphone was immediately apparent. It was the kind of direction that Odets, the writer, would have written an angry letter about, because there were more loose ends dangling than one finds on a $25 suit. He'd intended it to be a play and worked on it between assignments; then Wald and studio chief Goetz asked him to make it into a movie with himself directing. An ego as large as Odets' could not withstand that chance and so a cast was assembled and the picture begun. But there must have been many changes in the script on the set because there are so many errors in construction and motivation. Hayworth lives with her mother, Squire, who goes to see hard-drinking attorney Franciosa – a man just this side of bankruptcy, if we are to believe the shape of his office and the way in which he treats his clients. Hayworth and Young are lovers and have both been arrested for the murder of Hayworth's late husband, Ryder. Franciosa is hired to defend them. Into a flashback we see Hayworth being treated poorly by her drunken spouse, then her meeting old pal Young and taking up with him as an adulterous wife. Young goes to Hayworth's home and the two are together when Ryder walks in, grabs for his gun, and it goes off, killing Ryder. Now it's time for the trial, as poorly staged as you have ever seen. The sloppy, erratic Franciosa is miraculously transformed into a sleek, well-dressed Melvin Belli with the brilliant courtroom tactics of Clarence Darrow. The audience knows from the start that the death was an accident caused by Ryder himself so all elements of suspense are gone straightaway. It's only a question of whether or not Franciosa can convince the jury and judge Griffith that his cause is just. The prosecutor is Meisner, a tough man who is out to nail this immoral couple and will stop at nothing to do it. The jump from bum to sharp attorney is but the first jar to the senses. During the trial, the policeman brother of the slain man, McGuinn, is questioned on the stand while dressed in a business suit. There's a cut to the people in the courtroom watching and who should be there? McGuinn again, in his police uniform, interested in what he himself is saying. It happens again when Dunnock is noted in the background while her voice seems to be coming from the witness stand. Dunnock is a fine actress with many laudable talents but we suspect ventriloquism is not among them. In the middle of a scene on the same day, Franciosa is seen wearing two different suits, which makes him not only a terrific defense attorney but surely one of the world's greatest quick-change artists because he is able to totally substitute his entire outfit without anyone in the crowded courtroom having noticed] Franciosa is intense and every line of his dialog is read as though he were an Episcopalian minister warning about sin. Young has a tendency to be too glib and to go for the cutesy moves when his life is in danger of being snuffed by the state. Only Hayworth, of the three principals, is convincing. By this time, age and gravity had worn off her glamorous image and she was able to play the role of a wife who had spent years unhappily and was now seeking the chance to have a little joy in her life. The idea of having an adulterous couple as the protagonists turned many people off. From time to time, an excellent Odets line is heard but, as the director, he should have been crueler with the author's script. Odets' pal, Sanford Meisner, the driving force behind the Group Theater, overplays to a fault. His students – and they are legion – must have laughed themselves silly. Editor Fowler is not to be blamed for the mistakes as he could only work with the footage that was offered him. Surprising that veteran producer Wald could have let this get away.

p, Jerry Wald; d&w, Clifford Odets; ph, James Wong Howe (CinemaScope); m, Elmer Bernstein; ed, Hugh S. Fowler; art d, Lyle R. Wheeler, Howard Richmond; set d, Walter M. Scott,G. W. Berntsen; makeup, Ben Nye.

Drama   **(PR:C MPAA:NR)**

STORY WITHOUT A NAME   (SEE: WITHOUT WARNING, 1952)

STORY WITHOUT WORDS**½   (1981, Ital.) 59m Megavision-RAI c
(STORIA SENZA PAROLE)

Elisabeth Long, Lino Troisi, Lorraine de Selle, Dario Mazzoli, Tamara Trifflex, Aldo Donati.

An oddity for the sound age, this 16mm silent film visually relates a standard, lavishly decorated murder mystery which centers on an adulterous couple. While the technique is admirable for the 80s (only background music and incidental party sounds are used) the film can't hold its weight with the silents of the 20s. STORY WITHOUT WORDS is just that, and little more. On that basis alone it does not deserve any special attention.

d, Biagio Proietti; w, Proietti, Diana Crispo; ph, Alfio Contini; ed, Gisella Nuccitelli.

Mystery (PR:A MPAA:NR)

STOWAWAY** (1932) 54m UNIV bw

Fay Wray, Betty Francisco, Leon Waycoff [Ames], Roscoe Karns, Lee Moran, James Gordon, Maurice Black, Montagu Love, Knute Erickson, Paul Porcasi.

A love triangle forms when disenchanted dance hall girl Wray stows away on a cargo ship. Second mate Waycoff discovers her and agrees to keep her whereabouts secret, but first mate Love is less hospitable. Standard programmer fare which differs from others only in its change of location.

d, Phil Whitman; w, Norman Springer; ph, Leon Shamroy.

Drama (PR:A MPAA:NR)

STOWAWAY*** (1936) 86m FOX bw

Shirley Temple (Ching-Ching, Daughter of Missionaries), Robert Young (Tommy Randall), Alice Faye (Susan Parker), Eugene Pallette (The Colonel), Helen Westley (Mrs. Hope), Arthur Treacher (Atkins), J. Edward Bromberg (Judge Booth), Astrid Allwyn (Kay Swift), Allan Lane (Richard Hope), Robert Greig (Captain), Jayne Regan (Dora Day), Julius Tannen (First Mate), Willie Fung (Chang), Phillip Ahn (Sun Lo), Paul McVey (Second Mate), Helen Jerome Eddy (Mrs. Kruikshank), William Stack (Alfred Kruikshank), Honorable Wu (Latchee Lee).

A delightful Temple vehicle which has her cast as Ching-Ching, a ward of a group of murdered missionaries. She finds refuge in Young's car, which is then loaded onto an ocean liner. When Young weds Faye, the couple decide to adopt Temple as their own, but soon separate and file for divorce. Temple turns on the charm and convinces Young and Faye to remain husband and wife. The little moppet's most memorable scene was her impersonating Al Jolson, Eddie Cantor, and Ginger Rogers (dancing with a Fred Astaire doll). It is worth it just to hear Shirley speak Chinese. Songs include "Good Night, My Love," "One Never Knows, Does One" (sung by Faye), "You Gotta S-M-I-L-E to Be H-A-P-P-Y," "I Wanna Go to the Zoo" (Mack Gordon, Harry Revel, sung by Temple), "That's What I Want for Christmas" (Irving Caesar, Gerald Marks, sung by Temple).

p, Buddy G. DeSylva; d, William A. Seiter; w, William Conselman, Arthur Sheekman, Nat Perrin (based on a story by Samuel G. Engel); ph, Arthur Miller; ed, Lloyd Nosler; md, Louis Silvers; art d, William Darling; set d, Thomas Little; cos, Royer.

Musical/Comedy (PR:AAA MPAA:NR)

STOWAWAY GIRL*** (1957, Brit.) 87m PAR bw (GB: MANUELA)

Trevor Howard (James Prothero), Leslie Weston (Bleloch), Donald Pleasence (Evans), Jack McGowran (Tommy), Warren Mitchell (Moss), Harcourt Curacao (Wellington Jones), Barry Lowe (Murphy), Pedro Armendariz (Mario Constanza), Juan Carolilla (Official), John Rae (Ferguson), Roger Delgado (Stranger), Elsa Martinelli (Manuela Hunt), Harold Kasket (Pereira), Max Butterfield (Bliss), Andy Ho (Cook), Peter Illing (Agent), Armando Guinle (Patron), Michael Peake (Coca-Cola Man).

Howard plays the skipper of an old freighter on its last legs, when Martinelli is smuggled on board by the bullying engineer, Armendariz. Howard and Martinelli quickly develop a romance, in spite of the remonstrations of Armendariz who wants the girl for himself. Howard becomes so enthralled with the girl he forgets his duties as the ship's captain, causing a fire that both destroys the freighter and separates the lovers forever. Performances are sincere and poignant, molded by a keen hand in direction.

p, Ivan Foxwell; d, Guy Hamilton; w, William Woods, Hamilton, Foxwell; (based on the novel by Woods; ph, Otto Heller; m, William Alwyn; ed, Alan Osbiston; md, Muir Mathieson; art d, John Howell; cos, Beatrice Dawson.

Drama (PR:A MPAA:NR)

STOWAWAY IN THE SKY** (1962, Fr.) 82m Filmsonor-Films Montsouris/Lopert c (LE VOYAGE EN BALLON, VOYAGE IN A BALLOON)

Pascal Lamorisse (Pascal), Andre Gille (Grandfather), Maurice Baquet (Tou-Tou), Jack Lemmon (Narrator).

A visually stunning adventure from the director of the classic short THE RED BALLOON (1956, Fr.). Again filled with aerial photography (a process he called Helivision due to his use of helicopters), this picture offers some awe-inspiring views of the Eiffel Tower, the Arc de Triomphe, and numerous other Parisian sights. The story is a simple one–a young boy stows away in his grandfather's 60-foot balloon, with a few suspenseful scenes thrown in for good measure (a crash landing). What undermines the poetic nature of

the film is a voice-over added by Jack Lemmon (his Jalem company brought the film to the States). Choosing not to dub or subtitle, Lemmon had S.N. Behrman author a narrative which he reads with childlike (childish?) enthusiasm from the point of view of the youngster. Watch it with cotton in your ears.

d&w, Albert Lamorisse (English narration, S. N. Behrman); ph, Maurice Fellous, Guy Tabary (Dyaliscope, Helivision, Eastmancolor; aer ph, Lamorisse); m, Jean Prodromides; ed, Pierre Gillette; art d, Pierre Thevenet.

Children's Adventure (PR:AA MPAA:NR)

STRAIGHT FROM THE HEART** (1935) 75m UNIV bw

Mary Astor (Marian Henshaw), Roger Pryor (Andy MacLean), Baby Jane Quigley (Maggie Haines), Carol Coombe (Mrs. Haines), Andy Devine (Edwards), Henry Armetta (Ice Cream Man), Grant Mitchell (Austin), Virginia Hammond (Mrs. Austin), Robert McWade (Boss Tim Reglan), Doris Lloyd (Miss Carter), Hilda Vaughn (Miss Nellie), Louise Carter (Mother in Breadline), Willard Robertson (District Attorney), Douglas Fowley ("Speed" Spelvin, the Reporter), Clara Blandick (Mrs. Anderson, the Neighbor), Rollo Lloyd (Grant), Esther Howard (Tired Mother), Frank Reicher (Coroner), William B. Davidson (Prosecuting Attorney), Yola D'Avril, Georgette Rhodes (French Girls in Taxi), James Flavin (Policeman), Howard C. Hickman (Police Sergeant), Warner Richmond (Cop), Jack Mulhall (Reporter), Marion Lord (Blowsy Mother), Franklin Parker, Stanley Price (Reporters), Phil Tead (Ward Heeler), Joan Standing (Mother of Crippled Boy), Veda Buckland (Mother), Bernard Suss (Clerk), Jimmy Butts (Neighbor's Baby), Arther Howe (Austin's Son), Shirley Jean Rickert (Austin's Daughter), Bestor Aber (Newsboy), William Norton Bailey, Tom O'Grady (Men), Samuel T. Godfrey (Stenographer), Dorothy D. Vernon, Beth Hazelton, Louise Lester, Lillian Castel, Kathryn Sheldon (Women), Ronnie Cosbey (Crippled Boy), Helen Parrish (Neighbor Girl), George Ernest, Donald Haines (Neighbor Boys), Velma Gresham (Nurse).

Politician Pryor cons Astor into helping him blackmail the incumbent mayor in order to further his own political career. He tries to use Baby Jane as evidence for a paternity suit, but Astor soon catches on that the mayor is innocent of the charges and comes to his defense. Pryor redeems himself by the finale, and he and Astor begin a future together.

p, B.F. Zeldman; d, Scott R. Beal; w, Doris Anderson (based on a story by Anderson); ph, Charles Stumar; ed, Ted Kent.

Drama (PR:A MPAA:NR)

STRAIGHT FROM THE SHOULDER** (1936) 65m PAR bw

Ralph Bellamy (Curt Hayden), Katherine Locke (Gail Pyne), David Holt (Johnny Hayden), Andy Clyde (J.M. Pyne), Purnell Pratt (James McBride), Onslow Stevens (Mr. Wendl), Chick Chandler (Fly), Rollo Lloyd (Mr. Blake), Bert Hanlon (Baldy), Paul Fix (Trigger Benson), Noel Madison (Trim).

An interesting twist to the gangster film is brought to the screen in STRAIGHT FROM THE SHOULDER, as young Holt is holed up in his dad Bellamy's mountain cabin, with a gang of mobsters awaiting his father's return. Bellamy, a witness to a mob shootout, is a threat to the mobsters, who not surprisingly want him dead. The boy overhears their plan to kill his father and, in the middle of the night, takes their guns and fills them with melted lead in order to cause them to backfire.

p, A. M. Botsford; d, Stuart Heisler; w, Madeleine Ruthven (based on a story by Lucian Cary); ph, Al Gilks; ed, Everett Douglas.

Crime Drama (PR:A MPAA:NR)

STRAIGHT IS THE WAY* (1934) 59m MGM bw

Franchot Tone (Benny), May Robson (Mrs. Horowitz), Karen Morley (Bertha), Gladys George (Shirley), Nat Pendleton (Skippy), Jack LaRue (Monk), Raymond Hatton (Mendel), William Bakewell (Dr. Wilkes), C. Henry Gordon.

A totally unconvincing gangster film which has Tone trying to play a Jewish gangster from New York's East Side. Upon his release from prison he finds that his former girl friend is now the moll of a rival Italian hood, so Tone decides to kill the mobster before he goes straight. A remake of the silent FOUR WALLS.

p, Lucien Hubbard; d, Paul Sloane; w, Bernard Schubert (based on the play "Four Walls" by Dana Burnet, George Abbott); ph, Lucien Andriot; ed, William S. Gray; cos, Dolly Tree.

Crime (PR:A MPAA:NR)

STRAIGHT ON TILL MORNING** (1974, Brit.) 96m Hammer/International Co-Production s c

Rita Tushingham (Brenda Thompson), Shane Briant (Peter), Tom Bell (Jimmy Lindsay), Annie Ross (Liza), Katya Wyeth (Caroline), James Bolam (Joey), Claire Kelly (Margo), Harold Berens (Mr. Harris).

A well-crafted but empty thriller which has Tushingham leaving the security of her Liverpool flat for London. She spends her time searching for a man to father her child and ends up with Briant, whom she soon discovers to be a psychotic killer.

p&d, Peter Collinson; w, Michael Peacock; ph, Brian Probyn (Technicolor); m, Roland Shaw; ed, Alan Pattillo; art d, Scott MacGregor; m/l, title song, Annie Ross (sung by Ross).

Crime/Drama   **(PR:O   MPAA:R)**

STRAIGHT, PLACE AND SHOW**

(1938) 66m FOX bw (GB: THEY'RE OFF)

The Ritz Brothers (*Themselves*), Richard Arlen (*Denny*), Ethel Merman (*Linda*), Phyllis Brooks (*Barbara Drake*), George Barbier (*Drake*), Sidney Blackmer (*Braddock*), Will Stanton (*Truck Driver*), Ivan Lebedeff, Gregory Gaye, Rafael Storm (*Russians*), Stanley Fields (*Slippery Sol*), Tiny Roebuck (*Terrible Turk*), Ben Welden (*Promoter*), Ed Gargan (*Detective*), Pat McKee (*Referee*).

Merman was billed below the Ritz Brothers in this madcap 1930s comedy which had the brothers inheriting a racehorse, but lacking the necessary $1,000 entry fee. When they uncover a plot by a gang of Russian jockeys to sabotage the race, the brothers disguise themselves as the Reds and take their place. It's sure not A DAY AT THE RACES. Includes the tunes "With You On My Mind," "Why Not String Along With Me?" (Lew Brown, Lew Pollack; sung by Merman), "International Cowboys" (Ray Golden, Sid Kuller, Jule Styne). (See RITZ BROTHERS series, Index.)

p, Darryl F. Zanuck, David Hempstead; d, David Butler; w, M. M. Musselman, Allen Rivkin, Lew Brown (based on a play by Damon Runyan, Irving Caesar); ph, Ernest Palmer; ed, Irene Morra; md, Louis Silvers; art d, Bernard Herzbrun, Lewis Creber; cos, Gwen Wakeling; ch, Nicholas Castle, Geneva Sawyer.

Musical/Comedy   **(PR:A   MPAA:NR)**

STRAIGHT SHOOTER*   (1940) 54m Victory-Principal bw

Tim McCoy ("*Lightning*" *Bill Carson*), Julie Sheldon (*Margaret Martin*), Ben Corbett (*Magpie*), Ted Adams (*Brainard*), Reed Howes (*Slade*), Forrest Taylor (*Luke*), Budd Buster [George Selk] (*Sheriff Long*), Carl Mathews (*Lane*), Wally West [Hal Taliaferro], Jack Ingram.

McCoy is hired to hunt down a gang of bandits who made off with a bag of government bonds and killed an agent in the process. He catches up with the thieves, locates the hidden loot, and brings them back to face the law. Technically and conceptually shabby.

p, Sam Katzman; d, Sam Newfield; w, Joseph O'Donnell, Basil Dickey (based on a story by Dickey); ph, Art Reed; ed, Holbrook N. Todd.

Western   **(PR:A   MPAA:NR)**

STRAIGHT TIME****   (1978) 114m First Artists-Sweetwall/WB c

Dustin Hoffman (*Max Dembo*), Theresa Russell (*Jenny Mercer*), Harry Dean Stanton (*Jerry Schue*), Gary Busey (*Willy Darin*), M. Emmet Walsh (*Earl Frank*), Sandy Barron (*Manny*), Kathy Bates (*Selma Darin*), Edward Bunker (*Mickey*), Fran Ryan (*Cafe Owner*), Rita Taggart (*Carol Schue*), Jacob Busey (*Henry Darin*), Tina Menard (*Hotel Manager*), Stephanie Ericson-Baron (*Bar Patron*), Dave Kelly (*Counter Man*), Don Sommese (*Waiter*), Kit Lee Wong (*Grocer*), Peter Kwong (*Grocery Clerk*), Betty Jane Howarth (*Employment Clerk*), Ronald L. Mellinger (*Jail Guard*), Michael Blakley (*1st Beach Boy*), John Colton (*2nd Beach Boy*), John Gilgreen (*Bank Guard*), Mary Craven, Peter Jurasik (*Bank Tellers*), Enid Hendershot (*Girl at Bank*), James Ray (*Jewelry Store Manager*), Stuart I. Berton (*1st Salesman*), Barry Cahill (*2nd Salesman*), Susan Sherman, Francesca Drown (*Saleladies*), Emily La Rue (*Girl*), Ernest Taylor III (*Job Applicant*), Bob Jarvis (*Police Officer*), Corey Rand (*Carlos*).

A gripping, disturbing, and totally unglamorized portrait of a professional thief who thrives on the thrill and danger of armed robbery. Hoffman, in one of the best performances in his career, plays a thief who is released from prison after a six-year sentence for armed robbery. Unable to contact his parole officer by phone, Hoffman checks into a cheap Los Angeles hotel, and spends the night wandering the streets, relishing his freedom. The next morning he takes a bus to the parole office where he is confronted with Walsh, a slimy bureaucrat who enjoys telling racist, sexist jokes to the office help. Walsh treats Hoffman like an unruly child and warns him that he should have gone to the halfway house instead of a hotel. Hoffman tells Walsh that he tried to call and left a message with the secretary regarding his whereabouts, but Walsh says he didn't get the message. Walsh tells Hoffman he doesn't like his "attitude" and that he'd better shape up if he wants to stay on the streets. Hoffman apologizes and reaffirms his desire to go straight. Walsh relents and says that if Hoffman can find a good place to live and a decent job in one week, he won't have to stay at the halfway house. The next day Hoffman goes to an employment agency where he meets Russell, an attractive young employee. Hoffman confesses he's an ex-con and tells her that he is not allowed to drive a car without written permission and that he can't handle money. Russell, who is intrigued by Hoffman, finds him a minimum-wage position working at a can company. Hoffman asks her if they can go out and celebrate if he gets the job and she

agrees. Meanwhile, Hoffman calls Busey, his old friend and an ex-con, a lunkish and somewhat dull amateur crook who has a wife, Bates, and a young son (played by actor Busey's own son), all living on the poverty level. Busey is glad to see Hoffman, and Hoffman enjoys a meal with the family and watches as his friend wrestles with his boy (the kid seems destined for the same fate as his father). When Busey goes to put his son to bed, Bates asks Hoffman not to come around anymore because she doesn't want Busey to slip back into a life of crime (and besides, Hoffman is in violation of his parole by just associating with another ex-con). Hoffman understands, but Busey continues to see Hoffman on the sly. One day, while Busey visits Hoffman at his hotel, Busey pulls out his heroin paraphernalia and shoots up (he's been keeping his habit a secret from Bates). Hoffman is annoyed ("That can get me three more years, man."), but lets his friend satisfy his habit. Hoffman gets the job at the can company and works hard for his meager wages. He takes Russell out on a date and she becomes attracted to his intensity and interested in his stories about life behind bars. One day Hoffman comes home from work to find Walsh searching his room. The parole officer finds a burnt book of matches under the bed (used by Busey to heat up his heroin) and he immediately checks Hoffman's arms for track marks. Despite the fact that none are evident, Walsh handcuffs Hoffman to the bed and goes to make a phone call. He leaves the door open and a little girl from across the hall stands in the doorway staring at Hoffman. Hoffman is embarrassed and uncomfortable under the girl's gaze and smiles nervously saying, "We're just playing a game." Hoffman soon finds himself being booked, showered, deloused, and back behind bars. Days later he is released and Walsh tells him that his urine tested clean–he is free to go, but back to a halfway house. Walsh acts like he's doing Hoffman a favor and lets it slip that the results were known days ago but he was too busy to get back to Hoffman. On the ride to the halfway house, Hoffman finally snaps and assaults Walsh while they drive down the freeway. He forces the car to the shoulder and drags the parole officer out of the vehicle. Hoffman handcuffs Walsh to a cyclone fence and then pulls down the man's pants leaving him hanging bare-bottomed in the middle of traffic. Hoffman ditches the car and goes to Busey's house and borrows his station wagon. He then meets an old friend who owns a bar and borrows an ancient pistol that was taken from a drunken customer. Hoffman enters a small grocery store and robs the place. Later that night he meets with Russell and tells her the truth about his last few days. She decides to let him live at her place, despite his fugitive status. Hoffman borrows her car and goes to meet a connection who tells him of a high-stakes poker game played by a bunch of old men–an easy score worth at least $10,000. Hoffman then goes to Burbank to meet with Stanton, a former crook who has married a good woman, reformed, and now runs a successful painting and contracting business. Sitting in the back yard at a picnic table eating hot dogs and hamburgers hot off the grill, surrounded by his big suburban house and kidney- shaped swimming pool, Stanton tells Hoffman of his new-found legitimate success. When his wife leaves to get more beer, Stanton leans over to Hoffman and hisses, "Get me outa here. I can't make this scene anymore." Stanton joins Hoffman in the poker game robbery. The plan goes awry, however, when the guy who was supposed to bring the shotgun shows up late and empty-handed. Hoffman flies into a rage and beats the man up, leaving Stanton to patch things up. On his way home, Hoffman spots a shotgun on the wall of a closed pawnshop. To circumvent the alarm system, he easily breaks into the laundromat next door and burrows through the connecting wall where he grabs the shotgun. Stanton saws off the barrel, adapts a smaller stock for the weapon in his nice suburban garage, and the men rob a bank. Stanton allows Hoffman 30 seconds to take what he can from the cash drawers while he stands guard over the employees and customers armed with the shotgun and a stopwatch -swearing and threatening in order to scare the daylights out of any potential hero. When Stanton yells that the time is up, Hoffman continues his frenzied grabbing and takes another 30 seconds until he gets all the money. The men make off with a tidy sum, but Stanton warns Hoffman never to take that much time again. For his next robbery, Hoffman chooses an exclusive Beverly Hills jewelry store and brings Russell with him to case the place. While he pretends to be interested in buying a watch for Russell, Hoffman checks out the doors, cameras, alarms, employees, and any other item that may cause trouble during a robbery. Stanton is a bit intimidated by the store's location since there is an average of 20 cops per square mile in Beverly Hills. Hoffman tells him there is a three-minute response time and that they'd clear out after a minute and a half. Stanton agrees to the scheme, but is very angry when on the day of the robbery, Hoffman shows up with Busey as the getaway driver. Obviously inexperienced, Busey asks Hoffman dozens of stupid questions about what he's supposed to do. Busey drops Hoffman and Stanton off in front of the store and then waits around back with the motor running. Stanton covers the door while Hoffman walks to the back of the store, sets down his leather bag, pulls out goggles and heavy gloves, dons them, and then produces a large hammer. A saleslady asks him what he's doing and he calmly asks her to stand back. He brings the hammer down on the glass jewel case and Stanton–at the front of the store–produces the shotgun and tells everyone to stand still. Hoffman goes down the row of glass display cases breaking all the glass while the alarm bells scream. He then goes back and pulls the jewels from the cases. When the time is up, Stanton yells for them to go, but Hoffman keeps going like a shark in a feeding frenzy. Stanton grabs at Hoffman and Hoffman pushes him off and continues grabbing jewelry. After what seems to be an eternity, Hoffman finally heads for the back door (Stanton sarcastically screams, "Why don't you steal the clock too?"). The two step into the alley and Busey and the car are gone. The thieves are forced to escape on foot through the back yards of Beverly Hills, but the police soon catch up with them and Stanton is killed. Hoffman shoots the cop and makes good his escape. Sweaty and desperate looking, Hoffman shows up at Russell's place of work and hustles her off to her car. He drives with her to Busey's home and leaves her in the car. He finds Busey–who explains he waited for three minutes longer than was agreed upon and then got scared and left. Hoffman tells him that Stanton is dead. Busey practically sobs apologizing, when Hoffman relents and asks for a hug. As Busey embraces him, Hoffman shoots his friend dead. Hoffman and Russell then head out to the desert. During the ride he realizes that she won't be able to take life on the run and leaves her at a roadside diner with money and instructions on how to take the bus back to Los Angeles. "Why can't I go with you?" she asks. "Because I'm gonna get caught." He drives off into the desert and the film ends with a montage of Hoffman's mug shots going all the way back to when he was 12. Based on a novel by ex-convict Edward Bunker entitled *No Beast So Fierce*, STRAIGHT TIME was an obsessive labor of love for its star, who had purchased the rights to the novel in 1972. Hoffman struck a deal with First Artists which would give him the right to direct the film and supervise the final cut. To research his role Hoffman had himself booked at Los Angeles County Jail and went through the procedure all inmates go through (this was later re-created for the film in an almost documentary-like fashion). Hoffman also managed to sneak into San Quentin prison and mingle with the prisoners for several hours incognito to get the feel of prison life. The actor also interviewed ex-cons and visited their homes. During production, however, Hoffman found that acting and directing was too much for him so he hired his old friend Grosbard to take over the helm. When the filming was completed, First Artists' president Phil Feldman took control of the film and refused Hoffman his right to final cut (Feldman was the same man who tampered with Sam Peckinpah's THE WILD BUNCH, cutting over 20 minutes of character development behind the director's back, further emphasizing the graphic bloodletting). Hoffman sued for damages; the studio–which thought the film a disaster–dumped the movie into release, where it received bad reviews and little box office. Hoffman's case was thrown out and to this day the actor speaks little of it. Hoffman has nothing to be ashamed of. STRAIGHT TIME is a powerful film which shows a criminal as he is. The film offers no tired explanations for Hoffman's behavior, no fingers are pointed, no apologies or excuses are offered. Hoffman is a habitual criminal and that is the way he is. Though the parole system is taken to task for the "Catch 22"-type restrictions given to ex-cons, this is not presented as an excuse for Hoffman's return to crime–only a match that ignites the fuse already inside the man. The performances in STRAIGHT TIME are nothing less than superb. Walsh is perfect as the slimy parole officer who couldn't care less about his charges. Busey once again proves his versatility and is unforgettable as the pathetic addict. Russell is fine as the naive girl willing to let Hoffman drift through her life and Stanton practically steals the film as the ex-thief yearning to escape from the boredom of his suburban life style. Grosbard's direction is straightforward and professional, with the highlight being the jewelry store robbery which will have viewers on the edge of their seats. Though STRAIGHT TIME was a financial and critical failure, it stands as one of the finest, most accurate, and honest portrayals of crime and criminals ever committed to film.

p, Stanley Beck, Tim Zinneman; d, Ulu Grosbard, (uncredited) Dustin Hoffman; w, Alvin Sargent, Edward Bunker, Jeffery Boam (based on the novel *No Beast So Fierce* by Bunker); ph, Owen Roizman (Technicolor); m, David Shire; ed, Sam O'Steen, Randy Roberts; prod d, Stephen Grimes; art d, Dick Lawrence; set d, Marvin March; cos, Bernie Pollack; m/l, "Two of Us," "Doin' Fine" (Shire, Norma Helms); stunts, Everett Creach, Dick Ziker.

Crime   Cas.   (PR:O MPAA:R)

STRAIGHT TO HEAVEN**   (1939) 55m Million Dollar Pictures bw

Nina Mae McKinney, Lionel Monogas, Jackie Ward, James Baskett, Percy Verwagen.

McKinney stars in this all-black feature as the wife of Monogas, an innocent man framed on trumped-up murder charges. She goes after mob head Verwagen and with the help of detective Baskett is able to clear her husband's name. A fine performance from McKinney, an alluring actress who was often billed as "the black Garbo."

d, Arthur Leonard.

Crime   (PR:A MPAA:NR)

STRAIGHTAWAY*   (1934) 60m COL bw

Tim McCoy, Sue Carol, William Bakewell, Ward Bond, Lafe McKee, Francis McDonald, Samuel S. Hinds, Arthur Rankin, Charles Sullivan.

McCoy finds himself in a bind when he is threatened with a murder rap if his younger brother takes the checkered flag at an upcoming auto race. Filled with stock footage of endless cars lapping each other and crashing off walls, ineptly edited with shots of the principals. Not worth a pit stop.

d, Otto Brower; w, Lambert Hillyer (based on a story by Hillyer); ph, Dan Clark; ed, Otto Mayer.

Crime/Action   (PR:A MPAA:NR)

STRAITJACKET, 1963   (SEE: SHOCK CORRIDOR, 1963)

STRAIT-JACKET**½   (1964) 89m COL bw

Joan Crawford (*Lucy Harbin*), Diane Baker (*Carol*), Leif Erickson (*Bill Cutler*), Howard St. John (*Raymond Fields*), John Anthony Hayes (*Michael Fields*), Rochelle Hudson (*Emily Cutler*), George Kennedy (*Leo Krause*), Edith Atwater (*Mrs. Fields*), Mitchell Cox (*Dr. Anderson*), Lee Yeary (*Frank Hardin*), Patricia Krest (*Stella Fulton*), Vickie Cos (*Carol Aged 3*), Patty Lee (*1st Little Girl*), Laura Hess (*2nd Little Girl*), Robert Ward (*Shoe Clerk*), Lyn Lundgren (*Beauty Operator*), Howard Hoffman.

Crawford is cast in this Robert Bloch-scripted (PSYCHO) tale of a crazed axe-murderer. Released after 20 years in an insane asylum, (for lopping the heads off her husband and his lover), Crawford returns home to her dear daughter, Baker, who witnessed the slayings when she was only three. Heads begin to roll again, but this time it's Baker dressed up like Mom. Before it's too late, her plan is uncovered and Crawford's sanity is reaffirmed. Guaranteed to give you the creeps now and then, but not nearly scary enough to sustain any respectable level of fright. Produced and directed by William Castle, who has always found some way to bring in an audience–this time it was free cardboard axes and a great slogan, "It's only a movie...It's only a movie." One of the victims, Mitchell Cox, was actually a vice-president of Pepsi-Cola, and Crawford a member of the board, which seems especially ironic considering that today Columbia Pictures is a division of a rival soda company, Coca-Cola.

p&d, William Castle; w, Robert Bloch; ph, Arthur Arling; m, Van Alexander; ed, Edwin Bryant; prod d, Boris Leven; set d, Frank Tuttle; spec eff, Richard Albain; makeup, Ben Lane (Joan Crawford's makeup, Monte Westmore).

Horror   Cas.   (PR:O MPAA:NR)

STRANDED**   (1935) 76m WB bw

Kay Francis (*Lynn Palmer*), George Brent (*Mack Hale*), Patricia Ellis (*Velma Tuthill*), Donald Woods (*John Wesley*), Barton MacLane (*Sharkey*), Robert Barrat (*Stan Januaschek*), June Travis (*Jennie Holden/Mary Rand*), Shirley Grey (*Marvel Young*), Henry O'Neill (*Mr. Tuthill*), Ann Shoemaker (*Mrs. Tuthill*), Frankie Darro (*Jimmy Rivers*), William Harrigan (*Updike*), Joseph Crehan (*Johnny Quinn*), John Wray (*Mike Gibbons*), Edward McWade (*Tim Powers*), Gavin Gordon (*Jack*), Mary Forbes (*Grace Dean*), Florence Fair (*Miss Walsh*), Burr Carruth (*Old Man*), Emmett Vogan (*Officer*), Harry C. Bradley (*Conductor*), Samuel R. McDaniel (*Porter*), Eily Malyon (*Old Maid*), John Kelly (*Sailor*), Joan Gay (*Dane*), Mae Busch (*Lizzie*), Edwin Mordant (*Surgeon*), Harrison Greene (*Blustery Man*), Eleanor Wesselhoeft (*Mrs. Young*), Wally Wales (*Peterson*), Wilfred Lucas (*Man Worker*), Glen Cavender (*Kolchak*), Joe King (*Dan Archer*), Frank Sheridan (*Boone*), Emma Young (*Chinese Girl*), Mia Liu (*Japanese Girl*), Rita Rozelle (*Polish Girl*), Louise Seidel (*Danish Girl*), Frank LaRue (*Doctor*), Lillian Harmer (*Desk Attendant*), Zeffie Tilbury (*Old Hag*), Lillian Worth (*Blonde*), Georgia Cooper (*Floor Nurse*), Adrian Rosley (*Headwaiter*), Spencer Charters (*Boatman*), Junior Coghlan (*Page*), Jack Richardson, Stan Cavanagh (*Taxi Drivers*), Edwin Stanley (*Police Surgeon*), Edward Keane (*Doctor*), Niles Welch (*Safety Engineer*), Walter Clyde (*Assistant*), Milton Kibbee (*Pat, the Timekeeper*), Marbeth Wright (*Operator*), Donald Downen (*Clerk*), Claudia Coleman (*Madame*), Patrick Moriarity (*Steve Brodie*), Sarah Padden (*Workman's Wife*), Dick French (*Clerk*), Jessie Arnold (*Scrubwoman*), Henry Otho (*Worker*), Vesey O'Davoren (*Butler*), Tom Wilson (*Immigrant*), Philo McCullough (*Immigration Officer*), Richard Loo (*A Groom*), Frank Marlowe (*Rollins, an Agitator*), Leo White (*Haines, a Drunken Worker*), Adrian Morris (*Rivet Boss*).

A weak romancer which stars Francis as a welfare worker for the San Francisco-based Traveler's Aid, and Brent as the chief foreman for the construction of the Golden Gate Bridge. After having a crush on him nine years earlier, Francis gets her chance to pursue the relationship. They struggle to find time to be together, but are both too busy, though they do manage to become engaged by the film's finale. Filled with tedious newsreel footage of the bridge's construction and some weak Socialist preachiness, which was in vogue at the time.

d, Frank Borzage; w, Delmer Daves, Carl Erickson (based on the story "The Lady With a Badge" by Frank Wead, Ferdinand Reyher); ph, Sid Hickox; ed, William Holmes; md, Leo F. Forbstein; art d, Anton Grot, Hugh Reticker; cos, Orry-Kelly.

Romance   (PR:A MPAA:NR)

STRANDED**½   (1965) 90m Compton bw

Juleen Compton (*Raina*), Gary Collins (*Bob*), Gian Pietro Calasso (*Olivier*), Alkis Yanakis (*Nicos*).

A likable independent feature which is basically a plotless meander through the life of Compton (who also wrote and directed), an American girl living in Greece. From her opening attempt at suicide (she calmly walks into the sea), we follow her as she experiences life with her friends and lovers. Film relies chiefly on the charm of Compton to sustain audience interest.

p,d&w, Juleen Compton; ph, Demos Sakeyyariose; m, John Sakellarides; ed, A. Siaskas, Claude Plouganio.

Drama (PR:O MPAA:NR)

STRANDED, 1967 (SEE: VALLEY OF MYSTERY, 1967)

STRANDED IN PARIS (SEE: ARTISTS AND MODELS ABROAD, 1938)

STRANGE ADVENTURE* (1932) 62m Chadwick/MON bw (AKA: WAYNE MURDER CASE)

Regis Toomey (*Lt. Mitchell*), June Clyde (*Toodles Reporter*), Lucille La-Verne (*Mrs. Sheen Housekeeper*), William V. Mong (*Silas Wayne*), Jason Robards, Sr (*Dr. Bailey*), Eddie Phillips (*Claude Wayne*), Dwight Frye (*Robert Wayne*), Isabelle Vecki (*Sarah Boulter*), Alan Roscoe (*Stephen Boulter*), Nadine Dore (*Gloria*), Snowflake [Fred Toones] (*Jeff*), William J. Humphrey (*Coroner*), Harry Myers (*Officer Kelly*), Eddy Chandler (*Policeman*).

Detective Toomey and newsgirl Clyde solve a mystery in which nearly everyone involved is suspect. The innocent ones are getting killed one by one, but eventually the pair of sleuth's get to the bottom.

p, Trem Carr; d, Phil Whitman, Hampton Del Ruth; w, Lee Chadwick (based on a story by Arthur Hoerl); ph, Leon Shamroy.

Mystery Cas. (PR:A MPAA:NR)

STRANGE ADVENTURE, A*½ (1956) 70m REP bw

Joan Evans (*Terry Dolgin*), Ben Cooper (*Harold Norton*), Marla English (*Lynn Novack*), Jan Merlin (*Al Kutner*), Nick Adams (*Phil Davis*), Peter Miller (*Luther Dolgin*), Paul Smith (*Carl Johnson*), Emlen Davies (*Mrs. Norton*), Frank Wilcox (*Public Defender*), Thomas Browne Henry (*Criminal Attorney*), John Maxwell (*Insurance Lawyer*), Steve Wayne (*Western Union Messenger*).

Cooper's love for hot rods and life in the fast lane gets him in trouble when he gets mixed up with Evans, an out-of-towner. He is forced by her and a pair of accomplices to drive them to their mountain hideout after they've knocked off an armored car.

p, William J. O'Sullivan; d, William Witney; w, Houston Branch; ph, Bud Thackery; ed, Howard Smith; md, R. Dale Butts; art d, Frank Arrigo; cos, Adele Palmer.

Crime (PR:A MPAA:NR)

STRANGE ADVENTURES OF MR. SMITH, THE*½ (1937, Brit.) 71m George Smith/RKO bw

Gus McNaughton (*Will Smith/Black Patch*), Norma Varden (*Mrs. Broadbent*), Eve Gray (*Mrs. Maidie Smith*), Aubrey Mallalieu (*Mr. Broadbent*), Billy Shine (*Rodney Broadbent*), Hal Walters (*Lobby*), Isobel Scaife (*Birkenstraw*), Michael Ripper.

McNaughton is a pavement artist who tries to convince his new wife, Gray, that he is really a successful businessman. He assumes a new identity, but is then suspected of murdering the pavement artist (himself). His identity is discovered by his curious mother-in-law, but the marriage is saved when a patron of the arts leaves him 10,000 pounds.

p, George Smith; d, Maclean Rogers; w, H. F. Maltby, Kathleen Butler; ph, Geoffrey Faithfull.

Comedy (PR:A MPAA:NR)

STRANGE AFFAIR* (1944) 78m COL bw

Allyn Joslyn (*Bill Harrison*), Evelyn Keyes (*Jacqueline Harrison*), Marguerite Chapman (*Marie Dumont*), Edgar Buchanan (*Lt. Washburn*), Nina Foch (*Freda Brenner*), Hugo Haas (*Domino*), Shemp Howard (*Laundry Truck Driver*), Frank Jenks (*Sgt. Erwin*), Erwin Kalser (*Dr. Brenner*), Tonio Selwart (*Leslie Carlson*), John Wengraf (*Rudolph Kruger*), Erik Rolf (*Johansen*), Carole Mathews (*Gloria*), Edgar Dearing (*Motor Cop*), Ray Teal (*Truck Driver*).

Joslyn is the creator of a detective cartoon strip who successfully applies his deductive powers to the solving of real police cases. His involvement perturbs the police, mainly because he's always right. When a fund-raising organizer dies at a benefit, Joslyn amends the police report stating that the cause of death was a heart attack. He proves that the man was poisoned and again makes the cops look like fools.

p, Burt Kelly; d, Alfred E. Green; w, Oscar Saul, Eva Greene, Jerome Odlum (based on the story "Stalk the Hunter" by Saul); ph, Franz F. Planer; m, Marlin Skiles; ed, Richard Fantl; md, M. W. Stoloff; art d, Lionel Banks, Walter Holscher; cos, Jean Louis.

Mystery (PR:A MPAA:NR)

STRANGE AFFAIR, THE* (1968, Brit.) 106m PAR c

Michael York (*Peter Strange*), Jeremy Kemp (*Detective Sgt. Pierce*), Susan George (*Frederika "Fred" March*), Jack Watson (*Daddy Quince*), George A. Cooper (*Superintendent Kingley*), Barry Fantoni (*Charley Small, Informer*), Artro Morris (*Inspector Evans*), Nigel Davenport (*Defense Attorney*), Madge Ryan (*Aunt Mary*), George Benson (*Uncle Bertrand*), George Selway (*Sgt. Clancy*), Michael Gover (*Detective Chief Superintendent Bryan*), Terence de Marney (*Mahon*), Jeremy Wilkin (*P.C. Wills*), Richard Pearson (*Constable*), Patrick Connor (*Sgt. Mac*), George Ghent (*Sgt. Perry*), David Glaisyer (*Roddy Quince*), Richard Vanstone (*Arthur Quince*), Robin Tolhurst (*Air Hostess*), Rita Webb (*Bedraggled Woman*), Patrick Newell (*Victim*), Richard Warner (*Magistrate*), Philip Ryan, Dave Carter (*Building Site Workmen*), Bernard Stone, Janet Lees Price, Toba Laurence (*Neighbors*), John Paul, The Blue Mountain Boys (*Pub Group*).

York is the Strange of the title who gets mixed up with Scotland Yard detective Kemp. The inspector is trying to put a gang of drug smugglers behind bars, but due to Britain's overly strict laws in favor of the private citizen, he has a tough time doing so. He threatens to blackmail York unless he plants some heroin on one of the smugglers. York agrees, but only gets himself in worse trouble when he is the one who gets arrested. In the meantime, York is carrying on with George, who is part of a porno ring that has her aunt and uncle film her sexual encounters from behind a one-way mirror.

p, Howard Harrison, Stanley Mann; d, David Greene; w, Mann (based on the novel by Bernard Toms); ph, Alex Thomson (Techniscope, Technicolor); m, Basil Kirchin; ed, Brian Smedley-Aston; prod d, Brian Eatwell; art d, Nicholas Pollock; set d, Peta Button; cos, Susan Yelland; makeup, George Blackler.

Crime (PR:O MPAA:R)

STRANGE AFFAIR OF UNCLE HARRY, THE (SEE: UNCLE HARRY, 1945)

STRANGE AFFECTION½** (1959, Brit.) 88m George Minter/Brenner bw (GB: THE SCAMP)

Richard Attenborough (*Stephen Leigh*), Dorothy Alison (*Barbara Leigh*), Colin Petersen (*Tod Dawson*), Terence Morgan (*Mike Dawson*), Jill Adams (*Julie Dawson*), Maureen Delaney (*Mrs. Perryman*), Margaretta Scott (*Mrs. Blundell*), David Franks (*Eddie*), Geoffrey Keen (*Headmaster*), Charles Lloyd Pack (*Beamish*), June Cunningham (*Annette*), Sam Kydd (*Shopkeeper*), Victor Brooks (*Inspector Birch*), Cyril Wheeler (*Constable Simpson*), Kenneth Edwards (*Chairman of Juvenile Court*), David Evans, Marc Sheldon (*Bar Customers*), Sidney Vivian (*Drunken Reveller*), Hugh Russell (*1st Boy*), Peter Soule (*2nd Boy*), Kenneth Collins (*Cheeky Boy*), Garry Leeman (*Colebrook*), Oliver McGreevy (*Building Foreman*), Roger Avon (*Constable*).

Shaky direction and a cliche-ridden script mar any possibilities for this human interest story about a neglected boy, charmfully portrayed by 10-year-old Petersen, who is a victim of his father's drunkenness and neglect. Saving grace has Attenborough and Alison as neighbors who take an interest in the boy, and try to give him something to believe in despite his wretched home life. In a moment of self defense, the fiery Petersen knocks his father over the head. Thinking his dad has been killed, Petersen runs to the protection of Attenborough. But the boy proves innocent of his father's death and is given the chance to stay with Attenborough for good.

p, James Lawrie; d&w, Wolf Rilla (based on the play "Uncertain Joy" by Charlotte Hastings); ph, Freddie Francis; m, Francis Chagrin; ed, Bernard Gribble.

Drama (PR:A MPAA:NR)

STRANGE ALIBI* (1941) 63m WB-FN/WB bw

Arthur Kennedy (*Joe Geary*), Joan Perry (*Alice Delvin*), Jonathan Hale (*Chief Sprague*), John Ridgely (*Tex*), Florence Bates (*Katie*), Charles Trowbridge (*Governor Phelps*), Cliff Clark (*Capt. Reddick*), Stanley Andrews (*Lt. Pagle*), Howard da Silva (*Monson*), Wade Boteler (*Capt. Allen*), Ben Welden (*Durkin*), Dick Rich (*Benny McKaye/Big Dog*), Paul Phillips (*Crips Vossen*), Joe King (*Warden Morrel*), Paul Stanton (*Prosecutor*), Joe Downing.

Kennedy isn't given much to work with in this familiar tale of a hard-working decent city cop who discovers that one of his higher-ups is also a top mob figure. He gets pinned with his chief's murder when the mob feels he's getting too wise. Kennedy can't be stopped, however, and he escapes from jail to expose the underworld wrongdoings. Given a better script, Kennedy's fine performance might have meant something.

d, D. Ross Lederman; w, Kenneth Gamet (based on the story "Give Me Liberty" by Leslie T. White); ph, Allen G. Siegler; ed, Frank Magee; cos, Howard Shoup.

Crime (PR:A MPAA:NR)

STRANGE AWAKENING, THE (SEE: FEMALE FIENDS, 1958, Brit.)

STRANGE BARGAIN**½   (1949) 68m RKO bw

Martha Scott (Georgia Wilson), Jeffrey Lynn (Sam Wilson), Henry [Harry] Morgan (Lt. Richard Webb), Katherine Emery (Edna Jarvis), Richard Gaines (Malcolm Jarvis), Henry O'Neill (Timothy Herne), Walter Sande (Sgt. Cord), Michael Chapin (Roddy Wilson), Arlene Gray (Hilda Wilson), Raymond Roe (Sydney Jarvis), Robert Bray (McTay).

An engrossing suspenser which has financially troubled bookkeeper Lynn getting in hot water with the police when he strikes a deal with his boss Gaines. He is told that the business is bankrupt and that his boss is going to commit suicide. Gaines goes on to offer $10,000 to Lynn if he will dispose of the gun in order to assure that Gaines' family gets the insurance claim. Lynn agrees, but soon becomes the chief suspect as the police try to pin a guilty verdict on him. The finale reveals, however, that Gaines didn't actually commit suicide, but was murdered. The real culprit is discovered and Lynn is let off the hook.

p, Sid Rogell; d, Will Price; w, Lillie Hayward (based on a story by J.H. Wallis); ph, Harry J. Wild; ed, Frederic Knudtson; md, Constantin Bakaleinikoff; art d, Albert S. D'Agostino, Carroll Clark.

Crime/Drama   (PR:A   MPAA:NR)

STRANGE BEDFELLOWS**½   (1965) 99m Fernwood/UNIV c

Rock Hudson (Carter Harrison), Gina Lollobrigida (Toni Vincente), Gig Young (Richard Bramwell), Edward Judd (Harry Jones), Terry-Thomas (Assistant Mortician), Arthur Haynes (Carter's Taxi Driver), Howard St. John (J.L. Stevens), Nancy Kulp (Aggressive Woman), David King (Toni's Taxi Driver), Peggy Rea (Mavis), Joseph Sirola (Petracini), Lucy Landau (Jolly Woman), Bernard Fox (Policeman), Edith Atwater (Mrs. Stevens), James McCallion (Old Man), Hedley Mattingly (Bagshott), John Orchard (Radio Dispatcher), Frederic Worlock (Lawyer), Arthur Gould Porter (Chief Mortician), Alan Caillou (Magistrate), Simon Scott (Slade), Henry Corden (Interpreter), Maurice Dallimore (Gentleman in Rain), George Robotham, John Dahein (Stuntmen), Dinah Anne Rogers (Secretary), Kanan Awni (Sheik).

An entertaining comedy with Hudson and Lollobrigida as the title characters, and Young as a PR man hired to mend their unstable marriage. Young has to work wonders on Hudson's saucy image in order to secure his promotion to the head of an oil company. One may falsely believe this one was filmed in London, but a perceptive eye (and a close look at the credits) will reveal that it was actually shot on a detailed Universal back lot.

p&d, Melvin Frank; w, Frank, Michael Pertwee (based on the story by Frank, Norman Panama); ph, Leo Tover (Technicolor); m, Leigh Harline; ed, Gene Milford; art d, Alexander Golitzen, Joseph Wright; set d, John McCarthy, John Austin; cos, Peter Saldutti, Sally Wood, Jean Louis; makeup, Bud Westmore.

Comedy   (PR:A-C MPAA:NR)

STRANGE BEHAVIOR (SEE: DEAD KIDS, 1981, Aus./New Zealand)

STRANGE BOARDERS*½   (1938, Brit.) 74m Gainsborough/GB bw

Tom Walls (Tommy Blythe), Renee Saint-Cyr (Louise Blythe), Googie Withers (Elsie), Ronald Adam (Barstow), C.V. France (Col. Anstruther), Nina Boucicault (Mrs. Anstruther), Leon M. Lion (Luke), C. Denier Warren (Fry), Irene Handl (Mrs. Dewar), Marda Vanne (Mrs. Greatorex), George Curzon (Sir Charles), Tyrell Davis (Hayes), Martita Hunt (Miss Pitter), George Hayes, Bryan Powley, Marie Wright, Arthur Goullet, Dino Galvini, Leo [Pokorny] von Pokorny, Fred Groves, Robert Nainby, John Turnbull, Douglas Stewart, Hay Plumb, Bernard Meresfield, Albert Chevalier.

Walls plays a top-notch secret service man who is called upon to solve a mystery involving the death of a bag lady whose bags contained secret airplane blueprints. He takes a room in the boarding house where she lived and soon learns that nearly every one of his neighbors is part of an espionage ring. The manner in which Walls unravels the case is overly familiar, adding nothing new to the genre this time around.

p, Edward Black; d, Herbert Mason; w, Sidney Gilliat, A. R. Rawlinson (based on the novel The Strange Boarders Of Paradise Crescent by E. Phillips Oppenheim); ph, Jack Cox; ed, Michael Gordon.

Mystery   (PR:A   MPAA:NR)

STRANGE BREW***   (1983) 90M MGM-UA c

Dave Thomas (Doug McKenzie), Rick Moranis (Bob McKenzie), Max von Sydow (Brewmeister Smith), Paul Dooley (Claude Elsinore), Lynne Griffin (Pam Elsinore), Angus MacInnes (Jean LaRose), Tom Harvey (Inspector), Douglas Campbell (Henry Green), Brian McConnachie (Ted), Len Doncheff (Jack Hawkland), Jill Frappier (Gertrude), David Beard (Judge), Thick Wilson (Prosecutor), Robert Windsor (Bailiff), Eric House (John Elsinore), Sid Lynas (Angry Man at Moie), Ron James (Man in Movie), Dora Dainton (Woman in Movie), David Clement (Man in Alley), Paddy Sampson (Pensioner), Roger Dunn (Beer Store Clerk), Diane Douglass (Receptionist), J. Winston Carroll (Fire Chief), James Conroy (Bald Con), Glenn Beck (Prison Guard), Desh Bandhu (Parking Attendant), Ilija Ilijevski (Emcee at Oktoberfest), Mary Charlotte Wilcox, Maggie Butterfield (Nurses), Thom Bell, Christopher Benson, John Stoneham (orderlies), David Rigby, Denis Forest, John Kelly, Dick Grant, George Stinton (Policemen), Mel Blanc (Voice of Mr. McKenzie).

Thomas and Moranis bring their "SCTV" comedy skit to the big screen with an equal amount of vigor and beer. While many of their television sketches lasted only a couple of minutes, STRANGE BREW drags them out to an hour and a half. Bob and Doug McKenzie do all the things they have done on TV–wear toques and plaid shirts, pontificate while under the influence of cheap Canadian beer, and call each other "hoseheads." No, there's nothing intelligent here–just a couple of likable fellows trying to stop mad brewer von Sydow from gaining control of the world. If you want intellect, go watch THE SEVENTH SEAL; von Sydow starred in that, too, before he got big with Bob and Doug. Filmed in Hoserama.

p, Louis M. Silverstein; d, Dave Thomas, Rick Moranis; w, Thomas, Moranis, Steven DeJarnatt; ph, Steven Poster (Metrocolor); m, Charles Fox; ed, Patrick McMahon; prod d, David L. Snyder; art d, Suzanna Smith, Debra Gjendem; set d, Gustave Meunier, Elena Kenney; cos, Larry Wells; spec eff, Henry Piersig, Eric Allard; m/l, "Strange Brew," Ian Thomas; makeup, L. Gill, K. Graham.

Comedy   **Cas.**   (PR:C   MPAA:PG)

STRANGE CARGO**   (1929) 75m Pathe bw

Lee Patrick (Diana Foster), June Nash (Ruth), George Barraud (Bruce Lloyd), Cosmo Kyrle Bellew (Sir Richard Barclay), Russell Gleason (Hungerford), Frank Reicher (Dr. Stecker), Claude King (Yacht Captain), Ned Sparks (Yacht First Mate), Josephine Brown (Mrs. Townsend), Charles Hamilton (Boatswain), Warner Richmond (Neil Stoker), Andre Beranger (1st Stranger), Otto Matiesen (2nd Stranger), Harry Allen (Short).

The cargo of the title is a dead man's body, and it's the captain of the ship who wants some answers and begins looking for them. A standard mystery entry which is notable for being Pathe's first all-talking feature.

d, Benjamin Glazer (sound), Arthur Gregor (silent); w, Glazer Horace Jackson (based on a story by Glazer, Melchior Lengyel); ph, Arthur Miller; ed, Paul Weatherwax, Jack Ogilvie.

Mystery   (PR:A   MPAA:NR)

STRANGE CARGO*½   (1936, Brit.) 68m Huntington/PAR bw

Kathleen Kelly (Sonia), George Mozart ('Orace), Moore Marriott (Capt. Burch), George Sanders (Roddy Burch), Richard Norris (Travers), Geoffrey Clarke (Rev. Twiddell), Kenneth Warrington (Capt. Mandera), Julien Vedey (Customs Officer), Alvin Saxon's Murray Club Band, Matt Davidson and Adele, Conway Palmer, Harry Lane.

Kelly is a dance hall girl who stows away on an English cargo ship and winds up in the middle of a Caribbean revolution as a murder suspect. With the help of Sanders, the captain's son, Kelly proves her innocence. The pair also prevent a group of mercenaries from supplying Santa Lucian rebels with ammunition which was to be smuggled onto the island in piano cases on the ship.

p&d, Lawrence Huntington; w, Gerald Elliott.

Crime/Drama   (PR:A   MPAA:NR)

STRANGE CARGO***   (1940) 105m MGM bw

Clark Gable (Andre Verne), Joan Crawford (Julie), Ian Hunter (Cambreau), Peter Lorre (Cochon), Paul Lukas (Hessler), Albert Dekker (Moll), J. Edward Bromberg (Flaubert), Eduardo Ciannelli (Telez), Victor Varconi (Fisherman), John Arledge (Dufond), Frederic Worlock (Grideau), Paul Fix (Benet), Bernard Nedell (Marfeu), Francis McDonald (Moussenq), Betty Compson (Suzanne), Charles Judels (Renard), Jack Mulhall (Dunning), Dewey Robinson (Georges), Harry Cording, Richard Alexander, Bud Fine, James Pierce, Hal Wynants, Christian Frank, Mitchell Lewis, Stanley Andrews, Dick Cramer, Ray Teal, Jack Adair (Guards), Gene Coogan, Eddie Foster, Frank Lackteen, Harry Semels (Convicts), Art Dupuis (Orderly), Stanley Andrews (Constable), William Edmunds (Watchman).

Gable and Crawford's eighth film together is a sensitively told Christ allegory, portrayed in an atmospheric manner that well conveys the story's spirituality. Crawford plays a club entertainer working in a cafe located near the infamous Devil's Island prison. She meets Gable, a prisoner, who later escapes and hides out in Crawford's dressing room. Gable is taken back into custody, but Crawford loses her job when the cafe owner learns of the incident. Back on the island, Dekker, another prisoner, has arranged an escape for a group of convicts. They include Lukas, Ciannelli, Arledge, Bromberg, as well as the despicable Lorre (whom the others call "M'sieu Pig"), and Hunter, a strange individual with an intense spirituality to him. Gable joins the escape, and again links up with Crawford. She goes with the men, and it gradually develops that Hunter has an unusual gift. At first the group of hard-core criminals hates the man because of his odd demeanor, but as men die off Hunter comforts them, exuding a strange power that helps each man accept his fate. Even the hardened Dekker and the repulsive Lorre are swayed by Hunter's influence, and die peacefully. Gable, however, refuses to believe in Hunter's Christ-like healing powers, and in frustration pushes the man overboard. Gable sees Hunter clinging to some driftwood and realizes that he cannot let this truly decent individual die, so he leaps into the water to rescue the man. Gable comes to understand that he must change his own views, and with Crawford promising to wait for him, he returns to prison to finish his sentence. This was Gable's follow-up to GONE WITH THE WIND, and his performance is a good one. Hunter's role is more difficult, but he creates a man whose deep-rooted spirituality never becomes sappy. The role was originally to have been played by Melvyn Douglas, but Hunter got the part, essaying the role perfectly. Crawford, sans glamorous makeup and with a wardrobe of only three dresses (which reportedly cost less than $40), brings a toughness to her character, accepting of her life yet determined to make it better at the end. Borzage's direction wisely avoids bathos, using murky images, along with intelligent use of light and shadow, to create a special film. STRANGE CARGO unfortunately was ill-received by the American religious community. The Catholic Legion of Decency initially gave the picture a "C" (Condemned) rating, claiming STRANGE CARGO "...presents a naturalistic concept of religion contrary to the teachings of Christ, irreverent use of Scripture, and lustful complications in dialog and situations." Following some cuts made by MGM, the Legion changed its rating to A-2, unobjectional for adults. Others, however, took harsher measures, and the film was banned in many cities across the country including Detroit and Providence, Rhode Island.

p, Joseph L. Mankiewicz; d, Frank Borzage; w, Lawrence Hazard, Lesser Samuels (based on the book *Not Too Narrow...Not Too Deep* by Richard Sale, adapted by Anita Loos); ph, Robert Planck; w, Franz Waxman; ed, Robert J. Kern; art d, Cedric Gibbons.

Drama   (PR:C MPAA:NR)

STRANGE CASE OF CLARA DEANE, THE*   (1932) 78m PAR bw

Wynne Gibson (*Clara Deane*), Pat O' Brien (*Frank Deane*), Frances Dee (*Nancy*), Dudley Digges (*Detective Garrison*), George Barbier (*Ware*), Russell Gleason (*Norman*), Florence Britton (*Miriam*), Lee Kohlmar (*Herzman*), Arthur Pierson (*Lew Severen*), Clara Blandick (*Mrs. Lyons*), Cora Sue Collins (*Nancy as a Child*).

A thoughtless programmer which insults its audience by assuming that they are as dumb as the characters in the film. Gibson is a hard-working dress designer who gets mixed up with O'Brien, a no-good scoundrel who acquires his cash by questionable means. They decide to marry, but during the ceremony–one they obviously cannot afford–detective Digges puts two and two together. The husband and wife are eyed with criminal suspicion until Gibson is arrested and sent to prison for 30 years. She is innocent, however, and it is O'Brien who is the guilty one. Before she is put away, Gibson gives birth to a daughter who is put up for adoption thanks to O'Brien's callousness. When Gibson is finally released after serving half her term, she tracks down her daughter and the pair are reunited.

d, Louis Gasnier, Max Marcin; w, Marcin (based on the play by Arthur M. Brilant); ph, Henry Sharp.

Drama   (PR:A MPAA:NR)

STRANGE CASE OF DR. MANNING, THE*

(1958, Brit.) 75m Winwell/REP bw (GB: MORNING CALL)

Ron Randell (*Nick Logan*), Greta Gynt (*Annette Manning*), Bruce Seton (*Inspector Brown*), Charles Farrell (*Karver*), Virginia Keily (*Vera Clark*), Garard Green (*Stevens*), Wally Patch (*Wally*), Peter Noble (*TV Announcer*), Peter Fontaine (*Fred Barnes*), Brian Summers (*Freddie*), David Lander (*Dr. Manning*), John Watson, Robert Raglan (*Plain clothesmen*).

When the title character (Lander) is kidnaped, his wife, Gynt, calls in private eye Randell and Scotland Yard investigator Seton. She tries to deliver the ransom money, but the interference of investigators makes it difficult. Eventually the doctor is murdered by his kidnaper, the vengeful brother of a woman killed by Lander in a car wreck years earlier. Released in Britain one year previously to a minuscule audience. U.S. Sources credit John Bash and Alfred Strauss as producers, though their names were simply tagged on in place of the film's actual British producers.

p, Derek Winn, Bill Luckwell; d, Arthur Crabtree; w, Paul Tabori, Luckwell, Tom Waldron (based on a story by Leo Townsend); ph, James Harvey; ed, John Ferris; md, John Bath; art d, John Stoll.

Crime Drama   (PR:A MPAA:NR)

STRANGE CASE OF DR. MEADE*

(1939) 64m COL bw (AKA: OUTSIDE THE LAW)

Jack Holt (*Dr. Meade*), Beverly Roberts (*Bonnie*), Paul Everton (*Dr. Hazard*), Noah Beery, Jr (*Mart*), John Qualen (*Stoner*), Charles Middleton (*Lacey*), Helen Jerome Eddy (*Mrs. Lacey*), Arthur Aylesworth (*Reuben*), Barbara Pepper (*Mattie*), Vic Potel (*Steve*), Harry Woods (*Harper*), George Cleveland (*Thurber*), Claire DuBrey (*Mrs. Thurber*), Hollis Jewell (*Thad*), Jay Ward (*Rufe*).

Holt, a New York doctor, goes south for rest and recreation, but finds himself working again when he meets backwoods nurse Roberts. It seems her doctor-boss doesn't believe in the progress of medical science and wants to treat an epidemic with old-fashioned herbs. Holt runs up against much resentment, but successfully controls the epidemic.

d, Lewis D. Collins; w, Gordon Rigby (based on the story by Rigby, Carlton Sand); ph, James S. Brown, Jr.; ed, Dwight Caldwell.

Drama   (PR:A MPAA:NR)

STRANGE CASE OF DR. RX, THE*   (1942) 66m UNIV bw

Patric Knowles (*Jerry Church*), Lionel Atwill (*Dr. Fish*), Anne Gwynne (*Kit Church*), Samuel S. Hinds (*Dudley Crispin*), Mona Barrie (*Mrs. Dudley Crispin*), Shemp Howard (*Sgt. Sweeney*), Paul Cavanagh (*John Crispin*), Edmund MacDonald (*Inspector Hurd*), Mantan Moreland (*Horatio, Butler*), John Gallaudet (*Ernie Paul*), William Gould (*Nason*), Leyland Hodgson (*Butler*), Mary Gordon (*Mrs. Scott*), Jan Wiley (*Lily*), Ray Corrigan (*Gorilla*), Boyd Davis (*Police Commissioner*), Gary Breckner (*Announcer*), Matty Fain (*Zarini*), Eddy Chandler (*Policeman*), Victor Zimmerman (*Kirk*), Harry Harvey (*Night Club Manager*), Paul Bryar (*Bailiff*), Joe Recht (*1st Newsboy*), Drew Demarest (*Club Waiter*), Jack Kennedy, Jack C. Smith (*Policemen*), Leonard Sues (*2nd Newsboy*).

A slipshod whodunit which has a mysterious killer trying to get away with a plot to kill off acquitted murderers who were saved from judicial justice by lawyer Hinds. The strangest case of all is the script and how anyone is supposed to make sense of it. Shemp Howard, on hiatus from The Three Stooges, tries unsuccessfully to add some comedy.

p, Jack Bernhard; d, William Nigh; w, Clarence Upson Young; ph, Woody Bredell; ed, Bernard W. Burton; cos, Vera West.

Mystery   (PR:A MPAA:NR)

STRANGE CONFESSION   (SEE: IMPOSTER, THE, 1944)

STRANGE CONFESSION**   (1945) 60m UNIV bw

Lon Chaney, Jr (*Jeff Carter, Chemist*), Brenda Joyce (*Mary Carter*), J. Carrol Naish (*Roger Graham*), Milburn Stone (*Stevens*), Lloyd Bridges (*Dave*), Addison Richards (*Dr. Williams*), Mary Gordon (*Mrs. O'Connor*), George Chandler (*Harper*), Gregory Muradian (*Tommy Carter*), Wilton Graff (*Brandon*), Francis McDonald (*Hernandez*), Jack Norton (*Inebriated Boarder*), Christian Rub (*Mr. Moore*).

Chaney stars as a chemist who is upset with his boss' (Naish) business practices. Naish sends the chemist to South America in order to continue some experiments, but while Chaney is away he steals a valuable formula and Chaney's wife. Tired of being in the jungle, Chaney returns home and decapitates Naish. The story is told in flashback as Chaney is trying to convince his attorney friend to defend him. Based on an "Inner Sanctum" mystery.

p, Ben Pivar; d, John Hoffman; w, M. Coates Webster (based on an "Inner Sanctum" mystery story by Jean Bart); ph, Maury Gertsman; ed, Russell Schoengarth; md, Frank Skinner; art d, John B. Goodman, Abraham Grossman; Cos, Vera West.

Mystery   (PR:A MPAA:NR)

STRANGE CONQUEST**   (1946) 63m UNIV bw

Jane Wyatt (*Dr. Mary Palmer*), Lowell Gilmore (*Dr. Paul Harris*), Peter Cookson (*William Sommers*), Julie Bishop (*Virginia Sommers*), Milburn Stone (*Bert Morrow*), Samuel S. Hinds (*Dr. A.L. Graves*), Abner Biberman (*Molugi*).

Gilmore and Cookson are rival doctors searching for a fever cure in the middle of a tropical jungle. Distressed with his failure, Cookson offers to let Gilmore test his cure on him, and dies in the process. It is then that Gilmore realizes Cookson was right all along, causing him to assume his rival's identity in order to finish the testing. While science takes a step forward, romance gets its feet tangled as Wyatt, Gilmore's girl, and Bishop, Cookson's wife, both vie for the same man. A remake of THE CRIME OF DR. HALLET.

p, Marshall Grant; d, John Rawlins; w, Roy Chanslor (based on the story by Lester Cole, Carl Dreher); ph, Charles Van Enger; ed, Philip Cahn; md, Paul Sawtell; art d, Jack Otterson, Martin Obzina.

Drama   (PR:A MPAA:NR)

STRANGE CONSPIRACY, THE
(SEE: PRESIDENT VANISHES, THE, 1934)

STRANGE DEATH OF ADOLF HITLER, THE*½

(1943) 72m UNIV bw

Ludwig Donath (*Franz Huber/Adolf Hitler*), Gale Sondergaard (*Anna Huber*), George Dolenz (*Herman Marbach*), Fritz Kortner (*Bauer*), Ludwig Stossel (*Graub*), William Trenk (*Col. Von Zechwitz*), Joan Blair (*Duchess*

Eugenie), Ivan Triesault (*Hohenberg*), Rudolph Anders (*Mampe*), Erno Verebes (*Godeck*), Merrill Rodin (*Hansl Huber*), Charles Bates (*Viki Huber*), Kurt Katch (*Karl*), Hans Schumm (*Profe*), Fred Giermann (*Heinrich Himmler*), Richard Ryen (*Palzer*), John Mylong (*Gen. Halder*), Kurt Kreuger (*Youth Leader*), Lester Sharpe (*Dr. Kaltenbruch*), Trude Berliner (*Frau Reitler*), Hans von Twardowski (*Judge*), Wolfgang Zilzer (*Attorney*), George Sorel, Gene Stutenroth [Roth], Hans von Morhart.

A bottom-rung exploitation film about a plot to do away with Hitler and replace him with a yes-man. The poor soul that the Nazis pick is Donath, a Viennese official, who goes under the knife to have his face altered. Donath's wife, an avowed Hitler hater, carries out her plan to shoot the Fuhrer, but ends up killing her husband, and then getting killed herself. An interesting conspiracy concept, which receives no help from its illogical script.

p, Ben Pivar; d, James Hogan; w, Fritz Kortner (based on the story by Kortner and Joe May); ph, Jerome Ash; ed, Milton Carruth; art d, John B. Goodman; Cos, Vera West.

Drama   (PR:A MPAA:NR)

STRANGE DECEPTION*½   (1953, Ital.) 99m Excelsa/Casino bw (IL CRISTO PROIBITO; AKA: THE FORBIDDEN CHRIST)

Raf Vallone (*Bruno*), Elena Varzi (*Nella*), Alain Cuny (*Mastro Antonio*), Gino Cervi (*The Sexton*), Rina Morelli (*Bruno's Mother*), Anna Maria Ferrero (*Maria*), Philippe Lemaire (*Pinin*), Gualtiero Tumiati (*Bruno's Father*), Ernesta Rosmino (*The Old Woman*), Luigi Tosi (*Andrea*).

More aptly titled THE FORBIDDEN CHRIST, this stark prisoner of war drama casts Vallone as a brutish Italian soldier released from a Russian camp. Upon learning that his brother had been informed on and then killed, Vallone sets out to find the betrayer. Cuny, the village carpenter, takes responsibility for the death and is killed by Vallone, who learns as the man is dying that he was actually innocent and merely sacrificing himself in the killer's place. Vallone is stunned and against the wishes of Cuny, continues his search, which leads to the frightened Lemaire, the real betrayer. The Christ-like sacrifice of Cuny digs at Vallone, however, and he is unable to kill Lemaire. Heavy on religious symbolism, STRANGE DECEPTION is a remarkable achievement for Malaparte; a well-known Italian novelist who scripted and directed this film, but he never again equalled this powerful success. (In Italian; English subtitles.)

p, Eugenio Fontano; d&w, Curzio Malaparte, ph, Gabor Pogany; m, Malaparte; art d, Leonida Maroulis.

Drama   (PR:O MPAA:NR)

STRANGE DOOR, THE*½   (1951) 81m UNIV bw

Charles Laughton (*Sire Alan de Maletroit*), Boris Karloff (*Voltan*), Sally Forrest (*Blanche de Maletroit*), Richard Stapley (*Denis de Beaulieu*), Michael Pate (*Talon*), Paul Cavanagh (*Edmond de Maletroit*), Alan Napier (*Count Grassin*), William Cottrell (*Corbeau*), Morgan Farley (*Rinville*), Charles Horvath (*Turec*), Edwin Parker (*Moret*).

A weak gothic horror film starring Laughton who seeks revenge on his brother for marrying Laughton's childhood sweetheart. Laughton imprisons his brother, Cavanagh, and convinces Cavanagh's grown daughter that her fatther is dead. He plans to make the girl's life miserable (the mother, Laughton's love, died years ago in childbirth) by marrying her off to a hard-drinking swine, Stapley. His plans go awry and everyone ends up in the dungeon. As Laughton is about to crush the whole clan with the movable cell walls, Karloff comes to their aid and releases them before they are flattened. Laughton and Karloff both seem to be competing to see who can be the hammiest in this low-budget, derivative horror film.

p, Ted Richmond; d, Joseph Pevney; w, Jerry Sackheim (based on the story "The Sire de Maletroit's Door" by Robert Louis Stevenson); ph, Irving Glassberg; ed, Edward Curtiss; md, Joseph Gershenson; art d, Bernard Herzbrun; set d, Russell A. Gausman, Julia Heron; cos, Rosemary Odell; spec eff, David S. Horsley; makeup, Bud Westmore.

Horror   (PR:A MPAA:NR)

STRANGE EVIDENCE*   (1933, Brit.) 71m LFP/PAR bw

Leslie Banks (*Francis Relf*), Carol Goodner (*Marie/Barbara Relf*), George Curzon (*Stephen Relf*), Frank Vosper (*Andrew Relf*), Norah Baring (*Clare Relf*), Haidee Wright (*Mrs. Relf*), Lyonel Watts (*Henry Relf*), Lewis Shaw (*Larry*), Diane Napier (*Jean*), Merle Oberon, Miles Malleson.

A slow-moving, melodramatic tale of an unfaithful wife, Goodner, who favors her cousin over her invalid husband. She does, however, have enough class not to accept the advances of her lecherous brother-in-law. When her husband is poisoned she is the most likely suspect, but facts surface and point to the brother-in-law. One of the last bit roles played by beautiful, dark-haired Oberon, before producer Korda began grooming her for stardom.

p, Alexander Korda; d, Robert Milton; w, Miles Malleson (based on a story by Lajos Biro); ph, Robert Martin; ed, Stephen Harrison.

Crime Drama   (PR:A MPAA:NR)

STRANGE EXPERIMENT*½   (1937, Brit.) 74m FOX British bw

Donald Gray (*James Martin*), Ann Wemyss (*Joan*), Mary Newcomb (*Helen Rollins*), Ronald Ward (*Waring*), Henry de Vries (*Prof. Bauer*), Alastair Sim (*Lawler*), James Carew (*Dr. Rollins*), Eric Hales, Lilian Talbot, Joan Pereira, Henry Caine, Charles Howard, Arnold Bell.

Gray is a scientist who inadvertently gets involved in a plot to make phony pearls. When he reconsiders and tries to quit the gang he is knocked out and left for dead. He is finally discovered, undergoes an experimental brain operation, and fakes amnesia in order to catch the criminals. His plan, as ridiculous as it seems, leads him to the gang and he successfully foils the scheme.

p, John Findlay; d, Albert Parker; w, Edward Dryhurst (based on the play "Two Worlds" by Hubert Osborne, John Golden).

Crime   (PR:A MPAA:NR)

STRANGE FACES*   (1938) 66m UNIV bw

Frank Jenks (*Nick Denby*), Dorothea Kent (*Maggie*), Andy Devine (*Hobbs*), Leon Ames (*Joe Gurney/William Evans*), Mary Treen (*Lorry May*), Spencer Charters (*Sheriff*), Joe King (*Lt. Hannigan*), Robert Emmett Keane (*Editor Hammond*), Frank M. Thomas (*Ward*), Frances Robinson (*Girl in Cafe*), Stanley Hughes (*Young Man in Cafe*), Eddie Anderson (*William*), Irving Bacon (*Meggs*), Charles Middleton (*Lincoln*), Hobart Cavanaugh (*Man*), Jack (*William*), Norton (*Drunk*), Rolfe Sedan (*Waiter*), Syd Saylor (*Mechanic*), Harry Tyler (*Deputy*), Renie Riano (*Mrs. Keller*), Frank Otto (*Clerk*), Frank Jaquet (*Henry Evans*), Ben Hall (*Gas Station Attendant*), Donald Brodie (*Attendant*), Eddy Waller (*Jeb*), Billy Wayne (*Taxi Driver*), Eddy Chandler (*Bartender*), Heinie Conklin (*Counterman*), Virginia Robinson (*Woman*), Broderick O'Farrell (*Conductor*), Kernan Cripps (*Detective*), Art Yeoman (*Mechanic*), John Estes (*Bell Hop*), Frank O'Connor, Bill Edwards, Charles Francis (*Men*), Stanley Orr (*Clerk*).

An oddball plot doesn't help this lackluster crime comedy about a pair of reporters—one male (Jenks), one female (Kent)—who are trying to crack a case. The crime involves mobster Ames who has found a look-a-like from Jenks' newspaper publicity section, and killed the fellow in order to assume his identity. Jenks and Kent spend more time battling each other than they do the killer, but finally bring him to justice.

p, Burt Kelly; d, Errol Taggart; w, Charles Grayson (based on a story by Cornelius Reese, Arndt Guisti); ph, Elwood Bredell; ed, Charles Maynard.

Crime/Comedy   (PR:A MPAA:NR)

STRANGE FASCINATION*½   (1952) 80m COL bw

Cleo Moore (*Margo*), Hugo Haas (*Paul Marvan*), Mona Barrie (*Diana*), Rick Vallin (*Carlo*), Karen Sharpe (*June*), Marc Krah (*Shiner*), Genevieve Aumont (*Yvette*), Patrick Holmes (*Walter*), Maura Murphy (*Mary*), Brian O'Hara (*Douglas*), Anthony Jochim (*Investigator*), Dr. Ross Tompson (*Dr. Tompson*), Maria Bibikoff (*Nurse*), Gayne Whitman (*Mr. Lowell*), Roy Engel (*Mr. Frim*), Robert Knapp (*Jack*).

Hugo Haas, Hollywood's oddest choice for an auteur, does it again with this strangely unfascinating drama about a concert pianist (Haas, not surprisingly), who hits a streak of bad luck. He can tolerate his financial misfortune, but when his vivacious blonde wife, Moore, walks out on him, he resorts to drastic measures. He mangles his hand in the hopes of collecting insurance money, but even that fails. The finale has him playing a one-handed piano piece. As with Haas' other films, this is interesting to watch because it is so melodramatic, not because it is a *good* film.

p,d&w, Hugo Haas; ph, Paul Ivano; m, Vaclav Divina, Jacob Gimpel; ed, Merrill G. White; md, Adolf Heller; art d, Rudi Feld.

Drama   (PR:A MPAA:NR)

STRANGE FETISHES, THE zero   (1967) 66m Americana
Entertainment Association bw (AKA: THE STRANGE FETISHES OF THE GO-GO GIRLS)

Sammy Arena (*Bill Shawn*), Sandy O'Hara, Taylor March.

A demented horror film about a madman who is strangling go-go dancers and threatening others. The crimes began after the death of a television host who was killed in a fight with the station manager. The manager is then murdered by the madman when the manager discovers the host's body has disappeared and in its place is a pool of acid. Not worth the time it takes to read this.

p&d, Enrico Blancocello.

Horror   (PR:O MPAA:NR)

STRANGE FETISHES OF THE GO-GO GIRLS
                    (SEE: STRANGE FETISHES, THE, 1967)

STRANGE GAMBLE**   (1948) 61m UA bw

William Boyd (Hopalong Cassidy), Andy Clyde (California Carlson), Rand Brooks (Lucky Jenkins), Elaine Riley (Nora), William Leicester, Joan Barton, James Craven, Joel Friedkin, Herbert Rawlinson, Robert Williams, Albert Morin, Lee Tung Foo.

The final entry in the HOPALONG CASSIDY series which began 13 years earlier. Boyd is a government agent sent West to investigate a gang of counterfeiters who are copying both U.S. and Mexican bills. With only two clues–the name "Mordigan" and the drawing of a comet–Boyd is able to track down the perpetrators. Boyd not only acted in this one, but served as the film's executive producer–a role he had for the final 12 HOPALONG CASSIDY pictures (SEE HOPALONG CASSIDY series, Index.)

p, Lewis J. Rachmil; d, George Archainbaud; w, Doris Schroeder; ph, Mack Stengler; ed, Fred W. Berger; art d, Jerome Pycha, Jr.

Western   **(PR:A   MPAA:NR)**

STRANGE HOLIDAY**   (1945) 61m Elite/PRC bw (AKA: THE DAY
                                                    AFTER TOMORROW)

Claude Rains (John Stephenson), Bobbie Stebbins (John, Jr.), Barbara Bates (Peggy Lee), Paul Hilton (Woodrow), Gloria Holden (Mrs. Jean Stephenson), Milton Kibbee (Sam Morgan), Walter White, Jr (Farmer), Wally Maher (Truck Driver), Martin Kosleck (Examiner), Priscilla Lyon (Betty), David Bradford (Boy Friend), Tommy Cook (Newsboy), Griff Barnett (Hegan), Ed Max (1st Detective), Paul Dubov (2nd Detective), Helen Mack (Secretary), Charles McAvoy (Guard).

An obvious piece of American propaganda produced in 1942 as a morale booster for the workers of General Motors. The project was shelved until Arch Oboler sold it to Metro, where it was shelved again. Not until Oboler and Rains bought it back in 1945 was it released, though independently. The story plays on the emotions of the day with Rains starring as a businessman who returns from a long hunting trip to find that the U.S. government and the Constitution have been thrown out the window by fascists. An interesting picture which lost much of its momentum by being released when the victorious soldiers were coming home.

p, A.W. Hackel, Edward Finney; d&w, Arch Oboler; ph, Robert Surtees; m, Gordon Jenkins; ed, Fred Feitshans, Jr.; art d, Bernard Herzbrun; spec eff, Howard Anderson, Ray Mercer.

Drama   **(PR:A   MPAA:NR)**

STRANGE HOLIDAY*½   (1969, Aus.) 75m Mass-Brown c

Jaeme Hamilton (Briant), Mark Healey (Doniphan), Jaime Messang (Moco), Van Alexander (Gordon), Carmen Duncan (Kate), Tony Allyn.

A group of boys shipwrecked on a deserted island get some unexpected visitors when a few months later another group of shipwreck survivors make it to shore. Some of them are British prisoners and pose a threat, but they are eventually captured or killed by the kids and surviving crew members.

pd&w, Mende Brown (based on the novel Deux Ans en Vacane by Jules Verne; ph, (Eastmancolor).

Adventure   **(PR:A   MPAA:NR)**

STRANGE ILLUSION**   (1945) 87m PRC bw (AKA: OUT OF THE
                                                         NIGHT)

James Lydon (Paul Cartwright), Warren William (Brett Curtis), Sally Eilers (Virginia Cartwright), Regis Toomey (Dr. Vincent), Charles Arnt (Prof. Muhlbach), George H. Reed (Benjamin), Jayne Hazard (Dorothy Cartwright), Jimmy Clark, Mary McLeod, Pierre Watkin, John Hamilton, Sonia Sorrel, Vic Potel (People).

Lydon stars as a suspicious young man who believes that his mother, Eilers, is responsible for the death of his father when she decides to remarry soon after. Lydon's plan is to trick his mother and future stepfather into believing he is insane, with the hopes of catching them off guard. He is committed to an asylum where he nearly does go insane, but gets out in time to prove that his mother's lover was the killer. Slow-moving and unbelievable, but a gruesome film noir atmosphere makes up for it.

p, Leon Fromkess; d, Edgar G. Ulmer; w, Adele Commandini (based on a story by Fritz Rotter); ph, Philip Tannura; ed, Carl Pierson; md, Leo Erdody; art d, Paul Palmentola; set d, Elias H. Reif; cos, Harold Bradow.

Crime Drama   **(PR:A   MPAA:NR)**

STRANGE IMPERSONATION**   (1946) 68m REP bw

Brenda Marshall (Nora Goodrich), William Gargan (Stephan Lindstrom), Hillary Brooke (Arline Cole), George Chandler (J.W. Rinse), Ruth Ford (Jane Karaski), H.B. Warner (Dr. Mansfield), Lyle Talbot (Inspector

Malloy), Mary Treen (Nurse), Cay Forester (Miss Roper), Richard Scott (Detective).

A convoluted tale about a female chemist, Marshall, who plans to try out her newly invented anesthesia on herself, with the help of her assistant Brooke. She is injected with the drug and her life takes a turn for the worst. Her fiance, Gargan, runs off, she is blackmailed, and a devastating explosion deforms Marshall's face. But it's only a dream induced by the anesthesia. Director Anthony Mann has some fun with Marshall's dream, but the picture never quite satisfies.

p, William Wilder; d, Anthony Mann; w, Mindret Lord (based on the story by Anne Wigton, Lewis Herman); ph, Robert W. Pittack; ed, John F. Link; md, Alexander Laszlo.

Drama   **(PR:A   MPAA:NR)**

STRANGE INCIDENT   (SEE: OX-BOW INCIDENT, THE, 1943)

STRANGE INTERLUDE***   (1932) 110m MGM bw (GB: STRANGE
                                                       INTERVAL)

Norma Shearer (Nina Leeds), Clark Gable (Ned Darrell), Alexander Kirkland (Sam Evans), Ralph Morgan (Charlie Marsden), Robert Young (Gordon), May Robson (Mrs. Evans), Maureen O'Sullivan (Madeline), Henry B. Walthall (Prof. Leeds), Mary Alden (Maid), Tad Alexander (Gordon as a Boy).

Shearer, the pampered daughter of academic Walthall, has loved the boy next door all her life, and the two plan to marry. WW 1 intervenes, and father Walthall persuades his daughter to defer the wedding until the cessation of international hostilities. The boy goes off to battle, where he is killed. Distraught, and regretful because she had not a single night of happiness with her beloved, Shearer–blaming her father for his interference– leaves the family home to take a job as a nurse in a hospital for wounded veterans. Their work throws her in close contact with a manly young doctor, Gable, and his best friend, the pleasant but weak-willed Kirkland. Gable advises the unhappy young woman to restructure her life, to marry and have children. Shearer concurs. Her choice for a bridegroom lies between two suitors, Kirkland and Morgan, a novelist with an Oedipal attachment to his mother. She chooses Kirkland, for whom she has maternal affection. Told by Kirkland's mother Robson that insanity runs in his family, Shearer is reluctant to have him father the children she so desperately wants. This is all right with Kirkland, who is repulsed by the very thought of physical love. Shearer is faced with another difficult choice: who will father her child? Manly Gable is the answer to her problem. The child born, Kirkland is overjoyed, thinking the boy to be the seed of his loins. Gable has fallen in love with Shearer and nobly sustains her secret, hovering on the fringes of the little family, a virtual lap dog to his beloved, albeit a strong, silent one. The boy, Alexander, grows to manhood loving his surrogate father, Kirkland, but suspicious and resentful of his real father, Gable. Both Shearer and Gable suffer terrible pangs of regret at the lad's dislike of Gable. One-time suitor Morgan also hovers about the nuclear family, serving as comic relief to the unremittingly somber story. The boy grows up to be Young. At college, Young falls in love with O'Sullivan. The fiercely possessive Shearer attempts to prevent the marriage of the young couple by telling O'Sullivan that mental illness runs in the lad's family. Gable realizes that the well-kept secret of the young man's parentage must come out; he reveals the secret and comforts the young woman. The happy Young's rowing team wins a crucial regatta; the enthusiastically rooting Kirkland–still believing himself to be the boy's father–suffers a stroke from the excitement. Shearer resigns herself to self-sacrifice, caring for Kirkland at the cost of her own potential happiness with Gable. O'Neill's talky tragedy–with a megalithic five hours of stage time–is hopelessly truncated in this misdirected cinematic version, notable mostly for being the film that pasted on actor Gable's first mustache. The picture mingles on-screen synchronous dialog with voiced-over thoughts of the characters. These asides were prerecorded and played for the on-camera performers, most of whom–Gable was the exception–felt compelled to register appropriate facial expressions. After a time, audiences began to giggle as the actors adjusted their faces to correspond to their off-screen voices; the film appeared almost to be part-talky, part-silent. Both the writing and the directing of the film reflect the surgical skills of Gable's physician character in that a mighty struggle was being made to reduce the corpus of the massive play. Little effort was expended on anything else. Gable's restrained performance as the he-man-turned-wimp through love is effective, and served to gain him some stature. All the adult characters age two decades in the picture, and all handle it well. Shearer, married to production chief Irving Thalberg, was still the queen of the lot at the time the film was made. Gable was delighted to gain the prestigious role; as a struggling, unsuccessful young Broadway hopeful, he had seen his long-time friend Earle Larimore become the darling of the theater-going intellectuals in the play, and he relished his own chance of attaining similar stature. He needn't have worried; he was ultimately to become the king of cinema. In Britain, the film was retitled STRANGE INTERVAL, and japesters said that censors had removed the lewd.

d, Robert Z. Leonard; w, Bess Meredyth, C. Gardner Sullivan (based on the play by Eugene O'Neill); ph, Lee Garmes; ed, Margaret Booth; cos, Adrian.

Drama   **(PR:C   MPAA:NR)**

STRANGE INTERVAL (SEE: STRANGE INTERLUDE 1932)

STRANGE INTRUDER** (1956) 82m AA bw

Edmund Purdom (*Paul Quentin*), Ida Lupino (*Alice*), Ann Harding (*Mary Carmichael*), Jacques Bergerac (*Howard*), Gloria Talbott (*Meg*), Carl Benton Reid (*James Carmichael*), Douglas Kennedy (*Parry*), Donald Murphy (*Adrian*), Ruby Goodwin (*Violet*), Mimi Gibson (*Libby*), Eric Anderson (*Johnny*), Marjorie Bennett (*Joady*).

Purdom agrees to honor a war buddy's final request to kill his two children so that his widow and her lover cannot raise them. A confused Purdom changes his mind when he meets the wife, Lupino, and her family, and grows to care for them instead. Far-fetched but handled well.

p, Lindsley Parsons; d, Irving Rapper; w, David Evans, Warren Douglas (based on the novel *The Intruder* by Helen Fowler); ph, Ernest Haller; m, Paul Dunlap; ed, Maurice Wright; md, Dunlap; m/l, "Bad For Each Other," Carroll Coates.

Drama (PR:A MPAA:NR)

STRANGE INVADERS** (1983) 94m EMI/Orion c

Paul LeMat (*Charles Bigelow*), Nancy Allen (*Betty Walker*), Diana Scarwid (*Margaret*), Michael Lerner (*Willie Collins*), Louise Fletcher (*Mrs. Benjamin*), Wallace Shawn (*Earl*), Fiona Lewis (*Waitress/Avon Lady*), Kenneth Tobey (*Arthur Newman*), June Lockhart (*Mrs. Bigelow*), Charles Lane (*Prof. Hollister*), Lulu Sylbert (*Elizabeth*), Joel Cohen (*Tim*), Dan Shor (*Teen Boy*), Dey Young (*Teen Girl*), Jack Kehler (*Gas Station Attendant*), Mark Goddard (*Detective*), Thomas Kopache (*State Trooper*), Bobby Pickett (*Editor*), Jonathan Ulmer (*Room Service Waiter*), Ron Gillham (*First Alien*), Al Roberts (*Man in Dark Glasses*), Edwina Fellows (*Nurse*), Patti Medwid (*Room Service Waitress*), Nancy Johnson, Betsy Pickering (*Stewardesses*).

An offbeat science-fiction film that came and left the theaters before anyone knew it existed. LeMat plays a professor who was once married to, but is now divorced from, an alien invader disguised as a female human (Scarwid). She and a horde of aliens landed on Earth during the 1950s, infiltrating a small midwestern town, and at the same time, beaming the townspeople to their spaceship via small, blue spheres. After three decades, the aliens decide to return to their planet, but must make sure all of their kind, including Scarwid and her half-human daughter by LeMat, are included. As Scarwid now lives in New York City, the aliens, who assumed the dress and mannerisms of the midwesterners they beamed away, arrive in Manhattan in their farm clothers. LeMat figures out their scheme, and fights to keep his daughter on Earth. Allen plays a reporter for a tabloid newspaper who befriends him for a story. There are a few grotesque scenes, but the picture as a whole self-consciously recalls, in terms of atmosphere and plot, the films of the 1950s, such as INVASION OF THE BODY SNATCHERS or IT CAME FROM OUTER SPACE. Behind all of it lies a subtle humor. An engrossing science-fiction entry which is an improvement over Laughlin and Condon's previous STRANGE BEHAVIOR.

p, Walter Coblenz; d, Michael Laughlin; w, William Condon, Laughlin; ph, Louis Horvath (DeLuxe Color); m, John Addison; ed, John W. Wheeler; prod d, Susanna Moore; art d, Emad Helmy, Mischa Petrow; set d, Gus Meunier; cos, Moore; spec eff, Chuck Comisky, Ken Jones, Larry Benson, John Muto, Robert Skotak, Martin Malivoire, Stephan Dupuis, Martin Coblenz; make-up, Ken Brooke.

Science Fiction Cas. (PR:O MPAA:PG)

STRANGE JOURNEY* (1946) 65m FOX bw

Paul Kelly, Osa Massen, Hillary Brooke, Lee Patrick, Bruce Lester, Gene Stutenroth [Roth], Fritz Leiber, Kurt Katch.

A lame adventure film about a gangster, Kelly, and his wife crash-landing on a remote Caribbean island. They soon discover they are not alone when they find a group of shipwrecked Nazis, who along with Kelly, begin risking their lives to uncover a uranium deposit.

p, Sol M. Wurtzel; d, James Tinling; w, Charles Kenyon, Irving Elman (based on a story by Kenyon); ph, Benjamin Kline; ed, William F. Claxton; art d, Art Peterson.

Adventure (PR:A MPAA:NR)

STRANGE JOURNEY, 1966 (SEE: FANTASTIC VOYAGE, 1966)

STRANGE JUSTICE* (1932) 72m (King/RKO) bw

Marian Marsh, Reginald Denny, Richard Bennett, Norman Foster, Irving Pichel, Thomas E. Jackson, Nydia Westman, Larry Steers.

A scheme by bankers Denny and Pichel leads to their faking a murder. As a result, an innocent man is sent to prison. As the convict is about to be executed, the "dead" man arrives and clears the man's name. A confusing script and inept direction make this film inadequate viewing.

p, J.G. Bachmann; d, Victor Schertzinger; w, William A. Drake; ph, Merritt Gerstad; m, Schertzinger.

Crime Drama (PR:A MPAA:NR)

STRANGE LADY IN TOWN**½ (1955) 112m WB c

Greer Garson (*Dr. Julia Winslow Garth*), Dana Andrews (*Dr. Rork O'Brien*), Cameron Mitchell (*David Garth*), Lois Smith (*Spurs O'Brien*), Walter Hampden (*Father Gabriel Mendoza*), Pedro Gonzales-Gonzales (*Trooper Martinez-Martinez*), Joan Camden (*Norah Muldoon*), Anthony Numkena [Earl Holliman] (*Tomasito Diaz*), Jose Torvay (*Bartolo Diaz*), Adele Jergens (*Bella Brown*), Bob Wilke (*Karg*), Frank de Kova (*Anse Hatlo*), Russell Johnson (*Shadduck*), Gregory Walcott (*Scanlon*), Douglas Kennedy (*Slade Wickstrom*), Ralph Moody (*Gen. Lew Wallace*), Nick Adams (*Billy the Kid*), Jack Williams (*Rebstock*), The Trianas (*Flamenco Dance Specialty*), Joey Costarello (*Alfred*), Bob Foulk (*Joe*), Jose Lopez (*Pueblo Indian*), Louise Lorimer (*Mrs. Wallace*), Helen Spring (*Mrs. Harker*), Joe Hamilton (*Mr. Harker*), George Wallace (*Curley*), Marshall Bradford (*Sheriff*), Antonio Triana, Luisa Triana (*Flamenco Dancers*).

LeRoy turns out an interesting western set in Santa Fe in 1879. Garson plays a lady doctor who arrives in town only to find that she is looked down upon by those who don't believe she can handle the job. She is courted by Andrews, a fellow doctor who is less experienced than she, and harrassed by Wilke, whose girl friend is under treatment. She eventually proves to the community that she is worthy, with the support of a local group of unprejudiced Mexicans and Indians.

p&d, Mervyn LeRoy; w, Frank Butler; ph, Harold Rosson (CinemaScope, Warner Color); m, Dmitri Tiomkin; ed, Folmar Blangsted; art d, Gabriel Scognamillo; cos, Emile Santiago; ch, Peggy Carroll; m/l, "Strange Lady in Town," Tiomkin, Ned Washington (sung by Frankie Laine with Mitch Miller and His Orchestra).

Western (PR:A MPAA:NR)

STRANGE LAWS (SEE: CHEROKEE STRIP, THE, 1937)

STRANGE LOVE OF MARTHA IVERS, THE**½
(1946) 116m PAR bw

Barbara Stanwyck (*Martha Ivers*), Van Heflin (*Sam Masterson*), Lizabeth Scott (*Toni Marachek*), Kirk Douglas (*Walter O'Neil*), Judith Anderson (*Mrs. Ivers*), Roman Bohnen (*Mr. O'Neil*), Darryl Hickman (*Sam Masterson as a Boy*), Janis Wilson (*Martha Ivers as a Girl*), Ann Doran (*Secretary*), Frank Orth (*Hotel Clerk*), James Flavin (*1st Detective*), Mickey Kuhn (*Walter O'Neil as a Boy*), Charles D. Brown (*Special Investigator*), Matt McHugh (*Bus Driver*), Walter Baldwin (*Dempsey the Garage Owner*), Catherine Craig (*French Maid*), Sayre Dearing, Harry Leonard (*Crap Shooters*), William Duray (*Waiter*), Payne B. Johnson (*Bellboy*), Max Wagner (*2nd Detective*), Tom Fadden (*Taxi Driver*), Gladden James (*John O. Butler*), Bert Roach, Ricky Ricardi, Billy Burt, Gene Ashley (*Men*), Robert E. Homans (*Policeman*), John Kellogg (*Plainclothesman*), Al Murphy (*Waiter*), Kay Deslys (*Jail Matron*), Bob Perry (*Bartender*), Olin Howland (*Newspaper Clerk*), Blake Edwards (*Sailor*), Betty Hill (*Waitress*), Tom Dillon (*Detective*), Tom Schamp, Kernan Cripps (*Policemen*), Thomas Louden (*Lynch the Butler*), Tommy Ryan.

A dark and somewhat perverse melodrama which stars Stanwyck as the wicked Martha Ivers, a wealthy and powerful woman who has gained control of the small town of Iverstown, Pennsylvania, after inheriting a large family fortune. She lives with her weakling husband, Douglas, a district attorney who is preparing to make a bid for mayor. What no one in the town knows, however, is that Stanwyck and Douglas share a deep secret. As a young girl, Stanwyck murdered her aunt, Anderson. In order to protect the family name, an innocent man was executed for the crime. Because Douglas witnessed the murder and was in the position to ruin Stanwyck, he was able to pressure her into marriage, thereby securing a comfortable future. Enter Heflin, a love from Stanwyck's past, who has returned to town after an 18-year absence to ask Douglas to help him effect the release of a young woman (Scott) who has been wrongly jailed. Douglas thinks Heflin also witnessed the murder by Stanwyck and that blackmail is his real reason for coming back. Douglas tries to scare Heflin off, but this only raises Heflin's curiosity, causing him to dig into the past murder case. From the information he gathers together, Heflin soon realizes that Stanwyck is indeed a murderess. By this time, Stanwyck's feelings of love for Heflin have resurfaced. Douglas, in a drunken rage, pushes a confrontation with Heflin and falls down a staircase. When Stanwyck suggests that Heflin kill Douglas, he refuses and leaves the pathetic husband and wife behind and goes off with Scott. With a gun Douglas has handed her, Stanwyck commits suicide. Douglas then takes the gun and does the same, securing their sick relationship even in death. A cruel *film noir* which, although it starts somewhat slowly, builds to a frenzied state of suspense in which all of the characters have a perverse hold over one another. The result is an often gripping film which shows the collaborative efforts of such talents as Wallis, Milestone, Rossen, Rozsa, Dreier, and Head. Oddly, this film also includes among its credits three future directors—screenwriter Rossen, assistant director Robert Aldrich and, as a bit player, Blake Edwards. Patrick received an Oscar nomination for his original story.

p, Hal B. Wallis; d, Lewis Milestone; w, Robert Rossen (based on the story "Love Lies Bleeding" by John Patrick); ph, Victor Milner; m, Miklos Rozsa;

ed, Archie Marshek; art d, Hans Dreier, John Meehan; set d, Sam Comer, Jerry Welch; cos, Edith Head; makeup, Wally Westmore; spec eff, Farciot Edouart; m/l, "Strange Love," Edward Heyman, Rozsa.

Crime Drama Cas. (PR:C MPAA:NR)

STRANGE LOVE OF MOLLY LOUVAIN, THE*½
(1932) 70m FN-WB bw (AKA: MOLLY LOUVAIN)

Ann Dvorak (Molly Louvain), Lee Tracy (Scotty Cornell), Richard Cromwell (Jimmie), Guy Kibbee (Pop), Leslie Fenton (Nick Grant), Frank McHugh (Skeets), Evalyn Knapp (Sally), Charles Middleton (Capt. Slade), Mary Doran (Dance Hall Girl), C. Henry Gordon (Martin), Willard Robertson (Sgt. Murdock), Harry Beresford (Taxi Driver), Harold Waldridge (Bellboy), William Burress (Policeman), Claire McDowell (Mrs. Schiller), Maurice Black (Sally's Pal), Richard Cramer (Detective), Ben Alexander (College Boy), Donald Dilloway (Ralph), Hank Mann (Harley), Thomas E. Jackson.

The strange thing about the love of the title lady is that it should be pluralized; she gets around a bit. Dvorak is a hotel clerk who meets and melts for ne'er-do-well playboy Dilloway, who dallies with her only long enough to impregnate her, and then leaves town. Dissolve to her liaison with the ill-fated Fenton, a salesman who has admired her for some time. He is really a crook but he is willing to take her complete with infant daughter as a package. She and Cromwell, the bellboy who has adored her since her hotel days, are in a stolen car with Fenton when he is stopped by a cop, whom he kills. Dvorak and her youthful swain, fearing charges of complicity, hide out in a rooming house also occupied by wisecracking newspaperman Tracy (in a familiar role, one he played many times). Unrecognizably blonde now, bleached brunette Dvorak finds herself getting romantically involved with the roving reporter, to the discomfiture of Cromwell. Tracy, hot for a scoop, is pursuing the runaway pair, unaware that they are right under his nose. The scheming scribbler hatches a plot: he has a friendly radio newsman broadcast that Dvorak's child is ill in order to bait her into the open. He is present, and appropriately surprised, when the lost lady ambles into a police station to give herself up. Realizing that he loves her, Tracy promises to help see her through her legal ordeal. Some good dialog, but with uneven cutting, perhaps due to censorship. This is not regarded as one of prolific director Curtiz's better efforts. Dvorak handled the comedic sequences well, but didn't quite come off as a tragic, circumstance-tossed heroine; she was fresh from MGM's chorus line, with only Howard Hughes' SKY DEVILS to her credit at this point.

p, Hal Wallis; d, Michael Curtiz [Mikhaly Kertesz]; w, Erwin Gelsey, Brown Holmes (based on the play "Tinsel Girl" by Maurine Watkins; ph, Robert Kurrle; ed, James Borby.

Drama (PR:A MPAA:NR)

STRANGE LOVERS*
(1963) 73m Mast/Gillman bw

"End of the Path": Walter Koenig (Bob Fuller), Sally le Cuyer (Jackie Hart), Elaine Kaye (Mrs. Hart), "Homo Means Man": Joe d'Agosta (George Lynn), Mark Bradley (Assailant), Jennifer Boles (Ann), "Segue": Arlene Hedrick (Yvonne Martin), Sylvia Brenner (Anita Rochland), Steve Hollister (Photographer).

A trilogy of shorts that attempts to deal with the issue of homosexuality in more of a psychological way than a physical one. The first segment, "End of the Path," deals with an emotionally distraught man whose past causes him to strike out and murder a woman who is coming on to him. "Homo Means Man" concerns a man leaving his wife in search of a male lover, but instead gets beat up and robbed. He turns to a female companion, attempts to seduce her, but is eventually brought back to his wife. "Segue" tells the story of a teen girl who is tempted by another woman to become her female lover. A male co-worker rapes her, which sends her running for refuge with the woman. Lacks depth, partly due to the length, but chiefly because of weak scripting.

p, Robert Stambler, William Mahan; d, Stambler; w, Stambler, Mahan, Nick Boretz, Alex Beaton; ph, Fouad Said; m, Warren Barker.

Drama (PR:O MPAA:NR)

STRANGE MR. GREGORY, THE**
(1945) 63m MON bw

Edmund Lowe (Gregory), Jean Rogers (Ellen Randall), Don Douglas (John Randall), Frank Reicher (Riker), Marjorie Hoshelle (Sheila Edwards), Robert Emmett Keane (District Attorney), Jonathan Hale (Blair), Frank Mayo (Inspector Hoskins), Fred Kelsey (Detective Lefert), Jack Norton (Drunk), Anita Turner (Maid), Tom Leffingwell (Judge).

A bizarre, but entertaining murder mystery about a magician who pretends to be his nonexistent brother after he is supposedly killed. There never was any murder, just a scheme to frame his true love's husband. He soon learns that it's difficult to pin a murder rap on someone when there's no body. The police end up killing him during a chase.

p, Louis Berkoff; d, Phil Rosen; w, Charles S. Belden (based on the story by Myles Connolly); ph, Ira Morgan; ed, Seth Larson; set d, Charles Thompson, Vin Taylor.

Crime/Mystery (PR:A MPAA:NR)

STRANGE MRS. CRANE, THE*
(1948) 60m EL bw

Marjorie Lord (Gina Crane), Robert Shayne (Floyd Durant), Pierre Watkin (Clinton Crane), James Seay (Mark Emery), Ruth Brady (Barbara Arnold), Claire Whitney (Edna Emmerson), Mary Gordon (Nora), Chester Clute (Marlow), Dorothy Granger (Jennette Woods), Charles Williams (McLean).

An implausible murder drama about the wife of a gubernatorial candidate falsely accused of killing her former partner in a confidence scam. It turns out that the real criminal has somehow managed to become jury foreman, who slips up by delivering to the judge an incriminating letter instead of the guilty verdict.

p, John Sutherland; d, Sherman Scott; w, Al Martin (based on the story by Frank Burt, Robert Libott); ph, Jack Greenhalgh; ed, Martin Cohn; md, Paul Smith; art d, Edward Jewell.

Crime/Drama (PR:A MPAA:NR)

STRANGE ONE, THE***
(1957) 100m Horizon/COL bw (GB: END AS A MAN)

Ben Gazzara (Jocko De Paris), Pat Hingle (Harold Knoble), [Peter] Mark Richman (Cadet Col. Corger), Arthur Storch (Simmons), Paul E. Richards (Perrin McKee), Larry Gates (Maj. Avery), Clifton James (Col. Ramey), Geoffrey Horne (Georgie Avery), James Olson (Roger Gatt), Julie Wilson (Rosebud), George Peppard (Robert Marquales).

Based on the play which followed "Take A Giant Step" into New York's Lyceum Theatre in the mid-1950s. It was not a hit when it was on Broadway, nor did it do much on the screen. Gazzara and many of the others were reprising their roles under the guidance of the same man who directed the stage version, Jack Garfein. Set in a southern military school, Gazzara is the student leader who wields his power over the younger students. He's abetted by Hingle and Olson, who take equal delight in causing pain for the frightened lowerclassmen, symbolized by Storch, a young man who is homosexual. Gates is one of the "adults" at the school (though many of the younger players seem too old for their roles) and knows how bad the situation is. He would like to get rid of Gazzara and Gazzara knows it, so he tries to discredit Gates every chance he can. Gazzara is the ultimate wise guy. He's mean, arrogant, and angry and has the run of the school until some of the younger students finally revolt (led by Peppard, in his motion picture debut.) Wilson is the only female in the cast, a role that never appeared in the novel or the play. She is a woman of loose morals and her part doesn't much matter in the proceedings but her voice does relieve the sound of all those baritones. Richards did some homosexual scenes which wound up on the cutting room floor due to the strict censorship of the Motion Picture Production Code at that time, which specifically stated that there could be no sexual perversion nor any inference of it on the screen. Garfein, who was married to sexpot Carroll Baker, made his directorial debut in films with this and did well, although the subject matter and the general darkness of the mood worked against making it a financial success. New Yorker Richman, a graduate pharmacist who gave up pills and potions for acting, was appearing in his second film after FRIENDLY PERSUASION. He later changed his name to Peter Mark Richman. Filmed also as SORORITY GIRL, 1957.

p, Sam Spiegel; d, Jack Garfein; w, Calder Willingham (based on his novel and play End as a Man); ph, Burnett Guffey; m, Kenyon Hopkins; ed, Sidney Katz; md, Hopkins; art d, Joseph C. Wright.

Drama (PR:O MPAA:NR)

STRANGE ONES, THE,
(SEE: LES ENFANTS TERRIBLES, 1952, Fr.)

STRANGE PEOPLE*
(1933) 64m CHES bw

John Darrow (Jimmy Allen, Auto Salesman), Gloria Shea (Helen Mason), Hale Hamilton (J.E. Burton), Wilfred Lucas (John Davis), J. Frank Glendon (Crandall the Butler), Michael Visaroff (Edwards the Caretaker), Jack Pennick (The Plumber), Jerry Mandy (The Barber), Lew Kelly (The Insurance Agent), Jane Keckley (Mrs. Reed), Walter Brennan (The Radio Repairman), Mary Foy (Mrs. Jones), Frank H. LaRue (Kelly), Stanley G. Blystone (Burke), Jay Wilsey (Guest), Gordon DeMain (Detective).

A variation on the standard horror plot involving a group of people, connected only by their prior association with a dead man, who are brought together to one house under mysterious circumstances. Hamilton has gathered together the 12 members of the group to prove that they had wrongly convicted a man of murder months ago when they served on the same jury. The complex, and sometimes confusing, plot contains more murders, more confessions, and even more startling revelations until it is discovered that the original victim the condemned man was supposed to have murdered a year ago is still alive. The film makes good use of some settings and props made famous by a couple of classic horror films from Universal Studios. The haunted house from James Whale's THE OLD DARK HOUSE served as the mystery house in STRANGE PEOPLE, while the graveyard set and the crooked staircases and cellar of the mansion in FRANKENSTEIN were also used for key scenes.

p, George R. Batcheller; d, Richard Thorpe; w, Jack Townley; ph, M.A.

Anderson; ed, Vera Wood; md, Abe Meyer; art d, Edward C. Jewell.

Mystery   (PR:A MPAA:NR)

STRANGE ROADS   (SEE: EXPOSED, 1932)

STRANGE SHADOWS IN AN EMPTY ROOM*
(1977, Can./Ital.) 99m Security Investment Trust Co./AIP c (AKA: SHADOWS IN AN EMPTY ROOM; BLAZING MAGNUM)

Stuart Whitman (*Capt. Tony Saitta*), John Saxon (*Sgt. Matthews*), Martin Landau (*Dr. George Tracer*), Tisa Farrow (*Julie Foster*), Carole Laure (*Louise Saitta*), Gayle Hunnicutt (*Margie Cohn*), Jean Leclerc (*Mystery Woman*), Jean Marchand (*Fred*), Anthony Forest, Andree St. Laurent, Peter MacNeil, Julie Wildman, James Tapp, Jerome Thibergien, Terence Ross, Dave Nichols, Jene Chandler.

The room may be empty but not nearly as much as the screenwriter's head when it came to writing the screenplay for this inadequate detective film. Whitman wants some answers to his kid sister's murder, but can't seem to get any cooperation from anyone involved. He scours most of Montreal, beating a few people senseless in the process, but only comes up with answers he doesn't want to hear. Far too violent, action-filled of course.

p, Edmondo Amati; d, Martin Herbert [Alberto De Martino]; w, Vincent Mann, Frank Clark; ph, Anthony Ford (Panavision, Eastmancolor); m, Armando Trovajoli; ed, Vincent P. Thomas; art d, Michael Proulux; cos, Louise Jobin, Luc Leflaquais; stunts, Tom Sutton.

Crime   **Cas.**   (PR:O MPAA:R)

STRANGE TRIANGLE½   (1946) 65m FOX bw (AKA: STRANGE ALIBI)

Signe Hasso (*Francine Huber*), Preston Foster (*Sam Crane*), Anabel Shaw (*Betty Wilson*), John Shepperd [Shepperd Strudwick] (*Earl Huber*), Roy Roberts (*Harry Matthews*), Emory Parnell (*Barney Shaefer*), Nancy Evans (*Hilda Shaefer*), Gladys Blake, Frank Pershing, Robert Malcolm, Jack Davis, Frank Wilcox, George Melford.

The extravagances of femme fatale Hasso lead to the downfall of a pair of business associates–traveling bank examiner Foster and bank manager Shepperd. Hasso is the wife of Shepperd and drives him into bankruptcy with her desire for luxury. She makes a play for Foster, who doesn't realize she is Shepperd's wife, and begins to bring him down before he stops her. The film is told in flashback by Foster, who is doing time in jail for the woman's murder.

p, Aubrey Schenck; d, Ray McCarey; w, Mortimer Braus, Charles G. Booth (based on a story by Jack Andrews); ph, Harry Jackson; m, David Buttolph; ed, Norman Colbert; md, Emil Newman; art d, James Basevi, Albert Hogsett; set d, Thomas Little, Fred J. Rode; spec eff, Fred Sersen.

Crime Drama   (PR:A MPAA:NR)

STRANGE VENEGEANCE OF ROSALIE, THE
(1972) 107m Cinecrest/FOX c

Bonnie Bedelia (*Rosalie*), Ken Howard (*Virgil*), Anthony Zerbe (*Fry*).

A novel story of a young Indian hitchhiker who gets businessman Howard to drive her to her remote cabin. In order to make sure she keeps his company she lets the air out of his tires and breaks his leg, nursing him back to health with the utmost of tenderness. The girl displays her violent capabilities when a motorcyclist tries to rob them and winds up dead, but still she remains gentle to Howard. A bizarre relationship that would have been more believable if there had been more rapport between them.

p, John Kohn; d, Jack Starrett; w, Anthony Greville-Bell, Kohn; ph, Ray Parslow; m, John Cameron; ed, Thom Noble; md, Cameron; art d, Roy Walker; makeup, Ricardo Vazquez.

Drama   (PR:C MPAA:PG)

STRANGE VOYAGE**   (1945) 67m Signal bw

Eddie Albert (*Chris Thompson*), Forrest Taylor (*Skipper*), Ray Teal (*Capt. Andrews*), Matt Willis (*The Hammer*), Martin Garralaga (*Manuel*), Elena Verdugo (*Carmelite*), Bobby Cooper (*Jimmy*), Clyde Fillmore (*The Sportsman*), Daniel Kerry (*Ben*), Henry Orosco (*The Father*).

Albert leads a group of sailors into the Mexican coastal area in search of a buried treasure. The film is heavy on action as Albert must calm the superstitions and fears that arise during storms at sea, sandstorms, octopuses, and sharks. Filmed by Signal Pictures, a production company composed of war veterans who worked in the film industry before shipping out to war.

p, Louise B. Appleton, Jr.; d, Irving Allen; w, Andrew Holt; ph, Jack H. Greenhalgh, Jr.; m, Lucian Moraweek; ed, Irving A. Applebaum; md, Lud Gluskin; art d, Ralph Berger.

Adventure   (PR:A MPAA:NR)

STRANGE WIVES*½   (1935) 75m UNIV bw

Roger Pryor (*Jimmy King*), June Clayworth (*Nadja*), Esther Ralston (*Olga*), Hugh O'Connell (*Warren*), Ralph Forbes (*Paul*), Cesar Romero (*Boris*), Francis L. Sullivan (*Bellamy*), Valerie Hobson (*Mauna*), Leslie Fenton (*Svengaart*), Ivan Lebedeff (*Dimitry*), Doris Lloyd (*Mrs. Sleeper*), Claude Gillingwater, Sr (*Guggins*), Carrie Daumery (*The Princess*), Walter Walker (*The General*), Greta Meyer (*Hilda*), Harry Cording (*Tribesman*), Buster Phelps, Dickie Jones (*Twins*), Phyllis Brooks (*The Actress*), Leonid Snegoff (*Head Waiter*), Anne O'Neal (*Secretary to Jim*), Bobby Gordon (*Elevator Boy*), Father Neal Dodd (*Minister*), Joseph Crehan (*Immigration Official*), George Hackathorne (*Guggin's Secretary*), Olaf Hytten (*Jim's Butler*), Jean Fenwick (*Jim's Secretary*), Nicholas Kobliansky (*Waiter*), Victor De Linsky (*Russian Priest*), Harry Cornell (*Man*), Ralph Brooks (*Chauffeur*), Cortez and Galante (*Dance Team*).

Pryor falls in love with Russian Clayworth, but besides gaining a wife, he learns that he has gained a whole family. He becomes stepfather to the entire clan and figures the only way to become independent of them is to make them famous. He also is up against a gutsy lover of Clayworth's who he cannot seem to avoid. A pleasant comedy which does not contain enough good moments to warrant its feature length.

p, Stanley Bergerman; d, Richard Thorpe; w, Gladys Unger, Barry Trivers, James Mulhauser (based on the novel *Bread Upon the Waters* by Edith Wharton); ph, George Robinson; ed, Edward Curtiss.

Comedy/Romance   (PR:A MPAA:NR)

STRANGE WOMAN, THE**   (1946) 100m Hunt Stromberg/UA bw

Hedy Lamarr (*Jenny Hager*), George Sanders (*John Evered*), Louis Hayward (*Ephraim Poster*), Gene Lockhart (*Isaiah Poster*), Hillary Brooke (*Meg Saladine*), Rhys Williams (*Deacon Adams*), June Storey (*Lena Tempest*), Moroni Olson (*Rev. Thatcher*), Olive Blakeney (*Mrs. Hollis*), Dennis Hoey (*Tim Hager*), Alan Napier (*Judge Saladine*), Ian Keith (*Lincoln Partridge*), Edward Biby (*Mr. Partridge*), Katherine York (*Miss Partridge*).

Of maligned Hedy Lamarr gives what may be her best performance in this star vehicle tailored for her talents. Fellow European Edgar Ulmer directed this adaptation of Ben Ames Williams' best seller with a strong hand and elicited a fine display of emotion from Lamarr's gorgeous–but usually icy–exterior, often going beneath the permafrost to reach heretofore unplumbed depths. Lamarr lives in the lusty, brawling town of Bangor, Maine, during the first half the 19th Century. Lumber is what makes Bangor prosper and Lamarr knows it. She is growing from a naive, frightened young girl into full-blown womanhood and this maturity causes her to leave the home of her drunken father, Hoey, and marry Lockhart, a well-to-do businessman who caters to the lumbermen. Lockhart has watched her grow with a lecherous eye and is thrilled when she decides to be his wife, even though she's at least 20 years younger than he. Underneath her cheery, amiable nature is a woman of cool, cruel, and conniving ideas. With Lockhart's money behind her, she is soon the social leader of the town. She donates money to causes, runs charity dinners, and does all the right things. Lockhart's son is Hayward. He's off at a university and Lamarr finds him attractive so she lures the weak-willed lad back from school, she entices him until he is addicted to her. Not satisfied with Hayward, Lamarr sets her chapeau for Sanders, the man who runs her husband's lumber interests. The fact that Sanders is set to marry her best friend, Brooke, doesn't matter to the predatory Lamarr. She wants Sanders so much that she tells Hayward she will marry him if he kills his father, Lockhart. Hayward mistakenly believes the shrew and manages to drown Lockhart. With the old man out of the way, Lamarr is now rich and independent so she tells Hayward to hit the road and if he insists on sticking around, she'll tell all. Her next move is to get Sanders; she succeeds in securing his love away from Brooke. Hayward becomes a drunk, increasingly depressed, and winds up by taking his own life. Sanders doesn't take long to recognize that he has married a strange woman. At one point, Lamarr inadvertently blurts out what she did to Lockhart through Hayward. Upon hearing that, Sanders beats a hasty rereat, lest he catch the next bite from this black widow. Sanders returns to the lumber camp and Brooke follows him there to offer balm and surcease. Lamarr travels to the camp with her coach and horses and when she sees Sanders reunited with Brooke, she is furious and attempts to kill them both by running them down. As she approaches the helpless couple, a carriage wheel hits a large boulder, overturns the carriage, and Lamarr is thrown from it and dies. Excellent period sets and costumes help to give this a patina of believability. Lamarr was behind the production with Hunt Stromberg and had a hand in every facet of the movie. The fact that Hayward, Sanders, Hoey, and Napier had British accents, while Lamarr sounded Viennese, didn't seem to bother anyone in this New England town.

p, Jack Chertok; d, Edgar Ulmer; w, Herb Meadows (based on the novel by Ben Ames Williams); ph, Lucien Andriot; m, Carmen Dragon; ed, James E. Newcom; art d, Nicolai Remisoff; cos, Natalie Visart; makeup, Joseph Stinton.

Historical Drama   (PR:C MPAA:NR)

STRANGE WORLD*   (1952) 85m UA bw

Angelica Hauff *(Elisa),* Alexander Carlos *(Edgar),* America Cabral *(Father),* Carmen Brown *(Dancer),* Kumatzaikuma *(Indian Chief),* Ary Jartul *(Ary),* Griyo Sobrinho *(Innkeeper),* W. Hardt *(Publisher).*

Given a semi-documentary feel, this adventure tale has Carlos returning to the South American jungles to find his long lost father and an Inca statue. His mission is a dangerous one and he eventually gets the ancient idol, but is less fortunate when it comes to his father who has been reduced to a shrunken head.

p, O.A. Bayer; d, Franz Eichhorn; w, Al O'Camp, Eichhorn, Bayer; ph, Edgar Eichhorn; m, W. Schultz Porto Alegro, Emil Velazco; ed, Rudolph Brent, Jose Canizares; art d, William Woller.

Adventure   **(PR:A MPAA:NR)**

STRANGE WORLD OF PLANET X, THE
                        (SEE: COSMIC MONSTERS, 1958, Brit.)

STRANGER, THE, 1940   (SEE: STRANGER FROM TEXAS, THE,
                                                                        1940)

STRANGER, THE****   (1946) 95m International Pictures/RKO bw

Edward G. Robinson *(Wilson),* Loretta Young *(Mary Longstreet),* Orson Welles *(Prof. Charles Rankin/Franz Kindler),* Philip Merivale *(Judge Longstreet),* Richard Long *(Noah Longstreet),* Byron Keith *(Dr. Jeff Lawrence),* Billy House *(Potter),* Konstantin Shayne *(Konrad Meinike),* Martha Wentworth *(Sara),* Isabel O'Madigan *(Mrs. Lawrence),* Pietro Sasso *(Mr. Peabody).*

Having created three box office flops in a row (THE MAGNIFICENT AMBERSONS, JOURNEY INTO FEAR, and IT'S ALL TRUE) the "boy genius," Orson Welles, was badly in need of a hit with which to right himself in the eyes of Hollywood. The result was THE STRANGER. Produced on schedule and under budget, it is the most restrained and conventional of Welles' films, but still a thrilling entertainment. The film begins in postwar Germany where a meeting of the War Crimes Commission is being held. It is decided by those present that a heinous Nazi war criminal, Shayne, should be released from prison in the hopes that he will lead the commission to his superior, the infamous Franz Kindler (Welles)–one of the architects of the genocide against the Jews. Robinson is assigned to follow Shayne and the chase begins. Shayne, a bug-eyed, seedy little man who always looks nervous, winds his way through Europe, Latin America, and finally to the small town of Harper, Connecticut, where Welles is living under the name of Charles Rankin. Robinson trails Shayne to Harper, which is a college town, and he sees the little man find Welles' name in the phone book. He then follows Shayne to the college, but loses him in the gymnasium. Shayne knows that Robinson is following him and ambushes the investigator in the gym by hitting him in the head with a gymnastic practice ring. Robinson is knocked cold. Shayne then goes to the address in the phone book, but finds only Young, Welles' fiancee, the daughter of a prominent judge in town. She and Welles are to marry later in the day. Young tells Shayne that Welles is a professor at the school and that he should be coming home any minute. Shayne leaves and meets Welles on the path. Welles is annoyed at Shayne's presence, and when he learns that the little man has been followed to Harper, he can barely repress his rage. Welles gleans what little information he can from Shayne and then leads him to a wooded area where he strangles him. He then hides the body in the brush, goes off to the church to be married, and during the reception returns to bury the body. Meanwhile, Robinson has come to and gone to the general store run by the obese House, who sits in a chair playing checkers while telling his customers to serve themselves. House tells Robinson, who is posing as an antique dealer, all about Welles' marriage to Young and learns that Welles is an expert on clocks and plans to fix the elaborate old clock in the town's 125-foot tower. Robinson decides that Welles must be his man because Kindler is an expert on clocks. Robinson manages to gain the trust of Young and her family and is invited to dinner. There, obviously for the benefit of Robinson, Welles launches into a passionate anti-German tirade that nearly convinces Robinson that Welles couldn't possibly be Franz Kindler. In his sleep, however, Robinson realizes the truth. When asked by Young's brother Long if he thought Karl Marx promoted freedom and equality, Welles responded: "But Marx wasn't a German. He was a Jew." "Who but a German would deny that Karl Marx was a German because he was a Jew?" Robinson later tells his superiors over the phone. Robinson has found his man. Feeling that he can trust Long, Robinson tells the young man who he is and asks for his help and Long agrees. Soon after, Welles catches Young's dog trying to dig up Shayne's body and he poisons the animal. Robinson figures out what the dog was up to and sends a search party to find Shayne's corpse. Knowing he is cornered, Welles confesses to Young that he has murdered the little man who came to the house on their wedding day, but he was a vicious blackmailer trying to ruin their lives because of an accident involving the death a girl Welles knew years ago. Confused, afraid, but still in love with her husband, Young agrees to keep her mouth shut. That evening Young is called to her father's house where Robinson waits. He shows her Nazi atrocity footage and tells her the truth about her husband in the hopes that she will help them. She refuses to believe him, though Robinson is convinced

that he's jarred her conscience and she'll see the light on her own. Welles realizes that he's losing Young and he arranges for her to be killed on the high ladder leading to the clock tower. The plan goes awry, however, and he is shocked to find Young alive and well at home. He finally reveals his true identity and what he had intended for her. Young screams: "Go ahead and kill me! Only when you do, don't lay you're hands on me. Use this!" and she offers him a poker from the fireplace. Welles drops the poker and flees to the clock tower to hide. Young leads Robinson to the clock tower for the final confrontation. Obviously insane and babbling to Robinson that he "was only following orders," Welles tries to escape. Welles drops his gun and Young picks it up and shoots at him several times, finally wounding him. Welles stumbles out onto the clock's platform and is impaled by one of the moving figures–an avenging angel holding a long sword. Dying, Welles manages to shake himself loose and falls to the sidewalk below. In THE STRANGER, Welles gives us one of the cinema's most realistic and chilling portrayals of a Nazi. Welles' Franz Kindler is not a cartoon character in uniform spouting propaganda, grinning evilly and clicking his heels. He is a smug, arrogant, cynical, amoral, and wholly self-confident creature who believes that he is superior to anyone he meets–he is evil incarnate. He is not a snarling, flamboyant evil, but a quiet, calm, cold evil that can infiltrate any community and destroy it. It is a chilling portrayal. Robinson is also quite good as the hunter determined to catch his prey. He represents the postwar world wanting to stamp out the threat of evil so that it may never happen again (Welles originally wanted to cast Agnes Moorehead in the role, but the studio wanted Robinson and got him). The rest of the cast registers strongly, especially House as the shopkeeper, but while Young is right for the part of the sheltered small-town girl, she overplays some of the more emotional scenes. Technically, as one expects with Welles, the film is superb. Though not as wildly creative as his other films, all the Welles trademarks are present, including superior lighting, inventive camera angles, strong transitions, and characters silhouetted in darkness (the scene where Robinson shows Young the atrocity footage has the light from the screen flickering the horror across the character's faces). There are also several little jokes from Welles, including a sign in the gymnasium that reads: "Use equipment at own risk" which is seen after Robinson gets knocked out by the practice ring, and a scene where Welles doodles a swastika on a pad of paper while talking on the phone at the height of the manhunt. Reports from all concerned indicate that the shooting of THE STRANGER went quite smoothly for a Welles film and even the construction of the clock tower, the largest outdoor set structure since D.W. Griffith's INTOLERANCE, went without a hitch. Welles himself provided the clock, which used to grace the Los Angeles County Courthouse until 1922 when the building was torn down. He had found it in the basement of the Los Angeles County Museum and had it installed in the tower. Though the critics, the public, and Welles himself were not happy with THE STRANGER, it proved he could make a tightly budgeted entertainment like everyone else in Hollywood and paved the way for one of his strangest films, THE LADY FROM SHANGHAI.

p, Sam P. Eagle [Sam Spiegel] d, Orson Welles; w, Anthony Veiller, (uncredited) John Huston, Welles (based on the story by Victor Trivas, Decla Dunning); ph, Russell Metty; m, Bronislau Kaper; ed, Ernest Nims; art d, Perry Ferguson; cos, Michael Woulfe

Drama   **Cas.**   **(PR:C MPAA:NR)**

STRANGER, THE, 1962   (SEE: INTRUDER, THE , 1962)

STRANGER, THE*   (1967, Algeria/Fr./Ital.) 104m DD-Master
              Marianne Casbah/PAR c (L'ETRANGER; LO STRANIERO)

Marcello Mastroianni *(Arthur Meursault),* Anna Karina *(Marie Cardona),* Bernard Blier *(Defense Counsel),* Georges Wilson *(Examining Magistrate),* Bruno Cremer *(Priest),* Pierre Bertin *(Judge),* Jacques Herlin *(Director of Home),* Marc Laurent *(Emmanuel),* Georges Geret *(Raymond),* Alfred Adam *(Prosecutor),* Jean-Pierre Zola *(Employer),* Mimmo Palmara *(Masson),* Angela Luce *(Madame Masson),* Saada Cheritel, Mohamed Ralem, Brahim Hadjadj *(Arabs),* Vittorio Duse *(Lawyer),* Joseph Marechal *(Salamano),* Jacques Monod, Valentino Macchi, Paolo Herzl.

Mastroianni plays the existential Meursault, a French clerk living in Algiers who one day, for no other reason than the brightness of the sun's rays, shoots and kills a young Algerian. He is brought to trial, where he is forced to answer questions about an affair he had shortly after the death of his mother, and explain why he failed to cry at his mother's funeral. While awaiting the guillotine, Mastroianni refuses to be swayed by the prison priest's beliefs, and then rejects his words of consolation, choosing instead to think about life and existence. As it so often happens when a great filmmaker brings the work of a great novelist to the screen, THE STRANGER is an utter failure, in terms of Camus. Visconti fails to come close to the style of Camus' words, as if he chose to make the film in the hopes of producing a failure. If so, that surely cannot explain why he fell to even lower depths with his version of Thomas Mann's A DEATH IN VENICE. THE STRANGER cannot expect to be judged solely on the basis of cinematic standards. He foolishly tackled one of the greatest pieces of writing in the 20th Century and turned out one of his poorest films. All that can be said in its favor lies in its stupendous technical achievements and the fine performances of Mastroianni (who somehow seems perfect as Meursault) and Karina.

p, Dino De Laurentiis; d, Luchino Visconti; w, Suso Cecchi D'Amico, Georges Conchon, Emmanuel Robles, Visconti (based on the novel by Albert Camus); ph, Giuseppe Rotunno (Technicolor); m, Piero Piccioni; ed, Ruggero Mastroianni; md, Bruno Nicolai; art d, Mario Garbuglia; cos, Piero Tosi; makeup, Mario Banchelli

Drama (PR:C-O MPAA:NR)

STRANGER AT MY DOOR** (1950, Brit.) 80m Leinster/Monarch bw

Valentine Dyall (*Paul Wheeler*), Joseph O'Conor (*Michael Foley*), Agnes Bernelle (*Laura Riordan*), Maire O'Neill (*Clarissa Finnegan*), Jill Raymond (*Kate*), Liam O'Leary (*Kelly*), Michael Moore (*Septimus Small*), Harry Hutchinson, W.E. Holloway, Michael Seavers, Alan Gore-Lewis, Charles Mansell, Dorothy Dewhurst, Madalene Burgess, Bea Duffell, Jimmy Page, Charles Vance, Malachy Keegan, Katherine Mora, Nigel Neilson.

A young Dubliner becomes a burglar in order to adorn his girl friend with gifts and luxuries. He soon discovers that she is paying off a blackmailer with the money. A gripping and surprisingly stark picture in which the main character learns a valuable, but expensive, lesson.

p, Paul King; d, Brendan J. Stafford, Desmond Leslie; w, Leslie; ph, Stafford.

Crime Drama (PR:A MPAA:NR)

STRANGER AT MY DOOR*** (1956) 85m REP bw

MacDonald Carey (*Hollis Jarret*), Patricia Medina (*Peg Jarret*), Skip Homeier (*Clay Anderson*), Stephen Wootton (*Dodie Jarret*), Louis Jean Heydt (*Sheriff John Tatum*), Howard Wright (*Doc Parks*), Slim Pickens (*Ben Silas, Horse Trader*), Malcolm Atterbury (*Rev. Hastings*), Fred Sherman.

Blessed with strong characterization, STRANGER AT MY DOOR tells the tale of a western preacher, Carey, who teaches outlaw Homeier the ways of the Lord. Homeier comes to Carey's farm, a fugitive looking for a hideaway, but soon finds that he is learning a set of morals and showing kindness to Carey's wife, Medina, and son, Wootton. A fine sampling of family entertainment, which does not spare any action to deliver its message.

p, Sidney Picker; d, William Witney; w, Barry Shipman (based on a story by shipman); ph, Bud Thackery; m, R. Dale Butts; ed, Howard Smith; art d, Frank Arrigo; cos, Adele Palmer.

Western (PR:A MPAA:NR)

STRANGER CAME HOME, THE (SEE: UNHOLY FOUR, THE 1954, Brit.)

STRANGER FROM ARIZONA, THE**½ (1938) 54m COL bw

Buck Jones (*Buck Weylan*), Dorothy Fay (*Ann*), Hank Mann (*Garrison*), Hank Worden (*Skeeter*), Roy Barcroft (*Thane*), Bob Terry (*Talbot*), Horace Murphy (*Sheriff*), Budd Buster (*Trickett*), Dot Farley (*Martha*), Walter Anthony (*Sandy*), Stanley Blystone (*Haskell*), Ralph Peters, Loren Riebe, Horace B. Carpenter, Silver the Horse.

An action-packed, slapstick western tale which has Jones coming from Arizona to help Fay, whose cattle are being snatched by an evil gang of rustlers. Jones mixes law and order with comedy and romance for this abovepar entry.

p, Monroe Shaff; d, Elmer Clifton; w, Shaff; ph, Eddie Linden; ed, Holbrook N. Todd.

Western (PR:A MPAA:NR)

STRANGER FROM PECOS, THE** (1943) 55m MON bw

Johnny Mack Brown (*Nevada*), Raymond Hatton (*Sandy*), Kirby Grant (*Tom*), Christine McIntyre (*Ruth*), Steve Clark (*Clem*), Sam Flint (*Ward*), Roy Barcroft (*Sheriff*), Robert Frazer (*Burstow*), Edmond Cobb (*Burt*), Charles King (*Harmond*), Bud Osborne (*Gus*), Artie Ortego (*Ed*), Tom London, Kermit Maynard, Milburn Morante, Lynton Brent, Carol Henry, George Morrell.

Brown swings his fists at a powerful cheat who is grabbing up people's mortgages after soaking them in poker games. Brown's pal, Hatton, purposely loses $3,000 to a rancher who earlier had his cash stolen, enabling the man to buy his property back.

p, Scott R. Dunlap; d, Lambert Hillyer; w, Jess Bowers [Adele Buffington]; ph, Harry Neumann; ed, Carl Pierson; md, Edward Kag; art d, Ernie Hickson.

Western (PR:A MPAA:NR)

STRANGER FROM TEXAS, THE** (1940) 54m COL bw (GB: THE STRANGER)

Charles Starrett (*Tom*), Lorna Gray [Adrian Booth] (*Joan*), Bob Nolan (*Bob*), Richard Fiske (*Ned*), Dick Curtis (*Springer*), Edmund Cobb (*Carver*), Al Bridge (*Jeff*), Jack Rockwell (*Sheriff*), Hal Taliaferro (*Clay*), Edward J. Le

Saint (*Murdock*), Buel Bryant, Art Mix, George Chesebro, Sons of the Pioneers.

Starrett prevents his umpteenth range war in this standard western, bringing a gang that loots ranches while the owners are out fighting to justice. Bob Nolan and The Sons Of The Pioneers deliver their usual tunes for our listening enjoyment.

p, Harry L. Decker; d, Sam Nelson; w, Paul Franklin (based on the story "The Mysterious Avenger" by Ford Beebe); ph, George Meehan; ed, Mel Thorsen; m/l, Bob Nolan, Tim Spencer.

Western (PR:A MPAA:NR)

STRANGER FROM VENUS, THE*½ (1954, Brit.) 75m Rich and Rich/Princess Pictures bw (AKA: IMMEDIATE DISASTER; THE VENUSIAN)

Patricia Neal (*Susan North*), Helmut Dantine (*Stranger*), Derek Bond (*Arthur Walker*), Cyril Luckham (*Dr. Meinard*), Willoughby Gray (*Tom*), Marigold Russell (*Gretchen*), Arthur Young (*Scientist*), Stanley Van Beer (*General*), Graham Stuart (*Police Chief*), Kenneth Edwards (*Charles Dixon*), David Garth (*1st Police Officer*), Nigel Green (*2nd Police Officer*), John Le Mesurier.

An uncredited remake of THE DAY THE EARTH STOOD STILL which again starred Neal as the lady who befriends an alien from Venus. He tells her that his people are concerned with the Earthlings' dismal future, but meets opposition from an unfriendly few. Cheaply filmed almost entirely on one hotel set in England.

p, Burt Balaban, Gene Martel; d, Balaban; w, Hans Jacoby (based on a story by Desmond Leslie); ph, Kenneth Talbot; m, Eric Spear; art d, John Elphick; makeup, Nel Taylor.

ScienceFiction Cas. (PR:A MPAA:NR)

STRANGER IN BETWEEN, THE**½ (1952, Brit.) 84m Independent Artists-British Film Makers/UNIV bw (GB: HUNTED)

Dirk Bogarde (*Chris Lloyd*), Jon Whiteley (*Robbie*), Elizabeth Sellars (*Magda Lloyd*), Kay Walsh (*Mrs. Sykes*), Frederick Piper (*Mr. Sykes*), Julian Somers (*Jack Lloyd*), Jane Aird (*Mrs. Campbell*), Jack Stewart (*Mr. Campbell*), Geoffrey Keen (*Detective Inspector Deaken*), Joe Linnane (*Pawnbroker*), Leonard White, Gerald Anderson, Denis Webb, Gerald Case, Katherine Blake, Molly Urquhart, Grace Arnold, Alec Finter, Harry Quashie, Ian Hunter.

Bogarde plays a murderer on the run (he had killed his wife's lover) who stumbles upon a little boy, Whiteley, who had run away from home. Feeling paternal, Bogarde allows the tyke to accompany him and they make an adventure of running from justice. Just as Bogarde is about to flee to safety, Whiteley falls ill and Bogarde turns himself in to get medical care for the boy.

p, Julian Wintle; d, Charles Crichton; w, Jack Whittingham (based on a story by Michael McCarthy); ph, Eric Cross; m, Hubert Clifford; ed, Ted Holliday; art d, Alex Vetchinsky.

DRAMA (PR:A MPAA:NR)

STRANGER IN HOLLYWOOD* (1968) 96m Roda/Emerson c

Sue Bernard (*Woman*), Scott Every (*Fiance*), Guy Mecoli, Mario Arezney, Grace Burnard, Phyllis Janus, Victor Smith, Anne Slipyj, Mary Clarke.

An uneventful tale of a woman who finds oil in Los Angeles and runs off to Hollywood to enjoy her new-found fortune. Discovering that there is not much to see, she returns home to her normal life.

p, Anne Slipyj; d&w, Rodion Slipyj; ph, Steve Salamandro (Eastmancolor); ed, Norm Vizents; art d, Ruth Brande.

Drama (PR:A-C MPAA:GP)

STRANGER IN MY ARMS**½ (1959) 88m UNIV bw

June Allyson (*Christina Beasley*), Jeff Chandler (*Pike Yarnell*), Sandra Dee (*Pat Beasley*), Charles Coburn (*Vance Beasley*), Mary Astor (*Mrs. Beasley*), Peter Graves (*Donald Beasley*), Conrad Nagel (*Harley Beasley*), Hayden Rorke (*Marcus Beasley*), Reita Green (*Bessie Logan*), Bartlett Robinson (*Col. Bert Wayne*), Howard Wendell (*Congressman*).

A bleary-eyed melodrama sure to warm the hearts of those who love this sort of film. Allyson stars as the overbearing mother of a son who, in an act of cowardice, killed himself while overseas. Mom is dead set on getting him a posthumous medal of honor, however, and is willing to bribe major Chandler to testify in his favor. Producer Ross Hunter rounded up the usual melodrama cast at Universal, plus took another novel from Wilder (WRITTEN ON THE WIND), but needed the likes of Douglas Sirk to direct this.

p, Ross Hunter; d, Helmut Kautner; w, Peter Berneis (based on the novel *And Ride A Tiger* by Robert Wilder); ph, William Daniels (CinemaScope); ed, Frank Gross; md, Joseph Gershenson; art d, Alexander Golitzen, Richard H. Riedel; cos, Bill Thomas.

Drama   **(PR:A   MPAA:NR)**

STRANGER IN THE HOUSE, 1967   (SEE: COP-OUT, 1967, Brit.)

STRANGER IN THE HOUSE, 1975
                          (SEE: BLACK CHRISTMAS, 1975, Can.)

STRANGER IN TOWN**   (1932) 63m WB bw

Charles "Chic" Sale (*Crickle*), Ann Dvork (*Marian*), David Manners (*Jerry*), Raymond Hatton (*Elmer Perkins*), Noah Beery, Sr (*Hilliker, Constable*), Maude Eburne (*Mrs. Petrick*), Lyle Talbot (*Brice*), John Larkin (*Jed*), Jessie Arnold (*Woman Customer*).

Grocery store owner Sale is forced to protect his Boilsville, Ark., business from the wicked ways of a rival chain-operated store. His fight gets complicated when his granddaughter falls in love with the competition, Manners.

p, Lucien Hubbard; d, Erle C. Kenton; W, Carl Erickson, Harvey Thew (based on the story "Competition" by Erickson); ph, Dev Jennings; ed, James Morley.

Drama/Comedy   **(PR:A   MPAA:NR)**

STRANGER IN TOWN, A**   (1943) 67m MGM bw

Frank Morgan (*John Josephus Grant*), Richard Carlson (*Bill Adams*), Jean Rogers (*Lucy Gilbert*), Porter Hall (*Judge Austin Harkley*), Robert Barrat (*Mayor Connison*), Donald MacBride (*Vinnie Z. Blaxton*), Walter Baldwin (*Tom Cooney*), Andrew Tombes (*Roscoe Swade*), Olin Howlin (*Homer Todds*), Chill Wills (*Charles Craig*), Irving Bacon (*Orrin Todds*), Eddie Dunn (*Henry*), Gladys Blake (*Birdie*), John Hodiak (*Hart Ridges*).

Morgan is a supreme court justice who takes a quiet fishing vacation in a small town, only to find that he has to carry out his duties to fight local corruption. The incumbent mayor and his powerful aides are making it tough on Carlson, an honest young lawyer who is a spokesman for the people. Carlson wants to run, and with the judge's help, does so and wins.

p, Robert Sisk; d, Roy Rowland; w, Isobel Lennart, William Kozlenko; ph, Sidney Wagner; m, Daniele Amfitheatrof, Nathaniel Shilkret; ed, Elmo Veron; art d, Cedric Gibbons.

Drama   **(PR:A   MPAA:NR)**

STRANGER IN TOWN**   (1957, Brit.) 73m Tempean/Eros bw

Alex Nicol (*John Madison*), Anne Page (*Vicky Leigh*), Mary Laura Wood (*Lorna Ryland*), Mona Washbourne (*Agnes Smith*), Charles Lloyd Pack (*Capt. Nash*), Bruce Beeby (*William Ryland*), John Horsley (*Inspector Powell*), Colin Tapley (*Henry Ryland*), Betty Impey (*Geraldine Nash*), Arthur Lowe.

Set in a quiet English village, STRANGER IN TOWN tells the story of a journalist who is trying to find the killer of an American composer who was murdered in the town. After turning up a series of clues, the journalist learns that the composer was actually a blackmailer who was killed by one of his frustrated victims, Pack.

p, Robert So Baker, Monty Baker, Sidney Roberts; d, George Pollock; w, Norman Hudis, Edward Dryhurst (based on the novel *The Univited* by Frank Chittenden); ph, Geoffrey Faithfull.

Crime   **(PR:A   MPAA:NR)**

STRANGER IN TOWN, A*   (1968, U.S./Ital.) 86m Primex
                    Italiana-Taka/MGM c (UN DOLLARO TRA I DENT)

Tony Anthony (*The Stranger*), Frank Wolff (*Aguila*), Iolanda Modio (*Cica*), Gia Sandri (*Maruka*), Raf Baldassarre, Aldo Berti, Enrico Capoleoni, Antonio Marsina, Arturo Corso, Salvatore Puntillo, Ivan Scratt [Ivan Scratuglia], Rossella Bergamonti, Fortunato Arena, Ugo Carbone, Loris Bazzocchi, Angela Minervini, Lars Bloch.

A lame spaghetti western, long on brutality, which stars Anthony as the mysterious "Stranger" who arrives in town, guns down a bandit who murdered a troop of Mexican soldiers, and then leaves just as unexpectedly as he came. It seems the bandit had plans for getting his hands on a U.S. gold shipment, which the soldiers were supposed to receive. Another Sergio Leone inspired ripoff. The type of film that would need two Clint Eastwoods to save it.

p, Carlo Infascelli; d, Vance Lewis [Luigi Vanzi]; w, Jone Mang [Giuseppe Mangione], Warren Garfield; ph, Marcello Masciocchi (Eastmancolor); m, Benedetto Ghiglia; ed, Mario Lucidi; art d, Carmelo Patrono.

Western   **(PR:C   MPAA:R)**

STRANGER IS WATCHING, A**   (1982) 92m MGM/UA c

Kate Mulgrew (*Sharon Martin*), Rip Torn (*Artie Taggart*), James Naughton (*Steve Peterson*), Shawn von Schreiber (*Julie Peterson*), Barbara Baxley (*Lally*), Stephen Joyce (*Detective*), James Russo (*Ronald Thompson*), Frank Hamilton (*Bill Lufts*), Maggie Task (*Mrs. Lufts*), Roy Poole (*Kurner*), Stephen Strimpell, Jason Robards III.

A thriller which casts Torn as a psychopathic killer who kidnaps and scares the daylights out of 11-year-old von Schreiber and journalist Mulgrew, who happens to be in love with the girl's father, Naughton. Torn keeps his prisoners hostage in the dark, dingy bowels of New York's Grand Central Station. The entire film has a sadistic bent to it, but curiously only a few murders–not nearly enough to sustain the interest of fans of this sort. Cunningham also directed the mega-money maker FRIDAY THE 13th, but none of its subsequent offspring.

p, Sidney Beckerman; d, Sean S. Cunningham; w, Earl MacRauch, Victor Miller (based on the novel by Mary Higgins Clark); ph, Barry Abrams (Metrocolor); m, Lalo Schifrin; ed, Susan E. Cunningham; art d, Virginia Field; spec eff, Connie Brink; makeup, Andrew Ciannella.

Horror   **Cas.**   **(PR:O   MPAA:R)**

STRANGER KNOCKS, A**   (1963, Den.) 81m Flamingo/Trans-Lux bw
                              (EN FREMMED BANKER PA)

Birgitte Federspiel (*The Woman*), Preben Lerdorff-Rye (*The Stranger*), Victor Montell (*Man from Village*).

It is shortly after WW II and a man on the run is trying to hide along a desolate piece of land bordered by the North Sea. The lone cottage contains a tough woman who takes him in and permits him to stay. He preys upon her loneliness and listens to her woes about being alone because fellow members of the Danish resistance killed her husband. The physical attraction overwhelms the two cottage occupants and they become lovers. While in an embrace, she spots a distinctive scar on his arm–a mark which shows he is the traitor who turned in her husband and had him tortured and killed. The stunned woman gets him to confess his crime and kills him as he tries to flee. But his guilt is erased with his death and she must now carry the guilt of murder.

p, Annelise Hovmand, Johan Jacobsen; d, Jacobsen; w, Finn Methling; ph, Ake Borglund, Jacobsen; m, Erik Fiehn; set d, Hovmand.

Drama   **(PR:C   MPAA:NR)**

STRANGER ON HORSEBACK**   (1955) 66m UA c

Joel McCrea (*Rick Thorne*), Miroslava (*Amy Lee Bannerman*), Kevin McCarthy (*Tom Bannerman*), John McIntire (*Josiah Bannerman*), Nancy Gates (*Caroline Webb*), John Carradine (*Col. Streeter*), Emile Meyer (*Sheriff Nat Bell*), Robert Cornthwaite (*Arnold Hammer*), Jaclynne Greene (*Paula Morison*), James Bell (*Vince Webb*), Walter Baldwin.

McCrea plays a judge who not only hands down the sentences, but also makes sure they are followed by use of his six-shooters. He is a traveling judge and when he hits town, he finds the place controlled by McIntire. Even though the townspeople back the land baron, McCrea brings his brat son, McCarthy, to trial for murder. Despite the town's fear of McIntire, McCrea rounds up enough witnesses to make sure that justice is served. Even McIntire comes to his side as does Miroslava just when he is ready to put his guns away again.

p, Robert Goldstein; d, Jacques Tourneur; w, Herb Meadow, Don Martin (based on a story by Louis L, Amour); ph, Ray Rennahan (Ansco Color); m, Paul Dunlap; ed, William Murphy.

Western   **(PR:A   MPAA:NR)**

STRANGER ON THE PROWL**½   (1953, Ital.) 82m
          Tirrenia-Riviera/UA bw (IMBARCO A MEZZANOTE; UN HOMME A
                              DETRUIRE; GB: ENCOUNTER)

Paul Muni (*The Man*), Joan Lorring (*Angela*), Vittorio Manunta (*Giacomo Fontana*), Luisa Rossi (*Giacomo's Mother*), Aldo Silvani (*Peroni*), Franco Balducci (*Morelli*), Enrico Glori (*Signor Pucci*), Arnoldo Foa (*The Inspector*), Elena Manson (*The Storekeeper*), Alfredo Varelli (*Castelli*), Fausta Mazzunchelli (*Giacomo's Sister*), Cesare Trapani (*Giacomo's Friend*), Leon Lenoir (*Mancini*), Linda Sini (*Signora Raffetto*), Giulio Marchetti (*Signor Raffetto*), Noel Calef (*Flute-Player*), Henri Alekan (*Priest on Bicycle*), Nando Bruno, Ave Ninchi.

It had been almost seven years since Muni's last film, ANGEL ON MY SHOULDER, and–with COMMANDOS STRIKE AT DAWN (1954) in the interim–it would be another six years before his final movie, THE LAST ANGRY MAN. Made in Italy at Tirrenia Studios with locations in Pisa, Livorno and Taranto, the movie was directed and cowritten by Losey. But alleged leftist Losey was in the midst of a squabble with the HUAC group so he used two *noms de cinema* in order to be able to get distribution in the U.S. The picture took 86 days to shoot. Muni did not like working away from the U.S. and let everyone know it. He's a bum who has to get away from where he is. In order to secure enough money to book passage on a freighter, he wants to sell his prized possession, a gun. Leaving the country will be illegal but that doesn't concern him as there are people who want his scalp in Italy. Nobody cares to purchase the revolver and he is getting desperate, as well as hungry. He walks into a store and tries to steal a bit of cheese to staunch his gnawing stomach pains. When the storekeeper, Manson, begins to scream for help, Muni attempts to keep her quiet and accidentally strangles her to death. The murder is seen by waif Manunta, who takes the opportunity to steal some milk for himself. Manunta decides to team up with Muni. The chase is on and Muni is shot and wounded by police. Then he and Manunta are given shelter by Lorring, who works as a maid in a rich home. Lorring and Muni have a short sexual fling but both realize that it can't go on. Muni and Manunta leave and the cops are soon on the trail. Muni is eventually killed by the police and Rossi, Manunta's laundress mother who has been sick with fear for most of the movie, clasps her son in her arms. Though much of the cast is Italian, the picture was shot in English, although some of the accents are thicker than manicotti and may be lost on U.S. ears. Muni had played the man on the run before when he was a fugitive from a chain gang. This film added nothing to his career. It originally came in at three hours, then was twice-edited until this final cut. We have to believe that there was a great deal more to the script Muni read which caused him to come back to the screen after having been away so long.

p, Noel Calef; d, Andrea Forzano [Joseph Losey]; w, Ben Barzman [Losey] (based on a story, "La Bouteille de Lait," by Calef); ph, Henri Alekan; m, G. C. Sonzogno; ed, Thelma Connelli; art d, Antonio Valente.

Drama   (PR:A-C MPAA:NR)

STRANGER ON THE THIRD FLOOR***½   (1940) 64m RKO bw

Peter Lorre *(Stranger)*, John McGuire *(Michael Ward)*, Margaret Tallichet *(Jane)*, Charles Waldron *(District Attorney)*, Elisha Cook, Jr. *(Joe Briggs)*, Charles Halton *(Meng)*, Ethel Griffies *(Mrs. Kane)*, Cliff Clark *(Martin)*, Oscar O'Shea *(Judge)*, Alec Craig *(Defense Attorney)*, Otto Hoffman *(Police Surgeon)*, Charles Judels *(Nick)*, Frank Yaconelli *(Jack)*, Paul McVey *(Lt. Jones)*, Robert Dudley *(Postman)*, Frank O'Connor, James Farley, Don Kelly *(Officers)*, Herbert Vigran, Robert Waldon, Terry Belmont 'Lee Bonnell', Gladden James *(Reporters)*, Harry C. Bradley *(Court Clerk)*, Greta Grandstedt *(Chambermaid)*, Katherine Wallace *(Woman)*, Bud Osborne *(Bartender)*, Broderick O'Farrell *(Minister)*, Emory Parnell, Jack Cheatham, Dell Henderson *(Detectives)*, Henry Roquemore *(Boss McLean)*, Jane Keckley *(Landlady)*, Bess Wade *(Charwoman)*, Ralph Sanford *(Truck Driver)*, Betty Farrington *(Stout Woman)*, Ray Cooke *(Drug Store Attendant)*, Don Kerr *(Bit)*, William Edmunds, Frank Hammond *(Janitors)*, Lee Phelps, Max Hoffman, Lynton Brent *(Taxi Drivers)*, Bobby Barber *(Italian Man)*.

This fascinating film has been hailed as the first *film noir*, and it certainly has all the *noir* elements, including shadowy compositions and a plot that emphasizes bizarre psychology. McGuire is a reporter who walks into a diner and finds the proprietor dead on the floor, his throat slashed. He identifies taxi driver Cook as the man he had seen running from the diner just ahead of McGuire, and his testimony convicts the cabbie, who protests that he was simply there to pay a small debt and panicked when he found the body. Cook is sentenced to die in the electric chair, but McGuire has doubts about the man's guilt. His fiancee, Tallichet, encourages him to continue to investigate and that night he encounters a strange looking man on the stairs (Lorre) and begins to think he might be the killer. His abrasive neighbor, Halton, whom McGuire had once, in a moment of anger, threatened to kill, is noticeably quiet that night and McGuire begins to wonder if he might be dead. Before he can check it out, though he falls asleep and has a weird dream in which he finds Halton murdered and is himself arrested for the crime. he is convicted on the strength of circumstantial evidence much the same as Cook was, and sentenced to the chair. As he is strapped in Halton walks into the execution room and laughs. McGuire awakens with a start and goes next door to check on Halton. As he feared, the old man is dead, his throat slashed just like the diner owner's. McGuire calls the police, but his discovery of the previous corpse, plus his threat to kill Halton, lead them to arrest him. Tallichet takes over the investigation and walks the streets all day trying to find the man who matches the description of Lorre McGuire had given her. Finally, in a diner, she overhears a man ask for two raw hamburgers. She looks around and sees the object of her quest feeding the two patties to a stray dog. She walks up to him and strikes up a conversation, asking if she can walk with him. He tells her that he has escaped from a place where they put him in a straitjacket and poured ice water on him. She realizes that she is dealing with an escaped lunatic and before she can figure out what to do he tells her of the other murders and then starts after her. She runs across the street and he follows, but is hit by a truck and killed, but not before making a full confession of his crimes to the bystanders. The happy ending sees McGuire and Tallichet about to be married and accepting a free ride in Cook's cab. The performances are average for a B movie and Lorre is on screen too briefly to make a big impression, but the film still remains in the memory on the strength of its weird plot and the bizarre dream sequence that takes up a good chunk of the film's brief running time. The camera work by Musuraca is superb, as claustrophobic as any *film noir* a decade later, every street a threat of unexpected, horrible death. Screenwriter Ingster made his debut as a director here and shows his heavy debt to the German expressionist films of the 1920s. He never again directed anything nearly as interesting as this neglected demi-classic.

p, Lee Marcus; d, Boris Ingster; w, Frank Partos; ph, Nicholas Musuraca; m, Roy Webb; ed, Harry Marker; art d, Van Nest Polglase; spec eff, Vernon L. Walker.

Crime   (PR:C MPAA:NR)

STRANGER RETURNS, THE**   (1968, U.S./Ital./Ger./Span.) 90m Primex Italiana-Juven tus-Reverse/MGM c (UN UOMO, UN CAVALLO, UNA PISTOLA)

Tony Anthony *(The Stranger)*, Dan Vadis *(En Plein)*, Daniele Vargas *(Good Jim)*, Marco Guglielmi *(The Preacher)*, Jill Banner *(Caroline)*, Ettore Manni *(Stafford)*, Marina Berti *(Ethel)*, Raf Baldassarre, Anthony Freeman, Renato Mambor, Franco Scala, Mario Dionisi, Armando Mangolini, Silvana Fiorini, Arturo Danesi, Filippo Antonelli.

A western that has plenty of detailed action, gore actually, to mask a thin plot. A greedy postal inspector informs a gang that a shipment of gold is coming in. They kill him. Anthony, with pink parasol in hand, finds the dead man, and hunts the bandits. Anthony takes on the postal inspector's identity and tries to infiltrate the gang but is captured. He finds out that Vargas is in cahoots with the criminals. The coach arrives and Vadis kills everyone aboard only to discover that the real coach has not yet arrived. The gold is hidden in the framework and painted over. With help from a priest, Anthony saves Vargas' daughter from being raped, kills the gang, and takes the coach. The pair take the bodies into town for a reward and he gives it to the priest. On the way out of town, it is discovered that the stranger has the real stagecoach, so he must give it to the U.S. Cavalry and he goes back to get his share of the reward from the priest. Sequel to STRANGER IN TOWN.

p, Roberto Infascelli, Massimo Gualdi; d, Vance Lewis [Luigi Vanzi]; w, Bob Ensescalle, Jr., Jone Mang (based on a story by Tony Anthony); ph, Marcello Masciocchi (Metrocolor); m, Stelvio Cipriani; ed, Renzo Lucidi.

Western   (PR:A MPAA:R)

STRANGER THAN LOVE   (SEE: STRANGE LOVERS, 1963)

STRANGER WALKED IN, A   (SEE: LOVE FROM A STRANGER, 1947)

STRANGER WORE A GUN, THE**½ (1953) 83m Scott-Brown/COL c

Randolph Scott *(Jeff Travis)*, Claire Trevor *(Josie Sullivan)*, Joan Weldon *(Shelby Conroy)*, George Macready *(Jules Mourret)*, Alfonso Bedoya *(Degas)*, Lee Marvin *(Dan Kurth)*, Ernest Borgnine *(Bull Slager)*, Pierre Watkin *(Jason Conroy)*, Joseph Vitale *(Dutch Mueller)*, Clem Bevans *(Jim Martin)*, Paul Maxey *(Poley)*, Frank Scannell *(Red Glick)*, Reed Howes *(Harve Comis)*, Roscoe Ates *(Milt Hooper)*, Edward Earle *(Jeb)*, Guy Wilkerson *(Ike)*, Mary Newton *(Shelby Conroy)*, Mary Lou Holloway, Franklyn Farnum, Barry Brooks, Tap Canutt, Al Haskell, Frank Hagney, Frank Ellis, Francis McDonald, Phil Tully, Al Hill, Harry Mendoza, Terry Frost, Diana Dawson, Richard Benjamin, Herbert Rawlinson, Britt Wood, Harry Seymour, James Millican, Jack Woody, Rayford Barnes, Rudy Germaine, Edith Evanson, Guy Teague.

The early 1950s spawned a multitude of 3-D films and this one followed right along. Scott, a spy for William Quantrill's raiders during the Civil War, heads out to Arizona after the conflict, hoping to lose that black mark on his reputation. He takes up with Macready and both watch and plot as Weldon and her father, Watkin, ship gold via the stagecoach line. Scott decides to go honest and instigates a feud between Macready and Mexican bandit Bedoya. After that smoke clears, Scott and Macready remain, and the two of them shoot it out in a top-notch action sequence in a flaming saloon. Scott not only gets his man, but also Trevor, who has been waiting there for him all the time. He also gets the credit as the associate producer on the film.

p, Harry Joe Brown; d, Andre De Toth; w, Kenneth Gamet (based on the novel *Yankee Gold* by John M. Cunningham); ph, Lester H. White (3-D, Technicolor); ed, Gene Havlick, James Sweeney; art d, George Brooks.

Western   (PR:A MPAA:NR)

STRANGERS, THE**   (1955, Ital.) 80m Sveva-Junior-Italiafilm/Titanus-Fine Arts bw (VIAGGIO IN ITALIA; AKA: JOURNEY TO ITALY; THE LONELY LADY; A TRIP TO ITALY; THE LONELY WOMAN)

Ingrid Bergman *(Katherine Joyce)*, George Sanders *(Alexander Joyce)*, Maria Mauban *(Marie)*, Paul Muller *(Paul Dupont)*, Leslie Daniels *(Tony Burton)*, Natalia Ray *(Natalie Burton)*, Anna Proclemer *(The Prostitute)*, Jackie Frost *(Betty)*.

Sanders and Bergman star as a married couple who travel to Naples to inspect the house they recently inherited. With their marriage already strained, the couple decide on a complete separation in their new surroundings, only to discover the need they have for each other. Strong performances by Bergman and Sanders do little to offset the plodding direction and weak script.

p&d, Roberto Rossellini; w, Rossellini, Vitaliano Brancati; ph, Enzo Sarafin;

m, Renzo Rossellini; ed, Jolanda Benvenuti.

Romance   (PR:A   MPAA:NR)

STRANGERS, 1970   (SEE: I NEVER SANG FOR MY FATHER, 1970)

STRANGERS ALL*   (1935) 70m RKO bw

May Robson (*Mom Carter*), Preston Foster (*Murray Carter*), Florine McKinney (*Lily Carter*), William Bakewell (*Dick Carter*), James Bush (*Lewis Carter*), Samuel S. Hinds (*Mr. Green*), Clifford Jones (*Pat Gruen*), Suzanne Kaaren (*Frances Farrell*), Leon Ames (*Mr. Walker*), Reginald Barlow (*Judge*), Paul Stanton (*Prosecuting Attorney*).

Weak, weak story that falls completely flat. Robson is the mother of three sons and one daughter who, having nothing in common, are "strangers." One son is the hard worker, who keeps food on the table; another thinks of himself as a great thespian; while the other boy is bent on saving the world from greedy capitalists. The daughter fits right in with the group, as she goes off to college and comes back married without telling anyone about it.

p, Cliff Reid; d, Charles Vidor; w, Milton Krims (based on a play by Marie M. Bercovici); ph, John Boyle; ed, Jack Hively.

Drama   (PR:A   MPAA:NR)

STRANGERS CAME, THE   (SEE: YOU CAN'T FOOL AN
                                 IRISHMAN, 1950, Ire.)

STRANGER'S GUNDOWN, THE*½   (1974, Ital.) 107m New Line
Cinema c (DJANGO DE BASTARDO; DJANGO IL BASTARDO; AKA:
DJANGO THE BASTARD)

Lu Kamante, R. Rassimov.

The Stranger slowly tracks down his prey, sticking crosses with his targets' names on in the middle of the street, predating them for the day he plans to get his revenge. And there are plenty of people he wants in the grave, including a pair of troublesome brothers who are so mean they toss a dynamite stick back and forth for fun–it's lighted, of course. But the Stranger, whose gun never seems to stop shooting, gets them in the end and walks off, remaining anonymous. This film was a sequel to THE STRANGER and just one of more than 30 Italian westerns that used the "Django" character.

p, Herman Cohen, Anthony Steffen, Teodoro Corra; d, Sergio Garroni; w, Garroni, Antonio De Teffe; ph, Gino Santini; m, M. Mancuso.

Western   (PR:C   MPAA:PG)

STRANGER'S HAND, THE½**   (1955, Brit.) 86m Independent Film
Producers/Distributor's Corporation of America bw (AKA: MANO DEL-
LA STRANIERO)

Trevor Howard (*Maj. Court*), Alida Valli (*Roberta*), Richard Basehart (*Joe Hamstringer*), Eduardo Ciannelli (*Dr. Vivaldi*), Richard O'Sullivan (*Roger Court*), Stephen Murray (*British Consul*), Giorgio Constantini (*Pescovitch*).

British novelist Graham Greene was well known for his mystery thrillers, but this film falls short on the thrill side. A father, a member of British Intelligence, has not seen his son in four years and arranges a meeting in Venice. However, he does not show up. The kid, while waiting, gets a call from his dad. Valli, a hotel receptionist, takes pity on the kid and talks her American boy friend, Basehart, into helping. It turns out the father, Howard, had spotted a colleague who was dazed and in trouble. While trying to help, he himself is captured and drugged. Basehart goes on the search after the police come up empty. The villains have done such a good job of tranquilizing the patients, even the son doesn't recognize his father. The drugged agents are taken on a boat bound for an Iron Curtain country. Since the police have no jurisdiction, Basehart hides on board and starts a fire, getting the attention of the authorities, who free the prisoners.

p, John Stafford, Graham Greene; d, Mario Soldati; w, Guy Elmes, Georgio Bassani (based on the story by Graham Greene); ph, Enzo Serafin; ed, Tom Simpson; md, Nino Rota.

Spy Drama   (PR:A   MPAA:NR)

STRANGERS HONEYMOON   (SEE: STRANGERS ON A
                                 HONEYMOON, 1937, Brit.)

STRANGERS IN LOVE**   (1932) 76m PAR bw

Fredric March (*Buddy Drake/Arthur Drake*), Kay Francis (*Diana Merrow*), Stuart Erwin (*Stan Kenney*), Juliette Compton (*Muriel Preston*), George Barbier (*Mr. Merrow*), Sidney Toler (*McPhail*), Earle Foxe (*J.C. Clark*), Lucien Littlefield (*Prof. Clark*), Leslie Palmer (*Bronson*), Gertrude Howard (*Snowball, Servant*), Ben Taggart (*Crenshaw*), John M. Sullivan (*Dr. Selous*).

March effectively plays a pair of twin brothers (one nice, one nasty) in this romantic comedy. Nasty March has forged his father's will, leaving out his

brother and forcing him to live a deprived life. When nice March arrives to seek help from his brother, they argue and the excitement brings on a heart attack that kills nasty March. Nice March takes on his brother's identity, his problems, and at the upbeat ending, his voluptuous secretary-girl friend, Francis. March had already turned in an Oscar-winning performance in something of a dual role in DR. JEKYLL AND MR. HYDE, and Paramount hoped for similar results with this film. Though he was able to create two distinct personalities, this picture was not much of a vehicle for his talent. Even the process photography – which allowed two Marches to appear on the screen simultaneously – was not very well done.

d, Lothar Mendes; w, William Slavens McNutt, Grover Jones (based on the novel *The Shorn Lamb* by William J. Locke); ph, Henry Sharp.

Drama/Comedy   (PR:A   MPAA:NR)

STRANGERS IN THE CITY½**   (1962) 83m EM bw

Robert Gentile (*Felipe Alvarez*), Camilo Delgado (*Jose Alvarez*), Rosita de Triana (*Antonia Alvarez*), Creta Margos (*Elena Alvarez*), Robert Corso (*Caddy*), Bob O'Connell (*Dan*), John Roeburt (*Grocer*), Ruth Kuzab (*Jo*), Kenny Delmar (*Mr. Lou*).

A gripping but sometimes overly melodramatic story about a Puerto Rican family struggling in a Manhattan ghetto. The father, Delgado, is entrenched in his old ways and cannot understand how the system in the U.S. works. He loses his job so his son and daughter go looking for work. The son encounters prejudice and gangs. The daughter, de Triana, gets a job in a factory and, trying to better herself, gets used by the boss. The son fights a gang leader and they become friends. He then finds out about his sister's activities and drags her from the creeps she's been hanging around with. The mother confronts her daughter's boss and accidentally kills him in a fight. All of these events have been eating away at Delgado, filling him with anger and confusion. When his wife returns, he accuses her of cheating on him, struggles with her, and pushes her into the bathtub, inadvertently electrocuting her. Reeling with guilt, he takes poison. Though this film falls victim to emotional overkill, independent filmmaker Carrier, nonetheless, presents a revealing look at immigrant life in New York.

p, d&w, Rick Carrier (based on a story by Carrier, Elgin Ciampi); ph, Carrier (Scanoscope; m, Robert Prince; ed, Stan Russell; m/l, "Strangers," Carrier.

Drama   (PR:A   MPAA:NR)

STRANGERS IN THE HOUSE***   (1949, Fr.) 95m Flag/Lopert bw
                                (LES INCONNUS DANS LA MAISON)

Raimu (*Hector Loursat*), Juliette Faber (*Nicole Loursat, His Daughter*), Jacques Baumer (*Rogissart*), Jean Tissier (*Ducup*), Lucien Coedel (*Jo*), Noel Roquevert (*Commissioner Binet*), Helena Manson (*Mme. Manu*), Andre Reybas (*Emile Manu*), Marcel Mouloudji (*Luska*), Marc Dolnitz (*Edmond Dossin*), Tania Fedor (*Mme. Dossin*), Jacques Denoel (*Destrivaux, Jr.*), Pierre Ringel (*Daillat, Jr.*), Pierre Fresnay (*The Narrator*).

A wandering film with an artsy flavor, this tells the story of a group of small-town youths bored with life. Their lives center on small crimes, drinking, and just talking. They steal a car one night and run over a strange man. He blackmails them, but the next day is found dead and it appears Reybas is the killer. His girl friend's father is Raimu, a bitter lawyer, who gave up practicing law 20 years earlier after his wife had left him. However, Raimu agrees to take the case, and in a slow, deliberate style, he proves the boy's innocence. In the flashy climax, he denounces the town's parents, castigating them for their irresponsibility and selfishness, and finally produces the real murderer. This film was made in occupied France by the French arm of UFA, and predictably it presents an extremely critical protrait of French society. It remains, however, a stylish film, notable for one of the last screen appearances by the great French actor, Raimu. (In French; English subtitles.)

d, Henri Decoin; w, Henri-Georges Clouzot (based on the novel by George Simenon); ph, Jules Kruger; m, Roland-Maunuel; English titles, Herman G. Weinberg.

Crime   (PR:C   MPAA:NR)

STRANGERS IN THE NIGHT***   (1944) 56m REP bw

William Terry (*Johnny Meadows*), Virginia Grey (*Dr. Leslie Ross*), Helen Thimig (*Hilda Blake*), Edith Barrett (*Ivy Miller*), Anne O'Neal (*Nurse Thompson*).

Terry is a Marine sergeant stationed in the South Pacific who passes the day by sending love letters to a girl named Rosemary Blake. When he returns stateside, he tries to track her down but learns from her mother, Thimig, that she has gone away. Barrett, a friend of Thimig's, tells Terry that there is no Rosemary Blake–that Thimig created a daughter for herself because she didn't have a real one. Thimig kills Barrett for revealing the truth, and then tries to do the same to Terry. The fanatical mother is killed, however, when a giant painting of her "daughter" falls from the wall and kills her. An early picture from Anthony Mann, who is best known for his nine pictures with Jimmy Stewart, including WINCHESTER '73 (1950) and THE GLENN MILLER STORY (1954). In STRANGERS IN THE NIGHT one can already see his interest in intensely emotional characters who teeter on the edge of sanity. A fine film and a must for Anthony Mann fans.

p, Rudolph E. Abel; d, Anthony Mann; w, Bryant Ford, Paul Gangelin (based on a story by Phillip MacDonald); ph, Reggie Lanning; ed, Arthur Roberts; md, Morton Scott; art d, Gano Chittenden.

Drama (PR:A-C MPAA:NR)

STRANGERS MAY KISS***½ (1931) 85m MGM bw

Norma Shearer (*Lisbeth Corbin*), Robert Montgomery (*Steve*), Neil Hamilton (*Alan*), Marjorie Rambeau (*Geneva*), Irene Rich (*Celia*), Hale Hamilton (*Andrew*), Conchita Montenegro (*Spanish Dancer*), Jed Prouty (*Harry*), Albert Conti (*Count De Bazan*), Henry Armetta, George Davis (*Waiters*), Bess Flowers (*Dining Extra*), Karen Morley, Wilbur Mack (*Dining Companions*), Kane Richmond (*Bit*), Raymond Milland (*Admirer*).

An excellent film version of a novel by Ursula Parrott, this is the story of Shearer's undying love for newspaper reporter Hamilton. She follows him to Mexico, but he leaves her to cover a story in China. Distraught, she travels to Europe, where she plays with a series of lovers, but remains obsessed with Hamilton. Tired of her vagabonding, she returns to New York, ostensibly to marry Montgomery, her suitor since childhood, who has kept his love for her alive with a sense of humor and a well-exercized drinking arm. Re-enter Hamilton, ready to marry Shearer until he hears of her European dalliances. Shearer contemplates suicide (in the novel she goes through with it), but Hamilton reconsiders and they tie the happy knot. This was the second Parrott work that provided the basis for a Shearer film, following in the wake of THE DIVORCEE, which was based on *Ex-Wife*.

d, George Fitzmaurice; w, John Meehan (based on the novel by Ursula Parrott); ph, William Daniels; ed, Hugh Wynn; art d, Cedric Gibbons; cos, Adrian.

Drama (PR:A MPAA:NR)

STRANGER'S MEETING* (1957, Brit.) 64m Parroch/RANK bw

Peter Arne (*Harry Belair*), Delphi Lawrence (*Margot Sanders*), Conrad Phillips (*David Sanders*), Barbara Archer (*Rosie Foster*), David Ritch (*Giovanni*), David Lodge (*Fred*), Selma Vaz Dias (*Magda Mayer*), Victor Maddern (*Willie Fisher*), John Kelly (*Michael O'Hara*), Doris Hare (*Nellie*), Kathleen Williams (*Mrs. Williams*), Lesley Nunnerley (*Miss Parke*), Reginald Hearne (*Taxi Driver*), George Tovey (*Van Driver*), Ernest Brightmore (*Policeman*), Norman Rossington (*Barrow Boy*), Arthur Sullivan (*Johnny*), Arthur Gomez (*Nightclub Manager*), Dorita Curtis-Hayward (*Landlady*).

Arne is an acrobat wrongly jailed for the murder of his partner. He escapes from prison, is injured in the process, and hides out in an inn. He learns that the real killer is Archer, a former member of the circus who killed out of jealousy. Arne gets her confession just moments before she is killed by a fall down a staircase.

p, Jack Parsons, E. Smedley Aston; d, Robert Day; w, David Gordon; ph, Arthur Grant.

Crime (PR:A MPAA:NR)

STRANGERS OF THE EVENING** (1932) 70m Tiffany bw

ZaSu Pitts (*Sybil, Servant*), Eugene Pallette (*Detective Brubacher*), Lucien Littlefield (*Frank Daniels*), Tully Marshall (*Robert Daniels*), Miriam Seegar (*Ruth*), Theodore von Eltz (*Dr. Raymond Everette*), Warner Richmond (*Chandler*), Harold Waldridge (*Tommy*), Mahlon Hamilton (*Nathan Frisbee*), Alan Roscoe (*Sutherland*), Charles Williams (*1st Man*), William Scott (*2nd Man*), James Burtis (*Nolan*), Francis Sayles (*Roberts*), Hal Price (*Policeman*).

With too many laughs (intentionally and unintentionally provoked) to be a straight mystery, this comedic adventure anticipated, somewhat clumsily, more recent forays into macabre humor. When Seegar's father disappears and seemingly reappears as a corpse, Seegar and von Eltz get mixed up in a political cover-up perpetrated by undertaker Richmond. The mystery unravels and Littlefield resurfaces alive, but not before the big fight scene and some ghostly encounters in a graveyard. This was the first directorial credit for Humberstone, who had long labored as an assistant. He was aided by the skillful camerawork of Edeson and fine performances by Littlefield, Pallette, and Pitts.

p, Sam Bischoff; d, H. Bruce "Lucky" Humberstone; w, Stuart Anthony, Warren B. Duff (based on the book *The Illustrious Corpse* by Tiffany Thayer); ph, Arthur Edeson; ed, Martin G. Cohn, Dave Berg; md, Val Burton; set d, Ralph M. De Lacy; cos, Elizabeth Coleman.

Comedy Cas. (PR:A MPAA:NR)

STRANGERS ON A HONEYMOON**½ (1937, Brit.) 66m GAU bw

Constance Cummings (*October Jones*), Hugh Sinclair (*Quigley*), Noah Beery, Sr (*Redbeard*), Beatrix Lehmann (*Elfrida*), David Burns (*Lennie*), Butler Hixon (*Sam Wasser*), Maurice Freeman (*Uncle Elmer*), James Arnold (*Bridegroom*), Anne Tucker McGuire (*Bride*), Edmund Breon (*Sir Gregory*),

Percy Parsons, Edward Ryan, Skelton Knaggs, Conway Palmer.

A tired story, helped by some snappy one-liners. Cummings is an orphan raised by her aunt and uncle. Knowing how phony the wealthy can be, she tells a rich prospective beau that she would rather marry a man of lesser means. He tries to force himself on her, but she turns him down and a bum (Sinclair) comes out of the weeds after hearing the whole affair. The marriage is set to take place despite the girl's opposition. However, when she arrives for the ceremony, the dissipated would-be groom gives her the choice of marrying him or Sinclair, whom he has brought along with him. She chooses Sinclair and it is revealed that he is in fact, an English lord. More trouble awaits the new couple, but they prevail at the end of this film set in Canada.

p, Haworth Bromley; d, Albert de Courville; w, Ralph Spence, Bryan Wallace, Sidney Gilliat, Laird Doyle, Julian Houston (based on the novel *The Northing Tramp* by Edgar Wallace); ph, Mutz Greenbaum; ed, C. Randell.

Comedy (PR:A MPAA:NR)

STRANGERS ON A TRAIN***** (1951) 101m WB bw

Farley Granger (*Guy Haines*), Ruth Roman (*Anne Morton*), Robert Walker (*Bruno Antony*), Leo G. Carroll (*Sen. Morton*), Patricia Hitchcock (*Barbara Morton*), Laura Elliott (*Miriam*), Marion Lorne (*Mrs. Antony*), Jonathan Hale (*Mr. Antony*), Howard St. John (*Capt. Turley*), John Brown (*Prof. Collins*), Norma Varden (*Mrs. Cunningham*), Robert Gist (*Hennessey*), John Doucette (*Hammond*), Howard Washington (*Waiter*), Dick Wessell (*Baggage Man*), Edward Clark (*Mr. Hargreaves*), Al Hill ("*Ring the Gong*" *Concessionaire*), Leonard Carey (*Butler*), Edna Holland (*Mrs. Joyce*), Dick Ryan (*Minister*), Tommy Farrell, Rolland Morris (*Miriam's Boy Friends*), Louis Lettieri (*Boy*), Murray Alper (*Boatman*), John Butler (*Blind Man*), Roy Engle, Joel Allen (*Policemen*), Eddie Hearn (*Sgt. Campbell*), Mary Alan Hokanson (*Secretary*), Janet Stewart, Shirley Tegge (*Girls*), Georges Renavent, Odette Myrtil (*Mons. and Mme. Darville*), Charles Meredith (*Judge Dolan*), Minna Phillips, Monya Andre (*Dowagers*), Laura Treadwell (*Mrs. Anderson*), J. Louis Johnson (*Butler*), Sam Flint, Ralph Moody (*Men*), Joe Warfield (*Seedy Man*), Harry Hines (*Man Under Merry- Go-Round*), Alfred Hitchcock (*Man Boarding Train with Bass Fiddle*).

Gripping all the way, this is a Hitchcock thriller which clutches happenstance and two men, completely different, drawing them inexorably together and toward an uncommon goal–murder. Hitchcock opens this electrifying film by showing two sets of male feet, those of Granger and Walker, hurrying towards a train. Granger wears conservative-looking shoes, Walker black-and-white spectator shoes, and from their very movements, the sure gait of Granger, the anxious steps of Walker, the viewer can easily tell, once the two are shown fully on camera, their distinctively separate personalities. When on the train the two men meet in the club car, have drinks, and share some chit-chat; then Walker asks Granger if he can join him in his compartment to carry on their "interesting" discussion. Walker quickly reveals an astounding amount of information about tennis pro Granger to Granger, telling him that he has read a great deal about him and his life in various publications. Walker then tells Granger that he knows all about his money-grubbing wife Elliott and how he has been separated from her and is now in love with Roman, the daughter of a U.S. senator, Carroll, and how Elliott refuses to give him a divorce so he can marry Roman and be happy. He has a similar problem, says Walker. He has a rich father he hates, Hale, a stern disciplinarian who is displeased at this playboy life style. (Walker has been kicked out of three colleges for drinking and gambling.) Both of them are in the same boat, he says, but there's one way to solve their problems. He proposes, *in theory*, of course, that they each murder the person vexing the other person's life. If he, Walker, murdered Elliott, and Granger murdered his father, there would be no way to link the killings, neither man having a motive for murdering a total stranger. Walker smiles at his insidiously simple plan but Granger is appalled at the idea and tells Walker that he's crazy. Well, Walker shrugs, it was only an idea. Yet when Granger gets to Washington he hears from Walker, who phones him and tells him that they must quickly go through with their plan. Granger tells him he has agreed to no plan and hangs up on the obviously deranged Walker. But the would-be killer has no intention of letting the idea drop. He keeps after Granger until the tennis pro confides in Roman that he's dealing with some sort of maniac. On one occasion, Granger looks out to the street to see Walker standing in the shadows, smoking a cigarette, smiling in his direction (one of the creepiest scenes Hitchcock was ever to film). Walker calls again and tells Granger that the next night will be perfect for killing his father and gives him instructions on how to enter the enormous mansion where his father lives, describing which room to go to, and how to murder Hale. Granger this time does not object to the madman's scheme but takes down the details and prepares to go through with the bizarre murder scheme, or so it seems. The next evening Granger goes to Walker's huge mansion, enters, and makes his way upstairs and down long hallways to a master bedchamber. He stands over a bed with a sleeping form in it, leans forward, and says: "Mr. Anthony, Mr. Anthony wake up, I want to speak to you about your son...about Bruno." In a frightening flash the covers are thrown back and the lamp next to the bed flashes on to reveal Walker, fully clothed, grinning maniacally. (This, too, is a shocking scene, guaranteed to raise the little hairs on the back of the neck.) As Granger steps back in horror, Walker calmly sits up and accuses Granger of going back on their arrangement. Walker tells Granger that he concluded that Granger didn't have the heart to carry out his end of the bargain and therefore he arranged this little test. But now Walker insists Granger go through with his end of the double murder scheme and tells him that if he falters, he, Walker, has a way of making him live up to his commitment. Again Granger tells him he needs psychiatric help and departs. Now Walker decides that he must kill Granger's wife to get the tennis pro to act. He follows Elliott to an amusement park and takes a boat ride to an island where lovers spoon. Elliott, though accompanied by two young men, sees the dapper Walker out of the corner of her eye and is flattered that he is following her, encouraging him with suggestive movements. He grabs her when she becomes separated from her friends and first pretends that he's interested in her romantically. She flirts with Walker and he gets closer, pretending to embrace her but placing his hands around her throat and strangling her. Elliott's thick-lensed glasses fall from her face as she struggles with the madman and (in one of his most inventive camera angles ever) the actual killing is seen through a lens of the spectacles as they lie on the grass, an upward and strangely distorted perspective of murder which is, of course, a distortion of the human character. Having killed Elliott, Walker quickly leaves the island and later reports to Granger that he has done his job and now Granger must live up to his end of a bargain only Walker has made. Granger knows he cannot call police when he reads of his wife's murder because he would be implicated. All he can do is tell the persistent Walker to stay away from him and Roman's family. This, of course, goads the lunatic into crashing a high society party Carroll and Roman give, appearing in tuxedo and without an invitation, compelling the nervous Granger to allow him to stay. At the party Walker jocularly tells murder tales to interested society matrons, one of whom, Varden, encourages him, witlessly thinking his macabre tales interesting. He tells her how easy it would be to strangle a person and demonstrates the technique by placing his hands about Varden's throat as she gives him a silly smile. Just then, Roman's younger sister, Patricia Hitchcock (the director's daughter), appears and stares at oddball Walker. She wears glasses similar to his murder victim on the island and bears a striking resemblance to Elliott. Suddenly, Walker, his hands stil about Varden's throat, beneath which a large diamond necklace is glimmering, fixes his stare on Patricia Hitchcock, and is lost in a memory trance that takes him back to the island. His grip around Varden's throat begins to tighten and he actually starts to choke the woman right there in the middle of the crowded party, reliving his murder of Elliott. (Here it is not a portrayal of the axiom that the murderer revisits the scene of his crime but actually re-creates it in his haunted memory.) Varden, now terrified, begins to scream loudly and the guests turn in horror to see Walker strangling her. He is jarred by her screams from his grim reverie, looking away from Patricia Hitchcock, the catalyst of that memory, and, dropping his hands from Varden's throat, mumbles some apology about having too much to drink. She coughs and sputters and complains loudly to host Carroll. By then Walker has walked into the library and plopped down on the couch as Granger orders him to leave the house. Walker closes his eyes and tells him that he is exhausted. Carroll marches into the library and tells his future son-in-law to get Walker out of his house immediately before he is ruined politically, and Walker later leaves, appearing to be offended by Carroll's lack of hospitality. The insidious Walker will not let up on Granger now, calling him incessantly on the phone to remind him that he must now kill his father, pursuing him everywhere. At one point Granger is in a car, driving, when he sees Walker, all in black, standing before the pristine, white-marbled Jefferson Memorial, appearing to be a hideous blot on a spotless historical monument. (Of course, Hitchcock is able to encompass many great American monuments in this film, shot on location in Washington, D.C., fulfilling his penchant for including such nationally symbolic places: in SABOTEUR he had portrayed Boulder Dam, the Brooklyn Navy Yards, and the Statue of Liberty; in NORTH BY NORTHWEST it was the U.N. Building in New York and Mt. Rushmore in South Dakota.) On the phone Walker reminds Granger that he really desired to have his wife dead: "But Guy, you *wanted* it–we planned it together. You're just as much in it as I am....You're a free man now." In one of their clandestine meetings where Granger practically pleads with Walker to leave him alone and reminding him that he never once agreed to a double murder scheme, he stands behind iron-barred gates encircling a Washington mansion, respectability, law and order ironically symbolized in a shot preceding the scene, one showing the lighted dome of the Senate House in the distance. As the two men talk, Hitchcock displays them with the shadows of the bars on their faces, both now psychological prisoners of the lethal machinations hatched in Walker's demented brain. "You've got me acting like a criminal now," Granger tells him and warns him emphatically to leave him alone. Walker ignores him, blithely reminding him that he possesses his monogrammed lighter, having "accidentally" picked it up on the train during their first meeting, one where Granger had made the mistake of encouraging Walker in the first place by being amused at his murder schemes, humoring him by telling him, "Of course, I agree with all your *theories*." Walker dogs Granger's life thereafter, even following him to tennis matches to stare down at him like a dark sentinel beckoning from hell. In one of the most spectacularly terrifying scenes master filmmaker Hitchcock ever created, Walker is shown as the ultimate menace in broad, blinding sunlight. Hitchcock, while showing Granger nervously playing a tennis match, moving frantically on the court, suddenly changes the perspective to encompass a huge crowd looking down on the match, hundreds of heads moving back and forth in unison as the spectators follow the course of the ball being batted back and forth on the court, all the heads moving except one which the camera closes in on, Walker, incongruously dressed in a business suit, head motionless, eyes riveted downward not on the moving ball but on Granger. Walker now demands that Granger kill his father. His only rationale to Granger's objections is a total indifference to human life: "What is a life or two, Guy? Some people are better off dead." Of course the berserk killer doesn't mean the one soul he cherishes in life, his mother, Lorne, who foolishly dotes upon Walker as if he were an 8 year-old. But the severe Hale must go and go right away. Granger can bear his secret no longer and confides the details to Roman, saying how Walker proposed that "I'd do his murder, he'd do mine." He then explains the swap killings Walker envisioned and how Walker actually went through with murdering his wife Elliott. Before the couple can figure out what to do next, Granger gets another call from Walker who tells him that he must pay for reneging on their arrangement and he is going to plant his monogrammed lighter on the island near the amusement park so that police still looking into the Elliott killing will quickly conclude that she was murdered by her irate husband. He is a suspect, anyway, having been shown at the beginning of the film arguing with Elliott in a music shop where she worked and later overheard telling Roman on the phone that Elliott will not give him a divorce, the tennis player so angry that he blurted: "I'd like to break her foul, useless little neck...I said I could strangle her!" Granger, hearing that Walker intends to implicate him in Elliott's murder, races to the amusement park, as does Walker. En route, Walker drops the monogrammed lighter by accident so that it falls into a sewer and he desperately forces his hand and arm through the grating, reaching painfully downward to retrieve the lighter from a ledge, spectators watching and softly urging him on, and here Hitchcock devilishly uses innocent bystanders to unwittingly encourage a homicidal maniac to carry out his heinous plans. Hitchcock's cameras almost side with the killer, showing him struggling to get to the lighter, with closeups on his fingers straining to reach it, shots that aim downward into the sewer and upward from it to show Walker's malignant looking face. He is finally triumphant and gets a little cheer from those watching him. As he stands up Walker gives the crowd a sort of sinister little grin and goes on his evil way. At the amusement park Granger catches up with his alter ego, Walker, both of them struggling for the lighter on a merry- go-round. As they fight, the operator of the machine shouts at them to stop and has a heart attack on the spot, falling forward and onto the controls which makes the merry-go-round accelerate, terrifying the few children riding on the machine. They are gotten off just as the ride increases in speed, all except one little terrified child whom Granger tries to reach while Walker, now as completely out of control as the machine, attempts to kill him. The shots of the whirling, dizzying merry-go-round, shown from ground level, boomshot level, and with furious cuts to the stationary horses with their grinning painted mouths, their hooves going furiously up and down, is a thing of sheer terror. The merry-go-round takes a weird angle as its terrific speed begins to break up the mechanism, boards splintering away and hurled by the speed of the machine outward. The horses also break away and are thrown forth like real steeds dashing outward, breaking free of their stationary positions. The whole machine begins to wobble and break apart, its mechanism screeching like a dying animal. Granger makes a last dive for the little child, picks it up, and leaps to safety at the very last second with Walker being trapped by the collapsing machine and crushed by its weight when it crashes inward on itself. With police surrounding him–they have been summoned by the double-dealing Walker to find the lighter he intended to plant–Granger tries to explain what happened, that Walker, lying on the ground, most of his body covered by wreckage, has tried to frame him for a murder he committed. The barely alive psychopath opens his eyes briefly and smiles, lying to the last that he had nothing to do with Granger's wife and doesn't know Granger. Desperate, Granger begs Walker to clear him, to tell the listening police that he intended to plant his lighter in the park so that he would be arrested for murdering Elliott. Walker tells him that he is "being ridiculous," and that he intended to do no such thing. He dies and it appears that Granger is doomed, but Hitchcock's camera closes in on Walker's clenched fist. Slowly the killer's hand opens and there, in the palm of Walker's hand, is the lighter, proving the dead man's guilt. Granger is next shown on a train traveling with Roman. He is approached by a total stranger trying to make light conversation but he dummies up, not taking a chance at meeting another Walker. Hitchcock closes this superbly crafted, brilliantly acted thriller with showing the train speeding away. STRANGERS ON A TRAIN ranks with the top of Hitchcock's most accomplished works, a masterpiece film that is so carefully constructed, its characters so well developed, that the viewer is quickly intimate and comfortable with the story long before Walker turns killer. This is the mark of a pantheon director who can easily and quickly set the plot and cause the viewer to become involved, as well as empathic toward those on the screen enacting the tale. The apprehensions and fears come later as everything begins to go a little haywire. Though there is a slight suggestion at homosexuality here, the basic thrust of this startling film is to show two men who are, in many ways, one. As Highsmith said in her original novel: "Nothing could be without its opposite that was bound up with it....Each was what the other had not chosen to be, the cast-off self, what he thought he hated but, perhaps, in reality loved...Two people in each person. There's also a person exactly the opposite of you, like the unseen part of you, somewhere in the world, and he waits in ambush." After reading the novel, Hitchcock paid Highsmith $7,500 for the rights to film the book and then went about having a rough draft written for the screen, later bringing in the renowned mystery-detective writer Raymond Chandler to do the finished script. The two did not get along well. At first Hitchcock insisted that he work at Chandler's side, working out every detail of the film as he, Hitchcock, envisioned it, a routine that soon had the brilliant, booze-sipping Chandler nervous and often upset. He complained to friends and his agent that Hitchcock was "smothering" him and he came to dread the appearance of the director, who was driven daily by limousine from Los Angeles to La Jolla, where Chandler lived, to work on the script. At one point, Chandler was standing at a window and sipping his morning drink when Hitchcock arrived by limousine. Said Chandler loudly to his secretary, "Look at the fat bastard trying to get out of his car." His secretary replied, "He can hear you." Snorted Chandler, "What do I care?" The author, who had written great *film noir* screenplays such as DOUBLE INDEMNITY and THE BLUE DAHLIA, found it impossible to continue working with Hitchcock. He finished a first draft and sent it to the director but heard nothing back which caused Chandler to write to a friend: "Not even a phone call. Not one word of criticism or appreciation. Silence. Blank silence then and since...,There are always things that need to be discussed. There are always places where a writer goes wrong, not being himself a master of the camera. There are always difficult little points which require the meeting of minds, the accommodation of points of view. I had none of this. I find it rather strange. I find it rather ruthless. I find it almost incomparably rude." Oddly, Chandler had complained when Hitchcock was with him, working out the script, then carped because the director left him too much alone. Hitchcock himself later remembered that his experience with Chandler "was not very happy. After a while I had to give up working with him. Sometimes when he was trying to get the idea for a scene, I would offer him a suggestion. Instead of giving that some thought, he would remark to me, very discontentedly, 'If you can go it alone, why the hell do you need me?' He refused to work with me as a director." Chandler's script nevertheless was the basic one employed by Hitchcock, although the director later asked his favorite writer, Ben Hecht, to come in and "spruce it up." Hecht was busy at the time writing several other screenplays but he assigned Ormonde, who worked for him, to clean up some of the dialog and tighten some scenes which he, Hecht, then looked over and edited before Hitchcock began shooting. Granger is exellent as the innocent victim of the evil plot of the movie and the supporting cast members shine in their roles, even Hitchcock's daughter, Patricia. But, daughter or no, the director showed her no favoritism on the set. During the production she told an interviewer: "We never discussed STRANGERS ON A TRAIN at home. On the set he gives me direction as well as criticism. I might as well be Jane Jones instead of Patricia Hitchcock." But the compelling character of this film was that superlative actor Walker whose sly and smiling ways, coupled to his mechanical way of killing (although only one body is produced in this chiller, a mimimum record for Hitchcock), terrified every viewer who saw the film when it was released and who sees it today. He is not only Hitchcock's most frightening character in any of his films but one of the most horrific creations in any film; he is Hyde with no trace of Jekyll at all. Hitchcock was asked in Jay Robert Nash's *The Innovators* how the director came to cast Walker, the one-time all-American boy of movies, as a homicidal maniac. "It was type casting," replied Hitchcock. "I think that somebody once said the better the heavy, the better the story. The menace coming from an individual is a pretty strong thing. If you take the premise of STRANGERS OF A TRAIN, well, you do have an insane man and a very dangerous one. He says, if you kill my father, I'll kill your wife for you. And the other guy finds himself caught up with this evil, insane person." In the same interview, Hitchcock recalled how strange Walker was in real life: "I remember one night we had him at a party, God rest his soul....a little party after the picture's showing at our house and my wife gave him brandy. Someone said: 'Oh, you should never do that, never give him brandy, because he'll be gone.' And he was gone, too. He had two or three. Then he took my wife aside and talked about me. He said: 'You know, I love him, but I hate him at the same time!' This was Robert Walker. It's scary, isn't it? In our own home!" Everything about STRANGERS ON A TRAIN is vivid and vital and it proved, after Hitchcock's two previous films, UNDER CAPRICORN and STAGE FRIGHT, both disappointments, to be a slambang success at the box office, bringing the director back into the limelight as a producer of masterpieces. Walker, who had had minimal impact up to the time of this film suddenly became an important star and it was thought that he would emerge as one of Hollywood's more accomplished dramatic actors. But, after performing in one more film, MY SON JOHN, (1951), a contrived but intriguing drama about Communists infiltrating the American family, he died prematurely of a heart attack, probably brought on by heavy drinking. His fascinating portrayal of Bruno Anthony lingers in the imagination, however, and one wonders what Walker might have accomplished had he lived. Remade as ONCE YOU KISS A STRANGER.

p&d, Alfred Hitchcock; w, Raymond Chandler, Czenzi Ormonde, Whitfield Cook (based on the novel by Patricia Highsmith); ph, Robert Burks; m, Dimitri Tiomkin; ed, William H. Ziegler; md, Ray Heindorf; art d, Ted Haworth; set d, George James Hopkins; cos, Leah Rhodes; spec eff, H.F. Koenekamp; makeup, Gordon Bau.

Thriller/Crime Drama   Cas.   (PR:C-O MPAA:NR)

STRANGER'S RETURN**   (1933) 88m MGM bw

Lionel Barrymore (*Grandpa Storr*), Miriam Hopkins (*Louise Storr*), Franchot Tone (*Guy Crane*), Stuart Erwin (*Simon, Farmhand*), Irene Hervey (*Nettie Crane*), Beulah Bondi (*Beatrice*), Grant Mitchell (*Allan Redfield*), Tad Alexander (*Widdie*), Aileen Carlyle (*Thelma Redfield*).

Hopkins flees New York to get away from her husband and settles in the Midwest with her grandfather, Barrymore. There she falls in love, but her new beau is a family man who is unwilling to forsake his wife and child, even for the passion he feels for Hopkins. All the while Hopkins is playing footsie, Barrymore is dispensing advice and trying to keep his farm out of the hands of the greedy relatives who are just waiting for him to die. He exposes their intentions and leaves the land to Hopkins. Phil Stong, the author of *State Fair*, wrote the novel this film is based on and contributed to the screenplay.

d, King Vidor; w, Brown Holmes, Phil Stong (based on the novel by Stong); ph, William Daniels; ed, Ben Lewis, Dick Fantl; art d, Frederic Hope; set d, Edwin B. Willis.

Drama   (PR:A MPAA:NR)

STRANGERS WHEN WE MEET½**   (1960) 117m Bryna-Quine/COL c

Kirk Douglas (*Larry Coe*), Kim Novak (*Maggie Gault*), Ernie Kovacs (*Roger Altar*), Barbara Rush (*Eve Coe*), Walter Matthau (*Felix Anders*), Virginia Bruce (*Mrs. Wagner*), Kent Smith (*Stanley Baxter*), Helen Gallagher (*Betty Anders*), John Bryant (*Ken Gault*), Roberta Shore (*Linda Harder*), Nancy Kovack (*Marcia*), Carol Douglas (*Honey Blonde*), Paul Picerni (*Gerandi*), Ernest Sarracino (*Di Labbia*), Harry Jackson (*Bud Ramsey*), Bart Patton (*Hank*), Robert Sampson (*Bucky*), Ray Ferrell (*David Coe*), Douglas Holmes (*Peter Coe*), Timmy Molina (*Patrick Gault*), Betsy Jones Moreland (*Mrs. Gerandi*), Audrey Swanson (*Mrs. Baxter*), Cynthia Leighton (*Mrs. Ramsey*), Judy Lang (*Ad Lib Girl*), Sharyn Gibbs (*Girl at Beach*), Charles Victor, Joe Palma, Tom Anthony, Sheryl Ellison, Mark Beckstrom (*Bits*), Sue Ane Langdon (*Daphne*), Ruth Batchelor (*Waitress*), Dick Crockett (*Charlie*), Lorraine Crawford (*Redhead*).

Another sex-in-suburbia soap that had already been closely examined in PEYTON PLACE and partly limned in NO DOWN PAYMENT. It looks gorgeous but is essentially empty in many ways. The star of the film is the house that's being built all through the story and we have been told that the director, Quine, got the home as part payment for having worked on the movie. The attractive house was co-designed by art director Ross Bellah and architect Carl Anderson and when a structure becomes the focal point for a movie, you know that the story is in trouble. Douglas is a gifted architect married to Rush, who spends most of her early scenes twittering about the family budget and neglecting Douglas. One day, he is taking one of his sons to school and he meets Novak, who is doing the same thing. She's married to Bryant, who doesn't have any sexual desire for Novak (a lie right there]). The two married people begin to have an affair. Douglas is asked by Kovacs to design a house. Kovacs is a successful writer with a quirky outlook on life (he delivers the only comedy in this relentless story) that sees him attempting to bed down every woman who comes his way. The hilltop house begins construction and Douglas and Novak keep their affair going through a series of illicit rendezvous, with many of their meetings taking place in a public cocktail lounge. (Another lie. Any couple intent on keeping its trysts secret would not be so foolish as to meet in such a busy place.) Their liaisons are noted by Matthau, a lecher who lives close by and is married to Gallagher in a loveless union. Douglas and Novak are very happy when they are together and she would like to make their relationship permanent but there is no way he will leave his family. There is a dinner party; Bryant and Novak are invited and the strain on the lovers is evident. Douglas tells Kovacs about what's happening in his life and Kovacs is jealous. While he's slept with many women, he's never known deep, passionate love for one and wishes he could be in Douglas' situation. Matthau thinks that he can move in on Rush and makes his feelings known to her but she rebuffs him. Douglas is offered a huge commission to build an entire city in Hawaii. He doesn't tell Rush, but instead goes to Novak and asks if she wants to go there with him. She declines and thinks it's better that they both stay married. Douglas comes home just as the rejected Matthau is leaving his house. When Douglas goes inside and Rush tells him what Matthau was there for, he runs after Matthau and punches him in the nose. Matthau takes the blow philosophically and asks Douglas: "How are we any different from each other?" This gives Douglas pause and he must now make a serious decision. Does he leave Rush or stay? Novak and Douglas meet at their usual hangout and he tells her that he will be leaving for the Aloha islands with Rush to try to make a go of their marriage. Novak understands and the picture ends with the thought that the next time they see each other, they'll be strangers when they meet. A slow-moving movie that is filled with emotional outbursts, but you are always aware that the characters are acting and never are drawn into the story. In small roles, note Nancy Kovack, who later gave up acting when she married conductor Zubin Mehta, and Sue Ane Langdon, a good comedienne who always does well with her roles, no matter how small. She is married to another excellent comic actor, Dick Gautier. Real estate values being what they are in Southern California, the house Douglas built for Kovacs should be worth about what the gross receipts for this movie were.

p&d, Richard Quine; w, Evan Hunter (based on his novel); ph, Charles Lang, Jr. (CinemaScope, Eastmancolor); m, George Duning; ed, Charles Nelson;

art d, Ross Bellah; set d, Louis Diage; md, Morris Stoloff; cos, Jean Louis; makeup, Ben Lane.

Drama   **(PR:C MPAA:NR)**

STRANGEST CASE, THE   (SEE: CRIME DOCTOR'S STRANGEST CASE, 1943)

STRANGLEHOLD**   (1931, Brit.) 66m Teddington/WB bw

Isobel Elsom (*Beatrice*), Garry Marsh (*Bruce*), Allan Jeayes (*King*), Dorothy Bartlam (*Grace*), Derrick de Marney (*Phillip*), Hugh E. Wright (*Briggs*), Henry Vibart (*Farren*), Minnie Rayner (*Cook*), Frank Bertram, Pat Baring, Kenji Takase.

Jeayes is a half-Chinese doctor who has fallen in love with a Chinese girl, only to have her end up in the arms of Marsh. The doctor decides to seek revenge by ruining Marsh's marriage. Jeayes does show some compassion, though, when he saves the life of Marsh's son at the picture's finale.

p&d, Henry Edwards; w, Hugh G. Esse.

Drama   **(PR:A MPAA:NR)**

STRANGLEHOLD**   (1962, Brit.) 73m Argo/RANK bw

Macdonald Carey (*Bill Morrison*), Barbara Shelley (*Chris Morrison*), Philip Friend (*Steffan*), Nadja Regin (*Lilli*), Leonard Sachs (*The Dutchman*), Mark Loerering (*Jimmy Morrison*), Susan Shaw (*Actress*), Josephine Brown (*Grace*).

A film star who specializes in gangster roles goes off the deep end and begins to believe that his character's actions are his own. Ultimately he believes that he is responsible for killing an actress who actually poisoned herself. An interesting idea that receives a lifeless treatment.

p, Jack Lamont, David Henley; d, Lawrence Huntington; w, Guy Elmes, Joy Garrison (based on a story by Elmes).

Crime   **(PR:A MPAA:NR)**

STRANGLER, THE*   (1941, Brit.) 75m ABF/Pathe bw (GB: EAST OF PICCADILLY)

Judy Campbell (*Penny Sutton*), Sebastian Shaw (*Tamsie Green*), Niall McGinnis (*Joe*), Henry Edwards (*Inspector*), George Pughe (*Oscar Juloff*), Martita Hunt (*Ma*), George Hayes (*Mark Struberg*), Cameron Hall (*George*), Edana Romney (*Sadie Jones*), Bunty Payne (*Tania*), Charles Victor (*Editor*), Fredrick Piper (*Ginger Harris*), June Corda.

A silk-stocking strangler is loose in London's Soho district in this outdated mystery yarn. Campbell plays a lady crime reporter who deduces that the murders are being committed by a visiting American millionaire, played by Pughe. That is not the case, however, and just before the millionaire is executed Campbell and a detective story writer who has joined her find the real killer.

p, Walter C. Mycroft; d, Harold Huth; w, J. Lee Thompson, Lesley Storym (based on the novel by Gordon Beckles); ph, Claude Friese-Greene.

Crime   **(PR:C MPAA:NR)**

STRANGLER, THE*½   (1964) 89m AA bw

Victor Buono (*Leo Kroll*), David McLean (*Lt. Benson*), Diane Sayer (*Barbara*), Davey Davison (*Tally*), Ellen Corby (*Mrs. Kroll*), Michael Ryan (*Posner*), Baynes Barron (*Sgt. Clyde*), Russ Bender (*Dr. Sanford*), Jeanne Bates (*Clara, Nurse*), Wally Campo (*Eggerton*), Mimi Dillard (*Thelma*), Byron Morrow (*Dr. Morton*), John Yates (*Intern*), James Sikking (*Artist*), Selette Cole (*Helen*), Robert Cranford (*Jack Rosten*), Victor Masi (*Attendant*).

Boston was being plagued by mysterious murders when this was released and it was strictly an exploitation film made to capitalize on that hysteria. Buono is evilly superb as a mild lab technician completely dominated and warped by his mother. He loves dolls and hates women, racking up 10 murders before his love of dolls gives him away before he can kill number 11.

p, Samuel Bischoff, David Diamond; d, Burt Topper; w, Bill S. Ballinger; ph, Jacques Marquette; m, Marlin Skiles; ed, Robert S. Eisen; art d, Hal Pereira, Eugene Lourie; set d, Sam Comer, James Payne; makeup, Wally Westmore.

Horror   **(PR:C MPAA:NR)**

STRANGLER OF THE SWAMP**   (1945) 60m PRC bw

Rosemary La Planche (*Maria*), Robert Barrat, Blake Edwards, Charles Middleton, Effie Parnell, Nolan Leary, Frank Conlan, Theresa Lyon, Virginia Farmer.

La Planche's grandfather is murdered and she takes over his ferry business. The village she comes to is continually frightened, always fearful of a vengeful ghost that was hanged earlier for a murder he did not do. The ghost comes back once in a while and kills people for revenge. He will only stop

when someone will give up his life willingly. Edwards (before he hit it big as a director and before he wed Julie Andrews) is next on the ghost's list, but La Planche offers herself instead to save her lover. The ghost is satisfied by La Planche's offer and finally finds peace, sparing both their lives. An unsatisfactory ending for a picture somewhat muddled by fuzzy images of the ghost (Middleton). PRC was a poor cousin even among the Poverty Row family of studios, but occasionally sparks of inspiration appeared in the studio's very B pictures. Director Wisbar had made an extremely stylish fantasy film, FAHRMAN MARIA, in Germany before coming to Hollywood. STRANGLER OF THE SWAMP is basically a remake of that film (with an upbeat ending added) and though Wisbar didn't come close to re-creating the excellence of the original, his inventive use of lighting, camera, and sets certainly covered over the usual production deficiencies that accompanied the low-budget films made by PRC.

p, Raoul Pagel; d, Frank Wisbar; w, Wisbar, Harold Erickson (based on a story by Wisbar, Leo McCarthy); ph, James S. Brown, Jr.; ed, Hugh Winn; md, Alex Steinert; art d, Edward C. Jewell; set d, Glenn P. Thompson.

Horror   **(PR:A MPAA:NR)**

STRANGLERS OF BOMBAY, THE**   (1960, Brit.) 80m Hammer/COL bw

Guy Rolfe (*Capt. Lewis*), Allan Cuthbertson (*Capt. Connaught-Smith*), Andrew Cruickshank (*Col. Henderson*), George Pastell (*High Priest*), Marne Maitland (*Patel Shari*), Jan Holden (*Mary*), Paul Stassino (*Silver*), Tutte Lemkow (*Ram Das*), David Spenser (*Gopali*), Michael Nightingale (*Flood*), Margaret Gordon (*Mrs. Dorothy Flood*), Ewen Solon (*Camel Vendor*), John Harvey (*Burns*), Roger Delgado (*Bundar*), Marie Devereux (*Karim*), Steven Scott (*Walters*), Jack McNaughton (*Cpl. Roberts*).

People are disappearing by the thousands en route to 1820s India, and it's up to Rolfe to find out why. A sadistic cult is carrying out the abductions and not only do they initiate children into their group, but they also perform grisly dismemberments. Rolfe finally solves the mystery, but loses fellow officer Cuthbertson in the process. A slight departure from the normal Hammer-horror fare, this picture is said to be based on actual events. Hammer called the camera process on this one "Strangloscope."

p, Anthony Hinds; d, Terence Fisher; w, David Z. Goodman; ph, Arthur Grant (MegaScope); m, James Bernard; ed, Alfred Cox.

Horror/Drama   **(PR:C MPAA:NR)**

STRANGLER'S WEB*½   (1966, Brit.) 55m Merton Park/AA bw

John Stratton (*Lewis Preston*), Pauline Munro (*Melanie*), Griffith Jones (*Jackson Delacorte*), Gerald Harper (*Inspector Murray*), Maurice Hedley (*Amos Colfax*), Michael Balfour (*John Vichelski*), Pauline Boty (*Nell Pretty*), Patricia Burke (*Norma Brent*), Barry Jackson (*Morton Bray*), Marianne Stone (*Alice Preston*).

A solicitor digs up some facts pertaining to the strangulation murder of a famed former actress. The clues lead to the London mansion of a former actor whose past is entangled with the dead woman's. More of the usual–none of which is very insightful or inventive.

p, Jack Greenwood; d, John Moxey; w, George Baxt.

Crime   **(PR:A-C MPAA:NR)**

STRATEGIC AIR COMMAND***   (1955) 114m PAR c

James Stewart (*Lt. Col. Robert "Dutch" Holland*), June Allyson (*Sally Holland*), Frank Lovejoy (*Gen. Ennis C. Hawkes*), Barry Sullivan (*Lt. Col. Rocky Samford*), Alex Nicol (*Ike Knowland*), Bruce Bennett (*Gen. Espy*), Jay C. Flippen (*Doyle*), James Millican (*Gen. Castle*), James Bell (*Rev. Thorne*), Richard Shannon (*Aircraft Commander*), Rosemary DeCamp (*Mrs. Thorne*), John R. McKee (*Capt. Symington*), Henry Morgan (*Sgt. Bible*), Don Haggerty (*Major Patrol Commander*), Glenn Denning (*Radio Operator*), Max Power (*Reporter*), Len Hendry (*General's Aide*), David Vaile (*Capt. Brown*), Vernon Rich (*Capt. Johnson*), Harlan Warde (*Duty Officer*), Helen Brown (*Nurse*), Strother Martin (*Airman*), Anthony Warde (*Colonel*), William Hudson (*Forecaster*), Robert House Peters, Jr (*Air Force Captain*), Henry Richard Lupino (*Lieutenant Controller*), William August Pullen (*Controller Okinawa*), Stephen E. Wyman (*Technical Sergeant*).

A smash hit movie, mainly due to the sensational airplane footage that showed how it was to fly in a previously unseen fashion. Not a war movie, not even an action picture, it's a made-up tale about a St. Louis Cardinals third baseman who is ordered back to service and put into the SAC. Stewart is the veteran hot-corner man who must give up a high salary when he's called into the Air Force (this actually did happen to superstar Ted Williams during the Korean fracas and probably resulted in his not breaking Babe Ruth's home-run record). Like Williams, Stewart already put in his time during the battles of WW II and thinks that the authorities have singled him out because he's an athletic star. He'd much prefer hot grounders to hot jets and makes his feelings loud and clear. Nevertheless, he must do his country's bidding and acquiesces. He is an experienced pilot and they need men like him to handle the new B-36 and B-47 jets that have the capability to deliver the atomic bomb wherever the President orders it to be dropped.

Stewart's wife is Allyson (for the third time, as she had also been his wife in THE GLENN MILLER STORY, also directed by Mann, and in the STRATTON STORY) and she is expecting a child. Once in the service, Stewart settles into his job and grows to respect Lovejoy, a tough but fair commanding officer who combines a gruff manner with a soft side. There is no question that the SAC is important to the nation's security and Stewart soon comes to appreciate that, despite Allyson's whining that her husband's job is keeping her from him. She has a baby daughter now and thinks that a father should be around. The middle of the film depicts what the SAC planes actually do. There's refueling in midair, there's an emergency landing in Greenland when Stewart's plane inexplicably catches on fire, there's the problem of men who love to fly and wives who wish they wouldn't. When Stewart finishes his brief tour, he is so impressed by what the SAC is doing that he decides to call his baseball career ended and hang up his spiked shoes in favor of Air Force boots. (We suspect he couldn't hit the outside curve ball anymore.) A fairly sappy story, totally contrived, with dialog they wouldn't dare use on TV's "One Life to Live" or "All My Children." What makes it so much fun to watch is the spectacular aerial scenes as shot by Thomas Tutwiler with Paul Mantz at the plane's controls. Mantz, who was one of the best movie pilots ever, died in a crash while making FLIGHT OF THE PHOENIX. His long-time partner was Frank Tallman (their company was TallMantz Aviation) who also died in a light-plane accident. Due to the nature of the movie, the SAC lent support and planes to the production so if there was anything at all that might have had a negative aspect, it was never seen. A far more exciting film could have been made had there been any antagonists. This was more of a staged documentary than anything else and served to quash the complaints of the taxpayers who were carping about the billions spent on defense. Stewart himself was a flier and loved making the movie. Lay's story was Oscar-nominated.

p, Samuel J. Briskin; d, Anthony Mann; w, Valentine Davies, Beirne Lay, Jr. (based on a story by Lay); ph, William Daniels (VistaVision, Technicolor); m, Victor Young; ed, Eda Warren; md, Young; art d, Hal Pereira, Earl Hedrick; cos, Edith Head; spec eff, John P. Fulton; m/l, "The Air Force Takes Command," Young, Ned Washington, Maj. Tommy Thomson, Jr., aerial ph, Thomas Tutwiler.

Aviation Drama   (PR:A   MPAA:NR)

STRATEGY OF TERROR*½   (1969) 90m Roncom/UNIV c (AKA: IN DARKNESS WAITING)

Hugh O'Brian (*Lt. Matt Lacey*), Barbara Rush (*Karen Lownes*), Neil Hamilton (*Mr. Harkin*), Frederick O'Neal (*Jacques Serac*), Will Corry (*Wally Pitt*), Harry Townes (*Richard*), Jan Merlin (*Jon*), Eric Morris (*Tippo*), Mort Mills (*Victor Pelling*).

This was originally made for television's ill-fated "Kraft Suspense Hour" and was later released for theatrical showings. Ineffective on both the large and small screen. A right winger, out to protect the U.S., is set to assassinate four U.N. under-secretaries. Rush is a newspaper reporter who discovers the story, but her tale is not believed by policeman O'Brian. After she is attacked, he joins her in the hunt for the killer and along the way they fall in love. Limited action and too much talking mar the film: Right-winger Hamilton loquaciously stands by his actions, and African delegate O'Neal goes on and on about the importance of the U.N. to the safety of the world. No one is safe from being bored by this.

p, Arthur H. Nadel; d, Jack Smight; w, Robert L. Joseph; ph, Bud Thackery; m, Lyn Murray; ed, Sam E. Waxman.

Mystery   (PR:A   MPAA:NR)

STRATTON STORY, THE*½   (1949) 106m MGM bw

James Stewart (*Monty Stratton*), June Allyson (*Ethel Stratton*), Frank Morgan (*Barney Wile*), Agnes Moorehead (*Ma Stratton*), Bill Williams (*Gene Watson*), Bruce Cowling (*Ted Lyons*), Eugene Bearden (*Western All-Stars Pitcher*), Bill Dickey, Jimmy Dykes (*Themselves*), Cliff Clark (*Higgins*), Mary Lawrence (*Dot*), Dean White (*Luke Appling*), Robert Gist (*Larnie*), Mervyn Shea (*White Sox Catcher*), Mitchell Lewis (*Conductor*), Michael Ross (*Pitcher*), James Nolan, Peter Crouse (*Reporters*), Florence Lake (*Mrs. Appling*), Anne Nagel (*Mrs. Piet*), Barbara Woodell (*Mrs. Shea*), Alphonse Martel (*Headwaiter*), Holmes Herbert (*Doctor*), Robert Graham, Eugene Persson (*Boys*), Lee Tung Foo (*Waiter*), Syd Saylor, George Melford, George Ovey, William Bailey, Cy Stevens, Polly Bailey, Vangie Beilby, Mabel Smaney, Jessie Arnold (*People in Theater*), Roy Partee (*Western Pitcher*), Kenneth Tobey (*Detroit Player*), Pat Flaherty (*Western Manager*), Capt. F. G. Somers (*Giants Manager*), Fred Millican (*All-Star Catcher*), Pat Orr, John "Ziggy" Sears, Jack Powell, Joe Rue (*Umpires*), John Kerr (*Yankee Coach*), Dwight Adams, George Vico, Lou Novikoff (*Detroit Ball Players*), Charles P. Smith (*Theater Usher*), William Bassett (*Stratton Baby*).

This was the first of the three movies Stewart and Allyson made together. In each, they were husband and wife and in two of the three, Stewart was a baseball player. This time, it's a film based upon the true and heroic struggle of pitcher Monty Stratton to come back to professional sports after his leg had been amputated due to a hunting accident. Although some liberties were taken with the story to make it play on screen, it hewed more closely to the facts than most biographies and therein lay its success. As

director, producer Cummings wisely selected Wood, who had already shown he knew his way around a diamond by his work on PRIDE OF THE YANKEES, an excellent picture about the short life of Yankee first-sacker Lou Gehrig. Stewart is pitching in a semi-pro game in Texas when Morgan, a one-time baseball player, sees him. Morgan is now a jobless hobo, but he knows talent when he sees it, and tells Stewart that he would be wise to consider a career of hurling the horsehide. Stewart finds the idea attractive but he feels he doesn't know the fine points that separate sandlotters from stars and Morgan says he'd be willing to teach him everything he knows. Morgan moves onto Stewart's farm, helps out with the chores, and spends his off-hours coaching Stewart over the winter. Spring approaches and Stewart is gaining confidence in his abilities. His mother, Moorehead, thinks it's all a lot of nonsense that grown men can earn a living playing a little boy's game and she's against the idea. Nevertheless, Stewart and Morgan leave the farm and thumb their way to California, where the White Sox are holding their training camp. Once there, Morgan introduces Stewart to his old pal, Jimmy Dykes, manager of the Chisox (playing himself as only he can). The skipper allows Stewart to have a trial and the lanky right-hander is so impressive that he's given a conditional contract. At the same time, love rears its head when Stewart meets Allyson and the two are soon gooney-eyed about each other. Stewart has to face the powerful Yankee team in his first mound chore and is sent reeling by the strength of their Louisville Sluggers. It's still too soon for the Big Leagues and Dykes wisely sends him down to the minors to learn his craft. While toiling in the lower depths, he shows his pitching ability and it isn't long before the phone rings for him to return to the Windy City. Before he does that, Stewart proposes to Allyson and is accepted. They marry and he arrives in Chicago with Allyson in tow. His rookie year is sensational. Allyson gives birth to a son and Stewart doesn't suffer from the "sophomore jinx," amassing a handful of impressive victories and a fine earned-run average. It looks as though there's another Cy Young in the offing until Stewart is hunting on the family property when his gun goes off and sends the ammo into his leg. In order to save his life, the leg must go, and it does. Stewart is terribly depressed. Just when he thought he had it all, it was over. He mopes around and feels sorry for himself and refuses to even try to rehabilitate himself. Meanwhile, their son is growing and beginning to walk. Stewart watches the child with interest and sees how difficult it is for the little guy to walk. He takes a step, falls down, gets up and tries again. The sight of the boy is inspirational to Stewart and he vows to give it all he's got. An artificial leg is attached and Stewart begins the painful process of learning how to walk again. The progress is slow and Stewart, at first, is just content to be able to move around. Now Allyson provides him with a prod. If he can walk, why can't he pitch? Stewart begins to warm up, sees that he can still whip the sphere up there with speed and deception and arranges to play in an exhibition game. When he overpowers the other batters, Stewart regains all of his old confidence and is ready to go back to work. An inspiring picture about a man who wouldn't give up, THE STRATTON STORY was originally cast with Van Johnson in the lead and one wonders how the picture would have done with the redhead in the role. Many times, in sports films, the choice of the actor is ludicrous (Tony Perkins as Jimmy Piersall is a good example), but there's no faulting Stewart here. He was obviously an athletic man and his moves on the mound are flawless and believable. MGMogul Mayer balked at Stewart because the young actor demanded a piece of the picture's profits and that was anathema to the diminutive studio chief. He grumpily agreed and the result was a smash hit that touched the hearts of the country. Adding to the reality was the casting of Bill Dickey and pitcher Gene Bearden as themselves, plus using the names of some ballplayers who were current at the time (although these were played by actors). Story writer Morrow won an Oscar and the movie made the Ten Best List for the year. True, there was a bit of sentimentality but it never sank into a morass and always maintained a dignified attitude. Baseball fans loved the movie but one did not have to know the difference between "hit and run" and "run and hit" to appreciate the story of a man who overcame circumstances to find happiness.

p, Jack Cummings; d, Sam Wood; w, Douglas Morrow, Guy Trosper (based on a story by Morrow); ph, Harold Rosson; ed, Ben Lewis; md, Adolph Deutsch; art d, Cedric Gibbons, Paul Groesse; set d, Edwin B. Willis, Ralph S. Hurst; cos, Helen Rose; spec eff, A. Arnold Gillespie, Warren Newcombe; makeup, Jack Dawn.

Sports Drama Biography   (PR:AA   MPAA:NR)

STRAUSS' GREAT WALTZ*½   (1934, Brit.) 80m GAU bw (GB: WALTZES FROM VIENNA)

Jessie Matthews (*Rasi*), Esmond Knight ("*Shani*" *Strauss, Jr.*), Frank Vosper (*The Prince*), Fay Compton (*The Countess Von Stahl*), Edmund Gwenn (*Johann Strauss the Elder*), Robert Hale (*Ebezeder*), Hindle Edgar (*Leopold*), Marcus Barron (*Drexler*), Charles Heslop (*Valet*), Sybil Grove (*Mme. Foucheft*), Betty Huntley Wright (*Lady's Maid*), Billy Shine, Jr, Bertram Dench, B. M. Lewis, Cyril Smith, Berinoff and Charlot.

Dull costume drama directed by a young Alfred Hitchcock during what he has called "the lowest ebb" of his career. STRAUSS' GREAT WALTZ was a musical based on a stage play which detailed young Johann's efforts to establish himself as a composer despite his famous father's dismay at being dethroned by his own son. When a wealthy countess commissions the young composer to put some of her verse to music, "The Blue Danube" is born, making him a sensation. While there are some clever moments, Hitchcock was obviously bored with the assignment and it must have shocked his peers when his next film, THE MAN WHO KNEW TOO MUCH (1934), demonstrated a brillance nowhere to be seen in STRAUSS' GREAT WALTZ.

p, Tom Arnold; d, Alfred Hitchcock; w, Alma Reville, Guy Bolton (based on the musical "Great Waltz" by Heinz Reichert, Dr. A. M. Willner, Ernst Marischka); ph, Glen MacWilliams; m, Johann Strauss the Elder, Johann Strauss the Younger; set d, Alfred Junge, Peter Proud.

Musical   **(PR:A MPAA:NR)**

STRAW DOGS zero   (1971, Brit.) 118m ABC Pictures-Talent
                                              Associates- Amerbroco/Cinerama c

Dustin Hoffman (*David Sumner*), Susan George (*Amy Sumner*), Peter Vaughan (*Tom Hedden*), T. P. McKenna (*Maj. Scott*), Del Henney (*Charlie Venner*), Ken Hutchison (*Scutt*), Colin Welland (*Rev. Hood*), Jim Norton (*Cawsey*), Sally Thomsett (*Janice*), Donald Webster (*Riddaway*), Len Jones (*Bobby Hedden*), Michael Mundell (*Bertie Hedden*), Peter Arne (*John Niles*), Robert Keegan (*Harry Ware*), June Brown (*Mrs. Hedden*), Chloe Franks (*Emma Hedden*), Cherina Mann (*Mrs. Hood*), David Warner (*Henry Niles*).

This is, from beginning to end, a disgusting tale which will appeal either to sadists or masochists, depending upon which end of the club these viewers like to be. There is absolutely nothing to recommend this abysmal film which is another Peckinpah paean to violence, one where the misguided director revels in every kind of physical abuse that can be heaped upon a human being. It's a disgrace to call this a movie–it's a filmic exercise in raw brutality which says little for the sensibilities of either Peckinpah or his cast and crew members, for all are responsible for creating this pus-oozing open sore of a film. To escape violence in America, Hoffman, a retiring mathematician, moves with his wife, George, to a Cornish village where she promptly allows a scabrous thug to have sex with her behind Hoffman's back. This encourages the other thugs of the village (people other than thugs don't seem to live within a hundred miles) to begin terrorizing the couple, killing their pets brutally and finally gang raping George and this, plus protecting a simpleton killer in his house, leads nonviolent Hoffman to kill all of the thugs in one ghastly way or another. Knives, shotguns, burning gasoline, and other torture weapons obsess Peckinpah as he draws out the agony of this story and needlessly dwells upon every sickening act of violence his oddball perception can devise. All of the gory, gratuitous mayhem is centered upon Hoffman's so- called desire to protect his household. At one point he shouts at his attackers: "This is where I live. This is me. I will not allow violence against my house." So he carries the violence outside and winds up burning down most of his house anyway. All of the actors, especially Hoffman, are nothing more than stooges to Peckinpah's notions of perversity, degradation, and dungheap characterization. In language, in action, the whole story is rotten through and through and anyone wasting a minute watching this putrid, wholly offensive and nauseating snotball of a film must ask themselves some serious questions concerning psychiatric help, as well as questioning the fiscal irresponsibility of paying to watch about two hours of a running sewer disgorging human waste. Williams, who authored the book on which this monstrosity is based, took one look at the movie Peckinpah produced and said: "I will never again sell one of my books to an American. It was horrific to see what they have done to my work. They've added a rape scene, an act of buggery, and lots of violence that was not in the book. A girl sitting next to me in the cinema vomited during one of the worst scenes and had to leave." Peckinpah tried to defend this insult to the medium by stating in the *New York Times*: "We're violent by nature. We're going to survive by being violent." Well, Peckinpah survived by being violent and made money doing it, blood money. Five minutes were cut from the original film so STRAW DOGS could receive an "R" MPAA rating instead of a much-deserved "X" before its American release.

p, Daniel Melnick; d, Sam Peckinpah; w, David Zelag Goodman, Peckinpah (based on the novel *The Siege of Trencher's Farm* by Gordon M. Williams); ph, John Coquillon (Eastmancolor); m, Jerry Fielding; ed, Paul Davies, Roger Spottiswoode, Tony Lawson; prod d, Ray Simm; art d, Ken Bridgeman; set d, Peter James; cos, Tiny Nicholls; makeup, Harry Frampton.

Crime   **Cas.**   **(PR:0 MPAA:R)**

STRAW MAN, THE**   (1953, Brit.) 74m Hedgerley/UA bw

Dermot Walsh (*Mal Farris*), Clifford Evans (*Jeff Howard*), Lana Morris (*Ruth Hunter*), Amy Dalby (*Lucy Graham*), Ronald Ward (*Clay Rushlow*), Josephine Stuart (*Miss Ward*), Peter Williams (*Inspector Conrad*), Philip Saville (*Link Hunter*).

Evans is an insurance company detective who is assigned to a case involving a wealthy, well-insured client and his recently murdered mistress. The man's wife, Morris, hires her own detective, Walsh, to uncover any wrongdoing. Evans, however, suspects that Walsh and Morris are behind the murder. Backed into a corner, Walsh attempts to kill Evans but is instead killed by Morris, who is trying to protect her own skin. Evans isn't easily fooled and is able to prove that Morris is responsible for the mistress' death.

p,d&w, Donald Taylor (based on the novel by Doris Miles Disney); ph, Gerald Gibbs.

Crime   **(PR:A MPAA:NR)**

STRAWBERRY BLONDE, THE***½   (1941) 97m WB bw

James Cagney (*Biff Grimes*), Olivia de Havilland (*Amy Lind*), Rita Hayworth (*Virginia Brush*), Alan Hale (*Old Man Grimes*), George Tobias (*Nick Pappalas*), Jack Carson (*Hugo Barnstead*), Una O'Connor (*Mrs. Mulcahey*), George Reeves (*Harold*), Lucile Fairbanks (*Harold's Girl Friend*), Edward McNamara (*Big Joe*), Herbert Heywood (*Toby*), Helen Lynd (*Josephine*), Peter Ashley (*Young Man*), Roy Gordon (*Bank President*), Tim Ryan (*Street Cleaner/Foreman*), Eddy Chandler, Jack Mower, John Sheehan, David Thursby (*Street Cleaners*), Addison Richards (*Official*), Frank Mayo, Max Hoffman, Jr., Pat Flaherty (*Policemen*), Peggy Diggins, Susan Peters, Ann Edmonds, Margaret Carthew (*Girls*), Jack Daley (*Bartender*), Bob Perry, Harrison Greene (*Hangers-On*), Dick Wessel, William "Billy" Newell, Frank Melton, Harry Seymour (*Men*), Dorothy Vaughan (*Woman*), Richard Clayton (*Dandy*), Herbert Anderson (*Boy*), Frank Orth (*Baxter*), James Flavin (*Boat Inspector*), George Campeau (*Sailor*), Abe Dinovitch (*Singer*), Paul Phillips (*Fellow*), George Humbert (*Guiseppi*), Creighton Hale (*Secretary*), Carl Harbaugh (*Workman*), Lucia Carroll (*Nurse*), Russell Hicks (*Treadway*), Wade Boteler (*Warden*).

Charming remake of ONE SUNDAY AFTERNOON (1933) which sees Cagney as a correspondence-school dentist struggling to make ends meet at the turn-of-the-century. On a Sunday afternoon, Cagney–who has recently been released from prison on a charge yet unrevealed–enjoys a game of horseshoes with his old friend Tobias, a Greek barber who mangles the English language. When a nearby band begins playing the song "And the Band Played On," the tune sparks bad memories for Cagney. The telephone rings and it is a man looking to have a sore tooth pulled. Despite the fact that the man is an alderman, Cagney refuses to work on a Sunday. When it is learned that the alderman is none other than Carson, Cagney's arch-enemy, Cagney immediately agrees to see him. While Cagney plots his revenge on Carson, Tobias worriedly tries to talk him out of it. In a flashback we see how Cagney came to hate Carson. Cagney, the son of neighborhood scalawag Hale, is among the many young men who have a hopeless crush on the local beauty queen, Hayworth, a strawberry blonde who enjoys flirting with every man she meets. Cagney's friend Carson, the local sharpie who is always cheating toward success, arranges to meet Hayworth and her friend de Havilland in the park. Needing a second male, Carson enlists Cagney. The boys rent a carriage and race to the park. When Cagney sees de Havilland, who is wearing her prim nurses uniform, he tries to back out of the date but Carson tells him that he can have Hayworth. As it turns out, Carson and Hayworth end up walking off into the bushes together while Cagney is stuck with de Havilland who reveals that she is a free-thinking, modern woman who wouldn't hesitate to kiss a boy without being engaged. "So you don't believe in the institution of marriage!" a shocked Cagney proclaims, adding, "Don't you want to meet a nice man and have children some day?" De Havilland declares that she would, but what's marriage anyhow, "...just a tradition started by the caveman and encouraged by florists and jewelers." "You mean...!" Cagney declares, surmising that de Havilland would consider having children without the benefit of marriage. "Exactly!" de Havilland responds with a risque click of the teeth and a wink. Cagney abruptly ends the date and makes Carson leave with him (Carson stumbles out of the brush straightening his clothes, whining that he and Hayworth were "Just getting acquainted!"). Carson declares he'll make things up to Cagney if he'll go on another date–this time he can have Hayworth. Cagney agrees and when the couples are separated at a boat ride, he gets to spend the day with Hayworth–who milks him for all he's worth (dinner, dancing, carriage ride). Hayworth soon learns that Cagney is quite poor and that he's spent all his money on her. Before they part she gives him a kiss and the head-over-heels in love Cagney runs off not realizing that he's just been kissed off. Three weeks later Cagney prepares himself for their next date (which Hayworth agreed to rather absent-mindedly), but he is informed by de Havilland that that afternoon Hayworth married Carson (who is rapidly making a name for himself by swindling half the citizens of New York). Quite on the rebound Cagney decides to take de Havilland up on her free-thinking and is shocked when she pulls away and confesses it was all a put-on–she's really quite conventional. Cagney asks her if she wants to go steady and she agrees. Soon after they are married and Cagney works long and hard at his lessons from the dentist correspondence school– barely making ends meet. Years later he runs into Hayworth, who invites the couple to dinner at her and Carson's huge mansion. Hayworth and Carson's marriage was not exactly made in heaven. He has become a sniveling, overweight, complacent snob, and Hayworth has become bored with him. Because she knows Cagney and de Havilland are struggling financially, she forces her husband to offer Cagney a vice presidency position in his contracting firm. Carson reluctantly agrees and Cagney warily accepts (he also gets a foreman position for his terminally unemployed father Hale). During dinner the mansion's new electric light blows a fuse, leaving everyone in the dark. During the blackout Hayworth makes her way to Cagney and kisses him passionately–but Cagney thinks that de Havilland was the one who kissed him. Six months later Cagney is climbing the walls because his vice presidency position gives him nothing to do other than read the day's newspapers and sign documents he doesn't understand. When a building Carson's company had constructed collapses because cheap materials were used (Hale is killed in the accident), the company is hauled before the courts and Cagney is made the fall-guy. He's sent to prison for five years and vows revenge on Carson. The film then returns to the Sunday afternoon where Cagney decides to give Carson a lethal dose of laughing gas when he comes in to have his tooth pulled. When Carson and Hayworth arrive, Cagney is a bit surprised to find him even more pathetic than he was five years ago and Hayworth more shrewish than ever. Deciding that life with Hayworth is punishment enough, Cagney doesn't gas Carson, but instead pulls his tooth without benefit of anesthetic. After they leave, Cagney goes for a walk with de Havilland and both are overjoyed when she tells him she's going to have a baby. THE STRAWBERRY BLONDE is a delightful romantic comedy which combines a strong cast, great production values, and a good musical score with professional direction by Walsh in a skillfull entertainment. The beautiful Hayworth was actually a replacement for Warner Bros.' starlet Ann Sheridan, who balked at the script and refused to participate and demanded better roles. With the costumes already designed and ready, director Walsh and studio head Jack Warner were in a quandary. Walsh immediately thought of Hayworth, the darling of Columbia Pictures head Harry Cohn. Cohn was delighted to have his rising starlet appear in a Cagney film and gladly lent her to Warners. While Cagney, Hayworth, and Carson are fine in their various roles, it is de Havilland who steals the film. Demonstrating a flair for comedy little tapped in her previous roles, de Havilland is wonderfully cute and spunky in the scenes where she and Cagney are courting. Another standout scene is where she explains her free-thinking ways to the very prim and proper Hayworth, delighting in shocking her friend. Her sexually aggressive winks and her bouncy swagger while trying to convince Cagney of her independence is endearing and hilarious. Director Walsh would remake the film again in 1948 as ONE SUNDAY AFTERNOON, this time as a musical, but THE STRAWBERRY BLONDE remains the definitive version.

p, Jack L. Warner, Hal B. Wallis; d, Raoul Walsh; w, Julius J. Epstein, Philip G. Epstein (based on the play "One Sunday Afternoon" by James Hogan); ph, James Wong Howe; m, Heinz Roemheld; ed, William Holmes; art d, Robert Haas; cos, Orry- Kelly; makeup, Perc Westmore.

Romantic Comedy   **Cas.**   **(PR:A MPAA:NR)**

STRAWBERRY ROAN**   (1933) 59m UNIV bw

Ken Maynard, Ruth Hall, Harold Goodwin, Frank Yaconelli, Charles King, William Desmond, James Marcus, Jack Rockwell, Robert Walker, Ben Corbett, Bill Patton, Art Mix, Roy Bucko, Buck Bucko, Bud McClure, "Tarzan.".

Maynard was a big western star and this was one of his most popular films. In it, he plays a stubborn rodeo star, ready to show that he hasn't been beaten yet. King, who played a villain in later westerns, this time provided the laughs, while Hall was Maynard's flame. In the late 1940s Maynard found himself down and Gene Autry, who was in many of his early films, bought the story from Maynard to help out his buddy. The 1948 film used the title from the earlier production, but that was about all.

p, Ken Maynard; d, Alan James; w, Nate Gatzert; ph, Ted McCord.

Western   **Cas.**   **(PR:A MPAA:NR)**

STRAWBERRY ROAN*½   (1945, Brit.) 84m BN/Anglo-American bw

Billy [William] Hartnell (Chris Lowe), Carole Raye (Molly Lowe), Walter Fitzgerald (Morley), Sophie Stewart (Mrs. Morley), John Ruddock (Dibben), Wylie Watson (Bill Gurd), Petula Clark (Emily), Joan Maude (Gladys Moon), Joan Young (Mrs. Dibben), Ellis Irving (Auctioneer), Kynaston Reeves (Dealer), Norman Shelley (Dr. Lambert), Jack Simpson and His Sextet, Patric Curwen (Vicar), Pat Geary, Charles Doe, Gordon Begg, Percy Coyte, Charles Paton, Richard Turner, Janet Morrison, Josie Huntley Wright, Patricia Stainer, Ernest Barrow, Vi Gould, Strawberry Roan the Heifer Calf.

Trying to show that the land is everything, this simple plot fails. A young farmer marries a former showgirl used to the finer things in life and he gives her a young heifer. Her free-spending lifestyle not only causes them to lose money, but makes him forget his work also. As their life crumbles around them, they fight and she rides off. She takes a tumble off the horse and dies. Now, not only is he broke, but guilt-ridden over his dead wife and is forced to work for a neighbor.

p, Louis H. Jackson; d, Maurice Elvey; w, Elizabeth Baron (based on a novel by A.G. Street); ph, James Wilson.

Drama   **(PR:A MPAA:NR)**

STRAWBERRY ROAN, THE**½   (1948) 79m COL c

Gene Autry (Himself), Gloria Henry (Connie Bailey), Jack Holt (Walt Bailey), Dick Jones (Joe Bailey), Pat Buttram (Hank), Rufe Davis (Chuck), John McGuire (Bud Williams), Eddy Waller (Steve), Redd Harper (Andy), Jack Ingram (Pete Lucas), Eddie Parker (Jake), Ted Mapes (Smitty), Sam Flint (Dr. Nelson), Champion the Horse.

Autry bought the rights for this story from old western star Ken Maynard and it was also his first venture into the world of color. Instead of Autry being the star, the story focuses on his horse Champion. As the film shows off the horse's color nicely, the plot revolves around Holt's intention of killing it. He vows to get the horse because the first time the horse was ever ridden, it injured Holt's son. Autry takes the horse and runs. He is charged with rustling and now there is a reward for his capture. But Autry is cleared when the crippled boy learns to ride again with the help of the singing cowboy and, of course, the horse.

p, Armand Schaefer; d, John English; w, Dwight Cummins, Dorothy Yost (based on a story by Julian Zimet); ph, Fred H. Jackman (Cinecolor); m, Paul Mertz; ed, Henry Batista; md, Mischa Bakaleinikoff; art d, Harold MacArthur; set d, George Montgomery.

Western   **(PR:A MPAA:NR)**

STRAWBERRY STATEMENT, THE**   (1970) 103m MGM c

Bruce Davison (Simon), Kim Darby (Linda), Bud Cort (Elliot, the Coxswain), Murray MacLeod (George), Tom Foral (Coach), Danny Goldman (Charlie), Kristina Holland (Irma), Bob Balaban (Elliot, the Organizer), Kristin Van Buren (Filing Room Girl), Israel Horovitz (Dr. Benton), James Simon Kunen (Chairman), James Coco (Grocer), Eddra Gale (Dean's Secretary), Michael Margotta (Swatch), Bob Benjamin (Man), Jeannie Berlin (Clipboard Girl), Carol Bagdasarian (Telephone Girl), Jon Hill, Jess Walton, Andrew Parks (Students), Booker Bradshaw (Lucas), Drew Eshelman (Tim), Greta Pope (Song Leader), David Dukes (Guard), Ed Greenberg (Bearded Leader), Kertia Thomas, Debbie Muller, Bruce Neckels (Student Speakers), Larry Canaga, Justin Christopher, Diann Henrichsen, Robin Menken, Christopher Pray, John R. Pray, Paul Willson (Guerilla Theater Troupe), Henry Leff (Police Inspector), Bert Remsen (Policeman), Joe Quinn (Professor), Pat May, Bill Boelk, Randy Thornally, Pat Rooney, (Red Mountain Jug Band), Jack Schmidt (University President), King Moody (Television Newscaster), Bill Striglos (Television Technician), Joseph Reale (Jock), Nancy Burnett, Margo Winkler, Ruth Silveira, Julie Payne (Women).

Davison is a college student who joins the protest movement only to meet a certain girl. Instead he becomes passionately involved in all the protests and sometimes gets beat up and accused of being a communist. The shock value comes from the violent means the police use to break up all the sit-ins and protests. Good intentions with the story, but it tries to do too many things at once and fails to make a real statement. Songs include: "The Circle Game" (Joni Mitchell, sung by Buffy Sainte-Marie), "Something in the Air" (John Keene, performed by Thunderclap Newman), "Helpless" (Neil Young, performed by Crosby, Stills, Nash & Young), "Our House" (Graham Nash, performed by Crosby, Stills, Nash & Young), "Suite Judy Blue Eyes" (Stephen Stills, performed by Crosby, Stills, Nash & Young), "Long Time Gone" (David Crosby, performed by Crosby, Stills, Nash & Young), "The Loner," "Down by the River" (Young, sung by Young), "Give Peace a Chance" (John Lennon, Paul McCartney), "Concerto in D Minor" (Alessandro Marcello), "Thus Spake Zarathustra (Richard Strauss).

p, Irwin Winkler, Robert Chartoff; d, Stuart Hagmann; w, Israel Horovitz (based on a novel by James Simon Kunen); ph, Ralph Woolsey (Metrocolor); m, Ian Freebairn-Smith; ed, Marjorie Fowler, Roger J. Roth, Fredric Steinkamp; art d, George W. Davis, Preston Ames; set d, Robert R. Benton, Chuck Pierce; cos, Norman Burza, Ricky Roberts; spec eff, J.D. Day; makeup, Jerry Cash.

Drama   **Cas.**   **(PR:C MPAA:R)**

STRAY DOG***½ (1963, Jap.) 122m Shin Toho/Toho International bw   (NORA INU)

Toshiro Mifune (Murakami, the Detective), Takashi Shimura (Sato, the Head Detective), Ko Kimura (Yuro, the Criminal), Keiko Awaji (Harumi, His Girl), Reisaburo Yamamoto (Hondo, the Suspect), Noriko Sengoku (Girl).

A gripping, but somewhat flawed, Kurosawa film which details the efforts of a young police detective, Mifune, to recover his pistol which was stolen from him on a crowded bus. Though he could be issued a new sidearm (the film is set shortly after WW II and firearms are very scarce), Mifune becomes obsessed with finding the gun, taking personal responsibility for all the crimes committed with it, including murder. Eventually the criminal is tracked down and the gun recovered, but it is obvious that Mifune had really been chasing his own criminal impulses (Shimura, Mifune's commanding officer, says he would have become a thief if he had not gone into police work) and was vicariously experiencing the killer's deeds. Kurosawa has little to say about STRAY DOG and feels he failed because he was more concerned with technique than character. While this is definitely arguable, the techniques employed by the director are more problematic than the script or performances. A sloppy pace, indifferent narration, and an unbearably long montage sequence showing Mifune scouring the underworld for his gun while posing as a returned veteran (nearly 10 minutes of dissolves, double-exposures, etc.), distract the viewer from the fascinating character study and threatens to collapse the whole film under its ponderous weight. Technical errors notwithstanding, STRAY DOG is still a powerful film and well worth seeing.

p, Sojiro Motoki; d, Akira Kurosawa; w, Ryuzo Kikushima, Kurosawa (based on a novel by Kurosawa); ph, Asakazu Kakai; m, Fumio Hayasaka; ed, Yoshi Sugihara; art d, So Matsuyama.

Crime   **(PR:A-C MPAA:NR)**

STREAMERS*½   (1983) 118m UA Classics c

Matthew Modine (Billy), Michael Wright (Carlyle), Mitchell Lichtenstein (Richie), David Alan Grier (Roger), Guy Boyd (Rooney), George Dzundza (Cokes), Albert Macklin (Martin), B.J. Cleveland (Pfc. Bush), Bill Allen (Lt. Townsend), Paul Lazar (MP Lieutenant), Phil Ward (MP Sgt. Kilick), Terry McIlvain (Orderly), Todd Savell (MP Sgt. Savio), Mark Fickert (Dr. Banes), Dustye Winniford (Staff Sergeant), Robert S. Reed (MP).

A very underrated Robert Altman film that did not receive the attention it deserved. The film is set in a military barracks with a group of Army recruits going back and forth from being macho to baring their souls. Things seem to close in on all the young men and we can feel their claustrophobia. All of them try to assimilate and start with a clean slate. A compelling film about human emotions.

p, Robert Altman, Nick J. Mileti; d, Altman; w, David Rabe (based on the play by Rabe); ph, Pierre Mignot (Movielab Color); ed, Norman Smith; prod d, Wolf Kroeger; art d, Steve Altman; cos, Scott Bushnell.

Drama   **Cas.**   **(PR:O MPAA:R)**

STREAMLINE EXPRESS**   (1935) 72m REP bw

Evelyn Venable (Patricia Wells), Victor Jory (Jimy Hart), Esther Ralston (Elaine Vinson), Ralph Forbes (Fred Arnold), Sidney Blackmer (Gilbert Landon), Erin O'Brien-Moore (Mrs. Forbes), Clay Clement (John Forbes), Lee Moran (Larry Houston), Vince Barnett (Jones), Wade Boteler, Theodore von Eltz, Harry Tyler, Libby Taylor.

A look at people's lives as they travel by train across the country and how many people will settle for less than what their heart desires. One vignette concerns Venable who says she will marry Forbes even though she is in love with Jory. Another has Clement and Ralston eloping as Barnett races against time to get his wife to California so their baby can be born there and they can inherit some money. Also along for the ride are a woman trying to save her marriage and the customary drunk.

p, George Yohalem; d, Leonard Fields; w, Fields, Dave Silverstein, Olive Cooper (based on a story by Goerge Yohalem); ph, Ernest Miller; ed, Joseph Lewis.

Drama   **(PR:A MPAA:NR)**

STREET ANGEL**   (1928) 102m FOX bw

Janet Gaynor (Angela), Charles Farrell (Gino), Alberto Rabagliati, Gino Conti (Policemen), Guido Trento (Neri, Police Sergeant), Henry Armetta (Mascetto), Louis Liggett (Beppo), Milton Dickinson (Bimbo), Helena Herman (Andrea), Natalie Kingston (Lisetta), David Kashner (The Strong Man), Jennie Bruno (Landlady).

Gaynor is a poor Neapolitan waif who steals to obtain medicine for her sick mother. She hides out from the police with a circus and there meets artist Farrell, who poses her for a portrait of the Madonna. Finally caught, she is sent to jail, and after her term she wanders into a church and sees her picture on the wall. She also sees Farrell, pining over his imprisoned love, and the two are reunited. More sentiment and gauzed photography from a leading practitioner of the treacle school, director Borzage, who was following up his "film of the year" in 1927, SEVENTH HEAVEN, with this unfortunate thing. Dated though it is today, STREET ANGEL cemented the pairing of six-foot-two Farrell with the tiny (five foot) Gaynor. So charmed were film audiences by these two basically all-American performers that they were accepted convincingly as Frenchman and Frenchwoman in SEVENTH HEAVEN and Italians in STREET ANGEL.

d, Frank Borzage; w, Marion Orth, Philip Klein, Henry Roberts Symonds (based on the novel Cristilinda by Monckton Hoffe); ph, Ernest Palmer; ed, Barney Wolf.

Drama   **(PR:A MPAA:NR)**

STREET BANDITS**   (1951) 54m REP bw

Penny Edwards (Mildred Anderson), Robert Clarke (Fred Palmer), Ross Ford (Tom Reagan), Roy Barcroft (Monk Walter), John Eldredge (L.T. Mitchell), Helen Wallace (Martha Palmer), Arthur Walsh (Arnold Black), Harry Hayden (William Carrington), Emmett Vogan (Brownell), Jane Adams (Jane Phillips), Charles Wagenheim (Gus), Richard Bartlett (Johnny), Norman Field (Dr. Sawyer), Robert Long (Judge), Dick Cogan (Clerk).

Routine story that inspires routine emotions. A pair of young lawyers want to make some quick cash, so they decide to take the case of slot machine mobster Barcroft. But Ford finds this unacceptable and against his morals so he turns the job down. Clarke's new bride, Edwards, also is unhappy. Clarke still takes the case and even gets wounded when Barcroft kills his partner. Clarke is able to clear his name eventually and vows never to take on another racketeering case again.

p, William Lackey; d, R.G. Springsteen; w, Milton Raison; ph, John MacBurnie; m, Stanley Wilson; ed, Arthur Roberts; art d, Frank Arrigo; cos, Adele Palmer.

Drama   **(PR:A MPAA:NR)**

STREET CORNER*   (1948) 62m Wilshire/Viro bw

Joseph Crehan (Dr. James Fenton), Marcia Mae Jones (Lois Marsh), John Treul (Bob Mason), Billie Jean Eberhart (Irene), John Duncan (Hal), Jean Fenwick (Mrs. Marsh), Don Brodie (Mr. Marsh), Greti DuPont (A Midwife), Jan Sutton (Kitty Mae), Milton Ross (Tom Brennan), Jean Andren (Dr. Fenton's Nurse), Stuart Holmes (Judge), Sam Ash (District Attorney), Eddie Gribbon (Taxi Driver).

A film that shows what can happen when high school kids have sex, told in narration style by the girl's doctor. Jones is the girl who has a fling after her graduation dance and becomes pregnant. Not only is she terrified to tell her mother about her problem, but her boy friend also is killed in an accident on his way to marry her. Her problems are compounded when she gets an abortion from a sleazy doctor.

p, George McCall; d, Albert Kelley; w, Jack Jungmeyer (based on a story by Kelley); ph, Virgil Miller; m, Bernard Katz; ed, John Faure.

Drama   **(PR:C MPAA:NR)**

STREET CORNER   (SEE: BOTH SIDES OF THE LAW, 1953, Brit.)

STREET FIGHTER**   (1959) 71m North Star/Brenner-States Rights bw

Vic Savage [A.N. White], Ann Atmar, Marlene Robbins, Ahmed Bey.

An independently produced "teenage delinquency" picture which is admirable in its intent but cinematically doesn't amount to much. It's the story of a young "tough" who goes through life lashing out at whatever opposes him. He soon realizes that emotions must be controlled when a girl he likes is senselessly murdered. With this tragedy, the ruffian becomes an adult, and learns to deal with life in a civilized manner. The film's "message" may be a bit heavy-handed, but some gutsy performances make it easier to swallow.

p, Bradley N. Nichols, Karl G. Kappel; d&w, A.N. White.

Drama   **(PR:A MPAA:G)**

STREET GANG   (SEE: VIGILANTE, 1983)

STREET GIRL**   (1929) 91m RKO bw

Betty Compson (Frederika "Freddie" Joyzelle, Violinist), John Harron (Mike Fall), Ned Sparks (Happy Winter), Jack Oakie (Joe Spring), Guy Buccola (Pete Summer), Joseph Cawthorn (Keppel, Cafe Owner), Ivan Lebedeff (Prince Nicholaus of Aragon), Eddie Kane (Club Manager), Doris Eaton and Radio Pictures Beauty Chorus, Raymond Maurel and the Cimini Male Chorus, Gus Arnheim and His Cocoanut Grove Ambassador Band.

Compson was a silent film star and one of her unknown talents at the time was her violin playing ability which she displays in this early talkie. A nice jazz quartet is making a meager living when two of them take Compson in from the street. She does all their domestic chores and becomes their very astute business manager. And when she joins the boys for some songs their fortunes really take off, going from $100 a week to $3,000. She even has an affair with one of the band members. The film has a realistic touch. The picture was remade twice by RKO as THAT GIRL FROM PARIS (1937) and FOUR JACKS AND A JILL (1942).

p, William LeBaron; d, Wesley Ruggles; w, Jane Murfin (based on the play "Viennese Charmer" by W. Carey Wonderly); ph, Lee Tover; md, Victor Barabelle; cos, Max Ree; ch, Pearl Eaton; m/l, "My Dream Melody" (sung by Betty Compson), "Broken Up Tune" (sung by Doris Eaton), "Huggable and Sweet," Oscar Levant, Sidney Clare.

Musical   **(PR:A MPAA:NR)**

STREET IS MY BEAT, THE*½   (1966) 93m Harann/Emerson bw

Shary Marshall (Della Martinson), Todd Lasswell (Phil Demarest), John Harmon (Mr. Martinson), Anne MacAdams (Mrs. Martinson), Tom Irish (Johnny Gibson), Beverly Oliver (Sally), Bob Brown (McGruber), Susan Cummings (Cora), J. Edward McKinley (Danby).

Teenager Marshall has a mother who tries to control her life. Marshall meets the older Lasswell who proposes marriage and promises to take her away from her miserable home life. He even gives her parents $200 for their consent to the marriage. After a good start, she learns Lasswell is involved in prostitution and she is arrested when she is tricked into helping him. She spends time in prison and cannot find a job upon her release. She returns to Lasswell and he makes her into a prostitute. When she finds him with another girl she leaves. Booze takes its toll on her life and she becomes a low-class prostitute working in cheap dives. During a fight with a drunk, she falls into the street and is hit by a car. At the hospital she reconciles with her parents and they tell her they will help her make a new beginning.

p, Alan P. Magerman, Jack Paller, Irvin Berwick; d, Berwick; w, Harold Livingston, Berwick (based on a story by Jack Kevan, Berwick); ph, Joseph V. Mascelli; m, Harrose; ed, Gerard Wilson; art d, David Towbin; m/l, "The Street Is My Beat" (sung by Marilyn Michaels).

Drama (PR:C MPAA:NR)

STREET MUSIC**½ (1982) 92m Pacificon c

Elizabeth Daily (*Sadie*), Larry Breeding (*Eddie*), Ned Glass (*Sam*), Marjorie Eaton (*Mildred*), W.F. Walker (*Jasper*), Miriam Phillips (*Hattie*), D'Alan Moss (*Monroe*), Sam Morford (*Slim*), John Romano (*Potts*), David Parr (*Simmons*).

A heartwarming independent feature about a young couple–singer Daily and her lackadaisical boy friend Breeding–who organize a group of elderly tenants in danger of losing their housing. An impressive directorial effort with some commanding performances, and a choice San Francisco location in the seedy Tenderloin district.

p, Richard Bowen; d, Jenny Bowen; ph, Richard Bowen; m, Ed Bogus, Judy Munson; ed, Lisa Fruchtman, Diana Pelligrini; art d, Don De Fina.

Drama Cas. (PR:A-C MPAA:R)

STREET OF CHANCE** (1930) 76m PAR bw

William Powell (*John B. Marsden/Natural Davis*), Jean Arthur (*Judith Marsden*), Kay Francis (*Alma Marsden*), Regis Toomey ("*Babe*" *Marsden*), Stanley Fields (*Dorgan*), Brooks Benedict (*Al Mastick*), Betty Francisco (*Mrs. Mastick*), John Risso (*Tony*), Joan Standing (*Miss Abrams*), Maurice Black (*Nick*), Irving Bacon (*Harry*), John Cromwell (*Imbrie*).

This is a tale inspired by the story of gambler Arnold Rothstein who was murdered amid a great deal of publicity. In this story, Toomey is a California card player who comes into town thinking his gambler brother Powell is a stockbroker. But Powell really is the notorious Natural Davis, a gambler of some repute. Powell is having marital troubles and swears off gambling to take a second honeymoon with his wife. But he decides to gamble once more to keep Toomey from following in his footsteps. Powell plays a crooked deal to break his brother. But others lose money in the same game and vow to break Powell. And they do. The final scene has Powell, Toomey, and the doctor riding in the back of an ambulance. The doctor says Powell will pull through. He offers 50 to 1 odds that he will not. The doctor says: "It's a bet." Powell dies. The film was remade in 1937 as HER HUSBAND LIES.

p, David O. Selznick; d, John Cromwell; w, Howard Estabrook, Leonore J. Coffee (based on a story by Oliver H.P. Garrett); ph, Charles Lang; ed, Otho Lovering; cos, Travis Banton; titles, Gerald Geraghty.

Drama (PR:A MPAA:NR)

STREET OF CHANCE*** (1942) 74m PAR bw

Burgess Meredith (*Frank Thompson*), Claire Trevor (*Ruth Dillon*), Louise Platt (*Virginia Thompson*), Sheldon Leonard (*Detective Joe Marucci*), Frieda Inescort (*Alma Diedrich*), Jerome Cowan (*Bill Diedrich*), Adeline de Walt Reynolds (*Grandma Diedrich*), Arthur Loft (*Sheriff Lew Stebbins*), Clancy Cooper (*Burke*), Paul Phillips (*Schoeder*), Keith Richards (*Intern*), Ann Doran (*Miss Peabody*), Cliff Clark (*Policeman Ryan*), Edwin Maxwell (*Stillwell, the District Attorney*), Gladden James (*Mr. Clark*), Reed Porter (*Counterman*), Kenneth Chryst, Kernan Cripps (*Taxi Drivers*), Sonny Boy Williams (*Small Boy*), Helen MacKellar (*Mrs. Webb, the Landlady*), Ruth Gillette (*Blonde*), Harry Tyler (*Proprietor of Clothing Store*), Besse Wade (*Landlady*), Ralph Dunn (*Fireman*), James C. Morton (*Bartender*), Milton Kibbee (*Barber*), George Watts (*Proprietor of Pawnshop*), Gloria Williams (*Woman*).

Low-budget drama comes off as a high-budget piece that keeps up the pace and interest throughout. Meredith suffers amnesia and the story unfolds through his eyes. He flees someone who is shadowing him and ends up in a boarding house where the receptionist recognizes him. As each new person enters his life Meredith, along with the audience, picks up clues to his identity. It turns out he is running from a chilling murder he cannot remember committing and only an old, paralyzed woman can clear him. Meredith is superb as the man who does not know his past and does not want to know after he finds out who he really is. This is an important early example of the *film noir* genre because it helped define it.

p, Sol C. Siegel; d, Jack Hively; w, Garrett Fort (based on the novel *The Black Curtain* by Cornell Woolrich); ph, Theodor Sparkuhl; m, David Buttolph; ed, Arthur Schmidt; art d, Hans Dreier, Haldane Douglas.

Drama (PR:A MPAA:NR)

STREET OF DARKNESS*½ (1958) 60m REP bw

Robert Keys (*Brett Marshall*), John Close (*Matt Flood*), James Seay (*Jesse Flores*), Julie Gibson (*Danielle Dubois*), Sheila Ryan (*Carmen Flores*), Dub Taylor (*Duffy Taylor*), Henry Rowland (*Inspector*), Richard Crockett (*Coke*), Val Winter (*Miles Barton*), Edwin Nelson (*Slavo*), Walter Hamlin (*Owen*), Steve Raines (*Flaky*), Pork Chops and Kidney Stew (*Themselves*).

A group of former Army mates reunite in New Orleans and decide to track down a buried treasure. Bert Reynolds appeared in a similar picture in 1969 titled IMPASSE, which was a vast improvement on this one. An adventurous tale which never amounts to much.

p, Robert Keys; d, Robert Walker; w, Malvin Wald, Maurice Tombragel; ph, Les White; ed, J.R. Whittredge, Robert J. Oswald; md, Frank Worth; m/l, Irving Bibo, Worth.

Adventure/Drama (PR:A MPAA:NR)

STREET OF MEMORIES** (1940) 70m FOX bw

Lynne Roberts (*Catherine Foster*), Guy Kibbee (*Harry Brent*), John McGuire (*Joe Mason*), Ed Gargan (*Mike Sullivan*), Hobart Cavanaugh (*Mr. Foster*), Jerome Cowan (*Mr. Grower*), Charles Waldron (*Mr. Havens*), Sterling Holloway (*Student Barber*), Scotty Beckett (*Tommy*), Adele Horner (*Mary Ann*), Pierre Watkin (*Dr. Thornton*).

New faces at 20th Century-Fox got a chance to show their stuff in this simple vehicle. McGuire is a drifting farm worker with amnesia who frequently gets into trouble with the police. He wanders into a small town and meets Roberts who takes care of him. They get married and in a brawl, a knock on the head restores his memory. He is the son of a Chicago businessman and now cannot remember who or how he married Roberts. After some time, his mind comes into focus and he discovers that he really does love Roberts. This was Hubbard's first film since joining Fox. This was Traube's first feature directing job and the first screenplay from Lees and Rinaldo. And newcomers Roberts and McGuire handled the leads.

p, Lucien Hubbard; d, Shepard Traube; w, Robert Lees, Frederic I. Rinaldo; ph, Charles Clarke; ed, Nick de Maggio; md, Emil Newman; art d, Richard Day, George Dudley; cos, Herschel.

Drama (PR:A MPAA:NR)

STREET OF MISSING MEN** (1939) 63m REP bw

Charles Bickford (*Cash*), Harry Carey (*Putnam*), Tommy Ryan (*Tommy*), Mabel Todd (*Dove*), Guinn "Big Boy" Williams (*T-Bone*), Nana Bryant (*Mrs. Putnam*), Ralph Graves (*Reardon*), John Gallaudet (*Kinsella*), Regis Toomey (*Parker*).

A story about revenge stars Bickford as a man just leaving prison after five years in the pen. His vengeance is aimed at Carey, a newspaper editor whose efforts against Bickford and organized crime resulted in Bickford's conviction. Bickford leaves prison bent on getting even with Carey, but when he finally meets Carey face to face, he changes his mind about killing him. Bickford decides to destroy the newspaper instead. After going to work for Carey, he has a change of heart, however, and loses his life in a gallant effort to save the newspaper from organized crime. Before starring in this picture, Carey was a big star in westerns, giving up the gun in this film for a pen.

p, Armand Schaefer; d, Sidney Salkow; w, Frank Dolan, Leonard Lee (based on a story by Eleanor Griffen, William Rankin); ph, Ernest Miller; m, Cy Feuer; ed, Ernest Nims.

Drama (PR:A MPAA:NR)

STREET OF MISSING WOMEN (SEE: CAFE HOSTESS, 1940)

STREET OF SHADOWS (SEE: SHADOW MAN, 1953, Brit.)

STREET OF SINNERS*** (1957) 76m UA bw

George Montgomery (*John Dean*), Geraldine Brooks (*Terry*), Nehemiah Persoff (*Leon*), Marilee Earle (*Nancy*), William Harrigan (*Gus*), Stephen Joyce (*Ricky*), Clifford David (*Tom*), Diana Milay (*Joan*), Sandra Rehn (*Frances*), Danny Dennis (*Short Stuff*), Ted Irwin (*1st Sergeant*), Melvin Decker (*Tiny*), Lou Gilbert (*Sam*), Barry McGuire (*Larry*), Elia Clark (*Boy*), Jack Hartley (*Fire Captain*), Billy James (*Joey*), Liza Balesca (*Sam's Wife*), Eva Gerson (*Tiny's Mother*), John Holland (*Harry*), Bob Duffy (*Motor Cop*), Joey Faye (*Pete*), Fred Herrick (*2nd Sergeant*), Charlie Jordan (*Customer*), John Barry (*Utility Bartender*), Wolf Barzell (*Tiny's Father*), Stephen Elliot (*Harry*).

Excellent action and well-paced story about the trials and tribulations of a first-year police officer sustain interest throughout the script. Montgomery is the rookie cop and on the first day has a run-in with Persoff, owner of a tavern and also ruler of many connections on the street. Montgomery doesn't back down even though his veteran partner, who is retiring, advises him to relax on the rules. But Montgomery stays tough, although the local youths are all against him and he becomes a target. He suffers even more when a drunk woman, commits suicide by jumping from his window. He gets suspended and through his own efforts, solves a killing and unlock's Persoff's hold on everyone in the neighborhood.

p&d, William Berke; w, John McPartland (based on a story by Philip Yordan); ph, J. Burgi Contner; m, Albert Glasser; ed, Everett Sutherland; md, Glasser.

Drama (PR:A MPAA:NR)

STREET OF WOMEN*½   (1932) 70m WB bw

Kay Francis (*Natalie Upton*), Alan Dinehart (*Larry Baldwin*), Marjorie Gateson (*Lois Baldwin*), Roland Young (*Link Gibson*), Gloria Stuart (*Doris Baldwin*), Allen Vincent (*Clarke Upton*), Louise Beavers (*Mattie the Maid*), Adrienne Dore (*Frances*), William Burress (*Doctor*), Wilbur Mack (*Mayor*).

Taken from the novel by Polan Banks, this script moves too slowly and the dialog is too wooden to tell the story of a father and daughter in love with a brother and sister. Dinehart is an architect with a mistress on the side, to relieve the tension from his society-minded wife and a daughter who adores him. The mistress, Francis, has a brother Vincent who falls for his daughter. He goes to South America, comes back and gets in an auto wreck with his girl. Dinehart's partner, in helping Gateson, shows how Dinehart is flaunting his mistress to everyone and Gateson is being laughed at. She obtains a quickie divorce to free Dinehart who now becomes a brother-in-law to his son-in-law. Too many angles for the audience to keep track of.

p, Hal B. Wallis; d, Archie Mayo; w, Charles Kenyon, Mary McCall, Jr., Brown Holmes (based on the novel by Polan Banks); ph, Ernest Haller; ed, Jim Gibbons; md, Leo F. Forbstein; set d, W. Sloane, J. Sloane.

Drama   (PR:A MPAA:NR)

STREET PARTNER, THE   (SEE: SECRET PARTNER, THE, 1961, Brit.)

STREET PEOPLE zero   (1976, U.S./Ital.) 92m Aetos Produzioni Cinematografiche/AIP c

Roger Moore (*Ulysses*), Stacy Keach (*Phil*), Ivo Garrani (*Salvatore Francesco*), Ettore Manni (*Bishop Lopetri*), Ennio Balbo (*Continenza*), Fausto Tozzi (*Nicoletta*), Pietro Martellanz (*Pano*), Romano Puppo (*Fortunate*).

Senseless violence and dramatic car chase scenes don't help the script for this low-budget mobster film that stars Moore as the son of a Mafioso head, and Keach as his racing car buddy. Between the two of them, most of the picture is taken up, with Moore and Keach cutting loose their guns in Italy and San Francisco. When hitman Moore isn't shooting at somebody, his driver, Keach, is running over some innocent pedestrian during the many car chase scenes. Weak story involves Moore and Keach in charge of finding out which rival Don is using the ploy of hiding pure heroin in crosses imported from Italy, disguised as gifts to his church in San Francisco.

p, Manolo Bolognini, Luigi Borghese; d, Maurice Lucidi; w, Ernest Tidyman, Gianfranco Bucceri, Randall Kleiser, Roberto Leoni, Niccola Badalucco, Lucidi (based on a story by Bucceri, Leoni); ph, Aiace Parolin (Movielab Color); m, Luis Enriquez; ed, Renzo Lucidi; art d, Gastone Carsetti; set d, Luigi Urbani; ch, William Garroni (car scenes); stunts, Remo De Angeles.

Crime   Cas.   (PR:O MPAA:R)

STREET SCENE**   (1931) 80m UA bw

Sylvia Sidney (*Rose Maurrant*), William Collier (*Sam Kaplan*), Estelle Taylor (*Anna Maurrant*), Beulah Bondi (*Emma Jones*), Max Montor (*Abe Kaplan*), David Landau (*Frank Maurrant*), Matt McHugh (*Vincent Jones*), Russell Hopton (*Steve Sankey*), Greta Grandstedt (*Mae Jones*), Tom H. Manning (*George Jones*), Adele Watson (*Olga Olsen*), John Qualen (*Karl Olsen*), Anna Konstant (*Shirley Kaplan*), George Humbert (*Filippo Fiorentino*), Allan Fox (*Dick McGann*), Eleanor Wesselhoeft (*Greta Fiorentino*), Nora Cecil (*Alice Simpson*), Louis Natheaux (*Harry Easter*), Lambert Rogers (*Willie Maurrant*), Virginia Davis (*Mary Hildebrand*), Helen Lovett (*Laura Hildebrand*), Kenneth Selling (*Charlie Hildebrand*), Conway Washburne (*Dan Buchanan*), Howard Russell (*Dr. John Wilson*), Richard Powell (*Officer Harry Murphy*), Walter James (*Marshal James Henry*), Harry Wallace (*Fred Cullen*), Monti Carter, Jane Mercer, Margaret Robertson, Walter Miller.

Elmer Rice's Pulitzer Prize-winning play about the lives and loves of the people who live on one West Side Manhattan street proved to have national appeal under the fine hand of helmer Vidor. Goldwyn never shrank from controversy and there were a few parts of the play that might have been a problem with national audiences but the producer hired Rice to do his own adaptation, thus insuring the integrity of the work. To keep the quality, eight of the original cast were hired to reprise their roles including Bondi, who here made her screen debut, and went on to have a long and satisfying film career. Practically all of the shooting was done on a huge street set. It's summer and the windows are open. The people can't bear to stay in their stifling apartments so the action takes place outside. Right now, the big topic of conversation is the love affair between mature woman Taylor and Hopton, a man who collects for the milk company. Taylor's husband, Landau, may be the only person in the street who doesn't know what's going on, but he has his own theory and is just waiting to catch them. The sun rises and Taylor's daughter, Sidney, is going off to work. Landau has to travel to Connecticut for the day (or so he says). Sidney's beau is Montor and after Landau leaves, he sees Hopton surreptitiously make his way to Taylor's flat. The shades come down (an odd occurrence and easily noticeable as every other shade is up to allow some fresh air to waft into the apartments) and, within a few seconds, Landau is back. He goes up to the apartment. Screams are heard, noises of a fight, then a single shot rings out. The people on the

street turn their eyes to the sound, the shade comes up and Hopton stands at the window. Then there's another shot and Hopton disappears. An instant later, Landau comes running out of the brownstone with the gun in his hand. He has the look of a crazed man and the street people shrink back when he tells them to scatter. Landau turns the corner and disappears down an alley as police cars and ambulances rush into the street. A crowd gathers and they wait to see what will happen next. Sidney gets there just in time to see Taylor being brought out by the ambulance attendants on a stretcher. She's dead and so is Hopton. Montor's sister is Konstant, a friend of Sidney's. She takes the bereaved daughter in her arms and tries to ease the pain. Officer Powell enters with Landau, who approaches Sidney and begs her forgiveness, saying that he had been drinking and didn't know what he was doing. The street begins to crowd with the curious, the scandal-lovers, the press, the flotsam who love to be where death is (not unlike the crowds that clamored to dip bits of cloth in the blood of the man who was murdered by federal agents outside the Biograph Theater in Chicago on July 22, 1934. Whether or not that corpse belonged to John Dillinger is still open for discussion). Sidney's brother, Rogers, arrives and the two will leave. Montor says he wants to be with her but she realizes that he is not the man she should be with. He's just another of the street people who could have made a difference and even stopped the murders if he'd said anything. But he didn't, and she wants no more of him. Sidney and Rogers look at their neighbors for a lingering moment, then walk away. The picture moves very quickly, with nary a wasted word. Although somewhat dated by the standards of the 1980s, it must be judged by the folkways and mores of the 1930s, when it was a stunning achievement. The play ran more than two years and is still revived often. An added dimension was composer Newman's main theme, which has since been used often in many films, whenever filmmakers want to have the underscoring feeling of New York. It ranks, to this day, as one of the most evocative pieces of music ever written and immediately conjures up the sight and strength of the crowded streets, the hustle, the oppressive claustrophobia of the Big Apple. The others who came from the stage were Montor, Wesselhoeft, McHugh, Humbert, Konstant, Landau, Manning, Qualen, and Washburne. Sidney was a second thought as Goldwyn had tried to get Nancy Carroll for the role that Erin O'Brien-Moore had done on Broadway. Carroll could not escape commitments to Paramount and studio boss B.P. Schulberg (father of Budd Schulberg) offered Sidney instead. Legend has it that he was "interested" in promoting Sidney's career and thought this would be a good move for the young actress. It was.

p, Samuel Goldwyn; d, King Vidor; w, Elmer Rice (based on his play); ph, George Barnes; m, Alfred Newman; ed, Hugh Bennett; art d, Richard Day.

Drama   Cas.   (PR:C MPAA:NR)

STREET SINGER, THE**   (1937, Brit.) 86m BN/Wardour-British National bw

Arthur Tracy (*Richard King*), Arthur Riscoe (*Sam Green*), Margaret Lockwood (*Jenny Green*), Hugh Wakefield (*Hugh Newman*), Emile Boreo (*Luigi*), Ellen Pollock (*Gloria Weston*), Wally Patch (*Policeman*), Ian MacLean (*Police Inspector*), John Deverell (*James, Butler*), Rawicz and Landauer (*The Pianists*), Car Hyson Dancers, Lew Stone and His Band.

Tracy was a big name in Britain for his radio shows and was good enough to carry his appeal to the big screen. In this lightweight musical that produces a few tears, Tracy has a fight with his lady singing partner during a stage show and runs outside, still dressed for the part he played as a beggar. He comes across Lockwood, an orphan, now a ward of an ex-magician. She takes pity on him and takes him home, thinking he is poor and without food. The contrast of his lifestyle and the slums she and her uncle live in slap him in the face and he realizes what he has. The two fall in love and he replaces his former leading lady with Lockwood.

p, Dora Nirva; d, Jean de Marguenat; w, Reginald Arkell (Based on a story by Paul Schiller, de Marguenat); ph, Henry Harris; m, Rawicz, Landauer.

Musical   (PR:A MPAA:NR)

STREET SONG*½   (1935, Brit.) 64m REA/RKO bw

John Garrick (*Tom Tucker*), Rene Ray (*Lucy*), Wally Patch (*Wally*), Lawrence Hanray (*Tuttle*), Johnny Singer (*Billy*).

Pet shop owner Ray befriends street singer Garrick, who has gotten himself involved with the criminal element. Ray helps him out by getting him a singing spot on radio, but his career is cut short when he is arrested for a crime he didn't commit. Ray's brother, Singer, hunts down the real crook and Garrick gets his freedom and a singing career.

p, Julius Hagen; d, Bernard Vorhaus; w, Vorhaus, Paul Gangelin.

Musical   (PR:A MPAA:NR)

STREET WITH NO NAME, THE*½**   (1948) 91m FOX bw

Mark Stevens (*Cordell*), Richard Widmark (*Alec Stiles*), Lloyd Nolan (*Inspector Briggs*), Barbara Lawrence (*Judy Stiles*), Ed Begley (*Chief Harmatz*), Donald Buka (*Shivvy*), Joseph Pevney (*Matty*), John McIntire (*Cy Gordon*), Walter Greaza (*Lt. Staller*), Howard Smith (*Commissioner Demory*), Bill Mauch (*Mutt*), Sam Edwards (*Whitey*), Don Kohler (*FBI Agent*

Atkins), Roger McGee *(Joe)*, Vincent Donahue *(Cholly)*, Phillip Pine *(Monk)*, Buddy Wright *(Giveno)*, Larry Anzalone *(Sparring Partner)*, Robert Karnes *(Dave)*, Bob Patten *(Danker)*, Joan Blair *(Valentine Leval)*, Kitty McHugh *(Waitress)*, Jack Herrick *(Pug)*, Joe Haworth *(Sgt. Bryant)*, Randy Stuart *(Helen)*, Marion Marshall *(Singer)*, Mike Kilian *(Police Sergeant)*, Edmund Cobb *(Desk Sergeant)*, Philip Van Zandt *(Manager of Bonding Company)*, Al Thompson *(Hotel Clerk)*, George Leonard *(Ticket Taker)*, Don Jessee *(Scar-Faced Tough)*, Joe McTurk *(Fight Manager)*, Billy Wayne *(Fight Trainer)*, Wally Rose, Wally Scott *(Ring Managers)*, Kid Wagner *(Old Pug)*, Charles Tannen *(Cab Driver)*, Fred Graham *(Bank Clerk)*, Michael Sheridan, Lyle Latell *(Officers)*, Sammy Shack *(Bartender)*, Robert B. Williams *(Sergeant)*.

Another of the spate of semidocumentary crime films from the late 1940s (HOUSE ON 92ND STREET, NAKED CITY, etc.). Stevens is an FBI agent called in and sent undercover when a woman is killed in the holdup of a nightclub. The chief suspect in the case is arrested, bailed out, and murdered, and the FBI soon learns that he was innocent and had been framed. Stevens is given the identity of a drifter and sent to hang out at a gym where he meets Widmark, a promoter. Later, when his wallet is stolen and then recovered at the scene of a robbery, he is arrested and taken to jail, but is soon out on bail posted by Widmark. He is inducted in Widmark's gang and learns the plans for their next holdup. Stevens gets word of the plan to police chief Begley, who sets a trap. An informant within the police department tips off Widmark, and the crime is cancelled. Widmark suspects that his wife, who has threatened to do just such a thing, has tipped off the cops, and he savagely beats her (this was Widmark's follow-up to pushing an old woman down the stairs in her wheelchair in KISS OF DEATH). Stevens takes a bullet from Widmark's Luger and sends it to the police to be checked against the bullet used in the nightclub murder. Widmark finds the fingerprints on his gun and gives them to his police informant, commissioner Smith, who runs them down and identifies them as belonging to an FBI agent. Widmark quickly figures out that Stevens is the man and prepares to kill him during their next holdup. Before he can murder the agent, though, Begley and the police burst in and gun him down, having cracked Smith and learned of the job. An exciting and tense film, with good performances and a tight, well-planned script. Widmark had made a huge impression as the psychotic Tommy Udo in KISS OF DEATH the year before and this film was designed chiefly to capitalize on that success. His character in this film is just as disturbed, but without the twitches and other affectations from the earlier role. Here his character is paranoid about drafts from windows, airborne germs, and fresh air. He constantly uses an inhaler while he talks. But he is smart, organizing his gang of thieves under "scientific lines." The scene in which he beats his wife, Lawrence, was originally even more brutal and had to be cut to get by the censor. Seven years later the same story was transposed to occupied Japan and directed by Samuel Fuller as HOUSE OF BAMBOO.

p, Samuel C. Engel; d, William Keighley; w, Harry Kleiner; ph, Joe MacDonald; ed, William Reynolds; md, Lionel Newman; art d, Lyle Wheeler, Chester Gore; set d, Thomas Little; cos, Kay Nelson; spec eff, Fred Sersen; makeup, Ben Nye, Tommy Tuttle.

Crime **(PR:C-O MPAA:NR)**

STREETCAR NAMED DESIRE, A***** (1951) 125m WB/FOX bw

Vivien Leigh *(Blanche DuBois)*, Marlon Brando *(Stanley Kowalski)*, Kim Hunter *(Ste lla Kowalski)*, Karl Malden *(Mitch)*, Rudy Bond *(Steve Hubbell)*, Nick Dennis *(Pablo Go nzales)*, Peg Hillias *(Eunice Hubbell)*, Wright King *(Young Collector)*, Richard Garrick *(Do ctor)*, Ann Dere *(The Matron)*, Edna Thomas *(Mexican Woman)*, Mickey Kuhn *(Sailor)*, Chester Jones *(Street Vendor)*, Marietta Canty *(Black Woman)*, Charles Wagenheim *(1st Passerby)*, Maxie Thrower *(2nd Passerby)*, Lyle Latell *(Policeman)*, Mel Archer *(Foreman)*.

This movie classic of a stage classic gets better with every viewing. The play opened in New York just before Christmas, 1947, with a 23-year-old Brando playing opposite a 38-year-old Jessica Tandy as "Blanche." It was a huge hit and stayed two years. Kazan directed the play that also saw Malden, Hunter, Bond, Dennis, Hillias, and Thomas trek westward to make the movie. When the play closed, Brando made his movie debut in THE MEN and impressed everyone with his "method" acting, but it was this reprise of his dynamic stage presentation of the brutish Pole that established him as a star. The play had been produced by Irene Mayer Selznick (now there are two movie names to recall) and the rights were acquired by former agent Feldman, who hired Saul to adapt Williams' play for the screen. Then Williams himself came in to write the final screenplay. The Mississippian, born Thomas Lanier Williams, had already mined gold with his first produced play, "The Glass Menagerie", which was made into a memorable movie by Feldman and Jerry Wald. He wanted Kazan to do the film but the short director balked as he didn't enjoy repeating the creative process on projects and preferred new challenges. Williams used his considerable gift of gab to turn Kazan around and the director ultimately agreed to go to work. They hired the aforementioned actors but the studio chiefs felt Tandy was wrong for the role. Not that she wasn't a brilliant actress, it was merely that hardly anyone west of 10th Avenue knew who she was. Leigh had been starring in the London presentation of the play (directed by her husband, Lawrence Olivier) and since she already knew the part, she was engaged for the job. Trouble began immediately because of a clash of acting techniques. Whereas Leigh was an advocate of the classical style, the others had all been trained in "The Stanislavsky Method." She brought her own, somewhat rigid, ideas with her, thus forcing early confrontations with Kazan. Brando was living the role and Leigh was quoted as saying she thought he was "a slob" off-camera, so the tension was thick as New Orleans humidity on the set. To assuage the Production Code, some changes had to be made in the script. In the play, Blanche's first husband (whom she recalls wistfully) was homosexual. That was deleted entirely and substituted with what would appear to be a case of mental instability. Also, at the end of the play, Stella decides to stay with Stanley even after he's raped her sister. For the screen she is seen to have made the decision to leave the lout. Neither deletion harmed the screen version although anyone who saw the Ann-Margaret remake for television in the 1980s was surprised by the revelations of the gay theme and the decision for the sister to tough it out, rather than exit, thus leaving Stanley to his own devices. Leigh arrives in New Orleans and, in order to get to sister Hunter's seedy apartment, has to take a streetcar named Desire (there is a Desire Street in the Crescent City, hence the title), then another named Cemetery and finally alight at a French Quarter area ironically named Elysian Fields. Leigh meets her pregnant sister and they are thrilled to see each other. The two could not be more unalike. Hunter is an earthy woman, lustful, happy in her marriage to Brando, a rough macho man who plays poker, drinks too much, and considers bowling a close second to sex. Leigh, on the other hand, is ethereal, flighty as delicate as a soap bubble, and deeply neurotic. Despite the tacky surroundings, Leigh attempts to maintain a facade of gentility, although there is something vaguely false about her pretentiousness. Brando enters and spots Leigh for what she is, a liar. The two sisters had been left a large estate (Belle Reve) and he wants to know what happened to it because, according to the Napoleonic Code of Louisiana, as Hunter's husband, he is entitled to his half of her half of the proceeds. He presses the question but Hunter steps in and pleads to allow Leigh to have a bit of rest before anything else. Hunter, who is much younger, sees that Leigh is teetering on the edge of a breakdown and wants to give her sister the benefit of every doubt. Brando won't put up with the "ya-dah-dah" and continues going for Leigh's jugular. Leigh admits that she had to sell the family home and Brando demands to see the bill of sale and to get their share of the money from it. When Leigh can't produce the papers, Brando goes through her huge steamer trunk and finds jewels and clothing and furs, the price of which could never have been paid by the money earned through schoolteaching. Leigh finally admits that a series of mortgages were taken on the property and when she couldn't pay them, the place was foreclosed. Brando is like a crack prosecuting attorney as he worms clues from Leigh's fanciful tales. Then he begins to ask a few questions, through friends, in the town where Leigh taught. The small apartment is tiny for two, but absolutely claustrophobic for three and Brando resents the long baths Leigh takes, the fact that she keeps the lights so low, and, most of all, her la-de-da ways. Over Hunter's objections, Brando will not alter his lifestyle and continues to have his pals over for their poker-playing marathons. Malden is one of the players, a bachelor who lives with his mother, has a bit more couth than the others, and is a sincere person. When Malden meets Leigh, he is entranced by her and we can see him begin to change as he attempts to be what he isn't, a man of sophistication. Brando can't stand to see his buddy being taken in by Leigh, whom he knows to be a fraud. The game goes on and Brando downs beer after beer. Leigh wants the radio on and Brando doesn't. When Hunter steps in on Leigh's behalf, Brando hits Hunter, wrecks the radio, and lets Malden know that he thinks he's a fool. Everyone exits. Hunter and Leigh go upstairs to the apartment of Hillias to spend the night. Brando is alone in the apartment and can't bear it. He knows that he did wrong, so he goes outside and yells for Hunter to come back. "Stella]" he screams. No response. "Stella?" Still no response. Finally, a great big and painful "STELLLLLAAAAA]" and suddenly Hunter is there. She looks down the iron staircase at Brando, then slowly walks down toward him. Brando drops to his knees, crying with happiness, puts his head against her swollen stomach, wraps his arms around her waist. The two kiss passionately and he takes her inside their apartment while the neighbors look on. Later, information about Leigh begins to trickle in: Leigh's first marriage and her husband's suicide (for no apparent reason in the film, although the homosexuality is explored in the play, thus motivating the gunshot), the scores of sexual liaisons she had with men who came through the small town, the scandal it caused there, and her eventual discharge from the school where she worked, the result of having seduced one of the young boy students. Leigh's penchant for teenagers is now out in the open. Whether her sexual needs led to her accepting money from the men whom she pleasured is a possibility (which pays off later in one of the play's more famous lines) and Brando is not content to keep this information to himself. Malden has been courting Leigh and Brando decides to put an end to that, thereby ending Leigh's chance of respectability, as Malden is seriously considering marriage. He tells Malden the truth, all of it, and the balding bachelor takes it hard. Brando has made an error in judgment. His telling Malden means that Leigh has nowhere else to go, so she will have to remain a permanent house guest. Hunter's labor pains commence and she is off to the hospital to have their child. For the first time, Leigh and Brando will have to spend time together. Hunter is in the throes, Malden won't come back, it's just the two of them. There's a battle of wits between the two and she is frightened of him. He is aggressive, he is sure of himself, he is all man, and he is frustrated as he's not made love to Hunter for the past several weeks in deference to her condition. Brando moves in on Leigh. She attempts to keep him at arm's length, but it's a lost cause. His strength and passion overcome her and she is raped, after he tells her "We've had this date from the beginning." The rape sends Leigh off the diving board and into the primordial morass of madness. She is no longer in touch with reality, her surroundings, nothing. Garrick, a doctor, and Dere, a heavyset matron, arrive to take Leigh away. They are employees of the only place Leigh can go now, a mental hospital. She madly believes they have come to escort her to see one of her old boy friends, a man who is rescuing her from this life, a man who will treat her with the respect to which she's always responded. Garrick nods to Dere that a straitjacket won't be necessary. He offers Leigh his arm in a gallant gesture and Leigh wistfully smiles and says, "Whoever you are, I have always depended on the kindness of strangers." And without saying goodbye to Hunter, she walks out. Hunter watches, turns to the pleased Brando, who has finally gotten this moth out of his hair, and quietly says: "Don't you ever, ever touch me again]" Brando attempts to talk to her but she is adamant, picks up the newborn babe, and goes up to Hillias' apartment, while assuring her child that they will never go back to Brando. She is upstairs in the equally dismal flat as Brando stands below and begins to scream her name. "Stella]" he shouts. "Stella]" "STELLLAAAAA]" And Hunter's face remains a mask as she listens but makes no move to return. The picture ends and one wonders if she ever did go back and did it last. No matter. The movie is done and we have been wrung dry with some of the best ensemble acting ever seen, a script that unpeeled many emotions, direction that was sensitive, and a musical score by newcomer Alex North that was superb. Two of the most famous southern belles were played by British Leigh. And in both cases, she won an Oscar for the job. The first was, of course, "Scarlett O'Hara" in GONE WITH THE WIND (1939) and this time, her portrayal was vastly different, though not any less powerful. Hunter, who just doesn't seem to work enough for us, won an Oscar as Best Supporting Actress. Malden won as Best Supporting Actor. Day won for his art direction (which was so authentic you could practically see the roaches crawling up the walls) and Hopkins for his set decoration (every item, from the fringed lamps to the ancient radio, was on the money). Also nominated were Brando (who lost to Humphrey Bogart for THE AFRICAN QUEEN), Kazan (who lost to George Stevens for A PLACE IN THE SUN), Stradling (who lost to William Mellor for A PLACE IN THE SUN), North (who lost to Franz Waxman for A PLACE IN THE SUN), Williams (who lost to Michael Wilson and Harry Brown for A PLACE IN THE SUN), and the movie itself, which was bested by AN AMERICAN IN PARIS. What a year that was for movies. All the aforementioned plus SEVEN DAYS TO NOON, DEATH OF A SALESMAN, BRIGHT VICTORY, THE BLUE VEIL, DETECTIVE STORY, DECISION BEFORE DAWN, and QUO VADIS. Leigh won as Best Actress at the Venice Film Festival and the New York Film Critics chose this as Best Picture, plus awards for Leigh and for Kazan's direction. The movie grossed more than $4 million and if that doesn't sound like much in this day of stratospheric box-office recipts, try to recall what it cost to go to the movies in those days. Brando was paid $75,00 for his labors in this one as opposed to his fee of $3 million for having acted in just three scenes in THE FORMULA. Despite the fact that this was the role that made him a star, Brando never liked playing Kowalski and the identification with the part has haunted him ever since, in much the same way Robert Ryan felt about his role as the anti-Semitic bigot in CROSS-FIRE. Brando's personal feelings aside, let all of us just be glad he did do it. It remains one of the most affecting portrayals ever affixed on film.

p, Charles K. Feldman; d, Elia Kazan; w, Tennessee Williams, adapted by Oscar Saul (based on the play by Williams); ph, Harry Stradling; m, Alex North; ed, David Weisbart; md, Ray Heindorf; art d, Richard Day; set d, George James Hopkins; cos, Lucinda Ballard.

Drama   **Cas.**   **(PR:C-O MPAA:NR)**

STREETFIGHTER, THE   (SEE: HARD TIMES, 1975)

STREETS OF GHOST TOWN*   (1950) 54m COL bw

Charles Starrett (Steve Woods/The Durango Kid), Smiley Burnette (Himself), George Chesebro (Bill Donner), Mary Ellen Kay (Doris Donner), Stanley Andrews (Sheriff), Frank Fenton (Bart Selby), Don Reynolds (Tommy Donner), John Cason (John Wicks), Jack Ingram (Kirby), Ozie Waters and His Colorado Rangers.

A muddled plot that needed help from lots of action to make it passable. In this confusing western, Starrett and laughable Burnette, along with Andrews, are looking for one million in gold left in a ghost town. When not battling ghosts, they review the story in flashback of how the gold got there and how the gang stole it. Starrett finally finds the loot and kills the rest of the gang. Burnette sings "Streets of Laredo," and Ozie Waters and His Colorado Rangers pipe in with "Oh, Susanna." (See DURANGO KID series, Index.)

p, Colbert Clark; d, Ray Nazarro; w, Barry Shipman; ph, Fayte Browne; ed, Paul Borofsky; art d, Charles Clague.

Western   **(PR:A MPAA:NR)**

STREETS OF LAREDO½**   (1949) 92m PAR bw

William Holden (Jim Dawkins), Macdonald Carey (Lorn Reming), Mona Freeman (Rannie Carter), William Bendix (Wahoo Jones), Stanley Ridges (Maj. Bailey), Alfonso Bedoya (Charley Calico), Ray Teal (Cantrel), Clem Bevans (Pop Lint), James Bell (Ike), Dick Foote (Pipes), Joe Dominguez (Francisco), Grandon Rhodes (Phil Jessup), Perry Ivins (Mayor Towson), James Davies, Bob Kortman (Rangers), Byron Foulger (Artist), Margarita Martin (Maria), Joaquin Elizondo (Mexican), Wade Crosby (Bartender), Carl Andre, Mike Lally, William Hamel (Townsmen).

Paramount put its rising young star of the late 1940s, William Holden, into this standard western vehicle just as they had put their rising young star of the 1930s, Fred MacMurray, into the same story in 1936 in TEXAS RANGERS. The film concerns three men on the wrong side of the law, Holden, Bendix, and Carey. One day the three happen upon pretty young Freeman, just as she is being harassed by unsavory tax collector Bedoya, and rescue her. A couple of years later she has grown up enough for Holden and Carey to take a romantic interest in her, but she only has eyes for the mustachioed Carey. The men become separated during a fight and Bendix and Holden join a band of Texas Rangers on the trail of Carey. The two men plan to use this convenient cover to find their partner and rejoin him. As they ride, though, they experience changes of heart and go straight, becoming real Rangers. Holden is assigned to bring in Carey, but he refuses out of loyalty to his old comrade. He is locked up while Bendix takes on the job. Bendix joins Carey's new gang but his old cohort uncovers his mission and kills him. Bendix's death is the impetus Holden needs to turn against his old friend, and he takes up the chase. Carey, meanwhile, has suffered a bullet wound and is being cared for by Freeman. Holden catches up to the outlaw and the two men have a gunfight. Carey is by far the better gunman and is about to kill Holden when Freeman finally sees the dark side of her Lothario and shoots him dead. Holden was only three films away from SUNSET BOULEVARD and the beginning of his reign as a major star, but he didn't know that and was becoming restless in vehicles like this routine–if "A" level–oater. His contract for the film included a clause that stated that the actor would not work after 6 p.m. When once asked to do so in order that they could finish with a particular set, he flew into a rage at the assistant director who came to fetch him from his dressing room. Director Fenton told him off and Holden, grumbling, did the scene. Later he apologized to the assistant. The finished film suffered from some confusing cutting, but the performances of the leads and the nice color photography made it worthwhile entertainment.

p, Robert Fellows; d, Leslie Fenton; w, Charles Marquis Warren (based on a story by Louis Stevens, Elizabeth Hill); ph, Ray Rennahan (Technicolor); m, Victor Young; ed, Archie Marshek; md, Young; art d, Hans Dreier, Henry Bumstead; set d, Sam Comer, Bertram Granger; cos, Mary Kay Dodson; m/l, "Streets of Laredo," Jay Livingston, Ray Evans; makeup, Wally Westmore, Carl Silvera, Roland Ray.

Western   **(PR:A-C MPAA:NR)**

STREETS OF NEW YORK*½   (1939) 73m MON bw

Jackie Cooper (Jimmy), Martin Spellman (Gimpy), Sidney Miller (Jiggsy), Buddy Pepper (Flatfoot), Bobby Stone (Beansy), David Durand (Spike), Robert Tucker (Howie), William Tucker (Sammy), George Cleveland (Pop O'Toole), Robert Emmett Keane (Roger Wilson), Robert Emmett O'Connor (Burke), Dick Purcell (Tap Keenan), George Irving (Judge Carroll), Marjorie Reynolds (Anne), William Gould.

Former child star Cooper led an assorted cast of other former child stars around in fighting gangsters. Cooper is a studious law student at night, who owns a newsstand during the day. Some young thugs want a piece of the action along with the mob, but Cooper and his crippled pal Spellman won't yield. The story starts to focus on the troubles of Cooper and Spellman and gives full character development, but then slides into meaningless gun battles for action. A good start, but a fading finish.

p, William T. Lackey; d, William Nigh; w, Robert D. Andrews; ph, Harry Neumann; ed, Russell Schoengarth; md, Edward Kay; art d, E.R. Hickson.

Drama   **(PR:A MPAA:NR)**

STREETS OF SAN FRANCISCO**   (1949) 60m REP bw

Robert Armstrong (Willard Logan), Mae Clarke (Hazel Logan), Gary Gray (Frankie Fraser), Wally Cassell (Ben Driscoll), Richard Benedict (Harry Walker), John Harmon (Sammy Hess), J. Farrell MacDonald (Pop Lockhart), Ian MacDonald (Luke Fraser), Charles Meredith (Eckert), Eve March (Joyce Quinn), Denver Pyle (Ed Quinn), Charles Cane (John O'Halloran), William A. Henry (Nichols), Claire DuBrey (Mrs. Partridge), Martin Garralaga (Rocco).

Gray is the son of a mob leader who has committed a murder. Policeman Armstrong tries to bring in the father and he puts up such a fight, that he is killed. Armstrong, trying to do the right thing, takes Gray into his home, even though the kid flat-out hates cops and doesn't hide his feelings. But under Armstrong's guidance, he slowly comes around. Gray almost falls back on his old ways when his father's old gang shows up and tries to turn him against his new father figure. But the kid resists in the climax and goes straight for good.

p, Sidney Picker; d, George Blair; w, John K. Butler (based on a story by Adele Buffington, Gordon Kahn); ph, John MacBurnie; m, Stanley Wilson; ed, Harry Keller; art d, Frank Hotaling; set d, John McCarthy, Jr., Charles Thompson; cos, Adele Palmer; spec eff, Howard Lydecker, Theodore Lydecker.

Drama (PR:A MPAA:NR)

STREETS OF SIN (SEE: NOT WANTED, 1949)

STREETS OF SINNERS (SEE: STREET OF SINNER, 1957)

STRICTLY CONFIDENTIAL (SEE: BROADWAY BILL, 1934)

STRICTLY CONFIDENTIAL zero (1959, Brit.) 62m
Alliance-Twickenham/RANK bw

Richard Murdoch (*Comdr. Bissham-Ryley*), William Kendall (*Maj. Rory McQuarry*), Maya Koumani (*Maxine Millard*), William Hartnell (*Grimshaw*), Colin Rix (*Warder*), Ellis Irving (*Capt. Sharples*), Larry Burns (*Barman*), Bruce Seton (*Inspector Shearing*), Paul Bogdan (*Rizzi*), Norman Pitt (*Muspratt*), Neil Hallatt (*Basil Wantage*), Jean Trend (*Elsie*), Llewellyn Rees (*Mellinger*), Harry Ross (*Hot Dog Man*), Beresford Egan (*O'Connor*), Denis Wood.

Lowbrow slapstick comedy with pitiful dialog and scattered direction. Kendall and Murdoch have just been released from jail and decide to team up. They think they have it made when a rich young widow hires them to run her factory. She has no idea about their past and they don't realize she is using them to play around with the shareholders. The idea never catches on and the film slowly dies. Luckily for the audience it was only 62 minutes of misery.

p, Guido Coen; d, Charles Saunders; w, Brock Williams; ph, Jimmy W. Harvey; m, Malcolm Lockyer; ed, Peter Pitt.

Comedy (PR:A MPAA:NR)

STRICTLY DISHONORABLE*½ (1931) 94m UNIV bw

Paul Lukas (*Count Di Ruva, "Gus"*), Sidney Fox (*Isabelle Parry*), Lewis Stone (*Judge Dempsey*), George Meeker (*Henry Greene*), William Ricciardi (*Tomasso*), Sidney Toler (*Mulligan*), Samuel Bonello, Carlo Schipa (*Waiters*), Natalie Moorhead (*Lilli*), Joe Torilla (*Cook*), Joseph W. Girard (*Officer*), Aldo Franchetti.

Preston Sturges' second stage play (written when he was still in his twenties and while recovering from an operation) became a Broadway hit and was filmed twice: this one and the remake in 1951 that starred Janet Leigh and Ezio Pinza. Screenwriter Lehman wisely stuck close to the original and the laughs were many as Lukas portrays a rakehell opera-singer. In an illegal speakeasy one night, he meets young southerner Fox, who is engaged to be married to boorish Meeker. Lukas lets her know that his intentions are strictly dishonorable but it matters not to petite Fox, who is, by this time, disgusted with her aggravating suitor. The speak is owned by Ricciardi (reprising his role in the play, as did Meeker) and frequented by Toler, a cop who turns the other way when he sees the illegal alcohol being poured in his own glass. Stone almost steals the movie as a one-time judge who has given up the law in favor of tippling. When Fox leaves Meeker and has no place to stay, Lukas offers her the use of his apartment, making certain she knows that he is a bounder, a cad, and a ne'er-do-well. Fox still wants to be with him and he almost does the dirty deed until Stone points out that she is little more than a child and he would be remiss if he allowed himself to fall prey to passion. Lukas leaves Fox in his apartment and goes up to Stone's apartment to spend the night, then realizes that he loves Fox, that his intentions have suddenly switched to honorable, and the only thing he can do now is marry her. The synopsis, admittedly, doesn't sound like much but the writing is sharp, the characters are well drawn, and the comedy timing is on a par with the best movies of the era. Watching the patrician Stone as a drunk is worth the price of admission. Fox had a brief career that began with BAD SISTER in 1931. She died at the age of 32 after having appeared in THE MOUTHPIECE, MURDERS IN THE RUE MORGUE, ONCE IN A LIFETIME, and MIDNIGHT, among others.

p, Carl Laemmle, Jr.; d, John M. Stahl; w, Gladys Lehman (based on the play by Preston Sturges); ph, Karl Freund, Jackson Rose; ed, Arthur Taveres, Maurice Pivar.

Comedy (PR:A-C MPAA:NR)

STRICTLY DISHONORABLE* (1951) 86m MGM bw

Ezio Pinza (*Augustino Caraffa*), Janet Leigh (*Isabelle Perry*), Millard Mitchell (*Bill Dempsey*), Gale Robbins (*Marie Donnelly*), Maria Palmer (*Countess Lili Szadvany*), Esther Minciotti (*Mme. Maria Caraffa*), Silvio Minciotti (*Uncle Nito*), Arthur Franz (*Henry Greene*), Sandro Giglio (*Tomasso*), Hugh Sanders (*Harry Donnelly*), Mario Siletti (*Luigi*).

Preston Sturges' smash stage comedy was well done in this film version through the talents of opera singer Pinza and the looks of Leigh. He plays, strangely enough, an opera singer not only known for his lungs but his love

for women. Leigh arrives on the scene straight off the Mississippi farm. She has been infatuated with Pinza from day one and just when Leigh and he meet, he has been fighting with a publisher because Pinza has axed Robbins' singing career. Pinza and Leigh are forced to marry for convenience, but really want to make it an ideal marriage despite the conniving efforts of Palmer, who once was a flame of Pinza's. All turns out right in the end for the rich opera star and simple farm girl. Some of the songs include: "Everything I Have Is Yours" (Harold Adamson, Burton Lane), "I'll See You in My Dreams" (Gus Kahn, Isham Jones).

p,d&w, Melvin Frank, Norman Panama (based on the play by Preston Sturges); ph, Ray June; ed, Cotton Warburton; md, Lennie Hayton; art d, Cedrie Gibbons, Hans Peters; set d, Edwin B. Willis, Hugh Hunt; cos, Helen Rose; makeup, William Tuttle.

Comedy (PR:A MPAA:NR)

STRICTLY DYNAMITE zero (1934) 71m RKO bw

Jimmy Durante (*Moxie Slaight*), Lupe Velez (*Vera*), Norman Foster (*Nick Montgomery*), William Gargan (*Georgie Ross*), Marian Nixon (*Sylvia Montgomery*), Eugene Pallette (*Sourwood Sam*), Minna Gombell (*Miss LeSeur*), Sterling Holloway (*Fleming*), Four Mills Brothers (*Specialty*), Stanley Fields, Tom Kennedy (*Bodyguards*), Leila Bennett, Franklin Pangborn, Berton Churchill, Jackie Searl, Irene Franklin, Mary Kornman.

Oddly enough in this picture Durante plays a radio funny man who starts running out of jokes and that is exactly what the film does, in about the first 15 minutes. The film relied too much on Durante referring to his famous "Schnozzola" and his sometimes funny butchering of the English language. While searching for more laughs, Durante hires Foster. But Foster's wife winds up getting involved with Durante's partner, Velez. The film was plagued with a slew of writers' contributions and it was a clear case of too many cooks spoiling the broth. The Mills Brothers add about the only touch of class. Songs include: "Swing It Sister," "Oh Me] Oh My] Oh You]" (Harold Adamson, Burton Lane), "Money in My Clothes" (Irving Kahal, Sammy Fain), "I'm Putty in Your Hands" (Jimmy Durante, Adamson), "Hot Patatta" (Durante).

p, Pandro S. Berman; d, Elliott Nugent; w, Maurine Watkins, Milton Raison, Jack Harvey, Ralph Spence (based on a play by Robert T. Colwell, Robert A. Simon); ph, Edward Cronjager; ed, George Crone; cos, Walter Plunkett.

Musical (PR:A MPAA:NR)

STRICTLY FOR PLEASURE (SEE: PERFECT FURLOUGH, THE, 1958)

STRICTLY FOR THE BIRDS* (1963, Brit.) 63m Independent
Artists/RANK bw

Tony Tanner (*Terry Blessing*), Joan Sims (*Peggy Blessing*), Graham Stark (*Hartley*), Jeanne Moody (*Claire*), Alan Baulch (*Alfie*), Toni Palmer (*Bridget*), Valerie Walsh (*Maxine*), Carol Cleveland (*Sandra*), Bernard Goldman (*Mendoza*), Murray Kash (*Mario*), Tony Hawes (*Joe*).

A gambler tries to strike it rich at the racetrack but gets taken by a gorgeous blonde who also happens to be a crook. One of this picture's familiar faces is the buxom Cleveland, who would soon become one of the regulars on the legendary British television program "Monty Python's Flying Circus."

p, E. Smedley Aston; d, Vernon Sewell; w, Tony Hawes.

Comedy (PR:C MPAA:NR)

STRICTLY ILLEGAL* (1935, Brit.) 69m Leslie Fuller/GAU bw
(AKA: HERE COMES A POLICEMAN)

Leslie Fuller (*Bill the Bookie*), Betty Astell (*Mrs. Bill*), Georgie Harris (*Bert the Runner*), Cissie Fitzgerald (*Lady Percival*), Glennis Lorimar (*The Girl*), Mickey Brantford (*The Boy*), Ernest Sefton (*The Colonel*), Alf Goddard (*The Cop*), Humberston Wright (*The Reverend*), Syd Courtenay, T. Arthur Ellis.

An amusing Leslie Fuller outing which casts him as a bookie who mistakenly believes he has killed a police officer. He disguises himself as a priest and soon gets conned into saying the wedding mass for Fitzgerald, who is preparing a royal ceremony for her daughter. In the meantime, another crook-in-priest's-clothing appears and steals Fitzgerald's jewelry. The chase is on—one phony priest chasing another. It all leads up to a madcap case of mistaken identities during a clergymens convention. The film was recut in 1940 and distributed as the 45-minute HERE COMES A POLICE-MAN.

p, Joe Rock; d, Ralph Ceder; w, Syd Courtenay, Georgie Harris (based on the play "The Naughty Age" by Con West, Herbert Sargent).

Comedy (PR:A MPAA:NR)

STRICTLY IN THE GROOVE zero (1942) 60m UNIV bw

Mary Healy (*Sally Monroe*), Richard Davies (*Bob Saunders*), Leon Errol (*Durham*), Shemp Howard (*Pops*), Grace McDonald (*Dixie*), Ozzie Nelson (*Ozzie*), Franklin Pangborn (*Cathcart*), Russell Hicks (*R.C. Saunders*),

Martha Tilton (*Martha*), Eddie Johnson (*Skat*), Charles Lang (*Russ Monroe*), Jimmie Davis (*Jimmie*), Ken Stevens (*Ken*), Jimmy Wakely Trio [Jimmy Wakely, Cyrus Bond, Eddie Snyder], Diamond's Solid-Aires [Leo Diamond, Abe Diamond, Buddy Raye, Maurice Fineman, Jerry Geller], Dinning Sisters [Ella Lucille, Eugenia Doy, Virginia Moy], Holmes Herbert (*Commissioner*), Tim Ryan (*Prof. Blake*), Ralph Dunn (*Big Boy*), Helen Deverell (*Pearl*), Oscar Loraine (*Chef*), Lloyd Ingraham (*McClelland*), Neeley Edwards (*Angry Man*), Frances Morris (*Phone Girl*), Charles Moore (*Cactus*), Drew Demarest (*Hotel Clerk*), Grace Lenard (*Woman*), Jim Lucas, Joey Ray (*Waiters*), Francis Sayles (*Guest*), Jack Gardner (*Desk Clerk*), Gerald Pierce (*Bell Hop*), Caroline Cooke (*Dowager*).

Weak script is wrapped around 16 songs in less than an hour, too many tunes for that length of time. Story centers on Davies, a college student who flunks out after spending more time with his band than his studies. This doesn't please his father, Hicks, a rich owner of a successful hotel chain, so Hicks sends Davies away to an Arizona dude ranch. Davies takes his band along, and there at the ranch he meets Healy, the owner of a competitor hotel. While she struggles to keep her place open, she and Davies also fall in love, much to the dismay of Hicks. Ozzie Nelson and His Orchestra appear, prior to his successful "Ozzie and Harriet" TV series. Songs include: "Chisholm Trail," "Buffalo Gal" sung by the Jimmy Wakely Trio), "Happy Cowboy" (Bob Nolan, sung by the Jimmy Wakely Trio), "It Makes No Difference Now" (Jimmie Davis, Floyd Tillman), "Sweethearts or Strangers" (Davis, Lou Wayne), "You Are My Sunshine" (Davis, Charles Mitchell, sung by Davis and the Jimmy Wakely Trio reprised " (sung Ozzie Nelson and His Orchestra), "Be Honest with Me" (Gene Autry, Fred Rose), "Elmer's Tune (Elmer Albrecht, Sammy Gallop, Dick Jurgens), "The Pretty Girl Milking Her Cow (sung by the Dinning Sisters and The Jimmy Wakely Trio), "Ridin' On" (Jimmy McHugh, Harold Adamson, sung by Kenny Stevens and the Diamond Solid-Aires), "Dancing on Air" (Milton Rosen, Everett Carter, sung by Martha Tilton with Ozzie Nelson and His Orchestra), "I Never Knew" (Tom Pitts, Ray Egan, Roy J. Marsh, sung by Ozzie Nelson and His Orchestra), "Somebody Else is Taking My Place" (Dick Howard, Bob Ellsworth, Russ Morgan, sung by Ozzie Nelson and His Orchestra), "Miss You" (Charles Tobias, Harry Tobias, sung by Mary Healy with Ozzie Nelson and His Orchestra), "I'll Remember April" (Don Raye, Gene De Paul, sung by Healy, with the Diamond Solid-Aires).

p, Joseph G. Sanford; d, Vernon Keays; w, Kenneth Higgins, Warren Wilson; ph, John W. Boyle; ed, Edward Curtis; art d, Jack Otterson.

Musical   (PR:A   MPAA:NR)

STRICTLY MODERN   (1930) 63m FN-WB bw

Dorothy Mackaill (*Kate*), Sidney Blackmer (*Heath Desmond*), Julanne Johnston (*Aimee Spencer*), Warner Richmond (*Judge Bartlett*), Mickey Bennett (*Bobby Spencer*), Katherin Clare Ward (*Mrs. Spencer*), Lotti Williams.

Film based on the play "Cousin Kate" tells the modest story of a women writer who has never found love. Blackmer and Johnston (Mackaill's cousin) are set to get married. But she starts laying down the law and two days before the big day, Blackmer decides he has had enough. He changes his mind and takes the train back to town. On the way, however, he starts exchanging glances with Mackaill, who is on the way to the wedding. They don't know one another at all and decide they are meant for each other. All is well at the end with the two going off together, along with Johnston and her long-time admirer, Richmond, who suffers a black eye at the hand of Mackaill in the end.

d, William A. Seiter; w, Ray Harris, Gene Towne, J. Morris (based on the play "Cousin Kate" by Hubert Henry Davies); ph, Sid Hickox; titles, Harris, Towne.

Drama   (PR:A   MPAA:NR)

STRICTLY PERSONAL*   (1933) 71m PAR bw

Marjorie Rambeau (*Annie Gibson*), Edward Ellis (*Soapy Gibson*), Dorothy Jordan (*Mary*), Eddie Quillan (*Andy*), Louis Calhern (*Magruder*), Dorothy Burgess (*Bessie*), Olive Tell (*Mrs. Castleman*), Hugh Herbert (*Wetzel*), Jean Barry (*Hope Jennings*), Rollo Lloyd (*Jerry O'Connor*), Charles Sellon (*Hewes*), Ben Hall (*Holbrook*), Gay Seabrook (*Giggles*), Harvey Clark (*Biddleberry*), DeWitt Jennings (*Capt. Reardon*), Helen Jerome Eddy (*Mrs. Lovett*), Thomas E. Jackson (*Flynn*), Hazel Jones (*Lelia*).

Confusing low budget picture stars Rambeau and Ellis as a pair who are trying to run a lonely hearts club in California. Ellis is on the run, however, as an escapee from jail. He goes as far as having his face changed by a plastic surgeon in his attempts at covering his tracks. But mobster Calhern knows his true identity, and blackmails the pair into letting him join the club. When he does, he starts running the show, turning the place into a scandalous rendezvous. The daughter of one of Ellis' prison buddies shows up, and when Calhern forces himself on her, he gets shot. The confusing finish points some fingers, but never reveals the real killer.

d, Ralph Murphy; w, Willard Mack, Beatrice Banyard, Casey Robinson (based on a story by Wilson Mizner, Robert T. Shannon); ph, Milton Krasner; ed, Joseph Kane.

Drama   (PR:A   MPAA:NR)

STRICTLY UNCONVENTIONAL*   (1930) 72m MGM bw (AKA: THE CIRCLE)

Catherine Dale Owen (*Elizabeth Champion-Cheney*), Paul Cavanagh (*Ted*), Tyrell Davis (*Arnold Champion-Cheney*), Lewis Stone (*Clive Champion-Cheney*), Ernest Torrence (*Lord Porteus*), Alison Skipworth (*Lady Catherine Champion-Cheney*), Mary Forbes (*Mrs. Anna Shenstone*), Wilfred Noy (*Butler*), William O'Brien (*Footman*).

Low budget and limited sets did not help the sound version of Somerset Maugham's "The Circle." It tells the story, in a limited way, of a woman who is married to a hard-working and straitlaced man, but falls for a Canadian visitor. The man's mother, whom he hasn't seen in 30 years because she took off with her lover, comes to the house and she crosses paths with her husband, the father of the wife's husband. Upon learning of Owen's intentions, Skipworth points out her own mistakes and warns her not to do it. Davis is told by his father romance his wife and put some spark back into his love life. This appeases Owen for a while, but the rough Canadian and his lifestyle appeals to her even more, so she eventually takes off with her lover.

d, David Burton; w, Sylvia Thalberg, Frank Butler, Somerset Maugham (based on the play "The Circle" by Maugham); ph, Oliver Marsh, William Daniels; ed, Margaret Booth; art d, Cedric Gibbons; cos, David Cox.

Drama   (PR:A   MPAA:NR)

STRIKE!**   (1934, Brit.) 69m GAU bw (GB: RED ENSIGN)

Leslie Banks (*David Barr*), Carol Goodner (*June Mackinnon*), Frank Vosper (*Lord Dean*), Alfred Drayton (*Manning*), Donald Calthrop (*Macleod*), Allan Jeayes (*Emerson*), Campbell Gullan (*Hannay*), Percy Parsons (*Casey*), Fewlass Llewellyn (*Sir Gregory*), Henry Oscar (*Raglan*).

Banks is a shipbuilder who wants to build a new cargo ship but is unable to convince his board of directors to back the project. Undaunted, he begins construction with his own money, although it means having to deal with a competitor who would like to force him out of business. When his own money runs out, he forges the signature of the chairman of the board on a check and goes to jail, but his ship is launched. Superficially not terribly interesting, but patient audiences will be rewarded with an intriguing character drama. Though one of Powell's early efforts, he is already showing his talent.

p, Jerome Jackson; d, Michael Powell; w, L. duGarde Peach (based on a story by Powell, Jackson); ph, Leslie Rowson; art d, Alfred Junge.

Drama   (PR:A   MPAA:NR)

STRIKE IT RICH*   (1933, Brit.) 72m BL bw

George Gee (*Eddie Smart*), Gina Malo (*Mary*), Davy Burnaby (*Humphrey Wells*), Betty Astell (*Janet Wells*), Ernest Sefton (*Sankey*), Cyril Raymond (*Slaughter*), Wilfrid Lawson (*Raikes*), Hal Walters, Ethel Warwick.

Absurd farce about a wimpy clerk in a firm that specializes in hair restoration who has a turn-around in his character after a meeting with a phrenologist (someone who studies human character by the shape of the skull). Gee, the clerk, invests in nutmeg, and then becomes head of the firm. Dumb subject unfolds into 72 minutes of pure agony.

p, Herbert Smith; d, Leslie Hiscott; w, Michael Barringer.

Comedy   (PR:A   MPAA:NR)

STRIKE IT RICH**   (1948) 81m AA bw

Rod Cameron (*Duke Massey*), Bonita Granville (*Julie Brady*), Don Castle (*Tex Warren*), Stuart Erwin (*Delbert Lane*), Lloyd Corrigan (*Matt Brady*), Ellen Corby (*Mrs. Harkins*), Emory Parnell (*Carlton*), Harry Tyler (*Pap Jonathan*), Virginia Dale (*Mabel*), William Haade (*Bull*), Edward Gargan (*Mack*), Robert Dudley (*Postmaster*).

Set in the late 1920s and early 1930s, this story has its humorous moments about oil wildcatters, some of whom strike it rich. It focuses on a group of three who like to use their fists at a moment's notice, guzzle booze, or go after oil with a vengeance. Cameron, one of the trio, doesn't like the way they do things, so he leaves with his new wife Granville. Right after he leaves, his former partners hit it big and are instantly rich men. Broke, the conniving Cameron finds a law forcing his past buddies to share their wealth. This doesn't sit well with Granville, so she leaves him until he changes his ways. In the end, he helps another independent group of oil wildcatters.

p, Jack Wrather; d, Lesley Selander; w, Francis Rosenwald; ph, Henry Sharp; m, Rudy Schrager; ed, William Ziegler; md, David Chudnow; art d, Lewis H. Creber, Gano Chittenden; set d, Earl Woodin; cos, Jack Perkins; makeup, Don Cash.

Comedy   (PR:A   MPAA:NR)

STRIKE ME DEADLY   (SEE: CRAWLING HAND, THE, 1963)

STRIKE ME PINK***   (1936) 99m UA bw

Eddie Cantor (*Eddie Pink*), Ethel Merman (*Joyce Lenox*), Sally Eilers (*Claribel Hayes*), Parkyakarkus [Harry Einstein] (*Harry Parke*), William Frawley (*Copple*), Helen Lowell (*Ma Carson*), Gordon Jones (*Butch Carson*), Brian Donlevy (*Vance*), Jack LaRue (*Thrust*), Sunnie O'Dea (*Sunnie*), Rita Rio [Dona Drake] (*Rita*), Edward Brophy (*Killer*), Sidney H. Fields (*Chorley*), Don Brodie (*Marsh*), Charles McAvoy (*Selby*), Stanley Blystone (*Miller*), Duke York (*Smiley*), Charles Wilson (*Hardin*), Clyde Hagar (*Pitchman*), The 1936 Goldwyn Girls (*Gail Sheridan, Vicki Vann, Kay Hughes, Elaine Johnson*), Eugenia [Jinx] Falkenberg, Gail Goodson, Eleanor Huntley, Dorothy Dugan, Marcia Sweet, Mary Gwynne, Charlotte Russell, Blanca Vischer, Germaine Greer [Joan Barclay], Anya Taranda, Monte Vandergrift, Fred Kohler, Jr, Nick Lukats, Howard Christie, Wade Boteler, Tammany Young, Lee Phelps, Robert E. Homans, Harry C. Bradley, The Flying Kitchens.

This was the last of five films Cantor did for Samuel Goldwyn and like all the others, this contained the Cantor trademarks: brisk songs, decent dialog, and plenty of writers to make it go. Cantor is a shy little tailor who after reading the book *Man or Mouse: What Are You?*, changes his ways and becomes a big shot around town by running an amusement park. The mob wants part of the action because the park contains slot machines, but Cantor, along with the authorities, provides some laughs, gets the crooks arrested, and resumes his now successful career. Of the four songs, three featured Merman. Songs included: "The Lady Dances," "Shake it Off With Rhythm," "You Have Me High, You Have Me Low," "Calabash Pipe."

P, Sam Goldwyn; d, Norman Taurog; w, Frank Butler, Walter DeLeon, Francis Martin, Philip Rapp (based on the novel *Dreamland* by Clarence Buddington Kelland); ph, Gregg Toland, Merritt Gerstad, Ray Binger; m, Harold Arlen; ed, Sherman Todd; md, Alfred Newman; art d, Richard Day; cos, Omar Kiam; ch, Robert Alton; m/l, Arlen, Lew Brown.

Musical   **(PR:A   MPAA:NR)**

STRIKE UP THE BAND*½   (1940) 120m MGM bw

Mickey Rooney (*Jimmy Connors*), Judy Garland (*Mary Holden*), Paul Whiteman and Orchestra (*Themselves*), June Preisser (*Barbara Frances Morgan*), William Tracy (*Phillip Turner*), Ann Shoemaker (*Mrs. Connors*), Larry Nunn (*Willie Brewster*), George Lessey (*Mr. Morgan*), Francis Pierlot (*Mr. Judd*), Harry McCrillis (*Booper Barton*), Margaret Early (*Annie*), Sarah Edwards (*Miss Hodges*), Elliot Carpenter (*Henry*), Virginia Brissac (*Mrs. May Holden*), Howard Hickman (*The Doctor*), Virginia Sale (*Music Teacher*), Milton Kibbee (*Mr. Holden*), Mickey Martin, Charles Smith (*Boys*), Sherrie Overton, Margareet Marquis, Maxine Cook (*Girls*), Phil Silvers (*Pitch Man*), Billy Wayne (*Clown*), Joe Devlin (*Attendant*), Don Castle (*Charlie*), Enid Bennett (*Mrs. Morgan*), Helen Jerome Eddy (*Mrs. Brewster*), Harlan Briggs (*Doctor*), Dick Allen (*Policeman*), Jimmie Lucas, Jack Albertson (*Barkers*), Earle Hodgins (*Hammer Concessionaire*), Harry Harvey (*Shooting Gallery Concessionaire*), Jack Baxley (*Ice Cream Concessionaire*), Harry Lash, Jack Kenny (*Hot Dog Concessionaires*), Roland Got (*House Boy*), Lowden Adams (*Butler*), Margaret Seddon, Margaret McWade (*Old Ladies*), Louise LaPlanche, Lois James, Helen Seamon, Mary Jo Ellis, Naida Reynolds, Linda Johnson, Wallace Musselwhite, Myron Speth, Douglas Wilson, Sidney Miller, Vendell Darr (*Students*), Jack Mulhall, Henry Roquemore (*Men*), Leonard Sues (*Trumpet Player*).

In 1928, Edgar Selwyn produced a Broadway show by George S. Kaufman and Morrie Ryskind with music by George and Ira Gershwin. The name of the hit musical was "Strike Up the Band." Any similarity between that play and this picture is impossible to discern, other than the title and the title song. After Rooney and Garland had such a hit with BABES IN ARMS, the studio sought a follow-up and this was the answer. Rooney was the leading box-office star of 1939, 1940, and 1941 and was riding the crest of his exuberant talents. He'd already been identified as Andy Hardy, won a special Oscar for BOYS TOWN, and, at the age of 20, Brooklyn-born Joe Yule, Jr., had already been in movies 14 years, having made his debut as a midget in the featurette NOT TO BE TRUSTED. Garland was another child star, slightly younger than Rooney, but already tired of the movies and rebelling against the long hours and hard work and lack of any real childhood other than appearing before the cameras. Berkeley was again called upon to direct and made the picture look 10 times more expensive than the budget allowed by dint of imaginative camera angles, superb choreography, and, of course, the protean talents of Rooney, who could literally do anything, and in this movie, he did. Rooney and Garland are attending Riverwood High where she works in the library after school and he spends his off-hours practicing his drums. Rooney wants to be the man who smacks the skins in a dance band and his widowed mother, Shoemaker, yearns for her son to drop the drumsticks and pick up the scalpel for a career behind the surgical mask. Rooney and Shoemaker have a scene wherein he carefully explains the meaning of music in his life (and what could have been a mawkish moment works, as Rooney is so sincere that we can believe he means what he says) and his doting mother backs off and gives her blessing to his desires. Rooney gets a bunch of his pals together ("Hey, Kids! Let's start a band!") to form an orchestra. (The fact that each of them plays an instrument that complements the other is one of those Hollywood conveni-

ences that no one questions. The truth is that there would have been 12 drummers and one violinist.) Preisser is to be the Jo Stafford out front. Rooney has a method to his musical madness because he knows the big band "King of Jazz" Paul Whiteman is sponsoring a contest to determine the best high school band in the land. Rooney thinks they can win the prize and sets to serious rehearsals. They need about $200 to take the train to Chicago where the contest is being held so they take a job at a dance, then Rooney and the others do a skit at a local fraternal organization. Garland would like to be the band's singer but Lessey, Preisser's wealthy father, lurks in the background, and if they need any money, he will probably supply it. Garland sticks by Rooney through it all and just when they are about to leave for Chicago, one of the boys falls ill. It's Nunn and he needs an operation right away or they can play his coda. Since his mother, Eddy, doesn't have any money, Rooney does the right thing and gives her the prized $200 to cover the trip. The band understands his motivation and all looks lost until Whiteman and his band just happen to come to the town to play at a private function. Rooney and his gang sneak into the party, set themselves up on the bandstand while Whiteman and the others are off-stage, and when the maestro walks in, he's greeted by the swinging sounds of Rooney at the drums and the others at their stations. Whiteman is impressed and lends them the money to get to the Windy City for the contest. The band gets there, wins the contest, and Rooney is tapped for a job as drummer with another band. He is ambitious and energetic but he is also loyal and, after a chat with Whiteman, Rooney decides to stick with the guys and ride their comet all the way. Some excellent touches abound. In a scene between Rooney and Garland, he's trying to explain an idea he has for a number and uses a bowl of fruit to illustrate. The fruit becomes little puppet models (created by Henry Rox) that are animated (by George Pal) and go into "Do the Conga" (written by Roger Edens, Freed's veteran right-hand man). Edens also wrote "Drummer Boy," "Nell Of New Rochelle" (a parody of an old-time melodrama), and collaborated with producer Freed on "Our Love Affair." Other songs include: "Sing, Sing, Sing" (Louis Prima), "Heaven Will Protect the Working Girl" (A. Baldwin Sloane, Edgar Smith), "I Just Can't Make My Eyes Behave" (Gus Edwards, Will Cobb), "The Curse of an Aching Heart" (Al Piantadosi, Henry Fink), "The Sidewalks of New York "(James Blake, Charles Lawlor), "Over the Waves" (Juventino Rosas), "The Light Cavalry Overture" (Franz von Suppe), "Walking Down Broadway" (arranged by Edens), with Ray Henderson's "Five Foot Two, Eyes Of Blue" and Charles K. Harris's "After The Ball" as background music. The idea for the fruit-puppets was allegedly supplied by director Vincente Minnelli, who married Garland about five years after. Edens wrote a parody of "I Ain't Got Nobody" for Garland to sing in which she decries the fact that Juliet had Romeo and studio boss Mayer has Leo the Lion. The movie falls down in act two and there may be just a little too much razzle-dazzle with a few spectacular numbers that go on too long. Rooney was a perfectionist and it shows. He plays drums, xylophone, dances, sings, tosses off quips, and handles the drama with ease. Garland is more ad-libby and had to be coerced into rehearsing, so when they were both on screen, it became evident which of the two was better prepared and Rooney gets the lion's share of screen time. In small roles, note Phil Silvers as a pitch man and another burlesque comic, Jack Albertson, in what may have been his debut. It wasn't until 1954 when he again teamed with Silvers in TOP BANANA. The movie made nothing but money.

p, Arthur Freed; d, Busby Berkeley; w, John Monks, Jr., Fred Finklehoffe (uncredited, Herbert Fields, Kay Van Riper); ph, Ray June; ed, Ben Lewis; md, Georgie Stoll; art d, Cedric Gibbons, John S. Detlie; set d, Edwin B. Willis; cos, Dolly Tree, Gile Steele; makeup, Jack Dawn.

Musical/Comedy   **Cas.**   **(PR:AAA   MPAA:NR)**

STRIKERS, THE   (SEE: ORGANIZER, THE, 1964, Fr./Ital./Yugo.)

STRIP, THE***   (1951) 85m MGM bw

Mickey Rooney (*Stanley Maxton*), Sally Forrest (*Jane Tafford*), William Demarest (*Fluff*), James Craig (*Delwyn "Sonny" Johnson*), Kay Brown (*Edna*), Louis Armstrong and Band (*Band*), Tommy Rettig (*Artie*), Tom Powers (*Detective Bonnabel*), Jonathan Cott (*Behr*), Tommy Farrell (*Boynton*), Myrna Dell (*Paulette Ardrey*), Jacqueline Fontaine (*Frieda*), Vic Damone, Monica Lewis, Jack Teagarden (*Singers*), Robert Foulk, John McGuire, Russell Trent, Fred Graham, Don Haggerty, William Tannen (*Deputies*), Frank Hyers (*Sergeant*), John Maxwell, Sherry Hall, Tom Quinn (*Doctors*), Fred Datig, Jr, Dan Foster, Jeff Richards (*GI's*), Dolores Castle, Joyce Jameson (*Girls*), Art Lewis (*Sam*), Samuel London (*Fred*), Larry Hudson, Roger Moore, Sam Finn, Tay Dunne, Bert Davidson, Don Kerr, Sig Frohlich (*Clerks in Bookie Joint*), Helen Spring (*Elderly Secretary*), Alex Frazer (*Horticulturist*), Lester Dorr (*Police Surgeon*), Robert Malcolm (*Deputy*), Earle Hodgins (*Technician*), Bette Arlen, Betty Jane Howarth (*Charleston Dancers*), Carl Saxe, Joel Allen (*Two Boy Friends*), Wilson Wood (*Patron*), Dee Turnell, Carmen Clifford, Ward Ellis, Jack Regas, Leo Scott, Bert May (*Specialty Dancers*).

The title of this low-budget crime-musical has nothing to do with an ecdysiast. Rather, it refers to an area in Los Angeles that is not part of the city environs. It's run by the county and thus subject to a different police force and fire department. The taxes are structured differently and there are some other minor changes. It runs along Sunset Boulevard and about a mile south but it's the famed Boulevard that's known as "the Sunset Strip" that was ballyhooed in the Warner Bros. TV series, "77 Sunset Strip," a totally fictitious address. Rooney is a drummer who comes home from a Korean stint and seeks employment slapping the snare. When he can't find a job right away, he gets involved with Craig, a heavy Hollywood bookmaker, and begins making a few bucks in the business. Then he meets Forrest, who works as a dancer-cigarette girl in the Demarest-owned nightclub. Forrest wants to be an actress, and since Craig does business with some of the movie studio executives, Rooney generously (but unwisely) introduces the two. Rooney has had it with booking bets and gets a job drumming at Demarest's club. Craig is not content to help a young actress; he wants more of her for himself, and when Rooney sees Craig moving in on the woman he loves, he states his displeasure and is rewarded by a thrashing. Forrest steps in to protect Rooney and shoots and kills Craig and is mortally wounded herself. She's still alive and Rooney tries to protect her by claiming that he killed Craig, but the cops are hip to the truth. When Forrest gives up the ghost, Rooney tells the truth and is released to go back to playing jazz, an unhappy man who lost the one woman he ever cared for. It's a typical "later" Rooney part, the little guy who gets into trouble not of his own accord and manages to barely survive. He'd done it several times and always managed to bring a fresh feeling to the role, no matter how stale the material. In between the crime beats, there are many musical scenes with cameos by Vic Damone, Monica Lewis (who married Universal Studios biggie Jennings Lang), Louis Armstrong, Jack Teagarden, and many others. Tunes from various writers included: "Ain't Misbehavin'" (by Fats Waller, Andy Razaf, performed by Rooney, Armstrong), "Basin Street Blues" (Spencer Williams, performed by Armstrong, Teagarden), "Shadrack" (Robert MacGimsey, performed by Armstrong), "Rose Room" (Art Hickman, Harry Williams, performed by Armstrong), "La Bota" (Charles Wolcott, Haven Gillespie II, sung by Lewis), "Don't Blame Me" (Jimmy McHugh, Dorothy Fields, sung by Damone), and the 1935 hit "Give Me a Kiss to Build a Dream On" (Harry Ruby, Oscar Hammerstein II, Bert Kalmar, performed by Armstrong and reprised often). Rooney played his own drums and showed that he could sit behind a set of traps with ability. The whole picture is told in flashback from the moment when Craig's dead body is discovered and Forrest is breathing her last. Putting it into flashback form made no sense and eased any edge-of-the-seat suspense that might have been engendered had they opted for a straight-line narrative.

p, Joe Pasternak, d, Leslie Kardos; w, Allen Rivkin; ph, Robert Surtees; m, Georgie Stoll; ed, Albert Akst; art d, Cedric Gibbons, Leonid Vasian; set d, Edwin B. Willis, Alfred E. Spencer; cos, Helen Rose; spec eff, A. Arnold Gillespie, Warren Newcombe; ch, Nick Castle; makeup, William Tuttle.

Crime/Musical   **(PR:C   MPAA:NR)**

STRIP-TEASE   (SEE: SWEET SKIN, 1965, Fr./Ital.)

STRIP TEASE MURDER*   (1961, Brit.) 66m Danziger/PAR bw

John Hewer (*Bert Black*), Ann Lynn (*Rita*), Jean Muir (*Diana*), Kenneth J. Warren (*Branco*), Carl Duering (*Rocco*), Michael Peake (*Martin*), Wanda Hudson (*Angelina*), Leon Cortez (*Lou*).

Lurid low-budget exploitation item has Hewer a strip-club operator who turns sleuth when his girl friend is electrocuted for a crime she didn't commit. Sleazy fun if not taken too seriously.

p, Ralph Ingram, John Elton; d, Ernest Morris; w, Paul Tabori.

Crime   **(PR:C-O   MPAA:NR)**

STRIPES*   (1981) 106m COL c

Bill Murray (*John*), Harold Ramis (*Russell*), Warren Oates (*Sgt. Hulka*), P.J. Soles (*Stella*), Sean Young (*Louise*), John Candy (*Ox*), John Larroquette (*Capt. Stillman*), John Voldstad (*Aide*), John Diehl (*Cruiser*), Lance LeGault (*Col. Glass*), Roberta Leighton (*Anita*), Conrad Dunn (*Psycho*), Judge Reinhold (*Elmo*), Antone Pagan (*Hector*), Glenn-Michael Jones (*Leon*), Bill Lucking (*Recruiter*), Fran Ryan (*Dowager*), Joseph P. Flaherty, Nick Toth (*Guards*), Dave Thomas (*Master of Ceremonies*), Robert Klein (*Cheerleader*), Robert J. Wilke (*Gen. Barnicke*), Lois Areno (*Stillman's Girl Friend*), Samuel Briggs (*Corporal*), Joseph X. Flaherty (*Sgt. Crocker*), Hershel B. Harlson (*Shoeshine Man*), Timothy Busfield (*Soldier with Mortar*), Solomon Schmidt (*Store Owner*), Craig Schaefer (*Soldier Outside Motor Pool*), Arkady Rakhman (*Immigrant*), Pamela Bowman (*Cruiser's Girl*), Gino Gottarelli, Gene Scherer, Dawn Clark, Juanita Merritt, Susan Mechsner, Sue Bowser, Linda Dupree, Leslie Henderson, Gerald J. Counts, Yetim Buntsis, Semyon Veyts, Larry R. Gillette, Glen Leigh Marshall, Dale Prince, Larry Odell Lane, Joyce D. Helmus, David A. Mullins, Bruce E. Ellis, David D. Platko, Phillip A. Urbansky, William R. Sykes, Bill Paxton, J.A. Crawford, Michael Flynn, Norman Mont-Eton, Mark S. Markowicz, Jeff Viola, Robert Dulaine.

An often funny satire of the peacetime Army that is just as often tasteless. That lack of taste didn't hurt the box office one whit as it proved to be a large hit with the younger audiences, mostly due to Murray's personal charm and increasingly larger following. It's the male side of PRIVATE BENJAMIN as Murray, a loser in life, decides to believe the glamorous ads and commercials put forth by the advertising agencies that handle the U.S. Army, and joins up, with buddy Ramis along for the ride. The two of them are a modern

Willie and Joe (BACK AT THE FRONT (1952)) who soon learn that they should never trust advertising. Oates is the tough drill sergeant at basic training, a man who makes Lou Gossett (from AN OFFICER AND A GENTLEMAN) look like Bambi. The platoon in which Ramis and Murray serve is what you might expect: a collection of misfits which includes rotund Candy, who joined the Army because he thought it would help him lose weight. There's a trip to Italy, the robbery of an armored vehicle (they want to take their sweethearts, Soles and Young, into West Germany for some fun and games), a mistaken alarm that almost sets off a war when the guys are told to cross the border into communist Czechoslavakia, a mud-wrestling match between Candy and a quintet of topless waitresses, and, the best sequence, a close-order drill by the incorrigible platoon when they finally get it all together and are whipped into shape by Murray, through the use of rock 'n' roll rhythms. The Army does not come out looking bad and the result is a warm feeling as you stroll out of the theater. Army life has often been satirized better, and although there are many laughs here, there are even more to be found in any given rerun of Phil Silvers' show "You'll Never Get Rich." Many of TV's "Second City" actors appear, including Ramis, Candy, Flaherty, and Thomas. In a small role, note Judge Reinhold, who went on to great acclaim in BEVERLY HILLS COP. Rough language, nudity, and a general lack of decorum make this the kind of film kids will love to see, but probably shouldn't.

p, Ivan Reitman, Dan Goldberg, d, Reitman; w, Len Blum, Goldberg; Harold Ramis; ph, Bill Butler (Metrocolor); m, Elmer Bernstein; ed, Eva Ruggiero, Michael Luciano, Harry Keller; prod d, James H. Spencer; cos, Richard Bruno; ch, Ronn Forella, Arthur Goldweit.

Comedy   **Cas.**   **(PR:O   MPAA:R)**

STRIPPER, THE* (1963) 95m FOX bw (GB: WOMAN OF SUMMER)

Joanne Woodward (*Lila Green*), Richard Beymer (*Kenny Baird*), Claire Trevor (*Helen Baird*), Carol Lynley (*Miriam Caswell*), Robert Webber (*Ricky Powers*), Louis Nye (*Ronnie Cavendish*), Gypsy Rose Lee (*Mme. Olga*), Michael J. Pollard (*Jelly*), Sondra Kerr (*Edwina*), Susan Brown (*Mrs. Mulvaney*), Marlene De Lamater (*Sandra Mulvaney*), Gary Pagett (*Dizzy*), Ralph Lee (*Sonny*), Bing Russell (*Mr. Mulvaney*).

Jerry Wald's swan song was not a proper way to end such an illustrious career. This was a mess, although it had several good creative talents behind it. William Inge's 1959 play "A Loss of Roses" was a flop so one can only question why it was acquired as a motion picture property. Supposedly written for Marilyn Monroe, it's the familiar Kansas territory of Inge's background and perhaps they felt that Monroe might be too spectacular for the prairie, even after her success in the film version of Inge's "Bus Stop." Inge must have liked the word "bus," for he used it again in his original screenplay BUS RILEY'S BACK IN TOWN, although he used the pseudonym of William Gage for that. Woodward is the stripper, a woman who couldn't make it in movies and is now working in a traveling troupe as a dancer. Her lover and the show's manager is Webber. The group arrives in the tiny Kansas town where Woodward spent some of her formative years and Webber uses the opportunity to skip out on her with all of the money from the group. Stranded Woodward moves in with old friend Trevor, a widow with a 19-year-old son, Beymer. It isn't long before Beymer is casting moon-eyes at Woodward, even though she's older and far wiser than he is. Beymer is seeing Lynley but calls a halt to their relationship and rashly proposes marriage to Woodward. She likes the attention but, deep inside, knows that it's an infatuation, little more. Webber comes back to the town with an offer for Woodward to work. He's booked a stag show and needs a stripper. Will she do it? Despite misgivings, she does and Beymer is at the show. He is at once repelled and attracted by what he sees. He can't bear the thought of the woman he thinks he loves being subjected to the lecherous leers of the men who watch her, so he again asks for her hand. She refuses once more and decides that it's time for her to take stock of herself and quit show business and settle down. Woodward's character is pathetic, the script is anemic and smacks of TEA AND SYMPATHY in the older woman-young man situation (although there is no question about Beymer's male identity), and the entire picture lacks conviction. Beymer is better than his role and so is Lynley. Woodward looks foolish in her bouffant hair style that is years out of sync. Louis Nye and Gypsy Rose Lee do well with what little humor they are given and Michael J. Pollard has some good moments. The working titles for this film were "A Woman in July" and "Celebration."

p, Jerry Wald; d, Franklin J. Schaffner; w, Meade Roberts (based on the play "A Loss of Roses" by William Inge); ph, Ellsworth Fredricks (CinemaScope); m, Jerry Goldsmith; ed, Robert Simpson; art d, Jack Martin Smith, Walter M. Simonds; set d, Walter M. Scott, Stuart A. Reiss, Norman Rockett; cos, Travilla; ch, Alex Romero; makeup, Ben Nye.

Drama   **(PR:O   MPAA:NR)**

STRIPTEASE LADY   (SEE: LADY OF BURLESQUE, 1943)

STROKER ACE zero   (1983) 96m UNIV/WB c

Burt Reynolds (*Stroker Ace*), Ned Beatty (*Clyde Torkle*), Jim Nabors (*Lugs*), Parker Stevenson (*Aubrey James*), Loni Anderson (*Pembrook Feeney*), John Byner (*Doc Seegle*), Frank O. Hill (*Dad Seegle*), Cassandra Peterson (*Girl with Lugs*), Bubba Smith (*Arnold*), Warren Stevens (*Jim Catty*), Alfie Wise (*Charlie*), Jim Lewis (*Crew Chief*), Jonathan Williams (*Man*), Donna Fowler (*Reporter*), Hunter Bruce (*Little Ace*), Cary Guffey (*Little Doc*), Linda Vaughn (*Miss Hurst Shifter*), Debbie Casperson (*Miss Leonard Fuel*), Valerie Mitchell (*Miss Winston*), Madonna Christian (*Girl in Bar*), Terri Ann Bantle (*Autograph Seeker*), B. J. France (*Hotel Guest*), Chip Kaye, Kevin McCorkle (*Customers*), Terry Beaver (*Director*), Neil Bonnett, Dale Earnhardt, Harry Gant, Terry Labonte, Benny Parsons, Kyle Petty, Tim Richmond, Ricky Rudd, Cale Yarborough (*Nascar Drivers*), Bill Connell, Bill Dollar, Chris Economaki, David Hobbs, Ken Squier (*Announcers*), Harold Kinder, Ernie Moore (*Flagmen*), Bill Brodrick (*Winner's Circle Coordinator*), Victor Langdon, Phil Mattingly (*Plainclothesmen*), Wallace Merck (*Rednecks*), Bill D. Brown (*Radio Announcer*), Carl Hill (*Nascar Official*), Charles E. Brown (*Barker*).

Reynolds hits new lows as he mugs his way through this film playing a race car driver who's under the control of chicken-franchise owner Beatty. His love interest is Anderson, playing a squeaky-clean virgin. Reynolds also teams up with old pal Hal Needham, in a script filled with "good ol' boy" humor and car crackups.

p, Hank Moonjean; d, Hal Needham; w, Needham, Hugh Wilson (based on the novel *Stand On It* by William Neely, Robert K. Ottum); ph, Nick McLean (Technicolor); m, Al Capps; ed, Carl Kress, William Gordean; art d, Paul Peters; cos, Norman Salling.

Comedy   Cas.   (PR:C MPAA:PG)

STROMBOLI**   (1950, Ital.) 81m Be-Ro-RKO bw

Ingrid Bergman (*Karin Bjorsen*), Mario Vitale (*Antonio*), Renzo Cesana (*The Priest*), Mario Sponza (*The Lighthouse Keeper*).

The off-screen activities of the star and the director were far more interesting than this Neo-Realistic picture. Rossellini had made some wonderful movies with OPEN CITY and PAISAN, both of which he shot "on the run," in that he rewrote the scripts as he did the films. It didn't work here. Bergman had been married to Dr. Peter Lindstrom (father of newswoman Pia Lindstrom), and when she met the director, sparks flew and they began a steamy love affair that was news across the world. Dr. Lindstrom tried to save his marriage by airplaning to Italy but it was too late. He insulted the director and would not give Bergman a divorce. She was pregnant, and, after she gave birth, Lindstrom finally capitulated. But there was a groundswell of anger against Bergman's "wanton ways" and women's groups began to boycott the picture. Contrast that to 1986, when Amy Irving gave birth to Steven Spielberg's child and Tatum O'Neal had a baby by tennis star John McEnroe and it barely rated a mention on "Entertainment Tonight." The movie was a giant travelog of the island of Stromboli with a bit of sex and drama thrown in whenever the audience got tired of watching sunsets over the mountains. Bergman is a Czechoslavakian refugee who is in a displaced person's camp in Italy. She can't bear the life there so, in order to escape, she marries Vitale, a discharged soldier, and he brings her to his home island of Stromboli, a speck in the Tyrrhenian Sea. Life is hard and bleak on the island and Bergman does her best to adjust but it's a chore. The people of Stromboli distrust newcomers and the other women pay little attention to Bergman's attempts to be friendly. Desperate for someone to talk with, she approaches Cesana, the parish priest, but even he is aloof and only offers her sayings from the Bible and empty phrases about keeping her faith strong. Vitale is a fisherman and out to sea often so she hungers for companionship. She eventually finds Sponza, a lighthouse keeper who is stuck at his post, and the two become friends. Vitale wishes she would be like the Strombolian women, eager to please their men and asking nothing but an occasional smile in return. Vitale thinks that Bergman and Sponza may be more than friends and beats her for his imaginary fears. Then, in order to keep her locked up, he nails boards to the windows of their small house. Bergman learns she is expecting and the thought of staying on this island and having many babies with Vitale is too horrendous to imagine, so she plans to escape. With Sponza aiding her, she flees the house and makes her way up the side of the mountain of Stromboli, an active volcano. Up there, she is trapped by a lava flow and the fumes render her unconscious. When she awakens, she seems to have taken some sort of energy from the volcano and descends to the village where she thinks she can make a go of her life and her marriage. The picture was heavily edited for the U.S. market and there were many untied plot points. Alfred Werker took the more than 40 cans of film and tried to prune it to a palatable length but he could only snip, not effect miracles. The result is a boring attempt at "verismo" (sort of like "truth" in Italian) that looks as though it was ad-libbed. Bergman had two children by Rossellini, the daughter being Isabella, who is now an actress. Bergman's penchant for affairs with her co-stars has been documented often. This was, perhaps, the first with a director.

p&d, Roberto Rossellini; w, Rossellini, Art Cohn, Renzo Cesana, Sergio Amedei, C.P. Callegari; ph, Otello Martelli; m, Renzo Rossellini; ed, Roland Gross, Jolanda Benvenuti [uncredited, Alfred Werker, U.S. version]; md, C.

Bakaleinikoff.

Drama   Cas.   (PR:C-O MPAA:NR)

STRONGER SEX, THE**   (1931, Brit.) 80m Gainsborough/Ideal bw

Colin Clive (*Warren Barrington*), Adrianne Allen (*Mary Thorpe*), Gordon Harker (*Parker*), Martin Lewis (*John Brent*), Renee Clama (*Joan Merivale*), Elsa Lanchester (*Thompson*).

Clive's first film after FRANKENSTEIN has him married to a cuckolding wife, then sacrificing his own life to save his wife's lover from a mine disaster. Lanchester and Clive would be together again four years later when he would bring her to screeching life in THE BRIDE OF FRANKENSTEIN.

p, Michael Balcon; d&w, V. Gareth Gundrey (based on a play by J. Valentine); ph, William Shenton.

Drama   (PR:A MPAA:NR)

STRONGER THAN DESIRE*½   (1939) 80m MGM bw

Virginia Bruce (*Elizabeth Flagg*), Walter Pidgeon (*Tyler Flagg*), Lee Bowman (*Michael McLain*), Ann Dvorak (*Eva McLain*), Ilka Chase (*Jo Brennan*), Rita Johnson (*Barbara Winter*), Richard Lane (*Jerry Brody*), Ann Todd (*Susan Flagg*), Paul Stanton (*Assistant District Attorney Galway*), Ferike Boros (*Mrs. D'Amoro*), Donald Douglas (*Clark*), Thomas Jackson (*Thompson*), John Hamilton (*Judge*), Margaret Bert (*Nursemaid*), Leonard Carey (*Albert*), Barbara Bedford (*Miss Watson*), Lester Dorr, Reed Hadley, Tom Neal, Phil Tead, Jack Hatfield (*Reporters*), Mariska Aldrich (*Matron*).

Poor script about a housewife bored with life in the remake of EVELYN PRENTICE. Bruce's husband is a workaholic so she turns to Bowman for fun. He in turn blackmails her and in a fight she shoots him. But it is his wife who is found with the weapon and she is up for the rap. Bruce gets her husband to defend the woman and in the end both confess to the crime. Pidgeon handles the courtroom scenes well, getting his own wife in the end to confess to the crime.

p, John W. Considine, Jr.; d, Leslie Fenton; w, David Hartz, William Ludwig (based on the novel *Evelyn Prentice* by W.E. Woodward); ph, William Daniels; ed, W. Donn Hayes.

Drama   (PR:A MPAA:NR)

STRONGER THAN FEAR   (SEE: EDGE OF DOOM, 1950)

STRONGER THAN THE SUN**   (1980, Brit.) 101m BBC c

Francesca Annis (*Kate*), Tom Bell (*Alan*).

Timely film deals with the dangerous specter of the nuclear age and has some striking resemblance to the American film SILKWOOD that starred Meryl Streep and Cher. Annis suspects a radioactive leak at the Yorkshire plant where she works. Her boy friend first tells her to go public with her information, but then pulls out when the pressure gets too intense. When he does, Annis starts going off the deep end as no one will believe her story and madness finally consumes her. This film was directed by Michael Apted who also directed the fine COAL MINER'S DAUGHTER.

p, Margaret Matheson; d, Michael Apted; w, Stephen Poliakoff; ph, Elmer Cossey; m, Howard Blake; ed, David Martin; cos, Amy Roberts.

Drama   (PR:A MPAA:NR)

STRONGEST MAN IN THE WORLD, THE***   (1975) 92m WD/BV c

Kurt Russell (*Dexter*), Joe Flynn (*Dean Higgins*), Eve Arden (*Harriet*), Cesar Romero (*A.J. Arno*), Phil Silvers (*Krinkle*), Dick Van Patten (*Harry*), Harold Gould (*Dietz*), Michael McGreevey (*Schuyler*), Dick Bakalyan (*Cookie*), William Schallert (*Quigley*), Benson Fong (*Ah Fong*), James Gregory (*Chief Blair*).

Disney and producer Bill Anderson do it again at the famed Medfield campus. This time some of the students discover a formula to give humans super strength. It takes a poke at the hype put out by cereal companies and with the school in financial trouble, Flynn gives the formula to one company. The school and its weightlifting team compete against another school sponsored by the No. 1 cereal company that has relied on slick advertising to reach its lofty position. Russell mistakenly eats the cereal and gains the super strength needed to bring his school to victory. This was the third in a trilogy that included *THE COMPUTER WORE TENNIS SHOES* and *NOW YOU SEE HIM AND NOW YOU DON'T* (1972). It was also the last film by Flynn who passed away after the picture was completed.

p, Bill Anderson; d, Vincent McEveety; w, Herman Groves, Joseph L. McEveety; ph, Andrew Jackson (Technicolor); m, Robert F. Brunner; ed, Cotton Warburton; art d, John B. Mansbridge, Jack Senter; cos, Chuck Keehne.

Comedy   Cas.   (PR:A MPAA:G)

STRONGHOLD** (1952, Mex.) 72m Producionne Mexico/Lippert bw

Veronica Lake *(Mary Stevens)*, Zachary Scott *(Don Miguel Navarro)*, Arturo de Cordova *(Don Pedro Alvarez)*, Rita Lacedo, Alfonso Bedoya, Yadiro Jiminez, Fanny Schiller, Gilberto Gonzalez, Carlos Muzquiz, Frederick A. Mack, Rock Galbin, Gustavo Rojo, Irene Ajay, Felipe de Alba.

Thin story line and overly talky script hinder any attempt at drama in this film about the Mexican revolution against Emperor Maximillian. After Lake and her mother leave the U.S. to visit the silver mines they own in Mexico, they are kidnaped by a band of thieves led by aristocrat de Cordova. Though Lake initially tries to protect her silver interests, she falls in love with de Cordova and begins to sympathize with his efforts to fight for the Mexican peasants' cause. Mine overseer Scott, in an attempt to stop de Cordova, blows up a dam, which floods the mines and forces the revolutionaries to surface. De Cordova is set to be executed, but the peasants come to his rescue.

p, Olallo Rubio, Jr.; d, Steve Sekely; w, Wells Root; ph, Stanley Cortez; ed, Charles L. Kimball; md, Antonio Diaz Conde.

Drama   **(PR:A   MPAA:NR)**

STRONGROOM** (1962, Brit.) 80m Theatrecraft/Union bw

Derren Nesbitt *(Griff)*, Colin Gordon *(Mr. Spencer)*, Ann Lynn *(Rose Taylor)*, Keith Faulkner *(Len)*, Morgan Sheppard *(Alec)*, John Chappell *(John Musgrove)*, Hilda Fenemore, Diana Chesney *(Charladies)*, Ian Colin *(Creighton)*, Kevin Stoney *(Police Sergeant)*, Duncan Lewis *(Mortuary Attendant)*, Lockwood West *(Police Inspector)*, Pamela Conway *(Secretary)*, Colin Tapley *(Haynes)*, John Dearth *(Hopkins)*, Frank Seton *(Gatekeeper)*, Anna Turner *(Mrs. Snape)*, Keith Campbell *(Snape)*, Duncan McIntyre *(Duty Sergeant)*, Jack Stewart *(Sgt. McIntyre)*, Colin Rix *(P.C. Harper)*, Michael Peake *(Inspector Gregg)*.

A suspenseful, taut crime drama, with a cast of unknowns, is about three small-time crooks who decide to rob a bank during an Easter holiday. They force bank director Gordon and clerk Lynn into an airtight vault and leave them to suffocate. To avoid facing a murder rap, the crooks decide to call the cops and leave the keys nearby. But while on the way to call the police, Sheppard is killed in a car accident. Gordon and Lynn are drawn to one another. Nesbitt and Faulker race back and try to free the pair, but they are caught by police, and Lynn is found dead.

p, Guido Coen; d, Vernon Sewell; w, Richard Harris, Max Marquis (based on an idea by Harris); ph, Basil Emmott; m, Johnny Gregory; ed, John Trumper; art d, Duncan Sutherland.

Crime Drama   **(PR:A   MPAA:NR)**

STRUGGLE, THE* (1931) 87m UA bw

Hal Skelly *(Jimmie Wilson)*, Zita Johann *(Florrie)*, Charlotte Wynters *(Nina)*, Jackson Halliday *(Nan Wilson)*, Evelyn Baldwin *(Johnnie Marshall)*, Edna Hagan *(Mary)*, Claude Cooper *(Sam)*, Arthur Lipson *(Cohen)*, Charles Richman *(Mr. Craig)*, Helen Mack *(A Catty Girl)*, Scott Moore *(A Gigolo)*, Dave Manley *(A Mill Worker)*.

One of the greatest directors who ever lifted a megaphone, David Wark Griffith, was 56 when he made this, his last movie, and it was a shame that he had to bow out with such a dud. He lived until 1948, but the stigma of this film followed him around and he never worked again. In Hollywood, you're only as good (or as bad) as your last movie, and this was one of the bad ones. While still in his thirties, Griffith made a Biograph short with a similar theme, A DRUNKARD'S REFORMATION. He'd been out of the business for a year after having done ABRAHAM LINCOLN, and when his treasurer surprised him with the news that the company had a few bucks in the till, Griffith borrowed some money from a bank, talked UA into advancing some money in return for the right to distribute, and set out to make this film. Prohibition was the rage and Griffith was against it, so he co-wrote the screenplay with Emerson and Loos that tells the story of mill worker Skelly, a man who can't get a legal drink so he takes to downing the illegal hooch. The stuff is tainted and he begins to abuse his wife, Johann, and his child. After Skelly goes through delirium tremens and seems to have kicked Demon Rum out of his life, he and his wife have an argument when she wants him to wear a silly tie and that's enough to send him back to the bottle and the ruination of his life. It's so over-the-top that it was eventually re-released as a comedy. Griffith struggled mightily with sound but the addition of voices and effects only served to harm his pictures. Made in New York, it has some good scenes in the Bronx and a few realistic moments shot in Connecticut at a mill, although most of the dialog between Skelly and Johann (a stage actress making her debut in a remarkably inept fashion) is ludicrous. From time to time, there are flashes of the old Griffith brilliance but it's a generally sad closing to a career. The money in Griffith's company came from an overpayment to the IRS which was returned a few years later. The treasurer put the cash in some stocks that weathered the market's crash and so, in 1931, when everything was cheaper than it had been a few years before, they cashed in and had enough to make the movie. Lots of inadvertent laughs, the kind no creator wants to hear when in the midst of a dramatic scene.

p&d, D.W. Griffith; w, Anita Loos, John Emerson, Griffith; ph, Joseph

Ruttenberg; ed, Barney Rogan.

Drama   **(PR:A-C   MPAA:NR)**

STRYKER* (1983, Phil.) 84m HCI International/New World c

Steve Sandor *(Stryker)*, Andria Savio *(Delha)*, William Ostrander *(Bandit)*, Michael Lane *(Kardis)*, Julie Gray *(Laurenz)*, Monique St. Pierre *(Cerce)*, Ken Metcalfe *(Trun)*, Jon Harris III *(Oiric)*, Joe Zucchero *(Bazil)*, Michael De Mesa, Catherine Schroeder, Tony Carreon, Pete Cooper, Corey Casey, Camille Ships.

Water is the sought-after commodity among post-nuclear war victims in this obvious rip-off of the popular Mad Max films. Between graphic fight scenes, the authorities are trying to decide to share the water or to keep it for themselves. When not battling, they drool over their women, including former Playboy playmate St. Pierre, who has perfected the art of standing around. The film utilizes stock documentary footage of an atomic test mushroom set off in the U.S.

p&d, Cirio H. Santiago; w, Howard R. Cohen (based on a story by Leonard Hermes); ph, Ricardo Remias (Technicolor); m, Ed Gatchalian, Susan Justin; ed, Bas Santos, Rudy Cabrales; prod d, Pol Dimalanta; art d, Arthur and Ramon Nicdao; spec eff, J.S. Domingo; makeup, Puzon, Mercador.

Science Fiction   **Cas.**   **(PR:O   MPAA:R)**

STUCK ON YOU zero (1983) 88m Troma c

Irwin Corey *(Judge Gabriel)*, Virginia Penta *(Carol)*, Mark Mikulski *(Bill)*, Albert Pia *(Artie)*, Norma Pratt *(Bill's Mother)*, Daniel Herris *(Napoleon)*, Denise Silbert *(Cavewoman)*, Eddie Brill *(Caveman)*, June Martin *(Eve)*, John Bingham *(Adam)*, Robin Burroughs *(Isabella)*, Carl Sturmer *(Columbus)*, Julie Newdow *(Pocahontas)*, Pat Tallman *(Guenevere)*, Mr. Kent *(King Arthur)*, Barbie Kielian *(Josephine)*, Louis Homyak *(Lance)*, Ben Kellman *(Indian Chief)*.

Every pathetic cliche is used in this worthless film that focuses more on bodily functions than anything else. In between belches, Corey is an angel who comes to Earth as a judge to earn his wings, a la IT'S A WONDERFUL LIFE. To do so, he must get Penta and Mikulski back together. As they stand before him, the film flashes back to the couple's happier moments.

p, Lloyd Kaufman, Michael Herz; d, Herz, Samuel Weil; w, Stuart Strutin, Warren Leight, Don Perman, Darren Kloomok, Melanie Mintz, Anthony Gittleson, Duffy Ceaser Magesis, Herz, Kaufman, Jeff Delman; ph, Kaufman (Guffanti Color); ed, Kloomok, Richard Haines; art d, Barry Shapiro; cos, Rosa Alfaro, Walter Steihl.

Comedy   **(PR:O   MPAA:R)**

STUCKEY'S LAST STAND* (1980) 92m Summer Camp/Royal Oak c

Whit Reichert *(Whit)*, Ray Anzalone *(Russ)*, Will Shaw *(Will)*, Tom Murray *(Pete)*, Richard Cosentino *(Duke)*, Marilyn Terschluse *(Billie)*, Jeanne L. Austin *(Marianne)*, John Zimmerman *(Gordon)*, Dan Dierdorf *(Angry Father)*, Pat Ball *(Angry Mother)*.

While MEATBALLS was a zany, offbeat look at summer camps, this film doesn't come close. Stuckey's is a camp for wealthy 9-year-olds run by inept counselor Anzalone and his staff. Reichert tells the story in flashback during a session with his psychiatrist. all the usual gags are tossed in, including a counselor's efforts to get in tight with Terschluse. Dialog is insipid, and actors possess limited acting ability.

p,d&w, Lawrence G. Goldfarb; ph, Anthony J. Fitzsimmons; m, Carson Whitsett; ed, Fitzsimmons, Ethan Edwards; art d, Julia Norris.

Comedy   **Cas.**   **(PR:C   MPAA:PG)**

STUD, THE** (1979, Brit.) 90m Brent Walker/Trans-American c

Joan Collins *(Fontaine Khaled)*, Oliver Tobias *(Tony Blake)*, Emma Jacobs *(Alex Khaled)*, Sue Lloyd *(Vanessa)*, Walter Gotell *(Ben Khaled)*, Mark Burns *(Leonard)*, Natalie Ogle *(Maddy)*, Felicity Buirski *(Deborah)*, Doug Fisher *(Sammy)*, Tony Allyn *(Hal)*, Peter Lukas *(Ian Thane)*, Constantin De Goguel *(Lord Newton)*, Guy Ward *(Peter)*, Minah Bird *(Molly)*, Hilda Fenemore *(Mum)*, Bernard Stone *(Dad)*, Hugh Morton *(Staton)*, Howard Nelson *(Sandro)*, Sarah Lawson *(Anne Khaled)*, Leonard Trolley *(Doctor)*, Jeremy Child *(Lawyer Scott)*, Franco De Rosa *(Franco)*, Shango Baku *(Flowers)*, Tania Rogers *(Janine)*, Michael Barrington *(Vicar)*, Rynagh O'Grady *(Meter Maid)*, Edmond Warwick *(Tailor)*, Robert Tayman *(Mario)*, Giorgio Bosso *(Chef)*.

When Collins made it big in the television series "Dynasty," everyone rushed out to get still shots from this film to use in one magazine or another. THE STUD was kept all in the family: It was based on Collins' sister Jackie's book and produced by then-husband Ron Kass. Too mild to qualify as soft-core pornography, the implausible story line also makes it of little interest to artsy types. Collins uses her sexual control over nightclub manager Tobias, who runs the club owned by her husband. If Tobias wants to keep his job, he must keep Collins and others satisfied. This first-time film by Brent Walker Film Productions was made on a budget of $1 million, most of which appears to have been spent on set design. Followed by THE BITCH, 1979.

p, Ronald S. Kass; d, Quentin Masters; w, Jackie Collins, Dave Humphries, Christopher Stagg (based on Collins' novel); ph, Peter Hannan; ed, David Camplin; md, Biddu; art d, Michael Bastow; m/l, Biddu, Sammy Cahn.

Drama   **Cas.**   **(PR:O MPAA:R)**

STUDENT BODIES*   (1981) 86m Universal Southwest Cinema/PAR c

Kristen Riter (Toby), Matthew Goldsby (Hardy), Richard Brando (The Breather), Joe Flood (Mr. Dumpkin), Joe Talarowski (Principal Peters), Mimi Weddell (Miss Mumsley), Carl Jacobs (Dr. Sigmund), Peggy Cooper (Ms. Van Dyke), Janice E. O'Malley (Nurse Krud), The Stick (Malvert the Janitor), Kevin Mannis (Scott), Sara Eckhardt (Patti), Brian Batytis (Wheels), Cullen G. Chambers (Charles), Joan Browning Jacobs (Mrs. Hummers), Angela Bressler (Julie), Kay Ogden (Ms. LeClair), Douglas Cotner (Mr. Hummers), Charles I. Trotter (Announcer), Jonathan Walling (Al), Keith Singleton (Charlie), Dario O. Jones (Mawamba), Thomas D. Cannon II (Ralph), Oscar James (Coach), Robyn Flanery (Joan), Tammie M. Tignor (Dagmar), Anita Taylor (Bertha), John M. Armstrong (Joe), Brenda Maduzia (Punker), Dorothy Rich (Mrs. Peters), Anne Bell (Teacher), Kathryn Reve Doster (Sue), Janice Elaine Berridge (Student).

Just when you thought it was safe to leave the house, another spoof of horror films surfaces. Potentially funny situations are humorless, and the gags are repetitive. Like other films of this genre, it's the horny teenagers who get killed before their moment of glory. The "producer" of the film even comes on and tells the audience that since the film will contain no sex or violence, the only thing to do to get that wonderful "R" rating is swear. He does. The film had good intentions but not enough material to carry it off. It was written and directed by Mickey Rose, Who had co-written such Woody Allen classics as BANANAS, WHAT'S UP TIGER LILY? and TAKE THE MONEY AND RUN. The film was plagued by production problems, as evidenced by the producing credit given to the nonexistent Allen Smithee (actually Michael Ritchie).

p, Allen Smithee; (Michael Ritchie); d&w, Mickey Rose; ph, Robert Ebinger (Movie Lab Color); m, Gene Hobson; ed, Kathryn Ruth Hope; prod d, Donald Nunley; COS, Kristin Nelson.

Horror Spoof   **Cas.**   **(PR:O MPAA:NR)**

STUDENT BODY, THE*   (1976) 84m Brandywine/Surrogate c

Warren Stevens (Dr. Blalock), Jillian Kesner (Carrie), Janice Heiden (Chicago), June Fairchild (Mitzi), Peter Hooten (Carter), Alan McRae (John), David Ankrum (LeRoy), Judith Roberts (Mrs. Blalock), Vic Jolley (Vernon), Faith Barnhardt (Sharon), Holmes Osborne (Joe), Sanford Lee (Phil), Gary Gitchell, Joseph Kanter, Harry Effertz, Cindy Jaco, Debora Layman, Jack Poessiger, Robert Elliott.

THE STUDENT BODY is precisely the type of picture that college students watch at their dormitories while consuming large amounts of alcohol. Only then, after being numbed by beer, do pictures like this become clear. This one has a group of delinquent girls frolicking around a college campus while reaping the benefits of liquor, sex, and sleepless nights.

p, Ed Carlin; d, Gus Trikonis; w, Hubert Smith; ph, Gary Graver (CFI Color); m, Don Bagley, Steve Michaels; ed, Jerry Cohen; art d, Mike Bennett.

Comedy   **(PR:O MPAA:R)**

STUDENT NURSES, THE*   (1970) 85m New World c

Elaine Giftos (Sharon), Karen Carlson (Phred), Brioni Farrell (Lynn), Barbara Leigh (Priscilla), Reni Santoni (Victor Charlie), Richard Rust (Les), Lawrence Casey (Jim Caspar), Darrell Larson (Greg), Paul Camen (Mark), Richard Stahl (Dr. Warshaw), Scottie MacGregor (Miss Boswell), Pepe Serna (Luis), John Pearce (Patient), Mario Aniouv (Ralpho), Ron Gans (Psychiatrist), El Teatro Popular (Themselves).

An exploitation film with a conscience focuses on the lives of four nurses in their final year of nursing school who eventually go their separate ways. Giftos falls for a terminally ill patient. Carlson accidentally gives a patient an overdose of drugs, but Dr. Casey saves her from being reprimanded. They fall in love, but their romance ends when she discovers he performed an abortion on her friend Leigh who had been made pregnant by a drug addict. Farrell's story is somewhat implausible: She gets mixed up with a revolutionary and takes off with him when he and his accomplice kill a policeman. STUDENT NURSES, with a budget of $120.000, was the cheapest movie made by Roger Corman's New World Pictures to date when it was released in 1970. The film even inspired a bet between Corman and New World publicity head Jon Davison that Davison co uld make an even cheaper film (Corman limited the budget to $60,000). The result was HOLLYWOOD BOULEVARD, directed by Joe Dante and Allan Arkush, which featured New World stock footage, a running commentary by Corman veteran Dick Miller and guest appearances by Godzilla and the Fly. Followed by PRIVATE DUTY NURSES.

p, Charles S. Swartz, Stephanie Rothman; d, Rothman; w, Don Spencer (based on a story by Swartz, Rothman); ph, Stevan Larner (Movielab Color);

ed, Stephen Judson; art d, David Nichols.

Drama   **(PR:O MPAA:R)**

STUDENT PRINCE, THE½**   (1954) 107m MGM c

Ann Blyth (Kathie), Edmund Purdom (Prince Karl, sung by Mario Lanza), John Ericson (Count Von Asterburg), Louis Calhern (King of Karlsburg), Edmund Gwenn (Prof. Juttner), S. Z. "Cuddles" Sakall (Joseph Ruder), Betta St. John (Princess Johanna), John Williams (Lutz), Evelyn Varden (Queen), John Hoyt (Prime Minister), Richard Anderson (Lucas), Roger Allen (Von Fischtenstein), Steve Rowland (Feuerwald), Chris Warfield (Richter), Gilbert Legay (Von Buhler), Archer MacDonald (Head Corps Servant), Charles Davis (Hubert), John Qualen (Willie Klauber).

A remake of the 1927 picture based on the musical by Romberg and Donnelly and the straight play by Meyer-Foerster, this was a pleasant trifle with some good songs that were sung by Mario Lanza, but came out of the mouth of Purdom. Lanza had been scheduled to play the German prince, but his weight was always fluctuating, and when his temper began to rise and fall with the speed of his avoirdupois the decision was made to toss him out and use Purdom. Since Lanza had already pre-recorded the tunes, that wasn't too tough, although the sound of the round tenor tones coming out of Purdom's slim chest did seem ludicrous, for a while. After the shock of it was over, the picture had its moments. Purdom is a prince with all the accoutrements of the royal purple. His valet is Williams and his tutor is Glenn. Purdom's father is the king, Calhern, who feels that his son needs to go out and see what the real world is like before he comes back to the princess, St. John, with whom a marriage has been arranged. He goes to Heidelberg where he meets Blyth, the daughter of innkeeper Sakall. They fall in love, but when Calhern falls ill and dies, Purdom must return and assume his position as king. Since there is no way for him to take a peasant as his bride, he must say farewell to Blyth. Unrequited love is the theme and 1954 audiences liked their love requited, so the picture didn't fare as well as the studio had hoped. Purdom got lots of build-up and later starred in THE EGYPTIAN, yet his career never did take off. The Romberg-Donnelly songs (with some revised lyrics by Paul Francis Webster) were "Golden Days," "Serenade," "Deep in My Heart," "To the Inn We're Marching," "Drink, Drink, Drink," and a song that causes gales of laughter these days because the meaning was quite different then,– a group of costumed boys lock arms and sing "Come Boy s, Let's All Be Gay, Boys." Webster and Nicholas Brodszky added three new tunes to the score, none of which was up to the original. They were "I'll Walk With God," "Beloved," and "Summertime In Heidelberg." Also heard was the traditional "Gaudeamus Igitur." Blyth had just come off another musical remake, ROSE MARIE. The editing by Ruggiero was a standout and Pan's choreography was properly rousing, but the time had passed for such corn by 1954.

p, Joe Pasternak; d, Richard Thorpe; w, William Ludwig, Sonya Levien (based on the operetta by Dorothy Donnelly, Sigmund Romberg and the novel and play by Wilhelm Meyer-Foerster); ph, Paul C. Vogel (Cinema-Scope, Ansco Color); m, Romberg; ed, Gene Ruggiero; md, George Stoll; ch, Hermes Pan.

Musical   **(PR:A MPAA:NR)**

STUDENT ROMANCE   (SEE: STUDENT'S ROMANCE, THE, 1936)

STUDENT TEACHERS, THE**   (1973) 84m New World c

Susan Damante, Brooke Mills, Brenda Sutton, Nora Heflin, Dick Miller, John Kramer, James Millhollin, Johnny Ray McGhee, Rich Duran, Douglas D. Anderson, Bob Harris, Charles Dierkop, Jac Emel, Tom Mohler, Rose Cypress, Gary Morgan, Ruth Warshawsky, Brad Jewett, Susan Madigan, Tracy Bogart, Gail Davies, Max Anderson, Amy Trachtenberg, Leslie Oliver, Paul Livadery, Chuck Norris, Vincent Barbi, Nick Dimitri, Jane Rosenfeld, Nancy Friedman.

One of the more watchable exploitationers to come from Roger Corman's New World camp. This time the adventures of a trio of student teachers supply the quota of soft-core, grade school tittilation. There is little here of any importance, but some feminist critics have a field day with films like this. Throughout the 1970s Corman found that there were basically two divisions of soft-core pictures – the "student/teacher" films, THE STUDENT TEACHERS, SUMMER SCHOOL TEACHERS (1976) and the "nurse" films, PRIVATE DUTY NURSES (1972), NIGHT CALL NURSES (1972), YOUNG NURSES (1973), and CANDYSTRIPE NURSES (1974). All of these pictures seem to be an offshoot of the 1970 film STUDENT NURSES, which managed to combine both "genres."

p, Julie Corman; d, Jonathan Kaplan; w, Danny Opatoshu; ph, Steven Katz (Metrocolor); m, David Nichtern; ed, George Van Noy; art d, Jim Newport.

Comedy   **Cas.**   **(PR:O MPAA:R)**

STUDENT TOUR**   (1934) 80m MGM bw

James [Jimmy] Durante (Hank), Charles Butterworth (Prof. Lippincott), Maxine Doyle (Ann Lippincott), Phil Regan (Bobby), Florine McKinney (Lilith), Douglas Fowley (Mushy), Monte Blue (Jeff), Betty Grable (Cayenne), Fay McKenzie (Mary Lou), Bobby Gordon (Jackie), Mary Anita

Loos *(Dolores)*, Pauline Brooks *(Peggy)*, Herman Brix [Bruce Bennett] *(Hercules)*, Nelson Eddy *(Himself)*, Florence and Alvarez *(Dance Team)*, Mary Jane Irving, Dorothy Short, Jean Seal, Edna Mae Jones, Susanne Thompson, Joan Sheldon, Maxine Nash, Joan Arlen, Vivien Reid, June Storey, Ercell Wood, Midgie Dare, Clarice Wood, Dixie Dean, Jerry Franks, George Bruggerman, Bryant Washburn, Jr, Dale Van Sickel, David O'Brien, Jack Lubell, Dudley James, Carlyle Blackwell, Jr, Lyman Williams *(Students)*, Lynn Cowan *(Master of Ceremonies)*, Helen Chan *(Sun Toy)*, Eddie Hart *(Stewart)*, Dutch Slickenmeyer *(Officer)*, Herbert Pryor *(Grouch)*, Minerva Urecal *(Wife)*, Carl Stockdale *(Dean)*, Linda Parker, Margo Early *(Students)*, Arthur Hoyt *(Assistant to Dean)*, Dora Clemant *(Wardrobe Woman)*, Dewey Robinson *(War Lord)*, Nick Copeland *(Waiter)*, Frank Tang, Luke Chan *(Chinese Prisoners)*, Sam Flint *(Captain)*, June Gittelson *(Fat Girl)*, Tom Tameriz *(Indian Prince)*, Arthur Wanzer *(Elderly Man)*, Florence Roberts *(Elderly Woman)*, Red Berger *(Mailman)*, Harry Strathey, Harry Wheat *(Business Men)*, E. Alyn Warren *(Saga)*, Robert Stevenson *(Bartender)*, Fred Malatesta *(French Manager)*, Dick Farham *(Assistant Manager)*, Charles Fallon *(Croupier)*, Sherry Hall *(Radio Announcer)*, Mischa Auer *(Sikhi Cop)*, Edward LeSaint *(Old Graduate)*, A. Barr Smith *(English Coxswain)*, Robert Adair *(English Trainer)*, Herbert Evans *(English Coach)*, Neville Clark *(Capt. English Crew)*, Otto Frisco, Eddie Daas, James Bell *(Indian Fagirs)*, Sam Lewis *(Jewish Hindu)*, Jamiel Hasson *(Indian Policeman)*.

All the elements are there, but this slapped-together musical still falls short. A college rowing crew, coached by Durante, is set to compete in a rowing event. But the grades come out and all the team members have flunked a philosophy class. Comedian Butterworth teams with Durante and plays the philosophy professor. His ugly-duckling daughter, Doyle, accompanies the team on its round-the-world trip, hoping to hook a husband. She doesn't have much luck until they hit England, whe she takes off her glasses and catches the eye of one of the rowers. Then aspiring starlet Betty Grable appeared in STUDENT TOUR. Eddy also had made two obscure appearances in films before being showcased in STUDENT TOUR. It was his final "guest appearance" before hitting the big time in NAUGHTY MARIETTA IN 1935. STUDENT TOUR, though a B film, had the look of an expensive major production. Yet, it had a lower payroll, fewer sets, and used MGM's second-string character actors in principal roles. Songs by Arthur Freed and Nacio Herb Brown include "A New Moon is Over My Shoulder" (Sung by the Chorus, and by Phil Regan and Maxine Doyle), "The Snake Dance" (sung by the chorus, and by Florine McKinney), "From Now On" (sung by Doyle), "The Carlo" (sung by Nelson Eddy), "Fight 'Em" (sung by the chorus, and by Doyle). "I Just Say it with Music" was penned and sung by Jimmy Durante.

p, Monta Bell; d, Charles F. Reisner; w, Ralph Spence, Philip Dunne (based on a story by George Seaton, Arthur Bloch, Samuel Marx); ph, Joseph Valentine; ed, Frank Hull; md, Jack Virgil; art d, Cedric Gibbons; ch, Chester Hale.

Musical   **(PR:A   MPAA:NR)**

STUDENT'S ROMANCE, THE*   (1936, Brit.) 70m BIP/Alliance bw

Grete Natzler *(Princess Helene)*, Patric Knowles *(Max Brandt)*, W.H. Berry *(Pedell)*, Carol Goodner *(Veronika)*, Mackenzie Ward *(Karl)*, Iris Ashley *(Desiree)*, Steve Geray *(Mickey)*, Hugh Dempster *(Bruno)*, Ivan Samson *(Grand Duke)*, Robert Nainby *(Karl's Uncle)*, Norma Varden *(Wife)*, Wallace Lupino *(Sportsman)*, Haver and Lee *(Hans and Otto)*.

Set in Austria, the film version of the operatta "I Lost My Heart in Heidelberg" does not do it justice. The time is 1825 and a songwriter, a Heidelburg Student, is down on his luck and being pressed to pay off his debts. A young woman, who is madly in love with him, bails him out without his knowledge. While she pines for him, he falls for the town newcomer, Natzler. It turns out she is the daughter of the Grand Duke, in town to announce her marriage to another man with a title. The group sings a few boring songs and trades a couple of wooden jokes, and real love wins out in the end.

p, Walter C. Mycroft; d, Otto Kanturek; w, Fritz Lohner, Clifford Grey, Richard Hutter, Norman Watson, Bruno Hardt Wardon (based on the operetta "I lost My Heart in Heidelberg" by Beda, Ernst Neubach); ph, Bryan Langley; ed, Kanturek; m/l, Hans May, Grey.

Musical   **(PR:A   MPAA:NR)**

STUDIO MURDER MYSTERY, THE*   (1929) 62m FP/PAR bw

Fredric March *(Richard Hardell)*, Neil Hamilton *(Tony White, Studio Gag Writer)*, Florence Eldridge *(Blanche Hardell)*, Warner Oland *(Rupert Borka, Film Director)*, Doris Hill *(Helen MacDonald)*, Eugene Pallette *(Detective Lieutenant Dirk)*, Chester Conklin *(George, Studio Gateman)*, Lane Chandler *(Bill Martin)*, Gardner James *(Ted MacDonald)*, Guy Oliver *(MacDonald, Studio Watchman)*, E. H. Calvert *(Grant)*, Donald MacKenzie *(Capt. Coffin)*, Jack Luden *(Bob)*, Lawford Davidson *(Al Hemming)*, Mary Foy *(Miss O'Brien)*.

This film, made cheaply and requiring only a couple of sets, uses old gags and trite suspense situations to tell the story. March plays an actor who keeps flubbing his lines to the chagrin of director Oland. After trying to

perfect a murder sequence, his life is actually threatened by his wife (played by Eldridge, March's real-life spouse), March's girl friend, the director and the girl friend's brother.

d, Frank Tuttle; w, Tuttle, Ethel Doherty (based on the book by A. Channing and Carmen Ballen Edington); ph, Victor Milner; ed, Merrill White.

Mystery   **(PR:A   MPAA:NR)**

STUDIO ROMANCE   (SEE: TALENT SCOUT, 1937)

STUDS LONIGAN*½   (1960) 103m Longridge Enterprises/UA bw

Christopher Knight *(Studs Lonigan)*, Frank Gorshin *(Kenny Killarney)*, Venetia Stevenson *(Lucy Scanlon)*, Carolyn Craig *(Catherine Banahan)*, Jack Nicholson *(Weary Reilly)*, Robert Casper *(Paulie Haggerty)*, Dick Foran *(Patrick Lonigan)*, Katherine Squire *(Mrs. Lonigan)*, Jay C. Flippen *(Father Gilhooey)*, Helen Westcott *(Miss Julia Miller)*, Kathy Johnson *(Frances Lonigan)*, Jack Kruschen *(Charlie the Greek)*, Suzi Carnell *(Eileen)*, Mme. Spivy *(Mother Josephine)*, James Drum *(Jim Doyle)*, Rita Duncan *(Kitty)*, Val Hidey *(Burlesque Stripper)*, Opal Eurard *(Mrs. Reilly)*, Mavis Neal *(Mrs. Haggerty)*, Ben Gary *(Various Roles)*, Stanley Adams, Steven Ritch, George Keymas *(Gangsters)*, Phil Arnold *(Dentist)*, John Graham *(Judge)*, Don Garrett, Casey MacGregor *(Policemen)*, Brian O'Hara *(Funeral Mourner)*, Snubby Pollard *(Vendor)*, Marty Crail *(Bartender)*, Darlene Hendrix, Josie Lloyd, Suzanne Sidney *(New Year's Eve Party Girls)*, Kathie Browne, Judy Howard, Elaine Walker, Lorelei Vitek *(Girls at Wild Party)*.

Author James T. Farrell's trilogy about Irish hero growing up on Chicago's poverty-stricken South Side during the 1920s was a valiant effort, but lacked depth. Knight is too inexperienced to handle the lead role, but Gorshin shines in a supporting role. So does Westcott, as the schoolteacher he leans on when he's in trouble, who herself leads an empty and desperate life. Producer Yordan went too far trying to be artistic, rather than concentrating on a story about people struggling to make something themselves, despite great odds. Art direction, props and costumes give production an authentic look, but dialog at times seems too contemporary for the era. Jack Nicholson appears here in one of his earliest screen roles.

p, Philip Yordan; d, Irving Lerner; w, Yordan (based on the novel by James T. Farrell); ph, Arthur H. Feindel; m. Gerrald Goldsmith; ed, Verna Fields; art d, Jack Poplin.

Drama   **(PR:A   MPAA:NR)**

STUDY IN SCARLET, A**   (1933) 71m KBS/World Wide

Reginald Owen *(Sherlock Holmes)*, Anna May Wong *(Mrs. Pyke)*, June Clyde *(Eileen Forrester)*, Alan Dinehart *(Thaddeus Merrydew, Lawyer)*, John Warburton *(John Stanford)*, Warburton Gamble *(Dr. John H. Watson)*, J.M. Kerrigan *(Jabez Wilson)*, Alan Mowbray *(Inspector Lestrade)*, Doris Lloyd *(Mrs. Murphy)*, Billy Bevan *(Will Swallow)*, Leila Bennett *(Daft Dolly)*, Cecil Reynolds *(Baker)*, Wyndham Standing *(Capt. Pyke)*, Halliwell Hobbs *(Malcolm Dearing)*, Tetsu Komai *(Ah Yet)*, Temple Pigott *(Mrs. Hudson)*, Hobart Cavanaugh *(Publican)*, Olaf Hytten *(Butler)*, Lelia Bennett *(Dolly)*.

This Holmes film features Owen as the title detective who solves a handful of murders in his usual cunning and sometimes offbeat way. A robbery is committed, and all of a sudden dead bodies are turning up one after another. Owen trades quips with Gamble, who plays Dr. Watson. He discovers an underground crime syndicate is wiping out the competition so it can keep all the action to itself. The actors did a commendable job and photography and set decoration is first-rate. The film had an English flavor despite its being made in the U.S. Owen also wrote the dialog and continuity. (See: SHERLOCK HOLMES series, Index)

p, Burt Kelly, Samuel Bischoff, William Saul; d, Edwin L. Marin; w, Robert Florey, Reginald Owen (based on the novel by Sir Arthur Conan Doyle); ph, Arthur Edeson; ed, Rose Loewenger; md, Val Burton; art d, Ralph M. DeLacy.

Mystery   **Cas.**   **(PR:A   MPAA:NR)**

STUDY IN TERROR, A**   (1966, Brit./Ger.) 95m Compton-Tekli Sir Nigel-Planet/COL c (SHERLOCK HOLMES GROSSTER FALL; AKA: FOG)

John Neville *(Sherlock Holmes)*, Donald Houston *(Dr. John H. Watson)*, John Fraser *(Lord Edward Carfax)*, Anthony Quayle *(Dr. Murray)*, Robert Morley *(Mycroft Holmes)*, Barbara Windsor *(Annie Chapman)*, Adrienne Corri *(Angela)*, Frank Finlay *(Inspector Lestrade)*, Judi Dench *(Sally)*, Cecil Parker *(Prime Minister)*, Georgia Brown *(Saloon Singer)*, Barry Jones *(Duke of Shires)*, Kay Walsh *(Cathy Eddowes)*, Edina Ronay *(Mary Kelly)*, Terry Downes *(Chunky)*, Peter Carsten *(Max Steiner)*, Charles Regnier *(Joseph Beck)*, Dudley Foster *(Home Secretary)*, John Cairney *(Michael Osborne)*, Christiane Maybach *(Polly Nichols)*, Avis Bunnage *(Landlady)*, Barbara Leake *(Mrs. Hudson)*, Patrick Newell *(P.C. Benson)*, Norma Foster *(Liz Stride)*, Donna White *(1st Streetwalker)*.

Neville is cast as Sherlock Holmes in this thriller about a manhunt for Jack the Ripper in London's misty East End. Film takes the stance that Jack was well educated and did his slashing with medical finesse. A STUDY IN

TERROR was the second Sherlock Holmes film to be made in color. It also was unique in that it put the fictional detective on a real crime that occurred in the 1880s, Holmes' era; made him a younger character accustomed to action; and dealt with a story line that was more sexually explicit than previous Holmes films. Co-production status of West German has not been confirmed. The film was released in the U.S. as FOG. (See SHERLOCK HOLMES series, Index.)

p, Henry Lester; d, James Hill; w, Donald and Derek Ford (based on characters created by Sir Arthur Conan Doyle); ph, Desmond Dickinson; (Eastmancolor r); m, John Scott; ed, Henry Richardson; prod d, Alex Vetchinsky; cos, Motley; spec eff, Wally Veevers; makeup, Tom Smith.

Mystery   **Cas.**   **(PR:A   MPAA:NR)**

STUETZEN DER GESELLSCHAFT   (SEE: PILLARS OF SOCIETY, 1936, Ger.)

STUN MAN, THE**   (1980) 129m FOX c

Peter O'Toole (*Eli Cross*), Steve Railsback (*Cameron*), Barbara Hershey (*Nina Franklin*), Allen Goorwitz (*Sam*), Alex Rocco (*Jake*), Sharon Farrell (*Denise*), Adam Roarke (*Raymond Bailey*), Philip Bruns (*Ace*), Chuck Bail (*Chuck Barton*), John Garwood (*Gabe Cameramen*), Jim Hess (*Henry*), John B. Pearce (*Garage Guard*), Michael Railsback (*Burt*), George D. Wallace (*Father*), Dee Carroll (*Mother*), Leslie Winograde (*Sister*), Don Kennedy (*Lineman*), Whitey Hughes, Walter Robles, A. J. Bakunas, Gregg Berger, Ross Reynolds, Robert Caruso, Frank Avila, Stafford Morgan, John Alderman, James Avery, Leigh Webb, Frank Beetson, Jack Palinkas, Garrett McPherson, Nelson Tyler, Larry Dunn, Deanna Dae Coleman, Louis Gartner, Gordon Ross, Marion Wayne, William Joseph Arno (*Assistant Directors*).

A truly unique movie blessed with a giant performance by O'Toole, a literate script, high-energy direction, and a notable score. There have been many fine movies made about movies, but seldom have any reached the heights this one did. Against the story of a company making a WW I epic there is a secondary tale that grabs the imagination and holds on tightly to it. Based on a 1970 novel, the movie was made two years before and couldn't get a release until Fox picked it up. O'Toole had made a number of dreadful pictures before signing to appear here as a megalomaniacal director (and many of them will recognize themselves) who tyrannizes his writer (the same again) and plays with his actors, manipulating their lives in reality the way he does it in the story they are shooting. Railsback is a veteran on the run. He's being hunted by local sheriff Rocco when he comes upon the movie company which is shooting on the beach in front of the same turn-of-the-century-style hotel so well-known from SOME LIKE IT HOT. The hotel is the Del Coronado, which sits on Coronado Island, just across a scarifying bridge from San Diego. The number one stunt man on the movie is killed in an accident and O'Toole, who has shielded Railsback from Rocco, prevails on the young man to take the place of the dead stunt man. Railsback is not sure he wants to risk his life, but O'Toole convinces him with the promise of good money and protection. Railsback knows he has to lay low and can probably blend into the large movie crew and cast so he stays on. His hair is colored to match the blond man who died and he is thrust into the world of moviemaking, a world he soon discovers, not as glamorous as he thought it might be. The egos, the harangues, the fatigue, the nonsense, the danger, and the fun are soon demonstrated to him. Railsback finds the co-star of the film, Hershey, attractive and quirky. He thinks he loves her, then is stunned to learn that she and O'Toole have had a long-standing relationship, although O'Toole is so epicene that he appears to be ambisextrous. Railsback gets his stunt training from Bail, who plays a stunt coordinator and who is, in fact, just that, and one of the best in the movie business. The picture they are shooting goes on and the audience sees how movie magic is done while the off-screen story continues. Soon, Railsback is wondering if O'Toole will stop at nothing to get the shot he wants and he thinks that the dead stunt man may have died due to O'Toole's quest for reality. There's a particularly dangerous stunt coming up, one that requires Railsback to drive a vintage car off a bridge and to have it fall many feet into a river. Railsback thinks that he might die in the stunt and refuses to do it. O'Toole keeps upping the ante, but Railsback thinks he may not swim away from this alive. Further, he believes that O'Toole may, in fact, be doing this deliberately and intending to kill him. When the price gets high enough, Railsback agrees to do it and the stunt goes off. He crashes through the bridge and goes into the water, barely managing to get out before he drowns. Once it's over, he's just swum to the river bank when O'Toole arrives in a helicopter, smiling devilishly as he's done throughout the film, and invites Railsback to join him for a libation. Railsback tells him off and will be on his way, somewhat richer and a great deal wiser. Real life versus reel life is the theme and Marcus' script is a marvel of wit, with most of the bon mots being handed to O'Toole, who bites them off with precision. His script, O'Toole and director Rush (who also did the adaptation of the script from the novel) were all nominated for Oscars. The movie is tough, funny, mystifying and enigmatic, and how much more does anyone want from 129 minutes? Frontiere's score is infectious and contributes greatly to the mood of the movie. Filmed in 1978.

p&d, Richard Rush; w, Lawrence B. Marcus, Rush (based on the novel by Paul Brodeur); ph, Mario Tosi (Metrocolor), m, Dominic Frontiere; ed, Jack

Hofstra, Caroline Ferriol; art d, James Schoppe; set d, Richard Spero; cos, Rosanna Norton; m/l, Frontiere, Norman Gimbel.

Drama   **Cas.**   **(PR:O   MPAA:R)**

STUNT PILOT**   (1939) 61m MON bw

John Trent (*Tailspin Tommy*), Marjorie Reynolds (*Betty Lou*), Milburn Stone (*Skeeter*), Jason Robards, Sr (*Smith*), George Meeker (*Martin*), Pat O'Malley (*Sheehan*), Wesley Barry (*Glen*), George Cleveland (*Sheriff*), Mary Field (*Ethel*), Todd Sterling (*Charlie*), Buddy Cox (*Bobby*), Johnny Day (*Tex*).

This was the second film in a series about a daring group of pilots who this time head to Hollywood to fly planes and make movies. Aviator Trent is filming a movie that features a dogfight scene. However, someone has replaced blanks in his gun with live ammunition which results in his killing Meeker. O'Malley plays the director who eventually is implicated for making the switch. The story line was adapted from the comic strip "Tailspin Tommy" by Hal Forrest. (See TAILSPIN TOMMY Series, Index)

p, Paul Malvern; d, George Waggner; w, Joseph West, Scott Darling (based on a story based on the newspaper strip "Tailspin Tommy" by Hal Forrest); ph, Fred B. Jackman, Jr.; m, Fleming Allan, Carl Winge; ed, Carl Pierson.

Adventure   **(PR:A   MPAA:NR)**

STUNTS½   (1977) 90m Spiegel-Bergman-New Line/New Line c (AKA: WHO IS KILLING THE STUNTMAN.)

Robert Forster (*Glen Wilson*), Fiona Lewis (*B.J. Parswell*), Joanna Cassidy (*Patti Johnson*), Darrell Fetty (*Dave*), Bruce Glover (*Chuck Johnson*), James Luisi (*Blake*), Richard Lynch (*Pete*), Candice Rialson (*Judy Blake*), Malachi Throne (*Earl*), Ray Sharkey (*Pauley*), Gary Davis (*Billy Wilson*), Janet Hadland, H.B. Hagerty, Dave Shelley Stunt People: Phil Adams, Dick Butler, Joie Chitwood, Deanne Coleman, Gary Davis, Larry Dunn, Ted Duncan, Bud George, Beau Gibson, Lee Pulford, Dar Robinson, Chuck Tamburro.

A thin plot, lots of action, a fair script, and no comparison to a much better movie made about the same subject, THE STUNT MAN. When stunt man Davis is killed, his professor brother, Forster, who has given up the classroom for the life of a man who risks his body making movies, thinks that there may have been some foul play involved. Luisi is the smarmy producer of the picture. He's married to nymphomaniac Rialson (who starred in a few soft-porn movies, including CANDY STRIPE NURSES). Luisi is against what Forster wants to do: replace his late brother and get to the bottom of the death. But the others on the film insist that he be allowed to take the job. Forster meets some old pals, Glover and his wife Cassidy, plus Sharkey, an irrepressible lothario who spends his off-hours pursuing women. Lewis is hanging around the set writing an article about stunt men and she and Forster are immediately at odds. Davis was killed in a stunt that failed and Forster means to do it right. The others in the fraternity give Davis a proper funeral and toss his beloved motorcycle into the sea as a tribute. Forster, Sharkey, Glover, and Cassidy make a Musketeer-like pact to turn off the life-support equipment if any of them is ever permanently disabled. The truth about Davis is slowly revealed. He'd been sleeping with Luisi's wife, Rialson, who stars in the movie they are shooting, thereby causing Forster to wonder if Luisi didn't arrange for Davis' death. In order to show his mettle, Forster does a dazzling array of stunts, each more difficult and dangerous than the one before, and Lewis is amazed by his bravery. This is soon transformed into admiration, then physical attraction. Glover is set to do a very dangerous bit where he must fall several stories from a building while Forster and the others are going up the sheer side of it. Glover is frightened of the risk and Forster volunteers to change places with him for the leap. Glover uses Forster's gear for the climb up (he's better at going up than going down) and the switch will be made at the apex of the scale. Glover's rigging breaks (was it meant to break for Forster?) and he plunges to the earth. They race him to the hospital but the news is grim. Glover can't sustain life on his own and has been attached to the very life support system they spoke of earlier. Forster unplugs the machine and lets Glover expire. The shooting goes on and Sharkey is killed while doing a stunt that would normally be a piece of cake for such an experienced man. Forster now realizes that both Glover's and Sharkey's deaths were supposed to be his. The final stunt of the movie, the one Davis was killed doing, is intricate. It requires Forster to be in a moving car and grab for a rope that's lowered from an overhead helicopter. Rialson, in the meantime, has been soundly thrashed by Luisi, who has good reason to be jealous. Lewis finds the bruised and bloodied Rialson and is told that Luisi is the maniac who has been killing the stunt people (it was indicated right from the start so there is hardly a mystery). Forster is already into his final stunt when Lewis tries to race to the location shooting to warn him. Forster has gone up the rope and is holding on to the chopper's rail. Luisi has deliberately removed some of the holding bolts from the runner and it is beginning to loosen, having but a few seconds left before it separates from the helicopter. On the ground, Lewis shouts to Forster that Luisi is the culprit. Forster grabs on to a stronger section of the chopper and sees Luisi trying to get away in his open car. Forster jumps from the copter and into the car. The two men fight as the convertible careens across the road. Forster is tossed out by the whiplash movement of the car and Luisi, trying to regain control of the auto, is not fast enough. The car crashes and he is burned to ashes. It's an unbelievable story and could have used a stronger hand than Lester's to shape the script. Lester has had an interesting career. When given a bad script, he always seems to make it better. When given a good script, he somehow makes it worse.

p, Raymond Lofaro, William Panzer; d, Mark L. Lester; w, Dennis Johnson, Barney Cohen, (based on a story by Lofaro, from an idea by Robert Shaye, Michael Harpster); ph, Bruce Logan, Bob Bailin; m, Michael Kamen; ed, Corky Ehlers; stunts, Paul Nuckles.

Drama   **Cas.**   **(PR:C-O MPAA:PG)**

SUB-A-DUB-DUB   (SEE: HELLO DOWN THERE 1969)

SUBJECT WAS ROSES, THE**   (1968) 107m MGM c

Patricia Neal (*Nettie Cleary*), Jack Albertson (*John Cleary*), Martin Sheen (*Timmy Cleary*), Don Saxon (*Nightclub Master of Ceremonies*), Elaine Williams (*Woman*), Grant Gordon (*Man in Restaurant*).

Frank Gilroy's Pulitzer-Prize drama was beautifully realized in this film adaptation. Sheen and Albertson came from the stage to reprise their roles (with Albertson winning a Best Supporting Actor Oscar and proving he was much more than a lone comedy burlesque comic) and Neal replaced Irene Dailey (who starred in the play), securing a Best Actress nomination. What was even more miraculous was that Neal was working after having survived a series of strokes while filming SEVEN WOMEN (she was replaced by Anne Bancroft in that film). WW II has just ended and Sheen returns home from the battle to live with parents Neal and Albertson. In the years since he's been away the marriage of his parents has disintegrated into rancor, disagreements, and highly charged hostility. Before he left, Sheen was the apple of Neal's eye and only had a passing relationship with Albertson, who is the Irish equivalent of Willy Loman in DEATH OF A SALESMAN. Now that he's matured, he is like Mark Twain's comment about his father, and now has a closer tie to Albertson, finding that they are on a par. Sheen can't bear to see his parents at such loggerheads and attempts to mediate their differences without standing in either's corner. Sheen and Albertson have a day together at their vacation cottage in the country and Sheen stops to buy some roses for Neal on the way back home, then tells Albertson that it might be nice if it seemed as though the flowers came from the father, not the son. The flowers are given to Neal and she is genuinely appreciative of the gift and decides to go out with both of them and have some family fun together, as in the good old days. They travel to a nightclub where Saxon is the typical master of ceremonies and Albertson begins to drink too much. Later, at their residence, he is close to slobbering and tries to reawaken the sexual attraction they once had. Albertson's clumsy pawing at Neal turns her off and she rejects his lovemaking tries. Albertson is outraged and Neal further compounds the situation by taking revenge. She smashes the vase of roses and thinks that the move will hurt Albertson. He then tells her that he didn't buy them at all, that it was Sheen who had the idea and he wouldn't have done it. Dissolve. It's now Sunday morning and Albertson prepares to go to church and wants Sheen to join him. War has taken a toll on Sheen and he no longer embraces organized Catholicism and refuses to join Albertson in worship. Albertson goes off by himself and Neal begins a subtle campaign of sabotage against Albertson. Sheen sees through this and confronts his mother by saying that he will not side with her in any dispute. Nor will he take a position with Albertson. Above all, Sheen wants to be Swiss in this war, totally neutral. Neal can't handle Sheen's attitude, so she exits, then returns home to find Sheen drunk and arguing with Albertson in much the same way he had argued with her. Sheen, despite the booze he's ingested, makes some sense. This situation will never get better as long as things remain the same. He thinks that his parents must work out their marital differences without using him as a referee so he tells them that he is going to leave, find his own apartment, and strike out on his own. Neal and Albertson feel sad because they'd been looking forward to his return for the duration of the war, but they can see the wisdom in his choice and resign themselves to the fact that he will be moving out. Then Sheen has second thoughts and says that perhaps he should give himself a bit more time in adjusting to civilian life and that it might be better if he stayed. But by this time, Neal and Albertson have found one thing upon which they agree, that Sheen's first inclination was correct and that he must go out in the world. The family comes closer together with this decision and the movie ends with the three of them sharing a happy breakfast and love pouring out from all sides. It was not a hit, despite the terrific acting, sharp writing, and outstanding direction from Grosbard, who also staged the play. Never does the emotion explode into oratory, so almost every scene has an underlying tension that continues to bubble. Two songs sung by Judy Collins liven the lean score by Pockriss: "Albatross" (written by Collins) and "Who Knows Where The Time Goes?" (Sandy Denny). Realistically shot in New York City and Spring Lake, New Jersey.

p, Edgar Lansbury; d, Ulu Grosbard; w, Frank D. Gilroy (based on his play); ph, Jack Priestley (Metrocolor); m, Lee Pockriss; ed, Jerry Greenberg; md, Pockriss; art d, George Jenkins; set d, John Godfrey; cos, Anna Hill Johnstone; m/l, Sandy Denny, Judy Collins; makeup, Mike Maggi.

Drama   **(PR:C MPAA:NR)**

SUBMARINE ALERT*   (1943) 67m PAR bw

Richard Arlen (*Lee Deerhold*), Wendy Barrie (*Ann Patterson*), Nils Asther (*Dr. Arthur Huneker*), Roger Pryor (*G.B. Fleming*), Abner Biberman (*Comdr. Toyo*), Marc Lawrence (*Vincent Belga*), John Miljan (*Mr. Bambridge/Capt. Hargas*), Patsy Nash (*Tina*), Ralph Sanford (*Freddie Grayson*), Dwight Frye (*Henry Haldine*), Edward Earle (*Dr. Barclay*), William Bakewell (*Engineer*), Stanley Smith (*Clerk*).

The film was released a year after production was finished and, as a result, the technology depicted in the film was no longer novel or unusual. The story involves spies who are jamming the radio airwaves resulting in the sinking of American tankers by a Japanese submarine. Arlen plays one of a group of radio engineers who are "fired" from their jobs so they can work undercover for the FBI to infiltrate the gang jamming the airwaves. Arlen is soon recruited by the gang. When he realizes the sabotaging methods, he tries to stop them until the FBI moves in. He is aided and romanced by Barrie, also undercover for the authorities.

p, William Pine, William Thomas; d, Frank McDonald; w, Maxwell Shane; ph, Fred Jackman, Jr.; ed, William Zeigler.

Spy Drama   **(PR:A MPAA:NR)**

SUBMARINE BASE*   (1943) 65m PRC bw

John Litel (*Jim Taggart*), Alan Baxter (*Joe Morgan*), Fifi D'Orsay (*Maria*), Eric Blore (*Spike*), Iris Adrian (*Dorothy*), Jacqueline Dalya (*Judy*), Georges Metaxa (*Kroll*), Luis Alberni (*Styx*), Rafael Storm (*Felipo*), George Lee (*Cavanaugh*), Anna Demetrio (*Angela*), Lucien Prival (*Mueller*).

A former gangster redeems himself by helping to defeat the Nazis on a remote island. Litel plays a criminal hiding out on the island who at first seems to aid the Nazis by giving them a place to re fuel their submarines. When a ship is sunk, Baxter washes up on shore. He is a former New York City policeman, now in the merchant marines, who recognizes Litel as a gangster on the run, and tension soon builds between the two. By the end Litel is working against the Nazis and when that is discovered, he is shot. The reformed Litel dies in the arms of Baxter.

p, Jack Schwartz; d, Albert Kelley; w, Arthur St. Clair, George Merrick; ph, Marcel Le Picard; m, Charles Dant; ed, Holbrook N. Todd; md, Dant; art d, Frank Sylos.

War Drama   **(PR:A MPAA:NR)**

SUBMARINE COMMAND½   (1951) 87m PAR bw

William Holden (*Cmdr. White*), Nancy Olson (*Carol*), William Bendix (*C.P. Boyer*), Don Taylor (*Lt. Cmdr. Peter Morris*), Arthur Franz (*Lt. Carlson*), Darryl Hickman (*Ens. Wheelwright*), Peggy Webber (*Mrs. Alice Rice*), Moroni Olsen (*Rear Adm. Joshua Rice*), Jack Gregson (*Cmdr. Rice*), Jack Kelly (*Lt. Barton*), Don Dunning (*Quartermaster Perkins*), Jerry Paris (*Sgt. Gentry*), Charles Meredith (*Adm. Tobias*), Philip Van Zandt (*Gavin*), Gordon Polk (*Ralph*), Walter Reed (*Chief O'Flynn*), Noel Neill (*Mrs. Sue Carlson*), Fred Zendar, John V. Close (*Frogmen*), George Wallace (*Chief Herb Bixby*), Richard Berggren (*Clem*), Harold Fong (*Korean Officer*), Jerry James (*Man*).

Holden joined most of the male leads of the 1940s and 1950s (such as John Wayne, Clark Gable, Tyrone Power, Cary Grant, etc.) by taking command of a submarine in a film. As the executive officer of the undersea craft *Tiger Shark* on the last day of WW II he is forced to make a crash dive when a squadron of Japanese planes attacks, leaving his wounded skipper and quartermaster on deck to drown. An hour later word comes that the war is over. Although other officers tell Holden he did the right thing, his own conscience and chief torpedoman Bendix torture him for his decision to dive. With the war over the ship is decommissioned and Holden takes over duties ashore. He is still plagued by Bendix and his own self-doubts. Although his wife, Olson, tries to understand and help him, she fails on both counts. Then the Korean War breaks out and the *Tiger Shark* and Holden are pulled out of mothballs and sent off the coast of Korea. Holden performs a few intrepid acts that restore his self- respect and gain him the respect of the crew. The fourth and last teaming of Holden and Olson (the first was SUNSET BOULEVARD '1950', the film is reasonably entertaining within the narrow confines of its genre, with the sequences between the wars with Holden battling his conscience and boredom the most interesting. The action sequences were little more than cliches familiar to anyone who has seen a few of these underwater dramas (how many crewmen have been trapped abovedecks while their submarine crash- dives in these things?) During shooting, Holden and Taylor became drinking buddies. Once, the pair, in uniform, walked over to the set where another friend, Ronald Reagan, was making a picture. The two appeared in a crowd scene, taking home the minimum pay of an extra. Another time the drinking duo performed a dangerous stunt that involved diving off a ship and swimming to the sub, throwing director Farrow into fits when he found out. Far from Holden's best work, he still does an admirable job despite, as he later recalled, being drunk the whole time.

p, Joseph Sistrom; d, John Farrow; w, Jonathan Latimer (based on a story by Latimer); ph, Lionel Lindon; m, David Buttolph; ed, Eda Warren; art d, Hal Pereira, Henry Bumstead.

War Drama   (PR:A   MPAA:NR)

SUBMARINE D-1**   (1937) 100m FN-WB bw

Pat O'Brien (*Butch Rogers*), George Brent (*Lt. Comdr. Matthews*), Wayne Morris (*Sock McGillis*), Doris Weston (*Ann Callam*), Frank McHugh (*Lucky*), Henry O'Neill (*Adm. Thomas*), Dennie Moore (*Arabella*), Veda Ann Borg (*Dolly*), Regis Toomey (*Tom Callam*), John Ridgely (*Lt. Junior Grade*), Owen King (*Lt. Senior Grade*), Wally Maher (*Listener*), Jerry Fletcher (*Lt. Mason*), Dick Wessel, Ralph Dunn, Jeffrey Sayre, Don DeFore, Dick French, Allan Kenward, Sol Gorss, Don Turner, John Shea, Mike Lally, Billy Vincent, Eric Pettit, Gordon Clifford (*Sailors*), Don Briggs (*Instructor*), Eddie Fetherston (*Disagreeable Sailor*), Walter Miller (*Salvage Officer*), John Elliott, Jim Farley (*Fathers*), Walter Clyde (*Orderly*), Lee Phelps (*Marine Orderly*), Allan Cavan (*Skipper*), Walter Clyde (*Orderly*), Loia Cheaney, Fern Barrey (*Wives*).

Almost documentary in style, the film relates everything about submarines and those aboard, right down to the authentic uniforms and machinery. The Navy went out of its way to accomodate director Bacon so he could go behind the scenes to depict how the latest model operated. Along the way, during maneuvers, the boys stop off for rest and relaxation, chasing women in every port. This was the perfect recruiting tool for the Navy, stirring up the patriotism in the audiences as they watched the men work the new equipment with perfection. Ronald Reagan had a small role in the film, but he ended up on the cutting room floor.

p, Lou Edelman; d, Lloyd Bacon; w, Frank Wead, Warren Duff, Lawrence Kimble (based on the story *Submarine 262* by Wead); ph, Arthur Edeson; m, Max Steiner; ed, William Holmes; md, Leo F. Forbstein; spec eff, Byron Haskin, H.F. Koenekamp.

Action Drama   (PR:A   MPAA:NR)

SUBMARINE PATROL**   (1938) 95m FOX bw

Richard Greene (*Perry Townsend III*), Nancy Kelly (*Susan Leeds*), Preston Foster (*Lt. John C. Drake*), George Bancroft (*Capt. Leeds*), Slim Summerville (*Ellsworth "Spotts" Ficketts*), Joan Valerie (*Anne*), John Carradine (*McAllison*), Warren Hymer (*Rocky Haggerty*), Henry Armetta (*Luigi*), Douglas Fowley (*Brett*), J. Farrell McDonald (*"Sails" Quincannon*), Dick Hogan (*Johnny Miller*), Maxie Rosenbloom (*Sgt. Joe Duffy*), Ward Bond (*Olaf Swanson*), Robert Lowery (*Sparks*), Charles Tannen (*Kelly*), George E. Stone (*Irving*), Moroni Olsen (*Capt. Wilson*), Jack Pennick (*Guns McPeck*), Elisha Cook, Jr (*"Professor" Pratt*), Harry Strang (*Grainger*), Charles Trowbridge (*Rear Adm. Joseph Maitland*), Victor Varconi (*Chaplain*), Murray Alper (*Sailor*), E.E. Clive (*Mr. Pringle*).

Director John Ford would later achieve acclaim for his westerns, but he didn't do too badly with this sea adventure either. Foster plays a naval officer demoted and put in charge of a decrepit sub chaser manned by a misfit group, including irresponsible playboy Greene. Foster and veteran sailor McDonald have their work cut out for them trying to get the old hulk and the men in shipshape condition. Later, when Foster calls for volunteers for a dangerous mission, all crew members respond and heroically sink several enemy subs. Along the way the apathetic Greene learns his responsibilit ies to his fellow sailors and, in the process, wins the love of Kelly, the daughter of a tough, old ship owner. SUBMARINE PATROL was directed by Ford just prior to his classic STAGECOACH.

p, Darryl F. Zanuck; d, John Ford; w, Rian James, Darrell Ware, Jack Yellen (based on the novel *the splinter fleet* by John Milholland); ph, Arthur Miller; ed, Robert Simpson; md, Art Lange; art d, William Darling, Hans Peters; set d, Thomas Little; cos, Gwen Wakeling.

Action Drama/Adventure   Cas.   (PR:A   MPAA:NR)

SUBMARINE RAIDER*   (1942) 65m COL bw

John Howard (*Chris Warren*), Marguerite Chapman (*Sue Curry*), Bruce Bennett (*1st Officer Russell*), Warren Ashe (*Bill Warren*), Eileen O'Hearn (*Vera Lane*), Nino Pipitone (*Capt. Yamanada*), Philip Ahn (*1st Officer Kawakami*), Larry Parks (*Sparksie*), Rudy Robles (*Steward Seffi*), Roger Clark (*Grant Duncan*), Forrest Tucker (*Pulaski*), Eddie Laughton (*Shannon*), Stanley Brown (*Levy*), Jack Shay (*Oleson*), Gary Breckner (*Brick Brandon*).

Unconvincing script and poor special effects sink this submarine film from the start. Quickly made, it is based on the Japanese attack on Pearl Harbor. It relates fictional events that occurred before the attack, particularly a story line involving Chapman, who ends up on a submarine after the pleasure boat she was on has been sunk. The sub tries to warn the U.S. base about the upcoming attack, but to no avail. The scenes involving the submarine and plane battle are excellent, but the rest of the battle scenes are strictly mediocre.

p, Wallace MacDonald; d, Lew Landers; w, Aubrey Wisberg; ph, Franz F. Planer; ed, William Lyon.

War Drama   (PR:A   MPAA:NR)

SUBMARINE SEAHAWK**½   (1959) 83m AIP bw

John Bentley (*Paul Turner*), Brett Halsey (*David Shore*), Wayne Heffley (*Dean Stoker*), Steve Mitchell (*Andy Flowers*), Henry McCann (*Ellis*), Frank Gerstle (*Capt. Boardman*), Paul Maxwell (*Bill Hallohan*), Jan Brooks (*Ellen Turner*), Mabel Rea (*Maisie*), Leon Tyler (*Ed*), Nicky Blair (*Sam*), Hal Bogart, Don Fenwick (*Radio Operators*), Frank Watkins (*Sonar Operator*), Marilyn Hanold (*Nancy*), Dolores Domasin (*Waitress*), Robin Priest (*Medic*), Frank Ray (*Shore Patrol*), Brian Wood (*Courier*), Scott Peters, Ted Fish, Vince Williams, Alan Aric, Howard Hampton (*Sailors*).

Bentley stars as a Navy tactical instructor with little command experience who is made commander of the submarine *Seahawk*. His crew as well as executive officer Maxwell, who had expected to be promoted to the position Bentley now holds, resent Bentley's inexperience and his consistent orders to stand by rather than to sink Japanese aircraft carriers in the sub's vicinity. During the course of the film they discover that Bentle y was on orders to wait for other U.S. forces to arrive and that the Seahawk is to join a large maneuver to clear the Japanese out of the area. The film is a typical war feature, heavy on the action and stock character types and complete with library footage of WW II battles. Originally released on a double bill with AIP's PARATROOP COMMAND.

p, Alex Gordon; d, Spencer G. Bennet; w, Lou Rusoff, Owen Harris; ph, Gilbert Warrenton; m, Alexander Laszlo; ed, Ronald Sinclair.

War Drama   (PR:A   MPAA:NR)

SUBMARINE X-1**½   (1969, Brit.) 89m Mirisch-Oakmont/UA c

James Caan (*Lt. Comdr. Bolton*), Rupert Davies (*Vice Adm. Redmayne*), David Sumner (*Lt. Davies*), William Dysart (*Lt. Gogan*), Norman Bowler (*Sub-Lt. Pennington*), Brian Grellis (*Chief Petty Officer Barquist*), Paul Young (*Leading Seaman Quentin*), John Kelland (*Sub-Lt. Willis*), Kenneth Farrington (*Chief Petty Officer Knowles*), George Roubicek (*Redmayne's Flag Officer*), Keith Alexander (*Sub-Lieutenant*), Carl Rigg (*Chief Petty Officer Kennedy*), Nicholas Tate (*Leading Seaman on X-1*), Steve Kirby (*Leading Seaman on X-2*), Dennis Mayers (*Sub-Lieutenant on X-1*), Keith Alexander (*Sub-Lieutenant on X-3*), Diana Beevers (*W.R.N.S. Officer*), Paul Hansard (*Comdr. Steiner*), Hans De Vries (*German Lieutenant*), Richard Steele (*Captain in Redmayne's Office*), Desmond Jordan (*Naval Doctor*), George Pravda (*Capt. Erlich*).

It took two years from the time this action film was made until it was released in the U.S. Lensed in beautiful Scotland, with interiors at Boreham Woods Studio in London, it's a WW II submarine story and, since this was already 24 years after the war ended, there was little interest in the picture as it offered nothing new. Caan is a Canadian sub commander in 1943. His sub is sunk and most of his men drown when he attempts to take on a behemoth German battleship and comes off second best. There's an official inquiry and Caan is cleared of negligence, but the men who survived still hold him accountable and let their feelings show. Caan gets another assignment from admiral Davies. The development of mini-subs (four-man crews) has made it necessary to train sailors for the assignment of sailing these new ships. Caan must train the crews for three subs and secrecy is of utmost importance. The subs will be heavily laden with explosives but no one yet knows what the exact mission is. Some of the men are the survivors of Caan's last fiasco and rankle under Caan's martinet attitude, for they know how incompetent he truly is. They are training in a secret area and are under surveillance by Nazi recon planes. German troops parachute into the area and are repelled, but now the mission must get under way immediately as the enemy knows something is going on. They get the assignment: knock out the *Lindendorf*, the same ship that sunk Caan's last command. In the open sea they'd never have a chance, but since the battleship is currently undergoing minor work and resting in a fjord in Nazi-occupied Norway they must sink it right away. The three subs depart, snake their ways through mine fields, battle off Nazi underwater frogmen, and come closer to their quarry. One of the subs is destroyed by depth charges, the second is forced to the surface and the men are taken aboard the Linden dorf for questioning. They are about to be tortured into revealing the nature of their mission when the third sub manages to set off its explosives and sends the battleship to a watery grave. Location work at Loch Ness (but no sign of the Monster). Good cinematography, underplayed acting. Caan, who can take on the nature of those around him like a chameleon (the New York-born actor's Chicago accent in THIEF was flawless), is even more enigmatic than his British compatriots, so he borders on somnambulism, except when he is showing himself to be a strict disciplinarian. Director Graham may, or may not, have had a hand in the story with Champion. He did not get a credit for it.

p, John C. Champion; d, William Graham; w, Donald S. Sanford, Guy Elmes (based on a story by Champion, Edmund H. North); ph, Paul Beeson (DeLuxe Color); m, Ron Goodwin; ed, John S. Smith; art d, Bill Andrews; spec eff, Bowie Films; makeup, George Blackler.

War Drama   (PR:A   MPAA:G)

SUBMARINE ZONE (SEE: ESCAPE TO GLORY, 1941)

SUBMERSION OF JAPAN, THE (SEE: TIDAL WAVE 1975, Jap./U.S.)

SUBSTITUTION* (1970) 73m Boxoffice International c

Chuck Sailor (Henry Hedon), Patrice Nastasia (Alice Hedon), James Paulin (Fred Letcher), Marnie Kay (Dottie Letcher), Pam Collins, Kevin Johnston, Pat Duran, Leslie Schootz, Bernie Schootz, Fran Briggs, Jim Muntz, Carol Shiada, Diane Hunter, Renee Ray, Dana Schootz, Mary Bauer.

Sailor and Nastasia are bored with each other sexually. His buddy tells him to visit the Mahariji and Sailor skeptically goes. His first night back after getting help, he is in bed waiting for his wife. Doubts start crossing his mind about the whole thing, then out steps the most sexually attractive woman he has ever seen and she gives him the night of his life. And it continues with the same routine every night; his wife goes to the bathroom to get ready and out steps another gorgeous woman. The mystic has convinced Sailor to use his imagination and his wife has also done the same with her husband.

p&d, Walt Davis; m, Jonathan; makeup, Valli.

Comedy (PR:O MPAA:NR)

SUBTERFUGE* (1969, US/Brit.) 89m Interel-VTR-Commonwealth United/Commonwealth United Entertainment c

Gene Barry (Donovan), Joan Collins (Anne Langley), Richard Todd (Col. Victor Redmayne), Tom Adams (Peter Langley), Suzanna Leigh (Donetta), Michael Rennie (Goldsmith, CIA agent), Marius Goring (Shevik), Scott Forbes (Pannell), Colin Gordon (Kitteridge), Guy Deghy (Dr. Lundgren), Dermot Kelly (Van Driver), Stuart Cooper (Dubrossman), John Welsh (Heiner), Clifford Earl (Policeman), Ron Pember (Photographer), Gary Clifford (Michael Langley), Jane Blackburn (Aunt Mary), Harry Locke, Fred Peisley (Tramps), Sidney Vivian (Taxi Driver), Robert Raglan (Fennimore), Graham Lines (Immigration Officer), Bill Nagy (Embassy Attache), John Clifford (Government Chauffeur), Freda Dowie (Waitress), Charles Lamb (Caretaker), Marian Diamond (Schoolteacher), Carmen Dene, Lyn Marshall, Donna Reading, Valerie Hudson (Club Waitresses), Stella Sands (Nude).

Barry is the hero in the this stilted action film that pays special attention to Collins' physical attributes. A CIA agent on assingment in England, Barry is trying to ferret out a double agent. As assorted characters come under suspicion, he has time for a fling with Collins, the wife of one of the agents being investigated. Collins also has to "suffer" the kidnaping of her son, but judging from her appearance, a few visits to the beauty salon and shopping trip have eased her upset.

p, Trevor Wallace, Peter Snell; d, Peter Graham Scott; w, David Whitaker; ph, Roy Fuller (Eastmancolor); m, Cyril Ornadel; ed, Bill Lewthaite; art d, Roy Fouracre; md, Ornadel; m/l, "No Escape," Ornadel, Norman Newell (sung by Malcolm Roberts), "Love Looks Good on You," Ornadel, Peter Callander (sung by Marmalade).

Crime Drama Cas. (PR:A MPAA:NR)

SUBTERRANEANS, THE* (1960) 89m MGM bw

Leslie Caron (Mardou Fox), George Peppard (Leo Percepied), Janice Rule (Roxanne), Roddy McDowall (Yuri Gligoric), Anne Seymour (Charlotte Percepied), Jim Hutton (Adam Moorad), Scott Marlowe (Julien Alexander), Arte Johnson (Arial Lavalerra), Ruth Storey (Analyst), Bert Freed (Bartender), Gerry Mulligan (Joshua Hoskins), Carmen McRae (Herself), Andre Previn (Himself), Paul Sand (Poet), Nanette Fabray (Society Woman), Shelly Manne, Red Mitchell, Art Farmer, Dave Bailey, Buddy Clark, Russ Freeman, Art Pepper, Bob Enevoldsen, William R. Perkins, Frank Hamilton.

Jack Kerouac's "beat" novel came to the screen with some significant changes in plot and character and the result was disappointing. Peppard is a Columbia graduate and former Olympic champion who has turned his attention to noveling and searches for the meaning of life in San Francisco's legendary North Beach. He comes across a coffee house coterie of beatniks and is taken by free spirit Caron (in the novel her character was black). They fall for each other, roll around the sack for a while, and when she becomes pregnant, decide to join society once again–together (they split painfully in the book). Reputedly producer Freed intended to use a pair of unknown recent college graduates to write and direct the film, but changed his mind, slotting in Thom and McDougall instead. Beautifully poetic in its best moments and like something written by a dyslexic William Faulkner at its worst, THE SUBTERRANEANS would have been better left on paper. The jazz that played so important a part in the book is carried over into the film's soundtrack. Andre Previn wrote most of the numbers and they were interpreted by a number of leading jazz musicians. Songs include: "Wanderin'," "Leo In Bar," "Roxanne at Ariels's" (Andre Previn), "Should I" (Nacio Herb Brown, Arthur Freed), "Coffee Time" (Harry Warren, Freed), "Look Ma, No Clothes," "Analyst."

p, Arthur Freed, d, Ranald McDougall; w, Robert Thom (based on the novel by Jack Kerouac); ph, Joseph Ruttenberg (CinemaScope, Metrocolor); m,

Andre Previn; ed, Ben Lewis; art d, George W. Davis, Urie McCleary; set d, Henry Grace, Hugh Hunt; cos, Moss Mabry; spec eff, Lee LeBlanc; makeup, William Tuttle.

Drama (PR:C MPAA:NR)

SUBURBAN WIVES* (1973, Brit.) 90m Blackwater/Scotia International Films c

Eva Whishaw (Sarah), Maggie Wright (Irene), Peter May (John), Barry Linehan (John's Boss), Nicola Austine (Jean), Claire Gordon (Sheila), James Donnelly (Bookmaker), Heather Chasen (Kathy), Dennis Hawthorne (Kathy's Husband), Gabrielle Drake (Secretary), Yokki Rhodes (Yokki), Ian Sinclair (Water-Skiing Instructor), Jane Cardew (Carole), Robin Culver (Photographer), Pauline Peart (Mavis), Richard Thorpe (Sarah's Husband), Brian Miller (Husband's Friend), Sidonie Bond (Jill), Timothy Parkes (Jill's Husband), Mia Martin (Helene).

When it first came out this was a porno film, but some scenes were edited to make it more a palatable "R". It takes a satirical look at the sex lives of some bored housewives and the situations they get themselves into. It is told in narrative style by ambitious newspaperwoman Whishaw, who relates the tales of eight couples: her biggest story to date. The film suffered from editing, as some of the stories are loosely tied together and nothing flows well. Music adds much to the satire.

p, Morton Lewis; d&w, Derek Ford; ph, Bill Holland, Roy Poynter; m, Terry Warr; ed, Terry Keefe.

Drama (PR:O MPAA:R)

SUBVERSIVES, THE*** (1967, Ital.) 105m Ager bw (I SOVVERSIVO)

Ferruccio De Ceresa (Ludovico), Lucio Dalla (Ermanno), Giorgio Arlorio (Sebastiano), Giulio Brogi (Ettore), P.P. Capponi (Muzio), Marija Tocinowsky (Giulia), Fabienne Fabre (Giovanna).

A tightly made, well-knit drama that uses the death of Italy's Communist leader, Palmiero Togliatti, as a connecting device for four stories showing idealism losing force as the party enters a new phase. The fervor and romance of revolution are slowly dying as the party assumes its place in contemporary Halian society and individual concerns take precedence. The film reveals how Togliatti's death affects different people from diverse backgrounds. In one story, a man's wife falls into a lesbian relationship with one of his old girl friends while he attends the funeral. Another has a Venezuelan radical in bed with his rich lover, only to leave her to go back to his homeland and help "the cause." And a philosophy student decides to take a rebel stand in another of the sections. THE SUBBERSIVES was directed by the team of Paolo and Vittorio Taviani, who had 10 years of excellent filmmaking to their credit at the time.

d&w, Paolo and Vittorio Taviani; ph, Gianni Nazisi, Giuseppe Ruzzolino; m, Giovanni Fusco.

Drama (PR:C MPAA:NR)

SUBWAY EXPRESS* (1931) 68m COL bw

Jack Holt (Inspector Killian), Aileen Pringle (Dale Tracy), Fred Kelsey (Kearney), Alan Roscoe (Edward Tracy, Stock Broker), Jason Robards, Sr (Borden), Sidney Bracey (Stevens), Selmer Jackson (Mason), William Humphrey (Mr. Cotton), Ethel Wales (Mrs. Cotton), Lilliane Leighton (Mrs. Mullins), James Goss (Detective Mulvaney), Mason Williams (Prize Fighter), Harry Semels (Tony), Robert St. Angelo (Zippe), John Kelly (Motorman), Bertha Blackman, Robert Linden, Dorothy Bay, Bob Kortman, Sally St. Claire, Mary Gordon, Earl Seid, Ginger Connolley.

Too talky, turtle-paced, and just plain boring is this story of a killing done on the New York subway system. The killer rigged the wiring to cause a powerful enough shock to do someone in. As everyone on the train is being quizzed, the audience just wishes the end would come soon, and after the third round of questioning Holt finds the killer. Finally, for what it's worth, the action takes place entirely within the subway system.

d, Fred Newmeyer; w, Earl Snell (based on a play by Eva Kay Flint, Martha Madison); ph, Joseph Walker; ed, Arthur Huffsmith.

Mystery (PR:A MPAA:NR)

SUBWAY IN THE SKY½** (1959, Brit.) 85m Orbit/UA bw

Van Johnson (Maj. Baxter Grant), Hildegarde Neff (Lilli Hoffman), Albert Lieven (Carl von Schecht), Cec Linder (Capt. Carson), Katherine Kath (Anna Grant), Vivian Matalon (Stefan), Carl Jaffe (Adler), Chuck Keyser (Harwell), Edward Judd (Molloy), Gaylord Cavallaro (Switchboard Operator), Brian Wilde (Policeman), Bill Edwards, Michael Bell (G.I.'s), Kerrigan Prescott (Sentry), James Maxwell (Officer), Gerda Larsen (Stewardess), Tom Watson (Corporal).

An intriguing crime tale set in Berlin with Johnson starring as a military medic accused of trafficking in stolen drugs. He escapes from the M.P.'s and hides out in a flat his wife rented, unaware that she has sublet it to Neff, a steamy night club singer. Johnson pleads with Neff to help him and – for reasons that can only be attributed to romance - she agrees. Johnson is convinced that his wife somehow stole the key to his military drug supply, but the real culprit is soon identified as his malicious stepson, Matalon. Neff, who undertook a career change in the 1960s as a cabaret singer and songwriter, delivers one tune, "It Isn't Love."

p, Sydney Box, John Temple-Smith, Patrick Filmer-Sankey; d, Muriel Box; w, Jack Andrews (based on the play by Ian Main); ph, Wilkie Cooper; ed, Jean Barker; art d, George Provis.

Crime   (PR:C   MPAA:NR)

SUBWAY RIDERS   (1981) 118m Hep/Mainline c

Robbie Coltrane (Detective Fritz Langley), Charlene Kaleina (Claire Smith), Cookie Mueller (Penelope Trasher), John Lurie (The Saxophonist), Amos Poe (Writer Ant), Susan Tyrrell (Eleanor Langley), Bill Rice (Mr. Gollstone), Leigh Taylor (Susannah), Babs Egan (Maid), M. DeMuro, S. Moss, C. Yee, F. Kutlik, S. Vermont, A. Mashkov, J. Zaloga (Victims), Paul Ricci (Bodessa Owner), Emilio Cubero (The Poet), Lance Loud (1st Client), Tony Schafrazi (Last Client), Henry Benvenutti (Super), Nina Gaidarova (Upstairs Girl), Lindzee Smith (Mugger), Ed Buck (Vulture), Emily Poe (Cola-Marie), Glenn O'Brien (C.O.D. Isherwood), Chris Kosburg (Boy in Bed), Jane (Bartender), Tom Wright (On the Waterfront).

Mostly boring underground detective film shot on 16mm in New York City has Lurie a homicidal sidewalk saxophonist who murders his listeners, then flees on the subway. Detective Coltrane investigates and encounters a variety of New Wave low-lifes. A few good supporting performances, particularly Tyrrell (one of the few professionals in the cast) as the heroin addict wife of Coltrane, and some clever lines can't overcome a basically tedious story filled with long, dreary monologs and self-conscious references to a pack of B movies. Lurie later appeared in STRANGER THAN PARADISE (1984) and Lance Loud had earlier appeared as the homosexual son who comes out of the closet in the milestone documentary "An American Family". The best thing here is definitely the score, composed by some of the leading figures in the avant garde music scene.

P, Johanna Heer, Amos Poe; d&w, Poe; ph, Heer (TVC Color); ed, Orlando Gallini, Heer, Poe; m/l, "Urban Landscape No. 3 - The Tunnel," "Urban Lands cape No. 4," "1984," Robert Fripp, performed by Fripp, "10 Themes for Subway Riders," "The Writers Theme," "Composition in B Minor," Ivan Kral, performed by Kral, "Harlem Nocturne," Earle Hagen, "Demented," J. Lurie, "Conquest of Rar," J. Lurie, E. Lurie, A. Fier, "Do the Wrong Things," J. Lurie, S. Piccolo, performed by the Lounge Lizards; makeup, Claudia Porcelli.

Crime   (PR:O   MPAA:NR)

SUCCESS   (SEE: AMERICAN SUCCESS COMPANY, THE, 1979)

SUCCESS AT ANY PRICE**   (1934) 75m RKO bw

Douglas Fairbanks, Jr (Joe Martin), Genevieve Tobin (Agnes Carter), Frank Morgan (Raymond Merritt), Colleen Moore (Sarah Griswold), Edward Everett Horton (Fisher), Allen Vincent (Jeffery Halliburton), Nydia Westman (Dinah McCabe), Henry Kolker (Hadfield), Spencer Charters (Crawford), William B. Davidson (Ryan, Private Detective).

Writer John Howard Lawson was one of the blacklisted "Hollywood Ten" (the group of movie people convicted of contempt of Congress for refusing to reveal past political associations before Joseph McCarthy's House Committee on Un-American Activities), and this film shows his total disdain for and disgust with capitalism. Fairbanks is after the American dream - success - and nothing will stop him on his way to the top. He has no feeling for anyone or anything as he uses every trick in the book, legal or illegal, to make more and more money. But it all catches up with him and he sees suicide as the only way to escape. He fails in his attempt to do himself in, but ends up with Moore (who has always been there for him) when he finally came to his senses.

d, J. Walter Ruben; w, John Howard Lawson, Howard J. Green (based on the play "Success Story" by Lawson); ph, Henry W. Gerrard; ed, George Hively.

Drama   (PR:A   MPAA:NR)

SUCCESSFUL CALAMITY, A**½   (1932) 72m WB bw

George Arliss (Henry Wilton), Mary Astor (Emmie Wilton), Evalyn Knapp (Peggy Wilton), Grant Mitchell (Connors, Butler), David Torrence (Partington), William Janney (Eddie Wilton), Hardie Albright (George Struthers), Hale Hamilton (John Belden), Fortunio Bonanova (Pietro Rafaelo), Randolph Scott (Larry), Nola Luxford (Mary), Murray Kinnell (Curtis), Richard Tucker (Lawrence), Barbara Leonard (Pauline), Harold Minjur (Valet), Leon Waycoff [Ames] (Barney Davis), Oscar Apfel.

A lightweight comedy that stretches reality a little to keep its bright outlook. Arliss is a rich man who comes home after a long trip and finds everything in his house in disarray, as his kids totally ignore him and expect him to carry the load all the time. So, when he walks through the door, he announces he has lost all his money and they have to start living like

paupers. The kids don't whine about it, but start pitching in, in the most funny of ways–his son goes for a job as a pilot and his daughter is willing to marry a jerk she doesn't like. Even the butler donates his saved-up money. After learning that his family does care about one another, Arliss lets them go on for a while being poor before striking it "rich" again.

p, Lucien Hubbard; d, John G. Adolfi; w, Austin Parker, Maude Howell, Julien Josephson (based on a play by Clare Kummer); ph, James Van Trees; ed, Howard Bretherton.

Comedy   (PR:A   MPAA:NR)

SUCCESSFUL FAILURE, A**½   (1934) 62m MON bw

William Collier, Sr, Lucille Gleason, Russell Hopton, Gloria Shea, William Janney, Jameson Thomas, George Breakston, Richard Tucker, Clarence Wilson, Francis McDonald.

Collier is a veteran newspaperman who buckles under the pressure that his inconsiderate family lays on him. Eventually he loses his job, but finds himself a success in a new career - radio. An innocuous programmer which provides a little cheer and a couple of smiles.

d, Arthur Lubin; w, Marion Orth (based on a story by Michael Kane); ph, Jerry Ash; ed, Jack Ogilvie.

Comedy   (PR:A   MPAA:NR)

SUCH A GORGEOUS KID LIKE ME*
(1973, Fr.) 100m Les Films du Carrosse/COL c (UNE BELLE FILLE COMME MOI; GB: A GORGEOUS BIRD LIKE ME)

Bernadette Lafont (Camille Bliss), Claude Brasseur (Monsieur Murene), Charles Denner (Arthur), Guy Marchand (Sam Golden), Andre Dussollier (Stanislas Previne), Philippe Leotard (Clovis Bliss), Anne Kreis (Helene), Gilberte Geniat (Isobel Bliss), Daniele Girard (Florence Golden), Martine Ferriere (Prison Secretary), Michel Delahaye (Monsieur Marchal), Annick Fourgerie (Schoolmistress), Gaston Ouvrard (Old Prison Warder), Jacob Weizbluth (Alphonse).

A black comedy which is one of Truffaut's darker, and therefore often ignored, pictures about women and their magical hold over men. Lafont, who first appeared in Truffaut's 1957 short LES MISTONS (THE BRATS), takes up where she left off some 15 years earlier. In LES MISTONS she was tormented by a quintet of young boys who were very much in love with her. Here Lafont is able to take revenge on her tormentors. The picture starts with a sociologist, Dussollier, preparing to write a book called Criminal Women (which he never gets to publish). He visits a women's prison and decides to interview convicted murderess Lafont, passing up offers to interview a woman who dismembered her victims or another who would strangle them using only one hand. With his tape recorder, Dussollier captures Lafont's story, though her words sometimes differ from the pictures on the screen. He learns that she didn't commit the murder that she is in prison for (a child filmmaker has the proof on film but refuses to let Dussollier see it because it is still in "rushes"–its unedited form). Through Lafont's interview, Dussollier discovers that she has been surrounded by murders or murder attempts–she is indirectly responsible for the deaths of her father and her mother-in-law, and was unsuccessful in her attempts to kill attorney Brasseur and husband Leotard with rat poison. She is eventually acquitted of her crime and rises to become a famed singer, not because of her voice (which is wretched) but because of the publicity that surrounds her case. Backstage at one of her performances, when she is confronted with both Leotard and Dussollier, she shoots and kills Leotard. Exercising the power she holds over her men, Lafont hands the gun to Dussollier and lets him take the blame. SUCH A GORGEOUS KID LIKE ME is not the type of film that most audiences want to see from Truffaut. Most preferred instead to watch DAY FOR NIGHT (1973), his next film (and an admittedly superior one–a livelier and brighter picture). SUCH A GORGEOUS KID LIKE ME, though it may not initially seem Truffautesque, has roots in a number of his previous films. Truffaut compares this film to THE WILD CHILD (1969)– "For me, [Lafont's! ... the female replica of THE WILD CHILD where you have somebody who is wild and somebody who is trying to educate her." Lafont's murderous female character is also seen in JULES AND JIM (1961), THE BRIDE WORE BLACK (1967), and to a lesser non-violent extent in THE STORY OF ADELE H. (1975). While it may not be an audience pleaser, SUCH A GORGEOUS KID LIKE ME is a definite must for those who are interested in learning about the "total" Truffaut–the dark side as well as the well-known persona.

p, Marcel Berbert; d, Francois Truffaut; w, Truffaut, Jean-Loup Dabadie (based on the novel by Henry Farrell); ph, Pierre William Glenn (Eastmancolor); m, Georges Delerue; ed, Yann Dedet; art d, Jean-Pierre Kohut [Svelko]; cos, Monique Dury.

Drama   (PR:O   MPAA:R)

SUCH GOOD FRIENDS*   (1971) 101m Sigma/PAR c

Dyan Cannon (*Julie Messinger*), James Coco (*Dr. Timmy Spector*), Jennifer O'Neill (*Miranda Graham*), Ken Howard (*Cal Whiting, Photographer*), Nina Foch (*Mrs. Wallman*), Laurence Luckinbill (*Richard Messinger*), Louise Lasser (*Marcy Berns*), Burgess Meredith (*Bernard Kalman*), Sam Levene (*Uncle Eddie*), William Redfield (*Barney Halstead*), James Beard (*Dr. Mahler*), Rita Gam (*Doria Perkins*), Nancy Guild (*Molly Hastings*), Elaine Joyce (*Marion Spector*), Nancy R. Pollack (*Aunt Harriet*), Doris Roberts (*Mrs. Gold*), Lee Sabinson (*Dr. Bleiweiss*), Clarice Taylor (*Mrs. McKay*), Virginia Vestoff (*Emily Lapham*), Richard B. Shull (*Clarence Fitch*), Lawrence Tierney (*Guard*), Bette Howard, Michael Giordano III, Oscar Grossman, T.J. Hargrave, Joel Veigg, Joseph Papp and The Shakespeare Theatre in the Park.

A zero of a comedy about a modern couple who have problems. Luckinbill has to go into the hospital for minor surgery and Cannon discovers her husband's little black book, full of the names of her friends. Cannon decides to get even and engage in some extramarital affairs of her own. While she is trading partners, Luckinbill's mole-removal surgery has become a comedy of errors and he dies. This film was directed by the legendary Otto Preminger, but instead of being contemporary, it is just utterly contemptible. Still, it provides a look at a tough-skinned New York life style that Big Apple resident Preminger well understood. The main screenwriting credit went to Esther Dale, the pseudonym used by Elaine May (and borrowed from the capable character actress), who disdained screenwriting credits for films she hadn't directed. Novelist-screenwriter Joan Didion is also said to have contributed to the screenplay, but her work was uncredited.

p&d, Otto Preminger; w, Esther Dale [Elaine May], David Shaber (based on the novel by Lois Gould); ph, Gayne Rescher (Movielab); m, Thomas Z. Shepard; ed, Harry Howard; prod d, Rouben Ter-Arutunian; cos, Hope Bryce Preminger, Ron Talsky; m/l, "Suddenly, It's All Tomorrow," Shepard, Robert Brittan (sung by O.C. Smith); makeup, Saul Meth.

Comedy   **(PR:O   MPAA:R)**

SUCH IS LIFE**½   (1936, Brit.) 80m Incorporated Talking Films/National Provincial bw (AKA: MUSIC AND MILLIONS)

Gene Gerrard (*Jack Rayner*), Claude Dampier (*Green*), Jean Colin (*Betty Blair*), Eve Gray (*Vicky*), Frank Birch (*Mockett*), McArthur Gordon (*Chapman*), Aubrey Mallalieu (*Sallust*), Paul Sheridan (*Mandeville*), Billie Carlyle (*Secretary*), Robert Ashley, William Daunt, Bill Holland, John Mann, Chela & Dorvay.

Returning from vacation, millionaire Gerrard finds that a talented ne'er-do-well has homesteaded his posh London flat in his absence. Impressed by Dampier's gall, Gerrard takes him on as personal secretary. His life style altered by his new employee's manic personality, Gerrard falls in love with a pretty typist and, posing as a humble clerk in a talent agency he has purchased, helps her find stardom as a singer.

p, Reginald Gottwaltz, Brandon Fleming; d, Randall Faye; w, Fleming; ph, Geoffrey Faithfull.

Comedy   **(PR:A   MPAA:NR)**

SUCH IS THE LAW**   (1930, Brit.) 88m Stoll/BUT bw

Janice Adair (*Marjorie Marjoribanks*), C. Aubrey Smith (*Sir James Whittaker*), Lady Tree (*Granny*), Kate Cutler (*Mother*), Carl Harbord (*Vivian Fairfax*), Bert Coote (*Sir George*), Rex Maurice (*Philip Carberry*), Pamela Carme (*Mrs. Marjoribanks*), Aileen Despard, Frank Goldsmith, Winifred Oughton, Charles Fancourt. Cast from THE PRICE OF DIVORCE: Wyndham Standing, Frances Day, Miriam Seegar, Rex Maurice, Nancy Price, Gibb McLaughlin, Maud Gill, Frances Rose Campbell, Johnny Ashby, James Fenton.

Coming on the coat tails of sound, SUCH IS THE LAW is an attempt by producer Oswald Mitchell to recoup the losses of his unreleased silent THE PRICE OF DIVORCE (1928). He simply framed that silent tale with a talkie dealing with a mother telling her daughter a story whi ch will save her marriage. Mitchell was inventive, but his hard work was to no avail, since the public didn't like the story–with or without sound.

p, Oswald Mitchell; d, Sinclair Hill; w, Leslie Howard Gordon (based on a story by Reginald Fogwell); ph, Desmond Dickinson.

Drama/Romance   **(PR:A   MPAA:NR)**

SUCH MEN ARE DANGEROUS**   (1930) 83m FOX bw

Warner Baxter (*Ludwig Kranz*), Catherine Dale Owen (*Elinor Kranz*), Albert Conti (*Paul Strohm*), Hedda Hopper (*Muriel Wyndham*), Claude Allister (*Fred Wyndham*), Bela Lugosi (*Dr. Erdmann*).

A German businessman commits suicide by jumping out of a plane. Or does he? Baxter is the unattractive jumper whom Owen has married only for his money. Baxter disappears and undergoes plastic surgery in the Alps, but not only does his face undergo a radical change, so too does his personality. He shows up in Paris, still wealthy, because he left himself plenty of money under a different name. He even courts his widow, who he throws money

at, buying a kiss from her at a charity event and letting someone else do the honors. The story is decent, but the changes in Baxter's character are too unbelievable: A surgeon can't instill a personality through his knife.

d, Kenneth Hawks; w, Ernest Vajda (based on a story by Elinor Glyn); ph, L. W. O'Connell, George Eastman; m, Dave Stamper; ed, Harold Schuster; art d, Stephen Goosson; cos, Sophie Wachner.

Drama   **(PR:A   MPAA:NR)**

SUCH MEN ARE DANGEROUS   (SEE: RACERS, THE, 1955)

SUCH THINGS HAPPEN   (SEE: LOVE IS A RACKET, 1932)

SUCH WOMEN ARE DANGEROUS*½   (1934) 81m FOX bw

Warner Baxter (*Michael Shawn*), Rosemary Ames (*Helen Hallock, Secretary*), Rochelle Hudson (*Vernie Little*), Mona Barrie (*Wanda Paris*), Herbert Mundin (*Wilson*), Henrietta Crosman (*Aunt Sophie Travers*), Lily D. Stuart (*Ellison*), Irving Pichel (*Stanley*), Jane Barnes (*Nancy Ryan*), Matt Moore (*George Ryan*), Richard Carle, Murray Kinnell, Frank Conroy, Fred Santley, John Sheehan, Bodil Rosing.

Moralistic in tone, this picture has trouble telling its story. It wants to show how an innocent playboy can end up with a murder charge because he has left behind so many vindictive women who want to see him done in even though he is innocent. It drags considerably in the courtroom sequences, with too much time spent on objections and questioning, instead of on developing the characters.

p, Al Rockett; d, James Flood; w, Jane Storm, Oscar M. Sheridan, Lenore Coffee (based on the story "Odd Thursday" by Vera Caspary).

Drama   **(PR:A   MPAA:NR)**

SUCKER, THE***   (1966, Fr./Ital.) 101m Les Films Corona-Explorer/Royal c (LE CORNIAUD; COLPO GROSSO MA NON TROPPO; AKA: THE SUCKER...OR HOW TO BE GLAD WHEN YOU'VE BEEN HAD!)

Bourvil (*Antoine Marechal*), Louis de Funes (*Leopold Saroyan*), Walter Chiari (*La Souris*), Venantino Venantini (*Stutterer*), Beba Loncar (*Ursula*), Daniela Rocca (*Gina*), Lando Buzzanca (*Lino*), Jose-Luis de Vilallonga (*Maurel*), Saro Urzi (*Tagliella*), Pierre Roussel (*Mario Costa*), Michel Galabru (*Martial*), Jean Lefebvre (*Storekeeper*), Henri Genes, Henri Virlogeux, Jacques Eyser, Jacques Ary, Guy Delorme, Yvon Jeanclaude, Alida Chelli, Bernard Meusnier, Jean Meyer, Jean Droze, Jean-Marie Bon, Jacques Ferriere, Bob Lerick, Louis Viret.

A decent Italian comedy with Bourvil outwitting gangsters who have tried to use him. He is on his way out of Paris for a vacation when he gets into a car accident. De Funes, with whom he collided, wants to make it up to him, so he offers to let Bourvil drive his Cadillac to Bordeaux and enjoy his vacation. But Bourvil does not know the car is loaded with contraband, including jewels in the battery fluid and heroin in the tailfins. He is followed by de Funes and another gang but he is totally oblivious to them as they shoot at each other. He picks up a couple of female hitchhikers and just keeps driving along. Finally, he realizes he is being used and leads the gangs to the police. And his vacation gets an even bigger boost when he finds the world's largest diamond in the steering wheel.

p, Yves Laplanche, Enzo Provenzale; d, Gerard Oury; w, Oury, Marcel Jullian, Georges Tabet, Andre Tabet (based on a story by Oury); ph, Henri Decae (Franscope, Eastmancolor); m, Georges Delerue; ed, Albert Jurgenson; art d, Robert Giordani, Francesco Ciarletta.

Comedy   **(PR:A   MPAA:NR)**

SUCKER MONEY*½   (1933) 70m Progressive bw (GB: VICTIMS OF THE BEYOND)

Mischa Auer (*Swami Yormurda*), Phillis Barrington (*Clare Walton*), Ralph Lewis (*John Walton*), Earl McCarthy (*Jimmy Reeves*), Fletcher Norton (*Lukis*), Mae Busch (*Mame*), Mona Lisa, Al Bridge, Anita Faye.

The spiritualist con games are examined here as newspaper reporter McCarthy is after Auer and his gang of phonies. Barrington is a wealthy man's daughter. She has fallen under Auer's power and is involved in an oil scam. As events turn against him, the mystic and his gang get rough. A big chase scene after a murder provides the suspense at the end. The film shows lots of seance action, and attempted to expose the fake spiritualism game. The film was co-directed by Dorothy Reid. She was the widow of silent film star Wallace Reid who died in the early 1920s from complications incurred because of a long drug habit. After her husband died, Dorothy Reid tried to expose the evil of drug use in the film industry. After this campaign, she decided to work against another ill, the mystic racket.

p, Willis Kent; d, Dorothy Reid, Melville Shyer; w, Kent (based on a story by Kent); ph, James Diamond, William Nobles; ed, S. Roy Luby.

Crime Drama   **Cas.**   **(PR:A   MPAA:NR)**

SUCKER ... OR HOW TO BE GLAD WHEN YOU'VE BEEN HAD! THE

(SEE: SUCKER, THE 1966)

SUDAN**½   (1945) 76m UNIV c

Maria Montez (Naila), Jon Hall (Merab), Turhan Bey (Herua), Andy Devine (Nebka), George Zucco (Horadef), Robert Warwick (Maatet), Phil Van Zandt (Setna), Harry Cording (Uba), Peter George Lynn (Bata), Charles Arnt (Khafra the Horse Trader), Ray Teal (Slave Trader), Hans Herbert, Dick Dickinson (Buyers), Bob Barron (Jailer), Gene Stutenroth, Art Miles (Executioners), Charles Morton (Soldier), Tor Johnson (Slaver), Ed Hyans (Master of Ceremonies), James Dime, George Magrill (Guards), Art Foster (Wrestler), Jimmy Lucas, Byron Ruggles, Charles McAvoy (Bettors), Dave Kashner (Crack Bull Whip), Artie Ortego (Starter), Dink Trout (Potter), Duke Johnson (Juggler), Phil Dunham, Alix Nagy, Dan White (Men), Joe Bernard (Horse Owner), Shirley Hunter (Herita), Kay Yorke (Nephytis), Jack Chefe (Mestat), Roy Darmour (Horse Owner), Mary O'Brien (Nephytis), Ann Roberts, Maxine Leeds, Kathleen O'Malley, Rita Benjamin, Rosemarie Babbick, Vivian Mason (Girls), June Pickrell (Old Woman), Belle Mitchell (Woman), Clarke Stevens, Robert Strong (Sentries), Al Ferguson (King), Lloyd Ingraham (Elderly Man).

It's another one of Montez's patented "sand and sex" movies, with lots of dancing girls, brief costumes, and the ubiquitous desert lurking outside the tent. Montez is the new queen of her land of Khemmis (someplace near ancient Egypt) because her father has been assassinated. She is determined to uncover who did the dirty deed and her oily chamberlain, Zucco, suggests that the crime was committed by Bey, who leads a pack of slaves who've recently escaped. Montez believes Zucco (not yet knowing that it was the wily Manchester-born character man who actually killed old daddums) and doffs her royal robes in favor of peasant gear in order to masquerade as a civilian and personally wreak revenge on Bey. She thinks she can trap Bey and take his life and Zucco is all for it, hoping that she will somehow get killed out there so he can assume the throne. On the off-chance that she might actually survive the rigors of the desert, Zucco will take no chances, so he hires Warwick, a slave trader, to kidnap her and dump her body out where the camels roam. Montez, however, is made of stronger stuff and manages to escape her fate with the help of Hall and Devine, two itinerant Egyptian hobo-pickpockets who also steal horses when they can find a willing buyer. Devine and Hall don't know that Montez has the blue blood of royalty pounding in her lovely veins and treat her as they would any woman on the run, with humor and a touch of disdain. Just when it seems they've gotten away, they are re-captured by Warwick and his henchmen. Their deaths are imminent when Bey, at the forefront of his band of slaves, sweeps into the village where the executions are to take place and saves them all, exhibiting lots of derring-do and looking like a Turkish Errol Flynn. (Bey was actually born in Vienna of a Turkish father and Czech mother.) Montez appreciates Bey's intervention but she is still convinced that he was the man who slew her beloved father, although she doesn't tell him that. The group returns to the capital city and, once there, Montez reveals her power by having Bey clapped in jail. No sooner is that accomplished than Zucco shows his true colors (yellow on yellow) and marshals his powers to have Montez tossed in the same prison. Hall and Devine have watched Montez and Bey and realize that the two love each other. Both will die unless they take action and so they arrange to break Bey out of jail, then all flee to the mountains where Bey has been gathering his forces for an eventual assault on Zucco's army. Zucco then uses pain to extract the location of Bey's headquarters from Montez and takes her and his men to the hideout. In a spectacular finish that sees Montez miraculously spared, there are several thousand rocks just waiting to be released on anyone who comes that way; Bey lets the boulders fly and the advancing evil-doers are crushed into fodder. This time, Bey gets the female star and Hall is only used as comedic counterpoint with Devine. Hall had gained some weight and was no longer the svelte leading man he was in ALOMA OF THE SOUTH SEAS, ARABIAN-KNIGHTS, ALI BABA AND THE FORTY THIEVES, and a host of other costume pieces. Dominican-born Montez was only 25 when this was made but her career was already waning. She had weight problems and eventually embarked on a too-strenuous diet and died of a heart attack in her tub at the age of 31. Most of her movies were good examples of well-made B pictures and usually coined money. She ended her career overseas in a series of second-rate French and Italian movies, with her final appearance being in THE PIRATE'S REVENGE (LA VENDETTA DEL CORSARO).

p, Paul Malvern; d, John Rawlins; w, Edmund L. Hartmann; ph, George Robinson (Technicolor); m, Milton Rosen; ed, Milton Carruth; md, Rosen; art d, John B. Goodman, Richard H. Riedel; set d, Russell A. Gausman, Leigh Smith; spec eff, John P. Fulton; m/l, "The Call To Love," "Proud and Free," Rosen, Everett Carter.

Historical Adventure   (PR:A-C MPAA:NR)

SUDDEN BILL DORN*½   (1938) 60m UNIV bw

Buck Jones (Sudden Bill Dorn), Noel Francis (Lorna Kent), Evelyn Brent (Diana), Frank McGlynn, Sr (Cap Jinks), Harold Hodge (Mike Bundy), Ted Adams (Montana), William Lawrence (Hank Smith), Lee Phelps (Ben Fairchild), Tom Chatterton (Rock Morgan), Carlos Valdez (Don Francis), Ezra Paulette (Curly O'Connor), Red Hightower (Bud Williams), Charles

LeMoyne (Sheriff), Adolph Milar (Tony).

A small town goes astray when gold is discovered nearby. This atmosphere of looseness and lawlessness is soon brought to order with the arrival of Jones and his pocketful of heroics. Plenty of action, but pacing is a bit off.

p, Buck Jones; d, Ray Taylor; w, Frances Guihan (based on the story by Jackson Gregory); ph, Allen Thompson.

Western   (PR:A MPAA:NR)

SUDDEN DANGER**½   (1955) 85m AA bw

Bill Elliott (Lt. Doyle), Tom Drake (Curtis), Beverly Garland (Phyllis), Dayton Lummis (Witkins), Helene Stanton (Vera), Lucien Littlefield (Dave), Minerva Urecal (Mrs. Kelly), Lyle Talbot (Woodruff), Frank Jenks (Kenny), Pierre Watkin (Caldwell), John Close (Duncan), Ralph Gamble (Dr. Hastings).

When a sportswear manufacturer's death is ruled a suicide, detective Elliott does some snooping which incriminates the dead woman's blind son, Drake, whose blindness was caused by his mother's carelessness. But the youth manages an operation to cure his blindness and tries to clear his name. Drake finds his mother's former business partner is the real culprit. Strong efforts in all production matters makes for an entertaining melodrama.

p, Ben Schwalb; d, Hubert Cornfield; w, Daniel B. Ullman, Elwood Ullman (based on a story by Daniel Ullman); ph, Ellsworth Fredericks; m, Marlin Skiles; ed, William Austin.

Crime   (PR:A MPAA:NR)

SUDDEN FEAR***½   (1952) 110m RKO bw

Joan Crawford (Myra Hudson), Jack Palance (Lester Blaine), Gloria Grahame (Irene Neves), Bruce Bennett (Steve Kearney), Virginia Huston (Ann Taylor), Touch "Mike" Connors (Junior Kearney).

Despite a slow start, this winds up to be a fine suspense thriller that was good enough to merit recognition from the Academy when they gave Crawford, Palance, and Lang's cinematography Oscar nominations. Crawford is a wealthy San Francisco heiress who is also a successful playwright. She's casting her new opus in New York and meets Palance, who is auditioning for the romantic lead. She doesn't think he's right for the part but he is romantically right for her, and when they meet again, on her train trip back to California, he turns on his charm. By the time they reach Bagdhad by the Bay, they are in love and are soon husband and wife. Palance takes some time away from Crawford to have a little rendezvous with his former flame, Grahame. He tells her that he married Crawford for security (an actor's life is not a secure one), not because of any unbridled passion. He further informs Grahame that she had better not try to break up the marriage. He has plans of his own. Grahame has ways of finding out what Crawford has in mind for her inheritance and learns that the playwright intends to cede all of her late father's money to a foundation devoted to eliminating heart disease. She will then have to live on her writing income, and since she has confidence in her own talents, that's no problem for her...but it is for Palance. Grahame and Palance meet later in Crawford's study and discover that she's made a new will which only allots $10,000 per annum to Palance. But even that small stipend will cease when and if he remarries after her death. As they talk, they don't realize Crawford's dictating machine is on and their conversation is being recorded. They also don't notice that the will is unsigned. It seems that Crawford's lawyer, Bennett, has never trusted Palance and he drafted the will himself, without her ever knowing about it. A new will has since been written to supercede this one and, in that document, Palance has been more than generously remembered. Grahame knows her way around the law and notes the date on the "new" will that is so miserly. It won't take effect until the following Monday, and if Palance is to benefit by the California statutes in existence when a person dies with no will, he should knock Crawford off posthaste. The two depart and Crawford comes in later, sees that the dictating machine has been on, and listens back to the entire conversation of Palance and Grahame. She goes to bed that night but can't sleep, as she is in fear for her life. After a day or so, she surreptitiously breaks into Grahame's flat and locates the fatal poison that she thinks they will try to kill her with. She also finds a gun in good working order. Now she leaves a message, from Grahame, for Palance to meet at the woman's apartment. To make sure Grahame won't be there, she sends Grahame a message ordering her to wait for Palance at a garage in the neighborhood. Her playwright's mind is working overtime as she is putting all the pieces in place. Palance arrives and Crawford is waiting for him with the loaded gun but there's one flaw in her "play," she doesn't have the ability to shoot Palance down. She races out and runs down the hilly San Francisco street. Palance gets into his car and chases after her. As bad luck would have it, Grahame finally got tired of waiting for Palance and is now coming up the hill toward her apartment. The two women are dressed alike, with a coat and the same color scarves around their necks. Palance thinks Grahame is Crawford and heads his car straight for her. By the time he sees who he's aiming at and she sees who the aimer is, it's too late. Palance jerks the steering wheel and slams into Grahame, then dies himself as the car crashes. Crawford has seen the whole thing. Palance and Grahame are both dead and Crawford is free to do whatever she chooses as she walks away from the scene of the accident-murder. Crawford rides the roller coaster of emotions from dewy-eyed love to hatred, hurt, pain, and, eventually, triumph. Making his movie debut was Mike Connors, still using the nom de cinema his agent, Henry Willson, gave him after learning it was the young athlete's nickname at UCLA. Willson was also the man who changed Roy Fitzgerald to Rock Hudson and Arthur Gelien to Tab Hunter. Leading man Palance, one of the new breed of "method actors" who had studied at the Actor's Studio in New York which hatched Marlon Brando and other introspective, inner-directed thespians, proved to unnerve old line movie star Crawford. He was moody and distant during the production and alarmed the actress when, to build up his emotional state, would run madly about the sound stage. Crawford was also annoyed that Palance would cue her lamely when off-camera and she finally told director Miller: "I wish you would tell him that when he's not on camera he should act as though he is." The film was an enormous success, earning back many times its cost of $720,000. Crawford wisely elected to take 48 percent of the profits instead of her $200,000 salary, earning much more than that amount. She received her third Oscar nomination (the others being MILDRED PIERCE for which she won an Oscar and POSSESSED), but she lost out to Shirley Booth in COME BACK, LITTLE SHEBA.

p, Joseph Kaufman; d, David Miller; w, Lenore Coffee, Robert Smith (based on the novel by Edna Sherry); ph, Charles Lang, Jr.; m, Elmer Bernstein; ed, Leon Barsha; md, Bernstein; art d, Boris Leven; set d, Edward G. Boyle; cos, Sheila O'Brien; m/l, "Afraid," Elmer Bernstein, "Sudden Fear," Irving Taylor, Arthur Altman; makeup, Edwin Allen, Josef Norin.

Suspense/Drama (PR:A-C MPAA:NR)

SUDDEN FURY* (1975, Can.) 95m Film Can/Ambassador c

Dominic Hogan (*Fred*), Gay Rowan (*Janet*), Dan Hennessy (*Al*), Hollis McLaren (*Laura*), David Yorston (*Dan*), Sean McCann (*Polanski*), Eric Clavering (*Gas Station Attendant*), Steve Weston, Robin Ward, Gary Huckstep.

Intriguing melodrama that has Hogan getting violently upset when his wife will not help him buy some land that he hopes will pull him out of a financial bind. The final blow between the two comes while on a drive through Northern Ontario. Hogan loses control of the car and crashes. He just leaves his injured wife behind and takes off. Hennessy, a concerned stranger, happens along and finds himself offering more help than he had planned. Though the plot is rather simple, the filmmakers and actors take full advantage of the backwoods setting and heighten the suspense. McCauley provides an excellent soundtrack to enhance the plot.

p, Ben J. Caza; d&w, Brian Damude; ph, James Kelly (Eastmancolor); m, Mathew McCauley; ed, David Nicholson.

Drama/Thriller (PR:C MPAA:PG)

SUDDEN IMPACT*½ (1983) 117m WB c

Clint Eastwood (*Harry Callahan*), Sondra Locke (*Jennifer Spencer*), Pat Hingle (*Chief Jannings*), Bradford Dillman (*Capt. Briggs*), Paul Drake (*Mick*), Audrie J. Neenan (*Ray Parkins*), Jack Thibeau (*Kruger*), Michael Currie (*Lt. Donnelly*), Albert Popwell (*Horace King*), Mark Keyloun (*Officer Bennett*), Kevyn Major Howard (*Hawkins*), Bette Ford (*Leah*), Nancy Parsons (*Mrs. Kruger*), Joe Bellan (*Burly Detective*), Wendell Wellman (*Tyrone*), Mara Corday (*Coffee Shop Waitress*), Russ McCubbin (*Eddie*), Robert Sutton (*Carl*), Nancy Fish (*Historical Society Woman*), Carmen Argenziano (*D'Ambrosia*), Lisa Britt (*Elizabeth*), Bill Reddick (*Police Commissioner*), Lois de Banzie (*Judge*), Matthew Child (*Alby*), Michael Johnson, Nick Dimitri (*Assassins*), Michael Maurer (*George Wilburn*), Pat DuVal (*Bailiff*), Christian Phillips, Steven Kravitz (*Hawkins' Cronies*), Lloyd Nelson (*Desk Sergeant*), Christopher Pray (*Detective Jacobs*), James McEachin (*Detective Barnes*), Maria Lynch (*Hostess*), Ken Lee (*Loomis*), Morgan Upton (*Bartender*), John X. Heart (*Policeman*), Harry Demopoulas (*Dr. Barton*), Lisa London (*Young Hooker*), Tom Spratley (*Senior Man*), Eileen Wiggins (*Hysterical Customer*), John Nowak (*Bank Robber*), Dennis Royston, Melvin Thompson, Jophery Brown, Bill Upton (*Young Guys*), David Gonzales, Albert Martinez, David Rivers, Robert Rivers (*Gang Members*).

After a few setbacks at the box office (BRONCO BILLY, HONKY-TONK MAN, and FIREFOX all decent films, none of which made money by normal Eastwood standards, i.e. blockbusters), Eastwood returned to the popular character of "Dirty" Harry Callahan and directed himself in the role for the first time. The result is a brooding, disturbing film wherein Eastwood examines the darker aspects of the Dirty Harry character (a man whose motivations were always hotly debated by the left-leaning critics who saw him as Richard Nixon's law-and-order avenger) and comes up with a noir-ish, grim, but strangely hopeful film that sees Eastwood come to grips with his character. After being told to leave town for a while by his superiors because his feud with a local crime lord is wreaking havoc on all of San Francisco, Eastwood ventures to a small seaside town for a little peace and quiet. There he becomes embroiled in a brutal series of murders committed by Locke, a young artist who, along with her sister, was raped by a group of local men a few years back. The experience left Locke's sister a complete catatonic, and herself tortured by demons that not only come out through her haunting artwork, but now have manifested themselves in the murders

of the men who raped her. Eastwood investigates the killings, and during his stay in the town, meets and falls in love with Locke, not knowing that it is she who is committing the murders. Eventually he does find out, and after dispatching the last of the rapists, Eastwood is left with the moral dilemma of whether to turn in his love. Fans of the earlier "Dirty Harry" films would expect their hero to do the right thing and grimly turn her over to the police, but Eastwood does not. Instead he holds her close to him and together these disturbed, complex people face an uncertain future. Perhaps Harry sensed that they were two sides of the same coin with only the law separating them. Harry's obsession with dispensing justice to clever criminals who use civil rights as a shield has alienated him from a mainstream society which applauds the removal of the problem at the same time they gasp with horror at the method of disposal. So too is Locke alienated by the loneliness she feels at having been violated and then watching helplessly as the local law officals do nothing (one of the rapists was the son of the police chief). Just as Harry is driven to dispense justice despite what the law says, so is Locke, only she is not protected by a badge. It is at the last moment of SUDDEN IMPACT that Harry realizes that he is no better than she, and instead of pretending to be "holier than thou," he embraces his dark side and, perhaps, purges his demons. The end of SUDDEN IMPACT is hauntingly ambiguous and should, if Eastwood is honest to his character, be the end of the "Dirty Harry" films.

p&d, Clint Eastwood; w, Joseph C. Stinson (based on a story by Earl E. Smith, Charles B. Pierce, based on characters created by Harry Julian Fink, R.M. Fink); ph, Bruce Surtees (Panavision, Technicolor); m, Lalo Schifrin; ed, Joel Cox; prod d, Edward Carfagno; set d, Ernie Bishop; cos, Glenn Wright.

Crime/Drama Cas. (PR:O MPAA:R)

**SUDDEN MONEY*½ (1939) 66m PAR bw

Charles Ruggles (*Sweeney Patterson*), Marjorie Rambeau (*Elsie Patterson*), Charley Grapewin (*Grandpa Casey Patterson*), Broderick Crawford ("Doc" *Finney*), Billy Lee (*Junior Patterson*), Evelyn Keyes (*Mary Patterson*), Phillip Warren (*Eddie Dunn*), Joyce Mathews (*Yolo*), Richard Denning (*Johnny Jordan*), Mary Parker (*Ellen*), Richard Tucker (*Mr. Hinds*), James Burke (*McPherson*), Charles Halton (*Mr. Wixby*), Ethel Wales (*Miss Perkins*), Alex Melesh (*Prof. Tito*), John Gallaudet (*Phil*), John Kelly (*Butch*), Homer Dickinson (*Herbie*), Joe Yule (*Joe*), Billy Engle (*Peewee*), Douglas Wood (*Mr. Jordan*), Eddie Marr (*Diamond*), Mack Gray (*Duke*), Donald Kerr (*Ted*), William B. Davidson (*Sam*), Stanley Price, Dick Elliott, Robert Brister (*Gamblers*).

Unexciting, routine drama has Ruggles and brother-in-law Crawford winning a handsome sum in the lottery, and finding themselves popular with the rest of the family. But the money does not last very long: a blessing as far as this picture is concerned.

p, William C. Thomas; d, Nick Grinde; w, Lewis Foster (based on a play by Milton Lazarus); ph, Henry Sharp; ed, Ellsworth Hoagland; cos, Edith Head.

Comedy/Drama (PR:A MPAA:NR)

SUDDEN TERROR½ (1970, Brit.) 95m Anglo-EMI/NG c (AKA: EYEWITNESS)

Mark Lester (*Ziggy*), Lionel Jeffries (*Colonel*), Susan George (*Pippa*), Tony Bonner (*Tom*), Jeremy Kemp (*Galleria*), Peter Vaughan (*Paul*), Peter Bowles (*Victor*), Betty Marsden (*Mme. Robiac*), Anthony Stamboulish (*Tacherie*), John Allison (*Boutique Boy*), Tom Eytle (*President*), Joseph Furst (*Local Station Sergeant*), Robert Russell (*HQ Sergeant*), Maxine Kalil (*Anne Marie*), David Lodge (*Policeman in Jeep*), Jonathan Burn (*Waiter*), Christopher Robbie (*1st Policeman*), Jeremy Young (*Monk*).

Young Lester witnesses the assassination of an African leader by phony policemen, and must hide from them while trying to persuade his parents and the real police of the truth about what he has seen. Well made, but it's been done before. Nice shots of Malta where the filming was done.

p, Paul Maslansky; d, John Hough; w, Ronald Harwood (based on the novel *Eyewitness* by Mark Hebden); ph, David Holmes, Ernest Robinson (Technicolor); m, Fairfield Parlor, Van Der Graaf Generator; ed, Geoffrey Foot; md, David Symonds; prod d, Herbert Westbrook; set d, Arthur Taksen.

Suspense Cas. (PR:A MPAA:GP)

SUDDENLY*½ (1954) 75m UA bw

Frank Sinatra (*John Baron*), Sterling Hayden (*Tod Shaw*), James Gleason (*Pop Benson*), Nancy Gates (*Ellen Benson*), Kim Charney (*Pidge*), Paul Frees (*Benny Conklin*), Christopher Dark (*Bart Wheeler*), Willis Bouchey (*Dan Carney*), Paul Wexler (*Slim Adams*), Jim Lilburn (*Jud Hobson*), Charles Smith (*Bebop*), Ken Dibbs (*Wilson*), Clark Howatt (*Haggerty*), Dan White (*Burge*), Richard Collier (*Hawkins*), Roy Engel, Ted Stanhope (*Drivers*), Charles Waggenheim (*Kaplan*), John Bernardino (*Trooper*).

Sinatra followed his Oscar-winning performance in FROM HERE TO ETERNITY with this chilling portrayal of a crazed, cold-blooded assassin determined to kill the President. The film takes place in the sleepy California town of Suddenly. The local sheriff, Hayden, is informed by wire that the President of the U.S. will be arriving in town by train. The President is on a fishing trip and his party will take motor vehicles into the mountains from the train station. The whole operation is top secret and Hayden is instructed to keep it quiet until the Secret Service arrives. When the agents do arrive, their commander, Bouchey, sends his men to secure all the shops and houses near the train station to ensure that no one is lurking about. When Bouchey inquires about a big house on a hill overlooking the train station, Hayden informs him that it is the home of his girl friend, Gates (she's a widow), her young son Charney, and her father-in-law, Gleason. When Hayden mentions that Gleason used to be in the Secret Service, Bouchey smiles and says Gleason used to be his boss. Meanwhile, three men dressed like federal agents (Sinatra, Frees, and Dark) arrive in a car. Their leader, Sinatra, sees the house on the hill and tells his driver to go there. While Gleason tinkers with their broken television set, Gates answers the door. Sinatra says that he and his men are FBI agents who have come to secure the house while the President is in town. Gleason is a bit suspicious of the men, but he has been retired for several years and assumes that procedures have changed somewhat. The doorbell rings and it is Hayden and Bouchey (Bouchey has come to visit Gleason). The Secret Service men's reunion is short-lived, however, because Bouchey spots Sinatra and immediately realizes who he is. Before Bouchey can draw his gun, Sinatra guns him down and wounds Hayden in the arm. Sinatra and his men are assassins who have come to kill the President. Sinatra gathers the hostages into the living room and tells them that if there are any false moves, "The kid gets it." He then instructs Frees and Dark to put the kitchen table in front of the living room window–a window that offers a perfect view of the train depot. Sinatra then tells them to bolt his rifle tripod to the table so that it will be perfectly still. Sinatra reveals that he has been paid $500,000 by an unnamed source to kill the President. Hayden taunts Sinatra by telling him that he'll never get away with it. Sinatra responds, "I just make my plans and carry them out." Hayden retorts: "That's what John Wilkes Booth thought, too." "Booth!?" Sinatra sneers, "Hah, I'm no actor. Bustin' my leg on a stage so I can yell 'Down with the tyrant!' If Booth wasn't such a ham he might've made it." Unimpressed, Hayden responds: "The guy who killed Garfield didn't make it, either. Nobody made it." During this period Lilburn, the television repairman, arrives (the family had called him earlier in the day). He, too, is held hostage. In addition to Hayden and Gleason's taunting remarks, the boy, Charney, taunts the killers and calls them cowards. Frees and Dark would like to slap the kid, but Sinatra takes a liking to the boy and enjoys his spunk. At one point Charney produces his cap pistol and shoots Sinatra and the assassin laughs it off. Eventually Sinatra sends Frees down to the station to see if the train is expected to arrive on time. Frees is spotted by an alert deputy, but the lawman is gunned down. Frees is cornered by the Secret Service, but is killed before they can get any information out of him. Sinatra and Dark hear the gunfire and realize what has happened to Frees. As the situation becomes more intense, Sinatra's calm begins to unravel. He orders Lilburn to fix the television set and he begins to babble about the days before the war when he was a nobody. He hated crowds because they made him feel inferior. Then WW II came and they gave him a gun. It made him feel powerful. He killed 27 men during the war. Hayden comments, "You'd rather kill a man than love a girl." Enraged, Sinatra viciously kicks Hayden on his wounded arm. While Sinatra and Hayden argue, Gleason slyly suggests that Lilburn ground the TV set to the kitchen table so that the "reception" will be clearer. Lilburn understands and wires the electricity onto the metal table. Sinatra continues babbling: "Without the gun I'm nothing, and I never had anything before I got one. First time I got one in my hands and killed a man I got some self-respect. I was somebody. Without the gun you would never have spit at me. You would have never even noticed me. But because of the gun you'll remember me as long as you live." The train whistle blows and Sinatra prepares for the assassination. Gleason "accidentally" spills a glass of water at the foot of the metal table. Sinatra goes to look in the gunsight, but is distracted for a moment. Dark then goes to check the sight and is electrocuted–his finger spasms on the trigger sending bursts of gunfire at the train station. The Secret Service heads for the house. Sinatra kicks the wiring away from the table, shoots Lilburn, and pushes Dark's body away from the rifle. He leans over to take aim when Hayden hits him in the back with a heavy ashtray. Gleason tries to wrestle Sinatra to the ground, but is knocked cold by the assassin. Young Charney grabs a fallen pistol and takes a wild shot at Sinatra but he misses and tries to toss the gun to Hayden. Hayden sees Sinatra about to shoot the boy and dives for Charney, knocking him to safety. Determined to kill the President, Sinatra goes back to the rifle, but the train doesn't stop and zooms right on through the station. Sinatra is shocked and deeply disappointed. He begins repeating, "It didn't stop!" over and over. Robbed of his quarry, Sinatra turns on the family. Gates, who is closest to the pistol, shoots Sinatra. Hayden gets to his feet, grabs the gun, and finishes off the assassin. The terror is over. SUDDENLY, made nine years before President John F. Kennedy was assassinated, was chillingly prophetic. Sinatra's performance as the psychopathic killer is one of his best. He perfectly conveys the warped sensibilities of the assassin and we know quite well that he couldn't care less if he gets paid or caught–the act of killing is what drives this man and he'd do it for free. It is one of the most powerful portrayals of a psychopath ever commited to film. Sinatra totally dominates the screen and is ably supported by Hayden. The rest of the cast turns in workmanlike, if unremarkable, performances and director Allen knows where to put the camera to milk the claustrophobic atmosphere for all its worth. A few years after the Kennedy assassination Sinatra was

told that the President's killer, Lee Harvey Oswald, had watched SUDDENLY only days before committing his crime. Sinatra forced United Artists to withdraw both SUDDENLY and his 1962 political thriller, THE MANCHURIAN CANDIDATE (which also involves an assassination), from distribution, ostensibly to prevent other warped minds from being so inspired, but one must assume that Sinatra wished to disassociate himself and his image from these now-controversial films. It's really too bad because both films demonstrate the man's considerable acting talent and are now quite difficult to see. A bizarre footnote: SUDDENLY was recently subjected to the "colorization" process that enables black-and- white films to be made color on videotape. As a good example of how carefully these films are handled by video distributors looking to make a quick buck, Frank Sinatra, known for decades as "Ol' Blue Eyes," has *brown* eyes in the colorized version of SUDDENLY.

p, Robert Bassler; d, Lewis Allen; w, Richard Sale; ph, Charles Clarke; m, David Raksin; ed, John F. Schreyer; art d, Frank Sylos; set d, Howard Bristol; cos, Jack Masters; makeup, Bill Buell.

Crime   **Cas.**   **(PR:C   MPAA:NR)**

SUDDENLY, A WOMAN!   (1967, Den.) 91m PMK c (GUDRUN)

Laila Andersson (*Gudrun*), Jorgen Buckhoj (*Manne*), Poul Reichhardt (*Mr. Hollund*), Nils Asther (*Mr. Rossen*), Birgitte Federspiel (*Mrs. Brunn*), Elsa Kourani (*Mrs. Hollund*), Yvonne Ingdal (*Office Girl*), Constance (*Dancer*), Albert Watson.

A minor effort by the American expatriate Marion Gering (he presented this film), who tried to revive his less than brilliant career by making films in Europe. Here Andersson plays a young woman whose attractive looks nab a number of possible suitors including her boss, a wealthy tycoon, and her lesbian landlady. But her only romantic interest is the boy, Buckhoj, she has known since childhood. Her suitors do not take rejections in the most graceful manner.

p, Morton Schyberg; d, Anker; w, Tom Rowe (English dialog), Anker, Mette Budtz-Jorgensen (based on the novel *Gudrun* by Johannes Vilhelm Jensen); ph, Henning Bendtsen (Eastmancolor); m, Ib Glindermann; art d, Kai Rasch.

Drama   **(PR:O   MPAA:NR)**

SUDDENLY IT'S SPRING½   (1947) 87m PAR bw

Paulette Goddard (*Mary Morely*), Fred MacMurray (*Peter Morely*), Macdonald Carey (*Jack Lindsay*), Arleen Whelan (*Gloria Fay*), Lillian Fontaine (*Mary's Mother*), Frank Faylen (*Harold Michaels*), Frances Robinson (*Capt. Rogers*), Victoria Horne (*Lt. Billings*), Georgia Backus (*Maj. Cheever*), Jean Ruth (*WAC Corporal*), Roberta Jonay (*WAC Sergeant*), Willie Best (*Train Porter*), Griff Barnett (*Train Conductor*), Isabel Randolph (*Dowager in Elevator*), Paul Lees (*Elevator Operator*), Ella Ethridge, Helen Dickson, Jack Davidson, Beulah Parkington (*People in Elevator*), Archie Twitchell/ Richard Brandon (*Capt. Jergens*), William Newell (*Pier Manager*), Frances Morris (*Red Cross Worker*), Isabel Withers (*Woman Reporter*), Eddie Johnson, Eddie Coke (*Photographers*), Eddie Acuff (*Man*), Stanley Blystone, Crane Whitley (*Hotel Detectives*), Charles Quirk, Chester Clute (*Workmen*), William Hall (*MP in Phone Booth*), James Milligan, Len Hendry (*MPs*), Paul Oman, James Dundee (*Violinists*), Pat McVey, Perc Launders, George Lynn (*Reporters*), John Kellogg (*Newsreel Man*), Joleen Kelly (*Waitress*).

A pleasant romantic comedy with a switch on an old formula. MacMurray and Goddard had been a husband-wife team of lawyers before the outbreak of WW II. They weren't getting along and decided to call it quits but had to wait until after the fracas was over to file the papers because Goddard went into the Women's Army Corps to serve her nation. Now that peace is upon the land, she's not sure that she wants to divorce MacMurray. Whelan is MacMurray's new sweetie and does her best to get MacMurray to demand the papers be signed. At the same time, Carey is one of MacMurray's clients and has the hots for Goddard, but he won't move in until the final documents have been duly signatured. The more MacMurray pressures Goddard, the less she is likely to agree to the divorce. Several romantic complications later, the two are reconciled and Whelan and Carey are left out in the cold. It's a lightweight piece and the jokes are sound but the underpinning is weak and far too predictable. The same plot has been seen too many times before on the movie screen and will probably continue to be seen on television for ever and ever. Binyon had been writing superior screenplays for years, such as IF I HAD A MILLION, THIS IS THE ARMY, YOU BELONG TO ME, and many more. This was his first producer's assignment. He later tried his hand at directing with THE SAXON CHARM, AARON SLICK FROM PUNKIN CRICK, and several others before his death at 73 in 1978. Binyon is supposedly the ex-Variety editor who wrote the world-famous headline when the stock market crashed, "Wall Street Lays An Egg." Sources differ as to whether the role of Capt. Jergens was played by Archie Twitchell or Richard Brandon.

p, Claude Binyon; d, Mitchell Leisen; w, P. J. Wolfson, Binyon (based on the story "Sentimental Journey" by Wolfson); ph, Daniel L. Fapp; m, Victor Young; ed, Alma Macrorie; art d, Hans Dreier, John Meehan; set d, Sam Comer, Grace Gregory; cos, Mary Kay Dodson; spec eff, Farciot Edouart.

Comedy   **(PR:A   MPAA:NR)**

SUDDENLY, LAST SUMMER**½   (1959, Brit.) 114m
Horizon-Academy-Camp/COL bw

Elizabeth Taylor (*Catherine Holly*), Montgomery Clift (*Dr. John Cukrow-icz*), Katharine Hepburn (*Mrs. Violet Venable*), Albert Dekker (*Dr. Hockstader*), Mercedes McCambridge (*Mrs. Holly*), Gary Raymond (*George Holly*), Mavis Villiers (*Mrs. Foxhill*), Patricia Marmont (*Nurse Benson*), Joan Young (*Sister Felicity*), Maria Britneva (*Lucy*), Sheila Robbins (*Dr. Hockstader's Secretary*), David Cameron (*Young Blond Intern*), Roberta Woolley (*Patient*).

This bizarre and often distasteful movie at the end of the 1950s was an omen of things to come, as it went far beyond the realm of decency and out into a world that the average filmgoer had no idea existed. The one-act play on which the film was based consisted essentially of monologs by two women and was the second half of a Williams' bill collectively known as the "Garden District" when originally presented Off-Broadway (the opening half was entitled "Something Unspoken"). Robert Lansing starred in the role played here by Clift, Anne Meacham did the Taylor part, and Hortense Alden was in the Hepburn slot. In 1958, when the play was produced, it was strong stuff, although since it took place in one set, it was mostly imagined, rather than depicted. Williams and Vidal adapted the play and expanded it to an overblown length. It's surely "adult" material and anyone under the age of consent should be kept away from it, although the degeneracy is indicated far more than it is shown. Clift is a brain surgeon working in the tacky Louisiana State Hospital under Dekker. He specializes in lobotomies but finds it difficult going in these awful conditions. Dekker is the physician-supervisor of the facility and tells Clift that wealthy Hepburn, a resident of the New Orleans millionaire's row known as "The Garden District," is interested in Clift and his methods. She also has indicated in her letter that she is more than cognizant of the asylum's financial woes and might be willing to help. Dekker is hoping for that as she is known to be filthy rich. Clift goes to Hepburn's ivy-covered house where the widow says she is considering the establishment of a memorial fund in the name of her late son, Sebastian, who died suddenly last summer. He'd been a sensitive poet who wrote one poem each year, usually after coming home from his annual trip abroad. Hepburn had always accompanied him on these journeys, but on that fateful trip, her son chose his cousin, Taylor, to be his companion. As Hepburn takes Clift for a tour of the house and environs, she tells him more about her dead boy. The poem he wrote was about their vacations and he was ever so talented. She goes over, in patient detail, some of their experiences together and Clift just reacts, wondering why she has called for him to visit her. Now the truth emerges. Taylor came home from the trip in a maddened condition. She screamed and shouted and was vulgar, and a beefy nurse had to accompany her home on the ocean liner lest she harm herself or anyone else. Since returning to Louisiana, she's been incarcerated in a private asylum. Hepburn wonders if Clift's work with lobotomies might be applied to Taylor. The poor girl has a terrible nightmare locked in her memory, and if the operation were successful, wouldn't this be erased? Clift is not so sure, as the brain is a delicate organ. Hepburn tries to seal the deal by stating that she would be willing to donate a large sum to the state facility if Clift would operate on Taylor. Something about Hepburn's manner disturbs him and he wonders how much of what she's told him is the truth. She'd said that she couldn't take her son to Europe because of a minor stroke, although there is no vestige of it when they meet. Later, Clift visits Taylor. She is lucid, not mad at all, and tells him that she went to Europe with her cousin because she was having some personal problems that had set tongues to wagging. Her cousin asked her to go with him (not because Hepburn had a stroke) and they went to a small town on the coast of Spain. There Taylor realized what the Hepburn-son relationship was. (This is shown in flashback during a few visits from Clift.) Hepburn, knowing her son was a homosexual, used to find young boys for him to play with. She would use herself as bait, get the boys to where they were passionate, then her son would move in and have his way with them. Clift listens with amazement, still trying to learn what it was that caused Taylor to have a temporary mental lapse. He decides against a brain operation, feeling that she is already on her way to becoming mentally stable. Hepburn doesn't want to hear this and pressures Dekker. If Clift does the brain surgery, she'll come up with the money; if he doesn't, she won't. Hepburn begins to work on Taylor's mother, McCambridge, and her brother, Raymond, trying to persuade them to convince Taylor that she would be lots happier after the surgery. Clift rightly believes that Hepburn is just too assertive about this and brings Taylor to Hepburn's home, where the denouement is revealed. It seems that Sebastian (who is not billed in the movie and is only seen in a fleeting glimpse) had spent the summer debauching several young men and they'd finally had enough. They were poor, hungry, and angry. They turned on him like a pack of wolves, jumped on his body, ripped his clothes off his back, tore at his skin, and ate his dead body on the spot. (This is what is indicated. Taylor says they "seemed to devour him" and that can be taken as a metaphor.) Once the truth is bared, Hepburn's mind snaps and she begins talking to Clift as though he were her late son. The picture ends, and none too soon. An incident like this supposedly did happen in Africa when some rich homosexuals were turned upon by the Moroccans they had been toying with. Clift was working on the movie with no insurance (which is usually required) because he failed two medical examinations due to his use of controlled substances. At the same time, Hepburn was away from her beloved Tracy and worried about his health; Taylor, despite having just taken Eddie Fisher away from Debbie Reynolds, was still mourning

husband Mike Todd, who'd died in a tragic plane crash that also took the life of writer Art Cohn; director Mankiewicz was suffering from a bad skin ailment that caused him to wear gloves during shooting. Dekker was making his last film and died in a strange way, hanging himself accidentally as part of a weird sexual practice that saw him paint his body in many colors. Clift continued his drug use while they were shooting this in England (on a magnificent set that duplicated the New Orleans "feel" perfectly) and the result was a wooden, glassy-eyed performance. He was to make REFLECTIONS IN A GOLDEN EYE with Taylor, which would have been their fourth film together, but his death ended those plans. The speeches written by Williams and Vidal were long and Clift had no ability to memorize or concentrate, so the takes were brief and the talk had to be cut in half. After a few days of shooting, both Spiegel and Mankiewicz wanted to replace him but old friend Taylor warned them of the consequences of doing that and pleaded for him to stay. At the end of shooting, once Mankiewicz assured Hepburn that she was no longer needed, she spat in his face because she didn't appreciate his treatment of her, Clift, and everyone else. Hepburn and Taylor were both nominated for Oscars but probably cancelled each other out in the voting and Simone Signoret, who was better than both of them, managed to win for ROOM AT THE TOP. Hepburn was good but seemed to be in a different movie than everyone else and was more intent on delivering her lines than reacting to the other players. She had worked with Mankiewicz before on WOMAN OF THE YEAR, for Spiegel in THE AFRICAN QUEEN, and with cinematographer Hildyard in SUMMERTIME, so it would appear that she should have been comfortable. The production design by Oliver Messel, the art direction by William Kellner, and the set decoration by Scott Slimon were all commendable. It was the first time that homosexuality and cannibalism had ever been seen by a mainstream studio as being a commercial venture. Let's hope that it remains the last time those two practices will be presented in tandem.

p, Sam Spiegel; d, Joseph L. Mankiewicz; w, Gore Vidal, Tennessee Williams (based on the play by Williams); ph, Jack Hildyard; m, Buxton Orr, Malcolm Arnold; ed, Thomas G. Stanford, William W. Hornbeck; md, Orr; prod d, Oliver Messel; art d, William Kellner; set d, Scott Slimon; cos, Messel, Jean Louis, Norman Hartnell, Joan Ellacott; spec eff, Tom Howard; makeup, David Aylott.

Drama   Cas.   (PR:O MPAA:NR)

SUED FOR LIBEL**   (1940) 66m RKO bw

Kent Taylor (*Steve*), Linda Hayes (*Maggie*), Lillian Bond (*Muriel Webster*), Morgan Conway (*Pomeroy*), Richard Lane (*Smiley*), Roger Pryor (*Corbin*), Thurston Hall (*Hastings*), Emory Parnell (*Walsh*), Roy Gordon (*Col. White*), Keye Luke (*Chang Howe*), Edward Earle (*Judge*), Jack Arnold (*Dr. Baller*), Leona Roberts (*Mrs. Trent*), Solly Ward.

When radio announcer Taylor mistakenly broadcasts that a powerful broker is guilty of murder, the radio station and the newspaper that owns it are sued for libel. This motivates Taylor, and reporters Hayes and Lane to do some snooping to try to get out of the mess. After two more murders, with Taylor the main suspect in one of them, the trio uncover evidence that pins all three murders on one person. Suspense is maintained through the use of a number of various angles, with a climax that is totally unexpected.

p, Cliff Reid; d, Leslie Goodwins; w, Jerry Cady (based on a story by Wolfe Kaufman); ph, Jack MacKenzie; ed, Desmond Marquette; md, Roy Webb; art d, Van Nest Polglase; cos, Renie.

Crime/Mystery   (PR:A MPAA:NR)

SUEZ***½   (1938) 104m FOX bw

Tyrone Power (*Ferdinand de Lesseps*), Loretta Young (*Empress Eugenie*), Annabella (*Toni*), J. Edward Bromberg (*Said*), Joseph Schildkraut (*La Tour*), Henry Stephenson (*Count de Lesseps*), Sidney Blackmer (*Du Brey*), Maurice Moscovich (*Mohammed Ali*), Sig Rumann (*Sgt. Fellerin*), Nigel Bruce (*Sir Malcolm Cameron*), Miles Mander (*Benjamin Disraeli*), George Zucco (*Prime Minister*), Leon Ames (*Louis Napoleon*), Rafaela Ottiano (*Maria De Teba*), Victor Varconi (*Victor Hugo*), Jacques Lory (*Millet*), Odette Myrtil (*Duchess*), Frank Reicher (*Gen. Chargarnier*), Carlos J. de Valdez (*Count Hatzfeld*), Albert Conti (*Fevier*), Brandon Hurst (*Liszt*), Marcelle Corday (*Mme. Paquineau*), Egon Brecher (*Doctor*), Alphonse Martel (*Gen. St. Arnaud*), C. Montague Shaw (*Elderly Man*), Leonard Mudie (*Campaign Manager*), Jean Perry (*Umpire*), Robert Graves (*Official*), Christina Mantt (*Maid*), Anita Pike (*Julia*), Louis LaBey (*Servant*), Frank Lackteen (*Swami*), Alberto Morin (*Achmed*), Michael Visaroff, Louis Vincenot, Fred Malatesta (*Jewel Merchants*), Denis d'Auburn, Jerome De Nuccio, Tony Urchal (*Wrestlers*), Jean De Briac (*Engineer*), George Sorel (*Assistant*), Jacques Vanaire (*Old Engineer*).

Typically lavish Hollywood biography that bears even less relation to the truth than usual for the genre. Power is Ferdinand de Lesseps, the son of nobility and an engineer. For a time he romances Young, but she is desired by French president– later emperor–Louis Napoleon (Ames). Power goes off to Egypt, where his father is French consul. Power is enchanted with the country and one of the friends he makes is Annabella, the half- Egyptian, half-French daughter of a French soldier. She falls in love with him but he still loves Young. One day, while walking across the desert, Power is struck with an idea, a canal connecting the Red Sea to the Mediterranean. He returns to France to seek government backing for his project, and there runs into Young, who by this time has become Ames' mistress. She agrees to help him approach Ames with the idea, if he in return will convince his father to help dissolve the Assembly. Young swears, of course, that the government would be recalled as soon as possible. Power agrees, but once the government is out of the way, Ames declares himself emperor and makes Young his empress. Power's father dies from the shock of his betrayal and Power abandons his canal idea. The backing comes through, though, and Power starts work, fighting the heat and the Bedouins. With only 10 miles to be dug, though, the French cut off the finances and Power is forced to approach the British with the canal. The prime minister-elect, Mander, agrees to consider funding it and Power returns to Egypt once again. A desert windstorm known as a Black Simoon comes up and Power is injured, but Annabella manages to lash him to a post before she herself is picked up and carried off to her death by the wind. The storm having subsided, word comes from England that Power will be able to finish his dream. Inane dialog is the biggest culprit in this ridiculous view of 19th-Century French politics, but Power somehow pulls off the feat of making lines like "I wanted to do something for France, but now I think I can do something for the world!" sound like something a person might actually say. Young is impressively cool and detached as she trades away love for position and power, even lying to her former lover in order to become empress. Annabella makes a good impression, too, as she must have on Power, who married her soon after the filming. Director Dwan later admired her professionalism, especially during the sandstorm sequence, and told Peter Bogdanovich for his book on Dwan, *The Last Pioneer*:"I got about a hundred of those huge airplane prop fans we used to make a wind and lined them up, but I had to discard them because the sand would cut the skin off the cast. Instead we used ground cereal that we threw in front of the blades. The people had to move through that all day long, and I'm telling you, that was an ordeal. Everybody got beaten up good– particularly Ty Power and Annabella. In one scene, he was supposed to be unconscious and she is whipped away by the wind while trying to save him. We had to put her on a wire and fling her through the air. It was drastic." When the film was shown in France, the descendants of de Lesseps sued Fox, claiming that the engineer had been 54 when he first went to Egypt, and never had an affair with the Empress Eugenie. A French court threw out the case, determining that the film brought more honor to France than dishonor on the family. The film follows the formula of the other Zanuck biographical bowdlerizations: smart sets, great costumes, romance, fine special effects, and complete disregard of fact. Original release prints were sepia tinted.

p, Darryl F. Zanuck, Gene Markey; d, Allan Dwan, Otto Brower; w, Philip Dunne, Julien Josephson (based on a story by Sam Duncan); ph, J. Peverell Marley; ed, Barbara McLean; md, Louis Silvers; art d, Bernard Herzbrun, Rudolph Sternad; set d, Thomas Little; cos, Royer; spec eff, Fred Sersen.

Biography   **(PR:A   MPAA:NR)**

SUGAR HILL**   (1974) 90m AIP c (AKA: VOODOO GIRL, THE,
                                                Zombies of Sugar Hill)

Marki Bey (*Diana "Sugar" Hill*), Robert Quarry (*Morgan*), Don Pedro Colley (*Baron Samedi*), Richard Lawson (*Valentine*), Betty Anne Rees (*Celeste*), Zara Culley (*Mama Maitresse*), Larry D. Johnson (*Langston*), Charles Robinson (*Fabulous*), Rich Hagood (*Tank Watson*), Ed Geldhart (*O'Brien*), Thomas C. Carroll (*Baker*), Albert J. Baker (*George*), Raymond E. Simpson (*King*), Charles Krohn (*Capt. Merrill*), Jack Bell (*Parkhurst*), Peter Harrell III (*Police Photographer*), Walter Price (*Preacher*), Judy Hanson (*Masseuse*), Tony Brubaker (*Head Zombie*).

Better than average blaxploitation picture has Bey seeking vengeance against the gangsters responsible for murdering her boyfriend. To accomplish her deed, she gets help from Colley, a man skilled in voodoo. An army of zombies is called up from the grave and proves more than even the tough mobsters can handle. Suspenseful, exciting, and a different approach to the vengeance theme.

p, Elliott Schick; d, Paul Maslansky; w, Tim Kelly; ph, Bob Jessup (Movielab Color); m, Nick Zesses, Dino Fekaris; ed, Carl Kress.

Thriller/Crime   **(PR:C   MPAA:PG)**

SUGARFOOT**½   (1951) 80m WB c (AKA: SWIRL OF GLORY)

Randolph Scott (*Sugarfoot*), Adele Jergens (*Reva Cairn*), Raymond Massey (*Jacob Stint*), S.Z. Sakall (*Don Miguel*), Robert Warwick (*J.C. Crane*), Arthur Hunnicutt (*Fly-Up-the-Creek Jones*), Hugh Sanders (*Asa Goodhue*), Hope Landin (*Mary*), Hank Worden (*Johnny-Behind-the-Stove*), Gene Evans (*Billings*), Edward Hearn, John Hamilton, Cliff Clark, Kenneth MacDonald, Dan White, Paul Newlan, Philo McCullough.

Far too much talk for a western entry, as Scott plays a former Confederate soldier who tries to start life anew in Arizona. He sets up a cozy little ranch only to discover that an old enemy, Massey, has the rest of the town eating out of his hand. But Scott soon proves that he is not one to be pushed around, and takes care of Massey and his henchmen in customary style. Jergens is the saloon singer Scott falls for; she and Scott manage to carry a good portion of the film on their performances alone.

p, Saul Elkins; d, Edwin L. Marin; w, Russell Hughes (based on a novel by

Clarence Buddington Kelland); ph, Wilfrid M. Cline (Technicolor); m, Max Steiner; ed, Clarence Kolster; art d, Stanley Fleischer; m/l, "Oh, He Looked Like He Might Buy Wine," Ray Heindorf, Sammy Cahn (sung by Adele Jergens).

Western   **(PR:A   MPAA:NR)**

SUGARLAND EXPRESS, THE***   (1974) 109m UNIV c

Goldie Hawn (*Lou Jean Poplin*), Ben Johnson (*Capt. Tanner*), Michael Sacks (*Officer Slide*), William Atherton (*Clovis Poplin*), Gregory Walcott (*Officer Mashburn*), Steve Kanaly (*Jessup*), Louise Latham (*Mrs. Looby*), Harrison Zanuck (*Baby Langston*), A.L. Camp (*Mr. Nocker*), Jessie Lee Fulton (*Mrs. Nocker*), Dean Smith (*Russ Berry*), Ted Grossman (*Dietz*), Bill Thurman (*Hunter*), Kenneth Hudgins (*Standby*), Buster Danials (*Drunk*), Jim Harrell (*Mark Fenno*), Frank Steggall (*Logan Waters*), Roger Ernest (*Hot Jock No. 1*), Guich Koock (*Hot Jock No. 2*), Merrill L. Connally (*Looby*), Gene Rader (*Gas Jockey*), Gordon Hurst (*Hubie Nocker*), George Hagy (*Sparrow*), Big John Hamilton (*Big John*), Kenneth Crone (*Deputy*), Judge Peter Michael Curry (*Judge*), Charles Conaway (*Attorney*), Robert Golden, Ruby Robbins (*Mechanics*), Charlie Dobbs (*Cop*), Gene Lively (*Reporter*), John L. Quinlan III (*Bailiff*), Bill Scott (*Station Man*), Ralph E. Horwedel (*Dispatcher*), Edwin "Frog" Isbell (*Jelly Bowl*).

This is Steven Spielberg's first effort at the helm in feature filmmaking (the earlier DUEL being a made-for-TV movie), and contains much of the raw sense of adventure, though without the technical gadgetry, that would make his later films so popular and such good clean fun. After his success with THE SUGARLAND EXPRESS he went on to direct the highly profitable, beloved, and much imitated JAWS in 1975. This film is based on a true story and features Hawn playing a woman who helps her husband, Atherton, escape from prison. She needs him to help her keep her baby and fight the forces who would put the child up for adoption. What ensues is one long chase across America's highways. Throughout the film, more and more police, and the media, want in on the action. Spielberg exhibits that he still had a bit to learn in the world of filmmaking. The film moves well and never loses its gripping tension, but the lighthearted tone of the beginning takes a dive into an abyss that shocks many viewers. With this role, Hawn further proved she was an actress of some talent and not just an attractive woman to be taken lightly.

p, Richard D. Zanuck, David Brown; d, Steven Spielberg; w, Hal Barwood, Matthew Robbins (based on a story by Spielberg, Barwood, Robbins); ph, Vilmos Zsigmond (Panavision, Technicolor); m, John Williams; ed, Edward M. Abroms, Verna Fields; art d, Joseph Alves, Jr.; spec eff, Frank Brendel; stunts, Cary Loftin.

Adventure/Drama   **Cas.**   **(PR:C   MPAA:PG)**

SUGATA SANSHIRO   (SEE: JUDO SAGA, 1965, Jap.)

SUICIDE BATTALION**½   (1958) 79m Zuma/AIP bw

Michael Connors (*Maj. Matt McCormack*), John Ashley (*Tommy Novello*), Jewell Lian (*Elizabeth Ann Mason*), Russ Bender (*Harry Donovan*), Bing Russell (*Lt. Chet Hall*), Scott Peters (*Wally Skilzowski*), Walter Maslow (*Marty Green*), John McNamara (*Col. Craig*), Clifford Kawada (*Col. Hiosho*), Bob Tetrick (*Bill*), Marjorie Stapp (*Beverly*), Jan Englund (*Annette*), Isabel Cooley (*Julie*), Hilo Hattie (*Mama Lily*), Sammy Tong (*Papa Lily*), Gordon Barnes (*Peter Hendry*), Art Gilmore (*Capt. Hendry*), Jackie Joseph (*Cho Cho*).

Fairly taut thriller that features Connors, Ashley, and a number of others as Americans fighting behind enemy lines in the Philippines during WW II. Their mission is to make sure important U.S. documents are destroyed before the enemy gets them. The papers are hidden in a vault where the Americans were based before they fled. Although plot development is a bit confusing, the action moves well, with enough eccentric characters to provide interest.

p, Lou Rusoff; d, Edward L. Cahn; w, Rusoff; ph, Floyd Crosby; m, Ronald Stein; ed, Robert S. Eisen; md, Stein; art d, Don Ament.

War   **(PR:A   MPAA:NR)**

SUICIDE CLUB, THE   (SEE: TROUBLE FOR TWO, 1936)

SUICIDE FLEET**   (1931) 84m RKO-Pathe bw

Bill Boyd (*Baltimore Clark*), Robert Armstrong (*Dutch Herman*), James Gleason (*Skeets O'Riley*), Ginger Rogers (*Sally*), Harry Bannister (*Commander*), Frank Reicher (*Capt. Holtzman*), Henry Victor (*Capt. Von Stuben*), Ben Alexander (*Kid the Lookout*), Hans Joby (*Schwartz*), Yola D'Avril, Nanette Faro (*French Girls in Tangier*), James Pierce (*Recruit*), Harry Tenbrook (*Jim the Shore Patrolman/Tangier*), Charles Sullivan (*Sullivan the Sailor*), Tom Keene (*Officer*), Harry Strang (*Shore Patrolman/Havana*), Joe Dominguez, Harry Semels (*Havana Merchants*), James Burtis (*Sailor*), John Kelly, Charles Delaney (*Sailors at Sally's*).

Three Coney Island vendors, Boyd, Armstrong, and Gleason, are all in love with the same girl, Rogers. The men become shipmates when they are inducted into the Navy. They serve on a decoy ship and their mission is to draw German submarines out of the water. They entertain themselves by visiting bars in every port and flirt with Rogers while at their home base.

p, Charles R. Rogers; d, Albert Rogell; w, Lew Lipton, F. McGrew Wills (based on the story "Mystery Ship" by Comdr. Herbert A. Jones); ph, Sol Polito; ed, Joe Kane; md, Kane; Arthur Lange; art d, Carroll Clark; cos. Gwen Wakeling.

War/Drama   **(PR:A   MPAA:NR)**

SUICIDE LEGION**½ (1940, Brit.) 54m Wilcox/Film Alliance bw (GB: SUNSET IN VI ENNA)

Tullio Carminati *(Toni)*, Lilli Palmer *(Gelda)*, John Garrick *(Adolph)*, Geraldine Hislop *(Wanda)*, Davina Craig *(Deaf Lady)*, Hubert Harben *(Austrian General)*, Edgar Driver *(Toni's Batman)*, Alice O'Day *(Maddalena)*, Eileen Munro *(Superintendent of V.A.D.)*.

Well made but routine British programmer features Carminati as an Italian soldier who brings Palmer home as his Austrian bride. Soon war breaks out between the two countries and Palmer's brother enters Italy as a spy. He hides out with Palmer but Carminati, loyal to his country, shoots his brother-in-law. Palmer is embittered towards her husband; she is interned as an enemy alien during the war. The two lose touch during the fighting and when the war is over Carminati searches for his wife. He finally finds her in a cheap Egyptian cafe where she works as a dancer. This film was cut from its original 73 minutes for U.S. release. High in production values, with some intelligent performances, the story is too familiar and cliched to completely work though it does have some good moments. Popular actor/singer Carminati – born in Dalmatia – had returned to Europe only two years before this film's 1937 London release after a ten-year stint as a leading man in Hollywood films and on Broadway. Among his songs are "Sunset in Vienna" and We'll Never Run Short of Love."

p, Herbert Wilcox; d, Norman Walker; w, Marjorie Gaffney, Harrison Owens (based on a story by Florence Tranter); ph, F. A. Young; m, Lerner, Goodhart, Hoffman.

Drama   **(PR:C   MPAA:NR)**

SUICIDE MISSION**½   (1956, Brit.) 70m North Sea/COL bw

Anthony Oliver *(Narrator)*, Leif Larson, Michael Aldridge, Atle Larsen, Per Christiansen, T. W. Southam, Oscar Egede Nissen.

Set in the Shetland Islands during WW II, SUICIDE MISSION is a dramatic re-creation of a North Sea crossing by a group of daring Norwegians. Many of those who were actually part of the adventure appear in the film, lending a realistic portrayal to their mission. The Norwegians are seen traveling in mid-winter over a distance of 500 miles in order to deliver ammunition and soldiers to their Nazi-occupied country. The stock footage is often graphic and adds a chilling emotion to these "actors'" exploits, especially in knowing that just a few years earlier they were carrying out this mission for their lives instead of the cameras.

p&d, Michael Forlong; w, David Howarth, Sidney Cole, Forlong (based on the novel *The Shetland Bus* by Howarth); ph, Per G. Johnson, Mattis Mathiesen; ed, Lee Doig.

War/Drama   **(PR:C   MPAA:NR)**

SUICIDE RUN   (SEE: TOO LATE THE HERO, 1970)

SUICIDE SQUADRON*½   (1942, Brit.) 83m RKO/REP-RKO bw (GB: DANGEROUS MOONLIGHT)

Anton Walbrook *(Stefan Radetzky)*, Sally Gray *(Carole Peters)*, Derrick de Marney *(Mike Carroll)*, Keneth Kent *(de Guise)*, Percy Parsons *(Bill Peters)*, J. H. Roberts *(Resident Physician)*, Cecil Parker *(Specialist)*, Guy Middleton *(Shorty)*, John Laurie *(British Commander)*, Frederick Valk *(Polish Bomber Commander)*, Philip Friend *(Pete)*, Michael Rennie *(Pilot)*, Robert Beatty, Marion Spencer, Lesley Gordon, Conway Palmer, Cynthia Heppner, Alan Keith.

Polish flying officer Walbrook, facing suicide in attempting to repel the Luftwaffe aircraft during the German invasion of Poland at the onset of WW II, is tricked by his flying companions into journeying to Rumania and safety (they regard him as more valuable for his musical talents than for his aerial skills). Before his departure, he met and quickly married American journalist Gray, with whom he reunites during a musical concert tour of the U.S. to raise funds for the Polish resistance. Disturbed by the valiant sacrifices of his one-time flying compatriots, he opts for combat, joining the brave remnants of that group in the Polish Squadron of Britain's Royal Air Force over the objections of his rediscovered wife. His very Irish friend, de Marney, attempts unsuccessfully to reconcile the two; following a fierce argument, de Marney is killed in combat. Blaming himself for his problems, Walbrook – out of ammunition – deliberately crashes his fighter plane into a German bomber. Recovering, but with his memory gone, he again meets his wife, Gray. She seats him at a piano and urges him to play. The amnesiac Walbrook recovers his wits and his wife as the strains of Addinsell's "Warsaw Concerto" fill the theater. At the time the film was made, England

had quota restrictions on the number of foreign – largely U.S.-made – pictures that could be exhibited domestically. American companies responded by financing films made in England, using English talent and facilities, and then lobbying hard for quota concessions. RKO moguls had little hope for successful U.S. distribution for this film; they leased domestic rights – for a limited period only – to Republic Pictures, whose executives had more faith in it. It did reasonably well; the "Warsaw Concerto" was the making of the movie, and was a milestone in cinema history: the disc record made from the soundtrack was the first soundtrack blockbuster seller in history. Well after Republic's lease ran out, RKO reissued the film.

p, William Sistrom; d, Brian Desmond Hurst; w, Shaun Terence Young, Hurst, Rodney Ackland (based on a story by Young); ph, Georges Perinal; m, Richard Addinsell; ed, Alan Jaggs; md, Muir Mathieson; art d, John Bryan.

War   **(PR:A   MPAA:NR)**

SUITOR, THE**½   (1963, Fr.) 83m CAPAC-Cocinor/Atlantic bw (LE SOUPIRANT)

Pierre Etaix *(Pierre, the Suitor)*, Laurence Ligneres *(Laurence)*, Claude Massot *(Father)*, Denise Peronne *(Mother)*, Karin Vesely *(Ilka)*, France Arnell *(Stella)*, Lucien Fregis *(Painter)*, Brigitte Juslin, Petit Bobo.

The first feature-length film to be directed by comedian/illusionist Etaix – who claims artistic kinship with silent comedian Harry Langdon – is a joy. Etaix also stars as the studious son of Peronne, who expresses concern about his reclusive habits, urging him to meet and marry an appropriate young woman. Hoping to please his mother, he instantly proposes to the convenient Vesely, a boarder from Sweden who is attempting to learn the French language. Unsuccessful in her linguistic efforts, she fails to comprehend the substance of his suit; thinking himself rejected, he journeys out into the world of the night, where he meets lush Ligneres. As eager for amour as he, the bibulous beauty entices Etaix to her apartment, where she attempts to seduce him. During this deviltry, he spies the gorgeous face of Arnell on Ligneres' television screen. Freeing himself from the latter's embraces, he races home to concentrate on his new video sweetheart, the rage of all Paris. He collects mementos and published pictures of Arnell and purchases an engagement ring for this yet unmet compulsion. Tricking his way into her dressing room, he is dismayed to discover that she is wed, with a son his own age. Returning home to resume his lonely life, he discovers that Vesely has applied herself to her study of the language and now recognizes his proposal for what it was. She accepts. Etaix had good training in comedy; he served as an assistant to Jacques Tati during the filming of MY UNCLE in 1958. His short THE ANNIVERSARY (1962) won an Academy Award.

p, Paul Claudon; d, Pierre Etaix; w, Etaix, Jean-Claude Carriere; ph, Pierre Levent; m, Jean Paillaud; ed, Pierre Gillette.

Comedy/Drama   **(PR:C   MPAA:NR)**

SUITABLE CASE FOR TREATMENT, A
                                                     (SEE: MORGAN, 1966, Brit.)

SULEIMAN THE CONQUEROR*½   (1963, Ital.) 99m Produzioni Astor/Medallion c (SOLIMANO IL CONQUISTATORE)

Edmund Purdom *(Ibrahim Pasha, Grand Vizier)*, Georgia Moll *(Vesna Orlovic)*, Alberto Farnese *(Gaspar)*, Luciano Marin *(Ivan)*, Loris Gizzi *(Suleiman)*, Stane Potokar *(Nicholas Orlovic)*, Evi Maltagliati *(Anna)*, Raf Baldassarre *(Boris)*, Nando Tamberlani *(Viennese Chancellor)*, John Mac-Douglas *(Giuseppe Addobbati)*, Silvio Bagolini, Amedeo Trilli.

In 1566 Suleiman the Magnificent (Gizzi), ruler of the Ottoman Empire which threatens to overwhelm all of Europe, rejects the advice of his Grand Vizier (Purdom) that he besiege Vienna. Instead, he chooses an easier target, the isolated Christian fortress town of Szigetvar commanded by Potokar. During the siege, Gizzi dies of a stroke, but the news of his death is suppressed by Purdom, who slaughters those who have witnessed it. Within the fortress, jealousy and intrigue reign among the defenders. Farnese, Potokar's lieutenant, orders Marin – his rival for the hand of Potokar's daughter Moll – to undertake a dangerous race for Vienna to get reinforcements for the beleaguered Christians. Repulsed by Moll after Marin's departure, the evil Farnese turns his coat and joins the forces of Purdom. Returning from Vienna, rebuffed in his request for troops, Marin is attacked by Farnese, whom Marin kills. Potokar, informed by Marin of his rebuff, orders that all noncombatants be evacuated to safer surroundings. Then he leads a suicidal attack against the Turks. In victory, the Turks are exhausted and ill; they retreat from Austria. Marin and Moll lead the women and children back to the now-secure fortress. Filmed in Yugoslavia with a mixed cast and crew of Yugoslavians and Italians. Purdom, whose looks and resonant voice brought him leading-man roles in big-budget Hollywood costume epics early in his cinema career, filtered down to foreign-made B-grade action costumers such as this one later on.

p&d, Vatroslav Mimica; w, Mimica, Mario Caiano, Michelangelo Frieri, Stipe Delic; ph, Guiseppe La Torre (Totalscope, Eastmancolor); m, Francesco De Masi.

Adventure   **(PR:A   MPAA:NR)**

SULLIVANS, THE****   (1944) 111m FOX bw (AKA: THE FIGHTING SULLIVANS)

Anne Baxter (*Katherine Mary*), Thomas Mitchell (*Mr. Sullivan*), Selena Royle (*Mrs. Sullivan*), Edward Ryan (*Al*), Trudy Marshall (*Genevieve*), John Campbell (*Frank*), James Cardwell (*George*), John Alvin (*Matt*), George Offerman, Jr. (*Joe*), Roy Roberts (*Father Francis*), Ward Bond (*Lieutenant*), Mary McCarty (*Gladys*), Bobby Driscoll (*Al as a Boy*), Nancy June Robinson (*Genevieve as a Child*), Marvin Davis (*Frank as a Boy*), Buddy Swan (*George as a Boy*), Billy Cummings (*Matt as a Boy*), Johnny Calkins (*Joe as a Boy*), John Nesbitt (*Admiral*), Addison Richards (*Naval Captain*), Selmer Jackson (*Damage Control Officer*), Mae Marsh (*Woman*), Leon Tyler (*Boy*), Elsa Peterson (*Nun*), Harry Strang (*C.P.O.*), Barbara Brown (*Nurse*).

The tragic tale of the Sullivans, five brothers who served together on the cruiser *Juneau* during WW II who were all killed at Guadalcanal, is turned into a sentimental slice of Americana which served to remind wartime Americans what it was they were fighting for. The story begins in the small town of Waterloo, Iowa, and we see the Sullivan boys as youngsters (Davis, Swan, Cummings, Calkins, and Driscoll). Their father, Mitchell, is a railroad employee and his wife, Royle, tends to the house and tries to keep an eye on her rambunctious boys. The joys of growing up in a small town are detailed with the boys doing everything from their daily chores to experimenting with smoking cigarettes (father Mitchell catches them smoking cornsilk and makes them try cigars instead–they all get sick). Eventually the boys grow to manhood (now played by Campbell, Cardwell, Alvin, Offerman, and Ryan) and one of their number, Ryan, meets a nice girl, Baxter, gets married, and starts a family. The cruel world invades the solitude of Waterloo one Sunday morning when the Japanese bomb Pearl Harbor. The patriotic boys all decide to join the Navy, and even Ryan, who has a young family to think of, is urged by Baxter to join his brothers. Since they have always been a team, the brothers insist on serving together and they are assigned duty on the *Juneau*. When the boys are all killed in the same battle, the news is taken with sadness but pride. Mitchell and Royle are comforted to know that their boys would have wanted to go down together. The tragic deaths of the Sullivans spurred the Navy to never again allow all the members of a family to serve together on the same ship. THE SULLIVANS is a moving film which brings home the tragedy of loss and the cost of war. The film successfully evokes small town life and brings to it a level of character and understanding that goes well beyond anything seen in an "Andy Hardy" movie. The casting of relative unknowns in the roles of the brothers lends an almost documentary quality to the film because the faces are fresh and unfamiliar. The most familiar face in the film, that of veteran character actor Thomas Mitchell, is perfect casting and serves to enhance the role of father-figure and loving patriarch of the Sullivan clan. Because he is such a recognizable performer, Mitchell lends an air of authority and reassurance to the center of the film. While THE SULLIVANS is a very entertaining, warm film full of nostalgia for small town life and values, it also serves as a tribute to those men who give their lives in war and the families that must suffer the loss. The title was changed to THE FIGHTING SULLIVANS shortly after the film's release to improve its box office draw.

p, Sam Jaffe; d, Lloyd Bacon; w, Mary C. McCall, Jr. (based on a story by Edward Doherty, Jules Schermer); ph, Lucien Andriot; m, Cyril J. Mockridge; ed, Louis Loeffler; md, Alfred Newman; art d, James Basevi, Leland Fuller; spec eff, Fred Sersen.

Drama   (PR:A MPAA:NR)

SULLIVAN'S EMPIRE*   (1967) 85m UNIV c

Martin Milner (*John Sullivan, Jr.*), Linden Chiles (*Patrick Sullivan*), Don Quine (*Kevin Sullivan*), Clu Gulager (*Juan Clemente*), Arch Johnson (*John Sullivan, Sr.*), Karen Jensen (*Doris Wheeler*), Bernie Hamilton (*Amando*), Lee Bergere (*Rudi Andujar*), Than Wyenn (*Inspector Huante*), Jeanette Nolan (*Miss Wingate*), Miguel de Anda (*Driver*), Ken Renard (*Clerk*), Marianne Gordon (*2nd Girl*), Eileen Wesson (*3rd Girl*), Mark Miranda (*Boy*), Ruben Moreno (*Carlos*), Nadine Nardi (*Ramona*), Robert de Coy (*Chico*), Pepe Callahan (*Bartender*), Peter Pascal (*Pilot*), Sergio Mendes and Brazil '66.

Originally made as a pilot for a television series, then unfortunately transferred to the big screen, this picture has stock actors, stock shots which don't emphasize the dramatics, a ludicrous plot, and unsuitable characters who are not provided with enough motivation. Johnson plays a wealthy industrialist who walked out on his three sons when they were all still toddlers. Even so, the young men congregate from various points around the world to help the old man out of a jam. His plane crashed while flying near his Brazilian estate. The sons search for their father through the jungle, turning up a plot by his business partner to get control of the empire. A far-fetched ending has lady helicopter flyer Nolan rescuing all four of the men, who have been captured by guerrillas. Should have been left on television.

p, Frank Price; d, Harvey Hart, Thomas Carr; w, Frank Chase; ph, Hal A. McAlpin (Technicolor); m, Lalo Schifrin; ed, Robert F. Shugrue; art d, Russell Kimball; set d, John McCarthy, Ralph Sylos; cos, Burton Miller; makeup, Bud Westmore.

Adventure   (PR:A MPAA:NR)

SULLIVAN'S TRAVELS*****   (1941) 91m PAR bw

Joel McCrea (*John L. Sullivan*), Veronica Lake (*The Girl*), Robert Warwick (*Mr. Lebrand*), Wiliam Demarest (*Mr. Jones*), Franklin Pangborn (*Mr. Casalais*), Porter Hall (*Mr. Hadrian*), Byron Foulger (*Mr. Valdelle*), Margaret Hayes (*Secretary*), Robert Greig (*Sullivan's Butler*), Eric Blore (*Sullivan's Valet*), Torben Meyer (*The Doctor*), Victor Potel (*Cameraman*), Richard Webb (*Radio Man*), Charles Moore (*Chef*), Almira Sessions (*Ursula*), Esther Howard (*Miz Zeffie*), Frank Moran (*Tough Chauffeur*), George Renavent (*Old Tramp*), Harry Rosenthal (*The Trombenick*), Alan Bridge (*The Mister*), Jimmy Conlin (*Trusty*), Jan Buckingham (*Mrs. Sullivan*), Robert Winkler (*Bud*), Chick Collins (*Capital*), Jimmie Dundee (*Labor*), Pat West (*Counterman, Roadside Lunch Wagon*), J. Farrell Macdonald (*Desk Sergeant*), Edward Hearn (*Cop, Beverly Hills Station*), Arthur Hoyt (*Preacher*), Paul Newlan (*Truck Driver*), Roscoe Ates (*Counterman, Owl Wagon*), Robert Dudley (*One-Legged Bum*), Monte Blue (*Cop in Slums*), Harry Tyler (*R.R. Information Clerk*), Dewey Robinson (*Sheriff*), Madame Sul-te-wan (*Harmonica Player*), Jess Lee Brooks (*Black Preacher*), Harry Seymour (*Entertainer in Air-Raid Shelter*), Chester Conklin (*Old Bum*), Frank Mils (*Drunk in Theater*), Edgar Dearing (*Cop, Mud Gag*), Emory Parnell (*Man at R.R. Shack*), Julius Tannen (*Public Defender*), Gus Reed (*Mission Cook*), Perc Launders (*Yard Man*), Billy Bletcher (*Entertainer in Hospital*).

This brilliant and often devastating profile of Hollywood and the real world beyond the rosy perception of tinseltown, is Sturges' greatest film, although the inspired, humor-gifted, and socially incisive Sturges would put many masterpieces on celluloid. McCrea, in one of his best roles, essays a successful Hollywood film director who has made nothing but lightweight films such as SO LONG, SARONG. He suddenly gets the notion that he should make a searing drama about human suffering. His studio bosses, Warwick and Hall, laugh and tell him that such a proposal is ridiculous, that McCrea has no idea about human suffering since he has never suffered himself. This gives him an idea. He decides to suffer. He will don hobo clothes, and, with only 10 cents in his pocket, will go forth into the land of poverty and learn for himself what it means to suffer. Warwick and Hall, knowing they can't change McCrea's mind, go along with the eccentric director but decide to turn McCrea's nomadic adventure into a publicity stunt that will benefit the studio. In addition to a publicity entourage, McCrea is provided with a luxury van moving alongside the walking McCrea, a van equipped with all the luxuries in the world and one which carries his butler, Grieg, and valet, Blore, who both urge their employer to give up this mad idea, telling him that the poor insist upon their privacy and don't want him intruding upon it. To escape his retinue, McCrea hitches a ride with a young teenager who wheels his jalopy down the road so fast that he quickly loses the van but almost kills himself and McCrea in his hair-raising, speed-seeking race to get to the next town. McCrea gratefully gets out of the jalopy and begins walking. He gets a job chopping wood for two elderly sisters who feed him and fuss over him, becoming so possessive of him–he's their first visitor in years–that he must escape their "protective custody" by climbing out of a window. He promptly falls into a rain barrel full of ice water and catches a terrible cold, returning to his estate in Los Angeles to recuperate. He is utterly disillusioned but he hasn't given up his idea of discovering what it means to suffer. McCrea starts out again, shabbily dressed, and stops at a diner where he meets alluring Lake who is a failed actress. He tells her he "used to be" a director and will introduce her to famous director Ernest Lubitsch. She scoffs at that, saying that all she wants is a ride home. McCrea leaves and returns in a limousine, which upsets Lake because she thinks he is nothing more than a bum and has stolen the car. Police arrest McCrea as he is driving home and he has no way of proving that the car is his. The limousine has been reported stolen since he forgot to leave a note for Blore and Grieg that he was taking the car. The butler and valet are called to the station where they identify McCrea as their boss and *now* Lake believes McCrea. When she learns that he truly is a film director she insists upon accompanying him on his journey. McCrea demeans his comedies, saying that making people laugh in life is not the work of a serious artist. He tells Lake that he must learn about the suffering of people so he can produce films of serious drama. Lake is dressed like a boy and follows McCrea through flophouses and missions where they see the seamy side of life and very little to inspire McCrea. When they run out of food they are reduced to eating out of garbage cans and finally McCrea reluctantly concludes that it's time to return to civilization. But before he and Lake can go West a vicious hobo steals his shoes, replacing them with his old worn-out shoes. McCrea sends Lake back to L.A., telling her he will talk to Lubitsch about her career when he returns himself. That night McCrea goes through a hobo camp and hands out bills. The same man who has stolen his shoes jumps McCrea, knocks him out, and throws him aboard a freight train heading south. The tramp himself is killed by another train as he flees across the tracks and his horribly disfigured body is found later. Inside of one shoe is found McCrea's identification and news is flashed that famous director McCrea has been killed. McCrea's bitchy wife, who had earlier refused to divorce him marries someone else, now that the director is presumed dead. McCrea, meanwhile, suffering amnesia from the tramp's blow to his head, gets off the train and runs into a railroad guard who begins to shove him around. He knocks the guard down and is arrested and sentenced to a chain gang for six years. He lives a miserable existence working on the chain gang and, even though the amnesia wears off and he can now remember who he is, he has no way of proving his real identity. The prisoners are given a rare break one night and taken to an old Baptist church where black parishioners sit with the chain gang prisoners and all are treated to an old Mickey Mouse cartoon. Though there is misery and poverty all around him, McCrea sees the downtrodden movie viewers laughing and laughing at Mickey's crazy antics. He himself starts to laugh uncontrollably and he suddenly realizes the value of comedy and its importance to the public, especially to those who have nothing in their lives to laugh about. Now dedicated to the idea of somehow getting out of the chain gang and returning to Hollywood to make comedies, McCrea hits upon the brilliant idea of confessing to his own murder, claiming that he, a hobo, killed the famous director, John L. Sullivan, for his money and his picture appears in papers nationwide. He is identified by his trusty servants as the real director and released. He is now free to make his comedies as well as marry the beautiful Lake who is waiting for him when he returns to Tinseltown. Though the plot may sound a bit contrived, everything in this wonderful film works. And it presents a spectacular array of human emotions and diversified situations which allow for Sturges' magical direction and script to quickly turn all the sharp corners with his characters. Sturges produced a wonderful comedy-drama, a one-of- a-kind film for which he was noted. He was basically a writer with a good sense of camera use and visuals, and a man who was always experimenting with techniques. Here, unlike many of his other films, which were made for sheer entertainment he does attempt a message. He later stated (as quoted in *Between Flops* by James Curtis): "SULLIVAN'S TRAVELS is the result of an urge, an urge to tell some of my fellow filmwrights that they were getting a little too deep-dish and to leave the preaching to the preachers." The director wrote SULLIVAN'S TRAVELS with McCrea in mind and the actor does a splendid job with the role of the inquisitive director, a part that would always remain McCrea's favorite. One day at the Paramount commissary, Sturges approached McCrea who was having lunch and simply told him, "I've written a script for you." McCrea couldn't believe it, replying: "No one writes a script for me. They write a script for Gary Cooper and, if they can't get him, they use me." In a short time the director proved his statement by tossing a copy of SULLIVAN'S TRAVELS into McCrea's lap. Sturges also specifically wanted the 20-year-old Lake in the role of the waif-like girl after seeing her in I WANTED WINGS. Paramount executives thought she was wrong for the part, suggesting a host of other actresses, including Lucille Ball, Claire Trevor, Ida Lupino, Frances Farmer, Betty Field, and even hoofer Ruby Keeler. The studio finally agreed to let Lake do the role but only if Sturges would deliver the film within 45 days and not go over a budget of $600,000. Lake proved to be as energetic as McCrea in the film, but she hid the fact from Sturges that she was six months pregnant when he began shooting the film. In her biography, Lake later admitted: "Keeping my pregnancy from Preston hung over my head like a cumbersome weight. I certainly didn't want to upset him and the fever with which he approached the film. And yet I was scared to death that my condition would cause a problem later on and make completion of the film an impossibility. I had to do something and do it quickly so I told his wife Louise." Mrs. Preston was also pregnant and told Lake to inform her mercurial husband and she did; Sturges blew up and, according to Lake, "it took physical restraint to keep him from boiling over at me." When he calmed down, the director immediately designed a floppy bum's costume for Lake, rewrote some scenes to explain her attire, and had Edith Head design gowns that would not show the actress' condition. Sturges added scenes and changed dialog within minutes as he went along directing at a furious pace and many of the startling scenes that found their way into the movie came as spur-of-the-moment inspirations to the writer-director. "When I started writing it, I had no idea what Sullivan was going to discover," Sturges later said. "Bit by bit I took everything away from him–health, fortune, name, pride, and liberty. When I got down to there I found he still had one thing left: The ability to laugh. So, as a purveyor of laughs, he regained the dignity of his profession and returned to Hollywood to make laugher." Sturges brought the film in for $676,687 and was nine days over schedule. It was a great hit.

p, Preston Sturges; ph, John Seitz; m, Leo Shuken, Charles Bradshaw; ed, Stuart Gilmore; md, Sigmund Krumgold; art d, Hans Dreier, Earl Hedrick; cos, Edith Head; spec eff, Farciot Edouart; makeup, Wally Westmore; cartoon clip, "Playful Pluto," Walt Disney Productions.

Comedy/Drama   **Cas.**   **(PR:C MPAA:NR)**

SULT   (SEE: HUNGER, 1968, Den./Swed.)

SULTAN'S DAUGHTER, THE*½   (1943) 64m MON bw

Ann Corio (*Patra*), Charles Butterworth (*Sultan*), Tim Ryan (*Tim*), Irene Ryan (*Irene*), Eddie Norris (*Jimmy*), Fortunio Bonanova (*Kuda*), Jack LaRue (*Rata*), Gene Stutenroth [Gene Roth] (*Ludwig*), Cris-Pin Martin (*Merchant*), Joseph J. Greene (*Benson*), Gene Oliver, Freddy Fisher and His Orchestra.

Silly premise has sometime ecdysiast Corio as the daughter an Arab sultan and the object of American Norris' romantic desires. During WW II, an agent for the German government is after the sultan's oil fields, and tries to go behind his back by making a deal with Bonanova, the sultan's right-hand man. Corio walks through her role in a stiff manner – strange for a stripper – providing none of the warmth the role called for. Irene and Tim Ryan are around to provide for laughs, but they are not given enough of a chance. Monogram's mimi-moguls had announced their intention of upgrading their product beyond their customary quickie westerns; this was one of

the first results of that decision. Songs include: "I'm Always the Girl," "The Sultan's Daughter," "Clickety-Clack-Jack," and "I'd Love to Make Love to You."

p, Philip S. Krasne, James S. Burkett; d, Arthur Dreifuss; w, Milton M. Raison, Tim Ryan; ph, John Alton; m, Karl Hajos; ed, Martin G. Cohn; md, Hajos; art d, Neil Maguire, Dave Milton; ch, Nico Charisse; m/l, Hajos, Mort Greene.

Musical   **(PR:A MPAA:NR)**

SUMMER AND SMOKE*   (1961) 118m PAR c

Laurence Harvey (*John Buchanan*), Geraldine Page (*Alma Winemiller*), Rita Moreno (*Rosa*), Una Merkel (*Mrs. Winemiller*), John McIntire (*Dr. Buchanan*), Thomas Gomez (*Papa Zacharias*), Pamela Tiffin (*Nellie*), Malcolm Atterbury (*Rev. Winemiller*), Lee Patrick (*Mrs. Ewell*), Casey Adams (*Roger*), Earl Holliman (*Archie Kramer*), Harry Shannon (*Dr. Burke*), Pattee Chapman (*Cynthia*), Jester Hairston (*Thomas*), Pepe Hern (*Nico*), Elektra Rozanska (*Mrs. Anderson*), Dick Ryan (*Dr. Hodges*), Winnie Chandler (*Mrs. Bassett*), Linda Knutson (*Twyla*), Robert Slade (*John*), Rico Alaniz (*Knife Thrower*), John Frank (*Mr. Gilliam*), Marjorie Bennett (*Saleslady*), Susan Roberts (*Betty Lou*), Pamela Duncan (*Pearl*), Margaret Jane Blye (*Dusty*), Charles Watts (*Dignitary-Bandleader*), Cheryl Anderson (*Alma as a Girl*), Almira Sessions (*Woman*).

In 1952, Geraldine Page starred in this Williams play. It took nine years for it to get to the screen, and if it weren't for Page's luminous performance, there would not be much to recommend the movie. Williams had dealt with this character before in THE GLASS MENAGERIE, under another name. She is supposedly based on his sister, who ultimately went insane. What the title means is anybody's guess. Director Glenville staged the London version of the show and was brought in to handle the movie but didn't have much understanding of the oppressive southern upbringing depicted in the script. Perhaps his direction made sense when Englishmen and women spoke the lines in the West End but it failed here, except for Page, who was nominated as Best Actress, and Merkel, who was nominated as Best Supporting Actress. Bernstein's music captured the era and the surroundings and he, too, received an Academy nomination. It's just before WW I and Page lives in a tiny town in Mississippi where she must be above suspicion, as her father, Atterbury, is the town's minister. She is sexually repressed, flighty, neurotic, and seemingly on the edge of a breakdown. Her neighbor is Harvey, a doctor. His father, McIntire, is also a doctor, although the two men have differing opinions of how to conduct their practices. Page has always loved Harvey, ever since they were quite small. She is coy around him and continues to be shy, despite the fact that they were in diapers together. Harvey considers Page only a friend and prefers the company of lively Moreno, who works in her father's (Gomez) noisy dance hall. She is a happy young woman, uncomplicated, the opposite of Page, who persists in attempting to get close to him so he eventually takes her out for a night at Gomez's casino. Afterward, he mistakes her affection for him and tries to seduce her. She is unable to handle the direct frontal assault, tells him off, and runs away, leaving Harvey confused by her seesaw behavior. With Page out of his life, Harvey decides to become engaged to Moreno. He times it so his father is out of town and he can throw a large party as a celebration. Page watches the goings-on from her house and sees the party get wilder, then she phones McIntire and tells him that his home is being abused. McIntire rushes home, has a confrontation with Gomez, and is accidentally killed when a gun goes off. Harvey is stunned by what's happened and decides to mend his wicked ways, settle down, and take over his father's successful practice. Time passes and Page watches as Harvey seems to have become a solid citizen. Meanwhile, her passion becomes unbridled and she directly approaches him and offers herself for his pleasure. By this time, Harvey is a changed man and he only sees Page as a spiritual companion. Harvey has now met Tiffin, a sweet young woman to whom he becomes affianced. When Page hears that, she takes a walk in the local park where she meets Holliman, a traveling salesman just passing through (not unlike the traveling men who came to the small Mississippi town where Blanche Dubois lived and entertained them. Holliman doesn't know anyone, is lonely, and so is Page. She takes the young man by the hand and they go off to spend the night at Gomez's Moon Lake casino. Maybe, just maybe, they will wind up with each other at the salesman's motel. We'll never know. Like so many of the works of Williams, it deals with tension, with repression, with awakening, and, ultimately, with disintegration. Most of what makes happens is in Page's face, a magnificent instrument which she plays like Pablo Casals handles the cello. After many Academy nominations for Best Supporting Actress (HONDO, YOU'RE A BIG BOY NOW, PETE 'N' TILLIE), as well as for Best Actress in this, SWEET BIRD OF YOUTH, and INTERIORS, she finally won for her 1985 triumph, THE TRIP TO BOUNTIFUL.

p, Hal B. Wallis; d, Peter Glenville; w, James Poe, Meade Roberts (based on the play by Tennessee Williams); ph, Charles Lang, Jr. (Panavision, Technicolor); m, Elmer Bernstein; ed, Warren Low; art d, Hal Pereira, Walter Tyler; set d, Sam Comer, Arthur Krams; cos, Edith Head; spec eff, John P. Fulton; makeup, Wally Westmore.

Drama   **(PR:C-O MPAA:NR)**

SUMMER CAMP zero   (1979) 85m Borson/Seymour Borde c

Michael Abrams, Jake Barnes, Bud Bogart, Louise Carmona, Verkina Flower, Brenda Fogarty, Barbara Gold, Shelly Hart, Walt Hill, Ray Holland, Peter Lovett, Debra Marx, John C. McLaughlin, Matt Michaels, George Mills, Collene O'Neil, Dustin Pacino, Jr, Harry Reardon, Alexis Schreiner, Valdesta, Ralph von Albertson, Robert Wald, Bonnie Werchan.

Worthless piece of exploitation in which a camp that is suffering from some severe money problems invites old campers, not quite grown up, to come stay at the camp. The idea is that maybe the parents will open their pocketbooks for the camp. It doesn't look as if anyone bothered to devise a script or to coach the "actors" through their performances.

p, Mark Borde; d, Chuck Vincent; w, Avrumie Schnitzer (based on a story by Borde Schnitzer); ph, Ken Gibb; m, Sparky Sugarman; ed, Mark Ubell; ch, Dino Joseph Giannetta.

Comedy   **Cas.**   **(PR:O MPAA:R)**

SUMMER FIRES   (SEE: MADEMOISELLE, 1966, Fr./Brit.)

SUMMER FLIGHT   (SEE: STOLEN HOURS, 1963)

SUMMER HOLIDAY*½   (1948) 92m MGM c

Mickey Rooney (*Richard Miller*), Gloria DeHaven (*Muriel McComber*), Walter Huston (*Nat Miller*), Frank Morgan (*Uncle Sid*), Jackie "Butch" Jenkins (*Tommy Miller*), Marilyn Maxwell (*Belle*), Agnes Moorehead (*Cousin Lily*), Selena Royle (*Mrs. Miller*), Michael Kirby (*Arthur Miller*), Shirley Johns (*Mildred Miller*), Hal Hackett (*Wint*), Anne Francis (*Elsie Rand*), John Alexander (*Mr. McComber*), Virginia Brissac (*Miss Hawley*), Howard Freeman (*Mr. Peabody*), Alice MacKenzie (*Mrs. McComber*), Don Garner (*Gilbert Ralston*), Ruth Brady (*Crystal*), Emory Parnell (*Bartender*), Wally Cassell (*Salesman*), Terry Moore (*Hatcheck Girl*), Francis Stevens, Budd Fine (*Farmers*), Louise Colombet, Blanche Rose, Margaret Fealey, Nell Spaugh (*Old Painting Characters*), Oliver Blake (*Scorekeeper*), Margaret Bert (*Mrs. Nichols*).

A good musical version of O'Neill's "Ah, Wilderness]" However, good wasn't good enough and the movie lost almost $1.5 million. It took over 100 days to shoot at a cost of more than $2.2 million, a lot of money in those days. The overrun was caused by many factors, not the least of which was a union strike that took place in the middle of shooting that caused the company to shut down. The O'Neill play opened in October, 1933, and starred George M. Cohan, Gene Lockhart, and Elisha Cook, Jr., in the male leads. It ran nearly 300 performances. The 1935 movie version was a classic with Rooney as the young lad. He came back here to play the older brother, with Butch Jenkins in his former slot. It's the early 1900s in New England. Huston is the father of a lovely family, with Royle as his wife, Rooney as their oldest son, and Jenkins as their youngest. Huston is the local newspaper editor, a staunch upholder of Yankee tradition while Royle is the doting mother. Also living in the comfortable household are Moorehead, an old maid aunt, and bachelor uncle Morgan, a tippler. Rooney is extraordinarily bright, his high school's leading scholar, and a boy with big ideas about how to change the world. He adores DeHaven, a neighbor, but has been forbidden to see her because her conservative father, Alexander, caught them innocently kissing and he thinks that Rooney will be the key to his daughter's downfall. He insists she write Rooney a note to call off their budding romance. Rooney is hurt and decides to strike out on his own, meets dance hall girl Maxwell, and makes a pass at her. On a date, he gets drunk, spends every cent he has, and when he's out of money, is tossed out of the bar where they've been drinking. He comes home staggering and Huston (in a "Judge Hardy" scene) sends him to his room. The two reconcile later and Rooney swears that he didn't do anything untoward with Maxwell and that there will be no repercussions. He will never ever get involved with such a woman again] Later, DeHaven and Rooney are allowed to continue their relationship and Morgan, who has been courting the distaff half of the single population in the house, decides to stow his booze, and the moment he does that, Moorehead is his forever. A sweet movie with good work by all the actors, it failed to catch fire at the box office, although it is often played in revival houses to great applause. Mamoulian's last film prior to this was RINGS ON HER FINGERS in 1942. Then he took some time off to direct such musicals on stage as "Oklahoma]" and "Carousel," returned to pictures for this, then went away from the screen until his 1957 version of SILK STOCKINGS. More than a decade later, Bob Merrill wrote the score and David Merrick produced yet another musical version of "Ah, Wilderness" on Broadway. It was "Take Me Along," starring Jackie Gleason in the expanded role of the drunken uncle, Robert Morse in Rooney's second part, Walter Pidgeon as the father, and the superb comedienne Arlene Golonka as the loose woman played by Maxwell. It ran 448 performances and did lots better than this picture. Harry Warren and Ralph Blane wrote a good, not great, score that almost captured the elusive charm of O'Neill. Songs include: "It's Our Home Town" (sung by Huston, Rooney, DeHaven), "Afraid to Fall in Love" (Rooney, DeHaven), "All Hail, Danville High" (ensemble), "The Stanley Steamer" (Rooney, DeHaven, Moorehead, Huston, Royle, Morgan), "It's Independence Day" (ensemble), "I Think You're the Sweetest Kid I've Ever Known," "Weary Blues" (Maxwell). Fine orchestrations by Robert Franklyn, Conrad Salinger, and Sid Cutner. The script supervisor was a very

young Les Martinson who went on to direct many TV shows and films, including PT-109. Further, the cinematographer was, according to Mamoulian, color blind, and the sound man, whose sister was the widow of Irving Thalberg, was deaf. Hard to believe because Doug Shearer owned Oscars for SAN FRANCISCO and STRIKE UP THE BAND. There were three other songs written and shot for the movie but which wound up on the cutting room floor. They were "Spring Isn't Everything," "Never Again," and "Omar and the Princess," which also had an elaborate dance sequence.

p, Arthur Freed; d, Rouben Mamoulian; w, Frances Goodrich, Albert Hackett, Irving Brecher, Jean Holloway (based on the play "Ah, Wilderness]" by Eugene O'Neill); ph, Charles Schoenbaum (Technicolor); m, Harry Warren; ed, Albert Akst; md, Lennie Hayton; art d, Cedric Gibbons, Jack Martin Smith; set d, Edwin B. Willis, Richard Pefferle; cos, Irene, Walter Plunkett; ch, Charles Walters; makeup, Jack Dawn.

Musical/Comedy   **(PR:AA MPAA:NR)**

SUMMER HOLIDAY½   (1963, Brit.) 109m Ivy-Elstree/AIP c

Cliff Richard (*Don*), Lauri Peters (*Barbara*), Melvyn Hayes (*Cyril*), Una Stubbs (*Sandy*), Teddy Green (*Steve*), Pamela Hart (*Angie*), Jeremy Bulloch (*Edwin*), Jacqueline Daryl (*Mimsie*), Madge Ryan (*Stella*), Lionel Murton (*Jerry*), Christine Lawson (*Annie*), Ron Moody (*Orlando*), David Kossoff (*Magistrate*), Wendy Barry (*Shepherdess/Dancer*), Nicholas Phipps (*Wrightmore*), The Shadows (*Themselves*), Lindsay Dolan, Richard Farley, Terry Gilbert, Ian Kaye, Vincent Logan, John MacDonald, Paddy McIntyre, Leon Pomerantz, Ben Stevenson, Anne Briley, Leander Fedden, Sarah Hardenberg, Derina House, Eithne Milne, Sheila O'Neill, Joan Palethorpe (*Dancers*).

A popular British singer of the early 1960s, Richard starred as one of four mechanics trying to use one of London's famous double-decker buses to run a travel service across the European continent. As they start on their test trip they run into a girl rock group's car and demolish it; they then offer to drive the girls to their destination of Athens. Along the way they pick up another girl, Peters, who is posing as a boy in order to hide from her mother and press agent. She is really a popular American singing star with a taxing schedule that won't allow her a vacation. So, against her mother's wishes, she took one. Peters and Richard soon develop a romance, which runs into conflicts when the mother accuses Richard of abducting her daughter. But everything turns out for the best in the end. Performances are all sufficient for their meager demands, with a story that is mainly an excuse for some nifty European scenery and well-integrated music and dance numbers. Richard – no actor, but with a pleasant voice and personality – had done well previously in THE YOUNG ONES and in EXPRESSO BONGO with Laurence Harvey. Songs include: "Bachelor Boy" (Bruce Welch, Cliff Richard); "All at Once," "A Stranger in Town," "A Swinging Affair," "Yugoslav Wedding" (Peter Myers, Ronald Cass); "Dancing Shoes," "Foot Tapper" (Bruce Welch, Hank B. Marvin); "Summer Holiday" (Bruce Welch, Brian Bennett), "Les Girls," "Round and Round" (Bruce Welch, Hank B. Marvin, Brian Bennett); "The Next Time" (Buddy Kaye, Philip Springer); "Big News" (Mike Conlin, Cliff Richard, Ronald Cass).

p, Kenneth Harper; d, Peter Yates; w, Peter Myers, Ronald Cass; ph, John Wilcox (CinemaScope, Technicolor); m, Stanley Black; ed, Jack Slade; md, Black; art d, Syd Cain; cos Oliver Plunkett; spec eff, George Blackwel l; ch, Herbert Ross; m/l, Myers, Cass, Cliff Richard, Bruce Welch, Brian Bennett, Hank B. Marvin, Philip Springer, Buddy Kaye, Mike Conlin; makeup, John O'Gorman.

Musical/Comedy   **(PR:A MPAA:NR)**

SUMMER INTERLUDE   (SEE ILLICIT INTERLUDE, 1954, Swed.)

SUMMER LIGHTNING**   (1933, Brit.) 78m British and
                                                           Dominions/UA bw

Ralph Lynn (*Hugo Carmody*), Winifred Shotter (*Millicent Keable*), Dorothy [Chili] Bouchier (*Sue Brown*), Horace Hodges (*Lord Emsworth*), Helen Ferrers (*Lady Emsworth*), Esme Percy (*Baxter*), Miles Malleson (*Beach*), Gordon James (*Pillbream*), Joe Monkhouse (*Pigman*).

Light-hearted farce that has Lynn as secretary to the pompous lord, Hodges, while in love with the latter's pretty niece Shotter. Because his monetary situation makes marriage impossible, Lynn comes up with a plan to steal Hodges' prize pig, and then return it with the hope of getting on Hodges' good side.

p, Herbert Wilcox; d, Maclean Rogers; w, Miles Malleson (based on the novel by P.G. Wodehouse); ph, F.A. Young.

Comedy   **(PR:A MPAA:NR)**

SUMMER LIGHTNING, 1948   (SEE: SCUDDA-HOO] SCUDDA-HAY],
                                                           1948)

SUMMER LOVE**½   (1958) 85m UNIV bw

John Saxon (*Jim Daley*), Molly Bee (*Alice*), Rod McKuen (*Ox Bentley*), Judy Meredith (*Joan Wright*), Jill St. John (*Erica Landis*), John Wilder (*Mike Howard*), George "Foghorn" Winslow (*Thomas Daley III*), Fay Wray (*Beth Daley*), Edward C. Platt (*Dr. Thomas Daley*), Shelley Fabares (*Twinkie Daley*), Gordon Gebert (*Tad Powers*), Beverly Washburn (*Jackie*), Bob Courtney (*Half-Note Harris*), Troy Donahue (*Sax Lewis*), Hylton Socher (*Fingers Porter*), Marjorie Durant (*Hilda*), Walter Reed (*Mr. Reid*), Rock Murphy, Robert Bain, Plas Johnson, Jr, David Pell, Alvin Stoller, Ray Sherman, Mike Pacheco, Jimmy Daley's Ding-A-Lings.

Aimed solely at providing some musical entertainment to the bobbing teenagers of the late 1950s, this sequel to ROCK PRETTY BABY brings in pretty much the same cast, up to their usual antics of teenage romances and having fun. Saxon stars as the head of a music group which gets a job at a summer camp, making for some tough going for Saxon when he finds himself the object of two very pretty girls, Meredith and St. John. Poet-songster McKuen's soul-searching, self-involved verses made him a minor guru to the young university intelligentsia in later years. Seven songs include: "Summer Love" and "To Know You Is to Love You" (Henry Mancini, Bill Carey).

p, William Grady, Jr.; d, Charles Haas; w, William Raynor, Herbert Margolis; ph, Carl E. Guthriel, Clifford Stine; m, Henry Mancini; ed, Tony Martinelli; md, Joseph Gershenson; art d, Alexander Golitzen, Philip Barber; m/l, Rod McKuen, Bill Carey, Malvina Reynolds, Everett Carter, Milton Rosen.

Musical/Comedy   (PR:A MPAA:NR)

SUMMER LOVERS*½   (1982) 98m Filmways-Orion c

Peter Gallagher (*Michael Papas*), Daryl Hannah (*Cathy Feathererst*), Valerie Quennessen (*Lina*), Barbara Rush (*Jean Feathererst*), Carole Cook (*Barbara Foster*), Hans Van Tongeren (*Jan Tolin*), Lydia Lenosi (*Aspa*), Vladimiros Kiriakos (*Yorghos*), Carlos Rodriguez Ramos (*Cosmo*), Henri Behar (*Phillippe*), Rika Dialina (*Monica*), Andreas Filipidis (*Andreas*), Peter Pye (*Joe Saunders*), Janis Benjamin (*Trish Saunders*).

A shallow and meaningless picture that has Hannah and Gallagher as rich-kid lovers who decide to spend a summer at a Greek island villa. Their romancing is temporarily interrupted by a lady archaeologist, Quennessen, doing some digging on the island. She quickly fits into the scheme of things after she and Gallagher have a quick fling. There is little in any of these characters to make them likable or appealing to an ordinary person, who would only dislike them more for being spoiled kids who can spend their summers traveling around Europe. A horrible disco soundtrack is added to make this picture that much more sickening. Kleiser, who directed GREASE and THE BLUE LAGOON, apparently attempted to blend the two in this highly audible idiocy.

p, Mike Modor; d&w, Randal Kleiser; ph, Peter Collister, Timothy Galfas, Dimitri Papacostandis (Technicolor); m, Basil Poledouris; ed, Robert Gordon; prod d, Bruce Weintraub.

Drama/Comedy   Cas.   (PR:O MPAA:R)

SUMMER MADNESS   (SEE: SUMMERTIME, 1955)

SUMMER MAGIC**½   (1963) 109m Disney/BV c

Hayley Mills (*Nancy Carey*), Burl Ives (*Osh Popham*), Dorothy McGuire (*Margaret Carey*), Deborah Walley (*Cousin Julia*), Eddie Hodges (*Gilly Carey*), Jimmy Mathers (*Peter Carey*), Michael J. Pollard (*Digby Popham*), Wendy Turner (*Lallie Joy Popham*), Una Merkel (*Maria Popham*), Peter Brown (*Tom Hamilton*), James Stacy (*Charles Bryant*), O. Z. Whitehead (*Mr. Perkins*), Eddie Quillan (*Mailman*), Norman Leavitt (*Barber*), Paul E. Burns (*Drinker*), Harry Holcombe (*Henry Lord*), Jan Stine (*Mr. Perkins' Son*), Hilda Plowright (*Mary*), Marcy McGuire (*Ellen*).

Light and unpretentious Disney fare that flaunts nothing more than nearly two hours of escapist entertainment, but at times it's so cute that it's almost sickening. McGuire plays a recent widow forced to move from her expensive Boston home to a small town in Maine out of monetary necessity. With her teenage daughter, Mills, and Hodges and Mathers, her young sons, she finds an old broken-down house. They fix it up and manage to make it look like a very pleasant country home. Willing to go out of his way to lend a hand is the local postmaster, Ives, who must be the sweetest man ever to grace the giant screen, who is also responsible for collecting rent for the absent landlord, but hasn't the heart to ask the poor woman for any money. The actual owner of the house does show up unannounced, but keeps his identity a secret, giving him time to fall for Mills and to allow the family to stay at the house as long as they desire. A number of songs are thrown in, all as memorable as the saccharine story: "The Ugly Bug Ball," "Railroad Rag," "Flitterin'," "Beautiful Beulah," "The Pink of Perfection," "Summer Magic," "Femininity," and "On the Front Porch." Reworking of *MOTHER CAREY'S CHICKENS*.

p, Walt Disney, Ron Miller; d, James Neilson; w, Sally Benson (based on the novel Mother Carey's Chickens by Kate Douglas Wiggin); ph, William Snyder (Technicolor); m, Buddy Baker; ed, Robert Stafford; art d, Carroll

Clark, Robert Clatworthy; set d, Emile Kuri, Frank R. McKelvy; cos, Bill Thomas; spec eff, Peter Ellenshow; m/l, Richard M. and Robert B. Sherman; makeup, Pat McNalley.

Comedy   Cas.   (PR:AAA MPAA:NR)

SUMMER OF '42****   (1971) 102m WB c

Jennifer O'Neill (*Dorothy*), Gary Grimes (*Hermie*), Jerry Houser (*Oscy*), Oliver Conant (*Benjie*), Katherine Allentuck (*Aggie*), Christopher Norris (*Miriam*), Lou Frizzell (*Druggist*), Walter Scott (*Dorothy's Husband*), Maureen Stapleton (*Voice of Hermie's Mother*), Robert Mulligan (*Narrator, Older Hermie*).

People who actually recall 1942 will more greatly appreciate the waves of nostalgia that bathe this drama, although many of the emotions are constant and can be applied to anyone of any age, as proven by the fact that the movie made over $20 million on first release. It's a tale of the emotional and sexual awakenings of teenagers recounted in an affectionate, rather than a satirical, manner. Set on a tiny island off New England (which could have been Block Island), the screenplay is a fond remembrance of times gone by. Director Mulligan (as the adult Hermie) narrates his recollections and all of the names used in the story were the real names of the people involved (or so claimed screenwriter Raucher, who wrote the screenplay in less than two weeks). Grimes is the 15-year-old and we see his life on the tranquil island, where the horrors of war seemed a million miles away. Grimes and his friends – Houser and Conant – pal around together, get into minor scrapes, go see movies like NOW, VOYAGER (there's a clip from the Bette Davis/Paul Henreid movie in this. Easy to do as it was also out of Warner Bros.) and spend a great deal of time poring over a sex manual that gives explicit, though not necessarily pornographic, details about intercourse. Houser reads the manual as though it were the Bible and he a seminary student. Grimes is more interested in the practical aspects of sex and yearns for O'Neill, an "older woman" in her 20s. O'Neill is married to soldier Scott and bids him farewell as he goes off to fight in the war. Once he's gone, Grimes makes himself useful to the beauteous O'Neill (a former model in her fourth film) by offering to help her carry groceries, etc. She finds Grimes amusing and eventually invites him in to have coffee and doughnuts, out of no motivation but loneliness. Grimes interprets this as something more, but holds back and just dreams of an eventual liaison with O'Neill. As the story goes on, various memory-joggers are introduced so we always know the year we are in. Ice cream costs 12 cents for two scoops, radio soap operas are the rage, and everyone talks about the war. Grimes and Houser meet two teenage girls, Norris and Allentuck (Maureen Stapleton's 16-year-old daughter, making her film debut. Stapleton also did the voice of Grimes' mother), and take them to the movies. Grimes is aggressive and, while never taking his eyes off the screen, he thinks he is toying with Allentuck's breast. He is disappointed when Houser later tells him that he was only playing with the girl's arm] Grimes spends a day with O'Neill and carries heavy packages for her up to the attic. Each time he looks at her, it is with such passion that he seems about to explode. Houser has arranged a nighttime beach party with Norris and Allentuck. Grimes thinks that this just might be the night when he ceases to be a virgin so he goes to the pharmacy of Frizzell to buy contraceptives. Frizzell does a smashing cameo as the understanding and bemused druggist. Houser already has himself covered because his older brother left him a contraceptive with the admonition to use it well. Things never work out the way one expects and while Houser and Norris go behind a large sand dune and exercise their passions, Grimes and Allentuck spend a serene evening toasting marshmallows. The next day, Grimes goes to visit O'Neill, opens the door and walks in, and doesn't see her. But he does spot the official Army telegram informing O'Neill that Scott has been killed in action. O'Neill, with tears in her eyes, walks into the room and puts her head on his shoulder. They begin to move with Legrand's music (which won an Oscar) and what follows is a 17-minute lovemaking sequence that has only sound effects and music as she takes him into the bedroom and they sleep with each other (very tastefully shot). The next day, Grimes comes back to O'Neill's home and finds that she's left and only a short note remains. The letter says that she had to go and wishes him all the best and hopes that he will always recall their relationship. (Obviously Raucher recalled it well. He was interviewed about using the woman's real name but he said that he didn't worry about her bringing a lawsuit against him. She would have been in her middle 50s by the time this movie was made.) Mulligan's voice recaps the summer of '42 with the movies they saw, the rain that came down, the times they raided the local Coast Guard station, and the fact that he became a man. One source says the film was shot on the Mendocino coast, another source claims it was done at Fort Bragg. We called director Mulligan's office and were told that it was shot in both places in northern California. Scripter Raucher and cinematographer Surtees were nominated for Oscars and lost that year, respectively, to Paddy Chayefsky for THE HOSPITAL and to Oswald Morris for his camerawork on FIDDLER ON THE ROOF. Legrand also took a British Film Academy Award for his music. The language and the sexual situations should keep any youngsters away, but their parents and grandparents will enjoy the movie. If this film had actually been made in 1942, it couldn't have been as bold, but the story might have remained the same. O'Neill's career has been an odd one. Following the success of this film, she appeared in several turkeys. Then, the Brazilian-born (of American parents) actress had a succession of personal problems which have contributed to her being off the screen for more years than she's been on. The sequel to this was CLASS OF '44, which also featured Houser, Grimes, and Conant and was nowhere nearly as successful or intelligent. Raucher later novelized SUMMER OF '42.

p, Richard A. Roth; d, Robert Mulligan; w, Herman Raucher; ph, Robert Surtees (Technicolor); m, Michel Legrand; ed, Folmar Blangsted; md, Legrand; prod d, Albert Brenner; set d, Marvin March.

Drama   **Cas.**   **(PR:O MPAA:PG)**

SUMMER OF SECRETS**   (1976, Aus.) 100m Secret Picture
                                              Productions/Greater Union c

Arthur Dignam *(Doctor)*, Rufus Collins *(Bob)*, Neil Campbell *(Kym)*, Andrew Sharp *(Steve)*, Kate Fitzpatrick *(Rachel)*.

The director of THE ROCKY HORROR PICTURE SHOW, Sharman, tried to dig up some of the same elements which made the earlier picture such a success, but failed to provide the humor and absurdity that made the earlier film a hit. As in that picture, two young lovers, Campbell and Sharp, are shipwrecked on an almost deserted island. Dignam is the crazed doctor who is working on a way to bring his wife, Fitzpatrick, back from the dead. Half the financing for the film came from the Australian Film Commission, again unsuccessfully pushing for more domestic products.

p, Michael Thornhill; d, Jim Sharman; w, John Aitken; ph, Russell Boyd; m, Cameron Allen; art d, Jane Norris.

Comedy   **(PR:O MPAA:NR)**

SUMMER OF '64   (SEE: GIRLS ON THE BEACH, 1965)

SUMMER OF THE SEVENTEENTH DOLL
                        (SEE: SEASON OF PASSION, 1960, Brit./Aus.)

SUMMER PLACE, A**   (1959) 130m WB c

Richard Egan *(Ken Jorgenson)*, Dorothy McGuire *(Sylvia Hunter)*, Sandra Dee *(Molly Jorgenson)*, Arthur Kennedy *(Bart Hunter)*, Troy Donahue *(Johnny Hunter)*, Constance Ford *(Helen Jorgenson)*, Beulah Bondi *(Mrs. Hamilton Hamble)*, Jack Richardson *(Claude Andrews)*, Martin Eric *(Todd Hasper)*, Peter Constanti *(Captain)*, Junius Matthews *(Mr. Hamble)*, Gertrude Flynn *(Mrs. Carter)*, Marshall Bradford *(Dr. Matthias)*, Phil Chambers *(Sheriff)*, Robert Griffin *(Englehardt)*, Arthur Space *(Ken's Attorney)*, George Taylor *(Bart's Attorney)*, Roberta Shore *(Anne Talbert)*, Ann Doran *(Mrs. Talbert)*, Dale J. Nicholson *(Minister)*, Lewis Martin *(Doctor)*, Helen Wallace *(Wife)*, Everett Glass *(Dean)*, Eleanor Audley *(Mrs. Harrington)*, Richard Deacon *(Pawnbroker)*, Howard Hoffman *(Alvin Frost)*, Justice of the Peace, Nancy Matthews, Susan Odin, Cheryl Holdridge, Bonnie Franklin *(Young Girls in Dormitory)*.

A highly stylized and overly glossy soap opera which could do nothing to overcome the basic shallowness of the characters being portrayed. Two steamy and controversial – by the late 1950s' standards – love affairs are offered. One – for grownups – is between Egan and McGuire; the other – aimed at teenagers – is with Dee and Donahue. McGuire is married to Kennedy, a drunken louse who mourns the loss of his former wealth. Donahue is their teenage son. The wealthy Egan and family come back to the small New England town where he was an impoverished lifeguard 20 years earlier and where he carried on a lusty affair with McGuire. They resume their affair again, only this time they are discovered. No problem: they just get divorces from their respective spouses and marry each other. Meanwhile, Egan's daughter, Dee, is carrying on with Donahue, and mother Ford looms over Dee's shoulder worrying about whether she is still a virgin. Though there is an attempt to make these situations seem highly dramatic, the performances are little more than stereotypes, a result of the wretched dialog. This film was surprisingly frank about sex and illicit romantic affairs, much more so than PEYTON PLACE had been just two years earlier. However, A SUMMER PLACE did not receive nearly the criticism of the earlier film. Novelist Wilson had experienced a cinematic hit in THE MAN IN THE GRAY FLANNEL SUIT (1956). This film, pandering as it did to both old and young, also did well at the box office, and the title song became a popular classic. Famed architect Frank Lloyd Wright was responsible for the habitat of the title. This was Donahue's first featured screen role.

p,d,&w, Delmer Daves (based on the novel by Sloan Wilson); ph, Harry Stradling (Technicolor); m, Max Steiner; ed, Owen Marks; art d, Leo K. Kuter.

Drama   **(PR:C MPAA:NR)**

SUMMER RUN**½   (1974) 96m Movie and Music Corporation of
                                              Texas/Lighthouse c

Andy Parks *(Harry Ross)*, Tina Lund *(Kristina)*, Dennis Redfield *(Felix Zipper)*, Gail Joy *(Sam)*, Judith Nugent *(Debbie)*, Juliet Berto *(Juliet)*, Leon Capetanos, Froda Rassmussen, John Broderick, Phyllis Altenhaus.

Looking almost like a travelog, this film follows the adventures of Parks as

he backpacks through Europe, providing the scenic wonders of seven different countries. Though only on summer vacation, Parks meets a young Norwegian girl, with whom he falls in love. They share enough experiences to make their bond more than just a casual affair. He is then faced with the problem of whether or not to return to school in the U.S. or to stick it out with the girl. Though there is not much of a narrative, the picture manages to maintain interest through the development of the relationship, with Parks having the right type of energy for his role.

p, Steven Graham; d&w, Leon Capetanos; ph, Klaus Konig (Metrocolor); m, Patrick Ferrell; ed, Antranig Mahakian, Lewis Teague.

Drama   **(PR:A MPAA:PG)**

SUMMER SCHOOL TEACHERS**   (1977) 86m New World c

Candice Rialson *(Conklin T)*, Pat Anderson *(Sally)*, Rhonda Leigh Hopkins *(Denise)*, Will Carney *(Jeremy)*, Grainger Hines *(Bob)*, Christopher Barrett *(Jeff)*, Dick Miller *(Sam)*, Vince Barnett *(Principal Adams)*, Norman Bartold *(Agwin)*, Michael Greer *(John John Lacey)*, Barbara Peil *(Janice)*, Merie Earle *(Ethel)*, Ka-Ron Sowell Brown *(Jessie)*, Cecil Elliott *(Freida)*, John Kerry *(Hiram)*, C. D. Smith *(Cy)*, Brian Enright *(Slick)*, Walter O. Miles *(Mr. Carter)*, Beach Dickerson *(Apartment Manager)*, Gary Morgan *(Roger)*, Ken Smedberg *(James)*, Bill Thornbury *(Arthur)*, Mike McHenry *(Hal)*, Michael Miller *(Neighbor)*.

An adolescent fantasy tale which, unlike a film such as PORKY'S, (1981), shows women having intelligence and moral sense instead of merely serving as implements of eroticism. Three attractive midwestern woman take teaching positions at a southern California high school. Rialson is a physical-education teacher who coaches a girl's football team and gets suspended for stealing a crooked coach's financial books. Anderson is an art teacher who allows a student to take nude photos of her that eventually get published in a magazine, bringing about a suspension for both herself and the photographer. Hines Hopkins teaches a chemistry class and becomes romantically linked with Carney, a likeable student who gets mixed up in a stolen car ring. After a number of misadventures Hopkins and Carney crack the ring and get Rialson's and Anderson's suspensions lifted. Produced by Julie Corman, the wife of guerrilla producer/director Roger Corman. Sequel to THE STUDENT TEACHERS.

p, Julie Corman; d&w, Barbara Peters; ph, Eric Saarinen (Metrocolor); m, J. J. Jackson; ed, Barbara Pokras; art d, Marty Bercaw; makeup, Leigh Mitchell; stunts, Whitey Hughes.

Comedy   **(PR:O MPAA:R)**

SUMMER SOLDIERS**½   (1972, Jap.) 107m Teshigahara c

Keith Sykes *(Jim)*, Lee Reisen *(Relko)*, Kazuo Kitamura *(Tachikawa)*, Toshiko Kobayashi *(Mrs. Tachikawa)*, Shoichi Ozawa *(Tanikawa)*, Tetsuko Kuroyanagi *(Mrs. Tanikawa)*, Hideo Kanze *(Shimezu)*, Tamao Nakamura *(Mrs. Shimezu)*, Hishashi Igawa *(Ota)*, Kunie Tanaka *(Fujimura)*, Takeshi Kato *(Driver)*, Greg Antonacci *(Miguel)*, Barry Cotton *(Daryl)*, John Nathan *(Pete)*.

A strange, interesting, gentle, and intensely contemporary film (for its time) which explores the relationships between the dedicated and the dropouts during the Vietnam conflict. Cross cultures come into play as well in the picture as Japanese "host families" afford a succession of one-night shelters to GIs who have elected to desert from the U.S. armed forces while on leave in Tokyo. Sykes, whose motive for deserting is no more than exhaustion, is counterposed against Antonacci, an anti-war ideolog. The Japanese "Deserters' Aid Committee" members interact with the two, with one another, and with other deserters in interesting, telling, and often amusing ways. A non-judgmental film which raises more questions than it answers and seemingly takes no political stance, the screenwriter and the director preferring to explore the attitudes, compulsions, and involvements of all the characters. The dialog is a combination of English and subtitled Japanese. Director Teshigahara made a considerable splash with his WOMAN IN THE DUNES in 1964.

p, Yukio Tomizawa; d, Hiroshi Teshigahara; w, John Nathan; ph, Teshigahara; m, Toru Takemitsu; ed, Fusako Shuzui.

Drama   **(PR:C MPAA:NR)**

SUMMER STOCK***½   (1950) 109m MGM c (GB: IF YOU FEEL
                                              LIKE SINGING)

Judy Garland *(Jane Falbury)*, Gene Kelly *(Joe D. Ross)*, Eddie Bracken *(Orville Wingait)*, Gloria DeHaven *(Abigail Falbury)*, Marjorie Main *(Esme)*, Phil Silvers *(Herb Blake)*, Ray Collins *(Jasper G. Wingait)*, Carleton Carpenter *(Artie)*, Nita Bieber *(Sarah Higgins)*, Hans Conried *(Harrison I. Keath)*, Paul E. Burns *(Frank)*, Carol Haney, Dorothy Tuttle, Arthur Loew, Jr, Dick Humphreys, Jimmy Thompson, Bridget Carr, Joanne Tree, Jean Coyne, Jean Adcock, Rena Lenart, Joan Dale, Betty Hannon, Elynne Ray, Marilyn Reiss, Carol West, Eugene Freedley, Don Powell, Joe Roach, Albert Ruiz *(Members of Stock Company)*, Roy Butler, Henry Sylvester, George Bunny, Frank Pharr *(Townsmen)*, Cameron Grant, Jack Daley, Reginald Simpson *(Producers)*, Michael Chapin, Teddy Infuhr *(Boys)*, Almira Sessions *(Constance Fliggerton)*, Kathryn Sheldon *(Amy Fliggerton)*, Jack Gargan

(Clerk), Eddie Dunn (Sheriff), Erville Alderson (Zeb), Bette Arlen, Bunny Waters (Showgirls).

A tuneful throwback to old-fashioned musicals of the "you've got the barn, I've got the instruments, let's put on a show" genre. Garland's last movie for MGM was fraught with problems. She'd already spent some time in a Boston hospital to withdraw from drug dependency and had gained some weight. Because of her lateness, her disappearances from the set, and her general unwillingness to rehearse, the picture took far longer to shoot than it should have and her yo-yo weight changed, so there's a definite difference between the svelte Garland and the porky one within the picture. Producer Pasternak tried to get rid of her but studio chief Louis B. Mayer insisted she stay on, out of loyalty. She'd made millions for the studio and the tiny studio chief knew that she would be totally destroyed if they fired her. After completion of shooting, she was asked to replace June Allyson in ROYAL WEDDING. Allyson had become pregnant so Garland came in, but it was no go. She was tardy, ill, not prepared, and was herself replaced by Jane Powell. In SUMMER STOCK, Garland owns a New England farm and is having difficulty keeping up the payments. The crops are waiting to be harvested in the field and her sister, DeHaven, is due to come in and help. DeHaven arrives with a whole summer-stock company led by Kelly. Garland's housekeeper is Main and she doesn't much like this arrival of a bunch of actors. Garland is the beloved of Bracken, the goony son of local businessman Collins, who is trying to help Garland through her financial woes. DeHaven is a would-be actress and thinks that they might be able to raise some money by putting on a show in the large barn on the property. Garland is totally against it but the performers will help with the harvesting and the farm's chores in order to pay for their room and board. Kelly and DeHaven are an item and she is hoping that this show will be her springboard as an actress. Kelly and his pals have no money at all but since they are willing to work, Garland allows them to stay, thus incurring the wrath of both Bracken and Collins, who share Main's feelings about people who act for a living. Kelly becomes attracted to Garland but she maintains a businesslike attitude – even though she shares his feelings – because she knows that Kelly and DeHaven have been seeing each other on a personal level. When DeHaven and Kelly have an argument and she goes back to New York, Kelly is stuck for a leading lady and you have one guess as to who steps in. Meanwhile, Bracken leaves Connecticut to go to Manhattan and bring DeHaven back. Garland is thrust into the hectic rehearsals and she and Kelly can no longer hide their magnetism for each other. Bracken arrives with DeHaven on the night the show is to open. He's fetched her in order to break up the budding Kelly/Garland romance but he's too late. The show goes on, is a smash, and DeHaven and Bracken begin to look at each other in a new light, so everyone winds up in pairs. The film took eight months to shoot, about twice what was scheduled. The simplistic plot was aided by several excellent songs by Harry Warren and Mack Gordon which included: "Friendly Star" (sung by Garland), "Mem'ry Island" (sung by DeHaven and Conried), "Dig-Dig-Dig For Your Di nner" (Kelly, with Phil Silvers), "If You Feel Like Singing, Sing" (Garland), "Howdy Neighbor" (Garland, then as the finale by everyone), "All For You" (Kelly, Silvers), "Blue Jean Polka," "Portland Fancy" (Kelly, Garland) and "You, Wonderful You" (with lyrics by Jack Brooks, Saul Chaplin). The old hit "Get Happy" (by Ted Koehler, Harold Arlen) was thrown in because they thought the picture needed a lift. It remains Liza Minnelli's favorite performance by her mother. Garland wore leotards, a man's tuxedo jacket, and a black hat. Also heard was "Heavenly Music" (by Saul Chaplin, performed by Kelly and Silvers). It was four years until Garland worked again after this when she made the memorable A STAR IS BORN. Gene Kelly was reputed to have had the patience of a a saint when it came to working with the difficult Garland; he has never said a word against her. Producer Pasternak had a rose delivered to Garland's dressing room every morning and she never knew who it was from. Later, when she was working at London's Palladium, the rose was again delivered and Garland pressed the British delivery person and finally learned who did it. In a small role, note Arthur Loew, Jr., grandson of Marcus Loew, the man who united Metro, Goldwyn, and Mayer in 1924.

p, Joe Pasternak; d, Charles Walters; w, George Wells, Sy Gomberg (based on a story by Gomberg); ph, Robert Planck (Technicolor); ed, Albert Akst; md, Johnny Green, Saul Chaplin; art d, Cedric Gibbons, Jack Martin Smith; cos, Walter Plunkett, Helen Rose; ch, Nick Castle, Gene Kelly, Walters; m/l, Mack Gordon, Warren, Jack Brooks, Chaplin, Harold Arlen, Ted Koehler.

Musical/Comedy   **(PR:A   MPAA:NR)**

SUMMER STORM*   (1944) 105m UA-Angelus bw

George Sanders (Fedor Petroff), Linda Darnell (Olga), Anna Lee (Nadina), Edward Everett Horton (Count Volsky), Hugo Haas (Urbenin), Lori Lahner (Clara), John Philliber (Polycarp), Sig Rumann (Kuzma), Andre Charlot (Mr. Kalenin), Mary Servoss (Mrs. Kalenin), John Abbott (Lunin), Robert Greig (Gregory), Paul Hurst (Orloff, Gendarme), Charles Trowbridge (Doctor), Byron Foulger (Clerk in Newspaper Office), Charles Wagenheim (Postman), Frank Orth (Cafe Proprietor), Elizabeth Russell, Ann Staunton (Dinner Guests), Nina Koschetz (Gypsy Singer), Jimmy Conlin (Passerby at Mailbox), Kate MacKenna (Woman with Umbrella), Fred Nurney (Judge in Kharkov), Sarah Padden (Beggar Woman), Sharon McManus (Beggar Child), Gabriel Lionoff (Priest), Mike Mazurki (Policeman), Woody Charles (Young Lackey), Joyce Gates (Gypsy Girl), Rex Evans, Kenneth Jones, Anita Venge,

Francis Morris, John Kelly.

A dark, brooding drama based on Chekhov's "The Shooting Party," this marked the first time the Russian had been adapted for the screen. Made for less the $400,000, it's a flashback to 1912, in pre-revolutionary Russia (where star Sanders was born). Darnell is a grasping peasant who is determined to rise above her station. She uses her smoldering beauty and her feminine wiles to entice middle-aged farmer Haas to marry her. Her main reason is to flee her stern father. Haas knows full well he can't handle Darnell so he looks the other way as she embarks on a series of affairs. Sanders is a judge engaged to Lee. While vamping him, Darnell is also courting rich Horton, who plies her with jewels, gowns, and frippery. In the end, Darnell is murdered by Sanders, who – for her – has tossed away a promising career in law and the love of a good woman in Lee. Haas is arrested and convicted for the crime and Sanders keeps mum about it, enlisting the aid of his maid, Lahner, who also maintains the secret. Finally, Sanders can't take the guilt anymore (it's 10 years later when he wakes up to that) and confesses that he is the killer. He tries to escape but is killed by the cops. Excellent sets and costumes make this very realistic and Sirk's European style of direction is perfect for the material, but with the heroine being a ruined and ruinous woman and all of the men being playthings for her, it's not easy to find anyone to like in the picture. A good movie that sank.

p, Seymour Nebenzal; d, Douglas Sirk; w, Rowland Leigh, Sirk, Robert Thoeren (based on the story "The Shooting Party" by Anton Chekhov); ph, Archie Stout, Eugen Shuftan; m, Karl Hajos; ed, Gregg Tallas; md, Hajos; art d, Rudi Feld; cos, Max Pretzfelder.

Drama   **(PR:C   MPAA:NR)**

SUMMER TALES   (SEE: LOVE ON THE RIVIERA, 1964, Fr./Ital.)

SUMMER TO REMEMBER, A*   (1961, USSR) 80m
        Mosfilm/Kingsley International-M.J.P. Enterprises bw (SERYOZHA)

Borya Barkhatov (Seryozha), Sergey Bondarchuk (Korostelyov), Irina Skobtseva (Maryana), Natasha Chechyotkina (Lidka), Seryozha Metelitsyn (Vaska), Yura Kozlov (Zhenka), Alyosha Dotsenko (Shurik), L. Sokolova (Vaska's Mother), Vasiliy Merkuryev (Uncle Kostya), A. Panova (Aunt Pasha), K. Frolova (Zhenka's Aunt), Nikolay Sergeyev (Lukyanych), Valentin Bryleyev, V. Brovkin, Ye. Gulyayeva, P. Vinnik, M. Zharova, Ye. Zhdanova, P. Kiryutkin, Ye. Kudryashov.

An almost lyrical look at the the relationship between a young boy and his new stepfather. The man treats the boy with an unusual amount of kindness which continues to grow until their attachment becomes so strong the boy cannot bear to be separated from his stepfather. More engrossing to Western eyes than the simple plot line are the views of day-to-day life on the collective farm– as seen from the perspective of the boy–which is managed by the stripling's Stakhanovite stepfather. A first feature film from a talented young team of directors who linked up as film students, making their diploma film together. Actor Bondarchuk is also a talented director of epic films such as the four-part WAR AND PEACE (1968) and WATERLOO (1971). (In Russian; English subtitles.)

d, Georgiy Daneliya, Igor Talankin; w, Vera Panova, Daneliya, Talankin, M. Kachalova (based on the story "Seryozha" by Panova); ph, Anatoliy Nitochkin; m, Boris Chaykovskiy; ed, P. Chechyotkina; md, A. Roytman; art d, V. Nisskaya; spec eff, B. Pluzhnikov, N. Spiridonova; makeup, K. Yarmolyuk.

Drama   **(PR:A   MPAA:NR)**

SUMMER WISHES, WINTER DREAMS**   (1973) 87m Rastar-Gilbert
                                                          Cates/COL c

Joanne Woodward (Rita Walden), Martin Balsam (Harry Walden), Sylvia Sidney (Mrs. Pritchett), Dori Brenner (Anna), Win Forman (Fred Goody), Tresa Hughes (Betty Goody), Peter Marklin (Joel), Ron Rickards (Bobby Walden), Charlotte Oberley (Waitress), Minerva Pious (Mrs. Bimberg), Helen Ludlam (Grandmother), Grant Code (Grandfather), Sol Frieder (Mr. Goldblatt), Gaetano Lisi (Student in Theater), Nancy Andrews (Mrs. Pat Hungerford), Lee Jackson (Carl Hurlbutt), David Thomas (Chauffeur), Marian Swan (Nurse), Dennis Wayne (Dancer in Dream).

Some very captivating performances on the part of Woodward, Balsam, and – after a 17-year hiatus from films – Sidney (the latter starred in Fritz Lang's FURY back in 1936) are given almost nothing of a story. That just might be the point in this attempt to show the emptiness in the lives of a successful middle-age couple, Balsam and Woodward, who have only middle-class material pleasures. Upon the death of Sidney, Woodward's mother, the pair head to France and the battlefield where Balsam faced the scariest moments of his life, where he supposedly learned to really value his existence. The reasons for coming here are to recapture that sense of vitality, the importance of an existence free from danger. Balsam–in what might be viewed as a reprise of the Lew Ayres role in 1930's ALL QUIET ON THE WESTERN FRONT–had spent the night with three German corpses during WW II. Now a successful oculist, his problems– and those of wife Woodward -center about such things as whether she should redecorate their apartment. The tedium of their current lives is faithfully replicated in what becomes a tedious picture.

p, Jack Brodsky; d, Gilbert Cates; w, Stewart Stern; ph, Gerald Hirschfeld (Technicolor); m, Johnny Mandel; ed, Sidney Katz; prod d, Peter Dohanos; cos, Anna Hill Johnstone.

Drama   (PR:A   MPAA:PG)

SUMMERDOG**   (1977) 90m Film Foundry/Salisbury c

James Congdon (*Peter*), Elizabeth Eisenman (*Carol*), Oliver Zabriskie (*Adam*), Tavia Zabriskie (*Becky*), Don Rutledge (*Caleb*), Estelle Harris (*Mrs. Baleeka*), Tony Capra (*Mr. Baleeka*).

Kids always seem to have a place in their heart for movies about homely mutts. This time the dog is named Hobo and he is adopted by a vacationing family. Clean wholesome family entertainment.

p&d, John Clayton; w, George LaFollette-Zabriskie, Sherry LaFollette-Zabriskie; ph, Bill Godsey; m, Michael Gibson; ed, Julie Tanser.

Children's Film   **Cas.**   (PR:AAA   MPAA:G)

SUMMERFIELD**½   (1977, Aus.) 95m Clare Beach/Greater Union c

Nick Tate (*Simon Robinson*), John Walters (*David Abbott*), Elizabeth Alexander (*Jenny Abbott*), Michelle Jarman (*Sally Abbott*), Charles Tingwell (*Dr. Miller*), Geraldine Turner (*Betty Tate*), Max Cullen (*Jim Tate*), Sheila Florance (*Miss Gleeson*), Isabel Harley (*Miss Tucker*), Joy Westmore (*Mrs. Shields*), Adrian Wright (*Peter Flynn*), Barry Donnelly (*Sgt. Potter*), David Smeed (*Mark*), Max Fairchild (*Joe Baxter*).

A small island off the coast of Australia is the setting for some strange happenings in which newly arrived schoolteacher, Tate, finds himself. Called upon to replace the schoolteacher who has mysteriously disappeared, Tate goes about trying to put together the elements that will explain the absence of the missing man. The locals are unwilling to lend him any support and appear unusually cold to his questioning. As he approaches the answers, Tate's interest increases despite hazards to his own well-being. A slow pace is maintained, fitting the island atmosphere. The action picks up as the puzzle is pieced together.

p, Pat Lovell; d, Ken Hannam; w, Cliff Green; ph, Mike Molloy (Panaflex, Eastmancolor); m, Bruce Smeaton; ed, Sarah Bennet; art d, Grace Walker.

Mystery   (PR:O   MPAA:NR)

SUMMERPLAY   (SEE: ILLICIT INTERLUDE 1954, Swed.)

SUMMER'S CHILDREN*½   (1979, Can.) 95m Kohanyi-Haig bw

Tom Hauff (*Steve*), Paully Jardine (*Jennie*), Don Francks (*Albert*), Kate Lynch (*Kathy*), Patricia Collins (*Elaine*), Ken James (*Tony*).

A serious sortie into brother-sister incest – with a heavy debt to Jean Cocteau – this Canadian first effort deals with charming siblings, Hauff and Jardine, who separate following a passionate – but off-camera – sexual encounter. Hauff goes to a large city where he meets and makes love to Lynch. After settling in with the latter he learns that his sister resides in the same city and that she now practices prostitution. Tracking her down through the low haunts of the city – a process which brings him into contact with various low-life types such as racetrack tout, Francks, and lesbian, Collins – he finally reunites with her and makes his peace with the taboo attraction that initially drove them apart. Partly financed by the Canadian Film Development Corporation.

p, Julius Kohanyi, Don Haig; d, Kohanyi; w, Jim Osborne; ph, Joe Seckeresh; ed, M.C. Manne.

Drama   (PR:O   MPAA:NR)

SUMMERSKIN***   (1962, Arg.) 96m Producciones Angel/Angel bw
(PIEL DE VERANO)

Alfredo Alcon (*Martin*), Graciela Borges (*Marcela*), Franca Boni (*Joujou*), Luciana Possamay (*Adela*), Juan Jones (*Marcos*), Pedro Laxalt, Rafael Salzano, Juan Carlos, Carrasco, Rosita Miranda.

A realization of an old adage which holds that all one needs to cure a malaise is a good.... Boni is the geriatric Joujou, once a renowned beauty and mistress of famous men whose current millionaire lover has a sick son, the moribund Martin (Alcon). The elderly eccentric importunes her grand-daughter, Borges, to help make the dying boy's last days happy ones, promising her the reward of a trip to Europe and a new wardrobe. Although the slender, sick boy repulses her, Borges agrees to bring him what joy she can. The prescription pays off: Alcon gains weight and vitality with his growing interest in romance. His recovery is such that he accedes to the seductive wiles of his servant, Possamay. Discovering that he enjoys the process he persuades Borges to make love and spends the summer in an idyllically hyperaesthetic state of mind. When Alcon's physicians declare him cured of his apparently terminal ailment the ecstatic youth proposes to Borges. She confesses her opportunistic bargain with her grandmother and rejects his offer. Depressed, Alcon commits suicide. A cruel, clever look at

the ironies of romantic entanglements by Torre-Nilsson, one of South America's foremost directors. (In Spanish; English subtitles.)

p&d, Leopoldo Torre-Nilsson; w, Beatriz Guido, Torre-Nilsson (based on the story *Convalencia* by Guido); ph, Oscar Melli; m, Robert Schumann, Claudio Monteve Monteverdi; ed, Jacinto Cascales; set d, Oscar Lagomarsino.

Drama   (PR:C   MPAA:NR)

SUMMERSPELL***   (1983) 90m Lina Shanklin c

Dorothy Holland (*Bernice Wisdom*), Jennifer Mayo (*Daughter*), Frank Whiteman (*Lowell Wisdom*), Michael Holmes, Joan Crosby, Kay Freeman, G. Hagen, Coleman Creel, Bert Transwell, Wright.

Perhaps the best American independent feature of 1983; at least this was popular sentiment after the film received critical acclaim at the Munich Film Festival. Made for only $80,000 and taking over three years to complete, a finely tuned web of family relations is unfolded which focuses on the internal strife which is bound to tear the family apart. Taking place on two days during a family reunion during a Fourth of July celebration, the concentration is on Holland and Whiteman as they prepare to greet their relatives at the patriarchal home in what is destined to be the last full-family meeting. The head of the family, Whiteman's father, is quickly nearing death. The patriarch is the only reason Whiteman has chosen to remain at the family home and take over the arduous duties of running the place. No other family members were capable of the task. Though the script tends to be overly talky, an effort has been made to combine the Texas background with the unfolding dramatic situation, with effective results.

p, Lina Shanklin, Joanne D'Antone; d&w, Shanklin; ph, Robert Enwit; m, T. Marcus; ed, Gloria Whittemore.

Drama   (PR:C   MPAA:NR)

SUMMERTIME****   (1955) 100m LFP-Lopert/UA c (GB: SUMMER MADNESS)

Katharine Hepburn (*Jane Hudson*), Rossano Brazzi (*Renato Di Rossi*), Isa Miranda (*Signora Fiorina*), Darren McGavin (*Eddie Jaeger*), Mari Aldon (*Phyl Jaeger*), Jane Rose (*Mrs. McIlhenny*), MacDonald Parke (*Mr. McIlhenny*), Gaitano Audiero (*Mauro*), Andre Morell (*Englishman*), Jeremy Spenser (*Vito*), Virginia Simeon (*Giovanna*).

One of the rare times when the movie is better than the material. Based loosely on Arthur Laurents' play, "The Time Of The Cuckoo," SUMMERTIME is a romance set in one of the most romantic cities in the world, Venice. Since Venetians are precluded from making any changes on their buildings' exteriors, to visit Venice today is to see the same setting Lean used so magnificently. Matter of fact, study paintings of the city from 500 years ago and it will still appear the same way. Progress, thankfully, has no place in Venice. This is a rich-looking film (probably due to the real backgrounds) though it was brought in for under $1 million. Unrequited love stories have always been a staple of film drama and this falls into that BRIEF ENCOUNTER milieu that sees a couple that can never bring their temporary affair into permanence. Hepburn is an Ohio old maid who works as a secretary (although no secretary, no matter how much she earns, can afford the kinds of clothes Hepburn wears in this movie) and has saved her money for a trip to "Disneyland for adults," Venice. She's traveling alone and on her first night there she wanders around the city and sees lovers walking hand in hand and her loneliness is written on her famed cheekbones. She immediately meets Audiero, a charming child who hustles tourists, and he becomes her guide to the wonders of the city. The next day they go seeing the sights and meet Brazzi, a married man who owns an antique shop, although she doesn't know he's married at first. The two fall in love and there's a whirlwind montage as they walk, hand in hand, through the twisting streets of the main island. (In case you didn't know it, Venice is made up of more than 100 islands, not all of them inhabited. Some of the other major islands are Torchello [the oldest!], Murano [where they make and sell Venetian glass!], Burano [where they make the lace!, and Lido, the beach island where all the great hotels sit on the Adriatic.) While waiting for Brazzi in the Piazza San Marco (the hub of the tourist area where the pigeons rival those in London's Trafalgar Square in number and aggressiveness), she is approached by Spenser, a young man who tells her that Brazzi will be late. When she questions Spenser she learns that he is Brazzi's son and that her lover has a whole family he's never mentioned. Although hurt by this revelation, Hepburn realizes that this is the most romantic interlude of her spinsterish existence; she is not about to end it now. She goes off with Brazzi to Burano (where all the houses of the fishermen are painted in bright colors) and spends a perfect few days of love and happiness, although the reality of the situation is gnawing at her. At the conclusion, she leaves on the train and the vision of her face – as she bids farwell to the man who was the one great love of her life – is haunting. She is happy and sad at the same time. Happy that she had the affair, sad that it must end. It's touching, warm, often funny, and lushly photographed. There is one scene when Hepburn falls into the Grand Canal as she is shooting some eight-millimeter movies. Audiero, realizing that Hepburn can swim but the camera can't float, saves the camera. That spot is still pointed out by the tour guides who take rubberneckers around the city. Special kudos to the art director's staff (the assistants to Korda were W. Hutchinson and Ferdinand Bellan), and to Cicognini's excellent musical score. No matter how well Venice is shot, there is nothing to compare with the feeling of being there; although this movie comes as close to capturing the essence of the city as you will ever see. The story of the American woman being taken in by the married Venetian happens regularly in real life. Venetian men are a breed unto themselves and proud that they bear no psychological resemblance to Italians from any other city. Lean had also directed BRIEF ENCOUNTER so the story was familiar to him, although the terrain was vastly altered. There are places where the picture could have used some pruning, especially in the travelog portions, though that's carping by comparison to the affectionate scenes between Hepburn and Brazzi, who emerge as the best middle-aged couple (short of Hepburn and Tracy) of the 1950s. Hepburn and Lean were both nominated for Oscars.

p, Ilya Lopert; d, David Lean; w, Lean, H.E. Bates (based on the play "The Time of the Cuckoo" by Arthur Laurents); ph, Jack Hildyard (Eastmancolor); m, Alessandro Cicognini; ed, Peter Taylor; art d, Vincent Korda; makeup, Cesare Gamberelli.

Romance   **Cas.**   **(PR:A-C   MPAA:NR)**

SUMMERTIME KILLER**   (1973) 100m AE c

Karl Malden (*John Kiley*), Christopher Mitchum (*Ray Casster*), Olivia Hussey (*Tonia Alfredi*), Raf Vallone (*Lazaro Alfredi*), Claudine Auger (*Michele Dobvien*).

Mitchum is a young killer who is out to revenge his father's murder by the mob years earlier. He begins hunting down and murdering mafia kingpins and kidnaping Hussey, the daughter of mobster Vallone. Vallone and his men try to track down Mitchum, as does detective Malden. In the meantime Mitchum and Hussey have fallen head-over-heels in love. It all amounts to nothing more than an overlong television episode with some location shooting in Madrid, Rome, and Lisbon.

p&d, Antonio Isasi; w, R. Buckley, B. Degas; ph, Juan Gelpi.

Crime   **(PR:C   MPAA:PG)**

SUMMERTREE**   (1971) 89m Bryna/COL c

Michael Douglas (*Jerry McAdams*), Jack Warden (*Herb McAdams*), Brenda Vaccaro (*Vanetta*), Barbara Bel Geddes (*Ruth McAdams*), Kirk Callaway (*Marvis*), Bill Vint (*Tony*), Jeff Siggens (*Bennie*), Rob Reiner (*Don*), William Smith (*Draft Lawyer*), Garry Goodrow (*Ginsberg*), Dennis Clark Fimple (*Shelly*), June Fairchild (*Girl in Dorm*), Richard Stahl (*Man in Conservatory*).

Kirk Douglas produced this highly contrived film in which his son, Michael, starred as a young man faced with a number of confusing questions during the late 1960s. His parents, Warden and Bel Geddes, make attempt to understand their son, yet seem incapable of bridging the generation gap. Responsibility is pointed at them when their dead son's face flickers across the TV screen in news footage from the Vietnam conflict. Warden heatedly talks his son out of fleeing to Canada to avoid the draft, the father going to extremes to keep his son inside the country. All Douglas really wanted to do was play music and reach out to the young black youth he had befriended. Somehow beneath all the heavy drama and guilt-bearing situations is an emptiness reminiscent of a made-for-TV film.

p, Kirk Douglas; d, Anthony Newley, Don Record; w, Edward Hume, Stephen Yafa (based on the play by Ron Cowen); ph, Richard C. Glouner (Eastmancolor); m, David Shire; ed, Maury Winetrobe; art d, Ned Parsons; cos, Thomas Welsh; m/l, "Having the Time of Our Lives," David Shire, Richard Maltby (sung by Hamilton Camp); makeup, Carl Silvera.

Drama   **Cas.**   **(PR:A   MPAA:PG)**

SUMURU   (SEE: MILLION EYES OF SUMURU, THE, 1967 Brit.)

SUN ABOVE, DEATH BELOW**½   (1969, Jap.) 87m Toho c
                                                         (SOGEKI)

Yuzo Kayama (*Toru Matsushita*), Ruriko Asaoka (*Akiko*), Masayuki Mori (*Katakura*).

Professional killer, Kayama, finds himself the object of a member of his own trade. He accepts the challenge rather than flee the country, as his girl friend, Asaoka, urges. He successfully out-maneuvers his opponent, but not before his beloved is killed, making his efforts seem pretty worthless.

d, Hiromichi Horikawa; w, Hidekazu Nagahara; ph, Kiyoshi Hasegawa (Eastmancolor); m, Riichiro Manabe; art d, Shinobu Muraki.

Drama/Crime   **(PR:C   MPAA:NR)**

SUN ALSO RISES, THE****   (1957) 129m FOX c

Tyrone Power (*Jake Barnes*), Ava Gardner (*Lady Brett Ashley*), Mel Ferrer (*Robert Cohn*), Errol Flynn (*Mike Campbell*), Eddie Albert (*Bill Gorton*), Gregory Ratoff (*Count Mippipopolous*), Juliette Greco (*Georgette*), Marcel Dalio (*Zizi*), Henry Daniell (*Doctor*), Bob Cunningham (*Harris*), Danik Patisson (*The Girl*), Robert J. Evans (*Pedro Romero*), Rebecca Iturbi (*Frances Cohn*), Eduardo Noriega (*Mr. Braddock*), Jacqueline Evans (*Mrs.*

Braddock), Carlos Muzquiz (*Montoya*), Carlos David Ortigos (*Manager of Romero*), Lilia Guizar (*English Girl*), Lee Morgan (*American at Bullfight*), Ninos Cantores De Morelia (*Boy Choir Group*).

Author Hemingway's paean of praise and hopelessness to the Lost Generation in the wake of WW I may be the most faithful of all Hemingway's many transcriptions to the screen. Power is the fitful postwar expatriate drifting around Europe aimlessly, seeking excitement and thrills to compensate for his war-wound-induced impotence ("It's a rotten way to be wounded"). In the company of sultry prostitute Greco, Power threads his way through the bistros of Paris, simulating enjoyment of the adventurous life despite his enforced celibacy. He falls in with beautiful aristocrat Gardner, who once--as a volunteer--had helped him recover from his wounds during the war. Gardner is being pursued by amorous Greek tycoon Ratoff, and also by a young would-be writer (thought to be patterned after F. Scott Fitzgerald), Ferrer, a former acquaintance. Power and Gardner--still in love with each other, despite his condition and despite the intervening hiatus--make an unsuccessful attempt to be alone as the constant partying continues. One event that Power wants to experience is the famed running of the bulls at Pamplona in Spain during the San Fermin fiesta (the bulls that will soon fight in the *corrida* are released to run in the streets in a rites-of-passage tradition, the brave young men of the area racing before them, trying not to get gored). Power sets off with his trusted friend, fellow expatriate Albert, arriving in Pamplona only to find that Gardner, Ferrer, and Ratoff have preceded him there. The group is joined by carefree Scottish playboy Flynn, Gardner's former fiance. Through the hilarity and ostensible fun, tensions mount, with all the men lusting after gorgeous Gardner, and Gardner wanting only Power, whom she can never possess in a satisfactory physical manner. Albert and Flynn resolve their dilemma by remaining drunk most of the time, and actually run with the bulls in their besotted state, miraculously without personal injury. Gardner finds herself interested in young matador Evans, and the jealous Ferrer--a collegiate boxing champion--beats up the bullfighter. His actions only serve to enrage Gardner. When Evans demonstrates his courage by performing superbly in the bull ring despite his injuries, Gardner elopes with him. The remaining members of the group head in different directions. Power goes to Biarritz to recuperate from the drunken festivities knowing that he will hear from Gardner again. She telephones him from Madrid where, destitute, she has abandoned Evans. Power joins her and the picture ends with the two hoping to find some way to fulfill what both realize to be their mutual destiny. While the film has many flaws, producer Zanuck was determined at least to follow the novel as closely as possible. He admired Hemingway greatly--he had once said, "If I could have been anybody else, I'd like to have been Hemingway"--whom he had met in Paris, introduced by screenwriter Viertel, years before. Zanuck and Hemingway both wintered in Sun Valley for a number of years and were great friends, but their friendship had been flawed by Hemingway's reaction to Zanuck's production of THE SNOWS OF KILIMANJARO, which, the author stated, "\$e3should have been called 'The Snows of Zanuck'." The producer planned to avoid further remonstrances. Zanuck did the casting for the film. At 43, Power was old for the role (this was to be the actor's second-to-last film, and his last for Fox; Power died of a heart attack the following year). This was also Flynn's penultimate picture (except for one unreleased and unfinished personally produced one, which got trapped in litigation) and his self-parody is a joy, the best thing in the film. The fourth-billed Flynn for the first time in years--over his weak protests--here accepted less than the top spot in the credits, an honor he had been accorded ever since his success in CAPTAIN BLOOD. Power's habitually petulant at-rest facial expression here seems wrong; a contrapuntal masculinity would have served the story better. Ferrer is fine in his part as the resentful introvert. His wife Audrey Hepburn, who joined him on location in both Pamplona and in Morelia, Mexico (which doubled for the Spain location), was the one who suggested Greco for the role of the sympathetic prostitute to Zanuck. Greco was then singing at the Waldorf-Astoria in New York City. She had a substantial cult following in Europe, where she had appeared in movies, but this was her U.S. film debut. She and producer Zanuck had an on-location romance which was to sustain long past the picture's release. Touted as a Zanuck "find," Evans--who played the matador--had been a clothing manufacturer. He had actually been "found" by Norma Shearer, whose late husband, Irving Thalberg, he had portrayed in THE MAN WITH A THOUSAND FACES (not yet released at the time). Evans later became production chief at Paramount. Zanuck, goaded by the mischievous Flynn, actually ran with the bulls himself at Pamplona, but only after carefully timing himself to make certain he could stay ahead of them. The picture was reported to have cost \$5 million, but it made money for the studio.

p, Darryl F. Zanuck; d, Henry King; w, Peter Viertel (based on the novel by Ernest Hemingway); ph, Leo Tover (CinemaScope, DeLuxe Color); m, Hugo Friedhofer, Alexander Courage; ed, William Mace; md, Lionel Newman, Ramon Hernandez; art d, Lyle R. Wheeler, Mark-Lee Kirk; set d, Walter M. Scott, Paul S. Fox, Jack Stubbs; cos, Charles LeMaire, Fontana Sisters; bullfight ch, Miguel Delgado; makeup, Jack Obringer.

Drama   **(PR:C   MPAA:NR)**

SUN ALWAYS RISES, THE   (SEE: OUTCRY, 1949, Ital.)

SUN COMES UP, THE**   (1949) 93m MGM c

Jeanette MacDonald (*Helen Lorfield Winter*), Lloyd Nolan (*Thomas I. Chandler*), Claude Jarman, Jr (*Jerry*), Percy Kilbride (*Mr. Willie B. Williegoode*), Lewis Stone (*Arthur Norton*), Nicholas Joy (*Victor Alvord*), Margaret Hamilton (*Mrs. Pope*), Esther Somers (*Susan, the Maid*), Dwayne Hickman (*Hank Winter*), Teddy Infuhr (*Junebug*), Barbara Billingsley (*Nurse*), Charles Trowbridge (*Dr. Gage*), John A. Butler (*Doorman*), Ida Moore (*Sally*), Paul E. Burns (*Dr. Sample*), Guy Wilkerson (*Man*), Peter Roman (*Love*), Mickey McGuire (*Cleaver*), Lassie, Cameron Grant, John Sheffield, Douglas Carter, Wilson Wood, Barry Norton (*Music Lovers*), Timmy Hawkins, Alan Dinehart III, Michael Dill, Charles Bates Perry, Jimmy Crane, Bobby Beyers (*Orphans*), Henry Sylvester, John Beck, Ed Peil, Sr, Frank Pharr (*Ad Lib Bits*), Cy Stevens, Cosmo Sardo, Stuart Holmes, George Calliga, Albert Pollet, Ed Agresti (*Musicians*), Cecil Stewart (*Accompanist*), Jessie Arnold (*Woman*).

Time to take out the handkerchiefs again as MacDonald (in her last screen appearance before devoting herself totally to a music career) plays a war widow whose recent loss of her son has forced her to a retreat in the backwoods of Georgia. A boy from the local orphanage, Jarman, who comes to help her with chores in the company of Lassie begins to yank on her motherly instincts. Despite her efforts to remain detached from the youth, after he narrowly escapes being killed in a fire at the orphanage, – Lassie performing the heroics, – she takes the boy in for good. A fine cast of character actors heads up the support, allowing director Thorpe to effectively blend drama, comedy, and action. But the emphasis is upon the sentiment inherent in a boy, a dog, and a widow. Young Jarman, who had scored well in the 1946 hit THE YEARLING (also based on a work of author Rawlings) was a bit long in the tooth for the role requirement here. Twenty-year-old Previn's musical score – his first – wa s heavy-handed and tended to obscure the performances. MacDonald sings a number of songs, some of them backed up by a chorus of "orphans": "Tes Yeux" (Rene Alphonse Rabey); "Un Bel Di" from the opera "Madame Butterfly" (Giacomo Puccini, Luigi Illica); "Als die Alte Mutter" (Antonin Dvorak, Adolf Heyduck); the English-language variation of the latter, "Songs My Mother Taught Me" (Dvorak, Natalie MacFarren); "Cousin Ebenezer" (Andre Previn, William Katz); "Romance" (Anton Rubinstein, Paul Bourget).

p, Robert Sisk: d, Richard Thorpe; w, William Ludwig, Margaret Fitts (based on short stories by Marjorie Kinnan Rawlings); ph, Ray June (Technicolor); m, Andre Previn; ed, Irvine Warburton; art d, Cedric Gibbons, Randall Duell; set d, Edwin B. Willis, Hugh Hunt; cos, Irene.

Drama   (PR:AAA MPAA:NR)

SUN DEMON, THE   (SEE: HIDEOUS SUN DEMON, THE 1959)

SUN IS UP, THE   (SEE: A BOY...A GIRL, 1969)

SUN NEVER SETS, THE*   (1939) 98m UNIV bw

Douglas Fairbanks, Jr (*John Randolph*), Basil Rathbone (*Clive Randolph*), Barbara O'Neil (*Helen Randolph*), Lionel Atwill (*Hugo Zurof*), Virginia Field (*Phyllis Ransome*), C. Aubrey Smith (*Sir John Randolph*), Melville Cooper (*Cosey*), Mary Forbes (*Mrs. John Randolph*), John Burton (*Simon Randolph*), Arthur Mullinor (*Uncle Gerald Randolph*), Theodor Von Eltz (*Delafons*), Douglas Walton (*Carpenter*), Cecil Kellaway, Sidney Bracy (*Colonial Officials*), Harry Cording.

Despite an excellent cast with such names as Fairbanks and Rathbone heading the cast, the material handed them is so wretched they would have been better off staying home and letting some non-actors off the street take over their parts. A very poor piece of British Empire propaganda has Fairbanks and Rathbone as brothers on the coast of Africa fighting against Atwill, a demented munitions baron with a station who has dreams of taking over the world. Atwill's role name, Zurof, is an obvious modification of the name of sinister munitions magnate, Basil Zaharoff, who, in the latter part of the 19th Century, supplied guns to both sides in the Boer War. Producer/director Lee blamed the script for the failure of this big-budget epic which, in truth, resembled a low-budget serial. Critics contended that the fault was Lee's.

p&d, Rowland V. Lee; w, W.P. Lipscomb (based on a story by Jerry Horwin, Arthur Fitz-Richards); ph, George Robinson; m, Frank Skinner; ed, Ted Kent; md, Charles Previn; art d, Jack Otterson, R.H. Riedel; cos, Vera West.

War   (PR:A MPAA:NR)

SUN RISES AGAIN, THE   (SEE: OUTCRY, 1949, Ital.)

SUN SETS AT DAWN, THE½   (1950) 71m Holiday/EL bw

Sally Parr (*The Girl*), Philip Shawn (*The Boy*), Walter Reed (*The Chaplain*), Lee Fredericks (*Blackie*), Houseley Stevenson (*Pops*), Howard St. John (*The Warden*), Louise Lorimer (*The Warden's Wife*), Raymond Bramley (*The Deputy Warden*), Charles Meredith (*A.P.*), Jack Reynolds (*E.P.*), King Donovan (*National News Service*), Charles Arndt (*Globe Express*), Sam Edwards (*Herald*), Percy Helton (*Feature Syndicate*), Perry Ivans (*Forty-Six*).

An extremely dull picture in which Shawn plays a youth convicted of a crime he didn't commit, but who is destined to fry in the electric chair nonetheless. After various renditions of the story are recounted by reporters for the longest time, a last-minute twist of fate has the boy being saved when the real culprit is spotted.

p, Helen H. Rathvon, Paul H. Sloane; d&w, Sloane; ph, Lionel Lindon; m, Leith Stevens; ed, Sherman Todd; art d, William Flannery.

Drama   (PR:A MPAA:NR)

SUN SHINES, THE*½   (1939, Hung.) 80m Pegasus/Muvesz bw

Janos Olasz (*Michael Samson*), Alice Nagy (*Sarika*), Kalman Rozsahegyi (*Schoolmaster*), Manya Kiss (*Margit*), Gero Maly (*Ponge Juhasz*), Juliska Ligeti (*Postmistress*), Lily Berky (*Grandmother*), Lenke Egyed (*Juliska*), Sandor Pethes (*Railway Clerk*), Joseph Kurthy (*Parson*).

An overly stagey rendition of Zilahy's own play is the light-hearted story about a parson's daughter, Nagy, who falls in love with a poor peasant while she is rehearsing for a play. The youth spots her while she is in peasant garb and therefore takes her for one of his own class, but when he learns the truth, he doesn't think she takes him seriously. The youth almost weds another girl, but Nagy manages to convince him of her sincerity. Little adjustment is made in adapting this to the screen, resulting in a choppy looking and ill-paced rendition. Popular playwright Zihaly's works had been made into films before (his play "The General" was made into THE VIRTUOUS SIN, 1930, with Walter Huston and Kay Francis; THE FIREBIRD, 1934, was popular in his own country), but this was the first in which the author was directly involved in production. He was responsible for casting an amateur actor, Olasz – a gasworks employee – in the lead. Music is by the famed composer Kodaly.

d, Laszlo Kalmar; w, Lajos Zilahy (based on his play); m, Zoltan Kodaly, Bela Endre.

Drama   (PR:A MPAA:NR)

SUN SHINES BRIGHT, THE**   (1953) 90m Argosy/REP bw

Charles Winninger (*Judge William Pittman Priest*), Arleen Whelan (*Lucy Lee Lake*), John Russell Ashby (*Corwin*), Stepin Fetchit (*Jeff Poindexter*), Russell Simpson (*Dr. Lewt Lake*), Ludwig Stossel (*Herman Felsburg*), Francis Ford (*Feeney*), Paul Hurst (*Sgt. Jimmy Bagby*), Mitchell Lewis (*Sheriff Andy Redcliffe*), Grant Withers (*Buck Ramsey*), Milburn Stone (*Horace K. Maydew*), Dorothy Jordan (*Lucy's Mother*), Elzie Emanuel (*U.S. Grant Woodford*), Henry O'Neill (*Jody Habersham*), Slim Pickens (*Mink Sterling*), James Kirkwood (*General Fairfield*), Ernest Whitman (*Uncle Pleasant Woodford*), Trevor Bardette (*Rufe Ramseur, Lynch Mob Leader*), Eve March (*Mallie Cramp*), Hal Baylor (*Ramseur, Jr.*), Jane Darwell (*Mrs. Amora Ratchitt*), Ken Williams (*Maydew's Henchman*), Clarence Muse (*Uncle Zach*), Mae Marsh (*G.A.R. Lady at Ball*), Jack Pennick (*Beaker*), Patrick Wayne, Ken Williams.

Even the skilled handling of John Ford could do little to overcome the shortcomings in this story about a well-meaning Southern judge, Winninger, whose honest attitudes and simple ways prove more powerful than the prejudice he is up against. Shortly before election time Winninger aids in causes which could prove dangerous in the vote count against the Yankee carpetbagger who is after Winninger's post. He defends an innocent black youth against a lynch mob that accuses the boy of rape; then he provides for a prostitute who has fallen on hard times. These are just a few of the numerous good deeds that Winninger accomplishes in the short span of the film which has him winning the election by a single vote. But these characters are all stereotypes of the early twentieth-century South, the plot weaving them together to provide for an overabundance of sentiment at how good Winninger is despite the personal advantages in pursuing the opposite course. Winninger did well in the role originated by Will Rogers in Ford's 1934 picture JUDGE PRIEST. The director stated in an interview that THE SUN SHINES BRIGHT was his favorite picture, one that was true to life; that author Cobb drew his stories from the real world, and these stories were his best. He also said that his habit of the time was to make a commercially successful film and then to follow it with a little one like this which he truly liked. A few songs of the appropriate Civil War/Antebellum South period enliven the proceedings, including "Tenting On the Old Camp Ground" and "My Old Kentucky Home" (Stephen Foster).

p, John Ford, Merian C. Cooper; d, Ford; w, Laurence Stallings (based on several stories by Irvin S. Cobb); ph, Archie J. Stout; m, Victor Young; ed, Jack Murray; art d, Frank Hotaling; set d, John McCarthy, Jr., George Milo; cos, Adele Palmer.

Drama   (PR:A MPAA:NR)

SUN SHINES FOR ALL, THE**½   (1961, USSR) 91m
Mosfilm/Artkino bw (AKA: SOLNTSE SVETIT VSEM; THE SUN SHINES FOR EVERYBODY)

Valentin Zubkov (*Nikolay Savelyev*), Liliya Aleshnikova (*Svetlana*), Tatyana Konyukhova (*Tasya*), Yevgeniy Burenkov (*Koren*), Nikolay Sergeyev (*Maksim Petrovich*), Yelena Maksimova (*Pelageya Ivanovna*), Viktor Koltsov (*School Director*), Olya Narovchatova (*Katya*), Vitya Lobzov (*Yevsikov*),

Lyudmila Ovchinnikova, R. Rakitin, A. Lebedev, I. Ryabinin, O. Dolgova, M. Zharova, N. Pogodin, N. Smirnov, V. Seleznyov, S. Korenev, V. Pitsek, L. Chubarov, S. Gorokhova, N. Burenkova, P. Dolzhanov.

Blinded during WW II, schoolteacher Zubkov tries to adjust to civilian life with his disability. Things almost get to the point where he decides to throw in the towel; his wife leaves him and his teaching position is severely threatened because of his handicap. But he hangs on when he realizes that his new boss, Principal Burenkov, is the former soldier whose cowardice was responsible for the attack which caused his blindness. His desire to prove himself, and the love of the nurse who pampered him through the first days of his blindness, give him the strength to continue.

d, Konstantin Voinov; w, Semyon Freylikh, Yu. Vinokurova; ph, Anatoliy Kuznetsov; m, Veniamin Basner; ed, Z. Veryovkina; md, K. Eliasberg; art d, Boris Chebotaryov; cos, T. Kasparova; m/l, Basner, M. Matusovskiy; makeup, B. Baldin, L. Goremykina.

Drama   (PR:A MPAA:NR)

SUN SHINES FOR EVERYBODY, THE
                    (SEE: SUN SHINES FOR ALL, THE, 1961, USSR)

SUN VALLEY CYCLONE*½   (1946) 56m REP bw

Bill Elliott, Bobby Blake, Alice Fleming, Roy Barcroft, Monte Hale, Kenne Duncan, Eddy Waller, Tom London, Edmund Cobb, Edward Cassidy, George Chesebro, Rex Lease, Hal Price, Jack Kirk, Frank O'Connor, Jack Sparks.

"Wild Bill" Elliott added another RED RYDER series entry to his list starring as a western hero who tracks down the leader of a horse thieving ring. It seems the Army is being hit by this ring and Elliott is the only one who can stop them. (See RED RYDER Series, Index.)

p, Sidney Picker; d, R.G. Springsteen; w, Earl Snell; ph, Bud Thackery; ed, Harry Keller, Charles Craft; md, Richard Cherwin; art d, James Sullivan; set d, John McCarthy, Jr., Marie Arthur.

Western   (PR:A MPAA:NR)

SUN VALLEY SERENADE***½   (1941) 86m FOX bw

Sonja Henie (*Karen Benson*), John Payne (*Ted Scott*), Glenn Miller (*Phil Carey*), Milton Berle (*Nifty Allen*), Lynn Bari (*Vivian Dawn*), Joan Davis (*Miss Carstairs*), Nicholas Brothers (*Specialty*), William Davidson (*Murray*), Dorothy Dandridge (*Specialty*), Almira Sessions (*Nurse*), Mel Ruick (*Band Leader*), Forbes Murray (*Headwaiter*), Ralph Dunn (*Customs Officer*), Chester Clute (*Process Server*), Edward Earle, Edward Kane (*Men*), Lynne Roberts (*Receptionist*), Ann Doran (*Waitress*), Walter "Spec" O'Donnell (*Western Union Boy*), Bruce Edwards (*Ski Instructor*), John "Skins" Miller (*Sleigh Driver*), Fred Toones (*Porter*), Ernie Alexander (*Boy*), Sheila Ryan (*Telephone Operator*), William Forrest (*Husband*), Dora Clement (*Wife*), Herbert Gunn, Kenneth Alexander (*Ski Patrol Men*), The Modernaires (*Themselves*), Tex Beneke, Jimmy Priddy, "Chommy" Macgregor, Ernie Caceres, Hal McIntyre, Willie Schwarz, Al Klink, Ray Anthony, Johnny Best, Billy May, Maurice Purtill, Trigger Alpert, Paul Tanner, Frank D'Anolfo, Ralph Brewster, Mickey McMickle, Jack Lathrop (*The Glenn Miller Orchestra Members*), Paula Kelly, Ray Eberle (*Vocalists*), Pat Friday (*Vivian Dawn's Vocals*).

Glenn Miller had a very short career in films. This was his first and ORCHESTRA WIVES was his last before he went off on his ill-fated flight across the English Channel. It's set in the famous Idaho ski resort. The picture was said to be the brainchild of studio boss Darryl F. Zanuck, who had vacationed at Sun Valley and thought it might make a lovely setting for a musical. The Sun Valley Lodge ski resort, the actual location of many of the film's scenes, had opened for business only five years before the picture's release. It was the pet project of statesman W. Averell Harriman, then chairman of the board of the Union Pacific Railroad, who wanted this first major ski area in the U.S. in order to compete with the then-popular Canadian mountain resorts run by the Canadian Pacific. Harriman's publicists actively promoted the Lodge in the Hollywood community, offering junkets for major stars and executives in an attempt to make the massive – and costly – resort fashionable. This picture is evidence of the success of the promotional scheme. The Miller band is not getting enough work and has too much time off between gigs. Thrush Bari (who had her vocalizing looped by Pat Friday) helps get them an audition at Sun Valley and they are booked. The band's pianist is Payne, who had agreed to sponsor a Norwegian refugee some months before as part of a publicity stunt. The Norwegian arrives at Sun Valley and turns out to be Henie, a champion ice skater. Henie falls in love with her guardian and is aggressive about her intentions. Payne tries to hold her off, but finally realizes that he loves her as well. Bari is jealous of Payne's affection for Henie and quits, thus forcing Henie to have to appear in an ice show, which delights the audience. The plot is very thin but the songs and skating and the emergence of Henie as a full-fledged comedienne after two years off the screen, make the movie fun from start to finish. Berle chimes in with a good comedy role as the band's manager. A superb score by Harry Warren and Mack Gordon included: "Chattanooga Choo Choo" (danced by the Nicholas Brothers, sung by Dorothy Dandridge), "I know Why And So Do You," "It Happened In Sun Valley" (Bari dubbed by Friday), "The Kiss Polka," plus "In The Mood,"

Miller's theme song, written by Andy Razaf and Joe Garland. The final production number was skated by Henie on black ice that had been dyed. It took three days to shoot and, near the conclusion, Henie fell and was covered in the ebony goo. Choreographer Pan and director Humberstone asked for one more day of shooting to cover the end, but Mogul Zanuck refused so the number never actually ends. Instead, there's a dissolve from Henie skating to she and Payne skiing as the movie ends. "Chattanooga Choo Choo," Cronjager's cinematography, and Emil Newman's musical direction were nominated for Oscars. The actual location was used well and anyone unfamiliar with what happens at a ski resort will come away having felt they'd been there.

p, Milton Sperling; d, H. Bruce Humberstone; w, Robert Ellis, Helen Logan (based on a story by Art Arthur, Robert Harari); ph, Edward Cronjager; ed, James B. Clark; md, Emil Newman; art d, Richard Day, Lewis Creber; ch, Hermes Pan; m/l, Mack Gordon, Harry Warren, Andy Razaf, Joe Garland.

Musical   (PR:AA MPAA:NR)

SUNA NO KAORI   (SEE: NIGHT OF THE SEAGULL, THE, 1960, Jap.)

SUNA NO ONNA   (SEE: WOMAN IN THE DUNES, 1964, Jap.)

SUNBONNET SUE**½   (1945) 89m MON bw

Gale Storm (*Sue Casey*), Phil Regan (*Danny*), George Cleveland (*Casey, Tavern Owner*), Minna Gombell (*Mrs. Fitzgerald*), Raymond Hatton (*Joe Feeney*), Alan Mowbray (*Jonathan*), Charles Judels (*Milano*), Billy Green (*Flaherty*), Charles D. Brown (*Father Hurley*), Edna Holland (*Julia*), Gerald O. Smith (*Masters*), Jerry Franks, Jr (*Burke*).

A pleasant farce that supplies a good many musical numbers aimed at tugging memories of the good old days. Set in turn-of-the-century, Lower East Side New York. Storm plays a young woman who gets a kick out of singing and dancing in her father's seedy saloon. Her aunt, Gombell, sees this conduct as a possible threat to her social position, as some light may be thrown on her own Bowery beginnings. So the conniving lady sets up a fight that forces the tavern to be closed; and her niece must come live at her luxurious home. It doesn't take too long before Gombell's plans are seen through; before a settlement can be arranged tensions flare. Monogram was attempting to upgrade its product with this film in the wake of upheavals in the industry; the larger studios were in the process of being sued by the government for violations of the Sherman Anti-Trust act, charged with monopolizing distribution facilities. The time seemed ripe for lesser lights such as Monogram to try to join the giants. The studio threw major talent into the picture which might have been made by any of the larger studios. Producer Dunlap was an officer of the corporation; writer/director Murphy had scored with MRS. WIGGS OF THE CABBAGE PATCH in 1942. During the year, Monogram – as usual – cranked out more pictures than 20th Century-Fox, Paramount, Warner Bros., or Universal, but most of them were cheapies with limited distribution and short runs; the studio grossed only about $6 million during the year, compared to Fox's $178 million. Songs include: "School Days," "Sunbonnet Sue" (Gus Edwards, Will D. Cobb), "The Bowery" (Charles H. Hoyt, Percy Gaunt), "Yip-I-Addy-I-Ay" (Cobb, John H. Flynn), "Yoo Hoo, Ain't You Comin' Out Tonight?" (Carson Robison), "By The Light Of The Silvery Moon" (Ed Madden, Edwards), "If I Had My Way" (Lou Klein, James Kendis), "While Strolling Through The Park One Day" (Ed Haley), "Donegal," "Roll Dem Bones," "Look For The Rainbow" (Ralph Murphy, C. Harold Lewis).

p, Scott R. Dunlap; d, Ralph Murphy; w, Murphy, Richard A. Carroll (based on a story by Paul Gerard Smith, Bradford Ropes); ph, Harry Neumann; m, Edward J. Kay; ed, Richard Currier; md, Kay; art d, Ernest R. Hickson; cos, Lorraine MacLean; ch, Jack Boyle.

Musical/Comedy   (PR:A MPAA:NR)

SUNBURN**   (1979) 99m Tuesday/PAR c

Farah Fawcett[-Majors] (*Ellie*), Charles Grodin (*Jake*), Art Carney (*Marcus*), Joan Collins (*Nera*), William Daniels (*Crawford*), John Hillerman (*Webb*), Eleanor Parker (*Mrs. Thoren*), Keenan Wynn (*Mark Elmes*), Robin Clarke (*Karl*), Joan Goodfellow (*Joanna*), Jack Kruschen (*Gela*), Alejandro Rey (*Fons*), Jorge Luke (*Vasquez*), Seymour Cassel (*Dobbs*), Joanna Lehmann (*Mamie*), Alex Sharpe (*Kunz*), Bob Orrison (*Milan*), Deloy White (*Dr. Kellogg*), Steven Wilensky (*Elmer*), Joe L. Brown (*Milton*), Christa Walters, Youigi Rogi, Miguel Burciaga, George Belanger, Dick Subley, Ken Smith, Enrique Kahn, Delores Devine.

Private eye, Grodin, hires New York model, Fawcett, to pose as his wife while he investigates the murder of a wealthy industrialist down in sunny Acapulco. The feminine star is given little to do other than get a suntan and try and look captivating, but this is all for the best, leaving the real comic chores up to seasoned professionals Grodin and Carney, who are just great, the latter as the local sleazy detective. Fawcett's name appears on the on-screen title credits as Fawcett-Majors, but before the film's release she finalized her finish from former spouse Lee Majors by insisting that the press material and advertisements excise the offending half behind the hyphen. Various popular tunes transduce from a tape recorder during the course of the film, including "You Bet Your Love" (Herbie Hancock, Rubinson, Willis, Cohen, performed by Hancock).

p, John Daly, Gerald Green; d, Richard C. Sarafian; w, Daly Stephen Oliver, James Booth (based on the novel *The Bind* by Stanley Ellin); ph, Alex Phillips, Jr. (Panavision, Technicolor); m, John Cameron; ed, Geoff Foot; prod d, Ted Tester; art d, Augustin Ituarte; set d, Dick Purdy; cos, Moss Mabry; spec eff, Laurencio Cordero, Jesus Duran.

Comedy   **(PR:C   MPAA:PG)**

SUNDAY BLOODY SUNDAY***½   (1971, Brit.) 110m Vectia/UA c

Glenda Jackson *(Alex Greville)*, Peter Finch *(Dr. Daniel Hirsh)*, Murray Head *(Bob Elkin)*, Peggy Ashcroft *(Mrs. Greville)*, Tony Britton *(George Harding)*, Maurice Denham *(Mr. Greville)*, Bessie Love *(Answering Service Lady)*, Vivian Pickles *(Alva Hodson)*, Frank Windsor *(Bill Hodson)*, Thomas Baptiste *(Prof. Johns)*, Harold Goldblatt *(Daniel's Father)*, Hannah Norbert *(Daniel's Mother)*, Richard Pearson *(Middle-Aged Patient)*, June Brown *(Woman Patient)*, Caroline Blakiston *(Rowing Woman)*, Peter Halliday *(Her Husband)*, Douglas Lambert *(Man at Party)*, Marie Burke *(Aunt Astrid)*, Richard Loncraine *(Tony)*, Jon Finch *(Scotsman)*, Cindy Burrows *(Alex as a Child)*, Kimi Tallmadge *(Lucy Hodson)*, Russell Lewis *(Timothy Hodson)*, Emma Schlesinger *(Tess Hodson)*, Patrick Thornberry *(Baby John Stuart Hodson)*, Karl Ferber, Henry Danziger, Robin Presky, Gabrielle Daye, Royce Mills, John Rae, Joe Wadham, Robert Rietty, Liane Aukin, Edward Evans, George Belbin, Ellis Dale, Monica Vasilliou.

A strong drama about a menage a trois among homosexual Finch, heterosexual Jackson, and bisexual Head, who alternates between the other two. The homosexual aspect is never tawdry and neither Finch nor Head is ever seen to mince, to lisp, or to betray anything about sexual preference. In that, it's a breakthrough picture because it deals with affection and honest love, and doesn't go for any cheap exploitation. Written by *New Yorker* magazine movie critic, Gilliatt, it sometimes is too low-keyed in the attempt to avoid smarminess. Finch is a middle-aged bachelor doctor in London who shares his answering service with Jackson, a divorced woman who works at an employment agency. Both of them know Windsor and Pickles, a happy couple in the area, and both of them know--in the Biblical sense--Head, who is a middle-20s-aged designer of modern sculpture. Both Jackson and Finch are aware of each other because Head is an honest sort, almost naive in some ways. Windsor and Pickles have five children and need to get away, so Jackson and Head offer to stay at their home and tend the quintet while the parents go off to be part of an educational seminar. On Saturday morning Head excuses himself from Jackson and only says he's "going out." She knows that he's on his way to see Finch and the thought of it jars her off her strict diet, sending her into an orgy of fudge. At Finch's, the two men discuss an upcoming vacation to Italy, then Head returns to an annoyed Jackson, who resents having to share her lover with another man. (In the 1980s, no self-respecting woman would have been involved in such a triangle, due to the emergence of AIDS). That evening Finch is driving through the city and comes across an old lover who suggests they sleep together. Finch declines and goes home alone. The next day, Sunday, Head and Jackson take the kids to the park for an outing and the fun is ruined when the kids' dog is hit and killed by an automobile. A few days later, Jackson has dinner with her mother, Ashcroft, who complains about Jackson's desire to have everything. She says, "You keep throwing in your hand because you haven't got the whole thing. There *is* no whole thing." Jackson becomes increasingly depressed and decides to quit her counseling job at the agency. Before that, she meets 55-year-old Britton, an executive who can't find a job due to his age. He is a sad character and she decides to give him a little pleasure by taking him home to sleep with her. They are in bed when Head arrives, having left a party at Finch's that was marred by a quarreling provincial couple. Head is surprised to see Jackson in bed with Britton but he recovers from his shock quickly and admits that she is a grown woman and he has no hold on her. A day or so later, Head decides to make a brief business trip to the U.S., thus ruining Finch's carefully planned vacation for them. Finch is disappointed but he shrugs it off as he realizes that he is not Head's keeper. Later, Finch attends the bar mitzvah of his nephew (a lovely scene for anyone who has ever been to one of these functions that mark a Jewish boy's entrance into manhood) and enjoys his cultural heritage, recalling his own bar mitzvah. Head and Jackson have an argument and she decides that having only half of Head is worse than not having him at all. Head and Finch spend their final night with each other and Finch wonders if Head will actually miss Jackson or him. It's Sunday morning and Finch visits the Pickles/Windsor home. Outside, Jackson has arrived and she waits until Finch will leave. The two meet, have a brief conversation that betrays only a bit of their feelings, then Finch leaves. When Jackson goes home, she finds Head's pet bird and a note about what to feed him. The major problem with this is that it was not easy to see what an intelligent man like Finch and an equally intelligent (though somewhat desperate) woman like Jackson ever saw in Head. True, he was pretty to look at, but his character is not realized nearly as well as the others, so when the brace that holds up the see-saw is weak, it can only harm the two people at either end. Schlesinger said that he initiated the idea of the film based on some people he knew. Then he hired Gilliatt. She, on the other hand, claims total responsibility for the idea because she'd written a novel with a similar plot. The original actor selected to play the physician was Ian Bannen. When an illness laid him temporarily low, Finch was paged.

Jackson had turned down a role in THE DEVILS and Redgrave, who was slated to play in this, took that job. Casting Redgrave and Bannen would have put an entirely new perspective on the movie, though not necessarily better. Redgrave's acting trick of not blinking while she is on camera forces the eye to look at her. The three characters are terribly civilized about the whole thing, perhaps too civilized. Only Jackson betrays any heavy emotion and it comes like a thunderbolt because everyone else is underplaying. This falls short of greatness due to a lack of commitment on any of the actors' parts. Not that they are not committed to acting, it's just what they get to do is not enough. The movie made a few dollars over what it cost and secured many critical nods. Gilliatt, Schlesinger, Jackson, and Finch were nominated for Oscars. Schlesinger, Jackson, and Finch won British Film Academy nods and Gilliatt won the Writers Guild Award as well as the New York Film Critics Award. There's a standout set of cameos, led by Bessie Love as the woman who runs the answering agency, with Goldblatt and Norbert doing a wonderful scene as Finch's parents. Snatches from Mozart's "Cosi Fan Tutti" are sung by Barry McDaniel, Yvonne Minton, and Pilar Lorengar.

p, Joseph Janni; d, John Schlesinger; w, Penelope Gilliatt; ph, Billy Williams (DeLuxe Color); m, Ron Geesin, Wolfgang Amadeus Mozart; ed, Richard Marden; md, Douglas Gamley; prod d, Luciana Arrighi; art d, Norman Dorme; cos, Jocelyn Richards; makeup, Freddy Williamson.

Drama   **Cas.**   **(PR:O   MPAA:R)**

SUNDAY DINNER FOR A SOLDIER**½   (1944) 86m Fox bw

Anne Baxter *(Tessa Osborne)*, John Hodiak *(Eric Moore)*, Charles Winninger *(Grandfather Osborne)*, Anne Revere *(Agatha)*, Connie Marshall *(Mary Osborne)*, Chill Wills *(Mr. York)*, Robert Bailey *(Kenneth Normand)*, Bobby Driscoll *(Jeep Osborne)*, Jane Darwell *(Mrs. Dobson)*, Billy Cummings *(Michael Osborne)*, Marietta Canty *(Samanthy)*, Barbara Sears *(WAC Lieutenant)*, Larry Thompson, Bernie Sell *(M.P.s)*, Chester Conklin *(Photographer)*.

A touching little film that focuses on the attempts of a poor family living in Florida on a houseboat to invite a soldier to their meager floating home and supply him with a hearty meal. This is the family's sole purpose, and they scrimp and save until they finally have a chance to fulfill their desire when Hodiak, adorned in soldier's garb, comes walking along the beach. During the dinner, a romance develops between the soldier and the eldest girl Baxter, making the wait worthwhile for the poor family. Winninger is in his usual grouchy form as the grandfather of the four orphans for whom he must try to provide. Look for the brief appearance of Conklin, the arch-villain of hundreds of comic capers of the Keystone Cops.

p, Walter Morosco; d, Lloyd Bacon; w, Wanda Tuchock, Melvin Levy (based on the story by Martha Cheavens); ph, Joe MacDonald; m, Alfred Newman; ed, J. Watson Webb; art d, Lyle Wheeler, Russell Spencer; cos, Kay Nelson; spec eff, Fred Sersen.

Drama   **(PR:A   MPAA:NR)**

SUNDAY IN NEW YORK***   (1963) 105m Seven Arts/MGM c

Cliff Robertson *(Adam Tyler)*, Jane Fonda *(Eileen Tyler)*, Rod Taylor *(Mike Mitchell)*, Robert Culp *(Russ Wilson)*, Jo Morrow *(Mona Harris)*, Jim Backus *(Flight Dispatcher)*, Peter Nero *(Himself)*.

A fast, frantic, and sometimes funny sex comedy not unlike a thousand other sex comedies. Krasna's farce had been a fair success on Broadway and was perfect for the period. It's a lightweight piece with not much of a plot, but plenty of amusing lines in the middle of familiar situations. Robertson is an airline pilot from upstate New York who lives in a well-furnished Manhattan apartment. He has the weekend off and is looking forward to having some fun with his sweetheart, Morrow. Robertson's sister is Fonda, who has just had a tiff with her fiance, Culp, a wealthy yokel. He wanted to sleep with her before they were married and she was adamant about keeping pristine. Robertson tells her that she made the right move and that a man places a great deal of importance on his wife having been undeflowered. Robertson makes arrangements to see Morrow in another city and she goes there to meet him. When the airline calls to say that Robertson must now fly somewhere else, he can't locate Morrow to say he won't be there. Fonda explores Robertson's apartment and although he preaches about her staying pure, she finds some lingerie in his closet and realizes that he has one set of rules for him, and another for sisters. She leaves the apartment, gets on a bus, and meets Taylor. Her attitude has changed and she thinks it's about time she stopped being a virgin so she begins to work her wiles on Taylor. He sees how naive she really is and will not fall for her ploy, thus frustrating her even more. The two spend this Sunday in New York and fall in love fast (they have to; the whole movie is 105 minutes). Rain hits the city and they are drenched. They rush to Robertson's apartment, don bathrobes, and dry off. Then Culp shows up, thinks that Taylor is Robertson, and pleads with Fonda to come back as he's now willing to wait. Robertson enters, is surprised to see the trio, and Fonda introduces him as the co-pilot to her brother, who is, of course, not her brother at all, but a man she only met on a bus a few hours ago. The film ends as Culp storms out, believing that Fonda has done the deed with another. Taylor and Fonda profess their love and Robertson decides to marry Morrow. Peter Nero did the music and shows up in a cameo. He and Carroll Coates wrote the title tune, which turned out to be a hit with Mel Torme singing. Locations shot in New York, it's the equivalent of cinematic cotton candy. Robertson and Culp are not suited for comedy but Taylor shows a fine flair for it. Jim Backus does a bit as a flight schedule coordinator that could have been played by anyone. When you have someone as funny as Backus, give him something to do.

p, Everett Freeman; d, Peter Tewksbury; w, Norman Krasna (based on his play); ph, Leo Tover (Metrocolor); m, Peter Nero; ed, Fredric Steinkamp; md, Robert Armbruster; art d, George W. Davis, Edward Carfagno; set d, Henry Grace, George R. Nelson; cos, Orry-Kelly; m/l, "Sunday in New York," Nero, Carroll Coates, (sung by Mel Torme), "Hello," Nero, Roland Everett; makeup, William Tuttle, John Truwe.

Comedy   **(PR:C   MPAA:NR)**

SUNDAY IN THE COUNTRY*½   (1975, Can.) 90m
Impact-Quadrant/AIP c

Ernest Borgnine (*Adam Smith*), Michael J. Pollard (*Leroy*), Hollis McLaren (*Lucy*), Louis Zorich (*Dinelli*), Cec Linder (*Ackerman*), Vladimir Valenta (*Luke*), Al Waxman (*Sergeant*), Tim Henry (*Eddie*), Murray Westgate (*Conway*), Ralph Endersby (*Timmy Peterson*), Sue Petrie (*Jennifer Logan*), Ratch Wallace (*Policeman*), Mark Walker, Gary Reineke (*Highway Patrol*), Eric Clavering (*Station Master*), David Hughes (*Pastor*), Carl Banas (*Radio Announcer*), Franz Russell, Ruth Springford, Alan King, Laddie Dennis, Joan Hurley, Winnifred Springetti, Jonathan White, Jim Barron (*Churchgoers*).

Not the type of Sunday outing one would expect as Borgnine plays a peaceful farmer whose quest for revenge against a band of murderers leads to some of the most cruel torture scenes in the entire litany of cinema. Plenty of blood accompanies his deeds. Somehow the theme is maintained that Borgnine is in the right in a very distorted manner. This one should set gun-toting vigilantes' hearts pounding. Advertising for the picture compared it with STRAW DOGS (1971). It bears a closer resemblance to Ingmar Bergman's THE VIRGIN SPRING (1959). Funds for filming were provided in part by the Canadian Film Development Corporation.

p, David Perlmutter; d, John Trent; w, Robert Maxwell, Trent (based on a story by David Main); ph, Marc Champion; m, Paul Hoffert; ed, Tony Lower; art d, James Milton Parcher.

Crime   **(PR:O   MPAA:R)**

SUNDAY LOVERS**   (1980, Ital./Fr.) 125m Viaduc-Medusa/UA

"The French Method": Lino Ventura (*Francois Querole*), Robert Webber (*Henry Morrison*), Catherine Salviat (*Christine*), Denholm Elliott (*Parker*), Lynn Redgrave (*Lady Davina*), Priscilla Barnes (*Donna*), Rossana Podesta (*Clara*), Sylva Koscina (*Zaira*), Beba Loncar (*Marisa*), Catherine Spaak (*Carletta*), Kathleen Quinlan (*Lauri*), Dianne Crittenden (*Maggie*).

A large amount of international talent was gathered together to produce this fairly lame effort, comprising four supposedly lighthearted sketches centering on weekend sexual adventures from people in four different countries. None of these could be expected to express the sexual mores of its country of origin, and although each neatly makes a point in a limited amount of time, little wit or insight has been supplied to lift these sketches above a quick-tease portrayal. Perhaps the best of these vignettes has Ventura wishing to secure a business contract through the use of his personable secretary's charm, only to discover that he values this woman's personality and abilities much more than he does the big deal. The English episode has Moore playing a stud chauffeur who impersonates his employer with a different stewardess girl friend whenever his boss leaves London. One of his intended affairs becomes abruptly interrupted when society lady Redgrave steps onto the scene and wants the chauffeur for her own uses. Tognazzi plays the happily married man who is given a chance to pursue old affairs of the heart when his wife takes off for a weekend. The U.S. segment, written, directed, and starred in by Wilder, is the least amusing of the Four. Wilder plays a psychiatric patient who can't find fulfilling sexual relationships until he meets another patient in the hospital where he is staying. A weekend of lovemaking is followed by the woman's declaration that she is in love with another.

"The French Method": p, Leo Fuchs; d, Edouard Molinaro; w, Francis Veber; ph, Claude Agostini; m, Manuel de Sica; ed, Robert Isnardon; "An Englishman's Home": p, Fuchs; d, Bryan Forbes; w, Leslie Bricusse; ph, Claude Lecomte; m, de Sica; ed, Philip Shaw; "Armando's Notebook": p, Fuchs; d, Dino Risi; w, Age and Scarpelli; ph, Tonino Delli Colli; m, de Sica; ed, A. Galitti; "Skippy": p, Fuchs; d&w, Gene Wilder; ph, Jerry Hirschfield; m, de Sica; ed, Chris Greenbury.

Comedy   **(PR:O   MPAA:R)**

SUNDAY PUNCH**½   (1942) 76m MGM bw

William Lundigan (*Ken Burke*), Jean Rogers (*Judy Galestrum*), Dan Dailey, Jr (*Olaf Jensen*), Guy Kibbee (*Pops Muller*), J. Carrol Naish (*Matt Basler*), Connie Gilchrist (*Ma Galestrum*), Sam Levene (*Roscoe*), Leo Gorcey (*Biff*), Rags Ragland (*Killer*), Douglass Newland (*Baby Fitzroy*), Anthony Caruso (*Nat Cucci*), Tito Renaldo (*Jose*), Michael Browne (*Al*), Dane Clark (*Bill*), Dick Wessel (*Moxie*), Dave Willock (*Milkman*), Lester Matthews (*Smith*), Alfred Hall (*Butler*), Floyd Shackleford (*Doorman*), Duke York, Sammy

Shack (*Fighters*), Edward Earle (*Clerk*), Marcia Ralston (*Blonde*), Pat West (*Announcer*), Robin Raymond (*Vivian*), Ava Gardner (*Ringsider*).

Living in a boardinghouse full of boxers can have its unusual moments, as chorine Rogers discovers. Lundigan is one of the fighters who ends up getting knocked out by Dailey (back when he was still a junior), a Swedish janitor turned pug. However, it's the man on the mat who wins the girl's heart rather than the champ. An entertaining, minor B comedy with a script by Fay and Michael Kanin. Watch for Gardner in a brief appearance.

p, Irving Starr; d, David Miller; w, Fay and Michael Kanin, Allen Rivkin (based on a story by the Kanins); ph, Paul Vogel; ed, Albert Akst; art d, Cedric Gibbons.

Comedy   **(PR:A   MPAA:NR)**

SUNDAY TOO FAR AWAY***   (1975, Aus.) 90m South Australian c

Jack Thompson (*Foley*), Peter Cummins (*"Black" Arthur*), Reg Lye (*Old Garth*).

The hard-drinking, hard-working world of Australian sheep shearers in the 1950s is depicted in this historically important and quite entertaining film. Thompson is the top shearer who leads a strike while maintaining his own position. The film was sent to Cannes and through some adroit maneuvers it was invited to the Director's Fortnight where it became a sensation, the first Australian film to gain any recognition abroad and one that paved the way for such later successes as THE LAST WAVE, BREAKER MORANT, and MAD MAX. Many of the shearing scenes were shot in the same shearing barn that Fred Zinneman used in THE SUNDOWNERS (1960). The title derives from an old Australian verse about the frustrations of being the wife of a shearer; "Friday too tired/Saturday too drunk/Sunday too far away." His role won Thompson the Best Actor prize at the Australian Film Awards of 1974-75.

d, Ken Hannam; w, John Dingwall; ph, Geoff Burton (Eastmancolor).

Drama   **Cas.**   **(PR:C   MPAA:NR)**

SUNDAYS AND CYBELE***   (1962, Fr.) 110m Terra-Fides-Orsay-Les
Films du Trocadero/Davis-Royal COL bw (LES DIMANCHES DE VILLE D'AVRAY; CYBELE)

Hardy Kruger (*Pierre*), Patricia Gozzi (*Francoise [Cybele]*), Nicole Courcel (*Madeleine*), Daniel Ivernel (*Carlos*), Michel de Re (*Bernard*), Andre Oumansky (*Nurse*), Anne-Marie Coffinet, Alain Bouvette, Rene Clermont, Malka Ribovska, Jocelyne Loiseau, Renee Duchateau, Raymond Pelissier, Martine Ferriere, Maurice Garrel, France Anglade, Albert Hugues, Florence Blot, Gilbert Edard, Antoine Tudal, Paul Bonifas, Serge Bourguignon, Dominique Maurin, Jacques Prevot, Jacques Roibiolles, Jacques Tessier, Roger Trapp, Lisette Lebon, Denise Peronne, Bibiane Stern.

After killing a young girl on a bombing mission, pilot Kruger returns to France from the Indochinese War. He takes up residence in a small town near Paris and becomes friendly with Gozzi, a 12-year-old girl who lives in a convent orphanage. The nuns assume that Kruger is her father; the pilot, who suffers from bouts of amnesia, lets the charade continue as he and girl begin spending their Sundays together. A close, warm friendship builds between the two and they decide to spend Christmas together in the woods. However, friends of Courcel, the nurse with whom Kruger lives, are suspicious of this unusual man-child relationship and call the police. Gozzi tells Kruger her real name as a Christmas gift. She is Cybele, which means "Goddess of the Earth". The police intrude on their celebration and–believing Kruger wants to assault the girl–they shoot and kill him. When Gozzi is asked her name, she replies that she no longer has one. A sensitive subject is dealt with in style and grace here, resulting in a warm, often poignant film. The chemistry between Kruger and Gozzi is marvelous, the true heart of the picture. However, the "arty" presentation distracts, some shots calling more attention to themselves than to the story. The film won an Oscar as Best Foreign Film of 1962. (In French; English subtitles.)

p, Romain Pines; d, Serge Bourguignon; w, Bourguignon, Antoine Tudal, Bernard Eschasseriaux (based on the novel *Les Dimanches de Ville d'Avray* by Eschasseriaux); ph, Henri Decae; m, Maurice Jarre; ed, Leonide Azar; art d, Bernard Evein.

Drama   **Cas.**   **(PR:C   MPAA:NR)**

SUNDOWN**½   (1941) 90m UA bw

Gene Tierney (*Zia*), Bruce Cabot (*Capt. Bill Crawford*), George Sanders (*Maj. Coombes*), Sir Cedric Hardwicke (*Bishop Coombes*), Harry Carey (*Dewey*), Joseph Calleia (*Pallini*), Reginald Gardiner (*Lt. Turner*), Carl Esmond (*Kuypens*), Marc Lawrence (*Hammud*), Jeni Le Gon (*Miriami*), Emmett Smith (*Kipsang*), Dorothy Dandridge (*Kipsang's Bride*), Gilbert Emery (*Ashburton*), Horace Walker (*Lecherous Old Man*), Edward Das (*Pindi*), Prince Modupe (*Miriami's Sweetheart*), Hassan Said (*Arab Reader*), Wesley Gale, Jester Hairston (*Native Boys*), Curtis Nero (*Corporal of Askaris*), Al Duval (*Magabul*), Kenny Washington (*Sgt. Kumakwa*), Woodrow [Woody] Strode (*Tribal Policeman*), Walter Knox (*Father*), William Broadus (*Village Headman*), Ivan Browning (*Signal Man*), William Dunn (*Kipsang's Victim*), Tetsu Komai (*Kuypens' Shenzi Aide*), Frederick Clark

(Ibraham), Darby Jones *(Camel Man)*, Blue Washington *(Askari Veteran)*, Laurence La Mar *(Shenzi Informer)*, Frank Clark, George Lincoln *(Pilots)*, St. Luke's Choristers.

In Africa, at the onset of WW II Nazis try to get the local tribes to rebel against the British colonials. Cabot is a local commissioner who, with the help of military man Sanders, discovers the German plot to run guns to the natives. Tierney plays the adopted daughter of an Arab who now runs some trading caravans and trading posts. She agrees to help the British and joins Esmond, the local undercover Nazi chief, in order to find out more about his plans. Despite some thrilling action sequences, this is little more than a standard B-western plot with an exotic setting and with touches of the British style of imperialism, with a bit of wartime patriotism thrown in for good measure. The Nazis are evil personified and the British represent all that is good in the world. The direction is to the point and the cast does a good job with the material. Some fine photography makes good use of the sets and locations.

p, Walter Wanger; d, Henry Hathaway; w, Barre Lyndon, Charles G. Booth (based on a story by Lyndon); ph, Charles Lang; m, Miklos Rozsa; ed, Dorothy Spencer; art d, Alexander Golitzen; cos, Walter Plunkett; spec eff, Ray O. Binger.

War/Adventure   **(PR:C   MPAA:NR)**

SUNDOWN IN SANTA FE*½   (1948) 60m REP bw

Allan Lane, Eddy Waller, Roy Barcroft, Trevor Bardette, Jean Dean, Rand Brooks, Russell Simpson, Lane Bradford, B. G. Norman, Minerva Urecal, Joseph Crehan, Kenne Duncan, Bob Wilke, "Black Jack.".

Allan "Rocky" Lane gets involved with the capture of the man who planned the assassination of President Lincoln. A rare western which delves into a historically significant theme instead of the usual cattle thieving and horse rustling.

p, Melville Tucker; d, R. G. Springsteen; w, Norman S. Hall; ph, John MacBurnie; m, Stanley Wilson; ed, Irving M. Schoenberg; art d, Frank Hotaling; set d, John McCarthy, Jr., Charles Thompson; makeup, Bob Mark.

Western   **(PR:A   MPAA:NR)**

SUNDOWN JIM½**   (1942) 53m FOX bw

John Kimbrough *(Jim Majors)*, Virginia Gilmore *(Tony Black)*, Arleen Whelan *(Catherine Barr)*, Joseph Sawyer *(Moffitt)*, Paul Hurst *(Broderick)*, Moroni Olson *(Andrew Barr)*, Don Costello *(Dobe Hyde)*, LeRoy Mason *(Brick Brand)*, Lane Chandler *(Nat Oldroyd)*, James Bush *(Ring Barr)*, Charles Tannen *(Dan Barr)*, Cliff Edwards *(Stable Proprietor)*, Paul Sutton *(Dale)*, Eddy Waller *(Clem Black)*, Tom Fadden *(Stage Coach Driver)*, Frank McGrath *(Outlaw)*.

Average western programmer features Kimbrough brought in to clean up a snowy mountain from the usual assortment of bad guys. The direction is good, with a sense of excitement due to more than the usual number of gunfights included in the short running time. The studio was considering a series with Kimbrough when this was made but ended up dropping his option shortly before the film's release.

p, Sol M. Wurtzel; d, James Tinling; w, Robert F. Metzler, William Bruckner (based on a story by Ernest Haycox); ph, Glen MacWilliams; ed, Nick De Maggio; md, Emil Newman.

Western   **(PR:A   MPAA:NR)**

SUNDOWN KID, THE**   (1942) 59m REP bw

Don "Red" Barry *(Red Tracy/Red Brannon)*, Ian Keith *(J. Richard Spencer)*, Helen MacKellar *(Lucy Randall)*, Linda Johnson *(Lynn Parsons)*, Emmett Lynn *(Pop Tanner)*, Wade Grosby *(Vince Ganley)*, Ted Adams *(Jim Dawson)*, Fern Emmett *(Mrs. Peabody)*, Bud Geary *(Nick Parker)*, Bob Kortman *(Luke Reed)*, Kenne Duncan *(Tex Bronner)*, Kenneth Harlan, Jack Ingram, Jack Rockwell, Joe McGuinn, Cactus Mack.

Undercover Pinkerton agent Barry goes to prison to find out about a counterfeiting operation. He ends up joining the gang and they grow suspicious of him after awhile. The gang is trying to steal rich recluse Mackellar's property. Barry stops them, of course, and turns out to be the woman's long lost son. Average western with standard production values.

p, Eddy White; d, Elmer Clifton; w, Norman S. Hall (based on a story by Hall); ph, Ernest Miller; m, Mort Glickman; ed, William Thompson; art d, Russell Kimball.

Western   **Cas.**   **(PR:A   MPAA:NR)**

SUNDOWN ON THE PRAIRIE*   (1939) 59m MON bw

Tex Ritter *(Tex)*, Horace Murphy *(Ananias)*, Dorothy Fay *(Ruth)*, Karl Hackett *(Hendricks)*, Charles King *(Dorgan)*, Hank Worden *(Hank)*, Frank Ellis *(Chuck)*, Wally West *(Slim)*, Ernie Adams *(Blackie)*, Frank LaRue *(Graham)*, Edward Piel, Sr *(John)*, Bud Osborne, Dave O'Brien, Bob Terry, the Musical Tornadoes [featuring] Juanita Street, White Flash the Horse.

Low-class Ritter western finds the singing cowboy riding the range on the lookout for some border smugglers. Hackett and King are the bad guys and Fay the love interest. Production values are below standard western quality.

p, Edward Finney; d, Al Herman; w, William Nolte, Edmund Kelso; ph, Bert Longenecker; ed, Fred Bain; m/l, "Sundown on the Prairie," Al Von Tilzer, Harry MacPherson, "Dust on My Saddle," Dwight Butcher, "Cactus Pete," Lew Porter, Johnny Lange.

Western   **(PR:A   MPAA:NR)**

SUNDOWN RIDER, THE½**   (1933) 65m COL bw

Buck Jones *(Camp O'Neill)*, Barbara Weeks *(Molly McCall)*, Pat O'Malley *(Lafe Armstrong)*, Wheeler Oakman *(Laughing Maxey)*, Niles Welch *(House-man)*, Bradley Page *(Jim Hunter)*, Frank LaRue *(Sheriff Rand)*, Ward Bond *(Gabe Powers)*, Ed Brady, Harry Todd, Silver the Horse.

Action-packed western features Jones who literally gets branded as a cattle rustler. The law is after him but eventually Jones gets even with bad guy Bond and gives him a branding as well. Plenty of bullets fly and there is some good looking two-fisted action as well. Weeks' role as the love interest is relatively minor for a western programmer. Some good direction adds to the excitement.

d&w, Lambert Hillyer (story by Jack Neville); ph, John Boyle.

Western   **(PR:AA   MPAA:NR)**

SUNDOWN RIDERS**   (1948) Film Enterprises c

Russell Wade, Jay Kirby, Andy Clyde *(Sundown Riders)*, Evelyn Finley *(Donna Fraser)*, Jack Ingraham *(Tug Wilson)*, Marshal Reed *(Bob Casey)*, Hal Price *(Yeager)*, Steve Clark *(Mr. Fraser)*, Ted Mapes *(Gilson)*, Bud Osborne *(Loco)*, Henry Wills *(Curly)*, Jack Shannon *(Jed)*, Ted Wells *(Bill)*, Cliff Parkinson *(Evans)*, George Fuller *(Sam)*, Chief Many Treaties *(Indian Charlie)*, Cactus Mack Peters *(Walker)*, Elmer Napier *(Pioneer)*, Emily Crittenden *(Pioneer's Daughter)*.

This typical story featuring Wade, Kirby and Clyde as a trio of cowpoke heros differed little in story from other program westerns. They take on a group of outlaws and after the usual amount of fights and gun play, come out on top. What is unusual here is the film was shot by an independent company on 16mm and in Kodachrome, which was cheaper than Technicolor. The final cost was only $30,000 and shot in just eight days, a budget much cheaper than most black and white westerns. The idea was to make 16mm films for domestic distribution as well as the natural market of schools, hospitals, and the like. Good though the idea seemed it never took off and the planned series of six by this small Denver company was eventually cancelled. Kirby and Clyde were from the HOPALONG CASSIDY series. Kirby, along with Wade (who came up with the 16mm distribution idea) and cinematographer Stensvold each had a profit sharing clause in their contracts, anticipating a time when profit sharing would become a standard practice in Hollywood.

p, H.V. George; d, Lambert Hillyer; w, Rodney J. Graham; ph, Alan Stensvold (Kodachrome); ed, Ella Brouner.

Western   **(PR:A   MPAA:NR)**

SUNDOWN SAUNDERS**   (1937) 63m Supreme/William Steiner bw

Bob Steele *(Sundown Saunders)*, Catherine Cotter *(Bess Preston)*, Earl Dwire *(Sheriff Baker)*, Ed Cassidy *(Taggart)*, Jack Rockwell *(Preston)*, Milburn Moranti *(Smokey)*, Frank Ball *(Manning)*, Hal Price *(Lewis)*, Charles King, Horace Murphy, Edmund Cobb, Bob McKenzie, Jack Kirk, Herman Hack.

After winning a ranch during a pony race, Steele finds that outlaw Cassidy will try anything to take the ranch. Though the story is routine, there are a few unusual twists within the script. However the direction (by Steele's father) is of lower quality and constricted by budget restraints. Cotter is the love interest, dripping with saccharine, and Dwire an apt sheriff.

p, A.W. Hackel; d&w, Robert N. Bradbury (based on a story by Bradbury); ph, Bert Longnecker; ed, S. Roy Luby.

Western   **Cas.**   **(PR:A   MPAA:NR)**

SUNDOWN TRAIL**   (1931) 56m RKO-Pathe bw

Tom Keene!!George Duryea]!, Marion Shilling, Nick Stuart, Hooper Atchley, Louise Beavers, Stanley Blystone, Alma Chester, William Welsh, Murdock McQuarrie.

Keene's first western has him playing a ranch foreman who co-inherits the property he works on. The other inheritor is Shilling, an Eastern woman who despises the West and fosters similar feelings for Keene. After an episode with some rustlers she changes her mind and ends up in Keene's arms. Stuart is Keene's outlaw buddy who decides to take the straight and narrow. Typical low-budget western with some good direction. This was the first of RKO's 12 westerns with Keene. In this series there were more people doing the camera work than in any other series and five producers worked on the 12 entries.

p, Fred Allen; d&w, Robert Hill; ph, Ted McCord; m/l, "I Built a Gal," Arthur Lange, Hill.

Western   **(PR:A MPAA:NR)**

SUNDOWN VALLEY**   (1944) 55m COL bw

Charles Starrett (*Steve Denton*), Dub Taylor (*Cannonball*), Jeanne Bates (*Sidney Hawkins*), Jessie Arnold (*Mom Johnson*), Clancy Cooper (*Hodge Miller*), Jack Ingram (*Bart Adams*), Wheeler Oakman (*Cab Baxter*), Joel Friedkin (*Joe Calloway*), Grace Lenard (*Sally Jenks*), Eddie Laughton (*Tom Carleton*), Forrest Taylor (*Gunsight Hawkins*), Jimmy Wakely and Saddle Pals.

Oakman and his Nazi cohorts are out to stop all functions at a western gunsight plant. They did not count on Starrett being the manager who fights them off with plenty of rootin' tootin' action and fisticuffs. The strange plot was directed by Kline, normally a cinematographer for numerous program westerns, who took directing chores here in a cost-cutting move. The small budget is reflected in the abundance of action which was an attempt to cover many of the film's weaknesses.

p, Jack Fier; d, Benjamin Kline; w, Luci Ward (based on a story by Ward); ph, George Meehan; ed, Aaron Stell; art d, Lionel Banks.

Western   **(PR:A MPAA:NR)**

SUNDOWNERS, THE**½   (1950) 83m EL c (GB: THUNDER IN THE DUST)

Robert Preston (*Kid Wichita*), Robert Sterling (*Tom Cloud*), Chill Wills (*Sam Beard*), John Litel (*John Gaul*), Cathy Downs (*Mrs. Boyce*), Jack Elam (*Boyce*), Don Haggerty (*Elmer Gaul*), Stanley Price (*Fletcher*), Clem Fuller (*Turkey*), Frank Cordell (*Strake*), Dave Kashner (*Batson*), John Barrymore, Jr (*Jeff Cloud*).

Not to be confused with the far superior Fred Zinnemann movie of the same name, this is a routine western distinguished only by Hoch's camerawork. There are three brothers in the Cloud family. The eldest is Preston, a desperado. His kid brother is John Barrymore, Jr. (in his movie debut) who loves Preston and wants to emulate him. The middle brother is Sterling, who is adored by Downs, but she is married to Elam. When Preston kills Elam, that paves the way for Sterling and Downs to cement their relationship. There's a rivalry between cattlemen, there are rustling raids, lots of gun play, a feud between Preston, who dominates the family, and Sterling, who wants to have his own section of land on which to live peacefully. Despite Preston being the star, it is he who gets gunned down at the end in order to bring serenity back to the land. Western fans will find much to like in this typical range war epic but it doesn't really provide much for anyone else. Barrymore was 18 at the time he made this and was using the "junior" designation in his name. That continued until 1956, then he decided to bill himself as John Drew Barrymore. He went to Europe and made a series of forgettable costumers until 1964, when he returned to the U.S. Late in the 1960s, he opted out of show business for a while for a life of meditation in the desert. A few years after that he came back to Hollywood and can be seen from time to time in small roles on TV.

p, Alan LeMay; d, George Templeton; w, LeMay; ph, Winton C. Hoch (Technicolor); m, Al Colombo; ed, Jack Ogilvie; md, Irvin Talbot; art d, John Goodman.

Western   **(PR:A MPAA:NR)**

SUNDOWNERS, THE****   (1960) 133m WB c

Deborah Kerr (*Ida Carmody*), Robert Mitchum (*Paddy Carmody*), Peter Ustinov (*Venneker*), Glynis Johns (*Mrs. Firth*), Dina Merrill (*Jean Halstead*), Chips Rafferty (*Quinlan*), Michael Anderson, Jr (*Sean*), Lola Brooks (*Liz*), Wylie Watson (*Herb Johnson*), John Meillon (*Bluey*), Ronald Fraser (*Ocker*), Mervyn Johns (*Jack Patchogue*), Molly Urquhart (*Mrs. Bateman*), Ewen Solon (*Bob Halstead*), Dick Bentley, Gerry Duggan, Peter Carver, Leonard Teale, Alastair Williamson, Ray Barrett, Mercia Barden.

A splendid, sprawling saga of Australia, well acted, beautifully shot, and perhaps the best movie to come out of the island continent. Set in the 1920s, it's the story of a single family and how they interact with the pioneers around them, how they extract a living from the land, how they live and love and cope. Lennart's adaptation of the Cleary novel is dotted with wit, sly philosophy, and solid, motivated action. The phrase in the title refers to those people who roam the land and live wherever they stop when the sun sets. Mitchum is married to Kerr and the two travel the land with their son, Anderson. They have no money, no assets, just a great love between the three and a continuing hope that things will get better. Mitchum works when he can, picks up a few dollars here and there (in Australia, they refer to their money as dollars, not pounds and shillings), and keeps moving. Kerr and Anderson are getting a bit tired of this Bedouin existence and yearn for a place where they can hang their hats. Mitchum can't bear the thought of that and takes a job leading more than a thousand sheep on a long trek to Cawndilla in the west of Australia. Since there are so many head, Mitchum has to hire another man to help and that's Ustinov, a one-time ship's captain. The journey is arduous and filled with incidents. They stop and visit with another group of "Sundowners" who have given up the road for a

permanent abode. Kerr and Anderson envy the new life led by Urquhart's family but Mitchum pays it no mind, preferring the open road. They continue and just manage to escape the wrath of a forest fire, then finally deliver their sheep and collect their fee. Kerr is getting tired and tells Mitchum she'd like to rest a while, so they take jobs on a large "station" (which is what they call ranches in Australia) and she hopes that this will allow them to amass enough cash to finally buy their own spread. Kerr signs on as a cook, Mitchum takes a position as a sheep shearer, and Anderson becomes a gofer. Ustinov, who has jealously guarded his bachelorhood, becomes enamored of Johns, a vivacious hotelkeeper who likes him just as well. Ustinov takes employment picking wool and it appears that they are settling in to a routine. Mitchum doesn't much like the new pals that Kerr and Anderson have found and thinks that the new situation is splitting the closeness of his family. The season for shearing comes to a close and Mitchum elects to follow the sun once more. Ustinov is torn between staying with Johns and departing with the Mitchum trio. His deep-seated desire to remain single overtakes his passion for Johns, so he leaves. Mitchum had won a race horse on a bet and that steed is taken in tow as the group climbs into their wagon and exits. On the ride, Anderson practices riding the horse (aptly named "Sundowner") and gets to be a fairly good jockey. There's a small race track out in the country and Mitchum thinks their horse might have a chance as the competition wouldn't be too stiff this far away from a major city. Anderson rides the horse and it's a better animal than they'd figured, winning the race in a walk. Mitchum is thrilled and dreams of making a fortune by visiting these tiny tracks in the outback and cleaning up. And that they do, gathering enough money to put down on a farm. It appears that their traveling is finally over, then Mitchum risks all that hard earned cash gambling and loses the bundle, putting them right back where they started. Mitchum feels awful about what he's done and Kerr and Anderson are downright shattered. There's a big race, for a large purse, coming up. The horse will be running against animals quite a bit better than the swaybacks and nags he's faced in the past. Mitchum says that if Sundowner wins the race, there will surely be prospective claimers and he'll sell the horse. They'll take the purse and the proceeds from the horse's sale and buy that farm of their dreams. The race is run and the horse wins again. Afterward, Kerr realizes how much her son and husband love the animal and says that they'll keep him. Before they can collect their purse, the track officials claim that the horse interfered with another horse and is therefore disqualified. Once again, they are back where they were before. Ustinov climbs into the wagon with Kerr and Anderson. Mitchum grabs the reins, Sundowner is attached to the rear of the wagon, and off they go, ready to seek new adventures. Kerr was nominated for an Oscar, as were Johns, Zinnemann, Lennart, and the picture itself. Every aspect of the movie was first-rate and all the smaller roles were wonderfully cast, including Australia's favorite actor, Chips Rafferty, as the sheep-shearing foreman. Rafferty was in just about every Australian movie made in the 1940s, 1950s and 1960s, with his most famous appearance being in THE OVERLANDERS, which was about a cattle drive from north to south while the whole country was perched for an invasion from the Japanese. Zinnemann's company criss-crossed the Australian landscape, from Cooma, in the Snowy River area of New South Wales, to Port Augusta, on the Gulf of Spencer, to Carriewerloo, in the interior. Kerr plays with little makeup and her natural beauty shines through the dust that accumulates on her face. Johns is a delight in her small but telling role and Ustinov does his usual excellent job. The prolific Ustinov used his off-screen time well, writing short stories for magazines, proofreading the galleys of his novel, *The Loser*, and re-writing his play "Romanoff and Juliet" into the film he made right after finishing this. Zinnemann is a tireless researcher and spent three months scouring the country for the right locations, then purchasing thousands of sheep for the movie. Sheep are very tractable animals and need to be told what to do. (It's amazing to watch one small Australian sheep dog push hundreds of the creatures around.) A sheep was trained as a leader and managed to handle the other 4,999, under Zinnemann's ovine direction. THE SUNDOWNERS is a true "family" film that doesn't ever seem that way. It's big, funny, tender, and humane all at the same time. And there are darned few movies that can claim that.

p, Fred Zinnemann, Gerry Blattner; d, Zinnemann; w, Isobel Lennart (based on the novel by Jon Cleary); ph, Jack Hildyard (Technicolor); m, Dimitri Tiomkin; ed, Jack Harris; art d, Michael Stringer; set d, Frants Folmer, Terrence Morgan; cos, Elizabeth Haffenden; makeup, George Frost.

Drama   **(PR:A MPAA:NR)**

SUNFLOWER*½   (1970, Fr./Ital.) 101m C.C. Champion-Les Films Concordia/AE c (LES FLEURS DU SOLEIL; I GIRASOLI)

Sophia Loren (*Giovanna*), Marcello Mastroianni (*Antonio*), Lyudmila Savelyeva (*Mascia*), Galina Andreyeva (*Soviet Woman Official*), Anna Carena (*Antonio's Mother*), Germano Longo (*Ettore*), Nadya Serednichenko (*Woman in Sunflower Field*), Glauco Onorato (*Returning Veteran*), Silvano Tranquilli (*Russian-Italian Worker*), Marisa Traversi (*Prostitute*), Gunar Zilinskiy (*Russian Ministry Official*), Carlo Ponti, Jr. (*Giovanna's Baby*), Giorgio Basso, Umberto Di Grazie, Gianni Bortolotti, Giuliano Girardi, Pippo Starnazza, Dino Peretti.

In this dull grade Z soap opera, Loren plays an Italian woman who marries Mastroianni only 12 days before WW II breaks out. Mastroianni tries to evade the draft by faking insanity, but this ruse is easily uncovered by officials. He is sent to the Russian front, where the cold weather and lack of food takes its toll on the troops. He is taken in by Savelyeva, a Russian girl, and the two later marry. Years go by, and still Loren waits for word on her husband's fate. He has been declared missing in action, but Loren is determined to find out what really happened. She goes to Russia, looking through military cemeteries, searching records, and showing Mastroianni's picture to anyone who will listen. Eventually she finds Savelyeva, and finally Mastroianni. Loren leaves him to his new life, and returns to Italy where she marries Longo, an older factory worker who loves her. The two have a son (played in an undistinguished film debut by the real-life son of Loren and producer Ponti), and the years go by. Mastroianni remains obsessed after Loren's visit, and gets permission from authorities to visit Italy. He and Loren reunite to discuss their past, but her baby's cry shatters any illusions the two might be fostering. Mastroianni returns to his Russian wife, while Loren remains with Longo, and the film takes predictable step after step towards its unexceptional conclusion. De Sica's direction is perfunctory, a shallow effort from a cinematic master. One sequence has Loren walking through a field of oh-so-symbolic sunflowers as she hopes and dreams of Mastroianni. Loren's performance is lethargic, showing no insight whatsoever to an already cardboard character. This was the first Italian feature shot in Moscow, and the shots of the Soviet capital are one of the film's few redeeming qualities. Despite the sap that flowed fast and furious between every sprocket hole of this film, THE SUNFLOWER did fairly good box office. (In Italian; English subtitles.)

p, Carlo Ponti, Arthur Cohn; d, Vittorio De Sica; w, Tonino Guerra, Cesare Zavattini, Georgiy Mdivani; ph, Giuseppe Rotunno (Technicolor); m, Henry Mancini; ed, Adriana Novelli; art d, Piero Poletto, David Vinitskj; cos, Enrico Sabbatini.

Drama (PR:A MPAA:G)

SUNNY½ (1930) 67m FN bw

Marilyn Miller (Sunny), Lawrence Gray (Tom Warren), Joe Donahue (Jim Deming), Mackenzie Ward (Wendell-Wendell), O.P. Heggie (Peters), Inez Courtney ("Weenie"), Barbara Bedford (Marcia Manners), Judith Vosselli (Sue), Clyde Cook (Sam), Barry Allen (The Barker), William Davidson (1st Officer), Ben Hendrickson, Jr (2nd Officer).

The play was a huge hit on Broadway and the film company thought they could transfer Miller's magic to the screen. They were wrong. Miller is a horseback performer from England who stows away on an ocean liner going to New York. It goes without saying that she is discovered but there is a passenger list of friendly people and she's soon welcomed as one of them, sings and dances for her supper and cabin, and winds up getting married before they reach the U.S., so she has no problem with the officials at Ellis Island. There are several set pieces including a fox hunt in England, a comedy sequence in a gym, a fancy dress ball, etc. Miller never could quite show her stuff on film the way she did it on stage and her career in movies was brief, with the highlights being this, SALLY, and HER MAJESTY LOVE. June Haver played her in LOOK FOR THE SILVER LINING, her cinema biography. In Jerome Kern's biography, TILL THE CLOUDS ROLL BY, she was impersonated by Judy Garland. The score for the play and this picture was by Kern, Otto Harbach, and Oscar Hammerstein II. It included: "Sunny," "Who?" "D'ya Love Me?" "Two Little Love Birds," and "I Was Alone" and most of them were done by Miller. Joe Donahue plays her cloddish boy friend and Lawrence Gray is the man who loses her to Donahue. Kosloff's choreography is a highlight in this otherwise stagy film that never comes close to showing what it was about Miller that made her a star.

d, William A. Seiter; w, Humphrey Pearson, Henry McCarthy (based on the musical play by Otto Harbach, Oscar Hammerstein II, Jerome Kern); ph, Ernest Haller; m, Harbach, Hammerstein II, Kern; ed, Leroy Stone; md, Erno Rapee; ch, Theodore Kosloff.

Musical/Comedy (PR:A MPAA:NR)

SUNNY** (1941) 98m RKO bw

Anna Neagle (Sunny Sullivan), Ray Bolger (Bunny Billings), John Carroll (Larry Warren), Edward Everett Horton (Henry Bates, Lawyer), Grace Hartman (Juliet Runnymede), Paul Hartman (Egghead), Frieda Inescort (Elizabeth Warren), Helen Westley (Aunt Barbara), Benny Rubin (Maj. Montgomery Sloan), Muggins Davies (Muggins), Richard Lane (Reporter), Martha Tilton (Queen of Hearts), Torben Mayer (Head Waiter).

Simplistic remake of the 1930 original features Neagle as the star of a circus that is performing at Mardi Gras. She meets Carroll, the son of a wealthy automobile manufacturer, and promptly falls in love. Of course his upper crust family disapproves but love conquers all and they marry at the film's end. The story was old and unbelievable by the time of this remake resulting in a lesser feature. However, the beautiful Kern score is always a treat and the talented Bolger's dancing is great fun. Direction is less than supportive with a flat, ho-hum style that injected little into the production. Songs (with lyrics by Oscar Hammerstein II) include: "Who?" (sung by Anna Neagle and John Carroll), "D'ya Love Me?" "Sunny" (sung by Carroll), and "Two Little Bluebirds."

p&d, Herbert Wilcox; w, Sig Herzog (based on the musical comedy by Otto

Harbach, Oscar Hammerstein II); ph, Russell Metty; m, Jerome Kern; ed, Elmo Williams; md, Anthony Collins; art d, L.P. Williams; spec eff, Vernon L. Walker; ch, Leon Leonidoff.

Musical (PR:A MPAA:NR)

SUNNY SIDE OF THE STREET** (1951) 71m COL c

Frankie Laine (Himself), Billy Daniels (Himself), Terry Moore (Betty Holloway), Jerome Courtland (Ted Mason), Toni Arden (Herself), Audrey Long (Gloria Pelley), Dick Wesson (Dave Gibson), Lynn Bari (Mary), William Tracy (Al Little), Willard Waterman (John Stevens), Jonathan Hale (Cyrus Pelley), Amanda Blake (Susie Manning), Benny Payne (Himself), Paul Dubov (Miller), Peter Price (Wilbur).

Empty-headed feature has TV studio receptionist Moore trying to help crooner Courtland get his big break in the new medium. With the help of Laine and Daniels (playing themselves) he manages to get a few commercial jobs. His big break comes when some executives discover that Courtland is the school chum of a big sponsor's daughter. The best thing about this picture is the songs. The best are "I Get a Kick out of You" (Cole Porter), "On the Sunny Side of the Street" (Dorothy Fields, Jimmy McHugh), and "Let's Fall in Love" (Ted Koehler, Harold Arlen). Other songs include "I'm Gonna Live Till I Die" (Al Hoffman, Mann Curtis) and "I May Be Wrong but I Think You're Wonderful" (Harry Ruskin, Henry Sullivan). Other than the songs, this feature is strictly by the book and boring. Shot in color, this early TV-themed film would have audiences in 1951 believing that color TV reception was a widespread thing.

p, Jonie Taps; d, Richard Quine; w, Lee Loeb (based on a story by Harold Conrad); ph, Ellis W. Carter (Supercinecolor); ed, Jerome Thoms; md, George Duning; art d, Walter Holscher.

Musical (PR:A MPAA:NR)

SUNNY SIDE UP** (1929) 80m FOX bw/c

Janet Gaynor (Molly Carr), Charles Farrell (Jack Cromwell), El Brendel (Eric Swenson), Marjorie White (Bee Nichols), Frank Richardson (Eddie Rafferty), Sharon Lynn (Jane Worth), Mary Forbes (Mrs. Cromwell), Joe E. Brown (Joe Vitto), Alan Paull (Raoul), Peter Gawthorne (Lake), Jackie Cooper (Tenement Boy).

After their great success as a team in silent movies, the U.S. eagerly awaited Gaynor and Farrell's first talkie and they were not disappointed. There had been several sound musicals by this time, most of which were "backstage" stories. This attempted to break away from the cliche and establish a cliche of its own. They took a standard "Cinderella" tale, added some tunes by De Sylva, Brown, and Henderson (who had a movie made about their lives in 1956, THE BEST THINGS IN LIFE ARE FREE) and one bizarre, spectacular production number that was partly tinted in "Multicolor" and had the patrons lining up in droves to plunk down their cash. Farrell is a member of the snobbish 400 in New York, the heir to huge wealth and a bit of a stuffed shirt at first. He is vacationing for the summer at Southampton strumming his ukulele and living the life Riley would like to live, if he had Farrell's family's money. Gaynor is a poor shopgirl who dwells in a rundown tenement in the city and is apparently happy with her lot. The two meet and he falls hard for her and wants to make her part of his life, over and above the disdain of his snooty pals and the icy mien of his mother, Forbes. In order to perpetrate the charade that she is as wealthy as he is, Gaynor enlists the aid of her friends, White, Brendel, and Richardson, to pose as her personal maid, her valet, and her chauffeur. Meanwhile, Farrell is being pursued by Lynn, a flapper in the same social circle and it seems as though she will eventually put her talons into him. The relationship between Farrell and Gaynor is almost severed until she performs at a charity ball and he comes to the realization that she is the woman for him. Lots of music and production numbers which include: "I'm a Dreamer" (Gaynor), "If I Had a Talking Picture of You" (Gaynor, Farrell, then reprised by children in a kindergarten class), "You've Got Me Pickin' Petals off o' Daisies" (Richardson, White), "It's Great to Be Necked" (White, in a parody of Harry Lauder's material), "You Find the Time, I'll Find the Place" (Lynn), "Sunny Side Up" (Gaynor), and the huge production number, "Turn on the Heat" wherein 36 comely women, led by Lynn, are dressed like Eskimos. Their igloos melt and they doff their furs and the frozen set becomes the tropics, with palm trees rising full-grown from the ground. Eventually the whole thing catches on fire and the women dive into a swimming pool. Busby Berkeley would have loved this number as staged by Seymour Felix. The fact that Gaynor and Farrell had very little musical talent didn't disturb audiences who were just happy that their voices had any quality at all. Joe E. Brown chimes in with some good comedy as a lower East Side undertaker who handles the M.C. chores for the street's block party.

p, William Fox; d, David Butler; w, Buddy De Sylva, Ray Henderson, Lew Brown, Butler; ph, Ernest Palmer, John Schmitz; m, De Sylva, Henderson, Brown; ed, Irene Morra; md, Howard Jackson, Arthur Kay; art d, Harry Oliver; cos, Sophie Wachner; ch, Seymour Felix; m/l, De Sylva, Brown, Henderson.

Musical/Comedy (PR:A MPAA:NR)

SUNNY SKIES*   (1930) 75m TIF bw

Benny Rubin (*Benny Krantz*), Marceline Day (*Mary Norris*), Rex Lease (*Jim Grant*), Marjorie "Babe" Kane (*Doris*), Greta Granstedt (*College Widow*), Wesley Barry (*Sturrle*), Robert Randall (*Dave*), James Wilcox (*Smith*), Harry Lee.

Old hokum plot about college kids and the big game. Lease is a college kid who donates some blood to save his roommate's (Rubin) life. The next day he is out on the football field winning the big game despite his weakened condition. Oddly enough, this nonsense is a musical comedy. Overly sentimental and smothered with sap. Rubin's performance teeters between comedy and pathos without the talent to pull it off. The budget was bare bones and that was well reflected in the production values. Songs include: "Sunny Days" (sung by Rex Lease), "I Must Have You" (sung by Babe Kane), "Wanna Find a Boy" (sung by Kane), "Must Be Love."

d, Norman Taurog; w, Erle Snell, George Cleveland (based on a story by A.P. Younger); ph, Paul Meyers, Arthur Reeves; ed, Clarence Kolster.

Musical   **(PR:A MPAA:NR)**

SUNNYSIDE*   (1979) 100m AIP c

Joey Travolta (*Nick Martin*), John Lansing (*Denny Martin*), Stacey Pickren (*Donna Rosario*), Andrew Rubin (*Eddie Reaper*), Michael Tucci (*Harry Cimoli*), Talia Balsam (*Ann Rosario*), Chris Mulkey (*Reggie Flynn*), Joan Darling (*Mrs. Martin*), Richard Beauchamp (*Hector*), Heshimu Cumbuka (*Ice*), Jonathan Gries (*Wild Child*), E. Lamont Johnson (*Rage*), David Byrd (*Roy*).

John Travolta's younger brother tried to emulate his sibling's success with SATURDAY NIGHT FEVER in this nonsense. The younger Travolta makes his film debut playing a street kid trying to help his neighborhood by trying to do in "The Savage Warlocks," a local street gang. Once he finishes that Travolta plans to move to Manhattan and settle down with Pickren. Travolta can do a mean imitation of his brother but not much more in this poorly scripted mess. The film is loaded with bad dialog and implausible situations. The direction is unbelievably bad, injecting high camera angles that ultimately work against the little drama found here. The producers apparently wanted to cash in on the musical bonanza SATURDAY NIGHT FEVER created for the soundtrack album business, packing this film with plenty of forgettable pop tunes.

p, Robert L. Schaffel; d, Timothy Galfas; w, Galfas, Jeff King (based on a story by King, Schaffel); ph, Gary Graver (Movielab Color); m, Alan Douglas, Harold Wheeler; ed, Eric Albertson, Herbert H. Dow.

Drama   **(PR:O MPAA:R)**

SUNRISE AT CAMPOBELLO***   (1960) 144m WB c

Ralph Bellamy (*Franklin D. Roosevelt*), Greer Garson (*Eleanor Roosevelt*), Hume Cronyn (*Louis Howe*), Jean Hagen (*Missy Le Hand*), Ann Shoemaker (*Sara Roosevelt*), Alan Bunce (*Al Smith*), Tim Considine (*James Roosevelt*), Zina Bethune (*Anna Roosevelt*), Pat Close (*Elliot Roosevelt*), Robin Warga (*Franklin D. Roosevelt, Jr.*), Tommy Carty (*Johnny Roosevelt*), Lyle Talbot (*Mr. Brimmer*), David White (*Mr. Lassiter*), Herb Anderson (*Daly*), Frank Ferguson (*Dr. Bennett*), Walter Sande (*Capt. Skinner*), Janine Grandel (*Marie*), Otis Greene (*Edward*), Ivan Browning (*Charles*), Al McGranary (*Sen. Walsh*), Jerry Crews (*Speaker*), William Haddock (*Mr. Owens*), Floyd Curtis (*Mailman*), Jack Henderson (*Joe*), Ruth March (*Miss Garroway*), Ed Prentiss (*Barker*), Francis DeSales (*Riley*), Craig Curtis (*Newsboy*), Don Dillaway (*Sloan*), Fern Barry, Mary Benoit, Jack Perrin (*Campaign Workers*).

After a distinguished career in movies, Dore Schary decided to try his typewriter for the stage and the result was this play about FDR's first physical crisis, from 1921 through 1924. The play won the Antoinette Perry Award after opening in January, 1958, and giving 857 performances with Bellamy in the lead. Schary wisely decided to bring Bellamy and the same director who steered his play, Donehue, along with him for the screen version. The result is a heartwarming (though somewhat slanted) look at the early years of the only man who was elected to the highest office in the U.S. four times. Bellamy was superb as Roosevelt, capturing almost every nuance of a man who was the most photographed and listened-to politician of his generation. Surpassing Bellamy, though, is Garson, who didn't *play* Eleanor Roosevelt, she *became* her. It's 1921 and the Roosevelt family is vacationing on the small island of Campobello, off New Brunswick. The Roosevelts are a patrician group, with plenty of money and no worries at all, though the matriarch's son, Bellamy, has an eye toward public service and is the assistant secretary of the Navy, above the wishes of his mother, Shoemaker, who would prefer that he spend his time clipping coupons and alternating between Campobello and the family's estate at Hyde Park. Bellamy goes out sailing on an August day and comes home not feeling well, but quipping, "Home is the sailor, home from the sea," as he walks into the house and greets his family. He takes to bed to get over a "chill" and when his legs suddenly become paralyzed, he's whisked to the hospital where he soon learns from doctor Ferguson that he's the victim of polio and will never again walk. Shoemaker insists that he give up his political aspirations and Bellamy is too prone to argue until his pal, Cronyn, begins to light a fire under the bed-ridden man. Cronyn is a chain-smoking, asthmatic behind-the-

scenes type who thinks that Bellamy would be better off if he gave up feeling sorry for himself and got on with life. In this, Garson concurs and the three of them form a triumvirate. Garson accompanies Bellamy to various political functions, in between tending their five children, Considine, Bethune, Warga, Carty, and Close. Cronyn thinks that Bellamy has got the stuff that leaders are made of, although Bellamy doesn't share that opinion at first. With raw courage pushing him forward, Bellamy learns to get up from his wheelchair and use his powerful arms to drag him on crutches, while his useless legs are encased in heavy metal braces. The culmination of the film comes when Bunce is to be nominated for the 1924 Democratic presidential candidate and chooses Bellamy to place his name on the slate. Bunce, playing "The Happy Warrior" (Al Smith), is a Catholic and the centrists in the party are against his candidacy, feeling that the religious issue will see him go down to ignominious defeat. (They were right. Smith lost by a landslide but no one knows for sure how much the "Papist" charges had to do with it.) In the dramatic conclusion, Bellamy has to walk the 10 longest steps in his life, from his wheelchair to the dais. He pulls himself up out of his metal prison, grabs for his crutches, and makes it across the chasm where he gives the nominating speech. The crowd screams with happiness, the band plays "The Sidewalks of New York" (Smith's theme) and there's not a dry eye in the theater as the movie ends on an inspirational moment. It was only eight years later that Roosevelt came into office to rebuild a country which had fallen upon hard times under the naive regimes of Calvin Coolidge and Herbert Hoover. Poignant, powerful, and perceptive, the movie was somehow overlooked by the Motion Picture Academy, except for Garson's magnificent performance which earned her an Oscar nomination, losing to Elizabeth Taylor in BUTTERFIELD 8, a gross miscarriage of taste. Taylor had done far better in other roles but had recently suffered a near-fatal medical problem and the consensus is that they gave the statuette to her more out of sentiment than anything else. Garson used some prosthetic teeth to better stimulate Eleanor Roosevelt's looks but she needn't have because her acting was from within. She was able to emulate Eleanor's unique, often quavery voice, and she submerged her own inimitable persona into that of the president's wife to such a degree that one forgot Garson was ever MRS. MINIVER or MRS. PARKINGTON or Irene Forsyte in THE FORSYTE SAGA, or Calpurnia in JULIUS CAESAR. It was a performance that should be studied by actors forever. The movie was released in September, 1960, just as the Kennedy-Nixon race was going strong. The Catholic issue was still important to some voters and Schary knocked that out of the box with a denunciation of racism and bigotry in his screenplay. Since Schary was a staunch Democrat, we can only assume that the timing of the movie's release was calculated for maximum power at the polls, as well as at the box office. Bunce played the same role on stage and was seldom seen west of the Hudson River, preferring the Broadway arena and also making his name on the popular radio show "Ethel and Albert," where he costarred with writer Peg Lynch. His role on that show was originated in 1944 by a young actor named Richard Widmark, who eventually found employment elsewhere.

p, Dore Schary; d, Vincent J. Donehue; w, Schary (based on his play); ph, Russell Harlan (Technicolor); m, Franz Waxman; ed, George Boemler; art d, Edward Carrere; cos, Marjorie Best.

Biography Drama   **Cas.**   **(Pr:A MPAA:NR)**

SUNRISE TRAIL½**   (1931) 65m TIF bw

Bob Steele, Blanche Mehaffey, Jack Clifford, Eddie Dunn, Germaine De Neel, Fred Burns, Dick Alexander.

Pretty good early talkie for Steele finds him working undercover for the local sheriff. He is out to stop a rustler and ends up falling for barmaid Mehaffey along the way. The action is fast and furious, made all the more interesting by Steele's rather small stature. Most of the brutes tower over the hero and are quickly knocked over by him without much trouble.

p, Trem Carr; d, J.P. McCarthy; w, Wellyn Totman (based on a story by Totman); ph, Archie Stout; ed, Charles A. Post.

Western   **(PR:A MPAA:NR)**

SUNSCORCHED**   (1966, Span./Ger.) 78m Balcazar P.C.-Creole Film-produktion/Featu re Film Corp. of America c (TIERRA DE FUEGO; VERGELTUNG IN CATANO)

Mark Stevens (*Sheriff Jess Kinley*), Mario Adorf (*Abel Dragna*), Marianne Koch (*Anna-Lisa*), Frank Oliveras (*Luke*), Antonio Iranzo (*Charlie*), Oscar Pellicer, Julio Pena, Albert Bessler, Mario Via, Vivian Dodds, Felipe Pena, Luis Rivera, Jesus Puche.

Stevens is the sheriff in a small Missouri town. The locals all think he is a coward when he does not stand up against the bad guys. But Koch, who loves Stevens, remains loyal. Adorf is the outlaw's headman who threatens to expose Stevens' former association with the gang should he try anything. The gang attacks a widow and a minister, killing the minister's son but Stevens fights back and kills the murderer. However the people are still unhappy and remove his authority. Stevens' past is finally revealed and his wife leaves him. Koch is killed and Stevens goes after the remaining outlaws. He kills them all and regains both the townspeople's respect and his wife's affections.

p, Ronald Rietti; d, Mark Stevens, Jesus Jaime Balcazar; w, Stevens, Irving Dennis, Alfonso Balcazar, Jose Antonio de la Loma (based on a story by Stevens); ph, Francisco Marin (Techniscope, Eastmancolor); m, Michel Auzepi, Silvestre Enzo; ed, Steven Collins; art d, Juan Alberto Soler.

Western **(PR:O MPAA:NR)**

SUNSET BOULEVARD***** (1950) 110m PAR bw

William Holden *(Joe Gillis)*, Gloria Swanson *(Norma Desmond)*, Erich von Stroheim *(Max von Mayerling)*, Nancy Olson *(Betty Schaefer)*, Fred Clark *(Sheldrake)*, Lloyd Gough *(Morino)*, Jack Webb *(Artie Green)*, Cecil B. DeMille, Hedda Hopper, Buster Keaton, Anna Q. Nilsson, H.B. Warner, Sidney Skolsky, Ray Evans, Jay Livingston, Bernice Mosk *(Themselves)*, Franklyn Farnum *(Undertaker)*, Larry Blake, Charles Dayton *(Finance Men)*, Eddie Dew *(Assistant Coroner)*, Roy Thompson *(Shoeshine Boy)*, Michael Brandon 'Archie Twitchell', Kenneth Gibson *(Salesmen)*, Peter Drynan *(Tailor)*, Ruth Clifford *(Sheldrake's Secretary)*, Bert Moorhouse *(Gordon Cole)*, E. Mason Hopper *(Doctor/Courtier)*, Yvette Vedder *(Girl on Telephone)*, Virginia Randolph, Gertrude Astor, Frank O'Connor, Eva Novak *(Courtiers)*, Al Ferguson *(Phone Standby)*, Stan Johnson *(1st Assistant Director)*, William Sheehan *(2nd Assistant Director)*, Julia Faye *(Hisham)*, Ralph Montgomery *(1st Prop Man)*, Gertrude Messinger *(Hair Dresser)*, John Skins Miller *(Hog Eye, Electrician)*, John Cortay *(Young Policeman)*, Robert Emmett O'Connor *(Jonesy, Old Policeman)*, Gerry Ganzer *(Connie)*, Joel Allen *(2nd Prop Man)*, Tommy Ivo *(Boy)*, Emmett Smith *(Man)*, Ottola Nesmith *(Woman)*, Jay Morley *(Fat Man)*, Howard Negley *(Captain of Police)*, Ken Christy *(Captain of Homicide)*, Len Hendry *(Police Sergeant)*, Arthur A. Lane, Archie R. Dalzell *(Camera Operators)*, James Hawley, Edward Wahrman *(Camera Assistants)*, Sanford E. Greenwald *(Newsreel Cameraman)*, Howard Joslin *(Police Lieutenant)*, Creighton Hale.

No other film about Hollywood comes near the devastating and utterly fascinating portrait drawn by Wilder in this fantastic film, a searing and uncompromising look at the community's zealously guarded nostalgia. And beneath it all is raging vanity, madness, and murder. This is Wilder's most important work, a haunting and utterly unforgettable profile of an aging silent film star who lives in a dream world that turns gradually into a nightmare and a young man half her age who is engulfed by the demented siren's illusionary past. The movie opens with a a jolt; the body of young man Holden is seen floating face down in Swanson's pool next to her mansion, with three bullet holes in him. Holden, though dead, is narrating the grim opening, saying, "the poor dope–he always wanted a pool, and, in the end, he got himself a pool." Holden posthumously recounts how, six months earlier, he had been grinding out a film script, not having much luck with his profession, authoring only a few B film scripts. He is running out of money and the finance company wants his car because he has failed to make payments. He slips outside to move his car from a used car lot where a friend has kept it and drives to Paramount Studios where he sees producer Clark, trying to sell a sports film entitled BASES LOADED. Reader Olson enters the office and reports that Holden's script is "from hunger." When she learns that Holden, who is present, is the author, Olson apologizes but she continues to criticize the film, calling it trite. Clark turns down Holden and even refuses to loan him $300 after telling him a sob story. Holden goes to Schwab's Drugstore. Even his slick agent, Gough, refuses him the money, telling him he should write, that the best things ever written were written out of hunger and poverty. Holden drives along Sunset Boulevard thinking about leaving Hollywood and returning to a $35-a-week newspaper job in Dayton, Ohio. He suddenly spots the two men from the finance company who are out searching for his car and he speeds off, gets a flat, and pulls into the driveway of a great, run-down mansion which Holden begins to inspect, believing the owners have moved out after seeing an ancient touring car on blocks in the garage, one bearing 1932 license plates. "It was a great big elephant of a place," Holden states, "the kind of place crazy movie people built in the crazy Twenties." He likens the dilapidated place to "that old woman in GREAT EXPECTATIONS, Miss Havisham, in her rotting wedding dress and her torn veil, taking it out on the world for giving her the go-by." A woman's voice, full of authority, calls down to him, asking why he has kept her waiting so long, and ordering him into the house. A severe-looking, bald-headed butler, von Stroheim, waves Holden inside and he is shown into the august presence of silent screen star Swanson. She thinks he is the man who is going to bury her cherished pet monkey, recently deceased. He tells her that he is not the pet mortician and that his car broke down in her driveway. Then he recognizes the fiftyish woman (Swanson was 52 at the time), saying: "You're Norma Desmond. You used to be in silent pictures. You used to be big." She lifts her chin with arrogance and indignity, replying: "I *am* big! It's the pictures that got small!" Holden begins to walk away, saying, "I knew there was something wrong with them." "They're dead," Swanson shouts after him, "they're finished! There was a time when they had the eyes of the whole world on them. But oh, no, they had to have the ears of the world, too! They opened their big mouths and out came talk, talk, talk." Holden looks at her suspiciously and retorts: "That's where the popcorn business came in. You buy yourself a bag and plug up your ears." Swanson rails against the front offices of the studios and how they "took the idols and smashed them, the Fairbankses, the Gilberts, the Valentinos! Who've we got now–just some nobodies!" Later she graphically illustrates her hatred for talking pictures by telling Holden, who symbolizes the writers who put words into the mouths of actors, "You made a rope of words and strangled this business!" Holden tells her not to blame him, he's only a writer. This interests Swanson and she quickly offers him a job working on a script she intends to use for her return to the films, a reworking of SALOME, and when Holden asks if she will play the role, she rears up her head and says, "Who else?" "I was only asking," Holden says. "I didn't know you were planning a comeback." "I *hate* that word," spits Swanson, "it's *return*, a return to the millions of people who have never forgiven me for deserting the screen." Holden takes the writing job and lives in the mansion while Swanson glares at him through dark glasses and the somber, silent von Stroheim waits on him. In the roccoco living room–a vast expanse of antique furniture–is a huge organ which whines as the wind whistles through it. Swanson insists that Holden stay with her while working on the script, living in a room over the garage and, destitute, the scriptwriter moves in. He is thus a prisoner of Swanson and her strange past. When von Stroheim shows Holden to his room he tells him just how important Swanson used to be as a silent screen star: "She was the greatest of them all. In one week she received 17,000 fan letters. There was a maharaja who came all the way from India to beg for one of her silk stockings. Later he strangled himself with it!" He thinks von Stroheim is "slightly cuckoo, too; the whole place was sort of stricken with a creeping paralysis...and, of course she had a pool, who didn't then? Mabel Normand and John Gilbert must have swum in it 10,000 midnights ago, and Vilma Banky and Rod La Rocque...it was empty now, or was it?" He notices the rats scurrying about the pool. The next day he finds von Stroheim playing the organ in the main house to amuse Swanson. Holden goes to work on Swanson's script but when he throws out some scenes, telling her that the public doesn't want to see her in *every* scene, she insists the scenes be put back in the script and that her public wants to see her in everything and that's why she still receives enormous fan mail begging her for her autographed photos. Holden puts the scenes back in the script and tells himself: "You don't yell at a sleepwalker. That's it, she was still sleepwalking along the dizzy heights of her lost career. One subject: her celluloid self. The great Norma Desmond! How could she breathe in that house so crowded with Norma Desmond?" The camera pans many tables all laden with endless photos of Swanson shown in her heyday. A few times a week von Stroheim pulls up an enormous oil painting to reveal a huge screen and the butler then runs Desmond's old silent movies. Swanson gets excited about the woman on the screen, herself. At one point she is so entranced with a scene from one of her old movies (this was QUEEN KELLY, actually shot in 1928 and directed by von Stroheim, which the director loaned to Wilder for this film) that she leaps up into the shaft of light from the projector, yelling: "Have they forgotten what a star looks like? I'll be up there again, so help me!" She turns slowly to let the blinding light from the projector bathe her aging face, closing her eyes, ecstatic to be under this tiny limelight in her own living room. On other occasions, Swanson is shown playing bridge with a group of old friends Holden calls "the waxworks, dim figures from the silent days." (This, perhaps is the cruelest line in the movie, as Holden is talking about Buster Keaton, Anna Q. Nilsson, and H.B. Warner, all great stars of silent films, all shown sitting about the card table playing bridge with Swanson.) The actress allows Holden's car to be towed away, his last method of escape. Swanson tells him that they don't need another car, anyway, that she has her Isotta- Fraschini touring car which she paid $28,000 for when new and how it features leopard skin seats and a gold phone. Holden succumbs, allowing Swanson to buy him expensive clothes and hand him pocket money and jewelry. He has become a kept man, a replacement for her pet monkey. He goes to Swanson's ornate bedroom and sees her bed, shaped like a boat, made of gold leaf (this bed used to be owned by Gladys Desloys, silent star, borrowed for the film), and tells himself that the setting befits that of a silent movie queen, "poor devil, still waving to a parade which has long since passed her by." He has learned by then that no fans write to Swanson, that it is the loyal von Stroheim who writes the fan letters and mails them to her to keep up her spirits. Swanson gives a New Year's party just for Holden, having him wear a new tuxedo she has purchased for him. A full orchestra has been hired for the occasion and a great banquet of food and champagne awaits on tables. Swanson and Holden begin to dance across the enormous living room, the actress pulling the writer close to her, then looking down at her beautiful floor appreciatively, saying, "Valentino used to say, 'there's nothing like tile for the tango.'" Then he discovers there will be no guests, just Swanson and he, and realizes that she is seducing him. He tries to joke her out of the notion, saying, "Come midnight, how about blindfolding the orchestra and smashing glasses over Max's (von Stroheim) head?" She does not appreciate his little jokes and later gives him some expensive jewelry. He tells her he can't take the gifts. She tells him that she has $10 million and "oil wells in Bakersfield...pumping...pumping!" Holden tells her that he's all wrong for her, she needs a Valentino. Swanson jumps up from a lounge and grits her teeth: "You're saying you don't want me to love you. Say it?" She slaps him and runs off. Holden grabs his coat and goes out to Schwab's drugstore and later to a party given by his friend Webb. There he meets Olson again and she tells him that she's resurrected one of his old stories which he had earlier submitted to Paramount and has some producer interested in it, that she wants him to work with her on the script. Olson is as ambitious in getting her scripts filmed as Holden used to be and she pushes him hard to develop the script. Holden calls Swanson's mansion and tells von Stroheim to pack his bags but finds that Swanson is being treated by a doctor. He leaves the party and returns to the mansion to find the one-time star has attempted suicide, slashing both wrists over his rejection of her. "What kind of silly thing was that to do?" Holden asks Swanson. "Loving you was the silly thing," she says. He wants to comfort her and tells her that "you're the only person in this stinking town who's been good to me." As the orchestra downstairs continues playing "Auld Lang Syne," Holden sits on Swanson's bed and leans forward as she pulls him downward into an embrace that is more like a web closing over his form. Later, Swanson has the pool filled and sits outside watching Holden swim. She sends her script of SALOME to Cecil B. DeMille at Paramount, expecting that the great director will accept it. While out driving with her a few evenings later, Holden goes into Schwab's drugstore to get Swanson some cigarettes and runs into Olson, who asks him to help her with that script, that Clark likes the idea and wants to back the film. Olson tells him that she's tracked him down to a Crestview number but that someone with an accent has always hung up on her. (von Stroheim, again protecting his mistress). Holden tells her that he won't work on the script and rejoins Swanson who tries to cheer up Holden later by doing impersonations of old film stars, including Mabel Normand and Charlie Chaplin (a technique later used by Judy Garland when trying to cheer up her alcoholic husband James Mason in A STAR IS BORN). All Holden can do is think about Olson and the script she wants him to write with her but he concludes that "audiences don't know that a writer writes the script; they think the actors make it up as they go along." Then Paramount calls, but since it's not DeMille, Swanson refuses to talk to an assistant. "*I've* waited 20 years for this call, now *they* can wait!" she says, and later has von Stroheim, in full livery, drive her to Paramount Studios, believing DeMille is about to produce her movie, SALOME. As they proceed toward the studio, von Stroheim, studying Swanson in a rear view mirror, sees her applying her makeup and tells her, "You will pardon me, madam, but the shadow over the left eye is not quite correct." She fixes the makeup. At the studio gate a young guard does not recognize her, refusing to admit her car but Swanson sees an older guard, O'Connor, who tells the other guard that Swanson doesn't need a pass. He opens the gate and Swanson has the car stop a moment to talk with O'Connor, "And teach your friend some manners because without me he wouldn't have a job, there wouldn't be a Paramount Studios." O'Connor agrees and passes her through with a smile, then calls DeMille at the sound stage where he is shooting, to tell him that Swanson is coming to see him. DeMille is perplexed and then upset when he learns that Paramount has been calling Swanson to rent her exotic antique car for a picture and DeMille quickly concludes that she is there thinking he has called her to make a deal on her miserable script. He doesn't want to hurt her feelings so he placates her, telling her she will hear from him soon. This is a fascinating scene in that it shows DeMille directing SAMSON AND DELILAH. He is interrupted by an unfeeling assistant who tells him that Swanson is there and adds, "She must be about a million years old." DeMille gives him a little smile and says: "I'd hate to think where that puts me. I'm old enough to be her father." DeMille thinks out loud about how to deal with her and the assistant suggests that he give Swanson an excuse. "I can give her the brush," he says, and DeMille replies with great feeling: "Thirty million fans have given her the brush–isn't that enough?...You didn't know Norma Desmond as a little girl of 17 with more courage, wit, and heart than ever came together in one youngster." When the assistant says that "she was terrible to work with," DeMille adds, "only toward the end. You know a dozen press agents working overtime can do terrible things to the human spirit." DeMille greets Swanson at the sound stage door calling her "young fellow," and they embrace. (This was, Swanson reminded Wilder, DeMille's salutation to Swanson during the 1920s.) "The last time I saw you," Swanson says, "it was at someplace gay and I was waving to you, dancing on a table." He smiles at her and says: "A lot of people were. Lindbergh had just landed in Paris." While DeMille continues his rehearsal, Swanson sits in his director's chair and one of the old lighting technicians turns a kleig light on her and the older members of the cast of the film DeMille is making flock to her. DeMille returns to her, ordering the light put back to its correct position and he tries to tell her about the mixup on the phone call she received from Paramount but can't bring himself to tell her that she will not be making SALOME with him, especially when she begins to cry and tells him how much it means to her to be back at the old studio. She tells him that she doesn't care about her pay for the film but her temperament blurts out with the line, "Remember I work only between 10 and 4:30." Outside, waiting in the car, Holden hears von Stroheim tell him that the entire building across from the sound stage used to be Swanson's dressing room. "That didn't leave much room for Wallace Reid," quips Holden. Von Stroheim then tells Holden that he had the office upstairs, where the readers department now is, and that "my walls are covered with black patent leather." Holden looks up to the readers department and sees Olson walking along the balcony toward her office. He runs up to see her. Olson still tries to persuade Holden to work with her and it is evident that she is emotionally involved with him, even though she's engaged to Webb. Holden still puts her off and goes back with Swanson who begins a merciless physical regimen to get ready for a starring role that will never come. She later reproaches Holden for going out at night and taking her car. He lies to her, saying he drove to the beach, but he has been working with Olson on the script and fears telling Swanson lest she try to commit suicide once more. When Holden returns one night to the mansion von Stroheim tells him to be careful so that Swanson will not see him coming home so late. Holden asks von Stroheim how long he is going to protect Swanson from the truth. "You must understand," von Stroheim replies, "I discovered her at 16. I made her a star and I cannot let her be destroyed." He explains that he directed all of Swanson's early films. "There were three young directors who showed promise in those days," von Stroheim proudly states. "D.W. Griffith, Cecil B. DeMille, and Max von Mayerling." The third person, of course, is himself (and he really means Erich von Stroheim, and he is correct in his statement; von Stroheim *was* that important). Holden looks at von Stroheim and says: "and she's turned you into a servant." "It was I who asked to come back," von Stroheim says, defending Swanson, "humiliating as it may seem. I could have continued my career, only I found everything unendurable after she'd left me. You see, I was her first husband." Holden is shocked by this revelation. He again tries to break with the clutching Swanson when he learns that Olson is in love with him. Swanson by then has discovered the liaison, finding a copy of the script Olson and Holden have been working on, seeing their names on the title page, side by side. She calls Olson and tells her in a faked voice that Holden is a kept man, just as Holden walks in on her, taking the phone away and telling Olson that it's all true and she can "come out and see for yourself. The address is ten-thousand-eighty-six Sunset Boulevard." Olson arrives at the address and discovers that Holden is a kept man, Holden himself letting her in and escorting her into the huge foyer and living room, saying casually: "Ever been in one of these Hollywood palazzas....That's when they were making 18,000 a week and no taxes. Careful of these tiles, they're slippery. Valentino used to dance here." He confesses how Swanson "got herself a companion–an older woman, a young man who's not doing so well." Olson doesn't want to hear it, just tells him to get his things so they can leave. She asks him to leave with her if he loves her. "Look, sweetie," replies the cynical Holden. "I got a good deal here, long-term contract with no options...It's not very admirable, but you and Arty 'Webb' can be admirable." Olson turns away, saying she can't look at him anymore. "How about looking for the exit?" he tells her and takes her to the door. Before Olson silently leaves, he switches on the pool lights and tells her that if she ever wants to take a swim she's welcome. Olson goes and Holden turns to see Swanson looking down at him from the balcony next to her bedroom. He walks up the stairs and past her without looking at her, and then begins to take only the clothes he came with, leaving all of Swanson's gifts behind. Holden tells her he's going. "I don't qualify for the job," he tells her. Holden begins to leave and Swanson tells him that she will shoot herself. "You'd be killing yourself for an empty house," Holden responds. "The audience left 20 years ago." Holden tells her DeMille doesn't want her; Paramount only wanted to rent her car. Von Stroheim enters the room and Holden tells him to stop pretending that the fan mail Swanson gets is real, asking the sad-faced servant to be honest with Swanson. Says von Stroheim resolutely, "Madam is the greatest star of them all." With eyes wide and looking only backward on her golden days, Swanson says, "You heard him." "You're a woman of 50," Holden tells her. "Now grow up. There's nothing tragic about being 50 unless you try to be 25!" But he sees she is lost to her reveries and begins to walk out. Swanson rolls her eyes after him, hissing, "No one ever leaves Norma Desmond." She runs after him, gun in hand, calling to Holden from the balcony as he walks down the circular stairway before her. She goes after him, following him outside, calling his name, but Holden doesn't turn around, keeps going. As he walks toward the pool, Swanson fires but Holden keeps walking though hit, and she fires again and again, until he turns and falls into the pool, dead. When von Stroheim runs up to Swanson she is in a daze, looking skyward into the night and whispering, "The stars are ancient, aren't they?" The next morning Holden (shown in an underwater shot looking up at his body, his face down in the water toward the camera) is fished out of the pool by police. He is still narrating from the world of the dead: "Well, this is where you came in, back at that pool again, the one I always wanted. It's dawn now and they must have photographed me a thousand times. And they got a couple of pruning hooks from the garden and fished me out...ever so gently. Funny, how gentle people get with you once you're dead. They beached me like a harpooned baby whale and started to check the damage just for the record." He describes how the crowds have assembled before the mansion, even the newsreel people and these are shown swarming about the estate, the newsreel photographers bringing equipment into the house and setting it up at the base of the stairs. Even from the world of the dead, Holden thinks of pathetic Swanson, saying how the publicity will kill her, envisioning the headlines, "Forgotten Star A Slayer, Aging Actress, Yesterday's Glamor Queen." Inside, the police wait for Swanson to come down from her bedroom. Hedda Hopper (herself) is shown on a phone reporting the story from an upstairs bedroom. Police are grilling the actress in her boudoir but she is busy making up her face and turns when she hears the word "cameras." She tells von Stroheim to tell "Mr. DeMille" that she will be down shortly to play her scene. Von Stroheim nods and the police do, too, the detective in charge telling an officer to have a car ready outside. Swanson's mind has obviously snapped, she is now back at Paramount making films and is about to do the most important scene of her star-studded career. Von Stroheim marches downstairs with great authority and goes to the newsreel cameramen, asking if their equipment is set up and if their lights are ready and they tell him that all is ready. He looks up toward the balcony. Von Stroheim, directing his last great scene, shouts, "Quiet everybody!" Then he turns to the newsmen and says, "Lights!" Above, a confused Swanson tells him she doesn't understand the scene and von Stroheim tells her, "This is the staircase of the palace." She nods in understanding, "Oh, yesss, yesss, down below, they're waiting for the princess." She sweeps her sequined gown about her with one hand, eyes wide, then begins to descend the stairs. "Cameras! Action!" yells von Stroheim. Almost as if she is floating, Swanson begins to slowly go down the stairs, policemen, reporters, all standing transfixed by her bizarre performance, as if the people on the stairs are all wax figures or props in a macabre movie, Swanson slowly wending her way downward as she glides toward von Stroheim's cameras, von Stroheim looking up at his once brilliant star with an expression of excruciating pain on his face. He is in agony. And, as Swanson moves down the stairs, Holden's voice is heard: "So they were turning again. Those cameras, which can be strangely merciful, had taken pity on Norma Desmond. The dream she had clung to so desperately had enfolded her." She reaches the bottom of the stairs, raising her arms, eyes wide, lost in the part of Salome. She suddenly stops and says that she can't go on with the scene because she is too happy, overjoyed at making a picture again. "You don't know how much I've missed all of you," she tells the dumbfounded newsmen and police; to Swanson they are her ghostly legions of co-workers and adoring fans come back to laud her once more. "And I promise you I'll never desert you again," she says, eyes wider, mouth open, glistening teeth, a stare into nowhere, "because after SALOME we'll make another picture and another...You see, this is my life! It always will be! Nothing else! Just us, the cameras, and those wonderful people out there in the dark!" She is staring straight into the camera now, to the overall viewer, her hand with long fingernails like talons stretched forward. She gives von Stroheim a serious look and says, "All right, Mr. DeMille, I'm ready for my close-up." Swanson pulls her shoulders back and begins to approach the camera slowly, eyes almost bursting out of her sockets, a huge toothy smile, jaw jutting, her arm undulating as if floating on the surface of a rippling pool, as music, soft and sweet, as was heard in the Levant thousands of years earlier, fuses with her movements, and she comes closer and closer and closer to the camera. As she does Wilder lets the enormous close-up of Swanson, almost overwhelming the camera now, go slowly out of focus, brightening her countenance so that, in a few seconds, her image is that of youth and one that is copied from the image produced in the silent era, soft focus, hot light, a blur of glamor and insanity and death as Swanson, in those last few seconds of this masterpiece, slips visually backward into the time of her heyday, into the very past she has yearned to once more embrace, magically escaping real life to live forever inside the illusion. Wilder captured the tragic and pathetic past that truly was Hollywood for the silent stars in SUNSET BOULEVARD. The film excels in ordinary and extraordinary passions and Swanson gives one of many razor-sharp insights into the whole film with her line: "We didn't need dialog. We had faces then. They don't have faces anymore, maybe one, Garbo."

This was a comeback for Swanson, an enormous return to the screen, the actress achieving here what her tragic character in SUNSET BOULEVARD could not. "After nine years of obscurity," Swanson would say later in her autobiography, *Swanson on Swanson*, "I was in the glaring spotlight again, thanks to Billy Wilder and a brilliant script." She arrived in Hollywood but did not get the attention she had received once in the 1920s when tens of thousands turned out to cheer her in a mammoth parade. Montgomery Clift had been scheduled to play the role of the young writer, but at the last moment, had backed out, saying, "I don't think I could be convincing making love to a woman twice my age." Wilder exploded when he heard the news, saying, "If he's any kind of actor he could be convincing making love to any woman!" The real reason why Clift refused the part was that he felt that by appearing on screen at his age with the 52-year-old Swanson he would further encourage the thousands of older women who wrote daily to him, begging to let them be his "mother." He desperately wanted to escape the image of a "mama's boy." Holden was the next choice but he was extremely nervous about acting in the role, although he gives a superlative performance as the reluctant gigolo, though his remarks about Swanson and the silent era often slip in their delivery from the cynical to the ruthless. Swanson felt insulted when she heard that Clift refused to appear opposite her because he felt himself too young. Holden was really 31 instead of the 25-year-old he was supposed to be playing, Swanson pointed that out to Wilder and she balked at being made older than the 50-year-old *she* was supposed to be playing, saying "can't you use makeup on Mr. Holden instead, to make him look more youthful?" He was youthful enough, presenting just the right amount of age, savvy, and sarcasm to pull off the slick part, projecting a wonderful air of cocksuredness, while dismissing the glories of the Hollywood past as Wilder himself had when first arriving in the film colony, under not too dissimilar circumstances. "I'm scared," Holden told his wife when he accepted this role. "I've agreed to do this picture and I'm not sure I can deliver." He delivered one of the finest performances of his career, and was nominated for an Oscar as Best Actor, losing to Jose Ferrer (for CYRANO DE BERGERAC) that year, but recouping for this performance by winning an Oscar for STALAG 17. Swanson, too, deservedly earned a nomination for Best Actress but lost out to Judy Holiday for BORN YESTERDAY. No one of her time better understood the glorious, fabulous, and exotic 1920s in Hollywood and the exciting, eccentric people who made it famous and infamous, than Swanson. There is much of Norma Desmond, the screen Norma Desmond, that is Swanson and she gave over that hard-earned image to the film, letting Wilder use up her silent career, even showing her in von Stroheim's QUEEN KELLY. But she was never the neurotic, mentally disturbed creature that Norma Desmond was offscreen. Before Swanson was chosen, however, Wilder and Brackett talked about the possibility of using Mary Pickford, Mae Murray, Pola Negri, or even Mae West, for the Desmond role. They concluded that these temperamental glamor queens of the 1920s had personalities and careers that were too close to home in the Desmond persona and would appear to be burlesquing themselves. But none of them could have come close to the magnificent portrayal Swanson gave and an understanding of the character that was so penetrating that she astounded the critics, the public, and even her peers. Swanson later admitted that she fell in love with SUNSET BOULEVARD and "hated to have the picture end. None had ever challenged or engrossed me more. The final mad scene raised problems. I had to descend a grand staircase crowded with extras and a few people like Hedda Hopper, in a state of derangement, and Billy Wilder wanted me to come down on the side of the stairway where the steps were narrowest. On high heels I would have tripped for sure. I played the scene barefoot. I imagined a steel ramrod in me from head to toe holding me together and descended as if in a trance." When Wilder yelled "cut!" Swanson burst into tears and all on the set gave the actress a thunderous applause and cheered. Wilder and the rest could not wait to give the actress a victory party later so they immediately threw a party that hour on the set to celebrate one of the greatest scenes ever put on film. "We were in a great state of emotion," Swanson commented. "...Norma Desmond had taken her leave." Some nights later MGM mogul Louis B. Mayer gave Swanson a lavish sit-down dinner for 20 and then the party went to the luxurious Paramount screening room where 300 of Hollywood's greatest stars and directors sat waiting to watch the first important screening of SUNSET BOULEVARD. The studio had specifically made sure that the most famous of the silent stars–those still alive–were present. Keaton, Warner, Nilsson, those "waxworks" figures in the film, were present but so too were Mickey Neilan and the great Mary Pickford with Charles "Buddy" Rogers. The normally restrained reaction at such screenings was discarded at the fabulous finish and the entire audience leapt to their feet to cheer Swanson. She was surrounded by her peers who wept openly at a performance by a silent screen actress who was better than almost anything the sound era had to offer. Younger actresses rushed up to Swanson to lavish congratulations on her, including Barbara Stanwyck, who dropped to her kness, picked up Swanson's dress, and kissed its hem as a sign of adoring appreciation. But mostly, the fallen stars of the silent screen stood close to Swanson, as if to tell her that she had appeared for all of them in SUNSET BOULEVARD. "I could read in all their eyes a single message of elation," Swanson said. "If she can do it, why should we be terrified? She's shown us that it can be done!" Swanson looked around for Mary Pickford, asking for her. A prodcuer told her: "She can't show herself, Gloria. She's overcome. We all are." Some people in Hollywood became incensed when seeing SUNSET BOULEVARD, chiefly the moguls running the studios, not the least of whom was MGM head Mayer. He saw the film at the special private showing at the Paramount lot that night and went blind crazy with anger, taking Wilder aside after the showing and yelling at him: "You bastard! You have disgraced the industry that made you and fed you! You should be tarred and feathered and run out of Hollywood!" One person not at the Paramount screening was the enigmatic Erich von Stroheim whose part was undoubtedly closer to his own career than Swanson's part was to her real life. The eccentric von Stroheim had been all the things (except Desmond's husband) he claimed to be in the movie, one of the greatest directors of the silent era, having helmed such masterpieces as GREED, BLIND HUSBANDS, FOOLISH WIVES, THE WEDDING MARCH, THE MERRY WIDOW. Wilder had used von Stroheim seven years earlier in his WW II film, FIVE GRAVES TO CAIRO, where he had convincingly played Field Marshal Erwin Eugen Rommel, but here Wilder asked him to do a part that was largely autobiographical, one where he would have to hold up his real self as an icon of the past and this, for von Stroheim, opened many old wounds. He had not lived in Hollywood for a long time, but resided in Europe where he was treated as a master filmmaker (and rightly so). Hollywood was a Mecca that had crumbled for von Stroheim two decades earlier. His part is the most bitter of all and the most self-humiliating, one which von Stroheim thereafter referred to as "that goddamned butler role!" Here Wilder was asking von Stroheim to enact what Hollywood always thought of him, a mad director. Not only that, but he was asked to play a lackey, a manservant, not even a fallen aristocrat, nor a down-on-his heels German officer, which had always been his on-screen persona. But the great director needed the money and took the role, then tried to help Wilder by making many suggestions on everything from dialog to props. His amazing memory of Hollywood lore contributed mightily to the overall look of authenticity in the film. It was he who suggested using his film with Swanson, QUEEN KELLY. Some of the plot elements of SUNSET BOULEVARD can be found, interestingly enough, in the von Stroheim film. In QUEEN KELLY, as in Wilder's film, an older woman, terrified of aging, is holding on to a younger man who is kept in the luxury of a palace, and the climax arrives when the older woman announces her wedding to the reluctant gigolo-lover at a party which causes a fatal confrontation. Both older women in the two films are insanely jealous of their men and where Holden falls dead in a swimming pool at the hands of Swanson in SUNSET BOULEVARD, Swanson drowns in a lake to commit suicide in QUEEN KELLY. Both women live in baroque mansions, smoke exotic weeds–the queen cigars, Norma Desmond Turkish Abdullas–and both dote on ornate mirrors and photographs of themselves surrounding them in every room of their mansions. To make the irony complete, Swanson had played the innocent girl in QUEEN KELLY 22 years earlier in the silent days while Olson plays the innocent girl in SUNSET BOULEVARD. Von Stroheim, therefore, in suggesting Wilder use a clip from his silent film QUEEN KELLY to show Desmond-Swanson as the silent film star of old, also loaned Wilder the essential plot elements for SUNSET BOULEVARD. During the production Wilder, never one to shower compliments on anyone, turned to von Stroheim and said, "Von, you were always 10 years ahead of your time." Von Stroheim never blinked an eye when correcting Wilder in his one word response, "Twenty." One scene von Stroheim found particularly embarrassing was where he was required to drive Swanson to Paramount Studios. He confessed that he could not drive. He pretended to, however, the camera staying close on him as he sits behind the steering wheel, turning it, but all the while the ancient Isotta-Fraschini was being towed by a truck. Some of von Stroheim's ideas for the film were rejected by Wilder. At one point von Stroheim proposed that he be shown washing and later ironing Swanson's underwear. No, said Wilder, that was too much. This suggestion may not have been as perverse or bizarre as later thought, but merely a memory von Stroheim had of another, earlier film, THREE FACES EAST, a film in which he unpacks Constance Bennett's bags, taking great pains to remove her lingerie without creating wrinkles. The mansion serving as Swanson's palace was an actual 25-room French-Italian villa built in 1908 by a wealthy Mexican dignitary, situated not on Sunset Boulevard, but on Wilshire Boulevard and Lorraine Avenue and was then owned by J. Paul Getty. The use of the building (torn down in the late 1950s) was arranged for by Wilder himself. The director agreed to build the pool used in the film and leave it as part payment for the use of the house. Wilder was not to be outdone by von Stroheim in the department of bizarre scenes. He actually opened SUNSET BOULEVARD with one of the most outlandish sequences on film, one which was later dropped. Instead of being found dead floating in the pool, Holden is seen in a morgue. Wilder originally showed a row of slabs in the county morgue, panning the bodies stretched out until coming to the final slab where two bare feet protrude from beneath a sheet. A tag is put on the big toe of one of the feet and suddenly a corpse sits up. It's Holden and he begins to have a conversation with the other cadavers, explaining why he is there. When this scene was first shown at a preview, audiences howled with laughter at the ridiculous scene and Wilder cut it before general release. But certainly the most grotesque scene in this film is the one showing the elaborate burial of Swanson's pet monkey in her back yard by moonlight, as a solemn von Stroheim carries forth the deceased animal adorned in silk. How Wilder planned to stage this macabre scene baffled his assistants when they read over his script. One of them went to the director and asked how to manage the strange burial and Wilder shrugged and replied, "You know, the usual monkey-funeral sequence."

p, Charles Brackett; d, Billy Wilder; w, Wilder, Brackett, D.M. Marshman, Jr. (based on the story "A Can of Beans" by Brackett, Wilder); ph, John F. Seitz; m, Franz Waxman, "Salome's Dance of the Seven Veils," Richard Strauss; ed, Doane Harrison, Arthur Schmidt; art d, Hans Dreier, John Meehan; set d, Sam Comer, Ray Moyer; cos, Edith Head; spec eff, Gordon Jennings, Farciot Edouart; m/l, "The Paramount-Don't-Want-Me Blues," Jay Livingston, Ray Evans; makeup, Wally Westmore, Karl Silvera.

Drama   **Cas.**   **(PR:C-O MPAA:NR)**

SUNSET COVE*   (1978) 87m Cal-Am c

Jay B. Larson (Dexter), Karen Fredrik (Joyce), John Carradine (Judge Winslow), John Durren (Kragg), Burr Schmidt (Mayor Nix), Ray Andrews (Mike), Steven Fisher (Chubby), Shirley Ann Broger (Mimi), Jane Ralston (Joanne), Mark Flynn (Bart), Will Walker (John).

A group of teenie-bopping beach bums decide to take time off from their beer and tan fests to fight some condominium developers who want to buy their favorite beach strip. The local sheriff is in with the businessmen but the kids fight back with sexual blackmail. Not for all filmgoers, to say the least.

p, Harry Hope; d, Al Adamson; w, Cash Maintenant, Budd Donnelly; ph, Gary Graver (CFI Color); m, Bruce Stewart; ed, Ron Moler.

Teenage Drama   **(PR:O MPAA:R)**

SUNSET IN EL DORADO*½   (1945) 65m REP bw

Roy Rogers (Himself), George "Gabby" Hayes (Gabby), Dale Evans (Lucille Wiley), Hardie Albright (Cecil Phelps), Margaret Dumont (Aunt Dolly), Roy Barcroft (Buster Welch), Tom London (Sheriff Gridley), Stanley Price (Lyle Fish), Rob Wilke (Curley Roberts), Ed Cassidy (U.S. Marshal), Dorothy Granger (Maisie), Bob Nolan and the Sons of the Pioneers, Edmund Cobb, Hank Bell, Jack Kirk, Gino Corrado, Frank Ellis, Tex Cooper, Bert Morehouse, Joe McGuinn, Tex Terry, Bud Osborne, Trigger the Horse.

After growing bored with her mundane job, Evans quits and heads to an old ghost town where her grandmother had been a notorious dancehall queen. In a dream sequence that takes up much of the film, Evans sees herself as her famous ancestor and meets the various characters of her Old West life. Among them is, of course, Rogers, a nice-guy cowboy. The unusual plot is not particularly well handled, with a faulty script and middling direction. There is some action but a larger emphasis on the songs, a feature that was beginning to become rather noticeable in Rogers' films of this period. Despite the weakness this series entry did pretty well at the box office.

p, Louis Gray; d, Frank McDonald; w, John K. Butler (based on a story by Leon Abrams); ph, William Bradford; ed, Tony Martinelli; md, Morton Scott; art d, Frank Hotaling; ch, Larry Ceballos.

Western   **(PR:A MPAA:NR)**

SUNSET IN THE WEST½**   (1950) 67m REP c

Roy Rogers (Himself), Estelita Rodriguez (Carmelita), Penny Edwards (Dixie Osborne), Gordon Jones (Splinters), Will Wright (Sheriff Osborne), Pierre Watkin (MacKnight), Charles LaTorre (Nick Corella), William J. Tannen (John Kimball), Gaylord Pendleton (Walter Kimball), Paul E. Burns ("Blink" Adams), Dorothy Ann White (Dot), Foy Willing and the Riders of the Purple Sage, Trigger the Horse.

Pretty good Rogers' series entry features him as a deputy sheriff. He comes onto a gunrunning gang who use the local railroads and some unwilling agents to ply their trade. Rogers stops them, of course, with a terrific climactic gun battle. A good script and good direction made this one of Rogers' best films before he made the switch to TV. Willing's title song, crooned by the star, featured an unusual novelty: lyrics in both English and Spanish.

p, Eddy White; d, William Witney; w, Gerald Geraghty; ph, Jack Marta (Trucolor); m, R. Dale Butts; ed, Tony Martinelli; art d, Frank Hotaling; spec eff, Howard Lydecker, Theodore Lydecker; m/l, "Rollin' Wheels," "Sunset in the West," Foy Willing (sung by Roy Rogers), "When a Pretty Girl Passes By," Jack Elliott, Aaron Gonzales (sung by Estelita Rodriguez).

Western   **(PR:A MPAA:NR)**

SUNSET IN VIENNA   (SEE: SUICIDE LEGION, 1940, Brit.)

SUNSET IN WYOMING*½   (1941) 65m REP bw

Gene Autry, Smiley Burnette, Maris Wrixon, George Cleveland, Robert Kent, Sarah Edwards, Monte Blue, Dick Elliott, John Dilson, Stanley Blystone, Eddie Dew, Fred Burns, Reed Howes, Ralph Peters, Syd Saylor, Tex Terry, Lloyd Whitlock, Herman Hack, Champion the Horse.

Lesser Autry effort finds him away from the Wild West, a recurring factor in several of his pictures of the time. A lumber king is stripping the land of timber, thus causing a real potential for flooding. It's up to Autry to show the man a thing or two about conservation. This lands him at a country club party for the rich where everyone wears tie and tails, including comedy sidekick Burnette. The predictable humor results in this unoriginal, weak outing for the cowboy star.

p, Harry Grey; d, William Morgan; w, Ivan Goff, Anne Morrison Chapin (based on a story by Joe Blair); ph, Reggie Lanning; m, Raoul Kraushaar; ed, Tony Martinelli; md, Kraushaar.

Western   **(PR:A MPAA:NR)**

SUNSET MURDER CASE*   (1941) 59m George Hirliman bw

Sally Rand (Kathy O'Connor), Reed Hadley (Oliver Helton), Dennie Moore (Lou Fleming), Esther Kane (Penny), Paul Sutton (Bapti Stephani), Stanley Price (Luigi), Vince Barnett (Martin), Esther Muir (Lora Wynne), Frank O'Connor (Tom O'Connor), George Douglas (Carlo Rossmore), Lona Andre (Nita Madera), Mary Brodel (Jane Baird), Bruce Mitchell (Everett), Eddie Gordon (Rankin), Lester Dorr (Editor), Bill Duray (Interne), Monte Carter (Staufer), Henry King and Orchestra.

An awful gangster film which features famed fan dancer Rand, though she doesn't dance in this one. The routine and extremely corny story involves Rand's detective father O'Connor who is shot down by some mobsters. Rand vows her revenge and achieves it without much trouble. Direction and script are completely amateurish in this independent production. The cast matches the poor production values with uniformly bad ensemble work.

d, Louis Gasnier; w, Arthur Hoerl, Paul Franklin (based on a story by Harold Joyce); ph, Mack Stengler; m, Hugo Riesenfeld, (Sam Coslow); ed, Martin G. Cohn.

Crime   **(PR:C MPAA:NR)**

SUNSET OF A CLOWN   (SEE: THE NAKED NIGHT, 1956, Swed.)

SUNSET OF POWER½**   (1936) 66m UNIV bw

Buck Jones (Cliff Lea), Dorothy Dix (Ruth Brannum), Charles B. Middleton (Neil Brannum), Donald Kirk (Page Cothran), Ben Corbett (Red), Charles King (Coley), William Lawrence (Bud Rolfe), Joe Delacruzo (Indian Joe), Nina Campana (Rosita), Eumenco Blanco (Andreas), Murdock McQuarrie, Alan Sears, Monte Vandergrift, Glenn Strange, Silver the Horse.

Hard-bitten cattle rancher Middleton wants his daughter, Dix, to be just as tough and driven as he is. Jones, along with King and Corbett (forming one of the earliest trios in western movie history), help him out when they discover the ranch foreman is a rustler. There are some nice characterizations here not normally found in program westerns as well as some good gun play, making this a better-than-average series entry for Jones. Also, Jones' attempt at a more mature approach to his films results in a more realistic view of the West than his previous work offered.

p, Buck Jones; d, Ray Taylor; w, Earle Snell (based on a story by J.E. Grinsted); ph, Allen Thompson, Herbert Kirkpatrick; ed, Bernard Loftus.

Western   (PR:A MPAA:NR)

SUNSET ON THE DESERT**   (1942) 63m REP bw

Roy Rogers *(Roy/Sloane)*, George "Gabby" Hayes *(Gabby Whittaker)*, Lynne Carver *(Ann)*, Frank M. Thomas *(Judge Kirby)*, Beryl Wallace *(Julie Craig)*, Glenn Strange *(Louie)*, Douglas Fowley *(McCall)*, Fred Burns *(Prentiss)*, Roy Barcroft *(Nelson)*, Henry Wills *(Eddie)*, Forrest Taylor *(Belknap)*, Bob Nolan, Bob Woodward, Edward Cassidy, Pat Brady, Cactus Mack, The Sons of the Pioneers, Trigger the Horse.

Rogers plays a double role as both hero and villain. A group of outlaws led by the bad Rogers mistakes good guy Roy as their leader. He goes along with them in hopes of eventually turning them over to the authorities, but the villainous lookalike shows up before Rogers can carry out his plan. After a bit of fisticuffs and a few gunshots, however, Rogers delivers the gang to the law. An average entry for Rogers with a few tunes, none especially memorable, mixed in as usual.

p&d, Joseph Kane; w, Gerald Geraghty; ph, Reggie Lanning; ed, Lester Orlebeck; md, Cy Feuer; m/l, Bob Nolan, Tim Spencer.

Western   **Cas.**   (PR:AA MPAA:NR)

SUNSET PASS**½   (1933) 64m PAR bw

Randolph Scott *(Ash Preston)*, Tom Keene *(Jack Rock)*, Kathleen Burke *(Jane Preston)*, Harry Carey, Jr *(John Hesbitt)*, Noah Beery, Jr *(Marshal Blake)*, Leila Bennett, Fuzzy Knight, Kent Taylor, George Barbier, Vince Barnett, Patricia Farley, Charles Middleton, Tom London, Christian J. Frank, Frank Beal, Al Bridge, Bob Kortman, James Mason.

Scott is a government agent out to break up a gang of rustlers in this western. One of 10 Paramount B-westerns with an A-western appearance starring Scott in a Zane Grey story mostly directed by Hathaway made during the early 1930s when the studio was near bankruptcy. The studio solved its financial problems during those bank-holiday Depression times by cleverly melding footage from its high-budget silents starring Jack Holt (whose contract with the studio had lapsed) with entirely new close-action shots using the same costumes worn by different actors. In this film, as in the others of the series, the uncredited Holt is seen in the costly location long shots; the close-up cuts are of Scott. All of the synchronous sound takes were thus made under tightly controlled studio conditions. While many other companies routinely used stock footage and cuts from earlier films, Paramount made the technique a way of life for its westerns during this period. The matches were well done; the Scott-starring Grey westerns are among the best of the genre, and author Grey himself attested that of all the actors who had portrayed his protagonists, Scott came closest to his visualized ideal. Holt's silent version of this film had been released four years previously; a third version followed in 1946. Director Hathaway later went on to make such noted pictures as CALL NORTHSIDE 777 (1948) and TRUE GRIT (1969).

p, Adolph Zukor; d, Henry Hathaway; w, Jack Cunningham, Gerald Geraghty (based on the novel by Zane Grey); ph, Archie Stout; art d, Earl Hedrick.

Western   (PR:A MPAA:NR)

SUNSET PASS**   (1946) 58m RKO bw

James Warren *(Rocky)*, Nan Leslie *(Jane)*, John Laurenz *(Chito)*, Jane Greer *(Helen)*, Robert Barrat *(Curtis)*, Harry Woods *(Cinnabar)*, Robert Clarke *(Ash)*, Steve Brodie *(Slagle)*, Harry Harvey *(Doab)*, Slim Balch, Roy Bucko, Steve Stevens, George Plues, Clem Fuller, Bob Dyer, Artie Ortego, Buck Bucko *(Posse Men)*, Slim Hightower, Boyd Stockman, Glen McCarthy *(Robbers)*, Carl Faulkner *(Passenger)*, Frank O'Connor *(Station Agent)*, Florence Pepper, Vonne Lester *(Dancers)*, Robert Bray, Dennis Waters *(Bank Clerks)*, Maria Dodd, Dorothy Curtiss *(Women at Station)*.

This third version of the Zane Grey novel is a simple, straightforward B-western. Warren plays the frontier lawman who, with the assistance of sidekick Laurenz, tries to crack a group of train robbers who work along the Arizona borderline. Complications arise when love interest Leslie's younger brother proves to be one of the gang. The film boasts good direction, but the leads' less than dynamic characterizations result in a typical programmer.

p, Herman Schlom; d, William Berke; w, Norman Houston (based on the novel by Zane Grey); ph, Frank Redman; m, Paul Sawtell; ed, Samuel E. Beetley; md, C. Bakaleinikoff; art d, Albert S. D'Agostino, Lucius Croxton; set d, Darrell Silvera, William Stevens; m/l, Sawtell.

Western   (PR:A MPAA:NR)

SUNSET RANGE**   (1935) 60m FD bw

Hoot Gibson, Mary Doran, James C. Eagles, Walter McGrail, John Elliott, Eddie Lee, Ralph Lewis, Kitty McHugh, Martha Sleeper, Fred Gilman.

When Doran's brother uses her trunk to hide some money he stole from his outlaw gang, she finds herself in trouble. The brother has just bought a ranch for Doran, and the outlaws want her to sell it and give them their money back. Fortunately Gibson and sidekick Elliott come to the rescue,

saving her after she was kidnaped. A strictly by-the-book western, SUNSET RANGE used a tie-in contest with a national toothpaste company in order to draw crowds to the theater.

d, Ray McCarey; w, Paul Schofield; ph, Gilbert Warrenton; ed, Ralph Dietrich.

Western   **Cas.**   (PR:A MPAA:NR)

SUNSET SERENADE***   (1942) 58m REP bw

Roy Rogers *(Roy)*, George "Gabby" Hayes *(Gabby)*, Helen Parrish *(Sylvia Clark)*, Onslow Stevens *(Gregg Jackson)*, Joan Woodbury *(Vera Martin)*, Frank M. Thomas *(Clifford Sheldon)*, Roy Barcroft *(Bart Reynolds)*, Jack Kirk *(Sheriff Praskins)*, Dick Wessel, Rex Lease, Jack Ingram, Fred Burns, Budd Buster, Jack Rockwell, Bob Nolan and the Sons of the Pioneers, Trigger the Horse.

When Easterner Parrish arrives at her recently purchased ranch, villain Stevens tries to cheat her out of it. It is up to Rogers to sing a few numbers and save the day as well. Woodbury plays Stevens' girl friend who ends up in a catfight with Parrish. Some good dialog and strong direction make this a pretty good outing for Rogers, one of the better entries in his series.

p&d, Joseph Kane; w, Earl Felton (based on a story by Robert Yost); ph, Bud Thackery; ed, Arthur Roberts; md, Morton Scott, art d, Russell Kimball; m/l, "Song of the San Joaquin," "I'm a Cowboy Rockefeller," "I'm Headin' for the Home Corral," Tim Spencer, Bob Nolan.

Western   **Cas.**   (PR:A MPAA:NR)

SUNSET TRAIL**   (1932) 62m TIF bw

Ken Maynard, Ruth Hiatt, Philo McCullough, Frank Rice, Buddy Hunter, Dick Alexander, Frank Ellis, Slim Whitaker, Jack Rockwell, Lew Meehan, Bud Osborne, Bud McClure, Tarzan the Horse.

Typical cowboy story has Maynard and a friend protecting a lady rancher from some bad men. When the villains kill Maynard's pal, he goes after them with the usual fighting and gunplay. Routine fare for the genre with standard production values.

p, Phil Goldstone; d, B. Reeves Eason; w, Bennett Cohen; ph, Arthur Reed; ed, S. Roy Luby.

Western   **Cas.**   (PR:A MPAA:NR)

SUNSET TRAIL***   (1938) 60m PAR bw

William Boyd *(Hopalong Cassidy)*, George "Gabby" Hayes *(Windy)*, Russell Hayden *(Lucky)*, Charlotte Wynters *(Ann Marsh)*, Jane Clayton *(Dorrie Marsh)*, Robert Fiske *(Monte Keller)*, Kathryn Sheldon *(Abigail Snodgrass)*, Maurice Cass *(E. Prescott Furbush)*, Anthony Nace *(Steve Dorman)*, Kenneth Harlan *(John Marsh)*, Alphonse Ethier *(Superintendent)*, Glenn Strange *(Bouncer)*, Jack Rockwell *(Stage Driver)*, Tom London *(Patrol Captain)*, Claudia Smith *(Mary Rogers)*, Jim Toney, Fred Burns, Jerry Jerome, Jim Corey, Frank Ellis, Horace B. Carpenter.

An entertaining Boyd western that boasts some unusually fine photography. When a rancher is murdered Boyd goes undercover as an Eastern dude in order to fool and capture the villains. Some good humor in the screenplay with a fun performance by Boyd. (See HOPALONG CASSIDY Series, Index.)

p, Harry Sherman; d, Lesley Selander; w, Norman Houston (based on a story by Clarence E. Mulford); ph, Russell Harlan; ed, Robert Warwick; art d, Lewis J. Rachmil.

Western   (PR:A MPAA:NR)

SUNSHINE AHEAD**   (1936, Brit.) 64m Baxter and Barter/UNIV bw

Eddie Pola *(The Producer)*, Betty Astell *(The Girl)*, Leslie Perrins *(The Critic)*, Eve Lister *(The Secretary)*, Jack Payne and His Band, Leonard Henry, Harry S. Pepper, Harold Ramsay, Ruth Naylor, Troise and His Mandoliers, The Two Leslies, Doris Arnold, George Baker, Webster Booth, The Sherman Fisher Girls, Dan Carlos, Rios and Santos, The Harmonica Band.

Pola is a producer who decides to hold a radio broadcast outdoors. Despite some problems from jealous critic Perrins the show goes off well in this programmer designed to showcase popular radio stars of the time.

p, John Baxter; d, Wallace Orton; w, Con West, Geoffrey Orme; ph, Jack Barker.

Musical   (PR:A MPAA:NR)

SUNSHINE BOYS, THE****   (1975) 111m UA c

Walter Matthau *(Willy Clark)*, George Burns *(Al Lewis)*, Richard Benjamin *(Ben Clark)*, Lee Meredith *(Nurse in Sketch)*, Carol Arthur *(Doris)*, Rosetta LeNoire *(Nurse)*, F. Murray Abraham *(Mechanic)*, Howard Hesseman *(Commercial Director)*, Jim Cranna *(TV Director)*, Ron Rifkin *(TV Floor Manager)*, Jennifer Lee *(Helen)*, Fritz Feld, Jack Bernardi *(Men at Audi-*

tion), Garn Stephens (*Stage Manager*), Santos Morales (*Desk Clerk*), Archie Hahn (*Assistant at Audition*), Sid Gould (*Patient*), Tom Spratley (*Card Player*), Rashel Novikoff (*Woman in Hotel*), Sammy Smith (*Man on Street*), Dan Resin (*Mr. Ferranti*), Milt Kogan (*Doctor*), Bob Goldstein (*Waiter*), Phyllis Diller, Steve Allen (*Themselves*), Walter Stocker (*TV Executive*), Duchess Dale (*Ben's Secretary*), Bill Reddick Announcer, Eddie Villery (*Delivery Boy*), Gary K. Steven (*Boy*).

One of Neil Simon's best movies comes from his 1972 play that was not nearly the hit he had with other works. Jack Benny had been slated to star with old pal Burns (who, at the age of 79, was making his first movie appearance in 35 years and won the Best Supporting Actor Oscar, which was the only fly in the ointment of ONE FLEW OVER THE CUCKOO'S NEST, the film that swept everything else that year) but died in December, 1974, so Matthau took the job. Over the objections of his advisors, Matthau took the job and showed his comedic talents again, no mean task when playing opposite a master like Burns. The play and film are based on the lives of Smith and Dale, whose "Dr. Kronkheit" sketch is a classic they performed in their dotage on the Ed Sullivan TV show after having done it in vaudeville for decades. Matthau is a retired comic who is barely making a living doing bits on commercials that his nephew, Benjamin, an agent, has secured for him. He's auditioning for a silly potato chip TV spot for advertising director Hesseman when he blows his lines and decides that this isn't show business and he no longer wants to be a part of it. There's a nostalgic TV special coming up and Benjamin books Matthau on it, hoping that he will put aside his rancor toward his former partner, Burns, and unite this last time for the benefit of all those people who never saw them in the flesh. Burns and Matthau haven't been talking for years and the mere mention of Burns is enough to send Matthau's blood pressure soaring. But he buries his enmity and agrees to see his erstwhile friend. The two men meet and it's easy to see that they hate as well as love each other. They talk about all of their compatriots who've since died, the times they had together, and finally get down to rehearsing the sketch that made them household words way back when they were known as "The Sunshine Boys." Battles begin immediately as they argue over the first words of the sketch. There's a knock at the door and the disagreement is whether or not the opening line was "Come in" or "Enter." They fight bitterly about that and it almost winds up with blows thrown. Benjamin calms down his uncle and the men go in to do the special, being directed by Cranna. In the sketch is Meredith, a stacked blonde who plays the nurse. (The woman who played it with them years ago is so old she's gone through the change of life, twice.) No sooner does rehearsal for the camera begin when Matthau and Burns argue again. They manage to run through most of the sketch (which is not as funny as Smith and Dale's) and when Burns insists on using a line that Matthau hates, Matthau stalks off and has a heart attack. He's taken to the hospital, plays some funny dialog with nurse LeNoire, and eventually gets better. Benjamin is married to Lee and she can't bear the thought of having irascible Matthau live with them so Matthau goes off to spend his final days at the Actors' Home in New Jersey. When Burns comes to see him, the two men begin reminiscing and remember the good times they shared. The heart is then warmed and a tear invades the eye as Burns announces that he is going to move into the home as well and they will again be together. A solid movie with stellar performances from all. In a small role as a garage mechanic, note F. Murray Abraham who won his Oscar for AMADEUS. Playing a doctor is actor Milt Kogan, who specializes in playing doctors (he did it in E.T. plus many more) perhaps because he is actually a doctor. Kogan always wanted to act but his parents insisted he go to medical school. After graduating and opening a practice, he spent his evenings acting, received excellent reviews for his work in various Los Angeles stage shows, and now divides his time between the office, where most of his patients are fellow actors, and performing. The associate producer was Roger Rothstein, who later became producer, then executive producer on many of Simon's movies. Director Ross' ex-ballerina wife, Nora Kaye, functioned as his assistant. The movie was made in New York, New Jersey, and California and started Burns into his second movie career. Simon and art director Brenner were nominated for Oscars, as was Matthau. Simon's one-liners were never delivered better or with more of a reason. In many of his works, ordinary people are seen to be incredibly witty. Here, since the two leads are supposed to be comics, the jokes make more sense.

p, Ray Stark; d, Herbert Ross; w, Neil Simon (based on his play); ph, David M. Walsh (Panavision, Metrocolor); ed, Margaret Booth, John F. Burnett; prod d, Albert Brenner; set d, Marvin March; cos, Pat Norris, Seth Banks; makeup, Dick Smith.

Comedy   **Cas.**   **(PR:A-C   MPAA:PG)**

SUNSHINE SUSIE   (SEE: OFFICE GIRL, THE, 1931, Brit.)

SUNSTRUCK**½   (1973, Aus.) 90m BEF c

Harry Secombe (*Stanley Evans*), Maggie Fitzgibbon (*Shirley Marshall*), John Meillon (*Mick Cassidy*), Dawn Lake (*Sal Cassidy*), Peter Whittle (*Pete Marshall*), Dennis Jordan (*Steve Cassidy*), Bobby Limb, Jack Allen, Roger Cox, Norman Erskine, Tommy Mack, John Armstrong, Stuart Wagstaff, Jess Ashby, Max Brouggy, Benita Collings, Charles McCallam.

Simple but warm-hearted story of a teacher (Secombe) who migrates to Australia after a failed romance. He gets a position teaching in a small

outback village with a classroom ranging from ages 7 to 15. After getting homesick for his old school choir a local official suggests that Secombe start a choir with his new students. The official (Meillon) also plays Cupid when he fixes Secombe up with Fitzgibbon, an earthy, hard-working local woman. Secombe projects a naive earnestness in his role and is given good support from the cast. The production credits are suitable.

p, Jack Neary, James Grafton; d, James Gilbert; w, Grafton; ph, Brian West; m, Peter Knight; ed, Anthony Buckley.

Romance/Drama   **(PR:A   MPAA:NR)**

SUPER COPS, THE***   (1974) 95m MGM/UA c

Ron Leibman (*Dave Greenberg*), David Selby (*Bob Hantz*), Sheila E. Frazier (*Sara*), Pat Hingle (*Lt. Novik*), Dan Frazer (*Capt. Krasna*), Joseph Sirola (*Lt. O'Shaughnessy*), Arny Freeman (*Judge Kellner*), Bernard Kates (*D.A. Heller*), Alex Colon (*Carlos*), Charles Turner (*Joe Hayes*), Ralph Wilcox (*John Hayes*), Al Fann (*Frank Hayes*), David Greenberg (*Det. Basoff*), Robert Hantz (*Det. Neel*), Norman Bush (*Billy*), Arthur French (*Victor*), Tamu (*Girl*), Hector Troy (*Angel*), Charles White (*Old Sarge*), Ralph Strait (*Instructor*), Joseph P. McCartney (*Lt. -- Gym Instructor*), Pat Corley (*Capt. Busch*), Albert Henderson (*Capt. Arbow*), Barton Heyman (*Lt. Stratton*).

Falling somewhere between THE FRENCH CONNECTION and SERPICO, THE SUPER COPS is a cartoon-like action film based on the true-life exploits of two New York City cops who were dubbed "Batman and Robin" by the press. Fighting red tape and harassment by their peers, Leibman and Selby go after the pushers and dope dealers in the Bedford-Stuyvesant ghetto. Using unorthodox methods, the two make a record number of arrests, using the help of sympathetic prostitute Frazier. Direction is fast and furious with good performances by Leibman and Selby. Their interpretation of the roles gives the action a necessary realistic edge that gives the story credibility. Watch for Greenberg and Hantz, the two real-life super cops, in bit parts as detectives.

p, William Belasco; d, Gordon Parks; w, Lorenzo Semple, Jr. (based on the book by L. H. Whittemore); ph, Dick Kratina (Metrocolor); m, Jerry Fielding; ed, Harry Howard; art d, Stephen Hendrickson.

Action/Crime   **(PR:O   MPAA:R)**

SUPER DRAGON   (SEE: SECRETA AGENT SUPER DRAGON, 1966, Fr./Ital./Ger./Monaco)

SUPER DUDE   (SEE: HANGUP, 1974)

SUPER FUZZ*   (1981) 97m Transcinema-TV, Inc./AE c (AKA: SUPERSNOOPER)

Terence Hill (*Dave Speed*), Ernest Borgnine (*Willy Dunlop*), Joanne Dru (*Rosy Labouche*), Marc Lawrence (*Torpedo*), Julie Gordon (*Evelyn*), Lee Sandman (*Chief McEnroy*), Herb Goldstein (*Silvius*), Don Sebastian (*Dingo*), Sal Borghese (*Paradise Alley*), Claudio Ruffini (*Tragedy Row*), Sergio Smacchi (*Slot Machine*), Woody Woodbury, Dow Stout, Jack McDermott, Charles D. Thomas, Charles Buie, Bobby Gale, Ben Taylor, Florence McGee.

After being exposed to radiation, spaghetti-western veteran Hill gains extraordinary powers that make him invincible to crooks, thieves, and hoodlums. With his partner, Borgnine, the supercharged cop goes after mobster Lawrence, catches bullets with his teeth, and jokes it up in the face of some awful special effects and stupid gags. The film reeks of its low budget and quickie status, bad performances both in front of and behind the camera.

p, Maximilian Wolkoff; d, Sergio Corbucci; w, Corbucci, Sabatino Ciuffini; ph, Silvano Ippoliti (Technicolor); m, La Bionda; ed, Eugene Alabiso; prod d, Marco Dentici; spec eff, Dino Galiano, Cass Gillespie; makeup, Maurice St. Just.

Comedy   **Cas.**   **(PR:C   MPAA:PG)**

SUPER INFRAMAN, THE   (SEE: INFRA-MAN 1975, Hong Kong)

SUPER SLEUTH***   (1937) 75m RKO bw

Jack Oakie (*Willard "Bill" Martin*), Ann Sothern (*Mary Strand*), Eduardo Ciannelli (*Prof. Horman*), Alan Bruce (*Larry Frank*), Edgar Kennedy (*Lt. Garrison*), Joan Woodbury (*Doris Dunne*), Bradley Page (*Ralph Waring*), Paul Guilfoyle (*Gibbons, Film Director*), Willie Best (*Warts*), William Corson (*Beckett*), Alec Craig (*Eddie, Doorman*), Richard Lane (*Barker*), Paul Hurst (*Motorcycle Cop*), George Rosener (*Policeman*), Fred Kelsey (*Jailer*), Robert E. O'Connor (*Casey, Cop*), Philip Morris (*Sullivan*), Dick Rush (*Grimes*), Dewey Robinson (*Film Gangster*).

A clever and original comedy features Oakie as a movie detective who takes his onscreen persona too seriously. He decides that his movie profession is the real career for him instead of acting and takes up sleuthing in Los Angeles. The egotistical star finds himself in hot water when he takes on a blackmail/murder case that's been baffling the cops. Unwittingly Oakie hires Ciannelli to help him, not realizing that this is the very man he's after.

Oakie is marvelous in the role with some fine comic moments. The support from Sothern as the studio publicist trying to retrieve the fantasy-minded star is equally good. The film is blessed with a clever script, and fine direction, which deftly handles both the comic and suspense elements. Filmed before as GENIUS AT WORK.

p, Edward Small; d, Ben Stoloff; w, Gertrude Purcell, Ernest Pagano (based on a play by Harry Segall); ph, Joseph H. August; ed, William Hamilton; art d, Van Nest Polglase; spec eff, Vernon L. Walker

Comedy/Mystery   **(PR:A   MPAA:NR)**

SUPER SPOOK**   (1975) 103m Levitt-Pickman c

Leonard Jackson (Super Spook), Bill Jay (Hi-Yo), Tony King (Sgt. Sandwich), Bob Reed (Rev. Ignatius Dooley Tile), Virginia Fields (Bag Woman), Marcella Lowery (Bag Woman's Daughter), Sam McKnight (Big D.).

Jackson stars in this comic blaxploitation picture as a private detective who has none of the talents or laurels of Shaft, the character played by Richard Roundtree in the 1971 movie of the same name. He and his sidekick, Jay, do their best to rid Harlem of its undesirables, but that proves to be too large a task for these bumbling misfits. A harmless picture which, like the rest in the genre, quickly became dated.

p, Ed Dessisso; d, Anthony Major; w, Dessisso, Leonard Jackson, Bill Jay, Tony King, Anthony Major (based on an original idea by Major); ph, Jim Walker; m, Rheet Taylor; ed, Sandy Tung.

Crime/Comedy   **(PR:O   MPAA:R)**

SUPER VAN*   (1977) 91m Empire Releasing c

Mark Schneider (Clint Morgan), Katie Saylor (Karen Trenton), Morgan Woodward (T.B. Trenton), Len Lesser (Banks), Skip Riley (Vince), Bruce Kimball (Sarge), Tom Kindle (Boseley), Ralph Seeley (Clint's Father), Richard Sobek (Grinder).

Utter nonsense designed to cash in on the van craze of the 1970s. The title vehicle comes complete with solar power and laser beams, which come in handy to stop some motorcycle gang members and engage in some standard chases and smash-ups. The plot is too slight to even be noticed in this vehicle for vehicles. Strictly for the drive-in crowd. Filmed around St. Joseph, Missouri, which was known for holding "van-ins" at the height of their popularity. Noted van authority George Barris designed the Super Van for the film.

p, Sal A. Capra, Sandy Cohen; d, Lamar Card; w, Neva Friedenn, Robert Easter (based on a story by John Arnoldy); ph, Irv Goodnoff; m, Andy DeMartino, Mark Gibbons, Bob Stone; ed, Steve Butler; spec eff, Harry Woolman; m/l, "Ridin' High," Stone; stunts, Von Deeming.

Action   **(PR:C   MPAA:PG)**

SUPERARGO**   (1968, Ital./Span.) 95m GV-Sec/Izaro c (IL RE DEI CRIMINALI; SUPERARGO E I GIGANTI SENZA VOLTO; SUPERARGO EL GIGANTE; AKA: SUPERARGO THE GIANT: THE KING OF THE CRIMINALS)

Guy Madison, Ken Wood [Giovanni Cianfriglia], Liz Barrett [Luisa Baratto], Diana Loris, Harold Sambrel [Aldo Sambrell], Thomas Blank [Blanco].

Wood plays the wrestler-turned-superhero who dons his bulletproof leotard to fight off villain Madison. Madison plays an evil mad scientist who's been kidnaping top athletes and replacing their hearts with electronic devices. This way Madison can keep his musclebound forces under his control for his nefarious schemes. Minor Italian muscle picture, a popular genre in that country during the 1960s. One of many in the successful "Superargo" series.

p, Oliver Wells; d, Paul Maxwell [Paolo Bianchini] w, Richard Lovelace [Julio Buchs] ph, Geoffrey Packett [Godofredo Packo]

Action   **(PR:A   MPAA:NR)**

SUPERARGO VERSUS DIABOLICUS**
(1966, Ital./Span.) 88m Liber Balcazar P.C.-S.E.C./COL c (SUPERARGO CONTRO DIABOLIKUS; SUPERARGO CONTRA DIABOLICUS: SUPERARGO EL HOMBRE ENMASCARADO)

Ken Wood [Giovanni Cianfriglia] (Superargo), Gerard Tichy (Diabolicus), Loredana Nusciak, Monica Randal, Francisco Castillo Escalona, Emilio Messina, Valentino Macchi, Geoffrey Copleston, Giulio Battiferri.

An advertising campaign that stressed the film was "not a cartoon!" says it all for this adventure in the Italian"Superargo" series. Here musleman Wood, playing the wrestling superhero with the invincible leotard, takes on mad scientist Tichy. Typically, Tichy wants to take over the world. His plan is to make artificial gold but Wood stops him. Tichy is destroyed when his escape rocket has a computer malfunction and explodes. The film is wonderfully stupid, generating unintentional laughter with its inept acting and direction. Tichy's underground laboratory is surprisingly well designed considering the film's low-budget look.

p, Ottavio Poggi, J.J. Balcazar; d, Nick Nostro; w, Balcazar (based on a story

by Mino Giarda); ph, Francisco Marin (Cromoscope, Eastmancolor); m, Franco Pisano; ed, Teresa Alcocer; art d, Juan Alberto Soler; set d, Cimino, Gabriele D'Angelo, Pierluigi Basile; makeup, Anacleto Giustini.

Action   **(PR:A   MPAA:G)**

SUPERBEAST zero   (1972) 90m A&S/UA c

Antoinette Bower (Dr. Alix Pardee, Pathologist), Craig Littler (Dr. Bill Fleming), Harry Lauter (Stewart Victor), Vic Diaz (Diaz), Jose Romulo (Vigo), John Garwood (Cleaver), Manny Oheda (Dr. Rojas), Bruno Punzalan (Datu), Alex Flores (Sloco), Roderick Paulate (Pepe), Ricardo Santos (Benny), Nanita (Lupe).

When pathologist Bower gets lost in the Philippine jungle she accidentally stumbles onto the secret laboratory of Littler. He is conducting some experiments that supposedly cure criminals of their psychopathic tendencies, but instead turn them into beasts. The unoriginal plot is developed in a confusing directorial style by writer-director Schenck. It was released with the equally bad DAUGHTERS OF SATAN.

p,d&w, George Schenck; ph, Nonong Rasca (DeLuxe Color); m, Richard LaSalle; ed, Tony DiMarco; md, LaSalle; art d, Hernando Balon; set d, Mario Carmona; makeup, John Chambers, Fred C. Blau, Jr.

Science Fiction/Horror   **(PR:O   MPAA:R)**

SUPERBUG, SUPER AGENT zero   (1976, Ger.) Barbara/Central Park c

Robert Mark, Heidi Hansen, George Goodman, Kathrin Ogen.

This German children's film tries some one-upmanship on Disney's THE LOVE BUG, but instead is an unabashed rip-off. The computerized Volkswagon of this film–dubbed "Dodo the Beetle"–is able to do just about anything Herbie the Love Bug can do including talk, swim, and disguise itself. What it can't do is entertain, particularly with the handicaps with which this film is pockmarked. The production is amateurish on all counts, from the inept direction and editing to the lackadasical attitude of the cast. Avoid.

d&w, Rudolf Zehetgruber.

Action/Adventure   **(PR:AAA   MPAA:G)**

SUPERCHICK zero   (1973) 94m Marimark/Crown International c

Joyce Jillson (Tara B. True), Louis Quinn (Garrick), Thomas Reardon (Ernest), Tony Young (Johnny), Timothy Wayne-Brown (Davey), John Carradine (Igor Smith), Junero Jennings (Simms), James Carrol Jordan (Marine), Jack Wells (Himself), Steve Drexel (Pete), Norman Bartold (Old Policeman), Phil Hoover (Tommy Hooks), John Donovan (The Bag-Man), Lilyan MacBride (Old Lady on Plane), Gus Peters (The Flasher), Dale Ishimoto (Yuki), Fuji (Aki), Myron Griffin (Tom Slauson), Uschi Digart (May Day), Marland Proctor (The Pilot), Gary Crutcher (Young Policeman), Ralph Campbell (The Butler), Flo Gerrish (Funky Jane), Jana Scott (2nd Stewardess), Mary Gavin, Shuji Nozawa.

While in the air she's a brown-haired stewardess serving coffee to happy passengers. But once she hits the ground Jillson doffs her wig, letting her natural blonde hair and natural unrestrainable erotic instincts take over. For she is SUPERCHICK, the stewardess-cum-karate expert and crime fighter, who also has enormous sexual appetites. Her adventures take her around the country in an episodic romp that culminates with Our Heroine foiling a skyjacking. Using plenty of stock footage of airplanes to pad out the empty plot, SUPERCHICK lacks the campy sense of humor that might have made this work. The film seems to be just more proof that one doesn't necessarily need talent to make films: only backers. Of notable interest only to those who will enjoy viewing the further degradation of aging actor Carradine, who here portrays a geriatric pervert who exhorts SUPERCHICK to flagellate him in the confines of his private dungeon. In a small part is Digart, an underground poster princess of the 1970s.

p, John Burrows; d, Forsyth; w, Gary Crutcher; ph, Paul Hipp (DeLuxe Color); m, Allan Alper; ed, Ed Forsyth; md, Alper; art d, Budd Costello; makeup, Ray Sebastian II; stunts, Eric Cord.

Action/Adventure   **Cas.**   **(PR:O   MPAA:R)**

SUPERDAD*½   (1974) 96m Disney/BV c

Bob Crane (Charlie McCready), Barbara Rush (Sue McCready), Kurt Russell (Bart), Joe Flynn (Cyrus Hershberger), Kathleen Cody (Wendy McCready), B. Kirby, Jr (Stanley), Joby Baker (Klutch), Dick Van Patten (Ira Hershaw), Judith Lowry, Ivor Francis, Jonathan Daly, Naomi Stevens, Nicholas Hammond, Jack Manning, Jim Wakefield, Ed McCready, Larry Gelman, Steve Dunne, Allison McKay, Leon Belasco, Sarah Fankboner, Christina Anderson, Ed Begley, Jr, Don Carter, Joy Ellison, Ann Marshall, Mike Rupert.

Most of Disney's live-action features could not live up to the studio's animated films and SUPERDAD is a good example why. The plot is too simplistic and hopelessly outdated, featuring Crane as a father who wants to get closer to his teenage daughter. He takes the advice of a TV commentator and starts doing things with Cody, much to her chagrin. Crane starts acting like a teenager and participating in "typical" teen activities with Cody's crowd. Russell, who got his start in Disney pictures before graduating to more quality films, is the boy friend whom Cody knew from childhood and who becomes Crane's main competitor. The teenagers portrayed here are little different from those in Disney's films of the 1950s, a mythical group of fun-loving types who don't resemble real-life teenagers at all. The direction and performances are earnest despite the obvious dishonesty of the material.

p, Bill Anderson; d, Vincent McEveety; w, Joseph L. McEveety (based on a story by Harlan Ware); ph, Andrew Jackson (Technicolor); m, Buddy Baker; ed, Ray de Leuw; art d, John B. Mansbridge, William J. Creber; cos, Shelby Tatum; m/l, "These Are the Best Times," Shane Tatum (sung by Bobby Goldsboro).

Comedy   **(PR:AAA   MPAA:G)**

SUPERFLY***   (1972) 96m WB c

Ron O'Neal (Youngblood Priest), Carl Lee (Eddie), Sheila Frazier (Georgia), Julius W. Harris (Scatter), Charles McGregor (Fat Freddie), Nate Adams (Dealer), Polly Niles (Cynthia), Yvonne Delaine (Mrs. Freddie), Henry Shapiro (Robbery Victim), K.C (Pimp), Jim Richardson (Junkie), Sig Shore (Deputy Commissioner), The Curtis Mayfield Experience.

This interesting feature is one of the few Hollywood films that is an honest look at the life of those black Americans in the ghetto. O'Neal plays a Harlem cocaine pusher whose success has gained him the respect and envy of the neighborhood. He wants to retire from the business and enjoy the comforts this life has brought him but first he must pull off one last million dollar dope deal. Using his connection in the corrupt police department, he scores the cocaine deal and leaves the business to retire to the good life with his girl friend. The moral ambiguity of the film may disturb some viewers but the film smacks of realistic grit throughout. Parks, one of the few blacks to direct in Hollywood, had a real feeling for the Harlem locations and the language of its residents. There's also some good action sequences and a fine score by Mayfield that counterpoints the story well. SUPERFLY was financially backed by a group of Harlem businessmen marking the first time a black-oriented film was financed by blacks. It was also one of the first to use a nonwhite cast and crew. Director Parks was the son of Gordon Parks, Sr., the director of the"Shaft" movies Sequel: SUPERFLY T.N.T..

p, Sig Shore; d, Gordon Parks, Jr.; w, Phillip Fenty; ph, James Signorelli (Technicolor); m, Curtis Mayfield; ed, Bob Brady; md, Marvin Stuart; cos, Nate Adams; m/l, "Superfly," "Freddie's Dead," Mayfield (sung by Mayfield); makeup, James Farabee.

Crime Drama   **Cas.**   **(PR:O   MPAA:R)**

SUPERFLY T.N.T.*   (1973) 87m PAR c (AKA: SUPER FLY T.N.T.)

Ron O'Neal (Youngblood Priest), Roscoe Lee Browne (Dr. Lamine Sonko), Sheila Frazier (Georgia), Robert Guillaume (Jordan Gaines), Jacques Sernas (Matty Smith), William Berger (Lefevre), Roy Bosler (Customs Man), Silvio Nardo (George), Olga Bisera (Lisa), Dominic Barto (Rand), Minister Dem (General), Jeannie McNeill (Riding Instructress), Dan Davis (Pilot), Luigi Orso (Crew Chief), Ennio Catalfamo (Photographer), Francesco Rachini (Warehouse Custodian), George Wang, Fernando Piazza, Ferrucio Brusarosco (Poker Players), Rik Boyd (Rik).

A poor sequel to SUPERFLY, this time directed by star O'Neal. After leaving the Harlem drug racket, O'Neal and girl friend Frazier retire to Rome. There O'Neal gets involved in the black revolution of a fictional white-ruled African nation. O'Neal's direction can't match the original, showing no sense of style or any knowledge of even rudimentary camera setups. His acting also falters, giving a lackluster performance that is disappointing considering the charisma he projected so well in the original. Shot on a cheap budget by Hollywood standards, the screenplay is by Haley, author of The Autobiography of Malcolm X and the highly acclaimed Roots.

p, Sig Shore; d, Ron O'Neal; w, Alex Haley (based on an original story by Shore and O'Neal); ph, Robert Gaffney (Movielab Color); m, Osibisa; ed, Bob Brady; prod d, Giuseppe Bassan.

Action Drama   **(PR:O   MPAA:R)**

SUPERMAN***   (1978) 143m WB c

Marlon Brando (Jor-El), Gene Hackman (Lex Luthor), Christopher Reeve (Superman/Clark Kent), Ned Beatty (Otis), Jackie Cooper (Perry White), Glenn Ford (Pa Kent), Trevor Howard (1st Elder), Margot Kidder (Lois Lane), Jack O'Halloran (Non), Valerie Perrine (Eve Teschmacher), Maria Schell (Vond-Ah), Terence Stamp (Gen. Zod), Phyllis Thaxter (Ma Kent), Susannah York (Lara), Jeff East (Young Clark Kent), Marc McClure (Jimmy Olsen), Sarah Douglas (Ursa), Harry Andrews (2nd Elder), Lee Quigley (Baby Kal-El), Aaron Smolinski (Baby Clark Kent), Diane Sherry (Lana Lang), Jeff Atcheson (Coach), Jill Ingham (Perry's Secretary), Rex Reed (Himself), Weston Gavin (Mugger), George Harris II (Patrolman Mooney), Rex Everhardt (Desk Sergeant), Jayne Tottman (Little Girl), Larry Hagman (Major), Paul Tuerpe (Sgt. Hayley), Phil Brown, Bill Bailey (State Senators), Chief Tug Smith (Indian Chief), Roy Stevens (Warden), Kirk Alyn, Noel Neill (Couple on Train), Bob Dahdah (Newspaper Customer), Vass Anderson, John Hollis, James Garbutt, Michael Gover, David Neal, William Russell, Penelope Lee, John Stuart, Alan Cullen, Larry Lamb, James Brockington, John Cassady, John F. Parker, Antony Scott, Ray Evans, Su Shifrin, Miguel Brown, Vincent Marzello, Benjamin Feitelson, Lise Hilboldt, Leueen Willoughby, Pieter Stuyck, Stephen Kahan, Ray Hassett, Randy Jurgenson, Matt Russo, Colin Skeaping, Bo Rucker, Paul Avery, David Maxt, Michael Harrigan, John Cording, Raymond Thompson, Oz Clarke, Frank Lazarus, Brian Protheroe, Lawrence Trimble, Robert Whelan, David Calder, Norwick Duff, Keith Alexander, Michael Ensign, Graham McPherson, David Yorston, Robert O'Neill, Robert MacLeod, John Ratzenberger, Alan Tilvern, Burnell Tucker, Norman Warwick, Chuck Julian, Colin Etherington, Mark Wynter.

"You'll believe a man can fly" stated the advertising and audiences agreed when the much ballyhooed SUPERMAN finally opened as the big Christmas movie of 1978. Two years in the making, the film's final cost reportedly ranged between $40 to $55 million. The great expense and enormous publicity on the film's making belie the fact that this is a simple story of a great 20th Century American myth. The film opens with an elaborate setting as Brando, playing the future hero's father, sentences three outlaws (Stamp, O'Halloran, and Douglas) to a cosmic jail. The story of planet Krypton's destruction is faithfully retold and the baby Jor-El is sent off to planet Earth. There he is found by Ford and Thaxter and raised to young adulthood. East, in a fine performance as the young Clark Kent, is confused by his superpowers (he outraces a train that Neill, Lois Lane of the 1950s TV "Superman" series, is riding), and when Ford dies, East is compelled by a magic crystal to head to the Arctic. The crystal transforms into an enormous ice palace where East learns his true identity and purpose. Twelve years pass and the film finally buckles down to the real heart of the story. Reeve plays the Clark Kent/Superman role, a mild-mannered reporter on the Daily Planet. (Film critic Rex Reed makes a cameo appearance as the paper's film critic.) When ace reporter Kidder gets herself in trouble in a helicopter, Reeve makes his debut as Superman, rescuing her and changing the face of law enforcement forever. Flying about in his tights and cape, Reeve next saves Air Force One from crashing and is proclaimed a great and mysterious hero. Kidder, of course, falls for the Man of Steel, not knowing he's her bumbling co-worker. Reeve grants her an interview ("I fight for truth, justice, and the American way," he tells her) and takes her on a romantic night flight around the city. Meanwhile, ace badman Hackman and his sidekick Beatty (a wonderful comic pairing) are out to take over the world using two atomic bombs. He traps Reeve using a chunk of Kryptonite, a poisonous substance that weakens Superman, and sets off his bombs. But Hackman's assistant, Perrine (again, an excellent comic caricature), feels a soft spot for Reeve and rescues him after he promises to stop the bomb aimed at her mother's hometown first. Reeve does but the other bomb goes off, setting off an earthquake in which Kidder is killed. Reeve is overwrought with emotion at her death and circles the Earth at reverse speed, causing a backwards rotation that brings Kidder back to life. He hand-delivers Hackman and Beatty to prison officials and flies off to new adventures. Structurally SUPERMAN has several problems. It tries to encompass the entire myth, creating several story lines along the way until the Superman character finally emerges. The overlong prolog gets bogged down at points, although the photography of East's boyhood is beautiful, shot on location in the Canadian farmlands. The entire film itself runs much too long at 2 hours, 23 minutes (with another 40 minutes added to the television showing), with the more tedious and elongated moments found in the pre-Metropolis epilog. Once Reeve takes the screen, SUPERMAN becomes highly engaging, full of charm and excitement. A worldwide hunt had been conducted by the producers to find the right man for the role. If the lead could not be believed, the entire film would be an extremely expensive flop. Among the actors considered for Clark Kent/Superman were Robert Redford, Burt Reynolds, Nick Nolte, Kris Kristofferson, Sylvester Stallone, Ryan O'Neal, and even Clint Eastwood and Charles Bronson. But after the signing of Brando and Hackman, the father son Salkind production team decided that an unknown actor would better suit the film. The search went on for several months (at one point a New York dentist was considered) until they finally chose Reeve, a veteran of soap operas and Broadway. He took the role very seriously, working out to fit the part until he had added 30 pounds and added two inches to his chest (Reeve's workouts were supervised by David Prowse, the man who filled Darth Vader's suit in STAR WARS). The Salkinds couldn't have picked a finer man for the job. Reeve was absolutely marvelous, giving real sensitivity to his dual characters. He projected a naive charm and a good sense of humor without any of the campiness that worked on TV's "Batman" series. Audiences believed a man could fly because they believed in Reeve. Brando's part in the film is probably more noted for his salary than performance. For 13 days of work he received $3 million which came down to roughly $27,000 for a day's work (Brando graciously offered a free day for necessary retakes). The script was from an original story by Puzo, author of Godfather which was based on the D. C. Comics Superman legend. Contributing to the final script were Puzo, Newman and Benton (writers of BONNIE AND CLYDE, and a minor Broadway musical "It's a Bird...It's a Plane...It's Superman" in 1966), as well as Newman's wife, Leslie. Donner's direction manages to tie up the episodes of the story, working best in the film's more intimate moments rather than the larger set pieces. (Donner had gotten his start directing action sequences for the kiddie TV show "The

Banana Splits.") The special effects were surprisingly routine. Reeve's flying looked good, but a STAR WARS-jaded film public needed more than that. A dam burst is particularly bad, a highly dramatic sequence that was dramatically damaged by the painfully obvious model. The film was dedicated to Unsworth, the great British cinematographer who passed away after shooting was completed.

p, Pierre Spengler; d, Richard Donner; w, Mario Puzo, David Newman, Leslie Newman, Robert Benton (based on the story by Puzo, from the comic strip created by Jerry Siegel, Joel Shuster); ph, Geoffrey Unsworth (Panavision, Technicolor); m, John Williams; ed, Stuart Baird; prod d, John Barry; cos, Yvonne Blake, Colin Chilvers, Roy Field, Derek Meddings, Zoran Perisic, Denys Coop, Les Bowie; m/l, "Can You Read My Mind," John Williams, Leslie Bricusse (sung by Margo Kidder); makeup, Philip Rhodes, Basil Newall, Kay Freeborn, Graham Freeborn, Nick Maley, Sylvia Croft, Connie Reeve, Louis Lane, Jamie Brown.

Fantasy/Adventure   Cas.   (PR:AAA MPAA:PG)

SUPERMAN AND THE MOLE MEN**   (1951) 67m Lippert bw (GB:
SUPERMAN AND THE STRANGE PEOPLE)

George Reeves (*Clark Kent/Superman*), Phyllis Coates (*Lois*), Jeff Corey (*Luke Benson*), Walter Reed (*Bill Corrigan*), J. Farrell MacDonald (*Pop Shannon*), Stanley Andrews (*Sheriff*), Ray Walker (*John Craig*), Hal K. Dawson (*Weber*), Frank Reicher (*Hospital Superintendent*), Beverly Washburn (*Child*), Stephen Carr (*Eddie*), Paul Burns (*Doc Saunders*), Margia Dean (*Mrs. Benson*), Byron Foulger (*Jeff Reagan*), Irene Martin (*Esther Pomfrey*), John Phillips (*Matt*), Phil Warren (*Deputy*), John Baer (*Intern*), Adrienne Marden (*Nurse*), Billy Curtis, Jack Banbury, Jerry Marvin, Tony Baris (*Creatures*).

Before Christopher Reeve there was George Reeves as the Man of Steel. This short feature was Reeves' debut in the Superman role which he reprised the next year in his popular television series. Here he helps out the innocent "mole men" of the underworld who are disturbed when oilmen start drilling into their homes. It's a simplistic allegory for the rights of all men –Reeves gives a wind-up speech about accepting others and their differences– directed with a certain crudity but retaining a certain innocent feeling that worked out nicely. SUPERMAN AND THE MOLE MEN later turned up on the TV series as a two part episode titled "Unknown People."

p, Robert Maxwell, Barney A. Sarecky; d, Lee Sholem; w, Richard Fielding!!Robert Maxwell]! ph, Clark Ramsey; ed, Al Joseph; spec eff, Ray Mercer.

Fantasy/Adventure   (PR:A MPAA:NR)

SUPERMAN AND THE STRANGE PEOPLE
(SEE: SUPERMAN AND THE MOLE MEN, 1951)

SUPERMAN II***½   (1980) 127m WB c

Gene Hackman (*Lex Luthor*), Christopher Reeve (*Clark Kent/Superman*), Ned Beatty (*Otis*), Jackie Cooper (*Perry White*), Sarah Douglas (*Ursa*), Margot Kidder (*Lois Lane*), Jack O'Halloran (*Non*), Valerie Perrine (*Eve Teschmacher*), Susannah York (*Lara*), Clifton James (*Sheriff*), E. G. Marshall (*The President*), Marc McClure (*Jimmy Olsen*), Terence Stamp (*Gen. Zod*), Leueen Willoughby (*Leueen*), Robin Pappas (*Alice*), Roger Kemp (*Spokesman*), Roger Brierley, Anthony Milner, Richard Griffiths (*Terrorists*), Melissa Wiltsie (*Nun*), Alain DeHay (*Gendarme*), Marc Boyle (*C.R.S. Man*), Alan Stuart (*Cab Driver*), John Ratzenberger, Shane Rimmer (*Controllers*), John Morton (*Nate*), Jim Dowdell (*Boris*), Angus McInnes (*Warden*), Antony Sher (*Bellboy*), Elva May Hoover (*Mother*), Hadley Kay (*Jason*), Todd Woodcroft (*Father*), John Hollis (*Krypton Elder*), Gordon Rollings (*Fisherman*), Peter Whitman (*Deputy*), Bill Bailey (*J. J.*), Dinny Powell (*Boog*), Hal Galili (*Man at Bar*), Marcus D'Amico (*Willie*), Jackie Cooper (*Dino*), Richard Parmentier (*Reporter*), Don Fellows (*General*), Michael J. Shannon (*President's Aide*), Tony Sibbald (*Presidential Imposter*), Tommy Duggan (*Diner Owner*), Pamela Mandell (*Waitress*), Pepper Martin (*Rocky*), Eugene Lipinski (*News Vendor*), Cleon Spencer, Carl Parris (*Kids*).

This superior sequel to the original SUPERMAN is a wonderful time, poking fun at its American mythic qualities, yet never dipping into camp comedy. Reeve reprises his role as the bumbling reporter-cum-Man of Steel with marvelous success. It opens with a fury. Terrorists have taken over the Eiffel Tower and threaten to blow it up with a nuclear bomb. Kidder, ever the inquisitive reporter, tries to interview the terrorists and finds herself in more trouble than she had hoped. Fortunately Reeve comes to save the day, rescuing Kidder and flinging the bomb into outer space. But this sets off a nuclear explosion that frees Stamp, Douglas, and O'Halloran from the cosmic prison they had been sentenced to in SUPERMAN. The sequel goes into full stride as they come to take over Earth, not knowing their fellow Kryptonian is that planet's hero. While on an undercover reporting assignment to Niagara Falls, Kidder begins to suspect that her bumbling colleague, Clark Kent, just may be Superman. She's proven right when Reeve's hand isn't burned in a fireplace and the two go to the Arctic Fortress of Solitude. There Reeve goes through a mystical baptism of light that saps his superpowers. The couple goes to a little diner after making love and Reeve is surprised that he can be beaten up. He finds the evil trio have taken

over the world and returns to the Fortress in an attempt to regain his powers. He does, though his regained strength has its limits. Reeve and the three villains engage in a spectacular sky battle over Metropolis (actually New York City) and he ultimately tricks them back to his fortress, thus saving the world from their destructive lust for power. And just to set things right, Reeve returns to the truck stop and takes care of the rowdy who pushed him around earlier. SUPERMAN II succeeds, in that it has a good story line with a clear line of progression. The romance between Reeve and Kidder is charming and dealt with in a sensitive, believable manner. Reeve's deep kiss at the film's end which causes Kidder to forget his secret is less believable. Other problems come from occasional stretched out moments of unnecessary comedy, such as various comic reactions by citizens during the sky battle. However, direction is smooth and efficent, instilling excitement and a good sense of whimsy into the story. During all the publicity for SUPERMAN, it was revealed that some of the sequel was being shot along with the original film. Though Lester is given credit as director for SUPERMAN II, movie insiders suggested that SUPERMAN's director Richard Donner had a lot to do with the sequel before being fired from the production. The off-camera politics don't effect the final production, though. SUPERMAN II is a good time at the movies, a rare instance of a sequel that equals the original.

p, Pierre Spengler; d, Richard Lester; w, Mario Puzo, David Newman, Leslie Newman (based on a story by Puzo, from characters created by Jerry Siegel, Joe Shuster); ph, Geoffrey Unsworth, Robert Paynter (Panavision, Technicolor); m, Ken Thorne (from original material composed by John Williams); ed, John Victor-Smith; prod d, John Barry, Peter Murton; art d, Maurice Fowler; cos, Yvonne Blake, Susan Yelland; spec eff, Colin Chilvers, Roy Field, Zoran Perisic; makeup, Stuart Freeborn.

Fantasy/Adventure   Cas   (PR:A MPAA:PG)

SUPERMAN III**   (1983) 123m WB c

Christopher Reeve (*Clark Kent/Superman*), Richard Pryor (*Gus Gorman*), Jackie Cooper (*Perry White*), Margot Kidder (*Lois Lane*), Annette O'Toole (*Lana Lang*), Annie Ross (*Vera Webster*), Pamela Stephenson (*Lorelei Ambrosia*), Robert Vaughn (*Ross Webster*), Marc McClure (*Jimmy Olsen*), Nancy Roberts (*Unemployment Clerk*), Graham Stark (*Blind Man*), Henry Woolf (*Penguin Man*), Gordon Rollings (*Man in Cap*), Peter Wear (*Bank Robber*), Justin Case (*Mime*), Bob Todd (*Dignified Gent*), Terry Camilleri (*Delivery Man*), Stefan Kalipha (*Data School Instructor*), Helen Horton (*Miss Henderson*), Lou Hirsch (*Fred*), Bill Reimbold (*Wages Man*), Shane Rimmer (*State Policeman*), Al Matthews (*Fire Chief*), Barry Dennen (*Dr. McClean*), Enid Saunders (*Minnie Bannister*), Kevin Harrison Cork (*D. J.*), Robert G. Henderson (*Mr. Simpson*), Paul Kaethler (*Ricky*), R. J. Bell (*Mr. Stokis*), Pamela Mandell (*Mrs. Stokis*), Peter Whitman (*Man at Cash Point*), Ronnie Brody (*Husband*), Sandra Dickinson (*Wife*), Philip Gilbert (*Newsreader*), Pat Starr (*White-Coated Scientist*), Gordon Signer (*Mayor*), John Bluthal (*Pisa Vendor*), George Chisholm (*Street Sweeper*), David Fielder (*Olympic Runner*), Robert Beatty (*Tanker Captain*), Chris Malcolm, Larry Lamb (*Miners*), Gavan O'Herlihy.

Considering the standards set by the first two SUPERMAN films, SUPERMAN III is a disappointment. The story's mythic qualities were pretty well gone by this film and the filmmakers had to rely on Pryor as the audience grabber. Reeve plays the reporter/ super hero as a confused individual this time, trying to figure out the dual aspects of his personality. For a while he decides to give up doing nice things for the world and takes up with old girl friend O'Toole (another reason for this new romance is Kidder was tired of playing Lois Lane and would only consent to a cameo for this film). Reeve finally gets his act together when bad guy Vaughn tries to use his corporate holdings, along with computer whiz Pryor, to take over the world. The result is nothing more than a tired gag-fest with fight scenes that owe more to video game technology than the Man of Steel's super powers. As usually is the case, Pryor steals the show with his manic performance that rises well above the material. Pryor consistently chooses projects that are below his enormous talents and comes out looking good every time. Reeve's performance is okay but not quite up to his earlier SUPERMAN work. Lester's direction injects nothing new into the material, giving the feeling that this was nothing more than an exercise in comedy set pieces for him. After Lois Lane discovered Clark Kent's identity in SUPERMAN II, a part of the legend was over and SUPERMAN III confirmed this with a resounding note.

p, Pierre Spengler; d, Richard Lester; w, David Newman, Leslie Newman (based on characters created by Jerry Siegel, Joe Shuster); ph, Robert Paynter (Panavision); m, Ken Thorne, John Williams; ed, John Victor Smith; prod d, Peter Murton; art d, Brian Ackland-Snow, Charles Bishop, Terry Ackland-Snow; cos, Vangie Harrison; spec eff, Roy Field, Colin Chilvers, Martin Gutteridge, Brian Warner; m/l, Giorgio Moroder; makeup, Engelen, Freeborn.

Fantasy/Adventure   Cas.   (PR:A MPAA:PG)

SUPERNATURAL**½   (1933) 65m PAR bw

Carole Lombard (*Roma Courtney*), Randolph Scott (*Grant Wilson*), Vivienne Osborne (*Ruth Rogen*), Alan Dinehart (*Paul Bavian*), H. B. Warner (*Dr. Houston*), Beryl Mercer (*Mme. Gourjan*), William Farnum (*Robert "Nickey" Hammond*), Willard Robertson (*Warden*), George Burr MacAnnon (*Max*),

Lyman Williams (*Ghost of John Courtney*).

The Halperin brothers, who made WHITE ZOMBIE, took a crack at the spooky again with this film and the result was ho-hokum. Lombard is a rich heiress who has lost her brother. She's contacted by phony spiritualist Dinehart who says that he can put the bereaved sister in touch with the dead man's ghost. Dinehart plans a seance and has a mask made of the late sibling which he uses to show Lombard that the man was murdered by Farnum, who is Lombard's guardian and totally innocent of any wrongdoing. What Dinehart wants to do is get the decent Farnum out of the way, thus clearing a path for him to move in and grab Lombard's money. Lombard falls for the ruse and tearfully exits. Warner is a doctor who truly believes that the the spirit of a murderer can get inside the body of a living person and cause that person to continue behaving illegally. He visits Osborne, a convicted murderess who was involved in a killing in Greenwich Village which made her the darling of the tabloids. She awaits her execution and doesn't much care about what happens to her dead body so she gives Warner the right to perform his experiments on her corpse, once the electric chair has shocked her into death. She is in jail because Dinehart betrayed her and she hopes that whatever Warner does will help put Dinehart in the grave as well. Osborne is executed and Warner immediately begins his work. There's another seance and Dinehart takes the opportunity of darkness to slay Farnum. The moment that happens, the drapes rustle (even though there's no wind) and Osborne's ghost invades Lombard's body. Suddenly, the formerly placid Lombard becomes the distaff version of Dr. Jekyll and Mr. Hyde as her face contorts and we can see that there is something amiss behind that gorgeous phiz. Lombard has a large yacht and invites Dinehart to spend some time aboard with her. Once on the ship, Lombard tries to throttle Dinehart with her hands. Meanwhile, the dead brother, Williams, contacts Warner, who is ill, and tells him what's happening. Through this, Lombard's boy friend, Scott, is found and told where she and Dinehart are at this moment. Lombard is about to kill Dinehart on the boat when Scott arrives and momentarily takes her mind off her strangulation attempts. Dinehart races out of the yacht's main room, runs on deck, and gets tangled in the ship's ropes, thus strangling himself to death. Osborne's ghost leaves Lombard's body and Williams' ghost arrives and riffles the pages of a magazine to an ad about a Bermuda honeymoon. Scott and Lombard realize what Williams is trying to say, kiss, and the picture ends. Lombard hated this movie, hated the thought of doing anything about the dead, and warned director Halperin that strange things might happen. While filming, one of California's frequent earthquakes hit the area and Lombard gleefully told Halperin, "See? I warned you." The dialog director on this movie was Sidney Salkow, who went on to become one of the better B moviemakers, with credits that included many of THE LONE WOLF pictures, as well as THE ADVENTURES OF MARTIN EDEN, SITTING BULL, RAIDERS OF THE SEVEN SEAS, TWICE TOLD TALES, and many more. His first picture was WOMAN DOCTOR in 1939, when he was 30 years old.

p, Victor Halperin, Edward Halperin; d, Victor Halperin; w, Harvey Thew, Brian Marlow (based on the story by Garnett Weston); ph, Arthur Martinelli.

Mystery   **(PR:A-C   MPAA:NR)**

SUPERSNOOPER   (SEE: SUPER FUZZ, 1981)

SUPERSONIC MAN*   (1979, Span.) 85m Almena c

Michael Coby, Cameron Mitchell, Diana Polakov, Richard Yesteran, Frank Brana, Javier de Campos, Tito Garcia, Quique Camoiras, Luis Barboo, Angel Ter.

Inept, quickie SUPERMAN rip-off with reminders of old muscle movies tossed in for good measure. Coby is a private eye-cum -superhero complete with a Superman-styled outfit (he wears a mask to boot). His female cohort is Lois Lane look-alike, Polakov, and Mitchell is the mad scientist that Coby must stop from carrying out the standard evil plans. This film has every SUPERMAN motifclearly in place, from his otherworldly beginnings to the big city settings of New York. Despite the rip-off qualities, the film does have some fairly good special effects, but that's not nearly enough to make this worth watching.

p, Tonino Moi, Dick Randall, Faruk Alatan; d, Piquer Simon!!Juan Piquer]! w, Moi, Simon; ph, John!!Juan]iMarine (Dinavision, Eastmancolor-Supercol-or); m, Gino Peguri, Juan Luis Izaguirre, Carlos Attias; ed, Pedro del Rey; set d, Emil!!Emilio]iRuiz, Frank (Francisco) Prosper; spec eff, Prosper, Ruiz, Jack Elkubi, Miguel Villa.

Fantasy/Adventure   **(PR:A   MPAA:NR)**

SUPERSPEED**½   (1935) 56m COL bw

Norman Foster (*Randy Rogers*), Florence Rice (*Billie Devlin*), Mary Carlisle (*Nan Gale*), Charley Grapewin (*Terry Devlin*), Arthur Hohl (*Philip Morton*), Robert Middlemass (*Wilson Gale*), George McKay (*George Stone*).

Entertaining programmer about rivalries in the motorcar and motorboat worlds. When a young man invents a "superspeed" formula for the car of the same name, it works well. However, the evil plant manager tries to sabotage the invention. The young man's affections are also subject to the whims of Rice and Carlisle, the daughter of an automobile manufacturer

and a motorboat racer respectively. The film climaxes in an exciting motorboat race, nicely photographed by western vet, Kline. Some good thrills with a fast-paced direction and well-acted performances.

d, Lambert Hillyer; w, Harold Shumate (based on a story by Shumate); ph, Benjamin Kline; ed, Otto Meyer.

Action   **(PR:A   MPAA:NR)**

SUPERZAN AND THE SPACE BOY***   (1972, Mex.) 130m Tikal Internacional bw (SUPERZAN Y EL NINO DEL ESPACIO)

Giovanni Lanuza (*Superzan*), Caro Laniesti (*Carmen*), Claudio Lanuza (*Silio*), Freddy Pecherelly (*Beto*).

This episodic space adventure is a little long, but otherwise it's a good children's film that will entertain the younger set. The story involves a golden boy from another planet who arrives on Earth. He wants to help the people here improve their lives and create a world of global harmony. However, the doctor he goes to only wants to use the boy as a tool to take over the world. Two superpowers, one good and one evil, slug it out and in the process, the laboratory is destroyed. The boy's father summons him back to his home planet, for Earth is not yet ready for their message and support. The film has occasional overindulgences in morality statements and sentimental moments, but overall this is a nice children's film with some good direction that makes it entertaining.

d&w, Rafael Lanuza; ph, Antonio Ruiz.

Fantasy   **(PR:AAA   MPAA:NR)**

SUPPORT YOUR LOCAL GUNFIGHTER***   (1971) 92m Cherokee-Brigrade/UA c

James Garner (*Latigo Smith*), Suzanne Pleshette (*Patience Barton*), Jack Elam (*Jug May*), Joan Blondell (*Jenny*), Harry Morgan (*Taylor Barton*), Marie Windsor (*Goldie*), John Dehner (*Col. Ames*), Henry Jones (*Ez*), Chuck Connors (*Swifty Morgan*), Dub Taylor (*Doc Schultz*), Kathleen Freeman (*Mrs. Perkins*), Ellen Corby (*Abigail*), Dick Curtis (*Bud Barton*), Herb Vigran (*Fat*), John Wheeler (*Croupier*), Mike Wagner (*Bartender*), Ben Cooper (*Colorado*), Willis Bouchey (*McLaglen*), Grady Sutton (*Storekeeper*), Walter Burke (*Morris*), Gene Evans (*Butcher*), Terry Wilson (*Thug*), Roy Glenn (*Headwaiter*), Virginia Capers (*Maid*), Pedro Gonzales-Gonzales (*Ortiz*).

A follow up film (though not a sequel) to SUPPORT YOUR LOCAL SHERIFF finds Garner playing a con artist running off from his madame bride-to-be, Windsor. He ends up in the small western town of Purgatory where the citizens mistake him for a famous gunslinger. Garner decides to let them think what they want and proceeds to take Purgatory for everything he can. Elam once more is his sidekick and Pleshette is the love interest who wants to start a Ladies Finishing School in New York state. Garner's tongue in cheek comic style works nicely with some fun support in Elam's great clowning. Though not quite the film its predecessor was, this still has an enormous amount of gleeful fun, with good direction that kids around affectionately with the Western cliches.

p, William Finnegan; d, Burt Kennedy; w, James Edward Grant; ph, Harry Stradling, Jr. (Deluxe Color); m, Jack Elliott, Allyn Ferguson; ed, Bill Gulick; art d, Phil Barber; set d, Chester L. Bayhi; cos, Lambert Marks, Pat Norris; spec eff, A. D. Flowers; makeup, Tom Tuttle.

Western Comedy   **Cas**   **(PR:A   MPAA:G)**

SUPPORT YOUR LOCAL SHERIFF***½   (1969) 96m Cherokee/UA c

James Garner (*Jason McCullough*), Joan Hackett (*Prudy Perkins*), Walter Brennan (*Pa Danby*), Harry Morgan (*Mayor Olly Perkins*), Jack Elam (*Jake*), Bruce Dern (*Joe Danby*), Henry Jones (*Preacher Henry Jackson*), Walter Burke (*Fred Johnson*), Dick Peabody (*Luke Danby*), Gene Evans (*Tom Danby*), Willis Bouchey (*Thomas Devery*), Kathleen Freeman (*Mrs. Danvers*), Gayle Rogers (*Bar Girl*), Richard Hoyt (*Gunfighter*), Marilyn Jones (*Bordello Girl*).

A great spoof of western movie cliches features Garner as a stranger who stops off at a small town en route to Australia, a running joke that works well through the rest of the film. He's hired as the new sheriff, taking the job as he can't afford the booming gold town's inflationary prices. Elam, the town drunk, is hired as a deputy. After arresting Dern and having the outlaw help build the new jail, Dern's father, Brennan, gets angry and summons the rest of his family to rescue the wayward son. A climactic street shootout is held with Garner winning as he holds them off with a seemingly empty cannon. Unlike the later BLAZING SADDLES (1974), SUPPORT YOUR LOCAL SHERIFF has a good time with the western cliches but still shows respect for the formula western. Garner's performance is a marvelous study in underplaying, his expressive face saying all that needs to be said. Brennan is hilarious in a self parody of his role in MY DARLING CLEMINTINE (1946).

p, William Bowers; d, Burt Kennedy; w, Bowers; ph, Harry Stradling, Jr. (Deluxe); m, Jeff Alexander; ed, George W. Brooks; art d, Leroy Coleman; set d, Hugh Hunt; cos, Norman Burza, Florence Hackett; spec eff, Marcel

Vercoutere; makeup, Stan Smith.

Western/Comedy/Satire   Cas.   (PR:A MPAA:G)

SUPPOSE THEY GAVE A WAR AND NOBODY CAME?**
(1970) 113m ABC/Cinerama c (AKA: WAR GAMES)

Brian Keith (*Warrant Officer Nace*), Tony Curtis (*Sgt. Shannon Gambroni*), Ernest Borgnine (*Sheriff Harve*), Ivan Dixon (*Sgt. Jones*), Suzanne Pleshette (*Ramona*), Tom Ewell (*Billy Joe Davis*), Bradford Dillman (*Capt. Myerson*), Arthur O'Connell (*Mr. Kruft, Bank Official*), John Fiedler (*Maj. Purvis*), Don Ameche (*Col. Flanders*), Robert Emhardt (*Lester Calhoun*), Maxine Stuart (*Zelda*), Christopher Mitchum (*Alturi*), Pamela Britton (*Sgt. Graham*), Grady Sutton (*Rev. Dinwood*), Cliff Norton (*Herman Hyde*), Jeanne Bates (*Mrs. Flanders*), Eddie Firestone (*Deputy Goulash*), William Bramley (*Deputy Henry*), Sam G. Edwards (*Deputy Sam*), Buck Young (*Deputy Ron*), Paul Sorensen (*Deputy Randy*), David Cass (*Deputy Dave*), John Lasell (*Dr. Hillery*), Dorothy Green (*Mrs. Kruft*), Pamela Branch (*Mrs. Purvis*), Janet E. Clark (*Mrs. Davis*), Jean Argyle (*Mrs. Calhoun*), Monty Margetts (*Mrs. Dinwood*), Paula Stewart (*1st Prostitute*), Carolyn Williamson (*2nd Prostitute*), John James Bannon (*1st Military Policeman*), Vince Howard (*2nd Military Policeman*), Stanley W. Barrett (*Green Beret*).

In a small town in the deep South the local citizens, led by Ewell, a right-wing militia man, accept the offer when Ameche extends a friendly invitation from his Army base. A dance is arranged to foster good community-military relations but this erupts into a free-for-all between the two sides when Curtis is arrested after he's caught necking with Pleshette. His buddies decide to rescue him and Ewell calls out his militia. The film ends with Ewell losing not only the fight but his high position in town, which is a relief to the locals. SUPPOSE THEY GAVE A WAR... suffers from a direction and script that never can quite decide which way they want to go. At times this plays as farce, while other parts come off as serious drama. The acting is never convincing, with a myriad of styles that add to the confusion.

p, Fred Engel; d, Hy Averback; w, Don McGuire, Hal Captain (based on a story by Captain); ph, Burnett Guffey (DeLuxe Color); m, Jerry Fielding; ed, John F. Burnett; prod d, Jack Poplin; set d, James W. Payne; spec eff, Larry Hampton; m/l, "Mama Two March," Fielding, David McKechnie; makeup, Gary Liddiard, Robert Bau; stunts, Paul Baxley.

Comedy/Drama   (PR:A MPAA:GP)

SUPREME KID, THE***½ (1976, Can.) 90m Seventh Wave/Cinepix c

Frank Moore (*Ruben*), Jim Henshaw (*Wes*), Don Granberry (*Wilbur*), Helen Shaver (*Girl*), Gordon Robertson (*Frankie*).

Two drifters who hate authority figures bum around Canada, encountering nasty cops and seedy bikers, giving each equal time. The lackadaisical, episodic plot line is dotted with various characters and adventures, and works in an offbeat way. It's not entirely successful but has enough good moments and an upbeat ending that satisfies. This independent film was shot in 16mm, then blown up to 35mm.

d&w, Peter Bryant; ph, Tony Westman (Eastmancolor); m, Howie Vickers; ed, Homer Powell, Sally Paterson.

Comedy   (PR:C MPAA:NR)

SUPREME SECRET, THE** (1958, Brit.) 56m GHW/Church and Chapel bw (AKA: GOD SPEA KS TODAY)

Hugh David, Meredith Edwards, Anthony Green, Harry Fowler.

Another dose of predictable religious pontification is to be found in this drama dealing with a young lad who gets involved with some mission workers after he's caught in a dockside robbery. The film was cut down to a half-hour and rereleased in 1965 under the title GOD SPEAKS TODAY.

d, Norman Walker; w, Lawrence Barratt.

Drama   (PR:A MPAA:NR)

SUR LA COUR   (SEE: CRIME OF MONSIEUR LANGE, THE, 1964, Fr.)

SUR LA ROUTE DE SALINA   (SEE: ROAD TO SALINA, 1971, Fr./Ital.)

SURCOUF, LE DERNIER CORSAIRE
(SEE: SEA PIRATE, THE, 1967, Fr./Ital./Span.)

SURF, THE   (SEE: OCEAN BREAKERS, 1949, Swed.)

SURF PARTY*   (1964) 69m AP/FOX bw

Bobby Vinton (*Len Marshal*), Patricia Morrow (*Terry Wells*), Jackie De Shannon (*Junior Griffith*), Kenny Miller (*Milo Talbot*), Lory Patrick (*Sylvia Dempster*), Richard Crane (*Sgt. Wayne Neal*), Jerry Summers (*Skeet Wells*), Martha Stewart (*Pauline Lowell*), The Astronauts, The Routers (*Them-

selves), Mickey Dora, John Fain, Pam Colbert, Donna Russell, Lloyd Kino.

"Hey gang, let's go down to the beach and hang ten]" That's exactly what Arizona teens Morrow, De Shannon, and Miller do as they head for Malibu. There they find lots of romance (including naughty fun by 1964 standards), big waves, and the Polish Prince (Vinton) running a surf shop. Inane stuff that was pretty hot in its time but now plays as entertaining camp. Song include: "If I Were an Artist," "That's What Love Is," "Surf Party" ("By" Dunham, Bobby Beverly), "Fire Water," "Glory Wave," "Crack-Up," "Never Comin' Back," "Great White Water" (Dunham, Haskell), "Pearly Shells" (Lani Kai, Jericho Brown, Dunham).

p&d, Maury Dexter; w, Harry Spaulding; ph, Kay Norton; m, Jimmie Haskell; ed, Jodie Capelan; set d, Harry Reif; makeup, Ted Coodley.

Comedy/Drama   (PR:A MPAA:NR)

SURF TERROR   (SEE: BEACH GIRLS AND THE MONSTER, THE, 1965)

SURFTIDE 77*   (1962) 60m Volcan/Olympic International c (AKA: CALL SURFTIDE 77; CALL GIRL 77; SURFTIDE 777)

Tom Newman (*Bernard Bingbang*), Bob Cresse (*Agatha Bungworthy/Townsend Bungworthy*), Virginia Gordon (*Vultura*), Dwayne Winton (*Lt. Ricketts*), Victor Tayback (*Arms Cooper*).

Cresse, a rich woman, hires private eye Newman to find her heiress niece, whose left breast carries a butterfly birthmark. During Newman's search he's nearly killed by Gordon and he ends up at a Hollywood strip party but still the niece cannot be found. Finally Newman learns that Cresse really is a man in woman's clothing and is out to kill the niece. Watch for Tayback, of TV's "Alice", in an early appearance.

p, H. Duane Weaver; d, R. L. Frost.

Comedy   (PR:O MPAA:NR)

SURFTIDE 777   (SEE: SURFTIDE 77, 1962)

SURGEON'S KNIFE, THE** (1957, Brit.) 84m Gibraltar/GN bw

Donald Houston (*Dr. Alex Waring*), Adrienne Corri (*Laura Shelton*), Lyndon Brook (*Dr. Ian Breck*), Jean Cadell (*Henrietta Stevens*), Sydney Tafler (*Dr. Hearne*), Mervyn Johns (*Mr. Waring*), Marie Ney (*Matron Fiske*), Ronald Adam (*Maj. Tilling*), John Welsh (*Inspector Austen*), Beatrice Varley (*Mrs. Waring*), Noel Hood (*Sister Slater*), Andre Van Gysegham (*Mr. Dodds*), Frank Forsyth (*Anaesthetist*), Tom Bowman (*Surgeon*), Susan Westerby (*Miss Jenner*), Betty Shale (*Garsten*).

Houston is a lower-class individual who manages to climb the ladder of success with his surgical skills. However, an error on his part causes a patient to die in surgery. In order to save his status the doctor kills the two people present at the operation. He gets carried away with his murderous success and prepares to do in his wife, but he himself is killed before he carries out this nefarious plan. Standard melodrama without enough built-up suspense to be terrifying.

p, Charles A. Leeds; d, Gordon Parry; w, Robert Westerby (based on the novel *The Wicked Flee* by Anne Hocking); ph, Lionel Banes.

Crime   (PR:C MPAA:NR)

SURPRISE PACKAGE**   (1960) 100m COL bw

Yul Brynner (*Nico March*), Bill Nagy (*Johnny Stettina*), Mitzi Gaynor (*Gabby Rogers*), Lionel Burton, Barry Foster (*Two U.S. Marshals*), Eric Pohlmann (*Stefan Miralis*), Noel Coward (*King Pavel II*), George Coulouris (*Dr. Hugo Panzer*), "Man Mountain" Dean (*Igor Trofim*), Warren Mitchell (*Klimatis*), Guy Deghy (*Tibor Smolny*), Lyndon Brook (*Stavrin*).

Brynner is a big-time mob boss who's deported from the U.S. to Greece. A king (Coward, who performs his part merely as an extension of his well-known personality) lives on a Greek island, exiled from his homeland. He's got the valuable crown jewels and Brynner is willing to pay $1 million for them, loot he stashed away before his deportation. He wires "da boys" to send him the money, but they send him Gaynor instead, "A gift from da boys." This would-be comedy is directed with a fast pace but it only spins its wheels. The plot is confusing and the ensemble carries an "aren't we funny?" air. Donen and his cast were all capable of much better than this disappointment.

p&d, Stanley Donen; w, Harry Kurnitz (based on *A Gift from the Boys* by Art Buchwald); ph, Christopher Challis; m, Benjamin Frankel; ed, James Clark; m/l, "Surprise Package," Sammy Cahn, James Van Heusen (sung by Noel Coward).

Comedy   (PR:C MPAA:NR)

SURRENDER*½   (1931) 69m FOX bw

Warner Baxter (Sgt. Dumaine), Leila Hyams (Axelle), Ralph Bellamy (Capt. Elbing), William Pawley (Goulot), C. Aubrey Smith (Count Reichendorf), Alexander Kirkland (Dietrich), Howard Phillips (Claverie), Bert Hanlon (Vandaele), Tom Ricketts (Gottlieb), Bodil Rosing (Dominica), George Andre Beranger (Fichet), Frank Swales (Hugo), Joseph Sauers!!Sawyer]i (Muller), Albert Burke (Audemard), Jack Conrad (Sylvestre), William von Brincken, Albert Burke, J. Carrol Naish.

Poorly made drama involving Baxter as a POW during WW I. He's a Frenchman being held in a German prison camp. Meanwhile, at a nearby castle a proud father dreams of the day his four sons will march into Paris for a great German victory. One son is engaged to Hyams, but she is trying to have an affair with Baxter. The drama is poorly written and often confusing, though Bellamy gives a good performance as a prison guard. Surrender is what cast and director did with this muddled story.

d, William K. Howard; w, S.N. Behrman, Sonya Levien (based on the play "Axelle" by Pierre Benoit); ph, James Wong Howe; ed, Paul Weatherwax; art d, Anton Grot.

War Drama   (PR:A   MPAA:NR)

SURRENDER½**   (1950) 90m REP bw

Vera Ralston (Violet Barton), John Carroll (Gregg Delaney), Walter Brennan (William Howard), Francis Lederer (Henry Vaan), William Ching (Johnny Hale), Maria Palmer (Janet Barton), Jane Darwell (Mrs. Hale), Roy Barcroft (Deputy), Paul Fix (Williams), Esther Dale (Aunt May), Edward Norris (Wilbur), Howland Chamberlain (Manager), Norman Budd (Carson), Nacho Galindo (Grigo), Jeff York (Canning), Mickey Simpson (Pete), Dick Elliott (Sen. Clowe), Ralph Dunn (Jailer), Virginia Farmer (Mrs. Brown), J. Louis Johnson (Butler), Elizabeth Dunne (Elderly Woman), Cecil Elliott (Mrs. Schultz), Glenn Strange (Lon the Deputy), Kenne Duncan (Rider), Paul Stader (Gentleman Gambler), Wesley Hopper (Barney Gale), Tex Terry (Shotgun Guard), Charles Morton (Doorman), Doris Cole (Colette), Al Rhein (Dealer), Al Murphy (Cashier), Tina Menard (Flower Vendor), Frank Dae (Elderly Gentleman), Petra Silva (Maria), Tony Roux (Chocolate Vendor), Shelby Bacon (Georgie), Fred Hoose (Assistant Editor).

In a small town near the Mexican border Ralston is a wanted woman. To escape the law she marries Ching, an important newspaperman. Ching is also the best friend of Carroll, owner of the local gambling hall. Carroll can see through Ralston's charade and keeps a close eye on her. When Ralston's other husband, Lederer, shows up and claims bigamy, she kills him. Evidence points to Ching but Ching believes Carroll did the killing to protect his marriage. Ralston confesses and tries to escape across the border with Carroll, but the two are shot by sheriff Brennan. Despite some fairly corny dialog, SURRENDER isn't a bad little film. Dwan's direction moves the story well and the cast is highly competent.

p, Herbert J. Yates; d, Allan Dwan; w, James Edward Grant, Sloan Nibley (based on a story by Grant); ph, Reggie Lanning; m, Nathan Scott; ed, Richard L. Van Enger; art d, James Sullivan; set d, John McCarthy, Jr., Charles Thompson; cos, Adele Palmer; spec eff, Howard and Theodore Lydecker; m/l, "Surrender," Jack Elliott, John Carroll.

Western   (PR:C   MPAA:NR)

SURRENDER--HELL!**   (1959) 85m AA bw

Keith Andes (Col. Donald D. Blackburn), Susan Cabot (Delia), Paraluman (Pilar), Nestor De Villa (Maj. Bulao).

Andes is an Army lieutenant given the awesome assignment of organizing Filipino headhunters into a guerrilla force to fight the Japanese during WW II. Based on a diary kept by the man who actually carried out the mission, Col. Donald D. Blackburn, the script is hopelessly cliche-ridden and does little justice to the real man and his ordeal. However, there is romance coupled with interesting native dances and fascinating views of the Philippines, where the film was made. Cast wins plaudits all around, including some highly talented Filipinos.

p, Edmund Goldman; d&w, John Barnwell (based on the novel Blackburn's Headhunters by Philip Harkins, from the diaries of Col. Donald D. Blackburn); ph, Miguel Accion; m, Francisco Buencamino, Jr.; ed, Hugo Grimaldi; art d, Richard Abelardo

War   (PR:C   MPAA:NR)

SURVIVAL, 1962   (SEE: PANIC IN YEAR ZERO] 1962)

SURVIVAL, 1965   (SEE: GUIDE, THE, 1965, U.S./India)

SURVIVAL zero   (1976) 85m FOX c

Suzanne Benton (Suzanne), Barbara Blake (Barbara), Hampton Fancher (Hampton), Anne Francis (Anne), Dee Hartford (Dee), David Maure (David), Chuck McCann (Chuck), Sheree North (Sheree), Barry Sullivan (Barry), Jessie Wills (Jessie), Otis Young (Otis).

Ridiculous psychodrama has cast gathering for a dinner party, then discussing reasons for their continued existence. At the end of the evening they take a vote to see which two will be allowed to live. An almost infallible rule of thumb is to avoid any film where the actors play characters with their own names.

p&d, Michael I. Campus; w, John F.F. Black (based on a short story by Campus).

Drama   (PR:C   MPAA:NR)

SURVIVAL RUN*   (1980) 90m Film Ventures International c

Peter Graves, Ray Milland, Vincent Van Patten, Pedro Armendariz, Jr, Alan Conrad, Anthony Charnota, Gonzalo Vega, Cosie Costa, Randi Meryl, Marianne Sauvage, Robby Weaver, Danny Ades, Susan Pratt O'Hanlon.

Wretched stuff about a group of innocent teenagers off on a weekend of fun. Their van breaks down in the desert and they go looking for help. Unfortunately for them, they stumble onto Graves and Milland. The kids see the pair making a shady $2 million deal so Graves and Milland go after them. Some wild violence and naked flesh follow in this poorly imagined exploitation piece which commits the cardinal sin in the genre of toning down the grisly parts the fans come to see.

p, Lance Hool; d, Larry Speigel; w, Speigel, G. M. Cahill (based on a story by Cahill, Fredric Shore); ph, Alex Phillips, Jr. (Deluxe Color); m, Gary William Friedman; ed, Chris Greenbury.

Crime/Action   Cas.   (PR:O   MPAA:R)

SURVIVE! zero   (1977, Mex.) 85m PAR c

Pablo Ferrel (Raul), Hugo Stiglitz (Francisco), Luz Maria Aguilar (Mrs. Madero), Fernando Larranga (Madero), Norma Lazareno (Sylvia), Lorenzo de Rodas, Gloria Chavez, Jose Elias Moreno, Carlos Camara, Fernando Palaviccini, Sara Guash.

In the early 1970s an airplane carrying 45 passengers crashed in the Andes mountains. To live, the 16 survivors were forced to eat their dead compatriots. This quick exploitation piece capitalizes on that tragedy, emphasizing the more grisly aspects rather than the psychological impact of cannibalism. With an inept production, poorly dubbed for American audiences, SURVIVE! merely exploits a deeply human tragedy. The film was immediately snapped up by Alan Carr for American distribution and he made a good chunk of money with it. Director Cardona is also known for CULT OF THE DAMNED (1970).

p,d&w, Rene Cardona, Jr. (based on the book by Clay Blair, Jr.); m, Gerald Fried; ed, Marshall M. Borden

Drama   (PR:O   MPAA:R)

SURVIVOR*   (1980, Aus.) 93m Ginnane c

Robert Powell (Keller), Jenny Agutter (Hobbs), Joseph Cotten (The Priest), Angela Punch McGregor (Beth Rogan), Peter Sumner (Tewson), Ralph Cotterill (Slater), Adrian Wright (Goodwin).

Powell is the pilot of a 747 that crashes, and he is the only survivor. Strange things start to happen to him then in this interesting import. An excellent cast helps along this creepy story, sold straight to cable TV in the U.S.

p, Anthony I. Ginnane; d, David Hemmings; w, David Ambrose.

Horror   (PR:C-O   MPAA:NR)

SURVIVORS, THE**   (1983) 102m Rastar/COL c

Walter Matthau (Sonny Paluso), Robin Williams (Donald Quinelle), Jerry Reed (Jack Locke), James Wainwright (Wes Huntley), Kristen Vigard (Candice Paluso), Annie McEnroe (Doreen), Anne Pitoniak (Betty), Bernard Barrow (TV Manager), Marian Hailey (Jack's Wife), Joseph Carberry (Detective Matt Burke), Skipp Lynch (Wiley), Marilyn Cooper (Waitress), Meg Mundy (Mace Lover), Sanford Seeger (Knife Wielding Old Man), Yudie Bank (Accosted Old Lady), Michael P. Moran (Gun Salesman), Norma Pratt (Armed Little Lady), John DeBallo (Salesman), Del Hinkley (Wes Man No.1), Morgan Upton (Cost-Conscious Survivalist), John Goodman (Commando), Regina David (Nose Biter), Francisco Prado (Illegal Alien), J. B. Waters (Interviewer), Indira Manjrekar (Indian Woman), Tiffany Clark, Marc Stevens (Themselves).

Williams plays a young executive whose business day begins with a visit to the boss' office. When Williams opens the door the boss is nowhere to be found, but a large parrot sits perched atop the big man's chair. The confused employee looks at the bird quizzically and the trained parrot informs the man that he is fired. Thinking this a joke, Williams confronts the boss' secretary who calmly informs him that the parrot does indeed speak for the boss and that the parrot is used by high-level executives who find the firing of employees stressful. The stunned Williams now faces the unemployment line. Unfortunately, this rather unique and funny scene is the high point of THE SURVIVORS, leaving the rest of the film a mishmash of undeveloped characters and unfunny jokes. Back in the unemployment line, Williams meets Matthau, a former gas station owner whose business was blown up.

The two become friends and have lunch together. At the diner, Williams and Matthau witness a robbery and happen to catch a glimpse of the culprit, Reed. Reed, who claims he is a professional hit man for the mob, is determined to kill the pair because they have seen his face. Meanwhile, the basically wimpy Williams becomes obsessed with macho impulses and decides to enroll in a survivalist training school deep in the woods. Through a variety of unbelievable and confusing circumstances, Reed, Matthau, and Williams all wind up shooting it out among the survivalists. Considering the personnel involved, THE SURVIVORS should have been a very funny movie. Director Ritchie has successfully satirized American politics in THE CANDIDATE (1972), beauty contests in SMILE (1975), little-league baseball in THE BAD NEWS BEARS (1976), and even football in SEMI-TOUGH (1977), but in this film he doesn't seem to know what he's after. Williams, Matthau, and Reed struggle with the material and they do manage to root out some bright moments, but overall THE SURVIVORS is a bewildering stew of half-baked ideas strewn haphazardly across the screen. A frustrating movie.

p, William Sackheim; d, Michael Ritchie; w, Michael Leeson; ph, Billy Williams (Metrocolor); m, Paul Chihara; ed, Richard A. Harris; prod d, Gene Callahan; art d, Jay Moore; cos, Ann Roth.

Comedy   **Cas.**   **(PR:C-O   MPAA:R)**

SUSAN AND GOD*   (1940) 115m MGM bw (GB: THE GAY MRS.
                                                              TREXEL)

Joan Crawford (*Susan Trexel*), Fredric March (*Barry Trexel*), Ruth Hussey (*Charlotte*), John Carroll (*Clyde Rochester*), Rita Hayworth (*Leonora Stubbs*), Nigel Bruce (*Hutchins Stubbs*), Bruce Cabot (*Michael O'Hara*), Rose Hobart (*Irene Burrows*), Rita Quigley (*Blossom Trexel*), Romaine Callender (*Oliver Leeds*), Marjorie Main (*Mary*), Aldrich Bowker (*Patrick*), Constance Collier (*Lady Wiggam*), Herbert Evans (*Bronson*), Cece Broadhurst (*Cowboy Joe*), Richard O. Crane (*Bob*), Don Castle (*Attendant*), Henryetta Yates (*Fifi*), Oscar O'Shea (*Sam the Bartender*), Claude King (*J.F.*), Jane Drummond (*Rose*), Dan Dailey (*Homer*), Louis Payne (*Dave*), Sam Harris (*Amos*), Bobby Hale (*Tom*), Keith Hitchcock (*Scotchman*), Edward Paysen (*Athlete*), Phil Tead (*Customer*), Edward Gargan (*Cab Driver*), Eleanor Soohoo, Rama Bai (*Native Women*), Harold Landon (*Christopher*), David Oliver (*Man at Bar*), Gloria De Haven (*Enid*), Joan Leslie, Susan Peters, William Lechner, David Tillotson (*Guests*).

Anita Loos wrote an adaptation of the successful drama by Rachel Crothers that was actually better than the play's script. It had been specifically tailored for Gertrude Lawrence on the stage and after the property was acquired by MGM, it was offered to Norma Shearer, who declined because she didn't want to be seen as the mother of a teenage child. Crawford eagerly jumped in and made the transformation from 1930s siren to honest-to-goodness actress with this role. Crawford and Shearer never liked each other and often competed for roles, which were usually handed to Shearer because she was sleeping with the studio boss, Irving Thalberg. (Lest you think that's gossip, be aware that Shearer and Thalberg were happily married.) Crawford is a flighty society lady who has been living an "in name only" marriage with husband March, an intelligent man who has taken to tippling because his wife is so inner-directed that she has no time for anyone else but herself. Crawford returns home from abroad and is filled to the brim with the tenets of a new faith that's sweeping the upper crust in Europe. It involves purging oneself, with a public confession, of all sins, real or imagined, that one has ever done. This religious zealousness causes Crawford's bored society friends to think she's gone off her 14-karat rocker. As happens with anyone bubbling with a new fervor, she makes herself disgusting by meddling in the lives of people who would prefer she mind her own business. Her "good deed" attitude and "holier than thou" demeanor cause a problem between friends Bruce and Hayworth. Despite all of her preaching, Crawford's own domestic life is in disarray. March is hitting the bottle, her daughter, Quigley, is not able to cope with Crawford and her life in general and is becoming more and more introspective. March tries to understand what's driving Crawford to this new religion and wants it to be an indication that she is finally growing up and able to look away from the mirror and out at other people. But he soon understands that it's just another in a series of fads that Crawford has embraced over the years. March is living apart from Crawford and asks that the family be united again, if only for Quigley's well-being. Crawford moves back in and it takes a while until she sees what her selfishness and preoccupation have done to her marriage and child. She eventually learns to live the words she's been espousing instead of just mouthing them for other people. March had been off the screen for more than a year after completing TRADE WINDS. He'd always preferred New York and the stage and the small apartment he shared with wife Florence Eldridge at the Stanhope Hotel on Fifth Avenue. The husband's role in the play (originally done by Paul Kelly) was not nearly so important as it was in the film so we can only surmise that it was expanded in order to attach March to the film. Some sharp lines from Loos and a bit of satire of the kind of Christianity put forth by Dr. Frank Buchman, in his Oxford Theory of total confession. The religion satirized was similar in many ways to several branches of Protestantism still pounding the pulpit today, so the movie is not dated. Hayworth does well as the young wife of Bruce, having been lent by Columbia for the job when Cukor asked for her. It was her 18th film using the name of Hayworth. For her first 10 movies, she used her real name of Cansino.

p, Hunt Stromberg; d, George Cukor; w, Anita Loos (based on the play by Rachel Crothers); ph, Robert Planck; m, Herbert Stothart; ed, William H. Terhune; art d, Cedric Gibbons; cos, Adrian.

Drama   **(PR:A   MPAA:NR)**

SUSAN LENOX--HER FALL AND RISE*½**
   (1931) 74m MGM bw(GB: THE RISE OF HELGA; RISING TO FAME)

Greta Garbo (*Susan Lenox*), Clark Gable (*Rodney*), Jean Hersholt (*Ohlin*), John Miljan (*Burlingham*), Alan Hale (*Mondstrum*), Hale Hamilton (*Mike Kelly*), Hilda Vaughn (*Astrid*), Russell Simpson (*Doctor*), Cecil Cunningham (*Mme. Panoramia*), Ian Keith (*Robert Lane*), Helene Millard, Marjorie King, Theodore Von Eltz.

The only teaming of Garbo and Gable ("Don't miss the one and only Garbo in the arms of Clark Gable" the ads proclaimed), SUSAN LENOX--HER FALL AND RISE was based on a rather racy novel that caused a sensation some 15 years before. Garbo plays the illegitimate daughter of a poor, brutish farmer, Hersholt. He decides to arrange a marriage between her and a more wealthy farmer, Hale. Garbo detests Hale and runs away rather than face married life with the brute. During her flight she discovers a cabin inhabited by Gable, a handsome and romantic engineer. The two are immediately attracted to each other and romance blooms. Unfortunately, Garbo learns that her father is out searching for her, and she must flee once again. Gable is away on a job at the time and never learns of her departure. In desperation, Garbo hooks up with a carnival train and becomes the concubine of the owner, Miljan, to earn her keep. Gable eventually resurfaces, and when he learns of her unfaithfulness, he is crushed. He dissolves their relationship and goes off to South America. Having lost the man she really loves, Garbo leaves the carnival and decides to make a new life for herself. She changes her name to Susan Lenox and spends her paltry savings on exotic clothes. She eventually becomes the mistress of a prominent politician, Hamilton, but this soon ends when Hamilton's political enemies discover Garbo's true identity and use it to ruin him. Left with no place to go, Garbo travels to South America to search for Gable. She eventually finds him, now a pathetic, booze-soaked sot who feels sorry for himself, working deep in the jungle on a construction project. She begs him to come home with her and tries to convince him that she has changed, but he'll have none of it and knocks a pesky prostitute down a flight of stairs as if to emphasize his point (this a shockingly brutal act). Garbo catches the eye of a wealthy industrialist, Keith, and he offers her the chance to leave the jungle with him. Given the perfect opportunity to prove her love for Gable, Garbo rejects Keith's offer and elects to stay in the jungle with her true love. Now convinced of her sincerity, Gable accepts Garbo's love and the pair go off together to start life anew. Chosen solely because Garbo wanted to work with the handsome young actor, Gable was a bit miscast in SUSAN LENOX--HER FALL AND RISE. The script was weak (rumor had it that as many as 24 different screenwriters took a whack at it) and didn't really provide the proper vehicle for a Garbo-Gable sizzler. Gable's role was better suited for the less-rugged John Gilbert, and the viewer has a hard time believing that Gable would be that destroyed and bitter over losing Garbo. Gable agreed to be in the film because it would improve his standing at the box office, and he used the opportunity to see how one of MGM's biggest stars threw her weight around (she walked off the set six times). Problems aside, the film is a fine, fast-paced melodrama with a strong cast that never bores. Perhaps more in reaction to the sensational novel it was based on, the British censors removed a few minutes of what they considered objectionable in the film and changed the title to THE RISE OF HELGA.

d, Robert Z. Leonard; w, Wanda Tuchock, Zelda Sears, Leon Gordon, Edith Fitzgerald (based on the novel by David Graham Phillips); ph, William Daniels; ed, Margaret Booth.

Romance   **(PR:C   MPAA:NR)**

SUSAN SLADE*½**   (1961) 116m WB c

Troy Donahue (*Hoyt Brecker*), Connie Stevens (*Susan Slade*), Dorothy McGuire (*Leah Slade*), Lloyd Nolan (*Roger Slade*), Brian Aherne (*Stanton Corbett*), Grant Williams (*Conn White*), Natalie Schafer (*Marian Corbett*), Kent Smith (*Dr. Fain*), Bert Convy (*Wells Corbett*), Guy Wilkerson (*Slim*).

This juicy little soap opera features Stevens as a naive 17- year-old who has an affair with mountaineer Williams. She winds up pregnant and things are complicated when the would-be father is killed falling off Mt. McKinley. Her parents take her to Guatemala with the plan that her mother, McGuire, will pretend the child is hers when they return. But her father, Nolan, succumbs to a heart attack, so Stevens and McGuire return to California. There Stevens is proposed to by Convy, the rich son of her late father's employer, and by Donahue, an embittered would-be novelist, whose father had committed suicide after embezzling funds from Convy's father. Stevens rejects both men but when her baby is badly burned in an accident she confesses to the child's origin. Convy withdraws his proposal but Donahue, who has finally sold his first novel, accepts with open arms. Corny but entertaining in its own fashion. The photography is quite lush, giving this the needed gloss that makes it work. Just enjoy this one for what it is.

p,d&w, Delmer Daves (based on the novel *The Sin of Susan Slade* by Doris Hume); ph, Lucien Ballard (Technicolor); m, Max Steiner; ed, William

Ziegler; art d, Leo K. Kuter; set d, William L. Kuehl; cos, Howard Shoup; makeup, Gordon Bau.

Drama   (PR:C   MPAA:NR)

SUSAN SLEPT HERE**   (1954) 98m RKO c

Dick Powell (*Mark, Screen Writer*), Debbie Reynolds (*Susan*), Anne Francis (*Isabella*), Alvy Moore (*Virgil*), Glenda Farrell (*Maude, Mark's Secretary*), Horace McMahon (*Maizel, Cop*), Herb Vigran (*Hanlon, Cop*), Les Tremayne (*Harvey, Mark's Lawyer*), Mara Lane (*Marilyn*), Maidie Norman (*Georgette, Mark's Maid*), Rita Johnson (*Dr. Rawley, Psychiatrist*), Ellen Corby (*Waitress*), Benny Rubin (*Janitor*), Barbara Darrow (*Legal Secretary*), Sue Carlton (*Cashier*), Oliver Blake (*Motel Manager*), Louella O. Parsons (*Telephone Voice*).

A would-be comedy has Powell playing a screenwriter who is doing research for a film about juvenile delinquents. Two policeman buddies drop off 18-year-old Reynolds to help him get a better handle on the subject. She proves to be more than Powell can handle and complications arise when his girl friend, Francis, grows jealous. The premise is terrific and seemingly good material for director Tashlin. However, the film is a real mess that is more ugly than funny. There are a few humorous moments in this pseudo-sex farce, but it's a surprisingly bad outing considering all the talent involved.

p, Harriet Parsons; d, Frank Tashlin; w, Alex Gottlieb (based on the play "Susan" by Gottlieb, Steve Fisher); ph, Nicholas Musuraca (Technicolor); m, Leigh Harline; ed, Harry Marker; md, Constantine Bakaleinikoff; ch, Robert Sidney; m/l, "Hold My Hand," Jack Lawrence, Richard Myers (sung by Don Cornell), "Susan Slept Here," Lawrence.

Comedy   Cas.   (PR:C   MPAA:NR)

SUSANNA   (SEE: SHEPHERD OF THE OZARKS, 1942)

SUSANNA PASS*½   (1949) 67m REP c

Roy Rogers (*Himself*), Dale Evans (*Kay "Doc" Parker*), Estelita Rodriguez (*Rita*), Martin Garralaga (*Carlos Mendoza*), Robert Emmett Keane (*Martin Masters*), Lucien Littlefield (*Russell Masters*), Douglas Fowley (*Del Roberts*), David Sharpe (*Vince*), Robert Bice (*Bob Oliver*), Foy Willing and The Riders of the Purple Sage, Trigger the Horse.

When a fish hatchery suffers a series of explosions, game warden Rogers investigates. He finds out that bad guys are after the oil deposits beneath the hatchery's lake and will do anything they can to get at it. This is one of the rare poor films for Rogers with a predictable and often improbable plot. Film marked the return of his off-screen leading lady, Evans, to the popular series after several seasons apart.

p, Edward J. White; d, William Witney; w, Sloan Nibley, John K. Butler; ph, Reggie Lanning (Trucolor); ed, Tony Martinelli; md, Morton Scott; art d, Frank Hotaling; m/l, "Brush Those Tears Away," Oakley Haldeman, Al Trace, Jimmy Lee (performed by Roy Rogers, Dale Evans, Foy Willing and The Riders of the Purple Sage), "Susanna Pass," "A Good, Good Mornin'" (performed by Rogers, Evans, Willing and his Riders), "Two Gun Rita" (performed by Estelita Rodriguez).

Western   (PR:A   MPAA:NR)

SUSANNAH OF THE MOUNTIES**½   (1939) 77m FOX bw

Shirley Temple (*Susannah Sheldon*), Randolph Scott (*Inspector Angus "Monty" Montague*), Margaret Lockwood (*Vicky Standing*), Martin Good Rider (*Little Chief*), J. Farrell MacDonald (*Pat O'Hannegan*), Maurice Moscovich (*Chief Big Eagle*), Moroni Olsen (*Supt. Andrew Standing*), Victor Jory (*Wolf Pelt*), Lester Matthews (*Harlan Chambers*), Leyland Hodgson (*Randall*), Herbert Evans (*Doctor*), Charles Irwin (*Sgt. McGregor*), John Sutton (*Cpl. Piggot*), Chief Big Tree (*Chief*), Jack Luden (*Williams*), Harold Goodwin (*Orderly*).

Once again Temple plays an orphan, this time having lost her parents in an Indian attack. She's adopted by rugged Mountie Scott and his sweetheart, Lockwood. The Blackfoot tribe continues to attack and Scott is nearly burned to death by the savages. Shirley solves all the problems in her own unique fashion, and teaches Scott how to tap dance as well. This is a lesser vehicle for Temple, probably her last good feature. Still the child star is engaging despite the slightness of the film, and the kids will still eat it up like candy. Temple was rapidly becoming a big girl by 1939 and the era of her cute little musicals was coming to a halt.

p, Kenneth Macgowan; d, William A. Seiter; w, Robert Ellis, Helen Logan (based on a story by Fidel La Barba and Walter Ferris from the novel *Susannah, A Little Girl of the Mounties* by Muriel Denison); ph, Arthur Miller; ed, Robert Bischoff; md, Louis Silvers.

Children's Adventure   (PR:AAA   MPAA:NR)

SUSIE STEPS OUT**   (1946) 65m Comet/UA bw

David Bruce (*Jeffrey Westcott*), Cleatus Caldwell (*Clara Russell*), Howard Freeman (*Mr. Starr*), Grady Sutton (*Dixon*), Margaret Dumont (*Mrs. Starr*), Percival Vivian (*Papa Russell*), John Berkes (*Wilkins*), Joseph J. Greene (*Bailey*), Nita Hunter (*Susie Russell*), Harry Baris, Emmett Vogan.

All the cliches of "radio musical" movies are adapted to the infant medium of television for this minor programmer. Caldwell works for an ad agency but is fired after a mixup with the boss' wife. Her father (Vivian), a cello player, becomes ill and the family has no income until little sister Hunter poses as a nightclub singer and ends up a TV star. Simplistic and typical for this sort of film, with standard production values and reasonably good performances. Songs include: "When You're Near," "When Does Love Begin?" (Hal Borne, sung by David Bruce), "For the Right Guy," "I'm So Lonely" (Borne), "Bob-Bob That Did It" (Borne, Eddie Cherkose).

p, Buddy Rogers, Ralph Cohn; d, Reginald LeBorg; w, Elwood Ullman (added dialog by Fred Freiberger, original story by LeBorg, Kurt Neumann); ph, Robert Pitack; ed, Lynn Harrison; md, Hal Borne; art d, George Van Marter; set d, Al Greenwood.

Musical   (PR:A   MPAA:NR)

SUSPECT, THE***   (1944) 85m UNIV bw

Charles Laughton (*Philip*), Ella Raines (*Mary*), Dean Harens (*John*), Stanley C. Ridges (*Huxley*), Henry Daniell (*Mr. Simmons*), Rosalind Ivan (*Cora*), Molly Lamont (*Mrs. Simmons*), Raymond Severn (*Merridew*), Eve Amber (*Sybil*), Maude Eburne (*Mrs. Packer*), Clifford Brooke (*Mr. Packer*).

Though Laughton's classic roles were past him by 1944, in THE SUSPECT the esteemed actor proved once more why his talents were highly respected in the film community. It is Victorian London at the turn of the century. Laughton is an amiable shopkeeper married to Ivan, a mean-spirited woman who constantly is complaining about something. After meeting Raines, a stenographer, Laughton falls in love, and decides to kill his shrewish wife. He beats Ivan to death with a cane, then manages to convince the authorities that she died after severely injuring herself in a staircase fall. With Ivan out of the way, Laughton is free to marry the beautiful young stenographer. Ridges is a police detective who finds Laughton's story a bit shady, as does Daniell, Laughton's neighbor. Daniell decides to blackmail Laughton, but soon the meddling neighbor comes to an untimely end of his own. Ridges pushes on with his investigation and Laughton eventually succumbs to the pressure, confessing to both murders. Siodmak, who had been a successful German director until forced to flee by the growing power of Nazi rule, develops his story well, creating a double-edged morality within his story. Laughton is initially presented as a kind and caring man. His crimes are heinous, but because the character is shown in such a sympathetic light, the questions of right and wrong become ambiguous. Laughton is excellent in the compassionate portrait of a man caught up in a nightmare of his own making. The story is loosely based on the case of Dr. Crippen, a London surgeon who, in an infamous case that shocked society, murdered his wife, then cut her body into small pieces before disposing of them.

p, Islin Auster; d, Robert Siodmak; w, Bertram Milhauser, Arthur T. Hormen (based on the novel *This Way Out* by James Ronald); ph, Paul Ivano; m, Frank Skinner; ed, Arthur Hilton; md, Martin Obzina; cos, Vera West.

Crime   (PR:C   MPAA:NR)

SUSPECT, 1961   (SEE: RISK, THE, 1961, Brit.)

SUSPECTED   (SEE: TEXAS DYNAMO, 1950)

SUSPECTED ALIBI   (SEE: SUSPENDED ALIBI, 1956, Brit.)

SUSPECTED PERSON**½   (1943, Brit.) 78m ABF/PRC bw

Clifford Evans (*Jim Raynor*), Patricia Roc (*Joan Raynor*), David Farrar (*Inspector Thompson*), Anne Firth (*Carol*), Robert Beatty (*Franklin*), Eric Clavering (*Dolan*), Leslie Perrins (*Tony Garrett*), Eliot Makeham (*David*), John Salew (*Jones*), Billy Hartnell (*Saunders*), Anthony Shaw, Terry Conlin.

Good little suspense programmer from England finds Evans as an innocent man who accidentally comes across some money stolen from an American bank. The two men who stole the money come to England and Scotland Yard follows their every move. Roc, Evans' sister, tries to make him give up the money. The direction is well paced for the fare, with a good sense for suspense. This sort of thriller was director-writer Huntington's bread and butter.

p, Warwick Ward; d&w, Lawrence Huntington; ph, Gunther Krampf, Ronald Anscombe; ed, Flora Newton.

Suspense   (PR:A   MPAA:NR)

SUSPENDED ALIBI★★ (1957, Brit.) 64m ACT Films/RANK bw (AKA: SUSPECTED ALIBI)

Patrick Holt (*Paul Pearson*), Honor Blackman (*Lynn Pearson*), Valentine Dyall (*Inspector Kayes*), Naomi Chance (*Diana*), Lloyd Lamble (*Waller*), Andrew Keir (*Sandy Thorpe*), Frederick Piper (*Mr. Beamster*), Viola Lyel (*Mrs. Beamster*), Bryan Coleman (*Bill Forrest*), Wally Patch (*Porter*), Jeanette Hutchinson (*Secretary*), Tony Winterbottom (*Bobby*), Madoline Thomas (*Granny*), Edgar Wreford (*Prison Chaplain*), John Baker (*Post Supervisor*), Ian Whittaker (*Telegraph Boy*), Brown Derby (*Sgt. Roberts*), Vincent Lawson (*Coroner*), Walter Horsburgh (*Customs Official*), Richard McNeff (*Police Constable*).

Holt is having an affair with Chance, and when he finally decides to break it off he goes to a friend to help him establish an alibi while he was visiting his mistress, then later discovers the friend has been murdered. He is arrested for the crime, condemned by his own alibi and slated to hang. Keir is a crime reporter who won't give up on the case, and he eventually uncovers the evidence that frees Holt. Okay crime drama passes the time pleasantly.

p, Robert Dunbar; d, Alfred Shaughnessy; w, Kenneth R. Hayles; ph, Peter Hennessey.

Crime   (PR:A   MPAA:NR)

SUSPENSE★★   (1930, Brit.) 75m British International bw

Mickey Brantford (*Pvt. Reggie Pettigrew*), Cyril McLaglen (*Sgt. McCluskey*), Jack Raine (*Capt. Wilson*), D. Hay Petrie (*Scruffy*), Fred Groves (*Pvt. Lomax*), Percy Parsons (*Pvt. Alleluia Brett*), Syd Crossley (*Cpl. Brown*), Hamilton Keene (*Officer*).

Dated WW I drama has a group of British forces hiding in the trenches along the German lines. The typical war-movie characters abound, including the tough-as-nails sergeant and the shell-shocked kid. Poorly lit, with stripped-down dialog, SUSPENSE has some good moments, but all in all, is a pale shadow of ALL QUIET ON THE WESTERN FRONT. The ensemble isn't bad considering the film's weaknesses. Groves, in particular, turns in a fine performance, but McLaglen was considerably less convincing as a soldier in this than was his brother Victor, the perennial sergeant in countless other films.

p,d&w, Walter Summers (based on the play by Patrick MacGill); ph, T. Sparkuhl, Hal Young; ed, Walter Sovkis, Emile de Ruello.

War   (PR:C   MPAA:NR)

SUSPENSE★★½   (1946) 100m MON bw

Belita (*Roberta Elba*), Barry Sullivan (*Joe Morgan*), Albert Dekker (*Frank Leonard*), Eugene Pallette (*Harry*), Bonita Granville (*Ronnie*), Edith Angold (*Nora*), George Stone (*Max*), Billy Nelson, Robert Middlemass, Lee "Lasses" White (*Woodsmen*), Byron Foulger (*Cab Driver*), Leon Belasco (*Pierre*), Nestor Paiva, Dewey Robinson (*Men with Blond*), Marian Martin (*Blond*), George Chandler (*Louie*), Frank Scannell (*Monk*), Sidney Melton (*Smiles*), Bobby Ramos (*Vocalist*), Jack Chefe (*Waiter*), Billy Grey (*Small Boy*), Norma Jean Nilsson (*Little Girl*), Paul Kruger (*Stranger*), Bernard Sell (*Peanut Vendor*), Charlie Wilson (*Police Officer*), Chris-Pin Martin (*Mexican Waiter*), Hugh Prosser (*Photographer*), Ernie Adams (*Watchman*), Kid Chrissell (*Workman*), Capt. Summers (*Truck Driver*), Don Clarke, Jack Richardson, Charles Sherlock, Joey Cappo, Jack Kenney (*Poker Players*), Edward Brian (*Reporter*), Parker Gee, Martha Clemmons, Jo Ann Deen, Harisse Brin (*Spectators*), Kristine Miller, Beverly Haney, Beverly Hawthorne, Virginia Owen, Zaz Vorka, Alice Kirsten, Phyllis Henry, Barbara Swanson, Marie Icido, Mercedes, Susanne Rosser, Evelyn Moriarity (*Models*), Tiny Lipson (*Man in Audience*), Bobby Barber (*Delicatessen Man*), Dave Shore (*Clerk*), Miguelito Valdez (*Himself*), Members of the Bobby Ramos Band.

Okay crime story with the added attraction of music, ice skating, and what must have been the highest budget that Monogram put behind a picture up to that time. Two of the King Brothers produced this melange of styles from an original script by Yordan. Sullivan is a one-time hot shot who has had a few bad rolls of the dice so he must seek honest employment. He takes a job hustling peanuts for the ice skating show run by Dekker. Not content to hawk the food, Sullivan insinuates himself with his boss, makes some good suggestions and one of them turns out to be a spectacular trick that Dekker's wife, Belita, performs. She finds Sullivan more than passingly interesting and it's only a short time before the two are cheating behind Dekker's back. Dekker didn't get to be an important impresario by luck, though, and he soon smells what's happening between Sullivan and Belita so he takes her off to a vacation in the mountains, where they own a cabin. At the same time, Sullivan's old flame, Granville, comes back into his life. She's just arrived from Chicago and would like to resume their once-torrid affair, but Sullivan will have no part of her and the torch she is carrying burns fiercely. Sullivan drives to the mountains, ostensibly to discuss some business with Dekker, but it's really to see Belita. Dekker invites Sullivan to stay the night, rather than drive back to town in the dark. It's a ruse on Dekker's part. He yawns, tells them he's tired, and says he's going to sleep. Instead, he peeks and sees that Belita and Sullivan are magnetized to each other and kiss passionately. When Sullivan and Belita go ice skating the

next day, a shot rings out that misses them both. But the sound of the rifle crack is so strong that an avalance begins and inundates the small frozen pond and the surrounding area. Belita and Sullivan manage to escape the angry snow, then get back to the cabin where they find that Dekker and a rifle are missing. They surmise that it was Dekker who fired the shot and was then crushed by the avalanche. Back in the city, Sullivan becomes the boss of the ice show and he and Belita practically melt the ice around them with the heat of their passion. Belita is disturbed that Dekker's body was never found and the memory bothers her. She eventually discovers that Dekker didn't die in the avalanche. He was murdered by Sullivan and his corpse was placed in a large roll-top desk that Sullivan burned at a later time, thus destroying the evidence. When she finds that out, she can't bear to be with Sullivan any longer and Sullivan has his own plans about how to deal with a recalcitrant mistress. The big number in the show is Belita's leap through a circle of razor-sharp swords. If any of the blades is loose, or even slightly out of kilter, she would be killed. Prior to a show, Sullivan arranges for one of the swords to be loose enough to get her. Belita's eagle eye spots the sword and she slips it back into place. Sullivan sees that she's too smart for him and walks out of the arena. He's hated being the show's ringmaster anyhow and it's time for him to move on. As he walks down the darkened street, Granville, the spurned woman, steps out of the shadows and guns him down in as unlikely and unmotivated an ending as anyone would want. Nick Castle does some good ice skating choreography and Belita, who was one of many skaters who were all the rage at the time, handles her chores well. Miguelito Valdez, who plays a singer in the ice show, does his own song, "Candido." The production number tunes were "Ice Cuba," "East Side Boogie" (Tommy Reilly) and "With You in My Arms" (by Dunham and Alexander) and both were done by Bobby Ramos and his orchestra. Belita's real name was Gladys L. Jepson-Turner and she was born in England. She'd been skating since infancy and was a headliner in the "Ice Capades" before making her first film, ICE CAPADES in 1941. Other films include THE MAN ON THE EIFFEL TOWER, SILK STOCKINGS, and THE TERRACE.

p, Maurice King, Frank King; d, Frank Tuttle; w, Philip Yordan; ph, Karl Struss; m, Daniele Amfitheatrof; ed, Otho Lovering, Dick Heermance; art d, F. Paul Sylos; set d, George J. Hopkins; cos, Robert Kalloch; spec eff, Jack Shaw, Ray Mercer; ch, Nick Castle.

Mystery/Musical   (PR:A-C   MPAA:NR)

SUSPICION★★★½   (1941) 99m RKO bw

Cary Grant (*Johnnie Aysgarth*), Joan Fontaine (*Lina McLaidlaw*), Sir Cedric Hardwicke (*Gen. McLaidlaw*), Nigel Bruce (*Beaky Thwaite*), Dame May Whitty (*Mrs. McLaidlaw*), Isabel Jeans (*Mrs. Newsham*), Heather Angel (*Ethel the Maid*), Auriol Lee (*Isobel Sedbusk*), Reginald Sheffield (*Reggie Wetherby*), Leo G. Carroll (*Capt. Melbeck*), Maureen Roden-Ryan (*Winnie the Maid*), Carol Curtis-Brown (*Jessie Barham*), Constance Worth (*Mrs. Fitzpatrick*), Violet Shelton (*Alice Barham*), Pax Walker (*Phoebe the Maid*), Leonard Carey (*Jenner the Butler*), Gertrude Hoffman (*Mrs. Wetherby*), Kenneth Hunter (*Sir Gerald*), Clyde Cook (*Photographer*), Faith Brook (*Alice Barham*), Dorothy Lloyd (*Miss Wetherby*), Rex Evans (*Mr. Bailey*), Edward Fielding (*Antique Shop Proprietor*), Hilda Plowright (*Postmistress*), Ben Webster (*Registrar*), Gavin Gordon (*Bertram Sedbusk*), Nondas Metcalf (*Phyllis Swinghurst*), Lumsden Hare (*Inspector Hodgson*), Clara Reid (*Mrs. Craddock*), Vernon Downing (*Benson*), Billy Bevan (*Ticket Taker*), Alec Craig (*Hogart Club Bit*), Aubrey Mather (*Mr. Webster*), Elsie Weller (*Miss Wetherby*).

Fully three-fourths of this, Hitchcock's second U.S. movie after REBECCA, is excellent. It then falls apart and has a tacked-on ending that was a sop to RKO, who felt that there was no way Grant could be shown to be a murderer. Anthony Berkeley Cox, under the pseudonym of "Frances Iles," had written a successful murder mystery titled *Before the Fact*. It referred to what happened before a murder, but since there was no murder seen in the picture, the name was changed to suspicion, which was far too generic but fit what was seen. Hitchcock borrowed Fontaine from David O. Selznick and she won an Oscar for her work here, although there are those who feel she received the statuette for her work the year before in REBECCA and that the Academy was making up to her for having given the Best Actress nod to Ginger Rogers in KITTY FOYLE. Working from a script co-written by Hitchcock's wife, Reville, long-time associate Harrison, and superior playwright Raphaelson, Hitchcock built the suspense slowly, deliciously, and filled the screen with spine-tingling moments. Unfortunately, the film's climax wasn't the equal of the foundation that Hitchcock had laid and the result was a picture that fizzled out in the finale. Despite that, it did well at the box office and returned a neat profit. In the novel, the Grant character is, in fact, a killer, which made far more sense. In order to keep to the Hollywood theory of a "happy ending," that development was tossed aside for an ending which sent audiences out crinkling their noses. Grant is a cad, a rogue, a wastrel; Fontaine is the protected spinster who lives in a large English manor house. Her parents, Hardwicke and Whitty (and this was one of the rare times in films when a "sir" and a "dame" played husband and wife), are unbearably stuffy and she is nearing the age when "old maid" would be her designation, so she escapes the oppressive house by marrying Grant, even though she's been forewarned that he is a fortune hunter, a rakehell, and an incorrigible playboy. Grant becomes involved in an embezzlement and then Bruce, playing his usual lovable but bumbling self, dies in Paris, in a fashion that leads Fontaine to believe that Grant may have done the geezer in. From that moment, Fontaine begins to suspect that she is next on Grant's list and everything he does seems to be pointed in that direction. The good humor of the first half vanishes and the tension mounts. Fontaine doesn't know what to do, as she has no proof that her smiling, attentive husband is a killer. One night, she is up in her room and Grant is bringing her a nightly glass of milk. (Hitchcock actually put a lit bulb inside the milk so it glowed as Grant carried it to Fontaine.) She thinks it's poisoned and doesn't know how to handle the situation. It isn't, of course, and the lit bulb is a trick Hitch uses to put the audience on the seat edge. Later, the two of them are driving along a rocky cliff high above the crashing surf. She leaps from the car because she thinks he is about to throw her out. He stops the car, saves her from falling off the cliff, and she finally realizes that he loves her. The original ending had the milk poisoned. Fontaine was to drink it, but not before asking Grant to mail a letter for her. In that missive were all of her suspicions and a note saying that if she died, her husband was the killer. Hitchcock claimed that the studio made him alter the ending, but there is some evidence that he came up with the change. Despite the fact that it was a U.S. picture, all of the actors, save Fontaine, who was born in the Far East to British parents, were from England. The actual script was not as good as the mood created by Hitchcock and Stradling, a murky, fearful aura of murder lurking behind every staircase. The movie and Waxman's score were nominated for Oscars, losing to HOW GREEN WAS MY VALLEY and Bernard Herrmann for ALL THAT MONEY CAN BUY (AKA: THE DEVIL AND DANIEL WEBSTER).

d, Alfred Hitchcock; w, Samson Raphaelson, Joan Harrison, Alma Reville (based on the novel *Before the Fact* by Frances Iles [Anthony Berkeley Cox]); ph, Harry Stradling, Clark; m, Franz Waxman; ed, William Hamilton; art d, Van Nest Polglase, Clark; set d, Darrell Silvera; cos, Edward Stevenson; spec eff, Vernon L. Walker.

Suspense   **Cas.**   **(PR:A-C MPAA:NR)**

SUSPIRIA***   (1977, Ital.) 97m Seda Spettacoli/International
                                                              Classics-FOX c

Jessica Harper (*Susy Banyon*), Joan Bennett (*Madame Blank the School Head*), Alida Valli (*Miss Tanner the Ballet Mistress*), Udo Kier (*Frank*), Flavio Bucci (*Daniel*), Stefano Casini (*Sara*), Miguel Bose (*Mark*), Barbara Magnolfi (*Olga*), Susanna Javicoli (*Sonia*), Margherita Horowitz (*A Teacher*), Jacopo Mariani (*Albert*), Fulvio Mingozzi (*Taxi Driver*), Renato Zamengo (*Caroline*), Rudolf Schundler (*Milius*), Eva Axen (*Pat*), Giuseppe Transocchi (*Pavlo*).

Innocent American student Harper arrives in Germany to enroll in a dance academy. She arrives in the middle of a dark, stormy evening when two girls turn up murdered. That's just the beginning of her troubles. It seems that this place is really a witches' coven headed by Bennett (best known for her work with Fritz Lang and her role in the TV Gothic-Horror soap opera "Dark Shadows") and Valli. This is a stylish and often gross shocker that is definitely not for everyone. Some of the horrors include maggots falling onto sleeping young ladies, blood draining in a steel mesh trap, and assorted bats and witches. The story is fairly ridiculous, but the visual effects more than make up for that. A must for genre fans.

p, Claudio Argento; d, Dario Argento; w, Dario Argento, Daria Nicolodi; ph, Lucian Tovoli (Technicolor); m, The Goblins, Dario Argento; ed, Franco Fraticelli; art d, Giuseppe Bassan; cos, Pierangelo Cicoletti.

Horror   **(PR:O MPAA:R)**

SUSUZ YAZ   (SEE: DRY SUMMER, 1967, Turk.)

SUTTER'S GOLD**   (1936) 69m UNIV bw

Edward Arnold (*John Sutter*), Lee Tracy (*Pete Perkin*), Binnie Barnes (*Countess Elizabeth Bartoffski*), Katherine Alexander (*Mrs. Anna Sutter*), Addison Richards (*James Marshall*), Montagu Love (*Capt. Kettleson*), John Miljan (*Gen. Juan Batista Alvarado*), Robert Warwick (*Gen. Rotscheff*), Harry Carey (*Kit Carson*), Mitchell Lewis (*King Kamehameh*), William Janney (*John Sutter, Jr.*), Ronald Cosbey (*John Sutter, Jr. at Age 8*), Nan Grey (*Ann Eliza Sutter*), Joanne Smith (*Ann Eliza Sutter at Age 3*), Billy Gilbert (*Gen. Ramos*), Aura De Silva (*Senora Alvarado*), Allen Vincent (*Alvarado, Jr.*), Harry Cording (*Lars*), Sidney Bracey (*Smythe*), Bryant Washburn (*Capt. Petroff*), Gaston Glass (*Lt. Bacalenakoff*), Oscar Apfel, Richard Cramer, George Irving, Frank Reicher, Jim Thorpe, Morgan Wallace, Don Briggs, Charles Farr, Harry Stubbs, Neeley Edwards, Alfred J. Smith, Jose Robio, Priscilla Lawson, Paul Weigel, Russ Powell, William Gould, John Bleifer, Pedro Regas, William Ruhl.

Lavish but dull story of the man on whose land gold was discovered in California and how it destroyed him. Arnold is John Sutter, a political refugee from Switzerland who travels to New York, then through Canada and to Hawaii before ending up in California, where he obtains land grants that give him all the land for seven-days' ride in all directions. When gold is discovered in the water-race for a sawmill he owns, his empire disintegrates. Workers desert him, people stake their own claims out of his lands, his buildings are torn down for their wood, his crops and orchards are burned, and his son is murdered trying to defend the family holdings. Arnold catches gold fever as well, and deserts his wife (Alexander) in favor of a

Russian countess, Barnes. He loses everything, though, and after returning to Alexander he spends the rest of his days as an embittered old man endlessly pestering the government to give him some sort of compensation. Based on a best-selling biography by Blaise Cendrars, the film was originally to have been directed by Sergei Eisenstein during his extended visit to Hollywood some years earlier, but the deal fell through, as did all the projects that had been lined up for the great Russian director. Howard Hawks then took over the project, but as the costs rocketed, Hawks was replaced by James Cruze–director of the profitable silent classic THE COVERED WAGON (1923)–who eventually got screen credit. Universal Studios head Carl Laemmle sank more than $2 million into this film, when the studio's usual product cost less than $100,000. The film bombed on its initial release, was pulled, re-edited, re-released to even less interest, then taken out of circulation entirely. The disaster was the final straw to Universal stockholders, and they forced "Uncle Carl" to sell his interest in the company. Arnold's performance is lackluster and the film is too episodic to generate much interest. Barnes is rather good as the countess who almost lures Arnold away from his wife, but that subplot comes and goes too quickly to make a difference. Fortunately the studio had a big hit that same year with SHOWBOAT, and this saved the disastrous reception of SUTTER'S GOLD from sinking the company entirely. The cautious studio production chiefs were not to experience a financial disaster of such magnitude until 1978 with their costly failure THE WIZ. In reality, SUTTER'S GOLD more closely resembles the United Artists calamity of 1980, Michael Cimino's HEAVEN'S GATE, in its episodic style, lavish landscapes, and poor character development. Originally released at 94 minutes, segments of the picture were seen in other of the studio's films, including MUTINY ON THE BLACKHAWK (1939).

p, Edmund Grainger; d, James Cruze; w, Jack Kirkland, Walter Woods, George O'Neil (based on the biography by Blaise Cendrars and a story by Bruno Frank); ph, George Robinson, John P. Fulton.

Western   **(PR:A MPAA:NR)**

SUZANNE*   (1980, Can.) 114m RSL/Ambassador c

Jennifer Dale (*Suzanne McDonald*), Winston Rekert (*Nicky Callaghan*), Gabriel Arcand (*Georges Laflamme*), Ken Pogue (*Andrew McDonald*), Michelle Rossignol (*Yvette McDonald*), Marianne McIsaac (*Kathy*), Michael Ironside (*Jimmy*), Gina Dick (*Marilyn*), Pierre Curzi (*Pierre*), Gordon Thompson (*Greg*), Helen Hughes (*Brenda Callaghan*), Adam Chase (*Andre*).

An inept drama about a 20-year romance set in Montreal. It begins in 1944 with a religious parade that sets up a feeling of cultural restraints on daily living. The film then flashes forward to 1955 and gets to the meat of the story. Dale is a young woman with stern parents (her mother is Quebecois, her father a Scot) who's involved with Rekert. He's a rough sort who gets her pregnant and is then arrested for petty theft. He is sentenced and Dale marries Arcand. 10 years later Rekert returns and nearly destroys their happiness, but when he sees how happy his son is, Rekert decides to fade away. This is a poorly written and badly directed film, showing no sense for dramatic construction. There are moments when the drama seems like it could break through and become something meaningful, but the production qualities always nip it in the bud. Despite the mediocrity of the filmmaking, the acting isn't too bad. This cast clearly deserved better material. Though set in the past, the English-French cultural conflict which acts as the backdrop for the film mirrors the heightened tension in the province of Quebec at the time the film was made, a time of the ascendency of separatist leader Rene Levesque.

p, Robert Lantos; d, Robin Spry; w, Spry, Ronald Sutherland (based on the novel *Snow Lark* by Sutherland); ph, Miklos Lente; m, Francois Couisineau, Luc Plamondon; ed, Fima Noveck; art d, Vianney Gauthier; cos, Louise Jobin.

Drama   **Cas.**   **(PR:C MPAA:NR)**

SUZY***   (1936) 99m MGM bw

Jean Harlow (*Suzy Trent*), Franchot Tone (*Terry Moore*), Cary Grant (*Andre Charville*), Benita Hume (*Mme. Diane Eyrelle*), Lewis Stone (*Baron Charville*), Reginald Mason (*Capt. Barsanges*), Inez Courtney (*Maisie*), Greta Meyer (*Mrs. Schmidt*), David Clyde (*Knobby McPherson*), Elspeth Dudgeon (*Mrs. Boggs*), Tyler Brooke (*Raoul the Airman*), Robert Livingston (*Pierre, an Officer*), Dennis Morgan (*Lt. Charbret*), Christian Rub (*Pop Gaspard the Pianist*), George Spelvin (*Gaston*), Juan De La Cruz (*Clubfoot*), Luana Walters (*Check Room Girl*), Drew Demorest (*Aviator*), George Davis (*Bartender*), Frank Dawson (*Albert the Butler*), Charles McNaughton (*Peter*), Theodor von Eltz (*Suave Producer of Revue*), Una O'Connor (*Mrs. Bradley the Landlady*), Tempe Pigott (*Old Woman*), Forrester Harvey, John Rogers (*Counter Man*), Harry Cording (*Chauffeur*), Adrienne d'Ambricourt (*Cab Driver*), Joseph R. Tozer (*Colonel*), Hugh Huntley (*Adjutant*), Robert A'dair (*Landon*), Stanley Morner (*Officer*), Charles Judels (*Producer*).

Harlow's only film with Grant (and her fourth with Tone) had a few fine moments but was generally not up to the talents of those involved. The screenwriters worked with the title and some of the incidents of the novel, although it generally dispensed with the original premise. In 1914 London, Harlow is working as a showgirl. She's in love with Tone, who is an inventor from Ireland. He's currently working for an engineering firm owned by

Meyer, a German national. Tone and Harlow marry and, instead of checking into a hotel, he proudly takes his new wife to see his latest invention. While at the factory, Harlow notes that Meyer is having a late-night meeting with Hume and she wonders why these two women would choose to do business at that hour. Hume is a spy and Meyer thinks that Tone might be aware of the fact that Hume and Meyer are in cahoots in a cabal against England. Tone is unaware of the alliance though. Meyer tells Hume to knock off Tone. Later, Harlow and Tone are at his apartment and preparing to spend their first night together when Hume enters, her face covered so she can't be identified. She shoots Tone, then throws the gun on the floor and flees. Harlow thinks that there is nothing she can do for her bridegroom so she panics and also runs, rather than face the police who, she believes, will blame her for Tone's death. Harlow races across the channel to Paris and moves in with Courtney, who helps her get work at a local nightspot. Harlow thinks she is a widow and doesn't know that Hume wasn't a good enough shot to kill Tone. He's now recovered from his wound and wonders where his wife is. Further, Meyer and all of her fellow spies have been arrested, with the sole exception being Hume. The assassination at Sarajevo leads to WW I and Harlow is stuck in Paris, where she meets dashing aviator Grant, a French pilot whose dash and derring-do are legendary in Europe. Grant woos and wins Harlow and they are married almost instantly. Grant comes from a noble family and his father, Stone, is not so sure that he approves of this blonde his son has taken to be a wife. Harlow is engaging and soon wins Stone over, especially since she is totally faithful to Grant, who starts to cheat on her before the wedding bed has gotten cold. In London, Tone has perfected a new airplane and there is only one man with the skill and the guts to fly it, Grant. But Grant has been hurt in an air battle and is currently recovering in the hospital. Tone comes to Paris and is shocked to see Harlow. She explains that she thought Hume had plugged him for keeps, otherwise she would have stayed and nursed him back to health. Tone is adamant and questions that statement, calling her a fortune hunter and denouncing her for departing when he was bleeding. Harlow is now a bigamist, although Tone doesn't let on that she and he are still married. One of Grant's many amours is Hume, who he doesn't know is a spy. Harlow isn't aware of Hume and Grant until she sees a photo of the two in a local publication. She shows this to Tone and lets him know that she thinks it was Hume who fired the shots in reel one. Grant has recovered and flown off to Hume's country mansion for a tryst. He is having a last fling before returning to the war. Tone and Harlow know this and race along the road in an attempt to head him off. Before any of this can happen, Hume's thug shoots Grant and she and her aide race away. Grant's airplane is at the chateau and Tone climbs into it and chases Hume's car. Since Grant's plane is battle-equipped, he machine-guns the fleeing car and kills the two. Next, he goes after some overhead German Spads, shoots three of them down in flames and winds up in a crash landing at Hume's home. Harlow races to him and informs Tone that Grant is dead. They decide that Grant should be honored as the man who brought down the planes and uncovered Hume's plot. Grant's body is put in the pilot's seat and he is posthumously awarded a medal for his work. Tone and Harlow are reunited when he finally believes Harlow is really contrite about what happened and wants to make this second chance work. That's a lot of story for 99 minutes but it never feels crammed, just brisk. Good air footage, some nice funny scenes, and even a hit song, "Did I Remember?" (Walter Donaldson, Harold Adamson), which was nominated for an Oscar.

p, Maurice Revnes; d, George Fitzmaurice; w, Dorothy Parker, Alan Campbell, Horace Jackson, Lenore Coffee (based on the novel by Herbert Gorman); ph, Ray June; m, Dr. William Axt; ed, George Boemler; art d, Cedric Gibbons, Gabriel Scognamillo, Edwin B. Willis; cos, Dolly Tree.

War Drama   **(PR:C   MPAA:NR)**

SVALT   (SEE: HUNGER, 1965, Den./Swed./Nor.)

SVEGLIATI E UCCIDI   (SEE: WAKE UP AND DIE, 1967, Fr./Ital.)

SVENGALI**½   (1931) 76m WB bw

John Barrymore (Svengali), Marian Marsh (Trilby), Bramwell Fletcher (Billee), Donald Crisp (The Laird), Lumsden Hare (Taffy), Carmel Myers (Honori), Luis Alberni (Gecko), Paul Porcasi (Manager).

A remake of the silent TRILBY which starred Wilton Lackaye as Svengali and Clara Kimball Young as Trilby. Lackaye had also starred in the stage play drawn from du Maurier's novel. The emphasis has changed here to give Barrymore the lion's share of the picture and make the man who manipulated the woman the star. Marsh is a beautiful blonde who has lived with several artists and currently earns her living as a nude model. Barrymore is a music teacher with the ability to hypnotize. He's seen early as Myers' teacher (she shows that she has a good voice, and it was really hers) and then falling for Marsh. Marsh would like to quit taking off her clothes for a living and settle down with Fletcher, a wealthy Englishman who is infatuated with her, but knows that his upper-crust family will not approve of any alliance. Barrymore gets to Marsh and begins working on her voice. She starts singing, giving concerts, and achieving some notable success as he pulls her strings and makes her do everything he wants. When he does his hypnotic shtick, Barrymore's eyes are obliterated and substituted by gaping white holes that mesmerize the young woman. The relation-

ship deepens as Marsh is unable to perform unless Barrymore is there. In the end, both Barrymore and Marsh die, leaving audiences only the insipid Fletcher on screen. It's not quite a love story, not a great tragedy, not a comedy. Matter of fact, it's difficult to figure out what it is. Barrymore postures, gesticulates, and leaves molar marks all over the excellent sets. The following year, Barrymore did a similar role in THE MAD GENIUS. The only parts of the picture worth citing are the makeup and the excellent cinematography by McGill, which was nominated for an Oscar.

d, Archie Mayo; w, J. Grubb Alexander (based on the novel Trilby by George du Maurier); ph, Barney McGill; ed, William Holmes.

Drama   **Cas.**   **(PR:A-C   MPAA:NR)**

SVENGALI**   (1955, Brit.) 82m Alderdale/MGM c

Hildegarde Neff (Trilby O'Ferrall), Donald Wolfit (Svengali), Terence Morgan (Billy Bagot), Derek Bond (The Laird), Paul Rogers (Taffy), David Kossoff (Gecko), Hubert Gregg (Durien), Noel Purcell (Patrick O'Ferrall), Alfie Bass (Carrell), Harry Secombe (Barizel), Peter Illing (Police Inspector), Joan Haythorne (Mrs. Bagot), Hugh Cross (Dubose), David Oxley (Dodor), Richard Pearson (Lambert), Toots Pounds (Mama Martin), Michael Craig (Zouzou), Rica Fox, Neville Phillips, Arnold Bell, Joan Heal, Martin Boddey, Cyril Smith, Marne Maitland, The Voice of Madame Elisabeth Schwarzkopf.

Neff made her British film debut in this remake that doesn't come up to the standards of the 1931 original. She's the artist's model, taken from a Partician bar, who comes under Wolfit's spells and becomes a famous singer. The film is unnecessarily talky and has a few superfluous scenes. The second half picks up a bit, building some good suspense, but the outstanding feature of this SVENGALI is the visual aspect, based on illustrations from the original book. The production began with character actor Robert Newton in the part of Svengali, but when he walked out Wolfit was brought in as his replacement.

p, George Minter; d&w, Noel Langley (based on the novel Trilby by George du Maurier); ph, Wilkie Cooper (Eastmancolor); m, William Alwyn; ed, John Pomeroy; md, Alwyn; art d, Fred Pusey; cos, Beatrice Dawson.

Romance   **(PR:C   MPAA:NR)**

SVIRACHUT   (SEE: CLOWN AND THE KIDS, THE, 1968, U.S./Bulgaria)

SWALLOWS AND AMAZONS***   (1977, Brit.) 92m EMI/LDS c

Virginia McKenna (Mrs. Walker), Ronald Fraser (Uncle Jim), Brenda Bruce (Mrs. Dixon), Jack Woolgar (Old Billy), John Franklyn-Robbins (Young Billy), The Swallows: Simon West (John), Zanna Hamilton (Susan), Sophie Neville (Titty), Stephen Grendon (Roger), The Amazons: Kit Seymour (Nancy), Lesley Bennett (Peggy).

In the 1920s four children known as the Swallows go for a holiday in England's Lake District. There they meet two tomboys known as the Amazons and together the children have some good adventures. The film is of a simple nature but well made, using the locations with good effect. The intended youth audience should probably be thrilled with this nice little piece, well-directed and carried off with amazingly good ability by its mostly child cast.

p, Richard Pilbrow; d, Claude Whatham; w, David Wood (based on the book by Arthur Ransome); ph, Denis Lewiston (Technicolor); m, Wilfred Josephs; ed, Michael Bradsell; art d, Simon Holland.

Children's Drama   **(PR:AAA   MPAA:NR)**

SWAMP COUNTRY**   (1966) 98m Patrick-Sandy c

Rex Allen (Sheriff), Baker Knight (Baker), Carole Gilbert (Nora Cox), Sue Casey (Mrs. Cox), David DaLie (Dave Wetzel), Lyle Waggoner (Deputy), Kiva Lawrence (Mary Richmond), Marian Patrick (Nora's Sister), R.L. Armstrong (Hysmith), Vincent Barbi (Head of the Bootlegging Syndicate).

When a mobster's girl (Lawrence) is found dead in a motel, DaLie, an ex-big-game hunter is the prime suspect. He runs off and is chased by Allen through Okefenokee Swamp. Gilbert, the sheriff's girl, is warned about the man. Knight, a singer and rival for Gilbert's affections, is kidnaped by some bootleggers who think he's ratting on them. He's saved by the sheriff and DaLie saves Gilbert's younger sister from a panther. She agrees to help DaLie prove his innocence and, eventually, Armstrong is proven to be the murderer. The sheriff comes to realize that Gilbert loves Knight after he attends a local dance. Songs include: "Wasted Love," "Man With A Plan," "Swamp Country," "The Misfits," "You Turn and Walk Away" (Baker Knight, sung by Knight).

p&d, Robert Patrick; w, David DaLie; ph, Mario Tosi (Techniscope, Technicolor); m, Michael Terresco.

Drama/Action   **(PR:O   MPAA:NR)**

SWAMP DIAMONDS   (SEE: SWAMP WOMEN, 1956)

SWAMP FIRE*½   (1946) 69m PAR bw

Johnny Weissmuller *(Johnny Duval)*, Virginia Grey *(Janet Hilton)*, Buster Crabbe *(Mike Kalavich)*, Carol Thurston *(Toni Rousseau)*, Edwin Maxwell *(Capt. Moise)*, Pedro De Cordoba *(Tim Rousseau)*, Pierre Watkin *(Mr. Hilton)*, Marcelle Corday *(Grandmere Rousseau)*, David Janssen, William Edmunds, Charles Gordon, Frank Fenton.

The two great Olympic swimming stars-turned-movie-heroes meet on the silver screen and prove the pool isn't the only place where they can share a rivalry. Weissmuller is a war-shocked Navy veteran who now runs a boat at the mouth of the Mississippi River. He's got a little romance going with Thurston, but is challenged for her love by nasty trapper Crabbe. The two fight it out both on land and in the alligator-filled swamp, until good inevitably triumphs over evil. Ineptly made, with an undersized performance by Weissmuller, this routine story saves itself by throwing in action at every possible moment. Aside from his "Tarzan" films and the "Jungle Jim" series (in addition to a few cameo roles), this was Weissmuller's only leading role. Watch for an early screen appearance by Janssen.

p, William Pine, William Thomas; d, Pine; w, Geoffrey Homes; ph, Fred Jackman, Jr.; m, Rudy Schrager; ed, Howard Smith; art d, F. Paul Sylos.

Adventure   (PR:A   MPAA:NR)

SWAMP THING**   (1982) 90m Swampfilms/EM c

Louis Jourdan *(Arcane)*, Adrienne Barbeau *(Alice Cable)*, Ray Wise *(Dr. Alec Holland)*, David Hess *(Ferret)*, Nicholas Worth *(Bruno)*, Don Knight *(Ritter)*, Al Ruban *(Charlie)*, Dick Durock *(Swamp Thing)*, Ben Bates *(Arcane Monster)*, Nannette Brown *(Dr. Linda Holland)*, Reggie Batts *(Jude)*, Mimi Meyer *(Secretary)*, Karen Price *(Messenger)*, Bill Erickson *(Young Agent)*, Dov Gottesfeld *(Commando)*, Tommy Madden *(Little Bruno)*.

SWAMP THING tries its best to play as a camp parody of 1950s creature features, complete with hokey dialog and men running around in rubber monster-suits. The difference between this and its mentors lies in sincerity. The 1950s filmmakers honestly believed they were making something of merit, while this merely runs around pretending to be a camp fest. Wise is a scientist who is working on a secret government experiment to combine plant and animal cells. Bad guy Jourdan and his cohorts try to steal the formula Wise creates and accidentally get it all over the scientist. A monster-movie chase follows, with cheap green latex abounding. Barbeau, who had the dubious distinction of doing her first topless film with this piece, gives some heart to her role as the government agent trying to outwit Jourdan in capturing the title creature. Director Craven built up quite a reputation with some effective little shockers like LAST HOUSE ON THE LEFT and THE HILLS HAVE EYES, but none of the talent demonstrated in them is evident here. SWAMP THING does have its moments, though, and is often funny in spite of itself. Off screen, Barbeau was married to horror film director John Carpenter.

p, Benjamin Melniker, Michael E. Uslan; d&w, Wes Craven (based on DC Comics characters); ph, Robin Goodwin (Technicolor); m, Harry Manfredini; ed, Richard Bracken; prod d, Robb Wilson King; art d, David Nichols, King, Rhoda Neal; cos, Patricia Bolomet, Bennett Choate, Paul A. Simmons; makeup, William Munns; stunts, Ted Duncan.

Horror   **Cas.**   (PR:C   MPAA:PG)

SWAMP WATER**½   (1941) 90m FOX bw (GB: THE MAN WHO CAME BACK)

Walter Brennan *(Tom Keefer)*, Walter Huston *(Thursday Regan)*, Anne Baxter *(Julie)*, Dana Andrews *(Ben)*, Virginia Gilmore *(Mabel McKenzie)*, John Carradine *(Jesse Wick)*, Mary Howard *(Hannah)*, Eugene Pallette *(Jeb McKane)*, Ward Bond *(Tim Dorson)*, Guinn "Big Boy" Williams *(Bud Dorson)*, Russell Simpson *(Marty McCord)*, Joe Sawyer *(Hardy Ragan)*, Paul Burns *(Tulle McKenzie)*, Matt Willis *(Miles Tonkey)*, Dave Morris *(Barber)*, Frank Austin *(Fred Ulm)*, Edward Clark *(Dekle)*, Red Larkin *(Clem Hooper)*, Charles Miller *(Fiskus)*, Mae Marsh *(Mrs. McCord)*, Sherman Sanders *(Caller)*.

Actors have played the same role in more than one movie. Cagney did George M. Cohan in YANKEE DOODLE DANDY and THE SEVEN LITTLE FOYS. Edward Arnold played Diamond Jim Brady in DIAMOND JIM and LILLIAN RUSSELL. This was the first time Brennan played this role, then he did it again in a total remake of this picture called LURE OF THE WILDERNESS, a rare item in cinema history. It was Renoir's first U.S. picture and they handed him a difficult assignment because the story had to do with an area and a collection of people who were not familiar to most Americans. Brennan has been falsely accused of a murder, tried, convicted, and sent to jail. He's escaped and taken refuge in the overgrown swamps of Georgia. He was to be hanged but fought his way out and is determined to bring the real culprit to justice. But first, he has to make himself scarce. Andrews is Huston's oldest son. He is out searching for his lost hound when he meets the fugitive Brennan. The escapee fears that Andrews will turn him in and there's a tense moment as Brennan thinks about killing Andrews.

Then Brennan tells Andrews how he was railroaded and Andrews believes him. The two men begin trapping animals for their pelts, with Brennan handling the snares and Andrews selling the furs. Brennan has told Andrews to give his share of the proceeds to his daughter, Baxter. Andrews has been seeing Gilmore and she knows what's going on. When she believes that Andrews is falling for Baxter, Gilmore tells the authorities of Brennan's hideout and Andrews is questioned, but refuses to give away the information. Andrews is now enamored of Baxter and solves the crime when he learns that the testimony against Brennan was perjury to protect the true killers of the man Brennan was supposed to have slain. Now that he's cleared, Brennan is taken out of the tangled vegetation and marshy waterways and brought back to civilization. Renoir's direction and Marley's moody camera are superior to the dialog from Nichols, who was one of the best screenwriters around but failed to put much down on paper for this one.

p, Irving Pichel; d, Jean Renoir; w, Dudley Nichols (based on a story by Vereen Bell); ph, Peverell Marley; m, David Buttolph; ed, Walter Thompson; art d, Thomas Little; cos, Gwen Wakeling.

Drama   (PR:A   MPAA:NR)

SWAMP WOMAN zero   (1941) 62m George R. Batcheller/PRC bw

Ann Corio *(Annabelle)*, Jack LaRue *(Pete)*, Jay Novello *(Brand)*, Richard Deane *(Jeff)*, Mary Hull *(Lizbet)*, Earl Gunn *(Jed)*, Ian McDonald *(Rance)*, Guy Wilkerson *(Abner)*, Jimmy Aubrey *(Tod)*, Frank Hagney *(Guard)*, Lois Austin, Carlin Sturdevant.

Awful programmer features Corio as a saloon singer returning to her hometown in Florida. Her old boy friend, LaRue, is now engaged to Hull, Corio's niece. As if that weren't enough, a man on the run (Deane) arrives and causes more trouble. Eventually, Corio proves that nasty guy Novello is responsible for the crime Deane was accused of, and she gets back LaRue to boot. The script and direction are both hopelessly bad, even at a camp level. This plays like amateur night at the movies, and Corio, best known as a burlesque stripper, has more than her share of problems due to her untrained voice.

p, George Merrick, Max Alexander; d, Elmer Clifton; w, Arthur G. Durlam (based on a story by Fred McConnell); ph, Edward Linden; ed, Charles Henkel.

Drama   (PR:A   MPAA:NR)

SWAMP WOMEN*   (1956) 73m Woolner Brothers/Favorite Films of California c (AKA: S WAMP DIAMONDS; CRUEL SWAMP)

Carole Mathews *(Lee)*, Marie Windsor *(Josie)*, Jil Jarmyn *(Billie)*, Beverly Garland *(Vera)*, Touch [Mike] Connors *(Bob)*, Susan Cummings, Lou Place, Jonathan Haze, Edward Nelson.

A policewoman (Mathews) is sent undercover to a Louisiana women's prison in order to infiltrate the evil "Nardo Gang." These naughty ladies have stolen some jewels and it's up to Mathews to help them escape prison and discover where the loot is hidden. The gang is led by Windsor, with flirty Jarmyn and nasty Garland as her compatriots in crime. The girls get out but lose their boat in the muddy bayou when it sinks. Fortunately they run into geologist Connors (billed as "Touch," Mike's nickname from his UCLA basketball days) who is traveling with his girl friend and a guide. The gang knocks him out, kills the guide, and throws the hapless girl friend to the alligators. That will teach Connors to pick up strangers. He has to fight off their wanton lusts and, eventually, the diamonds are found. Garland grabs the guy and the jewels while the other women sleep. Fortunately, Mathews saves the day and walks off arm in arm with Connors. This is one of those "so bad it's good" types, featuring plenty of "rough" dialog from the ladies and some inept direction by Corman, "the King of the B's" Some seemingly doped-up alligators are supposed to provide danger, though in one sequence it's obvious Connors is doing battle with a giant lizard in the very safe atmosphere of a swimming pool. "Danger and death were just a slip away from the stars and technicians who made up the location unit," claimed a thundering press release. The same might be said for an audience member who falls asleep and tumbles from his seat to the floor.

p, Bernard Woolner; d, Roger Corman; w, David Stern; m, Willis "Bill" Holman.

Drama/Adventure   (PR:A   MPAA:NR)

SWAN, THE***   (1956) 112m MGM c

Grace Kelly *(Princess Alexandra)*, Alec Guinness *(Prince Albert)*, Louis Jourdan *(Dr. Nicholas Agi)*, Agnes Moorehead *(Queen Maria Dominika)*, Jessie Royce Landis *(Princess Beatrix)*, Brian Aherne *(Father Hyacinth)*, Leo G. Carroll *(Caesar)*, Estelle Winwood *(Symphorosa)*, Van Dyke Parks *(George)*, Christopher Cook *(Arsene)*, Robert Coote *(Capt. Wunderlich)*, Doris Lloyd *(Countess Sigenstoyn)*, Edith Barrett *(Beatrix's Maid)*.

Even though HIGH SOCIETY was released afterward, this was Kelly's last film before ascending the throne of Monaco on April 18, 1956. It's a dusty old property that MGM pulled out in order to take advantage of the realities in Kelly's life. It's early in the century and she is a young woman of noble parentage. Kelly's mother, Landis, is eager to marry her off to Guinness, the crown prince. Kelly is being tutored by Jourdan and falls in love with him during the strains of a Kaper tune, "The Swan Waltz," but it's for naught. Landis' brother is Aherne, who has given up the royal ermine for the monk's cloth and he is against Landis' obvious attempt to marry off Kelly. He thinks his niece should be allowed to make her own decisions of the heart. Landis' sister, Winwood, is a dotty old woman who has all the best comedy lines as she comments on the shenanigans in a pixilated fashion, sort of like the female version of Cecil Kellaway in so many movies. Guinness comes to see Kelly and doesn't pop the question, so Jourdan is enlisted to play a love rival, thus causing Guinness to finally ask for her hand and be granted it. The story was written in 1922 and was vaguely about the Hapsburgs and, in 1956, seemed out-of-synch with what was going on in the world, though not necessarily what was transpiring in Kelly's life. She had gone from a Philadelphia debutante to model to award-winning actress and was now about to become a queen. This movie would have been immeasurably helped by songs and screamed to be treated as a musical rather than a straight comedy-drama. It's the stuff that operettas are made of and many of the anti-monarchist jokes are totally lost on modern audiences. The Biltmore estate in North Carolina stands in for the European castle, just as it stood in for the home of the President's adviser in BEING THERE. Grace Kelly soared over the material and lent a credibility to an otherwise hard-to-swallow tale. It was made originally as ONE ROMANTIC NIGHT in 1930 with Lillian Gish in the lead. THE SWAN is for unabashed romantics only.

p, Dore Schary; d, Charles Vidor; w, John Dighton (based on the play by Ferenc Molnar); ph, Joseph Ruttenberg, Robert Surtees (CinemaScope, Eastmancolor); m, Bronislau Kaper; ed, John Dunning; art d, Cedric Gibbons, Randall Duell; set d, Edwin B. Willis, Henry Grace; cos, Helen Rose.

Romance (PR:A MPAA:NR)

SWAN LAKE, THE**   (1967) 111m United Productions of America-Seven Arts c

Rudolf Nureyev, Dame Margot Fonteyn, The Vienna State Opera Ballet.

This excellent adaption of the famous ballet differs from other ballet films in its imaginative use of cinematic technique. Rather than just portray the dancing, the camera is used in overhead shots and a good amount of closeups on the dancers. Transitions are well handled and the entire work is a visual delight. Unlike many dance films, this is not a heavy-handed or somber work. Instead it shows us a group of people dancing for the sheer joy of the art, clearly having a good time with what they're doing. The choreography was by Nureyev. The production which is said to have cost more than a $1 million to make, included the participation of the Vienna Symphony Orchestra and 60 dancers from the Vienna State Opera Ballet. It was filmed on soundstages in Munich.

d, Truck Branss; w, Peter Ilyich Tchaikovsky; ph, Gunther Anders (Eastmancolor); m, Tchaikovsky; ed, Marina Runne; md, John Lanchbery; set d&cos, Nicholas Georgiadis; ch, Rudolf Nureyev.

Ballet (PR:AAA MPAA:NR)

SWANEE RIVER*   (1939) 84m FOX c

Don Ameche (Stephen Foster), Andrea Leeds (Jane), Al Jolson (E.P. Christy), Felix Bressart (Henry Kleber), Chick Chandler (Bones), Russell Hicks (Andrew McDowell), George Reed (Old Joe), Richard Clarke (Tom Harper), Diane Fisher (Marion Foster), Charles Halton (Pond), George Breakstone (Ambrose), Al Herman (Tambo), Charles Trowbridge (Mr. Foster), George Meeker (Henry Foster), Leona Roberts (Mrs. Foster), Charles Tannen (Morrison Foster), Harry Hayden (Erwin), Clara Blandick (Mrs. Griffin), Nella Walker (Mrs. McDowell), Esther Dale (Temperance Woman), The Hall Johnson Choir (Themselves).

Ameche had already played the man who gave us the telephone and now he was to have an even more difficult task as one of America's premier songwriters, Stephen Foster. The problem was that Foster was a drunk, treated his wife and child badly, never provided for his family, and died at a young age (37) in the charity ward at Bellevue Hospital in New York. He'd earned a good deal of royalty money from 1849 through 1860 but drank it all away and died a pauper. The last song he wrote is not in this film. It was "Beautiful Dreamer" and was composed a few days before his death. The screenwriters considered the true story, then threw most of it away in order to fashion a more commercial biography. Pittsburgh-born Ameche (actually, Ameche was born in Kenosha, Wisconsin; Foster was from Pennsylvania) falls in love with the South and with southerner Leeds (the truth was that Foster's wife was also from Pittsburgh) in Kentucky. He begins writing songs, sells one of them to Jolson (as the famous minstrel man E.P. Christy, who did, in fact, make Foster famous). During the War Between the States, Ameche is accused of being a sympathizer to the Gray cause. He travels to New York with Leeds and child in tow, goes off on more toots than a railroad engine, and she leaves him. Jolson is about to give a performance with his troupe when he learns that Ameche has died of drink and so he does "Swanee River" for a tearful audience. Other songs by Foster are "My Old Kentucky Home, "Ring the Banjo, and "Jeannie with the Light Brown Hair" (sung by Ameche). Jolson gets to sing the aforementioned classic, "Swanee River," plus "Oh, Susanna," and "Camptown Races." The Hall Johnson Choir sings "Old Black Joe" and "Here Comes The Heavin' Line." Foster's "Suite For Small Orchestra" is also heard. Musical director Silvers

and director Lanfield wrote "Curry A Mule," William Davis wrote "Gwine Down The River," and Hall Johnson wrote "The Mule Song." Good production values, nice acting, but a flawed and untrue script.

p, Darryl F. Zanuck; d, Sidney Lanfield; w, John Taintor Foote, Philip Dunne; ph, Bert Glennon (Technicolor); ed, Louis Loeffler; md, Louis Silvers; art d, Richard Day, Joseph C. Wright; cos, Royer; ch, Nick Castle, Geneva Sawyer.

Musical/Biography Cas.   (PR:A-C MPAA:NR)

SWAP MEET zero   (1979) 84m Dimension c

Ruth Cox (Nancy), Debi Richter (Susan), Danny Goldman (Ziggy), Cheryl Rixon (Annie), Jonathan Gries, Dan Spector, Loren Lester.

It's a good old time at the town swap meet, where everybody meets to trade items and get a few cheap laughs. There are lots of cars, big bad bruisers, and teenagers who know more about sex than the adults. It is all delivered with lots of energy and completely mindless. There's plenty of cheap sexual humor, which is no surprise, and the same stock characters who easily could be transplanted into any of a dozen quickie exploitation features like this. A real waste of time aimed strictly for the drive-in crowds who aren't concerned with cinematic quality to begin with.

p, Steve Krantz; d, Brice Mack; w, Krantz; ph, (CFI Color); m, Hemlock; art d, Donald Harris.

Comedy (PR:O MPAA:R)

SWAPPERS, THE zero   (1970, Brit.) 84m Salon/Trans-American c (GB: THE WIFE SWAPPERS)

James Donnelly (Paul), Larry Taylor (Leonard), Valerie St. John (Ellen), Denys Hawthorne (Cliff), Bunty Garland (Sheila), Sandra Satchwith (Carol), Fiona Fraser (Marion), Joan Hayward (Jean), Stacy Harris (Psychiatrist), David Gell (Narrator).

A "study" of the hip phenomenon of mate-swapping which consists of a number of documentary-style episodes linked by an outrageously deadpan American psychologist. The first episode has a young wife being ordered to swim naked to a houseboat where she is forced to stay the night. The next episode has a husband and wife, Donnelly and St. John, looking for sexual satisfaction and finding it in swapping. Of course, St. John is shy at first, but before long becomes addicted to the kinky practice. In another episode a couple find adventure on a weekend cruise. There's also an "interview" with a woman who turns to prostitution to help her husband pay the bills. He gets carted off to prison for his involvement while she is allowed to continue selling herself. The picture is filled with people trying to avoid being "square," but who now seem ridiculous doing so. The film, narrated by one David Gell, claims to be an "in-depth" study revealing the reasons behind swapping. All it really reveals is the gross lack of filmmaking ability that director Ford and his counterparts possess.

p, Stanley Long; d, Derek Ford; w, Ford, Long; ph, Michael Francis, Trevor Brooker, Richard Pope, Albert Lloyd (Eastmancolor); m, Michael Eaton, John Fiddy; ed, Dorak Film Services. m/l, "The Wife Swappers," sung by Jay Dee.

Drama (PR:O MPAA:R)

SWARM, THE*   (1978) 116m WB c

Michael Caine (Brad Crane), Katharine Ross (Helena), Richard Widmark (Gen. Slater), Richard Chamberlain (Dr. Hubbard), Olivia de Havilland (Maureen Schuster), Ben Johnson (Felix), Lee Grant (Anne MacGregor), Jose Ferrer (Dr. Andrews), Patty Duke Astin (Rita Bard), Slim Pickens (Jud Hawkins), Bradford Dillman (Maj. Baker), Fred MacMurray (Clarence), Henry Fonda (Dr. Krim), Cameron Mitchell (Gen. Thompson), Christian Juttner (Paul Durant), Morgan Paull (Dr. Newman), Alejandro Rey (Dr. Martinez), Don "Red" Barry (Pete Harris), Doria Cook (Mrs. Durant), Robert Varney (Mr. Durant), Patrick Culliton (Sheriff Morrison), Chris Petersen (Hal), Arthur Space (Engineer), John Williams (Launching Officer), Mara Cook (Secretary), Stephen Powers (Radarman), Steve Marlo (1st Pilot), Ernie Orsatti (Duty Officer), John Furlong (Cameraman), Jerry Toomey (Eddie), Joey Eisnach (Bee Boy), Chris Capen (Lieutenant), Tony Haig (2nd Officer), Bill Snider (2nd Radarman), Arell Blanton (Sergeant), George Simmons (Nurse), Trent Dolan (Radio Sergeant), Phil Montgomery (Mechanic), Marcia Nicholson (Captain), Art Balinger (Radio Announcer), Frank Blair (Himself), Chuck Hayward (Standby Engineer), Michael Seehan (1st Airman), Howard Culver (2nd Airman), Glenn Charles Lewis (Chemical Warfare Guard), Jim Mills.

THE SWARM is a real B movie in every sense of the term. Somehow disaster-movie king Allen convinced top Hollywood stars (including five Oscar winners) to appear in this nonsense. Caine is an entomologist who's trying to stop a swarm of killer bees as they attack Houston. General Widmark wants to use the military on the tiny creatures (actually dots painted onto film, the ultimate in cheap special effects) but, of course, this wouldn't be right. After all, the film runs almost two hours and there's a lot of people to be stung. After many deaths and a few explosions, Caine discovers that the warning system of the military base is similar to the bees' mating call. This system is used to draw the swarm over the ocean, where they are burned to death with some oil, placed there just for the occasion. One can only wonder why stars of this cast's quality would consent to doing such trash. THE SWARM is a worthless, poorly made, and utterly laughable film that has gained a minor cult status with "bad film" fans. Ultimately, it was the studio that was stung by THE SWARM. Warner brothers sunk $13 million into the production and another $8 million into advertising. All in all, the film grossed only $10 million, making one wonder what Allen, the cast, and Warner Bros. thought they were trying to pull off.

p&d, Irwin Allen; w, Sterling Silliphant (based on a novel by Arthur Herzog); ph, Fred J. Koenekamp (Panavision/Technicolor); m, Jerry Goldsmith; ed, Harold F. Kress; prod d, Stan Jolley; set d, Stuart Reiss; cos, Paul Zastupnevich; spec eff, L.B. Abbott, Van Der Veer Photo Effects, Howard Jensen; stunts, Paul Stader.

Disaster   Cas.   (PR:C   MPAA:PG)

SWASHBUCKLER*   (1976) 101m UNIV c (GB: THE SCARLET BUCCANEER)

Robert Shaw (*Ned Lynch*), James Earl Jones (*Nick Debrett*), Peter Boyle (*Lord Durant*), Genevieve Bujold (*Jane Barnet*), Beau Bridges (*Maj. Folly*), Geoffrey Holder (*Cudjo*), Avery Schreiber (*Polonski*), Tom Clancy (*Mr. Moonbeam*), Anjelica Huston (*Woman of Dark Visage*), Bernard Behrens (*Sir James Barnet*), Dorothy Tristan (*Alice*), Mark Baker (*Lute Player*), Kip Niven (*Willard Culverwell*), Tom Fitzsimmons (*Corporal*), Louisa Horton (*Lady Barnet*), Sid Haig (*Bald Pirate*), Robert Ruth (*Bearded Pirate*), Robert Morgan (*Peglegged Pirate*), Jon Cedar (*Pirate Gun Captain*), Diana Chesney (*Landlady*), Manuel DePina (*Barnet Servant*), Tom Lacy (*Chaplain*), Alfie Wise (*Sailor*), Harry Basch (*Barman Man*).

A travesty of the Errol Flynn movies of the 1930s and 1940s, SWASHBUCKLER has a lot more swash than buckle. There's little substance here, as the creators couldn't make up their minds whether this was a parody or for real. Jones and Shaw (who was already 49 years of age and a few years past it for this kind of bravura) are two pirates who come to Jamaica in an attempt to rid the island of the tyrannical pervert, Boyle, who runs the place. Boyle is obviously a homosexual and painted in such broad, black strokes that any attempt at sincere villainy is lost. One thing about the pirate picture of yore is that the bad guys had a real commitment to their roles and here it doesn't exist. Bujold provides the love interest as the daughter of Behrens. Bridges is a Leslie Howard "Scarlet Pimpernel"-type of fop and Schreiber provides the only real comedy as one of the supporting numbskulls. The only person missing was Marty Feldman. Director Goldstone had already proven he could ruin a good story when he made THE GANG WHO COULDN'T SHOOT STRAIGHT and he did it again with this silly, inane treatment of what might have been some fun under the helm of a better director. Although, it must be admitted, he didn't have much of a script with which to work. In England, they named this THE SCARLET BUCCANNEER, perhaps trying to get some of the people who went to see a far better picture, THE CRIMSON PIRATE. Some tasteless gay jokes, heaving bosoms, lots of blood, a total waste except for some of the supporting players. Note Anjelica Huston, winner of the Oscar for her work in PRIZZI'S HONOR. This was so early in her career that her character didn't even have a name, just "Woman of Dark Visage." Her first picture was SINFUL DAVEY when she was 17. Then she did a bit in A WALK WITH LOVE AND DEATH, followed by THE LAST TYCOON. A great deal of action, but staged in such a phony fashion that it fails to stir the imagination. Although it initially was given a "PG" rating by the MPAA, the rating for SWASHBUCKLER later was changed to "R" and children should be blindfolded.

p, Jennings Lang; d, James Goldstone; w, Jeffrey Bloom (based on a story by Paul Wheeler); ph, Philip Lathrop (Panavision, Technicolor); m, John Addison; ed, Edward A. Biery; prod d, John Lloyd; set d, Hal Gausman; cos, Burton Miller; ch, Geoffrey Holder; stunts, Buddy Van Horn, Victor Paul.

Comedy   (PR:O   MPAA:PG/R)

SWASTIKA SAVAGES   (SEE: HELL'S BLOODY DEVIL'S, 1970)

SWEATER GIRL*½   (1942) 77m PAR bw

Eddie Bracken (*Jack Mitchell*), June Preisser (*Susan Lawrence*), Phillip Terry (*Martin Lawrence*), Nils Asther (*Prof. Henri Menard*), Frieda Inescort (*Mrs. Menard*), Betty Rhodes (*Louise Menard*), Kenneth Howell (*Miles Tucker*), Johnnie Johnston (*Johnny Arnold*), William Henry ("*Happy*" *Dudley*), Ella Neal (*Patsy Connors*), Minerva Urecal (*Melinda*), Charles D. Brown (*Lt. McGill*), Isabel Withers (*Mrs. McGill*), Robert Cherry (*Freddy*), William Cabanne (*Ambulance Doctor*), Eddy Chandler, George Offerman, Jr, Tommy Hicks, Joel Dean, Leonard Sues.

This campus comedy takes a fairly unusual twist for the genre and ends up getting quickly muddled. A group of well-scrubbed college kids are working hard to put on a musical revue, when suddenly the gang starts dropping like flies. They know the killer is among the group, but just who is it? The usual hijinks go on with Bracken eventually exposing the murderer before the surprised audience. The mix between comedy and murder is more than a little uneasy, resulting in a lower quality programmer. The film was best remembered for the song "I Don't Want to Walk Without You" by Styne and

Loesser. It became a big hit in wartime America and propelled the film careers of its composers. Songs include: "I Don't Want to Walk Without You" (Frank Loesser, Jule Styne, sung by Johnnie Johnston, reprised by Betty Rhodes), "I Said No" (Loesser, Styne, sung by Rhodes), "What Gives Out Now" (Loesser, Styne, sung by Eddie Bracken, June Preisser), "Sweater Girl" (Loesser, Styne, sung by Bracken).

p, Sol C. Siegel; d, William Clemens; w, Eve Greene, Robert Blees (based on a story by Beulah Marie Dix, Bertram Millhauser); ph, John Mescall; ed, Alma Macrorie; ch, Dave Gould; m/l, Frank Loesser and Jule Styne.

Musical/Mystery   (PR:A   MPAA:NR)

SWEDENHIELMS*½   (1935, Swed.) 92m Svenskfilmindustri bw

Gosta Ekman (*Rolf Swedenhielm*), Karin Swanstrom (*Marta Boman*), Bjorn Berglund (*Rolf, Jr.*), Hakan Westergren (*Bo*), Tutta Rolf (*Julia*), Ingrid Bergman (*Astrid*), Sigurd Wallen (*Eriksson*), Nils Ericsson, Adele Soderblom, Mona Geijer-Falkner, Hjalmar Peters.

Swedish scientist Ekman is a poor man who lives only for his work. His three grown children (Berglund, Westergren, and Rolf) have been raised in large part by Swanstrom, Ekman's housekeeper and sister-in-law. His eldest son Westergren is engaged to Bergman (quite good in this early appearance), a rich girl who is quite willing to support her fiance. When Westergren refuses this offer out of pride, Bergman appeals to Ekman, who tells her his son must do what his feelings tell him to. Ekman learns that his foster brother, Wallen, with whom he holds a longstanding grudge, has some promissory notes with Ekman's forged signature. These could be embarrassing, particularly since the culprit appears to be Westergren. Ekman is embarassed and nearly gives up the Nobel prize he is to be awarded when his son is about to be exposed as a forger. Westergren admits he was trying to protect his brother (Berglund), whom he suspected of the phony signature. The real culprit is Swanstrom, who had been frustrated by the financial impracticality of the family. She explains that this was the only way to get money to run a proper household. All is resolved and Ekman goes back to his research. This is a well-made Swedish feature, played with feeling and holding the delicate balance between the drama and comedy of the situations with great skill. The photography is quite good, with direction and acting to match. Packed with emotion, the film maintains a consistently high level that never falters. (In Swedish.)

d, Gustaf Molander; w, Stina Bergman (based on the play by Hjalmar Bergman); ph, Ake Dahlquist; m, Helge Lindberg.

Comedy/Drama   (PR:A   MPAA:NR)

SWEDISH MISTRESS, THE*   (1964, Swed.) 77m Svensk Filmindustri/Janus bw (ALSKAR INNAN)

Bibi Andersson (*Girl*), Per Myrberg (*Boy*), Max von Sydow (*Married Man*), Ollegard Wellton (*His Wife*), Birgitta Valberg (*Elderly Woman*).

While at a scientific gathering in Stockholm, Andersson begins an affair with von Sydow, an older married man. He refuses to give up his wife for her, which causes Andersson much anguish. She tells her boy friend, Myrberg, about the affair, then leaves both men for a new job in Rome. She's about to board the train to take her to Italy when she's met by von Sydow. He tells her that he really needs her and the two spend the night together. But in the morning, Andersson realizes that this is not what she wants and breaks off the affair so she can begin her new life. This film was released in 1962, but was not shown in the U.S. until two years later.

d&w, Vilgot Sjoman; ph, Lars Bjorne (AgaScope); ed, Lennart Wallen; set d, P.A. Lundgren; cos, Mago.

Drama   (PR:O   MPAA:NR)

SWEDISH WEDDING NIGHT*½   (1965, Swed.) 95m Minerva Royal bw (BROLLOPSBESVAR)

Jarl Kulle (*Hilmer Westlund*), Lena Hansson (*Siri Westlund*), Christina Schollin (*Hildur Palm*), Edvin Adolphson (*Victor Palm*), Isa Quensel (*Hilma Palm*), Catrin Westerlund (*Irma Palm*), Tor Isedal (*Rudolph Palm*), Peter Thelin (*Gummar Palm*), Lars Ekborg (*Simon*), Margareta Krook (*Mary*), Yvonne Lombard (*Svea*), Georg Arlin (*Johan Borg*), Ove Tjernberg (*Ivar*), Lars Passgard (*Martin*), Lars Lind (*Soren*), Sigge Fischer (*Philip*), Tommy Nilsson (*Loony- Anders*), Ulla Edin (*Rullan*), Claes Esphagen (*Wallinder*), John Norrman (*Bjuhr*), Sten Mattsson (*Hagstrom*), Thor Zackrisson (*Karlsson*), Gosta Krantz (*Nisse Johansson*), Jessie Flaws (*Mary Lou*), Frithiof Bjarne (*Beef Manager*), Lasse Poysti (*Pedlar*), Julia Caeser (*Cafe Proprietor*), Ake Falck (*Narrator*).

Kulle, a butcher, marries Schollin, a woman young enough to be his daughter. She's also pregnant, courtesy of Passgard, a young farmhand she loves. Passgard works for her father but will not marry her. After the wedding there is a great feast and many of the guests become drunk. They begin to spill their private secrets and Passgard hangs himself from a tree. Kulle takes home his bride, but being too inebriated to carry out his husbandly duties, he lets his best friend take care of the business. (In Swedish; English subtitles).

p, Tore Sjoberg, Lorens Marmstedt; d, Ake Falck; w, Lars Widding (based on the book *Brollopsbesvar* by Stig Halvard Dagerman); ph, Rune Ericson; m, Georg Riedel; ed, Ingemar Ejve; art d, Rolf Bohman.

Drama   (PR:C MPAA:NR)

SWEENEY**   (1977, Brit.) 97m Euston/EMI c

John Thaw (*Regan*), Dennis Waterman (*Carter*), Barry Foster (*McQueen*), Ian Bannen (*Baker*), Colin Welland (*Chadwick*), Diane Keen (*Bianca*), Michael Coles (*Johnson*), Joe Melia (*Brent*), Brian Glover (*Mac*), Lynda Bellingham (*Janice*), Morris Perry (*Commander*), Paul Angelis (*S.S. Man*), Nick Brimble (*Burtonshaw*), John Alkin (*Daniels*), Bernard Kay (*Matthews*), Anthony Scott (*Codaly*), Anthony Brown (*Superintendent*).

This big-screen adaptation of a popular British television program is simply a routine cops-and-robbers flick with pretentions at political intrigue. Thaw and Waterman are a pair of London dicks who are investigating a series of murders. The case leads them to some oil dealings that carry political implications. Violent, with occasional glimpses of wit, this is all routine and told without much flair. Some good London scenery is used without much effect.

p, Ted Childs; d, David Wickes; w, Ranald Graham (based on a television series created by Ian Kennedy Martin); ph, Dusty Miller (Technicolor); m, Denis King; ed, Chris Burt; art d, Bill Alexander.

Crime   (PR:O MPAA:NR)

SWEENEY TODD. THE DEMON BARBER OF FLEET STREET
       (SEE: DEMON BARBER OF FLEET STREET, THE, 1939. Brit.)

SWEENEY 2***½   (1978, Brit.) 108m Euston/EMI c

John Thaw (*Regan*), Dennis Waterman (*Carter*), Denholm Elliott (*Jupp*), Georgina Hale (*Switchboard Lady*), Nigel Hawthorne (*Dilke*), Lewis Fiander (*Gorran*), James Warrior (*Jellyneck*), John Flanagan (*Willard*), David Casey (*Goodyear*), Derrick O'Connor (*llewlyn*), John Alkin (*Daniels*), Michal Jackson (*Soames*), Ken Hutchison (*Hill*), Brian Gwaspari (*White*), John Lyons (*Duncan Mead*), Brian Hall (*Morris Haughton*), Matthew Scurfield (*Jefferson*), Anna Gael (*Mrs. Hill*), Lynn Dearth (*Mrs. White*), Fiona Mollison (*Mrs. Haughton*), Sarah Atkinson (*Mrs. Mead*), George Mikell, Marc Zuber, Leon Lissek, Stefan Gryff, Diana Weston, Anna Nygh, George Innes, Roddy McMillan.

This far better follow-up to SWEENEY finds Thaw and Waterman on the trail of some bank robbers. The thieves support their families on a Mediterranean isle by making periodic visits to London banks for armed withdrawals. The plot is pretty farfetched but the film is quite engaging, directed with style and humor. The acting is uniformly good though some of the British accents may be difficult for American audiences to decipher. The police investigation has a realistic feel to it, a factor rarely found in most modern cop films.

p, Ted Childs; d, Tom Clegg; w, Troy Kennedy Martin; ph, Dusty Miller (Technicolor); m, Tony Hatch; ed, Chris Burt; art d, Bill Alexander.

Crime   (PR:O MPAA:NR)

SWEEPINGS*   (1933) 80m RKO bw

Lionel Barrymore (*Daniel Pardway*), Alan Dinehart (*Thane Pardway*), Eric Linden (*Fred Pardway*), William Gargan (*Gene Pardway*), Gloria Stuart (*Phoebe Pardway*), Gregory Ratoff (*Abe Ullman*), Ninetta Sunderland (*Abigail Pardway*), Helen Mack (*Mamie Donohue*), Ivan Lebedeff (*Prince Niko*), George Meeker (*Bert Pardway*), Franklin Pangborn (*Photographer*), Chick Chandler (*Gene's Friend*), Esther Muir.

After the Chicago fire Barrymore builds a department store that becomes a major business. He wants his sons to take over but each proves to be spoiled by wealth and his daughter is too much of a socialite to care. Finally he turns his empire over to Ratoff, the man who helped him start the store. Despite Barrymore's usual good standards, this is a slow and stuffy film without much merit. The drama is sapped by the film's all too serious presentation that unintentionally draws sympathy for the children who are presented as selfish. The film was remade by RKO again in 1939 under the title THREE SONS.

p, Pandro S. Berman; d, John Cromwell; w, Lester Cohen, Howard Estabrook, H.W. Hanemann (based on the novel by Cohen); ph, Edward J. Cronjager; m, Max Steiner ed, George Nichols, Jr.

Drama   (PR:A MPAA:NR)

SWEEPSTAKE ANNIE**   (1935) 81m Liberty bw

Tom Brown, Marian Nixon, Wera Engels, Inez Courtney, Ivan Lebedeff, Lucien Littlefield, Dorothy Peterson, William Janney, Carol Tevis.

Studio script girl Nixon is the sole support for her lazy family. She wins some good money in a sweepstakes, gives the folks some of the cash and then moves in with her friend Courtney. Brown is her boy friend who at first leaves her when she sticks by her family. But when some nasty guys try to get her newly gotten riches, Brown stops them and marries the girl himself.

A standard production with routine plotting, though the cast is somewhat better than the material.

p, M.H. Hoffman; d, William Nigh; w, W. Scott Darling (based on a story by Evelyn Law); ph, Harry Neumann; ed, Mildred Johnston; m/l, J. Walter Leopold.

Comedy   (PR:A MPAA:NR)

SWEEPSTAKE RACKETEERS (SEE: UNDERCOVER AGENT, 1939)

SWEEPSTAKES**   (1931) 75m RKO-Pathe bw

Eddie Quillan (*Bud Doyle*), James Gleason (*Sleepy Jones*), Marian Nixon (*Babe Ellis*), Lew Cody (*Wally Weber*), Paul Hurst (*Bartender*), Fred Burton (*Pop Blake*), King Baggott (*Weber's Trainer*), Billy Sullivan (*Speed Martin*), Lillian Leighton (*Ma Clancy*), Mike Donlin (*The Dude*), Tom Jackson.

Quillan is a jockey who is unfairly barred from racing. He becomes a singing waiter in Tijuana but soon finds himself back in the saddle again, winning the climactic race. His horse always gives an extra burst of speed when he hollars "Whoop-te-do!" and Quillan does this often and loud. This is a silly little programmer, though Quillan handles his comedy role in a good fashion. Production credits are up to standards.

p, Charles E. Rogers; d, Albert Rogell; w, Lew Lipton, Ralph F. Murray (based on a story by Lipton); ph, Edward Snyder; ed, Joe Kane; m/l, "How About Me Calling You My Sweetheart," Ted Snyder, Mort Harris.

Comedy   (PR:A MPAA:NR)

SWEEPSTAKES WINNER**½   (1939) 59m FN-WB bw

Marie Wilson (*Jenny Jones*), Johnnie Davis (*Downey*), Allen Jenkins (*Bailey*), Charley Foy (*Jinx*), Jerry Colonna (*Nick*), Frankie Burke (*Chalky*), Vera Lewis (*Mrs. McCarthy*), Granville Bates (*Reynolds*), Eddie Kane (*Blake*), Bert Hanlon (*Poolroomer*), George Lloyd (*Dutch*), Sidney Bracey (*Simpkins*), Charles Irwin, John Harron, Reid Kilpatrick, Ken Niles (*Announcers*), Sam McDaniel (*Mose*), Bernice Pilot (*Martha*).

Somewhat amusing programmer finds waitress Wilson receiving $1,000 from her grandfather. She wants to buy a horse with it and gives the cash to racing tout Jenkins. He promptly loses the cash but gives her a ticket for the Irish Sweepstakes and sells her an old nag. Both turn out winners for the horse regains its old form and her ticket pays off big. The direction is standard for minor B work but the acting is not bad, giving the script some credibility.

p, Bryan Foy; d, William McGann; w, John Krafft, Albert DeMond (based on a story by DeMond, Hugh Cummings); ph, Arthur Edeson; ed, Frank Magee.

Comedy   (PR:A MPAA:NR)

SWEET ADELINE**½   (1935) 87m WB bw

Irene Dunne (*Adeline Schmidt*), Donald Woods (*Sid Barnett*), Hugh Herbert (*Rupert Rockingham*), Ned Sparks (*Dan Herziq*), Joseph Cawthorn (*Oscar Schmidt*), Louis Calhern (*Maj. Jim Day*), Winifred Shaw (*Elysia*), Nydia Westman (*Nellie Schmidt*), Dorothy Dare (*Dot, the Band Leader*), Phil Regan (*Singer*), Don Alvarado (*Renaldo*), Jack Mulhall (*Bob*), Noah Beery, Sr (*Sultan*), Martin Garralaga (*Dark Young Man*), Emmett Vogan (*Captain*), Howard Dickinson (*Civilian*), Eddie Shubert (*Eddie*), Nick Copeland (*Prop Man*), Ferdinand Munier (*Gen. Hawks*), William V. Mong (*Cobbler, a Spy*), Johnny Eppelite (*Young Jolson*), Mary Treen (*Girl*), Milton Kibbee (*Stagehand*), Joseph Bernard (*Waiter*), Charles Hickman (*Manx*), Howard H. Mitchell (*Bartender*), Landers Stevens, William Arnold (*Men*), David Newell (*Young Man*), Evelyn Wynans (*Woman*), Harry Tyler (*Louise*).

This dull programmer has one big thing in its favor, a wonderful score by Kern and Hammerstein. Otherwise the film was a minor talkie featuring Dunne as a girl of the gay 'nineties who enchants the men who come to her father's Hoboken biergarten. Woods plays the songwriter with whom she finally finds true love. LeRoy's direction is by the book and without much life. Some of the songs include: "Here Am I," "Don't Ever Leave Me," "Why Was I Born?," and "'Twas Not So Long Ago" (by Jerome Kern, Oscar Hammerstein II), and "We Were So Very Young," "Out of the Blue," and "Lonely Feet."

p, Edward Chodorov; d, Mervyn LeRoy; w, Erwin S. Gelsey (based on the stage musical by Jerome Kern, Oscar Hammerstein II); ph, Sol Polito; ed, Harold McLernon; md, Leo F. Forbstein; art d, Robert Haas; cos, Orry-Kelly; ch, Bobby Connolly.

Musical   (PR:A MPAA:NR)

SWEET ALOES   (SEE: GIVE ME YOUR HEART, 1936)

SWEET AND LOWDOWN*½   (1944) 76m FOX bw

Benny Goodman and His Band *(Themselves)*, Linda Darnell *(Trudy Wilson)*, Lynn Bari *(Pat Sterling)*, Jack Oakie *(Popsy)*, James Cardwell *(Johnny Birch)*, Allyn Joslyn *(Lester Barnes)*, John Campbell *(Dixie Zang)*, Roy Benson *(Skeets McCormick)*, Dickie Moore *(Gen. Carmichael)*, Buddy Swan *(Tony Birch)*, Beverly Hudson *(Helen Birch)*, Dorothy Vaughan *(Mrs. Birch)*, George Lessy *(Norman Wilson)*, Ray Mayer *(Coroner)*, Billy Dawson *(Maj. Ellis)*, Harry McKim *(Col. Wiseman)*, Robert Emmett Keane *(Tivoli Owner)*, Hope Landin *(Matron)*, Cara Williams *(Blonde)*, Roger Clark *(Friend)*, William Colby *(Escort)*, Terry Moore *(Snub-Nosed Girl)*, The Pied Pipers.

Cardwell plays a young trombone player who gets a chance to play with the Benny Goodman Orchestra, but the success immediately goes to his head. Pushed by Darnell, he tries to start up his band, but with disastrous results. He goes back to his old factory job, only to get another chance with good ole' Benny. Acting and plot are bad but the music is quite hot. Musical numbers include: "I'm Making Believe," "Chug-Chug-Choo-Choo-Chug," "Hey Bub, Let's Have a Ball," "Ten Days with a Baby" (by Mack Gordon, James V. Monaco), "I Found a New Baby" (by Jack Palmer, Spencer Williams), "Jersey Bounce" (by Robert B. Wright, Bobby Plater, Tiny Bradshaw, Edward Johnson), "Let's Dance" (by Fanny Baldridge, Gregory Stone, Joseph Bonine), "The World is Waiting for the Sunrise" (by Gene Lockhart, Ernest Seitz), "Mozart's Clarinet Quintet" (performed by Goodman and strings), "No Love, No Nothing" (by Leo Robin, Harry Warren), "Rachel's Dream" (by Benny Goodman), and "I Yi Yi Yi Yi, I Like You Very Much" (by Gordon, Warren).

p, William Le Baron; d, Archie Mayo; w, Richard English (based on a story by English, Edward Haldeman); ph, Lucien Ballard; ed, Dorothy Spencer; md, Emil Newman, Charles Henderson; art d, Lyle Wheeler, Maurice Ransford; spec eff, Fred Sersen.

Musical   (PR:A   MPAA:NR)

SWEET AND SOUR**½   (1964, Fr./Ital.) 93m Compagnia Cinematografica Antonio Cervi-Les Films Number One/Pathe bw (DRAGEES AU POIVRE; CONFETTI AL PEPE)

Guy Bedos *(Gerard)*, Jean-Pierre Marielle *(Rakanowski)*, Sophie Daumier *(Jackie)*, Francis Blanche *(Franz)*, Jean-Marc Bory *(Reporter)*, Anna Karina *(Giselle)*, Simone Signoret *(Genevieve)*, Jean-Paul Belmondo *(Raymond)*, Alexandra Stewart *(Anna)*, Jacques Dufilho *(Mons. Alphonse)*, Francois Perier *(Legrand)*, Jean Richard *(Lepetit)*, Monica Vitti *(She)*, Roger Vadim *(He)*, Romolo Valli *(Mons. X)*, Francoise Brion *(Striptease Girl)*, Claude Brasseur *(Plumber)*, Sophie Desmarets *(The Pianist)*, Anne Doat *(Journalist)*, Daniel Laloux *(Gaby)*, Rita Renoir *(Ethnologist/Striptease Girl)*, Francesca Solleville *(Singer)*, Jean-Baptiste Thierree *(Gregoire)*, Marina Vlady *(Radio-Taxi-Girl)*, Elisabeth Wiener *(Frederique)*, Georges Wilson *(Casimir)*, Jean Babilee *(Oscar)*, Jacques Seiler *(Police Officer)*, Pascale Roberts, Valerie Lagrange, Andrea Parisy *(Striptease Girls)*.

A bit of fun is poked at the likes of Jean-Luc Godard, Alain Resnais, and other prominent filmmakers of the early 1960s in France, as a group of young film worshipers go about making short films that are really quite silly. It is a reflection of the type of enthusiasm that the members of the New Wave had for film, and the movie laughs with these directors instead of at them.

p, Pierre Kalfon; d, Jacques Baratier; w, Guy Bedos, Baratier, Eric Olivier; ph, Henri Decae; m, Ward Swingle; ed, Nena Baratier; art d, Jacques Noel, Raymond Gabutti; ch, Jean Babilee.

Comedy   (PR:A   MPAA:NR)

SWEET BEAT*   (1962, Brit.) 56m Flamingo/Constitution bw (AKA: THE AMOROUS SEX)

Julie Amber *(Ronnie Martin)*, Sheldon Lawrence *(Bill Lacey)*, Irv Bauer *(Dave Lefferts)*, Leonie Page *(Tina Miller)*, David Browning *(Gerry Turner)*, Al Burnett, Billy Myles, The Mellowkings, Cindy Mann, Miss Jeri Lee, Delilah, Fred Parris and His Satins, Lee Allen and His Band.

Amber wins a local beauty contest and is sent to London for the semifinals. Her real goal is to become a singer, so when she loses the contest she accepts an offer to travel to New York for a recording session. She soon realizes that she has been duped by "producer" Bauer who wants to seduce her. She is nearly forced into becoming a stripper when her boy friend, Lawrence, comes to New York to save her. The film's theme song is sung by Tony Crombie, and many of the popular musical entertainers of the time are featured.

p, Jeffrey S. Kruger; d, Ronnie Albert; w, Ron Ahran; ph, S.D. Onions; ed, Jay Dea; md, Malcolm Lockyer.

Drama/Musical   (PR:A   MPAA:NR)

SWEET BIRD OF YOUTH***½   (1962) 120m Roxbury-MGM/MGM c

Paul Newman *(Chance Wayne)*, Geraldine Page *(Alexandra Del Lago)*, Shirley Knight *(Heavenly Finley)*, Ed Begley *("Boss" Finley)*, Rip Torn *(Thomas J. Finley, Jr.)*, Mildred Dunnock *(Aunt Nonnie)*, Madeleine Sherwood *(Miss Lucy)*, Philip Abbott *(Dr. George Scudder)*, Corey Allen *(Scotty)*, Barry Cahill *(Bud)*, Dub Taylor *(Dan Hatcher)*, James Douglas *(Leroy)*, Barry Atwater *(Ben Jackson)*, Charles Arnt *(Mayor Henricks)*, Dorothy Konrad *(Mrs. Maribelle Norris)*, James Chandler *(Prof. Burtus H. Smith)*, Mike Steen *(Deputy)*, Kelly Thordsen *(Sheriff Clark)*, William Forrest *(Benny Taubman)*, Roy Glenn *(Charles)*, Davis Roberts *(Fly)*, Robert Burton *(Director)*.

An emasculated picture about a castrated hero (in the play, he was thus rewarded), this is a tame version of the slimy story Williams wrote for the stage. Newman, Page, Sherwood, and Torn repeated their Broadway roles. On the screen, the parts played by Sidney Blackmer, Diana Hyland, and Martine Bartlett were done by Begley (who won an Oscar for Best Supporting Actor), Knight, and Dunnock. Brooks, who had already bowdlerized CAT ON A HOT TIN ROOF, does it again here but, one must admit, he was under orders, as the seaminess of the play was deemed unfit for general movie audiences and he had to make the changes in order to secure approval from the Production Code, which was still in effect. Page is a marvel in her role and really the only reason to see this picture. She was honored by an Oscar nomination, as was Knight, for her small supporting part that was not nearly as good as what Hyland had done on stage. Newman is a handsome, masculine man who thinks he has what it takes to make it on the silver screen. All he needs now is a break, but it has not yet come. In Florida, he meets Page, a fading movie star who is at the end of her tether. Her last movie is, she is certain, a dismal flop. She is now one of the dregs of humanity. When she meets Newman and he gives her a ride to his home town, she begs him for more gin. Later, when they stay in a motel together, she demands an oxygen inhalator. Then she asks Newman if he can find her some hashish to smoke. In order to keep the virile Newman at her side, she tells him that she can help him get his start in Hollywood. She knows everyone there and will introduce him to the right people. They travel to Newman's home town before going back to California. Newman wants to see his one-time girl friend, Knight, who is the apple of her father's (Begley) eye. Begley is a corrupt politician who runs the area and hates Newman with a passion because the last time he came through town Newman left Knight pregnant and she had to get an abortion. (In the play, she was liberally diseased with syphilis by her lover and had to have her ovaries removed.) Begley wants to get even with Newman for what he did to Knight, so he plots revenge with his lackey son, Torn. Despite what Newman did to her, Knight can't keep away from Newman, and her aunt, Dunnock, arranges trysts between the two. At the same time, Page is unburdening herself to Newman and giving him details about her sordid past. He records all of these with an eye toward using them to blackmail her at a later date if she doesn't come across with the Hollywood introductions she's promised him. When Page is delighted to learn that her comeback movie has been both critically and publically lauded, she stops using the drugs and booze, gets herself together, and plans to exit the small town as soon as possible. Newman doesn't much like being abandoned by Page and lets her know that he has information which she might not like revealed. She is staying at the small hotel in the center of town and outside the inn there's a large political rally taking place for Begley. It disintegrates into a brawl as Begley's former mistress steps forward (Sherwood) to tell one and all about her back-street life with Begley and the fact that Knight once once had an illegal operation. Page realizes that Newman's life may be precarious so she offers to take him with her, but he declines and thinks he can make a go of it with Knight, whom he does love. Later, Newman is outside the Begley house when Torn and some of his hoodlum cronies find him as he's trying to get to Knight. They beat him senseless and mar his face as badly as the boxing scenes in SOMEBODY UP THERE LIKES ME. Knight sees this and understands that Newman took his life in his hands to be near her, so she defies the wishes of her irate father and she and the bloody Newman leave together as Begley fumes and Dunnock beams. That "happy ending" was in direct contrast with the play's powerful finish that saw Newman pay for his sins by being castrated. Everyone in here is a sleazeball and it makes one think twice about going below the Mason-Dixon line. This is a mean bunch of people and Page, despite her drinking, drugging, painful reaching out for the arms of younger men, is the only one of the leads with a modicum of decency. All of the well-known Williams themes are intermingled here: violence, the same mob mentality seen in SUDDENLY, LAST SUMMER when a group of Spanish boys killed and then ate the homosexual who used them, the bird-like relatives (often seen in many of his plays), and the perpetual neuroses of the female characters. The best scene is Page's as she gets a phone call from Broadway columnist Walter Winchell (who isn't really heard). He tells her that her movie comeback has succeeded and her magnificently manipulative face goes through a series of emotions that should stand as an acting lesson for anyone who wants to don the sock and buskin for a living. She begins with self-doubt, becomes unsure and cynical, finally accepts what she's hearing, and marches through a possibility of hope, then into glowing happiness. Torn is excellent as the Begley son and exudes evil out of every pore of his skin. Begley is even more malevolent, perhaps too much so, in a parody of Huey Long and every other redneck bigot ever seen. The addition of color was not needed as Williams just seems to play better in black and white and gray.

p, Pandro S. Berman; d&w, Richard Brooks (based on the play by Tennessee Williams); ph, Milton Krasner (CinemaScope, Metrocolor); ed, Henry Berman; md, Robert Armbruster; art d, George W. Davis, Urie McCleary; set d, Henry Grace, Hugh Hunt; cos, Orry-Kelly; spec eff, Lee Le Blanc; makeup, William Tuttle.

Drama   (PR:O MPAA:NR)

SWEET BODY, THE   (SEE: SWEET BODY OF DEBORAH, THE, 1969, Ital./Fr.)

SWEET BODY OF DEBORAH, THE*   (1969, Ital./Fr.) 95m Zenith Cinematografica-Flora- C.C.F. LUX/WB-Seven Arts c (IL DOLCE CORPO DI DEBORAH; L'ADORABLE CORPS DE DEBORAH; AKA: THE SOFT BODY OF DEBORAH; THE SWEET BODY)

Carroll Baker (Deborah), Jean Sorel (Marcel), George Hilton (Robert), Evelyn Stewart (Susan), Luigi Pistilli (Philip), Michel Bardinet (Police Commissioner), Renato Montalbano (Telephone Man), Mirella Pamphili (Telephone Clerk), Domenico Ravenna (Doctor), Valentino Macchi (Garage Attendant), Giuseppe Ravenna (Maitre d').

An intricate scheme by Sorel to kill his wife, Baker, backfires when she develops her own plan with the next-door neighbor to kill Sorel. All this plotting is an attempt to collect insurance money, allowing for lots of gore and the chance to show off Baker's body.

p, Mino Loy, Luciano Martino; d, Romolo Guerrieri; w, Ernesto Gastaldi (based on the story by Gastaldi, Martino); ph, Marcello Masciocchi (Techniscope, Technicolor); m, Nora Orlandi; ed, Eugenio Alabiso; art d, Amedeco Fago; cos, Balestra; makeup, Mario Van Riel.

Suspense   (PR:O MPAA:R)

SWEET CHARITY*½**   (1969) 157m UNIV c

Shirley MacLaine (Charity Hope Valentine), Sammy Davis, Jr (Big Daddy), Ricardo Montalban (Vittorio Vitale), John McMartin (Oscar Lindquist), Chita Rivera (Nickie), Paula Kelly (Helene), Stubby Kaye (Herman), Barbara Bouchet (Ursula), Alan Hewitt (Nicholsy), Dante D'Paulo (Charlie), John Wheeler (Rhythm of Life Dancer), John Craig (Man in Fandango Ballroom), Dee Carroll (Woman on Tandem), Tom Hatten (Man on Tandem), Sharon Harvey (Young Woman on Bridge), Charles Brewer (Young Man on Bridge), Richard Angarola (Maitre d'), Henry Beckman, Jeff Burton (Policemen), Ceil Cabot (Married Woman), Alfred Dennis (Waiter at Chile Hacienda), David Gold (Panhandler), Nolan Leary (Manfred), Diki Lerner (Man with Dog on Bridge), Buddy Lewis (Appliance Salesman), Joseph Mell (Man on Bridge), Geraldine O'Brien (Lady on Bridge), Alma Platt (Lady with Hat on Bridge), Maudie Prickett (Nurse on Bridge), Chet Stratton (Waiter), Robert Terry (Doorman), Roger Til (Greeter at Pompeii Club), Buddy Hart, Bill Harrison (Baseball Players), Suzanne Charny (Lead Frug Dancer), Bick Goss (Drummer Boy), Chelsea Brown, Ray Chabeau, Bryan Da Silva, Lynn Fields, Dick Fitzell, Ellen Halpin, Dick Korthaze, April Nevins, Maris O'Neill, Lee Roy Reams, Sandy Roveta, Charleen Ryan, Juleste Salve, Patrick Spohn, Jerry Trent, Ben Vereen, Bud Vest, Lorene Yarnell (Frug Dancers), John Frayer, Dom Salinaro, Paul Shipton, Walter Stratton (Patrons at Dancehall), Larry Billman, Herman Boden, Dick Colacino, Lynn McMurrey, Ted Monson, Ed Robinson (Waiter-Dancers), Leon Bing, Sue Linden, Jackie Mitchell, Carroll Roebke (Models), Kathryn Doby, Al Lanti, Gloria Mills, Louise Quick, Victoria Scruton, Tiffni Twitchell, Renata Vaselle, Adele Yoshioka (Dancers in "Big Spender" Number), Chuck Harrod, Charles Lunard, Jerry Mann, Frank Radcliff (Singers), Marie Bahruth, Toni Basil, Carol Birner, Donald Bradburn, Lonnie Burr, Cheryl Christiansen, Marguerite De Lain, Jimmy Fields, Ben Gooding, Carlton Johnson, Kirk Kirksey, Lance Le Gault, Trish Mahoney, Walter Painter, Bob Thompson, Jr, Bonnie G. West, Kay York (Dancers in "Rhythm of Life" Number), Leon Alton, Norman Stevans (Conversions).

A very good musical that could have been and *should* have been a great musical. Fosse was making his movie debut as a director and showed some restraint in cinematic trickery but still couldn't bring the same verve to the movie that he did when directing the stage version. The play was based on the Italian movie "Nights of Cabiria" and was adapted by Neil Simon. It opened in New York in January, 1966, and ran more than two years with Gwen Verdon in the lead, supported by Helen Gallagher, Thelma Oliver, James Luisi, John Wheeler, Arnold Soboloff, and John McMartin, who was the only Broadway actor to be used in the film. Ross Hunter was the original producer but when he and Fosse had the usual Hollywood "creative differences," Hunter was replaced by Arthur. The Italian movie was a lovely, gentle picture that was powerful in its simplicity. This musical is overblown and strives for the blockbuster status it didn't achieve. MacLaine is a dime-a-dance hostess in a tacky New York ballroom. Despite her tough life, she is an optimist who always sees the bright side of things. Her latest boy friend is D'Paulo, a hoodlum who takes all of her hard-earned savings, pushes her off a low bridge in Central Park, and absconds with the cash. MacLaine is down but not out. She feels cheated because she has a tattoo with his name on her arm, but that can all be worked out if she ever falls in love with another guy named "Charlie." MacLaine is walking along the street one evening and comes across dashing Italian movie star Montalban in a furious argument with Bouchet, his exquisite lover. Bouchet leaves

Montalban on the street and he turns to gamine MacLaine and asks if she would like to be his date in the nightclub where he was about to take Bouchet. MacLaine is honored, goes to the club, then back to his place for a bite to eat. Just as it seems that MacLaine and Montalban have found affection, Bouchet returns, totally contrite about her earlier behavior. MacLaine hides in one of the closets and spends the evening there while Montalban and Bouchet make up. MacLaine tries to secure straight employment at an employment agency in a tall building but it doesn't work out. On her way down, the elevator has a power failure and she is stuck with McMartin in close quarters. He's a mild-mannered insurance clerk named Oscar and terribly claustrophobic. She calms his fears and the two of them hit it off. McMartin is a nice, pleasant man who is as interesting as dust at first but MacLaine sees something in him and realizes that he has the stability she may have been searching for all these years. He thinks she's a bank employee and probably would never make a move if he knew she toiled in a dance hall. MacLaine's close friends, Kelly and Rivera, can't believe that she sees anything in McMartin and tell her that mixed marriages never work (squares and showbiz types). Even after McMartin learns what she does for a living, he still wants to marry her. Then he goes to her place of employment, meets her pals, and sees the tattoo she carries and he backs out, giving Kelly and Rivera the opportunity to say, "I told you so." With McMartin out of her life, MacLaine takes a moment out to consider her life. She strolls into Central Park, to the same bridge she once was thrown off. A band of hippies approach and hand her a fresh new flower. She stares at the daisy, smells it, and takes new energy from it. The picture ends as MacLaine is renewed and ready to face life again. Cy Coleman and Dorothy Fields wrote a fine score for the play, with two new songs for the movie. The specially written tunes were "My Personal Property" (sung by MacLaine) and "It's a Nice Face" (sung by MacLaine to McMartin in the elevator scene). The others are "Hey, Big Spender" (MacLaine, Kelly, Rivera and the other ballroom girl), "Rich Man's Frug" (instrumental, danced by several girls with Suzanne Charny as the lead, a tune later used in a commercial), "If My Friends Could See Me Now" (MacLaine), "There's Gotta Be Something Better Than This" (MacLaine, Rivera, Kelly), "Rhythm of Life" (Sammy Davis, Jr. as a hippie religious cult leader in an extraneous number), "Sweet Charity" (McMartin), "I'm a Brass Band" (MacLaine), "I Love to Cry at Weddings" (Stubby Kaye and ensemble), and "Where Am I Going?" (MacLaine). A fast eye will note several members of the chorus and ensemble who went on to distinguish themselves in later years. They include Ben Vereen, choreographers Toni Basil and Walter Painter, mime star Lorene Yarnell, Broadway dancer Lee Roy Reams (who starred in Merrick's stage version of "42nd Street") and Chelsea Brown, who played on TV's "Laugh-In." Peter Stone, who wrote the book for many a Broadway play (1776 and "Woman of the Year" among them), does okay by this but he had Simon's stage book to work with and there were many jokes to use. The scene in the elevator was particularly funny. MacLaine works very hard at not seeming to work hard and the result is that she looks like she's working hard. It's a studied performance that goes for the tear ducts and the laugh-lines and never quite reaches either. The location work was done in New York with interiors in California. In all, a pleasing family movie (it was rated "G"), that never goes beyond being anything more than that.

p, Robert Arthur; d, Bob Fosse; w, Peter Stone (based on the play by Neil Simon, Cy Coleman, Dorothy Fields, adapted from the screenplay "Notti Di Cabiria" by Federico Fellini, Tullio Pinelli, Ennio Flaiano); ph, Robert Surtees (Panavision, Technicolor); m, Coleman; ed, Stuart Gilmore; md, Joseph Gershenson; art d, Alexander Golitzen, George C. Webb; set d, Jack D. Moore; cos, Edith Head; ch, Bob Fosse; makeup, Bud Westmore.

Musical/Comedy   (PR:A MPAA:G)

SWEET CREEK COUNTY WAR, THE*½   (1979) 99m Imagery/Key International c

Richard Egan (Judd Firman), Albert Salmi (George W. Breakworth), Nita Talbot (Firetop Alice Dewey), Slim Pickens (Jitters Pippin), Robert J. Wilke (Lucas K. Derring), Joe Orton (Lyle Derring), Ray Cardi (Rowdy Derring), Tom Jackman (Virgil Harper).

An old oater theme is given modern production techniques and looks none the better for it. Characters are all stereotypes and plot development is handled in a strictly routine fashion. Egan plays a sheriff who has decided to retire to a ranch, but discovers he must fight a crooked businessman. Old cowboy entries are at least fun to watch just for seeing how the great character actors do their bits. This does not even have that, though Pickens has a role.

p, Ken Byrnes, J. Frank James; d&w, James; ph, Gregory von Berblinger; m, Richard Bowden; ed, Ronald Sinclair; prod d, Allen H. Jones; cos, Peggy Sjulstad.

Western   Cas.   (PR:A MPAA:PG)

SWEET DEVIL*½   (1937, Brit.) 79m GFD bw

Bobby Howes (Tony Brent), Jean Gillie (Jill Turner), William Kendall (Edward Bane), Syd Walker (Belton), Ellis Jeffreys (Lady Tonbridge), Glen Alyn (Sylvia Tonbridge), Anthony Ireland (Flores), Hazel Terry (Rose), Sylvia Leslie (Frances), Syd Crossley (Police Constable), The Four New Yorkers.

A cheery musical romp which stars Howes and Kendall as business partners, the latter planning to marry his typist, Gillie. Howes advises Kendall to fire Gillie before proposing, but when the typist loses her job she attempts suicide. Howes pulls her from the river and brings her back to his apartment to recover. It takes a great deal of brandy to bring Gillie around, getting her drunk enough to spoil a VIP party Howes throws later that evening. Howes' high society fiancee walks out on him and he proposes instead to Gillie. An enjoyable picture as illogical as it is entertaining.

p, Jack Buchanan; d, Rene Guissart; w, Ralph Spence, Geoffrey Kerr (based on the play "Quelle Drole de Gosse").

Musical/Romance   **(PR:A   MPAA:NR)**

SWEET DIRTY TONY   (SEE: CUBA CROSSING, 1980)

SWEET ECSTASY**   (1962, Fr.) 75m Paris Inter Productions-Contact Organization-Les Films du Griffon/Audubon bw (DOUCE VIOLENCE; AKA: SWEET VIOLENC E)

Elke Sommer (Elke), Pierre Brice (Maddy), Vittoria Prada (Barbara), Christain Pezey (Olivier), Claire Maurier (Claire), Jenny Astruc (Mick), Michele Bardollet (Choutte), Robert Darane (Charlie), Agnes Spaak (Dominique), Albert Dinan (Popoff), Robert Bar, Mitsouko.

The idle youths of Paris are under scrutiny as Pezey becomes part of a group who want to have as much fun as possible. When he refuses to allow Sommer to seduce him because he needs to be in love with someone to sleep with them, tensions begin to erupt. This eventually leads the young folk to realize how wasted their lifes really are.

p, Joel Lifschultz; d, Max Pecas; w, Jacques Aucante, Grisha M. Dabat, Pecas; ph, Marc Fossard (CinemaScope); m, Charles Aznavour; ed, Paul Cayatte; art d, Bob Luchaire; m/l, Aznavour, Georges Garvarentz, Clement Nicolas (sung by Johnny Hallyday).

Drama   **(PR:C MPAA:NR)**

SWEET HUNTERS**   (1969, Panama) 115m General Productions c

Sterling Hayden (Allan), Maureen McNalley (Clea), Susan Strasberg (Lis), Stuart Whitman (Prisoner), Andrew Hayden (Bob).

A small family consisting of Sterling Hayden as the father, McNalley, the mother, and son, Andrew Hayden, live on a remote tropical island. Sterling Hayden is totally engrossed in birds, leaving his wife to a lonely and almost desperate existence. An escaped prisoner is believed to be hiding on the island, which fills McNalley with excitement. She goes about leaving little knick-knacks for him until they eventually meet, at which point they have a quick fling. The atmosphere of the island is made to seem oppressive and having this effect on the characters. Problems come when the director dwells too much on the scenery and not enough in the development of the plot or the characters.

p, Claude Giroux; d, Ruy Guerra; w, Guerra, Philippe Dumarcay, Gerard Zinzz; ph, Ricardo Arnonovitch (Eastmancolor); ed, Kenout Peltier; art d, Bernard Evein.

Drama   **(PR:C MPAA:NR)**

SWEET INNISCARRA*½   (1934, Brit.) 72m COL bw

Sean Rogers (Gerald O'Carroll), Mae Ryan (Kate).

Rogers is a millionaire determined to make Ryan love him. To win her over he pretends to be a schoolmaster. A lighthearted romance set against the picturesque background of 1930s Ireland.

p,d&w, Emmett Moore.

Romance   **(PR:A MPAA:NR)**

SWEET JESUS, PREACHER MAN*   (1973) 103m Capitol Cinema-Entertainment Pyramid/MGM c

Roger E. Mosley (Holmes/Lee), William Smith (Martelli), Michael Pataki (State Sen. Sills), Tom Johnigarn (Eddie Stoner), Joe Tornatore (Joey), Damu King (Sweetstick), Marla Gibbs (Beverly Solomon), Sam Laws (Deacon Greene), Phil Hoover (George Orr), Paul Silliman (Roy), Chuck Lyles (Detroit Charlie), Norman Fields (Police Captain), Della Thomas (Foxey), Amentha Dymally (Mrs. Greene), Patricia Edwards (Marion Hicks), Chuck Douglas, Jr (Lenny Solomon), Vincent LaBauve (Bobby Thompson), Chuck Wells (Eli Stoner), Betty Coleman (Maxine Gibbs), Lillian Tarry (Mother Gibbs), Lou Jackson (Randy Gibbs), T.C. Ellis (Earl Saunders), Lee Frost (1st Policeman), JoAnn Bruno (Widow Foster), Rev. K.D. Friend (Funeral Minister), Billy Quinn (Sweetstick's Bodyguard), Bob Angelle, John Washington, Bruce Hall, Don Senette, Dan Black, Curtiss Price (Militants).

Poorly produced and acted black exploitation picture has Mosley going undercover as a preacher. He works for one mob boss who wants to know what his rival is doing.

p, Daniel B. Cady; d, Henning Schellerup; w, John Cerullo, M. Stuart Madden, Abbey Leitch; ph, Paul E. Hipp (Metrocolor); m, Horace Tapscott;

ed, Warren Hamilton, Jr.; set d, Merolyn Ravetz; spec eff, Harry Woolman, Rick Helmer.

Crime   **(PR:O   MPAA:R)**

SWEET KILL   (SEE: AROUSERS, THE, 1973)

SWEET KITTY BELLAIRS**   (1930) 72m WB c

Claudia Dell (Sweet Kitty Bellairs), Ernest Torrence (Sir Jasper Standish), Walter Pidgeon (Lord Varney), June Collyer (Julia Standish), Perry Askam (Capt. O'Hara), Lionel Belmore (Col. Villiers), Arthur Edmund Carewe (Capt. Spicer), Flora Finch (Gossip), Douglas Gerrard (Tom Stafford), Christianne Yves (Lydia, Maid).

A costume drama set in 18th Century England had the added advantage of Technicolor to heighten all the colorful gowns and settings, which by the standards of 1930, are extremely professional. The simple plot concerns a love affair between Dell, an impetuous flirt, and bandit Askam, when the lady takes a trip to Bath. Humor and song are interspersed with the action, but the music was aimed at sophisticates; that is, people not into jazz. Songs by Bobby Dolan and Walter O'Keefe include: "Tally-Ho," "Highwayman Song," "Song of the City of Bath," "Drunk Song," "Pump Song," "Dueling Song," "My Love," "You-oo, I Love You," "Peggy's Leg."

d, Alfred E. Green; w, Hermann Harrison, J. Grubb Alexander (based on the play by David Belasco from the novel The Bath Comedy by Agnes and Egerton Castle); ph, Watkins McDonald (Technicolor).

Musical/Comedy   **(PR:A MPAA:NR)**

SWEET LIGHT IN A DARK ROOM***   (1966, Czech.) 93m Barrandov-Ceskoslovensky/Prome nade bw (ROMEO, JULIA A TMA; AKA: ROMEO, JULIET AND DARKNESS)

Ivan Mistrik (Pavel), Dana Smutna (Hanka), Jirina Sejbalova (Pavel's Mother), Frantisek Smolik (Grandfather), Blanka Bohdanova (Kubiasova), Eva Mrazova (Alena), Karla Chadimova (Josefka), Miroslav Svoboda (Wurm), Karlicka Svobodova (Marticka Wurmova), Vladimar Raz (Class Master), Milos Nedbal (Headmaster), Anna Meliskova (Kubrychtova), Vaclav Lohnisky (Railwayman), Josef Kozak (Janitor), Ladislav Kazda (Melicar), Jiri Kodet (Vojta), Jindrich Narenta (Bubi), Josef Vorel, Ivo Gubel, Pavel Bartl (Gestapo Agents), Vera Tichankova (Farmer's Wife), Alexandra Myskova (Wurmova), Marie Maresova, Ela Poznerova (Neighbors), Vera Vachova (Irena), Zuzana Fisarkova (Melicharova), Stanislav Langer (Doctor), Ladislav Mrkvicka (Bubenik), Ladislav Gzela (Neighbor), Jan Pelikan (Old Man), Ruda Princ (Trash Collector), Jan Skopecek (Secret Agent), Vaclav Sloup (Student).

Set in Prague during the Nazi occupation, Mistrik plays a student who hides a Jewish girl who had escaped when her family was taken to the ghetto. Eventually he falls in love with her. Problems arise when his mother becomes overly suspicious and the death of an S.S. general leads to increased Nazi harassment. The girl flees from her shelter because she feels she has become too great of a burden, and is quickly shot down by an S.S. patrol. Director Weiss himself had been forced to leave Czechoslovakia during the Nazi occupation of that country. He returned after WW II to become the leading Czech filmmaker of his generation.

d, Jiri Weiss; w, Weiss, Jan Otcenasek (based on Romeo, Julia a Tma by Otcenasek); ph, Vaclav Hanus; m, Jiri Srnka; ed, Miroslav Hajek; art d, Karel Skvor.

War Drama   **(PR:A MPAA:NR)**

SWEET LOVE, BITTER**   (1967) 92m Film 2/Film 2-Peppercorn Wormser-UM bw (AKA: IT WON'T RUB OFF, BABY]; BLACK LOVE– WHITE LOVE)

Dick Gregory (Richie "Eagle" Stokes), Don Murray (David Hillary), Diane Varsi (Della), Robert Hooks (Keel Robinson), Jeri Archer (Candy), Barbara Davis (Girl in Bar), Bruce Glover, Carla Pinza.

Embittered, black saxophonist Gregory befriends Murray, a white college professor who blames himself for the recent death of his wife, and subsequently drowns his sorrows in alcohol. Gregory and Murray's drinking binges develop into a friendship based on personal understanding. A third member to the group is added when Hooks, a cafe owner, gives Murray a job as a waiter and, in general, keeps the two men from going overboard. Eventually Murray gets back on his feet again and returns to his teaching job. When Gregory comes to visit Murray, a white cop stops him and then beats him up for being a vagrant. Murray, paralyzed by his inability to do something, witnesses the whole incident. Later Murray tells Gregory, but Gregory shrugs it off and goes on another drinking binge. Soon thereafter, he dies of a heroin overdose. Murray is left to blame himself for another death. Though a sincere attempt was made to depict the problems surrounding black-white relationships, the characters in the film are shallow and lack definition.

p, Lewis Jacobs; d, Herbert Danska; w, Danska, Jacobs (based on Night Song by John Alfred Williams); ph, Victor Solow; m, Mal Waldron; ed, Gerald Kleppel.

Drama   (PR:C   MPAA:NR)

SWEET MAMA*   (1930) 56m FN bw (GB: CONFLICT)

Alice White (*Goldie*), David Manners (*Jimmy*), Kenneth Thomson (*Joe Palmer*), Rita Flynn (*Lulu*), Lee Moran (*Al Hadrick*), Richard Cramer (*Elmer*), Robert Elliott (*Mack, City Detective*), Lew Harvey (*Gangster*), Lee Shumway.

A ridiculous film starring White who proves to be more than the mob can handle, putting all the crooks, who really don't come off as being too bad, where they belong. She does it so her beau will go straight and be able to stay that way. White is horribly miscast, as was just about everyone, making this well-worn story that much worse.

d, Edward Cline; w, Earl Baldwin (based on the story by Baldwin, Frederick Hazlitt Brennan); ph, Sid Hickox; ed, Frederick Y. Smith, Edward Schroeder.

Crime   (PR:A   MPAA:NR)

SWEET MUSIC*½   (1935) 90m WB bw

Rudy Vallee (*Skip Houston*), Ann Dvorak (*Bonnie Haydon*), Ned Sparks (*Ten Percent Nelson, Press Agent*), Helen Morgan (*Herself*), Robert Armstrong (*Dopey Malone*), Allen Jenkins (*Barney Cowan, Publicity Man*), Alice White (*Lulu Betts*), Joseph Cawthorn (*Sidney Selzer*), Al Shean (*Sigmund Selzer*), William B. Davidson (*Billy Madison*), Phillip Reed (*Grant, Announcer*), Henry O'Neill (*Louis Trumble*), Addison Richards (*Mr. Thomas*), Russell Hicks (*Mayor*), Clay Clement (*Mr. Johnson*), Jack Norton (*Drunk*), Mary Treen (*Girl at Train*), Eddie Kane (*Restauranteur*), Dave O'Brien (*Bit*), Milt Kibbee, Rudy Vallee's Connecticut Yankees, Frank and Milt Britton Orchestra.

A fiery backstage romance between Vallee and Dvorak acts as an excuse to string along a bunch of musical numbers. The songs are adequate, with Vallee doing most of the singing–a good thing considering his acting ability. Songs include: "Fare Thee Well Annabelle," "The Snake Charmer" (Mort Dixon, Allie Wrubel), "Sweet Music" (Al Dubin, Harry Warren), "Good Green Acres Of Home," "Ev'ry Day," "Don't Go On A Diet," "Winter Overnight," "There's A Different You In Your Heart," and "Seltzer Theme Song" (Irving Kahal, Sammy Fain).

p, Sam Bischoff; d, Alfred E. Green; w, Jerry Wald, Carl Erickson, Warren Duff (based on a story by Wald); ph, James Van Trees; ed, Herbert Leonard; art d, Robert Haas; ch, Bobby Connolly.

Musical   (PR:A   MPAA:NR)

SWEET NOVEMBER**   (1968) 114m Gina/WB-Seven Arts c

Sandy Dennis (*Sara Deever*), Anthony Newley (*Charlie Blake*), Theodore Bikel (*Alonzo*), Burr DeBenning (*Clem Batchman*), Sandy Baron (*Richard*), Marj Dusay (*Carol*), Martin West (*Gordon*), Virginia Vincent (*Mrs. Schumacher*), King Moody (*Digby*), Robert Gibbons (*Sam Naylor*).

A tear-jerker starring Dennis who plays a woman suffering from an incurable disease. Knowing that she doesn't have too much more time in this world, she takes in a different man every month to sublet her apartment with her. The only stipulations are that they must have a hang-up that she might be able to cure, and that they leave at the end of the month. The November apartment mate, Newley, poses a problem, however, when they fall in love. He begs to stay, but Dennis forces him to leave. Dennis is good in the role, but the character she portrays is difficult to take seriously.

p, Jerry Gershwin; Elliott Kastner; d, Robert Ellis Miller; w, Herman Raucher; ph, Daniel L. Fapp (Technicolor); m, Michel Legrand; ed, James Heckert; art d, John Robert Lloyd; set d, Ralph S. Hurst; cos, Ann Roth; m/l, "Sara's Theme," Legrand, "Sweet November," Leslie Bricusse, Anthony Newley (sung by Newley); makeup, Gordon Bau.

Drama   (PR:A   MPAA:NR)

SWEET REVENGE   (SEE: DANDY, THE ALL AMERICAN GIRL, 1976)

SWEET RIDE, THE*½   (1968) 111m FOX c

Tony Franciosa (*Collie Ransom*), Michael Sarrazin (*Denny McGuire*), Jacqueline Bisset (*Vicki Cartwright, Actress*), Bob Denver (*Choo-Choo Burns, Jazz Pianist*), Michael Wilding (*Mr. Cartwright*), Michele Carey (*Thumper*), Lara Lindsay (*Martha*), Norma Crane (*Mrs. Cartwright*), Percy Rodriguez (*Lt. Atkins*), Warren Stevens (*Brady Caswell, TV Producer*), Pat Buttram (*Texan*), Michael Forest (*Barry Green*), Lloyd Gough (*Parker*), Stacy King (*Big Jane*), Corinna Tsopei (*Tennis Girl*), Charles Dierkop (*Mr. Clean, Cyclist*), Arthur Franz (*Psychiatrist*), Seymour Cassel (*Surfer/Cyclist*), Paul Condylis (*Sgt. Solomon*), Ralph Lee (*Scratch*), Lou Procopio (*Diablo*), Linda Gamble, Sam Chew, Jr.

The film is anything but what the title claims, as a group of beach dwellers who live on Malibu Beach are brought together to show the pointlessness of their lifestyle. It takes the fatal beating of Bisset to make beach bum Sarrazin come to his senses; he wanted to have a meaningful relationship with her, but she was too wrapped up in shallow sexual encounters to handle it. Sarrazin then decides to put meaning into his life by getting a job at a hardware store. Denver co-stars as a flaky jazz musician who is Sarrazin's roommate, as is Franciosa, the tennis pro who lives off the admiration of the other inhabitants of the beach. There was a possibility for a good movie in this script, but the film came out being as bland as the characters it was trying to expose.

p, Joe Pasternak; d, Harvey Hart; w, Tom Mankiewicz (based on the novel by William Murray); ph, Robert B. Hauser (Panavision, DeLuxe Color); m, Pete Rugolo; ed, Philip W. Anderson; art d, Jack Martin Smith, Richard Day; set d, Walter M. Scott, Stuart A. Reiss; m/l, "Sweet Ride," Lee Hazlewood (sung by Dusty Springfield), "Never Again," Moby Grape (sung by Moby Grape).

Drama   (PR:C   MPAA:R)

SWEET ROSIE O'GRADY***   (1943) 74m FOX c

Betty Grable (*Madeleine Marlowe*), Robert Young (*Sam Mackeever*), Adolphe Menjou (*Morgan*), Reginald Gardiner (*Duke Charles*), Virginia Grey (*Edna Van Dyke*), Phil Regan (*Composer*), Sig Rumann (*Joe Flugelman*), Alan Dinehart (*Arthur Skinner*), Hobart Cavanaugh (*Clark*), Frank Orth (*Cabby*), Jonathan Hale (*Mr. Fox*), Stanley Clements (*Danny*), Byron Foulger (*Rimplemayer*), Lilyan Irene (*Gracie*), Milton Parsons (*Madison*), Hal K. Dawson (*Poindexter*), George Chandler (*Kelly*), Charles Trowbridge (*Husband*), St. Brendan's Choir (*Themselves*), Leo Diamond and His Solitaires (*Themselves*), Oliver Blake (*White the Artist*), Cyril Ring, Herbert Vigran, Perc Launders (*Photographers*), Dorothy Granger (*Singer*), Mary Gordon, Connie Leon (*Charwomen*), Gabriel Canzona (*Hurdy Gurdy Man with Monkey*), Edward Earle, James Metcalfe, Bruce Warren, John Dilson, Paul Maxey, Sam Wren, Hooper Atchley (*Salesmen*), Joe King (*Burl Ship Official*).

Alice Faye was supposed to play the lead but decided to get married instead so the chore went to Fox's other blonde, Betty Grable, who shined. She's a Brooklynite who is masquerading as something other than that. A star who has just come home from England where she nabbed great notices on the musical-comedy stage as well as the interest of British nobleman Gardiner, Grable comes back to New York where Young, a one-time boy friend, is now a reporter for the *Police Gazette* (which was, in the 1880s, a combination of *Playboy* and the *National Enquirer*). Young is under orders from Menjou, his editor, to expose the truth about Gable. She is, in fact, a former beer-hall performer who toiled in New York's Bowery for Rumann. Young prints the truth about Grable and she gets back by saying that he only did it because she spurned him. The chance to become a peeress of the realm is ruined but Grable realizes that she loves and always has loved Young and the two of them wind up together, naturally, at the end. The slim story is greatly enhanced by many songs, most written by Harry Warren and Mack Gordon. The Warren-Mack songs include: "My Heart Tells Me," "My Sam" (sung by Grable), "Oh Where is the Groom?" (sung by Grable, chorus), "The Wishing Waltz" (a production number that features choreographer Hermes Pan), "Going to the Country Fair," "Get Your Police Gazette." Other songs include: "Battle Cry" (Maude Nugent, sung by Irene), "Sweet Rosie O'Grady" (Nugent, sung by Grable, Young, Menjou), "Sidewalks of New York" (Charles Lawlor, James Blake), "Two Little Girls in Blue" (Charles Graham, sung by Grable, chorus), "Little Annie Rooney" (Michael Nolan, sung by Young, Grable, Orth), "Heaven Will Protect the Working Girl" (Edgar Smith, A.B. Sloane, sung by Young, Grable), "Waiting at the Church" (Fred W. Leigh, Henry E. Pether, sung by Grable, chorus). Although Young sings, he is no Don Ameche or John Payne and they wisely keep his light baritone to a minimum. The picture made a good deal of money and will be pleasantly forgotten. Good color work, nice sets, and costumes all contribute to the authentic period flair. Remade as THAT WONDERFUL URGE.

p, William Perlberg; d, Irving Cummings; w, Ken Englund (based on stories by William R. Lipman, Frederick Stephani, Edward Van Every); ph, Ernest Palmer (Technicolor); ed, Robert Simpson; md, Alfred Newman, Charles Henderson; art d, James Basevi, Joseph C. Wright; set d, Thomas Little, Frank E. Hughes; spec eff, Fred Sersen; ch, Hermes Pan.

Musical/Comedy   (PR:A   MPAA:NR)

SWEET SIXTEEN* (1983) 90m Productions Two/Century International c

Bo Hopkins (*Dan*), Susan Strasberg (*Joanne*), Don Stroud (*Billy*), Dana Kimmell (*Marci*), Aleisa Shirley (*Melissa*), Don Shanks (*Jason*), Steve Antin (*Hank*), Logan Clarke (*Jimmy*), Michael Pataki (*George*), Patrick Macnee (*John*), Larry Storch (*Earl*), Henry Wilcoxon (*Greyfeather*), Sharon Farrell (*Kathy*).

Another teenage slasher picture. This one has all the boy friends of sweet 16-year-old Shirley being found hacked to death. It's all the fault of some crazed schizophrenic, as usual, and Shirley's being punished for her sexual awakening. Fair direction and a decent cast (most notably Hopkins as the sheriff) make this one at least partly watchable.

p&d, Jim Sotos; w, Erwin Goldman; ph, James L. Carter; m, Tommy Vig; ed, Drake Silliman; makeup, Jim Gillespie, Debbie Gillespie.

Horror   Cas.   (PR:O   MPAA:R)

SWEET SKIN** (1965, Fr./Ital.) 96m Lambor-Variety/Times Film bw
(AKA: STRIP-TEASE)

Krista Nico (*Ariane*), Dany Saval (*Dodo Voluptuous/Berthe*), Darry Cowl
(*Paul*), Jean Sobieski (*Jean-Loup*), Renee Passeur (*The Rich Woman*), Jean
Tissier (*The Painter*), Alice Cocea (*Middle Class Lady/Jean-Loup's Aunt*),
Umberto Orsini (*Dancer/Ariane's Dance Partner*), Yves Barsacq, Badin,
Jean-Pierre Zola, Norma Dugo, Marcello Oliveto.

A ballet dancer turns to the strip-tease when out of a job. Although a popular
success, mainly because she refuses to uncover her breasts, a stilted affair
makes her realize what she has become, so she decides to return to the
ballet.

p, Jules Borkon; d, Jacques Poitrenaud; w, Poitrenaud, Jacques Sigurd
(based on an idea by Alain Moury); ph, Raymond Lemoigne; m, Serge
Gainsbourg; ed, Gilbert Natot.

Drama   (PR:O   MPAA:NR)

SWEET SMELL OF LOVE** (1966, Ital./Ger.) 81m La Regina
Produzione- Thor/William Rowland bw (UNA VERGINE PER UN BAS-
TARDO; VERGINE PER UN BASTARDO; DAS BETT EINER JUNG-
FRAU)

Marisa Solinas (*Maria*), Dan Harrison (*Philip*), Henrik Reinkwell (*Kurt*),
Georg Hauke, Gianluigi Crescenzi.

Thief Harrison double-crosses his partner, Reinkwell, by absconding with a
cache of money and jewels both of them were to divide. Harrison takes
refuge on a small island where he meets and falls for Solinas, who shuns his
advances. Reinkwell catches up with his former partner in crime, but
Harrison kills him, leaving the body behind for Solinas and her mute friend
to bury. Harrison eventually marries Solinas, but leaves the island the
morning after the wedding.

p, Joseph Justman; d, Edward Dein [Ubaldo Ragona]; w, Dein, Karlheinz
Deikert; ph, Franco Delli Colli; m, Ugo Calise; ed, Giancarlo Cappelli.

Crime/Drama   (PR:A   MPAA:NR)

SWEET SMELL OF SUCCESS**** (1957) 96m Norma-Curtleigh/UA
bw

Burt Lancaster (*J.J. Hunsecker*), Tony Curtis (*Sidney Falco*), Susan Harri-
son (*Susan Hunsecker*), Martin Milner (*Steve Dallas*), Sam Levene (*Frank
D'Angelo*), Barbara Nichols (*Rita*), Jeff Donnell (*Sally*), Joseph Leon
(*Robard*), Edith Atwater (*Mary*), Emile Meyer (*Harry Kello*), Joe Frisco
(*Herbie Temple*), David White (*Otis Elwell*), Lawrence Dobkin (*Leo Bartha*),
Lurene Tuttle (*Mrs. Bartha*), Queenie Smith (*Mildred Tam*), Autumn
Russell (*Linda*), Jay Adler (*Manny Davis*), Lewis Charles (*Al Evans*), The
Chico Hamilton Quintet.

Curtis is a Broadway flack, whose income depends on the exposure he gets
for his public-relations clients in the syndicated newspaper column of the
influential Lancaster, whose clout is boundless, sufficient to influence
presidents, to start wars. Lancaster's column of gossip, opinion, and planted
publicity items is read by nearly every commuter in the country. Curtis,
beholden to the powerful press pundit for his livelihood, panders to
Lancaster's every whim. Lancaster spends his evenings sipping coffee in a
posh hangout for the famous and wealthy, his regular table his own domain.
A bachelor–and, by implication, not interested in women in any romantic
way–Lancaster's demeanor is stern, his eyeglassed appearance forbidding,
his manner terse and phlegmatic. Asked to perform a favor by the ruthless
columnist, Curtis–against his own judgment–must reluctantly comply.
Lancaster–whose protective attitude about his sister, Harrison, seems more
than merely brotherly–wants Curtis to find a way to break up his sister's
budding romance with musician Milner, whose jazz ensemble performs in
the area. Unable to accomplish the task–for Milner is a cleancut young man
with no bad habits who might make an excellent husband for the girl–Curtis
is cut off from inclusion in Lancaster's columns. Desperate, he seeks a
solution. He inveigles cigarette girl Nichols into bedding down with another
slimy columnist in return for a suggestion that the young musician is a
pot-smoking Communist in the next day's newspaper. Fired from his gig as
a result, Milner appeals to Lancaster who, evincing sympathy, uses his
considerable influence to regain Milner's job for him, asking in return that
Milner stop seeing Harrison. Milner, realizing the extent to which he is
being manipulated, refuses. Lancaster, not wishing to alienate his sister,
backs off, but later extracts a promise from her that she will not see Milner
again. She breaks her promise, meeting Milner at a secluded river's-edge
spot, where he persuades her that she is being manipulated by her
possessive older brother. Harrison resumes her relationship with Milner on
the sly. When Lancaster discovers the couple's rebellious reunion, the
enraged columnist contacts Curtis, promising that if he can break up the
romance, he will have a three-month entry to Lancaster's column for his
clients. Unable to bring himself to resist the lucrative offer, Curtis plants
marijuana in Milner's topcoat pocket, and then calls sadistic policeman
Meyer, alerting the latter to the coat's contents. Meyer slowly pulls on the
shot-loaded gloves he wears when he brutalizes his collars and waits for

Milner to emerge from the nightclub. As Curtis celebrates, he receives a call
from Harrison, who seems suicidal. He races to the apartment she shares
with Lancaster, and affectionately tries to talk the half-dressed girl out of
self-destruction while sitting on her bed. Lancaster arrives and assumes the
worst. As Curtis tries to plead his case, Lancaster throws him out of the
apartment, then asks Harrison to explain. Knowing of Curtis' involvement
in Milner's plight, she refuses to exonerate him. Lancaster calls the brutal
Meyer and tells him that Curtis set up Milner. Meyer again pulls on his
sinister gloves as Curtis shouts defiance at him from an overpass. Harrison
packs a suitcase and walks out of her brother's apartment forever, out into
the morning sunlight. This remarkable, believable picture contains a
brilliant performance by Curtis, as the sleazy–yet sometimes compassionate-
-striver in thrall, through his own choosing, to a self-made slavemaster.
Curtis' casting had been something of a joke to this point in his career–a joke
epitomized by his well- known line "Yonda lies da castle of my fodda" in
THE BLACK SHIELD OF FALWORTH–but here he was in his milieu, and
he performed perfectly. Lancaster is wonderful as the perverse pundit, his
enormous ego demanding obedience, fueled as it is by his influence over the
millions who read his column. Nichols is superb as the girl who is used and
humiliated by Curtis because of her affection for him. Great things occur in
small compass in this picture of pallored night people, shot almost entirely
indoors, a chillingly realistic realization of the misuse of power possible for
the media. A stunning work by Lancaster's own production company, with
British director Mackendrick demonstrating amazing skill and comprehension of Odets' superb script, and cinematographer Howe handling the
lighting of Carrere's *verite* sets with his usual skill. Filmmakers learned
from this picture, which teaches the further lesson that movies can be
successful even when their denominator is not the lowest common one.

p, James Hill; d, Alexander Mackendrick; w, Clifford Odets, Ernest Lehman
(based on the short story "Tell Me About It Tomorrow" by Lehman); ph,
James Wong Howe; m, Elmer Bernstein; ed, Alan Crosland, Jr.; md,
Bernstein; art d, Edward Carrere; m/l, Chico Hamilton, Fred Katz.

Drama   (PR:C-O   MPAA:NR)

SWEET STEPMOTHER   (SEE: KIND STEPMOTHER, 1936, Hung.)

SWEET SUBSTITUTE** (1964, Can.) 81m Larry Kent/Joseph Brenner
bw (AKA: CARESSED)

Robert Howay (*Tom*), Angela Gann (*Elaine*), Lanny Beckman (*Bill*), Carol
Pastinsky (*Kathy*), Bob Silverman (*Al*), Bill Hartley, Mitzi Hurd, Virginia
Dunsaith.

An inexpensively made Canadian feature centering on a high-school boy,
Howay, whose obsession with sex keeps him from thinking of much else. A
sweet but plain girl, who helps him with his homework, gives in to his urges
resulting in her pregnancy. He then goes off to college to have an affair with
a more attractive girl. Though the theme has been reworked innumerable
times, a certain freshness is added by the performances of the young actors.
The competent camera work heightens the reality of the story. The film was
shot on location in Vancouver.

p,d,&w, Larry Kent; ph, Richard Bellamy; m, Jack Dale; ed, Sheila Reljac;
graphics, Sonja Arentzson.

Drama   (PR:C   MPAA:NR)

SWEET SUGAR zero (1972) 85m Dimension c (AKA: CHAINGANG
GIRLS)

Phyllis Elizabeth Davis (*Sugar*), Ella Edwards (*Simone*), Timothy Brown
(*Ric*), Pamela Collins (*Dolores*), Cliff Osmond (*Burgos*), Angus Duncan (*Dr.
John*), James Whitworth (*Mario*), Jackie Giroux, Darl Severns, Albert Cole,
James Houghton, Elvira Oropeza, Ramon Coll, Nicholas Baker, Juan
Antillon Baker, Frank Garcia, Diane Rojas, Antonio Casas Figueroa, Ana
Maria Rivera, Nicky Jacobstahl, Luis Jimenez, Laurencio Cordero.

A vile exploitationer about a group of white female slaves who live on a
sugar cane plantation in Costa Rica. Davis objects to the way she is treated
by Duncan, the sadistic plantation owner, and tries to organize an escape.
By time the girls actually do get away one man has been skewered with a
sword, another burned at the stake, and a third has a hand lopped off. It's
all supposed to be acceptable, however, since they're the bad guys and
deserve all they get. Then the filmmakers try to pass off their perverse
treatment of women by letting the girls emerge victorious at the finale. A
waste of time from the director of the equally pathetic WEREWOLVES ON
WHEELS (1971).

p, Charles S. Swartz; d, Michel Levesque; w, Don Spencer (based on a story
by R.Z. Samuel); ph, (Metrocolor); m, Don Gere.

Adventure   (PR:O   MPAA:R)

SWEET SURRENDER* (1935) 80m Broadway/UNIV bw

Frank Parker (*Danny O'Day*), Tamara (*Delphine Marshall/Maizie Mar-
shall*), Helen Lynd (*Dot Frost*), Russ Brown (*Jerry Burke*), Arthur Pierson
(*Nick Harrington*), Otis Sheridan (*James P. Hargrave*), Jules Epailly
(*Rozan*), William Adams (*Edgar F. Evans*), Alois Havrilla (*Himself*), Abe

Lyman (Himself), Jack Dempsey (Himself), Frank S. Moreno (Antonio Grebato), James Spottiswood (Horace Allen), Lena Powers (Mrs. Horace Allen), Lee Timmons (Larry Forbes), The Tune Twisters, Sara Mildred, The Strauss Dancers, The Nador Singers.

A haphazard script, which includes antiwar propaganda, gangsters, and mistaken identity, features dancer Tamara and her crooning boy friend, Parker, on a Europe-bound luxury liner. On board they encounter a woman posing as the dancer, also played by Tamara. The imposter has some nasty plans that require her to snoop around places she shouldn't be. The film is a big thud, with the only highlights coming from the glimpses inside Jack Dempsey's famous restaurant. Songs include: "Love Makes the World Go Round," "Take This Ring," "I'm So Happy I Could Cry," "The Day You Were Born," and "Twenty Four Hours a Day" (Edward Heyman, Dana Suesse, James Hanley, Arthur Swanstrom).

p, Bill Rowland, Monte Brice; d, Brice; w, John V.A. Weaver, Edward C. Lilley, Charles Beahan (based on a story by Herbert Fields); ph, William Miller; ed, Leo Zochling; addl. m/l, Mabel Wayne, Neville Fleeson.

Musical **(PR:A MPAA:NR)**

SWEET SUZY* (1973) 82m Signal 166 c (AKA: BLACKSNAKE)

Anouska Hempel (Lady Susan), David Warbeck (Walker), Percy Herbert (Overseer), Milton McCollin (Joshua), Thomas Baptiste (Isiah), Bernard Boston (Capt. Daladier), Vikki Richards (Slave Girl), Dave Prowse (Walker's Brother).

Hempel stars in this period sexploitationer from Russ Meyer as the tyrannical female leader of a Caribbean island in the early 1800s. She rules with a steel hand, bestowing violence on those who oppose her. McCollin, a brash young slave, decides to fight Hempel by organizing a revolt. Also woven into the story line is Warbeck's search for his brother, Prowse, who was married to the maniacal ruler. A second-rate Meyer film which translates into a first-rate time waster.

p&d, Russ Meyer; w, Meyer, Len Neubauer (based on a story by Meyer, A. James Ryan); ph, Arthur Ornitz (Movielab Color); m, Bill Loose, Al Teeter; ed, Fred Baratta; art d, Rick Heatherly.

Adventure **(PR:O MPAA:R)**

SWEET TRASH*½ (1970) 79m Clover c

Patrick Shea, William Conners, Mary McGee.

A New York dockworker is unknowingly made part of the loan shark business through his association with prostitutes and shady businessmen. The man is led to drink when he is unable to accept the life he has made for himself.

p, Daniel Cady, John Hayes; d&w, Hayes; ph, Paul Hipp.

Drama/Crime **(PR:O MPAA:NR)**

SWEET VIOLENCE (SEE: SWEET ECSTASY, 1962, Fr.)

SWEET WILLIAM**½ (1980, Brit.) 92m Kendon/World Northal c

Sam Waterson (William), Jenny Agutter (Ann), Anna Massey (Edna), Geraldine James (Pamela), Daphne Oxenford (Mrs. Walton), Rachel Bell (Mrs. Kershaw), David Wood (Vicar), Tim Pigott-Smith (Gerald), Emma Bakhle (Daisy), Sara Clee (Actress), Arthur Lowe (Capt. Walton), Peter Dean (Roddy), Victoria Fairbrother (Sheila), Ivor Roberts (Uncle Walter), Joan Cooper (Aunt Bee).

Waterson plays a wild Scotsman who has had two marriages and several affairs and encounters without the slightest twinge of guilt. Deep down he's really a romantic, something that is discovered by Agutter, one of the women he sees. He takes up with her when her regular beau is away on a trip to the U.S. Though thematically concerned with sex, no explicit scenes are ever shown, an amazing feature in this day when screen sex runs rampant. Waterson's depiction of the character is an honest one, making him totally believable in the situation.

p, Jeremy Watt; d, Claude Whatham; w, Beryl Bainbridge (based on the novel by Bainbridge); ph, Les Young; ed, Peter Coulson; prod d, Eileen Diss.

Drama **Cas.** **(PR:O MPAA:R)**

SWEETHEART OF SIGMA CHI** (1933) 77m MON bw (GB: GIRL OF MY DREAMS)

Mary Carlisle (Vivian), Buster Crabbe (Bob North), Charles Starrett (Morley), Florence Lake (Dizzy), Eddie Tamblyn (Coxswain), Sally Starr (Madge), Mary Blackford (Bunny), Tom Dugan (Trainer), Burr McIntosh (Professor), Major Goodsell (Coach), Grady Sutton (Pledge), Purnell Pratt (Doctor), Franklin Parker (House Prexy), Ted Fio-Rito and His Orchestra, Leif Erickson, Betty Grable, Bill Carey, Muzzy Marcelino, The Three Midshipmen, The Blue Keys (Themselves).

A college movie that concentrates on the romances between the coeds and the fraternity guys. Carlisle plays the hard-to-get, though very flirtatious,

girl who succumbs to the embraces of Crabbe, fraternity rowing star. Starrett also makes a pretty good bid for Carlisle's affections. Pleasant and unpretentious, with a few witty bits of humor added for flavor. Songs include: "Fraternity Walk," "It's Spring Again" (George Waggner, Ed Ward), "Five Minutes More" (Jule Styne, Sammy Cahn), "Sweetheart of Sigma Chi" (Byron D. Stokes, F. Dudleigh Vernor).

d, Edward L. Marin; w, Luther Reed, Albert E. DeMond, George Waggner (based on a story by Waggner); ph, Gilbert Warrenton; ed, J. Edwin Robbins.

Musical/Drama **(PR:A MPAA:NR)**

SWEETHEART OF SIGMA CHI** (1946) 76m MON bw

Phil Regan (Lucky Ryan), Elyse Knox (Betty Allen), Phil Brito (Phil Howard), Ross Hunter (Ted Sloan), Tom Harmon (Coach), Paul Guilfoyle (Frankie), Anne Gillis (Sue), Edward Brophy (Arty), Fred Colby (Bill Ryan), Alan Hale, Jr (Mike Mitchell), David Holt (Tommy Carr), Marjorie Hoerner (Margie), William Beaudine, Jr (Charlie), Emmett Vogan, Jr (Emmett), Ruth Allen (Ruth), Robert Arthur (Harry Townsend), Fred Datig, Jr (Fred), Slim Gaillard Trio, Frankie Carle Orchestra.

A remake of the 1933 film which starred Buster Crabbe and Mary Carlisle, only given a lot more attention in the tunes department, with situations and music more in accordance with the times. Hunter plays the star rowing champ, recently returned to school after doing a stint overseas, and the aim of Knox's affections, which he has been avoiding for some unknown reason. Also included is a scheme by local hoods to fix a boat race–there being a lot of big money being placed on the side. Songs include: "Sweetheart of Sigma Chi" (F. Dudleigh Vernon, Byron D. Stokes), "Penthouse Serenade" (Will Jason, Val Burton, sung by Phil Regan), "It's Not I'm Such a Wolf, It's Just You're Such a Lamb" (Merle Maddern, Lanier Darwin, sung by Phil Brito), "And Then It's Heaven" (Edward Seiler, Sol Marcus, Al Kaufman; sung by Brito), "Cement Mixer" (Slim Gaillard, Lee Ricks, sung by Gaillard), "Yeproc-Heresi" (Gaillard, sung by Gaillard), "Bach Meets Carle" (a Bach pastiche by Frankie Carle), "Five Minutes More" (Jule Styne, Sammy Cahn; sung by Brito).

p, Jeffrey Bernerd; d, Jack Bernhard; w, Michel Jacoby (based on the story by George Waggner); ph, L.W. O'Connell; ed, William Austin; md, Edward J. Kay.

Musical **(PR:A MPAA:NR)**

SWEETHEART OF THE CAMPUS* (1941) 67m COL bw (GB: BROADWAY AHEAD)

Ruby Keeler (Betty Blake), Ozzie Nelson (Ozzie Norton), Harriet Hilliard (Harriet Hale), Gordon Oliver (Terry Jones), Don Beddoe (Sheriff Denby), Charles Judels (Victor Demond), Kathleen Howard (Mrs. Minnie Sparr), Byron Foulger (Dr. Bailey), George Lessey (Dr. Hale), Frank Gaby (Dr. Grimsby), Leo Watson (Tom Tom), The Four Spirits of Rhythm.

Keeler's final starring role was a far cry from some of the successful ventures she shared in Busby Berkeley musicals. Here she's teamed with the Nelsons (of TV and radio fame) as the singer in Ozzie's band. The setting is a college campus which is suffering from monetary woes, but somehow Ozzie's band manages to attract enough attention to increase the enrollment and keep the school from having to shut down. Crotchety old Howard would like nothing better than to see the school close. The same sentiments should be shared by the audience. Songs include: "When the Glee Club Swings the Alma Mater" (Charles Newman, Walter G. Samuels), "Where" (Jacques Krakeur), "Tom, Tom the Elevator Boy" (Samuels), "Tap Happy," "Zig Me Baby with a Gentle Zag," and "Here We Go Again" (Eddie Cherkose, Jacques Press).

p, Jack Fier; d, Edward Dmytryk; w, Robert D. Andrews, Edmund Hartmann (based on the story by Andrews); ph, Franz F. Planer; m, M.W. Stoloff; ed, William Lyon; art d, Lionel Banks; ch, Louis Da Pron.

Musical **(PR:A MPAA:NR)**

SWEETHEART OF THE FLEET** (1942) 65m COL bw

Joan Davis (Phoebe Weyms), Jinx Falkenburg (Jerry Gilbert), Joan Woodbury (Kitty Leslie), Blanche Stewart (Brenda), Elvia Allman (Cobina), William Wright (Lt. Philip Blaine), Robert Stevens (Ens. George "Tip" Landers), Tim Ryan (Gordon Crouse), George McKay (Hambone Skelly), Walter Sande (Daffy Bill), Charles Trowbridge (Comdr. Hawes), Tom Seidel (Bugsy), Dick Elliott (Chumley), Irving Bacon (Standish), Lloyd Bridges (Sailor), Stanley Brown (Call Boy), Boyd Davis (Mayor), John Tyrell (Bell Boy), Gary Breckner (Radio Announcer).

Davis plays an agent for an ad agency who comes up with a scheme to promote a "Blind Date" service. This includes having two popular singers appearing in a USO show for the Navy. No one knows what these two girls look like and for good reason because they are really ugly. So Davis comes up with the plan to have two attractive models lip syncing while the singers sing from behind stage. Her plan almost backfires when the singers meet a couple of sailors and decide to elope with them. Mild entertainment that depends heavily upon the comic talents of Davis, who comes through for the most part. Songs include: "I Surrender Dear" (Harry Barris, Gordon

Clifford), "We Did It Before and We Can Do It Again," "All Over the Place" (Charles Tobias, Cliff Friend), "When Johnny Comes Marching Home."

p, Jack Fier; d, Charles Barton; w, Albert Duffy, Maurice Tombragel, Ned Dandy (based on the story by Duffy); ph, Philip Tannura; ed, Richard Fantl; md, M.W. Stoloff.

Musical/Comedy   **(PR:A   MPAA:NR)**

SWEETHEART OF THE NAVY*½   (1937) 63m GN bw

Eric Linden (Harris), Cecilia Parker (Joan), Roger Imhof (Commander), Bernadene Hayes (Maggie), Jason Robards, Sr (Bumper), Cully Richards (Shorty), Etta McDaniel (Cook), Don Barclay (Pudge), Art Miles, Edward Waller, John T. Murray, Henry Roquemore, Benny Burt, Fred Murray, Vance Carroll, Reed Howes.

Dive singer Parker gets herself out of a jam through the efforts of docked sailors who come to her rescue. Prominent among them are Linden as the level-headed chap who almost tosses his Navy career aside to make sure Parker's name is cleared. Not much of anything exciting happens though Parker makes an interesting cafe singer.

p, Bennie F. Zeidman; d, Duncan Mansfield; w, Carroll Graham (based on the story by Garrett Graham, Jay Strauss); ph, Edward Snyder; ed, Edward Schroeder; art d, Paul Palmentola; ch, Max Scheck; m/l, "Sweetheart of the Navy," "Want You to Want Me," Jack Stern, Harry Tobias (sung by Cecilia Parker).

Drama   **(PR:A   MPAA:NR)**

SWEETHEARTS***½   (1938) 120m MGM c

Jeanette MacDonald (Gwen Marlowe), Nelson Eddy (Ernest Lane), Frank Morgan (Felix Lehman), Ray Bolger (Hans the Dancer), Florence Rice (Kay Jordan), Mischa Auer (Leo Kronk), Fay Holden (Hannah the Dresser), Terry Kilburn (Gwen's Brother, Junior), Betty Jaynes (Una Wilson), Douglas McPhail (Harvey Horton), Reginald Gardiner (Norman Trumpett), Herman Bing (Oscar Engel), Allyn Joslyn (Dink Rogers), Raymond Walburn (Orlando Lane), Lucile Watson (Mrs. Marlowe), George Barbier (Benjamin Silver), Kathleen Lockhart (Aunt Amelia Lane), Gene Lockhart (Augustus Marlowe), Berton Churchill (Sheridan Lane), Olin Howland (Appleby the Box Office Man), Gerald Hamer (Harry), Marvin Jones (Boy in Lobby), Dorothy Gray (His Girl Friend), Emory Parnell (Fire Inspector), Maude Turner Gordon (Dowager), Jac George (Violinist), Roger Converse (Usher), Reed Kilpatrick (Radio Announcer), Wilson Benge (2nd Valet to Ernest), George Ernest (1st Call Boy), Billy McCullough (2nd Call Boy), Lee Phelps (Doorman at St. Regis), Pat Gleason, Ralph Malone, David Kerman, Jack Gardner (Reporters), Ralph W. Berry, Rollin B. Berry, Chester L. Berolund, Leo Berolund (Lawyer Twins), Mira McKinney, Grace Hayle (Telephone Operators), Hal K. Dawson (Morty, Stage Manager), Forrester Harvey (Tailor's Assistant), Gayne Whitman (Commentator), Margaret Irving (Madame), Irving Bacon (Assistant Director), Barbara Pepper, Marjorie "Babe" Kane (Telephone Operators), Jimmy Conlin (Property Man), Dick Rich (1st Stage Hand), Ralph Sanford (2nd Stage Hand), James Flavin (Theater Doorman), Richard Tucker, Edwin Stanley, Edward Earle, Brent Sargent (Men in Lobby), Betty Ross Clarke, Dorothy Christy, Suzanne Kaaren, Lulu May Bohrman (Women in Lobby), Hal Cooke, Jenifer Gray (Mr. Silver's Secretaries), Fred Santley (Music Vendor), Don Barclay (Taxi Driver from Bridgeport), Arthur "Pop" Byron (Policeman), James Farley (Carriage Starter), Bruce Mitchell (Stage Hand), George Cooper, Frank Mills (Electricians), Mary Howard, Joan Barclay, Sharon Lewis, Vivian Reid, Lucille Brown, Valerie Day, Ethelreda Leopold (Chorus Girls), Lester Dorr (Dance Director), Anne Wigton (Saleswoman), Dalies Frantz (Pianist "Badinage"), Paul Marquardt (Conductor of Marine Band), Paul Kerby (Orchestra Conductor), Joe A. Devlin (New York Taxi Driver), Ralph Brooks, Brooks Benedict (Extras in Radio Audience), Toby Wing (Telephone Operator), Cyril Ring (Waiter).

For their very first three-color Technicolor movie, MGM chose the old chestnut "Sweethearts" out of the 1913 era. Knowing that modern audiences wouldn't sit still for an ancient story about the orphan who was raised by a laundry operator only to find out that she was a crown princess and therefore eligible to marry a prince, they took that tale and made it the show-within-the-movie, in order to utilize much of Victor Herbert's score. The original "Sweethearts" opened in 1913 for a brief run of 136 performances, then went out on tour where it still is playing somewhere even as you read this. The studio hired Dorothy Parker and her husband, Alan Campbell, and they wrote an entirely new backstage story with many sharp lines of dialog and a story that made logical sense, something operettas seldom did. MacDonald and Eddy are happily married stars of the Broadway stage. They have been husband and wife for the same amount of time their latest hit has been playing, six years. While they have been presenting Herbert's "Sweethearts," the Broadway lights have been twinkling with the likes of Helen Hayes in "Victoria Regina," and Lunt And Fontanne in "Idiot's Delight." MacDonald and Eddy are truly sweethearts on and off stage and are as beloved as any couple can be. They are preparing to spend their sixth wedding and show anniversary in the usual fashion, with a performance, when they both suddenly come to the conclusion that they would like to take a rest. Although their show is doing business, they are constantly called upon to keep ballyhooing it in order to keep the stiles

turning. True to the stage, they have been rejecting movie offers for quite a while but the thought of sunshine in California and a more civilized schedule of less than eight arduous shows each week is beginning to sound inviting. Morgan is the show's producer and invites them to come to a "small party for friends" as part of the anniversary celebration. At first, they are reluctant, but Morgan plays the role of the crushed and disappointed party giver to the hilt and they finally agree. Meanwhile, Gardiner is the Hollywood agent who comes to the theater annually to try to sign them to a movie contract and, despite their negative stances, he is undaunted. The "little party" turns out to be a huge affair, with a full orchestra and a coast-to-coast radio hookup so MacDonald and Eddy have to sing for the hundreds assembled. Later, MacDonald and Eddy go to their capacious townhouse where their permanent guests include their uncles and aunts plus her bratty brother, Kilburn. They'd like to go to sleep but the relatives insist they sit up and talk. Now their secretary, Rice, walks in and wonders how they can be awake at this early morning hour because they have such a breakneck schedule later that day. It turns out they've been committed for several appointments, including interviews and a recording session. Walburn comes in. He's yet another of the relatives and traveling with a band of "Pirates Of Penzance" players who have run out of money and must now put up at the house. Eddy writes a check to send Walburn and his troupe back on the road while Rice pays the armada of taxi drivers who have carted the actors in from their unsuccessful stop in Bridgeport. Disgusted with all the activity around them, MacDonald and Eddy realize they must put a stop to this and get as far away as they can from the freeloading and demanding relatives. Where can that be? Hollywood. Morgan, playwrite Auer, composer Bing, and the others who earn their livings from the voices of Eddy and MacDonald are thrown into a panic. Morgan has an idea that just might work. Auer's new play is based on the premise that a woman who is deeply in love with a man harbors a jealousy that is constantly smoldering. If the situation is played right, she can be convinced that she has a rival for her man's affections. MacDonald is led to believe that Auer's new play is based on a real-life affair going on between Eddy and their secretary, Rice. It's all untrue, of course, but Morgan and the others will do anything to keep the show going. Eddy and MacDonald have a rip-roaring fight (witnessed in rehearsal by a columnist who thought it was real. He duly reported that the two stars hated each other to a breathless public), part, and each goes out on tour with their own show and different co-stars. Later, in two locations, both are reading the reviews of Auer's new play and the notice is a slam which says that it's hard to believe anyone could fall for such a sham of a story (which is the exact thing that MacDonald fell for!). Both Eddy and MacDonald have been reading the same trade paper in separate cities. Both reach for the phone at the same time to attempt to call the other with the information that they've been duped and, of course, both phones are busy because they're dialing each other. Eddy and MacDonald are reunited, walk into Morgan's office with their movie contracts and tell him that they are leaving. He begins to sob, pleads with them to stay, then Eddy and MacDonald break out in smiles. They'll stay and they'll sign for another six years. What could be more fun than starring in a Broadway show with the mate you love? The Parker-Campbell script was witty, wise, and had many satirical moments without ever stepping into farce. Almost all of the songs were by Victor Herbert, with new lyrics written by Chet Forrest and Bob Wright, who did the same thing with Borodin's music for KISMET. Tunes include: "Wooden Shoes" (performed by Ray Bolger, in his 3rd role after a successful stage career), a snip of "Angelus" (with original lyrics by Robert Smith), "Every Lover Must Meet His Fate" (Eddy, MacDonald, male chorus), "Happy Day" (chorus), "Sweethearts" (Eddy, MacDonald), "Pretty as a Picture" (MacDonald, Eddy, female chorus), "Game of Love" (Eddy, MacDonald), "Badinage" (MacDonald), "On Parade" (Eddy, male chorus), "In the Convent" (MacDonald, Betty Jaynes). Other songs were added including: "Auld Lang Syne" (MacDonald, Eddy, and chorus), "The Message of the Violet" from "The Prince of Pilsen" (written by Gustav Luders, Frank Pixley, performed by MacDonald, Eddy, Gene Lockhart), "Keep It Dark" also from "The Prince of Pilsen" (Luders, Pixley, performed by Eddy, MacDonald, Lockhart, Berton Churchill, Lucile Watson), "Little Gray Home in the West" (by Hermann Lohr, D. Eardley-Wilmot, performed by Eddy, MacDonald), "Give My Regards to Broadway" (George M. Cohan, instrumental), "Sidewalks of New York" (Charles Lawlor, James Blake), "St. Louis Blues" (W.C. Handy, instrumental), "Missouri Waltz" (Fredrick Knight Logan, James Royce Shannon, instrumental), "Home, Sweet Home" (by Henry Bishop, sung by cast). Also heard as background music were "Tea for Two" by Irving Caesar and Vincent Youmans and "Night and Day" by Cole Porter. With all that music, it's amazing they had any time at all for a plot, but they did. The young woman who played MacDonald's understudy in "Sweethearts" was Betty Jaynes. She married the young man who played Eddy's understudy, Doug McPhail. He had a good career going for him with appearances in BABES IN ARMS and BROADWAY MELODY OF 1940 but it was short-lived and he took to drink, then committed suicide in 1944 at the age of 34. A large budget, plenty of time lavished for production numbers, and a sense of great fun all combine to make this a most enjoyable experience. The movie was nominated for Best Score (Stothart) and Best Sound Recording (Doug Shearer, Norma's brother) and won an Oscar for Marsh and Davey's color cinematography, which was a new field that was being covered for the first time by the Academy voters.

p, Hunt Stromberg; d, W. S. Van Dyke II; w, Dorothy Parker, Alan Campbell (based on the operetta by Harry B. Smith, Fred DeGresac, Robert B. Smith, Victor Herbert); ph, Oliver Marsh, Allen Davey (Technicolor); m, Victor

Herbert, adapted by Herbert Stothart; ed, Robert J. Kern; art d, Cedric Gibbons; set d, Edwin B. Willis; cos, Adrian; spec eff, Slavko Vorkapich; ch, Albertina Rasch.

Musical/Comedy (PR:A MPAA:NR)

SWEETHEARTS AND WIVES*½ (1930) 77m FN bw

Billie Dove (*Femme de Chambre*), Sidney Blackmer (*Anthony Peel*), Clive Brook (*Reginald De Brett*), Leila Hyams (*Angela Worthington*), Fletcher Norton (*Maitre d'Hotel*), John Loder (*Sam Worthington*), Crauford Kent (*Sir John Deptford*), Albert Gran (*Police Inspector*), Alphonse Martell (*Gendarme*), Rolfe Sedan (*Waiter*).

After a murder is committed in a shady French inn a number of the guests go searching about for a necklace that was in the possession of the murdered woman. This includes Hyams as a witchy woman who switches places with maid Dove in order to have a better chance of locating the necklace. This was supposed to be a comedy, but the little humor there is comes off as very forced.

d, Clarence Badger; w, Forest Halsey (based on the play "Other Men's Wives" by Walter Hackett); ph, John F. Seitz; ed, Jack Rollins.

Comedy (PR:A MPAA:NR)

SWEETHEARTS OF THE U.S.A.* (1944) 63m MON bw (GB: SWEETHEARTS ON PARADE)

Una Merkel (*Patsy*), Parkyakardus "Harry" Einstein (*Parky*), Donald Novis (*Don Clark*), Lillian Cornell (*Helen Grant*), Judith Gibson (*Loretta*), Joel Friend (*Bill Craige*), Cobina Wright, Sr (*Mrs. Carver*), Marion Martin (*Josephine*), Vince Barnett (*Clipper*), Ralph Sanford (*Gilhooley*), Joseph Kirk (*Napoleon*), Georgann Smith, Joe Devlin, Edmund Cobb, Dorothy Bradshaw, Charles Williams, Jan Garber Orchestra, Phil Ohman Orchestra.

Merkel plays a worker in a defense factory who is knocked out cold, and it is her dream while in this condition that becomes the plot for this movie. As it turns out, it's not really a dream worth sharing. Parkyakarkus plays a dick on the trail of bank robbers. Very silly and very bad. Songs include: "Sweethearts of the USA," "All the Latins Know is Si Si," "You Can't Brush Off a Russian," "We're the Ones," "Hold On to Your Hat," and "That Reminds Me" (Charles Newman, Lew Pollack).

p, Lester Cutler; d, Lew Collins; w, Arthur St. Claire, Sherman Lowe, Mary Sheldon (based on the story by Sheldon); ph, Ira Morgan; ed, George M. Merrick; md, David Chudnow.

Comedy/Musical (PR:A MPAA:NR)

SWEETHEARTS ON PARADE*½ (1930) 65m Christie/COL bw

Alice White (*Helen*), Lloyd Hughes (*Bill*), Marie Prevost (*Nita*), Kenneth Thomson (*Harrison Hendricks*), Ray Cooke (*Hank*), Wilbur Mack (*Parker*), Ernest Wood (*Denham*), Max Asher (*Store Manager*).

Hughes plays a marine who falls in love with an innocent young White while on leave in New York City. Away on a cruise, he comes back to find that a shiftless millionaire has taken to his girl–so much so that he's asked her to marry him. Thinking practically instead of passionately, White accepts the millionaire's offer, only to discover that he's already wed to another. But Hughes and pals are quick to see that justice is done. Little variation on a tired theme, even by 1930s standards. Songs include: "Sweethearts on Parade" (Carmen Lombardo, Charles Newman), "Dream of Me" (Irving Bibo, Henry Cohen), "Yearning Just for You" (Joe Burke, Benny Davis), "Misstep" (Bibo).

p, Al Christie; d, Marshall Neilan; w, Colin Clements (based on a story by Al Cohn, James A. Starr); ph, Gus Peterson; ed, Sidney Walsh.

Drama/Musical (PR:A MPAA:NR)

SWEETHEARTS ON PARADE, 1944 (SEE: SWEETHEART OF THE U.S.A., 1944)

SWEETHEARTS ON PARADE*½ (1953) 90m REP c

Ray Middleton (*Cam Ellerby*), Lucille Norman (*Kathleen Townsend*), Eileen Christy (*Sylvia*), Bill Shirley (*Bill Gamble*), Estelita (*Lolita Lamont*), Clinton Sundberg (*Dr. Harold Wayne*), Harry Carey, Jr (*Jim Riley*), Irving Bacon (*Sheriff Doolittle*), Leon Tyler (*Tommy Wayne*), Marjorie Wood (*Wardrobe Woman*), Mara Corday (*Belle*), Ann McCrea (*Flo*), Tex Terry (*Zebe*), Emory Parnell (*Mayor*).

Middleton and Shirley are part of a traveling medicine show that finds itself in the town of Middleton's former sweetheart, Norman, mother to budding young beauty Christy. The girl soon becomes interested in the spectacle of the medicine show, and especially in her father's partner, Shirley. An overabundance of songs, awkwardly inserted into the plot, hampers the development of much of a plot–or anything else for that matter. Songs include: "You Naughty, Naughty Man" (I. Kennick, G. Bicknell), "Young Love" (Von Suppe), "Romance" (Anton Rubenstein), "Ah, So Pure" (Flotow, Kathleen Mavourneen), "If" (F. Crouch), "Blue Juniata" (M.D. Sullivan),

"Mating Time" (Strauss), "In the Evening by the Moonlight" (James Bland), "Flow Gently Sweet Afton" (Spillman), "Molly Darling" (Will S. Hayes), "Regnava Nil Silencio" (Donizetti), "Sweet Genevieve" (George Cooper, Henry Tucker), "Nelly Bly" (Stephen Foster), "Extension for Romance" (Robert Armbruster), "Then You'll Remember Me" (M.W. Balfe), "Ah Non Guin Ge" (V. Bellini), "I Wish I Was Single Again" "Ah, Rovin'," "Wanderin'," "Cindy," and "Love is a Pain."

d, Allan Dwan; w, Houston Branch (based on his story); ph, Reggie Lanning (Trucolor); ed, Fred Allen; md, Robert Armbruster; art d, James Sullivan; ch, Nick Castle.

Musical (PR:A MPAA:NR)

SWEETIE** (1929) 95m PAR bw

Nancy Carroll (*Barbara Pell*), Helen Kane (*Helen Fry*), Stanley Smith (*Biff Bentley*), Jack Oakie (*Tap-Tap Thompson*), William Austin (*Prof. Percy "Pussy" Willow*), Stuart Erwin (*Axel Bronstrup*), Wallace MacDonald (*Bill Barrington*), Charles Sellon (*Dr. Oglethorpe*), Aileen Manning (*Miss Twill*).

Though drifting far from a realistic rendition of college life, SWEETIE is an enjoyable little picture that is light on plot line but heavy in the charm category. This includes two song numbers which could easily be considered musical classics. The first of these has Kane spouting off "He's So Unusual" to her oaf of a boy friend who's more interested in football than in her. Then Jack Oakie does an imitation of Al Jolson with black-face and bent knee to a song entitled "Alma Mammy." Yarn centers around Carroll as a Broadway star *and* the new owner of a North Carolina college which has a small girls' school just a few miles away. Carroll's sweetheart, Smith, is a student at the college, and subsequent star of the football team. Trouble arises when Carroll is more concerned with eloping than with her college, while Smith refuses to let his teammates down in the upcoming big game against their rival school. The owner then goes about finding ways to keep her beau off the playing field. But she doesn't succeed. Songs include: "My Sweeter Than Sweet," "The Prep Step," "I Think You'll Like It," "Alma Mammy" (sung by Jack Oakie), "Bear Down Pelham" (Richard A. Whiting, George Marion, Jr.), "He's So Unusual" (Al Lewis, Abner Silver, Al Sherman), "Sweetie" (sung by Helen Kane).

d, Frank Tuttle; w, George Marion, Jr., Lloyd Corrigan; ph, Alfred Gilks; m, Richard Whiting; ed, Verna Willis; ch, Earl Lindsay; m/l, Whiting, George Marion, Jr.

Musical (PR:A MPAA:NR)

SWELL GUY** (1946) 87m UNIV bw

Sonny Tufts (*Jim Duncan*), Ann Blyth (*Marian Tyler*), Ruth Warrick (*Ann Duncan*), William Gargan (*Martin Duncan*), John Litel (*Arthur Tyler*), Thomas Gomez (*Dave Vinson, Correspondent*), Millard Mitchell (*Steve*), Mary Nash (*Sarah Duncan*), Howard Freeman (*Botsworth*), Donald Devlin (*Tony Duncan*), John Craven (*Mike O'Conner*), Pat McVey (*Ray Link*), Vince Barnett (*Sam Burns*), Charles Lane (*Ben Tilwell*), Garry Owen (*Ernie*), Frank Ferguson (*Eddie*), David Clarke (*Frank*), Eugene Persson (*Jackie*), George Beban, Jr (*George*).

Tufts stars as an unscrupulous war correspondent who comes back to the town where his brother and sister-in-law live, and wreaks havoc upon the entire population, while posing as a hero. He takes the citizens' money in crap games, makes advances toward his sister-in-law, and a number of other things which he is allowed to get away with because of his status as war hero. When Tufts attempts to leave the town after stealing funds from a veterans' drive, he meets his death performing the first heroic deed of his life–saving his nephew. Tufts isn't always convincing in his role, but the remainder of the cast all give competent performances. Major problems are due to the director's inability to gain firm control of the material.

p, Mark Hellinger; d, Frank Tuttle; w, Richard Brooks (based on the play "The Hero" by Gilbert Emery); ph, Tony Gaudio, David S. Horsley; m, Frank Skinner; ed, Edward Curtiss; art d, John B. Goodman.

Drama (PR:A MPAA:NR)

SWELLHEAD, THE** (1930) 70m TIF bw

James Gleason (*Johnny Trump, Sportswriter*), Johnny Walker (*Bill "Cyclone" Hickey*), Marion Shilling (*Mamie Judd*), Natalie Kingston (*Barbara Larkin*), Paul Hurst (*Mugsy*), Freeman Wood (*Clive Warren*), Lillian Elliott (*Mrs. Callahan*).

A simple story about a factory girl, Shilling, who falls in love with an overconfident, underimpressive prizefighter, Walker. Shilling engages sportswriter Gleason to manage the boxer. Walker's attitude causes Gleason to walk out and the boxer's career takes a nosedive. Gleason is finally persuaded to return as Walker's manager and Walker begins to win again, paving the way for the romantic clinch between the boxer and his girl.

d, James Flood; w, Richard Cahoon, Adele Buffington, James Gleason (based on the story "Cyclone Hickey" by A.P. Younger); ph, Jackson Rose, Art Reeves; ed, Cahoon.

Sports Drama (PR:A MPAA:NR)

SWELL-HEAD*   (1935) 62m COL bw

Wallace Ford (Terry McCall), Dickie Moore (Billy Malone), Barbara Kent (Mary Malone), J. Farrell MacDonald (Umpire), Marion Byron (Bessie), Sammy Cohen (Casey Cohen), Frank Moran (The Rube), Mike Donlin (Brick Baldwin).

Overly talky, stupid story about an egomaniacal baseball player who comes down to earth after being hit by a fast ball in the head. Apparently the pitch knocked some sense into him–and the causes of his problems out of the way. But this thing just doesn't make much sense.

p, Bryan Foy; d, Ben Stoloff; w, William Jacobs (based on a story by Gerald Beaumont); ph, Joseph A. Valentine; ed, Arthur Hilton.

Comedy   (PR:A MPAA:NR)

SWEPT AWAY...BY AN UNUSUAL DESTINY IN THE BLUE SEA OF AUGUST**½   (1975, Ital.) 116m Medusa/Cinema 5 c (AKA: SWEPT AWAY)

Giancarlo Gianninni (Gennarino), Mariangela Melato (Raffaella).

Aboard a chartered yacht, a group of wealthy north Italians discuss a variety of topics as they bask in the sun. Melato, a snob, takes particular delight in taunting Gianninni, a Sicilian deckhand. She laughs at his Communist ideas and the smelly shirt he wears. This is the last man in the world she could ever possibly want to be shipwrecked with on a deserted isle and yet... SWEPT AWAY is a wild romp, and a film that certainly lives up to its elongated title. The two are indeed grabbed up by destiny when they are shipwrecked. None of Melato's high-class manners can help Melato and she grows dependent on the vulgar sailor. He in turn takes delight in putting this woman in her place. As she grows to rely more on the man for basic survival the inevitable happens and the two make love. Eventually they are rescued but not without repercussions. Despite himself, Gianninni has fallen in love with this beautiful capitalist. And though Melato has some shared feelings, she knows quite well where her place is. This was the fourth film of director Wertmuller's to be released in this country, and in it she continues to explore some of her favorite themes in a much broader fashion. Politics and the battle between the sexes are ever present throughout the story, but laced with a delightfully satiric bite that draws out laughter amidst the simply presented ideas. The two leads are perfectly matched, playing well off of and with one another. It is their chemistry that makes the unbelievable nature of the story totally natural and honest. In lesser hands the story never would have worked.

p, Romano Cardarelli; d&w, Lina Wertmuller; ph, Giulio Battiferri, Giuseppe Fornari, Stefano Ricciotti; m, Piero Piccioni; set d&cos, Enrico Job.

Drama/Comedy   **Cas.**   (PR:O MPAA:R)

SWIFT VENGEANCE   (SEE: ROOKIE COP, THE, 1939)

SWIFTY*½   (1936) 59m Diversion bw

Hoot Gibson (Swifty), June Gale (Helen), George F. Hayes (Dan Hughes), Ralph Lewis (Alec McNeil), Bob Kortman (Clam Givens), William Gould (Cheevers), Wally Wales (Price McNeil), Lafe McKee (Sandy), Art Mix (Squid), Duke Lee, Starlight the Horse.

Good-hearted cowpoke Gibson is accused in the murder of a local rancher, but he escapes hanging in time to run down the real culprit as well as win the heart of the girl whose father he was supposed to have killed. Pretty fair as far as these things go.

p, Walter Futter; d, Alan James; w, Bennett Cohen, Walton Farrar, Roger Allman (based on the story by Stephen Payne); ph, Art Reed; ed, Carl Himm.

Western   **Cas.**   (PR:A MPAA:NR)

SWIMMER, THE**½   (1968) 94m Horizon-Dover/COL c

Burt Lancaster (Ned Merrill), Janet Landgard (Julie Hooper), Janice Rule (Shirley Abbott), Tony Bickley (Donald Westerhazy), Marge Champion (Peggy Forsburgh), Nancy Cushman (Mrs. Halloran), Bill Fiore (Howie Hunsacker), John Garfield, Jr (Ticket Seller), Kim Hunter (Betty Graham), Rose Gregorio (Sylvia Finney), Charles Drake (Howard Graham), Bernie Hamilton (Chauffeur), House Jameson (Mr. Halloran), Jimmy Joyce (Jack Finney), Michael Kearney (Kevin Gilmartin), Richard McMurray (Stu Forsburgh), Jan Miner (Lillian Hunsacker), Diana Muldaur (Cynthia), Keri Oleson (Vernon), Joan Rivers (Joan), Cornelia Otis Skinner (Mrs. Hammar), Dolph Sweet (Henry Biswanger), Louise Troy (Grace Biswanger), Diana Van Der Vlis (Helen Westerhazy), Alva Celauro (Muffie), Lisa Daniels (Matron at the Biswangers' Pool), John Gerstad (Guest at the Bunkers' Pool), Marilyn Langner (Enid Bunker), Ray Mason (Bunkers' Party Guest).

A weird movie that is compelling, boring, anti-materialistic, and enigmatic. Based on a short story by John Cheever that appeared in The New Yorker, it's been expanded into an episodic screenplay that is buoyed by the music of a 22-year-old making his scoring debut, Marvin Hamlisch. It's a summer day in Connecticut as Lancaster, in swim trunks, finds himself several miles from the home in which he lives. Rather than walk to his house, the ad-man decides to swim across the suburb by diving into the pools of the people

whom he knows. Each pool is owned by someone whose life he has touched, and by the time the picture is over, the audience knows everything about Lancaster through these homes he's visited. His life is a mess and it's squeezed out in little strips as he stops at the homes of many. First, it's the comfortable house of Hunter and Drake. He tells Hunter that he used to have a crush on her and she takes that news with a stoical attitude, offering him nothing in return. At Skinner's house, she is so angry at him for something he once did that she won't let him onto her property. At the next pool, he meets Landgard (making her film debut), who once was a baby-sitter for his daughters. Landgard is a seductive type who says that she loved him when she was a teenager. Lancaster asks her to come back to his house to baby-sit and the grown-up girl looks at him as though he's nuts. He continues his journey to the homes of Van Der Vlis and Bickley, Champion and McMurray, Miner and Fiore, Cushman and Jameson, and Troy and Sweet. In each place, he is confronted by bits of information that puzzle him. The people are hostile, make remarks about his failed marriage, about the children who have turned their backs on him, and each of these revelations comes as almost a shock to him, as though he's been somewhere far away and never knew these occurrences happened. When he meets his one-time mistress, Rule, and she says she never loved him, Lancaster is shattered. It begins to rain as Lancaster finds his own home, a shabby place where no one has lived for years. Where has he been? Where has the time gone? What is the truth? The questions are never answered, just the way many of the stories in the New Yorker leave loose ends dangling. Sydney Pollack directed the Lancaster-Rule scene. The picture was shot in Westport, Connecticut, and probably did well there but it failed to get much attention anywhere else because of the odd subject matter. Well made but mystifying.

p, Frank Perry, Roger Lewis; d, Perry, (uncredited) Sydney Pollack; w, Eleanor Perry (based on the short story by John Cheever); ph, David Quaid, Michael Nebbia (Technicolor); m, Marvin Hamlisch, ed, Sidney Katz, Carl Lerner, Pat Somerset; art d, Peter Dohanos; cos, Anna Hill Johnstone, Elizabeth Stewart; makeup, John Kiras.

Drama/Fantasy   (PR:C MPAA:M/PG)

SWINDLE, THE**½   (1962, Fr./Ital.) 92m Titanus-S.G.C./Astor bw (IL BIDONE)

Broderick Crawford (Augusto), Richard Basehart (Picasso), Franco Fabrizi (Roberto), Giulietta Masina (Iris, Picasso's Wife), Lorella De Luca (Patrizia, Augusto's Daughter), Giacomo Gabrielli (Vargas), Sue Ellen Blake (Anna, Crippled Girl), Alberto De Amicis (Rinaldo, Drug Dealer), Irene Cefaro (Marisa, Girl at Party), Xenia Valderi (Luciana, Rinaldo's Girl), Mara Werlen (Maggie), Maria Zanolli (Stella Florina, Swindled Woman), Ettore Bevilaqua (Swindled Man), Mario Passante.

To many people the films of Fellini are an obnoxious blend of tiresome episodes filled with ugly characters and extreme symbolism. Others find these same elements to be a magical universe filled with the forces influencing an individual's fate. They appreciate the revealing caricatures, lively costumes and sets, and extenuating sounds which create a poetic vision. The latter camp will find much to entertain themselves with THE SWINDLE, a film similar in many respects to its predecessor, LA STRADA, in its depiction of a man who goes through life almost blind to its wonders and with little pity for other humans. Crawford plays a petty thief who teams up with Basehart and Fabrizi to accomplish a number of schemes based on swindling poor people out of their money. Fabrizi is the first to back out of these schemes–not to redeem himself–but to go on to "better" things. Of the three, his character is the least sympathetic because his acts of thievery are done so casually. In a moment of enlightenment, Basehart forsakes this life style to return to his wife Masina who as in LA STRADA looks on the events with her large round eyes. She is the direct opposite of the soulless Fabrizi. This leads Crawford to assemble another bunch to assist in his operations; it is these same men who eventually stone their cohort to death in the touching final scenes, Crawford is dressed in the robes of a bishop in order to execute a scheme when he is approached by an invalid, Blake, who takes him for the real thing, bending down to kiss his hand. Crawford finally feels remorse for his exploits, realizing that he has been taking advantage of people who are driven by pure faith. But by this time it's too late for him to repent. His associates are unsympathetic to his change of heart and stone him to death. A very dark vision that isn't always pleasant to look at, but is nonetheless fascinating.

p, Mario Derecchi; d, Federico Fellini; w, Fellini, Ennio Flaiano Tullio Pinelli (based on a story by Fellini, Flaiano); ph, Otello Martelli; m, Nino Rota; ed, Mario Serandrei, Giuseppe Vari; set d, Dario Cecchi.

Drama   (PR:A MPAA:NR)

SWING AND SWAY   (SEE: SWING IN THE SADDLE, 1944)

SWING FEVER*½   (1943) 80M MGM bw

Kay Kyser (Lowell Blackford), Marilyn Maxwell (Ginger Gray), William Gargan (Waltzy Malone), Nat Pendleton (Killer Kennedy), Maxie Rosenbloom (Rags), Curt Bois (Nick), Morris Ankrum (Dan Conlon), Andrew Tombes (Clyde L. Star), Lou Nova (Kid Mandell), Clyde Fillmore (Mr. Nagen), Ish Kabibble [M.A. Bogue] (Ish), Pamela Blake (Lois), Lena Horne, Merriel Abbott& Her Abbott Dancers (Specialties), Kay Kyser's Orchestra,

Sully Mason, Julie Conway, Trudy Irwin *(Themselves)*, Harry Babbitt *(Harry)*, Katharine [Karen] Booth, Kathleen Williams, Ava Gardner *(Girls)*, Mike Mazurki, Sammy Stein *(Wrestlers)*, Mantan Moreland *(Woodie)*, William Bishop *(Soldier)*, Dan Tobey *(Announcer)*, Murray Alper *(Burly Attendant)*, Charles Sullivan *(Cop)*.

Kyser stars as a young composer who also knows how to hypnotize people. Maxwell helps trick him into using this skill on a boxer in order to fix a fight. Second rate production with Kyser proving he should stick to orchestra conducting instead of trite roles such as this. Musical numbers include: "Mississippi Dream Boat" (Lew Brown, Ralph Freed, Sammy Fain), "I Planted a Rose," "One Girl and Two Boys" (Freed, Brown, Nacio Herb Brown), "You're So Different" (Fain; sung by Lena Horne), "Sh! Don't Make a Sound" (Sunny Skylar), "Thinking of You" (Walter Donaldson).

p, Irving Starr; d, Tim Whelan; w, Nat Perrin, Warren Wilson (based on a story by Matt Brooks, Joseph Hoffman); ph, Charles Rosher; ed, Ferris Webster; md, Georgie Stoll, David Snell; art d, Cedric Gibbons, Stephen Goosson; set d, Edwin A. Willis; ch, Ernst Matray, Maria Matray.

Musical Comedy (PR:A MPAA:NR)

SWING HIGH* (1930) 95m Pathe bw

Helen Twelvetrees *(Maryan)*, Fred Scott *(Garry)*, Dorothy Burgess *(Trixie)*, John Sheehan *(Doc May)*, Daphne Pollard *(Mrs. May)*, George Fawcett *(Pop Garner)*, Bryant Washburn *(Ringmaster Joe)*, Nick Stuart *(Billy)*, Sally Starr *(Ruth)*, Little Billy *(Maj. Tiny)*, William Langan *(Babe)*, Stepin Fetchit *(Sam)*, Chester Conklin *(Sheriff)*, Ben Turpin *(Bartender)*, Robert Edeson *(Doctor)*, Mickey Bennett *(Mickey)*.

A very trying account of circus life has Twelvetrees as part of a sister aerialist team who fights to keep her lover, Scott, out of the hands of vamp Burgess. A number of circus features were added to draw interest or a few laughs, but failed on both counts. Songs include: "Do You Think I Could Grow on You?," "It Must Be Love," "With My Guitar and You," "Shoo the Hoodoo Away," "There's Happiness over the Hill" (Mack Gordon, Abner Silver, Ted Snyder).

p, E.B. Derr; d, Joseph Santley; w, Santley, James Seymour (based on their story); ph, Dave Abel; ed, Daniel Mandell; md, Josiah Zuro; art d, Carroll Clark; set d, Ted Dickson; cos, Gwen Wakeling.

Drama (PR:A MPAA:NR)

SWING HIGH, 1944 (SEE: JIVE JUNCTION, 1944)

SWING HIGH, SWING LOW* (1937) 92m PAR bw

Carole Lombard *(Maggie King)*, Fred MacMurray *(Skid Johnson)*, Charles Butterworth *(Harry)*, Jean Dixon *(Ella)*, Dorothy Lamour *(Anita Alvarez)*, Harvey Stephens *(Harvey Dexter)*, Cecil Cunningham *(Murphy)*, Charlie Arnt *(Georgie)*, Franklin Pangborn *(Henri)*, Anthony Quinn *(The Don)*, Charles Judels *(Tony)*, Harry Semels *(Chief of Police)*, Ricardo Mandia *(Interpreter)*, Enrique DeRosas *(Judge)*, Chris-Pin Martin *(Sleepy Servant)*, Charles Stevens *(Panamanian at Cock Fight)*, Ralph Remley *(Musselwhite)*, Lee Bowman, Nick Lukats *(Men in Nightclub)*, Darby Jones *(Black Santa Claus)*, Eumenio Blanco *(Interpreter)*, George W. Jimenez *(Justice of Peace)*, Oscar Rudolph *(Elevator Boy)*, George Sorel *(Manager)*, Jack Daley *(Dock Policeman)*, Gino Corrado *(Italian)*, Tiny Newland *(Army Lieutenant)*, William Arnold *(Croupier)*, Frank Whitson, Nick Kobliansky, Louis Natheaux *(Gamblers)*, William Wright *(Attendant)*, Esther Howard *(Customer)*, Spencer Chan *(Cook)*, Donald Kerr *(Radio Technician)*, Richard Kipling *(Army Surgeon)*, Lee Cooley *(Radio Announcer)*, Bud Flanagan [Dennis O'Keefe] *(Purser)*.

This was the second film version of the play "Burlesque." In the first, DANCE OF LIFE, and third, WHEN MY BABY SMILES AT ME, as well as in the play, the lead actor is a comic-dancer but MacMurray, who had many talents, couldn't get his feet to move on cue, so the occupation was changed to trumpeter. (MacMurray was an accomplished saxophonist, having appeared with a band known as the California Collegians, but someone must have felt that a trumpet was sexier than a sax.) Lombard gets to sing for the first time on screen, as she plays a performer sailing from New York to Central America. She meets MacMurray on the liner and they disembark at Panama where they visit a local hot spot. In the cabaret, a local rake, Quinn, makes a pass a Lombard and MacMurray decks him. After the battle, MacMurray is arrested and Lombard, who was set to leave on the ship, is stranded. MacMurray's roomie is hypochondriac Butterworth. Lombard and Butterworth extract MacMurray from the local hoosegow and the three of them move into a small place together. With Lombard's help, MacMurray goes to work at Cunningham's nightclub. It's not long before MacMurray becomes a hit in the Canal Zone, marries Lombard, and is offered a plumb job back in New York. He leaves Lombard in Panama and goes north with Lamour, a local singer with whom he'd worked. In a flash, he's a smash in the Big Apple and spends his off-hours with the tempestuous Latin on his arm. Lombard comes north, sees the situation, and announces that she's had it, thus sending MacMurray directly to the bottle and the skids. Later, when Lombard learns that MacMurray is hitting the hooch, she goes to him and gets him sober for an important radio audition. He gets the job and realizes Lombard is the only woman in the world for him. Songs from

many writers include: "Swing High, Swing Low" (Burton Lane, Ralph Freed), "Panamania," "I Hear a Call to Arms" (Sam Coslow, Al Siegel), "If It Isn't Pain, Then It Isn't Love" (Leo Robin, Ralph Rainger), "Spring is in the Air" (Charles Kisco, Freed), "Lonely Senorita" (Robin, Julian Oliver). MacMurray's trumpet playing was actually by William Candreva and Frank Zinziv. DANCE OF LIFE, the original film of this story, was released in 1929 with Hal Skelly in the MacMurray role and Nancy Carroll in the Lombard part. Note Lee Bowman as one of the men in the nightclub. Quinn was a pal of Lombard's, having just worked with her on THE PLAINSMAN. He spoke only Spanish in the picture.

p, Arthur Hornblow, Jr.; d, Mitchell Leisen; w, Virginia Van Upp, Oscar Hammerstein II (based on the play "Burlesque" by George Manker Watters, Arthur Hopkins); ph, Ted Tetzlaff; ed, Eda Warren; md, Boris Morros; art d, Hans Dreier, Ernst Fegte; set d, A.E. Freudeman; cos, Travis Banton; spec eff, Farciot Edouart; m/l, Burton Lane Ralph Freed, Al Siegel, Sam Coslow, Ralph Rainger, Leo Robin, Charles Kisco.

Musical/Drama **Cas.** (PR:A-C MPAA:NR)

SWING HOSTESS*½ (1944) 76m PRC bw

Martha Tilton, Charles Collins, Iris Adrian, Betty Brodel, Earle Bruce, Philip Van Zandt, Emmett Lynn, Cliff Nazarro, Harry Holman, Paul Porcasi, Terry Frost, Claire Rochelle.

Tilton, who rode the crest to fame as Benny Goodman's vocalist, takes a role as an out-of-work big band singer. After being turned down for a job in a band, she takes work as a switchboard operator for a juke box company. She falls in love with a bandleader who hires her to handle the vocal chores. A mediocre story which is watchable only because of its jumping soundtrack. Songs include: "I'll Eat My Hat," "Let's Capture This Moment," "Say It with Love," "Music to My Ears," "Highway Polka," "Got an Invitation" (Jay Livingston, Ray Evans, Lewis Bellin).

p, Sigmund Neufeld; d, Sam Newfield; w, Louise Rousseau, Gail Davenport; ph, Jack Greenhalgh; ed, Holbrook N. Todd; md, David Chudnow.

Musical (PR:A MPAA:NR)

SWING IN THE SADDLE** (1944) 69m COL bw (GB: SWING AND SWAY)

Jane Frazee, Guinn "Big Boy" Williams, Slim Summerville, Sally Bliss, Mary Treen, Red River Dave, Carole Mathews, Byron Foulger, Hoosier Hot Shots, Nat King Cole Trio, Jimmy Wakely and His Oklahoma Cowboys, Cousin Emmy.

A horse opera which features Frazee and Bliss as a couple of actresses who wander out west to dig up the identity of a secret admirer. They end up working in a kitchen which allows them to continue snooping as they warble a number of tunes. Songs include: "Amor," (Sunny Skylar, Gabriel Ruiz), "Hey Mabel" (Fred Stryker), "By the River Sainte Marie" (Edgar Leslie, Harry Warren), "She Broke My Heart in Three Places" (Oliver Drake), "When It's Harvest Time in Peaceful Valley" (Robert Martin, Raymond McKee), and "There'll Be a Jubilee" (Phil Moore).

p, Jack Fier; d, Lew Landers; w, Elizabeth Beecher, Morton Grant, Bradford Ropes (based on a story by Maurice Leo); ph, George Meehan, Glen Gano; ed, Aaron Stell; art d, Lionel Banks, Charles Clague.

Musical/Western (PR:A MPAA:NR)

SWING IT BUDDY (SEE: SWING IT, PROFESSOR, 1937)

SWING IT, PROFESSOR½** (1937) 62m Ambassador bw (GB: SWING IT BUDDY)

Pinky Tomlin *(Prof. Artemis Roberts)*, Paula Stone *(Teddy Ross)*, Mary Kornman *(Joan Dennis)*, Milburn Stone *(Lou Morgan)*, Pat Gleason *(Brickhead)*, Gordon Elliott *(Randall)*, Gentle Maniacs, Four Singing Tramps, Four Squires.

Delightful comedy in which Tomlin plays a university music professor who refuses to recognize the validity of jazz. His stubbornness causes him to lose his job, leading to a hobo camp and eventually a nightclub where Tomlin decides that the stuff isn't all that bad. The performance of Tomlin, both in acting and singing, is what gives this production its light touch. A creative use of the camera in both shot selection and camera placement are a big plus in the development of the plot. Songs include: "I'm Sorta Kinda Glad I Met You," "An Old-Fashioned Melody," and "Richer Than a Millionaire" (Al Heath, Connie Lee, Buddy LeRoux).

p, Maurice Conn; d, Marshall Neilan; w, Nicholas H. Barrows, Robert St. Clair (based on a story by Connie Lee); ph, Jack Greenhalgh; ed, Martin G. Cohn, Richard G. Wray; md, Bakaleinikoff; art d, E.H. Reif; ch, George Grandee.

Comedy/Musical (PR:A MPAA:NR)

SWING IT SAILOR* (1937) 63m GN bw

Wallace Ford (*Pete Kelly*), Ray Mayer (*Husky Stone*), Isabel Jewell (*Myrtle Montrose*), Mary Treen (*Gertie Burns*), Cully Richards (*Shaunus O'Shay*), Tom Kennedy (*Policeman*).

Mayer plays a dimwitted soldier in love with the sexy Jewell, but his best buddy Ford decides he wants to have his chance at the gal as well. A feud between the two Navy boys is brought to an end when Jewell pulls the wool over both their eyes by taking off with somebody else, leaving Mayer and Ford to continue their affair with the Navy. Inane.

p, David Diamond; d, Raymond Cannon; w, Clarence Marks, Diamond; ph, Richard Fryer; ed, Gene Milford.

Comedy **Cas.** **(PR:A MPAA:NR)**

SWING IT SOLDIER*½ (1941) 66m UNIV bw (GB: RADIO REVELS OF 1942)

Ken Murray (*Jerry*), Frances Langford (*Patricia*), Don Wilson (*Brad*), Blanche Stewart (*Brenda*), Elvia Allman (*Cobina*), Hanley Stafford (*Maxwellton*), Susan Miller (*Clementine*), Senor Lee (*Himself*), Iris Adrian (*Dena*), Lewis Howard (*Bill*), Thurston Hall (*Oscar Simms*), Kitty O'Neil (*Mrs. Simms*), Lew Valentine (*Dr. Browning*), Peter Sullivan (*Elevator Boy*), Tom Dugan (*Sergeant*), Skinnay Ennis and His Orchestra, Kenny Stevens, Louis Da Pron, Stop, Look, and Listen, Three Cheers.

Langford plays a pregnant disc jockey whose husband is a soldier stationed overseas. A look-alike twin allows her to take some time off. This gives Murray, the soldier buddy asked to look after Langford by her husband, a real headache. Mainly an excuse to present some tunes. These include: "Annie Laurie," "Rug Cuttin' Romeo" (sung by Susan Miller), "My Melancholy Baby" (Ernie Burnett, George A. Norton, sung by Frances Langford), "I'm Gonna Swing My Way to Heaven" (Eddie Cherkose, Jacques Press, sung by Langford), "Got Love" (sung by Langford).

p, Joseph G. Sanford; d, Harold Young; w, Dorcas Cochran, Arthur V. Jones; ph, Elwood Bredell; ed, Ted J. Kent; ch, Reginald Le Borg.

Musical/Comedy **(PR:A MPAA:NR)**

SWING OUT, SISTER** (1945) 60m UNIV bw

Rod Cameron (*Geoffry*), Billie Burke (*Jessica*), Arthur Treacher (*Chumley*), Frances Raeburn (*Donna*), Jacqueline De Wit (*Pat*), Samuel S. Hinds (*Rufus*), Fuzzy Knight (*Clutch*), Milburn Stone (*Tim*), Edgar Dearing (*Motorcycle Cop*), Sam Flint (*Mr. Bradstreet*), Constance Purdy (*Mrs. Bradstreet*), Selika Pettiford (*Organ Specialty*), Irene Thomas, Tony Rae (*Jitterbugs*), Dee Carroll (*Hat Check Girl*), Harry Strang (*Policeman No. 2*), Bill Davidson (*Doorman*), Chester Clute (*Mr. Gaston*), Rex Evans (*Butler*), Eddie Kane (*Waiter*), Eddie Hart (*Bruiser*), Leo Diamond Quintet.

Raeburn stars as a young singer who makes a living singing in a nightclub, while her folks think she is on her way to becoming an opera star. To coincide with her confusion in musical inclination, Raeburn can't decide whether she wants the owner of the nightclub, Stone, or orchestra leader Cameron as her beau. Raeburn's indecision lasts long enough to provide for some pleasant entertainment. Songs include: "Emperor Waltz" (Johann Strauss II), "Only in Dreams," "Love Is a Bluebird on the Wing," "All I Want to Do Is Swing," "Happy-Go-Lucky-Lady," and "Swing It Mr. Chumbly."

p, Bernard W. Burton; d, Edward Lilley; w, Henry Blankfort (based on the story by Eugene Conrad, Edward Dein); ph, Paul Ivano; ed, Edward Curtiss; art d, John B. Goodman.

Musical/Drama **(PR:A MPAA:NR)**

SWING OUT THE BLUES** (1943) 73m COL bw

Bob Haymes (*Rich Cleveland*), Lynn Merrick (*Penelope Carstairs*), Pete Peterson, Till Risso, Al Torrieri, Don Germano (*The Vagabonds*), Janis Carter (*Dena Marshall*), Tim Ryan (*Dudley Gordon*), Joyce Compton (*Kitty Grogan*), Arthur Q. Bryan (*Larry Stringfellow*), Kathleen Howard (*Aunt Amanda*), John Eldredge (*Gregg Talbot*), Dick Elliott (*Malcolm P. Carstairs*), Lotte Stein (*The Duchess*), Tor Johnson (*Weightlifter*).

Haymes heads a musical foursome whose careers are in jeopardy when he takes to the altar with a socialite. Problems develop when the group's agent, Carter, connives to wreck the wedding plans. Light entertainment that has its moments, with Haymes in good singing voice. Songs include: "It Can't Be Love," "Prelude to Love" (sung by Haymes), "We Should Be Ever So Quiet," "Beethoven's Minuet," "Tahitian War Chant," "Rockabye Baby" (Effie I. Crockett), "Dark Eyes" (English version of "Otchichonria," lyrics by A. Salami, sung by the Vagabonds).

p, Sam White; d, Mal St. Clair; w, Dorcas Cochran (based on a story by Doris Malloy); ph, Arthur Martinelli; ed, Jerome Thoms; md, M.W. Stoloff; art d, Lionel Banks.

Musical/Comedy **(PR:A MPAA:NR)**

SWING PARADE OF 1946** (1946) 73m MON bw

Gale Storm, Phil Regan, Edward Brophy, Mary Treen, John Eldredge, Russell Hicks, Leon Belasco, Windy Cook, The Three Stooges, Connie Boswell, Louis Jordan, Will Osborne.

Storm stars in this songfest as an aspiring singer who falls in love with club owner Regan. Regan's father mistakes Storm's identity and tries to get her to serve a summons on Regan's club. Romance wins out, however, and Storm and Regan become a pair–both in music and in love. Songs include Connie Boswell singing "Stormy Weather" (Harold Arlen, Ted Koehler) and "Just a Little Fond Affection" (Elton Box, Desmond Cox, Lewis Ilda), Louis Jordan and His Tympany Five with "Don't Worry About the Mule" (William Davis, Duke Groner, Charles Stewart), and Will Osborne and His Orchestra delivering "A Tender Word Will Mend It All" (Doris Fisher, Allan Roberts). Other Songs include: "On the Sunny Side of the Street" (Dorothy Fields, Jimmy McHugh), "Oh, Brother" (Matt Melneck, Allie Wrubel), "After All This Time" (Paul DeFur, Ken Thompson), "Caledonia" (Fleecie Moore).

p, Lindsley Parsons, Harry A. Romm; d, Phil Karlson; w, Tim Ryan (based on a story by Edmund Kelso); ph, Harry Neumann; ed, Richard Currier; md, Edward J. Kay; art d, Ernest R. Hickson; ch, Jack Boyle.

Musical **(PR:A MPAA:NR)**

SWING SHIFT MAISIE*½ (1943) 87m MGM bw (GB: THE GIRL IN OVERALLS)

Ann Sothern (*Maisie Ravier*), James Craig (*Breezy McLaughlin*), Jean Rogers (*Iris Reid*), Connie Gilchrist (*Maw Lustvogel, Landlady*), John Qualen (*Horatio Curley*), Fred Brady (*Judd Evans*), Marta Linden (*Emmy Lou Grogan*), Donald Curtis (*Joe Peterson*), Celia Travers (*Helen Johnson*), Pierre Watkin (*Judge*), Lillian Yarbo (*Myrtle Lea*), Wiere Brothers (*Schmitt Brothers*), Pamela Blake (*Billie*), Jacqueline White (*Grace*), Betty Jaynes (*Ruth*), Kay Medford (*Ann*), Katharine Booth (*Louise*), John Hodiak (*Clerk*), Rose Hobart (*Lead Woman*), Jack Mulhall (*Doctor*), William Bishop (*Flier*), James Davis (*Detective*).

Uninspiring outing from the MAISIE series has Sothern in the title role getting a job in an aircraft plant. She falls head-over-heels for pilot Craig, but is unable to keep him landed when aspiring actress Rogers gets her claws into him. Even the charm and talent of Sothern can't help this lifeless production. This was square-jawed Hodiak's second film after switching to the movies from radio, a change made easier by the fact that Hollywood needed men during WW II, and Hodiak had been excused from service because of hypertension. (See MAISIE series, Index.)

p, George Haight; d, Norman Z. McLeod; w, Mary C. McCall, Jr., Robert Raiff (based on the characters created by Wilson Collison); ph, Harry Stradling; m, Lennie Hayton; ed, Elmo Veron; art d, Cedric Gibbons.

Comedy **(PR:A MPAA:NR)**

SWING, SISTER, SWING** (1938) 63m UNIV bw

Ken Murray (*"Nap" Sisler*), Johnny Downs (*Johnny*), Kathryn Kane (*"Snookie"*), Eddie Quillan (*Chick*), Ernest Truex (*Prof. Orlando Beebee*), Edna Sedgwick (*Nona*), Nana Bryant (*Hyacinth*), Esther Howard (*Mrs. Fredericks*), Herbert Heywood (*Mr. Beagle*), Clara Blandick (*Ma Sisler*), Ted Weems Orchestra (*Themselves*), James Flavin (*Pilot*), Emmett Vogan (*Theatrical Agent*), Esther Howard (*Mrs. Fredericks*), Hugh Stovall, LeRoy Atkins (*Black Specialty Act*), Fred Santley, Eddie Fetherston (*Photographers*), John Ward (*Nate Raymond*), Alan Davis (*Stafford*), Clara Blore (*Woman Dancer*), John Hiestand (*Announcer*), Lloyd Ingraham (*Station Agent*), Alice Weaver (*Girl*), Art Yeoman (*Reporter*), Joe Niemeyer (*Dance Instructor*).

Unpretentious filler that has Downs and Kane as two kids from a small town who come to New York to dance their way to fame, using the jitterbug as their steppingstone. Their quick success is met with an equally quick departure home. But the kids had fun during their short trip. Songs include: "Baltimore Bubble," "Gingham Gown," "Just a Bore," "Wasn't It You," "Kaneski Waltz" (Frank Skinner, Charles Henderson).

p, Burt Kelly; d, Joseph Santley; w, Charles Grayson (based on the story "Swing Fever" by Kelly); ph, Elwood Bredell; ed, Frank Gross; md, Charles Previn; art d, Jack Otterson; ch, Matty King.

Musical Comedy **(PR:A MPAA:NR)**

SWING, TEACHER, SWING (SEE: COLLEGE SWING, 1938)

SWING THAT CHEER* (1938) 63m UNIV bw

Tom Brown (*Bob Potter*), Robert Wilcox (*Larry Royal*), Andy Devine (*Doc Saunders*), Constance Moore (*Marian Stuart*), Ernest Truex (*Prof. Peabody*), Margaret Early (*Betty Wilson*), Raymond Parker (*Jay Hill*), Samuel S. Hinds (*Coach McGann*), Stanley Hughes (*Winston*), Doodles Weaver (*Bennett*), David Oliver (*Intern*).

Another college football yarn that can't go beyond the routine. Brown and Wilcox play buddies whose heroics on the field make for a dispute when the fullback gets all the credit, while his blocking buddy remains in the shadows.

To remedy this, the blocker decides to play hurt and see how well the team does without him. The outcome is far too obvious.

p, Max H. Golden; d, Harold Schuster; w, Charles Grayson, Lee Loeb (based on a story by Thomas Ahearn, F. Maury Grossman); ph, Elwood Bredell; ed, Edward Curtiss.

Comedy **(PR:A MPAA:NR)**

SWING TIME*½** (1936) 105m RKO bw

Fred Astaire *(John "Lucky" Garnett)*, Ginger Rogers *(Penelope "Penny" Carrol)*, Victor Moore *(Dr. Cardetti, "Pop")*, Helen Broderick *(Mabel Anderson)*, Eric Blore *(Mr. Gordon)*, Betty Furness *(Margaret Watson)*, George Metaxa *(Ricardo Romero)*, Landers Stevens *(Judge Watson)*, John Harrington *(Dice Raymond)*, Pierre Watkin *(Al Simpson)*, Abe Reynolds *(Schmidt)*, Gerald Hamer *(Eric Facannistrom)*, Edgar Dearing *(Policeman)*, Harry Bowen, Harry Bernard *(Stagehands)*, Donald Kerr, Jack Good, Ted O'Shea, Frank Edmunds, Bill Brand *(Dancers)*, Frank Jenks *(Red)*, Ralph Byrd *(Hotel Clerk)*, Charles Hall *(Taxi Driver)*, Jean Perry *(Roulette Dealer)*, Olin Francis *(Muggsy)*, Floyd Schackleford *(Romero's Butler)*, Joey Ray *(Announcer)*, Jack Rice *(Wedding Guest)*, Howard Hickman *(1st Minister)*, Ferdinand Munier *(2nd Minister)*, Fern Emmett *(Maid)*, Frank Mills *(Croupier)*, Dale Van Sickel *(Diner)*, Dennis O'Keefe, Bess Flowers, Ralph Brooks *(Dance Extras)*, Jack Good *(Dancer)*, Blanca Vischer, Sailor Vincent, Baby Marie Osborne.

An engaging bit of fluff marked the sixth pairing of Astaire and Rogers and the first (and only) under the helm of George Stevens. The plot is thinner than a philandering husband's excuse but it mattered not as the actors went through their paces with such *bonhomie* and verve that audiences suspended heaps of disbelief and just sat back and enjoyed. Astaire is a gambler-dancer who is engaged to marry Furness. When he shows up late for the wedding, Furness' father, Stevens (George Stevens' father in real life), tells the dandy that he'd better not come back unless he can earn $25,000 to prove that he's not just a fop layabout. Once he meets Rogers, his main problem is to keep from earning the 25 grand because he falls hopelessly, and predictably, in love with Rogers. She's a dance teacher at the academy run by Blore. He's the type of nefarious dance master who will do anything to sell lessons and there's a very funny scene as Rogers attempts to teach Astaire, who is pretending to be a clod just so he can stay with her longer. Blore watches Astaire's inept hoofing and fires Rogers on the spot, thinking that she has no ability to teach and because she won't take money from such a hopeless prospective student. Astaire mends that fence by going into an incredibly complex routine that leaves both Blore and Rogers breathless with awe. In the course of events, Astaire and Rogers wind up together and so do Blore and Rogers' sharp-tongued pal, Broderick (who had played with Astaire in "The Band Wagon" on Broadway for a year). Moore, who'd worked with Astaire before in "Funny Face," comes back to play Fred's sidekick and chimes in with some other comedy. The picture was announced as "I Won't Dance" (due to Astaire's hit tune in "Roberta"), then altered to "Never Gonna Dance," and finally, under Stevens' suggestion, was changed to SWING TIME. It's a smart, hip movie that recreates the nightclub era of the "Roaring Twenties" with superb sets, lots of excellent dancing, and not enough of a score from Jerome Kern and Dorothy Fields. There were only six songs, and it was about 30 minutes before the first one was heard. This may have been due to the fact that another song, "It's Not in the Cards," had been shot, then mostly cut from the film. Astaire does his first and only "blackface" number in this film, a tribute to Bill Robinson called "Bojangles of Harlem." It's a huge production number with two dozen chorines, half in white, the other half in black. Then Astaire dances with three shadows of himself, dancing in and out of synch with the other images. The intelligence and the placing of the other Kern-Fields tunes is what makes them stand out. Rogers is washing her hair and it's filled with shampoo when Astaire sits down at the piano to sing the haunting and romantic "The Way You Look Tonight." When Rogers is attempting to teach Astaire to dance, she launches into "Pick Yourself Up" and he joins her. In the sarcastic love song "A Fine Romance" (with some of Fields' best lyrics), the irony is outstanding as Rogers tries her best to get Astaire's attention and he looks more like Stan Laurel than himself in the number. (Stevens had worked with Laurel when he was the cameraman on LEAVE 'EM LAUGHING.) A stunning musical tour de force was "Waltz in Swing Time," which was exactly that as the two manage to combine a pair of dances in one number, and the "Never Gonna Dance" number is the visual highlight. There are two levels of the stage and Astaire indicates that if he can't dance with Rogers, he'll never dance again. The entire story of the film is recapitulated in song and dance (with snatches of the songs that came before) and perfectionist Astaire (and Stevens, who is known for overshooting) kept on going until more than 40 attempts were made. Rogers' feet began to hurt and eventually bleed from all the pounding. The result was worth the pain. "The Way You Look Tonight" won the Oscar as Best Song and Pan's choreography was nominated. Although Kern gets credit for "Waltz in Swing Time," there is reason to believe that the instrumental was, in fact, composed by Robert Russell Bennett, Kern's favorite orchestrator. If there had been a better script or even a few more tunes, it would have elevated this film to a higher status. Lindsay's script was extensively rewritten by Scott after the Broadway playwright returned to New York, following his three-month stint at RKO. Lindsay felt that Scott should have received solo credit for the screenplay but the producers thought otherwise, so they shared the credit. Furness eventually abandoned movies to become a TV commentator and spokeswoman.

p, Pandro S. Berman; d, George Stevens; w, Howard Lindsay, Allan Scott (based on a story by Erwin Gelsey); ph, David Abel; m, Jerome Kern; ed, Henry Berman; md, Nathaniel Shilkret; art d, Van Nest Polglase, Carroll Clark; set d, Darrell Silvera; cos, Bernard Newman, John Harkrider; spec eff, Vernon Walker; ch, Hermes Pan; makeup, Mel Burns.

Musical/Comedy **Cas.** **(PR:AA MPAA:NR)**

SWING YOUR LADY* (1938) 72m WB bw

Humphrey Bogart *(Ed Hatch)*, Penny Singleton *(Cookie Shannon)*, Frank McHugh *(Popeye Bronson)*, Louise Fazenda *(Sadie Horn)*, Nat Pendleton *(Joe "Hercules" Skopapoulos)*, Allen Jenkins *(Shiner Ward)*, Leon Weaver *(Waldo Davis)*, Frank Weaver *(Ollie Davis)*, Loretta "Elviry" Weaver *(Mrs. Davis)*, Ronald Reagan *(Jack Miller)*, Daniel Boone Savage *(Noah Wulliver)*, Hugh O'Connell *(Smith the Referee)*, Tommy Bupp *(Rufe Horn)*, Sonny Bupp *(Len Horn)*, Joan Howard *(Mattie Horn)*, Sue Moore *(Mabel)*, Olin Howland *(Hotel Proprietor)*, Sammy White *(Specialty)*, Tex Driscoll *(Man on Porch)*, Spec O'Donnell *(Boy in Overalls)*, Irving Bacon *(Photographer)*, Vic Potel *(Clem)*, Roger Gray, John "Skins" Miller, Foy Van Dolsen, Frank Pharr *(Hillbillies)*, George Ovey *(Telegraph Operator)*, Georgia Simmons *(Mountain Woman)*, June Gittleson *(Fat Waitress)*.

Bogart approached his role in this silly musical comedy with the same enthusiasm as a mass murderer being dragged down the hall to the gas chamber. The straight Broadway play had been a fair success in New York but the movie suffered from being opened up as all of the holes and lack of motivation were exposed for everyone to see. Bogart is a promoter traveling in Kentucky with his one asset, a numskull wrestler played by Pendleton. Also in the entourage is Pendleton's trainer, McHugh, Bogart's aide, Jenkins, and Bogart's girl friend, Singleton. (The Pendleton character was plainly Greek, a parody of "The Weeping Greek from Cripple Creek," George Zaharias, who made a fortune wrestling around the country in those years before marrying Babe Didrickson, the greatest female athlete of the century.) They are just about out of money and have no ideas, as this hinterlands tour has been a bust. When their car is stuck in a morass of mud and slime, they figure this is the end of the line. Along comes Fazenda, a muscular Amazon who works as a blacksmith. She lifts the car out of the goo with ease and Bogart has a light bulb flash over his head: a match between Fazenda and Pendleton. It should pack in the customers. (Fazenda was an ex-Keystone Komedienne and built like a Sherman Tank.) Pendleton is not there when Fazenda performs her lift, and when he meets her later, he realizes that this is the woman for him. She tells him that they are to meet in a wrestling match but he doesn't let on to Bogart that he knows. When Bogart informs him, Pendleton is adamant about it. He won't lay hands on the woman he loves. Fazenda is angered because she was to receive $100 for her role and wanted to buy some furniture with it. Although Fazenda looks like a whale with long hair, there is yet another man who loves her, Savage. When he hears that Pendleton and Fazenda are getting closer, he begins taking shots at the wrestler with his long rifle. This gives Bogart another idea. He'll match Savage and Pendleton in the big wrestling bout. Since there is no love lost between the two, it'll be billed as a "grudge" (the best kind of wrestling match if one is to believe promoters) and the winner will win Fazenda, who will get the money which has been allocated. There's a dance at the local arena and Fazenda tells Bogart that she doesn't much care who wins the match, she is going to leave Savage anyhow and marry Pendleton. Bogart panics and tells Fazenda that Pendleton is married with a large family and couldn't marry her. Fazenda believes Bogart, walks up to Pendleton, who is expecting a kiss, and picks him up, body-slams him to the floor, then exits in a huff. It's the night of the big match and Pendleton is depressed because his sweetie has departed. Bogart tells Pendleton that the match is fixed and that he must take the fall in front of the local crowd which has packed the arena to the topmost rows. Just before the opening bell, Bogart gets a telegram from a New York impresario. This match is now big news across the country, and Madison Square Garden, the center of all wrestling then and now, is offering big money to whoever wins this bout. The bell rings and Bogart frantically tries to tell Pendleton to forget about taking a dive, now he wants him to win. Pendleton is so preoccupied with his heartbreak about losing Fazenda that he is in a daze. The bout goes on and Savage is making the superior Pendleton look bad, much to the delight of the crowd and to the amazement of sports reporter Reagan. Fazenda screams at Pendleton to stop fooling around and get down to business. Seeing her buoys Pendleton's spirits (just as seeing Talia Shire in ROCKY gave Sylvester Stallone the strength to come back in his title bout) and he makes short work of Savage. After the match is over, the local townspeople scream for Fazenda to be "awarded" to Pendleton, but she sadly tells her pals that it's impossible, as Pendleton is already spoken for. This causes Bogart to have to tell her the truth. Once that's out in the open, the entire group goes north to New York in the old car and the picture ends. There are several hillbilly numbers in the movie, mostly done by the popular Weaver Brothers and Elviry act. Leon and Cicero Weaver and their sister eventually made a few more movies at Republic Studios, but their career was short-lived. The tunes by Jack Scholl and M.K. Jerome include: "Mountain Swingeroo" (sung by the Weavers and Singleton, with a brief dance sequence by Singleton and White), "The Old Apple Tree" (Singleton, the Weavers), "Hillbilly from Tenth Avenue" (Singleton), "Dig Me a Grave in

Old Missouri" and "Swing Your Lady" (Weavers). The orchestrations for the undistinguished tunes were by Hugo Freidhofer and helped matters a bit. It was one of the rare movies in Bogart's career that lost money, and rightly so. There is some amusement in the picture and none of it came from Bogart, who resented being cast in such a B movie. The depictions of the local hillbillies in Kentucky are just what one might expect. They wear overalls, drink from jugs marked XXX, then, after draining the jugs, use the empty vessels to make music. Director Enright specialized in mindless movies and directed such memorable efforts as EARTHWORM TRACTORS, THE SINGING MARINE, NAUGHTY BUT NICE, and SIN TOWN among others. Singleton was appearing in her first movie with that name. Prior to this, she'd been known as Dorothy McNulty in GOOD NEWS, LOVE IN THE ROUGH, AFTER THE THIN MAN, VOGUES OF 1938, and SEA RACKETEERS. A good vaudeville performer, she attained national prominence in the "Blondie" films, then became involved in the union movement and was eventually elected to an office in The American Guild of Variety Artists. Although Hal Wallis gets the credit for this, he was really the man in charge of many Warner movies at the time and his associate, Sam Bischoff, actually oversaw the day-to-day shooting.

p, Hal B. Wallis; d, Ray Enright; w, Joseph Schrank, Maurice Leo (based on the story "Toehold on Artemus" by H.R. Marsh and the play by Kenyon Nicholson, Charles Robinson); ph, Arthur Edeson; m, Adolph Deutsch; ed, Jack Killifer; md, Leo F. Forbstein; art d, Esdras Hartley; cos, Howard Shoup; ch, Bobby Connolly.

Musical/Comedy   **(PR:A   MPAA:NR)**

SWING YOUR PARTNER*½   (1943) 72m REP bw

Roger Clark (*Johnny Murphy*), Esther Dale (*Caroline Bird*), Judy Clark (*Judy*), Charles Judels (*Digby*), Rosemary LaPlanche (*Secretary*), Sam Flint (*Teal*), Forbes Murray (*Morningside*), Elmer Jerome (*Duffy*), Lulubelle & Scotty, Vera Vague, Dale Evans, Ransom Sherman, Harry "Pappy" Cheshire, Richard Lane, George "Shug" Fisher, The Tennessee Ramblers, Peppy & Peanuts.

Thinly spun plot acts as a veil for a number of performances by once popular country music stars. Dale plays the owner of a dairy who goes undercover to figure out what's going on in her factory. Songs include: "Cheese Cake," "Swing Your Partner" (Charles Henderson), "Cracker Barrel County" (Frank Loesser, Jule Styne), "Kiss Your Partner" (Dick Sanford, John Redmond, Frank Weldon), "Shug, Shug Yodel" (George "Shug" Fisher), "In the Cool of the Evening" (Walter Bullock, Styne).

p, Armand Schaefer; d, Frank McDonald; w, Dorrell Stuart McGowen; ph, Bud Thackery; m, Morton Scott; ed, Richard Van Enger; art d, Russell Kimball; md, Scott; ch, Josephine Earl.

Musical   **(PR:A   MPAA:NR)**

SWINGER, THE**½   (1966) 81m PAR c

Ann-Margret (*Kelly Olsson*), Tony Franciosa (*Ric Colby*), Robert Coote (*Sir Hubert Charles*), Yvonne Romain (*Karen Charles*), Nydia Westman (*Aunt Cora*), Craig Hill (*Sammy Jenkins*), Milton Frome (*Mr. Olsson*), Mary LaRoche (*Mrs. Olsson*), Horace McMahon (*Detective Sgt. Hooker*), Clete Roberts (*Himself*), Myrna Ross (*Sally*), Corinne Cole (*Sir Hubert's Secretary*), Bert Freed (*Police Captain*), Romo Vincent (*Jack Happy*), Steven Geray (*Man with Fish*), Larry D. Mann (*John Mallory*), Lance Le Gault (*Warren*), Diki Lerner (*Svengali*), Barbara Nichols (*Blossom LaTour*).

Ann-Margret plays a naive girl from Minnesota who wants to become a writer. The editors at the publication she sends her stories to, *Girl-Lure Magazine*, don't think her material is up to their standards of excitement and sexual exploitation. So Ann-Margret writes a story that will please publishers Franciosa and Coote by lifting lines out of other girlie publications, saying that this is a description of her own life style. To prove it she stages an orgy and has her neighbor cop make a bust to heighten the luridity of the situation. This makes Franciosa believe it to be his duty to reform Ann-Margret, which he goes about doing only to learn her true background. A humorous satire against an overly sex-oriented culture, with Ann-Margret in a role that takes advantage of her bombshell image to take some stabs at what it represents.

p&d, George Sidney; w, Lawrence Roman; ph, Joseph Biroc (Technicolor); m, Marty Paich; ed, Frank Santillo; art d, Hal Pereira, Walter Tyler; set d, Robert K. Benton, Arthur Krams; cos, Edith Head; spec eff, Paul K. Lerpae; ch, David Winters; m/l, "Oh, So Bad," Marty Paich, "Once," Paich, Mel Torme, "The Swinger," Andre and Dory Previn (all sung by Ann-Margret), other songs by Johnny Mercer, Harold Arlen, Richard Rodgers, Lorenz Hart, Billy Rose Edward Heyman; makeup, Wally Westmore.

Comedy   **(PR:A   MPAA:NR)**

SWINGER'S PARADISE**   (1965, Brit.) 83m Ivy/AIP c (GB: WONDERFUL LIFE)

Cliff Richard (*Johnnie*), Walter Slezak (*Lloyd Davis*), Susan Hampshire (*Jenny*), The Shadows [Hank B. Marvin, Bruce Welch, Brian Bennett, John Rostill] (*Mood Musicians*), Melvyn Hayes (*Jerry*), Una Stubbs (*Barbara*),

Derek Bond (*Douglas Leslie*), Joseph Cuby (*Miguel*), Richard O'Sullivan (*Edward*), Gerald Harper (*Sheik/Scotsman/Harold*).

British pop star Cliff Richard turns out his third peppy musical comedy as a singer who, with his band, is stranded in the Canary Islands. Slezak, a stereotypical film director, comes to the island to make a picture and Richard falls for leading lady Hampshire. He decides to make his own musical version of the film, sneakily using the equipment and the cast. Richard's film and Slezak's are equally rancid, but when they combine their two pictures, they wind up with a smash hit. A silly piece of fluff which boasts a decent soundtrack. Songs include: "Wonderful Life," "A Girl in Every Port," "Home," "A Little Imagination," "On the Beach," "In the Stars," "We Love a Movie," "Do You Remember," "What I Gotta Do," "All Kinds of People," "A Matter of Moments," "Youth and Experience" (performed by Richard and The Shadows), "Theme from Young Lovers," "Walkin'" (performed by the Shadows).

p, Kenneth Harper; d, Sidney J. Furie; w, Peter Myers, Ronald Cass; ph, Ken Higgins (Techniscope, Technicolor); m, Stanley Black; ed, Jack Slade; prod d, Stanley Dorfman; art d, Herbert Smith; cos, Cynthia Tingey; ch, Gillian Lynne; m/l, Myers, Cass, Cliff Richard, Hank B. Marvin, Brian Bennett, Bruce Welch.

Comedy/Musical   **(PR:A   MPAA:NR)**

SWINGIN' AFFAIR, A*   (1963) 85m Bengal International/Emerson Film Enterprises bw (AKA: A SWINGING AFFAIR)

William Wellman, Jr, Arline Judge, Dick Dale and the Del Tones, Sandra Gale Bettin.

Sappy story has Wellman as a college student who becomes a boxer to raise money for school. He meets with quite a bit of success but never loses sight of his original aim or the waitress who is waiting for him. Too bad the knocks to Wellman's head didn't knock any acting ability into him.

p, Gunther Collins; d, Jay O. Lawrence; w, Collins.

Drama   **(PR:A   MPAA:NR)**

SWINGIN' ALONG*½   (1962) 74m FOX c (AKA: DOUBLE TROUBLE)

Tommy Noonan (*Freddy Merkle*), Pete Marshall (*Duke*), Barbara Eden (*Carol Walker*), Connie Gilchrist (*Aunt Sophie*), Carol Christensen (*Ginny*), Alan Carney (*Officer Sullivan*), Mike Mazurki (*Bookie*), Tommy Farrell (*Georgie*), Lennie Bremen (*Willie*), Don Diamond (*Tony*), Ted Knight (*Priest*), Terry Miele (*Mrs. Crenshaw*), Frank Wilcox (*Psychiatrist*), Sandra Warner (*Secretary*), Art Baker (*TV Announcer*), Gregg Martell (*Man in Manhole*), Norman Leavitt (*Cab Driver*), Edith Evanson (*Woman*), Jimmy Ames, Robert Foulk (*Piano Movers*), Blossom Rock [Marie Blake] (*Woman in Apartment No. 1*), Earl Holmes (*Western Union Boy*), Sophania Whitney (*Woman in Apartment No. 4*), Ray Charles, Roger Williams, Bobby Vee (*Themselves*).

The final teaming of Noonan and Marshall before the former went on to do semi-porn films with Jayne Mansfield and her husband, Mickey Hartigay. Here Noonan plays an inept delivery boy who tries his hand at a variety of creative projects, never meeting with much success. When his motorcycle is destroyed, he decides to give songwriting a shot, and, under the gaze of con man Marshall, he enters a tune in a contest. The piece he has written is temporarily lost, but entered into the contest by a well-meaning priest. To everyone's surprise it wins. High points of picture are the appearances of singers Ray Charles and Bobby Vee.

p, Jack Leewood; d, Charles Barton; w, Jameson Brewer; ph, Arthur E. Arling (CinemaScope, DeLuxe Color); m, Arthur Morton; ed, Betty Steinberg; art d, Duncan Cramer, George Van Marter; set d, Walter M. Scott, Lou Hafley; m/l, "Song of the City," Walter Kent, Walton Farrar; makeup, Bén Nye.

Comedy   **(PR:A   MPAA:NR)**

SWINGIN' MAIDEN, THE**   (1963, Brit.) 98m Gregory, Hake and Walker/Anglo-Amalgam ated-COL c (GB: THE IRON MAIDEN)

Michael Craig (*Jack Hopkins*), Anne Helm (*Kathy Fisher*), Jeff Donnell (*Mrs. Fisher*), Alan Hale, Jr (*Paul Fisher*), Noel Purcell (*Adm. Sir Digby Trevelyan*), Cecil Parker (*Sir Giles Trent*), Roland Culver (*Lord Upshott*), Joan Sims (*Mrs. Fred*), Judith Furse (*Mrs. Webb*), John Standing (*Humphrey*), Brian Oulton (*Vicar*), Sam Kydd (*Fred*), Richard Thorp (*Harry Markham*), Brian Rawlinson (*Village Policeman*), Tom Gill (*Rally Official*), Duke of Bedford (*Himself*), Jim Dale, George Woodbridge, Ian Wilson, Douglas Ives, David Aylmer, Peter Burton, Michael Nightingale, Raymond Glendenning, Cyril Chamberlain, Peter Jesson, Anton Rodgers, Anthony Baird, Bill Cartwright, Peter Byrne, Middleton Woods, Peter Wells, Eric Corrie, Jonathon Kydd.

The early days of commercial aircraft acts as the setting for a rivalry between Craig and Standing for a contract from tycoon Hale. Craig designs engines more out of dedication while Standing and family are mainly out for the money. The clash makes for some hilarious goings on as Craig's flying machine tends to be more of a menace than a development in aviation, but it all ends happily as Craig wins the contract and the girl. The Duke of Bedford lent his stately home and grounds to the film and attractive they are.

p, Peter Rogers; d, Gerald Thomas; w, Vivian A. Cox, Leslie Bricusse (based on a story by Harold Brooks, Kay Bannerman); ph, Alan Hume (Eastmancolor); m Eric Rogers; ed, Archie Ludski, Rogers; art d, Carmen Dillon; cos, Joan Ellacott; makeup, W. T. Partleton, Basil Newall.

Comedy   (PR:A   MPAA:NR)

SWINGIN' ON A RAINBOW*   (1945) 72m REP bw

Jane Frazee (Lynn Ford), Brad Taylor (Steve Ames), Harry Langdon (Chester Willoby), Minna Gombell (Minnie Regan), Amelita Ward (Barbara Marsden), Tim Ryan (Huston Greer), Paul Harvey (Thomas Marsden), Wendell Niles (Radio Announcer), Richard Davies (Jimmy Rhodes), Helen Talbot (Myrtle).

Frazee plays a songwriter who tries to gain compensation from a man who has made a hit out of one of her songs without her permission. She hangs out in his apartment to wait for his return, and winds up writing songs with the next door neighbor, Taylor, by matching his knocks against the wall. Pretty tough going.

p, Eddy White; d, William Beaudine; w, Olive Cooper, John Grey (based on a story by Cooper); ph, Marcel LaPicard; ed, Fred Allen; m/l, Kim Gannon, Walter Kent, Jack Elliott; art d, Russell Kimball, Gano Chittenden.

Comedy   (PR:A   MPAA:NR)

SWINGIN' SUMMER, A**   (1965) 81m National Talent
                                              Consultants/United Screen Arts c

William Wellman, Jr (Rick), Quinn O'Hara (Cindy), James Stacy (Mickey), Martin West (Turk), Raquel Welch (Jeri), Mary Mitchell (Shirley), Robert Blair (Tony), Allan Jones (Mr. Johnson), Lili Kardell (Sandra), Diane Bond, Diane Swanson, Irene Sale, Kathy Francis, Laurie Williams (The Girls), Reno Carell, Buck Holland, Glenn Stensel (The Hoods), The Righteous Brothers, The Rip Chords, Donnie Brooks, Gary Lewis and the Playboys, Jody Miller.

The son of famous director William Wellman stars, along with Stacy and O'Hara, in this innocent feature in which the three attempt to make money by starting up a dance pavilion at a lake resort. O'Hara goes behind the back of her boy friend, Wellman, to get assistance from her father to back the project. Wellman finds out and goes into a proud youth routine: he wanted to make it on his own. This blows over soon, leaving West as the only obstacle with which to contend: he's jealous of Wellman's success with O'Hara and attempts to destroy the dance hall. Some great classic bands in The Righteous Brothers and Gary Lewis and the Playboys are among the musical talent. Songs include: "Red Hot Roadster," "Justine," "Penny the Poo," "Out to Lunch," "Nitro," and "Ready to Groove." Film debut for Raquel Welch.

p, Reno Carell; d, Robert Sparr; w, Leigh Chapman (based on a story by Carell); ph, Ray Fernstrom (Techniscope, Technicolor); m, Harry Betts; ed, James T. Heckert, William E. Lee; ch, Michael Blodgett.

Musical/Comedy   Cas.   (PR:A   MPAA:NR)

SWINGING BARMAIDS, THE*½   (1976) 88m Premier c (AKA:
                                              EAGER BEAVERS)

Bruce Watson, Laura Hippe, Katie Saylor, Renie Radich, William Smith, Zitto Kazann, Dyanne Thorne, James Travis, Ray Glavin, John Alderman, Judith Roberts, Andre Tayir, Dick Yarmy, Milt Kogan, M.J. Kane.

There's a psycho killer on the loose again and this time he has an appetite for barmaids. Smith is a tough cop who's determined to stop the bloodshed and make the world safe again for girls. Will the killer strike again? Will the barmaids swing again? Will the audience wake up in time to see the ending? The screenplay is by Roger Corman alumnus Charles B. Griffith (BUCKET OF BLOOD, 1959, and THE LITTLE SHOP OF HORRORS, 1960, among others), and never quite succeeds.

p, Ed Carlin; d, Gus Trikonis; w, Charles B. Griffith.

Crime   (PR:O   MPAA:R)

SWINGING FINK   (SEE: RAT FINK, 1965)

SWINGING PEARL MYSTERY, THE
                                              (SEE: THE PLOT THICKENS, 1936)

SWINGING SET   (SEE: GET YOURSELF A COLLEGE GIRL, 1964)

SWINGING THE LEAD**   (1934, Brit.) 63m Weiner, MacKane and
                                              Rogers/UNIV bw

Billy [William] Hartnell (Freddy Fordum), Moira Lynd (Joan Swid), Gibb McLaughlin (Inigo Larsen), Marie Ault (Mrs. Swid), George Rogers (Ben-

jamin Brown), Nita Harvey (Peggy).

A harmless comedy about a zany gang of criminals who get their hands on a secret formula that changes people's personalies. A rival gang tries to swipe the drug, as do the police, leading to a madcap chase.

p, Paul Weiner; d, David MacKane; w, George Rogers.

Comedy   (PR:A   MPAA:NR)

SWINGTIME JOHNNY*   (1944) 60m UNIV bw

The Andrews Sisters (Themselves), Harriet Hilliard (Linda), Peter Cookson (Jonathan), Tim Ryan (Sparks), Matt Willis (Monk), William "Bill" Phillips (Steve), Tom Dugan (Gruff Character), Ray Walker (Mike), Marion Martin (Blonde), John Hamilton (Caldwell), John Sheehan (Raffle Wheel Barker), Syd Saylor (Sea Food Barker), Jack Rice (Bill), Emmett Vogan (Chairman of the Board), Herbert Heywood (Pop), Alphonse Martell (Pierre), Mitch Ayres and His Orchestra.

The Andrews Sisters shift from nightclubs to an ammunitions factory as they decide to do their duty for the war effort. Luckily, most people did not approach the war like these gals, who use every conceivable situation to spout off another tune. A slight plot has them trying to help owner Cookson keep his factory running despite efforts of a saboteur. Songs include: "Boogie Woogie Bugle Boy" (Don Raye, Hughie Prince), "Sweet and Low," "Poor Nell" (Everett Carter, Milton Rosen), "You Better Give Me Lots of Loving" (Kermit Goell, Fred Spielman), "I May Be Wrong but I Think You're Wonderful" (Henry Sullivan, Harry Ruskin), "Boogie Woogie Choo Choo" (Johnny Murphy, Roy Jordan), "When You and I Were Young Maggie" (J.A. Butterfield, George W. Johnson).

p, Warren Wilson; d, Edward F. Cline; w, Clyde Bruckman (based on a story by Wilson); ph, Jerome Ash; m, Vic Schoen; ed, Edward Curtiss; art d, John B. Goodman; cos, Vera West.

Musical   (PR:A   MPAA:NR)

SWIRL OF GLORY   (SEE: SUGARFOOT, 1951)

SWISS CONSPIRACY, THE*   (1976, U.S./Ger.) 89m WB-S.J.
                                              International c

David Janssen (David), Senta Berger (Denise), John Ireland (McGowan), Elke Sommer (Rita), John Saxon (Hayes), Ray Milland (Hurtil), Anton Diffring (Franz), Arthur Brauss (Korsak), Curt Lowens (Andre), David Hess (Tony), Inigo Gallo (Hans), Sheila Ruskin (Corinne), Irmgard Frost (Florelle).

An extraordinary cast of talented players turn up in this tedious thriller about the world of numbered bank accounts. Janssen is hired to protect some of the bank customers from evil types who would like to take their money away. The most interesting conspiracy here is the one the producers cooked up to foist this star-heavy tedium on the public.

p, Maurice "Red" Silverstein; d, Jack Arnold; w, Norman Klenman, Philip Saltzman, Michael Stanley (based on a novel by Stanley).

Crime   Cas.   (PR:C   MPAA:PG)

SWISS FAMILY ROBINSON½**   (1940) 92m RKO bw

Thomas Mitchell (William Robinson), Edna Best (Elizabeth Robinson), Freddie Bartholomew (Jack Robinson), Terry Kilburn (Ernest Robinson), Tim Holt (Fritz Robinson), Baby Bobby Quillan (Francis Robinson), Christian Rub (Thoren), John Wray (Ramsey), Herbert Rawlinson (Captain).

A close rendition of the famous novel about a London family sidetracked on its voyage to Australia by a storm that leaves the group shipwrecked. They are the only ones from the ship who remain alive, and, under pressure of father Mitchell, they learn to adapt to a tropical environment, liking it so much they decide to stay when a ship comes to rescue them. Though technically efficient, convincingly acted, and having a number of subtle messages, SWISS FAMILY ROBINSON was still a hefty loss to RKO.

p, Gene Towne, Graham Baker; d, Edward Ludwig; w, Walter Ferris, Towne, Baker (based on the novel by Johann David Wyss); ph, Nicholas Musuraca; ed, George Crone; cos, Edward Stevenson; spec eff, Vernon L. Walker.

Drama/Adventure   (PR:AAA   MPAA:NR)

SWISS FAMILY ROBINSON*½**   (1960) 126m Disney/BV c

John Mills (Father), Dorothy McGuire (Mother), James MacArthur (Fritz), Janet Munro (Roberta), Sessue Hayakawa (Pirate Chief), Tommy Kirk (Ernst), Kevin Corcoran (Francis), Cecil Parker (Capt. Moreland), Andy Ho (Auban), Milton Reid (Big Pirate), Larry Taylor (Battoo).

Disney's version of the famous novel is a superior adventure that improves on the ponderous classic. Wyss was a Swiss professor who wrote the story his father dictated. It was his one important work and was filmed twice before, as a 15-episode silent serial in 1925, then in 1940 by RKO with Thomas Mitchell, Freddie Bartholomew, and Edna Best. Neither compares with this $4.5 million version that was a box-office bonanza for the Burbank lot. Many liberties were taken from the book and all were improvements, as this turned into a merry cartoon-like romp with lots of explosions, action, and virtually nobody being killed or even hurt. In that respect, it resembled the average "Pluto" or "Goofy" short. Shot on the paradise island of Tobago (which is now part of the independent country of Trinidad And Tobago), it was a miracle they ever got it done, as there were many production problems. It took 22 weeks to make, partly due to the fact that the sun goes down around six every night, winter or summer (it's near the equator and the closer one gets to that line, the less difference there is in the day's length), and they had to quit at dusk. Mills, McGuire, and their three sons, MacArthur, Kirk, and Corcoran, are running from Napoleon and trying to find someplace to live in the South Seas. (There were four sons in the original and no villains other than natural catastrophes.) They are chased by pirates and their ship is pounded by an angry sea. The crew of the ship has left the sinking vessel and the only passengers are the Robinson family. The ship crashes on the island's rocks and the family emerges to find that they are on a tropical Eden. Since the ship, which is only halfsubmerged, is filled with food and gear, the family takes all of it to the island and they prepare to settle in. Animals abound, though many of them totally wrong for the South Seas where they are supposed to be. (How in the world could an elephant, a zebra, a tiger, ostriches, monkeys, and an anaconda have ever made it to such a place from the continents where they live?) Comfort is no problem as they build an elaborate tree house with an elevator, running water, and even a stove. Further, they erect a stone building in an impregnable position atop a hill, just in case the pirates, led by silent star Sessue Hayakawa, decide to come after them. Once they've stripped the ship, they blow it up so nobody will know they are there. They build a small boat and begin to sail around the island to get the lay of the land. When their boat cracks up, they see Parker, an English sea captain, and a small boy (who turns out to be a girl, Munro) being held by the pirates, who are arguing about how to dispose of their prisoners. Munro is rescued and Parker heroically stays behind as ransom bait. Back at the tree house, Munro is brought into the house and the family celebrates Christmas Eve, then Kirk and MacArthur each become jealous of the other's attentions to Munro. Before that can erupt, the pirates arrive. Mills has prepared for such an emergency by stocking up all of the ship's weapons. They have grenades made with explosive powder inside coconut shells, land mines, traps, etc. The pirates attack time and again (although no one is hurt), and when it seems that all is lost as the family are running out of ammo, Parker, who has been ransomed, arrives with a ship filled with sailors and saves the day. The family has the opportunity to leave the island but chooses to stay. MacArthur and Munro are in love and Kirk decides to leave with Parker and seek an education in Europe. Exciting, funny, and filled with Disney's family touches, it's a tongue-in-cheek movie that avoids the usual sappy sentiment of so-called "family" films and concentrates on sheer entertainment. Annakin's direction is slow at times and could have benefitted from a slight speeding up of the speeches. The scenery is lush, colorful, and the success of the picture made Tobago a tourist haven for many years afterward. The guides taking people around the small island still point with pride to the locations used in the making of this movie.

p, Bill Anderson; d, Ken Annakin; w, Lowell S. Hawley (based on the novel by Johann Wyss); ph, Harry Waxman (Panavision, Technicolor); m, William Alwyn; ed, Peter Boita; prod d, John Howell; md, Muir Mathieson; art d, Howell; set d, Jack Stephens; cos, Julie Harris; spec eff, Dan Lee, Walter Stones; makeup, Bill Lodge.

Historical Adventure   Cas.   (PR:AAA MPAA:G)

SWISS HONEYMOON*   (1947, Brit.) 63m IA/New Realm bw

Percy Marmont (The Man), Pat Mainwaring (The Girl).

Marmont and Mainwaring make the title trip and see all the natural wonders of the Swiss Alps before getting stranded on a snowy mountainside. Of course, rescue is not far off in this glorified travelog. Not a film likely to ever turn up on the revival circuit, and for good reason.

p, W.M. Sibley; d, Jan Sikorski, Henry C. James; w, Sibley; ph, Sikorski.

Drama   (PR:A MPAA:NR)

SWISS MISS*   (1938) 72m HR/MGM bw

Stan Laurel, Oliver Hardy (Themselves), Walter Woolf King (Victor Albert), Della Lind (Anna Hoepfel Albert), Adia Kuznetzoff (Franzelhuber), Eddie Kane (Village Tradesman), Anita Garvin (His Bickering Wife), Franz Hug (Flag Thrower), Eric Blore (Edward Morton), Ludovico Tomarchio (Anton Luigi), Sam Lufkin, Tex Driscoll (Bearded Swiss Peasants), Charles Judels (Emile, Cheese Factory Proprietor), George Sorel (Joseph the Chauffeur), Harry Semels (Organ-Grinder), Etherine Landucci (Accordian Player with Gorilla), Gustav von Seyffertitz, Conrad Seideman (Gardeners), Joseph Struder, Louis Struder, Otto Jehle, Fritz Wolfesberger (Yodeling, Horn-Blowing, and Sideline Music Performers), Bob O'Conner, Michael Mark (Astonished Swiss Villagers), Jean De Briac (Enrico the Waiter), Agostino Borgato (Man with Mule-Drawn Cart), Jacques Vanaire, James Carson, Ed Searpa (Alpen Hotel Waiters), Winstead "Doodles" Weaver (Driver of the Ancient Taxi), Hal Gerard, Nick Copeland, George Granlich, Earl Douglas, Alex Melesh, Jack Lubell, Eddie Brian, Eddie Johnson (Bellboys at the Alpen

Hotel), Baldwin Cooke, Ed Brandenburg (Alpen Hotel Atmosphere People), Jack Hill, Lester Dorr (Swiss Dress Extras for the Alpenfest), Val Raset (Dancer), Ham Kinsey (Stunt Double for Stan Laurel), Cy Slocum (Stunt Double for Oliver Hardy), Charles Gamora (Gorilla), Dinah (Mule).

One of L&H's less effective outings has them as mousetrap salesmen in Switzerland thinking that to be the most logical place to display their wares because it's a country of cheese. It turns out not to be so, and they wind up as waiters at a Swiss chalet where their usual ineptitude causes havoc. The kitchen scenes give open opportunity to display L&H's comic ability, but none of it seems very funny. This isn't their fault, but due to a poorly conceived script and an even worse manner of staging the story. All the action takes place during a music festival, so there are plenty of people going about singing, including King and Lind as a couple with King trying to ditch his wife, only to have L&H play cupid. The wonderfully bizarre nature of the settings and some of the scenes were damaged by the fact that Laurel reportedly had been ill during the production, and he certainly looks it, being drawn and overweight and appearing tired much of the time. Also, Roach, who was born in Switzerland, allegedly changed certain gags and killed one routine completely, no doubt helping to bury the whole thing in a Swiss snowslide of audience antipathy. (See LAUREL AND HARDY series, Index.)

p, Hal Roach; d, John G. Blystone, Roach; w, James Parrott, Charles Rogers, Felix Adler, Charles Melson (based on a story by Jean Negulesco, Charles Rogers, Stan Laurel, Roach); ph, Norbert Brodine, Art Lloyd; ed, Bert Jordan; md, Marvin Hatley; art d, Charles D. Hall; set d, William L. Stevens; ch, Val Raset.

Comedy   Cas.   (PR:AAA MPAA:NR)

SWISS TOUR   (SEE: FOUR DAYS LEAVE, 1949)

SWITCH, THE*   (1963, Brit.) 69m RFD bw

Anthony Steel (Bill Craddock), Zena Marshall (Caroline Markham), Conrad Phillips (John Curry), Dermot Walsh (Inspector Tomlinson), Susan Shaw (Search Officer), Dawn Beret (Janice Lampton), Jerry Desmonde (Customs Chief), Arnold Diamond (Jean Lecraze).

When Marshall is kidnaped by a vicious gang of wristwatch smugglers, it's up to brave customs officer Steel to come to the rescue. Audiences are likely to check their watches frequently during this lifeless crime thriller.

p, Philip Ridgeway, Lance Comfort; d, Peter Maxwell; w, Ridgeway, Colin Fraser (based on a story by Ridgeway).

Crime   (PR:C MPAA:NR)

SWITCHBLADE SISTERS**   (1975) 91m Centaur c (AKA: THE JEZEBELLES; THE JEZEBELS; PLAYGIRL GANG)

Robbie Lee, Joanne Nail, Monica Gayle, Kitty Bruce, Janice Karman, Marlene Clark, Michael Miller.

A gang of female ex-cons go on a spree of robbery and murder in this vaguely feminist exploitation film. Decent trashy fun which includes Lenny Bruce's daughter Kitty for added interest.

p, John Prizer; d, Jack Hill; w, F.X. Maier; ph, (CFI Color).

Crime   Cas.   (PR:O MPAA:R)

SWORD AND THE DRAGON, THE**   (1960, USSR) Valiant c (ILYA MOUROMETZ)

Boris Andreyev (Ilya Mporometz), Andrei Abrikosov (Prince Vladimir), Natalie Medvedeva (Princess Apraxia), Ninel Myshkova (Vasilisa), Shukur Burkhanov (Kalin-Tsar).

Imaginatively staged enactment of the life of a Russian hero from the Middle Ages known for his daring against three-headed dragons and other equally terrifying creatures. The special effects are fantastic.

p&d, Alexander Ptushko; w, V. Kotochnev.

Fantasy   (PR:A MPAA:NR)

SWORD AND THE ROSE, THE**   (1953) 91m Disney/RKO c (GB: WHEN KNIGHTHOOD WAS IN FLOWER)

Richard Todd (Charles Brandon), Glynis Johns (Princess Mary Tudor), James Robertson Justice (King Henry VIII), Michael Gough (Duke of Buckingham), Jane Barrett (Lady Margaret), Peter Copley (Sir Edwin Caskoden), Rosalie Crutchley (Queen Katherine of Aragon), D.A. Clarke-Smith (Cardinal Wolsey), Ernest Jay (Lord Chamberlain), John Vere (Lawyer Clerk), Phillip Lennard (Chaplain), Bryan Coleman (Earl of Surrey), Philip Glasier (Royal Falconer), Jean Mercure (King Louis XII of France), Gerard Oury (Dauphin of France), Fernand Fabre (De Longueville, Ambassador of France), Robert Le Beal (Royal Physician), Gaston Richer (Antoine Duprat, Grand Chancellor), Helen Goss (Princess Claude), Patrick Cargill, Anthony Sharpe (French Diplomats), Caven Watson (Capt. Bradhurst), Richard Molinas (Father Pierre), Hal Osmond (Costermonger),

Norman Pierce (*Innkeeper*), Douglas Bradley-Smith (*Squire*), Ewen Solon (*Guardsman*), Rupert Evans, Paddy Ryan (*Bargemen*), Thomas Heathcoate (*Wrestling Second*), Arthur Brander (*1st Mate*), Russell Waters (*Sailor*), John Serrett (*French Squire*), Bob Simmons (*French Champion*).

Historically inaccurate but bursting with Disney energy and charm, this is an account of the love life of Mary Tudor, sister to King Justice VIII, as she shuns the advances of a nobleman in order to wed a commoner. Johns plays the woman of royalty who falls for commoner Todd, forcing him to stay in England by making him captain of the guards. To help her brother's plans of a reconciliation with France, she weds the king of France, knowing that his ill-health will lead him to a quick grave. When Johns attempts to return to England, the Lord of Buckingham, played by Gough, pursues her in an attempt to coerce her to the altar. But the woman only has eyes for Todd, who shows up in time. For his efforts, Henry allows his sister to marry the commoner and bestows on him a large portion of land. The king, as played by Justice, is much more hearty and gusty than was the real thing, while Johns gives a very passionate portrayal of the sister. A lot of effort went into the costumes and settings, but the picture remains drab.

p, Perce Pearce; d, Ken Annakin; w, Lawrence E. Watkin (based on the novel *When Knighthood Was in Flower* by Charles Major); ph, Geoffrey Unsworth (Technicolor); m, Clifton Parker; ed, Gerald Thomas; art d, Carmen Dillon; cos, F. Arlington Valles; ch, David Paltenghi; makeup, Geoff Rodway.

Historical Drama   **(PR:A   MPAA:NR)**

SWORD AND THE SORCERER, THE*   (1982) 100m Group 1 c

Lee Horsley (*Talon*), Kathleen Beller (*Alana*), Simon MacCorkindale (*Mikah*), George Maharis (*Machelli*), Richard Lynch (*Cromwell*), Richard Moll (*Xusia*), Anthony DeLongis (*Rodrigo*), Robert Tessier (*Verdugo*), Nina Van Pallandt (*Malia*), Anna Bjorn (*Elizabeth*), Jeff Corey (*Craccus*), Joe Regalbuto (*Darius*), Christopher Cary (*King Richard*), Russ Marin, Earl Maynard, George Murdock, John Davis Chandler, Emily Yancy, Christopher Cary, Peter Breck, Alan Caillou, Michael Evans, Jay Robinson, Simmy Bow, Reb Brown, Eric Cord, Jo-Jo D'Amore, Steve Davis, Anthony Farrar, Greg Finley, George Fisher, Tammi Furness, Hubie Kerns, Lennie Geer, Michael Holt, James Jarnigan, Edgy Lee, Charlie Messenger, Shelley Taylor Morgan, Christina Nigra, Buckley Norris, Patrick O'Moore, Thomas Rosales, Gina Smika, Alvah Stanley, Mark Steffan, William Watson, Barry Chase, Corinne Calvet.

A complex medieval plot has Horsley leading 1 group to regain control of the kingdom now ruled by a sadistic knight who murdered the previous ruler. Lots of gore and some decent artistic effects may gain the interest of modern moviegoers. If not, then the scantily clad cast is there to drag them in.

p, Brandon and Marion Chase; d, Albert Pyun; w, Pyun, Thomas Karnowski, John Stuckmeyer; ph, Joseph Mangine (DeLuxe Color); m, David Whittaker; ed, Marshall Harvey; art d, George Costello; spec eff, John Carter, Harry Woolman, Terry Woolman; makeup, Greg Cannom.

Fantasy/Adventure   **Cas.**   **(PR:O   MPAA:R)**

SWORD IN THE DESERT***½   (1949) 100m UNIV bw

Dana Andrews (*Mike Dillon*), Marta Toren (*Sabra*), Stephen McNally (*David Vogel*), Jeff Chandler (*Kurta*), Philip Friend (*Lt. Ellerton*), Hugh French (*Maj. Sorrell*), Liam Redmond (*McCarthy*), Lowell Gilmore (*Maj. Stephens*), Stanley Logan (*Col. Bruce Evans*), Hayden Rorke (*Capt. Beaumont*), George Tyne (*Dov*), Peter Coe (*Tarn*), Paul Marion (*Jeno*), Marten Lamont (*Capt. Fletcher*), David Wolfe (*Gershon*), Campbell Copelin (*Sgt. Chapel*), Art Foster (*Sgt. Rummins*), Gilchrist Stuart (*Radio Operator*), Emil Rameau (*Old Man*), Jack Webb (*Hoffman*), Jerry Paris (*Levitan*), Shepherd Menken, Joseph Turkel, Sam Resnik, Russ Kaplan (*Haganah Soldiers*), Dennis Dengate (*Driver*), Martin Garralaga (*Ahmed the Great*), James Craven (*Brig. Gen. Vincent*), Robin Hughes (*Soldier*), George Dockstader, Paul Brinegar (*British Soldiers*).

An exciting, though historically muddled film, SWORD IN THE DESERT is the first motion picture to deal with the struggles between Jewish factions and the British in the creation of the state of Israel. It is 1947, and a group of Jews are illegally smuggled into Palestine on a freighter piloted by American captain Andrews. Through underground channels, they make their way to a rebel headquarters in the desert, where a plot to overthrow British rule is hatched. Chandler is a rebel leader, and Toren broadcasts propaganda against the British using an underground radio station. Eventually British authorities discover the location of the rebel base, then swoop in to capture the band. They are held at a British headquarters, but on Christmas Eve other Jewish resisters stage a raid to rescue their comrades. The story is well told in an exciting panorama with Andrews, Chandler, and Toren giving especially strong performances. Studio executives were particularly impressed with Chandler, and put him under an exclusive seven-year contract after this film. The problems in this picture lie in the decidedly one-sided view taken in the story. The Jewish forces are portrayed as heroic freedom fighters, in complete solidarity, while the British are pictured as nothing more than stiff-upper- lipped villains. The creation of Israel (and its continued struggle for survival) is a complex, multifaceted subject that deserves far more than the simplistic politics

portrayed here.

p, Robert Buckner; d, George Sherman; w, Buckner; ph, Irving Glassberg; m, Frank Skinner; ed, Otto Ludwig; art d, Bernard Herzbrun, Alexander Golitzen; set d, Al Fields; spec eff, Nick Carmona; makeup, Emile La Vigne.

War Drama   **(PR:C   MPAA:NR)**

SWORD IN THE STONE, THE***½   (1963) 75m Disney/BV c

Voices: Rickie Sorenson (*Wart*), Sebastian Cabot (*Sir Ector*), Karl Swenson (*Merlin the Magician*), Junius Matthews (*Archimedes, Merlin's Pet Owl*), Alan Napier (*Sir Pelinore*), Norman Alden (*Kay*), Wart's Foster Brother, Martha Wentworth (*Mad Madame Mim/Granny Squirrel*), Barbara Jo Allen (*Scullery Maid*), Ginny Tyler (*Little Girl Squirrel*), The Mellomen, Richard Reitherman, Robert Reitherman.

The legend of King Arthur, via the novel of T.H. White, was treated with modern touches by the Disney studios to appeal to the funny bone. This works well, but dampens the mystical quality of the legend. In fact, when the lad Arthur pulls the sword out of the stone and is thus made king of England, he does so just to pry open a door. Concentration is on Merlin's training of Arthur to become king, entailing the turning of the boy into a fish, a squirrel, and a bird. In each instance, the animal comes upon a hazardous situation which he must get out of by using his head instead of his brawn. Thus a valuable lesson is learned which appears to be pretty much the purpose of this project, though it goes about it in an almost preachy manner. Arthur is portrayed as a modern youth, as mischievous and clumsy as all kids; thus the lessons he learns can be easily transmitted to children viewers. High point of the picture is the antics of Merlin; at one point he's hilariously funny in his absent-mindedness, and the next he shows his cunning, defeating Mad Madam Mim in a battle of the sorcerers. Though well-received when it came out, and grossing $4.5 million, THE SWORD IN THE STONE has sunk out of sight since it came out in the early 1960s. It is seldom mentioned in discussions of Disney's work and no character in it evolved into a Disney favorite. Arthur is portrayed as a modern youth, as mischievous and clumsy as all kids; thus the lessons he learns can be easily transmitted to children viewers. High point of the picture is the antics of Merlin; at one point he's hilariously funny in his absent-mindedness, and the next he shows his cunning, defeating Mad Madam Mim in a battle of the sorcerers. Though well-received when it came out, and grossing $4.5 million, THE SWORD IN THE STONE has sunk out of sight since it came out in the early 1960s. It is seldom mentioned in discussions of Disney's work and no character in it evolved into a Disney favorite. Songs include: "A Most Befuddling Thing," "Blue Oak Tree," "Mad Madam Mim," "That's What Makes the World Go Round," "Higitus Figitus," and "The Legend of the Sword in the Stone" (Richard and Robert B. Sherman).

d, Wolfgang Reitherman; w, Bill Peet (based on a book by T.H. White); m, George Bruns; ed, Donald Halliday; art d, Ken Anderson; animators, Franklin Thomas, Milt Kahl, Oliver Johnston, Jr., John Lounsbery, Hal King, Eric Larson, Cliff Nordberg, Hal Ambro, Dick Lucas; backgrounds, Walt Peregoy, Bill Layne, Albert Dempster, Anthony Rizzo, Ralph Hulett, Fil Mottola.

Animated Feature   **(PR:AAA   MPAA:G)**

SWORD OF ALI BABA, THE*   (1965) 81m UNIV c

Peter Mann (*Ali Baba*), Jocelyn Lane (*Amara*), Peter Whitney (*Abou*), Gavin MacLeod (*Hulagu Khan*), Frank Puglia (*Prince Cassim*), Frank McGrath (*Pindar*), Greg Morris (*Yusuf*), Frank DeKova (*Old Baba*), Morgan Woodward (*Captain of Guard*), Irene Tsu (*Halu*).

This is an extension of the 1951 film THE PRINCE WHO WAS A THIEF, and uses far too much footage from the earlier ALI BABA AND THE FORTY THIEVES as well as from some Maria Montez epics. Fifteen years after an ordeal which forced Mann, as Ali Baba, to escape from the evil Mongol MacLeod, Mann returns with his thieves to Baghdad to lay claim to Lane and start a revolt against the Mongol oppressors. Puglia was in the original ALI BABA AND THE FORTY THIEVES and was called back for this film to help tie in the two films.

p, Howard Christie; d, Virgil W. Vogel, Arthur Lubin; w, Oscar Brodney, Edmund Hartmann; ph, William Margulies (Eastmancolor); m, Frank Skinner; ed, Gene Palmer; art d, Alexander Golitzen, William D. DeCinces; set d, John McCarthy, Julia Heron; cos, Helen Colvig; makeup, Bud Westmore.

Adventure   **(PR:A   MPAA:NR)**

SWORD OF DOOM, THE**   (1967, Jap.) 122m Toho bw
                                          (DAIBOSATSU TOGE)

Tatsuya Nakadai (*Ryunosuke Tsukue*), Toshiro Mifune (*Toranosuke Shimada*), Yuzo Kayama (*Hyoma Utsuki*), Michiyo Aratama (*Ohama*), Ichiro Nakaya (*Bunnojo Utsuki*), Yoko Naito, Kei Sato.

Usual samurai fare in which Nakadai plays a ruthless master who lives by the rule of the sword and dies by it as well, members of his own family doing the killing. Before he reaches that point he commits enough careless murders to satisfy any follower of samurai. A secondary plot has Kayama taking up the sword to get vengeance against Nakadai for murdering his brother. Drawing card Mifune is a disappointment, in that his impressive person appears only briefly in the film.

p, Sanezumi Fujimoto; d, Kihachi Okamoto; w, Shinobu Hashimoto (based on the novel *Daibosatsu Toge* by Kaizan Nakazato); ph, Hiroshi Murai (Tohoscope); m, Masaru Sato.

Drama   **(PR:C-O   MPAA:NR)**

SWORD OF EL CID, THE   (1965, Span./Ital.) 86m Alexandria
Produzione-Cintora, S.L.-Victor Torruella/PRC-Eldorado c (LA SPADA
DEL CID; LAS HIJAS DEL CID)

Roland Carey (*Bernardo*), Sandro Moretti (*Ramon*), Chantal Deberg (*Maria Sol*), Iliana Grimaldi (*Bianca*), Jose Luis Pellicena (*Felix Munoz*), Daniela Bianchi (*Elvira*), Ray Miles, Jeff Russel, Luis Induni, Andres Mejuto, Fernando Cebrian, Andrea Fantasia.

The ruler of Catalonia is discovered to be an impostor who killed his own brother to obtain the throne, but hadn't accounted for a son of the brother who would claim the power. With the aid of soldiers from Castile, the throne is captured by the rightful owner with a royal wedding cementing the bond between Castile and Catalonia.

d, Miguel Iglesias; w, Jose Luis Navarro, Victor Torruella, Ferdinando Baldi, Alfredo Giannetti, Antonio Navarro Linares, Iglesias; ph, Francisco Marin (Supercinescope, Eastmancolor); m, Carlo Savina; art d, Juan Alberto Soler.

Adventure/Drama   (PR:A   MPAA:NR)

SWORD OF HONOUR*½   (1938, Brit.) 83m BUT bw

Geoffrey Toone (*Bill Brown*), Sally Gray (*Lady Moira Talmadge*), Dorothy Dickson (*Mrs. Stanhope*), Donald Gray (*Stukeley*), Wally Patch (*Pomeroy Brown*), Peter Gawthorne (*Lord Carhampton*), Frederick Culley (*Duke of Honiton*), Maire O'Neill (*Biddy*), Gordon Begg (*Grandpa Brown*), Cyril Smith (*Bright*), Patrick Susands (*Adjutant*), Tommy Woodrooffe (*Commentator*), Humphrey Morton, Brian Coleman, Patrick Parsons [Patrick Holt], Charles Eaton.

Toone is the scion of an old army family sent to the military college at Sandhurst. Severely reprimanded for mistreating a horse, he drops out and devotes himself to horse racing. When, as a jockey, he rides the winner of the Grand National, he returns to Sandhurst in triumph, his horsemanship proved, and wins the title award. Silly drama of little interest.

p&d, Maurice Elvey; w, Gerald Elliott (based on a story by Dudley Sturrock).

Drama   (PR:A   MPAA:NR)

SWORD OF LANCELOT**   (1963, Brit.) 116m Emblem/UNIV c (GB:
LANCELOT AND GUINEVERE)

Cornel Wilde (*Sir Lancelot*), Jean Wallace (*Queen Guinevere*), Brian Aherne (*King Arthur*), George Baker (*Sir Gawaine*), Archie Duncan (*Sir Lamorak*), Adrienne Corri (*Lady Vivian*), Michael Meacham (*Sir Modred*), Iain Gregory (*Sir Tors*), Mark Dignam (*Merlin*), Reginald Beckwith (*Sir Dragonet*), John Barrie (*Sir Bedivere*), Richard Thorpe (*Sir Gareth*), Joseph Tomelty (*Sir Kaye*), Graham Stark (*Rian*), Geoffrey Dunn (*Edric*), Walter Gotell (*Sir Cedric*), Peter Prowse (*Brandagorus*), Christopher Rhodes (*Ulfus*), John Longden (*King Leodogran*), Bob Bryan (*Sir Dorjak*), Violetta Farjeon (*French Serving Maid*).

Producer-director-star Wilde tried to tackle the Lancelot legend in this independent effort, and put his wife, Wallace, in the role of the adulteress Queen Guinevere, while he played the knight whose loyalty to his king was forsaken in his pursuit of her bed. Concentration in this version of the legend is on the torrid affair between Wilde and Wallace, with the king finally discovering his wife's extramarital play through the gossip of Meacham. Wilde is banished from the court and Wallace escapes a beheading by going to a nunnery. They are reunited years later when Wilde returns to avenge the murder of the king at the hands of Meacham. The exterior scenes were shot in Yugoslavia.

p, Bernard Luber; exec p&d, Cornel Wilde; w, Richard Schayer, Jefferson Pascal (based on *Le Morte d'Arthur* by Thomas Malory); ph, Harry Waxman (Panavision, Eastmancolor); m, Ron Goodwin; ed, Frederick Wilson; art d, Maurice Carter, Jack Maxsted; set d, Leonard Townsend; cos, Terence Morgan II; makeup, George Blackler.

Adventure/Drama   (PR:A   MPAA:NR)

SWORD OF MONTE CRISTO, THE½**   (1951) 80m (FOX) c

George Montgomery (*Capt. Renault*), Paula Corday (*Lady Christiane*), Berry Kroeger (*Minister Charles La Roche*), William Conrad (*Maj. Nicolet*), Rhys Williams (*Major of Varonne*), Steve Brodie (*Sergeant*), Robert Warwick (*Marquis de Montableau*), David Bond (*Louis Napoleon III*), Lillian Bronson (*Pepite*), Acquanetta (*Felice*), Trevor Bardette (*Navarre*), Crane Whitley (*Hansmann*), Leonard Mudie (*Court Physician*), John Davidson (*Artist*), George Baxter (*Mocquard*), Steven Darrell (*Courdelay*), Ken McDonald (*Chamberlain*), Henry Corden (*Bouchard*), Michael Vallon (*Viard*), Stuart Holmes (*Chatelain*).

Period piece with Kroeger as an evil chief minister in the court of Napoleon III. Kroeger wants a valuable sword which belonged to the Count of Monte Cristo and is the key to uncovering his vast fortune. However, the sword is in the hands of Corday, a masked saviour of the liberty of the French people, who plans to use the sword to start a revolt. Montgomery plays a captain who switches sides when he realizes the government is evil. Delivered in a formula-type manner with stereotypical performances. This film explored

two important themes which run through the swashbuckling adventure dramas, that of the masked avenger and the importance of the female fighter for justice against some type of evil government. In THE SWORD OF MONTE CRISTO, both elements were combined in the character played by Corday, a courtier by day and masked avenger by night.

p, Edward L. Alperson; d&w, Maurice Geraghty (based on the novel by Alexandre Dumas); ph, Jack Greenhalgh (Supercinecolor); m, Raoul Kraushaar; ed, Francis D. Lyon; art d, Martin Obzina.

Adventure   (PR:A   MPAA:NR)

SWORD OF SHERWOOD FOREST½**   (1961, Brit.) 80m
Hammer-Yeoman/COL c

Richard Greene (*Robin Hood*), Peter Cushing (*Sheriff of Nottingham*), Niall MacGinnis (*Friar Tuck*), Sarah Branch (*Maid Marian Fitzwalter*), Richard Pasco (*Earl of Newark*), Nigel Green (*Little John*), Jack Gwillim (*Hubert Walter, Archbishop of Canterbury*), Vanda Godsell (*Prioress*), Dennis Lotis (*Alan A'Dale*), Desmond Llewelyn (*Wounded Traveler*), Edwin Richfield (*Sheriff's Lieutenant*), Brian Rawlinson (*1st Falconer*), Patrick Crean (*Ollerton*), Oliver Reed (*Melton*), Derren Nesbitt (*Martin*), Reginald Hearne (*1st Man of Arms*), Jack Cooper (*Master of Archery*), Adam Keane (*Retford*), Charles Lamb (*Old Bowyer*), Aiden Grennell (*1st Veteran Outlaw*), James Neylin (*Roger*), Barry De Boulay (*Officer*), John Hoey (*Old Jack*), Anew McMaster (*Judge*), John Franklin (*Archbishop's Secretary*), Maureen Halligan (*Portress*).

Yet another rendition of the Robin Hood legend, this time given the Hammer studio's knack for creating atmosphere, an old hand at playing the famous thief in Greene, who portrayed him on the television series, and a truly vicious villain in Peter Cushing. Greene goes undercover to infiltrate the group headed by Cushing and the evil earl, Pasco, discovering their plan to murder the Archbishop of Canterbury, Gwillim, and then go on to take over Bawtry Castle. But Greene organizes his band of men to rescue Gwillim and Branch, then continues to quell the insurrection by defeating Pasco's small army. Director Fisher was not too comfortable with the battle scenes, but knew how to set the right mood and to get appropriate caricatures out of his players.

p, Sidney Cole, Richard Greene; d, Terence Fisher; w, Alan Hackney; ph, Ken Hodges (Megascope, Eastmancolor); m, Alun Hoddinott; ed, Lee Doig; art d, John Stoll; cos, John McCorry; m/l, Stanley Black (sung by Dennis Lotis); makeup, Gerry Fletcher; tech adv, Ivor Collin, Patrick Crean, Jack Cooper.

Adventure   (PR:A   MPAA:NR)

SWORD OF THE AVENGER*   (1948) 76m EL bw

Ramon Del Gado (*Roberto Bolagtas*), Sigrid Gurie (*Maria Louisa*), Ralph Morgan (*Don Adolfo*), Duncan Renaldo (*Fernando*), Leonard Strong (*Ming Tang*), David Leonard (*Ignacio*), Tim Huntley (*Rodrigo*), Trevor Bardette (*Miguel*), Belle Mitchell (*Aunt*), Lee Baker (*Duke of Herrara*), Cy Kendall (*Count Velasquez*).

Del Gado plays a sailor for the Spanish crown of the 1800s who is imprisoned by the Philippine government. Given a cruel prison sentence, he escapes by a tunnel to seek vengeance. The nice sepia tint is wasted in this mundane effort.

p&d, Sidney Salkow; w, Julius Evans; ph, Clyde De Vinna (sepiatone); m, Eddison von Ottenfeld; ed, Mel Thorsen.

Adventure   (PR:A   MPAA:NR)

SWORD OF THE CONQUEROR*½   (1962, Ital.) 95m Titanus/UA c
(ROSMUNDA E ALBOINO)

Jack Palance (*Alboino*), Eleonora Rossi-Drago (*Rosamunde*), Guy Madison (*Amalche*), Mirella D'Angelo (*Falisco*), Andrea Bosic (*King Cunimondo*), Edy Vessel (*Mathilde*), Ivan Palance (*Ulderico*), Vittorio Sanipoli (*Wolfango*), Raf Baldassarre, Guido Celano, Guido Manfredi, Alfredo Marchetti, Elio Folgaresi, Olga Romanelli, Vittorio Vaser, Franco Jamonte, Joe Camel, Spartaco Nale, Renato Mori, Giovanni Vari, Lamberto Antinori, Roberto Altamura, Calisto Calisti, Aldo Pini.

Two warring tribes in 6th-Century France have a temporary truce when Palance, as king of Lombard, agrees to keep from attacking the Gepidae if Rossi-Drago, daughter to the Gepidaen king, marries him. She refuses on the grounds that she is already betrothed to Madison; in fact she already has a child by him, but this is kept secret. When Madison is put in jail, Rossi-Drago agrees to marry Palance, but a couple of instances of backstabbing never allows this wedding to take place. Instead a bloody battle occurs, with Madison the hero when he brings additional forces to give the Gepidaens a victory. Although the settings are convincing and the mounting and photography are all first class, the characters portrayed and the subsequent dialog dubbed into English border on the totally ridiculous.

p, Gilberto Carbone; d, Carlo Campogalliani; w, Roberto Gianviti, Alessandro Ferrau, Campogalliani (based on a story by Paola Barbara, Primo Zeglio); ph, Raffaele Masciocchi (CinemaScope, Eastmancolor); m, Carlo Rustichelli; ed, Mario Serandrei; art d, Giorgio Giovannini; set d, Massimo

Tavazzi; cos, Giuliana Ghidini.

Adventure/Drama   (PR:C   MPAA:NR)

SWORD OF VENUS* (1953) 73m RKO bw (GB: ISLAND OF MONTE
CRISTO)

Robert Clarke (*Dantes*), Catherine McLeod (*Claire*), Dan O'Herlihy (*Danglars*), William Schallert (*Valmont, Attorney*), Marjorie Stapp (*Duchess de Villefort*), Merritt Stone (*Fernand*), Renee de Marco (*Suzette*), Eric Colmar (*Geriot*), Stuart Randall (*Hugo*).

Haphazard and stilted production that has Clarke playing the son of the famous Count of Monte Cristo and the victim of a scheme by O'Herlihy to get at his wealth. Clarke is framed for a murder, than forced into a wedding that will turn all his money over to the window. But Clarke escapes just in time to clear himself. Boring.

p, Aubrey Wisberg, Jack Pollexfen; d, Harold Daniels; w, Wisberg, Pollexfen; ph, John L. Russell, Jr.; m, Charles Koff; ed, W. Donn Hayes.

Adventure   (PR:A   MPAA:NR)

SWORDSMAN, THE*½   (1947) 81m COL c

Larry Parks (*Alexander MacArden*), Ellen Drew (*Barbara Glowan*), George Macready (*Robert Glowan*), Edgar Buchanan (*Angus MacArden*), Ray Collins (*Mac-Ian*), Marc Platt (*Murdoch Glowan*), Michael Duane (*Colin Glowan*), Holmes Herbert (*Lord Glowan*), Nedrick Young (*Bruce Glowan*), Robert Shayne (*Ronald MacArden*), William [Billy] Bevan (*Old Andrew*), Lumsden Hare (*Rev. Douglas*), Tom Stevenson (*Gordon Glowan*), Harry Allen (*Charles*).

Parks and Drew attempt a romance while the clans of their respective families are busy feuding. A peace treaty is momentarily broken by hothead members of Drew's clan, but peace soon prevails, with Drew and Parks marrying to the applause of everyone. Performers sound ridiculous trying to mimic Scottish accents, and what is supposed to be Scotland looks like anything but.

p, Burt Kelly; d, Joseph H. Lewis; w, Wilfrid H. Pettit; ph, William Snyder (Technicolor); m, Hugo Friedhofer; ed, Al Clark; md, M. W. Stoloff; art d, Stephen Goosson, A. Leslie Thomas; set d, Wilbur Menefee, Sidney Clifford; cos, Jean Louis.

Drama   (PR:A   MPAA:NR)

SWORDSMAN OF SIENA, THE* (1962, Fr./Ital.) 96m Monica
-C.C.M.-CIPRA/MGM c (LE MERCENAIRE; LO SPADACCINO DI
SIENA; IL MERCENARIO)

Stewart Granger (*Thomas Stanwood*), Sylva Koscina (*Orietta Arconti*), Christine Kaufman (*Serenella Arconti*), Riccardo Garrone (*Don Carlos*), Tullio Carminati (*Father Giacomo*), Alberto Lupo (*Paresi*), Fausto Tozzi (*Hugo*), Tom Felleghi (*Spanish Captain*), Carlo Rizzo (*Gino*), Claudio Gora (*Leoni*), Marina Berti (*Countess of Osta*), Fanfulla, Giulio Marchetti, Ignazio Dolce.

A costume drama from the 1500s features Granger as a mercenary soldier in the Italian town which is under ruthless Spanish nobleman Garrone's thumb. Though paid to work for the bad guys, Granger soon switches and helps the underground movement which is plotting to overthrow Garrone. The head of the movement is Koscina, daughter of the former ruler, and the woman whom Garrone has chosen as his bride. After the maximum amount of swordfights, Granger and company liberate their town during the annual horserace. Believability is streched when Granger goes through the heroism bits, but otherwise he handles his role in an appropriately suave fashion.

p, Jacques Bar; d, Etienne Perier, Baccio Bandini; w, Michael Kanin, Fay Kanin, Alec Coppel, Sandro Continenza, Dominique Fabre (based on a story by Anthony Marshall); ph, Tonio Delli Colli (CinemaScope, Metrocolor); m, Mario Nascimbene; ed, Robert Isnardon, Monique Isnardon; md, Carlo Rustichelli, Franco Ferrara; art d, Alberto Boccianti.

Adventure   (PR:A   MPAA:NR)

SWORN ENEMY½** (1936) 62m MGM bw

Robert Young ("*Hank*" *Sherman*), Florence Rice (*Margaret Gattle*), Joseph Calleia (*Joe Emerald*), Lewis Stone (*Dr. Simon Gattle*), Nat Pendleton ("*Steamer*" *Krupp*), Harvey Stephens (*District Attorney Paul Scott*), Samuel S. Hinds (*Eli Decker*), Edward Pawley ("*Dutch*" *McTurk*), John Wray (*Lang*), Cy Kendall (*Simmons*), Leslie Fenton (*Steve Sherman*), Robert Gleckler (*Hinkle*), George Regas (*Greek*), Duke York (*Al*), Lillian Harmer (*Landlady*), King Mojave (*Gibbons*), Guy Kingsford, Wallace Gregory, Ed Hart, Anthony Quinn (*Gangsters*), George Chandler (*Lunchstand Man*), Harry Tyler (*Nick*), Jack Daley (*Cop*), Charley Keppen (*Fight Announcer*), George Guhl (*Guard*), Al Hill (*Morris*), Norman Ainsley (*Bergen the Chauffeur*), Tom Mahoney, Robert E. Homans (*Policemen*), William Orlamond (*Kreel*).

Well produced B crime drama that has Young as a chauffeur-law student getting involved in a scheme to pin down local crook Calleia, the man

responsible for his boss' murder, his brother's injury, and a number of other crimes. By posing as a fight promoter, and using Rice's charms, Young becomes trusted enough to go to Calleia's home, locating the necessary information to pin a number of crimes onto Calleia and his gang. A young Anthony Quinn plays a gang member. Although the material is fairly routine, efficient pacing and good performances make for an entertaining outing.

p, Lucien Hubbard; d, Edwin L. Marin; w, Wells Root (based on the story by Richard Wormser); ph, Lester White; m, Edward Ward; ed, Frank Hull; art d, Frederic Hope.

Crime/Drama   (PR:A   MPAA:NR)

SYLVIA* (1965) 115m PAR bw

Carroll Baker (*Sylvia West*), George Maharis (*Alan Macklin*), Joanne Dru (*Jane Phillips*), Peter Lawford (*Frederick Summers*), Viveca Lindfors (*Irma Olanski, Librarian*), Edmond O'Brien (*Oscar Stewart*), Aldo Ray (*Jonas Karoki*), Ann Sothern (*Grace Argona, Penny Arcade Cashier*), Lloyd Bochner (*Bruce Stamford III*), Paul Gilbert (*Lola Diamond*), Nancy Kovack (*Big Shirley*), Paul Wexler (*Peter Memel*), Jay Novello (*Father Gonzales*), Connie Gilchrist (*Molly Baxter*), Alan Carney (*Gus*), Shirley O'Hara (*Mrs. Karoki*), Anthony Caruso (*Muscles*), Gene Lyons (*Gavin Cullen*), Val Avery (*Pudgey*), Manuel Padilla (*Pancho*), Majel Barrett (*Anne*), Bob Random.

Maharis plays a private detective who Lawford hires to dig up the shady past of his fiancee, Baker, now a successful poet. Starting with her poetry and leading through various points across the country, Maharis learns that Baker started out as a prostitute after being raped by her stepfather when she was 14. She escaped from a life on the streets by blackmailing a customer and then wisely investing the money. A variety of colorful characters are interviewed, giving Maharis a picture of a woman he has yet to meet; when he does he falls in love with her, refusing to tell Lawford the truth he has learned about her past. But Baker exposes herself to Lawford, then decides that she cannot marry him, hooking up with Maharis instead. Baker is not as sophisticated as the part calls for, but Maharis' subdued, sensitive performance and the various character actors carry the picture.

p, Martin H. Poll; d, Gordon Douglas; w, Sydney Boehm (based on the novel by E.V. Cunningham); ph, Joseph Ruttenberg; m, David Raksin; ed, Frank Bracht; art d, Hal Pereira, Roland Anderson; set d, Sam Comer, Arthur Krams; cos, Edith Head; spec eff, Paul K. Lerpae; m/l, "Love and Learn," Ira Gershwin, Harold Arlen, "Sylvia," Paul Francis Webster, David Raksin (sung by Paul Anka); makeup, Wally Westmore.

Drama   (PR:O   MPAA:NR)

SYLVIA AND THE GHOST (SEE: SYLVIA AND THE PHANTOM,
1950, Fr.)

SYLVIA SCARLETT½** (1936) 97m RKO bw

Katharine Hepburn (*Sylvia Scarlett*), Cary Grant (*Jimmy Monkley*), Brian Aherne (*Michael Fane*), Edmund Gwenn (*Henry Scarlett*), Natalie Paley (*Lily*), Dennie Moore (*Maudie Tilt*), Lennox Pawle (*Drunk*), Daisy Belmore, Nola Luxford, Daisy Goodill, Elsa Buchanan, Lilyan Irene, Kay Deslys, May Beatty, Thomas A. Braidon, Elspeth Dudgeon, Ellis McKenzie, Roger Roughton, Ethel Rawson, Alec Harford, Frank Moran, Colin Campbell, Connie Lamont, Lorimer Johnston, Gwendolyn Logan, Montague Shaw, Elsie Mackay, Patricia Caron, Robert Hale, Mme. Borget, Carmen Beretta, Harrington Reynolds, Violet Seaton, Pat Somerset (*Bits*), George Nardelli (*Frenchman*), Dina Smirnova (*Russian*), E.E. Clive, Edward Cooper, Olaf Hytten (*Customs Inspectors*), Bunny Beatty (*Maid*), Peter Hobbes, Jack Vanair, Leonard Mudie (*Stewards*), Adrienne D'Ambricourt (*Stewardess*), Gaston Glass, Michael S. Visaroff (*Pursers*), Harold Entwistle (*Conductor*), Lionel Pape (*Sgt. Major*), Robert [Bob] Adair (*Turnkey*), Harold Cheevers (*Bobby*).

A curious movie that lost a fortune at the box office, this was well ahead of its time, as it featured Hepburn spending most of the movie clothed as a male, thus presaging VICTOR/VICTORIA and TOTTSIE and SOME LIKE IT HOT in the cross-dressing department. Gwenn is Hepburn's father, and his wife has just passed away. He is a compulsive gambler and hasn't much left in his pocket so he decides to leave France and go to England where, perhaps, he can smuggle in some expensive stolen lace. Hepburn wants to leave with him but the cops are looking for her, as she is the person who purloined the lace, and they'll catch her if she stays. However, all the borders are being watched so she must masquerade as a boy in order to get across the channel. Her hair is cut short and she takes a masculine name and tries her best to swagger and be "butch" as they board the ship. Gwenn drinks too much on board and reveals the lace robbery to cockney Grant, who is, himself, a jewel smuggler. In order to take attention away from himself, Grant informs the customs cops that Gwenn is a smuggler. To keep from being jailed, Gwenn has to give the officials every cent he has. Later, Hepburn spots Grant aboard a train and decks him with a blow for what he's done. Grant is contrite and gives Gwenn and Hepburn some money to cover their losses, but he explains that he had to do what he did or risk being caught himself. Now he offers to take them in as part of his future schemes, still unaware that Hepburn is a female. They try a few ploys but none work, then Grant squires Gwenn to a large home where his pal, Moore, is a maid. The wealthy family is away on a trip and Grant uses his charm to convince Moore to steal the jewels in the house. Hepburn arrives and talks Moore out of it and Moore, thankful for being saved from a life of crime and finding Hepburn attractive, kisses her (this may be one of the rare instances where two women kissed on screen in more than just a friendly buss). Moore has saved a bit of money and wants to be a singer, so Hepburn talks her into investing her money in backing a show. At the same time, Moore and Gwenn fall in love with each other and marry. They move their operations to a small seaside town and are rehearsing their show when local rich artist Aherne comes around and makes fun of their efforts. Hepburn lets him know that she thinks he's a boor, and when he is forced to agree, he asks them all to his mansion for a soiree. Hepburn finds Aherne both handsome and interesting and Grant thinks Aherne's girl friend, Paley, is attractive. Aherne is starting to doubt his masculinity because the male Hepburn is magnetizing him. His line "I don't know what it is that gives me a queer feeling when I look at you" brings down the house. When Aherne sees Hepburn pilfer a dress, he finally comes to the realization that he is a she. He is about to make a move on her when Paley comes in and he assures the Russian that he still loves her. Gwenn's wife, Moore, takes up with another man and leaves him. This sets the old geezer to drinking and he goes outside during a heavy downpour. The following day, Grant and Hepburn find him dead. She is distraught and the two decide that they can find some solace with each other. Before they depart, both confess their true loves. Hepburn loves Aherne and Grant wants Paley. Paley senses Aherne's feeling about Hepburn, so she tries to drown herself but is rescued by Hepburn, thus impressing Aherne with her bravery. Then Paley leaves with Grant. Hepburn and Aherne board the same passenger train as the couple, and while they are chasing them, realize how much they love each other and get off the train to find their happiness together while Grant and Paley continue on the train and begin their first spat. Paley was a real Russian, the daughter of a grand duke who was the uncle to the slain Czar Nicholas (who had his own movies made about him and his so-called "survivor," Anastasia). She had appeared with Maurice Chevalier in FOLIES BERGERE. The major problem with this movie is that they were never certain if they were making a comedy or a drama so it's a hit-and-miss proposition. Despite that, it's become a cult movie and is often shown at festivals. Hepburn made an interesting boy and could have done a terrific "Peter Pan."

p, Pandro S. Berman; d, George Cukor; w, Gladys Unger, John Collier, Mortimer Offner (based on the novel *The Early Life and Adventures of Sylvia Scarlett* by Compton Mackenzie); ph, Joseph August; ed, Jane Loring; md, Roy Webb; art d, Van Nest Polglase, Sturges Carne; cos, Muriel King, Bernard Newman; makeup, Mel Burns.

Drama/Comedy   (PR:A-C MPAA:NR)

SYLVIA AND THE PHANTOM**½
    (1950, Fr.) 90m DIF bw (SYLVIE ET LE FANTOME) (GB: SYLVIA AND THE GHOST)

Odetta Joyeux *(Sylvie)*, Francois Perier *(Ramure)*, Louis Salou *(Anicet)*, Julien Carette *(Hector)*, Pierre Larquey *(The Baron)*, Jean Desailly *(Frederick)*, Rognoni *(Antique Dealer)*, Jacques Tati *(Alain de Francigny)*, Paul Demange *(Counsellor)*, Claude Marcy *(Countess)*, Gabrielle Fontan *(Mariette)*, Marguerite Cassan *(Marthe)*.

Originally made in 1946 but not making it to the U.S. until 1950, after Autant-Lara met with international success with his DEVIL IN THE FLESH. SYLVIA is a lighthearted, though cutting, look at the French aristocracy. Joyeux plays a 16-year-old girl enamored of the image of a former nobleman whose portrait hangs in her castle home. In order to give his daughter a successful birthday party, her father sells the painting, then pays someone to impersonate the dead nobleman. Two other possible suitors of Joyeux also pose as the man from the picture. Further confusion is added when the ghost of the real thing pops into the scene, invisible to the rest of the characters. The premier French comedy director Tati shows up in a small role. (In French; English subtitles.)

p, Andre Paulve; d, Claude Autant-Lara; w, Jean Aurenche (based on the play by Alfred Adam); ph, Philippe Agostini; m, Rene Cloerec; ed, Madeleine Gug.

Comedy/Drama   (PR:A MPAA:NR)

SYLVIE AND THE PHANTOM
    (SEE: SYLVIA AND THE PHANTOM, 1950, Fr.)

SYMPATHY FOR THE DEVIL   (SEE: ONE PLUS ONE, 1969, Brit.)

SYMPHONIE FANTASTIQUE*½
    (1947, Fr.) 85m L'Atelier Francais/A.F. bw

Jean-Louis Barrault *(Hector Berlioz)*, Renee Saint-Cyr *(Marie Martin)*, Lise Delamare *(Henriette)*, Jules Berry *(Schlessinger)*, Bernard Blier *(Charbonnel)*, Gilbert Gil *(Louis Berlioz)*, Catherine Fontenay *(Hector's Mother)*.

Boring account of the life of famed composer Berlioz, which concentrates on the strife between the composer and his wife when he is unable to support her. He takes off to be with another woman who gives him the environment

he needs in which to compose his masterpieces. Settings look good and Berlioz's compositions are nice to hear, but otherwise it is pretty dull going. The Berlioz music includes pieces from "Damnation of Faust," "Requiem," "Benvenuto Cellini," "Symphonie Funebre et Triomphale," and "Symphonie Fantastique." (In French; English subtitles.)

p, L'Atalier; d, Christian-Jaque; w, J.P. Feydeau, H.A. Legrand; ph, Armand Chirard; md, Maurice-Paul Guillot; art d, Andrei Andrieu.

Drama   (PR:A MPAA:NR)

SYMPHONIE PASTORALE***½
    (1948, Fr.) 105m Pathe/Films International bw (LA SYMPHONIE PASTORALE)

Michele Morgan *(Gertrude)*, Pierre Blanchar *(Pastor Martin)*, Line Noro *(Amelie Martin)*, Louvigny *(Casteran)*, Jean Desailly *(Jacques Martin)*, Andre Clement *(Piette)*, Rosine Luguet *(Charlotte)*.

Pierre Bost and Jean Aurenche made a career of adapting famous books for the screen, several of these for Delannoy which provided Francois Truffaut the material to base his cutting attack in the famous *Cahiers du Cinema* articles "A Certain Tendency of the French Cinema." Truffaut criticized Bost and Aurenche for their literal adaptations of novels without getting down to the thematic essence. Like their other works, SYMPHONIE PASTORALE is an adaptation from a novel by Andre Gide, but it could hardly be a source for Truffaut to criticize, as even Gide found the film very enjoyable. Morgan plays an orphaned blind girl brought into the home of pastor Blanchar. He nurtures and raises the girl, eventually falling in love with Morgan and becoming oblivious to his wife. Blanchar provides the girl with an image of a totally harmonious world, something that is best revealed in the second movement of Beethoven's Sixth Symphony, also known as the "Symphonie Pastorale." The preacher's son, Desailly, comes back from school and also falls in love with Morgan. He gets her an operation that restores her sight. But the pastor never wanted her to have the operation because she would no longer be dependent upon him. But once Morgan regains her sight she witnesses the problems in the lives of the people around her. Desailly wants to marry her, but Blanchar persuades his son that she would never accept. In a state of confusion, the guilt-ridden Morgan leaves the protection of the pastor's home, and drowns herself in a nearby creek. A powerful story that unfolds in a timely fashion as the pastor's passion for the young girl deepens, with him becoming blind to the world around him. Morgan's performance was touching enough to win her the Best Actress award at Cannes. She prepared for the role by observing the characteristics of the blind at a hospital. But her piercing blue eyes were the strongest element in capturing the essence of the blind girl's inner nature. (In French; English subtitles.)

d, Jean Delannoy; w, Pierre Bost, Jean Aurenche, Delannoy (based on the novel *Two Symphonies* by Andre Gide); ph, Roger Corbeau, Armand Thirard; m, Georges Auric; ed, Suzanne Fauvel; set d, Rene Renoux; English titles, Justin O'Brien.

Drama   (PR:C MPAA:NR)

SYMPHONY FOR A MASSACRE**½
    (1965, Fr./Ital.) 115m C.I.C.C.-P.E.C.F.-Dear-Ultr a/Seven Arts-Goldstone bw (SYMPHONIE POUR UN MASSACRE; SINFONIA PER UN MASSACRO; AKA: THE MYSTIFIERS)

Michel Auclair *(Clavet)*, Claude Dauphin *(Valoti)*, Jose Giovanni *(Moreau)*, Charles Vanel *(Paoli)*, Jean Rochefort *(Jabeke)*, Michele Mercier *(Madeleine Clavet)*, Daniela Rocca *(Helene Valoti)*.

Four gangsters agree to share the purchase and sale of a large shipment of drugs. But Rochefort becomes greedy and takes the drugs. He then must kill his former partners. But a vengeance-seeking widow, Mercier, kills him in the end, proving that one should not double-cross one's buddies.

p, Julien Derode; d, Jacques Deray; w, Jose Giovanni, Claude Sautet, Deray (based on "Les Mystifies" by Alain Reynaud-Fourton); ph, Claude Renoir; m, Michel Magne; ed, Paul Cayatte; art d, Leon Barsacq.

Crime   (PR:A MPAA:NR)

SYMPHONY IN TWO FLATS*½
    (1930, Brit.) 86m GAU-Gainsborough/Sono Art-World Wide

Ivor Novello *(David Kennard)*, Jacqueline Logan *(Leslie Fullerton)*, Cyril Ritchard *(Leo Chavasse)*, Renee Clama *(Elsie)*, Minnie Rayner *(Mabel)*, Maidie Andrews *(Miss Trebelly)*, Clifford Heatherley *(Wainright)*, Ernest A. Dagnall *(Bradfield)*, Alex Scott-Gatty *(Dr. Mortimer)*, Jack Payne and the BBC Dance Band.

Sappy story features Novello playing a blind musician who hopes to win a competition with a piece he submitted. When prize time comes his devoted wife, Logan, does not have the heart to tell him he lost. Neighbor Ritchard, partially to appease Logan, gives Novello a hefty check so he will think he won the competition. But the musician soon learns he did not win and immediately accuses his wife of infidelity. He leaves and only returns when his compositions start to become well received. Performances are adequate. But the biggest drawback is that the British stuck close to the stage version and the pacing is ponderous. Benita Hume played the wife in the British version and Jacqueline Logan took the role in the U.S. version.

p, Michael Balcon; d, V. Gareth Gundrey; w, Gundrey, Angus Macphail (based on the play by Ivor Novello).

Drama   **(PR:A   MPAA:NR)**

SYMPHONY OF LIFE**½   (1949, USSR) 102m Mosfilm/Artkino bw

Vladimir Druzhnikov (*Andrei Balashov*), Marina Landinina (*Natasha Malinina*), Boris Andreyev (*Yakov Burmak*), Sergei Kalinin (*Korney*), Helena Savitskaya (*Kapitolina*), Vladimir Zeldin (*Boris Olenich*), Vera Vassilieva (*Nastenka*).

Druzhnikov plays a young musician who retreats to Siberia from his position at a conservatory after a war injury makes it impossible for him to continue at the music academy. He is inspired to keep composing by the contact he has with the native Siberians, the people he grew up with. Druzhnikov turns in a fine performance, and Andreyev and Vassilieva contribute some nice comic moments. (In Russian; English subtitles.)

d, Ivan Piriev; w, Eugene Pomischikov, Nicolai Rozhekov; ph, Valentine Pavlov; m, Nikolai Kriukov.

Drama   **(PR:A   MPAA:NR)**

SYMPHONY OF LIVING**½   (1935) 75m IN/CHES bw

Evelyn Brent (*Paula Greig*), Al Shean (*Adolph Greig*), Charles Judels (*Rozzini*), John Darrow (*Richard Greig*), Albert Conti (*Mancini*), Lester Lee (*Carl Rupert*), Gigi Parrish (*Carmen Rozzini*), Richard Tucker (*Michael Rupert*), John Harron (*Herb Livingston*), Ferike Boros (*Mary Schultz*), Ferdinand Schumann-Heink.

Based on an actual event but given a bit of Hollywood flair to hype up the sentiment, this picture has Shean as an aging musician who has devoted his entire life to music, but who has lost out on his big chance due to an injury. His two children do little to help him out after the accident that destroys his career. His daughter, Brent, marries a millionaire and has a son who proves to have his grandfather's gift for music. Through a fluke Shean becomes his grandson's music teacher, although this familial relationship is unknown to either Brent or her son. When Brent divorces her husband, they fight for custody of the son, but the judge rules that the rightful guardian should be the grandfather. Except for Brent, who is ill-fit to play the part of the bitchy daughter, the cast does a convincing job. One of the highlights of this picture is the classical music, including Offenbach's "Orpheus in Hades."

p, Maury M. Cohen; d, Frank Strayer; w, Charles Spencer Belden; ph, M.A. Anderson; m, Jacques Offenbach; ed, L.C. Clark; md, Lee Zahler.

Drama Cas   **(PR:A   MPAA:NR)**

SYMPHONY OF SIX MILLION**
                         (1932) 85m RKO bw (GB: MELODY OF LIFE)

Ricardo Cortez (*Dr. Felix Klauber*), Irene Dunne (*Jessica*), Anna Appel (*Hannah Klauber*), Gregory Ratoff (*Meyer Klauber*), Lita Chevret (*Birdie Klauber*), Noel Madison (*Magnus Klauber*), Helen Freeman (*Miss Spencer*), Julie Haydon (*Nurse-Receptionist*), Josephine Whittell (*Mrs. Gifford*), Oscar Apfel (*Doctor*), Harold Goodwin (*Intern*), John St. Polis (*Dr. Schifflen*), Eddie Phillips (*Birdie's Husband*), Lester Lee (*Felix as a Boy*).

Cortez plays a young Jewish surgeon who takes his blade to his father, Ratoff, to remove a tumor but fails under the pressure, leaving his father dead. Reluctant to go to the operating table again, Cortez is forced back into surgery when his girl friend persuades him to operate on her. But this time the operation is successful, giving the young man back his self-confidence. Although the surgery scene is handled in a convincing style, it is hard to believe any doctor would be allowed to operate on any member of his family, but that is what allows this film to go into its forced sentiment. The performances are all wooden and have little resemblance to real people. Max Steiner's first complete score tends to be a bit heavy handed. This was also the first film for Ratoff. It cost RKO $270,000 to produce.

p, Pandro S. Berman; d, Gregory La Cava; w, Bernard Schubert, J. Walter Ruben, James Seymour (based on the novel by Fannie Hurst); ph, Leo Tover; m, Max Steiner; ed, Archie Marshek; art d, Carroll Clark.

Drama   **(PR:A   MPAA:NR)**

SYMPTOMS*½   (1976, Brit.) 81m Bryanston c

Angela Pleasence, Lorna Heilbron, Peter Vaughan, Ronald O'Neil, Raymond Huntley, Michael Grady, Nancy Nevinson, Marie-Paul Mailleux.

Pleasence plays the lesbian owner of a secluded English country house. The arrival of a few visitors soon prompts a gory murder when Pleasence falls into a jealous rage. A truly chilling atmosphere is created, but its effectiveness is lost when the gore takes over.

p, Jean L. Dupuis; d, Joseph Larraz; w, Larraz, Stanley Miller; ph, Trevor Wreen; m, John Scott.

Horror   **(PR:O   MPAA:R)**

SYNANON***   (1965) 105m COL bw (GB: GET OFF MY BACK)

Edmond O'Brien (*Chuck Dederich*), Chuck Connors (*Ben*), Stella Stevens (*Joaney*), Alex Cord (*Zankie Albo*), Richard Conte (*Reid*), Eartha Kitt (*Betty Coleman*), Barbara Luna (*Mary*), Alejandro Rey (*Chris*), Richard Evans (*Hopper*), Gregory Morton (*Vince*), Chanin Hale (*Arline*), Casey Townsend (*Pruddy*), Larry Kert (*Bob Adamic*), Bernie Hamilton (*Pete*), Mark Sturges (*Joe Mann*), Lawrence Montaigne (*The Greek*), Patricia Houston (*Carla*), John Peterson, James Middleton, Anthony Daddio, Dan Spaccarelli, Herb Rosen, Candy Latson, William Crawford, Charles Haden, Matthew Notkins.

A realistic portrayal of drug addicts trying to kick the habit is obtained by Quine and company through the use of the actual rehabilitation house which served as the inspiration for the film, Synanon House, in Santa Monica, California. Cord is an ex-con who is unable to conform to the strict rules of the center, and quickly initiates an affair with the former prostitute, Stevens, assigned to watch over his recovery. This arouses the jealousies of fellow inmate Connors, whose impingement upon the couple forces them to flee from the house. However, Cord is not fully cured of his addiction and seeks out more junk as soon as the need arises. He dies from an overdose in a sleazy hotel room, and Stevens goes back to continue with her own treatment. A realistic atmosphere is achieved through semi-documentary-type techniques; this adds to the effectiveness in portraying the troubles of an addict trying to reform. In a commendable performance, O'Brien plays the former alcoholic, Charles Dederich, who opened the house despite the hostility of the local citizens. Some of the actual residents of Synanon House also appear in the film.

p&d, Richard Quine; w, Ian Bernard, S. Lee Pogostin (based on a story by Barry Oringer, Pogostin); ph, Harry Stradling; m, Neal Hefti; ed, David Wages; art d, Philip Jefferies; set d, William Kiernan; cos, Kathleen McCandless; makeup, Ben Lane.

Drama   **(PR:C   MPAA:NR)**

SYNCOPATION*½   (1929) 83m RKO bw

Barbara Bennett (*Flo*), Bobby Watson (*Benny*), Morton Downey (*Lew*), Ian Hunter (*Winston*), Dorothy Lee (*Peggy*), Osgood Perkins (*Hummel*), Veree Teasdale (*Rita*), MacKenzie Ward (*Henry*), Fred Waring and His Pennsylvanians.

RKO's first talkie musical was not a very impressive debut, employing an already tired formula for the Hollywood musical, a genre which had only been in existence since the advent of sound. This yarn has Bennett and Watson as a vaudeville team whose togetherness continues off the stage. When Hunter, a hotshot millionaire, steps into the scene, Bennett starts to find things about her mate that drive her to drop him for a bit. A reunion is not long in coming, however, with the two heading for the altar after their ordeal. Some of the musical numbers are fairly entertaining, especially those featuring Fred Waring and His Pennsylvanians, but the acting is less than exceptional, as is the story. Songs include: "Jericho" (Leo Robin, Richard Myers), "Mine Alone" (Herman Ruby, Myers), "Do Something," and "I'll Always Be in Love with You" (Bud Green, Sammy Stept, Ruby).

p, Robert Kane; d, Bert Glennon; w, Frances Agnew, Paul S. Haschke (based on the novel *Stepping High* by Gene Markey); ph, Dal Clawson, George Weber, Frank Landi; ed, Edward Pfitzenmeier.

Musical   **(PR:A   MPAA:NR)**

SYNCOPATION**   (1942) 88m RKO bw

Adolphe Menjou (*George Latimer*), Jackie Cooper (*Johnnie*), Bonita Granville (*Kit Latimer*), George Bancroft (*Mr. Porter*), Ted North (*Paul Porter*), Todd Duncan (*Rex Tearbone*), Connee Boswell (*Cafe Singer*), Frank Jenks (*Smiley Jackson*), Jessie Grayson (*Ella*), Mona Barrie (*Lillian*), Lindy Wade (*Paul Porter as a Child*), Peggy McIntyre (*Kit Latimer as a Child*), Harry James, Gene Krupa, Charlie Barnet, Alvino Rey, Joe Venuti, Jack Jenney, The Hall Johnson Choir.

A rather spotty story served the purpose of presenting some of the hottest musical talent of the day in Gene Krupa and Benny Goodman, to name just a few. Cooper is a young trumpet player who takes a liking to Granville, a girl who shares his enthusiasm for music but is suffering a broken heart from the childhood sweetheart she just lost in WW I. After gaining the girl's trust, Cooper starts about some real romancing, before getting his band together to have a go at making it. Musical numbers included: Goin' Up the River" (Dave Torbett, Leith Stevens), "You Made Me Love You" (Joseph McCarthy, James V. Monaco), "Only Worry for a Pillow," "Chicago Ragtime" (Stevens), "Under a Falling Star" (Rich Hall, Stevens, sung by Connie Boswell), and "Slave Market" (Hall Johnson).

p&d, William Dieterle; w, Philip Yordan, Frank Cavett) based on thestory "The Band Played On" by Valentine Davies); ph, J. Roy Hunt; ed, John Sturges; md, Leith Stevens; art d, Albert S. D'Agostino, Al Herman.

Musical   **(PR:A   MPAA:NR)**

SYNDICATE, THE**   (1968, Brit.) 63m ABF-Pathe/Schoenfeld c

William Sylvester *(Burt Hickey)*, June Ritchie *(Mari Brant)*, Robert Urquhart *(George Brant)*, Christian Doermer *(Kurt Hohmann)*, John Bennett *(Dr. Singh)*, John De Villiers *(Schultz)*, Omari Suleman *(Kamahru)*, Sal Davis *(Shafiq)*, Bill Dixson *(Englishman)*.

The search for uranium in the wilds of Kenya leads to an outbreak of greed and backstabbing, as one of the members in a group headed by Doermer is actually a spy for a powerful company. The culprit turns out to be Doermer himself, something the other members uncover just as a large uranium deposit is discovered.

p, Harry Field; d, Frederic Goode; w, Geoffrey Hays (based on the novel by Denys Rhodes); ph, George Stevens (Technicolor); m, Edwin Astley; ed, Frederick Ives, John Blair.

Adventure   **(PR:A   MPAA:NR)**

SYSTEM, THE**   (1953) 90m WB bw

Frank Lovejoy *(John Merrick)*, Joan Weldon *(Felice Stuart)*, Bob Arthur *(Rex Merrick)*, Paul Picerni *(David Wiley)*, Donald [Don] Beddoe *(Jerry Allen)*, Jerome Cowan *(Brady)*, Dan Seymour *(Marty)*, Sarah Selby *(Liz Allen)*, Fay Roope *(Roger Stuart)*, Frank Richards *(Charley)*, Victor Perrin *(Little Harry)*, Henry Corden *(Specs)*, Howard Negley *(Sen. Ketteridge)*, Al

Gordon *(Reuben)*, Bruno VeSota *(Angelo)*, Richard Garrick *(Tasker)*.

Lovejoy plays a hotshot bookie who becomes the center of an investigation by a newspaper reporter trying to expose the evils of organized crime. The investigation later develops into a committee designed by politicos to investigate the syndicate. Though at first refusing to budge from his stance of silence, the death of a young robber and subsequent suicide of his son, lead Lovejoy to supply the committee with all the information it desires. In the process he winds up in prison himself, but with a possibly bright future because Weldon, daughter of the publisher who supported the investigation, promises to remain faithful until Lovejoy's release from jail. The plot stretches believability quite a bit to drag out some sentiment, otherwise everything is handled in a completely routine fashion.

p, Sam Bischoff; d, Lewis Seiler; w, Jo Eisinger (based on the story "Investigation" by Edith and Samuel Grafton); ph, Edwin Du Par; m, David Buttolph; ed, Clarence Kolster; art d, John Beckman.

Crime/Drama   **(PR:A   MPAA:NR)**

SYSTEM, THE, 1966   (SEE: GIRL GETTERS, THE, 1966, Brit.)

SZEGENYLEGENYEK (NEHEZELETUEK)
                    (SEE: ROUND UP, THE, 1969, Hung.)